January 26–28, 2011
Austin, Texas, USA

Association for
Computing Machinery

Advancing Computing as a Science & Profession

POPL'11

Proceedings of the 38th Annual ACM SIGPLAN-SIGACT Symposium on

Principles of Programming Languages

Sponsored by:

ACM SIGPLAN

In cooperation with:

ACM SIGACT

Supported by:

Google, IBM Research, Intel, Microsoft Research, Mozilla, NEC, NSF, & Computer Science Dept., University of Texas at Austin

Association for
Computing Machinery

Advancing Computing as a Science & Profession

The Association for Computing Machinery
2 Penn Plaza, Suite 701
New York, New York 10121-0701

Notice to Past Authors of ACM-Published Articles

ACM intends to create a complete electronic archive of all articles and/or other material previously published by ACM. If you have written a work that has been previously published by ACM in any journal or conference proceedings prior to 1978, or any SIG Newsletter at any time, and you do NOT want this work to appear in the ACM Digital Library, please inform permissions@acm.org, stating the title of the work, the author(s), and where and when published.

ISBN: 978-1-4503-0490-0

Additional copies may be ordered prepaid from:

ACM Order Department
PO Box 11405
New York, NY 10286-1405

Phone: 1-800-342-6626 (USA and Canada)
+1-212-626-0500 (all other countries)
Fax: +1-212-944-1318
E-mail: acmhelp@acm.org

Printed in the USA

Foreword

Welcome to the Thirty-Eighth Symposium on Principles of Programming Languages, held January 26–January 28, 2011, in Austin, Texas. This volume contains 49 papers selected from 209 submissions.

The POPL'11 PC made an attempt to increase the number of accepted papers while maintaining very high quality and to increase the thoroughness of the reviews. Twenty-five PC members spent 10 weeks reviewing the papers; the reviews were forwarded to the authors who were allowed to respond. Then the PC members discussed the papers electronically during a period of two weeks. Finally all PC members flew to Maryland for two days to discuss the papers. This required a lot of effort from the PC members and additional external reviewers. Indeed, 379 reviewers produced 140,000 lines of reviews. In certain cases, the reviews reveal significant technical errors and other major problems in the submitted papers. I am totally amazed by the devotion of each of the PC members and the external reviewers.

Program Committee members were allowed to submit papers, but such papers were accepted only if there was a consensus among the PC members and the external reviewers that the paper is strong enough to be included in POPL. Six out of sixteen submissions co-authored by PC members were accepted.

I thank everyone who contributed to the success of POPL'11. I thank the authors, attendees, the steering committee, additional reviewers, and the invited speakers. Special thanks goes to Thomas Ball, the program general chair for steering the boat and making the procedure most efficient and enjoyable. I thank Alex Aiken, Kathleen Fisher, Peter O'Hearn and Greta Yorsh for great advice whenever I needed it. I also thank Jeff Foster for hosting the POPL in person PC meeting in Maryland and for organizing the post PC meeting workshop. Matthew Might organized the workshops. The POPL treasurer Bor-Yuah Evan Chang raised money for student travel. I thank Swarat Chaudhuri for publicity and maintaining the POPL homepage. I thank Eddie Kohler for the HOTCRP system, and the TAU system team and Shachar Itzhaky for maintaining it. I thank Lisa M. Tolles of Sheridan Printing Company. Finally, I thank my assistant Gilit Zohar-Oren for incredible help throughout the process.

Mooly Sagiv
POPL'11 Program Chair
Tel Aviv, Israel

Table of Contents

Session 2.2: Semantic Models and Translations
Session Chair: Philippa Gardner *(Imperial College)*

Session 3.1: Shape Analysis
Session Chair: Radhia Cousot *(École Normale Supérieure)*

Session 3.2: Type Abstractions
Session Chair: Derek Dreyer *(MPI-SWS)*

Invited Talk
Session Chair: Steve Zdancewic *(University of Pennsylvania)*

Session 4.1: Separation Logic
Session Chair: Hongseok Yang *(Queen Mary)*

Session 4.2: Automata

Session Chair: Kathleen Fisher *(AT&T Laboratorie)*

Session 5.1: Synthesis

Session Chair: Viktor Kuncak *(EPFL)*

Session 5.2: Algebra

Session Chair: Jeff Foster *(University of Maryland)*

Session 6.1: Model Checking

Session Chair: Azadeh Farzan *(University of Toronto)*

Session 6.2: Types

Session Chair: Stephen Freund *(Williams College)*

Invited Talk

Session Chair: Thomas Ball *(Microsoft Research)*

Session 7.1: Complexity

Session Chair: Madhusudan Parthasarathy *(University of Illinois)*

Session 7.2: Medley

Session Chair: Jan Vitek *(Purdue University)*

Session 8.1: Compilation

Session Chair: Dan Grossman *(University of Washington)*

Session 8.2: Verification

Session Chair: Sumit Gulwani *(Microsoft Research)*

Sessions 8.1 + 8.2

Session Chair: Michael Hicks *(University of Maryland)*

POPL'11 Symposium Organization

General Chair: Thomas Ball *(Microsoft Research, USA)*

Program Chair: Mooly Sagiv *(Tel Aviv University, Israel)*

Publicity Chair: Swarat Chaudhuri *(Pennsylvania State University, USA)*

Treasurer: Bor-Yuh Evan Chang *(University of Colorado, Boulder, USA)*

Steering Committee Chair: Manuel Hermenegildo *(IMDEA Software, Spain)*

Steering Committee:
Philip Wadler *(University of Edinburgh, UK)*
Kathleen Fisher *(AT&T Labs Research, USA)*
Graham Hutton *(University of Nottingham, UK)*
Chandra Krintz *(University of California, USA)*
Thomas Ball *(Microsoft Research, USA)*
Mooly Sagiv *(Tel Aviv University, Israel)*
Manuel Hermenegildo *(IMDEA Software, Spain)*
Jens Palsberg *(University of California, Los Angeles, USA)*
Zhong Shao *(Yale University, USA)*
Benjamin Pierce *(University of Pennsylvania, USA)*

Program Committee:
Radhia Cousot *(École Normale Supérieure, France)*
Oege de Moor *(Oxford University Computing Laboratory, UK)*
Derek Dreyer *(MPI-SWS, Germany)*
Azadeh Farzan *(University of Toronto, Canada)*
Kathleen Fisher *(AT&T Laboratories, USA)*
Matthew Fluet *(Rochester Institute of Technology, USA)*
Jeff Foster *(University of Maryland, USA)*
Stephen Freund *(Williams College, USA)*
Philippa Gardner *(Imperial College, UK)*
Dan Grossman *(University of Washington, USA)*
Sumit Gulwani *(Microsoft Research, USA)*
Tim Harris *(Microsoft Research, USA)*
Naoki Kobayashi *(Tohoku University, Japan)*
Viktor Kuncak *(EPFL, Switzerland)*
Ken McMillan *(Cadence Research Laboratories, USA)*
Anders Møller *(Aarhus University, Denmark)*
Peter Müller *(ETH Zurich, Switzerland)*
Aleks Nanevski *(IMDEA Software, Spain)*
David Naumann *(Stevens Institute of Technology, USA)*
Prakash Panangaden *(McGill University, Canada)*
G. Ramalingam *(Microsoft Research, USA)*
Jan Vitek *(Purdue University, USA)*
Eran Yahav *(IBM Research, USA)*
Hongseok Yang *(Queen Mary, UK)*
Steve Zdancewic *(University of Pennsylvania, USA)*

POPL'11 Additional Reviewers

Samson Abramsky
Umut Acar
Vikram Adve
Yehuda Afek
Amal Ahmed
Sameer Ajmani
Jonathan Aldrich
Rajeev Alur
Todd Anderson
Torben Amtoft
Andrew Appel
Krzysztof R. Apt
Mohamed-Faouzi Atig
Robert Atkey
Arthur Baars
Roland Backhouse
Gogul Balakrishnan
Anindya Banerjee
Franco Barbanera
Rida Bazzi
Amir Ben-Amram
Michael Benedikt
Jesper Bengtson
Nick Benton
Josh Berdine
Lars Bergstrom
Lennart Beringer
Lorenzo Bettini
Lars Birkedal
Bruno Blanchet
Ras Bodik
Hans Boehm
Aaron Bohannon
Ahmed Bouajjani
Pierre Boudes
Chandrasekhar Boyapati
Julian Bradfield
Edwin Brady
Paul Brauner
Nathan Bronson
Steve Brookes
Roberto Bruni
Antonio Bucciarell
Tevfik Bultan
Sebastian Burckhardt
Jacob Burnim
Jan Van den Bussche
Luis Caires
Cristiano Calcagno
Magnus Carlsson
Luke Cartey
Giuseppe Castagna
Bor-Yuh Evan Chang
Swarat Chaudhuri
James Cheney
Olaf Chitil
Adam Chlipala
Vincenzo Ciancia
Dave Clarke
Byron Cook
Keith D. Cooper
Manuel Costa
Bruno Courcelle
Karl Crary
Vijay D'Silva
Nils Anders Danielsson
Olivier Danvy
Anupam Datta
Jack Davidson
Rowan Davies
Nachum Dershowitz
Isil Dillig
Thomas Dillig
Thomas Dinsdale-Young
Robert Dockins
Julian Dolby
Evelyn Dusterwald
Stefan Edelkamp
Laura Effinger-Dean
Cindy Eisner
Ãšlfar Erlingsson
Javier Esparza
Patrick Eugster
Manuel Fahndrich
Paolo Faraboschi
Eitan Farchi
Matthias Felleisen
John Field
Andrzej Filinski
Jean-Christophe Filliâtre
Robby Findler
Cormac Flanagan
Bryan Ford
Cédric Fournet
Richard A. Frost
Pierre Ganty
Richard Garner
Gauthier van den Hove
David Gay
Roberto Giacobazzi
Benjamin Goldberg
Denis Gopan
Alexey Gotsman
Eric Goubault
Clemens Grabmayer
David Greaves
Michael Greenberg
Jeroen Groenendijk
Guy Gueta
Bhargav Gulavani
Philip Guo
Sam Guyer
Christian Haack
Sebastian Hack
Jurriaan Hage
William Harris
Masahito Hasegawa
Peter Hawkins
Chris Hayden
Fritz Henglein
Tom Henzinger
Michael Hicks
Mark Hillebrand
Ralf Hinze
Aquinas Hobor
Martin Hofmann
Tom Hvitved
Pierre Hyvernat
Danko Ilik
Neil Immerman
Jun Inoue
Bart Jacobs
Radha Jagadeesan
Suresh Jagannathan
Alan Jeffrey
Ranjit Jhala
Patricia Johann
Neil D. Jones
Richard Jones
Simon Peyton Jones
Christophe Joubert
Vineet Kahlon
Michael Kaminski
Elham Kashefi
Khoo Yit Phang
Sarfraz Khurshid
Nick Kidd
Oleg Kiselyov
Casey Klein
Guy Korland
Eric Koskinen
Dexter Kozen
Sriram Krishamurthi
Michael Kuperstein
Orna Kupferman
Shuvendu Lahiri
Jim Laird
Akash Lal
Patrick Lam
Peter Lammich
Julia L. Lawall
Gary T. Leavens
Daan Leijen
Xavier Leroy
Richard Lethin
Paul Blain Levy
Percy Liang
Ben Liblit
Daniel Licata
Jia Limin
Annie Liu
Ben Livshits
Alexey Loginov
Francesco Logozzo
Bertram Ludaescher
Ian Mackie
P. Madhusudan
Sergio Maffeis
Rupak Majumdar
Yitzhak Mandelbaum

Roman Manevich
Mark Marron
Matthieu Martel
Laurent Mauborgne
Karl Mazurak
Stephen McCamant
Bill McCloskey
Guy McCusker
Paul-Andre Mellies
David Melski
Maged Michael
Arie Middelkoop
Ana Milanova
Todd Millstein
Antoine Miné
Mike Mislove
Paolo Missier
John C. Mitchell
Torben Mogensen
Eugenio Moggi
Alberto Momigliano
Luc Moreau
Greg Morrisett
Georg Moser
Elliot Moss
Shin-Cheng Mu
Markus Müller-Olm
Andrzej Murawski
Andrew Myers
Kedar Namjoshi
Mayur Naik
George Necula
Lasse Nielsen
Henrik Nilsson
Tobias Nipkow
Aditya Nori
Peter O'Hearn
Alexander Okhotin
Luke Ong
Joel Ouaknine
Scott Owens
Catuscia Palamidessi
Jens Palsberg
Sungwoo Park
Sascha Parduhn
Matthew Parkinson
Gennaro Parlato
Wolfgang Paul
David Pearce
Simon Perdrix
Leaf Petersen
Erez Petrank
Brigitte Pientka
Benjamin C. Pierce
Ruzica Piskac
Marco Pistore
Corin Pitcher
Andrew Pitts
Filip Pizlo
Polyvios Pratikakis
Shaz Qadeer
Alexander Rabinovich
Komondoor V Raghavan
Sriram K. Rajamani
Hridesh Rajan
Kaushik Rajan
Norman Ramsey
Jean-Francois Raskin
Lawrence Rauchwerger
Razieh Nokhbeh Zaeem
Uday Reddy
Jason Reed
Didier Rémy
Tom Ridge
Martin Rinard
Noam Rinetzky
Xavier Rival
Patrick Rondon
Andreas Rossberg
Tom Rothamel
Abhik Roychoudhury
Andrey Rybalchenko
Andrei Sabelfeld
Dave Sands
Sriram Sankaranarayanan
Joao Sariava
Vivek Sarkar
Vladimiro Sassone
Raluca Sauciuc
Max Schaefer
David Schmidt
Jan Schwinghammer
Helmut Seidl
Peter Selinger
Koushik Sen
Peter Sewell
Thomas Sewell
Ohad Shacham
Chung-chieh Shan
Natarajan Shankar
Zhong Shao
Nir Shavit
Jeremy Siek
KC Sivaramakrishnan
Alexandra Silva
Axel Simon
Rishabh Singh
Yannis Smaragdakis
Douglas R. Smith
Geoffrey Smith
Pawel Sobocinski
Mary Lou Soffa
Armando Solar-Lezama
Manu Sridharan
Saurabh Srivastava
Ian Stark
Sam Staton
Martin Steffen
Chris Stone
Kristian Stovring
Bjarne Stroustrup
Aaron Stump
Zhendong Su
Eijiro Sumii
Philippe Suter
Kasper Svendsen
Nikhil Swamy
Doaitse Swierstra
Wouter Swierstra
Nicolas Tabareau
Walid Taha
Ankur Taly
Ross Tate
Gadi Taubenfeld
Tachio Terauchi
Jacob Thamsborg
Peter Thiemann
Nikolai Tillmann
Ashish Tiwari
Terkel K. Tolstrup
Mads Torgersen
Stavros Tripakis
Thomas Tuerk
Hiroshi Unno
Shmuel Ur
Taarmo Uustalu
Viktor Vafeiadis
Benoit Valiron
Tijs van der Storm
Moshe Y. Vardi
Martin Vechev
Arnaud Venet
Victor Vianu
Jurgen Vinju
Mirko Viroli
Janis Voigtländer
Dennis Volpano
Dimitrios Vytiniotis
Philip Wadler
David Walker
Mitch Wand
Stephanie Weirich
Edwin Westbrook
Mark Wheelhouse
Reinhard Wilhelm
Benjamin Wood
James Worrell
Tobias Wrigstad
Dana Xu
Greta Yorsh
Santiago Zanella
Andreas Zeller
Florian Zuleger

POPL 2011 Sponsor & Supporters

Sponsor: ACM SIGPLAN

In cooperation with: SIGACT

Supporters: Google, IBM Research, Intel, Microsoft Research, mozilla.org, NEC, NSF, The University of Texas at Austin

Computer Science Department

Verified Squared: Does Critical Software Deserve Verified Tools?

Xavier Leroy *

INRIA Paris-Rocquencourt

Xavier.Leroy@inria.fr

Abstract

The formal verification of programs have progressed tremendously in the last decade. Principled but once academic approaches such as Hoare logic and abstract interpretation finally gave birth to quality verification tools, operating over source code (and not just idealized models thereof) and able to verify complex real-world applications [6, 8, 15, 18]. In this talk, I review some of the obstacles that remain to be lifted before source-level verification tools can be taken really seriously in the critical software industry: not just as sophisticated bug-finders, but as elements of absolute confidence in the correctness of a critical application.

Categories and Subject Descriptors D.2.4 [*Software Engineering*]: Software/Program Verification; D.3.1 [*Programming Languages*]: Formal Definition and Theory; D.3.4 [*Programming Languages*]: Processors; F.3.1 [*Logics and meanings of programs*]: Specifying and Verifying and Reasoning about Programs; F.3.2 [*Logics and meanings of programs*]: Semantics of Programming Languages

General Terms Languages, Verification

Extended abstract of invited talk

Critical software Software is critical when human lives are at stake and there is no simple, safe failure mode. I take the paradigmatic example of electronic flight control systems ("fly-by-wire") in aircraft, which provides a fascinating glimpse of what software perfection may look like. Impressive reliability has been achieved so far—but at tremendous costs—by following meticulous development and certification processes, as codified in DO-178 regulations for instance. These processes rely on (qualitative) review, (quantitative) analysis, and (black-box) testing at multiple levels of the design, complemented with strong traceability between high-level requirements and actual implementation. In this domain, verification tools have great potential to facilitate and strengthen the results of analysis phases, while at the same time remove the need for some costly tests [15].

Trust in compilers and code generators With a few notable exceptions, most verification tools operate over the source code: generally C code, possibly Scade/Simulink block diagrams. The guarantees provided by these tools are therefore vulnerable to *miscompilation*: compiler bugs that cause wrong executable code to be silently generated from correct sources. DO-178 recognizes this issue and mandates that either the compiler/code generator is qualified to the same level of assurance as the code it compiles, or the generated code is certified as if hand-written [9]. Neither requirement can be fully achieved in the case of a conventional C compiler. Even when possible, e.g. for Scade-to-C code generators, qualification of a compiler generally comes at the cost of inefficiencies in the generated code.

An obvious alternative is compiler verification: apply mechanized program proof to the compiler itself and prove semantic preservation (the generated code behaves as prescribed by the semantics of the source program). For example, CompCert [10, 11] is a lightly-optimizing, multi-pass compiler for a large subset of C that was programmed and proved semantically preserving using Coq. From the results of the CompCert experiment, the formal verification of realistic compilers appears within reach of today's proof technology, and generates (arguably) unprecedented confidence in the compilation process and, indirectly, in source-level verification. At the same time, much remains to be done in this area, such as verifying more of the "first miles" (preprocessing, parsing) and the "last miles" (assembing and linking, or even connections with micro-architecture verification), and proving compilers for source languages significantly different from C.

Trust in verification tools While unsound verification tools still have value as bug-finders, verification-based certification of critical software demands formal evidence that the results of the verification tools are sound with respect to concrete executions. The general principles for stating and proving these soundness results are well known; some approaches, such as classic abstract interpretation, even ensure soundness by construction of the analysis. Mechanization of these principles appear well within reach [2, 5, 17]. Perhaps the biggest challenge to extend these efforts to realistic verification tools is the need to prove some of the fairly complex algorithms involved in the implementation of abstract domains and theorem provers.

Verified vs. validated Not all parts of a compiler or verifier need to be proved: only those parts that affect soundness, but not those part that only affect termination, precision of the analysis, or efficiency of the generated code. Leveraging this effect, complex algorithms can often be decomposed into an untrusted implementation followed by a formally-verified validator that checks the computed results for soundness and fails otherwise. (Failure is not an option in flight, but is an option at compile-time and verification-time.) In static analysis, for example, it is much easier to prove the code that checks that an abstract value X is a post-fixpoint of an operator F than to prove the correctness of the fixpoint iteration

* Partially supported by ANR grant Arpège U3CAT.

POPL '11 January 26–28, Austin, TX, USA

ACM 978-1-4503-0490-0/11/01.

that computes X. Likewise, in a compiler, translation validation of the results of an untrusted compilation pass can provide soundness guarantees as strong as formal verification of this pass, provided the validator is proved sound [12, 13, 16]. While often effective to reduce the overall proof effort, validation a posteriori is not a silver bullet either: many compiler passes are no easier to validate than to prove correct once and for all. Between full compiler verification and full translation validation lies a continuum of combined approaches that remain to be systematically explored.

Mechanized semantics Formal verification of compilers and program verifiers does not eliminate all sources of uncertainty, but reduces the issue of trusting these tools to (primarily) the issue of trusting the formal semantics used for the source and target languages. Extensive manual reviews and testing of these semantics remains a necessity. As a further difficulty, different tasks favor different styles of semantics: big-step semantics or definitional interpreters are perhaps the easiest to review by hand, while verification of type-checkers, abstract interpreters, and compilers favor Wright-Felleisen small-step semantics, collecting semantics, and transition semantics with explicit contexts, respectively. Finally, there is also a strong tension between low-level operational semantics, easy to mechanize but difficult to work with, and higher-level approaches such as type- or step-indexed logical relations that provide much nicer reasoning principles but are expensive to set up [1, 4]. Agreement on one reference semantics for, say, the C language is therefore unlikely to happen. Instead, we should strive for systematic, mechanized proofs of equivalence or implication between these various semantics. Such proofs, as well as tool verification in general, considerably strengthen the confidence we can have in these semantics.

Multiple languages Many applications combine sources written in several languages, such as Scade/Simulink, C, and assembly for control/command systems. Also, implementations of high-level languages combine compiled code with run-time systems written in a lower-level language. Verifying the correctness of the whole system requires a delicate combination of proofs, some coming from the verification of the individual sources, others coming from the verification of the compilers involved. In this situation, whole-program semantic preservation result such as those of CompCert do not directly apply, and finer-grained approaches are needed: possibly proof-preserving compilation [3, 14] combined with separation logics.

Floating-point woes "It makes me nervous to fly an airplane since I know they are designed using floating-point arithmetic." A. Householder, the author of this famous quote, should be even more nervous because modern airplanes *fly* using floating-point arithmetic. Floating-point is, today, the biggest source of infidelities between the semantics used for verification and the code that actually runs, owing to fundamental aspects of floating-point arithmetic (limited precision, limited range) that are further aggravated by sloppy language specifications (C leaves unspecified the precision of intermediate floating-point results) and dubious compiler optimizations (reassociation during vectorization, for instance). Good static analyzers manage to conservatively approximate most of these floating-point artefacts, at significant cost. Program logics and deductive program provers still have some way to go in this direction: just specifying simple numerical routines in a floating-point accurate manner is already a challenge [7].

Conclusions The formal verification of development and verification tools for critical software appears worthwhile: first, to strengthen the confidence we can have in the results of verification tools, and therefore to make a stronger case for their adoption; second, because it raises scientifically-challenging issues, shedding new light on well-researched areas and exposing new problems at their frontiers. The POPL community has, obviously, much to contribute to this endeavor: feel free to join!

References

[1] A. J. Ahmed. Step-indexed syntactic logical relations for recursive and quantified types. In *Programming Languages and Systems, 15th European Symposium on Programming, ESOP 2006*, volume 3924 of *Lecture Notes in Computer Science*, pages 69–83. Springer, 2006.

[2] A. W. Appel and S. Blazy. Separation logic for small-step Cminor. In *Theorem Proving in Higher Order Logics, 20th Int. Conf. TPHOLs 2007*, volume 4732 of *Lecture Notes in Computer Science*, pages 5–21. Springer, 2007.

[3] G. Barthe, B. Grégoire, C. Kunz, and T. Rezk. Certificate translation for optimizing compilers. *ACM Transactions on Programming Languages and Systems*, 31(5), 2009.

[4] N. Benton and C.-K. Hur. Biorthogonality, step-indexing and compiler correctness. In *International Conference on Functional Programming 2009*, pages 97–108. ACM Press, 2009.

[5] F. Besson, D. Cachera, T. P. Jensen, and D. Pichardie. Certified static analysis by abstract interpretation. In *Foundations of Security Analysis and Design*, volume 5705 of *Lecture Notes in Computer Science*, pages 223–257. Springer, 2009.

[6] B. Blanchet, P. Cousot, R. Cousot, J. Feret, L. Mauborgne, A. Miné, D. Monniaux, and X. Rival. A static analyzer for large safety-critical software. In *Programming Language Design and Implementation 2003*, pages 196–207. ACM Press, 2003.

[7] S. Boldo, J.-C. Filliâtre, and G. Melquiond. Combining Coq and Gappa for certifying floating-point programs. In *Intelligent Computer Mathematics, Calculemus/MKM 2009*, volume 5625 of *Lecture Notes in Computer Science*, pages 59–74. Springer, 2009.

[8] G. Klein, J. Andronick, K. Elphinstone, G. Heiser, D. Cock, P. Derrin, D. Elkaduwe, K. Engelhardt, R. Kolanski, M. Norrish, T. Sewell, H. Tuch, and S. Winwood. seL4: formal verification of an operating-system kernel. *Communications of the ACM*, 53(6):107–115, 2010.

[9] A. J. Kornecki and J. Zalewski. The qualification of software development tools from the DO-178B certification perspective. *CrossTalk*, Apr. 2006.

[10] X. Leroy. Formal verification of a realistic compiler. *Communications of the ACM*, 52(7):107–115, 2009.

[11] X. Leroy. A formally verified compiler back-end. *Journal of Automated Reasoning*, 43(4):363–446, 2009.

[12] G. C. Necula. Translation validation for an optimizing compiler. In *Programming Language Design and Implementation 2000*, pages 83–95. ACM Press, 2000.

[13] A. Pnueli, M. Siegel, and E. Singerman. Translation validation. In *Tools and Algorithms for Construction and Analysis of Systems, TACAS '98*, volume 1384 of *Lecture Notes in Computer Science*, pages 151–166. Springer, 1998.

[14] Z. Shao, V. Trifonov, B. Saha, and N. Papaspyrou. A type system for certified binaries. *ACM Transactions on Programming Languages and Systems*, 27(1):1–45, 2005.

[15] J. Souyris, V. Wiels, D. Delmas, and H. Delseny. Formal verification of avionics software products. In *FM 2009: Formal Methods*, volume 5850 of *Lecture Notes in Computer Science*, pages 532–546. Springer, 2009.

[16] J.-B. Tristan and X. Leroy. Verified validation of Lazy Code Motion. In *Programming Language Design and Implementation 2009*, pages 316–326. ACM Press, 2009.

[17] H. Tuch, G. Klein, and M. Norrish. Types, bytes, and separation logic. In *34th symposium Principles of Programming Languages*, pages 97–108. ACM Press, 2007.

[18] J. Yang and C. Hawblitzel. Safe to the last instruction: automated verification of a type-safe operating system. In *Programming Language Design and Implementation 2010*, pages 99–110. ACM Press, 2010.

Points-To Analysis with Efficient Strong Updates

Ondřej Lhoták Kwok-Chiang Andrew Chung
D. R. Cheriton School of Computer Science
University of Waterloo
Waterloo, Ontario, Canada
{olhotak,kachung}@uwaterloo.ca

Abstract

This paper explores a sweet spot between flow-insensitive and flow-sensitive subset-based points-to analysis. Flow-insensitive analysis is efficient: it has been applied to million-line programs and even its worst-case requirements are quadratic space and cubic time. Flow-sensitive analysis is precise because it allows strong updates, so that points-to relationships holding in one program location can be removed from the analysis when they no longer hold in other locations. We propose a "Strong Update" analysis combining both features: it is efficient like flow-insensitive analysis, with the same worst-case bounds, yet its precision benefits from strong updates like flow-sensitive analysis. The key enabling insight is that strong updates are applicable when the dereferenced points-to set is a singleton, and a singleton set is cheap to analyze. The analysis therefore focuses flow sensitivity on singleton sets. Larger sets, which will not lead to strong updates, are modelled flow insensitively to maintain efficiency. We have implemented and evaluated the analysis as an extension of the standard flow-insensitive points-to analysis in the LLVM compiler infrastructure.

Categories and Subject Descriptors D.3.4 [*Programming Languages*]: Processors; D.2.4 [*Software Engineering*]: Software/Program Verification

General Terms Algorithms, Design, Experimentation, Languages, Performance, Verification

Keywords points-to analysis, flow sensitivity, strong updates, Andersen's analysis, LLVM

1. Introduction

One of the design decisions facing a developer selecting a subset based points-to analysis is flow sensitivity. On one hand, flow-insensitive analyses are well understood, and techniques have been developed that make them quite efficient and scalable (e.g. [2, 12, 15, 19, 25, 27], among many others). On the other hand, flow-sensitive analyses promise potentially more precise results. Recently, there has been a resurgence of interest in techniques that reduce the previously prohibitive cost of flow sensitivity [14, 22, 31, 32].

This paper proposes a hybrid subset-based analysis algorithm that has desirable properties of both flow-insensitive and flow-sensitive analyses. This "Strong Update" analysis provides the key precision benefit that flow sensitivity brings, strong updates. However, its performance is comparable to that of flow-insensitive analysis: in the worst case, it requires quadratic space and cubic time, and in practice, it is almost as fast as flow-insensitive analysis. More precisely, the strong update analysis requires $O(VA)$ space and $O(EV^2)$ time, where V is the number of pointer variables in the program, A is the number of variables whose address is taken (i.e. possible pointer targets), and E is the number of edges in the interprocedural control flow graph.

The idea that enables this good compromise is the realization that the precise points-to sets that matter most are also cheap to propagate, even flow sensitively. A strong update can only be performed if the may-point-to set of the dereferenced pointer corresponds to exactly one (runtime) target; otherwise, the analysis could not guarantee that any one of the possible targets is definitely overwritten. A necessary condition for this case is that the points-to set must be a singleton (i.e., contain one abstract target). When one strong update improves the precision of a given points-to set, the more precise set may enable a chain of further strong updates. Thus in order to be precise overall, an analysis must model these small sets precisely. Yet singleton sets are also very cheap to represent and propagate. In particular, it is possible to propagate singleton sets flow-sensitively without significantly increasing the asymptotic complexity of an otherwise flow-insensitive analysis or its practical running time.

Thus our strong update points-to analysis can be summarized as follows. It is a flow-insensitive subset-based analysis extended with flow-sensitive modeling of singleton sets, which are used to enable strong updates. The analysis maintains sound flow-insensitive points-to sets for all pointers. In addition, it provides flow-sensitive points-to sets for those pointers and at those program points where the sets are singletons. When a flow-sensitive set is available, the analysis uses it, possibly to perform a strong update. When no flow-sensitive set is available (because it is not a singleton), the analysis falls back to the flow-insensitive information. Although we have described the analysis here as a combination of two separate analyses, both analyses are intertwined in the actual algorithm and performed at the same time so that they can query each other. Thus the flow-sensitive analysis improves the precision of the flow-insensitive analysis, and the flow-insensitive analysis provides a fall-back to the flow-sensitive analysis when necessary.

This paper makes the following contributions:

- It identifies and discusses the characteristics of flow-sensitive analyses that give rise to improved precision over flow-insensitive analyses. It argues that strong updates are the most important such characteristic.

POPL'11, January 26–28, 2011, Austin, Texas, USA.

- It presents the hybrid strong update analysis algorithm, first as a system of constraints, and then as an algorithm extending the flow-insensitive algorithm.
- It shows that the worst-case complexity of the strong update analysis is the same as that of the flow-insensitive analysis, quadratic in space and cubic in time.
- It describes an implementation of the strong update analysis in the LLVM compiler infrastructure [24]. The implementation is available for download at `http://plg.uwaterloo.ca/~olhotak/su`.
- It experimentally evaluates the implementation on the SPECINT 2000 and SPECCPU 2006 benchmark suites [33], shows that its practical performance is comparable to that of the flow-insensitive analysis, and that it performs 98% of the strong updates and propagates more precise sets than a flow-insensitive analysis at 98% of the loads at which a fully flow-sensitive analysis would.

The paper is organized as follows. Section 2 presents background material. It first defines the form of the intermediate representation on which the analyses work. It then presents a high level specification, in the form of subset constraints, of three existing analyses: a flow-insensitive analysis and a flow-sensitive analysis without and with strong updates. Section 3 presents the high-level decisions guiding the design of the strong update analysis. It discusses the key benefits of flow sensitivity and assumptions about the intermediate representation that make analyses easier to express. It then presents, at the same high level of subset constraints, the strong update analysis for comparison with the existing flow-insensitive and flow-sensitive analyses. Section 4 presents the strong update analysis algorithm in detail. It also proves the worst-case complexity results. Section 5 presents details of the implementation of the strong update analysis in LLVM as an extension of the flow-insensitive analysis already existing in that framework. Section 6 presents results of an experimental evaluation of the strong update analysis measuring both its practical efficiency and the benefits to precision. The results show that the performance of the strong update analysis is comparable to that of the flow-insensitive analysis, and that the analysis provides the same benefits as a fully flow-sensitive analysis at 98% of stores and loads. Section 7 surveys other work related to efficient flow-sensitive points-to analysis. Finally, Section 8 concludes.

2. Background

This section defines the program model and the notation that will be used throughout the rest of the paper, briefly reviews flow-insensitive subset-based points-to analysis (often called Andersen's analysis [1]), and specifies a flow-sensitive extension of that analysis.

The program model commonly used in the points-to analysis literature and in the points-to analysis implementation in LLVM represents the program using a control flow graph containing the four kinds of pointer-manipulating instructions shown in the left column of Figure 1. More complicated statements that manipulate pointers (such as statements containing multiple levels of indirection) are decomposed into these basic instructions. The ADDROF instruction is used to model all statements that cause a pointer p to point to some new target a. This includes not only statements that take the address of a variable, but also statements that allocate new objects dynamically, in which case the pointer target is the statement at which the allocation takes place, the allocation site. The COPY instruction is used to model all copying of one pointer to another, including the interprocedural copying of arguments to procedure parameters due to procedure calls. The STORE and LOAD instructions model dereferencing of and writes and reads through pointers.

$p = \&a$	$\{a\} \subseteq pt(p)$	[ADDROF]
$p = q$	$pt(q) \subseteq pt(p)$	[COPY]
$*p = q$	$\forall a \in pt(p) \,.\, pt(q) \subseteq pt(a)$	[STORE]
$p = *q$	$\forall a \in pt(q) \,.\, pt(a) \subseteq pt(p)$	[LOAD]

Figure 1. Constraints for flow-insensitive subset-based points-to analysis

For simplicity of presentation, we follow the LLVM convention of separating variables into two disjoint sets of top-level and address-taken variables. The set $\mathcal{A}$ is defined to contain all possible targets of a pointer, including address-taken variables and dynamic allocation sites. The set $\mathcal{P}$ contains all top-level pointer variables. The instructions in Figure 1 are restricted to operate only on top-level pointers $p, q \in \mathcal{P}$, except for the ADDROF instruction that takes the address of an address-taken variable $a \in \mathcal{A}$. If a program contains a variable v violating this restriction (i.e. it has its address taken, and is also used in a copy, store, or load instruction), the program is transformed into an equivalent program that replaces v with a separate top-level pointer p_v and target variable a_v by adding the instruction $p_v = \&a_v$ and replacing all occurrences of v in the original program with $*p_v$. The set of all variables is denoted $\mathcal{V} = \mathcal{P} \cup \mathcal{A}$. We use a, b, and c to range over $\mathcal{A}$, p, q, and r to range over $\mathcal{P}$, and v and w to range over $\mathcal{V}$.

The flow-insensitive points-to relation $pt : \mathcal{V} \rightarrow 2^{\mathcal{A}}$, is defined as the least solution to the subset constraints shown in Figure 1. For each pointer in the program, it provides a set of targets to which the pointer may point. The solution can be computed by initializing all points-to sets to the empty set, then iteratively choosing a subset constraint that is violated and propagating the contents of the points-to set on the left-hand-side of the constraint into the right-hand-side, thereby satisfying the constraint. In formal terms, this process is equivalent to applying a monotone function on the cartesian product lattice of the powerset lattices $2^{\mathcal{A}}$ associated with each of the individual points-to sets. The height of this lattice is finite. The constraints therefore have a unique least solution, and the iterative process converges to it [10].

The concretization of a given points-to analysis result is defined as all execution states in which the C expression $v == \&a$ evaluates to false for all v and a for which $a \notin pt(v)$.

The feature that distinguishes a flow-sensitive analysis from a flow-insensitive one is that the flow-sensitive analysis takes control flow between instructions into account and computes a possibly different result for each program point. The subset-based points-to analysis can be extended to be flow-sensitive as shown in Figure 2. Each instruction is annotated with a label $\ell \in \mathcal{L}$ to indicate its position in the control flow graph. The points-to relation is extended with an extra parameter that dictates the program point at which the points-to information applies. The notation $\overline{\ell}$ and $\underline{\ell}$ indicates the program points immediately before and after the instruction labelled ℓ, respectively. For example, $pt[\underline{\ell}](v)$ gives the points-to set of pointer v after the instruction labelled ℓ. The subset constraints modelling the four kinds of instructions are similar to those in the flow-insensitive analysis, except they now relate a points-to set before each instruction with a points-to set after that instruction. The new CFLOW constraints model the effect of control flow: whenever ℓ_2 follows ℓ_1 in the control flow graph, the points-to sets before ℓ_2 contain everything contained in the points-to sets after ℓ_1. The new PRESERVE constraint accounts for the fact that any pointers not affected by an instruction maintain the values that they had before the instruction executed. For each pointer v not in the kill set of the instruction, the points-to set after the instruction contains all the targets that were in the points-to

$$\begin{array}{llr}
\ell : p = \&a & \{a\} \subseteq pt[\overline{\ell}](p) & \text{[AddrOf]} \\
\ell : p = q & pt[\overline{\ell}](q) \subseteq pt[\underline{\ell}](p) & \text{[Copy]} \\
\ell : *p = q & \forall a \in pt[\overline{\ell}](p) \,.\, pt[\overline{\ell}](q) \subseteq pt[\underline{\ell}](a) & \text{[Store]} \\
\ell : p = *q & \forall a \in pt[\overline{\ell}](q) \,.\, pt[\overline{\ell}](a) \subseteq pt[\underline{\ell}](p) & \text{[Load]} \\
\ell_1 \in pred(\ell_2) & \forall v \in \mathcal{V} \,.\, pt[\underline{\ell_1}](v) \subseteq pt[\overline{\ell_2}](v) & \text{[CFlow]} \\
\ell \in \mathcal{L} & \forall v \in \mathcal{V} \setminus kill(\ell) \,.\, pt[\overline{\ell}](v) \subseteq pt[\underline{\ell}](v) & \text{[Preserve]}
\end{array}$$

Figure 2. Constraints for flow-sensitive subset-based points-to analysis

set before the instruction. For a simple implementation of a flow-sensitive analysis, it is sufficient (and sound) to define all the kill sets to be empty, so that the PRESERVE subset constraints apply to every pointer at every instruction.

Following past work on flow-sensitive points-to analysis, we focus on path-insensitive analysis (i.e. the analysis ignores condition expressions in conditional branches). Path-sensitive analyses are a different compromise in the tradeoff between analysis precision and efficiency, and they are beyond the scope of our study.

Additional precision can be obtained using strong updates, which are implemented in the analysis by defining kill sets that are not empty. A strong update occurs when it is known that an instruction completely overwrites a previous value of a given pointer. In this case, the pointer is listed in the kill set of the instruction to prevent the PRESERVE constraints from propagating the previous value of the pointer through the instruction.

To soundly include an abstract pointer v in the kill set, we must be sure that the instruction definitely writes to v, and that the abstract pointer v represents no more than a single concrete pointer in the execution of the program. For example, if v is a dynamic allocation site, an instruction may overwrite one but not all of the objects allocated there, so it would be unsound to include v in the kill set. In Section 5, we will define a set $singletons \subseteq \mathcal{V}$ of abstract pointers corresponding to a single concrete pointer at run time.

Precise kill sets to implement strong updates are defined in Figure 3. Each of the ADDROF, COPY, and LOAD instructions overwrites a target top-level pointer p, so that pointer is in the kill set. For a STORE instruction $*p = q$, the kill set depends on the points-to set of p before the instruction. If its size is greater than 1, the analysis cannot determine which of the targets will be overwritten, so the kill set is empty (because no specific target is certain to be overwritten). If its size is exactly 1, and the unique target a is in *singletons*, then the instruction will definitely overwrite a, so a is in the kill set.

For correctness, we must also consider the case when the points-to set of p is empty. It is tempting but incorrect to suggest that in this case, the instruction cannot have any effect (except to dereference a null pointer, halting the program), so the kill set should be empty. Such a definition would violate the monotonicity of the subset constraints, which would invalidate the guarantee of a unique least solution and cause the analysis to loop forever on some programs without converging to a fixed point. Concretely, suppose the points-to set of p before $\ell : *p = q$ were empty, so that PRESERVE constraints would be created at ℓ for all variables. Later, some target a might be added to the points-to set of p and therefore to the kill set of ℓ. This would entail the removal of the PRESERVE constraint for a. But this constraint might have been responsible for causing a to be in the points-to set of p in the first place, so fully removing the constraint would require removing a from the points-to set of p, thus forcing the constraint to be added back again. Thus the analysis would loop forever.

When the points-to set of p is empty, the correct definition of the kill set is $\mathcal{V}$, the set of all variables. As a result, no PRESERVE constraints are generated until the points-to set of p becomes non-empty. No subset constraints ever need to be removed after they

$$kill(\ell : p = \ldots) \triangleq \{p\}$$

$$kill(\ell : *p = q) \triangleq \begin{cases} \{\} & \text{if } |pt[\overline{\ell}](p)| > 1 \\ \{\} & \text{if } pt[\overline{\ell}](p) = \{a\} \wedge a \notin singletons \\ \{a\} & \text{if } pt[\overline{\ell}](p) = \{a\} \wedge a \in singletons \\ \mathcal{V} & \text{if } pt[\overline{\ell}](p) = \{\} \end{cases}$$

Figure 3. Definition of kill sets

$$\begin{array}{l}
1 : p_a = \&a \\
2 : p_b = \&b \\
3 : p_c = \&c \\
4 : *p_a = p_b \\
5 : *p_a = p_c
\end{array}$$

Figure 4. Example of straight-line code on which flow sensitivity improves precision

are generated, so the non-monotonicity of the constraints and non-termination of the analysis are avoided. Suggesting that a dereference of an empty points-to set kills the values of all pointers may be surprising, but it is sound. If p can only point to null, dereferencing p causes the program to abort, and therefore the values of any pointers before the null dereference cannot be observed anywhere in the program after the dereference. Since the statements after the null dereference are unreachable, from the point of view of abstract interpretation, their points-to sets should be $\perp$, and indeed, in the points-to domain, this value corresponds to all points-to sets being empty.

3. Design Overview

In this section, we present the design objectives for the strong update points-to analysis. We begin with a discussion of the beneficial effects of flow sensitivity in a points-to analysis that are desirable in our strong update analysis. We then discuss the performance trade-offs that are made to achieve those precision improvements.

3.1 Benefits of flow sensitivity

The advantage of flow sensitivity can be classified into two benefits: handling of straight-line code and strong updates. Of the two, strong updates generally provide the greater improvement in precision. The strong update algorithm that we will present aims to provide the benefit of strong updates at a cost comparable to that of a flow-insensitive analysis.

The flow-sensitive points-to analysis that was presented in Figure 2 provides some improvement in precision even without strong updates (i.e. when all of the kill sets are defined to be empty). If the program being analyzed contains code that is not inside any loop and can never be executed more than once, a flow-sensitive analysis can determine that facts established at the end of such code do not yet hold at the beginning of such code. For example, consider the short program in Figure 4. The program sets pointer a to point to b in line 4 and then to c in line 5. A flow-insensitive analysis would report that $pt(a) = \{b, c\}$. A flow-sensitive analysis, even one without strong updates, would determine that after line 4, a does not yet point to c: $pt[\underline{4}](a) = \{b\}$. Thus flow sensitivity improves precision for this program even without strong updates.

However, this benefit is brittle: if the same code appeared inside a loop, the analysis would determine that $pt[\ell](a) = \{b, c\}$ at all points ℓ. More generally, we can show that the points-to sets at every point inside a given loop are always identical:

Proposition 1. *Suppose that there is a cycle in the interprocedural control flow graph leading from ℓ_1 to ℓ_2 and back to ℓ_1. Then if all the kill sets are empty, $pt[\underline{\ell_1}](v) = pt[\underline{\ell_2}](v)$ for every variable v.*

Proof. The cycle in the control flow graph induces a similar cycle of CFLOW and PRESERVE constraints $pt[\underline{\ell_1}](v) \subseteq \cdots \subseteq pt[\underline{\ell_2}](v) \subseteq \cdots \subseteq pt[\underline{\ell_1}](v)$. Thus $pt[\underline{\ell_1}](v) = pt[\underline{\ell_2}](v)$. □

Most of the code of most programs is found inside loops. Many compiler optimizations target loops because loop bodies are where the most frequently executed code appears. Even many long straight-line sequences of code occur inside a large outer loop. For example, long-running programs such as web servers or database servers run most of their code inside an outer loop that handles individual requests. Relying on code to be outside of any loop is also brittle. For example, when a program is incorporated into a benchmark suite, it is generally invoked from a test harness that executes it multiple times, in a loop. In all of these cases, due to Proposition 1, a flow-sensitive analysis without strong updates would compute the same points-to sets at all program points inside the loop. That is, its result would be no more precise than that of a flow-insensitive analysis.

We therefore focus the design of the strong update analysis algorithm on providing the benefits of strong updates at low cost. The benefit of precisely handling straight-line code is minimal, and it is difficult to achieve without an expensive analysis that maintains distinct, large points-to sets at different program points. On the other hand, we will show how to achieve the more significant benefit of strong updates within the quadratic space and cubic time bounds of a flow-insensitive analysis.

3.2 Using SSA form for strong updates of top-level variables

The kill sets from Figure 3 define strong updates of both top-level variables (the first definition in the figure) and of address-taken pointer targets (the second definition). It is well known that the effect of strong updates of top-level variables can be easily achieved by first converting the program to Static Single Assignment (SSA) form [9]. In SSA form, every variable is written to only once. Conversion to SSA form requires identifying all of the writes to a variable. Therefore, for a program with pointers, SSA conversion requires points-to information to enumerate the indirect writes to variables through pointers, so full SSA conversion cannot be done before the points-to analysis. However, since top-level variables cannot be accessed through pointers, it is possible to convert the top-level variables into SSA form prior to points-to analysis. Specifically, we require the program to be converted to strict SSA form, which enforces that every use of a variable is dominated by its (unique) definition. We can show that for a program whose top-level variables are in strict SSA form, a flow-insensitive analysis provides the precision of flow-sensitive analysis with strong updates for top-level variables:

Proposition 2. *Given a program whose top-level variables are in strict SSA form, a top-level variable p whose unique definition is at ℓ_d, and an arbitrary label ℓ_u at which p is used, a flow-sensitive points-to analysis with strong updates will determine that $pt[\overline{\ell_u}](p) = pt[\underline{\ell_d}](p)$.*

Proof. Since the program is in strict SSA form, there is a path in the ICFG from ℓ_d to ℓ_u, so $pt[\underline{\ell_d}](p) \subseteq \cdots \subseteq pt[\overline{\ell_u}](p)$ (using CFLOW and PRESERVE constraints and the fact that no instruction other than ℓ_d kills p). Notice that in the constraints in Figure 2, whenever the points-to set $pt[\ell](p)$ of a top-level variable p appears on the right-hand side of a constraint, either there is a definition of p at ℓ, or the left-hand side of the constraint also contains the same top-level variable (i.e., the constraint is $pt[\ell'](p) \subseteq pt[\ell](p)$, where ℓ' is some other label). The only label ℓ for which there can be a constraint whose left-hand side is not a points-to set of p is ℓ_d, the unique definition of p. Therefore, every path $\{a\} \subseteq \cdots \subseteq pt[\overline{\ell_u}](p)$ of constraints from a pointer target $\&a$ to $pt[\overline{\ell_u}](p)$ must pass through $pt[\underline{\ell_d}](p)$. Since the analysis finds the least solution, the only pointer targets in $pt[\overline{\ell_u}](p)$ will be ones for which there is such a path, and are therefore also in $pt[\underline{\ell_d}](p)$. That is, $pt[\overline{\ell_u}](p) \subseteq pt[\underline{\ell_d}](p)$. Since we also showed that $pt[\underline{\ell_d}](p) \subseteq pt[\overline{\ell_u}](p)$, we conclude that $pt[\overline{\ell_u}](p) = pt[\underline{\ell_d}](p)$. □

$\ell : p = \&a$	$\{a\} \subseteq pt(p)$	[ADDROF]
$\ell : p = q$	$pt(q) \subseteq pt(p)$	[COPY]
$\ell : *p = q$	$\forall a \in pt(p) \,.\, pt(q) \subseteq pt[\underline{\ell}](a)$	[STORE]
$\ell : p = *q$	$\forall a \in pt(q) \,.\, pt[\overline{\ell}](a) \subseteq pt(p)$	[LOAD]
$\ell_1 \in pred(\ell_2)$	$\forall a \in \mathcal{A} \,.\, pt[\underline{\ell_1}](a) \subseteq pt[\overline{\ell_2}](a)$	[CFLOW]
$\ell \in \mathcal{L}$	$\forall a \in \mathcal{A} \setminus kill(\ell) \,.\, pt[\overline{\ell}](a) \subseteq pt[\underline{\ell}](a)$	[PRESERVE]

Figure 5. Constraints for flow-sensitive subset-based points-to analysis on SSA form

As a result of Proposition 2, we can merge all of the flow-sensitive points-to sets $pt[*](p)$ of p into a single flow-insensitive points-to set $pt(p)$ without reducing the precision of the analysis. The subset constraints after this simplification are shown in Figure 5. Note that the CFLOW and PRESERVE constraints for a top-level variable p reduce to the trivial $pt(p) \subseteq pt(p)$ and are therefore not needed. While this analysis is as precise as the flow-sensitive analysis, it has regained some of the simplicity of the flow-insensitive analysis. The space required to store the points-to sets has been reduced from $O(|\mathcal{V}||\mathcal{L}||\mathcal{A}|)$ to $O(|\mathcal{P}||\mathcal{A}| + |\mathcal{A}|^2|\mathcal{L}|)$.

SSA transformation has also been used as a preparatory step for sparse analysis of top-level variables [17], which follows def-use chains between top-level variables instead of paths in the control flow graph. SSA form simplifies these def-use chains.

3.3 Quadratic-space representation of points-to sets of pointer targets

To achieve space requirements that are quadratic in the size of the program, we must further reduce the $|\mathcal{A}|^2|\mathcal{L}|$ term in the above bound, which is due to the size of the points-to sets $pt[\underline{\ell}](a)$ of address-taken variables. The strong update algorithm does this by taking advantage of the following insights:

- Most of the precision benefit of flow-sensitivity comes from strong updates.
- A strong update requires the points-to set of the dereferenced pointer to contain at most one pointer target.
- A singleton points-to set is cheap to store and manipulate.
- Any larger points-to sets will not directly enable strong updates, so there is little benefit in spending much space or time storing them.

Therefore, the strong update analysis stores points-to sets of pointer targets flow sensitively when they are singletons, and only flow insensitively when they are larger.

To implement this, we define the singleton-set lattice $\mathcal{S}$ as shown in Figure 6. An element of this lattice is either the empty set, a singleton set, or $\top$ indicating some larger set. For each program point ℓ and for each pointer target a, the analysis stores an element of this lattice $su[\underline{\ell}](a)$. However, unlike in a constant propagation analysis, the value of $\top$ in the strong update analysis does not immediately imply that a pointer can point to anything. Instead, the analysis *also* stores a flow-insensitive points-to set $pt(a)$ for each pointer target a to be used when the flow-sensitive analysis indicates $\top$. The STORE constraint updates both $pt(a)$ and $su[\underline{\ell}](a)$ if

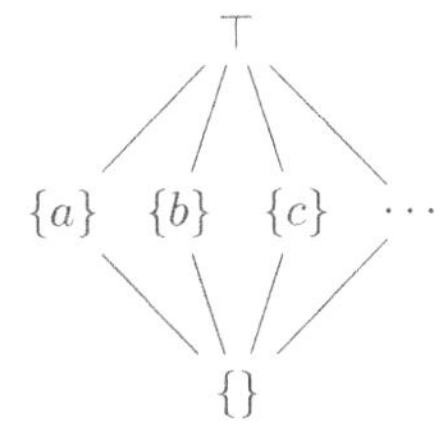

Figure 6. The singleton-set lattice $\mathcal{S}$

$\ell : p = \&a$	$\{a\} \subseteq pt(p)$	[ADDROF]
$\ell : p = q$	$pt(q) \subseteq pt(p)$	[COPY]
$\ell : *p = q$	$\forall a \in pt(p) \, . \, pt(q) \sqsubseteq su[\underline{\ell}](a)$ $\forall a \in pt(p) \, . \, pt(q) \subseteq pt(a)$	[STORE]
$\ell : p = *q$	$\forall a \in pt(q) \, . \, ptsu[\overline{\ell}](a) \subseteq pt(p)$	[LOAD]
$\ell_1 \in pred(\ell_2)$	$\forall a \in \mathcal{A} \, . \, su[\underline{\ell_1}](a) \sqsubseteq su[\overline{\ell_2}](a)$	[CFLOW]
$\ell \in \mathcal{L}$	$\forall a \in \mathcal{A} \setminus kill(\ell) \, . \, su[\overline{\ell}](a) \sqsubseteq su[\underline{\ell}](a)$	[PRESERVE]

$$\text{Where } ptsu[\overline{\ell}](a) \triangleq \begin{cases} su[\overline{\ell}](a) & \text{if } su[\overline{\ell}](a) \neq \top \\ pt(a) & \text{if } su[\overline{\ell}](a) = \top \end{cases}$$

Figure 7. Constraints for Strong Update Analysis

the points-to set of the variable q being stored is a singleton (and sets $su[\underline{\ell}](a)$ to $\top$ if it is not). When the LOAD constraint needs the points-to set of a at $\overline{\ell}$, it first looks for a possible singleton by consulting $su[\overline{\ell}](a)$; if this returns $\top$, it falls back on the points-to set $pt(a)$. This is implemented by the *ptsu* function in Figure 7. Only the small *su* sets need to be propagated flow-sensitively along the control flow edges of the program, so the CFLOW and PRESERVE constraints act only on these sets. The possibly large *pt* sets are stored only once for the whole program. As a result, the space bound of this representation is $O(|\mathcal{P}||\mathcal{A}| + |\mathcal{A}|^2 + |\mathcal{L}||\mathcal{A}|)$, reflecting the space requirements of the points-to sets of $\mathcal{P}$, the points-to sets of $\mathcal{A}$, and the sets *su*, respectively.

Of course, it is possible to construct examples on which this simplification loses precision compared to a fully flow-sensitive analysis.

```
p = &a;
*p = &b;
if(*) *p = &c; else *p = &d;
q = *p;
r = *q;
```

Both the strong update analysis and the flow-sensitive analysis will perform strong updates at all three stores. At the final load, $su[\overline{\ell}](a) = \top$ due to the control flow merge, so the flow-insensitive points-to set $pt(a) = \{b, c, d\}$ will be propagated to r in the strong update analysis, whereas the flow-sensitive analysis would propagate $\{c, d\}$. However, as we will see in Section 6, such examples are very rare in practice.

Although the asymptotic complexity of the strong update representation is low, we should also consider actual behaviour on realistic programs. In most programs, only a small number of pointer targets a will have singleton points-to sets at a given label. Thus the representation of the sets $su[\underline{\ell}]$ at each program point ℓ should be worst-case linear not only in $|\mathcal{A}|$, but also in the (much smaller) subset of pointer targets a for which $su[\underline{\ell}](a)$ is a singleton. Since $su[\underline{\ell}](a) = \top$ for most values of a, we use a map storing only those pointer targets whose associated value is not $\top$, and default to $\top$ when we do not find a particular pointer target in the table. There is one other special case, however. Following a store through a pointer p whose points-to set is empty, $su[\underline{\ell}](a) = \{\}$ for all values of a. Therefore, in our implementation, we use a boolean flag to indicate this special value. When the flag is true, $su[\underline{\ell}](a) = \{\}$ for all values of a. When the flag is false, a map stores the values of $su[\underline{\ell}](a)$ other than $\top$, and $\top$ is returned when a pointer target is not found in the map. This hybrid representation is compact in all of the common use cases. As we will see in Section 6, the mean number of entries in each map is less than 2.2 in all of the SPEC benchmarks.

3.4 Sparse Allocation of Labels

Almost all practical flow-sensitive analyses share the representation of flow-sensitive facts for successive program points at which the facts cannot change, and the same can be done for the strong update analysis. We do this by removing redundant labels from the program representation. In our discussion thus far, every instruction was assigned its own unique label ℓ. However, most instructions do not change the points-to sets of address taken variables $a \in \mathcal{A}$. The only instructions whose outgoing *su* value is different from its incoming *su* value are STORE instructions, instructions with multiple control flow predecessors (i.e. control flow merges), and the very first instruction in the program.

When it is certain that the *su* sets at one instruction are identical to those at its predecessor, we assign both instructions the same label. Specifically, we relabel the instructions in the program in the following way. First, every STORE instruction is assigned a unique label. Second, at every control flow merge point, we add a new no-op instruction and give it a unique label. The *su* value computed at this label will be the join of the *su* values at the control flow predecessors. Third, we add a no-op instruction at the very beginning of the program and also give it a unique label. The *su* value computed at this label will be $\lambda a.\top$, meaning that no flow-sensitive information is known. Finally, we label every other instruction with the label of its (unique) control flow predecessor. As a result, every label in the program can be classified as either a store, a merge, or a clear (the beginning of the program). In particular, every LOAD instruction in the program is now labelled with the same label as the most recent instruction at which the *su* value may have changed.

After this relabelling process, it is necessary to update the references to program points in the constraints from Figure 7. The notation $\overline{\ell}$ and $\underline{\ell}$ for the program points immediately before and after the instruction at ℓ may no longer designate the appropriate program points when there are multiple instructions with the same label ℓ. Instead of distinguishing $su[\overline{\ell}]$ and $su[\underline{\ell}]$, the strong update analysis algorithm defines one strong update value $su[\ell]$ for each label ℓ. The value $su[\ell]$ is defined to describe the program state at the point immediately after the first instruction at label ℓ. By construction, this first instruction is always a STORE or a no-op. Because a STORE instruction is always the first instruction at its label, the $su[\underline{\ell}]$ in the STORE constraint from Figure 7 is equivalent to $su[\ell']$, where ℓ' is the new label of the instruction. Similarly, because a LOAD instruction always comes after the first instruction at a label, the $ptsu[\overline{\ell}]$ in the LOAD constraint is equivalent to $ptsu[\ell']$, where ℓ' is the new label of the instruction. Thus, in the remainder of this paper, we no longer use the notation $\overline{\ell}$ and $\underline{\ell}$, but use simply ℓ to refer to the program point immediately after the first instruction with label ℓ.

4. Strong Update Analysis Algorithm

This section presents the strong update analysis algorithm used to solve the constraints of Figure 7. The algorithm is an extension of the flow-insensitive subset-based points-to analysis algorithm already implemented in LLVM and other compilers. We therefore begin with a brief review of that algorithm, and follow it with an explanation of the extensions that enable strong updates.

The original flow-insensitive algorithm that solves the constraints of Figure 1 is shown in Figure 8. The core data structure,

1 **foreach** AddrOf constraint $p = \&a$ **do** $pt(p) \cup= \{a\}$; $worklist \cup= \{p\}$ **od**
2 **foreach** Copy constraint $p = q$ **do** $graph \cup= \{q \rightarrow p\}$ **od**
3 **while** $worklist \neq \{\}$ **do**
4 remove a variable v from *worklist*
5 $\Delta \leftarrow pt(v) \setminus oldpt(v)$
6 $oldpt(v) \leftarrow pt(v)$
7 **foreach** Store constraint $*v = q$ **do foreach** $a \in \Delta$ **do** AddEdge(q, a) **od od**
8 **foreach** Load constraint $p = *v$ **do** ProcessLoad(p, Δ) **od**
9 **foreach** $v \rightarrow w \in graph$ **do**
10 $pt(w) \cup= \Delta$
11 **if** $pt(w)$ changed **then** $worklist \cup= \{w\}$ **fi**
12 **od**
13 **od**
14 **proc** ProcessLoad(p, Δ)
15 **foreach** $a \in \Delta$ **do** AddEdge(a, p) **od**
16 **endproc**
17 **proc** AddEdge(v, w)
18 **if** $v \rightarrow w \notin graph$ **then** $graph \cup= \{v \rightarrow w\}$; $pt(w) \cup= pt(v)$; **if** $pt(w)$ changed **then** $worklist \cup= \{w\}$ **fi fi**
19 **endproc**

Figure 8. Original Flow-insensitive Points-to Analysis Algorithm in LLVM

graph, maintains a set of edges corresponding to the subset constraints being solved. The presence of the edge $v \rightarrow w$ corresponds to the subset constraint $pt(v) \subseteq pt(w)$. The *graph* is initialized with the constraints corresponding to Copy instructions in Line 2, and the constraints induced by Store and Load instructions are added to it as they are discovered during the analysis. The *worklist* keeps track of the variables $v \in \mathcal{V}$ whose points-to set has grown since the variable was last processed. The body of the main loop in Lines 3 to 13 is executed for each such variable. In Lines 9 to 12, the new elements are propagated along the edges in the constraint *graph*; as a result, all of the subset constraints with v on their left-hand side become satisfied. Any other variables whose points-to sets grow in the process are added to the worklist. Lines 7 and 8 and the ProcessLoad and AddEdge helper procedures add new subset constraints induced by Store and Load instructions to the *graph*. Whenever a new constraint $v \rightarrow w$ is added, the AddEdge procedure immediately propagates the existing contents of $pt(v)$ into $pt(w)$ in Line 18. This is necessary because the normal propagation in Lines 9 to 12 propagates only the part of the points-to set that was added since the last propagation. The algorithm maintains the invariant that if for any variable v, there may be a constraint $pt(v) \subseteq pt(w)$ that is not satisfied, then v is on the worklist. Therefore, once the worklist empties, all of the constraints are satisfied. Every iteration increases the size of $oldpt(v)$, and since every *oldpt* is a subset of $\mathcal{A}$, the iteration must eventually terminate.

The extended algorithm that enables strong updates and solves the constraints of Figure 7 is shown in Figure 9. The lines marked with asterisks are additions to the original flow-insensitive algorithm. Lines not marked with asterisks are identical to or only trivially changed from corresponding lines in the flow-insensitive algorithm of Figure 8.

An important change is in the worklist: in the strong update algorithm, the worklist holds not only variables v whose subset constraints need to be reprocessed, but additionally labels ℓ whose *su* constraints need to be reprocessed. More precisely, the algorithm maintains the following invariants:

1. If there is a constraint $pt(v) \subseteq pt(w)$ that is not satisfied, then v is on the worklist.
2. If there is a Load or Store instruction dereferencing p that induces subset constraints not already in *graph*, then p is on the worklist.
3. If there is a constraint $ptsu[\ell](a) \subseteq pt(p)$ induced by a Load that is not satisfied, then a is on the worklist.
4. If there is a constraint of the form $su[\ell](a) \sqsubseteq su[\ell'](a')$ that is not satisfied, then ℓ is on the worklist.
5. If there is a Store instruction ($\ell : *p = q$) that induces the constraint $pt(q) \sqsubseteq su[\ell](a)$ and this constraint is not satisfied, then ℓ is on the worklist.

The first two invariants were already present in the original flow-insensitive points-to analysis algorithm. Invariant 3 is a variation of Invariant 1 adapted to the modified constraint involving *ptsu* that is induced by a Load instruction. Invariants 4 and 5 ensure that all violated constraints involving *su* are tracked by the worklist and eventually satisfied. We will explain how the invariants are maintained shortly.

First, however, we explain how the algorithm processes a label ℓ appearing on the worklist. As was explained in Section 3.4, each label is associated with either a clear, a control flow merge, or a unique store instruction $\ell : *p = q$. The first two possibilities are handled in the obvious manner in Lines 17 and 18. The interesting case is that of a Store instruction. If $pt(p)$ is empty, then $su[\ell]$ remains at $\bot$ (i.e. $\lambda a.\{\}$), as was explained in Section 2, so nothing needs to be done (Line 20). Note that it is not possible for $pt(p)$ to be empty when $su[\ell]$ is not $\bot$, because all of the code that modifies $su[\ell]$ is conditional on $pt(p)$ being non-empty, and $pt(p)$ never shrinks, so once it is non-empty, it can never become empty again. When $pt(p)$ is non-empty, the algorithm needs to establish the constraints $\forall a \in pt(p) \,.\, pt(q) \sqsubseteq su[\ell](a)$ due to the Store instruction. The algorithm first converts $pt(q)$ into an element of the singleton set lattice of Figure 6, substituting $\top$ if $pt(q)$ is not a singleton set; this is done by the PtToSu procedure. Then a strong or weak update is done to $su[\ell]$. If the points-to set of p is a singleton $\{a\}$, the target a of p is certain to be overwritten by the store, so the algorithm simply assigns PtToSu(q) to $su[\ell](a)$, overwriting the existing value (which came from the control flow predecessor of ℓ in Line 21). This is a strong update (Line 24). If $pt(p)$ is not a singleton, weak updates to all the locations a to which p may be pointing are performed, by joining PtToSu(q) with the existing value of $su[\ell](a)$ which came from the control flow predecessor of ℓ (Line 25).

The processing of Load instructions is updated to take advantage of the flow-sensitive information available in *su* in Lines 34

```
1    foreach AddrOf constraint p = &a do pt(p) ∪= {a}; worklist ∪= {p} od
2    foreach Copy constraint p = q do graph ∪= {q → p} od
3    while worklist ≠ {} do
4      remove a variable v or a label ℓ from worklist
5      if a variable v was removed then
6        Δ ← pt(v) \ oldpt(v)
7        oldpt(v) ← pt(v)
8*       foreach Store constraint ℓ : *v = q do worklist ∪= {ℓ} od
9*       worklist ∪= affected[v]
10       foreach Store constraint ℓ : *v = q do foreach a ∈ Δ do AddEdge(q, a) od od
11       foreach Load constraint ℓ : p = *v do ProcessLoad(ℓ, p, Δ) od
12       foreach v → w ∈ graph do
13         pt(w) ∪= Δ
14         if pt(w) changed then worklist ∪= {w} fi
15       od
16*    else // a label ℓ was removed
17*      if ℓ is a clear then su[ℓ] ← λa.⊤
18*      else if ℓ is a merge then su[ℓ] ← ⊔_{ℓ'∈pred(ℓ)} su[ℓ']
19*      else // ℓ is a store *p = q
20*        if pt(p) = {} then continue fi
21*        su[ℓ] ← su[pred(ℓ)]
22*        if |pt(q)| ≤ 1 then affected[q] ∪= {ℓ} else affected[q] \= {ℓ} fi
23*        if pt(p) = {a} and a ∈ singletons
24*          then su[ℓ](a) ← PtToSu(q)  // strong update
25*          else foreach a ∈ pt(p) do su[ℓ](a) ⊔= PtToSu(q) od fi // weak update
26*      fi
27*      if su[ℓ] changed then
28*        worklist ∪= succ(ℓ)
29*        foreach Load constraint ℓ : p = *q do ProcessLoad(ℓ, p, pt(q)) od
30*      fi
31   fi od
32   proc ProcessLoad(ℓ, p, Δ)
33     foreach a ∈ Δ do
34*      if su[ℓ](a) = ⊤
35         then AddEdge(a, p)
36*        else pt(p) ∪= su[ℓ](a); if pt(p) changed then worklist ∪= {p} fi fi
37   od endproc
38   proc AddEdge(v, w)
39     if v → w ∉ graph then graph ∪= {v → w}; pt(w) ∪= pt(v); if pt(w) changed then worklist ∪= {w} fi fi
40   endproc
41*  proc PtToSu(q)
42*    if |pt(q)| ≤ 1 and pt(q) ⊆ singletons then return pt(q) else return ⊤ fi
43*  endproc
```

Figure 9. Strong Update Points-to Analysis Algorithm

and 36. These lines simply implement the *ptsu* function and the modified LOAD constraint that uses it from Figure 7. Whereas in the original flow-insensitive algorithm, a subset constraint $a \to p$ was added to *graph* unconditionally, it is now done only when $su[\ell](a)$ is $\top$; otherwise, only $su[\ell](a)$ is propagated to $pt(p)$.

The algorithm must ensure that it maintains the invariants enumerated earlier. Invariants 1 and 2 are guaranteed by the existing code from the original flow-insensitive algorithm and by the similar addition of p to the *worklist* in Line 36. Invariant 3 for a LOAD $\ell : *p = q$ can be violated when, for some $a \in pt(p)$, either $su[\ell](a)$ changes, or $su[\ell](a) = \top$ and $pt(a)$ changes. The first case is handled by Line 29, which calls ProcessLoad, which updates $pt(p)$ to restore the invariant in Line 36. The second case is handled the same way as in the original flow-insensitive algorithm: when $su[\ell](a)$ becomes $\top$, an edge $a \to p$ is added to *graph* in Line 35, which establishes the invariant and ensures that it remains established in response to changes in $pt(a)$ using the normal propagation code of Lines 12 to 15. Invariant 4 applies to constraints modelling control flow in the program. Line 28 restores the invariant by ensuring that whenever $su[\ell]$ changes, every control-flow successor of ℓ is added to the *worklist*. Invariant 5 is the most complicated. For a given STORE $\ell : *p = q$, the invariant can be invalidated when either $pt(p)$ or $pt(q)$ grows. Growth of $pt(p)$ is detected by the loop on Line 8. Growth of $pt(q)$ is handled by Line 9, by adding all *affected* stores to the *worklist*. The *affected* array is used to keep track of all the STORES $\ell : *p = q$ whose invariant may be invalidated by a change in $pt(q)$. These are all stores whose right-hand side is q, but excluding those for which $pt(q)$ was already seen to be a non-singleton in Line 22 and whose *su* values are therefore already $\top$. Line 22 ensures that the *affected* array is correctly maintained.

The invariants ensure that when the *worklist* is empty, all of the constraints of Figure 7 are satisfied. A variable v is added to the worklist only when $pt(v)$ grows. A label ℓ is added to the worklist only when some $su[\ell']$ grows or when ℓ labels a STORE $*p = q$ and either $pt(p)$ or $pt(q)$ has grown. Since each $pt(v)$ and $su[\ell]$ can grow only a finite number of times, the algorithm eventually terminates at a fixed point that satisfies all of the constraints. Since each update of $pt(v)$ or $su[\ell]$ is the application of a monotone function, and since the algorithm begins with all of these values at $\bot$, the fixed point at which it converges is the least fixed point of all the constraints.

4.1 Worst-case complexity

As we have already discussed in Section 3.3, the strong update algorithm maintains the quadratic space bound of the flow-insensitive points-to analysis algorithm. We will now show that the strong update algorithm also maintains the cubic time bound of the flow-insensitive algorithm.

For the worst-case analysis, we assume that the set propagation operation $s_1 \cup= s_2$ takes time proportional to the size of the set being propagated (i.e. $O(|s_2|)$ time).

Lemma 1. *The total number of times that a variable is removed from the worklist is $O(|\mathcal{V}||\mathcal{A}|)$, and the sum of the sizes of all the sets Δ computed in Line 6 is also $O(|\mathcal{V}||\mathcal{A}|)$.*

Proof. A given variable v is added to the worklist only when $pt(v)$ changes. Since the maximum size of $pt(v)$ is $|\mathcal{A}|$, and elements are never removed from $pt(v)$, $pt(v)$ can only change $|\mathcal{A}|$ times. Moreover, the sum of all the increases in the size of $pt(v)$ is at most $|\mathcal{A}|$. Thus a variable is added to the worklist $O(|\mathcal{V}||\mathcal{A}|)$ times and the sum of the sizes of Δ is also $O(|\mathcal{V}||\mathcal{A}|)$. □

Lemma 2. *The total number of times that a label is removed from the worklist is $O(E|\mathcal{A}|)$, where E is the number of edges in the interprocedural control flow graph.*

Proof. A given label ℓ is added to the worklist only when $su[\ell']$ changes for some $\ell' \in pred(\ell)$, or, if ℓ is a store $*p = q$, when $pt(p)$ or $pt(q)$ changes. The total number of times that the former can happen is at most $2E|\mathcal{A}|$, since for any given $a \in \mathcal{A}$, $su[\ell'](a)$ can change at most twice (from an empty set to a singleton, then to $\top$). The total number of times that the latter can happen is $2|\mathcal{A}|$ for any given store, or a total of $2|\mathcal{L}||\mathcal{A}|$ times. Since every label in the control flow graph has a predecessor (else it would not be reachable), $|\mathcal{L}| < E$, and so the total number of times that a label can be added to the worklist is $O(E|\mathcal{A}|)$. □

Theorem 1. *The worst-case running time of the strong update algorithm is $O(E|\mathcal{V}|^2)$, where E is the number of edges in the interprocedural control flow graph. Thus it is cubic in the size of the program being analyzed.*

Proof. By Lemma 1, the block from Line 6 to 15 is executed at most $O(|\mathcal{V}||\mathcal{A}|)$ times. Most of the lines in this block take at most $O(\max\{|\mathcal{V}|, |\mathcal{L}|\})$ time. The only exceptions are Lines 10 and 13, which take $O(|\mathcal{L}||\Delta|)$ and $O(|\mathcal{V}||\Delta|)$ time. Since the sum of the sizes of all the Δ sets is $O(|\mathcal{V}||\mathcal{A}|)$, the total time spent in these lines is $O(|\mathcal{V}||\mathcal{A}|(|\mathcal{L}| + |\mathcal{V}|))$. Since $|\mathcal{V}|$ is in $O(|\mathcal{L}|)$, the total amount of time spent in the block from Line 6 to 15 is $O(|\mathcal{V}||\mathcal{A}||\mathcal{L}|)$.

By Lemma 2, the block from Line 17 to 26 is executed at most $O(E|\mathcal{A}|)$ times. All of the operations in it complete in $O(|\mathcal{A}|)$ time, so the total time spent in this block is $O(|\mathcal{A}|^2|\mathcal{L}|)$.

For each load $\ell : p = *q$, ProcessLoad is called only when $su[\ell]$ or $pt(q)$ changes, each of which can happen $O(|\mathcal{A}|)$ times. Each call to ProcessLoad completes in $O(\mathcal{A})$ time. Therefore the total time spent in ProcessLoad is $O(|\mathcal{A}|^2|\mathcal{L}|)$.

AddEdge does a propagation taking $O(|\mathcal{A}|)$ time, but only when a new edge is added to *graph*, which can happen at most $O(|\mathcal{V}|^2)$ times, so the total time spent in AddEdge is $O(|\mathcal{V}|^2|\mathcal{A}|)$.

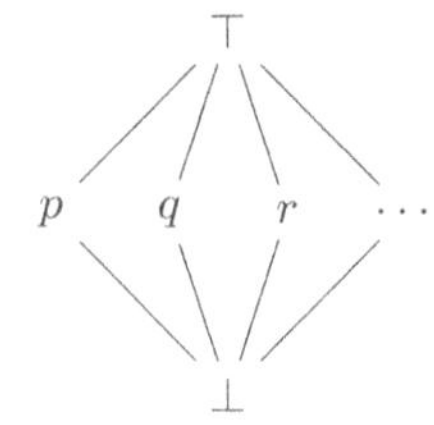

Figure 10. The top-level variable equivalence lattice

All of the bounds on the total time spent in each section of the algorithm are in $O(E|\mathcal{V}^2|)$, so the overall algorithm completes in $O(E|\mathcal{V}^2|)$ time. □

In general graphs, the number of edges can be up to quadratic in the number of vertices. However, it is well known that control flow graphs are very sparse, since most instructions have one successor, some have two (conditional branches), and few rare ones have more (switch statements and indirect function calls). Other complexity analyses of flow-sensitive points-to analysis also rely on this empirical fact [13].

4.2 An improvement: equivalence to top-level variables

The precision of the strong update algorithm can be further improved "for free" by a small extension to the lattice from which $su[\ell](a)$ values are chosen. Given a store $*p = q$ where $pt(p) = \{a\}$, the lattice presented so far (and shown in Figure 6) can represent the fact that $pt(a)$ is a singleton set after the store, if $pt(q)$ happens to be a singleton set. However, the analysis can be easily extended to track that $pt(a) = pt(q)$ even when $pt(q)$ is not a singleton, and this extension has no effect on the asymptotic complexity. In the extended analysis, $su[\ell]$ maps each address taken variable a to a pair $\langle\alpha, \beta\rangle$. The α component is a value from the singleton set lattice, as in the original analysis. The β component is an element of the lattice shown in Figure 10: it is either a top-level variable p, or $\top$ or $\bot$. For example, the pair $su[\ell](a) = \langle\{b\}, p\rangle$ indicates that at ℓ, $pt(a) = \{b\} = pt(p)$, while $su[\ell](a) = \langle\top, p\rangle$ indicates that although $pt(p)$ may not be a singleton set, $pt(a) = pt(p)$.

To adapt the algorithm to this extended lattice, only minor changes are needed. The if statement in Line 42 is updated to return $\langle pt(q), q\rangle$ in the then clause and $\langle\top, q\rangle$ in the else clause. To take advantage of the additional information, an extra else-if clause is added to the if statement in Line 34. When $su[\ell](a)$ is $\langle\top, q\rangle$ but not $\langle\top, \top\rangle$, this new clause calls AddEdge(q, p) so that the contents of $pt(q)$ (which the *su* information says are equal to $pt(a)$) are propagated to $pt(p)$.

This simple extension increases the height of the lattice that $su[\ell](a)$ ranges over from 3 to only 4, so it does not affect the asymptotic complexity of the algorithm and has a negligible effect on actual running times. Knowing that $pt(a) = pt(p)$ when $pt(p)$ is not a singleton may not directly enable additional strong updates, but it can yield some improvement in analysis precision.

4.3 Constraint optimization

For flow-insensitive points-to analysis, several techniques have been developed to speed up the analysis by simplifying the subset constraints [12, 15, 16, 26, 28]. With suitable modifications, these techniques can also be used for strong update analysis. We have adapted and implemented strong update versions of the three techniques used in LLVM: Hash-based Value Numbering (HVN), HVN with Union (HU), and Hybrid Cycle Detection (HCD).

4.3.1 HVN and HU

Both HVN and HU, as well as the earlier Off-line Variable Substitution (OVS) [28], are intended to simplify the original constraints before the constraint solving begins. All three of the techniques perform the following two steps:

1. Identify top-level pointers whose points-to sets are known to be equal.
2. Merge the nodes representing these top-level pointers and update all the subset constraints to refer to the newly merged node.

The techniques differ in how aggressive they are in Step 1: each technique finds possibly different sets of pointers that are provably equal.

All three techniques are based on the idea of a *subset graph* [28] (also called the *pointer assignment graph* [25] and the *offline constraint graph* [16]). Nodes in the graph are top-level pointers p, addresses $\&a$, and dereferences $*q$, and edges in the graph correspond to the ADDROF, COPY, and LOAD statements from Figure 1. For each node of the subset graph, we can define a subset-graph points-to set pt_{SG} as follows: $pt_{SG}(p) = pt(p)$, $pt_{SG}(\&a) = \{a\}$, $pt_{SG}(*q) = \bigcup_{a \in pt(q)} pt(a)$. All three techniques depend only on the following property of the subset graph.

Proposition 3. *For every top-level pointer p, $pt(p)$ is the union of $pt_{SG}(\alpha)$, where α ranges over all predecessors of p in the subset graph.*

The techniques merge pointers appearing in a common cycle in the subset graph and pointers having similar ancestors in the subset graph. The three techniques differ in their precise definition of similar ancestors and the method used to compute them. HU finds more pointer equivalences than HVN, but HU takes cubic time while HVN takes only quadratic time. Therefore, LLVM uses the more aggressive HU, but precedes it with a pass of HVN to reduce the size of the input to HU and therefore its cost.

Thanks to the use of SSA form as described in Section 3.2, the strong update algorithm models top-level pointers flow-insensitively. Therefore, the strong update analysis can merge top-level pointers (Step 2 above) in the same way as the flow-insensitive algorithm. It is only Step 1 that must be adapted to the strong update algorithm, since the increased precision may cause different pointers to have equal points-to sets than in a flow-insensitive analysis.

The only change needed is to separate dereference nodes by program point label (i.e. change nodes of the form $*q$ to the form $\ell : *q$), since in the strong update algorithm, the result of a load from $*q$ depends on the location ℓ of the load. The definition of pt_{SG} is changed to include the label ℓ as follows: $pt_{SG}(\ell : *q) = \bigcup_{a \in pt(q)} ptsu[\ell](a)$. This updated definition satisfies Proposition 3, so OVS, HVN, and HU can be safely applied without further modifications.

4.3.2 HCD

Unlike OVS, HVN, and HU, the HCD technique is intended to find subset constraint cycles that do not arise until the analysis begins to solve the constraints. Suppose there is a path $*p \to q \to \ldots \to r$ in the subset graph and a store $*p = r$. Before constraint solving, HCD creates a data structure compactly recording all such paths. During constraint solving, when some address a is added to $pt(p)$, the following constraint cycle is created: $pt(a) \subseteq pt(q) \subseteq \ldots \subseteq pt(r) \subseteq pt(a)$. When this happens, the top-level pointers on the path from q to r can be merged. HCD also "merges" the address node a with the top-level pointers q to r, but we must be careful in interpreting the meaning of "merging" an address a and a top-level pointer p. HCD merges *only* the representation of the points-to sets $pt(p)$ and $pt(a)$. It does *not* merge the notion of the address a; ADDROF constraints involving $\&a$ are not changed. If two addresses a and b are both merged with p, although $pt(a)$ is known to equal $pt(b)$, the addresses a and b are still distinct, and membership of a in a given points-to set is still independent of the membership of b in that points-to set. When merging a top-level pointer p with an address a, by convention, we can always choose the top-level pointer p as the representative of the merged node. This has the advantage that none of the instructions from Figure 1 involving p need to be rewritten with a, and preserves the property that all instructions involve only top-level pointers (except the right-hand side of ADDROF, of course).

The strong update analysis analogue of an HCD path is a path $\ell : *p \to q \to \ldots \to r$ and a store $\ell : *p = r$ at the same label ℓ. When a is added to $pt(p)$ during constraint solving, the following constraint cycle is created: $ptsu[\ell](a) \subseteq pt(q) \subseteq \ldots \subseteq pt(r) \subseteq ptsu[\ell](a)$. Thus the top-level pointers q to r can be merged. The flow-insensitive HCD also merges $pt(a)$ with $pt(q)$; the analogous merge of $su[\ell](a)$ and $pt(q)$ cannot be done in the strong update analysis because $su[\ell](a)$ is not a points-to set. However, such a merge is also unnecessary because unlike $pt(a)$ in the flow-insensitive analysis, which is of size $\Theta(|\mathcal{A}|)$, $su[\ell](a)$ has a constant size of only a few bytes.

5. Implementation

We have implemented the strong update algorithm by extending the existing flow-insensitive subset-based points-to analysis that is included in the LLVM compiler infrastructure [24], version 2.6. In the rest of this paper, we call this base analysis "flow-insensitive", even though some flow sensitivity is achieved by analyzing an intermediate representation in SSA form as discussed in Section 3.2. The base analysis is an implementation of the flow-insensitive algorithm of Figure 8 using sparse bit vectors to represent points-to sets, and with extensions for the constraint optimizations discussed in the previous section. Thus it was straightforward to extend the implementation to implement the strong update analysis algorithm, with only a few issues that we will explain in this section. Our implementation is publicly available at `http://plg.uwaterloo.ca/~olhotak/su`.

An implementation detail that is important for soundness is identifying which address-taken variables are completely overwritten by strong updates (i.e. what the *singletons* set should be). First, we strongly update only variables that are the same size as a pointer, because, for example, a store to an array of multiple pointers would only update one element of the array, so the analysis should not strongly update the whole array. Second, we strongly update only global variables and local variables of procedures that are not recursive (either directly or mutually through other procedures). A local variable of a recursive procedure can have many instances on the stack at the same time, and a store only updates one of those instances, so a strong update would be unsound. Recursive procedures are found by detecting cycles in the call graph built ahead of time by LLVM, which conservatively assumes that a procedure pointer could point to any procedure whose address has been taken. Finally, we never apply strong updates to dynamically allocated variables, since multiple instances of them can be created by repeating the allocation.

To test the correctness of the implementation, we enabled the LLVM transformations that take advantage of points-to information and used the analysis to compile the SPEC CINT 2000 and SPEC CPU 2006 benchmarks [33] that are written in C. The SPEC harness validated that all of the compiled benchmarks generated the correct output. On these benchmarks, with these test inputs, and for these LLVM transformations using the analysis results, our implementation of the strong update analysis is sound.

To compare the results of the strong update analysis with fully flow-sensitive analysis results, we also expressed the flow-sensitive analysis constraints of Figure 2 in Datalog. We used the LogicBlox Datalog implementation and applied the manual Datalog optimization techniques suggested by Bravenboer and Smaragdakis [3]. We extracted the input to the Datalog program from the LLVM points-to analysis to ensure that both analysis implementations were using the same input constraints. This setup enabled us to compare the strong update analysis results with fully flow-sensitive results.

6. Empirical Evaluation

We compared the strong update analysis with the original flow-insensitive points-to analysis by running both of them on the C benchmarks from the SPECINT 2000 and the SPECCPU 2006 suites [33]. The first column of Table 1 gives the name of the benchmarks, and the following four columns give various measurements of the size of each benchmark. Column 2 shows the number of lines of source code. The next three columns show the number of top-level pointers, the number of address-taken pointer targets, and the number of labels in the sparse labelling that was defined in Section 3.4. These counts are taken after applying the HVN and HU constraint simplifications discussed in Section 4.3.

The next three columns show the running times of the flow-insensitive analysis and the strong update analysis, and the relative time difference between them. The times shown are means of ten runs. The time differences have a geometric mean of a 5% slowdown and range from a speedup of 9% to a slowdown of 22%. The 9% speedup on 400.perlbench is due to the smaller points-to sets that need to be propagated as a result of the increased precision of the strong update analysis. These results confirm that the speed of the strong update analysis is comparable to that of the flow-insensitive analysis not only in theory, but also in practice.

For information only, the next two columns show the running times of two flow-sensitive analysis implementations that are not directly comparable with LLVM's built-in flow-insensitive analysis implementation and our strong update adaptation. The FS column shows the running time of the Datalog/LogicBlox implementation of the fully flow-sensitive analysis. This analysis runs on the same input constraints as the analyses in the FI and SU columns, and therefore produces comparable output (except for the added precision from flow sensitivity). However, this implementation is written in Datalog, whereas the LLVM implementation is written in C. On four of the benchmarks, the fully flow-sensitive analysis did not complete even after running for 48 hours. The HL [17] column shows the running time of Hardekopf and Lin's SSO semi-sparse analysis [17]. Ben Hardekopf provided an implementation and helped us make it run on the SPEC benchmarks. In theory, the HL analysis should compute the same output as the FS analysis, satisfying the constraints from Figure 2. Like the LLVM implementations of FI and SU, the HL analysis is written in C, but there are important differences that affect performance and make it impossible to directly compare the analysis output:

1. The LLVM implementation contains code that defines the sets of top-level variables ($\mathcal{P}$) and possible pointer targets ($\mathcal{A}$) and extracts ADDROF, COPY, STORE, and LOAD constraints out of the intermediate representation. The same extracted constraints are used as input to the FI, SU, and FS implementations. The HL implementation does not use this constraint generation code, but implements its own definition of $\mathcal{P}$ and $\mathcal{A}$ and its own extraction of an analogous but different set of constraints. Thus the inputs to the analysis are different, and the intermediate and final points-to sets are different in cases where top-level variables and pointer targets are modelled differently in the input constraints.
2. The LLVM implementation of FI and our adaptation SU use sparse bit vectors to represent points-to sets. The HL implementation uses binary decision diagrams (BDDs).
3. The SU implementation is built on top of the LLVM 2.6 version of the FI analysis. The HL implementation is built on top of LLVM 2.5.

The final column shows the space usage of the strong update analysis in terms of the number of tuples $\langle \ell, a, b, p\rangle$ such that $su[\ell](a) = \langle\{b\}, p\rangle$. This metric was chosen because it is proportional to the size of the *su* sets, the only data structure of significant size added in the transformation of the flow-insensitive analysis to the strong update analysis. This data structure is an array of maps, one for each label ℓ. The last column in the table shows the total number of entries in these maps. Each such entry records three 32-bit numbers representing a, b, and p. These maps could be implemented using different data structures. Even assuming a 2x space overhead for the map data structure, for the largest benchmark (403.gcc), the strong update analysis uses at most 6.1 MB more memory (268375 entries times 24 bytes) than the flow-insensitive analysis. The overall memory usage is lowered by the reduction in points-to set sizes due to the increased precision of the strong update analysis.

Table 2 compares the strong update analysis with the fully flow-sensitive analysis. The three columns under Stores – Strong Updates measure the number of store instructions in the program at which a strong update can be performed (i.e. the points-to set of the dereferenced pointer contains only one target, and this target is in the *singletons* set). As discussed in Section 3.1, strong updates are the main benefit of a flow-sensitive analysis compared to a flow-insensitive analysis. The FS column counts the number of stores at which the flow-sensitive analysis performs a strong update. In theory, the strong update analysis can perform a strong update at some subset of these stores; the size of this subset is shown in the SU column. In total (excluding the four benchmarks on which the flow-sensitive analysis does not complete), the strong update analysis performs 98% of the strong updates that the flow-sensitive analysis performs.

The right section of the table presents counts of loads in each benchmark. Load instructions are where any difference between analyses is observed because they are the only instructions in the LLVM IR in which address-taken variables are read. Every other instruction works directly only with top-level variables; if an address-taken variable is to be used, it must first be loaded into a top-level variable using a load instruction. The FS column in the table counts the number of loads $\ell : p = *q$ at which the flow-sensitive points-to set of $*q$ is strictly smaller than the flow-insensitive points-to set of $*q$ (i.e. $\cup_{a \in pt(q)} pt[\ell](a) \subsetneq \cup_{a \in pt(q), \ell' \in \mathcal{L}} pt[\ell'](a)$). At these loads, a smaller (i.e. more precise) set is propagated to p than would be if the analysis were flow-insensitive. The SU column presents the analogous counts for the strong update analysis (i.e. $\cup_{a \in pt(q)} ptsu[\ell](a) \subsetneq \cup_{a \in pt(q)} pt(a)$). In total, of all the loads at which the fully flow-sensitive propagates more precise sets than a flow-insensitive analysis would, on 98% of them the strong update analysis does too.

The benefit that a given client analysis derives from flow sensitivity in the points-to analysis needs to be evaluated separately for each proposed client. Our study has shown that the strong update analysis improves points-to precision at 98% of program points at which a flow sensitive analysis does. Thus we conclude that if a client analysis benefits from flow sensitivity in the points-to analysis, then it will similarly benefit from the strong update analysis.

Benchmark	kSLOC	$\|\mathcal{P}\|$	$\|\mathcal{A}\|$	$\|\mathcal{L}\|$	Analysis Time (s) FI	SU	slowdown	FS	HL [17]	Space SU
164.gzip	8.6	1740	971	2818	0.13	0.14	3%	7	0.50	1347
175.vpr	17.8	7241	2896	7025	0.51	0.54	6%	46	1.02	7552
176.gcc	230.5	104663	24518	117121	41.86	45.79	9%	—	97.72	142152
181.mcf	2.5	1092	262	821	0.08	0.08	6%	3	0.42	1745
186.crafty	21.2	4145	2345	10671	0.40	0.41	2%	45	0.76	1037
197.parser	11.4	6741	2442	8509	0.76	0.92	21%	1206	2.39	9262
253.perlbmk	87.1	45803	11544	49584	13.75	16.74	22%	—	52.88	37284
254.gap	71.5	53285	11560	45431	8.81	9.47	8%	7029	11.47	55112
255.vortex	67.3	34531	14305	30759	4.39	4.52	3%	1665	7.68	17802
256.bzip2	4.7	951	577	1590	0.08	0.09	1%	3	0.46	325
300.twolf	20.5	13423	3255	11650	1.20	1.25	4%	100	1.88	12004
400.perlbench	169.9	89661	21441	93792	66.99	60.71	-9%	—	306.70	70229
401.bzip2	8.3	3265	915	3243	0.28	0.30	9%	10	0.67	4161
403.gcc	521.1	240239	55012	272420	190.17	213.01	12%	—	3526.02	268375
429.mcf	2.7	1096	260	823	0.08	0.09	12%	2	0.44	1744
433.milc	15.0	5269	2343	5954	0.43	0.45	5%	30	1.04	4260
445.gobmk	197.2	54022	43881	41769	23.42	23.33	0%	7223	41.80	12391
456.hmmer	36.0	20240	4982	17186	2.10	2.22	6%	229	3.11	19713
458.sjeng	13.9	2591	1551	6544	0.26	0.27	2%	20	0.62	1687
462.libquantum	4.4	1742	912	1652	0.14	0.14	4%	5	0.49	534
464.h264ref	51.6	26884	6817	22951	3.35	3.41	2%	547	3.28	18685
470.lbm	1.2	337	150	322	0.05	0.05	-4%	2	0.42	228
482.sphinx3	25.1	12410	4013	10332	1.01	1.06	5%	115	2.51	11778

Table 1. Benchmark characteristics, analysis running times and space requirements of strong update and flow-insensitive analysis

Benchmark	Stores Total	Strong Updates SU	FS	%	Loads Total	More Precise SU	FS	%
164.gzip	246	235	235	100%	564	12	12	100%
175.vpr	916	802	802	100%	3757	16	16	100%
176.gcc	26776	23061	—	—	88050	690	—	—
181.mcf	304	204	207	99%	780	3	3	100%
186.crafty	509	405	423	96%	1493	13	13	100%
197.parser	2024	1355	1584	86%	5147	6	6	100%
253.perlbmk	14926	9175	—	—	41091	54	—	—
254.gap	12182	10060	10067	100%	39089	358	361	99%
255.vortex	4511	3786	3942	96%	17815	48	48	100%
256.bzip2	30	29	29	100%	270	0	0	100%
300.twolf	1829	1446	1446	100%	9718	0	0	100%
400.perlbench	25196	16899	—	—	79543	105	—	—
401.bzip2	316	220	237	93%	2139	22	22	100%
403.gcc	62134	40215	—	—	204112	149	—	—
429.mcf	300	199	202	99%	784	3	3	100%
433.milc	944	893	893	100%	2360	0	0	100%
445.gobmk	2206	1931	1955	99%	7043	3	4	75%
456.hmmer	2880	2216	2267	98%	13925	142	152	93%
458.sjeng	120	114	115	99%	677	0	0	100%
462.libquantum	171	140	147	95%	736	0	0	100%
464.h264ref	2143	1778	1844	96%	18944	354	363	98%
470.lbm	53	45	45	100%	134	0	0	100%
482.sphinx3	1906	1542	1549	100%	7471	17	17	100%

Table 2. Comparison of strong update and flow-sensitive analysis

7. Related Work

The study of flow-sensitive pointer analyses has a long history. Choi et al. [6] presented an early flow-sensitive alias pair analysis as an instantiation of the standard dataflow analysis framework [23]. The analysis was applied on a Sparse Evaluation Graph [5]; that is, a control flow graph with irrelevant nodes removed. In order to improve efficiency further, Choi et al. [7] devised one of the first extensions of SSA form [9] to represent indirect writes through pointers. Their Factored SSA (FSSA) form allowed "preserving" definitions, analogous to weak updates that may or may not overwrite the value of a variable.

Chow et al. [8] proposed a different extension of SSA form for handling pointers, Hashed SSA (HSSA) form. This intermediate representation added two new kinds of nodes. A χ node was placed after every store to indicate that address-taken variables may or may not have been updated (similar to a preserving definition). A μ node was used to indicate a possible use of an address-taken variable by a load.

Emami et al. [11] defined a points-to analysis that was not only flow-sensitive but also context-sensitive. Each points-to relationship was annotated as either possible or definite to enable strong updates. Like earlier analyses, the analysis was implemented as a dataflow analysis on the control flow graph.

Wilson and Lam [37] presented a context-sensitive pointer analysis based on partial transfer functions (PTF) summarizing the effects of procedures. Each PTF was constructed using a flow-sensitive analysis, which was efficient because it was intra-procedural. The PTFs were then combined to obtain context-sensitive interprocedural results. They presented experimental results on programs of up to 5 kLOC. This work sparked a line of similar points-to analyses that were flow-sensitive intra-procedurally and generated procedure summaries that could be instantiated at call sites [29, 35, 36]. However, these analyses performed strong updates only on top-level variables.

Hasti and Horwitz [18] proposed a technique that iteratively builds SSA form for variables with known aliasing, then performs alias analysis to increase the set of variables for which aliasing is known. It remains an open question whether the fixed point of this technique matches the results of a fully flow-sensitive alias analysis.

Hind and Pioli [20, 21] performed an empirical study of the benefits of flow sensitivity in alias analysis as well as of techniques to improve its performance. They found that flow sensitivity improves precision for a small subset of pointers.

Goyal [13] derived a flow-sensitive points-to analysis algorithm that uses a fine-grained worklist to run in asymptotically cubic time and cubic space in the worst case. The worst-case cubic bounds are likely to be achieved on typical programs because the algorithm explicitly generates a full points-to graph for each program point, and points-to graphs are typically quadratic in size. In contrast, the strong update algorithm is similar in both structure and empirical behaviour to flow-insensitive analysis, which has been shown to run in quadratic time in practice [30]. We are not aware of any implementation or empirical evaluation of Goyal's algorithm, but Staiger-Stöhr [31, 32] designed and implemented a similar algorithm with the same asymptotic complexity.

Zhu and Calman [38] took initial steps towards using Binary Decision Diagrams (BDDs) [4] to efficiently represent flow-sensitive points-to sets.

Tok et al. [34] presented a technique to speed up flow-sensitive dataflow analysis on a control flow graph using computed def-use chains for address-taken variables. As the analysis discovers new def-use chains, the chains are used to reorder the instructions in the worklist to reduce the analysis time.

Hardekopf and Lin [17] presented a semi-sparse algorithm to improve the running time of a fully flow-sensitive subset-based points-to analysis. The analysis was sparse in that it did not process control flow graph nodes as a whole, but instead followed def-use chains to directly find the stores that produce the values for each load. Because def-use chains for address-taken variables are not known until the analysis completes, the analysis was semi-sparse in that it was sparse only on top-level variables. The analysis used BDDs to keep the memory requirements of full flow sensitivity manageable. It was the first fully flow-sensitive subset-based points-to analysis that scaled to benchmarks of hundreds of kLOC.

8. Conclusion

We have presented a subset-based points-to analysis algorithm that combines the key advantages of flow-insensitive and flow-sensitive analyses. Like a flow-sensitive analysis, the algorithm enables strong updates, which are the main precision benefit of flow sensitivity. Like a flow-insensitive analysis, the strong update algorithm requires, in the worst case, quadratic space and cubic time. We have shown that its running time in practice is comparable to that of the flow-insensitive analysis. We have also shown that the strong update analysis performs 98% of the strong updates of a fully flow-sensitive analysis, and propagates more precise points-to sets at 98% of the loads at which a fully flow-sensitive analysis does. These benefits of the algorithm stem from the notion that it is the precise points-to sets that enable strong updates (and therefore further precision), yet it is also these sets that can be manipulated efficiently. Thus the strong update algorithm focuses attention on these sets to gain the precision benefits of flow sensitivity and the efficiency benefits of flow insensitivity.

Acknowledgements

We thank Ben Hardekopf for his assistance with the semi-sparse analysis of [17]. We are grateful to the anonymous POPL reviewers for their particularly constructive suggestions that helped improve this paper. This research was supported by the Natural Sciences and Engineering Research Council of Canada.

References

[1] L. O. Andersen. *Program Analysis and Specialization for the C Programming Language*. PhD thesis, DIKU, University of Copenhagen, May 1994. (DIKU report 94/19).

[2] M. Berndl, O. Lhoták, F. Qian, L. Hendren, and N. Umanee. Points-to analysis using BDDs. In *Proceedings of the ACM SIGPLAN 2003 Conference on Programming Language Design and Implementation*, pages 103–114, 2003.

[3] M. Bravenboer and Y. Smaragdakis. Strictly declarative specification of sophisticated points-to analyses. In *OOPSLA '09: Proceeding of the 24th ACM SIGPLAN Conference on Object Oriented Programming Systems Languages and Applications*, pages 243–262, 2009.

[4] R. E. Bryant. Symbolic boolean manipulation with ordered binary-decision diagrams. *ACM Comput. Surv.*, 24(3):293–318, 1992.

[5] J.-D. Choi, R. Cytron, and J. Ferrante. Automatic construction of sparse data flow evaluation graphs. In *Proceedings of the 18th ACM SIGPLAN-SIGACT Symposium on Principles of Programming Languages*, pages 55–66, 1991.

[6] J.-D. Choi, M. Burke, and P. Carini. Efficient flow-sensitive interprocedural computation of pointer-induced aliases and side effects. In *Proceedings of the 20th ACM SIGPLAN-SIGACT Symposium on Principles of Programming Languages*, pages 232–245, 1993.

[7] J.-D. Choi, R. Cytron, and J. Ferrante. On the efficient engineering of ambitious program analysis. *IEEE Trans. Software Eng.*, 20(2):105–114, 1994.

[8] F. Chow, S. Chan, S.-M. Liu, and R. Lo. Effective representation of aliases and indirect memory operations in SSA form. In *Compiler Construction: 6th International Conference, CC'96*, volume 1060 of *Lecture Notes in Computer Science*, pages 253–267, 1996.

[9] R. Cytron, J. Ferrante, B. K. Rosen, M. N. Wegman, and F. K. Zadeck. An efficient method of computing static single assignment form. In *Proceedings of the 16th ACM SIGPLAN-SIGACT Symposium on Principles of Programming Languages*, pages 25–35, 1989.

[10] B. A. Davey and H. A. Priestly. *Introduction to Lattices and Order*. Cambridge Mathematical Textbooks. Cambridge University Press, first edition, 1990.

[11] M. Emami, R. Ghiya, and L. J. Hendren. Context-sensitive interprocedural points-to analysis in the presence of function pointers. In *Proceedings of the ACM SIGPLAN '94 Conference on Programming Language Design and Implementation*, pages 242–256, 1994.

[12] M. Fähndrich, J. S. Foster, Z. Su, and A. Aiken. Partial online cycle elimination in inclusion constraint graphs. In *Proceedings of the ACM SIGPLAN '98 Conference on Programming Language Design and Implementation*, pages 85–96, 1998.

[13] D. Goyal. Transformational derivation of an improved alias analysis algorithm. *Higher Order Symbol. Comput.*, 18(1-2):15–49, 2005.

[14] B. Hardekopf. *Pointer Analysis: Building a Foundation for Effective Program Analysis*. PhD thesis, University of Texas at Austin, May 2009.

[15] B. Hardekopf and C. Lin. The ant and the grasshopper: fast and accurate pointer analysis for millions of lines of code. In *PLDI '07: Proceedings of the 2007 ACM SIGPLAN Conference on Programming Language Design and Implementation*, pages 290–299, 2007.

[16] B. Hardekopf and C. Lin. Exploiting pointer and location equivalence to optimize pointer analysis. In H. R. Nielson and G. Filé, editors, *Static Analysis, 14th International Symposium, SAS 2007*, volume 4634 of *Lecture Notes in Computer Science*, pages 265–280, 2007.

[17] B. Hardekopf, and C. Lin,. Semi-sparse flow-sensitive pointer analysis. In *POPL '09: Proceedings of the 36th Annual ACM SIGPLAN-SIGACT Symposium on Principles of Programming Languages*, pages 226–238, 2009.

[18] R. Hasti and S. Horwitz. Using static single assignment form to improve flow-insensitive pointer analysis. In *Proceedings of the ACM SIGPLAN '98 Conference on Programming Language Design and Implementation*, pages 97–105, 1998.

[19] N. Heintze and O. Tardieu. Ultra-fast aliasing analysis using CLA: a million lines of C code in a second. In *Proceedings of the ACM SIGPLAN'01 Conference on Programming Language Design and Implementation*, pages 254–263, 2001.

[20] M. Hind and A. Pioli. Assessing the effects of flow-sensitivity on pointer alias analyses. In *Static analysis: 5th International Symposium, SAS '98*, volume 1503 of *Lecture Notes in Computer Science*, pages 57–81, 1998.

[21] M. Hind and A. Pioli. Which pointer analysis should I use? In *Proceedings of the 2000 ACM SIGSOFT International Symposium on Software Testing and Analysis*, pages 113–123, 2000.

[22] V. Kahlon. Bootstrapping: a technique for scalable flow and context-sensitive pointer alias analysis. In *PLDI '08: Proceedings of the 2008 ACM SIGPLAN Conference on Programming Language Design and Implementation*, pages 249–259, 2008.

[23] J. B. Kam and J. D. Ullman. Monotone data flow analysis frameworks. *Acta Inf.*, 7:305–317, 1977.

[24] C. Lattner and V. Adve. LLVM: A compilation framework for lifelong program analysis & transformation. In *CGO '04: Proceedings of the International Symposium on Code Generation and Optimization*, page 75, 2004.

[25] O. Lhoták and L. Hendren. Scaling Java points-to analysis using Spark. In G. Hedin, editor, *Compiler Construction, 12th International Conference*, volume 2622 of *LNCS*, pages 153–169, Apr. 2003.

[26] D. J. Pearce, P. H. J. Kelly, and C. Hankin. Online cycle detection and difference propagation: Applications to pointer analysis. *Software Quality Journal*, 12(4):311–337, 2004.

[27] F. M. Q. Pereira and D. Berlin. Wave propagation and deep propagation for pointer analysis. In *CGO '09: Proceedings of the 2009 International Symposium on Code Generation and Optimization*, pages 126–135, 2009.

[28] A. Rountev and S. Chandra. Off-line variable substitution for scaling points-to analysis. In *Proceedings of the ACM SIGPLAN '00 Conference on Programming Language Design and Implementation*, pages 47–56, 2000.

[29] A. Salcianu. *Pointer Analysis for Java Programs: Novel Techniques and Applications*. PhD thesis, Massachusetts Institute of Technology, Sept. 2006.

[30] M. Sridharan and S. J. Fink. The complexity of andersen's analysis in practice. In J. Palsberg and Z. Su, editors, *Static Analysis, 16th International Symposium, SAS 2009*, volume 5673 of *Lecture Notes in Computer Science*, pages 205–221, 2009.

[31] S. Staiger-Stöhr. Implementing sparse flow-sensitive andersen analysis. Technical Report 2009/03, Universität Stuttgart, 2009.

[32] S. Staiger-Stöhr. *Kombinierte statische Ermittlung von Zeigerzielen, Kontroll- und Datenfluss*. PhD thesis, Universität Stuttgart, 2009.

[33] Standard Performance Evaluation Corporation. URL `http://www.spec.org/`.

[34] T. B. Tok, S. Z. Guyer, and C. Lin. Efficient flow-sensitive interprocedural data-flow analysis in the presence of pointers. In A. Mycroft and A. Zeller, editors, *Compiler Construction, 15th International Conference, CC 2006*, volume 3923 of *Lecture Notes in Computer Science*, pages 17–31, 2006.

[35] F. Vivien and M. Rinard. Incrementalized pointer and escape analysis In *Proceedings of the ACM SIGPLAN'01 Conference on Programming Language Design and Implementation*, pages 35–46, 2001.

[36] J. Whaley and M. Rinard. Compositional pointer and escape analysis for Java programs. In *Proceedings of the 1999 ACM SIGPLAN Conference on Object-Oriented Programming Systems, Languages, and Applications*, pages 187–206, 1999.

[37] R. P. Wilson and M. S. Lam. Efficient context-sensitive pointer analysis for C programs. In *Proceedings of the Conference on Programming Language Design and Implementation*, pages 1–12, 1995.

[38] J. Zhu. Towards scalable flow and context sensitive pointer analysis. In *DAC '05: Proceedings of the 42nd Annual Conference on Design automation*, pages 831–836, 2005.

Pick Your Contexts Well: Understanding Object-Sensitivity

The Making of a Precise and Scalable Pointer Analysis

Yannis Smaragdakis
Department of Computer Science,
University of Massachusetts,
Amherst, MA 01003, USA
and Department of Informatics,
University of Athens, 15784, Greece
yannis@cs.umass.edu—smaragd@di.uoa.gr

Martin Bravenboer
LogicBlox Inc.
Two Midtown Plaza
Atlanta, GA 30309, USA
martin.bravenboer@acm.org

Ondřej Lhoták
David R. Cheriton School of
Computer Science
University of Waterloo
Waterloo, ON N2L 3G1, Canada
olhotak@uwaterloo.ca

Abstract

Object-sensitivity has emerged as an excellent context abstraction for points-to analysis in object-oriented languages. Despite its practical success, however, object-sensitivity is poorly understood. For instance, for a context depth of 2 or higher, past scalable implementations deviate significantly from the original definition of an object-sensitive analysis. The reason is that the analysis has many degrees of freedom, relating to which context elements are picked at every method call and object creation. We offer a clean model for the analysis design space, and discuss a formal and informal understanding of object-sensitivity and of how to create good object-sensitive analyses. The results are surprising in their extent. We find that past implementations have made a sub-optimal choice of contexts, to the severe detriment of precision and performance. We define a "full-object-sensitive" analysis that results in significantly higher precision, and often performance, for the exact same context depth. We also introduce "type-sensitivity" as an explicit approximation of object-sensitivity that preserves high context quality at substantially reduced cost. A type-sensitive points-to analysis makes an unconventional use of types as context: the context types are not dynamic types of objects involved in the analysis, but instead upper bounds on the dynamic types of their allocator objects. Our results expose the influence of context choice on the quality of points-to analysis and demonstrate type-sensitivity to be an idea with major impact: It decisively advances the state-of-the-art with a spectrum of analyses that simultaneously enjoy speed (several times faster than an analogous object-sensitive analysis), scalability (comparable to analyses with much less context-sensitivity), and precision (comparable to the best object-sensitive analysis with the same context depth).

Categories and Subject Descriptors F.3.2 [*Logics and Meanings of Programs*]: Semantics of Programming Languages—Program Analysis
; D.3.1 [*Programming Languages*]: Formal Definitions and Theory—Semantics

General Terms Algorithms, Languages, Performance

POPL'11, January 26–28, 2011, Austin, Texas, USA.

1. Introduction

Points-to analysis (or *pointer analysis* in our context) is one of the most fundamental static program analyses. Points-to analysis consists of computing a static abstraction of all the data that a pointer expression (or just a variable, without loss of generality) can point to during program run-time. The analysis forms the basis for practically every other program analysis and is closely inter-related with mechanisms such as call-graph construction, since the values of a pointer determine the target of dynamically resolved calls, such as object-oriented dynamically dispatched method calls or functional lambda applications. By nature, the entire challenge of points-to analysis is to pick judicious approximations. Intractability lurks behind any attempt to track program control- or data-flow precisely. Furthermore, the global character and complicated nature of the analysis make it hard to determine how different analysis decisions interact with various language features. For object-oriented and functional languages, *context-sensitivity* is a general approach that achieves tractable and usefully high precision. Context-sensitivity consists of qualifying local program variables, and possibly (heap) object abstractions, with context information: the analysis collapses information (e.g., "what objects this method argument can point to") over all possible executions that result in the same context, while separating all information for different contexts. Two main kinds of context-sensitivity have been explored: *call-site sensitivity* [18, 19] and *object-sensitivity* [13].

Ever since the introduction of object-sensitivity by Milanova et al. [13], there has been accumulating evidence [3, 7, 8, 10, 14] that it is a superior context abstraction for object-oriented programs, yielding high precision relative to cost. The success of object-sensitivity has been such that, in current practice, object-sensitive analyses have almost completely supplanted traditional call-site sensitive/*k*CFA analyses for object-oriented languages. This paper is concerned with understanding object-sensitivity in depth, formalizing it conveniently, and exploring design choices that produce even more scalable and precise analyses than current practice.

What is object-sensitivity at a high level? Perhaps the easiest way to describe the concept is by analogy and contrast to the better-known call-site sensitivity. A call-site sensitive/*k*CFA analysis uses method call-sites (i.e., labels of instructions that may call the method) as context elements. That is, in OO terms, the analysis separates information on local variables (e.g., method arguments) per call-stack (i.e., sequence of *k* call-sites) of method invocations that led to the current method call. Similarly, the analysis separates information on heap objects per call-stack of method invocations that led to the object's allocation. For instance, in the code example below, a 1-call-site sensitive analysis (unlike a *context-insensitive* analysis) will distinguish the two call-sites of method `foo` on lines 7 and 9. This means that the analysis will treat `foo` separately for two cases: that of its argument, `o`, pointing to anything `someobj1` may point to, and that of `o` pointing to anything `someobj2` may point to.

```
1  class A {
2    void foo(Object o) { ... }
3  }
4
5  class Client {
6    void bar(A a1, A a2) { ...
7      a1.foo(someobj1);
8      ...
9      a2.foo(someobj2);
10   }
11 }
```

In contrast, object-sensitivity uses object allocation sites (i.e., labels of instructions containing a `new` statement) as context elements. (Hence, a better name for "object-sensitivity" might have been "allocation-site sensitivity".) That is, when a method is called on an object, the analysis separates the inferred facts depending on the allocation site of the receiver object (i.e., the object on which the method is called), as well as other allocation sites used as context. Thus, in the above example, a 1-object-sensitive analysis will analyze `foo` separately depending on the allocation sites of the objects that `a1` and `a2` may point to. It is not apparent from the above fragment neither whether `a1` and `a2` may point to different objects, nor to how many objects: the allocation site of the receiver object may be remote and unrelated to the method call itself. Similarly, it is not possible to compare the precision of an object-sensitive and a call-site sensitive analysis in principle. In this example, it is not even clear whether the object sensitive analysis will examine all calls to `foo` as one case, as two, or as many more, since this depends on the allocation sites of all objects that the analysis itself computes to flow into `a1` and `a2`.

Note that our above description has been vague: "the analysis separates ... facts depending on the allocation site of the receiver object ... as well as other allocation sites". What are these "other allocation sites"? The first contribution of our paper consists of recognizing that there is confusion in the literature regarding this topic. The original definition of object-sensitivity (see [13], Fig.6, p.12.) defines the context of a method call to be the allocation site of the receiver object *obj*, the allocation site of the allocator object (*obj'*) of *obj*, (i.e., the receiver object of the method that made the allocation of *obj*), the allocation site of the allocator object of *obj'*, and so on. Nevertheless, subsequent "object-sensitive" analyses (e.g., [5, 8, 10, 20], among many) maintain the fundamental premise of using allocation sites as context elements, yet differ in which allocation sites are used. For instance, the 2-object-sensitive analysis in the PADDLE framework [7, 9] uses as method context the allocation site of the receiver object and the allocation site of the *caller* object (i.e., an object of class `Client`, and not `A`, in our example).

In this paper, we offer a unified formal framework that captures the object-sensitive analyses defined in the literature and allows a deeper understanding of their differences. Additionally, we implement an array of object-sensitive analyses and draw insights about how the choice of context relates to scalability and precision. We discover that the seemingly simple difference of how an analysis context is chosen results in large differences in precision and performance. We use the name *full-object sensitivity* to refer to (a slight generalization of) the original statement of object-sensitivity by Milanova et al. We argue that full-object sensitivity is an excellent choice in the design space, while the choice of context made in past actual implementations is sub-optimal and results in substantial loss of precision. Concretely, a practical outcome of our work is to establish a 2-full-object-sensitive analysis with a 1-object sensitive heap (shortened to "2full+1H") as an analysis that is often (though not always) feasible with current technology and impressively precise.

Perhaps even more importantly, our understanding of the impact of context on the effectiveness of an analysis leads to defining a new variant that combines scalability with good precision. Namely, we introduce the idea of a *type-sensitive* analysis, which is defined to be directly analogous to an object-sensitive analysis, yet approximates (some) context elements using types instead of full allocation sites. In contrast to past uses of types in points-to analysis (e.g., [1, 15, 21] and see Ryder [17] for several examples) we demonstrate that the types used as contexts should *not* be the types of the corresponding objects. Instead, the precision of our type-sensitive analysis is due to replacing the allocation site of an object *o* (which would be used as context in an object-sensitive analysis) with an upper-bound of the dynamic type of *o*'s allocator object. The result is a substantial improvement that establishes a new sweet spot in the practical tradeoff of points-to analysis precision and performance.

In summary, our work makes the following contributions:

- We offer a better understanding of the concept and variations of object-sensitive points-to analyses. Our understanding relies on a precise formalism that captures the different object-sensitive analyses, as well as on informal insights.
- We identify the differences in past object-sensitive analyses and analyze the influence of these differences on precision and performance. We argue that full-object-sensitivity is a substantially better choice than others used in actual practice. We validate the impact of full-object-sensitivity for the case of a context depth of 2. The difference is significant in terms of precision and scalability. Our results help establish a 2full+1H analysis as the state-of-the-art for precision in object-oriented programs, among analyses that are often practically feasible.
- We introduce type-sensitivity, as a purposeful collapsing of the context information of an object-sensitive analysis, in order to improve scalability. We discuss what is a good type-sensitive context and show that the straightforward option (of replacing an object by its type) is catastrophically bad. Instead, we identify an excellent choice of type context and demonstrate that it yields a surprisingly ideal combination of precision and scalability. A type-sensitive analysis for a context depth of 2 is several times (2x to unboundedly high) faster than a corresponding object-sensitive analysis, while keeping almost the same precision. In fact, the run-time performance and scalability of a type-sensitive analysis often exceed those of a cheap object-sensitive analysis of a lower context depth, while yielding vastly more precision.

2. Formalizing Object-Sensitivity and Variations

We formalize analyses using an abstract interpretation over a simplified base language that closely captures the key operations that practical points-to analyses perform. For this, we use Featherweight Java [6] in "A-Normal" form. A-Normal Featherweight Java is identical to ordinary Featherweight Java, except that arguments to a function call must be atomically evaluable. For example, the body `return f.foo(b.bar());` becomes `b1 = b.bar(); f1 = f.foo(b1); return f1;`. This shift does not change the expressive power of the language or the nature of the analysis, but it simplifies the semantics and brings the language closer to the intermediate languages that practical points-to analysis implementations operate on. Our formalism is an imperative variant (with a call stack instead of continuations) of the corresponding formalism of Might, Smaragdakis and Van Horn [12], which attempts a unified treatment of control-flow analysis (in functional languages) and points-to analysis (in imperative/OO languages).

The grammar below describes A-Normal Featherweight Java. Some of the Featherweight Java conventions merit a reminder: A class declaration always names a superclass, and lists fields (distinct from those in the superclass) followed by a single constructor and a list of methods. Constructors are stylized, always taking in as many parameters as total fields in the class and superclasses, and consisting of a call to the superclass constructor and assignment of the rest of the fields, all in order.

$$\text{Class} ::= \texttt{class}\ C\ \texttt{extends}\ C'\ \{\overrightarrow{C''\ f\ ;}\ K\ \vec{M}\}$$

$$K \in \text{Konst} ::= C\ (\overrightarrow{C\ f})\{\texttt{super}(\vec{f'})\ ;\ \overrightarrow{\texttt{this}.f'' = f''';}\}$$

$$M \in \text{Method} ::= C\ m\ (\overrightarrow{C\ v})\ \{\ \overrightarrow{C\ v\ ;}\ \vec{s}\ \}$$

$$s \in \text{Stmt} ::= v = e\ ;^{\ell} \mid \texttt{return}\ v\ ;^{\ell}$$

$$e \in \text{Exp} ::= v \mid v.f \mid v.m(\vec{v}) \mid \texttt{new}\ C\ (\vec{v}) \mid (C)v$$

$v \in$ Var is a set of variable names

$f \in$ FieldName is a set of field names

$C \in$ ClassName is a set of class names

$m \in$ MethodCall is a set of method invocation sites

$\ell \in$ Lab is a set of labels

Every statement has a label, to provide a convenient way of referencing program points. The function $succ$: Lab $\rightharpoonup$ Stmt yields the subsequent statement for a statement's label.

2.1 Concrete Semantics

We express the semantics using a small-step state machine. Figure 1 contains the state space. A state consists of a statement, a data stack (for local variables), a store, a call-stack (recording, for each active method invocation, the statement to return to, the context to restore, and the location that will hold the return value), and a current context. Following earlier work [12], our concrete semantics anticipates abstraction in that variables and fields are mapped to context-sensitive addresses, and the store maps such addresses to objects. The purpose served by the concept of a context-sensitive address is to introduce an extra level of indirection (through the store). In the usual concrete semantics, every dynamic instance of a variable or field will have a different context, making context-sensitive addresses extraneous. Nevertheless, the existence of the store makes it easy to collapse information from different program paths, as long as variables or fields map to the same context-sensitive address.[1] In addition to being a map from fields to context-sensitive addresses, an object also stores its creation context. There are two different kinds of context in this state space: a context for local (method) variables, and a heap context, for object fields. At a first approximation, one can think of the two contexts as being the same sets. Any infinite sets can play the role of context. By picking specific context sets we can simplify the mapping from concrete to abstract, as well as capture the essence of object-sensitivity.

The semantics are encoded as a small-step transition relation $(\Rightarrow) \subseteq \Sigma \times \Sigma$, shown in Figure 2. There is one transition rule for each expression type, plus an additional transition rule to account for return. Evaluation consists of finding all states reachable from an initial state (typically a single call statement with an empty store and binding environment). We use standard functions $cons$, car, cdr, and $first_n$ to construct and deconstruct lists/stacks. For convenience, we define a lookup of a variable in a stack to mean a lookup in the top component of the stack, e.g., $st(v)$ means $(car(st))(v)$. We also use helper functions

$$\mathcal{M} : Obj \times \text{MethodCall} \rightharpoonup \text{Method}$$

$$\mathcal{F} : \text{ClassName} \to \text{FieldName}^*.$$

[1] To prevent misunderstandings, we note that the extra level of indirection is the only purpose of the store in our semantics. Specifically, our store is not intended for modeling the Java heap and our stack is not modeling the Java local variable stack (although it has similar structure, as it is a map over local variables). For instance, the store is used to also map local variables to actual values, which is the purpose of a Java stack.

$$\varsigma \in \Sigma = \text{Stmt} \times Stack \times Store \times CallStack \times Context$$

$$st \in Stack = (\text{Var} \rightharpoonup ContSensAddr)^*$$

$$\sigma \in Store = ContSensAddr \to Obj$$

$$o \in Obj = HContext \times (\text{FieldName} \rightharpoonup ContSensAddr)$$

$$cst \in CallStack = (\text{Stmt} \times Context \times ContSensAddr)^*$$

$$a \in ContSensAddr = (\text{Var} \times Context) + (\text{FieldName} \times HContext)$$

$c \in Context$ is an infinite set of contexts

$hc \in HContext$ is an infinite set of heap contexts.

Figure 1. State-space for A-Normal Featherweight Java.

Variable reference

$$([\![v = v'\ ;^{\ell}]\!], st, \sigma, cst, c) \Rightarrow (succ(\ell), st, \sigma', cst, c), \text{ where}$$
$$\sigma' = \sigma + [st(v) \mapsto \sigma(st(v'))].$$

Return

$$([\![\texttt{return}\ v\ ;^{\ell}]\!], st, \sigma, cst, c) \Rightarrow (s, cdr(st), \sigma', cdr(cst), c'), \text{ where}$$
$$(s, c', a_{ret}) = car(cst) \qquad \sigma' = \sigma + [a_{ret} \mapsto \sigma(st(v))].$$

Field reference

$$([\![v = v'.f\ ;^{\ell}]\!], st, \sigma, cst, c) \Rightarrow (succ(\ell), st, \sigma', cst, c), \text{ where}$$
$$(\_, [f \mapsto a_f]) = \sigma(st(v')) \qquad \sigma' = \sigma + [st(v) \mapsto \sigma(a_f)].$$

Method invocation

$$([\![v = v_0.m(\vec{v'})\ ;^{\ell}]\!], st, \sigma, cst, c) \Rightarrow (s_0, st', \sigma', cst', c'),$$
where
$$M = [\![C\ m\ (\overrightarrow{C\ v''})\ \{\overrightarrow{C'\ v'''\ ;}\ \vec{s}\}]\!] = \mathcal{M}(o_0, m)$$
$$o_0 = \sigma(st(v_0)) \qquad o_i = \sigma(st(v'_i))$$
$$(hc_0, \_) = o_0 \qquad c' = merge(\ell, hc_0, c)$$
$$a'_i = (v''_i, c') \qquad a''_j = (v'''_j, c')$$
$$\sigma' = \sigma + [a'_i \mapsto o_i] \qquad cst' = cons((succ(\ell), c, st(v)), cst)$$
$$st' = cons([v''_i \mapsto a'_i, v'''_j \mapsto a''_j], st).$$

Object allocation

$$([\![v = \texttt{new}\ C\ (\vec{v'})\ ;^{\ell}]\!], st, \sigma, cst, c) \Rightarrow (succ(\ell), st, \sigma', cst, c),$$
where
$$o_i = \sigma(st(v'_i)) \qquad hc = record(\ell, c)$$
$$\vec{f} = \mathcal{F}(C) \qquad a_i = (f_i, hc)$$
$$o' = (hc, [f_i \mapsto a_i]) \qquad \sigma' = \sigma + [st(v) \mapsto o'] + [a_i \mapsto o_i].$$

Casting

$$([\![v = (C')\ v']\!], st, \sigma, cst, c) \Rightarrow (succ(\ell), st, \sigma', cst, c), \text{ where}$$
$$\sigma' = \sigma + [st(v) \mapsto \sigma(st(v'))].$$

Figure 2. Concrete semantics for A-Normal Featherweight Java.

The former takes a method invocation point and an object and returns the object's method that is called at that point (which is not known without knowing the receiver object, due to dynamic dispatch). The latter returns a list of all fields in a class definition, including superclass fields.

Our semantics is parameterized by two functions that manipulate contexts:

$$record : \mathsf{Lab} \times Context \to HContext$$
$$merge : \mathsf{Lab} \times HContext \times Context \to Context$$

The *record* function is used every time an object is created, in order to store a creation context with the object. The *merge* function is used on every method invocation. Its first argument is the current call statement label, while the second and third arguments are the context of allocation of the method's receiver object and the current (caller's) context, respectively. The key for different flavors of context sensitivity is to specify different *record* and *merge* functions for contexts.

For a simple understanding of the concrete semantics that yields the natural behavior one expects, we can define contexts as just natural numbers:

$$Context = HContext = \mathbb{N}.$$

In that case, we need to ensure that the *record* and *merge* functions never return a duplicate context. For instance, if we consider labels to also map to naturals we can capture the entire history of past context creation by defining $record(\ell, c) = 2^{\ell} \cdot 3^{c}$ and $merge(\ell, hc, c) = 5^{\ell} \cdot 7^{hc} \cdot 11^{c}$. A different choice of context that is closer to idealized (infinite context) object-sensitive semantics consists of defining a context as a list of labels:

$$Context = HContext = \mathsf{Lab}^*,$$

yielding a straightforward *record* function, while the *merge* function can ignore its second argument:

$$record(\ell, c) = cons(\ell, c)$$
$$merge(\ell, hc, c) = cons(\ell, c).$$

These definitions enable every variable to have a different address for different invocations, and every object field to have a different address for each object allocated, as expected.[2]

2.2 Abstract Semantics

It is now straightforward to express object-sensitive points-to analyses by abstract interpretation [4] of the above semantics for an abstract domain that maintains only finite context.

The abstract state space is shown in Figure 3. The main distinctions from the concrete state-space are that the set of contexts is finite and that the store can return a *set* of objects, instead of a single object. Generally, the abstract semantics closely mirror the concrete.

The abstract semantics are encoded as a small-step transition relation $(\leadsto) \subseteq \hat{\Sigma} \times \hat{\Sigma}$, shown in Figure 4. There is one abstract transition rule for each expression type, plus an additional transition rule to account for return. We assume the usual properties for $\sqcup$ of a map to sets (i.e., merging of the sets for the same value).

We similarly define abstract versions of the context-manipulating functions:

$$\widehat{record} : \mathsf{Lab} \times \widehat{Context} \to \widehat{HContext}$$
$$\widehat{merge} : \mathsf{Lab} \times \widehat{HContext} \times \widehat{Context} \to \widehat{Context}$$

[2] Technically, this is true only because the FJ calculus has no iteration, so object allocations from the same statement can only occur after a recursive call. Thus, the string of labels for method calls is enough to ensure that objects have a unique context.

$$\hat{\varsigma} \in \hat{\Sigma} = \mathsf{Stmt} \times \widehat{Stack} \times \widehat{Store} \times \widehat{CallStack} \times \widehat{Context}$$
$$\widehat{st} \in \widehat{Stack} = (\mathsf{Var} \rightharpoonup \widehat{ContSensAddr})^*$$
$$\hat{\sigma} \in \widehat{Store} = \widehat{ContSensAddr} \to \mathcal{P}\left(\widehat{Obj}\right)$$
$$\hat{o} \in \widehat{Obj} = \widehat{HContext} \times (\mathsf{FieldName} \rightharpoonup \widehat{ContSensAddr})$$
$$\widehat{cst} \in \widehat{CallStack} = (\mathsf{Stmt} \times \widehat{Context} \times \widehat{ContSensAddr})^*$$
$$\hat{a} \in \widehat{ContSensAddr} = (\mathsf{Var} \times \widehat{Context}) + (\mathsf{FieldName} \times \widehat{HContext})$$
$$\hat{c} \in \widehat{Context} \text{ is a finite set of contexts}$$
$$\widehat{hc} \in \widehat{HContext} \text{ is a finite set of heap contexts.}$$

Figure 3. Object-sensitive analysis state-space for A-Normal Featherweight Java.

Variable reference

$$([\![v = v'\,;^{\ell}]\!], \widehat{st}, \hat{\sigma}, \widehat{cst}, \hat{c}) \leadsto (succ(\ell), \widehat{st}, \hat{\sigma}', \widehat{cst}, \hat{c}), \text{ where}$$
$$\hat{\sigma}' = \hat{\sigma} \sqcup [\widehat{st}(v) \mapsto \hat{\sigma}(\widehat{st}(v'))].$$

Return

$$([\![\texttt{return}\ v\ ;^{\ell}]\!], \widehat{st}, \hat{\sigma}, \widehat{cst}, \hat{c}) \leadsto (s, cdr(\widehat{st}), \hat{\sigma}', cdr(\widehat{cst}), \hat{c}'), \text{ where}$$
$$(s, \hat{c}', \hat{a}_{ret}) = car(\widehat{cst}) \qquad \hat{\sigma}' = \hat{\sigma} \sqcup [\hat{a}_{ret} \mapsto \hat{\sigma}(\widehat{st}(v))].$$

Field reference

$$([\![v = v'.f\ ;^{\ell}]\!], \widehat{st}, \hat{\sigma}, \widehat{cst}, \hat{c}) \leadsto (succ(\ell), \widehat{st}, \hat{\sigma}', \widehat{cst}, \hat{c}), \text{ where}$$
$$(\_, [f \mapsto \hat{a}_f]) = \hat{\sigma}(\widehat{st}(v')) \qquad \hat{\sigma}' = \hat{\sigma} \sqcup [\widehat{st}(v) \mapsto \hat{\sigma}(\hat{a}_f)].$$

Method invocation

$$([\![v = v_0.m(\overrightarrow{v'})\,;^{\ell}]\!], \widehat{st}, \hat{\sigma}, \widehat{cst}, \hat{c}) \leadsto (s_0, \widehat{st}', \hat{\sigma}', \widehat{cst}', \hat{c}'),$$

where

$$M = [\![C\ m\ (\overrightarrow{C\ v''})\ \{\overrightarrow{C'\ v'''\ ;}\ \vec{s}\}]\!] = \mathcal{M}(\hat{o}_0, m)$$
$$\hat{o}_0 \in \hat{\sigma}(\widehat{st}(v_0)) \qquad \hat{o}_i = \hat{\sigma}(\widehat{st}(v'_i))$$
$$(\widehat{hc}_0, \_) = \hat{o}_0 \qquad \hat{c}' = \widehat{merge}(\ell, \widehat{hc}_0, \hat{c})$$
$$\hat{a}'_i = (v''_i, \hat{c}') \qquad \hat{a}''_j = (v'''_j, \hat{c}')$$
$$\hat{\sigma}' = \hat{\sigma} \sqcup [\hat{a}'_i \mapsto \hat{o}_i] \qquad \widehat{cst}' = cons((succ(\ell), \hat{c}, \widehat{st}(v)), \widehat{cst})$$
$$\widehat{st}' = cons([v''_i \mapsto \hat{a}'_i, v'''_j \mapsto \hat{a}''_j], \widehat{st}).$$

Object allocation

$$([\![v = \texttt{new}\ C\ (\overrightarrow{v'})\,;^{\ell}]\!], \widehat{st}, \hat{\sigma}, \widehat{cst}, \hat{c}) \leadsto (succ(\ell), \widehat{st}, \hat{\sigma}', \widehat{cst}, \hat{c}),$$

where

$$\hat{o}_i = \hat{\sigma}(\widehat{st}(v'_i)) \qquad \widehat{hc} = \widehat{record}(\ell, \hat{c})$$
$$\vec{f} = \mathcal{F}(C) \qquad \hat{a}_i = (f_i, \widehat{hc})$$
$$\hat{o}' = (\widehat{hc}, [f_i \mapsto \hat{a}_i]) \qquad \hat{\sigma}' = \hat{\sigma} \sqcup [\widehat{st}(v) \mapsto \hat{o}'] \sqcup [\hat{a}_i \mapsto \hat{o}_i].$$

Casting

$$([\![v = (C')\ v']\!], \widehat{st}, \hat{\sigma}, \widehat{cst}, \hat{c}) \leadsto (succ(\ell), \widehat{st}, \hat{\sigma}', \widehat{cst}, \hat{c}), \text{ where}$$
$$\hat{\sigma}' = \hat{\sigma} \sqcup [\widehat{st}(v) \mapsto \hat{\sigma}(\widehat{st}(v'))].$$

Figure 4. Object-sensitivity abstract semantics for A-Normal Featherweight Java.

The abstract $\widehat{record}$ and $\widehat{merge}$ functions capture the essence of object-sensitivity: an object-sensitive analysis is distinguished by its storing a context together with every allocated object (via $\widehat{record}$), and by its retrieving that context and using it as the basis for the analysis context of every method dispatched on the object (via $\widehat{merge}$).

2.3 Analysis Variations and Observations

With the above framework, we can concisely characterize all past object-sensitive analyses, as well as discuss other possibilities. All variations consist of only modifying the definitions of $\widehat{Context}$, $\widehat{HContext}$, $\widehat{record}$, and $\widehat{merge}$.

Original Object Sensitivity. Milanova et al. [13] gave the original definition of object-sensitivity but did not implement the analysis for context depths greater than 1. Taken literally, the original definition prescribes that, for an n-object-sensitive analysis, the regular and the heap context consist of n labels:

$$\widehat{Context} = \widehat{HContext} = \mathsf{Lab}^n,$$

while $\widehat{record}$ just keeps the first n elements of the context defined in our concrete semantics, and $\widehat{merge}$ discards everything but the receiver object context:

$$\widehat{record}(\ell, \hat{c}) = cons(\ell, first_{n-1}(\hat{c}))$$
$$\widehat{merge}(\ell, \widehat{hc}, \hat{c}) = \widehat{hc}.$$

In practical terms, this definition has several consequences:

- The only labels used as context are labels from an object allocation site, via the $\widehat{record}$ function.
- On a method invocation, only the (heap) context of the receiver object matters.
- The heap context of a newly allocated object is derived from the context of the method doing the allocation, i.e., from the heap context of the object that is doing the allocation.

In other words, the context used to analyze a method consists of the allocation site of the method's receiver object, the allocation site of the object that allocated the method's receiver object, the allocation site of the object that allocated the object that allocated the method's receiver object, and so on. In the next section we discuss whether this is a good choice of context for scalability and precision.

Past Implementations of Object Sensitivity. For an object-sensitive analysis with context depth 1, the context choice is obvious. The $\widehat{merge}$ function has to use some of the receiver object context, or the analysis would not be object-sensitive (just call-site-sensitive), and the receiver object context consists of just the object's allocation site.

For analyses with context depth $n > 1$, however, the definitions of $\widehat{merge}$ and $\widehat{record}$ can vary significantly. Actual implementations of such analyses deviated from the Milanova et al. definition. Notably, the PADDLE framework [7, 9] (which provides the most-used such implementation available) merges the allocation site of the receiver object with multiple context elements *from the caller object context* when analyzing a method. This results in the following functions:

$$\widehat{record}(\ell, \hat{c}) = cons(\ell, first_{n-1}(\hat{c}))$$
$$\widehat{merge}(\ell, \widehat{hc}, \hat{c}) = cons(car(\widehat{hc}), first_{n-1}(\hat{c})).$$

The practically interesting case is of $n = 2$. (Higher values are well outside current technology if the analysis is applied as defined, i.e., the context depth applies to all program variables.) The above definition then means that every method is analyzed using as context a) the allocation site of the receiver object; and b) the allocation site of the caller object.

Heap Context, Naming, and Full-Object Sensitivity. The above analyses defined the heap context ($\widehat{HContext}$) and the regular/method context ($\widehat{Context}$) to be the same set, namely Lab^n. There are other interesting possibilities, however. Since the $\widehat{merge}$ function has access to a heap context and to a regular context (and needs to build a new regular context) the heap context can be shallower. For instance, Lhoták's exploration of object-sensitive analyses [7] studies in depth analyses where the heap context is always just a single allocation site:

$$\widehat{HContext} = \mathsf{Lab}$$
$$\widehat{Context} = \mathsf{Lab}^n$$
$$\widehat{record}(\ell, \hat{c}) = \ell$$
$$\widehat{merge}(\ell, \widehat{hc}, \hat{c}) = cons(\widehat{hc}, first_{n-1}(\hat{c})).$$

In fact, *the above definition is what is most commonly called an "object-sensitive analysis" in the literature*! The analyses we saw earlier are colloquially called "object-sensitive analyses with a context-sensitive (or object-sensitive) heap". That is, the points-to analysis literature by convention uses context to apply only to methods, while heap objects are represented by just their allocation site. Adding more context to object fields than just the object allocation site is designated with suffixes such as "context-sensitive heap" or "heap cloning" in an analysis description. Thus, one needs to be very careful with naming conventions. We summarize ours at the end of this section.

Another interesting possibility is that of keeping a *deeper* context for heap objects than for methods. The most meaningful case in practice is the one where the heap object keeps one extra context element:

$$\widehat{HContext} = \mathsf{Lab}^{n+1}$$
$$\widehat{Context} = \mathsf{Lab}^n$$
$$\widehat{record}(\ell, \hat{c}) = cons(\ell, \hat{c}).$$

(The $\widehat{merge}$ function can vary orthogonally, as per our earlier discussion.) For $n = 1$, this is Lhoták's "1obj+H" analysis, which is currently considered the best trade-off between scalability and precision [8], and to which we refer repeatedly in our experimental evaluation of Section 5.

This latest variation complicates naming even more. In Lhoták's detailed naming scheme, the above analysis would be an "n-object-sensitive analysis with an (n-)object-sensitive heap", while our standard n-object-sensitive analysis (with $\widehat{Context} = \widehat{HContext} = \mathsf{Lab}^n$) is called an "$n$-object-sensitive analysis with an $n-1$-object-sensitive heap". The reason for the off-by-one convention is historical: it is considered self-evident in the points-to analysis community that the static abstraction for a heap object will consist of at least its allocation site label. Therefore, the heap context is considered to be $n - 1$ labels, when the static abstraction of an object consists of n labels in total.

In the rest of this paper, we adopt the standard terminology of the points-to analysis literature. That is, we talk of an "n-object-sensitive analysis with an $n-1$-object-sensitive heap" to mean that $\widehat{Context} = \widehat{HContext} = \mathsf{Lab}^n$. Furthermore, to distinguish between the two dominant definitions of a $\widehat{merge}$ function (Milanova et al.'s, as opposed to that of the PADDLE framework) we refer to a *full-object-sensitive analysis* vs. a *plain-object-sensitive analysis*. A full-object-sensitive analysis is characterized by a $\widehat{merge}$ function:

$$\widehat{merge}(\ell, \widehat{hc}, \hat{c}) = \widehat{hc}.$$

That is, the "full" object abstraction of the receiver object is used as context for the method invoked on that object. In contrast, a plain-object-sensitive analysis merges information from the receiver and the caller objects:

$$\widehat{record}(\ell, \hat{c}) = cons(\ell, first_{n-1}(\hat{c}))$$

$$\widehat{merge}(\ell, \widehat{hc}, \hat{c}) = cons(car(\widehat{hc}), first_{n-1}(\hat{c})).$$

Thus, the original object-sensitivity definition by Milanova et al. is a full-object-sensitive analysis, while the practical object-sensitive analysis of the PADDLE framework is plain-object-sensitive. We abbreviate plain-object-sensitive analyses for different context and heap context depths to "*n*plain+*m*H" and full-object-sensitive analyses to "*n*full+*m*H". When the two analyses coincide, we use the abbreviation "*n*obj+*m*H".

Discussion. Finally, note that our theoretical framework is not limited to traditional object-sensitivity, but also encompasses call-site sensitivity. Namely, the $\widehat{merge}$ function takes the current call-site label as an argument. None of the actual object-sensitive analyses we saw above use this argument. Thus, our framework suggests a generalized interpretation of what constitutes an object-sensitive analysis. We believe that the essence of object-sensitivity is *not* in "only using allocation-site labels as context" but in "storing an object's creation context and using it at the site of a method invocation" (i.e., the functionality of the $\widehat{merge}$ function). We expect that future analyses will explore this direction further, possibly combining call-site and allocation-site information in interesting ways.

Our framework also allows the same high-level structure of an analysis but with different context information preserved. Section 4 pursues a specific direction in this design space, but generally we can produce analyses by using as context *any abstractions computable from the arguments to functions $\widehat{record}$ and $\widehat{merge}$* (with appropriate changes to the $\widehat{Context}$ and $\widehat{HContext}$ sets). For instance, we can use as context coarse-grained program location information (module identifiers, packages, user annotations) since these are uniquely identified by the current program statement label, ℓ. Similarly, we can make different context choices for different allocation sites or call sites, by defining the $\widehat{record}$ and $\widehat{merge}$ functions conditionally on the supplied label. In fact, there are few examples of context-sensitive points-to analyses that cannot be captured by our framework, and simple extensions would suffice for most of those. For instance, a context-sensitive points-to analysis that employs as context a static abstraction of the arguments of a method call (and not just of the receiver object) is currently not directly expressible in our formalism. (This approach has been fruitful in different static analyses, e.g., for type inference [1, 15].) Nevertheless, it is a simple matter to adjust the form of the $\widehat{merge}$ function and the "method invocation" rule in order to allow the method call context to also be a function of the heap contexts of argument objects.

3. Insights on Context Choice

With the benefit of our theoretical map of context choices for object-sensitivity, we next discuss what makes a scalable and precise analysis in practice.

3.1 Full-Object-Sensitivity vs. Plain-Object-Sensitivity

The first question in our work is how to select which context elements to keep—i.e., what is the best definition of the $\widehat{merge}$ function for practical purposes. We already saw the two main distinctions, in the form of full-object-sensitive vs. plain-object-sensitive analyses. Consider the standard case of a 2-object-sensitive analysis with a 1-object-sensitive heap, i.e., per the standard naming convention, $\widehat{Context} = \widehat{HContext} = \mathsf{Lab}^2$. The 2full+1H analysis will examine every method using as context the allocation site of the method's receiver object, and the allocation site of the allocator of this receiver object. (Recall that all information for method invocations under the same context will be merged, while information under different contexts will be kept separate.) In contrast the 2plain+1H analysis examines every method using as context the allocation site of the receiver object, and the allocation site of the caller object.

The 2full+1H analysis has not been implemented or evaluated in practice before. Yet with an understanding of how context is employed, there are strong conceptual reasons why one may expect 2full+1H to be superior to 2plain+1H. The insight is that context serves the purpose of yielding extra information to classify dynamic paths, at high extra cost for added context depth. Thus, for context to serve its purpose, it needs to be a good classifier, splitting the space of possibilities in roughly uniform partitions. When mixing context elements (allocation site labels) from the receiver and the caller object (as in the 2plain+1H analysis), the two context elements are likely to be correlated. High correlation means that a 2-object-sensitive analysis is effectively reduced to a high-cost 1-object-sensitive one. In a simple case of context correlation, an object calls another method on itself: the receiver object and the caller object are the same.[3] There are many more patterns of common object correlation—knowing that we are executing a method of object *p* almost always yields significant information about which object *q* is the receiver of a method call. Wrapper patterns, proxy patterns, the Bridge design pattern, etc., all have pairs of objects that are allocated and used together. For such cases of related objects, one can see the effect in intuitive terms: The traditional mixed context of a 2plain+1H analysis classifies method calls by asking objects "where were you born and where was your sibling born?" A 2full+1H analysis asks "where were you born and where was your parent born?" The latter is a better differentiator, since birth locations of siblings are more correlated.

3.2 Context Depth and Analysis Complexity

The theme of context element correlation and its effect on precision is generally important for analysis design. The rule of thumb is that context elements should be as little-correlated as possible for an analysis with high precision. To see this consider how context depth affects the scalability of an analysis. There are two opposing forces when context depth is increased. On the one hand, increased precision may help the analysis avoid combinatorial explosion. On the other hand, when imprecision will occur anyway, a deeper context analysis will be significantly less scalable.

For the first point, consider the question "when can an analysis with a deeper context outperform one with a shallower context?" Concretely, are there cases when a 2-object-sensitive analysis will be faster or more scalable than a 1-object-sensitive analysis (for otherwise the same analysis logic, i.e., both plain-obj or full-obj)? Much of the cost of evaluating an analysis is due to propagating matching facts. Consider, for instance, the "Variable reference" rule from our abstract semantics in Figure 4, which results in an evaluation of the form: $\hat{\sigma}' = \hat{\sigma} \sqcup [\widehat{st}(v) \mapsto \hat{\sigma}(\widehat{st}(v'))]$. For this evaluation to be faster under a deeper context, the lookup $\hat{\sigma}(\widehat{st}(v'))$ should return substantially fewer facts, i.e., the analysis context should result in much higher precision. Specifically two conditions need to be satisfied. First, the more detailed context should partition the facts well: the redundancy should be minimal between partitions in context-depth-2 that would project to the same partition with context depth 1. Intuitively, adding an extra level of context should not cause all (or many) facts to be replicated

[3] This case can be detected statically by the analysis, and context repetition can be avoided. This simple fix alone is not sufficient for reliably reducing the imprecision of a 2plain+1H analysis, however.

for all (or many) extra context elements. Second, fewer facts should be produced by the rule evaluation at context depth 2 relative to depth 1, when compared after projection down to depth-1 facts. In other words, going to context depth 2 should be often enough to tell us that some object does not in fact flow to a certain 1-context-sensitive variable, because the assignment is invalid given the more precise context knowledge.

In case of imprecision, on the other hand, the deeper context will almost always result in a combinatorial explosion of the possible facts and highly inefficient computation. When going from a 1obj+H analysis to a 2full+H or 2plain+H, we have every fact analyzed in up to N times more contexts (where N is the total number of context elements, i.e., allocation sites). As a rule of thumb, every extra level of context can multiply the space consumption and runtime of an analysis by a factor of N, and possibly more, since the N-times-larger collections of facts need to be used to index in other N-times-larger collections, with indexing mechanisms (and possibly results) that may not be linear.

It is, therefore, expected that an analysis with deeper context will perform quite well when it manages to keep precise facts, while exploding in runtime complexity when the context is not sufficient to maintain precision. Unfortunately, there are inevitable sources of imprecision in any real programming language—these include reflection (which is impossible to handle soundly and precisely), static fields (which defeat context-sensitivity), arrays, exceptions, etc. When this imprecision is not well-isolated and affects large parts of a realistic program, the points-to analysis will almost certainly fail (within any reasonable time and space bound). This produces a *scalability wall* effect: a given analysis on a program will either terminate quickly or will fail to terminate "ever" (in practical terms). Input characteristics of the program (e.g., size metrics) are almost never good predictors of whether the program will be easy to analyze, as this property depends directly on the induced analysis imprecision.

The challenge then becomes whether we can maintain high precision while reducing the possibility for a combinatorial blowup of analysis facts due to deeper context. We next introduce a new approach in this direction.

4. Type-Sensitivity

If an analysis with a deeper context by nature results in a combinatorial explosion in complexity, then a natural step is to reduce the base of the exponential function. Context elements in an object-sensitive analysis are object allocation sites, and typical programs have too many allocation sites, making the product of the number of allocation sites too high. Therefore, a simple idea for scalability is to use coarser approximations of objects as context, instead of complete allocation sites. This would collapse the possible combinations down to a more manageable space, yielding improved scalability. The most straightforward static abstraction that can approximate an object is a type, which leads to our idea of a *type-sensitive* analysis.

4.1 Definition of Type-Sensitive Analysis

A type-sensitive analysis is almost identical to an object-sensitive analysis, but *whereas an object-sensitive analysis would keep an allocation site as a context element, a type-sensitive analysis keeps a type instead.*[4] Consider, for instance, a 2-type-sensitive analysis with a 1-type-sensitive heap (henceforth "2type+1H"). The method context for this analysis consists of two types. (For now we do not care which types. We discuss later what types yield high precision.)

[4] Despite the name similarity, our type-sensitive points-to analysis has no relationship to Reppy's "type-sensitive control-flow analysis" [16], which uses types to filter control flow facts in a context-insensitive analysis.

Expressed in our framework, the 2type+1H analysis has:

$$\widehat{HContext} = \mathsf{Lab} \times \mathsf{ClassName}$$
$$\widehat{Context} = \mathsf{ClassName}^2.$$

Note again the contrast of the standard convention of the points-to analysis community and the structure of abstractions: the 2type+1H analysis also includes an allocation site label in the static abstraction of an object—this aspect is considered so essential that it is not reflected on the analysis name. Approximating the allocation site of the object itself by a type would be possible, but detrimental for precision.

Generally, type-contexts and object-contexts can be merged at any level, as long as the $\widehat{merge}$ function can be defined. An interesting choice is an analysis that merely replaces one of the two allocation sites of 2full+1H with a type, while leaving all the rest of the context elements intact. We call this a 1-type-1-object-sensitive analysis with a 1-object-sensitive heap, and shorten the name to "1type1obj+1H". That is, a 1type1obj+1H analysis has:

$$\widehat{HContext} = \mathsf{Lab}^2$$
$$\widehat{Context} = \mathsf{Lab} \times \mathsf{ClassName}.$$

The 2type+1H and the 1type1obj+1H analyses are the most practically promising type-sensitive analyses with a context depth of 2. Their context-manipulation functions can be described with the help of an auxiliary function

$$\mathcal{T} : \mathsf{Lab} \to \mathsf{ClassName},$$

which retrieves a type from an allocation site label. For 2type+1H, the context functions become:[5]

$$\widehat{record}(\ell, \hat{c} = [C_1, C_2]) = [\ell, C_1]$$
$$\widehat{merge}(\ell, \widehat{hc} = [\ell', C], \hat{c}) = [\mathcal{T}(\ell'), C],$$

while for 1type1obj+1H, the two functions are:

$$\widehat{record}(\ell, \hat{c} = [\ell', C]) = [\ell, \ell']$$
$$\widehat{merge}(\ell, \widehat{hc} = [\ell_1, \ell_2], \hat{c}) = [\ell_1, \mathcal{T}(\ell_2)],$$

In other words, the two analyses are variations of 2full+1H (and not of 2plain+1H), with some of the context information downgraded to be types instead of allocation site labels. The function $\mathcal{T}$ makes opaque the method we use to produce a type from an allocation site, which we discuss next.

4.2 Choice of Type Contexts

Just having a type as a context element does not tell us how good the context will be for ensuring precision—the choice of type is of paramount importance. The essence of understanding what constitutes a good type context is the question "what does an allocation site tell us about types?" After all, we want to use types as a coarse approximation of allocation sites, so we want to maintain most of the information that allocation sites imply regarding types.

The identity of an allocation site, i.e., an instruction "`new A()`" inside class `C`, gives us:

- the dynamic type `A` of the allocated object
- an upper bound `C` on the dynamic type of the *allocator* object. (Since the allocation site occurs in a method of class `C`, the allocator object must be of type `C` or a subclass of `C` that does not override the method containing the allocation site.)

[5] We use common list and pattern-matching notation to avoid long expressions. E.g., "$\widehat{record}(\ell, \hat{c} = [C_1, C_2])$" means "when the second argument, $\hat{c}$, of $\widehat{record}$ is a list of two elements, C_1 and C_2...".

A straightforward option would be to define the $\mathcal{T}$ function to return just the type of the allocation site, i.e., type `A` above. This is an awful design decision, however. To see why, consider first the case of a 2type+1H analysis. When we analyze a method context-sensitively and the first element of the context is the type of the receiver object, we are effectively wasting most of the potential of the context. The reason is that the method under analysis already gives us enough information about the type of the receiver object—i.e., the identity of the method and the type of the receiver are closely correlated. If, for instance, the method being analyzed is "`B::foo`" (i.e., method `foo` defined in class `B`) then we already have a tight upper bound on the dynamic type of the receiver object: the receiver object's type has to be either `B` or a subclass of `B` that does not override method `foo`. Since we want to pick a context that is less correlated with other information and yields meaningful distinctions, a 2type+1H analysis should have its $\mathcal{T}$ function return the type in which the allocation takes place, i.e., class `C` above.

A similar argument applies to a 1type1obj+1H analysis. In this analysis the method context consists of the receiver object, as well as a type. We want 1type1obj+1H to be a good approximation of 2full+1H, which would keep two allocation sites instead (that of the receiver object and that of the receiver object's allocator object). Thus the two allocation sites of 2full+1H give us the following information about types:

- the dynamic type of the receiver object
- an upper bound on the dynamic type of the receiver object's allocator object
- the dynamic type of the receiver object's allocator object
- an upper bound on the dynamic type of the receiver object's allocator's allocator object.

The first two pieces of information, above, come from the identity of the receiver object's allocation site, and, thus, are kept intact in a 1type1obj+1H analysis. The question is which of the last two types we would like to keep. The high correlation of the second and third bullet point above (upper bound of a type and the type itself) makes it clear that we want to keep the type of the last bullet. That is, in all scenarios, the function $\mathcal{T}(l)$, when l represents an instruction "`new A()`" inside class `C`, should return type `C` and not type `A`. We validate this understanding experimentally as part of the results of the next section.

5. Implementation and Evaluation

We implemented and evaluated several object-sensitive analyses for a context depth up to 2, which meets the limit of practicality for real-world programs. The questions we want to answer relate to the main new ideas presented so far:

- Is full-object-sensitivity advantageous compared to plain-object-sensitivity in terms of precision and performance, as argued in Section 3.1? (Recall that full-object-sensitive analyses had not been implemented in the past for context depth greater than 1.)
- Does the definition of function $\mathcal{T}$ matter, as predicted in Section 4.2?
- Does type-sensitivity achieve higher scalability than regular object-sensitive analyses while maintaining most of the precision?

5.1 Setting

Our implementation is in the context of the Doop framework [2, 3]. Doop uses the Datalog language to specify analyses declaratively. Additionally, Doop employs an *explicit* representation of relations, listing all the elements of tuples of related elements explicitly, as opposed to employing Binary Decision Diagrams (BDDs), which have often been used in points-to analysis [7, 8, 22, 23]. As we showed in earlier work [3] BDDs are only useful when the selected context abstractions introduce high redundancy, while analyses that take care to avoid unnecessary imprecision are significantly faster and scalable in an explicit representation. Doop is a highly scalable framework and implements very efficiently the most complex and precise context-sensitive analyses in current use [3]. Doop achieves functional equivalence (identical results) with Lhoták and Hendren's Paddle system [8], which is another feature-rich framework for precise analyses, but based on an entirely different architecture (using semi-declarative analysis specifications and BDDs to represent relations). This equivalence of results is useful for establishing that an analysis is correct and meaningful, which is a property far from granted for complex points-to analysis algorithms.

We use a 64-bit machine with a quad-core Xeon E5530 2.4GHz CPU (only one thread was active at a time). The machine has 24GB of RAM, but we have found no analysis that terminates (within two hours, but also occasionally allowing up to 12) after occupying more than 12GB of memory. Most analyses require less than 2GB, with only the longest running analyses (over 1000 seconds run time) occasionally needing more memory. This is indicative of the scalability wall described earlier: the explosion of contexts without a corresponding increase in precision makes an analysis intractable quite abruptly.

We analyzed the DaCapo benchmark programs, v.2006-10-MR2, with JDK 1.4 (j2re1.4.2_18). These benchmarks are the largest in the literature on context-sensitive points-to analysis.

We analyzed all benchmarks except hsqldb and jython with the full Doop functionality and support for language features, including native methods, reflection (a refinement of Livshits et al.'s algorithm [11] with support for reflectively invoked methods and constructors), and precise exception handling [2]. Generally our settings are a superset (i.e., more complete feature support) than prior published benchmarks on Doop [2, 3]. (The Doop language feature support is among the most complete in the literature, as documented in detail in the past [3].) Hsqldb and jython could not be analyzed with reflection analysis enabled—hsqldb cannot even be analyzed context-insensitively and jython cannot even be analyzed with the 1obj analysis. This is due to vast imprecision introduced when reflection methods are not filtered in any way by constant strings (for classes, fields, or methods) and the analysis infers a large number of reflection objects to flow to several variables. (E.g., in the theoretically worst case 244 sites in jython can be inferred to allocate over 1.1 million abstract objects.) For these two applications, our analysis has reflection reasoning disabled. Since hsqldb in the DaCapo benchmark code has its main functionality called via reflection, we had to configure its entry point manually.

5.2 Full-object-sensitivity vs. Plain-object-sensitivity

Figure 5 shows the precision comparison of a 2plain+1H and a 2full+1H analysis for a subset of the DaCapo benchmarks. For reference, we also include a context-insensitive, 1-object-sensitive and 1obj+1H analysis, and indicate how the metrics change from an analysis to the next more precise one. The metrics are a mixture of core points-to statistics and client analysis metrics, resembling the methodology of Lhoták and Hendren [8]. For ease of reference, we highlight (in bold) some of the most important metrics: the number of methods inferred to be reachable (including both application methods and methods in the standard Java library), the average var-points-to set (i.e., how many allocation sites a variable can refer to), the total number of call sites that are found to be polymorphic (i.e., for which the analysis cannot pinpoint a single method as the target of the dynamic dispatch), and the total number of casts that

		insensitive	1obj	1obj+H	2plain+1H	2full+1H
antlr	call-graph edges	43055	-559	-1216	-1129	-368
	reachable methods	**5758**	**-29**	**-37**	**-62**	**-21**
	total reachable virtual call sites	27823	-128	-96	-272	-139
	total polymorphic call sites	**1326**	**-38**	**-22**	**-38**	**-68**
	application reachable virtual call sites	16393	0	0	0	-9
	application polymorphic call sites	851	0	0	0	0
	total reachable casts	1038	-14	-15	-33	-6
	total casts that may fail	**844**	**-136**	**-94**	**-144**	**-64**
	application reachable casts	308	0	0	0	-1
	application casts that may fail	262	-8	-38	-66	-23
	average var-points-to	**216.71**	**24.7**	**15.1**	**8.5**	**8.2**
	average application var-points-to	327.27	20.8	15.3	8.8	8.5
chart	call-graph edges	44930	-1239	-2063	-2287	-765
	reachable methods	**8502**	**-76**	**-87**	**-115**	**-53**
	total reachable virtual call sites	23944	-233	-327	-368	-172
	total polymorphic call sites	**1218**	**-90**	**-24**	**-83**	**-119**
	application reachable virtual call sites	3649	0	-8	-47	-12
	application polymorphic call sites	110	-4	-13	-10	-4
	total reachable casts	1728	-22	-38	-58	-7
	total casts that may fail	**1457**	**-182**	**-252**	**-164**	**-120**
	application reachable casts	232	0	-4	-21	-1
	application casts that may fail	196	-17	-64	-32	-38
	average var-points-to	**98.35**	**36.0**	**20.1**	**9.4**	**6.7**
	average application var-points-to	55.35	27.2	14.4	5.0	2.8
eclipse	call-graph edges	36057	-1342	-2499	-1900	-803
	reachable methods	**6541**	**-67**	**-153**	**-83**	**-49**
	total reachable virtual call sites	18447	-291	-315	-356	-226
	total polymorphic call sites	**873**	**-96**	**-25**	**-38**	**-89**
	application reachable virtual call sites	5959	-101	-53	-31	-44
	application polymorphic call sites	292	-40	-9	-3	-3
	total reachable casts	1270	-21	-21	-27	-24
	total casts that may fail	**1001**	**-213**	**-103**	**-133**	**-51**
	application reachable casts	476	-3	-2	-8	0
	application casts that may fail	362	-61	-55	-58	1
	average var-points-to	**102.7**	**21.8**	**16.1**	**9.8**	**9.1**
	average application var-points-to	104.1	22.9	15.8	9.6	9.4
luindex	call-graph edges	24069	-663	-1155	-1119	-354
	reachable methods	**4742**	**-31**	**-34**	**-64**	**-20**
	total reachable virtual call sites	12675	-193	-117	-276	-130
	total polymorphic call sites	**507**	**-50**	**-22**	**-38**	**-66**
	application reachable virtual call sites	1267	-65	-29	-4	0
	application polymorphic call sites	39	-10	0	0	0
	total reachable casts	790	-14	-15	-33	-5
	total casts that may fail	**627**	**-129**	**-69**	**-96**	**-43**
	application reachable casts	63	0	-1	0	0
	application casts that may fail	46	-3	-18	-13	-2
	average var-points-to	**69.66**	**14.7**	**10.8**	**6.5**	**6.3**
	average application var-points-to	90.05	9.2	5.9	3.0	2.9
pmd	call-graph edges	30990	-527	-1329	-809	-1043
	reachable methods	**6158**	**-34**	**-44**	**-37**	**-62**
	total reachable virtual call sites	16029	-144	-163	-208	-280
	total polymorphic call sites	**576**	**-42**	**-26**	**-21**	**-107**
	application reachable virtual call sites	4545	-22	-87	-5	-83
	application polymorphic call sites	93	-2	-10	-4	-24
	total reachable casts	1260	-15	-15	-13	-27
	total casts that may fail	**1066**	**-137**	**-97**	**-94**	**-78**
	application reachable casts	531	-2	-2	0	-2
	application casts that may fail	485	-11	-43	-32	-21
	average var-points-to	**88.08**	**22.3**	**15.8**	**8.2**	**7.3**
	average application var-points-to	102.3	29.7	26.1	8.5	8.0

Figure 5. Precision metrics for 2plain+1H and 2full+1H for a subset of the DaCapo benchmarks. The last two metrics ("average ...") are in absolute numbers, the rest are given relative to the *immediately preceding* column (*not* relative to the numbers in the "insensitive" column). All metrics are end-user (i.e., context-insensitive) metrics. Var-points-to is the main relation of a points-to analysis, linking a variable to the allocation sites it may be referring to. (The average is over variables.) "Reachable methods" is the same as call-graph nodes, hence the first two metrics show how precise is the on-the-fly inferred call-graph. "Polymorphic call-sites" are those for which the analysis cannot statically determine a unique receiver method. "Casts that may fail" are those for which the analysis cannot statically determine that they are safe.

may fail at run-time (i.e., for which the analysis cannot statically determine that the cast is always safe). These metrics paint a fairly complete picture of relative analysis precision, although the rest of the metrics are useful for framing (e.g., for examining how the statistics vary between application classes and system libraries, for comparing to the total number of reachable call sites, etc.).

As can be seen in Figure 5, 2full+1H is almost always significantly more precise than 2plain+1H, even though both analyses have the same context depth. The difference in precision is quite substantial: For several metrics and programs (e.g., multiple metrics for pmd, or reduction in total polymorphic virtual call sites for many programs), the difference between full-object-sensitivity and plain-object-sensitivity is as large as any other single-step increment in precision (e.g., from 1-obj to 1obj+H).

Perhaps most impressively, this precision is accompanied by substantially improved performance. Figure 6 shows the running time of the analyses, together with two key internal complexity metrics: the number of edges in the context-sensitive callgraph (i.e., how many context-qualified methods are inferred to call how many other context-qualified methods) and the size of the context-sensitive var-points-to set, i.e., the total number of facts inferred that relate a context-qualified variable with a context-qualified allocation site.

The running time of 2full+1H is almost always much lower than that of 2plain+1H. The case of "chart" is most striking, with 2full+1H finishing in well under a third of the time of 2plain+1H, while achieving the much higher precision shown in Figure 5. The internal metrics show that 2full+1H makes excellent use of its context and has substantially lower internal complexity than 2plain+1H. Note that the statistics for context-sensitive var-points-to are quite low, explaining why the analysis is faster, since each variable needs to be examined only in a smaller number of contexts. A second reason why such internal metrics are important is that the performance of an analysis depends very much on algorithmic and data structure implementation choices, such as whether BDDs are used to represent large relations. Internal metrics, on the other hand, are invariant and indicate a complexity of the analysis that often transcends representation choices.

It is easy to see from the above figures that full-object-sensitivity makes a much better choice of context than plain-object-sensitivity, resulting in both increased precision and better performance. In fact, we have found the 2full+1H analysis to be a sweet spot in the current set of near-feasible analyses *in terms of precision*. Adding an extra level of context sensitivity for object fields, yielding a 2full+2H analysis, adds extremely little precision to the analysis results while greatly increasing the analysis cost.

In fact, for the benchmarks shown, 2full+1H is even significantly faster than the much less precise 1obj+H. Nevertheless, the same is not true universally. Of the 10 DaCapo benchmarks in our evaluation set, 2full+1H handles 6 with ease (the 5 shown plus "lusearch" which has very similar behavior to "luindex") but its running time explodes for the other 4. The 2plain+1H analysis explodes at least as badly for the 4 benchmarks, but a 1obj+H analysis handles 9 out of 10, and a 1-obj analysis handles all of them. In short, the performance (and internal complexity) of a highly-precise but deep-context analysis is bimodal: when precision is maintained, the analysis performs admirably. When, however, significant imprecision creeps in, the analysis does badly, since the number of contexts increases in combinatorial fashion.

Therefore, 2full+1H achieves excellent precision but is not a good point in the design space in terms of scalability. (In the past, the only fully scalable uses of object-sensitivity with depth > 1 have applied deep context to a small, carefully selected subset of allocation sites; we are interested in scalability when the whole program is analyzed with the precision of deep context.) This is the shortcoming that we expect to address with type-sensitive analyses.

5.3 Importance of Type Context Choice

In Section 4.2 we argued that, for judicious use of the extra context element, function $\mathcal{T}$ has to be defined so that it returns the enclosing type of an allocation site and not the type that is being allocated. Experimentally, this is very clearly the case. Figure 7 demonstrates this for two of our benchmark programs (the alphabetically first and last, which are representative of the rest). 1obj+H is shown as a baseline, to appreciate the difference. With the "wrong" type context, a 1type1obj+1H analysis is far more expensive and barely more precise than 1obj+H, while with the right type context the analysis is impressively scalable and precise (very close to 2full+1H, as we show later).

As can be seen, the impact of a good context is highly significant, both for scalability (in terms of time and internal metrics) and for precision. In our subsequent discussion we assume that all type-sensitive analyses use the superior context, as defined above.

5.4 Type-Sensitivity Precision and Performance

We found that type-sensitivity fully meets its stated goal: it yields analyses that are almost as precise as full-object-sensitive ones, while being highly scalable. In fact, type-sensitive analyses seem to clearly supplant other current state-of-the-art analyses—e.g., both 2type+1H and 1type1obj+1H seem overwhelmingly better than 1obj+H in both precision and performance for most of our benchmarks and metrics.

Our experiment space consists of the four precise analyses that appear feasible or mostly-feasible with current capabilities: 1obj+H, 2type+1H, 1type1obj+1H, and 2full+1H. Figure 8 shows the results of our evaluation for 8 of the 10 benchmark programs. (There is some replication of numbers compared to the previous tables, but this is limited to columns included as baselines.) We omit lusearch for layout reasons, since it behaves almost identically to luindex. We discuss the final benchmark, hsqldb, in text, but do not list it on the table because 2type+1H is the only of the four analyses that terminates on it.

Note that the first two analyses (1obj+H, 2type+1H) are semantically incomparable in precision but every other pair has a provably more precise analysis, so the issue concerns the amount of extra precision obtained and the running time cost. Specifically, 2full+1H is guaranteed to be more precise than the other three analyses, and 1type1obj+1H is guaranteed to be more precise than either 1obj+H or 2type+1H.

The trends from our experiments are quite clear:

- Although there is no guarantee, 2type+1H is almost always more precise than 1obj+H, hence the 2type+1H precision metrics (reported in the table relative to the preceding column, i.e., 1obj+H) are overwhelmingly showing negative numbers (i.e., an improvement). Additionally, 2type+1H is almost always (for 9 out of 10 programs) the fastest analysis in our set. In all but one case, 2type+1H is several times faster than 1obj+H—e.g., 5x faster or more for 4 of the benchmarks. The clear improvement of 2type+1H over 1obj+H is perhaps the most important of our experimental findings. Recall that 1obj+H is currently considered the "sweet spot" of precision and scalability in practice: a highly precise analysis, that is still feasible for large programs without exploding badly in complexity.
- 2type+1H achieves great scalability for fairly good precision. It is the only analysis that terminates for all our benchmark programs. It typically produces quite tight points-to sets, with antlr being a significant exception that requires more examination. In terms of client analyses and end-user metrics, the increase in pre-

		insensitive	1obj	1obj+H	2plain+1H	2full+1H
antlr	time (sec)	86.5	134.0	427.4	236.9	161.1
	context-sensitive callgraph edges (thousands)		1,484	966	1,428	2,458
	context-sensitive var-points-to (thousands)	13,143	8,147	49,237	24,980	9,279
chart	time (sec)	72.2	380.2	1199.2	**2496.0**	**688.2**
	context-sensitive callgraph edges (thousands)		1,463	1,087	9,564	7,469
	context-sensitive var-points-to (thousands)	7,054	19,942	83,354	107,221	22,854
eclipse	time (sec)	67.2	228.0	826.0	502.0	480.4
	context-sensitive callgraph edges (thousands)		1,921	1,278	2,103	5,341
	context-sensitive var-points-to (thousands)	5,754	9,962	64,586	65,435	22,574
luindex	time (sec)	37.9	63.2	179.3	123.9	124.3
	context-sensitive callgraph edges (thousands)		384	324	779	1,227
	context-sensitive var-points-to (thousands)	2,737	2,781	16,968	9,576	5,072
pmd	time (sec)	57.7	120.0	293.7	**392.6**	**160.0**
	context-sensitive callgraph edges (thousands)		553	418	3,610	1,614
	context-sensitive var-points-to (thousands)	4,392	5,314	24,902	35,628	6,770

Figure 6. Performance and complexity metrics for object-sensitive analyses. 2full+1H is almost always faster than 2plain+1H (some striking cases are highlighted). Additionally, 2full+1H makes good use of context and has often substantially lower internal metrics than 2plain+1H, and typically even than 1obj+H.

		1obj+H	1type1obj+1H	
			bad context	good context
antlr	call-graph edges	41280	-329	-1124
	reachable meths	**5692**	**-3**	**-78**
	reachable v-calls	27599	-2	-404
	poly v-calls	**1266**	**-51**	**-27**
	reach. v-calls in app	16393	0	-9
	poly v-calls in app	851	0	0
	reachable casts	1009	-1	-38
	casts that may fail	**614**	**-4**	**-157**
	reach. casts in app	308	0	-1
	casts in app may fail	216	0	-61
	avg var-points-to	**15.14**	**10.62**	**8.19**
	avg app var-points-to	15.25	9.02	8.51
	time (sec)	**427.4**	**376.7**	**114.2**
	c-s callgraph edge (K)	965	816	960
	c-s var-points-to (K)	49237	43030	7459

		1obj+H	1type1obj+1H	
			bad context	good context
xalan	call-graph edges	35908	-408	-1290
	reachable meths	**7237**	**-2**	**-86**
	reachable v-calls	19828	-2	-389
	poly v-calls	**1175**	**-52**	**-51**
	reach. v-calls in app	7709	0	0
	poly v-calls in app	726	-2	-6
	reachable casts	1264	-1	-37
	casts that may fail	**668**	**-5**	**-123**
	reach. casts in app	501	0	0
	casts in app may fail	250	-4	-23
	avg var-points-to	**14.94**	**14.03**	**9.57**
	avg app var-points-to	15.73	15.14	11.58
	time (sec)	**979.9**	**4398.9**	**831.0**
	c-s callgraph edge (K)	936	4915	2580
	c-s var-points-to (K)	96021	163916	38205

Figure 7. Precision, performance, and internal complexity metrics for a type-object-sensitive analysis with a good and a bad choice of context. The entries are the same as in Figures 5 and 6, with metric names condensed. As in Figure 5, all but the last two precision metrics are reported as differences relative to the *immediately preceding* column (i.e., we are showing how much more precision the good context yields over the already higher precision of the bad context, not over the baseline).

cision going from 1obj+H to 2type+1H is often greater than that of going from 2type+1H to 2full+1H. Overall, 2type+1H is an excellent approximation of 2full+1H given its low cost.

- Although not shown on the table, 2type+1H is not just faster than the three shown analyses but also faster than 1obj, for 7 out of 10 benchmark programs. The difference in precision between the two analyses is enormous, however. A good example is the hsqldb benchmark, omitted from Figure 8 since 2type+1H is the only analysis with a context-sensitive heap that terminates for it. 2type+1H processes hsqldb slightly faster than 1obj (404sec instead of 464sec). At the same time, all precision metrics are drastically better. The points-to sets are almost half the size (11.3 total vs. 22.1, and 13.2 for application vars only vs. 18.2). On other precision metrics the difference between 2type+1H and 1obj is much greater than that between 1obj and a context-insensitive analysis. For "application casts that may fail" alone, 2type+1obj eliminates 117 instances relative to 1obj.
- 1type1obj+1H is highly precise and its difference from 2full+1H is rarely significant. (It is illuminating to add the two columns and compare the cumulative difference of 1type1obj+1H from 1obj+1H, relative to the difference of the former from 2full+1H.)

At the same time, 1type1obj+1H avoids many of the scalability problems of 2full+1H: it terminates on 8 of 10 benchmarks (instead of 6 out of 10) and is always faster than 2full+1H, occasionally (e.g., chart) by a significant factor.

6. Conclusions

In this paper we strove for a better understanding of the concept of object-sensitivity in points-to analysis. Our exploration led to a precise formal modeling, to a complete mapping of past object-sensitive analyses in the literature, as well as to insights on how context affects the precision and scalability of an analysis. One concrete outcome of our work is to establish full-object-sensitivity (and especially a 2full+1H analysis) as a superior choice of context compared to others in past literature. Additionally, we have introduced the concept of type-sensitivity and applied our insights to pick an appropriate type to use as context of a points-to analysis. The result is a range of analyses, especially 2type+1H and 1type1obj+1H, that have very good to excellent scalability, while maintaining most of the precision of a much more expensive analysis. The new analyses we introduced are current sweet spots in the design space and represent a significant advancement of the state-of-the-art in points-to analysis.

		1obj+H	2type +1H	1type 1obj+1H	2full +1H
antlr	call-graph edges	41280	-1401	-52	-44
	reachable meths	**5692**	**-77**	**-4**	**-2**
	reachable v-calls	27599	-405	-1	-5
	poly v-calls	**1266**	**-70**	**-8**	**-28**
	reach.v-calls in app	16393	-9	0	0
	poly v-calls in app	851	0	0	0
	reachable casts	1009	-39	0	0
	casts that may fail	**614**	**-104**	**-57**	**-47**
	reach. casts in app	308	-1	0	0
	app casts may fail	216	-53	-8	-28
	avg var-points-to	**15.1**	**23.0**	**8.2**	**8.2**
	avg app v-points-to	15.3	41.7	8.5	8.5
	time (sec)	**427.4**	**78.8**	**114.2**	**161.1**
	c-s callgraph edge (K)	966	512	960	2,458
	c-s var-points-to (K)	49,237	4,029	7,459	9,279
bloat	call-graph edges	47792	-1797	-489	
	reachable meths	**6945**	**-85**	**-12**	
	reachable v-calls	25220	-404	-18	
	poly v-calls	**1406**	**-82**	**-85**	
	reach.v-calls in app	13879	-20	0	
	poly v-calls in app	953	-28	-58	
	reachable casts	2062	-43	-2	
	casts that may fail	**1546**	**-45**	**-120**	
	reach. casts in app	1346	-2	0	
	casts in app may fail	1134	13	-70	
	avg var-points-to	**32.5**	**21.8**	**18.6**	
	avg app var-points-to	42.6	31.9	29.1	
	time (sec)	**2307.2**	**432.7**	**2431.0**	
	c-s callgraph edge (K)	1,791	1,036	3,196	
	c-s var-points-to (K)	73,527	10,375	43,073	
chart	call-graph edges	41628	-2776	-191	-85
	reachable meths	**8339**	**-133**	**-27**	**-8**
	reachable v-calls	23384	-491	-39	-10
	poly v-calls	**1104**	**-155**	**-20**	**-27**
	reach. v-calls in app	3641	-30	-29	0
	poly v-calls in app	93	-8	-6	0
	reachable casts	1668	-55	-10	0
	casts that may fail	**1023**	**-39**	**-199**	**-46**
	reach. casts in app	228	-15	-7	0
	casts in app may fail	115	3	-66	-7
	avg var-points-to	**20.1**	**8.5**	**6.8**	**6.7**
	avg app var-points-to	14.4	4.0	2.8	2.8
	time (sec)	**1199.2**	**143.2**	**199.0**	**688.2**
	c-s callgraph edge (K)	1,087	974	1,252	7,469
	c-s var-points-to (K)	83,354	6,572	9,093	22,854
eclipse	call-graph edges	32216	-2575	-86	-42
	reachable meths	**6321**	**-127**	**-4**	**-1**
	reachable v-calls	17841	-577	-1	-4
	poly v-calls	**752**	**-77**	**-24**	**-26**
	reach. v-calls in app	5805	-74	-1	0
	poly v-calls in app	243	3	-7	-2
	reachable casts	1228	-51	0	0
	casts that may fail	**685**	**-58**	**-98**	**-28**
	reach. casts in app	471	-8	0	0
	casts in app may fail	246	-5	-44	-8
	avg var-points-to	**16.1**	**11.8**	**9.1**	**9.1**
	avg app var-points-to	15.8	13.0	9.5	9.4
	time (sec)	**826.0**	**178.0**	**301.1**	**480.4**
	c-s callgraph edge (K)	1,278	1,314	2,241	5,341
	c-s var-points-to (K)	64,586	9,232	17,154	22,574

		1obj+H	2type +1H	1type 1obj+1H	2full +1H
jython	call-graph edges	30370	-2091		
	reachable meths	**5754**	**-118**		
	reachable v-calls	16057	-830		
	poly v-calls	**768**	**-71**		
	reach. v-calls in app	7146	-492		
	poly v-calls in app	422	0		
	reachable casts	1272	-18		
	casts that may fail	**741**	**-11**		
	reach. casts in app	677	0		
	casts in app may fail	445	17		
	avg var-points-to	**21.2**	**19.1**		
	avg app var-points-to	30.7	31.4		
	time (sec)	**1215.7**	**2107.6**		
	c-s callgraph edge (K)	923	4,399		
	c-s var-points-to (K)	110,113	53,552		
luindex	call-graph edges	22251	-1368	-63	-42
	reachable meths	**4677**	**-78**	**-4**	**-2**
	reachable v-calls	12365	-400	-1	-5
	poly v-calls	**435**	**-66**	**-12**	**-26**
	reach. v-calls in app	1173	-4	0	0
	poly v-calls in app	29	4	-4	0
	reachable casts	761	-38	0	0
	casts that may fail	**429**	**-54**	**-66**	**-19**
	reach. casts in app	62	0	0	0
	casts in app may fail	25	3	-18	0
	avg var-points-to	**10.8**	**7.8**	**6.4**	**6.3**
	avg app var-points-to	5.9	4.2	2.9	2.9
	time (sec)	**179.3**	**67.7**	**80.8**	**124.3**
	c-s callgraph edge (K)	324	473	656	1,227
	c-s var-points-to (K)	16,968	2,848	3,892	5,072
pmd	call-graph edges	29134	-1720	-52	-80
	reachable meths	**6080**	**-86**	**-5**	**-8**
	reachable v-calls	15722	-475	-1	-12
	poly v-calls	**508**	**-83**	**-8**	**-37**
	reach. v-calls in app	4436	-84	0	-4
	poly v-calls in app	81	-17	0	-11
	reachable casts	1230	-40	0	0
	casts that may fail	**832**	**-63**	**-75**	**-34**
	reach. casts in app	527	-2	0	0
	casts in app may fail	431	-12	-26	-15
	avg var-points-to	**15.8**	**8.8**	**7.3**	**7.3**
	avg app var-points-to	26.1	8.9	8.0	8.0
	time (sec)	**293.7**	**78.2**	**128.1**	**160.0**
	c-s callgraph edge (K)	418	527	1,043	1,614
	c-s var-points-to (K)	24,902	3,370	5,901	6,770
xalan	call-graph edges	35908	-1553	-145	
	reachable meths	**7237**	**-65**	**-23**	
	reachable v-calls	19828	-355	-36	
	poly v-calls	**1175**	**-88**	**-15**	
	reach. v-calls in app	7709	35	-35	
	poly v-calls in app	726	-1	-7	
	reachable casts	1264	-34	-4	
	casts that may fail	**668**	**21**	**-149**	
	reach. casts in app	501	4	-4	
	casts in app may fail	250	52	-79	
	avg var-points-to	**14.9**	**12.1**	**9.6**	
	avg app var-points-to	15.7	14.4	11.6	
	time (sec)	**979.9**	**435.8**	**831.0**	
	c-s callgraph edge (K)	936	2,871	2,580	
	c-s var-points-to (K)	96,021	21,717	38,205	

Figure 8. Precision, performance, and internal complexity metrics for precise analyses. The entries are the same as in Figures 5 and 6, with metric names condensed. As in Figure 5, all but the last two precision metrics are reported as differences relative to the *immediately preceding* column. Empty entries are due to non-termination after 2 hours of running time. Some of the most interesting metrics are highlighted.

Acknowledgments

We thank the anonymous reviewers for their helpful comments, as well as Matt Might and David Van Horn for interesting discussions. This work was funded by the National Science Foundation under grants CCF-0917774 and CCF-0934631, as well as by the Natural Sciences and Engineering Research Council of Canada.

References

[1] Ole Agesen. The cartesian product algorithm: Simple and precise type inference of parametric polymorphism. In *Proceedings of the 9th European Conference on Object-Oriented Programming*, pages 2–26, London, UK, 1995. Springer-Verlag.

[2] Martin Bravenboer and Yannis Smaragdakis. Exception analysis and points-to analysis: Better together. In Laura Dillon, editor, *ISSTA '09: Proceedings of the 2009 International Symposium on Software Testing and Analysis*, New York, NY, USA, July 2009.

[3] Martin Bravenboer and Yannis Smaragdakis. Strictly declarative specification of sophisticated points-to analyses. In *OOPSLA '09: 24th annual ACM SIGPLAN conference on Object Oriented Programming, Systems, Languages, and Applications*, New York, NY, USA, 2009. ACM.

[4] Patrick Cousot and Radhia Cousot. Abstract interpretation: a unified lattice model for static analysis of programs by construction or approximation of fixpoints. In *Proceedings of the 4th ACM SIGACT-SIGPLAN symposium on Principles of programming languages*, POPL '77, pages 238–252, New York, NY, USA, 1977. ACM.

[5] Stephen Fink, Eran Yahav, Nurit Dor, G. Ramalingam, and Emmanuel Geay. Effective typestate verification in the presence of aliasing. In *ISSTA '06: Proceedings of the 2006 international symposium on Software testing and analysis*, pages 133–144, New York, NY, USA, 2006. ACM.

[6] Atsushi Igarashi, Benjamin C. Pierce, and Philip Wadler. Featherweight Java: a minimal core calculus for Java and GJ. *ACM Trans. Program. Lang. Syst.*, 23(3):396–450, 2001.

[7] Ondřej Lhoták. *Program Analysis using Binary Decision Diagrams*. PhD thesis, McGill University, January 2006.

[8] Ondřej Lhoták and Laurie Hendren. Evaluating the benefits of context-sensitive points-to analysis using a BDD-based implementation. *ACM Trans. Softw. Eng. Methodol.*, 18(1):1–53, 2008.

[9] Ondřej Lhoták and Laurie Hendren. Relations as an abstraction for BDD-based program analysis. *ACM Trans. Program. Lang. Syst.*, 30(4):1–63, 2008.

[10] Donglin Liang, Maikel Pennings, and Mary Jean Harrold. Evaluating the impact of context-sensitivity on Andersen's algorithm for Java programs. In Michael D. Ernst and Thomas P. Jensen, editors, *PASTE*, pages 6–12. ACM, 2005.

[11] Benjamin Livshits, John Whaley, and Monica S. Lam. Reflection analysis for Java. In Kwangkeun Yi, editor, *Proceedings of the 3rd Asian Symposium on Programming Languages and Systems*, volume 3780. Springer-Verlag, November 2005.

[12] Matthew Might, Yannis Smaragdakis, and David Van Horn. Resolving and exploiting the k-CFA paradox: Illuminating functional vs. object-oriented program analysis. In *Conf. on Programming Language Design and Implementation (PLDI)*. ACM, June 2010.

[13] Ana Milanova, Atanas Rountev, and Barbara G. Ryder. Parameterized object sensitivity for points-to analysis for Java. *ACM Trans. Softw. Eng. Methodol.*, 14(1):1–41, 2005.

[14] Mayur Naik, Alex Aiken, and John Whaley. Effective static race detection for Java. In *Proceedings of the 2006 ACM SIGPLAN Conference on Programming Language Design and Implementation (PLDI'06)*, pages 308–319, 2006.

[15] John Plevyak and Andrew A. Chien. Precise concrete type inference for object-oriented languages. In *Proceedings of the ninth annual conference on Object-oriented programming systems, language, and applications*, OOPSLA '94, pages 324–340, New York, NY, USA, 1994. ACM.

[16] John Reppy. Type-sensitive control-flow analysis. In *Proceedings of the 2006 ACM SIGPLAN Workshop on ML*, pages 74–83, September 2006.

[17] Barbara G. Ryder. Dimensions of precision in reference analysis of object-oriented programming languages. In Görel Hedin, editor, *Compiler Construction, 12th International Conference, CC 2003*, volume 2622 of *Lecture Notes in Computer Science*, pages 126–137. Springer, 2003.

[18] Micha Sharir and Amir Pnueli. Two approaches to interprocedural data flow analysis. In Steven S. Muchnick and Neil D. Jones, editors, *Program Flow Analysis*, pages 189–233, Englewood Cliffs, NJ, 1981. Prentice-Hall, Inc.

[19] Olin Shivers. *Control-Flow Analysis of Higher-Order Languages*. PhD thesis, Carnegie Mellon University, May 1991.

[20] Manu Sridharan and Rastislav Bodík. Refinement-based context-sensitive points-to analysis for Java. In *PLDI '06: Proc. of the 2006 ACM SIGPLAN conf. on Programming language design and implementation*, pages 387–400, New York, NY, USA, 2006. ACM.

[21] Vijay Sundaresan, Laurie Hendren, Chrislain Razafimahefa, Raja Vallée-Rai, Patrick Lam, Etienne Gagnon, and Charles Godin. Practical virtual method call resolution for Java. In *Proceedings of the Conference on Object-Oriented Programming Systems, Languages, and Applications*, pages 264–280. ACM Press, 2000.

[22] John Whaley, Dzintars Avots, Michael Carbin, and Monica S. Lam. Using Datalog with binary decision diagrams for program analysis. In Kwangkeun Yi, editor, *APLAS*, volume 3780 of *Lecture Notes in Computer Science*, pages 97–118. Springer, 2005.

[23] John Whaley and Monica S. Lam. Cloning-based context-sensitive pointer alias analysis using binary decision diagrams. In *PLDI '04: Proc. of the ACM SIGPLAN 2004 conf. on Programming language design and implementation*, pages 131–144, New York, NY, USA, 2004. ACM.

Learning Minimal Abstractions

Percy Liang
UC Berkeley
pliang@cs.berkeley.edu

Omer Tripp
Tel-Aviv University
omertrip@post.tau.ac.il

Mayur Naik
Intel Labs Berkeley
mayur.naik@intel.com

Abstract

Static analyses are generally parametrized by an abstraction which is chosen from a family of abstractions. We are interested in flexible families of abstractions with many parameters, as these families can allow one to increase precision in ways tailored to the client without sacrificing scalability. For example, we consider k-limited points-to analyses where each call site and allocation site in a program can have a different k value. We then ask a natural question in this paper: What is the minimal (coarsest) abstraction in a given family which is able to prove a set of client queries? In addressing this question, we make the following two contributions: (i) we introduce two machine learning algorithms for efficiently finding a minimal abstraction; and (ii) for a static race detector backed by a k-limited points-to analysis, we show empirically that minimal abstractions are actually quite coarse: it suffices to provide context/object sensitivity to a very small fraction (0.4–2.3%) of the sites to yield equally precise results as providing context/object sensitivity uniformly to all sites.

Categories and Subject Descriptors D.2.4 [*Software Engineering*]: Software/Program Verification

General Terms Measurement, Experimentation, Verification

Keywords heap abstractions, static analysis, concurrency, machine learning, randomization

1. Introduction

Static analyses typically have parameters that control the tradeoff between precision and scalability. For example, in a k-CFA-based or k-object-sensitivity-based points-to analysis [10–13, 20, 26], the parameter is the k value, which determines the amount of context sensitivity and object sensitivity. Increasing k yields more precise points-to information, but the complexity of the analysis also grows exponentially with k. Shape analysis [19] and model checkers based on predicate abstraction [3, 5] are parametrized by some number of predicates; these analyses also exhibit this tradeoff.

In many analyses, these tradeoffs are controlled by a small number of parameters, for instance, a single k value. Past studies (e.g., client-driven [7] and demand-driven [9] approaches) have shown that it is often not necessary to provide context sensitivity to each call site or object sensitivity to each allocation site. This motivates working with a larger family of abstractions parametrized by a separate k value for each site, akin to the parametric framework of Milanova et al. [12, 13]. More generally, we represent an abstraction as a binary vector (e.g., component j of the vector specifies whether site j should be treated context-sensitively). But how much context/object sensitivity is absolutely needed, and where is it needed?

In this paper, we formulate and tackle the following problem: Given a family of abstractions, find a minimal (coarsest) abstraction sufficient to prove all the queries provable by the finest abstraction in the family. Studying this problem is important for two reasons: (i) a minimal abstraction provides insight into which aspects of a program need to be modeled precisely for a given client; and (ii) reducing the complexity of the abstraction along some components could enable us to increase the complexity of the abstraction along other components more than before. For example, keeping the k values of most sites at zero enables us to use higher k values for a select subset of sites.

To find these minimal abstractions, we introduce two machine learning algorithms. Both treat the static analysis as a black box which takes an abstraction (and a set of client queries) as input and produces the set of proven queries as output. The first algorithm, StatRefine, starts with the coarsest abstraction, runs the static analysis on randomly chosen abstractions, and from these training examples detects statistical correlations between components of the abstraction and whether a query is proven; components highly correlated with proven queries are added (Section 4.1). The second algorithm, ActiveCoarsen, starts with the finest abstraction and samples coarser abstractions at random, incrementally reducing the abstraction to a minimal one (Section 4.2).

POPL'11, January 26–28, 2011, Austin, Texas, USA.

We also provide a theoretical analysis of our algorithms. Let p be the number of components of the abstraction family and s be the number of components in the largest minimal abstraction. We show that although the number of abstractions considered is exponential in p, we only need $O(s \log p)$ calls to the static analysis to find a minimal abstraction. The significance of this result is that when a very small abstraction suffices to prove the queries ($s \ll p$), our algorithms are much more efficient than a naïve approach, which would require $O(p)$ calls. Empirically, we found that minimal abstractions are indeed very small. This is an instance of *sparsity*, an important property in machine learning and statistics [4, 24], that very few components of an unknown vector are non-zero.

Our approach represents a significant departure from traditional program analysis, where iterative refinement techniques are the norm [2, 7, 22]. In particular, our methods exploit randomness to generate information in the form of statistical correlations. Also note that iterative refinement is in general not guaranteed to find a minimal abstraction, whereas our techniques do have this guarantee. We present one iterative refinement technique (DATALOGREFINE in Section 3.1) and show that it refines 18–85% of the components whereas the minimal abstractions found by our approach only refine 0.4–2.3% (Section 6).

All our empirical results are for a static race detection client [14] backed by a k-limited points-to analysis. Points-to information is used extensively by the race detector to determine which statements may be reachable, which statements may access the same memory locations, which statements may access thread-shared memory locations, and which statements may happen in parallel. Our points-to analysis is both context-sensitive and object-sensitive (see Section 5 for details).

2. Problem Formulation

Let $(\mathcal{A}, \preceq)$ be a poset corresponding to a family of abstractions, and let $\mathbb{Q}$ be a set of queries that we would like to prove. We assume we have access to a static analysis, $\mathbf{F} : \mathcal{A} \mapsto \{0,1\}^{\mathbb{Q}}$, which maps an abstraction $\mathbf{a} \in \mathcal{A}$ to a binary vector $\mathbf{F}(\mathbf{a})$ where component q is 0 if query q is proven and 1 if it is not.

We assume that $\mathbf{F}$ is monotone with respect to the abstraction family $(\mathcal{A}, \preceq)$, that is, if $\mathbf{a} \preceq \mathbf{a}'$, then $\mathbf{F}(\mathbf{a}) \succeq \mathbf{F}(\mathbf{a}')$. In other words, refining an abstraction (increasing $\mathbf{a}$) can only enable us to prove more queries (decrease $\mathbf{F}(\mathbf{a})$).

The focus of this paper is on the following problem:

Definition 1 (Minimal Abstraction Problem). *Given a family of abstractions $\mathcal{A}$ with a unique top element $\mathbf{1}$ (the most precise), output an abstraction $\mathbf{a} \preceq \mathbf{1}$ such that*

1. *$\mathbf{a}$ is correct—that is, $\mathbf{F}(\mathbf{a}) = \mathbf{F}(\mathbf{1})$; and*
2. *$\mathbf{a}$ is minimal—that is, such that $\{\mathbf{a}' \preceq \mathbf{a} : \mathbf{F}(\mathbf{a}') = \mathbf{F}(\mathbf{a})\} = \{\mathbf{a}\}$.*

In general, there could be multiple minimal abstractions, but we are content with choosing any one of them. Furthermore, we would like to find a minimal abstraction efficiently, i.e., minimizing the number of calls to $\mathbf{F}$.

2.1 Binary Abstractions

We now specialize to abstractions representable by binary vectors, that is, $\mathcal{A} = \{0,1\}^{\mathbb{J}}$ for some index set of *components* $\mathbb{J}$, where the partial order is component-wise inequality ($\mathbf{a} \preceq \mathbf{a}'$ iff $\mathbf{a}_j \le \mathbf{a}'_j$ for all $j \in \mathbb{J}$). The idea is that for an abstraction $\mathbf{a} \in \mathcal{A}$, $\mathbf{a}_j$ denotes whether component $j \in \mathbb{J}$ has been refined or not. It will also be convenient to treat $\mathbf{a} \in \mathcal{A}$ directly as a set of components (namely, $\{j \in \mathbb{J} : \mathbf{a}_j = 1\}$), so that we can use set notation (e.g., $\mathbf{a} \cup \{j\}$). We use $\emptyset$ and $\mathbb{J}$ to denote the coarsest and finest abstractions in the family, and we denote the *size* of abstraction $\mathbf{a}$ by $|\mathbf{a}|$.

Many commonly-used abstraction families are binary. In predicate abstraction [3, 5], $\mathbb{J}$ is the set of candidate abstraction predicates, and an abstraction $\mathbf{a}$ would specify a subset of these predicates to include in the analysis. Shape analysis [19] uses predicates on the heap graph, e.g., reachability from a variable. Similar to predicate abstraction, $\mathbf{a}_j = 1$ if predicate j is to be treated as an abstraction predicate.

2.2 k-limited Abstractions

In this paper, we focus on k-limited abstractions. Let $\mathbb{H}$ be the set of allocation sites and $\mathbb{I}$ be the set of call sites in a program. We use $\mathbb{S} = \mathbb{H} \cup \mathbb{I}$ to denote the set of *sites* of both types. Consider the family of abstractions defined by setting a non-negative integer k for each site $s \in \mathbb{S}$. In the case of k-CFA, this integer specifies that the k most recent elements of the call stack should be used to distinguish method calls and objects allocated at various sites. We denote this abstraction family as $\mathcal{A}^{\mathrm{K}} = \{0, 1, \ldots, k_{\max}\}^{\mathbb{S}}$, where $k_{\max}$ is the largest allowed k value.

At first glance, it may not be evident that the k-limited abstraction family $\mathcal{A}^{\mathrm{K}}$ is a binary abstraction family. However, we can represent $\mathcal{A}^{\mathrm{K}}$ using binary vectors as follows: Let $\mathbb{J} = \mathbb{S} \times \{1, \ldots k_{\max}\}$ be the set of components. We map each element $\mathbf{a} \in \mathcal{A} = \{0,1\}^{\mathbb{J}}$ in the binary abstraction family to a unique element $\mathbf{a}^{\mathrm{K}} \in \mathcal{A}^{\mathrm{K}}$ in the original k-limited abstraction family by $\mathbf{a}^{\mathrm{K}}_s = \sum_{k=1}^{k_{\max}} \mathbf{a}_{(s,k)}$. Essentially $\mathbf{a} \in \mathcal{A}$ is a unary encoding of the k values of $\mathbf{a}^{\mathrm{K}} \in \mathcal{A}^{\mathrm{K}}$. Note that multiple binary vectors $\mathbf{a}$ map onto the same $\mathbf{a}^{\mathrm{K}}$ (i.e., $(1,1,0)$ and $(1,0,1)$ both represent $k = 2$), but this is not important. It is crucial, however, that the mapping from $\mathcal{A}$ to $\mathcal{A}^{\mathrm{K}}$ respects the partial ordering within each family.

3. Deterministic Approaches

In this section, we discuss two deterministic approaches for finding small abstractions. Conceptually, there are two ways to proceed: start with the coarsest abstraction and refine, or start with the finest abstraction and coarsen. We present two algorithms: DATALOGREFINE (Section 3.1) and

SCANCOARSEN (Section 3.2), which operate in these two directions.

3.1 Refinement via Datalog Analysis

We first present the DATALOGREFINE algorithm, which assumes that static analysis $\mathbf{F}$ is expressed as a Datalog program P. The basic idea behind the algorithm is as follows: run the static analysis with the coarsest abstraction $\emptyset$ and look at queries which were not proven. DATALOGREFINE then inspects P to find *all* the components of the abstraction which could affect the unproven queries and refines exactly these components.

A Datalog program P consists of (i) a set of *relations* $\mathcal{R}$ (e.g., $\mathtt{ptsV} \in \mathcal{R}$, where $\mathtt{ptsV}(v, o)$ denotes whether variable v may point to abstract object o); (ii) a set of *input tuples* $\mathcal{I}$ (for example, $\mathtt{ptsV}(\mathtt{v5}, \mathtt{o7}) \in \mathcal{I}$); and (iii) a set of *rules* of the following form:

$$R_0(w_0) \Leftarrow R_1(w_1), \dots, R_m(w_m), \tag{1}$$

where for each $i = 0, \dots, m$, we have a relation $R_i \in \mathcal{R}$ and a tuple of variables w_i of the appropriate arity (e.g., when $R_0 = \mathtt{ptsV}$, $w_0 = (v, o)$).

Given a Datalog program, we derive new tuples from the input tuples $\mathcal{I}$ by using the rules. Formally, let a *derivation* be a sequence $t_1, \dots, t_n$ of tuples satisfying the following two conditions: (i) for each $i = 1, \dots, n$, either t_i is an input tuple ($t_i \in \mathcal{I}$) or there exist indices $j_1, \dots, j_m$ all smaller than i such that $t_i \Leftarrow t_{j_1}, \dots, t_{j_m}$ is an instantiation of a rule; and (ii) for each $j = 1, \dots, n-1$, tuple t_j appears on the right-hand side of an instantiation of a rule with some t_i ($i > j$) on the left-hand side.

In this formalism, each query $q \in \mathbb{Q}$ is a tuple. In race detection, the set of queries is

$$\mathbb{Q} = \{\mathtt{race}(p_1, p_2) : p_1, p_2 \in \mathbb{P}\}, \tag{2}$$

where $\mathbb{P}$ is the set of program points. For each query q, we define $\mathbf{F}(\mathbf{a})_q = 1$ if and only if there exists a derivation of q. In other words, $\mathbf{F}(\mathbf{a})_q = 0$ if and only if q is proven.

The abstraction $\mathbf{a}$ determines the input tuples $\mathcal{I}$. More specifically, let $\mathbf{A}(t, j)$ denote whether the value $\mathbf{a}_j$ of component j affects the input tuple $t \in \mathcal{I}$. For example, $\mathbf{A}(\mathtt{ptsV}(v, o), j) = 1$ for any $j = (s, k)$ and abstract object o where o can represent a concrete object allocated at allocation site $s \in \mathbb{H}$. Given $\mathbf{A}$, let $J^{\mathbf{A}}$ denote the components which are involved in a derivation of some (unproven) query:

$$J^{\mathbf{A}} \triangleq \{j \in \mathbb{J} : \exists t \in \mathcal{I}, q \in \mathbb{Q}, \mathbf{A}(t, j) = 1 \wedge t \rightsquigarrow q\}, \tag{3}$$

where $t \rightsquigarrow q$ denotes that there exists some derivation $t_1, \dots, t_n$ where $t_i = t$ for some i and $t_n = q$. The key point is that a component not in $J^{\mathbf{A}}$ cannot eliminate existing derivations of q, which would be necessary to prove q. Such a component is therefore irrelevant and not refined.

Computation via a Datalog Program Transformation We now define the DATALOGREFINE algorithm, which computes and returns $J^{\mathbf{A}}$ as the abstraction. DATALOGREFINE works by taking a Datalog program P as input and transforming it into another Datalog program P' whose output contains $J^{\mathbf{A}}$. Having this general transformation allows us to leverage existing Datalog solvers [25] to efficiently compute the set of relevant components $J^{\mathbf{A}}$ to refine.

The new program P' contains all the rules of P plus additional ones. For each Datalog rule of P taking the form given in (1), P' will contain m rules, one for each $i = 1, \dots, m$:

$$R'_i(t_i) \Leftarrow R'_0(t_0), R_1(t_1), \dots, R_m(t_m). \tag{4}$$

$R'_i(t_i)$ is true iff $R_i(t_i) \rightsquigarrow q$ for any query $q \in \mathbb{Q}$. We also add the following rule for each $R \in \mathcal{R}$, which aggregates the relevant components:

$$J^{\mathbf{A}}(j) \Leftarrow R'(t), \mathbf{A}(t, j). \tag{5}$$

It can be verified that $J^{\mathbf{A}}(j)$ is true exactly when $j \in J^{\mathbf{A}}$, where $J^{\mathbf{A}}$ is defined in (3).

Note that DATALOGREFINE is correct in that it outputs an abstraction $\mathbf{a}$ which is guaranteed to prove all the queries that $\mathbf{1}$ can, but $\mathbf{a}$ will most likely not be minimal.

k-limited Abstractions We now describe how we use DATALOGREFINE for k-limited abstractions. Recall that in our binary representation of k-limited abstractions (Section 2.2), the components are (s, k), where $s \in \mathbb{S}$ is a site and $0 \leq k \leq k_{\max}$. We start with the abstraction $\mathbf{a}_0 = \mathbf{0}$, corresponding to 0-CFA. We then iterate $k = 1, \dots, k_{\max}$, where at each iteration, we use $\mathbf{a}_{k-1}$ to construct the input tuples and call DATALOGREFINE to produce a set $J^{\mathbf{A}}$. We refine the sites specified by $J^{\mathbf{A}}$, setting $\mathbf{a}_k = \mathbf{a}_{k-1} \cup \{(s, k') : (s, k) \in J^{\mathbf{A}}, k = k'\}$. In this way, in each iteration we increase the k value of each site by at most one. Because we always refine all relevant components, after k iterations, $\mathbf{a}_k$ is guaranteed to prove the same subset of queries as k-CFA. The approach is the same for k-object-sensitivity.

3.2 Coarsening via Scanning

In the previous section, we started with the coarsest abstraction and refined it. We now introduce a simple algorithm, SCANCOARSEN, which does the opposite: it takes the most refined abstraction $\mathbf{a}$ and coarsens it, preserving correctness (Definition 1) along the way. To simplify presentation, suppose we have one query. We will revisit the issue of multiple queries in Section 4.4.

The idea behind the algorithm is quite simple: for each component, try removing it from the abstraction; if the resulting abstraction no longer proves the query, add the component back. The pseudocode of the algorithm is given in Figure 1. The algorithm maintains the invariant that $\mathbf{a}^{\mathrm{L}}$ is a

Coarsening via Scanning

```
SCANCOARSEN(a^L, a^U):
  if a^L = a^U: return a^U
  choose any component j ∈ a^U\a^L
  if F(a^U\{j}) = 0:   [try coarsening j]
    return SCANCOARSEN(a^L, a^U\{j})   [don't need j]
  else:
    return SCANCOARSEN(a^L ∪ {j}, a^U)   [need j]
```

Figure 1: Algorithm that finds a minimal abstraction.

subset of some minimal abstraction and $\mathbf{a}^{\text{U}}$ is a superset sufficient to prove the query. The algorithm requires $|\mathbb{J}|$ calls to $\mathbf{F}$, and therefore is only practical when the number of components under consideration is small.

Theorem 1 (Properties of SCANCOARSEN). *The algorithm* SCANCOARSEN($\emptyset, \mathbb{J}$) *returns a minimal abstraction* $\mathbf{a}$ *with* $O(|\mathbb{J}|)$ *calls to* $\mathbf{F}$.

Proof. Let $\mathbf{a}$ be the returned abstraction. It suffices to show that $\mathbf{F}(\mathbf{a}\backslash\{j\}) = 1$ for all $j \in \mathbf{a}$ (that is, we fail to prove the query with removal of any j). Take any $j \in \mathbf{a}$. Since j was kept, $\mathbf{F}(\mathbf{a}^{\text{U}}\backslash\{j\}) = 1$, where $\mathbf{a}^{\text{U}}$ corresponds to the value when j was considered. However, we also have $\mathbf{a} \subset \mathbf{a}^{\text{U}}$, so $\mathbf{F}(\mathbf{a}\backslash\{j\}) = 1$ by monotonicity of $\mathbf{F}$. □

4. Machine Learning Approaches

We now present two machine learning algorithms for finding minimal abstractions, which is the main theoretical contribution of this paper. The two algorithms are STATREFINE, which refines an abstraction by iteratively adding components (Section 4.1) and ACTIVECOARSEN, which coarsens an abstraction by removing components (Section 4.2).

At a high level, these two algorithms parallel their deterministic counterparts, DATALOGREFINE and SCANCOARSEN, presented in the previous section. However, there are two important distinctions worth noting: (i) the machine learning algorithms find a minimal abstraction much more effectively by exploiting *sparsity*, the property that a minimal abstraction contains a small fraction of the full set of components; and (ii) randomization is used to exploit this sparsity.

For clarity of presentation, we again focus on the case where we have a single query; Section 4.4 addresses the multiple-query setting.

4.1 Refinement via Statistical Learning

We call a component $j \in \mathbb{J}$ *dependent* if j appears in any minimal abstraction. Let $D \subset \mathbb{J}$ be the set of dependent components and let $d = |D|$. Note that D is the union of all minimal abstractions. Define s to be the size of the largest minimal abstraction, observing that $s \le d$. STATREFINE identifies dependent components by sampling n independent random abstractions and running the static analysis $\mathbf{F}$ on them. The component j associated with the most number of proven queries is then added to the abstraction, and we iterate. The pseudocode of the algorithm is given in Figure 2.

Refinement via Statistical Learning

```
Parameters:
  α: refinement probability
  s: size of largest minimal abstraction
  n: number of training examples per iteration

SAMPLE(α, a^L, a^U):
  a ← a^L
  for each component j ∈ a^U\a^L:
    a_j ← 1 with probability α
  return a

STATREFINE(a^L):
  if F(a^L) = 0 or |a^L| = s: return a^L
  for i = 1, ..., n:   [create training examples]
    a^(i) ← SAMPLE(α, a^L, J)
  for each j ∉ a^L:   [compute a score for each component]
    n_j ← |{i : a_j^(i) = 1, F(a^(i)) = 0}|
  j* ← argmax_{j∉a^L} n_j   [choose best component]
  return STATREFINE(a^L ∪ {j*})
```

Figure 2: Algorithm for finding a minimal abstraction by iteratively adding dependent components determined via statistical learning.

While DATALOGREFINE inspects the Datalog program backing $\mathbf{F}$ to compute the set of *relevant* components, STATREFINE relies instead on correlations with the output of $\mathbf{F}$ to find *dependent* components.[1] As Theorem 2 will show, with high probability, a dependent component can be found with n calls to $\mathbf{F}$, where n is only logarithmic in the total number of components $|\mathbb{J}|$.

We must also ensure that n depends only polynomially on s and d. The main technical challenge is to set the refinement probability α properly to achieve this. To appreciate this problem, suppose that $s = d$, so that $\mathbf{F}(\mathbf{a})$ consists of a simple conjunction ($\mathbf{F}(\mathbf{a}) = 0$ iff $\mathbf{a}_j = 1$ for each j in the minimal abstraction). If we set α to a constant, then it would take an exponential number of examples ($(\frac{1}{\alpha})^s$ in expectation) to even see an example where $\mathbf{F}(\mathbf{a}) = 0$. Fortunately, the following theorem shows that if α is set properly, then we obtain the desired polynomial dependence (see Appendix A for the proof):

Theorem 2 (Properties of STATREFINE). *Let d be the number of dependent components in $\mathbb{J}$ and s be the size of the largest minimal abstraction. Suppose we set the refinement probability* $\alpha = (\frac{d}{d+1})^d$ *and obtain* $n = \Theta(d^2(\log|\mathbb{J}| +$

[1] Note that dependent components are a subset of relevant components.

Coarsening via Active Learning

Parameters:
  α: refinement probability
  s: size of largest minimal abstraction

ACTIVECOARSEN($\mathbf{a}^{U}$):
  if $|\mathbf{a}^{U}| \le s+1$: return SCANCOARSEN($\emptyset, \mathbf{a}^{U}$)
  $\mathbf{a} \leftarrow$ SAMPLE($\alpha, \emptyset, \mathbf{a}^{U}$)
  if $\mathbf{F}(\mathbf{a}) = 0$:   [run static analysis]
    return ACTIVECOARSEN($\mathbf{a}$)   [reduced]
  else:
    return ACTIVECOARSEN($\mathbf{a}^{U}$)   [try again]

Figure 3: ACTIVECOARSEN returns a minimal abstraction $\mathbf{a}$ by iteratively removing a random α-fraction of the components from an upper bound. SAMPLE is defined in Figure 2.

$\log(s/\delta)))$ *training examples from* $\mathbf{F}$ *each iteration. Then with probability* $1-\delta$, STATREFINE($\emptyset$) *outputs a minimal abstraction with* $O(sd^2(\log|\mathbb{J}|+\log(s/\delta)))$ *total calls to* $\mathbf{F}$.

4.2 Coarsening via Active Learning

We now present our second machine learning algorithm, ACTIVECOARSEN. Like SCANCOARSEN, it starts from the finest abstraction $\mathbb{J}$ and tries to remove components from $\mathbb{J}$. But instead of doing this one at a time, ACTIVECOARSEN tries to remove a *random constant fraction* of the components at once. As we shall see, this allows us to hone in on a minimal abstraction much more quickly.

The pseudocode of the algorithm is given in Figure 3. It maintains an upper bound $\mathbf{a}^{U}$ which is guaranteed to prove the query. It repeatedly tries random abstraction $\mathbf{a} \preceq \mathbf{a}^{U}$. until $\mathbf{a}$ can prove the query ($\mathbf{F}(\mathbf{a}) = 0$). Then we set $\mathbf{a}^{U}$ to $\mathbf{a}$ and repeat.

Recall that SCANCOARSEN, which removes one component at a time, requires an exorbitant $O(|\mathbb{J}|)$ calls to the static analysis. The key idea behind ACTIVECOARSEN is to remove a constant fraction of components each iteration. Then we would hope to need only $O(\log_{1/\alpha}|\mathbb{J}|)$ iterations.

However, the only wrinkle is that it might take a lot of trials to sample an $\mathbf{a}$ that proves the query ($\mathbf{F}(\mathbf{a}) = 0$). To appreciate the severity of this problem, suppose $\mathbf{F}(\mathbf{a}) = \neg(\mathbf{a}^* \preceq \mathbf{a})$ for some unknown set $\mathbf{a}^*$ with $|\mathbf{a}^*| = s$; that is, we prove the query if all the components in $\mathbf{a}^*$ are refined by $\mathbf{a}$. Then there is only a α^s probability of sampling a random abstraction $\mathbf{a}$ that proves the query. The expected number of trials until we prove the query is thus $(\frac{1}{\alpha})^s$, which has an unfortunate exponential dependence on s. On the other hand, when we succeed, we reduce the number of components by a factor of α. There is therefore a tradeoff here: setting α too small results in too many trials per iteration, but setting α too large results in too many iterations. Fortunately, the following theorem shows that we can balance the two to yield an efficient algorithm (see Appendix A for the proof):

Theorem 3 (Properties of ACTIVECOARSEN). *Let s be the size of the largest minimal abstraction. If we set the refinement probability* $\alpha = e^{-1/s}$, *the expected number of calls to the analysis* $\mathbf{F}$ *made by* ACTIVECOARSEN($\mathbb{J}$) *is* $O(s\log|\mathbb{J}|)$.

4.3 Adapting the Refinement Probability

Until now, we have assumed that the size of the largest minimal abstraction s is known, and indeed Theorems 2 and 3 depend crucially on setting α properly in terms of s. In practice, s is unknown, so we seek a mechanism for setting α without this knowledge.

The intuition is that setting α properly ensures that queries are proven with a probability $p(\mathbf{F}(\mathbf{a}) = 0)$ bounded away from 0 by a constant. Indeed, in STATREFINE, following the prescribed setting of α, we get $p(\mathbf{F}(\mathbf{a}) = 0) = (\frac{d}{d+1})^d$; in ACTIVECOARSEN, we have $p(\mathbf{F}(\mathbf{a}) = 0) = (e^{-1/s})^s = e^{-1}$. (Interestingly, $(\frac{d}{d+1})^d$ is lower bounded by e^{-1} and tends exactly to e^{-1} as $d \to \infty$.)

The preceding discussion motivates a method that keeps $p(\mathbf{F}(\mathbf{a}) = 0) \approxeq e^{-1} \triangleq t$, which we call the *target probability*. We can accomplish this by adapting α as we get new examples from $\mathbf{F}$. The adaptive strategy we will derive is simple: if $\mathbf{F}(\mathbf{a}) = 0$, we decrease α; otherwise, we increase α. But by how much?

To avoid boundary conditions, we parametrize $\alpha = \sigma(\theta) = (1+e^{-\theta})^{-1}$, which maps $-\infty < \theta < \infty$ to $0 < \alpha < 1$. For convenience, let us define $g(\theta) = p(\mathbf{F}(\mathbf{a}) = 0)$. Now consider minimizing the following function:

$$\mathcal{O}(\theta) = \frac{1}{2}(g(\theta) - t)^2. \tag{6}$$

Clearly, the optimum value (zero) is obtained by setting θ so that $g(\theta) = t$. We can optimize $\mathcal{O}(\theta)$ by updating its gradient:

$$\theta \leftarrow \theta - \eta\frac{d\mathcal{O}}{d\theta}, \quad \frac{d\mathcal{O}}{d\theta} = (g(\theta) - t)\frac{dg(\theta)}{d\theta}, \tag{7}$$

where η is the step size. Of course we cannot evaluate $g(\theta)$, but the key is that we can obtain unbiased samples of $g(\theta)$ by evaluating $\mathbf{F}(\mathbf{a})$ (which we needed to do anyway); specifically, $\mathbb{E}[1 - \mathbf{F}(\mathbf{a})] = g(\theta)$. We can therefore replace the gradient with a stochastic gradient, a classic technique with a rich theory [18]. We note that $\frac{dg(\theta)}{d\theta} > 0$, so we absorb it into the step size η.[2] This leaves us with the following rule for updating θ given a random $\mathbf{a}$:

$$\theta \leftarrow \theta - \eta(1 - F(\mathbf{a}) - t). \tag{8}$$

[2] Note that we have not verified the step size conditions that guarantee convergence. Instead, we simply set $\eta = 0.1$ for our experiments, which worked well in practice.

4.4 Multiple Queries and Parallelization

So far, we have presented all our algorithms for one query. Given multiple queries, we could just solve each query independently, but this is quite wasteful, since the information obtained from answering one query is not used for other queries. We therefore adopt a *lazy splitting* strategy, where we initially place all the queries in one group and partition the groups over time as we run either STATREFINE or ACTIVECOARSEN. More specifically, we maintain a partition of $\mathbb{Q}$ into a collection of groups G, where each $g \in G$ is a subset of $\mathbb{Q}$. We run the algorithm independently for each $g \in G$. After each call to $\mathbf{F}(\mathbf{a})$, we create two new groups, $g_0 = \{q \in g : \mathbf{F}(\mathbf{a})_q = 0\}$ and $g_1 = \{q \in g : \mathbf{F}(\mathbf{a})_q = 1\}$, and set G to $(G \backslash \{g\}) \cup \{g_0, g_1\}$, throwing away empty groups. In g_0, we take the $\mathbf{F}(\mathbf{a}) = 0$ branch of the algorithm and in g_1, we take the $\mathbf{F}(\mathbf{a}) = 1$ branch.

We thus maintain the invariant that for any two queries $q_1, q_2 \in g$, we have $\mathbf{F}(\mathbf{a})_{q_1} = \mathbf{F}(\mathbf{a})_{q_2}$ for any $\mathbf{a}$ that we have run $\mathbf{F}$ on for g or any of g's ancestral groups. Conceptually, from the point of view of a fixed $q \in \mathbb{Q}$, it is as if we had run the algorithm on q alone, but all of the calls to $\mathbf{F}$ are shared by other queries. When the algorithm terminates, all the queries in one group share the same minimal abstraction. In Section 6, we will see that the number of groups is much smaller than the number of queries.

Our algorithms have been presented as sequential algorithms, but parallelization is possible. STATREFINE is trivial to parallelize because the n training examples are generated independently. Parallelizing ACTIVECOARSEN is slightly more intricate because of the sequential dependence of calls to $\mathbf{F}$. With one processor, we set α so that the target probability is e^{-1}. When we have m processors, we set the target probability to e^{-1}/m, so that the expected time until a reduction is approximately the same. The upshot of this is that α (monotonically related to t) is now smaller and thus we obtain larger reductions.

4.5 Discussion of Algorithms

Table 1 summarizes the properties of the four algorithms we have presented in this paper. One of the key advantages of the learning-based approaches (STATREFINE and ACTIVECOARSEN) is that they have a logarithmic dependence on $|\mathbb{J}|$ since they take advantage of *sparsity*, the property that a minimal abstraction has at most s components.

Both algorithms sample random abstractions by including each component with probability α, and to avoid an exponential dependence on s, it is important to set the probability α properly—for STATREFINE, so that the profile of an irrelevant component is sufficiently different from that of a relevant component; for ACTIVECOARSEN, so that the probability of obtaining a successful reduction of the abstraction is sufficiently large.

The algorithms are also complementary in several respects: STATREFINE is a Monte Carlo algorithm (the running time is fixed, but there is some probability that it does not find a minimal abstraction), whereas ACTIVECOARSEN is a Las Vegas algorithm (the running time is random, but we are guaranteed to find a minimal abstraction). Note that STATREFINE has an extra factor of d^2, because it implicitly tries to reason globally about all possible minimal abstractions which involve d dependent components, whereas ACTIVECOARSEN tries to hone in on one minimal abstraction. In practice, we found ACTIVECOARSEN to be more effective, and thus used it to obtain our empirical results.

5. Site-varying k-limited Points-to Analysis

We now present the static analysis ($\mathbf{F}(\mathbf{a})$ in our general notation) for the abstraction family $\mathcal{A}^{\text{K}}$ (defined in Section 2.2), which allows each allocation and call site to have a separate k value. Figure 4 describes the basic analysis. Each node in the control-flow graph of each method $m \in \mathbb{M}$ is associated with a simple statement (e.g., $v_2 = v_1$). We omit statements that have no effect on our analysis (e.g., operations on data of primitive type). For simplicity, we assume each method has a single argument and no return value. Our actual implementation is a straightforward extension of this simplified analysis which handles multiple arguments, return values, class initializers, and objects allocated through reflection.

Our analysis uses sequences of call sites (in the case of k-CFA) or allocation sites (in the case of k-object-sensitivity) to represent method contexts. In either case, abstract objects are represented by an allocation site plus the context of the containing method in which the object was allocated. Our abstraction $\mathbf{a}$ maps each site $s \in \mathbb{S}$ to the maximum length $\mathbf{a}_s$ of the context or abstract object to maintain. For example, k-CFA (with heap specialization) is represented by $\mathbf{a}_h = k+1$ for each allocation site $h \in \mathbb{H}$ and $\mathbf{a}_i = k$ for each call site $i \in \mathbb{I}$; k-object-sensitivity is represented by $\mathbf{a}_h = k$ for each allocation site $h \in \mathbb{H}$. The abstraction determines the input tuples $\mathtt{ext}(s, c, c')$, where prepending s to c and truncating at length $\mathbf{a}_s$ yields c'. For example, if $\mathbf{a}_{\mathtt{h2}} = 2$ then we have $\mathtt{ext}(\mathtt{h2}, [\mathtt{i3}, \mathtt{i7}], [\mathtt{h2}, \mathtt{i3}])$.

Our analysis computes the reachable methods (`reachM`), reachable statements (`reachP`), and points-to sets of local variables (`ptsV`), each with the associated context; the context-insensitive points-to sets of static fields (`ptsG`) and heap graph (`heap`); and a context-sensitive call graph (`cg`).

We briefly describe the analysis rules in Datalog. Rule (1) states that the main method m_{main} is reachable in a distinguished context []. Rule (2) states that a target method of a reachable call site is also reachable. Rule (3) states that every statement in a reachable method is also reachable. Rules (4) through (9) implement the transfer function associated with each kind of statement. Rules (10a) and (10b) populate the call graph while rules (11a) and (11b) propagate the points-to set from the argument of a call site to the formal argument of each target method. Rules (10a) and (11a) are used in the case of k-CFA whereas rules (10b) and (11b)

Algorithm	Minimal	Correct	# calls to $\mathbf{F}$
DATALOGREFINE	no	yes	$O(1)$
SCANCOARSEN	yes	yes	$O(\|\mathbb{J}\|)$
STATREFINE	prob. $1-\delta$	prob. $1-\delta$	$O(sd^2(\log\|\mathbb{J}\| + \log(s/\delta))$
ACTIVECOARSEN	yes	yes	$O(s\log\|\mathbb{J}\|)$ [in expectation]

Table 1: Summary showing the two properties of Definition 1 for the four algorithms we have presented in this paper. Note that the two machine learning algorithms have only a logarithmic dependence on $|\mathbb{J}|$, the total number of components, and a linear dependence on the size of the largest minimal abstraction s.

are used in the case of k-object-sensitivity. As dictated by k-object-sensitivity, rule (10b) analyzes the target method m in a separate context o for each abstract object o to which the distinguished `this` argument of method m points, and rule (11b) sets the points-to set of the `this` argument of method m in context o to the singleton $\{o\}$.

Race Detection We use the points-to information computed above to answer datarace queries of the form presented in (2), where we include pairs of program points corresponding to heap-accessing statements of the same field in which at least one statement is a write. We implemented the static race detector of [14], which declares a (p_1, p_2) pair as racing if both statements may be reachable, may access thread-escaping data, may point to the same object, and may happen in parallel. All four components rely heavily on the context- and object-sensitive points-to analysis.

6. Experiments

In this section, we apply our algorithms (Sections 3 and 4) to the k-limited analysis for race detection (Section 5) to answer the main question we started out with: how small are minimal abstractions empirically?

6.1 Setup

Our experiments were performed using IBM J9VM 1.6.0 on 32-bit Linux machines. All the analyses (the basic k-limited analysis, DATALOGREFINE, and the race detector) were implemented in Chord, an extensible program analysis framework for Java bytecode.[3] The machine learning algorithms simply use the race detector as a black box.

The experiments were applied to five multi-threaded Java benchmarks: an implementation of the Traveling Salesman Problem (`tsp`), a discrete event simulation program (`elevator`), a web crawler (`hedc`), a website downloading and mirroring tool (`weblech`), and a text search tool (`lusearch`).

Table 2 provides the number of classes, number of methods, number of bytecodes of methods, and number of allocation/call sites deemed reachable by 0-CFA in these benchmarks. Table 3 shows the number of races (unproven queries) reported by the coarsest and finest abstractions. Their difference is the set of queries $\mathbb{Q}$ that we want to prove with a minimal abstraction.

[3] `http://code.google.com/p/jchord/`

	# classes	# methods	# bytecodes	$\|\mathbb{H}\|$	$\|\mathbb{I}\|$
`tsp`	167	635	40K	656	1,721
`elevator`	170	637	42K	663	1,893
`hedc`	335	1,965	153K	1,580	7,195
`weblech`	559	3,181	225K	2,584	12,405
`lusearch`	627	3,798	266K	2,873	13,928

Table 2: Benchmark characteristics. $|\mathbb{H}|$ is the number of allocation sites, and $|\mathbb{I}|$ is the number of call sites. Together, these determine the number of components in the abstraction family $|\mathbb{J}|$. For k-CFA, $|\mathbb{J}| = k(|\mathbb{H}| + |\mathbb{I}|)$; for k-object-sensitivity, $|\mathbb{J}| = (k-1)|\mathbb{H}|$.

a	`tsp`	`elevator`	`hedc`	`weblech`	`lusearch`
$\emptyset$ (CFA)	570	510	21,335	27,941	37,632
$\mathbb{J}$ (CFA)	494	441	17,837	8,208	31,866
diff. ($\|\mathbb{Q}\|$)	76	69	3,498	19,733	5,766
$\emptyset$ (OBJ)	536	475	17,137	8,063	31,428
$\mathbb{J}$ (OBJ)	489	437	16,124	5,523	20,929
diff. ($\|\mathbb{Q}\|$)	47	38	1,013	2,540	10,499

Table 3: Number of races (unproven queries) reported using the coarsest abstraction $\emptyset$ (0-CFA/1-object-sensitivity) and the finest abstraction $\mathbb{J}$ (2-CFA/3-object-sensitivity for `tsp`, `elevator` and 1-CFA/2 object-sensitivity for `hedc`, `weblech`, `lusearch`). The difference is the set of queries under consideration (those provable by $\mathbb{J}$ but not by $\emptyset$).

6.2 Results

Table 4 summarizes the basic results for DATALOGREFINE and ACTIVECOARSEN. While both find abstractions which prove the same set of queries, ACTIVECOARSEN obtains this precision using an abstraction which is minimal and an order of magnitude smaller than the abstraction found by DATALOGREFINE, which is not guaranteed to be minimal (and is, in fact, far from minimal in our experiments).

Algorithms aside, it is noteworthy in itself that very small abstractions exist. For example, on `tsp`, we can get the same precision as 2-CFA by essentially using a "0.01-CFA" analysis. Indeed, our static analysis using this minimal abstraction was as fast as using 0-CFA, whereas 2-CFA took significantly longer.

Domains:

$$
\begin{array}{rcll}
\text{(method)} & m & \in & \mathbb{M} = \{m_{\text{main}}, ...\} \\
\text{(local variable)} & v & \in & \mathbb{V} \\
\text{(global variable)} & g & \in & \mathbb{G} \\
\text{(object field)} & f & \in & \mathbb{F} \\
\text{(method call site)} & i & \in & \mathbb{I} \\
\text{(allocation site)} & h & \in & \mathbb{H} \\
\text{(allocation/call site)} & s & \in & \mathbb{S} = \mathbb{H} \cup \mathbb{I} \\
\text{(statement)} & p & \in & \mathbb{P} \\
\text{(method context)} & c & \in & \mathbb{C} = \bigcup_{k \geq 0} \mathbb{S}^k \\
\text{(abstract object)} & o & \in & \mathbb{O} = \mathbb{H} \times \mathbb{C} \\
\text{(abstraction)} & \mathbf{a} & \in & \mathcal{A}^{\text{K}} = \{0, 1, \dots\}^{\mathbb{S}}
\end{array}
$$

Input relations:

$$
\begin{array}{llll}
\texttt{body} & \subset & \mathbb{M} \times \mathbb{P} & \text{(method contains statement)} \\
\texttt{trgt} & \subset & \mathbb{I} \times \mathbb{M} & \text{(call site resolves to method)} \\
\texttt{argI} & \subset & \mathbb{I} \times \mathbb{V} & \text{(call site's argument variable)} \\
\texttt{argM} & \subset & \mathbb{M} \times \mathbb{V} & \text{(method's formal argument variable)} \\
\texttt{ext} & \subset & \mathbb{S} \times \mathbb{C} \times \mathbb{C} & \text{(extend context with site)} \\
 & = & \multicolumn{2}{l}{\{(s, c, (s, c)[1..\min\{\mathbf{a}_s, 1+|c|\}]) : s \in \mathbb{S}, c \in \mathbb{C}\}}
\end{array}
$$

Output relations:

$$
\begin{array}{llll}
\texttt{reachM} & \subset & \mathbb{C} \times \mathbb{M} & \text{(reachable methods)} \\
\texttt{reachP} & \subset & \mathbb{C} \times \mathbb{P} & \text{(reachable statements)} \\
\texttt{ptsV} & \subset & \mathbb{C} \times \mathbb{V} \times \mathbb{O} & \text{(points-to sets of local variables)} \\
\texttt{ptsG} & \subset & \mathbb{G} \times \mathbb{O} & \text{(points-to sets of static fields)} \\
\texttt{heap} & \subset & \mathbb{O} \times \mathbb{F} \times \mathbb{O} & \text{(heap graph)} \\
\texttt{cg} & \subset & \mathbb{C} \times \mathbb{I} \times \mathbb{C} \times \mathbb{M} & \text{(call graph)}
\end{array}
$$

$$p ::= v = \texttt{new}\, h \mid v_2 = v_1 \mid g = v \mid v = g \mid v_2.f = v_1 \mid v_2 = v_1.f \mid i(v)$$

Rules:

$$
\begin{array}{llll}
\texttt{reachM}([], m_{\text{main}}). & & & (1) \\
\texttt{reachM}(c, m) & \Leftarrow & \texttt{cg}(*, *, c, m). & (2) \\
\texttt{reachP}(c, p) & \Leftarrow & \texttt{reachM}(c, m),\ \texttt{body}(m, p). & (3) \\
\\
\texttt{ptsV}(c, v, o) & \Leftarrow & \texttt{reachP}(c, v = \texttt{new}\, h),\ \texttt{ext}(h, c, o). & (4) \\
\texttt{ptsV}(c, v_2, o) & \Leftarrow & \texttt{reachP}(c, v_2 = v_1),\ \texttt{ptsV}(c, v_1, o). & (5) \\
\texttt{ptsG}(g, o) & \Leftarrow & \texttt{reachP}(c, g = v),\ \texttt{ptsV}(c, v, o). & (6) \\
\texttt{ptsV}(c, v, o) & \Leftarrow & \texttt{reachP}(c, v = g),\ \texttt{ptsG}(g, o). & (7) \\
\texttt{heap}(o_2, f, o_1) & \Leftarrow & \texttt{reachP}(c, v_2.f = v_1),\ \texttt{ptsV}(c, v_1, o_1),\ \texttt{ptsV}(c, v_2, o_2). & (8) \\
\texttt{ptsV}(c, v_2, o_2) & \Leftarrow & \texttt{reachP}(c, v_2 = v_1.f),\ \texttt{ptsV}(c, v_1, o_1),\ \texttt{heap}(o_1, f, o_2). & (9) \\
\\
\texttt{cg}(c_1, i, c_2, m) & \Leftarrow & \texttt{reachP}(c_1, i),\ \texttt{trgt}(i, m),\ \texttt{ext}(i, c_1, c_2). & (10a) \\
\texttt{cg}(c, i, o, m) & \Leftarrow & \texttt{reachP}(c, i),\ \texttt{trgt}(i, m),\ \texttt{argI}(i, v),\ \texttt{ptsV}(c, v, o). & (10b) \\
\texttt{ptsV}(c_2, v_2, o) & \Leftarrow & \texttt{cg}(c_1, i, c_2, m),\ \texttt{argI}(i, v_1),\ \texttt{argM}(m, v_2),\ \texttt{ptsV}(c_1, v_1, o). & (11a) \\
\texttt{ptsV}(c, v, c) & \Leftarrow & \texttt{reachM}(c, m),\ \texttt{argM}(m, v). & (11b)
\end{array}
$$

Figure 4: Datalog implementation of our k-limited points-to analysis with call-graph construction. Our abstraction $\mathbf{a}$ affects the analysis solely through ext, which specifies that when we prepend s to c, we truncate the resulting sequence to length $\mathbf{a}_s$. If we use rules (10a) and (11a), we get k-CFA; if we use (10b) and (11b), we get k-object-sensitivity.

Query Groups Recall from Section 4.4 that to deal with multiple queries, we partition the queries into groups and find one minimal abstraction for each group. The abstraction sizes reported so far are the union of the abstractions over all groups. We now take a closer look at the abstractions for individual queries in a group.

First, Table 5 shows that the number of groups is much smaller than the number of queries, which means that many queries share the same minimal abstraction. This is intuitive since many queries depend on the same data and control properties of a program.

Next, Figure 5 shows a histogram of the abstraction sizes across queries. Most queries required a tiny abstraction, only requiring a handful of sites to be refined. For example, for object-sensitivity on hedc, over 80% of the queries require just a single allocation site to be refined. Even the most demanding query requires only 9 of the 1,580 sites to be refined. Recall that refining 37 sites suffices to prove all the queries (Table 4). For comparison, DATALOGREFINE refines 906 sites.

7. Related Work

One of the key algorithmic tools that we used to find minimal abstractions is randomization. Randomization, a powerful idea, has been previously applied in program analysis, e.g., in random testing [8] and random interpretation [6].

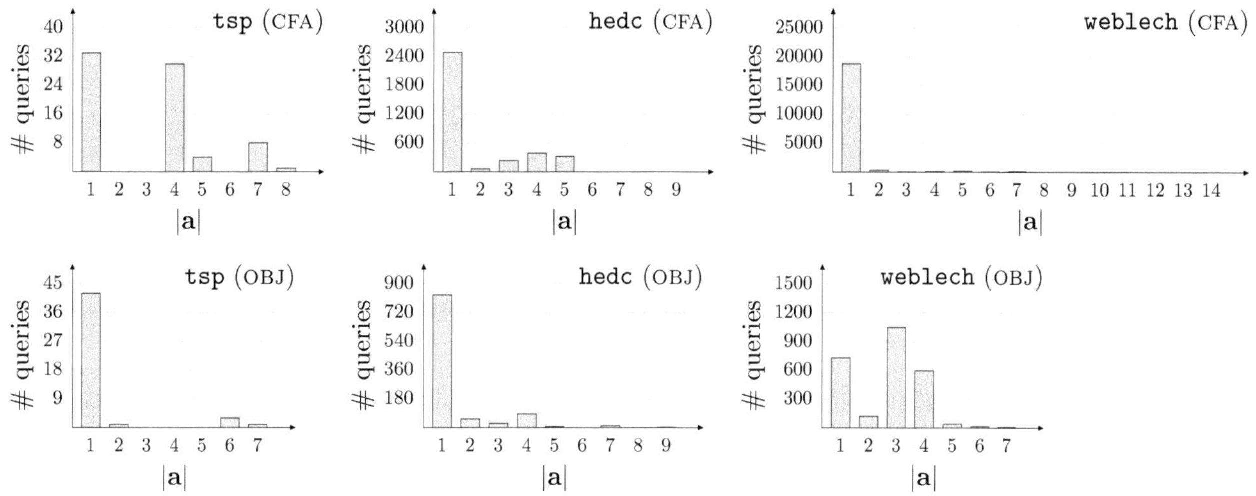

Figure 5: A histogram showing for each abstraction size |a|, the number of queries that have a minimal abstraction of that size (for three of the five benchmarks). Note that most queries need very small abstractions (some need only one site to be refined).

	$\|\mathbb{J}\|$	DATALOGREFINE	Minimal
tsp (CFA)	4,754	3,170 (67%)	27 (0.6%)
tsp (OBJ)	1,312	236 (18%)	7 (0.5%)
elevator (CFA)	5,112	3,541 (69%)	18 (0.4%)
elevator (OBJ)	1,326	291 (22%)	6 (0.5%)
hedc (CFA)	8,775	7,270 (83%)	90 (1.0%)
hedc (OBJ)	1,580	906 (57%)	37 (2.3%)
weblech (CFA)	14,989	12,737 (85%)	157 (1.0%)
weblech (OBJ)	2,584	1,768 (68%)	48 (1.9%)
lusearch (CFA)	16,801	14,864 (88%)	250 (1.5%)
lusearch (OBJ)	2,873	2,085 (73%)	56 (1.9%)

Table 4: This table shows our main results. $|\mathbb{J}|$ is the number of components (the size of the finest abstraction). The next two columns show abstraction sizes (absolute and fraction of $|\mathbb{J}|$) for the abstraction found by DATALOGREFINE and a minimal abstraction found by ACTIVECOARSEN. All abstractions prove the same set of queries. DATALOGREFINE refines anywhere between 18%–85% of the components, while the minimal abstraction is an order of magnitude smaller (0.4%–2.3% of the components).

	# groups	min.	mean.	max.
tsp (CFA)	10	1	8	26
tsp (OBJ)	5	1	9	22
elevator (CFA)	6	3	12	22
elevator (OBJ)	4	1	10	18
hedc (CFA)	63	1	56	546
hedc (OBJ)	43	1	24	300
weblech (CFA)	79	1	250	17,164
weblech (OBJ)	49	1	52	899
lusearch (CFA)	140	1	41	1,346
lusearch (OBJ)	72	1	146	5,104

Table 5: Recall that our learning algorithms group the queries (Section 4.4) so that all the queries in one group share the same minimal abstraction. The minimum, mean, and maximum size of a group is reported. In all cases, there is large spread of the number of queries in a group.

Our approach is perhaps more closely associated with machine learning, although there is an important difference in our goals. Machine learning, as exemplified by the PAC learning model [23], is largely concerned with prediction—that is, an algorithm is evaluated on how accurately it can learn a function that predicts well on future inputs. We are instead concerned with finding the smallest input on which a function evaluates to 0. As a result, many of the results, for example on learning monotone DNF formulae [1], are not directly applicable, though many of the bounding techniques used are similar.

One of the key properties that our approach exploited was sparsity—that only a small subset of the components of the abstraction actually matters for proving the desired query. This enabled us to use a logarithmic rather than linear number of examples. Sparsity is one of the main themes in machine learning, signal processing, and statistics. For example, in the area of compressed sensing [4], one also needs a logarithmic number of linear measurements to recover a sparse signal.

Past research in program analysis, and pointer analysis specifically, has proposed various ways to reduce the cost of the analysis while still providing accurate results. Parametrization frameworks provide a mechanism for the user to control the tradeoff between cost and precision of the analysis. Client-driven approaches are capable of computing an exhaustive solution of varying precision while demand-driven approaches are capable of computing a partial solution of fixed precision. Below we expand upon each of these topics in relation to our work.

Milanova et al. [12, 13] present a parametrized framework for a k-object-sensitive points-to analysis, where each local variable can be separately treated context-sensitively or context-insensitively, and different k values can be chosen for different allocation sites. Instantiations of the framework using k=1 and k=2 are evaluated on side-effect analysis, call-graph construction and virtual-call resolution, and are shown to be significantly more precise than 1-CFA while being comparable to 0-CFA in performance, if not better. Lhoták and Hendren [10, 11] present Paddle, a parametrized framework for BDD-based, k-limited alias analysis. They empirically evaluate various instantiations of Paddle, including conventional k-CFA, k-object-sensitivity and k-CFA with heap cloning, on the monomorphic-call-site and cast-safety clients, as well as using traditional metrics, and show that k-object-sensitivity is superior to other approaches both in performance and in precision.

Plevyak and Chien [15] use a refinement-based algorithm to determine the concrete types of objects in programs written in the Concurrent Aggregates object-oriented language. When imprecision in the analysis causes a type conflict, the algorithm can improve context sensitivity by performing *function splitting*, and object sensitivity through *container splitting*, which divides object creation sites and thus enables the creation of objects of different types at a single site. In a more recent study, Sridharan and Bodik [21] present a demand-driven, refinement-based alias analysis for Java, and apply it to a cast-safety client. Their algorithm computes an overapproximation of the points-to relation, which is successively refined in response to client demand. At each stage of refinement, the algorithm simultaneously refines handling of heap accesses and method calls along paths, establishing the points-to sets of variables that are relevant for evaluating the client's query.

Guyer and Lin [7] present a client-driven pointer analysis for C that adjusts its precision in response to inaccuracies in the client analysis. Their analysis is a two-pass algorithm: In the first pass, a low-precision pointer analysis is run to detect which statements lead to imprecision in the client analysis; based on this information, a fine-grained precision policy is built for the second pass, which treats these statements with greater context and flow sensitivity. This is similar to our DATALOGREFINE in spirit, but DATALOGREFINE is more general.

In contrast to client-driven analyses, which compute an exhaustive solution of varying precision, demand-driven approaches compute a partial solution of fixed precision. Heintze and Tardieu's demand-driven alias analysis for C [9] performs a provably optimal computation to determine the points-to sets of variables queried by the client. Their analysis is applied to call-graph construction in the presence of function pointers. A more recent alias analysis developed by Zheng and Rugina [27] uses a demand-driven algorithm that is capable of answering alias queries without constructing points-to sets.

Reps [16, 17] shows how to automatically obtain demand-driven versions of program analyses from their exhaustive counterparts by applying the "magic-sets transformation" developed in the logic-programming and deductive-database communities. The exhaustive analysis is expressed in Datalog, akin to that in our DATALOGREFINE approach, but unlike us, they are interested in answering specific queries of interest in the program being analyzed as opposed to all queries. For instance, while we are interested in finding all pairs of points (p_1, p_2) in a given program that may be involved in a race, they may be interested in finding all points that may be involved in a race with the statement at point p42 in the given program. The magic-set transformation takes as input a Datalog program which performs the exhaustive analysis along with a set of specified queries. It produces as output the demand-driven version of the analysis, also in Datalog, but which eliminates computation from the original analysis that is unnecessary for evaluating the specified queries. In contrast, our transformation takes as input a parametrized analysis expressed in Datalog and produces as output another analysis, also in Datalog, whose goal is to compute all possible parameters that may affect the output of the original analysis, for instance, all possible sites in a given program whose small k values may be responsible for a set of races being reported by the original analysis.

8. Conclusion

We started this study with a basic question: what is the minimal abstraction needed to prove a set of queries of interest? To answer this question, we developed two machine learning algorithms and applied them to find minimal k values of call/allocation sites for a static race detector. The key theme in this work is *sparsity*, the property that very few components of an abstraction are needed to prove a query. The ramifications are two-fold: Theoretically, we show that our algorithms are efficient under sparsity; empirically, we found that the minimal abstractions are quite small—only 0.4–2.3% of the sites are needed to prove all the queries of interest.

A. Proofs

Proof of Theorem 2. Note that the algorithm will run for at most s iterations, where s is the size of the largest minimal abstraction. If we set n so that STATREFINE chooses a dependent component each iteration with probability at least $1 - \delta/s$, then the algorithm will succeed with probability at least $1 - \delta$ (by a union bound).

Let us now focus on one iteration. The main idea is that a dependent component j is more correlated with proving the query ($\mathbf{F}(\mathrm{a}) = 0$) than one that is independent. This enables picking it out with high probability given sufficiently large n.

Recall that D is the set of dependent components with $|D| = d$. Fix a dependent component $j^+ \in D$. Let B_{j^-} be the event that $n_{j^-} > n_{j^+}$, and B be the event that B_{j^-} holds for any independent component $j^- \in \mathbb{J}\backslash D$. Note that if B does not happen, then the algorithm will correctly pick a dependent component (possibly j^+). Thus, the main focus is on showing that $P(B) \leq \delta/s$. First, by a union bound, we have

$$P(B) \leq \sum_{j^-} P(B_{j^-}) \leq |\mathbb{J}| \max_{j^-} P(B_{j^-}). \quad (9)$$

For each training example $\mathbf{a}^{(i)}$, define $X_i = (1 - \mathbf{F}(\mathbf{a}^{(i)}))(\mathbf{a}^{(i)}_{j^-} - \mathbf{a}^{(i)}_{j^+})$. Observe that B_{j^-} happens exactly when $\frac{1}{n}(n_{j^-} - n_{j^+}) = \frac{1}{n}\sum_{i=1}^{n} X_i > 0$. We now bound this quantity using Hoeffding's inequality,[4] where the mean is

$$\mathbb{E}[X_i] = p(\mathbf{F}(\mathbf{a}) = 0, \mathbf{a}_{j^-} = 1) - p(\mathbf{F}(\mathbf{a}) = 0, \mathbf{a}_{j^+} = 1),$$

and the bounds are $a = -1$ and $b = +1$. Setting $\epsilon = -\mathbb{E}[X_i]$, we get:

$$p(B_{j^-}) \leq e^{-n\epsilon^2/2}, \quad j^+ \in D, j^- \notin D. \quad (10)$$

Substituting (10) into (9) and rearranging terms, we can solve for n:

$$\delta/s \leq |\mathbb{J}|e^{-n\epsilon^2/2} \Rightarrow n \geq \frac{2(\log|\mathbb{J}| + \log(s/\delta))}{\epsilon^2}. \quad (11)$$

Now it remains to lower bound ϵ, which intuitively represents the gap (in the amount of correlation with proving the query) between a dependent component and an independent one. Note that $p(\mathbf{a}_j = 1) = \alpha$ for any $j \in \mathbb{J}$. Also, j^- is independent of $\mathbf{F}(\mathbf{a})$, so $p(\mathbf{F}(\mathbf{a}) = 0 \mid \mathbf{a}_{j^-} = 1) = p(\mathbf{F}(\mathbf{a}) = 0)$. Using these two facts, we have:

$$\epsilon = \alpha(p(\mathbf{F}(\mathbf{a}) = 0 \mid \mathbf{a}_{j^+} = 1) \quad p(\mathbf{F}(\mathbf{a}) = 0)). \quad (12)$$

Let C be the set of minimal abstractions of $\mathbf{F}$. We can think of C as a set of clauses in a DNF formula: $\mathbf{F}(\mathbf{a}; C) = \neg \bigvee_{c \in C} \bigwedge_{j \in c} \mathbf{a}_j$, where we explicitly mark the dependence of $\mathbf{F}$ on the clauses C. For example, $C = \{\{1,2\},\{3\}\}$ corresponds to $\mathbf{F}(\mathbf{a}) = \neg[(\mathbf{a}_1 \wedge \mathbf{a}_2) \vee \mathbf{a}_3]$. Next, let $C_j = \{c \in C : j \in c\}$ be the clauses containing j. Rewrite $p(\mathbf{F}(\mathbf{a}) = 0)$ as the sum of two parts, one that depends on j^+ and one that does not:

$$p(\mathbf{F}(\mathbf{a}) = 0) = p(\mathbf{F}(\mathbf{a}; C_{j^+}) = 0, \mathbf{F}(\mathbf{a}; C\backslash C_{j^+}) = 1) + p(\mathbf{F}(\mathbf{a}; C\backslash C_{j^+}) = 0). \quad (13)$$

Computing $p(\mathbf{F}(\mathbf{a}) = 0 \mid \mathbf{a}_{j^+} = 1)$ is similar; the only difference due to conditioning on $\mathbf{a}_{j^+} = 1$ is that the first term has an additional factor of $\frac{1}{\alpha}$ because conditioning divides by $p(\mathbf{a}_{j^+} = 1) = \alpha$. The second term is unchanged because no $c \notin C_{j^+}$ depends on $\mathbf{a}_{j^+}$. Plugging these two results back into (12) yields:

$$\epsilon = (1-\alpha)p(\mathbf{F}(\mathbf{a}; C_{j^+}) = 0, \mathbf{F}(\mathbf{a}; C\backslash C_{j^+}) = 1). \quad (14)$$

Now we want to lower bound (14) over all possible $\mathbf{F}$ (equivalently, C), where j^+ is allowed to depend on C. It turns out that the worst possible C is obtained by either having d disjoint clauses ($C = \{\{j\} : j \in D\}$) or one clause ($C = \{D\}$ if $s = d$). The intuition is that if C has d clauses, there are many opportunities ($d-1$ of them) for some $c \notin C_{j^+}$ to activate, making it hard to realize that j^+ is a dependent component; in this case, $\epsilon = (1-\alpha)\alpha(1-\alpha)^{d-1}$. If C has one clause, then it is very hard (probability α^d) to even activate this clause; in this case, $\epsilon = (1-\alpha)\alpha^d$.

Let us focus on the case where C has d clauses. We can maximize ϵ with respect to α by setting the derivative $\frac{d\epsilon}{d\alpha} = 0$ and solving for α. Doing this yields $\alpha = \frac{1}{d+1}$ as the optimal value. Plugging this value back into the expression for ϵ, we get that $\epsilon = \frac{1}{d+1}(\frac{d}{d+1})^d$. The second factor can be lower bounded by e^{-1}, so $\epsilon^{-2} = O(d^2)$. Combining this with (11) completes the proof. □

Proof of Theorem 3. Let $T(\mathbf{a}^{\mathrm{U}})$ be the expected number of calls that ACTIVECOARSEN($\mathbf{a}^{\mathrm{U}}$) makes to $\mathbf{F}$. The recursive computation of this quantity parallels the pseudocode of Figure 3:

$$T(\mathbf{a}^{\mathrm{U}}) \quad (15)$$
$$= \begin{cases} |\mathbf{a}^{\mathrm{U}}| & \text{if } |\mathbf{a}^{\mathrm{U}}| \leq s+1 \\ 1+\mathbb{E}[(1-\mathbf{F}(\mathbf{a}))T(\mathbf{a})+\mathbf{F}(\mathbf{a})T(\mathbf{a}^{\mathrm{U}})] & \text{otherwise,} \end{cases}$$

where $\mathbf{a} \leftarrow$ SAMPLE($\emptyset, \mathbf{a}^{\mathrm{U}}$) is a random binary vector. By assumption, there exists an abstraction $\mathbf{a}^* \preceq \mathbf{a}^{\mathrm{U}}$ of size s that proves the query. Define $\mathbf{G}(\mathbf{a}) = \neg(\mathbf{a}^* \preceq \mathbf{a})$, which is 0 when all components in $\mathbf{a}^*$ are active under the random $\mathbf{a}$. We have $p(\mathbf{G}(\mathbf{a}) = 0) = p(\mathbf{a}^* \preceq \mathbf{a}) = \alpha^s$. Note that $\mathbf{G}(\mathbf{a}) \geq \mathbf{F}(\mathbf{a})$, as activating $\mathbf{a}^*$ suffices to prove the query. We assume $T(\mathbf{a}) \leq T(\mathbf{a}^{\mathrm{U}})$ (T is monotonic), so we get an upper bound by replacing $\mathbf{F}$ with $\mathbf{G}$ and performing some algebra:

$$T(\mathbf{a}^{\mathrm{U}}) \leq 1 + \mathbb{E}[(1-\mathbf{G}(\mathbf{a}))T(\mathbf{a}) + \mathbf{G}(\mathbf{a})T(\mathbf{a}^{\mathrm{U}})] \quad (16)$$
$$\leq 1 + \alpha^s\mathbb{E}[T(\mathbf{a}) \mid \mathbf{a}^* \preceq \mathbf{a}] + (1-\alpha^s)T(\mathbf{a}^{\mathrm{U}}) \quad (17)$$
$$\leq \mathbb{E}[T(\mathbf{a}) \mid \mathbf{a}^* \preceq \mathbf{a}] + \alpha^{-s}. \quad (18)$$

Overloading notation, we write $T(n) = \max_{|\mathbf{a}|=n} T(\mathbf{a})$ to be the maximum over abstractions of size n. Note that $|\mathbf{a}|$ given $\mathbf{a}^* \preceq \mathbf{a}$ is s plus a binomial random variable N with expectation $\alpha(n-s)$.

Using the crude bound $T(n) \leq (1-\alpha^n)T(n-1) + \alpha^n T(n)\alpha^{-s}$, we see that $T(n) \leq \frac{\alpha^{-s}}{1-\alpha^n} \cdot n$; in particular, $T(n)$ is sublinear. Moreover, $T(n)$ is concave for large

[4] Hoeffding's inequality: if $X_1, \ldots, X_n$ are i.i.d. random variables with $a \leq X_i \leq b$, then $p(\frac{1}{n}\sum_{i=1}^{n} X_i > \mathbb{E}[X_i] + \epsilon) \leq \exp\left\{-\frac{2n\epsilon^2}{(b-a)^2}\right\}$.

enough n, so we can use Jensen's inequality to swap T and $\mathbb{E}$:

$$T(n) \le T(\mathbb{E}[s+N]) + \alpha^{-s} = T(s+\alpha(n-s)) + \alpha^{-s}. \quad (19)$$

Solving the recurrence, we obtain:

$$T(n) \le \frac{\alpha^{-s}\log n}{\log \alpha^{-1}} + s + 1. \quad (20)$$

From (20), we can see the tradeoff between reducing the number of iterations (by increasing $\log \alpha^{-1}$) versus reducing the number of trials (by decreasing α^{-s}).

We now set α to minimize the upper bound. Differentiate with respect to $x = \alpha^{-1}$ and set the derivative to zero: $\frac{sx^{s-1}}{\log x} - \frac{x^{s-1}}{\log^2 x} = 0$. Solving this equation yields $\alpha = e^{-1/s}$. Plugging this value back into (20) yields $T(n) = es\log n + s + 1 = O(s \log n)$. □

References

[1] D. Angluin. Queries and concept learning. *Machine Learning*, 2(4):319–342, 1988.

[2] T. Ball and S. Rajamani. The SLAM project: debugging system software via static analysis. In *Proceedings of ACM Symp. on Principles of Programming Languages (POPL)*, pages 1–3, 2002.

[3] T. Ball, R. Majumdar, T. Millstein, and S. Rajamani. Automatic predicate abstraction of C programs. In *Proceedings of ACM Conf. on Programming Language Design and Implementation (PLDI)*, pages 203–213, 2001.

[4] D. Donoho. Compressed sensing. *IEEE Trans. on Information Theory*, 52(4):1289–1306, 2006.

[5] S. Graf and H. Saidi. Construction of abstract state graphs with PVS. pages 72–83, 1997.

[6] S. Gulwani. *Program Analysis using Random Interpretation.* PhD thesis, UC Berkeley, 2005.

[7] S. Guyer and C. Lin. Client-driven pointer analysis. In *Proceedings of Intl. Static Analysis Symposium*, pages 214–236, 2003.

[8] D. Hamlet. Random testing. In *Encyclopedia of Software Engineering*, pages 970–978, 1994.

[9] N. Heintze and O. Tardieu. Demand-driven pointer analysis. In *Proceedings of ACM Conf. on Programming Language Design and Implementation (PLDI)*, pages 24–34, 2001.

[10] O. Lhoták and L. Hendren. Context-sensitive points-to analysis: is it worth it? In *Proceedings of Intl. Conf. on Compiler Construction*, pages 47–64, 2006.

[11] O. Lhoták and L. Hendren. Evaluating the benefits of context-sensitive points-to analysis using a BDD-based implementation. *ACM Transactions on Software Engineering and Methodology*, 18(1):1–53, 2008.

[12] A. Milanova, A. Rountev, and B. Ryder. Parameterized object sensitivity for points-to and side-effect analyses for Java. In *Proceedings of ACM Intl. Symp. on Software Testing and Analysis*, pages 1–11, 2002.

[13] A. Milanova, A. Rountev, and B. Ryder. Parameterized object sensitivity for points-to analysis for Java. *ACM Transactions on Software Engineering and Methodology*, 14(1):1–41, 2005.

[14] M. Naik, A. Aiken, and J. Whaley. Effective static race detection for Java. In *Proceedings of ACM Conf. on Programming Language Design and Implementation (PLDI)*, pages 308–319.

[15] J. Plevyak and A. Chien. Precise concrete type inference for object-oriented languages. In *Proceedings of ACM Conf. on Object-Oriented Programming, Systems, Languages, and Applications*, pages 324–340.

[16] T. W. Reps. Demand interprocedural program analysis using logic databases. In *Workshop on Programming with Logic Databases*, pages 163–196, 1993.

[17] T. W. Reps. Solving demand versions of interprocedural analysis problems. In *Proceedings of Intl. Conf. on Compiler Construction*, pages 389–403, 1994.

[18] H. Robbins and S. Monro. A stochastic approximation method. *Annals of Mathematical Statistics*, 22(3):400–407, 1951.

[19] M. Sagiv, T. W. Reps, and R. Wilhelm. Parametric shape analysis via 3-valued logic. *ACM Transactions on Programming Languages and Systems*, 24(3):217–298, 2002.

[20] O. Shivers. Control-flow analysis in Scheme. In *Proceedings of ACM Conf. on Programming Language Design and Implementation (PLDI)*, pages 164–174, 1988.

[21] M. Sridharan and R. Bodík. Refinement-based context-sensitive points-to analysis for Java. In *Proceedings of ACM Conf. on Programming Language Design and Implementation*, pages 387–400, 2006.

[22] M. Sridharan, D. Gopan, L. Shan, and R. Bodík. Demand-driven points-to analysis for Java. In *Proceedings of ACM Conf. on Object-Oriented Programming, Systems, Languages, and Applications*, pages 59–76, 2005.

[23] L. Valiant. A theory of the learnable. *Communications of the ACM*, 27(11):1134–1142, 1984.

[24] M. J. Wainwright. Sharp thresholds for noisy and high-dimensional recovery of sparsity using ℓ_1-constrained quadratic programming (lasso). *IEEE Transactions on Information Theory*, 55:2183–2202, 2009.

[25] J. Whaley. *Context-Sensitive Pointer Analysis using Binary Decision Diagrams.* PhD thesis, Stanford University, 2007.

[26] J. Whaley and M. Lam. Cloning-based context-sensitive pointer alias analysis using binary decision diagrams. In *Proceedings of ACM Conf. on Programming Language Design and Implementation (PLDI)*, pages 131–144, 2004.

[27] X. Zheng and R. Rugina. Demand-driven alias analysis for C. In *Proceedings of ACM Symp. on Principles of Programming Languages (POPL)*, pages 197–208, 1998.

Relaxed-Memory Concurrency and Verified Compilation

Jaroslav Ševčík[1] Viktor Vafeiadis[1,2] Francesco Zappa Nardelli[3] Suresh Jagannathan[4] Peter Sewell[1]

[1]University of Cambridge [2]MPI-SWS [3]INRIA [4]Purdue University
(work done while on sabbatical at Cambridge)

Dedicated to the memory of Robin Milner

Abstract

In this paper, we consider the semantic design and verified compilation of a C-like programming language for concurrent shared-memory computation above x86 multiprocessors. The design of such a language is made surprisingly subtle by several factors: the relaxed-memory behaviour of the hardware, the effects of compiler optimisation on concurrent code, the need to support high-performance concurrent algorithms, and the desire for a reasonably simple programming model. In turn, this complexity makes verified (or verifying) compilation both essential and challenging.

We define a concurrent relaxed-memory semantics for *ClightTSO*, an extension of CompCert's Clight in which the processor's memory model is exposed for high-performance code. We discuss a strategy for verifying compilation from ClightTSO to x86, which we validate with correctness proofs (building on CompCert) for the most interesting compiler phases.

Categories and Subject Descriptors C.1.2 [*Multiple Data Stream Architectures (Multiprocessors)*]: Parallel processors; D.1.3 [*Concurrent Programming*]: Parallel programming; F.3.1 [*Specifying and Verifying and Reasoning about Programs*]

General Terms Reliability, Theory, Verification

Keywords Relaxed Memory Models, Verifying Compilation, Semantics

1. Introduction

Context Multiprocessors are now ubiquitous, with hardware support for concurrent computation over shared-memory data structures. But building programming languages with well-defined semantics to exploit them is challenging, for several inter-linked reasons.

At the hardware level, most multiprocessor families (e.g., x86, Sparc, Power, Itanium, and ARM) provide only *relaxed* shared-memory abstractions, substantially weaker than sequentially consistent (SC) memory [Lam79]: some of the hardware optimisations they rely on, while unobservable to sequential code, can observably affect the behaviour of concurrent programs. Moreover, while for some multiprocessors it has long been clear what the programmer can rely on, e.g. the Sparc *Total Store Ordering* (TSO) model [Spa], for others it has been hard to interpret the vendor's informal-prose architecture specifications [SSZN$^+$09]. For x86, we recently proposed *x86-TSO* [SSO$^+$10, OSS09] as a rigorous and usable semantics; we review this in §2.

POPL'11, January 26–28, 2011, Austin, Texas, USA.

Compilers also rely on optimisations for performance, and again many common optimisations (e.g., common subexpression elimination, and so on) preserve the behaviour of sequential code but can radically change the behaviour of concurrent programs.

Hence, when designing a concurrent shared-memory programming language, where one must choose what memory semantics to provide, there is a difficult tension to resolve. A strong model (such as sequential consistency) will be relatively easy for programmers to understand but hard to implement efficiently, because compiler optimisations will not always be sound and because expensive processor-specific memory fences (or other synchronisation instructions) will be needed to enforce ordering in the target hardware. Another alternative is to forbid programs containing races and give SC semantics to the rest [AG96], relying on synchronisation from the implementations of lock and unlock. Precisely defining a non-SC programming language model is a technical challenge in itself, as witnessed by the complexities in establishing a Java memory model that admits all the intended optimisations [Pug00, MPA05, CKS07, SA08, TVD10], and the ongoing work on C++0x [BOS$^+$11].

However, when it comes to concurrent systems code and concurrent data structure libraries, for example as used in an OS kernel and in `java.util.concurrent` [Lea99], it seems that a weak model is essential. Compiler optimisations are not the main issue here: these low-level algorithms often have little scope for optimisation, and their shared-memory accesses should be implemented exactly as expressed by the programmer. But for good performance it is essential that no unnecessary memory fences are introduced, and for understanding and reasoning about these subtle algorithms it is essential that the language has a clear semantics. Moreover, such algorithms are intrinsically racy. Such code is a small fraction of that in a large system, but may have a disproportionate effect on performance [Boe05]. This is illustrated by an improvement to a Linux spinlock, where a one-instruction change to a non-SC primitive gave a 4% performance gain [Lin99]. Recognising this, both Java and C++0x aim to provide a strong model for most programming but with low-level primitives for expert use.

In the face of all this intertwined semantic subtlety, of source language, target language, compilation between them, and the soundness of optimisations, it is essential to take a mathematically rigorous and principled approach to relaxed-memory concurrency: to give mechanised semantics for source and target languages and to consider verified (or verifying) compilation between them. In the sequential setting, verifying compilation has recently been shown to be feasible by Leroy et al.'s CompCert, a verifying compiler from a sequential C-like language, Clight, to PowerPC assembly language [Com09, Ler09a, Ler09b, BL09]. In this paper, we consider verifying compilation in the setting of concurrent programs with a realistic relaxed memory model.

Contributions Our first contribution is the design and definition of *ClightTSO* (§3). ClightTSO is not intended to be a general-purpose programming language, but rather a language in which concurrent algorithms can be expressed precisely, and, more importantly, as a test case for reasoning about relaxed-memory computation. It essentially exposes the x86 or Sparc hardware load and store operations (and synchronisation primitives) to the programmer, so ClightTSO loads and stores inherit the hardware relaxed-memory TSO behaviour, but can be implemented without memory fences or atomic instructions. (As we discuss in §6, in a full language one would expect to augment these with thread-local accesses that the compiler is permitted to optimise away, for high-performance sequential code, but that is not our focus here.) The semantic design of ClightTSO turns out to involve a surprisingly delicate interplay between the relaxed memory model, the behaviour of block allocation and free, and the behaviour of pointer equality.

Our second contribution is one of *semantic engineering* (§4). Relaxed memory models are complex in themselves, and a verifying compiler such as CompCert is complex even in the sequential case; to make verifying compilation for a concurrent relaxed-memory language feasible we have to pay great attention to structuring the semantics of the source and target languages, and the compiler and any correctness proof, to separate concerns and re-use as much as possible. We factor out the TSO memory from each language and build small-step 'labellised' semantics, allowing most of the proof to be done by threadwise simulation arguments. A key question for each compiler phase is the extent to which it changes the memory accesses of the program. For most of our phases (8 of 15) the memory accesses of source and target are in exact 1:1 correspondence. Moreover, for four phases the memory accesses are identical except that some values that are undefined in the source take particular values in the target; and one phase (register allocation) has no effect on memory accesses except that it removes memory loads to dead variables. For all these, the correctness of the phase is unrelated to the TSO nature of our memory. That leaves two phases that change memory accesses substantially, and whose proofs must really involve the whole system, of all threads and the TSO memory.

Thirdly, we present evidence that our approach is effective (§5). We have implemented a compiler from ClightTSO to x86 multiprocessors, taking CompCert as a starting point, and have proved correctness (in Coq [Coq]) for key phases thereof. In addition, we have successfully run the compiler on a number of sequential and concurrent benchmarks, including an implementation of a non-trivial lock-free algorithm by Fraser [Fra03]. Finally, we reflect on the formalisation process and on the tools we used (§6), discuss related work, and conclude. The proof effort for each compiler phase was broadly commensurate with its conceptual difficulty: some have essentially no effect on memory behaviour, and needed only days of work; a few were much more substantial, really changing the intensional behaviour of the source and with proofs that involve the TSO semantics in essential ways.

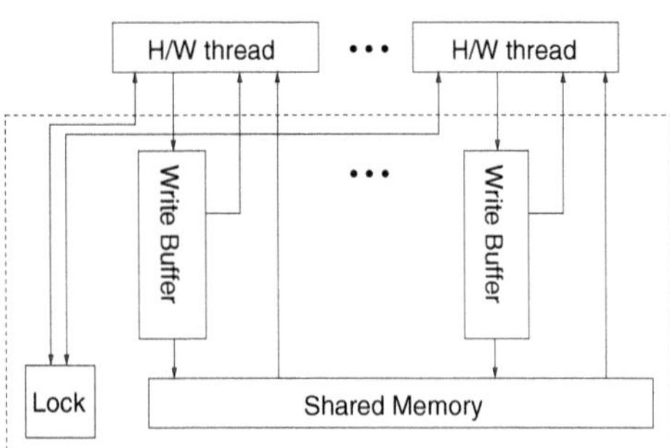

Figure 1. x86-TSO block diagram

2. Background: x86-TSO

We begin by recalling the relaxed-memory behaviour of our target language, x86 multiprocessor assembly programs, as captured by our x86-TSO model [SSO+10, OSS09]. The classic example showing non-SC behaviour in a TSO model is the store buffer (SB) assembly language program below: given two distinct memory locations x and y (initially holding 0), if two hardware threads (or processors) respectively write 1 to x and y and then read from y and x (into register EAX on thread 0 and EBX on thread 1), it is possible for both to read 0 *in the same execution*. It is easy to check that this result cannot arise from any SC interleaving of the reads and writes of the two threads, but it is observable on modern Intel or AMD x86 multiprocessors.

SB

Thread 0	Thread 1
MOV [x]←1 MOV EAX←[y]	MOV [y]←1 MOV EBX←[x]
Allowed Final State: Thread 0:EAX=0 ∧ Thread 1:EBX=0	

Microarchitecturally, one can view this behaviour as a visible consequence of store buffering: each hardware thread effectively has a FIFO buffer of pending memory writes (avoiding the need to block while a write completes), so the reads from y and x can occur before the writes have propagated from the buffers to main memory.

In addition, it is important to note that many x86 instructions involve multiple memory accesses, e.g. an increment INC [x]. By default, these are not guaranteed atomic (so two parallel increments of an initially 0 location might result in it holding 1), but there are 'LOCK'd' variants of them: LOCK INC [x] atomically performs a read, a write of the incremented value, *and* a flush of the local write buffer. Compare-and-swap instructions (CMPXCHG) are atomic in the same way, and memory fences (MFENCE) simply flush the local write buffer.

The x86-TSO model makes this behaviour precise in two equivalent ways: an abstract machine with an operational semantics, illustrated in Fig. 1, and an axiomatisation of legal executions, in the style of [Spa92, App. K] (the model covers the normal case of aligned accesses to write-back cacheable memory; it does not cover other memory types, self-modifying code, and so on). For the relationship between the model and the vendor documentation (and with empirical testing) we refer to our previous work [SSO+10, OSS09, SSZN+09].

3. ClightTSO

ClightTSO is a C-like language: imperative, with pointers and pointer arithmetic, and with storage that is dynamically allocated and freed, but not subject to garbage collection (GC)[1]. We choose this level of abstraction for several reasons. First, it is what is typically used for concurrent systems programming, for example in an OS kernel (where garbage collection may be infeasible), and many concurrent algorithms are expressed in C-like pseudocode. Second, it is an attractive starting point for research in relaxed-memory PL semantics and compilation because C source-level shared-memory accesses will often map 1:1 onto target accesses, without the complexity and cost of accesses required for GC. Last but not least, the work of Leroy et al. on CompCert gives us a verifying compiler for sequential programs, so by using that as a starting point we can focus on the issues involved in relaxed-memory concurrency.

Syntactically, ClightTSO is a straightforward extension of the CompCert Clight language [BL09], adding thread creation and

[1] Currently this is stack-allocated storage for function local variables, but our development is structured so that adding explicit `malloc` and `free` should be straightforward.

```
type, ty ::=  void | int (intsize, signedness)
 | float (floatsize) | pointer (ty) | array (ty, len)
 | function (ty*, ty) | struct (id, φ) | union (id, φ)
 | comp_pointer(id) | (ty)
fieldlist, φ ::=  nil | (id, ty)::φ
unary_operation, op1 ::=  ! | ~ | -
binary_operation, op2 ::=  + | - | * | / | % | & | | | ^ | << | >>
 | == | != | < | > | <= | >=
expr, e ::=  a^ty
expr_descr, a ::=  n | f | id | *e | &e | op1 e | e1 op2 e2 | (ty)e
 | e1?e2:e3 | e1&&e2 | e1||e2 | sizeof (ty) | e.id
opt_lhs ::=   | (id:ty)=
atomic_statement, as ::=  CAS | ATOMIC_INC | MFENCE
statement, s ::=  skip | e1=e2 | opt_lhs e'(e*) | s1;s2
 | if (e1) then s1 else s2 | while (e) do s | do s while (e)
 | for (s1;e2;s3)s | break | continue | return opt_e
 | switch (e)ls | l:s | goto l |  thread_create(e1, e2)
 | opt_lhs as(e*)
labeled_statements, ls ::=  default : s | case n:s;ls
fndefn_internal ::=  ty id(arglist){varlist s}
program ::=  dcls fndefns main=id
```

Figure 2. ClightTSO abstract syntax (excerpts)

some atomic read-modify-write primitives that are directly implementable by x86 LOCK'd instructions. An excerpt of the abstract syntax is given in Fig. 2, where one can see that programs consist of a list of global variable declarations, a list of function declarations, and the name of a `main` function. Function bodies are taken from a fairly rich language of statements and expressions.

Semantically, though, the addition of relaxed-memory concurrency has profound consequences:

TSO Most obviously, the ClightTSO load and store operations must have TSO semantics to make them directly implementable above x86, so we cannot model memory as (say) a function from locations to values. Instead, we use a derivative of the TSO machine in Fig. 1 (the abstract machine style is more intuitive and technically more convenient here than the axiomatic model).

Pointer equality C implementations are typically not memory-safe: one can use pointer arithmetic to corrupt arbitary state (including that introduced by compilation). But in order to specify an implementable language, C standards rule out many programs from consideration, giving them undefined behaviour. For example, the draft C1X standard states "*If an object is referred to outside of its lifetime, the behavior is undefined. The value of a pointer becomes indeterminate when the object it points to reaches the end of its lifetime*" [C1X, 6.2.4p2]. In Clight the memory state records what is allocated, with equality testing of pointers giving the undefined value (`Vundef`) if they do not refer to currently allocated blocks. However, in a relaxed-memory setting any appeal to global time should be treated with great caution, and the concept of "currently allocated" is no longer simple: different threads might have different views not only of the values in memory but also of what is allocated. For example, in x86-TSO one thread might free, re-allocate and use some memory while another thread compares against a pointer to it, with the writes of the first thread remaining within its buffer until after the comparison. One could make pointer comparison effectful, querying the x86-TSO abstract machine to see whether a pointer is valid w.r.t. a particular thread whenever it is used, but this would lead to a complex and unwieldy semantics. Moreover, comparing potentially dangling pointers for equality is useful in practice, e.g. in algorithms to free cyclic data structures. Accordingly, for ClightTSO we take pointer comparison to always be defined.

Block reuse In turn, this means that the ClightTSO semantics must permit re-use of pointers (again contrasting with Clight, in which allocations are always fresh), otherwise it would not be sound w.r.t. the behaviour of reasonable implementations. For example, in the program below `h` must be allowed to return `0` or `1`, as an implementation might or might not reuse the stack frame of `f` for `g`.

```
int* f() { int a; return &a; }
int* g() { int a; return &a; }
int h()  { return (f() == g()); }
```

Memory errors and buffering of allocations and frees A read or write of a pointer that is dangling w.r.t. that thread must still be a semantic error, so that a correct compiler is not obliged to preserve the behaviour of such programs. Now, implementations of memory allocation and free do not necessarily involve a memory fence or other buffer flush: at the assembly language level, stack allocation and free are simply register operations, while heap `malloc` and `free` might often be w.r.t. some thread-local storage. To test whether pointers are valid, therefore, we treat allocations and frees analogously to writes, adding them to the buffers of the TSO machine. This is a convenient common abstraction of stack and heap allocation (for the former, it essentially models the stack pointer).

An allocation must immediately return a block address to the calling thread, but they should not clash when they are unbuffered (when they hit the main memory of the TSO machine), so they must return blocks that are fresh taking into account pending allocations and frees from all threads. It is technically convenient if frees and writes also fail immediately, when they are added to the TSO machine buffer, so we also take all possible sequences of the pending allocations and frees into account when enqueuing them. Otherwise one would have latent failures, e.g. if two threads free a block and those frees are both held in buffers.

Finite memory A final novelty of ClightTSO, not directly related to concurrency, is that we support finite memory, in which allocation can fail and in which pointer values in the running machine-code implementation can be numerically equal to their values in the semantics. The latter is convenient for our correctness proofs, simplifying the simulations. It also means that pointer arithmetic works properly (mod 2^{32}) and may be helpful in the future for a semantic understanding of out-of-memory errors. The memory usage of a compiled program and its source may be radically different, as the compiler may be able to promote local variables to registers but will need extra storage for stack frames and temporaries. But (analogous to verifying rather than verified compilation), it would be reasonably straightforward to make the compiler emit and check, for each function, bounds on those. One could then reason about real space usage in terms of a source semantics annotated with these bounds.

Small-step semantics ClightTSO is a concurrent language, in which execution of an expression or a statement may involve multiple memory reads and hence multiple potential interaction points with other threads. We therefore need a small-step operational semantics for both expressions and statements. Conceptually this is routine, but it requires significant re-engineering (described in §5.1) of definitions and proofs w.r.t. CompCert, where Clight had a big-step semantics for expressions.

We use a frame-stack style, with thread states that can be an executing expression paired with an expression-holed continuation or an executing statement paired with a statement-holed continuation:

$$\begin{array}{lcl} \mathit{expr\_cont},\ \kappa_e & ::= & [op_1^\tau\ \_] \cdot \kappa_e \mid [\_^\tau = e_2] \cdot \kappa_s \mid [v^\tau = \_] \cdot \kappa_s \mid \ldots \\ \mathit{stmt\_cont},\ \kappa_s & ::= & \texttt{stop} \mid [\_\,;\, s_2] \cdot \kappa_s \mid \ldots \\ \mathit{state} & ::= & e \cdot \kappa_e |_\rho \\ & \mid & s \cdot \kappa_s |_\rho \\ & \mid & \ldots \end{array}$$

Here ρ is a thread-local environment mapping identifiers to their locations in allocated blocks. The semantics is also parameterised by an unchanging global environment of global variables and functions, and additional machinery is needed to deal with l-values, loops, and function calls, which we return to in §5.1. We also fix a left-to-right evaluation order.

Examples We give a flavour of the language with some very small examples of ClightTSO source programs.

SB The x86 visible-store-buffer behaviour can now be seen at the ClightTSO level, e.g. if the following threads are created in parallel then both could print 0 in the same execution.

```
                   int x=0; int y=0;
void *thread0(void *tid)    | void *thread1(void *tid)
{ x=1;                      | { y=1;
  printf("T0: %d\n", y);    |   printf("T1: %d\n", x);
  return(0); }              |   return(0); }
```

Spinlock using CAS More usefully, an efficient spinlock can be implemented directly in ClightTSO using CAS. Any integer variable can be used to represent the state of the spinlock, with lock and unlock as follows:

```
void lock(int *mutex)           | void unlock(int *mutex)
{ while (CAS(mutex, 0, 1))      | { *mutex = 0; }
    while (*mutex) ; }          |
```

The generated assembler mimics the optimised implementation of Linux spinlocks mentioned in Section 1: as shown by Owens [Owe10], the memory update performed by unlock does not need to be synchronising on x86-TSO.

A publication idiom The memory model supports the common publication idiom below:

```
              double channel; int flag = 0;
// sender                | // receiver
channel = 5.2;           | while (flag == 0);
flag = 1;                | printf ("%f\n", channel);
```

Since the store buffers are FIFO, when the receiver thread sees the update to `flag`, the contents of the `channel` variable must have been propagated into main memory, and as such must be visible to all other threads (that do not themselves have a pending write to `channel`). For contrast, in C++0x [Bec10, BOS+11] (which also targets non-TSO machines), `flag` must be accessed with sequentially consistent atomics, implemented with costly x86 LOCK'd instructions or fences, or with release/acquire atomics, implemented with normal stores and loads but with a much more involved semantics.

4. Verifying Compiler Strategy

Having discussed our x86 target language in §2, and the design and rationale of our ClightTSO source language in §3, we now consider the semantics and proof structure required to make a verifying compiler for a concurrent relaxed-memory language feasible.

Correctness statement The first question is the form of the correctness theorems that we would like the compiler to generate. We confine our attention to the behaviour of whole programs, leaving a compositional understanding of compiler correctness for relaxed-memory concurrency (e.g. as in the work of Benton and Hur for sequential programs [BH09]) as a problem for future work. We take the observable behaviour of both ClightTSO and x86-TSO programs to be labelled transition systems (LTS) with visible actions for call and return of external functions (e.g. OS I/O primitives), program exit, semantic failure, and an out-of-memory error, together with internal τ actions:

$$\mathit{event},\ \mathit{ev} ::= \texttt{call}\ \mathit{id}\ \mathit{vs} \mid \texttt{return}\ \mathit{typ}\ v \mid \texttt{exit}\ n \mid \texttt{fail} \mid \texttt{oom} \mid \tau$$

We split external I/O into call and return transitions so that blocking OS calls can be correctly modelled.

Now, how should the source and target LTS be related? As usual for implementations of concurrent languages, we cannot expect them to be (in some sense) equivalent, as the implementation may resolve some of the source-language nondeterminism (c.f. [Sew97]). For example, in our implementation, stack frames will be deterministically stack-allocated and the pointers in the block-reuse example above will always be equal. Hence, the most we should expect is that if the compiled program has some observable behaviour then that behaviour is admitted by the source semantics — some kind of *backward simulation*[2] result.

This must be refined further: compiled behaviour that arises from an erroneous source program need not be admitted in the source semantics (e.g. if a program mutates a return address on its stack, or tries to apply a non-function). We have to distinguish between such semantic errors (modelled with `fail`) and out-of-memory allocation errors (modelled by `oom`) so that we can correctly blame the source program in the former case. Moreover, the compiled program should only diverge, indicated by an infinite trace of τ labels, if the source program can. We express all this with the following notion of backward simulation between a source LTS S and a compiled target LTS T.

DEFINITION 1. *A family of relations* R^i : States(S) × States(T), *indexed by elements* i *of a well-founded order* $>$, *is a* measured backward simulation *if, whenever* $s\ R^i\ t$ *and* $t \xrightarrow{ev} t'$ *for* $ev \neq$ `oom`, *then either*

1. $\exists s'.\ s \xrightarrow{\tau}{}^{*} s' \xrightarrow{\texttt{fail}}$ *(s can reach a semantic error), or*
2. $\exists s', j.\ s \xrightarrow{\tau}{}^{*} \xrightarrow{ev} s' \wedge s'\ R^j\ t'$ *(s can do a matching step), or*
3. $\exists j.\ ev = \tau \wedge i > j \wedge s\ R^j\ t'$ *(t stuttered, with a decreasing measure).*

Given a measured backward simulation relating S and T, one can easily see that if S has no semantic failures then any (finite or infinite) completed trace of T, that does not include an out-of-memory error, is a trace of S.

The CompCert 1.5 proof strategy ClightTSO is an extension of sequential Clight, and its compiler has to deal with everything that a Clight compiler does, except for any optimisations that become unsound in the concurrent setting. We therefore arrange our semantic definitions and proof structure to re-use as much as possible of the CompCert development for sequential Clight, isolating the parts where relaxed-memory concurrency plays a key role.

CompCert 1.5 is around 55K lines of Coq subdivided into 13 compiler phases, each of which builds a semantic preservation proof between semantically defined intermediate languages. The

[2] Terminology: in CompCert "forward" and "backward" refer to the direction of the simulation with respect to the compiler phases, not to the direction of transitions. Thinking of compilation as "forwards", a forward simulation means that source behaviours can be matched by the target.

overall strategy is to build some kind of forward simulation for each phase; these can be composed together and combined with determinacy for the target language (PowerPC or ARM assembly) to give a backward simulation for a complete compilation. Forward simulations are generally easier to establish than backward simulations because compiler phases tend to introduce intermediate states; a forward simulation proof does not have to characterise and relate these.

As we shall see, this strategy cannot be used directly for compilation of concurrent ClightTSO to x86, but much can be adapted.

Decomposing the proof by compiler phases Our compiler is divided into similar (but not identical) phases to CompCert. The above notion of backward simulation also serves as the correctness criterion for each of our phases:

THEOREM 1. *The composition of two measured backward simulations is a measured backward simulation.* [Coq proof]

Labellisation and threadwise proof In our concurrent setting the languages are not deterministic, so the CompCert approach to building backward simulations is not applicable. However, for most of the phases we can re-use the CompCert proof, more-or-less adapted, to give forward simulation results for the behaviour of a single thread in isolation — and we can make our semantics deterministic for such. We therefore 'labellise' the semantics for each level (source, target, and each intermediate language). Instead of defining transitions

$$(s, m_{\mathrm{SC}}) \longrightarrow (s', m'_{\mathrm{SC}})$$

over configurations that combine a single-threaded program state s and an SC memory m_{SC} (as most sequential language semantics, including CompCert, do), we define the semantics of a single thread (split apart from the memory) as a transition system:

$$s \xrightarrow{te} s'$$

(together with extra structure for thread creation) where a thread event te is either an external event, as above, an interaction with memory me, an internal τ action, or the start or exit of the thread:

$thread\_event,\ te$ ::=
`ext` ev | `mem` me | τ | `start` $opt\_tid\ p\ vs$ | `exit`

The whole-system semantics of each level is a parallel composition roughly of the form

$$s_1 \mid \ldots \mid s_n \mid m_{\mathrm{TSO}}$$

of the thread states s_i and a TSO machine m_{TSO}. The threads interact with the TSO machine by synchronising on various events: reads or writes of a pointer p with a value v of a specified $memory\_chunk$ size, allocations and frees of a memory block at a pointer p, various error cases, and thread creation. These transitions are in the style of the 'early' transition system for value-passing CCS [Mil89]: a thread doing a memory read will have a transition for each possible value of the right type. For example, here is the ClightTSO rule for dereferencing a pointer:

$$\frac{\begin{array}{l}\texttt{access\_mode}\ ty' = \texttt{By\_value}\ c\\ typ = \texttt{type\_of\_chunk}\ c\\ \texttt{Val.has\_type}\ v\ typ\end{array}}{p \cdot [*\_^{ty'}] \cdot \kappa_e|_\rho \xrightarrow{\texttt{mem (read}\ p\ c\ v)} v \cdot \kappa_e|_\rho}\ \text{LOADBYVALUE}$$

External events of the threads (and of the TSO machine) are exposed directly as the whole-system behaviour.

This conceptually simple change separates concerns: compiler phases that do not substantially affect the memory accesses of the program can be proved correct per-thread, as described in §5.4 (and those results lifted to the whole system by a general result below), leaving only the two remaining phases that require proofs that really involve the TSO machine.

The TSO machine Our TSO machine is based on the x86-TSO abstract machine, with a main memory and per-thread buffers, but with several differences. The TSO machine must handle memory allocations and frees (which are buffered), and various memory errors; the main memory records allocation as in CompCert. We use the TSO semantics for software threads, not hardware threads, which is sound provided that the scheduler flushes the buffer during task switching. We use the same TSO machine for all the intermediate languages, and we uniformly lift threadwise LTSs to the parallel composition with the TSO machine.

Lifting threadwise forward simulations to whole-system backward simulations We convert forward threadwise simulations to whole-system backward simulations in two steps. First, we observe that a forward simulation from a receptive language to a determinate language implies the existence of backward simulation.

We say that two labels are of the same kind, written $te \asymp te'$ if they only differ in input values. In our case, $te \asymp te'$ if (i) te and te' are reads from the same memory location (but not necessarily with the same value), or (ii) te and te' are external returns, or (iii) $te = te'$.

DEFINITION 2. *A thread LTS is* receptive *if $s \xrightarrow{te} t$ and $te' \asymp te$ implies $\exists t'.\ s \xrightarrow{te'} t'$.*

DEFINITION 3. *A thread LTS is* determinate *if $s \xrightarrow{te} t$ and $s \xrightarrow{te'} t'$ implies $te \asymp te'$ and, moreover, if $te = te'$, then $t = t'$.*

DEFINITION 4. *A relation R between the states of two thread LTSs S and T is a* threadwise forward simulation *if there is a well-founded order $<$ on the states of S such that if given any $s, s' \in S$, $t \in T$ and label te, whenever $s \xrightarrow{te} s'$ and $s\ R\ t$, then either $te = \texttt{fail}$, or $\exists t'.\ t \xrightarrow{\tau}{}^{*} \xrightarrow{te} \xrightarrow{\tau}{}^{*} t' \wedge s'\ R\ t'$, or $te = \tau \wedge s'\ R\ t \wedge s' < s$.*

DEFINITION 5. *A relation R is a* threadwise backward simulation *if there is a well-founded order $<$ on T such that whenever $t \xrightarrow{te} t'$ and $s\ R\ t$, then either $\exists s'.\ s \xrightarrow{\tau}{}^{*} \xrightarrow{te} s' \wedge s'\ R\ t'$, or $\exists s'.\ s \xrightarrow{\texttt{fail}} s'$, or $te = \tau \wedge s\ R\ t' \wedge t' < t$. Moreover, if $t \not\rightarrow$ (t is stuck) and $s\ R\ t$, then $s \not\rightarrow$ or $\exists s'.\ s \xrightarrow{\texttt{fail}} s'$.*

Note the subtle asymmetry in handling errors: if a source state does an error or gets stuck, both the backward simulation and forward simulation hold. In contrast, the target states' errors must be reflected in the source to make the backward simulation hold. This is necessary to allow compilers to eliminate errors, but not to introduce them.

THEOREM 2. *If R is a threadwise forward simulation from S to T, S is receptive, and T is determinate, then there is a threadwise backward simulation that contains R.* [Coq proof]

Eliding details of initialisation and assumptions on global environments, we have:

THEOREM 3. *A threadwise backward simulation can be lifted to a whole-system measured backward simulation, for the composition of the threads with the TSO machine.* [Coq proof]

To establish correctness of compiler phases that remove dead variable loads and concretise undefined values, we have also proved variants of Theorems 2 and 3 for suitably modified Definitions 4 and 5.

The two non-threadwise proofs In ClightTSO (as in Clight) local variables are all in allocated blocks, but an early phase of the compiler identifies the variables whose addresses are not taken (by any use of the `&` operator) and keeps them in thread-local environments, changing loads and stores into (τ-action) environment accesses; moreover, individual stack allocations on function entry are merged into one large allocation of the entire stack frame. Conversely, a later phase does activation record layout, and thread-local state manipulation (τ actions) is compiled into memory accesses to the thread-local part of activation records. In both cases, the thread has different views of memory in source and target, and these views involve the TSO-machine buffering of loads, stores, allocations and frees. We return to this, which is the heart of our proof, in §5.2 and §5.3.

Finite memory revisited To be faithful to a real machine semantics, our x86 semantics uses finite memory and performs memory allocations only when threads are initialized (the stack of the thread is allocated). In Clight, however, small memory allocations happen whenever a variable is declared; as a result, the memory should be unbounded because the compiler can promote local variables to registers and thus a Clight program can have a footprint that would not fit in the x86 memory. In our intermediate languages, we switch from infinite to finite memory in the Csharpminor to Cstacked phase (§5.2), where we move local variables whose address is not taken to local environments, and perform one allocation (for the remaining local variables) per function call. Since our pointer type needs to accommodate both the finite and infinite nature of addresses, our pointers are composed of two parts: an unbounded block identifier and machine integer offset within the block. The lower-level language semantics uses only the finite memory in block 0—the memory refuses to allocate any other block. The higher level languages can allocate in any block. Note that one memory block can contain more than one memory object. A later phase (MachAbs to MachConc phase, §5.3) compiles away the allocations per function call pre-allocating a thread's stack when it is created.

The final phase: targetting x86 We target x86 because x86-TSO gives us a relatively simple and well-understood relaxed memory model for a common multiprocessor. CompCert 1.5 targets sequential PowerPC and ARM assembly language, but these have much more intricate concurrent behaviour which is still not fully understood (though c.f. [AMSS10]). We therefore need an x86 backend, described in §5.5, adopting parts of the new x86 backend of CompCert 1.8.

5. CompCertTSO

Following the strategy above, we have built a working compiler from ClightTSO to x86 assembly language with x86-TSO semantics, and have proved correctness of the most interesting phases. This shows (a) how we can reason about concurrent TSO behaviour, in the phases where that plays a key role, and (b) how our overall strategy enables relatively straightforward adaptation of the existing sequential proof, in the phases where concurrent memory accesses do not have a big impact. Our development, all mechanised in Coq, is available online[3].

The structure of our compiler, and of its proof, is shown in Fig. 3. The subdivision into phases between intermediate languages follows CompCert 1.5 as far as possible, with our major changes being:

- The source and target languages are ClightTSO and concurrent x86 assembly, not Clight and PowerPC or ARM assembly.

[3] `www.cl.cam.ac.uk/users/pes20/CompCertTSO`

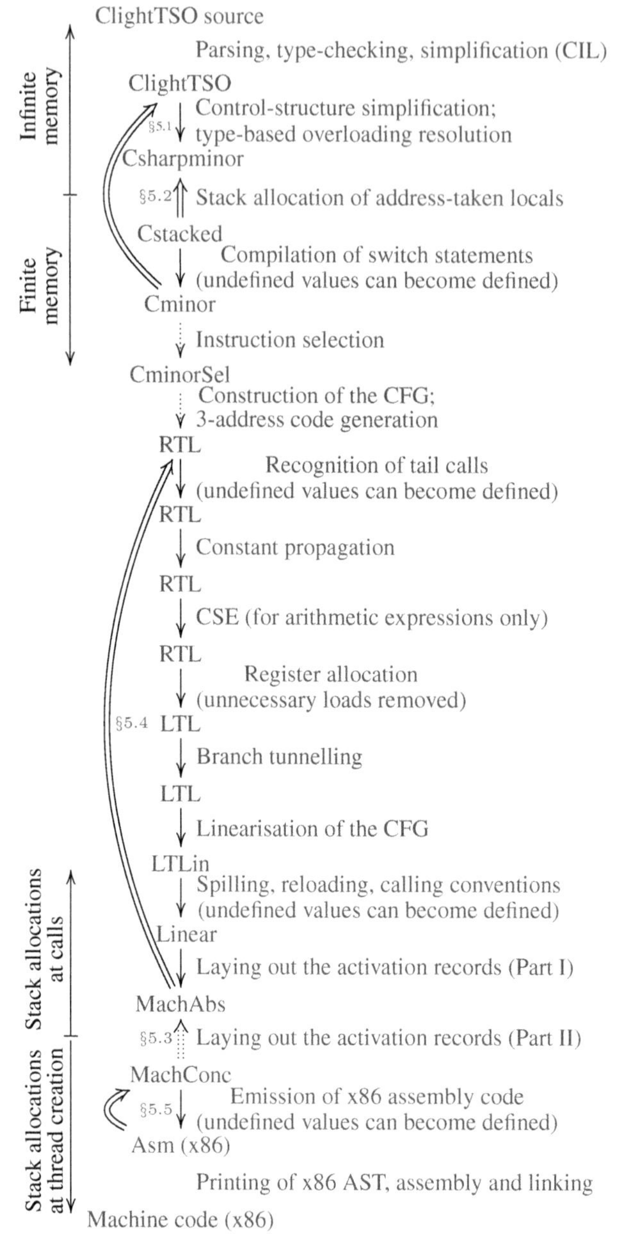

Our proof structure is indicated by single arrows for threadwise forward simulations; and straight double arrows for direct proofs of whole-system backward simulations. Arrows are solid if the proof is completed and dotted otherwise. The completed composite whole-system backward simulations (lifted with Theorems 2 and 3, and composed with Theorem 1) are shown with curved double arrows.

ClightTSO and Csharpminor perform a stack allocation for each individual variable in the program and assume an infinite memory, whereas the languages below have only finite memory. From Cstacked to MachAbs a stack allocation occurs for each non-empty stack frame (that is, almost every function call), whereas in MachConc and Asm only when a thread is created.

Figure 3. CompCertTSO phases

- The semantics is expressed with a TSO machine, which is common to all phases.
- We need a stack of memory-model-aware abstractions for the intermediate languages. While named after those of CompCert, their semantics are all adapted to labellised TSO semantics.
- The simulation from ClightTSO to the first intermediate language, Csharpminor, is a new proof above our small-step semantics.
- The CompCert phase that does stack allocation of some local variables (those whose address is taken by &), from Csharpminor to Cminor, is divided into two via a new intermediate language Cstacked. Cstacked has the same syntax as Csharpminor (and compilation to it is the identity on terms) but a memory semantics more like Cminor. The proof of the Csharpminor-to-Cstacked phase is a new direct whole-system backward simulation argument, dealing with the very different patterns of memory accesses in the two languages and how they interact with the TSO machine.
- The proofs of the middle phases of the compiler, from RTL to MachAbs with various optimisations, are relatively straightforward adaptations of the CompCert proofs to our per-thread labellised semantics and then lifted by the general results of the previous section.
- Our Mach-to-Asm phase generates x86 rather than PowerPC or ARM assembly.

The rest of this section discusses these in more detail. Our main results are as follows.

THEOREM 4. *Given a ClightTSO program, p, and its compilation to a Cminor program, p′, there is a measured backward simulation between the LTSes of p and p′.* [Coq proof]

THEOREM 5. *If an RTL program, p, has been successfully compiled to a Machabs program, p′, by the following phases: tail call recognition, constant propagation, restricted CSE, register allocation, branch tunnelling, linearisation, reloading and activation record layout, then there is a measured backward simulation between the LTSes of p and p′.* [Coq proof]

Proof outline: First, we construct threadwise forward simulations from ClightTSO to Csharpminor, from Cstacked to Cminor, and between each of the eight phases from RTL to MachAbs. (More precisely, for the tail call recognition and reloading phases we establish a threadwise forward simulation with undefs, and for the register allocation phase a lock-step threadwise forward simulation with unnecessary load removal.) Then, we turn these threadwise forward simulations to threadwise backward simulations by Theorem 2 (and by the analogous theorems for the threadwise forward simulation with undefs and for the lock-step threadwise forward simulation with unnecessary load removal). Then, by Theorem 3, we turn the threadwise backward simulations into whole-system measured backward simulations. In §5.2, we also establish a measured backward simulation from Cstacked to Csharpminor. Finally, by composing these measured backward simulations according to Theorem 1, we get the overall measured backward simulations.

At the time of writing, the remaining proofs required for a complete verifying compiler include our MachAbs-to-MachConc phase, which involves memory manipulations very similar to those of Csharpminor-to-Cstacked, and the forward simulations for compilation from Cminor to RTL, which should be relatively straightforward adaptations from CompCert. These have been sketched out in detail (in Coq), and we believe that the main intellectual challenges have all been addressed, though of course one can never be certain until the proof is complete.

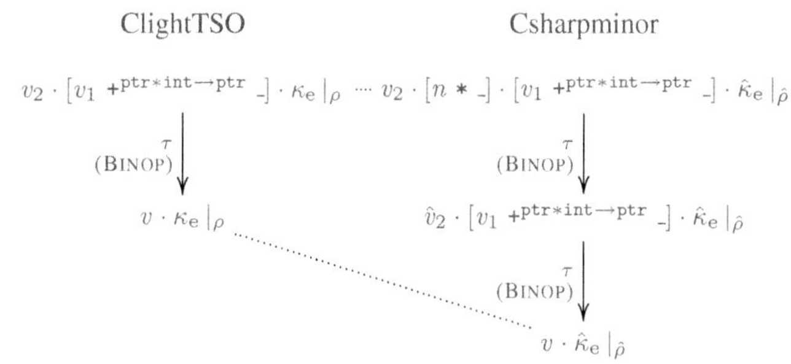

Here int = int(I32,Signed) and ptr = pointer(int). The type annotation in the multiplication (*) context is omitted.

Figure 4. Part of the simulation relating ClightTSO and Csharpminor evaluation for addition of an int and a pointer.

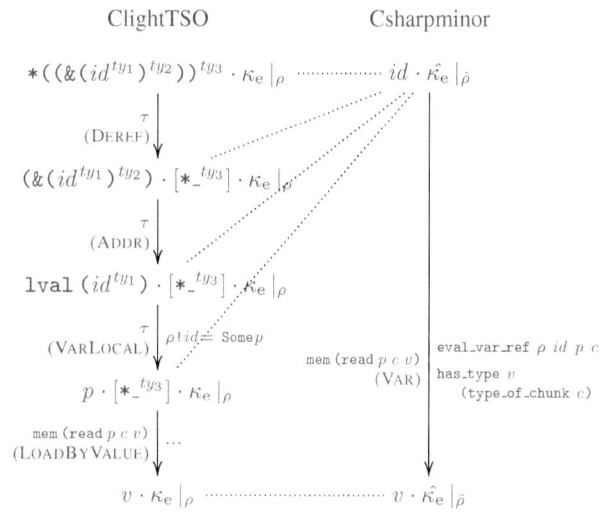

Figure 5. ClightTSO compilation can sometimes eliminate source-level transitions.

5.1 Small-stepping (ClightTSO to Csharpminor)

ClightTSO is compiled into Csharpminor, a high-level intermediate representation that has a simpler form of expressions and statements. Most notably, the translation unifies various looping constructs found in the source, compiles away casts, translates union and structs into primitive indexed memory accesses, and makes variable l-value and r-value distinctions explicit. High-level type information found in ClightTSO is compiled to a lower-level byte-aware memory representation. Accounting for these differences in the simulation is complicated by the relatively large size of the two languages: ClightTSO's definition has 90 rules, while Csharpminor has 56.

Because expression evaluation is defined by a small-step semantics, adapting the forward simulation proofs directly from CompCert (which uses a big-step expression evaluation semantics) was not feasible, and much of the proof, along with the simulation change, had to be written from scratch as a result. Since the two languages are relatively close, however, the revised simulation could sometimes simply map ClightTSO transitions directly to the corresponding Csharpminor ones; evaluation of constants, unary operations, and certain components of function call and return are such examples.

However, as we mentioned earlier, compilation often results in a ClightTSO term becoming translated to a sequence of lower-level simpler Csharpminor terms. To illustrate, the diagram shown in Fig. 4 shows the evaluation of a binary addition of an integer and a pointer. For ClightTSO, the multiplication of the integer operand by the representation size of the pointer type is performed implicitly, subsumed within the intrinsic definition of addition. In Csharpminor, an explicit binary multiplication operation is introduced. Notice that the continuations in the subsequent matching states are structurally quite different from each other as a result; the simulation relation must explicitly account for these differences.

Perhaps a more surprising consequence of using a small-step semantics is that the simulation relation may sometimes be required to match multiple ClightTSO transitions to a single Csharpminor one. For example, compilation from ClightTSO to Csharpminor eliminates various states defined in ClightTSO to deal with addressing and dereferencing. Consider the evaluation of an identifier that appears in an r-value context. In ClightTSO, the identifier is first translated into a pointer, and a separate step returns either the contents of the pointer (in case it references a scalar type) or the pointer itself (in case of e.g., arrays or structs). Compilation to Csharpminor removes this intermediate step, generating the appropriate access instruction directly, since the pointer type is statically known. This simplification generalizes to sequences of address-of and dereferencing operations. We depict the sequence of steps necessary to compute a variable's address, and then dereference it (if it is a scalar) in Fig. 5. The relation `eval_var_ref` states that variable `id`, in the context of local environment ρ, evaluates to pointer p that references an object with memory representation c. The value v read must have a type consistent with c as defined by relation `has_type`. Notice that ClightTSO requires four steps to perform this operation while compilation to Csharpminor requires only one. To account for such differences, the simulation relation forces Csharpminor transitions to stutter, incorporating a measure on ClightTSO expressions and continuations that allows matching of several intermediate ClightTSO states to a single Csharpminor one. Indeed, such a measure, suitably adapted, must be defined for most other compiler phases.

Besides memory read and write operations, the ClightTSO semantics also generates events for function argument and local variable allocation as part of the function calling sequence. The small-step semantics requires these operations be performed in stages. After all argument expressions and the function pointer have been evaluated, memory is allocated for each formal parameter, as well all local variables, in turn. Each distinct allocation is represented as a separate labelled transition. After allocation, the values of the actuals are written to the formals. On function exit, allocated storage is freed individually. The corresponding Csharpminor transitions are similar, albeit with a change in the underlying type representation used to guide memory allocation and writes.

5.2 Changing memory accesses (1) (Csharpminor to Cstacked)

Languages and Compilation The Csharpminor to Cstacked phase bridges the semantic gap to the next intermediate language, Cminor, by introducing a new semantics of the Csharpminor syntax. That is, the program transformation from Csharpminor to Cstacked is an identity function. However, the Cstacked memory semantics closely follows that of Cminor, which differs radically from Csharpminor.

To understand the motivation for introducing Cstacked, we summarise the main features of the following compilation phase (Cstacked to Cminor):

1. Local variable reads and writes are turned into explicit memory accesses or local state reads and updates. Note that in Csharpminor, as in C, it is legal to take the address of a local variable and even to pass it to another thread, so long as it is not accessed outside its lifetime. Variables whose address is never taken, however, are guaranteed to be thread-local, and the compiler lifts such variables from memory to local state. The remaining variables are kept in memory.
2. Individual local variable allocations are replaced with single stack-frame allocation.
3. Switch-case statements are compiled to switch-table statements.

Without the intermediate Cstacked phase, the first two steps change memory semantics: step 1 replaces memory accesses to local variables with local state manipulation that does not touch memory, and step 2 replaces the individual variable (de)allocations with a single stack-frame (de)allocation in Cminor.

To separate concerns, the Cstacked semantics only captures the memory effects of the transformation, i.e., its transitions simulate the compilation steps 1 and 2. Cstacked and Csharpminor only differ in handling local variables. The change is most evident in the types of local environments, which are part of the local state of threads. In Csharpminor, a local environment is a map from names to pointers and type information that essentially describes the size of a local variable in memory:

$var\_kind,\ vk ::= \texttt{scalar}\ memory\_chunk \mid \texttt{array}\ size$
$cshm\_env,\ cshe ::= \texttt{nil} \mid (\ id : (\ p\ ,\ vk)) :: cshe$

In Cstacked, a local environment consists of a stack frame pointer and a map that assigns to each name a value or an offset within the stack-frame:

$st\_kind,\ sk ::= \texttt{local}\ v \mid \texttt{stack\_scalar}\ memory\_chunk\ ofs$
$\mid \texttt{stack\_array}\ size\ ofs$
$cst\_items,\ csti ::= \texttt{nil} \mid (\ id : sk) :: csti$
$cst\_env,\ cste ::= (\ p\ ,\ csti)$

Note that Cstacked can keep values of local variables in the local environment (when the corresponding *st_kind* is `local`). This contrasts with Csharpminor, which stores the values of all local variables in memory.

The difference in the environment drives all the other changes from Csharpminor to Cstacked: we adjust the rules for assignment, the write of a function's return value, local variable reads, function entry, and function exit to handle local in-state variables and on-stack variables separately. The most significant change is in function entry, where we scan the function body for the `&` operator and compute the size of its stack frame together with offsets for on-stack local variables.

We illustrate the radical difference between the memory semantics of Csharpminor and Cstacked on the environment construction and parameter binding in function entry. Consider the following function:

```
int f(int i) {int j, k; g(i, &j, &k); return j+k;}
```

Fig. 6 shows the environment construction and argument binding transitions following an invocation of `f` with parameter 1. The states have the following meaning: the state `Call` $l\ f$ follows the evaluation of actual parameters l in the invocation of f; `Alloc` $l\ v\ e$ is an intermediate state for allocation of local variables v, where e is an accumulator for the environment and l is the list of values to be bound to the function's formal parameters; `Bind` $l\ p\ e$ is a state for binding parameter names p to values l in environment e. The `Alloc` to `Bind` transition retrieves the parameter names from the state's continuation, which we omit in this example for brevity. Note that

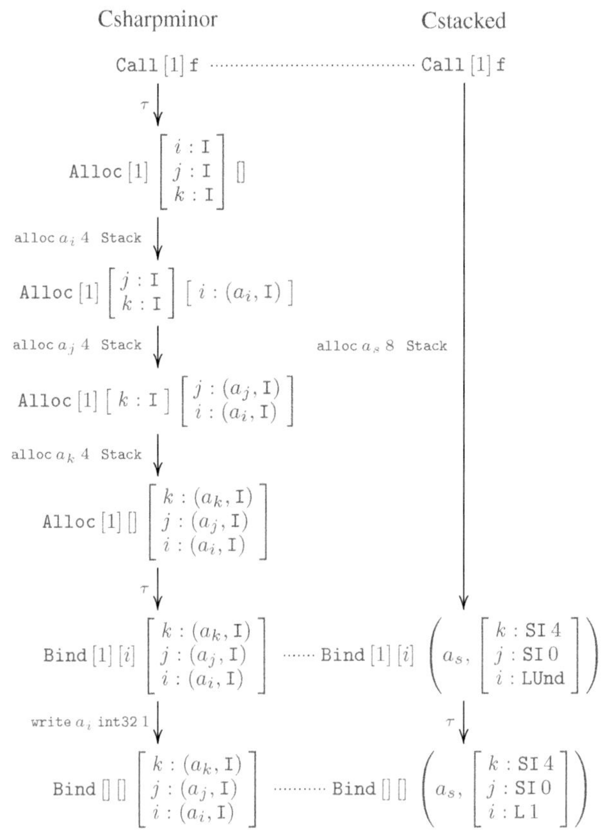

where I stands for `scalar int32`, LUnd for `local Vundef`, SI *ofs* for `stack_scalar int32` *ofs*, and L 1 for `local (Vint 1)`.

Figure 6. Function entry transitions in Csharpminor and Cstacked.

the states do not refer to memory directly. Instead, the transitions expose the memory interaction in the labels. In Csharpminor, the semantics of function entry allocates three different 4-byte blocks, one for parameter `i`, and two for variables `j` and `k`. In Cstacked (and in all languages between Cminor and MachAbstract), the function entry semantics allocates a single 8-byte stack frame for variables `j` and `k`. No memory is reserved for variable `i` because `i`'s value is kept in the thread-local local environment. The binding transitions are also different: Csharpminor writes the value 1 of parameter `i` to memory, but Cstacked simply stores the value in the environment. Indeed, note the difference in the environment entry for i in the last `Bind` states at the bottom of the figure: the Csharpminor entry only contains a pointer to memory, whereas the Cstacked entry contains the value of the variable.

Simulating Cstacked in Csharpminor Remember that the Csharpminor-Cstacked phase switches from infinite memory to finite memory. This is necessary to be able to simulate the creation of the Cstacked local environments by fresh memory allocation in Csharpminor so that the memory cannot be allocated even by future Cstacked allocations. We call the finite space used by Cstacked the *machine space*. The remaining (infinite) part of the Csharpminor memory space in other blocks is called *scratch space*. Our representation of pointers is of the form (b, ofs) where b is an integer block identifier and $ofs \in \{0, \ldots, 2^{32} - 1\}$ is an offset. In our semantics, the machine space pointers have block $b = 0$, the pointers with non-zero b are scratch space pointers. We simulate Cstacked transitions so that we preserve equality of pointer values in the states and the values in the (machine) memory:

- We simulate Cstacked stack frame allocation by allocations of individual variables at the same (machine) memory location as they have in Cstacked. Moreover, we allocate space for Cstacked local environments in globally fresh blocks in the scratch memory.
- Cstacked memory reads/writes are simulated by the same reads/writes in Csharpminor.
- Cstacked local environment accesses (which are τ events in Cstacked) are simulated by memory accesses to the corresponding Csharpminor scratch memory.
- We simulate Cstacked stack frame deallocation by freeing the individual variables, including the ones in non-machine memory, in Csharpminor.

The simulation relation on the states of the parallel composition of threads and the TSO machine consists of three main components: a thread state relation, a TSO buffer relation and a memory relation.

Relating thread states The main source of difficulty is relating the local environments of Cstacked and Csharpminor because the values of the local environments in Cstacked correspond to the memory contents of Csharpminor. Therefore, the thread state simulation must relate Cstacked thread state with Csharpminor thread state *and* memory.

In our TSO semantics, a thread's view of memory may differ from the real contents of the memory and from other threads' views of memory because of possibly pending writes, allocations and frees in store buffers of this and other threads. We consider local environments related for thread t if the values in the local environments in the Cstacked state are the same as the ones in the memory of Csharpminor's TSO machine with t's buffer applied. Moreover, we consider stack environments related if for each Cstacked environment item of the stack kind with offset *ofs*, the corresponding Csharpminor item's pointer equals the sum of Cstacked stack frame pointer and *ofs*. Since Cstacked and Csharpminor only differ in their environments, the thread state simulation relation is a natural lifting of the environment relation.

All thread transitions preserve such a relation because they can only affect the thread's buffer. However, the simulation of applying other threads' buffers to the main memory (unbuffering) requires a stronger relation. In particular, the state relation does not prevent unbuffering in one thread from interfering with another thread's state relation. To get non-interference for unbuffering, we keep track of memory partitioning among threads (this is also necessary to make sure that threads do not free each others' stack frames) by augmenting the state relation with the partitions they own in memory.

Relating buffers The buffer relation requires that a Cstacked (stack-frame) allocation corresponds to individual disjoint Csharpminor allocations (of individual variables) that must be in the stack-frame; Cstacked writes correspond to the same writes in Csharpminor buffer; frees in Cstacked buffer correspond to frees of subranges in Csharpminor. To relate frees, we must know the sizes of objects in memory because a free label does not contain a size; hence, we parametrise the buffer relation by the thread's partition. It is worth noting that the Csharpminor buffer may contain extra memory labels for the local environment manipulation, which are τ labels in Cstacked and thus do not appear in the Cstacked buffer. We only require the operations in the labels to be valid in the thread's partition.

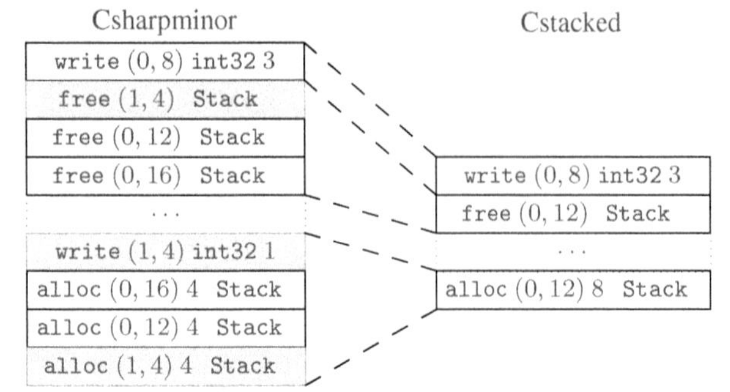

Figure 7. Buffer relation.

Fig. 7 illustrates the buffer relation. Assuming that the TSO machine inserts labels to the top of the buffer and applies the labels to memory from the bottom, the buffer contents might be generated by the function `f` from the beginning of this section, where the allocations correspond to the transitions from Fig. 6, the dotted part of the buffer is generated by the function `g`, the frees correspond to local variable deallocations at function exit, and the write label is issued by writing the return value to the caller's stack frame. The grey labels are the memory manipulation removed by the compiler, or, more precisely, they are the labels introduced by the backward simulation (note that they act on scratch memory).

In the simulation proof, the buffer relation says how to simulate Cstacked buffer application in Csharpminor while preserving the simulation relation. For example, if we are to simulate Cstacked buffer application of the `alloc` label, we apply the three corresponding allocations followed by the write from the Csharpminor buffer.

Relating TSO states The whole-system simulation relation states that there are Cstacked and Csharpminor partitionings, i.e., maps from thread ids to partitions such that

- The Csharpminor (resp. Cstacked) partitioning corresponds to the ranges allocated in the Csharpminor (resp. Cstacked) TSO machine's memory. Moreover, the partitionings must be pairwise disjoint and for each thread, the Csharpminor machine partitions must contain sub-ranges of Cstacked partitions. This is necessary to guarantee that any Cstacked allocation can be successfully simulated in Csharpminor[4].
- The values in the machine memory are the same in Cstacked and in Csharpminor. We need this property to establish that reads of the same address give the same value in Cstacked and in Csharpminor.
- Each thread's Cstacked and Csharpminor buffers are related.
- For each thread t, the states of t in Csharpminor and Cstacked are related in the partitions and memory updated by t's buffers.

The relation also imposes several consistency invariants: to guarantee that Cstacked writes do not overwrite Csharpminor scratch memory, we require scratch pointers only appear as pointers in Csharpminor environments. With these ingredients, the relation on the TSO states is a whole-system backward simulation relation.

[4] A simulation of successful allocation is an interesting (and lengthy) exercise because one must show that in Csharpminor, no possible partial application of other threads' buffers conflicts with the simulated allocations. The partial buffer applications create states that do not directly correspond to any Cstacked state (e.g., partially allocated environments), forcing us to invent a new simulation relation for this purpose.

5.3 Changing memory accesses (2) (MachAbs to MachConc)

In many respects, the simulation from MachAbs to MachConc is similar to the Csharpminor-Cstacked simulation. MachAbs and MachConc are again two different semantics for the same programs.

In MachAbs, the thread-local state consists of the current function being executed, the program counter, the stack pointer, the register file, the current stack frame, and a sequence of the stack frames for the function's callers. Instructions that manipulate local stack variables (`getstack`, `setstack`, `getparam`) perform a τ-step, which accesses only the thread-local stack frames. In contrast, MachConc allocates the stack frames in (global) memory; so the three aforementioned instructions generate read or write events for communicating with the TSO machine.

The proof is by whole-system measured backward simulation, which keeps track of which regions of MachConc's memory are local for a given thread (corresponding to the thread-local parts of the stack frames) and which regions correspond to the possibly shared parts of each thread's stack frames. For the thread-local parts, MachConc's memory is related to the corresponding thread's frames only after the thread's buffered updates have been applied, whereas for the shared parts, MachConc's memory is immediately related to MachAbs's memory (i.e., before any buffers have been applied). In addition, the MachConc and the MachAbs buffers for each thread are related in an element-wise manner if we ignore the thread-local writes from the MachConc buffers (as they do not correspond to any memory writes in MachAbs). Of course, deciding whether a buffered write is thread-local depends on its position inside the buffer, since preceding buffered allocations and frees can affect whether an address is local or shared. The full simulation relation also relates the states of each thread in the two semantics and contains several administrative properties, such as that the various thread-local and shared stack allocation ranges are pairwise disjoint, and that stack frames are aligned to 16 byte boundaries.

A distinguishing aspect of this simulation is that we compile away stack-allocations and frees. In MachAbs, each non-empty stack frame is allocated with a fresh address at function entry, and deallocated at function return. Concretely, however, no memory allocation takes place; the stack pointer is simply incremented or decremented accordingly. Therefore, in MachConc, each thread is allocated a stack when created, and the stack pointer is simply decremented at function entry and incremented at function return (x86 stacks grow downwards). If decrementing the stack pointer exceeds the allocated stack range, the semantics raises an 'Out of Memory' error. In concrete x86 executions, this would correspond to a segmentation fault due to stack overflow. Compiling away stack-allocations and frees makes the simulation relation slightly more intricate as the relations between buffers and between memories over the appropriate ranges are of equality on values; the MachAbs values are less defined than the corresponding MachConc ones. This is because a newly allocated stack frame in MachAbs will initially contain `Vundef` everywhere, whereas in MachConc the corresponding block, after decrementing the stack pointer, will contain whatever values happened to be there.

5.4 The 'easy' phases, including optimisations

We have enabled all the CompCert 1.5 optimisations that are sound under the TSO semantics. These are: constant propagation & partial evaluation, a restricted version of CSE (common subexpression elimination) that eliminates only common arithmetic expressions, but does not eliminate common memory loads, redundant load removal (as part of register allocation), branch tunneling, and tail call optimisation. The only CompCert 1.5 optimisation we do not perform is CSE for memory reads, because this is unsound under the TSO memory model as demonstrated by the following example (adapted from [Pug00]):

```
int x;
x = 0;  | void f (int *p) {int a = x, b = *p, c = x;
x = 1;  |   printf("%d%d%d", a, b, c);}
        | f(&x);
```

CSE would replace the assignment `c = x` with `c = a`, allowing the second thread to print 010, a behaviour that is not allowed by the TSO semantics.

Labellising CompCert's definitions of RTL, LTL, LTLin, Linear, MachAbs, and MachConc and establishing that they are determinate and receptive (so that they can be composed with the TSO machine) was straightforward because the CompCert 1.5 definitions of these languages were already fully small-step. Porting CompCert's forward simulation proofs to threadwise forward simulation proofs and lifting them to measured whole-system backward simulations using Theorems 2 and 3 was equally straightforward. (In the early days of the project, porting one phase took approximately two days, but by the end 3 hours were sufficient to port constant propagation and lift it to a measured whole-system backward simulation.) Elimination of redundant loads required a small adaptation of the forward-to-backward simulation infrastructure. Moreover, the tail call optimisation and the spilling/reloading phases may change some of the undefined values in the source semantics to particular values in the target semantics requiring us to prove another slightly more general version of Theorems 2 and 3.

5.5 The x86 backend

We adapted the x86 backend from CompCert 1.8 (CompCert 1.5 supported PowerPC and ARM only), with several notable differences in the semantics and proofs. Our x86 semantics is based on a well-tested HOL4 formalisation of part of the x86 instruction set [SSZN$^+$09, Section 3]. The structure of our instruction AST is closer to that of general x86 instructions, with their various combinations of immediate, register and addressing-mode arguments, than that of CompCert 1.8, which is a flatter AST supporting just the combinations used by the compiler. It does entail some additional complexity in the proof, however.

We replaced individual stackframe allocations with one-off stack space allocation at the start of the thread and direct stack pointer arithmetic. We detect stack overflow by checking that the stack pointer register stays inside the thread's stack space. If not, the semantics issues an explicit `oom` event.

Using the more realistic single stack space gives us the added benefit of direct access to function arguments and the return address. This contrasts with CompCert that accesses arguments through an indirect link to parent stackframe and models the return address with a virtual return-address register (similarly to PowerPC's real link register). The direct access to arguments buys us a slight performance advantage over CompCert, while the direct return address access enables a more honest modelling of x86.

Several parts of the x86 semantics are less realistic than we would wish. The most notable abstraction in the semantics is modelling register and memory contents by the high-level `value` datatype (as in CompCert), which is a discriminated union of pointers, integers, floats and undefined value, instead of the more appropriate bit-vector representation.

5.6 Running CompCertTSO

Despite not making any attempt at optimising the generated code results on simple sequential and concurrent benchmarks (mostly drawn from [Com09]) show that our generated code runs at about 75% of the performance of `gcc -O1`. As a more representative example, we have also successfully compiled Fraser's lock-free skiplist algorithm [Fra03]; we are roughly 69% of the performance of `gcc -O1` on this benchmark. Porting required only three changes, all to in-line assembly macros, two of which were replacing macros for `CAS` and `MFENCE` by the ClightTSO constructs.

6. Discussion

We reflect briefly on the impact of the tool chain and proof style that we employed to ease development of our compiler.

The main tool was Coq. Here we found the proof style advocated by SSREFLECT [GM07] to be helpful in ensuring proof robustness, but to retain backward compatibility with CompCert, we employed it selectively. Occasionally, we used specialised tactics to automate some of the more tedious proofs, such as the threadwise determinacy and receptiveness of all the languages.

To give the reader a flavour for the effort involved in the development, we list the number of lines of proof and specifications (definitions and statements of lemmas) for some of the important (and fully proven) phases of our compiler.

Phases	Specs	Proofs
TSO machine & memory	2079	2746
Simulations (§4)	1075	1810
ClightTSO definition	2010	186
ClightTSO-Csharpminor (§5.1)	1452	2379
Csharpminor-Cstacked (§5.2)	3481	8208
RTL-Linear (§5.4)	7141	5098
MachConc-Asm (§5.5)	2594	2803

Of those the RTL-Linear phases are adaptations of existing code (7 phases in total), as is the compiler part of MachConc-Asm; the rest is largely new. For comparison, CompCert 1.5 has roughly 31K lines of specifications and 23K lines of proofs for all the phases. The project has taken approximately 36 man-months.

The semantics of ClightTSO is given as an inductively defined relation, as usual and following Clight. To make it easier to check the integrity of the definition, we also implemented a functional characterisation of the threadwise single-step transition relation and proved that the two definitions are equivalent. By extracting the functional version into an OCaml program serving as an interpreter, we were able to test the semantics on sample ClightTSO programs. This revealed a number of subtle errors in our original definitions. It would also be worth testing our x86 semantics against processor behaviour, as we did for a HOL4 x86 semantics in previous work with Myreen [SSZN$^+$09].

A mechanised theorem is only useful if its statement can be understood, and for CompCertTSO the overall correctness theorem involves the ClightTSO and x86 semantics. We defined ClightTSO using Ott [SZNO$^+$10], a tool that generates Coq and LaTeX definitions from a single source; it also helped in enforcing naming conventions. The ClightTSO grammar and semantic rules, and the terms in examples are all parsed and automatically typeset.

7. Related Work

Research on verified compilation of sequential languages has a long history. Notable recent work includes CompCert, which we have already discussed in detail; Chlipala's compiler from a small impure functional language to an idealised assembly language, focussing on Coq proof automation [Chl10]; Myreen's JIT compiler from a bytecode to x86 [Myr10]; and Benton and Hur's compilation [BH09] from a simply typed functional language to a low-level SECD machine. This last differs from most other work in giving a compositional understanding of compiler correctness rather than just a relationship between the whole-program behaviours of source and target.

Verified compilation of concurrent languages has received much less attention. Perhaps the most notable example is the work of Lochbihler [Loc10] extending Jinja (a compiler from sequential Java to JVM, verified in Isabelle/HOL) to concurrency. As here, shifting to a small-step semantics required non-trivial proof effort, but the Jinja memory accesses in source and target are very closely related, so issues of relaxed-memory behaviour, memory layout, finite memory, and so on seem to have played no role. To the best of our knowledge, there is no prior work addressing verified compilation for a relaxed-memory concurrent language.

An alternative approach to extending CompCert with concurrency has been suggested by Hobor et al. [HAZN08]. They define a concurrent version of Cminor equipped with a concurrent separation logic. The idea is to do verifying compilation for programs that have been proved correct in such a logic, and their *oracle semantics* for concurrent Cminor (factored rather differently to ours) is intended to make that possible without extensive refactoring of the CompCert proofs. That is in some sense complementary to our work: we focus on intrinsically racy concurrent algorithms, whereas programs proved correct in that logic are known to be race free (as most application code is expected to be). However, we conjecture that an oracle semantics could be defined directly above the labellised semantics that we use.

ClightTSO is not intended as a proposal for a complete language: its load and store operations are loosely analogous to the C++0x *atomics* [Bec10, BOS+11] and Java *volatiles* [MPA05], and it has no distinguished class of memory operations which are supposed to be thread-local (and hence which a compiler is licenced to optimise between synchronisation points). It is closer to the pseudocode or C-with-macros that is commonly used for concurrent shared-memory algorithms, and the ClightTSO operations can be implemented efficiently, with simple x86 loads and stores. Volatiles and C++0x SC atomics need heavier implementations, though C++0x also has cheaper *low-level atomics* with weaker semantics that are cheaper to implement. Java and C++0x also have more complex semantics, albeit not specific to TSO processors (essentially x86 and Sparc).

8. Conclusion

The shift to commodity multicore processors has recently made relaxed-memory concurrent computation pervasive, but semantics and verification in this setting is a long-standing problem. As Lamport wrote in 1979 [Lam79]:

> *For some applications, achieving sequential consistency may not be worth the price of slowing down the processors. In this case, one must be aware that conventional methods for designing multiprocess algorithms cannot be relied upon to produce correctly executing programs. Protocols for synchronizing the processors must be designed at the lowest level of the machine instruction code, and verifying their correctness becomes a monumental task.*

This paper is a step towards putting them on a rigorous foundation, both for programming and verification.

Acknowledgements We thank Xavier Leroy for enlightening discussions and for making CompCert available. We acknowledge funding from EPSRC grants EP/F036345 and EP/H005633 and ANR grant ANR-06-SETI-010-02.

References

[AG96] S. V. Adve and K. Gharachorloo. Shared memory consistency models: A tutorial. *IEEE Computer*, 29(12):66–76, 1996.

[AMSS10] J. Alglave, L. Maranget, S. Sarkar, and P. Sewell. Fences in weak memory models. In *Proc. CAV*, 2010.

[Bec10] P. Becker, editor. *Programming Languages — C++. Final Committee Draft.* 2010. ISO/IEC JTC1 SC22 WG21 N3092.

[BH09] N. Benton and C.K Hur. Biorthogonality, step-indexing and compiler correctness. In *Proc. ICFP*, 2009.

[BL09] Sandrine Blazy and Xavier Leroy. Mechanized semantics for the Clight subset of the C language. *Journal of Automated Reasoning*, 43(3):263–288, 2009.

[Boe05] H.-J. Boehm. Threads cannot be implemented as a library. In *Proc. PLDI*, pages 261–268, 2005.

[BOS+11] M. Batty, S. Owens, S. Sarkar, P. Sewell, and T. Weber. Mathematizing C++ concurrency. In *Proc. POPL*, 2011.

[C1X] Programming languages – C (committee draft, WG14 N1494, ISO/IEC 9899:201x). `http://www.open-std.org/jtc1/sc22/wg14/www/docs/PostColorado.htm`.

[Chl10] A. Chlipala. A verified compiler for an impure functional language. In *Proc. POPL*, 2010.

[CKS07] P. Cenciarelli, A. Knapp, and E. Sibilio. The Java memory model: Operationally, denotationally, axiomatically. In *Proc. ESOP*, 2007.

[Com09] The Compcert verified compiler, v. 1.5. `http://compcert.inria.fr/release/compcert-1.5.tgz`, August 2009.

[Coq] The Coq proof assistant. `http://coq.inria.fr/`.

[Fra03] Keir Fraser. *Practical Lock Freedom.* PhD thesis, 2003. Also available as Tech. Report UCAM-CL-TR-639.

[GM07] G. Gonthier and A. Mahboubi. A small scale reflection extension for the coq system. Technical report, 2007.

[HAZN08] A. Hobor, A. W. Appel, and F. Zappa Nardelli. Oracle semantics for concurrent separation logic. In *Proc. ESOP*, 2008.

[Lam79] L. Lamport. How to make a multiprocessor computer that correctly executes multiprocess programs. *IEEE Trans. Comput.*, C-28(9):690–691, 1979.

[Lea99] D. Lea. *Concurrent Programming in Java. Second Edition: Design Principles and Patterns.* 1999.

[Ler09a] Xavier Leroy. Formal verification of a realistic compiler. *Communications of the ACM*, 52(7):107–115, 2009.

[Ler09b] Xavier Leroy. A formally verified compiler back-end. *Journal of Automated Reasoning*, 43(4):363–446, 2009.

[Lin99] 1999. Linux Kernel mailing list, thread "spin_unlock optimization(i386)", 119 messages, Nov. 20–Dec. 7th, `http://www.gossamer-threads.com/lists/engine?post=105365;list=linux`. Accessed 2009/11/18.

[Loc10] A. Lochbihler. Verifying a compiler for Java threads. In *Proc. ESOP'10*, 2010.

[Mil89] R. Milner. *Communication and Concurrency.* Prentice Hall International, 1989.

[MPA05] J. Manson, W. Pugh, and S.V. Adve. The Java memory model. In *Proc. POPL*, 2005.

[Myr10] M. O. Myreen. Verified just-in-time compiler on x86. In *Proc. POPL*, 2010.

[OSS09] S. Owens, S. Sarkar, and P. Sewell. A better x86 memory model: x86-TSO. In *Proc. TPHOLs*, 2009.

[Owe10] S. Owens. Reasoning about the implementation of concurrency abstractions on x86-TSO. In *Proc. ECOOP*, 2010.

[Pug00] W. Pugh. The Java memory model is fatally flawed. *Concurrency - Practice and Experience*, 12(6), 2000.

[SA08] J. Ševčík and D. Aspinall. On validity of program transformations in the Java memory model. In *ECOOP*, 2008.

[Sew97] P. Sewell. On implementations and semantics of a concurrent programming language. In *Proc. CONCUR*, July 1997.

[Spa] The SPARC architecture manual, v. 9. `http://developers.sun.com/solaris/articles/sparcv9.pdf`.

[Spa92] *The SPARC Architecture Manual, V. 8.* SPARC International, Inc., 1992. Revision SAV080SI9308. `http://www.sparc.org/standards/V8.pdf`.

[SSO+10] P. Sewell, S. Sarkar, S. Owens, F. Zappa Nardelli, and M. O. Myreen. x86-TSO: A rigorous and usable programmer's model for x86 multiprocessors. *C. ACM*, 53(7):89–97, 2010.

[SSZN+09] S. Sarkar, P. Sewell, F. Zappa Nardelli, S. Owens, T. Ridge, T. Braibant, M. Myreen, and J. Alglave. The semantics of x86-CC multiprocessor machine code. In *Proc. POPL*, 2009.

[SZNO+10] P. Sewell, F. Zappa Nardelli, S. Owens, G. Peskine, T. Ridge, S. Sarkar, and R. Strniša. Ott: Effective tool support for the working semanticist. *J. Funct. Program.*, 20(1):71–122, 2010.

[TVD10] E. Torlak, M. Vaziri, and J. Dolby. MemSAT: checking axiomatic specifications of memory models. In *PLDI*, 2010.

Mathematizing C++ Concurrency

Mark Batty Scott Owens Susmit Sarkar Peter Sewell Tjark Weber
University of Cambridge

Abstract

Shared-memory concurrency in C and C++ is pervasive in systems programming, but has long been poorly defined. This motivated an ongoing shared effort by the standards committees to specify concurrent behaviour in the next versions of both languages. They aim to provide strong guarantees for race-free programs, together with new (but subtle) relaxed-memory atomic primitives for high-performance concurrent code. However, the current draft standards, while the result of careful deliberation, are not yet clear and rigorous definitions, and harbour substantial problems in their details.

In this paper we establish a mathematical (yet readable) semantics for C++ concurrency. We aim to capture the intent of the current ('Final Committee') Draft as closely as possible, but discuss changes that fix many of its problems. We prove that a proposed x86 implementation of the concurrency primitives is correct with respect to the x86-TSO model, and describe our CPPMEM tool for exploring the semantics of examples, using code generated from our Isabelle/HOL definitions.

Having already motivated changes to the draft standard, this work will aid discussion of any further changes, provide a correctness condition for compilers, and give a much-needed basis for analysis and verification of concurrent C and C++ programs.

Categories and Subject Descriptors C.1.2 [*Multiple Data Stream Architectures (Multiprocessors)*]: Parallel processors; D.1.3 [*Concurrent Programming*]: Parallel programming; F.3.1 [*Specifying and Verifying and Reasoning about Programs*]

General Terms Documentation, Languages, Reliability, Standardization, Theory, Verification

Keywords Relaxed Memory Models, Semantics

1. Introduction

Context Systems programming, of OS kernels, language runtimes, etc., commonly rests on shared-memory concurrency in C or C++. These languages are defined by informal-prose standards, but those standards have historically not covered the behaviour of concurrent programs, motivating an ongoing effort to specify concurrent behaviour in a forthcoming revision of C++ (unofficially, C++0x) [AB10, BA08, Bec10]. The next C standard (unofficially, C1X) is expected to follow suit [C1X].

The key issue here is the multiprocessor relaxed-memory behaviour induced by hardware and compiler optimisations. The design of such a language involves a tension between usability and performance: choosing a very strong memory model, such as sequential consistency (SC) [Lam79], simplifies reasoning about programs but at the cost of invalidating many compiler optimisations, and of requiring expensive hardware synchronisation instructions (e.g. fences). The C++0x design resolves this by providing a relatively strong guarantee for typical application code together with various *atomic* primitives, with weaker semantics, for high-performance concurrent algorithms. Application code that does not use atomics and which is race-free (with shared state properly protected by locks) can rely on sequentially consistent behaviour; in an intermediate regime where one needs concurrent accesses but performance is not critical one can use *SC atomics*; and where performance is critical there are *low-level atomics*. It is expected that only a small fraction of code (and of programmers) will use the latter, but that code —concurrent data structures, OS kernel code, language runtimes, GC algorithms, etc.— may have a large effect on system performance. Low-level atomics provide a common abstraction above widely varying underlying hardware: x86 and Sparc provide relatively strong TSO memory [SSO+10, Spa]; Power and ARM provide a weak model with cumulative barriers [Pow09, ARM08, AMSS10]; and Itanium provides a weak model with release/acquire primitives [Int02]. Low-level atomics should be efficiently implementable above all of these, and prototype implementations have been proposed, e.g. [Ter08].

The current draft standard covers all of C++ and is rather large (1357 pages), but the concurrency specification is mostly contained within three chapters [Bec10, Chs.1, 29, 30]. As is usual for industrial specifications, it is a prose document. Mathematical specifications of relaxed memory models are usually either operational (in terms of an abstract machine or operational semantics, typically involving explicit buffers etc.) or axiomatic, defining constraints on the relationships between the memory accesses in a complete candidate execution, e.g. with a happens-before relation over them. The draft concurrency standard is in the style of a prose description of an axiomatic model: it introduces various relationships, identifying when one thread *synchronizes with* another, what a *visible side effect* is, and so on (we explain these in §2), and uses them to define a happens-before relation. It is obviously the result of extensive and careful deliberation. However, when one looks more closely, it is still rather far from a clear and rigorous definition: there are points where the text is unclear, places where it does not capture the intent of its authors, points where a literal reading of the text gives a broken semantics, several substantial omissions, and some open questions. Moreover, the draft is very subtle. For example, driven by the complexities of the intended hardware targets, the happens-before relation it defines is intentionally non-transitive. The bottom line is that, given just the draft standard text, the basic question for a language definition, of what behaviour is allowed for a specific program, can be a matter for debate.

Given previous experience with language and hardware memory models, e.g. for the Java Memory Model [Pug00, MPA05, CKS07, SA08, TVD10] and for x86 multiprocessors [SSZN+09, OSS09, SSO+10], this should be no surprise. Prose language definitions leave much to be desired even for sequential languages; for relaxed-memory concurrency, they almost inevitably lead to ambiguity, error and confusion. Instead, we need rigorous (but readable)

POPL'11, January 26–28, 2011, Austin, Texas, USA.

mathematical semantics, with tool support to explore the consequences of the definitions on examples, proofs of theoretical results, and support for testing implementations. Interestingly, the style of semantics needed is quite different from that for conventional sequential languages, as are the tools and theorems.

Contributions In this paper we establish a mathematically rigorous semantics for C++ concurrency, described in Section 2 and with further examples in Section 3. It is *precise*, formalised in Isabelle/HOL [Isa], and is *complete*, covering essentially all the concurrency-related semantics from the draft standard, without significant idealisation or abstraction. It includes the data-race-freedom (DRF) guarantee of SC behaviour for race-free code, locks, SC atomics, the various flavours of low-level atomics, and fences. It covers initialisation but not allocation, and does not address the non-concurrent aspects of C++. Our model builds on the informal-mathematics treatment of the DRF guarantee by Boehm and Adve [BA08]. We have tried to make it as *readable* as possible, using only minimal mathematical machinery (mostly just sets, relations and first-order logic with transitive closure) and introducing it with a series of examples. Finally, wherever possible it is a *faithful* representation of the draft standard and of the intentions of its authors, as far as we understand them.

In developing our semantics, we identified a number of issues in several drafts of the C++0x standard, discussed these with members of the concurrency subgroup, and made suggestions for changes. These are of various kinds, including editorial clarifications, substantive changes, and some open questions. We discuss a selection of these in Section 4. The standards process for C++0x is ongoing: the current version is at the time of writing the 'final committee draft', leaving a small window for further improvements. That for C1X is at an earlier stage, though the two should be compatible.

As a theoretical test of our semantics, we prove a correctness result (§5) for the proposed prototype x86 implementation of the C++ concurrency primitives [Ter08] with respect to our x86-TSO memory model [SSO+10, OSS09]. We show that any x86-TSO execution of a translated C++ candidate execution gives behaviour that the C++ semantics would admit, which involves delicate issues about initialisation. This result establishes some confidence in the model and is a key step towards a verified compilation result about translation of programs.

Experience shows that tool support is needed to work with an axiomatic relaxed memory model, to develop an intuition for what behaviour it admits and forbids, and to explore the consequences of proposed changes to the definitions. At the least, such a tool should take an example program, perhaps annotated with constraints on the final state or on the values read from memory, and find and display all the executions allowed by the model. This can be combinatorially challenging, but for C++ it turns out to be feasible, for typical test examples, to enumerate the possible witnesses. We have therefore built a CPPMEM tool (§6) that exhaustively considers all the possible witnesses, checking each one with code automatically generated from the Isabelle/HOL axiomatic model (§6). The front-end of the tool takes a program in a fragment of C++ and runs a symbolic operational semantics to calculate possible memory accesses and constraints. We have also explored the use of a model generator (the SAT-solver-based Kodkod [TJ07], via the Isabelle Nitpick interface [BN10]) to find executions more efficiently, albeit with less assurance. All of the examples in this paper have been checked (and their executions drawn) using CPPMEM.

Our work provides a basis for improving both standards, both by the specific points we raise and by giving a precisely defined checkpoint, together with our CPPMEM tool for exploring the behaviour of examples in our model and in variants thereof. The C and C++ language standards are a central interface in today's computational infrastructure, between what a compiler (and hardware) should implement, on the one hand, and what programmers can rely on, on the other. Clarity is essential for both sides, and a mathematically precise semantics is a necessary foundation for any reasoning about concurrent C and C++ programs, whether it be by dynamic analysis, model-checking, static analysis and abstract interpretation, program logics, or interactive proof. It is also a necessary precondition for work on compositional semantics of such programs.

2. C++0x Concurrency, as Formalised

Here we describe C++ concurrency incrementally, starting with single-threaded programs and then adding threads and locks, SC atomics, and low-level atomics (release/acquire, relaxed, and release/consume). Our model also covers fences, but we omit the details here. In this section we do not distinguish between the C++ draft standard, which is the work of the Concurrency subcommittee of WG21, and our formal model, but in fact there are substantial differences between them. We highlight some of these (and our rationale for various choices) in Section 4. Our memory model is expressed as a standalone Isabelle/HOL file and the complete model is available online [BOS]; here we give the main definitions, automatically typeset (and lightly hand-edited in a few cases) from the Isabelle/HOL source.

The semantics of a program p will be a set of allowed *executions* X. Some C++ programs are deemed to have *undefined behaviour*, meaning that an implementation is unconstrained, e.g. if any execution contains a data race. Accordingly, we define the semantics in two phases: first we calculate a set of pre-executions which are admitted by the operational semantics and are *consistent* (defined in the course of this section). Then, if there is a pre-execution in that set with a race of some kind, the semantics indicates undefined behaviour by giving NONE, otherwise it gives all the pre-executions. In more detail, a candidate execution X is a pair $(X_{\text{opsem}}, X_{\text{witness}})$, where the first component is given by the operational semantics and the second is an existential witness of some further data; we introduce the components of both as we go along. The top-level definition of the memory model, then, is:

$$
\begin{array}{l}
\text{cpp\_memory\_model } \mathit{opsem}\ (p : \mathsf{program}) = \\
\quad \textbf{let}\ \text{pre\_executions} = \{(X_{\text{opsem}}, X_{\text{witness}}).\\
\qquad\quad \mathit{opsem}\ p\ X_{\text{opsem}} \wedge \\
\qquad\quad \text{consistent\_execution}\ (X_{\text{opsem}}, X_{\text{witness}})\}\ \textbf{in} \\
\quad \textbf{if}\ \exists X \in \text{pre\_executions}. \\
\qquad (\text{indeterminate\_reads}\ X \neq \{\}) \vee \\
\qquad (\text{unsequenced\_races}\ X \neq \{\}) \vee \\
\qquad (\text{data\_races}\ X \neq \{\}) \\
\quad \textbf{then}\ \text{NONE} \\
\quad \textbf{else}\ \text{SOME pre\_executions}
\end{array}
$$

2.1 Single-threaded programs

We begin with the fragment of the model that deals with single-threaded programs, which serves to introduce the basic concepts and notation we use later.

As usual for a relaxed memory model, different threads can have quite different views of memory, so the semantics cannot be expressed in terms of changes to a monolithic memory (e.g. a function from locations to values). Instead, an execution consists of a set of *memory actions* and various relations over them, and the memory model axiomatises constraints on those.

For example, consider the program on the left below. This has only one execution, shown on the right. There are five actions, labelled (a)–(e), all by the same thread (their thread ids are elided). These are all non-atomic memory reads ($\mathsf{R_{na}}$) or writes ($\mathsf{W_{na}}$), with their address (x or y) and value (0,1, or 2). Actions (a) and (b) are the initialisation writes, (c) and (d) are the reads of the operands of the == operator, and (e) is a write of the result of ==. The evaluations of the arguments to == are *unsequenced* in C++ (as are arguments to functions), meaning that they could be in either order, or even overlapping. Evaluation order is expressed by the *sequenced-before* (sb) relation, a strict preorder over the actions, that here does not order (c) and (d). The two reads both *read from* the same write (a), indicated by the *rf* relation.

```
int main() {
  int x = 2;
  int y = 0;
  y = (x==x);
  return 0; }
```

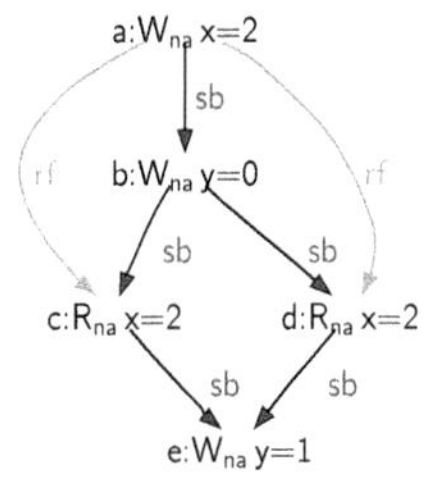

The set of actions and the sequenced-before relation are given by the operational semantics (so are part of the X_{opsem}); the *rf* relation is existentially quantified (part of the X_{witness}), as in general there may be many writes that each read might read from.

In a non-SC semantics, the constraint on reads cannot be simply that they read from the 'most recent' write, as there is no global linear time. Instead, they are constrained here using a *happens-before* relation, which in the single-threaded case coincides with sequenced-before. Non-atomic reads have to read from a *visible side effect*, a write to the same location that happens-before the read but is not happens-before-hidden, i.e., one for which there is no intervening write to the location in happens-before. We define the visible-side-effect relation below, writing it with an arrow. The auxiliary functions is_write and is_read pick out all actions (including atomic actions and read-modify-writes but not lock or unlock actions) that write or read memory.

$$
\begin{array}{l}
a \xrightarrow{\textit{visible-side-effect}} b = \\
\quad a \xrightarrow{\textit{happens-before}} b \wedge \\
\quad \text{is\_write } a \wedge \text{is\_read } b \wedge \text{same\_location } a\ b \wedge \\
\quad \neg(\exists c.\ (c \neq a) \wedge (c \neq b) \wedge \\
\qquad \text{is\_write } c \wedge \text{same\_location } c\ b \wedge \\
\qquad a \xrightarrow{\textit{happens-before}} c \xrightarrow{\textit{happens-before}} b)
\end{array}
$$

The constraint on the values read by nonatomic reads is in two parts: the reads-from map must satisfy a well-formedness condition (not shown here), saying that reads cannot read from multiple writes, that they must be at the same location and have the same value as the write they read from, and so on. More interestingly, it must respect the visible side effects, in the following sense.

$$
\begin{array}{l}
\text{consistent\_reads\_from\_mapping} = \\
\quad (\forall b.\ (\text{is\_read } b \wedge \text{is\_at\_non\_atomic\_location } b) \implies \\
\qquad (\textbf{if } (\exists a_{vse}.\ a_{vse} \xrightarrow{\textit{visible-side-effect}} b) \\
\qquad \textbf{then } (\exists a_{vse}.\ a_{vse} \xrightarrow{\textit{visible-side-effect}} b \wedge a_{vse} \xrightarrow{rf} b) \\
\qquad \textbf{else } \neg(\exists a.\ a \xrightarrow{rf} b))) \wedge \\
\quad [\ldots]
\end{array}
$$

If a read has no visible side effects (e.g. reading an uninitialised variable), there can be no *rf* edge. This is an *indeterminate read*, and the program is deemed to have undefined behaviour.

$$
\text{indeterminate\_reads} = \{b.\ \text{is\_read } b \wedge \neg(\exists a.\ a \xrightarrow{rf} b)\}
$$

A pre-execution has an *unsequenced-race* if there is a write and another access to the same location, on the same thread that are unsequenced.

$$
\begin{array}{l}
\text{unsequenced\_races} = \{(a, b). \\
\quad (a \neq b) \wedge \text{same\_location } a\ b \wedge (\text{is\_write } a \vee \text{is\_write } b) \wedge \\
\quad \text{same\_thread } a\ b \wedge \\
\quad \neg(a \xrightarrow{\textit{sequenced-before}} b \vee b \xrightarrow{\textit{sequenced-before}} a)\}
\end{array}
$$

Programs with an execution that contains an unsequenced race (ur), like the one below, have undefined behaviour.

```
int main() {
  int x = 2;
  int y = 0;
  y = (x == (x=3));
  return 0; }
```

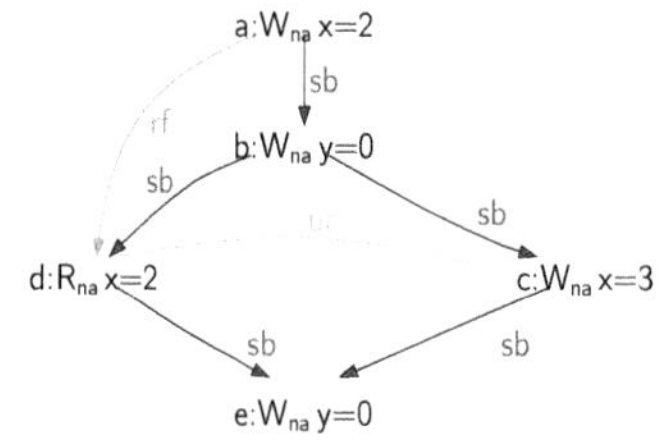

2.2 Threads, Data Races, and Locks

We now integrate C++-0x threads into the model. The following program spawns a thread that writes 3 to x and concurrently writes 3 into y in the original thread.

```
void foo(int* p) {*p = 3;}
int main() {
  int x = 2;
  int y;
  thread t1(foo, &x);
  y = 3;
  t1.join();
  return 0; }
```

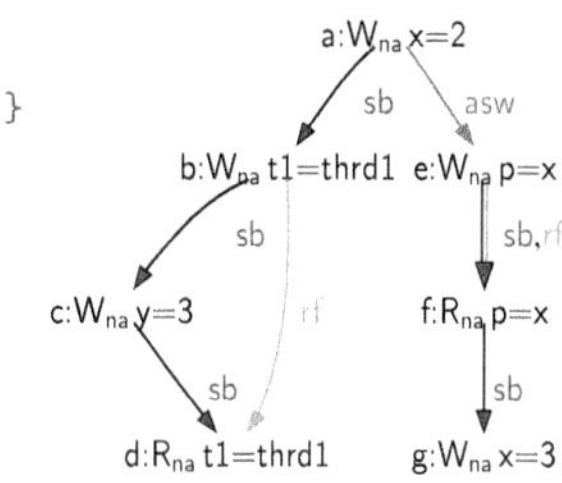

The thread creation gives rise to *additional-synchronizes-with* (asw) edges (here $a \xrightarrow{\text{asw}} e$) from sequenced-before-maximal actions of the parent thread before the thread creation to sequenced-before-minimal edges of the child. As we shall see, these edges are also incorporated, indirectly, into happens-before. They are generated by the operational semantics, so are another component of an X_{opsem}.

Thread creation gives rise to many memory actions (for passing function arguments and writing and reading the thread id) which clutter examples, so for this paper we usually use a more concise parallel composition, written `{{{ ... ||| ... }}}`:

```
int main() {
  int x = 2;
  int y;
  {{{  x = 3;
  |||  y = (x==3);
  }}};
  return 0; }
```

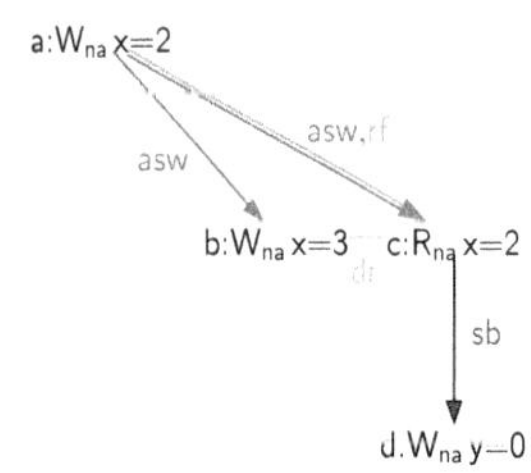

This example exhibits a *data race* (dr): two actions at the same location, on different threads, not related by happens-before, at least one of which is a write.

$$
\begin{array}{l}
\text{data\_races} = \{(a, b). \\
\quad (a \neq b) \wedge \text{same\_location } a\ b \wedge (\text{is\_write } a \vee \text{is\_write } b) \wedge \\
\quad \neg\,\text{same\_thread } a\ b \wedge \\
\quad \neg(\text{is\_atomic\_action } a \wedge \text{is\_atomic\_action } b) \wedge \\
\quad \neg(a \xrightarrow{\textit{happens-before}} b \vee b \xrightarrow{\textit{happens-before}} a)\}
\end{array}
$$

If there is a pre-execution of a program that has a data-race, then, as with unsequenced-races, that program has undefined behaviour.

Data races can be prevented by using mutexes, as usual. These give rise to *lock* and *unlock* memory actions on the mutex location, and a pre-execution has a relation, *sc*, as part of X_{witness} that totally orders such actions. A consistent_locks predicate checks that lock and unlock actions are appropriately alternating. Moreover, these actions on each mutex create *synchronizes-with* edges from every unlock to every lock that is ordered after it in *sc*. The synchronizes-with relation is a derived relation, calculated from a candidate execution, which contains mutex edges, the additional-synchronizes-with edges (e.g. from thread creation), and other edges that we will come to.

$$a \xrightarrow{\textit{synchronizes-with}} b =$$
(* – additional synchronisation, from thread create etc. – *)
$$a \xrightarrow{\textit{additional-synchronizes-with}} b \vee$$

$$(\text{same\_location}\ a\ b \wedge a \in \mathit{actions} \wedge b \in \mathit{actions} \wedge ($$
(* – mutex synchronization – *)
$$(\text{is\_unlock}\ a \wedge \text{is\_lock}\ b \wedge a \xrightarrow{sc} b) \vee$$
$$[\ldots]))$$

For multi-threaded programs with locks but without atomics, happens-before is the transitive closure of the union of the sequenced-before and synchronizes-with relations. The definition of a visible side effect and the conditions on the reads-from relation are unchanged from the single-threaded case.

2.3 SC Atomics

For simple concurrent accesses to shared memory that are not protected by locks, C++0x provides *sequentially consistent atomics*. Altering the racy example from above to use an atomic object `x` and SC atomic operations, we have the following, in which the concurrent access to `x` is not considered a data race, and so the program does not have undefined behaviour.

```
int main() {
  atomic_int x;
  x.store(2);
  int y = 0;
  {{{ x.store(3);
  ||| y = ((x.load())==3);
  }}};
  return 0; }
```

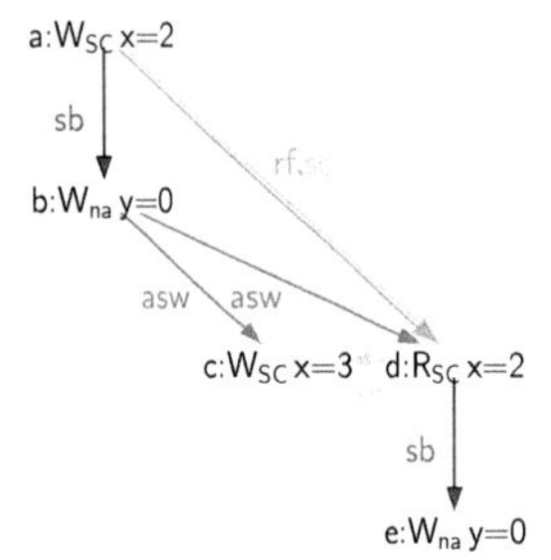

Semantically, this is because SC atomic operations are totally ordered by *sc*, and so can be thought of as interleaving with each other in a global time-line. Their semantics are covered in detail in [BA08] and we will describe their precise integration into happens-before in the following section.

Initialisation of an atomic object is by non-atomic stores (to avoid the need for a hardware fence for every such initialisation), and those non-atomic stores *can* race with other actions at the location unless the program has some synchronisation. Non-initialisation SC-atomic accesses are made with atomic read, write and read-modify-write actions that do not race with each other.

2.4 Low-level Atomics

SC atomics are expensive to implement on most multiprocessors, e.g. with the suggested implementations for an SC atomic load being `LOCK XADD(0)` on x86 [Ter08] and `hwsync; ld; cmp; bc; isync` on Power [MS10]; the LOCK'd instruction and the `hwsync` may take 100s of cycles. They also provide more synchronisation than needed for many concurrent idioms. Accordingly, C++0x includes several weaker variants: atomic actions are parametrised by a *memory order*, mo, that specifies how much synchronisation and ordering is required. The strongest ordering is required for MO_SEQ_CST actions (which is the default, as used above), and the weakest for MO_RELAXED actions. In between there are MO_RELEASE/MO_ACQUIRE and MO_RELEASE/MO_CONSUME pairs, and MO_ACQ_REL with both acquire and release semantics.

2.5 Types and Relations

Before giving the semantics of low-level atomics, we summarise the types and relations of the model. There are base types of action ids aid, thread ids tid, locations l, and values v. As we have seen already, actions can be non-atomic reads or writes, or mutex locks or unlocks. Additionally, there are atomic reads, writes, and read-modify-writes (with a memory order parameter mo) and fences (also with an mo parameter). We often elide the thread ids.

action =

$aid, tid{:}\mathrm{R}_{\mathrm{na}}\, l = v$	non-atomic read
| $aid, tid{:}\mathrm{W}_{\mathrm{na}}\, l = v$	non-atomic write
| $aid, tid{:}\mathrm{R}_{mo}\, l = v$	atomic read
| $aid, tid{:}\mathrm{W}_{mo}\, l = v$	atomic write
| $aid, tid{:}\mathrm{RMW}_{mo}\, l = v_1/v_2$	atomic read-modify-write
| $aid, tid{:}\mathrm{L}\ l$	lock
| $aid, tid{:}\mathrm{U}\ l$	unlock
| $aid, tid{:}\mathrm{F}_{mo}$	fence

The is_read predicate picks out non-atomic and atomic reads and atomic read-modify-writes; the is_write predicate picks out non-atomic and atomic writes and atomic read-modify-writes.

Locations are subject to a very weak type system: each location stores a particular kind of object, as determined by a *location-kind* map. The atomic actions can only be performed on ATOMIC locations. The non-atomic reads and writes can be performed on either ATOMIC or NON_ATOMIC locations. Locks and unlocks are *mutex* actions and can only be performed on MUTEX locations. These are enforced (among other sanity properties) by a well_formed_threads predicate; we elide the details here.

The X_{opsem} part of a candidate execution X consists of a set of thread ids, a set of actions, a location typing, and three binary relations over its actions: *sequenced-before* (sb), *additional-synchronized-with* (asw), and *data-dependency* (dd). We have already seen the first two: *sequenced-before* contains the intra-thread edges imposed by the C++ evaluation order, and *additional-synchronized-with* contains additional edges from thread creation and thread join (among others). Data dependence will be used for release/consume atomics (in §2.8). These are all relations that are decided by the syntactic structure of the source code and the path of control flow, and so the set of possible choices for an X_{opsem} can be calculated by the operational semantics without reference to the memory model (with reads taking unconstrained values).

The X_{witness} part of a candidate execution X consists of a further three binary relations over its actions: *rf*, *sc*, and *modification order* (mo). The *rf* reads-from map is a relation containing edges to read actions from the write actions whose values they take, and edges to each lock action from the last unlock of its mutex. The sequentially consistent order *sc* is a total order over all actions that are MO_SEQ_CST and all mutex actions. The modification order (mo) is a total order over all writes at each atomic location (leaving writes at different locations unrelated), and will be used to express coherence conditions. These relations are existentially quantified in the definition of cpp_memory_model, and for each X_{opsem} admitted by the operational semantics there may be many choices of an X_{witness} that give a consistent execution (each of which may or may not have a data race, unsequenced race, or indeterminate read).

The happens-before relation, along with several others, are derived from those in X_{opsem} and X_{witness}.

2.6 Release/Acquire Synchronization

An atomic write or fence is a *release* if it has the memory order MO_RELEASE, MO_ACQ_REL or MO_SEQ_CST. Atomic reads or fences with order MO_ACQUIRE, MO_ACQ_REL or MO_SEQ_CST, and fences with order MO_CONSUME, are *acquire* actions.

Pairs of a write-release and a read-acquire support the following programming idiom. Here one thread writes some data `x` (perhaps spanning multiple words) and then sets a flag `y` while the other spins until the flag is set and then reads the data.

```
// sender          | // receiver
x = ...            | while (0 == y);
y = 1;             | r = x;
```

The desired guarantee here is that the receiver must see the data writes of the sender (in more detail, that the receiver cannot see any values of data that precede those writes in modification order). This can be achieved with an atomic store of `y`, annotated MO_RELEASE, and an atomic load of `y` annotated MO_ACQUIRE. The reads and writes of `x` can be nonatomic.

In the model, any instance of a read-acquire that reads from a write-release gives rise to a *synchronizes-with* edge, e.g. as on the left below (where the *rf* edges are suppressed).

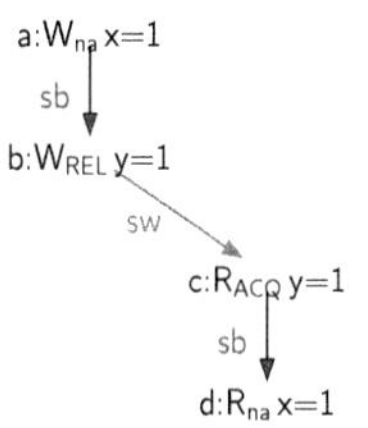

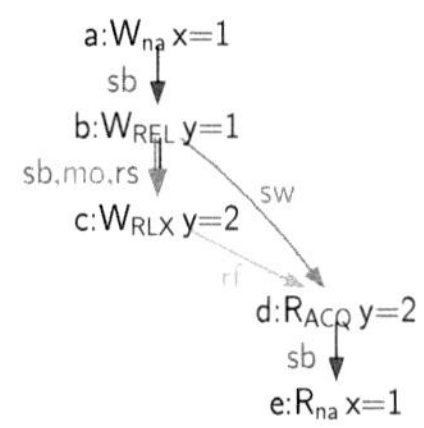

For such programs (in fact for any program without release/consume atomics), happens-before is still the transitive closure of the union of the sequenced-before and synchronizes-with relations, so here $a \xrightarrow{\textit{happens-before}} d$ and (d) is obliged to read from (a).

In this case, the read-acquire synchronizes with the write-release that it reads from. More generally, the read-acquire can synchronize with a write-release (to the same location) that is before the write that it reads from. To define this precisely, we need to use the modification order of a candidate execution and to introduce the derived notion of a *release sequence*, of writes that follow (in some sense) a write-acquire.

For example, in the fragment of an execution on the right above, the read-acquire (d) synchronizes with the write-release (b) by virtue of the fact that (d) reads from another write to the same location, (c), and (b) precedes (c) in the modification order (mo) for that location.

The modification order of a candidate execution (here $b \xrightarrow{\textit{modification-order}} c$) totally orders all of the write actions on each atomic location, in this case `y`. It must also be consistent with happens-before, in the sense below.

$$
\begin{array}{l}
\text{consistent\_modification\_order} = \\
\quad (\forall a.\ \forall b.\ a \xrightarrow{\textit{modification-order}} b \implies \text{same\_location}\ a\ b) \land \\
\quad (\forall l \in \text{locations\_of}\ \textit{actions}.\ \textbf{case}\ \textit{location-kind}\ l\ \textbf{of} \\
\qquad \text{ATOMIC} \rightarrow (\\
\qquad\quad \textbf{let}\ \textit{actions\_at\_l} = \{a.\ (\text{location}\ a = \text{SOME}\ l)\}\ \textbf{in} \\
\qquad\quad \textbf{let}\ \textit{writes\_at\_l} = \{a \in \textit{actions\_at\_l}.\ (\text{is\_store}\ a \lor \\
\qquad\qquad \text{is\_atomic\_store}\ a \lor \text{is\_atomic\_rmw}\ a)\}\ \textbf{in} \\
\qquad\qquad \text{strict\_total\_order\_over}\ \textit{writes\_at\_l} \\
\qquad\qquad (\xrightarrow{\textit{modification-order}}|_{\textit{actions\_at\_l}}) \land \\
\qquad\qquad (\text{* happens-before at the writes of } l \text{ is a subset of mo for } l\ \text{*}) \\
\qquad\qquad \xrightarrow{\textit{happens-before}}|_{\textit{writes\_at\_l}} \subseteq \xrightarrow{\textit{modification-order}} \land \\
\qquad\qquad [\ldots]) \\
\quad \|\ \_ \rightarrow (\\
\quad \textbf{let}\ \textit{actions\_at\_l} = \{a.\ (\text{location}\ a = \text{SOME}\ l)\}\ \textbf{in} \\
\quad (\xrightarrow{\textit{modification-order}}|_{\textit{actions\_at\_l}}) = \{\}))
\end{array}
$$

In the example, the release action (b) has a release sequence [(b),(c)], a contiguous sub-sequence of modification order on the location of the write-release. The release sequence is headed by the release and can be followed by writes from the same thread or read-modify-writes from any thread; other writes by other threads break the sequence. We represent a release sequence not by the list of actions but by a relation from the head to all the elements, as the order is given by modification order. In figures we usually suppress the reflexive edge from the head to itself.

$$
\begin{array}{l}
\text{rs\_element}\ \textit{rs\_head}\ a = \\
\quad \text{same\_thread}\ a\ \textit{rs\_head} \lor \text{is\_atomic\_rmw}\ a
\end{array}
$$

$$
\begin{array}{l}
a_{rel} \xrightarrow{\textit{release-sequence}} b = \\
\quad \text{is\_at\_atomic\_location}\ b \land \\
\quad \text{is\_release}\ a_{rel} \land (\\
\qquad (b = a_{rel}) \lor \\
\qquad (\text{rs\_element}\ a_{rel}\ b \land a_{rel} \xrightarrow{\textit{modification-order}} b \land \\
\qquad\quad (\forall c.\ a_{rel} \xrightarrow{\textit{modification-order}} c \xrightarrow{\textit{modification-order}} b \implies \\
\qquad\qquad \text{rs\_element}\ a_{rel}\ c)))
\end{array}
$$

A write-release *synchronizes-with* a read-acquire if both act on the same location and the release sequence of the release contains the write that the acquire reads from. In the example $b \xrightarrow{\textit{release-sequence}} c \xrightarrow{\textit{rf}} d$, so we have $b \xrightarrow{\textit{synchronizes-with}} d$. The definition below covers mutexes and thread creation (in additional-synchronizes-with) but elides the effects of fences.

$$
\begin{array}{l}
a \xrightarrow{\textit{synchronizes-with}} b = \\
\quad (\text{* -- additional synchronization, from thread create etc. -- *}) \\
\quad a \xrightarrow{\textit{additional-synchronizes-with}} b \lor \\
\\
\quad (\text{same\_location}\ a\ b \land a \in \textit{actions} \land b \in \textit{actions} \land (\\
\qquad (\text{* -- mutex synchronization -- *}) \\
\qquad (\text{is\_unlock}\ a \land \text{is\_lock}\ b \land a \xrightarrow{sc} b) \lor \\
\\
\qquad (\text{* -- release/acquire synchronization -- *}) \\
\qquad (\text{is\_release}\ a \land \text{is\_acquire}\ b \land \neg\,\text{same\_thread}\ a\ b \land \\
\qquad (\exists c.\ a \xrightarrow{\textit{release-sequence}} c \xrightarrow{\textit{rf}} b)) \lor \\
\qquad [\ldots]))
\end{array}
$$

The modification order and the sc order we saw earlier must also be consistent, in the following sense:

$$
\begin{array}{l}
\text{consistent\_sc\_order} = \\
\quad \textbf{let}\ \text{sc\_happens\_before} = \xrightarrow{\textit{happens before}}|_{\text{all\_sc\_actions}}\ \textbf{in} \\
\quad \textbf{let}\ \text{sc\_mod\_order} = \xrightarrow{\textit{modification-order}}|_{\text{all\_sc\_actions}}\ \textbf{in} \\
\quad \text{strict\_total\_order\_over all\_sc\_actions}\ (\xrightarrow{sc}) \land \\
\quad \xrightarrow{\text{sc\_happens\_before}} \subseteq \xrightarrow{sc} \land \\
\quad \xrightarrow{\text{sc\_mod\_order}} \subseteq \xrightarrow{sc}
\end{array}
$$

2.7 Constraining Atomic Read Values

The values that can be read by an atomic action depend on happens-before, derived from sequenced-before and synchronizes-with. We return to the execution fragment shown on the right in the previous subsection, showing a transitive reduction of happens-before that coincides with its constituent orderings.

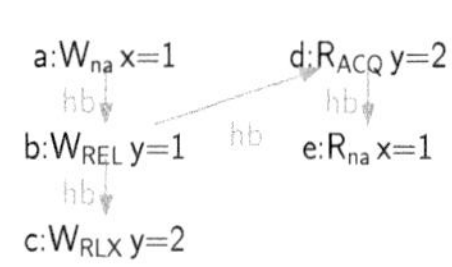

An atomic action must read a write that is in one of its *visible sequences of side effects*; in this case (d) either reads (b) or (c).

A visible sequence of side effects of a read is a contiguous subsequence of modification order, headed by a visible side effect of the read, where the read does not happen before any member of the sequence. We represent a visible sequence of side effects not as a list but as a set of actions in the tail of the sequence (we are not concerned with their order).

$$
\begin{array}{l}
\mathrm{visible\_sequence\_of\_side\_effects\_tail}\ \mathit{vsse\_head}\ b = \\
\quad \{c.\ \mathit{vsse\_head} \xrightarrow{\mathit{modification\text{-}order}} c\ \wedge \\
\quad \neg(b \xrightarrow{\mathit{happens\text{-}before}} c)\ \wedge \\
\quad (\forall a.\ \mathit{vsse\_head} \xrightarrow{\mathit{modification\text{-}order}} a \xrightarrow{\mathit{modification\text{-}order}} c \\
\qquad \Longrightarrow \neg(b \xrightarrow{\mathit{happens\text{-}before}} a))\}
\end{array}
$$

We define *visible-sequences-of-side-effects* to be the binary relation relating atomic reads to their visible-side-effect sets (now including the visible side effects themselves). The atomic read must read from a write in one of these sets.

We can now extend the previous definition of the consistent reads-from predicate to be the conjunction of the read-restrictions on nonatomic and atomic actions, and a constraint ensuring read-modify-write atomicity.

$$
\begin{array}{l}
\mathrm{consistent\_reads\_from\_mapping} = \\
\quad (\forall b.\ (\mathrm{is\_read}\ b \wedge \mathrm{is\_at\_non\_atomic\_location}\ b) \Longrightarrow \\
\qquad (\mathbf{if}\ (\exists a_{vse}.\ a_{vse} \xrightarrow{\mathit{visible\text{-}side\text{-}effect}} b) \\
\qquad \mathbf{then}\ (\exists a_{vse}.\ a_{vse} \xrightarrow{\mathit{visible\text{-}side\text{-}effect}} b \wedge a_{vse} \xrightarrow{\mathit{rf}} b) \\
\qquad \mathbf{else}\ \neg(\exists a.\ a \xrightarrow{\mathit{rf}} b)))\ \wedge \\
\quad (\forall b.\ (\mathrm{is\_read}\ b \wedge \mathrm{is\_at\_atomic\_location}\ b) \Longrightarrow \\
\qquad (\mathbf{if}\ (\exists (b', \mathit{vsse}) \in \mathit{visible\text{-}sequences\text{-}of\text{-}side\text{-}effects}.\ (b' = b)) \\
\qquad \mathbf{then}\ (\exists (b', \mathit{vsse}) \in \mathit{visible\text{-}sequences\text{-}of\text{-}side\text{-}effects}. \\
\qquad\qquad (b' = b) \wedge (\exists c \in \mathit{vsse}.\ c \xrightarrow{\mathit{rf}} b)) \\
\qquad \mathbf{else}\ \neg(\exists a.\ a \xrightarrow{\mathit{rf}} b)))\ \wedge \\
\quad (\forall (a, b) \in \xrightarrow{\mathit{rf}}.\ \mathrm{is\_atomic\_rmw}\ b \\
\qquad \Longrightarrow a \xmapsto{\mathit{modification\text{-}order}} b)\ \wedge \\
\quad [\ldots]
\end{array}
$$

A candidate execution is also required to be free of the following four execution fragments. This property is called coherence.

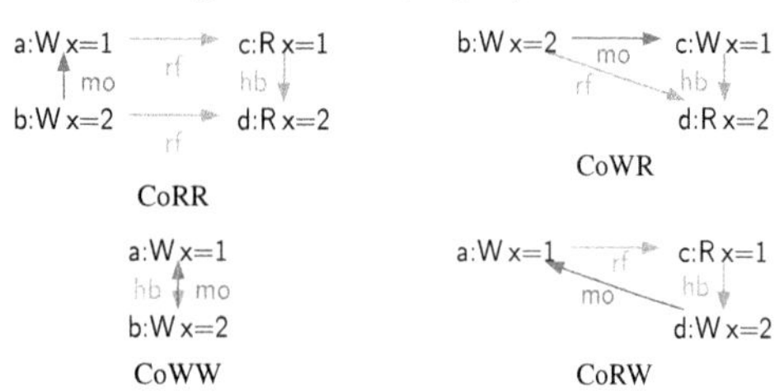

CoRR Two reads ordered by happens-before may not read two writes that are modification ordered in the other direction.

CoWR It is forbidden to read from a write that is happens-before-hidden by a later write in modification order.

CoWW Happens-before and modification-order may not disagree.

CoRW The union of the reads-from map, happens-before and modification-order must be acyclic.

Finally, we restrict SC reads: If there is no preceding write in sc order, then there is no extra restriction. Otherwise, they must read from the last prior write in sc order, from a non-atomic write that follows it in modification order, or from any non-SC atomic write.

2.8 Release/Consume Atomics

On multiprocessors with weak memory orders, notably Power, release/acquire pairs are cheaper to implement than sequentially consistent atomics but still significantly more expensive than plain stores and loads. For example, the proposed Power implementation of load-acquire, `ld; cmp; bc; isync`, involves an `isync` [MS10]. However, Power (and also ARM) does guarantee that certain dependencies in an assembly program are respected, and in many cases those suffice, making the `isync` sequence unnecessary. As we understand it, this is the motivation for introducing a *read-consume* variant of read-acquire atomics. On a stronger processor (e.g. a TSO x86 or Sparc), or one where those dependencies are not respected, read-consume would be implemented just as read-acquire.

Read-consume enables efficient implementations of algorithms that use pointer reassignment for commits of their data, e.g. read-copy-update [MW]. For example, suppose one thread writes some data (perhaps spanning multiple words) then writes the address of that data to a shared atomic pointer, while the other thread reads the shared pointer, dereferences it and reads the data.

`// sender`
`data = ...`
`p = &data;`
	`// receiver`
	`r1 = p`
	`r2 = *r1;     // data`

Here there is a dependency at the receiver from the read of `p` to the read of `data`. This can be expressed using a write-release and an atomic load of `p` annotated MO_CONSUME:

```
int main() {
  int data; atomic_address p;
  {{{ { data=1;
        p.store(&data, mo_release); }
  ||| printf("%d\n", *(p.load(mo_consume)) );
  }}};
  return 0; }
```

As we saw in §2.6, the semantics of release/acquire pairs introduced synchronizes-with edges, and happens-before includes the transitive closure of synchronizes-with and sequenced-before — for a release/acquire version of this example, we would have the edges on the left below, and hence $a \xrightarrow{\mathit{happens\text{-}before}} d$.

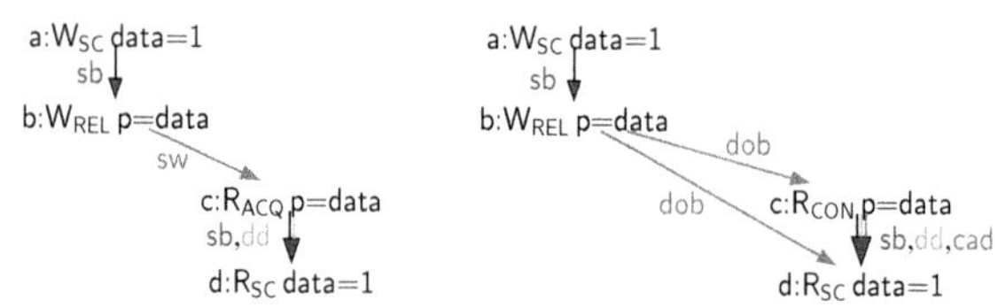

For release/consume, the key fact is that there is a *data dependency* (dd) from (c) to (d), as shown on the right. The (dd) edge is provided by the operational semantics and gives rise to a *carries-a-dependency-to* (cad) edge, which extends data dependency with thread-local reads-from relationships:

$$
\begin{array}{l}
a \xrightarrow{\mathit{carries\text{-}a\text{-}dependency\text{-}to}} b = \\
\quad a\ ((\xrightarrow{\mathit{rf}} \cap \xrightarrow{\mathit{sequenced\text{-}before}}) \cup \xrightarrow{\mathit{data\text{-}dependency}})^{+}\ b
\end{array}
$$

In turn, this gives rise to a *dependency-ordered-before* (dob) edge, which is the release/consume analogue of the release/acquire synchronizes-with edge. This involves release sequences as before (in the example just the singleton [(b)]):

$$
\begin{array}{l}
a \xrightarrow{\mathit{dependency\text{-}ordered\text{-}before}} d = \\
\quad a \in \mathit{actions} \wedge d \in \mathit{actions}\ \wedge \\
\quad (\exists b.\ \mathrm{is\_release}\ a \wedge \mathrm{is\_consume}\ b\ \wedge \\
\qquad (\exists e.\ a \xrightarrow{\mathit{release\text{-}sequence}} e \xrightarrow{\mathit{rf}} b)\ \wedge \\
\qquad (b \xrightarrow{\mathit{carries\text{-}a\text{-}dependency\text{-}to}} d \vee (b = d)))
\end{array}
$$

2.9 Happens-before

Finally, we can define the complete happens-before relation. To accommodate MO_CONSUME, and specifically the fact that release/consume pairs only introduce happens-before relations to dependency-successors of the consume, *not* to all actions that are sequenced-after it, the definition is in two steps. First, we define *inter-thread-happens-before*, which combines synchronizes-with and dependency-ordered-before, allowing transitivity with sequenced-before on the left for both and on the right only for synchronizes-with:

$$\xrightarrow{\textit{inter-thread-happens-before}} =$$
$$\textbf{let } r = \xrightarrow{\textit{synchronizes-with}} \cup \xrightarrow{\textit{dependency-ordered-before}} \cup (\xrightarrow{\textit{synchronizes-with}} \circ \xrightarrow{\textit{sequenced-before}}) \textbf{ in}$$
$$(\xrightarrow{r} \cup (\xrightarrow{\textit{sequenced-before}} \circ \xrightarrow{r}))^+$$

In any execution, this must be acyclic:

$$\mathrm{consistent\_inter\_thread\_happens\_before} = \mathrm{irreflexive}\,(\xrightarrow{\textit{inter-thread-happens-before}})$$

Happens-before (which is thereby also acyclic) is then just the union with sequenced-before:

$$\xrightarrow{\textit{happens-before}} = \xrightarrow{\textit{sequenced-before}} \cup \xrightarrow{\textit{inter-thread-happens-before}}$$

2.10 Putting it together

Given a candidate execution $X = (X_{\mathrm{opsem}}, X_{\mathrm{witness}})$, we can now calculate the derived relations:

release-sequence (§2.6), *hypothetical-release-sequence* (a variant of *release-sequence* used in the fence semantics), *synchronizes-with* (§2.2, §2.6), *carries-a-dependency-to* (§2.8), *dependency-ordered-before* (§2.8), *inter-thread-happens-before* (§2.8), *happens-before* (§2.1, §2.2, §2.3, §2.8), *visible-side-effect* (§2.1), and *visible-sequences-of-side-effects* (§2.7).

The definition of consistent_execution used at the start of Section 2 is then simply the conjunction of the predicates we have defined:

consistent_execution =	
well_formed_threads ∧	(§2.5, defn. elided)
consistent_locks ∧	(§2.2, defn. elided)
consistent_inter_thread_happens_before ∧	(§2.8)
consistent_sc_order ∧	(§2.6)
consistent_modification_order ∧	(§2.6)
well_formed_reads_from_mapping ∧	(§2.1, defn. elided)
consistent_reads_from_mapping	(§2.1, §2.7)

The acyclicity check on inter-thread-happens-before, and the subtlety of the non-transitive happens-before relation, are needed only for release/consume pairs:

Theorem 1. *For an execution with no consume operations, the* consistent_inter_thread_happens_before *condition of* consistent_execution *is redundant.*

Theorem 2. *If a consistent execution has no consume operations, happens-before is transitive.*

The proofs are by case analysis and induction on the size of possible cycles.

3. Examples

We now illustrate the varying strength of the different memory orders by showing the semantics of some 'classic' examples. In all cases, variants of the examples with SC atomics do not have the weak-memory behaviour. As in our other diagrams, to avoid clutter we only show selected edges, and we omit the C++ sources for these examples, which are available on-line [BOS].

Store Buffering (SB) Here two threads write to separate locations and then each reads from the other location. In Total Store Order (TSO) models both can read from before (w.r.t. coherence) the other write in the same execution. In C++0x this behaviour is allowed if those four actions are relaxed, for release/consume pairs and for release/acquire pairs. This behaviour is not allowed for the same program using sequentially consistent consistent atomics (with non-atomic initialisation).

Message Passing (MP) Here one thread (non-atomically) writes data and then an atomic flag while a second thread waits for the flag and then (non-atomically) reads data; the question is whether it is guaranteed to see the data written by the first. As we saw in §2.6, with a release/acquire pair it is. A release/consume pair gives the same guarantee iff there is a dependency between the reads, otherwise there is a consistent execution (on the left) in which there is a data race (here the second thread sees the initial value of x; the candidate execution in which the second thread sees the write x=1 is ruled out as that does not happen-before the read and so is not a visible side effect).

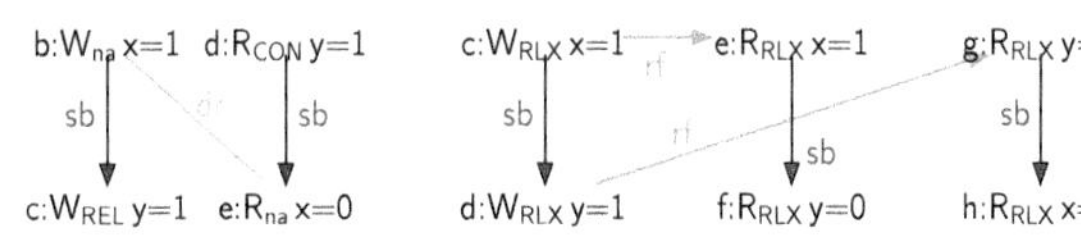

The same holds with relaxed flag operations.

In a variant in which all writes and reads are release/consumes or relaxed atomics, eliminating the race, and there are two copies of the reading thread, the two reading threads can see the two writes of the writing thread in opposite orders (as on the right above) — consistent with what one might see on Power, for example.

Load Buffering (LB) In this dual of the SB example the question is whether the two reads can both see the (sequenced-before) later write of the other thread in the same execution. With relaxed atomics this is allowed, as on the left:

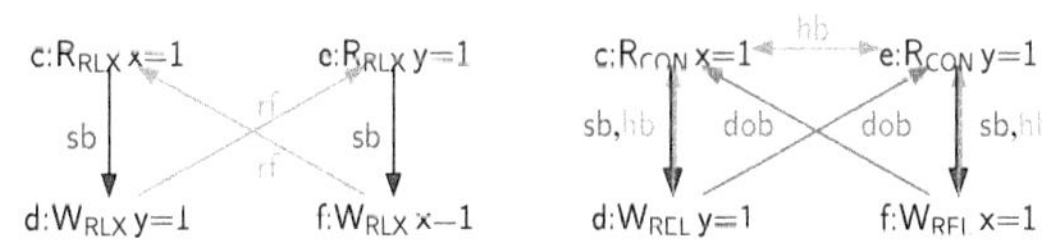

but with release/consumes (with dependencies) it is not (as on the right above), because inter-thread-happens-before would be cyclic. It is not allowed for release/acquire and sequentially consistent atomics (which are stronger than release/consumes with dependencies), because of the cyclic inter-thread-happens-before and stronger inter-thread ordering.

Write-to-Read Causality (WRC) Here the first thread writes to x; the second reads from that and then (w.r.t. sequenced-before) writes to y; the third reads from that and then (w.r.t. sequenced-before) reads x. The question is whether it is guaranteed to see the first thread's write.

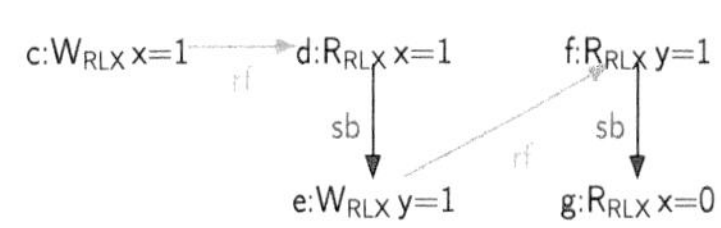

With relaxed atomics, this is not guaranteed, as shown above, while with release/acquires it is, as the *synchronizes-with* edges in the inter-thread-happens-before relation interfere with the required read-from map.

Independent Reads of Independent Writes (IRIW) Here the first two threads write to different locations; the question is whether the second two threads can see those writes in different orders. With relaxed, release/acquire, or release/consume atomics, they can.

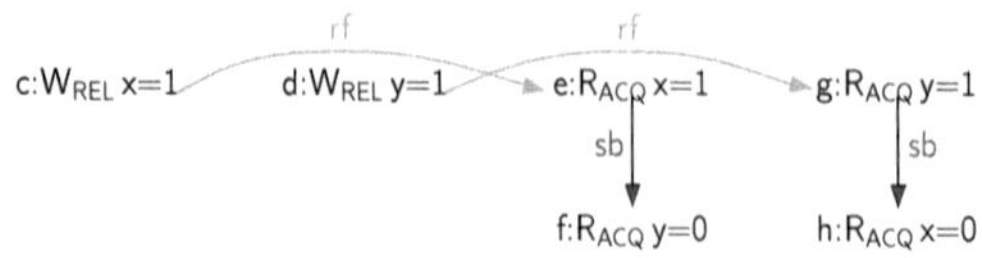

4. From standard to formalisation and back

We developed the model presented in Section 2 by a lengthy iterative process: building formalisations of various drafts of the standard, and of Boehm and Adve's model without low-level atomics [BA08]; considering the behaviour of examples, both by hand and with our tool; trying to prove properties of the formalisations; and discussing issues with members of the Concurrency subcommittee of the C++ Standards Committee (TC1/SC22/WG21). To give a flavour of this process, and to explain how our formalisation differs from the current draft (the final committee draft, N3092) of the standard, we describe a selection of debatable issues. This also serves to bring out the delicacy of the standard, and the pitfalls of prose specification, even when carried out with great care. We have made suggestions for technical or editorial changes to the draft for many of these points and it seems likely that they will be incorporated.

We begin with two straightforward drafting issues, easily fixed. Then there are three substantial semantic problems in N3092 where we have proposed solutions. Finally, there is an outstanding question that warrants further investigation.

'Subsequent' in visible sequences of side effects N3092 defines: *The visible sequence of side effects on an atomic object M, with respect to a value computation B of M, is a maximal contiguous sub-sequence of side effects in the modification order of M, where the first side effect is visible with respect to B, and for every subsequent side effect, it is not the case that B happens before it.* However, if every element in a vsse happens-before a read, the read should not take the value of the visible side effect. Following discussion, we formalise this without the *subsequent*.

Additional happens-before edges There are 6 places where N3092 adds happens-before relationships explicitly (in addition to those from sequenced-before and inter-thread-happens-before), e.g. between the invocation of a thread constructor and the function that the thread runs. As happens-before is carefully *not* transitively closed, such edges would not be transitive with (e.g.) sequenced-before. Accordingly, we instead add them to the synchronizes-with relation; for those within our C++ fragment, our operational semantics introduces them into additional-synchronizes-with.

Acyclicity of happens-before N3092 defines happens-before, making plain that it is not necessarily transitive, but does not state whether it is required to be acyclic (or whether, perhaps, a program with a cyclic execution is deemed to have undefined behaviour). The release/consume LB example of §3 has a cyclic inter-thread-happens-before, as shown there, but is otherwise a consistent execution. After discussion, it seems clear that executions with cyclic inter-thread-happens-before (or, equivalently, cyclic happens-before) should not be considered, so we impose that explicitly.

Coherence requirements The draft standard enforced only two of the four coherence requirements presented in §2.7, CoRR and CoWW. In the absence of CoRW and CoWR, the following executions were allowed.

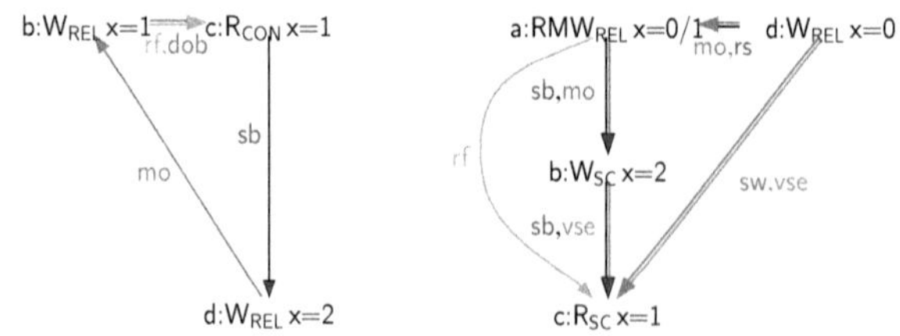

The execution on the left violates CoRW by containing a cycle of happens-before and modification order edges, allowed only due to the lack of transitivity of happens-before. The execution on the right violates CoWR by having a read from a write (the read-modify-write (a)) that is sequenced-before-hidden by (c). Actions (b) and (c) are shown as SC atomics for emphasis.

Furthermore, the draft standard refers to *'the'* visible sequence of side-effects, suggesting uniqueness. Nevertheless, it allows valid executions that have more than one, relying on the lack of transitivity of happens-before as in the CoRW execution above.

These behaviours are surprising and were not intended by the designers.

Sequential consistency for SC atomics The promise of sequential consistency to the non-expert programmer is a central design choice of C++0x and is stated directly by N3092: `memory_order_seq_cst` *ensures sequential consistency [...] for a program that is free of data races and uses exclusively* `memory_order_seq_cst` *operations.* Unfortunately N3092 allows the following non-sequentially consistent execution of the SB example with SC atomics (initialisation writes, such as (a) and (b), are non-atomic so that they need not be compiled with memory fences):

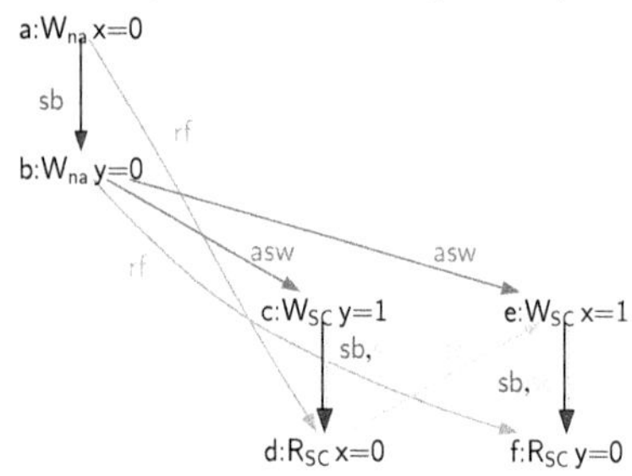

We devised a stronger restriction on the values that may be read by SC atomics, stated in §2.7, that does provide sequential consistency here.

Overlapping executions and thin-air reads In a C++0x program that gives rise to the relaxed LB example in §3, the written value 1 might have been concrete in the program source. Alternatively, one might imagine a *thin-air read*: the program below has the same execution, and here there is *no* occurrence of 1 in the program source.

```
int main() {
  int r1, r2;
  atomic_int x = 0;
  atomic_int y = 0;
  {{{ { r1 = x.load(mo_relaxed));
        y.store(r1,mo_relaxed); }
  ||| { r2 = y.load(mo_relaxed));
        x.store(r2,mo_relaxed); }
  }}}
  return 0; }
```

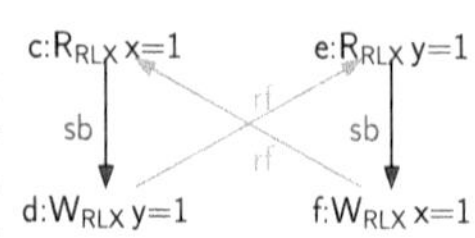

This would be surprising, and in fact would not happen with typical hardware and compilers. In the Java Memory Model [MPA05], much of the complexity of the model arises from the desire to outlaw thin-air reads, which there is essential to prevent forging of pointers. N3092 also attempts to forbid thin air reads, with:

An atomic store shall only store a value that has been computed from constants and program input values by a finite sequence of program evaluations, such that each evaluation observes the values of variables as computed by the last prior assignment in the sequence. This seems to be overly constraining. For example, two subexpression evaluations (in separate threads) can overlap (e.g. if they are the arguments of a function call) and can contain multiple actions. With relaxed atomics there can be consistent executions in which it is impossible to disentangle the two into any sequence, for example as below, where the SC-write of x must be between the two reads of x. In our formalisation we currently do not impose any thin-air condition.

```
int main() {
  atomic_int x = 0;
  int y;
  {{{ x.store(1);
  ||| { y = (x.load()==x.load()); }
  }}};
  return 0; }
```

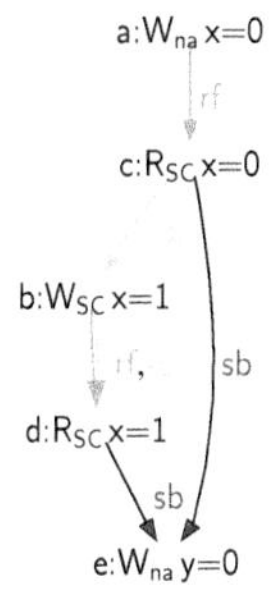

5. Correctness of a Proposed x86 Implementation

The C++0x memory model has been designed with compilation to the various target architectures in mind, and prototype implementations of the atomic primitives have been proposed. For example, the following table presents an x86 prototype by Terekhov [Ter08]:

Operation	x86 Implementation	
Load non-SC	mov	
Load Seq_cst	lock xadd(0)	OR: mfence, mov
Store non-SC	mov	
Store Seq_cst	lock xchg	OR: mov , mfence
Fence non-SC	no-op	
Fence Seq_cst	mfence	

This is a simple mapping from individual source-level atomic operations to small fragments of assembly code, abstracting from the vast and unrelated complexities of compilation of a full C++ language (argument evaluation order, object layout, control flow, etc.). Proposals for the Power [MS10] and other architectures follow the same structure, although, as they have more complex memory models than the x86, the assembly code for some of the operations is more intricate.

Verifying that these prototypes are indeed correct implementations of the model is a crucial part of validating the design. Furthermore, as they represent the atomic-operation parts of efficient compilers (albeit without fence optimisations), they can directly form an important part of a verified C++ compiler, or inform the design and verification of a compiler with memory-model-aware optimisations.

Here, we prove a version of the above prototype x86 implementation [Ter08] correct with respect to our x86-TSO semantics [SSZN+09, OSS09, SSO+10]. Following the prototype, we ignore lock and unlock operations, as well as forks and joins, all of which require significant runtime or operating system support in addition to the x86 hardware. We also ignore sequentially consistent fences, but cover all other fences. We do consider read-modify-write actions, implementing them with x86 LOCK'd read-modify-writes; and we include non-atomic loads and stores, which can map to multiple x86 loads and stores, respectively. The prototype mapping is simple, and x86-TSO is reasonably well-understood, so this should be seen as a test of the C++ memory model.

In x86-TSO, an operational semantics gives meaning to an assembly program by creating an *x86 event structure* E_{x86} (analogous to X_{opsem}) comprising a set of events and an intra-thread *program-order* relation (analogous to sequenced-before) that orders events according to the program text. Events can be reads, writes, or fences, and certain instructions (e.g. CMPXCHG) create *locked* sets of events that execute atomically. Corresponding to $X_{witness}$, there are *x86 execution witnesses* X_{x86} which comprise a reads-from mapping and a memory order, which is a partial order over reads and writes that is total on the writes. The remainder of the axiomatisations are very different: x86-TSO has no concept of release, acquire, visible side effect, etc.

Abstracting out the rest of the compiler To discuss the correctness of the proposed mapping in isolation, without embarking on a verification of some particular full compiler, we work solely in terms of candidate executions and memory models.

First, we lift the mapping between instructions to a nondeterministic translation $action\_comp$ from C++ actions to small x86 event structures, e.g. relating an atomic read-modify-write action to the events of the corresponding x86 LOCK'd instruction.

To define what it means for the mapping to be correct, suppose we have a C++ program p with no undefined behaviour and an X_{opsem} which is allowed by its operational semantics. We regard an abstract compiler evt_comp as taking such an X_{opsem} and giving an x86 event structure E_{x86}, respecting the $action\_comp$ mapping but with some freedom in the resulting x86 program order.

We say the mapping is correct if given such an abstract compiler, the existence of a valid x86-TSO execution witness for E_{x86} implies the existence of a consistent C++ execution witness $X_{witness}$ for the original actions X_{opsem}. We prove this by lifting such an x86 execution witness to a C++ consistent execution, as illustrated below.

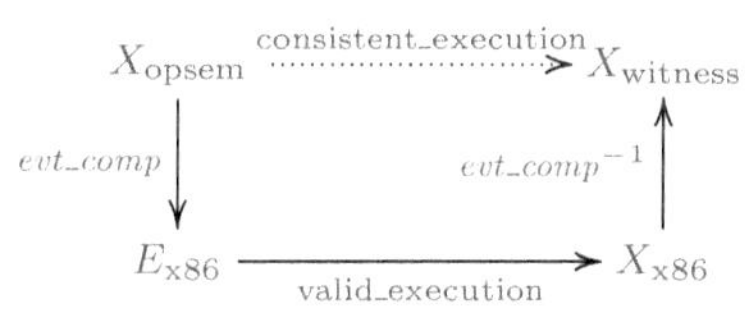

Below we show an X_{opsem} and E_{x86} that could be related by evt_comp. The dotted lines indicate some of the x86 program ordering decisions that the compiler must make, but which evt_comp does not constrain.

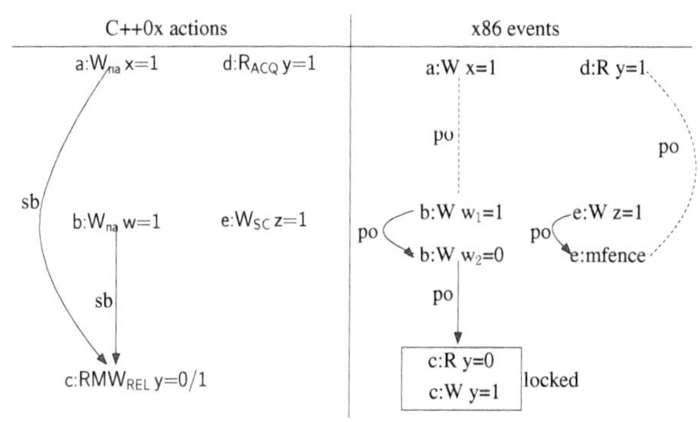

In more detail, we use two existentially quantified helper functions $locn\_comp$ and tid_comp to encapsulate the details of a C++ compiler's data layout, its mapping of C++ locations to x86 addresses, and the mapping of C++ threads to x86 threads.

Given a C++ location and value, $locn\_comp$ produces a finite mapping from x86 addresses to x86 values. The domain of the finite map is the set of x86 addresses that corresponds to the C++ location, and the mapping itself indicates how a C++ value is laid out across the x86 addresses. A well-formed $locn\_comp$ has the following properties: it is injective; the address calculation cannot depend on the value; each C++ location has an x86 address; different C++ locations have non-overlapping x86 address sets; and an atomic C++ location has a single x86 address, although a non-atomic location can have several addresses (e.g. for a multi-word object).

Finally, the evt_comp relation specifies valid translations, applying $action\_comp$ with a well-formed $locn\_comp$ and also constraining how events from different actions relate: no single x86 instruction instance can be used by multiple C++ actions, and the x86 *program-order* relation must respect C++'s *sequenced-before*. The detailed definitions, and the proof of the following theorem, are available online [BOS].

Theorem 3. *Let p be a C++ program that has no undefined behaviour. Suppose also that p contains no SC fences, forks, joins, locks, or unlocks. Then the x86 mapping is correct in the sense above. That is, if $actions$, sequenced-before, and location-kind are members of the X_{opsem} part of a candidate execution resulting from the operational semantics of p, then the following holds:*

$$\begin{array}{l} \forall comp\ locn\_comp\ tid\_comp\ X_{\text{x86}}. \\ \quad \text{evt\_comp}\ comp\ locn\_comp\ tid\_comp\ actions \\ \qquad\qquad sequenced\text{-}before\ location\text{-}kind \wedge \\ \quad \text{valid\_execution}\ (\cup_{a \in actions}(comp\ a))\ X_{\text{x86}} \Rightarrow \\ \quad \exists X_{\text{witness}}.\ \text{consistent\_execution}\ (X_{\text{opsem}}, X_{\text{witness}}) \end{array}$$

Proof outline. X_{x86} includes a reads-from map and a memory ordering relation that is total on all memory writes. To build X_{witness}, we lift a C++ reads-from map and modification order from these through $comp$ (e.g., $a \xrightarrow{rf} b$ iff $\exists (e_1 \in comp\ a)(e_2 \in comp\ b).\ e_1 \xrightarrow{x86\text{-}rf} e_2$). We create an sc ordering by restricting the X_{x86} memory ordering to the events that originate in sequentially consistent atomics, and linearising it using the proof technique from our previous triangular-race freedom work for x86-TSO [Owe10]. We then lift that through $comp$. The proof now proceeds in three steps:

1) We first show that if $a \xrightarrow{happens\text{-}before} b$ and there are x86 events e_1 and e_2 such that $e_1 \in comp\ a$ and $e_2 \in comp\ b$, then e_1 precedes e_2 in either X_{x86}'s memory order or program order. We have machine-checked this step in HOL-4 [HOL].[1]

This property establishes that, in some sense, x86-TSO has a stronger memory model than C++, and so any behaviour allowed by the former should be allowed by the latter. However, things are not quite so straightforward.

2) Check that X_{witness} is a consistent_execution. Most cases are machine checked in HOL; some are only pencil-and-paper. Many rely upon the property from 1. For example, in showing that (at a non-atomic location) if $a \xrightarrow{rf} b$ then $a \xrightarrow{visible\text{-}side\text{-}effect} b$, we note that if there were a write c to the same location such that $a \xrightarrow{happens\text{-}before} c \xrightarrow{happens\text{-}before} b$, then using the property from 1, there is an x86 write event in $comp\ c$ that would come between the events of $comp\ a$ and $comp\ b$ in X_{x86}, thus meaning that they would not be in X_{x86}'s reads-from map, contradicting the construction of X_{witness}'s reads from map.

3) In some cases, some of the properties required for 2 might be false. For example, in showing that $a \xrightarrow{rf} b$ implies $a \xrightarrow{visible\text{-}side\text{-}effect} b$, we need to show that $a \xrightarrow{happens\text{-}before} b$. Even though there is such a relationship at the x86 level, it does not necessarily exist in C++. In general, x86 executions can establish reads-from relations that are prohibited in C++. Similarly, for non-atomic accesses that span multiple x86 addresses, the lifted reads from-map might not be well-formed.

We show that if one of these violations of 2 arises, then the original C++ program has a data race. We find a minimum violation in X_{x86}, again using techniques from our previous work [Owe10]. Next we can remove the violation, resulting in a consistent X_{witness} for a prefix of the execution, then we add the bad action, note that it creates a data race, and allow the program to complete in any way. The details of this part are by pencil-and-paper proof. □

[1] The C++ model is in Isabelle/HOL, but x86-TSO is in HOL-4. We support the proof with a semi-automated translation from Isabelle/HOL to HOL-4.

Sequentially consistent atomics The proposal above includes two implementations of sequentially consistent atomic reads and writes; one with the x86 locked instructions, and the other with fence instructions on both the reads and writes. However, we can prove that it suffices either to place an mfence before every sc read, or after every sc write, but that it is not necessary to do both. In practice, placing the fence after the sc writes is expected to yield higher performance.

This optimisation is a direct result of using triangular-race freedom (TRF) [Owe10] to construct the sc ordering in proving Theorem 3. Roughly, our TRF theorem characterises when x86-TSO executions are not sequentially consistent; it uses a pattern, called a triangular race, involving an x86-level data race combined with a write followed, on the same thread, by a read without a fence (or locked instruction) in between. If no such pattern exists, then an execution X_{x86} can be linearised such that each read reads from the most recent preceding write.

Although the entirety of an execution witness X_{x86} might contain triangular races and therefore not be linearisable, by restricting attention to only sc reads and writes we get a subset of the execution that is TRF, as long as there is a fence between each sc read and write on the same thread. Linearising this subset guarantees the relevant property of X_{witness}'s sc ordering: that if a and b are sequentially consistent atomics and $a \xrightarrow{rf} b$, then a immediately precedes b in sc restricted to that address.

Compiler correctness Although we translate executions instead of source code, Theorem 3 could be applied to full source-to-assembly compilers that follow the prototype implementation. The following diagram presents the overall correctness property.

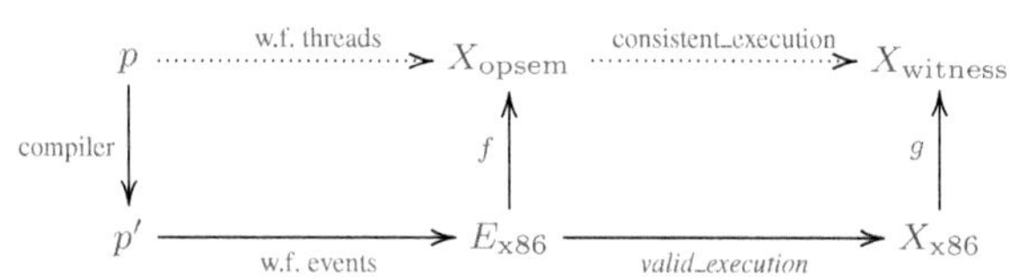

If, once we use f, we can then apply evt_comp to get the same event set back, i.e., informally, $evt\_comp(f(E)) = E$, then Theorem 3 ensures that the compiler respects the memory model, and so we only need to verify that it respects the operational semantics. Thus, our result applies to compilers that do not optimise away any instructions that evt_comp will produce. These restrictions apply to the code generation phase; the compiler can perform any valid source-to-source optimisations before generating x86 code.

6. Tool support for exploring the model

Given a relatively complex axiomatic memory model, as we presented in Section 2, it is often hard to immediately see the consequences of the axioms, or what behaviour they allow for particular programs. Our CPPMEM tool takes a program in a fragment of C++0x and calculates the set of its executions allowed by the memory model, displaying them graphically.

The tool has three main components: an executable symbolic operational semantics to build the X_{opsem} parts of the candidate executions X of a program; a search procedure to enumerate the possible X_{witness} for each of those; and a checking procedure to calculate the derived relations and predicates of the model for each $(X_{\text{opsem}}, X_{\text{witness}})$ pair, to check whether it is consistent and whether it has data races, unsequenced races or indeterminate reads.

Of these, the checker is the most subtle, since the only way to intuitively understand it is to understand the model itself (which is what the tool is intended to aid with), and thus bugs are hard to catch. It also has to be adapted often as the model is developed. We therefore use Isabelle/HOL code generation [Haf09] to build the checker directly from our Isabelle/HOL axiomatisation, to keep the checker and our model in exact correspondence and reduce the possibility for error.

The operational semantics Our overall semantics is stratified: the memory model is expressed as a predicate on the actions and relations of a candidate execution. This means we need an operational semantics of an unusual form to generate all such candidates. In a setting with a global SC memory, the values read by loads can be determined immediately, but here, for example for a program with a single load, in principle we have to generate a large set of executions, each with a load event with one of the possible values. We make this executable by building a symbolic semantics in which the values in actions can be either concrete values or unification variables (shown as $?v$). Control flow can depend on the values read, so the semantics builds a set of these actions (and the associated relations), together with constraints on the values, for each control-flow path of the program. For each path, the associated constraint is solved at the end; those with unsatisfiable constraints (indicating unreachable execution paths) are discarded.

The tool is designed to support litmus test examples of the kind we have seen, not arbitrary C++ code. These do not usually involve many C++ features, and the constraints required are propositional formulae over equality and inequality constraints over symbolic and concrete values. It is not usually important in litmus tests to do more arithmetic reasoning; one could imagine using an SMT solver if that were needed, but for the current constraint language, a standard union-find unifier suffices. The input program is processed by the CIL parser [NMRW02], extended with support for atomics. We use Graphviz [GN00] to generate output. We also allow the user to add explicit constraints on the value read by a memory load in a C++ source program, to pick out candidate executions of interest; to selectively disable some of the checks of the model; and to declutter the output by suppressing actions and edges.

As an example, consider the first program we saw, in §2.1. There are two possibilities: the reads of x either read the same value or different values, and hence the operational semantics gives the two candidate executions and constraints below:

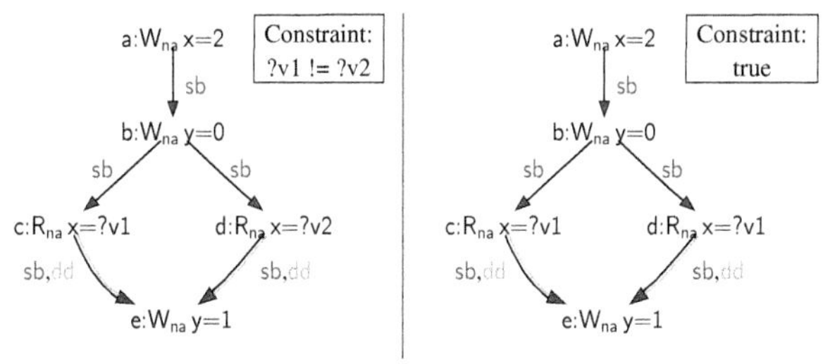

Later, the memory model will rule out the left execution, since there is no way to read anything but 2 at x.

The semantics maintains an environment mapping identifiers to locations. For loads, the relevant location is found in that, and a fresh variable $?v$ is generated to represent the value read.

Other constructs typically combine the actions of their subterms and also build the relations (sequenced-before, data-dependency, etc.) of X_{opsem} as appropriate. For example, for the `if` statement, the execution path splits and two execution candidates will be generated. The one for the true branch has an additional constraint, that the value returned by the condition expression is true (in the C/C++ sense , i.e. different from `0`), and the candidate for the false branch constrains the value to be false. There are also additional *sequenced-before* and *control-dependency* edges from the actions in the condition expression to actions in the branch.

Choosing instantiations of existential quantifiers Given the X_{opsem} part of a finite candidate execution, the X_{witness} part is existentially quantified over a finite but potentially large set. In the worst case, with m reads and n writes, all sequentially consistent (atomic), to the same location, and with the same value, there might be $O(m^{(n+1)} \cdot m! \cdot (m+n)!)$ possible choices of an *rf*, *modification-order* and *sc* relation. In practice, though, litmus tests are much simpler: there are typically no more than 2 or 3 writes to any one location, so we avoid coding up a sophisticated memory-model-aware search procedure in favour of keeping this part of the code simple. For the examples shown here, the tool has to check at most a few thousand alternatives, and takes less than 0.2 seconds. The most complex example we tested (IRIW with all SC) had 162,000 cases to try, and the overall time taken was about 5 minutes.

Checking code extracted from Isabelle We use Isabelle/HOL code generation to produce a checker as an OCaml module, which can be linked in with the rest of the CPPSEM tool. Our model is stated in higher-order logic with sets and relations. Restricted to finite sets, the predicates and definitions are almost all directly executable, within the domain of the code generation tool (which implements finite sets by OCaml lists). For a few cases (e.g importantly transitive closure), we had to write a more efficient function and an Isabelle/HOL proof of equivalence. The overall checking time per example is on the order of 10^{-3} seconds, for examples with around 10 actions.

6.1 Finite model generation with Nitpick/Kodkod

Given the X_{opsem} part of a candidate execution, the space of possible X_{witness} parts which will lead to valid executions can be explored by tools for model generation. We reused the operational semantics above to produce a X_{opsem} from a program, and then posed problems to Nitpick, a finite model generator built into Isabelle [BN10]. Nitpick is a frontend to Kodkod, a model generator for first order logic extended with relations and transitive closure based on a state-of-the-art SAT solver. Nitpick translates higher-order logic formulae to first-order formulae within Kodkod syntax. For small programs, Nitpick can easily find some consistent execution, or report that none such exists, in a few seconds. In particular, for the IRIW-SC example mentioned above, Nitpick takes 130 seconds to report that no execution exists, while other examples take around 5 seconds. Of course, Nitpick can also validate an execution X with both parts X_{opsem} and X_{witness} concretely specified, but this is significantly slower than running the Isabelle-extracted validator. The bottleneck here is the translation process, which is quite involved.

7. Related work

The starting points for this paper were the draft standard itself and the work of Boehm and Adve [BA08], who introduced the rationale for the C++0x overall design and gave a model for non-atomic, lock, and SC atomic operations, without going into low-level atomics or fences in any detail. It was expressed in informal mathematics, an intermediate point between the prose of the standard and the mechanised definitions of our model. The most closely related other work is the extensive line of research on the Java Memory Model (JMM) [Pug00, MPA05, CKS07, SA08, TVD10]. Java imposes very different constraints to C++ as there it is essential to prohibit thin-air reads, to prevent forging of pointers and hence security violations.

Turning to the sequential semantics of C++, Norrish has recently produced an extensive HOL4 model [Nor08], and Zalewski [Zal08] formalised the proposed extension of C++ concepts.

There is also a body of research on tool support for memory models, notably including (among others) the MEMSAT of Torlak et al. [TVD10], which uses Kodkod for formalisations of the JMM, and NEMOSFINDER of Yang et al. [YGLS04], which is based on Prolog encodings of memory models and included an Itanium specification. Building on our previous experience with the MEMEVENTS tool for hardware (x86 and Power) memory models [SSZN+09, OSS09, SSO+10, AMSS10], we designed CPPMEM to eliminate the need for hand-coding of the tool to reflect changes in the model, by automatically generating the checker code from the Isabelle/HOL definition. We made it practically usable for exploring our non-idealised (and hence rather complex) C++0x model by a variety of user-interface features, letting us explore the executions of a program in various ways.

8. Conclusion

We have put the semantics of C++ and C concurrency on a mathematically sound footing, following the current final committee draft standard as far as possible, except as we describe in §4. This should support future improvements to the standard and the development of semantics, analysis, and reasoning tools for concurrent systems code.

Having done so, the obvious question is the extent to which the formal model could be incorporated as a *normative* part of a future standard. The memory model is subtle but it uses only simple mathematical machinery, of various binary relations over a fixed set of concrete actions, that can be visualised graphically. There is a notational problem: one would probably have to translate (automatically or by hand) the syntax of first-order logic into natural language, to make it sufficiently widely accessible. But given that, we suspect that the formal model would be clearer than the current 'standardsese' for all purposes, not only for semantics and analysis.

Acknowledgements This work would not have been possible without discussions with members of the C++ Concurrency subcommittee and the `cpp-threads` mailing list, including Hans Boehm, Lawrence Crowl, Peter Dimov, Doug Lea, Nick Maclaren, Paul McKenney, Clark Nelson, and Anthony Williams. Jasmin Blanchette assisted us with the Nitpick tool. We acknowledge funding from EPSRC grants EP/F036345, EP/H005633, EP/H027351, and EP/F067909.

References

[AB10] S. V. Adve and H.-J. Boehm. Memory models: A case for rethinking parallel languages and hardware. *C. ACM*, 2010.

[AMSS10] J. Alglave, L. Maranget, S. Sarkar, and P. Sewell. Fences in weak memory models. In *Proc. CAV*, 2010.

[ARM08] ARM. *ARM Architecture Reference Manual (ARMv7-A and ARMv7-R edition)*. April 2008.

[BA08] H.-J. Boehm and S.V. Adve. Foundations of the C++ concurrency memory model. In *Proc. PLDI*, 2008.

[Bec10] P. Becker, editor. *Programming Languages — C++. Final Committee Draft*. 2010. ISO/IEC JTC1 SC22 WG21 N3092.

[BN10] Jasmin Christian Blanchette and Tobias Nipkow. Nitpick: A counterexample generator for higher-order logic based on a relational model finder. In *Proc. ITP*, 2010.

[BOS] `www.cl.cam.ac.uk/users/pes20/cpp`.

[C1X] JTC1/SC22/WG14 — C. `http://www.open-std.org/jtc1/sc22/wg14/`.

[CKS07] P. Cenciarelli, A. Knapp, and E. Sibilio. The Java memory model: Operationally, denotationally, axiomatically. In *Proc. ESOP*, 2007.

[GN00] E. R. Gansner and S. C. North. An open graph visualization system and its applications to software engineering. *Softw. Pract. Exper.*, 30(11):1203–1233, 2000.

[Haf09] Florian Haftmann. *Code Generation from Specifications in Higher-Order Logic*. PhD thesis, TU München, 2009.

[HOL] The HOL 4 system. `http://hol.sourceforge.net/`.

[Int02] Intel. A formal specification of Intel Itanium processor family memory ordering. `http://www.intel.com/design/itanium/downloads/251429.htm`, October 2002.

[Isa] Isabelle 2009-2. `http://isabelle.in.tum.de/`.

[Lam79] L. Lamport. How to make a multiprocessor computer that correctly executes multiprocess programs. *IEEE Trans. Comput.*, C-28(9):690–691, 1979.

[MPA05] J. Manson, W. Pugh, and S.V. Adve. The Java memory model. In *Proc. POPL*, 2005.

[MS10] P. E. McKenney and R. Silvera. Example POWER implementation for C/C++ memory model. `http://www.rdrop.com/users/paulmck/scalability/paper/N2745r.2010.02.19a.html`, 2010.

[MW] P. E. McKenney and J. Walpole. What is RCU, fundamentally? Linux Weekly News, `http://lwn.net/Articles/262464/`.

[NMRW02] George C. Necula, Scott McPeak, Shree Prakash Rahul, and Westley Weimer. Cil: Intermediate language and tools for analysis and transformation of c programs. In *Proc. CC*, 2002.

[Nor08] M. Norrish. A formal semantics for C++. Technical report, NICTA, 2008.

[OSS09] S. Owens, S. Sarkar, and P. Sewell. A better x86 memory model: x86-TSO. In *Proc. TPHOLs*, 2009.

[Owe10] S. Owens. Reasoning about the implementation of concurrency abstractions on x86-TSO. In *Proc. ECOOP*, 2010.

[Pow09] *Power ISA Version 2.06*. IBM, 2009.

[Pug00] W. Pugh. The Java memory model is fatally flawed. *Concurrency - Practice and Experience*, 12(6), 2000.

[SA08] J. Ševčík and D. Aspinall. On validity of program transformations in the Java memory model. In *ECOOP*, 2008.

[Spa] The SPARC architecture manual, v. 9. `http://developers.sun.com/solaris/articles/sparcv9.pdf`.

[SSO+10] P. Sewell, S. Sarkar, S. Owens, F. Zappa Nardelli, and M. O. Myreen. x86-TSO: A rigorous and usable programmer's model for x86 multiprocessors. *C. ACM*, 53(7):89–97, 2010.

[SSZN+09] S. Sarkar, P. Sewell, F. Zappa Nardelli, S. Owens, T. Ridge, T. Braibant, M. Myreen, and J. Alglave. The semantics of x86-CC multiprocessor machine code. In *Proc. POPL*, 2009.

[Ter08] A. Terekhov. Brief tentative example x86 implementation for C/C++ memory model. `cpp-threads` mailing list, `http://www.decadent.org.uk/pipermail/cpp-threads/2008-December/001933.html`, Dec. 2008.

[TJ07] E. Torlak and D. Jackson. Kodkod: a relational model finder. In *Proc. TACAS*, 2007.

[TVD10] E. Torlak, M. Vaziri, and J. Dolby. MemSAT: checking axiomatic specifications of memory models. In *PLDI*, 2010.

[YGLS04] Y. Yang, G. Gopalakrishnan, G. Lindstrom, and K. Slind. Nemos: A framework for axiomatic and executable specifications of memory consistency models. In *IPDPS*, 2004.

[Zal08] M. Zalewski. *Generic Programming with Concepts*. PhD thesis, Chalmers University, November 2008.

Formal Verification of Object Layout for C++ Multiple Inheritance

Tahina Ramananandro
INRIA Paris-Rocquencourt
Tahina.Ramananandro@inria.fr

Gabriel Dos Reis *
Texas A&M University
gdr@cs.tamu.edu

Xavier Leroy †
INRIA Paris-Rocquencourt
Xavier.Leroy@inria.fr

Abstract

Object layout — the concrete in-memory representation of objects — raises many delicate issues in the case of the C++ language, owing in particular to multiple inheritance, C compatibility and separate compilation. This paper formalizes a family of C++ object layout schemes and mechanically proves their correctness against the operational semantics for multiple inheritance of Wasserrab *et al.* This formalization is flexible enough to account for space-saving techniques such as empty base class optimization and tail-padding optimization. As an application, we obtain the first formal correctness proofs for realistic, optimized object layout algorithms, including one based on the popular "common vendor" Itanium C++ application binary interface. This work provides semantic foundations to discover and justify new layout optimizations; it is also a first step towards the verification of a C++ compiler front-end.

Categories and Subject Descriptors D.2.4 [*Software Engineering*]: Software/Program Verification—*Correctness proofs*; D.3.3 [*Programming Languages*]: Language Constructs and Features—*Classes and objects*; D.3.4 [*Programming Languages*]: Processors—*Compilers*; E.2 [*Data storage representations*]: Object representation; F.3.3 [*Logics and meanings of programs*]: Studies of program constructs—*Object-oriented constructs*

General Terms Languages, Verification

1. Introduction

One of the responsibilities of compilers and interpreters is to represent the data types and structures of the source language in terms of the low-level facilities provided by the machine (bits, pointers, etc.). In particular, for data structures that must be stored in memory, an appropriate *memory layout* must be determined and implemented. This layout determines the position of each component of a compound data structure, relative to the start address of the memory area representing this structure.

Many programming languages are implemented using straightforward memory layouts. In Fortran and C, for example, compound data structures are laid out consecutively in memory, enumerating their members in a conventional order such as column-major ordering for Fortran arrays or declaration order for C structures. Padding is inserted between the members as necessary to satisfy the alignment constraints of the machine. Higher-level languages leave more flexibility for determining data representations, but practical considerations generally result in simple memory layouts quite similar in principle to those of C structures, with the addition of tags and dynamic type information to guide the garbage collector and implement dynamic dispatch and type tests.

This paper focuses on data representation for objects in the C++ language. C++ combines the many scalar types and pointer types inherited from C with a rich object model, featuring multiple inheritance with both repeated and shared inheritance of base classes, object identity distinction, dynamic dispatch, and run-time type tests for some but not all classes. This combination raises interesting data representation challenges. On the one hand, the layout of objects must abide by the semantics of C++ as defined by the ISO standards [8]. On the other hand, this semantics leaves significant flexibility in the way objects are laid out in memory, flexibility that can be (and has repeatedly been) exploited to reduce the memory footprint of objects. A representative example is the "empty base optimization" described in section 2.

As a result of this tension, a number of optimized object layout algorithms have been proposed [6, 7, 13, 17], implemented in production compilers, and standardized as part of application binary interfaces (ABI) [3]. Section 2 outlines some of these algorithms and their evolution. These layout algorithms are quite complex, sometimes incorrect (see Myers [13] for examples), and often difficult to relate with the high-level requirements of the C++ specification. For example, the C++ "common vendor" ABI [3] devotes several pages to the specification of an object layout algorithm, which includes a dozen special cases.

The work reported in this paper provides a formal framework to specify C++ object layout algorithms and prove their correctness. As the high-level specification of operations over objects, we use the operational semantics for C++ multiple inheritance formalized by Wasserrab *et al* [19], which we have extended with structure fields and structure array fields (section 3). We then formalize a family of layout algorithms, independently of the target architecture, and axiomatize a number of conditions they must respect while leaving room for many optimizations (section 4). We prove that these conditions are sufficient to guarantee semantic preservation when the high-level operations over objects are reinterpreted as machine-level memory accesses and pointer manipulations (section 5). Finally, we formalize two realistic layout algorithms: one based on the popular "common vendor" C++ ABI [3], and its ex-

* Partially supported by NSF grants CCF-0702765 and CCF-1035058.
† Partially supported by ANR grant Arpège U3CAT.

POPL '11 January 26–28, Austin, TX, USA

tension with one further optimization; we prove their correctness by showing that they satisfy the sufficient conditions (section 6).

All the specifications and proofs in this paper have been mechanically verified using the Coq proof assistant. The Coq development is available online [15].

The contribution of this paper is twofold. On one hand, it is (to the best of our knowledge) the first formal proof of semantic correctness for realistic, optimizing C++ object layout algorithms, one of which being part of a widely used ABI. Moreover, we hope that large parts of our formalization and proofs can be reused for other, present or future layout algorithms. On the other hand, just like the subobject calculus of Rossie and Friedman [16] and the operational semantics for multiple inheritance of Wasserrab *et al* [19] were important first steps towards a formal specification of the semantics of (realistic subsets of) the C++ language, the work presented in this paper is a first step towards the formal verification of a compiler front-end for (realistic subsets of) C++, similar in principle and structure to earlier compiler verification efforts for other languages such as Java [9], C0 [10], and C [11].

2. Overview

2.1 The object layout problem

Generally speaking, an object layout algorithm is a systematic way to map an abstract, source-level view of objects down to machine-level memory accesses and pointer operations. At the source level, a C++ object is an abstract entity over which various primitive operations can be performed, such as accessing and updating a field, converting ("casting") an object or an object descriptor to another type, or dispatching a virtual function call. At the machine level, an object descriptor is a pointer p to a block of memory containing the current state of the object. The object layout scheme determines, at compile-time, how to reinterpret the source-level object operations as machine instructions:

- Accessing a field f defined in the class C of the object becomes a memory read or write at address $p + \delta$, where the constant offset δ is determined by the layout algorithm as a function of C and f.
- Dispatching a virtual function call is achieved by querying the dynamic type information attached to the object (typically, a virtual function table), a pointer to which is stored at a fixed offset relative to p.
- Converting to a base class (super-class) D of C is also achieved by adding an offset δ to the pointer p, making it point to the subobject of class D contained within. The offset δ can be statically determined in many cases, but owing to multiple virtual inheritance, it may have to be determined at run-time by querying the dynamic type information of the object.
- Accessing a field f defined in a base class D of C is achieved by converting p to D, then accessing f at a fixed offset from the resulting pointer.

For the generated machine operations to correctly implement the C++ semantics of object operations, the object layout scheme must satisfy a number of correctness conditions. First, when a scalar field is updated, the values of all other fields must be preserved. This immediately translates to the following requirement:

> *Field separation*: two distinct scalar fields, reachable through inheritance and/or fields from the same object, map to disjoint memory areas.

Moreover, the hardware architecture can impose *alignment constraints* on memory accesses: for example, loading a 32-bit integer is possible only from an address that is a multiple of 4. This leads to a second requirement:

> *Field alignment*: for any field f of scalar type t, the natural alignment of type t evenly divides its memory address.

Besides containing fields, C++ objects also have an *identity*, which can be observed by taking the address of an object and comparing it (using the == or != operators) with addresses of other objects of the same type. The C++ semantics specifies precisely the outcome of these comparisons, and this semantics must be preserved when the comparisons are reinterpreted as machine-level pointer comparisons:

> *Object identity*: two pointers to two distinct (sub)objects of the same static type A, obtained through conversions or accesses to structure fields, map to different memory addresses.

This requirement is further compounded by the fact that C++ operates under a simplistic separate compilation model inherited from C, and the fact that every class can be used independently to create complete objects, and every subobject in isolation is a potential target of most operations supported by any complete object of the same type.

Furthermore, some classes are considered to be *dynamic*: those classes that need dynamic type data to perform virtual function dispatch, dynamic cast, access to a virtual base, or other dynamic operations. The concrete representation for objects of these dynamic classes must include dynamic type data (usually as a pointer to a data structure describing the class), and such data must be preserved by field updates.

> *Dynamic type preservation*: any scalar field maps to a memory area that is disjoint from any memory area reserved to hold dynamic type data.

The separation conditions between two areas holding dynamic type data are weaker than the separation conditions for fields. Indeed, most layout algorithms arrange that the dynamic type data for a class C is shared with that of one of its dynamic non-virtual direct bases, called the *non-virtual primary base* of C and chosen during layout, in a way that preserves the semantics of virtual function dispatch and other dynamic operations.

> *Dynamic type data separation*: for any two dynamic classes, the memory areas of their respective dynamic type data must be disjoint, unless one of the classes is the non-virtual primary base of the other.

2.2 The historic layout scheme

Early C++ compilers such as Cfront (Stroustrup's C++-to-C translator) used a simple object layout algorithm that obviously satisfies the requirements listed above. In effect, all components of a class (fields, base classes, and dynamic data if needed) are laid out contiguously following a conventional order, inserting padding (unused bytes) between components and after the last component as necessary to satisfy alignment constraints. In this approach, each component (base or field) of a class C has its own memory area, disjoint from those of all other components of C. Moreover, each class is represented by at least one byte of data, even if it contains no fields nor dynamic type data. This trivially enforces the object identity requirement.

2.3 Tail padding optimization

The simple layout scheme just described is inefficient in space, because it never attempts to reuse padding to store useful data. Consider:

```
struct A     { int a; };
struct B : A { char b; };
struct C : B { char c; };
```

Assume the size and natural alignment of type int are 4 bytes. To ensure proper alignment of field a, 3 bytes of padding are inserted after field b in B, and 3 more bytes of padding are inserted after field c in C. (To understand why, consider arrays whose elements have type B or C.) Consequently, B has size 8 while C has size 12.

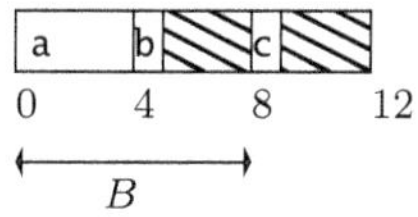

However, it is perfectly legitimate to reuse one of the 3 bytes of padding present at the end of B to hold the value of field c of C. In this case, C occupies only 8 bytes, for a nice space saving of 1/3. This layout trick is known as the *tail padding optimization*, and is used by many C++ compilers.

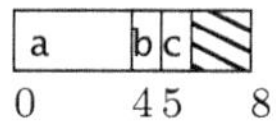

2.4 Empty base class optimization

Empty classes offer another opportunity for reusing space that is unused in a base class. Consider:

```
struct A          {};
struct B1 : A     {};
struct B2 : A     {};
struct C  : B1, B2 { char c1; char c2; };

C   c;
A * a1 = (A *) (B1 *) &c;
A * a2 = (A *) (B2 *) &c;
```

Here, the classes A, B1 and B2 are *empty*: they contain no field and need no dynamic type information. It is tempting to give them size 0, so that their instances occupy no memory space at all. However, this would violate the "object identity" requirement: as depicted to the right, the pointers a1 and a2 (to the two instances of A logically contained within C) would compare equal, while C++'s semantics mandate that they are different.

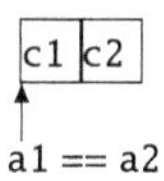

The layout algorithm must therefore insert (at least) one byte of padding in A, resulting in A, B1 and B2 having size 1. Following the naive approach outlined in section 2.2, C therefore occupies 4 bytes.

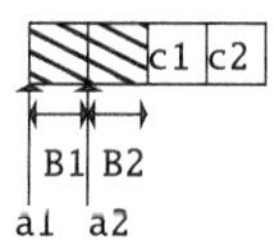

However, it is unnecessary to keep the fields c1 and c2 disjoint from the subobjects of types B1 and B2: the padding inserted in the latter to satisfy the object identity requirement can be reused to hold the values of fields c1 and c2, as shown to the right.

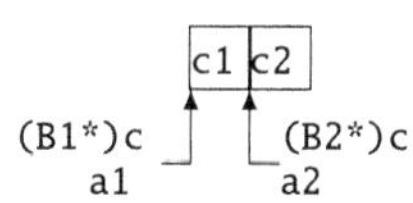

This technique is known as the *empty base class optimization*. It is implemented by many C++ compilers, but often in restricted cases only. Here is an example where GCC 4.3 misses an opportunity for reusing the tail padding of an empty base class.

```
struct A          {};
struct B1 : A     {};
struct B2 : A     {};
struct C  : B1, B2 { char c; };
struct D  : C      { char d; };
```

As in the previous example, B1 and B2 must be laid out at different offsets within C, to allow distinguishing the two A contained in C. Thus, C must have size at least 2. This lower bound can be achieved by placing c at offset 0, as explained above.

What about D? GCC places d at offset 2, resulting in a size of 3 for D. However, the second byte of C is just padding introduced to preserve the identity of empty base classes, and it can be reused to hold data such as field d. This optimized layout fits D in just two bytes.

Why empty classes matter Over the years, successful C++ software, such as the Standard Template Libraries (STL), has become dependent on C++'s ability to deliver efficient code based on simple techniques such as empty classes and inlining. Part of the success of the STL is based on its archetypical use of function objects: these are objects of classes with the function call operator overloaded. These objects typically do not carry any runtime data. Rather, their semantics is their static types. As an example, consider sorting an array of integers. The STL provides the following template:

```
template<typename Ran, typename Comp>
  void sort(Ran first, Ran last, Comp cmp);
```

The comparator cmp could be a pointer to function (like the qsort function in C), but in idiomatic C++ it is any object whose type overloads the function call operator.

```
struct MyGreater {
   typedef int first_argument_type;
   typedef int second_argument_type;
   typedef bool result_type;
   bool operator()(int i, int j) const {
      return i > j;
   }
};
```

The sort template can, then, be invoked as sort(t, t + n, MyGreater()). The comparator object constructed by MyGreater() is of interest not for its runtime data (it carries none), but for its type: the comparison function is not passed to the sorting routine through data, but through the type of the object. Consequently, it is directly called, and in most cases inlined since the body is a simple integer comparison, which typically reduces to a single machine instruction. This simple technique, a cornerstone of the STL success, is effective. One can think of it as a simulation of dependent types, where data is encoded at the level of types, therefore making data flow obvious.

The function object technique just described is at the basis of a composable component of the STL. Composition implies a protocol that parts being composed should adhere to. For example, if we want to combine two unary function objects, we need a mechanism to ensure that the result type of one function object agrees with the argument type of the other. To that end, the STL requires the existence of certain nested types, such as first_argument_type, second_argument_type and result_type in the MyGreater class above. To reduce clutter, the STL provides ready-to-use classes that define those types. In this case, idiomatically, one would write

```
struct MyGreater :
  std::binary_function<int,int,bool> {
    bool operator()(int i, int j) const {
       return i > j;
    }
};
```

The sole purpose of std::binary_function<int,int,bool> is to provide those nested types. It is an empty base class that introduces no data and no virtual functions. Its semantics is purely static. This usage, while not object-oriented programming by most popular definitions, is very common in modern C++ programs.

The pattern is not restricted to only one empty base class: a class can simulatenously inherit from several empty base classes. This is the case of bidirectional_input_iterator_tag, which inherits both from forward_iterator_tag and output_iterator_tag. A compiler that effectively supports C++ should not have to allocate space for such empty classes since their runtime semantics are completely irrelevant. While an optimization in C++03, the empty base optimization is considered so important that it is required in the next version dubbed C++0x [4].

3. Semantic model

To capture the expected behavior of C++ object operations, we build on the model of multiple inheritance introduced by Rossie and Friedman [16] and further developed and mechanized by Wasserrab *et al.* [19] using the Isabelle proof assistant. In this section, we briefly recall the main aspects of this model, referring the reader to [19] for full details, then describe how we extended it to handle fields that are themselves structures or arrays of structures, and finally use the model to given an operational semantics to a simple calculus of C++ objects.

3.1 Modeling multiple inheritance

A C++ class can inherit from several base classes. Consequently, a class D can inherit from another class A through several different ways. Consider for example:

```
struct A      { int a; };
struct B1: A          {};
struct B2: A          {};
struct C : A          {};
struct D : B1, B2, C {};
```

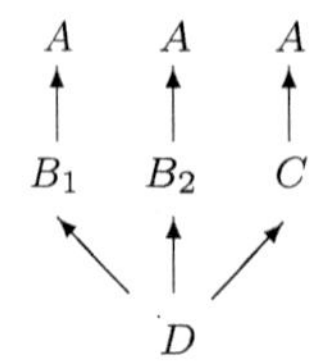

An instance of D contains as many copies of A as ways to inherit. Each copy of A is called a *subobject* of D, of static type A. In this example, D has three different subobjects of static type A, obtained through the base classes B1, B2 and C. This is called *non-virtual inheritance* by Stroustrup [5], *replicated inheritance* by Rossie and Friedman [16], or *repeated inheritance* by Wasserrab *et al* [19].

However, the programmer can elect to declare some base classes as *virtual*, as in the following example:

```
struct A      { int a; };
struct B1: virtual A {};
struct B2: virtual A {};
struct C : A          {};
struct D : B1, B2, C {};
```

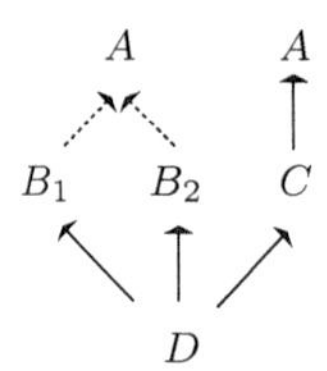

In this case, B1 and B2 contribute only one subobject of static type A to class D: the paths B1::A and B2::A designate the same subobject. This is called *virtual inheritance* [5] or *shared inheritance* [19]. Note, however, that C contributes another, distinct subobject A to D, since C inherits from A in a non-virtual manner.

Following Wasserrab *et al* [19], we capture this notion of subobject and these two flavors of inheritance as follows. A base class subobject of a given object is represented by a pair $\sigma = (h, l)$ where h is either Repeated or Shared, and l is a path in the non-virtual inheritance graph (the directed graph having classes as nodes and edges $U \to V$ if and only if V is a direct non-virtual base of U). More formally, we write $C \prec\!(\sigma)\!\overset{\mathcal{I}}{\rightarrowtail} A$ to mean that σ designates a base class subobject of class C, this subobject having static type A. This predicate is defined inductively:

$$C \prec\!(\mathsf{Repeated}, C :: \epsilon)\!\overset{\mathcal{I}}{\rightarrowtail} C$$

$$\frac{B \text{ direct non-virtual base of } C \qquad B \prec\!(\mathsf{Repeated}, l)\!\overset{\mathcal{I}}{\rightarrowtail} A}{C \prec\!(\mathsf{Repeated}, C :: l)\!\overset{\mathcal{I}}{\rightarrowtail} A}$$

$$\frac{B \text{ virtual base of } C \qquad B \prec\!((h, l))\!\overset{\mathcal{I}}{\rightarrowtail} A}{C \prec\!(\mathsf{Shared}, l)\!\overset{\mathcal{I}}{\rightarrowtail} A}$$

The fields of a full instance of a class C, then, are the pairs (σ, f) where $C \prec\!(\sigma)\!\overset{\mathcal{I}}{\rightarrowtail} A$ and f is a field defined in class A. In the first example above, the fields of D are $\{((\mathsf{Repeated}, \mathtt{D} :: \mathtt{B1} :: \mathtt{A} :: \epsilon), \mathtt{a});\ ((\mathsf{Repeated}, \mathtt{D} :: \mathtt{B2} :: \mathtt{A} :: \epsilon), \mathtt{a});\ ((\mathsf{Repeated}, \mathtt{D} :: \mathtt{C} :: \mathtt{A} :: \epsilon), \mathtt{a})\}$, while in the second example (involving virtual inheritance), they are $\{((\mathsf{Shared}, \mathtt{A} :: \epsilon), \mathtt{a});\ ((\mathsf{Repeated}, \mathtt{D} :: \mathtt{C} :: \mathtt{A} :: \epsilon), \mathtt{a})\}$.

3.2 Structure fields and structure array fields

In the original formalization of Wasserrab *et al* [19], fields are restricted to scalar types (arithmetic types or pointer types). We extended this formalization to support fields that are themselves structures or arrays of structures. To simplify presentation, we only consider arrays of structures, treating a structure field or variable `C x;` as a one-element array `C x[1];`.

In our formalization, a full object is always an element of a (possibly one-element) array of structures, which is either bound to a program variable, or dynamically created using **new**, or appears as a structure array field of a larger object. To designate a subobject of an array of structures, we therefore proceed in three steps:

1. select an array of structures contained in this array;
2. select an element of this sub-array;
3. select a base class subobject of this element (in the sense of section 3.1).

To select an array of structures contained in a larger array, we introduce the notion of an *array path* α from an array of n structures of type C to an array of n' structures of type C', written $C[n] \prec\!(\alpha)\!\overset{\mathcal{A}}{\rightarrowtail} C'[n']$. Array paths are defined inductively by the following rules:

$$\frac{i \leq n \qquad C \prec\!(\sigma)\!\overset{\mathcal{I}}{\rightarrowtail} A}{C[n] \prec\!(i, \sigma)\!\overset{\mathcal{CI}}{\rightarrowtail} A} \qquad\qquad \frac{n' \leq n}{C[n] \prec\!(\epsilon)\!\overset{\mathcal{A}}{\rightarrowtail} C[n']}$$

$$\frac{F = (f, D, m) \text{ is a structure field defined in } A \qquad C[n] \prec\!(i, \sigma)\!\overset{\mathcal{CI}}{\rightarrowtail} A \qquad D[m] \prec\!(\alpha)\!\overset{\mathcal{A}}{\rightarrowtail} C'[n']}{C[n] \prec\!((i, \sigma, F) :: \alpha)\!\overset{\mathcal{A}}{\rightarrowtail} C'[n']}$$

Then, a *generalized subobject* of type A of a full object of type $C[n]$ is a triple (α, i, σ) where α is an array path from $C[n]$ to some $C'[n']$ and $i \in [0, n')$ is an index in the array of type $C'[n']$ and σ is a base class subobject of C' of type A. We write $C[n] \prec\!((\alpha, i, \sigma))\!\rightarrowtail A$ and formally define this relation by:

$$\frac{C\,[n] \prec\!(\alpha)\!\overset{\mathcal{A}}{\rightarrowtail} C'\,[n'] \prec\!(i, \sigma)\!\overset{\mathcal{CI}}{\rightarrowtail} A}{C\,[n] \prec\!((\alpha, i, \sigma))\!\rightarrowtail A}$$

Consider for example:

```
struct Z                 {};
struct A : Z             {};
struct B                 { A a[4]; };
struct C1: virtual B {};
struct C2: virtual B {};
struct D : C1, C2        {};
struct E                 { D d[5]; };
E e[7];
```

The expression `(Z *) &(e[2].d[0].a[3])` denotes the generalized subobject (α, i, σ) within e, where

$$\alpha = (2, (\mathsf{Repeated}, \mathtt{E} :: \epsilon), \mathtt{d}) :: (0, (\mathsf{Shared}, \mathtt{B} :: \epsilon), \mathtt{a}) :: \epsilon$$
$$i = 3$$
$$\sigma = (\mathsf{Repeated}, \mathtt{A} :: \mathtt{Z} :: \epsilon)$$

The static type of a generalized subobject (α, i, σ) is the static type of the base class subobject σ. This generalized subobject denotes a full instance of class C if and only if σ is the trivial subobject of C of static type C, that is, $\sigma = (\mathsf{Repeated}, C :: \epsilon)$.

3.3 An operational semantics

Building on these notions of subobjects, we now give an operational semantics for a small 3-address intermediate language featuring a C++-style object model. The syntax of this language is as follows. (x ranges over variable names.)

$Stmt ::= x := op(x_1, \ldots, x_n)$	arithmetic
$\mid x :=$ `nullptr`	null pointer
$\mid x := x'$->$_C field$	field access
$\mid x$->$_C field := x'$	field assignment
$\mid x := \&x_1[x_2]_C$	array indexing
$\mid x := x_1 == x_2$	pointer equality test
$\mid x :=$ `static_cast`$\langle C' \rangle_C(x_1)$	static cast
$\mid x :=$ `dynamic_cast`$\langle C' \rangle_C(x_1)$	dynamic cast

Object operations are annotated with static types C (subscripted) as determined during type-checking. For instance, in field operations, C is the class that defines the field being accessed; in conversions, C is the static type of the argument of the conversion, and C' is the destination type. Our Coq formalization also includes some control structures (sequence, conditional, loops), which we omit for simplicity. Also omitted are virtual function calls, object creation and object destruction, which we have not fully formalized yet.

The operational semantics uses the following semantic objects:

$v ::= \mathsf{Atom}\ baseval$	base value
$\mid \mathsf{Ptr}\ \varnothing$	null pointer
$\mid \mathsf{Ptr}\ (objid, \alpha, n, \sigma)$	pointer to a subobject
$V ::= x \mapsto v$	variable environment
$\omega ::= (\alpha, n, \sigma, (f, t)) \mapsto v$	values of scalar fields
$H ::= objid \mapsto (C, n, \omega)$	object heap

The state of the execution is a pair (V, H) of an environment V mapping variable names to scalar values (either base values or pointers), and a heap H mapping top-level object identifiers $objid$ to their type $C[n]$ and their contents ω. The contents ω is, in turn, a mapping from scalar field designators (pairs of a generalized subobject (α, n, σ) and a field (f, t)) to scalar values.

The operational semantics is given as a transition relation $Stmt \vdash (V, H) \rightarrow (V', H')$ relating the state (V, H) before and the state (V', H') after executing $Stmt$. We show some representative rules.

$$\frac{V(x') = \mathsf{Ptr}(o, \alpha, i, \sigma) \qquad H(o) = (C, n, \omega) \qquad C[n] \prec\!(\alpha, i, \sigma)\!\succ\!\rightarrow A \qquad F \text{ is a scalar field of } A}{x := x'\text{->}_A F \vdash (V, H) \rightarrow (V\{x \leftarrow \omega(\alpha, i, \sigma, F)\}, H)}$$

$$\frac{V(x) = \mathsf{Ptr}(o, \alpha, i, \sigma) \qquad H(o) = (C, n, \omega) \qquad C[n] \prec\!(\alpha, i, \sigma)\!\succ\!\rightarrow A \qquad F \text{ is a scalar field of } A \qquad \omega' = \omega\{(\alpha, i, \sigma, F) \leftarrow V(x')\}}{x\text{->}_A F := x' \vdash (V, H) \rightarrow (V, H\{o \leftarrow (C, n, \omega')\})}$$

$$\frac{V(x') = \mathsf{Ptr}(o, \alpha, i, \sigma) \qquad H(o) = (C, n, \omega) \qquad C[n] \prec\!(\alpha, i, \sigma)\!\succ\!\rightarrow A \qquad F = (f, A', n') \text{ is an array field of } A \qquad p' = (o, \alpha +\!\!+ (i, \sigma, F) :: \epsilon, 0, (\mathsf{Repeated}, A' :: \epsilon))}{x := x'\text{->}_A F \vdash (V, H) \rightarrow (V\{x \leftarrow \mathsf{Ptr}\ p'\}, H)}$$

$$\frac{V(x_1) = \mathsf{Ptr}(o, \alpha, i, (\mathsf{Repeated}, A :: \epsilon)) \qquad H(o) = (A', n', \omega) \qquad A'[n'] \prec\!\alpha\!\succ\!\xrightarrow{A} A[n] \qquad 0 \leq i < n \qquad V(x_2) = \mathsf{Atom}\ j \qquad 0 \leq i + j < n \qquad p' = (o, \alpha, i + j, (\mathsf{Repeated}, A :: \epsilon))}{x := \&x_1[x_2] \vdash (V, H) \rightarrow (V\{x \leftarrow \mathsf{Ptr}\ p'\}, H)}$$

For reads and writes over scalar fields (first two rules above), the content map ω of the top-level object o being accessed is consulted or updated at the path (α, i, σ) to the subobject and the accessed field. In contrast, accessing a structure array field (third rule) and addressing an array element (fourth rule) just synthesize the appropriate subobject from that given in the object pointer. In the case of a structure array field, the given subobject (α, i, σ) is refined into the sub-subobject $(\alpha +\!\!+ (i, \sigma, F) :: \epsilon, 0, (\mathsf{Repeated}, A' :: \epsilon))$ designating the structure array. ($+\!\!+$ stands for list concatenation.) For array addressing, only the i part of the given subobject is modified. By lack of space, we omit the rules for static and dynamic casts, which are complicated but similar to those given by Wasserrab *et al* [19].

4. Formalization of a family of layout algorithms

In this section, we formalize the interface to a family of layout algorithms and sufficient conditions ensuring that they are semantically correct.

4.1 Platform-dependent parameters

Our formalization is independent of the characteristics of the hardware platform. It is parameterized by a set of scalar types, comprising arithmetic types (e.g. **int**, **short**, **char**, **float**, **double**, etc.) and pointer types. For each scalar type t, we take as parameters its size scsize_t and its natural alignment $\mathsf{scalign}_t$. The only assumptions we make about size and alignment is that they are positive and that all pointer types have the same size and alignment. The unit of size is not even specified: a natural choice is bytes, but bits could be used as well. Likewise, natural alignments are not required to be powers of 2.

As additional parameters, we also assume given a positive size dtdsize and a positive natural alignment dtdalign for dynamic type data. For simplicity, we assume that dynamic type data has the same size for all classes. This was not always the case in early compilers [17], but nowadays the trend is to store only a pointer to a class descriptor, thus incurring a constant access overhead (one or two more indirections) but significant improvements on the size of objects.

4.2 Interface of a layout algorithm

Let C be a class. We introduce the following notations:

- $\mathsf{dnvbases}_C$ is the set of direct non-virtual bases of C.
- vbases_C is the set of (direct or indirect) virtual bases of C.
- $\mathsf{scfields}_C$ is the set of scalar fields declared in C. Each such field is of the form (f, t) where f is an identifier and t is a scalar type.
- $\mathsf{stfields}_C$ is the set of structure array fields declared in C. Each such field is of the form (f, B, n) where f is an identifier, B is the structure type of the field, and $n > 0$ is the number of elements in the array.
- $\mathsf{fields}_C = \mathsf{scfields}_C \cup \mathsf{stfields}_C$ is the set of all fields declared in C.

For every class C in the program, a layout algorithm is expected to compute each of the following (as depicted in figure 1):

- pbase_C is the primary base of C, if any. More precisely, either $\mathsf{pbase}_C = \varnothing$, or $\mathsf{pbase}_C = \{B\}$ for some direct non-virtual base B of C.
- $\mathsf{dnvboff}_C : \mathsf{dnvbases}_C \rightarrow \mathbb{N}$ assigns offsets to the non-virtual direct bases of C.
- $\mathsf{fboundary}_C \in \mathbb{N}$ is an offset within C representing the boundary between non-virtual base data and field data.
- $\mathsf{foff}_C : \mathsf{fields}_C \rightarrow \mathbb{N}$ assigns offsets to the fields declared in C.
- $\mathsf{nvdsize}_C \in \mathbb{N}$ is the non-virtual data size of C: the data size of its non-virtual part.
- $\mathsf{nvsize}_C \in \mathbb{N}$ is the non-virtual size of C: the total size of its non-virtual part.

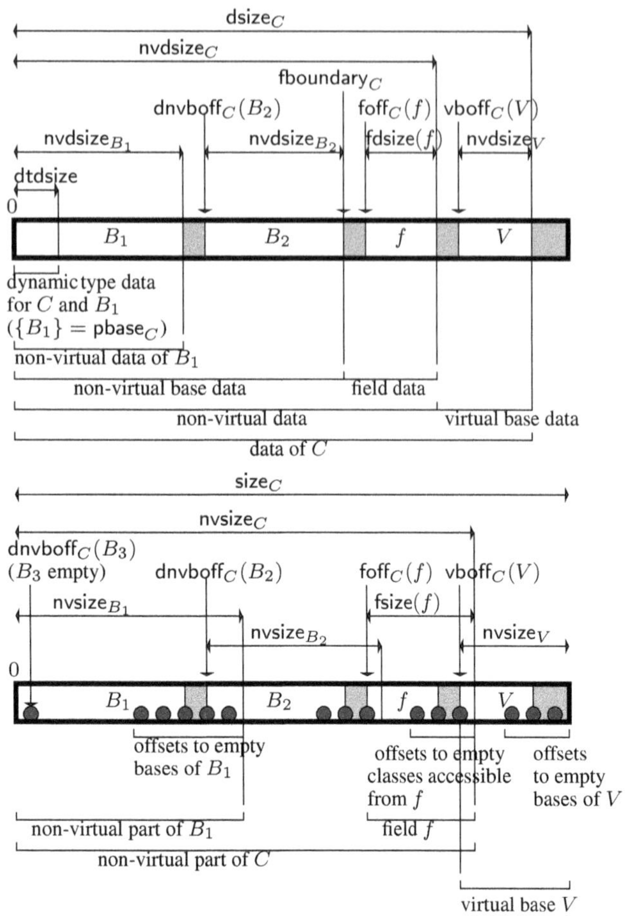

Figure 1. A proposed layout for a full instance of a dynamic class C having a primary non-virtual base B_1, a non-empty non-virtual base B_2, an empty non-virtual base B_3, a field f and a virtual base V. Grayed areas represent padding. Bullets represent offsets to (inheritance or field) subobjects of C of empty types. The top part depicts the layout parameters related to data; the bottom part, those related to object identity.

- $\mathsf{vboff}_C : \mathsf{vbases}_C \to \mathbb{N}$ gives the offsets of the virtual bases of C.
- $\mathsf{dsize}_C \in \mathbb{N}$ is the total data size of C.
- $\mathsf{size}_C \in \mathbb{N}$ is the total size of C. This is the quantity that **sizeof**(C) evaluates to.

For the purpose of our formalization, C can be considered as a virtual base of itself. Thus we introduce the notion of a class B being a *generalized virtual base* of C: either $B = C$, or B is a direct or indirect virtual base of C. Thanks to this notion, we can state that the layout of a full instance of C is composed of the layout of the non-virtual parts of the generalized virtual bases of C for this instance, with the non-virtual part of C starting at offset 0. Thus, we may safely extend the domain of vboff_C by taking $\mathsf{vboff}_C(C) = 0$.

4.3 Empty classes and dynamic classes

Our formalization leaves partially specified the notions of empty classes and dynamic classes, leaving their exact definitions to the layout algorithm, subject to the following conditions:

- An empty class must not contain any scalar field.
- An empty class must not contain any structure field of a non-empty class type.
- An empty class must not have any non-empty base.
- A dynamic class is not empty.
- If a class C has a virtual base, then C is dynamic
- If a class C has a non-virtual primary base B, then both C and B are dynamic.

In our formalization, the data size and the non-virtual data size of a class are of interest only if the class is not empty. Our way of classifying empty classes and dynamic classes can be understood as follows: the data of a class is composed of all its reachable scalar fields and dynamic type data; an empty class is a class that requires no data; and a dynamic class is a class that requires dynamic type data.

4.4 Computing offsets and compiling object operations

Once the quantities listed in section 4.2 have been computed by a layout algorithm, all the offsets mentioned in section 2.1 and required during compilation can be computed as follows. The offset $\mathsf{nvsoff}(C :: l)$ of a non-virtual, base class subobject $(\mathsf{Repeated}, C :: l)$ within the low-level representation of a subobject of static type C is:

$$\mathsf{nvsoff}(C :: \epsilon) = 0$$

$$\mathsf{nvsoff}(C :: B :: l') = \mathsf{dnvboff}_C(B) + \mathsf{nvsoff}(B :: l')$$

The offset $\mathsf{soff}_C(h, l)$ of the base class subobject (h, l) of C within the low-level representation of a full instance of C is computed as follows:

$$\mathsf{soff}_C(\mathsf{Repeated}, C :: l') = \mathsf{nvoff}(C :: l')$$

$$\mathsf{soff}_C(\mathsf{Shared}, B :: l') = \mathsf{vboff}_C(B) + \mathsf{nvsoff}(B :: l')$$

If l is an array path from $C[n]$ to $C'[n']$, then the offset $\mathsf{aoff}_C(l)$ of (the first element of) the array of n' elements of type C' designated by l within the low-level representation of an array of n elements of type C is determined by $\mathsf{aoff}_C(\epsilon) = 0$ and

$$\mathsf{aoff}_C((i, s, (f, A, m)) :: \alpha)$$
$$= i \cdot \mathsf{size}_C + \mathsf{soff}_C(s) + \mathsf{foff}_B(f, A, m) + \mathsf{aoff}_A(\alpha)$$
$$\text{(where } B \text{ is the static type of } s\text{)}$$

Finally, the offset $\mathsf{off}_C(\alpha, i, s)$ of a generalized subobject (α, i, s) within an array of structures of type C is computed as follows:

$$\mathsf{off}_C(\alpha, i, s) = \mathsf{aoff}_C(\alpha) + i \cdot \mathsf{size}_B + \mathsf{soff}_B(s)$$
$$\text{(where } B[m] \text{ is the destination type of } \alpha\text{)}$$

Using these offsets, we now outline a compilation scheme for the C++-like intermediate language of section 3.3. The target language is a conventional low-level intermediate language, featuring a flat, byte-addressed memory, pointer arithmetic, and explicit $\mathtt{load}(n, p)$ and $\mathtt{store}(n, p, x)$ operations to read and write n-byte quantities at address p. For field and array accesses, we have:

$$[\![x := x' \text{->}_C F]\!] = x := \mathtt{load}(\mathsf{scsize}_t, x' + \mathsf{foff}_C(F))$$
$$\text{(if } F = (f, t) \text{ is a scalar field of } C\text{)}$$

$$[\![x \text{->}_C F := x']\!] = \mathtt{store}(\mathsf{scsize}_t, x + \mathsf{foff}_C(F), x')$$
$$\text{(if } F = (f, t) \text{ is a scalar field of } C\text{)}$$

$$[\![x := x' \text{->}_C F]\!] = x := x' + \mathsf{foff}_C(F)$$
$$\text{(if } F \text{ is a structure array field of } C\text{)}$$

$$[\![x := \&x_1[x_2]_C]\!] = x := x_1 + \mathsf{size}_C \times x_2$$

$$[\![x := x_1 == x_2]\!] = x := x_1 == x_2$$

For static casts, we have two cases depending on whether inheritance is virtual or not. If $C \prec\!(\mathsf{Repeated}, l)\!\succ\!\xrightarrow{\mathcal{I}} A$ for a uniquely-defined path (Repeated, l) (conversion to or from a non-virtual base), the static cast is achieved by adjusting the pointer by a constant offset:

$$[\![x := \texttt{static\_cast}\langle A\rangle_C(x')]\!] = x := x' + \mathsf{nvsoff}(l)$$
$$[\![x := \texttt{static\_cast}\langle C\rangle_A(x')]\!] = x := x' - \mathsf{nvsoff}(l)$$

If $C \prec\!\langle(\mathsf{Shared}, B :: l)\rangle\!\overset{\mathcal{I}}{\mapsto} A$ and $(\mathsf{Shared}, B :: l)$ is unique (conversion through a virtual base), the offset of the virtual base B of C must be looked up in the dynamic type data:

$$[\![x := \texttt{static\_cast}\langle A\rangle_C(x')]\!] =$$
$$t := \texttt{load}(\mathsf{dtdsize}, x'); x := x' + \texttt{vboff}(t, B) + \mathsf{nvsoff}(l)$$

Finally, the code $[\![x := \texttt{dynamic\_cast}\langle A\rangle_C(x')]\!]$ for a dynamic cast is:

$$t := \texttt{load}(\mathsf{dtdsize}, x');$$
$$\textbf{if}\,(\texttt{dyncastdef}(t, A))\ \texttt{then}\ x := x' + \texttt{dyncastoff}(t, A)$$
$$\texttt{else}\ x := \texttt{NULL}$$

As shown in the last two cases, the target language features three operations over the run-time representation t of dynamic type data: $\texttt{vboff}(t, B)$ returns the offset appropriate for virtual base B; $\texttt{dyncastdef}(t, A)$ returns 1 if a dynamic cast to A is possible, 0 otherwise; and $\texttt{dyncastoff}(t, A)$ returns the offset appropriate for a dynamic cast to A.

In the semantics of our target language, we formalize these operations at an abstract level through queries to an "oracle". The actual concrete implementation (virtual table, dictionary, etc.) is left unspecified. However, we have formally proved that such an oracle can always be constructed from a well-founded class hierarchy.

4.5 Soundness conditions

We now state a number of soundness conditions over the results of the layout algorithm. Section 5 shows that these conditions are sufficient to guarantee semantic preservation.

Sizes The first set of conditions ensures that the total non-virtual size and total size of a class C are large enough to enclose all corresponding components of C.

(C1) $\mathsf{dnvboff}_C(B) + \mathsf{nvsize}_B \leq \mathsf{nvsize}_C$ if B direct non-virtual base of C

(C2) $\mathsf{foff}_C(f) + \mathsf{fsize}(f) \leq \mathsf{nvsize}_C$ if f field of C

(C3) $\mathsf{vboff}_C(B) + \mathsf{nvsize}_B \leq \mathsf{size}_C$ if B generalized virtual base of C

(C4) $\mathsf{dsize}_C \leq \mathsf{size}_C$

(C5) $0 < \mathsf{nvsize}_C$

The first two conditions ensure that the total non-virtual size of C is large enough to hold the non-virtual part of any non-virtual base of C (C1) as well as any field of C (C2). We write $\mathsf{fsize}(f)$ for the size of the field f, computed as follows:

$$\mathsf{fsize}(f) = \mathsf{scsize}_t \qquad \text{if } f \text{ has scalar type } t$$
$$\mathsf{fsize}(f) = n \cdot \mathsf{size}_B \qquad \text{if } f \text{ has array type } B[n]$$

Likewise, the total size of C must be large enough to hold a full instance of C, including any virtual base of C (C3), the non-virtual part of C itself (C3 again), and all data of C excluding its tail-padding (C4).

By contrast, it is not required that $\mathsf{nvdsize}_C \leq \mathsf{nvsize}_C$. More precisely, the non-virtual size of a class is an upper bound of the interval in which offsets to fields or subobjects within the non-virtual part of the class must appear. The non-virtual size plays no role in the correctness of data access. However, (C4) is used to show that the data of two disjoint cells of a structure array (or of two cells of distinct structure arrays) are disjoint, which guarantees that data access within an object does not affect other objects. Conversely, the non-virtual data size, and data sizes in general, play no role in the correctness of subobject identification.

The C++ standard [8] mandates that the total size of a class be positive. This is necessary to ensure that distinct elements of an array of structures have different offsets. We require a stronger condition, imposing that the total *non-virtual size* of a class be positive (C5). This is necessary to preserve object identity, as the following example demonstrates.

```
struct A           {};
struct B0: A       {};
struct B1: A       {};
struct C : B0, B1 {};
C[2] c;
A * a0 = (A*) (B1*) &c[0];
A * a1 = (A*) (B0*) &c[1];
```

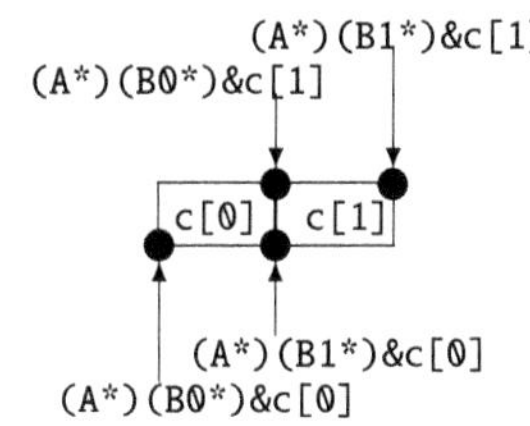

If the non-virtual size of `A` were 0, then (C1) would allow the non-virtual sizes of `B0` and `B1` to be 0, so that the non-virtual size of `C` could be 1. Thus, (C3) would allow the size of `C` to be 1. But in that case, assuming `B0` at offset 0 and `B1` at offset 1 in `C`, the pointers `a0` and `a1` would compare equal, even though they refer to logically different subobjects.

Field separation We now present a set of conditions sufficient to guarantee separation between scalar fields and, therefore, the "good variable" property (updating a field preserves the values of all other fields). These conditions are pleasantly local: they only involve the fields defined in the class C under consideration, as well as the layout quantities for its direct bases, but do not need to consider inherited fields nor indirect bases. They focus on *relevant* components of the class C under consideration. A base class is not relevant if, and only if, it is of an empty class type. A field is not relevant if, and only if, it is an array of structures of an empty type. We write $\mathcal{S} \# \mathcal{T}$ to say that two sets are disjoint ($\mathcal{S} \cap \mathcal{T} = \emptyset$).

(C6) $[\mathsf{dnvboff}_C(B_1), \mathsf{dnvboff}_C(B_1) + \mathsf{nvdsize}_{B_1}) \;\#\; [\mathsf{dnvboff}_C(B_2), \mathsf{dnvboff}_C(B_2) + \mathsf{nvdsize}_{B_2})$ if B_1, B_2 distinct non-empty non-virtual direct bases of C

(C7) $\mathsf{dnvboff}_C(B) + \mathsf{nvdsize}_B \leq \mathsf{fboundary}_C$ if B non-empty non-virtual direct base of C

(C8) $\mathsf{fboundary}_C \leq \mathsf{foff}_C(f)$ if f relevant field of C

(C9) $[\mathsf{foff}_C(f_1), \mathsf{foff}_C(f_1) + \mathsf{fdsize}(f_1)) \;\#\; [\mathsf{foff}_C(f_2), \mathsf{foff}_C(f_2) + \mathsf{fdsize}(f_2))$ if f_1 and f_2 are distinct relevant fields of C

(C10) $\mathsf{foff}_C(f) + \mathsf{fdsize}(f) \leq \mathsf{nvdsize}_C$ if f relevant field of C

(C11) $\mathsf{fboundary}_C \leq \mathsf{nvdsize}_C$

(C12) $[\mathsf{vboff}_C(B_1), \mathsf{vboff}_C(B_1) + \mathsf{nvdsize}_{B_1}) \;\#\; [\mathsf{vboff}_C(B_2), \mathsf{vboff}_C(B_2) + \mathsf{nvdsize}_{B_2})$ if B_1, B_2 distinct non-empty generalized virtual bases of C

(C13) $\mathsf{vboff}_C(B) + \mathsf{nvdsize}_B \leq \mathsf{dsize}_C$

Condition (C6) states the absence of overlap between the data of two distinct, *non-empty*, non-virtual direct bases of a class. To separate the data of direct non-virtual bases of C from the data of the fields of C, our formalization introduces a *boundary* $\mathsf{fboundary}_C$ such that every *non-empty* direct non-virtual base of C has its data laid out below this boundary (C7), and every *relevant* field f of C is laid out above this boundary (C8). It is however possible for the tail padding of a direct non-virtual base of C to straddle the data, or even the tail padding, of a field of C.

Define the *data size* $\mathsf{fdsize}(f)$ of a relevant field f as:

$$\begin{array}{ll}\mathsf{fdsize}(f) = \mathsf{scsize}_t & \text{if } f \text{ has scalar type } t \\ \mathsf{fdsize}(f) = (n-1)\cdot\mathsf{size}_B + \mathsf{dsize}_B & \text{if } f \text{ has array type } B[n]\end{array}$$

In other words, the tail padding of a structure array field is that of the last element of the array, while the tail padding of the first $n-1$ elements is part of the data area for this field (so that this data area is contiguous in memory). Then, condition (C9) states that the *data* areas of two distinct *relevant* fields f_1 and f_2 of C are disjoint. Note, however, that the tail padding of a field of C can be reused to hold some of the next fields of C.

The non-virtual data size of C, like the non-virtual size and the size of C, is not computed directly. Instead, it is constrained as follows: the data of any relevant field f of C is included in the non-virtual data of C (C10), and the non-virtual data of any direct non-virtual bases of C is embedded in the non-virtual data of C (C11). This condition is redundant if C has at least one relevant field.

Finally, as regards virtual inheritance, two distinct, non-empty, generalized virtual bases B_1 and B_2 of C are laid out in such a way that they do not overlap (C12). Recall that a generalized virtual base of C is C itself or a direct or indirect virtual base of C. Then, if B is a non-empty virtual base of C, then C is not empty (as it has a non-empty base), so the above condition holds for generalized virtual bases B and C, which guarantees that the data of the non-virtual part of the virtual base B does not overlap the data of the non-virtual part of C.

Finally, the data of C (excluding its tail-padding) contains the non-virtual data of any generalized virtual base B of C (C13). By contrast, since neither any scalar value nor any virtual function can be accessed from an irrelevant component, the data of an irrelevant component need not be disjoint from other fields or bases of the same type. Likewise, it is not required that an irrelevant field starts at the field boundary: it may also straddle non-virtual base data.

Field alignment The next set of conditions ensures that every field is laid out at an offset that is naturally aligned with respect to its type, even if the field appears in a base class or an array. Define the natural alignment $\mathsf{falign}(f)$ of a field f as $\mathsf{falign}(f) = \mathsf{scalign}_t$ if f has scalar type t, and $\mathsf{falign}(f) = \mathsf{align}_B$ if f has type $B[n]$.

Besides its alignment align_C, a class C has a *non-virtual alignment* $\mathsf{nvalign}_C$ used whenever C is laid out as a base of another class. This distinction allows the non-virtual part of C to be laid out under weaker alignment constraints than for a full instance of C, especially if the alignment of a full instance of C is constrained by that of a virtual base.

The conditions related to alignment are as follows. We write $p \mid q$ to mean that p evenly divides q.

(C14) $(\mathsf{falign}(f) \mid \mathsf{foff}_C(f))$ and $(\mathsf{falign}(f) \mid \mathsf{nvalign}_C)$ if f field of C

(C15) $(\mathsf{nvalign}_B \mid \mathsf{dnvboff}_C(B))$ and $(\mathsf{nvalign}_B \mid \mathsf{nvalign}_C)$ if B non-virtual base of C

(C16) $(\mathsf{dtdalign} \mid \mathsf{nvalign}_C)$ if C is dynamic

(C17) $(\mathsf{nvalign}_B \mid \mathsf{vboff}_C(B))$ and $(\mathsf{nvalign}_B \mid \mathsf{align}_C)$ if B is a generalized virtual base of C

(C18) $(\mathsf{align}_C \mid \mathsf{size}_C)$

In particular, (C17) implies that $(\mathsf{nvalign}_C \mid \mathsf{align}_C)$, as expected. (C16) ensures correctly-aligned accesses to the dynamic type data of a class. Finally, (C18) is used to show that an access to an element of an array of type C is correctly aligned. It is, however, not necessary for non-virtual sizes, as there are never any arrays composed only of non-virtual parts of a class.

Dynamic type data Similarly to compilers such as GCC, we chose to store the dynamic type data of a subobject at the beginning of the subobject. This leads to the following conditions for a dynamic class C:

(C19) $\mathsf{dtdsize} \leq \mathsf{fboundary}_C$

(C20) $\mathsf{pbase}_C = \varnothing \Rightarrow \mathsf{dtdsize} \leq \mathsf{dnvboff}_C(B)$ if B is a non-empty non-virtual direct base of C

(C21) $\mathsf{pbase}_C = \{B\} \Rightarrow \mathsf{dnvboff}_C(B) = 0$

Any relevant field must be laid out after the dynamic type data (C19). If C is dynamic but has no primary base, (C20) ensures that all non-empty non-virtual direct bases of C start after the dynamic type data of C. Finally, the primary base of a class is laid out at offset 0, so that the class and its primary base can share the same storage for their dynamic type data (C21).

As a consequence of (C20), (C21) and (C6), it follows that non-empty, direct, non-virtual bases of C other than its primary base are laid out at offsets at least $\mathsf{dtdsize}$.

Identity of subobjects The final set of conditions guarantees that two different subobjects of a class C of the same type B map to different offsets in memory. This identity requirement is achieved in two completely different ways, depending on whether B is empty or not. If B is non-empty, the requirement follows immediately from

(C22) C non-empty $\Rightarrow 0 < \mathsf{nvdsize}_C$

In practice, actual layout algorithms define empty bases in such a way that this condition automatically holds (a non-empty base contains at least one byte of field data or some dynamic type data), but we still need to include it in the specification.

If B is an empty base of C, neither condition (C22) nor the field separation conditions suffice to show that two different B subobjects map to distinct memory offsets. We therefore need specific conditions for empty bases.

Unfortunately, we found no local condition to ensure that two different subobjects of the same empty type are mapped to distinct offsets: we need to involve not only the layout parameters of the direct bases of the class C under consideration, but also those of all classes transitively reachable from C by inheritance or structure fields. Indeed, if we took a local interval-based condition similar to the one used for field separation – for instance, if we required the whole non-virtual zones (not only the data) of non-virtual bases to be disjoint –, then we would lose tail padding optimization, and fall back to a naive implementation similar to that of section 2.2.

Therefore, we have to compute, for any class C, the set eboffs_C of empty base offsets, i.e. the offsets of all empty classes reachable from C through inheritance or structure fields.

Similarly, we compute, for any class C, the set $\mathsf{nveboffs}_C$ of non-virtual empty base offsets, i.e. the offsets of all empty classes that are subobjects of direct non-virtual bases, or that are reachable through a field of C or a field of a non-virtual base. Define:

$$\omega + \mathcal{S} =_{\mathrm{def}} \{(A, \omega + o) \mid (A, o) \in \mathcal{S}\}$$

Then, the sets $\mathsf{nveboffs}_C$ of the *non-virtual empty base offsets* of C and eboffs_C of *empty base offsets* of C are defined as follows:

$$\mathsf{eboffs}_C =_{\mathrm{def}} \bigcup_{B \in \mathsf{vbases}_C \cup \{C\}} \mathsf{vboff}_C(B) + \mathsf{nveboffs}_B$$

$$\begin{array}{rl}\mathsf{nveboffs}_C =_{\mathrm{def}} & \text{if } C \text{ is empty then } \{(C,0)\} \text{ else } \varnothing \\ \cup & \displaystyle\bigcup_{B \in \mathsf{dnvbases}_C} \mathsf{dnvboffs}_C(B) + \mathsf{nveboffs}_B \\ \cup & \displaystyle\bigcup_{\substack{(f,B,n) \in \mathsf{stfields}_C \\ 0 \leq i < n}} \mathsf{foff}_C(f,B,n) + i \cdot \mathsf{size}_B + \mathsf{eboffs}_B\end{array}$$

For the purposes of the Coq proofs, those sets are described as (mutually) inductive predicates and intended to be computed separately by algorithms. From an implementation point of view, we can assume that those sets are computed incrementally: when it comes to computing those offsets for C, they are assumed to be computed for all of the bases and structure field types of C.

Now, we impose that the unions defining $\mathsf{nveboffs}_C$ and eboffs_C be disjoint:

(C23) $(\mathsf{dnvboff}_C(B_1) + \mathsf{nveboffs}_{B_1}) \# (\mathsf{dnvboff}_C(B_2) + \mathsf{nveboffs}_{B_2})$ if B_1, B_2 distinct non-virtual bases of C

(C24) $(\mathsf{dnvboff}_C(B_1) + \mathsf{nveboffs}_{B_1}) \# \bigcup_{0 \leq j < n} \mathsf{foff}_C(f, B_2, n) + j \cdot \mathsf{size}_{B_2} + \mathsf{eboffs}_{B_2}$ if B_1 non-virtual base of C and (f, B_2, n) structure field of C

(C25) $\bigcup_{0 \leq j_1 < n_1} \mathsf{foff}_C(f_1, B_1, n_1) + j_1 \cdot \mathsf{size}_{B_1} + \mathsf{eboffs}_{B_1} \# \bigcup_{0 \leq j_2 < n_2} \mathsf{foff}_C(f_2, B_2, n_2) + j_2 \cdot \mathsf{size}_{B_2} + \mathsf{eboffs}_{B_2}$ if (f_1, B_1, n_1) and (f_2, B_2, n_2) distinct structure fields of C

(C26) $(\mathsf{vboff}_C(B_1) + \mathsf{nveboffs}_{B_1}) \# (\mathsf{vboff}_C(B_2) + \mathsf{nveboffs}_{B_2})$ if B_1, B_2 distinct generalized virtual bases of C

In practice, whenever the algorithm tries to lay out a base or a field, it can check its empty base offsets against the empty base offsets laid out so far for the main class; whenever this check fails, the offset is incremented by the alignment of the component. As the algorithms in section 6 show, these checks can be simplified by imposing tighter layout constraints, at the cost of losing some tail padding optimizations.

5. Correctness proof

We now show that the conditions stated in section 4 are sufficient to guarantee the various separation, alignment and disjointness properties discussed in section 2.1, these properties being, in turn, sufficient to ensure semantic preservation during compilation. All the results below have been mechanically verified using the Coq proof assistant. We therefore only sketch the proofs, giving an idea of how the various conditions are used.

5.1 Field separation

Consider a generalized subobject p of static type A from an array of structures of type C, and a field f defined in class A. Define $\mathsf{Foff}_C(p, f)$ to be the offset of the field f of the subobject designated by p, within the representation of the array of type C:

$$\mathsf{Foff}_C(p, f) = \mathsf{off}_C(p) + \mathsf{foff}_A(f)$$

Theorem 1. *If p_1, p_2 are two generalized subobjects of static type A_1, A_2 within an array of structures of type C, and if f_1, f_2 are scalar fields of A_1, A_2 of types t_1, t_2 respectively, such that $(p_1, f_1) \neq (p_2, f_2)$, then the memory areas associated with these fields are disjoint:*

$$[\mathsf{Foff}_C(p_1, f_1), \mathsf{Foff}_C(p_1, f_1) + \mathsf{scsize}_{t_1}) \# [\mathsf{Foff}_C(p_2, f_2), \mathsf{Foff}_C(p_2, f_2) + \mathsf{scsize}_{t_2})$$

Proof. First we show that two distinct scalar fields reachable through base class subobjects s_1 and s_2 of a class C are disjoint. There are two cases. If $s_1 = s_2$, then $f_1 \neq f_2$ and (C9) concludes. Otherwise, we show that, if A_i is the static type of s_i, then each f_i is included (C8, C7, C11, C10) in the *field data zone* of A_i (the memory zone between offsets $\mathsf{fboundary}_{A_i}$ and $\mathsf{nvdsize}_{A_i}$ within A_i) such that the two field data zones of s_1 and s_2 are disjoint.

Then we show that if s_1 and s_2 are two distinct base class subobjects of C through non-virtual inheritance only, then their field data zones are disjoint. There are two cases. If one subobject, say s_1, is a subobject of the other s_2, then, A_2 denoting the static type of s_2, field f_2 is on the right-hand side of the field boundary of A_2 (C8), whereas f_1 is included in a direct non-virtual base of A_2, which is on the left-hand side of the field boundary of A_2 (C7), which concludes. Otherwise, s_1 and s_2 are subobjects of some classes A_1 and A_2 that are distinct direct non-virtual bases of some class A, so a similar inclusion scheme, combined with (C6), concludes.

Then, if s_1 and s_2 are distinct base class subobjects of C, we consider the generalized virtual bases of which s_1 and s_2 are non-virtual subobjects. If they are equal, then the non-virtual case above can be reused. Otherwise, (C12) concludes.

Finally, we can show our main theorem by induction on the length of the array path of, say, p_1. Then, for each i, (p_i, f_i) can be decomposed into (j_i, s_i, f'_i, P'_i) where j_i is an integer less than the size n of the array of type $C[n]$ from which p_1 and p_2 start, and s_i is a base class subobject of C of some static type B_i, and f'_i is a field of A_i such that either $(f'_i, P'_i) = (f_i, \varnothing)$ (no structure fields are traversed), or f'_i is a structure field of type $A_i[n_i]$ and $P'_i = \{p'_i\}$ for some generalized subobject p_i from the array $A_i[n_i]$. In that case, the array path of p'_1 is one element shorter than the one of p_1, which allows induction. There are five cases. If $j_1 \neq j_2$, then the scalar fields are included in distinct cells of the initial array. As two distinct fields of an array are necessarily disjoint, we conclude, additionally using (C13, C4). If $s_1 \neq s_2$, then fields f'_1 and f'_2 are included in disjoint field data zones; as fields f_1 and f_2 are included in the data zones of f_1 and f_2, this concludes. If $f'_1 \neq f'_2$, then their data zones are disjoint; as the data zone of each f_i is included in the data zone of f'_i (which may be the same, if $f'_i = f_i$). Otherwise, $f'_1 = f'_2$ is a structure field, and we may use the induction hypothesis.

It is legal to use all those conditions, as all considered classes are non-empty: as f_1 and f_2 are scalar fields, the classes defining them are non-empty, so are their derived classes, the structure fields containing them, and so on. □

5.2 Alignment

Theorem 2. *If p is a generalized subobject of static type A within an array of structures of type C, and if f is a scalar field of A of type t, then the access to f via p is correctly aligned:*

$$(\mathsf{scalign}_t \mid \mathsf{Foff}_C(p, f)) \text{ and } (\mathsf{scalign}_t \mid \mathsf{align}_C)$$

Proof. Easy induction on the path, using transitivity of the "evenly divides" relation, alignment conditions (C14, C15, C17), and additionally (C18) for array cell accesses. Access to the i-th cell of an array of structures of type B corresponds to shifting by $i \cdot \mathsf{size}_B$, which requires an alignment condition for size_B. □

Theorem 3. *If p is a generalized subobject of static type A within an array of structures of type C, and if A is dynamic, then the access to the dynamic data of p is correctly aligned:*

$$(\mathsf{dtdalign} \mid \mathsf{off}_C(p)) \text{ and } (\mathsf{dtdalign} \mid \mathsf{align}_C)$$

Proof. Same reasoning as above, additionally using (C16). □

5.3 Identity of subobjects

Theorem 4. *If p_1, p_2 are two different generalized subobjects of the same static type A within an array of structures of type C, then their corresponding offsets are distinct:*

$$p_1 \neq p_2 \Rightarrow \mathsf{off}_C(p_1) \neq \mathsf{off}_C(p_2)$$

Proof. There are two radically different sub-proofs depending on whether A is empty. If it is not empty, then the proof is similar to that of theorem 1, thanks to condition (C22). If A is empty, all those conditions no longer apply. By induction on the length of the array path of p_1, there are two cases. If p_1 and p_2 originate from the same cell of the array of structures of type C, then, (C23, C24, C25, C26) and the induction hypothesis conclude. Otherwise, we know that the two cells are entirely disjoint (not only their data), so we simply have to show that each p_i is included in its own cell, using (C1, C2, C3) and also (C5). □

5.4 Preservation of dynamic type data

The following theorem ensures that writing a scalar field does not change the dynamic type data of subobjects.

Theorem 5. *If p_1, p_2 are two generalized subobjects of static type A_1, A_2 within an array of structures of type C, and if A_1 is a dynamic class and if f_2 is a scalar field of A_2 of type t_2, then the memory area occupied by the dynamic type data of A_1 is disjoint from the memory area occupied by field f_2:*

$$\begin{array}{rl} & [\mathsf{off}_C(p_1), \mathsf{off}_C(p_1) + \mathsf{dtdata}) \\ \# & [\mathsf{Foff}_C(p_2, f_2), \mathsf{Foff}_C(p_2, f_2) + \mathsf{scsize}_{t_2}) \end{array}$$

Proof. The proof resembles that of theorem 1, except that data inclusions (not only field data inclusions) must be checked. (C19) ensures that dynamic type data is included in the data of a subobject, but it also ensures that it is disjoint from the field data zones if p_1 is a generalized subobject that is reachable from p_2 by inheritance and/or scalar fields. Conversely, if p_2 is reachable from p_1, then (C20, C21) must be additionally used. □

A dynamic class C may share its dynamic type data with one of its dynamic non-virtual bases B: the primary base of C. But the semantics of C++ guarantees that dynamic operations (e.g. dynamic cast, dynamic function dispatch) on a base class subobject s_2 of C give the same result as on a base class subobject s_1 of C if s_2 is reachable from s_1 (i.e. if s_1 *dominates* s_2 [19]). As the primary base B is a base of C, this sharing is semantically sound.

However, initialization of dynamic data has still to be checked. Even without a detailed semantics of object construction and destruction, which is out of the scope of this paper, we still have to know whether initializing the dynamic data of a subobject does not change the dynamic data of other subobjects. We proved formally that this is the case, except for two subobjects s_1 and s_2 such that s_2 can be reached by s_1 through primary bases only.

A *primary path* is a path in the primary path graph (where classes are the vertices, and (U, V) is an edge if and only if V is the primary base of U). Any non-virtual path $B :: l$ can be decomposed into a *reduced path* $\mathsf{red}(B :: l)$ such that:

- if $B :: l$ is primary, then $\mathsf{red}(B :: l) =_{\mathrm{def}} B :: \epsilon$;
- otherwise, $B :: l$ can be rewritten as $l_1 +\!\!+ B_1 :: B_2 :: l_2$ where B_2 is a non-virtual base of B_1 that is not the primary base of B_1, and $B_2 :: l_2$ is a primary path. Then, $\mathsf{red}(B :: l) =_{\mathrm{def}} l_1 +\!\!+ B_1 :: B_2 :: \epsilon$.

In other words, the reduced path of a non-virtual path l' is obtained by truncating the longest primary path on the right of l'.

Theorem 6. *Let $p_1 = (\alpha_1, i_1, (h_1, l_1))$, $p_2 = (\alpha_2, i_2, (h_2, l_2))$ be two generalized subobjects of static types A_1 and A_2 respectively, from an array of structures of type C. Assume A_1 and A_2 are dynamic classes. If $(\alpha_1, i_1) \neq (\alpha_2, i_2)$ or $\mathsf{red}(l_1) \neq \mathsf{red}(l_2)$, then the dynamic type data of the two subobjects are disjoint:*

$$\begin{array}{rl} & [\mathsf{off}_C(p_1), \mathsf{off}_C(p_1) + \mathsf{dtdata}) \\ \# & [\mathsf{off}_C(p_2), \mathsf{off}_C(p_2) + \mathsf{dtdata}) \end{array}$$

Proof. The proof proceeds like that of theorem 5, but replacing each l'_i with its reduced path $\mathsf{red}(l'_i)$. □

5.5 Semantic preservation

To conclude this section and exercise the theorems above, we now sketch a proof of semantic preservation for the compilation scheme given in section 4.4.

The semantics of the target language is given in terms of states (V', M), where V' maps variables to target values and M is a machine-level, byte-addressed memory state in the style of Tuch [18]. Target values v' are the union of base values $\mathsf{Atom}\ bv$, data pointers $\mathsf{Ptr}\ i$ (where i, an integer, is the address of a byte in memory), and pointers to dynamic type data $\mathsf{Vptr}(C, \sigma)$. Memory states are presented abstractly through the two partial operations $\mathtt{load}(i, n, M)$ and $\mathtt{store}(i, n, v', M)$ where i, an integer, is the address of a byte, and n is a byte count. By lack of space, we omit the operational semantics of the target language, referring the reader to the online supplement [15] instead.

We now define a predicate $(V, H) \triangleright (V', M)$ relating the execution states of the program before and after compilation. We start with the relation $H \vdash v \triangleright v'$ between source values and target values:

$$H \vdash \mathsf{Atom}\ bv \triangleright \mathsf{Atom}\ bv \qquad\qquad H \vdash \mathsf{Ptr}\ \varnothing \triangleright \mathsf{Ptr}\varnothing$$

$$\frac{H(o) = (C, n, \omega) \qquad C[n] \prec\!(\alpha, i, \sigma)\!\succ\!\!\rightarrow A}{H \vdash \mathsf{Ptr}(o, \alpha, i, \sigma) \triangleright \mathsf{Ptr}(\mathsf{objoff}(o) + \mathsf{off}_C(\alpha, i, \sigma))}$$

In the last rule, objoff is a partial mapping from source-level object identifiers o to memory addresses. It represents the initial placement of top-level objects in memory.

Agreement $(V, H) \triangleright (V', M)$ between a source state and a target state is, then, the conjunction of the following conditions:

1. Variable agreement: $H \vdash V(x) \triangleright V'(x)$ for all $x \in \mathrm{Dom}(V)$.
2. Alignment of top-level objects: $(\mathsf{align}_C \mid \mathsf{objoff}(o))$ if $H(o) = (C, n, \omega)$.
3. Separation between top-level objects: $[\mathsf{objoff}(o_1), \mathsf{objoff}(o_1) + n_1 \times \mathsf{size}_{C_1})\ \#$ $[\mathsf{objoff}(o_2), \mathsf{objoff}(o_2) + n_2 \times \mathsf{size}_{C_2})$ if $H(o_1) = (C_1, n_1, \omega_1)$ and $H(o_2) = (C_2, n_2, \omega_2)$ and $o_1 \neq o_2$.
4. Correct values for scalar fields: $H \vdash \omega(\alpha, i, \sigma, (f, t)) \triangleright$ $\mathsf{load}(\mathsf{objoff}(o) + \mathsf{off}_C(\alpha, i, \sigma) + \mathsf{foff}_A(f, t), \mathsf{scsize}_t, M)$ if $H(o) = (C, n, \omega)$ and $C[n] \prec\!(\alpha, i, \sigma)\!\succ\!\!\rightarrow A$ and (f, t) is a scalar field of A.
5. Correct values for dynamic data: $\mathsf{load}(\mathsf{objoff}(o) + \mathsf{off}_C(\alpha, i, \mathsf{red}(\sigma)), \mathsf{dtdsize}, M) = \mathsf{Vptr}(B, \mathsf{red}(\sigma))$ if $H(o) = (C, n, \omega)$ and $C[n] \prec\!\alpha\!\succ\!\!\xrightarrow{\mathcal{A}} B[m] \prec\!i, \sigma\!\succ\!\!\xrightarrow{\mathcal{CI}} A$ and A is a dynamic class.

Theorem 7. *Every execution step of the source program is simulated by one or several execution steps of the compiled code: if $(V_1, H_1) \triangleright (V'_1, M_1)$ and $Stmt \vdash (V_1, H_1) \rightarrow (V_2, H_2)$, then there exists a target state (V'_2, M_2) such that $[\![Stmt]\!] \vdash (V'_1, M_1) \xrightarrow{+} (V'_2, M_2)$ and $(V_2, H_2) \triangleright (V'_2, M_2)$.*

Proof. If $Stmt$ is an assignment to a scalar field, the existence of M_2 follows from theorem 2, which guarantees that the store is properly aligned and therefore succeeds. Theorem 1, combined with the "good variable" properties of the target memory model, shows part (4) of the agreement between the final states. Part (5) likewise follows from theorem 5 and the good variable properties.

If $Stmt$ is a pointer comparison, theorem 4 ensures that the address comparison generated by the compilation scheme produces the same boolean outcome.

The remaining cases follow more or less directly from the hypothesis $(V_1, H_1) \triangleright (V_1', M_1)$. □

6. Verification of representative layout algorithms

We now put our formalization into practice by using it to prove the correctness of two realistic, optimizing C++ object layout algorithms.

6.1 The common vendor C++ ABI

The first layout algorithm we study is the one specified in the "common vendor" C++ ABI [3], first introduced for Itanium and now used by the GCC compiler on many other platforms. Our algorithm is faithful to the ABI specification with one exception: we do not allow the use of nearly empty virtual bases as primary bases, an optimization of dubious value discussed in section 7.

Following the ABI, we define a class C to be dynamic if, and only if, it has a virtual function, or a non-virtual dynamic base, or a virtual base. In the latter case, C is considered dynamic as its dynamic type data is actually used to find the offsets of the virtual bases of C. Likewise, we define a class to be empty if, and only if, all the following conditions hold: it has no virtual function; it has no non-static fields; it has no virtual bases; all its direct non-virtual bases are empty. In particular, an empty class cannot be dynamic.

The layout algorithm is summarized below. (See [15] for the full pseudocode.) It takes as input a class C and the layout of all classes B mentioned in C (i.e. B is a direct or indirect base of C, or B is the type of a field of C, or depends on a base of C or of the type of a field of C). Besides the layout parameters listed in section 4.2, it also computes the set eboffs'_C of the offsets of all subobjects of an empty virtual base of C or an empty non-virtual direct base of C.

1. Start from $\mathsf{nvdsize}_C = 0$ and $\mathsf{nvalign}_C = \mathsf{nvsize}_C = 1$.
2. Arbitrarily choose a dynamic non-virtual direct base B, if any. This will be the primary base. Give it offset 0 within C, and update $\mathsf{nveboffs}_C$, $\mathsf{nvdsize}_C$, nvsize_C and $\mathsf{nvalign}_C$ to their B counterparts.
3. If there is no primary base but the class is dynamic, then reserve some space for the dynamic type data: update $\mathsf{nvdsize}_C$ and nvsize_C to $\mathsf{dtdsize}$, and $\mathsf{nvalign}_C$ to $\mathsf{dtdalign}$. Start at offset equal to the size of dynamic type data.
4. Then, for each non-primary non-virtual direct base B of C:
   - Try to give it an offset $\mathsf{dnvboff}_C(B)$ within C, starting from the least multiple of $\mathsf{nvalign}_B$ no less than $\mathsf{nvdsize}_C$. If there is a type conflict with empty base offsets, then try at a further offset by increasing $\mathsf{dnvboff}_C(B)$ by $\mathsf{nvalign}_B$, knowing that for $\mathsf{dnvboff}_C(B) \geq \mathsf{nvsize}_C$ there will be no conflict. However, if B is empty, first try 0 before trying any offset from $\mathsf{nvdsize}_C$.
   - Update nvsize_C to $\max(\mathsf{nvsize}_C, \mathsf{dnvboff}_C(B) + \mathsf{nvsize}_B)$, and $\mathsf{nvalign}_C$ to $\mathrm{lcm}(\mathsf{nvalign}_C, \mathsf{nvalign}_B)$.
   - If B is not empty, also update $\mathsf{nvdsize}_C$ to $\mathsf{dnvboff}_C(B) + \mathsf{nvsize}_B$: in this case, note that the whole non-virtual part of B (not only its data) is included in the data of C
5. Set $\mathsf{fboundary}_C$ to $\mathsf{nvdsize}_C$.
6. Then for each field, try to lay it out. Starting from $\mathsf{nvdsize}_C$, find a correctly aligned offset (incrementing by $\mathsf{falign}(f)$), and set $\mathsf{nvdsize}_C$ to $\mathsf{foffset}_C(f) + \mathsf{fsize}(f)$, so that the next field starts after the end of the whole previous field (not only its data). This explains why any class having a field, even an irrelevant one, is not empty.
7. Then for each virtual base, try to lay out its non-virtual part, the same way as for non-virtual bases, but updating align_C, size_C, etc. instead of $\mathsf{nvalign}_C$, nvsize_C, etc.

Type conflicts with empty base offsets are detected as follows. When trying to lay out an empty base B, check between B's non-virtual empty base offsets and the whole set of empty base offsets so far. When trying to lay out a non-empty base B, or a field of type $B[n]$, check between the base's or the field's non-virtual empty base offsets and the offsets of C so far reachable by inheritance only through an empty direct non-virtual base or an empty virtual base. In other words, ignore those offsets of bases reachable through fields, or through non-empty bases of C. Indeed, those offsets are guaranteed to be laid out in the data zone of C, as this algorithm ensures that a field, or a non-empty base, is wholly included (not only its data) in the data of C. As the data zone of already laid out relevant components is disjoint from the data zone of the current relevant component, there is no need to check whether those offsets are present in the empty base offsets of the current component.

These details about type conflict resolution were not present in the ABI specification [3]: it gave no clue about which offsets to empty subobjects need to be checked.

We proved that this algorithm satisfies all the conditions stated in section 4. Thus, it is semantically correct with respect to field access, dynamic operations and subobject identification.

6.2 A more efficient layout: empty member optimization

The previous algorithm misses several opportunities for saving space. Consider:

```
struct A0     {};
struct A: A0  {};
struct B      { char f; A a; };
struct C      { B b; char f; };
struct D: A   { A a; };
struct E: D   { char f; };
```

Running this example through GCC 4.3 (which follows the common vendor ABI), we obtain `sizeof(C) == 3` and `sizeof(E) == 3`. This indicates that field `f` of `C` is laid out completely disjointly from `b`, even though `b.a` contains no data (`A` is empty). The space for `b.a` could be reused, giving `sizeof(C) == 2`. Likewise, field `f` of `E` is laid out completely disjointly from the subobject `D`, which is considered as not empty even though `D::a` contains no data. The space for `D` could be reused, resulting in `sizeof(E) == 2`. This optimisation is justified insofar as an object of empty class has no source of observable behavior other than its address: it carries no runtime data. Consequently a conforming C++ implementation can systematically compile assignments to such objects as no-ops.

We propose an algorithm that performs these space optimizations by refining the notion of empty classes. Say that a class is empty if, and only if, all the following conditions hold:

- it has no virtual functions;
- it has no scalar fields;
- it has no virtual bases;
- all its direct non-virtual bases are empty;
- all its structure fields are of an empty type.

In particular, an empty class cannot be dynamic. (This definition of empty classes is the smallest that satisfies the conditions from section 4.3.) Then, the previous algorithm is modified as follows:

- When laying out an irrelevant component, all correctly aligned offsets starting from 0 are tried, until the offsets to empty subobjects do not clash, or nvsize_C is reached
- A field can start in the tail padding of the previous field: when a relevant field is being laid out, the data size is updated to $\mathsf{foff}_C(f) + \mathsf{fdsize}(f)$ instead of $\mathsf{foff}_C(f) + \mathsf{fsize}(f)$. Similarly for a non-empty base.

This requires a modification when checking for type conflicts with empty base offsets: the whole sets of offsets must be considered every time. Indeed, as there are no more conditions about the sizes of the fields or the non-virtual sizes of the bases, there are no more guarantees that an empty subobject reachable from an already laid out component will not clash with the current component being laid out. Similar modifications occur for fields, and virtual bases (in the latter case, checking against eboffs_C). As all offsets are checked, the auxiliary set eboffs'_C is no longer useful.

We proved this algorithm to be correct. In fact, the proof is easier than for the previous algorithm, as this algorithm is closer to the conditions stated in Section 4.

7. Limitations and extensions

Bit fields In our formalization, we did not specify the size unit, so that sizes and offsets can be expressed in bits instead of bytes. However, this may not be enough to fully implement bit fields, as they require specific alignment constraints. Consider:

```
struct A { int i: 29; int j: 2; int k: 3; }
```

On a 32-bit platform, fields `i` and `j` can be packed into a single 32-bit integer, and retrieved by shifting and masking from this integer. However, the field `k` should not be packed adjacent to `j`, otherwise two correctly-aligned memory accesses would be required to recover the value of `k`. Our alignment constraints over field offsets would have to be strengthened accordingly.

POD Our work does not consider the specificities of POD (*Plain Old Data*), and treats them in an ordinary way, not distinguishing them from general C++ structures. Roughly speaking, a POD structure is a structure with no inheritance, and no non-POD fields: as such, it is roughly equivalent to a C structure. The Standard mandates the layout of POD structures to be compatible with C, allowing in particular bitwise assignment between POD structures using memcpy. By contrast, our work considers that structures are always assigned to by memberwise assignments of fields. However, we suspect that constraining $\mathsf{nvdsize}_C = \mathsf{nvsize}_C = \mathsf{size}_C$ whenever C is a POD could help us prove the correctness of bitwise copy, even if a POD is inherited by another class.

Unions Just like structures, unions offer opportunities for reusing tail padding that is common to all of its members. The practical benefits are low: unions are used infrequently enough that treating them like POD is a reasonable choice. The main difficulty in extending our formalism to unions comes from the operational semantics, which must be instrumented to enforce the policy that, at any time, the only member of an union that can be accessed is the one most recently initialized.

Virtual primaries In our work, a class can share its dynamic type data only with a non-virtual primary base. However, the common vendor ABI [3] allows a class to share its dynamic type data with one of its virtual bases, as long as the latter has no fields. In practice, the layout of such a virtual base (called a *nearly empty virtual base*) is reduced to its dynamic type data, so that it can be shared with the dynamic type data of its derived class. However, such a layout would break the schema of laying out the non-virtual part of a class separately from the non-virtual parts from its virtual bases, as some non-empty virtual bases may be actually laid out in the non-virtual part of the class. Moreover, indirect primary virtual bases may appear several times in a class layout because they have been chosen as primary bases by different non-virtual bases. We do not know how to solve this layout ambiguity. In practice, the latter case also actually poses efficiency problems in most compilers, so much so that the "virtual primary" optimization is described as "an error in the design" of the common vendor ABI [3].

Alternate layout of dynamic type data Our work assumes that dynamic type data is laid out at the beginning of a class. Some C++ compilers such as Cfront or Compaq's compiler elect to place it at a different offset. That layout scheme has the property that a pointer to the complete object is also a pointer to the data of the primary base class subobject, which may not need dynamic type data. How frequently that situation occurs in practice is unclear. Moreover, it can lead to alignment padding that is more difficult to reuse in derived classes.

Bidirectional layout In our work as in production C++ compilers, object representation can only be extended on one side in derived classes. There are, however, some layouts [7] that may extend an object representation to both sides, so that for instance a class may share its dynamic type data with two of its bases. However, an efficient implementation of such layout would need to know the derived classes of a class in advance, which would impede separate compilation.

Reusing padding holes Our work assumes that the non-virtual data of a class is a contiguous memory zone. Consequently, holes arising from inter-field padding cannot be detected and reused, as in the following example:

```
struct A0    { }
struct A: A0 { char x; int y; };
struct B: A  { char z; };
```

There is some alignment padding between `A::x` and `A::y`, but in the layout of `B`, our formalization does not allow `z` to be stored in this unused space, as the data of `A` is considered to be contiguous.

Virtual table layout Our work focused so far on the representation of objects, leaving unaddressed the concrete representation of dynamic type data. Future work includes formalizing the layout of virtual tables as studied by Sweeney and Burke [17], as well as **this** pointer adjustment during virtual function dispatch. This would lead to mechanized verification of the implementation of dynamic operations such as virtual function dispatch and dynamic cast.

Object construction and destruction A related piece of future work is the formalization of object construction and destruction, especially the updates to the dynamic type data of objects that take place during this process.

8. Related work

Obviously, any C++ compiler includes an object layout algorithm. However, to the best of our knowledge, none has been reported as formally verified. Stroustrup [5] extensively discusses object layouts found in earlier C++ compilers. Although he explicitly stated "Objects of an empty class have a nonzero size" [5, p. 164], he did not consider empty base class optimization. Nor was that optimization implemented in Cfront. The nonzero size requirement was later clarified by the C++ standard [8, paragraph 10/5].

The empty base optimization, as a basis for efficient programming technique, was popularized by Myers [13]. He credited Jason Merrill for the possibility of optimizing empty *member* subobjects, as we consider in this paper. However, there was no proposed algorithm, and as we observed such an optimization requires careful assumptions about PODs (*Plain Old Data*). The empty base class optimization is explicitly mandated by the common vendor ABI [3], which is a practical basis of our formalization and improvements.

Our present work is based on the algebraic model of inheritance by Rossie and Friedman [16], and the operational semantics of Wasserrab *et al* [19]. These foundational papers do not consider concrete object layout algorithms. Rather, they purposefully focus on abstract object semantics independent of concrete machine representations.

There are other formalizations of aspects of the compilation of C++, but none of them considers concrete data representation. Chen [2] proposed a typed intermediate language for compiling multiple inheritance. This work formally describes which pointer adjustments are necessary for virtual function calls and conversions, including offset computations and thunks, and proves type soundness results about them. However, Chen's formalization, focusing only on an intermediate language, leaves largely unspecified the concrete object layout. The delicate issue of subobject identity is not addressed either.

Luo and Qin [12] proposed a separation logic-based formalism for reasoning about C++-style multiple inheritance. This paper does not address the thorny issues of concrete object layout. Rather, it relies on a syntactic form of field resolution close to the algorithm of Ramalingam and Srinivasan [14], itself a reformulation of the calculus of Rossie and Friedman [16]. Furthermore, Luo and Qin restricted themselves to non-virtual multiple inheritance only, considered a rather abstract storage model, and defined the semantics of field access through substitution.

In a completely different direction, Gil and Sweeney [6] proposed an arguably space and time-efficient bidirectional object layout scheme for multiple inheritance. The core of their algorithms is based on the assumption that the compiler knows the complete class hierarchy. That assumption holds only in special cases (e.g. in a closed world with whole program analysis), and is inadequate for most realistic C++ compilers at large, which must cope with a separate compilation model inherited from C. This theoretical work was followed up by an quantitative study by Sweeney and Burke [17]. They developed a formalism to characterize when compiler artifacts (to support runtime semantics of C++-style inheritance) are required. Their work influenced design choices in the memory layout of the IBM Visual Age C++ V5 compiler. The core of the bidirectional layout was later refined by Gil, Pugh, Weddell and Zibin [7] to a "language-independent" object layout algorithm for multiple inheritance. However, they explicitly exclude C++-style non-virtual multiple inheritance on the ground that it is "a rarity or [...] an abomination". It is not rare, and we cannot afford such assumption for formally verified layout algorithms in real world compilers for ISO standard C++.

Leaving C++ objects for the simpler world of C structures, Tuch [18] axiomatized a field separation property of structure layout and used it in a separation logic able to verify low-level system C code. The Clight formal semantics of Blazy and Leroy [1] defines a simple structure layout algorithm; the field separation, field alignment and prefix compatibility properties were mechanically verified.

9. Conclusions

C++ object layout is one of those seemingly-simple implementation issues that turn out to require a 18 000 line Coq development to start making formal sense. Between the few compilers in the past that over-optimized the layout, losing object identity in the process, and the great many contemporary compilers that err on the side of caution and miss opportunities for saving space, our formalization and mechanized verification delineate a design space of trustworthy, yet efficient layout algorithms, bringing more confidence in commonly-used ABIs and suggesting further safe optimizations.

This work is also a first step towards formally verifying a compiler front-end for a realistic subset of C++, even though much work remains to be done on other aspects of the C++ object model (virtual dispatch, construction and destruction, etc).

Acknowledgments

We are grateful to the anonymous reviewers for their very helpful suggestions to improve our results and their presentation. We thank Bjarne Stroustrup and Lawrence Rauchberger for their feedback, which helped us to keep our formalization connected to the realistic practices of C++ compilers.

References

[1] S. Blazy and X. Leroy. Mechanized semantics for the Clight subset of the C language. *Journal of Automated Reasoning*, 43(3):263–288, 2009.

[2] J. Chen. A typed intermediate language for compiling multiple inheritance. In *34th symp. Principles of Programming Languages*, pages 25–30. ACM, 2007.

[3] CodeSourcery, Compaq, EDG, HP, IBM, Intel, Red Hat, and SGI. Itanium C++ ABI, 2001. URL `http://www.codesourcery.com/public/cxx-abi`.

[4] B. Dawes. POD's Revisited; Resolving Core Issue 568 (Revision 2). Technical report, ISO/IEC SC22/JTC1/WG21, March 2007. URL `http://www.open-std.org/JTC1/SC22/WG21/docs/papers/2007/n2172.html`.

[5] M. A. Ellis and B. Stroustrup. *The Annotated C++ Reference Manual*. Addison-Wesley, 1990.

[6] J. Gil and P. F. Sweeney. Space and time-efficient memory layout for multiple inheritance. In *14th conf. on Object-Oriented Programming, Systems, Languages, and Applications (OOPSLA 1999)*, pages 256–275. ACM, 1999.

[7] J. Y. Gil, W. Pugh, G. E. Weddell, and Y. Zibin. Two-dimensional bidirectional object layout. *ACM Trans. Program. Lang. Syst.*, 30(5): 1–38, 2008.

[8] *International Standard ISO/IEC 14882:2003. Programming Languages — C++*. International Organization for Standards, 2003.

[9] G. Klein and T. Nipkow. A machine-checked model for a Java-like language, virtual machine and compiler. *ACM Trans. Prog. Lang. Syst.*, 28(4):619–695, 2006.

[10] D. Leinenbach, W. Paul, and E. Petrova. Towards the formal verification of a C0 compiler: Code generation and implementation correctness. In *Int. Conf. on Software Engineering and Formal Methods (SEFM 2005)*, pages 2–11. IEEE, 2005.

[11] X. Leroy. Formal verification of a realistic compiler. *Commun. ACM*, 52(7):107–115, 2009.

[12] C. Luo and S. Qin. Separation Logic for Multiple Inheritance. *Electron. Notes Theor. Comput. Sci.*, 212:27–40, 2008.

[13] N. Myers. The empty member C++ optimization. *Dr Dobb's Journal*, Aug. 1997. URL `http://www.cantrip.org/emptyopt.html`.

[14] G. Ramalingam and H. Srinivasan. A member lookup algorithm for C++. In *Programming Language Design and Implementation (PLDI'97)*, pages 18–30. ACM, 1997.

[15] T. Ramananandro. Formal verification of object layout for C++ multiple inheritance – Coq development and supplementary material, 2010. URL `http://gallium.inria.fr/~tramanan/cxx/`.

[16] J. G. Rossie and D. P. Friedman. An algebraic semantics of subobjects. In *10th conf. on Object-Oriented Programming, Systems, Languages, and Applications (OOPSLA 1995)*, pages 187–199. ACM, 1995.

[17] P. F. Sweeney and M. G. Burke. Quantifying and evaluating the space overhead for alternative C++ memory layouts. *Software: Practice and Experience*, 33(7):595–636, 2003.

[18] H. Tuch. Formal verification of C systems code: Structured types, separation logic and theorem proving. *Journal of Automated Reasoning*, 42(2):125–187, 2009.

[19] D. Wasserrab, T. Nipkow, G. Snelting, and F. Tip. An operational semantics and type safety proof for multiple inheritance in C++. In *21st conf. on Object-Oriented Programming, Systems, Languages, and Applications (OOPSLA 2006)*, pages 345–362. ACM, 2006.

Static Analysis of Multi-Staged Programs via Unstaging Translation *

Wontae Choi
Seoul National University, Korea
wtchoi@ropas.snu.ac.kr

Baris Aktemur
UIUC, USA & Ozyegin University, Turkey
Baris.Aktemur@ozyegin.edu.tr

Kwangkeun Yi
Seoul National University, Korea
kwang@ropas.snu.ac.kr

Makoto Tatsuta
National Institute of Informatics, Japan
tatsuta@nii.ac.jp

Abstract

Static analysis of multi-staged programs is challenging because the basic assumption of conventional static analysis no longer holds: the program text itself is no longer a fixed static entity, but rather a dynamically constructed value. This article presents a semantic-preserving translation of multi-staged call-by-value programs into unstaged programs and a static analysis framework based on this translation. The translation is semantic-preserving in that every small-step reduction of a multi-staged program is simulated by the evaluation of its unstaged version. Thanks to this translation we can analyze multi-staged programs with existing static analysis techniques that have been developed for conventional unstaged programs: we first apply the unstaging translation, then we apply conventional static analysis to the unstaged version, and finally we cast the analysis results back in terms of the original staged program. Our translation handles staging constructs that have been evolved to be useful in practice (typified in Lisp's quasi-quotation): open code as values, unrestricted operations on references and intentional variable-capturing substitutions. This article omits references for which we refer the reader to our companion technical report.

Categories and Subject Descriptors D.3.1 [*Programming Languages*]: Formal Definitions and Theory; D.3.3 [*Programming Languages*]: Language Constructs and Features; F.3.2 [*Logics and Meanings of Programs*]: Semantics of Programming Languages—Program analysis

General Terms Languages, Theory

* This work was supported by the Engineering Research Center of Excellence Program of Korea Ministry of Education, Science and Technology(MEST)/National Research Foundation of Korea(NRF) (Grant 2010-0001717).

PoPL'11, January 26–28, Austin, Texas, USA.

Keywords Multi-staged languages, Static analysis, Unstaging translation, Semantics preservation, Abstract interpretation, Projection

1. Introduction

Staged programming, which explicitly divides a computation into separate stages, is a unifying principle for the existing program-generation systems. Partial evaluation [21, 12], runtime code generation [16, 32, 26, 28], function inlining, and macro expansion [35, 18], are all instances of staged computation.

There can be arbitrarily many stages, determined by the nesting depth of program generations: stage 0 is for conventional non-staged programs, and a program of stage 0 generates a program of stage 1 that generates a program of stage 2, and so on. A program of stage 1 can be brought to stage 0 for execution.

The key aspect of multi-staged languages is to have code templates (program fragments) as first-class values. Code templates are freely passed, stored, composed with code of other stages, and executed when appropriate. For this reason, multi-staged programming is also called "meta-programming."

Multi-staged programming is commonplace in mainstream programming. Lisp(or Scheme)'s quasi-quotation system [35, 18] is a fully fledged multi-staged system that has been evolved to comply with the demands from multi-staged programming practices. C's macros and C++'s templates are multi-staged features. C#, JavaScript, PHP, and Python support a form of multi-staged programming, albeit a limited one. MetaOcaml [36] and Template Haskell [33] are extensions to ML and Haskell respectively to support multi-staged programming.

However, static analysis of multi-staged programs (in order to, for example, find bugs or optimize) is mostly unexplored. Aside from static typing systems such as [25, 4, 13, 31, 3, 37], there are, as far as we know, no studies on more general and more powerful semantic-based static analysis (*á la* abstract interpretation) for multi-staged programs.

The primary obstacle is the fact that the basic assumption of conventional static analysis no longer holds: the program text itself is no longer a fixed static entity, but rather a dynamically constructed value. Conventional static analysis can finitely estimate the set of constructed code fragments, but we reach a stalemate after that. If the program executes the generated code, how can we statically analyze the execution? The program text to analyze at this stage is not a usual text but a finitely abstracted representation of the possibly infinite set of generated code.

Contribution

- As a solution to the problem, we present a semantic-preserving translation of multi-staged call-by-value programs into unstaged programs and a static analysis framework based on this translation. We prove the translation is semantic-preserving in that every small-step reduction of a multi-staged program is simulated by the evaluation of its unstaged version.

  Thanks to this translation we can analyze multi-staged programs with existing static analysis techniques that have been developed for conventional unstaged programs: we first apply the unstaging translation, then we apply conventional static analysis to the unstaged version, and finally we cast the analysis results back in terms of the original staged program.
- We present a framework of safely projecting the static analysis results of unstaged translated version back in terms of the original staged program. Once the projection's safety condition is satisfied, we can use conventional static analysis for the unstaged language to achieve a static analysis for the multi-staged language.
- Our semantic-preserving translation handles staging constructs that have been evolved to be useful in practice (typified in Lisp's quasi-quotation): open code as values, unrestricted operations on references, and intentional variable-capturing substitutions. This article omits references, for which we refer the reader to our companion technical report.

We illustrate the problem and our solution using an example program. In the example, we use Lisp's quasi-quote syntax [35] for staging constructs: backquote expression `` `e `` denotes program e as data (a program of the next stage), inside which, if any, comma expression $,e'$ replaces itself by the code result from evaluating e'.

1.1 Problem

For example, consider the following two-staged program.

```
x := `0;
repeat
   x := `(,x + 2)
until cond;
run x
```

Variable x initially has code `` `0 ``. The `repeat` statement repeatedly assigns a new code value to x. The expression `` `(,x + 2) `` becomes a code value by plugging x's current contents into the place of "$,x$". Thus after one iteration x contains `` `(0 + 2) ``, after two iterations `` `(0 + 2 + 2) ``, and so on. Finally `run` x evaluates the x's code and returns a non-negative even integer.

Now consider statically estimating the above program. In order to estimate the value of the "`run` x" expression we must estimate the set of possible code values that may be assigned to x. Suppose that the number of iterations of the repeat statement is statically undecidable. Then flow-insensitive static analysis, for example, must somehow finitely estimate the set of all possible, infinitely many code values

$$\{`0, `(0+2), `(0+2+2), \cdots\}.$$

To finitely approximate the infinite set of code, suppose we use grammar-based abstraction [7, 29, 5]. Then the set of code for x would be approximated by a grammar:

$$S \to 0 \mid S{+}2.$$

However, in order to analyze the code run by the "`run` x" expression (at least by conventional analyses for unstaged programs), every code implied by the grammar must be exposed first; that is, the grammar must be concretized. Since the concrete image has infinitely many code values, such analysis is unrealizable. A different static analysis technique that can evade such concretization trap is necessary.

1.2 Solution

As a solution to the problem, we present a three-step approach: translate, analyze, and project. To make this three-step approach correct, we prove the translation semantic-preserving: the translated unstaged version simulates every evaluation step of the original staged program. And we show a sound condition for the projection to be correct, i.e., to be aligned with the correspondence induced by the translation.

Here we will demonstrate these steps with the motivating example just presented. Exact definitions, lemmas and theorems are presented in Sections 2, 3 and 4.

- **Translation**: The above example program is translated as

```
x := λρ.0;
repeat
   x := (λh.(λρ.(h ρ)+2)) x
until cond;
(x {})
```

  The translation works as follows.

  - Code is translated into a function that explicitly takes a record (for its environment) as an argument:

    $$`0 \longmapsto \lambda\rho.0$$

    Hence, the run expression is translated into a function application:

    $$\texttt{run}\ `0 \longmapsto (\lambda\rho.0)\{\}$$

    The function is applied to an empty record because only closed code can be run.
  - Free variables inside a code are translated to record access expressions. For example,

    $$`x \longmapsto \lambda\rho.\rho{\cdot}x$$

  - Code composition `` `(,x + 2) `` is translated to a function(for the resulting code)-generating application whose actual parameter is the part for the code-to-be-plugged expression:

    $$`(,x\ +\ 2) \longmapsto (\lambda h.(\lambda\rho.(h\ \rho)+2))\ x$$

    The code value of x will be plugged into its corresponding hole (the place of "h"). The "$\lambda\rho.(h\ \rho)$+2" stands for the resulting code. The application "$(h\ \rho)$" is for capturing the code's, if any, free variables by the current environment.
  - The evaluation of the unstaged version simulates that of the original staged program. For example, after one iteration of the repeat statement, x has $\lambda\rho.((\lambda\rho.0)\rho)+2$. After two iterations, $\lambda\rho.((\lambda\rho.((\lambda\rho.0)\rho)+2)\rho)+2$, and so on. These functions correspond to code values `` `(0+2) `` and `` `(0+2+2) `` after the same numbers of iterations in the original staged program.

- **Analysis**: Because the translation removes all the staging features, we can apply conventional static analysis techniques to translated results.

  For example, suppose we estimate the values of expressions by a simple flow-insensitive value analysis with 0CFA. (We can apply any elaborate static analysis technique, but just for illustration this simple analysis is sufficient.) We present the analysis results in set-constraint style [19, 20]. We write V_i or V_x for the values of expression i and variable x respectively. Let us first label some expressions including lambdas:

```
x := λρ1.0;
repeat
   x := (λh.(λρ2.(h ρ2)1 + 2)) x
until cond;
(x {})2
```

The analysis will deduce set constraints as follows. For brevity, we write "$\lambda\rho_i$" omitting the body expression for lambdas (0CFA-closure values).

From the first assignment statement,

$$V_x \ni \lambda\rho_1.$$

From the assignment inside the repeat statement, V_x can also contain the value of the application "(λh...) x", i.e., λh's body expression's value, which is $\lambda\rho_2$. Hence

$$V_x \ni \lambda\rho_2.$$

The parameter binding in the application "(λh....) x" gives

$$V_h \ni V_x, \quad \text{hence} \quad V_h \ni \lambda\rho_1 \ \text{and}\ V_h \ni \lambda\rho_2.$$

Application expression "(h ρ_2)$_1$" has values of called functions' body expressions. The called functions would be V_h, which has $\lambda\rho_1$ and $\lambda\rho_2$. Thus,

$V_1 \ni 0$ (* V_h has $\lambda\rho_1$ and $\lambda\rho_1$'s body's value is 0 *)
$V_1 \ni V_1{+}2$. (* V_h has $\lambda\rho_2$ and $\lambda\rho_2$'s body's value is $V_1{+}2$ *)

Similarly, from the application expression "$(x\ \{\})_2$",

$V_2 \ni 0$ (* V_x has $\lambda\rho_1$ and $\lambda\rho_1$'s body's value is 0 *)
$V_2 \ni V_1{+}2$. (* V_x has $\lambda\rho_2$ and $\lambda\rho_2$'s body's value is $V_1{+}2$ *)

The above constraints can be understood as inductive rules for value sets. For example, the (infinite) sets V_1 and V_2 are inductively defined as follows:

$$V_1 \rightarrow 0 \mid V_1{+}2$$
$$V_2 \rightarrow 0 \mid V_1{+}2$$

Thus we can conclude that V_1 and V_2 consist of all non-negative even integers.

- **Projection**: Finally, the analysis results for the unstaged version need to be cast back in terms of the original staged program. Because code (backquote) expressions are translated into lambdas, some lambdas in the above example analysis' results correspond to the code expressions in the original staged program. For example, analysis result V_h for variable h has $\lambda\rho_1$ and $\lambda\rho_2$ which respectively correspond to code expressions '0 and '(,x + 2). That is, code to be plugged into the place of ",x" can be '0 and, recursively, '(,x + 2).

  It is straightforward to keep track of which lambdas in the unstaged version correspond to which code expression in the staged original. We can, for instance, assign parameter names of such lambdas from a unique namespace to identify the corresponding code expression, such as, $\lambda\rho_i$ for the lambda translated from code expression 'e_i of index i.

  Regarding the projections, we cannot use arbitrary ones. Arbitrary projections of the static analysis results of the translated program can have images that fail to qualify as static analysis results of the original staged program. Projection from abstract semantics of the translated program to that of the subject program must be a safe approximation of its concrete counterpart (projection from concrete semantics of the translated program to that of the subject program). Section 4 presents the formalization of this condition and an analysis example.

Comparisons

- Translation: Davies and Pfenning's unstaging translation [13] works only for closed code. Their translation does not support open code and intentional variable-capturing substitution at stages > 0 ("unhygienic" macros). This feature, which may be unacceptable in a purely functional language, has long been used in practice (for example by Lisp's quasi-quote programmers) for efficiency programming convenience. Kameyama et.al [23]'s translation supports open code but they do not provide an observational equivalence; hence it is not adequate for our purpose: a round-about static analysis approach for multi-staged programs.

  Our unstaging translation is a refinement of [1]. We prove only two kinds of administrative reductions suffice whose exhaustive application reaches the admin-normal form. We also define an inverse translation that converts expressions in the admin-normal form back to the original staged expression.
- Static analysis: Most static analyses for multi-staged programs are string analyses for programs that generate code as strings, but they are limited to estimate only the shape, not the semantics, of generated code by using a grammar [7, 29, 5] or the parsing stack [15]. Such string analyses do not analyze the semantics of the generated code string.

  Multi-staged static type systems [13, 37, 25, 40] and their inference algorithms can be considered sound static analyses, but extending them for analyzing other behavior than types (*á la* effect type systems [27, 22, 39]) is also constrained by the aforementioned infinite-concretization trap. Any extension to estimate other properties than types is limited to those that can proceed without analyzing the semantics of the generated code. Existing multi-staged static type systems can evade the infinite concretization trap because typing the execution of the generated code (for expression such as `run` e) does not have to analyze the generated code itself but can just pick up the type from the generated code's type.

1.3 Organization

Section 2 defines the subject call-by-value multi-staged language λ_S and the target unstaged record language $\lambda_{\mathcal{R}}$. Section 3 defines and proves semantic-preservation of the unstaging translation from λ_S to $\lambda_{\mathcal{R}}$. Section 4 presents a condition for safe projection. Section 5 discusses related works. Section 6 concludes.

2. Languages

In this section we give the formal definitions of the subject staged language λ_S and the target record language $\lambda_{\mathcal{R}}$. For each, we present the syntax, operational semantics and the type system.

2.1 Multi-Staged Language λ_S

The language λ_S is a typed, call-by-value λ-calculus with staging annotations. It is based on λ^{sim}_{open} [25], simplified by removing hygienic code composition (i.e. λ^*), mutable reference, and the lift operation. Also, the `unbox` operator is restricted to 1 stage. In this work our focus is not on polymorphism. Thus, we omit let-bindings from the syntax; we use them in the examples as a syntactic sugar for application.

Definitions

$$\begin{array}{ll} \mathit{Value}^0 & v^0 ::= i \mid \lambda x.e \mid \texttt{fix}\ f\ x.e \mid \texttt{box}\ v^1 \\ \mathit{Value}^n\ (n > 0) & v^n ::= i \mid x \mid \lambda x.v^n \mid v^n v^n \mid \texttt{fix}\ f\ x.v^n \\ & \quad \mid \texttt{box}\ v^{n+1} \mid \texttt{unbox}\ v^{n-1}\ (n > 1) \\ & \quad \mid \texttt{run}\ v^n \end{array}$$

Operational Semantics ($n \geq 0$)

$$\text{(APP)} \quad \frac{e_1 \xrightarrow{n} e_1'}{e_1\ e_2 \xrightarrow{n} e_1'\ e_2} \qquad \frac{e \xrightarrow{n} e' \quad v \in \mathit{Value}^n}{v\ e \xrightarrow{n} v\ e'}$$

$$(\lambda x.e)\ v \xrightarrow{0} [x \overset{0}{\mapsto} v]e$$

$$(\texttt{fix}\ f\ x.e)\ v \xrightarrow{0} [x \overset{0}{\mapsto} v][f \overset{0}{\mapsto} \texttt{fix}\ f\ x.e]e$$

$$\text{(BOX)} \quad \frac{e \xrightarrow{n+1} e'}{\texttt{box}\ e \xrightarrow{n} \texttt{box}\ e'}$$

$$\text{(RUN)} \quad \frac{e \xrightarrow{n} e'}{\texttt{run}\ e \xrightarrow{n} \texttt{run}\ e'} \qquad \frac{v \in \mathit{Value}^1 \quad FV_0(v) = \varnothing}{\texttt{run}\ (\texttt{box}\ v) \xrightarrow{0} v}$$

$$\text{(UNB)} \quad \frac{e \xrightarrow{n} e'}{\texttt{unbox}\ e \xrightarrow{n+1} \texttt{unbox}\ e'} \qquad \frac{v \in \mathit{Value}^1}{\texttt{unbox}\ (\texttt{box}\ v) \xrightarrow{1} v}$$

$$\text{(ABS)} \quad \frac{e \xrightarrow{n+1} e'}{\lambda x.e \xrightarrow{n+1} \lambda x.e'}$$

$$\text{(FIX)} \quad \frac{e \xrightarrow{n+1} e'}{\texttt{fix}\ f\ x.e \xrightarrow{n+1} \texttt{fix}\ f\ x.e'}$$

Figure 1. Operational Semantics of λ_S.

Syntax

$$\begin{array}{ll} \mathit{Variable} & x, y, f \in \mathit{Vars}_S \\ & \\ \mathit{Exprs}_S & e ::= i \mid x \mid \lambda x.e \mid e\ e \mid \texttt{fix}\ f\ x.e \\ & \quad \mid \texttt{box}\ e \mid \texttt{unbox}\ e \mid \texttt{run}\ e \end{array}$$

The syntax of λ_S is given above. The language contains constants, variables, lambda abstraction, application, and the fixpoint operator `fix`. Finally, there are staging annotations: `box` is used to define code templates. `unbox` is the escape operator that defines a "hole" inside a code template which is filled in with another code template. `box` and `unbox` operators can be arbitrarily nested. `run` executes a code template.

Operational Semantics

λ_S has a small-step, call-by-value, operational semantics. Evaluation rules of the language are in Figure 1. The evaluation $e \xrightarrow{n} e'$ has the meaning that "the expression e is evaluated to e' at stage n."

Values are expressions that cannot be reduced further. Values are defined for all stages. At stage 0, values are constants, functions and code templates. A code template is a frozen expression within a `box` annotation. Inside code templates, holes denoted by the `unbox` are filled in by evaluating the unboxed expression to a code template. In other words, code templates are composed using the `unbox` operator. Only stage-1 holes can be filled in. Once all the holes are filled, a code template becomes a box-value. A code template can be evaluated at stage 0 by `run`. Code to `run` must not have any free variable. $FV_0(e)$ in the (RUN) rule denotes the set of free variables in stage-0 expression e, to which none of e's sub-expression of stage > 0 contributes.

λ_S extends lambda calculus conservatively. At stage 0, (APP) is the same as the traditional substitution-based call-by-value semantics. Alpha conversion and beta reduction are available at stage-0.

$$\text{(CONt)} \quad \Gamma_0 \ldots \Gamma_n \vdash_S i : \iota$$

$$\text{(VARt)} \quad \frac{\Gamma_n(x) = \mathrm{T}}{\Gamma_0 \ldots \Gamma_n \vdash_S x : \mathrm{T}}$$

$$\text{(ABSt)} \quad \frac{\Gamma_0 \ldots \Gamma_n + \{x : \mathrm{T}_1\} \vdash_S e : \mathrm{T}_2}{\Gamma_0 \ldots \Gamma_n \vdash_S \lambda x.e : \mathrm{T}_1 \to \mathrm{T}_2}$$

$$\text{(FIXt)} \quad \frac{\Gamma_0 \ldots \Gamma_n + \{x : \mathrm{T}_1\} + \{f : \mathrm{T}_1 \to \mathrm{T}_2\} \vdash_S e : \mathrm{T}_2}{\Gamma_0 \ldots \Gamma_n \vdash_S \texttt{fix}\ f\ x.e : \mathrm{T}_1 \to \mathrm{T}_2}$$

$$\text{(APPt)} \quad \frac{\Gamma_0 \ldots \Gamma_n \vdash_S e_1 : \mathrm{T}_1 \to \mathrm{T}_2 \quad \Gamma_0 \ldots \Gamma_n \vdash_S e_2 : \mathrm{T}_1}{\Gamma_0 \ldots \Gamma_n \vdash_S e_1\ e_2 : \mathrm{T}_2}$$

$$\text{(BOXt)} \quad \frac{\Gamma_0 \ldots \Gamma_n, \Gamma \vdash_S e : \mathrm{T}}{\Gamma_0 \ldots \Gamma_n \vdash_S \texttt{box}\ e : \Box(\Gamma \rhd \mathrm{T})}$$

$$\text{(UNBt)} \quad \frac{\Gamma_0 \ldots \Gamma_n \vdash_S e : \Box(\Gamma_{n+1} \rhd \mathrm{T})}{\Gamma_0 \ldots \Gamma_n, \Gamma_{n+1} \vdash_S \texttt{unbox}\ e : \mathrm{T}}$$

$$\text{(RUNt)} \quad \frac{\Gamma_0 \ldots \Gamma_n \vdash_S e : \Box(\varnothing \rhd \mathrm{T})}{\Gamma_0 \ldots \Gamma_n \vdash_S \texttt{run}\ e : \mathrm{T}}$$

Figure 2. Type System of λ_S.

Type System

Figure 2 shows a monomorphic type system for λ_S. A polymorphic type system is also available [25]. Types in λ_S are defined as below.

$$\begin{array}{lll} \mathit{Types}_S & \mathrm{T} & ::= \iota \mid \mathrm{T} \to \mathrm{T} \mid \Box(\Gamma \rhd \mathrm{T}) \\ \mathit{Type\ Environments}_S & \Gamma & \in \mathit{Vars}_S \overset{fin}{\to} \mathit{Types}_S \end{array}$$

We use T to denote type terms, ι for base types, $\mathrm{T} \to \mathrm{T}$ for function types, $\Box(\Gamma \rhd \mathrm{T})$ for code template types, Γ for type environments. A code template is given a box-type $\Box(\Gamma \rhd \mathrm{T})$ with the meaning that "the code template will evaluate to a value of type T if put in a context that provides the environment Γ." The type environment Γ in the box-type $\Box(\Gamma \rhd \mathrm{T})$ contains the types of the unbound variables in the code template.

A type environment Γ is a mapping from variables to types. $\Gamma + \{x : \mathrm{T}\}$ is a function update operation that defines a function as follows: $(\Gamma + \{x : \mathrm{T}\})(x) = \mathrm{T}$ and $(\Gamma + \{y : \mathrm{T}\})(x) = \Gamma(x)$ if $x \neq y$. A typing judgment has the form $\Gamma_0 \ldots \Gamma_n \vdash_S e : \mathrm{T}$ with the meaning that "a stage-n expression e, under type environments $\Gamma_0 \ldots \Gamma_n$, has type T." $\Gamma_0 \ldots \Gamma_n$ is a sequence of type environments. Each type environment corresponds to a stage where Γ_n is the current (i.e. most recent) type environment. For a proof of the soundness of this type system and its let-polymorphic extension, see [25].

2.2 The Record Calculus $\lambda_{\mathcal{R}}$

The language $\lambda_{\mathcal{R}}$ is a λ-calculus with record operations. As the target language of our translation, it is sufficient for the record expression to have only variables and values. As opposed to λ_S, we include let-bindings in $\lambda_{\mathcal{R}}$. This is to be able to syntactically distinguish several $\lambda_{\mathcal{R}}$ expressions during inverse translation (Section 3.3). The language is still monomorphic.

Syntax

$$\begin{array}{llll} \mathit{Variable} & \rho & \in & \mathit{Var}_P \quad \text{(record variables)} \\ & h & \in & \mathit{Var}_H \quad \text{(hole variables)} \\ & x, y, f & \in & \mathit{Var}_X = \mathit{Vars}_S \quad \text{(ordinary variables)} \\ & w & \in & \mathit{Var}_{\mathcal{R}} = \mathit{Var}_X \cup \mathit{Var}_P \cup \mathit{Var}_H \\ & & & \\ \mathit{Label} & \mathtt{x} & \in & \mathit{Label} = \{\mathtt{x} \mid x \in \mathit{Var}_X\} \\ & & & \quad \text{(ordinary variables in typewriter font)} \end{array}$$

Operational Semantics

$$(\text{APP}_{\mathcal{R}})\quad \frac{e_1 \xrightarrow{\mathcal{R}} e_1'}{e_1\ e_2 \xrightarrow{\mathcal{R}} e_1'\ e_2} \qquad \frac{e \xrightarrow{\mathcal{R}} e'}{v\ e \xrightarrow{\mathcal{R}} v\ e'}$$

$$(\lambda w.e)\ v \xrightarrow{\mathcal{R}} [w \mapsto v]e$$

$$(\texttt{fix}\ f\ x.e)\ v \xrightarrow{\mathcal{R}} [x \mapsto v][f \mapsto \texttt{fix}\ f\ x.e]e$$

$$(\text{LET}_{\mathcal{R}})\quad \frac{e_1 \xrightarrow{\mathcal{R}} e_1'}{\texttt{let}\ w = e_1\ \texttt{in}\ e_2 \xrightarrow{\mathcal{R}} \texttt{let}\ w = e_1'\ \texttt{in}\ e_2}$$

$$\texttt{let}\ w = v\ \texttt{in}\ e \xrightarrow{\mathcal{R}} [w \mapsto v]e$$

$$(\text{ACC}_{\mathcal{R}})\quad v_r \cdot \texttt{x} \xrightarrow{\mathcal{R}} v_r(\texttt{x})$$

Record Lookup

$$v_r(\texttt{x}) = \begin{cases} v & \text{if } v_r = v_r' + \{\texttt{x} = v\} \\ v_r'(\texttt{x}) & \text{if } v_r = v_r' + \{\texttt{y} = \_\} \text{ and } \texttt{x} \neq \texttt{y} \end{cases}$$

Figure 3. Operational Semantics of $\lambda_{\mathcal{R}}$.

$$(\text{CONt}_{\mathcal{R}})\quad \Gamma \vdash_{\mathcal{R}} i : \iota$$

$$(\text{VARt}_{\mathcal{R}})\quad \frac{\Gamma(w) = \texttt{T}}{\Gamma \vdash_{\mathcal{R}} w : \texttt{T}}$$

$$(\text{ABSt}_{\mathcal{R}})\quad \frac{\Gamma + \{w : \texttt{T}_1\} \vdash_{\mathcal{R}} e : \texttt{T}_2}{\Gamma \vdash_{\mathcal{R}} \lambda w.e : \texttt{T}_1 \to \texttt{T}_2}$$

$$(\text{FIXt}_{\mathcal{R}})\quad \frac{\Gamma + \{x : \texttt{T}_1\} + \{f : \texttt{T}_1 \to \texttt{T}_2\} \vdash_{\mathcal{R}} e : \texttt{T}_2}{\Gamma \vdash_{\mathcal{R}} \texttt{fix}\ f\ x.e : \texttt{T}_1 \to \texttt{T}_2}$$

$$(\text{APPt}_{\mathcal{R}})\quad \frac{\Gamma \vdash_{\mathcal{R}} e_1 : \texttt{T}_1 \to \texttt{T}_2 \quad \Gamma \vdash_{\mathcal{R}} e_2 : \texttt{T}_1}{\Gamma \vdash_{\mathcal{R}} e_1\ e_2 : \texttt{T}_2}$$

$$(\text{LETt}_{\mathcal{R}})\quad \frac{\Gamma \vdash_{\mathcal{R}} e_1 : \texttt{T}_1 \quad \Gamma + \{w : \texttt{T}_1\} \vdash_{\mathcal{R}} e_2 : \texttt{T}_2}{\Gamma \vdash_{\mathcal{R}} \texttt{let}\ w = e_1\ \texttt{in}\ e_2 : \texttt{T}_2}$$

$$(\text{EMPt}_{\mathcal{R}})\quad \Gamma \vdash_{\mathcal{R}} \{\} : \varnothing$$

$$(\text{UPDt}_{\mathcal{R}})\quad \frac{\Gamma \vdash_{\mathcal{R}} r : \texttt{T}_r \quad \Gamma \vdash_{\mathcal{R}} e : \texttt{T}}{\Gamma \vdash_{\mathcal{R}} r + \{\texttt{x} = e\} : \texttt{T}_r + \{\texttt{x} : \texttt{T}\}}$$

$$(\text{ACCt}_{\mathcal{R}})\quad \frac{\Gamma \vdash_{\mathcal{R}} r : \texttt{T}_r \quad \texttt{T}_r(\texttt{x}) = \texttt{T}}{\Gamma \vdash_{\mathcal{R}} r \cdot \texttt{x} : \texttt{T}}$$

Figure 4. Type System of $\lambda_{\mathcal{R}}$.

$$\begin{array}{lll} \mathit{Expr}_{\mathcal{R}} & e & ::= i \mid w \mid \lambda w.e \mid e\ e \mid \texttt{fix}\ f\ x.e \\ & & \mid r \mid r \cdot \texttt{x} \mid \texttt{let}\ w = e\ \texttt{in}\ e \\ \mathit{Value}_{\mathcal{R}} & v & ::= i \mid \lambda w.e \mid \texttt{fix}\ f\ x.e \mid v_r \\ \mathit{Record\ Value}_{\mathcal{R}} & v_r & ::= \{\} \mid v_r + \{\texttt{x} = v\} \\ \mathit{Record}_{\mathcal{R}} & r & ::= \{\} \mid \rho \mid r + \{\texttt{x} = x\} \mid r + \{\texttt{x} = v\} \end{array}$$

The record language $\lambda_{\mathcal{R}}$ has constants (i), variables (x), lambda abstractions, applications, a fixpoint operator `fix`, and let-expressions. As for the record operations there are empty records ($\{\}$), record variables (ρ), and the record update operation $r + \{\texttt{x} = \_\}$. For field names (or labels) in records, we use variables written in teletype font.

We separate variables into three disjoint sets: ordinary variables Var_X (which are the same as variables of λ_S), record variables Var_P, and hole variables Var_H. This syntactic distinction makes our presentation of the inverse translation in Section 3.3 easier. The operational semantics does not need to make a distinction; all variables are treated uniformly.

Operational Semantics

$\lambda_{\mathcal{R}}$ has a small-step, call-by-value operational semantics. The evaluation $e \xrightarrow{\mathcal{R}} e'$ means that "the expression e evaluates to expression e'". The operational semantics of $\lambda_{\mathcal{R}}$ is mostly standard. Evaluation rules and the definition of values are given in Figure 3.

Type System

A monomorphic type system for $\lambda_{\mathcal{R}}$ is given in Figure 4. Types are defined as follows:

$$\begin{array}{lll} \mathit{Type}_{\mathcal{R}} & \texttt{T} & ::= \iota \mid \texttt{T} \to \texttt{T} \mid \texttt{T}_r \\ \mathit{Record\ Type} & \texttt{T}_r & \in \mathit{Label} \xrightarrow{fin} \mathit{Type}_{\mathcal{R}} \\ \mathit{Type\ Environment}_{\mathcal{R}} & \Gamma & \in \mathit{Var}_{\mathcal{R}} \xrightarrow{fin} \mathit{Type}_{\mathcal{R}} \end{array}$$

There are base type and function types as usual. A record type is a mapping from field labels to types. Type environments are similar to those for λ_S.

3. Translation

In this section we present how staged expressions can be represented with record calculus expressions.

We begin with an observation: Boxed expressions are not executed – they remain frozen – until they are `run`. This notion is very similar to closures; closures are not executed until they are applied to an operand. This observation hints that boxed expressions can be represented as functions.

The second observation is that when an unboxed expression is replaced with a code template (see rule UNB in the operational semantics), the free variables in the code template may be captured by the surrounding expression. In other words, the surrounding boxed expression provides the code template with an environment that carries the "meaning" of the free variables in the code template. Combining the two observations, we can then represent a boxed expression as a function whose parameter is an environment. Providing an environment to a boxed expression (as in the case of unboxing) is then nothing but a function application where the operator is the boxed expression and the operand is the environment.

The next question is how to represent environments. The answer is trivial: as records. A variable occurrence then becomes a lookup in the current environment (i.e. record), and a binding is an update to the current environment (i.e. record).

Our translation at the type level translates code expression of type $\square(\Gamma \triangleright \texttt{T})$ into function expression of type $\underline{\Gamma} \to \underline{\texttt{T}}$, where $\underline{\Gamma}$ is a record type for Γ and $\underline{\texttt{T}}$ is a translated type for $\texttt{T}$.

To give a few examples, consider the expression `box` x. It can be represented as $\lambda\rho.\rho \cdot \texttt{x}$, where the value of `x` is being obtained from the environment ρ. The expression

$$\texttt{box}\ (\texttt{let}\ x = 42\ \texttt{in}\ \texttt{unbox}\ (\texttt{box}\ x))$$

can be represented as

$$\lambda\rho'.(\lambda\rho.\rho \cdot \texttt{x})\{\texttt{x} = 42\}.$$

Note how the `unbox` expression becomes a function application. As a special case, `run` becomes an application where the argument

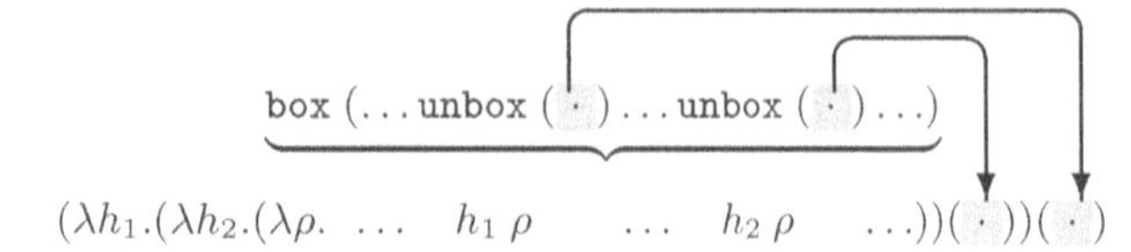

Figure 5. Illustration of the translation of a box expression with two unboxes.

is the empty environment, because only closed expressions can be executed. For example, **run** (box 42) becomes $(\lambda\rho.42)\{\}$.

To illustrate how variable capturing is handled, let us now take the following example.

$$\begin{array}{ll} \texttt{let} & a = \texttt{box}\ x \\ & b = \texttt{box}\ (\lambda x.\lambda y.(\texttt{unbox}\ a)+y) \\ \texttt{in} & (\texttt{run}\ b)\ 1\ 1 \end{array}$$

In the example, the value of b will be box $(\lambda x.\lambda y.x+y)$. Note how the variable x, which was free in box x, is captured. Continuing the evaluation, **run** b will reduce to the function $\lambda x.\lambda y.x+y$, resulting in a final value of 2.

Based on the translation described, the example above is translated as below:

$$\begin{array}{ll} \texttt{let} & a = \lambda\rho.\rho\cdot\mathrm{x} \\ & b = \lambda\rho.\lambda x.\lambda y.(a\ (\rho + \{\mathrm{x}=x, \mathrm{y}=y\}))+y \\ \texttt{in} & (b\ \{\})\ 1\ 1 \end{array}$$

Both box expressions are converted to a function that takes as parameter an environment, ρ. In the first line, the occurrence of x is free. So it is translated to a lookup operation in ρ. The occurrence of y in the second line is not free, hence it is left as it is. The unbox expression becomes a function application where the operand is the environment ρ updated with the bindings of x and y. Finally, the run expression is translated to an application to the empty record. When evaluated, the translation reduces to 2, too.

Order of Evaluation

In the staged calculus, unbox expressions inside box are evaluated to code templates. When translated to record calculus as discussed above, however, the contents of a box become guarded under a lambda abstraction and hence are not evaluated. Consider the following example

$$\begin{array}{l} \texttt{box}\ (\texttt{unbox}\ ((\lambda x.x)\ \texttt{box}\ 1)) \\ \xrightarrow{0} \texttt{box}\ (\texttt{unbox}\ (\texttt{box}\ 1)) \\ \xrightarrow{0} \texttt{box}\ 1 \end{array}$$

The translation of box (unbox $((\lambda x.x)$ box 1)) would be $\lambda\rho.((\lambda x.x)\ \lambda\rho.1)\rho$, which is already a value and does not evaluate further. So, the order of evaluation (in the call-by-value semantics) is perturbed by the translation. This would incur a serious problem in the presence of expressions with side-effects.

To preserve the order of evaluation, the translation has to move the expression inside unbox to the outside of the enclosing box, as illustrated in Figure 5. To do this, every unbox expression is replaced with a *hole variable* h and a *context* in the form of $(\lambda h.[\cdot])\ \underline{e}$, where $\underline{e}$ is the translation of the unboxed expression, is created so that the inside of the context can be filled in with the translation of the enclosing box. Because $\underline{e}$ is at the argument position of a function, the call-by-value semantics of the record calculus evaluates $\underline{e}$ first and then handles the rest. The correct translation of the example above is $(\lambda h.\lambda\rho.h\ \rho)\ ((\lambda x.x)\ \lambda\rho.1)$.

Our translation to preserve the order of evaluation is similar to Davies and Pfenning's [13]. They suggested the translation from the implicit modal language Mini-ML$^{\Box}$, which is similar to λ_S, to the explicit modal language Mini-ML$_e^{\Box}$. Their target language is still staged whereas ours is the record language with no staging. Kameyama et.al [23] also developed a similar translation that translates 2-staged programs to System F with tuples. More details on the related work are given in Section 5.

Admin Reductions

Let us examine the evaluation of the expression above in small steps.

$$\begin{array}{l} (\lambda h.\lambda\rho.h\ \rho)\ ((\lambda x.x)\ \lambda\rho.1) \\ \xrightarrow{\mathcal{R}} (\lambda h.\lambda\rho.(h\ \rho))\ (\lambda\rho.1) \\ \xrightarrow{\mathcal{R}} \lambda\rho.((\lambda\rho.1)\ \rho) \end{array}$$

The final value, $\lambda\rho.((\lambda\rho.1)\ \rho)$, is not directly the translation of box 1; there is still a reducible term, $(\lambda\rho.1)\ \rho$, inside a lambda. This residual term is seen because of the following fact: In the staged calculus, when an unbox expression evaluates to a code template, the code template immediately (i.e. in one step) replaces the unbox expression. On the other hand, in the record calculus, the unbox expression becomes an argument to a function, in which the argument is applied to an environment. Passing the argument to the function takes one step of evaluation (i.e. substitution). The application of the argument to the environment still remains, and is, in fact, the residual term that needs to be reduced via further action. This kind of a reduction is called an "admin reduction". Admin reductions simplify the record calculus terms and bring them to a form that is the direct result of a translation. In general, beta-reduction of an application where the operator is a lambda expression and the operand is a record is an admin reduction; this reduction may happen anywhere, including inside lambda abstractions. The example above is admin-reduced as follows, where the admin-reducible term is underlined. Note that the resulting term, $\lambda\rho.1$, is directly the translation of box 1.

$$\lambda\rho.(\underline{(\lambda\rho.1)\ \rho}) \xrightarrow{\mathcal{A}} \lambda\rho.1$$

There are two kinds of admin reductions. The first is the one explained above. The second is related to variable capture. Recall that when a code template replaces an unbox expression, the free variables are captured. A free variable becomes a lookup expression in the current environment after the translation. Such lookups need to be resolved (after a hole replacement). This is done by the second kind of admin reduction. Figure 6 shows a trace that belongs to the first example given in this section. Both kinds of admin reductions are used. Admin-reducible terms are again underlined. Figure 7 shows the evaluation of the original staged expression. Note that any term in Figure 7 translates to a term in Figure 6.

The formal definitions of the translation and admin reductions are given in the next section.

3.1 Translation Definition

The translation is presented in Figure 8. A translation judgment has the form $R \vdash e \mapsto (\underline{e}, K)$ with the meaning that "a λ_S expression e, under *environment stack* R, translates to the $\lambda_{\mathcal{R}}$ expression $\underline{e}$ and the *context stack* K."

An *environment* is a subset of a record expression that associates fields to variables. It keeps the information of which variables have been bound so far. Each stage has a corresponding environment, held in the environment stack. Hence, the translation of a stage-n expression involves a stack of length $n+1$. The rightmost (or topmost) environment in the stack corresponds to the current stage.

An expression that binds a variable updates the environment with the new binding. Lambda abstraction and **fix** are such ex-

$\mathtt{let}\ a\ =\ \lambda\rho.\rho\cdot\mathtt{x}$
$\quad\ \ b\ =\ (\lambda h.\lambda\rho.\lambda x.\lambda y.(h\ (\rho + \{\mathtt{x}=x, \mathtt{y}=y\}))+y)a$
$\mathtt{in}\ \ (b\ \{\})\ 1\ 1$
$\xrightarrow{\mathcal{R}}$
$\mathtt{let}\ b\ =\ (\lambda h.\lambda\rho.\lambda x.\lambda y.(h\ (\rho + \{\mathtt{x}=x, \mathtt{y}=y\}))+y)(\lambda\rho.\rho\cdot\mathtt{x})$
$\mathtt{in}\ \ (b\ \{\})\ 1\ 1$
$\xrightarrow{\mathcal{R}}$
$\mathtt{let}\ b\ =\ \lambda\rho.\lambda x.\lambda y.\underline{((\lambda\rho.\rho\cdot\mathtt{x})\ (\rho + \{\mathtt{x}=x, \mathtt{y}=y\}))}+y$
$\mathtt{in}\ \ (b\ \{\})\ 1\ 1$
$\xrightarrow{\mathcal{A}}$
$\mathtt{let}\ b\ =\ \lambda\rho.\lambda x.\lambda y.(\underline{((\rho + \{\mathtt{x}=x, \mathtt{y}=y\})\cdot\mathtt{x})})+y$
$\mathtt{in}\ \ (b\ \{\})\ 1\ 1$
$\xrightarrow{\mathcal{A}}$
$\mathtt{let}\ b\ =\ \lambda\rho.\lambda x.\lambda y.x+y$
$\mathtt{in}\ \ (b\ \{\})\ 1\ 1$
$\xrightarrow{\mathcal{R}} ((\lambda\rho.\lambda x.\lambda y.x+y)\ \{\})\ 1\ 1$
$\xrightarrow{\mathcal{R}} (\lambda x.\lambda y.x+y)\ 1\ 1$
$\xrightarrow{\mathcal{R}} (\lambda y.1+y)\ 1$
$\xrightarrow{\mathcal{R}} 1+1$
$\xrightarrow{\mathcal{R}} 2$

Figure 6. Reduction trace of the example expression after the unstaging translation. Admin-reducible terms are underlined.

$\mathtt{let}\ a\ =\ \mathtt{box}\ x$
$\quad\ \ b\ =\ \mathtt{box}\ (\lambda x.\lambda y.(\mathtt{unbox}\ a)+y)$
$\mathtt{in}\ \ (\mathtt{run}\ b)\ 1\ 1$
$\xrightarrow{0}$
$\mathtt{let}\ b\ =\ \mathtt{box}\ (\lambda x.\lambda y.(\mathtt{unbox}\ (\mathtt{box}\ x))+y)$
$\mathtt{in}\ \ (\mathtt{run}\ b)\ 1\ 1$
$\xrightarrow{0}$
$\mathtt{let}\ b\ =\ \mathtt{box}\ (\lambda x.\lambda y.x+y)$
$\mathtt{in}\ \ (\mathtt{run}\ b)\ 1\ 1$
$\xrightarrow{0} (\mathtt{run}\ (\mathtt{box}\ (\lambda x.\lambda y.x+y)))\ 1\ 1$
$\xrightarrow{0} (\lambda x.\lambda y.x+y)\ 1\ 1$
$\xrightarrow{0} (\lambda y.1+y)\ 1$
$\xrightarrow{0} 1+1$
$\xrightarrow{0} 2$

Figure 7. Reduction trace of the example staged expression. Any term in this trace translates to a term in Figure 6.

Definitions

Environment	$r ::= \{\} \mid \rho \mid r+\{\mathtt{x}=x\}$
Environment Stack	$R ::= \bot \mid R, r$
Context	$\kappa ::= ((\lambda h.[\cdot])\ \underline{e}) \mid ((\lambda h.\kappa)\ \underline{e})$
Context Stack	$K ::= \bot \mid K, \kappa$

Environment Lookup

$$r(\mathtt{x}) = \begin{cases} x & \text{if } r = r'+\{\mathtt{x}=x\} \\ r'(\mathtt{x}) & \text{if } r = r'+\{\mathtt{y}=\_\} \text{ and } \mathtt{x} \neq \mathtt{y} \\ \rho\cdot\mathtt{x} & \text{if } r = \rho \end{cases}$$

Term Translation

(TCON) $$R \vdash i \mapsto (i, \bot)$$

(TVAR) $$R, r \vdash x \mapsto (r(\mathtt{x}), \bot)$$

(TABS) $$\frac{R, r+\{\mathtt{x}=x\} \vdash e \mapsto (\underline{e}, K)}{R, r \vdash \lambda x.e \mapsto (\lambda x.\underline{e}, K)}$$

(TFIX) $$\frac{R, r+\{\mathtt{x}=x\}+\{\mathtt{f}=f\} \vdash e \mapsto (\underline{e}, K)}{R, r \vdash \mathtt{fix}\ f\ x.e \mapsto (\mathtt{fix}\ f\ x.\underline{e}, K)}$$

(TAPP) $$\frac{R \vdash e_1 \mapsto (\underline{e_1}, K_1) \quad R \vdash e_2 \mapsto (\underline{e_2}, K_2)}{R \vdash e_1\ e_2 \mapsto (\underline{e_1}\ \underline{e_2}, K_1 \bowtie K_2)}$$

(TBOX) $$\frac{R, \rho \vdash e \mapsto (\underline{e}, (K, \kappa))}{R \vdash \mathtt{box}\ e \mapsto (\kappa[\lambda\rho.\underline{e}], K)}\ \text{new } \rho$$

$$\frac{R, \rho \vdash e \mapsto (\underline{e}, \bot)}{R \vdash \mathtt{box}\ e \mapsto (\lambda\rho.\underline{e}, \bot)}\ \text{new } \rho$$

(TUNB) $$\frac{R \vdash e \mapsto (\underline{e}, K)}{R, r \vdash \mathtt{unbox}\ e \mapsto (h\ r, (K, (\lambda h.[\cdot])\ \underline{e}))}\ \text{new } h$$

(TRUN) $$\frac{R \vdash e \mapsto (\underline{e}, K)}{R \vdash \mathtt{run}\ e \mapsto (\mathtt{let}\ \ h = \underline{e}\ \mathtt{in}\ (h\{\}), K)}\ \text{new } h$$

Context Stack Merge Operator

$$\bot \bowtie K = K$$
$$K \bowtie \bot = K$$
$$(K_1, \kappa_1) \bowtie (K_2, \kappa_2) = (K_1 \bowtie K_2), (\kappa_1[\kappa_2])$$

Figure 8. Translation from $\lambda_{\mathcal{S}}$ to $\lambda_{\mathcal{K}}$.

pressions (see rules TABS and TFIX). A box expression starts a new environment by putting a fresh environment variable on top of the environment stack. Dually, unbox chops off the topmost environment from the stack.

The notion of a *context* was informally discussed in the previous section. A context $((\lambda h.[\cdot])\ \underline{e})$ corresponds to unbox e where $\underline{e}$ is the translation of the unboxed expression e. Contexts are used for putting the unboxed expression outside their enclosing box expressions so that the evaluation order is preserved. The variable that a context binds, that is h, is a fresh variable that replaces the original unbox in the translation. Note that there may be multiple unbox expressions at a particular stage, e.g. box (unbox (e_1) + unbox (e_2)). Therefore, contexts are defined recursively, as in $((\lambda h.\kappa)\ \underline{e})$. This way, a context is able to keep information about multiple unbox expressions in a stage, while still preserving their relative order of evaluation. Also note that unbox expressions can be nested, e.g. box (box (unbox (unbox e))). The translation, therefore, produces context stacks instead of a single context. Each context in the stack corresponds to a stage. The contexts in a stack are positioned in the following order: The context of the stage that is immediately lower than the current stage is positioned at the rightmost side; stages go lower (i.e. get closer to 0) as we go left. The stage closest to 0 is located at the leftmost side of the stack.

New contexts in the translation are populated by unbox expressions (see rule TUNB). A fresh hole variable is also generated as a placeholder for the unboxed expression. The translation of a box expression pulls the topmost context from the stack and puts the translated expression inside this context. The translation of expressions with no subexpressions (e.g. variables) results in empty context stacks, since there are no unbox contained within the expression. The translation of expressions with single subexpressions (e.g. abstraction) simply threads the context stack that results from the translation of the subexpression. The translation of expressions with more than one subexpression (e.g. application) merges the context stacks resulting from the translation of subexpressions. A context stack merge operation respects the order of appearance, hence serves the preservation of the order of evaluation.

When discussing the translation informally, we converted run to a function application, but in the formal definition we translate to a let-expression. The difference is merely syntactic; we want to be able to distinguish translations of `run` from `unbox` so that the inverse translation can properly translate expressions back.

3.2 Semantics Preservation

In this section we formally make the connection between semantics of λ_S and $\lambda_\mathcal{R}$ through the translation. For complete proofs for lemmas and theorems, we refer the reader to the companion technical report [6].

Recall that a translation yields a pair of an expression and a context stack. This pair can be constructed into a single expression using a context closure operation:

Definition 1. *(Context Closure) Let e be a $\lambda_\mathcal{R}$ expression and K be a context stack. The context closure $K(e)$ is defined as follows.*

$$K(e) = \begin{cases} K'(\kappa[e]) & \text{if } K = (K', \kappa) \\ e & \text{if } K = \bot \end{cases}$$

In Section 3 we discussed the need for admin reductions; here we give the formal definition:

Definition 2. *(Admin Reduction) Administrative reduction of an expression is a congruence closure of the following two rules:*

$$\textit{(APP)} \quad (\lambda\rho.e)\ r \xrightarrow{\mathcal{A}} [\rho \mapsto r]e$$

$$\textit{(ACC)} \quad \frac{r \neq \rho}{r \cdot \mathtt{x} \xrightarrow{\mathcal{A}} r(\mathtt{x})}$$

The definition of administrative reductions also extends to contexts and context stacks.

Note that an administrative reduction may happen anywhere, even under lambdas. Also note that an admin reduction is "safe" to perform, in the sense that no side-effecting or non-terminating expression is eliminated by an admin reduction. It is also straightforward to check that admin reductions terminate.

Definition 3. *(Admin-normal form) An expression e is said to be in admin-normal form iff there does <u>not</u> exist any e' such that $e \xrightarrow{\mathcal{A}} e'$.*

An important observation is that a translated expression does not contain any admin-reducible terms:

Lemma 1. *Let e be a λ_S expression such that $R \vdash e \mapsto (\underline{e}, K)$ for some R. Then, $K(\underline{e})$ is in admin-normal form.*

Proof. By structural induction on e [6]. □

Notation 1. *The Kleene closure of admin reductions is denoted as $\xrightarrow{\mathcal{A}^*}$.*

Notation 2. *We use $\xrightarrow{\mathcal{R};\mathcal{A}^*}$ to denote sequential application of one step of eager evaluation followed by <u>exhaustive</u> administrative reductions. Exhaustive admin reductions are those that bring an expression to the admin-normal form.*

Next, we show the relation between the operational semantics of λ_S and $\lambda_\mathcal{R}$: Given a λ_S expression e, we can first translate e, then evaluate it in record language semantics followed by application of admin reductions, and we will have obtained the translation of the expression that e evaluates to in the staged semantics. Furthermore, the admin reductions that we apply are exhaustive; we do not need to worry about oversimplification. This relation is formally stated in Theorem 1 and illustrated in Figure 9.

Two properties are critical to prove the semantic preservation. First, the translation preserves the substitution operation.

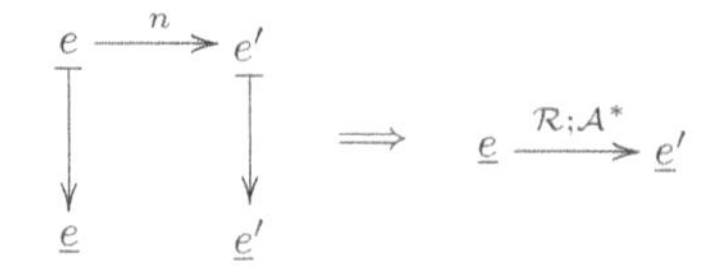

Figure 9. Relation between λ_S and $\lambda_\mathcal{R}$ operational semantics.

Type Term

$$\iota \mapsto \iota \qquad \frac{\mathrm{T}_1 \mapsto \underline{\mathrm{T}_1} \quad \mathrm{T}_2 \mapsto \underline{\mathrm{T}_2}}{\mathrm{T}_1 \to \mathrm{T}_2 \mapsto \underline{\mathrm{T}_1} \to \underline{\mathrm{T}_2}} \qquad \frac{\Gamma \mapsto \mathrm{T_r} \quad \mathrm{T} \mapsto \underline{\mathrm{T}}}{\Box(\Gamma \rhd \mathrm{T}) \mapsto \mathrm{T_r} \to \underline{\mathrm{T}}}$$

Record Type Term

$$\frac{\Gamma \mapsto \mathrm{T_r} \quad \mathrm{T} \mapsto \underline{\mathrm{T}}}{\Gamma + x : \mathrm{T} \mapsto \mathrm{T_r} + \{\mathrm{x} : \underline{\mathrm{T}}\}} \qquad \varnothing \mapsto \varnothing$$

Figure 10. Type Translation.

Lemma 2. *(Substitution Preservation) Assume e_1 is a stage-n λ_S expression, e_2 is a stage-0 λ_S expression with no free variables. Let $r_0 \ldots r_n \vdash e_1 \mapsto (\underline{e_1}, \kappa_p \ldots \kappa_1)$ for $p \leq n$ and $\{\} \vdash e_2 \mapsto (\underline{e_2}, \bot)$ where r_0 is such that $r_0(\mathtt{x}) = x$ for some variable x. Then*

- *If $n = 0$ then $r_0 \vdash [x \overset{0}{\mapsto} e_2]e_1 \mapsto ([x \mapsto \underline{e_2}]\underline{e_1}, \bot)$.*
- *If $n > p$ then $r_0 \ldots r_n \vdash [x \overset{n}{\mapsto} e_2]e_1 \mapsto (\underline{e_1}, \kappa_p \ldots \kappa_1)$.*
- *If $n = p$ then $r_0 \ldots r_n \vdash [x \overset{n}{\mapsto} e_2]e_1 \mapsto (\underline{e_1}, (\kappa_p', \kappa_{p-1} \ldots \kappa_1))$ where $\kappa_p' = [x \mapsto \underline{e_2}]\kappa_p$.*

Proof. By structural induction on expression e_1 [6]. □

Second, the translation preserves the variable-capturing reduction which happens in λ_S because of open code.

Lemma 3. *(Variable-Capturing Preservation) Assume e is a stage-n λ_S expression and S is a substitution where $S = [\rho \mapsto r]$. Let $r_0 \ldots r_n \vdash e \mapsto (\underline{e}, K)$ and $S(r_0 \ldots r_n) \vdash e \mapsto (\underline{e}', K')$. Then, $S\underline{e} \xrightarrow{\mathcal{A}^*} \underline{e}'$ and $SK \xrightarrow{\mathcal{A}^*} K'$.*

Proof. By structural induction on e [6]. The substitution operations ($S(r_0 \ldots r_n)$, $S\underline{e}$, and SK) are the usual compositional, homomorphic operations. □

Finally we give the simulation theorem that shows our translation is semantics-preserving. An illustration of this theorem is given in Figure 9.

Theorem 1. *(Simulation) Let e be a stage-n λ_S expression with no free variables such that $e \xrightarrow{n} e'$. Let $R \vdash e \mapsto (\underline{e}, K)$ and $R \vdash e' \mapsto (\underline{e}', K')$. Then $K(\underline{e}) \xrightarrow{\mathcal{R};\mathcal{A}^*} K'(\underline{e}')$.*

Proof. By induction on the evaluation $e \xrightarrow{n} e'$ using Lemma 1, Lemma 2 and Lemma 3. For complete proof, see [6]. □

Type Translation

A relation between the two languages exists not only between their operational semantics but also between their type systems. The translation preserves the typability of an expression: If a λ_S expression is typable in the λ_S type system, its translation is typable in the $\lambda_\mathcal{R}$ type system. The type translation is a straightforward conversion that converts all the box-types in a λ_S type to arrow types. (Figure 10)

Theorem 2. *(Type Correctness) Let e be a stage-0 λ_S expression with no free variables such that $\varnothing \vdash_S e : \mathrm{T}$. If $R \vdash e \mapsto (\underline{e}, \bot)$ then $\varnothing \vdash_\mathcal{R} \underline{e} : \underline{\mathrm{T}}$.*

Definitions

Hole Environment $H : Var_H \rightarrow Expr_{\mathcal{R}}$

Term Translation

(IVAR) $$H \vdash x \mapsto x$$

(IACC) $$H \vdash \underline{e}\cdot\mathtt{x} \mapsto x$$

(IABS) $$\frac{H \vdash \underline{e} \mapsto e}{H \vdash \lambda x.\underline{e} \mapsto \lambda x.e}$$

(IABS) $$\frac{H \vdash \underline{e} \mapsto e}{H \vdash \mathtt{fix}\ f\ x.\underline{e} \mapsto \mathtt{fix}\ f\ x.e}$$

(IAPP) $$\frac{H \vdash \underline{e_1} \mapsto e_1 \quad H \vdash \underline{e_2} \mapsto e_2 \quad \underline{e_1} \neq \lambda h.\underline{e} \quad \underline{e_2} \notin Record_{\mathcal{R}}}{H \vdash \underline{e_1}\ \underline{e_2} \mapsto e_1\ e_2}$$

(ICTX) $$\frac{H \cup \{h : \underline{e'}\} \vdash \underline{e} \mapsto e}{H \vdash ((\lambda h.\underline{e})\ \underline{e'}) \mapsto e}$$

(IBOX) $$\frac{H \vdash \underline{e} \mapsto e}{H \vdash \lambda\rho.\underline{e} \mapsto \mathtt{box}\ e}$$

(IUNB) $$\frac{H \vdash H(h) \mapsto e}{H \vdash h\ r \mapsto \mathtt{unbox}\ e}$$

(IRUN) $$\frac{H \vdash \underline{e} \mapsto e}{H \vdash \mathtt{let}\ h = \underline{e}\ \mathtt{in}\ (h\ \{\}) \mapsto \mathtt{run}\ e}$$

Figure 11. Inverse Translation from $\lambda_{\mathcal{R}}$ to $\lambda_{\mathcal{S}}$.

For a proof of this theorem, see [1, 38].

3.3 Inverse Translation

We have so far seen how a $\lambda_{\mathcal{S}}$ expression can be translated to a $\lambda_{\mathcal{R}}$ expression and how the two expressions relate. We can also translate a $\lambda_{\mathcal{R}}$ expression back to $\lambda_{\mathcal{S}}$. With such an inverse translation, we can not only translate a $\lambda_{\mathcal{S}}$ expression and evaluate the result using record language semantics as we saw in the previous section, but also translate the evaluation result back to $\lambda_{\mathcal{S}}$ without ever having to evaluate the original $\lambda_{\mathcal{S}}$ expression.

The definition of the inverse translation is in Figure 11. An inverse translation judgment is in the form $H \vdash \underline{e} \mapsto e$ with the meaning that "under the *hole environment* H, the $\lambda_{\mathcal{R}}$ expression $\underline{e}$ translates to the $\lambda_{\mathcal{S}}$ expression e."

A *hole environment* is a function that associates hole variables with expressions. Recall that a forward translation replaces an `unbox` expression with a hole variable h and moves the unboxed expression outside the enclosing `box`. A hole environment maps the hole variable to the expression that was moved out so that we can convert the hole variable back to an `unbox` expression. This is done in the (IUNB) rule. Note that in inverse translation we have a single environment as opposed to having a stack of environments (and stack of contexts) in the forward translation. There are two reasons for this: (1) There is no notion of stages in $\lambda_{\mathcal{R}}$. (2) All the hole variables are freshly generated by the forward translation and they are used only once each in unique locations. Hence, it suffices to use a single function to keep the information about hole variables and associated expressions.

The key points of the inverse translation are the following:

- Record lookup expressions are converted back to variables (rule IACC).
- A lambda abstraction that has a record variable as its parameter is converted to a `box` expression (rule IBOX).

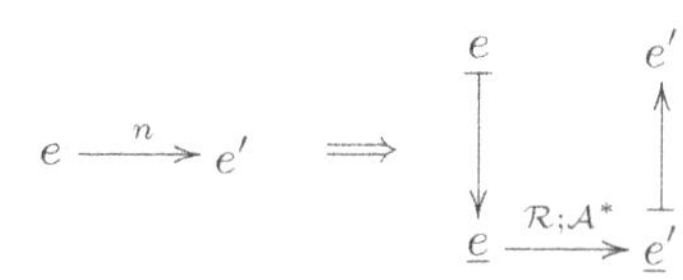

Figure 12. Given a $\lambda_{\mathcal{S}}$ expression e, we can evaluate its translation in the $\lambda_{\mathcal{R}}$ semantics and then translate the result back to obtain the result that we get from evaluation of the original expression e.

- A function application where the operator is a hole variable is converted to an `unbox` expression (rule IUNB).
- A new mapping is added to the hole environment when translating a function application where the operator is a lambda abstraction whose parameter is a hole variable (rule ICTX).

Note that the rules of inverse translation are not ambiguous; each rule matches a unique syntactic category. For instance, even though (IABS) and (IBOX) are both defined for lambda abstractions, in the former, the bound variable is a regular variable and in the latter it is a record variable. These two variables come from disjoint sets and are syntactically differentiable. Similarly, hole variables are syntactically distinguishable. This distinction of variables helps us have an unambiguous coverage of expressions.

To make the connection between forward translation and inverse translation, we first define how to interpret context stacks as hole environments.

Definition 4. *(From Contexts to Hole Environments) Let K be a context stack. The operation $\overline{K}$ defines a hole environment in the following way:*

$$\overline{K} = \begin{cases} \varnothing & \text{if } K = \bot \\ \overline{K'} \cup \overline{\kappa} & \text{if } K = K', \kappa \end{cases}$$
$$\overline{\kappa} = \begin{cases} \{h : e\} & \text{if } \kappa = (\lambda h.[\cdot])\ e \\ \overline{\kappa'} \cup \{h : e\} & \text{if } \kappa = (\lambda h.\kappa')\ e \end{cases}$$

The lemma below states that we can translate a $\lambda_{\mathcal{S}}$ expression to $\lambda_{\mathcal{R}}$ and then translate the result back to $\lambda_{\mathcal{S}}$ to obtain the same expression.

Theorem 3. *(Inversion) Let e be a $\lambda_{\mathcal{S}}$ expression and R be an environment stack. If $R \vdash e \mapsto (\underline{e}, K)$, then $H \vdash \underline{e} \mapsto e$ for any H such that $\overline{K} \subseteq H$.*

Proof. By induction on the structure of e [6]. □

Combining Theorem 1 with Theorem 3 gives a stronger result: not only that the evaluation of translated $\lambda_{\mathcal{R}}$-program simulate every reduction step of the original $\lambda_{\mathcal{S}}$-program but also that every intermittent $\lambda_{\mathcal{R}}$-expression occurring in the simulation steps can be projected back to its corresponding $\lambda_{\mathcal{S}}$-expression of the $\lambda_{\mathcal{R}}$-evaluation (Figure 12). The existence of such inversion facilitates our development of the projection step, which is the topic of the next section.

4. Projection

Among our three-step (translate, analysis, and project) approach to analyze multi-staged programs, the first two steps have sound foundations. Since we have proven that the translation is semantic-preserving, statically analyzing translated programs can replace analyzing the original subject programs. The analysis for the translated unstaged programs can be proven correct using a conventional static analysis framework such as abstract interpretation [9, 10].

The last step, projecting the analysis results back in terms of the original staged program, needs a condition for its safety. Arbitrary projections can have images that fail to qualify as static analysis results of the original staged program. For example, staged program `run '0` is translated into an application $(\lambda\rho.0)\{\}$, and the binding of the empty record to variable ρ has no counterpart in the original staged program's semantics. Hence, a projection whose image is only such an extra binding effect is clearly not a static analysis result of the original program.

A noticeable point about the safety of projections is that the safety is defined in reference to a static analysis of the original staged program. Checking whether the projection image qualifies to be a static analysis result of the original staged program needs the static analysis definition. This requirement is not a dilemma; static analysis can always be defined, though it may not be realizable.

A sufficient condition for projection safety is easy to see once we model static analysis in the abstract interpretation framework [9, 10]. Let e be a multi-staged program and $\underline{e}$ be its translated unstaged version. Let $[\![e]\!] \in D_S$ and $[\![\underline{e}]\!] \in D_R$ be their concrete semantics over concrete domains D_S and D_R respectively. Static analyses of e and $\underline{e}$ are computations of abstract (approximate) versions of the concrete semantics. Let $\widehat{[\![e]\!]} \in \hat{D}_S$ and $\widehat{[\![\underline{e}]\!]} \in \hat{D}_R$ be the abstract semantics. Each pair of concrete and abstract domains is Galois-connected by an adjoined pair of abstraction (α and $\underline{\alpha}$) and concretization functions (γ and $\underline{\gamma}$). A concrete (resp. abstract) projection π (resp. $\hat{\pi}$) is a monotonic function from D_R to D_S (resp. $\hat{D}_R$ to $\hat{D}_S$). The following diagram summarizes the setting:

$$\begin{array}{ccccc} e & \quad & [\![e]\!] \in D_S & \underset{\alpha}{\overset{\gamma}{\leftrightarrows}} & \hat{D}_S \ni \widehat{[\![e]\!]} \\ \big\downarrow & & \uparrow \pi & & \uparrow \hat{\pi} \\ \underline{e} & & [\![\underline{e}]\!] \in D_R & \underset{\underline{\alpha}}{\overset{\underline{\gamma}}{\leftrightarrows}} & \hat{D}_R \ni \widehat{[\![\underline{e}]\!]} \end{array}$$

A safety condition for the abstract projection $\hat{\pi}$ is as follows.

Theorem 4. *(Safe Projection) Let e and $\underline{e}$ be, respectively, a staged program and its translated unstaged version. If $[\![e]\!] \sqsubseteq \pi[\![\underline{e}]\!]$ and $\alpha \circ \pi \circ \underline{\gamma} \sqsubseteq \hat{\pi}$ then $\alpha[\![e]\!] \sqsubseteq \hat{\pi}\widehat{[\![\underline{e}]\!]}$.*

Proof. By the first condition and the abstraction function α's monotonicity (because of the Galois connection), $\alpha[\![e]\!] \sqsubseteq (\alpha \circ \pi)[\![\underline{e}]\!]$, which, by the monotonicity of α and π, and by the correctness of $\widehat{[\![\underline{e}]\!]}$, is $\sqsubseteq (\alpha \circ \pi \circ \underline{\gamma})\widehat{[\![\underline{e}]\!]}$, which, by the second condition, is $\sqsubseteq \hat{\pi}\widehat{[\![\underline{e}]\!]}$. □

These conditions are not particularly constraining. Concrete projection π that satisfies the first condition $[\![e]\!] \sqsubseteq \pi[\![\underline{e}]\!]$ always exists. Such π is the inverse translation function in Section 3.3 composed with an eraser function that first filters out from $[\![\underline{e}]\!]$, if any, extra things outside $[\![e]\!]$. Such composition satisfies the condition because (1) $[\![\underline{e}]\!]$ always includes $[\![e]\!]$ since the translated program $\underline{e}$ simulates every reduction step of e and (2) by Theorem 3. The second condition is analogous to the usual correctness condition for an abstract operation in the abstract interpretation framework.

Once the above conditions are satisfied, we can concentrate on defining an abstract analysis of $\lambda_{\mathcal{R}}$ programs without considering staged constructs. Analyzing the translated program and applying the abstract projection $\hat{\pi}$ to the analysis result achieves a safe analysis result of the original staged program.

4.1 Example

Consider the following staged program e. As in Section 1 we use Lisp's quasi-quote syntax [35] for staging constructs.

```
let x = '0                (* indexed as ρ1 *)
    y = '(,x + 2)         (* indexed as ρ2 *)
in run y
```

The translated version $\underline{e}$, is

```
let x = λρ1.0
    y = (λh.(λρ2.(h ρ2)+2)) x
in y{}
```

First we consider the three concrete components: concrete semantics $[\![e]\!]$ and $[\![\underline{e}]\!]$ and concrete projection π. The concrete semantics of the two programs are collecting semantics: collections of values of expressions and variables.

- $[\![e]\!]$: Collecting semantics $[\![e]\!]$ of the staged original has entries such as:

x	has	`'0`
y	has	`'(,x + 2)` where `,x` has `'0`
`(run y)`	has	2

- $[\![\underline{e}]\!]$: Collecting semantics $[\![\underline{e}]\!]$ of the translated version has entries such as:

x	has	$\langle\lambda\rho_1.0, \emptyset\rangle$ (* closure value *)
y	has	$\langle\lambda\rho_2.(h\ \rho_2)+2, \{h \mapsto \langle\lambda\rho_1.0, \emptyset\rangle\}\rangle$
h	has	$\langle\lambda\rho_1.0, \emptyset\rangle$
ρ_1	has	$\{\}$ (* empty record *)
ρ_2	has	$\{\}$
$(y\ \{\})$	has	2

- π: Projection π that satisfies $[\![e]\!] \sqsubseteq \pi[\![\underline{e}]\!]$ is straightforward: it forgets extra bindings (for h, ρ_1, ρ_2) and projects closure value $\langle\lambda\rho_i, \sigma\rangle$ to code expression i whose `unbox` (comma) expression's code are those projected from the environment σ.

  Projecting the closure values of $\lambda_{\mathcal{R}}$ into code values of λ_S is essentially identical to the inverse translation in Section 3.3. That is, π projects closure values as follows:

$\langle\lambda\rho_1.0, \emptyset\rangle$	to	`'0`
$\langle\ \lambda\rho_2.(h\ \rho_2)+2,\ \{h \mapsto \langle\lambda\rho_1.0, \emptyset\rangle\}\ \rangle$	to	`'(,x + 2)` where the `,x` position has `'0`

Now we consider the abstract components: $\widehat{[\![e]\!]}$, $\widehat{[\![\underline{e}]\!]}$, and $\hat{\pi}$. Note that the static analysis will compute $\widehat{[\![\underline{e}]\!]}$ and project its results by $\hat{\pi}$ back in terms of the abstract semantic domain of $\widehat{[\![e]\!]}$. The abstract semantics $\widehat{[\![e]\!]}$ of the original staged program is only a mathematical definition that will be referenced in checking the safety of $\hat{\pi}$.

- $\widehat{[\![e]\!]}$: For the abstract semantics $\widehat{[\![e]\!]}$ of the original staged program e, suppose we abstract a set of code values into a regular term grammar [17, 8].

  In a regular term grammar, each production's rhs is $f(t, ..., t)$ where the function symbol f is a code expression label ρ_i and each argument term t is either a code expression label or a nonterminal symbol of a grammar. The n-th argument term is for the code to be plugged into the n-th `unbox` expression inside the code expression ρ_i.

  For example, production rule

$$S \to \rho_2(\rho_1)$$

  means the set of code values from code expression ρ_2 whose only hole (`unbox` expression) is plugged by the code value from code expression ρ_1.

- $\widehat{[\![\underline{e}]\!]}$: Suppose our static analysis $\widehat{[\![\underline{e}]\!]}$ for the translated unstaged programs is defined in a flow-insensitive 0CFA manner. That is, because the analysis will be ignorant about the environment parts for closures, the best such analysis result for $\underline{e}$ would be:

x	has	$\lambda\rho_1.0$	ρ_1	has	$\{\}$
y	has	$\lambda\rho_2.(h\ \rho_2)+2$	ρ_2	has	$\{\}$
h	has	$\lambda\rho_1.0$	$(y\ \{\})$	has	2

- $\hat{\pi}$: Lastly, abstract projection $\hat{\pi}$ cast the above analysis results $[\![\hat{\underline{e}}]\!]$ back in terms of regular term grammars of $[\![\hat{e}]\!]$. Additionally, it filters out those for the translation-induced extra variables h, ρ_1, and ρ_2.

  Of the many ways to safely project 0CFA-closure values (those corresponding to code) into regular term grammars, a safe yet naive projection $\hat{\pi}$ projects 0CFA-closures as follows:

$$\begin{array}{rcl} \lambda\rho_1.\texttt{0} & \text{to} & S_1 \rightarrow \rho_1 \\ \lambda\rho_2.(h\ \rho_2)\texttt{+2} & \text{to} & S_2 \rightarrow \rho_2(S) \end{array}$$

  where the nonterminal S represents all code ($S \rightarrow S_1|S_2$). The argument term S in the production rule is for the values of the application expression ($h\ \rho_2$) that encodes the `unbox` (comma) expression inside code expression `'(,`x` + 2)`.

  Another more precise projection projects $\lambda\rho_2.(h\ \rho_2)\texttt{+2}$ differently:

$$\lambda\rho_2.(h\ \rho_2)\texttt{+2} \quad \text{to} \quad S_2 \rightarrow \rho_2(\rho_1)$$

  where the argument term ρ_1 in the production rule is from the analysis result for the h variable, not blindly the "universe"(S) nonterminal.

  Both the two abstract projections $\hat{\pi}$ satisfy the safety condition

$$\alpha \circ \pi \circ \underline{\gamma} \sqsubseteq \hat{\pi}.$$

  Let us check the more precise projection case. Note that the concretization image (by $\underline{\gamma}$) of a 0CFA-closure $\lambda\rho.body$ is the set of closure $\langle\lambda\rho.body, \sigma\rangle$'s for every possible environment σ for the free variables in $body$. The free variables' values are transitively the concretized images of their abstract values computed by $[\![\hat{\underline{e}}]\!]$. Thus, the image of $\alpha \circ \pi \circ \underline{\gamma}$ for $\lambda\rho_2.(h\ \rho_2)\texttt{+2}$ becomes

$$\begin{array}{rcl} \lambda\rho_2.(h\ \rho_2)\texttt{+2} & \stackrel{\underline{\gamma}}{\longmapsto} & \{\langle\lambda\rho_2.(h\ \rho_2)\texttt{+2}, \{h \mapsto \langle\lambda\rho_1.\texttt{0}, \emptyset\rangle\}\rangle\} \\ & \stackrel{\pi}{\longmapsto} & \texttt{'(,}x\texttt{ + 2)} \text{ where } ,x \text{ has } \texttt{'0} \\ & \stackrel{\alpha}{\longmapsto} & S \rightarrow \rho_2(\rho_1), \end{array}$$

  which is equivalent to the abstract projection $\hat{\pi}$'s image.

5. Related Work

A translation that makes the order of evaluation explicit was previously given by Davies and Pfenning [14]. The translation in Figure 8 follows the same principles. Their translation, however, is not an unstaging one. Recently, a program logic for Mini-$\text{ML}_e^{\square}$ was presented [2] which precisely captures the operational semantics, yet cannot be realizable as an automatic static analysis.

An unstaging translation was previously discussed by Kameyama et al. [23] but has several limitations for our purpose. Their translation is to System F with tuples, needs type and environment classifier [37] annotations, supports only two stages. Finally, they did not prove the translation's semantics preservation property.

Another idea of translation of staged expressions is given by Chen and Xi [4]. They convert boxed expressions to first-order abstract syntax expressions in a second-order language with recursion. An advantage of this representation is that inverse translation becomes straightforward. Chen and Xi use deBruijn indices to represent program variables inside code templates. This has the problem that a binding at a higher stage may disappear or occur unexpectedly [4]. (Such an example is given by Kim et al. [25, §6.4].)

Our translation is in principle similar to Minamide et al. [30]'s closure conversion where free variables inside lambdas become environment loop operations, though their translation is a type-directed one for conventional unstaged programs.

Our translation is an improvement of [1]: we refined the admin reductions to only two kinds and showed that these two admin reductions suffice to reach an admin-normal form that can be converted back to the corresponding staged expression using an inverse translation. The refined proof of semantic preservation and the existence of the inverse translation is new.

From the perspective of Cousot and Cousot's abstract interpretation-based program transformation framework [11], our unstaging translation can be seen as being derivable by an abstract interpretation of the staged language λ_S.

Most static analyses for multi-staged programs are string analyses for programs that generate code as strings (a.k.a. heterogeneous meta programs), but they are limited to estimate only the shape, not the semantics, of generated code by using a grammar [7, 29, 5] or the parsing stack [15]. Such string analyses can not analyze the semantics of the generated code string.

Multi-staged static type systems [13, 37, 25, 40] and their inference algorithms are limited forms of staged static analyses. Any extension to estimate other properties than types (*á la* effect type systems [27, 22, 39]) is limited to those that can proceed without analyzing the semantics of the generated code. Existing multi-staged static type systems do not have to analyze the generated code because code-generation expression's type comes with the type of the generated code.

Kamin et al. [24]'s data flow analysis of multi-staged programs combines static and dynamic techniques. Our approach is completely static. Smith et al. [34] presented a static analysis of code templates. Their language is two-staged and code templates are not first-class citizens. Variable bindings do not extend beyond the code templates they are defined in. Our approach does not have this limitation.

6. Conclusion

Static analysis of multi-staged programs is challenging because the basic assumption of conventional static analysis no longer holds: the program text itself is no longer a fixed static entity, but rather a dynamically constructed value.

In this article we have presented a semantic-preserving translation of multi-staged programs into unstaged ones and a static analysis framework based on this translation. Our static analysis approach has three steps: (1) we first apply the unstaging translation; (2) we apply conventional static analysis to the unstaged version; (3) we project the analysis results back in terms of the original staged program. As long as the unstaged static analysis is correct w.r.t. the unstaged semantics, and the projection is safe w.r.t the imaginary staged analysis, a sound static analysis for the original staged programs is obtained. Because directly defining a staged static analysis is difficult, our technique makes it possible to use the knowledge and experience in static analyses of conventional unstaged programs without having to develop staged analyses from scratch.

Our semantics-preserving translation handles staging constructs that have been evolved to be useful in practice (typified in Lisp's quasi-quotation): open code as values, unrestricted operations on references and intentional variable-capturing substitutions. We refer the reader to our companion technical report [6] for the mutable reference cases and complete proofs.

Acknowledgment

We thank Sam Kamin, Elsa Gunter and Peter Sestoft for their very valuable feedback on an earlier version of this paper. We thank Iksoon Kim, Ben Lickly, Cristiano Calcagno, Xavier Rival, and all the members of the ROPAS group in Seoul National University for criticism, discussion, correction, and encouragement.

References

[1] Baris Aktemur. *Improving Efficiency and Safety of Program Generation*. PhD thesis, University of Illinois at Urbana-Champaign, 2009.

[2] Martin Berger and Laurence Tratt. Program logics for homogeneous meta-programming. In *Proceedings of the 17th International Conference on Logic for Programming, Artificial Intelligence and Reasoning*, to appear, 2010.

[3] Cristiano Calcagno, Eugenio Moggi, and Walid Taha. Closed types as a simple approach to safe imperative multi-stage programming. In *ICALP '00: Proceedings of the 27th International Colloquium on Automata, Languages and Programming*, pages 25–36, London, UK, 2000. Springer-Verlag.

[4] Chiyan Chen and Hongwei Xi. Meta-programming through typeful code representation. In *ACM International Conference on Functional Programming*, pages 275–286. ACM, August 2003.

[5] Tae-Hyoung Choi, Oukseh Lee, Hyunha Kim, and Kyung-Goo Doh. A practical string analyzer by the widening approach. In *Proceedings of the Asian Symposium on Programming Languages and Systems*, volume 4729 of *Lecture Notes in Computer Science*, pages 374–388, Sydney, Austrailia, November 2006. Springer-Verlag.

[6] Wontae Choi, Baris Aktemur, and Kwangkeun Yi. Semantics preservation proof of an unstaging translation of lisp-like multi-staged languages. Technical Report ROSAEC-2010-009, ROSAEC Center, Seoul National University, 2010. `http://rosaec.snu.ac.kr/publish/2010/techmemo/ROSAEC-2010-009.pdf`.

[7] Aske Simon Christensen, Anders Mller, and Michael I. Schwartzbach. Precise analysis of string expressions. In *Proceedings of the Static Analysis Symposium*, pages 1–18. Springer-Verlag, 2003.

[8] Hubert Comon, Max Dauchet, Remi Gilleron, Florent Jacquemard, Denis Lugiez, Christof Löding, Sophie Tison, and Marc Tommasi. Tree automata techniques and applications, April 1999.

[9] P. Cousot and R. Cousot. Abstract interpretation: a unified lattice model for static analysis of programs by construction or approximation of fixpoints. In *Proceedings of The ACM SIGPLAN-SIGACT Symposium on Principles of Programming Languages*, pages 238–252, Los Angeles, California, 1977. ACM Press, New York, NY.

[10] P. Cousot and R. Cousot. Abstract interpretation frameworks. *Journal of Logic and Computation*, 2(4):511–547, 1992.

[11] Patrick Cousot and Radhia Cousot. Systematic design of program transformation frameworks by abstract interpretation. In *Proceedings of The ACM SIGPLAN-SIGACT Symposium on Principles of Programming Languages*, pages pp.178–190, January 2002.

[12] Olivier Danvy. Type-directed partial evaluation. In *Proceedings of The ACM SIGPLAN-SIGACT Symposium on Principles of Programming Languages*, pages 242–257. ACM, Jan 1996.

[13] Rowan Davies and Frank Pfenning. A modal analysis of staged computation. In *Proceedings of The ACM SIGPLAN-SIGACT Symposium on Principles of Programming Languages*, pages 258–270. ACM, 1996.

[14] Rowan Davies and Frank Pfenning. A modal analysis of staged computation. *Journal of the ACM*, 48(3):555–604, 2001.

[15] Kyung-Goo Doh, Hyunha Kim, and David Schmidt. Abstract parsing: static analysis of dynamically generated string output using LR-parsing technology. In *Proceeeding of the International Static Analysis Symposium*, 2009.

[16] Dawson R. Engler. VCODE:A retargetable, extensible, very fast dynamic code generation system. In *Proceedings of the SIGPLAN Conference on Programming Language Design and Implementation*, pages 160–170, New York, 1996. ACM.

[17] Ferenc Gécseg and Magnus Steinby. *Tree Automata*. Akadémiai Kiadó, 1984.

[18] Paul Graham. *On Lisp: an advanced techniques for Common Lisp*. Prentice Hall, 1994.

[19] Nevin Heintze. *Set Based Program Analysis*. PhD thesis, Carnegie Mellon University, October 1992.

[20] Nevin Heintze. Set based analysis of ML programs. In *Proceedings of the SIGPLAN Conference on Lisp and Functional Programming*, pages 306–317, 1994.

[21] Neil D. Jones, Carsten K. Gomard, and Peter Sestoft. *Partial evaluation and automatic program generation*. Prentice-Hall, 1993.

[22] Pierre Jouvelot and David K. Gifford. Algebraic reconstruction of types and effects. In *Proceedings of The ACM SIGPLAN-SIGACT Symposium on Principles of Programming Languages*, pages 303–310, 1991.

[23] Yukiyoshi Kameyama, Oleg Kiselyov, and Chung chieh Shan. Closing the stage : from staged code to typed closure. In *Proceedings of The ACM Symposium on Partial Evaluation and Program Manipulations*, pages 147–157, 2008.

[24] Sam Kamin, Baris Aktemur, and Michael Katelman. Staging static analyses for program generation. In *GPCE '06: Proceedings of the 5th international conference on Generative programming and component engineering*, pages 1–10, New York, NY, USA, 2006. ACM.

[25] Ik-Soon Kim, Kwangkeun Yi, and Cristiano Calcagno. A polymorphic modal type system for lisp-like multi-staged languages. In *Proceedings of The ACM SIGPLAN-SIGACT Symposium on Principles of Programming Languages*, pages 257–269, 2006.

[26] M. Leone and Peter Lee. Optimizing ML with run-time code generation. In *Proceedings of the ACM SIGPLAN'96 Conference on Programming Language Design and Implementation*, pages 137–148. ACM Press, June 1996.

[27] John M. Lucassen and David K. Gifford. Polymorphic effect systems. In *Proceedings of The ACM SIGPLAN-SIGACT Symposium on Principles of Programming Languages*, pages 47–57, 1988.

[28] H. Massalim. *An Efficient Implementation of Functional Operating System Services*. PhD thesis, Columbia University, 1992.

[29] Yasuhiko Minamide. Static approximation of dynamically generated web pages. In *Proceedings of the International Conference on World Wide Web*, pages 432–441, New York, NY, USA, 2005. ACM.

[30] Yasuhiko Minamide, Greg Morrisett, and Robert Harper. Typed closure conversion. In *Proceedings of The ACM SIGPLAN-SIGACT Symposium on Principles of Programming Languages*, pages 271–283. ACM, 1996.

[31] Aleksandar Nanevski and Frank Pfenning. Staged computation with names and necessity. *Journal of Functional Programming*, 15(6):893–939, 2005.

[32] Massimilian Poletto, Wilson C. Hsieh, Dawson R. Engler, and M. Frans Kasshoek. C and tcc:a language and compiler for dynamic code generation. *ACM Transactions on Programming Languages and Systems*, 21:324–369, March 1999.

[33] Tim Sheard and Simon Peyton Jones. Template meta-programming for Haskell. In *Proceedings of The Haskell Workshop*, October 2002. `http:/www.haskell.org/haskellwiki/Template_Haskell`

[34] Frederick Smith, Dan Grossman, Greg Morrisett, Luke Hornof, and Trevor Jim. Compiling for template-based run-time code generation. *Journal of Functional Programming*, 13(3):677–708, 2003.

[35] Guy L. Steele. *Common Lisp the Language, 2nd edition*. Digital Press, 1990.

[36] Walid Taha, Cristiano Calcagno, Xavier Leroy, and Ed Pizzi. MetaOCaml. `http:/www.metaocaml.org/`

[37] Walid Taha and Michael Florentin Nielsen. Environment classifiers. In *Proceedings of The ACM SIGPLAN-SIGACT Symposium on Principles of Programming Languages*. ACM, 2003.

[38] Makoto Tatsuta. Translation of multi-staged language. Technical Report NII-2010-003E, National Institute of Informatics, Tokyo, 2010. `http://research.nii.ac.jp/TechReports`.

[39] Mads Tofte and Jean-Pierre Talpin. Implementation of the typed call-by-value λ-calculus using a stack of regions. In *Proceedings of The ACM SIGPLAN-SIGACT Symposium on Principles of Programming Languages*, pages 188–201, January 1994.

[40] Edwin Westbrook, Mathias Ricken, Jun Inoue, Yilong Yao, Tamer Abdelatif, and Walid Taha. Mint: Java multi-stage programming using weak separability. In *Proceedings of The ACM SIGPLAN-SIGACT Symposium on Principles of Programming Languages*, 2010.

Static Analysis of Interrupt-driven Programs Synchronized via the Priority Ceiling Protocol

Martin D. Schwarz Helmut Seidl
Vesal Vojdani
Technische Universität München
Boltzmannstraße 3, D-85748 Garching, Germany
{schwmart,seidl,vojdanig}@in.tum.de

Peter Lammich Markus Müller-Olm
Westfälische Wilhelms-Universität Münster
Einsteinstraße 62, D-48149 Münster, Germany
{peter.lammich,markus.mueller-olm}@uni-muenster.de

Abstract

We consider programs for embedded real-time systems which use priority-driven preemptive scheduling with task priorities adjusted dynamically according to the immediate ceiling priority protocol. For these programs, we provide static analyses for detecting data races between tasks running at different priorities as well as methods to guarantee transactional execution of procedures. Beyond that, we demonstrate how general techniques for value analyses can be adapted to this setting by developing a precise analysis of affine equalities.

Categories and Subject Descriptors F.3.1 [*Logics and meaning of programs*]: Specifying and Verifying and Reasoning about Programs; F.3.2 [*Logics and meaning of programs*]: Semantics of Programming Languages—Program analysis; D.2.4 [*Software Engineering*]: Software/Program Verification

General Terms Algorithms, Theory, Verification

Keywords inter-procedural analysis, abstract domains, interrupt-driven concurrency

1. Introduction

There is an inherent tension in concurrent real-time software between synchronization, needed to preserve data consistency, and prioritized execution, needed to meet hard deadlines. Retaining execution of high-priority tasks within a predictable time frame, yet allowing lower priority tasks to complete critical sections, requires sophisticated synchronization primitives which limit the worst-case waiting time of high-priority tasks. Using common binary semaphores (mutexes) can result in a higher-priority task waiting an indefinite amount of time for a lower-priority task to complete, a situation known as *unbounded priority inversion*.

As an example of unbounded priority inversion, consider a low-priority task q_1 which acquires a lock needed by a high-priority task q_3. When q_3 is ready to execute, it will preempt q_1, but as soon as q_3 attempts to acquire the lock, it must wait for q_1 to complete its critical section. It is perfectly acceptable, and necessary for the sake of data consistency, that a high-priority task wait for a low-priority task to complete execution of a critical section; however, the problem is that an intermediate-priority task q_2 may preempt the low-priority task before it releases the lock. Then, q_2 is indirectly blocking the high-priority task q_3 for an arbitrary amount of time.

Since unbounded priority inversion defeats the possibility of meeting hard deadlines, operating systems for embedded systems provide more sophisticated synchronization primitives than common mutexes. Typically such primitives are based on priority inheritance: a lower-priority task which blocks a higher-priority task inherits the priority of that higher-priority task for the duration of the critical section which caused the blocking. This bounds the time a higher-priority task can be blocked. The *original ceiling priority protocol* [27] ensures that a higher-priority task can only be blocked for the duration of a single critical section.

In safety-critical systems, a simplification of this protocol, *the immediate ceiling priority protocol*, is often used. This variation is also known as the priority ceiling emulation protocol to distinguish it from the original inheritance-based ceiling protocol. Under this name, it is included in Safety Critical Java [13], a proposed subset of Real-Time Java. The immediate ceiling priority protocol is used by the OSEK/VDX operating system [22], which has been adopted by the automotive software architecture Autosar [3], an emerging global standard in the automotive domain. It is also present in the POSIX library, where it is called the Priority Protect Protocol. In this paper, we will follow the OSEK usage and simply call it the priority ceiling protocol (PCP). The PCP relies on the concept of resources. Each resource r obtains a ceiling priority, which is the maximal priority of tasks acquiring the resource r. The scheduling of tasks then follows the *dynamic priority* of tasks, i.e., the maximum of a task's static priority and the ceiling priorities of all resources it has acquired. In this way, a task acquiring a given resource will immediately inherit the priority of all tasks which could request that resource. As this blocks intermediate-priority tasks, unbounded priority inversion is avoided.

In this paper, we develop static analyses for programs synchronized via the PCP. We provide methods for uncovering subtle flaws due to the concurrency induced by interrupts. Specifically, we focus on data races and transactional behavior of procedures. Moreover, we explain how interprocedural value analyses can be enhanced to take priorities and interrupts into account. We exemplify this with an algorithm for inferring affine equalities. The PCP was engineered to run on uniprocessor systems, which are the *de facto* standard for embedded real-time systems.

The program in Figure 1 is used as a running example throughout the paper. It consists of one (main) task T and two interrupts I and I' with priorities 1, 2 and 3, respectively (higher numbers denote higher priorities). The program uses resources r and r'. Since

POPL'11 January 26–28, 2011, Austin, Texas, USA.

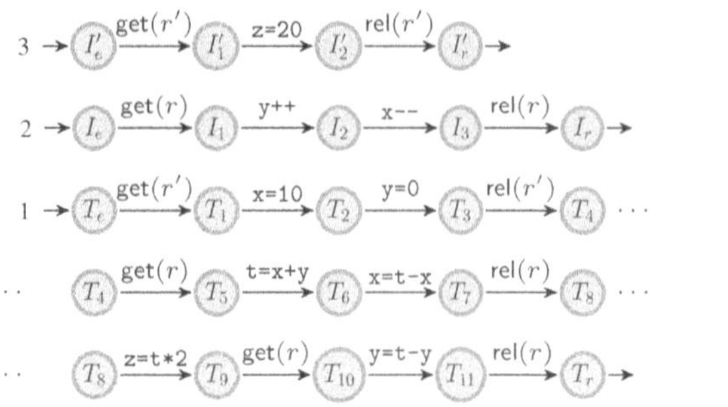

Figure 1. Example program.

r is used by T and I, its ceiling priority is 2, while r' is used by T and I', so its ceiling priority is 3. The interrupt I' of highest priority resets the variable z to the fixed value 20. The interrupt I increments the counter y and decrements the counter x. The main task T initializes the counters x and y; then, it attempts to swap their values by means of an auxiliary variable t, which receives the sum of x and y. Before completing the swap, the result $2 * t$ is stored in the variable z. This example is designed to exhibit both a data race and a nontransactional behavior.

The resource r' is held during the initialization of the main task; consequently, the dynamic priority of this part is 3 (the maximal priority), ensuring that no interrupts may occur. Then, the resource r with ceiling priority 2 is acquired, which will only protect against the interrupt I, while I' may still occur. Note that the interrupt I is unaware of the resource r', and yet acquiring resource r', protects a task from being interrupted by I because the static priority of I is less than the ceiling priority of r'. This effect is typical for priority based synchronization. An analysis which treats resources as locks, though, could not exclude the possibility of I interrupting the initialization code, resulting in false alarms.

The assignment $\mathtt{z} = \mathtt{t} * 2$ may overwrite the assignment in I' if I' occurs at T_8 (or earlier). Or it might itself be overwritten if I' occurs at T_9 (or later). This constitutes a *data race*. Moreover, at T_{10}, variable y is overwritten with a value that might have become outdated due to an occurrence of I. In the example, this will result in failing to correctly swap the variables x and y. Note that this occurs although all accesses to x and y are protected by the resource r. We call this *nontransactional* behavior.

The paper is organized as follows. In Section 2, we present a concrete semantics of PCP programs based on execution paths. We formally define the concepts of nontransactional behavior and data races for interrupt-driven programs. In Section 3, we show how to analyze resource sets to determine priorities and consequently possible interleavings. In Section 4, we use the resource framework to detect races, and in Section 5, nontransactional behavior. Section 6, shows how to extend the framework to allow data-flow analysis and we exemplify this by computing affine equations for the example program. Section 7 presents the experimental evaluation of our methods for race detection and transactionality. Finally, we discuss related work and conclude.

2. The Core PCP Model and its Semantics

Our model consists of one task $main$, with which program execution starts; a finite collection of interrupt routines Irpt, which we also call tasks, i.e., $\mathsf{Task} = \mathsf{Irpt} \cup \{main\}$; and auxiliary procedures Proc, which may be called by all tasks. The main task as well as the interrupt routines are distinguished procedures which may not be called otherwise. For the sake of the analysis, procedures are specified by means of control-flow graphs as in Figure 1.

Every procedure f has a designated entry node f_e and return node f_r. The collection of all control flow graphs of procedures in Proc is denoted by (N, E) where N is the set of nodes and E the set of edges. Let N_e and N_r denote the set of all entry and return nodes, respectively. Each edge is labeled either with a basic statement s, or with a call $f()$, $f \in \mathsf{Proc}$. For simplicity, we consider procedures without parameters only. Each basic statement s is either a basic command cmd, such as an assignment to a global variable, or a PCP statement, such as resource acquisition. Let Res denote the finite set of resources used by the program. For $r \in \mathsf{Res}$, the PCP statement $\mathsf{get}(r)$ acquires the resource r and $\mathsf{rel}(r)$ releases r. We assume that at the exit node of each task, all resources have been released. This can be enforced, e.g., by successively releasing all resources potentially used by the task.

Additionally, we assume that we are given functions $\mathcal{P} : \mathsf{Task} \to \mathbb{N}$ and $\mathcal{U} : \mathsf{Task} \to 2^{\mathsf{Res}}$ which map tasks to their *static* priorities from $\mathbb{N}$ and (super-)sets of the sets of resources possibly acquired during their execution. In particular, we assume that $\mathcal{P}(main) = 0 < \mathcal{P}(q)$ for each $q \in \mathsf{Irpt}$. To each resource $r \in \mathsf{Res}$, we then assign its *ceiling priority* $\mathcal{P}(r)$ which equals the maximal priority of a task acquiring r, i.e.,

$$\mathcal{P}(r) = \max\{\mathcal{P}(q) \mid r \in \mathcal{U}(q)\}$$

For a subset of resources $R \subseteq \mathsf{Res}$, we also write $\mathcal{P}(R)$ as a shorthand for $\max\{\mathcal{P}(r) \mid r \in R\}$ where $\mathcal{P}(\emptyset) = -\infty$.

2.1 Execution Paths

An execution path π of a PCP program is a sequence of control-flow edges labeled by basic statements into which subsequences corresponding to procedure calls or interrupts are nested. The nesting of a call to the procedure f is indicated by means of the start and end tags $\langle f \rangle$ and $\langle / f \rangle$, respectively. Interrupts are indicated analogously.

Same-level execution paths reaching a program point v (on the same level) are defined as follows:

- ϵ is an same-level execution path reaching the entry nodes q_e of procedures;
- $\pi(u, \mathsf{cmd}, v)$ is a same-level execution path reaching v if π is a same-level execution path reaching u;
- $\pi_1\langle f \rangle \pi_2 \langle / f \rangle$ is a same-level execution path reaching v if π_1 is a same-level execution path reaching u, $(u, f(), v)$ is a call edge, and π_2 is a same-level execution path reaching the return node f_r of f;
- $\pi_1\langle q \rangle \pi_2 \langle / q \rangle$ is a same-level execution path reaching v if π_1 is a same-level execution path reaching v, and π_2 is a same-level execution path reaching the return node q_r of an interrupt q.

Likewise, a (reaching) execution path reaching a program point v (not necessarily at the same level) is defined as follows.

- ϵ is an execution path reaching the entry point $main_e$ of the main task;
- $\bar{\pi}(u, \mathsf{cmd}, v)$ is an execution path reaching v if $\bar{\pi}$ is an execution path reaching u;
- $\bar{\pi}_1\langle f \rangle \pi_2 \langle / f \rangle$ is an execution paths reaching v if $\bar{\pi}_1$ is a execution path reaching u, $(u, f(), v)$ is a call edge and π_2 is an execution path reaching the return node f_r of f;
- $\bar{\pi}_1\langle q \rangle \pi_2 \langle / q \rangle$ is an execution path reaching v if $\bar{\pi}_1$ is an execution path reaching v, and π_2 is a same-level execution path reaching the return node q_r of an interrupt q;
- $\bar{\pi}\langle q \rangle$ is an execution path reaching the entry node q_e of q if $\bar{\pi}$ is an execution path reaching u and either there is a call edge $(u, q(), v)$ or q is an interrupt.

We write Π_S and Π_R for the set of same-level execution paths and reaching execution paths, respectively.

For same-level execution paths, we define the resource set after the path in terms of the resource set R before the path:

$$\begin{array}{lcll} \mathcal{R}(\epsilon, R) & = & R & \\ \mathcal{R}(\pi(u, \mathsf{cmd}, v), R) & = & \mathcal{R}(\pi, R) & \\ \mathcal{R}(\pi(u, \mathsf{get}(r), v), R) & = & \mathcal{R}(\pi, R) \cup \{r\} & \\ \mathcal{R}(\pi(u, \mathsf{rel}(r), v), R) & = & \mathcal{R}(\pi, R) \setminus \{r\} & \\ \mathcal{R}(\pi_1 \langle q \rangle \pi_2 \langle /q \rangle, R) & = & \mathcal{R}(\pi_1, R) & \text{if } q \in \mathsf{Task} \\ \mathcal{R}(\pi_1 \langle f \rangle \pi_2 \langle /f \rangle, R) & = & \mathcal{R}(\pi_2, \mathcal{R}(\pi_1, R)) & \text{if } f \notin \mathsf{Task} \end{array}$$

This definition is extended to (reaching) execution paths:

$$\begin{array}{lcll} \mathcal{R}(\bar{\pi}\langle f \rangle \pi, R) & = & \mathcal{R}(\pi, \mathcal{R}(\bar{\pi}, R)) & \text{if } f \notin \mathsf{Task} \\ \mathcal{R}(\bar{\pi}\langle q \rangle \pi, R) & = & \mathcal{R}(\pi, \emptyset) & \text{if } q \in \mathsf{Task} \end{array}$$

where π is a same-level execution path and $\bar{\pi}$ is a reaching execution path.

2.2 The Path Semantics

The concrete semantics collects, for each program point v, the set of execution paths reaching v taking static priorities and resource sets into account. Each task starts with an empty set of resources. We assume that procedures cannot be interrupted at their entry points. If a task is interrupted (while executing some procedure), its resource set before and after the interrupt is identical, while procedure calls may change the set of currently held resources.

Let p denote the maximal static priority of all tasks, and $[p]$ the interval $\{0, \ldots, p\}$. For a procedure f, let $[\![f]\!] : [p] \to (2^{\mathsf{Res}} \to 2^{\Pi_S})$ denote the function which assigns to each static priority i at which f can be called, a function which takes a resource set R before a call to f and returns the set of same-level execution paths of the procedure f including all execution paths of interrupts which possibly may have occurred. Likewise for $j > 0$, let $[\![j]\!] \subseteq \Pi_S$ denote the set of execution paths of all interrupts with static priority level j. For an edge e labeled with a basic statement, the concrete semantics is a function $[\![e]\!] : 2^{\mathsf{Res}} \to 2^{\Pi_S}$ which for each resource set R returns the singleton set $[\![e]\!](R) = \{e\}$.

In order to put up a constraint system to characterize the sets of same-level execution paths of procedures, we require composition operators which take resource sets and static priorities into account. The composition of mappings $M_1, M_2 : 2^{\mathsf{Res}} \to 2^{\Pi_S}$ must ensure that the sets of execution paths are concatenated according the attained sets of resources:

$$(M_2 \circ M_1)\ R = \{\pi_1\pi_2 \mid \pi_1 \in M_1(R), \pi_2 \in M_2(\mathcal{R}(\pi_1, R))\}$$

For interrupts, we need to filter out execution paths which cannot be interrupted due to high dynamic priorities. Let S_j denote the set of execution paths of interrupts of priority j. Then we define the application of S_j with a mapping $M : 2^{\mathsf{Res}} \to 2^{\Pi_S}$:

$$(S_j \bullet_j M)\ R = \{\pi_1\pi_2 \mid \pi_1 \in M(R), \pi_2 \in S_j, j > \mathcal{P}(\mathcal{R}(\pi_1, R))\}$$

where the priority condition checks that the acquired resources allow the interrupt to occur.

The functions $[\![f]\!] : [p] \to 2^{\mathsf{Res}} \to 2^{\Pi_S}, f \in \mathsf{Proc}$, and the sets $[\![j]\!]$ then can be characterized as the least solution of the following constraint system:

$$\begin{array}{llll} [\mathrm{S0}] & \mathbf{S}[f_e, i] \supseteq I & & \\ [\mathrm{S1}] & \mathbf{S}[v, i] & \supseteq [\![(u, s, v)]\!] \circ \mathbf{S}[u, i] & (u, s, v) \in E \\ [\mathrm{S2}] & \mathbf{S}[v, i] & \supseteq ([\![f]\!]\ i) \circ \mathbf{S}[u, i] & (u, f(), v) \in E \\ & [\![f]\!]\ i & \supseteq \mathcal{H}_f(\mathbf{S}[f_r, i]) & \\ [\mathrm{S3}] & [\![j]\!] & \supseteq ([\![q]\!]\ j\ \emptyset) & q \in \mathsf{Irpt}, \mathcal{P}(q) = j \\ & \mathbf{S}[u, i] & \supseteq [\![j]\!] \bullet_j \mathbf{S}[u, i] & u \notin N_e, j > i \end{array}$$

Here, the function I is given by $I(R) = \{\epsilon\}$. The auxiliary variable $\mathbf{S}[v, i]$ for a node v of some procedure f, and a static priority i describes the function which for a given resource set R at procedure start, returns the set of all same-level execution paths reaching v within f when executed within a task of static priority i. The auxiliary operator $\mathcal{H}_f$ takes a description M of the same-level execution paths of the procedure f and wraps it into the opening and closing tags corresponding to f, i.e,

$$\mathcal{H}_f(M)(R) = \{\langle f \rangle \pi \langle /f \rangle \mid \pi \in M(R)\}$$

For real-time systems, it is reasonable to assume that every procedure has at least one same-level execution path, i.e., that $[\![f]\!]\ i\ R$ is non-empty for every i and R. If this is the case, the set of all program points which are definitely unreachable can be computed by standard means and then removed from the control-flow graphs — implying that property (S) is satisfied:

(S) Each program point v of a procedure f is same-level reachable, i.e., $S[v, i](R) \neq \emptyset$ for every i and R.

This property therefore will henceforth be generally assumed.

In order to put up a constraint system to characterize the sets of reaching execution paths, we require an operator to apply the effects $M : 2^{\mathsf{Res}} \to 2^{\Pi_S}$ of edges or procedures to sets of reaching execution paths S, which takes attained sets of resources into account. We define

$$M @ S = \{\bar{\pi}_1\pi_2 \mid \bar{\pi}_1 \in S, \pi_2 \in M(\mathcal{R}(\bar{\pi}_1, \emptyset))\}$$

Likewise, the application of a set of same-level execution paths S_2 of interrupts of priority j to a set S_1 of reaching execution paths is defined by:

$$S_2 @_j S_1 = \{\bar{\pi}_1\pi_2 \mid \bar{\pi}_1 \in S_1, \pi_2 \in S_2, \mathcal{P}(\mathcal{R}(\bar{\pi}_1, \emptyset)) < j\}$$

The collecting semantics of sets of reaching execution paths then is given by the least solution of the following constraint system:

$$\begin{array}{llll} [\mathrm{R0}] & \mathbf{R}[main_e, 0] \supseteq \{\epsilon\} & & \\ [\mathrm{R1}] & \mathbf{R}[v, i] & \supseteq [\![(u, s, v)]\!] @ \mathbf{R}[u, i] & (u, s, v) \in E \\ [\mathrm{R2}] & \mathbf{R}[v, i] & \supseteq ([\![f]\!]\ i) @ \mathbf{R}[u, i] & (u, f(), v) \in E \\ & \mathbf{R}[f_e, i] & \supseteq \mathsf{enter}_f(\mathbf{R}[u, i]) & (u, f(), v) \in E \\ [\mathrm{R3}] & \mathbf{R}[u, i] & \supseteq [\![j]\!] @_j \mathbf{R}[u, i] & u \notin N_e, j > i \\ & \mathbf{R}[j] & \supseteq \mathsf{proj}_j(\mathbf{R}[u, i]) & u \notin N_e, j > i \\ & \mathbf{R}[q_e, \mathcal{P}(q)] & \supseteq \mathsf{enter}_q(\mathbf{R}[j]) & q \in \mathsf{Irpt}, \mathcal{P}(q) = j \end{array}$$

Here, the operator enter_f for a procedure $f \notin \mathsf{Task}$ when applied to a set S of reaching execution paths, appends the opening tag $\langle f \rangle$ to each reaching execution path in S, i.e.,

$$\mathsf{enter}_f(S) = \{\bar{\pi}\langle f \rangle \mid \bar{\pi} \in S\}$$

The operator proj_j when applied to a set S, extracts the set of all reaching execution paths $\bar{\pi}$ from S where the priority of the resource set $\mathcal{R}(\bar{\pi}, \emptyset)$ is less than j, i.e,

$$\mathsf{proj}_j(S) = \{\bar{\pi} \mid \bar{\pi} \in S, \mathcal{P}(\mathcal{R}(\bar{\pi}, \emptyset)) < j\}$$

The constraints $S0$, $R0$ provide values for entry points of all procedures in Proc, and the entry node of procedure $main$, respectively. $S1$ and $R1$ take care of all non-call edges, by applying the semantics of the edge, i.e., appending the edge to the collected sets of paths. Procedure calls are handled by the constraints $S2$ and $R2$. In $S2$ as well as the first part of $R2$, the same-level executions of the called procedure are composed with the executions before the call. Additionally, the second part of $R2$ describes execution paths entering procedures. The constraints $S3$ and $R3$ deal with interrupts. They correspond to implicitly introducing extra loop edges with *interrupt calls* at every node where an interrupt may occur, given that the dynamic priority of the executing task is sufficiently low. Interrupts are summarized by static priority levels. Similarly the entry sets of the reaching execution paths are summarized into one set for each static priority level. According to our assumption, entry nodes are excluded from constraints $S3$ and $R3$.

2.3 Data Races and Nontransactional Behavior

Let $Acc(\mathsf{cmd})$ and $Acc(f)$ denote the set of all variables accessed by the basic command cmd and same-level executions of procedure f, respectively. For clarity of presentation, we do not distinguish read and write accesses.

Then a *data race* at some global variable x occurs if program execution reaches an access to x at a dynamic priority j while x also might be accessed by some interrupt q of static priority exceeding j.

Definition 1. A PCP program contains a data race at variable x if there exists a reaching execution path

$$\bar{\pi}\;(u, \mathsf{cmd}, v)\;\langle q\rangle\;\pi\langle/q\rangle \quad\in\quad \mathbf{R}[v, i]$$

for a basic command cmd with $x \in Acc(\mathsf{cmd})$ and a same-level execution path π of the interrupt q with $x \in Acc(q)$.

In the example program of Figure 1, a data race occurs at the variable z. The interrupt I' has static priority 3 and accesses z while the main task T accesses z at a dynamic priority of 1 and can therefore be preempted by I' at T_8 or T_9. A possible run of the example program reaching the data race would be: $(T_e, \mathsf{get}(r'), T_1)\ \ldots\ (T_3, \mathsf{rel}(r'), T_4)\ \ldots\ (T_8, \mathtt{z} = \mathtt{t} * 2, T_9)$ $\langle I'\rangle(I'_e, \mathsf{get}(r'), I'_1)\ (I'_1, \mathtt{z} = 20, I'_2)\ (I'_2, \mathsf{rel}(r'), I'_r)\langle/I'\rangle$. There are no further data races in the example program since the variables x and y are only used by the interrupt I which has a static priority of 2 and all accesses to these variables occur at a dynamic priority of at least 2.

A procedure f is considered as *transactional* (or atomic) if during every execution of f, no interrupt may occur between the first and last access to global variables which accesses any of the globals accessed by f.

Definition 2. Formally, f is *nontransactional* at static priority j for a resource set R, if there exists a same-level execution path

$$\langle f\rangle\;\pi_1\;\langle q\rangle\;\pi\;\langle/q\rangle\;\pi_2\langle/f\rangle \quad\in\quad [\![f]\!](j)(R)$$

where the following holds:

- $\pi_1\pi_2 \in \mathbf{S}[f_r, j](R)$ is a same-level execution path which contains no interrupts;
- π is a same-level execution path of the interrupt q without further interrupts;
- π_1 and π_2 contain edges $(u_1, \mathsf{cmd}_1, v_1)$,$(u_2, \mathsf{cmd}_2, v_2)$ with $Acc(\mathsf{cmd}_1) \neq \emptyset \neq Acc(\mathsf{cmd}_2)$; and
- π contains an edge (u, cmd, v) with $Acc(\mathsf{cmd}) \cap Acc(f) \neq \emptyset$.

To exemplify this situation we use again the program of Figure 1. The first access of the main task T to a global occurs before program point T_2 while the last access is after T_{10}. In between, e.g., at program point T_8, the dynamic priority is 1. At this node, T can be preempted by the interrupt I which changes the variables x and y also used by T. Therefore T is *not* transactional. A possible run of the example program exhibiting this behavior would be: $\langle T\rangle\ (T_e, \mathsf{get}(r'), T_1)\ \ldots\ (T_7, \mathsf{rel}(r), T_8)\ \langle I\rangle\ (I_e, \mathsf{get}(r), I_1)\ \ldots$ $(I_3, \mathsf{rel}(r), I_r)\ \langle/I\rangle\ (T_8, \mathtt{z} = \mathtt{t} * 2, T_9) \ldots (T_{11}, \mathsf{rel}(r), T_r)\ \langle/T\rangle$.

3. Analyzing Resources

In this section, we present an analysis of sets of resources possibly held at a given program point. The results of this analysis are fundamental for determining the minimal dynamic priority guaranteed to hold at this program point, as well as all subsequent analyses of the program.

The analysis determines for each program point a set of possible resource sets. The complete lattice thus is given by $2^{2^{\mathsf{Res}}}$. Sets of sets are ordered by subset inclusion. At join points we therefore take the union of reaching sets.

For analyzing same-level executions, we associate to each procedure f an abstract semantics $[\![f]\!]^\sharp : 2^{\mathsf{Res}} \to 2^{2^{\mathsf{Res}}}$. Unlike the collecting semantics, $[\![f]\!]^\sharp$ does not depend on the static priority in which a call to f is made. The static priority determines the interrupts which may occur during the call of f, but interrupts do not modify the sets of currently held resources. In order to set up the corresponding abstract constraint system, we define an abstract semantics from $2^{\mathsf{Res}} \to 2^{2^{\mathsf{Res}}}$ for edges (u, s, v) labeled with basic statements. We define:

$$\begin{array}{lcl} [\![(u, \mathsf{cmd}, v)]\!]^\sharp(R) &=& \{R\} \\ [\![(u, \mathsf{get}(r), v)]\!]^\sharp(R) &=& \{R \cup \{r\}\} \\ [\![(u, \mathsf{rel}(r), v)]\!]^\sharp(R) &=& \{R \setminus \{r\}\} \end{array}$$

Additionally, we require an abstract composition operator $\circ^\sharp$ which, for abstract mappings $M_1, M_2 : 2^{\mathsf{Res}} \to 2^{2^{\mathsf{Res}}}$, returns the function defined by the following equation:

$$(M_2 \circ^\sharp M_1)(R) = \bigcup\{M_2(R') \mid R' \in M_1(R)\}$$

As with the concrete semantics we compute the effect of procedures depending on resource sets they are called with. The functions $[\![f]\!]^\sharp : 2^{\mathsf{Res}} \to 2^{2^{\mathsf{Res}}}$, $f \in \mathsf{Proc}$, then are given by the least solution of the following constraint system:

$$\begin{array}{lll} [\mathrm{S}^\sharp 0] & \mathbf{S}[f_e]^\sharp \sqsupseteq I^\sharp & f \in \mathsf{Proc} \\ [\mathrm{S}^\sharp 1] & \mathbf{S}[v]^\sharp \ \sqsupseteq [\![(u, s, v)]\!]^\sharp \circ^\sharp \mathbf{S}[u]^\sharp & (u, s, v) \in E \\ [\mathrm{S}^\sharp 2] & \mathbf{S}[v]^\sharp \ \sqsupseteq [\![f]\!]^\sharp \circ^\sharp \mathbf{S}[u]^\sharp & (u, f(), v) \in E \\ [\mathrm{S}^\sharp 3] & [\![f]\!]^\sharp \ \ \sqsupseteq \mathbf{S}[f_r]^\sharp & \end{array}$$

where the function $I^\sharp$ is given by $I^\sharp(R) = \{R\}$. No constraints have been included to deal with interrupts: the reason is that interrupts do not change sets of held resources.

For determining the sets of reaching resource sets, we require an abstract application operator $@^\sharp$ which applies a mapping $M : 2^{\mathsf{Res}} \to 2^{2^{\mathsf{Res}}}$ to a set of resource sets $S \in 2^{2^{\mathsf{Res}}}$ as follows:

$$M @^\sharp S = \bigcup\{M(R) \mid R \in S\}$$

For approximating the sets of resource sets reaching a node v at static priority level i, we consider the following constraint system:

$$\begin{array}{lll} [\mathrm{R}^\sharp 0] & \mathbf{R}[q_e, j]^\sharp \supseteq \{\emptyset\} & q \in \mathsf{Task}, j = \mathcal{P}(q) \\ [\mathrm{R}^\sharp 1] & \mathbf{R}[v, j]^\sharp \ \supseteq [\![(u, s, v)]\!]^\sharp @^\sharp \mathbf{R}[u, j]^\sharp & (u, s, v) \in E \\ [\mathrm{R}^\sharp 2] & \mathbf{R}[v, j]^\sharp \ \supseteq [\![f]\!]^\sharp @^\sharp \mathbf{R}[u, j]^\sharp & (u, f(), v) \in E \\ & \mathbf{R}[f_e, i]^\sharp \supseteq \mathbf{R}[u, i]^\sharp & (u, f(), v) \in E \end{array}$$

Note that the constraints $R^\sharp 0$ not only provides an abstract start value for the entry node of $main$, but also for the entry nodes of all interrupts $q \in \mathsf{Irpt}$. This is because every interrupt may occur, for example at the exit node of $main$, and will always start with the empty resource set. Note further that for reachability, we have kept the information i about the static priority at which a node is reached, in order to be able to determine its possible dynamic priorities.

In order to relate the concrete and abstract semantics of programs, we introduce appropriate abstraction functions $\alpha : (2^{\mathsf{Res}} \to 2^{\Pi_S}) \to (2^{\mathsf{Res}} \to 2^{2^{\mathsf{Res}}})$ and $\bar{\alpha} : 2^{\Pi_R} \to 2^{2^{\mathsf{Res}}}$. These are given by

$$\begin{array}{lcl} \alpha(M)(R) &=& \{\mathcal{R}(\pi, R) \mid \pi \in M(R)\} \\ \bar{\alpha}(X) &=& \{\mathcal{R}(\bar{\pi}, \emptyset) \mid \bar{\pi} \in X\} \end{array}$$

The following theorem states that the resource sets computed by the above constraint systems not only safely over-approximate the set of resources attained by the collecting semantics, but the computations are precise w.r.t. the concrete semantics.

Theorem 1. *1. Let $[\![f]\!]\ j, \mathbf{S}[v,j]$ and $[\![f]\!]^\sharp, \mathbf{S}[v]^\sharp$ denote the least solutions of the constraint systems S and $S^\sharp$, respectively. Then for every procedure f, static priority i, and program point v,*

$$\alpha([\![f]\!]\ j) = [\![f]\!]^\sharp \qquad \alpha(\mathbf{S}[v,j]) = \mathbf{S}[v]^\sharp$$

2. Let $\mathbf{R}[v,j]$ and $\mathbf{R}[v,j]^\sharp$ denote the least solutions of the constraint systems R and $R^\sharp$, respectively. Then for every program point v and possible static priority j,

$$\bar{\alpha}(\mathbf{R}[v,j]) = \mathbf{R}[v,j]^\sharp$$

Proof. For the proof, we observe that for every edge $e = (u,s,v)$,

$$\alpha([\![e]\!]) = [\![e]\!]^\sharp$$

Also for composition of functions $M_1, M_2 : 2^{\mathsf{Res}} \to 2^{\Pi_S}$, we have:

$$\alpha(M_2 \circ M_1) = \alpha(M_2) \circ^\sharp \alpha(M_1)$$

Since furthermore, the abstract functions $[\![e]\!]^\sharp$, as well as the operation $\circ^\sharp$ are completely distributive, i.e., commute with arbitrary least upper bounds, the first assertion of the theorem follows by fixpoint induction. A similar argument applies to the second statement of the theorem. □

Let n denote the sum of the number of program points and control flow edges, and o the number of resources used by the program. Recall that p is the number of static priority levels. Then the number of constraints in the systems $S^\sharp$ and $R^\sharp$ are bounded by $\mathcal{O}(p \cdot n)$. Since the height of the lattice $2^{\mathsf{Res}} \to 2^{2^{\mathsf{Res}}}$ is exponential in the number of resources, the least solution of these systems can be computed by a standard work-list algorithm in time $\mathcal{O}(p \cdot n \cdot 2^{co})$ for some constant c.

Typically, the number of resources used by embedded controllers are quite small. A practical implementation still may tabulate functions $[\![f]\!]^\sharp$ only for those (i, R) of static task priorities i and resource sets R for which the procedure f may be called at runtime. Also, elements in $2^{2^{\mathsf{Res}}}$ can be naturally modeled by Boolean functions which in turn can be efficiently operated on, if these are represented through ordered binary decision diagrams.

The example program in Figure 1 does not use any procedures, which means we have to look at the constraint $R^\sharp 0$ and $R^\sharp 1$ only. Furthermore, each node is only reached with the static priority of its task. Therefore we directly obtain the following results:

Node	$[I'_e, 3]$	$[I'_1, 3]$	$[I'_2, 3]$	$[I'_r, 3]$
Result	$\{\emptyset\}$	$\{\{r'\}\}$	$\{\{r'\}\}$	$\{\emptyset\}$

Node	$[I_e, 2]$	$[I_1, 2]$	$[I_2, 2]$	$[I_3, 2]$	$[I_r, 2]$
Result	$\{\emptyset\}$	$\{\{r\}\}$	$\{\{r\}\}$	$\{\{r\}\}$	$\{\emptyset\}$

Node	$[T_e, 1]$	$[T_1, 1]$	$[T_2, 1]$	$[T_3, 1]$	$[T_4, 1]$
Result	$\{\emptyset\}$	$\{\{r'\}\}$	$\{\{r'\}\}$	$\{\{r'\}\}$	$\{\emptyset\}$
Node	$[T_5, 1]$	$[T_6, 1]$	$[T_7, 1]$	$[T_8, 1]$	$[T_9, 1]$
Result	$\{\{r\}\}$	$\{\{r\}\}$	$\{\{r\}\}$	$\{\emptyset\}$	$\{\emptyset\}$
Node	$[T_{10}, 1]$	$[T_{11}, 1]$	$[T_r, 1]$		
Result	$\{\{r\}\}$	$\{\{r\}\}$	$\{\emptyset\}$		

3.1 Flow-independent Must-resource Analysis

One interesting class of PCP programs consists of all programs where the set of held resources at a program point v does only depend on the set of resources held at the entry point of a procedure f but not on the concrete execution path reaching v. More precisely, we demand that for every procedure f and set of resources R, the set $\mathbf{S}[v,j]^\sharp(R)$ is a singleton set $\{R'\}$. These programs are said to have *flow-independent* resource sets. Such programs can be analyzed more efficiently, while still being precise w.r.t our model.

The analysis presented above can be further abstracted to compute not all possible resource sets, but the set of definitely held resource. The domain is then simplified to 2^{Res} ordered by superset inclusion ($\supseteq$) and intersection as the least upper bound. Since every program point is reachable by some same-level execution path, no dedicated bottom element is required to denote unreachability. We consider the abstraction functions $\alpha_m : (2^{\mathsf{Res}} \to 2^{2^{\mathsf{Res}}}) \to (2^{\mathsf{Res}} \to 2^{\mathsf{Res}})$ and $\bar{\alpha}_m : 2^{2^{\mathsf{Res}}} \to 2^{\mathsf{Res}}$ given by:

$$\alpha_m(M)(R) = \bigcap M(R) \qquad \bar{\alpha}_m(S) = \bigcap S$$

where $\bigcap \emptyset$ is defined as Res. The resulting analysis is called *must resource* analysis. The abstract functions $[\![e]\!]^\sharp_m : 2^{\mathsf{Res}} \to 2^{\mathsf{Res}}$ for edges $e = (u,s,v)$ corresponding to this analysis are given by:

$$\begin{array}{lcl} [\![(u, \mathsf{cmd}, v)]\!]^\sharp_m(R) & = & R \\ [\![(u, \mathsf{get}(r), v)]\!]^\sharp_m(R) & = & R \cup \{r\} \\ [\![(u, \mathsf{rel}(r), v)]\!]^\sharp_m(R) & = & R \setminus \{r\} \end{array}$$

Note that these now are functions of the general format $g(R) = R \setminus K \cup G$ for suitable constant sets K, G. Let $\mathcal{F}$ denote the set of all these functions. This lattice is well known for *gen-kill* bit-vector analyses [12]. Since also the abstract composition of functions as used by the constraint system $S^\sharp$, for must resource analysis becomes ordinary composition of functions, must resource analysis for PCP programs can be performed by means of an interprocedural *gen-kill* approach. Similarly the abstract function application, becomes ordinary function application. Let $S^\sharp_m$ denote the constraint system over the complete lattice $\mathcal{F}$ corresponding to $S^\sharp$.

Theorem 2. *Assume that $[\![f]\!]^\sharp, \mathbf{S}[v]^\sharp$ and $[\![f]\!]^\sharp_m, \mathbf{S}[v]^\sharp_m$ are the least solutions of $S^\sharp$ and $S^\sharp_m$, respectively, where $\mathbf{S}[v]^\sharp(R) \neq \emptyset$ for all program points v, and resource sets R. Then for every procedure f, and program point v,*

$$\alpha_m([\![f]\!]^\sharp) = [\![f]\!]^\sharp_m \qquad \alpha_m(\mathbf{S}[v]^\sharp) = \mathbf{S}[v]^\sharp_m$$

The proof is analogous to the proof of Theorem 1. The non-emptiness assumptions are required as the functions from $\mathcal{F}$ only commute with *non-empty* least upper bounds (since $\bigcap \emptyset = \mathsf{Res}$).

In the analysis results of the example program of Figure 1 presented above every set of resource sets, has only one element. This is the case because the example program is flow-independent. Applying α_m in this case just removes the extra pair of set brackets. For the interrupt I' we obtain e.g.:

Node	$[I'_e, 3]$	$[I'_1, 3]$	$[I'_2, 3]$	$[I'_r, 3]$
Result	$\emptyset$	$\{r'\}$	$\{r'\}$	$\emptyset$

For programs with flow-independent resource sets satisfying assumption (S), we obtain:

Corollary 1. *Assume that all resource sets are flow-independent. Assume that $[\![f]\!], \mathbf{S}[v,i]$ and $[\![f]\!]^\sharp_m, \mathbf{S}[v]^\sharp_m$ are the least solutions of the constraint systems S and $S^\sharp_m$, respectively. Then for every program point v, possible static priority i and resource set R,*

$$\alpha([\![f]\!]\ i)(R) = \{[\![f]\!]^\sharp_m(R)\} \qquad \alpha(\mathbf{S}[v,i])(R) = \{\mathbf{S}[v]^\sharp_m(R)\}$$

The least solution to the system $S^\sharp_m$ can be computed in $\mathcal{O}(n \cdot o)$ if operations on resource sets (bit vectors) are counted for $\mathcal{O}(1)$. In case a program with flow-independent resource sets consisting solely of tasks, each program node needs to be analyzed for only a single context, the static priority of its task and the empty resource set. However, a node inside a procedure can be reached not only with different static priorities but also with several distinct resource sets. In order to deal with this situation, we propose to combine the summary functions $[\![f]\!]^\sharp_m$ (which can be computed in polynomial time) with the constraint system $R^\sharp$. This is possible since, by Corollary 1, the functions $[\![f]\!]^\sharp$ can be recovered from the functions $[\![f]\!]^\sharp_m$ by: $[\![f]\!]^\sharp(R) = \{[\![f]\!]^\sharp_m(R)\}$.

4. Data Races

In this section, we apply the results from the last section to detect data races in PCP programs. One can think of a task using its dynamic priority to defend against interfering interrupts. Interrupts use their static priority to attack other tasks. Note that it is the static priority of an interrupt q which decides whether q may interfere with the computation of another task executing at a given dynamic priority level. We there refer to the dynamic priority level protecting an access as *defensive priority* and the static priority level of an access as its *offensive priority*.

Definition 3. Assume that $\mathbf{R}[v,i]^\sharp$ denotes the least solution to the constraint system $R^\sharp$. We define:

$$\mathcal{P}_o(x) = \bigvee\{\mathcal{P}(q) \mid x \in Acc(q), q \in \mathsf{Irpt}\}$$
$$\mathcal{P}_d(x) = \bigwedge\{\mathcal{P}(R) \vee i \mid (u, \mathsf{cmd}, v) \in E, x \in Acc(\mathsf{cmd}), R \in \mathbf{R}[v,i]^\sharp \neq \emptyset\}$$

Where $\wedge$ and $\vee$ denote minimum and maximum, respectively.

These functions map global variables to their offensive and defensive priorities, respectively. We have:

Theorem 3. *If the program satisfies assumption (S), a data race occurs at x if and only if $\mathcal{P}_o(x) > \mathcal{P}_d(x)$.*

Proof. First we assume that we are given an execution path $\bar{\pi}(u,s,v)\langle q\rangle\pi\langle/q\rangle \in \mathbf{R}[v,i]$ for some static priority i where $\bar{\pi}$ is an execution path reaching program point u, π is a same-level execution path of the interrupt q, (u,s,v) accesses the global x and π also contains an access to x. Let $R = \mathcal{R}(\bar{\pi},\emptyset)$ denote the resource set held when reaching v along $\bar{\pi}(u,s,v)$, and $j = i \vee \mathcal{P}(R)$ denote the corresponding dynamic priority. Since the interrupt q may occur after the execution of $\bar{\pi}$, we have $j < \mathcal{P}(q)$. By Theorem 1, $R \in \mathbf{R}[v,i]^\sharp$. Therefore, $\mathcal{P}_d(x) \le j < \mathcal{P}(q) \le \mathcal{P}_o(x)$. Conversely assume that $\mathcal{P}_o(x) > \mathcal{P}_d(x)$. This means that there is an interrupt q of priority $\mathcal{P}_o(x)$ which has a same-level execution path π containing an access to the global x. Furthermore, there is an edge (u,cmd,v) accessing x together with a static priority i and resource set $R \in \mathbf{R}[v,i]^\sharp$ such that $\mathcal{P}(R) \vee i = \mathcal{P}_d(x) < \mathcal{P}(q)$. Since $\mathbf{R}[u,i]^\sharp$ gathers all resource sets possibly reaching u and cmd may not change resource sets, R is also contained in $\mathbf{R}[u,i]^\sharp$. Therefore by Theorem 1, there exists an execution path $\bar{\pi}$ reaching u at static priority i with $\mathcal{R}(\bar{\pi},\emptyset) = R$. It follows that $\bar{\pi}(u,\mathsf{cmd},v)\langle q\rangle\pi\langle/q\rangle$ is a reaching execution path from $\mathbf{R}[v,i]$, and we have a data race at x. □

If the program has flow-independent resource sets, and all accesses are reachable, an equivalent result can be achieved using the cheaper must-resource analysis $R^\sharp_m$. In a general setting this would still yield a safe over-approximation of data races. For the example program in Figure 1, $\mathcal{P}_o(x)$ and $\mathcal{P}_d(x)$ are as follows:

$$\mathcal{P}_o(x) = \mathcal{P}_o(y) = 2 \quad \mathcal{P}_o(z) = 3$$
$$\mathcal{P}_d(x) = \mathcal{P}_d(y) = 2 \quad \mathcal{P}_d(z) = 1$$

This means that x and y are safe, but there is a data race at z. Which is due to I' being possible at T_9. More generally we can say, that an access to x or y is safe at a defensive priority of 2 and higher, while z requires priority 3 or more.

5. Analyzing Transactionality

Nontransactional behavior occurs when a fragment of a program which is meant to be executed atomically is interrupted by a task which accesses data manipulated by this fragment. A write access of the interrupting task may result in inconsistent data for the program fragment, while a read access may supply the interrupt with inconsistent data. In the example in Figure 1 the main task switches the value of x and y and whenever accessing either one it holds the resource r guaranteeing exclusive access. However, it releases the resource between the two operations, which allows the interrupt I to modify x and y. However the old value of x is still stored in the local variable t which is used later to overwrite y. This is an instance of the nontransactional behavior described by Definition 2.

These problems are avoided if the defensive priority is sufficiently large not only for a single access, but for the whole program fragment in question. There are several subtle points to be taken into account. One point is, that a procedure may have leading and trailing parts which do not access globals. These parts should not influence the defensive priority of the procedure. Another one point is, that there can be calls to other procedures which might release a held resource and then, perhaps, acquire it again. This influences the defensive priority of the caller, no matter where in the callee the temporary decrease in priority occurs.

5.1 Tasks Without Procedures

Let us first consider PCP programs with tasks, but no procedure calls. Thus, transactional behavior may refer to tasks only. Assume that q is such a task with static priority j. Assume further that for every program point v of q, we are given a set $\mathbf{S}[v]^\sharp_m(\emptyset) \subseteq \mathsf{Res}$ of (definitely) held resources when reaching program point v. In particular, $\mathbf{S}[q_e]^\sharp_m(\emptyset) = \emptyset$. These sets allow to compute a (lower bound to) the dynamic priority of q when reaching program point v. This value is given by:

$$\mathcal{P}[v] = \mathcal{P}(q) \vee \mathcal{P}(\mathbf{S}[v]^\sharp_m(\emptyset))$$

Let $[p]_* = \{0,\dots,p\} \cup \{\infty\}$ equipped with the reverse natural ordering $\ge$. For convenience, we denote the componentwise ordering on pairs from $[p]^2_*$ by $\ge$ as well.

For each program point v, we determine values $\mathbf{S}[v]^\sharp_t \in [p]^2_*$ where the first component of $\mathbf{S}[v]^\sharp_t$ is the minimal dynamic priority attained on execution paths reaching v between the first and the last access to a global. It equals ∞ if and only if no global has been accessed so far. The second component is the minimal dynamic priority attained after the first access. The pairs $\mathbf{S}[v]^\sharp_t$ are characterized as the least solution (least w.r.t. to the ordering $\ge$) of the following constraint system:

$$\begin{array}{lll}
\mathbf{S}[q_e]^\sharp_t & \le & (\infty,\infty) \\
\mathbf{S}[v]^\sharp_t & \le & \textbf{let } (a_1,a_2) = \mathbf{S}[u]^\sharp_t \\
 & & \textbf{in let } a = \mathcal{P}[v] \wedge a_2 \\
 & & \textbf{in } (a_2, a) \\
 & & (u,s,v) \text{ control-flow edge with } Acc(s) \neq \emptyset \\
\mathbf{S}[v]^\sharp_t & \le & \textbf{let } (a_1,a_2) = \mathbf{S}[u]^\sharp_t \\
 & & \textbf{in let } a = \ \textbf{if } a_2 < \infty \textbf{ then } \mathcal{P}[v] \wedge a_2 \\
 & & \qquad\qquad \textbf{else } \infty \\
 & & \textbf{in } (a_1, a) \\
 & & (u,s,v) \text{ control-flow edge with } Acc(s) = \emptyset
\end{array}$$

Let $\mathcal{P}_d(q)$ be the first component of $\mathbf{S}[q_r]^\sharp_t$. Then the task q is transactional, if and only if $\mathcal{P}_d(q) \ge \mathcal{P}_o(x)$ holds for all globals x accessed by q. Where $\mathcal{P}_o(x)$ is the offensive priority of the global x as defined in Definition 3. In case that the PCP program has flow-independent resource sets, also the reverse implication holds. We will not prove these statements here, since they follow from

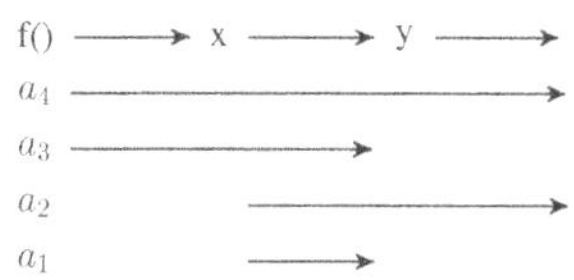

Figure 2. Priority ranges.

the corresponding properties of the more general interprocedural setting presented in the next subsection. Instead, we consider our introductory example.

Applying the analysis to the example program from Figure 1, we obtain the following results (showing only selected nodes):

Node	T_2	T_5	T_8	T_r	I_r	I'_r
Priorities	$(3,3)$	$(1,1)$	$(1,1)$	$(1,1)$	$(2,2)$	$(3,3)$

In each task, the return point is reachable from every program point of the task. Therefore, the defensive priorities are given by:

$$\mathcal{P}_d(T) = 1 \quad \mathcal{P}_d(I) = 2 \quad \mathcal{P}_d(I') = 3$$

We conclude that I' and I are transactional, since the sets of variables accessed by I and I' are disjoint, but T is not, since the offensive priority, e.g., of z exceeds 1. Note that if z is removed from the program, our analysis still detects that the task T does not swap x and y transactionally.

5.2 Tasks With Procedures

In presence of procedure calls, the dynamic priority when reaching a program point v of some procedure f, may depend on the static priority j of the task which executes f as well as the set R of resources held when f has been called. Let $\mathbf{S}[v]^\sharp_m(R)$ denote the set of resources which are (definitely) held when reaching program point v. Then (a lower bound to) the dynamic priority of v is given by $j \vee \mathcal{P}(\mathbf{S}[v]^\sharp_m(R))$.

Moreover, two values per program point do no longer suffice for analyzing transactionality, since we cannot exclude procedure parts before the first or after the last access to a global when a procedure is called. Therefore, we determine four values a_1, a_2, a_3, a_4. The first two components correspond to the two components which have been used in absence of procedures. Thus, the priority a_1 is the lowest priority attained between the first and the last access to some global variable, and a_2 is the lowest priority attained after the first access to a global. As before, a_1 receives the value of a_2 at every access to a global. At the return node of a procedure, the value of a_1 denotes the procedure's defensive priority.

Additionally, we compute the lowest priority obtained before the last access to a global variable in component a_3. For that, the component a_4 tracks the lowest priority encountered altogether. The component a_3 then receives the value of component a_4 at every access to a global. This is illustrated in Figure 2.

Let $\mathbb{D}$ denote the set of all quadruples $(a_1, a_2, a_3, a_4) \in [p]^4_*$ where $a_1 \geq a_2 \vee a_3$ and $a_4 \leq a_2 \wedge a_3$. Let the ordering on $\mathbb{D}$ again be the componentwise extension of the reverse natural ordering $\geq$ on quadruples. The minimal element w.r.t. this ordering thus is given by $(\infty, \infty, \infty, \infty)$ which signifies the empty set of same-level execution paths. The abstract effect $[\![(u,s,v)]\!]^\sharp_t : [p] \times 2^R \to \mathbb{D}$ of a control-flow edge (u, s, v) is defined by:

$$[\![(u,s,v)]\!]^\sharp_t(j,R) = \begin{cases} (\infty, j \vee \mathcal{P}(R), j \vee \mathcal{P}(R), j \vee \mathcal{P}(R)) & Acc(s) \neq \emptyset \\ (\infty, \infty, \infty, j \vee \mathcal{P}(R \backslash \{r\})) & s \equiv \mathsf{rel}(r) \\ (\infty, \infty, \infty, j \vee \mathcal{P}(R)) & \text{otherwise} \end{cases}$$

The tuple $[\![(u,s,v)]\!]^\sharp_t(j,R)$ collects the defensive priorities of the execution of s with resource set R at static priority j.

The following constraint system characterizes the defensive priorities for triples (u, j, R) of nodes u, static priority level j and resource sets R. The resource set R denotes the set of resources held, when the current procedure has been called. Similarly for non-task procedures, j denotes the static priority of the calling task.

$$\begin{array}{lll} [\mathrm{S}^\sharp_t 0] & \mathbf{S}[q_e, j, \emptyset]^\sharp_t \leq (\infty,\infty,\infty,j) & q \in \mathsf{Task}, j = \mathcal{P}(q) \\ & \mathbf{S}[f_e, j, R]^\sharp_t \leq (\infty,\infty,\infty, j \vee \mathcal{P}(R)) & f \notin \mathsf{Task}, j \in [p] \\ [\mathrm{S}^\sharp_t 1] & \mathbf{S}[v,j,R]^\sharp_t \leq ([\![(u,s,v)]\!]^\sharp_t\,(j, \mathbf{S}[u]^\sharp_m(R))) \circ^\sharp_t \mathbf{S}[u,j,R]^\sharp_t & \\ & & (u,s,v) \in E \\ [\mathrm{S}^\sharp_t 2] & \mathbf{S}[v,j,R]^\sharp_t \leq ([\![f]\!]^\sharp_t(j, \mathbf{S}[u]^\sharp_m(R))) \circ^\sharp_t \mathbf{S}[u,j,R]^\sharp_t & \\ & & (u, f(), v) \in E \\ [\mathrm{S}^\sharp_t 3] & [\![f]\!]^\sharp_t\, j\, R \leq \mathbf{S}[f_r, j, R]^\sharp_t & \end{array}$$

where abstract composition $\circ^\sharp_t : \mathbb{D} \times \mathbb{D} \to \mathbb{D}$ is defined by:

$$(b_1, b_2, b_3, b_4) \circ^\sharp_t (a_1, a_2, a_3, a_4) =$$
$$\begin{cases} (\infty,\infty,\infty,\infty) & a_4 \vee b_4 = \infty \\ (a_1, a_2, a_3, a_4 \wedge b_4) & a_2 = \infty = b_2 \\ (b_1, b_2, a_4 \wedge b_3, a_4 \wedge b_4) & a_2 = \infty \neq b_2 \\ (a_1, a_2 \wedge b_4, a_3, a_4 \wedge b_4) & a_2 \neq \infty = b_2 \\ (a_2 \wedge b_3, a_2 \wedge b_4, a_4 \wedge b_3, a_4 \wedge b_4) & a_2 \neq \infty \neq b_2 \end{cases}$$

Note that a quadruple represents an execution path containing an access to some global if and only if the second component is less than ∞. Let $(c_1, c_2, c_3, c_4) = (b_1, b_2, b_3, b_4) \circ^\sharp_t (a_1, a_2, a_3, a_4)$. The abstract composition then is defined by case distinction on whether the represented execution paths contain accesses to globals or not. Assume for example the fourth case, i.e., that $a_2 \neq \infty$ and $b_2 = \infty$. Thus, the right quadruple represents an execution path π containing an access, while the left quadruple represents execution paths π' which do not access globals. In this case, $c_1 = a_1$ because first and last accesses in $\pi\,\pi'$ both are contained in π. Furthermore, $c_2 = a_2 \wedge b_4$ as the dynamic priorities encountered during the entire path π' occur after the first access to a global. The third component is $c_3 = a_3$, since the last access to a global occurs in π. Finally, the fourth component is $c_4 = a_4 \wedge b_4$ since this component provides the minimal dynamic priority encountered during the whole path $\pi\,\pi'$. The other cases are analogous with the exception of the first case, which takes care of bottom values. We have:

Proposition 1. *The abstract composition* $\circ^\sharp_t : \mathbb{D} \times \mathbb{D} \to \mathbb{D}$ *is distributive in each argument, i.e., for all* $a, b, c \subset \mathbb{D}$,

$$\begin{array}{rcl} c \circ^\sharp_t (a \wedge b) & = & (c \circ^\sharp_t a) \wedge (c \circ^\sharp_t b) \\ (a \wedge b) \circ^\sharp_t c & = & (a \circ^\sharp_t c) \wedge (b \circ^\sharp_t c) \end{array}$$

Proof. Let $a = (a_1, a_2, a_3, a_4)$, $b = (b_1, b_2, b_3, b_4)$ and $c = (c_1, c_2, c_3, c_4)$. Consider the first assertion of the proposition If $a_2 = b_2$, then the same case of the composition applies to $c \circ^\sharp_t (a \wedge b)$ as well as to $c \circ^\sharp_t a$ and $c \circ^\sharp_t b$, and the assertion follows by idempotency, commutativity and associativity of the minimum $\wedge$. Accordingly, assume that w.l.o.g. $a_2 = \infty$ and $b_2 \neq \infty$. If $c_2 = \infty$, we obtain:

$$\begin{array}{lcl} c \circ^\sharp_t (a \wedge b) & = & (a_1 \wedge b1,\ a_2 \wedge b_2 \wedge c_2,\ a_3 \wedge b_3,\ a_4 \wedge b_4 \wedge c_4) \\ c \circ^\sharp_t a & = & (\ a_1\ ,\ a_2\ ,\ a_3\ ,\ a_4 \wedge c_4\ ) \\ c \circ^\sharp_t b & = & (\ b_1\ ,\ b_2 \wedge c_2\ ,\ b_3\ ,\ b_4 \wedge c_4\ ) \end{array}$$

By inspection of each component, the assertion can be verified. If on the other hand, $c_2 \neq \infty$, we obtain:

$$\begin{array}{lcl} c \circ^\sharp_t (a \wedge b) & = & (a_2 \wedge b_2 \wedge c_3,\ a_2 \wedge b_2 \wedge c_4,\ a_4 \wedge b_4 \wedge c_3,\ a_4 \wedge b_4 \wedge c_4) \\ c \circ^\sharp_t a & = & (\ c_1\ ,\ c_2\ ,\ a_4 \wedge c_3\ ,\ a_4 \wedge c_4\ ) \\ c \circ^\sharp_t b & = & (\ b_2 \wedge c_3\ ,\ b_2 \wedge c_4\ ,\ b_4 \wedge c_3\ ,\ b_4 \wedge c_4\ ) \end{array}$$

In order to prove the assertion, it only must be proven for the first two columns that:

$$a_2 \wedge b_2 \wedge c_3 = c_1 \wedge b_2 \wedge c_3 \qquad a_2 \wedge b_2 \wedge c_4 = c_2 \wedge b_2 \wedge c_4$$

Recall that $a_2 = \infty$. Since by assumption on the quadruples in $\mathbb{D}$, $c_1 \geq c_3$ and $c_2 \geq c_4$, these equalities hold. This completes the proof of the first assertion. The proof of the second assertion is analogous. □

Assume that $\mathbf{S}[v,j,R]^\sharp_t$ and $[\![f]\!]^\sharp_t\ j\ R$ is the least solution of the constraint system $S^\sharp_t$. Assume further that $\mathcal{P}_o(x)$ is the offensive priority of the global x as defined in Definition 3. Then we have:

Theorem 4. *Assume that assumption (S) is satisfied, i.e., all program points are reachable by some same-level execution path. For a procedure f of a program with control-flow independent resource sets, a static priority j and a resource set R, let $(a_1, a_2, a_3, a_4) = [\![f]\!]^\sharp_t(j, R)$. Then the procedure f called with resource set R at static priority level j is nontransactional, if and only if there exists a global variable $x \in Acc(f)$ with $\mathcal{P}_o(x) > a_1$.*

Proof. For a given static priority level j and an initial resource set R, we assign to each same-level execution path π not containing interrupts, a priority tuple $(b_1, b_2, b_3, b_4) = \alpha_t(\pi, j, R) \in \mathbb{D}$ where b_1 is the minimal dynamic priority between the first and the last access to a global in π; b_2 is the minimal dynamic priority after the first access to the end of π; b_3 is the minimal dynamic priority from the beginning of π to the last access to a global; and b_4 is the minimal dynamic priority through π. By the definition of $[\![(u,s,v)]\!]^\sharp_t$ and $\circ^\sharp_t$, the tuple $\alpha_t(\pi, j, R)$ is inductively defined by:

$$\alpha_t(\epsilon, j, R) = (\infty, \infty, \infty, j \vee \mathcal{P}(R))$$

$$\alpha_t(\pi_1(u,s,v), j, R) = [\![(u,s,v)]\!]^\sharp_t(j, \mathcal{R}(\pi_1, R)) \circ^\sharp_t \alpha_t(\pi_1, j, R)$$

$$\alpha_t(\pi_1\langle f\rangle\pi_2\langle/f\rangle, j, R) = \alpha_t(\pi_2, j, \mathcal{R}(\pi_1, R)) \circ^\sharp_t \alpha_t(\pi_1, j, R)$$

We extend the mapping α_t to sets $S \subseteq \Pi_S$ of same-level execution paths by:

$$\alpha_t(S, j, R) = \bigwedge\{\alpha_t(\pi, j, R) \mid \pi \in S\}$$

Note that according to this definition, $\alpha_t(S,j,R) = (\infty,\infty,\infty,\infty)$ if and only if $S = \emptyset$. Let $\mathbf{S}[v,j]'(R)$ denote the set of same-level execution paths at static priority j and initial resource set R reaching v which do not contain interrupts. These sets can be characterized by a constraint system S' which is obtained from constraint system S characterizing all same-level execution paths by removing the constraints $S3$. By definition, the operator $\circ^\sharp_t$ preserves the least element. Since by Proposition 1, $\circ^\sharp_t$ is also distributive in each argument, it follows that $\alpha_t(\mathbf{S}[v,j]'(R), j, R) = \mathbf{S}[v,j,R]^\sharp_t$ for all program points v.

Now assume that the procedure f is nontransactional at static priority level j and initial resource set R, i.e., there is an execution path $\langle f\rangle\ \pi_1\ \langle q\rangle\ \pi\ \langle/q\rangle\ \pi_2\langle/f\rangle \in [\![f]\!](j)(R)$ such that $\pi_1\pi_2 \in \mathbf{S}[f_r, j](R)$ is a same-level execution path containing no interrupts; π is a same-level execution path of the interrupt q; both π_1 and π_2 contain an edge accessing a global; and π contains an edge which accesses a global variable $x \in Acc(f)$. Thus in particular, $\mathcal{P}_o(x) \geq \mathcal{P}(q)$. Let $\alpha_t(\pi_1\pi_2, j, R) = (b_1, b_2, b_3, b_4)$. Since the interrupt q may occur between the two global accesses in π_1 and π_2, we have $\mathcal{P}(q) > b_1$. From the definition of α_t we obtain that:

$$(b_1, b_2, b_3, b_4) \geq (a_1, a_2, a_3, a_4) = [\![f]\!]^\sharp_t(j, R)$$

Therefore,

$$\mathcal{P}_o(x) \geq \mathcal{P}(q) > b_1 \geq a_1$$

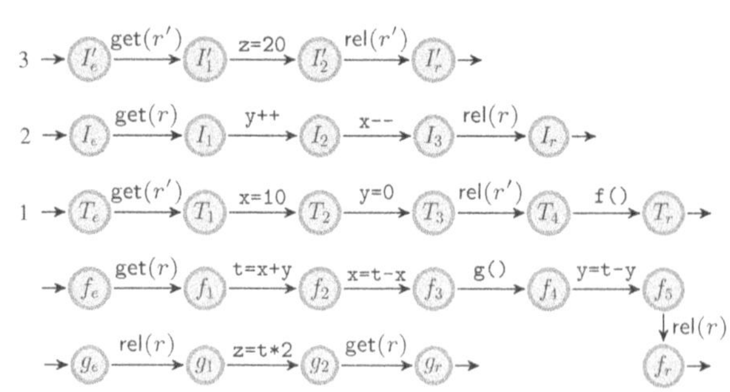

Figure 3. Example program with procedures.

Conversely assume that $[\![f]\!]^\sharp_t(j, R) = (a_1, a_2, a_3, a_4)$ and there is a global $x \in Acc(f)$ such that $\mathcal{P}_o(x) > a_1$. This means that $a_1 < \infty$, and that there is an interrupt q with $\mathcal{P}(q) = \mathcal{P}_o(x) > 0 = \mathcal{P}(main)$ which has a same-level execution path π which accesses x. Since $a_4 \leq a_1 < \infty$, Recall that

$$\begin{aligned}\mathbf{S}[f_r, j, R]^\sharp_t &= \alpha_t(\mathbf{S}[f_r, j]'(R), j, R) \\ &= \bigwedge\{\alpha_t(\pi', j, R) \mid \pi' \in \mathbf{S}[f_r, j]'(R)\}\end{aligned}$$

Therefore, there exists an interrupt-free same-level execution path $\pi' \in \mathbf{S}[f_r, j]'(R)$ such that a_1 equals the first component of $\alpha_t(\pi', j, R)$. Since $a_1 < \infty$, there exist at least two accesses to globals in π'. Moreover, π' can be factored into $\pi' = \pi_1\pi_2$ where π_1 and π_2 both contain at least one access to a global and the dynamic priority after π_1 equals a_1. Since $\mathcal{P}(q) > a_1$ interrupt q may occur between π_1 and π_2. Thus by Definition 2, f is not transactional when called at static priority j with resource set R. □

For programs with flow-dependent resource acquisition, this analysis still yields a safe over-approximation, i.e., transactional procedures may be considered as possibly nontransactional, but not the other way round. Alternatively, the flow-precise resource analysis $S^\sharp$ could be used to obtain more precise results.

Consider the example program of Figure 3 where the part of T after the initialization has been wrapped into the procedure f and the nodes T_9 to T_{10} of the original example program have into procedure g. The procedure g is transactional since it only contains one access to a global variable. The procedure f holds the resource r at all nodes between its first and last access to a global variable. However the call to g compromises the transactionality of f since it temporarily releases r. The analysis presented above captures this behavior. For the procedure g called at static priority 1 with resource set $\{r\}$ we obtain the following summary: $[\![g]\!]^\sharp_t(j, \{r\}) = (\infty, 1, 1, 1)$. When applied to the tuple reaching f_3 we have: $(\infty, 1, 1, 1) \circ^\sharp_t (2, 2, 1, 1) = (1, 1, 1, 1)$. Since tuple entries may not increase, this tuple is then carried over to f_r and with $\mathcal{P}_d(x) = 2$ we see that f is not transactional.

6. Linear Equalities For PCP Programs

The resource analysis presented in Section 3 need not explicitly deal with interrupts. The reason is that interrupts neither change sets of held resources nor affect the current priorities of tasks. Values of globals on the other hand, can be affected by interrupts.

Fortunately, summary-based interprocedural analyses [28] can be adapted to resource aware value analyses of PCP programs rather easily. As a prototypic example we extend the approach presented in [21] for analyzing *linear equalities* to take resources and interrupts into account. The goal of this analysis is to compute the linear closure of extended states of the collecting semantics.

For simplicity, we restrict ourselves to PCP programs with flow-independent resource sets.

Let $X = \{x_1, \ldots, x_k\}$ denote the set of global variables, where $k = |X|$ is the number of global variables. We consider affine assignments of the form $x_j := t_0 + \Sigma_{i=1}^{k} t_i \cdot x_i$ with $t_i \in \mathbb{Q}$. We write V for the complete lattice of linear subspaces of $(k+1)\times(k+1)$ matrices over the rationals $\mathbb{Q}$. Each matrix A describes the effect of an execution onto the global state. Thereby, each global state is represented by a vector $v = [v_0, \ldots, v_k]^\mathsf{T} \in \mathbb{Q}^{k+1}$ where $v_0 = 1$ and for $i > 0$, v_i records the value of the variable x_i. We write V' for the complete lattice of linear subspaces of $(k+1)$ vectors over the rationals $\mathbb{Q}$. The extra component v_0 allows to linearize affine transformations. A set $S \subseteq \mathbb{Q}^{(k+1)\times(k+1)}$ of transformation matrices is abstracted by the linear space $\mathbf{Span}\, S \in V$ of all linear combinations of matrices in S.

The concrete resource sensitive semantics $[\![(u,s,v)]\!]_l : 2^{\mathsf{Res}} \to \mathbb{Q}^{(k+1)\times(k+1)}$ of an edge is then given by:

$$
\begin{array}{ll}
[\![(u,s,v)]\!]_l(R) = & \\
\qquad \left[\begin{array}{c|c|c} 1 & 0 & 0 \\ \hline 0 & I_{j-1} & 0 \\ \hline t_0 & t_1 \quad \ldots & t_k \\ \hline 0 & 0 & I_{k-j} \end{array}\right] & s = x_j := t_0 + \Sigma_{i=1}^{k} t_i \cdot x_i \\
[\![(u,s,v)]\!]_l(R) = I_{k+1} & \text{otherwise}
\end{array}
$$

Where I_m denotes the m-dimensional identity matrix. Note, that the resource parameter is not used here, but might be in another instance of the framework and is therefore given for completeness.

The resource sensitive semantics of an execution path $\pi \in \Pi$ is defined as follows:

$$
\begin{array}{rcl}
[\![\epsilon]\!]_l & = & I_{k+1} \\
[\![e\pi']\!]_l & = & [\![\pi']\!]_l \cdot [\![e]\!]_l \\
[\![\langle f\rangle \pi_1 \langle/f\rangle \pi_2]\!]_l & = & [\![\pi_2]\!] \cdot [\![\pi_1]\!]_l \\
[\![\langle f_1\rangle \pi_1 \ldots \langle f_s\rangle \pi_s]\!]_l & = & [\![\pi_s]\!]_l \cdot \ldots \cdot [\![\pi_1]\!]_L
\end{array}
$$

The concrete resource sensitive collecting semantics $\mathbf{R}[u,i]_l : 2^{\mathsf{Res}} \to \mathbb{Q}^{k+1}$ of a program point u and static priority level i is then given by:

$$\mathbf{R}[u,i]_l(R) = \{[\![\bar{\pi}]\!](x) \mid R = \mathcal{R}(\bar{\pi}, \emptyset), x \in \mathbb{Q}^{k+1}, \bar{\pi} \in \mathbf{R}[u,i]\}$$

As in [21] we approximate this by its span, i.e.:

$$\mathbf{R}[u,i]_l^\sharp(R) - \mathbf{Span}(\mathbf{R}[u,i]_l(R))$$

We define the abstract semantics $[\![e]\!]_l^\sharp : 2^{\mathsf{Res}} \to V$ by $[\![e]\!]_l^\sharp(R) = \mathbf{Span}\{[\![e]\!]_l(R)\}$. Since in the end we are interested in equalities holding at a program point, we can model non-affine assignments, x_j =?, by assignments of all constant values. For the abstract semantics we therefore have:

$$
[\![x_j :=?]\!]_l^\sharp(R) = \mathbf{Span}\left\{ \left[\begin{array}{c|c|c} 1 & 0 & 0 \\ \hline 0 & I_{j-1} & 0 \\ \hline 0 & 0 & 0 \\ \hline 0 & 0 & I_{k-j} \end{array}\right], \left[\begin{array}{c|c|c} 1 & 0 & 0 \\ \hline 0 & I_{j-1} & 0 \\ \hline 1 & 0 & 0 \\ \hline 0 & 0 & I_{k-j} \end{array}\right] \right\}
$$

To each procedure f, we assign an abstract function $[\![f]\!]_l^\sharp : [p] \to 2^{\mathsf{Res}} \to V$ which summarizes the abstract effect of f. These effects are characterized by the least solution of the constraint system:

$$
\begin{array}{lll}
[\mathrm{S}_1^\sharp 0] & \mathbf{S}[f_e, i, R]_l^\sharp \supseteq I & \\
[\mathrm{S}_1^\sharp 1] & \mathbf{S}[v, i, R]_l^\sharp & \supseteq ([\![(u,s,v)]\!]_l^\sharp R) \circ_l^\sharp \mathbf{S}_l^\sharp[u, i, R]_l^\sharp \\
 & & \qquad (u,s,v) \in E \\
[\mathrm{S}_1^\sharp 2] & \mathbf{S}[v, i, R]_l^\sharp & \supseteq ([\![f]\!]_l^\sharp\, i\, (\mathbf{S}[u]_m^\sharp\, (R))) \circ_l^\sharp \mathbf{S}[u, i, R]_l^\sharp \\
 & & \qquad (u, f(), v) \in E \\
[\mathrm{S}_1^\sharp 3] & \mathbf{S}[u, i, R]_l^\sharp & \supseteq [\![j]\!]_l^\sharp \circ_l^\sharp \mathbf{S}[u, i, R]_l^\sharp \\
 & & \qquad u \notin N_e, j > i \vee \mathcal{P}(\mathbf{S}_m^\sharp[u]\,(R)) \\
[\mathrm{S}_1^\sharp 4] & [\![f]\!]_l^\sharp\, i\, R & \supseteq \mathcal{H}_f^\sharp(\mathbf{S}[f_r, i, R]_l^\sharp) \\
 & [\![j]\!]_l^\sharp & \supseteq [\![q]\!]_l^\sharp\, j\, \emptyset \qquad q \in \mathsf{Irpt}, \mathcal{P}(q = j)
\end{array}
$$

For two sets of matrices $M_1, M_2 \in V$, the operator $\circ_l^\sharp : V \times V \to V$ is defined as follows:

$$M_1 \circ_l^\sharp M_2 = \mathbf{Span}\{A_1 A_2 \mid A_1 \in M_1, A_2 \in M_2\}$$

By using the precomputed transformers for resource sets, we can statically check the priority condition including the resource set information and therefore, for this instance, we do not need a dedicated $\bullet_l^\sharp$ operator performing this check. Instead, we use $\circ_l^\sharp$ for interrupts as well. Since we consider global variables only, the operator $\mathcal{H}_f^\sharp$ which transforms the abstract semantics of a procedure into the abstract semantics of its call, is simply the identity. For tasks the resource set parameter R is always the empty set and the static priority i is the static priority of that task. Thus, if the program does not contain procedures, the summaries can be simplified to vector spaces of matrices.

In the second phase, we compute for every program point v and static priority i a mapping $\mathbf{R}_l^\sharp[v,i] : 2^{\mathsf{Res}} \to V'$. For any given resource set R, this mapping is meant to return the linear hull of all concrete states $x \in \mathbb{Q}^{k+1}$ possibly reaching program point v within a task with static priority i given the current resource set equals R. The set of all functions $2^{\mathsf{Res}} \to V'$ forms a complete lattice w.r.t. the partial ordering on functions induced by the partial ordering on V'. From a basis B of $R_l^\sharp[u,i](R)$ for a program point u with static priority i and resource set R, we obtain the set of valid equalities $t_0 + \sum_{i=1}^{k} t_i \cdot x_i = 0$ as the set of solutions of the system

$$t_0 \cdot b_0 + \ldots + t_k \cdot b_k = 0\,, \quad (b_0, \ldots, b_k) \in B$$

In order to describe the effect of a procedure f for this second phase, we rely on two ingredients:

- the summary $[\![f]\!]_m^\sharp$ computed by same-level must resource analysis, which records how the execution of f may change the sets of held resources, and
- the summary $[\![f]\!]_l^\sharp$ computed by the same-level analysis of linear transformations in the first phase, which for each static priority i and resource set before the call returns the vector space of possible linear transformations.

This yields the following constraint system:

$$
\begin{array}{llll}
[\mathrm{R}_1^\sharp 0] & \mathbf{R}[main_e\ ,0\,]_l^\sharp \sqsupseteq M_0 & & \\
[\mathrm{R}_1^\sharp 1] & \mathbf{R}[v,i]_l^\sharp & \sqsupseteq ([\![e]\!]_l^\sharp, [\![e]\!]_m^\sharp) @_l^\sharp \mathbf{R}[u,i]_l^\sharp & \\
 & & & e = (u,s,v) \in E \\
[\mathrm{R}_1^\sharp 2] & \mathbf{R}[v,i]_l^\sharp & \sqsupseteq (([\![f]\!]_l^\sharp\, i), [\![f]\!]_m^\sharp) @_l^\sharp \mathbf{R}[u,i]_l^\sharp & \\
 & & & (u, f(), v) \in E \\
 & \mathbf{R}[f_e, i]_l^\sharp & \sqsupseteq \mathsf{enter}_{f,l}^\sharp(\mathbf{R}[u,i]_l^\sharp) & (u, f(), v) \in E \\
[\mathrm{R}_1^\sharp 3] & \mathbf{R}[u,i]_l^\sharp & \sqsupseteq [\![j]\!]_l^\sharp @_{j,l}^\sharp \mathbf{R}[u,i]_l^\sharp & u \notin N_e, j > i \\
 & \mathbf{R}[j]_l^\sharp & \sqsupseteq \mathsf{proj}_{j,l}^\sharp(\mathbf{R}_l[u,i]) & u \notin N_e, j > i \\
 & \mathbf{R}[q_e, j]_l^\sharp & \sqsupseteq \mathsf{enter}_{q,l}^\sharp(\mathbf{R}[j]_l^\sharp) & q \in \mathsf{Irpt}, \mathcal{P}(q) = j
\end{array}
$$

Here, M_0 is the mapping which assigns the full vector space $\mathbb{Q}^{k+1}$ to the empty resource set $R = \emptyset$ and the zero space $\{\mathbf{0}\}$ to all resource sets $R \neq \emptyset$. The operator $@_l^\sharp : ((2^{\mathsf{Res}} \to V') \times (2^{\mathsf{Res}} \to 2^{\mathsf{Res}})) \times (2^{\mathsf{Res}} \to V') \to (2^{\mathsf{Res}} \to V')$ is defined by:

$$
\begin{array}{l}
((M, h) @_l^\sharp \phi)(R') = \\
\qquad \mathbf{Span}\{Ax \mid R' = h(R), A \in M(R), x \in \phi(R)\}
\end{array}
$$

Since we consider global variables only, the function $\mathsf{enter}_{f,l}^\sharp$ is the identity function, i.e., $\mathsf{enter}_{f,l}^\sharp\, \phi = \phi$.

In the constraint $R_l^\sharp 3$, a modified version of the application and the enter operator are required which take into account that an interrupt q can only be enabled if the static priority of q exceeds the dynamic priority at a given program point. Therefore, we define:

$$(M@^\sharp_{j,l}\phi)\, R = \mathbf{Span}\{Av \mid A \in M(\emptyset), v \in \phi(R), j > \mathcal{P}(R)\}$$

$$(\mathsf{proj}^\sharp_{j,l}\phi)\, R = \begin{cases} \mathbf{Span}\{v \in \phi(R') \mid j > \mathcal{P}(R')\} & \text{if } R = \emptyset \\ \{\mathbf{0}\} & \text{otherwise} \end{cases}$$

In any case we have the following theorem:

Theorem 5. *Assume that the PCP program has flow-independent resource sets and satisfies (S) Let furthermore* $\mathbf{S}[v,i], [\![f]\!]$ *and* $\mathbf{S}[v,i,R]^\sharp_l, [\![f]\!]^\sharp_l, \mathbf{S}[v]^\sharp_m, [\![f]\!]^\sharp_m$ *as well as* $\mathbf{R}[v,i]^\sharp_l$ *denote the least solutions of the constraint systems* S, $S^\sharp_l$, $S^\sharp_m$, *and* $R^\sharp_l$, *respectively. Then the following holds:*

1. *For every program point* v, *static priority* i, *resource set* R *and procedure* f,

$$\mathbf{Span}\{[\![\pi]\!]_l \mid \pi \in \mathbf{S}[v,i](R)\} = \mathbf{S}[v,i,R]^\sharp_l$$
$$\mathbf{Span}\{[\![\pi]\!]_l \mid \pi \in [\![f]\!]\, i\, R\} = [\![f]\!]^\sharp_l\, i\, R$$

2. *For every program point* v, *static priority* i *and resource set* R

$$\mathbf{Span}\{[\![\bar\pi]\!]_l(x) \mid \bar\pi \in \mathbf{R}[v,i], x \in \mathbb{Q}^{k+1}, \mathcal{R}(\bar\pi,\emptyset) = R\} = \mathbf{R}[v,i]^\sharp_l(R)$$

For the constraint system $S^\sharp_l$ we have at most $n \cdot p^2 \cdot 2^o$ constraints. Using the techniques from [21], this implies that the least solution can be computed in time $\mathcal{O}(n \cdot p^2 \cdot 2^o \cdot k^8)$. This is a smooth generalization of the results obtained in [21] to the case of programs with interrupts and resources. Note that a practical implementation may explore the given constraint systems in a demand-driven fashion such that only those resource sets are considered which actually are necessary for computing the reachability information as provided by the least solution of $R^\sharp_l$. For the special case of tasks only without auxiliary procedures, this means that the factor 2° can be dropped completely.

We exemplify our analysis for the example program in Figure 1. Due to their non-deterministic nature, interrupts may occur arbitrarily often, creating an infinite number of program executions for a given program point, each corresponding to linear transformations of the state vectors. Since we are only interested in the linear hull of these transformations, it suffices to maintain a basis of the generated sub-space of matrices. Accordingly, we obtain the following summaries for the interrupts I and I':

$$[\![I']\!]^\sharp_l(3,\emptyset) = \mathbf{Span}\left\{\begin{bmatrix} 1&0&0&0&0\\ 0&1&0&0&0\\ 0&0&1&0&0\\ 20&0&0&0&0\\ 0&0&0&0&1 \end{bmatrix}\right\}$$

$$[\![I]\!]^\sharp_l(2,\emptyset) = \mathbf{Span}\left\{\begin{bmatrix} 1&0&0&0&0\\ -1&1&0&0&0\\ 1&0&1&0&0\\ 0&0&0&1&0\\ 0&0&0&0&1 \end{bmatrix}, \begin{bmatrix} 1&0&0&0&0\\ -1&1&0&0&0\\ 1&0&1&0&0\\ 20&0&0&0&0\\ 0&0&0&0&1 \end{bmatrix}\right\}$$

These transformations can be applied to compute the subspace of possible values for each program point of the main task. For T_4, we obtain:

$$\mathbf{R}[T_4,1]^\sharp_l\emptyset = \mathbf{Span}\left\{\begin{bmatrix}1\\10\\0\\0\\0\end{bmatrix}, \begin{bmatrix}0\\1\\-1\\0\\0\end{bmatrix}, \begin{bmatrix}0\\0\\0\\1\\0\end{bmatrix}, \begin{bmatrix}0\\0\\0\\0\\1\end{bmatrix}\right\}$$

The second vector is due to the potential occurrence of the interrupt I. The interrupt I' has no impact, since I' is not enabled and there are no restrictions on the value of z, at T_4. From the basis we obtain the system of equalities:

$$\begin{array}{lllllll} 1\cdot t_0 & + & 10\cdot t_1 & & & & = 0 \\ & & 1\cdot t_1 & + & (-1)\cdot t_2 & & = 0 \\ & & & & 1\cdot t_3 & & = 0 \\ & & & & & 1\cdot t_4 & = 0 \end{array}$$

Solving this yields the equality $x + y = 10$. Overall we have the following equalities:

Node	Example Equalities
T_3	$x = 10,\ y = 0,\ x + y = 10$
T_4, T_5	$x + y = 10$
T_6	$t = x + y = 10$
T_7	$x - y + t = 0$
T_8	$z = 10$
$T_9, \ldots, T_r$	$z = 20,\ t = 10$
I'_2, I'_r	$z = 20$

This means that at the end of the main task T and the interrupt I', the equality $z = 20$ holds. Moreover, the equality $10 = x+y$ holds although interrupts may freely occur at nodes T_4 and T_5. Finally, the local variable t equals 10, once it has been written. Note that the equalities for z and t cannot be guaranteed in I, since I may occur at node T_3 where both variables may still be uninitialized.

Note that while this analysis directly fits into the framework, it is also possible to use analyses, which for example use infinite lattices, evaluate branching conditions, or even are unable to provide closed function summaries. For infinite lattices one would use a demand-driven local solver ([9]) and possibly widenings ([6]. The branching conditions could be added to the flow-graph and the framework semantics extended to treat them as nops while allowing the concrete analysis instance to fully evaluate them. Finally summary functions can be handled by tabulating them. This technique is used in the Goblint analyzer and proved to be very useful.

7. Implementation

The data race and transactionality analyses from Sections 4 and 5, respectively, have been implemented in the analyzer *Goblint* for multi-threaded C [31]. This analyzer framework is based on a local fixpoint engine and provides basic analyses such as constant propagation and alias analysis, which then can be enhanced with additional specific domains and transfer functions. The analyzer differentiates between read and write accesses in order to avoid read-read warnings. Beyond the path-based approach presented in sections 4 and 5, *Goblint* takes conditions into account whenever possible. By that, the analysis may exclude some unrealizable execution paths and therefore may raise less false alarms.

The test suite consists of sample programs from the *nxtOSEK* implementation [29] together with our own examples. Program `biped_robot` is part of the control software of a self-balancing two wheeled robot, which uses resources to synchronize the balancing with remote control commands. The programs `xxx_test` are examples for preemptive scheduling (`pe`), resource synchronization (`res`), time-triggered tasks (`tt`) and usb communication (`usb`). Each of these tests uses two tasks and one resource. Programs `example` and `example_fun` are from Figure 1 and Figure 3, respectively. Program `pingpong` consists of two tasks which alternately set a variable to "ping" and "pong" synchronizing via a single resource. Program `counter` consists of an interrupt which increases two fields of a struct if an integer flag is set and does nothing otherwise as well as a task which unsets the flag, then prints the struct and re-sets the flag. The integer flag itself is protected by the resource.

The results of running the analyzer on these examples are summarized in Table 1. We ran these experiments on a Intel(R) Core(TM)2 Quad CPU machine with 3.00GHz under Ubuntu 10.04. The analyzer verifies that the two programs `pingpong` and `usb_test` are free of data races. The data races in both versions of the example program are discovered, as well as the unsafe access to counters in `pe_test` and `tt_test`. The race warning in `biped_robot` occurs since re-running the initialization task is not ruled out. For `counter`, race warnings are produced for the fields

Program	Size	Time	Race	Trans.
biped_robot	151 lines	0,02 s	1	0
pe_test	97 lines	0,06 s	1	1
res_test	74 lines	0,03 s	0	1
tt_test	101 lines	0,07 s	1	1
usb_test	140 lines	0,04 s	0	0
example	38 lines	0,01 s	1	1
example_fun	51 lines	0,01 s	1	2
pingpong	53 lines	0,03 s	0	0
counter	58 lines	0,02 s	2	1

Table 1. Result of analyzing example programs

of the struct since they are accessed both by the task and the interrupt without protection with a resource. While we verify that the integer flag accesses are safe, the analysis presented here approximates conditional branching with non-deterministic branching and therefore does not relate the flag value with the accesses to the struct. Other analyses provided by the *Goblint* analyzer, however, may split the execution path based on the value of the flag and thus may separately analyze the cases for a set and an un-set flag.

Regarding transactionality, the analyzer verifies that the tasks of usb_test and pingpong are transactional. It discovers the violation of transactionality of the running example and also produces warnings for pe_test and tt_test where the race occurs between accesses to the counter. In res_test, a variable whose accesses are otherwise protected by a resource, is *read* after the release of the resource — thus violating our definition of transactionality. In biped_robot, on the other hand, the accesses to globals may be involved in data races, but are the only accesses to globals in their respective procedures. Accordingly, transactionality is not violated. For counter, a transactionality warning is produced, since the resource is released between un-setting and re-setting the flag.

All examples are small and therefore analyzed in negligible time. In order to get an intuition how the analyses scales, we evaluated the analyzer on the synthetic benchmarks chain_n. While the estimates for the asymptotic complexity of our analyses grow exponentially with the number of resources, they depend only linearly on the program size. Therefore, we do not expect the program size to be the major bottleneck for scalability but the number of resourced and interrupt levels. Thus, we vary these latter parameters in the benchmarks. For $n \geq 1$, program chain_n has globals $x_0, \ldots, x_n$, n interrupt levels and n resources which are used to successively copy the value of the variable x_i into the variable x_{i-1}. The running times of the analyzer for the instances $n = 100, 200, \ldots, 1000$ are shown in Figure 4. For each of them, the analyzer verified absence of data races and transactionality of all tasks. The increase in run time for these instances is slightly worse than linear. Even for 1000 interrupt levels and resources, the runtime is still quite acceptable. The source code of our analyses, all benchmarks, and a script to run them are available at http://goblint.in.tum.de/popl11.html.

8. Related Work

While the ceiling and inheritance protocols [4, 27] have been formally studied [7, 23], these papers focus on schedulability rather than data consistency; that is, one assumes the program is correctly synchronized and characterizes the impact of synchronization primitives on meeting hard deadlines as a function of resource usage. In contrast, we are interested in detecting erroneous use of these synchronization primitives.

Already simple analysis problems for concurrent programs with recursion and synchronization are undecidable [24]. Practical approaches therefore either over-approximate the interaction

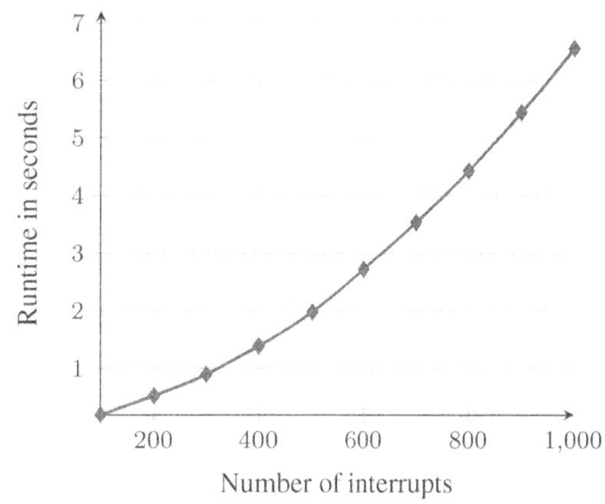

Figure 4. Runtimes of the analyzer on chain_n.

between threads, as in thread-modular model checking [10], or ignore synchronization altogether [5, 8]. Some also place restrictions on concurrency. In a number of papers, Kahlon et al. [14–16] discuss model checking of pushdown systems synchronized via locks where the usage of locks must be well nested. This approach has been generalized to pushdown systems with dynamic thread creation [19, 20]. With the exception, perhaps, of dynamically changing priorities, PCP programs extended with dynamic task creation can also be cast within the more general model of multi-set pushdown systems. For these, Atig et al. [2] show that control point reachability is decidable. Their approach is based on Petri net reachability and does not support the inference of more complicated invariants such as linear equalities.

Kidd et al. [18] observe that every priority preemptive system can be transformed into a pushdown system. Beyond that, they additionally represent the schedulers corresponding to synchronization protocols as exponentially large pushdown systems. In case of PCP as well as for priority inheritance with well-nested resource usage, these two systems can be combined into one pushdown system. From that, they conclude that reachability is decidable for PCP as well as for priority inheritance with well-nested resource usage. Our approach cannot be applied to priority inheritance directly, while for PCP, our analysis is exponential only in the number of resources (not in the number of interrupts).

Summarizing abstract effects of interrupts has also been considered by Regehr et al. [26] for analyzing stack overflow in assembly code. Their summaries describe the stack consumption of an interrupt together with the set of interrupts which become enabled/disabled by the execution. Their model does not deal with specific protocols such as PCP. Additionally, Regehr and Cooprider [25] present a transformation technique to turn interrupt-driven embedded code into thread-based code and apply off-the-shelf race detection tools to the transformed code. They introduce artificial interrupt locks to make interrupt disabling/(re-)enabling visible to the analysis. They assume fixed static priorities and suffer from the imprecision possibly incurred by the thread analyzer. In contrast, our approach directly exploits the properties of the PCP protocol for interrupt-driven concurrency and explicitly deals with dynamically changing priorities. This allows us to handle the set of possible interleavings precisely.

Flanagan et al. [11] present a type system for atomicity in concurrent Java programs. A transactional procedure as defined in this paper is atomic in their sense since every execution of a transactional procedure that is possibly interrupted has an equivalent serial execution, i.e., no interrupts occur during its execution. This atomicity condition is relaxed by Vaziri et al. [30], who provide a set of problematic access patterns and show that they are complete, i.e., the absence of all these patterns guarantee that the execution is serializable w.r.t. the critical variables and demarcated critical sections. Our notion of transactionality for a procedure f considers all, potentially accessed, global variables as critical for f where the critical section of f is the section between the first and last access to global variables. Kidd et al. [17] provide a static analysis for Java programs to verify the absence of such patterns in a given program. Artho et al. [1] give a static analysis to detect *stale-value* atomicity violations, i.e., accesses to outdated values of globals stored in a local variable that has escaped the critical section.

9. Conclusions

We have provided practical methods to analyze data races and transactionality in PCP programs. Moreover, our analysis of linear equalities can be considered as one instance of an analysis framework which generalizes the functional approach of [28] from programs with procedures to programs with procedures, interrupts, priorities and resources following the PCP protocol. Other instances of this framework can be obtained by providing specific domains V and V' for summary functions and abstract states, respectively, together with transfer functions for the basic statements and specific versions of the operators $\circ$, $\bullet_j$, $\mathcal{H}_f$, $@$, enter_f, $@_j$ and proj_j.

We have implemented the analyses of potential data races and transactionality within the static analyzer *Goblint* [31]. Preliminary experiments with typical examples as well as a scalable synthetic benchmark, are encouraging. Still, experiments with larger and more complicated real-world examples are desirable. We would also like to analyze further kinds of concurrency flaws in PCP programs and explore in how far the given approach can be generalized to more general programming models, e.g., PCP programs with task creation.

Acknowledgements

We thank Gordon Haak and Philipp Legrum for interesting us in PCP programs as well as providing example programs and valuable insights from a user's perspective. This work is supported by the joint DFG project OpIAT (MU 1508/1-1 and SE 551/13-1). The third author is partially supported by EstSF grant 8421.

References

[1] C. Artho, K. Havelund, and A. Biere. Using block-local atomicity to detect stale-value concurrency errors. In *ATVA'04*, vol. 3299 of *LNCS*, pp. 150–164. Springer, 2004.

[2] M. F. Atig, A. Bouajjani, and T. Touili. Analyzing asynchronous programs with preemption. In *FSTTCS'08*, vol. 2 of *LIPIcs*, pp. 37–48. Schloss Dagstuhl, 2008.

[3] Autosar consortium. *Autosar Architecture Specification, Release 4.0*, 2009. URL `http://www.autosar.org/`.

[4] T. P. Baker. Stack-based scheduling of realtime processes. *Real-Time Systems*, 3(1):67–99, 1991.

[5] A. Bouajjani, M. Müller-Olm, and T. Touili. Regular symbolic analysis of dynamic networks of pushdown systems. In *CONCUR'05*, vol. 3653 of *LNCS*, pp. 473–487. Springer, 2005.

[6] P. Cousot and R. Cousot. Comparing the Galois connection and widening/narrowing approaches to abstract interpretation, invited paper. In *PLILP'92*, pp. 269–295. Springer, 1992.

[7] B. Dutertre. Formal analysis of the priority ceiling protocol. In *RTSS'00*, pp. 151–160. IEEE Press, 2000.

[8] J. Esparza and A. Podelski. Efficient algorithms for pre* and post* on interprocedural parallel flow graphs. In *POPL'00*, pp. 1–11. ACM Press, 2000.

[9] C. Fecht and H. Seidl. A Faster Solver for General Systems of Equations. *Sci. Comput. Programming*, 35(2):137–161, 1999.

[10] C. Flanagan, S. N. Freund, S. Qadeer, and S. A. Seshia. Modular verification of multithreaded programs. *Theoretical Comput. Sci.*, 338 (1-3):153–183, 2005.

[11] C. Flanagan, S. N. Freund, M. Lifshin, and S. Qadeer. Types for atomicity: Static checking and inference for java. *ACM Trans. Prog. Lang. Syst.*, 30(4):1–53, 2008.

[12] M. S. Hecht. *Flow Analysis of Computer Programs*. Elsevier, 1977.

[13] T. Henties, J. J. Hunt, D. Locke, K. Nilsen, M. Schoeberl, and J. Vitek. Java for safety-critical applications. In *SafeCert'09*, ENTCS. Elsevier, 2010.

[14] V. Kahlon and A. Gupta. On the analysis of interacting pushdown systems. In *POPL'07*, pp. 303–314. ACM Press, 2007.

[15] V. Kahlon, F. Ivančić, and A. Gupta. Reasoning about threads communicating via locks. In *CAV'05*, vol. 3576 of *LNCS*, pp. 505–518. Springer, 2005.

[16] V. Kahlon, Y. Yang, S. Sankaranarayanan, and A. Gupta. Fast and accurate static data-race detection for concurrent programs. In *CAV'07*, vol. 4590 of *LNCS*, pp. 226–239. Springer, 2007.

[17] N. Kidd, P. Lammich, T. Touili, and T. Reps. A decision procedure for detecting atomicity violations for communicating processes with locks. In *SPIN'09*, vol. 5578 of *LNCS*, pp. 125–142. Springer, 2009.

[18] N. Kidd, S. Jagannathan, and J. Vitek. One stack to run them all — reducing concurrent analysis to sequential analysis under priority scheduling. In *SPIN'10*, vol. 6349 of *LNCS*, pp. 245–261. Springer, 2010.

[19] P. Lammich and M. Müller-Olm. Conflict analysis of programs with procedures, dynamic thread creation, and monitors. In *SAS'08*, vol. 5079 of *LNCS*, pp. 205–220. Springer, 2008.

[20] P. Lammich, M. Müller-Olm, and A. Wenner. Predecessor sets of dynamic pushdown networks with Tree-Regular constraints. In *CAV'09*, vol. 5643 of *LNCS*, pp. 525–539. Springer, 2009.

[21] M. Müller-Olm and H. Seidl. Precise interprocedural analysis through linear algebra. In *POPL'04*, pp. 330–341. ACM Press, 2004.

[22] OSEK/VDX Group. *OSEK/VDX Operating System Specification, Version 2.2.3*, 2005. URL `http://www.osek-vdx.org`.

[23] M. Pilling, A. Burns, and K. Raymond. Formal specifications and proofs of inheritance protocols for real-time scheduling. *Softw. Eng. J.*, 5(5):263–279, 1990.

[24] G. Ramalingam. Context-sensitive synchronization-sensitive analysis is undecidable. *ACM Trans. Prog. Lang. Syst.*, 22(2):416–430, 2000.

[25] J. Regehr and N. Cooprider. Interrupt verification via thread verification. *ENTCS*, 174(9):139–150, 2007.

[26] J. Regehr, A. Reid, and K. Webb. Eliminating stack overflow by abstract interpretation. *ACM Trans. Embedded Comput. Syst.*, 4(4): 751–778, 2005.

[27] L. Sha, R. Rajkumar, and J. P. Lehoczky. Priority inheritance protocols: an approach to real-time synchronization. *IEEE Trans. Comput.*, 39(9):1175–1185, Sept. 1990.

[28] M. Sharir and A. Pnueli. Two approaches to interprocedural data flow analysis. *Program Flow Analysis: Theory and Applications*, pp. 189–234, 1981.

[29] Takashi Chikamasa et al. *OSEK platform for* LEGO® MINDSTORMS ®, 2010. URL `http://lejos-osek.sourceforge.net/`.

[30] M. Vaziri, F. Tip, and J. Dolby. Associating synchronization constraints with data in an object-oriented language. In *POPL'06*, pp. 334–345. ACM Press, 2006.

[31] V. Vojdani and V. Vene. Goblint: Path-sensitive data race analysis. *Annales Univ. Sci. Budapest., Sect. Comp.*, 30:141–155, 2009.

A Parametric Segmentation Functor for Fully Automatic and Scalable Array Content Analysis

Patrick Cousot
École normale supérieure &
New York University
Courant Institute of Mathematical Sciences
cousot@ens.fr, pcousot@cs.nyu.edu

Radhia Cousot
Centre National de la Recherche Scientifique
École normale supérieure &
Microsoft Research, Redmond
radhia.cousot@ens.fr

Francesco Logozzo
Microsoft Research, Redmond
logozzo@microsoft.com

Abstract

We introduce FunArray, a parametric segmentation abstract domain functor for the fully automatic and scalable analysis of array content properties. The functor enables a natural, painless and efficient lifting of existing abstract domains for scalar variables to the analysis of uniform compound data-structures such as arrays and collections. The analysis automatically and semantically divides arrays into consecutive non-overlapping possibly empty segments. Segments are delimited by sets of bound expressions and abstracted uniformly. All symbolic expressions appearing in a bound set are equal in the concrete. The FunArray can be naturally combined via reduced product with any existing analysis for scalar variables. The analysis is presented as a general framework parameterized by the choices of bound expressions, segment abstractions and the reduction operator. Once the functor has been instantiated with fixed parameters, the analysis is fully automatic.

We first prototyped FunArray in Arrayal to adjust and experiment with the abstractions and the algorithms to obtain the appropriate precision/ratio cost. Then we implemented it into Clousot, an abstract interpretation-based static contract checker for .NET. We empirically validated the precision and the performance of the analysis by running it on the main libraries of .NET and on its own code. We were able to infer thousands of non-trivial invariants and verify the implementation with a modest overhead (circa 1%). To the best of our knowledge this is the first analysis of this kind applied to such a large code base, and proven to scale.

Categories and Subject Descriptors D.2.4 [*Software Engineering*]: Program Verification—formal methods, validation, assertion checkers; D.3.1 [*Programming Languages*]: Formal Definitions and Theory—semantics; F.3.1 [*Logics and Meanings of Programs*]: Specifying and Verifying and Reasoning about Programs—Mechanical verification, assertions, invariants; F.3.2 [*Logics and Meanings of Programs*]: Semantics of Programming Languages—Program analysis.

General Terms Algorithms, Design, Languages, Performance, Reliability, Security, Theory, Verification.

Keywords Abstract interpretation, Array abstraction, Array content analysis, Array property inference, Invariant synthesis, Static analysis, Program verification.

1. Introduction

Our goal is to augment static analyzers for very large programs with a new fully automatic static analysis determining properties of array elements with good precision but at low cost so as to scale up. The approach is in the context of abstract interpretation [7]. The first objective of the array content analysis is to reduce the false alarms due to accessing array elements which analysis is often imprecise, in particular because their proper initialization is unknown. The second objective is to allow for automatically proving user provided pre/post conditions and assertions of moderate complexity on arrays (such as the non relational property "all elements are initialized" but not the relational one "the array is sorted" as in [6]). To cope with verification, we want to be able to adjust the cost/precision ratio towards more or less precision, one extreme being the classical analysis by array smashing, the other being an element by element analysis of maximal precision and cost.

2. Motivating Example

Let us consider the example in Fig. **1**, extracted from the public constructor of the Random class of the .NET framework. The constructor initializes all the elements of the private array SeedArray to be ≥ -1. The initialization process is quite complex, relying on some number theory properties which are out-of-the scope of the paper. The precondition requires the parameter Seed not to be the smallest 32-bits integer, to prevent Math.Abs from throwing an OverflowException. Next, an array of 56 elements is allocated and assigned to SeedArray. The last array element is set to the value of Seed, whereas all the others are zero (because of .NET semantics). The first loop (Loop 1), sets *all* the elements of indexes $1 \dots 54$ to be ≥ -1 according to the non-contiguous indexing sequence: $21, 42, 8, \dots$, leaving the first and the last elements unchanged. Therefore the assertion at the end of Loop 1 holds. The next loop (Loop 2) shakes the values in the array, updating the last element of the array but not the first. To prove the second assertion one should prove that (i) the last element of SeedArray is definitely updated in the inner loop to a ≥ 1 value; and that (ii) the inner loop is executed at least once.

Array expansion The first and most precise approach for proving the two assertions: (i) expands the 56 cells of the array to 56 local variables; (ii) fully unrolls the loops. The example will then become intractable, even with up-to-date hardware and tools. We totally unrolled the first loop, we sliced the second loop according to some "interesting" variables (manually determined), and we tried to prove the second postcondition using Boogie [2] and the state-of-the-art SMT solver Z3 [10]. We let the verification process run for a whole week-end without getting an answer. The theorem prover

```
public Random(int Seed) {
 Contract.Requires(Seed != Int32.MinValue);
 int num2 = 161803398 - Math.Abs(Seed);
 this.SeedArray = new int[56];
 this.SeedArray[55] = num2;
 int num3 = 1;
 // Loop 1
 for (int i = 1; i < 55; i++) {
  int index = (21 * i) % 55;
  this.SeedArray[index] = num3;  // (*)
  num3 = num2 - num3;
  if (num3 < 0)  num3 += 2147483647;
  num2 = this.SeedArray[index];
 }
 Contract.Assert(Contract.Forall( // (**)
   0,this.SeedArray.Length - 1, i => a[i] >= -1));
 // Loop 2
 for (int j = 1; j < 5; j++) {
  // Loop 3
  for (int k = 1; k < 56; k++) {
   this.SeedArray[k] -= this.SeedArray[1 + (k + 30) % 55];
   if (this.SeedArray[k] < 0)
    this.SeedArray[k] += 2147483647;
  } }
 Contract.Assert(Contract.Forall(0,  // (***)
   this.SeedArray.Length, i => a[i] >= -1));
}
```

Figure 1. A motivating example taken from the core library of `.NET`. `Contract.{Requires, Assert, ForAll}` is the `CodeContracts` API (adopted in `.NET` from $v4.0$) to express preconditions, assertions and bounded universal quantifications [3].

was overcome by the large number of case splits it had to perform (because of conditionals in loop bodies and the lack of primitive support for the remainder operation which had to be axiomatized).

Array smashing At the opposite side of the precision spectrum there is the smashing of all the array elements into one summary location. It is immediate that this is not going to work. For instance in `Loop 1`, the value of `SeedArray[55]` is smashed with the others, concluding that any value can be written anywhere in the array.

Predicate abstraction The method of Qadeer and Flanagan [15] uses some easy syntactic heuristics to derive the predicates used for the abstraction, which unfortunately do not work here. For instance, one needs to know that $1 \leq$ `index` < 55 to determine that the last element of `SeedArray` is never overwritten in `Loop 1`, or that `num3` ≥ -1. Both properties cannot be inferred with syntactic heuristics.

Array Partitioning The array partitioning approach of Gopan, Reps and Sagiv [17] (later improved by Péron and Halbwachs [19]) separates the task of array partitioning from that of establishing array properties. Given a partition of the array into slices, the analysis populates the slices with some abstract value. The partitioning is done either syntactically or by some pre-analysis. The syntactic approach (used in the examples of [17, 19, 29]) simply does not work here (*e.g.* it cannot determine which array element is written at `(*)`), and in general it is unfeasible in the generic setting of the bytecode analysis, where high-level syntactic structures are compiled away. As a consequence, at the early stages of this work, we tried to implement the second pre-analysis approach in `Clousot` [14]. The idea was to first perform a preliminary analysis of indices to provide a restricted domain for each loop, and then to perform the array analysis (generalizing [19, Sect. 15]). Performance turned out to be extremely bad. The first pre-analysis generated *too many* partition slices (also noticed by Dillig *et al* [12, Sect. 4]). The second analysis needed to replay the index analysis (*e.g.* to distinguish the first iteration from all the others) and the partition analysis (*e.g.* to track how abstract values flowed between partitions). The analysis of the example induced a $28\times$ slowdown with respect to a run of `Clousot` without the array analysis. We have therefore developed a new approach (subject of this paper) in which: (i) the scalar analysis and the array analysis are performed at the same time (which is also more precise [8]); (ii) the array segmentation is automatically and semantically discovered by the analysis; and (iii) the segmentation admits possibly empty segments. In particular, possibly empty segments are a winning choice because they enable a compact representation for array partitions avoiding the exponential multiplication of slices of the aforementioned works (Sect. **4.4**). Yang *et al* remarked similar advantages when using possibly empty list segments for shape analysis [37].

Under-approximations and Templates The technique of Gulwani, McCloskey and Tiwari [18] is extremely powerful yet expensive. It requires: (i) the user to provide templates for the array invariants; and (ii) the abstract domain to perform under-approximations for the index variable. It can infer all the invariants of our example, provided some refinement in the handling of transition functions for quantified facts and in the under-approximation algorithm. Their technique uses uninterpreted functions and a guess & prove cycle to determine precedents for guards. Unfortunately, the abstract domain of uninterpreted functions exposes a double-exponential complexity [18], which seriously affects the analysis cost. According to [18, Sect.5.2], *at best* the quantified domain induces a 70% slowdown of their analyzer, and *at most* a 1800% slowdown (w.r.t. a normal run) on small examples. As a comparison, the functor abstract domain presented in this paper induces a mere 1% slowdown with respect to a normal `Clousot` run on huge, production quality libraries (*cf.* Sect. **12**), yet presenting a high precision.

Deductive methods Program verifiers *à la* ESC/Java 2 [5] or Spec# [1] require the user to provide loop invariants. In our running example, we needed to provide a few extra-annotations (9 to be exact) to help both tools prove the assertions in the code. First we have to add the invariant on the content of `SeedArray` to every loop in the code. Then, we added the loop invariant `num3` $\geq -1 \wedge$ `i` ≥ 1 to `Loop 1`, `j` ≥ 1 to `Loop 2` and `k` ≥ 1 to `Loop 3`. In general, such program verifiers are very powerful but the extra-annotations impose a burden that very few professional programmers are willing to pay for. Furthermore, deductive verification-based tools can *check* the correctness of a program fragment (*e.g.* a method), but they cannot *infer* facts to be used on larger pieces of code (*e.g.* class invariants to verify whole classes [26]).

Theorem prover-based The method of Kovács and Voronkov [23] uses a saturation theorem prover to generate loop invariants. The idea is to encode the changes to an array at the i-th iteration as a quantified fact and then to systematically apply resolution to derive a closed form (one not mentioning the loop iteration i). A problem with such a technique is termination, for instance to determine when the "right" loop invariant has been produced by a saturation step. This may require a human help (stopping the saturation process when a postcondition does not work: for instance if we remove the first assertion in Fig. **1**, then the process may go on forever). Furthermore, their method is based on the use of monotonic changes to the array (which is not the case for `Loop 1`) and it requires a pre-analysis of indexes (causing an extra slow-down).

The techniques of Jhala and McMillan [20, 30] and of Seghir, Podelski and Wies [35] make use of the loop postconditions to be proven in order to infer the quantified loop invariants. Suppose we remove (**) and (***) from the example. Then their techniques (unlike ours) cannot infer the postcondition that all the elements of SeedArray are initialized to a value ≥ -1 at the end of the Random constructor. In practice, such a postcondition is needed, for instance to prove that it is an object invariant for the class Random [26] and hence to prove the safety of the public methods. Furthermore, the techniques above do not always guarantee termination.

The fluid updates technique of Dillig, Dillig and Aiken [12] is very expressive and it can be extended to precisely track complex containers properties [13]. It is exposed to a potential exponential explosion too. Theoretically, their technique is the lifting to the reduced cardinal power [8] of a points-to analysis. Practically, every time an array is accessed or created, the points-to edges are modified, new constraints are added and calls to an SMT solver are issued to prove the (un-)feasibility of the edge(s) and simplify the constraints. This may negatively influence the performance of the analysis and also affect the precision (whenever the expressions go out of the language treated by the SMT solver, as for instance the reminder in Fig. **1**).

Our Approach Our analysis infers *all* the invariants for Fig. **1** without user interaction: no templates, no annotations nor partitions are required, no hypotheses are done on the structure of the source program. The invariants are inferred even if the assertions are removed from the code. The code is analyzed in (a little bit less than) 60 milliseconds (50 milliseconds for reading the bytecode, performing a stack analysis, heap analysis, non-null, and numerical analysis alone).

The analysis is an instance of FunArray, which we introduce in this paper. FunArray is a functor abstract domain which lifts existing analyses for scalar values to uniform compound data structures as arrays or collections. In this paper we will concentrate on arrays, but it is immediate to see how the results generalize to collections as found in mainstream object-oriented languages such as C# or Java as well as matrices when instantiating the functor on itself.

The FunArray analysis automatically divides the array into a sequence of possibly empty segments delimited by a set of segment bounds. The content of each segment is uniformly abstracted. The array analysis can be combined via a reduced product with an abstraction for scalar variables. Therefore the FunArray has three main parameters: (i) the expressions used to describe the segment bounds; (ii) the abstract domain used to abstract the segment values; and (iii) the abstract domain used to abstract scalar variables. When the three parameters above are chosen to be: (i) simple expressions in the form k or $\mathtt{x} + k$ where x is a variable and k is an integer [33]; (ii) and (iii) intervals [7] then for Loop 1 our analysis infers that all the values of the arrays with indexes in the range $1 \ldots 54$ are greater or equal to -1, and that the last element of the array is not overwritten. The FunArray uses the information to infer the segmentation below, which is enough to prove the assertion (**) (values in brackets are bounds, intervals denote the abstraction for the array elements in the bounds, see Sect. **4.3**).

```
{0} [-1,+oo] {55} [+oo,-oo] {56}.
```
(1)

For Loop 3, the analysis discovers that *all* the array elements, including the last one, have been overwritten with a value ≥ -1:

```
{0} [-1,+oo] {56}.
```
(2)

The loop invariant for Loop 2 is then the union of the two invariants above, that is (1) as the first segmentation subsumes the second one. If directly propagated after the loop, this invariant is too weak to prove the assertion (***). The imprecision is originated by the fact that we are not considering that the body of Loop 2 is executed at least once, so that SeedArray[55] is overwritten at least once (because of (1)). Standard static analysis techniques such as loop unrolling or backwards goal propagation [14, Sect. 6] can be used to recover the needed precision, and hence refine the abstract post-state of Loop 2 to (2). This highlights another advantage of our analysis, which benefits *for free* of precision refinement techniques applied to the analyzer.

3. Our Contribution

The main advantages of our analysis can be summarized as:

1. The array segmentation is automatically and semantically inferred during the analysis. By semantically, we mean that the subdivision of the array is done during the analysis using *semantic* information, unlike the aforementioned approaches which derive the partition by looking at the syntactic structure of the program. The segments are consecutive, without holes (a hole being just another segment). The segments derive from the way array elements are modified and accessed. Segments are delimited by bounds, in increasing order, denoted by sets of simple symbolic expressions with equal but unknown values;
2. The combinatorial explosion in the handling of disjunctions is avoided by considering symbolic segment bounds as well as possibly empty segments;
3. The relations between array indexes and array elements can be inferred by abstracting pairs made of the array index and the value of the corresponding array element (vs. abstracting array element values only);
4. The precision/cost ratio in the abstraction of the array content can be finely tuned using a functor abstract domain: the array content analysis is parameterized by the abstract domain representing symbolic segment bound expressions, the abstract domain abstracting the pairs (index, value) in segments, the abstract domain assigning values to segment bound expressions, and the reduction between those domains.
5. By instantiating the array segmentation abstract domains functor with different abstract domains, different static analyzers can be automatically generated with different cost/precision ratios allowing the cost versus precision tradeoff of the analysis to be tuned depending on the target application at no re-programming cost of the static analyzer.

We have first implemented our technique in a research prototype Arrayal, to quickly experiment with the algorithms and adjust the abstractions. Then we fully implemented it in Clousot, an industrial-quality static contract checker for .NET based on abstract interpretation. The functor abstract domain enabled a natural lifting of the abstract domains, already present in Clousot, to array contents. To the users, this is exposed as a simple checkbox in the development environment. We validated the precision of the analysis by using it to check its own implementation. The analysis is extremely fast: we estimated the cost of the array analysis on Clousot to be less than 1% of the total running time when running it on production code (Sect. **12**). To the best of knowledge, this is the first analysis of this kind applied to such a large scale.

4. Array Initialization

We explain the details of our technique on the initialization example of Fig. **2**, slightly more general than Loop 3. We illustrate how we avoid the combinatorial explosion on the partial initialization example of Fig. **3** and on the array rearrangement example of Fig. **4**.

4.1 Manual proof

A manual proof of the exit specification would involve a loop invariant at program point 2 stating that if $\mathtt{A.Length} = 0$ then $\mathtt{i} = 0$ and the array A is empty or else $\mathtt{A.Length} \geqslant 1$ in which case either $\mathtt{i} = 0$ and the array A is not initialized or else $\mathtt{i} > 0$

```
              void Init(int[] A) {
/* 0: */        int i = 0;
/* 1: */        while /* 2: */ (i < A.Length) {
/* 3: */          A[i] = 0;
/* 4: */          i = i + 1;
/* 5: */        }
/* 6: */      }
```

Figure 2. The fully initialized example. We want to prove that $\forall i \in [0, \texttt{A.Length}) : \texttt{A}[i] = 0$ at program point 6.

so that $\texttt{A[0]} = \texttt{A[1]} = \ldots = \texttt{A[i} - 1] = 0$. Formally the invariant $(\texttt{A.Length} = 0 \wedge \texttt{i} = 0) \vee (\texttt{A.Length} \geqslant 1 \wedge 0 \leqslant \texttt{i} \leqslant \texttt{A.Length} \wedge \forall j \in [0, \texttt{i}) : \texttt{A}[j] = 0)$ holds at point 2 [(1)].

This invariant shows that array content analyses must be able to: (i) express disjunctions of array descriptions; (ii) express properties of array segments (that is sequences of values of consecutive array elements); and (iii) relate the symbolic limits $0, \texttt{i}-1, \texttt{A.Length}-1$ of these segments to the scalar program variables.

4.2 Automatic proof and the meaning of the abstract invariant predicates

In our array segmentation analysis instantiated *e.g.* with constant propagation [22], we automatically get the abstract invariant predicates

```
p1 = A: {0 i} T {A.Length}?
p2 = A: {0} 0 {i}? T {A.Length}?
p6 = A: {0} 0 {A.Length i}?
```

where pi is the abstract invariant predicate at program point $i = 1, \ldots, 6$. In this example the properties of scalar variables need not be used. The abstract values for constant propagation can be _|_ (*i.e.*, bottom $\perp$, meaning unreachable), an integer constant (meaning equal to that constant), or T (*i.e.*, top $\top$, meaning unknown).

In the array environments such as `A: {0 i} T {A.Length}?` in p1, each array of the program (such as A) has its content described by a segmentation (such as `{0 i} T {A.Length}?`). From the symbolic segment bounds such as `{0 i}` and `{A.Length}?` we know that $\texttt{i} = 0$ (since all expressions in a bound are equal) and that $0 = \texttt{i} \leqslant \texttt{A.Length}$ (since the segment bounds are in increasing order, strictly increasing in absence of ?). The segments are not empty, except if the upper bound of the segment is marked with ?. The segments are consecutive without holes, since a hole can always be represented by a $\top$ segment (possibly empty if the hole may or may not be absent). Each segment uniformly describes the array elements within that segment bounds, lower bound included, upper bound excluded. In `{0 i} T {A.Length}?`, the array element abstract value is T, meaning in the constant propagation analysis, that the array values are unknown ($\top$). So the invariant p1 states that $\texttt{i} = 0 \leqslant \texttt{A.Length} \wedge \forall j \in [0, \texttt{A.Length}) : \texttt{A}[j] \in \mathbb{Z}$. In particular, when $\texttt{i} = \texttt{A.Length} = 0$, the interval $[0, \texttt{A.Length})$ is empty, so the quantified expression holds vacuously.

The invariant p2 states that $0 \leqslant \texttt{i} \leqslant \texttt{A.Length}$ (in absence of question marks ? these inequalities would be strict), that $\texttt{A[0]} = \texttt{A[1]} = \ldots = \texttt{A[i} - 1] = 0$ when $\texttt{i} > 0$ and that the values $\texttt{A[i]}, \texttt{A[i} + 1], \ldots, \texttt{A[A.Length} - 1]$ are unknown when $\texttt{A.Length} > \texttt{i}$. So the array is divided into consecutive non-overlapping segments, which may be empty and are delimited by symbolic expressions in increasing order. The abstraction of the array elements within one segment is uniform but different segments can have different abstract properties.

[(1)] This invariant can also be written $0 \leqslant \texttt{i} \leqslant \texttt{A.Length} \wedge \forall j \in [0, \texttt{i}) : \texttt{A}[j] = 0$ with the convention that $[0, -1] = \emptyset$ is the empty set in which case $\texttt{A}[j]$ is not evaluated, which is made explicit by a disjunction of cases (marked ? in segmentation bounds).

In order to avoid combinatorial explosion, disjunctions appear in restricted form only either as possible segment emptiness, or symbolic bounds which may have different values, or in the segment content analysis (see Sect. **11.1**). For example, the post-condition p6 expresses that either the array is empty (*i.e.* $\texttt{A.Length} = \texttt{i} = 0$) or else $\texttt{A.Length} = \texttt{i} > 0$ and all array elements are initialized to 0.

Please note that the case $\texttt{A.Length} < 0$ is excluded. This comes from the initial condition stating that $\texttt{A.Length} \geqslant 0$ since most programming languages like C, C# and Java do not allow arrays of negative size. We handle all such runtime errors including division by zero, index out of bounds, ...by stopping execution. This is a sound treatment of their undefined semantics in absence of runtime errors but may otherwise miss some other possible erroneous executions (following from the fact that execution goes on in practice with an undefined semantics).

4.3 Detailed unreeling of the initialization example analysis

We now consider the details of the analysis of the code of Fig. 2 with constant propagation. The initial condition $\texttt{A.Length} \geqslant 0$ is recorded in the segmentation of array A.

```
p0 = A: {0} T {A.Length}?
```

The assignment `i = 0;` sets the value of the scalar variable i to 0. The equality `i = 0` is valid after the assignment and so is recorded in the lower bound of the array segment. Initially $\texttt{p2} = \texttt{p3} = \ldots = \texttt{p5} = \perp$ denotes unreachability of the loop so that the abstract loop invariant is initially $\texttt{p2} = \texttt{p1} \sqcup \texttt{p5} = \texttt{p1}$ (using the join $\sqcup$ in the constant abstract domain for segments: $x \sqcup \perp = \perp \sqcup x = x$, $x \sqcup \top = \top \sqcup x = \top$, $i \sqcup i = i$, and $i \sqcup j = \top$ when $i \neq j$).

```
p2 = p1 = p0[i=0] = A: {0 i} T {A.Length}?
```

The loop is entered when `i < A.Length` so that the array, hence its only segment, cannot be empty so ? is dropped:

```
p3 = p2[i<A.Length] = A: {0 i} T {A.Length}
```

The analysis of the array assignment `A[i] = 0;` splits the array segment around the index i and assigns to the array element the value of expression 0 in the constant domain that is 0:

```
p4 = p3[A[i]=0] = A: {0 i} 0 {1 i+1} T {A.Length}?
```

Please note that the segment i ... i+1 is definitely not empty while the segment i+1 ... A.Length may be empty. The scalar variable assignment `i = i + 1;` is invertible since the old value of i is the new value of variable i decremented by 1. So the segment bounds involving variable i have to be modified accordingly:

```
p5 = p4[i=i+1] = A: {0 i-1} 0 {1 i} T {A.Length}?
```

The next approximation of the loop invariant is $\texttt{p2} = \texttt{p1} \sqcup \texttt{p5}$. This join first involves the unification of the segment $\{\texttt{0 i}\}\top\{\texttt{A.Length}\}$ of p1 and that $\{\texttt{0 i} - 1\}0\{\texttt{1 i}\}\top\{\texttt{A.Length}\}?$ of p5. Keeping only the expressions appearing in both segmentations, we get $\{\texttt{0 i}\}\top\{\texttt{A.Length}\}$ and $\{0\}0\{\texttt{i}\}\top\{\texttt{A.Length}\}?$. Splitting the bound $\{\texttt{0 i}\}$ we get $\{0\}\perp\{\texttt{i}\}?\top\{\texttt{A.Length}\}$ so that the union with $\{0\}0\{\texttt{i}\}\top\{\texttt{A.Length}\}?$ can now be performed segmentwise in the constant domain $\{0\}\perp \sqcup 0\{\texttt{i}\}(? \curlyvee \llcorner\!\lrcorner)\top \sqcup \top\{\texttt{A.Length}\}(\llcorner\!\lrcorner \curlyvee ?) = \{0\}0\{\texttt{i}\}?\top\{\texttt{A.Length}\}?$ since the segments may be empty in at least one of the cases (that is $\llcorner\!\lrcorner \curlyvee \llcorner\!\lrcorner = \llcorner\!\lrcorner$ for non-empty segments and otherwise $\llcorner\!\lrcorner \curlyvee ? = ? \curlyvee \llcorner\!\lrcorner = ? \curlyvee ? = ?$ for possibly empty ones). We get

```
p2 = p1 U p5 = A: {0} 0 {i}? T {A.Length}?
```

The next iteration is similar:

```
p3 = p2[i<A.Length] =  A: {0} 0 {i}? T {A.Length}
p4 = p3[A[i]=0] =  A: {0} 0 {i}? 0 {i+1} T {A.Length}?
p5 = p4[i=i+1] =  A: {0} 0 {i-1}? 0 {i} T {A.Length}?
p2 = p1 U p5 =  A: {0} 0 {i}? T {A.Length}?
```

```
void InitPartial(int[] A, int[] C) {
 Contract.Requires(A.Length == C.Length);

 int i = 0, j = 0;

 while (i < A.Length) {
  if (p(A[i])) // For some predicate p
    C[j++] = 1;
  i++;
 } }
```

Figure 3. Partial array initialization. Partition-based techniques use four partitions encoding the fact that at loop exit C may be empty, partially filled, almost-totally filled or totally filled. Our analysis: (i) compactly represents the same information with only one segmentation; and (ii) infers the segmentation automatically.

```
          void Rearrangement(int[] A) {
           Contract.Requires(A.length > 1);
           Contract.Requires(Contract.Forall(0,A.length,
             i => (-100 <= A[i] && A[i] <= 100)));
           int a = 0, b = A.length;
/* 1: */   while /* 2: */ (a < b) {
/* 3: */     if A[a] >= 0 then {
/* 4: */       a = a + 1;
/* 5: */     } else {
/* 6: */       b = b - 1;
/* 7: */       int x = A[a]; A[a] = A[b]; A[b] = x;
/* 8: */     } }
/* 9: */   }
```

Figure 4. The array in-situ rearrangement example.

so that we have reached a fixpoint. It remains to compute

```
p6 = p2[i>=A.Length] = A: {0} 0 {A.Length,i}?
```

where A.Length $=$ i since the segmentation of p2 provides the information that $0 \leqslant$ i $\leqslant$ A.Length.

The array content analysis always terminates since the only two reasons for non-termination are impossible:

1. The array might have infinitely many symbolic segments as in {0} ... ... {n-3} ... {n-2} ... {n-1} ... {n} which is prevented by segmentation unification and widening;
2. A segment might take successive strictly increasing abstract values which is prevented by the use of a widening/narrowing convergence acceleration for segment content analysis [7]. No widening was necessary for constant propagation which satisfies the ascending chain condition ($\perp \sqsubset i \sqsubset \top, i \in \mathbb{Z}$).

4.4 Partial Array Initialization

Full array initialization is a very well studied example, and array-partitioning techniques perform reasonably well on it [17, 19]. However, partial array initialization (Fig. 3) illustrates the multiplication of partitions which makes those techniques not-scalable. At the end of the loop, our analysis (instantiated with constant propagation) infers the following segmentation for C:

```
{0} 1 {j}? T {i,A.Length,C.Length}?
```

which compactly captures the fact that C may be empty (when $0 =$ j $=$ i), may be not initialized (when j $= 0$), may be partially initialized (when $0 <$ j $<$ i), may be fully initialized (when $0 <$ j $=$ i). Compare it with partition-based approaches where the abstract state at the end of the loop contains four disjuncts: one representing the concrete state when none of the C elements is initialized (j $= 0$), two representing the partial initialization of C distinguishing when j+1 $<$ C.Length or j $<$ C.Length, and one representing the total initialization (j == C.Length) ([17, 7.2]). We tried this example using our early implementation of [19] and we got a $2\times$ slow-down with respect to a normal run of Clousot (it is worth noting that the experimental results reported in [17] and those in [18] are even worse than our first implementation). For this example, Clousot lifted with the functor abstract domain was so fast that we were unable to measure its impact on the performances: the additional cost is in the order of magnitude the noise of the virtual machine (JIT, garbage collector ...) *i.e.* few milliseconds.

4.5 Array in-situ rearrangement example

The in-situ array rearrangement algorithm of Fig. 4 [4, 23] maintains an invariant

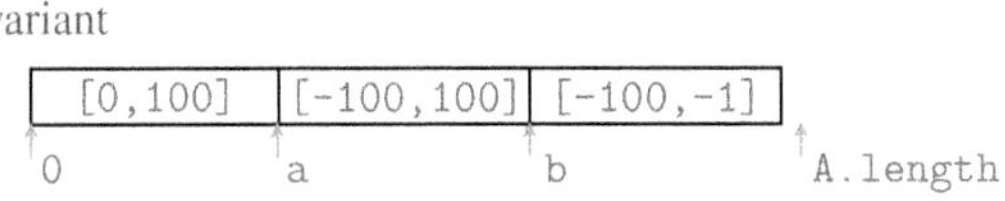

where positive numbers are on the left of a, the negative numbers are on the right, from b included, and in the middle, between a and $\mathtt{b} - 1$ the numbers remain to be handled. If A[a] is positive, the limit a is moved to the right. Otherwise, A[a] is exchanged with A[b-1] and b is moved to the left. The algorithm terminates when the central zone is empty. This invariant which is automatically inferred by the automatic array segmentation analysis illustrates the interest of using possibly empty segments:

```
p1 = (A: {0 a} [-100,100] {b A.length}
       a:[0,0] b:[2,+oo] A.length:[2,+oo])
p2 = (A: {0}[0,100]{a}?[-100,100]{b}?[-100,-1]{A.length}?
       a:[0,+oo] b:[0,+oo] A.length:[2,+oo])
p9 = (A: {0} [0,100] {b a}? [-100,-1] {A.length}?
       a:[0,+oo] b:[0,+oo] A.length:[2,+oo])
```

5. Abstract Domains and Functors

An *abstract domain* $\mathbf{D}$ includes a set $\overline{\mathcal{D}}$ of abstract properties as well as abstract functions and operations $\mathbf{D}.op$ for the partial order structure of abstract properties ($\sqsubseteq$), the join ($\sqcup$), the meet ($\sqcap$), convergence acceleration operators: widening (∇) and narrowing (Δ), the abstract property transformers involved in the definition of the semantics of the programming language: the abstract evaluation of program arithmetic and Boolean expressions, the assignment to scalar variables ... [7]. A monotonic concretization function γ provides the meaning of abstract properties in terms of concrete properties.

An *abstract domain functor* $\mathbf{D}$ is a function from the parameter abstract domains $\mathbf{D}_1, \ldots, \mathbf{D}_n$ to a new abstract domain $\mathbf{D}(\mathbf{D}_1, \ldots, \mathbf{D}_n)$. The term "functor" is mutated from OCaml terminology. The formal parameters $\mathbf{D}_1, \ldots, \mathbf{D}_n$ of the abstract domain functor $\mathbf{D}$ can be instantiated to various actual abstract domains without needing to rewrite the code of the static analyzer. So various abstractions can be experimented at no programming cost. The abstract domain functor $\mathbf{D}(\mathbf{D}_1, \ldots, \mathbf{D}_n)$ composes abstract properties $\overline{\mathcal{D}}_1, \ldots, \overline{\mathcal{D}}_n$ of the parameter abstract domains $\mathbf{D}_1, \ldots, \mathbf{D}_n$ to build a new class of abstract properties $\overline{\mathcal{D}}$ (*e.g.* abstract environments mapping program numerical variables to intervals) and operations (*e.g.* assignment of an interval to a variable). For short, we can omit the parameters writing $\mathbf{D}$ or *op* when the parameters $\mathbf{D}_1, \ldots, \mathbf{D}_n$ are clear from the context.

6. Concrete Semantics

We describe the elements of the semantics of programming languages to which our array content analysis does apply, that is scalar variables, simple expressions, and unidimensional arrays and corresponding assignments.

6.1 Scalar Variables Semantics The operational semantics of scalar variables with basic types (bool, char, int, float, *etc.*) is assumed to be concrete variable environments $\rho \in \mathcal{R}_v$ mapping variable names $\mathtt{i} \in \mathbb{X}$ to their values $\rho(\mathtt{i}) \in \mathcal{V}$ so that $\mathcal{R}_v \triangleq \mathbb{X} \mapsto \mathcal{V}$. In the following we let $\mathtt{A.Length} \in \mathbb{X}$ be the name denoting the length of the array A.

*6.2 **Simple Expressions Semantics*** The program simple expressions $\mathtt{e} \in \mathbb{E}$ containing only constant, scalar variables, and mathematical unary and binary operators have a semantics $[\![\mathtt{e}]\!]\rho$ in the concrete variable environment ρ so that $[\![\mathtt{e}]\!] \in \mathcal{R}_v \mapsto \mathcal{V}$. For simplicity, the values in our examples are chosen to be integers (so $\mathcal{V} = \mathbb{Z}$). The semantics of scalar variable assignment is as usual $[\![\mathtt{i := e}]\!]\rho \triangleq \rho[\mathtt{i} := [\![\mathtt{e}]\!]\rho]$ where $\rho[\mathtt{i} := v](\mathtt{i}) = v$ and $\rho[\mathtt{i} := v](\mathtt{j}) = \rho(\mathtt{j})$ when $\mathtt{j} \neq \mathtt{i}$.

*6.3 **Unidimensional Arrays Semantics*** The operational semantics of array variables (such as $\mathtt{A} \in \mathbb{A}$) are concrete array environments $\theta \in \mathcal{R}_a$ mapping array names $\mathtt{A} \in \mathbb{A}$ to their values $\theta(\mathtt{A}) \in \mathcal{A} \triangleq \mathcal{R}_v \times \mathbb{E} \times \mathbb{E} \times (\mathbb{Z} \mapsto (\mathbb{Z} \times \mathcal{V}))$ so that $\mathcal{R}_a \triangleq \mathbb{A} \mapsto \mathcal{A}$.

In order to be able to relate array element values to their indexes, we assume that the concrete value of an array A is a quadruple $a = (\rho, \mathtt{A.low}, \mathtt{A.high}, A) \in \mathcal{A}$, where:

- $\rho \in \mathcal{R}_v$ is a scalar variable environment (Sect. **6.1**);
- $\mathtt{A.low} \in \mathbb{E}$ is an expression (0 in our examples) which value $[\![\mathtt{A.low}]\!]\rho$ evaluated in the variable environment ρ yields the integer lower bound of the array;
- $\mathtt{A.high} \in \mathbb{E}$ ($\mathtt{A.Length}$ in our examples) is an expression which value $[\![\mathtt{A.high}]\!]\rho$ evaluated in the variable environment ρ yields the integer upper bound of the array;
- A maps an index $i \in [[\![\mathtt{A.low}]\!]\rho, [\![\mathtt{A.high}]\!]\rho)$ to a pair $A(i) = (i, v)$ of the index i and the corresponding array element value v.

The instrumented semantics of arrays makes explicit the fact that arrays relate indexes to indexed element values by considering array elements to be a pair of an index and an array element value. This instrumented semantics is in contrast with the classical semantics $a \in [\ell, h) \mapsto \mathcal{V}$ of arrays mapping indexes in $[\ell, h)$ to array element values in $\mathcal{V}$. The explicit inclusion of the array bounds is useful to handle arrays of parametric length such as JavaScript arrays or collections in managed languages. Nevertheless, the examples here consider arrays of fixed length, maybe unknown, with $\mathtt{A.low} = 0$. The inclusion of the concrete variable environment is also necessary to explain segments (which are sub-arrays whose bounds may symbolically coincide at different program points although they may take different concrete values over time, so that the length of the segment can vary during execution as shown *e.g.* in Sect. **4.3** by p1 and p5).

The semantics of an array element access A[e] is classical. The expression e is evaluated to an index i. The array variable A is evaluated to its array value $a = (\rho, \mathtt{A.low}, \mathtt{A.high}, A)$ where ρ is the concrete variable environment. It is a "buffer overrun" runtime error if $i < [\![\mathtt{A.low}]\!]\rho$ or $[\![\mathtt{A.high}]\!]\rho \leqslant i$, in which case the value of A[i] is undefined so that program execution is assumed to stop. Otherwise the index is in-bounds so $A(i) = (i, v)$ is well-defined and v is the value, in the classical sense, of the array element A[e]. Obviously storing (i, v) instead of v is useless but for the fact that the instrumented semantics can be used to make the array content analysis more precise.

Example 1 Let us consider the initialization example of Fig. **2** with the *additional* assumption that $\mathtt{A.Length} > 1$. At program point 6 the final values of the scalar variables are given by ρ_6 such that $\rho_6(\mathtt{i}) = \rho_6(\mathtt{A.Length}) = n$ where $n > 1$ is the unknown array length. The final value of A is $a_6 = (\rho_6, 0, \mathtt{A.Length}, A_6)$ with $A_6(i) = (i, 0)$ for all $i \in [0, n)$. Because ρ_6, 0, and A.Length are easily understood from the context, we write $\mathtt{A[}i\mathtt{]} = (i, 0)$ by abuse of notation where the value i of i is assumed to be in-bounds. □

In the analysis of the example of Fig. **2**, the pair $\mathtt{A[}i\mathtt{]} = (i, v)$ was first abstracted to v, which is the case for all non-relational abstract domains such as constant propagation which cannot establish a relation between the index i and the array element value v.

Array properties are sets of concrete array values and so belong to $\wp(\mathcal{A})$ (relations between array values are thus abstracted away).

We have no hypotheses on expressions but $\mathbb{Z} \subseteq \mathbb{E}$ and $\mathbb{X} \subseteq \mathbb{E}$ so that the expressions used in segment bounds can at least be integer constants or scalar variables, which is necessary in most programming languages to express bounds.

7. The Variable and Expression Abstract Domains

7.1 Scalar variable abstraction

We let $\mathbf{X}$ be an abstract domain encoding program variables including a special variable v_0 which value is assumed to be always zero so $\overline{\mathcal{X}} = \mathbb{X} \cup \{\mathrm{v}_0\}$ where $\mathrm{v}_0 \notin \mathbb{X}$. Operations include the equality comparison of variables.

Properties and property transformers of concrete variable environments in $\wp(\mathcal{R}_v)$ are abstracted by the variable environment abstract domain $\mathbf{R}(\mathbf{X})$ which depends on the variable abstract domain $\mathbf{X}$ (so that $\mathbf{R}$ is an abstract domain functor). The abstract properties $\overline{\rho} \in \overline{\mathcal{R}}$ are called abstract variable environments. The concretization $\gamma_v(\overline{\rho})$ denotes the set of concrete variable environments having this abstract property. It follows that $\gamma_v \in \overline{\mathcal{R}} \mapsto \wp(\mathcal{R}_v)$.

The static analysis of scalar variables may or may not be relational. For non-relational abstractions, $\wp(\mathcal{R}_v)$ is first abstracted to $\mathbb{X} \mapsto \wp(\mathcal{V})$ and $\overline{\mathcal{R}} \triangleq \mathbb{X} \mapsto \overline{\mathcal{V}}$ where the abstract domain $\mathbf{V}$ abstracts properties of values in $\mathcal{V}$ with concretization $\gamma_v \in \overline{\mathcal{V}} \mapsto \wp(\mathcal{V})$.

7.2 Expressions in simple normal form

The symbolic expressions appearing in segment bounds belong to the expression abstract domain $\mathbf{E}(\mathbf{X})$. The abstract properties $\overline{\mathcal{E}}$ consist in a set of symbolic expressions depending on the variables in $\overline{\mathcal{X}}$ restricted to a canonical normal form plus the bottom expression $\perp$ corresponding to unreachability and the top expression $\top$ abstracting all symbolic expressions which cannot be put in the considered normal form. The array bound expressions are assumed to be converted in canonical normal form (*e.g.* via auxiliary variables, so that `...A[B[i]]...` becomes `...{int x; x := B[i]; A[x]}...`). Different canonical forms for expressions correspond to different expression abstract domains $\mathbf{E}(\mathbf{X})$.

In our examples, and in the Clousot implementation, the abstract expressions $\overline{\mathcal{E}}$ are restricted to the normal form $\mathrm{v} + k$ where $\mathrm{v} \in \overline{\mathcal{X}}$ is an integer variable plus an integer constant $k \in \mathbb{Z}$ ($\mathrm{v}_0 + k$ represents the integer constant k). An alternative example of convenient normal form would be linear expressions $a.\mathrm{v} + b$ where v is a variable and $a, b \in \mathbb{Z}$ ($a = 0$ for constants).

7.3 Concretization

Given an abstract domain for scalar variables with concretization $\gamma_v \in \overline{\mathcal{R}} \mapsto \wp(\mathbb{X} \mapsto \mathbb{Z})$, the concretization $\gamma_e(\mathtt{e})\overline{\rho}$ of an expression $\mathtt{e} \in \overline{\mathcal{E}}$ depends on the abstract value $\overline{\rho} \in \overline{\mathcal{R}}$ of the scalar variables in $\overline{\mathcal{X}}$ and is the set of possible concrete values of the expression. So $\gamma_e \in \overline{\mathcal{E}} \mapsto \overline{\mathcal{R}} \mapsto \wp(\mathcal{V})$ such that $\gamma_e(\perp)\overline{\rho} \triangleq \emptyset$, $\gamma_e(\top)\overline{\rho} \triangleq \mathcal{V}$, $\gamma_e(\mathrm{v}_0 + i)\overline{\rho} \triangleq \{i\}$, and otherwise $\gamma_e(\mathrm{v} + i)\overline{\rho} \triangleq \{\rho(\mathrm{v}) + i \mid \rho \in \gamma_v(\overline{\rho})\}$.

7.4 Abstract operations on expressions in simple normal form

Simple operations are defined on symbolic expressions in normal form such as the check that an expression depends or not on a given variable, or the substitution of an expression for a variable in an expression followed by its reduction in normal form, returning $\top$ if impossible.

Given two expressions in normal form, we must be able to answer the question of their equality and inequality, which in the abstract is always true, false or unknown. These abstract equality and inequality tests of expressions may be more or less sophisticated. We consider below three cases of increasing complexity, which one is chosen can be a parameter of the analysis.

Syntactic comparisons In their simplest form the comparisons can be purely syntactic. For example $\mathtt{v} + i = \mathtt{v'} + j$ is true if and only if $\mathtt{v} = \mathtt{v'}$ and $i = j$, false if $\mathtt{v} = \mathtt{v'}$ and $i \neq j$ and unknown otherwise. Similarly $\mathtt{v} + i < \mathtt{v'} + j$ is true if and only if $\mathtt{v} = \mathtt{v'}$ and $i < j$, false if $\mathtt{v} = \mathtt{v'}$ and $i \geqslant j$ and unknown otherwise. The comparison of i and $\mathtt{v} + j$ where $\mathtt{v} \neq \mathtt{v}_0$ always has an unknown result. This is very simple, rapid, but rather imprecise.

Variable comparisons An immediate refinement consists in using the abstract information $\overline{\rho} \in \overline{\mathcal{R}}$ available on scalar variables. This is always possible since the corresponding abstract domains, whether relational or not, do have primitives to handle program conditional expressions.

For example assume that $\mathbf{R}(\mathbf{X})$ is an interval analysis, $\overline{\rho}(\mathtt{v}) = [a, b]$, and $\overline{\rho}(\mathtt{v'}) = [a', b']$. The comparison $\mathtt{v} + i < \mathtt{v'} + j$ is true when $\mathtt{v} = \mathtt{v'}$ and $i < j$ or $\mathtt{v} \neq \mathtt{v'}$ but (using the abstract variable environment) $b + i < a' + j$, false when $\mathtt{v} = \mathtt{v'}$ and $i \geqslant j$ or $\mathtt{v} \neq \mathtt{v'}$ but (using the abstract variable environment) $b' + j \leqslant a + j$ and unknown otherwise. Relational domains such as DBM [11] and Octagons [32] can directly answer such questions. In that case the expression abstract domain $\mathbf{E}$ is an abstract domain functor $\mathbf{E}(\mathbf{X}, \mathbf{R}(\mathbf{X}))$ depending on the variable abstract domain $\mathbf{X}$ and the variable environment abstract domain $\mathbf{R}(\mathbf{X})$.

Please note that comparison of expressions $\mathtt{e}, \mathtt{e'} \in \overline{\mathcal{E}}$ must be done for all possible variable abstract domains $\mathbf{R}$ which requires all of them to share a common abstract interface for expression comparison. A reasonable choice is to translate the comparison of normal expressions in $\overline{\mathcal{E}}$ to that of program expressions which anyway have to be evaluated in the abstract using $\mathbf{R}$.

Segmentation-based comparisons The information in the array segmentation can be used to symbolically compare expressions. In fact a segmentation $\{e^1_1 \ldots e^1_{m^1}\} \ldots \{e^2_1 \ldots e^2_{m^2}\}[?^2] \ldots \{e^n_1 \ldots e^n_{m^n}\}[?^n]$ maintains the information that $e^1_1 = \ldots = e^1_{m^1} \leqslant e^2_1 = \ldots = e^2_{m^2} \leqslant \ldots \leqslant e^n_1 = \ldots = e^n_{m^n}$ (where the i-th inequality is strict when $[?^{i+1}]$ is empty ␣ and not strict when $[?^{i+1}]$ is ?). In its simplest form, two expressions are known to be equal if they appear in the same segment bound, unequal if they appear in different segment bounds of the same array (strictly when separated by at least one ␣), and otherwise their comparison is unknown.

More sophisticated algorithms can be used depending on the allowed syntactic form of normal expressions.

For example, in the case of expressions of the restricted form $\mathtt{v} + i, i \in \mathbb{Z}$ where constant expressions are represented by the distinguished variable $\mathtt{v}_0$ which value is assumed to always be zero, we can use Pratt's algorithm [33] to compare their symbolic values. A graph matrix is constructed with an edge $(\mathtt{v}, \mathtt{v'})$ labelled $i - j$ whenever $\mathtt{v}+i \leqslant \mathtt{v'}+j$ (respectively $i-j+1$ when $\mathtt{v}+i < \mathtt{v'}+j$) is derived from a segmentation of some array. Equalities are represented by two inverse inequalities. Arcs between incomparable variables are marked $+\infty$ (including when $i - j$ or $i - j + 1$ overflows so that the relation is abstracted away). The Roy-Warshall-Floyd all-pairs shortest paths/transitive closure algorithm [34] is used to derive all possible comparisons derived by repeated application of the transitivity of comparisons. A cycle $(\mathtt{v}, \mathtt{v})$ for a variable $\mathtt{v}$ in the transitive closure matrix means impossibility, that is unreachability in the concrete. A constraint $\mathtt{v} + k \leqslant \mathtt{v'}$ holds when the label of arc $(\mathtt{v}, \mathtt{v'})$ is less than or equal to k in the transitive closure matrix.

Another similar example is Shostak algorithm [36] for comparison of linear expressions of the form $a.\mathtt{v} + b.\mathtt{v'} \leqslant c$ where $a, b, c \in \mathbb{Z}$.

8. Segment Bounds Abstract Domain Functor

The segment bound abstract domain functor $\mathbf{B}$ takes any of the expression abstract domains $\mathbf{E}$ discussed in Sect. **7.2** and produces an instantiated segment bound abstract domain $\mathbf{B}(\mathbf{E})$ whose abstract properties are sets of expressions $\overline{\mathcal{B}} \triangleq \wp(\overline{\mathcal{E}} \setminus \{\bot, \top\})$. The empty set $\emptyset$ denotes unreachability while non-empty sets $\{e_1 \ldots e_m\}$ of expressions $e_1, \ldots, e_m \in \overline{\mathcal{E}}$ are all equivalent symbolic denotations of some concrete value (generally unknown in the abstract except when one of the e_i is a constant).

8.1 Concretization

The concretization $\gamma_b \in \overline{\mathcal{B}} \mapsto \wp(\mathcal{R}_v)$ of segment bounds is the set of scalar variables concrete environments ρ making the concrete values of all expressions in the set to be equal $[\![e_1]\!]\rho = \ldots = [\![e_m]\!]\rho$. So $\gamma_b(\emptyset) = \emptyset$ and $\gamma_b(S) = \{\rho \mid \forall \mathtt{e}, \mathtt{e'} \in S : [\![\mathtt{e}]\!]\rho = [\![\mathtt{e'}]\!]\rho\}$ where $[\![\mathtt{e}]\!]\rho$ is the concrete value of expression $\mathtt{e}$ in the concrete environment ρ (for example $[\![\mathtt{v}_0 + c]\!]\rho \triangleq c$ and otherwise $[\![\mathtt{v} + c]\!]\rho = \rho(\mathtt{v}) + c$).

When normal expressions and segment bounds are simplified and compared in the context of variable abstract environments $\overline{\rho} \in \overline{\mathcal{R}}$ (Sect. **7.4**), the concretization can be chosen as $\gamma_b \in \overline{\mathcal{B}} \mapsto \overline{\mathcal{R}} \mapsto \wp(\mathcal{R}_v)$ such that $\gamma_b(S)\overline{\rho} = \{\rho \in \gamma_v(\overline{\rho}) \mid \forall \mathtt{e}, \mathtt{e'} \in S : [\![\mathtt{e}]\!]\rho = [\![\mathtt{e'}]\!]\rho\}$.

8.2 Abstract operations on segment bounds

The segment bound abstract domain operations include basic set operations (such as the empty and singleton constructors, test for emptiness, inclusion, strict inclusion, and equality, union, intersection) as well as a widening (when the normal form of expressions does not enforce the finiteness of the number of expressions which can all have the same concrete value). A simple widening limits the number of expressions that can appear to a maximum given as a parameter of the analysis.

In order to handle non-invertible assignments to scalar variables, the segment bounds abstract domain $\mathbf{B}(\mathbf{E})$ has an operation that eliminates from a set of expressions all the expressions that contain a given variable (using the check provided by the expression domain parameter $\mathbf{E}$ in Sect. **7.4**).

Similarly, to handle invertible assignments to scalar variables, an operation is available to substitute an expression for a variable in all expressions of a set, a resulting expression being eliminated from the set when the expression domain parameter cannot put it in normal form. After a side-effect free assignment `i=e;` or an equality test `i==e`, we have $\mathtt{i} = \mathtt{e}$ so `e'(e)` can be added to a segment bound containing the expression `e'(i)` provided the expression domain parameter $\mathbf{E}$ can put `e'(e)` in normal form.

Based on the comparison of expressions in sections Sect. **7.4** the segment bounds abstract domain functor can compare sets of equal expressions. For example $s < s'$ is true if there exists an expression e in s and expression e' in s' such that the expression domain parameter $\mathbf{E}$ can determine that $e < e'$ is true. $s < s'$ is false if the expression domain parameter $\mathbf{E}$ can determine that there exists $e \in s$ and $e' \in s'$ such that $e \geq e'$. Otherwise the comparison $s < s'$ has an unknown result.

9. Array Element Abstract Domain

The array element abstract domain $\mathbf{A}$ abstracts properties of pairs (index, value of indexed array element). The concretization is $\gamma_a \in \overline{\mathcal{A}} \mapsto \wp(\mathbb{Z} \times \mathcal{V})$.

Properties in $\wp(\mathbb{Z} \times \mathcal{V})$ may not or may be first abstracted to $\wp(\mathcal{V})$ when we do not want to relate array element values to their index. In the first case we have a relational analysis (*e.g.* in Sect. **11.1**), in the second a non-relational (*e.g.* in Sect. **4.3**).

10. Conversion between the Variable and Array Element Abstract Domains

In general the variable and array elements abstractions do differ so that a conversion from one to the other is needed.

A variable to array element abstract property conversion is involved in an assignment `A[i] = e;` (handled as `A[i] = (i,e);`), while an array element to variable property conversion is required in an assignment `x := A[i];`, and no conversion is required in `A[i] := A[j];` or `i = j;`. This is taken care of by a conversion abstract domain providing the two conversion functions. Therefore, the analysis must be parameterized by a conversion abstract domain functor $\mathbf{C}(\mathbf{A}, \mathbf{R})$ which contains two conversion functions from variable abstract properties in $\overline{\mathcal{R}}$ to abstract array elements properties in $\overline{\mathcal{A}}$ and inversely. This domain can also abstract `(i,e)` into `e` to get array content analyses not relating indexes to indexed array elements.

11. FunArray: The Array Segmentation Abstract Domain Functor

The array segmentation abstract domain $\mathbf{S}(\mathbf{B}(\mathbf{E}), \mathbf{A}, \mathbf{R})$ abstracts a set of possible array contents by consecutive, non-overlapping segments covering all array elements. The precision/cost ratio of the array segmentation analysis can be adjusted to a specific application domain by changing the abstraction $\mathbf{R}$ of scalar variable environments (Sect. **7.1**), the normal form $\mathbf{E}$ of symbolic expressions (Sect. **7.2**), hence that of the segment bounds $\mathbf{B}(\mathbf{E})$ (Sect. **8**), the abstraction $\mathbf{A}$ of the abstract array elements (Sect. **9**), as well as the various parameters of these abstract domains (such are the degree of refinement of expression comparison in $\mathbf{E}$ in Sect. **7.4**, hence of segment bounds comparison of $\mathbf{B}(\mathbf{E})$ (Sect. **8.2**) and the conversions (Sect. **10**).

11.1 Examples of array segmentation functor instantiations

To illustrate the possibility of relating the value of array elements to their index, let us consider the static analysis of

```
           int n = 10, i = 0;
           int[] A = new int[n];
/* 1: */   while /* 2: */ (i < n) {
/* 3: */     A[i] = 0;
/* 4: */     i = i + 1:
/* 5: */     A[i] = -16;
/* 6: */     i = i + 1:
/* 7: */   }
/* 8: */
```
(3)

typical of data transfer protocols where even and odd numbered packets contain data of different types *e.g.* [16, Sec. 6.6.3], [25]. We will combine parity (where `_|_` (*i.e.* $\bot$) is unreachable, `o` is odd, `e` is even, `T` (*i.e.* $\top$) is unknown) and intervals.

Example 2 The first abstraction is the reduced product [8] of parity and intervals where pairs of a parity and an interval denote the conjunction of both properties (with a reduction *e.g.* of bounds by parity (such as `(e,[0,9])` $\longrightarrow$ `(e,[0,8])`) and parity for constant intervals (such as `(T,[1,1])` $\longrightarrow$ `(o,[1,1])`)). In the following analysis of (3) this abstraction is used both for variables and array elements (hence ignoring their relationship to indexes since $[\![(i, e)]\!]\overline{\rho} = (parity([\![e]\!]\overline{\rho}), interval([\![e]\!]\overline{\rho}))$).

```
p1 = (A: {0 i} (T, [-oo,+oo]) {n 10},
      i: (e, [0,0]) n: (e, [10,10]))
p2 = (A: {0} (e, [-16,0]) {i}? (T, [-oo,+oo]) {n 10}?
      i: (e, [0,10]) n: (e, [10,10]))
p8 = (A: {0} (e, [-16,0]) {n 10 i}
      i: (e, [10,10]) n: (e, [10,10]))
```

The analysis of `i` starts with the initial value `(e,[0,0])` and is `(e,[0,2])` after one iteration which is widened to `(e,[0,+oo])` hence stable. The narrowing phase starts with the test `i < n` where `n in [10, 10]` so `i` is in `(e,[0,9])` hence `(e,[0,8])` by reduction through evenness. After one more iteration we get back `(e,[0,10])` to narrow `(e,[0,+oo])` which is `(e,[0,10])` and is a fixpoint. □

Example 3 The second abstraction is the reduced cardinal power [8] of intervals by parity whose abstract properties have the form `(o ->` i_o`,e ->` i_e`)` meaning that the interval is i_o (resp. i_e) when the parity is `o` (resp. `e`). In the following non-relational analysis of (3), we use the reduced product of parity and intervals for simple variables and the power of parity by interval for array elements (hence ignoring their relationship to indexes since $[\![(i, e)]\!]\overline{\rho}$ maps $parity([\![e]\!]\overline{\rho})$ to $interval([\![e]\!]\overline{\rho})$). For example `(o -> _|_,e -> [-16,0])` means that the indexed array elements must be even with value included between -16 and 0.

```
p1 = (A: {0 i} (o -> [-oo,+oo],e -> [-oo,+oo]) {n 10},
      i: (e, [0,0]) n: (e, [10,10]))
p2 = (A: {0} (o -> _|_,e -> [-16,0]) {i}?,
                (o -> [-oo,+oo],e -> [-oo,+oo]) {n 10}?,
      i: (e, [0,10]) n: (e, [10,10]))
p8 = (A: {0} (o -> _|_,e -> [-16,0]) {n i 10},
      i: (e, [10,10]) n: (e, [10,10]))
```

Observe that the abstraction is more powerful but the result is exactly the same as in the above analysis in Ex. **1** using the reduced product since `(o -> _|_,e -> [-16,0])` is exactly `(e, [-16,0])` on array elements. □

Example 4 The third abstraction also uses the reduced cardinal power of intervals by parity, but this time in a relational way for arrays thus relating the parity of an index to the interval of possible variation of the corresponding element (so $[\![(i, e)]\!]\overline{\rho}$ is a map of $parity([\![i]\!]\overline{\rho})$ to $interval([\![e]\!]\overline{\rho})$). We get

```
p1 =  (A: {0 i} (o -> [-oo,+oo],e -> [-oo,+oo]) {n 10},
       i: (e, [0,0]) n: (e, [10,10]))
p2 =  (A: {0} (o -> [-16,-16],e -> [0,0]) {i}?
           (o -> [-oo,+oo],e -> [-oo,+oo]) {n 10}?,
       i: (e, [0,10]) n: (e, [10,10]))
p8 =  (A: {0} (o -> [-16,-16],e -> [0,0]) {n 10 i},
       i: (e, [10,10]) n: (e, [10,10]))
```

so that the array elements with odd index are shown to be equal to -16 while those of even index are zero. □

11.2 Abstract Predicates

The array segmentation abstract predicates belong to $\overline{\mathcal{S}} \triangleq \{(\overline{\mathcal{B}} \times \overline{\mathcal{A}}) \times (\overline{\mathcal{B}} \times \overline{\mathcal{A}} \times \{\_, ?\})^k \times (\overline{\mathcal{B}} \times \{\_, ?\}) \mid k \geqslant 0\} \cup \{\bot\}$ and have the form

$$\{e_1^1 \ldots e_{m^1}^1\}\, P_1\, \{e_1^2 \ldots e_{m^2}^2\}[?^2]\, P_2 \;\ldots\; P_{n-1}\, \{e_1^n \ldots e_{m^n}^n\}[?^n]$$

where

- the segment bounds $\{e_1^i \ldots e_{m^i}^i\} \in \overline{\mathcal{B}}$, $i \in [1, n]$, $n > 1$, are finite non-empty sets of symbolic expressions in normal form $e_j^i \in \overline{\mathcal{E}}$ as respectively considered in Sect. **8** and Sect. **7.2**;
- the $P_i \in \overline{\mathcal{A}}$ are abstract predicates chosen in an abstract domain $\mathbf{A}$ denoting possible values of pairs (index, indexed array element) in a segment of Sect. **9**; and

- the optional question mark $[?^i]$ follows the upper bound of a segment. Its presence ? means that the segment might be empty. Its absence ␣ means that the segment cannot be empty. Because this information is attached to the segment upper bound (which is also the lower bound of the next segment), the lower bound $\{e_1^1 \ldots e_{m^1}^1\}$ of the first segment never has a question mark. $(\{␣, ?\}, \preccurlyeq, ␣, ?, \curlyvee, \curlywedge)$ is a complete lattice with ␣ $\prec$?.

The symbolic expressions $e_i^k \in \overline{\mathcal{E}}$ in a given segment bound depend on scalar variables but not on array elements hence `A[A[i]]` should be handled as `x=A[i]; A[x]` so that the auxiliary variable `x` can appear in a segment bound for array `A`. The consecutive segment bounds are in strictly increasing order in the concrete except when followed by a question mark meaning that the preceding block may be empty. There is no hole between segments (since this hole can always be viewed as another segment whose properties are unknown). The first block limit always contains an expression in normal form denoting the array lower bound while the last block always contains an expression in normal form denoting the array upper bound. Within one block the abstraction is uniform (but can be relational, since the array semantics of Sect. **6.3** can relate the array value `A[i]` to the index `i`). A possible refinement would be to introduce relationships between segment emptiness marks (so as to express that in `{0} 0{i}? T {n}?` both segments cannot be simultaneously empty), which we do not do for the sake of efficiency.

11.3 Concretization

Given the concretizations $\gamma_v \in \overline{\mathcal{R}} \mapsto \wp(\mathcal{R}_v)$ for the variable abstract domain and $\gamma_a \in \overline{\mathcal{A}} \mapsto \wp(\mathbb{Z} \times \mathcal{V})$ for the array elements abstract domain, the concretization γ_s of an abstract array segmentation is an array property so $\gamma_s \in \overline{\mathcal{S}} \mapsto \overline{\mathcal{R}} \mapsto \wp(\mathcal{A})$.

The concretization of a segment $B\ P\ B'\ [?]$ is the set of arrays whose elements in the segment $[B, B')$ satisfy the abstract property P ($<_␣$ stands for $<$ while $<?$ stands for $\leqslant$):

$$\begin{aligned}\gamma'_s(B\ P\ B'\ [?])\overline{\rho} \ \triangleq\ & \\ &\{(\rho, \ell, h, A) \mid \rho \in \gamma_v(\overline{\rho}) \wedge \forall \mathsf{e}_1, \mathsf{e}_2 \in B : \forall \mathsf{e}'_1, \mathsf{e}'_2 \in B' : \\ &\quad [\![\ell]\!]\rho \leq [\![\mathsf{e}_1]\!]\rho = [\![\mathsf{e}_2]\!]\rho <[?]\ [\![\mathsf{e}'_1]\!]\rho = [\![\mathsf{e}'_2]\!]\rho \leq [\![h]\!]\rho \wedge \\ &\quad\quad \forall i \in \big[[\![\mathsf{e}_1]\!]\rho, [\![\mathsf{e}'_1]\!]\rho\big) : A(i) \in \gamma_a(P)\}\end{aligned}$$

The concretization of an array segmentation $B_1 P_1 B_2 [?^2] P_2 \ldots P_{n-1} B_n [?^n]$ is the set of arrays whose elements in all segments $[B_i, B_{i+1}), i = 1, \ldots, n-1$ satisfy abstract property P_i and whose lower and upper bounds are respectively given by B_1 and B_n.

$$\begin{aligned}\gamma_s(B_1 P_1 B_2 [?^2] P_2 \ldots P_{n-1} B_n [?^n])\overline{\rho} \ \triangleq\ & \\ &\{(\rho, \ell, h, A) \in \bigcap_{i=1}^{n-1} \gamma'_s(B_i\ P_i\ B_{i+1} [?^{i+1}])\overline{\rho} \mid \\ &\quad \forall \mathsf{e}_1 \in B_1 : [\![\mathsf{e}_1]\!]\rho = [\![\ell]\!]\rho \wedge \forall \mathsf{e}_n \in B_n : [\![\mathsf{e}_n]\!]\rho = [\![h]\!]\rho\}\end{aligned}$$

and $\gamma_s(\bot) = \emptyset$.

11.4 Segmentation unification

Given two segmentations with *compatible* extremal segment bounds (in general for the same array), the objective of segmentation unification is to modify the two segmentations so that they coincide. By compatible we mean that the first (the last) segment bounds should have a non-empty intersection. In practice this is always the case as the first segment bound always contains `0` and the last segment bound always contains the symbolic name for the array length (*e.g.*, `A.Length`).

On the* best *unification The problem of segmentation unification admits a partially ordered set of solutions, in general not forming a lattice.

The minimal elements, hence the least precise unifications are those where all the segments are joined, and only the extremes are preserved.

Example 5 Let `a` and `b` be distinct variables. When unifying `{0}...{a b}` with `{0}...{a b c}`, both segmentations `{0}...{a}` and `{0}...{b}` are minimal solutions, but not comparable. □

The maximal elements, hence the most precise unifications are the coarsest common refinements of both segmentations.

Example 6 When unifying `{0}...{a}...{b}...{c}` with `{0}...{b}...{a}...{c}` both segmentations `{0}...{a}...{c}` and `{0}...{b}...{c}` are maximal , but not comparable solutions. □

In general, *a* solution is such that the bounds: (i) do appear in one or the other initial segmentation; and (ii) preserve the original orderings.

One segment can be empty in one segmentation (like `{0 i}`) and non-empty in the other one (like `{0}`P`{1,i}`). Therefore segmentation must include the splitting of empty segments (like `{0 i}` $\rightarrow$ `{0}`P'`{i}?`). Such an empty segment splitting is used in the comparison/join/meet/widening/narrowing of segments (which are not all commutative) so that the abstract value P' of the created empty segment must be chosen as the left/right neutral element of the considered operation (*e.g.* P' is $\bot$ for join, $\top$ for meet, $\bot$ on the left and $\top$ on the right of the partial order $\sqsubseteq$).

The segmentations involved in a unification are usually related to different program contexts:

Example 7 Assume we want to unify `{0 i-1}P1{i}` and `{0 i-2}P2{i}` (obviously in two different contexts). The coarsest common refinement is `{i-2}`$\bot$`{0}`$\bot$`{i-1}?P1{i}` for `{0, i-1}P1{i}` and `{i-2}`$\bot$`{0}?P2{i-1}P2{i}` for `{0,i-2}P2{i}` (which would yield the join `{i-2}`$\bot$`{0}?P2{i-1}?P1` $\cup$ `P2{i}`). However, it might be the case that `i` < 2 from the abstract variable environment, in which case the expression `i-2` in the lower bound of the first refined segmentation is undefined. □

Therefore, the well-definedness of the coarsest common refinement, if any, depends upon the abstract variable environment, too.

To sum up, we want the array segmentation analysis: (i) to have the possibility of being completely independent of the variable analysis (see Sect. **11.7**); (ii) to have a deterministic behavior in presence of several maximal common refinements. Therefore we present a segmentation unification which does not provide any guarantee on the maximality of the result, but instead one which: (i) is always well-defined in absence of knowledge of the contexts of the segmentations; (ii) does terminate; (iii) is deterministic.

The segmentation unification algorithm The first step of the algorithm is checking the compatibility of the two input segmentations to verify that they do have common lower and upper bounds.

Then, the unification proceeds recursively from left to right and maintains the invariant that the left part is already unified. We let $\top\!\!\!\!\bot_l$ (resp. $\top\!\!\!\!\bot_r$) denote the left (resp. right) neutral element.

1. $B[?_1]\ P_1\ B'_1[?'_1]\ldots$ and $B[?_2]\ P_2\ B'_2[?'_2]\ldots$ have same lower bounds and so keep the first segments as they are and go on with $B'_1[?'_1]\ldots$ and $B'_2[?'_2]\ldots$.
2. In case $(B \cup B_1)[?_1]\ P_1\ B'_1[?'_1]\ldots$ and $B[?_2]\ P_2\ B'_2[?'_2]\ldots$ with $B_1 \neq \emptyset$ and $B \cap B_1 = \emptyset$, let $\overline{B}_1$ be the set of expressions in B_1 appearing in the second segmentation blocks $B'_2, \ldots$.
   - 2.1 If $\overline{B}_1$ is empty then go on with $B[?_1]\ P_1\ B'_1[?'_1]\ldots$ and $B[?_2]\ P_2\ B'_2[?'_2]\ldots$ following case 1.
   - 2.2 Otherwise go on with $B[?_1]\ \top\!\!\!\!\bot_l\ B_1?\ P_1\ B'_1[?'_1]\ldots$ and $B[?_2]\ P_2\ B'_2[?'_2]\ldots$ as in case 1.
3. The symmetrical case is similar.
4. In case $(B \cup B_1)[?_1] P_1 B'_1[?'_1]\ldots$ and $(B \cup B_2)[?_2] P_2 B'_2[?'_2]\ldots$ with $B_1, B_2 \neq \emptyset$ and $B \cap B_1 = B \cap B_2 = \emptyset$, let $\overline{B}_1$ (resp.

$\overline{B}_2$) be the set of expressions in B_1 (resp. B_2) appearing in the second (resp. first) segmentation blocks $B'_2, \ldots$ ($B'_1, \ldots$).

4.1 If $\overline{B}_1$ and $\overline{B}_2$ are both empty, go on with $B[?_1]\, P_1\, B'_1[?'_1] \ldots$ and $B[?_2]\, P_2\, B'_2[?'_2] \ldots$ as in case 1.

4.2 Else if $\overline{B}_1$ is empty (so that $\overline{B}_2$ is not empty) then go on with $B[?_1]\, P_1\, B'_1[?'_1] \ldots$ and $B[?_2]\, \mathbb{I}_r\, \overline{B}_2?\, P_2\, B'_2[?'_2] \ldots$ (where $\mathbb{I}_r$ is the right neutral element).

4.3 The symmetrical case is similar.

4.4 Finally if $\overline{B}_1$ and $\overline{B}_2$ are both non-empty then go on with $B[?_1]\, \mathbb{I}_l\, \overline{B}_1?\, P_1\, B'_1[?'_1] \ldots$ and $B[?_2]\, \mathbb{I}_r\, \overline{B}_2?\, P_2\, B'_2[?'_2] \ldots$ as in case 1.

5. In case $B_1[?_1]\; P_1\; B'_1[?'_1] \ldots$ and $B_2[?_2]\; P_2\; B'_2[?'_2] \ldots$ with $B_1 \cap B_2 = \emptyset$, we cannot be on the first left segment block so we have on the left $B_0[?_0]\; P_0\; B_1[?_1]\; P_1\; B'_1[?'_1] \ldots$ and $B'_0[?'_0]\, P'_0\, B_2[?_2]\, P_2\, B'_2[?'_2] \ldots$ and go on by merging these consecutive blocks $B_0[?_0]\; P_0 \sqcup P_1\; B'_1[?_1 \curlywedge ?'_1] \ldots$ and $B'_0[?'_0]\; P'_0 \sqcup P_2\; B'_2[?_2 \curlywedge ?'_2] \ldots$.

6. Finally, at the end either we are left with the right limits that have both been checked to be equal or else we have $B_1[?_1]\; P_1\; B'_1[?'_1]$ and $B_2[?_2]$ with $B'_1 = B_2$. Because we have maintained the invariant that B_1 is always equal to B_2 in the concrete (so necessarily $[?'_1]\; =?$ since then $B_1 = B_2 = B'_1$), and so we end up with $(B_1 \cup B'_1 \cup B_2)[?_1]$ and $(B_1 \cup B'_1 \cup B_2)[?_2]$ □

Example 8 In the analysis of the example of Fig. **2**, we have to unify `{0 i} T {n}` and `{0 i-1} 0 {1 i} T {n}?` which becomes `{0}` $\perp$ `{i}? T {n}` and `{0} 0 {1 i} T {n}?` by 4.3 and we go on with `{i}? T {n}` and `{1 i} T {n}?` which, by the symmetric in 3 of 2.1 becomes `{i}? T {n}` and `{i} T {n}?` so we go on with `{n}` and `{n}?` which terminates the recursion by 6, thus returning `{0}`$\perp$`{i}? T {n}` and `{0} 0 {i} T {n}?`. Their array segmentation join is then `{0} 0 {i}? T {n}?` (taking the disjunction $\curlyvee$ of potential segment emptiness). □

The algorithm never adds any new expression to the segment bounds nor increments the total number of segment bounds in splits and so does terminate. The algorithm has a look-ahead of 1 (cf. case 5). It can be easily refined to provide a larger look-ahead at a price of an increased complexity. However, an advantage of the algorithm is that its behavior and output are deterministic. For instance, in the Ex. **6** our algorithm returns the non-maximal segmentation `{0}...{c}`. A 2-look-ahead algorithm should make the choice between the two maximal solutions.

In general, the algorithm can be easily adapted and refined to take into account specific knowledge when comparing segment bounds (for instance the total order induced by constants Sect. **12.2**).

11.5 Partial order/join/meet/widening/narrowing

For an array segmentation join $\mathbf{S}.\sqcup$, a $(\perp, \perp)$-segmentation unification is performed and then the array element abstract domain join $\mathbf{A}.\sqcup$ is applied segmentwise. For the meet $\mathbf{S}.\sqcap$, a $(\top, \top)$-segmentation unification is performed and then a segmentwise meet $\mathbf{A}.\sqcap$. For the widening $\mathbf{S}.\nabla$, a $(\perp, \perp)$-segmentation unification is performed and then a segmentwise widening $\mathbf{A}.\nabla$. Moreover, the widening merges consecutive segments with same abstract value. Widenings could also be used to limit the size of segment bound sets and/or the number of segments given as parameters of the analysis. For the narrowing $\mathbf{S}.\Delta$, a $(\top, \top)$-segmentation unification is performed and then a segmentwise narrowing $\mathbf{A}.\Delta$. For the partial order $\mathbf{S}.\sqsubseteq$, a $(\perp, \top)$-segmentation unification is performed before returning the conjunction of the segmentwise comparisons $\mathbf{A}.\sqsubseteq$. The potential segment emptiness indications must also be taken into account, that is $\llcorner = \llcorner \prec ? = ?$.

11.6 Abstract Transfer Functions

Abstract value of an indexed array element Assume that we have to evaluate $[\![$`A[e]`$]\!]\overline{\rho}$ for the array `A` abstracted by the segmentation $B_1 P_1 B_2[?^2] P_2 \ldots P_{n-1} B_n[?^n]$. The expression $B_1 \leqslant$ `e` $\leqslant B_n$ is evaluated in the abstract and a warning is emitted if the result is unreachable (dead code), false (definite error) or unknown (potential error). Let B_ℓ be the largest segment bound such that $B_\ell \leqslant$ `e` is true (B_1 otherwise) and B_h be the smallest segment bound such that `e` $< B_h$ is true (B_n otherwise, assuming that execution goes on only in absence of buffer overrun). The value of $[\![$`A[e]`$]\!]\overline{\rho}$ is then $\bigsqcup_{k=\ell}^{h-1} P_k$ where $\sqcup$ is the join in the domain $\mathbf{A}$ abstracting (index, value of indexed array element) pairs. A call to a conversion function of $\mathbf{C}$ is necessary if this abstract value in $\mathbf{A}$ must be converted to a variable abstract value in $\mathbf{R}$.

Assignment to an array element In an array element assignment `A[e] = e'` with abstract variable environment $\overline{\rho}$ where the array `A` is abstracted by the segmentation $B_1 P_1 B_2[?^2] P_2 \ldots P_{n-1} B_n[?^n]$, we first determine the range of segments such that $B_\ell \leqslant$ `e` $< B_h$ is definitely true. The segmentation of `A` can be thought of as being abstracted to $B_1 P_1 \ldots B_\ell[?^\ell](\bigsqcup_{k=\ell}^{h-1} P_k) B_h[?'] P_h \ldots P_{n-1} B_n[?^n]$ where $[?']$ is ? if all the $[?^{\ell+1}], \ldots, [?^h]$ are ? (so that the block $B_\ell \ldots B_h$ can then be empty) and $\llcorner$ otherwise. Of course it may happen that $h = \ell + 1$ in which case only one segment is concerned or $\ell = 1$ and $h = n$ in which case all segments are smashed. In all cases, the assignment is definitely in the segment $B_\ell \ldots B_h$ (may be at its borders). This segment is split. Let $P \in \overline{\mathcal{A}}$ be the abstraction of the value of the pair (`e`, `e'`) in $\mathbf{A}$. After the array element assignment, the array segmentation of `A` becomes $B_1 P_1 \ldots B_\ell[?^\ell](\bigsqcup_{k=\ell}^{h-1} P_k)$`{e}`$[?_l] P$`{e +` `1}`$(\bigsqcup_{k=\ell}^{h-1} P_k) B_h[?_r] P_h \ldots P_{n-1} B_n[?^n]$. $[?_l]$ is ? unless the segment bounds comparison discussed in Sect. **8.2** can determine that $B_\ell <$ `{e}` is always true. Similarly, $[?_r]$ is $\llcorner$ when `{e + 1}` $< B_h$ for sure and ? otherwise.

There are special cases. When the index expression `e` or `e+1` or both cannot be put in the normal form of $\mathbf{E}$, we have to merge the corresponding segments, to get $B_1 P_1 \ldots B_\ell[?^\ell](P \sqcup \bigsqcup_{k=\ell}^{h-1} P_k)$ $B_h[?'] P_h \ldots P_{n-1} B_n[?^n]$ in the worst case. This is the case of the assignment `(*)` in Fig. **1**. If the segment bounds comparison can determine that $B_\ell =$ `{e}` we get $B_1 P_1 \ldots (B_\ell \cup$ `{e}`$)[?_l] P$`{e +` `1}`$(\bigsqcup_{k=\ell}^{h-1} P_k) B_h[?_r] P_h \ldots P_{n-1} B_n[?^n]$. Similarly if `{e + 1}` $=$ B_h for sure, we get $B_1 P_1 \ldots B_\ell[?^\ell](\bigsqcup_{k=\ell}^{h-1} P_k)$`{e}`$[?_l] P($`{e+1}`$\cup B_h) P_h \ldots P_{n-1} B_n[?^n]$.

Test of an array element A test $c($`A[e]`$)$ of an array element `A[e]` can be done by getting the abstract value of (i, v) of `(e,A[e])` in $\mathbf{A}$, restricting the abstract value (i, v) by restricting i to the array bounds (execution is assumed to stop in case of buffer overrun) and v to the test $c(v)$, and assigning the restricted value back to the array element `A[e]`. For a simpler uniform treatment of tests involving both scalar variables and array elements, (i, v) in $\mathbf{A}$ can be converted to the variable abstract domain $\mathbf{R}$ and back after handling the test using $\mathbf{C}$.

Assumption for the content of an array For a statement in the form of `assume` $\forall i \in [a, b).\ c($`A[e]`$)$ (assuming $a \leq b$ are within the array bounds): (i) we infer an abstract segment value as in the previous case (let us call it `P`); (ii) we abstract the bounds a, b in the quantification to their best possible approximation `a, b` in the bounds abstract domain; (iii) we materialize the most generic abstract segmentation

```
A: {0} T {a}? P {b}? T {A.Length}?
```

and we use the scalar abstract domain to get rid of some of the uncertainties. Finally the so-obtained abstract predicate is intersected (using the meet operation) with the abstract value in the pre-state of A. For example, using the abstract domain of intervals:

```
/* (A: {0} T {A.Length}, k:[10,10], A.Length:[10, +oo]) */
assume forall i: [0, k) => A[i] >= 0;
/* (A: {0} [0, +oo] {k} T {A.Length}?, ...) */
```

In fact, the materialized abstract segment is

```
A: {0} T {0}? [0, +oo] {k}? T {A.Length}?,
```

which can be reduced using the abstract domain of scalars to:

```
A: {0} [0, +oo] {k} T {A.Length}?
```

The constant zero is trivially equal to itself and k is positive but it may be equal to the length of the array A. Finally the value in the pre-state of A is refined via the meet operation.

Invertible assignment to a scalar variable In an invertible assignment to a scalar variable $\mathtt{x} = \mathtt{f}(\mathtt{x}, \vec{\mathtt{y}})$ where $\vec{\mathtt{y}} = \mathtt{y}_1, \ldots, \mathtt{y}_m$, we have $x_{\text{new}} = f(x_{\text{old}}, \vec{y})$, where f is the value of f, x_{old} denotes the value of the variable x before assignment, x_{new} denotes the value of the variable x after assignment, f has no side effect so the values $\vec{y}$ of the variables $\vec{\mathtt{y}}$ are not changed, and $x_{\text{old}} = f^{-1}(x_{\text{new}}, \vec{y})$. For such an invertible assignment, all occurrences of the variable x in the expressions in the segment bounds must be replaced by the expression $f^{-1}(\mathtt{x}, \vec{\mathtt{y}})$ and the resulting expressions simplified into canonical normal form, if any, and dropped otherwise. In case a segment bound becomes empty because normalization is impossible, the two adjacent segments must be joined. For the example in Fig. **2**, we have:

```
/* (A: {0} 0 {i}? 0 {i+1} T {n}?, ...) */
i = i + 1;
/* (A: {0} 0 {i-1}? 0 {i} T {n}?, ...) */
```

Non-invertible assignment to a scalar variable In a non invertible assignment $\mathtt{x} = f(\mathtt{x}, \vec{\mathtt{y}})$, no inverse $x_{\text{old}} = f^{-1}(x_{\text{new}}, \vec{y})$ is available, for example in $\mathtt{x} = f(\vec{\mathtt{y}})$. For such a non invertible assignment $\mathtt{x} = \mathtt{e}$, all expressions in the segment bounds containing occurrences of the variable x must be eliminated from these segment bounds. In case a segment bound becomes empty, the two adjacent segments must be joined. Then the variable x and expression e are added to the segment bound containing an expression $\mathtt{e}'$ such that $[\![\mathtt{e}' == \mathtt{e}]\!]\overline{\rho}$ is definitely true in the abstract. In the simple purely syntactic case of Sect. **7.4**, $[\![\mathtt{e}' == \mathtt{e}]\!]\overline{\rho} = \mathit{true}$ is under-approximated by $\mathtt{e}' = \mathtt{e}$ so that x is added to all segment bounds containing e. For the example of Fig. **2** we have:

```
/* (A: {0} T {n}?, i: T n: T ) */
i = 0;
/* (A: {0 i} T {n}?, i: 0 n: T ) */
```

In case of an assignment $\mathtt{x} = f(\vec{\mathtt{y}}), \mathtt{x} \notin \vec{\mathtt{y}}$ where $y_i = f_i^{-1}(x_{\text{new}}, y_1, \ldots, y_{i-1}, y_{i+1}, \ldots, y_m)$ is available, the expression $\mathtt{e}(f_i^{-1}(x_{\text{new}}, y_1, \ldots, y_{i-1}, y_{i+1}, \ldots, y_m))$ can be added to all segment bounds containing an expression $\mathtt{e}(y_i)$ whenever simplification in canonical normal form is possible. For example:

```
/* (A: {0} 0 {i+5 j+7} T {10 n}, ...) */
i = j - 7;
/* (A: {0} 0 {i+14 j+7} T {10 n}, ...)  */
```

Comparison of scalar variable expressions The equality comparison e = e' (where e and e' have equivalent normal forms) together with the segment bounds comparison discussed in Sect. **8.2** that may be able to determine that $\mathtt{e} = B_i$[(2)] is always true will add e and e' to B_i. Moreover, if $\mathtt{e'} = B_j$ for sure and $i < j$ then the segmentation $B_1 P_1 B_2 [?^2] P_2 \ldots P_{n-1} B_n [?^n]$ will be reduced to $B_1 P_1 B_2 [?^2] P_2 \ldots P_{i-1} (B_i \cup B_{i+1} \cup \ldots \cup B_j \cup \{\mathtt{e}, \mathtt{e'}\}) [?^i] P_j \ldots P_{n-1} B_n [?^n]$ or to unreachability when one of the $[?^{i+1}], \ldots, [?^j]$ is $\_$ (since then $\mathtt{e} < \mathtt{e'}$). The comparison $\mathtt{e} \leqslant \mathtt{e'}$ has the same effect when $j < i$ or when $\mathtt{e} < \mathtt{e'}$ and $i = j$.

(2) Recall that $\mathtt{e} = B$ is $\exists \mathtt{e}' \in B : \mathtt{e} = \mathtt{e}'$.

```
               InitBackwards(int[] A) {
                 int i = A.Length;
/* 1: */         while /* 2: */ (0 < i) {
/* 3: */            i = i - 1;
/* 4: */            A[i] = 0;
/* 5: */         }
/* 6: */       }
```

Figure 5. Example of a backwards initialization. Array segmentation reduction is needed to prove the postcondition $\forall j \in [0, \mathtt{A.Length}).\ \mathtt{A}[j] = 0$.

Otherwise disequality $\mathtt{e} <> \mathtt{e'}$ and strict inequality $\mathtt{e} < \mathtt{e'}$ with $\mathtt{e} = B_i$ and $\mathtt{e'} = B_{i+1}$ can be used to remove a doubt ? on the possible emptiness of a segment $B_i P_i B_{i+1}?$ which becomes $B_i P_i B_{i+1}$.

11.7 Array segmentation reduction

A program analysis is the product of a segmentation analysis for arrays and the analysis of scalar variables. The two analyses can be completely independent which is an important feature for the array segmentation analysis to be easily inserted in any analyzer without having to make any hypothesis on the static analyzer. The consequence is that the result may not be as precise as possible. Let us illustrate this phenomenon on the program of Fig. **5**.

Using the independent product of interval abstractions for array elements and scalar variables, the post condition derived by the static analyzer with Sect. **7.4** at program point 6 is

```
(A: {0} [-oo,+oo] {i}? [0,0] {A.Length}?,
 i: [0,0] A.Length: [2,+oo])
```

It states that it is possible that i = 0 but the array segmentation analysis cannot prove that this is indeed always the case. It is in general always more precise to consider the reduced product of the array and variable analyses [8]. This consists in iterating reduction operators that propagate information for one abstract domain to the other. For example it may be useful to propagate the relational information of array segmentation (equality of expressions in a segment bounds and segment bounds in increasing order (strictly increasing in absence of ?)), unless a more precise relational domain is already used for scalar variables. In the other direction, the information provided by the scalar variable analysis can be propagated to segmentations. A possibly empty segment $\ldots B[?]\ P\ B'? \ldots$ can be reduced to a non-empty one $\ldots B[?]\ P\ B' \ldots$ if the scalar variables environment $\overline{\rho}$ implies $\exists \mathtt{e} \in B : \exists \mathtt{e}' \in B' : [\![\mathtt{e}]\!]\overline{\rho} < [\![\mathtt{e}']\!]\overline{\rho}$ is always *true* in the abstract (the abstract test returning either $\perp$, *true*, *false*, or *unknown*). Similarly, a possibly empty segment $\ldots B[?] P B'? \ldots$ may be definitely empty and reduced to the bound $\ldots (B \cup B')[?] \ldots$ when $\exists \mathtt{e} \in B : \exists \mathtt{e}' \in B' : [\![\mathtt{e}]\!]\overline{\rho} = [\![\mathtt{e}']\!]\overline{\rho} = \mathit{true}$.

In the reduction example of Fig. **5**, the fact that $\mathtt{i} \in [0, 0]$ implies that the segment {0} [-oo,+oo] {i} is empty, in which case the reduction automatically yields

```
(A: {0 i} [0,0] {A.Length},
 i: [0,0] A.Length: [2,+oo])
```

which is exactly the expected result at program point 6.

12. Implementation

12.1 CodeContracts and Clousot

CodeContracts allow the language-agnostic specification of contracts (preconditions, postconditions and object-invariants [3, 31]).

The CodeContracts API is included in `.NET` starting from $v4.0$. `Clousot` is an abstract interpretation-based static analyzer developed at MSR Redmond used to statically check: (i) contracts; and (ii) the absence of common runtime errors such as non-null dereferences or buffer overruns. `Clousot` is used both inside and outside Microsoft on large production projects. When a method is analyzed, its preconditions is turned into an assumption and its postcondition into an assertion. For each method call appearing in the method body, its precondition is turned into an assertion and the postcondition into an assumption. Object-invariants are assumed at the entry of public methods and asserted at the exit point (a detailed description of the object-invariants treatment is out-of-the scope of this paper). Further assertions are generated from the body text: *e.g.* when an array is accessed the indexing expression is better being in bounds. `Clousot` analyzes the bytecode, which presents several advantages (independence from the compiler, the language, the language version ...), but also some drawbacks (lack of program structure ...) [27]. After reading the bytecode, extracting the contracts, creating the control flow graph, and simplifying the program, a heap analysis is run so to resolve aliasing, and the program is turned into a scalar form. The heap analysis makes some assumptions on parameter aliasing, we refer the interested reader to [14]. On the top of the program scalar form several forward value analyses are run, and their results are used to discharge the assertions. Assertions are discharged using simple built-in decision procedures. If an assertion cannot be discharged, then the analysis is refined by using a more precise abstract domain or a goal-directed backward propagation. If refinement does not work, then a warning is reported to the user. Warnings are issued because of a lack of knowledge (*e.g.* missing postcondition, precondition too weak ...), incompleteness of the analysis (inevitable in all the static analyses), or because of too complex assertions (*e.g.* quadratic inequalities).

Before this work, quantified assertions over arrays (*e.g.* all the elements are non-null) were not understood by `Clousot` which reported warnings for assertions as *e.g.* the ones in Fig. **1**. Furthermore, the analysis was also very imprecise in handling array loads (and iterations over collections), so that each time a value was loaded from an array, nothing could be stated on that value, hence the worst case was assumed, degrading the analysis precision. Fixing those issues were a main request from `Clousot`'s users.

12.2 Implementation of `FunArray` in `Clousot`

We fully implemented `FunArray` in `Clousot`. To the user (typically a programmer with no background in formal methods) `FunArray` is exposed as a simple check-box in Visual Studio. When the check-box is enabled, the `FunArray` is transparently instantiated with the abstract domains in `Clousot`. The array analysis is orthogonal to the other components of `Clousot`, so that it can benefit of precision improvements for free. For instance, if a more precise scalar variable abstract environment is used, then the `FunArray` analysis is likely to get more precise.

Functor instantiation In the current implementation: (i) the abstract domain used for the segment elements is the disjoint union of intervals with non-nullness; (ii) the expressions used in the segment limits are the simple expressions of Sect. **7.2** augmented with explicit casts to model the fact that `a.Length` and `(int) a.Length` both denote the length of an array `a` in the bytecode; and (iii) the scalar numerical abstract domain is the one provided by `Clousot` in the particular run. Several numerical abstract domains are available in `Clousot`, among them: Pentagons [28] combined with Linear equalities [21], Subpolyhedra [24].

Clousot numerical domains are composed according to a tree topology [9]. Reduction is achieved via pushing or pulling of information. An abstract domain can *push* information to abstract domains of lower rank, and *pull* information from all other domains. The segmentation abstract domain is at the root of the tree. It pushes: bottom (contradiction), expression equality (when the two expressions appears in the same bound), array values (*e.g.*, in `x = a[i]`, if it determines that `a[i]!= null`, then it pushes the information `x != null`). It pulls: comparisons (`exp1 < exp2`, `exp1!= exp2`, `exp1 == exp2` ...), integer constants (all the variables which are known to be definitely constants), intervals (e.g. in `x = a[exp]`, which is the range for `exp`?), abstract values (*e.g.* in `a[i] = z`, which is the abstract value for `z`?).

The array analysis is currently implemented as a value analysis run *on the top of* the heap analysis, when in particular array aliasing has been resolved. As a consequence, the abstract transfer functions implemented in the analyzer are very similar to those described in Sect. **11**, with some adjustements to meet the peculiarietes of the `.NET` semantics and `Clousot` infrastructure.

Array creation When an array is created with the instruction `newarr A exp` then the segmentation

`{0} d { A.Length, exp }?`

is materialized, where `d` denotes the *abstraction* in the segment value abstract domain of the default value for the type of the array elements (*e.g.*, 0 is the default value for `int` and `null` is the default value for reference types). The so-materialized segmentation is then refined pulling some information from the scalar variables abstract domain. In the particular case, `Clousot` first asks the numerical abstract domain if $\texttt{exp} > 0$. If the answer is *true* then the uncertainity ? is dropped. If the answer is *false*, then it means that $\texttt{exp} == 0$ (as if $\texttt{exp} < 0$, then a buffer overrun occurs, causing the concrete execution to stop, and having some other `Clousot` analysis reporting the bug). Therefore the *empty* segmentation is returned. Otherwise, the original segmentation could not be refined, and it is returned as it is.

Assertions `Clousot` implements a very simple and specialized decision procedure to check whether an quantified assertion over arrays holds at a given program point. Given the statement $\texttt{assert}\ \forall i \in [\texttt{e1}, \texttt{e2}).\ c(\texttt{A}[i])$, `Clousot` uses the numerical abstract domain to provide a lower bound l for `e1` and an upper bound u for `e2` to be used to determine an upper-approximation v for the values of $\texttt{A}[i]$ in the range $[l, u)$. The expression $c(v)$, which does not contain any reference to array values, is then constructed and its truth is decided by the internal decision procedures commonly used in `Clousot`.

Example 9 Let us consider the example in Fig. **2**, and let us suppose that at the end of the method there was the statement $\texttt{assert}\ \forall i \in [0, \texttt{A.Length}).\ \texttt{A}[i] == 0$. `Clousot` infers the limits to be 0 and `A.Length`, and it uses the abstract state `p6` to determine that in such a range $v = \texttt{A}[i] = 0$. The consequent proof obligation $0 == 0$ is then trivially discharged. □

Function calls Function calls are not-inlined as `Clousot` relies on their contract instead. So they are turned into two instructions, an `assert` for the precondition, and an `assume` for the postcondition.

Segmentation Unification In the implementation we slightly refined the algorithm of Sect. **11.4** to cope with some *noise* produced by the bytecode representation and heap analysis. In general, in a segmentation done at bytecode level one will find many more extra-variables than those that one may expect, in particular when reasoning at the equivalent source code.

The first modification is the introduction of a *purification* step, which pre-processes the segmentations to remove those segment bounds (and hence segments) containing variables appearing only in one of the two segmentations. Of course those would have disappeared anyway with the original algorithm, but the *purification* step has the advantage of making the algorithm faster and more precise, as shown by the next example.

Example 10 Suppose we need to unify the segmentation {0} ... {a} ... {b}... {A.Length} with {0}... {b}... {A.Length}. The purification step removes {a} from the first segmentation, enabling the segmentation unification algorithm to produce a more precise result. Without purification, we would have needed a deeper look-ahead for the algorithm to prevent the abstraction of the bound {b}. □

The second modification is a refinement of the step 5 to take into account constants: If B_1 and B_2 contain a constant then we can use this information to materialize new bounds, as illustrated by the next example.

Example 11 Suppose we need to unify {0}...{25}...{26} ...{A.Length} with {0}... {20}... {30}... {A.Length}. The result of the unification is {0}...{20}...{25} ...{26} ...{30} ...{A.Length}. □

13. Experimental Evaluation

We validated the performances of the analysis by running on large, production quality libraries. We validated its precision by running it on its own implementation (Clousot is written in C#).

13.1 Analysis of large libraries

We report the experience of running Clousot on the main libraries of the .NET framework. The mscorlib.dll and System.dll libraries provide core functionalities such as basic types, optimized data structures, cryptographic primitives, date manipulation, interfaces with the operating system, *etc.* The other libraries focus on database interfacing (System.data.dll), bitmap manipulations (System.Drawings.dll), WEB contents (System.Web.dll), XML parsing and creation (System.Xml.dll). Libraries have been authored by several different programmers over the years, hence present all kinds of different programming styles and optimizations. We randomly inspected a large set of methods containing loops with arrays. For instance, this is how we picked the example in Fig. **1**. We found few cases of code as Fig. **2**, whereas Fig. **3** is a lot more common pattern. Other common idioms include the initialization using multiple loops, conditional initialization of an array prefix (or postfix) followed (or not) by the initialization of the remaining array segment (or a sub-segment). From our manual inspection we deduced that simple partitions based on the assumption that arrays are uniformly traversed from the first to the last element (*e.g.* [29]) simply do not apply to existing .NET code. Other syntactic-based partitioning heuristics do not apply as well (roughly because at bytecode level the structure of loops has been compiled away). We conclude that an array analysis technique in order to be effective should handle very efficiently the above cases.

At the beginning of this project, our first attempt was to implement the technique of [19] on the top of a semantic analysis to determine the array partitions. Performances turned out to be extremely bad: up to 100× slower w.r.t. a normal run of Clousot. The main reasons for the bad performance were: (i) the large number of generated slices (because of lack of possibly empty segments, unlike us); (ii) the need to re-run the analysis once the partition is discovered (*e.g.* to distinguish the first iteration from all the others); (iii) the cost of partition changes (detailed in [19, Sect. 5]). More generally, the problem of [17, 19] is that they abstract too much the concrete environment, *e.g.* by separating the array partitioning from the discovery of array partitions (we do it at the same time instead) and *e.g.* by forgetting the relative positioning of array slices (we have consecutive segments). The information lost because of the rough abstraction must then be recovered during the array analysis.

Next, we developed **FunArray** in which we made sure that: (i) the array analysis is run *at the same time* as the scalar variable analysis; and (ii) explicit partition enumeration is avoided by means of possibly empty segments, *i.e* at each program point there is at most *one* approximation for a given array. We first sketched the analysis in a research prototype (**Arrayal**), to experiment and adjust the algorithms and then we validated it by integrating it in Clousot.

Our analysis turned out to be extremely fast. We report the experimental results in Tab. **1**. For each library, we report the number of functions, the analysis time *without* the array analysis, the analysis time *with* the array analysis, the slowdown, and the number of inferred non-trivial array invariants in function postconditions. The libraries are not annotated with contracts, so we cannot report on it. In the experimental setting Clousot is run in its off-the-shelf configuration except for the iterative refinement which is switched off (as it is not needed for the particular experience). The workbench is a 2.4GHz Core 2 duo laptop running Windows 7 and .NET $v3.5$. The first observation is that the **FunArray** introduces a negligible analysis slowdown (less than 1%) whereas it discovers a thousands of non-trivial array invariants. More interestingly, we did not encountered any corner case causing the analysis time to blow up (unlike previous published similar techniques). This fact makes us comfortable to state that the analysis scales up well. We were also positively impressed by the fact that the analysis was able to handle complex initialization patterns such as the one in Fig. **1**, which were not considered at all during its design, meaning that the analysis is robust enough to handle *unexpected* code (a problem that unfortunately afflicts several static analyses usually developed for few coding patterns).

Lib	# func.	time	time w. arr.	Δ	# inv
mscorlib.dll	21 475	4:06	4:15	0:09	2 430
System.dll	15 489	3:40	3:46	0:06	1 385
System.data.dll	12 408	4:49	4:55	0:06	1 325
System.Drawings.dll	3 123	0:28	0:29	0:01	289
System.Web.dll	23 647	4:56	5:02	0:06	840
System.Xml.dll	10 510	3:59	4:16	0:17	807

Table 1. The execution time with and without the array analysis, the slow-down and the number of non-trivial array invariants. Time is in minutes. The incidence of array analysis is a mere 1%.

13.2 Analysis of annotated code

To validate the precision of the analysis in the context of contract checking we ran it against its own implementation in Clousot. Once again we run Clousot in the off-of-the-shelf configuration (and iterative refinement on). We implemented **FunArray** with a pair of *mutable* sequences, one for the bounds and the other for the array elements. Each sequence should only contain non-null elements. Sequences are implemented as partially filled arrays (to optimize cache hits). The class NonNullSeq abstracts sequences, allowing for in-place insertion, manipulation, update and removal of elements (13 methods in total). The object invariant of NonNullSeq states that all the elements in the partially filled array are non-null. The analysis of NonNullSeq *without* the functor analysis takes 5.36 seconds, reporting 11 warnings (out of 210 proof obligations). The analysis of NonNullSeq *with* the functor analysis takes 3.85 seconds, with 0 warnings! Therefore the more precise analysis is also faster. The reason why is that the array analysis induces a negligible slow-down and discover more facts on the program, which can be directly used to discharge the proof obligations, without moving to more refined analyses. Once NonNullSeq has been verified, then we considered the **FunArray** implementation (78 methods), where we were able to prove 61 further proof obligations, out of 1800 total (FunArray analysis cost was negligible). The remaining 8 warnings are issued by a possible violation of the precondition of the segment unification algorithm (out-of-reach of Clousot, and maybe of existing SMT solvers). Overall, our experience matched the feedback from our users (we do not have access to their code though): FunArray reduced the number of false positives at a negligeable cost.

14. Conclusions

Our main goal was to have a non-intrusive, precise and scalable static analysis for array contents. We achieved it through these core ideas: (i) to derive the segment bounds through array accesses in array element tests and assignments (so that we do not rely on the end-user or other analyses/tools to infer the segment bounds); (ii) to exploit segment unification for partial order, joins, meets, widenings, and narrowings; (iii) to carefully treat disjunction (via possibly empty segments, symbolic bounds with different instances, and relation of array values to indexes). Although expressiveness of array segmentation is limited, our analysis is self-contained without hidden hypotheses. It has proved to be simple enough to scale up in production-quality static analysis tools (whereas a previous attempt based on [17, 19] did not). We used it to validate its own implementation, effectively reducing to zero the false alarms.

The approach is applicable to matrices of higher dimensions by recursively instantiating the functor on an array instantiation. The work can be extended to relational properties among segments by using an auxiliary scalar variable to denote the value of any element of a segment and relating the values of these auxiliary scalar variables for different segments by a relational abstraction in the scalar environment. This would handle the partitioning in QuickSort. Intra-segment relational properties can also be considered by using several auxiliary scalar variables $\mathtt{x}_i, \mathtt{x}_j, \ldots$ to denote the values of elements indexed $i \leqslant j \leqslant \ldots$ within the segment and relating them in the scalar environment. This would handle sorting algorithms [6]. Of course inter-segments and intra-segment relational properties can be combined. The extra cost makes those relational analyses probably inappropriate in a general-purpose and scalable static verifier such as Clousot.

Acknowledgments We would like to thank Manuel Fähndrich for the insightful discussions and the support provided with the implementation of the decompilation of ForAll in Clousot. Work partly supported by the CMACS NSF Expeditions in Computing.

References

[1] M. Barnett, K. Leino, and W. Schulte. The Spec# programming system: An overview. *CASSIS'04*, LNCS 3362, 49–69. Springer, 2005.

[2] M. Barnett, B.-Y. Chang, R. DeLine, B. Jacobs, and K. Leino. Boogie: A modular reusable verifier for object-oriented programs. *FMCO'05*, LNCS 4111, 364–387. Springer, 2006.

[3] M. Barnett, M. Fähndrich, and F. Logozzo. Embedded contract languages. *SAC'10*. ACM, 2010.

[4] D. Beyer, T. A. Henzinger, R. Majumdar, and A. Rybalchenko. Path invariants. *PLDI'07*, 300–309. ACM, 2007.

[5] P. Chalin, J. Kinirya, G. Leavens, and E. Poll. Beyond assertions: Advanced specification and verification with JML and ESC/Java2. *FMCO'05*, LNCS 4111, 77–101. Springer, 2006.

[6] P. Cousot. Verification by abstract interpretation. *Verification – Theory & Practice*, LNCS 2772, 243–268. Springer, 2003.

[7] P. Cousot and R. Cousot. Abstract interpretation: a unified lattice model for static analysis of programs by construction or approximation of fixpoints. *4th POPL*, 238–252. ACM, 1977.

[8] P. Cousot and R. Cousot. Systematic design of program analysis frameworks. *6th POPL*, 269–282. ACM, 1979.

[9] P. Cousot, R. Cousot, J. Feret, L. Mauborgne, A. Miné, D. Monniaux, and X. Rival. Combination of abstractions in the Astrée static analyzer. *ASIAN*, LNCS 4435, 272–300. Springer, 2006.

[10] L. de Moura and N. Bjørner. Z3: An efficient SMT solver. *TACAS'08*, LNCS 4963, 337–340. Springer, 2008.

[11] D. Dill. Timing assumptions and verification of finite-state concurrent systems. *Automatic Verification Methods for Finite State Systems*, LNCS 407, 197–212. Springer, 1989.

[12] I. Dillig, T. Dillig, and A. Aiken. Fluid updates: Beyond strong vs. weak updates. *ESOP'10*, LNCS 6012, 246–266. Springer, 2010.

[13] I. Dillig, T. Dillig, and A. Aiken. Precise reasoning for programs using containers. *37th POPL*. ACM, 2011.

[14] M. Fähndrich and F. Logozzo. Static contract checking with abstract interpretation. *FoVeOOS'10*, LNCS. Springer, 2010.

[15] C. Flanagan and S. Qadeer. Predicate abstraction for software verification. *29th POPL*, 191–202. ACM, 2002.

[16] Garmin Int. Garmin device interface specification. Technical report, Garmin Int., Inc., Olathe, 2006. www.garmin.com/support/pdf/iop_spec.pdf.

[17] D. Gopan, T. Reps, and S. Sagiv. A framework for numeric analysis of array operations. *32nd POPL*, 338–350. ACM, 2005.

[18] S. Gulwani, B. McCloskey, and A. Tiwari. Lifting abstract interpreters to quantified logical domains. *35th POPL*, 235–246. ACM, 2008.

[19] N. Halbwachs and M. Péron. Discovering properties about arrays in simple programs. *PLDI'2008*, 339–348. ACM, 2008.

[20] R. Jhala and K. McMillan. Array abstractions from proofs. *CAV'07*, LNCS 4590, 193–206. Springer, 2007.

[21] M. Karr. Affine relationships among variables of a program. *Acta Inf.*, 6:133–151, 1976.

[22] G. Kildall. A unified approach to global program optimization. *1st POPL*, 194–206. ACM, 1973.

[23] L. Kovács and A. Voronkov. Finding loop invariants for programs over arrays using a theorem prover. *FASE'2009*, LNCS 5503, 470–485. Springer, 2009.

[24] V. Laviron and F. Logozzo. Subpolyhedra: A (more) scalable approach to infer linear inequalities. *VMCAI*, LNCS 5403, 229–244. Springer, 2009.

[25] S.-H. Lee and D.-H. Cho. Packet-scheduling algorithm based on priority of separate buffers for unicast and multicast services. *Electronics Letters*, 39(2):259–260, 2003.

[26] F. Logozzo. Class-level modular analysis for object oriented languages. *SAS'03*, LNCS 2694, 37–54. Springer, 2003.

[27] F. Logozzo and M. Fähndrich. On the relative completeness of bytecode analysis versus source code analysis. *CC'08*, LNCS 4959, 197–212. Springer, 2008.

[28] F. Logozzo and M. Fähndrich. Pentagons: a weakly relational abstract domain for the efficient validation of array accesses. *SAC*, 184–188. ACM, 2008.

[29] M. Marron, D. Stefanovic, M. Hermenegildo, and D. Kapur. Heap analysis in the presence of collection libraries. *PASTE'07*, 31–36. ACM, 2007.

[30] K. L. McMillan. Quantified invariant generation using an interpolating saturation prover. *TACAS'08*, LNCS 4963, 197–212. Springer, 2008.

[31] B. Meyer. *Eiffel: The Language*. Prentice Hall, 1991.

[32] A. Miné. The octagon abstract domain. *Higher-Order and Symbolic Computation*, 19:31–100, 2006.

[33] V. Pratt. Two easy theories whose combination is hard. Technical report, MIT, 1977. boole.stanford.edu/pub/sefnp.pdf.

[34] B. Roy. Transitivité et connexité. *Comptes-Rendus de l'Académie des Sciences de Paris, Sér. A-B*, 249:216–218, 1959.

[35] M. Seghir, A. Podelski, and T. Wies. Abstraction refinement for quantified array assertions. *SAS'09*, LNCS 5673, 3–18. Springer, 2009.

[36] R. Shostak. Deciding linear inequalities by computing loop residues. *JACM*, 28(4):769–779, 1981.

[37] H. Yang, O. Lee, J. Berdine, C. Calcagno, B. Cook, D. Distefano, and P. W. O'Hearn. Scalable shape analysis for systems code. *CAV'98*, LNCS 5123, 385–398. Springer, 2008.

Step-Indexed Kripke Models over Recursive Worlds

Lars Birkedal
IT University of Copenhagen, Denmark
birkedal@itu.dk

Bernhard Reus
University of Sussex, UK
bernhard@sussex.ac.uk

Jan Schwinghammer
Saarland University, Germany
jan@ps.uni-saarland.de

Kristian Støvring *
University of Copenhagen, Denmark
stovring@diku.dk

Jacob Thamsborg
IT University of Copenhagen, Denmark
thamsborg@itu.dk

Hongseok Yang
Queen Mary University London, UK
hyang@dcs.qmul.ac.uk

Abstract

Over the last decade, there has been extensive research on modelling challenging features in programming languages and program logics, such as higher-order store and storable resource invariants. A recent line of work has identified a common solution to some of these challenges: Kripke models over worlds that are recursively defined in a category of metric spaces. In this paper, we broaden the scope of this technique from the original domain-theoretic setting to an elementary, operational one based on step indexing. The resulting method is widely applicable and leads to simple, succinct models of complicated language features, as we demonstrate in our semantics of Charguéraud and Pottier's type-and-capability system for an ML-like higher-order language. Moreover, the method provides a high-level understanding of the essence of recent approaches based on step indexing.

Categories and Subject Descriptors D.3.1 [*PROGRAMMING LANGUAGES*]: Formal Definitions and Theory; F.3.1 [*LOGICS AND MEANINGS OF PROGRAMS*]: Specifying and Verifying and Reasoning about Programs

General Terms Languages, Theory, Verification

Keywords Kripke models, ultrametric spaces, step-indexed models, capability calculus, frame rules, indirection theory

1. Introduction

Over the last decade, there has been extensive research on modelling challenging features in programming languages, type systems and program logics, such as higher-order store and storable resource invariants, where modelling involves constructing recursively defined structures [15, 22, 29, 32, 41, 42]. One of the main aims of this research has been to develop a method for building semantic models such that (1) the method is simple enough to be understood by the designers of a type system or a program logic (who might have only limited knowledge of domain theory) but (2) the method is powerful enough to resolve the issue of constructing recursive structures.

Unfortunately, existing methods do not fully achieve this aim. Methods based on classical domain theory provide techniques for constructing recursive structures, but they require non-trivial mathematical knowledge from users. Methods based on step indexing [2, 4, 6, 11, 12], on the other hand, do not require sophisticated mathematics from the users; usually, the prerequisite is just familiarity with standard operational semantics of programs. However, the step-indexed methods only partially address the issue of constructing recursive structures. They change the original recursive equations that solutions have to satisfy to easier approximate ones, and construct structures that satisfy the approximate equations. We point out that solving the original recursive equations seems crucial in some applications, such as the semantics of various higher-order frame and anti-frame rules [44, 46]. Hence, in those applications, only domain-theoretic models, not step-indexed ones, have been developed.

In this paper, we propose a new method that brings together the benefits of both domain-theoretic and step-indexing methods. Our approach is based on a recent line of work where challenging features of programming languages and logics are modelled using a common solution: Kripke models over worlds that are recursively defined in a category of metric spaces [21, 44, 46]. This method transfers those worlds from the original domain-theoretic setup to an elementary, operational one based on step indexing.

Although our method does involve a modicum of metric space theory, it retains the flavour and simplicity of traditional step-indexed methods [2, 4, 6, 11, 12]. Unlike these step-indexed models, which only provide solutions to approximated versions of recursive equations, our approach provides solutions to the equations proper, i.e., we solve the equation up to isomorphism. In the paper, we demonstrate the benefits of our method by presenting the first semantic model of Charguéraud and Pottier's capability calculus [24]. This calculus is a substructural type system for a higher-order ML-like language with state. Our semantics justifies the typing rules of the calculus, and it also suggests a sound extension of the type system with a higher-order (deep) frame rule. The latter imposes a nontrivial soundness issue, because we need a recursively defined operation on a recursively-defined set of worlds to model the invariant-extension operator of higher-order framing. [1]

* Work carried out while employed at the IT University of Copenhagen.

[1] We have also used the new method to give an elementary *operational* model for a program logic for reasoning about higher-order store; this yields an alternative soundness proof to the earlier non-trivial domain-theoretic

POPL'11, January 26–28, 2011, Austin, Texas, USA.

Our method also provides a high-level understanding of the essence of step-indexed models. In particular, we show that the method can be specialized to Hobor et al.'s recent abstract description of step-indexed models [30], and explain the benefits of taking the metric viewpoint we suggest.

The remainder of the paper is organized as follows. In Section 2, we give an extensive introduction of our method, by developing a step-indexed Kripke model for ML references. In Section 3, we address the challenging problem of modelling Charguéraud and Pottier's capability type system, and show how our method gives rise to a step-indexed Kripke model of the calculus. Next, in Section 4, we consider the connection with the indirection theory of Hobor et al. [30], and point out what new insights our method brings to the work on step indexing. Finally, in Sections 5 and 6, we discuss related work and conclude the paper.

For space reasons, some proofs and details have been omitted. These can be found in the appendices of the long version of the paper, which is available at:

`http://www.itu.dk/people/birkedal/longessence.pdf`

2. Introductory Example: ML References

In this section, we give an extensive introduction of our method, using a programming language with impredicative polymorphism and general ML-like references, i.e., an extension of the call-by-value polymorphic lambda calculus with higher-order store. We do not give the syntax of this language as it is standard [36] but point out that we use v for values, e for expressions and τ for types, in particular $e[\tau]$ is application of a polymorphic term to a type.

First, we describe the general idea of interpreting the programming language with a Kripke-style possible-worlds model, where the set of worlds is recursively defined. Then, we review an existing model that realizes the idea in a domain-theoretic setting (based on an adequate denotational semantics of the language). Finally, we present a new step-indexed model (based purely on the operational semantics), and compare it with the domain-theoretic one.

A simple approach for modelling the polymorphic lambda calculus, without general references, is to interpret types as predicates (subsets) on some fixed set of values. To model the programming language of interest now, however, we need to extend this approach, because the language includes dynamic allocation of general references. Following earlier work on the semantics of dynamic allocation of simple integer cells [14, 32, 40, 48], we use an extension with Kripke-style possible worlds. In this extension, a type is interpreted as a predicate on values parameterized over worlds, and a world describes the type for each allocated location—a world $w \in W$ is a finite map from locations (modelled as natural numbers) to semantic types in T. The extension is described by the following recursive equations on the set W of worlds and the set T of semantic types:

$$V = \text{set of values, including locations}$$
$$W = \mathbb{N} \rightharpoonup_{fin} T \qquad T = W \to_{mon} Pred(V) \tag{1}$$

Note that in the equation for T, we impose a monotonicity requirement (with respect to an extension ordering of worlds). Intuitively, this requirement means that validity of semantic types is preserved in presence of a growing heap. The formal meaning of the monotonicity will be explained later in Section 2.2.

Once we are given the semantic domains W and T satisfying the above equations, we can interpret types as elements in T. In particular, the meaning of a reference type $\mathsf{ref}\,\tau$ can be defined roughly as

$$(\mathsf{ref}\,\tau)w = \{l \mid w(l) = \tau\},$$

i.e., for a world w, it is the set of locations l such that the semantic type recorded in the world at l is the same as τ. [2]

Observe that the natural model of types here is a *Kripke model over a recursively-defined set of worlds.* It is a Kripke model because the semantic types are parameterized over W. The problem is, of course, that for cardinality reasons there are no solutions to the above equations in the category of sets; unfolding the above equations we get $W = \mathbb{N} \rightharpoonup_{fin} (W \to_{mon} Pred(V))$ with W in a negative position, see also Ahmed [2].

To address this cardinality issue, existing methods based on step indexing, including the recent work by Hobor et al. [30], propose that we should give up solving the original recursive equations and instead solve approximate versions. As Hobor et al. show, solutions of the approximate equations are often sufficient for the applications of interest.

In this paper, we follow a different approach, which involves finding an appropriate simple category of metric spaces and solving the original recursive equations in the category. This approach has been developed in the setting of denotational semantics and domain theory. We show that the same approach can also be applied to operational semantics and step indexing. In the next subsections, we explain this point by giving a Kripke model of ML references, first using domain-theoretic methods, and then step indexing.

2.1 Review of Metric Spaces

Before describing our Kripke models, we review basic facts on the metric spaces, which will be used in the models; see, e.g., [47] for a thorough exposition. A **1-bounded ultrametric space** (X, d) is a metric space where the distance function $d : X \times X \to \mathbb{R}$ takes values in the closed interval $[0, 1]$ and satisfies the strong triangle inequality $d(x, y) \le \max\{d(x, z), d(z, y)\}$. An (ultra)metric space is **complete** if every Cauchy sequence has a limit. A function $f : X_1 \to X_2$ between metric spaces (X_1, d_1) and (X_2, d_2) is **non-expansive** if $d_2(f(x), f(y)) \le d_1(x, y)$ for all $x, y \in X_1$. It is **contractive** if there exists some $\delta < 1$ such that $d_2(f(x), f(y)) \le \delta \cdot d_1(x, y)$ for all $x, y \in X_1$.

The complete, 1-bounded, non-empty, ultrametric spaces and non-expansive functions between them form a Cartesian closed category $\mathbf{CBUlt}_{ne}$. Products are given by the set-theoretic product where the distance is the maximum of the componentwise distances. The exponential $(X_1, d_1) \to (X_2, d_2)$ has the set of non-expansive functions from (X_1, d_1) to (X_2, d_2) as underlying set, and distance function: $d_{X_1 \to X_2}(f, g) = \sup\{d_2(f(x), g(x)) \mid x \in X_1\}$. For any set S and space $(X, d) \in \mathbf{CBUlt}_{ne}$, the set of finite partial functions $S \rightharpoonup_{fin} X$ from S to X is again a complete, 1-bounded ultrametric space with distance function given by $d(f, g) = 1$, if the domains of f and g are not equal, and $d(f, g) = \max\{d(f(s), g(s)) \mid s \in \mathrm{dom}(f)\}$, if the domains of f and g are equal.

A functor $F : \mathbf{CBUlt}_{ne}^{op} \times \mathbf{CBUlt}_{ne} \longrightarrow \mathbf{CBUlt}_{ne}$ is **locally non-expansive** if $d(F(f, g), F(f', g')) \le \max\{d(f, f'), d(g, g')\}$ for all non-expansive f, f', g, g'. It is **locally contractive** if there exists $\delta < 1$ such that $d(F(f, g), F(f', g')) \le \delta \cdot \max\{d(f, f'), d(g, g')\}$ for all non-expansive f, f', g, g'. By multiplication of the distances of (X, d) with a non-negative shrinking factor $\delta < 1$, one obtains a new ultrametric space, $\delta \cdot (X, d) = (X, d')$ where $d'(x, y) =$

one [44]. Please see the appendix of the long version of the paper for this model.

[2] In both of the concrete models to be presented next, the interpretation of reference types is actually more complicated and involves certain "approximate equality" relations on semantic types. This is fairly standard for step-indexed models; that it is also required in the domain-theoretic setup is discussed by Birkedal et al. [21].

$\delta \cdot d(x, y)$. By shrinking, a locally non-expansive functor F yields a locally contractive functor $(\delta \cdot F)(X_1, X_2) = \delta \cdot (F(X_1, X_2))$.

It is well-known that one can solve recursive domain equations in $\mathbf{CBUlt}_{\mathrm{ne}}$ by an adaptation of the inverse-limit method from classical domain theory:

Theorem 2.1 (America-Rutten [9])**.** Let $F : \mathbf{CBUlt}_{\mathrm{ne}}^{\mathrm{op}} \times \mathbf{CBUlt}_{\mathrm{ne}} \to \mathbf{CBUlt}_{\mathrm{ne}}$ be a locally contractive functor. Then there exists a unique (up to isomorphism) $(X, d) \in \mathbf{CBUlt}_{\mathrm{ne}}$ such that $(X, d) \cong F((X, d), (X, d))$.

All the metric spaces we consider satisfy the following property:

Definition 2.2. A metric space is *bisected* if all non-zero distances are of the form 2^{-n} for some natural number $n \geq 0$.

The following notation is convenient when working with bisected metric spaces: in such a space, $x \stackrel{n}{=} y$ means that $d(x, y) \leq 2^{-n}$. We use two facts on $\stackrel{n}{=}$. First, each relation $\stackrel{n}{=}$ is an equivalence relation because of the ultrametric inequality. We are therefore justified in referring to the relation $\stackrel{n}{=}$ as "n-equality." Second, the distance of a bisected metric space is bounded by 1. In other words, the relation $x \stackrel{0}{=} y$ always holds.

Proposition 2.3. Let (X_1, d_1) and (X_2, d_2) be bisected metric spaces. A function $f : X_1 \to X_2$ is non-expansive if and only if $x_1 \stackrel{n}{=} x_1' \Rightarrow f(x_1) \stackrel{n}{=} f(x_1')$ holds for all $x_1, x_1' \in X_1$ and all natural numbers $n \geq 0$.

2.2 General Recipe and Domain-Theoretic Model

We now follow the idea outlined earlier and reformulate the recursive equations (1) in $\mathbf{CBUlt}_{\mathrm{ne}}$ to find solutions within this category. Concretely, the proposal suggests to use the recipe below:

1. Define a set V with a structure. The structure can be a preorder, or a uniform complete partial order, but does not have to be. Intuitively, V is a domain for semantic values.
2. Define an object $\mathit{Pred}(V)$ in $\mathbf{CBUlt}_{\mathrm{ne}}$. Elements in this object represent predicates on values.
3. Solve the recursive domain equation below in $\mathbf{CBUlt}_{\mathrm{ne}}$:
$$\hat{T} \;\cong\; \tfrac{1}{2} \cdot ((\mathbb{N} \rightharpoonup_{fin} \hat{T}) \to_{mon} \mathit{Pred}(V)) \,. \qquad (2)$$
4. Define T and W using $\hat{T}$:
$$W \;=\; N \rightharpoonup_{fin} \hat{T}, \qquad T \;=\; W \to_{mon} \mathit{Pred}(V). \qquad (3)$$

The function space in the equivalence in the third step consists of non-expansive and monotone functions, where monotonicity is imposed with respect to the following extension order on $\mathbb{N} \rightharpoonup_{fin} T$: For $w, w' \in \mathbb{N} \rightharpoonup_{fin} T$, we have $w \sqsubseteq w'$ iff the domain of w is included in the domain of w', and w and w' agree on the former. The $\frac{1}{2}$ is an example of a shrinking factor and, technically, ensures that the functor is locally contractive; it is a standard technique [9]. The equivalence is well-formed in $\mathbf{CBUlt}_{\mathrm{ne}}$, and it has a unique solution up to isomorphism by Theorem 2.1.

The recipe has been used by Birkedal, Støvring and Thamsborg [21], when they gave a relationally-parametric domain-theoretic model of a call-by-value language with impredicative polymorphism, general references and recursive types. They constructed the parameters V and $\mathit{Pred}(V)$ of the recipe using domain theory, choosing for V the cpo of values that is used in the standard "untyped" domain-theoretic interpretation of the language. This domain V comes with a family of projections $\pi_n : V \to V_\perp$ satisfying certain properties (so it becomes a uniform cpo). For the next parameter $\mathit{Pred}(V)$, Birkedal et al. used these projections to define $\mathit{Pred}(V)$ as the collection of *complete uniform* subsets of V. *Completeness* says that a subset P is closed under least upper bounds of chains, and *uniformity* that P is closed under all the projections (i.e., $\forall v \in P.\ \forall n > 0.\ \pi_n(v) \in P_\perp$). The set $\mathit{Pred}(V)$ can be viewed as a metric space in $\mathbf{CBUlt}_{\mathrm{ne}}$, by giving it an appropriate distance function along the lines of earlier work on interpreting recursive types and impredicative polymorphism [1, 7, 8, 23, 33].

Now, by simply following the recipe from the given ingredients (i.e. parameters V and $\mathit{Pred}(V)$) one obtains metric spaces T for semantic types and W for possible worlds, respectively. With this indexed semantic model of types, Birkedal et al. gave an interpretation of all the types of the programming language, and defined the typed meaning of expressions by proving the fundamental theorem of logical relations wrt. the untyped semantics of expressions. See [21] for a detailed treatment.[3]

2.3 Step-Indexed Model

Our new insight is that the recipe presented in Section 2.2 is not tied to domain theory and denotational semantics, but it can also be used with operational semantics. In this case, the first parameter of the recipe is the set *Val* of closed syntactic values from the operational semantics. The second parameter is the set of predicates on step-approximated values. Precisely, it is the collection $\mathit{UPred}(\mathit{Val})$ of subsets of $\mathbb{N} \times \mathit{Val}$ that are downwards closed in the first step ($\mathbb{N}$) component:

$$\mathit{UPred}(\mathit{Val}) \;=\; \{p \subseteq \mathbb{N} \times \mathit{Val} \mid \forall (k, v) \in p.\, \forall j \leq k.\, (j, v) \in p\}.$$

We call $p \in \mathit{UPred}(\mathit{Val})$ a **uniform predicate** on *Val*.

Note that we give a unary interpretation; in particular the model does not prove any program equivalences. This is just for simplicity of presentation, a relational, i.e., binary, model can be built along the same lines using $\mathit{UPred}(\mathit{Val} \times \mathit{Val})$.

The idea of considering predicates on step-approximated values is from step-indexed models [2, 4, 11, 12]. Here we go "a step further" and show that the collection $\mathit{UPred}(\mathit{Val})$ of such predicates can always be made into an object in $\mathbf{CBUlt}_{\mathrm{ne}}$. To do this, for $p \in \mathit{UPred}(\mathit{Val})$ and $k \in \mathbb{N}$, we use the notation $p_{[k]} = \{(m, v) \in p \mid m < k\}$, representing the k-th approximation of p. With this notation, we define a distance function d on $\mathit{UPred}(\mathit{Val})$, which measures "up-to-what-level" two predicates agree:

$$d(p, q) \;=\; \begin{cases} 2^{-\max\{k \mid p_{[k]} = q_{[k]}\}} & \text{if } p \neq q \\ 0 & \text{otherwise.} \end{cases}$$

Lemma 2.4. $(\mathit{UPred}(\mathit{Val}), d)$ is a well-defined object in $\mathbf{CBUlt}_{\mathrm{ne}}$. In fact, the construction in $\mathit{UPred}(\mathit{Val})$ does not depend on our choice of *Val*, and can be applied to any set X, giving a metric space $\mathit{UPred}(X)$ in $\mathbf{CBUlt}_{\mathrm{ne}}$.

Note that because of this lemma, we can consider uniform predicates $p \in \mathit{UPred}(X)$ on any set X.

Hence, the recipe in Section 2.2 is applicable for *Val* and $\mathit{UPred}(\mathit{Val})$, and gives rise to semantic domains $\hat{T}$, W and T that satisfy the recursive equations in (2) and (3). Note that by working in $\mathbf{CBUlt}_{\mathrm{ne}}$, we have solved the desired equations, even for a setting based on operational semantics. In the rest of this section, we use these domains and model the programming language with impredicative polymorphism and ML references.

For concreteness, we consider a language as in Dreyer et al. [27], except that we do not consider recursive types and we split the context for type variables and term variables in two. Term

[3] Notice that we use a small "trick" to construct the space of worlds W using Theorem 2.1. By solving the equation (2) we first obtain the space of semantic types, and we then define worlds in terms of semantic types. It is also possible to obtain W directly, as a solution of a recursive equation in a category of *pre-ordered* ultrametric spaces [20]. The latter technique is more general, but for this paper we do not need such pre-ordered spaces.

$$\llbracket \Xi \vdash \tau \rrbracket_\eta : W \to_{mon} \mathit{UPred}(\mathit{Val})$$

$$\llbracket \Xi \vdash 1 \rrbracket_\eta w = \{(k, ()) \mid k \in \mathbb{N}\}$$

$$\llbracket \Xi \vdash \mathsf{ref}\, \tau \rrbracket_\eta w = \{(k, l) \mid l \in \mathrm{dom}(w) \land w(l) \stackrel{k}{=} \llbracket \Xi \vdash \tau \rrbracket_\eta\}$$

$$\llbracket \Xi \vdash \alpha \rrbracket_\eta w = \eta(\alpha)(w)$$

$$\llbracket \Xi \vdash \forall \alpha.\tau \rrbracket_\eta w = \{(k, v) \mid \forall \tau' \in \mathit{SyntacticType}.\ \forall r \in T.\ \forall w' \sqsupseteq w.\ \forall i \le k.\ (i, v[\tau']) \in \mathcal{E}\llbracket \Xi, \alpha \vdash \tau \rrbracket_{\eta[\alpha \mapsto r]} w'\}$$

$$\llbracket \Xi \vdash \tau \to \tau' \rrbracket_\eta w = \{(k, v) \mid \forall v' \in \mathit{Val}.\ \forall w' \sqsupseteq w.\ \forall i \le k.\ (i, v') \in \llbracket \Xi \vdash \tau \rrbracket_\eta w' \Rightarrow (i, v\, v') \in \mathcal{E}\llbracket \Xi \vdash \tau' \rrbracket_\eta w'\}$$

$$\mathcal{E}\llbracket \Xi \vdash \tau \rrbracket_\eta w = \{(k, t) \mid \forall i \le k.\ \forall h, h'.\ \forall e'.\ \big(h :_k w \land (t \mid h) \longmapsto^i (e' \mid h') \land (e', h')\ \text{irreducible}\big) \Rightarrow \big(\exists w' \sqsupseteq w.\ h' :_{k-i} w' \land (k-i, e') \in \llbracket \Xi \vdash \tau \rrbracket_\eta w'\big)\}$$

$$h :_k w \iff \mathrm{dom}(h) = \mathrm{dom}(w) \land \forall i < k. \forall l \in \mathrm{dom}(w).\ (i, h(l)) \in w(l)(w)$$

(where $()$ is the unique element in the empty product, *SyntacticType* is the set of syntactic types, *Exp* is the set of closed syntactic expressions, and $(t \mid h)$ is a configuration of an expression t and a heap h. A heap h is a finite function from locations to closed syntactic values.)

Figure 1. Interpretation of types

judgments take the form

$$\Xi; \Gamma; \Sigma \vdash M : \tau$$

where Ξ is a context of type variables $\alpha_1, \dots, \alpha_n$; Γ is a context of typed term variables $x_1 : \tau_1, \dots, x_m : \tau_m$; and Σ is a context of typed locations $l_1 : \tau_1, \dots, l_k : \tau_k$. Detailed typing judgments and operational semantics can be found in the online appendix to Dreyer et al.

Types in this language are interpreted similar to those used in existing step-indexed models [2], but one can exploit the fact that W and T are solutions to the recursive equations above. The semantics of types in context is defined as a non-expansive function

$$\llbracket \Xi \vdash \tau \rrbracket : T^{|\Xi|} \to T$$

in $\mathbf{CBUlt}_{\mathrm{ne}}$. The definition is shown in Figure 1. In the figure, we use η for environments for Ξ, i.e., elements in the product space $T^{|\Xi|}$ in $\mathbf{CBUlt}_{\mathrm{ne}}$. Notice that in the case for $\llbracket \Xi \vdash \mathsf{ref}\, \tau \rrbracket$, we use k-equality in the space T and that $\mathcal{E}\llbracket \Xi \vdash \tau \rrbracket$ generalizes $\llbracket \Xi \vdash \tau \rrbracket$ from values to expressions.

Lemma 2.5. $\llbracket \Xi \vdash \tau \rrbracket$ is well-defined. In particular,

- for all $\eta \in T^{|\Xi|}$, $\llbracket \Xi \vdash \tau \rrbracket_\eta$ is non-expansive and monotone; and
- $\llbracket \Xi \vdash \tau \rrbracket$ is a non-expansive map on η's.

In Figure 2 we define interpretations of contexts and the logical relation interpretation of well-typed expressions. Using those definitions, we are ready to prove the main soundness result:

Theorem 2.6 (Fundamental Theorem of Logical Relations). If $\Xi; \Gamma; \Sigma \vdash t : \tau$, then $\Xi; \Gamma; \Sigma \vdash t :^{\log} \tau$.

One oddity is worth explaining: there is no coherence between the syntactic types that we substitute for type variables and the corresponding semantic types in the environment; this is the case both for the interpretation of universal types and in the definition of the logical relation. The explanation is simply that the syntactic types in values and expressions do not influence the computation; indeed, we could equally well have worked with a language without type-decorations as, e.g., Ahmed [3] does.

$$\llbracket \Xi \vdash \Gamma \rrbracket_\eta : W \to \mathit{UPred}(\mathit{Val}^{|\Gamma|})$$

$$\llbracket \Xi \vdash \emptyset \rrbracket_\eta w = \{(k, ()) \mid k \in \mathbb{N}\}$$

$$\llbracket \Xi \vdash \Gamma, x : \tau \rrbracket_\eta w = \{(k, \rho[x \mapsto v]) \mid (k, \rho) \in \llbracket \Xi \vdash \Gamma \rrbracket_\eta w \land (k, v) \in \llbracket \Xi \vdash \tau \rrbracket_\eta w\}$$

$$\llbracket \Sigma \rrbracket : \mathit{UPred}(W)$$

$$\llbracket \Sigma \rrbracket = \{(k, w) \mid \forall (l : \tau) \in \Sigma.\ (k, l) \in \llbracket \emptyset \vdash \mathsf{ref}\, \tau \rrbracket_{()} w\}$$

$$\begin{aligned}
&\Xi; \Gamma; \Sigma \vdash t :^{\log} \tau \iff \\
&\quad \exists \alpha_1, \dots, \alpha_n.\ \Xi = \alpha_1, \dots, \alpha_n \ \land \\
&\quad \forall \tau_1, \dots, \tau_n \in \mathit{SyntacticType}.\ \forall k \ge 0.\ \forall \eta.\ \forall \rho.\ \forall w. \\
&\qquad (\eta \in T^{|\Xi|} \ \land\ (k, \rho) \in \llbracket \Xi \vdash \Gamma \rrbracket_\eta w \ \land\ (k, w) \in \llbracket \Sigma \rrbracket) \\
&\qquad \Rightarrow ((k,\ (\rho(t))[\alpha_1{:=}\tau_1, \dots, \alpha_n{:=}\tau_n]) \in \mathcal{E}\llbracket \Xi \vdash \tau \rrbracket_\eta w)
\end{aligned}$$

(where $()$ is the unique environment for the empty context, and both $(-)[\alpha_1{:=}\tau_1, \dots, \alpha_n{:=}\tau_n]$ and $\rho(-)$ represent the applications of substitutions.)

Figure 2. Interpretation of contexts and well-typed expressions

We finally remark that it is not surprising that there is a connection between metric spaces and step-indexed models; this was already pointed out in [11]. The point is that it is useful not to forget this connection because it, e.g., allows us to define solutions to recursive world equations such as the ones in this section. (See also the discussion in Section 4.2.)

We do not present a formal relationship to existing models for this particular example, but rather show, in Section 4, how all the step-indexed models described via the indirection theory of Hobor et al. [30] can be obtained by a specialization of our general approach. In Section 4.2, we will also highlight the advantages of using metric spaces. Next, however, we consider another more substantial application to illustrate our method.

3. Application: A Step-indexed Model of Capabilities

Reasoning about higher-order stateful programs is notoriously difficult, and often involves the need to track aliasing information. A particular line of work that has been proposed to this end are substructural type systems with regions, capabilities and singleton types [5, 24, 26]. In this section, we give a step-indexed model for a substantial fragment[4] of Charguéraud and Pottier's capability calculus [24]. Our model provides an alternative soundness proof to the translation and progress and preservation results in [24, 38], and allows for the analysis of soundness of extensions. We illustrate this latter point by proving sound an extension of the language with higher-order frame rules [19, 44], and establish an explicit connection with models of separation logic *qua* our model, which shows that capabilities can be understood semantically as separation logic predicates, i.e., as predicates on heaps.

We believe that this step-indexed model provides an interesting application of the metric point of view that has been emphasized in the previous section. The model construction takes advantage of the fact that the recursive world equation can be *solved* (up to isomorphism), rather than merely *approximated*: the higher-order frame rules are modelled with the help of a recursive operation on worlds, and this operation is defined using the metric structure.

[4] We do not consider group regions.

$$v ::= x \mid () \mid \mathsf{inj}^i\, v \mid (v_1, v_2) \mid \mu f.\lambda x.t \mid l$$
$$t ::= v \mid (v\, t) \mid \mathsf{case}(v_1, v_2, v) \mid \mathsf{proj}^i\, v \mid \mathsf{ref}\, v \mid \mathsf{get}\, v \mid \mathsf{set}\, v$$

Figure 3. Syntax of values and expressions

$$\begin{array}{rll}
(\mu f.\lambda x.t)\, v \mid h \longmapsto & t[f := \mu f.\lambda x.t,\ x := v] \mid h & \\
\mathsf{proj}^i(v_1, v_2) \mid h \longmapsto & v_i \mid h & \text{for } i = 1,2 \\
\mathsf{case}(v_1, v_2, \mathsf{inj}^i v) \mid h \longmapsto & v_i\, v \mid h & \text{for } i = 1,2 \\
\mathsf{ref}\, v \mid h \longmapsto & l \mid h \cdot [l \mapsto v] & \text{if } l \notin \mathrm{dom}\, h \\
\mathsf{get}\, l \mid h \longmapsto & h(l) \mid h & \text{if } l \in \mathrm{dom}\, h \\
\mathsf{set}\, (l, v) \mid h \longmapsto & () \mid h[l := v] & \text{if } l \in \mathrm{dom}\, h \\
v\, t \mid h \longmapsto & v\, t' \mid h' & \text{if } t \mid h \longmapsto t' \mid h'
\end{array}$$

Figure 4. Operational semantics

While we do not model the anti-frame rule [38] here, the approach does scale to do that; this is demonstrated in recent work by Schwinghammer, Birkedal and Støvring [45].

3.1 A Calculus of Capabilities

In the following presentation, we keep close to the notation of Charguéraud and Pottier [24, 38]. Figures 3 and 4 give the syntax and operational semantics of the programming language that we consider. It is a standard call-by-value, higher-order language with general references, and polymorphic and recursive types. The only noteworthy point about the syntax is that expressions are restricted so that all sequencing is made explicit; this simplifies the presentation of the typing rules and semantics but is no real restriction. The term $\mu f.\lambda x.t$ stands for the recursive procedure f with body t and argument x. If f does not appear in t, we may simply write $\lambda x.t$.

The operational semantics is defined between configurations $(t \mid h)$ that consist of a (closed) expression t and a heap h. As in the previous section, a heap h is a finite map from locations to closed values. Also, we remind the reader of our notation $t[x{:=}v]$ that means the substitution of v for x in t. We use the notation $h \# h'$ to indicate that two heaps h and h' have disjoint domains, and we write $h \cdot h'$ for the union of two such heaps.

The types used in the system are given by the grammar in Figure 5. *Capabilities* C describe heap properties (much like the assertions of a Hoare-style program logic), *value types* τ classify values, and *memory types* θ (and the subset of computation types) describe properties of expressions and how their evaluation affects the heap. Because of the heap dependency, capabilities and memory types are linear, and correspondingly there is a distinction between value type environments and the more general linear environments.

A *region* σ is a static name that represents a value, and $[\sigma]$ is a singleton type that contains only this particular value. Capabilities are formed from *singleton capabilities* $\{\sigma : \theta\}$ by separating conjunction and existential quantification over regions. We also include capability variables γ and permit recursively defined capabilities. A singleton capability $\{\sigma : \theta\}$ asserts that the value denoted by σ has type θ, and moreover it represents the ownership of both this value and the fragment of the heap described by θ. Thus, it is similar to the points-to predicate of separation logic: for example, the capability $\{\sigma : \mathsf{ref}\, \tau\}$ means that σ denotes the address of a reference cell, and that the "owned" part of the heap stores a value of type τ at this address. Apart from singleton types, the value types include base types (here an empty type 0, the unit type 1, and int) and are closed under products, sums, and universal quantification over singletons, types and capabilities. The memory types extend value types by a type of references, and by the possibility to $*$-conjoin a capability. Like the pre- and postconditions used in Hoare logic, the arrow types make explicit which part of the heap is accessed when a procedure is called. For instance, the type $\forall \sigma, \sigma'.\, [\sigma] * \{\sigma : \mathsf{ref}\, [\sigma']\} \to [\sigma'] * \{\sigma : \mathsf{ref}\, [\sigma']\}$ can be given to a procedure that dereferences its argument.

Recursive capabilities and types are subject to a syntactic restriction: C must be *formally contractive* in γ for $\mu\gamma.C$ to be well-formed. By this we mean that the recursion must go through one of the type constructors $+$, $\times$, $\to$ or ref, or through the right-hand side of $\otimes$. This restriction ensures that the capability $\mu\gamma.C$ is the unique solution of the capability equation $\gamma = C$. Corresponding restrictions apply to recursively defined types $\mu\alpha.\tau$ and $\mu\beta.\theta$. We omit the straightforward inductive definition of formal contractiveness.

One interesting aspect of the type system is that each of the syntactic categories is equipped with an *invariant extension* operation, $\cdot \otimes C$. Intuitively, this operation conjoins C to the domain and codomain of every arrow type that occurs within its left hand argument, which means that the capability C is preserved by all functions of this type. This intuition is made precise by regarding capabilities and types modulo the structural equivalence given in Figure 6. This equivalence subsumes the "distribution axioms" for $\otimes$ that are used to express generic higher-order frame rules [19]. The first two groups of equations, equivalences (4)–(11), state that both $*$ and the derived operation $\circ$ on capabilities satisfy the axioms of a monoid, and that $*$ and $\otimes$ are actions of these monoids. Equivalences (15)–(30) describe the action by $\otimes$ on types. In particular, (25) shows the key case of the invariant extension described informally above.[5] Finally, the equivalences (34)–(38) for *focusing* let us build and deconstruct the capabilities over complex types in terms of capabilities over more primitive types.

The system also uses a subtyping relation, and Figure 7 gives some of the subtyping axioms. The typing rules are shown in Figure 8. Due to the use of linear environments and computation types (which in general contain embedded capabilities), the typing judgement $\Gamma \Vdash t : \chi$ is similar to a Hoare triple where Γ serves as a precondition and χ as a postcondition. This view explains the rules SHALLOW-FRAME and DEEP-FRAME; as in separation logic, these rules can be used to add an invariant C to a specification. The difference between SHALLOW-FRAME and DEEP-FRAME is that the former adds C only on the top-level, whereas the latter also extends all arrow types nested inside Γ and χ, via $\cdot \otimes C$. As with the higher-order frame rules in separation logic, this is useful for reasoning about information hiding [19].

3.2 Upwards Closed Uniform Predicates and Worlds

The main idea of the model that we present next is that types (as well as type contexts and capabilities) are parameterized by invariants. Thus, in this case the worlds will be predicates that, like the syntactic capabilities of the calculus, describe properties of the heap that all computations must preserve.

Recall that the set $UPred(X)$ of uniform predicates on a set X is defined by

$$UPred(X) \;=\; \{p \subseteq \mathbb{N} \times X \mid \forall (k, v) \in p.\, \forall j \leq k.\, (j, v) \in p\}.$$

The interpretation of types and capabilities is based on a variation on these uniform predicates. Let $(A, \sqsubseteq)$ be a partially ordered set. An *upwards closed* uniform predicate p on A is a predicate in $UPred(A)$ that is also upward closed in the second argument, i.e. if $(k, a) \in p$ and $a \sqsubseteq b$ then $(k, b) \in p$. We write $UPred^{\uparrow}(A)$ for

[5] Note that (13) and (14) let us move capabilities between assumptions – a form of ownership transfer.

Variables	$\xi ::= \alpha \mid \beta \mid \gamma \mid \sigma$
Capabilities	$C ::= C \otimes C \mid \emptyset \mid C * C \mid \{\sigma : \theta\} \mid \exists\sigma.C \mid \gamma \mid \mu\gamma.C \mid \forall\xi.C$
Value types	$\tau ::= \tau \otimes C \mid 0 \mid 1 \mid \mathsf{int} \mid \tau + \tau \mid \tau \times \tau \mid \chi \to \chi \mid [\sigma] \mid \alpha \mid \mu\alpha.\tau \mid \forall\xi.\tau$
Memory types	$\theta ::= \theta \otimes C \mid \tau \mid \theta + \theta \mid \theta \times \theta \mid \mathsf{ref}\,\theta \mid \theta * C \mid \exists\sigma.\theta \mid \beta \mid \mu\beta.\theta \mid \forall\xi.\theta$
Computation types	$\chi ::= \chi \otimes C \mid \tau \mid \chi * C \mid \exists\sigma.\chi$
Value environments	$\Delta ::= \Delta \otimes C \mid \varnothing \mid \Delta, x{:}\tau$
Linear environments	$\Gamma ::= \Gamma \otimes C \mid \varnothing \mid \Gamma, x{:}\chi \mid \Gamma * C$

Figure 5. Capabilities and types

VAR
$$\frac{(x : \tau) \in \Delta}{\Delta \vdash x : \tau}$$

UNIT
$$\frac{}{\Delta \vdash () : 1}$$

INJ
$$\frac{\Delta \vdash v : \tau_i}{\Delta \vdash (\mathsf{inj}^i\, v) : (\tau_1 + \tau_2)}$$

PAIR
$$\frac{\Delta \vdash v_1 : \tau_1 \qquad \Delta \vdash v_2 : \tau_2}{\Delta \vdash (v_1, v_2) : (\tau_1 \times \tau_2)}$$

RECFUN
$$\frac{\Delta, f : \chi_1 \to \chi_2, x : \chi_1 \Vdash t : \chi_2}{\Delta \vdash \mu f.\lambda x.t : \chi_1 \to \chi_2}$$

VAL
$$\frac{\Delta \vdash v : \tau}{\Delta \Vdash v : \tau}$$

APP
$$\frac{\Delta \vdash v : \chi_1 \to \chi_2 \qquad \Delta, \Gamma \Vdash t : \chi_1}{\Delta, \Gamma \Vdash (v\, t) : \chi_2}$$

PROJ-1
$$\frac{\Gamma \Vdash v : [\sigma] * \{\sigma : \tau_1 \times \theta_2\}}{\Gamma \Vdash \mathsf{proj}^1\, v : \tau_1 * \{\sigma : \tau_1 \times \theta_2\}}$$

PROJ-2
$$\frac{\Gamma \Vdash v : [\sigma] * \{\sigma : \theta_1 \times \tau_2\}}{\Gamma \Vdash \mathsf{proj}^2\, v : \tau_2 * \{\sigma : \theta_1 \times \tau_2\}}$$

CASE
$$\frac{\begin{array}{c}\Delta \vdash v_1 : (\exists\sigma_1.[\sigma_1] * \{\sigma : [\sigma_1] + 0\} * \{\sigma_1 : \theta_1\} * C) \to \chi \\ \Delta \vdash v_2 : (\exists\sigma_2.[\sigma_2] * \{\sigma : 0 + [\sigma_2]\} * \{\sigma_2 : \theta_2\} * C) \to \chi \\ \Delta, \Gamma \Vdash v : [\sigma] * \{\sigma : \theta_1 + \theta_2\} * C\end{array}}{\Delta, \Gamma \Vdash \mathsf{case}(v_1, v_2, v) : \chi}$$

$\forall$-INTRO
$$\frac{\Delta \vdash v : \tau}{\Delta \vdash v : \forall\xi.\tau}\ \xi \notin \Delta$$

$\forall$-ELIM-1
$$\frac{\Delta \vdash v : \forall\alpha.\tau}{\Delta \vdash v : \tau[\alpha := \tau']}$$

REF
$$\frac{\Gamma \Vdash v : \tau}{\Gamma \Vdash \mathsf{ref}\, v : \exists\sigma.[\sigma] * \{\sigma : \mathsf{ref}\,\tau\}}$$

GET
$$\frac{\Gamma \Vdash v : [\sigma] * \{\sigma : \mathsf{ref}\,\tau\}}{\Gamma \Vdash \mathsf{get}\, v : \tau * \{\sigma : \mathsf{ref}\,\tau\}}$$

SET
$$\frac{\Gamma \Vdash v : ([\sigma] \times \tau_2) * \{\sigma : \mathsf{ref}\,\tau_1\}}{\Gamma \Vdash \mathsf{set}\, v : 1 * \{\sigma : \mathsf{ref}\,\tau_2\}}$$

SHALLOW-FRAME
$$\frac{\Gamma \Vdash t : \chi}{\Gamma * C \Vdash t : \chi * C}$$

DEEP-FRAME
$$\frac{\Gamma \Vdash t : \chi}{(\Gamma \otimes C) * C \Vdash t : (\chi \otimes C) * C}$$

SUB
$$\frac{\Gamma \Vdash t : \chi_1 \qquad \chi_1 \le \chi_2}{\Gamma \Vdash t : \chi_2}$$

Figure 8. Typing of values and expressions

the set of all upwards closed uniform predicates on A, and define

$$p_{[k]} \;=\; \{(j, a) \in p \mid j < k\}.$$

As in Section 2.3 on $UPred(V)$, this restricts p to pairs with first component less than k. Note that $p_{[k]}$ is again upwards closed and uniform, so it belongs to $UPred^{\uparrow}(A)$ as well. We equip $UPred^{\uparrow}(A)$ with the same distance function d as $UPred(A)$ in Section 2.3. This makes $(UPred^{\uparrow}(A), d)$ an object of $\mathbf{CBUlt}_{\mathrm{ne}}$.

In our model, we use $UPred^{\uparrow}(A)$ with the following concrete instances for the partial order $(A, \sqsubseteq)$:

- $(Heap, \sqsubseteq)$ where $h \sqsubseteq h'$ iff $h' = h \cdot h_0$ for some $h_0 \# h$,
- $(Val, \sqsubseteq)$ where $u \sqsubseteq v$ iff $u = v$,
- $(Val \times Heap, \sqsubseteq)$ where $(u, h) \sqsubseteq (v, h')$ iff $u = v$ and $h \sqsubseteq h'$.

As in Section 2.3, *Val* is the set of closed values of the language, see Figure 3. We also use variants of the latter two instances where the set *Val* is replaced by the set of value substitutions, *Env*, and by the set of expressions, *Exp*.

On $UPred^{\uparrow}(Heap)$, ordered by subset inclusion, we have a complete Heyting BI algebra structure [17]. Meets and joins are given by set-theoretic intersections and unions, resp., and implication, separating conjunction and separating implication are given by

$$\begin{aligned}
(k, h) \in p \to q &\Leftrightarrow \forall j \le k.\, \forall h' \sqsupseteq h.\, (j, h') \in p \Rightarrow (j, h') \in q \\
(k, h) \in p_1 * p_2 &\Leftrightarrow \exists h_1, h_2.\, h = h_1 \cdot h_2 \wedge (k, h_i) \in p_i \\
(k, h) \in p \mathrel{-\!\!*} q &\Leftrightarrow \forall j \le k.\, \forall h' \# h.\, (j, h') \in p \Rightarrow (j, h \cdot h') \in q
\end{aligned}$$

The unit for $*$ is given by $I = \mathbb{N} \times Heap = \top$. Up to the natural number indexing, this is just the standard intuitionistic (in the sense that it is not "tight") model of separation logic [43].

Since the worlds are to represent invariants (for instance, describing the shape of data structures laid out in the heap) and since the language of Section 3.1 has general references (so these invariants talk about stored procedures and are themselves world-dependent), it is natural that worlds $w \in W$ must also double-act as functions $W \to UPred^{\uparrow}(Heap)$. Consequently, we solve in $\mathbf{CBUlt}_{\mathrm{ne}}$ the following recursive world equation:

$$W \;\cong\; \tfrac{1}{2} \cdot W \to UPred^{\uparrow}(Heap)\,. \tag{46}$$

Here, the function space is that of $\mathbf{CBUlt}_{\mathrm{ne}}$ and the $1/2$ denotes the scaling of the distance function on W. That W exists (and is uniquely determined up to isomorphism) follows from Theorem 2.1, applied to the locally contractive functor $F(X, Y) = \frac{1}{2} \cdot X \to UPred^{\uparrow}(Heap)$ on $\mathbf{CBUlt}_{\mathrm{ne}}$. Worlds are thus essentially *contractive* functions from worlds to $UPred^{\uparrow}(Heap)$, i.e. world dependent heap predicates. We define

$$Cap \;=\; \tfrac{1}{2} \cdot W \to UPred^{\uparrow}(Heap),$$

monoids

$$C_1 \circ C_2 \stackrel{def}{=} (C_1 \otimes C_2) * C_2 \tag{4}$$

$$(C_1 \circ C_2) \circ C_3 = C_1 \circ (C_2 \circ C_3) \tag{5}$$

$$C \circ \emptyset = C \tag{6}$$

$$(C_1 * C_2) * C_3 = C_1 * (C_2 * C_3) \tag{7}$$

$$C * \emptyset = C \tag{8}$$

$$C_1 * C_2 = C_2 * C_1 \tag{9}$$

monoid actions

$$(\cdot \otimes C_1) \otimes C_2 = \cdot \otimes (C_1 \circ C_2) \qquad \cdot \otimes \emptyset = \cdot \tag{10}$$

$$(\cdot * C_1) * C_2 = \cdot * (C_1 * C_2) \qquad \cdot * \emptyset = \cdot \tag{11}$$

action by $*$ on singleton

$$\{\sigma : \theta\} * C = \{\sigma : \theta * C\} \tag{12}$$

action by $*$ on linear environments

$$(\Gamma, x{:}\chi) * C = \Gamma, x{:}(\chi * C) \tag{13}$$

$$= (\Gamma * C), x{:}\chi \tag{14}$$

action by $\otimes$ on capabilities, types, and environments

$$(\cdot * \cdot) \otimes C = (\cdot \otimes C) * (\cdot \otimes C) \tag{15}$$

$$(\exists \sigma . \cdot) \otimes C = \exists \sigma . (\cdot \otimes C) \quad \text{if } \sigma \notin \mathit{RegNames}(C) \tag{16}$$

$$\emptyset \otimes C = \emptyset \tag{17}$$

$$\{\sigma : \theta\} \otimes C = \{\sigma : \theta \otimes C\} \tag{18}$$

$$0 \otimes C = 0 \tag{19}$$

$$1 \otimes C = 1 \tag{20}$$

$$\mathsf{int} \otimes C = \mathsf{int} \tag{21}$$

$$(\theta_1 + \theta_2) \otimes C = (\theta_1 \otimes C) + (\theta_2 \otimes C) \tag{22}$$

$$(\theta_1 \times \theta_2) \otimes C = (\theta_1 \otimes C) \times (\theta_2 \otimes C) \tag{23}$$

$$(\forall \xi . \theta) \otimes C = \forall \xi . (\theta \otimes C) \quad \text{if } \xi \notin \mathrm{fv}\, C \tag{24}$$

$$(\chi_1 \to \chi_2) \otimes C = (\chi_1 \circ C) \to (\chi_2 \circ C) \tag{25}$$

$$[\sigma] \otimes C = [\sigma] \tag{26}$$

$$(\mathsf{ref}\, \theta) \otimes C = \mathsf{ref}\, (\theta \otimes C) \tag{27}$$

$$\varnothing \otimes C = \varnothing \tag{28}$$

$$(\Gamma, x{:}\chi) \otimes C = (\Gamma \otimes C), x{:}(\chi \otimes C) \tag{29}$$

$$(\Gamma * C_1) \otimes C_2 = (\Gamma \otimes C_2) * (C_1 \otimes C_2) \tag{30}$$

region abstraction

$$\exists \sigma_1 . \exists \sigma_2 . \cdot = \exists \sigma_2 . \exists \sigma_1 . \cdot \tag{31}$$

$$\cdot * (\exists \sigma . C) = \exists \sigma . (\cdot * C) \tag{32}$$

$$\{\sigma_1 : \exists \sigma_2 . \theta\} = \exists \sigma_2 . \{\sigma_1 : \theta\} \quad \text{where } \sigma_1 \neq \sigma_2 \tag{33}$$

focusing

$$\{\sigma_1 : \mathsf{ref}\, \theta\} = \exists \sigma_2 . \{\sigma_1 : \mathsf{ref}\, [\sigma_2]\} * \{\sigma_2 : \theta\} \tag{34}$$

$$\{\sigma : \theta_1 \times \theta_2\} = \exists \sigma_1 . \{\sigma : [\sigma_1] \times \theta_2\} * \{\sigma_1 : \theta_1\} \tag{35}$$

$$\{\sigma : \theta_1 \times \theta_2\} = \exists \sigma_2 . \{\sigma : \theta_1 \times [\sigma_2]\} * \{\sigma_2 : \theta_2\} \tag{36}$$

$$\{\sigma : \theta_1 + 0\} = \exists \sigma_1 . \{\sigma : [\sigma_1] + 0\} * \{\sigma_1 : \theta_1\} \tag{37}$$

$$\{\sigma : 0 + \theta_2\} = \exists \sigma_2 . \{\sigma : 0 + [\sigma_2]\} * \{\sigma_2 : \theta_2\} \tag{38}$$

recursion

$$\mu \gamma . C = C[\gamma {:=} \mu \gamma . C] \tag{39}$$

$$\mu \alpha . \tau = \tau[\alpha {:=} \mu \alpha . \tau] \tag{40}$$

$$\mu \beta . \theta = \theta[\beta {:=} \mu \beta . \theta] \tag{41}$$

Figure 6. Structural equivalence

(first-order) frame axiom

$$\chi_1 \to \chi_2 \leq (\chi_1 * C) \to (\chi_2 * C) \tag{42}$$

free

$$C_1 * C_2 \leq C_1 \tag{43}$$

singletons

$$\tau \leq \exists \sigma . [\sigma] * \{\sigma : \tau\} \tag{44}$$

$$[\sigma] * \{\sigma : \tau\} \leq \tau * \{\sigma : \tau\} \tag{45}$$

Figure 7. Some subtyping axioms

and write $\iota : \mathit{Cap} \to W$ for the isomorphism in (46), and ι^{-1} for its inverse. By ordering the elements of *Cap* pointwise,

$$p \leq q \;\Leftrightarrow\; \forall w.\, p(w) \subseteq q(w),$$

we can lift the algebra structure on $\mathit{UPred}^{\uparrow}(\mathit{Heap})$.

Lemma 3.1. With the above ordering and the pointwise lifting of the algebra operations on $\mathit{UPred}^{\uparrow}(\mathit{Heap})$, the set *Cap* is a complete Heyting BI algebra.

The fact that *Cap* is a complete BI algebra immediately gives us a sound interpretation of $*$ on capabilities. (Moreover, it suggests that the syntax of capabilities could be extended with all the logical connectives of separation logic.) However, to interpret recursive capabilities we also need to know that the operations are non-expansive:

Lemma 3.2. The BI algebra operations on *Cap* are non-expansive functions, i.e., they are morphisms in $\mathbf{CBUlt}_{\mathrm{ne}}$:

$$\wedge, \vee, \to, *, -\!\!* : \mathit{Cap} \times \mathit{Cap} \to \mathit{Cap}$$

$$\textstyle\bigwedge_I, \bigvee_I : (I \to \mathit{Cap}) \to \mathit{Cap}$$

(For the last two operations, the indexing set I is given the discrete metric, i.e., the distance of any two different elements is 1.)

Proof sketch. One can first show the corresponding property for the operations on $\mathit{UPred}^{\uparrow}(\mathit{Heap})$ which is straightforward; the result then follows from the pointwise definition and the use of the sup-metric on *Cap*. To illustrate the non-expansiveness on $\mathit{UPred}^{\uparrow}(\mathit{Heap})$, we consider the case of separating conjunction: It suffices to show that $p \stackrel{n}{=} p'$ and $q \stackrel{n}{=} q'$ implies $p * q \stackrel{n}{=} p' * q'$. By definition of the n-equality, $p * q \stackrel{n}{=} p' * q'$ is equivalent to $(j, h) \in p * q \;\Leftrightarrow\; (j, h) \in p' * q'$ for all $j < n$, which follows easily from the assumptions that $p \stackrel{n}{=} p'$ and $q \stackrel{n}{=} q'$. □

Next, we define a 'composition' operation on the worlds W. This operation plays a role similar to the ordering by extension in the case where worlds are finite maps from locations to semantic types (cf. Section 2). However, it is more involved than a simple extension of worlds; rather, it corresponds to the syntactic abbreviation $C_1 \circ C_2 = C_1 \otimes C_2 * C_2$ from Figure 6, of conjoining C_1 and C_2 and additionally applying an invariant extension $\cdot \otimes C_2$ to C_1. Formally, $\circ : W \times W \to W$ is a non-expansive operation that for all $p, r, w \in W$ satisfies

$$\iota^{-1}(p \circ r)(w) \;=\; \iota^{-1}(p)(r \circ w) \,*\, \iota^{-1}(r)(w)\,.$$

Using the metric-space setup, we can define this operation by an easy application of Banach's fixed point theorem, as in [44]. Observe that it is here where we exploit that we have obtained a proper solution to the world equation (46) in $\mathbf{CBUlt}_{\mathrm{ne}}$.

We write *emp* for the image $\iota(\lambda w. I)$ of the BI unit under ι. Then it turns out that $\circ$ is associative and $p \circ \mathit{emp} = \mathit{emp} \circ p = p$ holds for all p, so $(W, \circ, \mathit{emp})$ is a monoid in $\mathbf{CBUlt}_{\mathrm{ne}}$. Now let (X, d) be an arbitrary ultrametric space. Using the composition operator on worlds, we consider a semantic analogue of the invariant extension operation, $\otimes : X^{(\frac{1}{2}\cdot W)} \times W \to X^{(\frac{1}{2}\cdot W)}$ defined by

$$(f \otimes w_0)(w) = f(w_0 \circ w) .$$

The following proposition is a slight generalization of [44, Lemma 5], and summarizes the key properties of $\circ$ and $\otimes$. In the following, these properties are used to justify some of the equivalences given in Figure 6.

Proposition 3.3 (Monoid and monoid action). Let (X, d) be an ultrametric space. Then $(W, \circ, emp)$ is a monoid in $\mathbf{CBUlt}_{ne}$, and the operation $\otimes : X^{(\frac{1}{2}\cdot W)} \times W \to X^{(\frac{1}{2}\cdot W)}$ is a (non-expansive) action of the monoid W on the ultrametric space of non-expansive functions from $\frac{1}{2} \cdot W$ to X, i.e., $f \otimes emp = f$ and $(f \otimes w_1) \otimes w_2 = f \otimes (w_1 \circ w_2)$.

3.3 Semantic Domains and Interpretation

In this section we give the interpretation of the capabilities, types and environments of the type system. The semantic domain corresponding to each syntactic category is a set of (contractively world-dependent) upwards closed and uniform predicates:

$$VT = \tfrac{1}{2} \cdot W \to UPred^{\uparrow}(Val)$$
$$MT = \tfrac{1}{2} \cdot W \to UPred^{\uparrow}(Val \times Heap) .$$

In particular, in each case there is an action of W by the operation $\otimes$, as described in Proposition 3.3. Note that $Cap = \frac{1}{2} \cdot W \to UPred^{\uparrow}(Heap)$ acts on itself, via the isomorphism ι between W and Cap. This operation plays a key role in explaining the higher-order frame (and also anti-frame) inference rules and the associated distribution axioms [44, 46]. Moreover, due to the shrinking factor $\delta = \frac{1}{2}$, this action is contractive in its right-hand side: for all $p, r \in Cap$, the assignment $r \mapsto p \otimes \iota(r)$ is a contractive endomap on Cap. This observation explains why the (syntactic) invariant extension can be assumed formally contractive in its second argument.

We also consider a further overloading of the separating conjunction. It is the below generalization $S * q$ to sets of the form $S \in UPred^{\uparrow}(A \times Heap)$ and $q \in UPred^{\uparrow}(Heap)$:

$$S * q = \{(k, (a, h \cdot h')) \mid (k, (a, h)) \in S \wedge (k, h') \in q \wedge h \# h'\}.$$

As for the separating conjunction on $UPred^{\uparrow}(Heap)$, this operation can be lifted pointwise to give a non-expansive operation on $S \in \frac{1}{2} \cdot W \to UPred^{\uparrow}(A \times Heap)$ and $r \in Cap$,

$$(S * r)(w) = S(w) * r(w) . \qquad (47)$$

This provides a second monoid action, with respect to the monoid structure given by the separating conjunction on Cap.

Proposition 3.4 (Monoid and monoid action). $(Cap, *, I)$ is a commutative monoid, and for any (pre-ordered) set A the operation in (47) is an action of this monoid on the space of non-expansive functions from $\frac{1}{2} \cdot W$ to $UPred^{\uparrow}(A \times Heap)$, i.e., $S * I = S$ and $(S * p) * q = S * (p * q)$.

The interpretation of capabilities and types is given in Figure 9. This interpretation depends on an environment η, which maps region names $\sigma \in RegName$ to closed values $\eta(\sigma) \in Val$, capability variables γ to semantic capabilities $\eta(\gamma) \in Cap$, and type variables α and β to semantic types $\eta(\alpha) \in VT$ and $\eta(\beta) \in MT$. As indicated above, the semantics of capabilities is defined in terms of the BI structure on Cap. The semantics of memory types uses the action of Cap on MT described in (47). It also makes explicit the aliasing information contained in memory types: for instance, the two components of a pair of type $\theta_1 \times \theta_2$ cannot overlap in the heap (a similar exclusion of sharing holds for referenced cells). In the interpretation of a value type τ considered as memory type, $[\![\tau]\!]$ on the right-hand side refers to the value type interpretation. Note that the computation types χ form a subset of the memory types, and thus obtain their interpretation in MT.

Let Env denote the finite maps from variables to closed values. Duplicable (heap-independent) environments are interpreted as contractive maps from W to $UPred^{\uparrow}(Env)$. Linear environments are modelled as contractive maps from W to $UPred^{\uparrow}(Env \times Heap)$. Conceptually, each of the entries in a linear environment owns a part of the heap, disjoint from that of the other entries.

With the exception of arrow types, the semantics of value types deserves little explanation; in all cases, the world is simply passed on, and the index is decreased (whenever justified by the operational semantics) to ensure that type constructors become contractive. The definition of arrow types is more intricate, and uses the following extension of memory types from values to expressions.

Definition 3.5. Let $S \in MT$. Then the function $\mathcal{E}(S) : W \to UPred^{\uparrow}(Exp \times Heap)$ is defined by $(k, (t, h)) \in \mathcal{E}(S)(w)$ iff

$$\forall j \leq k, t', h'. \, (t \mid h) \longmapsto^{j} (t' \mid h') \wedge (t' \mid h') \text{ irreducible}$$
$$\Rightarrow (k - j, (t', h')) \in S(w) * \iota^{-1}(w)(emp) .$$

Note that there is no scaling by $\frac{1}{2}$, i.e., $\mathcal{E}(S)$ is a non-expansive, but not a contractive, function of worlds. However, we do have a form of contractiveness on non-values:

Lemma 3.6. For all $S_1, S_2 \in MT$, expressions t and $h \in Heap$, if $w_1 \stackrel{n}{=} w_2$ in W, $S_1 \stackrel{n}{=} S_2$ and $t \notin Val$, then for all $k \leq n$,

$$(k, (t, h)) \in \mathcal{E}(S_1)(w_1) \Leftrightarrow (k, (t, h)) \in \mathcal{E}(S_2)(w_2) .$$

Proof. Let $w_1 \stackrel{n}{=} w_2$, and observe that this implies $S_1(w_1) \stackrel{n}{=} S_2(w_2)$ and $\iota^{-1}(w_1)(emp) \stackrel{n}{=} \iota^{-1}(w_2)(emp)$. Now assume that $(k, (t, h)) \in \mathcal{E}(S_1)(w_1)$ for some $k \leq n$. We must show that $(k, (t, h)) \in \mathcal{E}(S_2)(w_2)$. For this, suppose that $(t \mid h) \longmapsto^{j} (t' \mid h')$ for some $j \leq k$ where $(t' \mid h')$ is irreducible. The assumption $(k, (t, h)) \in \mathcal{E}(S_1)(w_1)$ yields $(k - j, (t', h')) \in S_1(w_1) * \iota^{-1}(w_1)(emp)$. In particular, $t' \in Val$ and therefore $t \neq t'$ by the assumption that $t \notin Val$. Thus we must have $j > 0$, and therefore $k - j < k \leq n$ which by the above observations means that $(k - j, (t', h')) \in S_2(w_2) * \iota^{-1}(w_2)(emp)$.

The direction from right to left is symmetric. □

We now explain the ideas behind the definition of arrow types in Figure 9 in more detail. First, the basic idea of our Kripke style semantics is that invariants added by the context are collected in the worlds. Thus, for a procedure application we realize this idea by interpreting the current world as a predicate $\iota^{-1}(w)(emp)$ on heaps, which is conjoined to the actual argument (computation) type $[\![\chi_1]\!]_\eta (w)$, as well as to the result (computation) type $[\![\chi_2]\!]_\eta (w)$ through the definition of $\mathcal{E}$. Second, by additionally conjoining r as an invariant we bake in the first-order frame property. Finally, the quantification over indices j less than k achieves that $[\![\chi_1 \to \chi_2]\!]_\eta \, w$ is in $UPred^{\uparrow}(Val)$. There are two explanations why we require that j be *strictly* less than k in the definition of $[\![\chi_1 \to \chi_2]\!]$. Technically, since $\iota^{-1}(w)(emp)$ is non-expansive but not contractive in w, we need the strict inequality to ensure the non-expansiveness of $[\![\chi_1 \to \chi_2]\!]$ as a function $\frac{1}{2} \cdot W \to UPred^{\uparrow}(Val)$. Moreover, the smaller index allows us to prove the typing rule for recursive functions, by induction on k. Intuitively, the use of $j < k$ for the arguments suffices since each procedure application consumes a step. The final $j + 1$ index on expressions in the interpretation of arrow types is justified by the above Lemma.

Proposition 3.7. The interpretation in Figure 9 is well-defined: all the $[\![\cdot]\!]$'s map into the declared sets, and the recursive definitions of capabilities and types have unique solutions.

Capabilities, $[\![C]\!]_\eta : \frac{1}{2}\cdot W \to \mathit{UPred}^{\uparrow}(\mathit{Heap})$

$$[\![C_1 \otimes C_2]\!]_\eta\, w = ([\![C_1]\!]_\eta \otimes \iota([\![C_2]\!]_\eta))w$$
$$[\![\emptyset]\!]_\eta\, w = \mathbb{N} \times \mathit{Heap}$$
$$[\![C_1 * C_2]\!]_\eta\, w = ([\![C_1]\!]_\eta * [\![C_2]\!]_\eta)w$$
$$[\![\{\sigma : \theta\}]\!]_\eta\, w = \{(k,h) \mid (k,(\eta(\sigma),h)) \in [\![\theta]\!]_\eta\, w\}$$
$$[\![\exists\sigma.C]\!]_\eta\, w = \textstyle\bigcup_{v\in \mathit{Val}} [\![C]\!]_{\eta[\sigma:=v]}\, w$$
$$[\![\gamma]\!]_\eta\, w = \eta(\gamma)(w)$$
$$[\![\mu\gamma.C]\!]_\eta\, w = \mathit{fix}(\lambda r.\ [\![C]\!]_{\eta[\gamma:=r]})w$$

Value types, $[\![\tau]\!]_\eta : \frac{1}{2}\cdot W \to \mathit{UPred}^{\uparrow}(\mathit{Val})$

$$[\![\tau \otimes C]\!]_\eta\, w = ([\![\tau]\!]_\eta \otimes \iota([\![C]\!]_\eta))w$$
$$[\![0]\!]_\eta\, w = \emptyset$$
$$[\![1]\!]_\eta\, w = \mathbb{N} \times \{()\}$$
$$[\![\mathsf{int}]\!]_\eta\, w = \mathbb{N} \times \{\underline{n} \mid n \in \mathbb{Z}\}$$
$$[\![\tau_1 + \tau_2]\!]_\eta\, w = \{(k, \mathsf{inj}^i v) \mid k>0 \Rightarrow (k-1,v) \in [\![\tau_i]\!]_\eta\, w\}$$
$$[\![\tau_1 \times \tau_2]\!]_\eta\, w = \{(k,(v_1,v_2)) \mid k>0 \Rightarrow (k-1,v_i) \in [\![\tau_i]\!]_\eta\, w\}$$
$$\begin{aligned}[\![\chi_1 \to \chi_2]\!]_\eta\, w = \{(k,v) \mid\ & \forall j<k.\ \forall r \in \mathit{Cap}.\\ & \forall (j,(v',h)) \in ([\![\chi_1]\!]_\eta * r)(w) * \iota^{-1}(w)(\mathit{emp}).\\ & (j{+}1,(v\,v',h)) \in \mathcal{E}([\![\chi_2]\!]_\eta * r)(w)\}\end{aligned}$$
$$[\![[\sigma]]\!]_\eta\, w = \mathbb{N} \times \{\eta(\sigma)\}$$
$$[\![\alpha]\!]_\eta\, w = \eta(\alpha)(w)$$
$$[\![\mu\alpha.\tau]\!]_\eta\, w = \mathit{fix}(\lambda S.\ [\![\tau]\!]_{\eta[\alpha:=S]})w$$
$$[\![\forall\alpha.\tau]\!]_\eta\, w = \textstyle\bigcap_{a\in VT} [\![\tau]\!]_{\eta[\alpha:=a]}\, w$$

Memory types, $[\![\theta]\!]_\eta : \frac{1}{2}\cdot W \to \mathit{UPred}^{\uparrow}(\mathit{Val}\times\mathit{Heap})$

$$[\![\theta \otimes C]\!]_\eta\, w = ([\![\theta]\!]_\eta \otimes \iota([\![C]\!]_\eta))\, w$$
$$[\![\tau]\!]_\eta\, w = \{(k,(v,h)) \mid h \in \mathit{Heap},\ (k,v) \in [\![\tau]\!]_\eta\, w\}$$
$$[\![\theta_1 + \theta_2]\!]_\eta\, w = \{(k,(\mathsf{inj}^i v, h)) \mid k>0 \Rightarrow (k-1,(v,h)) \in [\![\theta_i]\!]_\eta\, w\}$$
$$[\![\theta_1 \times \theta_2]\!]_\eta\, w = \{(k,(v_1,v_2),h_1\cdot h_2) \mid k>0 \Rightarrow (k-1,(v_i,h_i)) \in [\![\theta_i]\!]_\eta w\}$$
$$[\![\mathsf{ref}\,\theta]\!]_\eta\, w = \{(k,(l,h\cdot[l\mapsto v])) \mid k>0 \Rightarrow (k-1,(v,h)) \in [\![\theta]\!]_\eta w\}$$
$$[\![\theta * C]\!]_\eta\, w = ([\![\theta]\!]_\eta\, w) * ([\![C]\!]_\eta\, w)$$
$$[\![\exists\sigma.\theta]\!]_\eta\, w = \textstyle\bigcup_{v\in \mathit{Val}} [\![\theta]\!]_{\eta[\sigma:=v]}\, w$$
$$[\![\beta]\!]_\eta\, w = \eta(\beta)(w)$$
$$[\![\mu\beta.\theta]\!]_\eta\, w = \mathit{fix}(\lambda S.\ [\![\theta]\!]_{\eta[\beta:=S]})w$$

Duplicable environments, $[\![\Delta]\!]_\eta : \frac{1}{2}\cdot W \to \mathit{UPred}^{\uparrow}(\mathit{Env})$

$$[\![\Delta \otimes C]\!]_\eta\, w = ([\![\Delta]\!]_\eta \otimes \iota([\![C]\!]_\eta))w$$
$$[\![\varnothing]\!]_\eta\, w = \mathbb{N} \times \{[\,]\}$$
$$[\![\Delta, x{:}\tau]\!]_\eta\, w = \{(k,\rho[x\mapsto v]) \mid (k,\rho) \in [\![\Delta]\!]_\eta\, w \wedge (k,v) \in [\![\tau]\!]_\eta\, w\}$$

Linear environments, $[\![\Gamma]\!]_\eta : \frac{1}{2}\cdot W \to \mathit{UPred}^{\uparrow}(\mathit{Env}\times\mathit{Heap})$

$$[\![\Gamma \otimes C]\!]_\eta\, w = ([\![\Gamma]\!]_\eta \otimes \iota([\![C]\!]_\eta))w$$
$$[\![\varnothing]\!]_\eta\, w = \mathbb{N} \times (\{[\,]\} \times \mathit{Heap})$$
$$\begin{aligned}[\![\Gamma, x{:}\chi]\!]_\eta\, w = \{(k,(\rho[x\mapsto v], h\cdot h')) \mid\ & \\ & (k,(\rho,h)) \in [\![\Gamma]\!]_\eta\, w \wedge (k,(v,h')) \in [\![\chi]\!]_\eta\, w\}\end{aligned}$$
$$[\![\Gamma * C]\!]_\eta\, w = ([\![\Gamma]\!]_\eta\, w) * ([\![C]\!]_\eta\, w)$$

Figure 9. Interpretation

Proof sketch. We equip the set of values with the discrete metric, and then obtain a complete 1-bounded ultrametric on environments:

$$d(\eta,\eta') = \sup_\xi d(\eta(\xi),\eta'(\xi))\,. \qquad (48)$$

We then show by simultaneous induction on C, τ, and θ, the following properties:

1. $[\![C]\!]_\eta\, w$, $[\![\tau]\!]_\eta\, w$, and $[\![\theta]\!]_\eta\, w$ are upwards closed and uniform predicates;
2. $[\![C]\!]_\eta\, w$, $[\![\tau]\!]_\eta\, w$, and $[\![\theta]\!]_\eta\, w$ are non-expansive functions of η (with respect to the distance in (48)) and w (with respect to the metric on $\frac{1}{2}\cdot W$);
3. if C is formally contractive in ξ then $[\![C]\!]_{\eta[\xi:=(\cdot)]}$ is contractive;
4. if θ is formally contractive in ξ then $[\![\theta]\!]_{\eta[\xi:=(\cdot)]}$ is contractive.

These properties can be verified by a straightforward (but tedious) simultaneous induction, for instance using Lemma 3.6 and the non-expansiveness of separating conjunction to show the non-expansiveness of arrow types. The interpretation of recursive types and capabilities relies on our restriction to formally contractive equations, so that they are uniquely defined from Banach's fixed point theorem by the above properties 3 and 4. □

This interpretation respects the structural equivalence, i.e., whenever C_1 and C_2 are equivalent capabilities then $[\![C_1]\!] = [\![C_2]\!]$ (and similarly for value and memory types). The proofs of these facts are easy consequences of the definition of $[\![C]\!]$ and Propositions 3.3 and 3.4. Moreover, the interpretation validates the subtyping axioms, i.e., whenever $\theta_1 \le \theta_2$ then $[\![\theta_1]\!]_\eta\, w \subseteq [\![\theta_2]\!]_\eta\, w$ holds for all η and w. These proofs can be found in the appendix of the long version of the paper.

Recall that we have two kinds of judgments, one for typing of values and the other for the typing of expressions:

$$\Delta \vdash v : \tau \qquad\qquad \Gamma \Vdash t : \chi$$

The semantics of a value judgement simply establishes truth with respect to all worlds w, all environments η and all $k \in \mathbb{N}$:

$$\begin{aligned}&\models (\Delta \vdash v : \tau) \overset{def}{\iff}\\ &\quad \forall\eta.\ \forall w \in W.\ \forall k \in \mathbb{N}.\ \forall (k,\rho) \in [\![\Delta]\!]_\eta\, w.\ (k,\rho(v)) \in [\![\tau]\!]_\eta\, w\,.\end{aligned}$$

Here $\rho(v)$ means the application of the substitution ρ to v. The judgement for expressions mirrors the interpretation of the arrow case for value types, in that there is also a quantification over heap predicates $r \in \mathit{Cap}$:

$$\begin{aligned}&\models (\Gamma \Vdash t : \chi) \overset{def}{\iff}\\ &\quad \forall\eta.\ \forall w \in W.\ \forall k \in \mathbb{N}.\ \forall r \in \mathit{Cap}.\\ &\qquad \forall (k,(\rho,h)) \in ([\![\Gamma]\!]_\eta * r)w * \iota^{-1}(w)(\mathit{emp}).\\ &\qquad\quad (k,(\rho(t),h)) \in \mathcal{E}([\![\chi]\!]_\eta * r)(w).\end{aligned}$$

The universal quantifications allow us to have frame rules: the universal quantification over worlds w ensures the soundness of the deep frame rule, and the universal quantification over capabilities r validates the shallow frame rule.

We can now give the main result of this section, which expresses that the extension of the capability system with higher-order frame rules is sound. In particular, the below theorem implies type safety.

Theorem 3.8 (Soundness)**.** If $\Delta \vdash v : \tau$ then $\models (\Delta \vdash v : \tau)$, and if $\Gamma \Vdash t : \chi$ then $\models (\Gamma \Vdash t : \chi)$.

To prove the theorem, we show that each typing rule preserves the truth of judgements. These proofs are given in the appendix of the long version of the paper.

3.4 Observations

We conclude this section with some remarks on the model.

Structural equivalence. In previous work, where Pottier first introduced the anti-frame rule [38], the syntactic types are considered modulo the structural equivalence. This means that they are not inductively defined, and consequently Pottier avoids inductive proofs on their syntax. In contrast, our interpretation is given by induction on the structure of types and capabilities, and only after having established the interpretation do we consider the structural equivalence (and prove that our interpretation respects it).

Unique solutions proof principle. In practice, one may have to show type equivalences that do not easily follow from the structural equivalence. The metric structure of our model suggests a proof principle for this, by the uniqueness of solutions of contractive type equations: if two types are solutions of a common contractive fixed point equation, then we can conclude that they are equal.

Additional subtyping axioms. Our model satisfies some additional subtyping axioms that have not been mentioned in the literature before. These refer, e.g. to the duplication of value capabilities. In particular, our model implies the soundness of the axiom

$$[\sigma] * \{\sigma : \tau\} \leq [\sigma] * \{\sigma : \tau\} * \{\sigma : \tau\}.$$

A possible explanation why these axioms have not been noted before may be that previous soundness proofs for capability type systems (e.g. by translation [24] or progress and preservation [38]) rest on invariants that are stronger than necessary.

Classical interpretation. The capability calculus of Crary et al. [26] has a memory deallocation construct, and satisfies a "complete collection" property. Essentially, if a program of type $\tau * \emptyset$ terminates, then it does so in an empty heap. After dropping the subtyping axiom $C_1 * C_2 \leq C_1$ and adding a deallocation construct to our calculus, it would also satisfy this property. Our approach is flexible enough so that this can be shown by modifying the semantics and using the "classical" interpretation of separation logic. That is, the definition of worlds and capabilities would be based on $UPred(Heap)$ instead of $UPred^{\uparrow}(Heap)$, where the BI structure is given by $*$ and $-\!*$ as above but with unit $I = \omega \times \{[]\}$. However, this complete collection property is not only destroyed by the axiom $C_1 * C_2 \leq C_1$ but also by the inclusion of an anti-frame rule (which we do not consider in this paper, though).

Aliasing. Even though our model is based on the operational semantics, it gives a semantic understanding of capabilities. Let θ be any memory type, and consider the recursively defined memory type $mlist = \mu\beta.\mathsf{ref}\ 1 + \theta \times \beta$ of mutable lists from [24]. In *loc. cit.* it is mentioned (without proof) that this is the type of mutable *non-aliased* lists, and our semantics shows very directly that this is indeed the case: From the semantics of memory types in Figure 9, we see (for k large enough) that $(k, (l_1, h)) \in [\![mlist]\!]$ just in case that for some $n < k$, heap h can be split up into $2n$ disjoint parts:

$$h = [l_1 \mapsto (v_1, l_2)] \cdot h_1 \cdot [l_2 \mapsto (v_2, l_3)] \cdot h_2 \cdot \dots \cdot [l_n \mapsto ()] \cdot h_n,$$

with $(k-i, (v_i, h_i)) \in [\![\theta]\!]$, for all $1 \leq i < n$. Thus, all list entries live in disjoint parts of the heap and all locations l_i must be distinct; in particular, $mlist$ cannot contain cyclic lists.

A domain-theoretic model? Finally, it may be worthwhile to remark that we have tried to give a domain-theoretic ultrametric model of the calculus as well, but found this very difficult. In fact, this difficulty was one motivation for constructing the present step-indexed model. Very roughly, the projections that come with solutions to recursive domain equations disagree with, e.g., memory types. The step-indexed setting appears a bit more flexible in this respect.

4. Specialization to Indirection Theory

Hobor, Dockins and Appel [30] present a general *theory of indirection* for giving set-theoretic models of recursively defined structures. Faced with a recursive equation, Hobor et al. provide an approximate solution: this is a set together with a pair of functions characterized by the two axioms of indirection theory that elegantly capture the approximative nature of the solution.

Our approach to recursive equations is different. We provide an exact solution, but in a category of metric spaces instead of the category of sets and functions. In this section we argue that our approach is more general in the sense that, for the same recursive equation, one may build the approximative solution of Hobor et al. from our solution.

Before starting, we point out that this specialization to indirection theory is not unconditional. The construction presented by Hobor et al. is parameterized over a set-theoretic functor $F : \mathbf{Set} \to \mathbf{Set}$, and this functor must in a suitable sense have an extension to $\mathbf{CBUlt}_{ne}$ in order for our approach to apply. Fortunately, this condition holds for functors on **Set** built with standard constructors.

We now sketch how the specialization to indirection theory proceeds. The full story, including proofs, can be found in the appendix of the long version of the paper.

4.1 Indirection Theory

Assume that we are given a functor $F : \mathbf{Set} \to \mathbf{Set}$ and a non-empty set O. Let $2 = \{0, 1\}$ be the set of "truth values." Indirection theory begins from the desire to solve the equation

$$K \cong F(K \times O \to 2) \tag{49}$$

in **Set**, which is often impossible for cardinality reasons.[6] Instead, one obtains an approximate solution

$$K \underset{\mathsf{squash}}{\overset{\mathsf{unsquash}}{\rightleftarrows}} \mathbb{N} \times F(K \times O \to 2)$$

consisting of a set K and functions squash and unsquash satisfying:

1. $\mathsf{squash}(\mathsf{unsquash}\ k) = k$.
2. $\mathsf{unsquash}(\mathsf{squash}(m, \nu)) = (m, F(\mathsf{approx}_m)(\nu))$.

Here level $= \mathsf{fst} \circ \mathsf{unsquash} : K \to \mathbb{N}$, and the map $\mathsf{approx}_m : (K \times O \to 2) \to (K \times O \to 2)$ is defined, for each $m \in \mathbb{N}$, by

$$\mathsf{approx}_m(\psi)(k, o) = (\psi(k, o) \wedge \mathsf{level}(k) < m).$$

The idea is that elements of K have "levels," and that the function approx_m transforms a predicate on K to one that only holds for elements of level less than m. Notice that squash is a left inverse of unsquash, but in general not a right inverse: $\mathsf{unsquash}(\mathsf{squash}(m, \nu))$ is in some sense an approximation of (m, ν).

4.2 From Metric Spaces to Indirection Theory

Every set can be considered as a metric space by giving it the discrete metric d (i.e., $d(x, y) = 1$ if $x \neq y$). In this way, the category of non-empty sets can be viewed as a subcategory of $\mathbf{CBUlt}_{ne}$. We now assume that the functor $F : \mathbf{Set} \to \mathbf{Set}$ considered above has a so-called *plain lift* $\hat{F} : \mathbf{CBUlt}_{ne} \to \mathbf{CBUlt}_{ne}$. This means that $\hat{F}$ is a locally non-expansive functor which agrees with F on non-empty sets (and functions between them), and also that $\hat{F}$ satisfies some technical conditions given in the appendix of the long version of

[6] Unlike Hobor et al. we do not parameterize over the set of truth values. The generalization, while probably technically feasible, does not appear necessary for applications.

the paper. As noted above, plain lifts exist for all the standard constructors (see again the long version of the paper). In particular we have plain lifts of the functors of all the examples of Hobor et al.[7]

From Theorem 2.1 and Lemma 2.4, we easily obtain:

Theorem 4.1. Let $F : \mathbf{Set} \to \mathbf{Set}$ be a functor with a plain lift $\hat{F} : \mathbf{CBUlt}_{\mathrm{ne}} \to \mathbf{CBUlt}_{\mathrm{ne}}$. There is a non-empty, complete, 1-bounded ultrametric space X and an isomorphism

$$\Phi : X \cong \hat{F}\left(\tfrac{1}{2}(X \to \mathit{UPred}(O))\right),$$

where the function space consists of non-expansive maps.

We now show that one can use such an isomorphism to construct an approximate solution in the sense of indirection theory.

We deviate from Hobor et al. by building a solution that features only so-called *hereditary* maps from $K \times O$ to 2. This is a direct consequence of the downwards closedness required of members of $\mathit{UPred}(O)$, since hereditary predicates are, intuitively, "closed under approximation" in the K component. We regard this difference as an improvement since, in all applications to date, hereditariness is considered desirable and often necessary. This point is discussed further below.

Theorem 4.2. Let $F : \mathbf{Set} \to \mathbf{Set}$ be a functor with a plain lift $\hat{F} : \mathbf{CBUlt}_{\mathrm{ne}} \to \mathbf{CBUlt}_{\mathrm{ne}}$. We can, from the isomorphism of Theorem 4.1, build a set K, a subset of *hereditary* maps $K \times O \to_{her} 2$ of the full function space $K \times O \to 2$ and two maps

$$K \underset{\mathsf{squash}}{\overset{\mathsf{unsquash}}{\rightleftarrows}} \mathbb{N} \times F(K \times O \to_{her} 2)$$

satisfying Hobor et al.'s requirements for an approximate solution (items 1 and 2 above).

Advantages of metric solution approach. Having proved that our metric-space approach specializes to the indirection theory, we now proceed to argue some advantages of our approach in general.

Firstly, although we do not think that the step-indexed version of our metric-space approach is more expressive than standard step-indexed models, we believe that our version provides a good framework for doing step indexing with useful conceptual guidelines. This holds even if we disregard recursively defined worlds. Consider, e.g., the interpretation of recursive types in Figure 9 of Section 3. Under the aforementioned assumptions of formal contractiveness, we are free to interpret recursive types as actual fixed points – a conceptually pleasing thing to do. Another example is the $\otimes$ operator in the same section, which is also constructed using Banach's fixed-point theorem. A similar construction could possibly be pushed through either with hand-built approximate worlds as employed by Ahmed et al. [6], with the indirection theory of Hobor et al. [30] or the higher order μ described in Hobor's thesis [28]. But the precise course of action is much less immediate.

Secondly, in comparison with the indirection theory [30], our approach of solving recursive metric equations allows one to use a body of supporting theory on metric spaces and to construct a wider variety of possible worlds to be used in Kripke models. To illustrate this point, let us focus on the step-indexed model of ML references discussed in Section 2.3 and in Sections 2.1, 4.1 and 5 of [30]. In the model provided by indirection theory, types are arbitrary maps from worlds to values, modulo currying and nomenclature. But, as argued in [30, Section 5.1], we really want types that are both hereditary and monotone. In [30, Section 5.1], such types are elegantly identified using modal operators, but this does not change the problem that the types in a world may fail to meet these criteria. This is addressed in the last paragraph of [30, Section 10] where an alternative, and less straightforward, model with only hereditary types in the worlds is sketched. Alas, this means that one has to start the model construction all over again from scratch and it does not buy us monotonicity[8]. On the other hand, to obtain hereditary types with the metric approach we just use the downwards-closure condition on $\mathit{UPred}(V)$, verify Lemma 2.4 and apply Theorem 2.1. And to work with monotone types, we can apply a slightly stronger existence result [20, Proposition 5.4] for *pre-ordered* metric spaces. By a similar argument one can extend the approach to mixed variance functors discussed in [30, Section 10]: Indeed, in unpublished work we have used mixed-variance functors to verify that the metric-space approach scales to the elaborate worlds of [6].

Finally, we think that it is advantageous that the metric approach applies both to models based on domain theory and to models based on operational semantics.

5. Related and Future Work

Relational reasoning. We have focused on unary reasoning in this paper, but the techniques developed here also apply to relational reasoning. Relational reasoning principles about programs with higher-order store, such as logical relations for reasoning about contextual equivalence of programs, have been developed both based on domain theory (e.g., [15, 21]), and on step-indexed models (e.g., [6]). For such relational reasoning, the worlds are typically more sophisticated than the worlds we have discussed so far. This is because for relational reasoning worlds need to describe situations in which programs are contextually equivalent even though they use local states in different ways. One of us (Thamsborg) has recently phrased the state-of-the-art world model from [6] as a recursive world equation over a domain-theoretic model. He did this to obtain more abstract proof principles for program equivalences, which does not involve reasoning about step indices. Alternatively, Dreyer et al. [27] have shown how to extend the relational step-indexed model [6] to a model of a modal logic for more abstract reasoning about program equivalences. The latter modal logic has been derived from the step-indexed model. Even with this development, it is still a challenge to develop relational step-indexed models of Hoare Type Theory [35] and its new developments. It would be interesting to see whether the step-indexed metric space approach can be used to address this challenge.

Formalization. An often mentioned advantage of the traditional step-indexed approach is that it lends itself well to formalization in theorem provers. Indeed, impressive formalization work has been carried out in, e.g., Coq [10].

Thus, one may wonder whether our proposed metric approach hinders formalizations. It does not. Following the treatment in [20], Varming et al. have given a constructive formalization of the solutions of recursive metric-space equations in Coq [16], including the step-indexed model of ML references from Section 2.3.

Capabilities. In [5], Ahmed et al. presented a step-indexed model of a substructural type system, which is similar to the capability calculus considered in this paper. However, their model did not provide a satisfactory semantic analysis of capabilities. Ahmed et al. instrumented the operational semantics with abstract run-time entities corresponding to capabilities, and their model included those abstract entities, instead of giving a semantic analysis of what they really should denote. Moreover, they did not consider non-trivial combinations of capabilities such as $C_1 * C_2$ and did not

[7] With the possible exception of Example 2.7. The functor in that example is complex, and the presentation is a bit dense, so we are not sure whether the functor has a plain lift.

[8] It is worth noticing that since the publication of [30], Hobor et al. have given an even more expressive notion of indirection theory that guarantee monotone types too and works with mixed variance functors, see [10].

include frame rules, etc. The step-indexed model in this paper does not alter the operational semantics, interprets capabilities including $C_1 * C_2$, and justifies (shallow and deep) frame rules.

We point out that an alternative semantic model of the basic capability system could be obtained by combining the functional translation of Charguéraud and Pottier [24] with a semantic model of their purely functional target calculus. The functional translation in [24] does not, however, include higher-order frame rules and it is not immediate how to include those rules.

To extend our semantics to group regions is future work. Note that group regions are non-trivial, since they might grow over time but types need to be invariant (monotone) with respect to this growth. Further extensions will address, for instance, frame rules for more general (parameterized) invariants on local state [39].

Other operational techniques. We briefly mention two techniques other than step indexing that can be used to define logical relations based on operational semantics. First, *syntactic minimal invariance* [18, 25] is based on operational counterparts of the projection functions one obtains from solutions to recursive domain equations. As far as we know, this technique has not been developed for languages with store. Second, *biorthogonality* [13, 31, 37] is based on syntactically defined closure operators on relations. Biorthogonality has been developed for a language with integer store [37], but not (without also using step indexing) for languages with general recursive types or higher-order store. Voullion and Melliès [50] give an axiomatic setup that incorporates both techniques for a language without store. See also [34] by the same authors.

As an alternative to logical relations, techniques based on *bisimulation* can be used to show contextual equivalences for languages with store [49]. However, such techniques do not seem helpful for modelling expressive type systems such as the one considered in Section 3.

6. Conclusion

In this paper, we have argued that recursive features of programming languages, type systems and program logics, such as higher-order store, can be naturally interpreted via Kripke models over worlds that are recursively defined in a category of metric spaces. Interestingly, this can be carried out not only denotationally but also using operational semantics. Our method combines the simplicity of existing step-indexed models with the accuracy of domain-theoretic approaches for recursive domain equations. Unlike other step-indexed models, our method uses solutions of the original recursive equations, not their approximated versions. The benefits of this technique have been demonstrated in our new semantics of Charguéraud and Pottier's type-and-capability system [24], where solving an original recursive equation over worlds played a seemingly crucial role in modelling a recursively defined operator on worlds.

Additionally, we have shown that our metric approach can be specialized to Hobor et al.'s recent proposal [30] and argued that the metric approach has some advantages.

Acknowledgments

We would like to thank François Pottier, Aquinas Hobor, Robert Dockins, Andrew W. Appel and Carsten Varming for helpful discussions and insightful comments. Yang and Reus acknowledge support from the EPSRC.

References

[1] M. Abadi and G. D. Plotkin. A per model of polymorphism and recursive types. In *Proceedings of LICS*, pages 355–365, 1990.

[2] A. Ahmed. *Semantics of Types for Mutable State*. PhD thesis, Princeton University, 2004.

[3] A. Ahmed. Step-indexed syntactic logical relations for recursive and quantified types. In *Proceedings of ESOP*, pages 69–83, 2006.

[4] A. Ahmed, A. Appel, and R. Virga. A stratified semantics of general references. In *Proceedings of LICS*, pages 75–84, 2002.

[5] A. Ahmed, M. Fluet, and G. Morrisett. L3: A linear language with locations. *Fundam. Inf.*, 77(4):397–449, 2007.

[6] A. Ahmed, D. Dreyer, and A. Rossberg. State-dependent representation independence. In *Proceedings of POPL*, pages 340–353, 2009.

[7] R. M. Amadio. Recursion over realizability structures. *Information and Computation*, 91(1):55–85, 1991.

[8] R. M. Amadio and P.-L. Curien. *Domains and Lambda-Calculi*. Cambridge University Press, 1998.

[9] P. America and J. J. M. M. Rutten. Solving reflexive domain equations in a category of complete metric spaces. *J. Comput. Syst. Sci.*, 39(3):343–375, 1989.

[10] A. Appel, R. Dockins, and A. Hobor. Mechanized semantic library. `http://msl.cs.princeton.edu/`, 2009.

[11] A. W. Appel and D. A. McAllester. An indexed model of recursive types for foundational proof-carrying code. *ACM Trans. Program. Lang. Syst.*, 23(5): 657–683, 2001.

[12] A. W. Appel, P. Melliès, C. D. Richards, and J. Vouillon. A very modal model of a modern, major, general type system. In *Proceedings of POPL*, pages 109–122, 2007.

[13] N. Benton and C.-K. Hur. Biorthogonality, step-indexing and compiler correctness. In *Proceedings of ICFP*, pages 97–108, 2009.

[14] N. Benton and B. Leperchey. Relational reasoning in a nominal semantics for storage. In *Proceedings of TLCA*, pages 86–101, 2005.

[15] N. Benton, L. Beringer, M. Hofmann, and A. Kennedy. Relational semantics for effect-based program transformations: Higher-order store. In *Proceedings of PPDP*, pages 301–312, 2009.

[16] N. Benton, A. Kennedy, C. Varming, and L. Birkedal. Formalizing domains, ultrametric spaces and semantics of programming languages. Manuscript. Available at `http://www.itu.dk/people /birkedal/papers/formalizing-semantics.pdf`, 2010.

[17] B. Biering, L. Birkedal, and N. Torp-Smith. Bi-hyperdoctrines, higher-order separation logic, and abstraction. *ACM Trans. Program. Lang. Syst.*, 29(5), 2007.

[18] L. Birkedal and R. W. Harper. Constructing interpretations of recursive types in an operational setting. *Information and Computation*, 155:3–63, 1999.

[19] L. Birkedal, N. Torp-Smith, and H. Yang. Semantics of separation-logic typing and higher-order frame rules for Algol-like languages. *LMCS*, 2(5:1), 2006.

[20] L. Birkedal, K. Støvring, and J. Thamsborg. The category-theoretic solution of recursive metric-space quations. Technical Report ITU-2009-119, IT University of Copenhagen, 2009.

[21] L. Birkedal, K. Støvring, and J. Thamsborg. Realizability semantics of parametric polymorphism, general references, and recursive types. In *Proceedings of FOSSACS*, pages 456–470, 2009.

[22] N. Bohr and L. Birkedal. Relational reasoning for recursive types and references. In *Proceedings of APLAS*, pages 79–96, 2006.

[23] F. Cardone. Relational semantics for recursive types and bounded quantification. In *Proceedings of ICALP*, pages 164–178, 1989.

[24] A. Charguéraud and F. Pottier. Functional translation of a calculus of capabilities. In *Proceedings of ICFP*, pages 213–224, 2008.

[25] K. Crary and R. Harper. Syntactic logical relations for polymorphic and recursive types. *Electronic Notes in Theoretical Computer Science*, 172:259–299, 2007.

[26] K. Crary, D. Walker, and G. Morrisett. Typed memory management in a calculus of capabilities. In *Proceedings of POPL*, pages 262–275, 1999.

[27] D. Dreyer, G. Neis, A. Rossberg, and L. Birkedal. A relational modal logic for higher-order stateful ADTs. In *Proceedings of POPL*, pages 185–198, 2010.

[28] A. Hobor. *Oracle Semantics*. PhD thesis, Princeton University, 2008.

[29] A. Hobor, A. Appel, and F. Nardelli. Oracle semantics for concurrent separation logic. In *Proceedings of ESOP*, pages 353–367, 2008.

[30] A. Hobor, R. Dockins, and A. Appel. A theory of indirection via approximation. In *Proceedings of POPL*, pages 171–184, 2010.

[31] P. Johann and J. Voigtländer. A family of syntactic logical relations for the semantics of Haskell-like languages. *Information and Computation*, 207(2): 341–368, 2009.

[32] P. B. Levy. Possible world semantics for general storage in call-by-value. In *Proceedings of CSL*, pages 232–246, 2002.

[33] D. B. MacQueen, G. D. Plotkin, and R. Sethi. An ideal model for recursive polymorphic types. *Information and Control*, 71(1/2):95–130, 1986.

[34] P.-A. Melliès and J. Vouillon. Recursive polymorphic types and parametricity in an operational framework. In *Proceedings of LICS*, pages 82–91, 2005.

[35] A. Nanevski, G. Morrisett, and L. Birkedal. Polymorphism and separation in hoare type theory. In *Proceedings of ICFP*, pages 62–73, 2006.

[36] B. C. Pierce. *Types and Programming Languages*. The MIT Press, 2002.

[37] A. M. Pitts and I. D. B. Stark. Operational reasoning for functions with local state. In A. D. Gordon and A. M. Pitts, editors, *Higher-Order Operational Techniques in Semantics*, Publications of the Newton Institute, pages 227–273. Cambridge University Press, 1998.

[38] F. Pottier. Hiding local state in direct style: a higher-order anti-frame rule. In *Proceedings of LICS*, pages 331–340, 2008.

[39] F. Pottier. Generalizing the higher-order frame and anti-frame rules. Unpublished, July 2009.

[40] U. S. Reddy and H. Yang. Correctness of data representations involving heap data structures. *Science of Computer Programming*, 50(1–3):129–160, March 2004.

[41] B. Reus and J. Schwinghammer. Separation logic for higher-order store. In *Proceedings of CSL*, pages 575–590, 2006.

[42] B. Reus and T. Streicher. Semantics and logic of object calculi. In *Proceedings of LICS*, pages 113–124, 2002.

[43] J. C. Reynolds. Separation logic: A logic for shared mutable data structures. In *Proceedings of LICS*, pages 55–74, 2002.

[44] J. Schwinghammer, L. Birkedal, B. Reus, and H. Yang. Nested Hoare triples and frame rules for higher-order store. In *Proceedings of CSL*, pages 440–454, 2009.

[45] J. Schwinghammer, L. Birkedal, and K. Støvring. A step-indexed Kripke model of hidden state via recursive properties on recursively defined metric spaces. Manuscript. Available at `http://www.itu.dk/people/birkedal/papers/relpoms-antiframe-conf.pdf`, 2010.

[46] J. Schwinghammer, H. Yang, L. Birkedal, F. Pottier, and B. Reus. A semantic foundation for hidden state. In *Proceedings of FOSSACS*, pages 2–17, 2010.

[47] M. B. Smyth. Topology. In S. Abramsky, D. Gabbay, and T. S. E. Maibaum, editors, *Handbook of Logic in Computer Science*. Oxford University Press, 1992.

[48] I. Stark. Categorical models for local names. *LISP and Symbolic Computation*, 9(1):77–107, Feb. 1996.

[49] E. Sumii. A complete characterization of observational equivalence in polymorphic lambda-calculus with general references. In *Proceedings of CSL*, pages 455–469, 2009.

[50] J. Vouillon and P.-A. Melliès. Semantic types: a fresh look at the ideal model for types. In *Proceedings of POPL*, pages 52–63, 2004.

A Kripke Logical Relation Between ML and Assembly

Chung-Kil Hur * Derek Dreyer

Max Planck Institute for Software Systems (MPI-SWS)

{gil,dreyer}@mpi-sws.org

Abstract

There has recently been great progress in proving the correctness of compilers for increasingly realistic languages with increasingly realistic runtime systems. Most work on this problem has focused on proving the correctness of a particular compiler, leaving open the question of how to verify the correctness of assembly code that is hand-optimized or linked together from the output of multiple compilers. This has led Benton and other researchers to propose more abstract, compositional notions of when a low-level program correctly realizes a high-level one. However, the state of the art in so-called "compositional compiler correctness" has only considered relatively simple high-level and low-level languages.

In this paper, we propose a novel, extensional, compiler-independent notion of equivalence between high-level programs in an expressive, impure ML-like λ-calculus and low-level programs in an (only slightly) idealized assembly language. We define this equivalence by means of a biorthogonal, step-indexed, Kripke logical relation, which enables us to reason quite flexibly about assembly code that uses local state in a different manner than the high-level code it implements (*e.g.*, self-modifying code). In contrast to prior work, we factor our relation in a symmetric, language-generic fashion, which helps to simplify and clarify the formal presentation, and we also show how to account for the presence of a garbage collector. Our approach relies on recent developments in Kripke logical relations for ML-like languages, in particular the idea of possible worlds as state transition systems.

Categories and Subject Descriptors D.3.1 [*Programming Languages*]: Formal Definitions and Theory; D.3.3 [*Programming Languages*]: Language Constructs and Features; F.3.1 [*Logics and Meanings of Programs*]: Specifying and Verifying and Reasoning about Programs

General Terms Languages, Theory, Verification

Keywords Step-indexed Kripke logical relations, biorthogonality, compositional compiler correctness, garbage collection, self-modifying code

* This work was undertaken while the first author was at PPS, Université Paris Diderot, supported by Digiteo/Ile-de-France project COLLODI (2009-28HD) and Engineering Research Center of Excellence Program of Korea Ministry of Education, Science and Technology (MEST) / National Research Foundation of Korea (NRF) Grant R11-2008-007-01002-0.

POPL'11, January 26–28, 2011, Austin, Texas, USA.

1. Introduction

While compiler verification is an age-old problem, there has been remarkable progress in the last several years in proving the correctness of compilers for increasingly realistic languages with increasingly realistic runtime systems. Of particular note is Leroy's Compcert project [18], in which he used the Coq proof assistant to both program and verify a multi-pass optimizing compiler from Cminor (a C-like intermediate language) to PowerPC assembly. Dargaye [13] has adapted the Compcert framework to a compiler for a pure mini-ML language, and McCreight *et al.* [19] have extended it to support interfacing with a garbage collector. Independently, Chlipala [10, 12] has developed verified compilers for both pure and impure functional core languages, the former garbage-collected, with a focus on using custom Coq tactics to provide significant automation of verification.

That said, all of the aforementioned work has focused on proving the correctness of a *particular* compiler, leaving open the question of how to verify the correctness of assembly code that is hand-optimized or linked together from the output of multiple compilers. The issue is that compiler correctness results are typically established by exhibiting a fairly close simulation relation between source and target code, but code produced by another compiler may obey an entirely different simulation relation with the source program, and hand-optimized code might not closely simulate the source program at all. Thus, existing correctness proofs depend fundamentally on the "closed-world" assumption that one has control over how the whole source program is compiled.

In order to lift the closed-world assumption, Benton and Hur [5] suggest that what is needed is a more abstract, extensional notion of what it means for a low-level program to correctly implement a high-level one—a notion that is not tied to a particular compiler and that, moreover, offers as much flexibility in the low-level representation of high-level features as possible. When reasoning strictly about high-level programs, the canonical extensional notion of when one program implements the same functionality as another is *observational* (or *contextual*) equivalence, which says that the two programs exhibit the same (termination) behavior when placed into the context of an arbitrary enclosing well-typed high-level program. However, it is not clear how to define such a contextual notion of equivalence between high- and low-level programs, because there is no way to run both programs under the *same* context—one would need to quantify over *equivalent* high- and low-level program contexts, but when are two contexts equivalent? We are back to the original question.

Benton and Hur's solution is to define a *logical relation* between the high- and low-level languages (actually two relations, one for each direction of semantic approximation, employing a denotational semantics to represent the high-level side). Logical relations are inherently extensional—*e.g.*, two functions are logically related iff they map related arguments to related results, regardless of their private implementation details—and guarantee equivalent termination behavior under arbitrary contexts that are themselves logically related. While not as canonical as contextual equivalence, logical equivalence is nevertheless useful as long as one can establish that the logical relations are sufficiently populated—*i.e.,* that they relate enough programs/contexts of interest.

In the traditional setting where one is defining equivalence of programs in the same language, this "sufficient population" property is ensured by the *fundamental theorem of logical relations*, which states that all well-typed programs (and thus all well-typed contexts) are logically self-related. For mixed high-low relations, Benton and Hur demonstrate sufficient population by providing a simple, one-pass compilation translation from their high- to their low-level language and proving that all well-typed high-level programs are logically equivalent to their compilations. They also use the logical relations to show the relatedness of some simple hand-optimized low-level code with corresponding high-level programs.

Benton and Hur present their work as the first step towards "compositional compiler correctness". However, the source language they consider—the simply-typed λ-calculus with recursion—is purely functional, and the target language they consider—an SECD machine—is relatively high-level. Chlipala [11] has subsequently proposed a more syntactic approach to proving compositional compiler correctness, applicable to a richer, impure (albeit untyped) source language, but the target language he considers is also pretty high-level, namely a CPS variant of the source.

1.1 Contributions

In this paper, we study compositional equivalence of high- and low-level programs in a more realistic setting. Our high-level language is an expressive ML-like CBV λ-calculus, supporting abstract types, general recursive types, and general mutable references. Our low-level language is an (only slightly) idealized assembly language. Furthermore, our logical relation is designed to be sound in the presence of garbage collection, under some fairly abstract assumptions about the behavior of the garbage collector that are satisfied by both mark-and-sweep and copying collectors.

Following Benton and Hur, we define our equivalence using a *biorthogonal, step-indexed* logical relation. Biorthogonality is useful when reasoning about programs (such as low-level ones) whose behavior is *context-sensitive*, and step-indexing is useful in reasoning about semantically "cyclic" features like recursive types and higher-order state.

We depart from prior work, though, in that our relation is also a *Kripke* logical relation—*i.e.*, it is indexed by *possible worlds* that specify assumptions about the machine state. Possible worlds are useful in enforcing invariants about low-level data structures (*e.g.*, that a heap-allocated representation of a closure is immutable). They are also helpful in encoding a variety of runtime system invariants, such as the convention concerning callee-save registers and the notion of data liveness. Last but not least, possible worlds enable us to reason quite flexibly about assembly code that uses *local* state in a different manner than the high-level code it implements. An interesting example of this is *self-modifying* assembly code, whose correctness proof involves reasoning about low-level internal state changes—specifically, changes to the code itself—that clearly have no high-level counterpart. This is the essence of what we mean when we say that our relation is *extensional*.

Technically, our approach relies closely on recent developments in Kripke logical relations for ML-like languages, in particular the idea of possible worlds as *state transition systems*. This idea, which we review in Section 3.3, was proposed originally by Ahmed *et al.* [2] (in a somewhat different form) as a way to reason about representation independence for so-called "generative" abstract data types, whose private state undergoes a controlled series of state transitions during the execution of the program. Dreyer *et al.* [14] have subsequently generalized the idea in order to reason about "well-bracketed" state changes. By basing our high-low logical relations on this most recent work, we are able to cleanly model a variety of state transition systems that arise naturally in low-level code (*e.g.,* in self-modifying code).

Lastly, a novel feature of our logical relation is that, while it is defined by induction on an ML-like type structure, it is also defined in a *language-generic* fashion. That is, it may be instantiated to form an equivalence relation between any two languages (high- or low-level) that are capable of implementing various relevant linguistic constructs—*e.g.,* function application, plugging a continuation with a value, etc. Factoring the relation in this way helps to simplify and clarify the formal presentation. Moreover, it has the advantage that the relation becomes inherently symmetric and thus easier to use in proving high-low equivalences than Benton and Hur's asymmetric approximation relations.

2. HIGH and LOW

The high-level language **HIGH** is a System F-like polymorphic λ-calculus extended with existential, product and iso-recursive types, as well as ML-style general references (higher-order state). Figure 1 shows the syntax and the typing and evaluation judgments. The inference rules for typing and evaluation are standard, so we omit them (see the companion technical appendix [15] for details).

The low-level language **LOW** is an assembly language idealized in two ways: its word and memory sizes are infinite and its instructions are represented by abstract objects rather than by physical words. Its memory consists of four entities: code memory, register file, stack and heap. A code memory is a map from physical addresses (represented by natural numbers) to instructions. A register file is a map from registers to words. Words in turn are represented by natural numbers with an extra bit indicating whether the word is a pointer to a heap cell or not (useful for garbage collection purposes). There are 12 registers, half of which ($\mathrm{sp}, \mathrm{sv}_0, \ldots, \mathrm{sv}_4$) are specified as callee-save registers by our calling convention. Both a stack and a heap are random-access memories (*i.e.,* maps from addresses to words).

The instruction set includes standard instructions (`jmp`, `jnz`, `jneq`, `move`, `plus`, `minus`) supporting different addressing modes via lvalues and rvalues. The non-standard operations include `halt` for normal termination, `fail` for raising a runtime error, `jptr` for testing whether a value is a pointer or not, `setptr` for marking a pointer bit, and `isr`, `isw` for inspecting and updating instructions in code memory. Note that as instructions are not represented by words, we employ a bijection $\mathbb{E}$ and its inverse $\mathbb{D}$ (for $\mathbb{E}$ncode and $\mathbb{D}$ecode) to convert back and forth between instructions and words.

The dynamic semantics of **LOW** is standard and is given in Figure 1. A machine configuration (Φ, pc) is a pair consisting of a memory and a program counter; it halts, fails or evolves to another configuration (Φ', pc') by executing the instruction stored at pc in the code memory $\Phi.\mathrm{code}$.

3. The Key Ideas

In this section, we present the key ideas behind our work through the lens of an illustrative, challenging example. We will walk through the code of this example, suggest intuitively how to reason about it, and then explain how our Kripke logical relation formalizes this intuition. While we will initially ignore the question of how garbage collection affects matters, we will return to this issue at the end of the section and discuss how our logical relation enables reasoning in the presence of a garbage collector.

This section is intended to be accessible to a broad programming-languages audience, and hopefully to serve as a useful guide to the

HIGH – Syntax & Semantics

$$
\begin{array}{lcl}
\tau & ::= & \alpha \mid b \mid \tau_1 \times \tau_2 \mid \tau_1 \to \tau_2 \mid \forall\alpha.\,\tau \mid \exists\alpha.\,\tau \mid \mu\alpha.\,\tau \mid \mathsf{ref}\ \tau \\
e & ::= & x \mid \ell \mid \langle e_1, e_2\rangle \mid e.1 \mid e.2 \mid \lambda x{:}\tau.\,e \mid e_1\ e_2 \mid \Lambda\alpha.e \mid e\ \tau \mid \\
 & & \mathsf{pack}\ \langle\tau_1, e\rangle\ \mathsf{as}\ \tau_2 \mid \mathsf{unpack}\ e_1\ \mathsf{as}\ \langle\alpha, x\rangle\ \mathsf{in}\ e_2 \mid \\
 & & \mathsf{roll}_\tau\ e \mid \mathsf{unroll}\ e \mid \mathsf{ref}\ e \mid e_1 := e_2 \mid !e \mid e_1 == e_2 \mid \ldots \\
v & ::= & x \mid \ell \mid \langle v_1, v_2\rangle \mid \lambda x{:}\tau.\,e \mid \Lambda\alpha.e \mid \mathsf{pack}\ \langle\tau_1, v\rangle\ \mathsf{as}\ \tau_2 \mid \mathsf{roll}_\tau\ v \mid \ldots \\
K & ::= & \bullet \mid \langle K, e_2\rangle \mid \langle v_1, K\rangle \mid K.1 \mid K.2 \mid K\ e_2 \mid v_1\ K \mid K\ \tau \mid \mathsf{roll}_\tau\ K \mid \\
 & & \mathsf{unroll}\ K \mid \mathsf{pack}\ \langle\tau_1, K\rangle\ \mathsf{as}\ \tau_2 \mid \mathsf{unpack}\ K\ \mathsf{as}\ \langle\alpha, x\rangle\ \mathsf{in}\ e_2 \mid \\
 & & \mathsf{ref}\ K \mid K := e_2 \mid v_1 := K \mid !K \mid K == e_2 \mid v_1 == K \mid \ldots
\end{array}
$$

$\Sigma ::= \cdot \mid \Sigma, \ell{:}\tau$ with $\mathrm{ftv}(\tau) = \emptyset$ $\quad \Delta ::= \cdot \mid \Delta, \alpha \quad \Gamma ::= \cdot \mid \Gamma, x{:}\tau$

Static semantics : $\Sigma; \Delta; \Gamma \vdash e : \tau$

$\mathrm{HCVal} \overset{\mathrm{def}}{=} \{\, v \mid \mathrm{ftv}(v) = \emptyset \wedge \mathrm{fv}(v) = \emptyset \,\}$

$\mathrm{HHeap} \overset{\mathrm{def}}{=} \{\, h \in \mathrm{HLoc} \rightharpoonup_{\mathrm{fin}} \mathrm{HCVal} \,\}$

Dynamic semantics : $(h, e) \hookrightarrow (h', e')$

LOW – Syntax

$$
\begin{array}{lcl}
\mathrm{PConf} & \overset{\mathrm{def}}{=} & \{\, (\Phi, \mathrm{pc}) \in \mathrm{PMem} \times \mathrm{PAddr} \,\} \\
\mathrm{PMem} & \overset{\mathrm{def}}{=} & \{\, \Phi = (\mathrm{code}, \mathrm{reg}, \mathrm{stk}, \mathrm{hp}) \\
 & & \quad \in \mathrm{PCode} \times \mathrm{PRegFile} \times \mathrm{PStack} \times \mathrm{PHeap} \,\}
\end{array}
$$

$$
\begin{array}{lcl@{\qquad}lcl}
\mathrm{PCode} & \overset{\mathrm{def}}{=} & \mathrm{PAddr} \to \mathrm{Instruction} & \mathrm{PRegFile} & \overset{\mathrm{def}}{=} & \mathrm{Register} \to \mathrm{PWord} \\
\mathrm{PStack} & \overset{\mathrm{def}}{=} & \mathrm{PAddr} \to \mathrm{PWord} & \mathrm{PHeap} & \overset{\mathrm{def}}{=} & \mathrm{PAddr} \to \mathrm{PWord} \\
\mathrm{PAddr} & \overset{\mathrm{def}}{=} & \{\, a \in \mathbb{N} \,\} & \mathrm{PWord} & \overset{\mathrm{def}}{=} & \{\, w \in \{0, 1\} \times \mathbb{N} \,\}
\end{array}
$$

$$
\begin{array}{lcl}
r \in \mathrm{Register} & ::= & \mathrm{sp} \mid \mathrm{sv}_0 \mid \ldots \mid \mathrm{sv}_4 \mid \mathrm{wk}_0 \mid \ldots \mid \mathrm{wk}_5 \\
\mathrm{lv} \in \mathrm{PLvalue} & ::= & \lfloor r \rfloor \mid \langle a\rangle_{\mathrm{s}} \mid \langle r - o\rangle_{\mathrm{s}} \mid \langle a\rangle_{\mathrm{h}} \mid \langle r + o\rangle_{\mathrm{h}} \\
\mathrm{rv} \in \mathrm{PRvalue} & ::= & \mathrm{lv} \mid w \\
\iota \in \mathrm{Instruction} & ::= & \mathtt{fail} \mid \mathtt{halt} \mid \mathtt{jmp}\ \mathrm{rv} \mid \mathtt{jnz}\ \mathrm{rv}\ \mathrm{rv} \mid \mathtt{jneq}\ \mathrm{rv}\ \mathrm{rv}\ \mathrm{rv} \mid \\
 & & \mathtt{jptr}\ \mathrm{rv}\ \mathrm{rv} \mid \mathtt{setptr}\ \mathrm{lv} \mid \mathtt{move}\ \mathrm{lv}\ \mathrm{rv} \mid \mathtt{plus}\ \mathrm{lv}\ \mathrm{rv}\ \mathrm{rv} \mid \\
 & & \mathtt{minus}\ \mathrm{lv}\ \mathrm{rv}\ \mathrm{rv} \mid \mathtt{isr}\ \mathrm{lv}\ \mathrm{rv} \mid \mathtt{isw}\ \mathrm{rv}\ \mathrm{rv}
\end{array}
$$

LOW – Semantics

$$
|w| \overset{\mathrm{def}}{=} \pi_2(w) \quad \mathrm{isptr}(w) \overset{\mathrm{def}}{=} (\pi_1(w) = 1) \quad \underline{n} \overset{\mathrm{def}}{=} (0, n) \quad \widehat{a} \overset{\mathrm{def}}{=} (1, a)
$$

$$
\begin{array}{lcl@{\qquad}lcl}
\Phi(w) & \overset{\mathrm{def}}{=} & w & \Phi(\lfloor r \rfloor) & \overset{\mathrm{def}}{=} & \Phi.\mathrm{reg}(r) \\
\Phi(\langle a\rangle_{\mathrm{s}}) & \overset{\mathrm{def}}{=} & \Phi.\mathrm{stk}(a) & \Phi(\langle r - o\rangle_{\mathrm{s}}) & \overset{\mathrm{def}}{=} & \Phi.\mathrm{stk}(|\Phi(\lfloor r \rfloor)| - o) \\
\Phi(\langle a\rangle_{\mathrm{h}}) & \overset{\mathrm{def}}{=} & \Phi.\mathrm{hp}(a) & \Phi(\langle r + o\rangle_{\mathrm{h}}) & \overset{\mathrm{def}}{=} & \Phi.\mathrm{hp}(|\Phi(\lfloor r \rfloor)| + o)
\end{array}
$$

$$
\begin{array}{lcl}
\Phi[\lfloor r \rfloor \mapsto w] & \overset{\mathrm{def}}{=} & (\Phi.\mathrm{code}, \Phi.\mathrm{reg}[r \mapsto w], \Phi.\mathrm{stk}, \Phi.\mathrm{hp}) \\
\Phi[\langle a\rangle_{\mathrm{s}} \mapsto w] & \overset{\mathrm{def}}{=} & (\Phi.\mathrm{code}, \Phi.\mathrm{reg}, \Phi.\mathrm{stk}[a \mapsto w], \Phi.\mathrm{hp}) \\
\Phi[\langle r - o\rangle_{\mathrm{s}} \mapsto w] & \overset{\mathrm{def}}{=} & (\Phi.\mathrm{code}, \Phi.\mathrm{reg}, \Phi.\mathrm{stk}[|\Phi(\lfloor r \rfloor)| - o \mapsto w], \Phi.\mathrm{hp}) \\
\Phi[\langle a\rangle_{\mathrm{h}} \mapsto w] & \overset{\mathrm{def}}{=} & (\Phi.\mathrm{code}, \Phi.\mathrm{reg}, \Phi.\mathrm{stk}, \Phi.\mathrm{hp}[a \mapsto w]) \\
\Phi[\langle r + o\rangle_{\mathrm{h}} \mapsto w] & \overset{\mathrm{def}}{=} & (\Phi.\mathrm{code}, \Phi.\mathrm{reg}, \Phi.\mathrm{stk}, \Phi.\mathrm{hp}[|\Phi(\lfloor r \rfloor)| + o \mapsto w])
\end{array}
$$

$$
\begin{array}{lcl}
[\![\mathtt{fail}]\!]\,(\Phi, \mathrm{pc}) & \overset{\mathrm{def}}{=} & \mathit{fail} \\
[\![\mathtt{halt}]\!]\,(\Phi, \mathrm{pc}) & \overset{\mathrm{def}}{=} & \mathit{halt} \\
[\![\mathtt{jmp}\ \mathrm{rv}]\!]\,(\Phi, \mathrm{pc}) & \overset{\mathrm{def}}{=} & (\Phi, |\Phi(\mathrm{rv})|) \\
[\![\mathtt{jnz}\ \mathrm{rv}_1\ \mathrm{rv}_2]\!]\,(\Phi, \mathrm{pc}) & \overset{\mathrm{def}}{=} & \text{if } \Phi(\mathrm{rv}_2) \neq \underline{0} \\
 & & \text{then } (\Phi, |\Phi(\mathrm{rv}_1)|) \text{ else } (\Phi, \mathrm{pc} + 1) \\
[\![\mathtt{jneq}\ \mathrm{rv}_1\ \mathrm{rv}_2\ \mathrm{rv}_3]\!]\,(\Phi, \mathrm{pc}) & \overset{\mathrm{def}}{=} & \text{if } \Phi(\mathrm{rv}_2) \neq \Phi(\mathrm{rv}_3) \\
 & & \text{then } (\Phi, |\Phi(\mathrm{rv}_1)|) \text{ else } (\Phi, \mathrm{pc} + 1) \\
[\![\mathtt{jptr}\ \mathrm{rv}_1\ \mathrm{rv}_2]\!]\,(\Phi, \mathrm{pc}) & \overset{\mathrm{def}}{=} & \text{if } \mathrm{isptr}(\Phi(\mathrm{rv}_2)) \\
 & & \text{then } (\Phi, |\Phi(\mathrm{rv}_1)|) \text{ else } (\Phi, \mathrm{pc} + 1) \\
[\![\mathtt{move}\ \mathrm{lv}\ \mathrm{rv}]\!]\,(\Phi, \mathrm{pc}) & \overset{\mathrm{def}}{=} & (\Phi[\mathrm{lv} \mapsto \Phi(\mathrm{rv})], \mathrm{pc} + 1) \\
[\![\mathtt{setptr}\ \mathrm{lv}]\!]\,(\Phi, \mathrm{pc}) & \overset{\mathrm{def}}{=} & (\Phi[\mathrm{lv} \mapsto \widehat{|\Phi(\mathrm{lv})|}], \mathrm{pc} + 1) \\
[\![\mathtt{plus}\ \mathrm{lv}\ \mathrm{rv}_1\ \mathrm{rv}_2]\!]\,(\Phi, \mathrm{pc}) & \overset{\mathrm{def}}{=} & (\Phi[\mathrm{lv} \mapsto \underline{|\Phi(\mathrm{rv}_1)| + |\Phi(\mathrm{rv}_2)|}], \mathrm{pc} + 1) \\
[\![\mathtt{minus}\ \mathrm{lv}\ \mathrm{rv}_1\ \mathrm{rv}_2]\!]\,(\Phi, \mathrm{pc}) & \overset{\mathrm{def}}{=} & (\Phi[\mathrm{lv} \mapsto \underline{|\Phi(\mathrm{rv}_1)| - |\Phi(\mathrm{rv}_2)|}], \mathrm{pc} + 1) \\
[\![\mathtt{isr}\ \mathrm{lv}\ \mathrm{rv}]\!]\,(\Phi, \mathrm{pc}) & \overset{\mathrm{def}}{=} & (\Phi[\mathrm{lv} \mapsto \underline{\mathbb{E}(\Phi.\mathrm{code}(|\Phi(\mathrm{rv})|))}], \mathrm{pc} + 1) \\
[\![\mathtt{isw}\ \mathrm{rv}_1\ \mathrm{rv}_2]\!]\,(\Phi, \mathrm{pc}) & \overset{\mathrm{def}}{=} & ((\Phi.\mathrm{code}[\,|\Phi(\mathrm{rv}_1)| \mapsto \mathbb{D}(|\Phi(\mathrm{rv}_2)|)], \\
 & & \quad \Phi.\mathrm{reg}, \Phi.\mathrm{stk}, \Phi.\mathrm{hp}), \mathrm{pc} + 1)
\end{array}
$$

where $\mathbb{E}$: Instruction $\to \mathbb{N}$ is a bijection, and $\mathbb{D} = \mathbb{E}^{-1}$.

Dynamic semantics : $(\Phi, \mathrm{pc}) \hookrightarrow [\![\Phi.\mathrm{code}(\mathrm{pc})]\!]\,(\Phi, \mathrm{pc})$

Figure 1. Syntax and Semantics for the **HIGH** and **LOW** Languages (excerpt)

vast majority of readers who are not intimately familiar with recent developments in Kripke logical relations.

3.1 A Motivating Example

Our motivating example is based on Pitts and Stark's "awkward" example [22]. Their original example is almost blindingly simple—prove that the following **HIGH** terms are contextually equivalent:

$$
\begin{array}{lcl}
e & \overset{\mathrm{def}}{=} & \mathsf{let}\ x = \mathsf{ref}\ 0\ \mathsf{in}\ \lambda f{:}\mathsf{unit} \to \mathsf{unit}.\ (x := 1;\ f\ \langle\rangle;\ !x) \\
e' & \overset{\mathrm{def}}{=} & \lambda f{:}\mathsf{unit} \to \mathsf{unit}.\ (f\ \langle\rangle;\ 1)
\end{array}
$$

The first term, e, allocates a fresh memory location x, initially set to 0, and then returns a higher-order function. When called, the latter will set x to 1, invoke its callback argument f, and then return the contents of x. The second term, e', is similar, except that it does not bother allocating or updating any memory, and the function it defines always returns 1. Proving that e and e' are contextually equivalent is tantamount to showing that, in the former, whenever the callback invocation $f\ \langle\rangle$ returns, x points to 1.

After a moment's thought, it should hopefully be intuitively clear why the equivalence holds. The pointer x in e is initially set to 0, but once the function that e returns is applied for the first time, x will be set to 1 and will never be set back to 0. This is because e "owns" x as a piece of *local state* and the only thing e ever does to x after first allocating it is to set it to 1. Thus, the "awkward" example serves as an elegant distillation of (1) the ability of code to control some local state and impose arbitrary constraints on it, and (2) the ability of that local state to evolve over time in an *irreversible* (or *monotone*) way. Such irreversible changes to local state arise in a variety of real-world situations—*e.g.*, in "generative" ADTs (whose sets of inhabitants grow over time), and in data structure initialization [2]. It is thus rather remarkable that only recently have methods been developed for proving an equivalence as simple as the "awkward" example [8, 2, 23]. (More on that in Section 3.3.)

We are now ready to present our motivating example. We want to prove a variant of the awkward example, namely that the **HIGH** term e is implemented correctly by a **LOW** program p, where p's implementation follows the second **HIGH** term e' fairly closely. By itself, that would already be an interesting result—it would demonstrate the extensional equivalence of a high-level program with an "optimized" low-level program, where the optimization is based on the inability of high-level program contexts to observe e's manipulation of local state. But we will make it more interesting still with an added twist: the code of the function that p evaluates to will be *obfuscated* using a primitive form of encryption, and when first applied, the function will first decrypt and overwrite itself via *self-modifying code*.

The **LOW** program p is shown in Figure 2. Before we walk through the code, let us first note that p is parameterized by alloc, a code pointer to the memory allocation routine, and bg, the location in the code segment where p's code will be loaded and where its execution will begin—these parameters will be instantiated as part of linking and loading. (We will define the formal semantics of linking and loading for **LOW** programs in Section 7.)

bg: Create and return a closure. The evaluation of p is very simple: it does no interesting computation except to immediately create and return a closure value, just as the **HIGH** term e' does. The first 3 instructions starting at bg allocate a fresh one-word closure on the heap by invoking the alloc routine (passing it the size parameter 1 in register wk_5 and the return address $\mathrm{bg} + 3$ in register wk_4). We only need one word for the closure because the function we're implementing (e') is closed, so all we need to store in the closure is the naked code pointer. The alloc routine is assumed to return the pointer to a fresh one-word cell in wk_5, without modifying the contents of any registers except wk_4 and

$e \stackrel{\mathrm{def}}{=} \mathsf{let}\ x = \mathsf{ref}\ 0\ \mathsf{in}\ \lambda f{:}\mathsf{unit} \rightarrow \mathsf{unit}.\, x := 1; f\ \langle\rangle; !x$

$p \stackrel{\mathrm{def}}{=} \lambda\, \mathrm{alloc}, \mathrm{bg}.\ [$

bg	`move`	$\lfloor \mathrm{wk}_4 \rfloor$	$\underline{\mathrm{bg}+3}$		
	`move`	$\lfloor \mathrm{wk}_5 \rfloor$	$\underline{1}$		
	`jmp`	$\underline{\mathrm{alloc}}$			
bg + 3	`move`	$\langle \mathrm{wk}_5 + 0 \rangle_\mathrm{h}$	$\underline{\mathrm{bg}+5}$		
	`jmp`	$\lfloor \mathrm{wk}_0 \rfloor$			
bg + 5	`move`	$\lfloor \mathrm{wk}_3 \rfloor$	$\underline{\mathrm{bg}+10}$		
bg + 6	`isr`	$\lfloor \mathrm{wk}_4 \rfloor$	$\lfloor \mathrm{wk}_3 \rfloor$		
	`minus`	$\lfloor \mathrm{wk}_4 \rfloor$	$\lfloor \mathrm{wk}_4 \rfloor$	$\underline{666}$	
	`isw`	$\lfloor \mathrm{wk}_3 \rfloor$	$\lfloor \mathrm{wk}_4 \rfloor$		
	`plus`	$\lfloor \mathrm{wk}_3 \rfloor$	$\lfloor \mathrm{wk}_3 \rfloor$	$\underline{1}$	
bg + 10	$\mathbb{D}(\mathbb{E}(\texttt{jneq}$	$\mathrm{bg}+6$	$\lfloor \mathrm{wk}_3 \rfloor$	$\underline{\mathrm{bg}+21}$	$)+666)$
bg + 11	$\mathbb{D}(\mathbb{E}(\texttt{isw}$	$\underline{\mathrm{bg}+5}$	$\mathbb{E}(\texttt{jmp}\ \underline{\mathrm{bg}+12})$		$)+666)$
bg + 12	$\mathbb{D}(\mathbb{E}(\texttt{move}$	$\langle \mathrm{wk}_1 + 0 \rangle_\mathrm{h}$	$\underline{\mathrm{bg}+13}$		$)+666)$
bg + 13	$\mathbb{D}(\mathbb{E}(\texttt{plus}$	$\lfloor \mathrm{sp} \rfloor$	$\lfloor \mathrm{sp} \rfloor$	$\underline{1}$	$)+666)$
	$\mathbb{D}(\mathbb{E}(\texttt{move}$	$\langle \mathrm{sp} - 1 \rangle_\mathrm{s}$	$\lfloor \mathrm{wk}_0 \rfloor$		$)+666)$
	$\mathbb{D}(\mathbb{E}(\texttt{move}$	$\lfloor \mathrm{wk}_1 \rfloor$	$\lfloor \mathrm{wk}_2 \rfloor$		$)+666)$
	$\mathbb{D}(\mathbb{E}(\texttt{move}$	$\lfloor \mathrm{wk}_0 \rfloor$	$\underline{\mathrm{bg}+18}$		$)+666)$
	$\mathbb{D}(\mathbb{E}(\texttt{jmp}$	$\langle \mathrm{wk}_1 + 0 \rangle_\mathrm{h}$			$)+666)$
bg + 18	$\mathbb{D}(\mathbb{E}(\texttt{move}$	$\lfloor \mathrm{wk}_5 \rfloor$	$\underline{1}$		$)+666)$
	$\mathbb{D}(\mathbb{E}(\texttt{minus}$	$\lfloor \mathrm{sp} \rfloor$	$\lfloor \mathrm{sp} \rfloor$	$\underline{1}$	$)+666)$
bg + 20	$\mathbb{D}(\mathbb{E}(\texttt{jmp}$	$\langle \mathrm{sp} - 0 \rangle_\mathrm{s}$			$)+666)$

$]$

Figure 2. Motivating Example

wk_5. We then store in that cell the code pointer $\mathrm{bg} + 5$, before jumping to the return address, which we assume the linker/loader had passed to p originally in register wk_0. (The linker/loader has essentially the same calling convention as for ordinary functions, which is different from the one for alloc and is described below—see $\mathrm{bg} + 12$.) Although our calling convention is that return values are passed back to the caller in wk_5, our return value was already in wk_5 after the call to alloc, so we need not explicitly move anything into wk_5 before returning.

We now describe the implementation of the closure returned (in wk_5) by the evaluation of p. Initially, this closure contains just a code pointer to $\mathrm{bg} + 5$, but eventually that code pointer will be updated (see below).

$\mathrm{bg} + 5$: Decrypt and overwrite the code. The code from $\mathrm{bg} + 10$ on is obfuscated by the addition of 666 to the machine representation of each instruction. Eventually, once the code is decrypted, the function will be executable starting at the address $\mathrm{bg} + 13$. Before that time, however, the function must begin executing at $\mathrm{bg} + 5$, because the first step will be to decrypt and overwrite the obfuscated instructions. The reader can easily verify manually that the code starting at $\mathrm{bg} + 5$ will use register wk_3 to loop through the instructions $\mathrm{bg} + 10$ through $\mathrm{bg} + 20$. For each, it will use `isr` to read the instruction stored at wk_3 into wk_4, subtract 666 from it, and then write the decrypted instruction back to the code segment at address wk_3. When this loop is finished, the program counter will be at $\mathrm{bg} + 11$.

$\mathrm{bg} + 11$: Redirect the first instruction of the function. Having decrypted the code, we do not want future calls to this function to perform the decryption again. We therefore overwrite the first instruction (at $\mathrm{bg} + 5$) with a jump to $\mathrm{bg} + 12$.

$\mathrm{bg} + 12$: Update the code pointer. The **LOW** calling convention is that a function is passed its return address in wk_0, its argument in wk_2, and its own closure in wk_1. The decryption code starting at $\mathrm{bg} + 5$ did not touch any of these registers, so at $\mathrm{bg} + 12$ we know that wk_1 still stores a closure with a code pointer to $\mathrm{bg} + 5$. Having decrypted the code, we can now safely update this code pointer—$\langle \mathrm{wk}_1 + 0 \rangle_\mathrm{h}$—to point to $\mathrm{bg} + 13$, the address where the function begins its computation in earnest.

An important point: Why did we bother *both* redirecting the $\mathrm{bg} + 5$ instruction (to jump to $\mathrm{bg} + 12$) *and* updating the code pointer in the function closure? Would the latter alone not have been sufficient? The answer is that it depends. If p were only evaluated once, in which case only one closure for this function were ever generated, then yes, just updating the code pointer would be sufficient because $\mathrm{bg} + 5$ would become effectively dead code. But we would like our notion of high-low program equivalence to be preserved under a rich set of program contexts including those that evaluate the programs—here, p and e—more than once. Repeated evaluation of p will result in the creation of multiple closures for the function p defines, and merely updating the code pointer for one closure will not change the fact that other closures may still point to $\mathrm{bg} + 5$, so it is necessary to redirect the $\mathrm{bg} + 5$ instruction as well.

$\mathrm{bg} + 13$: Implement $\lambda f.\ (f\ \langle\rangle; 1)$. This is the implementation of the function proper. We first push our return address wk_0 onto the stack. We then invoke the callback argument (f in the **HIGH** code) by moving a pointer to f's closure into wk_1, moving the return address $\mathrm{bg} + 18$ into wk_0, and jumping to f's code pointer $\langle \mathrm{wk}_1 + 0 \rangle_\mathrm{h}$. (Note: f's argument type is unit, so there is no need to pass anything in the argument register wk_2.) When control is returned to $\mathrm{bg} + 18$, we store the result 1 in the result register wk_5, pop the return address off the stack, and jump to it.

3.2 Discussion of the Motivating Example

Why does p implement e? Intuitively, the reason is that the self-modifying aspects of p are not visible to p's clients because they do not affect its extensional behavior; and ultimately, once p has decrypted itself, it behaves essentially the same as the **HIGH** term e', which we have already argued is equivalent to e. Of course, this begs the question: how exactly do we know that p's clients cannot observe its self-modifications?

Interestingly, the answer is remarkably similar to the argument for why e and e' are equivalent, namely that what p does to its own code takes the form of irreversible changes to local state. Specifically, we take it as a given that p "owns" its own code, and since the evaluation of p will allocate a fresh memory cell for the closure it returns, p owns that closure as well. Thus, in reasoning about p, we can place restrictions on how its code and closure may evolve over time. Much as the local variable x in e starts out pointing to 0 and eventually points to 1, the code of p starts out in encrypted form, and if/when any closure it returns is first applied, it changes to decrypted form. In both cases, it is critical that we never revert to the earlier state. Similarly, the closure returned by the evaluation of p starts out with its code pointer set to $\mathrm{bg} + 5$, but if/when the closure is ever applied, it will be set to $\mathrm{bg} + 13$. In this case, it is not so essential for correctness that the code pointer never revert back to $\mathrm{bg}+5$, but it *is* essential that the closure's code pointer only be set to $\mathrm{bg} + 13$ when the code is in the decrypted state.

Given these restrictions on how the local state of p and e may evolve, it is but a short distance to a *bona fide* proof. Before sketching that proof, let us first review the recent work on Kripke logical relations that will put our reasoning on a solid footing.

3.3 Kripke Logical Relations and State Transition Systems

Logical relations are a well-established technique for reasoning about equivalence of higher-order programs. A logical relation is defined inductively on the type structure of the language: at base type the logical relation coincides with observable equality—*e.g.*, two programs of type int are logically related if they produce the same integer—and at higher type the relation is defined by interpreting each type operator by the appropriate logical connective—*e.g.*, two functions are related at type $\tau_1 \rightarrow \tau_2$ if relatedness of their arguments at type τ_1 *implies* relatedness of their results at type τ_2. The important feature about logical relations for our purposes is that they give considerable leeway to how related functions are implemented, so long as they produce related results. (As Benton and Hur [5] channeling Machiavelli put it, "the ends justify the means.")

In the presence of state, we cannot talk about the relatedness of two programs without making some assumptions and imposing some restrictions on how they manipulate state. This is where *Kripke logical relations* come in. Kripke logical relations are indexed by *possible worlds*, which represent a set of restrictions on the memories of the two programs under which the programs are guaranteed to behave equivalently. When we want to prove the relatedness of two programs under a world W, we suppose we are given arbitrary initial memories that are related by (*i.e.*, satisfy the restrictions of) W, and we proceed typically by showing that when evaluated under those memories the programs either (1) both diverge (don't terminate), or else (2) produce values and final memories that are related under some "future" world W' of W.

What does it mean for W' to be a future world of W? If in the course of evaluation the programs allocate fresh pieces of memory, W' may extend the initial world W with new restrictions governing the use of the freshly allocated memory. This approach allows us to establish whatever constraints we want on freshly allocated state that is kept *local*. (If the state is made globally accessible—*e.g.*, by being passed to the context at a ref type—then the state will have to obey the usual invariants dictated by the ref type.)

In traditional Kripke logical relations, such as those of Pitts and Stark [22], possible worlds essentially take the form of simple memory relations, *i.e.*, memory *invariants*. As we have seen in the "awkward" example, however, memory invariants are not necessarily enough; we need additionally the ability to describe assumptions about state that may change in a controlled and monotone way. (It is thus not a surprise that Pitts and Stark put forth the "awkward" example as an example for which their method was inadequate.)

To address this limitation, Ahmed *et al.* [2] proposed generalizing possible worlds to include the ability for a memory relation to *evolve*. Dreyer *et al.* [14] later streamlined and extended Ahmed *et al.*'s approach in various ways, and cast Ahmed *et al.*'s possible worlds as collections of *state transition systems (STS's)*. In the case of the "awkward" example, one can understand the restrictions placed on e's local variable x according to the following STS:

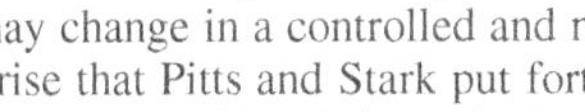

When this STS is first added to the initial world W, it starts out in the $x \hookrightarrow 0$ state, because after x is first allocated, it points to 0. However, under Dreyer *et al.*'s model, future worlds of W may not only place additional restrictions on fresh pieces of memory but also update the state of existing STS's in W. Thus, in some future world W', the above STS may be switched to the $x \hookrightarrow 1$ state, and memories satisfying W' would have to map x to 1. Furthermore, any future world of W' would have to remain in the $x \hookrightarrow 1$ state as there is no transition out of it. This corresponds to the intuitive reasoning about the example that we described in Section 3.1.

3.4 State Transition Systems for the Motivating Example

Using Kripke logical relations based on state transition systems, we can now roughly sketch the proof of equivalence of p and e.

We will prove that p and e are logically related in some initial world W_0 that includes some basic assumptions (in the form of STS's) about registers, the stack, etc. (See Section 7 for details.)

First, since we can assume p has just been loaded into memory, we can think of its code as a freshly allocated piece of memory, and we are therefore given the opportunity to extend W_0 with an STS governing p's code. For most programs, we would extend W_0 at this point with a one-state STS, representing the simple invariant that the code of the program never changes. For our motivating example, we instead extend W_0 with an STS of the form:

When the STS is in the left state, the associated memory relation will require that p's code be in its initial, encrypted form, and when the STS is in the right state, the memory relation will require that p's code be in decrypted form. Once decrypted, always decrypted.

When p and e are executed, the former allocates a fresh closure on the heap, setting its constituent code pointer to $\mathrm{bg} + 5$, and the latter allocates the local ref cell x, setting its contents to 0. Since both the closure and x are freshly allocated, we may at that point also extend the world with a new STS governing both of them:

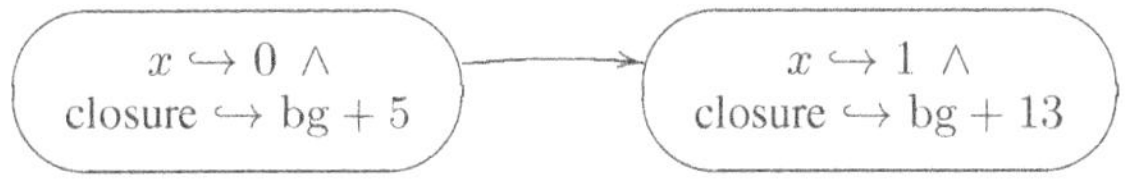

We have joined the assumptions about them into one STS because they change in lockstep: when the functions returned by p and e are applied for the first time, x gets updated to 1 and the closure's code pointer gets updated to $\mathrm{bg} + 13$ simultaneously.

As noted in Section 3.2, it should never be the case that the code is still encrypted while the closure returned by p points to $\mathrm{bg} + 13$. (The closure would behave in an unspecified manner if it were called in such a state.) When adding the second STS, it is therefore important that we outlaw this possibility up front so that we will not have to consider it later. Fortunately, Dreyer *et al.*'s model, on which our logical relation is based, allows us to define the second STS in such a way that we can only be in its right state if the first STS is also in its right state.

Let W be the world resulting from extending W_0 with the above two STS's. What remains to be shown is that the functions returned by p and e are related in world W. So, suppose that W' is a future world of W, and that we begin executing the high- and low-level functions in some corresponding high- and low-level memories that are related by W'. There are three cases to consider, depending on the states of the two STS's of interest in W' (the fourth case was outlawed, as described above):

Case 1: Code is encrypted, $x \hookrightarrow 0$, closure $\hookrightarrow \mathrm{bg} + 5$. In this case, we first decrypt the code, and then set x to 1 and the closure's code pointer to $\mathrm{bg} + 13$.

Case 2: Code is decrypted, $x \hookrightarrow 0$, closure $\hookrightarrow \mathrm{bg} + 5$. In this case, we set x to 1 and the closure's code pointer to $\mathrm{bg} + 13$.

Case 3: Code is decrypted, $x \hookrightarrow 1$, closure $\hookrightarrow \mathrm{bg} + 13$. In this case, we set x to 1 and don't touch the closure's code pointer.

In all three cases, we end up transitioning to a future world W'' in which both STS's of interest are in the right state, if they weren't already there in W'. After making the state transition, both the high- and low-level functions invoke their callback arguments. Assuming they return, they will do so with memories that satisfy some future world of W'', but in the STS's of interest, there is nowhere to transition to. So we know that x must still point to 1. The high- and low-level functions must therefore both return the same result, namely 1, along with memories that satisfy a future world of the starting world W'.

3.5 Well-Bracketed State Changes and Private Transitions

For simplicity, we have glossed over many details in the above proof sketch. One important detail is how we reason about the stack. When the functions invoke their unknown callback arguments, we need to know that the callback will return the stack—*i.e.*, the contents of the stack segment up to the stack pointer sp—as it found it. One approach would be to bake this condition into our logical relation for functions. However, as we explained in the introduction, we have set out to define our relation in a largely language-generic fashion, and it would not make sense to bake a low-level property about the stack into a language-generic relation.

Instead, we wish to build this condition into the initial world under which we relate high- and low-level programs, but the property we desire of the stack is not expressible in terms of STS's as we have described them so far. To account for stack-like behavior, we employ another aspect of Dreyer *et al.*'s possible worlds, namely the idea of *private* vs. *public* transitions [14]. Private transitions were introduced in order to reason about so-called "well-bracketed" state changes, of which the behavior of the stack is a perfect example.

The basic idea is to label local state transitions as either public or private. Functions may make either private or public transitions internally, but viewed extensionally (*i.e.*, end-to-end), they must appear to make a public transition. In the STS that we use to reason about the stack, the states of the STS correspond to the possible states of the stack; every state is accessible from every other state by a private transition, but the only public transitions are self-transitions. This grants logically-related functions plenty of flexibility in how they manipulate the stack, but requires that, when they return, they leave the stack exactly how they found it.

We also use private transitions to reason about callee-save registers, which logically-related functions are expected to return as they found them, even if they modify them internally.

3.6 Reasoning in the Presence of Garbage Collection

Another important detail we have glossed over is how the presence of a garbage collector affects our proof of equivalence of p and e. Let us assume that we are using a standard mark-and-sweep or copying collector. The main effect such a collector has on our reasoning is that, whenever we pass control to the allocator (or to an unknown function that may call the allocator), we need to make sure that (1) all data that we care about being able to access in the future is in the reachable portion of the heap, and (2) there are no dangling pointers in the reachable portion of the heap.

Typically, guaranteeing these two conditions is straightforward. In our example, there is one call to the allocator (at $\mathrm{bg}+2$) and one call to an unknown function (at $\mathrm{bg}+17$). In the case of the former, there is nothing interesting to show. But in the case of the latter, it is important that when we increment the stack pointer before invoking the callback, we set the contents at the top of the stack to a value from which no dangling pointer may be reached. Here, we store in that stack slot the return address $\lfloor \mathrm{wk_0} \rfloor$, which trivially satisfies this requirement.

So at an abstract level, reasoning in the presence of garbage collection is no big deal. What is more interesting is the technical question of how we actually implement this reasoning in the context of our logical relation. The central difficulty is that Kripke logical relations traditionally enjoy a *monotonicity* property, meaning that when two values are related in a world W, they are related in any future world of W. Monotonicity is essential when reasoning about unknown functions, such as the callback argument in our example. There, we were given the assumption that the callback argument was logically related in the world W', but we did not actually invoke it until we had transitioned to the future world W''. This step requires a use of monotonicity to show that the callback argument is still related in W''.

Unfortunately, garbage collection seems superficially to throw a wrench into monotonicity. For instance, in our logical relation we want to be able to relate a **HIGH** pair value $\langle v_1, v_2\rangle$ with a memory location pointing to a representation of that pair value on the heap. How can we expect those two value representations to be related in all future worlds if, at some point in the future, the memory location may get deallocated (or its contents moved by a moving collector) and later reused for storing something else?

Our solution is to employ *logical memories*, which form a layer of abstraction over physical memories. Pointers in a logical memory are never moved or deallocated. Their connection to reality is established by a component of the logical memory called the *lookup table*, which specifies for any given logical pointer whether it is live and, if so, what physical pointer it corresponds to. We say that a logical memory $\mathbf{M}$ *represents* a physical memory Φ only if $\mathbf{M}$'s lookup table describes a bijection between the reachable portions of $\mathbf{M}$ and Φ.

We maintain a global invariant on the logical memory, which must hold before and after calls to the allocator, requiring that all reachable data be live (and thus not dangling) according to the lookup table. Together with the definition of what it means for a logical memory to represent a physical one, this invariant guarantees the allocator's precondition—(2) above—that there are no reachable dangling pointers. After the allocator returns, the lookup table of the logical memory may have completely changed—*e.g.*, due to a semi-space collection—but the only other change to the logical memory will be its extension with a freshly allocated logical pointer. Thus, if any data we care about was reachable prior to allocation—condition (1) above—it will still be reachable post-allocation, and by the global invariant it will also still be live.

With logical memories in hand, we can adapt our logical relations accordingly so that they relate values in **HIGH** with *logical values* (*i.e.*, logical pointers or non-pointer data) in **LOW**. We also define our possible worlds to impose invariants on *logical* memories, not physical ones. In this way, we regain monotonicity, as well as a clean, abstract account of memory locations that gives the garbage collector significant flexibility in how it implements them and allows us to essentially ignore how it does so.

4. A Language-Generic Kripke Logical Relation

Figure 3 defines a Kripke logical relation between two languages that is parameterized by abstract specifications for those languages ($\in$ LangSpec), as well as by a specification for the possible worlds relating the memories of those languages ($\in$ WorldSpec).

4.1 Language Specifications

A language specification (upper left of Figure 3) must provide sets of values (Val), computations (Com), continuations (Cont), memories (Mem), and configurations (Conf), together with a number of operations on these sets. (Note that we are assuming here a standard stratification on sets, and that Val, Com, etc. are "smaller" than LangSpec.) Most of these operations take elements of some of these sets and return a predicate on another of the sets. In most cases, this is because there may be a number of different representations of the same thing—*e.g.*, in **LOW**, a pair value $\langle v_1, v_2\rangle$ is represented by a pointer that satisfies some conditions, but many pointers may satisfy those conditions.

"plugv" forms a configuration by plugging a value into a continuation under a given memory. "plugc" does the same, but plugging a computation instead of a value. "step" executes a configuration for one step of computation, resulting in either a new configuration, termination (*halt*), or failure (*fail*). "mdom" returns the domain of a memory, and "mdisj" takes two memories and returns a memory that contains their disjoint union, if it exists.

"oftype(τ)" determines whether a value is considered syntactically to have type τ under a certain memory. In our specification for **HIGH**, we include heap typings Σ in memories in order to define this predicate at ref type. For **LOW**, there is no notion of syntactic typing, but we find oftype convenient for expressing assumptions about the "syntactic" structure of closures (see Section 5).

$$
\begin{aligned}
&\mathrm{CType} \overset{\mathrm{def}}{=} \{\, \tau \mid \mathrm{ftv}(\tau) = \emptyset \,\}\\[4pt]
&\mathrm{LangSpec} \overset{\mathrm{def}}{=}\\
&\{\, (\mathrm{Val}, \mathrm{Com}, \mathrm{Cont}, \mathrm{Mem}, \mathrm{Conf},\\
&\quad \mathrm{plugv}, \mathrm{plugc}, \mathrm{step}, \mathrm{mdom}, \mathrm{mdisj},\\
&\quad \mathrm{oftype}, \mathrm{base}_b, \mathrm{pair}, \mathrm{app}, \mathrm{appty},\\
&\quad \mathrm{pack}, \mathrm{roll}, \mathrm{ref}, \mathrm{asgn}) \mid\\
&\quad \mathrm{Val}, \mathrm{Com}, \mathrm{Cont}, \mathrm{Mem}, \mathrm{Conf} \in \mathrm{Set} \;\wedge\\
&\quad \mathrm{plugv} \in \mathrm{Val} \times \mathrm{Cont} \times \mathrm{Mem} \to \mathbb{P}(\mathrm{Conf}) \;\wedge\\
&\quad \mathrm{plugc} \in \mathrm{Com} \times \mathrm{Cont} \times \mathrm{Mem} \to \mathbb{P}(\mathrm{Conf}) \;\wedge\\
&\quad \mathrm{step} \in \mathrm{Conf} \to \mathrm{Conf} \uplus \{\, \mathit{fail}, \mathit{halt} \,\} \;\wedge\\
&\quad \mathrm{mdom} \in \mathrm{Mem} \to \mathbb{P}(\mathrm{Val}) \;\wedge\\
&\quad \mathrm{mdisj} \in \mathrm{Mem} \times \mathrm{Mem} \to \mathbb{P}(\mathrm{Mem}) \;\wedge\\
&\quad \mathrm{oftype} \in \mathrm{CType} \to \mathbb{P}(\mathrm{Val} \times \mathrm{Mem}) \;\wedge\\
&\quad \mathrm{base}_b \in \llbracket b \rrbracket \to \mathbb{P}(\mathrm{Val} \times \mathrm{Mem}) \;\wedge\\
&\quad \mathrm{pair} \in \mathrm{Val} \times \mathrm{Val} \to \mathbb{P}(\mathrm{Val} \times \mathrm{Mem}) \;\wedge\\
&\quad \mathrm{app} \in \mathrm{Val} \times \mathrm{Val} \to \mathbb{P}(\mathrm{Com}) \;\wedge\\
&\quad \mathrm{appty} \in \mathrm{Val} \times \mathrm{CType} \to \mathbb{P}(\mathrm{Com}) \;\wedge\\
&\quad \mathrm{pack} \in \mathrm{CType} \times \mathrm{Val} \to \mathbb{P}(\mathrm{Val} \times \mathrm{Mem}) \;\wedge\\
&\quad \mathrm{roll} \in \mathrm{Val} \to \mathbb{P}(\mathrm{Val} \times \mathrm{Mem}) \;\wedge\\
&\quad \mathrm{ref} \in \mathrm{Val} \to \mathbb{P}(\mathrm{Val} \times \mathrm{Mem}) \;\wedge\\
&\quad \mathrm{asgn} \in \mathrm{Mem} \times \mathrm{Val} \times \mathrm{Val} \rightharpoonup \mathrm{Mem} \;\wedge\\
&\quad \forall M_1, M_2.\, \forall M \in \mathrm{mdisj}(M_1, M_2).\\
&\qquad \mathrm{mdom}(M) \supseteq \mathrm{mdom}(M_1) \uplus \mathrm{mdom}(M_2) \,\}
\end{aligned}
$$

For $\mathcal{L}_1, \mathcal{L}_2 \in \mathrm{LangSpec}$,

$$
\begin{aligned}
&\mathrm{WorldSpec} \overset{\mathrm{def}}{=}\\
&\{\, (\mathrm{World}, \mathrm{lev}, \mathcal{M}, \mathcal{B}, \mathcal{O}, \triangleright, \sqsupseteq, \sqsupseteq_{\mathrm{pub}}) \mid\\
&\quad \mathrm{World} \in \mathrm{Set} \;\wedge\\
&\quad \mathrm{lev} \in \mathrm{World} \to \mathbb{N} \;\wedge\\
&\quad \mathcal{M} \in \mathrm{World} \to \mathbb{P}(\mathcal{L}_1.\mathrm{Mem} \times \mathcal{L}_2.\mathrm{Mem}) \;\wedge\\
&\quad \mathcal{B} \in \mathrm{World} \to \mathbb{P}(\mathcal{L}_1.\mathrm{Val} \times \mathcal{L}_2.\mathrm{Val}) \;\wedge\\
&\quad \mathcal{O} \in \mathrm{World} \to \mathbb{P}(\mathcal{L}_1.\mathrm{Conf} \times \mathcal{L}_2.\mathrm{Conf}) \;\wedge\\
&\quad \triangleright \in \mathrm{World} \to \mathrm{World} \;\wedge\\
&\quad \sqsupseteq \in \mathbb{P}(\mathrm{World} \times \mathrm{World}) \;\wedge\\
&\quad \sqsupseteq_{\mathrm{pub}} \in \mathbb{P}(\mathrm{World} \times \mathrm{World}) \;\wedge\\
&\quad \sqsupseteq, \sqsupseteq_{\mathrm{pub}} \text{ are preorders} \wedge \sqsupseteq_{\mathrm{pub}} \subseteq \sqsupseteq \;\wedge\\
&\quad \forall W' \sqsupseteq W.\, \triangleright W' \sqsupseteq \triangleright W \;\wedge\\
&\quad \forall W' \sqsupseteq_{\mathrm{pub}} W.\, \triangleright W' \sqsupseteq_{\mathrm{pub}} \triangleright W \;\wedge\\
&\quad \forall W.\, \triangleright W \sqsupseteq_{\mathrm{pub}} W \;\wedge\\
&\quad \forall W' \sqsupseteq W.\, \mathrm{lev}(W') \le \mathrm{lev}(W) \;\wedge\\
&\quad \forall W.\, \mathrm{lev}(W) > 0 \implies \mathrm{lev}(\triangleright W) = \mathrm{lev}(W) - 1 \,\}
\end{aligned}
$$

$$
\begin{aligned}
\sqsupset_{\triangleright} &\overset{\mathrm{def}}{=} \{\, (W', W) \mid \mathrm{lev}(W) > 0 \wedge W' \sqsupseteq \triangleright W \,\}\\
\mathrm{WVRel} &\overset{\mathrm{def}}{=} \{\, R \in \mathbb{P}(\mathrm{World} \times \mathcal{L}_1.\mathrm{Val} \times \mathcal{L}_2.\mathrm{Val}) \,\}\\
R(W) &\overset{\mathrm{def}}{=} \{\, (\mathbf{v}_1, v_2) \mid (W, \mathbf{v}_1, v_2) \in R \,\}\\
\triangleright R &\overset{\mathrm{def}}{=} \{\, (W, \mathbf{v}_1, v_2) \mid \mathrm{lev}(W) > 0 \implies (\triangleright W, \mathbf{v}_1, v_2) \in R \,\}\\
\Box R &\overset{\mathrm{def}}{=} \{\, (W, \mathbf{v}_1, v_2) \mid \forall W' \sqsupseteq W.\, (W', \mathbf{v}_1, v_2) \in R \,\}\\
R_{\sqsupset_{\triangleright} W} &\overset{\mathrm{def}}{=} \{\, (W', \mathbf{v}_1, v_2) \mid W' \sqsupset_{\triangleright} W \wedge (W', \mathbf{v}_1, v_2) \in R \,\}\\
\overline{(R_1, R_2)} &\overset{\mathrm{def}}{=} \{\, (W, \mathbf{v}_1, v_2) \mid \forall (\mathbf{M}_1, M_2) \in \mathcal{M}(W).\, (\mathbf{v}_1, \mathbf{M}_1) \in R_1 \wedge (v_2, M_2) \in R_2 \,\}\\
&\quad \text{for } R_1 \in \mathbb{P}(\mathcal{L}_1.\mathrm{Val} \times \mathcal{L}_1.\mathrm{Mem}), R_2 \in \mathbb{P}(\mathcal{L}_2.\mathrm{Val} \times \mathcal{L}_2.\mathrm{Mem})\\
\mathrm{TyValRel} &\overset{\mathrm{def}}{=} \{\, (\tau_1, \tau_2, R) \mid \tau_1, \tau_2 \in \mathrm{CType} \wedge R \in \mathrm{WVRel} \,\}\\
\rho &\in \mathrm{TypeVar} \rightharpoonup \mathrm{TyValRel}\\
\rho.1(\tau) &\overset{\mathrm{def}}{=} \tau[\rho(\alpha).\tau_1/\alpha] \qquad\qquad \rho.2(\tau) \overset{\mathrm{def}}{=} \tau[\rho(\alpha).\tau_2/\alpha]\\
\mathrm{oftype}(\tau, \rho) &\overset{\mathrm{def}}{=} \Box\overline{(\mathcal{L}_1.\mathrm{oftype}(\rho.1(\tau)), \mathcal{L}_2.\mathrm{oftype}(\rho.2(\tau)))}\\
\mathcal{V}\llbracket \alpha \rrbracket\rho &\overset{\mathrm{def}}{=} \{\, (W, \mathbf{v}_1, v_2) \in \mathrm{oftype}(\alpha, \rho) \mid (W, \mathbf{v}_1, v_2) \in \Box\rho(\alpha).R \,\}\\
\mathcal{V}\llbracket b \rrbracket\rho &\overset{\mathrm{def}}{=} \{\, (W, \mathbf{v}_1, v_2) \in \mathrm{oftype}(b, \rho) \mid \exists x \in \llbracket b \rrbracket.\\
&\qquad (W, \mathbf{v}_1, v_2) \in \Box\overline{(\mathcal{L}_1.\mathrm{base}_b(x), \mathcal{L}_2.\mathrm{base}_b(x))} \,\}\\
\mathcal{V}\llbracket \tau \times \tau' \rrbracket\rho &\overset{\mathrm{def}}{=} \{\, (W, \mathbf{v}_1, v_2) \in \mathrm{oftype}(\tau \times \tau', \rho) \mid\\
&\qquad \exists (\mathbf{u}_1, u_2) \in \triangleright\mathcal{V}\llbracket \tau \rrbracket\rho(W).\, \exists (\mathbf{u}'_1, u'_2) \in \triangleright\mathcal{V}\llbracket \tau' \rrbracket\rho(W).\\
&\qquad (W, \mathbf{v}_1, v_2) \in \Box\overline{(\mathcal{L}_1.\mathrm{pair}(\mathbf{u}_1, \mathbf{u}'_1), \mathcal{L}_2.\mathrm{pair}(u_2, u'_2))} \,\}\\
\mathcal{V}\llbracket \tau' \to \tau \rrbracket\rho &\overset{\mathrm{def}}{=} \{\, (W, \mathbf{v}_1, v_2) \in \mathrm{oftype}(\tau' \to \tau, \rho) \mid \forall W' \sqsupset_{\triangleright} W.\, \forall (\mathbf{u}_1, u_2) \in \mathcal{V}\llbracket \tau' \rrbracket\rho(W').\\
&\qquad \forall \mathbf{e}_1 \in \mathcal{L}_1.\mathrm{app}(\mathbf{v}_1, \mathbf{u}_1).\, \forall e_2 \in \mathcal{L}_2.\mathrm{app}(v_2, u_2).\, (W', \mathbf{e}_1, e_2) \in \mathcal{E}\llbracket \tau \rrbracket\rho \,\}\\
\mathcal{V}\llbracket \forall\alpha.\, \tau \rrbracket\rho &\overset{\mathrm{def}}{=} \{\, (W, \mathbf{v}_1, v_2) \in \mathrm{oftype}(\forall\alpha.\, \tau, \rho) \mid \forall W' \sqsupset_{\triangleright} W.\, \forall (\tau_1, \tau_2, R) \in \mathrm{TyValRel}.\\
&\qquad \forall \mathbf{e}_1 \in \mathcal{L}_1.\mathrm{appty}(\mathbf{v}_1, \tau_1).\, \forall e_2 \in \mathcal{L}_2.\mathrm{appty}(v_2, \tau_2).\\
&\qquad (W', \mathbf{e}_1, e_2) \in \mathcal{E}\llbracket \tau \rrbracket\rho[\alpha \mapsto (\tau_1, \tau_2, R)] \,\}\\
\mathcal{V}\llbracket \exists\alpha.\, \tau \rrbracket\rho &\overset{\mathrm{def}}{=} \{\, (W, \mathbf{v}_1, v_2) \in \mathrm{oftype}(\exists\alpha.\, \tau, \rho) \mid\\
&\qquad \exists (\tau_1, \tau_2, R) \in \mathrm{TyValRel}.\, \exists (\mathbf{u}_1, u_2) \in \mathcal{V}\llbracket \tau \rrbracket\rho[\alpha \mapsto (\tau_1, \tau_2, R)](W).\\
&\qquad (W, \mathbf{v}_1, v_2) \in \Box\overline{(\mathcal{L}_1.\mathrm{pack}(\tau_1, \mathbf{u}_1), \mathcal{L}_2.\mathrm{pack}(\tau_2, u_2))} \,\}\\
\mathcal{V}\llbracket \mathsf{ref}\,\tau \rrbracket\rho &\overset{\mathrm{def}}{=} \{\, (W, \mathbf{v}_1, v_2) \in \mathrm{oftype}(\mathsf{ref}\,\tau, \rho) \mid \forall W' \sqsupseteq W.\, \forall (\mathbf{M}_1, M_2) \in \mathcal{M}(W').\\
&\quad (\mathbf{v}_1, v_2) \in \mathcal{B}(W') \;\wedge\\
&\quad \big(\exists (\mathbf{u}_1, u_2) \in \triangleright\mathcal{V}\llbracket \tau \rrbracket\rho(W').\, (\mathbf{v}_1, \mathbf{M}_1) \in \mathcal{L}_1.\mathrm{ref}(\mathbf{u}_1) \wedge (v_2, M_2) \in \mathcal{L}_2.\mathrm{ref}(u_2)\big) \;\wedge\\
&\quad \big(\forall (\mathbf{u}_1, u_2) \in \triangleright\mathcal{V}\llbracket \tau \rrbracket\rho(W').\, (\mathcal{L}_1.\mathrm{asgn}(\mathbf{M}_1, \mathbf{v}_1, \mathbf{u}_1), \mathcal{L}_2.\mathrm{asgn}(M_2, v_2, u_2)) \in \mathcal{M}(W')\big) \}\\
\mathcal{V}\llbracket \mu\alpha.\, \tau \rrbracket\rho &\overset{\mathrm{def}}{=} \mu(F_{\alpha,\tau,\rho})\\
F_{\alpha,\tau,\rho} &\overset{\mathrm{def}}{=} \lambda R.\, \{\, (W, \mathbf{v}_1, v_2) \in \mathrm{oftype}(\mu\alpha.\, \tau, \rho) \mid\\
&\qquad\quad \exists (\mathbf{u}_1, u_2) \in \mathcal{V}\llbracket \tau \rrbracket\rho[\alpha \mapsto (\rho.1(\mu\alpha.\, \tau), \rho.2(\mu\alpha.\, \tau), R)](W).\\
&\qquad\quad (W, \mathbf{v}_1, v_2) \in \Box\overline{(\mathcal{L}_1.\mathrm{roll}(\mathbf{u}_1), \mathcal{L}_2.\mathrm{roll}(u_2))} \,\}\\
\mu(F)(W) &\overset{\mathrm{def}}{=} F(\mu(F)_{\sqsupset_{\triangleright} W})(W)\\
\mathcal{K}\llbracket \tau \rrbracket\rho &\overset{\mathrm{def}}{=} \{\, (W, \mathbf{K}_1, K_2) \in \mathrm{World} \times \mathcal{L}_1.\mathrm{Cont} \times \mathcal{L}_2.\mathrm{Cont} \mid \forall W' \sqsupseteq_{\mathrm{pub}} W.\\
&\qquad \forall (\mathbf{v}_1, v_2) \in \mathcal{V}\llbracket \tau \rrbracket\rho(W').\, \forall (\mathbf{M}_1, M_2) \in \mathcal{M}(W').\\
&\qquad \forall C_1 \in \mathcal{L}_1.\mathrm{plugv}(\mathbf{v}_1, \mathbf{K}_1, \mathbf{M}_1).\, \forall C_2 \in \mathcal{L}_2.\mathrm{plugv}(v_2, K_2, M_2).\\
&\qquad (C_1, C_2) \in \mathcal{O}(W') \,\}\\
\mathcal{E}\llbracket \tau \rrbracket\rho &\overset{\mathrm{def}}{=} \{\, (W, \mathbf{e}_1, e_2) \in \mathrm{World} \times \mathcal{L}_1.\mathrm{Com} \times \mathcal{L}_2.\mathrm{Com} \mid\\
&\qquad \forall (\mathbf{K}_1, K_2) \in \mathcal{K}\llbracket \tau \rrbracket\rho(W).\, \forall (\mathbf{M}_1, M_2) \in \mathcal{M}(W).\\
&\qquad \forall C_1 \in \mathcal{L}_1.\mathrm{plugc}(\mathbf{e}_1, \mathbf{K}_1, \mathbf{M}_1).\, \forall C_2 \in \mathcal{L}_2.\mathrm{plugc}(e_2, K_2, M_2).\\
&\qquad (C_1, C_2) \in \mathcal{O}(W) \,\}
\end{aligned}
$$

Figure 3. Language Specifications, World Specifications, and a Language-Generic Kripke Logical Relation

The remaining operations define the various syntactic language forms that are referenced in the definition of the logical relation. One point of note: determining whether a value represents a particular canonical form may require one to consider an accompanying memory. It is easy to see why—*e.g.*, one cannot determine if a pointer to a pair of heap cells represents $\langle v_1, v_2 \rangle$ without inspecting the heap. Determining whether a computation represents a function application also may require inspecting the memory, but we have found it technically more convenient to assume that any memory inspection is somehow built into the notion of computation (see Section 5 to see how this works in the **LOW** specification).

4.2 World Specifications

A world specification (lower left of Figure 3) defines a set of possible worlds relating the memories of two languages specified by $\mathcal{L}_1$ and $\mathcal{L}_2$, together with a variety of operations on and relations indexed by those worlds. In order to understand some of these, it is necessary to first say a word about our use of *step-indexing*.

Appel and McAllester [3] introduced step-indexing in order to model recursive types in foundational proof-carrying code. The basic idea is to use a natural number index ("step level") to stratify what would otherwise be a circular construction. Step-indexing has also proven useful in modeling other semantically circular notions like higher-order state, which is how we use them here. Due to space considerations, since our step-indexed construction follows closely that of [2] and [14], we refer the interested reader to those previous works for the relevant background.

In the world specification, the important step-indexing-related bits are the lev function, which returns the step level of a given world, and the $\triangleright$ (pronounced "later") operator, which returns an approximated version of the given world at one lower step level. We use $\triangleright$ to ensure well-foundedness of the logical relation.

"$\mathcal{M}(W)$" is the memory relation associated with W, which specifies when two memories (from $\mathcal{L}_1$ and $\mathcal{L}_2$) satisfy the constraints of the STS's in W. "$\mathcal{B}(W)$" is a bijection on values representing memory locations in $\mathcal{L}_1$ and $\mathcal{L}_2$. This is used in defining the logical relation for ref type. "$\mathcal{O}(W)$" is an observation relation on configurations. For the possible worlds we employ in this paper, $\mathcal{O}(W)$ actually only depends on $\mathrm{lev}(W)$, and it is defined to relate configurations that either both terminate (without failure) or that both run for at least $\mathrm{lev}(W)$ steps of computation. When we prove that two programs are logically related, we will prove it in starting worlds of an arbitrary step level, thus ensuring that the programs are observably equivalent for arbitrarily many computation steps.

Finally, "$\sqsupseteq$" defines the general "future world" relation between worlds, and "$\sqsupseteq_{\mathrm{pub}}$" defines a restricted "public" version of that relation: if $W' \sqsupseteq_{\mathrm{pub}} W$, then for any STS in W, the new state of that STS in W' must be accessible from its old state in W only by public transitions (see Section 3.5). Both $\sqsupseteq$ and $\sqsupseteq_{\mathrm{pub}}$ are preorders.

4.3 Kripke Logical Relation

The right side of Figure 3 displays our Kripke logical relation, whose definition is parametric w.r.t. $\mathcal{L}_1$, $\mathcal{L}_2$, and an instance of WorldSpec thereon. In the definition, we adopt the convention that the entities (values, continuations, etc.) from $\mathcal{L}_1$ appear in boldface ($\mathbf{v}$, $\mathbf{K}$, etc.) and the entities from $\mathcal{L}_2$ appear in italics (v, K, etc.). The coincidence of the notation for $\mathcal{L}_2$ entities with the notation for the corresponding entities from **HIGH** is deliberate, for in the next section we will instantiate $\mathcal{L}_1$ and $\mathcal{L}_2$ with our specifications for **LOW** and **HIGH**, respectively. We abuse notation in this way in order to avoid the proliferation of more than two fonts.

Our logical relation is based very closely on Dreyer *et al.*'s [14], with the principal difference being that the relevant linguistic forms have been abstracted away in the language specifications $\mathcal{L}_1$ and $\mathcal{L}_2$. For instance, in the logical relation for arrow types, we do not construct the applications $\mathbf{v}_1\mathbf{u}_1$ and v_2u_2 directly, since $\mathcal{L}_1$ and $\mathcal{L}_2$ may not include an explicit application construct. Rather, we quantify over arbitrary computations $\mathbf{e}_1$ and e_2 drawn from $\mathcal{L}_1.\mathrm{app}(\mathbf{v}_1, \mathbf{u}_1)$ and $\mathcal{L}_2.\mathrm{app}(v_2, u_2)$, respectively.

The logical relation consists of a relation for values ($\mathcal{V}[\![\tau]\!]\rho$), one for continuations ($\mathcal{K}[\![\tau]\!]\rho$), and one for computations ($\mathcal{E}[\![\tau]\!]\rho$). Here, we assume that ρ is a relational interpretation of the free variables of τ, mapping them to arbitrary world-indexed value relations. For $\tau = \alpha$, $\mathcal{V}[\![\tau]\!]\rho$ is defined as the restriction of $\rho(\alpha)$ to triples $(W, \mathbf{v}_1, v_2)$ where $\mathbf{v}_1$ and v_2 are "well-typed" (according to $\mathcal{L}_i.\mathrm{oftype}$) and continue to be related in all future worlds of W. This last part, which is specified using the $\Box R$ operator defined at the top right of the figure, is key to ensuring monotonicity of the value relation. The pair and existential cases of the value relation also use the $\Box R$ operator in order to ensure monotonicity of data representations—*e.g.,* that if $\mathbf{v}_1$ represents a pair of $\mathbf{u}_1$ and $\mathbf{u}'_1$, it will continue to do so in all future worlds.

As in Appel *et al.* [4], the interpretation of recursive types is defined by induction on the "strictly future world" relation $\sqsupset_{\triangleright}$. This relation is well-founded because $W' \sqsupset_{\triangleright} W$ implies that W' has a lower step level than W. By defining the recursive type case this way, we can relate **HIGH** programs, where roll and unroll are explicit coercions, to **LOW** programs where they have been erased.

The ref type case relates two memory locations if dereferencing, assigning and testing them for pointer equality will always produce related results. The condition on pointer equality testing is guaranteed by the requirement that the locations be in the bijection of the world in which they are related.

The value relation is lifted to a relation on computations by the technique of *biorthogonality* (aka $\top\top$*-closure*) [22, 17]. The idea is to define two computations to be related if they behave in an observably equivalent manner when plugged into related continuations. Two continuations are in turn related if they behave in an observably equivalent manner when plugged with related values. By quantifying only over public future worlds in the definition of $\mathcal{K}[\![\tau]\!]\rho$, we ensure that computations may only make public transitions when viewed end-to-end, as per the discussion in Section 3.5.

This mind-bending technique is well-suited to languages where the evaluation of a computation is *context-sensitive* in the sense that it cannot be performed in ignorance of its continuation. Such is the case with **LOW**, where a computation always ends with a jump to its return address. As we shall see, the fact that the return address really is a valid return address, which is part of the contract between computation and continuation, will be encoded in the **LOW** implementation of plugc that we define in Section 5.

5. Implementing the Specifications

In order to instantiate our logical relations to relate **LOW** and **HIGH** entities, we must first show how to implement the abstract LangSpec interface for both languages.

For **HIGH**, the implementation of the interface is almost entirely straightforward, as all the required entities (values, computations) have direct correspondents in the **HIGH** language. The only slightly unusual bit is that we define **HIGH** memories to be pairs of heaps *and* heap typings Σ. The inclusion of the heap typing is necessary for defining oftype. For the remaining details, please see the companion technical appendix [15].

Low-Level Entities The implementation of LangSpec for **LOW** (Figure 4) is much more interesting. As described in Section 3.6, we employ a notion of *logical values* $\mathbf{v}$, which are either non-pointer words $\underline{w}$ or logical pointers $\widehat{l}$. Logical Lvalues are similar to physical PLvalues except that logical Lvalues include logical heap locations $\langle l : o\rangle_{\mathrm{h}}$ in place of physical ones $\langle a\rangle_{\mathrm{h}}$. We include the offset o because the logical heap is (for convenience) modeled two-dimensionally as a list of blocks.

LOW computations $\mathbf{e}$ are 4-tuples $(\mathrm{cpc}, \mathrm{kpc}, \mathrm{vloc}, \mathrm{data})$, where: cpc is the code address where the computation begins, kpc is the return address, vloc is the Lvalue where the return value will be stored, and data is a memory predicate that must be satisfied in order for the computation to be correctly executed. **LOW** continuations $\mathbf{K}$ are pairs $(\mathrm{kpc}, \mathrm{vloc})$, where: kpc is the code address where the continuation begins, and vloc is the Lvalue where the input to the continuation should be placed. It is worth noting that, unlike $\mathbf{e}.\mathrm{cpc}$ and $\mathbf{e}.\mathrm{kpc}$, the kpc in $\mathbf{K}$ must be a code address, not an Rvalue, because when we plug an $\mathbf{e}$ into a $\mathbf{K}$, we need to know that the value of $\mathbf{K}.\mathrm{kpc}$ will be the same before and after the execution of $\mathbf{e}$. Were $\mathbf{K}.\mathrm{kpc}$ an Rvalue, we would not know that.

Logical memories $\mathbf{M}$ are 6-tuples $(\mathrm{code}, \mathrm{reg}, \mathrm{stk}, \mathrm{hp}, \mathrm{tab}, \mathrm{shp})$, where: code is the code segment, reg is the register file (minus sp since it is determined by the size of the stack), stk is the stack, hp is the heap, tab is the lookup table (described in Section 3.6), and shp is the *system heap*, which is a separate portion of the heap controlled by the runtime system. The lookup table maps each logical pointer to a physical pointer and the size of the memory block starting at that address. The pointer is live iff the size is > 0. Note that reg, stk, and hp are all maps from various Lvalues to *logical* values, whereas the tab and shp are maps to physical values. In the proofs, we end up treating tab and shp as essentially black boxes, since they can be changed at whim by the allocator, whereas the allocator should not mess around with the logical portion of the memory represented by reg, stk, and hp.

Lastly, note that reg, stk, tab, and shp may all be undefined (undef). This is a useful technical device for defining the disjoint union of several partial memories: it enables us to specify that only one of those partial memories contains information about, say, the stack. (See the definition of "mdisj" below.)

Low-Level Representations of High-Level Constructs The bottom left of Figure 4 defines **LOW** representations of various high-level constructs, as required by the LangSpec interface. A pair of $\mathbf{v}_1$ and $\mathbf{v}_2$ is represented as a pointer to a pair of cells containing $\mathbf{v}_1$

$$
\begin{array}{lll}
\text{Loc} & \stackrel{\text{def}}{=} & \{\, \boldsymbol{l} \in \mathbb{N} \,\} \\
\text{Word} & \stackrel{\text{def}}{=} & \{\, w \in \mathbb{N} \,\} \\
\mathbf{v} \in \text{Val} & ::= & \underline{w} \mid \widehat{\boldsymbol{l}} \\
\text{lv} \in \text{Lvalue} & ::= & \lfloor r \rfloor \mid \langle a \rangle_{\text{s}} \mid \langle r - o \rangle_{\text{s}} \mid \langle \boldsymbol{l} : o \rangle_{\text{h}} \mid \langle r + o \rangle_{\text{h}} \\
\text{rv} \in \text{Rvalue} & ::= & \text{lv} \mid \mathbf{v} \\
\text{Com} & \stackrel{\text{def}}{=} & \{\, \mathbf{e} = (\text{cpc}, \text{kpc}, \text{vloc}, \text{data}) \\
 & & \quad \in \text{Rvalue} \times \text{Rvalue} \times \text{Lvalue} \times \mathbb{P}(\text{Mem}) \,\} \\
\text{Cont} & \stackrel{\text{def}}{=} & \{\, \mathbf{K} = (\text{kpc}, \text{vloc}) \in \text{PAddr} \times \text{Lvalue} \,\} \\
\text{CodeFrag} & \stackrel{\text{def}}{=} & \text{PAddr} \rightharpoonup_{\text{fin}} \text{Instruction} \\
\text{RegFile} & \stackrel{\text{def}}{=} & (\text{Register} \setminus \{\text{sp}\} \to \text{Val}) \uplus \{\, \text{undef} \,\} \\
\text{List } X & \stackrel{\text{def}}{=} & \{\, (x_0, \ldots, x_{n-1}) \mid n \in \mathbb{N} \wedge x_0, \ldots, x_{n-1} \in X \,\} \\
\text{Stack} & \stackrel{\text{def}}{=} & \text{List Val} \uplus \{\, \text{undef} \,\} \\
\text{Heap} & \stackrel{\text{def}}{=} & \text{Loc} \rightharpoonup_{\text{fin}} \text{List Val} \\
\text{Table} & \stackrel{\text{def}}{=} & (\text{Loc} \rightharpoonup_{\text{fin}} \mathbb{N} \times \text{PAddr}) \uplus \{\, \text{undef} \,\} \\
\text{SysHeap} & \stackrel{\text{def}}{=} & (\text{PAddr} \rightharpoonup \text{Word}) \uplus \{\, \text{undef} \,\} \\
\text{Mem} & \stackrel{\text{def}}{=} & \{\, \mathbf{M} = (\text{code}, \text{reg}, \text{stk}, \text{hp}, \text{tab}, \text{shp}) \\
 & & \quad \in \text{CodeFrag} \times \text{RegFile} \times \text{Stack} \times \text{Heap} \times \text{Table} \times \text{SysHeap} \,\} \\
\text{Conf} & \stackrel{\text{def}}{=} & \text{PConf} \\
\text{oftype}(\tau) & \stackrel{\text{def}}{=} & \{\, (\mathbf{v}, \mathbf{M}) \in \text{Val} \times \text{Mem} \mid \\
 & & \quad \forall \tau_1, \tau_2.\ \tau = \tau_1 \to \tau_2 \implies \exists \boldsymbol{l}, w.\ \mathbf{v} = \widehat{\boldsymbol{l}} \wedge \mathbf{M}.\text{hp}(\boldsymbol{l})(0) = \underline{w} \wedge \\
 & & \quad \forall \alpha, \tau'.\ \tau = \forall \alpha.\, \tau' \implies \exists \boldsymbol{l}, w.\ \mathbf{v} = \widehat{\boldsymbol{l}} \wedge \mathbf{M}.\text{hp}(\boldsymbol{l})(0) = \underline{w} \,\} \\
\text{base}_b(x) & \stackrel{\text{def}}{=} & \{\, (\mathbf{v}, \mathbf{M}) \in \text{Val} \times \text{Mem} \mid \mathbf{v} \text{ is a representation of } x \,\} \\
\text{pair}(\mathbf{v}_1, \mathbf{v}_2) & \stackrel{\text{def}}{=} & \{\, (\mathbf{v}, \mathbf{M}) \in \text{Val} \times \text{Mem} \mid \exists \boldsymbol{l}.\ \mathbf{v} = \widehat{\boldsymbol{l}} \wedge \\
 & & \quad \mathbf{M}.\text{hp}(\boldsymbol{l})(0) = \mathbf{v}_1 \wedge \mathbf{M}.\text{hp}(\boldsymbol{l})(1) = \mathbf{v}_2 \,\} \\
\text{app}(\mathbf{v}_1, \mathbf{v}_2) & \stackrel{\text{def}}{=} & \{\, \mathbf{e} \in \text{Com} \mid \exists \boldsymbol{l}.\ \mathbf{v}_1 = \widehat{\boldsymbol{l}} \wedge \\
 & & \quad \mathbf{e}.\text{cpc} = \langle \boldsymbol{l} : 0 \rangle_{\text{h}} \wedge \mathbf{e}.\text{kpc} = \lfloor \text{wk}_0 \rfloor \wedge \mathbf{e}.\text{vloc} = \lfloor \text{wk}_5 \rfloor \wedge \\
 & & \quad \mathbf{e}.\text{data} = \{\, \mathbf{M} \in \text{Mem} \mid \mathbf{M}.\text{reg}(\text{wk}_1) = \mathbf{v}_1 \wedge \mathbf{M}.\text{reg}(\text{wk}_2) = \mathbf{v}_2 \,\} \,\} \\
\text{appty}(\mathbf{v}, \tau) & \stackrel{\text{def}}{=} & \{\, \mathbf{e} \in \text{Com} \mid \exists \boldsymbol{l}.\ \mathbf{v} = \widehat{\boldsymbol{l}} \wedge \\
 & & \quad \mathbf{e}.\text{cpc} = \langle \boldsymbol{l} : 0 \rangle_{\text{h}} \wedge \mathbf{e}.\text{kpc} = \lfloor \text{wk}_0 \rfloor \wedge \mathbf{e}.\text{vloc} = \lfloor \text{wk}_5 \rfloor \wedge \\
 & & \quad \mathbf{e}.\text{data} = \{\, \mathbf{M} \in \text{Mem} \mid \mathbf{M}.\text{reg}(\text{wk}_1) = \mathbf{v} \,\} \,\} \\
\text{pack}(\tau, \mathbf{v}) & \stackrel{\text{def}}{=} & \{\, (\mathbf{v}', \mathbf{M}) \in \text{Val} \times \text{Mem} \mid \mathbf{v}' = \mathbf{v} \,\} \\
\text{roll}(\mathbf{v}) & \stackrel{\text{def}}{=} & \{\, (\mathbf{v}', \mathbf{M}) \in \text{Val} \times \text{Mem} \mid \mathbf{v}' = \mathbf{v} \,\} \\
\text{ref}(\mathbf{v}) & \stackrel{\text{def}}{=} & \{\, (\mathbf{v}', \mathbf{M}) \in \text{Val} \times \text{Mem} \mid \exists \boldsymbol{l}.\ \mathbf{v}' = \widehat{\boldsymbol{l}} \wedge \mathbf{M}.\text{hp}(\boldsymbol{l})(0) = \mathbf{v} \,\} \\
\text{asgn}(\mathbf{M}, \mathbf{v}_1, \mathbf{v}_2) & \stackrel{\text{def}}{=} & \begin{cases} \mathbf{M}[\boldsymbol{l} : 0 \mapsto \mathbf{v}_2]_{\text{hp}} & \text{if } \mathbf{v}_1 = \widehat{\boldsymbol{l}} \wedge |\mathbf{M}.\text{hp}(\boldsymbol{l})| > 0 \\ \text{undef} & \text{otherwise} \end{cases}
\end{array}
$$

$$
\begin{array}{lll}
|\mathbf{v}| & \stackrel{\text{def}}{=} & \begin{cases} w & \text{if } \mathbf{v} = \underline{w} \\ \boldsymbol{l} & \text{if } \mathbf{v} = \widehat{\boldsymbol{l}} \end{cases} \\
\mathbf{M}(\mathbf{v}) & \stackrel{\text{def}}{=} & \mathbf{v} \qquad \mathbf{M}(\lfloor r \rfloor) \stackrel{\text{def}}{=} \mathbf{M}.\text{reg}(r) \\
\mathbf{M}(\langle a \rangle_{\text{s}}) & \stackrel{\text{def}}{=} & \mathbf{M}.\text{stk}(a) \qquad \mathbf{M}(\langle r - o \rangle_{\text{s}}) \stackrel{\text{def}}{=} \mathbf{M}.\text{stk}(|\mathbf{M}.\text{reg}(r)| - o) \\
\mathbf{M}(\langle \boldsymbol{l} : o \rangle_{\text{h}}) & \stackrel{\text{def}}{=} & \mathbf{M}.\text{hp}(\boldsymbol{l})(o) \qquad \mathbf{M}(\langle r + o \rangle_{\text{h}}) \stackrel{\text{def}}{=} \mathbf{M}.\text{hp}(|\mathbf{M}.\text{reg}(r)|)(o) \\
\mathbf{M}[[T, S]] & \stackrel{\text{def}}{=} & (\mathbf{M}.\text{code}, \mathbf{M}.\text{reg}, \mathbf{M}.\text{stk}, \mathbf{M}.\text{hp}, T, S) \\
\mathbf{M}[\boldsymbol{l} : o \mapsto \mathbf{v}]_{\text{hp}} & \stackrel{\text{def}}{=} & (\mathbf{M}.\text{code}, \mathbf{M}.\text{reg}, \mathbf{M}.\text{stk}, \\
 & & \quad \mathbf{M}.\text{hp}[\boldsymbol{l} \mapsto (\mathbf{v}_0, \ldots, \mathbf{v}_{o-1}, \mathbf{v}, \mathbf{v}_{o+1}, \ldots, \mathbf{v}_{n-1})], \\
 & & \quad \mathbf{M}.\text{tab}, \mathbf{M}.\text{shp}) \\
 & & \quad \text{if } \ \mathbf{M}.\text{hp}(\boldsymbol{l}) = (\mathbf{v}_0, \ldots, \mathbf{v}_{n-1}) \wedge o < n \\
\text{phyv}(\mathbf{M})(\mathbf{v}) & \stackrel{\text{def}}{=} & \begin{cases} \underline{w} & \text{if } \mathbf{v} = \underline{w} \\ \widehat{a} & \text{if } \mathbf{v} = \widehat{\boldsymbol{l}} \wedge \mathbf{M}.\text{tab}(\boldsymbol{l}) = (n, a) \\ \text{undef} & \text{otherwise} \end{cases} \\
\text{phyh}(\mathbf{M}) & \stackrel{\text{def}}{=} & \biguplus_{\mathbf{M}.\text{tab}(\boldsymbol{l}) = (n,a) \ \wedge\ n > 0 \ \wedge\ \mathbf{M}.\text{hp}(\boldsymbol{l}) = (\mathbf{v}_0, \ldots, \mathbf{v}_{n-1})} [a \mapsto \text{phyv}(\mathbf{M})(\mathbf{v}_0), \ldots, \text{phyv}(\mathbf{M})(\mathbf{v}_{n-1})] \\
\mathbf{M} \text{ repr } \Phi & \stackrel{\text{def}}{=} & \Phi.\text{code} \supseteq \mathbf{M}.\text{code} \wedge \\
 & & \Phi.\text{reg} \supseteq \text{phyv}(\mathbf{M}) \circ \mathbf{M}.\text{reg} \wedge \Phi.\text{reg}(\text{sp}) = \underline{|\mathbf{M}.\text{stk}|} \wedge \\
 & & \forall j < |\mathbf{M}.\text{stk}|.\ \Phi.\text{stk}(j) = \text{phyv}(\mathbf{M})(\mathbf{M}.\text{stk}(j)) \wedge \\
 & & \Phi.\text{hp} \supseteq \text{phyh}(\mathbf{M}) \uplus \mathbf{M}.\text{shp} \wedge \\
 & & \forall \boldsymbol{l}, n, a.\ \mathbf{M}.\text{tab}(\boldsymbol{l}) = (n, a) \wedge n > 0 \Longrightarrow |\mathbf{M}.\text{hp}(\boldsymbol{l})| = n \\
\text{plugv}(\mathbf{v}, \mathbf{K}, \mathbf{M}) & \stackrel{\text{def}}{=} & \{\, (\Phi, \text{pc}) \in \text{Conf} \mid \mathbf{M} \text{ repr } \Phi \wedge \\
 & & \quad \text{pc} = \mathbf{K}.\text{kpc} \wedge \mathbf{M}(\mathbf{K}.\text{vloc}) = \mathbf{v} \,\} \\
\text{plugc}(\mathbf{e}, \mathbf{K}, \mathbf{M}) & \stackrel{\text{def}}{=} & \{\, (\Phi, \text{pc}) \in \text{Conf} \mid \mathbf{M} \text{ repr } \Phi \wedge \mathbf{M} \in \mathbf{e}.\text{data} \wedge \\
 & & \quad \underline{\text{pc}} = \mathbf{M}(\mathbf{e}.\text{cpc}) \wedge \mathbf{M}(\mathbf{e}.\text{kpc}) = \underline{\mathbf{K}.\text{kpc}} \wedge \mathbf{e}.\text{vloc} = \mathbf{K}.\text{vloc} \,\} \\
\text{step}(\Phi, \text{pc}) & \stackrel{\text{def}}{=} & R \quad \text{with } (\Phi, \text{pc}) \hookrightarrow R \\
\text{mdom}(\mathbf{M}) & \stackrel{\text{def}}{=} & \{\, \widehat{\boldsymbol{l}} \in \text{Val} \mid \boldsymbol{l} \in \text{dom}(\mathbf{M}.\text{hp}) \,\} \\
\text{mdisj}(\mathbf{M}_1, \mathbf{M}_2) & \stackrel{\text{def}}{=} & \{\, \mathbf{M} \in \text{Mem} \mid \\
 & & \quad \mathbf{M}.\text{code} \supseteq \mathbf{M}_1.\text{code} \uplus \mathbf{M}_2.\text{code} \wedge \\
 & & \quad \mathbf{M}.\text{hp} \supseteq \mathbf{M}_1.\text{hp} \uplus \mathbf{M}_2.\text{hp} \wedge \\
 & & \quad \text{nosh}(\mathbf{M}.\text{reg}, \mathbf{M}_1.\text{reg}, \mathbf{M}_2.\text{reg}) \wedge \\
 & & \quad \text{nosh}(\mathbf{M}.\text{stk}, \mathbf{M}_1.\text{stk}, \mathbf{M}_2.\text{stk}) \wedge \\
 & & \quad \text{nosh}(\mathbf{M}.\text{tab}, \mathbf{M}_1.\text{tab}, \mathbf{M}_2.\text{tab}) \wedge \\
 & & \quad \text{nosh}(\mathbf{M}.\text{shp}, \mathbf{M}_1.\text{shp}, \mathbf{M}_2.\text{shp}) \,\} \\
\text{nosh}(X, X_1, X_2) & \stackrel{\text{def}}{=} & (X_1 \neq \text{undef} \implies X_2 = \text{undef} \wedge X = X_1) \wedge \\
 & & (X_2 \neq \text{undef} \implies X_1 = \text{undef} \wedge X = X_2)
\end{array}
$$

Figure 4. The Implementation of LangSpec for **LOW**

and $\mathbf{v}_2$. pack$(\tau, \mathbf{v})$ and roll$(\mathbf{v})$ are represented the same as $\mathbf{v}$. References are represented directly as pointers. We also use oftype(τ) to enforce that values of arrow and universal type are represented by pointers to closures whose first cell is *not* a logical pointer. (This ensures that we can jump to the code address directly.)

The most interesting bit is the representation of app$(\mathbf{v}_1, \mathbf{v}_2)$ (and appty$(\mathbf{v}, \tau)$, which is similar). In order for a computation $\mathbf{e}$ to represent this application, $\mathbf{v}_1$ is assumed to be a pointer $\widehat{\boldsymbol{l}}$ to a closure. The starting address of the function application ($\mathbf{e}$.cpc) is thus taken to be the code address stored in the first cell of the closure, *i.e.*, $\langle \boldsymbol{l} : 0 \rangle_{\text{h}}$. Our calling convention is that, when the function is called, the return address should be stored in wk_0, and when the function returns, the return value should be stored in wk_5, so $\mathbf{e}$.kpc and $\mathbf{e}$.vloc reflect this convention. Finally, the memory predicate $\mathbf{e}$.data requires that when control is passed to $\mathbf{e}$.cpc, the function $\mathbf{v}_1$ and argument $\mathbf{v}_2$ are stored in wk_1 and wk_2.

Connecting Logical and Physical Memories The right side of Figure 4 defines the remaining elements of LangSpec, along with a number of auxiliary operations. The operations at the top right give shorthand for various lookup and update operations on logical memories. "phyv$(\mathbf{M})(\mathbf{v})$" returns the physical interpretation of $\mathbf{v}$ according to $\mathbf{M}$'s lookup table, if one exists, and "phyh$(\mathbf{M})$" returns the live portion of the physical heap according to $\mathbf{M}$'s lookup table. Note that the definition of phyh demands that the physical representations of logical memory blocks with distinct head pointers be disjoint, thus ensuring a proper bijection between the reachable parts of the physical and logical heaps.

"$\mathbf{M}$ repr Φ" says that $\mathbf{M}$ is a valid logical abstraction of Φ. The definition is fairly straightforward, making use of phyv and phyh as one would expect. The fourth line of the definition guarantees that the reachable heap is disjoint from the system heap, and the fifth condition just checks that the block sizes specified for live data in $\mathbf{M}$.tab are correct. Note that Φ may contain arbitrary other junk (in the code, stack, and heap segments) that is not described by $\mathbf{M}$.

Plugging Continuations Using $\mathbf{M}$ repr Φ, it is easy to specify how to plug continuations with values and computations. A configuration (Φ, pc) belongs to plugv$(\mathbf{v}, \mathbf{K}, \mathbf{M})$ if (1) $\mathbf{M}$ is a valid abstraction of Φ, (2) the program counter pc is set to the starting address of the continuation ($\mathbf{K}$.kpc), and (3) the value $\mathbf{v}$ is stored in the location where the continuation is expecting it ($\mathbf{K}$.vloc).

A configuration (Φ, pc) belongs to plugc$(\mathbf{e}, \mathbf{K}, \mathbf{M})$ if (1) $\mathbf{M}$ is a valid abstraction of Φ, (2) $\mathbf{M}$ satisfies the memory constraints demanded by $\mathbf{e}$, (3) the program counter pc is set to the starting address of the computation ($\mathbf{e}$.cpc), (4) the starting address of the continuation ($\mathbf{K}$.kpc) is stored in the place where the computation is expecting to find its return address ($\mathbf{e}$.kpc), and (5) the place where $\mathbf{e}$ will store its return value ($\mathbf{e}$.vloc) is the same place where $\mathbf{K}$ is expecting to find its input value ($\mathbf{K}$.vloc).

The remaining definitions (of step, mdom, and mdisj) are fairly self-explanatory. As mentioned earlier, the definition of

$$
\begin{array}{ll}
[\mathrm{bg} \Mapsto \mathrm{instrs}] & \stackrel{\mathrm{def}}{=} [\mathrm{bg} \mapsto \mathrm{instrs}(0), \ldots, \mathrm{instrs}(|\mathrm{instrs}| - 1)] \\
\{C\}_{\mathrm{code}} & \stackrel{\mathrm{def}}{=} (C, \mathrm{undef}, \mathrm{undef}, \emptyset, \mathrm{undef}, \mathrm{undef}) \in \mathrm{Mem} \\
\{H\}_{\mathrm{heap}} & \stackrel{\mathrm{def}}{=} (\emptyset, \mathrm{undef}, \mathrm{undef}, H, \mathrm{undef}, \mathrm{undef}) \in \mathrm{Mem} \\
\mathbf{v} \text{ live in } \mathbf{M} & \stackrel{\mathrm{def}}{=} \begin{cases} \top & \text{if } \mathbf{v} = \underline{w} \\ \exists n, a.\ \mathbf{M}.\mathrm{tab}(\boldsymbol{l}) = (n, a) \wedge n > 0 & \text{if } \mathbf{v} = \widehat{\boldsymbol{l}} \end{cases} \\
\mathrm{reach}_0(\mathbf{M}) & \stackrel{\mathrm{def}}{=} \{\, \boldsymbol{l} \mid \exists r \in \mathrm{Register}.\ \widehat{\boldsymbol{l}} = \mathbf{M}.\mathrm{reg}(r) \,\} \cup \\
& \quad\ \{\, \boldsymbol{l} \mid \exists j < |\mathbf{M}.\mathrm{stk}|.\ \widehat{\boldsymbol{l}} = \mathbf{M}.\mathrm{stk}(j) \,\} \\
\mathrm{reach}_{i+1}(\mathbf{M}) & \stackrel{\mathrm{def}}{=} \mathrm{reach}_i(\mathbf{M}) \cup \\
& \quad\ \{\, \boldsymbol{l} \mid \exists \boldsymbol{l}' \in \mathrm{reach}_i(\mathbf{M}).\ \exists j.\ \widehat{\boldsymbol{l}} = \mathbf{M}.\mathrm{hp}(\boldsymbol{l}')(j) \,\} \\
\mathrm{reach}(\mathbf{M}) & \stackrel{\mathrm{def}}{=} \bigcup_{i \in \mathbb{N}} \mathrm{reach}_i(\mathbf{M})
\end{array}
$$

$$
\begin{array}{l}
\mathrm{AllocSpec} \stackrel{\mathrm{def}}{=} \\
\{\, \mathcal{A} \in \mathrm{PAddr} \rightarrow \{\, (\mathrm{init}, \mathrm{alloc}, \mathrm{instrs}, I) \\
\qquad\qquad\qquad \in \mathrm{PAddr} \times \mathrm{PAddr} \times \mathrm{List\ Instruction} \times \\
\qquad\qquad\qquad\ \ \mathbb{P}(\mathrm{Table} \times \mathrm{SysHeap}) \,\} \mid \\
\quad \forall \mathrm{gcbg}, \Phi, \mathrm{pc}. \\
\quad\ \ \Phi.\mathrm{code} \supseteq [\mathrm{gcbg} \Mapsto \mathcal{A}(\mathrm{gcbg}).\mathrm{instrs}] \wedge \Phi.\mathrm{reg}(\mathrm{wk}_4) = \underline{\mathrm{pc}} \implies \\
\quad\ \ \exists \mathbf{M}', \Phi'. \\
\quad\quad (\Phi, \mathcal{A}(\mathrm{gcbg}).\mathrm{init}) \stackrel{*}{\hookrightarrow} (\Phi', \mathrm{pc}) \wedge \\
\quad\quad \Phi'.\mathrm{code} = \Phi.\mathrm{code} \wedge \mathbf{M}'.\mathrm{code} = [\mathrm{gcbg} \Mapsto \mathcal{A}(\mathrm{gcbg}).\mathrm{instrs}] \wedge \\
\quad\quad \mathbf{M}' \text{ repr } \Phi' \wedge \mathbf{M}' \in \mathcal{A}.GR(\mathrm{gcbg}) \wedge \mathbf{M}' \in \mathcal{A}.MR(\mathrm{gcbg}) \wedge \\
\quad \forall \mathrm{gcbg}, \mathbf{M}, \Phi, \mathrm{pc}, n. \\
\quad\ \ \mathbf{M} \text{ repr } \Phi \wedge \mathbf{M} \in \mathcal{A}.GR(\mathrm{gcbg}) \wedge \mathbf{M} \in \mathcal{A}.MR(\mathrm{gcbg}) \wedge \\
\quad\ \ \mathbf{M}.\mathrm{reg}(\mathrm{wk}_4) = \underline{\mathrm{pc}} \wedge \mathbf{M}.\mathrm{reg}(\mathrm{wk}_5) = \underline{n} \implies \\
\quad\ \ \exists \Phi', \mathbf{M}', T, S, w, \boldsymbol{l}, w_0, \ldots, w_{n-1}. \\
\quad\quad (\Phi, \mathcal{A}(\mathrm{gcbg}).\mathrm{alloc}) \stackrel{*}{\hookrightarrow} (\Phi', \mathrm{pc}) \wedge \\
\quad\quad \mathbf{M}' \text{ repr } \Phi' \wedge \mathbf{M}' \in \mathcal{A}.GR(\mathrm{gcbg}) \wedge \mathbf{M}' \in \mathcal{A}.MR(\mathrm{gcbg}) \wedge \\
\quad\quad \mathbf{M}' = \mathbf{M}[[T, S]][\mathrm{wk}_4 \mapsto \underline{w}]_{\mathrm{reg}}[\mathrm{wk}_5 \mapsto \widehat{\boldsymbol{l}}]_{\mathrm{reg}} \uplus \\
\qquad\qquad \{[\boldsymbol{l} \mapsto (\underline{w_0}, \ldots, \underline{w_{n-1}})]\}_{\mathrm{heap}} \,\} \\
\mathcal{A}.GR(\mathrm{gcbg}) \stackrel{\mathrm{def}}{=} \{\, \mathbf{M} \in \mathrm{Mem} \mid \forall \boldsymbol{l} \in \mathrm{reach}(\mathbf{M}).\ \widehat{\boldsymbol{l}} \text{ live in } \mathbf{M} \,\} \\
\mathcal{A}.MR(\mathrm{gcbg}) \stackrel{\mathrm{def}}{=} \{\, \mathbf{M} \in \mathrm{Mem} \mid (\mathbf{M}.\mathrm{tab}, \mathbf{M}.\mathrm{shp}) \in \mathcal{A}(\mathrm{gcbg}).I \wedge \\
\qquad\qquad\qquad\qquad\qquad \mathbf{M}.\mathrm{code} \supseteq [\mathrm{gcbg} \Mapsto \mathcal{A}(\mathrm{gcbg}).\mathrm{instrs}] \,\}
\end{array}
$$

Figure 5. Abstract Specification of the Memory Allocator

mdisj uses the undef option for reg, stk, tab, and shp to ensure that if a memory is split into disjoint pieces, each of these indivisible components can only appear in one of the pieces.

Possible Worlds The model of possible worlds that we use to implement WorldSpec is based very closely on Dreyer *et al.* [14]. For space reasons, we will therefore not present the details of the model in this paper and instead refer the reader to the appendix [15]. (See Section 8 for a more detailed discussion of how our model relates to Dreyer *et al.*'s.)

That said, there are a few salient aspects of the model that are needed for understanding the definition of compositional program equivalence that we will give in Section 7. In the model, worlds W are 3-tuples (k, ω, GR), where: k is W's step level, ω is a finite set of state transition systems (STS's) of the sort described in Section 3, and GR is a global invariant governing the entire memory. We call the STS's *islands* because they govern disjoint pieces of memory. Two memories are related by W if (1) they satisfy its global invariant GR, and (2) they can be split into disjoint memories (one for each island) such that the n-th pair of memories satisfies the "local" memory relation determined by the current state of the n-th island in ω. In our definition of program equivalence, we will use GR to enforce the property that all reachable data is live. We need to use a global invariant since reachability cannot be determined by looking at a local subheap. We use islands to express all other assumptions about memory.

6. Assumptions About the Memory Allocator

Figure 5 shows the assumptions we make about memory allocation and garbage collection, in the form of the specification AllocSpec. Given as input a starting physical address gcbg, the runtime system represented by $\mathcal{A}$ will return a 4-tuple (init, alloc, code, I), where: init is the starting address of the initialization routine that sets up the runtime system, alloc is the starting address of the allocator, code is the list of instructions defining the runtime system, which are assumed to be loaded at address gcbg, and I is a private invariant of the runtime system, which describes when a logical memory's lookup table is in sync with its system heap. The assumption about code is joined together with the private invariant I to form the memory predicate MR defined at the bottom of the figure.

Assuming init is invoked with the runtime system code in the right place, and with a return address placed in wk_4, its specification says it will return control in a memory that satisfies $MR(\mathrm{gcbg})$, along with the global invariant $GR(\mathrm{gcbg})$ that all reachable data is live.

Assuming that alloc is invoked in a physical memory Φ represented abstractly by the logical memory $\mathbf{M}$, that $\mathbf{M}$ satisfies the MR and GR properties, that the number of cells to be allocated (n) is stored in wk_5, and that the return address is stored in wk_4, the specification of alloc says that it will return a pointer to a fresh n-word block in wk_5, and that the memory it returns ($\mathbf{M}'$) will continue to satisfy all the aforementioned invariants. Moreover, while the lookup table and system heap of $\mathbf{M}'$ may be completely different from those of $\mathbf{M}$, the contents of $\mathbf{M}$ must remain otherwise unchanged. This does not of course prevent the allocator from having performed a GC: any logical pointer that was not reachable in $\mathbf{M}$ before the call to alloc may very well be marked as dead in the lookup table of the post-allocation $\mathbf{M}'$, but any pointer that was reachable in $\mathbf{M}$ will still be reachable in $\mathbf{M}'$ and thus, by the definition of GR, still be live.

Our specification of the runtime system provides considerable flexibility—for example, it should be satisfied by either a mark-and-sweep or a copying collector because the specification says nothing about the private invariant of the runtime system. However, it *does* assume that the collector places no restrictions (such as read or write barriers) on what the mutator does to live data. We believe it should be possible to adapt our approach to a wider range of collectors, but we leave that to future work.

7. Compositional Program Equivalence

The logical relation $\mathcal{E}[\![\tau]\!]\rho$ characterizes what it means for two *computations* to be logically equivalent, but ultimately what we really care about is whether a pair of **HIGH** and **LOW** *programs* are logically equivalent. What, one may wonder, is the difference between computations and programs? In short, a program is what you *write*, and a computation is what you *run*. That is, a program is a piece of relocatable code that must be linked with other programs and loaded into memory before it can be executed, whereas a computation describes the "next" thing to be executed in a running machine configuration. For the **HIGH** language, the distinction between computations and programs can be easily glossed over because the operational semantics of **HIGH** is defined directly on **HIGH** programs. For the **LOW** language, however, especially given the ability to write self-modifying code, it is important to distinguish the two notions. In this section, we explain what a **LOW** program is and how to define logical equivalence between **HIGH** and **LOW** programs, and we then present our key technical results.

7.1 Equivalence of HIGH and LOW Programs

As can already be seen from our motivating example in Section 3.1, we define a **LOW** program p to be a function from two code pointers to a list of instructions. The first of the code pointer inputs is assumed to be the address of the memory allocation routine, and the second is assumed to be the address where the list of instructions returned by the program will be loaded into memory.

$$\mathcal{H}.\mathrm{Prog} \stackrel{\mathrm{def}}{=} \{\, e \mid \mathrm{floc}(e) = \emptyset \,\}$$
$$\mathcal{L}.\mathrm{Prog} \stackrel{\mathrm{def}}{=} \{\, p \in \mathrm{PAddr} \times \mathrm{PAddr} \rightarrow \mathrm{List\ Instruction} \,\}$$

$$\mathcal{D}[\![\cdot]\!] \stackrel{\mathrm{def}}{=} \emptyset$$
$$\mathcal{D}[\![\Delta, \alpha]\!] \stackrel{\mathrm{def}}{=} \{\, (\rho, \alpha \mapsto R) \mid \rho \in \mathcal{D}[\![\Delta]\!] \wedge R \in \mathrm{TyValRel} \,\}$$

$$\mathcal{G}[\![\cdot]\!]\rho \stackrel{\mathrm{def}}{=} \{\, (W, \mathbf{v}, \emptyset) \mid W \in \mathrm{World} \wedge \mathbf{v} \in \mathcal{L}.\mathrm{Val} \,\}$$
$$\begin{aligned}\mathcal{G}[\![\Gamma, x : \tau]\!]\rho \stackrel{\mathrm{def}}{=} \{\, & (W, \mathbf{v}, (\gamma, x \mapsto v)) \mid \exists \mathbf{v}_1, \mathbf{v}_2. \\ & (W, \mathbf{v}, \langle\rangle) \in \square(\mathcal{L}.\mathrm{pair}(\mathbf{v}_1, \mathbf{v}_2), \mathcal{H}.\mathrm{Val} \times \mathcal{H}.\mathrm{Mem}) \wedge \\ & (W, \mathbf{v}_1, v) \in \mathcal{V}[\![\tau]\!]\rho \wedge (W, \mathbf{v}_2, \gamma) \in \mathcal{G}[\![\Gamma]\!]\rho \,\}\end{aligned}$$

$$W_k^\circ(\mathcal{A}, \mathrm{gcbg}) \stackrel{\mathrm{def}}{=} (k, [\iota^{\mathrm{regstk}}, \iota^{\mathrm{htyping}}, \iota^{\mathrm{gc}}(\mathcal{A}, \mathrm{gcbg})], GR^\circ(\mathcal{A}, \mathrm{gcbg}))$$

$$\begin{aligned}&\Delta; \Gamma \vdash \mathrm{bg} \approx_W e : \tau \stackrel{\mathrm{def}}{=} \\ &\quad \forall W' \sqsupseteq W.\ \forall \rho \in \mathcal{D}[\![\Delta]\!].\ \forall (\mathbf{v}, \gamma) \in \mathcal{G}[\![\Gamma]\!]\rho(W'). \\ &\qquad ((\underline{\mathrm{bg}}, \lfloor \mathrm{wk}_0 \rfloor, \lfloor \mathrm{wk}_5 \rfloor, \{\, \mathbf{M} \mid \mathbf{M}.\mathrm{reg}(\mathrm{sv}_0) = \mathbf{v} \,\}), \gamma\rho e) \in \mathcal{E}[\![\tau]\!]\rho(W') \\ &\quad \text{where } \gamma\rho e ::= e[\rho(\alpha).\tau_2/\alpha][\gamma(x)/x]\end{aligned}$$

$$\begin{aligned}&\Delta; \Gamma \vdash p \approx e : \tau \stackrel{\mathrm{def}}{=} \\ &\quad \emptyset; \Delta; \Gamma \vdash e : \tau \wedge \\ &\quad \forall \mathcal{A}, \mathrm{gcbg}, \mathrm{bg}.\ \forall k, W \sqsupseteq W_k^\circ(\mathcal{A}, \mathrm{gcbg}).\ \forall (\mathbf{M}, M) \in \mathcal{M}(W). \\ &\quad \forall \mathbf{M}'.\ \mathbf{M}' = \mathbf{M} \uplus \{[\mathrm{bg} \Mapsto p(\mathcal{A}(\mathrm{gcbg}).\mathrm{alloc}, \mathrm{bg})]\}_{\mathrm{code}} \implies \\ &\quad \exists W' \sqsupseteq W.\ \mathrm{lev}(W') = \mathrm{lev}(W) \wedge (\mathbf{M}', M) \in \mathcal{M}(W') \wedge \\ &\qquad\qquad \Delta; \Gamma \vdash \mathrm{bg} \approx_{W'} e : \tau\end{aligned}$$

Figure 6. Program Equivalence

When listing the code of a program (*e.g.*, in Figure 2), we write line numbers on selected lines of code (*e.g.*, bg + 3) to indicate the physical addresses where we expect the code to be loaded, but note that (1) these addresses are always relative to the second parameter of the program (typically named bg), so that the code is always relocatable, and (2) the notation is merely suggestive—the line numbers are not part of the actual program.

Now, concerning equivalence of **HIGH** and **LOW** programs: it is possible to define a notion of logical equivalence strictly between *closed* programs, but we will find it useful when reasoning about compiler correctness to generalize this relation to one on *open* programs. On the **HIGH** side, an open program is simply an expression e with free variables (and no free locations), but what is an open program on the **LOW** side? In order to answer this, we need to pick an environment-passing convention, specifying what is an official low-level representation of a high-level environment and where the low-level program expects to get its environment data. In Figure 6, we give a logical relation $\mathcal{G}[\![\Gamma]\!]\rho$ between low-level values and high-level environments. This relation specifies that a high-level environment γ should be represented as a linked list of low-level values that are componentwise related to the high-level values in the range of γ. We assume that the environment data is passed in the register sv_0—this assumption will be codified in the definition of the program equivalence relation $\approx$ (see below).

Before we define program equivalence, we must also specify the invariants on memories that are required for executing programs. These conditions are represented by the *initial* worlds W_k° in Figure 6. (The k in W_k° simply determines the step level but does not otherwise affect the definition.) The initial worlds consist of three islands and one global invariant: ι^{regstk} owns the register file and the stack in the **LOW** memory and requires that callee-save registers and stack be preserved before and after function calls (this is accomplished using a combination of private and public transitions as discussed in Section 3.5); ι^{htyping} requires that the heap typing in the **HIGH** memory should only grow in future worlds; $\iota^{\mathrm{gc}}(\mathcal{A}, \mathrm{gcbg})$ owns the lookup table and the system heap and enforces the private $\mathcal{A}.MR(\mathrm{gcbg})$ invariant of the runtime system (Figure 5); and the global invariant $GR^\circ(\mathcal{A}, \mathrm{gcbg})$ specifies that all reachable blocks in the **LOW** memory are live ($\mathcal{A}.GR(\mathrm{gcbg})$ in Figure 5) and that the **HIGH** memory satisfies its heap typing. All these components of W_k° are formally defined in the appendix [15].

We are now ready to define the program equivalence relation $\approx$. The judgment $\Delta; \Gamma \vdash p \approx e : \tau$ says that a **LOW** program p and a **HIGH** program e are equivalent if the following is true. First, let k be any starting step level, and let W be any future world of W_k° that does not already impose any invariants on the code segment of p. (This latter condition is guaranteed by the assumption that we are given initial memories $\mathbf{M}$ and M related by W, but where $\mathbf{M}$ does *not* contain the code segment of p. We use the notation $\mathbf{M}_1 \uplus \mathbf{M}_2$ here to denote the "smallest" memory in $\mathrm{mdisj}(\mathbf{M}_1, \mathbf{M}_2)$, in a sense defined formally in the appendix.)

Under these assumptions, we must be able to:

1. Extend W to a future world W' (of the same step level) such that W' relates $\mathbf{M}'$ and M, where $\mathbf{M}'$ is $\mathbf{M}$ extended with the code of p. Intuitively, this step affords p the opportunity to "own" its own code segment by extending W with an island governing it. Typically, this island will take the form of an invariant stating that p's code must never be modified, although in the case of self-modifying code we would instead define the island to be a state transition system (as described in Section 3.4).

2. Show that the **HIGH** *computation* e is related (under the world W' constructed in the previous step) to the **LOW** *computation* $\mathbf{e}$ that starts at the beginning (bg) of p's code segment. This subgoal is encapsulated in the *open computation equivalence* judgment $\Delta; \Gamma \vdash \mathrm{bg} \approx_{W'} e : \tau$ (Figure 6). This judgment says that, for any future world W'' of W', for any relational interpretation ρ of the type variables in Δ, and for any environments $\mathbf{v}$ and γ related under W'' by $\mathcal{G}[\![\Gamma]\!]\rho$, the **HIGH** computation $\gamma\rho e$ is logically related (by $\mathcal{E}[\![\tau]\!]\rho$, under W'') to the **LOW** computation starting at address bg. The other three components of the **LOW** computation stipulate, respectively, that (1) the computation expects to find its return address stored in wk_0, (2) the computation will store its resulting value in wk_5, and (3) the computation expects to find its environment stored in sv_0. One can think of this last assumption about sv_0 as having the effect of "closing" p, in much the same way that γ and ρ close e.

7.2 Compiler Correctness and Other Technical Results

Our first result is an *adequacy* theorem for our program equivalence relation $\approx$. The statement of the theorem refers to the following simple loader for the **LOW** language: $\mathrm{load}(\mathcal{A}, p)$ first runs the initialization routine of the memory allocator $\mathcal{A}$, then executes p, and finally halts as soon as it gets control back from p:

$$\begin{array}{llll} \multicolumn{4}{l}{\mathrm{load}(\mathcal{A}, p) ::= \mathrm{let}\ (\mathrm{init}, \mathrm{alloc}, \mathrm{gcinstrs}, \_) := \mathcal{A}(105),} \\ \multicolumn{4}{l}{\qquad\qquad\qquad \mathrm{instrs}^p := p(\mathrm{alloc}, 105 + |\mathrm{gcinstrs}|),} \\ \multicolumn{4}{l}{\qquad\qquad\qquad \mathrm{loadinstrs}^p := [} \\ (*\ 100\ *) & \mathtt{move} & \lfloor \mathrm{wk}_4 \rfloor & \underline{102} \\ & \mathtt{jmp} & \underline{\mathrm{init}} & \\ (*\ 102\ *) & \mathtt{move} & \lfloor \mathrm{wk}_0 \rfloor & \underline{104} \\ & \mathtt{jmp} & \underline{105 + |\mathrm{gcinstrs}|} & \\ (*\ 104\ *) & \mathtt{halt} & & \\ \multicolumn{4}{l}{] \mathbin{+\!\!+} \mathrm{gcinstrs} \mathbin{+\!\!+} \mathrm{instrs}^p \quad \mathrm{in}} \\ \multicolumn{4}{l}{\{\, (\Phi, 100) \in \mathrm{PConf} \mid \Phi.\mathrm{code} \supseteq [100 \Mapsto \mathrm{loadinstrs}^p] \,\}} \end{array}$$

The adequacy theorem states that closed **HIGH** and **LOW** programs that are equivalent according to $\approx$ must equi-terminate when loaded by the above loader.

Theorem 1 (Adequacy). For all $\emptyset; \emptyset \vdash p \approx e : \tau$,
$\forall \mathcal{A} \in \mathrm{AllocSpec}.\ \forall (\Phi, \mathrm{pc}) \in \mathrm{load}(\mathcal{A}, p).\ \forall h.$
both (Φ, pc) and (h, e) diverge or both halt without fail.

One might think that this adequacy result is weak because the loader does not inspect the result returned by the program p. How-

```
Papp(p1, p2) ::= λ alloc, bg.
let instrs1 := p1(alloc, bg + 4), c1 := |instrs1|,
    instrs2 := p2(alloc, bg + c1 + 6), c2 := |instrs2|   in  [
  bg                plus    ⌊sp⌋          ⌊sp⌋              2
                    move    ⟨sp − 2⟩s     ⌊wk0⌋
                    move    ⟨sp − 1⟩s     0
                    move    ⌊wk0⌋         bg + c1 + 4
                      instrs1
  bg + c1 + 4       move    ⟨sp − 1⟩s     ⌊wk5⌋
                    move    ⌊wk0⌋         bg + c1 + c2 + 6
                      instrs2
  bg + c1 + c2 + 6  move    ⌊wk0⌋         ⟨sp − 2⟩s
                    move    ⌊wk1⌋         ⟨sp − 1⟩s
                    move    ⌊wk2⌋         ⌊wk5⌋
                    minus   ⌊sp⌋          ⌊sp⌋              2
                    jmp     ⟨wk1 + 0⟩h
]
```

Figure 7. Compilation of Function Application

ever, together with the compositionality result below, one can link the program p with arbitrary well-behaved "test" programs and the linked programs are guaranteed to behave the same.

In order to show that our logical relations are sufficiently populated—an important desideratum, as we explained in the introduction—we have written a very naïve compiler from **HIGH** to **LOW** and proved that every source program is related to its compiled low-level program by our program equivalence. Specifically, we have implemented a low-level construct corresponding to each high-level construct and then defined the compiler purely inductively on the structure of source programs using these low-level constructs. For each construct, we have shown a corresponding "compatibility" lemma (following Pitts' terminology [21]), meaning that program equivalence is preserved under said construct. This implies that equivalent programs behave the same under arbitrary well-behaved contexts.

One example of a high-level construct is function application. Figure 7 shows its low-level realization as a simple linking program $\mathrm{Papp}(p_1, p_2)$. We assume here that p_1 is some program computing a value of function type $\tau' \to \tau$, and p_2 is some program computing a value of the argument type τ'.

The program begins by bumping up the stack pointer twice, pushing the return address (stored in wk_0) onto the first new stack slot, and clearing the second one with 0. The clearing instruction (at bg + 2) is needed because the stack slot at $\langle \mathrm{sp} - 1\rangle_{\mathrm{s}}$ might otherwise contain a dangling pointer; thus, in order to maintain the global invariant that all reachable data is live, we must clear $\langle \mathrm{sp} - 1\rangle_{\mathrm{s}}$ before passing control to p_1. When p_1 returns, we assume it returns a pointer to a function closure in wk_5, we store that pointer in the cleared stack slot, and we proceed to execute p_2. After p_2 returns, we move p_1's closure pointer into wk_1, the argument value (returned by p_2) into wk_2, and the original return address of $\mathrm{Papp}(p_1, p_2)$ into wk_0. We then pop off two stack slots and make a tail call to the code pointer stored in wk_1's closure.

The compatibility result for Papp can be seen as a compositionality result for our program equivalence relation.

Lemma 1 (Compatibility: App).

$$\Delta; \Gamma \vdash p_1 \approx e_1 : \tau' \to \tau \wedge \Delta; \Gamma \vdash p_2 \approx e_2 : \tau' \implies \Delta; \Gamma \vdash \mathrm{Papp}(p_1, p_2) \approx e_1\ e_2 : \tau$$

Another related construct of course is λ-abstraction. Figure 8 shows its low-level realization as the program $\mathrm{Pabs}(p)$. We assume here that p is a program implementing the body of a λ-abstraction, under the assumption that the argument of that abstraction is the first element in the linked list environment stored at sv_0.

```
Pabs(p) ::= λ alloc, bg.
let code := p(alloc, bg + 16), c := |code|   in  [
  bg           move    ⌊wk4⌋          bg + 3
               move    ⌊wk5⌋          2
               jmp     alloc
  bg + 3       move    ⟨wk5 + 0⟩h     bg + 6
               move    ⟨wk5 + 1⟩h     ⌊sv0⌋
               jmp     ⌊wk0⌋
  bg + 6       plus    ⌊sp⌋           ⌊sp⌋           2
               move    ⟨sp − 2⟩s      ⌊wk0⌋
               move    ⟨sp − 1⟩s      ⌊sv0⌋
               move    ⌊wk4⌋          bg + 12
               move    ⌊wk5⌋          2
               jmp     alloc
  bg + 12      move    ⟨wk5 + 0⟩h     ⌊wk2⌋
               move    ⟨wk5 + 1⟩h     ⟨wk1 + 1⟩h
               move    ⌊sv0⌋          ⌊wk5⌋
               move    ⌊wk0⌋          bg + c + 16
                 code
  bg + c + 16  move    ⌊sv0⌋          ⟨sp − 1⟩s
               minus   ⌊sp⌋           ⌊sp⌋           2
               jmp     ⟨sp − 0⟩s
]
```

Figure 8. Compilation of λ-Abstraction

The actual computation of the program is quite simple, because it merely allocates a closure representing the λ-abstraction and returns it (just like the example in Section 3.1). The closure consists of a code pointer (to bg + 6) and an environment pointer, which is of course just whatever environment was passed to $\mathrm{Pabs}(p)$ in sv_0. Whenever the closure is invoked (by jumping to bg + 6), it first saves the return address (stored in wk_0), as well as the callee-save register sv_0, by pushing them on the stack. It then pushes the argument value $\lfloor \mathrm{wk}_2 \rfloor$ onto the front of the environment linked-list headed by $\langle \mathrm{wk}_1 + 1\rangle_{\mathrm{h}}$ (which requires allocating two new memory cells), and stores a pointer to this extended environment in sv_0 before executing p. Finally, when p returns, it pops the stack twice, and restores the original contents of the callee-save sv_0, before jumping to the return address that was stored on the stack.

The compatibility result for Pabs is as follows:

Lemma 2 (Compatibility: Abs).

$$\Delta; \Gamma, x : \tau' \vdash p \approx e : \tau \implies \Delta; \Gamma \vdash \mathrm{Pabs}(p) \approx \lambda x{:}\tau'.\, e : \tau' \to \tau$$

Using Papp, Pabs, and all the other **LOW** program constructors, we can define a compiler $(\!|\Gamma \vdash e|\!)$ in a simple, syntax-directed fashion, *e.g.*,

$$(\!|\Gamma \vdash e_1\ e_2|\!) ::= \mathrm{Papp}((\!|\Gamma \vdash e_1|\!), (\!|\Gamma \vdash e_2|\!))$$
$$(\!|\Gamma \vdash \lambda x{:}\tau.\, e|\!) ::= \mathrm{Pabs}((\!|\Gamma, x{:}\tau \vdash e|\!))$$

and then establish the following compiler correctness result:

Theorem 2 (Compiler Correctness). For $\emptyset; \Delta; \Gamma \vdash e : \tau$,

$$\Delta; \Gamma \vdash (\!|\Gamma \vdash e|\!) \approx e : \tau$$

The theorem is easily provable by induction on e, using the appropriate compatibility lemma in each case.

Finally, we prove the self-modifying awkward program p_{awk} is equivalent to the high-level awkward program e_{awk} from Figure 2.

Theorem 3. $\emptyset; \emptyset \vdash p_{\mathrm{awk}} \approx e_{\mathrm{awk}} : (\mathsf{unit} \to \mathsf{unit}) \to \mathsf{int}$

As a corollary, we can see that for any $\emptyset; \emptyset; \emptyset \vdash e : \mathsf{unit} \to \mathsf{unit}$, both $e_{\mathrm{awk}}\ \ e$ and $\mathrm{load}(\mathcal{A}, \mathrm{Papp}(p_{\mathrm{awk}}, (\!|\emptyset \vdash e|\!)))$ equi-terminate. Similarly, for any $\emptyset; \emptyset; \emptyset \vdash e : ((\mathsf{unit} \to \mathsf{unit}) \to \mathsf{int}) \to \tau$, both $e\ e_{\mathrm{awk}}$ and $\mathrm{load}(\mathcal{A}, \mathrm{Papp}((\!|\emptyset \vdash e|\!), p_{\mathrm{awk}}))$ equi-terminate.

Detailed proofs of all these results appear in the companion technical appendix [15].

8. Related and Future Work

There is a huge body of work on compiler correctness and semantics for low-level code. We focus on the most closely related work.

Compositional Compiler Correctness As explained in the introduction, the overall motivation of our work is very similar to that of Benton and Hur [5], and our use of logical relations to build an extensional, compositional notion of equivalence between high- and low-level languages is inspired directly by their work. However, there are significant differences between our work and theirs.

First, they define a relation between a purely functional PCF-like language and an SECD machine, whereas we relate a more expressive, impure, ML-like high-level language to an assembly language that is significantly more low-level and realistic than SECD. Reasoning about compositional equivalence in our setting is significantly more complex, not least because we must deal with reasoning about the heap and the presence of a garbage collector. We make essential use of Kripke logical relations for this purpose.

That said, there is a sense in which our setting makes the problem easier. One of Benton and Hur's goals was to develop a model of low-level programs that would admit program equivalences (such as commutativity of addition) whose validity depend on the purely functional nature of the source language. Toward this end, they related low-level programs to *denotations* of high-level programs, so that one could use domain-theoretic reasoning to establish the purely functional equivalences of interest. These half-operational, half-denotational relations were of necessity asymmetric. In particular, they employ biorthogonality—but only on the low-level side of the relation—as well as step-indexing—but only in defining one direction of approximation (in the other direction, they use an admissible closure operation). As a result, proving in their setting that a high- and low-level program are *equivalent* really involves doing two proofs (one for each direction of approximation) using very different technical machinery.

In our work, we sidestep this problem because the ML-like lack of effect encapsulation in our high-level language causes it to have a relatively weak equational theory that simply does not admit the kinds of purely functional equivalences that Benton and Hur were interested in. Nevertheless, as our motivating example illustrates, there are still plenty of interesting equivalences in our setting, particularly involving uses of local state. Moreover, our logical relations, being entirely operational and defined in language-generic fashion, are inherently symmetric, making them easier to use.

More recently, Benton and Hur [6] have generalized their technique to a compiler for a polymorphic (yet still purely functional) language, but their logical relations are still asymmetric.

Chlipala [11] proposes a syntactic approach to proving compositional compiler correctness. His idea is to establish a set of criteria for high-low compilation relations, such that the results of different compilers can be correctly linked so long as their compilation relations satisfy these criteria. However, the criteria are still syntactic, and thus he cannot reason for instance about our motivating example, wherein the high-low equivalence depends on semantic reasoning about local state. Moreover, Chlipala only considers a fairly high-level target language that is a CPS version of the source.

Jaber and Tabareau [16] propose an alternative approach to compositional compiler correctness based on type preservation. Instead of proving compiler correctness directly, they prove that the compiler is type-preserving, but their source language has such a rich type system (with dependent refinement types) that this effectively implies correctness. Like Benton and Hur, they compile a purely functional language to an SECD machine, but their correctness result only applies to terminating programs.

None of the aforementioned work considers a target language that supports garbage collection.

Kripke Logical Relations Our logical relation is based closely on Dreyer, Neis and Birkedal's (hereafter, DNB) [14], which was in turn a refinement and generalization of Ahmed, Dreyer and Rossberg's [2]. (Of course, these are but the latest in a long line of work on Kripke logical relations spanning decades—see *loc. cit.*, as well as Pitts and Stark [22], for further pointers to the literature.)

DNB's main goal was to show how a Kripke model based on state transition systems could be extended in orthogonal ways to exploit the *absence* of certain features, namely higher-order state and/or control effects. For the **HIGH** language considered here, in which there are no control operators, DNB showed how to extend their baseline model with *private transitions* (Section 3.5) and demonstrated the utility of private transitions in reasoning about a variety of challenging contextual equivalences involving local state. For our purposes, private transitions have proved useful in formalizing the "well-bracketing" assumptions about the stack and callee-save registers, assumptions which indeed rely on the absence of control operators. Extending the **HIGH** language with control operators would thus necessitate a significant change to our Kripke model, precisely because the compilation strategy for **HIGH** would need to change as well. We leave this problem to future work.

Despite the close connection, our logical relation diverges from DNB's in several ways. First and foremost, whereas DNB's relation was only designed to reason about high-level programs, the whole point of our model is to allow us to relate high- and low-level programs. As a result, we have no "fundamental theorem of logical relations" because one cannot even state such a theorem for a relation between two languages. Instead, we prove a *compiler correctness* result, whose proof mirrors that of the usual fundamental theorem. Our consideration of low-level programs has also led us to make a clear distinction between *programs* and *computations*, and between the notions of equivalence thereon. This seems to us an interesting and important distinction that is worth investigating further.

Dealing with low-level programs introduces significant technical complexity. In order to isolate this complexity, we factor the presentation of our relation generically w.r.t. a language specification "interface" LangSpec. This helps to clarify the structure of our Kripke logical relation, bringing into relief its essentially symmetric high-level structure, as well as the components of the model that are language-dependent (namely the two implementations of LangSpec, where most of the complexity lies). Although we have in this paper only instantiated our model so as to relate **HIGH** and **LOW** programs, one may also instantiate the model to relate **HIGH** and **HIGH** programs, or **LOW** and **LOW** programs. The former model would be largely similar to Dreyer *et al.*'s; the latter would enable one to reason about equivalence of low-level programs directly, which may prove useful in reasoning about correctness of low-level optimizations, although this remains to be explored.

As far as possible worlds are concerned, although ours are largely similar to DNB's, we have extended their worlds in one relatively straightforward way: in addition to *local* invariants (expressed in our possible worlds by *islands*), our worlds also permit one to express a *global* invariant. We exploit this added functionality to encode the allocator's invariant that all reachable data are live (Sections 3.6 and 6).

Lastly, as far as the high-level structure of the logical relation is concerned, ours is also quite similar to DNB's, except that our interpretation of reference types is somewhat different. Various approaches to interpreting reference types have been proposed in the literature; our present interpretation is in a more "extensional" style than either DNB's or Ahmed *et al.*'s [2], in the sense that it avoids dependence on too many details of how possible worlds are structured. This enables us to present it, as we have, in a more "world-generic" fashion. Among existing accounts, our present formulation is fairly close to the denotational one given by Birkedal, Støvring and Thamsborg [7], but the jury is still out on which of these formulations is most felicitous.

Although the primary benefit of presenting our logical relation language- and world-generically is to clarify its (admittedly complex) structure, it also enables us to prove a few "structural" lemmas generically as well, most notably *monotonicity*. (That we can prove monotonicity generically should not be surprising, given that it is essentially baked into the logical relation via the quantification over future worlds in certain cases and the use of the □ operator in others.) Most of the interesting theorems, however, cannot be stated, let alone proven, without talking about the details of the LangSpec's for **HIGH** and **LOW**.

Garbage Collection Torp-Smith *et al.* [24] prove the correctness of a Cheney copying collector using separation logic. They specify the behavior of a correct garbage collector in terms of an isomorphism between the reachable portions of the initial and final heaps. Our specification is broadly similar in that we express the reachable portion of the heap in our logical memories. We construct our entire LangSpec for **LOW** around these logical memories.

Building on the work of Torp-Smith *et al.*, McCreight *et al.* [20] develop a garbage collector interface that is general enough to characterize a variety of different collectors, including incremental copying collectors with read and write barriers. They prove in Coq that various collectors implement this interface, and that various mutator programs respect it. In more recent work, McCreight *et al.* [19] extend Leroy's Compcert compiler [18] with support for garbage collection, by building the mutator-collector interface into the design of a new intermediate language, GCminor. They prove semantics preservation (mostly) for a compiler from a purely functional, typed language—Dminor—to GCminor, but (as in Compcert) not compositional correctness.

Self-Modifying Code Cai *et al.* [9] provide one of the only formal accounts of how to verify self-modifying code. They use Hoare-style separation-based reasoning to enable local reasoning about modifications to code, in much the same way that standard separation logic enables local reasoning about the heap. We adopt a similar approach, using possible worlds to impose local invariants on—and, more generally, to establish local state transition systems governing—both the heap and the code segment. Ours is the first relational model for reasoning about (compositional) equivalence of self-modifying programs.

Future Work Given our ability to reason about self-modifying code, one direction for future work is to adapt this functionality to reason about more practical applications, such as a just-in-time compiler or a dynamic linker/loader.

We have shown compositionality of our high-low relation by showing that it is closed under the linking constructs expressible at the level of our **HIGH** language, such as function application. In future work, we would like to prove that our relation is also compositional w.r.t. a more realistic linking language.

The concrete logical relation we have presented here assumes a uniform data representation. It is possible in principle to define the meaning of language forms like $\mathrm{pair}(\mathbf{v}_1, \mathbf{v}_2)$ in a non-uniform way—*e.g.*, to enable flattening—but it is not currently possible in our language-generic framework to define such language forms in a *type*-specialized manner. We leave a serious examination of this issue to future work.

Lastly, it is unclear how to scale our techniques to reason about compositional correctness of a *multi-phase* compiler because the step-indexed logical relations we define are not obviously transitive. This is a well-known problem with step-indexed logical relations [1], and it seems a fresh idea is needed to circumvent it.

Acknowledgments

We would like to thank Jacob Thamsborg for pointing out a very subtle technical oversight in an earlier draft of this paper.

References

[1] A. Ahmed. Step-indexed syntactic logical relations for recursive and quantified types. In *ESOP*, 2006.

[2] A. Ahmed, D. Dreyer, and A. Rossberg. State-dependent representation independence. In *POPL*, 2009.

[3] A. Appel and D. McAllester. An indexed model of recursive types for foundational proof-carrying code. *TOPLAS*, 23(5):657–683, 2001.

[4] A. Appel, P.-A. Melliès, C. Richards, and J. Vouillon. A very modal model of a modern, major, general type system. In *POPL*, 2007.

[5] N. Benton and C.-K. Hur. Biorthogonality, step-indexing and compiler correctness. In *ICFP*, 2009.

[6] N. Benton and C.-K. Hur. Realizability and compositional compiler correctness for a polymorphic language. Technical Report MSR-TR-2010-62, Microsoft Research, Apr. 2010.

[7] L. Birkedal, K. Støvring, and J. Thamsborg. A relational realizability model for higher-order stateful ADTs. Submitted for publication, 2010.

[8] N. Bohr. *Advances in Reasoning Principles for Contextual Equivalence and Termination*. PhD thesis, IT University of Copenhagen, 2007.

[9] H. Cai, Z. Shao, and A. Vaynberg. Certified self-modifying code. In *PLDI*, 2007.

[10] A. Chlipala. A certified type-preserving compiler from lambda calculus to assembly language. In *PLDI*, 2007.

[11] A. Chlipala. Syntactic proofs of compositional compiler correctness, 2009. Submitted for publication.

[12] A. Chlipala. A verified compiler for an impure functional language. In *POPL*, 2010.

[13] Z. Dargaye. *Vérification formelle d'un compilateur pour langages fonctionnels*. PhD thesis, Université Paris 7 Denis Diderot, July 2009.

[14] D. Dreyer, G. Neis, and L. Birkedal. The impact of higher-order state and control effects on local relational reasoning. In *ICFP*, 2010.

[15] C.-K. Hur and D. Dreyer. Technical appendix for this paper, 2010. URL: `http://www.mpi-sws.org/~dreyer/papers/lrmlasm/`.

[16] G. Jaber and N. Tabareau. Krivine realizability for compiler correctness. In *LOLA*, 2010.

[17] J.-L. Krivine. Classical logic, storage operators and second-order lambda-calculus. *Annals of Pure and Applied Logic*, 68:53–78, 1994.

[18] X. Leroy. A formally verified compiler back-end. *Journal of Automated Reasoning*, 43(4):363–446, 2009.

[19] A. McCreight, T. Chevalier, and A. Tolmach. A certified framework for compiling and executing garbage-collected languages. In *ICFP*, 2010.

[20] A. McCreight, Z. Shao, C. Lin, and L. Li. A general framework for certifying garbage collectors and their mutators. In *PLDI*, 2007.

[21] A. Pitts. Typed operational reasoning. In B. C. Pierce, editor, *Advanced Topics in Types and Programming Languages*, chapter 7. MIT Press, 2005.

[22] A. Pitts and I. Stark. Operational reasoning for functions with local state. In *HOOTS*, 1998.

[23] E. Sumii. A complete characterization of observational equivalence in polymorphic lambda-calculus with general references. In *CSL*, 2009.

[24] N. Torp-Smith, L. Birkedal, and J. C. Reynolds. Local reasoning about a copying garbage collector. *TOPLAS*, 30(4), 2008.

A Typed Store-Passing Translation for General References

François Pottier
INRIA
Francois.Pottier@inria.fr

Abstract

We present a store-passing translation of System F with general references into an extension of System F_ω with certain well-behaved recursive kinds. This seems to be the first type-preserving store-passing translation for general references. It can be viewed as a purely syntactic account of a possible worlds model.

Categories and Subject Descriptors D.3.3 [*Programming Languages*]: Language Constructs and Features—Dynamic storage management; F.3.3 [*Logics and Meanings of Programs*]: Studies of Program Constructs—Type structure

General Terms Languages, Theory

1. Introduction

Motivation Building a semantic model of a programming language amounts to translating it into some mathematical meta-language. An important constraint in the design of such an interpretation is that it must explain (that is, translate away) computational effects such as non-termination and state, which do not exist in mathematics. Non-termination is often handled using the tools of domain theory, which was created for this purpose. State is usually dealt with in the style of Strachey [32] by making the store explicit and interpreting commands as functions that map stores to stores. Another important consideration is that the model should exploit the type discipline of the programming language. This enables it to serve as a tool in establishing type soundness and in proving typed contextual equivalence laws.

As a result of these considerations, building a semantic model of a rich programming language can be a challenging task. It is common wisdom among compiler writers that when one is faced with a complex translation task, one should decompose it into a succession of independent phases, connected via suitably chosen intermediate languages.

In this paper, we study one instance where this wisdom might be applicable in the construction of a semantic model. We focus on a particular programming language, namely a version of System F equipped with general references, and on a particular aspect of its semantics, namely the store-passing transformation, whose purpose is to explain (translate away) references. We isolate this transformation, just as if it were a phase in a compiler, and present it as a translation of our typed, imperative source language into a typed, purely functional intermediate language.

POPL'11, January 26–28, 2011, Austin, Texas, USA.

In so doing, we move the frontier between syntax and semantics. We suggest that a model of the imperative source language might be obtained through the composition of the store-passing transformation with a model of the purely functional intermediate language. This makes the construction of the model more modular, and may help explain it to researchers who are familiar with syntactic techniques. This also extends the family of known type-preserving transformations: to the best of our knowledge, until now, it was an open question how to define a type-preserving store-passing translation for general references.

Which intermediate language? In this endeavor, an important part of the difficulty is to find out what the typed intermediate language should be, and to keep it minimal. It would be nice if it could be a well-studied calculus, such as System F or F_ω. However, these calculi are strongly normalizing, whereas our source language is not: general references allow recursion through the store. Thus, one more ingredient is needed. In order to find out what this ingredient should be, let us first review some of the semantic models of general references.

Possible worlds models A reference is a dynamically-allocated memory cell, whose value can be read and modified at any time. We consider *general* references, which means that a reference can hold a value of any type, including a function, or the address of some other reference. Furthermore, we are interested in *weak* references. That is, we are interested in a type discipline whereby updates are type-invariant, de-allocation is forbidden, and aliasing is permitted.

The presence of references precludes a naïve interpretation of types as sets of values. A sentence such as: "the address 100 is an integer reference" does not make sense on its own. It implicitly relies on the assumption that the address 100 is currently allocated, that some integer value is currently stored there, and on the knowledge that these facts will continue to hold in the future.

To reflect this, several semantic models of weak references in the literature follow the "possible worlds" approach [2, 10, 16, 34]. There, the interpretation of a type is parameterized over a world, which represents the current state of the store. Worlds are equipped with a partial ordering: $w_1 \leq w_2$ means that w_2 is a possible future world of w_1, that is, every address that is allocated in w_1 is also allocated in w_2, with the same type. Bounded universal quantification over worlds is used to express the idea that a value that is valid now is also valid in every possible future world. Bounded existential quantification is used to express the idea that a command has the effect of transforming the current world into some possible future world.

At the heart of these possible worlds models of general references is a circularity. As stated above, semantic types are open-ended: they are parameterized over a world. However, worlds too must be open-ended: they must describe the store now and in every possible future. One way of achieving this is to define a world as a map of memory addresses to semantic types. This makes the definitions of worlds and semantic types mutually recursive, and creates a need to either solve a recursive domain equation *world* ≅ *world* → ... [10] or work with approximate solutions of it [2, 14]. An alternative is to define a world as a map of memory addresses to syntactic types [16]. Then, the circularity appears when worlds and types must be interpreted as semantic objects, and again a recursive domain equation must be solved.

A calculus with recursive kinds In this paper, we are not interested in solving or approximating recursive domain equations. Our purpose is to argue that a certain syntactic program transformation (namely, a store-passing translation) produces well-typed terms. Drawing inspiration from the possible worlds models, we wish to parameterize and to quantify types over worlds. Thus, we need worlds to be types (of a particular kind). That is, *world* should be a kind. Because we need *world* ≅ *world* → ..., we should look for an intermediate calculus that supports *recursive kinds*. This is the key ingredient that was alluded to above.

Should we propose an extension of F_ω with *arbitrary* recursive kinds? Such a system would have Turing-complete computation at the type level. That sounds rather wild. Do we need non-terminating computation at the type level? Yes. We do wish to allow certain forms of non-terminating computation at the type level, because we find it natural to view a recursive type as a λ-term whose infinite reduction produces, in the limit, an infinite tree. This is a form of non-terminating but *productive* computation.

Is there a way of ensuring that every type-level computation is productive in such a sense? Yes. Nakano [21, 22], for instance, presents a type system that controls recursion so as to guarantee productive computation. This system has recursive types but requires every cycle in the type structure to cross a "later" modality, written •. We re-use this system off-the-shelf, at the kind level; therefore, Nakano's terms and types become our types and kinds.

By adopting Nakano's system, we rule out certain recursive kinds. For instance, the recursive equation *world* = *world* → ... is in fact invalid, because it does not involve the modality. Fortunately, the modified equation *world* = • *world* → ... is permitted, and still fits our purposes. This equation states that a world is a *contractive* function: it is able to produce some output independently of its argument. This intuitively seems to correspond to the fact that if one attempts to describe the shape of the store, one will be able to provide a non-empty prefix of a description before one hits a self-reference to the shape of the store. For instance, one might say: *"the store currently contains one cell, which contains one function, whose argument must be a store that is a possible future of the current store..."*

The ultrametric-space techniques of Birkedal *et al.* [9, 10] and of Schwinghammer *et al.* [30] served as inspiration for the present work, so it is no surprise that there is a close analogy between these works and ours. Their $\frac{1}{2}$ scaling factor becomes the • modality. Their construction of world composition as the fixed point of a contractive map [30, Lemma 13] becomes a recursive definition that happens to be permitted in Nakano's system. The fact that world composition is associative [30, Lemma 14] becomes an assertion about the equality of two Böhm trees and can be automatically checked (§4.4).

In recent work, spurred in part by an earlier version of the present paper, Birkedal *et al.* [8] construct a metric model of a version of Nakano's system. This gives firm footing to the correspondence between • and $\frac{1}{2}$. Birkedal *et al.* note that their work provides the basis for a semantic model of the typed calculus that is presented here. Whether and how this model can be exploited in useful ways remains to be determined.

Contributions The contributions of this paper are: (i) the design of FORK, an extension of system F Omega with well-behaved Recursive Kinds; (ii) a type-preserving encoding of general references into this calculus.

Paper outline We first recall Nakano's system (§2), and build upon it in the definition of FORK (§3). Then, we explain how a version of System F equipped with general references can be encoded into FORK. We prove that the encoding is type-preserving and semantics-preserving[1] (§4). A prototype implementation of a FORK type-checker, the complete source code for the encoding of references, as well as the machine-checked proof of semantic preservation, are available online [28]. Some proofs are omitted and can be found in the extended version of this paper [29].

$$\frac{\kappa_1' \leq \kappa_1 \qquad \kappa_2 \leq \kappa_2'}{\kappa_1 \to \kappa_2 \leq \kappa_1' \to \kappa_2'} \qquad \frac{\kappa \leq \kappa'}{\bullet\kappa \leq \bullet\kappa'} \qquad \kappa \leq \bullet\kappa$$

$$\bullet(\kappa_1 \to \kappa_2) \lesseqgtr \bullet\kappa_1 \to \bullet\kappa_2$$

Figure 1. FORK: properties of the subkind relation

$$K \vdash \alpha : K(\alpha) \qquad \frac{K; \alpha : \kappa_1 \vdash \tau : \kappa_2}{K \vdash \lambda\alpha.\tau : \kappa_1 \to \kappa_2}$$

$$\frac{K \vdash \tau_1 : \kappa_1 \to \kappa_2 \qquad K \vdash \tau_2 : \kappa_1}{K \vdash \tau_1\ \tau_2 : \kappa_2} \qquad \frac{K \vdash \tau : \kappa_1 \qquad \kappa_1 \leq \kappa_2}{K \vdash \tau : \kappa_2}$$

Figure 2. FORK: kind assignment

2. Nakano's system

We now recall the definition and properties of Nakano's system [21, 22]. Our version of the system is close to Nakano's S-$\lambda\bullet\mu^+$. It is slightly simplified in that it is restricted to finite types (without distinction between positively and negatively finite types) and (as a result) it does not have a $\top$ type. Despite this difference, we refer to it as "Nakano's system".

There are two levels in Nakano's system, which are usually referred to as "types" and "terms". Nakano's "types" and "terms" are the *kinds* and *types* of FORK, respectively, so this is how we refer to them.

Kinds The kinds are *co-inductively* defined as follows:

$$\kappa ::= \star \mid \kappa \to \kappa \mid \bullet\kappa$$

A kind κ is a possibly infinite tree. In the prototype implementation [28], kinds are finitely represented via a set of mutually recursive defining equations. (Thus, only regular kinds can be defined.)

A kind κ is *well-formed* iff every infinite path through κ crosses a • constructor infinitely often. A kind is *finite* iff every infinite path through κ enters the domain of an arrow infinitely often. We restrict our attention to kinds that are well-formed and finite. (The finiteness condition is used in the proof of Lemma 2.4, where it serves to rule out types that produce an infinite stream of λ's, and therefore do not have a head normal form.) In the implementation, this requirement is enforced by checking that every occurrence of a kind name in the right-hand side of its defining equation(s) lies under a • constructor *and* in the domain of an arrow.

[1] More precisely, we prove that the encoding preserves convergence, and sketch how one might prove that it also preserves divergence.

Subkinding Kinds come with a *subkind* relation $\leq$. We omit its definition, which is somewhat technical (the reader is referred to [27]) and is irrelevant as long as the following properties hold. The subkind relation is reflexive, transitive, and satisfies the laws in Figure 1, where $\lesseqgtr$ means that the relation holds in both directions. The subkind relation satisfies the following inversion lemma:

Lemma 2.1 *If $\kappa_1 \rightarrow \kappa_2 \leq \kappa'_1 \rightarrow \kappa'_2$ holds, then, for some $n \in \mathbb{N}$, both $\kappa'_1 \leq \bullet^n \kappa_1$ and $\bullet^n \kappa_2 \leq \kappa'_2$ hold.* ◇

(We write $\bullet^n \kappa$ for n applications of $\bullet$ to κ.) When kinds are finitely represented as a set of mutually recursive defining equations, it is decidable whether two kinds κ_1 and κ_2 are in the subkind relation. In fact, it is possible to decide whether there exists $n \in \mathbb{N}$ such that $\kappa_1 \leq \bullet^n \kappa_2$ holds, and to compute the least such n when one exists [27]. The prototype implementation [28] takes advantage of this fact to perform bottom-up kind synthesis.

Types Types are pure λ-terms:

$$\tau ::= \alpha \mid \lambda\alpha.\tau \mid \tau\ \tau$$

We write $\tau_1 \longrightarrow \tau_2$ when τ_1 β-reduces to τ_2. Reduction is permitted under arbitrary contexts.

A kind environment K is a sequence of bindings of the form $\alpha : \kappa$. The judgement $K \vdash \tau : \kappa$ means that, within such an environment K, the type τ has kind κ. The rules that define it (Figure 2) are standard.

Recursion The judgement $\vdash Y : (\bullet\kappa \rightarrow \kappa) \rightarrow \kappa$, where Y is Curry's fixed point combinator $\lambda f.((\lambda x.f\ (x\ x))\ (\lambda x.f\ (x\ x)))$, is derivable. (The variable x receives the recursive kind $\kappa' = \bullet(\kappa' \rightarrow \kappa)$.) We introduce the notation $\mu\alpha.\tau$ as syntactic sugar for $Y\ (\lambda\alpha.\tau)$. This gives rise to the derived reduction rule:

$$\mu\alpha.\tau \longrightarrow [\alpha \mapsto \mu\alpha.\tau]\tau$$

and to the derived kind assignment rule:

$$\frac{K; \alpha : \bullet\kappa \vdash \tau : \kappa}{K \vdash \mu\alpha.\tau : \kappa}$$

The prototype implementation [28] has built-in support for recursive type definitions, based on the above rules. In fact, it supports mutually recursive type definitions.

Properties The system enjoys the following *degradation* and *subject reduction* properties.

Lemma 2.2 *$K \vdash \tau : \kappa$ implies $\bullet K \vdash \tau : \bullet\kappa$.* ◇

Lemma 2.3 *$K \vdash \tau_1 : \kappa$ and $\tau_1 \longrightarrow \tau_2$ imply $K \vdash \tau_2 : \kappa$.* ◇

A type of the form $\lambda\alpha_1 \ldots \alpha_m.\alpha\ \tau_1 \ldots \tau_n$ is a *head normal form*. Types are solvable: they admit head normal forms [21, 22, 27].

Lemma 2.4 *If $K \vdash \tau : \kappa$ then τ has a head normal form.* ◇

It is worth noting that this holds under any environment K, that is, in the presence of type variables of arbitrary kind. Together, Lemmas 2.3 and 2.4 imply that every type admits a maximal Böhm tree, that is, one that does not contain any occurrence of $\perp$ (the undefined Böhm tree). These two lemmas have been checked by the author using the Coq proof assistant [27].

Type equality We take *type equality*, a relation between types, to be *Böhm tree equivalence up to η* [7, §10.2.25] [15]. Several alternative characterizations of this relation are known. It is the greatest consistent λ-theory. It coincides with the equational theory of Scott's D_∞ model. It is the greatest compatible semi-sensible relation, that is, it coincides with the observational congruence obtained by observing solvability.

We write $\tau_1 \equiv \tau_2$ when τ_1 and τ_2 are in the type equality relation. In this paper, this relation is used only when both $K \vdash \tau_1 : \kappa$ and $K \vdash \tau_2 : \kappa$ hold for some environment K and kind κ. This has the following beneficial consequence:

Lemma 2.5 *The relation $\equiv$, restricted to well-kinded types, is semi-decidable.* ◇

Proof. We outline a simple semi-algorithm. This semi-algorithm maintains a conjunction G of goals, where a *goal* is an equation $\tau_1 \equiv \tau_2$ between two head normal forms. The free variables of a goal are implicitly viewed as universally quantified.

A goal g can be decomposed into a conjunction of sub-goals, written $\langle g \rangle$, as per the following equations. A case applies only if no prior case applies. We write $\tau\!\downarrow$ for the principal head normal form of τ.

$$\begin{array}{lll}
\langle \lambda\alpha.\tau_1 \equiv \lambda\alpha.\tau_2 \rangle & \text{is } \langle \tau_1 \equiv \tau_2 \rangle & \\
\langle \lambda\alpha.\tau_1 \equiv \tau_2 \rangle & \text{is } \langle \tau_1 \equiv \tau_2\ \alpha \rangle & \text{if } \alpha \# \tau_2 \\
\langle \tau_1 \equiv \lambda\alpha.\tau_2 \rangle & \text{is } \langle \tau_1\ \alpha \equiv \tau_2 \rangle & \text{if } \alpha \# \tau_1 \\
\langle \tau_1\ \tau'_1 \equiv \tau_2\ \tau'_2 \rangle & \text{is } \langle \tau_1 \equiv \tau_2 \rangle \wedge \tau'_1\!\downarrow \equiv \tau'_2\!\downarrow & \\
\langle \alpha \equiv \alpha \rangle & \text{is true} & \\
\langle \tau_1 \equiv \tau_2 \rangle & \text{is false} &
\end{array}$$

We write $\langle G \rangle$ for the conjunction of sub-goals obtained by applying $\langle \cdot \rangle$ to every goal in G.

Consider the problem of deciding whether $\tau_1 \equiv \tau_2$ holds. Enumerate the potentially infinite sequence defined by $G_0 = (\tau_1\!\downarrow \equiv \tau_2\!\downarrow)$ and $G_{k+1} = \langle G_k \rangle$. If some G_k is found to be empty, report "yes". If some G_k is found to be false, report "no".

If $\tau_1 \not\equiv \tau_2$ holds, then this semi-algorithm reports "no". If $\tau_1 \equiv \tau_2$ holds and τ_1 and τ_2 have a finite Böhm tree, then it reports "yes". If $\tau_1 \equiv \tau_2$ holds and τ_1 and τ_2 have an infinite Böhm tree, then the semi-algorithm diverges. □

In the prototype implementation [28], this semi-algorithm is improved in two ways.

First, G_{k+1} is defined as $\langle G_k \rangle \setminus \bigcup_{j \leq k} G_j$. That is, any goal that has already appeared during an earlier step is considered valid. Goals are compared up to renaming of their free variables.

Second, an equation of the form $\tau_1\ \tau'_1 \equiv \tau_2\ \tau'_2$, where one of the two sides is *not* a head normal form, is heuristically decomposed into $\tau_1 \equiv \tau_2 \wedge \tau'_1 \equiv \tau'_2$. (This is done in addition to the default behavior, which is to reduce both sides to head normal form before decomposing them.) This can have the effect of replacing a difficult goal, which would lead the semi-algorithm into a sequence of ever-growing goals, with a conjunction of simpler goals that the semi-algorithm is able to prove.

The semi-algorithm thus improved remains sound. Indeed, when it succeeds, the set of goals that have been examined forms an *hnf bisimulation up to η and up to context,* as studied by Lassen [15], which implies that these goals are valid. The semi-algorithm remains incomplete, but is strong enough to prove all of the equations required by the encoding presented in §4.

Why do we require types to be well-kinded? If we were to remove this condition, every type would be permitted. Still, the fact that $\equiv$ is a consistent λ-theory would be sufficient to prove that FORK is type-safe (§3). However, type equality would then become undecidable, and (as a result) type-checking would become undecidable as well. This would make it pragmatically more difficult to build well-typed FORK terms, as we do in §4. If we do insist that types are well-kinded, on the other hand, then every type is solvable and (as a result) type equality and type-checking are semi-decidable, a pragmatically valuable property.

Another potential reason why kinds should be well-formed and types should be well-kinded is that these conditions make it possible to interpret kinds in a category of ultrametric spaces and to interpret types as inhabitants of kinds, in the style of Birkedal *et al.* [8].

$$\kappa ::= \star \mid \kappa \to \kappa \mid \bullet \kappa \qquad \text{(co-inductively; see §2)}$$

$$\begin{aligned} \tau ::= {} & \alpha \mid \lambda\alpha.\tau \mid \tau\ \tau && \text{(see §2)} \\ & \mid \to \mid () \mid (,) \mid \forall_\kappa \mid \exists_\kappa && \text{(type constants)} \end{aligned}$$

$$\begin{aligned} t ::= {} & x \mid \lambda x.t \mid t\ t && \text{(functions)} \\ & \mid () && \text{(unit)} \\ & \mid (t,t) \mid \text{let } (x,x) = t \text{ in } t && \text{(pairs)} \\ & \mid \Lambda\alpha.t \mid t\ \tau && \text{(universals)} \\ & \mid \text{pack } \tau, t \text{ as } \tau && \text{(existentials)} \\ & \mid \text{unpack } \alpha, x = t \text{ in } t \end{aligned}$$

$$\Gamma ::= \emptyset \mid \Gamma; \alpha : \kappa \mid \Gamma; x : \tau$$

Figure 3. FORK: kinds, types, terms

$$\begin{array}{ll} 1. & K \vdash () : \star \\ 2. & K \vdash \to : \bullet\star \to \bullet\star \to \star \\ 3. & K \vdash (,) : \bullet\star \to \bullet\star \to \star \\ 4. & K \vdash \forall_\kappa : (\kappa \to \bullet^n \star) \to \bullet^n \star \\ 5. & K \vdash \exists_\kappa : (\kappa \to \bullet^n \star) \to \bullet^n \star \end{array}$$

Figure 4. FORK: kind assignment: constants

VAR
$$\Gamma \vdash x : \Gamma(x)$$

ABS
$$\frac{\Gamma \vdash \tau_1 : \bigcirc\star \qquad \Gamma; x : \tau_1 \vdash t : \tau_2}{\Gamma \vdash \lambda x.t : \tau_1 \to \tau_2}$$

APP
$$\frac{\Gamma \vdash t_1 : \tau_1 \to \tau_2 \qquad \Gamma \vdash t_2 : \tau_1}{\Gamma \vdash t_1\ t_2 : \tau_2}$$

UNIT
$$\Gamma \vdash () : ()$$

(,)-INTRO
$$\frac{\Gamma \vdash t_1 : \tau_1 \qquad \Gamma \vdash t_2 : \tau_2}{\Gamma \vdash (t_1, t_2) : (\tau_1, \tau_2)}$$

(,)-ELIM
$$\frac{\Gamma \vdash t_1 : (\tau_1, \tau_2) \qquad \Gamma; x_1 : \tau_1; x_2 : \tau_2 \vdash t_2 : \tau}{\Gamma \vdash \text{let } (x_1, x_2) = t_1 \text{ in } t_2 : \tau}$$

$\forall$-INTRO
$$\frac{\Gamma; \alpha : \kappa \vdash t : \tau \qquad \alpha \# \Gamma}{\Gamma \vdash \Lambda\alpha.t : \forall_\kappa (\lambda\alpha.\tau)}$$

$\forall$-ELIM
$$\frac{\Gamma \vdash t : \forall_\kappa \tau_1 \qquad \Gamma \vdash \tau_2 : \bigcirc\kappa}{\Gamma \vdash t\ \tau_2 : \tau_1\ \tau_2}$$

$\exists$-INTRO
$$\frac{\Gamma \vdash t : \tau_1\ \tau_2 \qquad \Gamma \vdash \exists_\kappa \tau_1 : \bigcirc\star \qquad \Gamma \vdash \tau_2 : \bigcirc\kappa}{\Gamma \vdash \text{pack } \tau_2, t \text{ as } \exists_\kappa \tau_1 : \exists_\kappa \tau_1}$$

$\exists$-ELIM
$$\frac{\Gamma \vdash t_1 : \exists_\kappa \tau_1 \qquad \alpha \# \Gamma, \tau_2 \qquad \Gamma; \alpha : \kappa; x : (\tau_1\ \alpha) \vdash t_2 : \tau_2}{\Gamma \vdash \text{unpack } \alpha, x = t_1 \text{ in } t_2 : \tau_2}$$

CONVERSION
$$\frac{\Gamma \vdash t : \tau_1 \qquad \Gamma \vdash \tau_2 : \bigcirc\star \qquad \tau_1 \equiv \tau_2}{\Gamma \vdash t : \tau_2}$$

Figure 5. FORK: type assignment

3. FORK

In System F_ω, a system of simple finite kinds is used to classify types. In FORK, instead, Nakano's system is used. As a result, FORK is an extension of F_ω. FORK retains type safety, but abandons strong normalization.

Kinds and types Kinds and types (Figure 3) are as presented previously (§2), except a number of type constants are introduced, as is standard in F_ω. These constants are assigned kinds by the axioms in Figure 4.

$$\begin{array}{rcl} (\lambda x.t_1)\ t_2 & \longrightarrow & [x \mapsto t_2]t_1 \\ \text{let } (x_1, x_2) = (t_1, t_2) \text{ in } t & \longrightarrow & [x_1 \mapsto t_1, x_2 \mapsto t_2]t \\ (\Lambda\alpha.t)\ \tau & \longrightarrow & [\alpha \mapsto \tau]t \\ \text{unpack } \alpha, x = & & \\ (\text{pack } \tau_2, t_1 \text{ as } \tau_1) \text{ in } t_2 & \longrightarrow & [\alpha \mapsto \tau_2, x \mapsto t_1]t_2 \\ C[t_1] & \longrightarrow & C[t_2] \\ & & \text{if } t_1 \longrightarrow t_2 \end{array}$$

Figure 6. FORK: reduction semantics

It may come as a surprise that the function and product type constructors have kind $\bullet\star \to \bullet\star \to \star$, as opposed to $\star \to \star \to \star$ in F_ω. This means that these constructors are *contractive* in both arguments. An intuitive reason why they should be viewed as contractive is precisely that they are type *constructors*, as opposed to type *operators:* they produce syntax. For instance, an application of the function type constructor to two arbitrary types τ_1 and τ_2 yields a type that is well-defined down to depth 1—it has an arrow at its root— regardless of how τ_1 and τ_2 might behave. The FORK axioms are more liberal than their F_ω counterparts, and crucially so. For instance, the former allow the recursive type $\mu\alpha.\alpha \to \alpha$ to have kind $\star$, while the latter would make this type ill-kinded. Naturally, the encoding of general references into FORK (§4) relies on the existence of such recursive types.

Because the function and product type constructors have kind $\bullet\star \to \bullet\star \to \star$, one cannot expect the types that classify values to always have kind $\star$, as in F_ω. Instead, in FORK, the types that classify values have kind $\bullet^n \star$, for some $n \in \mathbb{N}$. We write $K \vdash \tau : \bigcirc\kappa$ when $K \vdash \tau : \bullet^n \kappa$ holds for some $n \in \mathbb{N}$.

The universal and existential type constructors $\forall_\kappa$ and $\exists_\kappa$ are not considered contractive. Because the types that classify values can have kind $\bullet^n \star$ for any $n \in \mathbb{N}$, it is natural for these two constants to admit every kind of the form $(\kappa \to \bullet^n \star) \to \bullet^n \star$, as opposed to just $(\kappa \to \star) \to \star$ in F_ω.

The properties stated in the previous section (§2) remain valid in the presence of type constants of arbitrary kind.

Type assignment The syntax of terms t and type environments Γ is standard (Figure 3). A type environment Γ can play the role of a kind environment K.

The type assignment judgement $\Gamma \vdash t : \tau$ is defined in Figure 5. The typing rules are identical to their F_ω counterparts up to a few details, which we now discuss.

The type conversion rule (CONVERSION) relies on the notion of type equality that was defined earlier (§2).

The types that classify values have kind $\bigcirc\star$. This is reflected in the following definition and lemma:

Definition 3.1 *The empty type environment is well-formed. The type environment $\Gamma; \alpha : \kappa$ is well-formed if Γ is well-formed and $\alpha \# \Gamma$. The type environment $\Gamma; x : \tau$ is well-formed if Γ is well-formed and $\Gamma \vdash \tau : \bigcirc\star$.* ◇

Lemma 3.2 *If Γ is well-formed, then $\Gamma \vdash t : \tau$ implies $\Gamma \vdash \tau : \bigcirc\star$.* ◇

In the following, we restrict our attention to well-formed type environments.

The type application rule ($\forall$-ELIM) states that a universally quantified variable of kind κ can be instantiated with a type of kind $\bigcirc\kappa$. The rule $\exists$-INTRO is similarly relaxed. This makes sense thanks to the following type substitution lemma, which is later exploited in the proof of subject reduction:

$$
\begin{aligned}
C &::= \lambda x.[] \mid [] \; e \mid e \; [] \mid \\
&\quad ([], e) \mid (e, []) \mid \pi_i \; [] \\
S &::= [] \mid S[\text{bind } ([], e)]
\end{aligned}
$$

$$
\begin{aligned}
(\lambda x.e_1) \; e_2 &\rightarrow [x \mapsto e_2]e_1 \\
\pi_i \; (e_1, e_2) &\rightarrow e_i \\
C[e] &\rightarrow C[e'] \\
&\quad \text{if } e \rightarrow e'
\end{aligned}
$$

$$
\begin{aligned}
(s, S, e_1) &\rightarrow (s, S, e_2) \\
&\quad \text{if } e_1 \rightarrow e_2 \\
(s, S, \text{bind } (e_1, e_2)) &\rightarrow (s, S[\text{bind } ([], e_2)], e_1) \\
(s, S[\text{bind } ([], e_2)], \text{return } e_1) &\rightarrow (s, S, e_2 \; e_1) \\
(s, S, \text{new } e) &\rightarrow (s\{\ell \mapsto e\}, S, \text{return } \ell) \\
&\quad \text{where } \ell = |s| \\
(s, S, \text{read } \ell) &\rightarrow (s, S, s(\ell)) \\
&\quad \text{if } \ell < |s| \\
(s, S, \text{write } (\ell, e)) &\rightarrow (s\{\ell \mapsto e\}, S, \text{return } ()) \\
&\quad \text{if } \ell < |s|
\end{aligned}
$$

Figure 7. System F: untyped reduction semantics

Lemma 3.3 *Let* $\Gamma_1 \vdash \tau_1 : \bigcirc\kappa$. *If* $\Gamma_1; \alpha : \kappa; \Gamma_2$ *is well-formed, then* $\Gamma_1; [\alpha \mapsto \tau_1]\Gamma_2$ *is well-formed. Furthermore,* $\Gamma_1; \alpha : \kappa; \Gamma_2 \vdash t : \tau_2$ *implies* $\Gamma_1; [\alpha \mapsto \tau_1]\Gamma_2 \vdash [\alpha \mapsto \tau_1]t : [\alpha \mapsto \tau_1]\tau_2$. ◇

It is possible to give a syntax-directed presentation of the type system, where the conversion rule is merged with the other rules. This allows type-checking to be performed in a standard bottom-up fashion. That is, provided every Λ-bound variable carries an explicit kind and every λ-bound variable carries an explicit type, the knowledge of Γ and t is sufficient to reconstruct a type τ (if one exists) such that $\Gamma \vdash t : \tau$ holds. The prototype implementation of FORK follows this scheme.

Type soundness FORK is equipped with a standard reduction semantics (Figure 6). Reduction is permitted under an arbitrary context. *Values* are defined as follows:

$$v ::= \lambda x.t \mid () \mid (v, v) \mid \Lambda\alpha.v \mid \text{pack } \tau, v \text{ as } \tau$$

The system enjoys the following properties:

Lemma 3.4 (Subject reduction) $\Gamma \vdash t_1 : \tau$ *and* $t_1 \longrightarrow t_2$ *imply* $\Gamma \vdash t_2 : \tau$. ◇

Definition 3.5 *A term t is* well-typed *iff* $\Gamma \vdash t : \tau$ *holds, where* Γ *binds only type variables (no term variables).* ◇

Lemma 3.6 (Progress) *A well-typed term either reduces or is a value.* ◇

Theorem 3.7 (Type soundness) *A well-typed term either diverges or reduces (in zero or more steps) to a value.* ◇

4. Encoding general references into FORK

4.1 The source calculus

The source language of the encoding is a monadic presentation of System F with general references. It is due to Peyton Jones and Wadler [25, §5.3].

The terms are the standard terms of System F, extended with the monadic constants return and bind; with the constants new, read, and write for allocating, reading and writing references; and with memory locations ℓ, which we take to be natural numbers.

$$
\begin{aligned}
e ::= \; & x \mid \lambda x.e \mid e \; e \mid \Lambda\alpha.e \mid e \; T \mid () \mid (e, e) \mid \pi_i \; e \mid \\
& \text{return} \mid \text{bind} \mid \text{new} \mid \text{read} \mid \text{write} \mid \ell
\end{aligned}
$$

F-VAR
$$E_1; x : T; E_2 \vdash x : T$$

F-ABS
$$\frac{E; x : T_1 \vdash e : T_2}{E \vdash \lambda x.e : T_1 \rightarrow T_2}$$

F-APP
$$\frac{E \vdash e_1 : T_1 \rightarrow T_2 \qquad E \vdash e_2 : T_1}{E \vdash e_1 \; e_2 : T_2}$$

F-∀-INTRO
$$\frac{E; \alpha \vdash e : T}{E \vdash \Lambda\alpha.e : \forall\alpha.T}$$

F-∀-ELIM
$$\frac{E \vdash e : \forall\alpha.T_1}{E \vdash e \; T_2 : [\alpha \mapsto T_2]T_1}$$

F-UNIT
$$E \vdash () : ()$$

F-(,)-INTRO
$$\frac{E \vdash e_1 : T_1 \qquad E \vdash e_2 : T_2}{E \vdash (e_1, e_2) : (T_1, T_2)}$$

F-(,)-ELIM
$$\frac{E \vdash e : (T_1, T_2)}{E \vdash \pi_i \; e : T_i}$$

F-RETURN
$$E \vdash \text{return} : \forall\alpha.\alpha \rightarrow M \; \alpha$$

F-BIND
$$E \vdash \text{bind} : \forall\alpha.\forall\beta.(M \; \alpha, \alpha \rightarrow M \; \beta) \rightarrow M \; \beta$$

F-NEW
$$E \vdash \text{new} : \forall\alpha.\alpha \rightarrow M \; (\text{ref } \alpha)$$

F-READ
$$E \vdash \text{read} : \forall\alpha.\text{ref } \alpha \rightarrow M \; \alpha$$

F-WRITE
$$E \vdash \text{write} : \forall\alpha.(\text{ref } \alpha, \alpha) \rightarrow M \; ()$$

Figure 8. System F: typing rules

The types are:

$$T ::= \alpha \mid () \mid T \rightarrow T \mid (T, T) \mid \forall\alpha.T \mid M \; T \mid \text{ref } T$$

where M is the monad. The definition of the typing judgement $E \vdash e : T$ appears in Figure 8. This definition concerns programs whose execution has not begun and (hence) that do not contain memory locations. A definition of the encoding of locations is needed only as part of the semantics preservation argument (§4.10).

The operational semantics is defined for type-erased terms, that is, terms where the type abstraction and type application constructs have been erased. The semantics, which appears in Figure 7, is organized in two layers, following Moggi and Sabry [19]. First, *simplification* of terms is defined: it is the compatible closure of β-reduction. Then, *reduction* of configurations is defined, where a configuration is a triple of a store s, an evaluation stack S, and a term e, which represents a computation (that is, it presumably has a type of the form $M \; T$). Because memory locations are natural numbers, a store is just a list of terms. We write *nil* for the empty store. We write $|s|$ for the length of the store s. We write $s(\ell)$ for the term found in the store s at location ℓ. We write $s\{\ell \mapsto e\}$ for the extension or update of the store s at location ℓ with the term e. An evaluation stack is just a list of suspended applications of bind.

In the following, we present an encoding of this calculus into FORK. We begin with a series of definitions of FORK kinds, types, and terms (§4.2–§4.6), whose well-formedness has been machine-checked by the prototype implementation of FORK [28]. Then, we define the encoding (§4.7 and §4.8), a type-directed transformation of the source calculus into FORK. Finally, we prove that the encoding is type-preserving (§4.9) and semantics-preserving (§4.10).

4.2 Fragments

In order to type-check the store, which is basically a sequence of values, we need sequences of base types, where a *base type* is a type of kind $\star$. Because the store grows with time, we often use

kind *fragment* =
  $\star \to \star$
type *fnil* : *fragment* =
  λ*tail. tail*
type @ : *fragment* $\to$ *fragment* $\to$ *fragment* =
  $\lambda f_1\, f_2$ *tail*. f_1 (f_2 *tail*)
type *snoc* : *fragment* $\to \star \to$ *fragment* =
  λf. λ*data*. λ*tail*. *f* (*data*, *tail*)

Figure 9. Fragments

type *array* : $\bullet$ *fragment* $\to \star$
type *index* : $\bullet$ *fragment* $\to \bullet \star \to \star$
term *array_empty* : *array fnil*
term *array_extend* :
  $\forall f$ *data*. *array f* $\to$ *data* $\to$ *array* (*f* '*snoc*' *data*)
term *array_read* :
  $\forall f$ *data*. *array f* $\to$ *index f data* $\to$ *data*
term *array_write* :
  $\forall f$ *data*. *array f* $\to$ *index f data* $\to$ *data* $\to$ *array f*
term *array_end_index* :
  $\forall f$. *array f* $\to \forall$*data*. *index* (*f* '*snoc*' *data*) *data*
term *index_monotonic* :
  $\forall f_1\, f_2$ *data*. *index* f_1 *data* $\to$ *index* (f_1 '@' f_2) *data*

Figure 10. Arrays

such a sequence to describe only part of the store, and concatenate multiple such sequences to obtain a description of the complete store. For this reason, we refer to such a sequence as a *fragment*.

Because we intend to parameterize types over fragments, to quantify over fragments, etc., fragments must be types (of a suitable kind), and the basic operations over fragments must be type operators.

This is done as follows (Figure 9). The kind *fragment* is $\star \to \star$. The empty fragment *fnil* is the identity function. Fragment concatenation @ is function composition. It is easy to check, with respect to type equality $\equiv$, that *fnil* is a left unit and right unit for @, and that @ is associative. The extension of a fragment *f* with a base type *data*, written *snoc f data* or more pleasantly *f* '*snoc*' *data*, is λ*tail*. *f* (*data*, *tail*). The type (*data*, *tail*) is the application of the "product" type constructor (,) (Figure 4) to the base types *data* and *tail*.

4.3 Arrays

We wish to represent the store as an array. Thus, FORK must support arrays. We need *heterogeneous* arrays: it must be permitted for different array elements to have different types. We need *safe* arrays: out-of-bound array accesses must be statically forbidden. (As Levy puts it, it "is unnatural [...] to specify what happens when we read a non-existent cell, something that can never occur in reality" [16].) We need *extensible* arrays: there must be a way of creating a new array by appending a new cell at the end of an existing array, and any valid index into the earlier array must remain a valid index into the new array.

The signature in Figure 10 fulfills these requirements. It introduces a couple of abstract type constructors for arrays and indices, as well as a number of operations over arrays.

The type *array f* describes a heterogeneous array whose elements are described by the fragment *f*. The type *index f data* represents the address of a cell of base type *data* within an array of type *array f*. The type operators *array* and *index* are contractive: as far as the user of the array abstraction is concerned, they can be thought of as type constructors.

kind *world* =
  $\bullet$ *world* $\to$ *fragment*
type *nil* : *world* =
  λx. *fnil*
type *o* : *world* $\to$ *world* $\to$ *world* =
  $\lambda w_1\, w_2\, x$. w_1 (w_2 '*o*' *x*) '@' w_2 *x*

Figure 11. Worlds

The zero length array, *array_empty*, is described by the fragment *fnil*. Array extension, *array_extend*, is described using the fragment extension operation, *snoc*. Reading and writing are permitted by *array_read* and *array_write*. Writing is type-invariant: the old and new array elements both have type *data*. The operation *array_end_index* returns the end index of an array of type *array f*. It is not a valid index into this array, but becomes a valid index once the array is extended with a new cell: this is expressed by the type $\forall$*data*. *index* (*f* '*snoc*' *data*) *data*. The operation *index_monotonic* witnesses the fact that a valid index into a smaller array is also a valid index into a larger array: this is expressed in terms of fragment concatenation. This operation is a coercion: its semantics is the identity.

There are two ways of making the types and operations described by this signature available in FORK.

The first way, which we follow, is to implement this signature. This can be done by representing array data as a tagless singly-linked list (that is, as a sequence of nested pairs) and by representing an array index as a pair of functions for reading and writing at this index. (The read function, for instance, encapsulates a sequence of pair projections.) The code is about a hundred lines [28]. It does not use any recursion: it is in fact expressed within F_ω. This implementation of arrays shows that, in principle, it is not necessary to extend FORK with primitive arrays. It is of course inefficient: reading and writing have linear time complexity.

The second way would be to extend FORK with primitive arrays, that is, to consider the signature of Figure 10 as a set of axioms, to extend the operational semantics of FORK with new reduction rules for arrays, and to extend its type soundness proof. This would allow a more efficient implementation of array access, although efficiency seems of little concern here.

4.4 Worlds

Our arrays are extensible *in width*. This helps us model dynamic allocation, that is, the fact that the store grows with time. There remains to model higher-order store, that is, the fact that the store can contain references and functions, whose type, in the encoding, depends on the shape of the store. This dependency means that, as the store grows in width, the type of an existing store cell evolves. We say that the store also grows *in depth*.

An example may help illustrate this phenomenon. Consider the ML program "let x_1 = ref ($\lambda x.x$) in let x_2 = ref 0 in x_1 := ($\lambda x.!x_2$)". When the reference cell x_1 is first allocated, it contains a function that has type int $\to$ int unconditionally. However, x_1 is later updated with a function that has type int $\to$ int only under a store where the cell x_2 exists and holds an integer value. Thus, the type of the contents of the cell x_1 evolves with time.

In order to reflect this, we introduce *worlds* (Figure 11). A world is an open-ended description of a store fragment. More precisely, a world is a fragment that is itself parameterized over a world. The kind *world* is recursive. It is well-formed, because the recursion goes through the "later" constructor $\bullet$. A world is a *contractive* function of a world: it produces some structure before it uses its argument.

The empty world *nil* is the constant function that returns the empty fragment. World composition, w_1 '*o*' w_2, can be described as

kind *stype* =
  • *world* → ⋆
type *box* : *stype* → *stype* =
  $\lambda a\ x.\ \forall y.\ a\ (x\ \text{'o'}\ y)$
type *unit* : *stype* =
  $\lambda x.\ ()$
type *pair* : *stype* → *stype* → *stype* =
  $\lambda a\ b\ x.\ (a\ x, b\ x)$
type *univ* : (*stype* → *stype*) → *stype* =
  $\lambda body\ x.\ \forall a.\ body\ a\ x$
type *arrow* : *stype* → *stype* → *stype* =
  $\lambda a\ b\ x.\ box\ a\ x \rightarrow box\ b\ x$
type *monad* : *stype* → *stype* =
  $\lambda a\ x.\ store\ x \rightarrow outcome\ a\ x$
type *outcome* : *stype* → *stype* =
  $\lambda a\ x.\ \exists y.\ (box\ a\ (x\ \text{'o'}\ y), store\ (x\ \text{'o'}\ y))$
type *store* : • *world* → ⋆ =
  $\lambda x.\ \forall y.\ array\ (x\ y)$
type *ref* : *stype* → *stype* =
  $\lambda a\ x.\ \forall y.\ index\ (x\ y)\ (a\ (x\ \text{'o'}\ y))$

Figure 12. Semantic types

the result of extending w_1 *in depth and in width* with w_2. Naturally, its definition is recursive. We invite the reader to check that it is well-typed in Nakano's system, using the derived kind assignment rule for recursive type definitions.

The empty world *nil* is a left unit and right unit for world composition. Furthermore, world composition is associative. This fact is non-obvious; fortunately, the semi-algorithm for type equality (§2) proves it (and others like it) without assistance.

In the following, by convention, the variable w has kind *world*, while the variables x and y have kind • *world*.

4.5 Semantic types

A type in the source language is translated to a *semantic type*, that is, a contractive function of worlds to base types (Figure 12).

Let a be a semantic type and x be a world. A value v of type $a\ x$ is valid now, in world x. Is it valid also in every future world? That is, is it the case that v also has type $a\ (x\ \text{'o'}\ y)$ for every y? In general, there is no guarantee that this is so. Where we need this to be the case, we are explicit about this requirement and use a value of type *box a x*, where the semantic type operator *box* builds in a universal quantification over future worlds. This operator is known as the *necessity modality* [5]. A semantic type of the form *box a* is known as *necessary* [5] or *hereditary* [14].

Remark There are semantic models (see e.g. [31]) where necessity is built into the world equation, so that (the analogue of) every type is hereditary. Here, this is not the case. FORK does not have a "monotonic arrow" at the kind level, so there seems to be no way of building necessity into worlds. We follow Appel *et al.* [5] and Hobor *et al.* [14] and explicitly use the *box* modality to keep track of which types are hereditary. ◇

It is worth noting that bounded quantification over all future worlds z (that is, $\forall z \geq x.\ \tau$) is expressed here in terms of ordinary quantification over a world extension y (that is, $\forall y.\ [z \mapsto x\ \text{'o'}\ y]\tau$). In this encoding, the associativity of world composition expresses the transitivity of the world ordering.

A hereditary value is valid in every future world, hence is hereditary in every future world. This is expressed by defining a coercion *forward* of type $\forall a\ x\ y.\ box\ a\ x \rightarrow box\ a\ (x\ \text{'o'}\ y)$.

The encoding of unit, pairs, and quantifiers is straightforward: the world parameter x is just passed down. The encoding of arrows states that functions require a hereditary argument and produce a hereditary result. This is expressed by the type $box\ a\ x \rightarrow box\ b\ x$.

Remark The reader might have expected instead the type $box\ (\lambda x.\ a\ x \rightarrow b\ x)$, which guarantees that the function itself is hereditary. This type is more general than $box\ a\ x \rightarrow box\ b\ x$.

However, this choice would cause a difficulty in the construction of certain functions, such as *new* (Figure 15). There, we must be able to argue that the argument v is hereditary, because this value will be written into the store, and the store holds hereditary values. If v has type *box a x*, the argument is trivial, whereas if it has type $a\ x$, it is not clear that v is hereditary.

Our current choice, on the other hand, does not seem to cause any difficulty. It leads to a style where every variable in the type environment has a boxed type (see Definition 4.2) and every expression has a boxed type (see the statement of Theorem 4.3). In short, the fact that the encoding $[\![T]\!]$ of a type T is not always hereditary does not hurt us: we use explicit boxes where needed.

Another route would be to set things up so that the encoding $[\![T]\!]$ of every type T is a hereditary semantic type. One would then build this information into the translation via coercions: wherever one abstracts over a semantic type variable a, one would also abstract over a coercion of type $\forall x.\ a\ x \rightarrow box\ a\ x$. It seems plausible that this would succeed; it could be investigated as part of future work.◇

The encoding of the monad is standard [16]. A computation requires a store in world x, and produces a pair of a (hereditary) result and a new store in some future world $x\ \text{'o'}\ y$. We use the abbreviation *outcome a x* for the type of such a pair.

A store in world w contains values that are valid in world w and in future worlds. That is, a store is an array of hereditary values. This is expressed by defining *store w* as $\forall x.\ array\ (w\ x)$. In other words, a store is of course of fixed *width*, but is polymorphic in *depth*.

A reference of type *ref a* in world x is, roughly speaking, an index that allows reading or writing data of type $a\ x$ within an array of type *store x*. More precisely, universal quantification over a world extension y is again used to guarantee that references are hereditary. By direct appeal to *index_monotonic*, it is possible to define a coercion *box_ref* of type $\forall a\ x.\ ref\ a\ x \rightarrow box\ (ref\ a)\ x$.

We have reviewed the encoding of every type constructor of the source language. Thus, any source-level type T is translated to a semantic type $[\![T]\!]$. (The inductive definition of this translation cannot be expressed within FORK.)

Definition 4.1 *The encoding* $[\![T]\!]$ *of a type* T *is defined as follows:*

$$\begin{aligned} [\![\alpha]\!] &= \alpha \\ [\![()]\!] &= unit \\ [\![T_1 \rightarrow T_2]\!] &= arrow\ [\![T_1]\!]\ [\![T_2]\!] \\ [\![(T_1, T_2)]\!] &= pair\ [\![T_1]\!]\ [\![T_2]\!] \\ [\![\forall\alpha.T]\!] &= univ\ (\lambda\alpha.[\![T]\!]) \\ [\![M\ T]\!] &= monad\ [\![T]\!] \\ [\![ref\ T]\!] &= ref\ [\![T]\!] \end{aligned}$$

where the combinators that appear in the right-hand sides of these equations are defined in Figure 12. ◇

4.6 Memory allocation

When a new reference is allocated, the width of the array that represents the store is increased by one. If the allocation takes place in world x, and if the newly created reference is initialized with a value v of type *box a x*, what is the new world after allocation?

This new world must be the composition of x and of a world of width one, which we refer to as a *cell*. That is, the new world must be $x\ \text{'o'}\ cell\ a\ x$, for an appropriate definition of *cell*, an operator that maps a and x to a world.

type *cell* : *stype* → • *world* → *world* =
  λa x y tail. (*a* (*x* '*o*' *cell a x* '*o*' *y*), *tail*)
term *store_extend* :
  ∀*x a. store x* → *box a x* → *store* (*x* '*o*' *cell a x*)
term *store_end_index* :
  ∀*x a. store x* → *ref a* (*x* '*o*' *cell a x*)

Figure 13. Memory allocation

The definition of *cell* appears in Figure 13. As above, the parameter *x* represents the world before allocation, or a past world. The parameter *y* represents a depth extension, or a future world, while *tail* represents a width extension. The type *cell a x y tail*, a type of kind ⋆, is a product of the types *a (...)* and *tail*. (This is consistent with our definition of fragment extension, *snoc*, in Figure 9.) The semantic type *a* is applied to the composite world *x 'o' (cell a x) 'o' y*, reflecting the manner in which the final world is obtained: starting in world *x*, first a memory cell is allocated, then the world is extended with *y*. Thus, the definition of *cell* is recursive.

It is worth noting that a value *v* of type *box a x* also has every type of the form *a (x 'o' cell a x 'o' y)*, simply because the latter is a polymorphic instance of the former. Thus, the value that is used to initialize the cell is indeed a suitable value for the cell in every future world *y*.

How do we ascertain that this definition of *cell* is right? The proof is in the fact that the terms *store_extend* and *store_end_index*, which respectively construct the new store and the address of the new reference, have the types shown in Figure 13. The definitions of these terms [28] are a couple lines each. Up to a number of suitable type abstractions and applications, *store_extend* is just *array_extend*, while *store_end_index* is just *array_end_index*.

4.7 Encoding the monadic constants

All of the infrastructure is now in place. We are in a position to encode the constants *return*, *bind*, *new*, *read*, and *write*. To do so, we must define five terms that admit the types shown in Figure 14 and that adequately implement the store-passing machinery.

We present and explain only the definitions of the term *new* (Figure 15). The definitions of *return*, *bind*, *read*, and *write* are omitted and can be found online [28]. We believe that the definition of *new* is representative, so that the reader who has studied it could (if he or she so wished!) reconstruct the other definitions as an exercise.

The structure of the definition of *new* is in large part imposed by its type. By definition of *box*, *univ*, *arrow*, and *monad* (Figure 12), the desired type for *new*:

box (*univ* (λ*a. a* '*arrow*' *monad* (*ref a*))) *nil*

is equal to:

∀*x.* ∀*a. box a x* → ∀*y. store* (*x* '*o*' *y*) → *outcome* (*ref a*) (*x* '*o*' *y*)

Thus, the definition of *new* begins with abstractions over a world *x*, a semantic type *a*, a value *v* of type *box a x*, a world *y*, and a store *s* of type *store xy*. The type *xy* is defined on the fly as a local abbreviation for *x 'o' y*.

It might seem strange that we must abstract over *two* successive world extensions, *x* and *y*. This is required by the monadic structure of the source language: the world *x* corresponds to the point in time where *ref* is applied to a value *v*, while the world *x 'o' y* corresponds to the point in time where the computation *ref v* is run.

After accepting these parameters, *new* must produce a result of type *outcome (ref a) xy*. By definition of *outcome* (Figure 12), this is equal to:

∃*z.* (*box* (*ref a*) (*xy* '*o*' *z*), *store* (*xy* '*o*' *z*))

term *return* :
  box (*univ* (λ*a. a* '*arrow*' *monad a*)) *nil*
term *bind* :
  box (*univ* (λ*a. univ* (λ*b.*
    (*monad a* '*pair*' (*a* '*arrow*' *monad b*)) '*arrow*' *monad b*
  ))) *nil*
term *new* :
  box (*univ* (λ*a. a* '*arrow*' *monad* (*ref a*))) *nil*
term *read* :
  box (*univ* (λ*a. ref a* '*arrow*' *monad a*)) *nil*
term *write* :
  box (*univ* (λ*a.* (*ref a* '*pair*' *a*) '*arrow*' *monad unit*)) *nil*

Figure 14. Encoding the monadic constants: declarations

term *new* : *box* (*univ* (λ*a. a* '*arrow*' *monad* (*ref a*))) *nil* =
  Λ *x a.*
  λ*v* : *box a x.*
  Λ *y.*
  type *xy* = *x* '*o*' *y* **in**
  λ*s* : *store xy.*
    type *c* = *cell a xy* **in**
    pack *c*, (
      box_ref [*a*] [*xy* '*o*' *c*] (*store_end_index* [*xy*] [*a*] *s*),
      store_extend [*xy*] [*a*] *s* (*forward* [*a*] [*x*] [*y*] *v*)
)
    as *outcome* (*ref a*) *xy*

Figure 15. Encoding the monadic constants: definition of *new*

This type is existentially quantified over a world extension *z*, which represents the new storage allocated by the computation. Here, this new storage is a single cell, which holds a value of semantic type *a*. So, according to our earlier discussion (§4.6), the concrete witness for *z* should be *cell a xy*. Thus, *c* is defined as a local abbreviation for *cell a xy*, and the construct **pack** *c*, ... **as** *outcome (ref a) xy* is used in order to build an existential package.

Inside this package should be a pair of a newly allocated memory location, at type *box (ref a) (xy 'o' c)*, and an extended store, at type *store (xy 'o' c)*.

The next available memory location is obtained by applying *store_end_index* (Figure 13) to suitable type arguments and to the current store *s*. This application has type *ref a (xy 'o' c)*. This is what was required, except a leading *box* is missing: we must justify that this memory location is valid not only now, but also in the future. This is achieved via an application of the coercion *box_ref*, which was mentioned earlier (§4.5).

It seems that the new store should be obtained by applying *store_extend* (Figure 13) to the current store *s* and to the initial value *v* of the newly allocated cell. However, there is a slight difficulty: *s* and *v* do not inhabit the same world. Indeed, *s* has type *store (x 'o' y)*, while *v* has type *box a x*. Thus, before *store_extend* can be applied, the value *v* must be moved from the world *x* into the world *x 'o' y*. Fortunately, *v* is hereditary, so this is easily achieved by applying the coercion *forward* (§4.5).

The definition of *new* is somewhat complex due to the many type annotations. However, by erasing all type abstractions, applications, and abbreviations, as well as all coercion applications, one finds that *new* is just λ*v.*λ*s.*(*store_end_index s*, *store_extend s v*). Thus, it is easy to informally convince oneself that the untyped translation that underlies our encoding is indeed a standard store-passing translation. A formal argument of semantics preservation appears further on (§4.10).

ENCODE-VAR
$$E_1; x : T; E_2 \vdash x \leadsto \Lambda y.x\ (w_{E_2}\ \text{`}o\text{`}\ y)\ : T$$

ENCODE-ABS
$$\frac{E; x : T_1 \vdash e \leadsto t\ : T_2}{E \vdash \lambda x.e \leadsto \Lambda w_x.\lambda x.t\ : T_1 \to T_2}$$

ENCODE-APP
$$\frac{E \vdash e_1 \leadsto t_1\ : T_1 \to T_2 \qquad E \vdash e_2 \leadsto t_2\ : T_1}{E \vdash e_1\ e_2 \leadsto t_1\ nil\ t_2\ : T_2}$$

ENCODE-∀-INTRO
$$\frac{E; \alpha \vdash e \leadsto t\ : T}{E \vdash \Lambda\alpha.e \leadsto \Lambda y.\Lambda(\alpha : stype).(t\ y)\ : \forall\alpha.T}$$

ENCODE-∀-ELIM
$$\frac{E \vdash e \leadsto t\ : \forall\alpha.T_1}{E \vdash e\ T_2 \leadsto \Lambda y.(t\ y\ [\![T_2]\!])\ : [\alpha \mapsto T_2]T_1}$$

ENCODE-UNIT
$$E \vdash () \leadsto \Lambda y.()\ : ()$$

ENCODE-(,)-INTRO
$$\frac{E \vdash e_1 \leadsto t_1\ : T_1 \qquad E \vdash e_2 \leadsto t_2\ : T_2}{E \vdash (e_1, e_2) \leadsto \Lambda y.(t_1\ y, t_2\ y)\ : (T_1, T_2)}$$

ENCODE-(,)-ELIM
$$\frac{E \vdash e \leadsto t\ : (T_1, T_2)}{E \vdash \pi_i\ e \leadsto \Lambda y.\text{let}\ (x_1, x_2) = t\ y\ \text{in}\ x_i\ : T_i}$$

Figure 16. System F-to-FORK encoding: pure fragment

4.8 Encoding terms

We have defined the encoding of the five monadic constants. There remains to encode the pure fragment of the source language, that is, the terms of System F. The encoding is type-directed. It takes the form of an encoding judgement $E \vdash e \leadsto t : T$, which enriches the System F typing judgement: that is, $E \vdash e : T$ holds iff $E \vdash e \leadsto t : T$ holds for a certain t. The definition of this judgement appears in Figure 16. Over pure terms, the encoding is essentially the identity. It introduces type abstractions and applications in order to introduce and/or eliminate the *box* modality.

4.9 Type preservation

The following definition and theorem state precisely in what way the encoding is type-preserving.

Definition 4.2 *With each variable x, we associate a world variable w_x. Then, with a System F type environment E, we associate a world w_E, as follows:*

$$\begin{aligned} w_\emptyset &= nil \\ w_{E;\alpha} &= w_E \\ w_{E;x:T} &= w_E\ \text{`}o\text{`}\ w_x \end{aligned}$$

The encoding $[\![E]\!]$ of a type environment E is given by:

$$\begin{aligned} [\![\emptyset]\!] &= \emptyset \\ [\![E;\alpha]\!] &= [\![E]\!]; \alpha : stype \\ [\![E; x : T]\!] &= [\![E]\!]; w_x : world; x : box\ [\![T]\!]\ w_{E;x:T} \end{aligned}$$ ◇

Every abstraction λx in the source program gives rise to a sequence of two abstractions, of the form $\Lambda w_x.\lambda x$, in the translated program. This accounts for the fact that the world at the time a function is defined and the world at the time this function is applied are distinct: the latter is in general an extension of the former. The parameter w_x represents this extension.

Theorem 4.3 (Type preservation) *$E \vdash e \leadsto t : T$ implies $[\![E]\!] \vdash t : box\ [\![T]\!]\ w_E$.* ◇

Proof. In this proof, we do not consider the cases of the constants return, bind, new, read, and write, which have been machine-checked [28]. There remains one case for each of the rules in Figure 16.

○ *Case* ENCODE-VAR. By hypothesis, under the environment $[\![E_1; x : T; E_2]\!]$, x has type:

$$box\ [\![T]\!]\ w_{E_1;x:T}.$$

By definition of *box*, this is:

$$\forall y.([\![T]\!]\ (w_{E_1;x:T}\ \text{`}o\text{`}\ y)).$$

Thus, the type application $x\ (w_{E_2}\ \text{`}o\text{`}\ y)$ has type:

$$[\![T]\!]\ (w_{E_1;x:T}\ \text{`}o\text{`}\ w_{E_2}\ \text{`}o\text{`}\ y),$$

that is,

$$[\![T]\!]\ (w_{E_1;x:T;E_2}\ \text{`}o\text{`}\ y).$$

Thus, the term $\Lambda y.x\ (w_{E_2}\ \text{`}o\text{`}\ y)$ has type:

$$\forall y.([\![T]\!]\ (w_{E_1;x:T;E_2}\ \text{`}o\text{`}\ y)),$$

that is,

$$box\ [\![T]\!]\ w_{E_1;x:T;E_2}.$$

○ *Case* ENCODE-ABS. By the induction hypothesis, under the environment $[\![E; x : T_1]\!]$, the term t has type $box\ [\![T_2]\!]\ w_{E;x:T_1}$. That is, under the type environment:

$$[\![E]\!]; w_x : world; x : box\ [\![T_1]\!]\ (w_E\ \text{`}o\text{`}\ w_x),$$

the term t has type:

$$box\ [\![T_2]\!]\ (w_E\ \text{`}o\text{`}\ w_x).$$

There follows that the term $\Lambda w_x.\lambda x.t$ has type:

$$\forall w_x.(box\ [\![T_1]\!]\ (w_E\ \text{`}o\text{`}\ w_x) \to box\ [\![T_2]\!]\ (w_E\ \text{`}o\text{`}\ w_x)),$$

By definition of the encoding and by definition of *box*, this type is:

$$box\ [\![T_1 \to T_2]\!]\ w_E.$$

○ *Case* ENCODE-APP. By the induction hypothesis, under the type environment $[\![E]\!]$, the term t_1 has type $box\ [\![T_1 \to T_2]\!]\ w_E$ and the term t_2 has type $box\ [\![T_1]\!]\ w_E$. By definition of *box* and by definition of the encoding, the former of these types is:

$$\forall w_x.(box\ [\![T_1]\!]\ (w_E\ \text{`}o\text{`}\ w_x) \to box\ [\![T_2]\!]\ (w_E\ \text{`}o\text{`}\ w_x)).$$

As a result, the application $t_1\ nil$ has type:

$$box\ [\![T_1]\!]\ w_E \to box\ [\![T_2]\!]\ w_E,$$

and the application $t_1\ nil\ t_2$ has type

$$box\ [\![T_2]\!]\ w_E.$$

○ *Case* ENCODE-∀-INTRO. By the induction hypothesis, under the type environment $[\![E]\!]; \alpha : stype$, the term t has type *box* $[\![T]\!]\ w_E$. Thus, the term:

$$\Lambda y.\Lambda(\alpha : \mathit{stype}).(t\ y)$$

has type

$$\forall y.\forall(\alpha : \mathit{stype}).([\![T]\!]\ (w_E\ \text{`}o\text{'}\ y)).$$

By definition of *univ*, this type is:

$$\forall y.(\mathit{univ}\ (\lambda\alpha.[\![T]\!])\ (w_E\ \text{`}o\text{'}\ y)),$$

that is, by definition of *box*:

$$\mathit{box}\ (\mathit{univ}\ (\lambda\alpha.[\![T]\!]))\ w_E,$$

that is, by definition of the encoding,

$$\mathit{box}\ [\![\forall\alpha.T]\!]\ w_E.$$

◦ *Case* ENCODE-∀-ELIM. By the induction hypothesis, under the type environment $[\![E]\!]$, the term t has type:

$$\mathit{box}\ [\![\forall\alpha.T_1]\!]\ w_E.$$

As we saw in the previous case, this type is:

$$\forall y.\forall(\alpha : \mathit{stype}).([\![T_1]\!]\ (w_E\ \text{`}o\text{'}\ y)).$$

Thus, the term $\Lambda y.(t\ y\ [\![T_2]\!])$ has type:

$$\forall y.(([\alpha \mapsto [\![T_2]\!]][\![T_1]\!])\ (w_E\ \text{`}o\text{'}\ y)).$$

Because the encoding of types is compositional (i.e., commutes with type substitution), this type is:

$$\forall y.([\![[\alpha \mapsto T_2]T_1]\!]\ (w_E\ \text{`}o\text{'}\ y)),$$

that is, by definition of *box*:

$$\mathit{box}\ [\![[\alpha \mapsto T_2]T_1]\!]\ w_E.$$

◦ *Cases* ENCODE-UNIT, ENCODE-(,)-INTRO, ENCODE-(,)-ELIM. Left to the reader. □

4.10 Semantics preservation

The encoding is semantics-preserving. This is true even in the absence of a well-typedness hypothesis. This is not surprising: one might be tempted to say that the encoding is "obviously" a store-passing translation, and that a store-passing translation is "obviously" semantics-preserving. Nevertheless, it is worth checking this fact. The results presented in this section have been machine-checked using Coq; the development can be found online [28].

Because the rules ENCODE-∀-INTRO and ENCODE-∀-ELIM in Figure 16 encode type abstractions and type applications in terms of type abstractions and type applications, it is possible to define an untyped version of the encoding, which transforms untyped terms into untyped terms. This untyped encoding is a function. In the following, we write e for an untyped term of the source calculus, and we write $[\![e]\!]$ for its untyped encoding.

It is easy to check, by examination of Figure 16, that the untyped encoding function is the identity over the pure fragment of System F. As an immediate corollary, every simplification step in the source calculus is simulated by one reduction step in the target calculus:

Lemma 4.4 $e_1 \rightarrow e_2$ *implies* $[\![e_1]\!] \longrightarrow [\![e_2]\!]$. ◇

We now wish to prove an analogous simulation diagram about the reduction of configurations. This requires defining the encoding of a memory location $[\![\ell]\!]$, the encoding of a store, the encoding of an evaluation stack, and the encoding of a configuration. These somewhat technical definitions are omitted, but can be found online [28].

It is then a matter of routine to check that one step of reduction in the source calculus is simulated by one or more steps of reduction in the target calculus. This is stated as follows.

In order to allow for some slack in the administrative reductions, the encoding of configurations is a relation, rather than a function. We write $(s, S, e) \rightsquigarrow t$ to indicate that the term t is an encoding of the configuration (s, S, e). Then, we have:

Lemma 4.5 (Simulation) *For a closed configuration* (s_1, S_1, e_1), *the following diagram holds:*

$$\begin{array}{ccc} (s_1, S_1, e_1) & \rightsquigarrow & t_1 \\ \downarrow & & \downarrow + \\ (s_2, S_2, e_2) & \rightsquigarrow & t_2 \end{array}$$

◇

It is worth noting that, in order to establish $t_1 \longrightarrow^+ t_2$, we exploit the fact that reduction of FORK terms is permitted under arbitrary contexts. We use this flexibility, in particular, to perform reduction inside the components of a pair.

As an immediate consequence, we find that convergence is preserved by the encoding.

Lemma 4.6 (Convergence) *Let* e_1 *be a closed term of the source calculus. If the start configuration* $(\mathit{nil}, [], e_1)$ *reduces (in many steps) to some configuration of the form* $(s, [], \mathit{return}\ e_2)$, *then the term* $[\![e_1]\!]\ [\![\mathit{nil}]\!]$ *reduces (in many steps) to the pair* $([\![e_2]\!], [\![s]\!])$. ◇

Proving that divergence is also preserved by the encoding is more difficult. Of course, by Lemma 4.5, the existence of an infinite reduction sequence out of the start configuration $(\mathit{nil}, [], e_1)$ implies the existence of an infinite reduction sequence out of its encoding $[\![e_1]\!]\ [\![\mathit{nil}]\!]$. However, this is not the desired property. Because reduction of FORK terms is permitted under arbitrary contexts, the relation $\longrightarrow$ is non-deterministic, and the existence of an infinite reduction sequence is not an appropriate definition of divergence. Instead, we would like to consider that the term $[\![e_1]\!]\ [\![\mathit{nil}]\!]$ diverges if and only if it does not have a head normal form. An analogous phenomenon arises in the source calculus, where simplification is permitted under arbitrary contexts.

Here is an informal sketch of how this problem might be solved. In each of the source and target calculi, define notions of standard (that is, leftmost) and internal reduction. Prove that divergence (that is, the absence of a head normal form) is equivalent to the existence of an infinite standard reduction sequence. In the target calculus, prove that standard reduction and internal reduction commute. Takahashi [33] proves these facts in the pure λ-calculus.

Then, refine Lemma 4.5, by showing that one standard reduction step in the source calculus is simulated by a mixture of at least one standard reduction step and an arbitrary number of internal reduction steps in the target calculus. Use this fact, together with the property that standard reduction and internal reduction commute, to conclude that, if a source configuration admits an infinite standard reduction sequence, then so does its encoding. We have not yet attempted to machine-check this development.

5. Related work

Several store-passing translations have appeared in the literature. Moggi's state monad [18] relies on a fixed store type: it does not support dynamic memory allocation. Parameterised monads [6] allow the type of the store to vary with time and can be used to model systems of strong references with memory allocation and de-allocation. Similarly, Hoare Type Theory [23] extends type theory with a monad that is indexed with pre- and post-conditions: $\{P\}x : A\{Q\}$ is the type of computations that expect a store in state P and produce a value x of type A together with a new store in state Q. Hoare Type Theory is very expressive, yet does not support weak references. O'Hearn and Reynolds [24] translate two variations of Algol 60 into a purely functional calculus with polymorphic and linear types, and compose this translation with a model of the target calculus to obtain models of the source languages. Charguéraud and Pottier [12] translate an expressive type-and-capability calculus, which supports strong references, into a purely functional calculus[2]. Pottier [26] extends Charguéraud and Pottier's work with an *anti-frame* rule that allows weak references to be defined in terms of strong references. However, it is not clear how Charguéraud and Pottier's store-passing translation could be extended to support the anti-frame rule. To the best of our knowledge, no typed store-passing translation for weak references has appeared in the literature.

The syntactic approach to type soundness [13, 35] deals with weak references via store types, which map memory addresses to types. The store type grows with time (this is part of the statement of subject reduction) and simultaneously describes the current store as well as all future stores. This is probably the simplest approach to type soundness for general references. However, it does not suggest how to design a type-preserving store-passing translation.

FORK is an ad hoc extension of System F_ω that allows non-terminating yet productive computation at the type level and (as a result) is able to express rich recursive types, far beyond the view of recursive types as regular trees that is commonly encountered in simpler type systems [4, 11]. There exist other calculi that permit productive computation at the type level: $\Pi\Sigma$ [3] and MiniAgda [1] come to mind. Perhaps these calculi could serve as target languages for a type-preserving store-passing translation of general references.

6. Directions for future work

In this paper, we have equipped the source and target calculi with pairs. Is it possible to equip both calculi with sums and extend the definition of the encoding? We believe so, up to a technical difficulty. In the definition of the encoding, we have exploited the commutation of *box* with respect to pairs: that is, a polymorphic pair can be transformed into a pair whose components are polymorphic. The term that performs this transformation can be defined in System F, and, a fortiori, in FORK; up to type erasure, it is the identity. If the calculi were extended with sums, then, analogously, we would need a coercion that transforms a polymorphic sum into a sum whose summands are polymorphic. Unfortunately, such a coercion cannot be defined, it seems, in System F. Instead, it must be added as an axiom, and one must move to a version of FORK equipped with subtyping, in the style of System F_η [17].

The typed store-passing translation that we have presented is not fully abstract: there are terms that inhabit the encoding of a source type, but do not encode any source term. In particular, there is "snapback:" it is permitted to duplicate or discard the store. Following O'Hearn and Reynolds [24], one could enrich FORK with linear types and refine the translation so as to encode the fact that the store is treated linearly. One might then hope to prove that the refined translation is fully abstract. Møgelberg and Staton [20] prove such a result for a store-passing translation that deals with local state. Their translation is simpler than the one considered here insofar as they fix the type of the store: all locations have the same type, and all locations are considered allocated (they initially hold a default value).

In this paper, only a limited meta-theoretic study of FORK has been carried out: we have established its type soundness with respect to an operational semantics. To go further, we suggest building semantic models of FORK, perhaps by following Birkedal *et al.* [8], and determining whether useful models of System F with general references can in fact be obtained by composition with the store-passing translation presented in this paper.

[2] In the absence of group regions in the source calculus, Charguéraud and Pottier's translation is type-preserving in a strong sense. When the source calculus has group regions, however, their translation is type-preserving only in a weaker sense: it uses map lookup and map update operations whose success is guaranteed by the type system of the source calculus but not by the type system of the target calculus. The success of these operations depends on the fact that the population of a group region can only grow with time. Thus, achieving type preservation in a strong sense might require a possible worlds machinery, as in the present paper.

Acknowledgments

I wish to thank Lars Birkedal, Paul-André Melliès, Bernhard Reus, Jan Schwinghammer, and Hongseok Yang for pleasant and inspiring discussions.

References

[1] Andreas Abel. MiniAgda: Integrating sized and dependent types. In *Workshop on Partiality And Recursion in Interactive Theorem Provers (PAR)*, July 2010.

[2] Amal Jamil Ahmed. *Semantics of Types for Mutable State*. PhD thesis, Princeton University, 2004.

[3] Thorsten Altenkirch, Nils Anders Danielsson, Andres Löh, and Nicolas Oury. $\Pi\Sigma$: Dependent types without the sugar. In *Functional and Logic Programming*, volume 6009 of *Lecture Notes in Computer Science*, pages 40–55. Springer, April 2010.

[4] Roberto M. Amadio and Luca Cardelli. Subtyping recursive types. *ACM Transactions on Programming Languages and Systems*, 15(4):575–631, September 1993.

[5] Andrew W. Appel, Paul-André Melliès, Christopher D. Richards, and Jérôme Vouillon. A very modal model of a modern, major, general type system. In *ACM Symposium on Principles of Programming Languages (POPL)*, pages 109–122, January 2007.

[6] Robert Atkey. Parameterised notions of computation. *Journal of Functional Programming*, 19(3–4):355–376, 2009.

[7] Henk P. Barendregt. *The Lambda Calculus, Its Syntax and Semantics*. Elsevier Science, 1984.

[8] Lars Birkedal, Jan Schwinghammer, and Kristian Støvring. A metric model of lambda calculus with guarded recursion. Presented at FICS 2010, July 2010.

[9] Lars Birkedal, Kristian Støvring, and Jacob Thamsborg. The category-theoretic solution of recursive metric-space quations. Technical Report ITU-2009-119, IT University of Copenhagen, 2009.

[10] Lars Birkedal, Kristian Støvring, and Jacob Thamsborg. Realizability semantics of parametric polymorphism, general references, and recursive types. *Mathematical Structures in Computer Science*, 2010. To appear.

[11] Michael Brandt and Fritz Henglein. Coinductive axiomatization of recursive type equality and subtyping. *Fundamenta Informaticæ*, 33:309–338, 1998.

[12] Arthur Charguéraud and François Pottier. Functional translation of a calculus of capabilities. In *ACM International Conference on Functional Programming (ICFP)*, pages 213–224, September 2008.

[13] Robert Harper. A simplified account of polymorphic references. *Information Processing Letters*, 51(4):201–206, 1994.

[14] Aquinas Hobor, Robert Dockins, and Andrew W. Appel. A theory of indirection via approximation. In *ACM Symposium on Principles of Programming Languages (POPL)*, January 2010.

[15] Soren B. Lassen. Bisimulation in untyped lambda calculus: Böhm trees and bisimulation up to context. In *Mathematical Foundations of Programming Semantics*, volume 20 of *Electronic Notes in Theoretical Computer Science*, pages 346–374. Elsevier Science, April 1999.

[16] Paul Blain Levy. Possible world semantics for general storage in call-by-value. In *Computer Science Logic*, volume 2471 of *Lecture Notes in Computer Science*. Springer, 2002.

[17] John C. Mitchell. Polymorphic type inference and containment. *Information and Computation*, 76(2–3):211–249, 1988.

[18] Eugenio Moggi. Notions of computation and monads. *Information and Computation*, 93(1), 1991.

[19] Eugenio Moggi and Amr Sabry. An abstract monadic semantics for value recursion. *Informatique théorique et applications*, 38(4):377–400, 2004.

[20] Rasmus Ejlers Møgelberg and Sam Staton. Full abstraction in a metalanguage for state. In *Workshop on Syntax and Semantics of Low Level Languages*, July 2010.

[21] Hiroshi Nakano. A modality for recursion. In *IEEE Symposium on Logic in Computer Science (LICS)*, pages 255–266, June 2000.

[22] Hiroshi Nakano. Fixed-point logic with the approximation modality and its Kripke completeness. In *International Symposium on Theoretical Aspects of Computer Software (TACS)*, volume 2215 of *Lecture Notes in Computer Science*, pages 165–182. Springer, October 2001.

[23] Aleksandar Nanevski, Greg Morrisett, and Lars Birkedal. Hoare type theory, polymorphism and separation. *Journal of Functional Programming*, 18(5–6), 2008.

[24] Peter W. O'Hearn and John C. Reynolds. From Algol to polymorphic linear lambda-calculus. *Journal of the ACM*, 47(1):167–223, 2000.

[25] Simon Peyton Jones and Philip Wadler. Imperative functional programming. In *ACM Symposium on Principles of Programming Languages (POPL)*, pages 71–84, January 1993.

[26] François Pottier. Hiding local state in direct style: a higher-order anti-frame rule. In *IEEE Symposium on Logic in Computer Science (LICS)*, pages 331–340, June 2008.

[27] François Pottier. A formalization of Nakano's type system. `http://gallium.inria.fr/~fpottier/fork/`, October 2009.

[28] François Pottier. The electronic FORK, July 2010. `http://gallium.inria.fr/~fpottier/fork/`.

[29] François Pottier. A typed store-passing translation for general references (extended version). November 2010.

[30] Jan Schwinghammer, Lars Birkedal, Bernhard Reus, and Hongseok Yang. Nested Hoare triples and frame rules for higher-order store. In *Computer Science Logic*, volume 5771 of *Lecture Notes in Computer Science*, pages 440–454. Springer, September 2009.

[31] Jan Schwinghammer, Hongseok Yang, Lars Birkedal, François Pottier, and Bernhard Reus. A semantic foundation for hidden state. In *International Conference on Foundations of Software Science and Computation Structures (FOSSACS)*, volume 6014 of *Lecture Notes in Computer Science*, pages 2–17. Springer, March 2010.

[32] Christopher Strachey. Fundamental concepts in programming languages. *Higher-Order and Symbolic Computation*, 13(1–2):11–49, April 2000.

[33] Masako Takahashi. Parallel reductions in λ-calculus. *Information and Computation*, 118(1):120–127, April 1995.

[34] Robert D. Tennent and Dan Ghica. Abstract models of storage. *Higher-Order and Symbolic Computation*, 13:119–129, 2000.

[35] Andrew K. Wright and Matthias Felleisen. A syntactic approach to type soundness. *Information and Computation*, 115(1):38–94, November 1994.

A Shape Analysis for Optimizing Parallel Graph Programs *

Dimitrios Prountzos[1] Roman Manevich[2] Keshav Pingali[1,2] Kathryn S. McKinley[1]
[1]Dept. of Computer Science, The University of Texas at Austin, Texas, USA.
[2]Institute for Computational Engineering and Sciences, The University of Texas at Austin, Texas, USA.
{dprountz@cs.utexas.edu,roman@ices.utexas.edu,pingali@cs.utexas.edu,mckinley@cs.utexas.edu }

Abstract

Computations on unstructured graphs are challenging to parallelize because dependences in the underlying algorithms are usually complex functions of runtime data values, thwarting static parallelization. One promising general-purpose parallelization strategy for these algorithms is optimistic parallelization.

This paper identifies the optimization of optimistically parallelized graph programs as a new application area, and develops the first shape analysis for addressing this problem. Our shape analysis identifies *failsafe* points in the program after which the execution is guaranteed not to abort and backup copies of modified data are not needed; additionally, the analysis can be used to eliminate redundant conflict checking. It uses two key ideas: a novel *top-down* heap abstraction that controls state space explosion, and a strategy for predicate discovery that exploits common patterns of data structure usage.

We implemented the shape analysis in TVLA, and used it to optimize benchmarks from the Lonestar suite. The optimized programs were executed on the Galois system. The analysis was successful in eliminating all costs related to rollback logging for our benchmarks. Additionally, it reduced the number of lock acquisitions by a factor ranging from 10× to 50×, depending on the application and the number of threads. These optimizations were effective in reducing the running times of the benchmarks by factors of 2× to 12×.

Categories and Subject Descriptors D.1.3 [*Programming Techniques*]: Concurrent Programming—Parallel Programming; D.1.3 [*Programming Techniques*]: Object-oriented Programming; F.3.2 [*Logics and Meanings of Programs*]: Program analysis

General Terms Algorithms, Languages, Performance, Verification

Keywords Abstract Interpretation, Compiler Optimization, Concurrency, Parallelism, Shape Analysis, Static Analysis, Amorphous Data-parallelism, Irregular Programs, Optimistic Parallelization, Synchronization Overheads, Cautious Operators.

* This work was supported by NSF grants 0833162, 0719966, 0702353, 0724966, and 0739601, as well as grants from the IBM and Intel Corporations.

POPL'11, January 26–28, 2011, Austin, Texas, USA.

1. Introduction

Computations on large, unstructured graphs are ubiquitous in many problem domains such as computational biology, machine learning, and data mining. They are difficult to parallelize because most dependences between computations in these algorithms are functions of values known only at runtime such as the structure of the (possibly mutating) graph; therefore, it is impossible to parallelize these algorithms statically using techniques such as shape analysis and points-to analysis [ ].

One general-purpose solution to parallelizing graph computations is optimistic parallelization: computations are performed speculatively in parallel, but the runtime system monitors conflicts between concurrent computations, and rolls back offending computations as needed. There are many implementations of this high-level idea such as thread-level speculation [ ], transactional memory [,], and the Galois system [ ]. For concreteness, our results are presented in the context of the Galois system but they are applicable to other systems as well.

In the Galois system, applications programmers write algorithms in sequential Java augmented with a construct called the *Galois unordered-set iterator*[1]. This iterator iterates in some unspecified order over a set of *active nodes*, which are nodes in the graph where computations need to be performed. The body of the iterator is considered to be an *operator* that is applied to the active node to perform the relevant computation, known as an *activity*. An activity may touch other nodes and edges in the graph, and these are collectively known as the *neighborhood* for that activity. These nodes and edges must be accessed by invoking methods from graph classes provided in the Galois library.

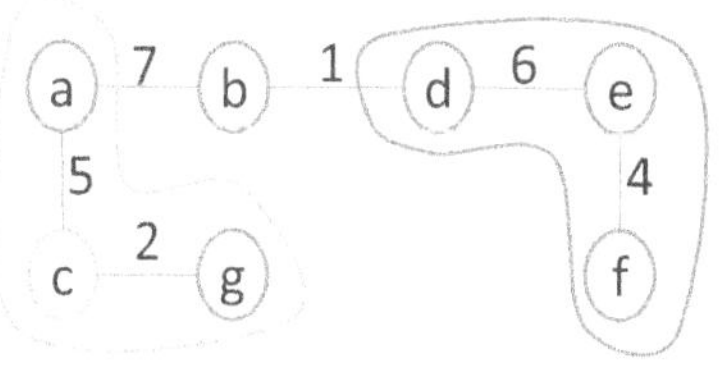

Figure 1. Neighborhoods in Boruvka's MST algorithm

We illustrate these concepts using Boruvka's minimal spanning tree (MST) algorithm [ ], the running example in this paper. The MST starts as a forest with each node in its own component. The algorithm iteratively contracts the graph by *non-deterministically* choosing a graph node, examining all edges incident on that node to find the lightest weight edge, and contracting that edge, which is

[1] The Galois system also supports ordered-set iterators, but we do not consider these in this paper.

added to the MST. The algorithm terminates when the graph has been contracted to a single node. Figure 1 shows an undirected graph. For active node **e**, the neighborhood of the corresponding activity consists of nodes **d**, **e** and **f**, and the edges between these nodes, since these are the edges that must be examined to find and contract the lightest weight edge connected to **e**.

In most algorithms, each neighborhood is a small portion of the overall graph, so it is possible to work on many active nodes concurrently provided the corresponding neighborhoods do not overlap. For example, in Figure 1, the neighborhood for the activity at node **c** is disjoint from the neighborhood for the activity at node **e**, so these activities can be performed in parallel. However, the activity at node **b** cannot be performed concurrently with the activity at **e** since the neighborhoods overlap.

In the Galois system, this concurrency is exploited by adding all graph nodes to the work-set and executing iterations of the Galois set-iterator speculatively in parallel. All concurrency control is performed within the library graph classes. Conceptually, an exclusive lock called an *abstract lock* is associated with each graph element, and this lock is acquired by an activity when it touches that element by invoking a graph API method. If the lock has already been acquired by another activity, a conflict is reported to the runtime system, which rolls back offending activities. To permit rollback, methods that modify the state of the graph also record undo actions that are executed on rollback. The idea of handling conflicts at the abstract data type level rather than at the memory level is also used in boosted TM systems [ ]. The Galois system has been used to parallelize complex graph algorithms in the Lonestar benchmark suite [ ].

Compared to static parallelization, optimistic parallelization has several overheads.

1. *Wasted work from aborted activities*: Because conflicts between activities are detected online, an activity may be rolled back after it has performed a lot of computation.
2. *Conflict checking*: Abstract locks must be acquired and released by activities, and this is an overhead even if no activities are ever aborted.
3. *Undo actions*: These must be registered for every graph API call that might mutate the graph.

In this paper, we present a novel shape analysis that can be utilized to reduce the overheads of conflict checking and registering undo actions (reducing the number of aborted activities is mainly a scheduling problem, and is dealt with elsewhere [ ]). Our main contributions are the following.

- *Shape Analysis*: We develop a novel shape analysis for programs with set and graph data structures, which infers properties for optimizing speculative parallel graph programs. We utilize the structure of stores arising in our programs to design a *hierarchy summarization abstraction*, which uses a finite set of reachability relations relative to a given property (the "object-is-locked" property), to abstract stores into shape graphs . Our abstraction assigns unary predicates *only to root objects*, capturing reachability facts from root objects to objects deeper in the heap. Thus, the size of an abstracted store is *linear in the number of variables*, and the number of abstracted stores at a program point depends on the number of explored variable-alias sets, which tends to be constant in our programs ($\approx$6). Therefore the number of abstract states explored by our analysis in practice is linear in the size of the program, circumventing the state-space explosion that is the bane of existing shape analyses.
- *Predicate Discovery*: We develop a simple yet effective technique for discovering predicates relevant for inferring the set objects that are always locked, at each program location, from data structure specifications and "footprints" of data structure method specifications.
- *Evaluation of effectiveness*: We implement our shape analysis in the TVLA framework and use a Java-to-TVLA front-end to analyze several benchmarks from the Lonestar Benchmark Suite [ ], a collection of real-world graph-based applications that exhibit irregular behavior. Our analysis takes at most 16 seconds on each benchmark and infers all available optimizations. These optimizations result in substantial improvements in running time, ranging from $2\times$ to $12\times$.

Several existing heap abstractions, including Canonical Abstraction [ ], Boolean heaps [ ], indexed predicate abstraction [ ], and generalized typestates [ ], abstract the heap by recording a set of unary predicates for **every object** and summarizing the heap by collapsing equivalence classes of objects with the same set of predicate values. Such abstractions achieve high precision, as they express every Boolean combination of intersection and union of objects satisfying those predicates. However, the size of a summarized heap can be exponential in the number of predicates, and the summarization of a set of stores can be doubly-exponential. We call these *bottom-up abstractions*, since they typically express reachability facts for objects in the depth of the heap relative to heap roots. Our experience with bottom-up abstraction shows that heaps are partitioned very finely, leading to state space explosion. As we discuss in Section 4, our *top-down abstraction* runs several orders of magnitude faster than an implementation of the bottom-up abstraction approach when analyzing our benchmarks.

The rest of the paper is organized as follows. Section 2 provides an overview of our optimizations and shape analysis on Boruvka's MST example. Section 3 presents our shape analysis via hierarchy summarization and predicate discovery. Section 4 describes the static analysis implementation and gives experimental results that demonstrate the effectiveness of the approach presented in this paper. Section 5 discusses related work.

2. Overview

This section introduces the programming model, the performance optimizations, and our shape analysis informally, using Boruvka's MST algorithm as the running example.

2.1 Boruvka's MST algorithm

Pseudocode for the algorithm is shown in Figure 2. The Galois iterator on line 25 iterates over the graph nodes in some non-deterministic order, performing edge contractions. In lines, 31-38 we examine the neighbors of the active node `a`, and identify the neighbor `lt`, which is connected to `a` by a lightest weight edge. In lines 44-59 we contract the two components by removing `lt` from the graph, and updating all of `lt`'s neighbors to become neighbors of `a`. This is done by the loop in lines 45-58. If a neighbor `n` of `lt` is already connected to `a`, we update the data value of the edge connecting them (lines 49-54). Otherwise, we add an edge connecting the two nodes (lines 55-57).

In Boruvka's algorithm, the neighborhood of an active node `a` consists of the immediate neighbors of `a` and `lt` and their related edges and data. In more complex examples like Delaunay mesh refinement, the neighborhood of an activity can be an unbounded subgraph.

2.2 Speculative Execution in Galois

The graph data structure `Graph<ND,ED>` is parameterized by data objects referenced by nodes and edges, respectively. The work list of active nodes is stored in a set `GSet<Node>`. The `Weight` ob-

```
class GaloisRuntime {
  @rep static set<Object> locks; // abstract locks
  // Flag options
  static int LOCK_UNDO=0; // acquire locks + log undo
  static int UNDO    =1; // log undo
  static int LOCK    =2; // acquire locks
  static int NONE    =3; // no locks and no undo
}

class Weight {
  static Weight MAX_WEIGHT;
  int v;
  // We record the end-points of the edge that
  // holds the weight in the input graph.
  final Node<Void> initSrc, initDst;
  int compareTo(Weight other);
}
class Boruvka {
  void main() {
    Graph<Void,Weight> g = ...// read from file
    GSet<Node> wl = new GSet<Node>();
    wl.addAll(g.getNodes(NONE), NONE);
    GBag<Weight> mst = new GBag<Weight>();

    // Galois iterator
    foreach (Node a : wl) { // in any order
L1:   Set<Node> aNghbrs = g.getNeighbors(a, LOCK);
      // Find neighbor incident to lightest edge
      Weight minW = Weight.MAX_WEIGHT;
      Node lt = null;
L2:   for (Node n : aNghbrs) { // Iterator nIter
        Edge e = g.getEdge(a, n, NONE);
        Weight w = g.getEdgeData(e, NONE);
        if (w.compareTo(minW) < 0) {
          minW = w;
          lt = n;
        }
      }
      if ( lt == null) // no neighbors
        continue;
      // Contract edge (a, lt)
L3:   g.getNeighbors(lt, LOCK); // avoids undo in L4
L4:   g.removeEdge(a, lt, NONE);
L5:   Set<Node> ltNghbrs = g.getNeighbors(lt, NONE);
L6:   for (Node n : ltNghbrs) { // Iterator nIter
        Edge e = g.getEdge( lt, n, NONE);
        Weight w = g.getEdgeData(e, NONE);
        Edge an = g.getEdge(a, n, NONE);
        if (an != null) { // merge edges
          Weight wan = g.getEdgeData(an, NONE);
          if (wan.compareTo(w) < 0)
            w = wan; // use minimal weight
L7:       g.setEdgeData(an, w, NONE);
        }
        else { // new neighbor for a
L8:       g.addEdge(a, n, w, NONE);
        }
      }
L9:   g.removeNode(lt, NONE);
L10:  mst.add(minW, NONE);
L11:  wl.add(a, NONE); // put node back on worklist
    } } }
```

Figure 2. Simplified implementation of Boruvka's algorithm.

jects, which record the weights of the MST edges and their end-points (nodes) in the original graph, are stored in another collection `GBag<Weight>`, which only allows addition operations in a concurrent context. The last argument to a data structure method is a flag that tells the runtime system whether the method should attempt to acquire abstract locks and whether it should log an inverse method call. The default value `LOCK_UNDO` is always a safe choice, ensuring correctness of speculative execution.

The Galois system protects user-defined data types, such as `Weight`, using a read-write lock (allowing concurrent read operations but at most one write operation) and maintaining backup copies of such objects.

Iterations of the Galois set iterator are executed speculatively in parallel, and this execution has transactional semantics: an iteration either completes and commits, or is rolled back and retried.

Syntactic Categories

TName	Types
OFld	Pointer fields
SFld	Set fields
Field	All fields
PVar	Pointer variables
BVar	Boolean variables
SVar	Set-valued variables
Var	All variables

Data Types (EBNF)

TypeDecl ::=	`class` *TName*{*FieldDecl** *MethodDef**}
FieldDecl ::=	[`@rep`] [`static`] *TName OFld*; |
	`@rep` [`static`] *set*⟨*TName*⟩ *SFld*;
MethodDef ::=	`@locks(`*Path**`)` `@op(`*Stmt**`)` `Java-code`
Stmt ::=	*Var* = *Expr* | *Var.Field* = *Expr*
Expr ::=	*Path* | *Path* + *Path* | *Path* − *Path* | `choose(`*Path*`)` |
	Path `in` *Path* | *Path* `notIn` *Path* |
	`isEmpty(`*Path*`)` | `new` *TName*((*Field* = *Var*)*)
Path ::=	$Var.(Var + Field[:SVar] + \texttt{rev}(Field)[:SVar])^{+}$

Figure 3. EBNF grammar for specified data structures. The notation $[x]$ means that x is optional.

2.3 Data Structure Specifications

Figure 3 shows the syntax for a lightweight specification of abstract data types (for all clients), defining their abstract state, abstract locks acquired by each method, and operational semantics of each method in terms of abstract fields. The set of variables, includes method parameters, the special `ret` parameter for returning values, static variables, and temporary variables used to define the semantics of methods. The formal semantics of this language can be found in the accompanying report [ ]. Our analysis operates in terms of these specifications, ignoring the internal details of library ADT's. We assume the correctness of the specifications; approaches such as [ ] can be used for their verification.

Figure 4 shows a graph type built from the `Node` and `Edge` types and the parametric types `ND` and `ED`, used to store user-defined data on the graph nodes and edges. In our example, nodes do not store any data objects and thus their `nd` fields are null. Figure 5 shows a bag, a set, and an iterator type.

Specifying Abstract Data Types. The `@rep` annotations in Figure 4 define the abstract state of a data structure in terms of *set-fields* [ ], i.e., fields whose values are sets of objects.

For example, the abstract state of `Graph` is given by a pair of sets — `ns` and `es` — representing the set of graph nodes and edges, respectively.[2] We represent an undirected edge by a single edge, directed arbitrarily.

`GaloisRuntime` contains a static (i.e., global) `locks` set, representing the set of abstract locks acquired by an iteration.[3]

Example 1. *Figure 6 shows an abstract store representing the input graph of Figure 1 where* `a` *references the active node* **a** *and* `lt` *references* **c** *— the node connected to* **a** *by the lightest edge, discovered on the second iteration after iterating over* **b**.

[2] The full specification includes additional first-order constraints.

[3] Galois implements a lock coarsening scheme by maintaining a single set of abstract locks, shared among all data structure instances.

```
class Graph<ND,ED> { // Undirected boosted graph
 @rep set<Node> ns; // graph nodes
 @rep set<Edge> es; // graph edges

 @locks(n.rev(src).dst, n.rev(dst).src)
 @op(nghbrs = n.rev(src).dst + n.rev(dst).src,
     ret = new Set<Node<ND>>(cont=nghbrs))
 Set<Node<ND>> getNeighbors(Node<ND> n, int opt);

 @locks(f.rev(src).dst.t, t.rev(src).dst.f)
 @op(f.rev(src):eft.dst.t, t.rev(src):etf.dst.f,
     ret = choose(eft + etf))
 Edge<ED> getEdge(Node<ND> f, Node<ND> t, int opt);

 @locks(f, t, f.rev(src).dst.t, t.rev(src).dst.f)
 @op(f.rev(src):eft.dst.t, t.rev(src):etf.dst.f,
     ret = (eft+etf) in es,
     ne = new Edge<ED>(src=f, dst=t, ed=d),
     es += ne)
 boolean addEdge(Node<ND> f, Node<ND> t, ED d,
                 int opt);

 @locks(n.rev(src).dst, n.rev(dst).src)
 @op(ret = n in ns, ns -= n,
     es -= n.rev(src) + n.rev(dst))
 boolean removeNode(Node<ND> n, int opt);

 @locks(f.rev(src).dst.t, t.rev(src).dst.f)
 @op(f.rev(src):eft.dst.t, t.rev(src):etf.dst.f,
     ret = (etf + eft) in es, es -= (etf + eft))
 boolean removeEdge(Node<ND> f, Node<ND> t, int opt);

 @locks(n)
 @op(ret = n.nd)
 ND getNodeData(Node<ND> n, int opt);

 @locks(e, e.src, e.dst)
 @op(ret = e.ed)
 ED getEdgeData(Edge<ED> e, int opt);

 @locks(e, e.src, e.dst)
 @op(e.ed = d)
 void setEdgeData(Edge<ED> e, ED d, int opt);

}

class Node<ND> {
 ND nd; // data object
}

class Edge<ED> {
  Node src; // edge origin
  Node dst; // edge destination
  ED ed;    // data object
}
```

Figure 4. Graph specification samples.

The figure does not show objects used by the internal (concrete) representation of specified data types. Instead, it uses the (@rep) set fields to indicate that an object is contained in a set field of a data structure.

Filled locks denote objects in `GaloisRuntime.locks`; hollow locks denote objects for which our analysis infers that lock protection is not required.

Path Language. We use a language of access path expressions (access paths for short) to denote the set of objects that can be obtained by following variables and fields in a store: a variable (x) denotes the object it references; a pointer field `e.f` denotes an object obtained by traversing the field `f` forward from an object denoted by the prefix expression `e`; a set field denotes any object stored in the set stored in a given object; a reverse field, written `rev(f)` or $\overleftarrow{f}$, denotes objects obtained by traversing field `f` backwards. We formalize path expressions in Section 3.

```
class GSet<E> { // boosted set
 @rep set<E> gcont;// set contents
 @locks(e)
 @op(ret = e in gcont)
 boolean contains(E e);
 @locks(e)
 @op(ret = e notIn gcont, gcont += e)
 boolean add(E e);
}

class GBag<E> {//boosted bag for reduction operations
 @rep set<E> bcont; // bag contents
 @locks() // No locks required!
 @op(bcont += e)
 void add(E e);
 @op(ret = new Set<E>(bcont))
 Set<E> toSet(); // used only in sequential code
}

interface Set<E> { // sequential set from java.util
 @rep set<E> cont; // set contents
}

interface Iterator<E> { // iterator from java.util
 @rep Set<E> all;     // underlying set
 @rep set<E> past;    // past iteration elements
 @rep E at;           // element at current iteration
 @rep set<E> future; // future iteration elements
}
```

Figure 5. Set, bag and iterator specification samples.

We use the notation `:x` inside a path expression to denote a set of intermediate objects during an access path traversal. We write + and - for set union and difference respectively.

Example 2 (Legend). *The following paths are derived from the abstract store in Figure 6:*

- *`a.rev(src)` represents the outgoing edges of `a`: $\{2,3\}$.*
- *`a.rev(dst)` represents the incoming edges of `a`: $\emptyset$.*
- *`a.rev(src).dst + a.rev(dst).src` represents all of the graph nodes adjacent to `a`: $\{b,c\}$.*
- *`a.rev(src):x.dst.lt` sets the temporary variable x to the edge from `a` to `lt`: $x = \{3\}$ (2 is not on a path from `a` to `lt`).*

Specifying Abstract Locks. A `@locks` annotation defines the set of abstract locks a method should acquire by a set of path expressions. To keep specifications succinct, access paths expressions in `@locks` stand for all of their prefixes (e.g., `n.rev(src).dst` stands for `n`, `n.rev(src)`, and `n.rev(src).dst`).

We call a node referenced by `n` along with its incident edges and adjacent nodes the immediate neighborhood of `n`. We specify the set of locks for such a neighborhood by `@locks(n.rev(src).dst, n.rev(dst).src)`.

Example 3 (Commutativity via abstract locks). *The `removeNode` method specifies locks for the immediate neighborhood of the node being removed. A call to `removeNode(c,LOCK)` attempts to lock the `Node` object `c`, the `Edge` objects referencing `c` via the `src` field or the `dst` field (the edges incident to `c`), and the `Node` objects that are neighbors of `c`. This ensures the concurrent method calls `removeNode(c,LOCK)` and `removeNode(e,LOCK)` will not cause their respective iterations to abort, since the immediate neighborhoods of `c` and `e` do not overlap.*

Specifying Method Semantics. An `@op` annotation defines the semantics of a method by a simple imperative language. The language allows a sequence of statements, using set expressions over method parameters, static fields, and temporary variables. Expressions of the form `a in b`, `a notIn b`, and `isEmpty(a)`, test whether `a` is contained in `b`, `a` is not contained in `b`, and whether `a` is an empty

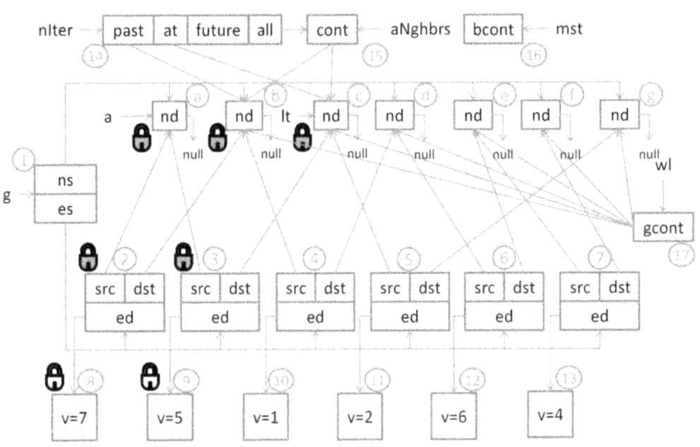

Figure 6. An abstract store arising at L2, using as input the graph from Figure 1. Object are shown by rectangles sub-divided by their fields; circles are used to name objects; locks show objects contained in the global `GaloisRuntime.locks` set. We label `Node` objects by the same labels used in Figure 1 and other objects by a running index.

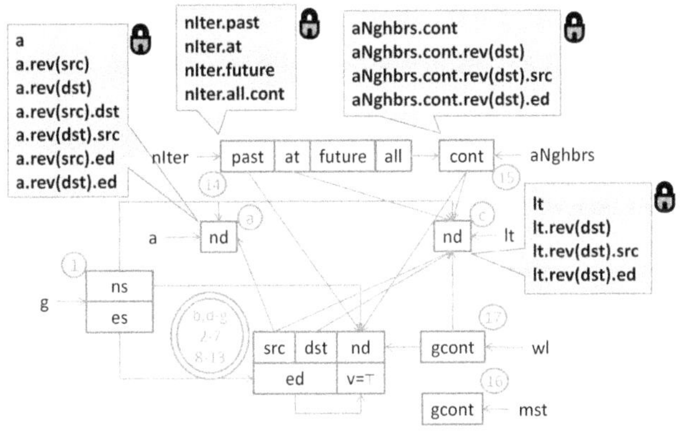

Figure 7. A shape graph obtained by applying hierarchy summarization abstraction to the store in Figure 6. Grey boxes represent sets of locked objects. $v=\top$ indicates that the numeric value of v has been abstracted away.

set, respectively. (We overload these expressions to treat reference variables as singleton sets.) Statements of the form `a += exp` and `a -= exp` are shorthand for `a = a + exp` and `a = a - exp`, respectively. `choose(exp)` non-deterministically chooses an object from a set denoted by `exp`.

2.4 Optimization Opportunities

Our static analysis enables the following optimizations.

Eliminating Usage of Concurrent Data Structures. The following conditions allow replacing a concurrent implementation of a data structure by a sequential implementation: the data structure is iteration private, or the data structure is never modified. We use a purity analysis [ ] to discover objects that are never modified inside an iteration (such as `Weight` in the running example).

Reducing Rollback Logging. Logging inverse method calls for iterations that commit represents wasted work, as the log is cleared when the iteration commits and the logged method calls are never used.

Our static analysis finds a minimal set of *failsafe points* — program locations in the client program such that an iteration reaching them cannot abort. The analysis computes an under-approximation of the set of objects that are always locked at a program location. If the set of locks computed for a location L subsumes the set of locks computed for all locations reachable from L, then L is a failsafe point. An iteration reaching a failsafe point will never fail to acquire a lock and therefore cannot abort. We eliminate logging inverse actions for method calls appearing after a failsafe point.

If no method call before a failsafe point modifies shared data structures, rollback logging is not needed anywhere in the iteration. Algorithms with this property are called *cautious* algorithms [ ].

Eliminating Redundant Locking. Our analysis can also be used to find method calls for which all locks have already been acquired by preceding method calls. Lock acquisitions can be eliminated for these calls. Furthermore, our analysis finds user-defined objects "dominated" by other locked objects, *i.e.*, objects that can only be accessed after a unique abstract lock is acquired. We eliminate lock operations for such objects as well.

2.5 Optimizing the Running Example by Static Analysis

We develop a sound static analysis to automatically infer available optimizations of the kind discussed above. The input to our analysis is a Java program with a single parallel loop, given by the `foreach` construct, operating over a library of specified boosted data structures. The output of our analysis is an assignment of option flags to each ADT method call and a list of (user-defined) types that do not need "transactional" protection.

The core component of our analysis is a shape analysis that under-approximates the set of objects that are always locked at a program point. Intuitively, our analysis abstracts stores into bounded-size shape graphs by collapsing all objects not referenced by variables together and recording for each root object a set of path expressions denoting the set of locked objects.

Figure 7 shows a shape graph obtained by applying our abstraction to the store in Figure 6. The object labeled by a double-circle shows the set of collapsed objects. The grey box pointing to **a** expresses the fact that the immediate neighborhood of **a** is locked, along with the `Weight` objects referenced by its incident edges. This shape graph represents an intermediate invariant inferred by our analysis at L2. The full invariant is given by a set of the shape graphs at that point, at the fixpoint.

Below, we provide sample invariants that our analysis infers for Figure 2 and the corresponding path expressions denoting sets of objects all of which are locked:

*Inv*1: At L2, the immediate neighborhood of a is locked:
`a + a.rev(dst).src + a.rev(src).dst.`

*Inv*2: At L4-L9, the immediate neighborhoods of a and lt are locked:
`a + a.rev(dst).src + a.rev(src).dst +`
`lt + lt.rev(dst).src + lt.rev(src).dst.`

*Inv*3: At L2 and L6, all graph nodes accessible by the iterator `nIter` (past, present, and future iterations) are locked:
`nIter.past + nIter.at + nIter.future.`

*Inv*4: At 33, 47, 50, and 53, the edges referenced by e and an and the nodes they reference are locked:
`e + an + e.src + e.dst + an.src + an.dst.`

*Inv*1 is part of the invariant needed to prove that L4 is a failsafe point (before executing the statement). *Inv*1 needs to be maintained from L2 and on. It is also used to eliminate locking in lines 32-33. *Inv*2 helps establish L4 as a failsafe point, since all accesses to nodes and edges in the second loop are to objects known to be locked. Also, it helps eliminate redundant locking at L9. *Inv*3 helps establish the failsafe point at L4 by the fact that the node referenced by n is locked at 46 and 48, and eliminate locking at 32. Finally, *Inv4* establishes that the calls to getEdgeData and setEdgeData in lines 33, 47, 50, and 53 do not lock new objects.

Additionally, our analysis infers that Weight objects are read-only, which enables eliminating all lock operations and backup copy maintenance for them. Points L7, L8, L10, L11 are after the failsafe point and do not require storing inverse actions. At L10, the calls to the add method of Bag do not require acquiring locks, and trivially commute.

We apply these optimizations to the code of Figure 2 by setting the LOCK option at L1 and L3, which eliminates rollback logging, and setting the NONE option in all other calls, eliminating both abstract locking and rollback logging.

This implementation of Boruvka's algorithm is cautious: our analysis infers that the failsafe point is L4 and that no modifications are made to the graph between L1 and L4. If we remove the statement at L3, the failsafe point is at L5, which requires logging an inverse method call for g.removeEdge(a, lt).[4]

3. A Shape Analysis for Graph Programs

This section presents our static analysis for enabling the optimizations described in previous sections. Our analysis considers only sequential executions, but the inferred properties apply to concurrent executions as well. We use a result by Filipovic et al. [ ] and the fact that our concurrent executions are strictly serializable to formally justify this [ ].

The core component of the analysis is a shape analysis that under-approximates the set of objects that are always locked, at each program location. This section is organized as follows: (1) we discuss the class of programs and stores that our shape analysis addresses; (2) we define Canonical Abstraction [ ] and partial join [ ] in our setting; (3) we define ***Hierarchy Summarization Abstraction*** (*HSA*); (4) we present a technique for discovering predicates relevant to our analysis; (5) we explain how the results of the shape analysis are used; (6) we contrast our abstraction with ***Backward Reachability Abstraction*** (*BRA*), a commonly used form of shape abstraction; (7) we discuss how our analysis can aid the programmer by providing non-cautiousness counterexamples; and finally (8) we discuss limitations of our analysis.

3.1 A Class of Programs and Stores

We analyze Java programs (excluding recursive procedures) where the implementation of specified data structures is replaced by the abstract fields in the @rep annotations and the semantics of methods is given by the @op annotations.

Figure 8 defines stores in terms of pointer fields and set-valued fields defined by the @rep annotations. We define the meaning of path expressions (recursively), which denote sets of objects reachable from a variable by following fields in specified directions and going through specified variables. The last definition in Figure 8 provides the meaning of variables assigned to intermediate objects along path expressions, such as f.rev(src):eft.dst.t.

Bounded-depth Hierarchical Stores. We define the set of types reachable from an object o (by forward paths) to be the set of types of all objects in $[\![o.p]\!]$ for all path expressions p.

This paper focuses on the class of *bounded-depth hierarchical stores* — stores where the set of types reachable from $[\![$o.f$]\!]$ is a proper subset of the set of types reachable from o, for every object o and field f. Such stores are acyclic — the length of any unidirectional path, i.e., a path where all fields are either forward or reverse, is linearly bounded by the number of program types.

3.2 Canonical Abstraction and Partial Join

We implement our shape analysis using the TVLA system [ ], which allows defining stores by first-order predicates, program statements by first-order transition formulae (formulae relating the values of predicates after a statement to those before), and abstract states by first-order *abstraction predicates*. The system automatically generates sound abstract operations and transformers, yielding a sound abstract interpretation for a given program.

TVLA uses Canonical Abstraction [ ], which abstracts stores into 3-valued logical structures. To focus our presentation on the important details of our analysis, we simplify our description of TVLA's abstraction and use *shape graphs* for abstract states instead of 3-valued structures.

Definition 3.1 (Shape Graph). *Let $P = AP \cup NAP$ be a set of predicates consisting of two disjoint sets of unary predicates called* abstraction predicates *(AP) and* non-abstraction predicates *(NAP). A shape graph G is a tuple (N^G, P^G, E^G) where N^G is a set of abstract objects, $P^G : N^G \to 2^P$ assigns predicates to objects, and $E^G : OFld \cup SFld \to N^G \times N^G$ is a set of* may-edges *for each field. We denote the set of shape graphs over P by ShapeGraph[P].*

We call the set of abstraction predicates assigned to an abstract node $v \in N^G$ its *canonical name*: $CName(v) \stackrel{\text{def}}{=} P^G(v) \cap AP$. A shape graph G is *bounded* if no two abstract nodes have the same canonical name. This means that the number of abstract nodes in a bounded shape graph is *exponentially bounded* by the number of abstraction predicates.

We define the abstraction function $\beta[P] : Store \to BGraph[P]$, which maps a store $\sigma = (S^\sigma, H^\sigma)$ into a bounded shape graph G as follows. We use the helper function $P^\sigma : T_O \to 2^P$, which evaluates the predicates in P for each object, and $\mu^{\sigma,G} : T_O \to N^G$, which maps store objects having an equal canonical name to an abstract node representing their equivalence class in G. The predicate assignment function assigns to abstract nodes the predicates common to all objects they represent, and a field edge exists between two abstract nodes if there exist two objects represented by the abstract nodes that are related by that field.

$$
\begin{aligned}
&\mu^{\sigma,G}(o_1) = \mu^{\sigma,G}(o_2) \iff P^\sigma(o_1) \cap AP = P^\sigma(o_2) \cap AP \\
&P^G(n) = \bigcap_{o \text{ s.t. } n=\mu^{\sigma,G}(o)} P^\sigma(o) \\
&E^G(f) = \{(n_1, n_2) \mid \exists o_1, o_2 \colon n_1 = \mu^{\sigma,G}(o_1), n_2 = \mu^{\sigma,G}(o_2). \\
&\qquad \begin{cases} o_2 = H^\sigma(f)(o_1), & f \in OFld; \\ o_2 \in H^\sigma(f)(o_1), & f \in SFld. \end{cases} \\
&\qquad \} .
\end{aligned}
$$

We say that a shape graph G' *subsumes* a shape graph G, written $G \sqsubseteq G'$, if there exists an onto function $\mu^{G,G'} : N^G \to N^{G'}$, such that $P^G(n) \supseteq P^{G'}(\mu^{G,G'}(n))$ for all $n \in N^G$, and $(n_1, n_2) \in E^G(f)$ implies that $(\mu^{G,G'}(n_1), \mu^{G,G'}(n_2)) \in E^{G'}(f)$ for all $n_1, n_2 \in N^G$, $f \in OFld \cup SFld$.

The meaning of a shape graph G is given by the function $\gamma[P] : ShapeGraph[P] \to 2^{Store}$ defined as $\gamma[P](G) = \{\sigma \mid \beta[P](\sigma) \sqsubseteq G\}$.

We say that two shape graphs G and G' are *congruent* if there exists a bijection between their sets of abstract nodes $\mu^{G,G'} : N^G \to N^{G'}$, which preserves the abstraction predicates: $P^G(n) \cap AP = P^{G'}(\mu^{G,G'}(n)) \cap AP$ for all $n \in N^G$. Two congruent shape graphs G and G' can be subsumed by a congruent shape graph $G'' = G \sqcup G'$, by intersecting corresponding predicate values and taking the union of corresponding edges using the bijections

[4] Swapping L4 and L5 makes the code cautious once again, but breaks sequential correctness, since in the Galois library it is illegal to remove an edge while iterating over the neighbors of a node incident to it.

Stores	
T_O	Objects
$\mathit{Stack} : \mathit{PVar} \to T_O \cup$ $\quad \mathit{SVar} \to 2^{T_O} \cup$ $\quad \mathit{BVar} \to \{\mathtt{T}, \mathtt{F}\}$	Stacks
$\mathit{Heap} : (T_O \times \mathit{OFld}) \to T_O \cup$ $\quad (T_O \times \mathit{SFld}) \to 2^{T_O}$	Heaps
$\mathit{Store} : \mathit{Stack} \times \mathit{Heap}$	Stores
$\sigma = (S^\sigma, H^\sigma)$	Store notation

Semantics of Path Expressions

$[\![\mathit{Path}]\!] : \mathit{Store} \to 2^{T_O}$

Base case. Variables:

$$[\![x]\!](\sigma) = \begin{cases} \{S^\sigma(x)\}, & x \in \mathit{PVar}; \\ S^\sigma(x), & x \in \mathit{SVar}. \end{cases}$$

Inductive case. $p \in \mathit{Path}$, $[\![p]\!](\sigma)$ is known, and e is a field or variable:

$$[\![p.e]\!](\sigma) = \begin{cases} [\![p]\!](\sigma) \cap [\![e]\!](\sigma), & e \in \mathit{PVar} \cup \mathit{SVar}; \\ \{H^\sigma(o,e) \mid o \in [\![p]\!](\sigma)\}, & e \in \mathit{OFld}; \\ \bigcup_{o \in [\![p]\!](\sigma)} H^\sigma(o,e), & e \in \mathit{SFld}; \\ \{o \in T_O \mid H^\sigma(o,f) \in [\![p]\!](\sigma)\}, & e = \mathtt{rev}(f), f \in \mathit{OFld}; \\ \{o \in T_O \mid H^\sigma(o,f) \cap [\![p]\!](\sigma) \neq \emptyset\}, & e = \mathtt{rev}(f), f \in \mathit{SFld}. \end{cases}$$

For an object $o \in T_O$ and path $p \in \mathit{Path}$, we define

$[\![o.p]\!](\sigma) = $ **let** y be fresh, $\sigma' = (S^\sigma[y \mapsto o, H^\sigma)$ **in** $[\![y.p]\!](\sigma')$

Meaning of intermediate variables:

The expression $x.p{:}v.q$ assigns to v the set of objects that are both on a path from x to q and in $x.p$. For $x \in \mathit{Var}$, $v \in \mathit{SVar}$, $p, q \in \mathit{Path}$

$[\![v]\!](\sigma) = [\![x.p]\!](\sigma) \cap \{o \in T_O \mid [\![o.q]\!](\sigma) \neq \emptyset\}$.

Figure 8. Stores and semantics of path expressions.

$\mu^{G'',G} : N^{G''} \to N^G$ and $\mu^{G'',G'} : N^{G''} \to N^{G'}$:

$$\begin{array}{rcl} N^{G''} & = & N^G \\ P^{G''}(n) & = & P^G(\mu^{G'',G}(n)) \cap P^{G'}(\mu^{G'',G'}(n)) \\ (n_1, n_2) \in E^{G''}(f) & \Leftrightarrow & (\mu^{G'',G}(n_1), \mu^{G'',G}(n_2)) \in E^G(f) \text{ or} \\ & & (\mu^{G'',G'}(n_1), \mu^{G'',G'}(n_2)) \in E^{G'}(f) \ . \end{array}$$

We use TVLA's partial join operator [ ], which merges congruent shape graphs into a single shape graph, and keeps non-congruent shape graphs in a set:

$$\{G\} \sqcup \{G'\} \stackrel{\text{def}}{=} \begin{cases} \{G \sqcup G'\}, & G \text{ and } G' \text{ are congruent;} \\ \{G, G'\}, & \text{else.} \end{cases}$$

The abstraction of a set of stores $\alpha[P] : 2^{\mathit{Store}} \to 2^{\mathit{BGraph}}[P]$ is defined as $\alpha[P](\Sigma) = \bigsqcup_{\sigma \in \Sigma} \beta[P](\sigma)$.

3.3 Hierarchy Summarization Abstraction

Our abstraction is defined relative to a set of *abstraction paths*, denoted by *AbsPaths*, which represent possible paths from variables to locked objects. The next subsection discusses a technique to discover a set of useful abstraction paths for a set of data structures.

Let $\sigma = (S^\sigma, H^\sigma)$ be a store. For a pointer variable x and an abstraction path p, we define a unary predicate expressing the fact that v is a root object referenced by x and **all** objects reachable from it by the path p are locked:

$$\mathit{ForwardReach}[x,p](v) \stackrel{\text{def}}{=} [\![x]\!]^\sigma = \{v\} \wedge [\![x.p]\!]^\sigma \subseteq [\![\mathtt{locks}]\!]^\sigma \ .$$

We encode hierarchy summarization abstraction via shape graphs and the set of predicates P^{HSA}, shown in Table 1, and the abstraction paths in Table 2. Since a pointer variable points to at most one node, the number of abstract nodes in a bounded shape graph $G \in \mathit{BGraph}[P^{HSA}]$ is equal to at most the number of heap roots + 1 (in the case where there exist non-root objects). The canonical names in such a shape graph are the sets of aliased pointer variables. We call such sets *aliasing configurations*. In practice, the average number of different aliasing configurations discovered by our analysis is a small constant (≈6), which means that the set of bounded shape graphs our analysis explores is linear in the number of program locations.

Figure 7 shows the result of applying $\beta[P^{HSA}]$ to the store in Figure 6 and the predicates in Table 1. Heap roots are labeled with path expressions that denote the sets of objects that are reachable from them and are definitely locked. At L2, we would expect that node **a**, its neighbors, and the edges connecting **a** are locked. This is specified by the path expressions labeling node **a**. For example, `a.rev(src).dst`, `a.rev(dst).src` refer to all the neighbors of **a**. Additionally, the current element that we are iterating over is node **c**, which is the lightest neighbor of **a**; this node has its single incoming edge and edge data locked. All other (non-root) nodes, edges, and `Weight` objects are collapsed by our abstraction.

Predicates	Meaning
Abstraction Predicates	
$\{x(v) \mid x \in \mathit{Var}\}$	x references v
Non-abstraction Predicates	
$\{\mathit{ForwardReach}[x,p](v) \mid x \in \mathit{Var}, p \in \mathit{AbsPaths}\}$	Hierarchy summarization predicates

Table 1. P^{HSA} predicates for hierarchy summarization abstraction.

Type	Abstraction Paths
Graph	es, es.src, es.dst, ns, $\mathtt{ns}.\overleftarrow{\mathtt{src}}$, $\mathtt{ns}.\overleftarrow{\mathtt{dst}}$, $\mathtt{ns}.\overleftarrow{\mathtt{dst}}\mathtt{.ed}$, $\mathtt{ns}.\overleftarrow{\mathtt{dst}}\mathtt{.ed}$, $\mathtt{ns}.\overleftarrow{\mathtt{src}}\mathtt{.dst}$, $\mathtt{ns}.\overleftarrow{\mathtt{dst}}\mathtt{.src}$, ns.nd, $\mathtt{ns}.\overleftarrow{\mathtt{src}}\mathtt{.dst.nd}$, $\mathtt{ns}.\overleftarrow{\mathtt{dst}}\mathtt{.src.nd}$, es.ed, es.src.nd, es.dst.nd
Node	a, lt, n, $\overleftarrow{\mathtt{src}}$, $\overleftarrow{\mathtt{dst}}$, $\overleftarrow{\mathtt{src}}\mathtt{.dst}$, $\overleftarrow{\mathtt{dst}}\mathtt{.src}$, nd $\overleftarrow{\mathtt{src}}\mathtt{.ed}$, $\overleftarrow{\mathtt{dst}}\mathtt{.ed}$, $\overleftarrow{\mathtt{src}}\mathtt{.dst.nd}$, $\overleftarrow{\mathtt{dst}}\mathtt{.src.nd}$
Edge	e, an, src, dst, ed, src.nd, dst.nd
Weight	$\overleftarrow{\mathtt{ed}}$, $\overleftarrow{\mathtt{ed}}\mathtt{.src}$, $\overleftarrow{\mathtt{ed}}\mathtt{.dst}$, $\overleftarrow{\mathtt{ed}}\mathtt{.src.nd}$, $\overleftarrow{\mathtt{ed}}\mathtt{.dst.nd}$
Set	cont, $\mathtt{cont}.\overleftarrow{\mathtt{src}}$, $\mathtt{cont}.\overleftarrow{\mathtt{dst}}$, $\mathtt{cont}.\overleftarrow{\mathtt{src}}\mathtt{.dst}$, $\mathtt{cont}.\overleftarrow{\mathtt{dst}}\mathtt{.src}$, $\mathtt{cont}.\overleftarrow{\mathtt{src}}\mathtt{.ed}$, $\mathtt{cont}.\overleftarrow{\mathtt{dst}}\mathtt{.ed}$, $\mathtt{cont}.\overleftarrow{\mathtt{src}}\mathtt{.dst.nd}$, $\mathtt{cont}.\overleftarrow{\mathtt{dst}}\mathtt{.src.nd}$, cont.nd
GSet	gcont, gcont.nd
GBag	bcont
Iterator	all, all.cont, all.cont.nd, past, at, future, past.nd, at.nd, future.nd

Table 2. Abstraction paths for the running example. We omit Java Generics parameters when no confusion is likely.

3.4 Predicate Discovery

We now describe heuristics for generating the set of abstraction paths from the data structures in a program, and show how it finds paths expressing the invariants described in Section 2. Our technique constructs paths in three phases: (a) building the *type dependence graph*, (b) discovering *variable-to-lock* paths in method specifications, and (c) combining variable-to-lock paths and all forward paths in the type dependence graph.

Definition 3.2 (Type Dependence Graph). *A* type dependence graph *for a program, contains a* type node N_T *for each program type* T*, labeled by the set of program variables of that type; and a* field edge *from type node* N_T *to type node* $N_{T'}$*, labeled by a field of type* T' *or* $set\langle T' \rangle$ *declared in type* T.

Figure 9 shows the type dependence graph for Figure 2. For the rest of this section, we fix the set of variables and fields, and define the set of well-formed path expressions, *WFPath*.

Definition 3.3 (Well-formed Path Expressions). *Define the* type-node pair *of a path expression element as follows:* $TNPair(x) = (N_T, N_T)$ *for a variable* x *of type* T; $TNPair(f) = (N_T, N_{T'})$ *for a field* f *of type* T' *or* $set\langle T' \rangle$ *declared in a type* T; *and* $TNPair(\overleftarrow{f}) = (N_{T'}, N_T)$ *for a reversed field expression* $\overleftarrow{f}$, *if* $TNPair(f) = (N_T, N_{T'})$.

Let p *be a path expression* $e_1.e_2.\ldots.e_k$ *and let the corresponding sequence of type-node pairs be* $(N_1, N'_1), \ldots, (N_k, N'_k)$. *We say that* p *is* well-formed *if the sequence of type-nodes* $N_1, N'_1, \ldots, N_k, N'_k$ *is an undirected path in the type dependence graph. We define the type-node pair of* p *to be* $TNPair(p) = (N_1, N'_k)$.

Example 4. *For example,* $nIter.at.\overleftarrow{gcont}.wl$ *is well-formed, whereas* $g.nd$ *and* $\overleftarrow{ed}.es$ *are not.*

In the sequel, we consider only well-formed path expressions. We say that a path expression p contains a cycle if the corresponding path in the type dependence graph contains a cycle. A forward path is a (well formed) path expression that contains no reversed field sub-expressions.

Definition 3.4 (Forward Closure). *The* forward closure *of a path expression* p*, written* $Forward(p)$*, is the set of all path expressions of the form* $p.p'$ *where* p' *is a forward path not containing program variables (*$p.p'$ *is well-formed) and* p' *does not introduce cycles other than ones already contained in* p*. The forward closure of a type* T *is the set of all forward paths starting from type* T*, not containing program variables.*

Path closures of sets of path expressions and types are obtained by taking the union of the closures of all set members.

Example 5. $Forward(Edge) = \{ed, src, dst, src.nd, dst.nd\}$ *and* $Forward(an.src.\overleftarrow{dst}) = \{an.src.\overleftarrow{dst}, an.src.\overleftarrow{dst}.ed\}$.

The forward closure of the types in the type dependence graph represent data access patterns where a sequence of method calls is used to obtain an object of type T from an object of a type T' higher in the hierarchy. For example, in lines 32-33 of Figure 2, a sequence of method calls is used to obtain an edge from the graph and a `Weight` from an edge. In particular, the forward closure gives us the paths needed to express *Inv*3 and *Inv*4.

However, these paths ignore the effect of methods, which create more intricate paths, such as the ones needed for *Inv*1 and *Inv*2. Those are discovered by "summarizing" method specifications, as explained next.

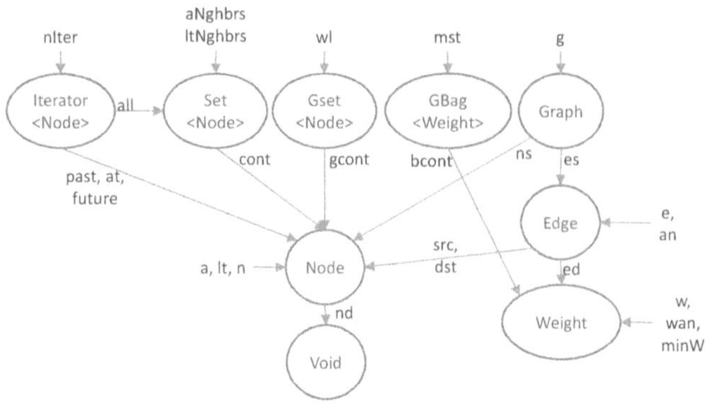

Figure 9. Type dependence graph for Figure 2.

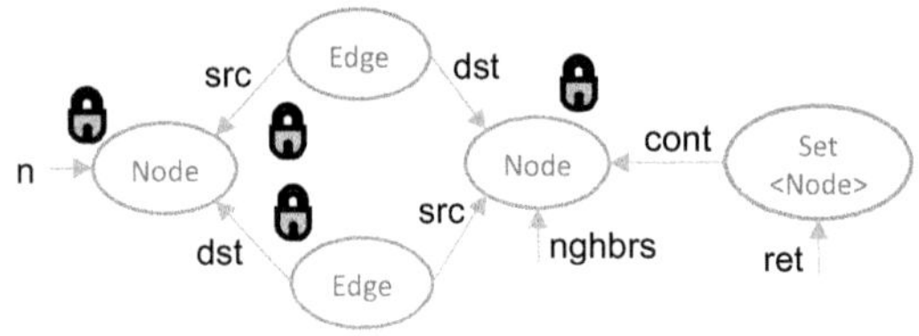

Figure 10. Footprint graph for `Graph.getNeighbors`. A lock is shown next to each node labeled by `locks`.

3.4.1 Discovering Paths in Method Footprints

We now explain how to find variable-to-lock paths, which represent possible paths between objects referenced by the method parameters (and returned value) and objects accessed by the `@locks` specification, after the `@op` specification "executes".

To find these paths, we construct a *footprint graph* for each method. Intuitively, this graph represents the set of objects accessed by the method, sometimes referred to as the "footprint" of the method. The idea of "footprint analysis" was defined by Calcagno et al. [ ] to infer method preconditions and postconditions. We put this idea to use for a different purpose.

We create a footprint graph by the following steps:

Handling statements We interpret the statements in `@op` in the order they appear. For each statement, we create a graph representing every path expression on the right-hand side of an assignment. This is done by creating a new node for each position in the expression, connecting them by the respective fields, and labeling nodes by the variables along the expression. If the left-hand side of the assignment is a pointer or set variable (`locks`), we use it to label the last node of each path graph. If it is a field of the type containing the method, we create a node of that type labeled by `this` and connect an edge field from that node to the last node of every path graph created for the right-hand side expression.

Creating `@locks` paths We create path graphs for all path expressions in `@locks` that do not already appear in `@op`.

Merging We merge nodes labeled by a common (pointer or set) variable.

Setting `locks` We label every node matching a path expression in `@locks` by `locks`.

Example 3.5. *Figure 10 shows the footprint graph for the* `getNeighbors` *method of* `Graph`*. The top node represents the outgoing edges of* `n`*, the lower node represents the incoming edges*

Type	Variable-to-Lock Paths
Graph	es, es.src, es.dst, ns, ns.$\overleftarrow{\texttt{src}}$, ns.$\overleftarrow{\texttt{dst}}$, ns.$\overleftarrow{\texttt{src}}$.dst, ns.$\overleftarrow{\texttt{dst}}$.src
Node	Var(Node), $\overleftarrow{\texttt{src}}$, $\overleftarrow{\texttt{dst}}$, $\overleftarrow{\texttt{src}}$.dst, $\overleftarrow{\texttt{dst}}$.src
Edge	Var(Edge), src, dst
Weight	$\overleftarrow{\texttt{ed}}$, $\overleftarrow{\texttt{ed}}$.src, $\overleftarrow{\texttt{ed}}$.dst
Set<Node>	cont, cont.$\overleftarrow{\texttt{src}}$, cont.$\overleftarrow{\texttt{dst}}$, cont.$\overleftarrow{\texttt{src}}$.dst, cont.$\overleftarrow{\texttt{dst}}$.src
GSet	gcont
GBag<E>	$\emptyset$

Table 3. Variable-to-Lock paths for the running example. `Var(T)` denotes an arbitrary variable to an object of type `T`.

of n. Both are connected to some neighbor of n. The node on the right represents the returned set containing the neighbors of n. We use this graph to obtain paths expressing that `getNeighbors` *has the effect of locking the immediate neighborhood of n.*

We define the function $VarToLock : TName \to 2^{WFPath}$ associating a set of variable-to-lock paths with each program type.

We create a set of variable-to-lock paths for every type node from all footprint graphs as follows. For each footprint graph, we take all the acyclic non-empty paths from a node labeled by a method parameter (including `this` and the return parameter `ret`) to any node labeled by `locks`. We associate these paths with the type node corresponding to the type of the parameter. We denote the set of variable-to-lock paths of type T by $VarToLock(T)$.

Table 3 shows the variable-to-lock paths that we get for the running example. These paths enable us to express *Inv*1 and *Inv*2.

We combine the sets of paths defined earlier to obtain the set of abstraction paths:

$$AbsPaths \stackrel{\text{def}}{=} \bigcup_{t \in TName} Forward(t) \cup Forward(VarToLock(t)) \ .$$

Here, expressions of the form `Var(T)` appearing in $VarToLock(t)$ are substituted by the set of paths $\{x \in Var \mid x \text{ is of type } T\}$.

3.5 Putting it All Together

Our overall static analysis consists of the following stages:

Preprocessing We use a lightweight purity analysis [ ] to detect objects that do not require concurrency control and fields that are never used inside the parallel loop, e.g., the `initSrc` and `initDst` fields of `Weight`. The remainder of the analysis does not consider path expressions in `@locks` containing unused fields and sets the `opt` flags of read-only objects to `NONE`.

Shape Analysis We execute a forward shape analysis using hierarchy summarization abstraction and TVLA-generated abstract transformers. The fixpoint is a set of bounded shape graphs at every program location.

Finding Redundant Locks We use abstract operations in TVLA to conservatively check whether every shape graph at a program location represents stores that lock all objects defined by a `@locks` specification of a method executing at that location. If so, we set the `opt` argument of that method call to `UNDO` (if it was not already set to `NONE`).

Finding Failsafe Points We perform a backward BFS traversal over the CFG (control flow graph) to find earliest program locations where all following method calls are labeled by `NONE` or `UNDO` (meaning they do not acquire locks). These program locations are the program failsafe points, We set the optimization argument of all method calls dominated by failsafe points to `NONE`.

Predicates	Meaning
Abstraction Predicates	
$\{x(v) \mid x \in Var\}$	x references v
$\{BackwardReach[x, p](v) \mid x \in Var, p \in AbsPaths\}$	Backward-reachability predicates

Table 4. Predicates for backward-reachability abstraction.

3.6 Backward Reachability Abstraction

A common abstraction idiom for shape abstraction uses *coloring*, which records a set of unary (object-)predicates with **every object** in the store. These predicates are used to partition the set of objects into equivalence classes. Examples are Canonical Abstraction [ ], Boolean heaps [ ], Indexed predicate abstraction [ ], and generalized typestates [ ].

These abstractions typically employ *backward reachability predicates* that use paths in the heap to relate objects to variables. For example, most TVLA-based analyses and analyses using Boolean heaps distinguish between disjoint data structure regions (e.g., list segments and sub-trees) by using transitive reachability from pointer variables. Indexed predicate abstraction [ ] uses predicates that assert that cache clients are contained in one of two lists (`sharer_list` and `invalidate_list`). Lam et al. [ ] use set containment predicates as the generalized typestate of an object.

We call such abstractions *bottom-up*, since they record properties of objects deep in the heap with respect to (shallow) root objects. These abstractions achieve high precision as they express every Boolean combination of intersection and union of objects satisfying the unary predicates. However, the size of an abstracted store can be exponential in the number of predicates, which might lead to state space explosion in cases where objects satisfy many different subsets of predicates.

We define backward reachability abstraction by using the set of abstraction paths presented earlier to define backward reachability predicates. For a pointer variable `x` and an abstraction path p, we define a unary predicate expressing the fact that v is a locked object reachable from `x` by the path p:

$$BackwardReach[x, p](v) \stackrel{\text{def}}{=} v \in [\![\texttt{locks}]\!]^{\sigma} \cap [\![x.p]\!]^{\sigma} \ .$$

We obtain a backward reachability abstraction $\beta[P^{BRA}]$ from the predicates shown in Table 4. *BRA* is strictly more precise than *HSA*. However, it can be very expensive — the number of abstract nodes in a shape graph obtained by $\beta[P^{BRA}]$ can be exponential in the number of backward-reachability predicates. State space explosion manifests when stores create overlaps between different interacting sets (set fields), which is often the case in our programs. Applying $\beta[P^{BRA}]$ to the store in Figure 6, will conflate all objects not locked and not referenced by a program variable. Compared to Figure 7, `Edge` objects 2 and 3, for example, will remain needlessly distinguished. Situations such as iterating over the neighbors of a node, exploring multiple neighborhoods simultaneously or sharing objects between multiple collections, cause the number of useless distinctions to increase.

3.7 Producing Non-Cautiousness Counterexamples

When the code of a parallel loop body is not cautious, our analysis can sometimes provide a counterexample to demonstrate the violation of the cautious property at appropriate program points. To find such counterexamples, we assume the small scope conjecture [ ], which says that counterexamples usually manifest in small graphs.

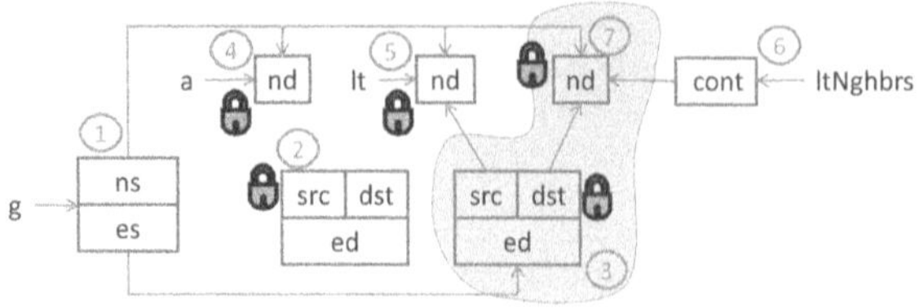

Figure 11. A counterexample at location L5 for the non-cautious implementation of BVK.

A graph with three nodes and two edges is sufficient to provide us with a counterexample for the case of BVK, as shown in Figure 11. The region of the graph where the violation happens is highlighted. This is the smallest counterexample found by our analysis, taking about 300 seconds to produce.

3.8 Limitations

We recognize the following limitations of our analysis.

Bounded-depth hierarchy. As discussed at the beginning of this section, we assume a class of stores where a finite-depth hierarchy property exists. This allows us to ensure a bound on the number of hierarchy summarization paths used to define our abstraction. This precludes us from handling benchmarks where data structures such as lists and trees are explicitly manipulated (and cannot be abstracted away by a `@rep` specification). Generalizing our analysis to handle recursive data structures may be done by considering abstraction paths with regular expressions over the pointer fields of the data structure.

Temporary violation of invariants. Our abstraction is geared to infer invariants of the form $\forall o.R(o) \implies p(o)$ where $R(o)$ expresses a heap region (by abstraction paths) and $p(o)$ is a property we wish to summarize for the objects in the region $R(o)$ (the is-locked property in our analysis). When the property p is temporarily violated for the objects in $R(o)$ and then restored, our analysis is not able to restore the invariant. For example, assume an invariant $\forall o.R(o) \implies p(o)$ holds at program point 1. Then a point 2 a single object in $R(o)$, referenced by a pointer variable x, is made to have $\neg p(o)$ and at point 3 it is removed from $R(o)$. In order to regain the invariant $\forall o.R(o) \implies p(o)$ at point 3, we may need to refine our abstraction in order to express an invariant such as $\forall o.(R(o) \wedge \neg \mathtt{x}(o)) \implies p(o)$.

4. Experimental Evaluation

The shape analysis described in Section 3 was implemented in TVLA, and used to optimize four benchmarks from the Lonestar suite [ ]. These benchmarks were chosen because they exhibit very diverse behavior. We describe them below.

- BVK: Boruvka's MST algorithm. This benchmark adds and removes nodes and edges from a graph.
- DMR: Delaunay mesh refinement. This benchmark uses iterative refinement to produce a quality mesh. In each iteration, a neighborhood of a bad triangle, called the *cavity* of that triangle, is removed from the mesh and replaced with new triangles. DMR uses a large number of collections with intricate patterns of data sharing, so it is a "stress test" for the analysis.
- SP: Survey propagation, a heuristic SAT solver. Most iterations only update node labels, but once in a while, an iteration removes a node (corresponding to a "frozen variable" [ ]) and its incident edges.

Prog.	IR Size	Graph Calls	Set Calls	Field Acc.	Optimal
BVK	340	17/20	4/4	23/23	✓
DMR	1,168	26/30	30/30	164/164	✓
SP	925	32/34	16/16	123/123	✓
PFP	479	6/8	3/3	28/28	✓

Table 5. Program characteristics and static analysis results. x/y measures Optimized/Total.

Analysis	Total SGs	Avg. # Abs. Nodes	Avg. # SGs CFG Location	Time (sec)
		BVK		
HSA	13,594	9	6.25	6
BRA	412,862	15	250	3,406
		DMR		
HSA	35,763	13	6.46	16
BRA	1,043,116	20	268	14,909
		SP		
HSA	25,421	13	6.26	12
BRA	394,765	21	158	12,446
		PFP		
HSA	17,692	10	6.96	7
BRA	71,800	17	45	972

Table 6. *HSA*, *BRA* performance statistics.(*SG: Shape Graph*)

- PFP: Preflow-push maxflow algorithm [ ]. This algorithm only updates labels of nodes and edges, and does not modify the graph structure.

4.1 Static Analysis Evaluation

Table 5 reports the results of static analysis of our benchmarks. We measure the size of benchmarks by the number of intermediate language (Jimple) instructions in the client program, excluding the code implementing the data structures accompanied by a specification. Columns 3 to 5 show the number of static optimization opportunities that our analysis enables. Galois protects application-specific objects (e.g., the cavity in DMR) using a variant of object-based STM, which can also benefit from our optimizations. Column 5 refers to those objects. In all cases, our analysis was precise enough to identify the maximum number of sites that were eligible for optimization, and it discovered the minimal set of latest failsafe points. The optimal result that we compare against was determined manually. Since our analysis is sound, we need to consider only the relatively few calls where the analysis does not suggest conflict detection or rollback logging optimizations.

4.1.1 Comparing Analyses: HSA vs. BRA

In Table 6, we compare our analysis using hierarchy summarization abstraction (*HSA*), with an analysis using backward reachability abstraction (*BRA*). The first column reports the total number of shape graphs (SG) explored by the analysis, which is a measure for the amount of work performed. We also report the average size of a shape graph, the average number of SG's per CFG location (our analysis uses roughly 1.43 CFG locations for a Jimple instruction) at the fixed point, and the running time of the analysis.

As expected, *HSA* generates a constant number of SG's at each program location, whereas in *BRA* the number of SG's increases as the benchmarks become more complex (from 45 SG's for PFP to 268 for DMR). The benefits of *HSA* are more striking as the complexity of the benchmark increases. For PFP, *BRA* generates roughly 6 times more SG's than *HSA*, per CFG location. For DMR, in which the number of collections increases, *BRA* produces 41 times more structures. Additionally, we observe that in *BRA* we have more refined and, consequently, larger SG's. For all benchmarks the average SG size in *BRA* is roughly 1.6 times larger than in *HSA*. These facts lead to a significant state space explosion, which translates to increased work performed by *BRA* (for DMR we see a 29-fold increase in the number of generated SG's), and to increased running times. Thus, *HSA* is as precise as *BRA* but more efficient.

4.2 Experimental Evaluation of Optimizations

This section provides detailed performance results for each benchmark. To evaluate the performance gains obtained by different levels of sophistication of the analysis, we considered the following variants for each benchmark.

- O1: Baseline version: accesses within parallel loops to *all* objects are protected.
- O2: Iteration-private objects are not protected.
- O3: O2+ dominated shared objects are not protected.
- O4: O3+ duplicate lock acquisitions and unnecessary undo operations are eliminated.

Even in the baseline version, we do not protect object accesses made outside of parallel loops since the analysis required to enable this is trivial. At level O2, iteration-private objects are identified and accesses to them are not protected; this optimization by itself can be accomplished by a combination of flow-insensitive points-to and escape analysis. Optimization levels O3 and O4 target shared data; for these levels, a shape analysis similar to ours is necessary.

We performed our experiments using the Galois runtime system and a Sun Fire X2270 Nehalem server running Ubuntu Linux version 8.04. The system contains two quad-core 2.93 GHz Intel Xeon processors, which share 24 GB of main memory. We used the Sun HotSpot 64-bit server JVM, version 1.6.0. Each variant was executed nine times in the same instance of the JVM. We drop the first two iterations to account for the overheads of JIT compilation, and report results for the run with the median running time.

Because of the don't-care non-determinism of unordered-set iterators, different executions of the same benchmark/input combination may perform different numbers of iterations. Since our optimizations focus on reducing the overhead of each iteration and not on controlling the total number of iterations, we focus on a performance metric called *throughput*, which is the number of committed iterations per millisecond. For completeness, we also present other measurements such as the total running time, the number of committed iterations, the abort ratio, etc. Table 7 shows detailed results for all benchmarks.

4.2.1 Boruvka's Algorithm

We do not provide results for level O2, since the number of iteration private objects is insignificant. The number of committed iterations is exactly the same across all thread counts (this is a natural property of the algorithm since each committed iteration adds one edge to the MST). The analysis is successful in reducing the number of locks per iteration, and it correctly infers that the operator implementation is cautious.

The Boruvka algorithm takes roughly 141 seconds to run if we use 1 thread and optimization level O1, and 75 seconds if we use 8 threads and optimization level O4. At optimization level O4, no undo's are logged and the number of acquired locks in each iteration is substantially reduced. However, overall speedup is limited by the high abort ratio (for example, for 8 threads, the abort ratio is between 68% and 75% for all levels of optimization). The abort ratio decreases as the optimization level increases because if the time to execute an iteration is reduced, the iteration holds its locks for a smaller amount of time, reducing the likelihood of conflicts. This high abort ratio is intrinsic to the algorithm. The MST is built bottom-up, so towards the end of the execution, only the top few levels of the tree remain to be built and there is not much parallel work.

A Non-Cautious Boruvka Implementation. As we discussed in Section 2, removing the call to *getNeighbors* at `L3` results in non-cautious iterations. Our analysis successfully infers that the failsafe point along this program path moves from `L3` to `L5`. The only difference in the inferred method flags is in `L4`, where the call to `removeEdge` requires the `UNDO` flag instead of `NONE`. This example shows the utility of our analysis for optimizing programs in which the operator implementation is not cautious.

4.2.2 Delaunay Mesh Refinement

The number of committed iterations for this application is fairly stable across thread counts and optimization levels. Lock acquisitions drop dramatically in going from O2 to O3. The analysis deduces correctly that the operator implementation is cautious, which is why the number of undo's per iteration drops to zero at optimization level O4 (the number of undo's per iteration is stable in going from O2 to O3 because the re-triangulated cavity is constructed in private storage and then stored into the shared graph). The abort ratio is very small even for 8 threads.

The reductions in the average number of acquired locks and logged undo's per iteration are reflected directly in the running time. DMR takes 171 sec. to run if we use 1 thread and optimization level O1, and only 5 sec. if we use 8 threads and optimization level O4. This is roughly a factor of 34 improvement in the running time, of which a factor of roughly 8 comes from optimizations and a scaling factor of roughly 4 comes from increasing the number of threads. Since the number of committed iterations is fairly stable across all optimization levels and thread counts, the same improvement factors can also be seen in throughput.

4.2.3 Survey Propagation

The number of committed iterations is fairly stable for this benchmark. The analysis is successful in reducing the number of locks per iteration. The number of undo's per iteration is fairly small even at optimization level O1 because the graph is mutated only when a variable is frozen, which happens in very few iterations. The analysis correctly infers that the operator implementation is cautious.

The SP algorithm takes roughly 180 seconds to run if we use 1 thread and optimization level O1, and 9 seconds if we use 8 threads and optimization level O4. Most of this benefit comes from the optimizations; at optimization level O4, we observe a speedup of roughly 1.6 on 8 threads. We see a 5.5× improvement in throughput for 8 threads when the optimization level goes from O1 to O4, and by 19% from O3 to O4.

4.2.4 Preflow-push Maximal Flow

A distinctive characteristic of PFP is its schedule sensitivity - because of don't-care non-determinism, different schedules can perform very different amounts of work. This can be seen in the 8-thread numbers: at optimization level O4, the program executes twice as many iterations on 8 threads as it does on a single thread. The number of undos per iteration is 0 for O3, since the graph structure is not mutated by the algorithm.

The preflow-push algorithm takes roughly 104 seconds to run if we use 1 thread and optimization level O1, and the best parallel time is 6.6 seconds if we use 4 threads and optimization level O4. This is a 16-fold improvement, of which roughly 6-fold im-

Th.	BVK			DMR				SP				PFP			
	O1	O3	O4	O1	O2	O3	O4	O1	O2	O3	O4	O1	O2	O3	O4
Lock Acquisitions/Iteration															
1	885	637	64	1,429	1,269	97	28	99	98	49	6	109	111	44	8
2	1,114	799	93	1,429	1,269	97	28	99	99	50	6	109	111	44	8
4	1,270	896	118	1,429	1,269	97	28	99	100	50	6	109	111	44	8
8	1,512	1,020	153	1,430	1,268	97	28	100	100	50	6	110	111	45	9
Undos/Iteration															
1	40.69	40.77	0.00	27.77	8.45	8.45	0.00	4.82	4.82	0.00	0.00	5.85	2.93	0.00	0.00
2	47.42	47.30	0.00	27.77	8.45	8.44	0.00	4.85	4.85	≈ 0.00	0.00	5.85	2.93	0.00	0.00
4	47.46	47.72	0.00	27.77	8.45	8.44	0.00	4.86	4.94	≈ 0.00	0.00	5.85	2.94	0.00	0.00
8	46.61	47.25	0.00	27.79	8.44	8.45	0.00	4.90	4.89	≈ 0.00	0.00	5.92	2.95	0.00	0.00
Committed Iterations (Millions)															
1	1.60	1.60	1.60	1.62	1.62	1.62	1.62	21.61	21.52	21.49	21.71	8.62	8.34	8.41	8.41
2	1.60	1.60	1.60	1.61	1.62	1.62	1.62	21.52	22.15	22.25	21.70	8.48	8.41	8.39	8.38
4	1.60	1.60	1.60	1.62	1.62	1.62	1.62	21.75	21.68	23.84	23.15	9.33	8.52	8.50	9.25
8	1.60	1.60	1.60	1.61	1.62	1.62	1.62	21.85	23.79	24.24	25.12	9.80	11.23	13.54	16.39
Abort Ratio %															
1	0.00	0.00	0.00	0.00	0.00	0.00	0.00	0.00	0.00	0.00	0.00	0.00	0.00	0.00	0.00
2	42.50	40.28	36.99	0.00	0.01	0.00	0.01	0.97	0.95	1.04	1.23	0.13	0.14	0.11	0.11
4	61.52	58.57	55.18	0.03	0.02	0.01	0.02	3.51	3.60	3.50	3.45	0.61	0.35	0.38	0.87
8	75.70	71.25	68.57	0.05	0.04	0.02	0.03	8.39	8.62	11.54	7.19	1.02	3.08	5.04	3.83
Running Time (sec)															
1	141	107	81	171	132	24	22	180	176	24	14	104	94	22	18
2	155	109	81	93	77	14	12	109	110	24	17	75	69	13	10
4	190	102	77	49	39	8	7	65	58	14	11	114	103	7.3	6.6
8	219	98	75	28	22	5	5	42	42	10	9	108	108	7.7	9.4
Throughput (Iterations/ms)															
1	11.38	15.01	19.65	9	12	68	75	120	122	893	1,533	83	89	389	463
2	10.34	14.71	19.72	17	21	118	131	198	201	934	1,274	113	122	659	798
4	8.41	15.62	20.87	33	41	212	234	333	371	1,729	2,074	82	83	1,167	1,402
8	7.31	16.38	21.40	57	73	323	347	515	573	2,404	2,868	91	104	1,762	1,739

Table 7. Performance metrics. BVK input is a random graph of 800,000 nodes and 5-10 neighbors per node. DMR input is a random mesh with 549,998 total triangles, 261,100 bad. SP input is a 3-SAT formula with 1,000 variables and 4,200 clauses. PFP input is a random graph of 262,144 nodes and capacities in the range [0, 10000].

provement comes from the optimizations, and an improvement of roughly 3-fold comes from exploiting parallelism.

4.2.5 Summary of Results

Our analysis eliminates all costs related to rollback logging for our benchmarks, and reduces the number of lock acquisitions by a factor ranging from 10× to 50×, depending on the application and the number of threads. These improvements translate to a noticeable improvement (ranging from 2× up to 12×) in the running time, which is consistent across different thread counts, and robust against pathologies of speculation (e.g. high abort ratio).

5. Related Work

Prior work on shape analysis has focused mostly on analyzing data structure implementations to infer heap structure. In contrast, we use data structure specifications to abstract away data structure representations, and we focus on unstructured graphs.

The Jahob system [ ] verifies that a data structure implementation meets its specification, and it uses the abstract state to simplify the verification of data structure clients. Our analysis assumes that a given specification is correct. Checking that the implementation and specification of the method semantics match and that the `@locks` specification ensures that only commutating methods can execute concurrently is an interesting challenge.

Maron et al. [ ] use specialized predicates to model sharing patterns between objects stored in data structures, and use this information to statically parallelize benchmarks from the JOlden suite and SPECjvm98 benchmarks. Our benchmarks operate on unstructured graphs and are not amenable to static parallelization. We exploit the fact that our execution model is speculative to avoid tracking correlations between different data structures, which increases the cost of the analysis considerably.

In the current Galois system, the optimizations described here are performed manually [ ]. Our shape analysis automates these optimizations, reducing the burden on the programmer and ensuring correctness of optimized code. Failsafe points extend the notion of cautious operators. Our running example shows that non-cautious code too can be optimized by turning conflict detection and rollback logging off for a subset of the calls, obtaining performance improvement similar to the cautious version. Additionally, in [ ] the system optimizes locking only after the failsafe point in contrast to our analysis, which optimizes locking regardless of whether an operator is cautious.

Prabhu et al. [ ] use value speculation to probabilistically reduce the critical path length in ordered algorithms. Their static analysis focuses mainly on array programs. Value speculation is orthogonal to our approach, and the benchmarks discussed in this paper do not benefit from value speculation. Furthermore, our heap abstractions are very different because we need to handle complex ADTs such as unstructured graphs.

Harris et al. [ ], Adl-Tabatabai et al. [ ], and Dragojevic et al. [ ] use compiler optimizations to reduce the overheads of transactional memory. They also handle immutable, and transaction local objects. Additionally, they describe extending traditional compiler optimizations such as common subexpression elimination (CSE) to reduce the overheads of logging. Although CSE helps to reduce repeated logging for a single object, its effectiveness for our benchmarks is limited by the extensive use of collections. Their approaches cannot capture global properties such as failsafe points. Other optimizations they propose are complementary to ours.

McCloskey et al. [ ], Hicks et al. [ ], and Cherem et al. [ ] describe analyses that infer locks for atomic sections. These techniques are overly conservative for our benchmarks since they would always infer that an iteration might touch the whole graph.

Acknowledgments

We would like to thank the anonymous referees, Noam Rinetzky, and Josh Berdine for their helpful comments.

References

[1] A. Adl-Tabatabai, B. T. Lewis, V. Menon, B. R. Murphy, B. Saha, and T. Shpeisman. Compiler and runtime support for efficient software transactional memory. In *PLDI*. ACM, 2006.

[2] A. Braunstein, M. Mèzard, and R. Zecchina. Survey propagation: An algorithm for satisfiability. *Random Structures and Algorithms*, 27(2):201–226, 2005.

[3] C. Calcagno, D. Distefano, P. W. O'Hearn, and H. Yang. Footprint analysis: A shape analysis that discovers preconditions. In *SAS*, 2007.

[4] S. Cherem, T. Chilimbi, and S. Gulwani. Inferring locks for atomic sections. In *PLDI*. ACM, 2008.

[5] T. Cormen, C. Leiserson, R. Rivest, and C. Stein, editors. *Introduction to Algorithms*. MIT Press, 2001.

[6] A. Dragojevic, Y. Ni, and A. Adl-Tabatabai. Optimizing transactions for captured memory. In *SPAA*, 2009.

[7] D. Eppstein. *Spanning trees and spanners*, pages 425–461. Elsevier, 1999.

[8] I. Filipovic, P. W. O'Hearn, N. Rinetzky, and H. Yang. Abstraction for concurrent objects. In *ESOP*, 2009.

[9] T. Harris and K. Fraser. Language support for lightweight transactions. In *OOPSLA '03*, 2003.

[10] T. L. Harris, M. Plesko, A. Shinnar, and D. Tarditi. Optimizing memory transactions. In *PLDI*. ACM, 2006.

[11] M. Herlihy and E. Koskinen. Transactional boosting: a methodology for highly-concurrent transactional objects. In *PPOPP*. ACM, 2008.

[12] M. Herlihy and J. Eliot B. Moss. Transactional memory: architectural support for lock-free data structures. In *ISCA*, 1993.

[13] M. Hicks, J. S. Foster, and P. Pratikakis. Lock inference for atomic sections. In *TRANSACT*, June 2006.

[14] D. Jackson. *Software Abstractions: Logic, Language, and Analysis*. The MIT Press, 2006.

[15] M. Kulkarni, M. Burtscher, C. Cascaval, and K. Pingali. Lonestar: A suite of parallel irregular programs. In *ISPASS*, 2009.

[16] M. Kulkarni, P. Carribault, K. Pingali, G. Ramanarayanan, B. Walter, K. Bala, and L. P. Chew. Scheduling strategies for optimistic parallel execution of irregular programs. In *SPAA '08*, 2008.

[17] M. Kulkarni, K. Pingali, B. Walter, G. Ramanarayanan, K. Bala, and L. P. Chew. Optimistic parallelism requires abstractions. In *PLDI*. ACM, 2007.

[18] V. Kuncak and M. C. Rinard. Decision procedures for set-valued fields. *Electr. Notes Theor. Comput. Sci.*, 131, 2005.

[19] V. Kuncak and M. C. Rinard. An overview of the jahob analysis system: project goals and current status. In *IPDPS*, 2006.

[20] S. K. Lahiri and R. E. Bryant. Predicate abstraction with indexed predicates. *ACM Trans. Comput. Log.*, 9(1), 2007.

[21] P. Lam, V. Kuncak, and M. C. Rinard. Generalized typestate checking using set interfaces and pluggable analyses. *SIGPLAN Notices*, 39(3), 2004.

[22] T. Lev-Ami and M. Sagiv. TVLA: A framework for implementing static analyses. In *SAS*, 2000.

[23] R. Manevich, S. Sagiv, G. Ramalingam, and J. Field. Partially disjunctive heap abstraction. In *SAS*, 2004.

[24] M. Marron, D. Stefanovic, D. Kapur, and M. V. Hermenegildo. Identification of heap-carried data dependence via explicit store heap models. In *LCPC*, pages 94–108, 2008.

[25] B. McCloskey, F. Zhou, D. Gay, and E. Brewer. Autolocker: synchronization inference for atomic sections. In *POPL*. ACM, 2006.

[26] M. Méndez-Lojo, D. Nguyen, D. Prountzos, X. Sui, M. A. Hassaan, M. Kulkarni, M. Burtscher, and K. Pingali. Structure-driven optimizations for amorphous data-parallel programs. In *PPOPP*. ACM, 2010.

[27] K. Pingali, M. Kulkarni, D. Nguyen, M. Burtscher, M. Mendez-Lojo, D. Prountzos, X. Sui, and Z. Zhong. Amorphous data-parallelism in irregular algorithms. regular tech report TR-09-05, The University of Texas at Austin, 2009.

[28] A. Podelski and T. Wies. Boolean heaps. In *SAS*, 2005.

[29] P. Prabhu, G. Ramalingam, and K. Vaswani. Safe programmable speculative parallelism. In *PLDI*, 2010.

[30] D. Prountzos, R. Manevich, K. Pingali, and K. S. McKinley. A shape analysis for optimizing parallel graph programs. Technical Report TR-10-27, UT Austin, `http://userweb.cs.utexas.edu/users/dprountz/UTCS-TR-10-27.pdf`, Jul 2010.

[31] L. Rauchwerger and D. A. Padua. The LRPD test: Speculative run time parallelization of loops with privatization and reduction parallelization. *IEEE Trans. Parallel Distrib. Syst.*, 10(2):160–180, 1999.

[32] M. Sagiv, T. Reps, and R. Wilhelm. Parametric shape analysis via 3-valued logic. *ACM Trans. Program. Lang. Syst.*, 24(3), 2002.

[33] A. Salcianu and M. C. Rinard. Purity and side effect analysis for java programs. In *VMCAI*, 2005.

[34] K. Zee, V. Kuncak, and M. Rinard. Full functional verification of linked data structures. In *PPOPP*. ACM, 2008.

Calling Context Abstraction with Shapes

Xavier Rival
INRIA Paris-Rocquencourt *
rival@di.ens.fr

Bor-Yuh Evan Chang
University of Colorado, Boulder
bec@cs.colorado.edu

Abstract

Interprocedural program analysis is often performed by computing procedure summaries. While possible, computing adequate summaries is difficult, particularly in the presence of recursive procedures. In this paper, we propose a complementary framework for interprocedural analysis based on a direct abstraction of the calling context. Specifically, our approach exploits the inductive structure of a calling context by treating it directly as a stack of activation records. We then build an abstraction based on separation logic with inductive definitions. A key element of this abstract domain is the use of parameters to refine the meaning of such call stack summaries and thus express relations across activation records and with the heap. In essence, we define an abstract interpretation-based analysis framework for recursive programs that permits a fluid per call site abstraction of the call stack—much like how shape analyzers enable a fluid per program point abstraction of the heap.

Categories and Subject Descriptors D.2.4 [*Software Engineering*]: Software/Program Verification; F.3.1 [*Logics and Meanings of Programs*]: Specifying and Verifying and Reasoning about Programs; F.3.2 [*Logics and Meanings of Programs*]: Semantics of Programming Languages—Program analysis

General Terms Languages, Verification

Keywords interprocedural analysis, context-sensitivity, calling context, shape analysis, inductive definitions, separation logic, symbolic abstract domain

1. Introduction

It seems there are few things, if any, more fundamental in programming than procedural abstraction. Hence, without qualification, interprocedural analysis is simply something that static program analyzers need to do well. Yet, precise interprocedural static analysis in presence of recursion is difficult—analyzers need to simultaneously abstract unbounded executions, unbounded calling context, and unbounded heap structures.

Broadly speaking, there are two main approaches to interprocedural analysis with different strengths and weaknesses. The first approach is to compute procedure summaries (e.g., [4, 16, 20]). These summaries are then used to modularly interpret function calls (i.e., derivatives of the *functional approach* [28]). This approach is exceedingly common, as modularity is important, if not a prerequisite, for scalability. Unfortunately, computing effective summaries is not easy for all families of properties. Intuitively, it is more complex to abstract relations between pairs of states than to abstract sets of states. The former is the essence of what needs to be done to compute procedure summaries, while the latter is what is more typical in program analysis.

The second approach is to perform whole program analysis that, at least conceptually, completely ignores procedural abstraction by inlining function calls. Therefore, the analysis only needs to abstract sets of states (instead of relations on pairs of states). While this kind of analysis yields context-sensitivity without the complexities of deriving procedure summaries, it is clear that the exponential blow-up makes scaling significantly more difficult. This blow-up then exerts negative pressure on the choice in precision of the state abstraction.

Certainly, these approaches are not entirely disjoint and overlap to some extent. However, in both situations, the typical result is a rather coarse abstraction of calling contexts. In the modular analysis situation, procedure summaries capture precisely what is touched by the function in question but assume the context to be arbitrary. For whole program analysis, the values of locals in the call stack above the current call are typically completely abstract. Coarse calling context abstraction makes it difficult to tackle, for example, recursive procedures where there are critical relations between successive activation records.

In this paper, we propose abstracting calling contexts precisely by directly modeling the call stack of activation records, that is, we explicitly push the call stack into the state on which we abstract. To do so, we exploit the fact that the call stack has a regular, inductive structure so that shape analysis techniques apply. Under the hood, we use separation logic formulas [21] with inductive definitions in order to elaborate precise and concise stack descriptions. We formalize our call stack abstraction inside the XISA shape analysis framework [5, 6], as we leverage this abstract domain, which is parametrized by inductive definitions.

While uncommon in practice, there has been prior work on directly abstracting the call stack [22] in the TVLA framework [27]. This approach requires careful choice of a set of predicates for the modeling of stack summaries. Instead, leveraging the natural inductive structure of the call stack and a framework built around inductive definitions, we seek to lower the configuration effort. In particular, we show that the inductive definitions for the summarization of the call stack can be derived automatically.

Overall, our motivation is to define global program analyses for programs with recursive functions that make use of a precise characterization of the calling context (including the status of the pending call returns). While we apply a shape domain to the abstraction of the call stack, our focus is not shape analysis per-se. Certainly, heap shapes continue to fit naturally into the framework, but there is

* Abstraction Project-team, shared with CNRS and École Normale Supérieure, Paris

POPL'11, January 26–28, 2011, Austin, Texas, USA.

```
void main() {
  dll* l; ...
  //l is a list (maybe not doubly-linked)
  l = fix(l, NULL);
}
dll* fix(dll* c, dll* p) {
  dll* ret;
  if (c != NULL) {
    c->prev = p;
▶   c->next = fix(c->next, c);
    if (check(c->data)) {
      ret = c->next; remove(c);
▷   }
    else { ret = c; }
  }
  else { ret = NULL; }
  return ret;
}
void remove(dll* n) {
  if (n->prev != NULL)
    n->prev->next = n->next;
  if (n->next != NULL)
    n->next->prev = n->prev;
  free(n);
}
```

(a) The recursive function fix.

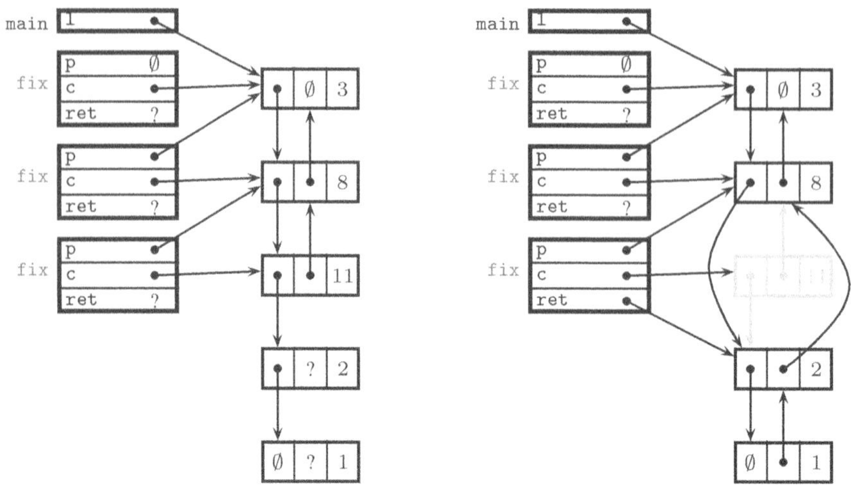

(b) After two recursive calls to fix and just about to make another recursive call at ▶.

(c) Before return from the second recursive call to fix at ▷.

Figure 1. An explanatory recursive program shown with diagrams depicting both the call stack and the heap at two points in its execution.

independent interest for numerical domains. In particular, the procedure summary approach has not been adapted to large classes of numerical domains, so the technique proposed in this paper takes steps towards a "plug-in" or product domain-style extension of base domains to precise interprocedural analysis.

If heap shapes are of interest, we assume our abstract domain has been instantiated with the appropriate inductive definitions describing them (e.g., they come from the user in the form of an inductive checker [6] corresponding to *structural consistency checking* code). That is, while we automatically derive a program-specific inductive definition to summarize call stacks, we do not try to infer inductive definitions for recursive heap structures. From a technical point of view, we exploit the fact that the call stack has a fixed recursive backbone—in contrast to user-defined recursive structures in the heap, which do not have a set shape. From a usability perspective, the stack of activations records is a low-level implementation mechanism for procedural abstraction and thus such inductive definitions would be problematic to expect from the user—in contrast to heap shapes, which are programmer-designed.

Finally, we clarify that we do not necessarily advocate a precise call stack abstraction in all situations. Rather our technique fills a gap in the analysis of programs with recursive procedures. In this paper, we make the following contributions:

- We define an abstract domain that models the call stack directly in an exact manner (Section 3) and with summarization (Section 4). The novel aspect of our approach is to leverage the inductive structure of the call stack by using a parametric shape domain based on separation logic and inductive definitions.
- We give an algorithm for automatically deriving inductive cases for call stack summarization (Section 5). That is, the inductive definition stack used to summarize the call stack is defined on the fly in a program-specific manner.
- We describe an analysis for programs with recursive procedures using this call stack abstraction (Section 6).
- We provide evidence through a case study that our call stack abstraction can be used to overcome precision issues in the modular approach (Section 7). That is, a less precise base domain with the call stack abstraction is sufficient for certain examples where a more precise one is needed with the modular approach.

2. Overview

In this section, we illustrate the main challenges in designing a precise abstraction of the calling context by following an example execution of the recursive function fix shown in Figure 1(a). Then, through this discussion, we preview our abstraction technique.

Consider the recursive function fix shown in Figure 1(a). This function takes as input a pointer c to a **dll** structure. A **dll** structure has three fields, next, prev, and data used to represent a doubly-linked list of integers. The function fix does two things: (1) it takes as input a singly-linked list (i.e., the prev links are unused or potentially invalid) and sets the prev field of each node to create a valid doubly-linked list; and (2) it implements a filtering operation where all nodes whose data field satisfies the check function are removed. It implements this functionality by a recursive walk using the c pointer. On each call, the p pointer points to the previous node where c->prev should be set. In particular, during the downward sequence of recursive calls, it updates c->prev to set up the doubly-linked list invariant. Then, on the upward sequence of returns, it removes all nodes whose data field satisfies check. To simplify our presentation, function fix also uses a local variable ret so that there is only one return site.

It is certainly possible to perform the filtering along the downward path of calls instead of upward path of returns, which in fact would likely make analysis easier. However, in this case, the developer has chosen to do the removal along the upward sequence, perhaps because she wants to call the library function remove. The remove function expects a doubly-linked list node, but the doubly-linked list invariant is not established until the downward sequence is complete. While this example is synthetic, it exemplifies in a small fragment many of the key challenges in analyzing recursive imperative programs: (1) state changes on both the downward call path and upward return path, (2) incomplete or temporary breakage of data structure invariants along the recursive call-return paths, and (3) interactions with heap state conceptually "belonging" to callers.

To illustrate the analysis challenges, let us consider the concrete program state at two points in an example execution. Figure 1(b) shows the concrete state right after two recursive calls to `fix` (i.e., `main` has called `fix`, which has called itself twice and is at the program point marked with ▶). To fix a convention, we say that the first call to `fix` from `main` is not recursive. Figure 1(c) depicts the concrete state just before the return of this same call and where the current node (pointed to by `c`) has just been removed (shown grayed out). In other words, `check`(11) evaluated to true and the state is at the program point marked with ▷. We can also see that between these two states, there have been two call-returns for the last two nodes in the list (where their prev fields have been set appropriately but neither node was removed). In addition to the list allocated in the heap shown in the right part of Figures 1(b) and 1(c), we show the call stack in the left part. In our picture, the call stack consists of sequence of activation records where each field is a local variable (e.g., `p`, `c`, and `ret` for activation records of `fix`).

Our approach to interprocedural analysis is essentially to abstract the notion of state depicted in Figures 1(b) and 1(c). Traditional shape analysis focuses on precise summarization of the heap, that is, the right part in the concrete state diagrams, while the call stack is elided or coarsely abstracted. In this paper, we define a precise abstraction of the call stack—the left part in the diagrams.

To gradually build up to our technique, let us consider an intuitive abstraction of the state shown in Figure 1(b) with only heap summarization:

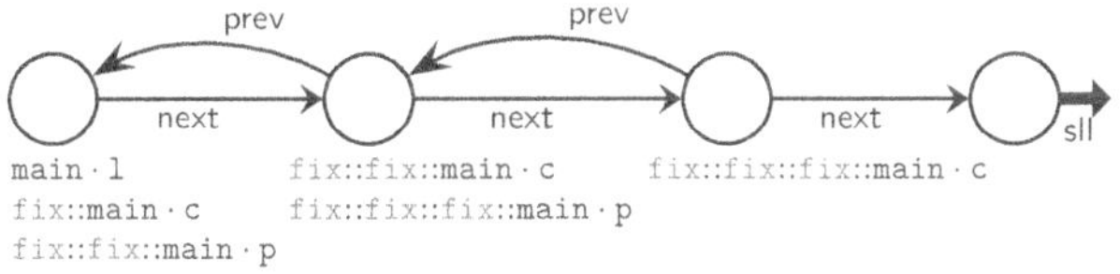

Here, the nodes represent heap addresses, the thin edges denote fields of a **dll** node (i.e., the edges labeled with next and prev), and the thick edge labeled sll represents a singly-linked list of **dll** nodes of undetermined length. The next and prev edges correspond to those fields of the first three nodes of the input list `l`; the `data` fields have been elided, as well as the prev field of the first node. The call stack is, in a sense, elided by fully qualifying variables with a call string (essentially, converting local variables into globals). For instance, the `l` variable of `main`'s activation record, `c` of the activation record for the first call to `fix`, and `p` of the activation record for the second call to `fix` all point to the first node.

Our first observation is that this kind of exact modeling of the call stack fits nicely in the separation logic-based abstraction shown above (depicted as a separating shape graph [18]) if we make the following simple extensions: (1) introduce a node for the base address of each activation record, (2) view local variables as fields of an activation record, and (3) link the activation records in a call stack together with a (conceptual) frame pointer field. Note that this representation does abstract low-level details, much like the diagram in Figure 1(b) (e.g., we do not capture contiguousness of activation records or low-level fields like the return address of each activation). This abstraction with heap summaries but an exact stack is formalized in Section 3.

At this point, we have an abstraction suitable for interprocedural analysis on non-recursive programs (but capable of precise reasoning with recursive data structures). However, for precise static analysis in the presence of recursive procedures as we propose, it is clear that we need to summarize the call stack to prevent our representation from growing unbounded. In particular, we need to abstract the concrete states both along the downward sequence of recursive calls and the upward sequence of returns. In our example, during the downward recursive call sequence, the structure of the activation records is actually quite regular: (1) the local variable `p` contains the same pointer value as `c->prev` in each activation record (even in the initial call where it is **NULL**), and (2) the `next` and `prev` fields of the already visited nodes (i.e., directly pointed to by the `c` variables in the call stack) define a valid doubly-linked list segment. It is not entirely a doubly-linked list, as `c->next` in the most recent activation record is not **NULL**. While the upward return sequence mostly preserves this pattern, there are wrinkles. In particular, in this case where a node is removed from the list, the `next` field of the previous element has been updated. In other words, the `next` field of the `c` of the second most recent activation record has been updated (i.e., `fix::fix::main · c` is updated when `fix::fix::fix::main` is still active).

Therefore, a suitable call stack abstraction must be able to precisely capture the following properties:

1. We must be able to track the *fragments* of the structure where the prev fields have been fixed. This property is needed so that we know that we obtain the doubly-linked list in the end. We also need this property to validate the call to `remove` (e.g., the prev field of the node to be removed is not dangling).
2. We must be able to track relations between the fields of each activation record and heap structures. In particular, we need to propagate invariants during the upward return sequence.

These properties can be expressed using an inductive statement since the structure of the call stack is itself inductive. Successive activation records must be disjoint regions of memory separate from each other and the heap. Thus, our second key observation is that a shape domain built on separation logic formulas with inductive definitions, such as the one described in our prior work [5, 6], seems well-suited not only for abstracting recursive heap structures precisely but also for abstracting call stacks crisply. In other words, a novel aspect of our approach is that we propose to use separation logic formulas to describe not only heap data structures but also the concrete call stack of activation records. Observe that the concrete states shown in Figures 1(b) and 1(c) are lower level than descriptions in many language semantics and most analyses.

While a shape domain based on inductive definitions seems adequate for abstracting the call stack, it is, informally speaking, necessary as well. Recall that in our example, the upward sequence of returns mostly preserves the pattern along the downward sequence of calls but not entirely. This observation indicates that the call stack abstraction must be fluid in the sense that there is a need for variation, for example, along the downward call sequence versus the upward return sequence. A similar kind of fluidity is obtained in shape analysis for heap abstraction with *materialization* [26, 27]. We observe that the classical summarization and materialization operations in shape analysis is exactly what we need at function call and function return to obtain this fluidity:

- At a function call site, the call stack grows by one activation record. We *summarize* (i.e., *fold*) the rest of call stack (excluding the new active activation record). In shape analysis, folding is done through either widening [6] or canonicalization [10, 27] operations. Folding allows us to continue the analysis with a bounded (and precise) description of the call stack. Moreover, the ability to create partial summaries is critical for addressing challenge 1 above.
- At a function return site, the compact description of the inactive activation records (i.e., the call stack excluding the most recent activation record) should be *materialized* to expose the

activation record of the caller. In shape analysis, materialization corresponds to unfolding [6, 10] or focus [27] operations. Materialization is essential for addressing challenge 2 above.

Therefore, the fundamental concepts in shape analysis provide the essential ingredients for the precise call stack abstraction that we desire. In Section 4, we describe our combined stack-heap state abstraction that makes use of an inductive predicate stack to precisely summarize recursive call stacks; the stack predicate is more complex than inductive predicates describing typical recursive data structures.

In general, shape domains require some level of parametrization to describe the structures or summaries of interest. For example, TVLA [27] uses instrumentation predicates, while separation logic-based analyzes rely on inductive definitions (either supplied by the analysis designer [2, 10] or the analysis user [6]). While asking the user to provide descriptions of user-defined structures seems quite natural, asking the user to describe the call stack does not. The call stack is not even a structure to which the user has direct access in any high-level language. However, at the same time, the inductive backbone (i.e., a stack structure) is fixed here. In Section 5, we describe a *subtraction* algorithm to automatically derive program-specific definitions of the stack predicate. Because the backbone is fixed, the challenge is in inferring the "node type" of activation records. This task is similar in spirit to Berdine et al. [2] in inferring the "node type" for a polymorphic doubly-linked list predicate.

3. Exact Call Stack Abstraction

Before we describe our approach for summarizing call contexts (see Section 4), we first formalize an exact abstraction of call stacks based on separation logic formulas.

Concrete Machine States. To begin, we describe the concrete machine states on which we abstract (see Figure 2(a)). A concrete state describes the status of a program at some point of its execution. An *environment* θ describes the set of program variables along with their machine addresses defined at a point in the execution of a program. It includes the global variables and the variables defined in each activation record in the call stack. The environment is given by the grammar in Figure 2(a): an environment encloses a stack of pairs made of a function name and a local variable to address binding before ending with a global variable binding. We write x for a generic variable drawn from $\mathbb{X}$ and use l and g to refer to local and global variable names, respectively. For any environment θ, we define a few functions to simplify our presentation. Let $\mathsf{callString}(\theta)$ denote the call string defined by θ (i.e., $p_n{::}\cdots{::}p_1{::}p_0$). Similarly, let $\mathsf{vars}(\theta)$ be the set of variables of environment θ. Finally, let $\mathsf{addrOf}(\theta) : \mathsf{vars}(\theta) \to \mathbb{V}$ be the function that gives the address of any variable in the environment. These functions can be defined by induction over the environment.

A *program state* s is a tuple made of an environment θ and a memory state σ. A memory state is a finite mapping from addresses to values (where the set of addresses is included in the set of values). Addresses that do not correspond to the address of any variable are *heap locations*, whereas addresses that correspond to the address of a variable defined in an activation record are *stack locations*.

3.1 Abstraction

The core of the abstraction is a spatial formula in separation logic describing the shape of memory. Spatial formulas can be seen equivalently as graphs [18]: (1) nodes, which are given symbolic names (e.g., α), abstract sets of values and (2) edges describe memory cells subject to certain constraints, such as "cell of address α contains value β" (i.e., $\alpha \mapsto \beta$). A graph G is the separating conjunction $*$ [21] of the memory regions represented by each of its

s	$::=$	$\langle\theta,\sigma\rangle$	program states ($\in \mathbb{S}$)
θ	$\in$	$\mathbb{E}$	environments
θ	$::=$	X	global variables
	$\mid$	$(p, X) :: \theta$	new activation record
σ	$\in$	$\mathbb{M} = \mathbb{V} \to_{\mathrm{fin}} \mathbb{V}$	memories
X	$::=$	$\cdot \mid X, x \mapsto a$	variable to address bindings
x, l, g	$\in$	$\mathbb{X}$	program variables
p	$\in$	$\mathbb{P}$	procedure names
a	$\in$	$\mathbb{V}$	values including addresses

(a) The concrete state.

G	$::=$	$\alpha \mapsto \beta$	points-to edge
	$\mid$	$\alpha\cdot\mathsf{f} \mapsto \beta$	points-to edge of a field
	$\mid$	$\alpha\cdot\mathsf{c}(\ldots)$	inductive edge
	$\mid$	$\alpha\cdot\mathsf{c}(\ldots) \mathrel{*\!\!=} \alpha'\cdot\mathsf{c}'(\ldots)$	segment edge
	$\mid$	$\mathsf{emp} \mid G_1 * G_2$	graphs
N	$\in$	$\mathbb{D}^\sharp_{\mathrm{num}}$	numerical constraints in a base domain
$\mathcal{A}$	$::=$	(G, N)	analysis state (i.e., abstract program state)
$\alpha, \beta, \ldots, \bar{\alpha}, g, \ldots$	$\in$	$\mathbb{V}^\sharp$	symbolic names (i.e., nodes)
$\mathsf{f}, \mathsf{g}, \ldots, \mathsf{fp}, l, \ldots$	$\in$	$\mathbb{F}$	field names (i.e., offsets)

(b) The abstract state.

Figure 2. Defining the concrete machine and abstract analysis states.

edges as shown in Figure 2(b); the empty graph is written emp. A points-to edge $\alpha \mapsto \beta$ describes a memory cell with abstract address α and contains the value abstracted by β. If we qualify the left-hand side of points-to with a field as in $\alpha\cdot\mathsf{f} \mapsto \beta$, we represent a memory cell whose address is α plus the offset of field f and whose content is β. We assume offsets are symbolic fields and thus use a relatively high-level Java-like model; a lower-level memory model could be mixed in without much difficulty by following our prior work [18]. An inductive edge $\alpha\cdot\mathsf{c}(\ldots)$ is an instance of inductive predicate c (with a distinguished traversal parameter α), while a segment edge $\alpha\cdot\mathsf{c}(\ldots) \mathrel{*\!\!=} \alpha'\cdot\mathsf{c}'(\ldots)$ is a partial derivation of an inductive predicate c. These edges summarize some set of memory cells as described by an inductive predicate allowing us to represent a potentially unbounded memory; Section 3.2 discusses these notions in greater depth. Concrete program states are then abstracted by an analysis state $\mathcal{A}$ consisting of a graph G and a numerical constraint N. A numerical constraint describes relations amongst symbolic names α and is drawn from some base domain $\mathbb{D}^\sharp_{\mathrm{num}}$, that is, the abstract domain described is parametrized by a standard sort of numerical domain. If we instantiate this abstraction with inductive definitions describing recursive heap data structures supplied by the user, we essentially obtain the shape domains in our prior work [5, 6].

To abstract the call stack in a concrete state $s = \langle\theta,\sigma\rangle$, we observe that the environment θ plays a significant role here. At the abstract level, we build it directly into the graph as follows:

- The address of each global is represented by a node. Thus, the set of global variable names are included in the set of symbolic names $\mathbb{V}^\sharp$.
- We introduce a node to represent the base address of each activation record. For the sake of clarity, we distinguish nodes representing activation record addresses by using a bar over the symbolic names as in $\bar{\alpha}$ and by drawing them with a bold, dotted border in diagrams. We also annotate them with the function to which they correspond (i.e., indicating the "type" of the activation record).

- Each local variable can be viewed as a field of its activation record. The set of field names $\mathbb{F}$ therefore includes local variable names. This representation is key in allowing locals to be summarized as part of the call stack (see Section 4).
- Lastly, we make explicit a *frame pointer* fp, which is simply a field of all activation records. Like in the physical memory at run time, the frame pointer fp points to the previous activation record in the call stack. To distinguish them clearly in the diagrams, frame pointer edges are drawn as dotted lines (and usually the fp label is omitted).

Thus, with the above observations, we encode the structure of the call stack in our shape domain in a faithful manner essentially as-is and without any significant modifications.

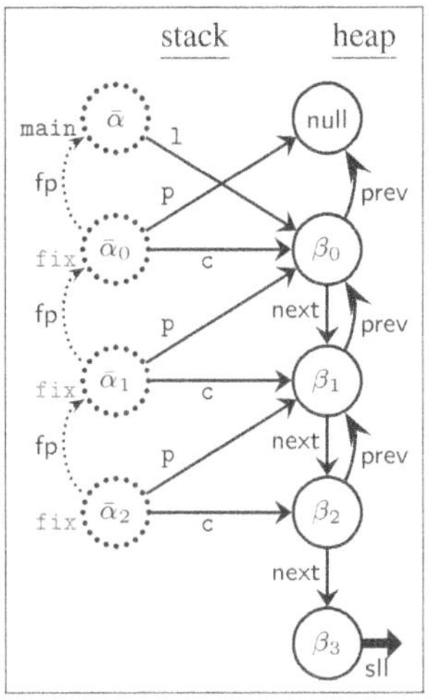

As an example, an abstraction of the concrete state from Figure 1(b) is shown inset. The $\bar{\alpha}$ nodes represent the base address of the activation records, and their outgoing points-to edges correspond to the call stack. Observe that the horizontal edges between the $\bar{\alpha}$ nodes and the β nodes are the stack cells for local variables. Meanwhile, the fp links connect the $\bar{\alpha}$ nodes to capture the actual stack structure. The heap is represented by the edges in the rightmost column: the vertical edges are the next and prev fields for the first three nodes and $\beta_3 \cdot \mathsf{sll}()$ summarizes an arbitrary singly-linked list. Note that this portion of the graph is the only part of the memory state that is captured by traditional shape analyses. We have elided a few edges from this figure, specifically the `ret` variable edges in the stack and the data fields in the heap.

Concretization. Like for concrete states, we define functions that compute the call string $\mathsf{callString}(G)$ and the set of variables it defines $\mathsf{vars}(G)$ given a graph G. These functions follow the chain of frame pointers to compute the desired result. We also define a function

$$\mathsf{addrOf}^\sharp(G) : \mathsf{vars}(G) \to \mathbb{V}^\sharp \times \mathbb{F}$$

that maps each variable to the points-to edge representing its cell (i.e., an abstract address-of mapping).

To define the concretization of a graph, we need a mapping between symbolic names and concrete values. Such mappings $\nu : \mathbb{V}^\sharp \to \mathbb{V}$ are called *valuations* [5] and allow us to abstract irrelevant details like concrete physical addresses. We first summarize the types of the concretizations (the names of the various domains are given in the inset):

$\mathbb{D}^\sharp_{\mathrm{graph}}$	graph domain
$\mathbb{D}^\sharp_{\mathrm{num}}$	numerical domain
$\mathbb{D}^\sharp = \mathbb{D}^\sharp_{\mathrm{graph}} \times \mathbb{D}^\sharp_{\mathrm{num}}$	shape domain

$$\begin{array}{rcll} \boldsymbol{\gamma}_{\mathrm{graph}} & : & \mathbb{D}^\sharp_{\mathrm{graph}} & \to \mathcal{P}(\mathbb{M} \times (\mathbb{V}^\sharp \to \mathbb{V})) \\ \boldsymbol{\gamma}_{\mathrm{num}} & : & \mathbb{D}^\sharp_{\mathrm{num}} & \to \mathcal{P}(\mathbb{V}^\sharp \to \mathbb{V}) \\ \boldsymbol{\gamma} & : & \mathbb{D}^\sharp & \to \mathcal{P}(\mathbb{E} \times \mathbb{M})\ . \end{array}$$

The concretization of a graph G yields a set of pairs consisting of a concrete memory σ and a valuation ν, while concretizing a numerical domain element N should give a set of valuations. Together, the concretization of the combined domain produces a set of pairs of a concrete environment θ and a concrete memory σ.

To concretize a graph, we take the concretization of each edge:

$$\begin{array}{lcl} \boldsymbol{\gamma}_{\mathrm{graph}}(\mathsf{emp}) & \stackrel{\mathrm{def}}{=} & \{ ([\cdot], \nu) \mid \nu \in (\mathbb{V}^\sharp \to \mathbb{V}) \} \\ \boldsymbol{\gamma}_{\mathrm{graph}}(G_1 * G_2) & \stackrel{\mathrm{def}}{=} & \{ (\sigma_1 \otimes \sigma_2, \nu) \mid (\sigma_1, \nu) \in \boldsymbol{\gamma}_{\mathrm{graph}}(G_1) \\ & & \quad \text{and } (\sigma_2, \nu) \in \boldsymbol{\gamma}_{\mathrm{graph}}(G_2) \}\ . \end{array}$$

We write $\otimes$ for the separating conjunction of concrete memories (i.e., the union of two memory maps with disjoint domains) and $[\cdot]$ for an empty concrete memory. The frame pointer fp fields are model fields, so they have no concrete correspondence, but otherwise, the concretization of a points-to edge is a single memory cell, written $[a_1 \mapsto a_2]$:

$$\begin{array}{lcl} \boldsymbol{\gamma}_{\mathrm{graph}}(\bar{\alpha}_1 \cdot \mathsf{fp} \mapsto \bar{\alpha}_2) & \stackrel{\mathrm{def}}{=} & \{ ([\cdot], \nu) \mid \nu \in (\mathbb{V}^\sharp \to \mathbb{V}) \} \\ \boldsymbol{\gamma}_{\mathrm{graph}}(\alpha \cdot \mathsf{f} \mapsto \beta) & \stackrel{\mathrm{def}}{=} & \{ ([\nu(\alpha, \mathsf{f}) \mapsto \nu(\beta)], \nu) \mid \\ & & \quad \nu \in (\mathbb{V}^\sharp \to \mathbb{V}) \} \\ \boldsymbol{\gamma}_{\mathrm{graph}}(\alpha \mapsto \beta) & \stackrel{\mathrm{def}}{=} & \{ ([\nu(\alpha) \mapsto \nu(\beta)], \nu) \mid \nu \in (\mathbb{V}^\sharp \to \mathbb{V}) \} \end{array}$$

where $\nu(\alpha, \mathsf{f})$ gives the base address α plus the offset of field f. We postpone defining the concretization of summary edges (i.e., inductive and segment edges) to Section 3.2.

Overall, the concretization of an analysis state $\mathcal{A}$ are the environment-memory pairs given by the graph and consistent with the numerical constraint:

$$\begin{array}{l} \langle \theta, \sigma \rangle \in \boldsymbol{\gamma}(G, N) \quad \text{iff} \quad \text{for some } \nu, \\ \quad \mathsf{callString}(\theta) = \mathsf{callString}(G) \quad \text{and} \quad \mathsf{vars}(\theta) = \mathsf{vars}(G) \\ \quad \text{and} \quad (\sigma, \nu) \in \boldsymbol{\gamma}_{\mathrm{graph}}(G) \quad \text{and} \quad \nu \in \boldsymbol{\gamma}_{\mathrm{num}}(N) \quad \text{and} \\ \quad \mathsf{addrOf}(\theta)(x) = \nu(\mathsf{addrOf}^\sharp(G)(x)) \quad \text{for all } x \in \mathsf{vars}(\theta)\ . \end{array}$$

Valuations ν connect the various components, capturing relations across disjoint memory regions and with the numerical constraint.

3.2 Inductive Summarization and Materialization

As alluded to in Section 3.1, we summarize a potentially unbounded memory using edges built on inductive definitions. At a high-level, an inductive definition consists of a set of *unfolding rules* or cases that specify how a memory region can be recognized through a recursive traversal. As stated earlier, our inductive edges come in two forms: (1) an *inductive edge* $\alpha \cdot \mathsf{c}(\ldots)$ describes a memory region that satisfies inductive definition c from α, and (2) a *segment edge* $\alpha \cdot \mathsf{c}(\ldots) \mathrel{*\!\!=} \alpha' \cdot \mathsf{c}'(\ldots)$ describes an incomplete structure, in particular, a memory region that can be derived by unfolding $\alpha \cdot \mathsf{c}(\ldots)$ a certain number of times up to a (missing) $\alpha' \cdot \mathsf{c}'(\ldots)$ sub-region [5]. Relations among pointers or numerical values between successive unfoldings of an inductive edge are captured by definitions with additional parameters. For instance, the relation between prev and next pointers in a doubly-linked list can be captured by the following inductive definition (written as a separation logic formula):

$$\begin{array}{l} l \cdot \mathsf{dll}(p) \stackrel{\mathrm{def}}{=} \big(\mathsf{emp} \wedge l \doteq \mathsf{null}\big) \vee \big(\exists n, d. \\ \qquad (l \cdot \mathsf{prev} \mapsto p * l \cdot \mathsf{next} \mapsto n * l \cdot \mathsf{data} \mapsto d \\ \qquad * \ n \cdot \mathsf{dll}(l)) \wedge l \neq \mathsf{null}\big) \end{array}$$

Unfolding. An inductive definition gives rise to a natural syntactic *unfolding* operation. Unfolding substitutes an inductive edge $\alpha \cdot \mathsf{c}(\ldots)$ or a segment edge $\alpha \cdot \mathsf{c}(\ldots) \mathrel{*\!\!=} \alpha' \cdot \mathsf{c}'(\ldots)$ with one inductive case of c's definition (and where all existentially-quantified variables are replaced with fresh nodes). For inductive edges, base cases correspond to a rule with no new inductive edge upon unfolding; for segment edges, the base case is unfolding to the empty segment (i.e., when $\alpha = \alpha'$ and $\mathsf{c} = \mathsf{c}'$). We write $G \rightsquigarrow_{\mathbf{unfold}} G'$ for an unfolding step from graph G to G', as well as $\rightsquigarrow^{\star}_{\mathbf{unfold}}$ for the reflexive-transitive closure of $\rightsquigarrow_{\mathbf{unfold}}$. Because the unfolding operation is so closely tied to the inductive definition, we often present an inductive definition by the unfoldings that it induces.

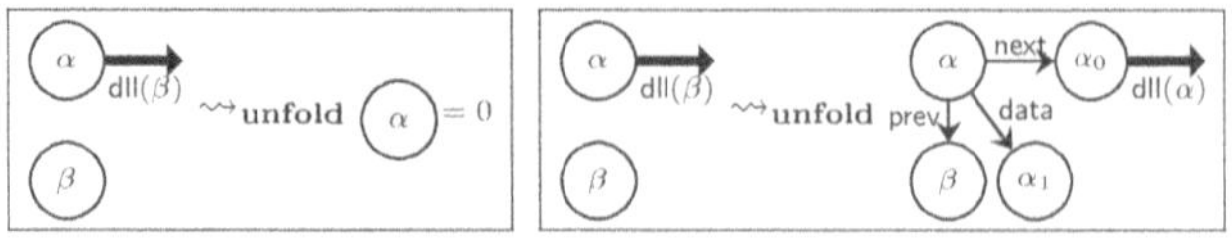

Figure 3. Unfolding operation induced by the dll definition.

For instance, in Figure 3, we present the doubly-linked list definition dll in this style.

The concretization of graphs containing inductive or segment edges is based on the concretization without them. In particular, the concretization of a graph G containing inductives is simply the join of the concretizations of all the graphs that can be derived from it by successive unfolding:

$$\gamma_{\text{graph}}(G) = \bigcup \{G' \in \mathbb{D}^\sharp_{\text{graph}} \mid G \rightsquigarrow^{\star}_{\textbf{unfold}} G'\} .$$

Unfolding and Analyzing Updates. Unfolding is the key operation for abstractly interpreting writes. To reflect an update $e_1 := e_2$, we traverse the graph to find the points-to edges (i.e., the memory cells) that correspond to the addressing expressions e_1 and e_2. If the points-to edges of interest already exist in the graph, then reflecting the update is simply a matter of swinging an edge. Because a graph is a separating conjunction of edges, this modification is a strong, destructive update. However, if the desired edges are not present, then we try to materialize them with the unfolding operation $\rightsquigarrow_{\textbf{unfold}}$. Unfolding to expose cells in a user-defined heap structure is necessarily heuristic, but the distinguished traversal parameter in our inductive predicates (i.e., α in $\alpha \cdot \mathsf{c}(\ldots)$) provide guidance (also see our prior work [5] for ways to make unfolding more robust). More crisply, we describe the abstract interpretation of an update with the following inference rule:

$$\boxed{\langle \mathcal{A}, \mathit{statement} \rangle \Downarrow \mathcal{A}'}$$

$$\frac{\langle \mathcal{A}, e_1 \rangle \Downarrow \langle \mathcal{A}', \alpha_1 \cdot f_1 \mapsto \beta_1 \rangle \quad \langle \mathcal{A}', e_2 \rangle \Downarrow \langle \mathcal{A}'', \alpha_2 \cdot f_2 \mapsto \beta_2 \rangle}{\langle \mathcal{A}, e_1 := e_2 \rangle \Downarrow \mathcal{A}''[G \to G(\mathcal{A}'')[\alpha_1 \cdot f_1 \mapsto \beta_2]]}$$

The abstract interpretation judgment $\langle \mathcal{A}, \mathit{statement} \rangle \Downarrow \mathcal{A}'$ says that in abstract state $\mathcal{A}$, evaluating statement *statement* produces a resulting state $\mathcal{A}'$ (as in a standard structured concrete operational semantics). This judgment is defined in terms of an auxiliary judgment $\langle \mathcal{A}, e \rangle \Downarrow \langle \mathcal{A}', \alpha \cdot f \mapsto \beta \rangle$ that evaluates an addressing expression e to a points-to edge in $\mathcal{A}$, which may yield a modified state $\mathcal{A}'$ as the result of unfolding. To reflect the update, we write $G(\mathcal{A})$ for looking up the graph component of $\mathcal{A}$, $\mathcal{A}[G \to G']$ for replacing the graph component of $\mathcal{A}$ with G', and $G[\alpha \cdot f \mapsto \beta]$ for updating the edge with source $\alpha \cdot f$ in G to point to β.

3.3 Towards Analyzing Calls and Returns

Our whole-program analysis is based on an abstract interpretation [7] of the program's interprocedural control-flow graph. We desire a sound analysis, which means at each step, the analysis applies locally-sound transfer functions. They cannot omit any possible concrete behavior. With just the abstraction described in this section, we can define an analysis for non-recursive programs (albeit a potentially computationally expensive one).

At a function call site in the concrete execution, a new activation record is pushed onto the call stack. Correspondingly at the abstract level, we push a new abstract activation record: (1) we create a new node representing the base address of the new activation record; and (2) we set the content

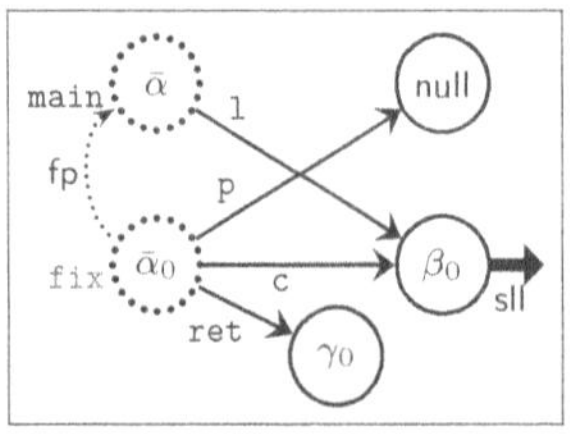

of its fields (i.e., the formal parameters and local variables) by assigning formal parameters to the actual arguments and by pointing local variables to fresh nodes. For example, consider again the code from Figure 1(a). At the call to `fix` from `main` (i.e., `fix(1, NULL)`) during the analysis, we push a new abstract activation record with base address $\bar{\alpha}_0$ with fields for parameters `c` and `p` and local variable `ret` as shown in the inset. The $\bar{\alpha}_0 \cdot \mathsf{fp}$ field is set to point to $\bar{\alpha}$, the base address of the activation record for `main`, while $\bar{\alpha}_0 \cdot \mathtt{c}$ is made to point to β_0 (as $\bar{\alpha} \cdot \mathtt{1} \mapsto \beta_0$) and $\bar{\alpha}_0 \cdot \mathtt{p}$ gets null. For the $\bar{\alpha}_0 \cdot \mathtt{ret}$ field, it is set to fresh node γ_0, which indicates it contains an arbitrary value. The $\beta_0 \cdot \mathsf{sll}()$ inductive edge states that β_0 is the head of a singly-linked list (of `dll` nodes), which existed before the call.

Now, if we continue analyzing the body of `fix`, we see that $\beta_0 \cdot \mathsf{sll}()$ would be unfolded along the path where $\beta_0 \neq$ null (i.e., `c != NULL`) before arriving at a recursive call to `fix`. It is clear that if we continue analyzing in the manner described above, we will keep on creating new activation records and never terminate. Thus, in order to ensure the termination of the analysis in the presence of recursive functions, we must apply a *widening* that is capable of summarizing the call stack.

As alluded to earlier, the key observation is that the call stack is itself an inductive structure. Specifically, it is a list of activation records where the frame pointer fp fields form the backbone. Based on this observation, we use a special inductive predicate stack to summarize recursive segments of the call stack (e.g., the sequence of `fix` calls—`fix`*::`main`). This inductive predicate stack is necessarily more complex than usual predicates for summarizing recursive heap structures and is described in detail in Section 4. Furthermore, the stack predicate must be program-specific because it depends on the program's interprocedural control-flow. Thus, its definition cannot be known before beginning the analysis. In Section 5, we detail an algorithm for deriving a definition of stack on the fly during the analysis.

Finally, at a function return site, the analysis proceeds like in a concrete execution by popping off the most recent activation. For instance, in the example above, on return from `fix` to `main`, we drop the node $\bar{\alpha}_0$ and its outgoing edges for fp, c, p, and ret, just like the disposal of heap cells. As an invariant of the analysis, we make sure the topmost activation record is always exposed (i.e., never summarized in a stack predicate). This invariant ensures that all program variables in scope (globals and locals) are directly accessible. As part of the transfer function for return, we need to make sure that the activation record of the caller function becomes exposed after the return, as now it is the topmost one. In the presence of call stack summarization that includes the caller, we need to unfold the stack predicate to expose the caller's activation record—using the $\rightsquigarrow_{\textbf{unfold}}$ operation with stack. As such, stack segments always go from callees to callers, that is, in the direction of the fp links.

4. Summarizing Call Stacks Inductively

As alluded to earlier, we summarize call stacks from recursive programs using an inductive predicate stack, exploiting their inherent inductive structure. The definition of stack is particularly interesting because it depends on the interprocedural control flow of the program being analyzed. To build intuition for a definition of stack, we first explore a number of examples that illustrate requirements for it. We consider analyzing simple recursive functions requiring no relations between successive activations, recursive procedures requiring simultaneous summarization of the stack and heap, nested recursion, and mutual recursion. Our algorithm for automatically deriving a stack definition on the fly during analysis is then described in Section 5.

Recursion without Heap Relations between Activations. Consider the simple program shown in inset (a) that constructs a list of random length using a recursive function `f`. For each call to function `f`, a new, uninitialized **list** node is allocated on the heap before the next recursive call. For simplicity in presentation, a **list** node has just one field: `next` for linking. Note that we elide the size-of argument to `malloc`, treating it as a high-level allocator with types. The `next` pointers are assigned during the sequence of returns. Inset (b) shows a graph (with no summarization) that describes the state of the program at the entry of the first recursive call to `f` (i.e., with the call string `f`::`f`::`main`), while inset (c) shows the state at the second recursive call (i.e., `f`::`f`::`f`::`main`). The repeated pattern is clear from these diagrams: all pending activations of `f` have a local variable `y` that point to a **list** node whose `next` field is arbitrary. This apparent pattern suggests the unfolding rule or case for the definition of `stack` shown in inset (d).

```
void main() { list* x = f(); }
list* f() {
  list* y;
  if (...) return NULL;
  else {
    y = (list*)malloc();
    y->next = f();
    return y;
  }
}
```

(a) List allocation.

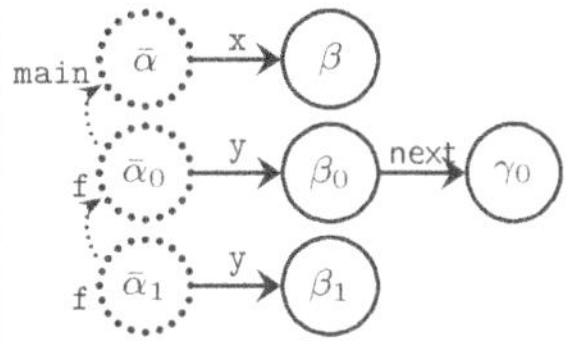

(b) After one recursive call.

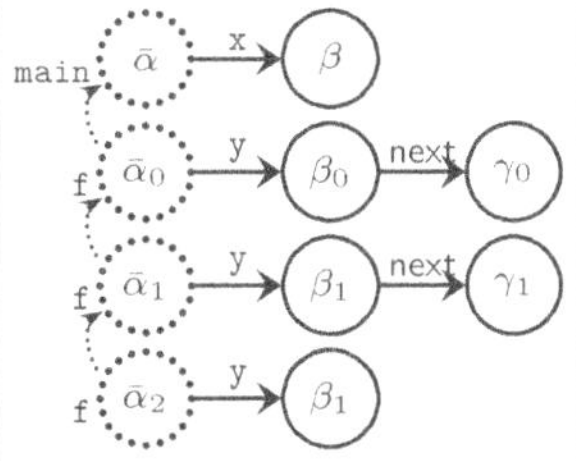

(c) After two recursive calls.

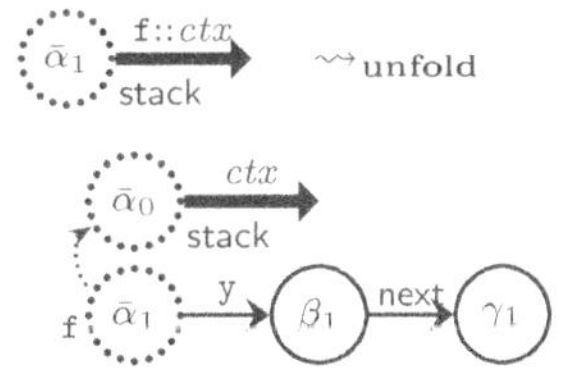

(d) An unfolding rule.

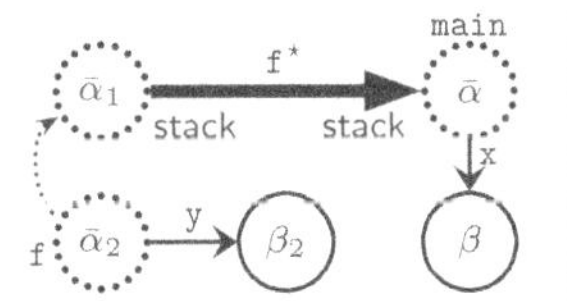

(e) Summary for entry to `f`.

Inductive edges of `stack` are labeled with a regular expression to convey the set of call strings to which the rule can be applied. Here, the regular expression `f`::ctx on this rule indicates that it can be applied only to a call stack where the topmost activation record corresponds to an `f` record, while the calling context ctx may be arbitrary. These constraints on the calling context can be expressed as an additional parameter to `stack`, so the labels are simply a shorthand. In other words, the first additional parameter to `stack` is a set of possible call strings expressed as a regular expression. In the case of rule definition, the label is a check for that regular expression pattern (e.g., `f`::ctx on the left-hand side of the example $\rightsquigarrow_{\text{unfold}}$). For an instance of the `stack` predicate, it gives an abstraction of the call string. As an example, using this rule, we can over-approximate all the possible states at the entry to function `f` after any number of recursive calls with the graph shown in inset (e). The `f`* label indicates that there are zero or more `f` activations between $\bar{\alpha}_0$ and $\bar{\alpha}$. Intuitively, these labels approximate the sequence of frame pointer links and the types of activation records along that sequence.

Recursion with Mixed Call Stack and Heap Summaries. In Figure 4, we present a slightly more involved example where an existing heap data structure is traversed recursively. Function `f` a recursive, non-destructive walk of a list (i.e., a singly-linked list consisting of **list** nodes). Before the first call to `f`, the memory state is abstracted by the graph shown in Figure 4(a). After the first call to `f` but before any recursive call, we have the graph shown in (b). In (c), we show the graph after the first recursive call at the entry point to `f`, while (d) shows the graph at the same point after two recursive calls. Just like in the previous example, there is a clear repeating pattern consisting of both stack and heap edges for each activation. However, unlike the previous example, there is an important relation between successive activation records through the heap: `x->next` of an activation record aliases `x` of the subsequent activation (e.g., $\bar{\alpha}_0 \cdot \mathtt{x} \mapsto \beta_0 * \beta_0 \cdot \mathsf{next} \mapsto \beta_1 * \bar{\alpha}_1 \cdot \mathtt{x} \mapsto \beta_1$). Such a relation can be captured with an additional parameter to the `stack` predicate, and thus we get the unfolding rule shown in Figure 4(e). The key difference between the unfolding rule here and the rule from the previous example is the parameter β_2 (shown highlighted in the figure) that says the `next` field from the value of $\bar{\alpha}_1 \cdot \mathtt{x}$ (i.e., β_1) points to an existing node given by parameter

```
void main() { list* l; ... /* make l·list() */ ...; f(l); }
void f(list* x) { if (x == NULL) return; else f(x->next); }
```

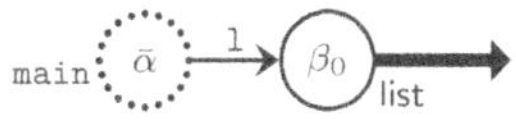

(a) Before the first call to `f`.

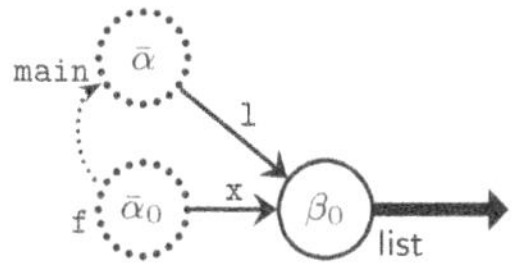

(b) After the first call to `f`.

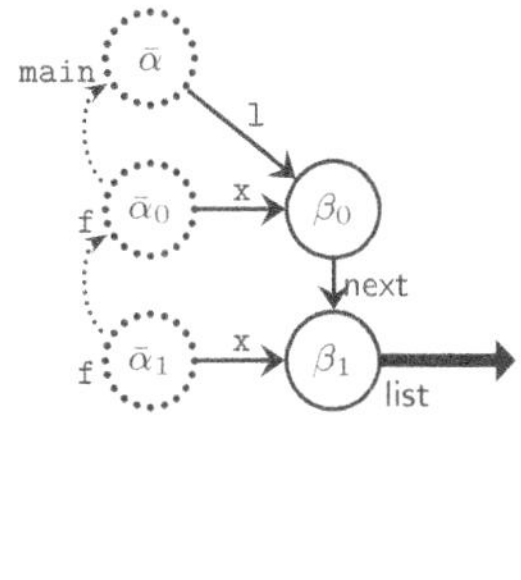

(c) After one recursive call.

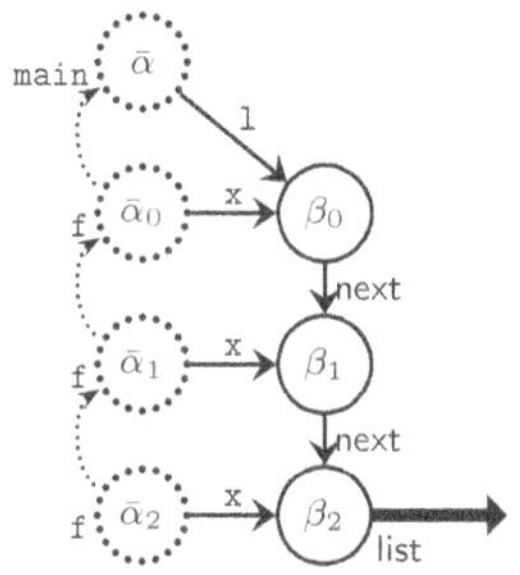

(d) After two recursive calls.

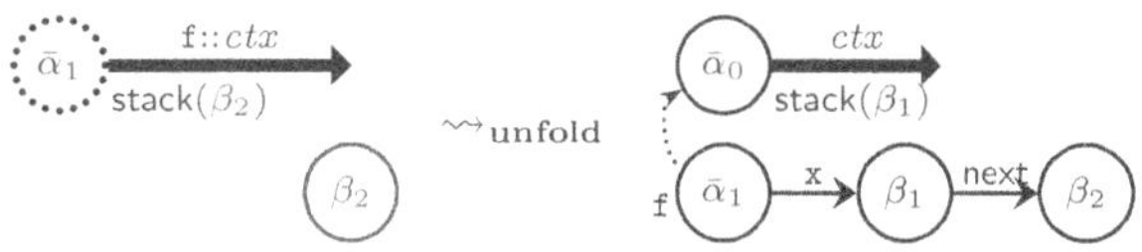

(e) An unfolding rule.

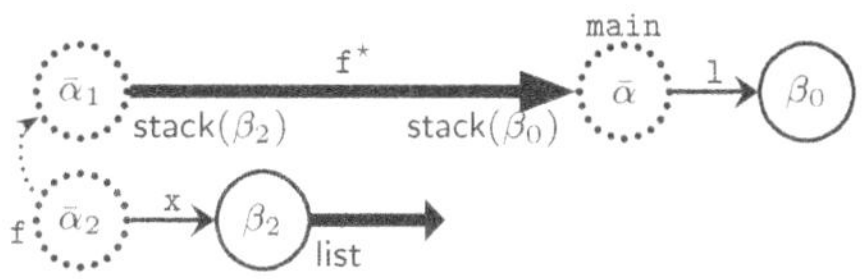

(f) Summary for the entry point to `f`.

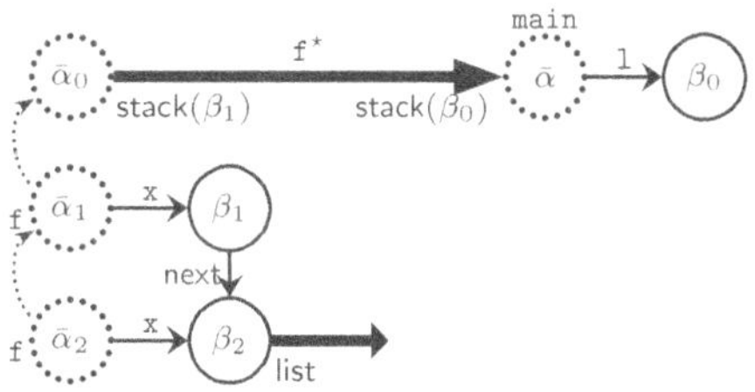

(g) Non-empty unfolding of the `stack` segment in (f).

Figure 4. Summarizing the memory states for recursive list traversal.

β_2. Using this inductive definition, we can summarize the possible states at the entry to function f using a stack segment edge (shown in Figure 4(f).

In the graph shown in Figure 4(f), the stack segment not only summarizes a portion of the call stack but also a fragment of the heap, specifically the list segment between β_0 and β_2. It also maintains the relation between the x pointers to elements in this list—the inductive definition of stack is quite powerful here. To get a better sense of this aspect, consider unfolding the stack segment in the summary shown in Figure 4(f). There are two cases:

- The segment is empty. This base case says there are no cells summarized by the segment and the ends are equal, that is, $\bar{\alpha}_1 = \bar{\alpha}$ and $\beta_2 = \beta_0$. This state is exactly the one at the entry point after the first call to f (i.e., with call string f::main) shown in Figure 4(b).
- The segment is non-empty. One step of unfolding yields the graph shown in Figure 4(g). Notice that one step of unfolding exposes the previous activation record with the desired relation between the previous activation's x and current activation's x. Overall, this inductive case summarizes the state after successive recursive calls (e.g., states shown in Figures 4(c) and (d)). For instance, replacing the stack segment in (g) with the empty segment (i.e., unfold it to empty), we get the state after one recursive call (c) where $\bar{\alpha}_0 = \bar{\alpha}$ and $\beta_1 = \beta_0$.

In both examples thus far in this section, we never defined a base case for the stack inductive definition. At the same time, it is not particularly meaningful to provide one, as the first function called in the program is main, which must be the first/oldest activation record. For our analysis, this absence of a base case for stack is actually never a problem, as the stack predicate is always used as a segment edge. For any segment, the base case is the empty segment.

Nested Recursion. The program below illustrates a nested recursion: main calls function f, which calls itself recursively a certain number of times, until it calls g, which then also calls itself recursively a certain number of times. There is no call to f from g.

```
void main() { t* x; f(x); }
void f(t* x) { if (...) f(x); else g(x); }
void g(t* x) { if (...) g(x); }
```

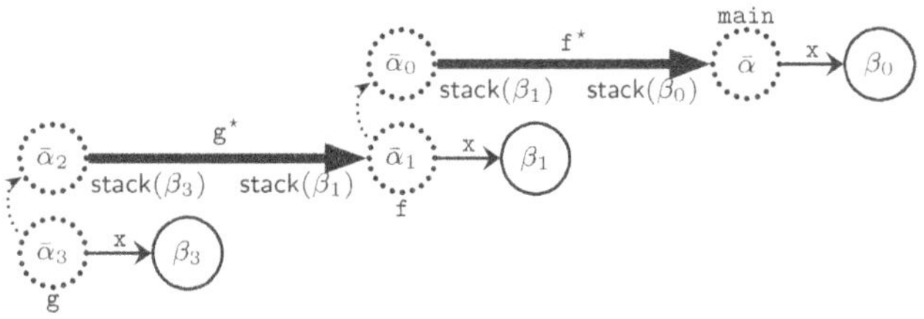

After a number of recursive calls, the layout of the call stack at the entry point to function g can be summarized by the above graph where the stack segments correspond to the sequence of recursive calls in g and to the sequence of recursive calls in f, respectively.

Mutual Recursion. In the program below, functions f and g are mutually recursive, so the call strings at the entry point to g are of the form g::f::(g::f)*::main.

```
void main() { t* x; f(x); }
void f(t* x) { if (...) g(x); }
void g(t* x) { if (...) f(x); }
```

As the cycles are of the form g::f::$\cdots$, the call stack of the above program at the entry point to g is summarized using the following rule:

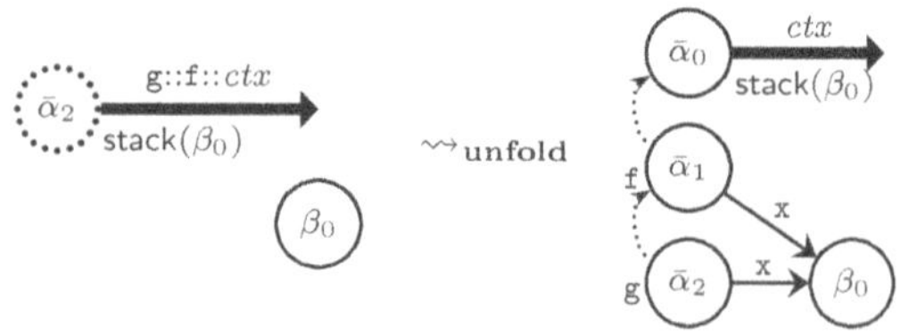

The cycles can be more complex. For example, for call stacks where the call strings are of the form g::(f*::g)*::main, the inductive stack rule for the (f*::g)* cycle would unfold into a call stack fragment, which would contain a summary for the inner f* cycle (i.e., another stack segment over the f* call string).

Defining **stack.** We can now state precisely the notion of an inductive definition suitable for abstracting the call stack:

- A *stack segment* is a segment edge. This edge is labeled with with a regular expression denoting a superset of the call strings that it describes.
- A *stack inductive definition* is an inductive definition stack such that each case unfolds a sequence of one or more activation records according to a call string.

As stack segments are simply segment edges of the stack definition, the concretization of graphs with stack segments follows from the definitions in Section 3. Notably, given the ability to parametrize inductive definitions by simple regular expressions, the meaning of stack summaries falls directly from the notion of inductive segments.

5. Inferring Call Stack Summarization Rules

In Section 4, we illustrated how the call stack corresponding to various forms of recursion is summarized by an inductive stack predicate. However, we also need to be able to derive a suitable definition for stack.

To obtain a terminating analysis, we require a widening operator capable of summarizing the call stack. To do so, it must fold fragments into stack segments. Yet, before beginning the analysis, the definition of stack cannot be known, as the interprocedural control flow of the program is still to be explored. This circularity means that the definition of stack must be derived on the fly during the analysis when recursive calls are found. In this section, we describe such an algorithm for defining a program-specific stack predicate on the fly.

Widening in Recursive Cycles. In this section, we consider a recursive function f, which directly calls itself. The technique we propose also applies to more complex cycles (e.g., mutual recursion). In general, when a function call is recursive, the interprocedural control-flow graph contains two cycles: one at the function entry (from the recursive call site) and one at the function exit (to the recursive return site). Thus, to ensure termination of the analysis in the presence of recursion, widening is applied at the entry and exit points of a recursive function.

We first describe, at a high-level, the steps that the analysis takes to compute an invariant at such a recursive widening point. The key operations are the widening on program states given some stack definition (see Section 6.1) and a *shape subtraction* to generate inductive rules of the stack predicate described later in this section.

Intuitively, deriving rules for stack comes from finding the difference between successive abstract program states at, for example, f's entry point after some number of recursive calls. Specifically, the analysis takes the following steps at f's entry point:

1. Compute a few abstract states by iterating over the recursive call cycle. In practice, unrolling a few iterations of a cycle is

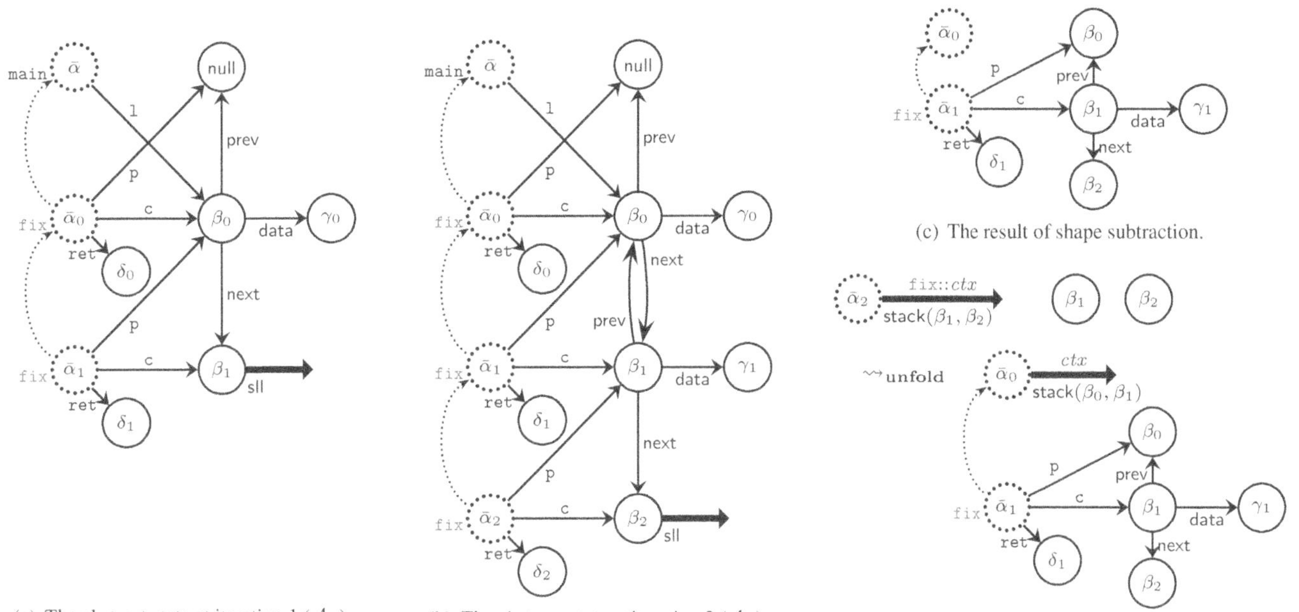

(a) The abstract state at iteration 1 ($\mathcal{A}_1$).

(b) The abstract state at iteration 2 ($\mathcal{A}_2$).

(d) An inferred rule for stack.

Figure 5. Inferring a stack rule from abstract states computed at the entry point to `fix` while analyzing the example in Figure 1(a).

often beneficial to get to stable behavior. Suppose we obtain three states $\mathcal{A}_0$, $\mathcal{A}_1$, and $\mathcal{A}_2$ from the first iterations, and we wish to extrapolate from $\mathcal{A}_1$ and $\mathcal{A}_2$.

2. We derive an inductive rule for stack from $\mathcal{A}_1$ and $\mathcal{A}_2$ using the shape subtraction algorithm.
3. We weaken $\mathcal{A}_2$ into a weaker $\mathcal{A}_2'$ using the rule derived in step 2. To perform this weakening step, we apply the widening operator over program states to $\mathcal{A}_1$ and $\mathcal{A}_2$ to produce $\mathcal{A}_2'$. The net result is that $\mathcal{A}_2'$ summarizes both $\mathcal{A}_2$ and $\mathcal{A}_1$ with a stack segment for the difference between them.
4. We perform widening iteration over the cycle until convergence to an invariant $\mathcal{A}_\infty$. The definition of the widening operator over program states guarantees convergence.

Note that the algorithm for inferring new inductive rules for stack in step 2 assists widening in obtaining quality invariants. It does not need to be sound or complete. In fact, it is possible to craft complicated examples where discovering a repeating pattern would be arbitrarily difficult. Instead, the goal should be that it is effective at discovering adequate rules in realistic situations.

Creating* stack *Rules by Shape Subtraction. At a high-level, we find the difference in the graphs between two successive state iterances $\mathcal{A}_1 = (G_1, N_1)$ and $\mathcal{A}_2 = (G_2, N_2)$ using shape subtraction. This difference gives the exposed or unfolded fragment in a new stack rule. In the following, suppose $\mathcal{A}_1$ corresponds to call string $\mathtt{f}::\mathtt{f}::ctx$ and $\mathcal{A}_2$ to $\mathtt{f}::\mathtt{f}::\mathtt{f}::ctx$.

The first step is to derive the graph part of the new rule. To do so, we want to isolate the edges that appear in G_2 but not in G_1. In other words, we want to partition G_2 into two disjoints sets of edges G_{common} and G_Δ such that informally speaking,

$$G_2 = G_{\text{common}} * G_\Delta \qquad \text{and} \qquad G_1 = G_{\text{common}} .$$

The above is informal because we must take care of matching symbolic node names (which correspond logically to existential variables). We illustrate the description of the algorithm by following the example from Section 2 (i.e., Figure 1). Figure 5(a) shows the abstract state at the entry point to `fix` obtained from one iteration over the recursive call cycle (i.e., after executing one recursive call); Figure 5(b) shows the abstract state after one more recursive call (i.e., after two recursive calls). The graph shown in Figure 5(c) shows the G_Δ computed from the states in (a) and (b).

In essence, shape subtraction works by performing a simultaneous traversal over G_1 and G_2 to identify matching structure (i.e., G_{common}). A node naming relation $\Psi \subseteq \mathbb{V}^\sharp \times \mathbb{V}^\sharp$ serves to track the correspondence between the nodes in G_1 and those in G_2, as well as to define the frontier of the traversal. To start the subtraction process, the node naming relation Ψ is initialized with root nodes of memory regions that we want to be in G_{common}. In particular, we pair the following for the initial Ψ: (1) nodes representing addresses of global variables, (2) base addresses of activation records in the context ctx (e.g., $(\bar{\alpha}, \bar{\alpha}) \in \Psi$ and $(\bar{\alpha}_0, \bar{\alpha}_0) \in \Psi$ for initializing the example subtraction in Figure 5), (3) the base address of the topmost activation record (e.g., $(\bar{\alpha}_1, \bar{\alpha}_2) \in \Psi$). This initialization states that G_{common} is any portion of memory reachable from the globals, activation records of the context, and the topmost activation. What remains, G_Δ, is the state difference between G_1 and G_2 that we wish to summarize with a stack segment. In the example, the only activation record node that does not appear in Ψ is the one for the second activation in G_2 (i.e., $\bar{\alpha}_1$ in Figure 5(b)). Observe that this node is exactly the base address of the activation that we wish to summarize.

At this point, the algorithm is rather straightforward. We collect together edges of the same kind whose the source nodes are in the node naming relation Ψ. Whenever two edges are matched, the target nodes (and any additional checker parameters) are added to Ψ. The matched edges are discarded from G_1 and G_2 and added to G_{common} (up to node renaming). For example, in Figure 5, the edges corresponding to field `l` of $\bar{\alpha}$ can be matched and consumed right after initialization. Then, the pair (β_0, β_0) is added to Ψ, and the prev edges from β_0 in both graphs can be consumed next. We iterate this "match and consume" traversal until G_1 is empty in which case G_2 has become G_Δ.

It is possible that G_1 fails to become empty, that is, we are unable to find a common fragment. This subtraction algorithm is much like the graph join algorithm [6] in that the result depends on the traversal order. Matching and consuming certain edge pairs too early may cause the algorithm to fail to produce an empty G_1 when another traversal order would have succeeded. Fortunately, in our experience, a simple breadth-first-style strategy suffices. First, we match fields from the topmost activation record, which are not pointed to by other activation records directly (e.g., from $(\bar{\alpha}_1, \bar{\alpha}_2)$). Then, we do the same for the fields from the context (e.g., from $(\bar{\alpha}, \bar{\alpha})$ and $(\bar{\alpha}_0, \bar{\alpha}_0)$). Nodes directly pointed to by the activation being summarized are considered last.

The graph result of shape subtraction G_Δ gives the unfolded edges for a stack unfolding rule, that is, the portion of memory that could be summarized by a stack segment (of length 1). As-is, such a rule does not express all the properties that are needed to describe the call stack precisely. In the Figure 5 example, we need to express aliasing relations between successive activations (cf., the difference between the list allocation and the list traversal examples in Section 4). These relations are captured by parameters on the stack definition. The parameters are given by the nodes at the boundary between the topmost activation and the activations being summarized. In this case, nodes β_1 and β_2 are this boundary and become parameters in the definition of the stack rule as shown in Figure 5(d). Finally, any relevant numerical constraints in the base domain is also captured in defining a stack rule. Once G_Δ has been computed, we simply take the projection of the numerical invariant N_2 onto the set of symbolic node names in G_Δ.

Shape subtraction on the graph portion can be seen as a restriction on frame inference [1]. Here, we are looking for an exact match as opposed to an entailment between two configurations. In spirit, the above algorithm potentially could be applied to derive other kinds of inductive definitions besides stack (cf., [14]). However, we make critical use of understanding the inductive structure of a call stack to get good results. For example, this background knowledge is used in initializing the node naming relation Ψ. We hypothesize that having some knowledge on the kind of inductive backbone of interest is key to getting high-quality definitions.

6. Applying Call Stack Summaries in Analysis

With the mechanism for deriving stack rules during analysis, we have all the pieces for analyzing recursive procedures with call stack summarization by following the outline in Section 3.3. In particular, sound transfer functions from intraprocedural inductive shape analysis [5, 6, 18] for basic program statements, like assignment (cf., Section 3.2), guard conditions for branching, loops, and memory allocation-deallocation, carry over in a straightforward manner. A slight difference is that instead of a fixed set of variables as in the intraprocedural case, we have both global and local variables. Local variables are fields of activation records in our graph, but all program variables in scope are easily accessible, as we ensure that the topmost activation is never summarized.

There are two remaining pieces to our interprocedural analysis. First, we want to see how widening with derived stack rules applies at the function entry and exit points in recursive call cycles (Section 6.1). Second, the soundness and termination of extensible inductive shape analysis [5, 6] relies on the assumption that all inductive definitions are fixed before the analysis starts. In this paper where the definition of stack is extended on the fly, we need to justify soundness and termination in the presence of such on-the-fly inductive rule generation (Section 6.2). We conclude this section with a summary of the reasons for termination and soundness for the overall analysis, as well as some empirical experience (Section 6.3).

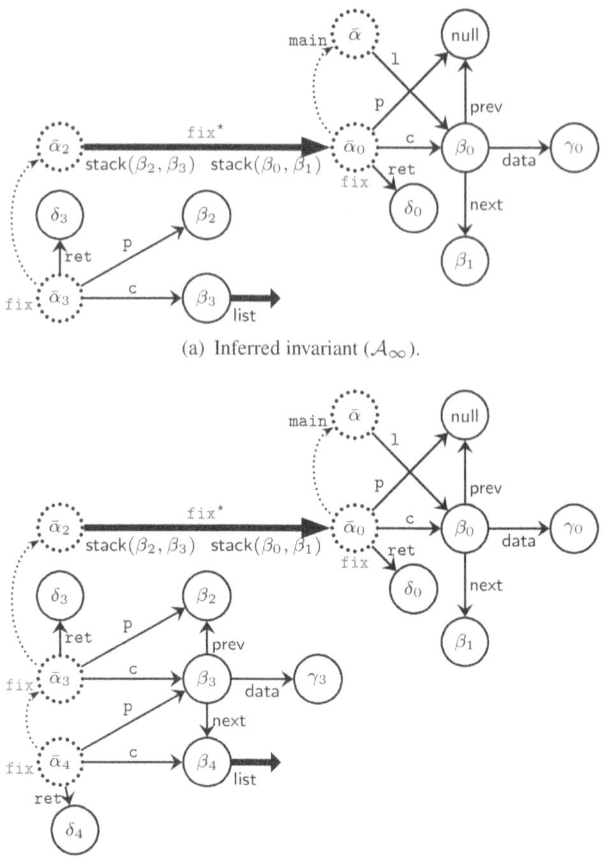

(a) Inferred invariant ($\mathcal{A}_\infty$).

(b) Next iteration, which confirms the inferred invariant ($\mathcal{A}_{\infty+1}$).

Figure 6. Widening at the entry point to fix in Figure 1(a).

6.1 Widening with Call Stack Summaries

After an appropriate inductive rule for stack has been derived (see Section 5), widening at function entry and exit points in a recursive call cycle is not particularly different than at loop heads. That is, the join $\sqcup$ and widen ∇ on graphs and program states [6] essentially carries over. We do not redefine these algorithms, but we discuss their main features here by following our example introduced in Section 2.

The join on separating shape graphs is stabilizing, so the only difference between join $\sqcup$ and widen ∇ is the operator applied to elements of the numerical base domain. At a high-level, the join on graphs is actually quite similar to the subtraction algorithm described in Section 5. They both work by a simultaneous match and consume traversal over two graphs from root nodes using a node naming relation (i.e., Ψ). Roughly speaking, the main difference is that join applies weakening to memory regions delineated by the traversal. For example, it folds fragments consisting of points-to edges (e.g., $\alpha \cdot \mathsf{next} \mapsto \beta$) into an instance of an inductive definition (e.g., $\alpha \cdot \mathsf{list}()$). Folding is in essence applying an unfolding rule in reverse [6].

Following the outline in Section 5, at the entry point to fix, we first obtain abstract states $\mathcal{A}_1$ and $\mathcal{A}_2$ from Figures 5(a) and (b), respectively. Subtraction is applied to them to get the stack rule in Figure 5(d). With this rule, widening on abstract states is applied to $\mathcal{A}_1$ and $\mathcal{A}_2$ to produce the state $\mathcal{A}_\infty$ shown in Figure 6(a), which summarizes both $\mathcal{A}_1$ and $\mathcal{A}_2$. Beginning at the entry point to fix with $\mathcal{A}_\infty$, we analyze until the next recursive call and returning to the entry point, we get the abstract state $\mathcal{A}_{\infty+1}$ shown

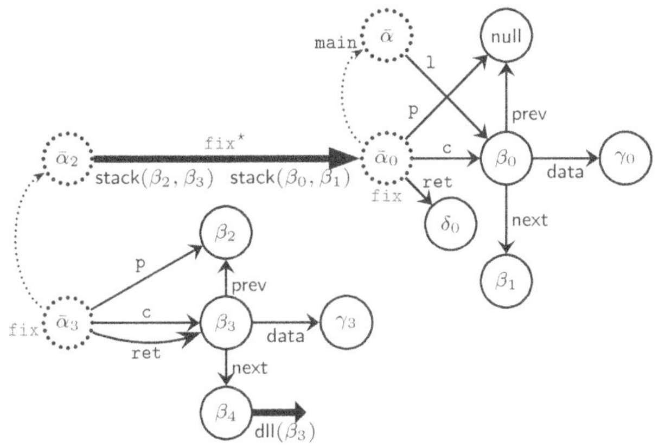

Figure 7. An invariant just before returning from a recursive call to `fix`.

in Figure 6(b). Observe that $\bar{\alpha}_3$ is the activation record that can be folded into the stack segment (using the Figure 5(d) rule). Thus, computing $\mathcal{A}_\infty \nabla \mathcal{A}_{\infty+1}$ yields $\mathcal{A}_\infty$, which confirms that $\mathcal{A}_\infty$ is an invariant that summarizes the set of all concrete states that can be observed at the entry to function `fix` (after one or more recursive calls).

The control point after the function exit before the return site of a recursive call is also on a cycle in the interprocedural control flow graph, so we perform widening iterations there. We perform widening at the point just before the topmost abstract activation record is discarded. In Figure 7, we show an abstract element summarizing concrete states that can be observed just before returning from a recursive call to `fix` (and where this call went along the path where c was not null and node c was not removed). Note that during the sequence of returns from recursive calls, the new dll edge appears, as upon function return, the tail of the structure has prev pointers set correctly so as to define a dll.

6.2 Introducing Inductive Rules on the Fly

As noted above, a source of complexity in summarizing the call stack with the stack predicate is that new inductive rules are generated on the fly. To reason about this aspect, we extend our framework with rule set extension. When the analysis starts, the set $\mathcal{R}$ is empty. Whenever a new recursive call site is discovered, a new rule is added to $\mathcal{R}$. Therefore, we consider $\mathcal{R}$ an element of a separate lattice, specifically the powerset of the set of rules. Each invariant is with respect to a set of rules $\mathcal{R}$, which determines the instance of the graph domain in use. Thus, our analysis state is actually an $(\mathcal{R}, G, N)$ tuple in the abstract domain $\mathbb{D}^\sharp$ defined below. For clarity, we annotate $\mathbb{D}^\sharp_{\text{graph}}$ with the set of rules $\mathcal{R}$ allowed for the inductive definition of stack as follows: $\mathbb{D}^\sharp_{\text{graph}\langle\mathcal{R}\rangle}$ (and similarly with $\boldsymbol{\gamma}_{\text{graph}\langle\mathcal{R}\rangle}$). We also define $\boldsymbol{\gamma}_{\langle\mathcal{R}\rangle}(G, N)$ as we did $\boldsymbol{\gamma}(G, N)$, except we now use $\boldsymbol{\gamma}_{\text{graph}\langle\mathcal{R}\rangle}$ in place of $\boldsymbol{\gamma}_{\text{graph}}$ (and similarly for the order $\sqsubseteq_{\langle\mathcal{R}\rangle}$ on states (G, N)).

$$\mathbb{D}^\sharp \stackrel{\text{def}}{=} \{ (\mathcal{R}, G, N) \mid G \in \mathbb{D}^\sharp_{\text{graph}\langle\mathcal{R}\rangle} \text{ and } N \in \mathbb{D}^\sharp_{\text{num}} \}$$

$$\boldsymbol{\gamma}(\mathcal{R}, G, N) \stackrel{\text{def}}{=} \{ s \mid s \in \boldsymbol{\gamma}_{\langle\mathcal{R}\rangle}(G, N) \}$$

$$(\mathcal{R}_0, G_0, N_0) \sqsubseteq (\mathcal{R}_1, G_1, N_1) \quad \text{iff} \quad \mathcal{R}_0 \subseteq \mathcal{R}_1 \text{ and } (G_0, N_0) \sqsubseteq_{\langle\mathcal{R}_1\rangle} (G_1, N_1)$$

The above ordering $\sqsubseteq$ is sound, as $\mathcal{R}_0 \subseteq \mathcal{R}_1$ implies that $\boldsymbol{\gamma}_{\text{graph}\langle\mathcal{R}_0\rangle}(G_0) \subseteq \boldsymbol{\gamma}_{\text{graph}\langle\mathcal{R}_1\rangle}(G_1)$. All transfer functions are as before, except for widening at the head of recursive functions, which also adds a new rule. Most importantly, as shown in Venet [29] that has similar a construction, this widening stabilizes if the process of adding rules is itself bounded. One possible bound is to allow at most one rule per call site.

The above construction also suggests applying more complex forms of widening to the set of rules $\mathcal{R}$, while preserving soundness. In the ordering $(\mathcal{R}_0, G_0, N_0) \sqsubseteq (\mathcal{R}_1, G_1, N_1)$ defined above, we stated that it must the case that $\mathcal{R}_0 \subseteq \mathcal{R}_1$. However, we could use a more sophisticated ordering on sets of rules. In particular, if we have two rules r_0 and r_1 where r_1 is weaker than r_0, then we could replace r_0 with r_1 in our set of rules while maintaining soundness. In terms of the analysis, this observation means that inductive rules for stack may be weakened during the course of the analysis. Surprisingly, we can use this process to improve what can be summarized. Suppose the analysis discovers a stack rule r to summarize the call stack at the entry of some function `f`. However, widening at the next iteration fails (i.e., is imprecise) due to rule r being too specific, we are allowed to weaken r to a coarser rule r' that may allow this widening step to succeed. This technique is potentially useful when the shape part of the rules is stable, but when the numeric contents of cells need to be computed by a non-trivial widening sequence, as can be seen in Section 7. To guarantee termination of the analysis with this process, the rule weakening step must be shown to stop in some way.

Benchmark	Recursive (ms)	Iterative (ms)
list traversal	11	4
list get n*th* element	22	4
list insertion n*th* element	48	16
list remove n*th* element	27	11
list deletion (memory free)	13	4
list append	20	13
list reverse	29	5

Table 1. Micro-benchmarks comparing analysis times for recursive and iterative versions of the same operation.

6.3 Termination, Soundness, and Empirical Experience

To ensure termination, the analysis algorithm applies widening to at least one point in each cycle in the set of abstract flow equations. In the case of whole program interprocedural analyses, the following is one set of such widening points: (1) loop heads for intraprocedural loops and (2) at the entry and at the exit of functions when analyzing a recursive call. At the end of the analysis, each program point is mapped to a finite set of abstract elements. As all transfer functions are sound, and there is at least one widening point on each cycle in the interprocedural control-flow graph, the analysis terminates and is sound:

> **Soundness.** *If concrete state s can be reached at program point ℓ and if the set of abstract elements computed for point ℓ is $\{ (\mathcal{R}^\ell_0, G^\ell_0, N^\ell_0), \ldots, (\mathcal{R}^\ell_n, G^\ell_n, N^\ell_n) \}$, then $s \in \boldsymbol{\gamma}(\mathcal{R}^\ell_i, G^\ell_i, N^\ell_i)$ for some $i \in 0..n$.*

Preliminary Empirical Experience. We have implemented shape subtraction and stack rule inference described in Section 5 in XISA [5, 6]. It discovers the appropriate stack rules for all of the examples given in Sections 2 and 4. In each case, the stack rule inference time is negligible. We also have implemented a prototype analyzer and ran it on a series of micro-benchmarks that compares the analysis time of some recursive functions against their iterative counterparts (Table 1). The tests were performed on a 2.4 GHz MacBook Pro with 8 GB of RAM and under a Linux 2.6.27 virtual machine. In all these cases, the memory usage is not significant (at most 6 MB).

While the analysis times on these micro-benchmarks are negligible, we do see that analyzing the recursive versions take about two to three times more time than their iterative counterparts. This slowdown is expected since the analysis of a recursive function involves not only the inference of a suitable stack definition but also two fixed-point computations (one over the call sites and one over the return sites). In contrast, the analysis of a single imperative loop requires only one fixed point computation. Note that in the case of list reverse, the imperative version is quite trivial (e.g., does not even require a segment summary in the loop invariant), while the stack inductive definition for the recursive version is just as complex as the other examples.

7. Case Study: Precision and Modularity

In this section, we look more closely at numerical properties, which are combined with shape properties in the presence of recursion. Figure 8(a) shows an example program that implements a filter equation over a doubly-linked list. Here, we replaced the integer data field with two floating point fields x and y. It walks through the structure and deletes the nodes where the x field is not in range $[-M, M]$. In the same pass, it integrates a filter equation by reading from the x fields and writing the result to the y fields; this computation is performed only for the nodes that are not deleted.

Let us first consider the purely numeric part of the code (i.e., the digital filter) and imagine that it is implemented using a while-loop instead of recursion. On this version of the program, the Astrée analyzer [3] can infer rather precise invariants using either the domain of Feret [11] or simply the interval domain with threshold widening. For instance, if we let $M = 5$, $a = 0.8$, and p is initially set to 0, then Astrée computes the range $[-85.00008, 85.00008]$ as an approximation for the terms of the sequence after 7 iterations using only the interval domain with threshold widening (on the iterative, purely numeric version). Even though Astrée does not support recursion, the basic techniques are applicable to the purely numeric part of the program shown in Figure 8(a).

On the other hand, using a modular approach to interprocedural analysis to reason precisely about the numeric part is quite challenging, as we must capture relations between the inputs and outputs in the abstract domain. For instance, to obtain the same properties as using the interval domain in the iterative version, we must use a complex domain like polyhedra [8]. For non-linear filters like those handled by Feret [11], even polyhedra would not be sufficient to achieve the same level of precision with the modular approach. In essence, relational abstract domains are sometimes required to achieve the same level of precision using the modular approach as non-relational domains on an iterative counterpart.

We now consider analyzing the program shown in Figure 8(a) using our call stack abstraction and by instantiating the base domain with intervals, that is, with a simple non-relational domain. When applied to this program, our analysis must infer inductive rules for stack at two call sites (as there are two recursive call sites). We consider only the second call site, as the other one is very similar, though slightly more complicated with respect to shape. Figure 8(b) depicts the abstract state after two recursive calls before summarization of the call stack is performed. Nodes that denote floating point values are annotated with an interval. In particular, we have that $\mathcal{I}_{\gamma_0} = \mathcal{I}_{\gamma_1} = [-M, +M]$, $\mathcal{I}_{\delta_0} = [-a \star M - \epsilon, +a \star M + \epsilon']$, and so on. The ϵ, ϵ' values account for rounding errors. To obtain an invariant, we first derive a stack rule shown in Figure 8(c). This rule allows us to fold the call stack at the first recursive call site. Interestingly, this rule does not work at the next iteration because the interval constraints over the floating point nodes have not yet stabilized. Instead, we weaken the stack as discussed in Section 6.2. In essence, this process amounts to the same series of widening steps on the numerical domain elements as

```
void filter(dll* l, float p) {
  if (l != NULL) {
    if (l->x < -M || l->x > M) {
      dll* n = l->next; remove(l); filter(n, p);
    }
    else {
      l->y = a * p + l->x; filter(l->next, l->y);
    }
  }
}
```

(a) Recursive implementation of a digital filter.

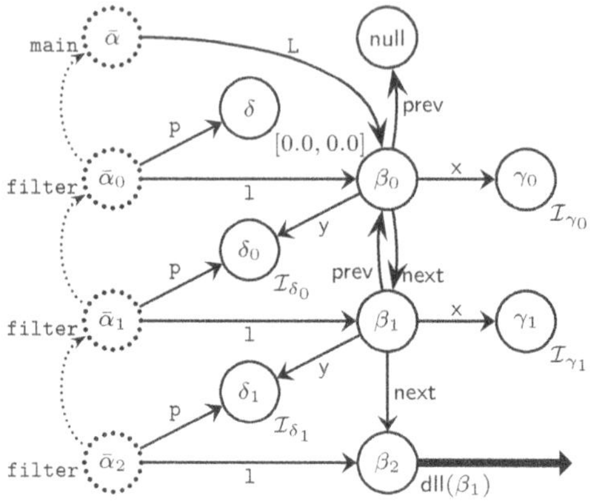

(b) An abstract state after two recursive calls.

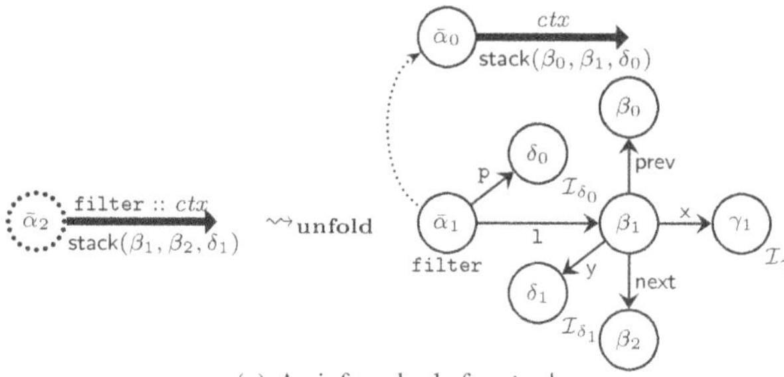

(c) An inferred rule for stack.

Figure 8. Obtaining numerical properties on a recursive program with the call stack abstraction.

in the analysis of the iterative program by Astrée, except they are applied when generating the stack summarization rule. Thus, it will lead to the computation of the same numerical invariants.

Recall that we are not advocating an abandonment of modular interprocedural analysis. As noted in Section 1, modularity is often the basis for scalability. When functions should be analyzed out of context (e.g., library API functions), then the modular approach seems ideal. Instead, we present interprocedural analysis by call stack summarization as an alternative that can be more effective in certain situations. A potentially hybrid approach could be to apply modular analysis except were call stack summarization is absolutely required. For example, call stack summarization is applied for a few intricate internal functions as part of a modular, tabulation-based analysis of the program.

8. Discussion: Interprocedural Shape Analysis

In this section, we consider known challenges in the context of interprocedural analysis of heap manipulating programs and comment on trade-offs.

8.1 Cutpoints

Modular shape analyses [4, 12, 13, 16, 23] typically infer an abstraction of the *effect* of a procedure on a portion of the heap. To make this effect abstraction precise, the analysis needs to carefully extract the fragment of the heap that may be modified during a call so that the rest of the heap is a *frame* [21]. Such an analysis must also abstract *cutpoints* [23] carefully to obtain precise results. Cutpoints are the locations at the border of the callee's reachable heap, that is, any node that is reachable from the callee's parameters (though not directly pointed-to by them) and reachable from a pending activation or a global (without following links inside the callee's reachable heap). It is important to track cutpoints precisely in a modular analysis, as they are used to reflect the effect of the callee in the caller's state on function return. Doing so can be challenging, as an unbounded number of cutpoints may arise either due to unbounded recursion or due to the traversal of unbounded heap structures. While there is no general solution for cutpoints today, several partial solutions have been proposed. For example, they focus on isolating their effect by proving cutpoint-freeness [24] or by proving that cutpoints are not live [17], or they reason up to a bounded number of them [23].

Our analysis based on call stack summarization also needs to cope with cutpoints so that the widening iteration reaches a precise fixed point. In the following, we consider how cutpoints impact our analysis in particular situations.

Summarizing Cutpoints. Cutpoints often arise when a field of a caller's activation record point into the heap space that may be modified by the callee (or a subsequent sub-call). This situation arises in the example in Section 2 (Figure 1). Such cutpoints may be unbounded, as each recursive call defines a set of local cutpoints and the number of recursive calls may be unbounded; however, they can be summarized as part of the call stack and re-exposed when recursive calls return. Observe that such cutpoints appear among the parameters in inductive rules for stack. Therefore, our approach can deal with an unbounded number of cutpoints by folding them as part of the call stack with finitely many parameters.

Case Splitting from Cutpoints. Another case is when the cutpoints stem from the global variables or from sections of the call stack that are not summarized (*e.g.*, as the activation record of main). Such cutpoints cause singularities in the call stack as in the example from Rinetzky et al. [23]. In that example, a singly-linked list is built by appending two singly linked lists while keeping a pointer to the element in the middle; then a destructive reverse function is applied to the whole structure. The state before the list reverse can be summarized as follows:

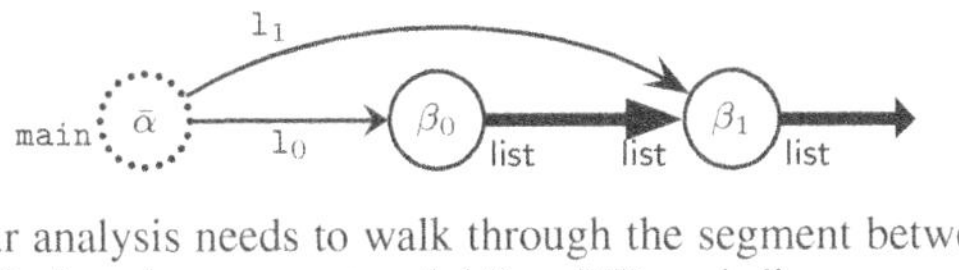

Now, our analysis needs to walk through the segment between β_0 and β_1 (using the segment unfolding [5]) and discovers a stack rule for summarizing the call stack. The generated rule is actually very similar to the one derived from the list traversal example of Section 4 (Figure 4(e)); it is essentially the same except for the direction of next pointers, which are switched by the reverse function. As we might predict, special care must be taken for the case where the reverse reaches node β_1. Applying widening here would cause the property that $\mathtt{l}_1$ points inside the list to be lost. A solution is to case split and not perform widening on that iteration. The trick here is a variation on a classical one: when a new behavior is observed (e.g., reaching β_1), postpone widening to the next iteration (cf., [3]).

To summarize, cutpoints induce a somewhat different set of issues compared with modular shape analyses, as our analysis abstracts only states and not effects. These issues can be alleviated using standard techniques to some extent.

8.2 Heap Partitioning and Cutpoints

Sharing can introduce more severe problems, as the example shown inset demonstrates. In this code, function f takes as input a doubly-linked list and performs a non-deterministic walk over it: at each step, depending on a random test, it either walks one step forward and calls itself recursively, or it walks one step backwards and calls itself recursively. The difficulty here is that this function may traverse several times the same elements of the doubly-linked list. Thus, at any time in a concrete execution, an element that has been visited in the past may be visited again in the future. This prevents the heap structure from being partitioned into sub-regions touched by successive recursive calls. This problem would also occur in the case of analyses that infer the footprint of procedures so as to compute their effect.

```
void f(dll* l) {
  if (...) { f(l->prev); }
  else { f(l->next); }
}
```

This sort of problem can arise even without procedures, so we consider this issue orthogonal to the cutpoint problem: cutpoints aim at describing the borders in the heap partition used to abstract successive calls, whereas the issue of this example is that no simple and good partitioning exists.

9. Related Work

The most closely related work to ours is Rinetzky and Sagiv [22]. They designed an analysis based on three-valued logic [27] where the call stack is abstracted together with the heap. Some earlier work had similar views (e.g., [9]). Rinetzky and Sagiv [22]'s concrete model is quite similar to ours. However, the abstraction is radically different, as we use separation logic and inductive definitions. In particular, we found that these tools are natural for abstracting the call stack. First, the call stack can be defined inductively, and second, there are built-in separation constraints between the call stack and the heap, as well as between successive activation records. Moreover, we found that the operations like function call, function return, and widening encode well in this abstraction.

Most interprocedural shape analyses take advantage of functions in order to achieve modularity. For instance, Jeannet et al. [16] abstracts input-output relations in the TVLA framework using three-valued structures with two occurrences of each element of the universe: one for the input state and one for the output state. The analysis of Rinetzky et al. [23, 24] is based on the tabulation of pairs of input-output three-valued structures. In Marron et al. [19], cutpoints are used in order to segment the abstract states and restrict the analysis to a precise approximation of the footprint of procedures. Similarly, separation logic-based modular analyses, such as Gotsman et al. [12], Calcagno et al. [4], or Gulavani et al. [13], isolate the footprint of procedures and compute the effect on the local heap (though in different manners). As we noted in Section 1, modularity in shape analysis has many advantages, especially when analyzing libraries or for scalability reasons. Our approach fills a gap to tackle a family of analysis problems, such as the combined analysis example of Section 7, where whole program analysis appears more suitable.

Another area of static analysis related to our work is that of context-sensitive analyses. The term "context sensitive" is used in many ways and may cover very different levels of abstraction, ranging from approaches that use call-strings to describe contexts [28] or an abstraction of the control flow history [25] to techniques where the call stack content is abstracted [15, 22]. Our technique uses a rather coarse abstraction of the call string and of the control flow history, so its precision can be further improved by applying those techniques [25, 28]. The analysis of Jeannet and Serwe [15] features a non-relational abstraction of the call stack in the sense that it discards the order of the activation records.

10. Conclusion

In this paper, we have explored a whole-program approach to interprocedural analysis over recursive programs. In particular, we have shown how to apply a shape analysis abstraction based on separation logic and inductive definitions to directly summarize call stacks along with heap structures. To automatically derive rules for call stack summarization, we exploited its built-in inductive structure. The XISA framework [5] turned out to be both expressive and robust in abstracting a very concrete model of calling contexts.

Acknowledgments

We would like to thank Josh Berdine, Noam Rinetzky, and Hongseok Yang for interesting discussions on interprocedural shape analysis and on the issues related to cutpoints. We also thank the anonymous reviewers for their helpful suggestions, including insightful comments on the whole-program versus modular approach.

References

[1] Josh Berdine, Cristiano Calcagno, and Peter W. O'Hearn. Symbolic execution with separation logic. In *Asian Symposium on Programming Languages and Systems (APLAS)*, pages 52–68, 2005.

[2] Josh Berdine, Cristiano Calcagno, Byron Cook, Dino Distefano, Peter W. O'Hearn, Thomas Wies, and Hongseok Yang. Shape analysis for composite data structures. In *Computer-Aided Verification (CAV)*, pages 178–192, 2007.

[3] Bruno Blanchet, Patrick Cousot, Radhia Cousot, Jérôme Feret, Laurent Mauborgne, Antoine Miné, David Monniaux, and Xavier Rival. A static analyzer for large safety-critical software. In *Programming Language Design and Implementation (PLDI)*, pages 196–207, 2003.

[4] Cristiano Calcagno, Dino Distefano, Peter W. O'Hearn, and Hongseok Yang. Compositional shape analysis by means of bi-abduction. In *Principles of Programming Languages (POPL)*, pages 289–300, 2009.

[5] Bor-Yuh Evan Chang and Xavier Rival. Relational inductive shape analysis. In *Principles of Programming Languages (POPL)*, pages 247–260, 2008.

[6] Bor-Yuh Evan Chang, Xavier Rival, and George C. Necula. Shape analysis with structural invariant checkers. In *Static Analysis (SAS)*, pages 384–401, 2007.

[7] Patrick Cousot and Radhia Cousot. Abstract interpretation: A unified lattice model for static analysis of programs by construction or approximation of fixpoints. In *Principles of Programming Languages (POPL)*, pages 238–252, 1977.

[8] Patrick Cousot and Nicolas Halbwachs. Automatic discovery of linear restraints among variables of a program. In *Principles of Programming Languages (POPL)*, pages 84–97, 1978.

[9] Alain Deutsch. On determining lifetime and aliasing of dynamically allocated data in higher-order functional specifications. In *Principles of Programming Languages (POPL)*, pages 157–168, 1990.

[10] Dino Distefano, Peter W. O'Hearn, and Hongseok Yang. A local shape analysis based on separation logic. In *Tools and Algorithms for the Construction and Analysis of Systems (TACAS)*, pages 287–302, 2006.

[11] Jérôme Feret. Static analysis of digital filters. In *European Symposium on Programming (ESOP)*, pages 33–48, 2004.

[12] Alexey Gotsman, Josh Berdine, and Byron Cook. Interprocedural shape analysis with separated heap abstractions. In *Static Analysis (SAS)*, pages 240–260, 2006.

[13] Bhargav S. Gulavani, Supratik Chakraborty, Ganesan Ramalingam, and Aditya V. Nori. Bottom-up shape analysis. In *Static Analysis (SAS)*, pages 188–204, 2009.

[14] Bolei Guo, Neil Vachharajani, and David I. August. Shape analysis with inductive recursion synthesis. In *Programming Language Design and Implementation (PLDI)*, pages 256–265, 2007.

[15] Bertrand Jeannet and Wendelin Serwe. Abstracting call-stacks for interprocedural verification of imperative programs. In *Algebraic Methodology and Software Technology (AMAST)*, pages 258–273, 2004.

[16] Bertrand Jeannet, Alexey Loginov, Thomas Reps, and Mooly Sagiv. A relational approach to interprocedural shape analysis. *ACM Trans. Program. Lang. Syst.*, 32(2), 2010.

[17] Jörg Kreiker, Thomas Reps, Noam Rinetzky, Mooly Sagiv, Reinhard Wilhelm, and Eran Yahav. Interprocedural shape analysis for effectively cutpoint-free programs. Technical report, Queen Mary University of London, 2010.

[18] Vincent Laviron, Bor-Yuh Evan Chang, and Xavier Rival. Separating shape graphs. In *European Symposium on Programming (ESOP)*, pages 387–406, 2010.

[19] Mark Marron, Manuel V. Hermenegildo, Deepak Kapur, and Darko Stefanovic. Efficient context-sensitive shape analysis with graph based heap models. In *Compiler Construction (CC)*, pages 245–259, 2008.

[20] Thomas Reps, Susan Horwitz, and Mooly Sagiv. Precise interprocedural dataflow analysis via graph reachability. In *Principles of Programming Languages (POPL)*, pages 49–61, 1995.

[21] John C. Reynolds. Separation logic: A logic for shared mutable data structures. In *Logic in Computer Science (LICS)*, pages 55–74, 2002.

[22] Noam Rinetzky and Mooly Sagiv. Interprocedural shape analysis for recursive programs. In *Compiler Construction (CC)*, pages 133–149, 2001.

[23] Noam Rinetzky, Jörg Bauer, Thomas Reps, Mooly Sagiv, and Reinhard Wilhelm. A semantics for procedure local heaps and its abstractions. In *Principles of Programming Languages (POPL)*, pages 296–309, 2005.

[24] Noam Rinetzky, Mooly Sagiv, and Eran Yahav. Interprocedural shape analysis for cutpoint-free programs. In *Static Analysis (SAS)*, pages 284–302, 2005.

[25] Xavier Rival and Laurent Mauborgne. The trace partitioning abstract domain. *ACM Trans. Program. Lang. Syst.*, 29(5), 2007.

[26] Mooly Sagiv, Thomas Reps, and Reinhard Wilhelm. Solving shape-analysis problems in languages with destructive updating. *ACM Trans. Program. Lang. Syst.*, 20(1):1–50, 1998.

[27] Mooly Sagiv, Thomas Reps, and Reinhard Wilhelm. Parametric shape analysis via 3-valued logic. *ACM Trans. Program. Lang. Syst.*, 24(3): 217–298, 2002.

[28] Micha Sharir and Amir Pnueli. Two approaches to interprocedural data flow analysis. In Steven S. Muchnick and Neil D. Jones, editors, *Program Flow Analysis: Theory and Applications*, chapter 7, pages 189–233. Prentice-Hall, 1981.

[29] Arnaud Venet. Abstract cofibered domains: Application to the alias analysis of untyped programs. In *Static Analysis (SAS)*, pages 366–382, 1996.

Precise Reasoning for Programs Using Containers

Isil Dillig
Department of Computer Science
Stanford University
isil@cs.stanford.edu

Thomas Dillig
Department of Computer Science
Stanford University
tdillig@cs.stanford.edu

Alex Aiken
Department of Computer Science
Stanford University
aiken@cs.stanford.edu

Abstract

Containers are general-purpose data structures that provide functionality for inserting, reading, removing, and iterating over elements. Since many applications written in modern programming languages, such as C++ and Java, use containers as standard building blocks, precise analysis of many programs requires a fairly sophisticated understanding of container contents. In this paper, we present a sound, precise, and fully automatic technique for static reasoning about contents of containers. We show that the proposed technique adds useful precision for verifying real C++ applications and that it scales to applications with over 100,000 lines of code.

Categories and Subject Descriptors D.2.4 [*Software Engineering*]: Software/Program Verication

General Terms Languages, Verification, Experimentation

1. Introduction

Containers are a family of general-purpose abstract data structures that provide functionality for inserting, retrieving, removing, and iterating over elements. Examples of containers include maps, lists, vectors, sets, multimaps, deques, as well as their combinations. We classify containers as either *position-dependent* or *value-dependent*: In position-dependent containers, each element e has a *position* that is used for inserting e into or reading e from the container. Position-dependent containers include vectors and lists, which support inserting and reading elements at a specified position, as well as queues and stacks, which allow inserting and reading elements at the first or last position. In contrast, value-dependent containers expose no notion of position, and each element is added and retrieved using its value. Instances of value-dependent containers include various kinds of maps, sets, bags, and multimaps. For instance, in a map, elements are inserted and looked up using a key; similarly, in a set, elements are inserted and found by the value of their elements rather than a position in the container.

Both kinds of containers are ubiquitous in modern programming, and many languages, such as C++, Java, and C#, provide a standard set of containers that programmers use as basic building blocks for the implementation of other more complex data structures and software. For this reason, successful verification of programs written in higher-level programming paradigms requires a fairly sophisticated understanding of how individual elements are modified as they flow in and out of containers. In fact, even basic safety properties often require reasoning about individual elements stored inside containers:

- To prove that the result of looking up a key k from a map m is non-null, we need to know that an element with key k is present in m and that the value associated with k is non-null.
- In languages with explicit memory management (such as C++), the safety of sequentially deallocating elements in a list or vector depends on the absence of aliasing pointers in the container.

As these examples illustrate, proving even simple properties may require a richer abstraction than treating container contents as sets. In the first example, we need to know not only which values are present in the map, but also which keys are associated with which values. Similarly, the second example requires proving the uniqueness of elements stored at different positions of the container. Hence, successful verification of these properties requires a detailed, per-element understanding of container contents.

We are interested in verifying properties of container-using programs, such as the examples above. We focus on verification of the client program, divorcing checking of the client from the separate problem of verifying the container implementation itself. We believe this separation is advantageous for several reasons:

1. *Understanding the contents of a container does not require understanding the container's implementation.*
   For example, while a map may be implemented as a hash table or a red-black tree, they both export the functionality of associating a key with a value. From the client's perspective, the difference between a hash map and a red-black tree lies primarily in the performance trade-off between various operations.
2. *Verifying container implementations requires different techniques and degrees of automation then verifying their clients.*
   Hence, separating these two tasks allows us to choose the verification techniques best-suited for each purpose. While we might need heavy-weight, semi-automatic approaches for verifying container implementations, we can still develop fully automatic and more scalable techniques for verifying their clients.
3. *There are orders of magnitude more clients of a container than there are container implementations.*
   This fact makes it possible to annotate a handful of library interfaces in order to analyze many programs using these containers.

We propose a precise and fully automatic technique for static reasoning about container contents. By separating the internal implementation of containers from their client-side use, our technique provides a uniform representation and analysis methodology for any position or value-dependent container. Rather than modeling containers as sets of values, our technique provides a per-element understanding of containers, enabling the abstraction to distinguish properties that hold for different elements. Our abstraction naturally models arbitrary nestings of containers, commonly used in

POPL'11, January 26–28, 2011, Austin, Texas, USA.

```
1: vector< map<string, int>* > exam_scores;
2:
3: for(int j=0; j<NUM_EXAMS; j++)
4: {
5:   map<string, int>* m = new map<string, int>();
6:   exam_scores.push_back(m);
7: }
8:
9: map<string, vector<int>*>::iterator it =
10:   student_scores.begin();
11: for(; it != student_scores.end(); it++)
12: {
13:   string student = it->first;
14:   vector<int>* scores = it->second;
15:   for(int k=0; k <NUM_EXAMS; k++)
16:   {
17:     (*exam_scores[k])[student] = (*scores)[k];
18:   }
19:}
```

Figure 1. Example illustrating key features of the technique

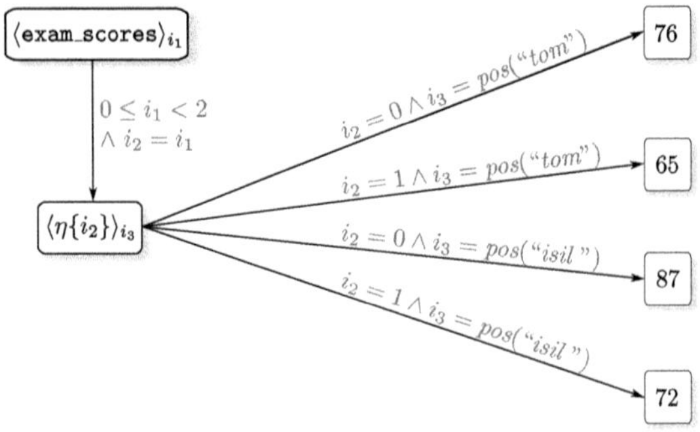

Figure 2. The representation of container `exam_scores` after the analysis of code from Figure 1

real programs. For example, our technique can reason precisely about a map of lists, expressing which lists are associated with which keys, which nested lists are shared or distinct, while also tracking the contents of the nested lists.

1.1 An Informal Overview

To develop a unified representation for containers, we model any container as a function that converts a *key* to an abstract *index* (an integer), which is then mapped to a value at that index. In this abstraction, a key corresponds to any term that is used for inserting an element into or reading an element from the container. For example, in a vector, keys are integers identifying a position in the vector; in a set, keys are the elements that are inserted into the set. For any container, keys are converted to abstract indices using a *key-to-index mapping*, but this mapping differs between position- and value-dependent containers: For position-dependent containers (such as a vector), the key-to-index mapping is the identity, as the key is the position in the data structure. For value-dependent containers, we leave the function converting keys to indices uninterpreted; clients of value-dependent containers cannot rely on elements being stored in any particular place, just that they are stored somewhere in the container.

A key advantage of introducing an extra level of indirection from keys to indices is that this strategy allows us to treat position- and value-dependent containers uniformly, while providing the ability to differentiate between distinct elements by using integer constraints on the indices. Specifically, we model containers using *indexed locations* of the form $\langle \alpha \rangle_i$ where the index variable i ranges over possible abstract indices of the container. *All* elements in the container are represented by a single abstract location $\langle \alpha \rangle_i$, but constraints on the index variable i allow distinctions to be made among the different elements of the container. This approach has been previously used for successful reasoning about array contents [1], and, as we shall see, our approach extends these benefits to both position- and value-dependent containers.

This combination of indexed locations and constraints on index variables allows for a much more detailed understanding of containers than representing their contents as a set. For example, if a container c's contents are modeled by the set of values $\{13, 5, 8\}$, this abstraction encodes that any element in c may have *any* of the values 13, 5, and 8, effectively mixing values associated with different elements. On the other hand, by representing c using an indexed abstract location $\langle \alpha \rangle_i$, we can qualify each of the values 13, 5, and 8 by constraints ϕ_1, ϕ_2, and ϕ_3, restricting which indices in $\langle \alpha \rangle_i$ may have which value. The latter abstraction encodes that only those values whose keys are consistent with the index constraint ϕ_i may have value v_i, and thereby retains the correlations between positions and values for position-dependent containers and key-value correlations for value-dependent containers.

To illustrate important features of our technique, consider the C++ code snippet in Figure 1. Here, the container `student_scores` maps each student to a vector of integers, indicating the score received by each student on every exam. To keep the example simple, suppose that there are only two students, Tom and Isil, and Tom received scores 76 and 65, and Isil received scores 87 and 72 on two exams. The code in Figure 1 builds a reverse mapping `exam_scores` where the i'th element in `exam_scores` is a map from each student to this student's score on the i'th exam.

Figure 2 shows a graphical representation of the facts established about the contents of `exam_scores` after analyzing the code from Figure 1. In this figure, nodes in the graph represent abstract locations, a directed edge from node A to B qualified by constraint ϕ indicates that B is one of the values stored in A and ϕ constrains at which index of A the value B may be stored. We highlight important features of the abstraction based on Figure 2:

1. **Abstract containers:** Observe that the vector `exam_scores` is qualified by an index variable i_1 and the maps nested inside `exam_scores` are also qualified by an index variable i_3. Both of these index variables allow us to select different elements in the container by constraining the values of i_1 and i_3.
2. **Memory allocations:** A key prerequisite for precise reasoning about nested containers is differentiating different allocations. In the figure, memory locations arising from the allocation at line 5 are described by $\eta\{i_2\}$, where i_2 is also an index variable. Hence, just as we use index variables to differentiate between elements in a container, we also use them for distinguishing different memory allocations arising from the same expression.
3. **Key-to-index mapping:** On the edge from $\langle \eta\{i_2\} \rangle_{i_3}$ to 76, index variable i_3 is equal to *pos("tom")*, where *pos* is an invertible, uninterpreted function representing the mapping from key *"tom"* to a unique, but unspecified index. On the other hand, since `exam_scores` is a position-dependent container, the key-to-index mapping is the identity function; hence, the outgoing edge from $\langle$`exam_scores`$\rangle_{i_1}$ is qualified by $0 \leq i_1 < 2$.
4. **Nesting of data structures:** On the edge from $\langle$`exam_scores`$\rangle_{i_1}$ to the nested maps modeled by $\langle \eta\{i_2\} \rangle_{i_3}$, i_2 is equal to i_1. This constraint indicates that there is a *unique* allocation for every index of the container `exam_scores` because there is exactly one i_2 for each i_1. Furthermore, together with the constraints on edges outgoing from $\langle \eta\{i_2\} \rangle_{i_3}$, the abstraction encodes that the map stored at position 0 of the vector `exam_scores` asso-

ciates key *tom* with value 76, but the map stored at position 1 of the vector associates *tom* with value 65.

5. **Iterators:** The indirection from keys to indices provides a natural way to model iterators by accessing every element in increasing order of their abstract indices. Since the key-to-index mapping is always an invertible function, the abstraction encodes that every element is visited exactly once. This abstraction is also consistent with the expected semantics that iteration order over value-dependent containers is, in general, unspecified (since *pos* is uninterpreted) while elements of position-dependent containers are visited according to their position.

The rest of this paper is organized as follows: Section 2 gives a small language in which we formalize our technique. Section 3 describes the analysis and states the soundness theorem. Section 4 describes some extensions that are useful for modeling containers in real applications, and Section 5 discusses our implementation. Section 6 presents experimental results, Section 7 surveys related work, and, finally, Section 8 concludes. To summarize, this paper makes the following key contributions:

- We present a unified, sound, and precise technique for client-side reasoning about contents of an important family of data structures known as containers.
- We describe a fully automatic static analysis for containers that provides a detailed, per-element understanding of their contents and that supports arbitrary nestings of containers.
- We show experimentally that our technique is scalable enough to analyze C++ programs ranging between 16,000 to 128,000 lines of code that make heavy use of containers.
- We demonstrate experimentally that precise reasoning about contents of containers reduces false alarms by an order of magnitude compared to an analysis that treats containers as sets of values when verifying the absence of null dereferences, memory leaks, and deleted memory accesses in C++ programs.

$$\frac{}{\Gamma \vdash c : \texttt{Int}} \qquad \frac{}{\Gamma \vdash \texttt{nil} : \texttt{Nil}} \qquad \frac{\Gamma(v) = \tau}{\Gamma \vdash v : \tau} \qquad \frac{\tau = \texttt{adt}(\tau') \quad \tau' \neq \texttt{Nil}}{\Gamma \vdash \texttt{new}\ \tau : \tau}$$

$$\frac{\Gamma \vdash v_1 : \texttt{adt}(\tau) \quad \Gamma \vdash v_2 : \texttt{Int}}{\Gamma \vdash v_1\texttt{.read}(v_2) : \texttt{maybe}(\tau)} \qquad \frac{\Gamma \vdash v_1 : \texttt{adt}(\tau) \quad \Gamma \vdash v_2 : \texttt{Int} \quad \Gamma \vdash v_3 : \tau_3,\ \tau_3 <: \texttt{maybe}(\tau)}{\Gamma \vdash v_1\texttt{.write}(v_2, v_3) : \texttt{Nil}}$$

$$\frac{\Gamma \vdash v : \texttt{adt}(\tau) \quad \Gamma[\texttt{Int}/v_1, \tau/v_2] \vdash e : \tau_e}{\Gamma \vdash \texttt{foreach}\ (v_1, v_2)\ \texttt{in}\ v\ \texttt{do}\ e\ \texttt{od} : \texttt{Nil}} \qquad \frac{\Gamma \vdash e_1 : \tau_1 \quad \Gamma \vdash e_2 : \tau_2}{\Gamma \vdash e_1; e_2 : \tau_2}$$

$$\frac{\Gamma \vdash v : \tau \quad \tau <: \texttt{maybe}(\tau') \quad \Gamma[\tau'/v] \vdash e_1 : \tau'' \quad \Gamma[\texttt{Nil}/v] \vdash e_2 : \tau''}{\Gamma \vdash \texttt{if}\ v \neq \texttt{nil}\ \texttt{then}\ e_1\ \texttt{else}\ e_2\ \texttt{fi} : \tau''} \qquad \frac{\Gamma \vdash e : \tau',\ \tau' <: \tau \quad \Gamma[\tau/v] \vdash e' : \tau''}{\Gamma \vdash \texttt{let}\ v : \tau = e\ \texttt{in}\ e' : \tau''}$$

Figure 3. Type checking rules

2. Language and Concrete Semantics

We first introduce a simple statically-typed language used to formalize our technique:

$$\begin{array}{lcl} \textit{Program } P & := & e^+ \\ \textit{Expression } e & := & v \mid c \mid \texttt{nil} \mid \texttt{new}^{\rho}\ \tau \mid e_1; e_2 \\ & & \mid \texttt{let}^{\rho}\ v : \tau = e\ \texttt{in}\ e' \\ & & \mid v_1\texttt{.read}(v_2) \mid v_1\texttt{.write}(v_2,\ v_3) \\ & & \mid \texttt{foreach}^{\rho_0}\ (v_1^{\rho_1}, v_2^{\rho_2})\ \texttt{in}\ v\ \texttt{do}\ e\ \texttt{od} \\ & & \mid \texttt{if}\ v \neq \texttt{nil}\ \texttt{then}\ e_1\ \texttt{else}\ e_2\ \texttt{fi} \end{array}$$

A program consists of one or more expressions. Expressions include variables v, non-negative integer constants c, the special constant `nil`, container allocations (`new` τ), sequencing $(e_1; e_2)$, and let expressions. A read operation v_1`.read`(v_2) reads the value of element with key v_2 from container v_1, and v_1`.write`$(v_2,\ v_3)$ writes value v_3 with key v_2 to container v_1. A `foreach` construct iterates over container v, binding the current key to v_1 and the value to v_2. Finally, an `if` expression evaluates expression e_1 or e_2, depending on whether variable v is `nil` or not. The `let`, `new` and `foreach` expressions are labeled with superscripts ρ which are globally unique expression identifiers. When irrelevant, we omit ρ.

Types in this language are defined by the grammar:

$$\textit{Type}\ \tau := \texttt{Int} \mid \texttt{Nil} \mid \texttt{pos\_adt}(\tau) \mid \texttt{val\_adt}(\tau) \mid \texttt{maybe}(\tau)$$

Base types in this language are `Int` and `Nil`. Position-dependent containers with elements of type τ have type `pos_adt`(τ), and value-dependent containers with value type τ have type `val_adt`(τ). To simplify the technical presentation, we require keys of value-dependent containers to be integers; Section 4 discusses how to extend our technique to keys with arbitrary types and custom equality operators. We also introduce a type `maybe`(τ) for elements whose type can be either `Nil` or τ. A subtyping relation is defined as:

$$\tau <: \tau \qquad \texttt{Nil} <: \texttt{maybe}(\tau) \qquad \tau <: \texttt{maybe}(\tau)$$

We write `adt`(τ) as shorthand for `pos_adt`$(\tau) \vee$ `val_adt`(τ). Type checking rules for this language are given in Figure 3.

Observe that this language allows arbitrary nestings of containers because the element type of a container can be another container. Also, while this language does not have explicit `contains` and `remove` operations that are commonly defined on containers, elements can be removed by writing `nil` and the presence of key `k` can be checked by testing whether the result of reading `k` is `nil`.

2.1 Operational Semantics

In the operational semantics of our language, we view memory as a two-dimensional array where each row stores a container, and each column identifies the index of a specific element in the container. We model scalar values (integers) as rows where only the 0'th column is used. A concrete memory location is a pair (l, i), where l is the *base location* (i.e., the row) and i is an offset (i.e, the column).

Figure 4 gives the operational semantics. The general structure of the rules are of the form $E, S, C \vdash e : l', S'$. Here, environment E maps program variables to base locations l, store S maps concrete memory locations (l, i) to an integer, identifying another base location or a constant, and C is a vector of integers denoting the current iteration number of each loop in scope. The judgment $E, S, C \vdash e : l', S'$ states that under environment E, store S, and counter vector C, expression e evaluates to value l', producing a new store S'. In Figure 4, we use the notation $S \backslash l$ to denote store S with binding l removed. In the rules, we also assume that type environment Γ is available to differentiate between position- and value-dependent containers.

Most of the rules in Figure 4 are straightforward; we only highlight important features of the language semantics. There are two key differences between position- and value-dependent containers that our language semantics tries to capture: First, position-dependent containers require filled positions of the container to be contiguous whereas value-dependent containers do not. Second, iteration over position-dependent containers visits elements in increasing order of their position, but iteration over value-dependent containers visits elements in arbitrary order in general.

To capture the first difference, observe that the language semantics requires position-dependent containers to use a contigu-

$$\frac{\begin{array}{l}E(v) = l\\ S(l,0) = l'\end{array}}{E,S,C \vdash v : l', S} \qquad \frac{}{E,S,C \vdash c : c, S} \qquad \frac{}{E,S,C \vdash \texttt{nil} : \texttt{NIL}, S} \qquad \frac{\begin{array}{c}l_n \notin dom(S)\\ S' = S[\forall i.(l_n,i) \leftarrow \texttt{NIL}]\end{array}}{E,S,C \vdash \texttt{new}\ \tau : l_n, S'} \qquad \frac{\begin{array}{l}E,S \vdash e : l, S'\\ E' = E[v \leftarrow l_n]\ \ (l_n \notin dom(S'))\\ S'' = S'[(l_n,0) \leftarrow l]\\ E',S'',C \vdash e' : l', S'''\end{array}}{E,S,C \vdash \texttt{let}\ v : \tau = e\ \texttt{in}\ e' : l',\ S'''\backslash l_n}$$

$$\frac{\begin{array}{l}E(v_2) = l_2\ \ S(l_2,0) = key\\ E(v_1) = l_1\ \ S(l_1,0) = l_1'\\ S(l_1', key) = l_{res}\end{array}}{E,S,C \vdash v_1\texttt{.read}(v_2) : l_{res}, S} \qquad \frac{\begin{array}{l}E(v_2) = l_2\ \ S(l_2,0) = key\\ E(v_3) = l_3\ \ S(l_3,0) = val\\ E(v_1) = l_1\ \ S(l_1,0) = l_1'\\ S' = S[(l_1', key) \leftarrow val]\end{array}}{E,S,C \vdash v_1\texttt{.write}(v_2,v_3) : \texttt{NIL}, S'}\ (v_1\texttt{val\_adt}) \qquad \frac{\begin{array}{l}E(v_2) = l_2\ \ S(l_2,0) = pos\\ E(v_3) = l_3\ \ S(l_3,0) = elem\\ E(v_1) = l_1\ \ S(l_1,0) = l_1'\\ S(l_1', pos-1) \neq \texttt{NIL}\ \ \textit{if}\ l_3 \neq \texttt{NIL} \wedge pos > 0\\ S(l_1', pos+1) = \texttt{NIL}\ \ \textit{if}\ l_3 = \texttt{NIL}\\ S' = S[(l_1', pos) \leftarrow elem]\end{array}}{E,S,C \vdash v_1\texttt{.write}(v_2,v_3) : \texttt{NIL}, S'}\ (v_1\texttt{pos\_adt})$$

$$\frac{\begin{array}{l}E(v) = l\ \ S(l,0) = l'\\ \Delta = \begin{array}{l}[(k_1,\vartheta_1),\ldots,(k_n,\vartheta_n)]\ \ where\ k_i < k_{i+1} \wedge\\ (k_i,\vartheta_i) \in \Delta \Leftrightarrow (S(l',k_i) = \vartheta_i \wedge \vartheta_i \neq \texttt{NIL})\end{array}\\ \Delta' = \begin{cases}\Delta & \textit{if}\ v\ \texttt{pos\_adt}\\ Permutation(\Delta) & \textit{if}\ v\ \texttt{val\_adt}\end{cases}\\ E' = E[v_1 \leftarrow l_k, v_2 \leftarrow l_v]\ \ l_k, l_v \notin dom(S)\\ E', S, (0{::}C) \vdash process((v_1,v_2)\ in\ \Delta')\ do\ e : S'\end{array}}{E,S,C \vdash \texttt{foreach}\ (v_1,v_2)\ \texttt{in}\ v\ \texttt{do}\ e\ \texttt{od} : \texttt{nil}, S'\backslash\{l_k,l_v\}} \qquad \frac{\begin{array}{l}E(v_1) = l_k\ \ E(v_2) = l_v\\ (k_i,\vartheta_i) = i\text{'th element of}\ \Delta\\ S' = S[l_k \leftarrow k_i, l_v \leftarrow \vartheta_i]\\ E, S', (i{::}C) \vdash e : l_e, S''\\ E, S'', ((i+1){::}C) \vdash process((v_1,v_2)\ in\ \Delta)\ do\ e : S'''\end{array}}{E, S, (i{::}C) \vdash process\ ((v_1,v_2)\ in\ \Delta)\ do\ e : S'''}\ (i < Size(\Delta))$$

$$\frac{i = Size(\Delta)}{E, S, (i{::}C) \vdash process\ ((v_1,v_2)\ in\ \Delta)\ do\ e : S} \qquad \frac{\begin{array}{l}E,S,C \vdash e_1 : l_1, S_1\\ E,S_1,C \vdash e_2 : l_2, S_2\end{array}}{E,S,C \vdash e_1; e_2 : l_2, S_2} \qquad \frac{\begin{array}{l}E(v) = l\ \ S(l,0) = l'\\ E,S,C \vdash e_1 : l_r, S'\ \ \textit{if}\ l' \neq \texttt{NIL}\\ E,S,C \vdash e_2 : l_r, S'\ \ \textit{if}\ l' = \texttt{NIL}\end{array}}{E,S,C \vdash \texttt{if}\ v \neq \texttt{nil}\ \texttt{then}\ e_1\ \texttt{else}\ e_2\ \texttt{fi} : l_r, S'}$$

Figure 4. Operational Semantics

ous region of memory whereas value-dependent containers may be sparse. In particular, it is legal to use any key when writing to a value-dependent container, but for position-dependent containers, the write operation is only defined if it does not create "holes" in the container, i.e., all elements with indices in range $[0, size)$ are non-`nil` and elements with indices at least *size* are `nil`. To capture the second difference, observe, in the `foreach rule`, that Δ is an ordered list of (key, value) pairs, but we construct an arbitrary permutation Δ' of Δ when iterating over value-dependent containers. Also, observe that the (key, value) pairs are pre-computed; hence, any changes to the container during the iteration do not affect the (key, value) pairs that are visited.

3. Abstract Semantics

In this section, we describe the abstract semantics that form the basis of our analysis. We first describe our abstract domain (Section 3.1) and then discuss our abstract model of containers (Section 3.2). In Section 3.3, we present the analysis, and in Section 3.4, we state the soundness theorem.

3.1 Abstract Domain and Preliminaries

Our abstraction differentiates between two kinds of *abstract memory locations*: *Basic locations*, β, represent a single concrete element, and *indexed locations*, $\langle\alpha\rangle_i$, represent containers. As mentioned in Section 1, although a single indexed location $\langle\alpha\rangle_i$ represents many concrete elements, our abstraction can reason about individual elements stored in the container by using constraints on the *index variable* i. The *abstract values* used in the analysis are:

$$\begin{array}{lcl}\textit{Abstract value}\ \pi & = & NIL \mid c \mid \delta\\ \textit{Abstract location}\ \delta & = & \beta^\rho \mid \langle\alpha\rangle_i\\ \textit{Allocation}\ \alpha & = & \eta_\rho\{\vec{i}\}\end{array}$$

Abstract values are *NIL*, integer constants c, basic locations β^ρ (where ρ indicates the program point where the location is introduced) and indexed abstract locations $\langle\alpha\rangle_i$. Allocations α are of the form $\eta_\rho\{\vec{i}\}$, where ρ is a label for the syntactic allocation expression $\texttt{new}^\rho\tau$. More interestingly, allocations are also qualified by a (potentially empty) vector of index variables to distinguish allocations arising from the same syntactic expression in different loop iterations. Hence, just as index variables allow us to refer to distinct elements in a container, index variables also distinguish allocations arising from the same program expression. Since loops may be nested, the number of index variables in $\eta_\rho\{\vec{i}\}$ is equal to the loop nesting depth of a $\texttt{new}^\rho\ \tau$ expression.

Unlike the concrete store that maps each concrete location to exactly one concrete value, the *abstract store* necessarily maps each abstract location to a *set* of possible abstract values. An *abstract value set* θ is a set of abstract value (π), constraint (ϕ) pairs:

$$\textit{Abstract value set}\ \theta := 2^{(\pi,\phi)}$$

Here, constraints ϕ select particular elements from indexed locations. For example, if the abstract value set for a container $\langle\alpha\rangle_i$ is $\{(7, i=0), (4, i=1), (NIL, i \geq 2)\}$, the abstraction encodes that the values of elements at indices 0 and 1 are 7 and 4 respectively, but all the other elements are `nil`.

In the rest of this paper, we assume that an abstract value set θ does not contain two pairs of the form (π,ϕ_1) and (π,ϕ_2); instead, θ contains π only once under $\phi_1 \vee \phi_2$.

3.1.1 Bracketing Constraints

The constraints we require are more elaborate than we have indicated so far. Since most static analyses overapproximate program behavior, the reader may expect that the constraints ϕ used in the abstraction are overapproximations. In other words, if ϕ^* is a constraint describing some subset of elements in the container during a concrete execution, then $\phi^* \Rightarrow \phi$ if ϕ is an overapproximation. Now, our analysis relies crucially on negating constraints to model certain constructs well, specifically updates to containers and path conditions. But, unfortunately, if ϕ is a *strict* overapproximation, then $\neg\phi$ is a strict underapproximation of $\neg\phi^*$, i.e., $\neg\phi^* \not\Rightarrow \neg\phi$. Clearly, for soundness, we need a negation operation that preserves overapproximations.

To solve this problem, all the constraints used in our abstraction are *bracketing constraints* $\langle\varphi_{may}, \varphi_{must}\rangle$, simultaneously representing over- and underapproximations of some set of concrete elements. A bracketing constraint is *well-formed* if $\varphi_{must} \Rightarrow \varphi_{may}$. The key benefit of bracketing constraints is that they preserve over- and underapproximations under negation:

$$\neg\langle\varphi_{may}, \varphi_{must}\rangle = \langle\neg\varphi_{must}, \neg\varphi_{may}\rangle$$

In other words, if φ_{may} and φ_{must} are over- and underapproximations for some fact F, then $\neg\varphi_{must}$ and $\neg\varphi_{may}$ are over- and underapproximations for $\neg F$ respectively. We briefly review some basic properties of bracketing constraints [1]:

$$\begin{array}{rcl}
\neg\langle\varphi_{may}, \varphi_{must}\rangle & = & \langle\neg\varphi_{must}, \neg\varphi_{may}\rangle \\
\langle\varphi_{may1}, \varphi_{must1}\rangle \wedge \langle\varphi_{may2}, \varphi_{must2}\rangle & = & \langle\varphi_{may1} \wedge \varphi_{may2}, \varphi_{must1} \wedge \varphi_{must2}\rangle \\
\langle\varphi_{may1}, \varphi_{must1}\rangle \vee \langle\varphi_{may2}, \varphi_{must2}\rangle & = & \langle\varphi_{may1} \vee \varphi_{may2}, \varphi_{must1} \vee \varphi_{must2}\rangle \\
SAT(\langle\varphi_{may}, \varphi_{must}\rangle) & \equiv & SAT(\varphi_{may}) \\
VALID(\langle\varphi_{may}, \varphi_{must}\rangle) & \equiv & VALID(\varphi_{must})
\end{array}$$

In this paper, any constraint ϕ is assumed to be a bracketing constraint unless explicitly stated otherwise. To make this clear, any time we do not use a bracketing constraint, we use the letter φ instead of ϕ. Furthermore, if the may and must conditions of a bracketing constraint are the same, we write a single constraint instead of a pair. For example, we abbreviate the bracketing constraint $\langle i = k, i = k\rangle$ as $i = k$. The constraints φ_{may} and φ_{must} we use inside bracketing constraints in this paper belong to the combined theory of linear integer arithmetic and uninterpreted functions.

3.2 Abstract Model of Containers

As discussed in Section 1, our abstraction models any position- or value-dependent container as a mapping from a key to an abstract index to a value stored at this index of the container. In this section, we detail the key-to-index and the index-to-value mappings.

3.2.1 Index Selection: From Keys to Indices

The most important requirement for the key-to-index mapping M for containers is that it obeys the following axiom:

$$\forall i_1, i_2.\, i_1 = i_2 \Rightarrow M^{-1}(i_1) = M^{-1}(i_2)$$

This axiom states that if two abstract indices are equal, then the keys associated with these indices must also be equal. This requirement is necessary for soundness; otherwise, two keys may be mapped to the same index, causing a value associated with key k_1 to be erroneously overwritten through inserts using a different key k_2. Hence, M has the property that its inverse mapping is a function. However, the question remains whether M is itself a function. In this regard, there are two sensible design alternatives:

1. For some containers that allow multiple values for the same key, such as multimaps, we can allow the same key to map to multiple indices such that M itself is not a function.
2. We can require M to be a function and model containers that allow multiple values per key using nested containers.

Without loss of generality, we choose (2) because our model can express arbitrary nestings of containers. Since both M and M^{-1} are functions, the key-to-index mapping is always a bijection (i.e., an invertible function). However, the key-to-index mapping for value-dependent containers differs from that of position-dependent containers: In particular, for value-dependent containers, M is an invertible *uninterpreted* function, while for position-dependent containers, M is the (interpreted) identity function. The intuition behind this choice is that if we insert an element e with key j into a position-dependent container, then e is guaranteed to be the j'th element when iterating over the container. On the other hand, if we insert element e with key j to a value-dependent container, we have no guarantees about where e will appear in the iteration order. Thus, we model the key-to-index mapping of value-dependent containers as an invertible uninterpreted function.

Formally, we define two index selection operators, $\diamondsuit$ and $\clubsuit$, for mapping keys to index constraints for position- and value-dependent containers respectively.

DEFINITION 1. **(Index Selection $\diamondsuit$ for Position-Dependent Container)** *Let θ_{key} be the set of possible abstract values associated with some key, and let i be an index variable. Then,*

$$\theta_{\text{key}} \diamondsuit\, i = \bigvee_{(\pi_j, \phi_j) \in \theta_{\text{key}}} (i = \pi_j \wedge \phi_j)$$

DEFINITION 2. **(Index Selection $\clubsuit$ for Value-Dependent Container)** *Let θ_{key} be the set of possible abstract values associated with some key, and let i be an index variable. Then,*

$$\theta_{\text{key}} \clubsuit\, i = \bigvee_{(\pi_j, \phi_j) \in \theta_{\text{key}}} (i = \text{pos}(\pi_j) \wedge \phi_j)$$

where pos *is an invertible uninterpreted function.*

Given an abstract value set θ_{key} representing a set of possible keys, the index selectors $\diamondsuit$ and $\clubsuit$ yield a constraint describing the possible indices associated with θ_{key}. In the definition of $\diamondsuit$, since the mapping M is the identity function, the index variable i is set equal to each possible value π_j of the key (i.e., $i = \pi_j$). On the other hand, in the definition of $\clubsuit$, the index variable i is equal to an invertible uninterpreted function *pos* of each key (i.e., $i = pos(\pi_j)$). Since the abstract value set associated with the key may contain more than one element, we take the disjunction of the constraints associated with each possible value of the key.

3.2.2 Element Selection: From Indices to Values

We now consider the problem of determining the value associated with a given index. More specifically, given an abstract value set θ associated with a container, we want to determine which elements of θ are consistent with some index constraint ϕ.

We begin with a simple example: Suppose that the abstract value set θ for a container $\langle\alpha\rangle_i$ is $\{(8, i = 1), (5, i = 2), (NIL, i > 2))\}$ and we want to determine the possible values of the element at index 2 in the container. To do this, we can substitute 2 for index variable i and remove all unsatisfiable elements from θ, which yields 5 as the only possible value for this element. We formalize this concept using an *element selection* operation $\bowtie$:

DEFINITION 3. **(Element Selection $\bowtie$)** *Let I denote the set of index variables mentioned in constraint ϕ, and let* QE *define a quantifier elimination procedure. Then,*

$$\theta \bowtie \phi = \left\{ (\pi_j, \phi'_j) \;\middle|\; \begin{array}{l} (\pi_j, \phi_j) \in \theta \wedge \text{SAT}(\phi_j \wedge \phi) \wedge \\ \phi'_j = \text{QE}(\exists I.\, (\phi_j \wedge \phi)) \end{array} \right\}$$

First, observe that the element selection operation $\bowtie$ filters out elements in θ inconsistent with ϕ because of the requirement $SAT(\phi_j \wedge \phi)$. Second, observe that the resulting constraint ϕ'_j is obtained by existentially quantifying and then subsequently eliminating all index variables used in ϕ from the constraint $\phi_j \wedge \phi$ because $\phi'_j = \text{QE}(\exists I.\, (\phi_j \wedge \phi))$. Existential quantifier elimination generalizes the simple substitution mechanism we sketched out informally in the example: Since the index constraint ϕ is not always a simple equality, we may not be able to substitute concrete values for the index variables; hence, we use existential quantifier elimination in the general case. Furthermore, it is not required that this

$$(1)\ \frac{\theta = \{NIL, true\}}{\mathbb{E},\mathbb{S},\mathbb{C} \vdash \texttt{nil} : \theta, \mathbb{S}} \qquad (2)\ \frac{\theta = \{c, true\}}{\mathbb{E},\mathbb{S},\mathbb{C} \vdash c : \theta, \mathbb{S}}$$

$$(3)\ \frac{\begin{array}{c}\mathbb{E}(v) = \beta\\ \mathbb{S}(\beta) = \theta\end{array}}{\mathbb{E},\mathbb{S},\mathbb{C} \vdash v : \theta, \mathbb{S}} \qquad (4)\ \frac{\begin{array}{c}\mathbb{E},\mathbb{S},\mathbb{C} \vdash e_1 : \theta_1, \mathbb{S}_1\\ \mathbb{E},\mathbb{S}_1,\mathbb{C} \vdash e_2 : \theta_2, \mathbb{S}_2\end{array}}{\mathbb{E},\mathbb{S},\mathbb{C} \vdash e_1; e_2 : \theta_2, \mathbb{S}_2}$$

$$(5)\ \frac{\begin{array}{l}\mathbb{E},\mathbb{S},\mathbb{C} \vdash e : \theta, \mathbb{S}'\\ \mathbb{E}[v \leftarrow \beta^\rho], \mathbb{S}'[\beta^\rho \leftarrow \theta], \mathbb{C} \vdash e' : \theta', \mathbb{S}''\end{array}}{\mathbb{E},\mathbb{S},\mathbb{C} \vdash \texttt{let}^\rho\ v : \tau = e \texttt{ in } e' : \theta', \mathbb{S}'' \backslash \beta^\rho}$$

$$(6)\ \frac{\begin{array}{l}\mathbb{E}(v) = \beta \quad \mathbb{S}(\beta) = \theta\\ \phi_{nil} = \bigvee_{(\pi_j,\phi_j)\in\theta}((\pi_j = NIL) \wedge \phi_j)\\ \mathbb{E},\mathbb{S},\mathbb{C} \vdash e_1 : \mathbb{S}_1 \quad \mathbb{E},\mathbb{S},\mathbb{C} \vdash e_2 : \mathbb{S}_2\\ \mathbb{S}' = (\mathbb{S}_1 \wedge \neg\phi_{nil}) \sqcup (\mathbb{S}_2 \wedge \phi_{nil})\end{array}}{\mathbb{E},\mathbb{S},\mathbb{C} \vdash \texttt{if } v \neq \texttt{nil then } e_1 \texttt{ else } e_2 : \mathbb{S}'}$$

Figure 5. Transformers not Directly Related to Containers

quantifier elimination procedure be exact since our technique uses bracketing constraints. In particular, since quantifier elimination in the theory of uninterpreted functions is not always exact, we may use quantifier-free over- and underapproximations [2].

EXAMPLE 1. *Consider the abstract value set*

$$\theta = \left\{ \begin{array}{l} (0, \langle 0 \leq i \leq 10, \text{false}\rangle), (1, \langle 0 \leq i \leq 10, \text{false}\rangle), \\ (\text{NIL}, \langle i > 10, i > 10\rangle) \end{array} \right\}$$

associated with container $\langle\alpha\rangle_i$. *To determine the possible values of those elements whose indices in the container are in the range* $[0, 2]$, *we compute:*

$$\theta \bowtie (0 \leq i \leq 2) = \{(0, \langle\text{true}, \text{false}\rangle), (1, \langle\text{true}, \text{false}\rangle)\}$$

The resulting set encodes that the possible values of elements in the range $[0, 2]$ *are either* 0 *or* 1, *but definitely not* NIL.

3.3 The Analysis

We describe the analysis as deductive rules of the form:

$$\mathbb{E}, \mathbb{S}, \mathbb{C} \vdash e : \theta, \mathbb{S}'$$

where $\mathbb{E}, \mathbb{S}$, and $\mathbb{C}$ are the abstract counterparts of the E, S, C environments used in the concrete semantics. In particular, the *abstract environment* $\mathbb{E}$ maps program variables to basic locations β^ρ, the *abstract store* $\mathbb{S}$ maps abstract memory locations δ to abstract value sets θ, and, finally, the counter vector $\mathbb{C}$ (a vector of integers) is used for distinguishing different loop iterations.

We present the analysis in three steps: First, we discuss the basic transformers not directly related to containers (Figure 5), then we describe the abstract semantics for reading from, writing to, and allocating containers (Figure 6), and, finally, we give the abstract semantics of the `foreach` construct (Figure 7).

Most of the transformers presented in Figure 5 are straightforward; we only discuss rule (6) in detail. In this rule, ϕ_{nil} describes under what condition v is *NIL*. After independently analyzing the then and else branches, we obtain the resulting abstract store $\mathbb{S}'$ by conjoining $\mathbb{S}_1$ and $\mathbb{S}_2$ with $\neg\phi_{nil}$ and ϕ_{nil} respectively and then taking their union.

In this rule, we use the notation $\mathbb{S} \wedge \phi$ as shorthand for the operation that conjoins ϕ with every constraint in $\mathbb{S}$:

$$\forall\delta \in dom(\mathbb{S}).\ (\mathbb{S} \wedge \phi)(\delta) = \{(\pi_j, \phi_j \wedge \phi) \mid (\pi_j, \phi_j) \in \mathbb{S}(\delta)\}$$

Read from Position Dependent Container

$$\frac{\begin{array}{l}\mathbb{E}(v_1) = \beta_1 \ \mathbb{E}(v_2) = \beta_2\\ \mathbb{S}(\beta_1) = \theta_1 \ \mathbb{S}(\beta_2) = \theta_2\\ \theta = \{\mathbb{S}(\langle\alpha\rangle_{i_j}) \bowtie ((\theta_2 \Diamond i_j) \wedge \phi_j) \mid (\langle\alpha\rangle_{i_j}, \phi_j) \in \theta_1)\}\end{array}}{\mathbb{E},\mathbb{S},\mathbb{C} \vdash v_1\texttt{.read}(v_2) : \theta, \mathbb{S}}$$

Read from Value Dependent Container

$$\frac{\begin{array}{l}\mathbb{E}(v_1) = \beta_1 \ \mathbb{E}(v_2) = \beta_2\\ \mathbb{S}(\beta_1) = \theta_1 \ \mathbb{S}(\beta_2) = \theta_2\\ \theta = \{\mathbb{S}(\langle\alpha\rangle_{i_j}) \bowtie ((\theta_2 \clubsuit i_j) \wedge \phi_j) \mid (\langle\alpha\rangle_{i_j}, \phi_j) \in \theta_1)\}\end{array}}{\mathbb{E},\mathbb{S},\mathbb{C} \vdash v_1\texttt{.read}(v_2) : \theta, \mathbb{S}}$$

Newval

$$\frac{\begin{array}{l}\theta'_w = \{(\pi_j, \phi_w \wedge \phi_j) \mid (\pi_j, \phi_j) \in \theta_w\}\\ \theta_p = \{(\pi_k, \neg\phi_w \wedge \phi_k) \mid (\pi_k, \phi_k) \in \mathbb{S}(\langle\alpha\rangle_i)\}\end{array}}{\mathbb{S} \vdash newval(\langle\alpha\rangle_i, \theta_w, \phi_w) : \theta'_w \cup \theta_p}$$

Update

$$\frac{\begin{array}{l}\theta_c = \{(\langle\alpha\rangle_{i_1}, \phi_1), \ldots, (\langle\alpha\rangle_{i_k}, \phi_k)\}\\ \mathbb{S} \vdash newval(\langle\alpha\rangle_{i_1}, \theta_{val}, (\theta_{key} \otimes i_1) \wedge \phi_1) : \theta_1\\ \ldots\\ \mathbb{S} \vdash newval(\langle\alpha\rangle_{i_k}, \theta_{val}, (\theta_{key} \otimes i_k) \wedge \phi_k) : \theta_k\\ \mathbb{S}' = \mathbb{S}[\langle\alpha\rangle_{i_1} \leftarrow \theta_1, \ldots, \langle\alpha\rangle_{i_k} \leftarrow \theta_k]\end{array}}{\mathbb{S} \vdash update(\theta_c, \theta_{key}, \theta_{val}) \textit{ with } \otimes : \mathbb{S}'} (\otimes \in \{\Diamond, \clubsuit\})$$

Write to Value Dependent Container

$$\frac{\begin{array}{l}\mathbb{E}(v_1) = \beta_1 \ \mathbb{E}(v_2) = \beta_2 \ \mathbb{E}(v_3) = \beta_3\\ \mathbb{S}(\beta_1) = \theta_1 \ \mathbb{S}(\beta_2) = \theta_2 \ \mathbb{S}(\beta_3) = \theta_3\\ \mathbb{S} \vdash update(\theta_1, \theta_2, \theta_3) \textit{ with } \clubsuit : \mathbb{S}'\end{array}}{\mathbb{E},\mathbb{S},\mathbb{C} \vdash v_1\texttt{.write}(v_2, v_3) : \{(NIL, true)\}, \mathbb{S}'}$$

Write to Position Dependent Container

$$\frac{\begin{array}{l}\mathbb{E}(v_1) = \beta_1 \ \mathbb{E}(v_2) = \beta_2 \ \mathbb{E}(v_3) = \beta_3\\ \mathbb{S}(\beta_1) = \theta_1 \ \mathbb{S}(\beta_2) = \theta_2 \ \mathbb{S}(\beta_3) = \theta_3\\ \mathbb{S} \vdash update(\theta_1, \theta_2, \theta_3) \textit{ with } \Diamond : \mathbb{S}'\end{array}}{\mathbb{E},\mathbb{S},\mathbb{C} \vdash v_1\texttt{.write}(v_2, v_3) : \{(NIL, true)\}, \mathbb{S}'}$$

Container Allocation

$$\frac{\begin{array}{l}\alpha = \eta_\rho\{\vec{i^\rho}\}, \ \vec{i^\rho} = [i_1^\rho, \ldots, i_n^\rho] \textit{ where } n = |\mathbb{C}|\\ \mathbb{S} \vdash newval(\langle\alpha\rangle_{i_0^\rho}, \{(NIL, true)\}, \vec{i^\rho} = \mathbb{C}) : \theta\end{array}}{\mathbb{E},\mathbb{S},\mathbb{C} \vdash \texttt{new}^\rho\ \tau : \{(\langle\alpha\rangle_{i_0^\rho}, \vec{i^\rho} = \mathbb{C})\}, \mathbb{S}[\langle\alpha\rangle_{i_0^\rho} \leftarrow \theta]}$$

Figure 6. Abstract Semantics for Container Operations

Rule (6) also uses a join operation on abstract stores defined as:

$$\begin{array}{c}\forall\delta \in (dom(\mathbb{S}_1) \cup dom(\mathbb{S}_2)).\ (\pi, \phi) \in (\mathbb{S}_1 \sqcup \mathbb{S}_2)(\delta) \Leftrightarrow\\ (\pi, \phi_1) \in \mathbb{S}_1(\delta) \wedge (\pi, \phi_2) \in \mathbb{S}_2(\delta) \wedge \phi = \phi_1 \vee \phi_2\end{array}$$

In this definition, we require that every abstract value π that is present in either $\mathbb{S}_1$ or $\mathbb{S}_2$ is also present in the other; if it is not explicitly there, we add it under constraint *false*.

3.3.1 Abstract Semantics for Container Operations

We now consider the abstract semantics for reading from containers, presented in Figure 6. In the first two rules of Figure 6, θ_2 represents the abstract value set for the key v_2, and each of the elements $\langle\alpha\rangle_{i_j}$ in abstract value set θ_1 are containers that the read operation may be performed on. We perform the key-to-index mapping using the $\Diamond$ operator for position-dependent containers and the $\clubsuit$ operator for value-dependent containers, as described in Section 3.2.1. In these rules, the constraints $((\theta_2 \Diamond i_j) \wedge \phi_j)$ and $((\theta_2 \clubsuit i_j) \wedge \phi_j)$

describe the positions in container $\langle\alpha\rangle_{i_j}$ from which we read the value. Finally, we perform the index-to-value mapping using the $\bowtie$ operation; the abstract value set θ describes all possible elements that may be obtained as a result of the read.

The now consider the rules in Figure 6 that describe the abstract semantics for writing to containers. The helper rule Newval computes the new abstract value set associated with container $\langle\alpha\rangle_i$ after writing θ_w at those indices of $\langle\alpha\rangle_i$ described by constraint ϕ_w. Since θ_w is written to only those locations that satisfy the index constraint ϕ_w, we conjoin ϕ_w with each element in θ_w to obtain θ'_w. Now, those elements in container $\langle\alpha\rangle_i$ that do not satisfy the index constraint ϕ_w are not modified by the write; hence the existing values $\mathbb{S}(\langle\alpha\rangle_i)$ are preserved under condition $\neg\phi_w$. Thus, θ_p represents all values in $\langle\alpha\rangle_i$ that are not affected by the write. Finally, the set of new values stored in container $\langle\alpha\rangle_i$ is obtained by taking the union of θ'_w (i.e.,the new value for the updated indices) and θ_p (i.e., values stored at all other indices).

The second helper rule, Update, uses Newval to compute the new abstract store after a write. In this rule, each element $\langle\alpha\rangle_{i_j}$ in θ_c represents a container that may be written to. The value set θ_{val} describes the possible values that may be written, and the constraint $((\theta_{key} \otimes i_j) \wedge \phi_j)$ (where $\otimes$ is either $\clubsuit$ or $\diamondsuit$) describes those indices of $\langle\alpha\rangle_{i_j}$ that are modified. For each container $\langle\alpha\rangle_{i_j}$ in θ_c, the Newval rule is invoked to compute the new value set θ_j after the write, and a new store $\mathbb{S}'$ is obtained by binding each $\langle\alpha\rangle_{i_j}$ to its new value set θ_j. The write rules for position- and value-dependent containers use the Update rule to compute the new abstract store after the write. As expected, the rule for position-dependent containers uses the $\diamondsuit$ operator while the rule for value-dependent containters uses $\clubsuit$. [1]

The last rule in Figure 6 describes the abstract semantics for container allocations. The abstract location arising from the allocation is labeled with the expression identifier ρ to differentiate allocation sites, and the vector of index variables $\vec{i^\rho}$ differentiates allocations arising from the same syntactic expression in different loop iterations. Since the counter vector $\mathbb{C}$ has as many entries as the loop nesting depth of the allocation expression, the number of variables in $\vec{i^\rho}$ is equal to the number of entries in $\mathbb{C}$. Observe that, in this rule, the constraint $\vec{i^\rho} = \mathbb{C}$ stipulates that each index variable in $\vec{i^\rho}$ is equal to the appropriate counter describing the iteration number of a loop. Finally, recall that the concrete semantics initializes the entries in a freshly allocated container to `NIL`, hence, the Newval rule is invoked to compute the new value set associated with container $\langle\alpha\rangle_{i^\rho_0}$ after initializing its elements to *NIL*.

EXAMPLE 2. *Consider the simple program:*

```
1: let^a v: val_adt(Int) = new^b val_adt(Int) in
2:   v.write(4, 87),
3:     let x = v.read(4) in
4:       let y = v.read(3) in nil
```

Assume $\mathbb{E}(\text{v}) = \beta^a$. *The abstract store after line 1 is given by:*

$$\mathbb{S} : [\beta^a \rightarrow \{(\langle\eta_b\rangle_i, \text{true})\}, \quad \langle\eta_b\rangle_i \rightarrow \{(\text{NIL}, \text{true})\}]$$

Here, η_b does not have any index variables because the allocation expression is not in a loop; the index variable i in $\langle\eta_b\rangle_i$ ranges over indices of the container. After the write at line 2, we have:

$$\mathbb{S} : \begin{bmatrix} \beta^a & \rightarrow & \{(\langle\eta_b\rangle_i, \text{true})\}, \\ \langle\eta_b\rangle_i & \rightarrow & \{(87, i = \text{pos}(4)), (\text{NIL}, i \neq \text{pos}(4))\} \end{bmatrix}$$

At line 3, the abstract value set for x *is:*

$$\begin{array}{rcl} \mathbb{S}(\langle\eta_b\rangle_i) \bowtie (i \clubsuit 4) & = & \mathbb{S}(\langle\eta_b\rangle_i) \bowtie (i = \text{pos}(4)) \\ & = & \{(87, \text{true})\} \end{array}$$

Similarly, at line 4 the abstract value set for y *is:*

$$\mathbb{S}(\langle\eta_b\rangle_i) \bowtie (i \clubsuit 3) \quad = \quad \{(\text{NIL}, \text{truc})\}$$

[1] Recall that the operational semantics are undefined if position-dependent containers are not used contiguously. Since checking this correct usage condition is an orthogonal problem to reasoning about container contents, the abstract semantics reason only about programs for which the operational semantics do not get "stuck".

Key, value pair at kth Iteration for pos_adt

$$\frac{\begin{array}{l} \mathbb{E}(v) = \beta \quad \mathbb{S}(\beta) = \theta_c \\ \theta_v = \{\mathbb{S}(\langle\alpha\rangle_{i_j}) \bowtie (i_j = k \wedge \phi_j) \mid (\langle\alpha\rangle_{i_j}, \phi_j) \in \theta_c\} \\ \theta_{k\times v} = \{((k, \pi_v), \phi_v) \mid \ (\pi_v, \phi_v) \in \theta_v \wedge \pi_v \neq \mathit{NIL}) \ \} \end{array}}{\vdash \mathit{elem}^\rho(v)@k : \theta_{k\times v}}$$

Key, value pair at kth Iteration for val_adt

$$\frac{\begin{array}{l} \mathbb{E}(v) = \beta \quad \mathbb{S}(\beta) = \theta_c \\ \theta_v = \{\mathbb{S}(\langle\alpha\rangle_{i_j}) \bowtie (i_j = k \wedge \phi_j) \mid (\langle\alpha\rangle_{i_j}, \phi_j) \in \theta_c\} \\ \theta_{k\times v} = \left\{ ((\pi_k, \pi_v), \phi_{kv}) \;\middle|\; \begin{array}{l} (\pi_v, \phi_v) \in \theta_v \wedge \pi_v \neq \mathit{NIL} \\ \wedge\, \phi_k = ((\mathit{pos}(\pi_k) = k) \\ \wedge\, (\phi_{kv} = (\phi_k \wedge \phi_v)[\mathit{pos}^\rho/\mathit{pos}]) \\ \wedge\, \mathit{SAT}(\phi_{kv}) \end{array} \right\} \end{array}}{\vdash \mathit{elem}^\rho(v)@k : \theta_{k\times v}}$$

Foreach

$$\frac{\begin{array}{l} \vdash \mathit{elem}^{\rho_0}(v)@k^{\rho_0} : \theta_{kv} \\ \theta_{key} = \{(\pi_{key}, \phi) \mid ((\pi_{key}, \pi_{val}), \phi) \in \theta_{kv}\} \\ \theta_{val} = \{(\pi_{val}, \phi) \mid ((\pi_{key}, \pi_{val}), \phi) \in \theta_{kv}\} \\ \mathbb{E}' = \mathbb{E}[v_1 \leftarrow \beta^{\rho_1}, v_2 \leftarrow \beta^{\rho_2}] \qquad \mathbb{S}' = \mathbb{S}[\beta^{\rho_1} \leftarrow \theta_{key}, \beta_2^{\rho_2} \leftarrow \theta_{val}] \\ \mathbb{E}', \mathbb{S}', (0{::}\mathbb{C}) \vdash \mathit{fix}\,(e, k^\rho) : \mathbb{S}'' \quad \theta = \{(\mathit{NIL}, \mathit{true})\} \end{array}}{\mathbb{E}, \mathbb{S}, \mathbb{C} \vdash \texttt{foreach}^{\rho_0}(v_1^{\rho_1}, v_2^{\rho_1})\ \texttt{in}\ v\ \texttt{do}\ e\ \texttt{od} : \theta, \mathbb{S}''\backslash\{\beta^{\rho_1}, \beta^{\rho_2}\}}$$

Fix

$$\frac{\begin{array}{l} \mathbb{E}, \mathbb{S}[c/k], (c{::}\mathbb{C}) \vdash e : \theta, \mathbb{S}', \quad \mathbb{S}' \sqsubseteq \mathbb{S}^* \\ \mathbb{E}, \mathbb{S}^*, ((c+1){::}\mathbb{C}) \vdash \mathit{fix}\,(e, k) : \mathbb{S}^* \end{array}}{\mathbb{E}, \mathbb{S}, (c{::}\mathbb{C}) \vdash \mathit{fix}\,(e, k) : \mathbb{S}^*}$$

Figure 7. Abstract Semantics for Iterating over Containers

3.3.2 Abstract Semantics for Iteration

The main idea behind the abstract semantics for iterating over containers is that *the j'th iteration of the loop accesses the key and value pairs stored at the j'th index* of the container. It is easy to see that this strategy is correct for position-dependent containers because (i) the concrete semantics requires an element with key j to be accessed during the j'th iteration and (ii) in our abstraction, the key-to-index mapping for position-dependent containers is the identity function. For value-dependent containers, recall that the operational semantics stipulates an arbitrary iteration order. Now, although the abstraction models iteration by visiting the element at the j'th index during the j'th iteration, it does not impose any restrictions on which key may be visited during the j'th iteration because the key-to-index mapping is an uninterpreted function (the constraint $j = \mathit{pos}(k)$ is satisfiable for any value of j and any key k). Furthermore, since *pos* is an invertible function, the abstraction encodes that for each different value of j, there is a different key k, indicating that no key may be visited multiple times.

Figure 7 gives the abstract semantics of the `foreach` construct. The first two rules compute the set of (key, value) pairs that may be visited during an arbitrary k'th iteration of the loop for position- and value-dependent containers respectively. Since the abstract semantics models iteration as visiting the k'th index during the k'th iteration, we retrieve the values stored in container $\langle\alpha\rangle_{i_j}$ under the index constraint $i_j = k$. Therefore, in the first two rules, the abstract value set θ_v describes the values that may be stored at index k. For position-dependent containers, the key during the k'th iteration of the loop is bound to k, as required by the operational semantics. In the first rule, we construct the set of possible key, value pairs for the k'th iteration as the set of all (k, π_v) such that π_v is non-nil and in θ_v. Observe that the (key, value) pairs in $\theta_{k\times v}$ respect the relationship between keys (i.e., positions) and values, as illustrated by the following example:

EXAMPLE 3. *Consider a position-dependent container $\langle\alpha\rangle_i$ such that $\mathbb{S}(\langle\alpha\rangle_i) = \{(44, i = 0), (3, i = 1), (\text{NIL}, i \geq 2)\}$. We compute the set of (key, value) pairs during the k'th iteration as:*

$$\theta_{k\times v} = \{((k, 44), k = 0), ((k, 3), k = 1)\}$$

Observe that the abstraction respects the relationship between positions and values; for example, the pair (1, 44) is infeasible.

The second rule in Figure 7 computes the (key, value) pairs during the k'th iteration for value-dependent containers. In this rule, the key during the k'th iteration is bound to all integers π_k such that $k = pos(\pi_k)$, as stipulated by constraint ϕ_k.[2] As in the position-dependent case, the relationship between keys and values are preserved because the rule filters out infeasible (key, value) pairs by checking the satisfiability of ϕ_{kv}. Finally, observe that the *pos* function is renamed to pos^ρ because elements may be visited in a different order in each loop.

The `foreach` rule first invokes the appropriate helper *elem* rule for computing the set of (key, value) pairs during an arbitrary k^{ρ_0}'th iteration. (The variable k is superscripted with the expression identifier ρ_0 for this loop in order to avoid naming conflicts.) The set θ_{kv} therefore describes the set of possible (key, value) pairs during an arbitrary iteration. The abstract value sets θ_{key} and θ_{val} are obtained by selecting the keys and the values from θ_{kv} respectively. The abstract environment $\mathbb{E}'$ binds variables v_1, v_2 to fresh locations β^{ρ_1} and β^{ρ_2}, and the abstract store $\mathbb{S}'$ binds β^{ρ_1} and β^{ρ_2} to θ_{key} and θ_{val}, since the operational semantics requires the (key, value) pairs to be computed before executing the body of the `foreach` construct. The `foreach` rule uses the helper *fix* rule to obtain the final store $\mathbb{S}''$.

In the *fix* (e, k) rule, c represents the current iteration number of the loop. Since the bindings for v_1 and v_2 are parametric on variable k, the rule replaces occurrences of k in $\mathbb{S}$ with concrete value c when evaluating the loop body e. In this rule, $\mathbb{S}^*$ is a sound store describing the cumulative effect of the loop, as $\mathbb{S}^*$ overapproximates the store after any loop iteration. Here, an abstract store $\mathbb{S}'$ overapproximates another abstract store $\mathbb{S}$, written $\mathbb{S} \sqsubseteq \mathbb{S}'$ according to Definition 5:

DEFINITION 4. (**Domain Extension** $\mathbb{S}_{\mapsto\mathbb{S}'}$) *An abstract store $S'' = \mathbb{S}_{\mapsto\mathbb{S}'}$ is a domain extention of $\mathbb{S}$ with respect to $\mathbb{S}'$ if the following condition holds: Let δ be any binding in $\mathbb{S}'$ and let (π_i, ϕ_i) be any element of $\mathbb{S}'(\delta)$.*

1. *If $\delta \in \mathbb{S} \wedge (\pi_i, \phi_i') \in \mathbb{S}(\delta)$, then $\delta \in \mathbb{S}_{\mapsto\mathbb{S}'} \wedge (\pi_i, \phi_i') \in \mathbb{S}_{\mapsto\mathbb{S}'}(\delta)$*
2. *Otherwise, $\delta \in \mathbb{S}_{\mapsto\mathbb{S}'} \wedge (\pi_i, \text{false}) \in \mathbb{S}_{\mapsto\mathbb{S}'}(\delta)$*

DEFINITION 5. (**Abstract Store Overapproximation** $\mathbb{S} \sqsubseteq \mathbb{S}'$) *Let $\mathbb{S}_1$ be the domain extension $\mathbb{S}_{\mapsto\mathbb{S}'}$, and let $\mathbb{S}_2$ be the domain extension $\mathbb{S}'_{\mapsto\mathbb{S}}$. Then, $\mathbb{S} \sqsubseteq \mathbb{S}'$ if for all $\delta \in \mathbb{S}_1$ and for all π_i such that $(\pi_i, \langle\varphi_{\text{may}}, \varphi_{\text{must}}\rangle) \in \mathbb{S}_1(\delta)$ and $(\pi_i, \langle\varphi'_{\text{may}}, \varphi'_{\text{must}}\rangle) \in \mathbb{S}_2(\delta)$:*

$$\varphi_{\text{may}} \Rightarrow \varphi'_{\text{may}} \quad \wedge \quad \varphi'_{\text{must}} \Rightarrow \varphi_{\text{must}}$$

According to this definition, a store $\mathbb{S}'$ overapproximates another abstract store $\mathbb{S}$ if, when they are extended to the same domain, any may constraint in $\mathbb{S}$ implies the corresponding may constraint in $\mathbb{S}'$, and any must constraint in $\mathbb{S}$ is implied by the corresponding must constraint in $\mathbb{S}'$. In other words, the overapproximation encoded in $\mathbb{S}'$ through the may constraints is *more* permissive than $\mathbb{S}$, and the underapproximation encoded by $\mathbb{S}'$ through the must constraints is *less* permissive than $\mathbb{S}$.

In the *fix* rule, it is easy to see that a trivial invariant store $\mathbb{S}^*$ always exists since the analysis creates a finite number of abstract locations for any given program, and an abstract store $\mathbb{S}_{triv}$ with constraint $\langle true, false\rangle$ mapping each possible abstract location to any other abstract location has the property $\forall\mathbb{S}.\ \mathbb{S} \sqsubseteq \mathbb{S}_{triv}$. To find a more useful invariant store than the trivial $\mathbb{S}_{triv}$, it is necessary to infer numeric invariants relating index variables associated with different containers or allocation sites. Since the focus of this paper is not invariant generation, we do not go into the details of how to find a "good" invariant store; various techniques based on abstract interpretation [3, 4] and quantifier elimination [1, 5] can be used for finding invariants. In particular, our previous work on array analysis [1] presents an algorithmic way of finding such invariants in this domain, and we use the algorithm from [1] in our implementation.

3.3.3 An Example Illustrating Key Features of the Analysis

In this section, we consider a small, but realistic, example illustrating some important features of the analysis. Consider the following program fragment:

```
1: let^a paper_scores: val_adt(pos_adt(Int)) =
2:    new^b val_adt(pos_adt(Int)) in
3:      foreach^c (pos, cur_paper) in papers
4:      do
5:        let^d scores: pos_adt(Int) = new^e pos_adt(Int) in
6:          paper_scores.write(cur_paper, scores)
7:      od;
8: let^f reviewed_paper = paper_scores.read(45) in
9:   if(reviewed_paper != nil)
10:     then reviewed_paper.write(0, 5) else nil
```

In this program fragment, `papers` is a position-dependent container whose elements are identifiers for all submitted papers to a conference. The code above creates a new value-dependent container `paper_scores` that maintains a mapping from each paper identifier to a list of scores associated with this paper. The code iterates over `papers` and, for each paper, allocates a new position-dependent container, `scores`, and inserts the (key, value) pair, `(cur_paper, scores)` into the map.

For simplicity, let us assume this particular conference was unpopular this year and had only 3 submissions with identifiers 21, 45, and 32, which are placed in `papers` in this order. Let us also assume that $\mathbb{E}(\texttt{papers})$ is β^p and $\mathbb{S}(\beta^p) = \{(\langle\eta_p\rangle_{i_1}, true)\}$. After the allocation at line 5 during some arbitrary k'th iteration of the loop, the abstract environment and stores are:

$$\mathbb{E}(\texttt{papers}) = \beta^p \;\; \mathbb{E}(\texttt{paper\_scores}) = \beta^a$$
$$\mathbb{E}(\texttt{scores}) = \beta^d \;\; \mathbb{E}(\texttt{cur\_paper}) = \beta^c$$

[2] Observe that the set of all possible π_k's is finite for any given program in our language; hence candidates for π_k are drawn from a finite set.

$$\begin{array}{lcl}
\mathbb{S}(\beta^p) & = & \{(\langle \eta_p \rangle_{i_1}, \mathit{true})\} \\
\mathbb{S}(\beta^a) & = & \{(\langle \eta_b \rangle_{i_2}, \mathit{true})\} \\
\mathbb{S}(\langle \eta_p \rangle_{i_1}) & = & \{(21, i_1 = 0), (45, i_1 = 1), \\
 & & (32, i_1 = 2), (\mathit{NIL}, i_1 \geq 3)\} \\
\mathbb{S}(\beta^c) & = & \{(21, k = 0), (45, k = 1), (32, k = 2)\} \\
\mathbb{S}(\langle \eta_b \rangle_{i_2}) & = & \{(\mathit{NIL}, \mathit{true})\} \\
\mathbb{S}(\beta^d) & = & \{(\langle \eta_e\{i_3\} \rangle_{i_4}, i_3 = k)\} \\
\mathbb{S}(\langle \eta_e\{i_3\} \rangle_{i_4}) & = & \{(\mathit{NIL}, i_3 = k)\}
\end{array}$$

Consider the write at line 6, which uses `cur_paper` as the key and the freshly allocated container `scores` as the value. Here, the possible values of `cur_paper` during the k'th loop iteration are given by $\mathbb{S}(\beta^c)$ above, which encodes that the value of `cur_paper` is 21 during the first iteration ($k = 0$), 45 during the second iteration ($k = 1$), and 32 during the third iteration ($k = 2$). The abstract value set for the value `scores` is given by $\mathbb{S}(\beta^d) = \{(\langle \eta_e\{i_3\} \rangle_{i_4}, i_3 = k)\}$. Here, the freshly allocated container is represented by $\langle \eta_e\{i_3\} \rangle_{i_4}$, which has two index variables i_3 and i_4, where i_3 distinguishes allocations from different loop iterations and i_4 differentiates elements stored in the container. The constraint $i_3 = k$ in $\mathbb{S}(\beta^d)$ encodes that we are considering the allocation that happened during the k'th iteration. Hence, the set of all possible (key, value) pairs that are written at line 6 in any k'th iteration are:

$$\left\{ \begin{array}{l}
((21, \langle \eta_e\{i_3\} \rangle_{i_4}), i_3 = k \wedge k = 0), \\
((45, \langle \eta_e\{i_3\} \rangle_{i_4}), i_3 = k \wedge k = 1), \\
((32, \langle \eta_e\{i_3\} \rangle_{i_4}), i_3 = k \wedge k = 2)
\end{array} \right\}$$

Now, if we eliminate the dependence on a particular iteration k, we obtain the set of all possible (key, value) pairs that may be written during any iteration of the loop:

$$W = \left\{ \begin{array}{l}
((21, \langle \eta_e\{i_3\} \rangle_{i_4}), i_3 = 0), \\
((45, \langle \eta_e\{i_3\} \rangle_{i_4}), i_3 = 1), \\
((32, \langle \eta_e\{i_3\} \rangle_{i_4}), i_3 = 2)
\end{array} \right\}$$

Observe that, while all the allocations at line 5 are represented by a single abstract container $\langle \eta_e\{i_3\} \rangle_{i_4}$, the index constraints stipulate that the allocations associated with each key are distinct from each other, since the values of i_3 are different for the keys 21, 45, and 32. Now, to process the write at line 6, we use the *update* rule from Figure 6 for each entry in W with $\theta_c = \{(\langle \eta_b \rangle_{i_2}, \mathit{true})\}$ (the location associated with container `paper_scores`), the key, value sets $\theta_{key}, \theta_{val}$ given by each entry in W ($\theta_{key} = \{(21, \mathit{true})\}$, $\theta_{val} = \{(\langle \eta_e\{i_3\} \rangle_{i_4}), i_3 = 0)\}$ etc.), and using the index selector ♣ since `paper_scores` is value-dependent. This yields:

$$\mathbb{S}(\langle \eta_b \rangle_{i_2}) = \left\{ \begin{array}{ll}
(\langle \eta_e\{i_3\} \rangle_{i_4}, & ((i_3 = 0 \wedge i_2 = \mathit{pos}(21)) \vee \\
 & (i_3 = 1 \wedge i_2 = \mathit{pos}(45)) \vee \\
 & (i_3 = 2 \wedge i_2 = \mathit{pos}(32))), \\
 & \\
(\mathit{NIL}, & i_2 \neq \mathit{pos}(21) \wedge \\
 & i_2 \neq \mathit{pos}(45) \wedge i_2 \neq \mathit{pos}(32))
\end{array} \right\}$$

The new abstract value set $\mathbb{S}(\langle \eta_b \rangle_{i_2})$ expresses that all containers stored in `paper_scores` are unique because the value of i_3 is different for each key. Now, let us consider lines 8-10 in the program fragment. To determine the result of the read at line 8, we compute:

$$\left\{ \begin{array}{ll}
(\langle \eta_e\{i_3\} \rangle_{i_4}, & ((i_3 = 0 \wedge i_2 = \mathit{pos}(21)) \vee \\
 & (i_3 = 1 \wedge i_2 = \mathit{pos}(45)) \vee \\
 & (i_3 = 2 \wedge i_2 = \mathit{pos}(32))), \\
 & \\
(\mathit{NIL}, & i_2 \neq \mathit{pos}(21) \wedge \\
 & i_2 \neq \mathit{pos}(45) \wedge i_2 \neq \mathit{pos}(32))
\end{array} \right\} \bowtie (i_2 = \mathit{pos}(45))$$

which, when simplified, yields $\{(\langle \eta_e\{i_3\} \rangle_{i_4}, i_3 = 1)\}$. Hence, if $\mathbb{S}(\texttt{reviewed\_paper}) = \beta^f$, then:

$$\mathbb{S}(\beta_f) = \{(\langle \eta_e\{i_3\} \rangle_{i_4}, i_3 = 1)\}$$

For the `if` expression at line 9, only the then branch is satisfiable since $\langle \eta_e\{i_3\} \rangle_{i_4}$ is not *NIL*. Finally, after the write at line 11, the values for the nested containers are given by:

$$\mathbb{S}(\langle \eta_e\{i_3\} \rangle_{i_4}) = \{(5, i_4 = 0 \wedge i_3 = 1), (\mathit{NIL}, i_4 \neq 0 \vee i_3 \neq 1)\}$$

Hence, this abstract store encodes that only the score at position 0 of the scores list associated with key 45 in `paper_scores` has been changed to 5, but the score lists associated with all other keys are unchanged.

3.4 Soundness of the Abstraction

In order to state the soundness theorem, we first need to define an abstraction function from concrete to abstract memory locations. Observe that if $\vec{i}$ denotes a vector of index variables used in some abstract location δ and σ is a concrete assignment to each of the index variables in $\vec{i}$, then the pair (δ, σ) represents one concrete memory location. Therefore, the abstraction function is a mapping from concrete locations to a pair consisting of an abstract memory location δ and a full assignment σ to all index variables used in δ:

$$\textit{Abstraction function } \alpha = \textit{Concrete loc } (l, i) \rightarrow (\delta, \sigma)$$

To make this abstraction function precise, it is necessary to augment the operational semantics with some additional bookkeeping machinery that was omitted from Figure 4 to avoid complicating the language semantics. First, for each concrete location (l, i) in store S, we need to determine the program point ρ that results in the binding of (l, i) in S; we write $\mathit{id}(l, i)$ to denote the program point ρ associated with the introduction of (l, i). Second, to be able to give a full assignment to the index variables in an abstract location, we need to determine the counter vector C when a concrete location was introduced. Hence, we assume an environment A maps each concrete location (l, i) to the counter vector C present when (l, i) was introduced in concrete store S. Since it is trivial to extend the operational semantics from Figure 4 to track $\mathit{id}(l, i)$ and $A(l, i)$, we assume this additional bookkeeping information is available. We can now define the abstraction function as follows:

DEFINITION 6. **(Abstraction Function)** *Let (l, k) be a concrete memory location, and let* $\mathrm{id}(l, k) = \rho$ *such that ρ labels expression e^ρ, and $A(l, k) = C$. Then, the abstraction of (l, k), written $\alpha(l, k)$, is:*

1. $(\langle \eta_\rho\{\vec{i_\rho}\} \rangle_{i_0^\rho}, \vec{i_\rho} = C \wedge i_0^\rho = k)$ if $e^\rho = \texttt{new}^\rho$ `pos_adt` τ
2. $(\langle \eta_\rho\{\vec{i_\rho}\} \rangle_{i_0^\rho}, \vec{i_\rho} = C \wedge i_0^\rho = \mathrm{pos}(k))$ if $e^\rho = \texttt{new}^\rho$ `val_adt` τ
3. $(\beta^\rho, \mathrm{true})$ otherwise

We extend this abstraction function from all concrete values v to all abstract values π in the following obvious way:

$$\alpha(v) = \left\{ \begin{array}{ll}
(\mathit{NIL}, \mathit{true}) & \mathit{if}\ v = \texttt{NIL} \\
(c, \mathit{true}) & \mathit{if}\ v\ \mathit{is\ integer\ constant}\ c \\
\alpha(l, k) & \mathit{if}\ v\ \mathit{is\ a\ memory\ location}(l, k)
\end{array} \right.$$

We write $\sigma(\phi)$ to denote the result of substituting each of the variables in ϕ with their concrete assignment specified by σ. In addition, we assume the substitution $\sigma(\phi)$ gives an interpretation to all function symbols pos^ρ in ϕ by replacing pos^ρ with the particular permutation it stands for in a given execution. Since it is trivial to extend the operational semantics to track which permutation was used for which loop, we assume this information is available.

DEFINITION 7. **(Value Agreement)** *Let v be a concrete value with $\alpha(v) = (\pi, \sigma)$, and let θ be an abstract value set. We say concrete value v agrees with abstract value set θ, written $v \sim \theta$, if:*

1. $(\pi, \langle \varphi_{\mathrm{may}}, \varphi_{\mathrm{must}} \rangle) \in \theta \wedge \mathrm{VALID}(\sigma(\varphi_{\mathrm{may}}))$
2. $\forall (\pi', \langle \varphi'_{\mathrm{may}}, \varphi'_{\mathrm{must}} \rangle) \in \theta.\ \mathrm{UNSAT}(\sigma(\varphi'_{\mathrm{must}}))\ \ (\pi' \neq \pi)$

In this definition, the first condition states the correctness of the overapproximation encoded by θ, and the second condition states the correctness of the underapproximation. If the abstract representation of v is (π, σ), then, for the overapproximation to be correct, π must be in θ under some constraint $\langle \varphi_{may}, \varphi_{must} \rangle$ and the may constraint φ_{may} must evaluate to *true* under the index assignment σ. (Recall that since the language from Section 2 has no inputs, the only variables in constraints are index variables; thus, φ_{may} always evaluates to a constant under σ.) The second condition of value agreement states the correctness of the underapproximation, requiring at most the abstract representation of v to be in θ, i.e., all other elements in θ should be infeasible under index assignment σ.

DEFINITION 8. **(State Agreement)** Let (v, E, S, C) be a *concrete state*, consisting of a concrete value v, concrete environment E, concrete store S and counter vector C, and let $(\theta, \mathbb{E}, \mathbb{S}, \mathbb{C})$ be an *abstract state* with abstract value set θ and abstract environment and store $\mathbb{E}, \mathbb{S}$ and counter vector $\mathbb{C}$. We say concrete state (v, E, S, C) agrees with abstract state $(\theta, \mathbb{E}, \mathbb{S}, \mathbb{C})$, written $(v, E, S, C) \sim (\theta, \mathbb{E}, \mathbb{S}, \mathbb{C})$, if the following conditions hold:

1. $v \sim \theta$ (according to Definition 7)
2. $\forall v \in dom(E).\ (v \in dom(\mathbb{E}) \wedge \mathbb{E}(v) = \alpha(E(v), 0))$
3. $\forall (l, k) \in dom(S).\ S(l, k) = l' \Rightarrow (\alpha(l, k) = (\delta, \sigma) \wedge l' \sim (\mathbb{S}(\delta) \bowtie \sigma))$
4. $\mathbb{C} = C$

THEOREM 1. **(Soundness)** Let P be any program. If $(E, S, C) \sim (\mathbb{E}, \mathbb{S}, \mathbb{C})$, then

$$E, S, C \vdash P : l, S' \\ \Rightarrow \\ \mathbb{E}, \mathbb{S}, \mathbb{C} \vdash P : \theta, \mathbb{S}' \wedge (l, E, S', C) \sim (\theta, \mathbb{E}, \mathbb{S}', \mathbb{C})$$

The proof is given in the appendix.

4. Extensions

The language we have used for the formal development requires keys of value-dependent containers to be integers, but, in real languages, keys may have arbitrary types. The techniques we have described so far are directly applicable when pointer values are used as keys because pointer equality is a form of integer equality. However, it is common to define custom equality predicates on some types, and determining whether two keys are equal may be more involved than simple integer equality. Consider the following C++ code snippet:

```
class Point {
  int x; int y; color c;
  Point(int x, int y, color c){
    this->x=x; this->y=y; this->c=c;
  };
  bool operator==(const Point & other) {
    return x == other.x && y == other.y;
  }
}
unordered_set<Point> points;
Point p1 = Point(5, 34, RED);  points.insert(p1);
Point p2 = Point(5, 34, BLUE); points.insert(p2);
```

Here, the type `Point` defines a custom equality operator that only checks the x and y coordinates for a point but disregards its color. In the above program, after the last insertion operation, there is only one element in the set even though two points with different colors are inserted. If we treat `p1` and `p2` as variables in the constraint language, our technique would conclude that the size of the set is 2 under constraint $p2 \neq p1$ and 1 under $p2 = p1$. To be more precise in the presence of custom equality predicates, we infer axioms characterizing when two objects are equal. Specifically, by analyzing the implementations of the custom equality predicates, we infer necessary and sufficient conditions $\langle \varphi^{=}_{may}, \varphi^{=}_{must} \rangle$ characterizing when two objects o_1 and o_2 may and must be equal. (Observe that treating `p1` and `p2` as variables in the constraint language as above is equivalent to the trivial and always sound equality condition $\langle true, false \rangle$). Now, in order to take into account what we know about the custom equality predicate, we add the axioms $\forall o_1, o_2.\ o_1 = o_2 \Rightarrow \varphi^{=}_{may}$ and $\forall o_1, o_2.\ \varphi^{=}_{must} \Rightarrow o_1 = o_2$ to the constraint solver. For instance, for the simple equality predicate for `Point`, we could utilize the axiom $\forall p_1, p_2.\ p_1 = p_2 \Leftrightarrow (p_1.x = p_2.x \wedge p_1.y = p_2.y)$, allowing the technique to conclude that the size of the set after the second insertion is 1.

In the technical development, we also assumed that the iteration order over value-dependent containers is arbitrary. While this is true in most cases, some value-dependent containers (such as a red-black-tree based map) may visit keys in a certain order during an iteration. We can encode such restrictions in the iteration order by analyzing the custom less than operators and inferring appropriate axioms about the *pos* function in a similar way as above.

5. Implementation

We have implemented the ideas presented in this paper in our Compass program verification framework for analyzing C and C++ programs. Compass utilizes a gcc and g++ based front-end called SAIL [6] which translates C and C++ code to a low-level representation, similar to 3-address code. Compass uses the Mistral SMT solver [7, 8] for solving and simplifying constraints generated during the analysis. Compass supports most features of C++, including classes, arrays, dynamic memory allocation, pointer arithmetic, references, single and multiple inheritance, and virtual method calls. Compass performs path-sensitive analysis and achieves context-sensitivity by computing polymorphic summaries of functions (and loops) and instantiates them in calling contexts [9].

6. Experimental Evaluation

To demonstrate the usefulness of the ideas presented in this paper, we evaluate the proposed technique in two different ways: In a first set of experiments, we perform a case study and prove the functional correctness of a set of small, but challenging programs manipulating containers. In a second set of experiments, we use this technique to prove memory safety properties of real C++ applications that heavily use containers, and we show that a precise understanding of data structure contents is beneficial in improving analysis results. For both sets of experiments, we annotated the containers provided by the C++ standard template library [10], either directly as position- or value-dependent containers or by nesting them inside already annotated STL containers.

6.1 Case Study

In our case study, we analyze fifteen small, but challenging, example programs totaling close to 1000 lines of code. All benchmarks are available at `http://www.stanford.edu/~tdillig/cont.txt`. The results of the case study are presented in Figure 8; we briefly discuss each of the programs from this table. The first two programs copy the contents of a vector and a map into another container of the same type and assert their element-wise equality. Program 3 builds the reverse map `r` of map `m` by inserting each (k, v) pair in `m` as the key-value pair (v, k) of `r`. Program 4 is modeled after the example in Section 1 and asserts the correctness of the entries in `exam_scores`. Program 5 inserts all the keys in a map `m` into a set `s` and asserts that `s` contains exactly the keys in `m`. Programs 6-8 illustrate nested containers by asserting properties about the composed data structures. Program 9 inserts numbers $[0, size)$ into a stack and a queue and asserts that the top of the stack is the last

	Program	Time	Memory
1	Vector copy	0.22s	<2 MB
2	Map copy	0.33s	<2 MB
3	Reverse mapping	0.14s	<2 MB
4	Example from Introduction	0.22s	<4 MB
5	Set containing map keys	0.62s	<2 MB
6	Map of lists	0.21s	<2 MB
7	Vector of sets	0.11s	<2 MB
8	Multimap	0.33s	<2 MB
9	Stack-queue relationship	0.19s	<2 MB
10	Singleton pattern correctness	0.23s	<5 MB
11	Prove map values non-null	0.30s	<2 MB
12	Prove non-aliasing between vector elements	0.31s	<2 MB
13	List containing key,value pairs of a map	1.14s	<2 MB
14	Set containing map keys with non-null values	0.44s	<2 MB
15	Relationship between keys and values in map	0.31s	<2 MB

Figure 8. Experimental Results of the Case Study

element in the queue. Program 10 emulates the singleton pattern through a `get_shared` method that uniquifies objects that are the same according to their custom equality predicate by using a set, and asserts the correctness of `get_shared`. Program 11 asserts that the values in a map are non-null, and Program 12 asserts that there is no aliasing between elements in a vector. Program 13 builds a list containing (key, value) pairs in a map and asserts that the list contains exactly the key, value pairs in the map. Program 14 builds a set containing all map keys with non-null values and asserts that the set contains exactly the keys with non-null values. Program 15 asserts various properties about the relationship between keys and values in a map. Compass is able to fully automatically verify all of these examples, while reporting errors in slightly modified, buggy versions of these programs. As shown in Figure 8, the running times for most of these examples are under a second and maximum memory consumption is consistently below 4 MB. We believe these examples illustrate that Compass can automatically verify interesting properties about the functional correctness of client programs using containers and their nestings.

6.2 Proving Memory Safety Properties

In a second set of experiments, we investigate the added benefits of precise reasoning about container contents when checking for memory safety properties in real C++ applications. Using Compass, we analyzed three applications ranging from 16,030 to 128,318 lines of C++ code: The first application is LiteSQL [11], which integrates C++ objects tightly with a database. The second application we analyzed is the widget library of the vector graphics program, Inkscape (which was used for the drawings in this submission) [12]. We chose this component of Inkscape because it illustrates how more complex abstract data types are implemented using standard containers as building blocks. The third application is Digikam, a stand-alone, fairly large, open-source photo management program [13].

Both LiteSQL and the Inkscape widget library use the C++ standard template library (STL), while Digikam uses container libraries of the QT framework [14]. Fortunately, since the containers in QT are interface-compatible with the ones in the STL, we were able to use the same set of container interface annotations for all three applications. As typical of many programs written in an object-oriented style, all of these applications make heavy use of containers, such as vectors, lists, maps, and their combinations.

To demonstrate the importance of precise, per-element reasoning about containers when checking for memory safety properties, we analyzed these applications in two different configurations: In the first configuration, we use the technique described in this paper, while in the second configuration, we track which set of elements a

LiteSQL 0.3.8		
Number of lines	16,030	
	Our technique	**Containers as sets**
Running time 1 CPU	4.5 min	5.8 min
Running time 8 CPUs	1.6 min	1.6 min
Maximum Memory	1.3 GB	1.5 GB
Null Dereference Errors		
Actual errors	2	2
False positives	2	68
Memory Leak Errors		
Actual errors	3	3
False positives	0	7
Access to Deleted Memory		
Actual errors	0	0
False positives	0	4
Total FP to error ratio	*0.75*	*15.8*

Inkscape 0.47 Widget Library		
Number of lines	37,211	
	Our technique	**Containers as sets**
Running time 1 CPU	7.2 min	6.1 min
Running time 8 CPUs	2.3 min	2.1 min
Maximum Memory	1.9 GB	1.8 GB
Null Dereference Errors		
Actual errors	1	1
False positives	0	24
Memory Leak Errors		
Actual errors	1	1
False positives	1	18
Access to Deleted Memory		
Actual errors	2	2
False positives	2	22
Total FP to error ratio	*0.75*	*16*

Digikam 1.2.0		
Number of lines	128,318	
	Our technique	**Containers as sets**
Running time 1 CPU	45.1 min	44.3 min
Running time 8 CPUs	8.7 min	10.3 min
Maximum Memory	12.0 GB	10.6 GB
Null Dereference Errors		
Actual errors	17	17
False positives	8	220
Memory Leak Errors		
Actual errors	8	8
False positives	1	45
Access to Deleted Memory		
Actual errors	3	3
False positives	0	6
Total FP to error ratio	*0.32*	*9.68*

Figure 9. Proving memory safety properties

container may store, but we do not reason about the relationship between positions and values for position-dependent containers, and we do not track the key-value relationships for value-dependent containers (i.e., we "smash" containers into a set of values).

Figure 9 summarizes the results of our experiments. For each of the three applications, we check the following memory safety properties: Null pointer dereferences, memory leaks (i.e., lack of unreachable memory), and accessing deleted memory. All of our experiments were performend on an 8-core 2.66 GHz Xeon workstation with 24GB of memory. In Figure 9, we provide the running times of the analyses both on a single core as well as on all eight cores. Since the analysis is summary-based, many functions can be analyzed in parallel to yield much better running times, ranging from 1.6 to 8.7 minutes on eight cores.

In Figure 9, observe that the technique presented in this paper improves the precision of the analysis over the second configuration which treats the container's contents as a set, in many cases by an order of magnitude. For example, the total false positive to error ratio for Digikam is 0.32 if the technique presented in this paper is used for the analysis, while this ratio increases to 9.68 with the second analysis configuration. This statistic means that there are roughly three actual error reports per false positive using our technique, while there is less than one actual error per nine false positives using the second, less precise configuration. We believe that this dramatic reduction in false positives illustrates the usefulness of our technique for analyzing real-world C++ applications.

Also, observe in Figure 9 that there are no significant differences in running time and memory consumption between the two analysis configurations. We believe that the statistics provided in Figure 9 illustrate that our technique adds useful precision without incurring significant extra computational resources.

7. Related Work

In this work, we share the goal of separating the verification of data structure implementations from the verification of their client-side use with the Hob verification framework [15–17]. Hob's main focus is to verify that the implementation of a data structure obeys its specification; on the client-side, Hob can be used to check that custom data structure invariants are obeyed by the client, such as the requirement that the data structure has no content before a certain method is called. While Hob addresses a more general class of abstract data structures than containers, the client-side abstraction of Hob is a *set abstraction* of data structures, which is less precise than the abstraction we consider. For instance, Hob's client-side reasoning about a map does not track the relationship between keys and values in a map or between positions and elements in a vector [17]. In contrast, we only consider the client-side use of a special, yet fundamental, class of data structures, and our focus is a fully automatic technique to improve analysis precision when analyzing real C++ programs that use containers.

Another work that addresses the client-side use of data structures is [18], which focuses on verifying that the client of a software component obeys the requirements of that component, such as the requirement that a data structure d is not modified during an iteration over d. Another work with a similar focus is [19], which uses predicate abstraction to verify that clients of the C++ standard template library (STL) obey the requirements for correct use of this library. Yet another work that is focused on usage of STL data structures is [20], which is an unsound bug finding tool for discovering incorrect usage of STL primitives. None of these efforts consider properties which require reasoning about the contents of containers, which is our focus. We believe that the problem of understanding container contents and the problem of verifying the correct usage of an ADT interface are orthogonal and complementary.

The idea of using numeric constraints to specify elements of unbounded data structures goes back to [21], which uses this idea for tracking may-alias pairs in lists. In our previous work on analysis of array contents, we use the combination of indexed locations and bracketing constraints to model arrays [1]. While this paper also uses some of the same underlying technical machinery as in [1], the contributions of this work include a formalization of the differences and similarities between different kinds of containers, and a precise and uniform analysis framework that both leverages what is the same and expresses what is different about containers.

In this paper, we observe that a key requirement for precise reasoning about nested containers is to differentiate between containers allocated in different loop iterations. The necessity to distinguish allocations arising from the same expression also arises in other contexts, such as static race detection in [22]. The technique described in [22] also uses a vector of loop counters to distinguish between distinct allocations.

The work described in [23] addresses the typestate verification problem for real-world Java programs, which make heavy use of containers. This work also reports on the challenge of achieving sufficient precision as objects flow in and out of containers; they utilize techniques such as *focus* and *blur*, developed by the shape analysis community based on 3-valued logic [24]. In contrast, our approach never performs explicit case splits on abstract containers and instead uses constraints to both specify different elements in the container as well as to perform updates on individual elements.

In this paper, we observe that differences among various position-dependent containers and different value-dependent containers are insignificant for developing a methodology for reasoning about their contents, although these differences may have significant performance implications. This paper does not address the problem of selecting efficient containers (which is considered in [25]) or estimating their computational complexity (addressed in [26]).

8. Conclusion

In this paper, we have presented a precise, scalable, and fully automatic technique for reasoning about contents of containers. We have demonstrated experimentally that precise client-side reasoning about containers is important for successful verification of memory safety properties in real C++ programs.

9. Acknowledgments

We would like to thank Roy Frostig for his help with extending our front-end for the C language to C++.

References

[1] Dillig, I., Dillig, T., Aiken, A.: Fluid Updates: Beyond Strong vs. Weak Updates. In: ESOP. (2010)

[2] Gulwani, S., Musuvathi, M.: Cover Algorithms. In: ESOP. (2008) 193–207

[3] Cousot, P., Halbwachs, N.: Automatic Discovery of Linear Restraints among Variables of a Program. In: POPL, ACM (1978) 84–96

[4] Karr, M.: Affine relationships among variables of a program. A.I. (1976) 133–151

[5] Kovacs, L., Voronkov, A.: Finding loop invariants for programs over arrays using a theorem prover. In: FASE 2009. (2009) 470–485

[6] Dillig, I., Dillig, T., Aiken, A.: SAIL: Static Analysis Intermediate Language. Stanford University Technical Report

[7] Dillig, I., Dillig, T., Aiken, A.: Cuts from Proofs: A Complete and Practical Technique for Solving Linear Inequalities over Integers. In: CAV. (2009)

[8] Dillig, I., Dillig, T., Aiken, A.: Small Formulas for Large Programs: On-line Constraint Simplification in Scalable Static Analysis. In: SAS. (2010)

[9] Dillig, I., Dillig, T., Aiken, A.: Sound, Complete and Scalable Path-sensitive Analysis. In: PLDI. (2008) 270–280

[10] http://www.sgi.com/tech/stl/: C++ standard template library

[11] http://sourceforge.net/apps/trac/litesql/: LiteSQL

[12] http://www.inkscape.org/: Inkscape

[13] http://www.digikam.org/: Digikam

[14] http://qt.nokia.com/products/: QT Framework

[15] Lam, P., Kuncak, V., Rinard, M.: Hob: A tool for verifying data structure consistency. In: Compiler Construction. 237–241

[16] Lam, P., Kuncak, V., Rinard, M.: Generalized Typestate Checking for Data Structure Consistency. In: VMCAI. (2005) 430–447

[17] Kuncak, V., Lam, P., Zee, K., Rinard, M.: Modular Pluggable Analyses for Data Structure Consistency. IEEE Transactions on Software Engineering **32**(12) (2006) 988–1005

[18] Ramalingam, G., Warshavsky, A., Field, J., Goyal, D., Sagiv, M.: Deriving Specialized Program Analyses for Certifying Component-client Conformance. In: PLDI. (2002) 94

[19] Blanc, N., Groce, A., Kroening, D.: Verifying C++ with STL Containers via Predicate Abstraction. In: IEEE/ACM Conference on Automated software engineering, ACM (2007) 521–524

[20] Gregor, D., Schupp, S.: STLlint: lifting static checking from languages to libraries. Software Practice and Experience **36**(3) (2006) 225

[21] Deutsch, A.: Interprocedural may-alias analysis for pointers: Beyond k-limiting. In: PLDI, ACM NY, USA (1994) 230–241

[22] Naik, M., Aiken, A.: Conditional Must not Aliasing for Static Race Detection. In: POPL. (2007) 338

[23] Fink, S., Yahav, E., Dor, N., Ramalingam, G., Geay, E.: Effective Typestate Verification in the Presence of Aliasing. TOSEM **17**(2) (2008) 1–34

[24] Reps, T.W., Sagiv, S., Wilhelm, R.: Static Program Analysis via 3-Valued Logic. In: CAV. (2004) 15–30

[25] Shacham, O., Vechev, M., Yahav, E.: Chameleon: Adaptive Selection of Collections. In: PLDI, ACM (2009) 408–418

[26] Gulwani, S., Mehra, K.K., Chilimbi, T.: Speed: Precise and efficient static estimation of program computational complexity. In: POPL. (2009) 127–139

[27] Gulwani, S., McCloskey, B., Tiwari, A.: Lifting abstract interpreters to quantified logical domains. In: POPL, ACM (2008) 235–246

Appendix: Proof of Soundness

In this section, we sketch the proof of soundness of the key rules from Section 3.3. The proof is a standard induction on the inference rules from Figures 5, 6, and 7. We only focus on the rules that involve containers.

A.1 Preliminaries

We first introduce some notation that is convenient to use in the proofs and state some assumptions.

DEFINITION 9. *($\sigma(\theta)$) Let θ be an abstract value set, and let σ be an assignment to (at least) the index variables in θ. Then:*

$$\sigma(\theta) = \{(\pi_j, \sigma(\phi_j) \mid (\pi_j, \phi_j) \in \theta \wedge \mathrm{SAT}(\sigma(\phi_j)\}$$

DEFINITION 10. *($\lceil\phi\rceil$, $\lfloor\phi\rfloor$) Let ϕ be the bracketing constraint $\langle\varphi_{\text{may}}, \varphi_{\text{must}}\rangle$. Then, $\lceil\phi\rceil = \varphi_{\text{may}}$ and $\lfloor\phi\rfloor = \varphi_{\text{must}}$.*

Throughout the proof, we assume that every abstract value π that can arise for a given program is present in every abstract value set θ; for values that have not been explicitly added to θ, we assume $(\pi, \mathit{false}) \in \theta$.

A.2 Proof of Key Rules

We first consider the read rule for position-dependent containers:

Let (l_c, k) denote the concrete location that the read is performed on (i.e, the result is obtained from $S(l_c, k)$). Let $\alpha(l_c, k) = (\delta, \sigma_c)$, and let $\alpha(S(l_c, k)) = (\pi, \sigma_\pi)$. In the rule, suppose:

$$\begin{array}{lcl} \theta_1 & = & \{\ldots, (\langle\alpha\rangle_{i_j}, \phi_j), \ldots\} \\ \theta_2 & = & \{\ldots, (\pi_k, \phi_k), \ldots\} \\ S(\langle\alpha\rangle_{i_j}) & = & \{\ldots, (\pi_{l_j}, \phi_{l_j}), \ldots\} \end{array}$$

By the assumption that the abstraction is correct before the read (i.e., $E, S, C \sim \mathbb{E}, \mathbb{S}, \mathbb{C}$), we have:

$$\begin{array}{lcl} (\langle\alpha\rangle_{i_j} = \delta) & \Rightarrow & \sigma_c(\lceil\phi_j\rceil) = \mathit{true} \\ (\langle\alpha\rangle_{i_j} \neq \delta) & \Rightarrow & \sigma_c(\lfloor\phi_j\rfloor) = \mathit{false} \\ \pi_k = k & \Rightarrow & \lceil\phi_k\rceil = \mathit{true} \\ \pi_k \neq k & \Rightarrow & \lfloor\phi_k\rfloor = \mathit{false} \\ \pi_{l_j} = \pi & \Rightarrow & \sigma_\pi(\sigma_c(\lceil\phi_{l_j}\rceil)) = \mathit{true} \\ \pi_{l_j} \neq \pi & \Rightarrow & \sigma_\pi(\sigma_c(\lfloor\phi_{l_j}\rfloor)) = \mathit{false} \end{array} \quad (*)$$

The resulting abstract value set θ is computed by the rule as:

$$\theta = S(\langle\alpha\rangle_{i_j}) \bowtie (\bigvee((i_j = \pi_k) \wedge \phi_k) \wedge \phi_j)$$

Now, assume, for contradiction, that $S(l_c, k) \not\sim \theta$. Then, either (i) $(\pi, \langle \mathit{true}, *\rangle) \notin \sigma_\pi(\theta)$, or (ii) $\exists \pi' \neq \pi.\ (\pi', \langle *, \mathit{true}\rangle) \in \sigma_\pi(\theta)$.

Assume (i). By (*), for $\delta = \langle\alpha\rangle_{i_j}$ and $\pi_k = k$, we have $\sigma_c(\lceil\phi_j\rceil) = \mathit{true}$ and $\lceil\phi_k\rceil = \mathit{true}$; thus,

$$\theta = S(\langle\alpha\rangle_{i_j}) \bowtie \langle(i_j = k \wedge \phi_j), *\rangle$$

By correctness of the abstraction before the read, we have:

$$(\pi, \langle\varphi_{may}, \varphi_{must}\rangle) \in \mathbb{S}(\langle\alpha\rangle_{i_j})$$

Furthermore since $\sigma_\pi(\sigma_c(\varphi_{may})) = \mathit{true}$ by (*) and since σ_c must assign i_j to k and $\sigma_c(\phi_j) = \mathit{true}$,

$$\sigma_\pi(\sigma_c(\varphi_{may} \wedge (i_j = k) \wedge \phi_j)) = \mathit{true}$$

Hence, assumption (i) is not possible.

Now, assume (ii). First, observe that if $\langle\alpha\rangle_{i_j} = \delta$ and $\pi_k = k$, then, from the last identity in (*), it follows that (ii) cannot hold. Now, if $\langle\alpha\rangle_{i_j} \neq \delta$, then $\sigma_c(\lfloor\phi_j\rfloor) = \mathit{false}$, and $\forall(\pi', \phi').\ \in \sigma_c(S(\langle\alpha\rangle_{i_j}) \bowtie (\bigvee((i_j = \pi_k) \wedge \phi_k) \wedge \phi_j))$, we have $\lfloor\phi'\rfloor = \mathit{false}$. Now, if $\pi_k \neq k$, we know from (*) that $\lfloor\phi_k\rfloor = \mathit{false}$, hence (ii) is again not possible.

An almost identical argument also applies to value-dependent containers; the only difference is that σ_c now assigns i_j to $\mathit{pos}(k)$ and θ is computed as:

$$\theta = S(\langle\alpha\rangle_{i_j}) \bowtie (\bigvee((i_j = \mathit{pos}(\pi_k) \wedge \phi_k) \wedge \phi_j)$$

Now, we consider a write $v_1.\mathtt{write}(v_2, v_3)$ to position-dependent container v_1. Let (l, k) denote the concrete memory location that is modified, and let v denote the concrete value that is written. From the operational semantics, we have:

$$S'(l, i) = \begin{cases} v & \text{if } i = k \\ S(l, i) & \text{otherwise} \end{cases} \quad (1)$$

Let:

$$\begin{array}{l} \alpha(l, i) = (\delta, \sigma_i) \\ \alpha(k) = (k, \mathit{true}) \\ \alpha(v) = (\pi_v^*, \sigma_v^*) \\ \alpha(S(l, i)) = (\pi_{e_i}, \sigma_{e_i}) \end{array}$$

In the write rule from Figure 6, let:

$$\begin{array}{lcl} \theta_1 & = & \{\ldots, (\langle\alpha\rangle_{i_j}, \phi_j), \ldots\} \\ \theta_2 & = & \{\ldots, (\pi_k, \phi_k), \ldots\} \\ \theta_3 & = & \{\ldots, (\pi_v, \phi_v), \ldots\} \\ \mathbb{S}(\langle\alpha\rangle_{i_j}) & = & \{\ldots, (\pi_{l_j}, \phi_{l_j}), \ldots\} \end{array}$$

By the assumption that the abstraction is correct before the write (i.e., $E, S, C \sim \mathbb{E}, \mathbb{S}, \mathbb{C}$), we know:

$$\begin{array}{lcl} (\pi_k = k) & \Rightarrow & \lceil\phi_k\rceil = \mathit{true} \\ (\pi_k \neq k) & \Rightarrow & \lfloor\phi_k\rfloor = \mathit{false} \\ (\pi_v = \pi_v^*) & \Rightarrow & \sigma_v^*(\lceil\phi_v\rceil) = \mathit{true} \\ (\pi_v \neq \pi_v^*) & \Rightarrow & \sigma_v^*(\lfloor\phi_v\rfloor) = \mathit{false} \\ (\delta = \langle\alpha\rangle_{i_j}) & \Rightarrow & \sigma_i(\lceil\phi_j\rceil) = \mathit{true} \\ (\delta \neq \langle\alpha\rangle_{i_j}) & \Rightarrow & \sigma_i(\lfloor\phi_j\rfloor) = \mathit{false} \\ \pi_{l_j} = \pi_{e_i} & \Rightarrow & \sigma_{e_i}(\sigma_i(\lceil\phi_{l_j}\rceil)) = \mathit{true} \\ \pi_{l_j} \neq \pi_{e_i} & \Rightarrow & \sigma_{e_i}(\sigma_i(\lfloor\phi_{l_j}\rfloor)) = \mathit{false} \end{array} \quad (*)$$

In the write rule, for each $\langle\alpha\rangle_{i_j}$, the new entry in new abstract store $\mathbb{S}'$ is computed as:

$$\begin{array}{lcl} \mathbb{S}'(\langle\alpha\rangle_{i_j}) & = \mathbb{S}[\langle\alpha\rangle_{i_j} \leftarrow & (\theta_3 \wedge (\theta_2 \Diamond i_j) \wedge \phi_j) \cup \\ & & \mathbb{S}(\langle\alpha\rangle_{i_j}) \wedge (\neg(\theta_2 \Diamond i_j) \vee \neg\phi_j)] \end{array} \quad (**)$$

where $\theta \wedge \phi$ is shorthand for conjoining ϕ with every constraint in θ, as described in Section 3.3.

Assume that the write rule is not sound. Then, using (1), either:

$$\begin{array}{ll} \text{(i)} & v \not\sim (\mathbb{S}'(\delta) \bowtie \sigma_i[k/i]) \quad \textit{or} \\ \text{(ii)} & S(l,i) \not\sim (\mathbb{S}'(\delta) \bowtie \sigma_i) \;\; \textit{for } i \neq k \end{array}$$

We first consider (i). Suppose $v \not\sim (\mathbb{S}'(\delta) \bowtie \sigma_i[k/i])$. Then, there are two possibilities:

$$\begin{array}{ll} 1a. & (\pi_v^*, \langle \textit{true}, * \rangle) \notin \sigma_v^*(\mathbb{S}'(\delta) \bowtie \sigma_i[k/i]) \\ 1b. & \exists \pi_v' \neq \pi_v^*.\ (\pi_v', \langle *, \textit{true} \rangle) \in \sigma_v^*(\mathbb{S}'(\delta) \bowtie \sigma_i[k/i]) \end{array}$$

Now, assume 1a and consider evaluating $\sigma_v^*(\mathbb{S}'(\delta) \bowtie \sigma_i[k/i])$. Under σ_v^*, we know from (*) that in (**), $\sigma_v^*(\theta_2)$ contains the pair $(\pi_v^*, \langle \textit{true}, * \rangle)$. Observe that $\sigma_i[k/i]$ must assign i_j to k. Hence, by using (*), we know that the constraint

$$\theta_2 \diamondsuit i_j = \bigvee ((i_j = \pi_k) \wedge \phi_k) \quad (***)$$

evaluates to $\langle \textit{true}, * \rangle$ under assignment $\sigma_i[k/i]$. Furthermore, under assignment $\sigma_i[k/i]$, (*) implies that $\lceil \phi_j \rceil$ is *true*; hence it follows that $(\pi_v^*, \langle \textit{true}, * \rangle) \in \sigma_v^*(\mathbb{S}'(\delta) \bowtie \sigma_i[k/i])$, contradicting assumption 1a.

Now assume 1b. Under assignment σ_v^*, we know from (*) that for any $(\pi_v', \phi_v') \in \theta_2$ such that $\pi_v' \neq \pi_v^*$, $\lfloor \phi_v' \rfloor$ is *false*. Since conjoining additional constraints cannot weaken *false*, it follows that $\forall \pi_v' \neq \pi_v^*.\ (\pi_v', \langle *, \textit{false} \rangle) \in \sigma_v^*(\mathbb{S}'(\delta) \bowtie \sigma_i[k/i])$, contradicting assumption 1b.

We know consider (ii), i.e., $S(l,i) \not\sim (\mathbb{S}'(\delta) \bowtie \sigma_i)$ for some i such that $i \neq k$. This corresponds to the case where the abstract semantics for `write` overwrites the existing value of the wrong key. Again, there are two possibilities:

$$\begin{array}{ll} 2a. & (\pi_{e_i}, \langle \textit{true}, * \rangle) \notin \sigma_{e_i}(\mathbb{S}'(\delta) \bowtie \sigma_i) \\ 2b. & \exists \pi_{e_i'} \neq \pi_{e_i}.\ (\pi_{e_i}, \langle *, \textit{true} \rangle) \in \sigma_{e_i}(\mathbb{S}'(\delta) \bowtie \sigma_i) \end{array}$$

Now, assume 2a. From (*), we know that under assignment σ_{e_i}, $(\pi_{e_i}, \langle \textit{true}, * \rangle)$. Now, by (**), we need to show that conjoining the constraint $(\neg(\theta_2 \diamondsuit i_j) \vee \neg \phi_j)$ cannot strengthen *true*. Observe that σ_i assigns i_j to i where $i \neq k$, and observe that $\pi_k \neq i \Rightarrow \sigma_i(\lfloor \phi_k \rfloor) = \textit{false}$; hence the sufficient condition for $\theta_2 \diamondsuit i_j$ is *false*. Thus, $\lceil \neg(\theta_2 \diamondsuit i_j) \rceil = \textit{true}$, which implies $(\pi_{e_i}, \langle \textit{true}, * \rangle) \in \sigma_{e_i}(\mathbb{S}'(\delta) \bowtie \sigma_i)$, contradicting 2a.

Finally, assume 2b. Under assignment σ_{e_i}, we know from (*) that for any $(\pi_{l_j}, \phi_{l_j}) \in \mathbb{S}(\langle \alpha \rangle_{i_j})$ such that $\pi_{l_j} \neq \pi_{e_i}$, $\lfloor \phi_{l_j} \rfloor$ is *false*. Since conjoining additional constraints cannot weaken *false*, assumption 2b is also infeasible.

The proof for value-dependent containers is almost identical. The only differences are that σ_i now assigns i_j to $pos(i)$ according to the definition of the abstraction function, and $\mathbb{S}'$ is computed as:

$$\begin{array}{ll} \mathbb{S}'(\langle \alpha \rangle_{i_j}) & = \mathbb{S}[\langle \alpha \rangle_{i_j} \leftarrow \quad (\theta_3 \wedge (\theta_2 \clubsuit i_j) \wedge \phi_j) \cup \\ & \qquad\qquad\qquad \mathbb{S}(\langle \alpha \rangle_{i_j}) \wedge (\neg(\theta_2 \clubsuit i_j) \vee \neg \phi_j)] \end{array}$$

We now consider the `foreach` rule. Since the *fix* rule stipulates that $\mathbb{S}^*$ is a correct invariant without giving a constructive algorithm, we only argue about the loop initialization, i.e., (key, value) pairs bound in the `foreach` rule of the abstract semantics correctly model the concrete execution. We focus on value-dependent containers. Let key_k be the concrete key visited during the k'th loop iteration such that $\alpha(key_k) = (key_k, \sigma_k)$ where σ_k gives interpretation to function symbols pos^ρ. In the abstract semantics, the value set θ_{key} during the k'th iteration is given by

$$\theta_{key} = \{\ldots, (\pi_k, k = pos^\rho(\pi_k)), \ldots\}$$

Suppose $key_k \not\sim \theta_{key}$. Then, either $(key_k, \langle \textit{true}, * \rangle) \notin \sigma_k(\theta_{key})$ or $\exists \pi_k \neq key_k.\ (\pi_k, \langle *, \textit{true} \rangle) \in \sigma_k(\theta_{key})$

But, under interpretation σ_k, we have:

$$\begin{array}{l} \pi_k = key_k \Rightarrow \sigma_k(pos^\rho) = k \\ \pi_k \neq key_k \Rightarrow \sigma_k(pos^\rho) \neq k \end{array}$$

Hence, $key_k \sim \theta_{key}$.

Blame for All

Amal Ahmed
Indiana University
amal@cs.indiana.edu

Robert Bruce Findler
Northwestern University
robby@eecs.northwestern.edu

Jeremy G. Siek
University of Colorado at Boulder
jeremy.siek@colorado.edu

Philip Wadler
University of Edinburgh
wadler@inf.ed.ac.uk

Abstract

Several programming languages are beginning to integrate static and dynamic typing, including Racket (formerly PLT Scheme), Perl 6, and C# 4.0 and the research languages Sage (Gronski, Knowles, Tomb, Freund, and Flanagan, 2006) and Thorn (Wrigstad, Eugster, Field, Nystrom, and Vitek, 2009). However, an important open question remains, which is how to add parametric polymorphism to languages that combine static and dynamic typing. We present a system that permits a value of dynamic type to be cast to a polymorphic type and vice versa, with relational parametricity enforced by a kind of dynamic sealing along the lines proposed by Matthews and Ahmed (2008) and Neis, Dreyer, and Rossberg (2009). Our system includes a notion of blame, which allows us to show that when casting between a more-precise type and a less-precise type, any cast failures are due to the less-precisely-typed portion of the program. We also show that a cast from a subtype to its supertype cannot fail.

Categories and Subject Descriptors D.3.3 [*Language Constructs and Features*]: Procedures, functions, and subroutines

General Terms Languages, Theory

Keywords casts, coercions, blame tracking, lambda-calculus

1. Introduction

The long tradition of work that integrates static and dynamic types includes the *partial types* of Thatte (1988), the *dynamic type* of Abadi et al. (1991), the *coercions* of Henglein (1994), the *contracts* of Findler and Felleisen (2002), the *dynamic dependent types* of Ou et al. (2004), the *hybrid types* of Gronski et al. (2006), the *gradual types* of Siek and Taha (2006), the *migratory types* of Tobin-Hochstadt and Felleisen (2006), the *multi-language* programming of Matthews and Findler (2007), and the *blame calculus* of Wadler and Findler (2009). Integration of static and dynamic types is a feature of .NET languages including Visual Basic and C#, is being explored for Javascript, Perl, Python, and Ruby, and is the subject of the recent STOP 2009 workshop held in conjunction with ECOOP.

POPL'11, January 26–28, 2011, Austin, Texas, USA.

A unifying theme in this work is to use casts to mediate between statically and dynamically typed code. Casts may be introduced by compiling to an intermediate language; the blame calculus may be regarded as either such an intermediate language or as a source language. The main innovation of the blame calculus is to assign positive and negative blame (to either the term *contained* in the cast or the context *containing* the cast), with associated notions of positive and negative subtype. These support the Blame Theorem, which ensures that when a program goes wrong, blame lies with the less-precisely-typed side of a cast (Wadler and Findler, 2009).

In this paper, we extend a fragment of the blame calculus to incorporate polymorphism, based on a notion of dynamic sealing. For simplicity, our fragment includes base types, function types, and the dynamic type, as found in gradual types, but omits subset types, as found in hybrid types. Our system adds the ability to cast a value of dynamic type to a polymorphic type and vice versa. We name this system the *polymorphic blame calculus*.

A fundamental semantic property of polymorphic types is *relational parametricity*, as introduced by Reynolds (1983). Our system uses dynamic sealing to ensure that values of polymorphic type satisfy relational parametricity. For instance, every function of type $\forall X.\, X \to X$ must either be the identity function (one which always returns its argument) or an undefined function (one which never returns a value), and this property holds true even for values of dynamic type cast to a polymorphic type. Relational parametricity underlies some program optimizations, notably *shortcut deforestation* as employed by the Glasgow Haskell Compiler (Gill et al., 1993). Our system may guarantee the validity of such optimizations even in the presence of dynamic types.

Dynamic sealing to enforce parametricity has a long history. Sealing for data abstraction goes back at least to Morris (1973). Cryptographic sealing for parametricity was introduced by Pierce and Sumii (2000). Extending casts to include seals, while demonstrating relational parametricity, was first explored in the context of multi-language programming by Matthews and Ahmed (2008). A practical implementation for Scheme contracts was described by Guha et al. (2007). Recently, Neis et al. (2009) used dynamic sealing to restore parametricity in a non-parametric language.

Our development is supported by the use of *type bindings* to control the scope of type variables, both statically and dynamically. Type bindings are closely related to constructs for generating new type names (Neis et al., 2009; Rossberg, 2003); an important difference is that our type bindings are immobile, that is, there is no scope extrusion. Our development also uses *static casts* to conceal and reveal the representations of type variables. Together with type bindings, static casts provide a syntactic means to preserve the type-hiding nature of type abstractions after they are instantiated. Static casts play an important role in the static semantics of our system but a lesser role in the dynamic semantics. As such, static casts are implicit in our main system (as in Neis et al. (2009)). However, we use an explicit version of the static casts as a technical device in our proof of the Subtyping Theorem. The explicit casts are closely related to the coercions of Rossberg (2003) and are reminiscent of the syntactic type abstractions of Grossman et al. (2000).

We present three technical results in this paper. The first result is the Jack-of-All-Trades Principle (Sections 6.3 and 11), which justifies the way we implement casts that instantiate polymorphic values. The second result is the Blame Theorem (Section 8), which states that when casting between a less-precise type and a more-precise type, any cast failures are due to the less-precisely-typed portion of the program. The final result is the Subtyping Theorem (Section 9), which states that a cast from a subtype to a supertype cannot lead to blame for that cast. We do not present a relational parametricity result; that result is forthcoming and will be an adaptation of the result by Matthews and Ahmed (2008).

The paper comes with a Redex model covering some of the systems in this paper, available online:
`http://plt.eecs.northwestern.edu/blame-for-all/`

This paper is an improved version of a paper in STOP 2009. The current paper is completely rewritten (and has lost one author and gained another). Among the more significant differences, we use type bindings as compared to a global store; and we prove the Subtyping Theorem, a conjecture in the earlier paper.

2. From untyped to typed

The blame calculus provides a framework for integrating typed and untyped programs. One scenario is that we begin with a program in an untyped language and we wish to convert it to a typed language.

Here is a simple untyped program.

$$\begin{array}{l}\texttt{let}\ pos^\star = \lceil \lambda x.\, x > 0 \rceil\ \texttt{in} \\ \texttt{let}\ app^\star = \lceil \lambda f.\, \lambda x.\, f\ x \rceil\ \texttt{in} \\ \lceil app^\star\ pos^\star\ 1 \rceil\end{array}$$

It returns $\lceil \texttt{true} \rceil : \star$. We indicate untyped code by surrounding it with ceiling brackets, $\lceil\cdot\rceil$. Untyped code is really uni-typed (a slogan due to Harper (2007)); it is a special case of typed code where every term has the dynamic type, $\star$. To aid the eye, we sometimes write variables of type $\star$ with a superscript $\star$.

Here is the same program, rewritten with types.

$$\begin{array}{l}\texttt{let}\ pos = \lambda x : \texttt{I}.\, x > 0\ \texttt{in} \\ \texttt{let}\ app = \Lambda X.\, \Lambda Y.\, \lambda f : X \to Y.\, \lambda x : X.\, f\ x\ \texttt{in} \\ app\ \texttt{I}\ \texttt{B}\ pos\ 1\end{array}$$

This program returns $\texttt{true} : \texttt{B}$.

As a matter of software engineering, when we add types to our code we may not want to do so all at once. Of course, it is trivial to rewrite a three-line program. However, the technique described here is intended to apply also when each one-line definition is replaced by a thousand-line module.

We manage the transition between untyped and typed code with a relatively new construct (Gronski et al., 2006; Siek and Taha, 2006) with an old name, "cast". Casts can be between any two compatible types. Roughly speaking, type A is compatible with type B when a value of type A can be coerced to type B. We are particularly interested in the case where either the source type is $\star$ (corresponding to importing untyped code into typed code), or where the target type is $\star$ (corresponding to importing typed code into untyped code). We introduce an order on types corresponding to precision, where $\star$ is the least precise type. We introduce a notion of *blame* associated with casts, so that we can prove the following result: if a cast between a less-precise type and a more-precise type fails, then blame falls on the less-precise side of the cast. An immediate corollary is that if a cast between untyped and typed code fails, blame lies with the untyped code—"well-typed programs can't be blamed".

A cast from a more-precise type to a less-precise type is called *widening*. Here is the above program rewritten to demonstrate widening. It is mostly untyped, but contains one typed component cast for use in an untyped context.

$$\begin{array}{l}\texttt{let}\ pos^\star = \lceil \lambda x.\, x > 0 \rceil\ \texttt{in} \\ \texttt{let}\ app = \Lambda X.\, \Lambda Y.\, \lambda f : X \to Y.\, \lambda x : X.\, f\ x\ \texttt{in} \\ \texttt{let}\ app^\star = app : \forall X.\, \forall Y.\, (X \to Y) \to X \to Y \Rightarrow^p \star\ \texttt{in} \\ \lceil app^\star\ pos^\star\ 1 \rceil\end{array}$$

It returns $\lceil \texttt{true} \rceil : \star$.

Every cast is annotated with a *blame label*, used to ascribe fault if the cast fails. The cast in the above program has blame label p.

Our notation is chosen for clarity rather than compactness. Writing the source type of the cast is redundant; the type of the source can always be inferred. In a practical language, we would expect the source type to be elided.

Of course, the untyped context may not satisfy the constraints required by the typed term. If in the above we replace

$$\lceil app^\star\ pos^\star\ 1 \rceil \qquad \text{by} \qquad \lceil app^\star\ 1\ pos^\star \rceil$$

it now returns $\texttt{blame}\ \overline{p}$. Blaming $\overline{p}$ (rather than p) indicates that the fault lies with the *context containing* the cast labelled p (rather than the *term contained* in the cast). This is what we expect, because the context is untyped.

Passing a polymorphically typed value into an untyped context requires an appropriate instantiation for the type parameters. As you might guess, in this case the type parameters X and Y are instantiated to $\star$. However you might not guess that instantiating to $\star$ always works, regardless of whether the target is $\star$ or something more precisely typed. One of the contributions of this paper is to prove the *Jack-of-All-Trades Principle*: if instantiating a type parameter to any given type yields an answer then instantiating that type parameter to $\star$ yields the same answer.

A cast from a less-precise type to a more-precise type is called *narrowing*. Here is the above program rewritten to demonstrate narrowing. It is mostly typed, but contains one untyped component cast for use in a typed context.

$$\begin{array}{l}\texttt{let}\ pos = \lambda x : \texttt{I}.\, x > 0\ \texttt{in} \\ \texttt{let}\ app^\star = \lceil \lambda f.\, \lambda x.\, f\ x \rceil\ \texttt{in} \\ \texttt{let}\ app = app^\star : \star \Rightarrow^p \forall X.\, \forall Y.\, (X \to Y) \to X \to Y\ \texttt{in} \\ app\ \texttt{I}\ \texttt{B}\ pos\ 1\end{array}$$

This returns $\texttt{true} : \texttt{B}$.

Of course, the untyped term may not satisfy the constraints required by the typed context. If in the above we replace

$$\lceil \lambda f.\, \lambda x.\, f\ x \rceil \qquad \text{by} \qquad \lceil \lambda f.\, \lambda x.\, x \rceil$$

it now returns $\texttt{blame}\ p$. Blaming p (rather than $\overline{p}$) indicates that the fault lies with the *term contained* in the cast labelled p (rather than the *context containing* the cast). This is what we expect, because the term is untyped.

To check for this error, the implementation must *seal* each value. That is, casting from type X to type $\star$ yields a value sealed with X, and attempting to cast from type $\star$ to type Y fails because the seals X and Y are distinct. One of the contributions of this paper is to work out the details of sealing in a setting with dynamic types. One consequence of sealing is that typed terms always satisfy appropriate parametricity properties, even when they are derived by casting from untyped terms.

We now begin our formal development.

3. Simply-typed lambda calculus

All the systems in this paper extend a vanilla call-by-value simply-typed lambda calculus, shown in Figure 1.

We let A, B, and C range over types. A type is either a base type ι or a function type $A \to B$. The base types include integers and Booleans, written $\mathtt{I}$ and $\mathtt{B}$ respectively. We let s and t range over terms. Terms include constants, primitive application, variables, abstractions, and application. The variables v and w range over values. A value is either a constant or an abstraction.

We write $\Gamma \vdash t : A$ if term t has type A in type environment Γ. A type environment maps variables to types. The function ty maps constants and primitive operators to their types. The function δ maps an operator and a tuple of values to a value, and must preserve types. That is, if $\mathrm{ty}(op) = \vec{A} \to B$ and $\cdot \vdash \vec{v} : \vec{A}$ then there is a w such that $\delta(op, \vec{v}) = w$ and $\cdot \vdash w : B$. Suitable choices of δ can specify arithmetic, conditional, and fixpoint operators.

We write $s \longrightarrow t$ to indicate that redex s reduces to t, and write $s \longmapsto t$ to indicate that reducing a redex inside s yields t. We let E range over evaluation contexts, which are standard.

4. Simply-typed blame calculus

Before proceeding to polymorphism, we review the fundamentals of the simply-typed blame calculus, shown in Figure 2. The blame calculus extends the simply-typed lambda-calculus with a dynamic type, written $\star$, and with four term forms: dynamic casts, grounded terms, type tests, and blame.

One can think of the dynamic type $\star$ as the sum of all the base types plus the function type.

$$\star = \mathtt{I} + \mathtt{B} + (\star \to \star)$$

Accordingly, the *ground types* are the base types together with the type $\star \to \star$. Every value of dynamic type is constructed by a cast from ground type to dynamic type, written $v : G \Rightarrow \star$. These casts can never fail, so they are not decorated with blame labels. For example, $id^\star = (\lambda x{:}\,\star\,.\,x) : \star \to \star \Rightarrow \star$ is a value of type $\star$. A test $s\ \mathtt{is}\ G$ returns true if s evaluates to a value grounded on G. For example, $(1 : \mathtt{I} \Rightarrow \star)\ \mathtt{is}\ \mathtt{I}$ returns true.

In general, a cast $s : A \Rightarrow^p B$ converts the value of term s from type A to type B. Casts are decorated with blame labels. We assume an involutive operation of negation on blame labels: if p is a blame label then $\bar{p}$ is its negation, and $\bar{\bar{p}}$ is the same as p. We write $s : A \Rightarrow^p B \Rightarrow^q C$ as shorthand for $(s : A \Rightarrow^p B) : B \Rightarrow^q C$.

A cast from A to B is permitted only if the types are *compatible*, written $A \prec B$. Every type is compatible with itself, the dynamic type is compatible with every type, and functions are compatible if their domain and range are compatible; note the contravariance in the function rule. For now, compatibility is symmetric, but this will change in Section 6.

Finally, the term $\mathtt{blame}\ p$ indicates a failure, identifying the relevant label. Blame terms may have any type.

We now briefly review the reduction rules. A cast from one function type to another reduces to a wrapper function that casts the argument, applies the original function, then casts the result—note the reversal in the argument cast, and the corresponding negating of the blame label (WRAP). A cast from a ground type to itself is the identity (ID). (The side condition $G \neq \star \to \star$ avoids overlap with (WRAP). For now, the only ground type other than $\star \to \star$ is ι, but this will change in Section 6.) A cast from type A to $\star$ factors into a cast from A to the unique ground type G that is compatible with A followed by a cast from G to $\star$ (GROUND). Here we see the reason for distinguishing between casts and ground terms: otherwise whenever the (GROUND) rule is applicable, it would be applicable infinitely many times. A cast from $\star$ to type A examines the ground G of the value of type $\star$. If G is compatible with A, the two casts collapse to a direct cast from G to A (COLLAPSE). If G is not compatible with A, the offending cast is blamed (CONFLICT). A test checks the ground of the value of type $\star$. If it matches the test returns $\mathtt{true}$, else it returns $\mathtt{false}$ (ISTRUE), (ISFALSE). An occurrence of $\mathtt{blame}\,p$ in an evaluation position causes the program to abort (ABORT).

For example, say $pos = \lambda x : \mathtt{I}.\, x > 0$. Then

$$\begin{array}{l} \quad (pos : \mathtt{I} \to \mathtt{B} \Rightarrow^p \star \to \star)\ (1 : \mathtt{I} \Rightarrow \star) \\ \longmapsto^* pos\ (1 : \mathtt{I} \Rightarrow \star \Rightarrow^{\bar{p}} \mathtt{I}) : \mathtt{B} \Rightarrow^p \star \\ \longmapsto^* pos\ 1 : \mathtt{B} \Rightarrow^p \star \\ \longmapsto^* \mathtt{true} : \mathtt{B} \Rightarrow \star \end{array}$$

The function cast factors into a pair of casts. The cast on the ranges retains the order and the blame label. The cast on the domains swaps the order and negates the blame label. The swap is required for types to work out. Negation of the blame label is required to assign blame appropriately, as can be seen by changing the argument:

$$\begin{array}{l} \quad (pos : \mathtt{I} \to \mathtt{B} \Rightarrow^p \star \to \star)\ (\mathtt{false} : \mathtt{B} \Rightarrow \star) \\ \longmapsto^* pos\ (\mathtt{false} : \mathtt{B} \Rightarrow \star \Rightarrow^{\bar{p}} \mathtt{I}) : \mathtt{B} \Rightarrow^p \star \\ \longmapsto^* \mathtt{blame}\ \bar{p} \end{array}$$

The inner cast fails, ascribing blame to the label $\bar{p}$ on the cast. Blaming $\bar{p}$ (rather than p) indicates that the fault in the original cast lies with the context containing the cast (rather than the term contained in the cast). That is, we blame the untyped context for failing to supply an integer rather than blame the typed function for failing to accept a boolean.

A cast from type dynamic to itself is the identity:

$$v : \star \Rightarrow^p \star \longmapsto v'$$

where v' is observationally equivalent to v. To see this, take $v = w : G \Rightarrow \star$. Then

$$\begin{array}{l} \quad w : G \Rightarrow \star \Rightarrow^p \star \\ \longmapsto w : G \Rightarrow^p \star \\ \longmapsto w : G \Rightarrow^p G \Rightarrow \star \end{array}$$

via (COLLAPSE) and (GROUND). And a cast from a ground type to itself produces either an equivalent value, via (ID) or (WRAP).

It is straightforward to define an embedding $\lceil \cdot \rceil$ from the untyped lambda calculus into the blame calculus.

$$\begin{array}{rcl} \lceil c \rceil & = & c : \mathrm{ty}(c) \Rightarrow \star \\ \lceil op(\vec{M}\,) \rceil & = & op(\lceil \vec{M} \rceil : \vec{\star} \Rightarrow^{\vec{q}} \vec{A}) : B \Rightarrow^r \star,\ \text{if}\ \mathrm{ty}(op) = \vec{A} \to B \\ \lceil x \rceil & = & x \\ \lceil \lambda x.\, M \rceil & = & (\lambda x{:}\,\star\,.\,\lceil M \rceil) : \star \to \star \Rightarrow^q \star \\ \lceil M\ N \rceil & = & (\lceil M \rceil : \star \Rightarrow^q \star \to \star)\ \lceil N \rceil \\ \lceil M\ \mathtt{is}\ G \rceil & = & \lceil M \rceil\ \mathtt{is}\ G \end{array}$$

For example, $\lceil \lambda x.\, x \rceil = (\lambda x{:}\,\star\,.\,x){:}\ \star \to \star \Rightarrow \star$.

5. Explicit binding

The traditional way to reduce a type application is by substitution, $(\Lambda X.\, t)\ A \longrightarrow t[X{:=}A]$. We begin by explaining why this cannot work in our case, and then introduce a variant of the polymorphic lambda calculus with an explicit binding construct.

5.1 The problem

A naive integration of casts and dynamic type with type substitution cannot ensure relational parametricity.

Say we wish to cast the untyped constant function

$$K^\star = \lceil \lambda x.\, \lambda y.\, x \rceil$$

to a polymorphic type. We consider two casts.

$$\begin{array}{l} K^\star : \star \Rightarrow^p \forall X.\, \forall Y.\, X \to Y \to X \\ K^\star : \star \Rightarrow^p \forall X.\, \forall Y.\, X \to Y \to Y \end{array}$$

Syntax

$$
\begin{array}{lll}
\text{Variables} & x, y & \\
\text{Constants} & c & \\
\text{Base types} & \iota & ::= \mathtt{I} \mid \mathtt{B} \\
\text{Types} & A, B, C & ::= \iota \mid A \to B
\end{array}
\qquad
\begin{array}{lll}
\text{Terms} & s, t & ::= c \mid op(\vec{t}) \mid x \mid \lambda x{:}A.\, t \mid t\ s \\
\text{Environments} & \Gamma & ::= \cdot \mid \Gamma, x : A \\
\text{Values} & v, w & ::= c \mid \lambda x{:}A.\, t \\
\text{Contexts} & E & ::= [\cdot] \mid op(\vec{v}, E, \vec{t}) \mid E\ s \mid v\ E
\end{array}
$$

Type rules

$$
\frac{\mathrm{ty}(c) = \iota}{\Gamma \vdash c : \iota}
\qquad
\frac{\Gamma \vdash \vec{t} : \vec{A} \quad \mathrm{ty}(op) = \vec{A} \to B}{\Gamma \vdash op(\vec{t}) : B}
\qquad
\frac{x : A \in \Gamma}{\Gamma \vdash x : A}
\qquad
\frac{\Gamma, x : A \vdash t : B}{\Gamma \vdash \lambda x{:}A.\, t : A \to B}
\qquad
\frac{\Gamma \vdash t : A \to B \quad \Gamma \vdash s : A}{\Gamma \vdash t\ s : B}
$$

Reduction rules

$$
\begin{array}{rll}
(\lambda x{:}A.\, t)\ v \longrightarrow t[x{:=}v] & (\textsc{Beta}) & \\
op(\vec{v}\,) \longrightarrow \delta(op, \vec{v}\,) & (\textsc{Delta}) &
\end{array}
\qquad
\frac{s \longrightarrow t}{E[s] \longmapsto E[t]} \quad (\textsc{Step})
$$

Figure 1. Simply-typed lambda calculus.

Syntax

$$
\begin{array}{lll}
\text{Blame labels} & p, q & \\
\text{Types} & A, B, C & ::= \iota \mid A \to B \mid \star \\
\text{Ground types} & G, H & ::= \iota \mid \star \to \star \\
\text{Terms} & s, t & ::= c \mid op(\vec{t}) \mid x \mid \lambda x{:}A.\, t \mid t\ s \mid s : A \Rightarrow^p B \mid s : G \Rightarrow \star \mid s\ \mathtt{is}\ G \mid \mathtt{blame}\ p \\
\text{Environments} & \Gamma & ::= \cdot \mid \Gamma, x : A \\
\text{Values} & v, w & ::= c \mid \lambda x{:}A.\, t \mid v : G \Rightarrow \star \\
\text{Contexts} & E & ::= [\cdot] \mid op(\vec{v}, E, \vec{t}) \mid E\ s \mid v\ E \mid E\ \mathtt{is}\ G \mid E : A \Rightarrow^p B \mid E : G \Rightarrow \star \\
\text{Untyped terms} & M, N & ::= c \mid op(\vec{M}\,) \mid x \mid \lambda x.\, M \mid M\ N \mid M\ \mathtt{is}\ G
\end{array}
$$

Type rules

$$
\frac{\Gamma \vdash s : A \quad A \prec B}{\Gamma \vdash (s : A \Rightarrow^p B) : B}
\qquad
\frac{\Gamma \vdash s : G}{\Gamma \vdash (s : G \Rightarrow \star) : \star}
\qquad
\frac{\Gamma \vdash s : \star}{\Gamma \vdash s\ \mathtt{is}\ G : \mathtt{B}}
\qquad
\Gamma \vdash \mathtt{blame}\ p : A
$$

Compatibility

$$
A \prec A \qquad A \prec \star \qquad \star \prec B \qquad \frac{A' \prec A \quad B \prec B'}{A \to B \prec A' \to B'}
$$

Reduction rules

$$
\begin{array}{rlr}
v : A \to B \Rightarrow^p A' \to B' \longrightarrow \lambda x'{:}A'.\, (v\ (x' : A' \Rightarrow^{\overline{p}} A) : B \Rightarrow^p B') & & (\textsc{Wrap}) \\
v : G \Rightarrow^p G \longrightarrow v & \text{if } G \neq \star \to \star & (\textsc{Id}) \\
v : A \Rightarrow^p \star \longrightarrow v : A \Rightarrow^p G \Rightarrow \star & \text{if } A \prec G \text{ and } A \neq \star & (\textsc{Ground}) \\
v : G \Rightarrow \star \Rightarrow^p A \longrightarrow v : G \Rightarrow^p A & \text{if } G \prec A & (\textsc{Collapse}) \\
v : G \Rightarrow \star \Rightarrow^p A \longrightarrow \mathtt{blame}\ p & \text{if } G \not\prec A & (\textsc{Conflict}) \\
(v : G \Rightarrow \star)\ \mathtt{is}\ G \longrightarrow \mathtt{true} & & (\textsc{IsTrue}) \\
(v : H \Rightarrow \star)\ \mathtt{is}\ G \longrightarrow \mathtt{false} & \text{if } G \neq H & (\textsc{IsFalse}) \\
E[\mathtt{blame}\ p] \longmapsto \mathtt{blame}\ p & \text{if } E \neq [\cdot] & (\textsc{Abort})
\end{array}
$$

Figure 2. Simply-typed blame calculus (extends Figure 1).

We expect the first cast to succeed and the second to fail, the latter because of parametricity. The parametricity property for the type $\forall X. \forall Y. X \to Y \to Y$ guarantees that a value of this type must be either the flipped constant function (which returns its second argument) or the undefined function (which never returns a value). So an attempt to cast the constant function (which returns its first argument) to this type should fail.

The traditional way to reduce a type application is by substitution. This cannot work in our case! To see why, consider reducing each of the above by substituting $X{:=}\mathtt{I}, Y{:=}\mathtt{I}$.

$$
\begin{array}{ll}
& (K^\star : \star \Rightarrow^p \forall X. \forall Y. X \to Y \to X)\ \mathtt{I}\ \mathtt{I}\ 2\ 3 \\
\longmapsto^* & (K^\star : \star \Rightarrow^p \mathtt{I} \to \mathtt{I} \to \mathtt{I})\ 2\ 3 \\
\longmapsto^* & 2
\end{array}
$$

$$
\begin{array}{ll}
& (K^\star : \star \Rightarrow^p \forall X. \forall Y. X \to Y \to Y)\ \mathtt{I}\ \mathtt{I}\ 2\ 3 \\
\longmapsto^* & (K^\star : \star \Rightarrow^p \mathtt{I} \to \mathtt{I} \to \mathtt{I})\ 2\ 3 \\
\longmapsto^* & 2
\end{array}
$$

Note how, in the second line of each reduction, the substitution has erased the difference between the two programs—the system has forgotten that the terms were once polymorphic.

Thus, we see that special run-time support is needed to enforce parametricity. In the literature, such run-time support is called *dy-*

Syntax

Types	A, B, C	$::=$	$\iota \mid A \to B \mid X \mid \forall X.\, B$
Terms	s, t	$::=$	$c \mid op(\vec{t}) \mid x \mid \lambda x{:}A.\, t \mid t\ s \mid \Lambda X.\, t \mid t\ A \mid \nu X{:=}A.\, t$
Environments	Γ	$::=$	$\cdot \mid \Gamma, x : A \mid \Gamma, X \mid \Gamma, X{:=}A$
	Δ	$::=$	$\cdot \mid \Gamma, X \mid \Gamma, X{:=}A$
Values	v, w	$::=$	$c \mid \lambda x{:}A.\, t \mid \Lambda X.\, v$
Contexts	E	$::=$	$[\cdot] \mid op(\vec{v}, E, \vec{t}) \mid E\ s \mid v\ E \mid \Lambda X.\, E \mid E\ A \mid \nu X{:=}A.\, E$

Type rules

$$\text{(TyAbs)}\ \frac{\Gamma, X \vdash t : B}{\Gamma \vdash \Lambda X.\, t : \forall X.\, B} \qquad \text{(TyApp)}\ \frac{\Gamma \vdash t : \forall X.\, B \quad \Gamma \vdash A}{\Gamma \vdash t\ A : B[X{:=}A]} \qquad \text{(New)}\ \frac{\Gamma, X{:=}A \vdash t : B \quad \Gamma \vdash A \quad X \notin \text{ftv}(B)}{\Gamma \vdash \nu X{:=}A.\, t : B}$$

$$\text{(Reveal)}\ \frac{\Gamma \vdash t : B \quad (X{:=}A) \in \Gamma}{\Gamma \vdash t : B[X{:=}A]} \qquad \text{(Conceal)}\ \frac{\Gamma \vdash t : B[X{:=}A] \quad (X{:=}A) \in \Gamma}{\Gamma \vdash t : B}$$

Reduction rules

$(\Lambda X.\, v)\ A \longrightarrow \nu X{:=}A.\, v$		(TyBeta)
$\nu X{:=}A.\, c \longrightarrow c$		(NuConst)
$\nu X{:=}A.\, (\lambda y{:}B.\, t) \longrightarrow \lambda y{:}B[X{:=}A].\, (\nu X{:=}A.\, t)$		(NuWrap)
$\nu X{:=}A.\, (\Lambda Y.\, v) \longrightarrow \Lambda Y.\, (\nu X{:=}A.\, v)$	if $Y \neq X$ and $Y \notin \text{ftv}(A)$	(NuTyWrap)

Figure 3. Polymorphic lambda calculus with type bindings (extends Figure 1).

Syntax

Types	A, B, C	$::=$	$\iota \mid A \to B \mid \star \mid X \mid \forall X.\, B$
Ground types	G, H	$::=$	$\iota \mid \star \to \star \mid X$
Terms	s, t	$::=$	$c \mid op(\vec{t}) \mid x \mid \lambda x{:}A.\, t \mid t\ s \mid s : A \Rightarrow^p B \mid s : G \Rightarrow \star \mid s\ \texttt{is}\ G \mid \texttt{blame}\ p \mid \Lambda X.\, t \mid t\ A \mid \nu X{:=}A.\, t$
Values	v, w	$::=$	$c \mid \lambda x{:}A.\, t \mid v : G \Rightarrow \star \mid \Lambda X.\, v$
Contexts	E	$::=$	$[\cdot] \mid op(\vec{v}, E, \vec{t}) \mid E\ s \mid v\ E \mid E\ \texttt{is}\ G \mid E : A \Rightarrow^p B \mid E : G \Rightarrow \star \mid \Lambda X.\, E \mid E\ A \mid \nu X{:=}A.\, E$

Compatibility

$$\frac{A \prec B}{A \prec \forall X.\, B}\ X \notin \text{ftv}(A) \qquad \frac{A[X{:=}\star] \prec B}{\forall X.\, A \prec B}$$

Reduction rules

$(v : G \Rightarrow \star)\ \texttt{is}\ G \longrightarrow \texttt{true}$	if $G \neq X$ for any X	(IsTrue)
$(v : H \Rightarrow \star)\ \texttt{is}\ G \longrightarrow \texttt{false}$	if $G \neq H$ and $H \neq X$ for any X	(IsFalse)
$(v : X \Rightarrow \star)\ \texttt{is}\ G \longrightarrow \texttt{blame}\ p_{\text{is}}$		(IsTamper)
$\nu X{:=}A.\, (v : G \Rightarrow \star) \longrightarrow (\nu X{:=}A.\, v) : G \Rightarrow \star$	if $G \neq X$	(NuGround)
$\nu X{:=}A.\, (v : X \Rightarrow \star) \longrightarrow \texttt{blame}\ p_\nu$		(NuTamper)
$v : A \Rightarrow^p (\forall X.\, B) \longrightarrow \Lambda X.\, (v : A \Rightarrow^p B)$	if $X \notin \text{ftv} A$	(Generalize)
$v : (\forall X.\, A) \Rightarrow^p B \longrightarrow (v\ \star) : A[X{:=}\star] \Rightarrow^p B$	if $B \neq \star$ and $B \neq \forall X'.\, B'$ for any X', B'	(Instantiate)

Figure 4. Polymorphic blame calculus (extends and updates Figures 1, 2 and 3).

namic sealing, which we review in Section 12. In particular, our approach is inspired by the dynamic sealing of Matthews and Ahmed (2008), the dynamic type generation of Neis et al. (2009), and the syntactic type abstraction of Grossman et al. (2000). Based on these ideas, we introduce an alternate semantics for the polymorphic lambda calculus as a step towards defining our polymorphic blame calculus.

5.2 Polymorphic lambda calculus with explicit binding

We avoid the problems above by introducing a polymorphic lambda calculus with explicit binding, shown in Figure 3. As usual, types are augmented by adding type variables X and universal quantifiers $\forall X.\, B$, and terms are augmented by adding type abstractions $\Lambda X.\, t$ and type applications $t\ A$. The key new construct is explicit type binding, $\nu X{:=}A.\, t$.

Type environments are augmented to include, as usual, type variables X and, more unusually, type bindings $X{:=}A$. As usual, we assume an implicit side condition when writing Γ, X or $\Gamma, X{:=}A$ that X is not in Γ.

The type rules for type abstraction and application are standard (TyAbs), (TyApp). The type rule for binding augments the type environment with the binding, and a side condition ensures that free type variables do not escape the binding (New). Two additional type rules, which are not syntax directed, permit a type variable to be replaced by its bound type, or vice versa, within the scope of a type binding (Reveal), (Conceal).

We now briefly consider the reduction rules. Our rule for type applications, instead of performing substitution, introduces an explicit type binding (TyBeta). Three new rules push explicit type bindings into the three value forms: constants (NuConst), value abstractions (NuWrap), and type abstractions (NuTyWrap). (Side conditions on the last rule avoid capture of type variables.) For example,

$$
\begin{array}{ll}
& (\Lambda X.\, \lambda x{:}X.\, (\lambda y{:}X.\, y)\ x)\ \mathtt{I}\ 2 \\
\longmapsto & (\nu X{:=}\mathtt{I}.\, \lambda x{:}X.\, (\lambda y{:}X.\, y)\ x)\ 2 \\
\longmapsto & (\lambda x{:}\mathtt{I}.\, \nu X{:=}\mathtt{I}.\, (\lambda y{:}X.\, y)\ x)\ 2 \\
\longmapsto & \nu X{:=}\mathtt{I}.\, (\lambda y{:}X.\, y)\ 2 \\
\longmapsto & \nu X{:=}\mathtt{I}.\, 2 \\
\longmapsto & 2
\end{array}
$$

by rules (TyBeta), (NuWrap), (Beta), (Beta) and (NuConst), respectively. Note that for the term $\nu X{:=}\mathtt{I}.\, (\lambda y{:}X.\, y)\ 2$ to be well-typed that 2 must be regarded as having type X—this is why the type rules permit both replacing a type variable by its binding and the converse.

As is well known, allowing type abstraction over terms with arbitrary effects can be problematic. As we will see in Section 6.4, the same issue arises here, due to raising of blame as a possible side effect. The usual solution is to restrict type abstraction to apply only to values, as in the value polymorphism restriction of SML (Wright, 1995). We would like to do the same here, and restrict our syntax to only include type abstractions of the form $\Lambda X.\, v$. However, this would not be consistent with the reduction (NuTyWrap), which may push the non-value type binding construct underneath a type abstraction. (A similar issue arises with the reduction (Generalize), introduced in Section 6.) Instead, therefore, we allow the body of a type abstraction to be any term (hence, the term form $\Lambda X.\, t$), but only consider a type abstraction to be a value if its body is a value (hence, the value form $\Lambda X.\, v$). This further requires, unusually, that we permit reduction underneath type abstractions (hence, the context form $\Lambda X.\, E$).

5.3 Relation to standard calculus

We relate the polymorphic lambda calculus with explicit binding to the standard polymorphic lambda calculus based on type substitution. We omit the definitions of the latter to save space. We define the erasure t° from the calculus with explicit bindings to the standard calculus as follows:

$$
\begin{array}{rlrl}
c^\circ = & c & (t\ s)^\circ = & t^\circ\ s^\circ \\
(op(\vec{t}))^\circ = & op(\vec{t}^{\,\circ}) & (\Lambda X.\, t)^\circ = & \Lambda X.\, t^\circ \\
x^\circ = & x & (t\ A)^\circ = & t^\circ\ A \\
(\lambda x{:}A.\, t)^\circ = & \lambda x{:}A.\, t^\circ & (\nu X{:=}A.\, t)^\circ = & t^\circ[X{:=}A]
\end{array}
$$

The only clause of interest is that for a binder, which is erased by performing the type substitution. We also define the application of an environment to a type $\Gamma(A)$ and the erasure of environments Γ°.

$$
\begin{array}{rlrl}
(\Gamma, x{:}B)(A) = & \Gamma(A) & (\Gamma, x{:}A)^\circ = & \Gamma^\circ, x{:}\Gamma(A) \\
(\Gamma, X)(A) = & \Gamma(A) & (\Gamma, X)^\circ = & \Gamma^\circ, X \\
(\Gamma, X{:=}B)(A) = & \Gamma(A[X{:=}B]) & (\Gamma, X{:=}A)^\circ = & \Gamma^\circ
\end{array}
$$

We can now state that the polymorphic lambda calculus with bindings correctly implements the standard calculus, that is, erasure preserves types and reductions.

Proposition 1 (Erasure). *If $\Gamma \vdash s : A$ then $\Gamma^\circ \vdash s^\circ : \Gamma(A)$, and if $s \longmapsto s'$ then either $s^\circ = s'^\circ$ or $s^\circ \longmapsto s'^\circ$.*

5.4 Type safety

It is straightforward to show the usual type safety results for the calculus with explicit binding. Typically these results are formulated with respect to closed terms and empty environments, but because we allow reduction under type abstractions and binding our results are formulated with regard to terms that may contain free type variables and environments that may contain type variables and bindings (but not term variables). We let Δ range over such environments.

With this caveat, we have the usual results for canonical forms, progress, and preservation.

Proposition 2 (Canonical forms). *If $\Delta \vdash v : C$ then either*

- *$v = c$ and $C = \iota$ for some c and ι, or*
- *$v = \lambda x{:}A.\, t$ and $C = A{\to}B$ for some x, t, A, and B, or*
- *$v = \Lambda X.\, w$ and $C = \forall X.\, A$ for some w, X, and A.*

Proposition 3 (Progress). *If $\Delta \vdash s : A$ then either $s = v$ for some value v or $s \longmapsto s'$ for some term s'.*

Proposition 4 (Preservation). *If $\Delta \vdash s : A$ and $s \longmapsto s'$ then $\Delta \vdash s' : A$.*

5.5 Relation to dynamic type generation

Neis et al. (2009) present a form for generating type names: $\mathsf{new}\, X \approx A\, \mathsf{in}\, t$. The main difference between our bindings and new is that new adds its binding to a global list of bindings, σ.

$$\sigma; \mathsf{new}\, X{\approx}A\, \mathsf{in}\, t \longrightarrow \sigma, X{\approx}A; t \qquad \text{if } X \notin \mathrm{dom}(\sigma)$$

Earlier versions of our system also used a global list of bindings, but two aspects of our system require the change to local bindings.

First, evaluation proceeds under Λ in our system, which makes it problematic to use the global binding approach. Let

$$s = (\lambda x{:}X.\lambda y{:}Y.x) : X{\to}Y{\to}X$$

and consider the following program and hypothetical reduction sequence.

$$
\begin{array}{lll}
& \epsilon; & \mathsf{let}\, f = \Lambda X.(\Lambda Y.s)\ X\, \mathsf{in}\, (f\ \mathtt{I}, f\ \mathtt{B}) \\
\longmapsto & Y{\approx}X; & \mathsf{let}\, f = \Lambda X.s\, \mathsf{in}\, (f\ \mathtt{I}, f\ \mathtt{B}) \\
\longmapsto & Y{\approx}X; & ((\Lambda X.s)\ \mathtt{I}, (\Lambda X.s)\ \mathtt{B}) \\
\longmapsto & Y{\approx}X, X{\approx}I; & (s, (\Lambda X.s)\ \mathtt{B})
\end{array}
$$

But the next step in the sequence is problematic. We would like to α-rename the X in $\Lambda X.\, s$, but that would lose the connection with Y. Also, Y should really get two different bindings. Local bindings solve this problem by binding $Y{:=}X$ locally, inside the ΛX.

Second, bindings play a role in enforcing parametricity, which we discuss in detail in Section 6.2. An earlier system, the λ_N-calculus by Rossberg (2003), uses local type bindings, but λ_N performs scope extrusion, that is, the type bindings float upwards. The type bindings in this paper are immobile because they can trigger errors and we want those errors to occur at predictable locations.

6. Polymorphic blame calculus

Now that we have established the machinery of explicit binding, we consider how to combine dynamic casts with polymorphism. The polymorphic blame calculus is shown in Figure 4. The syntax is simply the union of the constructs of the blame calculus and the polymorphic lambda calculus, and the type rules are the union of the previous type rules.

Two new cases for quantified types are added to the definition of type compatibility, one each corresponding to casts to and from quantified types. Note that these break the symmetry of compatibility enjoyed by the simply-typed blame calculus. We discuss compatibility in tandem with the corresponding reductions, in Sections 6.1 and 6.3.

The intuition behind parametric polymorphism is that functions must behave uniformly with regard to type variables. To maintain parametricity in the presence of dynamic types, we arrange that dynamic values corresponding to type variables must be treated abstractly. Recall that values of dynamic type have the form $v : G \Rightarrow \star$, where G is a ground type. A key difference in moving to polymorphism is that the ground types, in addition to including base types ι and the function type $\star{\rightarrow}\star$, now also include type variables X. A value of the form $v : X \Rightarrow \star$ is called a *sealed value*.

We now briefly consider the reduction rules. Tests are updated so that if the value is sealed then the test indicates blame rather than returning true or false (IsTrue), (IsFalse), (IsTamper); the reason for this change is discussed in Section 6.2. Two rules are added to push bindings into the one new value form, ground values (NuGround), (NuTamper); the motivation for these rules is also discussed in Section 6.2. Finally, the last two rules extend casts to the case where the target type or source type is a quantified type (Generalize), (Instantiate); these rules are discussed in Sections 6.1 and 6.3. A side condition on (Generalize) avoids capture of type variables, and a side condition of (Instantiate) avoids overlap with (Ground) and (Generalize). The rules (IsTamper) and (NuTamper) introduce two global blame labels, $p_{\mathtt{is}}$ and p_ν, which are presumed not to label any cast.

6.1 Generalization

Perhaps the two rules of greatest interest are those that cast to and from a quantified type. We begin by discussing casts to a quantified type, postponing the reverse direction to Section 6.3.

Rule (Generalize) casts a value to a quantified type by abstracting over the type variable and recursively casting the value; note that the abstracted type variable may appear free in the target type of the cast. Observe that the corresponding rule for compatibility asserts that if the cast on the left of this rule is compatible then the cast on the right is also compatible.

We now have enough rules in place to return to our examples from Section 5.1. Here is the first example[1]

$$
\begin{array}{ll}
 & (K^\star : \star \Rightarrow^p \forall X.\, \forall Y.\, X{\rightarrow}Y{\rightarrow}X)\ \mathtt{I}\ \mathtt{I}\ 2\ 3 \\
\longmapsto^* & (\Lambda X.\, \Lambda Y.\, K^\star : \star \Rightarrow^p X{\rightarrow}Y{\rightarrow}X)\ \mathtt{I}\ \mathtt{I}\ 2\ 3 \\
\longmapsto^* & (\nu Y{:=}\mathtt{I}.\, \nu X{:=}\mathtt{I}.\, K^\star : \star \Rightarrow^p X{\rightarrow}Y{\rightarrow}X)\ 2\ 3 \\
\longmapsto^* & \nu Y{:=}\mathtt{I}.\, \nu X{:=}\mathtt{I}. \\
 & \quad K^\star\ (2 : X \Rightarrow^{\bar{p}} \star)\ (3 : Y \Rightarrow^{\bar{p}} \star) : \star \Rightarrow^p X \\
\longmapsto^* & \nu Y{:=}\mathtt{I}.\, \nu X{:=}\mathtt{I}. \\
 & \quad K^\star\ (2 : X \Rightarrow \star)\ (3 : Y \Rightarrow \star) : \star \Rightarrow^p X \\
\longmapsto^* & \nu Y{:=}\mathtt{I}.\, \nu X{:=}\mathtt{I}.\, (2 : X \Rightarrow \star) : \star \Rightarrow^p X \\
\longmapsto^* & \nu Y{:=}\mathtt{I}.\, \nu X{:=}\mathtt{I}.\, 2 \\
\longmapsto^* & 2
\end{array}
$$

The first step applies (Generalize) twice, while the penultimate step applies (Collapse) and (Id). This yields 2, as expected.

The second example is similar, save for the last steps.

$$
\begin{array}{ll}
 & (K^\star : \star \Rightarrow^p \forall X.\, \forall Y.\, X{\rightarrow}Y{\rightarrow}Y)\ \mathtt{I}\ \mathtt{I}\ 2\ 3 \\
\longmapsto^* & \nu Y{:=}\mathtt{I}.\, \nu X{:=}\mathtt{I}.\, (2 : X \Rightarrow \star) : \star \Rightarrow^p Y \\
\longmapsto^* & \nu Y{:=}\mathtt{I}.\, \nu X{:=}\mathtt{I}.\, \mathtt{blame}\ p \\
\longmapsto^* & \mathtt{blame}\ p
\end{array}
$$

Here the penultimate step applies (Conflict), and the final step applies (Abort). This yields $\mathtt{blame}\ p$, as expected.

6.2 Parametricity

We now consider some further examples, with an eye to understanding how sealing preserves parametricity.

The parametricity property for the type $\forall X.\, X{\rightarrow}X$ guarantees that a value of this type must be either the identity function or the undefined function. Consider the following three untyped terms.

$$
\begin{array}{rl}
\mathit{id}^\star & = \lceil \lambda x.\, x \rceil \\
\mathit{inc}^\star & = \lceil \lambda x.\, x + 1 \rceil \\
\mathit{test}^\star & = \lceil \lambda x.\, \mathtt{if}\ (x\ \mathtt{is}\ \mathtt{I})\ \mathtt{then}\ (x+1)\ \mathtt{else}\ x \rceil
\end{array}
$$

Function *id* is parametric, because it acts uniformly on values of all types; while functions *inc* and *test* are not, since the former acts only on integers, while the latter acts on values of any type but behaves differently on integers than on other arguments. However, casting all three functions to type $\forall X.\, X{\rightarrow}X$ yields values that satisfy the corresponding parametricity property. Casting $\mathit{id}^\star$, as one might expect, yields the identity function, while casting $\mathit{inc}^\star$ and $\mathit{test}^\star$, perhaps surprisingly, both yield the only other parametric function of this type, the everywhere undefined function.

Here is the first example.

$$
\begin{array}{ll}
 & (\mathit{id}^\star : \star \Rightarrow^p \forall X.\, X{\rightarrow}X)\ \mathtt{I}\ 2 \\
\longmapsto^* & \nu X{:=}\mathtt{I}.\, \mathit{id}^\star (2 : X \Rightarrow^{\bar{p}} \star) : \star \Rightarrow^p X \\
\longmapsto^* & \nu X{:=}\mathtt{I}.\, 2 : X \Rightarrow \star \Rightarrow^p X \\
\longmapsto^* & 2
\end{array}
$$

The last step is by rules (Collapse) and (Id). No matter which type and value are supplied, the casts match up, so this behaves as the identity function.

Here is the second example.

$$
\begin{array}{ll}
 & (\mathit{inc}^\star : \star \Rightarrow^p \forall X.\, X{\rightarrow}X)\ \mathtt{I}\ 2 \\
\longmapsto^* & \nu X{:=}\mathtt{I}.\, \mathit{inc}^\star (2 : X \Rightarrow^{\bar{p}} \star) : \star \Rightarrow^p X \\
\longmapsto^* & \nu X{:=}\mathtt{I}.\, ((2 : X \Rightarrow \star \Rightarrow^q \mathtt{I}) + 1) : \mathtt{I} \Rightarrow^q \star \Rightarrow^p X \\
\longmapsto^* & \mathtt{blame}\ q
\end{array}
$$

The last step is by rules (Conflict) and (Abort); here q labels casts in $\mathit{inc}^\star$ introduced by embedding typed integer addition into the untyped lambda calculus. Regardless of what type and value are supplied the casts still don't match, so this behaves as the everywhere undefined function.

Here is the third example.

$$
\begin{array}{ll}
 & (\mathit{test}^\star : \star \Rightarrow^p \forall X.\, X{\rightarrow}X)\ \mathtt{I}\ 2 \\
\longmapsto^* & \nu X{:=}\mathtt{I}.\, \mathit{test}^\star (2 : X \Rightarrow^{\bar{p}} \star) : \star \Rightarrow^p X \\
\longmapsto^* & \nu X{:=}\mathtt{I}.\, \mathtt{if}\ (2 : X \Rightarrow \star)\ \mathtt{is}\ \mathtt{I}\ \mathtt{then}\ \cdots\ \mathtt{else}\ \cdots \\
\longmapsto^* & \mathtt{blame}\ p_{\mathtt{is}}
\end{array}
$$

The last step is by rules (IsTamper) and (Abort). Sealed values should never be examined, so rule (IsTamper) ensures that applying a type test to a sealed value *always* allocates blame. Rules (IsTrue) and (IsFalse) add side-conditions to ensure they do not overlap with (IsTamper). The use of explicit binding plays a central role: the test $(2 : \mathtt{I} \Rightarrow \star)\ \mathtt{is}\ \mathtt{I}$ returns true, while the test $(2 : X \Rightarrow \star)\ \mathtt{is}\ \mathtt{I}$ allocates blame to $p_{\mathtt{is}}$, even when X is bound to type $\mathtt{I}$. Regardless of what type and value are supplied, the test always fails, so this behaves as the everywhere undefined function.

An alternative choice might be for $(v : X \Rightarrow \star)\ \mathtt{is}\ G$ to always return false (on the grounds that a sealed value is distinct from any ground value). This choice would still retain parametricity, because under this interpretation the result of casting $\mathit{test}^\star$ would be the identity function. However, we would lose another key property; we want to ensure that casting can lead to blame but cannot otherwise change a value. In this case, casting converts $\mathit{test}^\star$ to the everywhere undefined function, which is acceptable, while converting it to the identity function would violate our criterion.

Finally, consider the polymorphic type $\forall X.\, X{\rightarrow}\star$. The parametricity property for this function states that it must be either a constant function (ignoring its argument and always returning the same value) or the everywhere undefined function. Let's see what

[1] Careful readers will spot that some reductions are shown out of order, so as to group related reductions together.

happens when we cast $id^\star$ to this type.

$$
\begin{array}{l}
(id^\star : \star \Rightarrow^p \forall X.\, X \to \star)\ \mathtt{I}\ 2 \\
\longmapsto^* \nu X{:=}\mathtt{I}.\, id^\star(2 : X \Rightarrow^{\overline{p}} \star) : \star \Rightarrow^p \star \\
\longmapsto^* \nu X{:=}\mathtt{I}.\, 2 : X \Rightarrow \star \Rightarrow^p \star \\
\longmapsto^* \nu X{:=}\mathtt{I}.\, 2 : X \Rightarrow \star \\
\longmapsto^* \mathtt{blame}\ p_\nu
\end{array}
$$

Here rule (NuTamper) plays a key role, ensuring that the attempt to pass a value grounded at type X through the binder for X must fail. In an earlier system we devised that did not have bindings (Ahmed et al., 2009), this term would in fact reduce to a value of type $\star$, violating a strict interpretation of the parametricity requirement. It was only a mild violation, because the value of type $\star$ was sealed, so any attempt to examine it would fail. Still, from both a theoretical and practical point of view the current system seems preferable, because it detects errors earlier, and even if the result of the offending cast is not examined.

6.3 Instantiation

Having considered casts to a quantified type, we now turn our attention to the reverse, casts from a quantified type.

Rule (Instantiate) casts a value from a quantified type by instantiating the quantified type variable to the dynamic type and recursively casting the result. Observe that the corresponding rule for compatibility asserts that if the cast on the left of this rule is compatible then the cast on the right is also compatible.

The rule always instantiates with the dynamic type. Often, we are casting to the dynamic type, and in that case it seems natural to instantiate with the dynamic type itself. However, is this still sensible if we are casting to a type other than the dynamic type? We show that there is a strong sense in which instantiating to the dynamic type is always an appropriate choice.

Let's look at some examples. Let K be a polymorphically typed constant function.

$$K = \Lambda X.\, \lambda x{:}X.\, \lambda y{:}X.\, x$$

Here is an example casting to dynamic type.

$$
\begin{array}{l}
(K : \forall X.\, X \to X \to X \Rightarrow^p \star \to \star \to \star)\ \lceil 2 \rceil\ \lceil 3 \rceil \\
\longmapsto^* (K\ \star : \star \to \star \to \star \Rightarrow^p \star \to \star \to \star)\ \lceil 2 \rceil\ \lceil 3 \rceil \\
\longmapsto^* \lceil 2 \rceil
\end{array}
$$

Unsurprisingly, instantiating polymorphically typed code to $\star$ works perfectly when casting typed code to untyped code.

Perhaps more surprisingly, it also works well when casting polymorphically typed code to a different type. Because every value embeds into the type $\star$, instantiating to $\star$ yields an answer if instantiating to any type yields an answer. Here is an example of casting to static type.

$$
\begin{array}{l}
(K : \forall X.\, X \to X \to X \Rightarrow^p \mathtt{I} \to \mathtt{I} \to \mathtt{I})\ 2\ 3 \\
\longmapsto^* (K\ \star : \star \to \star \to \star \Rightarrow^p \mathtt{I} \to \mathtt{I} \to \mathtt{I})\ 2\ 3 \\
\longmapsto^* 2
\end{array}
$$

This, of course, gives us exactly the same answer as if we had instantiated K to $\mathtt{I}$ instead of $\star$:

$$
\begin{array}{l}
(K\ \mathtt{I} : \mathtt{I} \to \mathtt{I} \to \mathtt{I} \Rightarrow^p \mathtt{I} \to \mathtt{I} \to \mathtt{I})\ 2\ 3 \\
\longmapsto^* 2
\end{array}
$$

In this sense, we say that $\star$ is a Jack-of-All-Trades: if instantiating to any type yields an answer, then so does instantiating to $\star$.

However, instantiating to $\star$ is something of a *laissez faire* policy, in that it may yield an answer when a strict instantiation would fail. For instance, consider a slight variant on the example above.

$$
\begin{array}{l}
(K : \forall X.\, X \to X \to X \Rightarrow^p \mathtt{I} \to \star \to \mathtt{I})\ 2\ \lceil \mathtt{true} \rceil \\
\longmapsto^* (K\ \star : \star \to \star \to \star \Rightarrow^p \mathtt{I} \to \star \to \mathtt{I})\ 2\ \lceil \mathtt{true} \rceil \\
\longmapsto^* 2
\end{array}
$$

Here, instantiating to $\mathtt{I}$ directly is more strict, yielding blame rather than a value.

$$
\begin{array}{l}
(K\ \mathtt{I} : \mathtt{I} \to \mathtt{I} \to \mathtt{I} \Rightarrow^p \mathtt{I} \to \star \to \mathtt{I})\ 2\ \lceil \mathtt{true} \rceil \\
\longmapsto^* \mathtt{blame}\ \overline{p}
\end{array}
$$

In other words, $\star$, though a Jack-of-All-Trades, is a master of none.

To formulate the relevant property precisely, we need to capture what we mean by saying that one term yields an answer if another does, so we formulate a notion of *contextual approximation* $\sqsubseteq$.

First, we define convergence and divergence. A term that neither converges nor diverges must allocate blame.

Definition 5. *A closed term s* converges, *written $s \Downarrow$, if $s \longmapsto^* v$ for some value v, and* diverges, *written $s \Uparrow$, if the reduction sequence beginning with s does not terminate.*

Next, we define a variant of contextual approximation, where a term that allocates blame approximates every term.

Definition 6. *Term s* approximates *term t, written $s \sqsubseteq t$, if for all evaluation contexts E we have*

- *$E[s] \Uparrow$ implies $E[t] \Uparrow$, and*
- *$E[s] \Downarrow$ implies $E[t] \Downarrow$.*

We can now state the principle.

Theorem 7 (Jack-of-All-Trades Principle). *If $\Delta \vdash v : \forall X.\, A$ and $A[X{:=}C] \prec B$ (and hence $A[X{:=}\star] \prec B$) then*

$$(v\ C : A[X{:=}C] \Rightarrow^p B) \quad \sqsubseteq \quad (v\ \star : A[X{:=}\star] \Rightarrow^p B).$$

We defer the proof until Section 11.

6.4 Evaluation under type abstraction

As noted in Section 5.2, an unusual feature of our presentation is that we evaluate underneath type abstractions. We now provide an example, promised there, of why such evaluation is necessary.

Parametricity guarantees that a term of type $\forall X.\, X$ cannot reduce to a value. One term with this type is $\Lambda X.\, \mathtt{blame}\ r$. In our calculus, this term is not a value, and it evaluates to $\mathtt{blame}\ r$. However, if we did not evaluate under type abstractions then this term would be a value.

We want it to be the case that $v : A \Rightarrow^p \star \Rightarrow^q A$ is equivalent to v for any value v of type A. (Among other things, it is easy to show that this is a consequence of the Jack-of-All-Trades Principle.) However, if $\Lambda X.\, \mathtt{blame}\ r$ is a value, this is not the case.

$$
\begin{array}{l}
(\Lambda X.\, \mathtt{blame}\ r) : \forall X.\, X \Rightarrow^p \star \Rightarrow^q \forall X.\, X \\
\longmapsto^* (\Lambda X.\, \mathtt{blame}\ r)\ \star : \star \Rightarrow^p \star \Rightarrow^q \forall X.\, X \\
\longmapsto^* (\nu X{:=}\star.\, \mathtt{blame}\ r) : \star \Rightarrow^p \star \Rightarrow^q \forall X.\, X \\
\longmapsto^* \mathtt{blame}\ r
\end{array}
$$

This is no good—a cast that should leave a value unchanged has instead converted it to blame!

The solution to this difficulty, as described in Section 5.2, is to permit evaluation under type abstractions, and to only regard terms of the form $\Lambda X.\, v$ as values. We conjecture that if we based our system on call-by-name rather than call-by-value that evaluation under type abstraction would not be necessary.

6.5 Type safety

The usual type safety properties hold for the polymorphic blame calculus.

Lemma 8 (Canonical forms). *If $\Delta \vdash v : C$, then*

1. *$v = c$ and $C = \iota$ for some c and ι, or*
2. *$v = w : G \Rightarrow \star$ and $C = \star$, for some w and G, or*
3. *$v = \lambda x{:}A.\, t$ and $C = A \to B$, for some x, t, A, and B, or*
4. *$v = \Lambda X.\, w$ and $C = \forall X.\, A$, for some w, X, and A.*

Compatibility $\boxed{A \prec B}$

$$A \prec A \qquad A \prec \star \qquad \star \prec B \qquad \frac{A' \prec A \quad B \prec B'}{A \to B \prec A' \to B'} \qquad \frac{A[X := \star] \prec B}{\forall X.A \prec B} \qquad \frac{A \prec B}{A \prec \forall X.B}\, X \notin \mathrm{ftv}(A)$$

Subtype $\boxed{A <: B}$

$$A <: A \qquad \frac{A <: G}{A <: \star} \qquad \frac{A' <: A \quad B <: B'}{A \to B <: A' \to B'} \qquad \frac{A[X := C] <: B}{\forall X.\, A <: B} \qquad \frac{A <: B}{A <: \forall X.\, B}\, X \notin \mathrm{ftv}(A)$$

Positive Subtype $\boxed{A <:^+ B}$

$$A <:^+ A \qquad A <:^+ \star \qquad \frac{A' <:^- A \quad B <:^+ B'}{A \to B <:^+ A' \to B'} \qquad \frac{A[X := \star] <:^+ B}{\forall X.\, A <:^+ B} \qquad \frac{A <:^+ B}{A <:^+ \forall X.\, B}\, X \notin \mathrm{ftv}(A)$$

Negative Subtype $\boxed{A <:^- B}$

$$A <:^- A \qquad \frac{A <:^- G}{A <:^- B} \qquad \star <:^- B \qquad \frac{A' <:^+ A \quad B <:^- B'}{A \to B <:^- A' \to B'} \qquad \frac{A[X := \star] <:^- B}{\forall X.\, A <:^- B} \qquad \frac{A <:^- B}{A <:^- \forall X.\, B}\, X \notin \mathrm{ftv}(A)$$

Naive Subtype $\boxed{A <:_n B}$

$$A <:_n A \qquad A <:_n \star \qquad \frac{A <:_n A' \quad B <:_n B'}{A \to B <:_n A' \to B'} \qquad \frac{A[X := \star] <:_n B}{\forall X.\, A <:_n B} \qquad \frac{A <:_n B}{A <:_n \forall X.\, B}\, X \notin \mathrm{ftv}(A)$$

Figure 5. Subtyping Relations

Proposition 9 (Preservation). *If $\Delta \vdash s : A$ and $s \longmapsto s'$, then $\Delta \vdash s' : A$.*

Proposition 10 (Progress). *If $\Delta \vdash s : A$, then either*

- *$s = v$ for some value v, or*
- *$s \longmapsto s'$ for some term s', or*
- *$s =$ `blame` p for some blame label p.*

Preservation and progress on their own do not guarantee a great deal because they do not rule out blame as a result. In sections 8 and 9 we characterize situations in which blame cannot arise.

7. Subtyping relations

Figure 5 presents the compatibility relation and four forms of subtyping—ordinary, positive, negative, and naive. Compatibility determines when it is sensible to attempt to cast one type to another type, and the different forms of subtyping characterize when a cast cannot give rise to certain kinds of blame. All five relations are reflexive, and all four subtyping relations are transitive.

Why do we need *four* different subtyping relations? Each has a different purpose. We use $A <: B$ to characterize when a cast from A to B cannot yield blame for that cast. One useful consequence is that casting from a quantified type $\forall X.\, B$ to any instance of that type $B[X{:=}A]$ never yields blame. However, while subtyping gives a strong guarantee, it arises relatively rarely in programs that integrate static and dynamic typing. What we wish to show for such programs is not that they never fail, but that when they do fail that blame always lies on the less precisely typed side of the cast, and this is the purpose of the other three relations. We use $A <:^+ B$ and $A <:^- B$ to characterize when a cast from A to B cannot yield either positive or negative blame, respectively, and we use $A <:_n B$ to characterize when A is a more precise type than B.

The definitions are related, in that $A <: B$ holds if $A <:^+ B$ and $A <:^- B$ (but not conversely), and $A <:_n B$ holds if and only if $A <:^+ B$ and $B <:^- A$. We tried to massage our definitions so that the first clause, like the second, would be an equivalence, but failed to do so.

Compatibility is written $A \prec B$. It is reflexive, and the dynamic type is compatible with every other type. The remaining three compatibility rules can be read off directly from the reductions (WRAP), (INSTANTIATE), and (GENERALIZE): replacing $\Rightarrow$ in the reductions yields the $\prec$ conditions in the rules. The casts on the left-hand side of the reductions correspond to the compatibilities in the conclusion of the rules, and the casts on the right-hand side correspond the hypotheses. Thus, the compatibility rules are designed to ensure that reducing compatible casts yield compatible casts.

Function compatibility is contravariant in the domain and covariant in the range, corresponding to the swapping in the (WRAP) rule. A polymorphic type $\forall X.\, A$ is compatible with type B if its instance $A[X{:=}\star]$ is compatible with B, corresponding to the (INSTANTIATE) rule. A type A is compatible with polymorphic type $\forall X.\, B$ if type A is compatible with B (assuming X does not appear free in A so there is no capture of bound variables), corresponding to the (GENERALIZE) rule.

Ordinary subtyping is written $A <: B$. It characterizes when a cast cannot give rise to blame. Every subtype of a ground type is a subtype of $\star$, because a cast from a ground type to $\star$ never allocates blame. As with all the relations, function subtyping is contravariant in the domain and covariant in the range. A polymorphic type $\forall X.\, A$ is a subtype of a type B if some instance $A[X{:=}C]$ is a subtype of B—this is the one way in which subtyping differs from all the other relations, which instantiate with $\star$ rather than an arbitrary type C. It is easy to see that $A <:^+ B$ and $A <:^- B$ together imply $A <: B$, but not conversely.

The next two relations are concerned with positive and negative blame. If reducing a cast with label p allocates blame to p we say it yields *positive* blame, and if it allocates blame to $\bar{p}$ we say it yields *negative* blame. The positive and negative subtyping relations characterize when positive and negative blame can arise. In the next section, we show that a cast from A to B with $A <:^+ B$ cannot give rise to positive blame, and with $A <:^- B$ cannot give rise to negative blame.

The two judgments are defined in terms of each other, and track the negating of blame labels that occurs in the contravariant

$\boxed{s \text{ sf } p}$

$$\frac{A <:^{+} B \quad s \text{ sf } p}{(s : A \Rightarrow^{p} B) \text{ sf } p} \qquad \frac{A <:^{-} B \quad s \text{ sf } p}{(s : A \Rightarrow^{\overline{p}} B) \text{ sf } p}$$

$$\frac{q \neq p \quad q \neq \overline{p} \quad s \text{ sf } p}{(s : A \Rightarrow^{q} B) \text{ sf } p} \qquad \frac{s \text{ sf } p}{(s : G \Rightarrow \star) \text{ sf } p}$$

$$\frac{s \text{ sf } p}{(s \texttt{ is } G) \text{ sf } p} \qquad \frac{q \neq p}{(\texttt{blame}\ q) \text{ sf } p}$$

$$\frac{}{c \text{ sf } p} \qquad \frac{\vec{t} \text{ sf } p}{(op(\vec{t})) \text{ sf } p} \qquad \frac{}{x \text{ sf } p}$$

$$\frac{t \text{ sf } p}{(\lambda x : A.\, t) \text{ sf } p} \qquad \frac{t \text{ sf } p \quad s \text{ sf } p}{(t\ s) \text{ sf } p}$$

$$\frac{t \text{ sf } p}{(\Lambda X.\, t) \text{ sf } p} \qquad \frac{t \text{ sf } p}{(t\ A) \text{ sf } p} \qquad \frac{t \text{ sf } p}{(\nu X{:=}A.\, t) \text{ sf } p}$$

Figure 6. Safety for $<:^{+}$ and $<:^{-}$

position of function types. We have $A <:^{+} \star$ and $\star <:^{-} B$ for every type A and B, because casting to $\star$ can never give rise to positive blame, and casting from $\star$ can never give rise to negative blame. We also have $A <:^{-} G$ implies $A <:^{-} B$, because a cast from a ground type to $\star$ cannot allocate blame, and a cast from $\star$ to any type cannot allocate negative blame.

We also define a naive subtyping judgment, $A <:_{n} B$, which corresponds to our informal notion of type A being more precise than type B, and is *covariant* for both the domain and range of functions.

8. The Blame Theorem

The Blame Theorem asserts that a cast from a positive subtype cannot lead to positive blame, and a cast from a negative subtype cannot lead to negative blame. The structure of the proof is similar to a type safety proof, depending on progress and preservation lemmas. However, the invariant we preserve is not well-typing, but instead a safety relation, t sf p, as defined in Figure 6. A term t is safe for blame label p with respect to $<:^{+}$ and $<:^{-}$, written t sf p, if every cast with label p has a source that is a positive subtype of the target, and every cast with label $\overline{p}$ has a source that is a negative subtype of the target; we assume that $p \neq p_{\texttt{is}}$ and $p \neq p_{\nu}$.

Lemma 11 (Blame progress). *If s sf p then $s \not\longmapsto \texttt{blame}\ p$.*

Lemma 12 (Blame preservation). *If s sf p and $s \longmapsto s'$, then s' sf p.*

Positive and negative subtyping are closely related to naive subtyping.

Proposition 13 (Factoring). *$A <:_{n} B$ iff $A <:^{+} B$ and $B <:^{-} A$.*

The proof of Proposition 13 requires four observations.

Lemma 14.
If $A <:^{+} B$ and $X \notin A$, then $X \notin B$.
If $A <:^{-} B$ and $X \notin B$, then $X \notin A$.
Given $X \notin B$, we have $A[X{:=}\star] <:^{+} B$ iff $A <:^{+} B$.
Given $X \notin A$, we have $A <:^{-} B[X{:=}\star]$ iff $A <:^{-} B$.

We may now characterize how positive, negative, and naive subtyping relate to positive and negative blame. Note that, typically, each cast in a source program has a unique blame label.

Corollary 15 (Blame Theorem). *Let t be a program with a subterm $s : A \Rightarrow^{p} B$ where the cast is labelled by the only occurrence of p in t, and $\overline{p}$ does not appear in t.*

$\boxed{s \text{ sf}^{<:} p}$

$$\frac{A <: B \quad s \text{ sf}^{<:} p}{(s : A \Rightarrow^{p} B) \text{ sf}^{<:} p} \qquad \frac{A <: B \quad s \text{ sf}^{<:} p}{(s : A \Rightarrow^{\overline{p}} B) \text{ sf}^{<:} p}$$

$$\frac{q \neq p \quad q \neq \overline{p} \quad s \text{ sf}^{<:} p}{(s : A \Rightarrow^{q} B) \text{ sf}^{<:} p} \qquad \frac{s \text{ sf}^{<:} p}{(s : G \Rightarrow \star) \text{ sf}^{<:} p}$$

$$\frac{s \text{ sf}^{<:} p}{(s \texttt{ is } G) \text{ sf}^{<:} p} \qquad \frac{q \neq p \quad q \neq \overline{p}}{(\texttt{blame}\ q) \text{ sf}^{<:} p}$$

$$\frac{}{c \text{ sf}^{<:} p} \qquad \frac{\vec{t} \text{ sf}^{<:} p}{(op(\vec{t})) \text{ sf}^{<:} p} \qquad \frac{}{x \text{ sf}^{<:} p}$$

$$\frac{t \text{ sf}^{<:} p}{(\lambda x : A.\, t) \text{ sf}^{<:} p} \qquad \frac{t \text{ sf}^{<:} p \quad s \text{ sf}^{<:} p}{(t\ s) \text{ sf}^{<:} p}$$

$$\frac{t \text{ sf}^{<:} p}{(\Lambda X.\, t) \text{ sf}^{<:} p} \qquad \frac{t \text{ sf}^{<:} p}{(t\ A) \text{ sf}^{<:} p} \qquad \frac{t \text{ sf}^{<:} p}{(\nu X{:=}A.\, t) \text{ sf}^{<:} p}$$

Figure 7. Safety for $<:$

- *If $A <:^{+} B$, then $t \not\longmapsto^{*} \texttt{blame}\ p$.*
- *If $A <:^{-} B$, then $t \not\longmapsto^{*} \texttt{blame}\ \overline{p}$.*
- *If $A <:_{n} B$, then $t \not\longmapsto^{*} \texttt{blame}\ p$.*
- *If $B <:_{n} A$, then $t \not\longmapsto^{*} \texttt{blame}\ \overline{p}$.*

The first two results are an immediate consequence of blame progress and preservation (Lemmas 11 and 12) while the second two results are an immediate consequence of the first two and factoring (Proposition 13).

Because our notion of more and less precise types is captured by naive subtyping, the last two clauses show that any failure of a cast from a more-precisely-typed term to a less-precisely-typed context must be blamed on the less-precisely-typed context, and any failure of a cast from a less-precisely-typed term to a more-precisely-typed context must be blamed on the less-precisely-typed term.

The Blame Theorem and Subtyping Theorem give no guarantees regarding the two global blame labels $p_{\texttt{is}}$ and p_{ν}. We are investigating an alternative design in which the is, Λ, and ν forms are individually labelled and the safety relations can guarantee the absence of blame going to those labels under suitable static conditions.

9. The Subtyping Theorem

The Subtyping Theorem asserts that a cast from a subtype to a supertype cannot lead to any blame whatsoever. As with the Blame Theorem, the structure of the proof is similar to that of a type safety proof, depending on progress and preservation lemmas. Again, we use a safety relation, $s \text{ sf}^{<:} p$, as defined in Figure 7. A term t is safe for blame label p with respect to $<:$, written $s \text{ sf}^{<:} p$, if every cast with label p or $\overline{p}$ has a source that is a subtype of the target; we assume that $p \neq p_{\texttt{is}}$ and $p \neq p_{\nu}$.

Lemma 16 (Subtyping progress). *If s sf p then $s \not\longmapsto \texttt{blame}\ p$.*

The preservation result is a little more complex than that for the Blame Theorem, because it involves approximation as introduced in Section 6.3.

Lemma 17 (Subtyping preservation). *If $s \text{ sf}^{<:} p$ and $s \longmapsto s'$, then either $s' \text{ sf}^{<:} p$ or there exists s'' such that $s'' \sqsubseteq s'$ and $s'' \text{ sf}^{<:} p$.*

The proof is by case analysis on $s \longrightarrow s'$ and $s \longmapsto s'$, where the case for (INSTANTIATE) depends on the Jack-of-All-Trades Principle. We may now characterize how subtyping relates to blame.

Syntax

Binding reference	P, Q	$::=$	$X \mid \overline{X}$
Terms	s, t	$::=$	$c \mid op(\vec{t}) \mid x \mid \lambda x{:}A.\,t \mid t\ s \mid \Lambda X.\,v \mid t\ A \mid \nu X{:=}A.\,t \mid s : A \Rightarrow^{P} B$
Values	v, w	$::=$	$c \mid \lambda x{:}A.\,t \mid \Lambda X.\,v \mid v : A \Rightarrow^{\overline{X}} X$
Contexts	E	$::=$	$[\,] \mid op(\vec{v}, E, \vec{t}) \mid E\ s \mid v\ E \mid E\ A \mid \nu X{:=}A.\,E \mid E : A \Rightarrow^{P} B$

Type rules

$$(\textsc{Reveal})\ \frac{\Gamma \vdash t : B \qquad (X{:=}A) \in \Gamma}{\Gamma \vdash (t : B \Rightarrow^{X} B[X{:=}A]) : B[X{:=}A]} \qquad (\textsc{Conceal})\ \frac{\Gamma \vdash t : B[X{:=}A] \qquad (X{:=}A) \in \Gamma}{\Gamma \vdash (t : B[X{:=}A] \Rightarrow^{\overline{X}} B) : B}$$

Reduction rules

$$(\Lambda X.\,v)\ A \longrightarrow \nu X{:=}A.\,(v : B \Rightarrow^{X} B[X{:=}A]) \quad \text{if } \Lambda X.\,v : \forall X.\,B \qquad (\textsc{TyBeta})$$

$$\nu X{:=}A.\,(v : B \Rightarrow^{\overline{Y}} Y) \longrightarrow (\nu X{:=}A.\,v) : B \Rightarrow^{\overline{Y}} Y \qquad (\textsc{NuSC})$$

$$v : \iota \Rightarrow^{P} \iota \longrightarrow v \qquad (\textsc{SCBase})$$

$$(\lambda x : A.\,t) : A \to B \Rightarrow^{P} A' \to B' \longrightarrow \lambda x{:}A'.\,(t[x{:=}(x : A' \Rightarrow^{\overline{P}} A)] : B \Rightarrow^{P} B') \qquad (\textsc{SCWrap})$$

$$(\Lambda X.\,v) : \forall X.\,B \Rightarrow^{P} \forall X.\,B' \longrightarrow \Lambda X.\,(v : B \Rightarrow^{P} B') \quad \text{if } X \neq P \text{ and } X \neq \overline{P} \qquad (\textsc{SCTyWrap})$$

$$v : X \Rightarrow^{P} X \longrightarrow v \quad \text{if } X \neq P \text{ and } X \neq \overline{P} \qquad (\textsc{SCSeal})$$

$$v : A \Rightarrow^{\overline{X}} X \Rightarrow^{X} A \longrightarrow v \qquad (\textsc{SCCancel})$$

Figure 8. Polymorphic lambda calculus with static casts (extends and updates Figures 1 and 3).

Syntax

Terms	s, t	$::=$	$c \mid op(\vec{t}) \mid x \mid \lambda x{:}A.\,t \mid t\ s \mid s{:}A \Rightarrow^{p} B \mid s{:}G \Rightarrow \star \mid s \texttt{ is } G \mid \texttt{blame}\ p \mid \Lambda X.\,t \mid t\ A \mid \nu X{:=}A.\,t \mid s{:}A \Rightarrow^{P} B$
Values	v, w	$::=$	$c \mid \lambda x{:}A.\,t \mid v : G \Rightarrow \star \mid \Lambda X.\,v \mid v : A \Rightarrow^{\overline{X}} X$
Contexts	E	$::=$	$[\,] \mid op(\vec{v}, E, \vec{t}) \mid E\ s \mid v\ E \mid E \texttt{ is } G \mid E{:}A \Rightarrow^{p} B \mid E{:}G \Rightarrow \star \mid \Lambda X.\,E \mid E\ A \mid \nu X{:=}A.\,E \mid E{:}A \Rightarrow^{P} B$

Reduction rules

$$v : \star \Rightarrow^{P} \star \longrightarrow v \qquad (\textsc{SCDyn})$$

Figure 9. Polymorphic blame calculus with static casts (extends and updates Figures 1, 2, 3, 4, and 8).

Corollary 18 (Subtyping Theorem). *Let t be a program with a subterm $s : A \Rightarrow^{p} B$ where the cast is labelled by the only occurrence of p in t, and $\overline{p}$ does not appear in t.*

- *If $A <: B$, then $t \not\longmapsto^{*}$ `blame` p and $t \not\longmapsto^{*}$ `blame` $\overline{p}$.*

The result is an immediate consequence of subtyping progress and preservation.

10. Static casts

The polymorphic lambda calculus with explicit bindings (Figure 3) includes two type rules that are not syntax directed, (Reveal) and (Conceal). In this section, we introduce the polymorphic lambda calculus with static casts, which extends the earlier calculus by adding two new constructs so that the two type rules in question become syntax directed. The result is a calculus which syntactically records exactly where type abstraction occurs, similar in some respects to that of Grossman et al. (2000). The more refined type information provided by the new calculus will be of use in the proof of the Jack-of-all-Trades Principle provided in the next section.

10.1 Polymorphic lambda calculus with static casts

We introduce the polymorphic lambda calculus with static casts in Figure 8. It proves convenient for the new constructs to use a notation similar to that for dynamic casts, and hence we call them static casts. Dynamic casts may fail and are decorated with a blame label. Static casts may not fail, and are decorated with a *binding reference*.

Static casts come in two forms, corresponding to the rules (Reveal) and (Conceal) in the polymorphic lambda calculus with explicit binding. Assume binding $X{:=}A$ appears in the environment Γ. We reveal the binding of a type variable with the construct

$$s : B \Rightarrow^{X} B[X{:=}A]$$

and we conceal the binding with the construct

$$s : B[X{:=}A] \Rightarrow^{\overline{X}} B.$$

For convenience in the reduction rules, we use the syntax

$$s : A \Rightarrow^{P} B$$

to range over both forms, where P is a binding reference that is either X or $\overline{X}$. We write $\overline{P}$ for the involution that adds an overbar when one is missing, or removes the overbar when one is present.

With the addition of static casts, we have a new value form. It is now the case that a value of type X always has the form

$$v : A \Rightarrow^{\overline{X}} X$$

where v has type A and X is bound to A in the environment.

The rule for type application is modified to also insert a suitable static cast (TyBeta). The static cast depends upon the type of the type abstraction; it is easy to annotate terms to preserve this information.

We introduce a reduction rule to push explicit bindings through the one new value form (NuSC). Surprisingly, the (NuSC) reduction rule requires no side conditions; the type system already ensures that $X \neq Y$ and $X \notin \text{ftv}(B)$. We also introduce reduction rules to perform static casts for each type constructor: base types (SCBase), functions (SCWrap), quantified types (SCTyWrap), and type variables (SCSeal). The rules to push a static cast through a base type (SCBase) or a type variable (SCSeal) both resemble the rule for dynamic casts (Id).

The rule to apply a static cast to a function (SCWrap) resembles the corresponding rule for dynamic casts (Wrap). Just as Wrap flips the cast on the arguments and negates the blame label, SCWrap also flips the static cast on the arguments and negates the binding reference. One notable difference between (SCWrap) and (Wrap) is that (SCWrap) does not introduce a new wrapper function to apply the cast, but instead performs substitution directly in the body of the lambda abstraction. This greatly simplifies the simulation relation used in the proof of the Jack-of-All-Trades Principle. The substitution-based approach is not viable for (Wrap) because a dynamic cast can fail, but works here because a static cast cannot fail.

The rule to apply a static cast to a quantified type (SCTyWrap) is simpler than the corresponding rules for applying a dynamic cast. For dynamic casts we require separate rules for universal quantifiers in the source (Instantiate) and in the target (Generalize); while for static casts it suffices to use a single rule to handle a universal quantifier in both the source and target (SCTyWrap), since one will be a substitution instance of the other.

Finally, if a static cast meets its negation, the two casts cancel (SCCancel).

10.2 Relation to explicit binding

We relate the polymorphic lambda calculus with static casts to the polymorphic lambda calculus with explicit binding. We define the erasure $t^\bullet$ from the calculus with static casts to the calculus with explicit binding as follows:

$$\begin{array}{rclrcl} c^\bullet &=& c & (\Lambda X.\, t)^\bullet &=& \Lambda X.\, t^\bullet \\ (op(\vec{t}))^\bullet &=& op(\vec{t^\bullet}) & (t\ A)^\bullet &=& t^\bullet\ A \\ x^\bullet &=& x & (\nu X{:=}A.\, t)^\bullet &=& \nu X{:=}A.\, t^\bullet \\ (\lambda x{:}A.\, t)^\bullet &=& \lambda x{:}A.\, t^\bullet & (t : A \Rightarrow^P B)^\bullet &=& t^\bullet \\ (t\ s)^\bullet &=& t^\bullet\ s^\bullet & & & \end{array}$$

Proposition 19 (Erasure). *If $\Gamma \vdash s : A$ then $\Gamma \vdash s^\bullet : A$, and if $s \longmapsto s'$ then either $s^\bullet = s'^\bullet$ or $s^\bullet \longmapsto s'^\bullet$.*

10.3 Type safety

It is straightforward to show the usual type safety results for the polymorphic lambda calculus with static casts. Notably, there is now one additional canonical form, for a term whose type is a type variable.

Proposition 20 (Canonical forms). *If $\Delta \vdash v : C$ then either*

- *$v = c$ and $C = \iota$ for some c and ι, or*
- *$v = \lambda x{:}A.\, t$ and $C = A \to B$ for some x, t, A, and B, or*
- *$v = \Lambda X.\, w$ and $C = \forall X.\, A$ for some w, X, and A.*
- *$v = w : A \Rightarrow^{\overline{X}} X$ and $C = X$ for some w, X, and A.*

Proposition 21 (Progress). *If $\Delta \vdash s : A$ then either $s = v$ for some value v or $s \longmapsto s'$ for some term s'.*

Proposition 22 (Preservation). *If $\Delta \vdash s : A$ and $s \longmapsto s'$ then $\Delta \vdash s' : A$.*

10.4 Polymorphic blame calculus with static casts

Given the above development, it is straightforward to augment the polymorphic blame calculus to include static casts, as shown in Figure 9. The syntax is just the union of the syntaxes of the previous calculi. Only one additional reduction rule is required, to apply a static cast to the dynamic type (SCDyn). Analogues of the previous results to relate the calculus with static casts to the one without are straightforward, as are analogues of the type safety results, and we omit the details.

11. The Jack-of-All-Trades Principle

We now provide the proof of Theorem 7, the Jack-of-All-Trades Principle. To prove the theorem we introduce a relation $s \precsim t$ that is contained in $\sqsubseteq$ and prove that $\precsim$ is a simulation. Examining the theorem gives our starting point for the relation.

$$v\ C : A[X{:=}C] \Rightarrow^p B \precsim v \star : A[X{:=}\star] \Rightarrow^p B.$$

As these terms reduce, this cast can break into many casts, but they will all have the general form

$$s : A \Rightarrow^p B \precsim t : A' \Rightarrow^p B$$

or the form

$$s : B \Rightarrow^{\bar{p}} A \precsim t : B \Rightarrow^{\bar{p}} A'$$

where $s \precsim t$, and A and A' are the same, except some types in A are replaced by $\star$ in A'. To make the latter specific, we introduce a few definitions.

Definition 23. *If Σ is a map from type variables to types, its* erasure *$\Sigma^\star$ is the map that takes each X in the domain of Σ to $\star$.*

Definition 24. *We say that type A* simulates *type A', written $A \precsim A'$, if there exists a type A'' and a map Σ such that $A = \Sigma(A'')$ and $A' = \Sigma^\star(A'')$.*

For example, if $A = (X \to X) \to B$ and $A' = \star \to \star$ we have $A \precsim A'$ by taking $A'' = Y \to Z$ and $\Sigma = Y{:=}X \to X, Z{:=}B$ (and hence $\Sigma^\star = Y{:=}\star, Z{:=}\star$). As a second example, consider what type A may simulate a type variable X, $A \precsim X$? The answer is that X is the only type that simulates X, so $A = X$.

The full definition of the relation $\precsim$ is given in Figure 10. The rules on the right-hand side make $\precsim$ a congruence and the remaining rules help us keep terms related as they reduce. We add the following side condition to the rule (LeftSC): the type variable in the binding reference does not appear anywhere in the program on the right-hand side of $\precsim$; this is because (LeftSC) arises from (LeftTyAbs), in which there is a type abstraction on the left that does not appear on the right.

Note that the simulation rules say nothing about types. But when the terms on each side of the conclusion are well typed then the terms in the hypothesis are as well. Furthermore, we have the following lemma.

Lemma 25. *If $s \precsim t$, $\Gamma \vdash s : A$, and $\Gamma' \vdash t : A'$, then $A \precsim A'$.*

The proof is a straightforward induction on $s \precsim t$.

An important property of $\precsim$ is that it relates values to terms that reduce to values.

Lemma 26 (Value on the left of $\precsim$). *If $v \precsim t$, then $t \longmapsto^* w$ and $v \precsim w$ for some value w.*

In the proof that $\precsim$ is a simulation, the case for (Beta) requires the following lemma regarding substitution.

Lemma 27 (Substitution preserves $\precsim$). *If $t \precsim t'$ and $v \precsim v'$, then $t[x{:=}v] \precsim t'[x{:=}v']$.*

The result is a consequence of the fact that $\precsim$ is a congruence.

We now show that $\precsim$ simulates both the reduction relation $\longrightarrow$ and the step relation $\longmapsto$, beginning with the former.

$$\frac{s \underset{\sim}{\sqsubset} t \quad A \underset{\sim}{\sqsubset} A'}{s : A \Rightarrow^{p} B \underset{\sim}{\sqsubset} t : A' \Rightarrow^{p} B} \quad (\textsc{PosCast})$$

$$\frac{s \underset{\sim}{\sqsubset} t \quad A \underset{\sim}{\sqsubset} A'}{s : B \Rightarrow^{\bar{p}} A \underset{\sim}{\sqsubset} t : B \Rightarrow^{\bar{p}} A'} \quad (\textsc{NegCast})$$

$$\texttt{blame}\, q \underset{\sim}{\sqsubset} t \quad (\textsc{Blame})$$

$$\frac{s \underset{\sim}{\sqsubset} t}{\Lambda Y.\, s \underset{\sim}{\sqsubset} t} \quad (\textsc{LeftTyAbs})$$

$$\frac{s \underset{\sim}{\sqsubset} t}{s : A \Rightarrow^{P} B \underset{\sim}{\sqsubset} t} \quad (\textsc{LeftSC})$$

$$\frac{s \underset{\sim}{\sqsubset} t}{\nu X{:=}A.\, s \underset{\sim}{\sqsubset} t} \quad (\textsc{LeftNu})$$

$$\frac{v \underset{\sim}{\sqsubset} w}{v \underset{\sim}{\sqsubset} w : G \Rightarrow \star} \quad (\textsc{RightGround})$$

$$\frac{v \underset{\sim}{\sqsubset} w}{(\Lambda X.\, v)\ \star \underset{\sim}{\sqsubset} w} \quad (\textsc{LeftTyApp})$$

$$c \underset{\sim}{\sqsubset} c \quad (\textsc{CongConst})$$

$$x \underset{\sim}{\sqsubset} x \quad (\textsc{CongVar})$$

$$\frac{s \underset{\sim}{\sqsubset} t \quad A \underset{\sim}{\sqsubset} A'}{\lambda x{:}A.\, s \underset{\sim}{\sqsubset} \lambda x{:}A'.\, t} \quad (\textsc{CongAbs})$$

$$\frac{s_1 \underset{\sim}{\sqsubset} t_1 \quad s_2 \underset{\sim}{\sqsubset} t_2}{s_1\, s_2 \underset{\sim}{\sqsubset} t_1\, t_2} \quad (\textsc{CongApp})$$

$$\frac{s \underset{\sim}{\sqsubset} t \quad A \underset{\sim}{\sqsubset} A'}{\Lambda Y.\, s \underset{\sim}{\sqsubset} \Lambda Y.\, t} \quad (\textsc{CongTypeAbs})$$

$$\frac{s \underset{\sim}{\sqsubset} t}{s\, A \underset{\sim}{\sqsubset} t\, A} \quad (\textsc{CongTypeApp})$$

$$\frac{s \underset{\sim}{\sqsubset} t}{s \,\mathtt{is}\, G \underset{\sim}{\sqsubset} t \,\mathtt{is}\, G} \quad (\textsc{CongIs})$$

$$\frac{s \underset{\sim}{\sqsubset} t}{s : A \Rightarrow^{p} B \underset{\sim}{\sqsubset} t : A \Rightarrow^{q} B} \quad (\textsc{CongCast})$$

$$\frac{v \underset{\sim}{\sqsubset} w}{v : G \Rightarrow \star \underset{\sim}{\sqsubset} w : G \Rightarrow \star} \quad (\textsc{CongGround})$$

$$\frac{s \underset{\sim}{\sqsubset} t \quad A \underset{\sim}{\sqsubset} A' \quad B \underset{\sim}{\sqsubset} B'}{s : A \Rightarrow^{P} B \underset{\sim}{\sqsubset} t : A' \Rightarrow^{P} B'} \quad (\textsc{CongSC})$$

$$\frac{t \underset{\sim}{\sqsubset} t' \quad A \underset{\sim}{\sqsubset} A'}{\nu X{:=}A.\, t \underset{\sim}{\sqsubset} \nu X{:=}A'.\, t'} \quad (\textsc{CongNu})$$

Figure 10. Simulation relation $\underset{\sim}{\sqsubset}$

Lemma 28. *($\underset{\sim}{\sqsubset}^{P}$ simulates $\longrightarrow$) Suppose $\Delta \vdash s : A$ and $\Delta' \vdash t : B$. If $s \underset{\sim}{\sqsubset} t$ and $s \longrightarrow s'$, then $t \longmapsto^{*} t'$ and $s' \underset{\sim}{\sqsubset} t'$ for some t'.*

The proof relies on the presence of bindings and static casts to preserve type information, especially the presence of type variables.

Lemma 29. *($\underset{\sim}{\sqsubset}^{P}$ simulates $\longmapsto$) Suppose $\Delta \vdash s : A$ and $\Delta' \vdash t : B$. If $s \underset{\sim}{\sqsubset} t$ and $s \longmapsto s'$, then $t \longmapsto^{*} t'$ and $s' \underset{\sim}{\sqsubset} t'$ for some t'.*

We then prove that $\underset{\sim}{\sqsubset}$ is contained in $\sqsubseteq$.

Lemma 30. *If $s \underset{\sim}{\sqsubset} t$, then $s \sqsubseteq t$.*

Proof. The proof is by case analysis on the reduction of s.
Suppose $E[s] \Uparrow$. Then $E[t] \Uparrow$ by Lemma 29.
Suppose $E[s] \Downarrow$. Then $E[t] \Downarrow$ by Lemmas 29 and 26. □

The proof of the main theorem follows from this lemma.

Proof of the Jack-of-All-Trades principle. We have

$$(v\ C : A[X{:=}C] \Rightarrow^{p} B) \underset{\sim}{\sqsubset} (v\ \star : A[X{:=}\star] \Rightarrow^{p} B)$$

and we conclude by applying Lemma 30. □

12. Related Work

Run-time sealing Matthews and Ahmed (2008) present semantics for a multi-language system (Scheme and ML) that enforces the parametricity of ML values with polymorphic type (with embedded Scheme values). Their system places boundaries between the two languages. Their boundaries roughly correspond to a combination of a static and dynamic cast in our system. The contributions of our work with respect to the work of Matthews and Ahmed (2008) is that 1) we tease apart the notion of dynamic casting and sealing, associating sealing with type abstraction instead of the interface between languages, and 2) we establish the blame and subtyping theorems and the Jack-of-All-Trades principle.

Syntactic type abstraction Grossman et al. (2000) develop a general theory of syntactic type abstraction in which multiple agents interact and have varying degrees of knowledge regarding the types at the interfaces between agents. Their general theory can be used to express the type abstraction in the polymorphic lambda calculus, as well as many other kinds of syntactic abstractions. They present two systems, a simple two-agent system and a multi-agent system. The two-agent system can handle a program with one type abstraction whereas the multi-agent system is needed for arbitrary programs, using one agent per type abstraction. However, the multi-agent system adds considerable complexity for generality that is unnecessary in our setting. The advantage of our system is that it scales up to handle arbitrary number of type abstractions while retaining much of the simplicity of the two-agent system.

Sulzmann et al. (2007) develop an extension of System F with type equality coercions. Their coercions closely resemble the static casts of this paper, including the reduction rules. Their system does not have an analogue of our type bindings and instead uses substitution to perform type application.

Integrating static and dynamic Tobin-Hochstadt and Felleisen (2006) formalize the interaction between static and dynamic typing at the granularity of modules and develop a precursor to the Blame Theorem. Wadler and Findler (2009) design the blame calculus drawing on the blame tracking of higher-order contracts (Findler and Felleisen, 2002), and prove the Blame Theorem.

Gronski et al. (2006) explore the interaction of type `Dynamic` with refinement types and first-class types, that is, allowing types to be passed to and returned from functions. This provides a form of polymorphism, but not relational parametricity.

In the language Thorn, Wrigstad et al. (2010) show how to integrate typed and untyped code, using *like types* to bridge the gap in a way that better enables compiler optimizations in statically typed regions of code. Their formal development includes classes and objects but not polymorphism.

13. Conclusion

We have extended the blame calculus with support for first-class parametric polymorphism, using explicit type binding to maintain relational parametricity for values of polymorphic type. Our calculus supports casts between the dynamic type and polymorphic types. When casting from a polymorphic type, our system instantiates the type variable with the dynamic type, a choice justified by the Jack-of-All-Trades Principle: if instantiating a type parameter to any given type yields an answer then instantiating that type parameter to the dynamic type yields the same answer. We proved this principle via a simulation argument that depended on the presence of type bindings and static casts. We have also proved the Blame Theorem, so in the new polymorphic blame calculus, "well-typed programs can't be blamed". Further, as a corollary of the Jack-of-All-Trades Principle, we have proved the Subtyping Theorem, showing that a traditional notion of subtyping is sound with respect to our operational semantics.

Looking forward, there are interesting questions regarding how to extend this work to subset and dependent types. Ultimately we hope to obtain a language with a full spectrum type system, supporting dynamic typing all the way to total correctness.

Acknowledgments

Our thanks to Jacob Matthews for his support and participation in early discussions of this work. Siek's work on this paper was supported by NSF grant 0846121 and by a Distinguished Visiting Fellowship from the Scottish Informatics and Computer Science Alliance. Findler's work was supported by NSF grant 0846012.

References

Martin Abadi, Luca Cardelli, Benjamin Pierce, and Gordon Plotkin. Dynamic typing in a statically typed language. *ACM Transactions on Programming Languages and Systems*, 13(2): 237–268, April 1991.

Amal Ahmed, Jacob Matthews, Robert Bruce Findler, and Philip Wadler. Blame for all. In *Workshop on Script-to-Program Evolution (STOP)*, pages 1–13, 2009.

Robert Bruce Findler and Matthias Felleisen. Contracts for higher-order functions. In *ACM International Conference on Functional Programming (ICFP)*, pages 48–59, October 2002.

Andrew Gill, John Launchbury, and Simon L. Peyton Jones. A short cut to deforestation. In *ACM Conference on Functional Programming Languages and Computer Architecture (FPCA)*, pages 223–232, September 1993.

Jessica Gronski, Kenneth Knowles, Aaron Tomb, Stephen N. Freund, and Cormac Flanagan. Sage: Hybrid checking for flexible specifications. In *Scheme and Functional Programming Workshop (Scheme)*, pages 93–104, September 2006.

Dan Grossman, Greg Morrisett, and Steve Zdancewic. Syntactic type abstraction. *ACM Transactions on Programming Languages and Systems*, 22(6):1037–1080, November 2000.

Arjun Guha, Jacob Matthews, Robert Bruce Findler, and Shriram Krishnamurthi. Relationally-parametric polymorphic contracts. In *Dynamic Languages Symposium (DLS)*, pages 29–40, 2007.

Robert Harper. *Practical Foundations for Programming Languages*. 2007. Working Draft.

Fritz Henglein. Dynamic typing: Syntax and proof theory. *Science of Computer Programming*, 22(3):197–230, 1994.

Jacob Matthews and Amal Ahmed. Parametric polymorphism through run-time sealing. In *European Symposium on Programming (ESOP)*, pages 16–31, 2008.

Jacob Matthews and Robert Bruce Findler. Operational semantics for multi-language programs. In *ACM Symposium on Principles of Programming Languages (POPL)*, pages 3–10, January 2007.

James H. Morris, Jr. Types are not sets. In *ACM Symposium on Principles of Programming Languages (POPL)*, pages 120–124, October 1973.

Georg Neis, Derek Dreyer, and Andreas Rossberg. Non-parametric parametricity. In *ACM International Conference on Functional Programming (ICFP)*, pages 135–148, September 2009.

Xinming Ou, Gang Tan, Yitzhak Mandelbaum, and David Walker. Dynamic typing with dependent types. In *IFIP International Conference on Theoretical Computer Science*, pages 437–450, August 2004.

Benjamin Pierce and Eijiro Sumii. Relating cryptography and polymorphism. Manuscript, 2000. URL `www.cis.upenn.edu/~bcpierce/papers/infohide.ps`.

John Reynolds. Types, abstraction, and parametric polymorphism. In R. E. A. Mason, editor, *Information Processing*, pages 513–523. North-Holland, 1983.

Andreas Rossberg. Generativity and dynamic opacity for abstract types. In *ACM Conference on Principles and Practice of Declarative Programming (PPDP)*, pages 241–252, 2003.

Jeremy G. Siek and Walid Taha. Gradual typing for functional languages. In *Scheme and Functional Programming Workshop (Scheme)*, pages 81–92, September 2006.

Martin Sulzmann, Manuel M. T. Chakravarty, Simon Peyton Jones, and Kevin Donnelly. System F with type equality coercions. In *ACM Workshop on Types in Languages Design and Implementation (TLDI)*, pages 53–66, 2007.

Satish Thatte. Type inference with partial types. In *International Colloquium on Automata, Languages and Programming (ICALP)*, volume 317 of *Lecture Notes in Computer Science*, pages 615–629. Springer-Verlag, 1988.

Sam Tobin-Hochstadt and Matthias Felleisen. Interlanguage migration: From scripts to programs. In *Dynamic Languages Symposium (DLS)*, pages 964–974, October 2006.

Philip Wadler and Robert Bruce Findler. Well-typed programs can't be blamed. In *European Symposium on Programming (ESOP)*, pages 1–16, March 2009.

Andrew K. Wright. Simple imperative polymorphism. *Higher-Order and Symbolic Computation*, 8(4):343–355, Dec. 1995.

Tobias Wrigstad, Francesco Zappa Nardelli, Sylvain Lebresne, Johan Östlund, and Jan Vitek. Integrating typed and untyped code in a scripting language. In *ACM Symposium on Principles of Programming Languages (POPL)*, pages 377–388, 2010.

Correct Blame for Contracts

No More Scapegoating

Christos Dimoulas
Northeastern University

Robert Bruce Findler
Northwestern University

Cormac Flanagan
University of California, Santa Cruz

Matthias Felleisen
Northeastern University

Abstract

Behavioral software contracts supplement interface information with logical assertions. A rigorous enforcement of contracts provides useful feedback to developers if it signals contract violations as soon as they occur and if it assigns blame to violators with precise explanations. Correct blame assignment gets programmers started with the debugging process and can significantly decrease the time needed to discover and fix bugs.

Sadly the literature on contracts lacks a framework for making statements about the correctness of blame assignment and for validating such statements. This paper fills the gap and uses the framework to demonstrate how one of the proposed semantics for higher-order contracts satisfies this criteria and another semantics occasionally assigns blame to the wrong module.

Concretely, the paper applies the framework to the *lax* enforcement of dependent higher-order contracts and the *picky* one. A higher-order dependent contract specifies constraints for the domain and range of higher-order functions and also relates arguments and results in auxiliary assertions. The picky semantics ensures that the use of arguments in the auxiliary assertion satisfies the domain contracts and the lax one does not. While the picky semantics discovers more contract violations than the lax one, it occasionally blames the wrong module. Hence the paper also introduces a third semantics, dubbed *indy*, which fixes the problems of the picky semantics without giving up its advantages.

Categories and Subject Descriptors D.3.1 [*Formal Definitions and Theory*]: Semantics; D.3.3 [*Language Constructs and Features*]: Constraints

General Terms Languages, Design, Reliability

Keywords Higher-order Programming, Behavioral Contracts, Blame Assignment

* Dimoulas and Felleisen were partly supported by AFOSR (FA9550-09-1-0110) and NSF (CRI 0855140 & CCF 0540818), Findler by NSF (0846012) and Flanagan by NSF (CNS-0905650).

POPL'11, January 26–28, 2011, Austin, Texas, USA.

1. Dependent Contracts: Lax or Picky?

Software engineers embrace behavioral[1] software contracts for two reasons. On one hand, contracts help explain and protect the interface of components, e.g., modules, classes, procedures, functions. On the other hand, programmers can use the familiar programming language to specify contracts, which makes it easy to read, write, and interpret them.

While both arguments obviously apply to contracts for first-order languages, Findler and Felleisen (2002)'s introduction of contracts for higher-order functions raises subtle, yet practically interesting questions. One particular question concerns dependent higher-order contracts—that is, contracts that can state assertions relating the potentially higher-order argument to the potentially higher-order result. Such contracts come with two distinct semantics in the literature. The first is the so-called *lax* semantics of Findler and Felleisen, which uses the argument in the assertion without monitoring the argument contract. In contrast, the second, *picky* semantics of Blume and McAllester (2006) monitors the argument contract during the evaluation of the component *and* during the evaluation of the assertion.

```
;; for some natural number n and real δ
(->d ([f (-> real? real?)][ε real?])
     (fp (-> real? real?))
     #:post-cond
     (for/and ([i (in-range 0 n)])
       (define x (random-number))
       (define slope
         (/ (- (f (- x ε)) (f (+ x ε)))
            (* 2 ε)))
       (<= (abs (- slope (fp x))) δ)))
```

Figure 1. A higher-order, dependent contract

To make this discussion concrete, consider the dependent function contract in figure 1. This Racket fragment (formerly known as PLT Scheme) (Flatt and PLT 2010) specifies a function that maps a real-valued function `f` (and a real number ε) to a real-valued function `fp`. The post-condition adds that for some number `n` of numbers `x`, the slope of `f` at `x` is within δ of the value of `fp` at `x`. A *picky* interpretation enforces that `f` and `fp` are applied to real numbers and produce such numbers during the evaluation of the post-condition; a *lax* interpretation does not check these specifications.

Greenberg et al. (2010) compare these two forms of dependent contracts (and relate contracts to Flanagan (2006)'s hybrid types). They come to the conclusion that *picky* contracts signal the same violations as *lax* contracts and possibly more. For example, `random-number` may actually produce a complex number and

[1] We use Beugnard et al. (1999)'s terminology.

Types	τ	$::=$	$o \mid \tau \rightarrow \tau$
	o	$::=$	$num \mid bool$
Terms	e	$::=$	$v \mid x \mid e\,e \mid \mu x{:}\tau.e \mid e{+}e$
		$\mid$	$e{-}e \mid e{\wedge}e \mid e{\vee}e \mid \texttt{zero?}(e)$
		$\mid$	$\texttt{if}\, e\, e\, e$
Values	v	$::=$	$0 \mid 1 \mid -1 \mid \ldots \mid \lambda x{:}\tau.e$
		$\mid$	$\texttt{tt} \mid \texttt{ff}$
E. Contexts	E	$::=$	$[\,] \mid E\,e \mid v\,E \mid E{+}e \mid v{+}E$
		$\mid$	$E{-}e \mid v{-}E \mid E{\wedge}e \mid v{\wedge}E$
		$\mid$	$E{\vee}e \mid v{\vee}E \mid \texttt{zero?}(E)$
		$\mid$	$\texttt{if}\, E\; e\; e$

Figure 2. PCF syntax

the contract may thus misapply f; the *picky* interpretation catches this potential problem, while the *lax* one doesn't. Our experience shows, however, that Greenberg et al. (2010)'s result doesn't truly settle the issue. When a *picky* contract signals a contract violation, it may blame the wrong party.

In this paper, we develop a third notion of contract monitoring and demonstrate that it satisfies an intuitive correctness criterion. We start from the observation that Greenberg et al. are correct in that a *picky* interpretation is important for dependent contracts. If the "dependency assertion" violates a contract, the computation may go wrong in all kinds of ways. The question is which party the monitoring system should blame for such a problem. The *picky* interpretation blames either the server or the client. Our new interpretation, dubbed *indy*, treats the contract as an independent party and blames it for problems where *picky* blames the wrong party.

To compare the three possible interpretations, we develop a unified semantic framework, based on a reduction semantics (Felleisen et al. 2009) for a PCF-like language with contracts. The three interpretations are expressed as three different, one-rule extensions that specify the semantics of dependent contracts. We then enrich the framework with the necessary information to track code ownership and contract obligations, two novel technical notions that might prove useful in other contexts. This enriched framework is used to formalize the following correctness criterion: a contract system should only blame a party if *the party controls the flow or return of values into the particular contract check that failed.*

We can prove that our new *indy* interpretation satisfies this criterion while *picky* fails to live up to it. Inspired by our theoretical result, we equip Racket with an *indy* dependent contract combinator, `->i`, in addition with the existing *lax* combinator, `->d`.

Finally, we explain how to use the framework to implement a tool that explains the responsibilities that contracts imposes. Specifically, the tool teases out contract obligations from complicated contracts and highlights them with colors. We have implemented the tool and include some screenshots to illustrate its usefulness.

2. Contract PCF

PCF (Plotkin 1977) is the starting point for our model; figure 2 summarizes the well-known syntactic domains. In this setting, a program is a closed term. Also, we equip the language with a standard type system and a call-by-value reduction semantics, though for lack of space, we omit the details (Plotkin 1975; Felleisen et al. 2009). Similarly, we use type annotations only when needed.

2.1 Adding Higher-Order Contracts

Adding plain higher-order contracts (Findler and Felleisen 2002) to PCF is straightforward: see figure 3. First, PCF is enriched with contracts, a contract type, and new terms for attaching contracts to terms and raising contract violations. Second, we extend our type system with rules for the extra terms. The resulting language is CPCF, PCF with contracts.

CPCF is equipped with two kinds of contracts: flat contracts, $\texttt{flat}(e)$, and higher-order contracts, $\kappa_1 \mapsto \kappa_2$. The former are predicates on base values. The latter combine a contract, κ_1, on the arguments of a function with a contract, κ_2, on the result of the function.

Contracts	κ	$::=$	$\texttt{flat}(e) \mid \kappa \mapsto \kappa$
Types	τ	$::=$	$\ldots \mid con(\tau)$
Terms	e	$::=$	$\ldots \mid \texttt{mon}_{l}^{l,l}(\kappa, e) \mid \texttt{error}^{l}$

$$\frac{\Gamma \vdash e : o \rightarrow bool}{\Gamma \vdash \texttt{flat}(e) : con(o)}$$

$$\frac{\Gamma \vdash \kappa_1 : con(\tau_1) \qquad \Gamma \vdash \kappa_2 : con(\tau_2)}{\Gamma \vdash \kappa_1 \mapsto \kappa_2 : con(\tau_1 \rightarrow \tau_2)}$$

$$\frac{\Gamma \vdash \kappa : con(\tau) \qquad \Gamma \vdash e : \tau}{\Gamma \vdash \texttt{mon}_{j}^{k,l}(\kappa, e) : \tau} \qquad \frac{}{\Gamma \vdash \texttt{error}^{l} : \tau}$$

Figure 3. CPCF: syntax and types

The most important new construct is the monitoring construct $\texttt{mon}_{j}^{k,l}(\kappa, e)$, which places a contract κ between a term e (the server) and its context (the client). It demands that any value that flows between e and its context is monitored for conformance with the contract. For a flat contract, the predicate is applied to the value; for a higher-order contract, the pieces of the contract are attached to the argument and range position of a wrapper function and the contract is monitored as the function flows through the program.

A monitor comes with three labels:[2] a pair of distinct blame labels k and l for the two parties to the contract and a contract label j, for the origin of the contract. In source code, the contract label j usually differs from k and l but under some circumstances it may be equal to either of the two. Labels are drawn from the enumerable set $\mathbb{L}$. The label l_o is used as the label of the whole program; $\bar{l}$ denotes a subset of $\mathbb{L}$. When a contract fails a contract error, $\texttt{error}^{l}$, is raised where l denotes the party responsible for the violation.

$$\textbf{E. Contexts} \quad E \quad ::= \quad \ldots \mid \texttt{mon}_{l}^{l,l}(\kappa, E)$$

$$\begin{array}{rcl}
E[\texttt{mon}_{j}^{k,l}(\kappa_1 \mapsto \kappa_2, v)] & \longmapsto & E[\lambda x.\texttt{mon}_{j}^{k,l}(\kappa_2, v\; \texttt{mon}_{j}^{l,k}(\kappa_1, x))] \\
E[\texttt{mon}_{j}^{k,l}(\texttt{flat}(e), v)] & \longmapsto & E[\texttt{if}\; (e\; v)\; v\; \texttt{error}^{k}] \\
E[\texttt{error}^{l}] & \longmapsto & \texttt{error}^{l}
\end{array}$$

Figure 4. CPCF: semantics

The introduction of contracts requires small changes to the reduction semantics. Figure 4 spells out the details, starting with the slight modification of the set of evaluation contexts. The bottom half shows the reduction rules for contract checking and blame assignment, adapted from Findler and Felleisen (2002)'s original semantics. A higher-order monitor is split into two parts:

1. a monitor for the argument with reversed blame labels;
2. a monitor for the result with the original blame labels.

[2] In an implementation, these labels are synthesized from the program text.

A first-order monitor is transformed to an `if` statement that checks whether the guarded value satisfies the contract's predicate. If the predicate is satisfied, the value is returned; otherwise a contract error is signaled using the first blame label to pinpoint the guilty party. Finally, when a contract error is raised the evaluation is aborted and the contract error is returned as the final result.

2.2 Adding Dependent Contracts

In contrast to conventional contracts for first-order functions, the higher-order contracts of the preceding section cannot express dependencies between arguments and results. Therefore Findler and Felleisen (2002) equip CPCF with a functional contract form that parameterizes the result contract over the argument:

$$\textbf{Contracts} \quad \kappa \quad ::= \quad \ldots \mid \kappa \overset{d}{\mapsto} (\lambda x.\kappa)$$

Findler and Felleisen (2002)'s reduction rule for these *dependent contracts* captures this intention:

$$E[\mathtt{mon}_j^{k,l}(\kappa_1 \overset{d}{\mapsto} (\lambda x.\kappa_2), v)] \quad \longmapsto_l \quad (lax)$$
$$E[\lambda x.\mathtt{mon}_j^{k,l}(\kappa_2, v\ \mathtt{mon}_j^{l,k}(\kappa_1, x))]$$

A dependent monitor acts like a higher-order monitor. The subtle difference is that the parameter x of the proxy function captures the free occurrences of x in the contract's postcondition κ_2. As a result, any argument to the proxy function is substituted for x in κ_2 and is then used in the argument position, suitably wrapped with an argument monitor.

Blume and McAllester (2006) observe that the precondition κ_1 is not enforced during the evaluation of postcondition κ_2. This gap opens the door for potential abuses of the argument in κ_2, i.e., uses that don't conform to κ_1. They rightly consider this a problem and, in turn, they propose the following change to the rule:[3]

$$E[\mathtt{mon}_j^{k,l}(\kappa_1 \overset{d}{\mapsto} (\lambda x.\kappa_2), v)] \quad \longmapsto_p \quad (picky)$$
$$E[\lambda x.\mathtt{mon}_j^{k,l}(\underline{\{\mathtt{mon}_j^{l,k}(\kappa_1, x)/x\}}\kappa_2, v\ \mathtt{mon}_j^{l,k}(\kappa_1, x))]$$

Specifically, every free occurrence of x in κ_2 is replaced with $\mathtt{mon}_j^{l,k}(\kappa_1, x)$. Thus, any argument to the function remains protected by κ_1 even inside κ_2. Note how the injected monitor carries the same blame labels as the monitor for the argument in the body of the function.[4]

Greenberg et al. (2010) compare the *lax* and *picky* contract systems and conclude that the former signals strictly fewer contract errors than a *picky* contract system. More precisely, for any program, the following statements hold:

- neither contract system signals a contract error;
- both raise an error and blame the same party; or
- the *picky* contract system discovers a contract violation and the *lax* system does not raise a contract error.

Their results characterizes two different philosophies of contract code. On the one hand, a *lax* contract system treats contracts as trusted code. Both parties have agreed to the contract and have presumably ensured that its evaluation doesn't violate any invariants. On the other hand, a *picky* contract system considers contracts to contain potentially faulty code. To enforce the contracts within this code, a *picky* system protects values that flow into the contracts.

The problem with the *picky* system is that it may blame the server or the client for violations of a contract κ when neither of them can control the flow of values into the responsible monitor. To illustrate this point and to provide an alternative, we introduce a third contract monitoring system that considers contracts as independent entities. When a dependent contract abuses a value according to κ_1, this revised system blames the contract for the violation.

Here is the reduction rule:

$$E[\mathtt{mon}_j^{k,l}(\kappa_1 \overset{d}{\mapsto} (\lambda x.\kappa_2), v)] \quad \longmapsto_i \quad (indy)$$
$$E[\lambda x.\mathtt{mon}_j^{k,l}(\underline{\{\mathtt{mon}_j^{l,j}(\kappa_1, x)/x\}}\kappa_2, v\ \mathtt{mon}_j^{l,k}(\kappa_1, x))]$$

The rule makes the contract responsible if it supplies an inappropriate value to a function argument during the evaluation of the "dependency." It accomplishes this switch of responsibility with the creation of a new monitoring expression for the argument with the contract label as the negative blame label. This new argument expression is substituted into the range part of the contract.[5]

For an example, consider this monitor expression:

$$\Pi^0 = \mathtt{mon}_j^{k,l}(\kappa, \lambda x.(\text{—0—}))\ \lambda x.(\text{—1—})$$

where

$$\kappa \quad = \quad \kappa_1 \overset{d}{\mapsto} (\lambda f.\mathtt{flat}(\lambda x.f\ (\lambda x.(\text{—2—})) > 0))$$
$$\kappa_1 \quad = \quad (\mathtt{P?} \mapsto \mathtt{P?}) \overset{d}{\mapsto} (\lambda g.\mathtt{flat}(\lambda x.g\ 3 > 0))$$

Here the server is the function $\lambda x.(\text{—0—})$, while the client is the context $[\ ]\ \lambda x.(\text{—1—})$. The mediating contract κ is a higher-order, dependent contract where P? checks for positive numbers, i.e., $\mathtt{P?} = \mathtt{flat}(\lambda x.x > 0)$ and $>$ has the standard recursive definition.

The argument $\lambda x.(\text{—1—})$ flows to the postcondition of κ and replaces f. To protect it from potentially misbehaving contract code, it is wrapped with a monitor that enforces κ_1:

$$\mathtt{mon}_j^{l,j}(\kappa_1, \lambda x.(\text{—1—}))\ .$$

Since κ_1 is a dependent contract, too, the story continues. When the postcondition is eventually checked, this proxy function for $\lambda x.(\text{—1—})$ is applied to $\lambda x.(\text{—2—})$. In that case, the latter flows to the postcondition of κ_1 and replaces g with another monitored domain contract.

Each of the three rules gives rise to a semantics for CPCF. In principal, we extend $\longmapsto$ with $\longmapsto_m$ where $m \in \{l, p, i\}$ to get the three complete reduction relations. Since there is no danger of ambiguity, we overload the symbol $\longmapsto_m$ and use it for the complete semantics.

2.3 Two More Flavors

The treatment of contracts as independent parties is compatible with some practical uses in our Racket implementation. First, contracts for Racket's unit system are given as part of the signature. Strickland and Felleisen (2009) show that linking such units may necessitate blaming the signature itself. Our framework finally provides a semantic explanation for this phenomenon.

Second, in Racket's first-order module system, contracts are specified via `provide/contract`, i.e., in the export interface of modules. This form combines identifiers with contracts and attaches contracts to these values as they flow across the module boundary. When things go wrong with the dependencies in such

[3] In principle, this reduction rule should use a `let` to preserve a strict call-by-value regime. But, due to the restrictions on our grammar for contracts, a straight substitution is technically correct and superior.

[4] An alternative definition for the *picky* rule is to *not* switch the blame labels on the internal monitor. Doing so does not affect our results.

[5] Morally, the monitor should not apply when the client is already labeled with the contract label. In that case, the value flow is entirely within the contract party and should strictly speaking not be monitored. To model this behavior, we would have to add the side condition $l \neq j$ and add a second rule:

$$E[\mathtt{mon}_j^{k,l}(\kappa_1 \overset{d}{\mapsto} (\lambda x.\kappa_2), v)] \quad \longmapsto_i \quad E[\lambda x.\mathtt{mon}_j^{k,l}(\kappa_2, v\ \mathtt{mon}_j^{l,k}(\kappa_1, x))] \quad \text{if } l = j$$

Both variants of *indy* satisfy the main theorem, which is why this paper focuses on the theoretically simpler approach.

contracts, the monitoring system considers the contract a part of the server module and blames the server module. We can express this idea—dubbed +*indy*—in our framework with the small change of using the module name as the contract label.

Finally, Typed Racket (Tobin-Hochstadt and Felleisen 2010, 2008) protects the interaction of typed and untyped modules with contracts derived from types. Since one of the basic assumptions of Typed Racket is that untyped modules stay unchanged, it implements this protection mechanism with `require/contract`. This contract form guarantees that values from an untyped module satisfy the specified contract. Put differently, the form protects the import boundary. If a programmer attached dependencies to these contracts, the code would have to be considered as a part of the client module. We can capture this semantics, dubbed −*indy*, by using the importing module's name as the contract label.

2.4 Comparing Contract Systems

Equipped with three additional contract monitoring systems, we can now explore their relationship. Consider this example:

$$\Pi^1 \;=\; \mathtt{mon}_*^{k,l}(\kappa, \lambda f.f\,42)\;\lambda x.x$$
$$\text{where } \kappa = (\mathtt{P?} \mapsto \mathtt{P?}) \overset{d}{\mapsto} (\lambda f.\mathtt{flat}(\lambda x.f\,0 > -1))$$

The example uses the placeholder $*$ for the contract label so that we can include +*indy* and −*indy*—the two additional flavors of *indy*—in our comparisons. As needed, we replace $*$ with k for +*indy*, with l for −*indy*, and a distinct label j for *indy*. Recall that the reduction rules for the *lax* and *picky* contract monitoring systems do not employ the contract label.

The evaluation of Π^1 yields the following results for the five different contract monitoring systems:

program	*	monitoring system	result
Π^1	—	*lax*	42
Π^1	—	*picky*	$\mathtt{error}^k$
Π^1	j	*indy*	$\mathtt{error}^j$
Π^1	k	+*indy*	$\mathtt{error}^k$
Π^1	l	−*indy*	$\mathtt{error}^l$

The table demonstrates several points. First, when a program yields a plain value according to the *lax* system, the *picky* system may still find a fault during contract checking and signal a violation. Second, the *picky* system here blames party k, the server component, for a contract violation. The specific violation is that f is applied to 0 in the dependency assertion, even though the domain contract promises that the function is only applied to positive numbers. Third, the *indy* system blames the contract itself, rather than the server. Fourth, the system based on the +*indy* rule agrees with the *picky* system, because it considers all code in a contract as part of the server. Finally, the −*indy* system blames party l; after all, the misapplication of f is internal to the client, which chooses to defy the restrictions on the domain of f.

Another example shows that *picky* can also blame the client when things go wrong with the contract:

$$\Pi^2 \;=\; \mathtt{mon}_*^{k,l}(\kappa, \lambda f.f\,\lambda x.x)\;\lambda g.g\,42$$
$$\text{where } \kappa = ((\mathtt{P?} \mapsto \mathtt{P?}) \overset{d}{\mapsto} (\lambda f.\mathtt{flat}(\lambda x.f\,0 > -1))) \mapsto \mathtt{P?}$$

Specifically, evaluating Π^2 yields the following results:

program	*	monitoring system	result
Π^2	—	*lax*	42
Π^2	—	*picky*	$\mathtt{error}^l$
Π^2	j	*indy*	$\mathtt{error}^j$
Π^2	k	+*indy*	$\mathtt{error}^k$
Π^2	l	−*indy*	$\mathtt{error}^l$

Again the *lax* system does not signal contract violations, while the other four report one. Here the *indy* system blames the contract itself rather than the client, which is blamed by the *picky* and −*indy* systems. The +*indy* system blames the server.

Together the two examples demonstrate that none of our new monitoring rules are logically related to *picky* if we take blame into account. In short, the introduction of contracts as independent parties calls for a comparison that takes into account why a contract violation is detected and why the accused party is blamed.

Note, however, that the *indy* contract system signals an error when the *picky* system signals an error and vice versa, though the errors aren't necessarily labeled with the same party.

PROPOSITION 1. $e \overset{*}{\longmapsto}_i \mathtt{error}^k$ *iff* $e \overset{*}{\longmapsto}_p \mathtt{error}^{k'}$

PROOF IDEA. By a straightforward bi-simulation argument. The bi-simulation used for the proof relates two expressions that are structurally identical except that their labels can differ. ∎

3. Tracking Ownership and Obligations

While the preceding section illuminates the problems of the *picky* contract system and the difficulty of comparing contract systems in general, it also implies a new way of thinking about contract violations. The first major insight is that the *picky* system may blame either the server module or the client module when, in fact, the contract itself is flawed. From here, it is obvious to inspect what a contract monitoring system would do if contracts were a part of the server, a part of the client, or a third party. Doing so produces the second major insight, namely, that none of these alternatives agrees with the *picky* semantics.

Putting the two insights together implies that we need a semantics that (1) for each party, keeps track of its contract obligations and (2) for each value, accounts for its origin. Once a semantics provides this additional information, we can check whether a contract system ever blames a party for violating an obligation if the party has no control over the value's flow into the contract. In this section, we equip CPCF's semantics with ownership and obligation information, which is maintained across reductions. In the next section, we use this information to state a contract correctness property and to measure how the various monitoring systems fare with respect to this property.

3.1 Ownership ...

To model an ownership relationship between parties and code, we extend CPCF with a new construct that relates terms and values to parties:[6]

$$\begin{array}{llcl} \textbf{Terms} & e & ::= & \ldots \mid \|e\|^l \\ \textbf{Values} & v & ::= & \ldots \mid \|v\|^l \end{array}$$

During reductions, terms and values come with a stack of owners, reflecting transfers from one party to another. The notations $\|e\|^{\vec{l_n}}$ and $\|e\|^{\overleftarrow{l_n}}$ are short-hands for such stacks, abbreviating $\|\ldots\|e\|^{l_1}\ldots\|^{l_n}$ and $\|\ldots\|e\|^{l_n}\ldots\|^{l_1}$, respectively. Ownership l for an expression means its result is attributed to l. In turn, a value with an ownership l originates from component l or is affected by a traversal through component l.

3.2 ...and Obligations

CPCF contracts consist of trees with flat contracts at the leafs. Exploiting the analogy with function types, Findler and Felleisen (2002) implicitly decompose these trees into obligations for servers

[6] The inspiration of *ownership* comes from the work of Zdancewic et al. (1999) on *principals*. For a comparison, see section 6.

(positive positions) and clients (negative positions). Their semantics tracks this connection via labels; errors use them to pinpoint contract violators.

Dimoulas and Felleisen use this idea for a static decomposition of contracts into server and client obligations. They define two functions from contracts to contracts that tease out the respective obligations. The one for teasing out server obligations replaces flat contracts in negative positions with $\top = \mathtt{flat}(\lambda x.\mathtt{tt})$ and then reconstructs the overall contract; analogously, the decomposition map for teasing out client obligations replaces flat contracts in positive positions with $\top$. For instance the contract of the Π^2 example in section 2 yields these decompositions:

	$((\mathtt{P?} \mapsto \mathtt{P?}) \stackrel{d}{\mapsto} (\lambda f.\mathtt{flat}(\lambda x.f\,0 > -1))) \mapsto \mathtt{P?}$
server	$((\top \mapsto \mathtt{P?}) \stackrel{d}{\mapsto} (\lambda f.\top)) \mapsto \mathtt{P?}$
client	$((\mathtt{P?} \mapsto \top) \stackrel{d}{\mapsto} (\lambda f.\mathtt{flat}(\lambda x.f\,0 > -1))) \mapsto \top$

Decomposition implies that each flat contract imposes obligations on a specific component, i.e., party to a contract. Since one and the same server may connect with many different clients and since *indy* systems may use the contract itself as a component, it is not just one party that is associated with a flat contract but many. Hence we modify the syntax of contracts to statically associate flat contracts and owners:

$$\textbf{Contracts}\quad \kappa \quad ::= \lfloor \mathtt{flat}(\|e\|^{l}) \rfloor^{\bar{l}} \mid \kappa \mapsto \kappa \mid \kappa \stackrel{d}{\mapsto} (\lambda x.\kappa)$$

In contrast with ownership, obligations come as sets of labels $\bar{l}$, not vectors. After all, there is no need to order obligations or to change them during an evaluation. Of course, a static attribute about a dynamic obligation calls for a way to determine whether such annotations are well-formed.

3.3 Well-formed Ownership and Obligations

Only some annotations make sense for a source program. Both ownership and contract monitors specify boundaries and, at the source level, these boundaries should coincide. We therefore introduce a well-formedness judgment to enforce these conditions for source programs. Before doing so, we present the simple typing rules for the two new constructs:

$$\frac{\Gamma \vdash e : o \rightarrow bool}{\Gamma \vdash \lfloor \mathtt{flat}(e) \rfloor^{\bar{l}} : con(o)} \qquad \frac{\Gamma \vdash e : \tau}{\Gamma \vdash \|e\|^{l} : \tau}$$

Concerning ownership annotations, a CPCF source program may contain those at only two places: in contract monitors and in flat contracts. Since contract monitors establish a boundary between the client component and the server component, we demand an ownership annotation on the server component and that a match of these annotation with the positive label of the monitor. Conversely, the context of such an expression must belong to the client. Finally, flat contracts must come with ownership labels consistent with the surrounding monitors because they are turned into plain code during the evaluation, and the semantics must track where they originated from.

We express this constraint with the well-formedness relation $l \vdash e$, which says that l "owns" e and checks that e is well-formed. Equivalently, l is the owner for the context of e. A closed expression e is a well-formed program if $l_o \vdash e$ where l_o is the label reserved for the owner of the program.

Figure 5 defines most of this well-formedness judgment. For terms that do not involve monitors and contracts the definition is a structural judgment, and base values and variables are well-formed under any owner. The actual key is the one for contract monitor, which we present separately. According to our informal description, a well-formed contract monitor is a boundary between

$\boxed{l \vdash e}$

$$\frac{l \vdash e_1 \quad l \vdash e_2}{l \vdash e_1\, e_2} \qquad \frac{l \vdash e}{l \vdash \lambda x.e} \qquad \frac{l \vdash e}{l \vdash \mu x.e}$$

$$\frac{l \vdash e_1 \quad l \vdash e_2 \quad l \vdash e_3}{l \vdash \mathtt{if}\ e_1\ e_2\ e_3}$$

$$\frac{l \vdash e_1}{l \vdash \mathtt{zero?}(e_1)}$$

$$\frac{l \vdash e_1 \quad l \vdash e_2}{l \vdash e_1 + e_2} \qquad \frac{l \vdash e_1 \quad l \vdash e_2}{l \vdash e_1 - e_2}$$

$$\frac{l \vdash e_1 \quad l \vdash e_2}{l \vdash e_1 \wedge e_2} \qquad \frac{l \vdash e_1 \quad l \vdash e_2}{l \vdash e_1 \vee e_2}$$

$$\frac{}{l \vdash \mathtt{n}} \qquad \frac{}{l \vdash \mathtt{tt}} \qquad \frac{}{l \vdash \mathtt{ff}} \qquad \frac{}{l \vdash x}$$

Figure 5. Ownership coincides with contract monitors

a client and a server, implying this shape for the judgment:

$$l \vdash \mathtt{mon}_{j}^{k,l}(\kappa, \|e\|^{k})$$

It says that if l owns the context and k is the blame label for the server, then the blame label for the client should be l *and* the wrapped expression e should come with an ownership annotation that connects it to k. Next, e must be well-formed with respect to its owner k, because it may contain additional contract monitors. But even with this antecedent, the well-formedness judgment is incomplete. After all, the contract κ that governs the flow of values between the server and the client contains code and this code must be inspected. Furthermore, we must ensure that all flat contracts within κ are obligations of the appropriate parties including the contract monitor itself, which is represented by the contract label j.

Putting everything together, we get this well-formedness rule for contract monitors in source programs:

$$\frac{k \vdash e \quad \{k\};\{l\};j \rhd \kappa}{l \vdash \mathtt{mon}_{j}^{k,l}(\kappa, \|e\|^{k})}$$

It relies on a secondary well-formedness judgment for contracts, to which we turn next.

$$\frac{\bar{l};\bar{k};j \rhd \kappa_1 \quad \bar{k};\bar{l};j \rhd \kappa_2}{\bar{k};\bar{l};j \rhd \kappa_1 \mapsto \kappa_2}$$

$$\frac{\bar{l};\bar{k}\cup\{j\};j \rhd \kappa_1 \quad \bar{k};\bar{l};j \rhd \kappa_2}{\bar{k};\bar{l};j \rhd \kappa_1 \stackrel{d}{\mapsto} (\lambda x.\kappa_2)}$$

$$\frac{j \vdash e}{\bar{k};\bar{l};j \rhd \lfloor \mathtt{flat}(\|e\|^{j}) \rfloor^{\bar{k}}}$$

Figure 6. Obligations coincide with labels on monitors

Roughly speaking, $\bar{k};\bar{l};j \rhd \kappa$ says that contract κ is well-formed for sets of positive and negative obligation labels $\bar{k}$ and $\bar{l}$, respectively, and the owner j of the contract monitor that attaches the contract to a boundary. As the definition in figure 6 shows, the two sets are swapped for the antecedents of higher-order (dependent) contracts. For the negative positions in the precondition of dependent contract label j is added to indicate that these are also obligations of the owner of the contract monitor. For flat contracts the positive obligation labels must coincide with the obligation labels of the contract.

Note that the well-formedness of flat contracts also enforces an ownership annotation. Specifically, the owner of the context—which, by assumption, is a contract monitoring construct labeled with j—is also the owner of the predicate in the flat contract. The antecedent of the rule recursively uses the well-formedness judgments for ownership to ensure that e itself is well-formed.

3.4 Ownership and Obligations Semantics

The final change to the CPCF model concerns the reduction semantics. Specifically, we change the reduction relations so that each reduction step keeps track of ownership rights and obligations. While ownership and obligations do not affect the semantics per se, the information is critical for characterizing the behavior of contract monitoring systems, as we show in the next section.

Our first step is to equip the grammar of evaluation contexts with a parameter that accounts for the owner of the hole. In the parameterized grammar, E^l, of figure 7 the parameter l points to the ownership annotations that is closest to the hole of the context.

$$
\begin{array}{llll}
\textbf{E. Contexts} & E^l & ::= & G^l \\
 & G^l & ::= & G^l\ e \mid v\ G^l \mid G^l + e \mid v + G^l \\
 & & \mid & G^l - e \mid v - G^l \mid G^l \wedge e \mid v \wedge G^l \\
 & & \mid & G^l \vee e \mid v \vee G^l \mid \texttt{zero?}(G^l) \\
 & & \mid & \texttt{if}\ G^l\ e\ e \mid \texttt{mon}_j^{k,l}(\kappa, G^l) \\
 & & \mid & \|F\|^l \mid \|G^l\|^{l'} \\
 & F & ::= & [\,] \mid F\ e \mid v\ F \mid F + e \mid v + F \\
 & & \mid & F - e \mid v - F \mid F \wedge e \mid v \wedge F \\
 & & \mid & F \vee e \mid v \vee F \mid \texttt{zero?}(F) \\
 & & \mid & \texttt{if}\ F\ e\ e \mid \texttt{mon}_j^{k,l}(\kappa, F)
\end{array}
$$

Figure 7. Parameterized evaluation contexts

Evaluation contexts are labeled with the label l_o—the label reserved for the whole program—if they do not contain an ownership constructs on the path from the hole to the root: $E^{l_o} ::= F$.

From now on, all reduction relations assume labeled evaluation contexts. This implies that newly created values are always assigned an owner. For the reduction relations concerning primitive operators and conditionals, the changes are straightforward and summarized in the top part of figure 8. For the rules concerning monitors with flat and plain higher-order contracts and their blame assignments, specified in the lower part of the same figure, we also know that they do not need to manipulate any ownership annotations. These reduction rules remain unchanged, modulo the labeled evaluation contexts. The obligation annotation on flat contracts is ignored. For details, see the bottom part of figure 8. We add one last simple rule separately:

$$E^l[\texttt{error}^k] \longmapsto_m \texttt{error}^k$$

Since the act of signaling errors erases the surrounding evaluation context, the format of this rule doesn't fit the table. Note that the context on the right is $[\,]^{l_o}$ and l may not equal l_o.

The reduction of β_v redexes typically demands several realignments with respect to ownership. To start with, the function and the argument may belong to different parties. Furthermore, the context brings together the operand and operator, and the semantics should keep track of this responsibility. Together, the two observations suggest the following relation:

$$E^l[\|\lambda x.e\|^{\vec{l_n}}\ v] \quad \longmapsto_m \quad E^l[\|\{\|v\|^{l\overleftarrow{l_n}}/x\}e\|^{\vec{l_n}}]$$

$E^l[\cdots]$	$\longmapsto_m$	$E^l[\cdots]$	
$\|\texttt{n}_1\|^{\vec{k}} + \|\texttt{n}_2\|^{\vec{l}}$	$\cdot$	$\texttt{n}$	where $n_1 + n_2 = n$
$\|\texttt{n}_1\|^{\vec{k}} - \|\texttt{n}_2\|^{\vec{l}}$	$\cdot$	$\texttt{n}$	where $n_1 - n_2 = n$
$\texttt{zero?}(\|0\|^{\vec{l}})$	$\cdot$	$\texttt{tt}$	
$\texttt{zero?}(\|\texttt{n}\|^{\vec{k}})$	$\cdot$	$\texttt{ff}$	if $n \neq 0$
$\|v_1\|^{\vec{k}} \wedge \|v_2\|^{\vec{l}}$	$\cdot$	v	where $v_1 \wedge v_2 = v$
$\|v_1\|^{\vec{k}} \vee \|v_2\|^{\vec{l}}$	$\cdot$	v	where $v_1 \vee v_2 = v$
$\texttt{if}\ \|\texttt{tt}\|^{\vec{l}}\ e_1 e_2$	$\cdot$	e_1	
$\texttt{if}\ \|\texttt{ff}\|^{\vec{l}}\ e_1 e_2$	$\cdot$	e_2	
$\texttt{mon}_j^{k,l}(\kappa_1 \mapsto \kappa_2, v)$	$\cdot$	$\lambda x.\texttt{mon}_j^{k,l}(\kappa_2, v\ \texttt{mon}_j^{l,k}(\kappa_1, x))$	
$\texttt{mon}_j^{k,l}(\lfloor\texttt{flat}(e)\rfloor^{\bar{l}'}, v)$	$\cdot$	$\texttt{if}\ (e\ v)\ v\ \texttt{error}^k$	

Figure 8. Ownership and obligation propagation

The relation says that after tagging the value with the ownership label l of the context, the value moves under the ownership annotations of the function. The result is a value whose innermost owner is l and whose outermost owner is l_1 of $\vec{l_n}$:

$$\|v\|^{l\overleftarrow{l_n}}$$

The properly annotated value is then substituted into the body e of the function for its parameter x. The result itself is owned by the same owner as the function.

Put differently, it is best to view function application as a form of communication between two components: the function and its context. The context picks the argument, declares itself its owner, and then passes it to the function. The function accepts the argument, adjusts its ownership, and integrates the result into its body.

Recursion is treated as a special form of function application:

$$E^l[\mu x.e] \quad \longmapsto_m \quad E^l[\{\|\mu x.e\|^l/x\}e]$$

The owner of the context l and user of the recursive function declares itself owner of $\mu x.e$ before substituting it in the body of the recursive function.

All the complexity of tracking ownership is due to dependent function contracts. Consider the simplest variant, *lax*:

$$
\begin{array}{ll}
E[\texttt{mon}_j^{k,l}(\kappa_1 \overset{d}{\mapsto} (\lambda x.\kappa_2), v)] \quad \longmapsto_l & (lax) \\
\qquad E[\lambda y.\texttt{mon}_j^{k,l}(\underline{\{y/x\}\kappa_2}, v\ \texttt{mon}_j^{l,k}(\kappa_1, y))] &
\end{array}
$$

For emphasis, this version of the reduction rule uses y as the parameter of the proxy function on the right hand side. The use of y as parameter demands that we also replace all occurrences of x in κ_2 with y so that when the proxy function is applied, the actual argument is substituted into the dependent range contract; without the substitution, the reduction would create free variables.[7]

Rewriting the *lax* rule in this way reveals that it encodes a masked function application. The problem is that, as discussed above, a function application must add the label of the responsible owner at the bottom of the stack, and this label is not available here. Instead, it is found at the flat leafs of the contract, which—according to the static semantics of the preceding subsection—must come with an ownership annotation. The solution is to introduce the substitution function $\{e/^c x\}\kappa$, which copies the ownership label from flat contracts to the substituted term.

[7] The value v is unaffected by this change of parameters, because we assume the usual hygiene condition (Barendregt 1984) for metavariables.

With this substitution function in place, it is easy to specify the three variants for the reduction of dependent functional contracts:

$$\frac{E^l[\cdots] \quad \ldots \quad E^l[\cdots]}{\begin{array}{ll} \mathtt{mon}^{k,l}_j(\kappa_1 \overset{d}{\mapsto} (\lambda x.\kappa_2), v) \longmapsto_l & \\ \quad \lambda x.\mathtt{mon}^{k,l}_j(\{x/^c x\}\kappa_2, v\ \mathtt{mon}^{l,k}_j(\kappa_1, x)) & (lax) \\ \mathtt{mon}^{k,l}_j(\kappa_1 \overset{d}{\mapsto} (\lambda x.\kappa_2), v) \longmapsto_p & \\ \quad \lambda x.\mathtt{mon}^{k,l}_j(\{\mathtt{mon}^{l,k}_j(\kappa_1, x)/^c x\}\kappa_2, v\ \mathtt{mon}^{l,k}_j(\kappa_1, x)) & (picky) \\ \mathtt{mon}^{k,l}_j(\kappa_1 \overset{d}{\mapsto} (\lambda x.\kappa_2), v) \longmapsto_c & \\ \quad \lambda x.\mathtt{mon}^{k,l}_j(\{\mathtt{mon}^{l,j}_j(\kappa_1, x)/^c x\}\kappa_2, v\ \mathtt{mon}^{l,k}_j(\kappa_1, x)) & (indy) \end{array}}$$

We conclude this section with the definition of the auxiliary substitution function:

$$\begin{array}{rcl} \{e/^c x\}\lfloor \mathtt{flat}(\|e'\|^{l'})\rfloor^{\bar{l}} & = & \lfloor \mathtt{flat}(\{\|e\|^{l'}/x\}\|e'\|^{l'})\rfloor^{\bar{l}} \\ \{e/^c x\}\kappa_1 \mapsto \kappa_2 & = & \{e/^c x\}\kappa_1 \mapsto \{e/^c x\}\kappa_2 \\ \{e/^c x\}\kappa_1 \overset{d}{\mapsto} (\lambda x.\kappa_2) & = & \{e/^c x\}\kappa_1 \overset{d}{\mapsto} (\lambda x.\kappa_2) \\ \{e/^c x\}\kappa_1 \overset{d}{\mapsto} (\lambda y.\kappa_2) & = & \{e/^c x\}\kappa_1 \overset{d}{\mapsto} (\lambda y.\{e/^c x\}\kappa_2) \\ & & \text{where } x \neq y \end{array}$$

The definition is total. The redefinition of the contract syntax enforces that flat contracts always have the annotations expected by the domain of the substitution function. This also guarantees that the reduction relations $\longmapsto_m$ are well-defined.

4. Correct Blame

Using ownership and obligation annotations, we can formulate what it means for a contract system to correctly blame a violator. After all, the tracking of ownership and obligations is entirely independent of the contract checking, and it is thus appropriate to use tracking as an independent specification of contract monitoring.

Values should be originating from one of the parties of the contract are checked only against flat pieces of the contract for which the party is responsible. Now we can phrase this property in terms of ownership and obligations: when the evaluation reaches a redex that checks a flat contract on a value, then the owner of the value must be the same as the positive party of the monitor and in addition the positive party is included in the obligations of the contract.

DEFINITION 2 (Blame Correctness). *A contract system m is* blame correct *if for all terms e_0 such that $l_o \vdash e_0$, and*

$$e_0 \longmapsto^*_m E^\dagger[\mathtt{mon}^{k,\dagger}_\dagger(\lfloor \mathtt{flat}(e_1)\rfloor^{\bar{l}}, v)]$$

$v = \|v_1\|^k$ *and* $k \in \bar{l}$. *The identity of the* $\dagger$ *labels is irrelevant.*

The definition says that when the reduction of a well-formed program reaches a state in which it checks a flat contract, then the server (positive) label of the monitor and the ownership label on the value must coincide and, furthermore, the set of obligations for the flat contract must contain this label. Conversely, if these obligations are not met, the monitor may blame k for a contract failure even though the party had no control over the flow of v into this monitor.

We can prove that the *indy* contract system and even the *lax* system are blame correct, while *picky* isn't. The proof of the positive theorem directly follows from a subject reduction theorem for ownership annotations. This latter theorem requires a complex proof, which is the subject of the second subsection. The third subsection explains how to prove the two main theorems. To start with, however, we clarify that ownership annotations and obligations do are orthogonal to semantics.

4.1 It is all about Information Propagation

The addition of ownership and obligation annotations does not affect the behavior of any programs. Our revised semantics simply propagates this information so that it can be used to characterize execution states. In order to formulate this statement, we use the symbol $\longmapsto^*_m{}^{cpcf}$ for the transitive-reflexive reduction relations of section 2 and $\longmapsto^*_m{}^{anno}$ for the relations of section 3.

PROPOSITION 3. *The following statements hold for $m \in \{l, p, c\}$.*

1. *Let e be a well-formed CPCF program: $l_o \vdash e$. Let $\bar{e}$ be the plain CPCF expression that is like e without annotations. If $e \longmapsto^*_m{}^{anno} e'$, then $\bar{e} \longmapsto^*_m{}^{cpcf} \bar{e}'$.*
2. *Let $\bar{e}$ be a plain CPCF program. There exists some labeled CPCF program e such that $l_o \vdash e$. Furthermore, if $\bar{e} \longmapsto^*_m{}^{cpcf} \bar{e}'$, then $e \longmapsto^*_m{}^{anno} e'$.*

PROOF IDEA. By a straightforward bi-simulation argument. ∎

One consequence of this proposition is that *picky* and *indy*signal still the same number of contract violations (proposition 1).

4.2 Subject Reduction

While $l \vdash e$ specifies when source programs are well-formed, the reduction semantics creates many expressions that do not satisfy these narrow constraints. For example, a well-formed program contains only monitor terms of the form $\mathtt{mon}^{k,l}_j(\kappa, \|e_0\|^k)$. A reduction sequence may contain programs with differently shaped monitors, however. In particular due to the reductions of higher-order dependent contracts, the monitored expressions may be applications, $\mathtt{mon}^{k,l}_j(\kappa, \|e_0\|^k\ e_r)$, or variables, $\mathtt{mon}^{k,l}_j(\kappa, x)$. Fortunately, such deviations are only temporary. In the case of the application the argument e_r is always well-formed under l and, when it is absorbed by $\|e_0\|^k$, the monitor expression is once again well-formed. In the case of the free variable we can show that x is always replaced with a value of the form $\|v_0\|^k$, which conforms to the standard form.

To formulate a subject reduction theorem, we must generalize both the judgment for well-formed programs, $l \vdash e$, and the one for well-formed contracts, $\bar{k}; \bar{l}; j \rhd \kappa$. First, we equip the two relations with an environment that records the label of bound variables:

$$\frac{l; \Gamma \uplus \{x : l\} \vdash e}{l; \Gamma \vdash \lambda x.e} \qquad \frac{l; \Gamma \setminus \{x\} \vdash e}{l; \Gamma \vdash \mu x.e}$$

With environments, it becomes possible to check variable occurrences in monitor terms.

Second, we add a rule for checking expressions that already have an owner:

$$\frac{k; \Gamma \vdash e}{l; \Gamma \vdash \|e\|^k}$$

While these terms show up only within monitors in source programs, they flow into many positions during evaluations. Using this new rule, we can check these cases, too.

All other rules—except those concerning monitors—propagate the environment and otherwise check expressions in the same way as the corresponding rules of the preceding section. The rule for variables ignores the environment. Variables not in monitor terms can be replaced with well-formed terms of any owner. For details, see figure 9.

The purpose of the environment is to check expressions without ownership annotations in monitor terms. Here is the key rule:

$$\frac{k; \Gamma \Vdash e \qquad \{k\}; \{l\}; j; \Gamma \rhd \kappa}{l; \Gamma \vdash \mathtt{mon}^{k,l}_j(\kappa, e)}$$

To check whether the wrapped expression is well-formed, it delegates to the auxiliary relation $k; \Gamma \Vdash e$. The contract is checked as before, though, with an environment.

With $k; \Gamma \Vdash e$, we can check the ordinary ownership terms but also applications and variables as introduced during reductions. For

$\boxed{j;\Gamma \vdash e}$

$$\frac{j;\Gamma \vdash e_1 \quad j;\Gamma \vdash e_2}{j;\Gamma \vdash e_1\ e_2} \qquad \frac{j;\Gamma \vdash e_1}{j;\Gamma \vdash \texttt{zero?}(e_1)}$$

$$\frac{}{j;\Gamma \vdash \texttt{error}^k} \qquad \frac{j;\Gamma \vdash e_1 \quad j;\Gamma \vdash e_2 \quad j;\Gamma \vdash e_3}{j;\Gamma \vdash \texttt{if}\ e_1\ e_2\ e_3}$$

$$\frac{j;\Gamma \vdash e_1 \quad j;\Gamma \vdash e_2}{j;\Gamma \vdash e_1 + e_2} \qquad \frac{j;\Gamma \vdash e_1 \quad j;\Gamma \vdash e_2}{j;\Gamma \vdash e_1 - e_2}$$

$$\frac{j;\Gamma \vdash e_1 \quad j;\Gamma \vdash e_2}{j;\Gamma \vdash e_1 \wedge e_2} \qquad \frac{j;\Gamma \vdash e_1 \quad j;\Gamma \vdash e_2}{j;\Gamma \vdash e_1 \vee e_2}$$

$$\frac{}{j;\Gamma \vdash \texttt{n}} \qquad \frac{}{j;\Gamma \vdash \texttt{tt}} \qquad \frac{}{j;\Gamma \vdash \texttt{ff}} \qquad \frac{}{j;\Gamma \vdash x}$$

$\boxed{\bar{k};\bar{l};j;\Gamma \rhd \kappa}$

$$\frac{\bar{l};\bar{k};j;\Gamma \rhd \kappa_1 \quad \bar{k};\bar{l};j;\Gamma \rhd \kappa_2}{\bar{k};\bar{l};j;\Gamma \rhd \kappa_1 \mapsto \kappa_2}$$

$$\frac{\bar{l};\bar{k} \cup \{j\};j;\Gamma \rhd \kappa_1 \quad \bar{k};\bar{l};j;\Gamma \rhd \kappa_2}{\bar{k};\bar{l};j;\Gamma \rhd \kappa_1 \overset{d}{\mapsto} (\lambda x.\kappa_2)}$$

$$\frac{j;\Gamma \vdash e \quad \bar{k} \subseteq \bar{k}'}{\bar{k};\bar{l};j;\Gamma \rhd \lfloor \texttt{flat}(\|e\|^j) \rfloor^{\bar{k}'}}$$

Figure 9. Obligations coincide with labels on monitors (2)

function applications, the label serves as ownership label for the operator and the operand, similar to the standard application rule:

$$\frac{k;\Gamma \vdash e_1 \quad k;\Gamma \vdash e_2}{k;\Gamma \Vdash \|e_1\|^k\ e_2}$$

For free variables, the environment serves as the source of the ownership label:

$$\frac{\Gamma(x) = k}{k;\Gamma \Vdash x}$$

After all, the variable in this position is going to be replaced by a value via a function application, and the substitution is going to use a value with the specified label. Finally, for a guarded term with an ownership annotation, it suffices to check if it is well-formed with respect to the specified owner:

$$\frac{k;\Gamma \vdash e}{k;\Gamma \Vdash \|e\|^k}$$

A well-formed program in the sense of the preceding section is a well-formed program in the sense of revised judgment, too.

PROPOSITION 4. *For all e and l, $l \vdash e$ implies $l;\varnothing \vdash e$.*

PROOF IDEA. By straightforward induction on the height of the derivation $l \vdash e$. ∎

A program that is well-formed according to $l;\Gamma \vdash e$ reduces to well-formed programs. This statement holds for a contract system using the *lax* reduction rule as well as for or those using *indy*.

THEOREM 5. *Let e be a program such that $l_o;\varnothing \vdash e$. Then:*

1. *if $e \longmapsto_l e_0$, then $l_o;\varnothing \vdash e_0$;*
2. *if $e \longmapsto_i e_0$, then $l_o;\varnothing \vdash e_0$.*

PROOF. (1) We proceed by case analysis on the reduction of e:

- $E^l[\|\texttt{n}_1\|^{\vec{k}} + \|\texttt{n}_2\|^{\vec{l}}] \longmapsto lE^l[\texttt{n}]$. By assumption $l_o;\varnothing \vdash e$, for which lemma 6 implies that $l;\varnothing \vdash \|\texttt{n}_1\|^{\vec{k}} + \|\texttt{n}_2\|^{\vec{l}}$. We can use the same label to check $\texttt{n}$ via the inference rules, i.e., $l;\varnothing \vdash \texttt{n}$. Hence, $l_o;\varnothing \vdash E^l[\texttt{n}]$.
- The cases for other primitive operations are similar to the first.
- $E^l[\mu x.e] \longmapsto_l E^l[\{\|\mu x.e\|^l/x\}e]$: By assumption and lemma 6, $l;\varnothing \vdash \mu x.e$. From lemma 7 we get that $l;\varnothing \vdash \{\|\mu x.e\|^l/x\}e$ and, in turn, $l_o;\varnothing \vdash E^l[\{\|\mu x.e\|^l/x\}e]$.
- $E^l[\|\lambda x.e_0\|^{\vec{k}}\ v] \longmapsto_l E^l[\|\{\|v\|^{l\overleftarrow{k}}/x\}e_0\|^{\vec{k}}]$: Again by assumption and lemma 6, we conclude that $l;\varnothing \vdash \|\lambda x.e_0\|^{\vec{k}}\ v$ and, therefore, $l;\varnothing \vdash \|\lambda x.e_0\|^{\vec{k}}$ and $l;\varnothing \vdash v$.

  Next we distinguish two cases, depending on the length of $\vec{k}$. First assume the vector is empty. In that case, the inference rules imply $l;\{x:l\} \vdash e_0$. Combining this judgment with $l;\varnothing \vdash v$, we may conclude that $l;\varnothing \vdash \{\|v\|^l/x\}e_0$ via lemma 8. Finally from here it is easy to get $l_o;\varnothing \vdash E^l[\{\|v\|^l/x\}e_0]$, the desired conclusion.

  Second, let k_1 be the first element of $\vec{k}$. In that case, the inference rules imply $k_1;\{x:k_1\} \vdash e_0$. Since $l;\varnothing \vdash v$ still holds, we conclude again via lemma 8 that $k_1;\varnothing \vdash \{\|v\|^{l\overleftarrow{k}}/x\}e_0$. Since k_1 is the outermost element of $\vec{k}$, we finally get the desired conclusion, $l_o;\varnothing \vdash E^l[\|\{\|v\|^{l\overleftarrow{k}}/x\}e_0\|^{\vec{k}}]$.
- $E^l[\texttt{mon}_j^{k,l}(\lfloor\texttt{flat}(e_c)\rfloor^{\bar{l}'}, v)] \longmapsto_l E^l[\texttt{if}\ (e_c\ v)\ v\ \texttt{error}^k]$: The assumptions imply $l;\varnothing \vdash \texttt{mon}_j^{k,l}(\lfloor\texttt{flat}(e_c)\rfloor^{\bar{l}'}, v)$ via lemma 6 and hence, $e_c = \|e_c'\|^j$ with $j;\varnothing \vdash e_c'$. Furthermore, the same reasoning yields $v = \|v_0\|^k$ and $k;\varnothing \vdash v_0$. Since the rules for well-formed expressions imply $l;\varnothing \vdash \texttt{if}\ (e_c\ v)\ v\ \texttt{error}^k$ is well-formed, the desired conclusion follows immediately.
- $E^l[\texttt{mon}_j^{k,l}(\kappa_1 \mapsto \kappa_2, v)] \longmapsto_l E^l[\lambda x.\texttt{mon}_j^{k,l}(\kappa_2, v\ \texttt{mon}_j^{l,k}(\kappa_1, x))]$: With the usual reasoning, we get $l;\varnothing \vdash \texttt{mon}_j^{k,l}(\kappa_1 \mapsto \kappa_2, v)$, $v = \|v_0\|^k$, and $k;\varnothing \vdash v_0$. The contract check yields two pieces of knowledge:

  $$\{l\};\{k\};j;\varnothing \rhd \kappa_1$$

  and

  $$\{k\};\{l\};j;\varnothing \rhd \kappa_2$$

  From an additional application of the inference rules for well-formedness we get $k;\{x:l\} \Vdash v\ \texttt{mon}_j^{l,k}(\kappa_1, x)$ and, with the help of lemma 9, $l;\{x:l\} \vdash \texttt{mon}_j^{k,l}(\kappa_2, v\ \texttt{mon}_j^{l,k}(\kappa_1, x))$. Finally from a last application of the inference rules for well-formedness we get $l;\varnothing \vdash \lambda x.\texttt{mon}_j^{k,l}(\kappa_2, v\ \texttt{mon}_j^{l,k}(\kappa_1, x))$.
- Finally, let $e = E^l[\texttt{mon}_j^{k,l}(\kappa_1 \overset{d}{\mapsto} (\lambda x.\kappa_2), v)]$ and observe that

  $$e \longmapsto_l E^l[\lambda x.\texttt{mon}_j^{k,l}(\{x/^c x\}\kappa_2, v\ \texttt{mon}_j^{l,k}(\kappa_1, x))].$$

  Via lemma 6 we derive $l;\varnothing \vdash \texttt{mon}_j^{k,l}(\kappa_1 \overset{d}{\mapsto} (\lambda x.\kappa_2), v)$. Thus, $v = \|v\|^k$ with $k;\varnothing \vdash v$, but also

  $$\{l\};\{k,j\};j;\varnothing \rhd \kappa_1$$

  and

  $$\{k\};\{l\};j;\varnothing \rhd \kappa_2\ .$$

  The rest of this argument uses the same strategy as the preceding case, except that we use lemmas 10 and 14 to derive the key result, $l;\{x:l\} \vdash \texttt{mon}_j^{k,l}(\{x/^c x\}\kappa_2, v\ \texttt{mon}_j^{l,k}(\kappa_1, x))$.

(2) The proof of part (2) differs from the proof of part (1) only in the case for monitors with dependent contracts. Therefore, let $e = E^l[\mathtt{mon}_j^{k,l}(\kappa_1 \overset{d}{\mapsto} (\lambda x.\kappa_2), v)]$ and recall that the contraction proceeds as follows:

$$e \longmapsto_i E^l[\lambda x.\mathtt{mon}_j^{k,l}(\{\mathtt{mon}_j^{l,j}(\kappa_1, x)/^c x\}\kappa_2, v\, \mathtt{mon}_j^{l,k}(\kappa_1, x))].$$

Once again, we derive $l;\varnothing \vdash \mathtt{mon}_j^{k,l}(\kappa_1 \overset{d}{\mapsto} (\lambda x.\kappa_2), v)$ via lemmas 6. Hence, $v = \|v\|^k$ with $k;\varnothing \vdash v$, but also

$$\{l\};\{k,j\};j;\varnothing \rhd \kappa_1$$

and

$$\{k\};\{l\};j;\varnothing \rhd \kappa_2 \,.$$

By the well-formedness, $k;\{x:l\} \Vdash v\, \mathtt{mon}_j^{l,k}(\kappa_1, x)$. Now, with the help of lemmas 12 and 14, we can derive

$$l;\{x:l\} \vdash \mathtt{mon}_j^{k,l}(\{\mathtt{mon}_j^{l,j}(\kappa_1, x)/^c x\}\kappa_2, v\, \mathtt{mon}_j^{l,k}(\kappa_1, x)) \,.$$

Thus we conclude the proof with another application of the inference rules for well-formedness. ∎

The proofs of the central lemmas depend on a series of auxiliary lemmas about the properties of well-formed terms and contracts, substitution, and contract substitution.

LEMMA 6. *If $l;\varnothing \vdash E^k[e]$ then $k;\varnothing \vdash e$.*

PROOF IDEA. By induction on the size of E^k. ∎

LEMMA 7. *If $l;\Gamma \vdash e$, $k;\Gamma \vdash e_0$, and $x \notin dom(\Gamma)$, $l;\Gamma \vdash \{\|e_0\|^k/x\}e$.*

PROOF IDEA. By induction on the height of $l;\Gamma \vdash e$. ∎

LEMMA 8. *If $l;\Gamma \uplus \{x:k\} \vdash e$, $v = \|v_0\|^k$ and $k;\Gamma \vdash v_0$, then*

$$l;\Gamma \vdash \{v/x\}e \,.$$

PROOF IDEA. By induction on the height of $l;\Gamma \uplus \{x:k\} \vdash e$. Note that $l;\Gamma \uplus \{x:k\} \vdash \mathtt{mon}_j^{k,l}(\kappa, x)$ is a base case. ∎

LEMMA 9. *If $l;\Gamma \vdash e$ and $x \notin dom(\Gamma)$, then $l;\Gamma \uplus \{x:k\} \vdash e$.*

PROOF IDEA. By induction on the height of $l;\Gamma \vdash e$. ∎

LEMMA 10. *If $\bar{k};\bar{l};j;\Gamma \rhd \kappa$ and $x \notin dom(\Gamma)$, then*

$$\bar{k};\bar{l};j;\Gamma \uplus \{x:l'\} \rhd \{x/^c x\}\kappa \,.$$

PROOF IDEA. By induction on the height of $\bar{k};\bar{l};l;\Gamma \rhd \kappa$. For the flat contracts case we employ lemma 11. ∎

LEMMA 11. *If $l;\Gamma \vdash e$ and $x \notin dom(\Gamma)$, $l;\Gamma \uplus \{x:k\} \vdash \{\|x\|^l/x\}e$.*

PROOF IDEA. First, we generalize the lemma's statement: If $l;\Gamma \vdash e$ and $x \notin dom(\Gamma)$, $l;\Gamma \uplus \{x:k\} \vdash \{\|x\|^j/x\}e$. Then we proceed by induction on the height of $l;\Gamma \vdash e$. ∎

LEMMA 12. *If $\bar{k};\bar{l};j;\Gamma \rhd \kappa$ and $k;\Gamma \uplus \{x:l\} \vdash \mathtt{mon}_j^{k,l}(\kappa', x)$, with $x \notin dom(\Gamma)$ then $\bar{k};\bar{l};j;\Gamma \uplus \{x:k\} \rhd \{\mathtt{mon}_j^{k,l}(\kappa', x)/^c x\}\kappa$*

PROOF IDEA. By induction on the height of $\bar{k};\bar{l};j;\Gamma \rhd \kappa$. For the flat contracts case we employ lemma 13. ∎

LEMMA 13. *If $l;\Gamma \vdash e$, $l;\Gamma \uplus \{x:k\} \vdash \mathtt{mon}_j^{k,l}(\kappa', x)$, & $x \notin dom(\Gamma)$, then $l;\Gamma \uplus \{x:k\} \vdash \{\|\mathtt{mon}_j^{k,l}(\kappa', x)\|^l/x\}e$*

PROOF IDEA. First, we generalize the lemma's statement as follows: If $l';\Gamma \vdash e$, $l;\Gamma \uplus \{x:k\} \vdash \mathtt{mon}_j^{k,l}(\kappa', x)$, & $x \notin dom(\Gamma)$, then $l';\Gamma \uplus \{x:k\} \vdash \{\|\mathtt{mon}_j^{k,l}(\kappa', x)\|^l/x\}e$ We proceed by induction on the height of $l';\Gamma \vdash e$. ∎

LEMMA 14. *If $\bar{k};\bar{l};j;\Gamma \rhd \kappa$, $\bar{k}' \subseteq \bar{k}$ and $\bar{l}' \subseteq \bar{l}$ then $\bar{k}';\bar{l}';j;\Gamma \rhd \kappa$.*

PROOF IDEA. By induction on the height of $\bar{k};\bar{l};j;\Gamma \rhd \kappa$. ∎

4.3 Main Theorems

When a program is well-formed, its monitors obviously satisfy the blame correctness criterion.

THEOREM 15. *$\longmapsto_l$ and $\longmapsto_i$ are blame correct.*

PROOF. This theorem is a straightforward consequence of theorem 5. To wit, the subject reduction theorem says that a program satisfies the subject including when its redex is a monitor term containing a flat contract. From the proof of the subject reduction theorem, we know that the subject implies

$$l;\varnothing \vdash \mathtt{mon}_j^{k,l}(\lfloor \mathtt{flat}(e_c) \rfloor^{\bar{l}'}, \|v\|^k)$$

The label on the context is the same as the client label by lemma 6 but we also need to know that the server label l is a member of the contract's obligations $\bar{l}'$. This has to be the case given that the monitor term is well-formed. Note how the proof is independent of the reduction semantics as long as it satisfies the subject reduction property. ∎

The *picky* contract system fails to satisfy an analogous theorem.

THEOREM 16. *There exists a program e such that $l_o \vdash e$ and*

$$e \overset{*}{\longmapsto}_p E^l[\mathtt{mon}_j^{k,l_2}(\lfloor \mathtt{flat}(e) \rfloor^{\bar{l}}, \|v\|^{l_1})]$$

but $k \neq l_1$.

PROOF. Here is one such program where $k \neq l_o$:

$$\Pi_l^3 = \mathtt{mon}_l^{k,l_o}(\kappa_l, \|\lambda h_1.h_1\ \lambda x.5\ (\lambda g.g\ 1)\|^k)\ (\lambda f.\lambda h_2.h_2\ \lambda x.6)$$

The restriction on the labels intuitively corresponds to the composition of the two different modules k and l_o through the contract κ_l. Note that Π_l^3 is a family of programs, one per label l. This label is the label of the contract monitor and, consequently, must be the owner of all embedded flat contracts. In principle, l could be the label of the client, the server, or any other non-top-level (l_o) label but in the end, our choice must obey subject reduction.

While Π_l^3 performs no interesting computation, its contract κ_l plays a critical role. To explain the contract though, it is best to start with the type of h_1:

$$[(num \to num) \to \{([num \to num] \to num) \to num\}] \to num$$

The type tells us that h_1 consumes a complex higher-order function and produces a number. Instead of plain numbers, however, we wish to deal with positive numbers only. We thus know that κ_l must have at least something like the following shape:

$$[(\mathrm{P?}_l \mapsto \mathrm{P?}_l) \mapsto \{([\mathrm{P?}_l \mapsto \mathrm{P?}_l] \mapsto \mathrm{P?}_l) \mapsto \mathrm{P?}_l\}] \mapsto \mathrm{P?}_l$$

Next we add two dependencies:

$$[(\mathrm{P?}_l \mapsto \mathrm{P?}_l) \overset{d}{\mapsto} (\lambda f.\{([\mathrm{P?}_l \mapsto \mathrm{P?}_l] \overset{d}{\mapsto} (\lambda g.\mathrm{P?}_l)) \mapsto \mathrm{P?}_l\})] \mapsto \mathrm{P?}_l$$

The two key points to notice are: (1) in this contract, g is in the scope of f and (2) while f originates in the server (wrapped expression), g originates in the client (context) and both flow into the contract.

Equipped with this informal and approximate understanding, we can now turn to the actual contract:

$$\begin{aligned}
\kappa_l &= ((\lfloor \mathrm{P?}_l \rfloor^{l_o} \mapsto \lfloor \mathrm{P?}_l \rfloor^k) \overset{d}{\mapsto} (\lambda f.\kappa_l^1)) \mapsto \lfloor \mathrm{P?}_l \rfloor^k \\
\kappa_l^1 &= ((\lfloor \mathrm{P?}_l \rfloor^k \mapsto \lfloor \mathrm{P?}_l \rfloor^{l_o}) \overset{d}{\mapsto} (\lambda g.\kappa_l^2)) \mapsto \lfloor \mathrm{P?}_l \rfloor^k \\
\kappa_l^2 &= \lfloor \mathtt{flat}(\|\lambda x.\mathtt{zero?}(f\ 1 - g\ 0)\|^l) \rfloor^k \\
\mathrm{P?}_l &= \mathtt{flat}(\|\lambda x.x > 0\|^l)
\end{aligned}$$

Note how κ_l^2 invokes f on a positive number and g on 0.

Now we show that l must be set to l_o in order to satisfy blame correctness. First, note that for for all $l \in \mathbb{L}$, $l_o \vdash \Pi_l^3$ if $k \neq l_o$. Second, the reduction of Π_l^3 eventually checks that 1 is greater than 0, i.e., that the post-condition contract κ_l^2 is satisfied:

$$\Pi_l^3 \overset{*}{\longmapsto}_p E_0^l[\mathtt{mon}_l^{l_o,k}(\lfloor \mathrm{P}?_l \rfloor^{l_o}, \| \| 1 \|^l \|^l)]$$

In order for the *picky* system to satisfy the blame correctness condition, l must be equal to l_o, which means the term looks like this:

$$E_0^{l_o}[\mathtt{mon}_{l_o}^{l_o,k}(\lfloor \mathrm{P}?_{l_o} \rfloor^{l_o}, \| \| 1 \|^{l_o} \|^{l_o})]$$

Unfortunately, the next few steps of the reduction process produces a state that is inconsistent with blame correctness. Specifically, κ_l^2 also checks that g's pre-condition holds for 0:

$$E_0^{l_o}[\mathtt{mon}_{l_o}^{l_o,k}(\lfloor \mathrm{P}?_{l_o} \rfloor^{l_o}, \| \| 1 \|^{l_o} \|^{l_o})] \overset{*}{\longmapsto}_p \\ E_1^{l_o}[\mathtt{mon}_{l_o}^{k,l_o}(\lfloor \mathrm{P}?_{l_o} \rfloor^{l_o}, \| \| 0 \|^{l_o} \|^{l_o})]$$

This last state, however, is inconsistent with the subject because k cannot equal l_o. Indeed, the next few reduction steps result in a failed check. The contract monitor blames k, which isn't the owner l_o of the value. The *picky* system fails to assign blame properly. ∎

In essence the proof of the theorem shows that there is no correct strategy for associating (pieces of) contracts with components in a picky semantics. No matter which labeling strategy we use, a contract violation may blame a component that has no control over the faulty value.

5. Consigliere

Our model introduces two concepts that are potentially useful for practical programmers: obligations and ownership. According to our judgments for well-formed contracts and expressions, a *contractual obligation* is a static property of contract text. When confronted with complex contracts, a programmer may benefit from displaying such information in the IDE. In contrast, *ownership information* is a dynamically evolving property, and it is particularly useful in a debugger for determining the creator and current owner of values as they flow from one component to another.

To test the practicality of displaying obligation information, we have implemented a tool that analyzes modules and contracts and annotates them with obligation information. The tool is a plug-in for DrRacket (Findler et al. 2002), our IDE for the Racket programming language. In this section, we refer to the tool as *consigliere*, though in DrRacket, it is simply a part of the *CheckSyntax* tool.

The *consigliere* tool operates on Racket modules in two different modes. In *server* mode, *consigliere* analyzes the module from the perspective of the supplier of services. It retrieves all the contracts that are attached to exported identifiers and uses

- *red* to tag the server's obligations;
- *green* to highlight the server's assumptions, i.e., the parts of the contract that the other party is responsible for; and
- *yellow* to signal that a part of the contract is both an assumption and an obligation.

In client mode, *consigliere* analyzes the module from the perspective of a consumer of services. Once it has the results, it proceeds as in server mode except that it uses red for the client's obligations and green for the client's assumptions.

For a simple example, consider the module in figure 10. The module `provide/contract` specification lists one exported function, `pick-one`. According to its contract, the function consumes a non-empty list of numbers and returns an number. A code inspection shows that the function actually returns a random element of the given list.

Figure 10. Obligations and assumptions for `one-of`

The top of figure 10 shows the result of using the tool in client mode. As expected, the non-empty list part of the contract is colored in red, because any user of `pick-one` is required to use a non-empty list of numbers as an argument. Also, because the client may assume that `pick-one` is a function and not some arbitrary value, *consigliere* colors the `->` contract constructor with green. The reverse reasoning explains the coloring of the lower part of figure 10, which shows the result of using *consigliere* in server mode.

For a second example, consider a `deriv` function with the contract from section 1. Its contract is significantly more complex than *pick-one*, because it comes with two higher-order components and a post-condition. Note that this contract uses the `->i` contract combinator, turning the contract provider into a party with obligations and assumptions. Here the contract provider is the server module, meaning `->i` is interpreted using the *+indy* semantics. Practically speaking, the obligations and assumptions of the server also include the obligations and assumptions of the contract provider.

The top screenshot of figure 11 shows the result of using the tool in client mode. The color assignment roughly follows the same contravariant traversal of pattern as the contract in figure 10. When it comes to the `#:post-cond` code, however, the color of the keyword indicates that the post-condition is an assumption for the client just like the other post-condition of the contract.

The lower screenshot depicts the server's obligations and assumptions, which are more interesting than the client's. The difference is due to the server's dual role as both a service provider *and* as the owner of the contract. Recall that the contract provider is responsible for meeting the pre-conditions of `f` and `fp` in the post-condition, while the server may assume that `f` and `fp` meet their post-conditions. As a result, the colors used for `f` from the server's perspective coincide with those used in the client mode. For `fp`, however, both parts are colored yellow because the obligation of the server is the contract provider's assumption and vice versa. Since the server is both the server and the contract provider party in this case, the user must be ready to treat the pre-condition and post-condition of `fp` either as an assumption or as an obligation depending on the use.

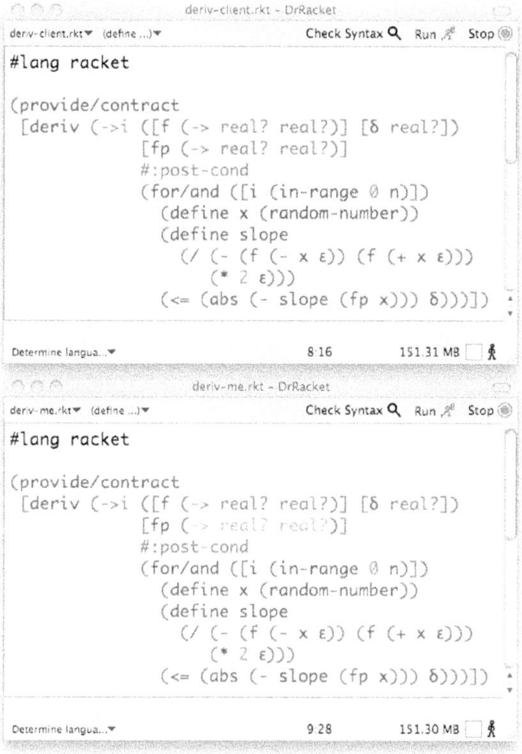

Figure 11. Obligations and assumptions for `deriv`

6. Related Work

Provenance is the book-keeping of origin, context and history information of data. It plays an important role for the correct and secure behavior of large software and hardware systems (Simmhan et al. 2005; Bose and Frew 2005). The study of provenance from a formal linguistic perspective is still at an initial stage (Cheney et al. 2009). Our notion of ownership is a means of keeping around some origin and context information about program values. So it can be viewed as a form of provenance. Also ownership can be used as a basis for studying formal properties of this kind of provenance. However our technique and its use to prove properties of contract systems is not related to any provenance tracking technology.

Tracking information flow in a computer system is a specialized kind of provenance. Secure information flow as pioneered by Denning (1976) is the restriction of flow of data in a computer system only between agents that have the appropriate level of clearance. There are both software and hardware techniques for imposing secure information flow. Our instrumentation of the dynamic semantics resembles techniques used for proving sound type systems that enforce secure information flow.

Zdancewic et al. (1999) introduce (program) principals as a means to prove type abstraction properties related to information flow with a syntactic proof technique. In a principal semantics, different principals "own" different components and exported values carry the principal of their component of origin. Since the principals semantics prevents reductions that involve values with different principals, a client component is obliged to use a server's functions on the server's values. In short, the semantics dynamically enforces a form of information hiding. It is now easy to see how a principals semantics supports a syntactic soundness proof for abstract types. If the interface between the server component and the client employs abstract types and if the type system soundly enforces type abstraction, stuck states become unreachable during computation.

Although both principals and ownership annotations point to the source of values and functions, the principal semantics differs substantially from our ownership semantics. Most importantly, principals may change the evaluation of a program; ownership does not. When a function from one server is applied to a value from a client or a different server, the principal semantics is stuck. In contrast, ownership annotations are simply propagated in our reduction rules; they do not affect computation. Ownership information is instead used to formulate a criteria for determining the correctness of blame assignment. We can imagine using an ownership semantics to formulate syntactic soundness proofs for type abstraction, while we do not see any advantages over the principals semantics for this application.

As explained in the introduction, Greenberg et al. (2010) study the full relationship between lax and picky contract systems on one hand and manifest contract systems on the other. For the latter, the type system propagates some of the contract constraints. While Gronski and Flanagan (2007) established a tight relationship for a world without dependent contracts, Greenberg et al. (2010) demonstrate that the full picture is rather complex. In particular, they show that as far as contract violations are concerned, manifest contracts sit strictly between lax contracts and picky contracts.

In general, this work extends our decade-old linguistic investigation of behavioral software contracts. Meyer (1988, 1991, 1992) introduced software contracts via the design of the Eiffel programming language and the creation of a contract-oriented software engineering curriculum. Since then contracts have been used both for extended static checking (Detlefs et al. 1998; Barnett et al. 2004) and runtime monitoring of higher-order programs (Findler and Felleisen 2002). Blume and McAllester (2006) introduce *picky* contract monitoring and explore a quotient model for higher-order contracts and use it to prove properties of Findler and Felleisen's higher-order contracts. Findler et al. (2004; 2006) propose an alternative view, namely, "contracts as projections," which relates contracts to Scott (1976)'s denotation model of types. Gronski and Flanagan (2007) relate Findler and Felleisen's higher-order contract to type casts. Their result motivates a type-oriented form of extended static checking (Knowles et al. 2006), which Greenberg et al. consider a manifest form of contract. Xu et al. (2009) use Blume and McAllester's ideas to develop static contract checking for Haskell using symbolic evaluation. Hinze et al. (2006) and Chitil et al. (2003) both introduce contracts to Haskell but end up with two different contract systems. The first performs eager contract checking while the second is lazy. Degen et al. (2010) compare eager and lazy contract checking for lazy languages through a series of formal properties but do not reach a definite conclusion.

Finally, in the context of JML (Leavens et al. 1999), Rudich et al. (2008) develop a method for proving the well-formedness of pure-method specifications and they discuss how their technique can benefit from automated theorem proving. The goal of this line of research is significantly different than ours. It concerns extraction of proof obligations for the verification of JML contracts internal consistency. Unfortunately, JML contracts capture only first-order properties, and it is unclear if their technique is applicable in a higher-order world. Furthermore, their static semantics lacks a formalization of the contract parties which plays an important role in our work.

7. Conclusion

This paper introduces a new semantics for dependent contracts in response to Greenberg et al. (2010)' s comparison of two alternatives. Our work acknowledges the motivation behind the *picky* contract system and turns the *lax* system into a choice for the confident programmer. Like the *picky* system, the new *indy* system protects arguments and results inside dependency assertions. In contrast to the *picky* system, each contract is treated as an independent party with its own obligations to meet.

Most importantly, we introduce a semantics that tracks value ownership and contract obligations, and we formulate the first ever correctness criterion for blame assignment. Our major theorems show that the *indy* system guarantees that contract monitors blame only components that are in control while the *picky* system fails to satisfy this intuitive correctness property for blame assignment.

Our results suggest several changes to the implementation of contracts in Racket. First, even though the *lax* semantics is blame correct, we now support the *indy* semantics for dependent contracts to ensure that only guilty parties are blamed. Second, by instantiating the contract party, we obtain flavors of an *indy* semantics that support the entire variety of Racket contracts in use: server-side contracts, client-side contracts, and contracts for ML-like modules where signatures have an independent existence.Third, the notion of well-formed contractual obligations is the basis of a DrRacket tool that can remind module programmers of their obligations and assumptions in complex, higher-order contracts.

Acknowledgments

Thanks to Matthew Flatt for suggesting how to exploit Racket's macro system to implement *consigliere*. We appreciate fruitful discussions with Riccardo Pucella, Sam Tobin-Hochstadt, Stevie Strickland and Carl Eastlund. We are grateful to the anonymous reviewers of POPL 2011 for their useful feedback.

References

H. P. Barendregt. *The Lambda Calculus – Its Syntax and Semantics*, volume 103 of *Studies in Logic and the Foundations of Mathematics*. North-Holland, 1984.

M. Barnett, K. R. M. Leino, and W. Schulte. The Spec# programming system: an overview. In *Construction and Analysis of Safe, Secure and Interoperable Smart Devices*, pages 49–69, 2004.

A. Beugnard, J.-M. Jézéquel, N. Plouzeau, and D. Watkins. Making components contract aware. *IEEE Computer*, 32(7):38–45, July 1999.

M. Blume and D. McAllester. Sound and complete models of contracts. *Journal of Functional Programming*, 16(4-5):375–414, 2006.

R. Bose and J. Frew. Lineage retrieval for scientific data processing: a survey. *ACM Computing Survey*, 37(1):1–28, 2005.

J. Cheney, S. Chong, N. Foster, M. Seltzer, and S. Vansummeren. Provenance: a future history. In *Proceeding of the 24th ACM SIGPLAN Conference Companion on Object Oriented Programming Systems Languages and Applications: Onward! Session (OOPSLA Onward!)*, pages 957–964, 2009.

O. Chitil, D. McNeill, and C. Runciman. Lazy assertions. In *Revised Papers of the 15th International Workshop on Implementation of Functional Languages (IFL)*, pages 1–19, 2003.

M. Degen, P. Thiemann, and S. Wehr. Eager and delayed contract monitoring for call-by-value and call-by-name evaluation. *Journal of Logic and Algebraic Programming*, page to appear, 2010.

D. E. Denning. A lattice model of secure information flow. *Communications of the ACM*, 19(5):236–243, 1976.

D. L. Detlefs, K. R. M. Leino, G. Nelson, and J. B. Saxe. Extended static checking. Technical Report 158, Compaq SRC Research Report, 1998.

C. Dimoulas and M. Felleisen. On contract satisfaction in a higher-order world. *ACM Transactions on Programming Languages and Systems*. accepted (with revisions) for publication.

M. Felleisen, R. B. Findler, and M. Flatt. *Semantics Engineering with PLT Redex*. MIT Press, 2009.

R. B. Findler and M. Blume. Contracts as pairs of projections. In *Proceedings of the 8th International Symposium on Functional and Logic Programming (FLOPS)*, pages 226–241, 2006.

R. B. Findler and M. Felleisen. Contracts for higher-order functions. In *Proceedings of the 7th ACM SIGPLAN International Conference on Functional Programming (ICFP)*, pages 48–59, 2002.

R. B. Findler, J. Clements, C. Flanagan, M. Flatt, S. Krishnamurthi, P. Steckler, and M. Felleisen. DrScheme: A programming environment for Scheme. *J. Funct. Program.*, 12(2):159–182, Mar. 2002.

R. B. Findler, M. Felleisen, and M. Blume. An investigation of contracts as projections. Technical Report TR-2004-02, University of Chicago, Computer Science Department, 2004.

C. Flanagan. Hybrid type checking. In *Proceedings of the 33th Annual ACM SIGPLAN-SIGACT Symposium on Principles of Programming Languages (POPL)*, pages 245–256, 2006.

M. Flatt and PLT. Reference: Racket. Technical Report PLT-TR-2010-1, PLT Inc., 2010. `http://racket-lang.org/tr1/`.

M. Greenberg, B. C. Pierce, and S. Weirich. Contracts made manifest. In *Proceedings of the 37th Annual ACM SIGPLAN-SIGACT Symposium on Programming Languages (POPL)*, pages 353–364, 2010.

J. Gronski and C. Flanagan. Unifying hybrid types and contracts. In *Proceedings of the 8th Symposium on Trends in Functional Programming (TFP)*, pages 54–69, 2007.

R. Hinze, J. Jeuring, and A. Löh. Typed contracts for functional programming. In *In Proceedings of the 8th International Symposium on Functional and Logic Programming (FLOPS)*, pages 208–235, 2006.

K. Knowles, A. Tomb, J. Gronski, S. N. Freund, and C. Flanagan. Sage: Unified hybrid checking for first-class types, general refinement types, and dynamic, 2006. URL `http://sage.soe.ucsc.edu/`.

G. T. Leavens, A. L. Baker, and C. Ruby. JML: A notation for detailed design. In H. Kilov, B. Rumpe, and I. Simmonids, editors, *Behavioral Specifications of Businesses and Systems*, pages 175–188. Kluwer Academic Publishers, 1999.

B. Meyer. Design by contract. In *Advances in Object-Oriented Software Engineering*, pages 1–50. Prentice Hall, 1991.

B. Meyer. *Eiffel: The Language*. Prentice Hall, 1992.

B. Meyer. *Object-oriented Software Construction*. Prentice Hall, 1988.

G. D. Plotkin. Call-by-name, call-by-value, and the λ-calculus. *Theoretical Computer Science*, 1(2):125–159, 1975.

G. D. Plotkin. LCF considered as a programming language. *Theoretical Computer Science*, 5(3):223–255, 1977.

A. Rudich, A. Darvas, and P. Müller. Checking well-formedness of pure-method specifications. In *Proceedings of the 15th International Symposium on Formal Methods (FM)*, pages 68–83, 2008.

D. S. Scott. Data types as lattices. *SIAM Journal of Computing*, 5(3):522–587, 1976.

Y. L. Simmhan, B. Plale, and D. Gannon. A survey of data provenance in e-science. *ACM SIGMOD Record*, 34(3):31–36, 2005.

T. S. Strickland and M. Felleisen. Contracts for first-class modules. In *Proceedings of the 5th Symposium on Dynamic Languages (DLS)*, pages 27–38. ACM, 2009.

S. Tobin-Hochstadt and M. Felleisen. Logical types for untyped languages. In *Proceedings of the 15th ACM SIGPLAN Internation Conference on Functional Programming (ICFP)*, pages 117–128, 2010.

S. Tobin-Hochstadt and M. Felleisen. The design and implementation of Typed Scheme. In *Proceedings of the 35th Annual ACM SIGPLAN-SIGACT Symposium on the Proncinles of Programming Languages (POPL)*, pages 395–407, 2008.

D. Xu, S. Peyton Jones, and K. Claessen. Static contract checking for Haskell. In *Proceedings of the 36th Annual ACM SIGPLAN-SIGACT Symposium on Programming Languages (POPL)*, pages 41–52, 2009.

S. Zdancewic, D. Grossman, and G. Morrisett. Principals in programming languages: A syntactic proof technique. In *Proceedings of the 4th ACM SIGPLAN International Conference on Functional Programming (ICFP)*, pages 197–207, 1999.

Generative Type Abstraction and Type-level Computation

Stephanie Weirich
University of Pennsylvania
Philadelphia, PA, USA
sweirich@cis.upenn.edu

Dimitrios Vytiniotis
Simon Peyton Jones
Microsoft Research
Cambridge, UK
{dimitris,simonpj}@microsoft.com

Steve Zdancewic
University of Pennsylvania
Philadelphia, PA, USA
stevez@cis.upenn.edu

Abstract

Modular languages support *generative type abstraction*, ensuring that an abstract type is distinct from its representation, except inside the implementation where the two are synonymous. We show that this well-established feature is in tension with the *non-parametric features* of newer type systems, such as indexed type families and GADTs. In this paper we solve the problem by using kinds to distinguish between parametric and non-parametric contexts. The result is directly applicable to Haskell, which is rapidly developing support for type-level computation, but the same issues should arise whenever generativity and non-parametric features are combined.

Categories and Subject Descriptors D.3.3 [*Language Constructs and Features*]: Abstract data types; F.3.3 [*Studies of Program Constructs*]: Type structure

General Terms Design,Languages

Keywords Haskell, Newtype deriving, Type functions

1. Introduction

Generative type abstraction allows programmers to introduce new type constants in their programs that are *isomorphic* to existing types; examples include ML's module system [Milner et al. 1997; Pierce 2005, Ch. 8], and Haskell's **`newtype`** construct [Peyton Jones et al. 2003]. Type generativity is important because it supports modularity by enforcing *abstraction*: the *implementor* of a module can move freely between the abstract and representation types, whereas to the *client* of the module the two types are completely distinct.

There is growing interest in languages that support some form of *type-level computation* including Haskell's type classes [Hall et al. 1996] and indexed type families [Kiselyov et al. 2010]. However, there is a fundamental tension between type-level computation and generative type abstraction, at least in the latter's more flexible forms. To summarize very briefly, the conflict is this:

- To maximize re-use and convenience, it is very desirable for the implementor to be able to treat the abstract type A and its concrete representation type C as synonymous – we call this *flexible type generativity*.
- However, given type-level function F the result of $(F\ A)$ and $(F\ C)$ may differ, so A and C cannot be synonymous.

Resolving this conflict is the subject of this paper. Specifically our contributions are:

- We show in Section 2 that the naive combination of type generativity and non-parametric type-level features can violate soundness; a problem that already manifests in the Glasgow Haskell Compiler, and affects not only type-level non-parametric functions, but also other forms of non-parametric constructs, such as *generalized algebraic datatypes* (GADTs) [Cheney and Hinze 2003; Hinze et al. 2002; Peyton Jones et al. 2006; Xi et al. 2003].
- We formalize a solution to this problem that reconciles flexible type generativity and non-parametric type functions in Section 3. Our language, FC_2, builds on GHC's existing core language, System FC [Sulzmann et al. 2007], which supports erasable type-level coercions. The key ingredient in our solution is to employ kinds decorated with *roles* to mark the distinctions that type contexts may make.
- We prove that FC_2 programs are type safe, provided that user axioms and definitions give rise to consistent axiom sets (Section 4).
- We give sufficient conditions for showing the consistency of an axiom set. For our proofs, we introduce a rewrite system for types that is novel in two dimensions: rewriting (i) is *role-sensitive*, and (ii) need not be strongly normalizing (Section 4.2).
- We present a Haskell-specific result: we show how Haskell source programs that may involve non-parametric type contexts and flexible type generativity can be translated to yield provably consistent FC_2 axiom sets. (Section 5)
- Our core language is an *improvement* of System FC since it permits safe flexible type generativity, but also *unsaturated* type functions. Perhaps surprisingly, our language is additionally a significant *simplification* of the original System FC, which *removes* several of the original coercion constructs that we have identified to be encodable (even in the original System FC). We discuss these differences in Section 6.2.

For the sake of concreteness we build our presentation around Haskell and System FC, since this setting allows us to demonstrate our points with real code, instead of using a hypothetical λ-calculus. However, we stress that our work is applicable whenever flexible type generativity and non-parametric type-level features are combined. For example, the very same issues could arise in extensions of the ML module system. We discuss related work in Section 7.

POPL'11, January 26–28, 2011, Austin, Texas, USA.

Some of the technical material has been elided from this version of the paper for space. Although this paper is self contained, more details are available at http://www.cis.upenn.edu/~sweirich/newtypes.pdf.

2. The problems with generative type abstraction

Generative type abstraction is an extremely useful mechanism for enforcing abstraction barriers and for refining interfaces. To see this benefit, let us consider the Haskell incarnation of type generativity, namely **newtype** definitions. In Haskell, the programmer may declare a **newtype** Age, with concrete representation type Int, thus:

```
newtype Age = MkAge Int
```

The implementor uses the "data constructor" MkAge to coerce an Int to an Age, and pattern matching to effect the inverse coercion. For example:

```
addAge :: Age → Int → Age
addAge (MkAge a) n = MkAge (a+n)
```

The client, in contrast, can be prevented from making such conversions, by using the module system to hide the MkAge constructor:

```
module AgeModule( Age, addAge, ... ) where
  -- Age definition and implementation
```

2.1 Coercion lifting

In describing MkAge, we wrote "data constructor" in quotes because although it behaves in many ways like a data constructor, its cost model is different. Specifically, a **newtype** definition guarantees that the abstract type really is represented by the concrete type, so the runtime conversion cost is zero. That would not be true if Age were instead declared with **data** instead of **newtype**.

So Age can be coerced to an Int, and vice versa, for free—i.e. without runtime cost—because it *is* an Int. Notationally, we say that Int $\sim$ Age, where we use $\sim$ for type equality[1]. But what about, say, Maybe Age?

```
data Maybe a = Nothing | Just a
```

Obviously, Maybe Age should be freely coercible to Maybe Int, because the two are represented identically. Alas, in Haskell 98 one would have to write

```
cvtAge :: Maybe Age → Maybe Int
cvtAge t = mapMaybe (λ(MkAge a) → a) t
-- mapMaybe :: (a → b) → Maybe a → Maybe b
```

This is unsavory for several reasons: (a) it is tedious for the programmer; (b) it may be difficult to implement the necessary "map" function; (c) it is hard for the compiler to eliminate a runtime call to the map function (let alone to guarantee to do so) especially if the map function is recursive. As an example of (b) consider the mapping function for the type T shown below, with co- and contravariance, and higher kinds:

```
data T a f = T1 a
           | T2 (a → Int)
           | T3 (f (T a f) (T a f))
```

These difficulties are frustrating, because we know that, say, T Age Maybe is represented identically to T Int Maybe. So, let us imagine a hypothetical extension of Haskell that provides lifted coercions; that is, it implements the following rule:

[1] There are too many sorts of "="!

> *Coercion lifting:* if for two types φ and ψ we have $\varphi \sim \psi$ (for example, if they are the abstract and concrete types of a **newtype** declaration), then $T\,\varphi \sim T\,\psi$ for any type constructor T.

In fact this extension is not so hypothetical, because such a rule is the basis of the so-called "newtype deriving" feature implemented by GHC. It is not difficult to use newtype deriving to define an identity function whose type is

```
cvt :: ∀{c}. c Int → c Age
```

ML supports coercion lifting even more directly: within a structure the abstract and the representation types are considered entirely interchangeable. For example in Standard ML one might say

```
signature AGE = sig
  type age
  val addAge : age → int → age
  ...
end

structure AgeModule :> AGE = struct
  type age = int
  fun addAge a n = a+n
  ...
end
```

Inside AgeModule the two types are synonymous, and so addAge need not convert in either direction.

However, the point of this paper is that the innocuous and obvious-seeming "lifting" of type identities becomes unsound when combined with type-level computation, as we show in the next section.

2.2 Type-level computation

One very popular extension to Haskell is that of Generalized Algebraic Data Types (GADTs) [Peyton Jones et al. 2006], with which we assume the reader is somewhat familiar. In GHC one could declare a GADT with two nullary constructors like this:

```
data K a where
  KAge :: K Age
  KInt :: K Int
```

Now, consider these definitions (using cvt from Section 2.1):

```
kint :: K Age          get :: K Age → String
kint = cvt KInt        get KAge = "Age"
```

Since get's type signature declares that its argument is of type K Age, the patterns in get are exhaustive. But consider the call (get kint). It is patently well typed, yet the pattern match in get will fail (recall that cvt is operationally the identity function), and if the compiler assumed otherwise a runtime crash could result.

In the last few years we have gone beyond GADTs, by extending GHC with type-level functions [Chakravarty et al. 2005a,b; Kiselyov et al. 2010]. The reader is urged to consult these papers for motivated examples of type functions, but for the purposes of this paper we content ourselves with a small but contrived example:

```
type family F a :: *
type instance F Age = Char
type instance F Int = Bool
```

Here the type function F maps the type Age to the type Char, but it maps Int to Bool.

However, the existence of such a type-level function threatens not just pattern exhaustiveness but type soundness itself. Consider the type Bool. This type is equivalent to F Int by the equation for F; and by coercion lifting that should be equivalent to `F Age`; and that is equivalent to `Char` by the other equation for F. Altogether we can coerce `Bool` to `Char`, which is obvious nonsense.

What went wrong? Maybe it should be illegal for a type function to behave differently on two coercible types, such as `Age` and `Int`? But in fact Haskell programmers often use **newtype**s precisely so that they can give a different type-class instance (for comparison, say) for `Age` than for the underlying `Int`. Type functions are no different; indeed, they are often introduced as an "associated type" of a type class [Kiselyov et al. 2010], and hence, just as the type class distinguishes between the abstract and concrete type, so must the type function.

How else might we fix the problem? Perhaps, in the definition of coercion lifting we should not allow T to range over type functions such as F or GADTs such as K? Indeed we should not, but that is not enough. Consider

```
data TF a = MkTF (F a)
```

Now, should coercion lifting allow us to coerce `TF Age` to `TF Int`? Obviously not! Otherwise we could write

```
to :: Bool → TF Int        from :: TF Age → Char
to b = MkTF b              from (MkTF c) = c
```

and now the composition `from ∘ cvt ∘ to` is well-typed (via coercion lifting) but obviously unsound. So in the the definition of coercion lifting, as well as type functions and GADTs we must exclude data types like `TF` that use their type arguments non-parametrically.

2.3 Summary

At this point it should be clear that a naive combination of:

- type-level dispatch, whether by GADTs or by type functions
- unrestricted coercion lifting

simply does not work. This interaction was far from obvious to us initially, and indeed GHC has a well-documented type-soundness bug[2] that arises *directly* from this unforeseen interaction. Yet both type-level dispatch and coercion lifting (suitably restricted) are valuable. The purpose of this paper is to show how they may be soundly combined.

This problem is important not only because it arises in GHC (which is our main source of motivation), but also because the same issues will arise in *any* type system that combines type-level dispatch and coercion lifting. Haskell is the first programming language that has pushed the type system far enough for these problems to arise in practice, but others may do so in the future. However, these different languages may expose the coercions between abstract and concrete types in different ways, possibly explicitly (as in Haskell) or implicitly (as in ML), in a way that is intimately connected with type inference. To avoid the complications associated with type inference, in this paper, we focus on an *intermediate language*, in which (runtime-erasable) coercions are explicit. Whether they come directly from the source program, or from elaboration by the type checker, is secondary.

3. The FC_2 language: codes versus types

Our goal is to resolve the tension between *generative types*, which allow programmers to express the intent that two types have identical representations, and *type functions*, which can distinguish two types even if they have the same underlying representation.

The inspiration for our solution comes from encodings of generic programming in dependently typed languages [Benke et al. 2003; Dybjer 2000]. These encodings use "codes" to represent types as a form of data. For example, the code `IntCode` may be the code for the type `Int`. Nonparametric functions branch on codes and thus have a different type from parametric functions. In this context, we can view `Age` and `IntCode` as two different codes that both map to the type `Int`. However, this encoding requires significant syntactic overhead as we must have a code for every type and must explicitly map codes to types when they are used to classify expressions.

However, the important distinction between codes and types is that they have *different definitions of equality*. In the encoding above, the codes `Age` and `IntCode` are different codes, but their interpretations are equal types. Therefore, we use this idea in FC_2 to define *roles*, which support different notions of equality for the same data. In this language, `Age` and `Int` are distinct when viewed at role *code* but equal when viewed at role *type*. Code equality is used to reason about the meaning of type-indexed functions and is finer-grained than type equality, which is used to determine which type coercions are safe. Importantly, FC_2 distinguishes type functions by what equivalences they respect. Parametric functions respect the role *type*, whereas functions that distinguish between `Age` and `Int` do not.

3.1 FC_2: an overview

These ideas are best explained in terms of an intermediate language that exposes the differences between the code and type roles and makes explicit the uses of the two kinds of equality mentioned above. Thus, the remainder of this section describes FC_2, our new variant of System FC [Sulzmann et al. 2007]—a model of the intermediate language used in GHC. As such, it is expressive enough to capture indexed type functions, **newtype** and **newtype deriving**, GADTs, existential and nested datatypes, and much more.

Figure 1 summarizes the syntax of FC_2, which, at the term level (e), is just the polymorphic lambda calculus with two extensions. First, FC_2 provides polymorphic datatypes, introduced by data constructors K. These datatypes are eliminated using a **case** construct that should be familiar from Haskell or ML-style functional programming—we describe how datatypes and **case** are typechecked in Section 3.5.

Second, FC_2 includes first-class proofs of type equality that witness safe coercions introduced during compilation. Programs in FC_2 can abstract over coercions reflecting a particular type equality (written $\Lambda c : \varphi_1 \sim \varphi_2 . e$), pass a coercion as an argument to such a function (written $e\,\gamma$), and use a coercion to cast a term from one type to another (written $e \triangleright \gamma$). These explicit coercions, written γ, make typechecking FC_2 programs *syntax-directed*—that is, the syntax of an FC_2 term encodes its typing derivation. Why is this important? The idea is that the compiler's front end performs perhaps-complex type inference on the source program, and records the proofs generated by inference directly in the syntax of the FC_2 intermediate language. The optimiser transforms FC_2 terms, perhaps radically. At any point one can check the consistency of the resulting FC_2 program using a simple, fast, syntax-directed typechecker; this consistency check has proven to be an extremely powerful aid to getting the compiler right. It is just as easy to find the type of an arbitrary FC_2 term, an ability that is used extensively inside GHC.

Figure 2 shows the typing rules for the terms of FC_2. The first five rules, EEVAR through ETAPP, are completely standard. We defer explanation of the remaining rules until we build up technical machinery having to do with FC_2's kind-level distinction between codes and types and the rules by which explicit coercions can themselves be combined. We describe these aspects of FC_2 next.

[2] `http://hackage.haskell.org/trac/ghc/ticket/1496`

η	$::=$	$\star \mid \kappa \to \eta$	kind
R	$::=$	$\mathsf{C} \mid \mathsf{T}$	role
κ	$::=$	η / R	kind and role
H	$::=$		type constants
	$\mid$	T	datatypes
	$\mid$	F	functions/newtypes
	$\mid$	$(\to)$	arrow
	$\mid$	$(\sim_\eta)$	equality
φ, σ, ψ	$::=$		codes and types
	$\mid$	a	variables
	$\mid$	H	constants
	$\mid$	$\varphi_1\, \varphi_2$	application
	$\mid$	$\forall a{:}\kappa.\varphi$	polymorphism
γ	$::=$		coercion proof
	$\mid$	$c\,\overline{\varphi}$	assumption
	$\mid$	φ	reflexivity
	$\mid$	$\mathbf{sym}\,\gamma$	symmetry
	$\mid$	$\gamma_1\,;\,\gamma_2$	transitivity
	$\mid$	$\gamma_1\,\gamma_2$	application
	$\mid$	$\mathbf{nth}\,k\,\gamma$	injectivity
	$\mid$	$\forall a{:}\kappa.\gamma_2$	polymorphism
	$\mid$	$\gamma @ \varphi$	instantiation
e	$::=$		expressions
	$\mid$	x	variable
	$\mid$	$\lambda x{:}\sigma.e$	abstraction
	$\mid$	$e_1\, e_2$	application
	$\mid$	$\Lambda a{:}\kappa.e$	type abstraction
	$\mid$	$e\,\varphi$	type application
	$\mid$	K	data constructor
	$\mid$	$\mathbf{case}_\sigma\; e\; \mathbf{of}\; brs$	case analysis
	$\mid$	$\Lambda c{:}\varphi_1 {\sim} \varphi_2.e$	proof abstraction
	$\mid$	$e\,\gamma$	proof application
	$\mid$	$e \rhd \gamma$	coercion
brs	$::=$	$\overline{K_i \Rightarrow e_i}^{\,i \in 1..n}$	branches
bnd	$::=$		binding
	$\mid$	$a{:}\kappa$	type variable
	$\mid$	$H{:}\eta$	type constant
	$\mid$	$c{:}\Delta.\,\varphi_1 \sim \varphi_2 / R$	coercion
	$\mid$	$x{:}\sigma$	term variable
	$\mid$	$K{:}\sigma$	data constructor
Γ	$::=$	$\cdot \mid \Gamma, bnd$	context
Δ	$::=$	$\cdot \mid a{:}\kappa, \Delta$	type context
ρ	$::=$	$e \mid \varphi \mid \gamma$	datacon argument
Θ	$::=$		telescopes
	$\mid$	$\cdot$	empty
	$\mid$	σ, Θ	expression type
	$\mid$	$a{:}\kappa, \Theta$	type variable
	$\mid$	$\varphi_1 \sim \varphi_2, \Theta$	equality
v	$::=$	$\lambda x{:}\sigma.e \mid \Lambda a{:}\kappa.e$	values
	$\mid$	$\Lambda c{:}\varphi_1 {\sim} \varphi_2.e$	
	$\mid$	$K\,\overline{\varphi}\,\overline{\rho}$	
τ	$::=$	$T \mid (\to) \mid (\sim_\eta)$	value types
	$\mid$	$\forall a{:}\kappa.\varphi \mid \tau\,\varphi$	

Figure 1. Syntax

$\boxed{\Gamma \vdash e : \sigma}$

$$\frac{x{:}\sigma \in \Gamma \quad \vdash \Gamma}{\Gamma \vdash x : \sigma}\ \textsc{EEVar}$$

$$\frac{\Gamma, x{:}\sigma_1 \vdash e : \sigma_2}{\Gamma \vdash \lambda x{:}\sigma_1.e : \sigma_1 \to \sigma_2}\ \textsc{EEAbs}$$

$$\frac{\Gamma \vdash e_1 : \sigma_1 \to \sigma_2 \quad \Gamma \vdash e_2 : \sigma_1}{\Gamma \vdash e_1\, e_2 : \sigma_2}\ \textsc{EEApp}$$

$$\frac{\Gamma, a{:}\kappa \vdash e : \sigma}{\Gamma \vdash \Lambda a{:}\kappa.e : \forall a{:}\kappa.\sigma}\ \textsc{ETAbs}$$

$$\frac{\Gamma \vdash e : \forall a{:}\kappa.\sigma \quad \Gamma \vdash \varphi : \kappa}{\Gamma \vdash e\,\varphi : \sigma[a \mapsto \varphi]}\ \textsc{ETApp}$$

$$\frac{\begin{array}{l} T{:}\overline{\kappa} \to \star \in \Gamma \\ K{:}\forall \overline{a}{:}\overline{\kappa}.\forall \Theta.T\,\overline{a} \in \Gamma \quad \vdash \Gamma \end{array}}{\Gamma \vdash K : \forall \overline{a}{:}\overline{\kappa}.\forall \Theta.T\,\overline{a}}\ \textsc{EDataCon}$$

$$\frac{\begin{array}{c} \Gamma \vdash e : T\,\overline{\varphi} \quad \Gamma \vdash \sigma : \star/\mathsf{T} \\ \text{for each } K_i \in \mathrm{Constr}_\Gamma(T) \\ K_i{:}\forall \overline{a}{:}\overline{\kappa}.\psi_i \in \Gamma \\ \psi_i[\overline{a} \mapsto \overline{\varphi}] = \forall \Theta_i.T\,\overline{\varphi} \\ \Gamma \vdash e_i : \forall \Theta_i.\sigma \end{array}}{\Gamma \vdash \mathbf{case}_\sigma\; e\; \mathbf{of}\; \overline{K_i \Rightarrow e_i}^{\,i} : \sigma}\ \textsc{ECase}$$

$$\frac{\Gamma, c{:}\varphi_1 \sim \varphi_2/\mathsf{C} \vdash e : \sigma}{\Gamma \vdash \Lambda c{:}\varphi_1 {\sim} \varphi_2.e : (\varphi_1 {\sim} \varphi_2) \Rightarrow \sigma}\ \textsc{ECAbs}$$

$$\frac{\begin{array}{c} \Gamma \vdash e : (\varphi_1 {\sim} \varphi_2) \Rightarrow \sigma \\ \Gamma \vdash \gamma : \varphi_1 \sim \varphi_2 \in \eta/\mathsf{C} \end{array}}{\Gamma \vdash e\,\gamma : \sigma}\ \textsc{ECApp}$$

$$\frac{\Gamma \vdash e : \sigma_1 \quad \Gamma \vdash \gamma : \sigma_1 \sim \sigma_2 \in \star/\mathsf{T}}{\Gamma \vdash e \rhd \gamma : \sigma_2}\ \textsc{ECoerce}$$

Figure 2. Typing rules

$\boxed{R_1 \preceq R_2}$

$$\frac{}{\mathsf{C} \preceq \mathsf{T}}\ \textsc{RSub} \qquad \frac{}{R \preceq R}\ \textsc{RRefl}$$

$\boxed{\Gamma \vdash \varphi : \kappa}$

$$\frac{a{:}\eta/R_1 \in \Gamma \quad R_1 \preceq R_2 \quad \vdash \Gamma}{\Gamma \vdash a : \eta/R_2}\ \textsc{PVar}$$

$$\frac{H{:}\eta \in \Gamma \quad \vdash \Gamma}{\Gamma \vdash H : \eta/R}\ \textsc{PConst}$$

$$\frac{\begin{array}{l} \Gamma \vdash \varphi_1 : (\eta_1/R_2 \to \eta_2)/R_1 \\ \Gamma \vdash \varphi_2 : \eta_1/min(R_1, R_2) \end{array}}{\Gamma \vdash \varphi_1\,\varphi_2 : \eta_2/R_1}\ \textsc{PApp}$$

$$\frac{\Gamma, a{:}\kappa \vdash \varphi : \star/R}{\Gamma \vdash \forall a{:}\kappa.\varphi : \star/R}\ \textsc{PAll}$$

$\boxed{\Gamma \vdash \overline{\varphi} : \overline{\kappa}}$

$$\frac{}{\Gamma \vdash \cdot : \cdot}\ \textsc{PNil} \qquad \frac{\Gamma \vdash \varphi : \kappa \quad \Gamma \vdash \overline{\varphi} : \overline{\kappa}}{\Gamma \vdash \varphi, \overline{\varphi} : \kappa, \overline{\kappa}}\ \textsc{PCons}$$

Figure 3. Kinding

3.2 FC_2 types and kinds

Types in FC_2 are classified by pairs κ of the form η/R, where the *kind* η ensures (as usual) that types are well-formed structurally, and the *role* R that determines the precision at which they can be analyzed. Codes (which distinguish `Age` and `Int`) have role C, whereas types (which identify them) have role T. This syntax is summarized at the top of Figure 1, while the kinding rules are in Figure 3.

The distinction between codes and types allows us to give informative kinds to type constructors:

- The `Maybe` type (Section 2.1) has kind $\star/\mathsf{T} \to \star$, indicating that `Maybe` treats its argument *parametrically*.
- The types `K`, `F`, and `TF` (Section 2.2) all use *type indexing* and therefore have kind $\star/\mathsf{C} \to \star$.

These kinds in turn support the key insight of this paper: *it is only safe to lift coercions through functions with parametric kinds.* So `Maybe Age` $\sim$ `Maybe Int` holds but `TF Age` $\not\sim$ `TF Int`.

The rules for constructing coercions are given in Section 3.3, but first we must deal with the kinding rules for types. The critical rule is PAPP in Figure 3, which deals with type application. It is quite conventional except for the treatment of roles. Consider these type declarations:

```
data TF1 a = MkTF1 (F (Maybe a)
data TF2 a = MkTF2 (Maybe (F a))
data TF3 a = MkTF3 (Maybe (Maybe a))
```

In the first two cases, type variable `a` is used non-parametrically (intuitively, under a type function), so `TF1` $: \star/\mathsf{C} \to \star$, and similarly for `TF2`. In contrast, `TF3` treats `a` parametrically, so `TF1` $: \star/\mathsf{T} \to \star$. The unusual "$min$" in rule PAPP achieves these kindings by combining the role of the context and the argument role of the function to get the role of the argument.

In fact, min is just the least upper bound induced by an inclusion relation $\mathsf{C}\preceq\mathsf{T}$ on roles (see the top of Figure 3). This inclusion makes explicit the fact that code equality implies type equality but not vice-versa. For example, consider

```
data TF4 a = MkTF4 (F a) a
```

Here `a` is used both non-parametrically (as an argument of `F`) and parametrically (as a plain argument of `MkTF4`). So `a` has role $\star/\mathsf{C}$, which makes sense; just because a type *can* be analyzed does not mean that it *must* be.

Despite these non-standard kinds, the types of FC_2 are mostly standard. Codes φ and types σ are drawn from the same syntax (see Figure 1), although we use two different metavariables as a reminder of the intended role. The type language includes type variables a, type constants H, applications $\varphi_1\ \varphi_2$, and polymorphic types $\forall a\!:\!\kappa.\sigma$.

Type constants, H, include datatypes T, and type functions F. For the most part, datatypes and type functions are treated uniformly, but there are two important distinctions:

- Datatypes must be injective, while type functions need not be. Injectivity is important because equalities between applications of injective functions imply equalities between their arguments; see rule CNTHT in Section 3.3.
- Datatypes are inhabited by values, but type functions are not—there are no values v with types that are headed by F. (There are *coerced values* with such types, but no raw values.) This distinction is key to the definition of consistency in Section 4.1.

Newtypes are not inhabited by raw values, so we treat them like type functions, ranged over by F. Unlike type functions, however, newtypes *are* injective at role C—after all, the essence of generativity is that newtypes create a fresh constant—but for now we will not take advantage of that fact, leaving it for discussion in Section 6.1.

The set of type constants also includes the familiar arrow type constructor $(\to)$, and a kind-indexed family of constructors $(\sim_\eta)$, which construct functions that abstract over coercions. The kinds of these constants are:

$$\begin{array}{lcl}(\to) & : & \star/\mathsf{T} \to \star/\mathsf{T} \to \star \\ (\sim_\eta) & : & \eta/\mathsf{C} \to \eta/\mathsf{C} \to \star/\mathsf{T} \to \star\end{array}$$

(We discuss in Sections 3.3 and 3.6 why the kind of $(\sim_\eta)$ must require role C for its first two arguments.) Type constants are generally applied prefix, but for these two constants we define infix syntactic sugar:

$$\begin{array}{lcl}\sigma \to \sigma' & \equiv & (\to)\ \sigma\ \sigma' \\ (\varphi_1 \sim \varphi_2) \Rightarrow \sigma & \equiv & (\sim_\eta)\ \varphi_1\ \varphi_2\ \sigma\end{array}$$

In the latter case, because the syntactic sugar lacks the η annotation, we only use this notation in contexts where the kind of φ_1 and φ_2 is irrelevant. Rule ECABS follows this convention—it shows that this family of type constructors is used to give a type to terms of the form $\Lambda c : \varphi_1 \sim \varphi_2.e$, which abstracts over an equality proof in the body e. Note that this rule applies only to code equalities; abstraction over type equalities is not needed for compilation of Haskell and permitting it, while straightforward, would require extra syntactic complexity.

Figure 3 defines the kinding rules for FC_2 using judgments of the form $\Gamma \vdash \varphi : \kappa$. Here, the context Γ maps type variables to their kind/role pairs and type constants and type functions to their kinds. This judgment relies on a judgment $\vdash \Gamma$ (shown in the extended version) that checks that contexts are well formed. These checks ensure that constants $(\to)$ and $(\sim_\eta)$ have the right kinds, that data constructors and term variables have well-formed types and that coercion axioms introduce equalities between well-formed codes and types.

Rule PCONST allows a type constant to play either role. Although a type constant may be given role C, its *kind* may well involve arguments with role T; for example, see the signature for $(\to)$ above. It follows that closed types can play both roles, independently of whether they contain newtypes or type functions. For example `(Int,Age)` $: \star/\mathsf{C}$ and `(Int,Age)` $: \star/\mathsf{T}$ both hold.

Together these kinding rules implement a subsumption relation that includes codes into the language of types:

LEMMA 1. *If* $\Gamma \vdash \varphi : \eta/\mathsf{C}$ *then* $\Gamma \vdash \varphi : \eta/\mathsf{T}$.

On the other hand, types have only one kind regardless of their role:

LEMMA 2. *If* $\Gamma \vdash \varphi : \eta_1/R_1$ *and* $\Gamma \vdash \varphi : \eta_2/R_2$ *then* $\eta_1 = \eta_2$.

Note that the kinding judgment, like term typing, is syntax-directed (see the remarks in Section 3.1). In particular, the role component R of the κ in this judgment is treated as *input* to the algorithm, and the η is an *output*—the context in which φ is used determines what the role should be. The only interesting case from this perspective is PAPP, in which φ_1 must be checked first to obtain R_2 so that the minimum of R_1 and R_2 can be passed as an input when checking φ_2.

3.3 Coercions and equality

In FC_2 a *coercion* is a proof term that witnesses the equality of two types. Coercions are used to change the type of a term, thus (Figure 2):

$$\frac{\Gamma \vdash e : \sigma_1 \quad \Gamma \vdash \gamma : \sigma_1 \sim \sigma_2 \in \star/\mathsf{T}}{\Gamma \vdash e \rhd \gamma : \sigma_2}\ \text{ECOERCE}$$

Here, γ is a *coercion* witnessing the equality $\sigma_1 \sim \sigma_2$ in role T; given that e has type σ_1, we can use γ to let us treat the term as hav-

$\boxed{\Gamma \vdash \gamma : \varphi_1 \sim \varphi_2 \in \kappa}$

$$\frac{\begin{array}{c}(c{:}\overline{a}{:}\overline{\kappa}.\,\varphi_1 \sim \varphi_2/R_1) \in \Gamma \\ \Gamma \vdash \varphi_1 : \eta/R_1 \quad \Gamma \vdash \overline{\psi} : \overline{\kappa} \quad R_1 \preceq R_2\end{array}}{\Gamma \vdash c\,\overline{\psi} : \varphi_1[\overline{a} \mapsto \overline{\psi}] \sim \varphi_2[\overline{a} \mapsto \overline{\psi}] \in \eta/R_2}\ \textsc{CAssm}$$

$$\frac{\Gamma \vdash \varphi : \kappa}{\Gamma \vdash \varphi : \varphi \sim \varphi \in \kappa}\ \textsc{CRefl}$$

$$\frac{\Gamma \vdash \gamma : \varphi_1 \sim \varphi_2 \in \kappa}{\Gamma \vdash \mathbf{sym}\,\gamma : \varphi_2 \sim \varphi_1 \in \kappa}\ \textsc{CSym}$$

$$\frac{\begin{array}{c}\Gamma \vdash \gamma_1 : \varphi_1 \sim \varphi_2 \in \kappa \\ \Gamma \vdash \gamma_2 : \varphi_2 \sim \varphi_3 \in \kappa\end{array}}{\Gamma \vdash \gamma_1\,;\,\gamma_2 : \varphi_1 \sim \varphi_3 \in \kappa}\ \textsc{CTrans}$$

$$\frac{\begin{array}{c}\Gamma \vdash \gamma_1 : \varphi_1 \sim \varphi_2 \in (\eta_1/R_2 \to \eta_2)/R_1 \\ \Gamma \vdash \gamma_2 : \psi_1 \sim \psi_2 \in \eta_1/min(R_1, R_2)\end{array}}{\Gamma \vdash \gamma_1\,\gamma_2 : \varphi_1\,\psi_1 \sim \varphi_2\,\psi_2 \in \eta_2/R_1}\ \textsc{CApp}$$

$$\frac{\begin{array}{c}\Gamma \vdash \gamma : T\,\overline{\varphi} \sim T\,\overline{\psi} \in \eta/\mathsf{T} \\ T{:}\overline{\kappa} \to \star \in \Gamma \\ \eta'/R_1 = nth\ k\ \overline{\kappa} \quad R_1 \preceq R_2\end{array}}{\Gamma \vdash \mathbf{nth}\,k\,\gamma : nth\ k\ \overline{\varphi} \sim nth\ k\ \overline{\psi} \in \eta'/R_2}\ \textsc{CNthT}$$

$$\frac{\Gamma, a{:}\kappa \vdash \gamma_2 : \varphi_1 \sim \varphi_2 \in \star/R}{\Gamma \vdash \forall a{:}\kappa.\gamma_2 : \forall a{:}\kappa.\varphi_1 \sim \forall a{:}\kappa.\varphi_2 \in \star/R}\ \textsc{CAll}$$

$$\frac{\begin{array}{c}\Gamma \vdash \gamma : \forall a{:}\kappa.\varphi_1 \sim \forall a{:}\kappa.\varphi_2 \in \star/R \\ \Gamma \vdash \psi : \kappa\end{array}}{\Gamma \vdash \gamma@\psi : (\varphi_1[a \mapsto \psi]) \sim (\varphi_2[a \mapsto \psi]) \in \star/R}\ \textsc{CInst}$$

$\boxed{\Gamma \vdash \overline{\gamma} : \overline{\varphi}_1 \sim \overline{\varphi}_2 \in \overline{\kappa}}$

$$\frac{\vdash \Gamma}{\Gamma \vdash \cdot : \cdot \sim \cdot \in \cdot}\ \textsc{CNil}$$

$$\frac{\begin{array}{c}\Gamma \vdash \gamma : \varphi_1 \sim \varphi_2 \in \kappa \\ \Gamma \vdash \overline{\gamma} : \overline{\varphi}_1 \sim \overline{\varphi}_2 \in \overline{\kappa}\end{array}}{\Gamma \vdash \gamma, \overline{\gamma} : \varphi_1, \overline{\varphi}_1 \sim \varphi_2, \overline{\varphi}_2 \in \kappa, \overline{\kappa}}\ \textsc{CCons}$$

Figure 4. Coercions

ing type σ_2. At compile time, these explicit coercions ensure that typechecking FC_2 programs is completely syntax directed. Such coercions have no run-time effect: they will be erased by the compiler before the program is run. Nevertheless, FC_2's operational semantics includes coercions, thereby allowing us to establish type safety using standard techniques (Section 3.6).

The translation of a source program into FC_2 may extend the type environment Γ with new equality axioms. For example, the `Age` **newtype** definition generates the axiom (where `mkAge` is a coercion constant c):

$$\texttt{mkAge} : \texttt{Age} \sim \texttt{Int}/\mathsf{T}$$

Note that ECoerce requires σ_1 and σ_2 to be equal when considered in role T, which is consistent with the idea that type equality determines when it is safe to coerce. On the other hand, source programs can also introduce code equalities. For example the type function `F` (Section 2.2) generates the two axioms:

$$\begin{array}{l}\texttt{axF1} : \texttt{F Int} \sim \texttt{Bool}/\mathsf{C} \\ \texttt{axF2} : \texttt{F Age} \sim \texttt{Char}/\mathsf{C}\end{array}$$

However, all code axioms can be used to prove type equalities, as code equality is a refinement of type equality.

More generally we permit axiom *schemes*. For example, the source language declaration

```
type instance F (Maybe a) = (a,a)
```

would create the axiom scheme

$$\texttt{axF3} : (a{:}\star/\mathsf{C}).\texttt{F (Maybe a)} \sim \texttt{(a,a)}/\mathsf{C}$$

In general, as shown in Figure 1, the context Γ includes bindings of the form $c{:}\Delta.\,\varphi_1 \sim \varphi_2/R$ for coercion axioms. The metavariable Δ stands for a type variable context: a list of quantified type variable bindings of the form $a{:}\kappa$. The same binding form is used both for axioms introduced at top level, and (with empty Δ) for local assumptions introduced in ECAbs (Figure 2).

Of course it is important to know that the top-level axioms are *consistent*—it would be unsound to assert that $\texttt{Bool} \sim \texttt{Char}/\mathsf{T}$, for example. Section 4 gives a sufficient set of conditions for ensuring that source programs generate consistent axioms.

Next, we need a way to compose coercions together to construct other coercions. Our goal is to have rules that allow the creation of composite coercions such as:

$$\begin{array}{lll}\texttt{List mkAge} & : & \texttt{List Age} \sim \texttt{List Int}/\mathsf{T} \\ \texttt{List axF2} & : & \texttt{List (F Int)} \sim \texttt{List Bool}/\mathsf{T}\end{array}$$

On the other hand, the coercion formation rules should disallow the formation of a coercion of the form $\gamma_3 : \texttt{F Age} \sim \texttt{F Int}/\mathsf{T}$, which creates the unsoundness described in Section 2.2.

Figure 1 gives the syntax of coercion terms, γ, and Figure 4 gives their typing rules. Coercions are typechecked using the judgment: $\Gamma \vdash \gamma : \varphi_1 \sim \varphi_2 \in \eta/R$, which asserts that the type of a coercion γ is an equality proposition $\varphi_1 \sim \varphi_2 \in \eta/R$. This proposition in turn implies that φ_1 and φ_2 both have kind η and are equal in role R. It is technically convenient to include η in the syntax of the judgement to enforce that both types have the same kind. However, this component is not always relevant, so we sometimes omit the $\in \eta$ part, as we have done in the examples above.

Rule CAssm instantiates an axiom scheme with types $\overline{\psi}$, using an auxiliary judgment $\Gamma \vdash \overline{\psi} : \overline{\kappa}$ defined at the bottom of Figure 3 to ensure that each variable is instantiated with a type of the matching kind and role. The notation $\overline{a} : \overline{\kappa}$ zips together a list of type variables and a list of kinds to create a type variable context Δ. These two lists must have the same length for the notation to be well-defined. The notation $\varphi[\overline{a} \mapsto \overline{\psi}]$ applies a multi-substitution of the types $\overline{\psi}$ for each of the corresponding variables in the list $\overline{a}$.

Rule CRefl shows that any type φ can be lifted to a reflexive coercion φ, while CSym and CTrans add symmetry and transitivity, ensuring that equality is an equivalence relation. The rules CApp and CAll extend equality compatibly over applications and polymorphic types; their structure is analogous to the corresponding kinding rules in Figure 3. Rule CApp is particularly important, because it implements the key coercion lifting idea we discussed in Section 2.1, using kinds to prevent the formation of the bogus coercion

$$\texttt{FmkAge} : \texttt{F Age} \sim \texttt{F Int}/\mathsf{T}$$

To see why, recall that `F` has kind $\star/\mathsf{C} \to \star$, but the `mkAge` axiom holds only at role T—type equalities cannot be lifted through code functions. Another example of a coercion that is correctly rejected by the application rule (because of the kind of $(\sim_\eta)$) is

$$(\sim_\star)\ \texttt{mkAge Int}\ \sigma$$

This coercion proves $(\texttt{Age} \sim \texttt{Int}) \Rightarrow \sigma \sim (\texttt{Int} \sim \texttt{Int}) \Rightarrow \sigma$, an equality that could be used to introduce a bogus assumption that $\texttt{Age} \sim \texttt{Int}/\mathsf{C}$ and satisfy it with reflexivity for `Int`.

As well as composing coercions to witness the equality of bigger types, it is also essential to do the reverse: to decompose equalities over complex types to give equalities of simpler types.

Decomposition is required by FC_2's operational semantics (Section 3.6), and it also makes the language usefully more expressive. Rule CINST allows equalities between polymorphic types to be instantiated. The other, more important decomposition rule is CNTHT, which decomposes the application of a datatype constant to arguments. For example, given a coercion γ : `List Int` $\sim$ `List a/T` we can use **nth** 0 γ to conclude that `Int` $\sim$ `a/T`. The soundness of this rule depends on the fact that datatypes are *injective*. In general, type functions are not, and hence CNTHT is restricted to datatypes T.

In rule CNTHT, the notation $T\,\overline{\varphi}$ abbreviates the multi-application $((T\,\varphi_1)\ldots\varphi_n)$ for $\varphi_1\ldots\varphi_n$ in $\overline{\varphi}$. In the conclusion of the rule, the notation $nth\ k\ \overline{\psi}$, accesses the kth element of the sequence of types, and $nth\ k\ \overline{\kappa}$, accesses the kind of the kth variable binding. Both of these notations are undefined if k is not less than the length of the sequence. The sequence of types $\overline{\kappa}$ is determined by the kind of the datatype, using the following notation.

DEFINITION 3. *We define* $\overline{\kappa} \to \eta$ *by induction on* $\overline{\kappa}$ *as follows:*

$$\begin{array}{rcl} \cdot \to \eta & = & \eta \\ \kappa, \overline{\kappa} \to \eta & = & \kappa \to (\overline{\kappa} \to \eta) \end{array}$$

The coercion judgment satisfies a number of sanity checking properties. First, coercions are between well-formed types.

LEMMA 4 (Coercion regularity). *If* $\Gamma \vdash \gamma : \varphi_1 \sim \varphi_2 \in \kappa$ *then* $\Gamma \vdash \varphi_1 : \kappa$ *and* $\Gamma \vdash \varphi_2 : \kappa$.

Next, each coercion proof is for one pair of codes/types.

LEMMA 5 (Unique types). *If* $\Gamma \vdash \gamma : \varphi_1 \sim \varphi_2 \in \eta/R$ *and* $\Gamma \vdash \gamma : \varphi_1' \sim \varphi_2' \in \eta'/R$ *then* $\varphi_1 = \varphi_1'$ *and* $\varphi_2 = \varphi_2'$ *and* $\eta = \eta'$.

Finally, equality for Cs is a refinement of that for Ts; that is, code equality implies type equality, but not vice versa.

LEMMA 6. *If* $\Gamma \vdash \gamma : \varphi_1 \sim \varphi_2 \in \eta/\mathsf{C}$ *then* $\Gamma \vdash \gamma : \varphi_1 \sim \varphi_2 \in \eta/\mathsf{T}$.

3.4 Coercion lifting

The application rule CAPP described in the previous section allows us to lift equalities through arbitrary type constructors; that is, for all datatypes T of kind $\star/\mathsf{T} \to \star$, we have a coercion that shows T `Age` $\sim$ T `Int` $\in \star/\mathsf{T}$.

In fact, this notion of coercion lifting is not restricted to datatypes (like `List`), but is available for more general contexts. More precisely, given an arbitrary type σ with free variable a of kind $\star/\mathsf{T}$, we can also create a coercion $\sigma[a \mapsto \texttt{Age}] \sim \sigma[a \mapsto \texttt{Int}] \in \star/\mathsf{T}$.

We create such coercions with the *lifting operation*. This operation replaces type variables by coercions in types to produce a new coercion, relying on the fact that the syntax of types is a subset of the syntax of coercions:

DEFINITION 7 (Lifting Operation). *Define the lifting operation, written* $\varphi[a \mapsto \gamma]$, *by induction on* φ.

$$\begin{array}{rcll} a[a \mapsto \gamma] & = & \gamma & \\ b[a \mapsto \gamma] & = & b & \textit{when } a \neq b \\ H[a \mapsto \gamma] & = & H & \\ (\varphi\,\psi)[a \mapsto \gamma] & = & (\varphi[a \mapsto \gamma])\ (\psi[a \mapsto \gamma]) & \\ (\forall b{:}\kappa.\sigma)[a \mapsto \gamma] & = & \forall b{:}\kappa.(\sigma[a \mapsto \gamma]) & \end{array}$$

The lifting operation produces a valid result as long as the role of the lifted coercion matches the role of the type variable in the type.

LEMMA 8 (Lifting). *If* $\Gamma, a{:}\eta/R \vdash \sigma : \kappa$ *and* $\Gamma \vdash \gamma : \varphi \sim \varphi' \in \eta/R$, *then* $\Gamma \vdash \sigma[a \mapsto \gamma] : \sigma[a \mapsto \varphi] \sim \sigma[a \mapsto \varphi'] \in \kappa$.

In other words, if a were used in some indexed context in σ, that is, if its role were C, then we would not be able to lift the coercion `Age` $\sim$ `Int` $\in \star/\mathsf{T}$ in σ. We generalize lifting to replace multiple type variables simultaneously in the obvious way, with notation $\sigma[\overline{a} \mapsto \overline{\gamma}]$.

3.5 Pattern matching and datatypes

FC_2 includes a formalization of recursive datatypes. These datatypes include all GHC extensions to standard datatypes: empty datatypes, nested datatypes, existential types, first-class polymorphism and GADTs. Both datatypes T and data constructors K must be declared in a context Γ before they can be used. For example, using the syntax for Γ in Figure 1, the declarations for the data constructors of `List` are:

$$\begin{array}{lcl} \texttt{List} & : & \star/\mathsf{T} \to \star \\ \texttt{Nil} & : & (a{:}\star/\mathsf{T}).\,\texttt{List}\ a \\ \texttt{Cons} & : & (a{:}\star/\mathsf{T}).\,a \to \texttt{List}\ a \to \texttt{List}\ a \end{array}$$

What about GADTs? Here's an example in Haskell:

```
data Rep a where
  Rint  :: Rep Int
  Rlist :: Rep a → Rep (List a)
```

Although a Haskell programmer writes the data constructors of a GADT with non-parametric result types, in the internal type system it is simpler in the formalization for the result type of a data constructor to take the form $(T\ a_1 \ldots a_n)$, where the $\overline{a}$ are the type parameters, using equality constraints to express the indexing, thus:

$$\begin{array}{ll} \texttt{Rep} & : \star/\mathsf{C} \to \star \\ \texttt{Rint} & : (a{:}\star/\mathsf{C}).(a \sim \texttt{Int}) \Rightarrow \texttt{Rep}\ a \\ \texttt{Rlist} & : (a{:}\star/\mathsf{C}).\forall (b : \star/\mathsf{C}).(a \sim \texttt{List}\ b) \Rightarrow \texttt{Rep}\,b \to \texttt{Rep}\ a \end{array}$$

Notice here that `Rep`'s kind expresses that its argument is an *index* (role C) rather than a *parameter* (role T). In fact, the C role for variable a falls out naturally because a appears as argument to the $(\sim_\star)$ constructor (in the type of `Rint` and `Rlist`), which in turn requires it to have role C.

More generally, we use the notation of *telescopes* [de Bruijn 1991] to conveniently express the types of data constructors. Figure 1 defines a telescope Θ like this:

$$\Theta ::= \cdot \mid a{:}\kappa, \Theta \mid \varphi_1 \sim \varphi_2, \Theta \mid \sigma, \Theta$$

A telescope is like a mini-context: a list of type variable bindings, equality propositions (between codes only) and types that classify each argument of the data constructor. (Note that a type variable context Δ is also a telescope.) We define the syntactic sugar $\forall\Theta.\sigma$ as follows:

DEFINITION 9 (Telescope syntactic sugar).

$$\begin{array}{rcl} \forall \cdot .\sigma & = & \sigma \\ \forall (a{:}\kappa, \Theta).\sigma & = & \forall a{:}\kappa.(\forall \Theta.\sigma) \\ \forall (\varphi_1 \sim \varphi_2, \Theta).\sigma & = & (\varphi_1 \sim \varphi_2) \Rightarrow (\forall \Theta.\sigma) \\ \forall (\sigma', \Theta).\sigma & = & \sigma' \to (\forall \Theta.\sigma) \end{array}$$

At each use of a data constructor (rule EDATACON), we check that the declaration of a data constructor is of the form

$$K{:}\forall \overline{a}{:}\overline{\kappa}.(\forall \Theta.\,T\,\overline{a})$$

where $\overline{a}{:}\overline{\kappa}$ lists the type parameters of the datatype, Θ describes the types of the arguments to the data constructor, and $T\,\overline{a}$ is syntactic sugar for the application of T to those parameters (i.e. $((T\ a_1)\ldots a_n)$). For example, the `List` type has a single parameter $a{:}\ \star/\mathsf{T}$, the constructor `Cons` has telescope $(a, \texttt{List}\ a, \cdot)$, and constructs type `List` a. Likewise, the `Rep` type has the parameter $a{:}\ \star/\mathsf{C}$, the telescope for `Rlist` is $(b{:}\ \star/\mathsf{C}, a \sim \texttt{List}\ b, (\texttt{Rep}\ b), \cdot)$, and the result type is `Rep` a.

$$\frac{\gamma_0 = \mathbf{sym}\,(\mathbf{nth}\;0\;\gamma) \quad \gamma_1 = \mathbf{nth}\;1\;\gamma}{((\lambda x{:}\sigma_1.e_1) \triangleright \gamma)\; e_2 \rightsquigarrow (\lambda x{:}\sigma_1.(e_1 \triangleright \gamma_1))\,(e_2 \triangleright \gamma_0)} \;\text{SSPUSH}$$

$$\frac{\Sigma \vdash \gamma : \forall a{:}\kappa.\sigma_1 \sim \forall a{:}\kappa.\sigma_2 \in \star/\mathsf{T}}{((\Lambda a{:}\kappa.e) \triangleright \gamma)\; \varphi \rightsquigarrow (\Lambda a{:}\kappa.(e \triangleright \gamma @ a))\; \varphi} \;\text{SSTPUSH}$$

$$\frac{\begin{array}{c}\Sigma \vdash \gamma : (\sim_\eta)\,\varphi_1\,\varphi_2\,\sigma \sim (\sim_\eta)\,\varphi_1'\,\varphi_2'\,\sigma' \in \star/\mathsf{T}\\ \gamma_0 = \mathbf{nth}\;0\;\gamma \quad \gamma_1 = \mathbf{sym}\,(\mathbf{nth}\;1\;\gamma) \quad \gamma_2 = \mathbf{nth}\;2\;\gamma\end{array}}{\begin{array}{l}((\Lambda c{:}\varphi_1 \sim \varphi_2.e) \triangleright \gamma)\;\gamma' \rightsquigarrow\\ \quad (\Lambda c{:}\varphi_1 \sim \varphi_2.(e \triangleright \gamma_2))\;(\gamma_0\,;\,\gamma'\,;\,\gamma_1)\end{array}} \;\text{SSCPUSH}$$

$$\frac{\begin{array}{c}\Sigma \vdash \gamma : T\,\overline{\varphi} \sim T\,\overline{\varphi}' \in \star/\mathsf{T}\\ K{:}\forall\,\overline{a}{:}\overline{\kappa}.\sigma \in \Sigma\end{array}}{\begin{array}{l}\mathbf{case}'_\sigma\;(K\,\overline{\varphi}\,\overline{\rho}) \triangleright \gamma\;\mathbf{of}\;brs \rightsquigarrow\\ \quad \mathbf{case}'_\sigma\;K\,\overline{\varphi}'\;(\overline{\rho} \triangleright \sigma[\overline{a} \mapsto nth\;\gamma])\;\mathbf{of}\;brs\end{array}} \;\text{SSKPUSH}$$

Figure 5. Operational Semantics (Push rules)

Telescope notation is also used for case expressions in rule ECASE (Figure 2). The type of the scrutinee of the case must be headed by a datatype constant T. Furthermore, for each data constructor that could create a T, there must be a corresponding branch. The (elided) function $\mathrm{Constr}_\Gamma(T)$ looks up the constructors of T from the context. After substituting for the parameters, the branch for data constructor K_i must abstract the same arguments as K_i and return the same result type as the entire case. To make sure that typechecking is syntax directed even when there are no branches (for empty datatypes), the case expression is annotated with its result type σ, and we must check that this type is well-formed in the current context.

3.6 Operational semantics: pushing coercions

The operational semantics of FC_2 is based on a small-step call-by-name operational semantics for a polymorphic lambda calculus. Although this language includes explicit type abstraction and application (as well as explicit coercion proof abstraction and application), types and coercions are not relevant at run time. All such abstractions and applications, as well as uses of coercions $e \triangleright \gamma$ may be erased prior to execution and so impose no run-time costs.

As alluded to above, this operational semantics preserves coercion proofs, which allows us to establish type safety using standard syntactic proofs of progress and preservation (described in the next section). The most important rules of the operational semantics are those that "push" coercions when they appear in active positions so that they do not interfere with reduction. Figure 5 shows the relevant pushing rules. (The complete rules of the operational semantics are listed in the extended version.) In some of the push rules, the coercion must be checked to constrain the types that it proves equal. This checking happens in a global context Σ that contains only the definitions of data constructors, data types, and coercion axioms. Note that these checks are not actually necessary at runtime, in a consistent context these checks will always succeed.

The first three rules show how in an application of a coerced abstraction, the term steps to a new application, where the coercion has been decomposed into a coercion for the body of the abstraction, and a coercion of the argument. For example, consider SSPUSH. Here, the γ is a coercion between some function types $\sigma_1 \to \sigma_1'$ and $\sigma_2 \to \sigma_2'$. The rule uses $\mathbf{nth}$ and $\mathbf{sym}$ to decompose γ into two coercions, one from $\sigma_2 \sim \sigma_1$ (the order is reversed to account for contra-variance) and one from $\sigma_1 \sim \sigma_2'$. These new coercions can be pushed to the body of the lambda and the function argument, exposing the reduction. Rules SSTPUSH and SSCPUSH work analogously.

$\boxed{\Gamma \vdash \overline{\rho} : \Theta}$

$$\frac{\vdash \Gamma}{\Gamma \vdash \cdot : \cdot} \;\text{TNIL}$$

$$\frac{\Gamma \vdash e : \sigma \quad \Gamma \vdash \overline{\rho} : \Theta}{\Gamma \vdash e, \overline{\rho} : (\sigma, \Theta)} \;\text{TCONSE}$$

$$\frac{\Gamma \vdash \varphi : \kappa \quad \Gamma \vdash \overline{\rho} : \Theta[a \mapsto \varphi]}{\Gamma \vdash \varphi, \overline{\rho} : (a{:}\kappa, \Theta)} \;\text{TCONST}$$

$$\frac{\Gamma \vdash \gamma : \varphi_1 \sim \varphi_2 \in \eta/\mathsf{C} \quad \Gamma \vdash \overline{\rho} : \Theta}{\Gamma \vdash \gamma, \overline{\rho} : (\varphi_1 \sim \varphi_2, \Theta)} \;\text{TCONSC}$$

Figure 6. Telescope rules

Note that SSCPUSH justifies the kind of $(\sim_\eta)$, which requires that the first two arguments be codes. If we had assigned $(\sim_\eta)$ the parametric kind $\eta/\mathsf{T} \to \eta/\mathsf{T} \to \star/\mathsf{T} \to \star$, then the coercions γ_0 and γ_1 in the rule would both be type coercions. However, type coercions cannot be composed with γ' to form a code coercion, which is the role required for the right hand side of the rule to typecheck.

The last rule, SSKPUSH, pushes the coercion of a data constructor in the scrutinee position of a case expression into coercions of the arguments of the data constructor. The arguments of a data constructor, notated ρ, can either be an expression, a type, or a coercion.

$$\rho ::= e \mid \varphi \mid \gamma$$

If the declared type of the data constructor K is $\forall\,\overline{a} : \overline{\kappa}.\forall\,\Theta.T\,\overline{a}$, and the type parameters are $\overline{\varphi}$, then we know that the arguments can be typed using $\Gamma \vdash \overline{\rho} : \Theta[\overline{a} \mapsto \overline{\varphi}]$ (see Figure 6). However, pushing the coercion changes the type parameters to be $\overline{\varphi}'$, so the new arguments must have type $\Theta[\overline{a} \mapsto \overline{\varphi}']$.

These new arguments are produced by coercing the list of arguments $\overline{\rho}$ with the coercion generated by *lifting* as described above. (The notation $\sigma[\overline{a} \mapsto nth\;\gamma]$ means that variable a_i is lifted to coercion $\mathbf{nth}\;i\;\gamma$.) Once this coercion has been defined by lifting, we use it to coerce the list of arguments of the data constructor with the following operation.

DEFINITION 10. *Define* argument coercion $\overline{\rho} \triangleright \gamma$ *by induction on* $\overline{\rho}$*:*

$$\begin{array}{lcl} \cdot \triangleright \gamma & = & \cdot \\ (e, \overline{\rho}) \triangleright \gamma_1 \to \gamma_2 & = & (e \triangleright \gamma_1), \overline{\rho} \triangleright \gamma_2 \\ (\varphi, \overline{\rho}) \triangleright \forall a{:}\kappa.\gamma_2 & = & \varphi, \overline{\rho} \triangleright \gamma_2 \\ (\gamma, \overline{\rho}) \triangleright (\gamma_1 \sim \gamma_2) \Rightarrow \gamma_3 & = & (\mathbf{sym}\,\gamma_1\,;\,\gamma\,;\,\gamma_2), \overline{\rho} \triangleright \gamma_3 \end{array}$$

Argument coercion coerces a list of arguments as described by the following lemma.

LEMMA 11. *If* $\Gamma \vdash \overline{\rho} : \Theta$ *and* $\Gamma \vdash \gamma : \forall\Theta.\sigma \sim \forall\Theta'.\sigma' \in \star/\mathsf{T}$ *then* $\Gamma \vdash (\overline{\rho} \triangleright \gamma) : \Theta'$

4. Type safety and consistency

The FC_2 language supports a straightforward proof of type safety based on the usual preservation and progress theorems. Importantly, the progress theorem holds only for *consistent* contexts—those that cannot equate `Int` and `Char`, for example. Below, we state the progress and preservation theorems and give a precise definition of consistency. In the next subsection, we formulate sufficient conditions for proving that a context is consistent.

4.1 Preservation and progress

The preservation proof for FC_2 is standard, relying on the usual regularity and substitution lemmas for the various judgement forms. For space reasons, we omit those definitions here and instead refer the reader to the extended version.

THEOREM 12 (Preservation). *If* $\Gamma \vdash e_1 : \sigma$ *and* $e_1 \rightsquigarrow e_2$ *then* $\Gamma \vdash e_2 : \sigma$.

The progress theorem holds only for *closed, consistent* contexts. A context is *closed* if it does not contain any term variable bindings. We use the metavariable Σ for closed contexts.

The definition of consistency and the canonical forms lemma (necessary to show the progress theorem) are both stated using the notions of uncoerced *values* and their types, *value types*. Value types include all types except those that are headed by a variable a or type function/newtype F. Formally, we define values v and value types τ, with the following grammars:

$$\begin{array}{lcl} \tau & ::= & T \mid (\rightarrow) \mid (\sim_\eta) \mid \forall a{:}\kappa.\varphi \mid \tau\,\varphi \\ v & ::= & \lambda x{:}\sigma.e \mid \Lambda a{:}\kappa.e \mid \Lambda c{:}\varphi_1 {\sim} \varphi_2.e \mid K\,\overline{\varphi}\,\overline{\rho} \end{array}$$

The canonical forms lemma tells us that the shape of a value is determined by its type:[3]

LEMMA 13 (Canonical Forms). *Say* $\Sigma \vdash v : \sigma$. *Then* σ *is a value type. Furthermore,*

1. *If* $\sigma = \sigma_1 \rightarrow \sigma_2$ *then* v *is* $\lambda x{:}\sigma_1.e$ *or* $K\,\overline{\varphi}\,\overline{\rho}$.
2. *If* $\sigma = \forall a{:}\kappa.\sigma'$ *then* v *is* $\Lambda a{:}\kappa.e$ *or* $K\,\overline{\varphi}\,\overline{\rho}$.
3. *If* $\sigma = (\varphi_1 {\sim} \varphi_2) \Rightarrow \sigma'$ *then* v *is* $\Lambda c{:}\varphi_1 {\sim} \varphi_2.e$ *or* $K\,\overline{\varphi}\,\overline{\rho}$.
4. *If* $\sigma = T\,\overline{\varphi}_1$ *then* v *is* $K\,\overline{\varphi}\,\overline{\rho}$.

In FC_2, not all irreducible forms are values. Evaluation can also produce a *coerced value* of the form $v \triangleright \gamma$, which erases to a value when coercions are dropped. To prove the progress theorem, we must reason about what sort of coercion γ could be so that we can appropriately apply the "push" rules in Figure 5. In the statement of the progress theorem, because γ coerces the value v, we know (by ECOERCE and canonical forms) that $\gamma : \tau \sim \sigma$—the left type is a value type τ. *Consistency* of the axiom set assures us that if σ is also a value type, it must have the same head form.

DEFINITION 14 (Consistency). *A context* Γ *is consistent if whenever* $\Gamma \vdash \gamma : \tau_1 \sim \tau_2 \in \eta/\mathsf{T}$ *it is the case that*

1. *If* τ_1 *is* $T\,\overline{\varphi}_1$ *then* τ_2 *is* $T\,\overline{\varphi}_2$.
2. *If* τ_1 *is* $(\rightarrow)\,\overline{\varphi}_1$ *then* τ_2 *is* $(\rightarrow)\,\overline{\varphi}_2$
3. *If* τ_1 *is* $(\sim_\eta)\,\overline{\varphi}_1$ *then* τ_2 *is* $(\sim_\eta)\,\overline{\varphi}_2$.
4. *If* τ_1 *is* $\forall a{:}\kappa.\sigma_1$ *then* τ_2 *is* $\forall a{:}\kappa.\sigma_2$.

Putting these observations together, we obtain:

THEOREM 15 (Progress). *If* Σ *is consistent and* $\Sigma \vdash e_1 : \sigma$ *and* e_1 *is not a value* v *or a coerced value* $v \triangleright \gamma$, *then there exists an* e_2 *such that* $e_1 \rightsquigarrow e_2$.

4.2 Determining consistency

Although the previous subsection gives a definition of when contexts are consistent, it does not provide any mechanism for determining whether a set of axioms leads to a consistent context.

This subsection defines *sufficient* conditions (written **Good** Γ) for establishing context consistency—these conditions are not the only way to show consistency (they are not *necessary*) but they are permissive enough to cover the axioms generated by compilation of type family declarations and newtype definitions.

[3] Note that all forms of value type must include *partial* applications of data constructors.

$$\boxed{\Gamma \vdash \varphi \rightsquigarrow \varphi' \in \kappa}$$

$$\frac{\begin{array}{l}\Gamma \vdash a : \overline{\kappa} \rightarrow \eta/R \\ \Gamma \vdash \overline{\varphi} \rightsquigarrow \overline{\varphi}' \in \overline{\kappa}/R\end{array}}{\Gamma \vdash a\,\overline{\varphi} \rightsquigarrow a\,\overline{\varphi}' \in \eta/R}\ \textsc{RVar}$$

$$\frac{\begin{array}{l}H{:}\overline{\kappa} \rightarrow \eta \in \Gamma \\ \Gamma \vdash \overline{\varphi} \rightsquigarrow \overline{\varphi}' \in \overline{\kappa}/R\end{array}}{\Gamma \vdash H\,\overline{\varphi} \rightsquigarrow H\,\overline{\varphi}' \in \eta/R}\ \textsc{RConst}$$

$$\frac{\Gamma, a{:}\kappa \vdash \sigma \rightsquigarrow \sigma' \in \star/R}{\Gamma \vdash \forall a{:}\kappa.\sigma \rightsquigarrow \forall a{:}\kappa.\sigma' \in \star/R}\ \textsc{RAll}$$

$$\frac{\begin{array}{l}H{:}\overline{\kappa}_1 \rightarrow (\overline{\kappa}_2 \rightarrow \eta) \in \Gamma \\ \Gamma \vdash \overline{\varphi}_1 \rightsquigarrow \overline{\varphi}_1' \in \overline{\kappa}_1/R \\ \Gamma \vdash \overline{\varphi}_2 \rightsquigarrow \overline{\varphi}_2' \in \overline{\kappa}_2/R \\ \Gamma \vdash c\,\overline{\psi} : H\,\overline{\varphi}_1' \sim \sigma \in \overline{\kappa}_2 \rightarrow \eta/R\end{array}}{\Gamma \vdash H\,\overline{\varphi}_1\,\overline{\varphi}_2 \rightsquigarrow \sigma\,\overline{\varphi}_2' \in \eta/R}\ \textsc{RRed}$$

$$\boxed{\Gamma \vdash \overline{\varphi} \rightsquigarrow \overline{\varphi}' \in \overline{\kappa}/R}$$

$$\frac{}{\Gamma \vdash \cdot \rightsquigarrow \cdot \in \cdot/R}\ \textsc{RNil}$$

$$\frac{\begin{array}{l}\Gamma \vdash \varphi \rightsquigarrow \varphi' \in \eta/min(R_1, R_2) \\ \Gamma \vdash \overline{\varphi} \rightsquigarrow \overline{\varphi}' \in \overline{\kappa}/R_1\end{array}}{\Gamma \vdash \varphi, \overline{\varphi} \rightsquigarrow \varphi', \overline{\varphi}' \in \eta/R_2, \overline{\kappa}/R_1}\ \textsc{RCons}$$

Figure 7. Type rewriting

As in the previous version of FC, we show consistency by (i) defining a rewrite system for types and (ii) proving that two types are joinable (share a common reduct) if and only if there is some coercion proof between those types. The rewrite system guarantees that value types preserve their head form throughout rewriting and therefore value types with different head forms can never be equated.

4.2.1 Rewriting and joinability

Figure 7 gives our rewrite relation, which is a variant of parallel reduction—it looks throughout the type, trying to fire reductions. The reduction of a type headed by a constant H is implemented in rule RRED. If, after the arguments to H have been reduced to $\overline{\varphi}'$, there is some instantiation of an axiom such that H applied to some prefix of the $\overline{\varphi}'$ matches the left-hand side of the coercion, then the type may reduce to the right-hand-side type (RRED). Importantly, rewriting (very much like coercibility) takes roles into account: rewriting occurs at some role R, which specifies what axioms are available. For example, at role T we can rewrite a newtype `Age` to its definition `Int`, but at role C, we cannot.

Notice that rules RCONST and RRED overlap. The term $H\,\overline{\varphi}$ may reduce using a matching axiom for H (via rule RRED), but not necessarily (via RCONST). With rule RCONST, the rewrite relation is reflexive.

LEMMA 16. *If* $\Gamma \vdash \varphi : \kappa$ *then* $\Gamma \vdash \varphi \rightsquigarrow \varphi \in \kappa$.

The *joinability* relation, below, is simply reduction to a common reduct after zero or more steps.

DEFINITION 17 (Joinable). *Two types are* joinable *if they share a common reduct. Define* $\Gamma \vdash \varphi_1 \Leftrightarrow \varphi_2 \in \kappa$ *if* $\Gamma \vdash \varphi_1 \rightsquigarrow^* \varphi \in \kappa$ *and* $\Gamma \vdash \varphi_2 \rightsquigarrow^* \varphi \in \kappa$.

Reflexivity of the rewrite relation is crucial for joinability of type applications with multiple arguments. Consider the axiom

$$\mathtt{c : F\ Int} \sim \mathtt{(F\ Int,\ F\ Int)}/\mathsf{C}$$

and the following two types:

$$\varphi_1 = \mathtt{T\ \ (F\ Int)\ \ (F\ Int,\ F\ Int)}$$
$$\varphi_2 = \mathtt{T\ \ (F\ Int,\ F\ Int)\ \ (F\ Int)}$$

We'd certainly like φ_1 and φ_2 to be reducible to a common reduct (after all, there exists a coercion term between them), but the first argument of `T` in φ_1 "lags behind" compared to the first argument of `T` in φ_2, whereas the second argument in φ_1 "advances ahead" compared to the second argument in φ_2. Reflexivity allows us to freeze the reduction of the second argument in φ_1 while reducing the first, and similarly for φ_2—which allows us to join the two types.

4.2.2 Soundness and completeness of the rewrite relation

We now give sufficient conditions on contexts which ensure that the rewrite relation of Figure 7 is sound and complete with respect to coercibility. Hence, these are sufficient conditions for consistency.

DEFINITION 18 (Good contexts). *We have* **Good** Γ *when the following conditions hold:*

1. *All axioms in* Γ *are of the form* $c : \Delta. F\,\overline{\varphi} \sim \psi/R$. *Let* $\overline{a} = dom(\Delta)$ *and* $\overline{\kappa}$ *be the corresponding kinds. For every well kinded* $\overline{\psi}$ *and result types* $\overline{\varphi}'$, *such that* $\Gamma \vdash (\overline{\varphi}[\overline{a} \mapsto \overline{\psi}]) \rightsquigarrow \overline{\varphi}' \in \overline{\kappa}'/R$ *it must be* $\overline{\varphi}' = \overline{\varphi}[\overline{a} \mapsto \overline{\psi}']$ *for some* $\overline{\psi}'$ *with* $\Gamma \vdash \overline{\psi} \rightsquigarrow \overline{\psi}' \in \overline{\kappa}/R$.
2. *There is no overlap between axioms. For each* $F\,\overline{\varphi}$ *there exists at most one prefix* $\overline{\varphi}_1$ *of* $\overline{\varphi}$ *such that there exist* c, ψ *and* $\overline{\psi}$ *where* $\Gamma \vdash c\,\overline{\psi} : F\,\overline{\varphi}_1 \sim \psi \in \kappa$. *This* c *is unique for every matching* $F\,\overline{\varphi}_1$.

The first condition above restricts the declared arguments of type functions to behave like patterns. It merely states that all the reductions that can possibly happen when we substitute types for Δ do not involve reductions from $\overline{\varphi}$ but only reductions *inside* those substituted types. This condition is a generalized (and more lenient) form of the current GHC restrictions on type family declarations, which only allow value types or variables as $\overline{\varphi}$. The second condition is simply a strong non-overlapping condition.

Interestingly, the first condition on the arguments to type functions restricts the kind that a type function may have. For example, recall the axioms for `F` from Section 2.2:

$$\mathtt{axF1 : F\ \ Int} \sim \mathtt{Bool}/\mathsf{C}$$
$$\mathtt{axF2 : F\ \ Age} \sim \mathtt{Char}/\mathsf{C}$$

For this to be a **Good** axiom set, the kind of `F` must be $\star/\mathsf{C} \to \star$ because the newtype `Age` is irreducible only in role C.

In the rest of this section, we sketch the proof that our conditions are sufficient for consistency. Soundness is a straightforward proof.

THEOREM 19 (Soundness). *If if* **Good** Γ *and* $\Gamma \vdash \varphi_1 \rightsquigarrow \varphi_2 \in \kappa$ *then there is some* γ *such that* $\Gamma \vdash \gamma : \varphi_1 \sim \varphi_2 \in \kappa$.

The three key lemmas of the completeness proof are that joinability is preserved under application and substitution and a local diamond property of rewriting.

LEMMA 20 (Application). *If* **Good** Γ *and* $\Gamma \vdash \varphi_1 \Leftrightarrow \varphi_1' \in (\eta_1/R_1 \to \eta_2)/R_2$ *and* $\Gamma \vdash \varphi_2 \Leftrightarrow \varphi_2' \in \eta_1/min(R_1, R_2)$ *then* $\Gamma \vdash \varphi_1\,\varphi_2 \Leftrightarrow \varphi_1'\,\varphi_2' \in \eta_2/R_2$.

THEOREM 21 (Local diamond property). *If* **Good** Γ *and* $\Gamma \vdash \varphi \rightsquigarrow \varphi_1 \in \kappa$ *and* $\Gamma \vdash \varphi \rightsquigarrow \varphi_2 \in \kappa$ *then there exists a* φ_3 *such that* $\Gamma \vdash \varphi_1 \rightsquigarrow \varphi_3 \in \kappa$ *and* $\Gamma \vdash \varphi_2 \rightsquigarrow \varphi_3 \in \kappa$.

LEMMA 22 (Substitution). *If* **Good** Γ *and* $\Gamma, a{:}\kappa, \Delta \vdash \sigma \rightsquigarrow^* \sigma' \in \kappa'$ *and* $\Gamma \vdash \varphi \rightsquigarrow^* \varphi' \in \kappa$, *then there is some* $\Gamma, \Delta \vdash \sigma[a \mapsto \varphi] \Leftrightarrow \sigma'[a \mapsto \varphi'] \in \kappa'$.

From these lemmas we see that joinability is complete.

THEOREM 23 (Completeness). *If* **Good** Γ *and* $\Gamma \vdash \gamma : \varphi_1 \sim \varphi_2 \in \kappa$ *then* $\Gamma \vdash \varphi_1 \Leftrightarrow \varphi_2 \in \kappa$.

THEOREM 24 (Consistency). *If* **Good** Γ *then* Γ *is consistent.*

Proof Suppose $\Gamma \vdash \gamma : \tau_1 \sim \tau_2 \in \star/R$, where τ_1 and τ_2 are two value types. By completeness, we have that those two types are joinable, i.e. that there is some φ such that $\Gamma \vdash \tau_1 \rightsquigarrow^* \varphi \in \star/R$ and $\Gamma \vdash \tau_2 \rightsquigarrow^* \varphi \in \star/R$. However, by inversion on the rewriting relation, we see that it preserves the head forms of value types (since there exist no axioms for those by the first condition of **Good** Γ). Thus, τ_1 and τ_2 (and φ) have the same head form.

A different novelty of our approach compared to previous work [Sulzmann et al. 2007] is that establishing the completeness theorem, and therefore type soundness, does not depend on strong normalization. Our definition of **Good** Γ that (i) forces the declared type family arguments to behave like patterns, and (ii) imposes strong (stronger than the previous work) non-overlapping conditions, is sufficient to show completeness.

With this new approach, a programmer can be confident that, even in the presence of possibly non-terminating type functions, if the compiler can show that the program is well-typed then the program will not crash. Although type checking is undecidable in general without strong normalization, there may be many programs that the compiler *can* actually type check, and this approach shows that those programs are type sound.

5. Compilation from source Haskell

In the previous sections we have informally presented the translations of Haskell source features such as datatype, type family, and **newtype** declarations into FC_2. We summarize them here:

$$\begin{array}{ll}
\mathbf{data}\ T\ \Delta\ \mathbf{where}\ \overline{K_i : \sigma} & \mapsto \\
\quad T : \forall\Delta.\star, \overline{K_i : \Delta.\sigma} & \\
\mathbf{type\ family}\ F : \overline{\eta/\mathsf{C}} \to \eta & \mapsto \\
\quad F : \overline{\eta/\mathsf{C}} \to \eta & \\
\mathbf{type\ instance}\ \Delta.F\ \overline{\varphi} = \psi & \mapsto \\
\quad cF : \Delta.F\ \overline{\varphi} \sim \psi \in \eta/\mathsf{C} & \\
\mathbf{newtype}\ \Delta.M\ \overline{a} = \mathtt{MkM}\ \varphi & \mapsto \\
\quad M : \Delta.\star, \mathtt{MkM} : \Delta.M\ \overline{a} \sim \varphi \in \star/\mathsf{T} &
\end{array}$$

In addition, uses of the data constructor of a **newtype**, both in terms and patterns, are translated to a use of the corresponding coercion in the obvious way. The important parts of these definitions are that (i) type families accept code arguments, (ii) type instances give rise to code equalities, and (iii) newtype definitions give rise to type equality axioms. The bindings generated in this way can be easily checked for well-formedness. If, in addition, the resulting context is **Good** (see Section 4.2)—the only possible problem is the potential to generate overlapping **type instance** declarations—then the context is consistent, which in turn guarantees type safety.

Notice that the source language features in this translation have been *already annotated* with their kinds. This is a reasonable assumption. Prior to type inference, which translates a source declaration to an FC_2 binding, we must have determined the kinds involved in the declarations. For the purposes of this paper, we assume that the kinds are given—in practice they would be the output of a kind inference process, potentially guided by the user to disambiguate role information and higher-order kinds.

Newtype deriving Generative type abstraction is achieved in Haskell using the **newtype deriving** mechanism, which allows type classes to be automatically lifted to new types. For instance, we may write

```
newtype Age = MkAge Int deriving Eq
```

The type class `Eq a` is a standard class in Haskell (signature, in ML terminology) that defines one method, `eq :: a → a → Bool`. For the type checker, a type class is nothing but a record type containing the method `eq`. The **deriving** line automatically generates an implementation of `Eq Age` from a pre-existing instance `Eq Int`. This can be done by simply applying a coercion `Eq Int` $\sim$ `Eq Age` to the old record. It is straightforward to construct this coercion: lift the `Age` $\sim$ `Int` axiom from the **newtype** definition over the `Eq` constructor and apply symmetry. Importantly, this lifting is safe because `Eq` has a *parametric kind* of the form $\star/\mathsf{T} \to \star$. However, if a type class has an *indexed kind* of the form $\star/\mathsf{C} \to \star$, **newtype deriving** is no longer sound. For example

```
class C x where
  op :: F x → x
instance C Int where ...
newtype Age = MkAge Int deriving C
```

It is unsound to lift the `C Int` implementation to a `C Age`, precisely because `x` has role C. The documented GHC bug mentioned earlier arises precisely as the result of such an unsound lifting over a non-parametric type class.

6. Discussion

6.1 Relaxing decomposition

Recall the coercion decomposition rule, CNTHT, from Figure 4. This rule allows us to deconstruct an equality of the form $\Gamma \vdash \gamma : T\,\overline{\varphi} \sim T\,\overline{\psi} \in \eta/\mathsf{T}$. In effect, it asserts that data constructors are injective. The rule is important because it is used in the operational semantics to ensure subject reduction. However, the decomposition rule may be somewhat restrictive for some Haskell source programs. Consider the following:

```
newtype M a = MkM (Maybe [a])
data Eq a b where EQ :: Eq a a
f :: Eq (M a) (M b) → a → b
f EQ x = x
```

Pattern matching against the `EQ` constructor introduces a coercion between `M a` and `M b`, which cannot be decomposed using the CNTHT rule to obtain `a` $\sim$ `b`, so this program cannot be typed. Nevertheless, *we know* that `M` is injective, because `M a` is defined to be equal to `Maybe [a]`, which is clearly injective.

On the other hand, the following **newtype** is *not* injective.

```
type instance G a = Char
newtype N a = MkN (G a)
```

Here, it is possible to derive $\Gamma \vdash \gamma :$ `N Int` $\sim$ `N Char` $\in \star/\mathsf{T}$, using the axiom for `G`, even though `Int` is not coercible to `Char`.

It turns out that **newtype** definitions are *always* injective with respect to code equality, but they might not be injective with respect to type equality (as illustrated by the two examples above). Thus it would be sound and potentially useful (but not necessary for type soundness) to introduce yet another decomposition rule for **newtype** definitions that takes advantage of injectivity with respect to codes (we use metavariable N newtypes):

$$\frac{\Gamma \vdash \gamma : N\,\overline{\varphi} \sim N\,\overline{\psi} \in \eta/\mathsf{C} \quad N{:}\overline{\kappa} \to \eta \in \Gamma \quad \eta'/R' = nth\ k\ \overline{\kappa}}{\Gamma \vdash \mathbf{nth}\, k\, \gamma : nth\ k\ \overline{\varphi} \sim nth\ k\ \overline{\psi} \in \eta'/R}\ \textsc{CNthN}$$

The only subtle part of this rule is that R is not related to R', since the equality $\Gamma \vdash \gamma : N\,\overline{\varphi} \sim N\,\overline{\psi} \in \eta/\mathsf{C}$ is a C-equality (and $min(\mathsf{C}, R') = \mathsf{C}$).

Arguably, decomposition for injective type functions is also desirable, were we able to effectively specify and check that property.

6.2 Other technical differences of FC_2 from System FC

The intermediate language FC_2 described in this paper is a significant modification of System FC [Sulzmann et al. 2007] due to the introduction of codes. However, FC_2 also makes a number of *technical simplifications*:

- The original System FC presentation includes *coercion kinds*, $\sigma_1 \sim \sigma_2$. The original coercion language includes three additional constructs, one to coerce coercions, and two more to decompose coercion kinds. By treating $(\varphi_1 \sim \varphi_2) \Rightarrow \varphi_3$ as the application of a constructor $(\sim_\eta)$ we no longer need any of these constructs in the operational semantics, nor have we identified any uses of these constructs that are not encodable.
- The operational semantics rules of FC_2 in Figure 5 not only use simpler coercion constructs, but are also expressed without need for substitutions, contrary to their original FC versions.
- FC_2 replaces the FC coercions **left** and **right**, which decomposed arbitrary type applications, by **nth**, which decomposes only the application of a datatype constructor. This allows us to lift a tiresome restriction in in System FC, namely that type functions were required to be saturated. Type family saturation was necessary in FC, in order to prevent the decomposition of equalities as `F` $a \sim$ `Maybe` $[a]$ via **left** or **right**. Allowing unsaturated functions increases the expressiveness of FC_2, because we can now abstract over type functoins, and also opens new directions for future research on type inference in the presence of unsaturated type functions.
- However, using **nth** instead of **left** and **right** does carry a small price. Generalizing the example from Section 6.1, should this program be well typed?

  ```
  data Eq a b where EQ :: Eq a a
  f :: Eq (p q) (r s) → q → s
  f EQ x = x
  ```

  To type it we must decompose a proof that $p\ q \sim r\ s$ to get a proof that $q \sim s$, which **right** could do, but **nth** cannot.

Some other differences are *presentational*:

- System FC used a common syntax for types and coercions, which is a convenient pun, but has turned out to be more confusing than helpful. In FC_2 we use a distinct syntax for types and coercions (Figure 1).
- In FC_2 we define top-level axiom schemes $c : \Delta.\, \varphi_1 \sim \varphi_2/R$ directly, and fully instantiate them at every occurrence with the form $c\ \overline{\gamma}$ (Figure 1). System FC instead defined a top-level axiom scheme as an equality between polytypes, thus $c : \forall\Delta.\varphi_1 \sim \forall\Delta.\varphi_2$. Here again FC is confusing (but not wrong) so in FC_2 we opt for telling the story more directly, albeit with slightly more syntax. Moreover the kinding rules for $\forall$ (PALL and CALL) can insist that the body of the forall has kind $\star$ as is conventional.

- Using telescopes in the treatment of datatypes simplifies the operational semantics rules but is also (only slightly) more expressive: The types of data constructors do not have to have their quantified variables preceding their coercion and term arguments. Instead, telescopes allow arbitrary interleavings.

7. Related work

Previous work on System FC [Sulzmann et al. 2007] discusses a significant amount of related work, in typed languages with explicit proof witnesses [Licata and Harper 2005; Shao et al. 2005], or in calculi that support coercions [Breazu-Tannen et al. 1991]. Below, we present related work in generativity and abstraction, type-indexed constructs and the separation between codes and types.

Generativity, abstraction, and module systems Generativity and abstraction has been studied extensively in the context of ML module systems [Milner et al. 1997]. Russo shows how generativity in module systems is connected to existential quantification [Russo 1999] and Dreyer [2005] has studied this connection in the presence of recursive modules. Montagu and Rémy [2009] refine this connection by introducing "open" existential types. Rossberg [2008] uses flexible generativity to explain ML-style module sealing.

Type abstraction can be understood in terms of dynamic name generation [Rossberg 2003; Vytiniotis et al. 2005], which can re-establish abstraction properties in languages with dynamic type analysis. Neis et al. [2009] prove a parametricity theorem in this setting. In addition, they use a translation from polymorphism to generative types to establish the parametric behavior of certain functions although they work in a non-parametric language.

Although many of these languages support type generativity and non-parametric features, they do not exhibit the soundness problems described in the paper, mainly due to the absence of type-level type dispatching. Nevertheless, the techniques developed in the aforementioned related work would be valuable in the formal study of the parametricity properties of FC_2.

Type-indexed types Although many systems for generic programming support dynamic computation based on types, very few systems allow the structure of *types* to be destructed to produce other types. However, such facility is often necessary to describe the *type* of generic programs. For example, Harper and Morrisett include a `Typerec` operator to their typed intermediate language λ_i^{ML} [Harper and Morrisett 1995], to describe type-directed optimizations. (They credit NuPRL's mechanism of "Universe Elimination" in NuPRL as the inspiration for this operation [Constable 1982; Constable and Zlatin 1984].)

To support generic programming in source languages, Hinze, Jeuring and Löh added Type-Indexed Datatypes [Hinze et al. 2002] to the Generic Haskell front end. In later work, Chakravarty et al. [2005b] introduced associated data families in GHC, which are type-indexed datatypes associated with type class instances. Extending this work, they later introduced associated type synonyms [Chakravarty et al. 2005a], which are proper type-level functions with instances associated with type class instances. Currently, the source language of GHC also supports standalone type-level type functions, often referred to as indexed type families [Kiselyov et al. 2010; Schrijvers et al. 2008], a feature that we have extensively used in our presentation.

Codes, types, and interpretations Our distinction between codes and types—and our terminology—is inspired by similar notions in intuitionistic type theory [Benke et al. 2003; Dybjer 2000; Martin-Löf 1975]. There, types (sets) are constructed as the recursive interpretation of codes, which inhabit inductively constructed *code universes*. A **`newtype`** definition can be viewed as giving rise to a new code, inhabiting an open universe of codes, and whose interpretation coincides with the interpretation of its definition.

Languages based on dependent type theory, such as Agda [Bove et al. 2009] or Coq [The Coq Team], naturally offer type-level computation to construct types, but they allow elimination of codes only, not types. Therefore, they do not exhibit the same soundness problem, as the expressiveness of these languages can readily enforce the distinction between types and codes. The disadvantage is the extra programming verbosity of explicit definitions and interpretations of codes. To better support generic programming, the dependently-typed language Epigram [Chapman et al. 2010] identifies types with their code universes.

The LX language [Crary and Weirich 1999] also uses universe constructions to solve problems with type-directed compilation. When the type translation in a compiler pass is not the identity then type dispatch must be compiled to code dispatch (so the generated code can dispatch on source types instead of target types). The interpretation of codes is then the type translation. To support universes, LX includes datakinds (for codes) and primitive recursive functions over datakinds (for their interpretation at types). In LX, source types `Age` and `Int` would be mapped to definable codes `AgeCode` and `IntCode`, and would be accompanied by an interpretation function such that `interp(AgeCode)` equals `Int` and `interp(IntCode)` equals `Int`. Therefore, the problem with generativity would not show up in that context. If one wanted to solve the problem in this paper along the LX lines, one would have to translate source Haskell types to void types that stand in as codes and handle the `interp()` function as any other type function. This function, as well as interpreting the codes as types, would have to be accompanied with suitable congruence axioms, like `interp(T t) ~ T (interp(t))`. Explicitly introducing these axioms means that coercions would be significantly more verbose. Our system dispenses with an explicit `interp()` function by conveniently using the roles in the judgements to determine whether we wish to derive an equality between codes or between their interpretations.

8. Conclusions and future work

In this paper we have identified a problem for the safe interaction of flexible type generativity and type-level computation. We have proposed a solution that distinguishes between indexed and parametric type contexts, by extending the language of kinds, and formalized the solution in the FC_2 language. We have several avenues for future research in mind, which we outline below.

Source language technology We would like to work on ways to expose the FC_2 expressive features to programmers. Specific directions are: enriching the kind declarations with the ability to declare parametric or indexed type-level constructs, introducing type family injectivity annotations, extending kind inference with roles, and extending type inference to support unsaturated functions using the more sophisticated kinds.

Enriching the universes of codes with terms We are currently working on enriching the universe of codes with constants or functions drawn from the *term* syntax, such as data constructors, in order to enable direct dependently-typed programming in Haskell.

More roles Lemma 6 asserts that the equivalence classes induced by T-equality are refined by C-equality. However, our approach readily extends to arbitrary lattices of roles with gradually more refined equivalence classes as we move down the $\preceq$ relation.

Consider, for example, a lattice with new roles C_1 and C_2, each lying between C and T, but incomparable with each other. These two roles model partial knowledge of newtype equalities. For example, perhaps C_1 identifies `Age` and `Int` but distinguishes a different newtype Moo from its definition Bool. Conversely, C_2 can identify Moo and Bool and distinguish Age and Int. These more precise roles could be used to give more precise types to nonparametric functions by identifying exactly which newtype equivalences they do and do not respect. However, we have not yet explored the practical implications of this precision.

Furthermore, one could explore adding a role above T. Type functions with kind $\star/\mathsf{T} \to \star$, are not necessarily parametric in FC_2. For example, because G below does not match *newtypes* it may be assigned either kind $\star/\mathsf{T} \to \star$ or $\star/\mathsf{C} \to \star$.

$$\texttt{axG1} : \texttt{G Int} \sim \texttt{Bool}/\mathsf{C}$$
$$\texttt{axG2} : \texttt{G Bool} \sim \texttt{Char}/\mathsf{C}$$

To distinguish truly parametric functions from those like G, we could add a role P, induced by the relation that equates all types of the same kind. As this equivalence is coarser than T, it could not (and should not) participate in coercions. However, this new role would provide a yet more descriptive kind for type functions.

Acknowledgements

We thank Brent Yorgey and the attendees of the Type System Wrestling sessions at MSR Cambridge for many useful discussions. We wrote this paper using the Ott tool. This work was partially supported by grants from DARPA (CSSG) and NSF (0910786) and a Sloan Foundation fellowship.

References

M. Benke, P. Dybjer, and P. Jansson. Universes for generic programs and proofs in dependent type theory. *Nordic J. of Computing*, 10(4):265–289, 2003. ISSN 1236-6064.

A. Bove, P. Dybjer, and U. Norell. A brief overview of agda — a functional language with dependent types. In *TPHOLs '09: Proceedings of the 22nd International Conference on Theorem Proving in Higher Order Logics*, pages 73–78, Berlin, Heidelberg, 2009. Springer-Verlag.

V. Breazu-Tannen, T. Coquand, C. A. Gunter, and A. Scedrov. Inheritance as implicit coercion. *Information and Computation*, 93:172–221, 1991.

M. M. T. Chakravarty, G. Keller, and S. Peyton Jones. Associated type synonyms. In *ICFP '05: Proceedings of the Tenth ACM SIGPLAN International Conference on Functional Programming*, pages 241–253, New York, NY, USA, 2005a. ACM.

M. M. T. Chakravarty, G. Keller, S. Peyton Jones, and S. Marlow. Associated types with class. *SIGPLAN Not.*, 40(1):1–13, 2005b. ISSN 0362-1340.

J. Chapman, P. Évariste Dagand, C. McBride, and P. Morris. The gentle art of levitation. In *Proceedings of the Fifteenth ACM SIGPLAN International Conference on Functional Programming (ICFP '10)*, Baltimore, MD, USA, September 2010. To appear.

J. Cheney and R. Hinze. First-class phantom types. CUCIS TR2003-1901, Cornell University, 2003.

R. L. Constable. Intensional analysis of functions and types. Technical Report CSR-118-82, Department of Computer Science, University of Edinburgh, June 1982.

R. L. Constable and D. R. Zlatin. The type theory of PL/CV3. *ACM Transactions on Programming Languages and Systems*, 6(1):94–117, Jan. 1984.

K. Crary and S. Weirich. Flexible type analysis. In *Proceedings of the Fourth ACM SIGPLAN International Conference on Functional Programming*, pages 233–248, Paris, France, Sept. 1999.

N. G. de Bruijn. Telescopic mappings in typed lambda calculus. *Inf. Comput.*, 91(2):189–204, 1991. ISSN 0890-5401.

D. Dreyer. Recursive type generativity. In *ICFP '05: Proceedings of the Tenth ACM SIGPLAN International Conference on Functional Programming*, pages 41–53, New York, NY, USA, 2005. ACM.

P. Dybjer. A general formulation of simultaneous inductive-recursive definitions in type theory. *Journal of Symbolic Logic*, 65(2):525–549, 2000.

C. V. Hall, K. Hammond, S. L. Peyton Jones, and P. L. Wadler. Type classes in Haskell. *ACM Transactions on Programming Languages and Systems*, 18(2):109–138, Mar. 1996.

R. Harper and G. Morrisett. Compiling polymorphism using intensional type analysis. In *POPL '95: Proceedings of the 22nd ACM SIGPLAN-SIGACT symposium on Principles of programming languages*, pages 130–141, New York, NY, USA, 1995. ACM. ISBN 0-89791-692-1.

R. Hinze, J. Jeuring, and A. Löh. Type-indexed data types. In B. M. Eerke Boiten, editor, *Proceedings of the Sixth International Conference on Mathematics of Program Construction (MPC 2002)*, pages 148–174, Dagstuhl, Germany, July 2002.

O. Kiselyov, S. Peyton Jones, and C. Shan. *Fun with type functions*. Springer, 2010.

D. R. Licata and R. Harper. A formulation of dependent ML with explicit equality proofs. Technical Report CMU-CS-05-178, Carnegie Mellon University Department of Computer Science, 2005.

P. Martin-Löf. An intuitionistic theory of types: Predicative part. In *Proceedings of the Logic Colloquium, 1973*, volume 80 of *Studies in Logic and the Foundations of Mathematics*, pages 73–118. North-Holland, 1975.

R. Milner, M. Tofte, and D. Macqueen. *The Definition of Standard ML*. MIT Press, Cambridge, MA, USA, 1997. ISBN 0262631814.

B. Montagu and D. Rémy. Modeling abstract types in modules with open existential types. In *POPL '09: Proceedings of the 36th annual ACM SIGPLAN-SIGACT Symposium on Principles of Programming Languages*, pages 354–365, New York, NY, USA, 2009. ACM.

G. Neis, D. Dreyer, and A. Rossberg. Non-parametric parametricity. In *ICFP '09: Proceedings of the 14th ACM SIGPLAN International Conference on Functional Programming*, pages 135–148, New York, NY, USA, 2009. ACM. ISBN 978-1-60558-332-7.

S. Peyton Jones et al. The Haskell 98 language and libraries: The revised report. *Journal of Functional Programming*, 13(1):0–255, Jan 2003. http://www.haskell.org/definition/.

S. L. Peyton Jones, D. Vytiniotis, S. Weirich, and G. Washburn. Simple unification-based type inference for GADTs. In *International Conference on Functional Programming (ICFP)*, Portland, OR, USA, Sept. 2006.

B. C. Pierce, editor. *Advanced Topics in Types and Programming Languages*. MIT Press, 2005.

A. Rossberg. Dynamic translucency with abstraction kinds and higher-order coercions. *Electr. Notes Theor. Comput. Sci.*, 218:313–336, 2008.

A. Rossberg. Generativity and dynamic opacity for abstract types. In *PPDP '03: Proceedings of the 5th ACM SIGPLAN International Conference on Principles and Practice of Declaritive Programming*, pages 241–252, New York, NY, USA, 2003. ACM. ISBN 1-58113-705-2.

C. V. Russo. Non-dependent types for Standard ML modules. In *PPDP '99: Proceedings of the International Conference PPDP'99 on Principles and Practice of Declarative Programming*, pages 80–97, London, UK, 1999. Springer-Verlag. ISBN 3-540-66540-4.

T. Schrijvers, S. Peyton Jones, M. Chakravarty, and M. Sulzmann. Type checking with open type functions. In *ICFP '08: Proceeding of the 13th ACM SIGPLAN international conference on Functional programming*, pages 51–62, New York, NY, USA, 2008. ACM.

Z. Shao, V. Trifonov, B. Saha, and N. Papaspyrou. A type system for certified binaries. *ACM Trans. Program. Lang. Syst.*, 27(1):1–45, 2005.

M. Sulzmann, M. M. T. Chakravarty, S. Peyton Jones, and K. Donnelly. System F with type equality coercions. In *TLDI '07: Proceedings of the 2007 ACM SIGPLAN International Workshop on Types in Languages Design and Implementation*, pages 53–66, New York, NY, USA, 2007. ACM.

The Coq Team. *Coq*. URL http://coq.inria.fr.

D. Vytiniotis, G. Washburn, and S. Weirich. An open and shut typecase. In *ACM SIGPLAN Workshop in Types in Language Design and Implementation*, Long Beach, CA, USA, Jan. 2005.

H. Xi, C. Chen, and G. Chen. Guarded recursive datatype constructors. In *POPL*, pages 224–235, 2003.

The Design of Kodu: A Tiny Visual Programming Language for Children on the Xbox 360

Matthew MacLaurin

Microsoft FUSE Labs / Microsoft Research

mmaclaurin@hotmail.com

Abstract

Kodu is a relatively new programming language (1) designed specifically for young children to learn through independent exploration. Kodu seeks to lower the barrier to entry for new programmers by presenting a radically simplified programming model which nevertheless has significant expressive power (2). Kodu is integrated in a real-time 3D gaming environment and is designed to compete with modern console games in terms of intuitive user interface and graphical production values. In this paper we will review key tradeoffs made in the design of the programming language and illustrate how it is one of very few languages designed using user interface design principles and methodologies, to the extent that the blend of subjective and objective factors considered in the language design[1] have succeeded in presenting a model of programming which is uniquely approachable and creatively empowering for non-technical users.

Categories and Subject Descriptors D.1.7 [**Programming Techniques**]: Visual Programming D.2.2 [**Software Engineering**]: Design Tools and Techniques – User interfaces; Computer-aided software engineering (CASE); Evolutionary prototyping, D.2.6 [**Software Engineering**]: Programming Environments – Graphical environments; Integrated environments; Interactive environments, D.3.2 [**Programming Languages**]: Language Classifications – Specialized application languages; Very high-level languages; Concurrent, distributed, and parallel languages

General Terms Design, Human Factors, Languages

Keywords games; game programming; 3d user interface; end-user authoring; K12 programming; programming early education; Kodu, Boku

1. Goals of Kodu

Kodu was initially inspired by the relatively easy access to programming – through a ROM-based BASIC interpreter – provided in early 1980s personal computers like the Commodore PET, Apple II, and the Radio Shack TRS-80. For programmers coming of age in that time, there was little to do with a computer *but* program or play simple games copied from magazine listings. Significantly, many programmers wrote their first lines of code in order to modify these "pre-fab" games to be more to their liking. We felt that this blend of play and learning had largely been lost, to the detriment of the programming community. Modern video games do not typically come with source code, cannot be reprogrammed on the fly and – particularly in the area of console games - require such advanced engineering that they present an intimidating barrier to entry.

It was our expectation that providing a more easily accessible, creatively powerful programming experience to young children would benefit the children in their cognitive development (3) and eventually increase the overall size and quality of the programming community. Ideally, more children would be drawn to programming as a creative tool for expressing their own ideas rather than an externally motivated career choice with limited personal relevance.

With Kodu, we set out to provide a new "first programming experience" that mirrored the early PC era: play games, fix them up, and eventually create your own from scratch. We realized very early that the kids of today have a very different context than we ourselves had in the 80s, particularly in regard to user interface and the games themselves, which often have art budgets comparable to those of the largest Hollywood films. We didn't want a 21st century language for building 1980s games; instead, we felt our new language should be able to achieve the same quality of work product that kids experience in commercial console games today. This indicated to us that we should pursue a higher level of abstraction than BASIC in order to meet kid's sophisticated expectations of game behavior while keeping the learning curve manageable. By coupling the language semantics with a real-time 3D game engine we sought to allow kids to leverage common gaming assumptions – such as physics – to focus on what was new about their own game designs.

2. Kodu Environment

Although our focus for Kodu was to create a new programming language, our chosen domain – 3d gaming – required that we also supply tools necessary for arranging and populating the game world. Kodu includes a full 3D gaming "development environment," include a terrain editor, layout tools, character menus, and other mechanisms which allow end-users to create the world "data" against which their code will operate.

Similarly, the Kodu runtime includes a full complement of fundamental game technology: camera controls, collision detection, physics, etc. Although implementing such basic game technology as a physics engine is a deep and fascinating endeavor for an advanced programmer, our interviews with children showed a clear focus on

POPL'11 January 26–28, 2011, Austin, Texas, USA.

new forms of gameplay which typically assume that physics already works. We decided to provide enough functionality out of the box that the problems the kids were trying to solve through programming were problems they already found interesting – their own game design ideas.

3. Design chronology

3.1 Inspirations

Once we had chosen our "north star" – to achieve the level of interactivity, ease of entry, and relative expressive power of 80s BASIC environments, we looked for modern inspirations of high-level systems with expressive power, even if they were not programming environments per se.

One such inspiration was the children's musical toy Music Blocks created by the toy company Neurosmith. This toy allows very small children to create a variety of different songs by changing the orientation and order of a set of electronic cubes on a rack. The attractive element of this toy was how the user interface ruled out the possibility of a syntax error: as long as the cubes are placed into the rack spaces, a song will result. There are no illegal combinations possible. We distilled this inspiration into a key creative image: a robot onto which the user places cards containing high level concepts such as "move," "see," "green," or "left," which then self-assemble into coherent behavioral statements. This crystalized a motivation to protect the user from having to memorize abstract grammatical structure or sequencing rules.

Another inspiration was the HyperCard environment created by Bill Atkinson at Apple Computer in the 1990s (4). In HyperCard, there was no distinction between the programming environment and the finished project. A user created a new program by interactively modifying an already running – albeit simplistic – program. We noticed that, in this model, a user is faced with a single level of abstraction – a program that can be modified - rather than the more daunting and complex concept of a program which creates programs which is presented in modern Interactive Development Environments (IDEs) such as Microsoft's Visual Studio or the Eclipse Foundation's eponymous product.

From more recent software history, we studied the "logical puzzle blocks" model presented by MIT's Scratch project and the menu-driven game programming environment in CMU's Alice (5). In seeking to contribute something beyond what these modern kid's programming tools had already achieved, we noticed that these environments closely modeled the syntax and level of abstraction of professional programming languages such as Java. We asked ourselves if we could use either higher-level language constructs or more deeply integrate common game engine concepts to allow our users to achieve more complex games in fewer lines of code than these other (excellent) environments. This became a key turning point in the language design as we realized that visually modeling the semantics of mainstream languages was not a goal because it had already been done quite effectively. Rather, we implicitly gave ourselves permission to invent a completely new language if we could convince ourselves that that language would more concisely express the ideas of a kid trying to design a new video game.

A full accounting of our inspirations is barely possible; some of the others included Smalltalk (6); Lisp and in particular the object-oriented dialect Dylan (7); interactive physics environments such as Crayon Physics; the event-driven model of programming popularized by the Apple Macintosh (8) and dataflow programming environments such as HookUp and Lego Mindstorms.

3.2 Vehicles

Our use of the gaming domain was implicit in our goal of speaking to kids existing motivations – making and playing games. The modern gaming world is overwhelmingly real-time and 3D, which led us to examine robotics literature, which deals extensively with controlling behavior in a real-time 3D environment. One particularly compelling example of this was Valentino Breitenberg's 1984 book Vehicles, which examines how surprisingly 'intelligent' behavior can be achieve by simple combinations of motors, wheels, lights, and light sensors, wired in different combinations.

In our first design exploration, we attempted to re-create the popular early video game Pac Man using a Breitenberg-style library of sensor and motor blocks within a wiring tool. We quickly discovered that even simple behaviors would quickly become very large, complex diagrams. Motors and sensors were too low-level to achieve the expressive power we were after. After a round of early paper prototyping work, we discarded this approach and went back to the drawing board.

3.3 Cards paradigm

Stephen Coy, one of the original Kodu team members, had recently completed a research prototype for a new graphical user interface for issuing commands to a computer. This prototype consisted of a virtual deck of cards representing OS concepts such as "printer" and "document." A user would construct a "hand" – like a poker hand – of these cards in a 3D environment and then "play" the hand and the system would infer a command. For example, selecting a card labeled "printer" and a card for a document would cause the document to be printed. The positive usability results from this internal Microsoft prototype motivated us to find a way to incorporate this "hand of cards" paradigm in our language design and user interface.

3.4 Behavior-based Robotics

As we continued to explore scenarios and design goals using paper prototyping, we found increasing relevance in the robotics literature of Rodney Brooks at MIT. Just as Brooks' subsumption architecture (9) reduced processing requirements for real-world robots, we realized these concepts could also be used to achieve greater expressive power for game designers. Based on these publications and more popular descriptions of robotic behavior programming Kodu co-founder Michael Miller designed a basic model for the language which is still in use today:

A **sensor** detects objects in the world. Sensors used in Kodu include physical analogs such as *see*, *hear* and *bump* (touch,) and also slightly more abstract sensors such as *timer*, which detects the passage of time, and *scored*, which detects changes to game scores. Sensors create sets of sensed objects which are available for further processing.

A **filter** reduces the set of objects detected by a sensor. A sensor produces a set, and the filter reduces that set. Filtering can be done on object types (apple, tree;) on object attributes such as color, or on situational characteristics such as distance (near, far) or quantity (many, few.)

A **selector** operates on the set emitted by the filter to select a single object for operation. In actual use the *nearest* selector is most commonly used; other selectors include *furthest* and *random*.

An **actuator** causes the executing robot (the subject) to take some action towards itself or the object provided by the selector (the object.)

Finally, a **modifier** further parameterizes the actuator, optionally incorporating information derived from the subject, object or global state.

A set of these primitives combine (2) to form a rule. Within that rule, the sensor, filters, and selectors form a *sensor clause* while the actuator and one or more modifiers form and *actuator clause*. At runtime, any sensor clause which detects at least one matching object in the environment causes the rules actuator clause to take effect, or "fire."

The core set of sensors, filters etc is based on primitive functionality oriented towards game design: sensors such as *see* and *hear*, filters that can reference object type (like *tree*) or *color*, and actuators like *move* with filters such as *towards* or *away*. *See – apple – nearest : move – towards* is a common "hello world" equivalent in Kodu.

Note that this approach does not mandate a particular order for the primitives in a rule. At this point in the design, we chose an order that provided the most direct mapping to English speech.

3.5 First User Interface

In designing Kodu, we gave equal weight to the design of the language itself and of the user interface used to create and edit Kodu programs. Our design process incorporated user interface design principles, such as *progressive disclosure (xxx)* (revealing elements after the user has made use of preceding elements) and methodologies such as *usability testing* (xxx) using both paper and interactive prototypes.

The first version of the Kodu user interface had the simple goal of allowing end users to create rules by combining the language primitives listed in the previous section. For this we chose a straightforward implementation of a grid where each row corresponds to a single rule and each column to a primitive type in the order *sensor – filter – selector – actuator – modifier*.

In Figure 1 we see a single rule consisting of nodes on a horizontal bar. Each node can be clicked (using an Xbox 360 controller) to open a menu allowing the user to select a primitive to be placed at that node. In this image the user has clicked on the Sensor node and is viewing a circular menu of sensors including See, Hear, and Touch as well as the now-defunct Remember and Stalled sensors.

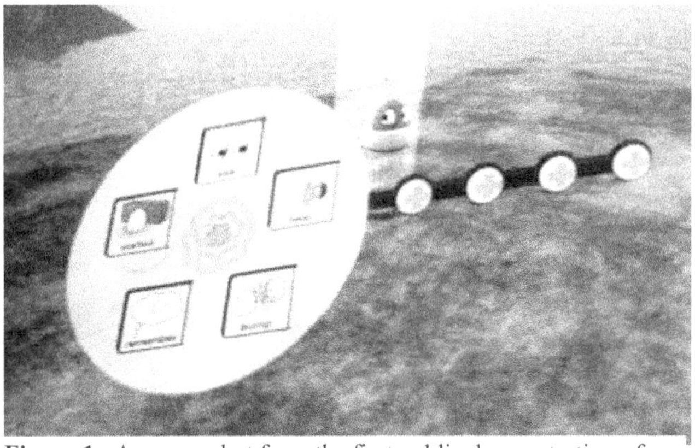

Figure 1. A screen shot from the first public demonstration of Kodu – then known as Boku – at Microsoft Research's Tech Fest in March of 2007.

Usability tests for the first user interface revealed a few problems. The first stemmed from our approach of having pre-allocated empty cells for each primitive type. Note that a user can add several filters to a rule:

```
See -            red -   apple -        nearest
sensor           filter  filter         selector
```

Since we couldn't know how many filters a user would need for a given rule, we simply left 3 filter spaces. This was usually enough; however, users new to the system tended to see it as a minimum requirement and felt compelled to add 3 filters to every rule. This often led to rules that were overly specific (see – red – apple – big) and could not select matching objects in the environment.

We needed a way to guide the user to create rules with the minimum effective number of primitives (such as filters) while allowing more advanced users to express more specific rules when necessary.

3.6 Rule Prioritization and Arbitration

In our previous example we considered the user interface for a single rule. Rules can be grouped together to form a page; in the user interface, this is depicted as a vertical stack of rules numbered in ascending order from top to bottom, with the topmost rule having the number 1. These numbers indicate the priority of the rules, with the highest priority rule appearing at the top of the screen.

For many simple programs, prioritization has no effect; rules are executed concurrently, with all sensors tested against the same world state. However, more subtle or complex behaviors are possible by programming conflicting rules and allowing prioritization to mask the results of some rules.

For example, one might create the Kodu program:

```
1. See - purple - move - away
2. See - apple - move - towards
```

In this example, the robot will move towards any apple and away from anything purple. In the case of a purple apple, the rule to move away from purple objects will take priority. A common use for this effect is to have a robot that patrols unless it sees an enemy, in which case it will give chase.

This ability to have multiple simple programs arbitrated by suppressing each other's outputs can be seen as a simplified version of Rodney Brook's subsumption architecture (10), with the difference that in Kodu suppression is based on a simple linear priority ordering rather than a hierarchical arrangement of behaviors.

3.7 Program Editor Revision

The next major revision of the program responded to two key issues. The first was the tendency of users to "fill in every slot" and create overly specific rules, as we mentioned earlier. The second issue was a problem of repetitiveness: in real-world design challenges, users tended to use the same selector almost exclusively: the *nearest* selector, which simply picks the closest object detected in the sensor clause. (ex *see – apple – nearest : move towards* vs. *see – apple – furthest – move – towards*)

This new design also recognized a natural hierarchy in the primitives: filters have a many-to-one mapping to sensors (the filters *red*, *blue*, etc apply to the *see* sensor) and modifiers have a similar relationship to actuators: the modifiers *toward* and *away* can similarly be seen as children of the *move* actuator.

Given this hierarchy, the team designed a new presentation which presented only two affordances: a sensor menu and an actuator menu. This streamlined presentation of an empty rule is shown below.

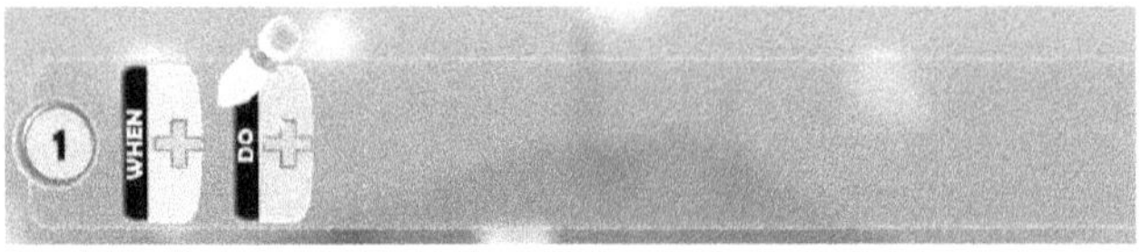

Figure 2. Revised Kodu rule editor focuses on the key sensor and actuator primitives.

In this simplified presentation, a more intuitive interpretation of the syntax emerged: the sensor and actuator are equivalent to a stimulus and a response, or to the classic if…then clause in most procedural languages. Based on polling of our usability test subjects, we settled on labels for each of these clauses of when (for the filter clause) and do (for the actuator clause.) These labels can be seen in Figure 2.

In this new presentation we also emphasize the hierarchical relationship between sensors and filters and between actuators and modifiers. In Figure 3, below, we see a filter clause (see – red – apple) with two filters and an actuator clause with a single modifier (move – toward.)

Figure 3. A fully populated rule in the new rule editor. Notice the clear grouping of sensor and actuator clauses. Less visible in this screenshot is that the sensor "tile" is larger than the filters and the actuator tile is larger than the modifier tiles.

Another significant change with this revision is that the selectors are no longer presented to the user. Since users almost universally chose the *nearest* selector, we made this the default. While the underlying architecture still allows for different types of selectors, the user interface no longer exposes this capability. As of this writing we are considering re-introducing the selector concept in the user interface as part of a deeper design investigation around set semantics, iteration, and concurrency, details of which are beyond the scope of this paper.

3.8 Consideration of State and Variables

At this point in the evolution of the language it was become clear that we needed a model for management of state. We considered adding classical variable types such as string and integers, but struggled to do it in a way which maintained the intuitiveness of the programming user interface.

Two insights guided this part of the design: the first was the general value in Rodney Brook's work (xxx) that reaction that state should be read from the environment and models were to be avoided. The second relied on personal correspondence with earlier implementers of prototype children's languages at Microsoft who had found that children seemed uninterested in abstractions (like variables) and more interested in real-world concepts (like seeing and moving.)

In the end, we decided to avoid typical presentation of variables in favor of reliance on world state. Although this was already a useful paradigm in robotics (11), Kodu has two advantages over the robotics field that made it even more useful. The first is that we could invent new actuators capable of *writing* state reliably into the simulation environment. Additionally our sensors, being virtual, are perfect and can be counted on to read state back from the environment instantly and without error.

A classic example of "Kodu style" state is object color. Characters can react to each other's color and also use the color actuator to change their own or each other's color. We've seen programs where characters signal their program state to each other by changing their own color, providing a lightweight synchronization mechanism that has the wonderful side effect of being visible to the user and therefore easier to understand and debug.

In the initial release of Kodu we also include a representation that has proven endlessly useful and, as all our language constructs, has an intuitive analog: the score. Kodu has primitives for setting, incrementing, decrementing, and testing scores. Although we present this in the curricula for the obvious reason – keeping track of who's winning – we were delighted to see our users use scores exactly as general-purpose integer variables, keeping track of iterations, resource counts, and even semaphores between characters.

3.9 State Machines and Structured Programming

Another classic "do we or don't we" moment arrived as sample programs started to use more complex real-world game designs. While prioritization and arbitration can achieve surprisingly subtle behavior, pages of rules can become unwieldy with more than 8 or so lines and our users wanted a way to encapsulate different modes of behavior.

Clearly this was an opportunity to introduce subroutines and structured programming. At the same time, jumping directly to those well-understood concepts would put severe pressure on our design goals of intuitive, discoverable user interface and minimal abstraction. Given the wonderfully English-like rules Kodu was currently composed of, the notion of shoe-horning in parameter passing and return address stacks threatened to take our user experience off the deep end and well beyond what a seven year old might willingly explore on their own.

In the end, we went with a minimal block structure with a real-world (i.e. non-abstract) metaphor: the page. Each Kodu program automatically presents one page of initially empty rules. Most new Kodu programmers will spend several hours without realizing that a robot can have more than one page. As they explore the set of actuators more deeply, they discover (or are shown) a *switch page* actuator that allows a robot to change from one page of rules to a completely different page of rules. No state is passed; again we rely on the environment to hold our "model". The icon for this actuator (a page icon with an arrow) is echoed elsewhere on the screen in a UI hint that shows the user how to move between pages in the editor.

4. Lessons: Kodu in the Real World

Kodu was first released on the Xbox 360 in June of 2009 and then for the PC (as a free download) in January of 2010. It is currently in use in 120 countries around the world and has been translated to several languages by enthusiastic users. Deployment environments range from single players on the Xbox at home (around 50,000 paid downloads by individuals) to a multi-school K12 collaborative Kodu system in Victoria Australia (12).

4.1 What worked

We attempted to provide a programming language so seamlessly embedded in a modern console gaming experience that children would voluntarily spend their leisure time learning to program their own games. Based on the downloads we've seen on the Xbox 360 and positive reviews in mainstream gaming press, we believe we have achieved that.

One result that pleasantly surprised us was that Kodu users in several school environments seem to be evenly divided between boys and girls. As our first pilot deployment was in an all-girls after-school program, our early user feedback may have guided us to an experience that appeals regardless of gender. This is an effect we are just beginning to investigate and would like to build on.

4.2 Missed opportunities

Although the team wanted to build a game-sharing server for Kodu, resource limitations prevented us from deploying it to end users. We feel that this limited the ability of kids to be motivated by each other's work, ultimately holding back the growth of the Kodu user base.

Feedback from some academic institutions has indicated a desire for a "ladder" from Kodu to mainstream professional programming languages. While we remain focused on the earliest possible programming experience rather than pure vocational preparation, we recognize the appeal of an integrated profession from Kodu to, say, C# or JavaScript.

4.3 Next steps

As of this writing we have a major Kodu upgrade scheduled to launch in fall of 2010. In early 2011 we plan to begin work on a global Kodu sharing server which will allow children to share their Kodu creations with classmates and students in other schools and countries.

We are also actively seeking partners in university to help us extend Kodu with specialized scenarios and more advanced language constructs. We have shared the Kodu source code with several university efforts, notably in support of Teale Fristoe's fuzzy logic extension for Kodu, in development at UC Santa Cruz. It is our hope that broadening the community of Kodu contributors will help it to reach its full potential as an easy-to-learn new language for young children.

5. References

1. **Microsoft FUSE Labs.** Kodu Web Site. [Online] [Cited: November 12, 2010.] http://fuse.microsoft.com/project/kodu.aspx.
2. **Stolee, K. T.** *Kodu language and grammar specification.* Redmond, WA, USA : Microsoft Research, 2010.
3. *"Let the players play!" & other earnest remarks about videogame authorship.* **Teske, Paul and Fristoe, Teale.** s.l. : International Society of the Learning Sciences, 2010. ICLS '10 Proceedings of the 9th International Conference of the Learning Sciences - Volume 1.
4. **Apple Computer, Inc.** *HyperCard Script Language Guide: The HyperTalk Language.* Reading, MA : Addison-Wesley Publishing Company, 1988.
5. **Matthew Conway, et al.** Alice: lessons learned from building a 3D system for novices. *CHI '00 Proceedings of the SIGCHI conference on Human factors in computing systems.* The Hague, The Netherlands : s.n., 2000.
6. **Goldberg, A.** *Smalltalk-80: the language and its implementation.* Boston, MA, USA : Addison-Wesley Longman Publishing Co., Inc., 1983. ISBN: 0-201-11371-6.
7. **Shalit, A.** *The Dylan reference manual.* Redwood City, CA, USA : Addison Wesley Longman Publishing Co., Inc., 1996. ISBN:0-201-44211-6.
8. *A declarative approach to event-handling in visual programming languages.* **Burnett, MM and al, et.** Seattle, WA, USA : s.n., 1992. Proceedings, 1992 IEEE Workshop on Visual Languages. pp. 34-40.
9. *New Approaches to Robotics.* **Brooks, RA.** 13, s.l. : Science, 1991, Vol. 253.
10. **Brooks, Rodney A.** *Intelligence Without Reason.* Cambridge, MA, USA : MIT, 1991.
11. **Brooks, Roney A.** Intelligence without representation. [book auth.] George F. Luger. *Computation & Intelligence.* Menlo Park, CA, USA : American Association for Artificial Intelligence, 1995.
12. *The impact of web 2.0 technologies in the clsassroom.* Department of Education and Early Childhood Development, State of Victoria. 2009.
13. *Kodu: end-user programmin gand design for games.* **MacLaurin, Matt.** s.l. : ACM, 2009. FDG '09: Proceedings for the 4th International Conference on Foundations of Digital Games.
14. *The early history of Smalltalk.* **Kay, Alan C.** s.l. : ACM, 1993. HOPL-II: The second ACM SIGPLAN conference on History of programming languages .
15. *Elephants don't play chess.* **Brooks, Rodney A.** 1-2, 1990, Robotics and Autonomous Systems, Vol. 6.

A Separation Logic for Refining Concurrent Objects

Aaron Turon * Mitchell Wand

Northeastern University

{turon, wand}@ccs.neu.edu

Abstract

Fine-grained concurrent data structures are crucial for gaining performance from multiprocessing, but their design is a subtle art. Recent literature has made large strides in verifying these data structures, using either atomicity refinement or separation logic with rely-guarantee reasoning. In this paper we show how the ownership discipline of separation logic can be used to enable atomicity refinement, and we develop a new rely-guarantee method that is localized to the definition of a data structure. We present the first semantics of separation logic that is sensitive to atomicity, and show how to control this sensitivity through ownership. The result is a logic that enables compositional reasoning about atomicity and interference, even for programs that use fine-grained synchronization and dynamic memory allocation.

Categories and Subject Descriptors D.2.4 [*Software Engineering*]: Software/Program Verification; F.3.1 [*Logics and Meanings of Programs*]: Specifying and Verifying and Reasoning about Programs

General Terms Algorithms, Verification

1. Introduction

1.1 The goal

This paper is about the semantic relationship between ownership, atomicity, and interference. We begin with a very simple data structure: the counter. Counters permit a single operation, `inc`:

```
int inc(int *C) {
  int tmp = *C;   *C = tmp+1;   return tmp;
}
```

Of course, this implementation only works in a sequential setting. If multiple threads use it concurrently, an unlucky interleaving can lead to several threads fetching the same value from the counter. The usual reaction to this problem is to use mutual exclusion, wrapping the operation with lock instructions. But as Moir and Shavit put it, "with this arrangement, we prevent the bad interleavings by preventing *all* interleavings" [20]. Fine-grained concurrent objects permit as many good interleavings as possible, without allowing any bad ones. The code

```
do { tmp = *C; } until CAS(C, tmp, tmp+1);
```

implements `inc` using an optimistic approach: it takes a snapshot of the counter without acquiring a lock, computes the new value of the counter, and uses compare-and-set (`CAS`) to safely install the new value. The key is that `CAS` compares `*C` with the value of `tmp`, *atomically* updating `*C` with `tmp + 1` and returning `true` if they are the same, and just returning `false` otherwise.

Even for this simple data structure, the fine-grained implementation significantly outperforms the lock-based implementation [17]. Likewise, even for this simple example, we would prefer to think of the counter in a more abstract way when reasoning about its clients, giving it the following specification:

$$\mathsf{inc}(c, \mathit{ret}) \triangleq \langle \forall x : c \mapsto x,\ c \mapsto x+1 \wedge \mathit{ret} = x \rangle$$

This specification says that, for any value x, inc atomically transforms a heap in which c points to x into one where c points to $x+1$, moreover ensuring that the value of *ret* (an out-parameter) is x.

We express both implementations and specifications in a single specification language, and say that φ *refines* (implements) ψ if for every context $C[-]$, each behavior of $C[\varphi]$ is a possible behavior of $C[\psi]$.[1] That is, no client can detect that it is interacting with φ rather than ψ, even if the client invokes φ's operations concurrently.

This paper presents a logic for proving such refinements, based on separation logic. The key idea is to use a notion of *ownership*, expressed through separation logic, to reason about both atomicity and interference. The key contributions are the semantics ("fenced refinement") and proof rules enabling this reasoning. We will be able to easily verify the counter given above (§4.1), as well as more complex nonblocking data structures (*e.g.* a nonblocking stack §6).

1.2 The approach

Since this paper is focused on verification rather than development, we will take the perspective of *abstraction*, which is converse to refinement: φ refines ψ iff ψ abstracts φ. The appeal of abstraction is that, to prove something about the behaviors of $C[\varphi]$ for a particular client C, it suffices to consider the behaviors of $C[\psi]$ instead—and ψ is usually much simpler than φ. For verifying data structures in a sequential setting, one is primarily interested in *data abstraction*, where ψ abstracts away representation details from φ. In a concurrent setting, we want simplicity in another respect as well: *atomicity abstraction*, where ψ appears to perform an operation in one atomic step even though φ takes many steps.

Refinement hinges on the power of the context $C[-]$: what can it observe, and with what can it interfere? The more powerful the context, the less freedom we have in implementing a specification. Concurrency changes not *what*, but *when*. In a first-order language, a sequential context can only interact with the state before or after

* Supported by a grant from Microsoft Research.

[1] We take the perspective, advanced by Filipović *et al.* [8], that linearizability [11] is a *proof technique* for refinement—and we choose not to use it. See §8 for more discussion.

POPL'11, January 26–28, 2011, Austin, Texas, USA.

running the program fragment in its hole. A concurrent context might do so at any time.

In his classic 1973 paper, "Protection in Programming Languages", Morris argued that "a programmer should be able to prove that his programs ... do not malfunction solely on the basis of what he can see from his private bailiwick" [22]. That paper and its contemporaries showed how to enable such reasoning by weakening the context, *e.g.* by hiding data through lexical scoping [22], protecting data by dynamic sealing [22] or by giving it an opaque (existential) type [15, 19]. A basic message of this paper is that these and other hiding techniques serve just as well to localize reasoning in a concurrent setting.

We present an approach for proving refinement/abstraction of concurrent objects using an ownership discipline to enforce hiding. As in any separation logic, the ownership discipline is *dynamic*: what is owned can vary over time and is often determined by runtime values in the heap. We derive two major benefits from our ownership discipline. First, it enables us to perform atomicity abstraction, under the basic principle that "if you don't own it, you can't see it". Thus an atomic step modifying only private data can be absorbed into an adjacent atomic step, to form a single *observably atomic* step.

> **Claim 1**: By making both atomicity and ownership explicit, we can clarify and exploit their relationship: observed atomicity is relative to ownership.

Atomicity abstraction stems from the notion of private data. The other benefit of ownership is to do with object instances, which are *shared* among concurrently-running methods.

> **Claim 2**: Because ownership limits possible interference, we can exploit it to give a *modular* and *dynamic* account of rely/guarantee reasoning.

Rely/guarantee reasoning [12] is a well-known technique for compositionally reasoning about interference: you prove that each thread guarantees certain behavior, as long as it can rely on other threads to interfere in a limited way. Traditionally, the rely constraint must be carried through the whole verification, even if it is only relevant to a small portion. Using ownership, we localize rely/guarantee reasoning to the definition of a concurrent object, since we know all interference must stem from the methods making up its definition. In our approach, rely/guarantee reasoning is done with respect to a hypothetical object instance; at runtime, there may be zero, one, or many such instances, each residing in its own region of the heap. A broadly similar form of rely/guarantee reasoning appeared in very recent work by Dinsdale-Young *et al.* [4]; we compare the approaches in §8.

To support our claims, we make the following contributions:

- We present a new specification language in the tradition of refinement calculi [1, 21], but tailored to separation logic-style reasoning (§2). We give it an operational semantics, which determines the meaning of refinement. Our notion of refinement captures safety properties only, but we expect most of our results to easily transfer to a model incorporating liveness.
- We adapt Brookes's transition trace model [2] to handle dynamic memory allocation, and use it to give our specification language a simple denotational semantics (§3). The semantics is adequate for the operational model, so it can be used to justify refinements. To our knowledge, this is the first model of separation logic that captures atomicity explicitly.
- On the strength of the denotational model, we are able to give many basic refinement laws (§4), and we show how these laws can be used to verify a simple nonblocking counter (§4.1). They are not strong enough, however, to handle more complex data structures—for that, we need ownership-based reasoning.
- In §5.2 we introduce our ownership discipline, formally captured by the notion of *fenced refinement*. The semantics of fenced refinement is a *hybrid* between trace semantics and input/output relations: traces for shared state, I/O for private state. We give laws of fenced refinement that justify our two claims above. Finally, we give a law DATA_2 relating fenced and standard refinement, which allows us to employ fenced refinement compositionally in correctness proofs. We sketch the soundness proof for this law in §7.
- We present a case study—the verification of a nonblocking stack—to demonstrate fenced refinement (§6).

This paper draws on several ideas from recent work, especially that of Vafeiadis *et al.* [27, 28] and Elmas *et al.* [5, 6]. We refer the reader to §8 for a detailed discussion of prior work.

Domains

$x, y, z \in$	VAR	variables
	LOC	locations
$v \in$	VAL	values
$\rho \in$	$\text{VAR} \rightharpoonup \text{VAL}$	environments
$\sigma \in$	$\Sigma \triangleq \text{LOC} \rightharpoonup \text{VAL}$	heaps
$o \in$	$\Sigma^{\lightning} \triangleq \Sigma \cup \{\lightning\}$	outcomes

Syntax

Specifications	φ, ψ, θ	$::=$	$\varphi;\psi \mid \varphi \parallel \psi \mid \varphi \vee \psi \mid \exists x.\varphi$
		$\mid$	$\mu X.\varphi \mid X \mid \textbf{let } f = F \textbf{ in } \psi$
		$\mid$	$F\ e \mid \langle \forall \overline{x} : p, q \rangle \mid \{p\}$
Procedures	F	$::=$	$f \mid \lambda x.\varphi$
Configurations	κ	$::=$	$\varphi, \sigma \mid o$
Predicates	p, q, r	$::=$	$\mathsf{true} \mid \mathsf{false} \mid \mathsf{emp} \mid e \mapsto e'$
		$\mid$	$e = e' \mid p * q \mid p \wedge q \mid p \vee q$
		$\mid$	$p \Rightarrow q \mid \forall x.p \mid \exists x.p$
Expressions	e	$::=$	$x \mid n \mid e + e' \mid (e, e')$

Figure 1.

2. Specifications

The standard view of refinement calculus is as follows [21]: we are broadly interested in "specifications", the most concrete of which are "programs". Thus, we have an expressive language of specifications φ (so it is easy to say *what* behavior is wanted), and a sublanguage of programs (that say *how* to produce such behavior). It will be possible, for instance, to write a specification that solves the halting problem, but this will not correspond to any program. The distinction between programs and general specifications is not important for our purposes here; suffice it to say that the implementations we will verify are clearly executable on a machine.

The language of specifications (Figure 1) includes traditional programming constructs like sequential composition $\varphi;\psi$ and parallel composition $\varphi \parallel \psi$, let-binding of first-order procedures, and recursion $\mu X.\varphi$. In addition, there are logical constructs like disjunction $\varphi \vee \psi$ and quantification $\exists x.\varphi$. These latter can be read operationally as nondeterminism: $\varphi \vee \psi$ either behaves like φ or behaves like ψ, and $\exists x.\varphi$ behaves like φ for some choice of x. The remaining specification constructs (shaded in gray) will be explained in §2.2.

In the largely-standard semantics given below, a specification interacts step-by-step with a heap σ. A *configuration* κ of the abstract machine is typically a pair φ, σ of the remaining specification to execute, and the current heap. In addition, there are two terminal configurations, called *outcomes*: either successful termination with heap σ, or else a *fault* $\lightning$. Faulting will be explained in §2.2; the important point at the moment is that faulty termination propagates up through sequential and parallel composition.

Operational semantics of specifications $\kappa \to \kappa'$

$$\frac{\varphi_1, \sigma \to \varphi_1', \sigma'}{\varphi_1; \varphi_2, \sigma \to \varphi_1'; \varphi_2, \sigma'} \qquad \frac{\varphi_1, \sigma \to \sigma'}{\varphi_1; \varphi_2, \sigma \to \varphi_2, \sigma'} \qquad \frac{\varphi_1, \sigma \to \lightning}{\varphi_1; \varphi_2, \sigma \to \lightning}$$

$$\frac{\varphi_1 \parallel \varphi_2, \sigma \to \kappa}{\varphi_2 \parallel \varphi_1, \sigma \to \kappa} \qquad \frac{\varphi_1, \sigma \to \varphi_1', \sigma'}{\varphi_1 \parallel \varphi_2, \sigma \to \varphi_1' \parallel \varphi_2, \sigma'}$$

$$\frac{\varphi_1, \sigma \to \sigma'}{\varphi_1 \parallel \varphi_2, \sigma \to \varphi_2, \sigma'} \qquad \frac{\varphi_1, \sigma \to \lightning}{\varphi_1 \parallel \varphi_2, \sigma \to \lightning}$$

$$\varphi_1 \vee \varphi_2, \sigma \to \varphi_1, \sigma \qquad \varphi_1 \vee \varphi_2, \sigma \to \varphi_2, \sigma$$

$$\frac{v \in \textsc{Val}}{\exists x.\varphi, \sigma \to \varphi[v/x], \sigma} \qquad \mu X.\varphi, \sigma \to \varphi[\mu X.\varphi/X], \sigma$$

$$\textbf{let } f = F \textbf{ in } \varphi, \sigma \to \varphi[F/f], \sigma \qquad (\lambda x.\varphi)e, \sigma \to \varphi[[\![e]\!]/x], \sigma$$

$$\frac{(\sigma, o) \in \mathsf{act}(p, q)}{\langle \forall \overline{x} : p,\ q \rangle, \sigma \to o} \qquad \frac{\sigma \models p * \mathsf{true}}{\{p\}, \sigma \to \sigma} \qquad \frac{\sigma \not\models p * \mathsf{true}}{\{p\}, \sigma \to \lightning}$$

A few other points of note:

- Variables x, y, z are immutable; only the heap is mutable.
- The domain of values $\textsc{Val}$ is unspecified, but at least includes locations, integers, and pairs.
- We assume a denotational semantics $[\![e]\!]^\rho : \textsc{Val}$ for expressions e, which is straightforward. We write $[\![e]\!]$ for $[\![e]\!]^\emptyset$.
- A composition $\varphi; \psi$ steps to ψ exactly when φ terminates.
- The first rule for $\parallel$ makes it symmetric.
- We abbreviate **let** $f = \lambda x.\varphi$ **in** ψ by **let** $f(x) = \varphi$ **in** ψ.

2.1 Heap predicates

To describe the remaining forms of specifications (shaded in gray), we first need to define *heap predicates* p. These are the usual predicates of separation logic: they make assertions about both program variables (*e.g.* $x = 3$) and the heap (*e.g.* $x \mapsto 3$). As such, the entailment relation $\sigma, \rho \models p$ holds when p is true both of the heap σ and the *environment* ρ, which gives the values of program variables:

Predicate semantics $\sigma, \rho \models p$

$\sigma, \rho \models \mathsf{emp}$ iff $\sigma = \emptyset$
$\sigma, \rho \models e \mapsto e'$ iff $\sigma = [[\![e]\!]^\rho \mapsto [\![e']\!]^\rho]$
$\sigma, \rho \models e = e'$ iff $[\![e]\!]^\rho = [\![e']\!]^\rho$
$\sigma, \rho \models p * q$ iff $\exists \sigma_1, \sigma_2.\ \sigma = \sigma_1 \uplus \sigma_2,\ \sigma_1, \rho \models p,\ \sigma_2, \rho \models q$
$\sigma, \rho \models p \vee q$ iff $\sigma, \rho \models p$ or $\sigma, \rho \models q$
$\sigma, \rho \models \forall x.p$ iff $\forall v.\ \sigma, \rho[x \mapsto v] \models p$

The predicates emp, $e \mapsto e'$ and $p * q$ come from separation logic. The predicate emp asserts that the heap is empty, while $e \mapsto e'$ asserts that the heap contains a *single* location e which contains the value e'. Thus $x \mapsto 3$ is satisfied when ρ takes x to the only location in σ, and σ maps that location to 3. The *separating conjunction* $p*q$ is satisfied by any heap separable into one subheap satisfying p and one satisfying q. Thus $x \mapsto 3 * y \mapsto 4$ asserts that the heap contains exactly two locations, containing 3 and 4. In particular, it implies that the locations $x \neq y$.

We write $\sigma \models p$ for $\sigma, \emptyset \models p$.

2.2 Actions, assertions, and assumptions

In separation logic, a Hoare triple $\{p\}C\{q\}$ for a command C asserts that, if $\sigma \models p$, then C running on σ

- will not fault (by, say, following a dangling pointer) and,
- if it terminates, will do so with a heap σ' such that $\sigma' \models q$.

Note that p and q may be quite specific about the shape of the heap, for example insisting that it consists of a single cell. A key idea of separation logic is that commands are *local*: what they do on a large heap is determined by what they do on smaller heaps. This idea leads to the *frame rule*, allowing $\{p*r\}C\{q*r\}$ to be inferred from $\{p\}C\{q\}$.

In our specification language, we forgo basic commands in favor of a single construct: the *action* $\langle \forall \overline{x} : p,\ q \rangle$. An action describes an *atomic* step of computation in terms of the strongest partial correctness assertion it satisfies (*cf.* Morgan's specification statements [21]). In other words, it permits every behavior that satisfies the triple $\{p\} - \{q\}$. The variables $\overline{x}$ are in scope for both p and q, and are used to link them together (as in inc above).

To understand the behavior of a simple action $\langle p,\ q \rangle$, it is helpful to think in terms of a specific starting heap σ. First, suppose that $\sigma \not\models p * \mathsf{true}$, meaning that no subheap of σ satisfies p. In this case, the behavior is unconstrained, and in particular the action is permitted to fault. Hence, faults arise when preconditions are not satisfied. On the other hand, if σ can be decomposed into subheaps $\sigma = \sigma_1 \uplus \sigma_2$ such that $\sigma_1 \models p$, then the action must take a step to some heap $\sigma_1' \uplus \sigma_2$ such that $\sigma_1' \models q$; it must establish the postcondition without modifying the frame σ_2, and cannot fault.

The semantics of actions is in essence that of Calcagno *et al.* [3]:

Action semantics $\mathsf{act}(p, q) \subseteq \Sigma \times \Sigma^{\lightning}$

$(\sigma, o) \in \mathsf{act}(p, q)$ iff $\forall \sigma_1, \sigma_2, \rho.$
if $\sigma = \sigma_1 \uplus \sigma_2$ and $\sigma_1, \rho \models p$
then $\exists \sigma_1'.\ o = \sigma_1' \uplus \sigma_2$ and $\sigma_1', \rho \models q$

Many familiar commands can be expressed as actions. The following are used in our examples, and provide some intuition for the semantics of actions:

$$\begin{aligned}
\mathsf{abort} &\triangleq \langle \mathsf{false},\ \mathsf{true} \rangle \\
\mathsf{miracle} &\triangleq \langle \mathsf{true},\ \mathsf{false} \rangle \\
\mathsf{skip} &\triangleq \langle \mathsf{emp},\ \mathsf{emp} \rangle \\
\mathsf{new}(x, \mathit{ret}) &\triangleq \langle \mathsf{emp},\ \mathit{ret} \mapsto x \rangle \\
\mathsf{put}(a, x) &\triangleq \langle a \mapsto -,\ a \mapsto x \rangle \\
\mathsf{get}(a, \mathit{ret}) &\triangleq \langle \forall x : a \mapsto x,\ a \mapsto x \wedge x = \mathit{ret} \rangle \\
\mathsf{cas}(a, \mathit{old}, \mathit{new}, \mathit{ret}) &\triangleq \\
&\left\langle \forall x : a \mapsto x,\ \begin{array}{l} (x \neq \mathit{old} \wedge \mathit{ret} = 0 \wedge a \mapsto x) \\ \vee\ (x = \mathit{old} \wedge \mathit{ret} = 1 \wedge a \mapsto \mathit{new}) \end{array} \right\rangle
\end{aligned}$$

where the predicate $a \mapsto -$ is shorthand for $\exists z.a \mapsto z$. The abort action can always fault, as its precondition is never satisfied. On the other hand, miracle never faults, but it also never takes any steps, as its postcondition is never satisfied. From the standpoint of the operational semantics, miracle *neither faults nor successfully terminates*; from a partial correctness standpoint, it satisfies every specification [21]. The skip action cannot fault, because any heap has a subheap that satisfies emp. Likewise, new cannot fault, and it furthermore ensures that *ret* is distinct from any address allocated in the frame. Finally, put, get and cas fault if a is unallocated. Notice that get and cas both quantify over a variable x in order to connect an observation made in the precondition to a constraint in the postcondition.

One common theme in these examples is the use of postconditions to filter possible behaviors, miracle being the most extreme case. For procedures like get, the postcondition is used to constrain the out-parameter *ret*. Where one might write **let** $x = \mathsf{get}(a)$ **in** φ as a program, we write $\exists x.\mathsf{get}(a, x); \varphi$ as a specification. Executions where x took on the wrong value simply disappear, neither terminating nor faulting.

One use of postcondition filtering is so common that we introduce shorthand for it: an *assumption* $[p]$ stands for the action $\langle \mathsf{emp},\ \mathsf{emp} \wedge p\rangle$. Because its precondition is emp, an assumption cannot fault, and because its postcondition implies emp as well, it cannot alter the heap; it is a refinement of skip. Since it is conjoined with emp, the predicate p cannot further constrain the heap; it is used only to constrain the value of variables. Assumptions are used for control flow: the specification **if** p **then** φ **else** ψ is sugar for $([p]; \varphi) \vee ([\neg p]; \psi)$.

Finally, *assertions* $\{p\}$ simply test a predicate: if some subheap satisfies p then the heap is left unchanged, and otherwise the assertion faults. Assertions provide a way to introduce a claim during verification while postponing its justification (*cf.* [5]).

We can write the fine-grained concurrent version of inc in our specification language as follows:

$$\begin{aligned}\mathsf{inc}'(c, ret) \triangleq \mu X.\ & \exists t.\mathsf{get}(c, t);\\ & \exists b.\mathsf{cas}(c, t, t+1, b);\\ & \textbf{if } b = 1 \textbf{ then } [ret = t] \textbf{ else } X\end{aligned}$$

3. Refinement: model theory

We have seen what specifications are, how they behave, and how they express common programming constructs. But the point of working with specifications is to *compare* them: we want to say when a relatively concrete specification "implements" a more abstract one. Informally, a specification φ implements ψ if no client can observe that it is interacting with φ instead of ψ, *i.e.*, every behavior of φ is a possible behavior of ψ. Formally, this situation is expressed as *refinement*:

Refinement $\varphi \sqsubseteq_{\mathsf{op}} \psi$

$$\varphi \sqsubseteq_{\mathsf{op}} \psi \text{ iff } \forall C, \sigma.\ \begin{cases} \text{if } C[\varphi], \sigma \ \lightning \text{ then } C[\psi], \sigma \ \lightning \\ \text{if } C[\varphi], \sigma \Downarrow \text{ then } C[\psi], \sigma \Downarrow \text{ or } C[\psi], \sigma \ \lightning \end{cases}$$

$$\text{where} \quad \kappa \ \lightning \ \text{ iff } \kappa \to^* \lightning \quad \text{and} \quad \kappa \Downarrow \ \text{ iff } \exists \sigma. \kappa \to^* \sigma$$

where C is a specification context (a specification with a hole) closing φ and ψ. The "op" stands for operational semantics. In this definition, we collapse the possible outcomes of a $C[\varphi], \sigma$ to three cases: nontermination, successful termination, and faulting termination. If the specification ψ can fault in a given context, then φ is relieved of any obligations for that context. In this way, faulting behavior is treated as "unspecified" behavior, and as we will soon see, it follows that abort is the most permissive specification ($\varphi \sqsubseteq_{\mathsf{op}}$ abort for all φ).

Ultimately, our goal is to give useful axioms and inference rules for proving such refinements. However, as usual, the quantification over all contexts in the definition of refinement makes it difficult to work with directly. As a stepping stone, in this section we give a denotational semantics for specifications, which will give us a sound (but not complete) denotational version $\sqsubseteq_{\mathsf{den}}$ of refinement. Readers primarily interested in the proof rules can read §4 first, taking the soundness of the rules on faith.

The denotational model is based on Brookes's transition trace model [2], which gave a fully abstract semantics for a parallel WHILE language. We adjust this model to deal with pointers and the heap, as well as faulting.

The challenge in giving a denotational model for concurrency is the semantics of parallel composition: to define $[\![\varphi \parallel \psi]\!]$ in terms of $[\![\varphi]\!]$ and $[\![\psi]\!]$ we must "leave room" for interference from ψ in the meaning of φ, and *vice-versa*. With transition traces, we give meaning to φ and ψ in terms of discrete timeslices of execution, between which we allow for arbitrary interference. To calculate the meaning of $\varphi \parallel \psi$, we need only interleave these timeslices.

In detail: we model the behavior of each specification as a set of transition traces. A *transition trace* is a finite sequence of *moves* (σ, σ'). Each move represents one timeslice of execution, which may correspond to zero, one, or some finite number of steps $\to$ in the operational semantics. A trace of φ like $(\sigma_1, \sigma_1')(\sigma_2, \sigma_2')$ arises from an execution where first $\varphi, \sigma_1 \to^* \varphi', \sigma_1'$, then some as-yet unknown specification in the environment changed the heap from σ_1' to σ_2, then $\varphi', \sigma_2 \to^* \varphi'', \sigma_2'$. A trace can be terminated by a fault, either on the part of the specification as in $(\sigma, \lightning)$, or on the part of its environment as in $(\lightning, \lightning)$:

Domains

$$\begin{array}{rcl} \text{MOVE} & \triangleq & \Sigma \times \Sigma \\ \text{FAULT} & \triangleq & \Sigma^{\lightning} \times \{\lightning\} \\ \text{TRACE} & \triangleq & \text{MOVE}^*; \text{FAULT}^? \end{array} \qquad \begin{array}{rcl} s, t, u & \in & \text{TRACE} \\ S, T, U & \subseteq & \text{TRACE} \end{array}$$

The transition traces of a specification can be read directly from the operational semantics:

Observed traces $t \in \mathcal{O}[\![\varphi]\!]$

$$\frac{}{(\lightning, \lightning) \in \mathcal{O}[\![\varphi]\!]} \qquad \frac{\varphi, \sigma \to^* o}{(\sigma, o) \in \mathcal{O}[\![\varphi]\!]} \qquad \frac{\varphi, \sigma \to^* \varphi', \sigma' \quad t \in \mathcal{O}[\![\varphi']\!]}{(\sigma, \sigma')t \in \mathcal{O}[\![\varphi]\!]}$$

The inference rules say, respectively: the environment might fault at any time; a terminating timeslice (whether successful or faulting) results in a singleton trace; a nonterminating timeslice allows the specification to resume later (under a possibly-changed heap).

An important insight in Brookes's model is that the transition traces of a specification are closed under *stuttering* (addition of a step (σ, σ)) and *mumbling* (merging of two steps with a common midpoint). Closure under stuttering means that the context of a specification cannot observe timeslices in which it does not change the heap; this justifies that skip is a unit for sequential composition. Closure under mumbling implies that, for example, $\langle p,\ r\rangle \sqsubseteq_{\mathsf{op}} \langle p,\ q\rangle ; \langle q,\ r\rangle$: the scheduler might give the latter specification a long enough timeslice to execute both actions, so that the behavior of the former is a possible behavior of the latter.

Our denotational semantics gives an alternative definition of $\mathcal{O}[\![\varphi]\!]$ that is *compositional* in the structure of φ. In giving the denotational semantics, we must explicitly apply stuttering and mumbling closure, which we do *via* the closure operator $\dagger$ (a quotient that blurs together observationally indistinguishable trace sets):

Closure $t \in T^\dagger$

$$\frac{t \in T}{t \in T^\dagger} \qquad \frac{st \in T^\dagger}{s(\sigma, \sigma)t \in T^\dagger} \qquad \frac{s(\sigma, \sigma')(\sigma', o)t \in T^\dagger}{s(\sigma, o)t \in T^\dagger}$$

$$\frac{}{(\lightning, \lightning) \in T^\dagger} \qquad \frac{t(\sigma, \lightning) \in T^\dagger}{t(\sigma, \sigma')u \in T^\dagger}$$

The unshaded rules for $\dagger$ appeared in Brookes's original paper. To them, we add two rules concerning faults. The first captures the fact

Denotational semantics of specifications $\quad [\![\varphi]\!]^\rho \subseteq \textsc{Trace}$

$$
\begin{aligned}
[\![\varphi;\psi]\!]^\rho &\triangleq ([\![\varphi]\!]^\rho ; [\![\psi]\!]^\rho)^\dagger \\
[\![\varphi \parallel \psi]\!]^\rho &\triangleq ([\![\varphi]\!]^\rho \parallel [\![\psi]\!]^\rho)^\dagger \\
[\![\varphi \vee \psi]\!]^\rho &\triangleq [\![\varphi]\!]^\rho \cup [\![\psi]\!]^\rho \\
[\![\exists x.\varphi]\!]^\rho &\triangleq \textstyle\bigcup_v [\![\varphi]\!]^{\rho[x\mapsto v]} \\
[\![\mathsf{let}\ f = F\ \mathsf{in}\ \psi]\!]^\rho &\triangleq [\![\psi]\!]^{\rho[f\mapsto [\![F]\!]^\rho]} \\
[\![F(e)]\!]^\rho &\triangleq [\![F]\!]^\rho\,([\![e]\!]^\rho) \\
[\![\mu X.\varphi]\!]^\rho &\triangleq \textstyle\bigcap\{T : T^\dagger = T,\ [\![\varphi]\!]^{\rho[X\mapsto T]} \subseteq T\} \\
[\![X]\!]^\rho &\triangleq \rho(X) \\
[\![\langle\forall\overline{x} : p,\ q\rangle]\!]^\rho &\triangleq \mathsf{act}(\rho(p), \rho(q))^\dagger \\
[\![\{p\}]\!]^\rho &\triangleq \{(\sigma,\sigma) \ :\ \sigma \in [\![p * \mathsf{true}]\!]^\rho\}^\dagger \\
&\quad\ \cup\ \{(\sigma,\lightning) \ :\ \sigma \notin [\![p * \mathsf{true}]\!]^\rho\}^\dagger
\end{aligned}
$$

Procedures:

$$[\![f]\!]^\rho \triangleq \rho(f) \qquad [\![\lambda x.\varphi]\!]^\rho \triangleq \lambda v.\,[\![\varphi]\!]^{\rho[x\mapsto v]}$$

Figure 2.

that the environment of a specification might cause a fault at any time. The second reflects that faulting on the part of a specification is *permissive*, so a specification that faults after some interactions t can be implemented by one that continues without faulting after t.

The reason $(\lightning,\lightning)$ steps are important is to handle cases like $(\mu X.X) \parallel \mathsf{abort}$. Without the $(\lightning,\lightning)$ steps, $\mathcal{O}[\![(\mu X.X)]\!]$ would be empty, but the semantics of the composition is nonempty. The effect of including $(\lightning,\lightning)$ in the closure is that every finite prefix of the behavior of a specification is included in its set of traces, but with the marker $(\lightning,\lightning)$ at the end signifying that the specification was terminated early by a fault on the part of the environment.

With those preliminaries out of the way, the denotational semantics is straightforward. Sequential composition is concatenation and parallel composition is nondeterministic interleaving. One caveat: when concatenating traces, a fault on the left wipes out everything on the right, since faulting causes early termination: $t(o,\lightning); u = t(o,\lightning)$. This rule applies to both sequential and parallel composition. Recursion is defined using the Tarskian least-fixed point over closed sets of traces; the order on trace sets is set inclusion. Disjunction and existential quantification are given by least upper bounds according to that ordering. Here, environments ρ map variables x to values v, specification variables X to closed sets of traces T, and procedure variables f to functions $\textsc{Val} \rightarrow 2^{\textsc{Trace}}$. Environments are ordered pointwise (over the subset order on closed sets of traces), leading to the following lemma.

Lemma 1. For each φ, the function $[\![\varphi]\!]$ from environments to trace sets is monotonic.

We connect the denotational semantics to refinement in two steps. First, we show that the denotational semantics gives the sames trace sets as the operational semantics, modulo $\dagger$-closure:

Lemma 2. If φ is a closed specification then $\mathcal{O}[\![\varphi]\!]^\dagger = [\![\varphi]\!]^\emptyset$.

This lemma is proved separately in each direction; the $\subseteq$ direction goes by induction on the rules defining $\mathcal{O}[\![-]\!]$, while $\supseteq$ goes by induction on the structure of φ.

We define a denotational version of refinement, and prove that it soundly approximates the operational version ("adequacy"):

Definition 1. $\varphi \sqsubseteq_{\mathsf{den}} \psi$ iff for all closing ρ, $[\![\varphi]\!]^\rho \subseteq [\![\psi]\!]^\rho$.

Theorem 1 (Adequacy)**.** If $\varphi \sqsubseteq_{\mathsf{den}} \psi$ then $\varphi \sqsubseteq_{\mathsf{op}} \psi$.

Some laws of refinement $\quad \varphi \sqsubseteq \psi$

$$\mathsf{miracle} \sqsubseteq \varphi \sqsubseteq \mathsf{abort} \qquad \varphi[e/x] \sqsubseteq \exists x.\varphi \sqsubseteq \varphi$$

$$\varphi \vee \varphi \sqsubseteq \varphi \sqsubseteq \varphi \vee \psi \qquad \mathsf{skip};\varphi \equiv \varphi \equiv \varphi;\mathsf{skip}$$

DstL	$(\varphi_1 \vee \varphi_2);\psi$	$\equiv$	$\varphi_1;\psi \vee \varphi_2;\psi$
DstR	$\psi;(\varphi_1 \vee \varphi_2)$	$\equiv$	$\psi;\varphi_1 \vee \psi;\varphi_2$
Str1	$\exists x.\varphi;\psi$	$\equiv$	$\varphi;(\exists x.\psi)$
Str2	$\exists x.\,\langle\forall\overline{y} : p,\ q\rangle$	$\sqsubseteq$	$\langle\forall\overline{y} : p,\ \exists x.q\rangle$
Frm	$\langle\forall\overline{x} : p,\ q\rangle$	$\sqsubseteq$	$\langle\forall\overline{x} : p * r,\ q * r\rangle$
Ext	$\langle\forall\overline{x} : p,\ p\rangle$	$\equiv$	$\{\exists\overline{x}.p\}$ (p exact)
Idm1	$\{p\};\{p\}$	$\equiv$	$\{p\}$
Idm2	$\{\exists\overline{x}.p\};\langle\forall\overline{x} : p,\ q\rangle$	$\equiv$	$\langle\forall\overline{x} : p,\ q\rangle$
Asm	$\langle\forall\overline{x} : p,\ q \wedge r\rangle$	$\equiv$	$\langle\forall\overline{x} : p,\ q\rangle ; [r]$ (r pure)

Ind $\dfrac{\varphi[\psi/X] \sqsubseteq \psi}{\mu X.\varphi \sqsubseteq \psi}$ $\qquad$ Csq1 $\dfrac{\forall\overline{x}.\ p \Rightarrow p' \qquad \forall\overline{x}.\ q' \Rightarrow q}{\langle\forall\overline{x} : p',\ q'\rangle \sqsubseteq \langle\forall\overline{x} : p,\ q\rangle}$ $\qquad$ Csq2 $\dfrac{q \Rightarrow p}{\{p\} \sqsubseteq \{q\}}$

NB: syntax appearing both in and outside a binder for x in a refinement (as in $\exists x.\varphi \sqsubseteq \varphi$) cannot mention x.

Figure 3.

Proof. Suppose $\varphi \sqsubseteq_{\mathsf{den}} \psi$. Let C be a specification context that closes φ and ψ. By the monotonicity of the semantics, one can show that $[\![C[\varphi]]\!]^\emptyset \subseteq [\![C[\psi]]\!]^\emptyset$. By Lemma 2, $\mathcal{O}[\![C[\varphi]]\!]^\dagger \subseteq \mathcal{O}[\![C[\psi]]\!]^\dagger$. It follows that if $C[\varphi], \sigma \lightning$ then $C[\psi], \sigma \lightning$, and that if $C[\varphi], \sigma \Downarrow$ then either $C[\psi], \sigma \lightning$ or $C[\psi], \sigma \Downarrow$. $\square$

4. Refinement: proof theory

With the denotational semantics in hand, it is easy to prove a number of basic refinement laws. These laws will be powerful enough to verify a basic nonblocking counter (§4.1), but to tackle more advanced examples we will need to employ ownership-based reasoning, the subject of §5.

We write $\sqsubseteq$ for axiomatic refinement, which is justified in terms of $\sqsubseteq_{\mathsf{den}}$, and we write $\equiv$ when the refinement goes in both directions. The benefit of the setup in the previous two sections is that *axiomatic refinement is a congruence*—which is what enables us to verify implementations in a stepwise, compositional manner.

Many of the rules in Figure 3 are familiar. The top group comes from first-order and Hoare logic; we leave those rules unlabeled and use them freely. The two Dst rules, giving the interaction between nondeterminism and sequencing, are standard for a linear-time process calculus [29]. Ind is standard fixpoint induction. Frm is the frame rule from separation logic, capturing the locality of actions. Csq1 is the consequence rule of Hoare logic.

The less familiar rules are still largely straightforward. Ext provides an important case where actions and assertions are equivalent: on *exact* predicates, which are satisfied by exactly one heap, and hence are deterministic as postconditions. The Str rules allow us to manipulate quantifier structure in a way reminiscent of scope extrusion in the π-calculus [25]; like the Dst rules, they express that the semantics is insensitive to *when* a nondeterministic choice is made. The Idm rules express the idempotence of assertions—recall that the precondition of an action acts as a kind of assertion. Asm allows us to move a guard into or out of a postcondition when that guard is *pure* (does not use emp or $\mapsto$). Csq2 tells us that assertions are antitonic, which follows from the permissive nature of faulting.

Theorem 2. The laws are sound: if $\varphi \sqsubseteq \psi$ then $\varphi \sqsubseteq_{\mathsf{op}} \psi$.

Proof. We prove soundness using the denotational semantics: we show that $\varphi \sqsubseteq \psi$ implies $\varphi \sqsubseteq_{\mathsf{den}} \psi$, which by Theorem 1 (adequacy) implies $\varphi \sqsubseteq_{\mathsf{op}} \psi$; most laws are very easy to show this way. The only nontrivial case, IND, uses the Knaster-Tarski fixpoint theorem in the standard way. □

As a simple illustration of the proof rules, we have:

Lemma 3.

$$\begin{array}{rll} & & \mathsf{get}(a, \mathit{ret}) \\ \text{definition} & \equiv & \langle \forall x : a \mapsto x,\ a \mapsto x \wedge x = \mathit{ret} \rangle \\ \text{CSQ}_1 & \sqsubseteq & \langle \forall x : a \mapsto x,\ a \mapsto x \rangle \\ \text{EXT} & \sqsubseteq & \{a \mapsto -\} \end{array}$$

This lemma shows that we can forget (abstract away) the constraint that get places on its out-parameter, allowing it to vary freely. But we cannot forget that $\mathsf{get}(a, \mathit{ret})$ faults when a is unallocated.

4.1 Example: a nonblocking counter

We now return to the example of an atomic counter:

$$\begin{array}{rcl} \mathsf{inc}(c,\ \mathit{ret}) & \triangleq & \langle \forall x : c \mapsto x,\ c \mapsto x + 1 \wedge \mathit{ret} = x \rangle \\ \mathsf{inc}'(c, \mathit{ret}) & \triangleq & \mu X.\ \exists t.\mathsf{get}(c, t); \\ & & \qquad \exists b.\mathsf{cas}(c, t, t+1, b); \\ & & \qquad \textbf{if } b = 1 \textbf{ then } [\mathit{ret} = t] \textbf{ else } X \end{array}$$

To show $\mathsf{inc}' \sqsubseteq \mathsf{inc}$, we first prove some useful lemmas about optimistic concurrency:

Lemma 4.

$$\begin{array}{rl} & \mathsf{cas}(a, t, e, b); [b = 1] \\ \text{def} \equiv & \left\langle \forall x : a \mapsto x,\ \begin{array}{r} (x \neq t \wedge b = 0 \wedge a \mapsto x) \\ \vee\, (x = t \wedge b = 1 \wedge a \mapsto e) \end{array} \right\rangle ; [b = 1] \\ \text{ASM} \equiv & \left\langle \forall x : a \mapsto x,\ \left(\begin{array}{r} (x \neq t \wedge b = 0 \wedge a \mapsto x) \\ \vee\, (x = t \wedge b = 1 \wedge a \mapsto e) \end{array} \right) \wedge b = 1 \right\rangle \\ \text{CSQ}_1 \sqsubseteq & \langle \forall x : a \mapsto x,\ a \mapsto e \wedge x = t \rangle \end{array}$$

Lemma 5. $\mathsf{cas}(a, t, e, b); [b \neq 1] \sqsubseteq \{a \mapsto -\}$.

Proof. Similar. □

Corollary 1.

$$\begin{array}{l} \mu X.\exists t.\mathsf{get}(a,t); \varphi; \\ \quad \exists b.\mathsf{cas}(a, t, e, b); \\ \quad \textbf{if } b = 1 \textbf{ then } \psi \\ \qquad\qquad \textbf{else } X \end{array} \sqsubseteq \begin{array}{l} \mu X.\exists t.\mathsf{get}(a,t); \varphi; \\ \left(\begin{array}{l} \left\langle \forall x : \begin{array}{l} a \mapsto x, \\ a \mapsto e \wedge x = t \end{array} \right\rangle ; \psi \\ \vee\, \{a \mapsto -\}; X \end{array} \right) \end{array}$$

Proof. Expand **if**, apply DSTR, and use Lemmas 4, 5. □

Lemma 6 (Optimism).

$$\begin{array}{l} \mu X.\exists t.\mathsf{get}(a,t); \varphi; \\ \quad \exists b.\mathsf{cas}(a, t, e, b); \\ \quad \textbf{if } b = 1 \textbf{ then } \psi \\ \qquad\qquad \textbf{else } X \end{array} \sqsubseteq \begin{array}{l} (\exists t.\mathsf{get}(a,t); \varphi)^*; \\ \exists t.\mathsf{get}(a,t); \varphi; \\ \langle \forall x : a \mapsto x,\ a \mapsto e \wedge x = t \rangle ; \psi \end{array}$$

where θ^* is shorthand for $\mu X.\mathsf{skip} \vee \theta; X$. Notice, too, that the scope of quantifiers continues over line breaks. The specification on the left captures a typical optimistic, nonblocking algorithm: take a snapshot of a cell a, do some work φ, and update a if it has not changed; otherwise, loop. The specification on the right characterizes the (partial correctness) effect of the algorithm: it performs some number of unsuccessful loops, and then updates a.

Proof. Apply Corollary 1. At a high level, the result follows by induction, using IDM_2 to remove assertions $\{a \mapsto -\}$. □

Applying Lemma 6 to inc' (letting φ be skip, which we drop), we have:

$$\begin{array}{rl} & \mathsf{inc}'(c, \mathit{ret}) \\ 1 \sqsubseteq & (\exists t.\mathsf{get}(c,t))^*; \\ & \quad \exists t.\mathsf{get}(c,t); \langle \forall x : c \mapsto x,\ c \mapsto x + 1 \wedge x = t \rangle ; [\mathit{ret} = t] \\ 2 \sqsubseteq & (\exists t.\{c \mapsto -\})^*; \\ & \quad \exists t.\{c \mapsto -\}; \langle \forall x : c \mapsto x,\ c \mapsto x + 1 \wedge x = t \rangle ; [\mathit{ret} = t] \\ 3 \sqsubseteq & \exists t.\{c \mapsto -\}; \langle \forall x : c \mapsto x,\ c \mapsto x + 1 \wedge x = t \rangle ; [\mathit{ret} = t] \\ 4 \sqsubseteq & \exists t.\ \langle \forall x : c \mapsto x,\ c \mapsto x + 1 \wedge x = t \rangle ; [\mathit{ret} = t] \\ 5 \sqsubseteq & \exists t.\ \langle \forall x : c \mapsto x,\ c \mapsto x + 1 \wedge \mathit{ret} = x \rangle \\ 6 \sqsubseteq & \langle \forall x : c \mapsto x,\ c \mapsto x + 1 \wedge \mathit{ret} = x \rangle \end{array}$$

Step (1) is the application of Lemma 6. In step (2), we abstract away the gets (the snapshots) using Lemma 3. In (3), we remove the first existential, extrude the remaining existential (STR_1) and apply IDM_2 inductively to coalesce the assertions; (4) applies IDM_1 to remove the remaining assertion; (5) applies ASM and CSQ_1; (6) removes the remaining existential.

The abstraction of get in step (2) is reminiscent of havoc abstraction [5], and it illustrates that the snapshots are not necessary for the safety of the algorithm (though essential for liveness).

Notice that we do not give and did not use any rules for reasoning about parallel composition. We certainly could give such rules (*e.g.*, an expansion law [18]), but that would be beside the point. Our aim is to reason about concurrent objects, which are defined by *sequential* methods that clients may choose to execute in parallel. Having proved the refinement, we can conclude that even for a concurrent client $C[-]$ we have $C[\mathsf{inc}'] \sqsubseteq C[\mathsf{inc}]$.

5. Ownership

In the previous section, we were able to reason about the non-blocking counter because it possesses a very helpful property: it works correctly *regardless of interference*. No matter what concurrent reads and writes occur to the counter, the inc' method will only modify the counter by atomically incrementing it. Such an implementation is possible because a counter can be represented in a single cell of memory, and so cas can be used to operate on the entire data structure at once. For more complex data structures, such as the stack we will study in §6, this will not be the case; such data structures cannot cope with arbitrary interference.

In this section, we will develop an ownership discipline that will enable reasoning about (lack of) interference. We will leverage the denotational semantics to give a meaning to, and find the consequences of, the ownership discipline. The resulting laws give voice to the key claims of the paper: atomicity is relative to ownership, and interference is modularized by ownership.

5.1 The discipline

The ownership discipline we have in mind is tied to the notion of a *concurrent object*, which is given by a collection of methods, one of which is a constructor. For example, imagine a counter that supported both incrementing and decrementing:

$$\begin{array}{l} \textbf{let } \mathsf{newcnt}(\mathit{ret}) = \mathsf{new}(0, \mathit{ret}) \textbf{ in} \\ \textbf{let } \mathsf{inc}(\ell,\ \mathit{ret}) = \cdots \textbf{ in} \\ \textbf{let } \mathsf{dec}(\ell,\ \mathit{ret}) = \cdots \textbf{ in } \varphi \end{array}$$

Intuitively, the representation of a counter can be described by a simple predicate: $\ell \mapsto x$. Notice that this predicate is specific to a counter located at address ℓ and with value x. A client

$$\varphi = \exists a.\mathsf{newcnt}(a); \exists b.\mathsf{newcnt}(b)$$

that called newcnt twice would expect to be left with a subheap satisfying $a \mapsto 0 * b \mapsto 0$.

More complex data structures are described by more complex predicates. Consider the specification of a thread-safe stack:

$$\begin{aligned}
&\textsf{let newStk}(ret) = \textsf{new}(0, ret)\ \textsf{in}\\
&\textsf{let push}(\ell, x) = \left\langle \forall h : \begin{array}{c}\ell \mapsto h,\\ \exists h'.\,\ell \mapsto h' * h' \mapsto (x, h)\end{array} \right\rangle\ \textsf{in}\\
&\textsf{let pop}(\ell, ret) = \left\langle \forall h, h', x : \begin{array}{c}\ell \mapsto h\\ * h \mapsto (x, h')\end{array}, \begin{array}{c}\ell \mapsto h'\\ * h \mapsto (x, h')\\ \wedge\ ret = x\end{array} \right\rangle\\
&\textsf{in}\ \varphi
\end{aligned}$$

In this representation, an instance of a stack consists of at least a memory cell s which points to the head of the stack (0 if the stack is empty). The contents of the stack is given by a linked list, which can be described by the following recursive predicate:

$$\begin{aligned}
\mathit{list}(\ell, \epsilon) &\triangleq \ell = 0\\
\mathit{list}(\ell, x \cdot xs) &\triangleq \exists \ell'.\ell \mapsto (x, \ell') * \mathit{list}(\ell', xs)
\end{aligned}$$

The second parameter to *list* is a sequence of list items; this sequence is "abstract" in the sense that it exists only at the level of the logic, not as a value in a program. Altogether, a stack located at ℓ with abstract contents x is described by the predicate $\exists a.\ \ell \mapsto a * \mathit{list}(a, x)$.

In general, the memory belonging to an instance of a concurrent object is described by a predicate $p[\ell, x]$ with free variables ℓ and x. The variable ℓ gives the location of the object, while x gives its abstract value. The predicate $\exists x.p[\ell, x]$ then describes a heap that contains an object instance at ℓ, with unknown contents. We call this latter predicate the *representation invariant* for a concurrent object, and use the metavariable I to designate such predicates. We introduce a new metavariable not just as a mnemonic, but also because we restrict representation invariants to be *precise*. A predicate is precise if, for every heap σ, there is at most one way to split $\sigma = \sigma_1 \uplus \sigma_2$ such that σ_1 satisfies the predicate. Thus, precise predicates serve to pick out ("fence" [7]) precisely the region of memory relevant to an object instance. For example, the invariant $I[\ell] = \exists a.\exists x.\ell \mapsto a * \mathit{list}(a, x)$ in some sense "discovers" the linked list associated with a stack, whatever its contents may be.

Our ownership discipline works as follows: a concurrent object is given (in the logic) a representation invariant $I[\ell]$ parameterized by location ℓ; an object instance at ℓ consists of the subheap described by $I[\ell]$. Clients may not access these subheaps directly, but must invoke methods of the object instead. Each method is parameterized by a location ℓ of the object to operate on, and is given access only to the subheap described by $I[\ell]$. Since multiple methods may be invoked on the same instance concurrently, this memory is shared between invocations. But because the object's methods are the *only* code with access to this memory, we may assume that any concurrent interference is due to one of these methods.

When a method begins executing, its view of the heap consists solely of some object instance $I[\ell]$. As it executes, the method may in addition allocate private memory, which is initially free from interference. If, however, the private memory is made reachable from the object instance, so that it falls into the region described by $I[\ell]$, it at that point becomes shared, and subject to interference. An implementation of push, for example, will first allocate a private linked list node, and only later actually link it into the list. Conversely, memory unlinked from the object instance becomes private to the method.

5.2 Fenced refinement

Now for the punchline: our ownership discipline enables partly-sequential reasoning about method bodies, through *fenced refinement* $I, \theta \vdash \varphi \sqsubseteq \psi$. As above, I describes a specific object instance; we leave the location ℓ implicit. Fenced refinement says that φ refines ψ under the assumption that all memory is either part of the shared instance described by I, or private. Moreover, interference on the shared memory is bounded by the specification θ (the "rely" [12]). Here are the key rules:

Some laws of fenced refinement $\qquad I, \theta \vdash \varphi \sqsubseteq \psi$

INV
$$I, \theta \vdash \{I\} \equiv \textsf{skip}$$

LIFT
$$\frac{\varphi \sqsubseteq \psi}{I, \theta \vdash \varphi \sqsubseteq \psi}$$

SEQL
$$I, \theta \vdash \langle \forall \overline{x} : p,\ q \rangle\ ; \langle \forall \overline{x} : q * p',\ r \rangle \sqsubseteq \{I * \exists \overline{x}.p\}; \langle \forall \overline{x} : p * p',\ r \rangle$$

STAB
$$\frac{\theta \sqsubseteq \langle \forall \overline{x} : q,\ q \rangle}{I, \theta \vdash \langle \forall \overline{x} : p,\ q \rangle\ ; \{\exists \overline{x}.q\} \sqsubseteq \langle \forall \overline{x} : p,\ q \rangle}$$

INV expresses that the representation invariant I always holds, so asserting it will always succeed. We check that the method itself maintains the invariant elsewhere, in the DATA$_2$ rule.

LIFT reflects the fact that fenced refinement is more permissive than standard refinement.

In fenced refinement, any data that is not part of the data structure instance fenced by I is private, and hence can be reasoned about sequentially. Suppose that, at some point, we know that $I * p$; that is, our view of the heap includes both a shared object instance described by I, and some other memory described by p. By our ownership discipline, we know that p is private. In this case, the execution of an action like $\langle p,\ q \rangle$ will *not* be visible to other threads, because it is operating on private memory. The SEQ rules permit atomicity abstraction: two sequenced atomic actions can be combined if one of them only operates on private data. We give one rule, SEQL, which combines two actions when the first (the Left) is unobservable. Notice that SEQL introduces the assertion $I * \exists \overline{x}.p$ as a verification condition for showing that the data operated on by the first action really is private. We omit the similar SEQR rule.

Finally, STAB allows as assertion $\{q\}$ to be removed if it is *stably* satisfied after an action. That is, the predicate q must be established by an action, and once established, must be maintained under any interference θ.

In addition to those rules, fenced refinement is also nearly a congruence: if $I, \theta \vdash \varphi \sqsubseteq \psi$ then $I, \theta \vdash C[\varphi] \sqsubseteq C[\psi]$ for any context C that does not contain parallel composition. It is not a congruence for parallel composition because of the sequential reasoning it permits on private data. Since we use fenced refinement only to reason about the method bodies implementing a concurrent object—which we assume to be sequential—this is all we need.

To give a semantics for fenced refinement, we want to *ignore* certain aspects of the denotational semantics. In some cases we throw away traces: for example, traces where the environment does not obey the rely θ should be discarded. A deeper issue is the distinction between private and shared memory. Because private memory cannot be observed or interfered with by concurrent threads, *we do not model it with a trace*. Instead, we view private memory in terms of "input-output" behavior, recording its value only at the beginning and end of a computation φ. As a consequence, sequential reasoning (*e.g.* SEQL) is valid for steps involving only private memory.

In short, the fenced semantics of method bodies is a hybrid between trace semantics and input-output relations. We thus define:

$$\text{FENCEDTRACE} \triangleq \Sigma^{\sharp} \times \text{TRACE} \times \Sigma^{\sharp}$$

A *fenced trace* contains three components: the initial state of private memory, a trace involving only the shared memory, and the final state of private memory. Suppose φ is a fragment of a method body. We calculate its fenced traces as follows:

Fenced projection $\llbracket I, \theta \vdash \varphi \rrbracket^{\rho} \subseteq \textsc{FencedTrace}$

$$\llbracket I, \theta \vdash \varphi \rrbracket^{\rho} \triangleq \left\{ (\mathrm{fst}(u),\ t',\ \mathrm{lst}(u)) \ :\ \begin{array}{l} t \uplus u \in \llbracket \varphi \rrbracket^{\rho},\ \ u \text{ seq} \\ t' \in \mathrm{rely}(\theta, I, \rho, t) \end{array} \right\}$$

where

$$\epsilon \uplus \epsilon \triangleq \epsilon \qquad (o_1, o_1')t \uplus (o_2, o_2')u \triangleq (o_1 \uplus o_2, o_1' \uplus o_2')(t \uplus u)$$

$$\frac{}{(o, o') \text{ seq}} \qquad \frac{u \text{ seq}}{(o, \mathrm{fst}(u))u \text{ seq}} \qquad \epsilon \in \mathrm{rely}(\theta, I, \rho, \epsilon)$$

$$\frac{\sigma, \rho \models I \qquad (\sigma', \mathrm{fst}(t)) \in \llbracket \theta \rrbracket^{\rho} \qquad t' \in \mathrm{rely}(\theta, I, \rho, t)}{(\sigma, \sigma')t' \in \mathrm{rely}(\theta, I, \rho, (\sigma, \sigma')t)} \qquad \frac{\sigma, \rho \models I \qquad o, \rho \not\models I}{(\sigma, \lightning) \in \mathrm{rely}(\theta, I, \rho, (\sigma, o)t)}$$

The functions $\mathrm{fst}(u)$ and $\mathrm{lst}(u)$ return the first and last heaps (or outcomes) that appear in a trace u.

Fenced projection separates each trace of φ into a part t dealing with the shared state and a part u dealing with the rest of the heap, which is presumed to be method-private. We do this by lifting $\uplus$ to traces. Notice that t and u have the same length and represent the same moves of φ; we are just splitting the heap involved in each move into a shared part and a private part.

The rely operator performs several tasks at once. First, it filters the traces t to include only those where the environment (1) maintains the invariant I and (2) obeys the rely θ. At the same time, it checks that the specification φ maintains the invariant as well, inserting faults when it does not. One effect is that the resulting trace, t', continually satisfies I, which means that is captures precisely the shared state; this shared state is unambiguous, due to the precision of I. It follows that the trace u, which carries the remaining state, contains exactly the private state. We therefore require u to be *sequential*, meaning that we filter any traces where the private data appears to have been interfered with at all.

Fenced projection gives us the fenced traces of a specification. *Fenced refinement* just compares these traces:

Semantics of fenced refinement $I, \theta \models \varphi \sqsubseteq \psi$

$$I, \theta \models \varphi \sqsubseteq \psi \quad \text{iff} \quad \forall \text{closing } \rho.\ \llbracket I, \theta \vdash \varphi \rrbracket^{\rho} \subseteq \llbracket I, \theta \vdash \psi \rrbracket^{\rho}$$

Theorem 3. The laws of fenced refinement are sound: if $I, \theta \vdash \varphi \sqsubseteq \psi$ then $I, \theta \models \varphi \sqsubseteq \psi$.

Proof. The semantics of fenced refinement was designed to make this theorem straightforward. Each law corresponds to one of the basic assumptions of fenced projection: Inv, that the invariant is satisfied; Stab, that the rely is obeyed; SeqL, that the private traces are sequential. The Lift rule expresses that fenced projection is monotonic. □

5.3 Enforcing ownership: hiding

So far, fenced refinement is just a fantasy: we have no way to deduce standard refinements from fenced refinements. To do so, we have to justify the assumptions made in fenced projection. The ownership discipline described in §5.1 is the desired policy; now we turn to the mechanism for carrying it out.

Consider the following specification:

$$\textsf{\textbf{let}}\ f(\mathit{ret}) = \langle \textsf{emp},\ \mathit{ret} \mapsto 0 \rangle\ \textsf{\textbf{in}}\ \exists x. f(x); \textsf{put}(x, 1)$$

Here we have a simple concurrent object with a constructor, f, and no methods. Its client, however, violates our ownership discipline by directly modifying an object instance, using put. If the assumptions of fenced refinement are to be met, such clients must somehow be ruled out.

Our solution is to introduce an abstraction barrier. We extend the language of specifications to include **abs** $\alpha.\varphi$, which binds the *abstraction variable* α in φ, and we likewise extend heaps to include *abstract cells* $\ell \overset{\alpha}{\mapsto} e$. Each location in the heap is either concrete ($\mapsto$) or abstract ($\overset{\alpha}{\mapsto}$), so the predicate $\ell \mapsto - \wedge \ell \overset{\alpha}{\mapsto} -$ is unsatisfiable. The purpose of abstract cells is to deny clients access to concurrent objects. Revisiting the misbehaved client above, we could instead write:

$$\textsf{\textbf{abs}}\ \alpha.\textsf{\textbf{let}}\ f(\mathit{ret}) = \left\langle \textsf{emp},\ \mathit{ret} \overset{\alpha}{\mapsto} 0 \right\rangle\ \textsf{\textbf{in}}\ \exists x. f(x); \textsf{put}(x, 1)$$

In this case, the client will *fault* when attempting the put, because put operates on concrete cells, but f allocates an abstract cell.

In general, the concrete representation of an object may involve multiple memory cells. When we introduce an abstraction variable, we also have an opportunity to switch to a more abstract representation, as in the following rule (applicable when $r[\ell, -]$ is precise):

Data₁

$$\frac{\textsf{\textbf{let}}\ f_i(\ell, x) = \langle \forall y : p_i * r[\ell, e_i],\quad q_i * r[\ell, e_i'] \rangle\ \textsf{\textbf{in}}\ \varphi}{\sqsubseteq\ \textsf{\textbf{abs}}\ \alpha.\ \textsf{\textbf{let}}\ f_i(\ell, x) = \left\langle \forall y : p_i * \ell \overset{\alpha}{\mapsto} e_i,\ q_i * \ell \overset{\alpha}{\mapsto} e_i' \right\rangle\ \textsf{\textbf{in}}\ \varphi}$$

As before, the predicate $r[\ell, z]$ is meant to describe an object instance located at ℓ with abstract contents z. Notice that the client φ is unconstrained, except for the implicit constraint that α cannot appear free in it. The idea is that, in applying this abstraction rule, we swap a concrete version of a concurrent object for an abstract one. Cases where the client might have accessed a concrete object instance directly will, in the context of the abstract object, result in a fault. Since a faulting specification is permissive (§3), this means that behaviors where the client performed such an access are irrelevant for this refinement; they are masked out by the fault. On the other hand, to ultimately verify that, say, **abs** $\alpha.\varphi \sqsubseteq \langle p, q \rangle$, it will be necessary to show that the client is well-behaved as long as the precondition p is satisfied. In short: when we introduce hiding, we can assume the client is well-behaved; when we verify a full program, we must check this assumption.

We define $\llbracket \textsf{\textbf{abs}}\ \alpha.\varphi \rrbracket^{\rho}$ as follows:

$$\llbracket \textsf{\textbf{abs}}\ \alpha.\varphi \rrbracket^{\rho} \triangleq \{ s : s \uplus_{\alpha} t \in \llbracket \varphi \rrbracket^{\rho},\ t \text{ seq},\ \mathrm{fst}(t) = \emptyset \}^{\dagger}$$

The notation $s \uplus_{\alpha} t$ denotes $s \uplus t$, but is only defined when *no* heap in s contains $\overset{\alpha}{\mapsto}$ cells, and *every* heap in t consists only of $\overset{\alpha}{\mapsto}$ cells (so it is not commutative!). Thus, as in fenced refinement, we are isolating in trace t the contents of the heap specific to an abstract variable. The operator works by *projecting away* the abstract resources, making them unavailable any external environment. In addition, it only includes those traces where no interference on those resources took place, since such interference is impossible due to the projection.

While **abs** hides abstract resources, we also need a way to realize an abstract data structure by a concrete one. We do this by extending the closure operator $\dagger$, as follows:

$$\frac{s \in T^{\dagger} \qquad t \text{ seq} \qquad \mathrm{fst}(t) = \emptyset}{s \uplus t \in T^{\dagger}} \qquad \frac{s; s' \in T^{\dagger} \qquad t \text{ seq} \qquad \mathrm{fst}(t) = \emptyset \qquad \mathrm{lst}(t) \not\subseteq \sigma}{(s \uplus t); (\sigma, \lightning) \in T^{\dagger}}$$

The first rule says that an implementation may always allocate more memory than its specification requires. The constraint that $\mathrm{fst}(u) = \emptyset$ requires the memory is freshly allocated. Notice that the rule also requires the allocated memory to be free from external interference (t seq).

Why is the freshly-allocated memory free from external interference? The key insight here is that the memory is *not* present in

$$\frac{\begin{array}{c}\textsc{Data}_2\\ r[\ell,-]\text{ precise} \qquad p_i\text{ pure} \qquad r[\ell,-],\ (\bigvee\overline{\theta_i}) \vdash \varphi_i \sqsubseteq \theta_i \qquad \theta_i \sqsubseteq \langle \forall y : r[\ell,y],\ r[\ell,e_i] \wedge p_i\rangle\end{array}}{\begin{array}{l}\textbf{let } f(\ell) = \langle \mathsf{emp},\ r[\ell,e]\rangle \textbf{ in}\\ \textbf{let } g_i(\ell,x) = \varphi_i \textbf{ in } \psi\end{array} \ \sqsubseteq\ \begin{array}{l}\textbf{abs } \alpha.\textbf{let } f(\ell) = \left\langle \mathsf{emp},\ \ell \overset{\alpha}{\mapsto} e\right\rangle \textbf{ in}\\ \overline{\textbf{let } g_i(\ell,x) = \left\langle \forall y : \ell \overset{\alpha}{\mapsto} y,\ \ell \overset{\alpha}{\mapsto} e_i \wedge p_i\right\rangle} \textbf{ in } \psi\end{array}}$$

Figure 4. Rely/guarantee reasoning

one possible behavior, s, of the specification T. Therefore, the environment cannot assume the memory will be present, and, indeed, if it tries to read or modify the memory and is interleaved with s rather than $s \uplus t$, it will fault. Although we know that the environment will fault if it attempts to interfere, the structure of transition trace semantics is such that arbitrary interference is always considered possible. Thus, we include a second new closure rule that says, in the presence of interference by the environment (which will ultimately result in a fault), the implementation is allowed to do anything (and in particular, may itself immediately fault).

Of course, we cannot extend † cavalierly: we must ensure that adequacy still holds. We sketch the proof that it does in §7.

The net effect of these definitions is to protect abstracted data from its client and environment, while allowing it to be implemented in a concrete way. As we mentioned above, when we introduce an abstraction through a rule like $\textsc{Data}_1$, we cause an ill-behaved client to fault where it would have blithely accessed concrete data. Ultimately, when we verify a whole program—including the client—we show it free from faults by showing that it refines some atomic action like $\langle \emptyset,\ p\rangle$. To do this we must eventually apply abstraction elimination: **abs** $\alpha.\varphi \sqsubseteq \varphi$, which by convention requires that α not appear in φ.

5.4 Refinements from fenced refinements: $\textsc{Data}_2$

Finally, we have the $\textsc{Data}_2$ rule in Figure 4, which allows us to derive standard refinements from fenced refinements, ensuring that the assumed ownership discipline is actually followed; "ownership is in the eye of the asserter" [23].

In $\textsc{Data}_2$, we are working with a concurrent object with constructor f and methods g_i. The predicate $r[\ell, y]$ describes a concrete object instance at location ℓ with abstract contents y. As in $\textsc{Data}_1$, the abstracted version of the object works on abstract cells $\ell \overset{\alpha}{\mapsto} y$ instead.

We introduce θ_i as a midpoint between φ_i and the specification $\langle \forall y : r[\ell,y],\ r[\ell,e_i] \wedge p_i\rangle$ because we want to keep the rely $\vee\overline{\theta_i}$ as simple as possible. In particular, methods usually operate on small portions of the object, while $r[\ell,y]$ refers to the entire object instance.

The definition of **abs** ensures that the client or environment of an object cannot interfere with it. But fenced refinement also assumes that (1) methods do not violate the invariant $r[\ell,-]$ and (2) methods do not violate the rely $\vee\overline{\theta_i}$.

- The invariant is maintained because each method body φ_i is a fenced refinement $\langle \forall y : r[\ell,y],\ r[\ell,e_i] \wedge p_i\rangle$, which clearly maintains the invariant.
- The rely is never violated because each method body φ_i is a fenced refinement of θ_i, and the rely permits the behavior of any of the θ_i's.

A key feature of $\textsc{Data}_2$ is its provision for modular and dynamic rely/guarantee reasoning. It is *modular* because we have isolated the memory involved (to $r[\ell,-]$) and the code involved (each φ_i)—we do not constrain the clients ψ, nor the contexts in which the data refinement holds. It is *dynamic* because it encompasses arbitrary allocation of new data structure instances—we get rely/guarantee reasoning for each individual instance, even though we do not know how many instances the client ψ will allocate.

As given, $\textsc{Data}_2$ only applies to methods whose action on the shared state is given in a single atomic step. The rule can easily be extended to allow methods which also take an arbitrary number of steps refining $\langle \forall y : r[\ell,y],\ r[\ell,y]\rangle$, which make internal adjustments to the object instance (often known as "helping" [10]) but look like skip to the client. We will not need this for our case study below, but it is necessary for related data structures such as queues.

The soundness proof for $\textsc{Data}_2$ is sketched in §7.

6. Case study: Treiber's nonblocking stack

Using fenced refinement, we will be able to verify a version of Treiber's nonblocking stack [26]:

$$\begin{aligned}
\mathsf{newStk}(ret) &= \mathsf{new}(0, ret)\\[1em]
\mathsf{push}(\ell, x) &= \exists n.\mathsf{new}((x,0), n);\\
&\quad\ \mu X.\ \exists t.\mathsf{get}(\ell, t);\\
&\qquad\qquad \mathsf{put}_2(n, t);\\
&\qquad\qquad \exists b.\mathsf{cas}(\ell, t, n, b);\\
&\qquad\qquad \textbf{if } b = 0 \textbf{ then } X\\[1em]
\mathsf{pop}(\ell, ret) &= \mu X.\ \exists t.\mathsf{get}(\ell, t); \{t \neq 0\};\\
&\qquad\qquad \exists n.\mathsf{get}_2(t, n);\\
&\qquad\qquad \exists b.\mathsf{cas}(\ell, t, n, b);\\
&\qquad\qquad \textbf{if } b = 0 \textbf{ then } X \textbf{ else } \mathsf{get}_1(t, ret)
\end{aligned}$$

The specifications get_i and put_i operate on the ith component of pairs, *e.g.*, $\mathsf{put}_2(a, x) \triangleq \langle \forall y : a \mapsto (y,-),\ a \mapsto (y,x)\rangle$. We have simplified pop so that it asserts that the stack is nonempty.

Stacks provide two new challenges compared to counters. First, the loop in push modifies the heap *every* time it executes, by calling put_2, rather than just at a successful cas; this makes atomicity nontrivial to show. Second, pop has a potential "ABA" problem [10]: it assumes that if the head pointer ℓ is unchanged (*i.e.* equal to t at the cas), then the tail of that cell is unchanged (*i.e.* equal to n at the cas). Intuitively this assumption is justified because stack cells are never changed or deallocated once they are introduced;[2] we must make such an argument within the logic.

First, we introduce the following procedures:

$$\begin{aligned}
\mathsf{getHd}(\ell, ret) &= \langle \forall x : \ell \mapsto x,\ \ell \mapsto x \wedge ret = x\rangle\\
\mathsf{pushHd}(\ell, t, n) &= \langle \forall x : \ell \mapsto x,\ \ell \mapsto n \wedge x = t\rangle\\
\mathsf{popHd}(\ell, t, n) &= \langle \forall x : \ell \mapsto x,\ \ell \mapsto n \wedge x = t\rangle
\end{aligned}$$

We apply Lemma 6 (Optimism) to push and pop:[3]

$$\begin{aligned}
\mathsf{push}(\ell, x) \sqsubseteq\ & \exists n.\mathsf{new}((x,0), n);\\
& (\exists t.\mathsf{getHd}(\ell, t); \mathsf{put}_2(n, t))^*;\\
& \exists t.\mathsf{getHd}(\ell, t); \mathsf{put}_2(n, t);\\
& \mathsf{pushHd}(\ell, t, n)
\end{aligned}$$

[2] We assume garbage collection here, but we can also verify a stack that manages its own memory using hazard pointers [16].

[3] Technically, for pop, we need a slight variant of the lemma allowing the existential $\exists n$ to scope over the cas.

$$\begin{aligned}\mathsf{pop}(\ell, ret) \sqsubseteq\ & (\exists t.\mathsf{getHd}(\ell, t); \{t \neq 0\}; \exists n.\mathsf{get}_2(t, n))^*;\\ & \exists t.\mathsf{getHd}(\ell, t); \{t \neq 0\}; \exists n.\mathsf{get}_2(t, n);\\ & \mathsf{popHd}(\ell, t, n); \mathsf{get}_1(t, ret)\end{aligned}$$

Notice that pop, after recording a pointer t to the current head node and checking that it is non-null, attempts to read the *tail* of that node (using get_2). In a sequential setting this would be unproblematic; in our concurrent setting, we must worry about interference. What if, between taking the snapshot t and getting its tail, the node t was popped from the stack, or worse, deallocated? Clearly the push and pop methods will give no such interference, but we must find an appropriate representation invariant I and interference description θ to explain that to the logic.

It turns out to be slightly tricky to formulate an appropriate representation invariant, because part of what we want to assert—that cells, even when popped, are neither altered nor deallocated—can involve memory that is no longer reachable from the head of the stack. In order to state the invariant, we need some way of remembering the addresses of cells which *used* to be part of the stack, but no longer are. To do this, we will introduce an internal abstract value α which caries a "ghost" parameter A, using DATA$_1$:

$$\begin{aligned}\mathsf{getHd}(\ell, ret) &= \left\langle \forall x, A : \begin{array}{l} \ell \overset{\alpha}{\mapsto} (x, A), \\ \ell \overset{\alpha}{\mapsto} (x, A) \wedge ret = x \end{array} \right\rangle \\ \mathsf{pushHd}(\ell, t, n) &= \left\langle \forall x, A : \begin{array}{l} \ell \overset{\alpha}{\mapsto} (x, A), \\ \ell \overset{\alpha}{\mapsto} (n, A) \wedge x = t \end{array} \right\rangle \\ \mathsf{popHd}(\ell, t, n) &= \left\langle \forall x, A : \begin{array}{l} \ell \overset{\alpha}{\mapsto} (x, A), \\ \ell \overset{\alpha}{\mapsto} (n, x \cdot A) \wedge x = t \end{array} \right\rangle\end{aligned}$$

In order to apply DATA$_1$, we have used the predicate $p[\ell, (x, A)] = \ell \mapsto x$. Notice that the parameter A does not appear in the concrete predicate. The idea is that the abstract A is a sequence of addresses of popped cells, while the concrete representation of A is simply—nothing!

We can now give a representation invariant I for stacks, along with a bound on interference, θ:

$$I[\ell] \triangleq \exists n.\exists A.\ \ell \overset{\alpha}{\mapsto} (n, A) * cells(A) * \exists x.list(n, x)$$

$$\begin{aligned} cells(\epsilon) &\triangleq \mathsf{emp} \\ cells(x \cdot A) &\triangleq x \mapsto - * cells(A)\end{aligned}$$

$$\begin{aligned}\theta \triangleq &\left\langle \forall x, A : \begin{array}{l} \ell \overset{\alpha}{\mapsto} (x, A), \\ \exists n.\ \ell \overset{\alpha}{\mapsto} (n, A) * n \mapsto (-, x) \end{array} \right\rangle \\ \vee &\left\langle \forall x, x_1, x_2, A : \begin{array}{l} \ell \overset{\alpha}{\mapsto} (x, A) * x \mapsto (x_1, x_2), \\ \ell \overset{\alpha}{\mapsto} (x_2, x \cdot A) * x \mapsto (x_1, x_2) \end{array} \right\rangle\end{aligned}$$

Notice that θ describes interference only in terms of the effect on the head of the stack. Implicitly (by framing) this means that the rest of the stack described by I—including the heap cells given by A—remain invariant under interference.

6.1 Proving push

We verify push using the refinements in Figure 5, which are fenced by I and θ. Step (1) just restates what we have done already. In step (2), we abstract getHd into the assertion $\{\ell \overset{\alpha}{\mapsto} (-, -)\}$ (as in §4.1), and then apply INV to abstract these assertions to skip (because they are implied by the invariant). In steps (3) and (5) we use SEQL to merge the calls to new and put_2 into a single atomic action, new; this introduces an assertion $\{I * \mathsf{emp}\}$, again implied by the invariant. Step (4) is just STR$_1$. Step (6) again applies SEQL, again producing a trivial assertion which we remove with INV. Step (7) applies STR$_2$, and step (8) is by CSQ$_1$.

$\mathsf{push}(\ell, x)$

1 $\sqsubseteq \exists n.\mathsf{new}((x, 0), n);$ $(\exists t.\mathsf{getHd}(\ell, t); \mathsf{put}_2(n, t))^*;$ $\exists t.\mathsf{getHd}(\ell, t); \mathsf{put}_2(n, t); \mathsf{pushHd}(\ell, t, n)$

2 $\sqsubseteq \exists n.\mathsf{new}((x, 0), n); (\exists t.\mathsf{put}_2(n, t))^*;$ $\exists t.\mathsf{put}_2(n, t); \mathsf{pushHd}(\ell, t, n)$

3 $\sqsubseteq \exists n.\mathsf{new}((x, -), n); \exists t.\mathsf{put}_2(n, t); \mathsf{pushHd}(\ell, t, n)$

4 $\sqsubseteq \exists n.\exists t.\mathsf{new}((x, -), n); \mathsf{put}_2(n, t); \mathsf{pushHd}(\ell, t, n)$

5 $\sqsubseteq \exists n.\exists t.\mathsf{new}((x, t), n); \mathsf{pushHd}(\ell, t, n)$

6 $\sqsubseteq \exists n.\exists t. \left\langle \forall z, A : \begin{array}{l} \ell \overset{\alpha}{\mapsto} (z, A), \\ \ell \overset{\alpha}{\mapsto} (n, A) * n \mapsto (x, t) \wedge z = t \end{array} \right\rangle$

7 $\sqsubseteq \left\langle \forall z, A : \begin{array}{l} \ell \overset{\alpha}{\mapsto} (z, A), \\ \exists n.\exists t.\ell \overset{\alpha}{\mapsto} (n, A) * n \mapsto (x, t) \wedge z = t \end{array} \right\rangle$

8 $\sqsubseteq \left\langle \forall z, A : \begin{array}{l} \ell \overset{\alpha}{\mapsto} (z, A), \\ \exists n.\ell \overset{\alpha}{\mapsto} (n, A) * n \mapsto (x, z) \end{array} \right\rangle$

Figure 5. High-level proof of push

6.2 Proving pop

We do not give the full proof of pop, but instead we show one important step in very careful detail (Figure 6). Recall that in pop, we take *two* snapshots every time we loop: one of the address of the current head node, and one of its tail. We will show that, although these snapshots take place at distinct points in time, they may as well have happened in a single atomic step. The justification is that no interference could change the tail between the two steps.

We have labeled each step with the rule it applies, except for the step (*), which applies the derived rule $\langle \forall \overline{x} : p, q \rangle \sqsubseteq \langle \forall \overline{x} : p \wedge r, q \wedge r \rangle$ for r pure. This rule follows from the frame rule and CSQ$_1$, because for pure r we have $p*(r \wedge \mathsf{emp}) \iff p \wedge r$.

The proof mostly consists of structural steps which we give for illustrative purposes; in practice, one would reason with more powerful derived rules. These steps serve to introduce enough names and frame to actually say what we want to say about the snapshots. The (*) step strengthens the precondition of the second snapshot by asserting that it has a fixed value t_2. The STAB step actually demonstrates that the tail of t has a stable value; strictly speaking, it requires a use of CSQ$_2$ to strengthen the assertion so that it matches the postcondition.

7. Soundness of data abstraction

7.1 The closure operator

The $\dagger$ operator acts as a homomorphism on the space of trace sets: if $T \subseteq U$ then $T^\dagger \subseteq U^\dagger$, but not conversely. To ensure that adequacy is preserved, we must show that this homomorphism acts properly as a quotient. It suffices to show that $\dagger$ has two properties (in addition to being a closure operator):

Lemma 7 (Strength [13])**.** For each semantic operator $\otimes$, we have $T^\dagger \otimes U^\dagger \subseteq (T \otimes U)^\dagger$.

Lemma 8 (Preservation of observation)**.**

1. $(\sigma, \lightning) \in T$ iff $(\sigma, \lightning) \in T^\dagger$
2. $\exists \sigma'.(\sigma, \sigma') \in T$ iff $\exists \sigma'.(\sigma, \sigma') \in T^\dagger$

Applying induction, strength says that if we apply $\dagger$ to each clause of our denotational semantics, the result will be no larger than had we calculated the semantics without $\dagger$, and only applied it at the top level. We then use preservation of observation to tell us that

$$
\begin{array}{rll}
& \exists t.\mathsf{getHd}(\ell, t); \exists n.\mathsf{get}_2(t, n); \varphi & \\
\text{defn} & \equiv \exists t. \left\langle \forall x, A : \ell \overset{\alpha}{\mapsto} (x, A),\ \ell \overset{\alpha}{\mapsto} (x, A) \wedge t = x \right\rangle ; & \exists n. \langle \forall y_1, y_2 : t \mapsto (y_1, y_2),\ t \mapsto (y_1, y_2) \wedge y_2 = n \rangle ; \varphi \\
\textsc{Frm} & \sqsubseteq \exists t. \langle \forall x, x_1, x_2, A : p,\ p \wedge t = x \rangle ; & \exists n. \langle \forall y_1, y_2 : t \mapsto (y_1, y_2),\ t \mapsto (y_1, y_2) \wedge y_2 = n \rangle ; \varphi \\
\textsc{Csq}_1 & \sqsubseteq \exists t. \langle \forall x, x_1, x_2, A : p,\ p \wedge t = x \wedge x_2 = x_2 \rangle ; & \exists n. \langle \forall y_1, y_2 : t \mapsto (y_1, y_2),\ t \mapsto (y_1, y_2) \wedge y_2 = n \rangle ; \varphi \\
\exists\ \text{intr} & \sqsubseteq \exists t.\exists t_2. \langle \forall x, x_1, x_2, A : p,\ p \wedge t = x \wedge t_2 = x_2 \rangle ; & \exists n. \langle \forall y_1, y_2 : t \mapsto (y_1, y_2),\ t \mapsto (y_1, y_2) \wedge y_2 = n \rangle ; \varphi \\
(*) & \sqsubseteq \exists t.\exists t_2. \langle \forall x, x_1, x_2, A : p,\ p \wedge t = x \wedge t_2 = x_2 \rangle ; & \exists n. \langle \forall y_1, y_2 : t \mapsto (y_1, y_2) \wedge y_2 = t_2,\ t \mapsto (y_1, y_2) \wedge y_2 = n \wedge y_2 = t_2 \rangle ; \varphi \\
\textsc{Csq}_1 & \sqsubseteq \exists t.\exists t_2. \langle \forall x, x_1, x_2, A : p,\ p \wedge t = x \wedge t_2 = x_2 \rangle ; & \exists n. \langle \forall y_1, y_2 : t \mapsto (y_1, y_2) \wedge y_2 = t_2,\ t \mapsto (y_1, y_2) \wedge y_2 = t_2 \wedge t_2 = n \rangle ; \varphi \\
\textsc{Asm} & \equiv \exists t.\exists t_2. \langle \forall x, x_1, x_2, A : p,\ p \wedge t = x \wedge t_2 = x_2 \rangle ; & \exists n. \langle \forall y_1, y_2 : t \mapsto (y_1, y_2) \wedge y_2 = t_2,\ t \mapsto (y_1, y_2) \wedge y_2 = t_2 \rangle ; [t_2 = n]; \varphi \\
\textsc{Ext} & \equiv \exists t.\exists t_2. \langle \forall x, x_1, x_2, A : p,\ p \wedge t = x \wedge t_2 = x_2 \rangle ; & \exists n. \{t \mapsto (-, t_2)\}; [t_2 = n]; \varphi \\
\textsc{Str}_1 & \equiv \exists t.\exists t_2.\exists n. \langle \forall x, x_1, x_2, A : p,\ p \wedge t = x \wedge t_2 = x_2 \rangle ; \{t \mapsto (-, t_2)\}; [t_2 = n]; \varphi & \\
\textsc{Stab} & \equiv \exists t.\exists t_2.\exists n. \langle \forall x, x_1, x_2, A : p,\ p \wedge t = x \wedge t_2 = x_2 \rangle ; [t_2 = n]; \varphi & \\
\text{Asm} & \equiv \exists t.\exists t_2.\exists n. \langle \forall x, x_1, x_2, A : p,\ p \wedge t = x \wedge t_2 = x_2 \wedge t_2 = n \rangle ; \varphi & \\
\textsc{Csq}_1 & \sqsubseteq \exists t.\exists t_2.\exists n. \langle \forall x, x_1, x_2, A : p,\ p \wedge t = x \wedge n = x_2 \rangle ; \varphi & \\
\therefore & \sqsubseteq \exists t.\exists n. \langle \forall x, x_1, x_2, A : p,\ p \wedge t = x \wedge n = x_2 \rangle ; \varphi & \text{where } p \triangleq \ell \overset{\alpha}{\mapsto} (x, A) * x \mapsto (x_1, x_2)
\end{array}
$$

Figure 6. Detailed atomicity abstraction for pop

applying the top-level $\dagger$ to a closed specification in context does not change the basic observables we are concerned with (§3): normal termination and faulting termination.

7.2 $\textsc{Data}_2$

As with the other refinement laws, we prove $\textsc{Data}_2$ by means of the denotational model. However, unlike the other laws, this proof is nontrivial.

In order to prove the law, we first show that if the hypotheses of the law hold, then

$$\textbf{let } f(\ell) = \overline{\langle \mathsf{emp},\ r[\ell, e] \rangle \textbf{ in let } g_i(\ell, x) = \varphi_i} \textbf{ in } \psi$$

simulates

$$\textbf{let } f(\ell) = \left\langle \mathsf{emp},\ \ell \overset{\alpha}{\mapsto} (e) \right\rangle \textbf{ in}$$
$$\overline{\textbf{let } g_i(\ell, x) = \left\langle \forall y : \ell \overset{\alpha}{\mapsto} (y),\ \ell \overset{\alpha}{\mapsto} (e_i) \wedge p_i \right\rangle} \textbf{ in } \psi$$

Simulation relates the concrete traces of the first specification to the abstract traces of the second. It is a generalization of fenced refinement: instead of dealing with a single object instance, we must track the arbitrary instances that may arise as a specification executes. For each object instance, we assume that the environment obeys the rely.

We prove the simulation result by induction on the structure of the *client* ψ. The noninductive cases include method calls, which interact with the concrete objects in known ways, and client actions, which cannot interact with the concrete objects. For the latter, we use the fact that in the second specification, the concrete objects do not exist at all—they are held abstract. Thus, if the client (which does not mention α) attempts to interact with them, it will fault, which as usual is permissive.

For inductive cases, we are assured inductively that the client itself never breaks the rely.

This simulation tells us that neither the methods nor the client can break the rely condition. To prove $\textsc{Data}_2$ we introduce **abs**, which further guarantees that the environment will not interfere at all.

An important lemma for showing simulation is *locality*:

Definition 2. T is *local* if, whenever $t(\sigma_1 \uplus \sigma_2, \sigma')u \in T$ either

- $\sigma' = \sigma_1' \uplus \sigma_2$ and $t(\sigma_1, \sigma_1')u \in T$ or
- $t(\sigma_1, \lightning) \in T$.

Lemma 9 (Locality)**.** For every φ, ρ, the set $[\![\varphi]\!]^\rho$ is local (assuming we take the fixpoint μ over only local trace sets).

Locality captures the idea that if, at some point, a specification is given fewer resources to execute with it will either fault, or it did not need those resources (so they are part of the frame for that step). We use this lemma when reasoning about steps that the client takes: we know that if we remove the concrete object instances, either the client would fault (and hence was ill-behaved) or else did not modify those instances.

The details of this and other proofs can be found online at

http://www.ccs.neu.edu/home/turon/sepref/

8. Evaluation and related work

In the last several years, there has been stunning progress in the formal verification of fine-grained concurrent data structures [4, 6, 9, 27], giving logics appropriate for hand verification as well as automated verification. We have sought in this work to clarify and consolidate this literature—the linchpin for us being the connection between ownership, atomicity, and interference. Our main contribution lies in making this connection, formalizing it with a new semantics for separation logic, and formulating proof rules based on the idea. While the logic resulting from our work offers some significant new features, more experience using it is required before its practicality or applicability can be compared to other approaches.

The most closely related work is "Concurrent Abstract Predicates," (CAP, [4]), a recent paper that also seeks to modularize reasoning about interference by using ownership and separation logic. CAP takes a radically different approach toward atomicity: rather than proving linearizability or refinement, in CAP one always uses *self-stable* predicates which are invariant under internal interference—thus sidestepping atomicity issues entirely. By contrast, we have focused on the semantic issues related to both atomicity and interference, and have shown both in terms of semantics and proof rules how these issues interact. It should be possible to apply our semantic insights to explain CAP in terms of contextual refinement as we have done.

Separation logic has also been used to localize rely/guarantee reasoning in Feng's work [7], from which we borrow the "fence" terminology. However, it does not appear possible to use that technique to both localize reasoning about interference to a group of methods and also let clients make use of the methods.

The *abstract predicates* in CAP are related to Bierman and Parkinson's work [24] investigating data abstraction in a sequential separation logic setting. In particular, Bierman and Parkinson use abstract predicates whose definition is known to the data structure implementation, but opaque to the client—a form of second-order existential quantification. There is clearly a close relationship to our abstract resources, but we do not define **abs** in terms of second-order quantification, because we need the ability to introduce faults and require sequentiality. The connections between these approaches certainly merits further investigation.

The basic form of our calculus clearly bears resemblance to Elmas *et al.*'s calculus of atomic actions [5, 6]. The key idea in that work is to combine Lipton's technique of *reduction* [14] for enlarging the grain of atomicity, with *abstraction* (*e.g.* weakening a Hoare triple) on atomic actions. The authors demonstrate that the combination of techniques is extremely powerful; they were able to automate their logic and use it to verify a significant number of data structures and other programs. A significant difference between their calculus and ours is what refinement entails, semantically. For them, refinement is ultimately about the *input-output relation* of a program, where for us, it is about the reactive, trace-based semantics. The distinction comes down to this: is refinement a congruence for parallel composition? For us it is, and this means that our system as a whole is compositional. We also demonstrate that reduction is not necessary for atomicity refinement, at least for the class of examples we have considered; we instead use ownership-based reasoning. Finally, aside from these points, we have shown how to incorporate separation logic into a calculus of atomic actions, enabling cleaner reasoning about the heap.

A significant departure in our work is that we have dispensed with linearizability, which is usually taken as the basic correctness condition for the data structures we are studying [11]. Here we are influenced by Filipović *et al.* [8], who point out that "programmers expect that the behavior of their program does not change whether they use experts' data structures or less-optimized but obviously-correct data structures." The authors go on to show that, if we take refinement as our basic goal, we can view linearizability as a sound (and sometimes complete) *proof technique*. But implicit in their proof of soundness—and indeed in the definition of linearizability—is the assumption that the heap data associated with data structures is never interfered with by clients. In a setting where clients are given pointers into those data structures, this is an assumption that should be checked. In contrast, we are able to give a comprehensive model including both data structures and their clients, and make explicit assumptions about ownership.

Our use of separation logic and rely/guarantee clearly derives from Vafeiadis *et al.*'s work [28], especially Vafeiadis's groundbreaking thesis [27]. In that line of work, it was shown how to combine separation logic and rely/guarantee reasoning, which provided a basis for verifying fine-grained concurrent data structures. While their logic for proving Hoare triples was proved sound, no formal connection to linearizability or refinement was made; there is only an implicit methodology for proving certain Hoare triples about data structures and concluding that those data structures are linearizable. We show how to make that methodology explicit, and moreover compositional, by tying it to data abstraction. As a byproduct, we get a modularized account of rely/guarantee. We also eliminate any need for explicit linearization points (which sometimes require prophecy variables) or annotations separating shared from private resources.

Finally, it should be noted that our semantics owes a debt both to Brookes [2] and to Calcagno *et al.* [3].

Acknowledgements Thanks to Dan Brown, Claudio Russo and Sam Tobin-Hochstadt for feedback and discussions. The first author was supported by a grant from Microsoft Research.

References

[1] R. J. Back and J. von Wright. *Refinement calculus: a systematic introduction*. Springer, 1998.

[2] S. Brookes. Full abstraction for a shared variable parallel language. *Information and Computation*, 127(2):145–163, 1996.

[3] C. Calcagno, P. W. O'Hearn, and H. Yang. Local action and abstract separation logic. In *LICS*, pages 366–378. IEEE Computer Society, 2007.

[4] T. Dinsdale-Young, M. Dodds, P. Gardner, M. Parkinson, and V. Vafeiadis. Concurrent abstract predicates. In *ECOOP*, June 2010.

[5] T. Elmas, S. Qadeer, and S. Tasiran. A calculus of atomic actions. In *POPL*, pages 2–15. ACM, 2009.

[6] T. Elmas, S. Qadeer, A. Sezgin, O. Subasi, and S. Tasiran. Simplifying linearizability proofs with reduction and abstraction. In *TACAS*, pages 296–311. Springer, 2010.

[7] X. Feng. Local rely-guarantee reasoning. In *POPL*, pages 315–327. ACM, 2009.

[8] I. Filipović, P. O'Hearn, N. Rinetzky, and H. Yang. Abstraction for concurrent objects. In *ESOP*, pages 252–266. Springer, 2009.

[9] L. Groves. Reasoning about nonblocking concurrency. *JUCS*, 15(1): 72–111, 2009.

[10] M. Herlihy and N. Shavit. *The Art of Multiprocessor Programming*. Morgan Kaufmann, 2008.

[11] M. P. Herlihy and J. M. Wing. Linearizability: a correctness condition for concurrent objects. *TOPLAS*, 12(3):463–492, 1990.

[12] C. B. Jones. Tentative steps toward a development method for interfering programs. *TOPLAS*, 5(4):596–619, 1983.

[13] A. Kock. Strong functors and monoidal monads. *Archiv der Mathematik*, 23:113–120, 1971. ISSN 1.

[14] R. J. Lipton. Reduction: a method of proving properties of parallel programs. *Commun. ACM*, 18(12):717–721, 1975.

[15] B. Liskov and S. Zilles. Programming with abstract data types. In *Symposium on Very high level languages*, pages 50–59. ACM, 1974.

[16] M. M. Michael. Hazard pointers: Safe memory reclamation for lock-free objects. *IEEE Transactions on Parallel and Distributed Systems*, 15:491–504, 2004. ISSN 1045-9219.

[17] M. M. Michael and M. L. Scott. Nonblocking algorithms and preemption-safe locking on multiprogrammed shared memory multiprocessors. *J. Parallel Distrib. Comput.*, 51(1):1–26, 1998.

[18] R. Milner. *A Calculus of Communicating Systems*. Springer-Verlag New York, Inc., 1982.

[19] J. C. Mitchell and G. D. Plotkin. Abstract types have existential type. *TOPLAS*, 10(3):470–502, 1988.

[20] M. Moir and N. Shavit. Concurrent data structures. In *Handbook of Data Structures and Applications, D. Metha and S. Sahni Editors*, pages 47–14–47–30, 2007. Chapman and Hall/CRC Press.

[21] C. Morgan and T. Vickers. *On the refinement calculus*. Springer, 1993.

[22] J. H. Morris, Jr. Protection in programming languages. *CACM*, 16(1): 15–21, 1973.

[23] P. W. O'Hearn. Resources, concurrency, and local reasoning. *Theor. Comput. Sci.*, 375(1-3):271–307, 2007.

[24] M. Parkinson and G. Bierman. Separation logic and abstraction. *POPL*, 40(1):247–258, 2005.

[25] D. Sangiorgi and D. Walker. *Pi-Calculus: A Theory of Mobile Processes*. Cambridge University Press, 2001.

[26] R. K. Treiber. Systems programming: coping with parallelism. Technical report, Almaden Research Center, 1986.

[27] V. Vafeiadis. *Modular fine-grained concurrency verification*. PhD thesis, University of Cambridge, 2008.

[28] V. Vafeiadis and M. Parkinson. A marriage of rely/guarantee and separation logic. In *CONCUR*, pages 256–271. Springer, 2007.

[29] R. J. van Glabbeek. The linear time - branching time spectrum. In *CONCUR*, pages 278–297. Springer, 1990.

Modular Reasoning for Deterministic Parallelism

Mike Dodds
University of Cambridge, UK
md466@cl.cam.ac.uk

Suresh Jagannathan
Purdue University, Indiana
(work done while on sabbatical at Cambridge)
suresh@cs.purdue.edu

Matthew J. Parkinson
Microsoft Research Cambridge, UK
mattpark@microsoft.com

Abstract

Weaving a concurrency control protocol into a program is difficult and error-prone. One way to alleviate this burden is *deterministic parallelism*. In this well-studied approach to parallelisation, a sequential program is annotated with sections that can execute concurrently, with automatically injected control constructs used to ensure observable behaviour consistent with the original program.

This paper examines the formal specification and verification of these constructs. Our high-level specification defines the conditions necessary for correct execution; these conditions reflect program dependencies necessary to ensure deterministic behaviour. We connect the high-level specification used by clients of the library with the low-level library implementation, to prove that a client's requirements for determinism are enforced. Significantly, we can reason about program and library correctness without breaking abstraction boundaries.

To achieve this, we use *concurrent abstract predicates*, based on separation logic, to encapsulate racy behaviour in the library's implementation. To allow generic specifications of libraries that can be instantiated by client programs, we extend the logic with higher-order parameters and quantification. We show that our high-level specification abstracts the details of deterministic parallelism by verifying two different low-level implementations of the library.

Categories and Subject Descriptors D.2.4 [*Software Engineering*]: Program Verification—Correctness proofs; D.3.3 [*Programming Languages*]: Language Constructs and Features—Concurrent programming structures

General Terms Languages, Theory, Verification

Keywords Separation Logic, Concurrent Abstract Predicates, Concurrency, Futures

1. Introduction

Writing safe and efficient concurrent programs is challenging because it requires programmers not only to parcel useful units of work into threads that can be executed in parallel, but also to weave suitable concurrency control to coordinate the access of these threads to shared data. To enable effective reasoning about concurrent programs, however, it is essential to devise *modular* abstractions whose implementations can be hidden behind well-defined interfaces, allowing clients to reason about correctness in terms of abstract, rather than concrete, behaviour.

In this paper, we consider the verification of one such concurrency construct: barriers. In *deterministic* parallelization, code regions in a sequential program are executed concurrently. While the parallelized program is internally nondeterministic, control constructs are used to ensure that it exhibits the same deterministic observable behaviour as its sequential counterpart. Automatic parallelization of this kind has been well-studied for loop-intensive numerical computations. However, it is also possible to extract parallelism from irregularly structured sequential programs, where program dependencies are not readily apparent [4, 22, 25].

One way to achieve deterministic parallelism is through compiler-injected barriers [19]. We can think of these barriers as resource management operations that enforce the original sequential order (aka program dependencies). A resource could be any program variable, data structure, memory region, lock, etc. for which ownership guarantees are essential in order to enforce deterministic semantics. We assume barrier implementations are provided as part of a library.

While the intuition behind using such barriers is quite simple, there are many possible implementations. Verifying that an implementation adheres to this intuition is challenging for several reasons.

First, the patterns of signalling in a barrier implementation are highly non-local. To access a resource, a barrier must wait until all logically preceding threads have indicated that it is safe to do so; these logically preceding threads represent sources in a dependency graph. This abstract view of resource-transfer does not fit with the structure of a highly concurrent implementation, making it difficult to avoid breaking abstraction boundaries.

Furthermore, compiler optimizations might strive to identify the earliest point in a thread's execution path from where a resource is no longer required. In some cases, this means threads can release resources without ever acquiring them, so that subsequent signalling of this resource by its ancestors to its descendants can bypass it altogether. An ancestor of a thread is a computation that logically precedes it under sequential execution, and a descendent is a computation that logically follows it. Implementations of barriers must allow a thread to renounce the acquisition of a resource in this way.

Finally, barriers may have to treat reads and writes differently to ensure preservation of sequential behaviour. Although many reads can be performed concurrently, they must be sequentialized with respect to writes. Moreover, reads must be sequentialized with respect to other reads, if there is an intervening write in the sequential order.

In this paper, we show how to reason in a modular way about implementations of such barriers. To do this, we use concurrent abstract predicates [6], a technique based on separation logic that enables abstract reasoning about concurrent modules. Our logic

POPL'11, January 26–28, 2011, Austin, Texas, USA.

allows us to reason about both high-level behavioural properties and low-level implementation details. This approach allows fine-grained reasoning about behaviour, meaning that each thread can be given access to exactly the behaviour it needs to run according to the abstract specification. This behavioural reasoning is *local*, meaning even non-local descriptions of the shared state can be encapsulated and abstracted.

By leveraging concurrent abstract predicates in this way, we take a first step towards the formal specification and verification of a system for deterministic parallelism. While full verification of compiler analyses, transformations, and library implementations is our ultimate goal, we focus here on just the verification problem for libraries. We present a high-level specification for reasoning about barriers for deterministic parallelism, independent of their low-level implementation. We prove that two low-level implementations of these barriers implement our high-level specification.

In the presence of runtime thread creation and dynamic (heap-allocated) data, our specification must also be both generic and dynamic, in the sense that it must be able to construct signals at runtime that protect arbitrary resources. To support the transfer of arbitrary resources between threads, we have extended the concurrent abstract predicates approach to support higher-order predicate parameters, and higher-order quantification. The controlled resources are represented by propositional arguments to abstract predicates.

We make the following contributions:

1. We develop a high-level abstract specification for reasoning about libraries that implement barriers used to enforce deterministic parallelism. This specification can express complex behaviours such as the dynamic construction of new barriers and out-of-order signalling between threads.
2. We provide proofs that two implementations of such barriers satisfy our high-level specification. The first implementation naïvely sequentializes signalling, while the second aggregates information from logically earlier threads to avoid this bottleneck.
3. We extend prior work on concurrent abstract predicates to support higher-order parameters and quantifications, following higher-order separation logic [3]. By allowing propositional parameters, we can define predicates that take invariants as arguments, to enable abstract reasoning about resource transfer.

An extended version of this paper containing full proofs is available as a technical report [9].

2. A Specification for Deterministic Parallelism

In this section, we describe the behaviour of a library providing barriers for enforcing deterministic parallelism. We define a high-level specifications for these barriers, which allow us to prove that programs parallelised using these barriers preserve sequential behaviour.

We assume that code sections believed to be amenable for parallelization have been identified, and the program split accordingly into threads. We assume a total logical ordering on threads, such that executing the threads serially in the logical order gives the same result as the original (unparallelised) program.

Barriers are associated with resources (e.g., program variables, data structures, etc.) that are to be shared between concurrently-executing program segments. There are two sorts of barriers. A *grant* barrier notifies logically later threads that the current thread will no longer use the resource. A *wait* barrier blocks until all logically prior threads have signalled that they will no longer use the resource (i.e., have issued grants). We assume barriers have been appropriately injected by a compiler to ensure that all salient data dependencies in the original program are respected.

Consider the following function `f`; here `*` corresponds to non-deterministic choice, so `sleep(*)` waits for an arbitrary period of time:

```
f(x,y,v) {
  if(x<10) {
    y:=y+v; x:=x+v;
  } else { sleep(*); }
}
```

Suppose now that we run two instances of `f` in sequence:

```
x:=0; y:=0; f(x,y,5); f(x,y,11);
```

When this program terminates, location `x` and `y` will both hold 16.

Here, the second call to `f` may have to wait for the first call to finish its arbitrarily long `sleep`, even though the first call will do nothing more once it wakes. We parallelise this function by constructing two new functions `f1` and `f2`. We run both concurrently, but require that `f1` passes control of `x` and `y` to `f2` *before* sleeping, allowing `f2` to continue executing.

```
f1(x,y,v,i) {                f2(x,y,v,i) {
  if(x<10) {                   wait(i);
    y:=y+v; x:=x+v;            if(x<10) {
    grant(i);                    y:=y+v; x:=x+v;
  } else {                     } else {
    grant(i);                    sleep(*);
    sleep(*);                } }
} }
x:=0; y:=0; i:=newchan(); f1(x,y,5,i)||f2(x,y,11,i);
```

The barriers in `f1` and `f2` ensure that the two threads wait exactly until the resources they require can be safely modified, without violating sequential program dependencies. The correct ordering is enforced by barriers that communicate through a channel; in the example, `newchan` creates the channel `i`. Assuming the barriers are correctly implemented, the resulting behaviour is equivalent to that of the original sequential program.

2.1 Verifying a Client Program

How can we verify that our parallelised program based on `f1` and `f2` has the same specification as the original sequential program? Typically, one would incorporate signalling machinery as part of a parallelization program analysis. Clients would then reason about program behaviour using the operational semantics of the barrier implementation. Validating the correctness of parallelisation with respect to the sequential program semantics would therefore require a detailed knowledge of the barrier implementation. Any changes to the implementation could entail reproving the correctness of the parallelisation analysis.

In contrast, we reason about program behaviour in terms of abstract specifications for `grant`, `wait` and `newchan`. Such an approach has the following advantages: (1) Implementors can modify their underlying implementation and be sure that relevant program properties are preserved by the implementation, and (2) client proofs (in this case, proofs involving compiler correctness) can be completed without knowledge of the underlying implementation.

We will reason about `f1` and `f2` using separation logic. We write the following assertion to denote that `x` points to value v and `y` to value v', and that `x` and `y` are distinct: $\mathtt{x} \mapsto v * \mathtt{y} \mapsto v'$. To reason about the parallel composition of threads, we use the PAR rule of concurrent separation logic [20]:

$$\frac{\{P_1\}\ C_1\ \{Q_1\} \qquad \{P_2\}\ C_2\ \{Q_2\}}{\{P_1 * P_2\}\ C_1 \parallel C_2\ \{Q_1 * Q_2\}}\ \textsc{Par}$$

Now, to reason about `f1` and `f2`, we must be able to encode the fact that `f1` can give up access to `x` and `y` by calling `grant(i)`, while `f2` can retrieve access to them by calling `wait(i)`. To use the parallel rule, we must be able to give the two threads star-separated preconditions.

We encode these two facts by defining two predicates, fut and req, corresponding to the *future resource*, the resource that can be acquired from logically earlier threads, and the *required resource*, the resource that must be supplied to logically later threads. We read these as follows:

- $\mathsf{fut}(i, P)$ – By calling `wait` on i, the thread will acquire a resource satisfying the assertion P.
- $\mathsf{req}(i, P)$ – By calling `grant` on i when holding a resource satisfying P, the thread will lose the resource P.

These predicates are *abstract*; each instantiation of the library will define them differently; the client program knows nothing about how they are actually defined. The client only depends on an abstract specification that captures the intuitive meaning of the predicates:

$$\{\mathsf{emp}\}\ \ i := \texttt{newchan()}\ \ \{\mathsf{req}(i,P) * \mathsf{fut}(i,P)\}$$
$$\{\mathsf{fut}(i,P)\}\ \ \texttt{wait}(i)\ \ \{P\}$$
$$\{\mathsf{req}(i,P) * P\}\ \ \texttt{grant}(i)\ \ \{\mathsf{emp}\}$$

(Note that this is a weaker version of our full specification, given in Fig. 2.)

The specification of `newchan` is noteworthy. This specification is implicitly universally quantified for all assertions P, meaning that we can construct a predicate for any assertion.[1] New fut and req predicates can be constructed at run-time using `newchan`, meaning we can construct an arbitrarily large number of channels for use in the program.

Given these two predicates, we can define the following specifications for `f1` and `f2`.

$$\left\{\begin{matrix} v_1 < 10 \land x \mapsto v_1 * y \mapsto v_2 \\ * \,\mathsf{req}\left(i, \begin{matrix} x \mapsto (v_1{+}v) * \\ y \mapsto (v_2{+}v) \end{matrix}\right) \end{matrix}\right\}\ \texttt{f1}(x,y,v,i)\ \{\mathsf{emp}\}$$

$$\left\{\begin{matrix} v_3 < 10 \land \\ \mathsf{fut}(i, x \mapsto v_3 * y \mapsto v_4) \end{matrix}\right\}\ \texttt{f2}(x,y,v,i)\ \left\{\begin{matrix} x \mapsto (v_3{+}v) \\ * \, y \mapsto (v_4{+}v) \end{matrix}\right\}$$

The specification for `f1` says that the thread must supply the req predicate with the resources x and y such that the value in x is less than 10. The specification for `f2` says that the thread can receive x and y with the value in x less than 10. Fig. 1 gives sketch-proofs for these two specifications.

Given this specification, the proof for the main program goes through as follows:

```
{x ↦ _ * y ↦ _}
x:=0; y:=0; i:=newchan();
{x ↦ 0 * y ↦ 0 * req(i, x ↦ 5 * y ↦ 5) * fut(i, x ↦ 5 * y ↦ 5)}
f1(x,y,5,i) || f2(x,y,11,i) // Parallel rule.
{x ↦ 16 * y ↦ 16}
```

This proof establishes that the post-condition for the parallelised version of the program is identical to the post-condition for the original sequential version.

[1] In the full specification, we impose an extra requirement that P is *stable*, meaning invariant under concurrent interference, but this holds trivially for unshared assertions such as $x \mapsto v * y \mapsto v'$.

```
{ v1 < 10 ∧ x ↦ v1 * y ↦ v2 *
  req (i, x ↦ (v1+v) * y ↦ (v2+v)) }
if(x<10) {
  y:=y+v; x:=x+v;
  { x ↦ (v1+v) * y ↦ (v2+v) *
    req (i, x ↦ (v1+v) * y ↦ (v2+v)) }
  grant(i); // Abstract spec.
  {emp}
} else ... // Contradiction as v1 < 10.
{emp}

{v3 < 10 ∧ fut (i, x ↦ v3 * y ↦ v4)}
if(x<10) {
  wait(i); // Abstract spec.
  {v1 < 10 ∧ x ↦ v3 * y ↦ v4}
  y:=y+v; x:=x+v;
  {x ↦ (v3+v) * y ↦ (v4+v)}
} else ... // Contradiction as v3 < 10.
{x ↦ (v3+v) * y ↦ (v4+v)}
```

Figure 1. Proofs for `f1` and `f2`.

2.2 Generalising to Many Threads

Suppose we want to run many copies of the function `f` in sequence, for example over an array of values `vs`. We might have the following sequential program:

```
for(j:=0; j<max; j++){ f(x,y,vs[j]); }
```

To parallelise this program, we want each call to `f` to run in a separate thread. To do this, `f` must be modified to contain calls to *both* `grant` and `wait`. Intuitively, each call to `f` receives the resource from logically earlier threads (those invoked in earlier loop iterations) with `wait`, then releases it to logically later threads (those invoked in later loop iterations) using `grant`.

To allow many threads to access the same resource in sequence, we can construct a *chain* of channels. A `wait` barrier called on a channel waits for `grant` barriers on *all* preceding channels. We use the ordering in chains of channels to model the logical ordering between a sequence of parallelised threads.

A chain initially consists of a singleton channel constructed using `newchan`. We introduce an operation `split` that allows us to insert a new channel into the chain. The specification of `split` takes a req predicate for an existing channel and creates a new fut and req predicate representing the new channel. The new channel is inserted into the chain immediately before the existing channel. We extend the req predicate with an additional argument identifying the preceding channel in the chain. The `split` operation's specification is given in Fig. 2.

There are two more potential sources of parallelism in `f`. First, in the original transformation involving `f1` and `f2`, we did not distinguish between the resources `x` and `y`. However, we need to gain access to `y` only if we take the first branch of the conditional. Otherwise we can release `y` to logically future threads. To realise this parallelism in the new version of `f`, we use two chains of channels: one for `x`, and one for `y`.

Second, we can exploit the ability to *renounce* access to a resource without acquiring it first. In the simple specification given

SPECS:

$$\{\mathsf{fut}(i,P)\}\quad \texttt{wait}(i)\quad \{P\}$$

$$\left\{\begin{array}{l}\mathsf{req}(i,i',P)\ *\\ P\vee\begin{pmatrix}\mathsf{fut}(i',P')\\ *\ (P' \mathrel{-\!\!*} P)\end{pmatrix}\end{array}\right\}\quad \texttt{grant}(i)\quad \{\mathsf{emp}\}$$

$$\left\{\begin{array}{l}\mathsf{req}(i,i',P)\\ *\ \mathsf{stable}(Q)\end{array}\right\}\ j,j' \texttt{:=split}(i)\ \left\{\begin{array}{l}\mathsf{req}(j,j',P)\\ \quad *\ \mathsf{fut}(j',Q)\\ *\ \mathsf{req}(j',i',Q)\end{array}\right\}$$

$$\{\mathsf{stable}(P)\}\ \ i\texttt{:=newchan()}\ \left\{\begin{array}{l}\mathsf{fut}(i,P)\\ *\ \mathsf{req}(i,\mathsf{nil},P)\end{array}\right\}$$

AXIOMS:

$$\begin{pmatrix}\mathsf{fut}(i,P) * (P \mathrel{-\!\!*} (P_1 * P_2))\\ *\ \mathsf{stable}(P_1) * \mathsf{stable}(P_2)\end{pmatrix} \implies \mathsf{fut}(i,P_1) * \mathsf{fut}(i,P_2)$$

Figure 2. Full abstract specification for deterministic parallelism.

above, we can only call `grant` if we hold the required resource. However, this is often not necessary. For example, if we take the second branch of the conditional in `f`, we do not need the resource `y`. It is safe to notify future threads that `y` is available, conditional on all logically prior threads releasing it, even though the thread itself never acquired access to the resource.

Renunciation can be a powerful technique for parallelisation. Suppose a thread is logically last in a chain of threads accessing a resource. Suppose the thread takes an execution path rendering it unnecessary to ever access the resource. Without renunciation, a call to `grant` will block until all earlier threads have finished with the resource. With renunciation, the thread can pass the barrier and continue executing, irrespective of the status of logically earlier threads.

To support renunciation, we modify the specification for `grant` (see Fig. 2). This new specification allows a thread to discharge a req using the preceding fut predicate. In other words, the thread gives up the ability to ever acquire the resource, and instead forwards this capability to future threads. When the resource becomes available from logically prior threads, the *next* thread in the logical order will receive it. The assertion $(P' \mathrel{-\!\!*} P)$ is used to convert the state supplied by the future to the state required by the next thread.[2]

In Fig. 2, we also add an *axiom* to our specification. This is a fact about the library predicates that clients of the library can make use of. The axiom allows resource splitting. This axiom asserts that when a thread can receive a resource P using identifier i, access to that resource can be split between two threads, potentially before the resource is available. The assertion $(P \mathrel{-\!\!*} (P_1 * P_2))$ asserts that P can be split into P_1 and P_2.

We now define `fp`, top of Fig. 3, a version of `f` which is safe to run in parallel with many copies of itself. This function takes arguments `ix` and `iy` representing the next points in the two channel sequences, and `ixp` and `iyp` representing the immediately prior points. We verify `fp` against the following specification:

$$\left\{\begin{array}{l}\mathsf{req}(\texttt{ix},\texttt{ixp},\texttt{x}\mapsto \_) * \mathsf{fut}(\texttt{ixp},\texttt{x}\mapsto \_)\ *\\ \quad \mathsf{req}(\texttt{iy},\texttt{iyp},\texttt{y}\mapsto \_) * \mathsf{fut}(\texttt{iyp},\texttt{y}\mapsto \_)\end{array}\right\}\ \texttt{fp(...)}\ \{\mathsf{emp}\}$$

A proof of this specification is given in Fig. 4. Note that we only assert basic memory safety in this specification. We could verify more complex properties by giving the fut and req predicates stronger invariants.

Line 14 of the proof is noteworthy. There, the precondition *does not* assert that the thread has access to $\texttt{y} \mapsto \_$; rather, it asserts it can acquire access by calling `wait`. Instead of doing this, the thread renounces access to the resource, giving it up without ever having it.

[2] A resource satisfies $P' \mathrel{-\!\!*} P$ iff its combination with any disjoint resource satisfying P' produces a resource satisfying P.

```
fp(x,y,v,ix,iy,ixp,iyp) {
  wait(ixp);
  if (x<10) {
    wait(iyp);
    y:=y+v; grant(iy);
    x:=x+v; grant(ix);
  } else {
    grant(ix); grant(iy);
    sleep(*);
} }


ixf:=newchan(); iyf:=newchan();
for(j:=0; j<max; j++){
  v:=vs[j];
  ixl:=ixn; (ixf,ixn):=split(ixf);
  iyl:=iyn; (iyf,iyn):=split(iyf);
  future( fp(x,y,v,ixn,iyn,ixl,iyl) );
}
wait(ixf); wait(iyf);
```

Figure 3. Example parallelisation of `f` and a client. The `future` annotation marks the call to `fp` as a source of deterministic parallelism.

```
1  { req(ix, ixp, x ↦ _) * fut(ixp, x ↦ _) *
     req(iy, iyp, y ↦ _) * fut(iyp, y ↦ _) }
2  fp(x,y,v,ix,iy,ixp,iyp) {
3    wait(ixp);
4    { x ↦ _ * req(ix, ixp, x ↦ _) *
       req(iy, iyp, y ↦ _) * fut(iyp, y ↦ _) }
5    if (x<10) {
6      wait(iyp);
7      { x ↦ _ * y ↦ _ *
         req(ix, ixp, x ↦ _) * req(iy, iyp, y ↦ _) }
8      y:=y+v; grant(iy);
9      { x ↦ _ * req(ix, ixp, x ↦ _) }
10     x:=x+v; grant(ix);
11   } else {
12     grant(ix);
13     { req(iy, iyp, y ↦ _) * fut(iyp, y ↦ _) }
14     grant(iy);
15     { emp }
16     sleep(*);
17 } }
18 { emp }
```

Figure 4. Proof for parallelised program `fp`.

```
g(x) {
  if(*) {
    sleep(*);
    read(x);
  }
  else {
    write(x);
} }
```

```
gp(x,r,rp,w,wp) {
  if(*) {
    grant(r);
    sleep(*);
    wait(rp);
    read(x);
    grant(w);
  } else {
    wait(rp); wait(wp);
    write(x);
    grant(r); grant(w);
} }
```

Figure 5. Example function g and its parallelisation.

The parallelised version of the main program is given at the bottom of Fig. 3. We give the following sketch-proof for this example. Here the predicates $\mathsf{req}(\mathtt{ixf}, \mathtt{ixn}, \mathsf{true})$ and $\mathsf{req}(\mathtt{iyf}, \mathtt{iyn}, \mathsf{true})$ are dummy req predicates used to represent the logically latest element of the sequential order. The predicate array stands for the array of values.

$$\left\{\mathsf{array}(\mathtt{vs},\mathtt{max})\right\}$$

```
ixf:=newchan(); iyf:=newchan();
```

$$\left\{\begin{array}{l}\mathsf{array}(\mathtt{vs},\mathtt{max}) * \mathsf{req}(\mathtt{ixf},\mathsf{nil},\mathsf{true}) * \mathsf{fut}(\mathtt{ixf}, x \mapsto \_) \\ \qquad * \mathsf{req}(\mathtt{iyf},\mathsf{nil},\mathsf{true}) * \mathsf{fut}(\mathtt{iyf}, y \mapsto \_)\end{array}\right\}$$

```
for(j:=0; j<max; j++){
  ixl:=ixn; (ixf,ixn):=split(ixf);
```

$$\left\{\begin{array}{l}\mathsf{array}(\mathtt{vs},\mathtt{max}) * \mathsf{req}(\mathtt{ixf},\mathtt{ixn},\mathsf{true}) * \mathsf{fut}(\mathtt{ixn}, x \mapsto \_) \\ \qquad * \mathsf{req}(\mathtt{ixn},\mathtt{ixl}, x \mapsto \_) * \mathsf{fut}(\mathtt{ixl}, x \mapsto \_) \\ \qquad * \mathsf{req}(\mathtt{iyf},\mathtt{iyn},\mathsf{true}) * \mathsf{fut}(\mathtt{iyn}, y \mapsto \_)\end{array}\right\}$$

```
  iyl:=iyn; (iyf,iyn):=split(iyf);
```

$$\left\{\begin{array}{l}\mathsf{array}(\mathtt{vs},\mathtt{max}) * \mathsf{req}(\mathtt{ixf},\mathtt{ixn},\mathsf{true}) * \mathsf{fut}(\mathtt{ixn}, x \mapsto \_) \\ \qquad * \mathsf{req}(\mathtt{ixn},\mathtt{ixl}, x \mapsto \_) * \mathsf{fut}(\mathtt{ixl}, x \mapsto \_) \\ \qquad * \mathsf{req}(\mathtt{iyf},\mathtt{iyn},\mathsf{true}) * \mathsf{fut}(\mathtt{iyn}, y \mapsto \_) \\ \qquad * \mathsf{req}(\mathtt{iyn},\mathtt{iyl}, y \mapsto \_) * \mathsf{fut}(\mathtt{iyl}, y \mapsto \_)\end{array}\right\}$$

```
  future( fp(x,y,vs[j],ixn,iyn,ixl,iyl) );
}
wait(ixf); wait(iyf); // GC dummy req predicates.
```

$$\left\{\mathsf{array}(\mathtt{vs},\mathtt{max}) * x \mapsto \_ * y \mapsto \_\right\}$$

We have shown that our parallelised version of the program is memory-safe. With a little more effort, we could verify the behaviour of the program. Crucially, even though this program features many threads running at once, with complex communication between threads, each individual thread is able to reason locally, without dealing with other threads or the implementation of the barriers.

2.3 Relating Reads and Writes

Further parallelism is available by refining read and write accesses to a resource. Consider the function g given in Fig. 5. It is safe for parallel threads to read x at the same time. However, it is important that writes to x are sequentialised, and that groups of reads are sequentialised *with respect to writes*. If two groups of reading threads are separated by a writing thread, the logically later group must wait for the writer to finish before reading.

To exploit this, we split reading and writing into two channels. We use `r` and `rp` for reads, and `w` and `wp` for writes. `w` and `r` are the outgoing channels, while `wp` and `rp` are the incoming channel. As soon as the thread nondeterministically takes the first branch of the conditional, it can use the read channel to signal that later threads can read. In contrast, a thread that wishes to write must wait for both the read and write channels. The parallelised program is given in Fig 5.

In separation logic, read and write access are often controlled by *fractional permissions* [5]. Each thread can hold either full permission, 1, on a location x, denoted $x \mapsto v$, or fractional permission $\pi \in (0..1)$, denoted $x \overset{\pi}{\longmapsto} v$. Full permission gives the thread exclusive permission to write, while fractional permission gives non-exclusive permission to read. Fractional permissions compose by addition, as follows:

$$x \overset{\pi}{\longmapsto} v * x \overset{\pi'}{\longmapsto} v \iff x \overset{\pi+\pi'}{\longmapsto} v \qquad \text{if } \pi+\pi' \leq 1.$$

We give the function gp the following specification:

$$\left\{\begin{array}{r}\mathsf{req}(\mathtt{r},\mathtt{rp}, x \overset{\frac{1}{2}\pi}{\longmapsto} \_) * \mathsf{fut}(\mathtt{rp}, x \overset{\pi}{\longmapsto} \_) * \\ \mathsf{req}(\mathtt{w},\mathtt{wp}, x \overset{\pi'+\frac{1}{2}\pi}{\longmapsto} \_) * \mathsf{fut}(\mathtt{wp}, x \overset{\pi'}{\longmapsto} \_) \\ \wedge\, \pi+\pi' = 1\end{array}\right\} \; \mathtt{gp(..)} \; \{\mathsf{emp}\}$$

This specification says that when a thread receives a fractional permission from the read channel, only half of it has to be sent on to future threads using the read channel. The other half can be supplied on the write channel. This allows a thread to keep the ability to read, while notifying future threads that they also can read.

Fig. 6 shows a sketch-proof for the program. We elide the writing branch of the conditional as it is straightforward. The most notable proof step is line 3, where the specification's resource-splitting axiom is used to divide up access to the fut predicate. Half is used to discharge the req predicate r, allowing logically later threads to read, while half is used to allow the current thread to read. In this way, many threads can simultaneously have fractional access to the resource.

1 $\left\{\begin{array}{l}\mathsf{fut}(\mathtt{rp}, \mathtt{x} \overset{\pi}{\longmapsto} \_) * \mathsf{fut}(\mathtt{wp}, \mathtt{x} \overset{\pi'}{\longmapsto} \_) \wedge \pi+\pi' = 1 \\ * \mathsf{req}(\mathtt{r},\mathtt{rp}, \mathtt{x} \overset{\frac{1}{2}\pi}{\longmapsto} \_) * \mathsf{req}(\mathtt{w},\mathtt{wp}, \mathtt{x} \overset{\pi'+\frac{1}{2}\pi}{\longmapsto} \_)\end{array}\right\}$

2 `if(*) {`

3 `  // Apply the future splitting axiom to rp.`

4 $\quad\left\{\begin{array}{l}\mathsf{fut}(\mathtt{rp}, \mathtt{x} \overset{\frac{1}{2}\pi}{\longmapsto} \_) * \mathsf{fut}(\mathtt{rp}, \mathtt{x} \overset{\frac{1}{2}\pi}{\longmapsto} \_) * \mathsf{fut}(\mathtt{wp}, \mathtt{x} \overset{\pi'}{\longmapsto} \_) \\ \qquad * \mathsf{req}(\mathtt{r},\mathtt{rp}, \mathtt{x} \overset{\frac{1}{2}\pi}{\longmapsto} \_) * \mathsf{req}(\mathtt{w},\mathtt{wp}, \mathtt{x} \overset{\pi'+\frac{1}{2}\pi}{\longmapsto} \_)\end{array}\right\}$

5 `  grant(r);`

6 $\quad\left\{\begin{array}{l}\mathsf{fut}(\mathtt{rp}, \mathtt{x} \overset{\frac{1}{2}\pi}{\longmapsto} \_) * \mathsf{fut}(\mathtt{wp}, \mathtt{x} \overset{\pi'}{\longmapsto} \_) \\ \qquad * \mathsf{req}(\mathtt{w},\mathtt{wp}, \mathtt{x} \overset{\pi'+\frac{1}{2}\pi}{\longmapsto} \_)\end{array}\right\}$

7 `  sleep(*); wait(rp);`

8 $\quad\left\{\mathtt{x} \overset{\frac{1}{2}\pi}{\longmapsto} \_ * \mathsf{fut}(\mathtt{wp}, \mathtt{x} \overset{\pi'}{\longmapsto} \_) * \mathsf{req}(\mathtt{w},\mathtt{wp}, \mathtt{x} \overset{\pi'+\frac{1}{2}\pi}{\longmapsto} \_)\right\}$

9 `  read(x); grant(w);`

10 $\quad\{\mathsf{emp}\}$

11 `} else { ... }`

12 $\{\mathsf{emp}\}$

Figure 6. Proof for parallelised program gp.

3. Verifying a Simple Implementation

So far, we have given an abstract specification for deterministic parallelism. The specification was independent of the implementation

```
grant(i) {                    wait(i) {
  if(i.prev!=nil)               while(i.bit!=1)
    wait(i.prev);                 skip;
  ⟨i.bit:=1⟩;                 }
}

split(i) {                    newchan() {
  n:=alloc(bit);                i:=alloc(bit);
  n.prev:=i.prev;               i.prev:=nil;
  n.bit:=0;                     i.bit:=0;
  i.prev:=n;                    return i;
  return (i,n);               }
}
```

Figure 7. Implementation of signalling library.

of the barrier. In this section, we show how such a specification can be justified by giving a simple implementation of the `wait` and `grant` barriers, and verifying our abstract specification against this concrete implementation.

The implementation is given in Fig. 7. This implementation supports resource transfer using a sequence of nodes, each of which has a `bit` field and a `prev` field. Each fut / req pair is associated with a single node, and the order of the sequence represents the logical ordering. The implementation requires that bits are set in sequential order. In §5 we consider a more sophisticated implementation that allows out-of-order signalling, and show that it also implements our abstract specification.

The `wait` barrier simply waits for the immediately preceding bit to be set. As bits are set in order, with logically earlier threads setting their bits before logically later ones, this suffices to show that all the earlier bits in the order have been set.

Recall from the previous section that our specification permits threads to renounce the ability to access a resource, meaning that `grant` can be called before `wait` within the same thread. To ensure that bits are set in sequential order, `grant` must wait for the previous bit to be set before setting its own bit. The implementation uses the `prev` field of the bit to call `wait`, and then sets its bit when it exits. Bits are set atomically by `grant`, denoted by $\langle - \rangle$.

The constructor functions `newchan` and `split` are implemented by allocating a new bit; `split` inserts a bit into the order by redirecting the `prev` pointer of the existing bit to point to the newly allocated bit. This allows computations to dynamically instantiate sub-computations that have internal deterministic parallelism.

3.1 Proof Approach

To prove the correctness of our module's functions, we use concurrent abstract predicates [6]. We extend this work with higher-order quantification, allowing us to prove specifications that abstract over the particular resource held by the predicate.

Concurrent abstract predicates extend standard separation logic with two new kinds of construct allowing explicit reasoning about sharing and interference. The first are *named shared regions*, denoted by boxed assertions of the form

$$\boxed{P}^{r}_{I}$$

This asserts that the region r contains a resource satisfying P, and nothing else. This region is shared between the current thread and an arbitrary number of other threads. The permitted state changes over the region are controlled by the *interference environment*, I.

The second are *capabilities*, resources controlling the updates that a thread can perform. In order to mutate the contents of a shared region, a thread requires a capability in its local state, denoted:

$$[\text{ACTION}]^{r}_{\pi}$$

This is a permission for the operation ACTION on the region r. The exact operation denoted by the name ACTION is determined by the interference environment for region r. Suppose that ACTION denoted the ability to rewrite the value in a shared address x from 0 to 1. Then we would have the following interference environment:

$$I(x) \quad \triangleq \quad (\text{ACTION}: \; x \mapsto 0 \quad \leadsto \quad x \mapsto 1)$$

A capability $[\text{ACTION}]^{r}_{\pi}$ controls both whether the operation is permitted to the local thread, and whether it can be performed by the environment. Following deny-guarantee [8], exactly what is allowed and denied is determined by the permission level, π. We write 1 if the thread can exclusively perform the action, $\mathsf{g}z$ if the thread and the environment can perform the action, and $\mathsf{d}z$ if neither the thread nor the environment can perform the action. The value $z \in (0..1)$ is used to track the amount of permission, allowing capabilities to be split and combined.

Updates performed by a thread must be permitted according to the capabilities held by the thread in local state. So-called *abstract updates*, those that do not modify the underlying heap-state, can be performed at any time by a thread. We write $P \Rrightarrow Q$ to denote that P can be abstractly updated to give Q.

As assertions describe shared states that can be updated by other threads, we need to be able to describe assertions that will remain true no matter what the environment does. We describe these assertions as *stable*. Capabilities specify exactly what behaviours the environment can perform, giving fine-grained control of stability. For example, the following assertion is stable, because I specifies that the only way region r can be mutated is by the ACTION operations, and the exclusive capability to perform this operation is held by the thread in local state:

$$\boxed{x \mapsto 0}^{r}_{I(x)} * [\text{ACTION}]^{r}_{1}$$

Our logic includes an assertion $\mathsf{stable}(P)$ that holds if P is stable.

An abstract specification for a module consists of abstract predicates, function specifications and axioms. To show that a concrete implementation of a module corresponds to a particular abstract specification, we must supply concrete definitions for the module's abstract predicates, and then show that the following three properties hold: (1) the module implementation satisfies the abstract specifications, given the concrete predicate definitions; (2) the predicate definitions are stable; and (3) the axioms hold, given the concrete predicate definitions.

For simplicity, we assume that resources are garbage collected, rather than being explicitly deallocated. This means that we can safely remove star-conjuncts from assertions, and we often use this to clean up the post-conditions for operations.

3.2 Verifying the Implementation

Next, we prove that the implementation satisfies the abstract specification. We give definitions to the fut and req predicates in Fig. 8. (In all our predicate definitions, we assume unbound variables are existentially quantified.)

The definition of $\mathsf{req}(i, i', P)$ captures three pieces of information: First, that there exists a shared bit at address i. Second, that i' is the immediate predecessor of i, and it can be read by the thread. Third, that the thread must supply the resource P before setting the bit at i.

In this definition, we use two auxiliary predicates: pa and box. The predecessor access predicate $\mathsf{pa}(i)$ asserts that i is either nil, or it is a shared bit that can be read. This ensures that the thread that holds req is able to access the preceding bit. The predicate $\mathsf{box}(i, P, \pi)$ asserts that the thread can exchange the resource P for

$$\mathsf{req}(i, i', P) \triangleq \boxed{i.\mathrm{bit} \mapsto 0}^{r}_{I(i)} * \mathsf{box}(i, P, 1) * i.\mathrm{prev} \mapsto i' * \mathsf{pa}(i')$$

$$\mathsf{pa}(i) \triangleq i = \mathsf{nil} \vee \boxed{i.\mathrm{bit} \mapsto \_}^{r}_{I(i)}$$

$$\mathsf{box}(i, P, \pi) \triangleq [\mathrm{PUT}]^{r'}_{1} * \boxed{\begin{array}{l} \boxed{i.\mathrm{bit} \mapsto 0}^{r}_{I(i)} * [\mathrm{SET}]^{r}_{\mathbf{d}\pi} \vee \\ \mathsf{box}(i, P_1, \pi_1) * \mathsf{box}(i, P_2, \pi_2) * \\ \quad P \mathrel{-\!\!*} (P_1 * P_2) \wedge \pi_1 + \pi_2 = \pi \end{array}}^{r'}_{J(i,P,\pi,r)}$$

$$\mathsf{fut}(i, P) \triangleq \mathsf{stable}(P) * [\mathrm{GET}]^{r'}_{1} * \boxed{\begin{array}{l} [\mathrm{SET}]^{r}_{\mathbf{d}\pi} * \boxed{i.\mathrm{bit} \mapsto 0}^{r}_{I(i)} \\ \vee P * \boxed{i.\mathrm{bit} \mapsto \_}^{r}_{I(i)} \end{array}}^{r'}_{J(i,P,\pi,r)}$$

Figure 8. Collected predicate definitions.

the permission $\mathbf{d}\pi$ on SET for the bit i. Hence, in order to acquire the full permission to set the shared bit, the thread must supply the resource P to the predicate $\mathsf{box}(i, P, 1)$. That is, the following abstract update holds:

$$\boxed{i.\mathrm{bit} \mapsto 0}^{r}_{I(i)} * \mathsf{box}(i, P, \pi) * P \implies \boxed{i.\mathrm{bit} \mapsto 0}^{r}_{I(i)} * [\mathrm{SET}]^{r}_{\mathbf{d}\pi}$$

Below, we prove that the abstract implication holds. For the moment, we just note that boxes are used to control the splitting of resources according to the splitting axiom. Note that, the definition of box is recursive, as it mentions the box predicate inside the shared region, and in the interference on the shared region. The fixed point exists by first finding a solution ignoring the interference environment, and then restricting the interference environment by the resulting solution.

Finally, we give a definition to $\mathsf{fut}(i, P)$. This assertion must capture one essential piece of information: that either the shared bit at i is zero, or the resource P is available for collection.

In these definitions, names surrounded with square brackets are capabilities. The semantics of such capabilities are defined by the interference environments. We define two environments. The first, $I(i)$ defines the interference over the shared bit i. This environment includes only a single operation, the ability to set the shared bit:

$$I(i) \triangleq (\mathrm{SET}:\ i.\mathrm{bit} \mapsto 0 \rightsquigarrow i.\mathrm{bit} \mapsto 1)$$

The interference environment $J(i, P, \pi, r)$ defines the interference over the resource-holding regions.

$$J(i,P,\pi,r) \triangleq \left(\begin{array}{l} \mathrm{PUT}: \left\{ \begin{array}{l} [\mathrm{SET}]^{r}_{\mathbf{d}\pi} \rightsquigarrow P \\ \begin{pmatrix} \mathsf{box}(i, P_1, \pi_1) * \mathsf{box}(i, P_2, \pi_2) * \\ P \mathrel{-\!\!*} (P_1 * P_2) \wedge \pi_1 + \pi_2 = \pi \end{pmatrix} \rightsquigarrow \mathsf{emp} \end{array} \right. , \\ \mathrm{GET}: \left\{ \begin{array}{l} P \rightsquigarrow \mathsf{emp} \\ [\mathrm{SET}]^{r}_{\mathbf{d}\pi} \rightsquigarrow \begin{pmatrix} \mathsf{box}(i, P_1, \pi_1) * \mathsf{box}(i, P_2, \pi_2) * \\ P \mathrel{-\!\!*} (P_1 * P_2) \wedge \pi_1 + \pi_2 = \pi \end{pmatrix} \end{array} \right. \end{array} \right)$$

Intuitively the first case for PUT allows the thread to push the resource P into the shared state, and retrieve a fractional permission to SET the shared bit. The first case for GET allows the thread to retrieve the resource P. The second cases are used in resource splitting; see below for details.

The first obligation for showing that our module implements the abstract specification is to use our program logic to prove the module functions' specifications. Proofs for `grant`, `wait` and `split` are given in Fig. 9. The proof of `newchan` is almost identical to the proof of `split`, and hence omitted.

The proof of `grant` operates by first appealing to the specification of `wait` to recover the full resource from a possible fut predicate. We also use the specification $\{\mathsf{pa(i)}\}$`wait`$(\mathsf{i})\{\mathsf{emp}\}$, which can be proved trivially. It then exchanges the resource and the box predicate for permission to set the shared bit. Finally it sets the shared bit and forgets all the remaining resource.

The proof of `wait` spins until the bit field is 1, which excludes the case where the resource is not present. As the resource can only be removed by the `wait` thread, this assertion is stable under interference. The thread uses the GET to recover the resource, and garbage-collects all the other resources.

The proof of `split` (and `newchan`) allocates a new piece of memory, sets the `pred` and `bit` fields to appropriate values, then creates the fut and req predicates by wrapping the new memory in a shared region.

The second obligation we must discharge is to show that the predicates are stable. To do this, we check each of the predicate definitions to make sure that each shared region assertion is invariant under permitted interference.

3.3 Resource Splitting Using Boxes

Our specification requires that we can split fut predicates according to the axiom given in Fig. 2.

We use the box predicate to support this splitting in our concrete implementation. Intuitively, each box initially shares its shared region with a fut predicate. Then, if that fut predicate is split, the box instead contains a pair of boxes representing the shared state for the two new fut predicates.

The definition of a predicate $\mathsf{box}(i, P, \pi)$, Fig. 8, either allows the thread to access the SET permission, or contains two boxes with resources P_1 and P_2 such that $P \mathrel{-\!\!*} P_1 * P_2$. In the proofs of the module's operations, we relied on the assumption that a predicate $\mathsf{box}(i, P, 1)$ and resource P can be exchanged for a permission to set the shared bit $i.\mathrm{bit}$. We now justify this assumption with a proof.

Our definition of box is the least fixed point of the recursive definition. We reason inductively, hence it suffices to prove that the entailment holds when box is defined as false, and under the assumption that the disjunction holds. The base case of the induction holds trivially as $\mathsf{box}(i, P, \pi)$ is false. In the first inductive case, we assume that the left disjunct in the shared region holds. The proof is given in Fig 10 **(a)**. In the second case, we assume that the property holds for $\mathsf{box}(i, P_1, \pi_1)$ and $\mathsf{box}(i, P_2, \pi_2)$. The proof is given in Fig. 10 **(b)**.

The proof given in Fig. 10 **(c)** shows that the future-splitting axiom holds for the concrete predicate definitions. We only show the left case for the disjunction; the right case is easy. This proof uses the GET action while at the same time creating new regions for the two new futures. This completes the proof that our simple implementation corresponds to our high-level specification.

4. Logic and Semantics

In this section, we present the syntax and semantics of our logic. It extends the previous work on concurrent abstract predicates [6] with higher-order parameters and quantification following the work of Biering *et al.* on higher-order separation logic [3].

Our assertion logic is a typed higher-order separation logic extended with predicates that denote the ability to change the state and a connective for expressing sharing. The syntax of the assertion

$\boxed{i.\mathsf{bit} \mapsto 0}^{r}_{I(i)} * \mathsf{box}(i, P, \pi) * P$

$\Longrightarrow$ *(defs & assumption)*

$\boxed{i.\mathsf{bit} \mapsto 0}^{r}_{I(i)} * P * [\mathrm{PUT}]^{r'}_{1} * \boxed{\boxed{i.\mathsf{bit} \mapsto 0}^{r}_{I(i)} * [\mathrm{SET}]^{r}_{\mathbf{d}\pi}}^{r'}_{J(i,P,\pi,r)}$

$\Longrightarrow$ *(action* PUT*)*

$\boxed{i.\mathsf{bit} \mapsto 0}^{r}_{I(i)} * [\mathrm{PUT}]^{r'}_{1} * [\mathrm{SET}]^{r}_{\mathbf{d}\pi} * \boxed{\boxed{i.\mathsf{bit} \mapsto 0}^{r}_{I(i)} * P}^{r'}_{J(i,P,\pi,r)}$

$\Longrightarrow$ *(GC)*

$\boxed{i.\mathsf{bit} \mapsto 0}^{r}_{I(i)} * [\mathrm{SET}]^{r}_{\mathbf{d}\pi}$

(a)

$\boxed{i.\mathsf{bit} \mapsto 0}^{r}_{I(i)} * \mathsf{box}(i, P, \pi) * P$

$\Longrightarrow$ *(defs and case split)*

$\boxed{i.\mathsf{bit} \mapsto 0}^{r}_{I(i)} * [\mathrm{PUT}]^{r'}_{1} * P * \boxed{\mathsf{box}(i, P_1, \pi_1) * \mathsf{box}(i, P_2, \pi_2) * P \mathbin{-\!\!*} (P_1 * P_2) \wedge \pi_1 + \pi_2 = \pi}^{r'}_{J(i,P,\pi,r)}$

$\Longrightarrow$ *(action* PUT*)*

$\boxed{i.\mathsf{bit} \mapsto 0}^{r}_{I(i)} * [\mathrm{PUT}]^{r'}_{1} * P * \boxed{\mathsf{emp}}^{r'}_{J(i,P,\pi,r)}$
$* P \mathbin{-\!\!*} (P_1 * P_2) \wedge \pi_1 + \pi_2 = \pi$
$* \mathsf{box}(i, P_1, \pi_1) * \mathsf{box}(i, P_2, \pi_2)$

$\Longrightarrow$ *(assumption and GC)*

$\boxed{i.\mathsf{bit} \mapsto 0}^{r}_{I(i)} * [\mathrm{SET}]^{r}_{\mathbf{d}\pi}$

(b)

$\mathsf{fut}(i, P) * (P \mathbin{-\!\!*} P_1 * P_2) *$
$\mathsf{stable}(P_1) * \mathsf{stable}(P_2)$

$\Longrightarrow$ *(def)*

$\mathsf{stable}(P_1) * \mathsf{stable}(P_2) * [\mathrm{GET}]^{r'}_{1} * \boxed{[\mathrm{SET}]^{r}_{\mathbf{d}\pi} * \boxed{i.\mathsf{bit} \mapsto 0}^{r}_{I(i)} \vee P * \boxed{i.\mathsf{bit} \mapsto \_}^{r}_{I(i)}}^{r'}_{J(i,P,\pi,r)}$

$\Longrightarrow$ *(action* GET*, creation of two new regions)*

$\boxed{\mathsf{box}(i, P_1, \pi_1) * \mathsf{box}(i, P_2, \pi_2) * P \mathbin{-\!\!*} (P_1 * P_2) \wedge \pi_1 * \pi_2 = \pi}^{r'}_{J(i,P,\pi,r)}$
$* [\mathrm{GET}]^{r'}_{1} * \mathsf{fut}(i, P_1) * \mathsf{fut}(i, P_2)$

$\Longrightarrow$ *(GC)*

$\mathsf{fut}(i, P_1) * \mathsf{fut}(i, P_2)$

(c)

Figure 10. Proofs of abstract updates

language is as follows:

$$
\begin{array}{rcl}
\tau & ::= & \mathsf{Int} \mid \mathsf{Frac} \mid \mathsf{Region} \mid \mathsf{Asn} \mid \tau \to \tau \\
P, Q, L, M, \Delta & ::= & \mathsf{false} \mid P \Rightarrow Q \mid \exists x{:}\tau.\, P \mid L\, M \mid \lambda x{:}\tau.\, M \\
& \mid & E \mid \mathsf{emp} \mid P * Q \mid P \mathbin{-\!\!*} Q \\
& \mid & L \mapsto M \mid \mathsf{stable}(P) \mid [\gamma(\vec{M})]^{r}_{\pi} \mid \boxed{\mathrm{P}}^{r}_{I} \\
I & ::= & \gamma(\vec{x}) : \exists \vec{y} : \vec{\tau}(P \rightsquigarrow Q) \mid I, I \\
\pi & ::= & 1 \mid \mathbf{d}L \mid \mathbf{g}L
\end{array}
$$

where r ranges over region names, γ over token names, and v over values. We lift expressions E from the programming language to the logic. Note that we use P, Q, Δ when the term is of type Asn. Terms are typed in the obvious way, and we will implicitly assume all definitions are well-typed.

Our propositions have three important aspects they describe: (1) the contents of the state, (2) the capability to change state, and (3) a partitioning of these contents and capabilities between local and shared regions.

For completeness, the full semantics of terms is given in Fig. 11. Below we will only describe the salient features of the semantics. A more thorough explanation can be found in [6].

Model We model propositions with Worlds that have three components: a local component, LWorld, that specifies the current local state and local capabilities; a shared component, SWorld, that specifies the current shared state and shared capabilities; and an interference environment, IEnv, that specifies the possible interference (or protocol) on the shared component of the world. The shared component is split into many named regions, each of which is modelled by an LWorld.

A local world, LWorld, is modelled by a partial heap, Heap, specifying the locally accessible state, and a capability mapping, Capab, mapping from actions in Action to permission to perform that action in DG. Each action is mapped to either a full permission 1, an exclusive permission to perform that action, that hence prohibits the environment from performing the action; a guarantee permission $\mathbf{g}z$, a non-exclusive permission to perform that action; a deny permission $\mathbf{d}z$, a non-exclusive prohibition on the action that also prevents the environment performing it; and an empty permission 0 that does not allow the action but does not prohibit the environment from performing it. Following Boyland [5], the z components of deny and guarantee are used to track how much permission is required to re-establish exclusive permission.

Members of Action comprise a Region, a Token and a sequence of Val arguments. An action's semantic meaning as interference over a shared region is defined by an interference environment, in the set IEnv. The definition of an interference environment as a relation over SWorld enforces the restriction that the interpretation of an action does not allow you to change the interference interpretation of any actions.

Model operations As we are building a separation logic we require a composition operator on worlds that will be used to interpret the separating conjunction and separating implication. We use the standard operation from separation logic for combining heaps, $h \oplus h'$, by disjoint partial function combination.

We use the deny-guarantee composition model [8] for DG. This has 0 as the unit of $\oplus$. It combines two guarantee (or deny) permissions by combining their fractional components to produce a guarantee (or deny) permission with the sum of the fractions. If the fractions sum to 1 then it lifts to 1. If the fractions sum to more than 1, then combination is undefined. This is then lifted to the function space in the obvious way.

We define the composition of LWorld as the combination on both components; and on World as the combination on the LWorld component, where the SWorld and IEnv components are equal.

We define other useful operations on the model that aid in the definition of the semantics: $\lfloor s \rfloor$ collapses all the shared regions into a single one; l_H gives the heap component of l; l_P gives the permission component of l; and $\lfloor\!\lfloor w \rfloor\!\rfloor$ collapses a world into a single heap.

Finally, we define the set of well-formed worlds, WFW. A world is well-formed iff all the regions and the local component can be combined, each capability is defined in the interference environment, and the capabilities only mention valid regions.

Types The types are semantically interpreted as in Figure 11. We use i for interpretations of the free variables in a term: it is a dependent product from a variable to the denotation of the type of that variable. We interpret propositions on the powerset of worlds.

Terms The interpretation of false, $\Rightarrow$, $\exists$, $*$, $\mathbin{-\!\!*}$, variables, function application, and function abstraction λ are standard.

The predicate emp specifies that the local component of the heap is empty and makes no restriction on the shared part, the

$\left\{\mathsf{req}(\mathtt{i}, i', P) * (P \vee (\mathsf{fut}(i', P') * P' -\!\!* P))\right\}$

```
grant(i) {
  if(i.prev!=nil) {
```

$\quad\quad\left\{\mathsf{req}(\mathtt{i}, i', P) * (P \vee (\mathsf{fut}(i', P') * P' -\!\!* P))\right\}$

```
    wait(i.prev); // wait() spec, or by pa.
```

$\quad\quad\left\{\mathsf{req}(\mathtt{i}, i', P) * P\right\}$

```
  } // Unfold definition.
```

$\quad\left\{\boxed{\mathtt{i.bit} \mapsto 0}^{r}_{I(\mathtt{i})} * \mathtt{i.prev} \mapsto i' * \mathsf{pa}(i') * \mathsf{box}(\mathtt{i}, P, 1) * P\right\}$

```
  // Push resource into the box.
```

$\quad\left\{\boxed{\mathtt{i.bit} \mapsto 0}^{r}_{I(\mathtt{i})} * \mathtt{i.prev} \mapsto i' * \mathsf{pa}(i') * [\mathrm{SET}]^{r}_{1}\right\}$

```
  <i.bit:=1>; // Action SET.
```

$\quad\left\{\boxed{\mathtt{i.bit} \mapsto 1}^{r}_{I(\mathtt{i})} * \mathtt{i.prev} \mapsto i' * \mathsf{pa}(i') * [\mathrm{SET}]^{r}_{1}\right\}$

```
} // Garbage collect.
```

$\left\{\mathsf{emp}\right\}$

$\left\{\mathsf{fut}(\mathtt{i}, P)\right\}$

```
wait(i){
```

$\quad\left\{\begin{array}{l}\mathsf{stable}(P) * [\mathrm{GET}]^{r'}_{1} * \\ \boxed{[\mathrm{SET}]^{r}_{d\pi} * \boxed{\mathtt{i.bit} \mapsto 0}^{r}_{I(\mathtt{i})} \vee P * \boxed{\mathtt{i.bit} \mapsto \_}^{r}_{I(\mathtt{i})}}^{r'}_{J(\mathtt{i}, P, \pi, r)}\end{array}\right\}$

```
  while(i.bit!=1){ skip; }
```

$\quad\left\{\mathsf{stable}(P) * [\mathrm{GET}]^{r'}_{1} * \boxed{P * \boxed{\mathtt{i.bit} \mapsto 1}^{r}_{I(\mathtt{i})}}^{r'}_{J(\mathtt{i}, P, \pi, r)}\right\}$

```
  // Abstract action GET.
```

$\quad\left\{P * \mathsf{stable}(P) * [\mathrm{GET}]^{r'}_{1} * \boxed{\boxed{\mathtt{i.bit} \mapsto 1}^{r}_{I(\mathtt{i})}}^{r'}_{J(\mathtt{i}, P, \pi, r)}\right\}$

```
} // Garbage collect.
```

$\left\{P\right\}$

$\left\{\mathsf{req}(\mathtt{i}, i', P) * \mathsf{stable}(Q)\right\}$

```
split(i) {
  n:=alloc(bit);
  n.prev:=i.prev; n.bit:=0; i.prev:=n;
```

$\quad\left\{\begin{array}{l}\boxed{\mathtt{i.bit} \mapsto 0}^{r}_{I(\mathtt{i})} * \mathsf{box}(\mathtt{i}, P, 1) * \mathtt{i.prev} \mapsto \mathtt{n} * \mathsf{pa}(i') \\ \quad * \mathsf{stable}(Q) * \mathtt{n.prev} \mapsto i' * \mathtt{n.bit} \mapsto 0\end{array}\right\}$

```
  // Construct region for new predicates.
```

$\quad\left\{\begin{array}{l}\boxed{\mathtt{i.bit} \mapsto 0}^{r}_{I(\mathtt{i})} * \mathsf{box}(\mathtt{i}, P, 1) * \mathtt{i.prev} \mapsto \mathtt{n} * \mathsf{pa}(i') * \\ \mathsf{stable}(Q) * \mathtt{n.prev} \mapsto i' * [\mathrm{SET}]^{r'}_{1} * \boxed{\mathtt{n.bit} \mapsto 0}^{r'}_{I(\mathtt{n})}\end{array}\right\}$

```
  // construct a new box for the future.
```

$\quad\left\{\begin{array}{l}\boxed{\mathtt{i.bit} \mapsto 0}^{r}_{I(\mathtt{i})} * \mathsf{box}(\mathtt{i}, P, 1) * \mathtt{i.prev} \mapsto \mathtt{n} * \mathsf{pa}(i') \\ * \mathtt{n.prev} \mapsto i' * \boxed{\mathtt{n.bit} \mapsto 0}^{r'}_{I(\mathtt{n})} * \mathsf{stable}(Q) * [\mathrm{GET}]^{r''}_{1} \\ \quad * [\mathrm{PUT}]^{r''}_{1} * \boxed{[\mathrm{SET}]^{r'}_{1} * \boxed{\mathtt{n.bit} \mapsto 0}^{r'}_{I(r')}}^{r''}_{J(n, Q, 1, r')}\end{array}\right\}$

```
  return (i,n);
} // Fold definitions.
```

$\left\{\begin{array}{l}\exists i_1, i_2.\, \mathrm{ret} = (i_1, i_2) \wedge \mathsf{req}(i_1, i_2, P) \\ \quad * \mathsf{fut}(i_2, Q) * \mathsf{req}(i_2, i', Q)\end{array}\right\}$

Figure 9. Proofs for `grant`, `wait` and `split`.

interference environment, or the capability. The points-to predicate $L \mapsto M$ specifies that the location L contains the value M in the local world, and that the heap contains nothing else.

The capability $[\gamma(\vec{M})]^{r}_{\pi}$ that says the local world contains the π permission on region r for action γ with parameters $\vec{M}$. The assertion $\mathsf{stable}(P)$ says that P will remain true given the permitted interference on the shared world. That is, if we start in a world satisfying P and take a step in R, then we must still satisfy P. The shared assertion $\boxed{P}^{r}_{I}$ says that the shared region r satisfies the assertion P and that region's interference is specified by I.

Interference We define several relations giving the possible updates to the shared world as a result of the thread and the environment. Following Jones [16], we call the interference permitted to the environment the *rely* and the interference permitted to the local thread the *guarantee*.

We define the semantics of the interference specfication as a relation of SWorlds. For a particular update $P \rightsquigarrow Q$, we specify that a part of the pre-state must satisfy P, and replacing that part with a part satisfying Q gives the post-state. We also allow the action to increase the number of regions in an unspecified way. This will allow actions both to repartition and to create new shared regions simultaneously.

We allow the dynamic creation of regions. The relations $\mathsf{R_c}$ and $\mathsf{G_c}$ model this creation. The first, $\mathsf{R_c}$, specifies the world-change if the environment creates a region. The environment can only create a region if it does not already exist. It adds a new shared region, and the relevant definition to the interference environment. The second, $\mathsf{G_c}$, specifies the world-change if the current thread created a region. This differs from the rely as all of the permissions on actions for the new region are given to the current thread.

The global rely relation, R, allows any action in the inference environment that is not explicitly prohibited with a deny permission or a full permission, as well as the creation of regions. We restrict R to well-formed worlds.

The global guarantee, G, allows any action for which there is either a full permission or a guarantee permission. The guarantee requires that the permissions and heap domain must be the same before and after the action, upto repartioning between regions. This ensures that permissions and heap cannot be created out of thin air. We also allow region creation, and restrict G to well-formed worlds.

Program logic We give the proof rules for our program logic in Figure 12. The judgements are of the form $\Delta; \Gamma \vdash \{P\}\ C\ \{Q\}$ where Δ is an assumption about the logical context, and Γ is an assumption about the procedures in the context of the form

$$\{P_1\}f_1\{Q_1\}, \ldots, \{P_n\}f_n\{Q_n\}.$$

We use Δ to encode the assumptions about the abstract predicates and their axioms

We assume a standard semantics of programs [6] where $(C, h) \xrightarrow{\eta} (C', h')$ denotes a successful reduction in the procedure context η (a mapping from procedure names to commands); and $(C, h) \xrightarrow{\eta} \mathit{fault}$ denotes a memory access problem. We then define the semantics of judgments as follows:

DEFINITION 1 (Configuration safety). *C, w, η, i, Q safe_0 always holds; and*
C, w, η, i, Q safe_{n+1} iff the following four conditions hold:

1. *$\forall w'.$ if $(w, w') \in \mathsf{R}^*$ then C, w', η, i, Q safe_n;*
2. *$\neg((C, \lfloor w \rfloor) \xrightarrow{\eta} \mathit{fault})$;*
3. *$\forall C', h'.$ if $(C, \lfloor w \rfloor) \xrightarrow{\eta} (C', h')$, then $\exists w'$ such that $(w, w') \in \mathsf{G}^*$, $h' = \lfloor w' \rfloor$ and C', w', η, i, Q safe_n; and*
4. *if C=**skip**, then $\exists w'$ such that $\lfloor w \rfloor = \lfloor w' \rfloor_H$, $(w, w') \in \mathsf{G}^*$, and $w' \in [\![Q]\!]_i$.*

Model

$$\pi \in \mathsf{DG} \triangleq \{1,0\} \uplus \{tz \mid z \in (0,1) \wedge t \in \{\mathbf{d},\mathbf{g}\}\} \quad a \in \mathsf{Action} \triangleq \mathsf{Region} \times \mathsf{Token} \times \mathsf{Val}^* \quad \rho \in \mathsf{Capab} \triangleq \mathsf{Action} \to \mathsf{DG}$$
$$h \in \mathsf{Heap} \triangleq \mathsf{Address} \to \mathsf{Val} \uplus \{\bot\} \quad l \in \mathsf{LWorld} \triangleq \mathsf{Heap} \times \mathsf{Capab} \quad s \in \mathsf{SWorld} \triangleq \mathsf{Region} \rightharpoonup \mathsf{LWorld}$$
$$\mathcal{I} \in \mathsf{IEnv} \triangleq \mathsf{Action} \rightharpoonup \mathcal{P}(\mathsf{SWorld} \times \mathsf{SWorld}) \quad w \in \mathsf{World} \triangleq \mathsf{LWorld} \times \mathsf{SWorld} \times \mathsf{IEnv}$$

Model operations

$$\bot \oplus v \triangleq v \oplus \bot \triangleq v \quad (t,z) \oplus (t,z') \triangleq 1 \text{ if } z+z'=1 \quad h_1 \oplus h_2 \triangleq \lambda v.\, h_1(v) \oplus h_2(v) \text{ if } \forall v.\, h_1(v) = \bot \vee h_2(v) = \bot$$
$$\pi \oplus 0 \triangleq 0 \oplus \pi \triangleq \pi \quad (t,z) \oplus (t,z') \triangleq (t, z+z') \text{ if } z+z' < 1 \quad \rho_1 \oplus \rho_2 \triangleq \lambda v.\, \rho_1(v) \oplus \rho_2(v) \text{ if } \forall v.\, \rho_1(v) \oplus \rho_2(v) \text{ defined}$$
$$(h_1,\rho_1) \oplus (h_2,\rho_2) \triangleq (h_1 \oplus h_2, \rho_1 \oplus \rho_2) \text{ if } h_1 \oplus h_2 \text{ and } \rho_1 \oplus \rho_2 \text{ are defined} \quad (h,\rho)_H \triangleq h \quad \lfloor s \rfloor \triangleq \oplus_{r \in \mathrm{dom}(s)} s(r)$$
$$(l_1,s_1,\mathcal{I}_1) \oplus (l_2,s_2,\mathcal{I}_2) \triangleq (l_1 \oplus l_2, s_1, \mathcal{I}_1) \text{ if } l_1 \oplus l_1 \text{ defined} \wedge s_1 = s_2 \wedge \mathcal{I}_1 = \mathcal{I}_2 \quad (h,\rho)_P \triangleq \rho \quad \llfloor (l,s,\mathcal{I}) \rrfloor \triangleq (l \oplus \lfloor s \rfloor)_H$$
$$\mathsf{WFW} \triangleq \{(l,s,\mathcal{I}) \mid (l \oplus \lfloor s \rfloor) \text{ defined} \wedge \mathrm{dom}((l \oplus \lfloor s \rfloor)_P) \subseteq \mathrm{dom}(\mathcal{I}) \wedge (\forall r.\, r \in \mathrm{dom}(s) \Leftrightarrow \exists \gamma, \vec{v}.\, (r,\gamma,\vec{v}) \in \mathrm{dom}(\mathcal{I}))\}$$

Types $\llbracket \mathsf{Int} \rrbracket \triangleq \mathbb{Z}$ $\llbracket \mathsf{Region} \rrbracket \triangleq \mathsf{Region}$ $\llbracket \tau_1 \to \tau_2 \rrbracket \triangleq \llbracket \tau_1 \rrbracket \to \llbracket \tau_2 \rrbracket$ $\llbracket \mathsf{Asn} \rrbracket \triangleq \mathcal{P}(\mathsf{World})$

Terms $\llbracket \mathsf{false} \rrbracket_i \triangleq \emptyset$ $\llbracket x \rrbracket_i \triangleq i(x)$

$$\llbracket P \Rightarrow Q \rrbracket_i \triangleq \{w \mid w \notin \llbracket P \rrbracket_i \vee w \in \llbracket Q \rrbracket_i\} \quad \llbracket L\, M \rrbracket_i \triangleq \llbracket L \rrbracket_i(\llbracket M \rrbracket_i) \quad \llbracket P * Q \rrbracket_i \triangleq \{w \oplus w' \mid w \in \llbracket P \rrbracket_i \wedge w' \in \llbracket Q \rrbracket_i\}$$
$$\llbracket \exists x \colon \tau.\, P \rrbracket_i \triangleq \textstyle\bigcup_{v \in \llbracket \tau \rrbracket} \cdot \llbracket P \rrbracket_{i[x \mapsto v]} \quad \llbracket \lambda x \colon \tau.\, M \rrbracket_i \triangleq \lambda v.\, \llbracket M \rrbracket_{i[x \mapsto v]} \quad \llbracket P \mathrel{-\!\!*} Q \rrbracket_i \triangleq \{w \mid \forall w' \in \llbracket P \rrbracket_i.\, w \oplus w' \in \llbracket Q \rrbracket_i\}$$
$$\llbracket \mathsf{emp} \rrbracket_i \triangleq \{((\emptyset,\rho),s,\mathcal{I})\} \quad \llbracket L \mapsto M \rrbracket_i \triangleq \{((\llbracket L \rrbracket_i \mapsto \llbracket M \rrbracket_i],\rho),s,\mathcal{I})\} \quad \left\llbracket [\gamma(\vec{M})]^r_\pi \right\rrbracket_i \triangleq \{((\emptyset,\rho),s,\mathcal{I}) \mid \rho(r,\gamma,\llbracket \vec{M} \rrbracket_i) \geq \pi\}$$
$$\llbracket \mathsf{stable}(P) \rrbracket_i \triangleq \{w \mid \forall w_1 \in \llbracket P \rrbracket_i.\, (w_1,w_2) \in \mathsf{R} \Rightarrow w_2 \in \llbracket P \rrbracket_i\} \quad \left\llbracket \boxed{P}^r_I \right\rrbracket_i \triangleq \{((\emptyset,\rho),s,\mathcal{I}) \mid (s(r),s,\mathcal{I}) \in \llbracket P \rrbracket_i \wedge \mathcal{I}(r) = \llbracket I \rrbracket_{i,r}\}$$

Interference

$$\llbracket \gamma(\vec{x}) : \exists \vec{y} : \vec{\tau}(P \rightsquigarrow Q) \rrbracket_{i,r}(r,\gamma',\vec{v}) \triangleq \left\{ s_1, s_2 \,\middle|\, \begin{array}{l} \exists \vec{v'} \in \llbracket \vec{\tau} \rrbracket, \mathcal{I}, l_0, l_1, l_2.\, (l_1,s_1,\mathcal{I}) \in \llbracket P \rrbracket_{i[\vec{x} \mapsto \vec{v}, \vec{y} \mapsto \vec{v'}]} \wedge (l_2,s_2,\mathcal{I}) \in \llbracket Q \rrbracket_{i[\vec{x} \mapsto \vec{v}, \vec{y} \mapsto \vec{v'}]} \\ \wedge \gamma = \gamma' \wedge s_1(r) = l_1 * l_0 \wedge s_2(r) = l_2 * l_0 \\ \wedge \forall r' \in \mathrm{dom}(s_1).\, r' \neq r \Rightarrow s_1(r') = s_2(r') \end{array} \right\}$$
$$\llbracket I, I' \rrbracket_{i,r} \triangleq \llbracket I \rrbracket_{i,r} \cup \llbracket I' \rrbracket_{i,r}$$
$$\mathsf{R_c} \triangleq \{(l,s,\mathcal{I}),(l,s',\mathcal{I} \cup \mathcal{I}') \mid r \notin \mathrm{dom}(s) \wedge s' = s[r \mapsto l'] \wedge \mathrm{rdom}(\mathcal{I}') = \{r\}\}$$
$$\mathsf{G_c} \triangleq \{(l,s,\mathcal{I}),(l',s',\mathcal{I} \cup \mathcal{I}') \mid r \notin \mathrm{dom}(s) \wedge s' = s[r \mapsto l_1] \wedge l \oplus \mathsf{all}(\mathcal{I}') = l_1 \oplus l' \wedge \mathrm{rdom}(\mathcal{I}') = \{r\}\}$$
$$\text{where} \quad \mathsf{all}(\mathcal{I}') \triangleq \bigoplus_{(r,\gamma,\vec{v}) \in \mathrm{dom}(\mathcal{I}')} (\emptyset, [r,\gamma,\vec{v} \mapsto 1]) \quad \text{and} \quad \mathrm{rdom}(\mathcal{I}) = \{r \mid (r,\_,\_) \in \mathrm{dom}(\mathcal{I})\}$$
$$\mathsf{R} \triangleq \left(\left\{(l,s,\mathcal{I}),(l,s',\mathcal{I} \cup \mathcal{I}') \,\middle|\, \exists a.\, (s,s') \in \mathcal{I}(a) \wedge (\lfloor s \rfloor \oplus l)_P(a) \notin \{1, \mathbf{d}z\} \wedge \mathrm{dom}(s') \setminus \mathrm{dom}(s) = \mathrm{rdom}(\mathcal{I}')\right\} \cup \mathsf{R_c}\right) \cap \mathcal{P}(\mathsf{WFW}^2)$$
$$\mathsf{G} \triangleq \left(\left\{\begin{array}{l}(l,s,\mathcal{I}), \\ (l',s',\mathcal{I} \cup \mathcal{I}')\end{array} \,\middle|\, \begin{array}{l} \exists a.\, (s,s') \in \mathcal{I}(a) \wedge (l'_P)(a) \in \{1,(\mathbf{g},\_)\} \wedge \mathrm{dom}(s') \setminus \mathrm{dom}(s) = \mathrm{rdom}(\mathcal{I}') \\ \wedge (\lfloor s \rfloor \oplus l)_P \oplus \mathsf{all}(\mathcal{I}') = (\lfloor s' \rfloor \oplus l')_P \wedge \mathrm{dom}((\lfloor s \rfloor \oplus l)_H) = \mathrm{dom}((\lfloor s' \rfloor \oplus l')_H) \end{array}\right\} \cup \mathsf{G_c}\right) \cap \mathcal{P}(\mathsf{WFW}^2)$$

Ancillary definitions

$$P \Longrightarrow_i^{\{p\}\{q\}} Q \triangleq \forall w \in \llbracket P \rrbracket_i.\, \exists h \in \llbracket p \rrbracket_i.\, \forall h_2 \in \llbracket q \rrbracket_i.\, \exists h'\, w_2.\, h \oplus h' = \llfloor w \rrfloor \wedge h_2 \oplus h' = \llfloor w_2 \rrfloor \wedge (w,w_2) \in \mathsf{G} \wedge w_2 \in \llbracket Q \rrbracket$$
$$\llbracket \Delta \rrbracket \triangleq \{i \mid \llbracket \Delta \rrbracket_i = \llbracket \mathsf{Asn} \rrbracket\} \qquad \Delta \models \Delta' \triangleq \llbracket \Delta \rrbracket \subseteq \llbracket \Delta' \rrbracket$$
$$\Delta \models P \Longrightarrow^{\{p\}\{q\}} Q \triangleq \forall i \in \llbracket \Delta \rrbracket.\, P \Longrightarrow_i^{\{p\}\{q\}} Q \qquad \Delta \models P \Longrightarrow Q \triangleq \forall i \in \llbracket \Delta \rrbracket.\, P \Longrightarrow_i^{\{\mathsf{emp}\}\{\mathsf{emp}\}} Q$$

Figure 11. Semantics of assertions

$$\frac{\vdash_{\mathsf{SL}} \{p\}\, C\, \{q\}}{\Delta;\Gamma \vdash \{p\}\, C\, \{q\}}\ (\textsc{Prim}) \qquad \frac{\Delta;\Gamma \vdash \{P_1\}\, C_1\, \{Q_1\} \quad \Delta;\Gamma \vdash \{P_2\}\, C_2\, \{Q_2\}}{\Delta;\Gamma \vdash \{P_1 * P_2\}\, C_1 \parallel C_2\, \{Q_1 * Q_2\}}\ (\textsc{Par}) \qquad \frac{\alpha \notin \Gamma, P, Q \quad \Delta;\Gamma \vdash \{P\}C\{Q\}}{(\exists \alpha.\Delta);\Gamma \vdash \{P\}C\{Q\}}\ (\textsc{Exists})$$

$$\frac{\{P\}\, f\, \{Q\} \in \Gamma}{\Delta;\Gamma \vdash \{P\}\, f\, \{Q\}}\ (\textsc{Call}) \qquad \frac{\vdash_{\mathsf{SL}} \{p\}\, C\, \{q\} \quad \Delta \models P \Longrightarrow^{\{p\}\{q\}} Q}{\Delta;\Gamma \vdash \{P\}\, \langle C \rangle\, \{Q\}}\ (\textsc{Atomic}) \qquad \frac{\Delta;\Gamma \vdash \{P\}\, C\, \{Q\} \quad \Delta \models \mathsf{stable}(R)}{\Delta;\Gamma \vdash \{P * R\}\, C\, \{Q * R\}}\ (\textsc{Frame})$$

$$\frac{\begin{array}{c}\Delta;\Gamma \vdash \{P_1\}\, C_1\, \{Q_1\} \quad \ldots \quad \Delta;\Gamma \vdash \{P_n\}\, C_n\, \{Q_n\} \\ \Delta; \{P_1\}\, f_1\, \{Q_1\}, \ldots, \{P_n\}\, f_n\, \{Q_n\}, \Gamma \vdash \{P\}\, C\, \{Q\}\end{array}}{\Delta;\Gamma \vdash \{P\}\ \mathrm{let}\ f_1 = C_1 \ldots f_n = C_n\ \mathrm{in}\ C\, \{Q\}}\ (\textsc{Let}) \qquad \frac{\begin{array}{c}\Delta';\Gamma \vdash \{P'\}\, C\, \{Q'\} \quad \Delta \models \Delta' \\ \Delta \models P \Longrightarrow P' \quad \Delta \models Q' \Longrightarrow Q\end{array}}{\Delta;\Gamma \vdash \{P\}\, C\, \{Q\}}\ (\textsc{Conseq})$$

Figure 12. Selected proof rules from [6]. All rules assume that the pre- and post-conditions of their judgements are stable.

DEFINITION 2 (Judgement Semantics). $\Delta; \Gamma \models \{P\}\, C\, \{Q\}$ *holds iff*

$$\forall n. \forall i \in [\![\Delta]\!] . \forall \eta \in [\![\Gamma]\!]_{n,i} .\ \models_{\eta,i,n+1} \{P\} C \{Q\},$$

where $[\![\Gamma]\!]_{n,i} \triangleq \{\eta \mid \forall \{P\} f \{Q\} \in \Gamma.\ \models_{\eta,i,n} \{P\} \eta(f) \{Q\}\}$ *and* $\models_{\eta,i,n} \{P\} C \{Q\} \triangleq \forall w \in ([\![P]\!]_i \cap \mathsf{WFW}).\ C, w, \eta, i, Q\ \mathit{safe}_n$.

Differences from the CAP paper [6]. The original paper treated the meaning of interference syntactically in the model, that is, the equivalent of IEnv was a map from action to syntactic definition of the actions. This was done to avoid a cyclic definition in World. In this paper, we have factored out the semantics of interference to be a separate component. We thus impose the restriction that the interference environment cannot update the interference environment. Note, this kind of update was not allowed before, but was not explicitly forbidden in the model, just in the interpretation. This small refactoring of the semantics allows higher-order quantification.

We extend the model from the original CAP paper to additionally contain deny permissions [8]. This is a straightforward extension to the original paper.

Finally, we take an intuitionistic model for the permissions. This enables permissions to leak. The library we are considering in this paper requires garbage collection to collect signals when they are no longer accessible.

5. Verifying a More Complex Implementation

The module implementation given in §3 imposes a strong sequential order on calls to `grant`. A `wait` only checks its immediate predecessor, so a call to `grant` must ensure its predecessor is set before setting its own bit. In this section, we consider an alternative implementation that allows out-of-order bit setting. We prove that this implementation also implements our abstract specification.

The new implementation uses the same data-structure as the simple implementation. Bits can be set by calls to `grant` in arbitrary order, but as a consequence, each call to `wait` must examine *all* prior bits before exiting. As this implementation uses the same data-structure as the first one, the `split` and `newchan` operations are identical. The `grant` and `wait` operations are defined as follows:

```
grant(i) {                 wait(i) {
  ⟨i.bit := 1⟩;              while (i!=nil) {
}                              while(i.bit=0){ skip; }
                               i := i.prev;
                           } }
```

As with the first implementation, each address has a `bit` field and a `prev` field. Calling `grant` sets the bit field for the current address from 0 to 1, then exits immediately. When `wait` is called, it blocks until every bit field earlier in the order is set. To do this, it chases `prev` fields, waiting for each `bit` field to go to 1 before accessing the preceding location. In this way, `wait` ensures that all previous threads have called `grant`.

The predicate definitions (given in Fig. 13) are similar to those for the simple implementation. The main difference is in the definition of the fut predicate. When the shared bit is set, the resource that is available to the thread may include a preceding fut predicate. So, if the current thread expects resource P, it may instead get a resource satisfying $(P' \mathrel{-\!\!*} P) * \mathsf{fut}(i', P')$, where i' is the immediately preceding location in the logical order.

The thread can then recover P' by checking the bit for i', which may include a fut predicate for the preceding location i''. Only when the thread has checked all the bits earlier in the order can it be confident it holds the full resource. In this way, our predicate definitions reflect the fact that the thread does not know exactly which threads have supplied a resource, and which have simply renounced access to it.

$$\mathsf{fut}(i, P) \triangleq [\mathrm{GET}]_1^{r'} * \boxed{\begin{array}{l} \left(\boxed{i.\mathrm{bit} \mapsto 0}^{r}_{I(i)} * \forall^* i'. [\mathrm{SET}(i')]^{r}_{\mathbf{d}\pi} \right) \vee \\ \left(\boxed{\begin{array}{l} i.\mathrm{bit} \mapsto 0 \vee \\ i.\mathrm{bit} \mapsto 1 * i.\mathrm{prev} \mapsto i' * \mathsf{pa}(i') \end{array}}^{r}_{I(r)} \right. \\ \left. * P \vee \exists P', i'. (\mathsf{fut}(i', P') * (P' \mathrel{-\!\!*} P)) \right) \end{array}}^{r'}_{J(i,P,\pi,r)}$$

$$\mathsf{req}(i, i', P) \triangleq \boxed{i.\mathrm{bit} \mapsto 0}^{r}_{I(i)} * i.\mathrm{prev} \mapsto i' * \mathsf{pa}(i') * \mathsf{box}(i, P, 1)$$

$$\mathsf{pa}(i) \triangleq i = \mathsf{nil} \vee \boxed{\begin{array}{l} i.\mathrm{bit} \mapsto 0 \vee \\ i.\mathrm{bit} \mapsto 1 * i.\mathrm{prev} \mapsto i' * \mathsf{pa}(i') \end{array}}^{r}_{I(i)}$$

$$\mathsf{box}(i, P, \pi) \triangleq \boxed{\begin{array}{l} \boxed{i.\mathrm{bit} \mapsto 0}^{r}_{I(i)} * \forall^* i. [\mathrm{SET}(i)]^{r}_{\mathbf{d}\pi} \vee \\ \mathsf{box}(i, P_1, \pi_1) * \mathsf{box}(i, P_2, \pi_2) * \\ \qquad P \mathrel{-\!\!*} (P_1 * P_2) \wedge \pi_1 + \pi_2 = \pi \end{array}}^{r'}_{J(i,P,\pi,r)} * [\mathrm{PUT}]_1^{r'}$$

Figure 13. Predicate definitions for out-of-order bit setting.

$\{\mathsf{fut}(\mathtt{i}, P)\}$

```
wait(i) {
  while (i!=nil) {
```

$\{\mathtt{i} \neq \mathsf{nil} \wedge (\mathsf{pa}(\mathtt{i}) * P \vee \exists P'. \mathsf{fut}(\mathtt{i}, P') * (P' \mathrel{-\!\!*} P))\}$

```
    while(i.bit=0) skip;
```

$\left\{ \boxed{\mathtt{i.bit} \mapsto \_ * \mathtt{i.prev} \mapsto i' * \mathsf{pa}(i')}^{r} * (P \vee \exists P'. \mathsf{fut}(i', P') * (P' \mathrel{-\!\!*} P)) \right\}$

```
    i := i.prev;
  }
```

$\{\mathtt{i} = \mathsf{nil} \wedge ((\mathsf{pa}(\mathtt{i}) * P) \vee (\exists P'. \mathsf{fut}(\mathtt{i}, P') * (P' \mathrel{-\!\!*} P)))\}$

`}` // $\mathsf{fut}(\mathtt{i}, \_)$ *is false if* $i = \mathsf{nil}$, *so...*

$\{P\}$

Figure 14. Proof for `wait`.

The req predicate is defined similarly to the first proof, with a recursive box predicate controlling access to bit-setting.

The interference environment for the shared bit, $I(i)$, is:

$$\mathrm{SET}(i'):\quad i.\mathrm{bit} \mapsto 0 \quad \rightsquigarrow \quad i.\mathrm{bit} \mapsto 1 * i.\mathrm{prev} \mapsto i' * \mathsf{pa}(i')$$

The environment $J(i, P, \pi, r)$ for resource-holding regions is:

$$\mathrm{PUT}: \begin{cases} [\mathrm{SET}(i')]^{r}_{\mathbf{d}\pi} \rightsquigarrow P \vee (\mathsf{fut}(i', P') * P' \mathrel{-\!\!*} P) \\ \begin{pmatrix} \mathsf{box}(i, P_1, \pi_1) * \mathsf{box}(i, P_2, \pi_2) \\ * P \mathrel{-\!\!*} (P_1 * P_2) \wedge \pi_1 + \pi_2 = \pi \end{pmatrix} \rightsquigarrow \mathsf{emp} \end{cases}$$

$$\mathrm{GET}: \begin{cases} P \rightsquigarrow \mathsf{emp} \\ (\forall^* i'. [\mathrm{SET}(i')]^{r}_{\mathbf{d}\pi}) \rightsquigarrow \begin{pmatrix} \mathsf{box}(i, P_1, \pi_1) * \mathsf{box}(i, P_2, \pi_2) * \\ P \mathrel{-\!\!*} (P_1 * P_2) \wedge \pi_1 + \pi_2 = \pi \end{pmatrix} \end{cases}$$

(Here the symbol $\forall^*$ is the iterated version of $*$.)

A proof for `wait` is given in Fig. 14. The most interesting step is line 5, where the resource is recovered from the shared region. We justify this step by the following proof. The other case, where a pa rather than fut is present, is trivial.

$$\left\{\mathsf{fut}(\mathtt{i}, P') * (P' \mathrel{-\!\!*} P)\right\}$$

// Unfold definitions.

$$\left\{\begin{array}{l}(P' \mathrel{-\!\!*} P) * [\mathrm{GET}]_1^{r'} * \\ \boxed{\begin{array}{l}\boxed{\mathtt{i}.\mathrm{bit} \mapsto 0}_{I(\mathtt{i})}^{r} * \forall^* i'.\,[\mathrm{SET}(i')]_{\mathrm{d}\pi}^{r} \vee \\ \boxed{\mathtt{i}.\mathrm{bit} \mapsto \_ * \mathtt{i}.\mathrm{prev} \mapsto i' * \mathsf{pa}(i')}_{I(\mathtt{i})}^{r} \\ * (P' \vee \exists P''.\,\mathsf{fut}(i', P'') * (P'' \mathrel{-\!\!*} P'))\end{array}}_{J(\mathtt{i},P',\pi,r)}^{r'}\end{array}\right\}$$

```
while(i.bit = 0) { skip; }
```

$$\left\{\begin{array}{l}(P' \mathrel{-\!\!*} P) * [\mathrm{GET}]_1^{r'} * \\ \boxed{\begin{array}{l}\boxed{\mathtt{i}.\mathrm{bit} \mapsto \_ * \mathtt{i}.\mathrm{prev} \mapsto i' * \mathsf{pa}(i')}_{I(\mathtt{i})}^{r} \\ * (P' \vee \exists P''.\,\mathsf{fut}(i', P'') * (P'' \mathrel{-\!\!*} P'))\end{array}}_{J(\mathtt{i},P',\pi,r)}^{r'}\end{array}\right\}$$

// Pull into local state and GC GET.

$$\left\{\begin{array}{l}\boxed{\mathtt{i}.\mathrm{bit} \mapsto \_ * \mathtt{i}.\mathrm{prev} \mapsto i' * \mathsf{pa}(i')}_{I(\mathtt{i})}^{r} * \\ (P' \vee \exists P''.\,\mathsf{fut}(i', P'') * (P'' \mathrel{-\!\!*} P')) * (P' \mathrel{-\!\!*} P)\end{array}\right\}$$

// Transitivity of $\mathrel{-\!\!*}$.

$$\left\{\begin{array}{l}\boxed{\mathtt{i}.\mathrm{bit} \mapsto \_ * \mathtt{i}.\mathrm{prev} \mapsto i' * \mathsf{pa}(i')}_{I(\mathtt{i})}^{r} * \\ \quad (P \vee \exists P''.\,\mathsf{fut}(i', P'') * (P'' \mathrel{-\!\!*} P))\end{array}\right\}$$

The proof for `grant`, `newchan` and `split` are similar to the proofs for the single-bit case. Once again, the proof of `grant` depends on the fact that fut can be split according to the resource held by it.

6. Related Work and Conclusions

Most work on combining separation logic with concurrency constructs has considered them as primitive in the logic. This begins with O'Hearn's work on concurrent separation logic [20], which takes statically allocated locks as a primitive. CSL has been extended to deal with dynamically-allocated locks [11, 14, 15] and re-entrant locks [12]. Others have extended separation logic or similar logics with primitive channels [13, 1, 24, 18], and event driven programs [17].

Concurrent abstract predicates [6] combine the explicit treatment of concurrent interference from rely-guarantee [16, 10, 23] and abstraction through abstract predicates [21], with a concurrent fiction of disjointness [7] supported by capabilities [8]. In this paper we have combined concurrent abstract predicates with higher-order separation logic [3]. We used our higher-order logic to define and verify a specification for barriers that enforce complex data and control dependencies in concurrent programs.

Although we have focussed in this paper on barrier constructs used for deterministic parallelism [25, 2, 4, 19], our logic is intended as a general approach to specifying concurrency constructs. Our syntactic approach has the advantage that concurrency constructs of different kinds combine transparently. For example, lock predicates defined in [6] can be transferred through our channel predicates without changing the semantics or proofs of correctness for either module. In addition, we can verify that concrete implementations of constructs satisfy their specification.

Acknowledgements Thanks to the anonymous referees, Richard Bornat, Matko Botinčan, Thomas Dinsdale-Young, Philippa Gardner, Neel Krishnaswami, Daiva Naudžiūnienė, Viktor Vafeiadis and John Wickerson.

References

[1] C. J. Bell, A. Appel, and D. Walker. Concurrent separation logic for pipelined parallelization. In *SAS*, 2009.

[2] E. D. Berger, T. Yang, T. Liu, and G. Novark. Grace: Safe multithreaded programming for C/C++. In *OOPSLA*, 2010.

[3] B. Biering, L. Birkedal, and N. Torp-Smith. BI-hyperdoctrines, higher-order separation logic, and abstraction. *TOPLAS*, 29(5), 2007.

[4] R. L. Bocchino, Jr., V. S. Adve, D. Dig, S. V. Adve, S. Heumann, R. Komuravelli, J. Overbey, P. Simmons, H. Sung, and M. Vakilian. A type and effect system for deterministic parallel Java. In *OOPSLA '09*, pages 97–116. ACM, 2009.

[5] J. Boyland. Checking interference with fractional permissions. In *SAS*, 2003.

[6] T. Dinsdale-Young, M. Dodds, P. Gardner, M. J. Parkinson, and V. Vafeiadis. Concurrent abstract predicates. In *ECOOP*, 2010.

[7] T. Dinsdale-Young, P. Gardner, and M. Wheelhouse. Abstraction and refinement for local reasoning. In *VSTTE*, 2010.

[8] M. Dodds, X. Feng, M. J. Parkinson, and V. Vafeiadis. Deny-guarantee reasoning. In *ESOP*, 2009.

[9] M. Dodds, S. Jagannathan, and M. J. Parkinson. Modular reasoning for deterministic parallelism. Computer laboratory technical report, University of Cambridge, 2010.

[10] X. Feng, R. Ferreira, and Z. Shao. On the relationship between concurrent separation logic and assume-guarantee reasoning. In *ESOP*, 2007.

[11] A. Gotsman, J. Berdine, B. Cook, N. Rinetzky, and M. Sagiv. Local reasoning for storable locks and threads. In *APLAS*, 2007.

[12] C. Haack, M. Huisman, and C. Hurlin. Reasoning about Java's Reentrant Locks. In *APLAS*, pages 171–187, 2008.

[13] C. A. R. Hoare and P. W. O'Hearn. Separation logic semantics for communicating processes. *ENTCS*, 212:3–25, 2008.

[14] A. Hobor, A. W. Appel, and F. Zappa Nardelli. Oracle semantics for concurrent separation logic. In *ESOP*, 2008.

[15] B. Jacobs and F. Piessens. Modular full functional specification and verification of lock-free data structures. Technical Report CW 551, Katholieke Universiteit Leuven, Dept. of Computer Science, 2009.

[16] C. B. Jones. Tentative steps toward a development method for interfering programs. *TOPLAS*, 5(4):596–619, 1983.

[17] N. R. Krishnaswami, L. Birkedal, and J. Aldrich. Verifying event-driven programs using ramified frame properties. In *TLDI*, 2010.

[18] K. R. M. Leino, P. Müller, and J. Smans. Deadlock-free channels and locks. In *ESOP*, 2010.

[19] A. Navabi, X. Zhang, and S. Jagannathan. Quasi-static Scheduling for Safe Futures. In *PPoPP*, pages 23–32. ACM, 2008.

[20] P. W. O'Hearn. Resources, concurrency and local reasoning. *TCS*, 2007.

[21] M. J. Parkinson and G. M. Bierman. Separation logic and abstraction. In *POPL*, pages 247–258, 2005.

[22] M. C. Rinard and M. S. Lam. Semantic Foundations of Jade. In *POPL*, pages 105–118. ACM, 1992.

[23] V. Vafeiadis. *Modular Fine-Grained Concurrency Verification*. PhD thesis, University of Cambridge, July 2007.

[24] J. Villard, É. Lozes, and C. Calcagno. Tracking heaps that hop with heap-hop. In *TACAS*, pages 275–279, 2010.

[25] A. Welc, S. Jagannathan, and A. Hosking. Safe Futures for Java. In *OOPSLA*, pages 439–435, 2005.

Expressive Modular Fine-Grained Concurrency Specification

Bart Jacobs * Frank Piessens

DistriNet Research Group, Department of Computer Science, Katholieke Universiteit Leuven, Belgium

{bart.jacobs,frank.piessens}@cs.kuleuven.be

Abstract

Compared to coarse-grained external synchronization of operations on data structures shared between concurrent threads, fine-grained, internal synchronization can offer stronger progress guarantees and better performance. However, fully specifying operations that perform internal synchronization modularly is a hard, open problem. The state of the art approaches, based on linearizability or on concurrent abstract predicates, have important limitations on the expressiveness of specifications. Linearizability does not support ownership transfer, and the concurrent abstract predicates-based specification approach requires hardcoding a particular usage protocol. In this paper, we propose a novel approach that lifts these limitations and enables fully general specification of fine-grained concurrent data structures. The basic idea is that clients pass the ghost code required to instantiate an operation's specification for a specific client scenario into the operation in a simple form of higher-order programming.

We machine-checked the theory of the paper using the Coq proof assistant. Furthermore, we implemented the approach in our program verifier VeriFast and used it to verify two challenging fine-grained concurrent data structures from the literature: a multiple-compare-and-swap algorithm and a lock-coupling list.

Categories and Subject Descriptors F.3.1 [*Logics and Meanings of Programs*]: Specifying and Verifying and Reasoning about Programs—Specification techniques

General Terms Verification

Keywords fine-grained concurrency, separation logic

1. Introduction

34 years after Owicki and Gries (O&G) proposed their resource-invariants-based (RI) method [12] and their interference-freedom-checks-based (IF) method [13] for the verification of parallel programs, doing so fully modularly is still an area of active research. For parallel programs, two kinds of modularity can be distinguished: thread-modularity and procedure-modularity.

Thread-modularity means that each thread can be verified separately, under a well-defined, concise set of assumptions on its environment. The RI method satisfies this criterion, since the resource invariants are the only shared assumptions among the threads. The IF method does not, since it requires each command of each thread to be checked for interference with each command of each other thread. The latter problem was solved by the rely-guarantee (RG) method [9], which summarizes each thread's interference assumptions and guarantees in a single rely, resp. guarantee condition.

Procedure-modularity means that each procedure, or each group of procedures that cooperate to implement an abstract data type, can be verified separately, again under a well-defined, concise set of assumptions on its environment that performs proper abstraction over implementation aspects. Neither the RI method nor RG satisfy this criterion. RI, because it requires auxiliary variable annotations that break modularity, as we will show; and RG, because it does not allow as-if-atomic operations on data structures to be treated just like atomic machine instructions, although this has been addressed recently with work on linearizability-based verification [6, 15].

In this paper, we propose an extension of the RI method that achieves procedure-modularity. The basic idea is simple: at each procedure call, the auxiliary variable updates required to enable verification of the client program are passed into the procedure as an extra argument. Correspondingly, the procedure's specification is parameterized by a precondition and a postcondition for the updates, and imposes a correctness condition on the updates in the form of a Hoare triple.

We first describe the approach informally in the context of an informal extension of the RI method with procedures. However, since the RI method imposes syntactic restrictions on which threads may mention specific variables, an extension with procedures requires more involved bookkeeping of variable occurrences. These details are not very interesting, and we do not develop this setting formally; rather, our formal system, like our implementation, uses separation logic [11, 14], where these issues do not occur.

We implemented the approach in our program verifier VeriFast and verified two challenging fine-grained concurrent data structures from the literature: a multiple-compare-and-swap (MCAS) algorithm [5], and a lock-coupling list.

The remainder of the paper is structured as follows. In §2 we recall the RI method. In §3 we show that this method is not procedure-modular. In §4, we informally present our approach for extending RI to achieve procedure-modularity. In §5, we describe how our approach may be lifted to a dynamic setting using separation logic and permission accounting. In §6, we introduce *ghost objects*, data structures constructed from auxiliary heap cells that enable partial information sharing. In §7, we describe how programs that use atomic machine instructions can be encoded straightforwardly into the system of this paper. In §8, we describe our proof of a concurrent set algorithm. In §9 we describe the verification tool. Finally, we discuss related work in §10.

2. The Owicki-Gries Method

Consider the simple parallel program used by O&G [12] to introduce their resource-invariant-based method, reproduced in Fig-

---

* This work was performed while Bart Jacobs was a Postdoctoral Fellow of the Research Foundation - Flanders (FWO)

POPL'11, January 26–28, 2011, Austin, Texas, USA.

```
resource r(x) : cobegin
    with r when true do x := x + 1
  //
    with r when true do x := x + 1
coend
```

Figure 1. A simple parallel program; can be verified with resource invariants and auxiliary variables

ure 1. It uses the parallel execution command

$$\textbf{cobegin}\ S_1 // \ldots // S_n\ \textbf{coend}$$

to run two threads that each increment variable x. Variable x is protected by resource r: the critical section command **with** r **when** B **do** S blocks until B is true and no other thread is using r.

In this simple language, data races can be avoided by imposing the following simple syntactic restrictions:

- An assignment to a variable x that belongs to a resource r is allowed only inside a critical section for r.
- An occurrence of a variable x outside of a critical section for a resource to which it belongs, if any, is allowed only if no other thread modifies the variable.

O&G propose the following axioms for parallel executions and critical sections, similar to the ones proposed by Hoare but with relaxed conditions on variable occurrences. The axioms assume that an assertion $I(r)$ has been defined for each resource r, called the resource's *resource invariant*.

Parallel Execution Axiom. If $\{P_1\}\ S_1\ \{Q_1\}$ and $\{P_2\}\ S_2\ \{Q_2\}$ and ...and $\{P_n\}\ S_n\ \{Q_n\}$ and no variable free in P_i or Q_i is changed in S_j $(i \neq j)$ and all variables in $I(r)$ belong to resource r, then $\{P_1 \wedge \cdots \wedge P_n \wedge I(r)\}$ **resource** r : **cobegin** $S_1 // \ldots // S_n$ **coend** $\{Q_1 \wedge \cdots \wedge Q_n \wedge I(r)\}$.

Critical Section Axiom. If $\{I(r) \wedge P \wedge B\}\ S\ \{I(r) \wedge Q\}$, and $I(r)$ is the invariant from the **cobegin** command, and no variable free in P or Q is changed in another process, then $\{P\}$ **with** r **when** B **do** S $\{Q\}$.

We would like to prove that if $x = 0$ before the program executes, then $x = 2$ after the program terminates. As O&G point out, this property cannot be verified using the above axioms directly. They propose to augment the program with *auxiliary variables* y and z, that track each thread's contribution to the value of x. Figure 2 shows the proof outline given by O&G for the augmented program.

```
{x = 0}
begin y := 0; z := 0;
  {y = 0 ∧ z = 0 ∧ I(r)}
  resource r(x, y, z) : cobegin
    {y = 0}
    with r when true do
      {y = 0 ∧ I(r)}
      begin x := x + 1; y := 1 end
      {y = 1 ∧ I(r)}
    {y = 1}
  //
    {z = 0}
    with r when true do
      {z = 0 ∧ I(r)}
      begin x := x + 1; z := 1 end
      {z = 1 ∧ I(r)}
    {z = 1}
  coend
  {y = 1 ∧ z = 1 ∧ I(r)}
end
{x = 2}
I(r) = {x = y + z}
```

Figure 2. Owicki and Gries' proof of the program of Figure 1. y and z are auxiliary variables.

Notice that the auxiliary variables are mentioned in assertions outside of the **with do** commands, even though they are protected by resource r; this is allowed provided that the thread that mentions a given variable is the only one that modifies that variable, per the Parallel Execution Axiom.

To regulate reasoning using auxiliary variables, O&G propose auxiliary variable sets and the Auxiliary Variable Axiom.

Definition. A set AV of program variables is an *auxiliary variable set* for a given program if variables in AV appear in the program only in assignments to variables in AV.

Auxiliary Variable Axiom. If AV is an auxiliary variable set for S, let S' be obtained from S by deleting all assignments to variables in AV. Then if $\{P\}\ S\ \{Q\}$ is true and P and Q do not refer to any variables from AV, $\{P\}\ S'\ \{Q\}$ is also true.

3. The Procedure-Modularity Problem

Now consider again the un-augmented program of Figure 1. Suppose we wish to encapsulate x and the operation on it, i.e. the increment operation, into a separate module. (Note: neither the programming language of O&G, nor their proof system, support procedures, since both impose syntactic conditions on the threads where variables occur, and this is not well-defined in the presence of procedures. In this section and the next, we informally introduce our approach, while glossing over this issue. In Section 5 we present our approach formally, using heap cells instead of global variables, thus eliminating this issue.) There are two ways to do this: using external synchronization (Figure 3a) and using internal synchronization (Figure 3b).

```
procedure incr() do x := x + 1
resource r(x) : cobegin
    with r when true do incr()
  //
    with r when true do incr()
coend
```

(a) External synchronization

```
procedure incr(r) do with r when true do x := x + 1
resource r(x) : cobegin
    incr(r)
  //
    incr(r)
coend
```

(b) Internal synchronization

Figure 3. Two modularized versions of the program of Figure 1

In the version that uses external synchronization, the module is easy to specify: procedure $incr$ satisfies the following specification: $\{x = X\}\ incr()\ \{x = X + 1\}$ where X is a logical variable; the specification holds for all values of X. Using this specification, both module and client program are easy to verify; the proof outline of Figure 2 is mostly unchanged. The reason is that the auxiliary variables can be added in the client program; no augmentation of the module is required.

procedure $incr(r, \rho)$ **do**
  with r **when** $true$ **do begin** $x := x + 1;\ \rho$ **end**
begin $y := 0; z := 0;$
  resource $r(x, y, z)$: **cobegin**
    $incr(r, y := 1)$
  //
    $incr(r, z := 1)$
  coend
end

Figure 4. The program of Figure 3b, augmented per our approach

For the version that uses internal synchronization, this is not the case. The updates of y and z need to be added inside the **with do** command, but this command is in the module and furthermore different updates need to be added for different call sites. One might then wonder whether insisting on internal synchronization is worthwhile; it is, because delegating synchronization to the module allows the module to perform *fine-grained synchronization*, for example by acquiring locks multiple times for smaller amounts of time, or by using atomic machine instructions such as compare-and-swap.

One can easily see that verifying this program with the Owicki-Gries method is impossible. Indeed, consider any augmentation of the program with auxiliary variable assignments, and any proof outline for the augmented program. Since the assignments inside the critical section occur in both threads, no variable modified inside the critical section may be mentioned by any thread's proof outline outside the critical section. Therefore, removing the critical section from the program does not invalidate the proof outline. Consequently, the proof outline cannot verify the triple $\{x = 0\} \cdot \{x = 2\}$.

4. Achieving Procedure-Modularity

In order to enable a modular specification of the module of Figure 3b, we propose to augment the program not just with auxiliary variables, but with a simple form of higher-order programming to allow the client program to pass auxiliary variable updates into the module. Specifically, we augment procedure $incr$ with a parameter ρ that ranges over *commands*, and its body so that it executes ρ after the update of x inside the critical section. In the client program, at each call of $incr$, the appropriate auxiliary variable update is specified as the value for parameter ρ. The augmented program is shown in Figure 4.

The specification of $incr$ is now more involved:

$$\frac{x \notin FV(P, U, Q) \qquad P \wedge I(r) \Rightarrow U(x+1) \qquad \{U(x)\}\ \rho\ \{Q \wedge I(r)\}}{\{P\}\ incr(r, \rho)\ \{Q\}}$$

The specification is universally quantified over the predicates P, Q, and U; it can be instantiated with appropriate predicates at each call site. Notice also that the specification is generic in the resource invariant. The resource invariant for the resource that protects a fine-grained concurrent data structure is chosen by the client of the data structure. This enables the client to specify the relationship between the state of the data structure and the auxiliary variables introduced by the client.

It is important to point out that although the specification of $incr$ looks like a proof rule, it is not part of the proof system and it does not affect the soundness of the proof system. Rather, it is a derived proof rule that must be verified starting from the proof rules of the proof system.

$\{P\}$
with r **when** $true$ **do begin**
  $\{P \wedge I(r)\}$
  $\{U(x + 1)\}$
  $x := x + 1;$
  $\{U(x)\}$
  ρ
  $\{Q \wedge I(r)\}$
end
$\{Q\}$

Figure 5. Proof outline for procedure $incr$

$\{x = 0\}$
begin $y := 0; z := 0;$
  $\{y = 0 \wedge z = 0 \wedge I(r)\}$
  resource $r(x, y, z)$: **cobegin**
    $\{y = 0\}$
    $incr(r, y := 1)$
      with $P \equiv y = 0; Q \equiv y = 1; U(X) \equiv X = 1 + z$
    $\{y = 1\}$
  //
    $\{z = 0\}$
    $incr(r, z := 1)$
      with $P \equiv z = 0; Q \equiv z = 1; U(X) \equiv X = y + 1$
    $\{z = 1\}$
  coend
  $\{y = 1 \wedge z = 1 \wedge I(r)\}$
end
$\{x = 2\}$
$I(r) = \{x = y + z\}$

Figure 6. Proof outline for the client program

It is easy to see that the implementation of $incr$ satisfies the specification; a proof outline is shown in Figure 5.

The proof of the client program is equally easy; see the proof outline in Figure 6.

5. Formal System

We presented our approach informally in the preceding sections. In order to achieve a well-defined approach, we need to resolve the problem of O&G's syntactic restrictions on which threads may mention which variables; these are not compatible with procedures. To do so, we move to a programming language without global variables, where threads share data only through the heap; and we use separation logic to reason about such programs. Specifically, we adopt the programming language and program logic of Gotsman et al. [4] for storable locks and threads, with a few modifications:

- We add support for auxiliary heap cells and passing closed commands into procedures as argument values.
- We do not treat local variables as resources.

A translation of the modularized Owicki-Gries example with internal synchronization of Figure 3 (b) to the more dynamic programming language is shown in Figure 7. The program consists of a procedure $incr$ and a main program. The main program allocates two consecutive memory cells and it initializes the first one (at address ℓ) for use as a lock, and releases it. (After a thread initializes a lock, it initially holds it.) The second cell (at address $\ell+1$) corresponds to the global variable x in the original program. The program then starts two threads, both of which increment the sec-

$$
\begin{array}{l}
\textbf{procedure } incr(\ell) \; = \\
\quad \textbf{acquire}(\ell); r := [\ell+1]; [\ell+1] := r+1; \textbf{release}(\ell) \\
\ell := \textbf{cons}(1,0); \textbf{init}(\ell); \textbf{release}(\ell); \\
t_1 := \textbf{fork } incr(\ell); \\
t_2 := \textbf{fork } incr(\ell); \\
\textbf{join}(t_1); \textbf{join}(t_2); \\
\textbf{acquire}(\ell); \textbf{finalize}(\ell)
\end{array}
$$

Figure 7. The Owicki-Gries example, translated into the dynamic programming language

ond cell, under protection of the lock. Finally, it joins both threads, acquires the lock, and decommissions it. (A thread may only decommission locks that it holds.) We wish to prove that when the program terminates, we have $\ell+1 \mapsto 2 * \mathbf{true}$.

The original proof by O&G used auxiliary global variables. In this section, we use *auxiliary heap cells* instead. Specifically, with each allocated real heap cell, say at address ℓ, we associate an infinite number of auxiliary heap cells, whose address is given by a pair of integers $\ell.\ell'$, where ℓ is the real address and ℓ' is the *ghost offset*.[1] In the example, we use the auxiliary heap cells at addresses $\ell.0$ and $\ell.1$ to track the contributions of thread 1 and 2 to the value of the cell at $\ell+1$, corresponding to auxiliary variables y and z in the original proof.

The proof system of Gotsman et al. requires that a *tag* A be associated with each lock, and a *lock invariant* I_A with each tag. We will associate the tag mylock with the lock of the example, and the following lock invariant with the tag:

$$
\begin{array}{l}
I_{\text{mylock}}(\ell) \; = \\
\qquad \exists C_0, C_1 \bullet \ell.0 \overset{1/2}{\mapsto} C_0 * \ell.1 \overset{1/2}{\mapsto} C_1 * \ell+1 \mapsto C_0 + C_1
\end{array}
$$

The lock invariant corresponds closely to the resource invariant of the original example. It states that the value of $\ell+1$ is the sum of the value of $\ell.0$ and $\ell.1$. In the original proof, syntactic restrictions ensured that auxiliary variable y could be modified only inside a critical section and only by the first thread; in the current proof, fractional permissions [1] achieve the same goal. Specifically, one half of the permission for each auxiliary heap cell becomes owned by the lock; the other half is retained by the corresponding thread.

As in the previous section, to verify procedure *incr*, we start by augmenting it with an auxiliary parameter ρ that ranges over auxiliary commands, and by augmenting its body with an occurrence of ρ after the update of $\ell+1$ but before the lock is released. As before, this parameter will serve to perform the auxiliary state updates required to preserve the lock invariant. The specification of procedure *incr* enforces that it does so:

$$
\frac{I_A(\ell) * P \Rightarrow \exists X \bullet \ell+1 \mapsto X * U(X) \qquad \forall X \bullet \{\ell+1 \mapsto X+1 * U(X)\}\; \rho \;\{I_A(\ell) * Q\}}{\{\pi A(\ell) * P\}\; incr(\ell,\rho)\; \{\pi A(\ell) * Q\}}
$$

The specification is universally quantified over the address ℓ of the lock, the tag A of the lock, the fraction π of the lock permission available to the procedure (any fraction will do), an additional precondition P and postcondition Q, and a predicate $U(X)$, parameterized over an integer X, that describes the resources (specifically, the auxiliary heap cells) owned by the lock besides the heap cell at address $\ell+1$, and states that those resources are in a state corresponding to value X of the heap cell at address $\ell+1$.

The specification has two premises. The first one states that the lock invariant $I_A(\ell)$ combined with the additional precondition P implies full permission to access the heap cell at address $\ell+1$, plus some extra state $U(X)$, where X is the value of the heap cell. The second premise states the correctness of the parameter ρ: it states that executing command ρ must re-establish the lock invariant after the update of $\ell+1$, and the remaining state must satisfy Q.

We again point out that this specification has the shape of a proof rule, but is not part of the proof system; as always when verifying programs with procedures, the specifications of the procedures must be derived using the proof rules of the system as part of the verification of the program.

A proof outline of the program is shown in Figure 8. Notice the following:

- The release of the lock consumes the lock invariant.
- A thread specification and thread specification arguments are associated with each **fork** operation for verification purposes. A fork with thread specification τ and arguments $\overline{n}$ consumes the precondition of τ and produces a thread permission $\mathsf{tid}_\tau(t,\overline{n})$, where t is the thread identifier.
- Joining a thread consumes the thread permission and produces the thread specification's postcondition.
- The acquisition of the lock produces the lock invariant. Merging the fractions of the auxiliary heap cells yields full information about $\ell+1$, per the following law:

$$
(a \overset{1/2}{\mapsto} v * \exists C \bullet a \overset{1/2}{\mapsto} C * P(C)) \Rightarrow a \mapsto v * P(v)
$$

5.1 Programming Language

The syntax of arithmetic expressions e, boolean expressions b, and commands c is given below. All commands return a value. Local variables are scoped, using **let** commands. The syntax $x := c; y := c'; c''$ is syntactic sugar for **let** $x := c$ **in let** $y := c'$ **in** c''. We assume a global table $pdef$ of procedure definitions. The recursion operator $(\mu f(\overline{x}) \bullet c)(\overline{e})$ applies the recursive function f with parameters $\overline{x}$ and body c to arguments $\overline{e}$. The scope of f is c, minus any command expressions in c. The syntax **letrec** $f(\overline{x}) = c$ **in** c' is syntactic sugar for $c'[(\mu f(\overline{x}) \bullet c)/f]$. All substitutions are capture-avoiding. A command is *closed* if it has no free variables $x \in \mathsf{Vars}$ and no free functions $f \in \mathsf{FuncNames}$. We assume a bijective encoding $\lfloor \cdot \rfloor$ of closed commands into integers. A command expression c denotes the encoding of c as an integer. A closure execution command $\mathbf{exec}(e)$ executes the closed command obtained by decoding the value of e. In the examples, we simply write ρ instead of $\mathbf{exec}(\rho)$. That is, a variable name used as a command denotes a closure execution.

$$
\begin{array}{rl}
& n \in \mathbb{Z}, x \in \mathsf{Vars}, p \in \mathsf{ProcNames}, f \in \mathsf{FuncNames} \\
e ::= & n \mid x \mid e+e \mid e-e \mid c \\
b ::= & e = e \mid e < e \\
c ::= & \mathbf{cons}(\overline{e}) \mid \mathbf{gcons}(e) \mid [e] \mid [e.e] \mid [e] := e \mid [e.e] := e \\
& \mid \mathbf{dispose}(e) \mid \mathbf{if}\ b\ \mathbf{then}\ c\ \mathbf{else}\ c \mid \mathbf{return}\ e \\
& \mid p(\overline{e}) \mid \mathbf{exec}(e) \mid \mathbf{let}\ x := c\ \mathbf{in}\ c \\
& \mid (\mu f(\overline{x}) \bullet c)(\overline{e}) \mid f(\overline{e}) \mid \mathbf{fork}\ c \mid \mathbf{join}(e) \\
& \mid \mathbf{init}_A(e) \mid \mathbf{acquire}(e) \mid \mathbf{release}(e) \mid \mathbf{finalize}(e) \\
pdef ::= & \mathbf{procedure}\ p(\overline{x}) = c
\end{array}
$$

The evaluation $[\![e]\!]$ of a closed expression e is defined as follows:

$$
[\![n]\!] = n \quad [\![e+e']\!] = [\![e]\!] + [\![e']\!] \quad [\![e-e']\!] = [\![e]\!] - [\![e']\!] \quad [\![c]\!] = \lfloor c \rfloor
$$

We define a small-step interleaving semantics. A configuration consists of a real heap h, a ghost heap g, and a thread map T. A real heap is a finite partial function from positive integers to integers. A ghost heap is a partial function from pairs of integers to integers. A thread map is a finite partial function from thread identifiers to closed *continuations*. The continuations κ and *contexts* ξ are

[1] We use the terms *auxiliary* and *ghost* interchangeably.

$\mathbf{procedure}\ \mathit{incr}(\ell, \rho) =$
$\quad \{\pi A(\ell) * P\}$
$\quad \mathbf{acquire}(\ell);$
$\quad \{\pi A(\ell) * \mathsf{locked}_A(\ell) * I_A(\ell) * P\}$
$\quad \{\pi A(\ell) * \mathsf{locked}_A(\ell) * \ell + 1 \mapsto X * U(X)\}$
$\quad r := [\ell + 1]; [\ell + 1] := r + 1;$
$\quad \{\pi A(\ell) * \mathsf{locked}_A(\ell) * \ell + 1 \mapsto X + 1 * U(X)\}$
$\quad \rho;$
$\quad \{\pi A(\ell) * \mathsf{locked}_A(\ell) * I_A(\ell) * Q\}$
$\quad \mathbf{release}(\ell),$
$\quad \{\pi A(\ell) * Q\}$
$\mathbf{threadspec}\ \mathit{thread1}(\ell)$
$\quad \mathbf{req}\ \frac{1}{2}\mathsf{mylock}(\ell) * \ell.0 \overset{1/2}{\mapsto} 0$
$\quad \mathbf{ens}\ \frac{1}{2}\mathsf{mylock}(\ell) * \ell.0 \overset{1/2}{\mapsto} 1$
$\mathbf{threadspec}\ \mathit{thread2}(\ell)$
$\quad \mathbf{req}\ \frac{1}{2}\mathsf{mylock}(\ell) * \ell.1 \overset{1/2}{\mapsto} 0$
$\quad \mathbf{ens}\ \frac{1}{2}\mathsf{mylock}(\ell) * \ell.1 \overset{1/2}{\mapsto} 1$

$\{\mathbf{emp}\}$
$\ell := \mathbf{cons}(1, 0);$
$\{\ell \mapsto 1 * (\circledast_{\ell' \in \mathbb{N}} \ell.\ell' \mapsto 0) * \ell + 1 \mapsto 0 * (\circledast_{\ell' \in \mathbb{N}} (\ell + 1).\ell' \mapsto 0)\}$
$\{\ell \mapsto 1 * \ell.0 \mapsto 0 * \ell.1 \mapsto 0 * \ell + 1 \mapsto 0 * \mathbf{true}\}$
$\mathbf{init}_{\mathsf{mylock}}(\ell); \mathbf{release}(\ell);$
$\{\mathsf{mylock}(\ell) * \ell.0 \overset{1/2}{\mapsto} 0 * \ell.1 \overset{1/2}{\mapsto} 0 * \mathbf{true}\}$
$t_1 := \mathbf{fork}$
$\quad \{\frac{1}{2}\mathsf{mylock}(\ell) * \ell.0 \overset{1/2}{\mapsto} 0\}$
$\quad \mathit{incr}(\ell, [\ell.0] := 1);$
$\qquad \text{with } U(X) = \ell.0 \mapsto 0 * \ell.1 \overset{1/2}{\mapsto} X$
$\quad \{\frac{1}{2}\mathsf{mylock}(\ell) * \ell.0 \overset{1/2}{\mapsto} 1\}$
$\{\frac{1}{2}\mathsf{mylock}(\ell) * \ell.1 \overset{1/2}{\mapsto} 0 * \mathsf{tid}_{\mathit{thread1}}(t_1, \ell) * \mathbf{true}\}$
$t_2 := \mathbf{fork}$
$\quad \{\frac{1}{2}\mathsf{mylock}(\ell) * \ell.1 \overset{1/2}{\mapsto} 0\}$
$\quad \mathit{incr}(\ell, [\ell.1] := 1);$
$\qquad \text{with } U(X) = \ell.0 \overset{1/2}{\mapsto} X * \ell.1 \mapsto 0$
$\quad \{\frac{1}{2}\mathsf{mylock}(\ell) * \ell.1 \overset{1/2}{\mapsto} 1\}$
$\{\mathsf{tid}_{\mathit{thread1}}(t_1, \ell) * \mathsf{tid}_{\mathit{thread2}}(t_2, \ell) * \mathbf{true}\}$
$\mathbf{join}(t_1);$
$\{\frac{1}{2}\mathsf{mylock}(\ell) * \ell.0 \overset{1/2}{\mapsto} 1 * \mathsf{tid}_{\mathit{thread2}}(t_2, \ell) * \mathbf{true}\}$
$\mathbf{join}(t_2);$
$\{\mathsf{mylock}(\ell) * \ell.0 \overset{1/2}{\mapsto} 1 * \ell.1 \overset{1/2}{\mapsto} 1 * \mathbf{true}\}$
$\mathbf{acquire}(\ell); \mathbf{finalize}(\ell)$
$\{(\exists C_0, C_1 \bullet \ell.0 \overset{1/2}{\mapsto} C_0 * \ell.1 \overset{1/2}{\mapsto} C_1 * \ell + 1 \mapsto C_0 + C_1)$
$\quad * \ \ell.0 \overset{1/2}{\mapsto} 1 * \ell.1 \overset{1/2}{\mapsto} 1 * \ell \mapsto \_ * \mathbf{true}\}$
$\{\ell.0 \mapsto 1 * \ell.1 \mapsto 1 * \ell + 1 \mapsto 2 * \ell \mapsto \_ * \mathbf{true}\}$

Figure 8. Proof outline for the example program

defined as follows:

$$\begin{array}{rcl} \kappa & ::= & c; \xi \mid n; \xi \\ \xi & ::= & \mathbf{let}\ x := [\,]\ \mathbf{in}\ c; \xi \mid \mathbf{done} \end{array}$$

The step relation $\rightsquigarrow$ is defined in Figure 9. In the step rules, symbols n match not just integer literals but other closed expressions as well, and denote their value. Notice that locks are implemented as a single heap cell that holds either the value 0, if the lock is not held, or the value 1, if the lock is held. We omit rules for **init** and **finalize**; we define them as equivalent to **return** 0 (i.e., a no-op) for purposes of the step relation. Throughout, $f[x := y]$ denotes function update; i.e. $f[x := y](x) = y$ and $f[x := y](z) = f(z)$ for $z \neq x$.

5.2 Simple Closures

We say a program has *simple closures* if there exists a partitioning of procedure parameters into closure parameters and non-closure parameters such that all **exec** commands are of the form $\mathbf{exec}(x)$ where x is a closure parameter, and all procedure call argument expressions for closure parameters are either command expressions or closure parameters. Applying the specification approach of this paper requires only simple closures. As we will see, simple closures admit a very simple proof system.

5.3 Proof System

The correctness of a command c is expressed in the form of a correctness judgment $\Gamma \vdash \{P\}\ c\ \{Q\}$, where Γ is a function environment and P and Q are *assertions*. An assertion describes a set of *permissions*. The set of permissions is defined as follows:

$$\hat{p} ::= \ell \mapsto v \mid \ell.\ell' \mapsto v \mid A(\ell) \mid \mathsf{locked}_A(\ell) \mid \mathsf{tid}_\tau(t, \overline{v})$$

A *permission bundle* is a total function from permissions to real numbers between 0, inclusive and 1, inclusive. We identify assertions with sets of permission bundles. That is, we treat assertions semantically. We denote the empty permission bundle (that maps all permissions to 0) as $\mathbf{0}$.

We define some syntax for assertions:

$$\begin{array}{l}
\mathbf{emp} = \{\mathbf{0}\} \\
\ell \overset{\pi}{\mapsto} v = \{\mathbf{0}[\ell \mapsto v := \pi]\} \\
\ell.\ell' \overset{\pi}{\mapsto} v = \{\mathbf{0}[\ell.\ell' \mapsto v := \pi]\} \\
\pi A(\ell) = \{\mathbf{0}[A(\ell) := \pi]\} \\
\pi \mathsf{tid}_\tau(t, \overline{v}) = \{\mathbf{0}[\mathsf{tid}_\tau(t, \overline{v}) := \pi]\} \\
P * Q = \{b \mid \exists b_1, b_2 \bullet b = b_1 + b_2 \wedge b_1 \in P \wedge b_2 \in Q\} \\
(\exists X \bullet P(X)) = \{b \mid \exists X \bullet b \in P(X)\} \\
(\circledast_{i \in \mathbb{N}} P(i)) = \{b \mid \exists B \bullet b = \Sigma_i B(i) \wedge \forall i \bullet B(i) \in P(i)\} \\
\quad \text{where } b = \Sigma_i B(i) \Leftrightarrow \\
\qquad (\forall \hat{p}, \varepsilon \bullet \exists n \bullet \forall i > n \bullet |b(\hat{p}) - \Sigma_{0 \leq j \leq i} B(j)(\hat{p})| < \varepsilon)
\end{array}$$

We say a permission bundle is *consistent* if there are no two points-to permissions with the same address and different values that both map to non-zero coefficients. We say one assertion A implies another one A', written $A \Rightarrow A'$, if for every *consistent* bundle $b \in A$, we have $b \in A'$.

The correctness judgment is defined inductively by the rules shown in Figure 10.

Notice that the proof rules for procedure calls and for closure executions simply require the correctness of the procedure or closure's body. It follows that a procedure that calls another procedure, or that executes a closure, does not, in isolation, have a closed proof tree. Rather, its proof tree is parameterized by the proof trees for the procedures called and closures executed. This simple approach is sufficient if the program has simple closures and an acyclic procedure call graph. Indeed, in that case, given a main command, one can inline all procedure calls to obtain an equivalent command that contains no procedure call or closure execution commands; the shape of the proof tree for the original main command will reflect the shape of the main command after inlining.

5.4 Soundness

We sketch how one can prove soundness of the program logic used. More details are in the technical report [7]; also, a machine-checked proof is at http://www.cs.kuleuven.be/~bartj/finegrained/.

Continuation step rules for relation $\langle h, g, \kappa\rangle \rightsquigarrow \langle h', g', \kappa'\rangle \mid \mathbf{abort}$

$\langle h, g, \mathbf{cons}(n_1, \ldots, n_m); \xi\rangle$	$\rightsquigarrow \langle h \cup \{\ell \mapsto n_1, \ldots, \ell + m - 1 \mapsto n_m\}, g \cup \{(\ell_1, \ell_2) \mapsto 0 \mid \ell \leq \ell_1 < \ell + m\}, \ell; \xi\rangle$	if $0 < \ell$ and $\{\ell, \ldots, \ell + m - 1\} \cap \mathrm{dom}(h) = \emptyset$
$\langle h, g, \mathbf{gcons}(n); \xi\rangle$	$\rightsquigarrow \langle h, g \cup \{(0, \ell') \mapsto n\}, \ell'; \xi\rangle$	if $0 < \ell' \wedge (0, \ell') \notin \mathrm{dom}(g)$
$\langle h, g, [n]; \xi\rangle$	$\rightsquigarrow$ if $n \in \mathrm{dom}(h)$ then $\langle h, g, h(n); \xi\rangle$ else **abort**	
$\langle h, g, [n.n']; \xi\rangle$	$\rightsquigarrow$ if $(n, n') \in \mathrm{dom}(g)$ then $\langle h, g, g((n, n')); \xi\rangle$ else **abort**	
$\langle h, g, [n] := v; \xi\rangle$	$\rightsquigarrow$ if $n \in \mathrm{dom}(h)$ then $\langle h[n := v], g, 0; \xi\rangle$ else **abort**	
$\langle h, g, [n.n'] := v; \xi\rangle$	$\rightsquigarrow$ if $(n, n') \in \mathrm{dom}(g)$ then $\langle h, g[(n, n') := v], 0; \xi\rangle$ else **abort**	
$\langle h, g, \mathbf{dispose}(n); \xi\rangle$	$\rightsquigarrow$ if $n \in \mathrm{dom}(h)$ then $\langle h \setminus_{\mathrm{dom}} \{n\}, g \setminus_{\mathrm{dom}} \{(n, \ell') \mid \mathbf{true}\}, 0; \xi\rangle$ else **abort**	
$\langle h, g, \mathbf{if}\ b\ \mathbf{then}\ c\ \mathbf{else}\ c'; \xi\rangle$	$\rightsquigarrow$ if $b = \mathsf{true}$ then $\langle h, g, c; \xi\rangle$ else $\langle h, g, c'; \xi\rangle$	
$\langle h, g, p(\overline{v}); \xi\rangle$	$\rightsquigarrow \langle h, g, c[\overline{v}/\overline{x}]; \xi\rangle$	if **procedure** $p(\overline{x}) = c$
$\langle h, g, \mathbf{exec}(\lfloor c \rfloor); \xi\rangle$	$\rightsquigarrow \langle h, g, c; \xi\rangle$	
$\langle h, g, \mathbf{return}\ n; \xi\rangle$	$\rightsquigarrow \langle h, g, n; \xi\rangle$	
$\langle h, g, \mathbf{let}\ x := c\ \mathbf{in}\ c'; \xi\rangle$	$\rightsquigarrow \langle h, g, c; \mathbf{let}\ x := [\,]\ \mathbf{in}\ c'; \xi\rangle$	
$\langle h, g, (\mu f(\overline{x}) \bullet c)(\overline{v}); \xi\rangle$	$\rightsquigarrow \langle h, g, c[(\mu f(\overline{x}) \bullet c)/f, \overline{v}/\overline{x}]; \xi\rangle$	
$\langle h, g, \mathbf{acquire}(n); \xi\rangle$	$\rightsquigarrow \langle h[n := 1], g, 0; \xi\rangle$	if $(n, 0) \in h$
$\langle h, g, \mathbf{acquire}(n); \xi\rangle$	$\rightsquigarrow$ **abort**	if $n \notin \mathrm{dom}(h)$
$\langle h, g, \mathbf{release}(n); \xi\rangle$	$\rightsquigarrow$ if $n \in \mathrm{dom}(h)$ then $\langle h[n := 0], g, 0; \xi\rangle$ else **abort**	
$\langle h, g, v; \mathbf{let}\ x := [\,]\ \mathbf{in}\ c; \xi\rangle$	$\rightsquigarrow \langle h, g, c[v/x]; \xi\rangle$	

Thread map step rules for relation $\langle h, g, T\rangle \rightsquigarrow \langle h', g', T'\rangle \mid \mathbf{abort}$

$\langle h, g, T\rangle$	$\rightsquigarrow \langle h', g', T[t := \kappa']\rangle$	if $(t, \kappa) \in T$ and $\langle h, g, \kappa\rangle \rightsquigarrow \langle h', g', \kappa'\rangle$
$\langle h, g, T\rangle$	$\rightsquigarrow$ **abort**	if $(t, \kappa) \in T$ and $\langle h, g, \kappa\rangle \rightsquigarrow \mathbf{abort}$
$\langle h, g, T\rangle$	$\rightsquigarrow \langle h, g, T[t := t'; \xi, t' := c; \mathbf{done}]\rangle$	if $(t, \mathbf{fork}\ c; \xi) \in T$ and $t' \notin \mathrm{dom}(T)$
$\langle h, g, T\rangle$	$\rightsquigarrow \langle h, g, T[t := v; \xi] \setminus_{\mathrm{dom}} \{t'\}\rangle$	if $(t, \mathbf{join}(t'); \xi) \in T$ and $(t', v; \mathbf{done}) \in T$
$\langle h, g, T\rangle$	$\rightsquigarrow$ **abort**	if $(t, \mathbf{join}(n); \xi) \in T$ and $n \notin \mathrm{dom}(T)$

Figure 9. Step rules for continuations κ and thread maps T. Note: **init** and **finalize** are no-ops.

$$\{\mathbf{emp}\}\ r := \mathbf{cons}(v_0, \ldots, v_n)\ \{\circledast_i\, r + i \mapsto v_i * (\circledast_{\ell' \in \mathbb{N}}\, (r + i).\ell' \mapsto 0)\} \qquad \{\mathbf{emp}\}\ r := \mathbf{gcons}(v)\ \{0.r \mapsto v\}$$

$$\{\ell \overset{\pi}{\mapsto} v\}\ r := [\ell]\ \{\ell \overset{\pi}{\mapsto} v \wedge r = v\} \qquad \{\ell.\ell' \overset{\pi}{\mapsto} v\}\ r := [\ell.\ell']\ \{\ell.\ell' \overset{\pi}{\mapsto} v \wedge r = v\} \qquad \{\ell \mapsto \_\}\ [\ell] := v\ \{\ell \mapsto v\}$$

$$\{\ell.\ell' \mapsto \_\}\ [\ell.\ell'] := v\ \{\ell.\ell' \mapsto v\} \qquad \{\ell \mapsto \_ * \circledast_{\ell' \in \mathbb{N}} \ell.\ell' \mapsto \_\}\ \mathbf{dispose}(\ell)\ \{\mathbf{emp}\} \qquad \{P\}\ r := \mathbf{return}\ v\ \{P \wedge r = v\}$$

$$\frac{\Gamma \vdash \{P \wedge b\}\ c\ \{Q\} \qquad \Gamma \vdash \{P \wedge \neg b\}\ c'\ \{Q\}}{\Gamma \vdash \{P\}\ \mathbf{if}\ b\ \mathbf{then}\ c\ \mathbf{else}\ c'\ \{Q\}} \qquad \frac{\mathbf{procedure}\ p(\overline{x}) = c \qquad \{P\}\ c[\overline{v}/\overline{x}]\ \{Q\}}{\{P\}\ p(\overline{v})\ \{Q\}} \qquad \frac{\{P\}\ c\ \{Q\}}{\{P\}\ \mathbf{exec}(c)\ \{Q\}}$$

$$\frac{\Gamma \vdash \{P\}\ r := c\ \{Q(r)\} \qquad \forall X \bullet \Gamma \vdash \{Q(X)\}\ c'[X/x]\ \{Q'\}}{\Gamma \vdash \{P\}\ \mathbf{let}\ x := c\ \mathbf{in}\ c'\ \{Q'\}} \qquad \frac{\mathbf{threadspec}\ \tau(\overline{x})\ \mathbf{req}\ P\ \mathbf{ens}\ Q \qquad \Gamma \vdash \{P[\overline{v}/\overline{x}]\}\ c\ \{Q[\overline{v}/\overline{x}]\}}{\Gamma \vdash \{P[\overline{v}/\overline{x}]\}\ r := \mathbf{fork}\ c\ \{\mathsf{tid}_\tau(r, \overline{v})\}}$$

$$\frac{\Gamma, \{P\}\ f(\overline{x})\ \{Q\} \vdash \{P\}\ c\ \{Q\}}{\Gamma \vdash \{P[\overline{v}/\overline{x}]\}\ (\mu f(\overline{x}) \bullet c)(\overline{v})\ \{Q[\overline{v}/\overline{x}]\}} \qquad \frac{\mathbf{threadspec}\ \tau(\overline{x})\ \mathbf{req}\ P\ \mathbf{ens}\ Q}{\{\mathsf{tid}_\tau(t, \overline{v})\}\ \mathbf{join}(t)\ \{Q[\overline{v}/\overline{x}]\}} \qquad \frac{\forall X \bullet \Gamma \vdash \{P(X)\}\ c\ \{Q(X)\}}{\Gamma \vdash \{\exists X \bullet P(X)\}\ c\ \{\exists X \bullet Q(X)\}}$$

$$\Gamma, \{P\}\ f(\overline{x})\ \{Q\}, \Gamma' \vdash \{P[\overline{v}/\overline{x}]\}\ f(\overline{v})\ \{Q[\overline{v}/\overline{x}]\} \qquad \{s \mapsto 1\}\ \mathbf{init}_A(s)\ \{A(s) * \mathsf{locked}_A(s)\}$$

$$\{\pi A(s)\}\ \mathbf{acquire}(s)\ \{\pi A(s) * \mathsf{locked}_A(s) * I_A(s)\} \qquad \{\mathsf{locked}_A(s) * I_A(s)\}\ \mathbf{release}(s)\ \{\mathbf{emp}\} \qquad \frac{\{P\}\ c\ \{Q\}}{\Gamma \vdash \{P\}\ c\ \{Q\}}$$

$$\{A(s) * \mathsf{locked}_A(s)\}\ \mathbf{finalize}(s)\ \{s \mapsto \_\} \qquad \frac{P \Rightarrow P' \qquad \Gamma \vdash \{P'\}\ c\ \{Q\} \qquad Q \Rightarrow Q'}{\Gamma \vdash \{P\}\ c\ \{Q'\}} \qquad \frac{\Gamma \vdash \{P\}\ c\ \{Q\}}{\Gamma \vdash \{P * R\}\ c\ \{Q * R\}}$$

Figure 10. Proof rules

The soundness theorem states that if for a command c we have $\{\mathbf{emp}\}\ c\ \{\mathbf{true}\}$, then $\langle \emptyset, \emptyset, \{(t, c; \mathbf{done})\}\rangle \not\rightsquigarrow^* \mathbf{abort}$ for any thread identifier t.

We do not define the semantics of the correctness judgment directly. Rather, we define an assertion transformer $\mathsf{valid}_\Gamma(c, Q)$ (similar to a weakest precondition operator, but we don't worry about whether it is the *weakest* precondition or not). We prove

$$(\Gamma \vdash \{P\}\ c\ \{Q\}) \Rightarrow (P \Rightarrow \mathsf{valid}_\Gamma(c, Q))$$

We can then define validity of a configuration. A configuration $\langle h, g, T\rangle$ is valid iff there exists a set of permissions P such that

- for every (ℓ, ℓ') with $0 < \ell$, if $(\ell, \ell') \in \mathrm{dom}(g)$ then $\ell \in \mathrm{dom}(h)$
- h equals the set of non-ghost points-to permissions in P plus one element $\ell \mapsto 0$ or $\ell \mapsto 1$ for each $A(\ell)$ permission in P
- g equals the set of ghost points-to permissions in P
- there is exactly one $\mathsf{tid}_\tau(t, \overline{v})$ permission for each thread $t \in \mathrm{dom}(T)$, and
- there is exactly one $\mathsf{locked}_A(\ell)$ permission for each $A(\ell)$ permission whose corresponding heap element equals 1, and
- there exists a permission bundle b_t for each thread t, and a permission bundle b_ℓ for each $A(\ell)$ permission for which there is no $\mathsf{locked}_A(\ell)$ permission, and a permission bundle b_C for the program's environment, which in particular contains the tid permission for the main thread, such that
  - the sum of all b_t and all b_ℓ and b_C equals $\{(\hat{p}, 1) \mid \hat{p} \in P\}$, and
  - for each thread $(t, \kappa) \in T$, $b_t \in \mathsf{valid}(\kappa, Q[\overline{v}/\overline{x}])$ where $\mathbf{threadspec}\ \tau(\overline{x})\ \mathbf{req} \cdots \mathbf{ens}\ Q$ and $\mathsf{tid}_\tau(t, \overline{v}) \in P$.
  - for each lock $A(\ell) \in P$ for which there is no $\mathsf{locked}_A(\ell) \in P$, $b_\ell \in I_A(\ell)$.

By correctness of the main program, the initial configuration is valid. We then prove that each execution step preserves configuration validity. The theorem then follows from the fact that **abort** is not a valid configuration.

5.5 Ghost erasure

After a program is verified, ghost code can be removed without invalidating the proof. Specifically, if all code that is removed is side-effect-free and terminates, then if the program after erasure aborts, the original program aborts. If the program has simple closures and the procedure call graph is acyclic, then non-termination can result only from non-terminating recursive functions. Removed code is side-effect-free if it affects only the ghost heap, provided that all ghost heap accesses are removed.

6. Ghost Objects

In the previous section we used fractional points-to assertions to enable a thread to maintain information about a shared object. The location is read-only while no thread has full permission, and the thread has full information: it knows the exact value.

Often, proofs require a more fine-grained type of tracking. A thread needs to maintain partial information about a value, while allowing other threads to modify the value in ways that preserve all threads' assumptions.

A general approach to this problem is rely-guarantee reasoning. However, in this paper we propose a different strategy. We propose the use of *ghost objects*. A ghost object is a data structure built from auxiliary heap cells, that represents some mathematical value, and that allows clients to obtain *handles* on the object that represent a condition on the value of the object. Handles represent partial information about the object. Correspondingly, they represent the permission to violate the condition, in the sense that the object does not allow violating the condition without handing in the handle.

A basic ghost object is a *ghost bag*. The abstract predicate $\mathsf{gbag}(b, B)$ represents a ghost bag with identifier b, currently holding the bag of integers B. The object provides the following operations:

$$\{\mathbf{emp}\}\ r := \mathit{create\_gbag}()\ \{\mathsf{gbag}(r, \emptyset)\}$$

$$\{\mathsf{gbag}(b, B)\}\ \mathit{gbag\_add}(b, v)\ \{\mathsf{gbag}(b, B \uplus \{v\}) * \mathsf{gbagh}(b, v)\}$$

$$\begin{array}{c}\{\mathsf{gbag}(b, B) * \mathsf{gbagh}(b, v)\}\\ \mathit{gbag\_remove}(b, v)\\ \{v \in B \wedge \mathsf{gbag}(b, B - \{v\})\}\end{array}$$

The predicate $\mathsf{gbagh}(b, v)$ represents the knowledge that the ghost bag b currently contains element v. It furthermore represents the permission to remove this element.

This ghost object can be implemented in terms of simple auxiliary heap cells. It does not need to be built into the proof system. A verified ghost bag implementation comes with our verification tool (see Section 9). Furthermore, based on ghost bags, a wide variety of ghost objects can be implemented easily.

7. Atomic Instructions

The programming language of the previous section does not include atomic machine instructions such as atomic compare-and-swap (CAS) instructions, which are available on most platforms. However, one can easily translate a program that uses atomics to a behaviorally equivalent (but less efficient) program of the formal language that uses locks by introducing an extra lock for each data structure of the program that is accessed using atomics, and then translating the atomic operations into code sequences that acquire the corresponding lock, perform the operation, and then release the lock. We will call such a lock an *atomic space* and its address an *atomic space identifier*, ranged over by s. (Note: our verification tool supports atomics and atomic spaces directly, and does not require a translation.)

A procedure corresponding to a CAS operation could look as follows, augmented with two ghost parameters ρ and ρ' for verification purposes:

$$\begin{array}{l}\mathbf{procedure}\ \mathit{cas}(s, \ell, o, n, \rho, \rho') =\\ \quad \mathbf{acquire}(s);\\ \quad v := [\ell];\\ \quad \mathbf{if}\ v = o\ \mathbf{then}\ ([\ell] := n; \rho)\ \mathbf{else}\ \rho';\\ \quad \mathbf{release}(s);\\ \quad \mathbf{return}\ v\end{array}$$

We can prove the following specification for it:

$$\frac{\begin{array}{c}I_A(s) * P \Rightarrow \exists X \bullet \ell \mapsto X * S(X)\\ \{S(o) * \ell \mapsto n\}\ \rho\ \{I_A(s) * Q(o)\}\\ \forall X \bullet X \neq o \Rightarrow \{S(X) * \ell \mapsto X\}\ \rho'\ \{I_A(s) * Q(X)\}\end{array}}{\{\pi A(s) * P\}\ r := \mathit{cas}(s, \ell, o, n, \rho, \rho')\ \{\pi A(s) * Q(r)\}}$$

We will use this procedure in the examples below, as well as procedures *load* and *store* corresponding to atomic loads and stores, respectively, specified as follows:

$$\frac{\begin{array}{c}I_A(s) * P \Rightarrow \exists X \bullet \ell \mapsto X * S(X)\\ \forall X \bullet \{S(X) * \ell \mapsto X\}\ \rho\ \{I_A(s) * Q(X)\}\end{array}}{\{\pi A(s) * P\}\ r := \mathit{load}(s, \ell, \rho)\ \{\pi A(s) * Q(r)\}}$$

$$\frac{\begin{array}{c}I_A(s) * P \Rightarrow \exists X \bullet \ell \mapsto X * S(X)\\ \forall X \bullet \{S(X) * \ell \mapsto v\}\ \rho\ \{I_A(s) * Q\}\end{array}}{\{\pi A(s) * P\}\ \mathit{store}(s, \ell, v, \rho)\ \{\pi A(s) * Q\}}$$

8. Abstraction: A Concurrent Set

In the example of the preceding sections, the data structure being manipulated was a simple cell, and its memory representation, $\ell + 1 \mapsto X$, was disclosed in the specification of the operation, *incr*. In this section, we show that our approach supports specifications that abstract over the representation of the concurrent data structure. Furthermore, we show that the approach allows abstract specification and verification of concurrent data structures built on top of other concurrent data structures. We do so by first showing a specification and implementation of a binary semaphore module implemented in terms of atomic machine instructions. We then show a specification, implementation, and proof of a concurrent set module implemented by hand-over-hand locking of a sorted linked list, that uses the semaphore module.

8.1 Semaphore Specification

The semaphore module defines an abstract predicate $\mathsf{sema}(\ell, v)$ which represents a semaphore at address ℓ whose value is v (either 0 or 1). The specification of the functions exported by the module can be given in terms of this predicate as follows:

$$\{\ell \mapsto 0\}\ \mathit{init\_sema}(\ell)\ \{\mathsf{sema}(\ell, 0)\}$$

$$\frac{I_A(s) * P \Leftrightarrow \exists v \bullet \mathsf{sema}(\ell, v) * S(v) \qquad \{S(0) * \mathsf{sema}(\ell, 1)\}\ \rho\ \{I_A(s) * Q\}}{\{\pi A(s) * P\}\ \mathit{sema\_acquire}(s, \ell, \rho)\ \{\pi A(s) * Q\}}$$

$$\frac{I_A(s) * P \Rightarrow \exists v \bullet \mathsf{sema}(\ell, v) * S(v) \qquad \forall v \bullet \{S(v) * \mathsf{sema}(\ell, 0)\}\ \rho\ \{I_A(s) * Q\}}{\{\pi A(s) * P\}\ \mathit{sema\_release}(s, \ell, \rho)\ \{\pi A(s) * Q\}}$$

$$\{\mathsf{sema}(\ell, \_)\}\ \mathit{finalize\_sema}(\ell)\ \{\ell \mapsto \_\}$$

Actually, to enable sharing of information about the state of a semaphore, the semaphore module defines a slightly different predicate $[\pi]\mathsf{sema}(\ell, v)$. Just $\mathsf{sema}(\ell, v)$ is shorthand for $[1]\mathsf{sema}(\ell, v)$. The module further exports the following lemmas:

$$[\pi_1 + \pi_2]\mathsf{sema}(\ell, v) \Rightarrow [\pi_1]\mathsf{sema}(\ell, v) * [\pi_2]\mathsf{sema}(\ell, v)$$
$$[\pi_1]\mathsf{sema}(\ell, v) * [\pi_2]\mathsf{sema}(\ell, v') \Rightarrow [\pi_1 + \pi_2]\mathsf{sema}(\ell, v) \wedge v' = v$$

where π_1 and π_2 range over positive real numbers.

8.2 Semaphore Implementation

The implementation of the semaphore module is straightforward:

```
predicate [π]sema(ℓ, v) = ℓ ↦^π v
procedure init_sema(ℓ) = skip
procedure sema_acquire(s, ℓ, ρ) =
  letrec iter() =
    r := cas(s, ℓ, 0, 1, ρ, skip);
    if r ≠ 0 then iter()
  in iter()
procedure sema_release(s, ℓ, ρ) =
  store(s, ℓ, 0, ρ)
procedure finalize_sema(ℓ) = skip
```

We omit the proof; it, too, is straightforward.

8.3 Set Specification

The set module exports three procedures:

$$\{\mathbf{emp}\}\ r := \mathit{create\_set}()\ \{\mathsf{set}(r, \emptyset)\}$$

$$\frac{I_A(s) * S \Leftrightarrow \exists V \bullet \mathsf{set}(o, V) * U(V) \qquad \forall V \bullet v \notin V \Rightarrow \{U(V) * P\}\ \rho\ \{U(V \cup \{v\}) * Q(1)\} \qquad \forall V \bullet v \in V \Rightarrow \{U(V) * P\}\ \rho'\ \{U(V) * Q(0)\}}{\{\pi A(s) * S * P\}\ r := \mathit{add}(s, o, v, \rho, \rho')\ \{\pi A(s) * S * Q(r)\}}$$

$$\frac{I_A(s) * S \Leftrightarrow \exists V \bullet \mathsf{set}(o, V) * U(V) \qquad \forall V \bullet v \in V \Rightarrow \{U(V) * P\}\ \rho\ \{U(V \setminus \{v\}) * Q(1)\} \qquad \forall V \bullet v \notin V \Rightarrow \{U(V) * P\}\ \rho'\ \{U(V) * Q(0)\}}{\{\pi A(s) * S * P\}\ r := \mathit{remove}(s, o, v, \rho, \rho')\ \{\pi A(s) * S * Q(r)\}}$$

Procedure *add* returns 1 if the element was not yet present, and 0 otherwise. Analogously, procedure *remove* returns 1 if the element was present, and 0 otherwise.

Notice that in the specification of *add* and *remove*, the first premise, which enables the procedure to separate the set out of the lock invariant, uses S instead of P. In earlier specifications, there was no separate S predicate and P was used for simplicity; however, using P means the procedure cannot perform further atomic operations on the set after the closure ρ or ρ' has been executed, since it consumes P and produces Q. Using a separate predicate S means the procedure can access the set both before and after executing the closure.

To simplify the presentation, the example module does not offer a procedure for disposing a set object. An implementation that supports disposal, verified using our verification tool, is available online.

8.4 Sugared Specifications

In the above specifications of procedures *add* and *remove*, the functional behavior is obscured somewhat by the fine-grained concurrency scaffolding. Fortunately, however, we can easily define an abbreviated notation for typical fine-grained specifications, which makes them look just like sequential specifications. We introduce the notation

$$\{\mathsf{object}(o, v)\}\ r := \mathit{foo}_{\mathrm{FG}}(o)\ \{\mathsf{object}(o, \mathrm{post}(v)) \wedge r = \mathrm{res}(v)\}$$

as an abbrevation for

$$\frac{I_A(s) * S \Leftrightarrow \exists v \bullet \mathsf{object}(o, v) * U(v) \qquad \forall v \bullet \{U(v) * P\}\ \rho\ \{U(\mathrm{post}(v)) * Q(\mathrm{res}(v))\}}{\{\pi A(s) * S * P\}\ r := \mathit{foo}(s, o, \rho)\ \{\pi A(s) * S * Q(r)\}}$$

Often, it is convenient to split the postcondition into multiple cases, with corresponding ghost command parameters and corresponding premises. We introduce

$$\{\mathsf{object}(o, v)\}$$
$$r := \mathit{foo}_{\mathrm{FG}}(o)$$
$$\left\{ \begin{array}{l} G_1(v) \wedge \mathsf{object}(o, \mathrm{post}_1(v)) \wedge r = \mathrm{res}_1(v) \vee \\ G_2(v) \wedge \mathsf{object}(o, \mathrm{post}_2(v)) \wedge r = \mathrm{res}_2(v) \end{array} \right\}$$

where G_i are pure assertions, as an abbreviation for

$$\frac{I_A(s) * S \Leftrightarrow \exists v \bullet \mathsf{object}(o, v) * U(v) \qquad \forall v \bullet G_1(v) \Rightarrow \{U(v) * P\}\ \rho_1\ \{U(\mathrm{post}_1(v)) * Q(\mathrm{res}_1(v))\} \qquad \forall v \bullet G_2(v) \Rightarrow \{U(v) * P\}\ \rho_2\ \{U(\mathrm{post}_2(v)) * Q(\mathrm{res}_2(v))\}}{\{\pi A(s) * S * P\}\ r := \mathit{foo}(s, o, \rho_1, \rho_2)\ \{\pi A(s) * S * Q(r)\}}$$

This notation allows the above specification for procedure *add* to be written as

$$\{\mathsf{set}(o, V)\}$$
$$r := \mathit{add}_{\mathrm{FG}}(o, v)$$
$$\{v \notin V \wedge \mathsf{set}(o, V \cup \{v\}) \wedge r = 1 \vee v \in V \wedge \mathsf{set}(o, V) \wedge r = 0\}$$

8.5 Set Implementation

The implementation of the set module is shown in Figure 11.

For node values, we implicitly perform an encoding of $\mathbb{Z} \cup \{-\infty, +\infty\}$ into $\mathbb{Z}$.

We use the following syntactic sugar: $n.\mathsf{next} = n + 1$, and $n.\mathsf{value} = n + 2$.

The set is implemented as a sorted linked list. For synchronization, one field of each node is converted into a semaphore that is used to perform hand-over-hand locking of consecutive nodes. This affords some degree of parallelism for concurrent operations on the set.

8.6 Set proof

The core of the proof of the set module is the definition of the set predicate; it serves as the invariant of the data structure, which holds before and after each atomic operation. This invariant must

```
procedure create_set() =
  lastNode := cons(0, 0, +∞);
  firstNode := cons(0, lastNode, −∞);
  init_sema(firstNode); return firstNode

letrec locate(n) =
  n' := [n.next]; v' := [n'.value];
  if v' < v then (
    sema_acquire(s, n'); sema_release(s, n);
    return locate(n')
  ) else return n
in

procedure add(s, o, v) =
  sema_acquire(s, o); n := locate(o);
  n' := [n.next]; v' := [n'.value];
  if v' = v then (
    sema_release(s, n); return 0
  ) else (
    n'' := cons(0, n', v); init_sema(n'');
    [n.next] := n''; sema_release(s, n); return 1
  )

procedure remove(s, o, v) =
  sema_acquire(s, o); n := locate(o);
  n' := [n.next]; v' := [n'.value];
  if v' = v then (
    sema_acquire(s, n');
    n'' := [n'.next]; [n.next] := n'';
    sema_release(s, n); return 1
  ) else (sema_release(s, n); return 0)
```

Figure 11. Implementation of the set module. Note: desugaring inlines *locate* into *add* and *remove*

enable each thread to retain, between the atomic operations that constitute a set operation, the information it needs about the state of the data structure.

For example, after locating a node, a thread must know this node will remain in the data structure. For this purpose, we track the set of nodes in the linked list using a ghost bag (see Section 6). We keep the identifier of the ghost bag in a ghost field of the first node. To refer to this ghost field, we use the syntactic sugar $o.\mathsf{bag} = o.1$.

Another consideration when defining the invariant is that we wish to retain the shape of the linked list even when a thread has taken ownership of a node's next field in preparation for inserting or removing the next node. Therefore, we use the ghost field at ghost offset 0 of each node as the oldNext field: $n.\mathsf{oldNext} = n.0$.

As usual, we use a recursive predicate lseg to describe the linked list:

$$\begin{array}{l}\mathsf{lseg}(b, f, v_f, \ell, v_\ell, \alpha, \beta) = \\ \quad (\alpha = \epsilon \wedge \beta = \epsilon \wedge f = \ell \wedge v_f = v_\ell) \vee \\ \quad (\exists \alpha', \beta', v_s, n, v_n \bullet \alpha = f \cdot \alpha' \wedge \beta = v_f \cdot \beta' \wedge \\ \qquad \mathsf{node}(b, f, v_s, v_f, n, v_n) * \mathsf{lseg}(b, n, v_n, \ell, v_\ell, \alpha', \beta'))\end{array}$$

where

$$\begin{array}{l}\mathsf{node}(b, n, v_s, v, n', v') = \\ \quad (v_s = 0 \wedge \mathsf{sema}(n, v_s) * n.\mathsf{next} \mapsto n' * n.\mathsf{oldNext} \mapsto n' * \\ \quad n.\mathsf{value} \overset{1/2}{\mapsto} v * n'.\mathsf{value} \overset{1/2}{\mapsto} v' * \mathsf{gbagh}(b, n) \wedge v < v') \vee \\ \quad (v_s = 1 \wedge [\tfrac{1}{2}]\mathsf{sema}(n, v_s) * n.\mathsf{oldNext} \overset{1/2}{\mapsto} n' * \\ \quad n.\mathsf{value} \overset{1/4}{\mapsto} v * n'.\mathsf{value} \overset{1/4}{\mapsto} v' \wedge v < v')\end{array}$$

The predicate $\mathsf{lseg}(b, f, v_f, \ell, v_\ell, \alpha, \beta)$ denotes the section of the sorted linked list from node f to node ℓ, excluding node ℓ. The other parameters are the ghost bag identifier b, the first value v_f, the last value v_ℓ, the list of nodes α, and the list of values β. The body of the predicate is a disjunction. The first disjunct describes the case where the first node equals the last node and therefore the section is empty.

The second disjunct describes the non-empty case. Specifically, it describes the first node using the predicate node and recursively calls the predicate to describe the subsection from the second node to the last node. This disjunct quantifies existentially over the tail α' of α, the tail β' of β, the value of the semaphore v_s of the first node, the next node n, and the value of the next node v_n.

Predicate node's body, too, is a disjunction; the first disjunct describes the case where the node is not locked; the second disjunct describes the case where the node is locked. In the latter case, full ownership of the n.next field and fractional ownership of the semaphore and the n.oldNext, n.value, and n'.value fields has been transferred to the thread that acquired the lock.

Notice that each node owns half of the value field of the next node. This means that when a thread locks a node, it knows not only that node's value but also the next node's value. This allows it to safely insert a new node in between, while maintaining the sortedness of the list.

The definition of the set predicate itself is now straightforward:

$$\begin{array}{l}\mathsf{set}(o, V) = \\ \quad \exists b, \ell, \alpha, \beta \bullet \mathsf{lseg}(b, o, -\infty, \ell, +\infty, \alpha, -\infty \cdot \beta) * \\ \qquad o.\mathsf{bag} \overset{-}{\mapsto} b * \mathsf{gbag}(b, \mathsf{elems}(\alpha)) * \mathbf{true} \wedge V = \mathsf{elems}(\beta);\end{array}$$

The definition uses the mathematical function $\mathsf{elems}(\alpha)$ which denotes the bag of the elements of the list α. It states that there is a sorted linked list starting at o, that starts with value $-\infty$ and ends with value $+\infty$ (which means that an insertion point can be found within the list for any finite value). It further states that the nodes of the list are exactly the elements in the ghost bag at o.**bag**, and that abstract value V of the set is exactly the bag of the values of the list.

The syntax $\ell \overset{-}{\mapsto} v$ is shorthand for $\exists \pi \bullet \ell \overset{\pi}{\mapsto} v$. That is, it denotes an unspecified fraction of the points-to permission. As applied in the set predicate, this allows threads to remember the connection between o and b.

The **true** conjunct allows us to leak memory locations (or fractions thereof) that we do not use; specifically, of the last node ℓ we use only one-half of field ℓ.value. We would need to be more precise if we wanted to support disposal of the set object.

The specification of local recursive function *locate* is as follows:

$$\left\{\begin{array}{l}\pi A(s) * S * o.\mathsf{bag} \overset{-}{\mapsto} b * \mathsf{gbagh}(b, n) * \\ {[\tfrac{1}{2}]}\mathsf{sema}(n, 1) * n.\mathsf{oldNext} \overset{1/2}{\mapsto} n' * n.\mathsf{next} \mapsto n' * \\ n.\mathsf{value} \overset{1/4}{\mapsto} v_n * n'.\mathsf{value} \overset{1/4}{\mapsto} v_{n'} \wedge v_n < v\end{array}\right\}$$

$$r := locate(n)$$

$$\left\{\begin{array}{l}\pi A(s) * S * o.\mathsf{bag} \overset{-}{\mapsto} b * \mathsf{gbagh}(b, r) * [\tfrac{1}{2}]\mathsf{sema}(r, 1) * \\ \exists n, v_r, v_n \bullet r.\mathsf{oldNext} \overset{1/2}{\mapsto} n * r.\mathsf{next} \mapsto n * \\ r.\mathsf{value} \overset{1/4}{\mapsto} v_r * n.\mathsf{value} \overset{1/4}{\mapsto} v_n \wedge v_r < v \wedge v \leq v_n\end{array}\right\}$$

Note that even though *locate* is shown outside of *add* and *remove*, after desugaring it is within the scope of the parameters of these procedures, and furthermore its proof can use the premises of these procedures' specifications, and in particular the first premise.

We show in Figure 12 the set implementation annotated with ghost commands. A full proof outline is in the technical report [7].

```
procedure create_set() =
  lastNode := cons(0, 0, +∞);
  firstNode := cons(0, lastNode, −∞);
  [firstNode.oldNext] := lastNode;
  init_sema(firstNode);
  b := create_gbag(); gbag_add(b, f); [firstNode.bag] := b;
  return firstNode

letrec locate(n) =
  n′ := [n.next]; v′ := [n′.value];
  if v′ < v then (
    sema_acquire(s, n′, skip);
    sema_release(s, n, skip);
    return locate(n′)
  ) else
    return n
in

procedure add(s, o, v, ρ, ρ′) =
  sema_acquire(s, o, skip);
  b := [o.bag]; n := locate(o);
  n′ := [n.next]; v′ := [n′.value];
  if v′ = v then (
    sema_release(s, n, ρ′);
    return 0
  ) else (
    n″ := cons(0, n′, v); [n″.oldNext] := n′;
    init_sema(n″); [n.next] := n″;
    sema_release(s, n,
      (gbag_add(b, n″); [n.oldNext] := n″; ρ));
    return 1
  )

procedure remove(s, o, v, ρ, ρ′) =
  sema_acquire(s, o, skip);
  b := [o.bag]; n := locate(o);
  n′ := [n.next]; v′ := [n′.value];
  if v′ = v then (
    sema_acquire(s, n′, skip);
    n″ := [n′.next]; [n.next] := n″;
    sema_release(s, n,
      (gbag_remove(b, n′); [n.oldNext] := n″; ρ));
    return 1
  ) else (
    sema_release(s, n, ρ′);
    return 0
  )
```

Figure 12. The set module, with ghost commands (highlighted)

8.7 Client program

In this subsection, to illustrate how the specification of the set module can be used to verify rich properties of client programs, we verify the example client program shown in Figure 13. The program starts by creating a set object o and a lock s for use by the set module to emulate its atomic operations. (Remember that this lock can be erased after verification if real atomic operations are used; see Section 7.) Then, the lock is initialized. From this time, the lock protects the set data structure. Finally, a producer thread is forked and the main thread turns into a consumer thread. The producer thread simply adds 1,2,3,... to the set. The consumer thread repeatedly performs the following experiment: it picks an arbitrary number (by allocating a heap cell and disposing it, just for the address) and tries to remove it. If the remove operation succeeds, it tries to remove it again and asserts that the latter remove operation fails. It always does, since the producer thread never adds the same number twice.

```
letrec
  producerThread(s, o, x) =
    add(s, o, x); producerThread(s, o, x + 1)
  consumer(s, o, x) =
    r := remove(s, o, x);
    if r = 1 then (r := remove(s, o, x); assert(r = 0))
  consumerThread(s, o) =
    // pick random number x
    x := cons(0); dispose(x);
    consumer(s, o, x); consumerThread(s, o)
in
o := create_set(); s := cons(1); init_space(s); release(s);
fork producerThread(s, o, 1);
consumerThread(s, o)
```

Figure 13. Example client program for the concurrent set module

Here is how our approach succeeds in verifying the **assert** command of this program. A proof outline for this program, including ghost commands, is shown in Figure 14. As always, the crucial step is coming up with an invariant; specifically, a lock invariant for the lock s. It is shown at the bottom of Figure 14. The proof uses three ghost fields of s: $s.\mathsf{set}$ (sugar for $s.0$) connects the lock to the set o; $s.\mathsf{prod}$ (sugar for $s.1$) records the last number added by the producer; and $s.\mathsf{cons}$ (sugar for $s.2$) records the last number removed by the consumer. The invariant states that the last value added by the producer is an upper bound for the set's elements; that the last value removed by the consumer is not greater than the last value added by the producer; and that the last value removed by the consumer is not in the set.

Once the invariant is established, the proof outline follows easily. As usual, each thread retains half of its associated ghost field: the producer thread retains half of $s.\mathsf{prod}$ and the consumer thread retains half of $s.\mathsf{cons}$. The producer passes the required update of $s.\mathsf{prod}$ into add as a ghost argument; analogously, the consumer passes the required update of $s.\mathsf{cons}$ into $remove$ as a ghost argument.

The specifications of add and $remove$ are instantiated as follows. For all calls, predicate S is instantiated with $s.\mathsf{set} \overset{-}{\mapsto} o$ and predicate $U(V)$ is instantiated with the invariant minus the set data structure itself:

$$U(V) = \exists p, c \bullet s.\mathsf{set} \overset{-}{\mapsto} o * s.\mathsf{prod} \overset{1/2}{\mapsto} p * s.\mathsf{cons} \overset{1/2}{\mapsto} c \land (\forall v \in V \bullet v \leq p) \land c \leq p \land c \notin V$$

where variables s and o are bound at the call site. The instantiations of P and Q are shown at the call sites in Figure 14. Given these instantiations, the premises of add and $remove$'s specifications can be verified easily.

9. Verification Tool

We implemented our approach in our program verification tool, VeriFast [8], and we used the tool to verify two challenging fine-grained concurrent data structures from the literature: a multiple-compare-and-swap algorithm [5] and a lock-coupling list [15].

VeriFast is a general-purpose verifier prototype for C programs, based on separation logic. It takes source code annotated with function specifications, loop invariants, predicate definitions, and other annotations, and reports either that the program is memory-safe, data-race-free, and complies with function specifications, or

$$\textbf{threadspec}\ \mathit{producerThread}(s, o, x) =$$
$$\quad \textbf{req}\ \tfrac{1}{2}\mathsf{space}(s) * s.\mathsf{set} \overset{-}{\mapsto} o * \exists p \bullet s.\mathsf{prod} \overset{1/2}{\mapsto} p \wedge p < x$$
$$\quad \textbf{ens false}$$
$$\textbf{threadspec}\ \mathit{consumerThread}(s, o) =$$
$$\quad \textbf{req}\ \tfrac{1}{2}\mathsf{space}(s) * s.\mathsf{set} \overset{-}{\mapsto} o * \exists c \bullet s.\mathsf{cons} \overset{1/2}{\mapsto} c$$
$$\quad \textbf{ens false}$$
$$\textbf{letrec}$$
$$\quad \mathit{producerThread}(s, o, x) =$$
$$\qquad \{\tfrac{1}{2}\mathsf{space}(s) * s.\mathsf{set} \overset{-}{\mapsto} o * \exists p \bullet s.\mathsf{prod} \overset{1/2}{\mapsto} p \wedge p < x\}$$
$$\qquad \mathit{add}(s, o, x, [s.\mathsf{prod}] := x, \textbf{skip});$$
$$\qquad\quad P = \exists p \bullet s.\mathsf{prod} \overset{1/2}{\mapsto} p \wedge p < x$$
$$\qquad\quad Q(r) = s.\mathsf{prod} \overset{1/2}{\mapsto} x$$
$$\qquad \{\tfrac{1}{2}\mathsf{space}(s) * s.\mathsf{set} \overset{-}{\mapsto} o * s.\mathsf{prod} \overset{1/2}{\mapsto} x\}$$
$$\qquad \mathit{producerThread}(s, o, x + 1)$$
$$\quad \mathit{consumer}(s, o, x) =$$
$$\qquad \{\tfrac{1}{2}\mathsf{space}(s) * s.\mathsf{set} \overset{-}{\mapsto} o * \exists c \bullet s.\mathsf{cons} \overset{1/2}{\mapsto} c\}$$
$$\qquad r := \mathit{remove}(s, o, x, [s.\mathsf{cons}] := x, \textbf{skip});$$
$$\qquad\quad P = \exists c \bullet s.\mathsf{cons} \overset{1/2}{\mapsto} c$$
$$\qquad\quad Q(r) = \exists c \bullet s.\mathsf{cons} \overset{1/2}{\mapsto} c \wedge (r = 1 \Rightarrow c = x)$$
$$\qquad \{\tfrac{1}{2}\mathsf{space}(s) * s.\mathsf{set} \overset{-}{\mapsto} o * \exists c \bullet s.\mathsf{cons} \overset{1/2}{\mapsto} c \wedge (r = 1 \Rightarrow c = x)\}$$
$$\qquad \textbf{if}\ r = 1\ \textbf{then}\ ($$
$$\qquad\quad r := \mathit{remove}(s, o, x, \textbf{skip}, \textbf{skip});$$
$$\qquad\qquad P = s.\mathsf{cons} \overset{1/2}{\mapsto} x$$
$$\qquad\qquad Q(r) = s.\mathsf{cons} \overset{1/2}{\mapsto} x \wedge r = 0$$
$$\qquad\quad \{\tfrac{1}{2}\mathsf{space}(s) * s.\mathsf{set} \overset{-}{\mapsto} o * s.\mathsf{cons} \overset{1/2}{\mapsto} x \wedge r = 0\}$$
$$\qquad\quad \textbf{assert}(r = 0))$$
$$\quad \mathit{consumerThread}(s, o) =$$
$$\qquad \{\tfrac{1}{2}\mathsf{space}(s) * s.\mathsf{set} \overset{-}{\mapsto} o * \exists c \bullet s.\mathsf{cons} \overset{1/2}{\mapsto} c\}$$
$$\qquad \mathit{// pick\ random\ number}\ x$$
$$\qquad x := \textbf{cons}(0); \textbf{dispose}(x);$$
$$\qquad \mathit{consumer}(s, o, x);$$
$$\qquad \mathit{consumerThread}(s, o)$$
$$\textbf{in}$$
$$\{\mathbf{emp}\}$$
$$o := \mathit{create\_set}();$$
$$\{\mathsf{set}(o, \emptyset)\}$$
$$s := \textbf{cons}(1);$$
$$\{\mathsf{set}(o, \emptyset) * s \mapsto 1 * \circledast_{\ell' \in \mathbb{N}} s.\ell' \mapsto 0\}$$
$$[s.\mathsf{set}] := o;$$
$$[s.\mathsf{prod}] := 0;$$
$$[s.\mathsf{cons}] := 0;$$
$$\{\mathsf{set}(o, \emptyset) * s \mapsto 1 * s.\mathsf{set} \mapsto o * s.\mathsf{prod} \mapsto 0 * s.\mathsf{cons} \mapsto 0 * \textbf{true}\}$$
$$\textbf{init}_{\mathsf{space}}(s); \textbf{release}(s);$$
$$\{\mathsf{space}(s) * s.\mathsf{set} \overset{-}{\mapsto} o * s.\mathsf{prod} \overset{1/2}{\mapsto} 0 * s.\mathsf{cons} \overset{1/2}{\mapsto} 0 * \textbf{true}\}$$
$$\textbf{fork}\ \mathit{producerThread}(s, o, 1);$$
$$\{\tfrac{1}{2}\mathsf{space}(s) * s.\mathsf{set} \overset{-}{\mapsto} o * s.\mathsf{cons} \overset{1/2}{\mapsto} 0 * \textbf{true}\}$$
$$\mathit{consumerThread}(s, o)$$

$$I_{\mathsf{space}}(s) =$$
$$\quad \exists o, p, c, V \bullet$$
$$\qquad s.\mathsf{set} \overset{-}{\mapsto} o * s.\mathsf{prod} \overset{1/2}{\mapsto} p * s.\mathsf{cons} \overset{1/2}{\mapsto} c *$$
$$\qquad \mathsf{set}(o, V) \wedge (\forall v \in V \bullet v \leq p) \wedge c \leq p \wedge c \notin V$$

Figure 14. Proof outline for the client program

it shows a symbolic execution trace that leads to a potential error. It symbolically executes each function in turn, using a separation logic formula as the symbolic representation of memory.

VeriFast supports ghost commands for creating and updating ghost cells. It also supports *lemma functions*, which are like ordinary C functions except they may contain only ghost commands and VeriFast checks that they terminate. It follows that calls of lemma functions are ghost commands. Thirdly, it supports *lemma function pointers* and *lemma function pointer calls*. These features are all that was needed to make it possible to apply our approach in VeriFast. More generally, any verification tool that supports ghost variables, ghost functions, and dynamic binding of ghost functions supports our verification approach. This means it should be easy to extend other verification tools, such as VCC [2] and Chalice [10], to support our approach.

We have used VeriFast to verify the concurrent set module used as the example for this paper. We also verified a multiple-compare-and-swap (MCAS) algorithm proposed by Harris et al. [5]. MCAS is built on top of a restricted-double-compare-single-swap (RDCSS) algorithm by the same authors. Our MCAS proof consists of a proof of RDCSS with respect to an abstract specification of RDCSS, and a proof of MCAS based on the abstract specification of RDCSS. We also verified a simple example client program for each algorithm. The annotation overhead, consisting of specifications as well as proof steps, is shown in the following table:

Program	LOC	LOAnn	Overhead	Time
lcset.c	72	610	847%	0.37s
lcset_client.c	27	266	985%	0.13s
rdcss.c	51	528	1035%	0.5s
mcas.c	63	1111	1763%	1.33s
mcas_client.c	34	230	676%	0.22s

In each case, the annotation overhead is in the order of 10 to 20 lines of annotation per line of code. Three things should be kept in mind when considering the overhead. Firstly, these are probably some of the most complex algorithms in existence. Secondly, we did not optimize the annotation requirements for lemma function pointers; it currently involves significant boilerplate. Thirdly, we show these results only as evidence that the specification approach is applicable to challenging algorithms; this paper is not about VeriFast.

Notice that the run-time of the verification tool is very acceptable: on the order of one second. This enables an interactive annotation insertion process.

The tool and the annotated example programs are available online at http://www.cs.kuleuven.be/~bartj/verifast/.

10. Related Work

To the best of our knowledge, our approach is the first that enables fully general modular specification and verification of fine-grained concurrent modules and their clients.

We are aware of two existing approaches for specification of fine-grained concurrent data structures, both based on a marriage of rely-guarantee and separation logic [17]: a linearizability-based approach, initially proposed in Vafeiadis' PhD thesis [15], and concurrent abstract predicates [3].

In the linearizability-based approach, the specification for a data structure operation is in the form of a piece of sequential code that operates on a ghost variable that holds the abstract state of the data structure. An implementation complies with the specification if for each execution trace, there is a total ordering of the operation invocations in the trace such that their return values equal the return values that would result if the operations' specifications were executed sequentially in this total order. In other words, there exists a linearization point between the start and end of each operation invocation such that the result values are as if each operation's specification was executed atomically at the linearization point.

Linearizability-based verification verifies that the data structure is linearizable, by verifying that there exists a linearization point for each operation. The approach can then verify client code as if the operations executed atomically.

A limitation of the linearizability-based approach is that it does not support the transfer of ownership of memory locations or other resources between the data structure and its client. For example, a queue implemented as a linked list where nodes are allocated by the client, passed into the module on enqueue, and passed back to the client on dequeue, cannot be specified by the linearizability-based approach. This is because the definition of linearizability assumes no memory is shared across the module boundary, and all interaction is in the form of invocation arguments and results. In contrast, in our approach ownership transfer is supported. For example, here is a specification for the enqueue and dequeue operations of the queue module suggested above:

$$\frac{\begin{array}{c} I_A(s) * S \Leftrightarrow \exists \alpha \bullet \mathsf{queue}(q, \alpha) * U(\alpha) \\ \forall \alpha \bullet \{U(\alpha) * P\}\ \rho\ \{U(\alpha \cdot n) * Q * \mathsf{node}(n)\} \end{array}}{\{\pi A(s) * S * P\}\ enqueue(s, q, n, \rho)\ \{\pi A(s) * S * Q\}}$$

$$\frac{\begin{array}{c} I_A(s) * S \Leftrightarrow \exists \alpha \bullet \mathsf{queue}(q, \alpha) * U(\alpha) \\ \forall n, \alpha \bullet \{U(n \cdot \alpha) * P * \mathsf{node}(n)\}\ \rho\ \{U(\alpha) * Q(n)\} \\ \{U(\epsilon) * P\}\ \rho'\ \{U(\epsilon) * Q(0)\} \end{array}}{\{\pi A(s) * S * P\}\ r := dequeue(s, q, \rho, \rho')\ \{\pi A(s) * S * Q(r)\}}$$

An important advantage of linearizability, however, is that powerful automation techniques have been built for it, e.g. [16].

Concurrent abstract predicates (CAP) extend separation logic with *shared regions*. Each shared region is associated with an *interference specification*, which is a set of action names with associated pre- and postconditions. A piece of local state can be converted into a shared region. This gives the thread full permission to perform the actions associated with the region. It may then pass fractions of these *action permissions* to other threads. Each assertion about a shared region must be stable with respect to the actions that other threads may perform.

The CAP authors [3] propose the following approach for modular specification of a fine-grained data structure. The module exposes the data structure to clients in the form of a number of concurrent abstract predicates, each of which give permission to perform a particular type of operation. For example, their example lock module exposes predicates $\mathsf{isLock}(x)$ and $\mathsf{Locked}(x)$, which give permission to acquire, resp. release lock x. Their example set module exposes predicates $\mathsf{in}(h, v)$ and $\mathsf{out}(h, v)$, which give permission to remove, resp. add element v.

This specification approach does not subsume ours. Whereas our approach enables fully general specification of data structure operations, this approach enforces restrictions on how the data structure may be used. Specifically, while the set module specification allows threads to concurrently add or remove distinct elements, it does not allow them to race to concurrently add or remove the same element. More generally, the choice of which predicates to expose is a trade-off between the restrictions on usage and the type of information a client can track. Indeed: the information content of a predicate imposes a restriction on what other threads can do. For example, if one thread holds an $\mathsf{in}(h, v)$ permission, other threads cannot remove this element.

To achieve a fully general specification, the choice of stable permissions must be done by the client, not by the module designer. In order to enable this, the client must be able to do atomic or unstable observations, not just non-atomic or stable ones. This is what linearizability enables by allowing operations to be treated like atomic instructions, and what our approach enables by allowing the insertion of ghost code into the critical section, and by allowing the client to choose the auxiliary variables and the lock invariant.

Note that our comparison is with the way the CAP logic is used in [3], not with other specification approaches based on the CAP logic that may be proposed in the future.

However, the CAP logic is a convenient alternative to the use of ghost objects to track partial information, and as such is complementary to our specification approach. Specifically, one could have a single auxiliary variable that holds the precise abstract state of the data structure, and then insert this variable into a shared region. For example, the ghost bags of Section 6 could be implemented more straightforwardly using shared regions than using a data structure built from auxiliary heap cells.

Acknowledgments

The authors would like to thank Cristiano Calcagno, Mike Dodds, Peter O'Hearn, Matthew Parkinson, Viktor Vafeiadis, and Hongseok Yang for helpful comments on drafts of this paper. This research is partially funded by the Interuniversity Attraction Poles Programme Belgian State, Belgian Science Policy, and by the Research Fund K.U.Leuven.

References

[1] Richard Bornat, Cristiano Calcagno, Peter O'Hearn, and Matthew Parkinson. Permission accounting in separation logic. In *POPL*, 2005.

[2] Markus Dahlweid, Michał Moskal, Thomas Santen, Stephan Tobies, and Wolfram Schulte. VCC: Contract-based modular verification of concurrent C. In *ICSE*, 2009.

[3] Thomas Dinsdale-Young, Mike Dodds, Philippa Gardner, Matthew Parkinson, and Viktor Vafeiadis. Concurrent abstract predicates. In *ECOOP*, 2010.

[4] Alexey Gotsman, Josh Berdine, Byron Cook, Noam Rinetzky, and Mooly Sagiv. Local reasoning for storable locks and threads. In *APLAS*, 2007.

[5] Tim Harris, Keir Fraser, and Ian A. Pratt. A practical multi-word compare-and-swap operation. In *16th International Symposium on Distributed Computing*, 2002.

[6] Maurice Herlihy and Jeanette Wing. Linearizability: A correctness condition for concurrent objects. *ACM TOPLAS*, 12(3), 1990.

[7] Bart Jacobs and Frank Piessens. Expressive modular fine-grained concurrency specification (extended version). Technical Report CW590, Dept. CS, K.U.Leuven, 2010.

[8] Bart Jacobs, Jan Smans, and Frank Piessens. A quick tour of the VeriFast program verifier. In *APLAS*, 2010.

[9] C. B. Jones. Specification and design of (parallel) programs. In *IFIP Congress*, 1983.

[10] K. Rustan M. Leino, Peter Müller, and Jan Smans. *Foundations of Security Analysis and Design V, FOSAD 2007/2008/2009 Tutorial Lectures*, volume 5705 of *LNCS*, chapter Verification of concurrent programs with Chalice. Springer, 2009.

[11] Peter W. O'Hearn, John Reynolds, and Hongseok Yang. Local reasoning about programs that alter data structures. In *CSL*, 2001.

[12] Susan Owicki and David Gries. Verifying properties of parallel programs: An axiomatic approach. *CACM*, 19(5):279–285, May 1976.

[13] Susan Owicki and David Gries. An axiomatic proof technique for parallel programs i. *Acta Inf.*, 6, 1976.

[14] J. C. Reynolds. Separation logic: a logic for shared mutable data structures. In *LICS*, 2002.

[15] Viktor Vafeiadis. *Modular fine-grained concurrency verification*. PhD thesis, Computer Laboratory, University of Cambridge, July 2007.

[16] Viktor Vafeiadis. Automatically proving linearizability. In *CAV*, 2010.

[17] Viktor Vafeiadis and Matthew Parkinson. A marriage of rely/guarantee and separation logic. In *CONCUR*, 2007.

The Tree Width of Auxiliary Storage

P. Madhusudan
University of Illinois at Urbana-Champaign, USA
madhu@illinois.edu

Gennaro Parlato
LIAFA, CNRS and University of Paris Diderot, France.
gennaro@liafa.jussieu.fr

Abstract

We propose a generalization of results on the decidability of emptiness for several restricted classes of sequential and distributed automata with auxiliary storage (stacks, queues) that have recently been proved. Our generalization relies on reducing emptiness of these automata to finite-state *graph automata* (without storage) restricted to monadic second-order (MSO) definable graphs of bounded tree-width, where the graph structure encodes the mechanism provided by the auxiliary storage. Our results outline a uniform mechanism to derive emptiness algorithms for automata, explaining and simplifying several existing results, as well as proving new decidability results.

Categories and Subject Descriptors F.1.1 [*Theory of Computation*]: Models of Computation: Automata; D.2.4 [*Software Engineering*]: Software/Program Verification: Model checking; F.4.3 [*Theory of Computation*]: Formal Languages: Decision problems

General Terms Algorithms, Reliability, Theory, Verification

Keywords model checking, automata, decision procedures, bounded tree-width

1. Introduction

Several classes of automata with auxiliary storage have been defined over the years that have a decidable emptiness problem. Classic models like pushdown automata utilizing a *stack* have a decidable emptiness problem [14], and several new models like restricted classes of multi-stack pushdown automata, automata with queues, and automata with both stacks and queues, have been proved decidable recently [8, 15, 17, 22].

The decidability of emptiness of these automata has often been motivated for *model-checking* systems. Software models can be captured using automata with auxiliary storage, as stacks can model the *control recursion* in programs while queues model *FIFO communication between processes*. In abstraction-based model-checking, data domains get abstracted from programs, resulting in automata models (e.g., the SLAM tool builds pushdown automata models using *predicate abstraction* [7], and the GETAFIX tool model-checks both single-stack and multi-stack automata models [18, 19]). The emptiness problem for these automata is the most relevant problem as it directly corresponds to checking reachability of an error state.

However, the various identified decidable restrictions on these automata are, for the most part, *awkward* in their definitions— e.g. emptiness of multi-stack pushdown automata where pushes to any stack is allowed at any time, but popping is restricted to the first non-empty stack is decidable! [8]. Yet, relaxing these definitions to more natural ones seems to either destroy decidability or their power. It is hence natural to ask: why do these automata have decidable emptiness problems? Is there a common underlying principle that explains their decidability?

We propose, in this paper, a general criterion that uniformly explains many such results— several restricted uses of auxiliary storage are decidable because they can be simulated by *graph automata* working on graphs that capture the storage as well as their sequential or distributed nature, and are also of bounded tree-width.

More precisely, we can show, using generalizations of known results on the decidability of *satisfiability* of monadic second-order logic (MSO) on bounded tree-width graphs [9, 23], that graph automata on *MSO-definable* graphs of bounded tree-width are decidable. Graph automata [24] are finite-state automata (without auxiliary storage) that accept or reject graphs using *tilings of the graph using states*, where the restrictions on tiling determine the graphs that get accepted. The general decidability of emptiness of graph automata on MSO-definable graphs follows since the existence of acceptable tilings is MSO-definable.

We proceed to show that several sequential/distributed automata with an auxiliary storage (we consider stacks and queues only in this paper), can be realized as *graph automata* working on single or multiple directed paths augmented with special edges to capture the mechanism of the storage. Intuitively, a symbol that gets stored in a stack/queue and later gets retrieved can be simulated by a graph automaton working on a graph where there is a special edge between the point where the symbol gets stored to the point where it gets retrieved. A graph automaton can retrieve the symbol at the retrieval point by using an appropriate tiling of this special edge.

The idea of converting automata with storage to graph automata without storage but working on specialized graphs is that it allows us to examine the *complexity* of storage using the *structure* of the graph that simulates it. We show that many automata with a tractable emptiness problem can be converted to graph automata working on MSO definable graphs of bounded tree-width, from which decidability of their emptiness follows.

We prove the simulation of the following classes of automata with auxiliary storage by graph automata working on MSO-definable bounded tree-width graphs:

- Multi-stack pushdown automata with bounded context-switching: This is the class of multi-stack automata where each computation of the automaton can be divided into k stages, where in each stage the automaton touches only one stack (proved decidable first in [22]). We show that they can be simulated by graph automata on graphs of tree-width $O(k)$.

POPL'11, January 26–28, 2011, Austin, Texas, USA.

- *Multi-stack pushdown automata with bounded phases:* These are automata that generalize the bounded-context-switching ones: the computations must be dividable into k phases, for a fixed k, where in each phase the automaton can push onto any stack, but can pop only from one stack (proved decidable recently in [15]). We show that graph automata on graphs of tree-width $O(2^k)$ (not $O(k)$ as in the above case) can simulate them.

- *Ordered multi-stack pushdown automata:* The restriction here is that there is a finite number of stacks that are ordered, and at any time, the automaton can push onto any stack, but pop only from the first non-empty stack. Note that the computation is not divided into phases, as in the above two restrictions. We show that automata on graphs of tree-width $O(n \cdot 2^n)$ (where n is the number of stacks) can simulate them.

- *Distributed queue automata on polyforest architectures:* Distributed queue automata is a model where finite-state processes at n sites work by communicating to each other using FIFO channels, modeled as queues. It was shown recently that when the architecture is a polyforest (i.e. the underlying *undirected* network graph of the architecture is a forest), the emptiness problem is decidable (and for other architectures, it is undecidable) [17]. We prove that graph automata working on graphs of tree-width (in fact, path-width) n, where n is the number of processes, can simulate distributed queue automata on polyforest architectures.

- *Distributed queue automata with stacks on forest architectures:* When we endow each process in a distributed queue automaton with a local stack, it turns out that if the automaton is *well-queuing* and the architecture is a forest, the emptiness problem is decidable [17]. The well-queuing condition demands that a process may dequeue from a queue only when its local stack is empty. Furthermore, it is known that simply dropping the well-queuing condition or dropping the condition that the architecture be a forest, makes emptiness undecidable [17]. We prove that graph automata that work on graphs that simulate both the local stacks and the queues can capture these automata, and for well-queuing automata over forest architectures, the graphs are of tree-width $O(n)$, where n is the number of processes.

The *graphs* on which the graph automata need to work to realize the above automata are also, surprisingly, uniform. For the first three classes of multi-stack automata, the graphs are simply a single word endowed with a set of *nesting edges relations*, one relation for each stack. For distributed queue automata, the graphs are composed of n distinct linear structures, one for each process, with queue edges connecting enqueing vertices to dequeuing vertices, and, if the processes have stacks, have nesting edges at each process to capture the local stack.

The tree-decompositions for these graphs as well as the proofs that the decompositions give bounded tree-width for the restrictions are involved, and are tailored to exploit the restriction placed on the automata.

The idea of interpreting stacks as nesting edges was motivated by the work relating *visibly pushdown automata* with *nested word automata* [1–3], where nesting edges capture a visible stack. Our work is also motivated by the work on bounded-phase multi-stack automata [15], in which we were involved, where tree-interpretations were used to show decidability of emptiness. Surveying the other known decidable automata restrictions led us to this uniform framework for proving decidability. The automata variants we study were often first proved to be decidable by different means— bounded context-switching multi-stack automata were shown to be decidable using regularity of *tuples* of reachable configurations [22], ordered multi-stack automata were shown decidable using manipulations of associated grammars, followed by a Parikh theorem [8], and distributed queue automata with stacks were shown decidable by reductions to bounded-phase automata [17].

Our theorems also lead to new consequences. First, automata with multi-stacks are decidable when their graphs are restricted to graphs of bounded tree-width, and in fact even bounded *clique-width* graphs [10, 11]; this result generalizes all the above multi-stack sequential automata. Second, several of our results extend to automata over infinite behaviors— for example, it follows easily that ordered multi-stack *Büchi* or *parity* automata on infinite words have a decidable emptiness problem. Third, several variants of the restrictions can be proved immediately decidable— for example, suppose we restrict multi-stack automata to k phases, where in each phase, there is only one stack that is *pushed* into (but arbitrary pops of stacks are allowed), then it easily follows that emptiness is decidable, as the *graphs* corresponding to these automata are precisely the same as those of bounded phase automata, save for the orientation of the linear and nesting edges, and hence has the same tree-width. Section 5 gives a summary of consequences of our general result.

Due to the variety of automata models we consider we do not give all definitions and proofs in the main text. The proofs for the boundedness of tree-width for various restrictions of multi-stack pushdown automata are given in the Appendix, while the proofs regarding distributed queue automata can be found in the technical report [20].

2. Logics, graphs, graph automata, tree-width, and emptiness

We start by defining, in this section, graph automata that work on edge-labeled finite directed graphs, and show that the emptiness problem for these automata is decidable over any MSO-definable class of graphs of bounded tree-width. This result is derived from classical results on interpretations of graphs on trees, and we sketch the derivations here.

Monadic second-order logic on graphs: Fix a finite alphabet (set) Σ. A Σ-labeled graph is a structure $(V, \{E_a\}_{a\in\Sigma})$, where V is a finite non-empty set of vertices, and each $E_a \subseteq V \times V$ is a set of a-labeled directed edges. We will assume, throughout this paper, that for any vertex v, there is at most one incoming a-labeled edge and at most one outgoing a-labeled edge.

We view graphs as logical structures, with V as the universe, and each set of edges E_a as a binary relation on vertices. Monadic second-order logic (MSO) is now the standard logic on these structures. We fix a countable set of first-order variables (we will denote these as x, y, etc.) and another countable set of set variables (denoted as X, Y, etc.). MSO is given by the following syntax:

$$\varphi ::= x = y \mid E_a(x,y) \mid x \in X \mid \varphi \vee \varphi \mid \neg\varphi \mid \exists x.\varphi \mid \exists X.\varphi$$

where $a \in \Sigma$. The semantics is the standard one, with first-order and set variables interpreted as vertices and sets of vertices.[1]

We say a class of Σ-labeled graphs $\mathcal{C}$ is MSO-definable, if there is an MSO formula φ such that $\mathcal{C}$ is the precise class of Σ-labeled graphs that satisfy φ.

Graph automata: Fix a *class* of Σ-labeled graphs $\mathcal{C}$. A graph automaton (GA) on $\mathcal{C}$ is a tuple $(Q, \{T_a\}_{a\in\Sigma}, \mathit{type})$, where Q is a finite set of states, each $T_a \subseteq Q \times Q$ is a *tiling relation*, and $\mathit{type} : Q \to 2^\Sigma \times 2^\Sigma$ is the type-relation.

[1] Note: In the literature, a variant of MSO (called MSO_2) has been considered where both vertices and edges are in a two-sorted universe and are related by an incidence relation; that version is stronger than ours, but we shall not need it for our exposition.

Intuitively, a graph automaton will accept a graph if there is a way to tile (label) the vertices by states so that the tiling relation is satisfied by vertices adjacent to each other, and further satisfies the type-relation. The type-relation associates each state to a pair (*In*, *Out*) of sets of labels, and in order for a state to decorate a vertex, we require its type to match the edges incident on it – the labels of incoming (and outgoing) edges must be precisely *In* (and *Out*).

Formally, we say that a graph automaton $(Q, \{T_a\}_{a\in\Sigma}, type)$ *accepts* a graph $(V, \{E_a\}_{a\in\Sigma})$ if there is a map $\rho : V \rightarrow Q$ that satisfies the following conditions:

- For every $(u, v) \in E_a$, with $a \in \Sigma$, $(\rho(u), \rho(v)) \in T_a$.
- For every u, $type(\rho(u)) = (In, Out)$, where $In = \{a \mid \exists v, (v, u) \in E_a\}$ and $Out = \{a \mid \exists v, (u, v) \in E_a\}$.

The language of a graph automaton GA over a class of graphs $\mathcal{C}$, denoted $L(GA)$, is the set of graphs in $\mathcal{C}$ that it accepts.

Note that the notion of an automaton "running" over the graph has been replaced by tiling constraints. Also, we have done away with initial or final states; we will capture these when needed using specially labeled edges in the sequel.

Our notion of graph automata is motivated by definitions of automata on graphs through tilings in the literature [24]. Graph automata can in fact be defined more powerfully (see [24]); however, for our purposes, the above definition will suffice. Most of our results will carry over to generalizations of the above definition.

Tree-width: We recall the definition of tree-width for graphs (see [12]). The tree-width of a graph intuitively captures how close a graph is to a tree.

Formally, a *tree-decomposition* of a graph (V, E) is a pair (T, bag), where $T = (N, \rightarrow)$ is a tree, and $bag : N \rightarrow 2^V$ is a function that satisfies:

- For every $v \in V$, there is a node $n \in N$ such that $v \in bag(n)$,
- For every edge $(u, v) \in E$, there is a node $n \in N$ such that $u, v \in bag(n)$, and
- If $u \in bag(n)$ and $u \in bag(n')$, for nodes $n, n' \in N$, then for every n'' that lies on the unique path connecting n and n', $u \in bag(n'')$.

The *width* of a tree decomposition is the size of the largest bag in it, minus one; i.e. $max_{n\in N}\{|bag(n)|\} - 1$.

The *tree-width* of a graph is the *smallest* of the widths of all of its tree decompositions.

It is easy to see that the tree-width of a tree is 1 while the tree-width of a k-clique is $k - 1$.

Emptiness of graph automata on graphs of bounded tree-width: We now show that emptiness of graph automata is decidable, when evaluated over graphs that are definable in MSO and are also of bounded tree-width.

First, we recall a classical result that the *satisfiability* problem for MSO is decidable on the class of *all* graphs of tree-width k (for a fixed k) [23]. Courcelle's classic theorem shows that checking if a *particular graph* G of tree-width k (for a fixed k) satisfies a fixed MSO formula is decidable in linear time. This result works by defining the graph in a labelled tree by MSO formulas, and by translating the MSO formula about graphs into one about trees, and using a tree-automaton for the MSO formula to check if the corresponding tree is accepted. It turns out the same proof can be used to prove the *satisfiability* theorem that we refer to above as well. Intuitively, we can interpret *all* graphs of tree-width k by using a uniform set of labeled binary trees whose labels only depend on k, translate the MSO formula on graphs to these labeled trees, and use the fact that satisfiability of MSO on trees is decidable.

THEOREM 2.1 (Seese [23]). *The problem of checking, given $k \in \mathbb{N}$ and $\varphi \in MSO$ over Σ-labeled graphs, whether there is a Σ-labeled graph G of tree-width at most k that satisfies φ, is decidable.*

Note that the above certainly does not imply that satisfiability of MSO is decidable on *any* class of graphs of bounded tree-width (take a non-recursive class of linear-orders/words for a counter-example). However, an immediate corollary is that satisfiability of MSO is also decidable on any MSO-definable class of graphs $\mathcal{C}$ of bounded tree-width (if $\varphi_{\mathcal{C}}$ defines the class of graphs, and φ is the MSO formula, we can instantiate the above theorem for $\varphi_{\mathcal{C}} \wedge \varphi$).

COROLLARY 2.2. *Let $\mathcal{C}$ be a class of MSO definable Σ-labeled graphs. The problem of checking, given $k \in \mathbb{N}$ and an MSO-formula φ, whether there is a graph $G \in \mathcal{C}$ of tree-width at most k that satisfies φ, is decidable.*

We can now prove that the emptiness problem for graph automata is decidable when restricted to bounded tree-width graphs over an MSO-definable class of graphs. Intuitively, we can write an MSO formula φ that checks whether there is a proper tiling of a graph by the graph automaton that respects the tiling and typing relations. This formula will essentially use an existential quantification of a set of sets X_a (for each $a \in \Sigma$) to "guess" a tiling, and check whether the tiling and typing is proper, using universal first-order quantification on vertices. We can then instantiate the above corollary with this formula to show decidability of graph automata emptiness. In fact, using a direct automaton construction on trees, we can show the complexity of graph-automata emptiness as well (see [20] for a gist of proof): to obtain our result:

THEOREM 2.3. *Let $\mathcal{C}$ be a class of MSO definable Σ-labeled graphs. The problem of checking, given $k \in \mathbb{N}$ and a graph automaton GA, whether there is some $G \in \mathcal{C}$ of tree-width at most k that is accepted by GA, is decidable, and decidable in time $|GA|^{O(k)}$.*

The above theorem will be the key result we will use to uniformly prove decidability results in this paper. For various restrictions of sequential and distributed automata with auxiliary storage, we will translate them to graph automata over MSO-definable graphs, show that the relevant graphs are of bounded tree-width, and use the above theorem to prove decidability of emptiness.

3. Multi-stack Pushdown Automata

In this section, we will show the decidability of emptiness of various restricted multi-stack pushdown automata (bounded context-switches, bounded phase, and ordered), by showing that they can be simulated by graph automata working over *multiply-nested word graphs* that are of bounded tree-width.

For any $n \in \mathbb{N}$, let $[n]$ denote the set $\{1, \ldots n\}$.

A multi-stack pushdown automaton is an automaton with finite control and equipped with a finite number of stacks. A transition of this automaton consists in pushing or popping a symbol from a specified stack and changing its control or simply an internal move that affects only the control state without alteration of the stacks' contents.

DEFINITION 3.1 (MULTI-STACK PUSHDOWN AUTOMATA). *For a fixed $n \in \mathbb{N}$, an n-stack* pushdown automaton *(n-PDA) is a tuple $M = (Q, q_0, \Gamma, \delta, Q_F)$, where Q is a finite set of states, $q_0 \in Q$ is the initial state, Γ is a finite stack alphabet, $Q_F \subseteq Q$ is the set of final states, and $\delta = \langle \delta_{push}, \delta_{pop}, \delta_{int}\rangle$ where*

- $\delta_{push} \subseteq (Q \times Q \times \Gamma \times [n])$ *is the set of push moves,*
- $\delta_{pop} \subseteq (Q \times \Gamma \times Q \times [n])$ *is the set of pop moves, and*

- $\delta_{int} \subseteq (Q \times Q)$ *is the set of internal moves.*

A multi-stack pushdown automaton (mPDA) is an n-stack pushdown automaton, for some $n \in \mathbb{N}$.

A *configuration* of an n-PDA $M = (Q, q_0, \Gamma, \delta, Q_F)$ is a tuple $\langle q, s_1, \ldots, s_n \rangle$ with $q \in Q$ and $s_j \in \Gamma^*$ is the content of stack j, for every $j \in [n]$. Let $C = \langle q, s_1, \ldots, s_n \rangle$ be a configuration of M. Then, C is the *initial* configuration if $q = q_0$ and $s_j = \epsilon$, for every $j \in [n]$. Moreover, C is a *final* configuration if $q \in Q_F$ and $s_j = \epsilon$, for every $j \in [n]$. Given two configurations $C = \langle q, s_1, \ldots, s_n \rangle$ and $C' = \langle q', s'_1, \ldots, s'_n \rangle$, there is a transition from C to C' on the action *act* from the behavior set $B_n = \{int, push_1, \ldots push_n, pop_1, \ldots, pop_n\}$, denoted $C \xrightarrow{act} C'$, if one of the following holds:

[Push γ onto stack j] $act = push_j$, and there exists γ such that $(q, q', \gamma, j) \in \delta_{push}$, $s'_j = \gamma.s_j$, and $s'_h = s_h$ for every $h \in [n] - j$.

[Pop γ from stack j] $act = pop_j$, and there exists γ such that $(q, \gamma, q', j) \in \delta_{pop}$, $s_j = \gamma.s'_j$, and $s'_h = s_h$ for every $h \in [n] - j$.

[Internal] $act = int$, and $(q, q') \in \delta_{int}$, and $s'_h = s_h$ for each $h \in [n]$.

A *run* of M is a sequence of transitions of M, $\rho = C_1 \xrightarrow{act_1} C_2 \ldots \xrightarrow{act_{m-1}} C_m$, where C_1 is initial and C_m is final.

For each such run ρ of M, we associate the behavior word $beh(\rho) = act_1.act_2 \ldots act_m$, and define the set of behaviors of M as the language $Beh(M) = \{\ beh(\rho) \mid \rho \text{ is a run of } M\ \}$. Note that the behaviors capture the way the automaton handles the stacks, noting the push and pop operations and the stack on which they are performed.

The *emptiness* problem for an mPDA M is the problem of checking if $Beh(M)$ is empty (or equivalently, whether there is a run of the mPDA).

Multiply-nested words: In the following we show that mPDAs can be naturally encoded as graph automata on a class of (edge-labelled) graphs that we call *multiply nested words*, and the emptiness problem on the former reduces to the emptiness problem on the latter. We start by defining multiply nested word graphs.

DEFINITION 3.2 (MULTIPLY NESTED WORDS). *For a given integer n, an n-nested word (n-NW) is a tuple $N = (V, Init, Final, L, \{E_j\}_{j \in [n]})$, where*

- *V is a finite set of vertices;*
- *$L \subseteq V \times V$ is a non-reflexive (successor) edge relation such that L^* is a linear ordering $<_L$ on the vertices of V;*
- *If x is the minimum element w.r.t. L, then $Init = \{(x, x)\}$; if x is the maximal element w.r.t. L, then $Final = \{(x, x)\}$;*
- *$E_j \subseteq V \times V$ is a nesting relation, for every $j \in [n]$. A nesting relation E_j is a relation that satisfies the following properties: for all $u, u', v, v' \in V$ and $j, j' \in [n]$,*
  - *if $E_j(u, v)$ then $u <_L v$ holds;*
  - *if $E_j(u, v)$ and $E_j(u, v')$ then $v = v'$; and if $E_j(u, v)$ and $E_j(u', v)$ then $u = u'$;*
  - *if $E_j(u, v)$ and $E_j(u', v')$ and $u <_L u'$ then either $v <_L u'$ or $v' <_L v$ holds*
  - *if $j \neq j'$, $E_j(u, v)$, and $E_{j'}(u', v')$, then u, v, u', v' are all different.*

A multiply nested word (mNW) is an n-nested word, for some $n \in \mathbb{N}$.

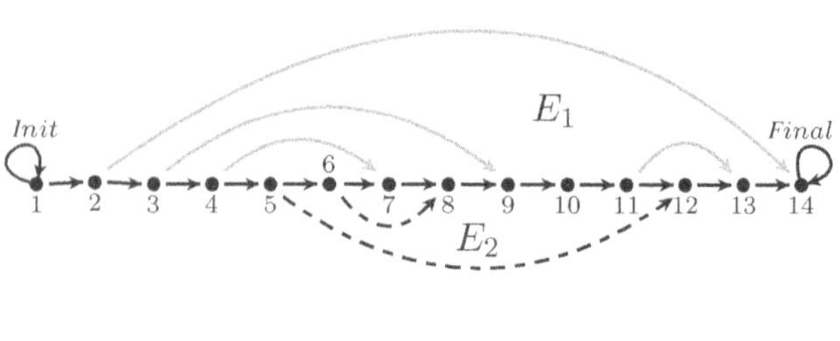

Figure 1. A 2 nested word graph.

Figure 1 illustrates a 2-nested word.

Intuitively, mNWs are meant to capture the behaviors of runs of mPDAs, where the stacks are compiled down to edges in the graph: the relation L relates consecutive actions in the run, while the nesting edge relation E_j captures the matching push-pop relation of stack j, for every stack index $j \in [n]$. The self-looping edges *Init* and *Final* capture the initial and final vertex with respect to L.

The properties of multiply nested words (Definition 3) can be easily stated in MSO:

PROPOSITION 3.3. *For any integer n, the class of n-NWs is MSO definable.*

We can define a 1-to-1 function nw from the set of behaviors of the n-PDA M to the class of n-NWs. Given an M run ρ with $beh(\rho) = a_1 a_2 \ldots a_m$, the corresponding nested word graph n-NW N is as follows. The set of vertices of N is $V = \{v_1, v_2, \ldots, v_m, v_{m+1}\}$, the relation L is such that $L(v_i, v_j)$ holds iff $j = i + 1$. The edge relation E_j is defined as follows. On the word $beh(\rho)$ there are intrinsic relations that match corresponding pushes and pops of the same stack, and since we assumed that all the stacks at the end of a run are empty, we have that in $beh(\rho)$ every symbol $push_j$ is matched with a future symbol pop_j and vice-versa. Thus the edge relation E_j is defined as: $E_j(v_i, v_h)$ holds if and only if $a_i = push_j$, $a_h = pop_j$ and the pair (i, h) is a matching pair of push and pop actions in $beh(\rho)$. It is easy to see that this is a 1-to-1 correspondence.

Given any n-PDA M, we can easily translate it to a graph automaton that accepts the mNWs corresponding to the behaviors of M. Intuitively, whenever the n-PDA pushes onto the i'th stack, the graph automaton decorates the corresponding node in the nested word graph with the symbol pushed, and when this symbol gets popped later, the graph automaton, using tiling conditions on the nested edge, will recover the symbol. Hence, by using tilings on the nested edges, the graph automaton can work *without a stack*, and capture the semantics of the n-PDA precisely. We hence have:

LEMMA 3.4. *For every n-PDA M, there is a (constructible) graph automaton GA on n-nested words such that $nw(Beh(M)) = L(GA)$. Hence $Beh(M) \neq \emptyset$ iff $L(GA) \neq \emptyset$.*

Note that 1-PDAs are basic pushdown automata, whose emptiness problem is decidable. The emptiness problem for n-PDA is well-known to be undecidable when $n > 1$ [14]. Thus, Lemma 3.4 can be used to show that the class of n-NWs, with $n > 1$, have unbounded tree-width.

LEMMA 3.5. *The class of 1-NWs has tree-width 2.*
For any integer $n > 1$, the class of n-NWs has unbounded tree-width.

Tree-decompositions of multiply nested words. In order to show restricted versions of mPDAs have a decidable emptiness problem, we will first define *canonical tree-decompositions* for multiply nested words, which we will use to prove bounds on tree-width and

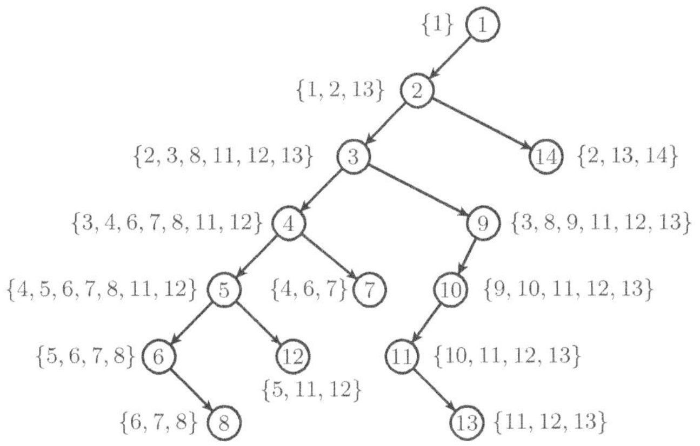

Figure 2. Tree decomposition of the graph illustrated in Figure 1.

hence prove emptiness for both bounded-phase automata as well as ordered automata (it turns out that bounded context-switching automata have a simpler tree decomposition).

DEFINITION 3.6 (CANONICAL TREE DECOMP. OF n-NWS). *For any n-NW $N = (V, Init, Final, L, \{E_j\}_{j\in[n]})$, the canonical tree-decomposition of N, can-td$(N) = (T, bag)$ is decomposition $T = (V, bag)$ defined as:*

- *The set of nodes of the tree T are the vertices V of the N.*
- *If $E_j(u, v)$ holds for any $j \in [n]$, then v is the right-child of u in T.*
- *if $L(u, v)$ holds and for all $j \in [n]$ and $z \in V$, $E_j(z, v)$ does not hold, then v is the left-child of u.*

The function bag associates the minimum set of vertices to each node of T that satisfies the following:

- *$v \in bag(v)$, for all $v \in V$.*
- *if u is the parent of v in T, then $u \in bag(v)$, for every $u, v \in V$.*
- *for $u, v \in V$, if $L(u, v)$ holds then $u \in bag(z)$, for all vertices z such that z is on the unique path from u to v in T.*

Figure 2 illustrates a tree-decomposition for the 2-nested graph in Figure 1.

In the above definition of the tree-decomposition of an n-NW N, the vertices of T are the same as the vertices of N. The root of T is the minimum vertex in N according to the linear ordering induced by L. The nesting-edge-successor of any node, if any, is always its right-child. Otherwise, a vertex v is the left-child of its linear predecessor. Notice that, since for each node v there exists at most one pair (u, j) such that $E_j(u, v)$ holds, and at most one vertex u such that $L(u, v)$ holds, the tree T is uniquely determined by N.

Note that the tree T captures all the nesting edges in: in fact if $E_j(u, v)$ holds then v must be the right-child of u, and hence $u, v \in bag(v)$. The successor relation L is not always local as the nesting-edge relation is: for example, if $L(u, v)$ and $E_j(z, v)$ hold for some j and z, then v is the right-child of z and not the left-child of u. However, the third property in the definition guaranties that all linear edges are captured by at least one bag, and also validates the requirement that nodes whose bags contain the same vertex in a tree decomposition be connected. Hence, it is clear that *can-td*(N) defines a unique tree decomposition for every n-NWs (though its width may not be bounded).

LEMMA 3.7. *For any multiply nested word graph N, can-td(N) is a tree-decomposition of N.*

3.1 Bounded context-switch emptiness

We show now that the multiply-nested words that correspond to bounded context-switching runs of a multi-stack automaton are of bounded tree-width, and hence admit a decidable emptiness problem.

For any $k \in \mathbb{N}$, we say that a behavior word $w \in B_n^*$ is a *k-context word*, if it belongs to $(\bigcup_{j\in[n]}\{int, push_j, pop_j\}^*)^k$. In other words, w can be factorized as at most k sub-words $w_1w_2 \dots w_h$ (with $h \leq k$) such that each w_i includes only actions of a single stack and internal actions. Let us define k-CS-*Beh*(M) to be the set of all k-context behavior words in *Beh*(M).

The emptiness problem for mPDAs restricted to k contexts is the problem of checking, given an mPDA M, whether the language k-CS-*Beh*(M) is empty.

As in the general case, the emptiness problem for mPDSs restricted to k contexts can be reduced to the emptiness problem for graph automata, where now the class of graphs to consider is that of mNWs restricted to k-context behaviors. For any $k, n \in \mathbb{N}$, a *k-context-switch n-nested word* is a tuple $N = (V, Init, Final, L, \{E_j\}_{j\in[n]})$ where N is a n-NW and $nw^{-1}(N)$ is a k-context behavior word.

The k-context restriction on multiply nested word graphs is easily expressible as an MSO formula ϕ; this formula will express that the graph can be factored into k segments and only nesting edges of one stack are incident on vertices of a single segment. Along with the MSO formula φ defining the class of mNWs, $\varphi \wedge \phi$ defines the class of all k-context mNWs. Moreover, a tree-decomposition where each stack is encoded as a subtree under the root (in the usual way, as in the canonical tree decomposition of 1-nested words), has width at most $k + 1$ (see Appendix A).

LEMMA 3.8. *For any $k, n \in \mathbb{N}$, the class of k-context n-NW graphs is MSO definable. Furthermore, for any k-context n-NW, there exists a tree-decomposition of width at most $k + 1$.*

From the fact that the emptiness problem for mPDAs restricted to k-contexts is effectively reducible to the emptiness problem for graph automata over k-context mNWs, and using Lemma 3.8, we can instantiate Theorem 2.3 to show the following:

THEOREM 3.9. *For any $k \in \mathbb{N}$, the emptiness problem for mPDAs restricted to k contexts is decidable, and decidable in time $O(|M|^{O(k)})$. For a fixed k, the emptiness problem is in* PTIME.

The original proof of decidability of reachability of multi-stack automata under a bounded number of context-switches was proved using tuples of automata to store the *configurations of stacks* [22]. The above proof is very different— it shows that the graph that captures the storage, i.e. multiple stacks with bounded context-switches, has bounded tree-width, and hence admits a decidable emptiness problem.

3.2 Bounded phase emptiness

Now we show that the multiply-nested words that correspond to bounded phase runs of a multi-stack automaton are of bounded tree-width (in fact, the canonical tree-decomposition gives bounded tree-width), and hence entails decidable emptiness.

A word $w \in B_n^*$ is a *phase* if it belongs to one of the sets $phase_j = (\{int, pop_j\} \cup \bigcup_{i\in[n]}\{push_i\})^*$, for some $j \in [n]$. A phase j describes any sequence of actions in which only internal actions, pushes to all stacks, and pops from stack j are permitted. A word $w \in B_n^*$ is a *k-phase* behavior word if it is the concatenation of at most k phases: that is, $w \in (\bigcup_{j\in[n]}(phase_j))^k$. We define the set k-*Phase-Beh*(M), for a mPDA M, as the set of all the k-phase words in *Beh*(M).

The emptiness problem for mPDAs restricted to k phase behaviors asks whether k-*Phase-Beh*(M) is an empty set. mPDAs restricted to bounded phases can be simulated by graph automata on a the class of bounded phase mNWs. For any $k, n \in \mathbb{N}$, a *k-phase n-nested word* N is an n-NW where $nw^{-1}(N)$ is a k-phase behavior word.

LEMMA 3.10. *For any $k, n \in \mathbb{N}$, the class of k-phase n-NW graphs is MSO definable. Moreover, the tree-decomposition nw-$td(N)$, where N is any k-phase n-NW, has tree-width at most $2^k + 2^{k-1} + 1$.*

From Lemma 3.10 and Theorem 2.3 to obtain the following theorem, which also matches the 2ETIME lower bound for this problem [16].

THEOREM 3.11. *For any $k \in \mathbb{N}$, the emptiness problem for mPDAs restricted to k phases is decidable, and decidable in time $|M|^{O(2^k)}$. When the number of phases is fixed, the emptiness problem is in* PTIME.

Proofs can be found in Appendix B.

3.3 Emptiness of ordered multi-stack automata

Turning to the orderedness restriction on multi-stack automata, we show that the multiply-nested words that correspond to ordered runs are of bounded tree-width (using the canonical tree-decomposition), and hence admits a decidable emptiness problem.

A run ρ of an nPDA is *ordered* if whenever a pop action happens on the stack $j \in [n]$, then all stacks of index less than j are empty: if $\rho = C_1 \xrightarrow{act_1} C_2 \ldots \xrightarrow{act_{m-1}} C_m$, then for every $i \in [m-1]$, if $act_i = pop_j$ and $C_i = \langle q, s_1, \ldots, s_n \rangle$ then $s_h = \epsilon$, for each $h < j$.

The set *ordered-Beh*(M), for a mPDA M, is the set of all the ordered words of *Beh*(M).

The emptiness problem for mPDAs restricted to ordered behaviors is the problem of checking the emptiness of *ordered-Beh*(M).

For any $n \in \mathbb{N}$, an *ordered n-nested word* N is an n-NW in which $nw^{-1}(N)$ is a ordered word.

LEMMA 3.12. *Let $n \in \mathbb{N}$. The class of ordered n-NW graphs is MSO definable. Furthermore, the tree-decomposition nw-$td(N)$, where N is any ordered n-NW, has width at most $(n+1) \cdot 2^{n-1} + 1$.*

From Lemma 3.12 and Theorem 2.3 we obtain the following theorem, which also matches the 2ETIME lower bound for this problem [6].

THEOREM 3.13. *The emptiness problem for mPDAs restricted to ordered runs is decidable, and decidable in time $|M|^{O(n.2^n)}$. When the number of stacks is fixed, the problem is decidable in* PTIME.

Proofs can be found in Appendix B.

4. Distributed Automata with Queues and Stacks

Distributed queue automata with stacks (DQSA) is an automaton model composed of a finite number of processes and a finite number of first-in-first-out (FIFO) channels using which they communicate, and where the local processes are endowed with a single local stack each. Each FIFO queue has a unique sender process that can enqueue onto it, and a unique receiver process that dequeues from it.

DEFINITION 4.1 (DISTRIBUTED QUEUE AUT. WITH STACKS). *A* distributed queue automaton with stacks *(DQSA) is a tuple $M = (P, Q, \Pi, \Gamma, Sender, Receiver, \{A_p\}_{p \in P})$ where P is a finite set of process names, Q is a finite set of queues, Π is a finite message alphabet, Γ is a finite stack alphabet, and Sender: $Q \to P$ and Receiver: $Q \to P$ are two maps that assign a unique* sender *process and* receiver *process for each queue, respectively. For every process $p \in P$, $A_p = (S_p, s_0^p, F_p, \delta_p)$ is the machine at site p, where S_p is a finite set of states, $s_0^p \in S_p$ is the initial state, $F_p \subseteq S_p$ is the set of final states, and $\delta_p = \langle \delta^p_{int}, \delta^p_{send}, \delta^p_{recv}, \delta^p_{push}, \delta^p_{pop} \rangle$ where*

- $\delta^p_{send} \subseteq (S_p \times Q^p_{send} \times \Pi \times S_p)$ *is the set of send moves, where* $Q^p_{send} = \{\, q \in Q \mid Sender(q) = p \,\}$;
- $\delta^p_{recv} \subseteq (S_p \times Q^p_{recv} \times \Pi \times S_p)$ *is the set of receive moves, where* $Q^p_{recv} = \{\, q \in Q \mid Receiver(q) = p \,\}$;
- $\delta_{push} \subseteq (S_p \times S_p \times \Gamma)$ *is the set of push moves;*
- $\delta_{pop} \subseteq (S_p \times \Gamma \times S_p)$ *is the set of pop moves;*
- $\delta^p_{int} \subseteq (S_p \times S_p)$ *is the set of internal moves.*

For the rest of the section we fix $M = (P, Q, \Pi, \Gamma, Sender, Receiver, \{A_p\}_{p \in P})$ to be a DQSA, where $A_p = (S_p, s_0^p, F_p, \delta_p)$ for every $p \in P$.

The semantics of DQSAs is as follows.

A *configuration* of a DQSA M is a tuple $\langle \{s_p\}_{p\in P}, \{\gamma_p\}_{p\in P}, \{\mu_q\}_{q\in Q} \rangle$ where for each $p \in P$, $s_p \in S_p$ and $\gamma_p \in \Gamma^*$ are the state and the stack content of process p respectively, and for each queue $q \in Q$, $\mu_q \in \Pi^*$ is the content of q. The configuration $C = \langle \{s_p\}_{p\in P}, \{\gamma_p\}_{p\in P}, \{\mu_q\}_{q\in Q} \rangle$ of M is the initial configuration if $s_p = s_0^p$ and $\gamma_p = \epsilon$ for each $p \in P$, and $\mu_q = \epsilon$, for each queue $q \in Q$. C is a *final* configuration if $s_p \in F_p$, for *every* process $p \in P$, and further all queues are empty, i.e. $\mu_q = \epsilon$, for each $q \in Q$, and all stacks are also empty, i.e. $\gamma_p = \epsilon$, for each $p \in P$.

Let the *actions of process* p be $B_p = \{int_p, push_p, pop_p\} \cup (\bigcup_{q\in Q}\{send_{(p,q)}\}) \cup (\bigcup_{q\in Q}\{recv_{(p,q)}\})$, and $B = \bigcup_{p\in P} B_p$ be the alphabet of all actions. For any two configurations $C = \langle \{s_p\}_{p\in P}, \{\gamma_p\}_{p\in P}, \{\mu_q\}_{q\in Q} \rangle$ and $C' = \langle \{s'_p\}_{p\in P}, \{\gamma'_p\}_{p\in P}, \{\mu'_q\}_{q\in Q} \rangle$, $C \xrightarrow{act} C'$, if $act \in B$ and one of the following holds:

[Send] $act = send_{(p,q)}$, and there is a move $(s_p, q, m, s'_p) \in \delta^p_{send}$ such that

- for each $\widehat{p} \neq p$, $s'_{\widehat{p}} = s_{\widehat{p}}$,
- $\mu'_q = m.\mu_q$, and for each $\widehat{q} \neq q$, $\mu'_{\widehat{q}} = \mu_{\widehat{q}}$.
- for each $\widehat{p}$, $\gamma'_{\widehat{p}} = \gamma_{\widehat{p}}$.

[Receive] $act = recv_{(p,q)}$, and there is a move $(s_p, q, m, s'_p) \in \delta^p_{recv}$ such that

- for each $\widehat{p} \neq p$, $s'_{\widehat{p}} = s_{\widehat{p}}$,
- $\mu_q = \mu'_q.m$, and for each $\widehat{q} \neq q$, $\mu'_{\widehat{q}} = \mu_{\widehat{q}}$.
- for each $\widehat{p}$, $\gamma'_{\widehat{p}} = \gamma_{\widehat{p}}$.

[Push] $act = push_p$, and there is a move $(s_p, s'_p, a) \in \delta^p_{push}$ such that

- for each $\widehat{p} \neq p$, $s'_{\widehat{p}} = s_{\widehat{p}}$,
- for each $\widehat{q}$, $\mu'_{\widehat{q}} = \mu_{\widehat{q}}$.
- $\gamma'_p = a.\gamma_p$, and for each $\widehat{p} \neq p$, $\gamma'_{\widehat{p}} = \gamma_{\widehat{p}}$.

[Pop] $act = pop_p$, and there is a move $(s_p, a, s'_p) \in \delta^p_{pop}$ such that

- for each $\widehat{p} \neq p$, $s'_{\widehat{p}} = s_{\widehat{p}}$,
- for each $\widehat{q}$, $\mu'_{\widehat{q}} = \mu_{\widehat{q}}$.
- $a.\gamma'_p = \gamma_p$, and for each $\widehat{p} \neq p$, $\gamma'_{\widehat{p}} = \gamma_{\widehat{p}}$.

[Internal] $act = int_p$, and there is a move $(s_p, s'_p) \in \delta^p_{int}$ such that

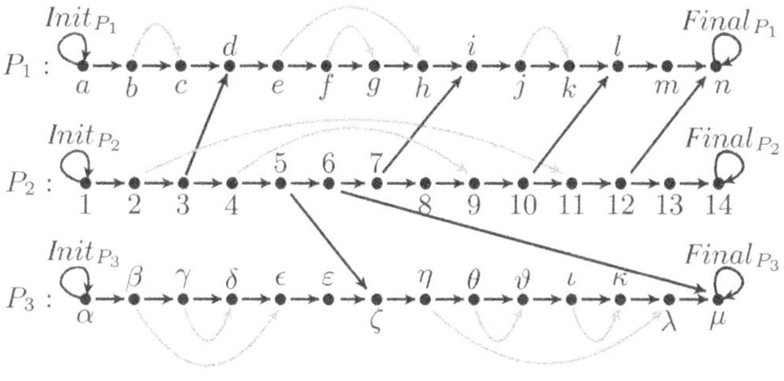

Figure 3. A stack-queue graph.

- for each $\widehat{p} \neq p$, $s'_{\widehat{p}} = s_{\widehat{p}}$,
- for each $\widehat{q}$, $\mu'_{\widehat{q}} = \mu_{\widehat{q}}$.
- for each $\widehat{p}$, $\gamma'_{\widehat{p}} = \gamma_{\widehat{p}}$.

Let $w = act_1 act_2 \ldots act_{m-1} \in B^*$. A *run* of M on w is a sequence $\rho = C_1 \xrightarrow{act_1} C_2 \ldots \xrightarrow{act_{m-1}} C_m$, where C_1 is initial and C_m is final.

The set of behaviors of M, $Beh(M)$ is the set of words $w \in B^*$ such that there is a run of M on w.

A *stack-queue graph* (SQG) captures the behaviors of DQSA as a graph. This graph captures the distributed behavior by modeling local behaviors of the process as *disjoint* linearly ordered sets of vertices with two additional kinds of edges: edges that capture the nesting relation matching pushes and pops of the local processes (like in a nested word), and edges that match send-events of one process with receive-events in others. Formally,

DEFINITION 4.2 (STACK-QUEUE GRAPHS). *A stack-queue graph (SQG) over $(P, Q, Sender, Receiver)$ (where P, Q are finite sets, Sender : $Q \to P$ and Receiver : $Q \to P$) is a tuple $SQG = (\{(V_p, Init_p, Final_p, L_p, E_p)\}_{p\in P}, \{E_q\}_{q\in Q})$, where*

- *$(V_p, Init_p, Final_p, L_p, E_p)$ is a 1-NW, for every $p \in P$;*
- *$V_p \cap V_{p'} = \emptyset$, for all $p, p' \in P$ with $p \neq p'$;*
- *$E_q \subseteq V_p \times V_{p'}$, for some $p, p' \in P$ with $p \neq p'$. Further, for all $u, x \in V_p$ and $v, y \in V_{p'}$, if $(u, v) \in E_q$ and $(x, y) \in E_q$ and $u <_{L_p} x$ holds, then $v <_{L_{p'}} y$.*
- *Any vertex $v \in \bigcup_{p\in P} V_p$ has at most one edge of $(\bigcup_{q\in Q}(E_q) \cup \bigcup_{p\in P}(E_p))$ incident on it.*

Figure 3 illustrates a stack-queue graph for three processes.

The properties defining stack-queue graphs (the definition above) can be easily expressed in MSO:

LEMMA 4.3. *For any tuple $(P, Q, Sender, Receiver)$, the class of stack-queue graphs over it is MSO definable.*

The class of stack-queue graphs represent all potential behaviors of any DQSA. The precise queue graphs corresponding to behaviors of a DQSA can be accepted by a graph automaton over queue graphs that decorates each of these graphs with the DQSA states and checks whether there is a run of the DQSA corresponding to the graph. Let us associate a function sqg that associates (as a $1-1$ correspondence), the stack-queue graph corresponding to any behavior w. Then,

LEMMA 4.4. *For any DQSA M over $(P, Q, Sender, Receiver)$, there is an effectively constructible graph automaton on stack-queue graphs over $(P, Q, Sender, Receiver)$ such that $sqg(Beh(M)) = L(GA)$.*

Stack-queue graphs are complex graphs, and several restrictions are required to make them tractable. In fact, they are of unbounded tree width:

LEMMA 4.5. *For any $(P, Q, Sender, Receiver)$, where $|P| > 2$ and $Q \neq \emptyset$, the class of stack-queue graphs over $(P, Q, Sender, Receiver)$ has an unbounded tree-width.*

The *architecture* of a DQSA M is the directed graph that describes the way its processes communicate trough queues: $Arch(M) = (\ P,\ \{\ (Sender(q), Receiver(q)) \mid q \in Q\ \}\ )$.

In [17], it is proved that if the underlying architecture is a directed tree (where each process hence has only one incoming queue) and if the processes are *well-queuing*, then the emptiness problem is decidable for DQSAs. The well-queuing assumption demands that each process may dequeue from an incoming queue only when its local stack is empty. The stack-queue graph in Figure 3 corresponds to such a well-queuing behavior. These properties (well-queuing and tree architectures) can be expressed in MSO.

Furthermore, we can prove that these restrictions cause the graphs to be of bounded tree-width. This proof is quite involved, and is given in the technical report [20]. The idea is to first define the notions of *graph decompositions and their widths* that extends the notion of tree-decompositions. If $\mathcal{H}$ is a class of graphs, then a $\mathcal{H}$-decomposition of a graph G is a graph $H \in \mathcal{H}$ where each node in H has an associated bag of vertices, where every edge in G is in the union of two adjacent bags in H, and where the nodes that contain a vertex of G are connected in H. We then show that stack-queue graphs over an architecture that is a directed tree can be decomposed with a small width onto a *nested word*. This process relies on the observation that the global run can be always be executed in a particular order where messages in queues never go beyond length 1. Then, by using the small tree-width of nested words, we obtain the following result.

LEMMA 4.6. *The set of all stack-queue graphs over a pair $(P, Q, Sender, Receiver)$ whose underlying architecture is a directed tree and are well-queuing, is MSO-definable, and furthermore, have tree-width bounded by $3n - 1$ where n is the number of processes.*

From Lemma 4.6, we have:

THEOREM 4.7. *The emptiness problem for a well-queuing DQSA M with tree-architectures is decidable. The problem is decidable in time $|M|^{O(n)}$, where n is the number of processes of M.*

In fact, the precise analysis of the tree-width that leads to the above theorem *improves* the complexity by one exponential over the one proved in [17], which gives an algorithm doubly exponential in n.

4.1 Distributed Queue Automata without stacks

Distributed Queue Automata without stacks (DQAs) are the same model as that of DQASs except that the local stacks at each process are not present. Even in this restricted setting, the emptiness problem is *undecidable*. We can capture behaviors using *queue graphs* that are composed of n linear orders, one for each process, with edges connecting matching sends and receives. Figure 4 illustrates a queue graph. In general, queue graphs of distributed queue automata without stacks are also of unbounded tree width. Formally, we define queue graph as a stack queue graph with an empty set of stack edges:

DEFINITION 4.8 (QUEUE GRAPHS). *A queue graph (QG) over $(P, Q, Sender, Receiver)$, is a tuple*

$$QG = (\{(V_p, Init_p, Final_p, L_p)\}_{p\in P}, \{E_q\}_{q\in Q}),$$

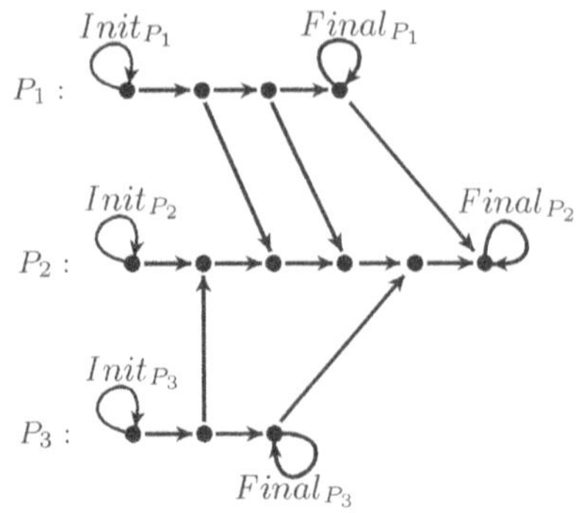

Figure 4. A queue graph.

where $(\{(V_p, Init_p, Final_p, L_p)\}_{p\in P}, \{E_p\}_{p\in P}, \{E_q\}_{q\in Q})$ *is a stack queue graph, where every* $E_p = \emptyset$*, for each* $p \in P$.

The properties defining queue graphs can be easily expressed in MSO:

LEMMA 4.9. *For any* $(P, Q, Sender, Receiver)$*, the class of queue graphs over it is MSO definable.*

Also, let qg be a function that associates to every behavior of a distributed queue automaton the corresponding queue graph.

LEMMA 4.10. *For every DQA* M*, there is a (constructible) graph automaton* GA *on queue graphs such that* $qg(Beh(M)) = L(GA)$.

In [17], it was proved that when the architecture of a DGA is a *polyforest* the emptiness problem is decidable. An architecture $Arch(M)$ of a DQA M is a *polyforest* if the underlying *undirected graph* is acyclic.

To bound the tree-width of queue graphs of *polyforest* architectures, we note that we can reverse any edge of the graph, without changing its tree-width. Hence, we can direct queuing edges in a way to make the underlying architecture a directed forest (note that since there are no stacks, the well-queuing assumption is satisfied vacuously, see [20]). This resulting graph hence can be interpreted on a linear word (using the same proof as for DQAS, except that now the nesting relation is not needed). Hence we obtain the following:

LEMMA 4.11. *Let* $(P, Q, Sender, Receiver)$ *be a tuple where* P *and* Q *are finite sets and* $Sender : Q \rightarrow P$ *and* $Receiver : Q \rightarrow P$*. Then the class of polyforest queue graphs over* $(P, Q, Sender, Receiver)$ *has tree-width (even path-width) bounded by* $|P|$.

Furthermore, from Lemma 4.10, Lemma 4.9 , and Theorem 2.3, we can conclude:

THEOREM 4.12. *The emptiness problem for polyforest DQAs is decidable, and decidable in time* $|M|^{O(n)}$*, where* n *is the number of processes of* M.

5. Conclusions and further results

The main contribution of this paper is to provide a uniform framework using which we can prove decidability of emptiness of a variety of automata with auxiliary storage. In this sense, our framework is the "mother" of several automata decidability results proved recently in the literature, where complex but awkward restrictions have been imposed to obtain decidability of emptiness. We also believe that our results can help in the search of new automaton models that have a tractable emptiness problem using the principles outlined by our framework.

There are several other results that follow immediately from our work, that we discuss below.

Under-approximation of abstracted programs using tree-width: The analysis of abstracted concurrent programs communicating through shared-variables is in general undecidable. These programs can be modeled as multi-stack pushdown automata. In the last few years, syntactic restrictions on the behaviors of those automata have been considered with the aim of making the analysis of such programs decidable, e.g. bounded context-switches [22], bounded-phases [15]), etc.

Since all the known syntactic restrictions correspond to graphs of bounded tree-width, we can consider the tree-width as a natural *semantic restriction* to consider for under-approximations. Given a multi-stack automaton and $k \in \mathbb{N}$, the problem of deciding whether there is a multiply nested word of tree-width k that is accepted by it is decidable, as shown in our framework, and hence can be used as an under-approximation technique to explore the state-space reached by a concurrent program. Note that this would cover all behaviors that explore k context-switches, and more, and yet has the same complexity.

Improvement in complexity for DQSAs: As mentioned earlier, Theorem 4.7 improves the complexity of the emptiness problem for a well-queuing DQSA M with tree-architectures to one exponential in the number of processes; the algorithm given in [17] is doubly exponential. This upper bound complexity matches the EXPTIME lower-bound for the emptiness problem on DQSAs [13].

Decidable emptiness problem for multi-stack pushdown automata with bounded* reverse-phase*: Our framework shows immediately the decidability of other restrictions placed on automata with auxiliary storage. For example, fix $k \in \mathbb{N}$ and consider multi-stack automata behaviors restricted to k *reverse-phases*, where in each reverse-phase, there is only one stack that is pushed into (but arbitrary pops of stacks are allowed). Then it easily follows that emptiness is decidable for this class, since the graphs corresponding to the runs of these automata are precisely the same as those of bounded-phase automata, save for the orientation of the linear and nesting edges, and hence has the same tree-width.

A general Parikh theorem: We can prove a general *Parikh theorem* [21] for all classes of automata that can be compiled to graph automata of bounded tree-width. The idea is to encode the graph into a tree using the tree-decomposition, with a unique vertex of the tree for every graph node. Since a depth-first traversal of the tree can be captured by a pushdown automata, we can build a context-free grammar that generates the graph nodes in some order. Using the classic Parikh theorem for context-free grammars, we can show that the labels of the graph nodes define a semi-linear set. This is a generalization of the technique using in [15], where a similar argument was used for proving a Parikh theorem for bounded-phase multi-stack automata.

Extension to infinite behaviors: Several of our results extend to automata over infinite behaviors. For example, consider ordered multi-stack *Büchi* or *parity* automata on infinite words. We can show that there are graph automata on multiply-nested infinite graphs (with appropriate Büchi and parity conditions) that can simulate these automata, and further that these graphs have bounded tree-width. This proves that the emptiness problem for this class of automata is decidable. (See [5] for recent results in this direction.) Similar results can be obtained by extending the tractable distributed automata presented in this paper to infinite words.

There are interesting temporal logics suitable for expressing properties of single-stack pushdown systems, like the logic CARET [4]). Natural extensions of temporal logics like CARET that allow to reason with multi-stack pushdown automata are also possible, and can be proved decidable for all multi-stack automata whose runs can be modeled by graphs of bounded tree-width.

Acknowledgments

This work was partially supported by the NSF CAREER grant #0747041 and the French ANR-09-SEGI project Veridyc.

References

[1] R. Alur and P. Madhusudan. Visibly pushdown languages. In L. Babai, editor, *STOC*, pages 202–211. ACM, 2004.

[2] R. Alur and P. Madhusudan. Adding nesting structure to words. In O. H. Ibarra and Z. Dang, editors, *Developments in Language Theory*, volume 4036 of *Lecture Notes in Computer Science*, pages 1–13. Springer, 2006.

[3] R. Alur and P. Madhusudan. Adding nesting structure to words. *J. ACM*, 56(3), 2009.

[4] R. Alur, K. Etessami, and P. Madhusudan. A temporal logic of nested calls and returns. In K. Jensen and A. Podelski, editors, *TACAS*, volume 2988 of *Lecture Notes in Computer Science*, pages 467–481. Springer, 2004.

[5] M. F. Atig. Global model checking of ordered multi-pushdown systems. In K. Lodaya and M. Mahajan, editors, *Proceedings of the 30th Conference on FSTTCS*, Leibniz International Proceedings in Informatics, Chennai, India, Dec. 2010. To appear.

[6] M. F. Atig, B. Bollig, and P. Habermehl. Emptiness of multi-pushdown automata is 2etime-complete. In M. Ito and M. Toyama, editors, *Developments in Language Theory*, volume 5257 of *Lecture Notes in Computer Science*, pages 121–133. Springer, 2008.

[7] T. Ball, R. Majumdar, T. D. Millstein, and S. K. Rajamani. Automatic predicate abstraction of C programs. In *PLDI*, pages 203–213, 2001.

[8] L. Breveglieri, A. Cherubini, C. Citrini, and S. Crespi-Reghizzi. Multi-push-down languages and grammars. *Int. J. Found. Comput. Sci.*, 7(3): 253–292, 1996.

[9] B. Courcelle. The expression of graph properties and graph transformations in monadic second-order logic. In G. Rozenberg, editor, *Handbook of Graph Grammars*, pages 313–400. World Scientific, 1997.

[10] B. Courcelle and S. Olariu. Upper bounds to the clique width of graphs. *Discrete Applied Mathematics*, 101(1-3):77–114, 2000.

[11] B. Courcelle, J. A. Makowsky, and U. Rotics. Linear time solvable optimization problems on graphs of bounded clique-width. *Theory Comput. Syst.*, 33(2):125–150, 2000.

[12] J. Flum and M. Grohe. *Parameterized Complexity Theory (Texts in Theoretical Computer Science. An EATCS Series)*. Springer-Verlag New York, Inc., Secaucus, NJ, USA, 2006.

[13] A. Heußner, J. Leroux, A. Muscholl, and G. Sutre. Reachability analysis of communicating pushdown systems. In C.-H. L. Ong, editor, *FOSSACS*, volume 6014 of *Lecture Notes in Computer Science*, pages 267–281. Springer, 2010.

[14] J. E. Hopcroft and J. D. Ullman. *Introduction to Automata Theory, Languages, and Computation*. Addison-Wesley, 1979.

[15] S. La Torre, P. Madhusudan, and G. Parlato. A robust class of context-sensitive languages. In *LICS*, pages 161–170. IEEE Computer Society, 2007.

[16] S. La Torre, P. Madhusudan, and G. Parlato. An infinite automaton characterization of double exponential time. In M. Kaminski and S. Martini, editors, *CSL*, volume 5213 of *Lecture Notes in Computer Science*, pages 33–48. Springer, 2008.

[17] S. La Torre, P. Madhusudan, and G. Parlato. Context-bounded analysis of concurrent queue systems. In C. R. Ramakrishnan and J. Rehof, editors, *TACAS*, volume 4963 of *Lecture Notes in Computer Science*, pages 299–314. Springer, 2008.

[18] S. La Torre, P. Madhusudan, and G. Parlato. Analyzing recursive programs using a fixed-point calculus. In M. Hind and A. Diwan, editors, *PLDI*, pages 211–222. ACM, 2009.

[19] S. La Torre, P. Madhusudan, and G. Parlato. Model-checking parameterized concurrent programs using linear interfaces. In T. Touili, B. Cook, and P. Jackson, editors, *CAV*, volume 6174 of *Lecture Notes in Computer Science*, pages 629–644. Springer, 2010.

[20] P. Madhusudan and G. Parlato. The tree width of automata with auxiliary storage. In *IDEALS Technical Report* `http://hdl.handle.net/2142/15433`, April 2010.

[21] R. Parikh. On context-free languages. *J. ACM*, 13(4):570–581, 1966.

[22] S. Qadeer and J. Rehof. Context-bounded model checking of concurrent software. In N. Halbwachs and L. D. Zuck, editors, *TACAS*, volume 3440 of *Lecture Notes in Computer Science*, pages 93–107. Springer, 2005.

[23] D. Seese. The structure of models of decidable monadic theories of graphs. *Ann. Pure Appl. Logic*, 53(2):169–195, 1991.

[24] W. Thomas. On logics, tilings, and automata. In J. L. Albert, B. Monien, and M. Rodríguez-Artalejo, editors, *ICALP*, volume 510 of *Lecture Notes in Computer Science*, pages 441–454. Springer, 1991.

Appendix

A. Tree-width of bounded-context multiply nested words

In this section we show that any k-context multiply nested word graph has a tree-width upper-bounded by $k + 1$.

LEMMA A.1. *For any $k \in \mathbb{N}$, the tree-width of any k-context mNW N is at most $k + 1$.*

The proof is simple, and we sketch the main idea. Let us create a tree-decomposition by creating a tree where the root has k subtrees, each subtree corresponding to a stack. For each stack s, we take the contexts that involve the stack s, remove the rest of the events, and build the tree (and the bags) as in the canonical tree-decomposition of a singly nested word (of width at most 2). These trees along with the root, and the bags associated with the nodes, capture all nesting edges and all linear edges, *except the linear edges that cross contexts* (which are at most $k - 1$ in number). Now, for every pair of nodes u and v, where v is the linear successor of u, and where u and v are in different contexts, let us add u to all nodes in the path from u to v. Clearly, the bag-sizes increase by at most $k - 1$, and the resulting tree-decomposition captures all edges and is of width at most $k + 1$.

B. On the tree-width of bounded-phase and ordered multiply nested words

In this section we give an upper-bound of the tree-width of both bounded-phase and ordered multiply nested word graphs. For a given k and n, the tree-width of any k-phase n-NW is $O(2^k)$, instead the tree-width of any ordered n-NW is $O(n \cdot 2^n)$.

We show such bounds by giving a general technique to upper-bound the width of the canonical tree decomposition $can\text{-}td(N)$, for any n-NW which is k-phase (Section B.1) or ordered (Section B.2).

Proof strategy: Our proof strategy is the following. First, notice that in any multiply nested word, the canonical tree decomposition we defined has all edges except the *pop-edges*, i.e. edges (u, v)

where v is a pop-node for some stack (other linear edges as well as all nesting edges are local in the tree decomposition). We define, first, a notion of an *extension* of a multiply nested word, which is the same as the multiply nested word except that every edge (u, v) where v is a pop-node is replaced by a *path* of nodes which, intuitively, connects u to v by taking a *backward* path along the linear order, all the way up to the push-node v' corresponding to v and then goes on to v. The crucial property of this expansion is that all edges between u and v become local in the tree. This backward path is constructed so that it utilizes nesting edges (of the same kind as the stack v is popping from) in order to reach v'.

This extension of a multiply nested word will be used in both the proofs of bounded phase words as well as ordered multi-stack words. We show that this extension preserves the bounded phase property as well as the ordered-ness property.

The extension of a multiply nested word N then helps us build a new tree-decomposition over the same tree as we need in the theorems; i.e. using a *different* set of bags but over the same tree T deriving from *can-td*(N). We show that this tree-decomposition certainly has width at least as the width of *can-td*(N), and hence establishing that the width of this tree decomposition is bounded by the appropriate bounds for bounded-phase multiply nested words and ordered multiply nested words is sufficient to prove our theorems.

We then define a notion of *generator trees* corresponding to *every node* of a multiply nested structure N. Intuitively, the generator tree of a node v consists of the copies of the node v in the extension of N, and a copy (v, h') of v is the child of a copy (v, h'), if (v, h') was created as a relabeling of (v, h) in a backward path that replaced a pop-edge. The generator tree is a technical structure that has certain structural properties (Lemma B.5 and Lemma B.6) that allows us to count the widths of the decompositions of both bounded phase words and ordered multiply nested words.

Proof outline: Throughout the section, every time we refer to N we mean the n-NW $N = (V, Init, Final, L, \{E_j\}_{j\in[n]})$. Moreover, whenever we refer to the ordering among N nodes, we always intend the linear ordering $<_L$. We also consider an ordering on L edges: if $e_1 = (a, b)$ and $e_2 = (c, d)$ with $e_1, e_2 \in L$, then $e_1 < e_2$ if $b <_L c$. Furthermore, T is the tree obtained as $(T, bag) =$ *can-td*(N). If $(u, v) \in E_j$ with $j \in [n]$, we say that u is a *push-j* node, v is a *pop-j* node, and that u and v are *matched*. Moreover, an L edge (u, v) is called a *pop-j* edge, if v is a pop-j node.

For any N, we define an n-NW $N' = (V', Init', Final', L', \{E'_j\}_{j\in[n]})$, called the *extension* of N, as follows. Intuitively, N' is obtained from N by replacing all the pop edges with a sequence of nodes. More precisely, consider a pop-j edge (u, v) and suppose that all the pop edges before (u, v) have already been replaced with paths to create a nested word N'. Then, the pop edge (u, v) is replaced with the "back-path" of N' starting from u and ending with the push node u' that matches v. The back-path is built in the following manner. Suppose we have reached a node b. Now, if b is a pop-j node — notice that v is also a pop-j node — then the next node in the back-path is a where a is the push-j node matched to b ($(a, b) \in E'_j$). (In this way we get closer to u', which must occur before a, and hence skipping all nodes between b and a.) Otherwise, the next node in the path will be the L' predecessor of b. In other words, the back-path from u to u' is formed by taking linear predecessors at each state, except taking nesting edges for the stack j. Obviously all the nodes in back-paths will be renamed so that they will be unique in N'.

Now we formally define the extension of a multiply nested word N, $Ext(N)$. We do this by defining a function $expand$ that takes the *first* pop-edge in a nested word, and replaces it by a back-path. We will first start with the nested word N, with renamed vertices. Then, we will apply $expand$ to it repeatedly till all pop-edges are replaced (and we reach a fixed-point). This fixed-point will be the extension of N. First, let us define back-paths formally.

Back-paths and extensions:
Let $\widehat{N} = (\widehat{V}, \widehat{Init}, \widehat{Final}, \widehat{L}, \{\widehat{E}_j\}_{j\in[n]})$ be a n-NW and let (u, v) be a pop-edge (i.e. v is a pop-node and u is the linear predecessor of v). Let $(v', v) \in \widehat{E}_j$ ($j \in [n]$). Then $BackPath_{\widehat{N}}(v)$ is the unique node sequence $v_1 \dots v_t$ such that

- $v_1 = u$ and $v_t = v'$, and
- For every $i \in [t-1]$, if v_i is a pop-j node, then v_{i+1} is the corresponding push-node, i.e. the node such that $(v_{i+1}, v_i) \in \widehat{E}_j$.
  Otherwise v_{i+1} is the linear predecessor of v (i.e. the node such that $(v_{i+1}, v_i) \in \widehat{L}$).

We now define the extension of a multiple nested word, using a systematic replacement of every pop-edge (u, v) by a linearly ordered sequence of nodes formed by a back-path from u to the push-node v' corresponding to v. Moreover, in the linearly ordered sequence that replaces the pop-edge, no node will have nesting edges incident on it. We will perform this surgery on all pop-edges, going from the left-most one to the right-most; this is important as back-paths for a pop-edge may utilize the extensions of pop-edges that occur to the left of it.

Let us fix a n-NW $N = (V, Init, Final, L, \{E_j\}_{j\in[n]})$. The extension of N will have vertices of the form (v, i) where $v \in V$ and $i \in \mathbb{N}$.

Let N_0 be the same as nested word N, except that each vertex $v \in V$ gets renamed to $(v, 1)$. In other words, $N_0 = (V \times \{1\}, Init_0, Final_0, L_0, \{E^0_j\}_{j\in[n]})$, where the various edges in N_0 are appropriately defined.

We now construct N_{i+1} from N_i using the following algorithm. Let $N_i = (V_i, Init_i, Final_i, L_i, \{E^i_j\}_{j\in[n]})$, where $V_i \subseteq V \times \mathbb{N}$. Let $((u, 1), (v, 1))$ be the first pop-edge of its kind (i.e. with indices 1) in N_i according to the linear ordering L_i (if no such pop-edge exists, then we set $N_{i+1} = N_i$, and reach a fixed-point). Then $N_{i+1} = (V_{i+1}, Init_i, Final_i, L_{i+1}, \{E^i_j\}_{j\in[n]})$ is defined as follows (note that the initial, final, and nesting edges do not change).

Let the back-path from $\langle u, 1\rangle$ be $BackPath_{N_i}(\langle u, 1\rangle) = \langle z_1, h_1\rangle \dots \langle z_t, h_t\rangle$. Note that any node occurs at most once in the back-path. Let us now relabel this path so that the nodes $\langle z_j, h_j\rangle$ get renamed to some $\langle z_j, h'_j\rangle$ so that they are not in V_i and do not get repeated in the back-path:

- $relabel_{V_i}(\epsilon) = \epsilon$
- $relabel_{V_i}(w, \langle x, m\rangle) = relabel_{V_i}(w), \langle x, m'\rangle$ where m' is the least positive integer such that $\langle x, m'\rangle \notin V_i$ and does not occur in $relabel_{V_i}(w)$.

Let $relabel_X(BackPath_{N'}(\langle u, 1\rangle)) = \langle z_1, h'_1\rangle \dots \langle z_t, h'_t\rangle$. Then, $V_{i+1} = (V_i \cup \{\langle z_i, h'_i\rangle \mid i \in [t]\})$ and the set L_{i+1} is:

$$L_{i+1} = (L_i \backslash \{(\langle u, 1\rangle, \langle v, 1\rangle)\}) \cup \{(\langle z_i, h'_i\rangle, \langle z_{i+1}, h'_{i+1}\rangle) \mid i \in [t]\}$$

$$\cup \{(\langle u, 1\rangle, \langle z_1, h'_1\rangle), (\langle z_t, h'_t\rangle, \langle v, 1\rangle)\}$$

Intuitively, we remove the linear edge from $\langle u, 1\rangle$ to $\langle v, 1\rangle)$ and replace it with the backward path from $\langle u, 1\rangle$, appropriately renamed.

We apply the above algorithm to systematically replace pop-edges by a linearly ordered set of nodes, left to right, till we reach a fixed-point, where there are no pop-edges of the form $(\langle u, 1\rangle, \langle v, 1\rangle)$. The final multiply nested word will be the *extension* of N.

Notice that, N' is the same as N except that pop edges of N are replaced by nodes that are neither the target nor the source of any nesting edges. Therefore, if N is a k-phase MNW then also N' is, and if N is an ordered n-NW then so is N':

LEMMA B.1. *Let N' be the extension of an n-NW N. Then, (1) N' is k-phase iff N is k-phase, (2) N' is ordered iff N is ordered.*

It is easy to prove that if $(\langle a,i\rangle,\langle b,j\rangle)$ is an edge in N', that is $(\langle a,i\rangle,\langle b,j\rangle) \in (L' \cup \bigcup_{h\in[n]} E'_h))$, then a and b are connected by an edge in T, which means that either a is the parent of b or vice-versa. By using N' we define a new tree decomposition of N whose underlying tree is T.

We define a map $bag' : V \to 2^V$ as follows. Map bag' associates the minimum set of vertices to each node of T according to the following rules:

1. $v \in bag'(v)$, for all $v \in V$.
2. if u is the parent of v in T, then $u \in bag'(v)$, for every $v \in V$.
3. if (u, v) is a pop edge of N, and $BackPath_{N'}(\langle u,1\rangle) = \langle u_1,h_1\rangle \ldots \langle u_t,h_t\rangle$, then $u \in bag'(u_i)$, for every $i \in [t]$.

Notice that the first and second condition defining the map bag (see Definition 3.6) and the first and second condition in the definition of bag' are the same. They only differ in the third one: if u' is such that $(u', v) \in E_j$, then condition three of Definition 3.6 says that u is added to $bag(z)$ for all nodes z lying along the unique shortest path in T between u and u'. Similarly the third condition of the definition above adds u to the bag' of all the T nodes along a path in T from u to u' which may not be the shortest. However, that path has to pass trough all the nodes of the shortest path between u' and u. Thus, (T, bag') is a tree decomposition of N, and more importantly for us $bag(z) \subseteq bag'(z)$, for every node z of T. Therefore, we can upper-bound the size of $bag(u)$ by considering the size of $bag'(u)$ for every $u \in V$, as stated in the next lemma.

LEMMA B.2. *Let N be an n-nested word, and $\mathcal{T} = (T, bag) = can\text{-}td(N)$. Then, $\mathcal{T}' = (T, bag')$ is a tree decompositions of N where $width(\mathcal{T}) \leq width(\mathcal{T}')$. Furthermore, for every $v \in V$, $|bag'(v)| \leq d_v + 1$, where $d_v = |\{\langle v,h\rangle \in V' \mid h \in \mathbb{N}\}|$.*

Generator Trees: A convenient way to calculate d_v (in the above lemma) is to represent the set of N' nodes $\{\langle v,h\rangle \in V' \mid h \in \mathbb{N}\}$ as a tree, for each $v \in V$. Let $\langle v,h\rangle$, with $h > 1$, be a node of N', and let $\langle u,1\rangle$ be the greatest push node of N' that occurs before $\langle v,h\rangle$. Intuitively, $\langle v,h\rangle$ is one of the node of the path between that have replaced the pop edge (u, v) of N. By definition of N', $\langle v,h\rangle$ is generated because there is another node $\langle v,h'\rangle$ with $h' < h$ in $BackPath(\langle u,1\rangle)$. We call $\langle v,h'\rangle$ the *generator* of $\langle v,h\rangle$. Note that for every node $\langle v,h\rangle$ with $h > 1$ there is a unique generator of it (though the vice-versa does not hold).

DEFINITION B.3 (GENERATOR TREES). *Let N' be the extension of an n-nested word N, and let V be the set of nodes of N. For every $v \in V$, we define a tree T_v as follows:*

- *$\langle v,1\rangle$ is the root of T_v.*
- *if $\langle v,h'\rangle$ is the generator of $\langle v,h\rangle$ then $\langle v,h\rangle$ is a child of $\langle v,h'\rangle$.*

For every $v \in V$, the tree T_v is called the generator tree *of v.*

Observe that, for a given N node v, all the nodes (v, h) in N' are also nodes of T_v, thus the value d_v corresponds to the number of nodes of T_v.

We can also associate a *stack* to every node of generator tree, except the root. If a node $\langle v,1\rangle$ is the first pop node after $\langle v,h\rangle$ (where $h > 1$), and if v is a pop node of stack j, then we say that j is the *stack* of $\langle v,h\rangle$. Intuitively, the stack associated with $\langle v,h\rangle$ is the stack whose popping led to a back-path that created $\langle v,h\rangle$.

In the following we give some properties of generator trees that will be instantiate later for the case in which N is bounded-phase and ordered. Intuitively, fix a stack j; then, any node in a multiply nested word can be touched only once on a backward path that is caused by a pop of stack j, except that when the node is a push onto stack j, in which case it may be touched twice. This is true because the backward path caused by a pop to stack j takes nesting edges of stack j as much as possible, hence skipping the nodes between the nesting edges it takes.

The first lemma states that if v is a push onto stack j, the root of the generator tree of v, namely $\langle v,1\rangle$, has at most $n+1$ children—at most two of these children may be of stack j, and all the other children must be of distinct stacks.

LEMMA B.4. *If $v \in V$ is a push-j node then the root $\langle v,1\rangle$ of T_v has at most two children of stack j. Moreover, for every $j' \neq j$, $\langle v,1\rangle$ has at most one child of stack j'.*

Proof By contradiction suppose that $(v, 1)$ has at least three children of stack j. Since a back-path goes always backward it contains distinct nodes. Therefore there must exist three pop-j edges in N, say $e_1 = (u_1, v_1), e_2 = (u_2, v_2), e_3 = (u_3, v_3)$, such that $\langle v,1\rangle$ is contained in $BackPath_{N'}(\langle u_i,1\rangle)$ for all $i \in [3]$. Suppose that e_1, e_2 and e_3, in the order, are the first three pop edges of N having the above property. It is easy to see that $\langle v_1,1\rangle$ is the matching pop of $\langle v,1\rangle$. Now, $BackPath_{N'}(\langle u_2,1\rangle)$ to reaches $\langle v,1\rangle$ must pass through $\langle v_1,1\rangle$ (a back-path always goes backward and since the E'_j relation is nested a back-path can never jump in between $\langle v,1\rangle$ and $\langle v_1,1\rangle$). Thus, when $BackPath_{N'}(\langle u_2,1\rangle)$ reaches $\langle v_1,1\rangle$, it goes directly to $\langle v,1\rangle$. This entails that the matching push of $\langle v_2,1\rangle$ occurs before $\langle v,1\rangle$. Now, $BackPath_{N'}(\langle u_3,1\rangle)$ must pass through $\langle v_2,1\rangle$ to reach $\langle v,1\rangle$. But, $\langle v_2,1\rangle$ is a pop-j node and thus the back-path jumps directly to the matching push of $\langle v_2,1\rangle$, which comes before $\langle v,1\rangle$. Since a back-path goes always backward, $\langle v,1\rangle$ can never be reached by $BackPath_{N'}(\langle u_3,1\rangle)$. This is a contradiction.

In similar way we prove that, if $j' \neq j$ then $\langle v,1\rangle$ has at most one child of stack j'. By contradiction, let $e_1 = (u_1, v_1)$ and $e_2 = (u_2, v_2)$ be the first two pop-j' edges of N such that $BackPath_{N'}(\langle u_1,1\rangle)$ and $BackPath_{N'}(\langle u_2,1\rangle)$ contain $\langle v,1\rangle$. If $BackPath_{N'}(\langle u_1,1\rangle)$ passes through $\langle v,1\rangle$ means that the push-j node matched by the $\langle v_1,1\rangle$ must occur before $\langle v,1\rangle$. Now $BackPath_{N'}(\langle u_2,1\rangle)$ must pass through $\langle v_1,1\rangle$ and hence jumps directly to the matched push j node matched with $\langle v_1,1\rangle$. Since such a node comes before $\langle v,1\rangle$ and back-paths never go forward we have that $\langle v,1\rangle$ cannot be reached by $BackPath_{N'}(\langle u_2,1\rangle)$. □

The second property we need is that for any node v, any non-root node in the generator tree of v has children whose stacks are distinct from each other. Moreover, if v is not a push, then the root also has children whose stacks are all distinct from each other.

LEMMA B.5. *Let $\langle z,h\rangle \in N'$. Then, if $h > 1$ or z is not a push node of N, then for every $j \in [n]$, the node $\langle z,h\rangle$ has at most one child of stack j in T_z.*

Proof If $h > 1$ then $\langle z,h\rangle$ must be a node of a path that has replaced a pop edge, say (u, v) of N. Suppose that $e_1 = (u_1, v_1)$ and $e_2 = (u_2, v_2)$ are the first two pop-j edges (in the order) of N such that $BackPath_{N'}(\langle u_1,1\rangle)$ and $BackPath_{N'}(\langle u_2,1\rangle)$ contain $\langle z,h\rangle$. Thus, $\langle z,h\rangle <_{L'} \langle u_1,1\rangle <_{L'} \langle v_1,1\rangle <_{L'} \langle u_2,1\rangle$. Since $BackPath_{N'}(\langle u_1,1\rangle)$ passes through $\langle z,h\rangle$ implies that the push-j node matched by the $\langle v_1,1\rangle$ occurs before $\langle z,h\rangle$. Now

$BackPath_{N'}(\langle u_2, 1\rangle)$ has to pass through $\langle v_1, 1\rangle$, which is a pop-j node, and hence jumps directly to the push-j node matched to $\langle v_1, 1\rangle$. Such a node appears before $\langle z, h\rangle$ and since back-paths only go backward we have that $\langle v, 1\rangle$ is never reached by $BackPath_{N'}(\langle u_2, 1\rangle)$ which contradicts the hypotheses.

The other case in which $\langle z, 1\rangle$ is not a push node is similar to the case above and we do not give it here.

□

B.1 Tree-width of bounded-phase multiply nested word graphs

In this section we show that the tree-width of any k-phase mNW N is $O(2^k)$.

From Lemma B.1, the extension N' of N is also a k-phase n-NW. Thus, we define $phase_{N'}$ to be the map that associates to every node $\langle v, h\rangle$ of N' its phase number.

The next lemma, which is a refinement of Lemma B.4, says that for any push-node v, the phase numbers of the children of the root of the generator tree of v are not less than that of the root, and further, all phase numbers of the children of the root are distinct from each other, save for one child. This bounds the number of children of the root to $k - j + 2$, if the root has phase j.

LEMMA B.6. *For every push node $v \in V$, the phase of the children of the root $\langle v, 1\rangle$ of T_v is greater or equal to the phase of $\langle v, 1\rangle$. Moreover, except for one child of $\langle v, 1\rangle$, all the other children have different phase number.*

Proof If $\langle v, h\rangle$ is a child of $\langle v, 1\rangle$, then $\langle v, 1\rangle <_{L'} \langle v, h\rangle$, and hence $phase_{N'}(\langle v, 1\rangle) \leq phase_{N'}(\langle v, h\rangle)$. Now, if the stack number of $\langle v, h\rangle$ is different from the stack number of $\langle v, 1\rangle$ then $phase_{N'}(\langle v, 1\rangle) < phase_{N'}(\langle v, h\rangle)$. Moreover, if $\langle v, h\rangle$ and $\langle v, h'\rangle$ are two children of $\langle v, 1\rangle$ with different stack number then $phase_{N'}(\langle v, h\rangle) \neq phase_{N'}(\langle v, h'\rangle)$. Thus, from Lemma B.4 we can conclude the proof. □

By using a similar argument of the previous proof, and Lemma B.5, we can show the following lemma, which says that for any v, the children of a non-root node (v, h) in the generator tree for v have distinct phases and have phases greater than the phase of (v, h). Moreover, this is also true for the root $(v, 1)$ provided v is not a push-node.

LEMMA B.7. *Let $\langle v, h\rangle \in N'$. Then, if $h > 1$ or v is not a push node of N, then for every child $\langle v, h'\rangle$ of $\langle v, h\rangle$ in T_v, $phase_{N'}(\langle v, h\rangle) < phase_{N'}(\langle v, h'\rangle)$. Moreover, for every phase number $p > phase_{N'}(\langle v, h\rangle)$, there is at most one child $\langle v, h'\rangle$ of $\langle v, h\rangle$ such that $phase_{N'}(\langle v, h'\rangle) = p$.*

By using the previous lemma we can upper-bound the number of nodes of the sub-tree of T_v rooted in any internal node of T_v, for every node v of N. Let $f : [k] \rightarrow \mathbb{N}$ defined as: $f(i) = 1 + \sum_{j=i+1}^{k} f(j)$ for every $i \in [k-1]$, and $f(k) = 1$. By a simple calculation it is easy to prove that $f(i) = 2^{k-i}$. Thus, we can upper-bound the number of nodes of any subtree of T_v rooted in an internal node $\langle v, h\rangle$ with $f(phase_{N'}(\langle v, h\rangle))$.

Now by instantiating Lemma B.6, we have that

$$d_v \leq 1 + f(1) + \sum_{i=1}^{k} f(i) = 2^k + 2^{k-1},$$

and by Lemma B.2 follows that the width of the tree decomposition $can\text{-}td(N)$ of N is at most $2^k + 2^{k-1} + 1$.

THEOREM B.8. *The tree-width of any k-phase mNW is at most $2^k + 2^{k-1} + 1$.*

B.2 Tree-width of ordered multiply nested word graph

In this section we show that the tree-width of any ordered n-nested words N is $O(n \cdot 2^{n-1})$. As in the previous section, we prove such a result by upper-bounding the number of nodes of each tree T_v, for every node v of N.

In the following we instantiate Lemma B.5 for ordered multiply nested words. We show that for any internal node (v, h) of the generator tree of a node v, the stacks of the children of v are strictly greater than that of v. The reason why the stack of a child of (v, h) cannot be lower than that of v is because of the ordered-ness of the stack accesses— if the back-path of a pop of stack j' leads through a pop of stack j, then we must have that $j \leq j'$ (the reason why it cannot $j \neq j'$ is also argued below). Hence, the depth of the tree gets bounded by the number of stacks, n, and each non-root node has at most $n - 1$ children.

LEMMA B.9. *If $\langle v, h\rangle \in N'$ is a stack j node with $h > 0$, then (1) the stack j' for any child of the node $\langle v, h\rangle$ is such that $j' > j$, and (2) the stacks for the children of the node $\langle v, h\rangle$ are all distinct.*

Proof Case (2) follows from Lemma B.4. Case (1) is proved by contradiction and we distinguish two cases, one when $j' < j$ and the other one for $j' = j$. Let $\langle v, h'\rangle$ be a child of $\langle v, h\rangle$, and suppose that $\langle v, h'\rangle$ is a stack j' node. Since $h, h' > 1$, $\langle v, h\rangle$ and $\langle v, h'\rangle$ are both lying on a two different paths that replace two different pop edges of N, say $e_1 = (u_1, v_1)$ and $e_2 = (u_2, v_2)$. Thus, we have that $\langle v, h\rangle <_{L'} \langle v_1, 1\rangle <_{L'} \langle u_2, 1\rangle <_{L'} \langle v, h'\rangle$. The fact that $BackPath_{N'}(\langle u_2, 1\rangle)$ has to visit $\langle v, h\rangle$ to reach the matching push-j' node of $\langle v_2, 1\rangle$ means that it occurs before the pop-j $\langle v_1, 1\rangle$.

Now if $j' < j$, it means that there is pop-j node that comes after a push-j' node that has not matched yet. Since $j' < j$, this contradicts the ordered-ness property of N' and hence N. Instead, if $j' = j$ then $BackPath_{N'}(\langle u_2, 1\rangle)$ will never visit $\langle v, h\rangle$ because between $\langle v, h\rangle$ and $\langle u_2, 1\rangle$ there is a pop-j node whose matching pop occurs before $\langle v, h\rangle$. □

For every $i \in [n]$, let us define the map $f : [n] \rightarrow \mathbb{N}$ as $f(i) = 1 + \sum_{j=i+1}^{k} f(j)$ if $i \in [n-1]$ and $f(n) = 1$. Notice that $f(i) = 2^{n-i}$. From Lemma B.9, It is easy see that $f(i)$ upper-bounds the number of nodes of any T_v subtree rooted in one of its internal node which is a stack i node.

Thus, from Lemma B.4 we can conclude that the following upper-bounds the number of nodes of any tree T_v.

$$1 + (n+1)f(1) = 1 + (n+1) \cdot 2^{n-1}.$$

Now from Lemma B.2 we can conclude with the main theorem of the section.

THEOREM B.10. *The tree-width of any ordered n-NW is at most $n \cdot 2^{n-1}$.*

Fresh-Register Automata

Nikos Tzevelekos
Oxford University Computing Laboratory
nikt@comlab.ox.ac.uk

Abstract

What is a basic automata-theoretic model of computation with names and fresh-name generation? We introduce Fresh-Register Automata (FRA), a new class of automata which operate on an infinite alphabet of names and use a finite number of registers to store fresh names, and to compare incoming names with previously stored ones. These finite machines extend Kaminski and Francez's Finite-Memory Automata by being able to recognise globally fresh inputs, that is, names fresh in the whole current run. We examine the expressivity of FRA's both from the aspect of accepted languages and of bisimulation equivalence. We establish primary properties and connections between automata of this kind, and answer key decidability questions. As a demonstrating example, we express the theory of the pi-calculus in FRA's and characterise bisimulation equivalence by an appropriate, and decidable in the finitary case, notion in these automata.

Categories and Subject Descriptors F.1.1 [*Computation by Abstract Devices*]: Models of Computation; D.3.1 [*Programming Languages*]: Formal Definitions and Theory—Semantics

General Terms Theory, Languages, Verification

1. Introduction

One of the most common and useful abstractions in programming is the assumption that entities of specific kinds can be created at will and, moreover, in such a manner that newly created entities are always *fresh* — distinct from any other such created thus far. This is, for example, the case with mutable reference cells, exceptions user-declared datatypes, *etc.* in languages like Standard ML [15]. Following a long tradition in computer science [20], we call these entities *names* and specify them as follows.

> Names can be created fresh dynamically and locally, compared for equality and communicated between agents or subroutines.

Apart from the uses mentioned above, names form the basis of calculi of mobile processes (e.g. the π-calculus [14]); appear in network protocols and secure transactions; and are generally essential in programming for identifying variables, channels, threads, objects, codes, and many other sorts of name in disguise. To our knowledge, there has not been in the literature a proposal of a basic automata-theoretic model of names, providing abstract machines underlying all these paradigms. We propose just such a model here.

POPL'11, January 26–28, 2011, Austin, Texas, USA.

Our model is based on the successful paradigm of ***Finite-Memory Automata (FMA)***, introduced by Kaminski and Francez in the early 90's [11]. Motivated by real-world problems (where codes, addresses, identifiers, *etc.* may have unbounded domains), those automata address a demand for a "natural" finite-state machine model over infinite alphabets. An FMA $\mathcal{A}$ is an automaton attached with a finite number of name-storing registers. Its structure looks identical to that of an ordinary finite-state automaton over a finite set of labels generated by indices in the range $1,\dots,n$, where n is the number of registers. However, $\mathcal{A}$ truly operates on the infinite set of inputs $\mathbb{A}$ (the set of names), with indices i referring to the names stored in the i-th register of $\mathcal{A}$. This simple idea lifts the automaton from finite to infinite alphabet.

There are two ways in which an FMA can access its registers: either by comparing an input name to a stored one, or by storing an input name in one of its registers but only in case it is *locally fresh*, that is, it does not already appear in any of them. Thus, FMA's are history-free: their computational steps rely solely on their current registers. Here we introduce ***Fresh-Register Automata (FRA)***, a finite-register automaton model which extends FMA's by *global freshness* recognition: an automaton can now accept (and store) an input name just in case it is fresh in the whole run. For example, a transition

$$q \xrightarrow{i^{\circledast}} q'$$

means that if $\mathcal{A}$ is at state q and the set of names that have appeared in its registers so far is H, then $\mathcal{A}$ can accept any name $a \notin H$, store it in its i-th register and proceed to q'. This history-sensitive feature precisely captures fresh-name creation.[1] Thus, e.g. the following language (not recognised by FMA's [11]) is recognised by a single-state FRA with one register.

$$\mathcal{L}_1 = \{\, a_1 \cdots a_k \in \mathbb{A}^* \mid \forall i \neq j.\, a_i \neq a_j \,\}$$

An intuitive way to view $\mathcal{L}_1$ is as the trace of a fresh-name generator: one which returns reference cells in SML, objects in Java, memory addresses in C, *etc.*

Research in FMA's and their formal languages has been extensive [2, 6, 11, 21, 25, 27]. It has been shown [11, 21] that FMA-recognisable languages are closed under union, intersection, concatenation and Kleene star; they are not closed under complement; emptiness of FMA's is decidable; and universality is undecidable. Our first contribution is to answer this series of questions for FRA's. We show that for emptiness and universality the situation remains the same as in FMA's. On the other hand, FRA-recognisable languages are still closed under union and intersection, but history-sensitiveness prohibits this for concatenation and Kleene star. Moreover, they are not closed under complement and, in fact, there is an FMA-recognisable language whose complement is not recognised by FRA's.

[1] Note that, although history-sensitive, the automaton does not have full access to the history H. In automata-theoretic jargon, the situation can be described as consulting an oracle who can decide the freshness of names.

Our main vehicle for studying equivalence between FRA's is bisimulation equivalence (also called *bisimilarity*). The notion is very relevant from the point of view of programming, and process calculi in particular, and in the case of FRA's it implies language equivalence. More importantly, we show that by examining FRA's at the *symbolic level*, i.e. as ordinary finite-state automata on the set of index-generated labels, it is possible to capture bisimilarity by an appropriate symbolic notion; we thus prove that FRA-bisimilarity is decidable. A symbolic bisimulation relates states of two automata in specific environments, the latter specifying how are the names which appear in their registers related.

As a demonstrating example, we express the π-calculus in the context of fresh-register automata. We introduce the *xπ-calculus* system: a presentation of the π-calculus with early transition semantics [14, 26], in which processes are states of an infinite FRA. Transitions are given by FRA-transitions and the system is finitely branching. More specifically, bound outputs are modelled by globally fresh transitions, while each input is decomposed into finitely many cases: either the incoming name is locally fresh or it already appears in the registers. This clean treatment of fresh and bound names is the main advantage of the xπ-calculus and allows for the finite representation, as ordinary FRA's, of finitary processes.[2] Moreover, we characterise strong bisimilarity by an appropriate symbolic notion in xπ. This gives an alternative proof of decidability of bisimilarity for finitary processes.

Motivation and related work

Programming languages The idea of studying names in higher-order languages and in isolation of other effects was first pursued by Pitts and Stark [24]. They introduced the ν-calculus, an extension of the simply-typed λ-calculus with references of unit type. Investigations on the ν-calculus were meticulously carried on by Stark in his PhD thesis [28], which exposed a rather unexpected complexity hidden behind names. It became evident that better models for languages with names were needed. To address this, new directions in denotational [1, 12, 13, 18] and operational [3, 10] models were explored, significantly advancing our understanding of computation with names but, at the same time, leaving basic questions unanswered. In particular, those works examined computation at the higher level, that of programs and program equivalence, leaving open the question of a basic, lower-level model.

Interestingly, in their initial paper on FMA's [11], Kaminski and Francez motivate their construction (also) by briefly presenting an idealised procedural language with names. There, names cannot be freshly created, but they can be read from the environment as inputs and stored in a finite memory. Moreover, stored names can flow inside the memory from one register to another and can also be compared for equality and thus trigger goto's. The authors explain that FMA's operate like acceptors for that simple imperative language with names. By analogy, FRA's describe the extension of the language with fresh-name generation.

Process calculi For mobile systems like the π-calculus [14], where processes can create locally, receive or send names, the use of ordinary labelled transition systems for its semantics is in many ways unsatisfactory: for example, infinite branching arises even in the case of very simple processes that receive a (locally fresh) name, or output a locally created (globally fresh) one. Such shortcomings naturally led to solutions involving representations of processes by formalisms which incorporate name-reasoning of some sort [4, 5, 16]. The most notable paradigm in this direction is that of *History-Dependent Automata (HD-Automata)* [16, 22], which are structures defined in a universe of *named sets* and *named functions*. HD-automata can succinctly represent the π-calculus, as HD-transitions match 'on-the-fly' names between the source, target, and label of π-calculus transitions, allowing thus for the use of representatives of processes and transitions, rather than all possible ones under e.g. permutation of fresh names. The stream of research on HD-automata has focussed both on foundational issues [17, 22] and on pragmatic applications [7]. The work presented here shares objectives with HD-automata, and to some extent can be viewed as a complementary attempt to the same question, albeit based on basic machines of "first principles".

Outline

In the next section we give the basic definitions on FRA's. Section 3 provides some useful bisimilar constructions. In Section 4 we recall FMA's and establish their connection to FRA's. We examine WFRA's, a weaker notion of FRA's focussing on global freshness, in Section 5. In Section 6 we prove some technical results regarding closure properties for FRA's, and in Section 7 we show that emptiness and bisimilarity are decidable using symbolic methods. Section 8 examines the π-calculus in the setting of FRA's.

2. Definitions

We distinguish between two sets of input symbols:

- an infinite set of *names*, $\mathbb{A}$, and
- a finite set of *constants*, $\mathbb{C}$.

Constants have an auxiliary role and are non-storable.[3] We let a, b, *etc.* range over names. We write $\mathbb{A}^*$ for the set of finite strings of names, and $\mathbb{A}^{\circledast}$ for its restriction to those containing pairwise distinct names. Strings $a_1 \cdots a_n$ will be typically represented by vectors $\vec{a}$, in which case $\mathsf{img}(\vec{a}) = \{a_1, \dots, a_n\}$.

For each $n \in \omega$, we write $[n]$ for the set $\{1, \dots, n\}$, and let

$$\mathbb{L}_n = \mathbb{C} \cup \{\, i, i^\bullet, i^{\circledast} \mid i \in [n] \,\}\,.$$

be the set of labels generated by $[n]$. Moreover, we define

$$\mathsf{Reg}_n = \{\, \sigma : [n] \to \mathbb{A} \cup \{\sharp\} \mid \forall i \neq j.\, \sigma(i) = \sigma(j) \implies \sigma(i) = \sharp \,\}$$

to be the set of *register assignments* of size n. We write $\mathsf{img}(\sigma)$ for the name-range of σ, i.e. $\mathsf{img}(\sigma) = \{\, a \in \mathbb{A} \mid \exists i.\, \sigma(i) = a \,\}$, and let $\mathsf{dom}(\sigma) = \{\, i \in [n] \mid \sigma(i) \in \mathbb{A} \,\}$. Whenever $a \notin \mathsf{img}(\sigma)$,

$$\sigma[i \mapsto a] = \{\, (i, a) \,\} \cup \{\, (j, \sigma(j)) \mid j \in [n] \setminus \{i\} \,\}$$

is an *update* of σ, for any $i \in [n]$.

Definition 1. A ***fresh-register automaton (FRA)*** of n registers is a quintuple $\mathcal{A} = \langle Q, q_0, \sigma_0, \delta, F \rangle$ where:

- Q is a finite set of states,
- q_0 is the initial state,
- $\sigma_0 \in \mathsf{Reg}_n$ is the initial register assignment,
- $\delta \subseteq Q \times \mathbb{L}_n \times Q$ is the transition relation,
- $F \subseteq Q$ is the set of final states.

$\mathcal{A}$ is called a ***register automaton (RA)*** if there are no q, q', i such that $(q, i^{\circledast}, q') \in \delta$.

Transitions containing labels of the form i are called *known* transitions; those of the form $i^\bullet$ are *locally fresh* ones; and *globally fresh* transitions involve $i^{\circledast}$. Thus, an RA is an FRA with no globally fresh transitions.[4]

Here is an informal reading of δ. Suppose $\mathcal{A}$ is at state q_1 with current register assignment σ. If input $\ell \in \mathbb{C} \cup \mathbb{A}$ arrives then:[5]

[2] A process is *finitary* if its it does not grow unboundedly in parallelism.

[3] In other presentations [11, 21] there is no such distinction, but symbols that appear in the initial register assignment can play the role of constants.

[4] This yields the same notion of register automaton as that of [21].

[5] Note that the same symbol, ℓ, is later used to range over elements of $\mathbb{L}_n$.

- If $\ell \in \mathbb{C}$ and $(q_1, \ell, q_2) \in \delta$ then $\mathcal{A}$ accepts ℓ and moves to q_2.
- If $\ell \in \mathbb{A}$ and $(q_1, i, q_2) \in \delta$ and $\sigma(i) = \ell$ then $\mathcal{A}$ accepts ℓ and moves to q_2.
- If $\ell \in \mathbb{A}$ and $(q_1, i^\bullet, q_2) \in \delta$ and ℓ is not stored in σ then $\mathcal{A}$ accepts ℓ, it sets $\sigma(i) = \ell$ and moves to q_2.
- If $\ell \in \mathbb{A}$ and $(q_1, i^\circledast, q_2) \in \delta$ and $\ell \notin \mathsf{img}(\sigma_0)$ and ℓ has not appeared in the current run then $\mathcal{A}$ accepts ℓ, it sets $\sigma(i) = \ell$ and moves to q_2.

The above is formally defined by means of configurations representing the intended current state of the automaton, which apart from states contains information on the current register assignment and the set of names having appeared thus far (the *history*). The latter component is necessary for globally fresh transitions.

Definition 2. A ***configuration*** of $\mathcal{A}$ is a triple $(q, \sigma, H) \in \hat{Q}$, with

$$\hat{Q} = Q \times \mathsf{Reg}_n \times \mathcal{P}_{\mathsf{fn}}(\mathbb{A})$$

and $\mathcal{P}_{\mathsf{fn}}(\mathbb{A})$ being the set of finite subsets of $\mathbb{A}$. From δ define a transition relation on configurations

$$\longrightarrow_\delta \subseteq \hat{Q} \times (\mathbb{C} \cup \mathbb{A}) \times \hat{Q}$$

as follows. For all $(q, \sigma, H) \in \hat{Q}$ and $(q, \ell, q') \in \delta$:

- If $\ell \in \mathbb{C}$ then $(q, \sigma, H) \xrightarrow{\ell}_\delta (q', \sigma, H)$.
- If $\ell = i$ and $\sigma(i) = a$ then $(q, \sigma, H) \xrightarrow{a}_\delta (q', \sigma, H \cup \{a\})$.
- If $\ell = i^\bullet$ and $a \notin \mathsf{img}(\sigma)$ then $(q, \sigma, H) \xrightarrow{a}_\delta (q', \sigma', H')$ with $\sigma' = \sigma[i \mapsto a]$ and $H' = H \cup \{a\}$.
- If $\ell = i^\circledast$ and $a \notin H \cup \mathsf{img}(\sigma_0)$ then $(q, \sigma, H) \xrightarrow{a}_\delta (q', \sigma', H')$ with $\sigma' = \sigma[i \mapsto a]$ and $H' = H \cup \{a\}$.

We write $\longrightarrow\!\!\!\!\twoheadrightarrow_\delta$ for the reflexive transitive closure of $\longrightarrow_\delta$.

We say that configuration $\hat{q}$ is *reachable* if $(q_0, \sigma_0, \emptyset) \xrightarrow{\vec{\ell}}\!\!\!\!\twoheadrightarrow_\delta \hat{q}$ for some $\vec{\ell} \in (\mathbb{A} \cup \mathbb{C})^*$. We call $\mathcal{A}$ a ***closed*** FRA if, for all reachable configurations (q, σ, H) and all $(q, i, q') \in \delta$, we have that $\sigma(i) \neq \sharp$. Finally, the set of strings *accepted* by $\mathcal{A}$ is:

$$\mathcal{L}(\mathcal{A}) = \{\, \vec{\ell} \in (\mathbb{A} \cup \mathbb{C})^* \mid (q_0, \sigma_0, \emptyset) \xrightarrow{\vec{\ell}}\!\!\!\!\twoheadrightarrow_\delta (q, \sigma, H) \wedge q \in F \,\}$$

and is called the *language* recognised by $\mathcal{A}$. Two automata are *equivalent* if they recognise the same language.

Remark 3. There is an equivalent definition of FRA's in which histories include $\mathsf{img}(\sigma_0)$ by default, and in which reachable configurations are the ones reached from $(q_0, \sigma_0, \mathsf{img}(\sigma_0))$. Here instead we have decided to separate the history of the run from its initial names, which appears to give a cleaner presentation but it is by no means a substantial point of difference. Note also that reachable configurations contain names that have appeared before one way or another: if (q, σ, H) is reachable then $\mathsf{img}(\sigma) \subseteq \mathsf{img}(\sigma_0) \cup H$.

Example 4. The reader can check that the language $\mathcal{L}_1$ $(= \mathbb{A}^\circledast)$ of the Introduction is recognised by the following FRA.

$$\mathcal{A}_0 = \langle \{q_0\}, q_0, \{(1, \sharp)\}, \{(q_0, 1^\circledast, q_0)\}, \{q_0\} \rangle$$

Note that the FRA $\mathcal{B} = \langle \{q_0\}, q_0, \{(1, \sharp)\}, \{(q_0, 1^\bullet, q_0)\}, \{q_0\} \rangle$ recognises the language:

$$\mathcal{L}_2 = \{\, a_1 \cdots a_k \in \mathbb{A}^* \mid k \in \omega \wedge \forall i.\, a_i \neq a_{i+1} \,\}$$

and is therefore not equivalent to $\mathcal{A}$.
A more elaborate example is the following. Let $\mathcal{A}$ be the FRA:

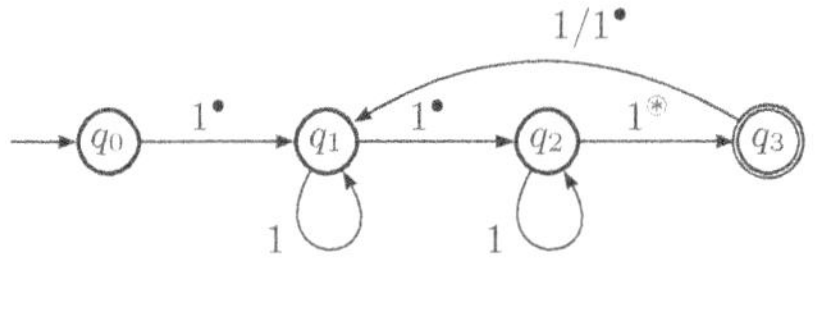

with initial assignment $\{(1, \sharp)\}$. The automaton works as follows. It receives a name a and then keeps receiving a until some $b \neq a$ arrives; then it keeps receiving b until a globally fresh c arrives; it then repeats from start. Thus, members of $\mathcal{L}(\mathcal{A})$ are of the form

$$a_0^{j_0}\, b_0^{k_0}\, c_0\, a_1^{j_1}\, b_1^{k_1}\, c_1\, a_2^{j_2}\, b_2^{k_2}\, c_2\, \ldots\, a_n^{j_n}\, b_n^{k_n}\, c_n$$

where, for all i, we have $j_i, k_i > 0$, $a_i \neq b_i$ and c_i differs from all symbols preceding it. Formally, setting

$$\mathcal{L}'(H) = \{\, a^{n_1} b^{n_2} c \mid n_i > 0 \wedge a \neq b \wedge c \notin H \cup \{a, b\} \,\}$$

we have that $\mathcal{L}(\mathcal{A}) = \bigcup_{i \in \omega} \mathcal{L}_i$, where we set $\mathcal{L}_0 = \mathcal{L}'(\emptyset)$ and $\mathcal{L}_{i+1} = \{\, \vec{a}\vec{b} \mid \vec{a} \in \mathcal{L}_i \wedge \vec{b} \in \mathcal{L}'(\mathsf{img}(\vec{a})) \,\}$.

Some basic results The languages of FMA's [11] are regular once constrained to a finite number of symbols. Moreover, the language accepted by an FMA is impervious to name-permutations that do not affect its initial register. These properties carry over to FRA's, and are proved as in [11].

Proposition 5. *Let $\mathcal{A} = \langle Q, q_0, \sigma_0, \delta, F \rangle$ be an FRA of n registers and $S \subseteq \mathbb{A}$ be finite. Then, $\mathcal{L}(\mathcal{A}) \cap S^*$ is a regular language.*

Proposition 6. *For $\mathcal{A}$ as above, if $\vec{a} \in \mathcal{L}(\mathcal{A})$ and $\pi : \mathbb{A} \xrightarrow{\cong} \mathbb{A}$ is such that $\pi(a) = a$ for all $a \in \mathsf{img}(\sigma_0)$ then $\pi(\vec{a}) \in \mathcal{L}(\mathcal{A})$.*

Bisimulation Bisimulation equivalence turns out to be a great tool for relating automata, even from different paradigms. It implies language equivalence and, in all our cases of interest, it is not too strict in this aspect. We choose it here as our main vehicle of study.

Definition 7. Let $\mathcal{A}_i = \langle Q_i, q_{0i}, \sigma_{0i}, \delta_i, F_i \rangle$ be FRA's with n_i registers, for $i = 1, 2$. A relation $R \subseteq \hat{Q}_1 \times \hat{Q}_2$ is called a ***simulation*** on $\mathcal{A}_1$ and $\mathcal{A}_2$ if, for all $(\hat{q}_1, \hat{q}_2) \in R$,

- if $\pi_1(\hat{q}_1) \in F_1$ then $\pi_1(\hat{q}_2) \in F_2$,
- if $\hat{q}_1 \xrightarrow{\ell}_{\delta_1} \hat{q}_1'$ then $\hat{q}_2 \xrightarrow{\ell}_{\delta_2} \hat{q}_2'$ for some $(\hat{q}_1', \hat{q}_2') \in R$.

R is called a ***bisimulation*** if both R and R^{-1} are simulations. We say that $\mathcal{A}_1$ and $\mathcal{A}_2$ are ***bisimilar***, written $\mathcal{A}_1 \sim \mathcal{A}_2$, if there is a bisimulation R such that $((q_{01}, \sigma_{01}, \emptyset), (q_{02}, \sigma_{02}, \emptyset)) \in R$.

Lemma 8. *If $\mathcal{A}_1 \sim \mathcal{A}_2$ then $\mathcal{L}(\mathcal{A}_1) = \mathcal{L}(\mathcal{A}_2)$.*

The above is proved using standard methods. Bisimilarity is also called *bisimulation equivalence*. For instance, the automaton $\mathcal{A}_0$ of example 4 is bisimilar to

$$\mathcal{B} = \langle \{q_0, q_1\}, q_0, \{(1, \sharp)\}, \{(q_0, 1^\bullet, q_1), (q_1, 1^\circledast, q_1)\}, \{q_0, q_1\} \rangle,$$

with a bisimulation witnessing this being the following,

$$\{((q_0, \sigma_0, \emptyset), (q_0, \sigma_0, \emptyset))\} \cup \{((q_0, \sigma_1, H_1), (q_1, \sigma_2, H_2)) \mid H_1 = H_2)\}$$

where $\sigma_0 = \{(1, \sharp)\}$.

3. Bisimilar constructions

In this section we demonstrate some bisimilar constructions which will be useful in the sequel. Starting from a fresh-register automaton $\mathcal{A} = \langle Q, q_0, \sigma_0, \delta, F \rangle$ of n registers, we effectively construct the following bisimilar automata.

- The closed FRA $\overline{\mathcal{A}}$, called the *closure* of $\mathcal{A}$.
- For any $\vec{a} \in \mathbb{A}^\circledast$ with $\mathsf{img}(\sigma_0) \cap \mathsf{img}(\vec{a}) = \emptyset$, the FRA $\mathcal{A} \uplus \vec{a}$. This is called the *extension* of $\mathcal{A}$ by $\vec{a}$, and its initial assignment is $\sigma_0 + \vec{a} = \sigma_0 \cup \{\, (i + n, a_i) \mid 1 \leq i \leq |\vec{a}| \,\}$.

Our presentation will focus on constructing the bisimilar automata and explaining the candidate bisimulation relation R, omitting the actual proof that R is a bisimulation, as these proofs are not difficult (but tedious) and follow directly from the constructions.

Closures For $\mathcal{A}$ as above with n registers we define its *closure* to be the n-register FRA $\overline{\mathcal{A}} = \langle Q', q_0', \sigma_0', \delta', F' \rangle$ given as follows. We set $Q' = Q \times \mathcal{P}([n])$, $q_0' = (q_0, \mathsf{dom}(\sigma_0))$, $\sigma_0' = \sigma_0$ and $F' = \{ (q, S) \mid q \in F \}$. Recall we want to construct an automaton which is closed, that is, whenever a configuration with state q and assignment σ is reached and (q, i, q') is a transition, then $\sigma(i) \in \mathbb{A}$ and therefore the transition is allowed. The extra component added in Q monitors the registers that have been assigned a name (note that once a register has been assigned a name it cannot return to the $\sharp$ state). Consequently, δ' will be designed in such a way so that this monitoring carries through and, moreover, the known transitions included in δ' are always allowed:

$$\begin{aligned}\delta' = &\{ ((q,S), \ell, (q', S)) \mid (q, \ell, q') \in \delta \wedge \ell \in \mathbb{C}) \} \\ &\cup \{ ((q,S), i, (q', S)) \mid (q, i, q') \in \delta \wedge i \in S) \} \\ &\cup \{ ((q,S), i^{\bullet}/i^{\circledast}, (q', S')) \mid (q, i^{\bullet}/i^{\circledast}, q') \in \delta \wedge S' = S \cup \{i\} \}\end{aligned}$$

Now, we can check that the following relation is a bisimulation

$$R = \{ ((q, \sigma, H), ((q, S), \sigma, H)) \mid \mathsf{dom}(\sigma) = S \}$$

and therefore that $\mathcal{A} \sim \overline{\mathcal{A}}$. Moreover, the reachable configurations of $\overline{\mathcal{A}}$ are of the form $((q, S), \sigma, H)$ with $\mathsf{dom}(\sigma) = S$, and therefore the automaton is closed.

Remark 9. If $\mathcal{A} = \langle Q, q_0, \sigma_0, \delta, F \rangle$ is a closed FRA then each path $q_0 \xrightarrow{\ell_1} q_1 \xrightarrow{\ell_2} \cdots \xrightarrow{\ell_m} q_m$ in $\mathcal{A}$ (where arrow notation represents δ) yields is a configuration path

$$(q_0, \sigma_0, \emptyset) \xrightarrow{\ell_1'}_{\delta} (q_1, \sigma_1, H_1) \xrightarrow{\ell_2'}_{\delta} \cdots \xrightarrow{\ell_m'}_{\delta} (q_m, \sigma_m, H_m)$$

according to the definition of $\longrightarrow_{\delta}$. For example, if $\ell_{j+1} = i$ then $\ell'_{j+1} = \sigma_j(i)$, $\sigma_{j+1} = \sigma_j$ and $H_{j+1} = H_j \cup \{\sigma_j(i)\}$. In this case, closedness of $\mathcal{A}$ guarantees that $\sigma_j(i) \neq \sharp$.

Name extension For $\mathcal{A}$ as above with n registers and $\vec{a} \in \mathbb{A}^{\circledast}$ a sequence of length m such that $\mathsf{img}(\sigma_0) \cap \mathsf{img}(\vec{a}) = \emptyset$, we define the extension $\mathcal{A} \uplus \vec{a}$ as the FRA with $n+m$ registers and description $\langle Q', q_0', \sigma_0', \delta', F' \rangle$ given as follows. We set

$$Q' = Q \times ([n] \to [n+m]) \times \mathcal{P}(\{n+1, \ldots, n+m\})$$

and $q_0' = (q_0, \iota, \{n+1, \ldots, n+m\})$, with ι the inclusion function, $F' = \{ (q, f, S) \in Q' \mid q \in F \}$ and $\sigma_0' = \sigma_0 + \vec{a}$. Finally:

$$\begin{aligned}\delta' = &\{ ((q,f,S), f(\ell), (q', f, S)) \mid \ell \in \mathbb{C} \wedge (q, \ell, q') \in \delta \} \\ &\cup \{ ((q,f,S), j, (q', f', S')) \mid (q, i^{\bullet}, q') \in \delta \wedge j \notin \mathsf{img}(f) \} \\ &\cup \{ ((q,f,S), j, (q', f', S')) \mid (q, i^{\circledast}, q') \in \delta \wedge j \in S \}\end{aligned}$$

where $f(i^{\bullet}) = f(i)^{\bullet}$, $f(i^{\circledast}) = f(i)^{\circledast}$, $f(\ell) = \ell$ for $\ell \in \mathbb{C}$, $f' = f[i \mapsto j]$ and $S' = S \setminus \{j\}$.
The transition relation in $\mathcal{A} \uplus \vec{a}$ proceeds as in $\mathcal{A}$ with the exception of locally/globally fresh transitions, where some extra care is needed. Since the registers of the new automaton contain more names than those of the initial one, fresh transitions in $\mathcal{A} \uplus \vec{a}$ can now capture fewer names. For example, if a is one of the added names then an $i^{\bullet}$ transition from the initial configuration could capture it before, but this is no more the case as a appears in σ_0'; instead, we need an explicit j transition for this purpose. This is what the second clause of the definition of δ' addresses. For this to work we need to introduce the component f to keep track of the correspondences between old and new registers that arise in the way just described. For globally fresh transitions a similar situation arises, only that this time we need only remember which of the names in the initial $\vec{a}$ have not appeared in the history thus far, which is what the component S achieves. Thus, the following is a bisimulation

$$R = \{ ((q, \sigma, H), ((q, f, S), \sigma', H)) \mid \sigma = \sigma' \circ f \wedge \mathsf{img}(\vec{a}) \subseteq H \uplus \sigma'(S) \}$$

and therefore $\mathcal{A} \sim \mathcal{A} \uplus \vec{a}$.

4. Finite-memory automata

We now present FMA's and examine their properties in relation to FRA's and RA's. In fact, RA's are equivalent to FMA's and in the literature they have been used as synonyms (e.g. compare [11] with [21]). The precise correspondence is stated in proposition 11, which is a folklore result.

Let us recall the original definition from [11]. A ***finite-memory automaton (FMA)*** of n registers is a sextuple $\mathcal{A} = \langle Q, q_0, \sigma_0, \rho, \delta, F \rangle$ where:

- Q is a finite set of states, with $q_0 \in Q$ initial, and $F \subseteq Q$ final.
- $\sigma_0 \in \mathsf{Reg}_n$ is the initial register assignment.
- $\rho : Q \rightharpoonup [n]$ is the *reassignment* (partial) function.
- $\delta \subseteq Q \times [n] \times Q$ is the transition relation.

The intuitive reading of δ is the following. Suppose $\mathcal{A}$ is at state q_1 with register assignment σ and let $(q_1, i, q_2) \in \delta$. If input $a \in \mathbb{A}$ arrives then:

- If $\sigma(i) = a$ then $\mathcal{A}$ accepts a and moves to state q_2.
- If $a \notin \mathsf{img}(\sigma)$ and $\rho(q_1) = i$ then $\mathcal{A}$ accepts a, it sets $\sigma(i) = a$ and moves to state q_2.

Formally, a configuration is now a pair $(q, \sigma) \in \hat{Q}$, where

$$\hat{Q} = Q \times \mathsf{Reg}_n\,,$$

and the transition relation $\longrightarrow_{\delta} \subseteq \hat{Q} \times \mathbb{A} \times \hat{Q}$ is defined as follows. For all $(q, \sigma) \in \hat{Q}$ and $(q, i, q') \in \delta$:

- If $\sigma(i) = a$ then $(q, \sigma) \xrightarrow{a}_{\delta} (q', \sigma)$.
- If $\rho(q) = i$ then, for all $a \notin \mathsf{img}(\sigma)$, $(q, \sigma) \xrightarrow{a}_{\delta} (q', \sigma[i \mapsto a])$.

The notions of reachable configurations and accepted strings and languages are defined just as in the case of FRA's.

Example 10. Recall the language $\mathcal{L}_2$ of example 4:

$$\mathcal{L}_2 = \{ a_1 \cdots a_k \in \mathbb{A}^* \mid \forall i.\, a_i \neq a_{i+1} \}$$

which is RA-recognisable. $\mathcal{L}_2$ is recognised by the FMA:

$$\mathcal{B} = \langle Q, q_0, \sigma_0, \{(q_0, 1), (q_1, 2)\}, \{(q_0, 1, q_1), (q_1, 2, q_0)\}, Q \rangle$$

where $Q = \{q_0, q_1\}$ and $\sigma_0 = \{(1, \sharp), (2, \sharp)\}$. Comparing this to $\mathcal{B}$ of example 4, the reader can observe how the differences between RA's and FMA's in reassignment have been addressed here by use of the extra register.

The main properties of FMA's and FMA-recognisable languages have been established as follows.

(a). Emptiness is decidable for FMA's [11] (i.e. is $\mathcal{L}(\mathcal{A}) = \emptyset$?), and in particular it is NP-complete [25].

(b). The languages accepted by FMA's are closed under union, intersection, concatenation and Kleene star; they are not closed under complement [11].

(c). Universality is undecidable [21] (i.e. is $\mathcal{L}(\mathcal{A}) = \mathbb{A}^*$?). Hence, the equivalence and containment problems are undecidable too (i.e. is $\mathcal{L}(\mathcal{A}) = / \subseteq \mathcal{L}(\mathcal{B})$?).

We shall see that the emptiness problem is also decidable for FRA's (proposition 24). Clearly, FRA's being extensions of FMA's implies that universality of the former is undecidable, and hence the same holds for equivalence and containment. In section 6 we will examine closure properties of FRA's and show that closure under concatenation and Kleene star are lost, closure under complement still fails, but closure under union and intersection prevail.

We now relate FMA's to the kind of automata we have introduced previously: in essence, FMA's are the same as RA's. The notions of simulation and bisimulation straightforwardly extend to FMA's. In fact, definition 7 applies to all machines operating on the infinite alphabet $\mathbb{C} \cup \mathbb{A}$ which have configuration graphs containing initial and final configurations. It therefore makes sense to extend these notions to RA-FMA pairs (and FRA-WFRA pairs later on).

Proposition 11. *For any FMA $\mathcal{A}$ of n registers there is an effectively constructible RA $\mathcal{B}$ of n registers such that $\mathcal{A} \sim \mathcal{B}$. Conversely, for any RA $\mathcal{B}$ of n registers there is an effectively constructible FMA $\mathcal{A}$ of $n+1$ registers such that $\mathcal{A} \sim \mathcal{B}$.*

Proof. Going from FMA's to FRA's is simple: we use the same set of states; we match each transition (q_1, i, q_2) with (q_1, i, q_2); and, additionally, for each transition (q_1, i, q_2) where $\rho(q_1) = i$ we add $(q_1, i^\bullet, q_2)$. The other direction is more elaborate but apparently the construction is already known [21], so we omit it. □

Corollary 12. *The universality, equivalence and containment problems are undecidable for RA's and FRA's.*

5. Weak fresh-register automata

In this section we examine a weaker version of FRA's by concentrating on the aspect of global freshness while relaxing that of local freshness. Even though this restriction leads us to machines that do not extend FMA's, we show that universality remains undecidable (proposition 17).

The machines we introduce operate on sets of labels

$$\mathbb{L}_n^{\mathsf{w}} = \mathbb{C} \cup \{\, i, i?, i^{\circledast} \mid i \in [n] \,\},$$

where $i?$ stands for "accept any name" transitions. Moreover, their registers are now taken from the sets $\mathsf{Reg}_n^{\mathsf{w}} = [n] \to \mathbb{A} \cup \{\sharp\}$.

Definition 13. A ***weak fresh-register automaton (WFRA)*** of n registers is a quintuple $\mathcal{A} = \langle Q, q_0, \sigma_0, \delta, F \rangle$ where:

- Q is a finite set of states, with $q_0 \in Q$ initial, and $F \subseteq Q$ final.
- $\sigma_0 \in \mathsf{Reg}_n^{\mathsf{w}}$ is the initial register assignment.
- $\delta \subseteq Q \times \mathbb{L}_n^{\mathsf{w}} \times Q$ is the transition relation.

The transition relation has the same intuitive meaning as in the case of FRA's, with the exception that in transitions of the form $(q_1, i?, q_2) \in \delta$ the automaton accepts any name a, stores it at its i-th cell and moves to state q_2. Formally, a configuration is now given as a triple $(q, \sigma, H) \in \hat{Q}$, where

$$\hat{Q} = Q \times ([n] \to (\mathbb{A} \cup \sharp)) \times \mathcal{P}_{\mathsf{fn}}(\mathbb{A}),$$

and the transition relation $\longrightarrow_\delta \subseteq \hat{Q} \times (\mathbb{C} \cup \mathbb{A}) \times \hat{Q}$ on configurations is defined as follows. For all $(q, \sigma, H) \in \hat{Q}$ and $(q, \ell, q') \in \delta$:

- if $\ell \in \mathbb{C}$ then $(q, \sigma, H) \xrightarrow{\ell}_\delta (q', \sigma, H)$;
- if $\ell = i$ and $\sigma(i) = a$ then $(q, \sigma, H) \xrightarrow{a}_\delta (q', \sigma, H')$;
- if $\ell = i?$ then $(q, \sigma, H) \xrightarrow{a}_\delta (q', \sigma', H')$;
- if $\ell = i^{\circledast}$ and $a \notin H \cup \mathsf{img}(\sigma_0)$ then $(q, \sigma, H) \xrightarrow{a}_\delta (q', \sigma', H')$;

with $\sigma' = \sigma[i \mapsto a]$ and $H' = H \cup \{a\}$. Reachable configurations and accepted strings/languages are defined exactly as in FRA's.

Example 14. Consider the following language,

$$\mathcal{L}_3 = \{\, a_1 \cdots a_k\, b_1 \cdots b_l \in \mathbb{A}^* \mid \forall i \neq j.\, a_i \neq a_j \wedge b_i \neq b_j \,\}$$

which is in fact the concatenation of $\mathbb{A}^{\circledast}$ with itself, and the WFRA:

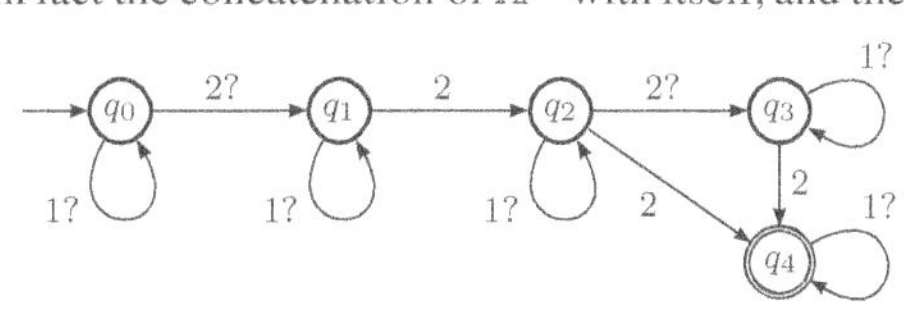

with 2 registers, both of them initially empty. Call the above $\mathcal{A}$. We claim that $\mathcal{L}(\mathcal{A}) = \mathbb{A}^* \setminus \mathcal{L}_3$, that is, $s \in \mathcal{L}(\mathcal{A}) \iff s \notin \mathcal{L}_3$ for all $s \in \mathbb{A}^*$. The forward implication is clear: if $s \in \mathcal{L}(\mathcal{A})$ then either the same name a appears three times in s (via the path $q_0q_1q_2q_4$), or names a_1 and a_2 appear each twice in s without interleaving (via the path $q_0q_1q_2q_3q_4$). In both cases, $s \notin \mathcal{L}'$.
For the opposite direction, let $s \notin \mathcal{L}_3$ and feed it to $\mathcal{A}$. Since $s \notin \mathbb{A}^{\circledast}$, we can write $s = s_1a_1s_2a_1s'$ with $s_1a_1s_2 \in \mathbb{A}^{\circledast}$. In $\mathcal{A}$, $s_1a_1s_2a_1$ leads control to q_2. Now, $s \notin \mathcal{L}_3$ implies that $a_1s' \notin \mathbb{A}^{\circledast}$ so there is some a_2 in a_1s' such that $a_1s' = a_1s_1'a_2s''$, $a_1s_1' \in \mathbb{A}^{\circledast}$ and a_2 appears in a_1s_1'. If $a_2 = a_1$ then $s_1'a_2$ leads $\mathcal{A}$ directly to q_4. Otherwise, it leads to q_4 via q_3.
The reader may want to verify that changing the labels of the loops at q_0 and q_1 above to $1^{\circledast}$, and the label from q_0 to q_1 to $2^{\circledast}$, leads to a WFRA $\mathcal{A}'$ that still satisfies $\mathcal{L}(\mathcal{A}') = \mathbb{A}^* \setminus \mathcal{L}_3$.

We show that any WFRA has a bisimilar FRA of the same number of registers. The idea is to simulate the non-linear memory (i.e. a set of registers that may contain names in common) of the WFRA by a linear memory plus a *reordering function* on the FRA part. For example, here is such a simulation:

$$\{(1,a),(2,b),(3,b)\} \longmapsto \begin{cases} \{(1,a),(2,b),(3,c)\} \\ \text{plus } (1 \mapsto 1,\ 2 \mapsto 2,\ 3 \mapsto 2) \end{cases}$$

The reordering functions will be attached to the states of the FRA. Moreover, we shall simulate any-transitions (i.e. of the form $i?$) of the WFRA by means of locally-fresh-transitions ($i^\bullet$) and known-transitions (j, for all j). In the end, defining the new transition relation gets a bit involved as one has to bear reorderings in mind, which need to be accounted for before making a transition and updated afterwards.

Lemma 15. *For any WFRA $\mathcal{A}$ of n registers there is an effectively constructible FRA $\mathcal{B}$ of n registers such that $\mathcal{A} \sim \mathcal{B}$.*

Proof. Let $\mathcal{A} = \langle Q, q_0, \sigma_0, \delta, F \rangle$; construct $\mathcal{B} = \langle Q', q_0', \sigma_0', \delta', F' \rangle$ as follows. We set $Q' = Q \times ([n] \to [n])$ and write elements of Q' as (q, f). Simulation of non-linear memory σ by linear memory σ' and reordering f is defined in the obvious manner: $\sigma = \sigma' \circ f$. Moreover, for each $i \in [n]$, the multiplicity of $\sigma(i)$, i.e. the number of times it appears in σ, is given by the size of $f^{-1}(f(i))$; we denote this by $\mu(i)$. We let (σ_0', f_0) be a simulation of σ_0 such that σ_0' contains no more names than σ_0, and set $q_0' = (q_0, f_0)$ and $F' = \{(q,f) \mid q \in F\}$. We now define δ':

$$\begin{aligned}
\delta' = {} & \{\, ((q,f), \ell, (q',f)) \mid (q,\ell,q') \in \delta \wedge \ell \in \mathbb{C} \,\} \\
\cup {} & \{\, ((q,f), f(i), (q',f)) \mid (q,i,q') \in \delta \,\} \\
\cup {} & \{\, ((q,f), f(i)^{\circledast}, (q',f)) \mid (q,i^{\circledast},q') \in \delta \wedge \mu(i) = 1 \,\} \\
\cup {} & \{\, ((q,f), j^{\circledast}, (q',f')) \mid (q,i^{\circledast},q') \in \delta \wedge \mu(i) > 1 \wedge j \notin \mathsf{img}(f) \} \\
\cup {} & \{\, ((q,f), f(i)^\bullet, (q',f)) \mid (q,i?,q') \in \delta \wedge \mu(i) = 1 \,\} \\
\cup {} & \{\, ((q,f), j^\bullet, (q',f')) \mid (q,i?,q') \in \delta \wedge \mu(i) > 1 \wedge j \notin \mathsf{img}(f) \} \\
\cup {} & \{\, ((q,f), j, (q',f')) \mid (q,i?,q') \in \delta \,\}
\end{aligned}$$

where $f' = f[i \mapsto j]$. The first line is straightforward. The second line says that receiving the name of the i-th register in $\mathcal{A}$ is simulated by receiving the $f(i)$-th name in $\mathcal{B}$. The same rationale is repeated in the third line, only that now we have to do a memory update and therefore we need to be careful with reorderings. In particular, storing the new name, say a, in the $f(i)$-th register should not be allowed when $\mu(i) > 1$: if this is the case and we set $\sigma'(f(i)) = a$ then a still appears in σ but no longer appears in σ', breaking thus the simulation. Nonetheless, if $\mu(i) > 1$ then there must be some j which is free in σ' (i.e. $j \notin \mathsf{img}(f)$) and we can safely store the new name in there, updating the reordering function accordingly. The last three lines of δ' implement the idea that receiving any name can be matched by receiving either a locally fresh name or one of the stored ones. Thus,

$$R = \{ ((q, \sigma, H), ((q, f), \sigma', H)) \mid \sigma = \sigma' \circ f \}$$

is a bisimulation and therefore $\mathcal{A} \sim \mathcal{B}$. □

We next show that the absence of locally fresh transitions in WFRA's renders them incapable of recognising FMA-recognisable languages. Combining this with the previous result we obtain that WFRA's are indeed strictly weaker than FRA's.

Lemma 16. *The language $\mathcal{L}_2 = \{a_1 \cdots a_k \mid \forall i.\, a_i \neq a_{i+1}\}$ of examples 4 and 10 is not WFRA-recognisable.*

Proof. Suppose $\mathcal{L}_2 = \mathcal{L}(\mathcal{A})$, for a WFRA $\mathcal{A}$ with n registers. Then, for any $s \in \mathbb{A}^{\circledast}$ of length $m > 1$, we have $ss \in \mathcal{L}(\mathcal{A})$. Let the following be the transition path in $\mathcal{A}$ accepting it,

$$q_0 \xrightarrow{\cdots} \cdots \xrightarrow{\cdots} q_0' \xrightarrow{\alpha_1} q_1' \xrightarrow{\alpha_2} \cdots \xrightarrow{\alpha_m} q_m'$$

with the subpath from q_0' to q_m' accepting the second copy of s. Then, none of the α's can be of the form $i^{\circledast}$ as their names have appeared before. Moreover, if $\alpha_i = j?$ then α_i can also accept the preceding symbol, contradicting the fact that $\mathcal{L}(\mathcal{A}) = \mathcal{L}_2$. Hence, all α's are in $[n]$. Choosing $m > n$ we arrive to a contradiction. □

Emptiness is decidable for WFRA's, by inheritance. More interestingly, the universality problem remains undecidable, and hence the same happens for equivalence and containment.

Proposition 17. *Universality is undecidable for WFRA's.*

Proof. The proof is by reduction from the Post Correspondence Problem, and follows the track of the analogous proof in [21]. In particular, we show that the locally fresh transitions of the RA's constructed in that proof can be replaced by WFRA-transitions. Unlike [21], here it is necessary to use the set $\mathbb{C}$. □

6. Closure properties

In order to establish closure properties of FRA's, and following the approach on FMA's in [11], it is useful to introduce a version of FRA's with *multiple assignment*, that is, automata that can store an input name at several of their registers at one step. In particular, assignments will now be taken from the sets $\mathsf{Reg}_n^{\mathsf{w}}$. The set of labels we shall use is the following.

$$\mathbb{L}_n' = \mathbb{C} \cup (\mathcal{P}([n]) \times \mathcal{P}([n]) \times (\{\bot\} \cup \mathcal{P}([n])))$$

Labels of the form $(S, T, \bot)$ are written simply (S, T), and when we write (S, T, A) we assume $A \neq \bot$. If we want to allow for $\bot$, we write $(S, T, A_\bot)$.

Definition 18. An ***MFRA*** of n registers is a quintuple $\mathcal{A} = \langle Q, q_0, \sigma_0, \delta, F\rangle$ where:

- Q is a finite set of states, $q_0 \in Q$ is initial and $F \subseteq Q$ are final.
- $\sigma_0 \in \mathsf{Reg}_n^{\mathsf{w}}$ is the initial register assignment.
- $\delta \subseteq Q \times \mathbb{L}_n' \times Q$ is the transition relation.

The intuitive reading of δ is the following. If $\mathcal{A}$ is at state q_1 with register assignment σ and input $\ell \in \mathbb{C} \cup \mathbb{A}$ arrives then:

- if $\ell \in \mathbb{C}$ and $(q_1, \ell, q_2) \in \delta$ then $\mathcal{A}$ accepts ℓ and moves to q_2.
- if $\ell \in \mathbb{A}$ and $(q_1, (S, T), q_2) \in \delta$ and $(\sigma[S \mapsto \ell])^{-1}(\ell) = T$, i.e. ℓ appears exactly in the registers in T after it is assigned to all registers in S, then $\mathcal{A}$ accepts ℓ, it sets $\sigma(S) = \{\ell\}$ and moves to state q_2.
- if $\ell \in \mathbb{A}$ and $(q_1, (S, T, A), q_2) \in \delta$, $(\sigma[S \mapsto \ell])^{-1}(\ell) = T$ and ℓ has not appeared in the history nor does it appear in $\sigma_0(A)$ then $\mathcal{A}$ accepts ℓ, it sets $\sigma(S) = \{\ell\}$ and moves to state q_2.

Thus, labels of the form (S, T) work in the same way as in *M-automata* [11], and the main novelty here is the inclusion of (S, T, A): in order for the transition to be allowed, the input name a must be fresh in the history and in the part of σ_0 specified by A. This addition allows us to model globally fresh transitions and also to combine automata unifying their initial assignments.

Formally, let $\hat{Q} = Q \times \mathsf{Reg}_n^{\mathsf{w}} \times \mathcal{P}_{\mathsf{fn}}(\mathbb{A})$ be the set of configurations and define $\longrightarrow_\delta \subseteq \hat{Q} \times (\mathbb{C} \cup \mathbb{A}) \times \hat{Q}$ as follows. For all $(q, \sigma, H) \in \hat{Q}$:

- If $(q, \ell, q') \in \delta$ with $\ell \in \mathbb{C}$ then $(q, \sigma, H) \xrightarrow{\ell}_\delta (q', \sigma, H)$.
- If $(q, (S, T), q') \in \delta$, $\sigma' = \sigma[S \mapsto a]$ and $\sigma'^{-1}(a) = T$ then $(q, \sigma, H) \xrightarrow{a}_\delta (q', \sigma', H \cup \{a\})$.
- If $(q, (S, T, A), q') \in \delta$, $\sigma' = \sigma[S \mapsto a]$, $\sigma'^{-1}(a) = T$ and $a \notin H \cup \sigma_0(A)$ then $(q, \sigma, H) \xrightarrow{a}_\delta (q', \sigma', H \cup \{a\})$.

Reachability and acceptance are defined as before. Note that plausible transition labels $(S, T, A_\bot)$ satisfy $S \subseteq T$. Moreover, if $S \neq T$ and $A_\bot \neq \bot$ then the transition can only be instantiated by a name $a \in \sigma_0([n] \setminus A)$ that has not yet appeared in the history but is still in some register.

Lemma 19. *For any FRA $\mathcal{A}$ of n registers there is an effectively constructible MFRA $\mathcal{B}$ of $n+1$ registers such that $\mathcal{A} \sim \mathcal{B}$*

The other direction is a bit more elaborate and we achieve it in two steps. Let us say that an MFRA $\mathcal{A}$ is *pure* if, for all transitions $(q, (S, T, A), q')$ of $\mathcal{A}$, $S = T$ and $A = [n]$.

Lemma 20. *For any MFRA $\mathcal{A}$ of n registers there is an effectively constructible pure MFRA $\mathcal{B}$ of $2n$ registers such that $\mathcal{A} \sim \mathcal{B}$.*

Lemma 21. *For any pure MFRA $\mathcal{A}$ of n registers there is an effectively constructible FRA $\mathcal{B}$ of n registers such that $\mathcal{A} \sim \mathcal{B}$.*

We can now establish the following closure properties. Closure under union and intersection is answered positively, while closure under concatenation, Kleene star or complement fails.

Proposition 22. *For FRA's $\mathcal{A}$ and $\mathcal{B}$, the languages $\mathcal{L}(\mathcal{A}) \cup \mathcal{L}(\mathcal{B})$ and $\mathcal{L}(\mathcal{A}) \cap \mathcal{L}(\mathcal{B})$ are FRA-recognisable.*

Proof. Assume MFRA's $\mathcal{A}' = \langle Q_1, q_{01}, \sigma_{01}, \delta_1, F_1\rangle \sim \mathcal{A}$ and $\mathcal{B}' = \langle Q_2, q_{02}, \sigma_{02}, \delta_2, F_2\rangle \sim \mathcal{B}$ of n, m registers respectively. For the union, construct an MFRA $\mathcal{C} = \langle Q, q_0, \sigma_0, \delta, F\rangle$ of $n+m$ registers, where

$$Q = \{q_0\} \uplus Q_1 \uplus Q_2\,, \quad \sigma_0 = \sigma_{01} + \sigma_{02}\,, \quad F = F_1 \cup F_2 \cup \phi(F_1 \cup F_2)$$

with $\phi : Q_1 \uplus Q_2 \to Q$ mapping q_{01} and q_{02} to q_0, and being elsewhere the identity. Finally:

$$\begin{aligned}\delta = {} & \{ (q'', \ell, q') \mid \ell \in \mathbb{C} \wedge (q, \ell, q') \in \delta_1 \cup \delta_2 \} \\ & \cup \{ (q'', (S \cup [m]^{+n}, T \cup [m]^{+n}, A_\bot), q') \mid (q, (S, T, A_\bot), q') \in \delta_1 \} \\ & \cup \{ (q'', ([n] \cup S^{+n}, [n] \cup T^{+n}, A_\bot^{+n}), q') \mid (q, (S, T, A_\bot), q') \in \delta_2 \}\end{aligned}$$

where $q'' \in \{q, \phi(q)\}$ and $S^{+n} = \{ i + n \mid i \in S \}$, for each $S \subseteq \omega$, and $\bot^{+n} = \bot$. It follows that $\mathcal{L}(\mathcal{C}) = \mathcal{L}(\mathcal{A}) \cup \mathcal{L}(\mathcal{B})$.
For the intersection, construct an MFRA $\mathcal{C} = \langle Q, q_0, \sigma_0, \delta, F\rangle$ of $n+m$ registers where $Q = Q_1 \times Q_2$, $q_0 = (q_{01}, q_{02})$, $\sigma_0 = \sigma_{01} + \sigma_{02}$, $F = F_1 \times F_2$ and, assuming $\bot \cup A_\bot = A_\bot$:

$$\begin{aligned}\delta = {} & \{ (q, \ell, q') \mid \ell \in \mathbb{C} \wedge \forall i \in [2].\, (\pi_i(q), \ell, \pi_i(q')) \in \delta_i \} \\ & \cup \{ (q, (S_1 \cup S_2^{+n}, T_1 \cup T_2^{+n}, A_{\bot 1} \cup A_{\bot 2}^{+n}), q') \mid \\ & \qquad \forall i \in [2].\, (\pi_i(q), (S_i, T_i, A_{\bot i}), \pi_i(q')) \in \delta_i \}\end{aligned}$$

It follows that $\mathcal{L}(\mathcal{C}) = \mathcal{L}(\mathcal{A}) \cap \mathcal{L}(\mathcal{B})$. □

Proposition 23. *There are FRA's $\mathcal{A}$ and $\mathcal{B}$ such that the language $\mathcal{L}(\mathcal{A}) * \mathcal{L}(\mathcal{B})$ is not FRA-recognisable. Moreover, there is an FRA $\mathcal{A}$ such that the language $\mathcal{L}(\mathcal{A})^*$ is not FRA-recognisable. Finally, there is an RA $\mathcal{B}$ such that the language $\mathbb{A}^* \setminus \mathcal{L}(\mathcal{B})$ is not FRA-recognisable.*

Proof. For the first part we show that the language $\mathcal{L}' = \mathcal{L}_1 * \mathcal{L}_1$ is not FRA-recognisable, where $\mathcal{L}_1 = \mathbb{A}^{\circledast}$. Suppose $\mathcal{L}'$ were recognised by an FRA $\mathcal{C}$ of n registers, so $ss \in \mathcal{L}(\mathcal{C})$ with s being a string of m distinct names. Let the following be the transition path in $\mathcal{C}$ accepting it,

$$q_0 \xrightarrow{\cdots} \cdots \xrightarrow{\cdots} q_0' \xrightarrow{\alpha_1} q_1' \xrightarrow{\alpha_2} \cdots \xrightarrow{\alpha_m} q_m'$$

with the subpath from q_0' to q_m', call it p, accepting the second copy of s. As all the symbols of s have already appeared before, none of the α's is of the form $i^{\circledast}$. Moreover, as all the symbols in s are distinct, there cannot be $i \in [n]$ and $j < j'$ such that $\alpha_j \in \{i, i^\bullet\}$ and $\alpha_{j'} = i$, as $\alpha_{j'}$ would then repeat a name already present in the subpath p. Moreover, there cannot be $i, i' \in [n]$ and $j < j' < j''$ such that $\alpha_j \in \{i, i^\bullet\}$, $\alpha_{j'} = i^\bullet$ and $\alpha_{j''} = i'^\bullet$. For suppose this were the case, and suppose that all α's between j and j' are not in $\{i, i^\bullet\}$, and that all α's between j' and j'' are not in $\{i'^\bullet \mid i' \in [n]\}$. Then, $s = s_1 a_1 s_2 a_2 s_3 a_3 s_4$ with a_1, a_2, a_3 corresponding to $\alpha_j, \alpha_{j'}, \alpha_{j''}$ respectively. But $i'^\bullet$ is also allowed to accept a_1, hence there is s_4' such that $s s_1 a_1 s_2 a_2 s_3 a_1 s_4' \in \mathcal{L}(\mathcal{C})$, contradicting $\mathcal{L}(\mathcal{C}) = \mathcal{L}'$. But now taking $m > n + 1$ we obtain a contradiction.
The second part is shown in a similar manner, taking as $\mathcal{A}$ the automaton accepting the language

$$\mathcal{L}_{2,a_0} = \{\, a_0 a_1 \ldots a_k \in \mathbb{A}^* \mid \forall i \neq j.\, a_i \neq a_j \,\}$$

for some chosen a_0. A similar argument to the above applies, that is, we assume $\mathcal{L}_{2,a_0}^* = \mathcal{L}(\mathcal{C})$ for some FRA $\mathcal{C}$ and select $a_0 s a_0 s \in \mathcal{L}_{2,a_0}^*$ of size big enough to yield a contradiction.
Finally, it suffices to show $\mathcal{L}' = \mathbb{A}^* \setminus \mathcal{L}(\mathcal{B})$ for an RA $\mathcal{B}$. By example 14 we have that $\mathcal{L}' = \mathbb{A}^* \setminus \mathcal{L}(\mathcal{A})$ for a WFRA $\mathcal{A}$ with no fresh transitions. From that, we obtain $\mathcal{B}$ by applying lemma 15. □

7. Symbolic methods

The automata we have introduced can be viewed in two different manners: either as ordinary finite-state automata operating on constant symbols and the symbols $1, 1^\bullet, 1^{\circledast}, \ldots, n^{\circledast}$ (for machines with n registers), or as machines which recognise languages from an alphabet comprising a finite set of constants and an infinite set of names. We use the term ***semantic level*** for the latter interpretation, and ***symbolic level*** for the former one. The semantic is of course the intended interpretation but, on the other hand, viewing our automata as operating on the finite alphabet $\mathbb{L}_n$ is much more convenient. In this section we examine methods from the symbolic level which characterise semantic notions. More specifically, we start by giving a simple proof of decidability of FRA-emptiness by reducing the problem to FSA-emptiness. We then proceed to our main point of focus, which is the definition of an appropriate notion of symbolic bisimilarity that is equivalent to the notion of bisimilarity we have been using thus far. As a corollary we prove that bisimilarity is decidable for FRA's.

Proposition 24. *The emptiness problem is decidable for FRA's.*

Proof. Given an FRA $\mathcal{A}$ of n registers, construct its closure $\overline{\mathcal{A}}$, and take $\mathcal{A}'$ to be the ordinary FSA with the same set of states, initial state, transition relation and final states as $\overline{\mathcal{A}}$, and operating on the set of labels $\mathbb{L}_n$. We claim that $\mathcal{L}(\overline{\mathcal{A}}) = \emptyset \iff \mathcal{L}(\mathcal{A}') = \emptyset$. Indeed, if $\overline{\mathcal{A}}$ accepts a string $s \in \mathbb{C} \cup \mathbb{A}^*$ then, the accepting path in $\overline{\mathcal{A}}$ yields a string $s' \in \mathbb{L}_n^*$, and $s' \in \mathcal{L}(\mathcal{A}')$. Conversely, if $\mathcal{A}'$ accepts a string s' then the accepting path in $\mathcal{A}'$ is also a path in $\overline{\mathcal{A}}$ ending in an accepting state. From remark 9, we have that the latter yields a string $s \in \mathcal{L}(\overline{\mathcal{A}})$. □

In order to define a symbolic notion of bisimulation equivalence which captures its semantical analogue, we introduce auxiliary structures which record the way in which two register assignments are related. In particular, they record the domains of the assignments and those indices on which the two assignments coincide. A symbolic bisimulation between two automata relates states of the automata in specific record environments. At each bisimulation step the records are updated according to the specific symbolic transitions taking place. This symbolic description is shown to accurately capture what happens at the semantical level.

We adapt Stark's notion of *span* [28]. We call

$$(S_1, \rho, S_2) \in \mathcal{P}([n_1]) \times \mathcal{P}([n_1] \times [n_2]) \times \mathcal{P}([n_2])$$

a ***typed span*** on (n_1, n_2) if:

- $(i,j), (i',j') \in \rho$ implies that $i = i' \iff j = j'$,
- $\mathsf{img}(\rho) \subseteq S_2$, where $\mathsf{img}(\rho) = \{\, i \in [n] \mid \exists j.\, (j,i) \in \rho \,\}$,
- $\mathsf{dom}(\rho) \subseteq S_1$, where $\mathsf{dom}(\rho) = \{\, j \in [n] \mid \exists i.\, (j,i) \in \rho \,\}$.

We write $[n_1] \rightleftharpoons [n_2]$ for the set of typed spans on (n_1, n_2). A perhaps more intuitive way to view a typed span (S_1, ρ, S_2) is as a triple of relations:

$$S_1 \hookleftarrow \mathsf{dom}(\rho) \xrightarrow{\cong} \mathsf{img}(\rho) \hookrightarrow S_2$$

By abuse of notation, we write ρ for the whole of (S_1, ρ, S_2), in which case we also use the notation $S_1(\rho) = S_1$ and $S_2(\rho) = S_2$. If $\rho : [n_1] \rightleftharpoons [n_2]$ and $(i,j) \in [n_1] \times [n_2]$ then $\rho[i \leftrightarrow j] : [n_1] \rightleftharpoons [n_2]$ is the typed span:

$$(S_1(\rho) \cup \{i\}, \rho \setminus \{(i',j') \mid i = i' \vee j = j'\} \cup \{(i,j)\}, S_2(\rho) \cup \{j\})$$

A typed span (S_1, ρ, S_2) relates register assignments σ_1 and σ_2 just in case ρ is a bijection between the parts of $[n_1]$ and $[n_2]$ that have common images under σ_1 and σ_2, while S_i keeps track of (the indices of) all names in σ_i. Formally, $\rho = \sigma_1 \leftrightarrow \sigma_2$ if:

$$\mathsf{dom}(\sigma_1) = S_1(\rho) \wedge \mathsf{dom}(\sigma_2) = S_2(\rho) \wedge \rho = \{(i,j) \mid \sigma_1(i) = \sigma_2(j)\}$$

In this case, $\|\rho\| = |S_1(\rho)| + |S_2(\rho)| - |\mathsf{dom}(\rho)|$ gives the total number of names in σ_1 and σ_2.

Suppose, for example, that we have related state q_1 of automaton $\mathcal{A}_1$ to state q_2 of $\mathcal{A}_2$ with respect to ρ. If (q_1, i, q_1') is a transition in $\mathcal{A}_1$ and $i \in \mathsf{dom}(\rho)$ then the name in register i of $\mathcal{A}_1$ (in the semantical scenario captured by the symbolic description) resides in register $\rho(i)$ of $\mathcal{A}_2$. Consequently, $\mathcal{A}_2$ can only simulate the transition by some $(q_2, \rho(i), q_2')$. On the other hand, if $(q_1, i^\bullet, q_1')$ is a transition in $\mathcal{A}_1$ then there are several factors to consider:

- Any private name of $\mathcal{A}_2$ can be captured by $i^\bullet$. Hence, $\mathcal{A}_2$ needs a simulating transition (q_2, j, q_2') for every $j \in S_2(\rho) \setminus \mathsf{img}(\rho)$.
- Moreover, $\mathcal{A}_2$ needs a transition for all names locally fresh to both $\mathcal{A}_1$ and $\mathcal{A}_2$. This can be some $(q_2, j^\bullet, q_2')$ but, under circumstances, it may also be some $(q_2, j^{\circledast}, q_2')$.

In order for $(q_2, j^{\circledast}, q_2')$ to capture all names locally fresh to $\mathcal{A}_1$ and $\mathcal{A}_2$, it must be the case that all names in history are present in the registers of $\mathcal{A}_1$ and $\mathcal{A}_2$ (so that global freshness coincide with mutual local freshness). If $\mathcal{A}_1$ has n_1 registers and $\mathcal{A}_2$ has n_2, and assuming that the initial register assignments for $\mathcal{A}_1$ and $\mathcal{A}_2$ contain the same names, the latter can only happen in case less than $n_1 + n_2$ names appear in the history.

We can therefore resolve the latter case by adding a component which counts the names in the history, up to $n_1 + n_2$. In the following we write n for n_1+n_2, and set $h^{++} = \lceil h+1 \rceil^n$ ($= h+1$ if $h < n$, and n otherwise).

Definition 25. Let $\mathcal{A}_i = \langle Q_i, q_{0i}, \sigma_{0i}, \delta_i, F_i \rangle$ be FRA's of n_i registers, for $i = 1, 2$, such that $\mathsf{img}(\rho_{01}) = \mathsf{img}(\rho_{02}) = H_0$. A ***symbolic simulation*** on $\mathcal{A}_1$ and $\mathcal{A}_2$ is a relation

$$R \subseteq Q_1 \times ([n] \cup \{0\}) \times ([n_1] \rightleftharpoons [n_2]) \times Q_2$$

such that, whenever $(q_1, h, \rho, q_2) \in R$, if $q_1 \in F_1$ then $q_2 \in F_2$ and if $(q_1, \ell, q_1') \in \delta_1$ then:

1. If $\ell \in \mathbb{C}$ then $(q_2, \ell, q_2') \in \delta_2$ for some $(q_1', h, \rho, q_2') \in R$.
2. If $\ell = i$ and $i \in \mathsf{dom}(\rho)$ then $(q_2, \rho(i), q_2') \in \delta_2$ for some $(q_1', h, \rho, q_2') \in R$.
3. If $\ell = i$ and $i \in S_1(\rho) \setminus \mathsf{dom}(\rho)$ then $(q_2, j^\bullet, q_2') \in \delta_2$ for some $(q_1', h, \rho[i \leftrightarrow j], q_2') \in R$.
4. If $\ell = i^\bullet$ then, for any $j \in S_2(\rho) \setminus \mathsf{img}(\rho)$, $(q_2, j, q_2') \in \delta_2$ for some $(q_1', h, \rho[i \leftrightarrow j], q_2') \in R$.
5. If $\ell = i^\bullet$ and $h = n$ or $\|\rho\| < h$ then $(q_2, j^\bullet, q_2') \in \delta_2$ for some $(q_1', h, \rho[i \leftrightarrow j], q_2') \in R$.
6. If $\ell \in \{i^\bullet, i^\circledast\}$ then $(q_2, j^\bullet, q_2') \in \delta_2$, or $(q_2, j^\circledast, q_2') \in \delta_2$, for some $(q_1', h^{++}, \rho[i \leftrightarrow j], q_2') \in R$.

Setting $(S_1, \rho, S_2)^{-1} = (S_2, \rho^{-1}, S_1)$, the inverse of R is:

$$R^{-1} = \{ (q_2, h, \rho, q_1) \mid (q_1, h, \rho^{-1}, q_2) \in R \}.$$

We say that R is a ***symbolic bisimulation*** if both R and R^{-1} are symbolic simulations. We say that $\mathcal{A}_1$ and $\mathcal{A}_2$ are ***symbolic bisimilar***, written $\mathcal{A}_1 \overset{s}{\sim} \mathcal{A}_2$, if there is a symbolic bisimulation R on $\mathcal{A}_1$ and $\mathcal{A}_2$ such that $(q_{01}, h_0, \rho_0, q_{02}) \in R$ with $h_0 = |H_0|$ and $\rho_0 = \sigma_{01} \leftrightarrow \sigma_{02}$.

In the following propositions let us assume the hypotheses of Definition 25. Let us also write $\hat{H}$ for $H \cup H_0$, and n for $n_1 + n_2$.

Proposition 26. *If R is a symbolic simulation on $\mathcal{A}_1$ and $\mathcal{A}_2$ then*

$$R' = \{ ((q_1, \sigma_1, H), (q_2, \sigma_2, H)) \mid (q_1, h, \rho, q_2) \in R \wedge \rho = \sigma_1 \leftrightarrow \sigma_2 \wedge h = \lceil |\hat{H}| \rceil^n \wedge \mathsf{img}(\sigma_i) \subseteq \hat{H} \}$$

is a simulation. Moreover, if R is a symbolic bisimulation then R' is a bisimulation.

Proposition 27. *If $\mathcal{A}_1$ and $\mathcal{A}_2$ are closed FRA's and R is a simulation on $\mathcal{A}_1$ and $\mathcal{A}_2$ then*

$$R' = \{ (q_1, h, \rho, q_2) \mid ((q_1, \sigma_1, H), (q_2, \sigma_2, H)) \in R \wedge \rho = \sigma_1 \leftrightarrow \sigma_2 \wedge h = \lceil |\hat{H}| \rceil^n \wedge (q_i, \sigma_i, H) \textit{ reachable} \}$$

is a symbolic simulation. Moreover, if R is a bisimulation then R' is a symbolic bisimulation.

Corollary 28. *Bisimilarity is decidable for FRA's.*

Proof. Let $\mathcal{A}_i = \langle Q_i, q_{0i}, \sigma_{0i}, \delta_i, F_i \rangle$ be FRA's of n_i registers, for $i = 1, 2$. Choose $\vec{a}_1, \vec{a}_2 \in \mathbb{A}^\circledast$ such that $\mathsf{img}(\vec{a}_i) = \mathsf{img}(\sigma_{0i}) \setminus \mathsf{img}(\sigma_{0\bar{i}})$, and form $\mathcal{A}_1' = \mathcal{A}_1 \uplus \vec{a}_2$ and $\mathcal{A}_2' = \mathcal{A}_2 \uplus \vec{a}_1$. Now close these and obtain closed FRA's $\overline{\mathcal{A}_i'}$. We have $\mathcal{A}_i \sim \overline{\mathcal{A}_i'}$. Moreover, by the previous propositions, $\overline{\mathcal{A}_1'} \sim \overline{\mathcal{A}_2'} \iff \overline{\mathcal{A}_1'} \overset{s}{\sim} \overline{\mathcal{A}_2'}$, and hence $\mathcal{A}_1 \sim \mathcal{A}_2 \iff \overline{\mathcal{A}_1'} \overset{s}{\sim} \overline{\mathcal{A}_2'}$. As the symbolic bisimulations between $\overline{\mathcal{A}_1'}$ and $\overline{\mathcal{A}_2'}$ live in a space bounded relatively to $|Q_1|, |Q_2|, n_1, n_2$, we can search it exhaustively for such relations. Hence, FRA-bisimilarity is decidable. □

8. Automata for the π-calculus

We briefly recall the definition of the π-calculus with early semantics and strong bisimulation [14, 26]. We use the fixed set $\mathbb{A}$ of names for *channel names*, and let p range over *process constants*. The set Π of π-calculus processes is given as follows,

$$P, Q ::= \mathbf{0} \mid \bar{a}b.P \mid a(b).P \mid [a = b]P \mid \nu a.P \mid P{+}Q \mid P \mid Q \mid p(\vec{a})$$

where $a, b \in \mathbb{A}$ and $\vec{a} \in \mathbb{A}^*$. Name binding is defined as usual (b is bound in $a(b).P$ and $\nu b.P$), and processes are equated up to α-equivalence. We write $\mathsf{fn}(P)$ for the set of names appearing free in P. Process constants are accompanied by *definitions* of the form $p(\vec{a}) = P$, where $\vec{a} \in \mathbb{A}^\circledast$ and $\mathsf{fn}(P) = \mathsf{img}(\vec{a})$. Moreover, each occurrence of p must be *guarded*, i.e. it must come in one of the forms $\bar{a}b.p(\vec{a})$ or $a(b).p(\vec{a})$.

The semantics of the calculus is *early* and is given via a labelled transition relation with labels:

$$\alpha ::= \bar{a}b \mid \bar{a}(b) \mid ab \mid \tau$$

Labels have free and bound occurrences of names, but they are not equated up to α-equivalence.

$$\mathsf{fn}(\bar{a}b) = \mathsf{fn}(ab) = \{a, b\} \quad \mathsf{fn}(\bar{a}(b)) = \{a\} \quad \mathsf{fn}(\tau) = \emptyset$$
$$\mathsf{bn}(\bar{a}b) = \mathsf{bn}(ab) = \emptyset \quad \mathsf{bn}(\bar{a}(b)) = \{b\} \quad \mathsf{bn}(\tau) = \emptyset$$

We write $\mathsf{n}(\alpha)$ for $\mathsf{fn}(\alpha) \cup \mathsf{bn}(\alpha)$. The transition relation is given by the following rules (plus symmetric counterparts).

$$\text{OUT}\ \frac{}{\bar{a}b.P \xrightarrow{\bar{a}b} P} \qquad \text{MATCH}\ \frac{P \xrightarrow{\alpha} P'}{[a = a]P \xrightarrow{\alpha} P'}$$

$$\text{INP}\ \frac{}{a(b).P \xrightarrow{ac} P\{c/b\}} \qquad \text{REC}\ \frac{P\{\vec{a}/\vec{b}\} \xrightarrow{\alpha} P'}{p(\vec{a}) \xrightarrow{\alpha} P'}\ {\scriptstyle p(\vec{b})=P}$$

$$\text{OPEN}\ \frac{P \xrightarrow{\bar{a}b} P'}{\nu b.P \xrightarrow{\bar{a}(b)} P'}\ {\scriptstyle a \neq b} \qquad \text{RES}\ \frac{P \xrightarrow{\alpha} P'}{\nu a.P \xrightarrow{\alpha} \nu a.P'}\ {\scriptstyle a \notin \mathsf{n}(\alpha)}$$

$$\text{SUM}\ \frac{P \xrightarrow{\alpha} P'}{P{+}Q \xrightarrow{\alpha} P'} \qquad \text{COMM}\ \frac{P \xrightarrow{\bar{a}b} P' \quad Q \xrightarrow{ab} Q'}{P \mid Q \xrightarrow{\tau} P' \mid Q'}$$

$$\text{PAR}\ \frac{P \xrightarrow{\alpha} P'}{P \mid Q \xrightarrow{\alpha} P' \mid Q}\ {\scriptstyle \mathsf{bn}(\alpha) \cap \mathsf{fn}(Q) = \emptyset}$$

$$\text{CLOSE}\ \frac{P \xrightarrow{\bar{a}(b)} P' \quad Q \xrightarrow{ab} Q'}{P \mid Q \xrightarrow{\tau} \nu b.(P' \mid Q')}\ {\scriptstyle b \notin \mathsf{fn}(Q)}$$

Note how the side-conditions impose global freshness on names created using the ν constructor.

Bisimulation is the standard notion of equivalence in the π-calculus; here we shall consider strong bisimulation. A relation $R \subseteq \Pi \times \Pi$ is called a ***simulation*** if, for all $(P_1, P_2) \in R$ and all α with $\mathsf{bn}(\alpha) \cap \mathsf{fn}(P_1, P_2) = \emptyset$, if $P_1 \xrightarrow{\alpha} P_1'$ then $P_2 \xrightarrow{\alpha} P_2'$ for some $(P_1', P_2') \in R$. R is called a ***bisimulation*** if both R and R^{-1} are simulations. We say that P and Q are ***π-bisimilar***, written $P \overset{\pi}{\sim} Q$, if there is a bisimulation R containing (P, Q).

We now define a version of the π-calculus with extended syntax that is directly representable by FRA's. Since transitions are multi-symbol, and our automata can recognise one symbol at a time, they will be decomposed to atomic ones. We add sets of *input* and *output* processes which cater for the intermediate stages in these decompositions. For example,

$$\bar{a}b.P \xrightarrow{\bar{a}b} P \quad \textit{decomposes to} \quad \bar{a}b.P \xrightarrow{\bar{a}} b.P \xrightarrow{b} P$$

where $b.P$ is an output process. Output [resp. input] processes are in the middle of sending [receiving] a name on a chosen channel.

Definition 29. The ***xπ-calculus*** syntax is given by the sets Π, Π_{out} and Π_{inp}, with elements:

$$P, Q ::= \mathbf{0} \mid \bar{a}b.P \mid a(b).P \mid [a = b]P \mid \nu a.P \mid P{+}Q \mid P \mid Q \mid p(\vec{a})$$
$$P_{\mathsf{out}} ::= b.P \mid \nu a.P_{\mathsf{out}} \mid P \mid P_{\mathsf{out}} \mid P_{\mathsf{out}} \mid P$$
$$P_{\mathsf{inp}} ::= (b).P \mid \nu a.P_{\mathsf{inp}} \mid P \mid P_{\mathsf{inp}} \mid P_{\mathsf{inp}} \mid P$$

where $a, b \in \mathbb{A}$ and $\vec{a} \in \mathbb{A}^*$. We write $\hat{\Pi}$ for $\Pi \cup \Pi_{\mathsf{out}} \cup \Pi_{\mathsf{inp}}$, and let $\hat{P}, \hat{Q}, \ldots$ range over its elements, which we equate up to α-equivalence. Name binding is defined as expected: b is bound in $\nu b.\hat{P}$, $a(b).P$ and $(b).P$.

It is handy to introduce here some very basic notions from the theory of nominal sets [8, 23]. We call *nominal structure* any structure which may contain names (i.e. elements of $\mathbb{A}$), and we denote by $\mathsf{Perm}(\mathbb{A})$ the set of finite permutations on $\mathbb{A}$ (i.e. bijections $\pi : \mathbb{A} \to \mathbb{A}$ such that $\pi(a) \neq a$ for finitely many $a \in \mathbb{A}$). For example, $\mathsf{id} = \{(a,a) \mid a \in \mathbb{A}\} \in \mathsf{Perm}(\mathbb{A})$. We shall define for each set X of nominal structures of interest a function

$$\_\cdot\_ : \mathsf{Perm}(\mathbb{A}) \times X \to X$$

such that $\pi \cdot (\pi' \cdot x) = (\pi \circ \pi') \cdot x$ and $\mathsf{id} \cdot x = x$, for all $x \in X$ and $\pi, \pi' \in \mathsf{Perm}(\mathbb{A})$. X will be called a ***nominal set*** if all its elements involve finitely many names, that is, for all $x \in X$ there is a finite set $S \subseteq \mathbb{A}$ such that $\pi \cdot x = x$ whenever $\forall a \in S.\pi(a) = a$. For example, $\mathbb{A}$ is a nominal set with action $\pi \cdot a = \pi(a)$, and so is $\mathcal{P}_{\mathsf{fn}}(\mathbb{A})$ with action $\pi \cdot S = \{\pi(a) \mid a \in S\}$. Also, any set of non-nominal structures is a nominal set with trivial action $\pi \cdot x = x$. More interestingly, if X is a nominal set then so is X^* with action $\pi \cdot x_1 \ldots x_n = (\pi \cdot x_1) \ldots (\pi \cdot x_n)$. Also, if X is a nominal set then so is the set $\bigcup_{n \in \omega}([n] \to X)$ with action $\pi \cdot f = \{(i, \pi \cdot x) \mid (i,x) \in f\}$.

Thus, $\Pi, \Pi_{\mathsf{out}}, \Pi_{\mathsf{inp}}, \hat{\Pi}$ are all nominal sets. For example,

$$\pi \cdot a(b).\, b\bar{c}.\,\mathbf{0} = a'(b').\, b'\bar{c}'.\,\mathbf{0}$$

where $a'{=}\pi(a)$, $b'{=}\pi(b)$, $c'{=}\pi(c)$ (note that permutations equally affect bound and free name occurrences). Similarly to X^*, we have that $X \times Y$ is a nominal set whenever X and Y are. Note that if X is a nominal set and $X' \subseteq X$ is such that $\pi \cdot x \in X'$, for all $x \in X'$ and $\pi \in \mathsf{Perm}(\mathbb{A})$, then X' is also a nominal set with the inherited action. Hence, the following set is a nominal set.

$$\hat{K} = \{\, (\sigma, \hat{P}) \mid \sigma \in \bigcup_{n \in \omega} \mathsf{Reg}_n \wedge \hat{P} \in \hat{\Pi} \wedge \mathsf{fn}(\hat{P}) \subseteq \mathsf{img}(\sigma) \,\} \quad (1)$$

We write K for the restriction of $\hat{K}$ to elements $(\sigma, \hat{P})$ with $\hat{P} \in \Pi$. Finally, from a nominal set X we can derive its set of *orbits*:

$$O(X) = \{O(x) \mid x \in X\} \quad \textit{where} \quad O(x) = \{\pi{\cdot}x \mid \pi \in \mathsf{Perm}(\mathbb{A})\}.$$

Note that each $O(x)$ is a nominal subset of X.

The technology of the previous paragraph is used for defining the transition system of the extended calculus. In contrast to the ordinary π-calculus, the transition relation we define is finitely branching, and this is achieved by considering processes-in-context and specifying channels by their context indices instead of their names. More specifically, we let $O(\hat{K})$ be the set of processes-in-context. Each such $O(\sigma, \hat{P})$ is written $\sigma \vdash \hat{P}$.

Since $\sigma \vdash \hat{P} = \pi{\cdot}\sigma \vdash \pi{\cdot}\hat{P}$, for any permutation π, what matters in $\sigma \vdash \hat{P}$ is not the specific names occurring in σ or P, but only their index in σ. For example,

$$\{(1,a),(2,c)\} \vdash a(b).\, b\bar{c}.\,\mathbf{0} = \{(1,a'),(2,c')\} \vdash a'(b).\, b\bar{c}'.\,\mathbf{0}$$

and in essence both of these are specified by an expression e.g. like $(\{(1,\circ),(2,\circ)\}, 1(b).\, b\bar{2}.\,\mathbf{0})$. Borrowing notation from FRA's, we build up on the indices idea and use transition labels of the form $i^\bullet / i^\circledast$ for fresh inputs/outputs.

Definition 30. The semantics of the xπ-calculus is given via a labelled transition system with set of states $O(\hat{K})$ and labels:

$$\alpha ::= i \mid i^\bullet \mid i^\circledast \mid \tau \mid \bar{i}j \mid \bar{i}j^\circledast \mid ij \mid ij^\bullet$$

where $i, j \in \omega$. The transition relation is given by the rules in Table 1.

Note that $\sigma \vdash \hat{P} \xrightarrow{\ell} \sigma' \vdash \hat{P}'$ implies $|\sigma| = |\sigma'|$. Some further remarks on reduction:

- Transitions restricted to Π use only τ and double labels, i.e. from $\{\, \bar{i}j, \bar{i}j^\circledast, ij, ij^\bullet \mid i,j \in \omega \,\}$.
- Inputs are decomposed as known inputs (INP2A) and locally fresh ones (INP2B), and are therefore finitely branching. The side-conditions impose that, whenever $\sigma \vdash P_{\mathsf{inp}} \xrightarrow{i^\bullet} \sigma' \vdash P$, then $\sigma' = \sigma[i \mapsto a]$, $a \notin \mathsf{img}(\sigma)$ and i is the least index such that $\sigma(i) \notin \mathsf{fn}(P)$.[6] Similar finiteness and minimisation apply to bound outputs (OPEN).
- Note that the CLOSE rule involves bound outputs, hence globally fresh transitions on the output side. On the input side, it is then necessary to have a matching locally fresh transition: global freshness implies local freshness.

Example 31. For each $a \in \mathbb{A}$, let $\sigma_a = \{(1,a)\}$ and

$$P_a = \nu b.\, p(ab) \quad \textit{with definition} \quad p(ab) = \bar{a}b.\, \nu c.\, p(bc)\,.$$

In the π-calculus, P_a induces an infinitely-branching, infinite-path transition graph:

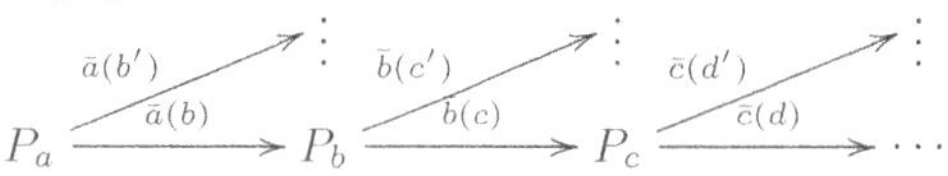

In the extended calculus, P_a induces the following transition graph,

$$\sigma_a \vdash P_a \xrightarrow{1} \sigma_a \vdash \nu b.\, b.\, \nu c.\, p(bc) \xrightarrow{1^\circledast} \sigma_b \vdash P_b \xrightarrow{1} \cdots$$

which is economic by branching once at each step. In fact, setting $P_{\mathsf{out}} = \nu b.\, b.\, \nu c.\, p(bc)$, and since $\sigma_a \vdash P_a = \sigma_b \vdash P_b$ and $\sigma_a \vdash P_{\mathsf{out}} = \sigma_b \vdash P_{\mathsf{out}}$ for all $a, b \in \mathbb{A}$, the graph above contains just two nodes:

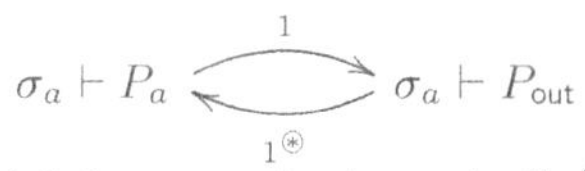

and using double labels we get simply $\sigma_a \vdash P_a$ with a loop labelled $11^\circledast$.

The way in which the two transition relations are related is given by the following lemma, which verifies the intuitions of Table 1.

Lemma 32. *Let σ, σ' be registers, and $\alpha, \hat{\alpha}$ be labels of π and xπ respectively. For all $P, P' \in \Pi$ with $\mathsf{fn}(P) \subseteq \mathsf{img}(\sigma)$:*

- *if $\sigma \vdash P \xrightarrow{\hat{\alpha}} \sigma' \vdash P'$ then $P \xrightarrow{\alpha} P'$,*
- *if $P \xrightarrow{\alpha} P'$ then $\sigma \vdash P \xrightarrow{\hat{\alpha}} \sigma' \vdash P'$;*

where either $\hat{\alpha} = \alpha = \tau$ and $\sigma = \sigma'$; or $\hat{\alpha} = \bar{i}j/ij$, $\alpha = \bar{a}b/ab$, $\sigma(i) = a$, $\sigma(j) = b$ and $\sigma' = \sigma$; or $\hat{\alpha} = \bar{i}j^\circledast/ij^\bullet$, $\alpha = \bar{a}(b)/ab$, $\sigma(i) = a$, $\sigma' = \sigma[j \mapsto b]$ and $j = \min\{j \mid \sigma(j) \notin \mathsf{fn}(P')\}$.

There is a straightforward passage from the xπ-calculus to FRA's: states are taken from $O(\hat{K})$, states from $O(K)$ are final, and the transition relation is the one given in Table 1 (omitting double transitions).[7] However, the usual (symbolic) notion of bisimulation between FRA's is not appropriate because it is defined for single-step transitions and, moreover, does not take into account the distinction between inputs and outputs. We therefore define the following notion.

Definition 33. A ***simulation*** is a relation

$$R \subseteq O(K) \times \bigcup_{n,m \in \omega}([n] \rightleftharpoons [m]) \times O(K)$$

[6] Although not essential, minimisation saves us from unnecessary branching.

[7] Note that this translation typically yields infinite FRA's — but we shall examine classes of processes where the resulting FRA's are finite in the end of this section.

$$\textsc{Inp1}\ \frac{}{\sigma \vdash a(b).P \xrightarrow{i} \sigma \vdash (b).P}\ {\scriptstyle \sigma(i)=a} \qquad \textsc{Match}\ \frac{\sigma \vdash P \xrightarrow{\alpha} \sigma \vdash \hat{P}'}{\sigma \vdash [a=a]P \xrightarrow{\alpha} \sigma \vdash \hat{P}'} \qquad \textsc{Sum}\ \frac{\sigma \vdash P \xrightarrow{\alpha} \sigma \vdash \hat{P}'}{\sigma \vdash P{+}Q \xrightarrow{\alpha} \sigma \vdash \hat{P}'}$$

$$\textsc{Inp2a}\ \frac{}{\sigma \vdash (b).P \xrightarrow{i} \sigma \vdash P\{a/b\}}\ {\scriptstyle \sigma(i)=a} \qquad \textsc{Inp2b}\ \frac{}{\sigma \vdash (b).P \xrightarrow{i^{\bullet}} \sigma[i \mapsto b] \vdash P}\ {\scriptstyle i=\min\{i \mid \sigma(i)\notin \mathsf{fn}(P)\},\ b\notin \mathsf{img}(\sigma)}$$

$$\textsc{Out1}\ \frac{}{\sigma \vdash \bar{a}b.P \xrightarrow{i} \sigma \vdash b.P}\ {\scriptstyle \sigma(i)=a} \qquad \textsc{Open}\ \frac{\sigma[i \mapsto a] \vdash P_{\mathsf{out}} \xrightarrow{i} \sigma[i \mapsto a] \vdash P}{\sigma \vdash \nu a.P_{\mathsf{out}} \xrightarrow{i^{\circledast}} \sigma[i \mapsto a] \vdash P}\ {\scriptstyle i=\min\{i \mid \sigma(i)\notin \mathsf{fn}(P)\},\ a\notin \mathsf{img}(\sigma)}$$

$$\textsc{Out2}\ \frac{}{\sigma \vdash b.P \xrightarrow{i} \sigma \vdash P}\ {\scriptstyle \sigma(i)=b} \qquad \textsc{Rec}\ \frac{\sigma \vdash P\{\vec{a}/\vec{b}\} \xrightarrow{\alpha} \sigma \vdash \hat{P}'}{\sigma \vdash p(\vec{a}) \xrightarrow{\alpha} \sigma \vdash \hat{P}'}\ {\scriptstyle p(\vec{b})=P} \qquad \textsc{Par1}\ \frac{\sigma \vdash P \xrightarrow{\alpha} \sigma \vdash \hat{P}'}{\sigma \vdash P \mid Q \xrightarrow{\alpha} \sigma \vdash \hat{P}' \mid Q}$$

$$\textsc{Res}\ \frac{(\sigma + a) \vdash \hat{P} \xrightarrow{\alpha} (\sigma' + a) \vdash \hat{P}'}{\sigma \vdash \nu a.\hat{P} \xrightarrow{\alpha} \sigma' \vdash \nu a.\hat{P}'}\ {\scriptstyle \alpha\neq(|\sigma|+1)} \qquad \textsc{Par2}\ \frac{\sigma \vdash \hat{P} \xrightarrow{i^{\bullet}/i^{\circledast}} \sigma[i \mapsto b] \vdash P'}{\sigma \vdash \hat{P} \mid Q \xrightarrow{j^{\bullet}/j^{\circledast}} \sigma[j \mapsto b] \vdash P' \mid Q}\ {\scriptstyle j=\min\{j \mid \sigma(j)\notin \mathsf{fn}(P',Q)\}}$$

$$\textsc{Comm}\ \frac{\sigma \vdash P \xrightarrow{\bar{i}j} \sigma \vdash P' \quad \sigma \vdash Q \xrightarrow{ij} \sigma \vdash Q'}{\sigma \vdash P \mid Q \xrightarrow{\tau} \sigma \vdash P' \mid Q'} \qquad \textsc{Close}\ \frac{(\sharp + \sigma) \vdash P \xrightarrow{\bar{i}1^{\circledast}} (b+\sigma) \vdash P' \quad (\sharp + \sigma) \vdash Q \xrightarrow{i1^{\bullet}} (b+\sigma) \vdash Q'}{\sigma \vdash P \mid Q \xrightarrow{\tau} \sigma \vdash \nu b.(P' \mid Q')}$$

$$\textsc{DblOut}\ \frac{\sigma \vdash P \xrightarrow{i} \sigma \vdash P_{\mathsf{out}} \xrightarrow{j/j^{\circledast}} \sigma' \vdash P'}{\sigma \vdash P \xrightarrow{\bar{i}j/\bar{i}j^{\circledast}} \sigma' \vdash P'} \qquad \textsc{DblInp}\ \frac{\sigma \vdash P \xrightarrow{i} \sigma \vdash P_{\mathsf{inp}} \xrightarrow{j/j^{\bullet}} \sigma' \vdash P'}{\sigma \vdash P \xrightarrow{ij/ij^{\bullet}} \sigma' \vdash P'}$$

Table 1. The transition relation for the xπ-calculus (symmetric counterparts of SUM, PAR, COMM, CLOSE omitted[8]).

such that if $(\sigma_1 \vdash P_1, \rho, \sigma_2 \vdash P_2) \in R$ then $\rho : [|\sigma_1|] \rightleftharpoons [|\sigma_2|]$ and $\sigma_1 \vdash P_1 \xrightarrow{\alpha} \sigma_1' \vdash P_1'$ implies that $\sigma_2 \vdash P_2 \xrightarrow{\alpha'} \sigma_2' \vdash P_2'$ for some $(\sigma_1' \vdash P_1', \rho', \sigma_2' \vdash P_2') \in R$ such that one of the following is the case, with $i \in \mathsf{dom}(\rho)$:

- $\alpha = \alpha' = \tau$ and $\rho' = \rho$;
- $\alpha = ij$, $j \in \mathsf{dom}(\rho)$, $\alpha' = \rho(i)\rho(j)$ and $\rho' = \rho$;
- $\alpha = ij$, $j \notin \mathsf{dom}(\rho)$, $\alpha' = \rho(i)k^{\bullet}$ and $\rho' = \rho[j \leftrightarrow k]$;
- $\alpha = ij^{\bullet}$, $\alpha' = \rho(i)k^{\bullet}$, $\rho' = \rho[j \leftrightarrow k]$ and,

  for all $k' \in S_2(\rho) \setminus \mathsf{img}(\rho)$, $\sigma_2 \vdash P_2 \xrightarrow{\rho(i)k'} \sigma_2 \vdash P_2'$ for some $(\sigma_1' \vdash P_1', \rho[j \leftrightarrow k'], \sigma_2 \vdash P_2') \in R$;
- $\alpha = \bar{i}j$, $j \in \mathsf{dom}(\rho)$, $\alpha' = \overline{\rho(i)}\rho(j)$ and $\rho' = \rho$;
- $\alpha = \bar{i}j^{\circledast}$, $\alpha' = \overline{\rho(i)}k^{\circledast}$ and $\rho' = \rho[j \leftrightarrow k]$.

R is called a ***bisimulation*** if both R and R^{-1} are simulations. We say that P_1 and P_2 are xπ***-bisimilar***, written $P_1 \overset{\times\pi}{\sim} P_2$, if there is a bisimulation R containing $(\sigma_{01} \vdash P_1, \sigma_{01} \leftrightarrow \sigma_{02}, \sigma_{02} \vdash P_2)$, for some σ_{01}, σ_{02} with $\mathsf{img}(\sigma_{01}) = \mathsf{fn}(P_1)$, $\mathsf{img}(\sigma_{02}) = \mathsf{fn}(P_2)$.

Proposition 34. *For all $P, Q \in \Pi$, $P \overset{\pi}{\sim} Q$ iff $P \overset{\times\pi}{\sim} Q$.*

Proof. The proof proceeds by showing that if R is a simulation for the π-calculus then

$$R' = \{ (\sigma_1 \vdash P_1, \rho, \sigma_2 \vdash P_2) \mid (P_1, P_2) \in R \wedge \rho = \sigma_1 \leftrightarrow \sigma_2 \}$$

is a simulation for xπ and, conversely, if R is a simulation for the xπ-calculus then

$$R' = \{ (P_1, P_2) \mid \exists \sigma_1, \sigma_2. (\sigma_1 \vdash P_1, \sigma_1 \leftrightarrow \sigma_2, \sigma_2 \vdash P_2) \in R \}$$

is a simulation for π. □

Note that the set of reducts of a given process-in-context is in general infinite. The following result provides sufficient conditions for excluding such infinite behaviours. We say that a process has *finite control* if no parallel compositions appear in its recursive definitions. A process is *ν-strict* if all its subprocesses of the form $\nu a.P$ satisfy $a \in \mathsf{fn}(P)$. Also, Q is a *descendant* of P if there is a series of π-transitions from P to Q.

Proposition 35. *If $P_0 \in \Pi$ has finite control and all its descendants are ν-strict, then there is some σ_0 and a finite $S \subseteq O(K)$ such that, for all $(\sigma \vdash P) \in S$, if $\sigma \vdash P \xrightarrow{\alpha} \sigma' \vdash P'$ then $(\sigma' \vdash P') \in S$, and $(\sigma_0 \vdash P_0) \in S$.*

Proof. Suppose (WLOG) that P_0 invokes definitions $p_i(\vec{a}_i) = P_i$, $i \in [N]$ for some N, and take $M = |P_0| \times \max\{ |P_i| \mid i \in [N] \}$ for the size function which counts a process' occurrences of $\mathbf{0}$'s, p's and names, free or bound (but not binding): e.g. $|\bar{a}b.P| = 2 + |P|$, $|a(b).P| = 1 + |P|$, $|\nu a.P| = |P|$, $|p(\vec{a})| = 1 + |\vec{a}|$ and $|\mathbf{0}| = 1$. If Q is a descendant of P then $|Q| \leq M$ as a process may only increase its size by recursion and, as P_0 has finite control, recursions cannot obtain size greater than $\max\{ |P_i| \mid i \in [N] \}$. But then, because all descendants of P_0 are ν-strict, their number of ν-abstractions is bounded by M, and hence they all have length (number of symbols or constructors) bounded relatively to M. They are still unboundedly many, due to different choices of free variables. But since each descendant can be matched with a context from Reg_M, the number of the resulting processes-in-context is bounded relatively to M. We collect all these in S. □

Corollary 36. *Bisimilarity is decidable in Π when restricted to processes with finite control.*

Proof. For any such processes $P_1, P_2 \in \Pi$, by the previous proposition and after equating processes up to non-strict ν-abstractions, we obtain xπ-transition graphs with sizes bounded relatively to P_1 and P_2. Clearly, $P_1 \overset{\times\pi}{\sim} P_2$ iff there is a bisimulation (in xπ) between those graphs. As those bisimulations live in a space bounded

[8] note: $\sigma{+}v = \sigma \cup \{(|\sigma|{+}1, v)\}$, $v{+}\sigma = \{(1,v)\} \cup \{(i{+}1, v') \mid (i, v') \in \sigma\}$.

relatively to the sizes of P_1 and P_2, we can search it exhaustively for such relations. □

Equating processes up to *structural congruence* [14], the above results can be further strengthened to processes with *finite degree of parallelism*, in a similar manner to [4].

9. Further directions

We have introduced an abstract computational paradigm and established its key properties, laying the ground for further research. The next logical step is to examine concrete applications of FRA's to the description of computation with names, either in the direction of mobile calculi or that of programming languages, relating this approach to existing higher-level approaches. A first such advance has been recently accomplished in [19] by constructing a model of a low-order restriction of Reduced ML (a fragment of ML with ground-type integer references) representable in a variant of FRA's where labels contain store information. This was achieved by representing the fully abstract game semantics of the language [18].

On the foundational side, the study of the π-calculus in FRA's revealed that there is a notion of polarity inherent in computation with names. In particular, the examined FRA's do not mix locally with globally fresh transitions, and this is clearly depicted in the partition $\hat{\Pi} = \Pi_{\mathsf{inp}} \uplus \Pi_{\mathsf{out}} \uplus \Pi$. A similar observation applies to FRA's describing Reduced ML [19]. There, the states are partitioned in P-states (for Proponent/Program) and O-states (for Opponent/Environment); only P-states are allowed to perform globally fresh transitions, and only O-states can do locally fresh ones. Intuitively, the only notion of freshness that can be observed on the program's side is local freshness, whereas the environment should be assumed to have the memory needed in order to observe global freshness. These observations suggest that a notion of *polarised FRA*, where states are partitioned as above, is relevant and should be further pursued. In the polarised setting, symbolic bisimulations are simplified as there is no longer need for an h component (cf. Definitions 25 and 33).

A potential criticism towards FRA's concerns the fact that they fail to satisfy closure under concatenation and Kleene star (cf. Section 6). We find these non-closure results rather expected as FRA's are history-sensitive machines. On the other hand, FRA's seem to be closed under the *nominal versions* of concatenation and Kleene star, as recently introduced by Gabbay and Ciancia [9]. The precise connections between FRA's and regular languages with name-restriction [9] are the subject of ongoing research.

Finally, some important questions have still not been answered. For example, we have not considered deterministic versions of FRA's, nor examined whether FRA's can be determinised. Assuming that in a deterministic FRA to each input string corresponds a unique path, we can see that e.g. the FRA accepting the language

$$\mathcal{L} = \{\, a_1 \cdots a_k a \mid a \in \{a_1, \dots, a_k\} \wedge \forall i \neq j.\, a_i \neq a_j \,\}$$

has no deterministic equivalent. Other directions for further research concern minimisation of FRA's (recently examined for FMA's [2]) and the evident connections to HD-automata. Moreover, several possible extensions of FRA's are of interest, e.g. variants with labels (data words), stores, or pushdown variants.

10. Acknowledgements

Thanks to Andrzej Murawski, Samson Abramsky, Vassilis Koutavas and Ulrich Schöpp for discussions and suggestions. Thanks also to the anonymous reviewers for their comments. Section 7 in particular is now much simpler due to a reviewer's suggestion.

A. Proofs from section 6

Proof of Lemma 19. Let $\mathcal{A} = \langle Q, q_0, \sigma_0, \delta, F\rangle$. The construction of $\mathcal{B} = \langle Q', q_0', \sigma_0', \delta', F'\rangle$ follows closely [11]. In particular, each transition of $\mathcal{A}$ involving a name induces an assignment of that name in the extra register of $\mathcal{B}$. If the transition were a fresh assignment then this would result in the name occurring in $\mathcal{B}$ just once after assignment, otherwise it would occur twice. As the actual extra register of $\mathcal{B}$ changes during this process we add an extra component in states to remember it.

We set $Q' = Q \times ([n+1] \xrightarrow{\cong} [n+1])$ and write elements of Q' as (q, π). Moreover, $q_0' = (q_0, \mathsf{id})$, $\sigma_0' = \sigma_0[n{+}1 \mapsto \sharp]$ and $F' = \{(q,\pi) \mid q \in F\}$. Finally:

$$\begin{aligned}\delta' = {} & \{\, ((q_1,\pi),\ell,(q_2,\pi)) \mid \ell \in \mathbb{C} \wedge (q_1,\ell,q_2) \in \delta \,\}\\ & \cup \{\, (q_1',(\{\pi(n{+}1)\},\{\pi(i),\pi(n{+}1)\}),(q_2,\pi)) \mid (q_1,i,q_2) \in \delta \,\}\\ & \cup \{\, (q_1',(\{\pi(n{+}1)\},\{\pi(n{+}1)\}),(q_2,\pi')) \mid (q_1,i^{\bullet},q_2) \in \delta \,\}\\ & \cup \{\, (q_1',(\{\pi(n{+}1)\},\{\pi(n{+}1)\},[n]),(q_2,\pi')) \mid (q_1,i^{\circledast},q_2) \in \delta \,\}\end{aligned}$$

where $q_1' = (q_1,\pi)$ and $\pi' = (\pi(i) \leftrightarrow \pi(n{+}1)) \circ \pi$ (we write $(k \leftrightarrow j)$ for the permutation that swaps k and j). We can show that the following relation is a bisimulation and therefore that $\mathcal{A} \sim \mathcal{B}$.

$$R = \{\, ((q,\sigma,H),((q,\pi),\sigma',H)) \mid \forall i \in [n].\, \sigma(i) = \sigma'(\pi(i)) \,\}$$

□

Proof of Lemma 20. Let $\mathcal{A} = \langle Q, q_0, \sigma_0, \delta, F\rangle$ and construct $\mathcal{B} = \langle Q', q_0', \sigma_0', \delta', F'\rangle$ as follows. The idea is to keep in the extra memory registers of $\mathcal{B}$ a copy of the initial configuration σ_0 which is never touched by assignments. Thus, whenever $\mathcal{A}$ wants to make a transition with label (S,T,A), $\mathcal{B}$ will simulate it by a transition $(S,S,[n])$ and transitions of the form $(S, T \cup T_a)$ where $T_a \subseteq \{n{+}1, ..., 2n\}$, $a \in \sigma_0([n] \setminus A)$ and a is not in the history. In order to accomplish this we need to enrich states with information regarding whether the names in $\mathsf{img}(\sigma_0)$ appear in the history. Therefore, we set $Q' = Q \times \mathcal{P}(\mathsf{img}(\sigma_0))$, $q_0' = (q_0, \emptyset)$, $\sigma_0' = \sigma_0 + \sigma_0$, $F' = \{(q,I) \mid q \in F\}$ and:

$$\begin{aligned}\delta' = {} & \{\, ((q,I),\ell,(q',I)) \mid \ell \in \mathbb{C} \wedge (q,\ell,q') \in \delta \,\}\\ & \cup \{\, ((q,I),(S,T),(q',I)) \mid (q,(S,T),q') \in \delta \,\}\\ & \cup \{\, ((q,I),(S,T \cup T_a),(q',I \cup \{a\})) \mid (q,(S,T),q') \in \delta \,\}\\ & \cup \{\, ((q,I),(S,S,[n]),(q',I)) \mid (q,(S,S,A),q') \in \delta \,\}\\ & \cup \{\, ((q,I),(S,T \cup T_{a'}),(q',I \cup \{a'\})) \mid (q,(S,T,A),q') \in \delta \,\}\end{aligned}$$

where $a \in \mathsf{img}(\sigma_0)$, $T_a = \{\, (n+i) \in [2n] \mid \sigma_0(i) = a \,\}$, $a' \in \sigma_0([n] \setminus A) \setminus I$, and $T_{a'}$ as T_a. We can check that

$$R = \{\, ((q,\sigma,H),((q,I),\sigma',H)) \mid I = H \cap \mathsf{img}(\sigma_0) \wedge \sigma' = \sigma + \sigma_0 \,\}$$

is a bisimulation and therefore that $\mathcal{A} \sim \mathcal{B}$. □

Proof of Lemma 21. Let $\mathcal{A} = \langle Q, q_0, \sigma_0, \delta, F\rangle$ and construct $\mathcal{B} = \langle Q', q_0', \sigma_0', \delta', F'\rangle$ by setting $Q' = Q \times ([n] \to [n])$ and selecting f_0, σ_0' such that $\mathsf{img}(\sigma_0) = \mathsf{img}(\sigma_0')$ and $\sigma_0 = \sigma_0' \circ f_0$. Moreover, set $q_0' = (q_0, f_0)$, $F' = \{(q,f) \mid q \in F\}$ and:

$$\begin{aligned}\delta' = {} & \{\, ((q,f),\ell,(q',f)) \mid \ell \in \mathbb{C} \wedge (q,\ell,q') \in \delta \,\}\\ & \cup \{\, ((q,f),i,(q',f')) \mid f(T \setminus S) = \{i\} \wedge (q,(S,T),q') \in \delta \,\}\\ & \cup \{\, ((q,f),i,(q',f')) \mid f^{-1}(i) \subseteq S \wedge (q,(S,S),q') \in \delta \,\}\\ & \cup \{\, ((q,f),i^{\bullet},(q',f')) \mid f^{-1}(i) \subseteq S \wedge (q,(S,S),q') \in \delta \,\}\\ & \cup \{\, ((q,f),i^{\circledast},(q',f')) \mid f^{-1}(i) \subseteq S \wedge (q,(S,S,[n]),q') \in \delta \,\}\end{aligned}$$

with $f' = f[S \mapsto i]$. Now, the following is a bisimulation

$$R = \{\, ((q,\sigma,H),((q,f),\sigma',H)) \mid \sigma = \sigma' \circ f \,\}$$

and hence $\mathcal{A} \sim \mathcal{B}$. □

B. Proofs from section 7

Proof of Proposition 26. It will suffice to check only non-constant transitions. So let $((q_1,\sigma_1,H),(q_2,\sigma_2,H)) \in R'$ due to some $(q_1,h,\rho,q_2) \in R$ and suppose that $(q_1,\sigma_1,H) \xrightarrow{a}_{\delta_1} (q_1',\sigma_1',H')$ with $H' = H \cup \{a\}$. We do case analysis on a. Below we write ρ' for $\rho[i \leftrightarrow j]$.

- $a \in \mathsf{img}(\sigma_1) \cap \mathsf{img}(\sigma_2)$, say $a = \sigma_1(i) = \sigma_2(j)$. Then, it is necessary that $(q_1,i,q_1') \in \delta_1$ and $\sigma_1' = \sigma_1$. Also, $\rho = \sigma_1 \leftrightarrow \sigma_2$ implies $(i,j) \in \rho$, so $(q_2,j,q_2') \in \delta_2$ for some $(q_1',h,\rho,q_2') \in R$. Thus, $(q_2,\sigma_2,H) \xrightarrow{a}_{\delta_2} (q_2',\sigma_2,H')$ and, noting that $\hat{H}' = \hat{H}$ so $h = \lceil|\hat{H}'|\rceil^n$, we can see that $((q_1',\sigma_1,H'),(q_2',\sigma_2,H')) \in R'$.
- $a \in \mathsf{img}(\sigma_1) \setminus \mathsf{img}(\sigma_2)$, say $a = \sigma_1(i)$. Then, again $(q_1,i,q_1') \in \delta_1$ and $\sigma_1' = \sigma_1$, but $i \in S_1(\rho) \setminus \mathsf{dom}(\rho)$. Thus, $(q_2,j^\bullet,q_2') \in \delta_2$ for some $(q_1',h,\rho',q_2') \in R$. Thus, $(q_2,\sigma_2,H) \xrightarrow{a}_{\delta_2} (q_2',\sigma_2',H')$, $\sigma_2' = \sigma_2[j \mapsto a]$. Noting that $\rho' = \sigma_1 \leftrightarrow \sigma_2'$ and $\hat{H}' = \hat{H}$, we have that $((q_1',\sigma_1,H'),(q_2',\sigma_2',H')) \in R'$.
- $a \in \mathsf{img}(\sigma_2) \setminus \mathsf{img}(\sigma_1)$, say $a = \sigma_2(j)$. Since $a \in \hat{H} \setminus \mathsf{img}(\sigma_1)$, we have some $(q_1,i^\bullet,q_1') \in \delta_1$, and $\sigma_1' = \sigma_1[i \mapsto a]$. Moreover, $j \in S_2(\rho) \setminus \mathsf{img}(\rho)$ and therefore $(q_2,j,q_2' \in \delta_2$ for some $(q_1',h,\rho',q_2') \in R$. Thus, $(q_2,\sigma_2,H) \xrightarrow{a}_{\delta_2} (q_2',\sigma_2,H')$ and we can see that $((q_1',\sigma_1',H'),(q_2',\sigma_2,H')) \in R'$.
- $a \in \hat{H} \setminus (\mathsf{img}(\sigma_2) \cup \mathsf{img}(\sigma_1))$, so $(q_1,i^\bullet,q_1') \in \delta_1$, and $\sigma_1' = \sigma_1[i \mapsto a]$. If $h < n$ then $\|\rho\| = |\mathsf{img}(\sigma_1) \cup \mathsf{img}(\sigma_2)| < |\hat{H}| = h$. Thus, $(q_2,j^\bullet,q_2) \in \delta_2$ for some $(q_1',h,\rho',q_2') \in R$, and so $(q_2,\sigma_2,H) \xrightarrow{a}_{\delta_2} (q_2',\sigma_2',H')$, $\sigma_2' = \sigma_2[j \mapsto a]$. We have $\rho' = \sigma_1' \leftrightarrow \sigma_2'$ and $h = \lceil|\hat{H}'|\rceil^n$, thus $((q_1',\sigma_1',H'),(q_2',\sigma_2',H')) \in R'$.
- $a \notin \hat{H}$ and say transition is due to $(q_1,i^\bullet/i^\circledast,q_1') \in \delta_1$, so $\sigma_1' = \sigma_1[i \mapsto a]$. Then, $(q_2,j^\bullet/j^\circledast,q_2') \in \delta_2$ for some $(q_1',h^{++},\rho',q_2') \in R$, so $(q_2,\sigma_2,H) \xrightarrow{a}_{\delta_2} (q_2',\sigma_2',H')$, $\sigma_2' = \sigma_2[j \mapsto a]$. We have that $h^{++} = \lceil|\hat{H}'|\rceil^n$, so $((q_1',\sigma_1',H'),(q_2',\sigma_2',H')) \in R'$.

Thus, R' is a simulation. If R is a symbolic bisimulation then, by symmetry, R' is a bisimulation. Finally, if $(q_{01},|H_0|,\sigma_{01} \leftrightarrow \sigma_{02},q_{02}) \in R$ then $((q_{01},\sigma_{01},\emptyset),(q_{02},\sigma_{02},\emptyset)) \in R'$. □

Proof of Proposition 27. We check non-constant transitions. Let $(q_1,h,\rho,q_2) \in R'$, due to some $((q_1,\sigma_1,H),(q_2,\sigma_2,H)) \in R$ and suppose that $(q_1,\ell,q_1') \in \delta_1$. We do case analysis on ℓ. Below we write H' for $H \cup \{a\}$, and ρ' for $\rho[i \leftrightarrow j]$.

- If $\ell = i$ then, by closure, $(q_1,\sigma_1,H) \xrightarrow{a}_{\delta_1} (q_1',\sigma_1,H')$ with $a = \sigma_1(i)$, and hence $(q_2,\sigma_2,H) \xrightarrow{a}_{\delta_2} (q_2',\sigma_2',H')$ for some $((q_1',\sigma_1,H'),(q_2',\sigma_2',H')) \in R$. If $i \in \mathsf{dom}(\rho)$, say $(i,j) \in \rho$, then $a \in \mathsf{img}(\sigma_2)$ and it must be $(q_2,j,q_2') \in \delta_2$, $\sigma_2' = \sigma_2$. We can see that $(q_1',h,\rho,q_2') \in R'$. If $i \in S_1(\rho) \setminus \mathsf{dom}(\rho)$ then $a \notin \mathsf{img}(\sigma_2)$ and there is some $(q_2,j^\bullet,q_2') \in \delta_2$, and $\sigma_2' = \sigma_2[j \mapsto a]$. We have that $(q_1',h,\rho',q_2') \in R'$.
- If $\ell = i^\bullet$ then, for each $a \notin \mathsf{img}(\sigma_1)$, $(q_1,\sigma_1,H) \xrightarrow{a}_{\delta_1} (q_1',\sigma_1',H')$, $\sigma_1' = \sigma_1[i \mapsto a]$, and therefore $(q_2,\sigma_2,H) \xrightarrow{a}_{\delta_2} (q_2',\sigma_2',H')$ for some $((q_1',\sigma_1',H'),(q_2',\sigma_2',H')) \in R$.

For any $j \in S_2(\rho) \setminus \mathsf{img}(\rho)$, $\sigma_2(j) \notin \mathsf{img}(\sigma_1)$, so we can take $a = \sigma_2(j)$. Then, we must have $(q_2,j,q_2') \in \delta_2$, $\sigma_2' = \sigma_2$, and we can check that $(q_1',h,\rho',q_2') \in R'$.

If $h = n$ or $\|\rho\| < h$ then we can choose $a \in \hat{H} \setminus (\mathsf{img}(\sigma_1) \cup \mathsf{img}(\sigma_2))$. Thus, we have some $(q_2,j^\bullet,q_2') \in \delta_2$, $\sigma_2' = \sigma_2[j \mapsto a]$. Noting that $\hat{H}' = \hat{H}$ and $\rho' = \sigma_1' \leftrightarrow \sigma_2'$, we get $(q_1',h,\rho',q_2') \in R'$.

Finally, if we choose $a \notin \hat{H}$ then there is some $(q_2,j^\bullet/j^\circledast,q_2') \in \delta_2$, and $\sigma_2' = \sigma_2[j \mapsto a]$. We have that $\rho' = \sigma_1' \leftrightarrow \sigma_2'$ and $\hat{H}' = \hat{H} \uplus \{a\}$, thus $h^{++} = \lceil|\hat{H}'|\rceil^n$. Hence, $(q_1',h^{++},\rho',q_2') \in R'$.

- If $\ell = i^\circledast$ then we work as in the last case above.

Thus, R' is a symbolic simulation. If R is a bisimulation then, by symmetry, R' is a symbolic bisimulation. Finally, if $((q_{01},\sigma_{01},\emptyset),(q_{02},\sigma_{02},\emptyset)) \in R$ then $(q_{01},|H_0|,\sigma_{01} \leftrightarrow \sigma_{02},q_{02}) \in R'$. □

References

[1] S. Abramsky, D. R. Ghica, A. S. Murawski, C.-H. L. Ong, and I. D. B. Stark. Nominal games and full abstraction for the nu-calculus. In *Proc. of LICS '04*, pages 150–159. IEEE Comp. Soc. Press, 2004.

[2] M. Benedikt, C. Ley, and G. Puppis. Minimal memory automata. *Alberto Mendelzon Workshop on Foundations of Databases*, 2010.

[3] N. Benton and V. Koutavas. A mechanized bisimulation for the nu-calculus. Tech. Rep. MSR-TR-2008-129, Microsoft Research, 2008.

[4] R. Bruni, F. Honsell, M. Lenisa, and M. Miculan. Modeling fresh names in the pi-calculus using abstractions. In *Proc. of CMCS '04*, volume 106, pages 25–41. Elsevier, 2004.

[5] S. Delaune, S. Kremer, and M. Ryan. Symbolic bisimulation for the Applied Pi Calculus. In *Proc. of FSTTCS '07*, volume 4855 of *LNCS*, pages 133–145, 2007.

[6] S. Demri and R. Lazic. LTL with the freeze quantifier and register automata. *ACM Trans. Comput. Log.*, 10(3), 2009.

[7] G. L. Ferrari, U. Montanari, and E. Tuosto. Model checking for nominal calculi. In *Proc. of FOSSACS '05*, volume 3441 of *LNCS*, pages 1–24, 2005.

[8] M. Gabbay and A. M. Pitts. A new approach to abstract syntax with variable binding. *Formal Asp. Comput.*, 13(3-5):341–363, 2002.

[9] M. J. Gabbay and V. Ciancia. Freshness and name-restriction in sets of traces with names. Submitted for publication, 2010.

[10] A. Jeffrey and J. Rathke. Towards a theory of bisimulation for local names. In *LICS*, pages 56–66, 1999.

[11] M. Kaminski and N. Francez. Finite-memory automata. *Theor. Comput. Sci.*, 134(2):329–363, 1994.

[12] J. Laird. A game semantics of local names and good variables. In *Proc. of FOSSACS '04*, volume 2987 of *LNCS*, pages 289–303, 2004.

[13] J. Laird. A fully abstract trace semantics for general references. In *Proc. of ICALP '07*, volume 4596 of *LNCS*, pages 667–679, 2007.

[14] R. Milner, J. Parrow, and D. Walker. A calculus of mobile processes, I and II. *Inf. Comput.*, 100(1):1–77, 1992.

[15] R. Milner, M. Tofte, and D. Macqueen. *The Definition of Standard ML.* MIT Press, 1997.

[16] U. Montanari and M. Pistore. An introduction to History Dependent Automata. *Electr. Notes Theor. Comput. Sci.*, 10, 1997.

[17] U. Montanari and M. Pistore. Structured coalgebras and minimal HD-automata for the pi-calculus. *Theor. Comput. Sci.*, 340(3):539–576, 2005.

[18] A. S. Murawski and N. Tzevelekos. Full abstraction for Reduced ML. In *Proc. of FOSSACS '09*, volume 5504 of *LNCS*, pages 32–47, 2009.

[19] A. S. Murawski and N. Tzevelekos. Algorithmic nominal game semantics. Submitted for publication, 2010.

[20] R. M. Needham. Names. In S. Mullender, editor, *Distributed systems*, pages 315–327. ACM Press/Addison-Wesley, 1993. 2nd edition.

[21] F. Neven, T. Schwentick, and V. Vianu. Finite state machines for strings over infinite alphabets. *ACM Trans. Comput. Logic*, 5(3):403–435, 2004.

[22] M. Pistore. *History Dependent Automata.* PhD thesis, University of Pisa, 1999.

[23] A. M. Pitts. Nominal logic, a first order theory of names and binding. *Inf. Comput.*, 186(2):165–193, 2003.

[24] A. M. Pitts and I. Stark. Observable properties of higher order functions that dynamically create local names, or: What's *new*? In *Proc. of MFCS '93*, number 711 in LNCS, pages 122–141, 1993.

[25] H. Sakamoto and D. Ikeda. Intractability of decision problems for finite-memory automata. *Theor. Comput. Sci.*, 231(2):297–308, 2000.

[26] D. Sangiorgi and D. Walker. *The pi calculus: A Theory of Mobile Processes.* Cambridge University Press, 2001.

[27] L. Segoufin. Automata and logics for words and trees over an infinite alphabet. In *Proc. of CSL '06*, vol. 4207 of *LNCS*, pages 41–57, 2006.

[28] I. Stark. *Names and Higher-Order Functions.* PhD thesis, University of Cambridge, 1994.

Vector Addition System Reachability Problem

A Short Self-Contained Proof

Jérôme Leroux
LaBRI, Université de Bordeaux, CNRS
leroux@labri.fr

Abstract

The reachability problem for Vector Addition Systems (VASs) is a central problem of net theory. The general problem is known decidable by algorithms exclusively based on the classical Kosaraju-Lambert-Mayr-Sacerdote-Tenney decomposition (KLMTS decomposition). Recently from this decomposition, we deduced that a final configuration is not reachable from an initial one if and only if there exists a Presburger inductive invariant that contains the initial configuration but not the final one. Since we can decide if a Preburger formula denotes an inductive invariant, we deduce from this result that there exist checkable certificates of non-reachability in the Presburger arithmetic. In particular, there exists a simple algorithm for deciding the general VAS reachability problem based on two semi-algorithms. A first one that tries to prove the reachability by enumerating finite sequences of actions and a second one that tries to prove the non-reachability by enumerating Presburger formulas. In this paper we provide the first proof of the VAS reachability problem that is not based on the KLMST decomposition. The proof is based on the notion of production relations inspired from Hauschildt that directly provides the existence of Presburger inductive invariants.

Categories and Subject Descriptors D.2.4 [*Software Engineering*]: Formal methods; D.2.2 [*Design Tools and Techniques*]: Petri nets

General Terms Theory, Verification

Keywords VAS, Petri, Presburger, Reachability

1. Introduction

Vector Addition Systems (VASs) or equivalently Petri Nets are one of the most popular formal methods for the representation and the analysis of parallel processes [EN94]. The reachability problem is central since many computational problems (even outside the parallel processes) reduce to the reachability problem. Sacerdote and Tenney provided in [ST77] a partial proof of decidability of this problem. The proof was completed in 1981 by Mayr [May81] and simplified by Kosaraju [Kos82] from [ST77, May81]. Ten years later [Lam92], Lambert provided a more simplified version based on [Kos82]. This last proof still remains difficult and the upper-bound complexity of the corresponding algorithm is just known non-primitive recursive. Nowadays, the exact complexity of the reachability problem for VASs is still an open-problem. Even an elementary upper-bound complexity is open. In fact, the known general reachability algorithms are exclusively based on the Kosaraju-Lambert-Mayr-Sacerdote-Tenney (KLMST) decomposition.

POPL'11, January 26–28, 2011, Austin, Texas, USA.

Recently [Ler09] we proved thanks to the KLMST decomposition that Parikh images of languages accepted by VASs are semi-pseudo-linear, a class that extends the Presburger sets. An application of this result was provided; we proved that a final configuration is not reachable from an initial one if and only if there exists a forward inductive invariant definable in the Presburger arithmetic that contains the initial configuration but not the final one. Since we can decide if a Presburger formula denotes a forward inductive invariant, we deduce that there exist checkable certificates of non-reachability in the Presburger arithmetic. In particular, there exists a simple algorithm for deciding the general VAS reachability problem based on two semi-algorithms. A first one that tries to prove the reachability by enumerating finite sequences of actions and a second one that tries to prove the non-reachability by enumerating Presburger formulas.

In this paper we provide a new proof of the reachability problem that is not based on the KLMST decomposition. The proof is based on the *production relations* inspired by Hauschildt [Hau90] and it provides directly that reachability sets are *Lambert sets*, a class of sets introduced in this paper that extend the class of Presburger sets and contained in the class of semi-pseudo-linear sets. In particular this paper provides a more precise characterization of the reachability sets of VASs.

Outline of the paper: Section 2 provides notations and classical definitions. Section 3 and Section 4 introduce classes of sets used in the sequel : *polytope conic sets* and *vector spaces* in the first one and *polytope periodic* sets, *Presburger* sets, *Lambert* sets, and *Petri* sets in the second one. Section 5 and Section 6 show that it sufficient to prove that the reachability relation of a Vector Addition system is a Petri relation in order to deduce the existence of forward inductive invariants definable in the Presburger arithmetic proving the non-reachability. In Section 7 we introduce the class of Vector Addition Systems and the central notion of production relations. We show in the next Section 8 that these relations are polytope periodic. In Section 9 we prove that the reachability relation of a Vector Addition System is a Petri relation. Finally in Section 10 we combine all the previous results to deduce the decidability of the Vector Addition System reachability problem based on Presburger inductive invariants.

2. Notations

We introduce in this section notations and classical definitions used in this paper.

We denote by $\mathbb{N}, \mathbb{N}_{>0}, \mathbb{Z}, \mathbb{Q}, \mathbb{Q}_{\geq 0}, \mathbb{Q}_{>0}$ the set of *natural numbers*, *positive integers*, *integers*, *rational numbers*, *non negative rational numbers*, and *positive rational numbers*. *Vectors* and *sets of vectors* are denoted in bold face. The ith *component* of a vector $\mathbf{v} \in \mathbb{Q}^d$ is denoted by $\mathbf{v}(i)$. We introduce $||\mathbf{v}||_\infty = \max_{1 \leq i \leq d} |\mathbf{v}(i)|$ where $|\mathbf{v}(i)|$ is the *absolute value* of $\mathbf{v}(i)$. The total order $\leq$ over $\mathbb{Q}$ is extended component-wise into an order $\leq$ over the set of vectors $\mathbb{Q}^d$. The addition function $+$ is also extended component-wise over $\mathbb{Q}^d$. Given two sets $\mathbf{V}_1, \mathbf{V}_2 \subseteq \mathbb{Q}^d$ we denote by $\mathbf{V}_1 + \mathbf{V}_2$ the set $\{\mathbf{v}_1 + \mathbf{v}_2 \mid (\mathbf{v}_1, \mathbf{v}_2) \in \mathbf{V}_1 \times \mathbf{V}_2\}$, and we denote by $\mathbf{V}_1 - \mathbf{V}_2$ the set $\{\mathbf{v}_1 - \mathbf{v}_2 \mid (\mathbf{v}_1, \mathbf{v}_2) \in \mathbf{V}_1 \times \mathbf{V}_2\}$. In the same way given $T \subseteq \mathbb{Q}$ and $\mathbf{V} \subseteq \mathbb{Q}^d$ we let $T\mathbf{V} = \{t\mathbf{v} \mid (t, \mathbf{v}) \in T \times \mathbf{V}\}$. We also denote by $\mathbf{v}_1 + \mathbf{V}_2$ and $\mathbf{V}_1 + \mathbf{v}_2$ the sets $\{\mathbf{v}_1\} + \mathbf{V}_2$ and $\mathbf{V}_1 + \{\mathbf{v}_2\}$, and we denote by $t\mathbf{V}$ and $T\mathbf{v}$ the sets $\{t\}\mathbf{V}$ and $T\{\mathbf{v}\}$. In the sequel, an empty sum of sets included in $\mathbb{Q}^d$ denotes the set reduced to the zero vector $\{\mathbf{0}\}$.

A *(binary) relation* R over $\mathbb{Q}^d$ is a subset $R \subseteq \mathbb{Q}^d \times \mathbb{Q}^d$. The *composition* of two relations R and S is the relation denoted by $R \circ S$ and defined as usual by the following equality:

$$R \circ S = \bigcup_{\mathbf{y} \in \mathbb{Q}^d} \left\{ (\mathbf{x}, \mathbf{z}) \in \mathbb{Q}^d \times \mathbb{Q}^d \mid (\mathbf{x}, \mathbf{y}) \in R \wedge (\mathbf{y}, \mathbf{z}) \in S \right\}$$

The *reflexive and transitive closure* of a relation R is denoted by R^*. In this paper, notions introduced over the sets are transposed over the relations by identifying $\mathbb{Q}^d \times \mathbb{Q}^d$ with $\mathbb{Q}^{2d}$.

An order $\sqsubseteq$ over a set S is said to be *well* if for every sequence $(s_n)_{n \in \mathbb{N}}$ of elements $s_n \in S$ we can extract a sub-sequence that is non-decreasing for $\sqsubseteq$, i.e. there exists a strictly increasing sequence $(n_k)_{k \in \mathbb{N}}$ of natural numbers in $(\mathbb{N}, \leq)$ such that $(s_{n_k})_{k \in \mathbb{N}}$ is non decreasing for $\sqsubseteq$. A *minimal element* of an ordered set $(S, \sqsubseteq)$ is an element $s \in S$ such that for every $t \in T$ the relation $t \sqsubseteq s$ implies $s = t$. Given a set $Y \subseteq S$ we denote by $\min_{\sqsubseteq}(Y)$ the *set of minimal elements* of the ordered set $(Y, \sqsubseteq)$. Let us recall that if $(S, \sqsubseteq)$ is well ordered then $X = \min_{\sqsubseteq}(Y)$ is finite and for every $y \in Y$ there exists $x \in X$ such that $x \sqsubseteq y$.

Let us consider an order $\sqsubseteq$ over a set S. We introduce the component-wise extension of $\sqsubseteq$ over the set of vectors S^d defined by $\mathbf{s} \sqsubseteq \mathbf{t}$ if $\mathbf{s}(i) \sqsubseteq \mathbf{t}(i)$ for every $i \in \{1, \ldots, d\}$.

Lemma 2.1 (Dickson's Lemma). *The ordered set $(S^d, \sqsubseteq)$ is well for every well ordered set $(S, \sqsubseteq)$.*

Example 2.2. *The set $(\mathbb{N}, \leq)$ is well ordered. Hence $(\mathbb{N}^d, \leq)$ is also well ordered. The set $(\mathbb{Z}, \leq)$ is not well ordered.*

3. Polytope Conic Sets

In this section we introduce the *polytope conic sets* and we provide a characterization of this class based on the *vector spaces*.

A *conic set* is a set $\mathbf{C} \subseteq \mathbb{Q}^d$ such that $\mathbf{0} \in \mathbf{C}$, $\mathbf{C} + \mathbf{C} \subseteq \mathbf{C}$ and such that $\mathbb{Q}_{\geq 0}\mathbf{C} \subseteq \mathbf{C}$. A conic set $\mathbf{C}$ is said to be *finitely generated* if there exists a finite sequence $\mathbf{c}_1, \ldots, \mathbf{c}_k$ of vectors $\mathbf{c}_j \in \mathbf{C}$ such that $\mathbf{C} = \mathbb{Q}_{\geq 0}\mathbf{c}_1 + \cdots + \mathbb{Q}_{\geq 0}\mathbf{c}_k$.

Definition 3.1. *A conic set $\mathbf{C}$ is said to be* polytope *if it is definable in* $\mathrm{FO}(\mathbb{Q}, +, \leq, 0, 1)$.

Example 3.2. *The conic set $\mathbf{C} = \{\mathbf{c} \in \mathbb{Q}_{\geq 0}^2 \mid \mathbf{c}(1) \leq \sqrt{2}\mathbf{c}(2)\}$ is not polytope.*

Example 3.3. *The conic set $\mathbf{C} = \{(0,0)\} \cup \mathbb{Q}_{>0}^2$ is polytope but it is not finitely generated.*

A *vector space* is a set $\mathbf{V} \subseteq \mathbb{Q}^d$ such that $\mathbf{0} \in \mathbf{V}$, $\mathbf{V} + \mathbf{V} \subseteq \mathbf{V}$ and such that $\mathbb{Q}\mathbf{V} \subseteq \mathbf{V}$. Let $\mathbf{X} \subseteq \mathbb{Q}^d$. The following set is a vector space called the *vector space generated* by $\mathbf{X}$.

$$\mathbf{V} = \left\{ \sum_{j=1}^{k} \lambda_j \mathbf{x}_j \mid k \in \mathbb{N} \text{ and } (\lambda_j, \mathbf{x}_j) \in \mathbb{Q} \times \mathbf{X} \right\}$$

Observe that this vector space is the minimal for the inclusion vector space that contains $\mathbf{X}$. Note that the vector space $\mathbf{V}$ generated by a conic set $\mathbf{C}$ satisfies the equality $\mathbf{V} = \mathbf{C} - \mathbf{C}$. Let us recall that every vector space $\mathbf{V}$ is generated by a finite set $\mathbf{X}$ with at most d vectors. The *rank* $\mathrm{rank}(\mathbf{V})$ of a vector space $\mathbf{V}$ is the minimal natural number $r \in \{0, \ldots, d\}$ such that there exists a finite set $\mathbf{X}$ with r vectors that generates $\mathbf{V}$. Note that $\mathrm{rank}(\mathbf{V}) \leq \mathrm{rank}(\mathbf{W})$ for every vector spaces $\mathbf{V} \subseteq \mathbf{W}$. Moreover if $\mathbf{V}$ is strictly included in $\mathbf{W}$ then $\mathrm{rank}(\mathbf{V}) < \mathrm{rank}(\mathbf{W})$.

The *(topological) closure* of a set $\mathbf{X} \subseteq \mathbb{Q}^d$ is the set $\overline{\mathbf{X}}$ of vectors $\mathbf{r} \in \mathbb{Q}^d$ such that for every $\epsilon \in \mathbb{Q}_{>0}$ there exists $\mathbf{x} \in \mathbf{X}$ satisfying $||\mathbf{r} - \mathbf{x}||_\infty < \epsilon$. A set $\mathbf{X}$ is said to be *closed* if $\overline{\mathbf{X}} = \mathbf{X}$. Note that $\overline{\mathbf{X}}$ is closed and this set is the minimal for the inclusion closed set that contains $\mathbf{X}$. Let us recall that a vector space $\mathbf{V}$ is closed and the closure of a conic set is a conic set. Since the classical topological interior of a conic set $\mathbf{C}$ is empty when the vector space generated by $\mathbf{C}$ is not equal to $\mathbb{Q}^d$ (the conic set is *degenerated*), we introduce the notion of interior of $\mathbf{C}$ relatively to the vector space $\mathbf{V} = \mathbf{C} - \mathbf{C}$. More precisely, a vector $\mathbf{c} \in \mathbf{C}$ is said to be in the *interior* of $\mathbf{C}$ if there exists $\epsilon \in \mathbb{Q}_{>0}$ such that $\mathbf{c} + \mathbf{v} \in \mathbf{C}$ for every $\mathbf{v} \in \mathbf{C} - \mathbf{C}$ satisfying $||\mathbf{v}||_\infty < \epsilon$. We denote by $\mathrm{int}(\mathbf{C})$ the set of *interior vectors* of $\mathbf{C}$. Let us recall that $\mathrm{int}(\mathbf{C})$ is non empty for every conic set $\mathbf{C}$, and $\overline{\mathbf{C}_1} = \overline{\mathbf{C}_2}$ if and only if $\mathrm{int}(\mathbf{C}_1) = \mathrm{int}(\mathbf{C}_2)$ for every conic sets $\mathbf{C}_1, \mathbf{C}_2$.

The following lemma characterizes the finitely generated cones. It proves that finitely generated conic sets are polytope.

Lemma 3.4. *Let $\mathbf{V} \subseteq \mathbb{Q}^d$ be a vector space. A conic set $\mathbf{C} \subseteq \mathbf{V}$ is finitely generated if and only if there exists a sequence $(\mathbf{h}_j)_{1 \leq j \leq k}$ of vectors $\mathbf{h}_j \in \mathbf{V} \backslash \{\mathbf{0}\}$ such that:*

$$\mathbf{C} = \bigcap_{j=1}^{k} \left\{ \mathbf{v} \in \mathbf{V} \mid \sum_{i=1}^{d} \mathbf{h}_j(i)\mathbf{v}(i) \geq 0 \right\}$$

Moreover in this case the following equality holds if and only if $\mathbf{V}$ is the vector space generated by $\mathbf{C}$:

$$\mathrm{int}(\mathbf{C}) = \bigcap_{j=1}^{k} \left\{ \mathbf{v} \in \mathbf{V} \mid \sum_{i=1}^{d} \mathbf{h}_j(i)\mathbf{v}(i) > 0 \right\}$$

Proof. This is a classical result of duality [Sch87]. □

Theorem 3.5. *A conic set $\mathbf{C} \subseteq \mathbb{Q}^d$ is polytope if and only if the conic set $\overline{\mathbf{C} \cap \mathbf{V}}$ is finitely generated for every vector space $\mathbf{V} \subseteq \mathbb{Q}^d$.*

Proof. Let us first consider a polytope conic set $\mathbf{C} \subseteq \mathbb{Q}^d$, let $\mathbf{V}$ be a vector space, and let us prove that $\overline{\mathbf{X}}$ is finitely generated where $\mathbf{X} = \mathbf{C} \cap \mathbf{V}$. Since $\mathbf{V}$ is generated by a finite set, we deduce that $\mathbf{V}$ and in particular $\mathbf{X}$ are definable in $\mathrm{FO}(\mathbb{Q}, +, \leq, 0, 1)$. Since this logic admits quantification elimination we deduce that there exists a quantifier free formula in this logic that denotes $\mathbf{X}$. Hence there exists a finite sequence $(A_j)_{1 \leq j \leq k}$ of finite sets $A_j \subseteq \mathbb{Q}^d \times \{>, \geq\} \times \mathbb{Q}$ such that $\mathbf{X} = \bigcup_{j=1}^{k} \mathbf{X}_j$ where:

$$\mathbf{X}_j = \bigcap_{(\mathbf{h}, \#, b) \in A_j} \left\{ \mathbf{x} \in \mathbb{Q}^d \mid \sum_{i=1}^{d} \mathbf{h}(i)\mathbf{x}(i) \# b \right\}$$

We can assume without loss of generality that $\mathbf{X}_j$ is non empty. Let us introduce the following set $\mathbf{R}_j$:

$$\mathbf{R}_j = \bigcap_{(\mathbf{h},\#,b)\in A_j} \left\{\mathbf{x} \in \mathbb{Q}^d \mid \sum_{i=1}^{d} \mathbf{h}(i)\mathbf{x}(i) \geq 0\right\}$$

Lemma 3.4 shows that $\mathbf{R}_j$ is finitely generated. In particular $\mathbf{R} = \sum_{j=1}^{k} \mathbf{R}_j$ is finitely generated. Thanks to Lemma 3.4, we deduce that $\mathbf{R}$ is closed. We are going to prove that $\overline{\mathbf{X}} = \mathbf{R}$. Let us first consider $\mathbf{x} \in \mathbf{X}$. For every $n \in \mathbb{N}$ we have $n\mathbf{x} \in \mathbf{X}$ since $\mathbf{X}$ is a conic set. Hence there exists $j \in \{1, \dots, k\}$ such that $n\mathbf{x} \in \mathbf{X}_j$ for an infinite number of $n \in \mathbb{N}$. We deduce that $\mathbf{x} \in \mathbf{R}_j$. Thus $\mathbf{X} \subseteq \mathbf{R}$ and we have proved that $\overline{\mathbf{X}} \subseteq \mathbf{R}$ by minimality of the closure of $\mathbf{X}$. For the converse inclusion, let $\mathbf{r} \in \mathbf{R}$. There exists a sequence $(\mathbf{r}_j)_{1\leq j\leq k}$ of vectors $\mathbf{r}_j \in \mathbf{R}_j$ such that $\mathbf{r} = \sum_{j=1}^{k} \mathbf{r}_j$. Since $\mathbf{X}_j$ is non empty, there exists $\mathbf{x}_j \in \mathbf{X}_j$. As $\mathbf{r}_j \in \mathbf{R}_j$ we deduce that $\mathbf{x}_j + \mathbb{Q}_{\geq 0}\mathbf{r}_j \subseteq \mathbf{X}_j$. Hence $\mathbf{x} + \sum_{j=1}^{k} \mathbb{Q}_{\geq 0}\mathbf{r}_j \subseteq \mathbf{X}$ where $\mathbf{x} = \sum_{j=1}^{k} \mathbf{x}_j$. In particular $\mathbf{x} + \mathbb{Q}_{\geq 0}\mathbf{r} \subseteq \mathbf{X}$. We deduce that for every $\epsilon \in \mathbb{Q}_{>0}$ we have $\epsilon\mathbf{x} + \mathbf{r} \in \mathbf{X}$. Therefore $\mathbf{r} \in \overline{\mathbf{X}}$. We have proved the other inclusion. Thus $\overline{\mathbf{X}} = \mathbf{R}$ is finitely generated.

Conversely, we prove by induction over r that the conic sets $\mathbf{C} \subseteq \mathbb{Q}^d$ such that $\text{rank}(\mathbf{C} - \mathbf{C}) \leq r$ and such that the conic set $\overline{\mathbf{C} \cap \mathbf{V}}$ is finitely generated for every vector space $\mathbf{V} \subseteq \mathbb{Q}^d$ are polytope. The case $r = 0$ is immediate since in this case $\mathbf{C} = \{\mathbf{0}\}$. Let us assume the induction proved for an integer $r \in \mathbb{N}$ and let us consider a conic set $\mathbf{C} \subseteq \mathbb{Q}^d$ such that $\text{rank}(\mathbf{C} - \mathbf{C}) \leq r + 1$ and such that the conic set $\overline{\mathbf{C} \cap \mathbf{V}}$ is finitely generated for every vector space $\mathbf{V} \subseteq \mathbb{Q}^d$. We introduce the vector space $\mathbf{W} = \mathbf{C} - \mathbf{C}$. Since $\overline{\mathbf{C}} = \overline{\mathbf{C} \cap \mathbf{V}}$ with $\mathbf{V} = \mathbb{Q}^d$, we deduce that $\overline{\mathbf{C}}$ is finitely generated. Lemma 3.4 shows that there exists a finite sequence $(\mathbf{h}_j)_{1\leq j\leq k}$ of vectors $\mathbf{h}_j \in \mathbf{W}\backslash\{\mathbf{0}\}$ such that the following equality holds:

$$\overline{\mathbf{C}} = \bigcap_{j=1}^{k} \left\{\mathbf{x} \in \mathbf{W} \mid \sum_{i=1}^{d} \mathbf{h}_j(i)\mathbf{x}(i) \geq 0\right\}$$

Since $\text{int}(\mathbf{C}) = \text{int}(\overline{\mathbf{C}})$ we get the following equality:

$$\text{int}(\mathbf{C}) = \bigcap_{j=1}^{k} \left\{\mathbf{x} \in \mathbf{W} \mid \sum_{i=1}^{d} \mathbf{h}_j(i)\mathbf{x}(i) > 0\right\}$$

In particular $\text{int}(\mathbf{C})$ is definable in $\text{FO}(\mathbb{Q}, +, \leq, 0, 1)$. As $\text{int}(\mathbf{C}) \subseteq \mathbf{C} \subseteq \overline{\mathbf{C}}$ we deduce the following decomposition where $\mathbf{W}_j = \{\mathbf{w} \in \mathbf{W} \mid \sum_{i=1}^{d} \mathbf{h}_j(i)\mathbf{w}(i) = 0\}$:

$$\mathbf{C} = \text{int}(\mathbf{C}) \bigcup_{j=1}^{k} (\mathbf{C} \cap \mathbf{W}_j)$$

Observe that $\mathbf{h}_j \in \mathbf{W}\backslash\mathbf{W}_j$ and in particular $\mathbf{W}_j$ is strictly included in $\mathbf{W}$. Thus $\text{rank}(\mathbf{W}_j) < \text{rank}(\mathbf{W}) \leq r + 1$. Note that $\mathbf{C}_j = \mathbf{C} \cap \mathbf{W}_j$ is a conic set such that $\text{rank}(\mathbf{C}_j - \mathbf{C}_j) \leq \text{rank}(\mathbf{W}_j) \leq r$ and such that $\overline{\mathbf{C}_j \cap \mathbf{V}}$ is a finitely generated conic set for every vector space $\mathbf{V}$. Thus by induction $\mathbf{C}_j$ is definable in $\text{FO}(\mathbb{Q}, +, \leq, 0, 1)$. We deduce that $\mathbf{C}$ is polytope. We have proved the induction. □

4. Presburger Sets, Lambert Sets, And Petri Sets

In this section we introduce the *Presburger* sets, *Lambert* Sets, and *Petri* Sets.

A *periodic set* is a subset $\mathbf{P} \subseteq \mathbb{Z}^d$ such that $\mathbf{0} \in \mathbf{P}$ and such that $\mathbf{P} + \mathbf{P} \subseteq \mathbf{P}$. A periodic set $\mathbf{P}$ is said to be *finitely generated* if there exists a finite sequence $\mathbf{p}_1, \dots, \mathbf{p}_k$ of vectors $\mathbf{p}_j \in \mathbf{P}$ such that $\mathbf{P} = \mathbb{N}\mathbf{p}_1 + \dots + \mathbb{N}\mathbf{p}_k$. A subset $\mathbf{S} \subseteq \mathbb{Z}^d$ is called a *Presburger set* if it can be denoted by a formula in the Presburger arithmetic $\text{FO}(\mathbb{Z}, +, \leq, 0, 1)$. Let us recall [GS66] that a subset $\mathbf{S} \subseteq \mathbb{Z}^d$ is Presburger if and only if it is a finite union of sets $\mathbf{b} + \mathbf{P}$ where $\mathbf{b} \in \mathbb{Z}^d$ and $\mathbf{P} \subseteq \mathbb{Z}^d$ is a finitely generated periodic set. The class of Lambert sets is obtained by weakening the finiteness property of the periodic sets $\mathbf{P}$.

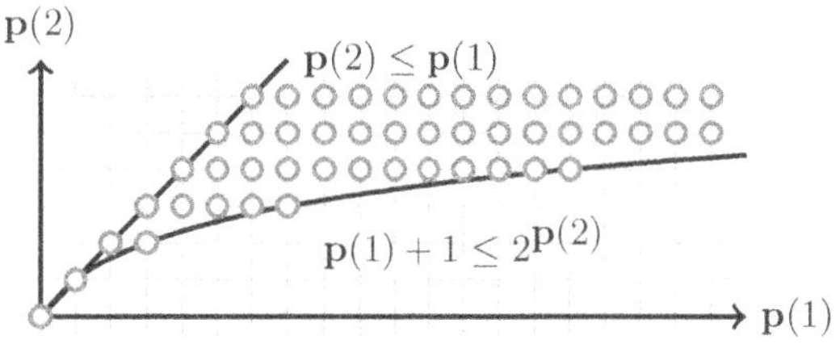

Figure 1. A polytope periodic set.

Definition 4.1. *A periodic set $\mathbf{P}$ is said to be* polytope *if the conic set $\mathbb{Q}_{\geq 0}\mathbf{P}$ is polytope.*

Remark 4.2. *Every finitely generated periodic set $\mathbf{P}$ is polytope since in this case $\mathbb{Q}_{\geq 0}\mathbf{P}$ is a finitely generated conic set and in particular a polytope conic set.*

Example 4.3. *The periodic set $\mathbf{P} = \{\mathbf{p} \in \mathbb{N}^2 \mid \mathbf{p}(1) \leq \sqrt{2}\mathbf{p}(2)\}$ is not polytope.*

Example 4.4. *The periodic set $\mathbf{P} = \{\mathbf{p} \in \mathbb{N}^2 \mid \mathbf{p}(2) \leq \mathbf{p}(1) \leq 2^{\mathbf{p}(2)} - 1\}$ is represented in Figure 1. Observe that $\mathbb{Q}_{\geq 0}\mathbf{P} = \{\mathbf{0}\} \cup \{\mathbf{c} \in \mathbb{Q}^2_{>0} \mid \mathbf{p}(2) \leq \mathbf{p}(1)\}$ is a polytope conic set. Thus $\mathbf{P}$ is a polytope periodic set.*

The following lemma shows that the class of polytope periodic sets is stable by finite intersections.

Lemma 4.5. *We have $(\mathbb{Q}_{\geq 0}\mathbf{P}_1) \cap (\mathbb{Q}_{\geq 0}\mathbf{P}_2) = \mathbb{Q}_{\geq 0}(\mathbf{P}_1 \cap \mathbf{P}_2)$ for every periodic sets $\mathbf{P}_1, \mathbf{P}_2 \subseteq \mathbb{Z}^d$.*

Proof. Observe that $\mathbf{P}_1 \subseteq \mathbb{Q}_{\geq 0}\mathbf{P}_1$ and $\mathbf{P}_2 \subseteq \mathbb{Q}_{\geq 0}\mathbf{P}_2$. Hence $\mathbf{P}_1 \cap \mathbf{P}_2 \subseteq \mathbf{C}$ where $\mathbf{C} = (\mathbb{Q}_{\geq 0}\mathbf{P}_1) \cap (\mathbb{Q}_{\geq 0}\mathbf{P}_2)$. As $\mathbf{C}$ is a conic set we deduce that $\mathbb{Q}_{\geq 0}(\mathbf{P}_1 \cap \mathbf{P}_2) \subseteq \mathbf{C}$. For the converse inclusion. Let $\mathbf{c} \in \mathbf{C}$. Since $\mathbf{c} \in \mathbb{Q}_{\geq 0}\mathbf{P}_1$, there exists $\lambda_1 \in \mathbb{Q}_{\geq 0}$ such that $\mathbf{c} \in \lambda_1\mathbf{P}_1$. Symmetrically there exists $\lambda_2 \in \mathbb{Q}_{\geq 0}$ such that $\mathbf{c} \in \lambda_2\mathbf{P}_2$. Let $n_1, n_2 \in \mathbb{N}_{>0}$ such that $n_1\lambda_1 \in \mathbb{N}$ and $n_2\lambda_2 \in \mathbb{N}$. Let $n = n_1 n_2$ and observe that $n\mathbf{c} \in n_2(n_1\lambda_1)\mathbf{P}_1 \subseteq \mathbf{P}_1$ since $\mathbf{P}_1$ is a periodic set. Symmetrically $n\mathbf{c} \in \mathbf{P}_2$. We have proved that $n\mathbf{c} \in \mathbf{P}_1 \cap \mathbf{P}_2$. Thus $\mathbf{c} \in \mathbb{Q}_{\geq 0}(\mathbf{P}_1 \cap \mathbf{P}_2)$ and we get the other inclusion. □

Lambert sets and *Petri sets* are central in this paper.

Definition 4.6. *A* Lambert set *$\mathbf{L} \subseteq \mathbb{Z}^d$ is a finite union of sets $\mathbf{b} + \mathbf{P}$ where $\mathbf{b} \in \mathbb{Z}^d$ and $\mathbf{P} \subseteq \mathbb{Z}^d$ is a polytope periodic set.*

Definition 4.7. *A* Petri set *is a subset $\mathbf{X} \subseteq \mathbb{Z}^d$ such that $\mathbf{X} \cap \mathbf{S}$ is a Lambert set for every Presburger set $\mathbf{S} \subseteq \mathbb{Z}^d$.*

Example 4.8. *Let us consider the periodic set $\mathbf{P} = \{(0,0)\} \cup \{(2^n, 1) \mid n \in \mathbb{N}\} \cup ((1,2) + \mathbb{N}^2)$. Observe that $\mathbb{Q}_{\geq 0}\mathbf{P}$ is the polytope conic set $\{(0,0)\} \cup \mathbb{Q}^2_{>0}$. We deduce that $\mathbf{P}$ is a Lambert set. Note that $\mathbf{P}$ is not a Petri set since $\mathbf{P} \cap (\mathbb{N} \times \{1\}) = \{(2^n, 1) \mid n \in \mathbb{N}\}$ is not a Lambert set.*

The class of Petri sets is between the class of Presburger sets and the class of Lambert sets. The previous Example 4.8 shows that the class of Petri sets is strictly included in the class of Lambert sets. The strict inclusion of the class of Presburger sets into the class of

Petri sets will be a direct consequence of a stronger result proved in this paper. In fact the *reachability relation of a Vector Addition System is proved to be a Petri relation* and we know that in general such a relation is not Presburger.

5. Linearizations

The linearization of a periodic set $\mathbf{P} \subseteq \mathbb{Z}^d$ is the periodic set $\text{lin}(\mathbf{P})$ defined by the following equality:

$$\text{lin}(\mathbf{P}) = (\mathbf{P} - \mathbf{P}) \cap \overline{\mathbb{Q}_{\geq 0}\mathbf{P}}$$

Lemma 5.1. *The linearization of a polytope periodic set is finitely generated.*

Proof. Let $\mathbf{V}$ be the vector space generated by $\mathbf{P}$ and let us introduce the conic set $\mathbf{C} = \overline{\mathbb{Q}_{\geq 0}\mathbf{P}}$. Note that $\mathbb{Q}_{\geq 0}\mathbf{P} \subseteq \mathbf{V}$ and since $\mathbf{V}$ is closed we get $\mathbf{C} \subseteq \mathbf{V}$. As $\mathbb{Q}_{\geq 0}\mathbf{P}$ is a polytope conic set we deduce that $\mathbf{C}$ is finitely generated. Hence there exists $\mathbf{c}_1, \ldots, \mathbf{c}_k \in \mathbf{C}$ such that $\mathbf{C} = \mathbb{Q}_{\geq 0}\mathbf{c}_1 + \cdots + \mathbb{Q}_{\geq 0}\mathbf{c}_k$. As $\mathbf{c}_j \in \mathbf{C} \subseteq \mathbf{V} = \mathbb{Q}_{\geq 0}\mathbf{P} - \mathbb{Q}_{\geq 0}\mathbf{P}$, by replacing $\mathbf{c}_j$ by a vector in $\mathbb{N}_{>0}\mathbf{c}_j$ we can assume that $\mathbf{c}_j \in \mathbf{P} - \mathbf{P}$ for every $j \in \{1, \ldots, k\}$.

We introduce the following set $\mathbf{R}$:

$$\mathbf{R} = \left\{ \mathbf{r} \in \mathbf{P} - \mathbf{P} \mid \mathbf{r} = \sum_{j=1}^{k} \lambda_j \mathbf{c}_j \;\; \lambda_j \in \mathbb{Q} \;\; 0 \leq \lambda_j < 1 \right\}$$

We observe that every vector $\mathbf{r} \in \mathbf{R}$ satisfies $||\mathbf{r}||_\infty \leq s$ where $s = \sum_{j=1}^{k} ||\mathbf{c}_j||_\infty$. Hence $\mathbf{R} \subseteq \{-s, \ldots, s\}^d$ and we deduce that $\mathbf{R}$ is finite.

Let $\mathbf{L}$ be the periodic set generated by the finite set $\mathbf{R} \cup \{\mathbf{c}_1, \ldots, \mathbf{c}_k\}$. Since this finite set is included in $\text{lin}(\mathbf{P})$ we deduce that $\mathbf{L} \subseteq \text{lin}(\mathbf{P})$. Let us prove the converse inclusion. Let $\mathbf{x} \in \text{lin}(\mathbf{P})$. Since $\mathbf{x} \in \mathbf{C}$, there exists a sequence $(\mu_j)_{1 \leq j \leq k}$ of rational elements $\mu_j \in \mathbb{Q}_{\geq 0}$ such that $\mathbf{x} = \sum_{j=1}^{k} \mu_j \mathbf{c}_j$. Let us introduce $n_j \in \mathbb{N}$ such that $\lambda_j = \mu_j - n_j$ satisfies $0 \leq \lambda_j < 1$. Let $\mathbf{r} = \sum_{j=1}^{k} \lambda_j \mathbf{c}_j$. As $\mathbf{r} = \mathbf{x} - \sum_{j=1}^{k} n_j \mathbf{c}_j$ we get $\mathbf{r} \in \mathbf{P} - \mathbf{P}$. Thus $\mathbf{r} \in \mathbf{R}$. From $\mathbf{x} = \mathbf{r} + \sum_{j=1}^{k} n_j \mathbf{c}_j$ we get $\mathbf{x} \in \mathbf{L}$. We have proved that $\text{lin}(\mathbf{P}) = \mathbf{L}$ is finitely generated. □

We observe that if the intersection $(\mathbf{b}_1 + \mathbf{P}_1) \cap (\mathbf{b}_2 + \mathbf{P}_2)$ is empty where $\mathbf{b}_1, \mathbf{b}_2 \in \mathbb{Z}^d$ and $\mathbf{P}_1, \mathbf{P}_2 \subseteq \mathbb{Z}^d$ are two polytope periodic sets then the intersection $(\mathbf{b}_1 + \text{lin}(\mathbf{P}_1)) \cap (\mathbf{b}_2 + \text{lin}(\mathbf{P}_2))$ may be non empty. In this section we show that a dimension is strictly decreasing.

Let us first introduce our definition of dimension. The *dimension* $\dim(\mathbf{X})$ of a non-empty set $\mathbf{X} \subseteq \mathbb{Z}^d$ is the minimal integer $r \in \{0, \ldots, d\}$ such that there exists $k \in \mathbb{N}_{>0}$, a sequence $(\mathbf{b}_j)_{1 \leq j \leq k}$ of vectors $\mathbf{b}_j \in \mathbb{Z}^d$, and a sequence $(\mathbf{V}_j)_{1 \leq j \leq k}$ of vector spaces $\mathbf{V}_j \subseteq \mathbb{Q}^d$ such that $\text{rank}(\mathbf{V}_j) \leq r$ and such that $\mathbf{X} \subseteq \bigcup_{j=1}^{k} \mathbf{b}_j + \mathbf{V}_j$. The dimension of the empty set is defined by $\dim(\emptyset) = -1$.

In the reminder of this section we prove the following Theorem 5.2. All other results or definitions introduced in this section are not used in the sequel.

Theorem 5.2. *Let $\mathbf{b}_1, \mathbf{b}_2 \in \mathbb{Z}^d$ and let $\mathbf{P}_1, \mathbf{P}_2$ be two polytope periodic sets such that the intersection $(\mathbf{b}_1 + \mathbf{P}_1) \cap (\mathbf{b}_2 + \mathbf{P}_2)$ is empty. The intersection $\mathbf{X} = (\mathbf{b}_1 + \text{lin}(\mathbf{P}_1)) \cap (\mathbf{b}_2 + \text{lin}(\mathbf{P}_2))$ satisfies:*

$$\dim(\mathbf{X}) < \max\{\dim(\mathbf{b}_1 + \mathbf{P}_1), \dim(\mathbf{b}_2 + \mathbf{P}_2)\}$$

We first characterize the dimension of a periodic set.

Lemma 5.3. *Let $\mathbf{V}$ be the vector space generated by a periodic set $\mathbf{P}$. Then $\text{rank}(\mathbf{V}) = \dim(\mathbf{P})$.*

Proof. Let $\mathbf{P}$ be a periodic set and let us first prove by induction over $k \in \mathbb{N}_{>0}$ that $\mathbf{P} \subseteq \bigcup_{j=1}^{k} \mathbf{V}_j$ implies that there exists $j \in \{1, \ldots, k\}$ such that $\mathbf{P} \subseteq \mathbf{V}_j$ for every sequence $(\mathbf{V}_j)_{1 \leq j \leq k}$ of vector spaces $\mathbf{V}_j \subseteq \mathbb{Q}^d$. The case $k = 1$ is immediate. Assume the property proved for an integer $k \in \mathbb{N}_{>0}$ and let us assume that $\mathbf{P} \subseteq \bigcup_{j=1}^{k+1} \mathbf{V}_j$. If $\mathbf{P} \subseteq \mathbf{V}_{k+1}$ the property is proved. So we can assume that there exists $\mathbf{p} \in \mathbf{P} \backslash \mathbf{V}_{k+1}$. Let us prove that $\mathbf{P} \subseteq \bigcup_{j=1}^{k} \mathbf{V}_j$. We consider $\mathbf{x} \in \mathbf{P}$. Observe that if $\mathbf{x} \notin \mathbf{V}_{k+1}$ then $\mathbf{x} \in \bigcup_{j=1}^{k} \mathbf{V}_j$. So we can assume that $\mathbf{x} \in \mathbf{V}_{k+1}$. We observe that $\mathbf{p} + n\mathbf{x} \in \mathbf{P}$ for every $n \in \mathbb{N}$ since the set $\mathbf{P}$ is periodic. We deduce that there exists $j \in \{1, \ldots, k+1\}$ such that $\mathbf{p} + n\mathbf{x} \in \mathbf{V}_j$. Naturally this integer j depends on n. However, since $\{1, \ldots, k+1\}$ is finite whereas $\mathbb{N}$ is infinite, there exists $j \in \{1, \ldots, k+1\}$ and $n < n'$ in $\mathbb{N}$ such that $\mathbf{p} + n\mathbf{x}$ and $\mathbf{p} + n'\mathbf{x}$ are both in $\mathbf{V}_j$. As $\mathbf{V}_j$ is a vector space, we deduce that $n'(\mathbf{p} + n\mathbf{x}) - n(\mathbf{p} + n'\mathbf{x})$ is in $\mathbf{V}_j$. Hence $\mathbf{p} \in \mathbf{V}_j$. As $\mathbf{p} \notin \mathbf{V}_{k+1}$ we deduce that $j \neq k+1$. As $\mathbf{V}_j$ is a vector space we deduce that $(\mathbf{p} + n'\mathbf{x}) - (\mathbf{p} + n\mathbf{x}) \in \mathbf{V}_j$. Hence $\mathbf{x} \in \mathbf{V}_j$. We have proved that $\mathbf{x} \in \bigcup_{j=1}^{k} \mathbf{V}_j$. Thus $\mathbf{P} \subseteq \bigcup_{j=1}^{k} \mathbf{V}_j$ and by induction there exists $j \in \{1, \ldots, k\}$ such that $\mathbf{P} \subseteq \mathbf{V}_j$. We have proved the induction.

Now, let us prove the lemma. We consider a periodic set $\mathbf{P}$ and we let $\mathbf{V}$ be the vector space generated by this set. Since $\mathbf{P} \subseteq \mathbf{V}$ we deduce that $\dim(\mathbf{P}) \leq \text{rank}(\mathbf{V})$. For the converse inclusion, since $\mathbf{P}$ is non empty we deduce that $\mathbf{P} \subseteq \bigcup_{j=1}^{k} \mathbf{b}_j + \mathbf{V}_j$ where $k \in \mathbb{N}_{>0}$, $\mathbf{b}_j \in \mathbb{Z}^d$ and $\mathbf{V}_j \subseteq \mathbb{Q}^d$ is a vector space such that $\text{rank}(\mathbf{V}_j) \leq \dim(\mathbf{P})$. Let us consider the set $J = \{j \in \{1, \ldots, k\} \mid \mathbf{b}_j \in \mathbf{V}_j\}$ and let us prove that $\mathbf{P} \subseteq \bigcup_{j \in J} \mathbf{V}_j$. Let $\mathbf{p} \in \mathbf{P}$ and $n \in \mathbb{N}$. Since $n\mathbf{p} \in \mathbf{P}$ there exists $j \in \{1, \ldots, k\}$ such that $n\mathbf{p} \in \mathbf{b}_j + \mathbf{V}_j$. Hence there exists $j \in \{1, \ldots, k\}$ and $n < n'$ in $\mathbb{N}$ such that $n\mathbf{p}$ and $n'\mathbf{p}$ are both in $\mathbf{b}_j + \mathbf{V}_j$. As $\mathbf{V}_j$ is a vector space we deduce that $n'\mathbf{p} - n\mathbf{p} \in \mathbf{V}_j$. Thus $\mathbf{p} \in \mathbf{V}_j$. Moreover as $\mathbf{b}_j \in n\mathbf{p} - \mathbf{V}_j \subseteq \mathbf{V}_j$ we deduce that $j \in J$. We have prove the inclusion $\mathbf{P} \subseteq \bigcup_{j \in J} \mathbf{V}_j$. From the previous paragraph we deduce that there exists $j \in J$ such that $\mathbf{P} \subseteq \mathbf{V}_j$. By minimality of the vector space generated by $\mathbf{P}$ we get $\mathbf{V} \subseteq \mathbf{V}_j$. Hence $\text{rank}(\mathbf{V}) \leq \text{rank}(\mathbf{V}_j)$. Since $\text{rank}(\mathbf{V}_j) \leq \dim(\mathbf{P})$ we have proved the inequality $\text{rank}(\mathbf{V}) \leq \dim(\mathbf{P})$. □

Next we prove a separation property.

Lemma 5.4. *Let $\mathbf{C}_{\leq}$ and $\mathbf{C}_{\geq}$ be two finitely generated conic sets that generates the same vector space $\mathbf{V}$ and such that the vector space generated by $\mathbf{C}_{\leq} \cap \mathbf{C}_{\geq}$ is strictly included in $\mathbf{V}$. Then there exists a vector $\mathbf{h} \in \mathbf{V} \backslash \{\mathbf{0}\}$ such that for every $\# \in \{\leq, \geq\}$, we have:*

$$\mathbf{C}_\# \subseteq \left\{ \mathbf{v} \in \mathbf{V} \mid \sum_{i=1}^{d} \mathbf{h}(i)\mathbf{v}(i) \# 0 \right\}$$

Proof. Lemma 3.4 shows that there exists two finite sets $\mathbf{H}_{\leq}, \mathbf{H}_{\geq}$ included in $\mathbf{V} \backslash \{\mathbf{0}\}$ such that:

$$\mathbf{C}_\# = \bigcap_{\mathbf{h} \in \mathbf{H}_\#} \left\{ \mathbf{v} \in \mathbf{V} \mid \sum_{i=1}^{d} \mathbf{h}(i)\mathbf{v}(i) \geq 0 \right\}$$

$$\text{int}(\mathbf{C}_\#) = \bigcap_{\mathbf{h} \in \mathbf{H}_\#} \left\{ \mathbf{v} \in \mathbf{V} \mid \sum_{i=1}^{d} \mathbf{h}(i)\mathbf{v}(i) > 0 \right\}$$

Assume by contradiction that the intersection $\text{int}(\mathbf{C}_{\leq}) \cap \text{int}(\mathbf{C}_{\geq})$ is non empty and let $\mathbf{c}$ be a vector in this set. Observe that there exists $\epsilon \in \mathbb{Q}_{>0}$ such that $\mathbf{c} + \mathbf{v} \in \mathbf{C}_{\leq} \cap \mathbf{C}_{\geq}$ for every $\mathbf{v} \in \mathbf{V}$ such that $||\mathbf{v}||_\infty < \epsilon$. We deduce that the vector space generated by $\mathbf{C}_{\leq} \cap \mathbf{C}_{\geq}$ contains $\mathbf{V}$ and we get a contradiction.

We deduce that the following intersection is empty where $\mathbf{H} = \mathbf{H}_{\leq} \cup \mathbf{H}_{\geq}$

$$\bigcap_{\mathbf{h} \in \mathbf{H}} \left\{ \mathbf{v} \in \mathbf{V} \mid \sum_{i=1}^{d} \mathbf{h}(i)\mathbf{v}(i) > 0 \right\}$$

The Farkas's lemma [Sch87] shows that there exists a non-zero function $f : \mathbf{H} \to \mathbb{Q}_{\geq 0}$ such that $\sum_{\mathbf{h} \in \mathbf{H}} f(\mathbf{h})\mathbf{h} = \mathbf{0}$. Let us introduce $\mathbf{a} = \sum_{\mathbf{h} \in \mathbf{H}_{\geq}} f(\mathbf{h})\mathbf{h}$ and $\mathbf{b} = \sum_{\mathbf{h} \in \mathbf{H} \setminus \mathbf{H}_{\geq}} f(\mathbf{h})\mathbf{h}$. Assume by contradiction that $\mathbf{a} = \mathbf{0}$. Since $\mathbf{a} + \mathbf{b} = \mathbf{0}$ we deduce that $\mathbf{b} = \mathbf{0}$. As f is not the zero function, there exists $\mathbf{h} \in \mathbf{H}$ such that $f(\mathbf{h}) \neq 0$. Note that either $\mathbf{h} \in \mathbf{H}_{\geq}$ or $\mathbf{h} \in \mathbf{H} \setminus \mathbf{H}_{\geq}$. In the first case we deduce that $\text{int}(\mathbf{C}_{\geq})$ is empty and in the second case we deduce that $\text{int}(\mathbf{C}_{\leq})$ is empty. Since both cases are impossible we get a contradiction. Thus $\mathbf{a} \neq \mathbf{0}$. For every $\mathbf{c} \in \text{int}(\mathbf{C}_{\geq})$ we have $\sum_{i=1}^{d} \mathbf{a}(i)\mathbf{c}(i) \geq 0$. Since the set $\{\mathbf{c} \in \mathbb{Q}^d \mid \sum_{i=1}^{d} \mathbf{a}(i)\mathbf{c}(i) \geq 0\}$ is closed we deduce that for every $\mathbf{c} \in \overline{\text{int}(\mathbf{C}_{\geq})} = \mathbf{C}_{\geq}$ the same inequality holds. Now let us consider $\mathbf{c} \in \text{int}(\mathbf{C}_{\leq})$. In this case $\sum_{i=1}^{d} \mathbf{b}(i)\mathbf{c}(i) \geq 0$. Since $\mathbf{a} + \mathbf{b} = \mathbf{0}$ we get $\sum_{i=1}^{d} \mathbf{a}(i)\mathbf{c}(i) \leq 0$. We deduce that this inequality holds for every $\mathbf{c} \in \mathbf{C}_{\leq}$. □

Remark 5.5. *The previous Lemma 5.4 is wrong if we remove the finitely generated condition on the conic sets $\mathbf{C}_{\leq}$ and $\mathbf{C}_{\geq}$. In fact let us consider the conic sets $\mathbf{C}_{\leq} = \{\mathbf{x} \in \mathbb{Q}_{\geq 0}^2 \mid \mathbf{x}(1) \leq \sqrt{2}\mathbf{x}(2)\}$ and $\mathbf{C}_{\geq} = \{\mathbf{x} \in \mathbb{Q}_{\geq 0}^2 \mid \mathbf{x}(2) \geq \sqrt{2}\mathbf{x}(2)\}$. Observe that $\mathbf{C}_{\leq} \cap \mathbf{C}_{\geq} = \{\mathbf{0}\}$. Hence the vector space generated by the intersection is strictly included in $\mathbb{Q}^2$. However there does not exist a vector $\mathbf{a} \in \mathbb{Q}^2 \setminus \{\mathbf{0}\}$ satisfying the separation property required by Lemma 5.4. This problem can be overcome by introducing the vector spaces of $\mathbb{R}^d$. We do not introduce this extension to simplify the presentation.*

We can now provide a proof of Theorem 5.2. We consider two vectors $\mathbf{b}_1, \mathbf{b}_2 \in \mathbb{Z}^d$ and two periodic sets $\mathbf{P}_1, \mathbf{P}_2 \subseteq \mathbb{Z}^d$ such that $(\mathbf{b}_1 + \mathbf{P}_1) \cap (\mathbf{b}_2 + \mathbf{P}_2) = \emptyset$. We introduce the intersection $\mathbf{X} = (\mathbf{b}_1 + \text{lin}(\mathbf{P}_1)) \cap (\mathbf{b}_2 + \text{lin}(\mathbf{P}_2))$. Observe that if $\mathbf{X}$ is empty the theorem is proved. So we can assume that there exists a vector $\mathbf{b}$ in this intersection. Let us denote by $\mathbf{V}_1$ and $\mathbf{V}_2$ the vector spaces generated by $\mathbf{P}_1$ and $\mathbf{P}_2$. Lemma 5.3 shows that $\text{rank}(\mathbf{V}_j) = \dim(\mathbf{P}_j)$ and from $\dim(\mathbf{b}_j + \mathbf{P}_j) = \dim(\mathbf{P}_j)$ we deduce that $\dim(\mathbf{b}_j + \mathbf{P}_j) = \text{rank}(\mathbf{V}_j)$. As $\mathbf{X}$ is included in $\mathbf{b} + \mathbf{V}$ where $\mathbf{V} = \mathbf{V}_1 \cap \mathbf{V}_2$, we deduce that if $\mathbf{V}$ is strictly included in $\mathbf{V}_j$ for one $j \in \{1, 2\}$ then $\dim(\mathbf{X}) \leq \text{rank}(\mathbf{V}) < \text{rank}(\mathbf{V}_j) = \dim(\mathbf{b}_j + \mathbf{P}_j)$ and the theorem is proved. So we can assume that $\mathbf{V}_1 = \mathbf{V}_2 = \mathbf{V}$. Let us consider the conic sets $\mathbf{C}_1 = \mathbb{Q}_{\geq 0}\mathbf{P}_1$ and $\mathbf{C}_2 = \mathbb{Q}_{\geq 0}\mathbf{P}_2$. Since $\mathbf{P}_1$ and $\mathbf{P}_2$ are polytope periodic sets, we deduce that $\mathbf{C}_1$ and $\mathbf{C}_2$ are finitely generated conic sets. Note that $\mathbf{C}_1, \mathbf{C}_2 \subseteq \mathbf{V}$. We introduce the intersection $\mathbf{C} = \mathbf{C}_1 \cap \mathbf{C}_2$.

Assume by contradiction that the vector space generated by $\mathbf{C}$ is equal to $\mathbf{V}$. Let us consider a vector $\mathbf{c}$ in the interior of $\mathbf{C}$. The characterization given by Lemma 3.4 shows that in this case $\text{int}(\mathbf{C}) = \text{int}(\mathbf{C}_1) \cap \text{int}(\mathbf{C}_2)$. Since $\text{int}(\mathbf{C}_j) = \text{int}(\mathbb{Q}_{\geq 0}\mathbf{P}_j)$ we deduce that $\mathbf{c} \in (\mathbb{Q}_{\geq 0}\mathbf{P}_1) \cap (\mathbb{Q}_{\geq 0}\mathbf{P}_2)$. Lemma 4.5 shows that $\mathbf{c} \in \mathbb{Q}_{\geq 0}(\mathbf{P}_1 \cap \mathbf{P}_2)$. By replacing $\mathbf{c}$ be a vector in $\mathbb{N}_{>0}\mathbf{c}$ we can assume that $\mathbf{c} \in \mathbf{P}_1 \cap \mathbf{P}_2$.

Let us prove that there exists $k_1 \in \mathbb{N}$ such that $\mathbf{b} + k_1\mathbf{c} \in \mathbf{b}_1 + \mathbf{P}_1$. From $\mathbf{b} \in \mathbf{b}_1 + \text{lin}(\mathbf{P}_1)$ we deduce that there exists $\mathbf{p}_1, \mathbf{p}_1' \in \mathbf{P}_1$ such that $\mathbf{b} = \mathbf{b}_1 + \mathbf{p}_1 - \mathbf{p}_1'$. Since $-\mathbf{p}_1'$ is in the vector space generated by $\mathbf{C}$ and $\mathbf{c}$ is in the interior of $\mathbf{C}$, there exists $n_1 \in \mathbb{N}$ large enough such that $n_1\mathbf{c} + (-\mathbf{p}_1') \in \mathbf{C}_1$. Hence there exists $n_1' \in \mathbb{N}_{>0}$ such that $n_1 n_1'\mathbf{c} - n_1'\mathbf{p}_1' \in \mathbf{P}_1$. Thus $n_1 n_1'\mathbf{c} - \mathbf{p}_1' \in (n_1' - 1)\mathbf{p}_1' + \mathbf{P}_1 \subseteq \mathbf{P}_1$. Hence $\mathbf{b} + k_1\mathbf{c} \in \mathbf{b}_1 + \mathbf{P}_1$ with $k_1 = n_1 n_1'$.

Symmetrically we deduce that there exists $k_2 \in \mathbb{N}$ such that $\mathbf{b} + k_2\mathbf{c} \in \mathbf{b}_2 + \mathbf{P}_2$. We have proved that $\mathbf{b} + (k_1 + k_2)\mathbf{c} \in (\mathbf{b}_1 + \mathbf{P}_1) \cap (\mathbf{b}_2 + \mathbf{P}_2)$ and we get a contradiction since this intersection is supposed to be empty.

We deduce that the vector space generated by $\mathbf{C}$ is strictly included in $\mathbf{V}$. Lemma 5.4 shows that there exists a vector $\mathbf{h} \in \mathbf{V} \setminus \{\mathbf{0}\}$ such that:

$$\mathbf{C}_1 \subseteq \left\{ \mathbf{v} \in \mathbf{V} \mid \sum_{i=1}^{d} \mathbf{h}(i)\mathbf{v}(i) \geq 0 \right\}$$

$$\mathbf{C}_2 \subseteq \left\{ \mathbf{v} \in \mathbf{V} \mid \sum_{i=1}^{d} \mathbf{h}(i)\mathbf{v}(i) \leq 0 \right\}$$

By replacing $\mathbf{h}$ by a vector in $\mathbb{N}_{>0}\mathbf{h}$ we can assume that $\mathbf{h} \in \mathbb{Z}^d$. Now let us consider $\mathbf{x} \in \mathbf{X}$. Since $\mathbf{x} - \mathbf{b}_1 \in \mathbf{C}_1$ we deduce that $\sum_{i=1}^{d} \mathbf{h}(i)(\mathbf{x}(i) - \mathbf{b}_1(i)) \geq 0$ and since $\mathbf{x} - \mathbf{b}_2 \in \mathbf{C}_2$ we deduce that $\sum_{i=1}^{d} \mathbf{h}(i)(\mathbf{x}(i) - \mathbf{b}_2(i)) \leq 0$. We introduce the integers $z_1 = \sum_{i=1}^{d} \mathbf{h}(i)\mathbf{b}_1(i)$ and $z_2 = \sum_{i=1}^{d} \mathbf{h}(i)\mathbf{b}_2(i)$. We have proved that $\mathbf{X}$ can be decomposed into a finite union of slices $\mathbf{X} = \bigcup_{z=z_1}^{z_2} \mathbf{X}_z$ where:

$$\mathbf{X}_z = \left\{ \mathbf{x} \in \mathbf{X} \mid \sum_{i=1}^{d} \mathbf{h}(i)\mathbf{x}(i) = z \right\}$$

Let us prove that $\dim(\mathbf{X}_z) < \text{rank}(\mathbf{V})$. If $\mathbf{X}_z$ is empty the relation is immediate. If $\mathbf{X}_z$ is non empty let us consider $\mathbf{x} \in \mathbf{X}_z$ and observe that $\mathbf{X}_z \subseteq \mathbf{x} + \mathbf{W}$ where:

$$\mathbf{W} = \left\{ \mathbf{v} \in \mathbf{V} \mid \sum_{i=1}^{d} \mathbf{a}(i)\mathbf{v}(i) = 0 \right\}$$

Note that $\mathbf{h} \in \mathbf{V} \setminus \mathbf{W}$. We deduce that $\mathbf{W}$ is strictly included in $\mathbf{V}$ and in particular $\text{rank}(\mathbf{W}) < \text{rank}(\mathbf{V})$. Hence $\dim(\mathbf{X}_z) < \text{rank}(\mathbf{V})$.

From $\mathbf{X} = \bigcup_{z=z_1}^{z_2} \mathbf{X}_z$ and $\dim(\mathbf{X}_z) < \text{rank}(\mathbf{V})$ for every z, we deduce that $\dim(\mathbf{X}) < \text{rank}(\mathbf{V})$ and the theorem is proved.

6. Presburger Invariants

Given a relation R over $\mathbb{Z}^d$ and two sets $\mathbf{X}, \mathbf{Y} \subseteq \mathbb{Z}^d$ we introduce the *forward image* $\text{post}_R(\mathbf{X})$ and the *backward image* $\text{pre}_R(\mathbf{Y})$ defined by the following equalities:

$$\begin{cases} \text{post}_R(\mathbf{X}) & = \bigcup_{\mathbf{x} \in \mathbf{X}} \{\mathbf{y} \in \mathbb{Z}^d \mid (\mathbf{x}, \mathbf{y}) \in R\} \\ \text{pre}_R(\mathbf{Y}) & = \bigcup_{\mathbf{y} \in \mathbf{Y}} \{\mathbf{x} \in \mathbb{Z}^d \mid (\mathbf{x}, \mathbf{y}) \in R\} \end{cases}$$

We say that a set $\mathbf{X} \subseteq \mathbb{Z}^d$ is a *forward invariant* for R if $\text{post}_R(\mathbf{X}) \subseteq \mathbf{X}$ and we say that a set $\mathbf{Y} \subseteq \mathbb{Z}^d$ is a *backward invariant* for R if $\text{pre}_R(\mathbf{Y}) \subseteq \mathbf{Y}$. In the reminder of this section we prove the following Theorem 6.1. All other results or definitions introduced in this section are not used in the sequel.

Theorem 6.1. *Let R^* be a reflexive and transitive Petri relation over $\mathbb{Z}^d$ and let $\mathbf{X}, \mathbf{Y} \subseteq \mathbb{Z}^d$ be two Presburger sets such that $R^* \cap (\mathbf{X} \times \mathbf{Y})$ is empty. There exists a partition of $\mathbb{Z}^d$ into a Presburger forward invariant that contains $\mathbf{X}$ and a Presburger backward invariant that contains $\mathbf{Y}$.*

We first prove the following lemma.

Lemma 6.2. *The sets $\text{post}_R(\mathbf{X})$ and $\text{pre}_R(\mathbf{Y})$ are Petri sets for every Petri relation $R \subseteq \mathbb{Z}^d \times \mathbb{Z}^d$ and for every Presburger sets $\mathbf{X}, \mathbf{Y} \subseteq \mathbb{Z}^d$*

Proof. Let us first prove that $\text{post}_R(\mathbf{X})$ is a Petri set. We consider a Presburger set $\mathbf{S} \subseteq \mathbb{Z}^d$. Observe that $\mathbf{X} \times \mathbf{S}$ is a Presburger relation. Since R is a Petri relation we deduce that $R \cap (\mathbf{X} \times \mathbf{S})$ is a Lambert relation. Hence this set can be decomposed into a finite union $\bigcup_{j=1}^{k}(\mathbf{a}_j, \mathbf{b}_j)+R_j$ with $k \in \mathbb{N}$, $(\mathbf{a}_j, \mathbf{b}_j) \in \mathbb{Z}^d \times \mathbb{Z}^d$ and R_j is a polytope periodic relation. We deduce that $\text{post}_R(\mathbf{X}) \cap \mathbf{S} = \bigcup_{j=1}^{k} \mathbf{b}_j + \mathbf{P}_j$ where $\mathbf{P}_j = \{\mathbf{v} \in \mathbb{Z}^d \mid \exists(\mathbf{u}, \mathbf{v}) \in R_j\}$. Since R_j is a periodic relation we deduce that $\mathbf{P}_j$ is a periodic set. Moreover since $\mathbb{Q}_{\geq 0}R_j$ is polytope we deduce that $\mathbf{C}_j = \{\mathbf{v} \in \mathbb{Q}^d \mid \exists(\mathbf{u}, \mathbf{v}) \in \mathbb{Q}_{\geq 0}R_j\}$ is polytope. Let us prove that $\mathbb{Q}_{\geq 0}\mathbf{P}_j = \mathbf{C}_j$. By construction we have $\mathbf{P}_j \subseteq \mathbf{C}_j$. Since $\mathbf{C}_j$ is conic we deduce that $\mathbb{Q}_{\geq 0}\mathbf{P}_j \subseteq \mathbf{C}_j$. For the converse inclusion let $\mathbf{v} \in \mathbf{C}_j$. There exists $\mathbf{u} \in \mathbb{Q}^d$ such that $(\mathbf{u}, \mathbf{v}) \in \mathbb{Q}_{\geq 0}R_j$. Hence there exists $\lambda \in \mathbb{Q}_{\geq 0}$ such that $(\mathbf{u}, \mathbf{v}) \in \lambda \mathbf{R}_j$. Let us consider $n \in \mathbb{N}_{>0}$ such that $n\lambda_j \in \mathbb{N}$ and observe that $(n\mathbf{u}, n\mathbf{v}) \in (n\lambda)R_j \subseteq R_j$ since R_j is periodic. Thus $n\mathbf{v} \in \mathbf{P}_j$ and we have proved that $\mathbf{v} \in \mathbb{Q}_{\geq 0}\mathbf{P}_j$. Hence $\mathbb{Q}_{\geq 0}\mathbf{P}_j = \mathbf{C}_j$ is a polytope conic set and we have proved that $\text{post}_R(\mathbf{X}) \cap \mathbf{S}$ is a Lambert set for every Presburger set $\mathbf{S} \subseteq \mathbb{Z}^d$. Hence $\text{post}_R(\mathbf{X})$ is a Petri set. From $\text{pre}_R(\mathbf{Y}) = \text{post}_{R^{-1}}(\mathbf{Y})$ with $R^{-1} = \{(\mathbf{y}, \mathbf{x}) \mid (\mathbf{x}, \mathbf{y}) \in R\}$ we deduce that $\text{pre}_R(\mathbf{Y})$ is a Petri set. □

Now, let us prove Theorem 6.1. We consider a reflexive and transitive Petri relation R^*. We introduce the notion of *separators*. A *separator* is a couple $(\mathbf{X}, \mathbf{Y})$ of Presburger sets such that the intersection $R^* \cap (\mathbf{X} \times \mathbf{Y})$ is empty. Since R^* is reflexive observe that $\mathbf{X} \cap \mathbf{Y}$ is empty. The Presburger set $\mathbf{D} = \mathbb{Z}^d \backslash (\mathbf{X} \cup \mathbf{Y})$ is called the *domain* of $(\mathbf{X}, \mathbf{Y})$. Let us observe that a separator $(\mathbf{X}, \mathbf{Y})$ with an empty domain is a partition of $\mathbb{Z}^d$ such that $\mathbf{X}$ is a Presburger forward invariant and $\mathbf{Y}$ is a Presburger backward invariant. In particular Theorem 6.1 is obtained thanks to the following Lemma 6.3 with an immediate induction.

Lemma 6.3. *Let $(\mathbf{X}_0, \mathbf{Y}_0)$ be a separator with a non-empty domain $\mathbf{D}_0$. There exists a separator $(\mathbf{X}, \mathbf{Y})$ with a domain $\mathbf{D}$ such that $\mathbf{X}_0 \subseteq \mathbf{X}$, $\mathbf{Y}_0 \subseteq \mathbf{Y}$ and $\dim(\mathbf{D}) < \dim(\mathbf{D}_0)$.*

Proof. We first observe that a couple $(\mathbf{X}, \mathbf{Y})$ of Presburger sets is a separator if and only if $\text{post}_{R^*}(\mathbf{X}) \cap \text{pre}_{R^*}(\mathbf{Y}) = \emptyset$ if and only if $\text{post}_{R^*}(\mathbf{X}) \cap \mathbf{Y} = \emptyset$ if and only if $\text{pre}_{R^*}(\mathbf{Y}) \cap \mathbf{X} = \emptyset$.

Since R^* is a Petri relation we deduce that $\text{post}_{R^*}(\mathbf{X}_0)$ is a Petri set. As $\mathbf{D}_0$ is a Presburger set, we deduce that $\text{post}_{R^*}(\mathbf{X}_0) \cap \mathbf{D}_0$ is a Lambert set. Hence $\text{post}_{R^*}(\mathbf{X}_0) \cap \mathbf{D}_0 = \bigcup_{j=1}^{k} \mathbf{b}_j + \mathbf{P}_j$ where $\mathbf{b}_j \in \mathbb{Z}^d$ and $\mathbf{P}_j \subseteq \mathbb{Z}^d$ is a polytope periodic set. We introduce the following Presburger set:

$$\mathbf{S} = \bigcup_{j=1}^{k} \mathbf{b}_j + \text{lin}(\mathbf{P}_j)$$

Observe that $\text{post}_{R^*}(\mathbf{X}_0) \cap \mathbf{D}_0 \subseteq \mathbf{S}$. We deduce that the set $\mathbf{Y} = \mathbf{Y}_0 \cup (\mathbf{D}_0 \backslash \mathbf{S})$ is such that $\text{post}_{R^*}(\mathbf{X}_0) \cap \mathbf{Y} = \emptyset$. Hence $(\mathbf{X}_0, \mathbf{Y})$ is a separator.

Symmetrically, since R^* is a Petri relation we deduce that $\text{pre}_{R^*}(\mathbf{Y})$ is a Petri set. As $\mathbf{D}_0$ is a Presburger set, we deduce that $\text{pre}_{R^*}(\mathbf{Y}) \cap \mathbf{D}_0$ is a Lambert set. Hence $\text{pre}_{R^*}(\mathbf{Y}) \cap \mathbf{D}_0 = \bigcup_{l=1}^{n} \mathbf{c}_l + \mathbf{Q}_l$ where $\mathbf{c}_l \in \mathbb{Z}^d$ and $\mathbf{Q}_l \subseteq \mathbb{Z}^d$ is a polytope periodic set. We introduce the following Presburger set:

$$\mathbf{T} = \bigcup_{l=1}^{n} \mathbf{c}_l + \text{lin}(\mathbf{Q}_l)$$

Observe that $\text{pre}_{R^*}(\mathbf{Y}) \cap \mathbf{D}_0 \subseteq \mathbf{T}$. We deduce that the set $\mathbf{X} = \mathbf{X}_0 \cup (\mathbf{D}_0 \backslash \mathbf{T})$ is such that $\text{pre}_{R^*}(\mathbf{Y}) \cap \mathbf{X} = \emptyset$. Hence $(\mathbf{X}, \mathbf{Y})$ is a separator.

Let us introduce the domain $\mathbf{D}$ of $(\mathbf{X}, \mathbf{Y})$. We have the following equality where $\mathbf{Z}_{j,l} = (\mathbf{b}_j + \text{lin}(\mathbf{P}_j)) \cap (\mathbf{c}_l + \text{lin}(\mathbf{Q}_l))$:

$$\mathbf{D} = \mathbf{D}_0 \cap (\bigcup_{\substack{1 \leq j \leq k \\ 1 \leq l \leq n}} \mathbf{Z}_{j,l})$$

As $(\mathbf{X}, \mathbf{Y})$ is a separator we deduce that $\text{post}_{R^*}(\mathbf{X}) \cap \text{pre}_{R^*}(\mathbf{Y})$ is empty. As $\mathbf{b}_j + \mathbf{P}_j \subseteq \text{post}_{R^*}(\mathbf{X}_0) \subseteq \text{post}_{R^*}(\mathbf{X})$ and $\mathbf{c}_l + \mathbf{Q}_l \subseteq \text{pre}_{R^*}(\mathbf{Y})$ we deduce that the intersection $(\mathbf{b}_j + \mathbf{P}_j) \cap (\mathbf{c}_l + \mathbf{Q}_l)$ is empty. Theorem 5.2 shows that $\dim(\mathbf{Z}_{j,l}) < \max\{\dim(\mathbf{b}_j + \mathbf{P}_j), \dim(\mathbf{c}_l + \mathbf{Q}_l)\}$. Since $\mathbf{b}_j + \mathbf{P}_j \subseteq \mathbf{D}_0$ and $\mathbf{c}_l + \mathbf{Q}_l \subseteq \mathbf{D}_0$ we deduce that $\dim(\mathbf{b}_j + \mathbf{P}_j) \leq \dim(\mathbf{D}_0)$ and $\dim(\mathbf{c}_l + \mathbf{Q}_l) \leq \dim(\mathbf{D}_0)$. We have proved that $\dim(\mathbf{D}) < \dim(\mathbf{D}_0)$. □

7. Vector Addition Systems

In this section we introduce the *Vector Addition Systems*, the *production relations* and a well order over the set of *runs* of Vector Addition Systems.

A *Vector Addition System (VAS)* is a finite subset $\mathbf{A} \subseteq \mathbb{Z}^d$. A *marking* is a vector $\mathbf{m} \in \mathbb{N}^d$. The semantics of vector addition systems is obtained by introducing for every word $w = \mathbf{a}_1 \dots \mathbf{a}_k$ of vectors $\mathbf{a}_j \in \mathbf{A}$ the relation $\xrightarrow{w}$ over the set of markings defined by $\mathbf{x} \xrightarrow{w} \mathbf{y}$ if there exists a word $\rho = \mathbf{m}_0 \dots \mathbf{m}_k$ of markings $\mathbf{m}_j \in \mathbb{N}^d$ such that $(\mathbf{x}, \mathbf{y}) = (\mathbf{m}_0, \mathbf{m}_k)$ and $\mathbf{m}_j = \mathbf{m}_{j-1} + \mathbf{a}_j$ for every $j \in \{1, \dots, k\}$. The word ρ is unique and it is called the *run* from $\mathbf{x}$ to $\mathbf{y}$ labeled by w. The marking $\mathbf{x}$ is called the *source* of ρ and it is denoted by $\text{src}(\rho)$, and the marking $\mathbf{y}$ is called the *target* of ρ and it is denoted by $\text{tgt}(\rho)$. The set of *runs* is denoted by Ω.

The *reachability relation* is the relation denoted by $\xrightarrow{*}$ over the set of markings defined by $\mathbf{x} \xrightarrow{*} \mathbf{y}$ if there exists a word $w \in \mathbf{A}^*$ such that $\mathbf{x} \xrightarrow{w} \mathbf{y}$. In the sequel we often used the fact that $\mathbf{x} \xrightarrow{w} \mathbf{y}$ implies $\mathbf{x} + \mathbf{v} \xrightarrow{w} \mathbf{y} + \mathbf{v}$ for every $\mathbf{v} \in \mathbb{N}^d$.

The *production relation* of a marking $\mathbf{m} \in \mathbb{N}^d$ is the relation $\xrightarrow{*}_{\mathbf{m}}$ over $\mathbb{N}^d$ defined by $\mathbf{r} \xrightarrow{*}_{\mathbf{m}} \mathbf{s}$ if $\mathbf{m} + \mathbf{r} \xrightarrow{*} \mathbf{m} + \mathbf{s}$. The *production relation* of a run $\rho = \mathbf{m}_0 \dots \mathbf{m}_k$ is the relation $\xrightarrow{*}_{\rho}$ defined by the following composition:

$$\xrightarrow{*}_{\rho} = \xrightarrow{*}_{\mathbf{m}_0} \circ \dots \circ \xrightarrow{*}_{\mathbf{m}_k}$$

The following Lemma 7.1 shows that $\xrightarrow{*}_{\rho}$ is periodic for every run ρ as a composition of periodic relations. Note that in Section 8 we prove that this periodic relation is polytope.

Lemma 7.1. *The relation $\xrightarrow{*}_{\mathbf{m}}$ is periodic.*

Proof. Let us assume that $\mathbf{r}_1 \xrightarrow{*}_{\mathbf{m}} \mathbf{s}_1$ and $\mathbf{r}_2 \xrightarrow{*}_{\mathbf{m}} \mathbf{s}_2$. Since $\mathbf{r}_1 \xrightarrow{*}_{\mathbf{m}} \mathbf{s}_1$ we deduce that $\mathbf{r}_1 + \mathbf{r}_2 \xrightarrow{*}_{\mathbf{m}} \mathbf{s}_1 + \mathbf{r}_2$. Moreover, since $\mathbf{r}_2 \xrightarrow{*}_{\mathbf{m}} \mathbf{s}_2$ we deduce that $\mathbf{r}_2 + \mathbf{s}_1 \xrightarrow{*}_{\mathbf{m}} \mathbf{s}_2 + \mathbf{s}_1$. Therefore $\mathbf{r}_1 + \mathbf{r}_2 \xrightarrow{*}_{\mathbf{m}} \mathbf{s}_1 + \mathbf{s}_2$. □

We introduce a well order over the set of runs based on the following Lemma 7.2

Lemma 7.2. *The following inclusion holds for every run ρ:*

$$(\text{src}(\rho), \text{tgt}(\rho)) + \xrightarrow{*}_{\rho} \subseteq \xrightarrow{*}$$

Proof. Assume that $\rho = \mathbf{m}_0 \dots \mathbf{m}_k$ with $\mathbf{m}_j \in \mathbb{N}^d$, and let $(\mathbf{r}, \mathbf{s})$ be a couple in the production relation $\xrightarrow{*}_{\rho}$. Since this relation is defined as a composition, there exists a sequence $(\mathbf{v}_j)_{0 \leq j \leq k+1}$ of vectors $\mathbf{v}_j \in \mathbb{N}^d$ satisfying the following relations with $\mathbf{v}_0 = \mathbf{r}$ and $\mathbf{v}_{k+1} = \mathbf{s}$:

$$\mathbf{v}_0 \xrightarrow{*}_{\mathbf{m}_0} \mathbf{v}_1 \cdots \mathbf{v}_k \xrightarrow{*}_{\mathbf{m}_k} \mathbf{v}_{k+1}$$

We introduce the vector $\mathbf{a}_j = \mathbf{m}_j - \mathbf{m}_{j-1}$ for every $j \in \{1, \ldots, k\}$. Since $\mathbf{m}_{j-1} \xrightarrow{\mathbf{a}_j} \mathbf{m}_j$ we deduce that $\mathbf{m}_{j-1} + \mathbf{v}_j \xrightarrow{\mathbf{a}_j} \mathbf{m}_j + \mathbf{v}_j$. Moreover, as $\mathbf{v}_j \xrightarrow{*}_{\mathbf{m}_j} \mathbf{v}_{j+1}$, there exists a word $w_j \in \mathbf{A}^*$ such that $\mathbf{m}_j + \mathbf{v}_j \xrightarrow{w_j} \mathbf{m}_j + \mathbf{v}_{j+1}$. We deduce that the following relation holds:

$$\mathbf{m}_0 + \mathbf{v}_0 \xrightarrow{w_0 \mathbf{a}_1 w_1 \ldots \mathbf{a}_k w_k} \mathbf{m}_k + \mathbf{v}_{k+1}$$

Therefore $(\mathbf{m}_0, \mathbf{m}_k) + (\mathbf{v}_0, \mathbf{v}_{k+1})$ is in the reachability relation. □

We introduce the order $\preceq$ over the set of runs defined by $\rho \preceq \rho'$ if the following inclusion holds:

$$(\mathrm{src}(\rho'), \mathrm{tgt}(\rho')) + \xrightarrow{*}_{\rho'} \subseteq (\mathrm{src}(\rho), \mathrm{tgt}(\rho)) + \xrightarrow{*}_{\rho}$$

In the reminder of this section we prove the following theorem. All other results or definitions introduced in this section are not used in the sequel.

Theorem 7.3. *The order $\preceq$ is well.*

The order $\preceq$ is proved well thanks to the *Higmann's Lemma*. We first recall this lemma. Let us consider an order $\sqsubseteq$ over a set S. We introduce the order $\sqsubseteq^*$ over the set of words over S defined by $u \sqsubseteq^* v$ where $u = s_1 \ldots s_k$ with $s_j \in S$ if there exists a sequence $(t_j)_{1 \leq j \leq k}$ with $t_j \in S$ and $s_j \sqsubseteq t_j$ and a sequence $(w_j)_{0 \leq j \leq k}$ of words $w_j \in S^*$ such that $v = w_0 t_1 w_1 \ldots t_k w_k$.

Lemma 7.4 (Higmann's Lemma). *The ordered set $(S^*, \sqsubseteq^*)$ is well for every well ordered set $(S, \sqsubseteq)$.*

We associate to every run $\rho = \mathbf{m}_0 \ldots \mathbf{m}_k$ the word $\alpha(\rho) = (\mathbf{a}_1, \mathbf{m}_1) \ldots (\mathbf{a}_k, \mathbf{m}_k)$ where $\mathbf{a}_j = \mathbf{m}_j - \mathbf{m}_{j-1}$. Note that $\alpha(\rho)$ is a word over the alphabet $S = \mathbf{A} \times \mathbb{N}^d$. We introduce the order $\sqsubseteq$ over this alphabet by $(\mathbf{a}, \mathbf{m}) \sqsubseteq (\mathbf{a}', \mathbf{m}')$ if $\mathbf{a} = \mathbf{a}'$ and $\mathbf{m} \leq \mathbf{m}'$. Since $\mathbf{A}$ is a finite set and $\leq$ is a well order over $\mathbb{N}^d$, we deduce that $\sqsubseteq$ is a well order over S. From the Higmann's lemma, the order $\sqsubseteq^*$ is well over S^*. We introduce the well order $\trianglelefteq$ over the set of runs defined by $\rho \trianglelefteq \rho'$ if $\alpha(\rho) \sqsubseteq^* \alpha(\rho')$, $\mathrm{src}(\rho) \leq \mathrm{src}(\rho')$ and $\mathrm{tgt}(\rho) \leq \mathrm{tgt}(\rho')$. The following lemma provides a useful characterization of this order.

Lemma 7.5. *Let $\rho = \mathbf{m}_0 \ldots \mathbf{m}_k$ be a run and let ρ' be another run. We have $\rho \trianglelefteq \rho'$ if and only if there exists a sequence $(\mathbf{v}_j)_{0 \leq j \leq k+1}$ of vectors in $\mathbb{N}^d$ such that $\rho' = \rho'_0 \ldots \rho'_k$ where ρ'_j is a run from $\mathbf{m}_j + \mathbf{v}_j$ to $\mathbf{m}_j + \mathbf{v}_{j+1}$.*

Proof. We introduce the sequence $(\mathbf{a}_j)_{1 \leq j \leq k}$ defined by $\mathbf{a}_j = \mathbf{m}_j - \mathbf{m}_{j-1}$.

Assume first that $\rho \trianglelefteq \rho'$. Since $\alpha(\rho) \sqsubseteq^* \alpha(\rho')$ we deduce that $\alpha(\rho') = w_0(\mathbf{a}_1, \mathbf{m}'_1) w_1 \ldots (\mathbf{a}_k, \mathbf{m}'_k) w_k$ where $w_j \in S^*$ and $\mathbf{m}'_j \geq \mathbf{m}_j$. We introduce the sequence $(\mathbf{v}_j)_{0 \leq j \leq k+1}$ defined by $\mathbf{v}_0 = \mathrm{src}(\rho') - \mathrm{src}(\rho)$, $\mathbf{v}_{k+1} = \mathrm{tgt}(\rho') - \mathrm{tgt}(\rho)$ and $\mathbf{v}_j = \mathbf{m}'_j - \mathbf{m}_j$ for every $j \in \{1, \ldots, k\}$. Observe that $\mathbf{v}_j \in \mathbb{N}^d$ for every $j \in \{0, \ldots, k+1\}$. We deduce that ρ' can be decomposed into $\rho' = \rho'_0 \ldots \rho'_k$ where ρ'_j is the run from $\mathbf{m}_j + \mathbf{v}_j$ to $\mathbf{m}_j + \mathbf{v}_{j+1}$ such that $\alpha(\rho'_j) = w_j$.

Conversely let $(\mathbf{v}_j)_{0 \leq j \leq k+1}$ be a sequence of vectors in $\mathbb{N}^d$ such that $\rho' = \rho'_0 \ldots \rho'_k$ where ρ'_j is a run from $\mathbf{m}_j + \mathbf{v}_j$ to $\mathbf{m}_j + \mathbf{v}_{j+1}$. We deduce that we have the following equality where $\mathbf{m}'_j = \mathbf{m}_j + \mathbf{v}_j$ and $\mathbf{a}'_j \in \mathbf{A}$:

$$\alpha(\rho') = \alpha(\rho'_0)(\mathbf{a}'_1, \mathbf{m}'_1)\alpha(\rho'_1) \ldots (\mathbf{a}'_k, \mathbf{m}'_k)\alpha(\rho'_k)$$

Observe that $\mathbf{a}'_j = \mathrm{tgt}(\rho'_{j-1}) - \mathbf{m}'_j = (\mathbf{m}_j + \mathbf{v}_j) - (\mathbf{m}_{j-1} + \mathbf{v}_j)$ and in particular $\mathbf{a}'_j = \mathbf{a}_j$. We deduce that $\alpha(\rho) \sqsubseteq^* \alpha(\rho')$. Moreover, since $\mathrm{src}(\rho) \leq \mathrm{src}(\rho')$ and $\mathrm{tgt}(\rho) \leq \mathrm{tgt}(\rho')$ we deduce that $\rho \trianglelefteq \rho'$. □

Since $\trianglelefteq$ is a well order, the following lemma shows that $\preceq$ is a well order. We have proved Theorem 7.3.

Lemma 7.6. *$\rho \trianglelefteq \rho'$ implies $\rho \preceq \rho'$.*

Proof. Assume that $\rho = \mathbf{m}_0 \ldots \mathbf{m}_k$. Lemma 7.5 shows that there exists a sequence $(\mathbf{v}_j)_{0 \leq j \leq k+1}$ of vectors in $\mathbb{N}^d$ such that $\rho' = \rho'_0 \ldots \rho'_k$ where ρ'_j is a run from $\mathbf{m}_j + \mathbf{v}_j$ to $\mathbf{m}_j + \mathbf{v}_{j+1}$. Lemma 7.2 shows that $(\mathrm{src}(\rho'_j), \mathrm{tgt}(\rho'_j)) + \xrightarrow{*}_{\rho'_j} \subseteq \xrightarrow{*}$. Hence $(\mathbf{v}_j, \mathbf{v}_{j+1}) + \xrightarrow{*}_{\rho'_j} \subseteq \xrightarrow{*}_{\mathbf{m}_j}$. We deduce that $(\mathbf{v}_0, \mathbf{v}_{k+1}) + \xrightarrow{*}_{\rho'} \subseteq \xrightarrow{*}_{\rho}$ by composition. Since $(\mathrm{src}(\rho'), \mathrm{tgt}(\rho')) = (\mathrm{src}(\rho), \mathrm{tgt}(\rho)) + (\mathbf{v}_0, \mathbf{v}_{k+1})$ we get $\rho \preceq \rho'$ from the previous inclusion. □

8. Polytope Production Relations

In this section we prove that production relations are polytope (Theorem 8.1). All other results or definitions introduced in the section are not used in the sequel.

Theorem 8.1. *Production relations are polytope.*

The following lemma shows that polytope periodic relations are stable by composition. In particular it is sufficient to prove that production relations $\xrightarrow{*}_{\mathbf{m}}$ are polytope for every marking $\mathbf{m} \in \mathbb{N}^d$ in order to deduce that production relations $\xrightarrow{*}_{\rho}$ are polytope for every run ρ.

Lemma 8.2. *We have $\mathbb{Q}_{\geq 0}(R_1 \circ R_2) = (\mathbb{Q}_{\geq 0} R_1) \circ (\mathbb{Q}_{\geq 0} R_2)$ for every periodic relations over $\mathbb{Z}^d$.*

Proof. We have $R_1 \subseteq \mathbb{Q}_{\geq 0} R_1$ and $R_2 \subseteq \mathbb{Q}_{\geq 0} R_2$. Thus $R_1 \circ R_2 \subseteq C$ where $C = (\mathbb{Q}_{\geq 0} R_1) \circ (\mathbb{Q}_{\geq 0} R_2)$. As C is a conic set we get $\mathbb{Q}_{\geq 0}(R_1 \circ R_2) \subseteq C$. For the converse inclusion, let us consider $(\mathbf{x}, \mathbf{z}) \in C$. There exists $\mathbf{y} \in \mathbb{Q}^d$ such that $(\mathbf{x}, \mathbf{y}) \in \mathbb{Q}_{\geq 0} R_1$ and $(\mathbf{y}, \mathbf{z}) \in \mathbb{Q}_{\geq 0} R_2$. There exists $\lambda_1, \lambda_2 \in \mathbb{Q}_{\geq 0}$ such that $(\mathbf{x}, \mathbf{y}) \in \lambda_1 R_1$ and $(\mathbf{y}, \mathbf{z}) \in \lambda_2 R_2$. We introduce $n_1, n_2 \in \mathbb{N}_{>0}$ such that $n_1 \lambda_1 \in \mathbb{N}$ and $n_2 \lambda_2 \in \mathbb{N}$ and we deduce that $n(\mathbf{x}, \mathbf{y}) \in R_1$ and $n(\mathbf{y}, \mathbf{z}) \in R_2$ with $n = n_1 n_2$. Hence $n(\mathbf{x}, \mathbf{z}) \in R_1 \circ R_2$. We deduce that $(\mathbf{x}, \mathbf{z}) \in \mathbb{Q}_{\geq 0}(R_1 \circ R_2)$. □

Theorem 3.5 shows that the conic set $\mathbb{Q}_{\geq 0} \xrightarrow{*}_{\mathbf{m}}$ is polytope if and only if the following conic set is finitely generated for every vector space $V \subseteq \mathbb{Q}^d \times \mathbb{Q}^d$:

$$\overline{(\mathbb{Q}_{\geq 0} \xrightarrow{*}_{\mathbf{m}}) \cap V}$$

We introduce the periodic relation $\xrightarrow{*}_{\mathbf{m},V}$ defined as the intersection $\xrightarrow{*}_{\mathbf{m}} \cap V$. Let us observe that $(\mathbb{Q}_{\geq 0} \xrightarrow{*}_{\mathbf{m}}) \cap V$ is equal to $\mathbb{Q}_{\geq 0} \xrightarrow{*}_{\mathbf{m},V}$. So, we just have to prove that the conic set $\overline{\mathbb{Q}_{\geq 0} \xrightarrow{*}_{\mathbf{m},V}}$ is finitely generated for every $\mathbf{m} \in \mathbb{N}^d$ and for every vector space $V \subseteq \mathbb{Q}^d \times \mathbb{Q}^d$.

We introduce the set $\Omega_{\mathbf{m},V}$ of runs ρ such that $(\mathrm{src}(\rho), \mathrm{tgt}(\rho)) - (\mathbf{m}, \mathbf{m})$ is in $(\mathbb{N}^d \times \mathbb{N}^d) \cap V$. Note that a couple $(\mathbf{r}, \mathbf{s}) \in \mathbb{N}^d \times \mathbb{N}^d$ satisfies $\mathbf{r} \xrightarrow{*}_{\mathbf{m},V} \mathbf{s}$ if and only if there exists a run $\rho \in \Omega_{\mathbf{m},V}$ such that $\mathrm{src}(\rho) = \mathbf{m} + \mathbf{r}$ and $\mathrm{tgt}(\rho) = \mathbf{m} + \mathbf{s}$. We introduce the set $\mathbf{Q}_{\mathbf{m},V}$ of markings $\mathbf{q}$ that occurs in at least one run $\rho \in \Omega_{\mathbf{m},V}$. In general the set $\mathbf{Q}_{\mathbf{m},V}$ is infinite. We consider the set $I_{\mathbf{m},V}$ of $i \in \{1, \ldots, d\}$ such that $\{\mathbf{q}(i) \mid \mathbf{q} \in \mathbf{Q}_{\mathbf{m},V}\}$ is infinite. We observe that if $i \in I_{\mathbf{m},V}$ there exists a sequence of markings in $\mathbf{Q}_{\mathbf{m},V}$ such that the ith component is strictly increasing. We are going to prove that there exists a sequence of markings in

$\mathbf{Q}_{\mathbf{m},V}$ such that every component in $I_{\mathbf{m},V}$ is strictly increasing. This property is proved by introducing the intraproductions. An *intraproduction* for $(\mathbf{m}, V)$ is a triple $(\mathbf{r}, \mathbf{x}, \mathbf{s})$ such that $\mathbf{x} \in \mathbb{N}^d$, $(\mathbf{r}, \mathbf{s}) \in (\mathbb{N}^d \times \mathbb{N}^d) \cap V$ and such that:

$$\mathbf{r} \xrightarrow{*}_{\mathbf{m}} \mathbf{x} \xrightarrow{*}_{\mathbf{m}} \mathbf{s}$$

Since $\xrightarrow{*}_{\mathbf{m}}$ is a periodic relation we deduce that the set of intraproductions is stable by addition. In particular $\mathbf{m} + n\mathbf{x}$ occurs in at least one run of $\Omega_{\mathbf{m},V}$ for every intraproduction $(\mathbf{r}, \mathbf{x}, \mathbf{s})$ and for every $n \in \mathbb{N}$. Hence, if $\mathbf{x}(i) > 0$ then $i \in I_{\mathbf{m},V}$. An *intraproduction* for $(\mathbf{m}, V)$ is said to be *total* if $\mathbf{x}(i) > 0$ for every $i \in I_{\mathbf{m},V}$.

Lemma 8.3. *There exists a total intraproduction for* $(\mathbf{m}, V)$.

Proof. Since finite sums of intraproductions are intraproductions, it is sufficient to prove that for every $i \in I_{\mathbf{m},V}$ there exists an intraproduction $(\mathbf{r}, \mathbf{x}, \mathbf{s})$ for $(\mathbf{m}, V)$ such that $\mathbf{x}(i) > 0$. We fix $i \in I$.

Let us first prove that there exists $\mathbf{q} \leq \mathbf{q}'$ in $\mathbf{Q}_{\mathbf{m},V}$ such that $\mathbf{q}(i) < \mathbf{q}'(i)$. Since $i \in I$ there exists a sequence $(\mathbf{q}_n)_{n\in\mathbb{N}}$ of markings $\mathbf{q}_n \in \mathbf{Q}_{\mathbf{m},V}$ such that $(\mathbf{q}_n(i))_{n\in\mathbb{N}}$ is strictly increasing. Since $(\mathbb{N}^d, \leq)$ is well ordered, we can extract for this sequence a subsequence that is non decreasing for $\leq$. We have proved that there exists $\mathbf{q} \leq \mathbf{q}'$ in $\mathbf{Q}_{\mathbf{m},V}$ such that $\mathbf{q}(i) < \mathbf{q}'(i)$.

As $\mathbf{q} \in \mathbf{Q}_{\mathbf{m},V}$ then $\mathbf{q}$ occurs in a run in $\Omega_{\mathbf{m},V}$. Hence there exists $(\mathbf{r}, \mathbf{s}) \in (\mathbb{N}^d \times \mathbb{N}^d) \cap V$ such that:

$$\mathbf{m} + \mathbf{r} \xrightarrow{*} \mathbf{q} \xrightarrow{*} \mathbf{m} + \mathbf{s}$$

Symmetrically, as $\mathbf{q}' \in \mathbf{Q}_{\mathbf{m},V}$ there exists $(\mathbf{r}', \mathbf{s}') \in (\mathbb{N}^d \times \mathbb{N}^d) \cap V$ such that:

$$\mathbf{m} + \mathbf{r}' \xrightarrow{*} \mathbf{q}' \xrightarrow{*} \mathbf{m} + \mathbf{s}'$$

Let us introduce $\mathbf{v} = \mathbf{q}' - \mathbf{q}$. We deduce:

- $(\mathbf{m} + \mathbf{r}') + \mathbf{r} \xrightarrow{*} \mathbf{q}' + \mathbf{r}$ from $\mathbf{m} + \mathbf{r}' \xrightarrow{*} \mathbf{q}'$.
- $\mathbf{q} + (\mathbf{v} + \mathbf{r}) \xrightarrow{*} (\mathbf{m} + \mathbf{s}) + (\mathbf{v} + \mathbf{r})$ from $\mathbf{q} \xrightarrow{*} \mathbf{m} + \mathbf{s}$.
- $(\mathbf{m} + \mathbf{r}) + (\mathbf{v} + \mathbf{s}) \xrightarrow{*} \mathbf{q} + (\mathbf{v} + \mathbf{s})$ from $\mathbf{m} + \mathbf{r} \xrightarrow{*} \mathbf{q}$.
- $\mathbf{q}' + \mathbf{s} \xrightarrow{*} (\mathbf{m} + \mathbf{s}') + \mathbf{s}$ from $\mathbf{q}' \xrightarrow{*} \mathbf{m} + \mathbf{s}'$.

Since $\mathbf{q}' + \mathbf{r} = \mathbf{q} + \mathbf{v} + \mathbf{r}$ and $\mathbf{q} + \mathbf{v} + \mathbf{s} = \mathbf{q}' + \mathbf{s}$, we have proved the following relations where $\mathbf{x} = \mathbf{s} + \mathbf{v} + \mathbf{r}$:

$$\mathbf{r} + \mathbf{r}' \xrightarrow{*}_{\mathbf{m}} \mathbf{x} \xrightarrow{*}_{\mathbf{m}} \mathbf{s} + \mathbf{s}'$$

As $(\mathbf{r}+\mathbf{r}', \mathbf{s}+\mathbf{s}') \in (\mathbb{N}^d \times \mathbb{N}^d) \cap V$ we deduce that $(\mathbf{r}+\mathbf{r}', \mathbf{x}, \mathbf{s}+\mathbf{s}')$ is an intraproduction for $(\mathbf{m}, V)$. Since $\mathbf{x}(i) > 0$ we are done. □

Let us introduce an additional element $\infty \notin \mathbb{N}$ and let $\mathbb{N}_\infty = \mathbb{N} \cup \{\infty\}$. A vector in $\mathbb{N}_\infty^d$ is called an *extended marking* and the set $I = \{i \in \{1, \ldots, d\} \mid \mathbf{m}(i) = \infty\}$ is called the set of *relaxed components* of an extended marking $\mathbf{m}$. Given a finite set $I \subseteq \{1, \ldots, d\}$ and a marking $\mathbf{m} \in \mathbb{N}^d$, we denote by $\mathbf{m}^I$ the extended marking defined by $\mathbf{m}^I(i) = \infty$ if $i \in I$ and $\mathbf{m}^I(i) = \mathbf{m}(i)$ if $i \notin I$. Given a word $w = \mathbf{a}_1 \ldots \mathbf{a}_k$ of vectors $\mathbf{a}_j \in \mathbf{A}$, we extend the relation $\xrightarrow{w}$ over the set of extended markings relaxed over a set I by $\mathbf{x} \xrightarrow{w} \mathbf{y}$ if there exists a word $\rho = \mathbf{m}_0 \ldots \mathbf{m}_k$ of extended markings relaxed over I such that $(\mathbf{x}, \mathbf{y}) = (\mathbf{m}_0, \mathbf{m}_k)$ and $\mathbf{m}_j(i) = \mathbf{m}_{j-1}(i) + \mathbf{a}_j(i)$ for every $j \in \{1, \ldots, k\}$ and for every $i \in \{1, \ldots, d\} \backslash I$. The word ρ is unique and it is called the *run* from $\mathbf{x}$ to $\mathbf{y}$ labeled by w.

We introduce the finite graph $G_{\mathbf{m},V} = (\mathbf{Q}, \mathbf{A}, E)$ where $\mathbf{Q} = \{\mathbf{q}^{I_{\mathbf{m},V}} \mid \mathbf{q} \in \mathbf{Q}_{\mathbf{m},V}\}$ and where $E = \{(\mathbf{p}^{I_{\mathbf{m},V}}, \mathbf{a}, \mathbf{q}^{I_{\mathbf{m},V}}) \mid \mathbf{p}, \mathbf{q} \in \mathbf{Q}_{\mathbf{m},V} \wedge \mathbf{q} = \mathbf{p} + \mathbf{a}\}$. We introduce the periodic relation $R_{\mathbf{m},V}$ of couples $(\mathbf{r}, \mathbf{s}) \in (\mathbb{N}^d \times \mathbb{N}^d) \cap V$ such that $\mathbf{r}(i) = \mathbf{s}(i) = 0$ for every $i \in \{1, \ldots, d\} \backslash I_{\mathbf{m},V}$ and such that there exists a cycle in $G_{\mathbf{m},V}$ on the state $\mathbf{m}^{I_{\mathbf{m},V}}$ labeled by a word $\mathbf{a}_1 \ldots \mathbf{a}_k$ where $\mathbf{a}_j \in \mathbf{A}$ such that $\mathbf{r} + \sum_{j=1}^k \mathbf{a}_j = \mathbf{s}$.

Lemma 8.4. *The periodic relation* $R_{\mathbf{m},V}$ *is Presburger.*

Proof. This is a classical result based on the fact that the Parikh image of a regular language is Presburger. □

Lemma 8.5. *The following equality holds:*

$$\overline{\mathbb{Q}_{\geq 0} R_{\mathbf{m},V}} = \overline{\mathbb{Q}_{\geq 0} \xrightarrow{*}_{\mathbf{m},V}}$$

Proof. Let us first prove the inclusion $\supseteq$. Let $(\mathbf{r}, \mathbf{s})$ such that $\mathbf{r} \xrightarrow{*}_{\mathbf{m},V} \mathbf{s}$. In this case there exists a word $w \in \mathbf{A}^*$ such that $\mathbf{m} + \mathbf{r} \xrightarrow{w} \mathbf{m} + \mathbf{s}$. Observe that $\mathbf{m} + n\mathbf{r}$ and $\mathbf{m} + n\mathbf{s}$ are in $\mathbf{Q}_{\mathbf{m},V}$ for every $n \in \mathbb{N}$. Hence $\mathbf{r}(i) > 0$ or $\mathbf{s}(i) > 0$ implies $i \in I_{\mathbf{m},V}$ and we deduce that $\mathbf{m}^{I_{\mathbf{m},V}} \xrightarrow{w} \mathbf{m}^{I_{\mathbf{m},V}}$. Therefore w is the label of cycle in $G_{\mathbf{m},V}$ on $\mathbf{m}^{I_{\mathbf{m},V}}$. We have proved that $(\mathbf{r}, \mathbf{s}) \in R_{\mathbf{m},V}$.

Now let us prove the inclusion $\subseteq$. We consider $(\mathbf{r}, \mathbf{s}) \in R_{\mathbf{m},V}$. In this case $(\mathbf{r}, \mathbf{s}) \in (\mathbb{N}^d \times \mathbb{N}^d) \cap V$ satisfies $\mathbf{r}(i) = \mathbf{s}(i) = 0$ for every $i \notin I_{\mathbf{m},V}$ and there exists a word $w = \mathbf{a}_1 \ldots \mathbf{a}_k$ of vectors $\mathbf{a}_j \in \mathbf{A}$ that labels a cycle in $G_{\mathbf{m},V}$ on $\mathbf{m}^{I_{\mathbf{m},V}}$ and such that $\mathbf{m} + \mathbf{r} + \sum_{j=1}^k \mathbf{a}_j = \mathbf{m} + \mathbf{s}$. Let us consider a total intraproduction $(\mathbf{r}', \mathbf{x}, \mathbf{s}')$ for $(\mathbf{m}, V)$. Given $p \in \mathbb{N}$ and $j \in \{0, \ldots, k\}$ we introduce the following vector $\mathbf{m}_{p,j}$:

$$\mathbf{m}_{p,j} = \mathbf{m} + \mathbf{r} + p\mathbf{x} + \mathbf{a}_1 + \cdots + \mathbf{a}_j$$

Let us first prove that there exists $p \in \mathbb{N}$ such that $\mathbf{m}_{p,j}(i) \in \mathbb{N}$ for every $i \in I_{\mathbf{m},V}$ and $j \in \{0, \ldots, k\}$. Let $i \in I_{\mathbf{m},V}$ and $j \in \{0, \ldots, k\}$, since $\mathbf{x}(i) > 0$, there exists $p_{i,j} \in \mathbb{N}$ such that $\mathbf{m}_{p,j}(i) \in \mathbb{N}$ for every $p \geq p_{i,j}$. We deduce that there exists $p \in \mathbb{N}$ such that $\mathbf{m}_{p,j}(i) \in \mathbb{N}$ for every $i \in I_{\mathbf{m},V}$ and $j \in \{0, \ldots, k\}$.

Now we prove that $\mathbf{m}_{p,j}(i) \in \mathbb{N}$ for every $i \in \{1, \ldots, d\} \backslash I_{\mathbf{m},V}$ and $j \in \{0, \ldots, k\}$. Let $j \in \{0, \ldots, k\}$. Since w is the label of a cycle on $\mathbf{m}^{I_{\mathbf{m},V}}$, there exists an extended marking $\mathbf{q}_j$ relaxed over $I_{\mathbf{m},V}$ such that the following relation holds:

$$\mathbf{m}^{I_{\mathbf{m},V}} \xrightarrow{\mathbf{a}_1 \ldots \mathbf{a}_j} \mathbf{q}_j$$

We deduce that for every $i \in \{1, \ldots, d\} \backslash I_{\mathbf{m},V}$ we have $\mathbf{m}(i) + \mathbf{a}_1(i) + \cdots + \mathbf{a}_j(i) = \mathbf{q}_j(i)$. Since $\mathbf{r}(i) = 0$ and $\mathbf{x}(i) = 0$ we get $\mathbf{m}_{p,j}(i) \in \mathbb{N}$.

We have proved that $\mathbf{m}_{p,j} \in \mathbb{N}^d$ for every $j \in \{0, \ldots, k\}$. Since $\mathbf{m}_{p,j} - \mathbf{m}_{p,j-1} = \mathbf{a}_j$ we deduce that $\rho_p = \mathbf{m}_{p,0} \ldots \mathbf{m}_{p,k}$ is a run. Note that $\mathbf{m}_{p,0} = \mathbf{m} + p\mathbf{x} + \mathbf{r}$ and $\mathbf{m}_{p,k} = \mathbf{m} + p\mathbf{x} + \mathbf{r} + \sum_{j=1}^k \mathbf{a}_j = \mathbf{m} + p\mathbf{x} + \mathbf{s}$. We have proved that the following relation holds:

$$\mathbf{m} + p\mathbf{x} + \mathbf{r} \xrightarrow{w} \mathbf{m} + p\mathbf{x} + \mathbf{s}$$

In particular $(\mathbf{r}, \mathbf{s})$ is in the production relation $\xrightarrow{*}_{\mathbf{m}'}$ where $\mathbf{m}' = \mathbf{m} + p\mathbf{x}$. Since a production relation is periodic we get $\mathbf{m}' + n\mathbf{r} \xrightarrow{*} \mathbf{m}' + n\mathbf{s}$ for every $n \in \mathbb{N}$. As $(p\mathbf{r}', p\mathbf{x}, p\mathbf{s}')$ is an intraproduction for $(\mathbf{m}, V)$ we get $\mathbf{m} + p\mathbf{r}' \xrightarrow{*} \mathbf{m}' \xrightarrow{*} \mathbf{m} + p\mathbf{s}'$. We deduce the relation $(\mathbf{m} + p\mathbf{r}') + n\mathbf{r} \xrightarrow{*} \mathbf{m}' + n\mathbf{r}$ from $(\mathbf{m} + p\mathbf{r}') \xrightarrow{*} \mathbf{m}'$, and the relation $\mathbf{m}' + n\mathbf{s} \xrightarrow{*} (\mathbf{m} + p\mathbf{s}') + n\mathbf{s}$ from $\mathbf{m}' \xrightarrow{*} (\mathbf{m} + p\mathbf{s}')$. We deduce that the following relation holds for every $n \in \mathbb{N}$:

$$\mathbf{m} + p\mathbf{r}' + n\mathbf{r} \xrightarrow{*} \mathbf{m} + p\mathbf{s}' + n\mathbf{s}$$

Hence $p(\mathbf{r}', \mathbf{s}') + \mathbb{N}(\mathbf{r}, \mathbf{s}) \subseteq \xrightarrow{*}_{\mathbf{m},V}$. Thus $(\mathbf{r}, \mathbf{s}) \in \overline{\mathbb{Q}_{\geq 0} \xrightarrow{*}_{\mathbf{m},V}}$. From the inclusion $R_{\mathbf{m},V} \subseteq \overline{\mathbb{Q}_{\geq 0} \xrightarrow{*}_{\mathbf{m},V}}$ we get the inclusion $\overline{\mathbb{Q}_{\geq 0} R_{\mathbf{m},V}} \subseteq \overline{\mathbb{Q}_{\geq 0} \xrightarrow{*}_{\mathbf{m},V}}$. □

Lemma 8.6. *The conic set $\overline{\mathbb{Q}_{\geq 0}\mathbf{P}}$ if finitely generated for every Presburger periodic set* $\mathbf{P}$.

Proof. Let us consider a Presburger periodic set $\mathbf{P}$. Since $\mathbf{P}$ is Presburger then $\mathbf{P} = \bigcup_{j=1}^{k} \mathbf{b}_j + \mathbf{P}_j$ where $\mathbf{b}_j \in \mathbb{Z}^d$ and $\mathbf{P}_j \subseteq \mathbb{Z}^d$ is a finitely generated periodic set. We introduce the finitely generated conic set $\mathbf{C} = \sum_{j=1}^{k}(\mathbb{Q}_{\geq 0}\mathbf{b}_j + \mathbf{C}_j)$ where $\mathbf{C}_j$ is the finitely generated conic set $\mathbf{C}_j = \mathbb{Q}_{\geq 0}\mathbf{P}_j$. Since $\mathbf{P} \subseteq \mathbf{C}$ and $\mathbf{C}$ is a conic set we deduce the inclusion $\mathbb{Q}_{\geq 0}\mathbf{P} \subseteq \mathbf{C}$. As $\mathbf{C}$ is finitely generated we deduce that $\mathbf{C}$ is closed. Hence $\overline{\mathbb{Q}_{\geq 0}\mathbf{P}} \subseteq \mathbf{C}$. For the other inclusion let $\mathbf{p} \in \mathbf{P}_j$. For every $n \in \mathbb{N}$ we have $\mathbf{b}_j + n\mathbf{p} \in \mathbf{P}$. Hence $\frac{1}{n}\mathbf{b}_j + \mathbf{p} \in \mathbb{Q}_{\geq 0}\mathbf{P}$ for every $n \in \mathbb{N}_{>0}$. We deduce that $\mathbf{p} \in \overline{\mathbb{Q}_{\geq 0}\mathbf{P}}$. Therefore $\mathbf{P}_j \subseteq \overline{\mathbb{Q}_{\geq 0}\mathbf{P}}$. We deduce that $\mathbf{C}_j \subseteq \overline{\mathbb{Q}_{\geq 0}\mathbf{P}}$. As $\mathbb{Q}_{\geq 0}\mathbf{b}_j \subseteq \mathbb{Q}_{\geq 0}\mathbf{P} \subseteq \overline{\mathbb{Q}_{\geq 0}\mathbf{P}}$ we have proved the inclusion $\mathbf{C} \subseteq \overline{\mathbb{Q}_{\geq 0}\mathbf{P}}$. Hence the previous inclusion is in fact an equality. □

Now, we can prove Theorem 8.1. Lemma 8.4 shows that $R_{\mathbf{m},V}$ is a Presburger periodic relation. Lemma 8.6 proves that the conic set $\overline{\mathbb{Q}_{\geq 0}R_{\mathbf{m},V}}$ is finitely generated. Lemma 8.5 shows that $\mathbb{Q}_{\geq 0} \xrightarrow{*}_{\mathbf{m},V}$ is finitely generated. Hence $(\mathbb{Q}_{\geq 0} \xrightarrow{*}_{\mathbf{m}}) \cap V$ is a finitely generated conic set for every vector space $V \subseteq \mathbb{Q}^d \times \mathbb{Q}^d$. Theorem 3.5 shows that the conic relation $\mathbb{Q}_{\geq 0} \xrightarrow{*}_{\mathbf{m}}$ is polytope. Hence $\xrightarrow{*}_{\mathbf{m}}$ is a polytope periodic relation.

9. Petri Reachability Relations

In this section we prove the following Theorem 9.1. All other results or definitions introduced in this section are not used in the sequel.

Theorem 9.1. *The reachability relation of a Vector Addition System is a Petri relation.*

We are interested in proving that $\xrightarrow{*}$ is a Petri relation. This problem is equivalent to prove that $\xrightarrow{*} \cap((\mathbf{m},\mathbf{n})+P)$ is a Lambert relation for every $(\mathbf{m},\mathbf{n}) \in \mathbb{N}^d \times \mathbb{N}^d$ and for every finitely generated periodic relation $P \subseteq \mathbb{N}^d \times \mathbb{N}^d$. We introduce the order $\leq_P$ over P defined by $p \leq_P p'$ if $p' \in p + P$. Since P is finitely generated we deduce that $\leq_P$ is a well order over P (Dickson's Lemma). We introduce the set $\Omega_{\mathbf{m},P,\mathbf{n}}$ of runs ρ such that $(\mathrm{src}(\rho), \mathrm{tgt}(\rho)) \in (\mathbf{m},\mathbf{n}) + P$. This set is well ordered by the relation $\preceq_P$ defined by $\rho \preceq_P \rho'$ if $\rho \preceq \rho'$, $(\mathrm{src}(\rho),\mathrm{tgt}(\rho)) - (\mathbf{m},\mathbf{n}) \leq_P (\mathrm{src}(\rho'),\mathrm{tgt}(\rho')) - (\mathbf{m},\mathbf{n})$. We deduce that $\min_{\preceq_P}(\Omega_{\mathbf{m},P,\mathbf{n}})$ is finite.

Lemma 9.2. *The following equality holds:*

$$\xrightarrow{*} \cap((\mathbf{m},\mathbf{n})+P) = \bigcup_{\rho \in \min_{\preceq_P}(\Omega_{\mathbf{m},P,\mathbf{n}})} (\mathrm{src}(\rho),\mathrm{tgt}(\rho)) + (\xrightarrow{*}_{\rho} \cap P)$$

Proof. Let us first prove $\supseteq$. Let $\rho \in \Omega_{\mathbf{m},P,\mathbf{n}}$. Lemma 7.2 shows that $(\mathrm{src}(\rho),\mathrm{tgt}(\rho)) + \xrightarrow{*}_{\rho} \subseteq \xrightarrow{*}$. Since $(\mathrm{src}(\rho),\mathrm{tgt}(\rho)) \in (\mathbf{m},\mathbf{n}) + P$ and P is periodic we deduce the inclusion $\supseteq$.

Let us prove $\subseteq$. Let $(\mathbf{x}',\mathbf{y}')$ in the intersection $\xrightarrow{*} \cap((\mathbf{m},\mathbf{n}) + P)$. There exists a run $\rho' \in \Omega_{\mathbf{m},P,\mathbf{n}}$ such that $\mathbf{x}' = \mathrm{src}(\rho')$ and $\mathbf{y}' = \mathrm{tgt}(\rho')$. Since $\preceq_P$ is a well order, there exists $\rho \in \min_{\preceq_P}(\Omega_{\mathbf{m},P,\mathbf{n}})$ such that $\rho \preceq_P \rho'$. We deduce that $(\mathbf{x}',\mathbf{y}')$ is in $(\mathrm{src}(\rho),\mathrm{tgt}(\rho)) + \xrightarrow{*}_{\rho}$. We get $(\mathbf{x}',\mathbf{y}') \in (\mathrm{src}(\rho),\mathrm{tgt}(\rho)) + (\xrightarrow{*}_{\rho} \cap P)$ and we have proved the inclusion $\subseteq$. □

Theorem 8.1 shows $\xrightarrow{*}_{\rho}$ is a polytope periodic relation. Since P is a finitely generated relation we deduce that P is a polytope periodic relation. Lemma 4.5 shows that the class of polytope periodic relations is stable by finite intersections. We deduce that $\xrightarrow{*}_{\rho} \cap P$ is polytope periodic relation. Thanks to the previous lemma we deduce that $\xrightarrow{*} \cap((\mathbf{m},\mathbf{n}) + P)$ is a Lambert relation for every $(\mathbf{m},\mathbf{n}) \in \mathbb{N}^d \times \mathbb{N}^d$ and for every finitely generated periodic relation $P \subseteq \mathbb{N}^d \times \mathbb{N}^d$. Therefore $\xrightarrow{*}$ is a Petri relation and we have proved Theorem 9.1.

10. Conclusion

The reachability problem for Vector Additions Systems consists to decide for a triple $(\mathbf{m},\mathbf{A},\mathbf{n})$ where $\mathbf{m},\mathbf{n}$ are two markings of a Vector Addition System $\mathbf{A}$ if there exists a word $w \in \mathbf{A}^*$ such that $\mathbf{m} \xrightarrow{w} \mathbf{n}$. The following algorithm decides this problem.

```
Reachability( m , A , n )
  k ← 0
  repeat forever
     for each word w ∈ A* of length k
        if m -w-> n
           return "reachable"
     for each Presburger formula ψ of length k
        if ψ(m) and ¬ψ(n) are true and
           ψ(x) ∧ y = x + a ∧ ¬ψ(y) unsat ∀a ∈ A
           return "unreachable"
     k ← k + 1
```

The correctness is immediate and the termination is guaranteed by the following Theorem 10.1.

Theorem 10.1. *For every pair of markings* $(\mathbf{m},\mathbf{n})$ *in the complement of the reachability relation of a Vector Addition System, there exists a partition of the set of markings into a Presburger forward invariant that contains* $\mathbf{m}$ *and a Presburger backward invariant that contains* $\mathbf{n}$.

Proof. Let us consider $\mathbf{X} = \{\mathbf{m}\}$ and $\mathbf{Y} = \{\mathbf{n}\}$ and let R^* be the reachability relation of the Vector addition system. Theorem 9.1 shows that R^* is a Petri relation. Since R^* is reflexive and transitive and such that $(\mathbf{X} \times \mathbf{Y}) \cap R^* = \emptyset$, Theorem 6.1 shows that there exists a partition of the set of markings into a Presburger forward invariant set that contains $\mathbf{X}$ and a Presburger backward invariant set that contains $\mathbf{Y}$. □

This algorithm does not require the classical KLMST decomposition. Note however that the complexity of this algorithm is still open. In fact, the complexity depends on the minimal size of a word $w \in \mathbf{A}^*$ such that $\mathbf{m} \xrightarrow{w} \mathbf{n}$ if $\mathbf{m} \xrightarrow{*} \mathbf{n}$, and the minimal size of a Presburger formula $\psi(\mathbf{x})$ denoting a forward invariant $\mathbf{M}$ such that $\mathbf{m} \in \mathbf{M}$ and $\mathbf{n} \notin \mathbf{M}$ otherwise. We left as an open question the problem of computing lower and upper bounds for these sizes. Note that the VAS exhibiting a large (Ackermann size) but finite reachability set given in [MM81] does not directly provide an Ackermann lower-bound for these sizes since Presburger forward invariants can over-approximate reachability sets.

As future work we are interested in providing complexity bounds on formulas in FO $(\mathbb{Q},+,\leq,0,1)$ denoting the polytope conic sets $\mathbb{Q}_{\geq 0} \xrightarrow{*}_{\mathbf{m}}$.

References

[EN94] J. Esparza and M. Nielsen. Decidability issues for petri nets - a survey. *Bulletin of the European Association for Theoretical Computer Science*, 52:245–262, 1994.

[GS66] Seymour Ginsburg and Edwin H. Spanier. Semigroups, Presburger formulas and languages. *Pacific Journal of Mathematics*, 16(2):285–296, 1966.

[Hau90] Dirk Hauschildt. *Semilinearity of the Reachability Set is Decidable for Petri Nets.* PhD thesis, University of Hamburg, 1990.

[Kos82] S. Rao Kosaraju. Decidability of reachability in vector addition systems (preliminary version). In *Proceedings of the Fourteenth Annual ACM Symposium on Theory of Computing, (STOC 1982), 5-7 May 1982, San Francisco, California, USA*, pages 267–281. ACM, 1982.

[Lam92] Jean Luc Lambert. A structure to decide reachability in petri nets. *Theoretical Computer Science*, 99(1):79–104, 1992.

[Ler09] Jérôme Leroux. The general vector addition system reachability problem by Presburger inductive invariants. In *LICS'09*, pages 4–13, 2009.

[May81] Ernst W. Mayr. An algorithm for the general petri net reachability problem. In *Conference Proceedings of the Thirteenth Annual ACM Symposium on Theory of Computation, (STOC 1981), 11-13 May 1981, Milwaukee, Wisconsin, USA*, pages 238–246. ACM, 1981.

[MM81] Ernst W. Mayr and Albert R. Meyer. The complexity of the finite containment problem for petri nets. *J. ACM*, 28(3):561–576, 1981.

[Sch87] Alexander Schrijver. *Theory of Linear and Integer Programming.* John Wiley and Sons, New York, 1987.

[ST77] George S. Sacerdote and Richard L. Tenney. The decidability of the reachability problem for vector addition systems (preliminary version). In *Conference Record of the Ninth Annual ACM Symposium on Theory of Computing, 2-4 May 1977, Boulder, Colorado, USA*, pages 61–76. ACM, 1977.

Automating String Processing in Spreadsheets Using Input-Output Examples

Sumit Gulwani
Microsoft Research, Redmond, WA, USA
sumitg@microsoft.com

Abstract

We describe the design of a string programming/expression language that supports restricted forms of regular expressions, conditionals and loops. The language is expressive enough to represent a wide variety of string manipulation tasks that end-users struggle with. We describe an algorithm based on several novel concepts for synthesizing a desired program in this language from input-output examples. The synthesis algorithm is very efficient taking a fraction of a second for various benchmark examples. The synthesis algorithm is interactive and has several desirable features: it can rank multiple solutions and has fast convergence, it can detect noise in the user input, and it supports an active interaction model wherein the user is prompted to provide outputs on inputs that may have multiple computational interpretations.

The algorithm has been implemented as an interactive add-in for Microsoft Excel spreadsheet system. The prototype tool has met the golden test - it has synthesized part of itself, and has been used to solve problems beyond author's imagination.

Categories and Subject Descriptors D.1.2 [*Programming Techniques*]: Automatic Programming; I.2.2 [*Artificial Intelligence*]: Program Synthesis

General Terms Algorithms, Human Factors

Keywords Program Synthesis, User Intent, Programming by Example (PBE), Version Space Algebra, Spreadsheet Programming, String Manipulation

1. Introduction

More than 500 million people worldwide use spreadsheets. These business *end-users* have myriad diverse backgrounds and include commodity traders, graphic designers, chemists, human resource managers, finance pros, marketing managers, underwriters, compliance officers, and even mailroom clerks – they are not professional programmers, but they need to create small, *often one-off*, applications to support business functions [5].

Unfortunately, the state of art in spreadsheet programming is far from satisfactory. Spreadsheet systems come with tons of features, but end-users struggle to find the correct feature or succession of commands to use from a maze of features to accomplish their task [9]. More significantly, programming is still required to perform tedious and repetitive tasks such as transforming entities like names/phone-numbers/dates from one format to another, data cleansing, extracting data from several text files or web pages into a single document, etc. Spreadsheet systems like Microsoft Excel allow users to write macros using a rich inbuilt library of string and numerical functions, or to write arbitrary scripts using a variety of programming languages like Visual Basic, or .Net. Since end-users are not proficient in programming, they find it too difficult to write desired macros or scripts.

We have performed an extensive case study of spreadsheet help forums and identified that string processing is one of the most common class of programming problems that end-users struggle with. This is not surprising given that languages like Perl, Awk, Python came into existence to support string/text processing, and that new languages like Java/C# provide a rich support for string processing. During our study of help forums, we also carefully studied how these users were describing the specification of the desired program to the experts on the other side of the help forums. It turns out that the most common form of specification was input-output examples. Since input-output examples may lead to underspecification, the interaction between the user and the expert often involved a few rounds of communication (over multiple days).

We describe a program synthesis system that is capable of synthesizing a wide range of string processing programs in spreadsheets from input-output examples. The synthesizer aims to replace the role of the forum expert, which not only removes a human from the loop, but also enables users to solve their problems in a few seconds as opposed to a few days. Our synthesis system, which is deployment ready, has the following important usability properties.

- Fully Automated: We do not require non-sophisticated end-users to provide annotations/hints of any form.
- Real Time: Our system takes less than 0.1 second on average per interactive round.
- Easy Interaction: Programming by examples is an interactive process where examples are added in each round to make the specification more precise. Our system helps identify the inputs for which the user should provide examples.
- Fast Convergence: Our system typically takes 1-4 rounds of iteration for convergence in practice.
- Noise Handling: If the user makes a small mistake in mostly correct specification, our system can still compute the likely solution and report the likely mistake.

This paper makes the following contributions.

1. We describe a string programming/expression language that is expressive enough to represent a wide variety of string manipulation tasks found during an extensive study of Excel online help

PoPL'11, January 26–28, 2011, Austin, Texas, USA.

forums, while at the same time also being restrictive enough to enable efficient program search over that space (Section 3).

2. We describe an algorithm with several novel concepts that can efficiently synthesize a set of programs in our language that are consistent with a given set of input-output examples (Section 4).
3. We describe extensions to the above algorithm that enable several usability properties (Section 5).
4. We discuss our experience with a ready-to-be-deployed prototype tool (Section 6).

2. Problem Definition

We start out by describing a representative case-study, picked up from an online Excel help forum, that illustrates a typical interaction between a user and an expert on help forums. We then use it to motivate the key technical problem that we address in this paper.

EXAMPLE 1. *The user intends to extract the following bold substrings from the respective strings:*

*1. John DOE 3 Data [TS]***865-000-0000** *- - 453442-00 06-23-2009*

2. A FF MARILYN 30'S **865-000-0030** *4535871-00 07-07-2009*

3. A GEDA-MARY 100MG **865-001-0020** *- - 5941-00 06-23-2009*

The user initially provides a few examples to the expert that are similar to the first example above. The expert provides a program P_1 that uses the logic of extracting 12 characters after the first occurrence of "]". The user runs program P_1 on other inputs in her spreadsheet and observes that it does not perform the desired extraction for the second example above and then presents that to the expert. The expert then provides a program P_2 that uses the logic of finding the first occurrence of "-" and extracting 3 characters on left of it and 8 characters on right of it. The user runs program P_2 on her spreadsheet and observes that it does not perform the desired extraction for the third example above and then presents that to the expert. The expert then provides a program P_3 that uses the logic of finding the first occurrence of a pattern of the form "???-????-???", where ? is supposed to match any character. The user runs program P_3 on her spreadsheet and is satisfied with the produced results, and the thread is closed.

One might wonder why did the expert not suggest a program P_4 which is similar to P_3, but ? is supposed to match any digit as opposed to any character. Or why did the expert not suggest a program P_5 which is similar to P_3, but the first three occurrences of ? are forced to match only 865. Even though programs P_3, P_4 and P_5 are semantically different, these programs may not yield different outputs on the inputs the user has in her spreadsheet. Hence these programs are observationally equivalent over the format of the inputs present in the spreadsheet.

We draw the following conclusions from this representative case study. First, the user is communicating her intent using input-output examples. Second, the user cannot be expected to provide representative inputs in the first round. Hence, an example based synthesis system must be interactive. However, in order to remain usable, the system should allow the user to interact easily and converge quickly (i.e., in a few rounds) to the desired intent [10]. In this paper, we describe such a program synthesis system. We present an algorithm for synthesizing string manipulation programs that are consistent with input-output examples. We also describe how the algorithm can be extended to enable easy interaction and fast convergence.

3. Expression Language for String Manipulation

We have identified a string expression language that is expressive enough to describe various string manipulation tasks succinctly, while at the same time concise enough to be amenable for efficient learning. There is a tradeoff between the expressiveness of a search space, and the complexity of finding simple consistent hypotheses within that space [6, 18]. In general, the more expressive a search space, the harder the task of finding consistent hypotheses within that search space. However, it is also worth-mentioning that the expressiveness-complexity tradeoff is not as simple as it seems, as an expressive language can sometimes make a simple theory fit the data, whereas restricting the expressiveness of the language means that any consistent theory must be very complex. Our string expression language seems to enjoy the right tradeoff. We present a core version of this language; extensions that enable easy adaptation of the underlying algorithm are mentioned later in Section 4.7.1.

The syntax and semantics of the string expressions P is formally described in Figure 1 and Figure 2 respectively. We use the notation ϵ to denote an empty string and $\perp$ to denote an undefined value. If any of the arguments to any constructor is $\perp$, then it returns $\perp$. The notation $s[t_1 : t_2]$ denotes the substring of s starting at location t_1 and ending at location t_2.

The string expressions P map an input state σ, which holds values for m string variables $v_1, \cdot\cdot, v_m$ (denoting the multiple input columns in a spreadsheet), to a single output string s.

$$P : (\texttt{String} \times \ldots \times \texttt{String}) \rightarrow \texttt{String}$$

The above formalism can also be used for string processing tasks that require generating a tuple of n strings as an output by simply solving n independent problems.

A *trace expression* refers to the $\texttt{Concatenate}(f_1, \cdot\cdot, f_n)$ constructor, which denotes the string obtained by concatenating the strings represented by $f_1, f_2, \cdot\cdot, f_n$ in that order. An *atomic expression* refers to `ConstStr` (denoting a constant string), `SubStr` or `Loop` constructors, which are explained below.

3.1 Substrings

The $\texttt{SubStr}(v_i, p_1, p_2)$ constructor makes use of two *position expressions* p_1 and p_2, each of which evaluates to an index within the string v_i. $\texttt{SubStr}(v_i, p_1, p_2)$ denotes the substring of string v_i that starts at index specified by p_1 and ends at index specified by p_2-1. If either of p_1 or p_2 refer to an index that is outside the range of string v_i, then the `SubStr` constructor returns $\perp$.

The position expression $\texttt{CPos}(k)$ refers to the kth index in a given string from the left side (or right side), if the integer constant k is non-negative (or negative). $\texttt{Pos}(r_1, r_2, c)$ is another position constructor, where r_1 and r_2 are some regular expressions and integer expression c evaluates to a non-zero integer. The `Pos` constructor evaluates to an index t in a given string s such that r_1 matches some suffix of $s[0 : t\text{-}1]$ and r_2 matches some prefix of $s[t : \ell\text{-}1]$, where $\ell = \texttt{Length}(s)$. Furthermore, t is the cth such match starting from the left side (or the right side) if c is positive (or negative). If not enough matches exist, then $\perp$ is returned.

We use notation $\texttt{SubStr2}(v_i, r, c)$ to denote the cth occurrence of regular expression r in v_i, i.e., $\texttt{SubStr}(v_i, \texttt{Pos}(\epsilon, r, c), \texttt{Pos}(r, \epsilon, c))$. We often denote $\texttt{SubStr2}(v_i, \texttt{CPos}(0), \texttt{CPos}(\text{-}1))$ by simply v_i.

Tokens and Regular Expressions A token is either some special token or is constructed from some character class C in two ways: $C+$ denotes a token that matches a sequence of *one or more* characters from C. $\neg C+$ denotes a token that matches a sequence of *one or more* characters that do not belong to C. We use the following collection of character classes C: Numeric Digits (0-9), Alphabets (a-zA-Z), Lowercase alphabets (a-z), Uppercase alphabets (A-Z), Accented alphabets, Alphanumeric characters, Whitespace characters, All characters. We use the following SpecialTokens.

- StartTok: Matches the beginning of a string.
- EndTok: Matches the end of a string.

$$
\begin{array}{rcl}
\text{String expr } P & := & \texttt{Switch}((\mathrm{b}_1, \mathrm{e}_1), \cdot\cdot, (\mathrm{b}_n, \mathrm{e}_n)) \\
\text{Bool b} & := & \mathrm{d}_1 \vee \cdot\cdot \vee \mathrm{d}_n \\
\text{Conjunct d} & := & \pi_1 \wedge \cdot\cdot \wedge \pi_n \\
\text{Predicate } \pi & := & \texttt{Match}(v_i, \mathrm{r}, k) \mid \neg\, \texttt{Match}(v_i, \mathrm{r}, k) \\
\text{Trace expr e} & := & \texttt{Concatenate}(\mathrm{f}_1, \cdot\cdot, \mathrm{f}_n) \\
\text{Atomic expr f} & := & \texttt{SubStr}(v_i, \mathrm{p}_1, \mathrm{p}_2) \\
& \mid & \texttt{ConstStr}(s) \\
& \mid & \texttt{Loop}(\lambda w : \mathrm{e}) \\
\text{Position p} & := & \texttt{CPos}(k) \mid \texttt{Pos}(\mathrm{r}_1, \mathrm{r}_2, \mathrm{c}) \\
\text{Integer expr c} & := & k \mid k_1 w + k_2 \\
\text{Regular Expression r} & := & \texttt{TokenSeq}(\mathrm{T}_1, \cdot\cdot, \mathrm{T}_m) \\
\text{Token T} & := & C+ \mid [\neg C]+ \\
& \mid & \text{SpecialToken}
\end{array}
$$

Figure 1. Syntax of String Expressions P. v_i refers to a free string variable, while w refers to a bound integer variable. k denotes an integer constant and s denotes a string constant.

- A token for each special character, such as hyphen, dot, semicolon, colon, comma, backslash, forwardslash, left/right parenthesis/bracket etc.

For better readability, we reference tokens by representative names. For example, AlphTok refers to a sequence of alphabetic characters, NumTok refers to a sequence of numeric digits, NonDigitTok refers to a sequence of characters that are not numeric digits, HyphenTok matches with the hyphen character.

Addition of more tokens may make the language more powerful. (These tokens may be added either by the user or can be mined by searching for frequently occurring substrings in a given spreadsheet.) However, to stay true to our goal of avoiding any user annotations, we aim to keep the language expressive without having to depend on addition of problem-specific tokens.

A regular expression $\mathrm{r} = \texttt{TokenSeq}(\mathrm{T}_1, \cdot\cdot, \mathrm{T}_n)$ is a sequence of tokens $\mathrm{T}_1, \cdot\cdot, \mathrm{T}_n$. We often refer to singleton token sequences $\texttt{TokenSeq}(\mathrm{T}_1)$ simply as T_1. We use the notation ϵ to denote an empty sequence of tokens. ϵ matches an empty string.

It is worth discussing our restricted choice of regular expressions. First, we allow for only a restricted form of the Kleene star operator. The Kleene star is restricted to one or more occurrences as opposed to zero or more occurrences (and that too at the innermost level). Second, we do not allow for the disjunction operator. These restrictions (together with the token partitioning optimization described in Section 4.2) enable us to efficiently enumerate regular expressions that match certain parts of a string. If we allowed arbitrary Kleene star and disjunction, we would lose this ability. Use of conditionals at the outer level allow us to recover some of the expressiveness lost due to restricted form of regular expressions.

The following two examples illustrate the expressive power of our substring constructor.

EXAMPLE 2. *The goal in this problem, taken from an Excel online help forum, is to extract the quantity of the purchase. Observe that characterizing the substring that is being extracted is non-trivial, in fact, not even possible using the character-class tokens that our language provides. However, characterizing the (left) position before the substring and the (right) position after the substring is relatively easy and also expressible in our language.*

$$
\begin{array}{rcl}
[\![\texttt{Switch}((\mathrm{b}_1, \mathrm{e}_1), \cdot\cdot, (\mathrm{b}_n, \mathrm{e}_n))]\!]\, \sigma & = & \text{if } ([\![\mathrm{b}_1]\!]\sigma) \text{ then } [\![\mathrm{e}_1]\!]\sigma \\
& & \vdots \\
& & \text{else if } ([\![\mathrm{b}_n]\!]\sigma) \text{ then } [\![\mathrm{e}_n]\!]\sigma \\
& & \text{else } \bot \\
[\![\mathrm{d}_1 \vee \ldots \vee \mathrm{d}_n]\!]\, \sigma & = & [\![\mathrm{d}_1]\!]\, \sigma \vee \ldots \vee [\![\mathrm{d}_n]\!]\, \sigma \\
[\![\pi_1 \wedge \ldots \wedge \pi_n]\!]\, \sigma & = & [\![\pi_1]\!]\, \sigma \wedge \ldots \wedge [\![\pi_n]\!]\, \sigma \\
[\![\texttt{Match}(v_i, \mathrm{r}, k)]\!]\, \sigma & = & \texttt{Match}(\sigma(v_i), \mathrm{r}, k) \\
[\![\texttt{Concatenate}(\mathrm{f}_1, \cdot\cdot, \mathrm{f}_n)]\!]\, \sigma & = & \texttt{Concatenate}([\![\mathrm{f}_1]\!]\, \sigma, \cdot\cdot, [\![\mathrm{f}_n]\!]\, \sigma) \\
[\![\texttt{Loop}(\lambda w : \mathrm{e})]\!]\, \sigma & = & \texttt{LoopR}(\lambda w : \mathrm{e}, 1, \sigma) \\
\texttt{LoopR}(\lambda w : \mathrm{e}, k, \sigma) & = & \text{let } t := [\![\mathrm{e}[k/w]]\!]\, \sigma \text{ in} \\
& & \text{if } (t = \bot) \text{ then } \epsilon \text{ else} \\
& & \texttt{Concatenate}(t, \texttt{LoopR}(\lambda w : \mathrm{e}, k{+}1, \sigma)) \\
[\![\texttt{SubStr}(v_i, \mathrm{p}_1, \mathrm{p}_2)]\!]\, \sigma & = & s[[\![\mathrm{p}_1]\!]\, s : [\![\mathrm{p}_2]\!]\, s], \text{where } s = \sigma(v_i). \\
[\![\texttt{ConstStr}(s)]\!]\, \sigma & = & s \\
[\![\texttt{CPos}(k)]\!]\, s & = & \begin{cases} k & \text{if } k \geq 0 \\ \texttt{Length}(s) + k & \text{otherwise} \end{cases} \\
[\![\texttt{Pos}(\mathrm{r}_1, \mathrm{r}_2, \mathrm{c})]\!]\, s & = & t \text{ such that } \exists\, t_1, t_2 \text{ s.t. } 0 \leq t_1 < t \leq t_2, \\
& & s[t_1 : t\text{-}1] \text{ matches } \mathrm{r}_1,\ s[t : t_2] \text{ matches } \mathrm{r}_2, \\
& & \text{and } t \text{ is the } \mathrm{c}^{th} \text{ such position (in increasing/} \\
& & \text{decreasing order if c is positive/negative.}
\end{array}
$$

Figure 2. Semantics of String Expressions P.

Input v_1	*Output*
BTR KRNL WK CORN 15Z	*15Z*
CAMP DRY DBL NDL 3.6 OZ	*3.6 OZ*
CHORE BOY HD SC SPNG 1 PK	*1 PK*
FRENCH WORCESTERSHIRE 5 Z	*5 Z*
O F TOMATO PASTE 6 OZ	*6 OZ*

The following string program identifies the left position to be the one before the occurrence of the first number, while the right position to be the one at the end of the string.
String Program (in our language):
$\mathit{SubStr}(v_1, \mathit{Pos}(\epsilon, \mathit{NumTok}, 1), \mathit{CPos}(-1))$

EXAMPLE 3 (Directory Name Extraction). *Consider the following example taken from an excel online help forum.*

Input v_1	*Output*
Company\Code\index.html	*Company\Code*
Company\Docs\Spec\specs.doc	*Company\Docs\Spec*

String Program:
$\mathit{SubStr}(v_1, \mathit{CPos}(0), \mathit{Pos}(\mathit{SlashTok}, \epsilon, -1))$

3.2 Loops

The string expression $\texttt{Loop}(\lambda w : \mathrm{e})$ refers to concatenation of $\mathrm{e}_1, \mathrm{e}_2, \ldots, \mathrm{e}_n$, where e_i is obtained from e by replacing all occurrences of w by i. n is the smallest integer such that evaluation of e_{n+1} yields $\bot$. It is also possible to define more interesting termination conditions (based on position expression, or predicates), but we leave out details for lack of space.

EXAMPLE 4 (Generate Abbreviation). *The goal here is to extract out all uppercase letters. This problem is taken from [21] and is presented as an example of* Advanced Text Formulas.

Input v_1	Output
International Business Machines	IBM
Principles Of Programming Languages	POPL
International Conference on Software Engineering	ICSE

String Program:
$\texttt{Loop}(\lambda w : \texttt{Concatenate}(\texttt{SubStr2}(v_1, \texttt{UpperTok}, w)))$.

EXAMPLE 5 (Split Odds). *The goal in this problem, taken from an Excel help forum, is to place each odd in a separate cell, while ignoring any extraneous numbers or parenthesis. We reduce the problem of generating multiple unbounded number of output strings to that of generating one output string where the multiple strings are separated by a unique symbol, say #.*

Input v_1	Output
(6/7)(4/5)(14/1)	6/7 # 4/5 # 14/1 #
49(28/11)(14/1)	28/11 # 14/1 #
() (28/11)(14/1)	28/11 # 14/1 #

String Program:
$\texttt{Loop}(\lambda w : \texttt{Concatenate}(\texttt{SubStr}(v_1, p_1, p_2), \texttt{ConstStr}(\text{"\# "})))$
where $p_1 \equiv \texttt{Pos}(\textit{LeftParenTok}, \texttt{TokenSeq}(\textit{NumTok}, \textit{SlashTok}), w))$
and $p_2 \equiv \texttt{Pos}(\texttt{TokenSeq}(\textit{SlashTok}, \textit{NumTok}), \textit{RightParenTok}, w)$.

EXAMPLE 6 (Remove excess spaces). *The goal in this problem, provided by the product team and also present in [21], is to remove all leading and trailing spaces and replace internal strings of multiple spaces by a single space. Notice how the loop expression prints out all but last sequence of non-whitespace characters (to not print any trailing whitespace in the output).*

Input v_1	Output
Oege de Moor	Oege de Moor
Kathleen Fisher AT&T Labs	Kathleen Fisher AT&T Labs

String Program:
$\texttt{Concatenate}(\texttt{Loop}(\lambda w : \texttt{Concatenate}(\texttt{SubStr}(v_1, p_1, p_2)), \texttt{ConstStr}(\text{" "})), \texttt{SubStr2}(v_1, \textit{NonSpaceTok}, -1))$
where $p_1 \equiv \texttt{Pos}(\epsilon, \textit{NonSpaceTok}, w)$, *and*
$p_2 \equiv \texttt{Pos}(\textit{NonSpaceTok}, \texttt{TokenSeq}(\textit{SpaceTok}, \textit{NonSpaceTok}), w)$.

3.3 Conditionals

The top-level string expression P is a **Switch** constructor whose arguments are pairs of (disjoint) boolean expressions b and trace expressions e. The value of P in a given input state σ is the value of the trace expression that corresponds to the boolean expression satisfied by σ. Boolean expressions b are represented in DNF form and are boolean combinations of predicates of the form $\texttt{Match}(v_i, \mathrm{r}, k)$, where r is some regular expression and k is some integer constant. $\texttt{Match}(v_i, \mathrm{r}, k)$ evaluates to true iff v_i contains at least k matches of regular expression r. We often denote $\texttt{Match}(v_i, \mathrm{r})$ by simply $\texttt{Match}(v_i, \mathrm{r}, 1)$.

Conditionals play a very important role in our string processing language. They allow us to appropriately interpret/process data that is in multiple formats. This is precisely the place where most existing (data cleansing) tools that allow string processing through tons of automated pre-canned features fail since they assume that the input is in a fixed structured format. Conditionals also allow us to express transformations that are beyond the expressive power of the underlying conditional-free part of our language.

EXAMPLE 7 (Conditional Concatenation). *The goal here is to concatenate the first and the second strings v_1 and v_2 in the input tuple as $v_1(v_2)$, only if both v_1 and v_2 are non-empty strings. Otherwise, the output should be empty string. This example is taken from an Excel online help forum.*

Input v_1	Input v_2	Output
Alex	Asst.	Alex(Asst.)
Jim	Manager	Jim(Manager)
Ryan	ϵ	ϵ
ϵ	Asst.	ϵ

String Program:
$\texttt{Switch}((b_1, e_1), (b_2, \epsilon))$, *where*
$b_1 \equiv \texttt{Match}(v_1, \textit{CharTok}) \wedge \texttt{Match}(v_2, \textit{CharTok})$,
$e_1 \equiv \texttt{Concatenate}(v_1, \texttt{ConstStr}(\text{"("}), v_2, \texttt{ConstStr}(\text{")"}))$,
$b_2 \equiv \neg\texttt{Match}(v_1, \textit{CharTok}) \vee \neg\texttt{Match}(v_2, \textit{CharTok})$.

EXAMPLE 8 (Mixed Date Parsing). *The goal here is to parse dates in multiple formats into day, month, and year. This example is taken from an internal mailing list. We show below the program for day extraction (Month and year extraction are solved similarly.)*

Input v_1	Output
01/21/2001	01
22.02.2002	02
2003-23-03	03

String Program:
$\texttt{Switch}((b_1, e_1), (b_2, e_2), (b_3, e_3))$, *where*
$b_1 \equiv \texttt{Match}(v_1, \textit{SlashTok})$, $b_2 \equiv \texttt{Match}(v_1, \textit{DotTok})$,
$b_3 \equiv \texttt{Match}(v_1, \textit{HyphenTok})$,
$e_1 \equiv \texttt{SubStr}(v_1, \texttt{Pos}(\textit{StartTok}, \epsilon, 1), \texttt{Pos}(\epsilon, \textit{SlashTok}, 1))$
$e_2 \equiv \texttt{SubStr}(v_1, \texttt{Pos}(\textit{DotTok}, \epsilon, 1), \texttt{Pos}(\epsilon, \textit{DotTok}, 2))$
$e_3 \equiv \texttt{SubStr}(v_1, \texttt{Pos}(\textit{HyphenTok}, \epsilon, 2), \texttt{Pos}(\textit{EndTok}, \epsilon, 1))$

EXAMPLE 9 (Name Parsing). *The goal in this problem, provided by the product team, is to parse names that occur in multiple formats and transform them into a uniform format.*

Input v_1	Output
Dr. Eran Yahav	Yahav, E.
Prof. Kathleen S. Fisher	Fisher, K.
Bill Gates, Sr.	Gates, B.
George Ciprian Necula	Necula, G.
Ken McMillan, II	McMillan, K.

String Program for extracting initial of the first name:
The logic used is that of extracting the initial of the first word not followed by a dot: $\texttt{SubStr}(v_1, p_1, p_2)$, *where*
$p_1 \equiv \texttt{Pos}(\epsilon, \texttt{TokenSeq}(\texttt{AlphTok}, \textit{NonDotTok}), 1)$, *and*
$p_2 \equiv \texttt{Pos}(\epsilon, \texttt{TokenSeq}(\texttt{LowerTok}, \textit{NonDotTok}), 1)$.

String Program for extracting last name:
The logic used is that of extracting the word followed by a comma, or the last word (if no comma exists): $\texttt{Switch}((b_1, e_1), (b_2, e_2))$,
where $b_1 \equiv \texttt{Match}(v_1, \texttt{CommaTok})$, $b_2 \equiv \neg\texttt{Match}(v_1, \texttt{CommaTok})$,
$e_1 \equiv \texttt{SubStr2}(v_1, p_1, p_2)$, $e_2 \equiv \texttt{SubStr2}(v_1, \texttt{AlphTok}, -1)$,
$p_1 \equiv \texttt{Pos}(\epsilon, \texttt{TokenSeq}(\texttt{AlphTok}, \texttt{CommaTok}), 1)$
and $p_2 \equiv \texttt{Pos}(\texttt{AlphTok}, \texttt{CommaTok}, 1)$

The above two programs can be concatenated together (after distributing conditionals at the top-level) along with some constant strings to yield the desired program.

EXAMPLE 10 (Phone Numbers). *The goal here is to parse phone numbers that occur in multiple formats and transform them into a uniform format, adding a default area code of "425" if the area code is missing. This example was provided by the product team.*

Input v_1	Output
323-708-7700	323-708-7700
(425)-706-7709	425-706-7709
510.220.5586	510-220-5586
235 7654	425-235-7654
745-8139	425-745-8139

String Program:
$\texttt{Switch}((b_1, e_1), (b_2, e_2))$, *where*

$$
\begin{array}{rcll}
\tilde{P} & := & \texttt{Switch}((\mathrm{b}_1, \tilde{\mathrm{e}}_1), \cdot\cdot, (\mathrm{b}_n, \tilde{\mathrm{e}}_n)) & \\
\tilde{\mathrm{e}} & := & \texttt{Dag}(\tilde{\eta}, \eta^s, \eta^t, \tilde{\xi}, W), & \\
 & & \quad \text{where } W : \tilde{\xi} \rightarrow 2^{\tilde{\mathrm{f}}} & \\
\tilde{\mathrm{f}} & := & \texttt{Loop}(\lambda w : \tilde{\mathrm{e}}) & \\
 & | & \texttt{SubStr}(v_i, \{\tilde{\mathrm{p}}_j\}_j, \{\tilde{\mathrm{p}}_k\}_k) & (1) \\
 & | & \texttt{ConstStr}(s) & \\
\tilde{\mathrm{p}} & := & \texttt{CPos}(k) & \\
 & | & \texttt{Pos}(\tilde{\mathrm{r}}_1, \tilde{\mathrm{r}}_2, \tilde{\mathrm{c}}) & \\
\tilde{\mathrm{r}} & := & \texttt{TokenSeq}(\tilde{\mathrm{T}}_1, \cdot\cdot, \tilde{\mathrm{T}}_n) &
\end{array}
$$

$$
\begin{array}{rcl}
[\![\texttt{Switch}((\mathrm{b}_1, \tilde{\mathrm{e}}_1), \cdot\cdot, (\mathrm{b}_n, \tilde{\mathrm{e}}_n))]\!] & = & \{\texttt{Switch}((\mathrm{b}_1, \mathrm{e}_1), \cdot\cdot, (\mathrm{b}_n, \mathrm{e}_n)) \mid \mathrm{e}_i \in [\![\tilde{\mathrm{e}}_i]\!]\} \\
[\![\texttt{Dag}(\tilde{\eta}, \eta^s, \eta^t, W)]\!] & = & \{\texttt{Concatenate}(\mathrm{f}_1, \cdot\cdot, \mathrm{f}_n) \mid \mathrm{f}_i \in [\![W(\xi_i)]\!], \\
 & & \quad \xi_1, \cdot\cdot, \xi_n \in \tilde{\xi} \text{ form a path between } \eta^s \text{ and } \eta^t\} \\
[\![\{\tilde{\mathrm{f}}_i\}_i]\!] & = & \{\mathrm{f} \mid \mathrm{f} \in [\![\tilde{\mathrm{f}}_i]\!]\} \\
[\![\texttt{Loop}(\lambda w : \tilde{\mathrm{e}})]\!] & = & \{\texttt{Loop}(\lambda w : \mathrm{e}) \mid \mathrm{e} \in [\![\tilde{\mathrm{e}}]\!]\} \\
[\![\texttt{SubStr}(v_i, \{\tilde{\mathrm{p}}_j\}_j, \{\tilde{\mathrm{p}}'_k\}_k)]\!] & = & \{\texttt{SubStr}(v_i, \mathrm{p}_1, \mathrm{p}_2) \mid \mathrm{p}_1 \in [\![\tilde{\mathrm{p}}_j]\!], \mathrm{p}_2 \in [\![\tilde{\mathrm{p}}'_k]\!]\} \\
[\![\texttt{ConstStr}(s)]\!] & = & \{\texttt{ConstStr}(s)\} \\
[\![\texttt{CPos}(k)]\!] & = & \{\texttt{CPos}(k)\} \\
[\![\texttt{Pos}(\tilde{\mathrm{r}}_1, \tilde{\mathrm{r}}_2, \tilde{\mathrm{c}})]\!] & = & \{\texttt{Pos}(\mathrm{r}_1, \mathrm{r}_2, \mathrm{c}) \mid \mathrm{r}_1 \in \tilde{\mathrm{r}}_1, \mathrm{r}_2 \in \tilde{\mathrm{r}}_2, \mathrm{c} \in \tilde{\mathrm{c}}\} \\
[\![\texttt{TokenSeq}(\tilde{\mathrm{T}}_1, \cdot\cdot, \tilde{\mathrm{T}}_n)]\!] & = & \{\texttt{TokenSeq}(\mathrm{T}_1, \cdot\cdot, \mathrm{T}_n) \mid \mathrm{T}_1 \in \tilde{\mathrm{T}}_1, \cdot\cdot, \mathrm{T}_n \in \tilde{\mathrm{T}}_n\}
\end{array}
$$

Figure 3. Syntax and semantics of a language/data-structure for succinctly describing huge sets of string expressions.

$$
\begin{array}{rcl}
\texttt{Intersect}(\texttt{Dag}(\tilde{\eta}_1, \eta_1^s, \eta_1^t, \tilde{\xi}_1, W_1), \texttt{Dag}(\tilde{\eta}_2, \eta_2^s, \eta_2^t, \tilde{\xi}_2, W_2)) & = & \texttt{Dag}(\tilde{\eta}_1 \times \tilde{\eta}_2, (\eta_1^s, \eta_2^s), (\eta_1^t, \eta_2^t), \tilde{\xi}_{12}, W_{12}), \text{ where} \\
 & & \tilde{\xi}_{12} = \{\langle(\eta_1, \eta_2), (\eta'_1, \eta'_2)\rangle \mid \langle\eta_1, \eta'_1\rangle \in \tilde{\xi}_1,\ \langle\eta_2, \eta'_2\rangle \in \tilde{\xi}_2\}, \text{ and} \\
 & & W_{12}(\langle(\eta_1, \eta_2), (\eta'_1, \eta'_2)\rangle) = \{\texttt{Intersect}(\tilde{\mathrm{f}}, \tilde{\mathrm{f}}') \mid \tilde{\mathrm{f}} \in W_1(\langle\eta_1, \eta'_1\rangle), \tilde{\mathrm{f}}' \in W_2(\langle\eta_2, \eta'_2\rangle)\}
\end{array}
$$

$$
\begin{array}{rcll}
\texttt{Intersect}(\texttt{SubStr}(v_i, \{\tilde{\mathrm{p}}_j\}_j, \{\tilde{\mathrm{p}}_k\}_k), \texttt{SubStr}(v'_i, \{\tilde{\mathrm{p}}'_\ell\}_\ell, \{\tilde{\mathrm{p}}_m\}_m)) & = & \{\texttt{IntersectPos}(\tilde{\mathrm{p}}_k, \tilde{\mathrm{p}}_m)\}_{k,m}) & \\
\texttt{Intersect}(\texttt{ConstStr}(s_1), \texttt{ConstStr}(s_2)) & = & \texttt{ConstStr}(s_1) \quad \text{if } s_1 = s_2 & \\
\texttt{Intersect}(\texttt{Loop}(\lambda w : \tilde{\mathrm{e}}_1), \texttt{Loop}(\lambda w : \tilde{\mathrm{e}}_2)) & = & \texttt{Loop}(\lambda w : \texttt{Intersect}(\tilde{\mathrm{e}}_1, \tilde{\mathrm{e}}_2)) & \\
\texttt{IntersectPos}(\texttt{CPos}(k_1), \texttt{CPos}(k_2)) & = & \texttt{CPos}(k_1) \quad \text{if } k_1 = k_2 & (2) \\
\texttt{IntersectPos}(\texttt{Pos}(\tilde{\mathrm{r}}_1, \tilde{\mathrm{r}}_2, \tilde{\mathrm{c}}), \texttt{Pos}(\tilde{\mathrm{r}}'_1, \tilde{\mathrm{r}}'_2, \tilde{\mathrm{c}}')) & = & \texttt{Pos}(\texttt{IntersectRegex}(\tilde{\mathrm{r}}_1, \tilde{\mathrm{r}}'_1), \texttt{IntersectRegex}(\tilde{\mathrm{r}}_2, \tilde{\mathrm{r}}'_2), \tilde{\mathrm{c}} \cap \tilde{\mathrm{c}}') & \\
\texttt{IntersectRegex}(\texttt{TokenSeq}(\tilde{\mathrm{T}}_1, \cdot\cdot, \tilde{\mathrm{T}}_n), \texttt{TokenSeq}(\tilde{\mathrm{T}}'_1, \cdot\cdot, \tilde{\mathrm{T}}'_m)) & = & \texttt{TokenSeq}(\tilde{\mathrm{T}}_1 \cap \tilde{\mathrm{T}}', \cdot\cdot, \tilde{\mathrm{T}}_n \cap \tilde{\mathrm{T}}'_m) \quad \text{if } n = m &
\end{array}
$$

Figure 4. The `Intersect` function. The `Intersect` function returns $\emptyset$ in all other cases not covered above.

$$
\begin{array}{l}
b_1 \equiv \mathtt{Match}(v_1, \mathit{NumTok}, 3),\ b_2 \equiv \neg\mathtt{Match}(v_1, \mathit{NumTok}, 3), \\
e_1 \equiv \mathtt{Concatenate}(\mathtt{SubStr2}(v_1, \mathit{NumTok}, 1), \mathtt{ConstStr}(\text{“-”}), \\
\qquad \mathtt{SubStr2}(v_1, \mathit{NumTok}, 2), \mathtt{ConstStr}(\text{“-”}), \\
\qquad \mathtt{SubStr2}(v_1, \mathit{NumTok}, 3)) \\
e_2 \equiv \mathtt{Concatenate}(\mathtt{ConstStr}(\text{“425-”}), \mathtt{SubStr2}(v_1, \mathit{NumTok}, 1), \\
\qquad \mathtt{ConstStr}(\text{“-”}), \mathtt{SubStr2}(v_1, \mathit{NumTok}, 2))
\end{array}
$$

4. Algorithm

In this section, we describe an algorithm for learning a string expression (in the language presented in Section 3) that is consistent with the provided input-output examples. In fact, the algorithm ends up learning a set of string expressions all of which are consistent with the provided input-output examples. This enables the algorithm to have several desirable properties discussed later.

The top-level structure of the algorithm is described in procedure `GenerateStringProgram` in Fig 7, which we explain below.

Step 1: The algorithm first computes (in the loop at Line 2), for each input-output pair (σ, s), a set of *all* trace expressions that map input σ to output s. We refer to this set as a *trace set*. This is done using the procedure `GenerateStr` (explained in Section 4.3). The set of such expressions can be huge; a key enabling technology is the data-structure (described in Section 4.1) for succinctly representing and manipulating such a huge set of expressions.

Step 2: If the target program does not contain any conditionals (i.e., it is expressible as a trace expression, then the algorithm can simply intersect the trace sets of all input-output examples. However, since this is not a valid assumption, the algorithm first partitions the examples so that inputs in the same partition are handled by the same conditional in the top-level `Switch` construct (and then intersect the trace sets for inputs in the same partition). Partitioning is performed (in Line 4) using the procedure `GeneratePartition` (explained in Section 4.5.1). Inputs in the same partition have the property that intersection of their trace sets is non-empty. The algorithm uses a greedy heuristic to minimize the number of such partitions by starting with singleton partitions and then iteratively merging those partitions that have the highest *compatibility score* (a notion defined in Sec 4.5.1).

Step 3: The algorithm then constructs (in the loop at Line 7) a boolean classification scheme as a function of the inputs that will place them in the appropriate partition. This is done using the procedure `GenerateBoolClassifier` (explained in Section 4.5.2). This boolean classification forms the top-level switch construct for the string program returned by the algorithm at Line 9.

Steps 2 and 3 are explained in detail in Sec 4.5. The `GenerateStr` procedure used in Step 1 is explained in Sec 4.3. It makes use of two key procedures `GenerateSubstring` and `GenerateLoop`, which are discussed in Sections 4.2 and 4.4 respectively. We start out by briefly describing the key data-structure (used by these procedures) and the operations that it supports.

4.1 Data-structure for Manipulating Sets of Expressions

Figure 3 describes our data-structure/language for succinctly representing huge sets of string expressions of various kinds and also presents its formal semantics.

$\tilde{P}$, $\tilde{\mathrm{e}}$, $\tilde{\mathrm{f}}$, $\tilde{\mathrm{p}}$, and $\tilde{\mathrm{r}}$ denote respectively a set of string programs, a set of trace expressions, a set of atomic expressions, a set of position expressions, and a set of regular expressions. They are represented using the data-structure shown in Fig 3. $\tilde{\mathrm{T}}$ and $\tilde{\mathrm{c}}$ represent a set

$$\text{Size}(\texttt{Switch}((b_1,\tilde{e}_1),\cdot\cdot,(b_n,\tilde{e}_n))) = \text{Size}(\tilde{e}_1)\times\cdot\cdot\times\text{Size}(\tilde{e}_n)$$

$$\text{Size}(\texttt{Dag}(\tilde{\eta},\eta^s,\eta^t,W)) = \texttt{size}(\eta^t)$$

$$\text{where } \texttt{size}(\eta) = \sum_{\eta'}(\texttt{size}(\eta')\times\sum_{\tilde{f}\in W(\langle\eta',\eta\rangle)}\text{Size}(\tilde{f}))$$

$$\text{and } \texttt{size}(\eta^s) = 1$$

$$\text{Size}(\texttt{SubStr}(v_i,\{\tilde{p}_j\}_j,\{\tilde{p}'_k\}_k)) = (\sum_j\text{Size}(\tilde{p}_j))\times(\sum_k\text{Size}(\tilde{p}'_k))$$

$$\begin{aligned}
\text{Size}(\texttt{Loop}(\lambda w:\tilde{e})) &= \text{Size}(\tilde{e})\\
\text{Size}(\texttt{ConstStr}(s)) &= 1\\
\text{Size}(\texttt{CPos}(k)) &= 1\\
\text{Size}(\texttt{Pos}(\tilde{r}_1,\tilde{r}_2,\tilde{c})) &= \text{Size}(\tilde{r}_1)\times\text{Size}(\tilde{r}_2)\times\text{Size}(\tilde{c})\\
\text{Size}(\texttt{TokenSeq}(\tilde{T}_1,\cdot\cdot,\tilde{T}_n)) &= \text{Size}(\tilde{T}_1)\times\cdot\cdot\times\text{Size}(\tilde{T}_n)
\end{aligned}$$

Figure 5. The Size function. The equations here also illustrate the huge representation savings that our data-structures provide compared to explicit representation.

of tokens and a set of integer expressions, and are represented explicitly.

The `Concatenate` constructor used in our string language is generalized to the `Dag` constructor $\texttt{Dag}(\tilde{\eta},\eta^s,\eta^t,\tilde{\xi},W)$, where $\tilde{\eta}$ is a set of nodes containing two distinctly marked source and target nodes η^s and η^t, $\tilde{\xi}$ is a set of edges over nodes in $\tilde{\eta}$ that induces a DAG, and W maps each $\xi\in\tilde{\xi}$ to a set of atomic expressions. The set of all `Concatenate` expressions represented by a $\texttt{Dag}(\tilde{\eta},\eta^s,\eta^t,\tilde{\xi},W)$ constructor include those whose ordered arguments belong to the corresponding edge on any path from η^s to η^t. The `Switch`, `Loop`, `SubStr`, `Pos`, and `TokenSeq` constructors have all been overloaded to accept a set of values of the corresponding type for its arguments with the expected semantics.

The data-structure supports the following two interesting operations, both of which are required for the partitioning procedure.

Intersection Operation Given two sets of expressions of the same kind, construct a set of expressions that are common to the two given sets. The intersection function is described in Fig 4. The most interesting part is the intersection of two DAGs, which is similar to intersection of two regular automatas. The challenge, compared to regular automata case, is to intersect the labels on the edges - in case of automata, the labels are simply a set of characters, while in our case, the labels are sets of string expressions. We intersect sets of string expressions using the intersection operation supported by the data-structure used for representing those sets of string expressions.

Size Operation Given a set of expressions of some kind, estimate the size of the set. The size function is described in Figure 5. Observe the succinctness benefits provided by the factorization used by each set construct.

4.2 Learning Substring Extraction Logics

In this section, we describe how to learn the set of all `SubStr` expressions in our language that can be used to extract a given substring from a given string. (This is an important component of the procedure `GenerateStr`.) The number of such expressions may be huge, in which case, explicit representation and computation of all these expressions would be infeasible with respect to both time and space. For example, following is a small sample of various logics for extracting "706" from the string "425-706-7709" (call it v_1).

- Second number: $\texttt{SubStr2}(v_1, \text{NumTok}, 2)$.
- Second last alphanumeric token: $\texttt{SubStr2}(v_1, \texttt{AlphNumTok}, -2)$.
- Substring between the first hyphen and the last hyphen: $\texttt{SubStr}(v_1, \texttt{Pos}(\text{HyphenTok}, \epsilon, 1), \texttt{Pos}(\epsilon, \text{HyphenTok}, -1))$.
- First number that occurs between hyphen on both ends. $\texttt{SubStr}(v_1, \texttt{Pos}(\text{HyphenTok}, \texttt{TokenSeq}(\text{NumTok}, \text{HyphenTok}), 1), \texttt{Pos}(\texttt{TokenSeq}(\text{HyphenTok}, \text{NumTok}), \text{HyphenTok}, 1))$.
- First number that is preceded by a number-hyphen sequence. $\texttt{SubStr}(v_1, \texttt{Pos}(\texttt{TokenSeq}(\text{NumTok}, \text{HyphenTok}), \text{NumTok}, 1), \texttt{Pos}(\texttt{TokenSeq}(\text{NumTok}, \text{HyphenTok}, \text{NumTok}), \epsilon, 1))$.

The `GenerateSubstring` procedure performs this task effectively, and is built around the following two key observations.

Decomposition into independent sub-problems The substring-extraction problem can be decomposed into two *independent* position-identification problems, each of which can be solved independently. Note the two independent calls to `GeneratePosition` procedure at Lines 3 and 4 in `GenerateSubstring` procedure in Figure 7. The solutions to the substring-extraction problem can also be maintained succinctly by independently representing the solutions to the two position-identification problems. Note the representation of the `SubStr` constructor in Eq. 1 in Figure 3.

Partitioning of Tokens into Indistinguishable Sets A given string does not often distinguish between several sets of tokens. Hence, for any position-identification problem, the choice of regular expressions for a given string can be restricted to using only one token from each set of indistinguishable tokens. We define this more formally below.

DEFINITION 1 (Indistinguishability). *We say that a token T_1 is* indistinguishable *from token T_2 with respect to a string s if the set of matches of token T_1 in s is same as the set of matches of token T_2 in string s.*

Note that indistinguishability is an equivalence relation.

DEFINITION 2 (Indistinguishability Partition). *Given a string s and a set of tokens, let $IParts_s$ denote the partition of tokens into indistinguishable sets, and let $Reps_s$ denote some set of representative tokens, one from each partition. We use the notation $IParts_s(T)$ to denote the set in which token T lies.*

We use this observation to restrict the choice of tokens used in constructing regular expressions to come from the set Reps_s at Lines 2 and 3 in procedure `GeneratePosition`. This significantly reduces the number of regular expressions that get considered at Lines 2 and 3 without affecting the completeness of the algorithm.

4.3 Learning Traces

In this section, we discuss how to learn the set of all trace expressions (i.e., `Concatenate` constructors) that can be used to generate a given output string from a given input state. The number of such expressions may be huge. For example, consider the problem of transforming phone numbers in Example 10. Consider the second input-output example, where the input state consists of one string "(425)-706-7709" and the output string is "425-706-7709". Figure 6 shows a small sampling of different ways of generating parts of the output string from the input string using `SubStr` and `ConstStr` constructors. (Each substring extraction task itself can be performed in a huge number of ways as explained in Sec 4.2). Following are three of the trace expressions represented in the figure, of which the second one (also shown in bold in the figure), would lead to the correct answer.

1. Extract the substring "425". Extract the substring "-706-7709".

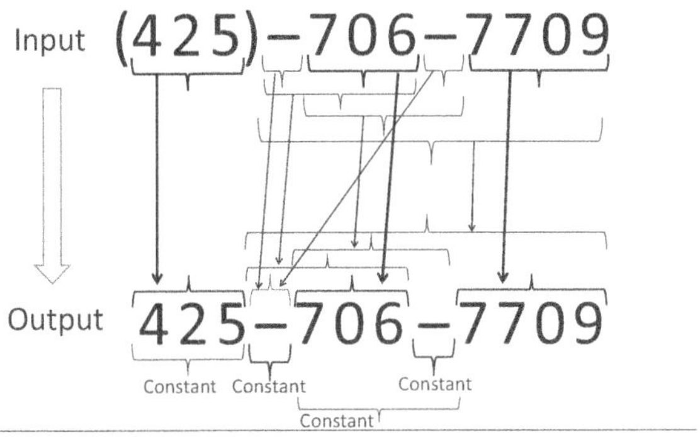

Figure 6. Small sampling of different ways of generating parts of an output string from the input string.

2. Extract the substring "425". Print constant "-". Extract the substring "706". Print constant "-". Extract the substring "7709".
3. Extract the substring "425". Extract the substring "-706". Print constant "-". Extract the substring "7709".

GenerateStr procedure performs this task effectively (by using the DAG data-structure introduced earlier to succinctly represent all trace expressions). It uses the following crucial observations.

Independence of (unknown) sub-problems First, observe that the logic for generating some substring of an output string is completely decoupled from the logic for generating another disjoint substring of the output string. Hence, the problem of generating the output string can be decoupled into independent sub-problems of generating different parts of the output string.

In particular, assume that we have an oracle (as in a PBD system like [11]) that provides us with the decomposition of a given output string into n disjoint adjacent substrings, where each disjoint substring gets generated by a different argument of the enclosing concatenate operator. Given such a decomposition, we can decompose the problem of identifying the trace expression for generating the output string, into n independent sub-problems of generating each of the disjoint adjacent substrings using at atomic expression constructor. These problems can not only be solved independently, but their solutions can also be stored independently to succinctly represent an exponential number of solutions in linear space. However, unfortunately, we do not apriori know the appropriate decomposition of the output string into various parts for which we can independently seek a solution. The naive strategy of enumerating all possible decompositions would not scale since the number of decompositions is exponential in the size of the output string.

Number of possible sub-problems is quadratic Second, observe that the total number of different substrings/parts of a string is quadratic (and not exponential) in the size of the output string. This leads to a succinct representation of all possible decompositions of a string using a DAG representation, and hence allows us to decompose the problem of generating the output string (using a trace expression) into a quadratic number of independent sub-problems of generating different substrings of the output string (using some atomic expression).

With the above two observations, we are now ready to explain the effective functioning of the procedure GenerateStr. The procedure GenerateStr generates a $\text{Dag}(\tilde{\eta}, \eta^s, \eta^t, \tilde{\xi}, W)$ constructor that represents the set of all trace expressions that can generate a given output string from a given input state. The key idea is to construct a node corresponding to each position within the output string and create an edge from a node corresponding to any position to a node corresponding to any later position. Observe that each edge here corresponds to some substring of the output. Each such edge is annotated with the set of all atomic expressions that can generate the corresponding substring (Lines 5 and 6 in procedure GenerateStr). The set of all such SubStr and Loop expressions is generated by Procedures GenerateSubstring and GenerateLoop respectively. The following theorem holds.

THEOREM 1. *Procedure GenerateStr(σ, s) computes the set of all trace expressions e with the following properties:*

A1. (Soundness) e generates the output string s from the input state σ, i.e., $[\![e]\!]\ \sigma = s$.

A2. (Completeness Restriction) Any loop that occurs in e is non-nested and executes at least twice on σ.

PROOF: The procedure GenerateSubstring(σ, s) generates the set of all SubStr expressions that can generate s from σ. The procedure GenerateLoop(σ, s, W) extends the mapping $W(k_1, k_4)$ with all Loop expressions that can generate $s[k_1, k_4]$ from σ and furthermore satisfy the restrictions in A2. Hence, the theorem follows.

4.4 Learning Loops

In this section, we discuss how to infer the set of all Loop constructors that can be used to generate some unknown part of a given output string s from a given input state σ. In the process, we would also identify the unknown part of the output string that the Loop constructor can generate. Procedure GenerateLoop performs this task effectively, and involves the following steps:

1. Guess three positions within the output string k_1, k_2, and k_3.
2. *Unify* the set of trace expressions that can generate $s[k_1 : k_2]$ with the set of trace expressions that can generate $s[k_2 : k_3]$ to obtain a new set of string expressions, say $\tilde{e}$ that uses the loop iterator w. The unification algorithm is explained below.
3. Obtain the set of substrings obtained by running the string expressions $\tilde{e}$ on input σ. If this set contains a singleton string that matches $s[k_1 : k_3]$ for some k_3, then we conclude that $s[k_1 : k_3]$ can be generated by Loop($\lambda w : \tilde{e}$). Otherwise ignore.

The unification algorithm is same as the intersection algorithm except with the following replacement to Eq. 2 in Figure 4.

$$\text{IntersectPos}(k_1, k_2) \quad = \quad (k_2 - k_1)w + k_1 \text{ if } k_1 \neq k_2$$

The key idea above is to guess a set of loop bodies by unifying the sets of trace expressions associated with the substrings $s[k_1 : k_2]$ and $s[k_2 : k_3]$, and then test the validity of the conjectured set of loops. For performance reasons, we do not recursively invoke GenerateLoop (in the call that it makes to GenerateStr). This allows us to discover all single loops. Nested loops may be discovered by controlling the recursion depth.

4.5 Learning Conditionals

In this section, we discuss how to generate the top-level Switch constructor, after having learned, for each input-output example, the set of all trace expressions that can generate the output string from the input state. There are two important components that enable learning of appropriate conditionals: partitioning of input-output examples into disjoint partitions, and learning classifiers based on inputs for those partitions. The classifiers provide the conditionals, while the intersection of the trace sets associated with various inputs in a partition yields the computational branch for the corresponding conditional.

4.5.1 Learning Partitions

In this section, we discuss how to appropriately classify the input-output examples into different partitions - the idea being that exam-

$\texttt{GenerateStringProgram}(S\texttt{: Set of } (\sigma, s) \texttt{ pairs})$
$T := \emptyset$;
foreach $(\sigma, s) \in S$
  $T := T \cup (\{\sigma\}, \texttt{GenerateStr}(\sigma, s))$;
$T := \texttt{GeneratePartition}(T)$;
$\tilde{\sigma}' := \{\sigma \mid (\sigma, s) \in S\}$;
foreach $(\tilde{\sigma}, \tilde{\mathrm{e}}) \in T$:
  let $B[\tilde{\sigma}] := \texttt{GenerateBoolClassifier}(\tilde{\sigma}, \tilde{\sigma}'\text{-}\tilde{\sigma})$
Let $(\tilde{\sigma}_1, \tilde{\mathrm{e}}_1), \ldots, (\tilde{\sigma}_k, \tilde{\mathrm{e}}_k)$ be the k elements in T in increasing order of $\texttt{Size}(\tilde{\mathrm{e}})$.
return $\texttt{Switch}((B[\tilde{\sigma}_1], \tilde{\mathrm{e}}_1), \ldots, (B[\tilde{\sigma}_k], \tilde{\mathrm{e}}_k))$;

$\texttt{GeneratePartition}(S\texttt{: Set of } (\sigma, s) \texttt{ pairs})$
while exists $(\tilde{\sigma}, \tilde{\mathrm{e}}), (\tilde{\sigma}', \tilde{\mathrm{e}}') \in T$ s.t. $\texttt{Comp}(\tilde{\mathrm{e}}, \tilde{\mathrm{e}}')$
  Let $(\tilde{\sigma}_1, \tilde{\mathrm{e}}_1), (\tilde{\sigma}_2, \tilde{\mathrm{e}}_2) \in T$ be s.t. $\texttt{CS}(\tilde{\mathrm{e}}_1, \tilde{\mathrm{e}}_2)$ is largest.
  $T := T - \{(\tilde{\sigma}_1, \tilde{\mathrm{e}}_1), (\tilde{\sigma}_2, \tilde{\mathrm{e}}_2)\} \cup \{(\tilde{\sigma}_1 \cup \tilde{\sigma}_2, \texttt{Intersect}(\tilde{\mathrm{e}}_1, \tilde{\mathrm{e}}_2))\}$;
return T;

$\texttt{GenerateBoolClassifier}(\tilde{\sigma}_1, \tilde{\sigma}_2\texttt{: Set of inputs})$
$\tilde{\sigma}_1' := \tilde{\sigma}_1$; $\texttt{b} := \texttt{false}$;
while $(\tilde{\sigma}_1' \neq \emptyset)$
  $\texttt{Old}\tilde{\sigma}_1' := \tilde{\sigma}_1'$;
  $\tilde{\sigma}_2' := \tilde{\sigma}_2$; $\tilde{\sigma}_1'' := \tilde{\sigma}_1'$; $\texttt{d} := \texttt{true}$;
  while $(\tilde{\sigma}_2' \neq \emptyset)$
    $\texttt{Old}\tilde{\sigma}_2' := \tilde{\sigma}_2'$;
    $\texttt{Preds} := \{\texttt{Match}(v_i, \texttt{r}, c), \neg\texttt{Match}(v_i, \texttt{r}, c) \mid [\![\texttt{Match}(v_i, \texttt{r}, c)]\!]\sigma, \sigma \in \tilde{\sigma}_1 \cup \tilde{\sigma}_2\}$;
    Let $\pi \in \texttt{Preds}$ be s.t. $\texttt{CSP}(\pi, \tilde{\sigma}_1'', \tilde{\sigma}_2')$ is largest.
    $\texttt{d} := \texttt{d} \wedge \pi$;
    $\tilde{\sigma}_1'' := \tilde{\sigma}_1'' - \{\sigma_1 \mid \sigma_1 \in \tilde{\sigma}_1'', \neg[\![\pi]\!]\sigma_1\}$;
    $\tilde{\sigma}_2' := \tilde{\sigma}_2' - \{\sigma_2 \mid \sigma_2 \in \tilde{\sigma}_2', \neg[\![\pi]\!]\sigma_2\}$;
    if $(\texttt{Old}\tilde{\sigma}_2' = \tilde{\sigma}_2')$ then FAIL.
  $\tilde{\sigma}_1' := \tilde{\sigma}_1' - \tilde{\sigma}_1''$; $\texttt{b} := \texttt{b} \vee \texttt{d}$;
  if $(\texttt{Old}\tilde{\sigma}_1' = \tilde{\sigma}_1')$ then FAIL.
return b;

$\texttt{GenerateStr}(\sigma\texttt{: Input state, } s\texttt{: Output string})$
$\tilde{\eta} := \{0, \ldots, \texttt{Length}(s)\}$;
$\eta^s := \{0\}$;
$\eta^t := \{\texttt{Length}(s)\}$;
$\tilde{\xi} := \{\langle i, j\rangle \mid 0 \leq i < j \leq \texttt{Length}(s)\}$;
Let W be the mapping that maps edge $\langle i, j\rangle \in \tilde{\xi}$ to the set $\{\texttt{ConstStr}(s[i : j-1])\} \cup \texttt{GenerateSubstring}(\sigma, s[i : j-1])$;
$W' := \texttt{GenerateLoop}(\sigma, s, W)$;
return $\texttt{Dag}(\tilde{\eta}, \eta^s, \eta^t, \tilde{\xi}, W')$;

$\texttt{GenerateLoop}(\sigma\texttt{: Input state, } s\texttt{: Output string, } W)$
$W' := W$;
foreach $0 \leq k_1, k_2, k_3 < \texttt{Length}(s)$:
  $\tilde{\mathrm{e}}_1 := \texttt{GenerateStr}(\sigma, s[k_1 : k_2])$; $\tilde{\mathrm{e}}_2 := \texttt{GenerateStr}(\sigma, s[k_2 : k_3])$;
  $\tilde{\mathrm{e}} := \texttt{Unify}(\tilde{\mathrm{e}}_1, \tilde{\mathrm{e}}_2)$;
  if $([\![\texttt{Loop}(\lambda w : \tilde{\mathrm{e}})]\!]\sigma = \{s[k_1 : k_4]\})$ for some k_4
    $W'(\langle k_1, k_4\rangle) := W'(\langle k_1, k_4\rangle) \cup \{\texttt{Loop}(\lambda w : \tilde{\mathrm{e}})\}$;
return W';

$\texttt{GenerateSubstring}(\sigma\texttt{: Input state, } s\texttt{: String})$
$\texttt{result} := \emptyset$;
foreach (i, k) s.t. s is substring of $\sigma(v_i)$ at position k
  $Y_1 := \texttt{GeneratePosition}(\sigma(v_i), k)$;
  $Y_2 := \texttt{GeneratePosition}(\sigma(v_i), k + \texttt{Length}(s))$;
  $\texttt{result} := \texttt{result} \cup \{\texttt{SubStr}(v_i, Y_1, Y_2)\}$;
return result;

$\texttt{GeneratePosition}(s\texttt{: String, } k\texttt{: int})$
$\texttt{result} := \{\texttt{CPos}(k), \texttt{CPos}(\text{-}(\texttt{Length}(s)\text{-}k))\}$;
foreach $\texttt{r}_1 = \texttt{TokenSeq}(\texttt{T}_1, \cdot\cdot, \texttt{T}_n)$ matching $s[k_1 : k\text{-}1]$ for some k_1:
  foreach $\texttt{r}_2 = \texttt{TokenSeq}(\texttt{T}_1', \cdot\cdot, \texttt{T}_m')$ matching $s[k : k_2]$ for some k_2:
    $\texttt{r}_{12} := \texttt{TokenSeq}(\texttt{T}_1, \cdot\cdot, \texttt{T}_n, \texttt{T}_1', \cdot\cdot, \texttt{T}_m')$;
    Let c be s.t. $s[k_1 : k_2]$ is the cth match for $\texttt{r}_{12}$ in s.
    Let c' be the total number of matches for $\texttt{r}_{12}$ in s.
    $\tilde{\texttt{r}}_1 := \texttt{generateRegex}(\texttt{r}_1, s)$;
    $\tilde{\texttt{r}}_2 := \texttt{generateRegex}(\texttt{r}_2, s)$;
    $\texttt{result} := \texttt{result} \cup \{\texttt{Pos}(\tilde{\texttt{r}}_1, \tilde{\texttt{r}}_2, \{c, \text{-}(c'\text{-}c\text{+}1)\})\}$;
return result;

$\texttt{generateRegex}(\texttt{r: Regular Expression, } s\texttt{: String})$
let r be of the form $\texttt{TokenSeq}(\texttt{T}_1, \cdot\cdot, \texttt{T}_n)$.
return $\texttt{TokenSeq}(\texttt{IParts}_s(\texttt{T}_1), \cdot\cdot, \texttt{IParts}_s(\texttt{T}_n))$;

Figure 7. Algorithm for learning string programs that are consistent with a given set S of input-output examples.

ples that end up in the same partition are those that require similar computational processing. We attempt to achieve this by requiring the partitioning to satisfy the following two properties.

- Utility: For each partition, there is at least one trace expression e that is consistent with all examples in that partition.
- Minimality: Number of partitions should be as small as possible.

Observe that the utility requirement can be satisfied trivially on its own by placing each example in its own partition, but then it would not lead to any generalization, which in turn would not lead to any convergence. The minimality requirement can be satisfied trivially on its own by placing all examples in the same partition, but it may lead to failure because there might not be any trace expression that can express the transformation for all the examples. It is the combination of these two requirements that leads to faster successful convergence.

It would be computationally expensive to try out all possible partitioning choices and select the one that contains smallest number of partitions. We present a partitioning algorithm (based on greedy algorithmic design pattern) that is not only efficient, but in practice, yields the smallest number of partitions.

The algorithm for learning partitions is described in procedure GeneratePartition in Figure 7. We start with singleton partitions that contain one input each, along with associated trace sets. We then merge two partitions only if their associated trace sets have at least one trace expression in common. (This criterion leads to satisfaction of the utility requirement). We refer to such trace sets as being compatible with each other.

DEFINITION 3 (Compatible). *We say that trace sets $\tilde{e}_1$ and $\tilde{e}_2$ are* compatible *with each other, denoted Comp($\tilde{e}_1, \tilde{e}_2$), if*

$$Comp(\tilde{e}_1, \tilde{e}_2) \stackrel{def}{=} \mathit{Intersect}(\tilde{e}_1, \tilde{e}_2) \neq \emptyset$$

Often there are multiple choices of pairs of partitions that can be merged with each other. We select a pair that has the highest *compatibility score*. The compatibility score is designed to facilitate partitioning decisions that, at least in practice, lead to the smallest number of partitions. The compatibility score has two components CS_1 and CS_2.

CS_1 measures agreement of two partitions with respect to the compatibility of their trace sets and their intersection with all other trace sets. In particular, if two trace sets $\tilde{e}_1$ and $\tilde{e}_2$ are both compatible with $\tilde{e}_3$, and so is $\texttt{Intersect}(\tilde{e}_1, \tilde{e}_2)$, then we bump up the compatibility score of $\tilde{e}_1$ and $\tilde{e}_2$. Also, if two trace sets $\tilde{e}_1$ and $\tilde{e}_2$ are both not compatible with $\tilde{e}_3$, then we bump up the compatibility score of $\tilde{e}_1$ and $\tilde{e}_2$. Note that in either of above-mentioned two cases, the potential of $\tilde{e}_1$ or $\tilde{e}_2$ to merge with $\tilde{e}_3$ is unchanged as a result of the intersection of $\tilde{e}_1$ and $\tilde{e}_2$. The idea is to select those partitions for merging that keep alive merging potential with other partitions in a later step, resulting in a smaller number of overall partitions.

CS_2 is used to produce a finer score in case there are ties on the CS_1 score. It gives preference to those pairs of trace sets whose relative size after intersection is largest. The idea is that a larger trace set is more likely to merge with other trace sets in a later step, resulting in a smaller number of overall partitions.

DEFINITION 4 (Compatibility score). *Let $\tilde{e}_1$ and $\tilde{e}_2$ be two compatible trace sets drawn from a set $T = \{\tilde{e}_{\sigma(1)}, \ldots, \tilde{e}_{\sigma(n)}\}$ of trace sets. We define the compatibility score of $\tilde{e}_1$ and $\tilde{e}_2$ with respect to T, denoted by $CS(\tilde{e}_1, \tilde{e}_2, T)$ as:*

$$CS(\tilde{e}_1, \tilde{e}_2, T) \stackrel{def}{=} (CS_1(\tilde{e}_1, \tilde{e}_2, T), CS_2(\tilde{e}_1, \tilde{e}_2))$$

where CS_1 and CS_2 are defined as follows:

$$CS_1(\tilde{e}_1, \tilde{e}_2, T) \stackrel{def}{=} \sum_{\tilde{e}_k \in T, k \neq 1, k \neq 2} z(\tilde{e}_1, \tilde{e}_2, \tilde{e}_k)$$

$$z(\tilde{e}_1, \tilde{e}_2, \tilde{e}_k) \equiv \begin{cases} 1 & if\ (Comp(\tilde{e}_1, \tilde{e}_k) = Comp(\tilde{e}_2, \tilde{e}_k) \\ & \quad = Comp(\texttt{Intersect}(\tilde{e}_1, \tilde{e}_2), \tilde{e}_k)) \\ 0 & otherwise \end{cases}$$

$$CS_2(\tilde{e}_1, \tilde{e}_2) \stackrel{def}{=} \frac{Size(\texttt{Intersect}(\tilde{e}_1, \tilde{e}_2))}{Max\{Size(\tilde{e}_1), Size(\tilde{e}_2)\}}$$

Comparison on compatibility scores (x,y), which are pairs of numbers, is defined using lexicographic ordering, i.e.,

$$(x_1, y_1) > (x_2, y_2) \stackrel{def}{=} (x_1 > x_2) \lor (x_1 = x_2 \land y_1 > y_2)$$

We repeat the merging process one by one until no more partitions can be merged.

4.5.2 Learning Classifiers for Partitions

In this section, we discuss how to generate classifiers for the various partitions generated using the algorithm `GeneratePartition` described above. A classifier for a partition is a boolean condition (over the set of predicates in our language) that returns true for all inputs in the partition and returns false for all inputs not in that partition. We attempt to learn not just any classifier, but a simple (small-sized) one.

Given a set of predicates, one simple approach can be to enumerate boolean formulas of increasingly large sizes and check if it can act as a classifier for some partition. However, this approach would be computationally expensive. We present a classifier learning algorithm (based on greedy algorithmic design pattern) that is not only efficient, but in practice, yields smallest classifiers.

The algorithm for learning classifiers is described in procedure `GenerateBoolClassifier` in Figure 7. We learn a boolean classifier in DNF form. The loop in line 2 learns a new conjunct d in each iteration with the property that none of the inputs in $\tilde{\sigma}_2$ satisfy d, but *several* inputs in $\tilde{\sigma}_1'$ do. $\tilde{\sigma}_1'$ is that monotonically decreasing subset of inputs from $\tilde{\sigma}_1$ that are not yet covered by the disjunctive boolean formula b learned so far. The loop in line 2 is repeated until $\tilde{\sigma}_1'$ becomes empty (or it does not change).

The loop in line 5 identifies a new predicate π in each iteration with the property that *several* inputs in $\tilde{\sigma}_1''$ satisfy π, but *several* inputs in $\tilde{\sigma}_2'$ do not satisfy π, and then adds it to the conjunct d. $\tilde{\sigma}_1''$ and $\tilde{\sigma}_2'$ are both those monotonically decreasing subsets of $\tilde{\sigma}_1'$ and $\tilde{\sigma}_2$ respectively that satisfy the conjunct d built so far. $\tilde{\sigma}_2$ is used to decide whether or not the loop in line 5 needs to be iterated any further, while $\tilde{\sigma}_1''$ is used to update $\tilde{\sigma}_1'$, which is required for the loop in line 2. Hence, the following theorem holds.

THEOREM 2. *If $\mathit{GenerateBoolClassifier}(\tilde{\sigma}_1, \tilde{\sigma}_2)$ does not fail and returns a boolean condition b, then all inputs in $\tilde{\sigma}_1$ satisfy b and none of the inputs in $\tilde{\sigma}_2$ satisfy b.*

To ensure learning of small boolean formulas, we ensure that the predicate π that is chosen at Line 8 is such that

- *several* inputs in $\tilde{\sigma}_2'$ do not satisfy π. This keeps $\tilde{\sigma}_2'$ smaller, which helps to terminate the inner loop at Line 5 faster, which leads to conjuncts d containing small number of predicates.
- *several* inputs in $\tilde{\sigma}_1''$ satisfy π. This keeps $\tilde{\sigma}_1''$ larger, which helps to keep $\tilde{\sigma}_1'$ smaller, which in turn helps to terminate the outer loop in Line 2 faster, which leads to fewer number of conjuncts.

To enable a selection that satisfies above-mentioned criterion, we choose a predicate with highest *classification score* (as defined below) with respect to the sets $\tilde{\sigma}_1''$ and $\tilde{\sigma}_2'$.

DEFINITION 5 (Classification Score of a Predicate). *Given two sets of inputs $\tilde{\sigma}_1$ and $\tilde{\sigma}_2$, and a unary predicate π over inputs, we define the classification score of π, denoted by $CSP(\pi, \tilde{\sigma}_1, \tilde{\sigma}_2)$, as:*

$$CSP(\pi, \tilde{\sigma}_1, \tilde{\sigma}_2) \stackrel{def}{=} Size(\{\sigma_1 \mid \sigma_1 \in \tilde{\sigma}_1, [\![\pi]\!]\sigma_1\}) \times Size(\{\sigma_2 \mid \sigma_2 \in \tilde{\sigma}_2, \neg[\![\pi]\!]\sigma_2\})$$

4.6 Correctness

If procedure `GenerateBoolClassifier` does not fail, the synthesis algorithm succeeds. In that case, the following theorem holds.

THEOREM 3 (Soundness). *The set $\tilde{P}$ of string expressions returned by $\mathit{GenerateStringProgram}(\{(\sigma_i, s_i)\}_i)$ are all consistent with each input-output pair (σ_i, s_i), i.e.,*

$$\forall P \in \tilde{P}\ \forall i: \ ([\![P]\!]\ \sigma_i) = s_i$$

The proof of theorem 3 follows from similar soundness properties of the involved procedures, of which the most interesting one has been stated in Theorem 2.

CONJECTURE 1 (Completeness). *If there exists a string expression in our language that is consistent with the given set of input-output pairs, the algorithm produces one.*

The above conjecture is true at the level of traces, i.e., if there exists a consistent trace expression (satisfying the restriction A2 in Theorem 1), then the algorithm generates it. However, the above conjecture may not be true in general. In practice though, we have observed our partitioning and classification procedures to always work, and it appears that there are some interesting theoretical properties of these procedures that might pave the way for proving the above conjecture under some general conditionals. This investigation is left for future work.

4.7 Discussion

4.7.1 Adaptability to Language Extensions

The algorithm can be easily adapted to deal with the following language extensions. The choice of tokens/predicates can be enriched arbitrarily as long as they can be efficiently enumerated. The choice of regular expressions is inextensible for reasons mentioned earlier. The substring construct can be extended further to allow for a constant index offset into the current choice of substrings. The loop construct can be enriched to allow for termination conditions based on position logic or conjunctions of predicates.

It may be possible to nest conditionals inside loops. The key algorithmic idea would be to recursively perform partitioning and classification, as is done at the top-level, instead of a simple unification. However, performance may be a concern.

4.7.2 General Principles

Here, we summarize some key general principles of our learning algorithm. The algorithm first learn traces and then infer loops/conditionals. This is unlike recent work on more-general program synthesis techniques (e.g., [19]) that attempt to learn everything at the same time, often leading to unscalablility.

For learning conditionals, the algorithm uses a greedy strategy based on scoring functions to first infer partitioning and then boolean classification. The standard way to learn conditionals in recent program synthesis work is to phrase this as a combinatorial search problem (using SAT/SMT solvers), which leads to solutions that may not scale in real-time settings like ours.

For learning traces, the algorithm uses DAG based data-structures that can represent and manipulate (intersection, evaluation, size/rank computation) huge sets of programs. This approach would work in general for any *term algebra*. The DAG based data-structure can be likened to BDDs, which can succinctly represent and manipulate (conjunction, disjunction, negation) huge sets of program states, and are popular in the verification community.

5. Usability Extensions

5.1 Active Interaction Model (for easier interaction)

A simple interaction model can be to ask the user to investigate the results of a synthesized program on other inputs in the spreadsheet and to report any discrepancy. However, this may be cumbersome in case of large spread-sheets. To enable easier interaction, we exploit the fact that our synthesis algorithm returns a set of programs $\tilde{P}$. The synthesis system can run $\tilde{P}$ on every input σ in the spreadsheet to generate a set of corresponding outputs $\tilde{s}$, i.e., $\tilde{s} = \{[\![P]\!]\sigma \mid P \in \tilde{P}\}$. The set $\tilde{s}$ can be computed directly without explicitly enumerating all programs in $\tilde{P}$. (This requires exploiting the structural decomposition of the underlying data-structures as is done in `Intersect` and Size methods - we leave out details for lack of space.) The synthesis system can then highlight any input (for user inspection) whose corresponding output set contains at least two strings. We refer to this as the *active interaction model*.

It is interesting to compare the above idea with the idea of *distinguishing inputs* that was introduced recently in the context of synthesis of bit-vector algorithms [8]. An application of that idea in our context would mean picking any two (semantically different) programs from $\tilde{P}$ and then synthesizing an input on which the two programs yield different outputs. Such an approach would not be effective in our setting since, as is illustrated by the case-study in Example 1, convergence does not require to narrow the choice of consistent programs down to a semantically unique program in the language. It is sufficient to narrow the choice down to that set of consistent programs that are equivalent with respect to the finite number of inputs in the spreadsheet.

5.2 Noise Handling

The algorithm declares failure when it fails to learn a boolean classification scheme. In that case, it can attempt to identify any noise (inadvertent error in one input-output example) as follows. The algorithm classifies an input-output example as a *potentially-noisy* if the input belongs to a singleton partition, but the boolean classification scheme fails to generate a boolean classifier for that singleton partition. For each potentially-noisy example, the algorithm ignores the corresponding partition, and re-learns the boolean classification scheme for other partitions. If it succeeds, it classifies the example as noisy and presents that to the user for validation, and can even suggest a fix by running the learned program on the input corresponding to the noisy example.

EXAMPLE 11. *Consider the following set of examples provided to our tool in one of the scenarios, in which the user failed to spell Kimberly correctly in the output column.*

Input v_1	*Input v_2*	*Output*
Otis	*Daniels*	*Otis, D.*
Kimberly	*Jones*	*Kimberley, J.*
Mary	*Leslie*	*Mary, L.*

The `GeneratePartition` algorithm groups the first and third example in one partition, while the second example belongs to a singleton partition. The `GenerateBoolClassifier` algorithm fails to generate a boolean classification scheme that distinguishes the two partitions. Ignoring the singleton partition enables `GenerateBoolClassifier` algorithm to succeed trivially (since there is only one partition). The algorithm declares the second example to be noisy and asks the user to investigate if she really meant "Kimberly, J." (which it generates by running the learned program on the noisy input).

5.3 Ranking of Multiple Solutions (for faster convergence)

Selecting an expressive language for inductive program synthesis systems raises an interesting dilemma. While it makes users who want to program sophisticated tasks happy, it may adversely impact users who want to program simple tasks but now may require to provide more bits for disambiguation of their intent (which manifests in the need to provide more examples and more rounds of interaction). The Occam's razor principle, which states that the simplest explanation is usually the correct one, comes to our rescue here. We define a comparison scheme between different string expressions by defining a partial order between them. Some of these choices are subjective, but have been observed to work well. (There is also a fascinating prospect of personalizing this partial order based on the user intent observed during last few scenarios).

A `Concatenate` constructor is simpler than another one if it contains smaller number of arguments or its arguments are pairwise simpler. Similarly for `TokenSeq` constructor. StartTok and EndTok are simpler than all other tokens (suggesting that extraction logics based on the start/end of strings are more common). A token corresponding to a character class is simpler than the one corresponding to a smaller character class. (We favor generality here.) `CPos` expressions are simpler than `Pos` expressions (giving preference to extraction logics based on constant offsets). A `SubStr` constructor is simpler than both `ConstStr` constructor (it is less likely for constant parts of an output string to also occur in the input) and `Concatenate` constructor (if there is a long substring match between input and output, it is more likely that the corresponding part of the output was produced by a single substring extraction logic).

Procedures `generateRegex`, `GenerateLoop`, `GenerateStr`, `GeneratePosition`, and `GenerateSubstring`, which generate a set of solutions, can take this ordering into account to produce an ordered set of solutions.

6. Prototype Tool

We have built the program synthesis system described in this paper as an add-in, called QuickCode, for Microsoft Excel 2010. Microsoft Excel is the most popularly used spreadsheet system in the world and is widely regarded to be the swiss army knife of all businesses.

The program synthesis system has two components: (a) the algorithm described in Section 4, which has been implemented in C# (it is less than 5000 lines of code), and (b) the usability extensions described in Section 5, which are supported using a simple, but cool, graphical user interface described below.

6.1 User Interface

The user first selects a rectangular region of spreadsheet containing both input and output columns. We treat the mostly populated columns as input columns, and less populated columns as output columns. However, we also provide the flexibility for the user to select multiple column ranges and identify explicitly which columns are inputs and which columns are outputs (since it may be the case that most cells in an input column have null entries, while our default treatment would be to regard it as an output column). We treat the rows that contain entries for an output column as input-output examples for the program to be learned for that column.

The user then presses the QuickCode button. The system then populates the spreadsheet as follows. It invokes the synthesis algorithm (procedure `GenerateStringProgram`) for each of the output column. For each output cell $\alpha_{r,c}$ (in row r and output column c), the system runs the generated set of programs for output column c on the input state specified in row r to generate an ordered set $\tilde{s}$ of possible outputs. The system populates the cell $\alpha_{r,c}$ as follows:

- If $\tilde{s}$ contains one string (the most common case), the system populates the cell with that string.
- If $\tilde{s}$ contains multiple strings, the system populates the cell with the first string (top ranked solution), but highlights it to point out to the user that there are multiple computational interpretations of the few examples provided by the user, and that the user may want to investigate the output of the highlighted cell.
- If $\tilde{s}$ is empty, the system populates the cell with ?? to draw the attention that the user should provide the output for that cell.

The user may then (repeatedly) fix contents of any cell by right-clicking on it, wherein a dialog box opens up that allows the user to choose from other strings in the corresponding sequence $\tilde{o}$, or to provide a new output altogether. After any such fix, the above learning process is automatically repeated with the extended set of input-output examples, and the contents of spreadsheet are automatically updated to reflect the new learned results.

6.2 Evaluation Metrics

Our synthesis system can be evaluated against several metrics stated below.

Algorithmic Performance: This is a measure of the effectiveness of the data-structures used by the algorithm. The algorithm was timed to take less than 0.1 seconds on average for a varied benchmark suite of more than 100 problem instances drawn from online help forums or obtained from Excel product team as representative examples. (The examples described in this paper form a representative part of this benchmark suite.) Each problem instance contained up to 10 input-output pairs (more than what the user would want to provide in any scenario) and each string in any pair contained up to 100 characters (more than what is typical of spreadsheet cells). Experiments were performed on a machine with Intel Core-2-Duo 2.8 GHz CPU, and 4 GB RAM.

Number of Interactive Rounds: This is a measure of the generalization power of the conditional learning part of the algorithm and the ranking scheme. We observed that the tool typically requires just one round of interaction, when the user is smart enough to give an example for each input format (which typically range from 1 to 3) to start with. It is heartening to note that this was indeed the case for most scenarios in our benchmarks, even though our algorithm can function robustly without this assumption. The maximum number of interactive rounds required in any scenario was 4 (with 2 to 3 being a more typical number). The maximum number of examples required in any scenario over all possible interactions was 10.

Success Ratio: We have not come across any problem instance that can be expressed in our language, but our algorithm fails to converge to the correct solution. This is a measure of the validity of the completeness hypothesis discussed in Section 4.6.

However, we have found several problem instances that cannot be expressed in our language. Most of these instances are related to semantic entity reasoning (such as transforming dates into day of the week). For syntactic string manipulation tasks, we have been more than pleasantly surprised at the expressiveness of our language. Few testing moments came in the middle of some internal demos to large audiences, where we were asked to try out modified scenarios on the spot (on real spreadsheet data). The tool successfully learned the desired transformations in all those cases.

Following are a few examples of scenarios where QuickCode was used by fellow colleagues to perform tasks beyond the imagination of the author.

EXAMPLE 12 (Synthesis of part of a future extension of itself). *The synthesis system is currently being extended with semantic knowledge of common entities that would allow the system to perform transformations that are beyond the realm of syntactic computations. One of the dictionaries that was recently added to the system was mapping from a country's international dialing code to the name of that country. Rishabh Singh performed this task, which he originally thought would take around an hour (in absence of any scripting), in less than a minute using the QuickCode add-in (after copying and pasting the data from Wikipedia into an Excel spreadsheet).*

Input v_1	*Input v_2*	*Output*
Albania	*355*	*case 355: return "Albania";*
Algeria	*213*	*case 213: return "Algeria";*

String Program:

$\texttt{Concatenate}(\texttt{ConstStr}(\text{"}case\ \text{"}), v_2, \texttt{ConstStr}(\text{": }return\ \text{""}),$
$v_1, \texttt{ConstStr}(\text{"";"}))$

The above examples were sufficient for QuickCode to populate the spreadsheet with the desired output for more than 200 rows, each containing data for a different country. The resultant code-fragment in the output column was copied and pasted in Visual Studio Development Environment as part of a switch statement, and it compiled!

EXAMPLE 13 (Filtering Task). *Ben Zorn wanted to estimate the total number of page-hits to links in the pictures directory from weekly statistics consisting of pairs of links and page-hits. He tried to use the QuickCode add-in by giving examples where the output column was a copy of the input page-hit column only if the input link column contained "pictures" in the path.*

Input v_1	*Input v_2*	*Output*
/um/people/sumitg/pictures/lake-tahoe/index.html	*192*	*192*
/um/people/sumitg/index.html	*104*	*0*
/um/people/sumitg/pubs/speed.html	*16*	*0*
/um/people/sumitg/pubs/popl10_synthesis.pdf	*13*	*0*
/um/people/sumitg/pictures/verona/index.html	*7*	*7*
/um/people/sumitg/pictures/kerela/target21.html	*3*	*3*

Quite surprisingly for the author, the QuickCode add-in worked successfully (without use of its hidden capability of being able to add new tokens - addition of "pictures" token would have done the trick). Closer investigation of the generated program revealed another trick for solving the same problem: all (and only) "pictures" links had 6 occurrences of the backslash token - a pattern that could not have been easy for the user to discover.

String Program:
$\texttt{Switch}((b_1, v_2), (b_2, \texttt{ConstStr}(0)))$, *where*
$b_1 \equiv \texttt{Match}(v_1, \mathit{SlashTok}, 6)$, *and* $b_2 \equiv \neg\texttt{Match}(v_1, \mathit{SlashTok}, 6)$.

EXAMPLE 14 (Arithmetic Task). *The synthesis engine currently does not support any arithmetic reasoning. Hence, we thought that a few examples found on Excel help forums, asking for computing the sum of all numbers in a string, had to wait. However, Bill Harris showed us a cute trick that almost did it.*

Input v_1	*Output*
Alpha 10 Beta 20 Charlie 30 Delta	*10+20+30*
POPL 9 CAV 7 PLDI 6 ESOP 4	*9+7+6+4*

String Program:

$$\texttt{Concatenate}(\texttt{Loop}(\lambda w : \texttt{Concatenate}(\texttt{SubStr}(v_1, p_1, p_2), \texttt{ConstStr}(\text{"}+\text{"}))), \texttt{SubStr2}(v_1, \mathit{NumTok}, -1))$$

where $p_1 \equiv \texttt{Pos}(\epsilon, \mathit{NumTok}, w)$ *and*
$p_2 \equiv \texttt{Pos}(\mathit{NumTok}, \texttt{TokenSeq}(\mathit{NonDigitTok}, \mathit{NumTok}), w)$.

It is interesting to note above how the loop constructor gets used to print all, but last, numbers, each followed by a plus sign (The position expression p_2 *ensures that there better be another number following the number to be extracted). The last integer is then concatenated separately. (The desired sum can now be obtained by formatting the output column as a number inside Excel.)*

7. Related Work

Work on learning concepts such as deterministic finite state automata [1], or regular transducers [20] from examples is not applicable in our setting because it requires making many more queries to the user, and most string processing tasks described in this paper are more expressive than what can be expressed by these concepts.

The most closely related work is that of automating text-editing using demonstrations or examples. These text-editor techniques may be lifted to the spreadsheet setting, but they would not work well because (a) the real spreadsheet scenarios are more challenging than what these techniques can handle, (b) the PBD interface, inherent to most of these techniques, requires users to provide much more information that is way beyond the usability bar in spreadsheets. We explain these issues below.

Text-editing using Demonstrations SMARTedit [11] is a Programming by Demonstration (PBD) system for learning text-editing commands, where the primitive program statements include moving the cursor to a new position and inserting/deleting text. However, there are two significant differences: (a) The language of programs considered is not as expressive as required in the spreadsheet setting. In particular, it does not provide support for conditionals, which are very important for data cleansing tasks in spreadsheets. Hence, it cannot be applied for the processing required in Examples 7, 8, 9, 10, 13. Also, its cursor movement logic is restricted to positions *either before or after* the kth occurrence of a *single* token, while scanning from *left side*. In contrast, our position extraction logic is much more powerful - it allows to identify positions based on k^{th} occurrence of *sequences* of tokens *both before and after* the desired position, while scanning from *left or right side*. As a result, the SMARTedit system cannot be applied for processing required in Examples 1, 3, 5, and 14. (b) More significantly, as for any PBD system, the user is required to provide a complete demonstration or trace, where the demonstration consists of a sequence of the editor state after each primitive action, really spelling out how to do the transformation, but on a given example. The user is also required to segment each iteration of an inner loop. Further, PBD based systems also have the drawback of being sensitive to the order in which the user chooses to perform actions. Our system is based on Programming by Example (as opposed to Demonstration) - it requires the user to only provide the final state (as opposed to also providing the intermediate states). This renders our system much more usable [10], however, at the expense of making the learning problem much more difficult, for which we do present an effective algorithm.

TELS [22] is another PBD system that records high-level actions similar to the actions used in SMARTedit, and implements a set of heuristics/expert rules for generalizing the arguments of each of the actions. However, TELS's dependence on heuristic rules to describe the possible generalizations makes it difficult to understand the hypothesis space clearly, as well as to imagine applying it to the different domain of spreadsheet applications.

Simultaneous editing [15] is another PBD-like system that allows the user to define a set of regions to edit, and then allows the user to make edits in one, while the system makes equivalent editing in all other records. The inference used in simultaneous editing is much less powerful since it does not support conditional or loopy edits (every editing action is applied uniformly to every record).

Text-editing using Examples Nix described a text-editing system that synthesizes *gap programs* based on examples [17]. A gap program is a collection of (pattern, replacement) pairs, where each pattern is composed of constants and variables that bind to the text in between the constants, and a replacement can be a constant string or a variable from the input pattern. Gap programs are not expressive enough to represent the solution of most of the string processing benchmark examples described in this paper.

Data Processing for Programmers The PADS project has enabled simplification of ad hoc data processing tasks for programmers by contributing along several dimensions: development of domain specific languages for describing text structure or data format [2, 3], learning algorithms for automatically inferring such formats [4], and a markup language to allow users to add simple annotations to enable more effective learning of text structure [23]. The learned format can then be used by programmers for documentation or implementation of custom data analysis tools. In contrast, the focus of this paper is to enable end-users (non-programmers) to perform small, often one-off, repetitive tasks on their spreadsheet data. Asking end-users to provide annotations for learning (relatively simple) text structure, and then develop custom tools to format/process the inferred structure is way above the expertise and usability bar for these users. Hence, we are interested in automating the entire end-to-end process, which includes not only learning the text structure from the inputs, but also learning the desired transformation from the outputs.

Algorithmic Techniques [6] provides a good survey of various program synthesis techniques: exhaustive search, logical reasoning, probabilistic inference, and version-space algebras. *Exhaustive search* based techniques would not scale for our problem setting since the underlying state space (even for programs of small bounded size) is huge. *Logical reasoning* techniques (such as those used in learning straight-line bit-vector programs from input-output examples [8], or loopy programs from logical specifications [19]) are not suited for various reasons: they are not as scalable (several minutes are acceptable for discovering a new bit-vector algorithm, but not for an interactive spreadsheet session); they cannot deal with noise in the user input; they cannot easily compute all solutions (required for providing various computational interpretations to the user for an ambiguous input).

The GenerateStr part of the synthesis algorithm presented in this paper is closest to the *version-space algebra* approach that involves maintaining a set of all hypotheses (drawn from a hypothesis space) that are consistent with a sequence of observed examples. Mitchell originally used this idea for refinement-based learning of boolean functions [16], while Lau et.al. extended the concept to learning more complex functions in a PBD setting [13]. Our synthesis algorithm shows how the concepts of version-space algebra can be lifted to the PBE (Programming by Example) setting, for a fairly expressive string expression language involving conditionals and loops. The idea of using DAGs as the version space for concatenate constructor is inspired by the use of a similar data-structure in a very different context of solving an important open problem related to *global value numbering* [7]. The novel concepts introduced in this paper are quite general - we feel that they might be used to create PBE versions of other version-space algebra based PBD systems (e.g., those that learn shell scripts [12] or imperative Python programs [14]).

8. Conclusion

General purpose computational devices, such as cell-phones, computers, are becoming accessible to people at large at an impressive rate. In the future, robots will become house-hold entities. But, unfortunately, programming general purpose platforms has never been easy, because we are still mostly stuck with the model of providing step-by-step, detailed, and syntactically correct instructions on *how* to accomplish a certain task, instead of simply describing *what* the task is. Program synthesis has the revolutionary potential to change this landscape, when targeted for the right set of people, for the right set of problems, and using the right interaction model.

In this paper, we have identified a killer application, that of automating string processing in spreadsheets, which hundreds of millions of end-users struggle with on a regular basis (as is evident from online help forums and talking to product groups). We have developed an efficient algorithm to help automate a variety of string processing tasks from input-output examples (which we found to be the most natural intent expression mechanism on help forums). We have paid special attention to usability issues and crossed the line from developing an academic-only technology to one that is ready to be deployed.

Acknowledgments

Thanks to Ben Zorn who had such a belief in the promise of this technology that he helped find connections in product teams even before a prototype could be built. Thanks to the Excel product team who kept engaging with us despite their initial skepticism whether such a "magical" technology can ever be possible. Thanks to Piali Choudhury for building a cool UI for the tool. Thanks to Bill Harris and Rishabh Singh for adding new features and taking the technology to another level, details of which are beyond the scope of this paper. Thanks to Ras Bodik, Venkie, and David Walker for useful discussions. Finally to my Excel-literate parents and spouse for the best (tear-rendering) compliment after playing with the tool: "For the first time, we understand what your research is about".

References

[1] D. Angluin. Learning regular sets from queries and counterexamples. *Inf. Comput.*, 75(2):87–106, 1987.

[2] K. Fisher and R. Gruber. PADS: a domain-specific language for processing ad hoc data. In *PLDI*, pages 295–304, 2005.

[3] K. Fisher, Y. Mandelbaum, and D. Walker. The next 700 data description languages. In *POPL*, pages 2–15, 2006.

[4] K. Fisher, D. Walker, K. Q. Zhu, and P. White. From dirt to shovels: fully automatic tool generation from ad hoc data. In *POPL*, 2008.

[5] M. Gualtieri. Deputize end-user developers to deliver business agility and reduce costs. In *Forrester Report for Application Development and Program Management Professionals*, April 2009.

[6] S. Gulwani. Dimensions in program synthesis. In *PPDP*. ACM, 2010.

[7] S. Gulwani and G. C. Necula. A polynomial-time algorithm for global value numbering. In *SAS*, pages 212–227, 2004.

[8] S. Jha, S. Gulwani, S. Seshia, and A. Tiwari. Oracle-guided component-based program synthesis. In *ICSE*, 2010.

[9] A. J. Ko, B. A. Myers, and H. H. Aung. Six learning barriers in end-user programming systems. In *VL/HCC*, pages 199–206, 2004.

[10] T. Lau. Why PBD systems fail: Lessons learned for usable AI. In *CHI 2008 Workshop on Usable AI*, Florence, Italy, 2008.

[11] T. Lau, S. Wolfman, P. Domingos, and D. Weld. Programming by demonstration using version space algebra. *Machine Learning*, 53(1-2), 2003.

[12] T. Lau, L. Bergman, V. Castelli, and D. Oblinger. Programming shell scripts by demonstration. In *Workshop on SCLAS, AAAI*, 2004.

[13] T. A. Lau, P. Domingos, and D. S. Weld. Version space algebra and its application to programming by demonstration. In *ICML*, 2000.

[14] T. A. Lau, P. Domingos, and D. S. Weld. Learning programs from traces using version space algebra. In *K-CAP*, pages 36–43, 2003.

[15] R. C. Miller and B. A. Myers. Interactive simultaneous editing of multiple text regions. In *USENIX Annual Technical Conference*, 2001.

[16] T. M. Mitchell. Generalization as search. *Artif. Intell.*, 18(2), 1982.

[17] R. P. Nix. Editing by example. *TOPLAS*, 7(4):600–621, 1985.

[18] S. Russell and P. Norvig. *Artificial Intelligence: A Modern Approach (2nd Edition)*. Prentice Hall, 2 edition, December 2002.

[19] S. Srivastava, S. Gulwani, and J. Foster. From program verification to program synthesis. In *POPL*, 2010.

[20] J. M. Vilar. Query learning of subsequential transducers. In *Proceedings of the 3rd International Colloquium on Grammatical Inference*, 1996.

[21] J. Walkenbach. *Excel 2010 Formulas*. John Wiley and Sons, 2010.

[22] I. H. Witten and D. Mo. TELS: learning text editing tasks from examples. In *Watch what I do: programming by demonstration*, pages 293–307. MIT Press, Cambridge, MA, USA, 1993.

[23] Q. Xi and D. Walker. A context-free markup language for semi-structured text. In *PLDI*, pages 221–232, 2010.

Predicate Abstraction and Refinement for Verifying Multi-Threaded Programs

Ashutosh Gupta Corneliu Popeea Andrey Rybalchenko

Institut für Informatik, Technische Universität München
Germany
{guptaa,popeea,rybal}@in.tum.de

Abstract

Automated verification of multi-threaded programs requires explicit identification of the interplay between interacting threads, so-called environment transitions, to enable scalable, compositional reasoning. Once the environment transitions are identified, we can prove program properties by considering each program thread in isolation, as the environment transitions keep track of the interleaving with other threads. Finding adequate environment transitions that are sufficiently precise to yield conclusive results and yet do not overwhelm the verifier with unnecessary details about the interleaving with other threads is a major challenge. In this paper we propose a method for safety verification of multi-threaded programs that applies (transition) predicate abstraction-based discovery of environment transitions, exposing a minimal amount of information about the thread interleaving. The crux of our method is an abstraction refinement procedure that uses recursion-free Horn clauses to declaratively state abstraction refinement queries. Then, the queries are resolved by a corresponding constraint solving algorithm. We present preliminary experimental results for mutual exclusion protocols and multi-threaded device drivers.

Categories and Subject Descriptors D.2.4 [*Software Engineering*]: Software/Program Verification; F.3.1 [*Logics and Meanings of Programs*]: Specifying and Verifying and Reasoning about Programs

General Terms Algorithms, Languages, Reliability, Verification.

Keywords Multi-threaded programs, safety, proof rule, modular reasoning, environment transitions, (transition) predicate abstraction, abstraction refinement, Horn clauses.

1. Introduction

The ubiquitous availability of parallel computing infrastructures facilitated by the advent of multicore architectures requires a shift towards multi-threaded programming to take full advantage of the available computing resources. Writing correct multi-threaded software is a difficult task, as the programmer needs to keep track of a very large number of possible interactions between the program threads. Automated program analysis and verification tools can support programmer in dealing with this challenge by systematically and exhaustively exploring program behaviours and checking their correctness.

Direct treatment of all possible thread interleavings by reasoning about the program globally is a prohibitively expensive task, even for small programs. By applying rely-guarantee techniques, see e.g. [17, 26], such global reasoning can be avoided by considering each program thread in isolation, using environment transitions to summarize the effect of executing other threads, and applying them on the thread at hand. The success of such an approach depends on the ability to automatically discover environment transitions that are precise enough to deliver a conclusive analysis/verification outcome, and yet do not keep track of unnecessary details in order to avoid sub-optimal efficiency.

In this paper we present a method that automates rely-guarantee reasoning for verifying safety of multi-threaded programs. Our method relies on an automated discovery of environment transitions using (transition) predicate abstraction [12, 28]. It performs a predicate abstraction-based reachability computation for each thread and interleaves it with the construction of environment transitions that over-approximate the effect of executing thread transitions using transition predicates. The success of our method crucially depends on an abstraction refinement procedure that discovers (transition) predicates. The refinement procedure attempts to minimize the amount of details that are exposed by the environment transitions, in order to avoid unnecessary details about thread interaction.

The crux of our refinement approach is in using a declarative formulation of the abstraction refinement algorithm that can deal with the thread reachability, environment transitions, and their mutual dependencies. We use Horn clauses to describe constraints on the desired (transition) predicates, and solve these constraints using a general algorithm for recursion-free Horn clauses. Our formalization can accommodate additional requirements that express the preference for modular predicates that do not refer to the local variables of environment threads, together with the preference for modular transition predicates that only deal with global variables and their primed versions.

We implemented the proposed method in a verification tool for multi-threaded programs and applied it on a range of benchmarks, which includes fragments of open source software, ticket-based mutual exclusion protocols, and multi-threaded Linux device drivers. The results of the experimental evaluation indicate that our declarative abstraction refinement approach can be effective in finding adequate environment transitions for the verification of multi-threaded programs.

This paper makes the following contributions:

POPL'11, January 26–28, 2011, Austin, Texas, USA.

1. the automatic, rely-guarantee based method for verifying multi-threaded programs using (transition) predicate abstraction;
2. the novel formulation of abstraction refinement schemes using Horn clauses, and its application for the (transition) abstraction discovery for multi-threaded programs;
3. the algorithm for solving recursion-free Horn clauses over linear arithmetic constraints;
4. the prototype implementation and its evaluation.

The rest of the paper is organized as follows. First, we illustrate our method in Section 2. In Section 3 we present necessary definitions. Section 4 presents a proof rule that provides a basis for our method, and shows how the proof rule can be automated using the connection to fixpoints and abstraction techniques. We present the main algorithm in Section 5. Section 6 focuses on the abstraction refinement using Horn clauses, while Section 7 presents a constraint solving algorithm for Horn clauses over linear inequalities. We discuss the experimental evaluation in Section 8. Related work is presented in Section 9.

2. Illustration

In this section we illustrate our algorithm using two multi-threaded examples. The first example does not have a modular proof, hence our algorithm reasons about relationship between the local variables of different threads. For the second example, our algorithm succeeds in finding a modular proof by applying an abstraction refinement procedure that guarantees the discovery of a modular abstraction whenever it exists.

2.1 Example LockBit

See Figure 1 for the program LockBit that consists of two threads. The threads attempt to access a critical section, and synchronize their accesses using a global variable lock . We assume that initially the lock is not taken, i.e., lock $=0$, and that the locking statement take_lock waits until the lock is released and then assigns the value of its second parameter to lock , thus taking the lock. We write $V = (\texttt{lock}, \texttt{pc}_1, \texttt{pc}_2)$ for the program variables, where $\texttt{pc}_1$ and $\texttt{pc}_2$ are local program counter variables of the first and second thread, respectively.

We start by representing the program using assertions φ_{init} and φ_{err} over program variables that describe the initial and error states of the program, together with assertions over unprimed and primed program variables ρ_1 and ρ_2 that describe the transition relations for program statements.

$$\begin{aligned}
\varphi_{init} &= (\texttt{pc}_1 = a \wedge \texttt{pc}_2 = p \wedge \texttt{lock} = 0) ,\\
\varphi_{err} &= (\texttt{pc}_1 = b \wedge \texttt{pc}_2 = q) ,\\
\rho_1 &= (\texttt{lock} = 0 \wedge \texttt{lock}' = 1 \wedge \texttt{pc}_1 = a \wedge \texttt{pc}_1{}' = b \wedge \rho_2^{=}) ,\\
\rho_1^{=} &= (\texttt{pc}_1 = \texttt{pc}_1{}') ,\\
\rho_2 &= (\texttt{lock} = 0 \wedge \texttt{lock}' = 1 \wedge \texttt{pc}_2 = p \wedge \texttt{pc}_2{}' = q \wedge \rho_1^{=}) ,\\
\rho_2^{=} &= (\texttt{pc}_2 = \texttt{pc}_2{}') .
\end{aligned}$$

The auxiliary assertions $\rho_1^{=}$ and $\rho_2^{=}$ state that the local variable of the first and second thread, respectively, is preserved during the transition.

To verify LockBit, our algorithm computes a sequence of ARETs (Abstract Reachability and Environment Trees). Each tree computation amounts to a combination of i) a standard abstract reachability computation that is performed for each thread and is called thread reachability, and ii) a construction and application of environment transitions. Abstract states represent sets of (concrete) program states, while environment transitions are binary relations of program states.

```
// Thread 1                  // Thread 2
a: take_lock(lock, 1);       p: take_lock(lock, 1);
b: // critical               q: // critical
```

Figure 1. Example program LockBit. Each thread waits until the lock is released, and then assigns the integer 1 to lock .

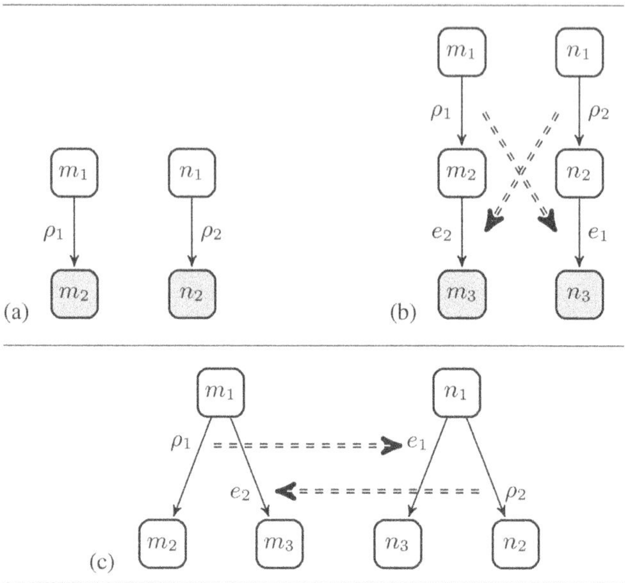

Figure 2. Reachability trees constructed using different abstraction functions. Edges are labeled with a transition. Nodes with gray background represent (spurious) error tuples: (m_2, n_2) from (a) and (m_3, n_3) from (b). No pair of states from (c) intersects φ_{err}.

First* ARET *computation The thread reachability computation for the first thread starts by computing an abstraction of the initial program states φ_{init} . Here, we use an abstraction function $\dot{\alpha}_1$, where the dot indicates that this function over-approximates sets of program states (and not sets of pairs of states, as will take place later) and the index 1 indicates that this abstraction function is used for the first thread. In this example, we assume that the abstraction function only tracks the value of the program counter of the first thread, i.e., $\dot{\mathcal{P}}_1 = \{\texttt{pc}_1 = a, \texttt{pc}_1 = b\}$, and is computed as follows: $\dot{\alpha}_1(S) = \bigwedge\{\dot{p} \in \dot{\mathcal{P}}_1 \mid \forall V : S \rightarrow \dot{p}\}$. We obtain the initial abstract state m_1 as follows:

$$m_1 = \dot{\alpha}_1(\varphi_{init}) = (\texttt{pc}_1 = a) .$$

Next, we compute an abstract successor of m_1 with respect to the transition ρ_1 using the strongest postcondition operator $post$ that is combined with $\dot{\alpha}_1$:

$$m_2 = \dot{\alpha}_1(post(\rho_1, m_1)) = (\texttt{pc}_1 = b) .$$

Similarly, we compute the thread reachability for the second thread. Using predicates over the program counter of the second thread, i.e., $\dot{\mathcal{P}}_2 = \{\texttt{pc}_2 = p, \texttt{pc}_2 = q\}$, we compute the following two abstract states:

$$\begin{aligned}
n_1 &= \dot{\alpha}_2(\varphi_{init}) &&= (\texttt{pc}_2 = p) ,\\
n_2 &= \dot{\alpha}_2(post(\rho_2, n_1)) &&= (\texttt{pc}_2 = q) .
\end{aligned}$$

For each thread, we organize the computed abstract states in a tree, see Figure 2(a).

We stop the ARET computation since we discover that the error states overlap with the intersection of the abstract state m_2 from the thread reachability of the first thread and n_2 from the second thread, i.e., $m_2 \wedge n_2 \wedge \varphi_{err}$ is satisfiable.

First abstraction refinement We treat the pair m_2 and n_2 as a possible evidence that the error states of the program can be reached. Yet, we cannot assert that the program is incorrect, since abstraction was involved when computing m_2 and n_2 .

We check if the discovered evidence is spurious by formulating a constraint that is satisfiable if and only if the abstraction can be refined to exclude the spuriousness. For each abstract state involved in the reachability of and including m_2 and n_2 we create an unknown predicate that denotes a set of program states. We obtain "m_1"(V), "n_1"(V), "m_2"(V), and "n_2"(V) , which correspond to m_1, n_1, m_2, and n_2, respectively. Then, we record the relation between the unknown predicates using constraints in the form of Horn clauses. For example, since m_1 was an abstraction of the initial program states, we require that "m_1"(V) over-approximates φ_{init} as well, and represent this requirement by a Horn clause $\varphi_{init} \rightarrow$ "m_1"(V) . As a result, we obtain the following set of clauses.

$$\begin{aligned} HC_1 = \{&\varphi_{init} \rightarrow \text{“}m_1\text{”}(V),\ \text{“}m_1\text{”}(V) \wedge \rho_1 \rightarrow \text{“}m_2\text{”}(V'),\\ &\varphi_{init} \rightarrow \text{“}n_1\text{”}(V),\ \text{“}n_1\text{”}(V) \wedge \rho_2 \rightarrow \text{“}n_2\text{”}(V'),\\ &\text{“}m_2\text{”}(V) \wedge \text{“}n_2\text{”}(V) \wedge \varphi_{err} \rightarrow \mathit{false}\} \end{aligned}$$

The last clause in HC_1 requires that the intersection of the refined versions of the abstract states m_2 and n_2 is disjoint from the error states of the program.

We check if the conjunction of the clauses in HC_1 is satisfiable using a SAT-based algorithm presented in [13]. (Section 7 presents an algorithm for solving Horn clauses over linear inequalities.) We obtain the following satisfying assignment SOL that maps each unknown predicate to an assertion of the program variables.

$$\begin{aligned} &\text{SOL}(\text{“}m_1\text{”}(V)) = (\texttt{pc}_2 = p) \quad \text{SOL}(\text{“}n_1\text{”}(V)) = (\texttt{pc}_1 = a)\\ &\text{SOL}(\text{“}m_2\text{”}(V)) = (\texttt{pc}_2 = p) \quad \text{SOL}(\text{“}n_2\text{”}(V)) = (\texttt{pc}_1 = a) \end{aligned}$$

The existence of SOL indicates that the discovered evidence is spurious. We use SOL to refine the abstraction functions and hence eliminate the source of spuriousness. We collect the predicates that appear in the solution for abstract states from the first thread, add them to the sets of predicates $\dot{\mathcal{P}}_1$, and perform a similar step for the second thread. The resulting sets of predicates are shown below.

$$\begin{aligned} \dot{\mathcal{P}}_1 &= \{\texttt{pc}_1 = a, \texttt{pc}_1 = b, \texttt{pc}_2 = p\}\\ \dot{\mathcal{P}}_2 &= \{\texttt{pc}_2 = p, \texttt{pc}_2 = q, \texttt{pc}_1 = a\} \end{aligned}$$

They guarantee that the same spuriousness will not appear during subsequent ARET computations.

Second* ARET *computation We re-start the ARET computation using the previously discovered predicates. Figure 2(b) shows the two trees computed with the refined abstraction functions where

$$\begin{aligned} m_1 &= (\texttt{pc}_1 = a \wedge \texttt{pc}_2 = p)\ , \quad n_1 = (\texttt{pc}_1 = a \wedge \texttt{pc}_2 = p)\ ,\\ m_2 &= (\texttt{pc}_1 = b \wedge \texttt{pc}_2 = p)\ , \quad n_2 = (\texttt{pc}_1 = a \wedge \texttt{pc}_2 = q)\ . \end{aligned}$$

Due to the first abstraction refinement step, $m_2 \wedge n_2 \wedge \varphi_{err}$ is unsatisfiable. The thread reachability computation for each thread does not discover any further abstract states.

The ARET computation proceeds by considering interleaving of the transitions from one thread with the transitions from the other thread. We account for thread interleaving by constructing and applying environment transitions. First, we construct an environment transition e_1 that records the effect of applying ρ_1 on m_1 in the first thread on the thread reachability in the second thread. This effect is over-approximated by using an abstraction function $\ddot{\alpha}_{1\triangleright 2}$. In this function, the double dot indicates that the function abstracts binary relations over states (and not sets of states). The index $1 \triangleright 2$ indicates that this function is applied to abstract effect of the first thread on the second thread. Initially, we use the empty set of transition predicates (over pairs of states) $\ddot{\mathcal{P}}_{1\triangleright 2} = \emptyset$ to define $\ddot{\alpha}_{1\triangleright 2}$. The environment transition e_1 is defined as

$$e_1 = \ddot{\alpha}_{1\triangleright 2}(m_1 \wedge \rho_1) = \mathit{true}\ ,$$

and it non-deterministically updates the program variables (since true does not impose any restrictions on the successor states of the transition).

Next, we add e_1 to the transitions of the second thread. Then, its thread reachability computation uses e_1 during the abstract successor computation, and creates an abstract state n_3 by applying e_1 on n_2 as follows:

$$n_3 = \dot{\alpha}_2(\mathit{post}(e_1 \wedge \rho_2^{=}, n_2)) = (\texttt{pc}_2 = q)\ .$$

The conjunct $\rho_2^{=}$ ensures that the local variable of the second thread is not changed by the environment transition.

Symmetrically, we use a function $\ddot{\alpha}_{2\triangleright 1}$ to abstract the effect of applying transitions in the second thread on the thread reachability of the first thread. The application of ρ_2 on n_1 results in the environment transition e_2 such that

$$e_2 = \ddot{\alpha}_{2\triangleright 1}(n_1 \wedge \rho_2) = \mathit{true}\ .$$

We apply e_2 to contribute an abstract successor m_3 of the abstract state m_2 to the thread reachability of the first thread:

$$m_3 = \dot{\alpha}_1(\mathit{post}(e_2 \wedge \rho_1^{=}, m_2)) = (\texttt{pc}_1 = b)\ .$$

We observe that the intersection of the abstract states m_3 and n_3 contains a non-empty set of error states, i.e., $m_3 \wedge n_3 \wedge \varphi_{err}$ is satisfiable, thus delivering a possible evidence for incorrectness.

Second abstraction refinement Similarly to the first abstraction refinement step, we construct a set of Horn clauses HC_2 to check if the discovered evidence is spurious. We consider predicates "m_1"(V), "n_1"(V), "m_2"(V), "n_2"(V), "m_3"(V), and "n_3"(V) that represent unknown sets of program states, together with "e_1"(V, V') and "e_2"(V, V') that represent unknown binary relations over program states.

$$\begin{aligned} HC_2 = \{&\varphi_{init} \rightarrow \text{“}m_1\text{”}(V),\ \text{“}m_1\text{”}(V) \wedge \rho_1 \rightarrow \text{“}m_2\text{”}(V'),\\ &\varphi_{init} \rightarrow \text{“}n_1\text{”}(V),\ \text{“}n_1\text{”}(V) \wedge \rho_2 \rightarrow \text{“}n_2\text{”}(V'),\\ &\text{“}m_1\text{”}(V) \wedge \rho_1 \rightarrow \text{“}e_1\text{”}(V, V'),\\ &\text{“}n_2\text{”}(V) \wedge \text{“}e_1\text{”}(V, V') \wedge \rho_2^{=} \rightarrow \text{“}n_3\text{”}(V'),\\ &\text{“}n_1\text{”}(V) \wedge \rho_2 \rightarrow \text{“}e_2\text{”}(V, V'),\\ &\text{“}m_2\text{”}(V) \wedge \text{“}e_2\text{”}(V, V') \wedge \rho_1^{=} \rightarrow \text{“}m_3\text{”}(V'),\\ &\text{“}m_3\text{”}(V) \wedge \text{“}n_3\text{”}(V) \wedge \varphi_{err} \rightarrow \mathit{false}\} \end{aligned}$$

The conjunction of clauses in HC_2 is satisfiable. We obtain the following satisfying assignment SOL.

$$\begin{aligned} &\text{SOL}(\text{“}m_1\text{”}(V)) = \mathit{true} && \text{SOL}(\text{“}m_2\text{”}(V)) = (\texttt{lock} = 1)\\ &\text{SOL}(\text{“}n_1\text{”}(V)) = \mathit{true} && \text{SOL}(\text{“}n_2\text{”}(V)) = (\texttt{lock} = 1)\\ &\text{SOL}(\text{“}m_3\text{”}(V)) = \mathit{false} && \text{SOL}(\text{“}e_1\text{”}(V, V')) = (\texttt{lock} = 0)\\ &\text{SOL}(\text{“}n_3\text{”}(V)) = \mathit{false} && \text{SOL}(\text{“}e_2\text{”}(V, V')) = (\texttt{lock} = 0) \end{aligned}$$

This solution constrains "m_2"(V) and "n_2"(V) to states where the lock is held $(\texttt{lock} = 1)$, while the environment transitions "e_1"(V, V') and "e_2"(V, V') are applicable only in states for which the lock is not held by the respective thread $(\texttt{lock} = 0)$.

We add the (transition) predicates that appear in the environment transition e_2 of the first thread to the set $\ddot{\mathcal{P}}_{2\triangleright 1}$, and, symmetrically, we add the predicates from e_1 to $\ddot{\mathcal{P}}_{1\triangleright 2}$. For the next ARET

```
// Thread 1                    // Thread 2
a: take_lock(lock, 1);         p: take_lock(lock, 2);
b: // critical                 q: // critical
```

Figure 3. Example program LockId .

computation we have the following set of predicates:

$$\dot{\mathcal{P}}_1 = \{\texttt{pc}_1 = a, \texttt{pc}_1 = b, \texttt{pc}_2 = p, \texttt{lock} = 1\}\ ,$$
$$\dot{\mathcal{P}}_2 = \{\texttt{pc}_2 = p, \texttt{pc}_2 = q, \texttt{pc}_1 = a, \texttt{lock} = 1\}\ ,$$
$$\ddot{\mathcal{P}}_{1\triangleright 2} = \{\texttt{lock} = 0\}\ ,$$
$$\ddot{\mathcal{P}}_{2\triangleright 1} = \{\texttt{lock} = 0\}\ .$$

Last* ARET *computation We perform another ARET computation and a subsequent abstraction refinement step. We add the predicate $\texttt{lock}' = 1$ to both $\ddot{\mathcal{P}}_{1\triangleright 2}$ and $\ddot{\mathcal{P}}_{2\triangleright 1}$, and proceed with the final ARET computation. Figure 2(c) shows the resulting trees. The application of thread transitions produces the following abstract states and environment transitions:

$$m_1 = \dot{\alpha}_1(\varphi_{init}) = (\texttt{pc}_1 = a \wedge \texttt{pc}_2 = p)\ ,$$
$$n_1 = \dot{\alpha}_2(\varphi_{init}) = (\texttt{pc}_1 = a \wedge \texttt{pc}_2 = p)\ ,$$
$$m_2 = \dot{\alpha}_1(post(\rho_1, m_1)) = (\texttt{pc}_1 = b \wedge \texttt{pc}_2 = p \wedge \texttt{lock} = 1)\ ,$$
$$n_2 = \dot{\alpha}_2(post(\rho_2, n_1)) = (\texttt{pc}_1 = a \wedge \texttt{pc}_2 = q \wedge \texttt{lock} = 1)\ ,$$
$$e_1 = \ddot{\alpha}_{1\triangleright 2}(m_1 \wedge \rho_1) = (\texttt{lock} = 0 \wedge \texttt{lock}' = 1)\ ,$$
$$e_2 = \ddot{\alpha}_{2\triangleright 1}(n_1 \wedge \rho_2) = (\texttt{lock} = 0 \wedge \texttt{lock}' = 1)\ .$$

The environment transitions e_1 and e_2 produce the abstract states m_3 and n_3 whose intersection does not contain any error states.

$$m_3 = \dot{\alpha}_1(post(e_2 \wedge \rho_{\overline{1}}^{=}, m_2)) = (\texttt{pc}_1 = a \wedge \texttt{lock} = 1)$$
$$n_3 = \dot{\alpha}_2(post(e_1 \wedge \rho_{\overline{2}}^{=}, n_2)) = (\texttt{pc}_2 = p \wedge \texttt{lock} = 1)$$

Neither thread nor environment transitions can be applied from the abstract states m_3 and n_3, while no further abstract states are found. Since each pair of abstract states from different threads yields an intersection that is disjoint from the error states, we conclude that LockBit is safe. The labeling of the computed trees can be directly used to construct a safety proof for LockBit, as Sections 4 and 5 will show.

2.2 Example LockId

Our second example LockId, shown in Figure 3, is a variation of LockBit. LockId uses an integer variable lock (instead of a single bit) to record which thread holds the lock. Due to this additional information recorded in the global variable, the example LockId has a modular proof, which does not refer to any local variables. We show how our algorithm discovers such a proof by only admitting modular predicates in the abstraction refinement step.

LockId differs from LockBit in its transition relation ρ_2:

$$\rho_2 = (\texttt{lock} = 0 \wedge \texttt{lock}' = 2 \wedge \texttt{pc}_2 = p \wedge \texttt{pc}_2{}' = q \wedge \rho_{\overline{1}}^{=})\ .$$

First* ARET *computation Similarly to LockBit, we discover that $m_2 \wedge n_2 \wedge \varphi_{err}$ is satisfiable, and compute the following set of Horn clauses:

$$HC_3 = \{\varphi_{init} \rightarrow \text{“}m_1\text{”}(V),\ \text{“}m_1\text{”}(V) \wedge \rho_1 \rightarrow \text{“}m_2\text{”}(V'),$$
$$\varphi_{init} \rightarrow \text{“}n_1\text{”}(V),\ \text{“}n_1\text{”}(V) \wedge \rho_2 \rightarrow \text{“}n_2\text{”}(V'),$$
$$\text{“}m_2\text{”}(V) \wedge \text{“}n_2\text{”}(V) \wedge \varphi_{err} \rightarrow false\}\ .$$

One possible satisfying assignment SOL is:

$$\text{SOL}(\text{“}m_1\text{”}(V)) = (\texttt{pc}_2 = p)\ ,\quad \text{SOL}(\text{“}n_1\text{”}(V)) = (\texttt{pc}_1 = a)\ ,$$
$$\text{SOL}(\text{“}m_2\text{”}(V)) = (\texttt{pc}_2 = p)\ ,\quad \text{SOL}(\text{“}n_2\text{”}(V)) = (\texttt{pc}_1 = a)\ .$$

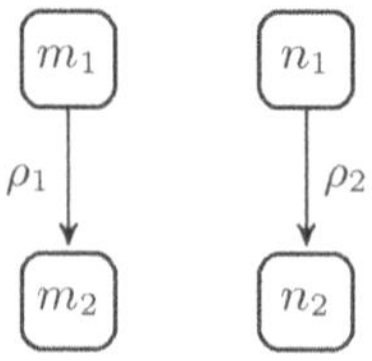

Figure 4. Tree that shows all the reachable abstract states found during the last ARET computation for LockId.

This assignment uses a predicate $\texttt{pc}_2 = p$ over the local variable of the second thread as a solution for the abstract state “m_1”(V) in the thread reachability of the first thread. By collecting and using the corresponding predicates, we will discover a non-modular proof.

To avoid the drawbacks of non-modular proofs, our algorithm does not use HC_3 and attempts to find modular predicates for abstraction refinement instead. We express the preference for modular predicates declaratively, using a set of Horn clauses in which the unknown predicates are restricted to the desired variables, as described in Sections 6. For the abstract states in the first thread, we require that the corresponding solutions are over the global variable lock and the local variable $\texttt{pc}_1$ of the first thread, i.e., we have the unknown predicates “m_1”$(\texttt{lock}, \texttt{pc}_1)$ and “m_2”$(\texttt{lock}, \texttt{pc}_1)$. Similarly, for the second thread we obtain “n_1”$(\texttt{lock}, \texttt{pc}_2)$ and “n_2”$(\texttt{lock}, \texttt{pc}_2)$. Instead of HC_3, we use a set of Horn clauses HC_4 shown below:

$$HC_4 = \{\varphi_{init} \rightarrow \text{“}m_1\text{”}(\texttt{lock}, \texttt{pc}_1),$$
$$\text{“}m_1\text{”}(\texttt{lock}, \texttt{pc}_1) \wedge \rho_1 \rightarrow \text{“}m_2\text{”}(\texttt{lock}', \texttt{pc}_1{}'),$$
$$\varphi_{init} \rightarrow \text{“}n_1\text{”}(\texttt{lock}, \texttt{pc}_2),$$
$$\text{“}n_1\text{”}(\texttt{lock}, \texttt{pc}_2) \wedge \rho_2 \rightarrow \text{“}n_2\text{”}(\texttt{lock}', \texttt{pc}_2{}'),$$
$$\text{“}m_2\text{”}(\texttt{lock}, \texttt{pc}_1) \wedge \text{“}n_2\text{”}(\texttt{lock}, \texttt{pc}_2) \wedge \varphi_{err} \rightarrow false\}\ .$$

The conjunction of clauses from HC_4 can be satisfied by an assignment SOL such that

$$\text{SOL}(\text{“}m_1\text{”}(\texttt{lock}, \texttt{pc}_1)) = true\ ,$$
$$\text{SOL}(\text{“}m_2\text{”}(\texttt{lock}, \texttt{pc}_1)) = (\texttt{lock} = 1)\ ,$$
$$\text{SOL}(\text{“}n_1\text{”}(\texttt{lock}, \texttt{pc}_2)) = true\ ,$$
$$\text{SOL}(\text{“}n_2\text{”}(\texttt{lock}, \texttt{pc}_2)) = (\texttt{lock} = 2)\ ,$$

which contains only modular predicates.

Last* ARET *computation We present the last ARET computation for LockBit, which uses on the following (transition) predicates collected so far:

$$\dot{\mathcal{P}}_1 = \{\texttt{pc}_1 = a, \texttt{pc}_1 = b, \texttt{lock} = 1\}\ ,$$
$$\dot{\mathcal{P}}_2 = \{\texttt{pc}_2 = p, \texttt{pc}_2 = q, \texttt{lock} = 2\}\ ,$$
$$\ddot{\mathcal{P}}_{2\triangleright 1} = \{\texttt{lock} = 0\}\ ,$$
$$\ddot{\mathcal{P}}_{1\triangleright 2} = \{\texttt{lock} = 0\}\ .$$

Figure 4 shows the resulting abstract reachability and environment trees constructed as follows:

$$m_1 = \dot{\alpha}_1(\varphi_{init}) = (\texttt{pc}_1 = a)$$
$$n_1 = \dot{\alpha}_2(\varphi_{init}) = (\texttt{pc}_2 = p)$$
$$m_2 = \dot{\alpha}_1(post(\rho_1, m_1)) = (\texttt{pc}_1 = b \wedge \texttt{lock} = 1)$$
$$n_2 = \dot{\alpha}_2(post(\rho_2, n_1)) = (\texttt{pc}_2 = q \wedge \texttt{lock} = 2)$$
$$e_1 = \ddot{\alpha}_{1\triangleright 2}(m_1 \wedge \rho_1) = (\texttt{lock} = 0)$$
$$e_2 = \ddot{\alpha}_{2\triangleright 1}(n_1 \wedge \rho_2) = (\texttt{lock} = 0)$$

The ARET construction is completed, since

$$\dot\alpha_1(post(e_2 \wedge \rho_{\bar 1}^{=}, m_1)) \rightarrow m_1\ , \quad \dot\alpha_1(post(e_2, m_2)) = \mathit{false}\ ,$$
$$\dot\alpha_2(post(e_1 \wedge \rho_{\bar 2}^{=}, n_1)) \rightarrow n_1\ , \quad \dot\alpha_2(post(e_1, n_2)) = \mathit{false}\ .$$

By inspecting pairs of abstract states from different trees we conclude that `LockId` is safe.

Furthermore no predicate in $\dot{\mathcal{P}}_1$ refers to the local variable of the second thread, the symmetric condition holds for $\dot{\mathcal{P}}_2$, and the predicates in $\ddot{\mathcal{P}}_{1\triangleright 2}$ as well as $\ddot{\mathcal{P}}_{2\triangleright 1}$ do not refer to any local variables. Thus, from the trees in Figure 4 we can construct a modular safety proof.

3. Preliminaries

In this section we briefly describe multi-threaded programs, their computations and correctness. We also introduce auxiliary definitions that we apply for reasoning about programs.

Programs We consider a *multi-threaded* program P that consists of $\mathsf{N} \geq 1$ concurrent threads. Let $1..\mathsf{N}$ be the set $\{1, \dots, \mathsf{N}\}$. We assume that the *program* variables $V = (V_G, V_1, \dots, V_\mathsf{N})$ are partitioned into *global* variables V_G that are shared by all threads, and *local* variables $V_1, \dots, V_\mathsf{N}$ that are only accessible by the threads $1, \dots, \mathsf{N}$, respectively.

The set of *global states* G consists of the valuations of global variables, and the sets of *local states* $L_1, \dots, L_\mathsf{N}$ consist of the valuations of the local variables of respective threads. By taking the product of the global and local state spaces, we obtain the set of *program states* $\Sigma = G \times L_1 \times \dots \times L_\mathsf{N}$. We represent sets of program states using assertions over program variables. Binary relations between sets of program states are represented using assertions over unprimed and primed variables. Let $\models$ denote the satisfaction relation between (pairs) of states and assertions.

The set of *initial* program states is denoted by φ_{init} , and the set of *error* states is denoted by φ_{err} . For each thread $i \in 1..\mathsf{N}$ we have a finite set of transition relations $\mathcal{T}_i$, which are abbreviated as *transitions*. Each transition $\rho \in \mathcal{T}_i$ can change the values of the global variables and the local variables of the thread i . Let $\rho_i^{=}$ be a constraint requiring that the local variables of the thread i do not change, i.e., $\rho_i^{=} = (V_i = V_i')$. Then, $\rho \in \mathcal{T}_i$ has the form

$$\rho^{\text{update}}(V_G, V_i, V_G', V_i') \wedge \bigwedge_{j \in 1..\mathsf{N} \setminus \{i\}} \rho_j^{=}\ ,$$

where the first conjunct represents the update of the variables in the scope of the thread i and the remaining conjuncts ensure that the local variables of other threads do not change. We write ρ_i for the union of the transitions of the thread i , i.e., $\rho_i = \bigvee \mathcal{T}_i$. The transition relation of the program is $\rho_\mathcal{T} = \rho_1 \vee \dots \vee \rho_\mathsf{N}$.

Computations A *computation* of P is a sequence of program states $s_1, s_2, \dots$ such that s_1 is an initial state, i.e., $s_1 \models \varphi_{init}$, and each pair of consecutive states s_i and s_{i+1} in the sequence is connected by some transition ρ from a program thread, i.e., $(s_i, s_{i+1}) \models \rho$. A *path* is a sequence of transitions. We write ϵ for the *empty* sequence.

Let $[z/w]$ be a substitution function such that $\varphi[z/w]$ replaces w by z in φ . Let $\circ$ be the *relational composition* function for binary relations given by assertions over unprimed and primed variables such that for assertions φ and ψ we have $\varphi \circ \psi = \exists V'' : \varphi[V''/V'] \wedge \psi[V''/V]$. Then, a *path relation* is a relational composition of transition relations along the path, i.e., for $\pi = \rho_1 \cdots \rho_n$ we have $\rho_\pi = \rho_1 \circ \ldots \circ \rho_n$. A path π is *feasible* if its path relation is not empty, i.e., $\exists V, V' : \rho_\pi$.

A program state is *reachable* if it appears in some computation. Let φ_{reach} denote the set of reachable states. The program is *safe* if *none* of its error states is reachable, i.e., $\varphi_{reach} \wedge \varphi_{err} \rightarrow \mathit{false}$.

For assertions $R_1, \dots, R_\mathsf{N}$ over V ,
and $E_1, \dots, E_\mathsf{N}$ over V and V'

CS1:	φ_{init}	$\rightarrow R_i$	for $i \in 1..\mathsf{N}$
CS2:	$R_i \wedge \rho_i$	$\rightarrow R_i'$	for $i \in 1..\mathsf{N}$
CS3:	$R_i \wedge E_i \wedge \rho_i^{=}$	$\rightarrow R_i'$	for $i \in 1..\mathsf{N}$
CS4:	$(\bigvee_{i \in 1..\mathsf{N}\setminus\{j\}} R_i \wedge \rho_i)$	$\rightarrow E_j$	for $j \in 1..\mathsf{N}$
CS5:	$R_1 \wedge \dots \wedge R_\mathsf{N} \wedge \varphi_{err}$	$\rightarrow \mathit{false}$	

program P is safe

Figure 5. Proof rule REACHENV for compositional safety proofs of multi-threaded programs. R_i' stands for $R_i[V'/V]$. REACHENV yields a pre-fixpoint characterization through Equations (1).

Auxiliary definitions We define a *successor* function *post* such that for a binary relation over states ρ and a set of states φ we have

$$post(\rho, \varphi) = \exists V'' : \varphi[V''/V] \wedge \rho[V''/V][V/V']\ .$$

We also extend the logical implication to tuples of equal length, i.e.,

$$(\varphi_1, \dots, \varphi_n) \rightarrow (\psi_1, \dots, \psi_n) = \varphi_1 \rightarrow \phi_1 \wedge \dots \wedge \varphi_n \rightarrow \phi_n\ ,$$

where each implication is implicitly universally quantified over the free variables occurring in it. From now on, we assume that tuples of assertions are partially ordered by the above extension of $\rightarrow$.

A *Horn clause* $b_1(w_1) \wedge \dots \wedge b_n(w_n) \rightarrow b(w)$ consists of relation symbols $b_1, \dots, b_n$, b, and vectors of variables $w_1, \dots, w_n$, w. For the algorithm SOLVELINEARHC in Section 7 we only consider Horn clauses over linear arithmetic. We say that b *depends* on the relation symbols $\{b_i \mid i \in 1..n \wedge b_i \neq (\leq)\}$. A set of Horn clauses is *recursion-free* if the transitive closure of the corresponding dependency relation is well founded.

4. Proof rule, fixpoints, and abstraction

In this section we develop the foundations for our verification algorithm. We present a compositional proof rule and then derive a corresponding characterization in terms of least fixpoints and their approximations. We present the ability of our proof rule to facilitate modular reasoning, when admitted by the program, without losing the ability for global reasoning otherwise.

Proof rule Figure 5 presents a proof rule REACHENV for compositional verification of program safety. The proof rule is inspired by the existing proof rules for compositional safety reasoning, see e.g. [5, 15, 16, 26]. Our formulation of REACHENV directly leads to a pre-fixpoint characterization, thus, providing a basis for the proof rule automation using abstraction and refinement techniques.

REACHENV relies on *thread reachability* assertions $R_1, \dots, R_\mathsf{N}$ that keep track of program states reached by threads $1, \dots, \mathsf{N}$ together with their respective *environment transitions* $E_1, \dots, E_\mathsf{N}$. The environment transition of each thread keeps track of modifications of program states by other threads. The auxiliary assertions used in our proof rule can refer to all program variables, that is, they are not restricted to a combination of global variables and local variables of a particular thread.

If the provided auxiliary assertions satisfy all premises of the proof rule, i.e., CS1, ..., CS5, then the program is safe. The premise CS1 requires that each thread reachability over-approximates the initial program states. CS2 ensures that the thread reachability of each thread is invariant under the application of the thread transitions. In addition, CS3 requires invariance under the environment transitions of the thread. The conjunct $\rho_i^{=}$ in CS3 selects the subset of the environment transition that does not modify the local variables of the thread. Given a thread j , the premise CS4 collects transitions that start from states in the thread reachability of other threads and combines them into the environment transition for j . Finally, CS5 checks that there is no error state that appears in each thread reachability set.

The proof rule REACHENV can be directly used to prove program safety following a two-step procedure. First, we need to identify candidate assertions for the thread reachability and environment transitions. Second, we need to check that these candidate assertions satisfy the premises of proof rule. The correctness of the conclusion is formalized by the following theorems.

THEOREM 1 (Soundness). *The proof rule* REACHENV *is sound.* ■

Proof. Let $R_1, \ldots, R_N$ and $E_1, \ldots, E_N$ satisfy the premises CS1, ..., CS5. We show that the program is safe. To prove safety, for each reachable state $s \models \varphi_{reach}$ we prove that $s \models R_1 \wedge \cdots \wedge R_N$ by induction over the length k of a shortest computation segment $s_1, \ldots, s_k$ such that $s_1 \models \varphi_{init}$ and $s_k = s$.

For the base case $k = 1$, the inclusion holds due to the premise CS1. For the induction step, we assume that the above statement holds for states reachable in $k \geq 1$ steps and prove the statement for their immediate successors. That is, let $s_k \models \varphi_{reach}$ and hence $s_k \models R_1 \wedge \cdots \wedge R_N$. If s_k does not have any successor, i.e., $\neg(\exists s_{k+1} : (s_k, s_{k+1}) \models \rho_T)$, then there are no more states to consider. Otherwise, we choose a successor state s_{k+1} of s_k that is reached by taking a transition in a thread i , i.e., $(s_k, s_{k+1}) \models \rho_i$. From CS2 follows that $s_{k+1} \models R_i$.

To show that $s_{k+1} \models R_j$ for each $j \in 1..N \setminus \{i\}$ we rely on the premises CS4 and CS3. By induction hypothesis $s_k \models R_i$ and due to CS4 we have $(s_k, s_{k+1}) \models E_j$. Now $s_{k+1} \in R_j$ follows from CS3. □

THEOREM 2 (Relative completeness). *The proof rule* REACHENV *is complete relative to first-order reasoning.* ■

Proof. Let P be safe. We define $R_1 = \cdots = R_N = \varphi_{reach}$ and $E_1 = \cdots = E_N = \varphi_{reach} \wedge \rho_T$. Then, the premises CS1, ..., CS5 are immediately satisfied. □

Modular and global proofs Reasoning about multi-threaded program is more complex than reasoning about sequential programs since thread interaction needs to be taken into account. Some programs admit modular reasoning that deals with each thread in isolation, i.e., assertions used in the proof only refer to the global variables and the local variables of one thread at a time.

The proof rule REACHENV facilitates *modular* reasoning about multi-threaded programs. If a program has a modular safety proof, then the following *modular* assertions satisfy the proof rule premises:

$$R_i = \exists V \setminus (V_G \cup V_i) : \varphi_{reach}\,, \qquad \text{for } i \in 1..N$$
$$E_i = \exists (V \cup V') \setminus (V_G \cup V_G') : \varphi_{reach} \wedge \rho_T\,. \qquad \text{for } i \in 1..N$$

REACHENV is *not* restricted to modular proofs. Since the assertions used in REACHENV can refer to each of the program variables, non-modular proofs can be directly used. In fact, the proof of Theorem 2 relies on non-modular assertions, since φ_{reach} may refer to local variables of different threads.

In Section 5 we will present our algorithm that can discover modular assertions for REACHENV if the program admits modular proofs, and delivers non-modular assertions otherwise.

Fixpoints The proof rule REACHENV in Figure 5 directly leads to a fixpoint-based characterization, which defines our algorithm in Section 5.

From the premises CS2, CS3, and CS4 we obtain a function F on N-tuples of assertions over the program variables and N-tuples of assertions over the unprimed and primed program variables such that

$$\begin{aligned} &F(S_1, \ldots, S_N, T_1, \ldots, T_N) = \\ &(post(\rho_1 \vee T_1 \wedge \rho_1^{=}, S_1), \ldots, post(\rho_N \vee T_N \wedge \rho_N^{=}, S_N), \\ &\textstyle\bigvee_{i \in 1..N \setminus \{1\}} S_i \wedge \rho_i, \quad \ldots, \bigvee_{i \in 1..N \setminus \{N\}} S_i \wedge \rho_i)\,. \end{aligned} \quad (1)$$

We formalize the relation between F and REACHENV as follows.

LEMMA 1. *Each pre-fixpoint of F satisfies the premises* CS2, CS3, *and* CS4 *of* REACHENV. *That is, if*

$$F(R_1, \ldots, R_N, E_1, \ldots, E_N) \rightarrow (R_1, \ldots, R_N, E_1, \ldots, E_N)$$

then $R_1, \ldots, R_N, E_1, \ldots, E_N$ *satisfies* CS2, CS3, *and* CS4 . ■

We define a distinguished tuple $\bot_F$:

$$\bot_F = (\varphi_{init}, \ldots, \varphi_{init}, \underbrace{false, \ldots, false}_{\text{N times}})\,. \quad (2)$$

Then, each pre-fixpoint of F that is greater than $\bot_F$ satisfies the premise CS1. By choosing a pre-fixpoint $(R_1, \ldots, R_N, E_1, \ldots, E_N)$ above $\bot_F$ such that $R_1 \wedge \ldots, R_N \wedge \varphi_{err} \rightarrow false$ we will satisfy all premises of the proof rule REACHENV, and hence prove the program safety.

Fixpoint abstraction Computing pre-fixpoints of F that satisfy CS1 and CS5 is a difficult task. We automate this computation using the framework of abstract interpretation [7], which uses over-approximation to strike a balance between reasoning precision and efficiency. To implement required over-approximation functions, we will use a collection of abstraction functions $\dot{\alpha}_i$ and $\ddot{\alpha}_{i \triangleright j}$, where $i \neq j \in 1..N$, that over-approximate sets and binary relations over programs states, respectively.

We define a function $F^{\#}$ that over-approximates F using given abstraction functions:

$$\begin{aligned} &F^{\#}(S_1, \ldots, S_N, T_1, \ldots, T_N) = \\ &\quad(\dot{\alpha}_1(post(\rho_1, S_1)) \vee \dot{\alpha}_1(post(T_1 \wedge \rho_1^{=}, S_1))\,, \\ &\quad\ldots \\ &\quad\dot{\alpha}_N(post(\rho_N, S_N)) \vee \dot{\alpha}_N(post(T_N \wedge \rho_N^{=}, S_N))\,, \\ &\quad\textstyle\bigvee_{i \in 1..N \setminus \{1\}} \ddot{\alpha}_{i \triangleright 1}(S_i \wedge \rho_i)\,, \\ &\quad\ldots \\ &\quad\textstyle\bigvee_{i \in 1..N \setminus \{N\}} \ddot{\alpha}_{i \triangleright N}(S_i \wedge \rho_i))\,. \end{aligned} \quad (3)$$

Let $\bot_{F^{\#}}$ be an over-approximation of F such that

$$\bot_{F^{\#}} = (\dot{\alpha}_1(\varphi_{init}), \ldots, \dot{\alpha}_N(\varphi_{init}), \underbrace{false, \ldots, false}_{\text{N times}})\,. \quad (4)$$

The least pre-fixpoint of $F^{\#}$ above $\bot_{F^{\#}}$ can be used to prove program safety by applying the following theorem, and is the key outcome of our algorithm in Section 5.

THEOREM 3 (Abstract fixpoint checking). *If the least pre-fixpoint of $F^{\#}$ above $\bot_{F^{\#}}$, say $(R_1, \ldots, R_N, E_1, \ldots, E_N)$, satisfies the premise* CS5 *then the program is safe.* ■

Proof. The theorem follows directly from the soundness of the proof rule REACHENV, Lemma 1, and over-approximations introduced by the applied abstraction functions. □

function MAIN
input
  P - program with N threads
vars
  $\dot{\mathcal{P}}_i, \dot{\alpha}_i$ - predicates for thread i and corresponding state abstraction function
  $\ddot{\mathcal{P}}_{i \triangleright j}, \ddot{\alpha}_{i \triangleright j}$ - transition predicates for pair of threads i, j and corresponding transition abstraction function
  $\mathcal{R}_i$ - abstract states of thread i
  $\mathcal{E}_i$ - abstract environment transitions of thread i
  $Parent$ - parent function for abstract states and environment transitions
  $ParentTId$ - parent thread function for abstract states and environment transitions
begin
1 **for** each $i \neq j \in 1..\mathsf{N}$ **do**
2   $\dot{\mathcal{P}}_i := \ddot{\mathcal{P}}_{i \triangleright j} := \emptyset$
3 **repeat**
4   **for** each $i \neq j \in 1..\mathsf{N}$ **do**
5     $\dot{\alpha}_i := \lambda S. \bigwedge\{\dot{p} \in \dot{\mathcal{P}}_i \mid \forall V : S \rightarrow \dot{p}\}$
6     $\ddot{\alpha}_{i \triangleright j} := \lambda T. \bigwedge\{\ddot{p} \in \ddot{\mathcal{P}}_{i \triangleright j} \mid \forall V, V' : T \rightarrow \ddot{p}\}$
7   ABSTREACHENV()
8   **if** exists $S_1 \in \mathcal{R}_1, \dots, S_\mathsf{N} \in \mathcal{R}_\mathsf{N}$ such that
9     $\exists V : S_1 \wedge \dots \wedge S_\mathsf{N} \wedge \varphi_{err}$
10   **then**
11   **try**
12   REFINE$(S_1, \dots, S_\mathsf{N})$
13   **with** UNSATISFIABLE
14   D := some S_i from $\{S_1, \dots, S_\mathsf{N}\}$
15   **return** "counterexample MKPATH(D)"
16   **else**
17   **return** "program P is safe with the proof
18       $\bigvee \mathcal{R}_1, \dots, \bigvee \mathcal{R}_\mathsf{N}, \bigvee \mathcal{E}_1, \dots, \bigvee \mathcal{E}_\mathsf{N}$"
19 **until** *true*
end.

Figure 6. Function MAIN for verifying safety of the multi-threaded program P.

procedure ABSTREACHENV
begin
1 $Parent := ParentTId := \bot$ (* the empty function *)
2 **for** each $i \in 1..\mathsf{N}$ **do**
3   $\mathcal{R}_i := \{\dot{\alpha}_i(\varphi_{init})\}$
4   $\mathcal{E}_i := \emptyset$
5 **repeat**
6   *finished* := *true*
7   **for** each $i \in 1..\mathsf{N}$ and $S \in \mathcal{R}_i$ **do**
8   (* states *)
9   **for** each $\rho \in \mathcal{T}_i \cup \mathcal{E}_i$ **do**
10   S' := **if** $\rho \in \mathcal{T}_i$ **then** $\dot{\alpha}_i(post(\rho, S))$
11   **else** $\dot{\alpha}_i(post(\rho \wedge \rho_i^{=}, S))$
12   **if** $\neg(\exists S'' \in \mathcal{R}_i\ \forall V : S' \rightarrow S'')$ **then**
13         $\mathcal{R}_i := \{S'\} \cup \mathcal{R}_i$
14         $Parent(S') := (S, \rho)$
15         $ParentTId(S') := i$
16   *finished* := *false*
17   **done**
18   (* environment transitions *)
19   **for** each $\rho \in \mathcal{T}_i$ and $j \in 1..\mathsf{N} \setminus \{i\}$ **do**
20       $\rho' := \ddot{\alpha}_{i \triangleright j}(S \wedge \rho)$
21   **if** $\neg(\exists \rho'' \in \mathcal{T}_j \cup \mathcal{E}_j\ \forall V, V' : \rho' \rightarrow \rho'')$ **then**
22         $\mathcal{E}_j := \{\rho'\} \cup \mathcal{E}_j$
23         $Parent(\rho') := (S, \rho)$
24         $ParentTId(\rho') := i$
25   *finished* := *false*
26   **done**
27   **done**
28 **until** *finished*
end

Figure 7. Procedure ABSTREACHENV implements ARET computation. We assume that the iterator statements in lines 7 and 9 make an immutable snapshot of their domains $\mathcal{R}_i$ and $\mathcal{E}_i$, respectively. For example, this implies that each addition of S' in line 12 is unnoticed in line 7 until the next iteration of the **repeat** loop.

The choice of the abstract domains, i.e., the range sets of the abstraction functions, determines if the least fixpoint of $F^{\#}$ yields a modular proof. Our abstraction discovery algorithm in Section 6 automatically chooses the abstraction such that modular proofs are preferred.

5. Thread reachability and environment transitions

In this section, we present our rely-guarantee based verification algorithm for proving safety properties of multi-threaded programs. The algorithm is based on Theorem 3 and consists of three main steps. The first step computes for each thread a tree that is decorated by abstract states and environment transitions, so-called ARET, and analyses the discovered abstract states. If an intersection with the error states of the program is found, then the second step generates a set of corresponding Horn clauses, see Section 6. At the third step, we solve the constraint defined by the conjunction of the generated Horn clauses and use the solutions to the refine the abstraction functions used for the ARET computation, see Section 7.

***Function* MAIN** The main function of our algorithm MAIN is shown in Figure 6. MAIN takes as input the multi-threaded program P . The **repeat** loop iterates through the three main steps of the algorithm. First, we construct the abstraction functions $\dot{\alpha}_i$ and $\ddot{\alpha}_{i \triangleright j}$ at lines 4–6 from a given set of (transition) predicates, which is empty initially. Next, the ARET computation is performed in line 7 using these abstraction functions. In lines 8–9, the abstract states in the computed ARET's are analyzed wrt. the safety property. In case of a positive outcome of this check, MAIN constructs and returns a safety proof in lines 17–18. If the safety check fails, then REFINE is executed on the violating abstract states. If REFINE terminates normally, and hence succeeds in eliminating the violation by refining the abstraction functions, then MAIN continues with the next iteration of the **repeat** loop. In case an UNSATISFIABLE exception is thrown, MKPATH from Figure 8 constructs a counterexample path that we report to the user.

***Procedure* ABSTREACHENV** See Figure 7 for the procedure ABSTREACHENV that implements ARET computation using the abstraction functions $\dot{\alpha}_i$ and $\ddot{\alpha}_{i \triangleright j}$. We use $Parent$ and $ParentTId$ to maintain information about the constructed trees, and initialize

```
function MkPath
input
  D - abstract state
begin
  match Parent(D) with
  | (S, ρ) ->
      π := MkPath(S)
      match Parent(ρ) with
      | (O, ρ_O) -> return π · ρ_O
      | ⊥ -> return π · ρ
  | ⊥ -> return ϵ                    (* the empty sequence *)
end
```

Figure 8. Function MkPath takes as input an abstract state D and returns a sequence of transitions that lead to D.

them with the empty function $\perp$ in line 1. $\mathcal{R}_i$ and $\mathcal{E}_i$ keep track of abstract states and environment transitions for a thread $i \in 1..\mathsf{N}$. $\mathcal{E}_i$ is initialized to an empty set in line 4, while $\mathcal{R}_i$ contains the abstraction of the initial program states computed for the thread i. The ARET computation is performed iteratively in the **repeat** loop, see lines 5–27.

The first part of the loop (see lines 7–17) implements a standard, least fixpoint computation over reachable states. At line 7, the algorithm picks an already reachable states $S \in \mathcal{R}_i$ in order to compute its abstract successors. After computing at lines 10–11 one successor of S, line 12 implements a fixpoint check, which succeeds if S' contains program states that have not been reached yet. The new states reachable in thread i are stored in $\mathcal{R}_i$. At line 14, the function *Parent* is updated to keep track of the child-parent relation between abstract states, while *ParentTId* maps the new reachable state to its parent thread.

The second part of the loop (see lines 19–26) performs a least fixpoint computation over environment transitions. Each time a transition from a thread i is picked at line 7, the abstraction of its effect computed in line 20 is propagated to each other thread j. Note however, that the propagation only happens for environment transitions that are not subsumed by the existing ones, which is checked in line 21. Additional environment transitions are recorded in line 22. Environment transitions are taken into consideration when computing abstract state reachability, see line 9.

Upon termination, which is guaranteed by the finiteness of our abstract domains, the function AbstReachEnv computes sets of abstract states $\mathcal{R}_1, \ldots, \mathcal{R}_\mathsf{N}$ and sets of environment transitions $\mathcal{E}_1, \ldots, \mathcal{E}_\mathsf{N}$.

6. Abstraction refinement

***Procedure* Refine** In Figure 9, we present the procedure Refine that takes as argument an error tuple and, if possible, refines the abstraction functions to include predicates that witness the fact that the error state is unreachable. The procedure Refine generates a set of Horn clauses corresponding to the error tuple (lines 1–4). Next, the Refine algorithm invokes a solving procedure for Horn clauses (lines 5–7). Lastly, the procedure Refine updates the abstraction functions using the solution of Horn clauses at lines 8–12. We consider the solution Sol and add the atomic predicates that appear in Sol("S"(V) to the set of predicates $\dot{\mathcal{P}}_i$. The index i is chosen to be that of the thread where S originated from. Similarly, the procedure updates the transition abstraction functions at line 12. Here, we only assume that SolveHC returns a correct solution to the set of Horn clauses received as argument. In

```
procedure Refine
input
  S_1, ..., S_N - abstract error tuple
begin
1   HC := {"S_1"(V) ∧ ··· ∧ "S_N"(V) ∧ φ_err → false}
2           ∪ MkHornClauses(S_1)
3           ...
4           ∪ MkHornClauses(S_N)
5   Sol := SolveHC(HC,
6                {"S"(V) | i ∈ 1..N ∧ S ∈ R_i} ∪
7                {"ρ"(V, V') | i ∈ 1..N ∧ ρ ∈ E_i})
8   for each i ∈ 1..N and S ∈ R_i do
9     Ṗ_i := PredsOf(Sol("S"(V))) ∪ Ṗ_i
10  for each j ∈ 1..N and ρ ∈ E_j do
11    i := ParentTId(ρ)
12    P̈_{i▷j} := PredsOf(Sol("ρ"(V, V'))) ∪ P̈_{i▷j}
end
```

Figure 9. Procedure Refine. The quotation function "·" creates a relation symbol from a given abstract state/abstract transition. The function *PredsOf* extracts atomic predicates from the solutions to the set of Horn clauses *HC*.

```
function MkHornClauses
input
  D - abstract state
begin
  i := ParentTId(D)
  return
    match Parent(D) with
    | (S, ρ) ->
      MkHornClauses(S) ∪
      begin
        match Parent(ρ) with
        | (O, ρ_O) ->
          {"O"(V) ∧ ρ_O → "ρ"(V, V'),
           "S"(V) ∧ "ρ"(V, V') ∧ ρ_i^= → "D"(V')}
          ∪ MkHornClauses(O)
        | ⊥ -> {"S"(V) ∧ ρ → "D"(V')}
      end
    | ⊥ -> {φ_init → "D"(V)}
end
```

Figure 10. Function MkHornClauses.

Section 7, we present a solving algorithm for recursion-free Horn clauses over the linear arithmetic domain.

***Function* MkHornClauses** The generation of the Horn clauses is started from lines 1–4 of Figure 9. One clause requires that the solutions corresponding to the abstract states from the error tuple do not intersect φ_{err} : $\{``S_1"(V) \wedge \cdots \wedge ``S_\mathsf{N}"(V) \wedge \varphi_{err} \rightarrow \mathit{false}\}$. The other clauses are generated by invoking $\textsc{MkHornClauses}(S_i)$ for $i \in 1..\mathsf{N}$. The function MkHornClauses generates Horn clauses for transitions considered during ARET computation as follows. If the abstract state D was produced by following a local transition, i.e., $\mathit{Parent}(D) =$

```
9              {"O"(V_G, V_i) ∧ ρ_O → "ρ"(V_G, V'_G) ,
10              "S"(V_G, V_i) ∧ "ρ"(V_G, V'_G) ∧
11               ρ_i^= → "D"(V'_G, V'_i)}
12           ∪ MKHORNCLAUSES(O)
13         | ⊥ -> {"S"(V_G, V_i) ∧ ρ → "D"(V'_G, V'_i)}
14       end
15     | ⊥ -> {φ_init → "D"(V_G, V_i)}
```

Figure 11. Modifications to MKHORNCLAUSES to admit only modular solutions.

```
// Thread 1                     // Thread 2
x:  cnt++;                      p: take_lock(lock,1);
    assume(cnt >= 1);           q: // critical
a:  take_lock(lock,1);
b:  // critical
```

$$\varphi_{init} = (\mathtt{pc}_1 = x \land \mathtt{pc}_2 = p \land \mathtt{lock} = 0 \land \mathtt{cnt} = 0)$$
$$\rho_{\overline{1}}^{=} = (\mathtt{pc}_1 = \mathtt{pc}_1{}' \land \mathtt{cnt} = \mathtt{cnt}')$$
$$\rho_{\overline{2}}^{=} = (\mathtt{pc}_2 = \mathtt{pc}_2{}')$$
$$\rho_0 = (\mathtt{pc}_1 = x \land \mathtt{pc}_1{}' = a \land \mathtt{lock} = \mathtt{lock}' \land \mathtt{cnt} + 1 = \mathtt{cnt}' \land 1 \leq \mathtt{cnt}' \land \rho_{\overline{2}}^{=})$$
$$\rho_1 = (\mathtt{pc}_1 = a \land \mathtt{pc}_1{}' = b \land \mathtt{lock} = 0 \land \mathtt{lock}' = 1 \land \mathtt{cnt} = \mathtt{cnt}' \land \rho_{\overline{2}}^{=})$$
$$\rho_2 = (\mathtt{pc}_2 = p \land \mathtt{pc}_2{}' = q \land \mathtt{lock} = 0 \land \mathtt{lock}' = 1 \land \rho_{\overline{1}}^{=})$$
$$\varphi_{err} = (\mathtt{pc}_1 = b \land \mathtt{pc}_2 = q)$$

Figure 12. `LockBitCnt` is an expanded version of the program `LockBit` .

(S, ρ) and $Parent(\rho) = \bot$, then one Horn clause corresponds to the application of the local transition at line 12: $\{$"S"$(V) \land \rho \to$ "D"$(V')\}$. Additional Horn clauses are generated recursively for the parent state S at line 5. If the abstract state D was produced by following an environment transition, i.e., $Parent(D) = (S, \rho)$ and $Parent(\rho) = (O, \rho_O)$, then two Horn clauses correspond to the generation of the environment transition (line 9) and to the application of the environment transition (line 10). Finally, if $Parent(D) = \bot$, then one Horn clause constrains the solution of "D"(V) at line 14: $\{\varphi_{init} \to$ "D"$(V)\}$. Note that solutions for unknown states are expressed in terms of all program variables V, while solutions for unknown transitions are expressed in terms of V and V' . Consequently, these solutions may lead to non-modular proofs even for a set of Horn clauses that has modular solutions.

Discovery of Modular Predicates We present modifications to our abstraction refinement algorithm that guarantee the discovery of modular solutions whenever they exist. With these modifications, solutions for unknown states originating in thread i can only be expressed in terms of V_G, V_i rather than the whole set of program variables V . Solutions for unknown transitions are restricted to the set of global variables V_G, V'_G . To implement these changes, we change line 1 from the REFINE procedure as follows:

```
1    HC := {"S_1"(V_G, V_1) ∧ ··· ∧ "S_N"(V_G, V_N) ∧ φ_err}
```

We also replace lines 9–14 from MKHORNCLAUSES with the fragment shown in Figure 11. The rest of the function MKHORNCLAUSES is unchanged. If the resulting Horn clauses have no solution, i.e., SOLVEHC throws an UNSATISFIABLE exception, then it may still be possible that a non-modular solution exists. In this case, we invoke the abstraction refinement once again, this time generating Horn clauses using the unmodified function MKHORNCLAUSES from Figure 10.

Example We illustrate the generation of Horn clauses using an expanded version of `LockBit` shown in Figure 12. This example contains an additional variable `cnt` local to the first thread. The initial symbolic state of the program φ_{init} constrains both `cnt` and `lock` to the value 0 . The transition relation of the first thread is extended with ρ_0, which increments `cnt` by 1 and assumes that the incremented value is greater than or equal to 1 . Similar to the example from Section 2, φ_{err} encodes the violation of the mutual exclusion property. We show in Figure 13(a) the reachability trees as computed by the ARET computation. The error tuple consists of m_4 and n_3 , i.e., $m_4 \land n_3 \land \varphi_{err}$ is satisfiable.

From this error tuple, MKHORNCLAUSES generates Horn clauses following the procedure from Figure 10. These Horn clauses are shown in Figure 13(b). The Horn clauses have unknown states "m_1"(V), "m_2"(V), "m_3"(V), "m_4"(V), "n_1"(V), "n_2"(V) , and "n_3"(V) . The unknown transitions are "e_1"(V, V') and "e_2"(V, V') .

Comparatively, we show in Figure 13(c) the Horn clauses generated with preference for modular solutions. The solutions for the unknown states of thread 1 can refer only to (V_G, V_1) , while the unknown states of thread 2 are restricted to (V_G, V_1) . The unknown transitions are "e_1"(V_G, V'_G) and "e_2"(V_G, V'_G) .

THEOREM 4 (Progress of abstraction refinement). *The procedure* REFINE *guarantees progress of abstraction refinement, i.e., the same set of Horn clauses is never discovered twice.* ■

7. Solving Horn clauses over linear inequalities

As presented in the previous section, REFINE calls the function SOLVEHC. In this section we present a function SOLVELINEARHC that can be used as an implementation of SOLVEHC takes as input a set of clauses *HC* over linear inequalities that is recursion-free.

To simplify the presentation of the algorithm, we make two additional assumptions on *HC*. First, we assume that for each pair of clauses $(\ldots) \to b(w)$ and $(\ldots) \to b'(w')$ from *HC* we have $b \neq b'$ and $b \neq (\leq) \neq b'$. Second, we assume that *HC* contains a clause $(\ldots) \to \mathit{false}$.

The additional assumptions are satisfied by the clauses generated in Section 6. In case SOLVELINEARHC is applied on a set of recursion-free Horn clauses over linear arithmetic that violates the two assumptions above, we can apply a certain renaming of relation symbols and introduction of additional clauses to meet the assumptions.

***Function* MKTREE** The function MKTREE generates a tree representation for a set of Horn clauses and is shown in Figure 15. For every relation appearing in the Horn clauses, the algorithm generates a corresponding tree node. The children of a node are maintained in a function *Children* as follows. Nodes that correspond to linear arithmetic relations have no children, see lines 11–12. A node that corresponds to an unknown relation with a relation symbol b has as children those nodes that represent relation symbols that depend on b . The *Label* attribute of the tree nodes is initialized to a linear arithmetic constraint for leaves of the tree in line 11, and to an unknown relation for internal tree nodes in line 13.

***Function* SOLVELINEARHC** See Figure 14 for the pseudocode of the procedure SOLVELINEARHC . This procedure creates a tree representation for *HC* at line 2. At line 3, we build a set containing

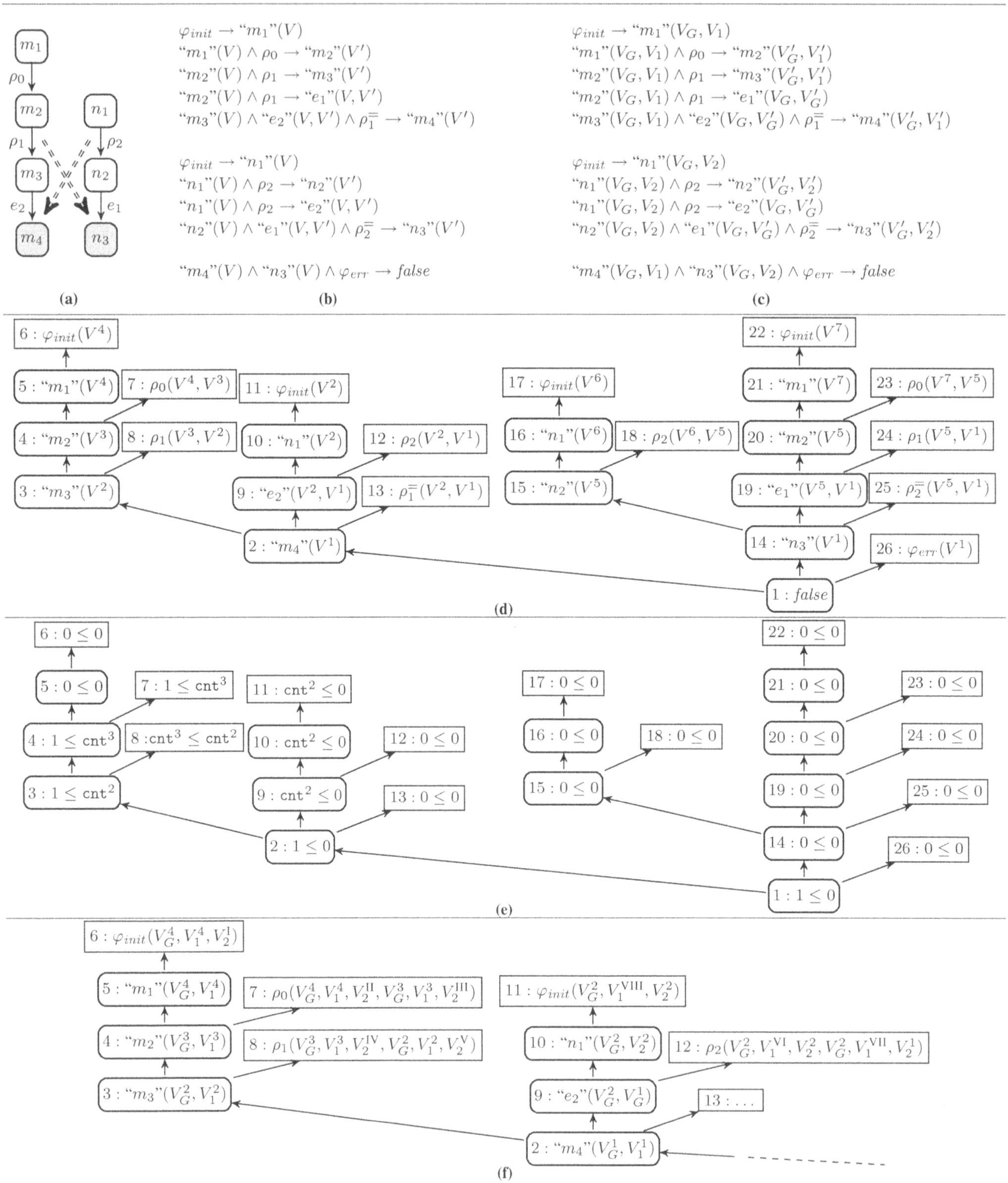

Figure 13. (a) Reachability trees constructed by ARET computation. (b) Corresponding Horn clauses generated using MKHORNCLAUSES. (c) Horn clauses generated with preference for modular solutions. (d) A tree representation of the clauses from (b) as generated by MKTREE. Each node shows its *Label* attribute. The superscript of the node name identifies the set of variables appearing in the attribute of the node. (e) The *Pred* map generated by SOLVELINEARHC from the clauses in (b). (f) The *Label* map generated by MKHORNCLAUSES from the clauses in (c).

all the *Label* attributes of leaf nodes and store this set in *Atoms* . The input set of Horn clauses is satisfiable if and only if $\bigwedge$ *Atoms* is unsatisfiable. If $\bigwedge$ *Atoms* is unsatisfiable, the test at lines 4–5 succeeds and returns a proof of unsatisfiability in the form of weights for each linear inequality. This test can be implemented using some linear arithmetic constraint solver. If the constraint solver fails to find a proof, an exception UNSATISFIABLE is thrown at line 12.

At line 7, SOLVELINEARHC calls the procedure ANNOTPRED , which is presented in Figure 16. This procedure recursively traverses the input tree in postorder. If this procedure is invoked for a leaf node n , it directly computes the value of $Pred(n)$ as a linear combination of atomic formulas with weights given by the *Proof* function (see line 2). If this procedure is invoked for an internal node n , the attribute *Pred* of n's children is computed using a recursive call at line 5. After completing the recursive call, $Pred(n)$ is calculated by adding the values of the *Pred* attributes of n's children.

Since there may be multiple nodes in the tree corresponding to the same unknown relation, the algorithm has to account for the *Pred* attributes of all these nodes. Therefore, at lines 8–9 we compute solutions for each $b(w)$ in *UnkRel* by taking conjunction of *Pred* of each node of the tree that is labeled with $b(u)$ for some u .

THEOREM 5. SOLVELINEARHC *computes a solution for a set of Horn clauses HC if and only if the conjunction of the clauses in HC is satisfiable.*

Example We illustrate the solving procedure using the same example from the previous section. Given the Horn clauses from Figure 13(b), MKTREE constructs a tree that is shown in Figure 13(d). This tree contains nodes which we label for convenience with identifiers from 1 to 26 . In Figure 13(d) we show the *Label* map of the tree. A witness of the unsatisfiability of $\bigwedge$ *Atoms* is given by the following atomic formulas:

$$\begin{array}{ccccc} (\mathtt{cnt}^3 \geq 1) & \wedge & (\mathtt{cnt}^3 = \mathtt{cnt}^2) & \wedge & (\mathtt{cnt}^2 = 0) \\ \Cap & & \Cap & & \Cap \\ Label(7) & & Label(8) & & Label(11) \end{array}$$

Our solver treats each linear equality as a conjunction of two linear inequalities. The equality $\mathtt{cnt}^2 = 0$ is split in two inequalities $\mathtt{cnt}^2 \leq 0 \wedge -\mathtt{cnt}^2 \leq 0$. The proof of unsatisfiability is:

$$(1 \leq \mathtt{cnt}^3) + (\mathtt{cnt}^3 \leq \mathtt{cnt}^2) + (\mathtt{cnt}^2 \leq 0) = (1 \leq 0).$$

This is encoded in the *Proof* map with values of 1 at locations corresponding to the three atomic formulas above and values of 0 for all the other atomic formula. Next, we show in Figure 13(e) the values for the *Pred* map as computed by ANNOTPRED . The final solution of the Horn clauses is built by a conjunction of the *Pred* attributes for nodes with the same unknown label. The resulting solution SOL is shown below.

$$\begin{array}{lclcl} \textsc{Sol}(``m_1"(V)) & = & \textsc{Sol}(``n_2"(V)) & = & (0 \leq 0) \\ \textsc{Sol}(``e_1"(V, V')) & = & & = & (0 \leq 0) \\ \textsc{Sol}(``m_2"(V)) & = & \textsc{Sol}(``m_3"(V)) & = & (1 \leq \mathtt{cnt}) \\ \textsc{Sol}(``n_1"(V)) & = & \textsc{Sol}(``e_2"(V, V')) & = & (\mathtt{cnt} \leq 0) \end{array}$$

Solving the clauses shown in Figure 13(c) Given the Horn clauses shown in this figure, MKTREE returns a tree representation with a similar *Children* map structure but with different *Label* attributes. The part of the tree that contributes to the proof of unsatisfiability is shown in Figure 13(f). The variable $\mathtt{cnt}^2$ does not appear in the subtree of the node 9 since $Label(9) = ``e_2"(V_G^2, V_G^1)$. Part of this subtree is the node 11. Let us name the variable at this node as $\mathtt{cnt}^{\mathrm{VIII}}$. The proof of unsatisfiability shown above does no longer hold, since the following formula is satisfiable:

$$(1 \leq \mathtt{cnt}^3) \wedge (\mathtt{cnt}^3 = \mathtt{cnt}^2) \wedge (\mathtt{cnt}^{\mathrm{VIII}} = 0)$$

However, the conjunction of the elements from the *Atoms* set is still unsatisfiable, indicating that a modular solution exists. We find that the following atoms contribute to a proof of unsatisfiability:

$$\begin{array}{ccc} \mathtt{lock}^2 = 1 & \wedge & \mathtt{lock}^2 = 0 \\ \Cap & & \Cap \\ Label(8) & & Label(12) \end{array}$$

After splitting the equalities in equivalent inequalities, our algorithm computes the following solution:

$$\begin{array}{ll} Pred(8) = (1 \leq \mathtt{lock}^2) & Pred(12) = (\mathtt{lock}^2 \leq 0) \\ Pred(3) = (1 \leq \mathtt{lock}^2) & Pred(9) = (\mathtt{lock}^2 \leq 0) \\ Pred(2) = (1 \leq 0) & \end{array}$$

From this *Pred* map, our algorithm derives a solution SOL in lines 8–9 and succeeds in computing modular predicates.

```
    function SOLVELINEARHC
    input
      HC - recursion-free Horn clauses over linear inequalities
      UnkRel - unknown relations
    vars
      Label - map from node to attribute
      Children - map from node to a set of nodes
      Pred - map from node to an atomic predicate
      Proof - weight function for inequalities
    begin
1     Label := Children := ⊥            (* the empty function *)
2     root := MKTREE(false)
3     Atoms := ⋃{Label(n) | Children(n) = ∅}
4     if exists Proof : Atoms → Q≥0 such that
5        ∑{Proof(b(u)) · b(u) | b(u) ∈ Atoms} = (1 ≤ 0)
6     then
7        ANNOTPRED(root)
8        for each b(w) ∈ UnkRel do
9           SOL(b(w)) := ⋀{Pred(n)[w/u] | Label(n) = b(u)}
10       return SOL
11    else
12       throw UNSATISFIABLE
    end
```

Figure 14. Function SOLVELINEARHC returns a solution for a set of recursion-free Horn clauses over linear arithmetic.

8. Experimental results

In this section, we describe a proof-of-concept implementation of our proposed algorithm as an extension of the model checker ARMC [29].

Tool description The verifier we built takes as input a number of functions (written in the C language) representing threads that should execute concurrently. The input file also contains the description of an initial state and a number of assertions to be proven correct. Our tool uses a frontend based on the CIL infrastructure [25] to translate a C program to its corresponding multi-threaded transition system that is formalized in Section 3. The main compo-

```
function MkTree
input
   g - relation, either b(u) or false
begin
   p, q := new nodes
   match g with
    | false ->
          {b_1(w_1) ∧ ··· ∧ b_n(w_n) → false, ...} := HC
          z_1, ..., z_n := fresh copies of w_1, ..., w_n
          σ := [z_1/w_1] ··· [z_n/w_n]
    | b(u) ->
          {b_1(w_1) ∧ ··· ∧ b_n(w_n) → b(w), ...} := HC
          z_1, ..., z_n, z := fresh copies of w_1, ..., w_n, w
          σ := [z_1/w_1] ··· [z_n/w_n][u/z]
   Label(p) := {b_i(w_i)σ | i ∈ 1..n ∧ b_i = (≤)}
   Children(p) := ∅
   Label(q) := g
   Children(q) :=
       {p} ∪ ⋃{MkTree(b_i(w_i)σ) | i ∈ 1..n ∧ b_i ≠ (≤)}
   return q
end
```

Figure 15. Function MkTree. Fresh copies are created consistent, e.g., fresh copies of $\{v_1, v_2\}$, $\{v_3, v_1\}$ returns $\{f_1, f_2\}$, $\{f_3 f_1\}$, where f_1, f_2, f_3 are fresh variables that do not appear anywhere else.

```
procedure AnnotPred
input
   n - node of Horn tree
begin
   if Children(n) = ∅ then
      Pred(n) := Σ{Proof(b(u))·b(u) | b(u) ∈ Label(n)}
   else
      for each n' ∈ Children(n) do
         AnnotPred(n')
      Pred(n) := Σ{Pred(n')|n' ∈ Children(n)}
end
```

Figure 16. Procedure AnnotPred.

nent of our tool is an implementation of our algorithm done using SICStus Prolog [33].

An important design decision in our implementation concerns the treatment of control-location and data variables. Even if both control-location variables and data variables can be handled uniformly by our algorithm, we found that different abstraction domains and refinement for the two domains can lead to significant improvement. In our implementation, the Refine procedure first splits the constraints into data variable constraints and control-location constraints. The splitting procedure preserves satisfiability/unsatisfiability of the original constraint since there is no atomic formula in the program transitions that relates both control variables and data variables. If the data constraints are satisfiable, the algorithm proceeds as in Figure 9. If the data constraints are unsatisfiable, our implementation relies on a specialized refinement procedure (described in [13]) that takes advantage of the simpler form of control counterexamples. For these counterexamples, control variables range over a finite domain and no atomic formula from the program transitions involves different control variables.

Benchmark programs We tested our prototype implementation using a collection of programs that have intricate correctness proofs for their safety assertions. The first four programs shown in Table 1 are derived from two buggy examples highlighted as figures in [20], together with their fixes from the Mozilla CVS repository. The property to verify is that two operations performed by different threads are executed in the correct order. The next three examples model the stopping procedure of a Windows NT Bluetooth driver [30]. Bluetooth2 contains two threads, one worker thread and another thread to model the stopping procedure of the driver. Bluetooth2-fixed and Bluetooth3-fixed are the fixed versions of the model with two and respectively three threads. Scull [6] is a Linux character device driver that implements access to a global memory area. The property to verify is that read and write operations are performed in critical section.

We also include some examples which are not particularly favorable to a modular reasoning approach. These examples are algorithms that establish mutual exclusion and mainly deal with global variables (no local computation is included in the critical region). The mutual exclusion property of the naïve version of the Bakery algorithm [22] holds only when assuming assignments are performed atomically. (Our verifier was able to confirm the bug present in the code without such atomicity assumption.) Bakery [18] is the complete version of the Bakery algorithm, while Lamport [19] is an algorithm with an optimized path in the absence of memory contention. Qrcu [23] is an algorithm implementing the Read-copy-update synchronization algorithm. It is an alternative to a readers-writer lock having wait-free read operations.

Performance of our tool To explain our experimental results, we first articulate a working hypothesis. This hypothesis suggests that, when verifying a program that does not have a modular proof, the algorithm with preference for modular solutions (denoted as *verification with bias*) is expected to pay a penalty by insisting to search for modular solutions that do not exist. On the other hand, for cases where a modular proof does exist, the non-biased verification could fail to find a modular proof and instead return a more detailed non-modular proof. Therefore, the hypothesis suggests that in these cases the biased verification is expected to succeed faster compared to the non-biased verification.

We report statistical data for each of the programs in Table 1. We show the number of lines of code (LOC) and whether a modular proof exists for a program (see Column 3). Our implementation has two modes. Column 4 shows the verification results, when using our algorithm with a preference for modular solutions. The last column of the table shows the verification results for the non-biased implementation of our algorithm. The results demonstrate that our approach to verification of multi-threaded programs is feasible and that the constraint solving procedure with bias is able to produce modular proofs more often than the non-biased verification. Furthermore, without the bias, the verification procedure times-out for Scull and QRCU examples showing the benefits of modular proofs.

As another experiment, we tested some of our smaller examples using two state-of-the-art model checkers for sequential C programs, Blast [14] and ARMC[31]. For each of the tested programs (Fig2-fixed, Fig4-fixed, Dekker, Peterson, and Lamport), we instrumented the program counter as explicit program variables ($\mathtt{pc}_1$ and $\mathtt{pc}_2$) and obtained a sequential model of the multi-threaded examples. Both Blast and ARMC eagerly consider all interleavings and obtained timeouts after 30 minutes for both Fig4-fixed and Lamport. Comparatively, our tool exploits the thread structure of these programs and obtains conclusive verification results fast.

Benchmark programs			Our algorithm			
Name	LOC	Has a modular proof?	With bias		No bias	
Fig2-cex[20]	33	No	×	0.2s	×	0.2s
Fig2-fixed[20]	38	Yes	✓-Modular	0.8s	✓-Modular	0.7s
Fig4-cex[20]	175	No	×	4.5s	×	3.7s
Fig4-fixed[20]	168	Yes	✓-Modular	1.5s	✓	11.1s
Bluetooth2[30]	90	No	✓	29.1s	✓	11.2s
Bluetooth2-fixed	90	No	✓	3.7s	✓	0.4s
Bluetooth3-fixed	90	No	✓	135s	✓	9.7s
Scull[6]	451	Yes	✓-Modular	128.5s	T/O	
Dekker[1]	39	No	✓	11.1s	✓	6s
Peterson[1]	26	No	✓	4.7s	✓	3.9s
Readers-writer-lock[10]	22	Yes	✓-Modular	0.2s	✓	0.4s
Time varying mutex[10]	29	No	✓	11.8s	✓	3.1s
Szymanski[32]	43	No	✓	32s	✓	8.8s
NaïveBakery[22]	22	Yes	✓-Modular	2.5s	✓	3s
Bakery[18]	37	No	✓	105.4s	✓	101s
Lamport[19]	62	No	✓	120.8s	✓	97s
QRCU[23]	120	Yes	✓-Modular	34.5s	T/O	

Table 1. "Has a modular proof?" indicates whether the program has a modular proof of correctness. "✓" and "×" indicate whether the program is proven safe or a counterexample is returned, while "T/O" stands for time out after 15 minutes. ✓-Modular indicates that a modular proof is found by our tool.

9. Related work

The main inspiration for our work draws from the rely-guarantee reasoning method [16, 17] and automatic abstraction refinement approach to verification [4].

The seminal work on rely-guarantee reasoning [16, 17] initially offered an approach to reason about multi-threaded programs by making explicit the interference between threads. Subsequently, rely-guarantee reasoning was used to tackle the problem of state explosion in verification of multi-threaded programs. Rely-guarantee reasoning was mechanized and firstly implemented in the Calvin model checker [10] for Java shared-memory programs. Calvin reduces the verification of the multi-threaded program to the verification of several sequential programs with the help of a programmer specified environment assumption. In [9], thread-modular model checking was proposed to infer automatically environment assumptions that propagate only global variable changes to other threads. The algorithm has low complexity, polynomial in the number of threads, but is incomplete and fails to discover environment assumptions that refer to the local states of a thread. Thread-modular verification is formalized by [21] in the framework of abstract interpretation as Cartesian product of sets of states.

The method of [15] uses a richer abstraction scheme that computes contextual thread reachability, where the context in which a thread executes includes information on both global and local states of threads. The context (or environment) is computed using bisimilarity quotients in steps that are interleaved with abstract reachability computations. The verification starts with the strongest possible environment assumption and, by refinement, the environment is weakened until it over-approximates the transitions of the other threads. In contrast, our approach refines iteratively the environment based on over-approximation, starting with the weakest environment and strengthening it at every iteration. For abstraction refinement, a counterexample from [15] is reduced to a concrete sequential path by replacing environment transitions with their corresponding local transitions.

The approach of [5] presents another solution to overcome the incompleteness of local reasoning. Guided by counterexamples, it refines the abstraction by exposing a local variable of a thread as a global variable. This refinement recovers the completeness of reasoning, but is applicable to finite-state systems and may compute an unnecessarily precise abstraction. In contrast, our refinement procedure relies on interpolation and includes predicates on local variables as needed during verification.

Another approach to overcome the state explosion problem of monolithic reasoning over multi-threaded programs is to translate the multi-threaded program to a sequential program assuming a bound on the number of context switches. This scheme was initially proposed and implemented in KISS [30], a multi-threaded checker for C programs, and later evolved to handle and reproduce even difficult to find Heisenbugs [24]. Monolithic reasoning can be greatly facilitated by using techniques evolved from partial-order reduction [11], like dynamic partial-order reduction [8] or peephole partial order reduction [34]. Yet another technique to fight state explosion is to factor out redundancy due to thread replication as proposed in counter abstraction [27] and implemented in the model checker Boom [2, 3]. We view these techniques as paramount in obtaining practical multi-threaded verifiers, but orthogonal to our proposal for automatic environment inference.

Acknowledgments

The first author was supported by the DFG Graduiertenkolleg 1480 (PUMA). We thank Byron Cook, Ruslán Ledesma Garza, and Peter O'Hearn for comments and suggestions.

References

[1] Y. Bar-David and G. Taubenfeld. Automatic discovery of mutual exclusion algorithms. In *DISC*, pages 136–150, 2003.

[2] G. Basler, M. Mazzucchi, T. Wahl, and D. Kroening. Symbolic counter abstraction for concurrent software. In *CAV*, pages 64–78, 2009.

[3] G. Basler, M. Hague, D. Kroening, C.-H. L. Ong, T. Wahl, and H. Zhao. Boom: Taking boolean program model checking one step further. In *TACAS*, pages 145–149, 2010.

[4] E. M. Clarke, O. Grumberg, S. Jha, Y. Lu, and H. Veith. Counterexample-guided abstraction refinement. In *CAV*, pages 154–169, 2000.

[5] A. Cohen and K. S. Namjoshi. Local proofs for global safety properties. *FMSD*, 34(2):104–125, 2009.

[6] J. Corbet, A. Rubini, and G. Kroah-Hartman. *Linux Device Drivers, 3rd Edition*. O'Reilly Media, Inc., 2005.

[7] P. Cousot and R. Cousot. Abstract interpretation: A unified lattice model for static analysis of programs by construction or approximation of fixpoints. In *POPL*, pages 238–252, 1977.

[8] C. Flanagan and P. Godefroid. Dynamic partial-order reduction for model checking software. In *POPL*, pages 110–121, 2005.

[9] C. Flanagan and S. Qadeer. Thread-modular model checking. In *SPIN*, pages 213–224, 2003.

[10] C. Flanagan, S. N. Freund, and S. Qadeer. Thread-modular verification for shared-memory programs. In *ESOP*, pages 262–277, 2002.

[11] P. Godefroid. *Partial-Order Methods for the Verification of Concurrent Systems - An Approach to the State-Explosion Problem*. PhD thesis, University of Liege, Computer Science Department, 1994.

[12] S. Graf and H. Saïdi. Construction of abstract state graphs with PVS. In *CAV*, pages 72–83, 1997.

[13] A. Gupta, C. Popeea, and A. Rybalchenko. Non-monotonic refinement of control abstraction for concurrent programs. In *ATVA*, pages 188–202, 2010.

[14] T. A. Henzinger, R. Jhala, R. Majumdar, and G. Sutre. Lazy abstraction. In *POPL*, pages 58–70, 2002.

[15] T. A. Henzinger, R. Jhala, and R. Majumdar. Race checking by context inference. In *PLDI*, pages 1–13, 2004.

[16] C. B. Jones. Tentative steps toward a development method for interfering programs. *ACM Trans. Program. Lang. Syst.*, 5(4):596–619, 1983.

[17] C. B. Jones. Specification and design of (parallel) programs. In *IFIP Congress*, pages 321–332, 1983.

[18] L. Lamport. A new solution of Dijkstra's concurrent programming problem. *Commun. ACM*, 17(8):453–455, 1974.

[19] L. Lamport. A fast mutual exclusion algorithm. *ACM Trans. Comput. Syst.*, 5(1):1–11, 1987.

[20] S. Lu, S. Park, E. Seo, and Y. Zhou. Learning from mistakes: a comprehensive study on real world concurrency bug characteristics. In *ASPLOS*, pages 329–339, 2008.

[21] A. Malkis, A. Podelski, and A. Rybalchenko. Thread-modular verification is cartesian abstract interpretation. In *ICTAC*, pages 183–197, 2006.

[22] Z. Manna and A. Pnueli. *Temporal verification of reactive systems: safety*. Springer-Verlag, 1995.

[23] P. McKenney. Using Promela and Spin to verify parallel algorithms. *LWN.net weekly edition*, 2007.

[24] M. Musuvathi, S. Qadeer, T. Ball, G. Basler, P. A. Nainar, and I. Neamtiu. Finding and reproducing Heisenbugs in concurrent programs. In *OSDI*, pages 267–280, 2008.

[25] G. C. Necula, S. McPeak, S. P. Rahul, and W. Weimer. CIL: Intermediate language and tools for analysis and transformation of C programs. In *CC*, pages 213–228, 2002.

[26] S. S. Owicki and D. Gries. An axiomatic proof technique for parallel programs I. *Acta Inf.*, 6:319–340, 1976.

[27] A. Pnueli, J. Xu, and L. D. Zuck. Liveness with (0, 1, infty)-counter abstraction. In *CAV*, pages 107–122, 2002.

[28] A. Podelski and A. Rybalchenko. Transition predicate abstraction and fair termination. In *POPL*, pages 132–144, 2005.

[29] A. Podelski and A. Rybalchenko. ARMC: The logical choice for software model checking with abstraction refinement. In *PADL*, pages 245–259, 2007.

[30] S. Qadeer and D. Wu. KISS: keep it simple and sequential. In *PLDI*, pages 14–24, 2004.

[31] A. Rybalchenko. The ARMC tool. *Available from http://www7.in.tum.de/~rybal/armc/*.

[32] B. K. Szymanski. A simple solution to Lamport's concurrent programming problem with linear wait. In *ICS*, pages 621–626, 1988.

[33] The Intelligent Systems Laboratory. *SICStus Prolog User's Manual*. Swedish Institute of Computer Science, 2001. Release 3.8.7.

[34] C. Wang, Z. Yang, V. Kahlon, and A. Gupta. Peephole partial order reduction. In *TACAS*, pages 382–396, 2008.

Geometry of Synthesis III

Resource Management Through Type Inference

Dan R. Ghica * Alex Smith
University of Birmingham, UK
{d.r.ghica,AIS523}@bham.ac.uk

Abstract

Geometry of Synthesis is a technique for compiling higher-level programming languages into digital circuits via their game semantic model. Ghica (2007) first presented the key idea, then Ghica and Smith (2010) gave a provably correct compiler into asynchronous circuits for Syntactic Control of Interference (SCI), an affine-typed version of Reynolds's Idealized Algol. Affine typing has the dual benefits of ruling out race conditions through the type system and having a finite-state game-semantic model for any term, which leads to a natural circuit representation and simpler correctness proofs. In this paper we go beyond SCI to full Idealized Algol, enhanced with shared-memory concurrency and semaphores (Ghica and Murawski, 2008).

Compiling ICA proceeds in three stages. First, an intermediate type system called Syntactic Control of Concurrency (SCC), (Ghica et al., 2006) is used to statically determine "concurrency bounds" on all identifiers in the program. Then, a program transformation called *serialization* is applied to the program to translate it into an equivalent SCC program in which all concurrency bounds are set to the unit. Finally, the resulting program can be then compiled into asynchronous circuits using a slightly enhanced version of the GoS II compiler, which can handle assignable variables used in non-sequential contexts.

Categories and Subject Descriptors F.3.3 [*Logics and Meanings of Programs*]: Studies of Program Constructs—Type structure

General Terms Theory, Languages

Keywords Automatic Synthesis, Event Logic, Syntactic Control of Interference, Game Semantics

1. Geometry of Synthesis

The problem of *hardware compilation*, synthesising digital circuits from behavioural specifications written in higher-level programming languages, turned out to be surprisingly difficult. Although the pioneering work of van Berkel and Saeijs (1988) and Page and Luk (1991); Luk et al. (1994) yielded promising initial results, more than a decade later this technology has yet to enter the mainstream of digital design. Several C-to-hardware compilers are available as commercial products from companies such as MENTOR, ALTERA, SYNOPSYS and others, but they all share a common weakness, providing poor support for handling of functions and procedures, at least when compared with modern conventional ("software") compilers.

The role of functions (and related concepts such as procedures, subroutines, methods, etc.) in modern languages and compilers is essential in several different ways. Through the functional interface a program will structure itself into reusable components, interact with code written in other programming languages (*foreign function interface*), and interact with run-time services of the operating systems (*application binary interface*). The functional subset of a modern language will usually be a variant of a typed lambda calculus and can handle functions as arguments (higher-order functions), anonymous functions (abstraction) and partial application (*currying*). Starting with Algol, at least in the idealized form of Reynolds (1981), such features are common enough to be taken for granted in most contemporary languages and compilers. However, this is not the case in hardware compilation. These methodological considerations are elaborated by Ghica (2009).

The Geometry of Synthesis (GoS) approach is concerned with remedying this situation by compiling higher level languages into hardware in a way that is consistent with a modern functional infrastructure having mature functional interface capabilities. The GoS approach starts from the widely accepted premise that circuit diagrams that are graph isomorphic should be behaviourally equal at the "right" level of abstraction, and builds on the work of Kelly and Laplaza (1980) and their seminal results regarding the representation of diagrams in the language of compact closed categories. Function objects can be encoded in the language of compact closed categories using just a disciplined accounting of boxes and wires, so the first key new insight provided by GoS is that function definition and (linear) application can be represented in hardware in a purely static way by an interconnection of circuits which is consistent with this discipline. The second insight is that in order to compile conventional programming languages, their imperative features and especially contraction (which allows multiple occurrences of identifiers) can be represented at the circuit level using game semantics (Ghica, 2007). In fact, the hardware compilation process is tantamount to a *reification* of game semantics into hardware (Ghica, 2009).

Contribution. In this paper we address what we perceive to be a key inconvenience in the GoS approach, namely restrictions on contraction in concurrent contexts. Ideally, we want to allow the programmer to write programs such as $\lambda f \lambda x.f(x); f(x)$ or $\lambda f \lambda x.f(x) || f(x)$. However, the type system which forms the basis of the programming language allows contraction only in sequential contexts, hence the first term is typeable but the second is not. The programmer needs to *serialize* the term by hand, writing some-

* supported by an EPSRC Advanced Research Fellowship

thing like $\lambda f_1 f_2 \lambda x_1 x_2.f_1(x_1)||f_2(x_2)$; in complicated terms this quickly becomes very difficult to handle. This becomes even more difficult if we want to apply this function to terms which themselves require transformation. For example, if applied to $\lambda c.c||c$, which needs itself to change to $\lambda c_1 c_2.c_1||c_2$, the original function should actually be $\lambda f_1 f_2 \lambda x_1 x_2 x_3 x_4.f_1 x_1 x_2||f_2 x_3 x_4$.

In this paper we give a systematic method of obtaining such terms, which we then know how to compile into hardware.

2. Type systems

In this section we will present a realistic shared-memory higher-order concurrent programming language with synchronisation primitives, and give several typing systems for the language. The first type system is *Idealized Concurrent Algol* (ICA), the most general one, which is essentially the simply-typed lambda calculus with special constants for state manipulation and concurrency. It represents an extension of the idealized Algol language proposed by Reynolds (1981) with parallel composition and semaphores (Ghica and Murawski, 2008).

The next typing system, *(Basic) Syntactic Control of Interference (SCI)* is an affine version of ICA in which contraction is disallowed over function application and parallel execution. SCI was initially proposed by Reynolds as a programming language which would facilitate Hoare-style correctness reasoning because covert interference between terms is disallowed (Reynolds, 1978, 1989). SCI turned out to be semantically interesting and it was studied extensively (Reddy, 1996; O'Hearn et al., 1999; McCusker, 2007, 2010). The restriction on contraction in SCI makes it particularly well suited for hardware compilation because any term in the language has a finite-state model and can therefore be compiled as a static circuit (Ghica, 2007; Ghica and Smith, 2010).

The third type system, *Syntactic Control of Concurrency* (SCC) is a half-way house between the unrestricted ICA and the constrained SCI (Ghica et al., 2006). In SCC, contraction is allowed in all contexts, but static bounds on the number of contractions in non-sequential contexts are enforced through the type system. In fact, SCC with all contraction bounds set to unit is equivalent to SCI. SCC has been initially proposed as a framework for model checking concurrent programs, because this language also enjoys a finite-state model property at all terms (Ghica and Murawski, 2006). Evidently, this property recommends it as a more flexible alternative to SCI for hardware compilation. Shared memory concurrency and semaphores cannot type in SCI because they require contraction in non-sequential contexts, but can be handled by the SCC system.

2.1 Idealized Concurrent Algol (ICA)

The primitive types of the language are commands, memory cells, semaphores and expressions. For simplicity we only consider boolean expressions, but finite-integer expressions can be added in a conceptually straightforward manner.

$$\sigma ::= \mathsf{com} \mid \mathsf{var} \mid \mathsf{sem} \mid \mathsf{exp}.$$

The type constructors are product and function:

$$\theta ::= \theta \times \theta \mid \theta \to \theta \mid \sigma.$$

Terms are described by typing judgements of the form

$$x_1 : \theta_1, \ldots, x_k : \theta_k \vdash M : \theta,$$

where we denote the set of identifier type assignments on the left by Γ. By convention, if we write Γ, Γ' it assumes that the two type assignments have disjoint sets of identifiers.

The term formation rules of the language are those of the simply typed lambda calculus:

$$\frac{}{x : \theta \vdash x : \theta}\ \text{Identity}$$

$$\frac{\Gamma \vdash M : \theta}{\Gamma, x : \theta' \vdash M : \theta}\ \text{Weakening}$$

$$\frac{\Gamma, x : \theta, y : \theta \vdash M : \theta'}{\Gamma, x : \theta \vdash M[x/y] : \theta'}\ \text{Contraction}$$

$$\frac{\Gamma, x : \theta' \vdash M : \theta}{\Gamma \vdash \lambda x.M : \theta' \to \theta}\ \text{Abstraction}$$

$$\frac{\Gamma \vdash M : \theta \to \theta' \qquad \Gamma \vdash N : \theta}{\Gamma \vdash MN : \theta'}\ \text{Application}$$

$$\frac{\Gamma \vdash M_i : \theta_i}{\Gamma \vdash \langle M_1, M_2 \rangle : \theta_1 \times \theta_2}\ \text{Product}$$

The constants of the language are described below:

$0, 1 : \mathsf{exp}$ are the boolean constants;

$\mathsf{skip} : \mathsf{com}$ is the only command constant ("no-op");

$\mathsf{asg} : \mathsf{var} \times \mathsf{exp} \to \mathsf{com}$ is assignment to memory cell, denoted by ":=" when used in infix notation;

$\mathsf{der} : \mathsf{var} \to \mathsf{exp}$ is dereferencing of memory cell, also denoted by "!";

$\mathsf{seq} : \mathsf{com} \times \mathsf{com} \to \mathsf{com}$ is command sequencing, denoted by ";" when used in infix notation;

$\mathsf{seq} : \mathsf{com} \times \mathsf{exp} \to \mathsf{exp}$ is sequencing of command with expression, denoted by ";" when used in infix notation, resulting in an expression with side effects;

$\mathsf{par} : \mathsf{com} \to \mathsf{com} \to \mathsf{com}$ is parallel composition of commands, denoted by "||" when used in infix notation;

$\mathsf{neg} : \mathsf{exp} \to \mathsf{exp}$ is boolean negation;

$\mathsf{or} : \mathsf{exp} \times \mathsf{exp} \to \mathsf{exp}$ is boolean disjunction;

$\mathsf{if} : \mathsf{exp} \times \mathsf{com} \times \mathsf{com} \to \mathsf{com}$ is branching;

$\mathsf{while} : \mathsf{exp} \times \mathsf{com} \to \mathsf{com}$ is iteration;

$\mathsf{grab} : \mathsf{sem} \to \mathsf{com}$ is semaphore grab;

$\mathsf{release} : \mathsf{sem} \to \mathsf{com}$ is semaphore release;

$\mathsf{newvar} : (\mathsf{var} \to \mathsf{com}) \to \mathsf{com}$ is local variable declaration in block command;

$\mathsf{newvar} : (\mathsf{var} \to \mathsf{exp}) \to \mathsf{exp}$ is local variable declaration in block expression;

$\mathsf{newsem} : (\mathsf{sem} \to \mathsf{com}) \to \mathsf{com}$ is semaphore declaration in block command;

$\mathsf{newsem} : (\mathsf{sem} \to \mathsf{exp}) \to \mathsf{exp}$ is semaphore declaration in block expression;

$\mathsf{rec}_\theta : (\theta \to \theta) \to \theta$ is a fix-point operator.

Local variable and semaphore binding is presented with a quantifier-style type in order to avoid introducing new variable binders in the language. Local variable declaration can be sugared into a more familiar syntax as $\mathsf{newvar}(\lambda x.M) \equiv \mathsf{newvar}\ x\ \mathsf{in}\ M$.

The language ICA is a highly expressive programming language in which a large variety of algorithms and programming constructs can be coded. Its operational semantics, which defines the imperative and shared-variable concurrency primitives in the usual way in the framework of a call-by-name lambda-calculus, along with a fully abstract game semantic model are given by Ghica and Murawski (2008).

2.2 Syntactic Control of Interference (SCI)

SCI is the affine version of ICA. It has the same type structure as ICA. However, since contraction in concurrent contexts is not allowed semaphores can play no meaningful role and can be omitted from the definition of the language. The only changes as compared to ICA are the removal of explicit contraction and a new rule for function application:

$$\frac{\Gamma \vdash M : \theta \to \theta' \qquad \Gamma' \vdash N : \theta}{\Gamma, \Gamma' \vdash MN : \theta'} \text{ Application (new)}$$

The immediate consequence of this restriction is that nested application is no longer possible, i.e. terms such as

$$f : \mathsf{com} \to \mathsf{com} \vdash f(f(\mathsf{skip}))$$

are illegal. Elimination of nested application means that the usual operational unfolding of recursion no longer preserves typing, therefore the rec_θ operator must be also eliminated. A restricted recursion operator can be reintroduced but we will not consider it here.

The second consequence of this restriction plays out in conjunction with the chosen types of sequential and parallel composition:

$$\mathsf{seq} : \mathsf{com} \times \mathsf{com} \to \mathsf{com}$$
$$\mathsf{par} : \mathsf{com} \to \mathsf{com} \to \mathsf{com}.$$

The uncurried type of seq allows the typing of normal imperative programs because contraction can be achieved via product formation. Terms such as $\lambda c.c; c$ are possible, but $\lambda c.c||c$ are not.

Despite its restrictions SCI is still expressive enough to allow many interesting programs. Its finite state model makes it perfectly suited for hardware compilation (Ghica, 2007; Ghica and Smith, 2010).

2.3 Syntactic Control of Concurrency (SCC)

The SCC type system allows contraction in all contexts but only when static bounds on the numbers of non-sequential contractions are respected. The types of the language are given by the grammar

$$\sigma ::= \mathsf{com} \mid \mathsf{exp} \mid \mathsf{var} \mid \mathsf{sem}$$
$$\gamma ::= \theta^n, \quad n \in \mathbf{N}$$
$$\theta ::= \sigma \mid \theta \times \theta \mid \gamma \to \theta.$$

If a bound in θ^n is unit we may omit it. SCC types have the following sub-typing relation

$$\frac{n_1 \le n_2 \qquad \theta_1 \le \theta_2}{\theta_1^{n_1} \le \theta_2^{n_2}} \qquad \frac{\gamma_2 \le \gamma_1 \qquad \theta_1 \le \theta_2}{\gamma_1 \to \theta_1 \le \gamma_2 \to \theta_2}$$

Type judgements have form

$$x_1 : \gamma_1, \ldots, x_k : \gamma_k \vdash M : \theta.$$

If a type assignment environment is $\Gamma = \{x_i : \theta_i^{n_i} \mid 1 \le i \le k\}$ we define

$$n \cdot \Gamma \stackrel{def}{=} \{x_i : \theta_i^{n \cdot n_i} \mid 1 \le i \le k\}.$$

The typing rules are like in ICA except for the management of bounds in contraction and function application, plus a new rule for sub-typing:

$$\frac{\Gamma, x : \theta^m, y : \theta^n \vdash M : \theta'}{\Gamma, x : \theta^{m+n} \vdash M[x/y] : \theta'} \text{ Contraction (new)}$$

$$\frac{\Gamma \vdash M : \theta^n \to \theta' \qquad \Gamma' \vdash N : \theta}{\Gamma, n \cdot \Gamma' \vdash MN : \theta'} \text{ Application (new)}$$

$$\frac{\Gamma \vdash M : \theta \qquad \theta \le \theta'}{\Gamma \vdash M : \theta'} \text{ Subtyping}$$

Note that $\lambda c.c||c$ is typeable in SCC, but the type is not the same as for $\lambda c.c; c$:

$$\dfrac{\dfrac{\dfrac{\dfrac{c{:}\mathsf{com} \vdash c{:}\mathsf{com} \qquad \vdash \mathsf{par}{:}\mathsf{com} \to \mathsf{com} \to \mathsf{com}}{c{:}\mathsf{com} \vdash \mathsf{par}\ c{:}\mathsf{com} \to \mathsf{com}} \qquad d{:}\mathsf{com} \vdash d{:}\mathsf{com}}{c{:}\mathsf{com}, d{:}\mathsf{com} \vdash \mathsf{par}\ c\ d : \mathsf{com}}}{c{:}\mathsf{com}^2 \vdash \mathsf{par}\ c\ c : \mathsf{com}}}{\vdash \lambda c{:}\mathsf{com}^2.\mathsf{par}\ c\ c : \mathsf{com}^2 \to \mathsf{com}}$$

As in SCI, a general fix-point combinator cannot be typed. All other constants are inherited from ICA and receive, where needed, unit bound, except that newvar and newsem are replaced by a family of constants which can accept a local variable (semaphore, respectively) for any given bound

$$\mathsf{newvar} : (\mathsf{var}^n \to \mathsf{com}) \to \mathsf{com}$$
$$\mathsf{newvar} : (\mathsf{var}^n \to \mathsf{exp}) \to \mathsf{exp}$$
$$\mathsf{newsem} : (\mathsf{sem}^n \to \mathsf{com}) \to \mathsf{com}$$
$$\mathsf{newsem} : (\mathsf{sem}^n \to \mathsf{exp}) \to \mathsf{exp}.$$

The SCC type system can be used to write a large variety of imperative, concurrent or higher order programs such as producer-consumer (Ghica and Murawski, 2006). In practice the restriction is felt mainly because general recursion is ruled out and in the definition of higher-order functions where concurrency bounds must be specified by the programmer. Without type inference the programmer needs to specify guarantees as well, which is inconvenient and will be also addressed in this paper. Consider for example a producer-consumer program where the producer and the consumer are given as arguments. In ICA such a program would have signature

$$\lambda prod : \mathsf{exp}.\lambda cons : \mathsf{exp} \to \mathsf{com}.M$$

whereas in SCC it must be given as, for example

$$\lambda prod : \mathsf{exp}.\lambda cons : \mathsf{exp}^1 \to \mathsf{com}.M,$$

which means that any argument consumer is not allowed to use its own argument more than once in non-sequential contexts.

EXAMPLE 2.1.

1. $\vdash \lambda f.\lambda x.f(f(x)) : (\mathsf{com}^n \to \mathsf{com})^{n+1} \to \mathsf{com}^{n^2} \to \mathsf{com}$
2. $\vdash \lambda f.\lambda x.f(x); f(x) : (\mathsf{com}^n \to \mathsf{com})^1 \to \mathsf{com}^n \to \mathsf{com}$
3. $\vdash \lambda f.\lambda x.f(x)||f(x) : (\mathsf{com}^n \to \mathsf{com})^2 \to \mathsf{com}^{2n} \to \mathsf{com}$
4. $\vdash \lambda f.f(f(\mathsf{skip})) : (\mathsf{com}^n \to \mathsf{com})^{n+1} \to \mathsf{com}$
5. $\vdash \lambda g.g(\lambda x.g(\lambda y.x)) : ((\mathsf{com}^n \to \mathsf{com})^n \to \mathsf{com})^{n+1} \to \mathsf{com}.$

In the above, n is a positive integer constant which must be provided by the environment (the user).

The term of "concurrency bound" is meant to encompass two kinds of run-time interleaving. The first is the genuine concurrency expressed in a term such as $f(x)||f(x)$ and the second is that occurring in a term such as $f(f(x))$. We feel justified in calling the latter "concurrent" because the computations associated with the two instances of f are interleaved during execution. In fact, in *loc. cit.* it is shown how a term of that form can be syntactically "pulled apart" using semaphores and side-effects into a term of shape $\cdots f \cdots || \cdots f \cdots || \cdots x \cdots$ which has precisely the same interleaving of effects as the original.

Note that some terms are not typeable, for example the application of term (5) to term (4) above. Many ICA programs have SCC typing; in fact all beta-normal form ICA programs and all ICA programs with beta-redexes of first order or base types are SCC typeable (Ghica et al., 2006, Lemma 10). *Loc. cit.* also gives a fully abstract game semantic model of SCC.

3. Type inference for SCC

SCC is an assume-guarantee type system where the assume bounds must be provided by the context but the guarantee can be computed via type inference, rather than being supplied by the programmer. In this section we will give a decidability result for SCC type inference. Without loss of generality we will restrict the algorithm to higher-order closed terms. ICA typing can be determined with a variant Hindley-Milner-style algorithm, and we assume it. It is well known that affine typing plus explicit contraction is as expressive as conventional typing and we will assume our ICA type inference algorithm uses this strategy. The details of such an algorithm are standard and will be omitted.

We further assume that each type $\theta \to \theta'$ is decorated with a fresh variable n, as in $\theta^n \to \theta'$, to form a skeleton for an SCC type. For instance, the type $(\mathsf{com} \to \mathsf{com}) \to \mathsf{com}$ will be annotated as $(\mathsf{com}^{n_1} \to \mathsf{com})^{n_2} \to \mathsf{com}$. The variables which occur in covariant positions in the type of the term are called *assumes* and those that occur in contravariant positions *guarantees*.

Once this annotated type expression is constructed the next step is to obtain a set of numeric constraints on the bounds. This is done by defining a function recursively on the derivation tree, which produces a set of constraints as a result. First we define the constraints at the level of the type system:

$$|\theta^n| = \{n\}$$
$$|\theta \times \theta'| = |\theta| \cup |\theta'|$$
$$|\theta^n \to \theta'| = \{n\} \cup |\theta'|$$
$$|\theta_1^{n_1} \geq \theta_2^{n_2}| = (n_1 \geq n_2) \wedge |\theta_1| \geq |\theta_2|$$
$$|\gamma_1 \to \theta_1 \geq \gamma_2 \to \theta_2| = |\gamma_2 \geq \gamma_1| \wedge |\theta_1 \geq \theta_2|$$
$$|\Gamma \geq \Gamma'| = \bigwedge_{\substack{x:\gamma \in \Gamma \\ x:\gamma' \in \Gamma'}} |\gamma \geq \gamma'|$$

The notation can be extended to $|\Gamma = \Gamma'|$ in the obvious way.

The required constraints are indicated as annotations on the derivation rules:

$$\frac{}{x : (\theta')^n \vdash x : \theta \blacktriangleright n \geq 1 \wedge |\theta' \geq \theta|}$$

$$\frac{}{\emptyset \vdash \mathsf{k} : \theta \blacktriangleright \bigwedge_{n \in |\theta|} n \geq 1}$$

$$\frac{\Gamma' \vdash M : \theta \blacktriangleright C}{\Gamma, x : (\theta')^n \vdash M : \theta \blacktriangleright |\Gamma = \Gamma'|}$$

$$\frac{\Gamma', x : \gamma \vdash M : \theta \blacktriangleright C}{\Gamma \vdash \lambda x : \gamma . M : \gamma \to \theta \blacktriangleright |\Gamma = \Gamma'|}$$

$$\frac{\Gamma' \vdash M_i : \theta_i \blacktriangleright C_i}{\Gamma \vdash \langle M_1, M_2 \rangle : \theta_1 \times \theta_2 \blacktriangleright |\Gamma = \Gamma'|}$$

The key rules are for contraction

$$\frac{\Gamma', x : \theta^{n_1}, y : \theta^{n_2} \vdash M : \theta' \blacktriangleright C}{\Gamma, x : \theta^n \vdash M[x/y] : \theta' \blacktriangleright |\Gamma = \Gamma'| \wedge n \geq n_1 + n_2}$$

and application

$$\frac{\Gamma \vdash M : \theta_1^k \to \theta_2 \blacktriangleright C \qquad \Delta \vdash N : (\theta_1)' \blacktriangleright C'}{\Gamma', \Delta' \vdash MN : \theta_2' \blacktriangleright |\Delta \leq \Delta'| \wedge |\Gamma = \Gamma'| \wedge \left(\bigwedge_{\substack{x:\theta^n \in \Delta \\ x:\theta^{n'} \in \Delta'}} n' \geq k \cdot n \right)}$$

Note that the environments Γ, Γ' and Δ, Δ' in each rule above differ only in the choice of variables used as bounds.

In Fig. 1 we show an example annotated derivation tree, for the term $\lambda f x . f(f(x))$.

Given a closed term M and its derivation tree, let $\mathcal{C}(M)$ be the constraint system generated from the conjunction of all the annotations in the derivation tree. For the example in Fig. 1, $\mathcal{C}(\lambda f x . f(f(x)))$ is

$$n_2 \geq n_4 + n_5 \wedge n_5 \geq n_1 \cdot n_7 \wedge n_6 \geq n_1 \wedge n_3 \geq n_1 \cdot n_8$$
$$\wedge n_8 \geq n_6 \cdot n_9 \wedge n_9 \geq 1 \wedge n_7 \geq 1 \wedge n_4 \geq 1$$

We say that a constraint system is *solved* for a given mapping of assumes into non-negative integer constants if constant bounds for all the guarantees consistent with the constraint system can be found if they exist. The mapping of guarantees into non-negative integers is the *solution* of the system.

The first result of this paper is:

> THEOREM 3.1. *For any closed ICA term M it is decidable whether $\mathcal{C}(M)$ can be solved, in which case a solution can be constructed.*

Proof. This theorem is proved by giving an algorithm for solving the constraint system then showing that the algorithm terminates.

We start by substituting all assumes with the provided constants. Note that all inequations in the constraint system have one of the following forms:

$$n \geq n' + n'' \quad n \geq n' \cdot n'' \quad n \geq n' \quad n \geq k,\ k \in \mathbb{N}.$$

We define the relation $n \succ n'$ if n appears on the left on a constraint and n' on the right. (In what follows, the order of arguments to $+$ and $\cdot$ is irrelevant for the purpose of working out if a constraint is of a particular form.) The algorithm is:

1. Construct the set $\mathcal{S}$ of solutions of the system in the abstract domain of positive integers formed by quotienting $\mathbb{Z}^{0,+}$ over the equivalence relation $a \equiv b \iff a = b \vee (a \geq 2 \wedge b \geq 2)$, defining $+, \cdot, \geq$ on this domain in the obvious way.
2. For all constraint systems in $\mathcal{S}$ repeat
   (a) Replace all variables assigned 0 (1, respectively) at (1) with 0 (1, respectively).
   (b) Add equations $n = 0$ or $n = 1$ respectively for each such replacement.
   (c) Delete all inequations of the form $n \geq 0 \cdot n'$, and replace all inequations of the form $n \geq 0 + n'$ and $n \geq 1 \cdot n'$ with $n \geq n'$.
   (d) Construct the $\succ$ relation on its set of variables.
   (e) Repeat until $\succ$ is well founded:
      i. Pick a cycle $n_1 \succ n_2 \cdots n_j \succ n_1$, or a single variable n_1 where $n_1 \succ n_1$ (treating it as a one-element cycle).
      ii. If the system contains any inequations of the form $n \geq n' + n''$, $n \geq n' + k$, $n \geq n' \cdot n''$, or $n \geq n' \cdot k$, where n, n', n'' are variables involved in the cycle and k is a constant discard the current solution and break to (2).
      iii. Pick a fresh variable n.
      iv. Replace all occurrences of n_i with n, adding equations of the form $n_i = n$ for each such replacement.
      v. Delete all inequations of the form $n \geq n$.
   (f) Repeat until all RHSs of all equations are constant expressions:
      i. Choose a $\succ$-minimal element n.

ii. Let E be the set of RHSes of inequations having n on the LHS, and which are all constants.

iii. Replace all occurrences of n on the RHS of any equation or inequation with the maximum element of E.

(g) Report the resulting set of equations and inequations as one possible solution to the constraint system.

Correctness. The key point of the correctness argument is that at step (2e), all remaining constraints of the form $n \geq n' + n''$ and $n \geq n' \cdot n''$ imply that $n > n'$ and $n > n''$, and thus $n \succ n'$ implies that $n \geq n'$. This has two consequences:

- In any cycle $n_1 \succ n_2 \cdots n_k \succ n_1$ all variables are greater than or equal to each other, and so must be equal, hence step (2(e)iii).
- Constraints as in step (2(e)ii) cannot be satisfied, and so show that the solution to the constraints in the $\{0, 1, \geq 2\}$ number system that is currently being tried is impossible.

If the dependency is well founded then given the form of the inequations in the system we can proceed to variable elimination via substitution in a straightforward way.

Termination. The algorithm contains three loops; the outside loop always terminates because it iterates over a finite set, and the inside loops always terminate because they always reduce either the number of variables, or the number of constraints. We take the empty relation to be trivially well founded. □

In our running example suppose we take the assume to be $n_1 = 2$, i.e. function f can use its argument in two concurrent contexts. Solving the system of constraints gives the following typing where the guarantees n_2, n_3 are given the smallest possible values:

$$\lambda f.\lambda x.f(f(x)) : (\mathsf{com}^2 \to \mathsf{com})^3 \to \mathsf{com}^4 \to \mathsf{com}.$$

This means that the term will use f in at most 3 non-sequential contexts and x in 4.

Finally, note that a purely symbolic solution of the constraint system, which does not require the assumes given as constants, is not always straightforward, so types cannot always be presented as in Ex. 2.1. The reason is that for some (pathological) terms, giving the type symbolically would require a large number of cases. There are even terms that type in some such cases but not others; one such example is the term

$$\lambda q.(\lambda g.g(\lambda x.g(qx)))(\lambda b.(\lambda k.((k(\lambda u.u))(\lambda l.((kb)$$
$$(\lambda t.(l(t\ \mathsf{skip})))))))(\lambda v.\lambda w.wv))$$
$$: (\mathsf{com}^m \to \mathsf{com}^n \to \mathsf{com})^{n^2} \to \mathsf{com},$$

which types only if $m \leq 1$.

4. Mapping to SCC(1): *serialisation*

Using GoS, we know how to compile into hardware terms that only use contraction in sequential contexts (Ghica and Smith, 2010). However, contraction in concurrent contexts cannot be compiled and must be replaced by systematic replication of resources.

We do that by translating any SCC-typed term into another SCC-typed term in which all bounds are set to the unit value. We call this type system SCC(1). Perhaps surprisingly, this is actually possible provided that we introduce new, multivariate binders for assignable variables. In this section we present the translation, which we call *serialisation* because it results in a term in which all identifiers are used sequentially.

First an informal introduction. Supposed that we want to compile the term in our running example, $\lambda f.\lambda x.f(f(x))$. We know that if $f : \mathsf{com}^2 \to \mathsf{com}$ then the term has type

$$(\mathsf{com}^2 \to \mathsf{com})^3 \to \mathsf{com}^4 \to \mathsf{com},$$

i.e. it uses 3 instances of f non-sequentially and 4 of x.

In hardware, contraction is used to mediate access to a shared piece of circuitry from several points in a client. When sharing is not possible then a circuit can be replicated as much as needed. We will take the same approach in the programming language, by replicating identifiers with bounds larger than the unit. The SCC bounds in fact tell us precisely how many instances of an identifier must be generated, because the bounds represent the maximum number of identifiers used in parallel at any given moment.

At the level of types, $\theta^n \to \theta'$ becomes $\theta \to \theta \to \cdots \to \theta'$; note that the expanded type must not be $\theta \times \theta \to \theta'$, as product allows contraction.

This means that our argument f must be changed to have type $\mathsf{com} \to \mathsf{com} \to \mathsf{com}$, and we will need three instances of it, f_1, f_2, f_3. The type of x does not change, but we will need 4 instances of it $x_1, \ldots, x_4$. The serialised form of the term is $\lambda f_1 f_2 f_3 x_1 x_2 x_3 x_4.f_1(f_2 x_1 x_2)(f_3 x_3 x_4)$.

An obstacle in the way of a straightforward transformation is the existence of storage types (var, sem) which can be used from non-sequential contexts. For example, how can the term

$$\mathsf{newvar}\ x.x := 0 \mid\mid x := 1 : \mathsf{com}$$
$$\equiv \mathsf{newvar}(\lambda x : \mathsf{var}^2.x := 0 \mid\mid x := 1) : \mathsf{com}$$

be serialized when the obvious serialization of the body of the loop is $\lambda x_1 x_2.x_1 := 0 \mid\mid x_2 := 1$? We can do that simply by generalising the local variable binder itself and allowing it to bind several identifiers to the same memory location.

We can now define the transformation in a systematic manner, inductively on the SCC type derivation inferred in the previous section. We denote the transformation operation by $\Longrightarrow$ and we define type level translation as

$$\overline{\sigma} = \sigma$$
$$\overline{\theta^1 \to \theta'} = \overline{\theta} \to \overline{\theta'}$$
$$\overline{\theta^n \to \theta'} = \overline{\theta} \to \overline{\theta^{n-1} \to \theta'}$$
$$\overline{\theta \times \theta'} = \overline{\theta} \times \overline{\theta'}.$$

For constants we define $\overline{k : \theta} = k : \theta$ except for

$$\overline{\mathsf{newvar} : (\mathsf{var}^n \to \mathsf{com}) \to \mathsf{com}}$$
$$= \mathsf{newvar}_\mathsf{n} : \overline{(\mathsf{var}^n \to \mathsf{com}) \to \mathsf{com}}$$
$$= \mathsf{newvar}_\mathsf{n} : (\underbrace{\mathsf{var} \to \cdots \to \mathsf{var}}_{\text{n times}} \to \mathsf{com}) \to \mathsf{com}.$$

Similarly for the other binders.

We need an ancillary transformation in cases when multiple variables could be assigned different SCC types. A simple example is $\lambda g.g(\lambda x.x); g(\lambda y.y||y)$, because both occurrences of g must be assigned the same SCC type, so its arguments have to have the same SCC type as well. Because the second argument is transformed to $\lambda y_1 y_2.y_1||y_2$, the first argument must receive a dummy variable and be rewritten to $\lambda x_2 x_1.x_1$. The subtype() construction inserts dummy variables whenever needed:

$$\mathrm{subtype}_{\theta \leq \theta}(M) \stackrel{def}{=} M$$

$$\mathrm{subtype}_{\theta_1^m \to \theta_3 \leq \theta_2^n \to \theta_3}(M) \stackrel{def}{=} \lambda x.\mathrm{subtype}_{\theta_1^{m+1} \to \theta_3 \leq \theta_2^n \to \theta_3}(M)$$

$$\mathrm{subtype}_{\theta_1^n \to \theta_3 \leq \theta_2^n \to \theta_3}(M) \stackrel{def}{=}$$
$$\lambda x_1 \ldots x_n.M\,(\mathrm{subtype}_{\theta_2 \leq \theta_1}(x_1) \ldots \mathrm{subtype}_{\theta_2 \leq \theta_1}(x_1))$$

$$\mathrm{subtype}_{\theta_3^n \to \theta_1 \leq \theta_3^n \to \theta_2}(M) \stackrel{def}{=}$$
$$\lambda x_1 \ldots x_n.\mathrm{subtype}_{\theta_1 \leq \theta_2}(Mx_1 \ldots x_n)$$

$$\dfrac{}{g : (\mathsf{com}^{n_6} \rightarrow \mathsf{com})^{n_7} \vdash g : \mathsf{com}^{n_6} \rightarrow \mathsf{com} \blacktriangleright n_7 \geq 1} \qquad \dfrac{}{x : \mathsf{com}^{n_9} \vdash x : \mathsf{com} \blacktriangleright n_9 \geq 1}$$

$$\dfrac{}{f : (\mathsf{com}^{n_1} \rightarrow \mathsf{com})^{n_4} \vdash f : (\mathsf{com}^{n_1} \rightarrow \mathsf{com}) \blacktriangleright n_4 \geq 1} \qquad g : (\mathsf{com}^{n_6} \rightarrow \mathsf{com})^{n_7}, x : \mathsf{com}^{n_8} \vdash g(x) : \mathsf{com} \blacktriangleright n_8 \geq n_6 \cdot n_9$$

$$f : (\mathsf{com}^{n_1} \rightarrow \mathsf{com})^{n_4}, g : (\mathsf{com}^{n_1} \rightarrow \mathsf{com})^{n_5}, x : \mathsf{com}^{n_3} \vdash f(g(x)) : \mathsf{com} \blacktriangleright n_5 \geq n_1 \cdot n_7 \wedge n_6 \geq n_1 \wedge n_3 \geq n_1 \cdot n_8$$

$$f : (\mathsf{com}^{n_1} \rightarrow \mathsf{com})^{n_2}, x : \mathsf{com}^{n_3} \vdash f(f(x)) : \mathsf{com} \blacktriangleright n_2 \geq n_4 + n_5$$

$$\vdash \lambda f \lambda x.f(f(x)) : (\mathsf{com}^{n_1} \rightarrow \mathsf{com})^{n_2} \rightarrow \mathsf{com}^{n_3} \rightarrow \mathsf{com}) \blacktriangleright true$$

Figure 1. Annotated SCC derivation tree for $\lambda fx.f(f(x))$

$$\dfrac{g : (\mathsf{com}^2 \rightarrow \mathsf{com}) \vdash g \Longmapsto g : \mathsf{com} \rightarrow \mathsf{com} \rightarrow \mathsf{com} \vdash g \qquad x : \mathsf{com}^1 \vdash x \Longmapsto x : \mathsf{com} \vdash x}{g : (\mathsf{com}^2 \rightarrow \mathsf{com}), x : \mathsf{com}^2 \vdash g(x) \Longmapsto g : \mathsf{com} \rightarrow \mathsf{com} \rightarrow \mathsf{com}, x_1, x_2 : \mathsf{com} \vdash g(x_1 x_2)}$$

$$f : (\mathsf{com}^2 \rightarrow \mathsf{com})^1 \vdash f \Longmapsto f_3 : \mathsf{com} \rightarrow \mathsf{com} \rightarrow \mathsf{com} \vdash f_3$$

$$f : (\mathsf{com}^2 \rightarrow \mathsf{com})^1, g : (\mathsf{com}^2 \rightarrow \mathsf{com})^2, x : \mathsf{com}^4 \vdash f(fx) \Longmapsto f_3, g, g' : \mathsf{com} \rightarrow \mathsf{com} \rightarrow \mathsf{com}, x_1, x_2, x_1', x_2' : \mathsf{com} \vdash f_3(g x_1 x_2)(g' x_1' x_2')$$

$$f : (\mathsf{com}^2 \rightarrow \mathsf{com})^3, x : \mathsf{com}^4 \vdash f(fx) \Longmapsto f_3, f_1, f_2 : (\mathsf{com} \rightarrow \mathsf{com} \rightarrow \mathsf{com}) \rightarrow \mathsf{com}, x_1, x_2, x_1', x_2' : \mathsf{com} \vdash f_3(f_1 x x)(f_2 x x)$$

$$\vdash \lambda fx.f(f(x)) \Longmapsto \ \vdash \lambda f_3 f_2 f_1 x_1 x_2 x_1' x_2'.f_3(f_1 x_1 x_2)(f_2 x_1' x_2')$$

Figure 2. Serialization of $\lambda fx.f(f(x))$

$$\text{subtype}_{\theta_1 \rightarrow \theta_2 \leq \theta_3 \rightarrow \theta_4}(M) \stackrel{def}{=} \text{subtype}_{\theta_3 \rightarrow \theta_2 \leq \theta_3 \rightarrow \theta_4}\left(\text{subtype}_{\theta_1 \rightarrow \theta_2 \leq \theta_3 \rightarrow \theta_2}(M)\right)$$

We define the transformation as follows:

$$\dfrac{}{x : \theta^n \vdash x : \theta \Longmapsto x : \overline{\theta} \vdash x : \overline{\theta}}$$

$$\dfrac{}{\vdash k : \theta \Longmapsto \overline{k} : \overline{\theta}}$$

$$\dfrac{\Gamma \vdash M : \theta_2 \Longmapsto \Gamma' \vdash M' : \overline{\theta_2}}{\Gamma, x : \theta_1^n \vdash M : \theta_2 \Longmapsto \Gamma', x_1 : \overline{\theta_1}, \ldots, x_n : \overline{\theta_1} \vdash M' : \overline{\theta_2}}$$

$$\dfrac{\Gamma, x : \theta_1^n \vdash M : \theta_2 \Longmapsto \Gamma', x_1 : \overline{\theta}_1, \ldots, x_n : \overline{\theta}_1 \vdash M' : \overline{\theta}_2}{\Gamma \vdash \lambda x.M : \theta_1^n \rightarrow \theta_2 \Longmapsto \Gamma' \vdash \lambda x_1 \cdots x_n.M' : \overline{\theta_1^n \rightarrow \theta_2}}$$

$$\dfrac{\Gamma \vdash M_i : \theta_i \Longmapsto \Gamma' \vdash M_i' : \overline{\theta_i}}{\Gamma \vdash \langle M_1, M_2 \rangle : \theta_1 \times \theta_2 \Longmapsto \Gamma' \vdash \langle M_1', M_2' \rangle : \overline{\theta_1 \times \theta_2}}$$

$$\dfrac{\Gamma \vdash M : \theta_1 \Longmapsto \Gamma' \vdash M' : \overline{\theta_1} \qquad \theta_1 \leq \theta_2}{\Gamma \vdash M : \theta_2 \Longmapsto \Gamma \vdash \text{subtype}_{\theta_1 \leq \theta_2}(M') : \overline{\theta_2}}$$

$$\dfrac{\begin{array}{l}\Gamma, x : \theta_1^{n_1}, y : \theta_1^{n_2} \vdash M : \theta_2 \\ \Longmapsto \Gamma', x_1 : \overline{\theta_1}, \ldots, x_{n_1} : \overline{\theta_1}, y_1 : \overline{\theta_1}, \ldots, y_{n_2} : \overline{\theta_1} \vdash M' : \overline{\theta_2}\end{array}}{\begin{array}{l}\Gamma, x : \theta_1^{n_1+n_2} \vdash M[x/y] : \theta_2 \\ \quad \Longmapsto \Gamma', x_1 : \overline{\theta_1}, \ldots, x_{n_1+n_2} : \overline{\theta_1} \vdash \\ \qquad M[x_{n_1+1}/y_1] \cdots [x_{n_1+n_2}/y_{n_2}] : \overline{\theta_2}\end{array}}$$

$$\dfrac{\begin{array}{c}\Gamma \vdash M : \theta_1^n \rightarrow \theta_2 \Longmapsto \Gamma' \vdash M' : \overline{\theta_1^n \rightarrow \theta_2} \\ \Delta \vdash N : \theta_1 \Longmapsto \Delta' \vdash N' : \overline{\theta_1}\end{array}}{\begin{array}{l}\Gamma, n \cdot \Delta \vdash MN : \theta_2 \\ \Longmapsto \Gamma', \Delta_1', \ldots, \Delta_n' \vdash M'(N'[\Delta_1'/\Delta']) \cdots (N'[\Delta_n'/\Delta']) : \overline{\theta_2}\end{array}}$$

In the last rule given an identifier type assignment Δ', by Δ_k' we understand an identifier type assignment isomorphic to Δ' where all the identifiers are fresh. The substitution $N'[\Delta_k'/\Delta']$ replaces all the identifiers in N' which occur in dom(Δ') with the corresponding fresh identifier from dom(Δ_k').

The correctness of the transformation is formulated as:

> THEOREM 4.1. *If $\Gamma \vdash M : \theta$ is a valid SCC term and $\Gamma \vdash M : \theta \Longmapsto \Gamma' \vdash M' : \theta'$ then $\Gamma' \vdash M' : \theta'$ is a valid SCC(1) term. Moreover, if M is a program then M may terminate if and only if M' may terminate.*

Proof. The proof of the first part of the theorem is by structural induction; that of the second, by showing that any sequence of reductions in the operational semantics of an SCC term corresponds to a sequence of reductions in the corresponding SCC(1) term, and vice versa. The small-step operational semantics of ICA is given in Ghica and Murawski (2008) and is the obvious one. We do not include it here for lack of space. SCC and SCI have essentially the same operational semantics as ICA.

Typing. As our induction hypothesis, we take the following (stronger) hypothesis: for $\Gamma \vdash M : \theta$ a valid SCC term, and $\Gamma \vdash M : \theta \Longmapsto \Gamma' \vdash M' : \theta'$, then $\Gamma' \vdash M' : \theta'$ is a valid SCC(1) term, $\theta' = \overline{\theta}$, and Γ' is Γ with all variables $x : \theta_1^n$ replaced with at most n copies of $x_i : \overline{\theta_1}$.

It is first necessary to prove that for any SCC type θ, $\overline{\theta}$ is an SCC(1) type, but this is obvious from the definition of type level translation, because it cannot produce any bounds greater than 1.

The base case is trivially true by definition for the second rule; for the first rule, the knowledge that the LHS is typed correctly implies that n is at least 1, and thus the typing is correct (via the identity axiom), $\theta' = \overline{\theta}$ by definition, and the use of 1 copy of x fulfils the requirement to have at most n copies with $n \geq 1$.

In the case of Contraction note that $N'[\Delta_k'/\Delta']$ must have the same SCC type as N' because it is a replacement of variables in N' with other variables of the same type. None of the $N'[\Delta_k'/\Delta']$ share free variables with M' by definition, and because the type of M' is $\overline{\theta_1^n \rightarrow \theta_2}$, the type of $M'(N'[\Delta_1'/\Delta'])$ is $\overline{\theta_1^{n-1} \rightarrow \theta_2}$ etc., until the type of $M'(N'[\Delta_n'/\Delta'])$ is $\overline{\theta_2}$, which proves the case of Contraction.

The key cases are Subtyping and Application.

For Application, observe that $N'[\Delta_k'/\Delta']$ must have the same SCC type as N' because it is a replacement of variables in N' with other variables of the same type. None of the $N'[\Delta_k'/\Delta']$ share free variables with M' by definition, and because the type of M' is $\overline{\theta_1^n \rightarrow \theta_2}$, the type of $M'(N'[\Delta_1'/\Delta'])$ is $\overline{\theta_1^{n-1} \rightarrow \theta_2}$, and so on, until the type of $M'(N'[\Delta_n'/\Delta'])$ is $\overline{\theta_2}$, proving that the eighth rule creates a correctly typed SCC(1) expression.

Correctness of Subtyping is proved by induction on the hypothesis, i.e. if $M' : \overline{\theta_1}$, then $\text{subtype}_{\theta_1 \leq \theta_2}(M') : \overline{\theta_2}$. Note that the cases in the definition of subtype mirror the cases in the definition of $\leq$ on SCC types (with the third and fourth cases being special cases of the fifth, needed to make the recursion well-founded), and thus $\text{subtype}_{\theta_1 \leq \theta_2}$ is defined whenever $\theta_1 < \theta_2$. The base case (the first definition) is degenerately true, the fifth case is true by definition, and the second, third, and fourth cases are obviously true if the type of x is taken to be $\overline{\theta_1}$, $\overline{\theta_2}$, and $\overline{\theta_3}$ respectively.

It is important to note also that this transformation is compositional on the syntax, i.e. for any term $\Gamma \vdash M : \theta$ and context $\mathcal{C}[-]$ such that $\emptyset \vdash \mathcal{C}[M] : \mathsf{com}$, if $\Gamma \vdash M\theta \Longrightarrow \Gamma' \vdash \widetilde{M'} : \theta'$ there exist context $\mathcal{C}'$ such that

$$\emptyset \vdash \mathcal{C}[M] : \mathsf{com} \Longrightarrow \emptyset \vdash \mathcal{C}'[M'] : \mathsf{com}. \quad (1)$$

Soundness. The following uses the operational semantics (OS) of SCC, which is essentially the same as that of ICA, the obvious combination of CBN lambda calculus, simple imperative language and parallel execution (Ghica and Murawski, 2008). The reduction rules are small-step and the semantics is non-deterministic because of possible race conditions. By "termination" of a program (closed term of com type) $M\Downarrow$ we mean may-termination, i.e. the existence of a chain of reductions leading to skip. We do not define the OS for lack of space.

The first step of the proof is to eliminate the multivariate binders from the SCC(1) term $\Gamma' \vdash M' : \theta'$; we do that simply by replacing all terms of form $\mathsf{new}_n(\lambda x_1 \ldots x_n.M)$ with $\mathsf{new}(\lambda x.M[x/x_i])$ where x is chosen fresh. We can do this because of the previous result (the correctness of typing). The resulting term is not pure SCC(1) but it must be operationally equivalent by the very definition of the multivariate binder. We denote this transformation by $\widetilde{M}$.

We define a logical relation $\Gamma \vdash M\mathcal{R}_\theta M'$ between SCC terms such that there exist Γ', θ' such that $\Gamma \vdash M : \theta \Longrightarrow \Gamma' \vdash \widetilde{M'} : \theta'$.

For programs, $\emptyset \vdash M\mathcal{R}_{\mathsf{com}}M'$ if and only if $M\Downarrow$ if and only if $\widetilde{M'}\Downarrow$. This is lifted to open terms in the usual manner, i.e. for all command contexts $\mathcal{C}$ which accept a term of type θ and trap free variables in Γ, $\mathcal{C}[M]\Downarrow$ if and only if $\mathcal{C}'[\widetilde{M'}]\Downarrow$. We can write this because of (1) and because there is no point in using multivariate binders in the context, so we eliminate them only in the original term.

We induct on the reduction rules of the operational semantics. The base cases (for identity and constants) are true by definition, as the transformation in those cases does not change them or their behaviour. The only new construct, the multivariate binder has been syntactically eliminated. Most in-context reductions are also trivial. In fact this is also the reason why the rules of the OS can be omitted, because this proof is entirely parametric on them.

The only interesting case is function application when the function has been reduced to a normal form:

$$(\lambda x.M)N, s \longrightarrow M[N/x], s'. \quad (2)$$

The serialised term is

$$(\mathrm{subtype}_{(\theta_1)^m \to \theta_2 \leq (\theta_1')^n \to \theta_2'}(\lambda x_1 \cdots x_m.M')) \\ (N_1') \cdots (N_n'), \quad (3)$$

where each N_k' is a copy of the same term but with free variables changed.

An argument on the definition of subtype() will show immediately that it is semantically innocuous, only introducing dummy variables and lambdas so that the types match.

Then we notice that the only difference between the two is that reduction 2 executes one reduction consisting of n substitutions, whereas reduction 3 executes n reductions consisting of one substitution each. □

The serialization of $\lambda fx.f(f(x))$ is shown in Fig. 2, with term types omitted for brevity.

5. Compilation and correctness

Here we will discuss compilation into asynchronous circuits using the Geometry of Synthesis approach.

Consider the typical implementation of a digital half-adder:

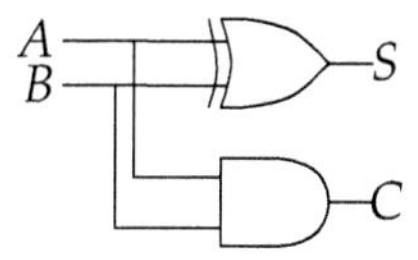

The inputs are A and B and outputs sum S and carry C:

$$S = A \oplus B, \qquad C = A \wedge B.$$

Suppose that the circuit is in an initial state, where $A = B = C = S = 0$ and we want to change the input values to $A = B = 1$. In a synchronous (clocked) circuit, the system clock has a period longer than the propagation delay of signals through wires and gates, and values are only considered meaningful on the falling (or raising) edge of the clock, giving them time to stabilise at the correct values of $S = 0, C = 1$. However, in an asynchronous (clock-less) circuit the new input signals will propagate along the wires and reach the four gate inputs at different times. Depending on the relative wire delays, there are 8 different orders in which this can happen. The two gates will see a sequence of four distinct inputs, and produce the corresponding outputs, before settling on the correct values. As inputs change from 0 to 1 on its inputs, the outputs of the AND gate are the sequence 001, which corresponds to a "clean" transition from 0 to 1. However, on the XOR gate, as the inputs change from 0 to 1 the outputs will see the sequence 010. Before settling on the correct value of 0, the circuit shows a spurious value of 1, a so-called *hazard*. If this adder is connected to other circuits then these circuits will consider the hazard value as a genuine value and propagate it, leading to more spurious values and ultimately a rather chaotic circuit behaviour.

In a nutshell, this is the main problem of asynchronous circuit design, and there exist a variety of theoretical and practical approaches to mitigating it (Hauck, 1995).

5.1 Event logic

A particularly interesting and clean solution was proposed by Sutherland (1989) in his seminal Turing Award lecture. At the foundation of his approach lies the observation that boolean logic is not particularly well suited to implementing asynchronous circuits, suggesting instead an *event logic*: a logic of pure control, dealing not with "true" and "false" but with the more fundamental notions that "something happened" or "nothing happened". The basic logical functions on events can be (efficiently) implemented as special gates or modules. At the level of physical implementation, an event is either a high-to-low or a low-to-high transition (*edge*) on a wire, the so-called *two-phase event encoding*.

XOR provides an OR-like function for events, producing an output event when an event arrives on any of the input ports.

C is the so-called Muller C-element (Miller, 1965, Chap. 10), a fundamental gate in asynchronous design. It has an AND-like functionality on events, producing an output when events arrive on both input ports.

TOGGLE steers events to its outputs alternately, starting with the dot.

SELECT steers its input event to the the output according to the value of input S.

CALL remembers which "client", R_1 or R_2, called more recently and it steers the matching D back to D_1 or D_2 as is the

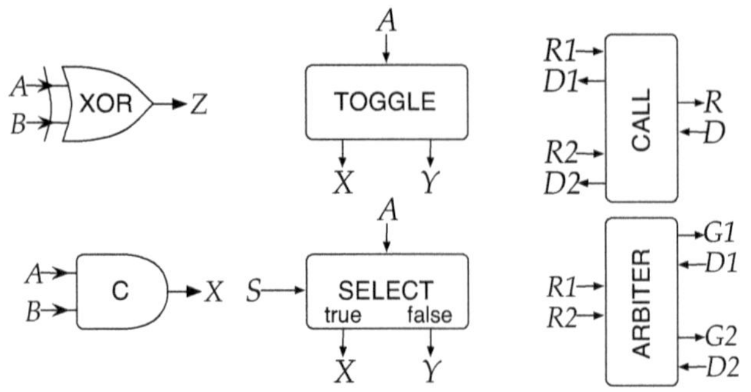

Figure 3. Logic modules for events

case. CALL can be generalised to the case where R, D, R_i, D_i represent sets of ports.

ARBITER grants service G_1 or G_2 to only one input request R_1 or R_2 at a time, delaying subsequent grants until the matching done event D_1 or D_2.

It also makes sense to consider as primitives $WIRE$, the simple connector, and $FORK$ the forking connector with one input and two outputs.

Ghica and Smith (2010) give a compositional trace model for event logic. Composition of event-logic circuits is rather subtle because the interaction between two circuits can lead to "unsafe" traces. We illustrate this with the following example.

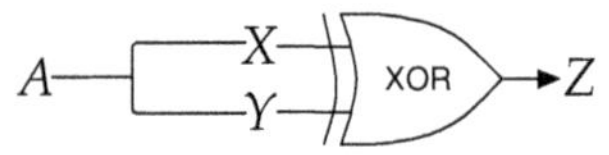

Given the obvious trace semantics for the two circuits, the composition $FORK; XOR$ might be expected to produce input-output traces of the form $(AZZ)^*$. However, if we consider traces including the internal channels X and Y, we can see that these observable traces might correspond to interactions $AXYZZ$, which are from a physical point of view unsafe: if events X and Y arrive very close to each other temporally, then it is possible that the sequence ZZ consists of two events that happen faster than the inertial delay of the wire or the gate and may be suppressed (Sparsø and Furber, 2001, Sec. 6.1.3).

However, composition disallows such unsafe traces. The set of traces of a composite system only contains those traces that can only be produced safely. Intuitively, the safe composition of two circuits involves only those traces in which, at the interface, each output produced by a circuit can be immediately consumed as an input by the other circuit. From this point of view, there are no safe traces in the composition above, i.e. $FORK; XOR = \emptyset$. This can be shown analysing all possible interactions. The interaction between the two is unsafe because after input A and interface event X the next output, on Y, cannot be consumed by XOR before it outputs on Z. AY is unsafe for a similar reasons. Since all interactions are prefixed by a sequence of events $A \cdot X$ or $A \cdot Y$ there are no safe interactions. This can be proved formally in the model of Ghica and Smith (2010).

On the other hand we can show that $FORK; C$ has the same behaviour as a wire connecting input A and output Z, and all interactions in the composite circuit are safe.

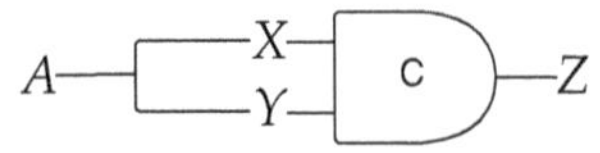

5.2 Compiling SCI into event logic

The game model for SCI can be represented using only the XOR, C, CALL, WIRE and FORK fragment of event logic.

The concrete representation of types follows the game-semantic model of the language so that each game-semantic *move* corresponds to a distinct port of a circuit. Concretely, the port structures generated during compilation is as follows:

com : the type of commands corresponds to one input port Q and one output port A. Intuitively, Q represents a request from the environment to execute the command and A and acknowledgment of termination.

exp : the type of expressions corresponds to one input port Q and two output ports T and F. As before, Q is a request to evaluate the expression while T and F are the two possible outcomes, true or false.

var : the type of variable corresponds to input ports Q, WT, WF and output ports T, F, A. Q is a read request, answered by T (true) or F (false), while WT (WF) is a request to write true (false) and is acknowledged by A.

$\theta_1 \times \theta_2$: the product type is the disjoint sum of the port structures corresponding to θ_1, θ_2.

$\theta_1 \to \theta_2$: the product type is the disjoint sum of the port structures corresponding to θ_1, θ_2 except that the input-output polarities associated with θ_1 are reversed.

The base-type constants are

skip : com 1 : exp

Note that in both cases the request Q is immediately propagated to the corresponding acknowledgment. The implementation of 0:exp is analogous.

The representations of games for the imperative language constants are given in Fig. 4, and are simply event logic representations of the game semantic model of SCI. The ports on this circuit are decorated in the same way as the types in the signature in order to make the correspondence obvious. The input-output behaviour of these circuits is operationally intuitive. We only discuss sequential composition, $\mathsf{seq} : \mathsf{com} \times \mathsf{com}' \to \mathsf{com}''$. The initial input request is Q'', corresponding to the return type com''. This request is simply propagated as an output request Q, corresponding to the operator requesting the evaluation of its first argument. When it acknowledges termination A, it is in turn simply propagated to Q', requesting the evaluation of the second argument. When it acknowledges termination A' the operator can acknowledge termination to the environment A''.

Here we only consider the representation of lazy sequential operators, such as $\mathsf{or}_l : \mathsf{exp} \times \mathsf{exp}' \to \mathsf{exp}''$:

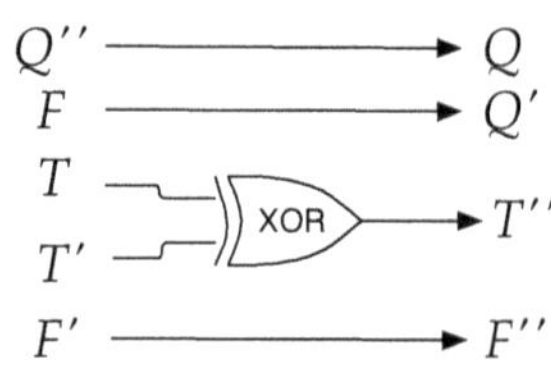

Parallel and (eager) sequential operators raise certain technical problems discussed in Ghica and Smith (2010). Note that this way of encoding boolean values using different ports, called *dual rail*, is standard in asynchronous circuit design and can be extended to integers.

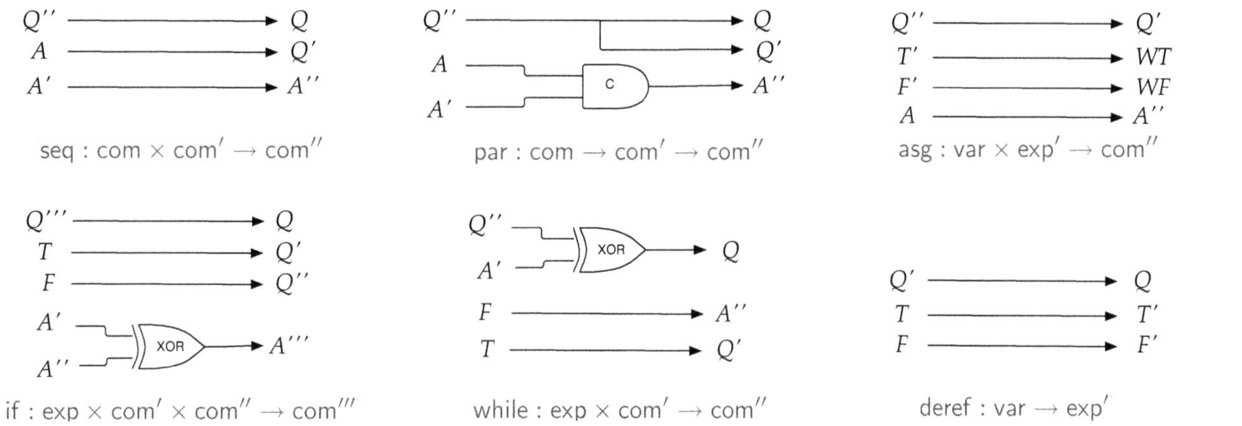

Figure 4. Event-logic circuits for SCI imperative constants

The CALL module is used to implement the family of diagonal strategies $\delta_\theta : \theta \to \theta' \times \theta''$ used in contraction. The implementation of $\delta_{\mathsf{com}} : \mathsf{com} \to (\mathsf{com}_1 \times \mathsf{com}_2)$ is simply the CALL module. Higher-order contraction is implemented using more complex generalised CALL module as shown in *loc. cit.*.

The local-variable binder newvar : $(\mathsf{var} \to \mathsf{com}') \to \mathsf{com}''$ can be also be implemented by taking advantage of the stateful nature of the CALL module.

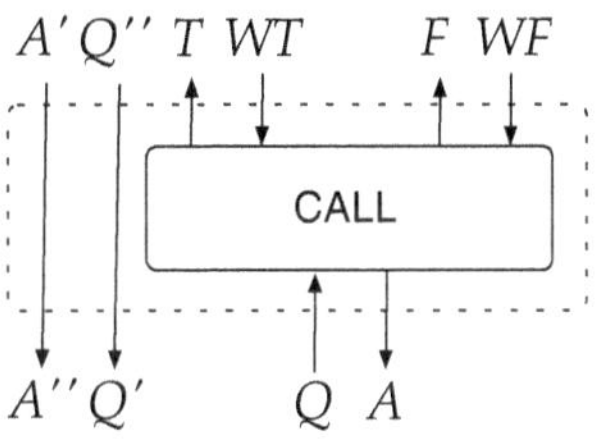

SCI terms can be interpreted inductively on the syntax, where terms are formed from constants, contraction (described above), function application, function declaration and free identifiers. Given circuits F, M which are compilations of terms $\Gamma \vdash_r F : \theta \to \theta'$ and, respectively, $\Delta \vdash_r M : \theta$, the circuit for $\Gamma, \Delta \vdash_r F(M) : \theta'$ is constructed as a certain interconnect for the two circuits, as discussed in Sec. 1 (connectors labelled by G, D, T, T' are multi-line input-output bundles).

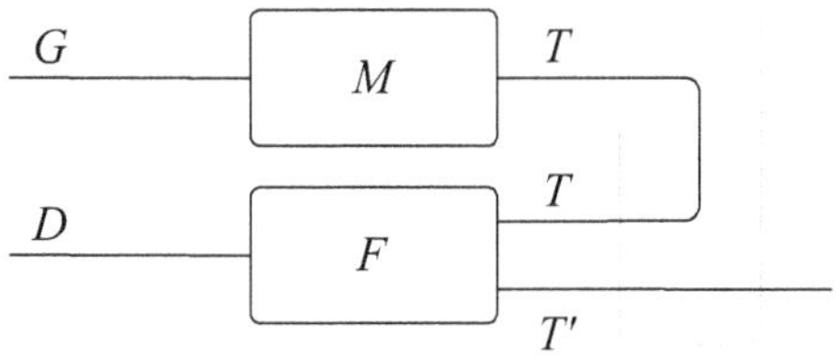

The greyed-out circuit connecting the argument to the function is the evaluation morphism, the uncurrying of the identity at type $\theta \to \theta'$. The entire construction can be expressed in the language of compact closed categories in a canonical way. Function declaration is the currying relabelling of ports discussed earlier, and free identifiers are the identity (wires).

A simple but useful program which illustrates the compilation of open higher-order programs is *in-place map,* which applies a function f to all elements of a data structure, modifying them in place. Consider an iterator over some data structure, provided with the following interface:

init : com initialise an iterator over the data structure;

curr : var get the current element in the data structure;

next : com advance the iterator to the next element;

more : exp return false if the end of the data structure has been reached and true otherwise.

Note that SCI being a call-by-name language these identifiers represent thunks, i.e. parameter-less procedures. The program for in-place map is:

$$\mathsf{init} : \mathsf{com}, \mathsf{curr} : \mathsf{var}, \mathsf{next} : \mathsf{com}, \mathsf{more} : \mathsf{exp} \vdash_r$$
$$\lambda f : \mathsf{exp} \to \mathsf{exp}.\mathsf{init}; \mathsf{while}\ (\mathsf{more})(\mathsf{curr} := f(!\mathsf{curr}); \mathsf{next}) : \mathsf{com}.$$

The structure of the resulting circuit is shown in Fig. 5, along with the concrete circuit, which is strikingly simple. Ports are annotated with the variable name for readability; top-level ports are *top.q* and *top.a*. For function $f : \mathsf{exp}' \to \mathsf{exp}$ the ports corresponding to the argument are primed. Technically, variable *curr* should go through a contraction circuit $\delta_{var} : \mathsf{var} \to \mathsf{var} \times \mathsf{var}$; however, because the first occurrence uses only the "write" ports and the second only the "read" ports, no connectors need to be actually reused and contraction can be omitted.

In *loc. cit.* we show that compiled circuits are both logically and physically correct, i.e. *delay-insensitive*. Any term is compiled into an event logic circuit that has the same input-output behaviour as the (sound) game semantic model of the language. Moreover, the circuits constructed by the compiler are always safe in the sense discussed earlier in Sec. 5.1.

5.3 Contraction and local variables in concurrent contexts

We can still use the method described above except that the local variable binder must handle the binding of multiple identifiers to the same memory cell. Moreover, the identifiers may occur in concurrent contexts. It also makes sense now to use semaphores.

In *loc. cit.* variable contraction can only be done in a sequential setting; the diagonal $\delta_{\mathsf{var}} : \mathsf{var} \to \mathsf{var}_1 \times \mathsf{var}_2$ is shown in Fig 6.

In the new setting, we do not have contraction of var-typed identifiers in the syntax but the simultaneous binding of several identifiers to the same memory cell amounts to the same thing in the implementation, if the identifiers belong to sequential contexts. This is not the case in non-sequential contexts, because the CALL module cannot handle concurrent request, which amount to a race condition. The standard solution in asynchronous design, which we will apply, is to guard the CALL modules by using n-way ARBITERs to mediate all inputs. Such circuits are not basic event

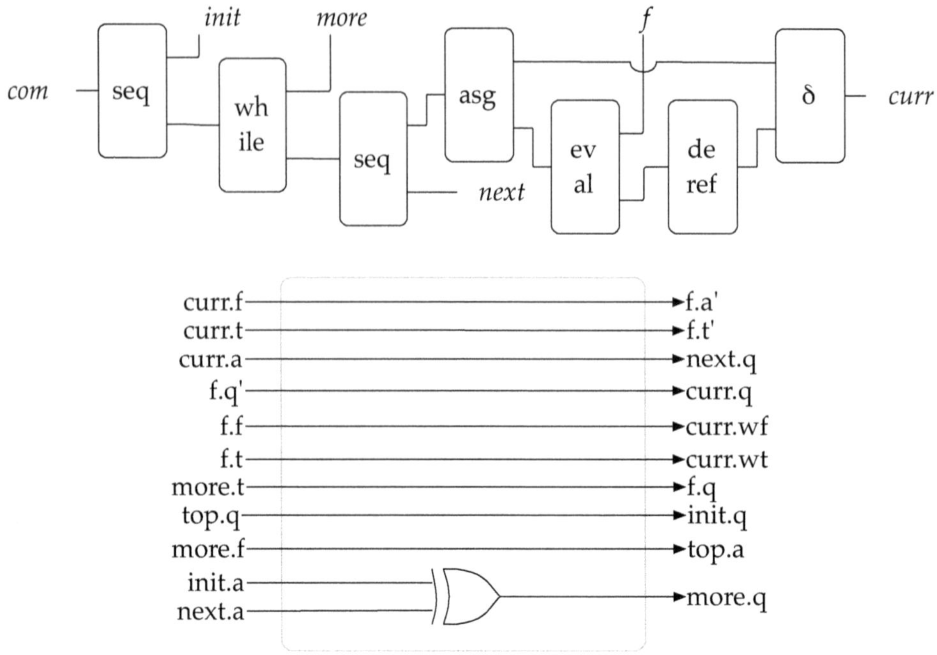

Figure 5. In-place map, overall structure and event-logic implementation

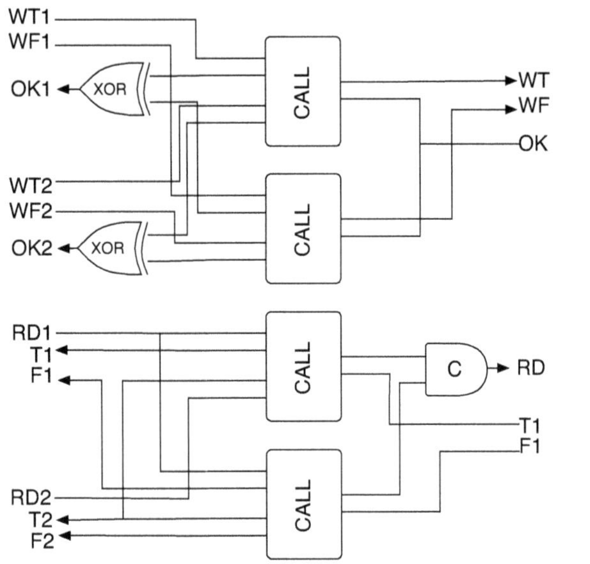

Figure 6. Event logic implementation for sequential contraction $\delta_{\mathsf{var}} : \mathsf{var} \rightarrow \mathsf{var}_1 \times \mathsf{var}_2$.

logic gates but can be constructed from the 2-way arbiters. In Fig. 7 we show a standard 3-way arbiter construction due to Seitz (1980). More efficient n-way arbiters can be designed however directly rather than compositionally from smaller arbiters (Martin, 1990). The new multivariate binding circuit is represented in Fig. 8.

We will not provide semantic-directed implementations for semaphores noting that they can be implemented in the language using shared memory in standard ways, e.g. the Peterson (1981) tie-breaker algorithm. As Murawski (2010) points out, the first-class semaphore provided in the original ICA is needed mostly for technical reasons related to definability and not algorithmic considerations.

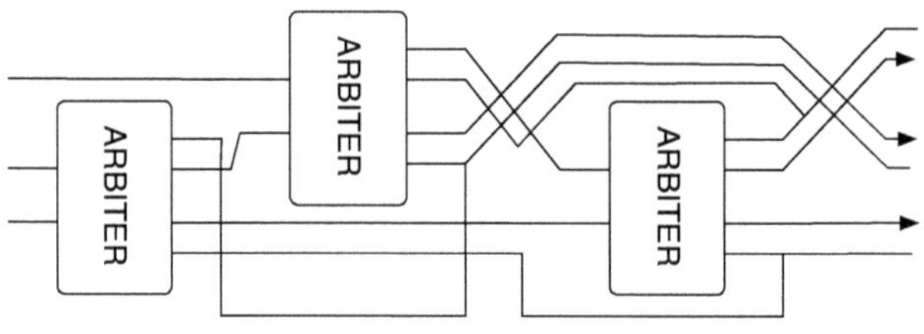

Figure 7. A 3-way arbiter

The correctness of the compilation is, as in Ghica and Smith (2010), the correctness of representation of the game model in event logic gates.

THEOREM 5.1. *Let M : com be an SCC(1) term and K its event-logic representation.*

Correctness: *If K receives an input event on its Q port it will produce an output event on its A port iff M terminates.*

Safety: *Circuit K is delay-insensitive.*

Proof. The proof of this theorem is a corollary of Thm. 5.3 in *loc. cit.*, which is essentially proving a logical relation between the input-output behaviour of any circuit and the game semantic model of the corresponding term. Since we are still within the SCC(1) game semantic model the proof stands, but it has to be extended with a new case, the family of variable binders for multiple identifiers. Because of the type of the multivariate binder ((var → var → com) → com) the concurrent usage of the variables does not violate the seriality constraint of the game model (Def. 2.7 in *loc. cit.*). The n-way arbiter then ensures that the underlying contraction circuit is actually used sequentially, because all read and write requests to the variable are serialized. The two XOR gates take mutually exclusive input events, therefore they are always used safely. □

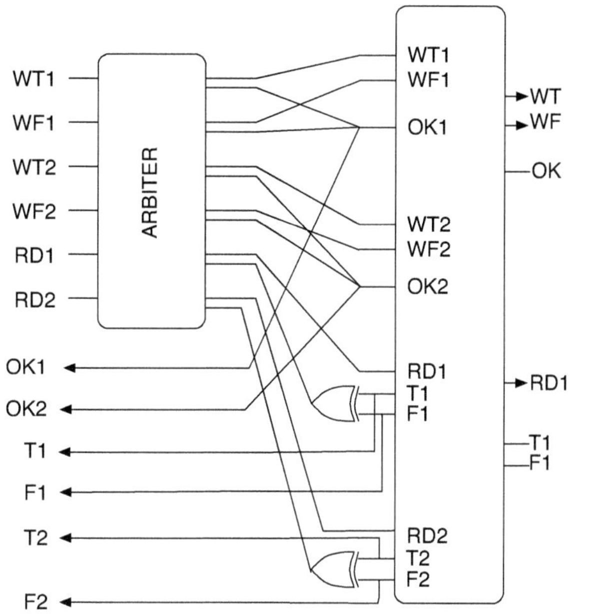

Figure 8. Event logic for contraction in concurrent contexts.

This, together with the correctness of type inference from ICA to SCC (Thm. 3.1) and program transformation from SCC to SCC(1) (Thm. 4.1) lead to the main result,

THEOREM 5.2. *Programs in ICA which have an SCC type can be effectively mapped into delay-insensitive event-logic circuits.*

5.4 Example

We show the compilation of three terms with identical ICA types but distinct SCC and serialised versions. The terms, the inferred SCC types and the SCC(1) versions are given below, assuming $f : \mathsf{com}^1 \to \mathsf{com}$.

$$\lambda fx.f(fx){:}(\mathsf{com}^1\to\mathsf{com})^2\to\mathsf{com}^1\to\mathsf{com} \Longrightarrow \lambda f_1 f_2 x.f_1(f_2 x)$$

$$\lambda fx.fx; fx{:}(\mathsf{com}^1\to\mathsf{com})^1\to\mathsf{com}^1\to\mathsf{com} \Longrightarrow \lambda fx.fx; fx$$

$$\lambda fx.fx||fx{:}(\mathsf{com}^1\to\mathsf{com})^2\to\mathsf{com}^2\to\mathsf{com} \Longrightarrow \lambda f_1 f_2 x_1 x_2.f_1 x_1; f_2 x_2$$

The compiled versions are in Fig. 9. The actual synthesised circuits are inside the grey box. The circuits marked F_i, X_i, F, X are instances of the argument that must be supplied by the designer to create a working circuits or, equivalently, arguments for f, x to lead to programs. Note the trade-offs in the last two designs. The second circuit contains two fairly expensive diagonal circuits but it only requires one instance of F and X, while the third consists only of connectors, but requires two instances of each of F and X;

6. Related and further work

There exist other higher-level approaches to hardware synthesis: SYSTEMC[1] or COWARE[2], hardware compilers based on process calculi, such as (van Berkel et al., 1991), or higher-order structural languages such as LAVA (Bjesse et al., 1998); these are interesting and useful, but conceptually different ways of approaching VLSI design.

[1] www.systemc.org

[2] www.coware.com

Hardware compilation in the behavioural style we are pursuing in GoS has a substantial literature which we cannot discuss extensively; some entry points to the literature are Budiu and Goldstein (2002); Buyukkurt et al. (2006). This line of work is in some sense parallel with ours and focuses almost exclusively on optimisation techniques such as automated parallelisation whereas we are concerned with problems of a structural nature. This difference of focus is discussed extensively in Ghica (2009).

Type inference for SCI has been studied before, but for a richer version of the type system which we do not need (Yang and Huang, 1998). A program transformation similar in spirit with our serialisation is *linearisation*, due to Kfoury (2000). The first main difference is that linearisation replicates every variable occurrence, without permitting contraction at all. The second one is that replication of variables of higher-order type does not have to be uniform, but can result in occurrences with different linearized types. The first difference is conceptually significant but technically rather minor, whereas the second one is conceptually minor but, perhaps surprisingly, technically significant resulting in the existence of normal forms which can be linearized but cannot be serialized. From the point of view of compiler support for separate compilation, foreign function calls and run-time services we consider it crucial to offer a consistent interface between a serialized term and its context, hence our decision. Also note that the soundness argument of Thm. 4.1 is simplified by the fact that serialization is uniform across copies of identifiers, leading to a very simple inductive step in the proof.

However, inside the serialised term itself perhaps a more flexible approach which mixes serialisation and linearization could be used at the expense of some complication in the algorithms. Even so, it is worth noting that non-typeable terms are somewhat pathological and unlikely to be found in algorithmically relevant programs. Combining serialization with a selective form of linearization can lead to interesting optimisations techniques. Various performance parameters can be calculated at compile-time, e.g. footprint (number of gates) or latency (longest delay). Linearisation of an identifier makes a trade-off between duplicating arguments to functions and using expensive contraction circuitry, as can be seen in Fig. 9. In this sense, serialization is the extreme scenario in which contraction is always favoured before replication. Introducing a controlled form of linearization will be investigated in further optimised implementations of the compiler.

Finally, the approach here can be extended to synchronous circuits using the *round abstraction* methodology for low-latency encoding of asynchronous specifications into synchronous circuits (Ghica and Menaa, 2010). This is forthcoming work.

References

Per Bjesse, Koen Claessen, Mary Sheeran, and Satnam Singh. Lava: hardware design in Haskell. In *ICFP*, pages 174–184, 1998.

Mihai Budiu and Seth Copen Goldstein. Compiling application-specific hardware. In *FPL*, pages 853–863, 2002.

Betul Buyukkurt, Zhi Guo, and Walid A. Najjar. Impact of loop unrolling on area, throughput and clock frequency in Roccc: C to VHDL compiler for FPGAs. In *ARC*, pages 401–412, 2006.

Dan R. Ghica. Geometry of Synthesis: a structured approach to VLSI design. In *POPL*, pages 363–375, 2007.

Dan R. Ghica. Function interface models for hardware compilation: Types, signatures, protocols. *CoRR*, abs/0907.0749, 2009.

Dan R. Ghica and Mohamed N. Menaa. On the compositionality of round abstraction. In *CONCUR*, pages 417–431, 2010.

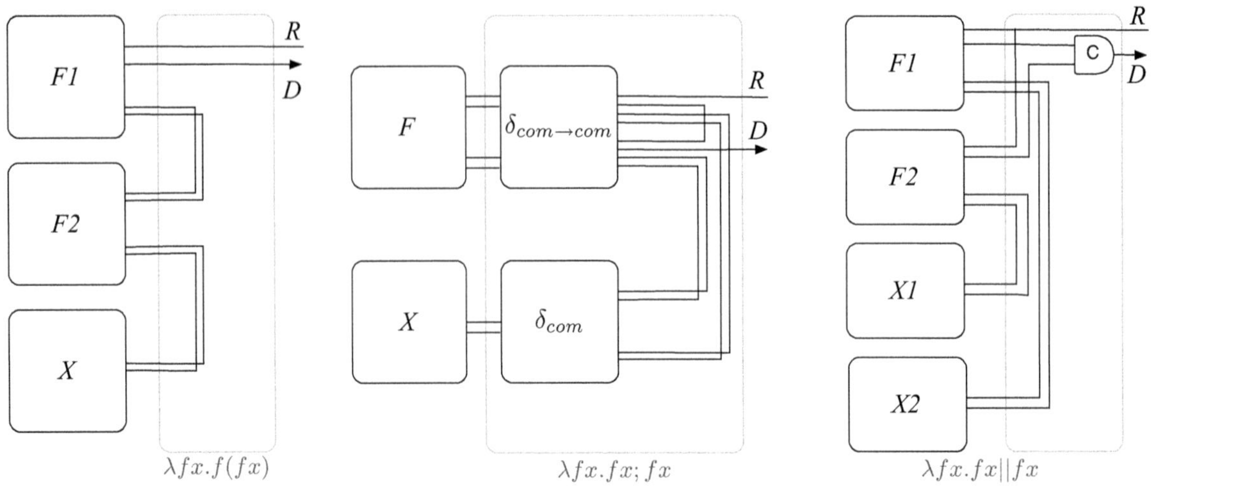

Figure 9. Three example circuits

Dan R. Ghica and Andrzej Murawski. Angelic semantics of fine-grained concurrency. *Annals of Pure and Applied Logic*, 151 (2-3):89–114, 2008.

Dan R. Ghica and Andrzej S. Murawski. Compositional model extraction for higher-order concurrent programs. In *TACAS*, pages 303–317, 2006.

Dan R. Ghica and Alex Smith. Geometry of Synthesis II: From games to delay-insensitive circuits. *Electr. Notes Theor. Comput. Sci.*, 265:301–324, 2010.

Dan R. Ghica, Andrzej S. Murawski, and C.-H. Luke Ong. Syntactic control of concurrency. *Theor. Comput. Sci.*, 350(2-3): 234–251, 2006.

S. Hauck. Asynchronous design methodologies: an overview. *Proceedings of the IEEE*, 83(1):69–93, Jan 1995.

G. M. Kelly and M. L. Laplaza. Coherence for compact closed categories. *Journal of Pure and Applied Algebra*, 19:193–213, 1980.

A. J. Kfoury. A linearization of the lambda-calculus and consequences. *J. Log. Comput.*, 10(3):411–436, 2000.

Wayne Luk, David Ferguson, and Ian Page. Structured hardware compilation of parallel programs. In Will Moore and Wayne Luk, editors, *More FPGAs*. Abingdon EE&CS Books, 1994.

A. J. Martin. *Developments in concurrency and communication*, chapter Programming in VLSI: From communicating processes to delay-insensitive circuits, pages 1–64. Addison-Wesley, 1990.

Guy McCusker. Categorical models of syntactic control of interference revisited, revisited. *LMS Journal of Computation and Mathematics*, 10:176–216, 2007.

Guy McCusker. A graph model for imperative computation. *Logical Methods in Computer Science*, 6(1), 2010.

R. E. Miller. *Sequential Circuits*. Wiley, NY, 1965.

Andrzej S. Murawski. Full abstraction without synchronization primitives. *Electr. Notes Theor. Comput. Sci.*, 265:423–436, 2010.

Peter W. O'Hearn, John Power, Makoto Takeyama, and Robert D. Tennent. Syntactic control of interference revisited. *Theor. Comput. Sci.*, 228(1-2):211–252, 1999.

Ian Page and Wayne Luk. Compiling Occam into FPGAs. In W. Moore and W. Luk, editors, *FPGAs*, pages 271–283. Abingdon EE&CS Books, 1991.

G. L. Peterson. Myths about the mutual exclusion problem. *Information Processing Letters*, 12:115–116, 1981.

Uday S. Reddy. Global state considered unnecessary: An introduction to object-based semantics. *Lisp and Symbolic Computation*, 9(1):7–76, 1996.

John C. Reynolds. Syntactic control of interference. In *POPL*, pages 39–46, 1978.

John C. Reynolds. The essence of Algol. In *Proceedings of the 1981 International Symposium on Algorithmic Languages*, pages 345–372. North-Holland, 1981.

John C. Reynolds. Syntactic control of inference, part 2. In *ICALP*, pages 704–722, 1989.

C. L. Seitz. Ideas about arbiters. *Lambda*, 1(1):10–14, 1980.

J. Sparsø and S. Furber, editors. *Principles of Asynchronous Circuit Design: A Systems Perspective*. European Low-Power Initiative for Electronic System Design. Kluwer Academic Publishers, 2001.

Ivan E. Sutherland. Micropipelines. *Commun. ACM*, 32(6):720–738, 1989. Turing Award Paper.

C. H. van Berkel and R. W. J. J. Saeijs. Compilation of communicating processes into delay-insensitive circuits. In *Proceedings of ICCD*, 1988.

Kees van Berkel, Joep Kessels, Marly Roncken, Ronald Saeijs, and Frits Schalij. The VLSI-programming language Tangram and its translation into handshake circuits. In *EURO-DAC*, pages 384–389, 1991.

Hongseok Yang and Howard Huang. Type reconstruction for syntactic control of interference, part 2. In *ICCL*, pages 164–173, 1998.

Multivariate Amortized Resource Analysis

Jan Hoffmann Klaus Aehlig Martin Hofmann
Ludwig-Maximilians-Universität München
{jan.hoffmann,aehlig,martin.hofmann}@ifi.lmu.de

Abstract

We study the problem of automatically analyzing the worst-case resource usage of procedures with several arguments. Existing automatic analyses based on amortization, or sized types bound the resource usage or result size of such a procedure by a sum of unary functions of the sizes of the arguments.

In this paper we generalize this to arbitrary multivariate polynomial functions thus allowing bounds of the form mn which had to be grossly overestimated by $m^2 + n^2$ before. Our framework even encompasses bounds like $\sum_{i,j \leq n} m_i m_j$ where the m_i are the sizes of the entries of a list of length n.

This allows us for the first time to derive useful resource bounds for operations on matrices that are represented as lists of lists and to considerably improve bounds on other super-linear operations on lists such as longest common subsequence and removal of duplicates from lists of lists. Furthermore, resource bounds are now closed under composition which improves accuracy of the analysis of composed programs when some or all of the components exhibit super-linear resource or size behavior.

The analysis is based on a novel multivariate amortized resource analysis. We present it in form of a type system for a simple first-order functional language with lists and trees, prove soundness, and describe automatic type inference based on linear programming.

We have experimentally validated the automatic analysis on a wide range of examples from functional programming with lists and trees. The obtained bounds were compared with actual resource consumption. All bounds were asymptotically tight, and the constants were close or even identical to the optimal ones.

Categories and Subject Descriptors F.3.2 [*Logics And Meanings Of Programs*]: Semantics of Programming Languages—Program Analysis; F.3.1 [*Logics and Meanings of Programs*]: Specifying and Verifying and Reasoning about Programs

General Terms Performance, Languages, Theory, Reliability

Keywords Functional Programming, Static Analysis, Amortized Analysis, Resource Consumption, Quantitative Analysis

1. Introduction

A primary feature of a computer program is its quantitative performance characteristics: the amount of resources like time, memory and power the program needs to perform its task.

POPL'11, January 26–28, 2011, Austin, Texas, USA.

Ideally, it should be possible for an experienced programmer to extrapolate from the source code of a well-written program to its *asymptotic* worst-case behavior. But it is often insufficient to determine the asymptotic behavior of program only. A conservative estimation of the resource consumption for a specific input or a comparison of two programs with the same asymptotic behavior require instead *concrete upper bounds for specific hardware*. That is to say, closed functions in the sizes of the program's inputs that bound the number of clock cycles or memory cells used by the program for inputs of these sizes on a given system.

Concrete worst-case bounds are particularly useful in the development of embedded systems and hard real-time systems. In the former, one wants to use hardware that is *just good enough* to accomplish a task in order to produce a large number of units at lowest possible cost. In the latter, one needs to guarantee specific worst-case running times to ensure the safety of the system.

The manual determination of such bounds is very cumbersome. Cf., e.g., the careful analyses carried out by Knuth in *The Art of Computer Programming* where he pays close attention to the concrete and best possible values of constants for the MIX architecture. Not everyone commands the mathematical ease of Knuth and even he would run out of steam if he had to do these calculations over and over again while going through the debugging loops of program development. In short, derivation of precise bounds by hand appears to be unfeasible in practice in all but the simplest cases.

As a result, *automatic methods for static resource analysis* are highly desirable and have been the subject of extensive research. On the one hand there is the large field of WCET (worst-case execution time) analysis [27] that is focused on (yet not limited to) the run-time analysis of sequential code without loops taking into account low-level features like hardware caches and instruction pipelines. On the other hand there is an active research community that employs type systems and abstract interpretation to deal with the analysis of loops, recursion and data structures [15, 3, 24].[1]

In this paper we continue our work [16] on the resource analysis of programs with recursion and inductive data structures. Our approach is as follows. 1. We consider *Resource Aware ML (RAML)*, a first-order fragment of OCAML that features integers, lists, binary trees, and recursion. 2. We define a big-step operational semantics that *formalizes the actual resource consumptions* of programs. It is parametrized with a resource metric that can be directly related to the compiled assembly code for a specific system architecture [23].[2] 3. We describe an elaborated *resource-parametric type system* whose type judgments establish concrete worst-case bounds in terms of closed, easily understood formulas. The type system allows for an efficient and completely automatic inference algorithm that is based on linear programming. 4. We *prove* the non-trivial soundness of the derived resource bounds with respect to the big-

[1] See §8 for a detailed overview of the state of the art.

[2] To obtain clock-cycle bounds for atomic steps one has to employ WCET tools [23].

step operational semantics. 5. We verify the practicability of our approach with a publically available implementation and a reproducible *experimental evaluation*.

As pioneered by Hofmann and Jost [18] to analyze the heap-space consumption of first-order functional programs, our type system relies on the potential-method of amortized analysis to take into account the interactions between different parts of a computation. This technique has been successfully applied to object-oriented programs [19, 20], to generic resource metrics [23, 7], to polymorphic and higher-order programs [24], and to Java-like bytecode by means of separation logic [4]. The main limitation shared by these analysis systems is their *restriction to linear resource bounds* which can be efficiently reduced to solving linear constraints.

A recently discovered technique [16, 17] yields an automatic amortized analysis for polynomial bounds while still relying on linear constraint solving only. The resulting extension of the linear system [18, 23] efficiently computes resource bounds for first-order functional programs that are sums $\sum p_i(n_i)$ of univariate polynomials p_i. For instance, it automatically infers evaluation-step bounds for the sorting algorithms quick sort and insertion sort that exactly match the measured worst-case behavior of the functions [17]. The computation of these bounds takes less then a second.

This analysis system for polynomial bounds has, however, two drawbacks that hamper the automatic computation of bounds for larger programs. First, many functions with multiple arguments that appear in practice have *multivariate* cost characteristics like $m \cdot n$. Secondly, if data from different sources is interlinked in a program then multivariate bounds like $(m+n)^2$ arise even if all functions have a univariate resource behavior. In these cases the analysis fails, or the bounds are hugely over-approximated by $3m^2 + 3n^2$.

To overcome these drawbacks, this paper presents an *automatic type-based amortized analysis for multivariate polynomial resource bounds*. We faced three main challenges in the development of the analysis.

1. The identification of multivariate polynomials that accurately describe the resource cost of typical examples. It is necessary that they are closed under natural operations to be suitable for local typing rules. Moreover, they must handle an unbounded number of arguments to tightly cope with nested data structures.
2. The automatic relation of sizes of data structures in function arguments and results, even if data that is scattered over different locations (like $n_1 + n_2 \leq n$ in the partitioning of quick sort).
3. The smooth integration of the inference of size relations and resource bounds to deal with the interactions of different functions while keeping the analysis technically feasible in practice.

To address challenge one we define *multivariate resource polynomials* that are a generalization of the resource polynomials that we used earlier [16]. To address challenges two and three we introduce a multivariate potential-based amortized analysis (§5 and §6). The local type rules emit only simple linear constraints and are remarkably modest considering the variety of relations between different parts of the data that are taken into account.

Our experiments with a prototype implementation[3] (see §7) show that our system automatically infers tight multivariate bounds for complex programs that involve nested data structures such as trees of lists. Additionally, it can deal with the same wide range of linear and univariate programs as the previous systems.

As representative examples we present in §7 the analyses of the dynamic programming algorithm for the length of the longest common subsequence of two lists and an implementation of insertion sort that lexicographically sorts a list of lists. Note that the latter example exhibits a worst-case running time of the form $O(n^2m)$ where n is the length of the outer list and m is the maximal length of the inner lists. The reason is that each of the $O(n^2)$ comparisons performed by insertion sort needs time linear in m.

We also implemented a more involved case study on matrix operations were matrices are lists of lists of integers. It demonstrates interesting capabilities like the precise automatic tracking of data sizes when transposing matrices or the automatic analyses of complex functions like the multiplication of lists of matrices of different (fitting) dimensions. Details are available on the web.

The main contributions we make in this paper are as follows.

1. The definition of multivariate resource polynomials that generalize univariate resource polynomials [16]. (in §4)
2. The introduction of type annotation that correspond to *global polynomial potential functions* for amortized analysis which depend on the sizes of several parts of the input. (in §5)
3. The presentation of *local type rules* that modify type annotations for global potential functions. (in §6)
4. The implementation of an efficient type inference algorithm that relies on *linear constraint solving* only.

2. Background and Informal Presentation

Amortized Analysis *Amortized analysis* with the *potential method* has been introduced [26] to manually analyze the efficiency of data structures. The key idea is to incorporate a non-negative potential into the analysis that can be used to pay (costly) operations.

To apply the potential method to statically analyze a program, one has to determine a mapping from machine states to potentials for every program point. Then one has to show that for every possible evaluation, the potential at a program point suffices to cover the cost of the next transition and the potential at the succeeding program point. The initial potential is then an upper bound on the resource consumption of the program.

Linear Potential One way to achieve such an analysis is to use linear potential functions [18]. Inductive data structures are statically annotated with a positive rational numbers q to define non-negative potentials $\Phi(n) = q \cdot n$ as a function of the size n of the data. Then a sound albeit incomplete type-based analysis of the program text statically verifies that the potential is sufficient to pay for all operations that are performed on this data structure during any possible evaluation of the program.

The analysis is best explained by example. Consider the function *filter*:$(int, L(int)) \to L(int)$ that removes the multiples of a given integer from a list of integers.

```
filter(p,l) = match l with | nil -> nil
        | (x::xs) -> let xs' = filter(p,xs) in
                        if x mod p == 0 then xs' else x::xs'
```

Assume that we need two memory cells to create a new list cell. Then the heap-space usage of an evaluation of *filter(p,ℓ)* is at most $2|\ell|$. To infer an upper bound on the heap-space usage we enrich the type of *filter* with a priori unknown potential annotations[4] $q_{(0,i)}, p_i \in \mathbb{Q}_0^+$.

$$filter:((int, L(int)), (q_{(0,0)}, q_{(0,1)})) \to (L(int), (p_0, p_1))$$

The intuitive meaning of the resulting type is as follows: to evaluate *filter(p,ℓ)* one needs $q_{(0,1)}$ memory cells per element in the list ℓ and $q_{(0,0)}$ additional memory cells. After the evaluation there are p_0 memory cells and p_1 cells per element of the returned list left. We say that the pair (p,ℓ) has potential

[3] See `http://raml.tcs.ifi.lmu.de` for a web interface, example programs, and the source code.

[4] We use the naming scheme of the unknowns that arises from the more general method introduced in this paper.

$\Phi((p,\ell),(q_{(0,0)},q_{(0,1)})) = q_{(0,0)} + q_{(0,1)} \cdot |\ell|$ and that $\ell' =$ *filter*(p,ℓ) has potential $\Phi(\ell',(p_0,p_1)) = p_0 + p_1 \cdot |\ell'|$. A valid potential annotation would be for instance $q_{(0,0)} = p_0 = p_1 = 0$ and $q_{(0,1)} = 2$. Another valid annotation would be $q_{(0,0)} = p_0 = 0$, $p_1 = 2$, and $q_{(0,1)} = 4$. It can be used to type the inner call of *filter* in an expression like *filter(a,filter(b,ℓ))*.

To infer the potential annotations one can use a standard type inference in which simple linear constraints are collected as each type rule is applied. For the heap-space consumption of *filter* the constraints would state that $q_{(0,0)} \geq p_0$ and $q_{(0,1)} \geq 2 + p_1$.

Univariate Polynomials An automatic amortized analysis can be also used to derive potential functions of the form $\sum_{i=0,\ldots,k} q_i\binom{n}{i}$ with $q_i \geq 0$ while still relying on solving linear inequalities only [16]. These potential functions are attached to inductive data structures via type annotations of the form $\vec{q} = (q_0,\ldots,q_k)$ with $q_i \in \mathbb{Q}_0^+$. For instance, the typing $\ell{:}(L(\mathit{int}),(4,3,2,1))$, defines the potential $\Phi(\ell,(4,3,2,1)) = 4 + 3|\ell| + 2\binom{|\ell|}{2} + 1\binom{|\ell|}{3}$.

The use of the binomial coefficients rather than powers of variables has several advantages. In particular, the identity $\sum_{i=0,\ldots,k} q_i\binom{n+1}{i} = \sum_{i=0,\ldots,k-1} q_{i+1}\binom{n}{i} + \sum_{i=0,\ldots,k} q_i\binom{n}{i}$ gives rise to a local typing rule for *list match* which allows to type naturally both, recursive calls and other calls to subordinate functions in branches of a pattern match.

This identity forms the mathematical basis of the *additive shift* $\triangleleft$ of a type annotation which is defined by $\triangleleft(q_0,\ldots,q_k) = (q_0+q_1,\ldots,q_{k-1}+q_k,q_k)$. For example, it appears in the typing *tail*:$(L(\mathit{int}),\vec{q}) \to (L(\mathit{int}),\triangleleft(\vec{q}))$ of the function *tail* that removes the first element from a list. The potential resulting from the contraction *xs*:$(L(\mathit{int}),\triangleleft(\vec{q}))$ of a list *(x::xs)*:$(L(\mathit{int}),\vec{q})$, usually in a pattern match, suffices to pay for three common purposes: (i) to pay the constant costs q_1 after and before the recursive calls, (ii) to fund, by $(q_2,\ldots,q_n)$, calls to auxiliary functions, and (iii) to pay, by $(q_0,\ldots,q_n)$, for the recursive calls.

To see how the polynomial potential annotations are used, consider the function *eratos*:$L(\mathit{int}) \to L(\mathit{int})$ that implements the sieve of Eratosthenes. It successively calls the function *filter* to delete multiples of the first element from the input list. If *eratos* is called with a list of the form $[2,3,\ldots,n]$ then it computes the list of primes p with $2 \leq p \leq n$.

```
eratos l = match l with | nil -> nil
           | (x::xs) -> x::eratos(filter(x,xs))
```

Note that it is possible in our system to implement the function *filter* with a destructive pattern match (just replace *match* with *matchD*). That would result in a filter function that does not consume heap-cells and in a linear heap-space consumption of *eratos*. But to illustrate the use of quadratic potential we use the *filter* function with linear heap-space consumption from the first example.[5] In an evaluation of *eratos(ℓ)* the function *filter* is called once for every sublist of the input list ℓ in the worst case. Then the calls of *filter* cause a worst-case heap-space consumption of $2\binom{|\ell|}{2}$. This is for example the case if ℓ is a list of pairwise distinct primes. Additionally, there is the creation of a new list element for every recursive call of *eratos*. Thus, the total worst-case heap-space consumption of the function is $2n + 2\binom{n}{2}$ if n is the size of the input list.

To bound the heap-space consumption of *eratos*, our analysis system automatically computes the following type.

$$\mathit{eratos}{:}(L(\mathit{int}),(0,2,2)) \to (L(\mathit{int}),(0,0,0))$$

Since the typing assigns the initial potential $2n+2\binom{n}{2}$ to a function argument of size n, the analysis computes a tight heap-space bound for *eratos*. In the pattern match, the additive shift assigns the type $(L(\mathit{int}),(2,4,2))$ to the variable *xs*. The constant potential 2 is then used to pay for the cons operation (i). The non-constant potential *xs*:$(L(\mathit{int}),(0,4,2))$ is shared between the two occurrences of *xs* in the following expression by using *xs*:$(L(\mathit{int}),(0,2,0))$ to pay the cost of *filter(xs)* (ii) and by using *xs*:$(L(\mathit{int})(0,2,2)$ to pay for the recursive call of *eratos* (iii).

To infer the typing, we start with an unknown potential annotation as in the linear case.

$$\mathit{eratos}{:}(L(\mathit{int}),(q_0,q_1,q_2)) \to (L(\mathit{int}),(p_0,p_1,p_2))$$

The syntax-directed type analysis then computes linear inequalities which state that $q_0 \geq p_0$, $q_1 \geq 2 + p_1$, and $q_2 \geq 2 + p_2$.

This analysis method works for many functions that admit a worst-case resource consumption that can be expressed by sums of univariate polynomials like $n^2 + m^2$. However, it often fails to compute types for functions whose resource consumption is bounded by a mixed term like $n^2 \cdot m$. The reason is that the potential is attached to a single data structure and does not take into account relations between different data structures.

Multivariate Bounds This paper extends type-based amortized analysis to compute mixed resource bounds like $2n \cdot \binom{m}{2}$. To this end, we introduce a global polynomial potential annotation that can express a variety of relations between different parts of the input. To give a flavor of the basic ideas we informally introduce this global potential in this section for pairs of integer lists.

The potential of a single integer list can be expressed as a vector $(q_0,q_1,\ldots,q_k)$ that defines a potential-function of the form $\sum_{i=0}^{k} q_i\binom{n}{i}$. To represent mixed terms of degree $\leq k$ for a pair of integer lists we use a triangular matrix $Q = (q_{(i,j)})_{0\leq i+j\leq k}$. Then Q defines a potential-function of the form $\sum_{0\leq i+j\leq k} q_{(i,j)}\binom{n}{i}\binom{m}{j}$ where m and n are the lengths of the two lists.

This definition has the same advantages as the univariate version of the system. Particularly, we can still use the additive shift to assign potential to sublists. To generalize the additive shift of the univariate system, we use the identity $\sum_{0\leq i+j\leq k} q_{(i,j)}\binom{n+1}{i}\binom{m}{j} = \sum_{0\leq i+j\leq k-1} q_{(i+1,j)}\binom{n}{i}\binom{m}{j} + \sum_{0\leq i+j\leq k} q_{(i,j)}\binom{n}{i}\binom{m}{j}$. It is reflected by two additive shifts $\triangleleft_1(Q) = (q_{(i,j)} + q_{(i+1,j)})_{0\leq i+j\leq k}$ and $\triangleleft_2(Q) = (q_{(i,j)} + q_{(i,j+1)})_{0\leq i+j\leq k}$ where $q_{(i,j)} := 0$ if $i + j > k$. The shift operations can be used like in the univariate case. For example, we derive the typing *tail1*: $((L(\mathit{int}),L(\mathit{int})),Q) \to ((L(\mathit{int}),L(\mathit{int})),\triangleleft_1(Q))$ for the function *tail1(xs,ys)=(tail xs,ys)*.

To see how the mixed potential is used, consider the function *dyade* that computes the dyadic product of two lists.

```
mult(x,l) = match l with | nil -> nil
                         | (y::ys) -> x*y::mult(x,ys)

dyade(l,ys) = match l with | nil -> nil
                   | (x::xs) -> (mult(x,ys))::dyade(xs,ys)
```

Similar to previous examples, *mult* consumes $2n$ heap cells if n is the length of input. This exact bound is represented by the typing

$$\mathit{mult}{:}\ ((\mathit{int},L(\mathit{int})),(0,2,0)) \to (L(\mathit{int}),(0,0,0))$$

that states that the potential is $0 + 2n + 0\binom{n}{2}$ before and 0 after the evaluation of *mult(x,ℓ)* if ℓ is a list of length n.

The function *dyade* consumes $2n + 2nm$ heap cells if n is the length of first argument and m is the length of the second argument. This is why the following typing represents a tight heap-space bound for the function.

$$\mathit{dyade}{:}\ ((L(\mathit{int}),L(\mathit{int})),\begin{pmatrix}0\ 0\ 0\\ 2\ 2\\ 0\end{pmatrix}) \to (L(\mathit{int},\mathit{int}),0)$$

[5] It is just more convenient to argue about heap space than to argue about evaluation steps.

To verify this typing of *dyade*, the additive shift $\lhd_1$ is used in the pattern matching. This results in the potential

$$(xs,ys)\text{: } ((L(int), L(int)), \begin{pmatrix} 2 & 2 & 0 \\ 2 & 2 & \\ 0 & & \end{pmatrix})$$

that is used as in the function *eratos*: the constant potential 2 is used to pay for the *cons* operation (i), the linear potential $ys{:}(L(int), (0, 2, 0))$ is used to pay the cost of *mult(ys)* (ii), the rest of the potential is used to pay for the recursive call (iii).

Multivariate potential is also needed to assign a super-linear potential to the result of a function like *append*. This is, for example, needed to type an expression like *eratos(append(ℓ_1,ℓ_2))*. Here, *append* would have the type

$$append\text{: } ((L(int), L(int)), \begin{pmatrix} 0 & 2 & 2 \\ 4 & 2 & \\ 2 & & \end{pmatrix}) \to (L(int), (0, 2, 2)).$$

The correctness of the bound follows from the convolution formula $\binom{n+m}{2} = \binom{n}{2} + \binom{m}{2} + nm$ and from the fact that *append* consumes $2n$ resources if n is the length of the first argument. The respective initial potential $4n + 2m + 2(\binom{n}{2} + \binom{m}{2} + mn)$ furnishes a tight bound on the worst-case heap-space consumption of the evaluation of *eratos(append(ℓ_1,ℓ_2))*, where $|\ell_1| = n$, $|\ell_2| = m$.

3. Resource Aware ML

RAML (Resource Aware ML) is a first-order functional language with ML-style syntax, booleans, integers, pairs, lists, binary trees, recursion and pattern match. In the implementation of RAML we already included a destructive pattern match that we could handle using the methods described here.

Syntax To simplify typing rules and semantics, we define the following *expressions of RAML* to be in *let normal form*. In the implementation we transform unrestricted expressions into a let normal form with explicit sharing before the type analysis.

$$\begin{aligned} e ::= {} & () \mid \mathit{True} \mid \mathit{False} \mid n \mid x \mid x_1 \ \mathit{binop}\ x_2 \mid f(x_1, \ldots, x_n) \\ & \mid \mathit{let}\ x = e_1\ \mathit{in}\ e_2 \mid \mathit{if}\ x\ \mathit{then}\ e_t\ \mathit{else}\ e_f \\ & \mid (x_1, x_2) \mid \mathit{nil} \mid \mathit{cons}(x_h, x_t) \mid \mathit{leaf} \mid \mathit{node}(x_0, x_1, x_2) \\ & \mid \mathit{match}\ x\ \mathit{with}\ (x_1, x_2) \to e \\ & \mid \mathit{match}\ x\ \mathit{with}\ \mid \mathit{nil} \to e_1 \mid \mathit{cons}(x_h, x_t) \to e_2 \\ & \mid \mathit{match}\ x\ \mathit{with}\ \mid \mathit{leaf} \to e_1 \mid \mathit{node}(x_0, x_1, x_2) \to e_2 \end{aligned}$$

$$\mathit{binop} ::= + \mid - \mid * \mid \mathit{mod} \mid \mathit{div} \mid \mathit{and} \mid \mathit{or}$$

We skip the standard definitions of integer constants $n \in \mathbb{Z}$ and variable identifiers $x \in$ VID. For the resource analysis it is unimportant which ground operations are used in the definition of *binop*. In fact, one can use here every function that has a constant worst-case resource consumption.

Simple Types We define the well-typed expressions of RAML by assigning a *simple type*, a usual ML type without resource annotations, to well-typed expressions. Simple types are data types and first-order types as given by the grammars below.

$$A ::= \mathit{unit} \mid \mathit{bool} \mid \mathit{int} \mid L(A) \mid T(A) \mid (A, A) \qquad F ::= A \to A$$

To each simple type A we assign a set of semantic values $[\![A]\!]$ in the obvious way. For example $[\![T(int, int)]\!]$ is the set of finite binary trees whose nodes are labeled with pairs of integers. It is convenient to identify tuples like (A_1, A_2, A_3, A_4) with the pair type $(A_1, (A_2, (A_3, A_4)))$.

A *typing context* Γ is a partial, finite mapping from variable identifiers to data types. A *signature* Σ is a finite, partial mapping of function identifiers to first-order types. The typing judgment $\Gamma \vdash_\Sigma e : A$ states that the expression e has type A under the signature Σ in the context Γ. The typing rules that define the typing judgment are standard and a subset of the resource-annotated typing rules from §5 if the resource annotations are omitted.

Programs Each *RAML program* consists of a signature Σ and a family $(e_f, y_f)_{f \in \mathrm{dom}(\Sigma)}$ of expressions with a distinguished variable identifier such that $y_f{:}A \vdash_\Sigma e_f{:}B$ if $\Sigma(f) = A \to B$.

We write $f(y_1, \ldots, y_k) = e'_f$ as an abbreviation to indicate that $\Sigma(f) = (A_1, (A_2, (\ldots, A_k) \cdots) \to B$ and $y_1{:}A_1, \ldots, y_k{:}A_k \vdash_\Sigma e'_f{:}B$. In this case, f is defined by $e_f =$ match y_f with $(y_1, y'_f) \to$ match y'_f with $(y_2, y''_f) \ldots e'_f$. Of course, one can use such function definitions also in the implementation.

Operational Semantics To prove the correctness of our analysis, we define a big-step operational semantics that measures the quantitative resource consumption of programs. It is parametric in the resource of interest and can measure every quantity whose usage in a single evaluation step can be bounded by a constant. The actual constants for a step on a specific system architecture can be derived by analyzing the translation of the step in the compiler implementation for that architecture [23].

The semantics is formulated with respect to a stack and a heap as usual: A value $v \in$ Val is either a location $\ell \in$ Loc, a boolean constant b, an integer n, a null value NULL or a pair of values (v_1, v_2). A *heap* is a finite partial mapping $\mathcal{H}$: Loc $\to$ Val from locations to values. A *stack* is a finite partial mapping $\mathcal{V}$: VID $\to$ Val from variables to values.

The operational evaluation rules define an evaluation judgment of the form $\mathcal{V}, \mathcal{H} \vdash e \rightsquigarrow v, \mathcal{H}' \mid (q, q')$ expressing the following. If the stack $\mathcal{V}$ and the initial heap $\mathcal{H}$ are given then the expression e evaluates to the value v and the new heap $\mathcal{H}'$. To evaluate e one needs at least $q \in \mathbb{Q}^+$ resource units and after the evaluation there are $q' \in \mathbb{Q}^+$ resource units available. The actual resource consumption is then $\delta = q - q'$. The quantity δ is negative if resources become available during the execution of e.

Fig. 1 shows the evaluation rules of the big-step semantics. There is at most one pair (q, q') such that $\mathcal{V}, \mathcal{H} \vdash e \rightsquigarrow v, \mathcal{H}' \mid (q, q')$ for a given expression e, a heap $\mathcal{H}$ and a stack $\mathcal{V}$. The non-negative number q is the (high) watermark of resources that are used simultaneously during the evaluation.

It is handy to view the pairs (q, q') in the evaluation judgments as elements of a monoid $\mathcal{Q} = (\mathbb{Q}_0^+ \times \mathbb{Q}_0^+, \cdot)$. The neutral element is $(0, 0)$ which means that resources are neither used nor restituted. The operation $(q, q') \cdot (p, p')$ defines how to account for an evaluation consisting of evaluations whose resource consumptions are defined by (q, q') and (p, p'), respectively. We define

$$(q, q') \cdot (p, p') = \begin{cases} (q + p - q',\ p') & \text{if } q' \le p \\ (q,\ p' + q' - p) & \text{if } q' > p \end{cases}$$

If resources are never restituted (as with time) then we can restrict to elements of the form $(q, 0)$ and $(q, 0) \cdot (p, 0)$ is just $(q + p, 0)$.

We identify a rational number q with an element of $\mathcal{Q}$ as follows: $q \ge 0$ denotes $(q, 0)$ and $q < 0$ denotes $(0, -q)$. This notation avoids case distinctions in the evaluation rules since the constants K that appear in the rules might be negative.

A notorious dissatisfying feature of classical big-step semantics is that it does not provide evaluation judgments for non-terminating evaluations. In a companion paper [17] we describe a big-step operational semantics for partial evaluations that agrees with the usual big-step semantics on terminating computations. It inductively defines statements of the form $\mathcal{V}, \mathcal{H} \vdash e \rightsquigarrow \mid q$ for a stack $\mathcal{V}$, a heap $\mathcal{H}$, $q \in \mathbb{Q}_0^+$ and an expression e. The meaning is that there is a partial evaluation of e with the stack $\mathcal{V}$ and the heap $\mathcal{H}$ that consumes q resources. This allows for a smooth extension of the soundness theorem (Theorem 1) to non-terminating evaluations (see [17]).

$$\frac{x \in \mathrm{dom}(\mathcal{V})}{\mathcal{V},\mathcal{H} \vdash x \rightsquigarrow \mathcal{V}(x),\mathcal{H} \mid K^{\mathrm{var}}} \text{ (E:VAR)} \qquad \frac{}{\mathcal{V},\mathcal{H} \vdash () \rightsquigarrow \mathrm{NULL},\mathcal{H} \mid K^{\mathrm{unit}}} \text{ (E:CONSTU)} \qquad \frac{n \in \mathbb{Z}}{\mathcal{V},\mathcal{H} \vdash n \rightsquigarrow n,\mathcal{H} \mid K^{\mathrm{int}}} \text{ (E:CONSTI)}$$

$$\frac{b \in \{\mathit{True}, \mathit{False}\}}{\mathcal{V},\mathcal{H} \vdash b \rightsquigarrow b,\mathcal{H} \mid K^{\mathrm{bool}}} \text{ (E:CONSTB)} \qquad \frac{\mathcal{V}(x) = v \qquad [y_f \mapsto v],\mathcal{H} \vdash e_f \rightsquigarrow v',\mathcal{H}' \mid (q,q')}{\mathcal{V},\mathcal{H} \vdash f(x) \rightsquigarrow v',\mathcal{H}' \mid K_1^{\mathrm{app}} \cdot (q,q') \cdot K_2^{\mathrm{app}}} \text{ (E:APP)}$$

$$\frac{x_1, x_2 \in \mathrm{dom}(\mathcal{V}) \qquad v = op(\mathcal{V}(x_1),\mathcal{V}(x_2))}{\mathcal{V},\mathcal{H} \vdash x_1 \; op \; x_2 \rightsquigarrow v,\mathcal{H} \mid K^{op}} \text{ (E:BINOP)} \qquad \frac{\mathcal{V}(x) = \mathit{True} \qquad \mathcal{V},\mathcal{H} \vdash e_t \rightsquigarrow v,\mathcal{H}' \mid (q,q')}{\mathcal{V},\mathcal{H} \vdash \mathit{if}\, x \,\mathit{then}\, e_t \,\mathit{else}\, e_f \rightsquigarrow v,\mathcal{H}' \mid K_1^{\mathrm{conT}} \cdot (q,q') \cdot K_2^{\mathrm{conT}}} \text{ (E:CONDT)}$$

$$\frac{\mathcal{V}(x) = \mathit{False} \qquad \mathcal{V},\mathcal{H} \vdash e_f \rightsquigarrow v,\mathcal{H}' \mid (q,q')}{\mathcal{V},\mathcal{H} \vdash \mathit{if}\, x \,\mathit{then}\, e_t \,\mathit{else}\, e_f \rightsquigarrow v,\mathcal{H}' \mid K_1^{\mathrm{conF}} \cdot (q,q') \cdot K_2^{\mathrm{conF}}} \text{ (E:CONDF)}$$

$$\frac{\mathcal{V},\mathcal{H} \vdash e_1 \rightsquigarrow v_1,\mathcal{H}_1 \mid (q,q') \qquad \mathcal{V}[x \mapsto v_1],\mathcal{H}_1 \vdash e_2 \rightsquigarrow v_2,\mathcal{H}_2 \mid (p,p')}{\mathcal{V},\mathcal{H} \vdash \mathit{let}\, x = e_1 \,\mathit{in}\, e_2 \rightsquigarrow v_2,\mathcal{H}_2 \mid K_1^{\mathrm{let}} \cdot (q,q') \cdot K_2^{\mathrm{let}} \cdot (p,p') \cdot K_3^{\mathrm{let}}} \text{ (E:LET)}$$

$$\frac{x_1, x_2 \in \mathrm{dom}(\mathcal{V}) \qquad v = (\mathcal{V}(x_1),\mathcal{V}(x_2))}{\mathcal{V},\mathcal{H} \vdash (x_1,x_2) \rightsquigarrow v,\mathcal{H} \mid K^{\mathrm{pair}}} \text{ (E:PAIR)} \qquad \frac{\mathcal{V}(x) = (v_1,v_2) \qquad \mathcal{V}[x_1 \mapsto v_1, x_2 \mapsto v_2],\mathcal{H} \vdash e \rightsquigarrow v,\mathcal{H}' \mid (q,q')}{\mathcal{V},\mathcal{H} \vdash \mathit{match}\, x \,\mathit{with}\, (x_1,x_2) \to e \rightsquigarrow v,\mathcal{H}' \mid K_1^{\mathrm{matP}} \cdot (q,q') \cdot K_2^{\mathrm{matP}}} \text{ (E:MATP)}$$

$$\frac{}{\mathcal{V},\mathcal{H} \vdash \mathit{nil} \rightsquigarrow \mathrm{NULL},\mathcal{H} \mid K^{\mathrm{nil}}} \text{ (E:NIL)} \qquad \frac{x_h, x_t \in \mathrm{dom}(\mathcal{V}) \qquad v = (\mathcal{V}(x_h),\mathcal{V}(x_t)) \qquad l \notin \mathrm{dom}(\mathcal{H})}{\mathcal{V},\mathcal{H} \vdash \mathit{cons}(x_h,x_t) \rightsquigarrow l,\mathcal{H}[l \mapsto v] \mid K^{\mathrm{cons}}} \text{ (E:CONS)}$$

$$\frac{\mathcal{V}(x) = \mathrm{NULL} \qquad \mathcal{V},\mathcal{H} \vdash e_1 \rightsquigarrow v,\mathcal{H}' \mid (q,q')}{\mathcal{V},\mathcal{H} \vdash \mathit{match}\, x \,\mathit{with} \mid \mathit{nil} \to e_1 \mid \mathit{cons}(x_h,x_t) \to e_2 \rightsquigarrow v,\mathcal{H}' \mid K_1^{\mathrm{matN}} \cdot (q,q') \cdot K_2^{\mathrm{matN}}} \text{ (E:MATNIL)}$$

$$\frac{\mathcal{V}(x){=}l \qquad \mathcal{H}(l){=}(v_h,v_t) \qquad \mathcal{V}[x_h{\mapsto}v_h, x_t{\mapsto}v_t],\mathcal{H} \vdash e_2 \rightsquigarrow v,\mathcal{H}' \mid (q,q')}{\mathcal{V},\mathcal{H} \vdash \mathit{match}\, x \,\mathit{with} \mid \mathit{nil} \to e_1 \mid \mathit{cons}(x_h,x_t) \to e_2 \rightsquigarrow v,\mathcal{H}' \mid K_1^{\mathrm{matC}} \cdot (q,q') \cdot K_2^{\mathrm{matC}}} \text{ (E:MATCONS)}$$

$$\frac{}{\mathcal{V},\mathcal{H} \vdash \mathit{leaf} \rightsquigarrow \mathrm{NULL},\mathcal{H} \mid K^{\mathrm{leaf}}} \text{ (E:LEAF)} \qquad \frac{x_0, x_1, x_2 \in \mathrm{dom}(\mathcal{V}) \qquad v = (\mathcal{V}(x_0),\mathcal{V}(x_1),\mathcal{V}(x_2)) \qquad l \notin \mathrm{dom}(\mathcal{H})}{\mathcal{V},\mathcal{H} \vdash \mathit{node}(x_0,x_1,x_2) \rightsquigarrow l,\mathcal{H}[l \mapsto v] \mid K^{\mathrm{node}}} \text{ (E:NODE)}$$

$$\frac{\mathcal{V}(x) = \mathrm{NULL} \qquad \mathcal{V},\mathcal{H} \vdash e_1 \rightsquigarrow v,\mathcal{H}' \mid (q,q')}{\mathcal{V},\mathcal{H} \vdash \mathit{match}\, x \,\mathit{with} \mid \mathit{leaf} \to e_1 \mid \mathit{node}(x_0,x_1,x_2) \to e_2 \rightsquigarrow v,\mathcal{H}' \mid K_1^{\mathrm{matTL}} \cdot (q,q') \cdot K_2^{\mathrm{matTL}}} \text{ (E:MATLEAF)}$$

$$\frac{\mathcal{V}(x){=}l \qquad \mathcal{H}(l){=}(v_0,v_1,v_2) \qquad \mathcal{V}[x_0{\mapsto}v_0, x_1{\mapsto}v_1, x_2{\mapsto}v_2],\mathcal{H} \vdash e_2 \rightsquigarrow v,\mathcal{H}' \mid (q,q')}{\mathcal{V},\mathcal{H} \vdash \mathit{match}\, x \,\mathit{with} \mid \mathit{leaf} \to e_1 \mid \mathit{node}(x_0,x_1,x_2) \to e_2 \rightsquigarrow v,\mathcal{H}' \mid K_1^{\mathrm{matTN}} \cdot (q,q') \cdot K_2^{\mathrm{matTN}}} \text{ (E:MATNODE)}$$

Figure 1. Evaluation rules of the big-step operational semantics.

The Cost-Free Resource Metric The type rules in §6 make use of the *cost-free* resource metric. This is the metric in which all constants K that appear in the rules are instantiated to zero. It follows that if $\mathcal{V},\mathcal{H} \vdash e \rightsquigarrow v,\mathcal{H}' \mid (q,q')$ then $q = q' = 0$. We will use the cost-free metric in §6 to pass on potential in the typing rule for let expressions.

Well-Formed Environments If $\mathcal{H}$ is a heap, v is a value, A is a type, and $a \in [\![A]\!]$ then we write $\mathcal{H} \vDash v{\mapsto}a : A$ to mean that v defines the semantic value $a \in [\![A]\!]$ when pointers are followed in $\mathcal{H}$ in the obvious way. We elide a formal definition of this judgment.

Note that if $\mathcal{H} \vDash v{\mapsto}a : A$ then v may well point to a data structure with some aliasing, but no circularity is allowed since this would require infinitary values a. We do not include them because in our functional language there is no way of generating such values; in principle our method can encompass circular data [19].

We also write $\mathcal{H} \vDash v : A$ to indicate that there exists a, necessarily unique, semantic value $a \in [\![A]\!]$ so that $\mathcal{H} \vDash v{\mapsto}a : A$. A stack $\mathcal{V}$ and a heap $\mathcal{H}$ are *well-formed* with respect to a context Γ if $\mathcal{H} \vDash \mathcal{V}(x) : \Gamma(x)$ holds for every $x \in \mathrm{dom}(\Gamma)$. We then write $\mathcal{H} \vDash \mathcal{V}{:}\Gamma$. Formal definitions can be found in the literature [24].

4. Resource Polynomials

A resource polynomial maps a value of some data type to a nonnegative rational number. Potential functions are always given by such resource polynomials.

In the case of an inductive tree-like data type, a resource polynomial will only depend on the list of entries of the data structure in pre-order. Thus, if $D(A)$ is such a data type with entries of type A, e.g., A-labelled binary trees, and v is a value of type $D(A)$ then we write $\mathrm{elems}(v) = [a_1, \ldots, a_n]$ for this list of entries.

An analysis of typical polynomial computations operating on a data structure v with $\mathrm{elems}(v) = [a_1, \ldots, a_n]$ shows that it consists of operations that are executed for every k-tuple $(a_{i_1}, \ldots, a_{i_k})$ with $1 \leq i_1 < \cdots < i_k \leq n$. The simplest examples are linear map operations that perform some operation for every a_i. Another example are common sorting algorithms that perform comparisons for every pair (a_i, a_j) with $1 \leq i < j \leq n$ in the worst case.

Base Polynomials For each data type A we now define a set $\mathcal{P}(A)$ of functions $p : [\![A]\!] \to \mathbb{N}$ that map values of type A to natural numbers. The resource polynomials for type A are then given as nonnegative rational linear combinations of these *base polynomials*. We define $\mathcal{P}(A)$ as follows.

$$\mathcal{P}(A) = \{a \mapsto 1\} \text{ if } A \text{ is an atomic type}$$

$$\mathcal{P}(A_1, A_2) = \{(a_1, a_2) \mapsto p_1(a_1) \cdot p_2(a_2) \mid p_i \in \mathcal{P}(A_i)\}$$

$$\mathcal{P}(D(A)) = \{v \mapsto \sum_{1 \le j_1 < \cdots < j_k \le n} \prod_{i=1}^{k} p_i(a_{j_i}) \mid k \in \mathbb{N}, p_i \in \mathcal{P}(A)\}$$

In the last clause $[a_1, \ldots, a_n] = \text{elems}(v)$. Every set $\mathcal{P}(A)$ contains the constant function $v \mapsto 1$. In the case of $D(A)$ this arises for $k = 0$ (one element sum, empty product).

For example, the function $\ell \mapsto \binom{|\ell|}{k}$ is in $\mathcal{P}(L(A))$ for every $k \in \mathbb{N}$; simply take $p_1 = \ldots = p_k = 1$ in the definition of $\mathcal{P}(D(A))$. The function $(\ell_1, \ell_2) \mapsto \binom{|\ell_1|}{k_1} \cdot \binom{|\ell_2|}{k_2}$ is in $\mathcal{P}(L(A), L(B))$ for every $k_1, k_2 \in \mathbb{N}$ and $[\ell_1, \ldots, \ell_n] \mapsto \sum_{1 \le i < j \le n} \binom{|\ell_i|}{k_1} \cdot \binom{|\ell_j|}{k_2} \in \mathcal{P}(L(L(A)))$ for every $k_1, k_2 \in \mathbb{N}$.

Resource Polynomials A *resource polynomial* $p : [\![A]\!] \to \mathbb{Q}_0^+$ for a data type A is a non-negative linear combination of base polynomials, i.e.,

$$p = \sum_{i=1,\ldots,m} q_i \cdot p_i$$

for $q_i \in \mathbb{Q}_0^+$ and $p_i \in \mathcal{P}(A)$. We write $\mathcal{R}(A)$ for the set of resource polynomials for A.

An instructive, but not exhaustive, example is given by $\mathcal{R}_n = \mathcal{R}(L(\mathit{int}), \ldots, L(\mathit{int}))$. The set $\mathcal{R}_n$ is the set of linear combinations of products of binomial coefficients over variables $x_1, \ldots, x_n$, that is, $\mathcal{R}_n = \{\sum_{i=1}^{m} q_i \prod_{j=1}^{n} \binom{x_j}{k_{ij}} \mid q_i \in \mathbb{Q}_0^+, m \in \mathbb{N}, k_{ij} \in \mathbb{N}\}$. These expressions naturally generalize the polynomials used in our univariate analysis [16] and meet two conditions that are important to efficiently manipulate polynomials during the analysis. First, the polynomials are non-negative, and secondly, they are closed under the discrete difference operators Δ_i for every i. The discrete derivative $\Delta_i p$ is defined through $\Delta_i p(x_1, \ldots, x_n) = p(x_1, \ldots, x_i + 1, \ldots, x_n) - p(x_1, \ldots, x_n)$.

As in [16] it can be shown that $\mathcal{R}_n$ is the largest set of polynomials enjoying these closure properties. It would be interesting to have a similar characterisation of $\mathcal{R}(A)$ for arbitrary A. So far, we know that $\mathcal{R}(A)$ is closed under sum and product (see Lemma 1) and are compatible with the construction of elements of data structures in a very natural way (see Lemmas 2 and 3). This provides some justification for their choice and canonicity. An abstract characterization would have to take into account the fact that our resource polynomials depend on an unbounded number of variables, e.g., sizes of inner data structures, and are not invariant under permutation of these variables. It seems that some generalization of infinite symmetric polynomials to subgroups of the symmetric group could be useful, but this would not serve our immediate goal of accurate multivariate resource analysis.

5. Annotated Types

The resource polynomials described in §4 are non-negative linear combinations of base polynomials. The rational coefficients of the linear combination are present as type annotations in our type system. To relate type annotations to resource polynomials we systematically describe base polynomials and resource polynomials for data of a given type.

If one considers only univariate polynomials then their description is straightforward. Every inductive data of size n admits a potential of the form $\sum_{1 \le i \le k} q_i \binom{n}{i}$. So we can describe the potential function with a vector $\vec{q} = (q_1, \ldots, q_k)$ in the corresponding recursive type. For instance can we write $L^{\vec{q}}(A)$ for annotated list types. Since each annotation refers to the size of one input part only, univariatly annotated types can be directly composed. For example, an annotated type for a pair of lists has the form $(L^{\vec{q}}(A), L^{\vec{p}}(A))$. See [16] for details.

Here, we work with multivariate potential functions, i.e., functions that depend on the sizes of different parts of the input. For a pair of lists of lengths n and m we have, for instance, a potential function of the form $\sum_{0 \le i+j \le k} q_{ij} \binom{n}{i}\binom{m}{j}$ which can be described by the coefficients q_{ij}. But we also want to describe potential functions that refer to the sizes of different lists inside a list of lists, etc. That is why we need to describe a set of indexes $I(A)$ that enumerate the basic resource polynomials p_i and the corresponding coefficients q_i for a data type A. These type annotations can be, in a straight forward way, automatically transformed into usual easily understood polynomials. This is done in our prototype to present the bounds to the user at the end of the analysis.

Names For Base Polynomials To assign a unique name to each base polynomial we define the *index set* $I(A)$ to denote resource polynomials for a given data type A. Interestingly, but as we find coincidentally, $I(A)$ is essentially the meaning of A with every atomic type replaced by *unit*.

$$I(A) = \{*\} \text{ if } A \in \{\mathit{int}, \mathit{bool}, \mathit{unit}\}$$

$$I(A_1, A_2) = \{(i_1, i_2) \mid i_1 \in I(A_1) \text{ and } i_2 \in I(A_2)\}$$

$$I(L(B)) = I(T(B)) = \{[i_1, \ldots, i_k] \mid k \ge 0, i_j \in I(B)\}$$

The *degree* $\deg(i)$ of an index $i \in I(A)$ is defined as follows.

$$\deg(*) = 0$$

$$\deg(i_1, i_2) = \deg(i_1) + \deg(i_2)$$

$$\deg([i_1, \ldots, i_k]) = k + \deg(i_1) + \cdots + \deg(i_k)$$

Define $I_k(A) = \{i \in I(A) \mid \deg(i) \le k\}$. The indexes $i \in I_k(A)$ are an enumeration of the base polyonomials $p_i \in \mathcal{P}(A)$ of degree at most k. For each $i \in I(A)$, we define a base polynomial $p_i \in \mathcal{P}(A)$ as follows: If $A \in \{\mathit{int}, \mathit{bool}, \mathit{unit}\}$ then

$$p_*(v) = 1.$$

If $A = (A_1, A_2)$ is a pair type and $v = (v_1, v_2)$ then

$$p_{(i_1,i_2)}(v) = p_{i_1}(v_1) \cdot p_{i_2}(v_2)$$

If $A = D(B)$ (in our type system D is either lists or binary node-labelled trees) is a data structure and $\text{elems}(v) = [v_1, \ldots, v_n]$ then

$$p_{[i_1,\ldots,i_m]}(v) = \sum_{1 \le j_1 < \cdots < j_m \le n} p_{i_1}(v_{j_1}) \cdots p_{i_m}(v_{j_m})$$

We use the notation 0_A (or just 0) for the index in $I(A)$ such that $p_{0_A}(a) = 1$ for all a. We have $0_{\mathit{int}} = *$ and $0_{(A_1,A_2)} = (0_{A_1}, 0_{A_2})$ and $0_{D(B)} = []$. If $A = D(B)$ for B a data type then the index $[0, \ldots, 0] \in I(A)$ of length n is denoted by just n. We identify the index (i_1, i_2, i_3, i_4) with the index $(i_1, (i_2, (i_3, i_4)))$.

For a list $i = [i_1, \ldots, i_k]$ we write $i_0{::}i$ to denote the list $[i_0, i_1, \ldots, i_k]$. Furthermore, we write ii' for the concatenation of two lists i and i'.

Lemma 1 *If $p, p' \in \mathcal{R}(A)$ then $p+p', p \cdot p' \in \mathcal{R}(A)$, and $\deg(p+p') = \max\{\deg(p), \deg(p')\}$ and $\deg(p \cdot p') = \deg(p) + \deg(p')$.*

By linearity it suffices to show this lemma for base polynomials. This is done by induction on A.

Corollary 1 *For every $p \in \mathcal{R}(A, A)$ there exists $p' \in \mathcal{R}(A)$ with $\deg(p') = \deg(p)$ and $p'(a) = p(a, a)$ for all $a \in [\![A]\!]$.*

This follows directly from Lemma 1 noticing that base polynomials $p \in \mathcal{P}(A, A)$ take the form $p_i \cdot p_{i'}$.

Lemma 2 *Let $a \in [\![A]\!]$ and $\ell \in [\![L(A)]\!]$. Let $i_0, \ldots, i_k \in I(A)$ and $k \geq 0$. Then $p_{[i_0,i_1,\ldots,i_k]}([]) = 0$ and $p_{[i_0,i_1,\ldots,i_k]}(a::\ell) = p_{i_0}(a) \cdot p_{[i_1,\ldots,i_k]}(\ell) + p_0(a) \cdot p_{[i_0,i_1,\ldots,i_k]}(\ell)$.*

To prove this, one decomposes the sum in the definition of $p_{[i_0,i_1,\ldots,i_k]}(a::\ell)$ into two summands, one corresponding to the case where the first position j_1 equals one, thus hits a and where it is greater than one, thus a is not considered. Note that $p_0(a) = 1$; this factor is there to achieve the format of the resource polynomials for types like $(A, L(A))$.

Lemma 3 characterizes concatenations of lists (written as juxtaposition) as they will occur in the construction of tree-like data. Note that, e.g., elems(node(a, t_1, t_2)) = a::elems(t_1) elems(t_2).

Lemma 3 *Let $\ell_1, \ell_2 \in [\![L(A)]\!]$. Then $\ell_1\ell_2 \in [\![L(A)]\!]$ and $p_{[i_1,\ldots,i_k]}(\ell_1\ell_2) = \sum_{t=0}^{k} p_{[i_1,\ldots,i_t]}(\ell_1) \cdot p_{[i_{t+1},\ldots,i_k]}(\ell_2)$.*

This can be proved by induction on the length of ℓ_1 using Lemma 2 or else by a decomposition of the defining sum according to which indices hit the first list and which ones hit the second.

Annotated Types and Potential Functions We use the indexes and base polynomials to define type annotations and resource polynomials. We then give examples to illustrate the definitions.

A *type annotation* for a data type A is defined to be a family

$$Q_A = (q_i)_{i \in I(A)} \text{ with } q_i \in \mathbb{Q}_0^+$$

We say Q_A is of *degree (at most)* k if $q_i = 0$ for every $i \in I(A)$ with $deg(i) > k$. An *annotated data type* is a pair (A, Q_A) of a data type A and a type annotation Q_A of some degree k.

Let $\mathcal{H}$ be a heap and let v be a value with $\mathcal{H} \vDash v \mapsto a : A$ for a data type A. Then the type annotation Q_A defines the *potential*

$$\Phi_{\mathcal{H}}(v{:}(A, Q_A)) = \sum_{i \in I(A)} q_i \cdot p_i(a)$$

Usually we define type annotations Q_A by only stating the values of the non-zero coefficients q_i. However, it is sometimes handy to write annotations $(q_0, \ldots, q_n)$ for a list of atomic types just as a vector. Similarly, we write annotations $(q_0, q_{(1,0)}, q_{(0,1)}, q_{(1,1)}, \ldots)$ for pairs of lists of atomic types sometimes as a triangular matrix.

If $a \in [\![A]\!]$ and Q is a type annotation for A then we also write $\Phi(a : (A, Q))$ for $\sum_i q_i p_i(a)$.

Examples The simplest annotated types are those for atomic data types like integers. The indexes for *int* are $I(int) = \{*\}$ and thus each type annotation has the form (int, q_0) for a $q_0 \in \mathbb{Q}_0^+$. It defines the constant potential function $\Phi_{\mathcal{H}}(v{:}(int, q_0)) = q_0$. Similarly, tuples of atomic types feature a single index of the form $(*, \ldots, *)$ and a constant potential function defined by some $q_{(*,\ldots,*)} \in \mathbb{Q}_0^+$.

More interesting examples are lists of atomic types like, e.g., $L(int)$. The set of indexes of degree k is then $I_k(L(int)) = \{[], [*], [*, *], \ldots, [*, ..., *]\}$ where the last list contains k unit elements. Since we identify a list of i unit elements with the integer i we have $I_k(L(int)) = \{0, 1, \ldots, k\}$. Consequently, annotated types have the form $(L(int), (q_0, \ldots, q_k))$ for $q_i \in \mathbb{Q}_0^+$. The defined potential function is $\Phi([a_1, \ldots, a_n]{:}(L(int), (q_0, \ldots, q_n)) = \sum_{0 \leq i \leq k} q_i \binom{n}{i}$.

The next example is the type $(L(int), L(int))$ of pairs of integer lists. The set of indexes of degree k is $I_k(L(int), L(int)) = \{(i, j) \mid i + j \leq k\}$ if we identify lists of units with their lengths as usual. Annotated types are then of the from $((L(int), L(int)), Q)$ for a triangular $k \times k$ matrix Q with non-negative rational entries. If $\ell_1 = [a_1, \ldots, a_n]$, $\ell_2 = [b_1, \ldots, b_m]$ are two lists then the potential function is $\Phi((\ell_1, \ell_2), ((L(int), L(int)), (q_{(i,j)}))) = \sum_{0 \leq i+j \leq k} q_{(i,j)} \binom{n}{i}\binom{m}{j}$.

Finally, consider the type $A = L(L(int))$ of lists of lists of integers. The set of indexes of degree k is then $I_k(L(L(int))) = \{[i_1, \ldots, i_m] \mid m \leq k, i_j \in \mathbb{N}, \sum_{j=1,\ldots,m} i_j \leq k - m\} = \{0, \ldots, k\} \cup \{[1], \ldots, [k-1]\} \cup \{[0, 1], \ldots\} \cup \cdots$. Let $\ell = [[a_{11}, \ldots, a_{1m_1}], \ldots, [a_{n1}, \ldots, a_{nm_n}]]$ be a list of lists and $Q = (q_i)_{i \in I_k(L(L(int)))}$ be a corresponding type annotation. The defined potential function is then $\Phi(\ell, (L(L(int)), Q)) =$

$$\sum_{[i_1,\ldots,i_l] \in I_k(A)} \sum_{1 \leq j_1 < \cdots < j_l \leq n} q_{[i_1,\ldots,i_l]} \binom{m_{j_1}}{i_1} \cdots \binom{m_{j_l}}{i_l}$$

In practice the potential functions are usually not very complex since most of the q_i are zero. Note that the resource polynomials for binary trees are identical to those for lists.

The Potential of a Context For use in the type system we need to extend the definition of resource polynomials to typing contexts. We treat a context like a tuple type.

Let $\Gamma = x_1{:}A_1, \ldots, x_n{:}A_n$ be a typing context and let $k \in \mathbb{N}$. The index set $I_k(\Gamma)$ is defined through

$$I_k(\Gamma) = \{(i_1, \ldots, i_n) \mid i_j \in I_{m_j}(A_j), \sum_{j=1,\ldots,n} m_j \leq k\}.$$

A *type annotation* Q of degree k for Γ is a family

$$Q = (q_i)_{i \in I_k(\Gamma)} \text{ with } q_i \in \mathbb{Q}_0^+.$$

We denote a *resource-annotated context* with $\Gamma; Q$. Let $\mathcal{H}$ be a heap and $\mathcal{V}$ be a stack with $\mathcal{H} \vDash \mathcal{V} : \Gamma$ where $\mathcal{H} \vDash \mathcal{V}(x_j) \mapsto a_{x_j} : \Gamma(x_j)$. The potential of $\Gamma; Q$ with respect to $\mathcal{H}$ and $\mathcal{V}$ is

$$\Phi_{\mathcal{V},\mathcal{H}}(\Gamma; Q) = \sum_{(i_1,\ldots,i_n) \in I_k(\Gamma)} q_{\vec{\imath}} \prod_{j=1}^{n} p_{i_j}(a_{x_j})$$

In particular, if $\Gamma = \emptyset$ then $I_k(\Gamma) = \{()\}$ and $\Phi_{\mathcal{V},\mathcal{H}}(\Gamma; q_{()}) = q_{()}$. We sometimes also write q_0 for $q_{()}$.

6. Type Rules

If $f : [\![A]\!] \to [\![B]\!]$ is a function computed by some program and $K(a)$ is the cost of the evaluation of $f(a)$ then our type system will essentially try to identify resource polynomials $p \in \mathcal{R}(A)$ and $\bar{p} \in \mathcal{R}(B)$ such that $p(a) \geq \bar{p}(f(a)) + K(a)$. The key aspect of such amortized cost accounting is that it interacts well with composition.

Proposition 1 *Let $p \in \mathcal{R}(A)$, $\check{p} \in \mathcal{R}(B)$, $\bar{p} \in \mathcal{R}(C)$, $f : [\![A]\!] \to [\![B]\!]$, $g : [\![B]\!] \to [\![C]\!]$, $K_1 : [\![A]\!] \to \mathbb{Q}$, and $K_2 : [\![B]\!] \to \mathbb{Q}$. If $p(a) \geq \check{p}(f(a)) + K_1(a)$ and $\check{p}(b) \geq \bar{p}(g(b)) + K_2(b)$ for all a, b, c then $p(a) \geq \bar{p}(g(f(a))) + K_1(a) + K_2(f(a))$ for all a.*

Notice that if we merely had $p(a) \geq K_1(a)$ and $\check{p}(b) \geq K_2(b)$ then no bound could be directly obtained for the composition.

Interaction with parallel composition, i.e., $(a, c) \mapsto (f(a), c)$, is more complex due to the presence of mixed multiplicative terms in the resource polynomials.

Proposition 2 *Let $p \in \mathcal{R}(A, C)$, $\bar{p} \in \mathcal{R}(B, C)$, $f : [\![A]\!] \to [\![B]\!]$, and $K : [\![A]\!] \to \mathbb{Q}$. For each $j \in I(C)$ let $p^{(j)} \in \mathcal{R}(A)$ and $\bar{p}^{(j)} \in \mathcal{R}(B)$ be such that $p(a, c) = \sum_j p^{(j)}(a) p_j(c)$ and $\bar{p}(b, c) = \sum_j \bar{p}^{(j)}(b) p_j(c)$.*

If $p^{(0)}(a) \geq \bar{p}^{(0)}(f(a)) + K(a)$ and $p^{(j)}(a) \geq \bar{p}^{(j)}(f(a))$ holds for all a and $j \neq 0$ then $p(a, c) \geq \bar{p}(f(a), c) + K(a)$.

In fact, the situation is more complicated due to our accounting for high watermarks as opposed to merely additive cost, and also due to the fact that functions are recursively defined and may be partial. Furthermore, we have to deal with contexts and not merely types. To gain an intuition for the development to come, the above simplified view should, however, prove helpful.

Type Judgments The declarative type rules for RAML expressions (see Fig. 2) define a *resource-annotated typing judgment* of the form $\Sigma; \Gamma; Q \vdash e : (A, Q')$ where e is a RAML expression, Σ is a resource-annotated signature (see below), $\Gamma; Q$ is a resource-annotated context and (A, Q') is a resource-annotated data type. The intended meaning of this judgment is that if there are more than $\Phi(\Gamma; Q)$ resource units available then this is sufficient to evaluate e. In addition, there are more than $\Phi(v{:}(A, Q'))$ resource units left if e evaluates to a value v.

Programs with Annotated Types *Resource-annotated first-order types* have the form $(A, Q) \to (B, Q')$ for annotated data types (A, Q) and (B, Q'). A *resource-annotated signature* Σ is a finite, partial mapping of function identifiers to *sets of* resource-annotated first-order types.

A RAML program with resource-annotated types consists of a resource-annotated signature Σ and a family of expressions with variables identifiers $(e_f, y_f)_{f \in \mathrm{dom}(\Sigma)}$ such that $\Sigma; y_f{:}A; Q \vdash e_f : (B, Q')$ for every function type $(A, Q) \to (B, Q') \in \Sigma(f)$.

Notations Families that describe type and context annotations are denoted with upper case letters $Q, P, R, \ldots$ with optional superscripts. We use the convention that the elements of the families are the corresponding lower case letters with corresponding superscripts, i.e., $Q = (q_i)_{i \in I}$, $Q' = (q'_i)_{i \in I}$, and $Q^x = (q^x_i)_{i \in I}$.

Let Q, Q' be two annotations with the same index set I. We write $Q \leq Q'$ if $q_i \leq q'_i$ for every $i \in I$. For $K \in \mathbb{Q}$ we write $Q = Q' + K$ to state that $q_{\vec{0}} = q'_{\vec{0}} + K \geq 0$ and $q_i = q'_i$ for $i \neq \vec{0} \in I$. Let $\Gamma = \Gamma_1, \Gamma_2$ be a context, let $i = (i_1, \ldots, i_k) \in I(\Gamma_1)$ and $j = (j_1, \ldots, j_l) \in I(\Gamma_2)$. We write (i, j) to denote the index $(i_1, \ldots, i_k, j_1, \ldots, j_l) \in I(\Gamma)$.

We write $\Sigma; \Gamma; Q \overset{\mathrm{cf}}{\vdash} e : (A, Q')$ to refer to cost-free type judgments where all constants K in the rules from Fig. 2 are zero. We use it to assign potential to an extended context in the let rule. More explanations will follow later.

Let Q be an annotation for a context Γ_1, Γ_2. For $j \in I(\Gamma_2)$ we define the *projection* $\pi^{\Gamma_1}_j(Q)$ of Q to Γ_1 to be the annotation Q' with $q'_i = q_{(i,j)}$. The essential properties of the projections are stated by Propositions 2 and 3; they show how the analysis of juxtaposed functions can be broken down to individual components.

Proposition 3 *Let $\Gamma, x{:}A; Q$ be an annot. context, $\mathcal{H} \vDash \mathcal{V} : \Gamma, x{:}A$, and $\mathcal{H} \vDash \mathcal{V}(x) \mapsto a : A$. Then it is true that $\Phi_{\mathcal{V},\mathcal{H}}(\Gamma, x{:}A; Q) = \sum_{j \in I(A)} \Phi_{\mathcal{V},\mathcal{H}}(\Gamma; \pi^{\Gamma}_j(Q)) \cdot p_j(a)$.*

Additive Shift A key notion in the type system is the *additive shift* that is used to assign potential to typing contexts that result from a pattern match or from the application of a constructor of an inductive data type. We first define the additive shift, then illustrate the definition with examples and finally state the soundness of the operation.

Let $\Gamma, y{:}L(A)$ be a context and let $Q = (q_i)_{i \in I(\Gamma, y:L(A))}$ be a context annotation of degree k. The *additive shift for lists* $\lhd_L(Q)$ of Q is an annotation $\lhd_L(Q) = (q'_i)_{i \in I(\Gamma, x:A, xs:L(A))}$ of degree k for a context $\Gamma, x{:}A, xs{:}L(A)$ that is defined through

$$q'_{(i,j,\ell)} = \begin{cases} q_{(i,j::\ell)} + q_{(i,\ell)} & j = 0 \\ q_{(i,j::\ell)} & j \neq 0 \end{cases}$$

Let $\Gamma, t{:}T(A)$ be a context and let $Q = (q_i)_{i \in I(\Gamma, t:T(A))}$ be a context annotation of degree k. The *additive shift for binary trees* $\lhd_T(Q)$ of Q is an annotation $\lhd_T(Q) = (q'_i)_{i \in I(\Gamma')}$ of degree k for a context $\Gamma' = \Gamma, x{:}A, xs_1{:}T(A), xs_2{:}T(A)$ that is defined by

$$q'_{(i,j,\ell_1,\ell_2)} = \begin{cases} q_{(i,j::\ell_1\ell_2)} + q_{(i,\ell_1\ell_2)} & j = 0 \\ q_{(i,j::\ell_1\ell_2)} & j \neq 0 \end{cases}$$

The definition of the additive shift is short but substantial. We begin by illustrating its effect in some example cases. To start with, consider a context $\ell{:}L(int)$ with a single integer list that features an annotation $(q_0, \ldots, q_k) = (q_{[]}, \ldots, q_{[0,\ldots,0]})$. The shift operation $\lhd_L$ for lists produces an annotation for a context of the form $x{:}int, xs{:}L(int)$, namely $\lhd_L(q_0, \ldots, q_k) = (q_{(0,0)}, \ldots, q_{(0,k)})$ such that $q_{(0,i)} = q_i + q_{i+1}$ for all $i < k$ and $q_{(0,k)} = q_k$. This is exactly the additive shift that we introduced in our previous work for the univariate system [16]. We use it in a context where ℓ points to a list of length $n+1$ and xs is the tail of ℓ. It reflects the fact that $\sum_{i=0,\ldots,k} q_i \binom{n+1}{i} = \sum_{i=0,\ldots,k-1} q_{i+1} \binom{n}{i} + \sum_{i=0,\ldots,k} q_i \binom{n}{i}$.

Now consider the annotated context $t{:}T(int); (q_0, \ldots, q_k)$ with a single variable t that points to a tree with $n+1$ nodes. The additive shift $\lhd_T$ produces an annotation for a context of the form $x{:}int, t_1{:}T(int), t_2{:}T(int)$. We have $\lhd_T(q_0, \ldots, q_k) = (q_{(0,i,j)})_{i+j \leq k}$ where $q_{(0,i,j)} = q_{i+j} + q_{i+j+1}$ if $i + j < k$ and $q_{(0,i,j)} = q_{i+j}$ if $i + j = k$. The intention is that t_1 and t_2 are the subtrees of t which have n_1 and n_2 nodes, respectively ($n_1 + n_2 = n$). The definition of the additive shift for trees incorporates the convolution $\binom{n+m}{k} = \sum_{i+j=k} \binom{n}{i}\binom{m}{j}$ for binomials. It is true that $\sum_{i=0,\ldots,k} q_i \binom{n+1}{i} = \sum_{i=0,\ldots,k-1} (q_i + q_{i+1}) \binom{n}{i} + q_k \binom{n}{k} = \sum_{i=0}^{k-1} \sum_{j_1+j_2=i} (q_i + q_{i+1}) \binom{n_1}{j_1}\binom{n_2}{j_2} + \sum_{j_1+j_2=k} q_i \binom{n_1}{j_1}\binom{n_2}{j_2}$.

As a last example consider the context $l_1{:}L(int), l_2{:}L(int); Q$ where $Q = (q_{(i,j)})_{i+j \leq k}$, l_1 is a list of length m, and l_2 is a list of length $n+1$. The additive shift results in an annotation for a context of the form $l_1{:}L(int), x{:}int, xs{:}L(int)$ and the intention is that xs is the tail of l_2, i.e., a list of length n. From the definition it follows that $\lhd_L(Q) = (q_{(i,0,j)})_{i+j \leq k}$ where $q_{(i,0,j)} = q_{(i,j)} + q_{(i,j+1)}$ if $i + j < k$ and $q_{(i,0,j)} = q_{(i,j)}$ if $i + j = k$. The soundness follows from the fact that for every $i \leq k$ it is true that $\sum_{j=1}^{k-i} q_{(i,j)} \binom{m}{i}\binom{n+1}{j} = \binom{m}{i}\big(\sum_{j=0}^{k-i-1} (q_{(i,j)} + q_{(i,j+1)})\binom{n}{i} + q_{(i,k-i)}\binom{n}{k}\big)$.

Lemmas 4 and 5 state the soundness of the shift operations.

Lemma 4 *Let $\Gamma, \ell{:}L(A); Q$ be an annotated context, $\mathcal{H} \vDash \mathcal{V} : \Gamma, \ell{:}L(A)$, $\mathcal{H}(\ell) = (v_1, \ell')$ and let $\mathcal{V}' = \mathcal{V}[x_h \mapsto v_1, x_t \mapsto \ell']$. Then $\mathcal{H} \vDash \mathcal{V}' : \Gamma, x_h{:}A, x_t{:}L(A)$ and $\Phi_{\mathcal{V},\mathcal{H}}(\Gamma, \ell{:}L(A); Q) = \Phi_{\mathcal{V}',\mathcal{H}}(\Gamma, x_h{:}A, x_t{:}L(A); \lhd_L(Q))$.*

This is a consequence of Lemma 2. One takes the linear combination of instances of its second equation and regroups the right hand side according to the base polynomials for the resulting context.

Lemma 5 *Let $\Gamma, t{:}T(A); Q$ be an annotated context, $\mathcal{H} \vDash \mathcal{V} : \Gamma, t{:}T(A)$, $\mathcal{H}(t) = (v_1, t_1, t_2)$, and $\mathcal{V}' = \mathcal{V}[x_0 \mapsto v_1, x_1 \mapsto t_1, x_2 \mapsto t_2]$. If $\Gamma' = \Gamma, x{:}A, x_1{:}T(A), x_2{:}T(A)$ then $\mathcal{H} \vDash \mathcal{V}' : \Gamma'$ and $\Phi_{\mathcal{V},\mathcal{H}}(\Gamma, t{:}T(A); Q) = \Phi_{\mathcal{V}',\mathcal{H}}(\Gamma'; \lhd_T(Q))$.*

We remember that the potential of a tree only depends on the list of nodes in pre-order. So, we can think of the context splitting as done in two steps. First the head is separated, as in Lemma 4, and then the list of remaining elements into two lists. Lemma 5 is then proved like the previous one by regrouping terms using Lemma 2 for the first separation and Lemma 3 for the second one.

Sharing Let $\Gamma, x_1{:}A, x_2{:}A; Q$ be an annotated context. The *sharing operation* $\curlyvee(Q)$ defines an annotation for a context of the form $\Gamma, x{:}A$. It is used when the potential is split between multiple occurrences of a variable. The following lemma shows that sharing is a linear operation that does not lead to any loss of potential.

Lemma 6 *Let A be a data type. Then there are non-negative rational numbers $c^{(i,j)}_k$ for $i, j, k \in I(A)$ and $\deg(k) \leq \deg(i, j)$ such that the following holds. For every context $\Gamma, x_1{:}A, x_2{:}A; Q$ and every $\mathcal{H}, \mathcal{V}$ with $\mathcal{H} \vDash \mathcal{V} : \Gamma, x{:}A$ it holds that $\Phi_{\mathcal{V},\mathcal{H}}(\Gamma, x{:}A; Q') = \Phi_{\mathcal{V}',\mathcal{H}}(\Gamma, x_1{:}A, x_2{:}A; Q)$ where $\mathcal{V}' = \mathcal{V}[x_1, x_2 \mapsto \mathcal{V}(x)]$ and $q'_{(\ell,k)} = \sum_{i,j \in I(A)} c^{(i,j)}_k q_{(\ell,i,j)}$.*

$$\frac{Q = Q' + K^{\text{var}}}{x{:}A; Q \vdash x : (A, Q')}\;(\text{T:VAR}) \qquad \frac{q_0 = K^{\text{unit}} \quad q'_0 = 0}{\emptyset; Q \vdash () : (\mathit{unit}, Q')}\;(\text{T:CONSTU}) \qquad \frac{n \in \mathbb{Z} \quad q_0 = K^{\text{int}} \quad q'_0 = 0}{\emptyset; Q \vdash n : (\mathit{int}, Q')}\;(\text{T:CONSTI})$$

$$\frac{b \in \{\mathit{True}, \mathit{False}\} \quad q_0 = K^{\text{bool}} \quad q'_0 = 0}{\emptyset; Q \vdash b : (\mathit{bool}, Q')}\;(\text{T:CONSTB}) \qquad \frac{op \in \{+, -, *, \mathit{mod}, \mathit{div}\} \quad q_{(0,0)} = K^{op} \quad q'_0 = 0}{x_1{:}\mathit{int}, x_2{:}\mathit{int}; Q \vdash x_1\ op\ x_2 : (\mathit{int}, Q')}\;(\text{T:OPINT})$$

$$\frac{P + K_1^{\text{app}} = Q \quad P' = Q' + K_2^{\text{app}} \quad (A, P) \to (A', P') \in \Sigma(f)}{x{:}A; Q \vdash f(x) : (A', Q')}\;(\text{T:APP}) \qquad \frac{op \in \{\mathit{or}, \mathit{and}\} \quad q_{(0,0)} = K^{op} \quad q'_0 = 0}{x_1{:}\mathit{bool}, x_2{:}\mathit{bool}; Q \vdash x_1\ op\ x_2 : (\mathit{bool}, Q')}\;(\text{T:OPBOOL})$$

$$\frac{\begin{array}{c}\Gamma_1; P \vdash e_1 : (A, P') \quad \Gamma_2, x{:}A; R \vdash e_2 : (B, R') \quad P + K_1^{\text{let}} = \pi_{\vec{0}}^{\Gamma_1}(Q) \quad P' = \pi_{\vec{0}}^{x:A}(R) + K_2^{\text{let}} \quad R' = Q' + K_3^{\text{let}} \\ \forall \vec{0} \neq j \in I(\Gamma_2){:}\ \ \Gamma_1; P_j \overset{\text{cf}}{\vdash} e_1 : (A, P'_j) \quad P_j = \pi_j^{\Gamma_1}(Q) \quad P'_j = \pi_j^{x:A}(R)\end{array}}{\Gamma_1, \Gamma_2; Q \vdash \mathit{let}\ x = e_1\ \mathit{in}\ e_2 : (B, Q')}\;(\text{T:LET})$$

$$\frac{\begin{array}{c}\Gamma; P \vdash e_t : (A, P') \quad P + K_1^{\text{conT}} = \pi_0^{\Gamma}(Q) \quad P' = Q' + K_2^{\text{conT}} \\ \Gamma; R \vdash e_f : (A, R') \quad R + K_1^{\text{conF}} = \pi_0^{\Gamma}(Q) \quad R' = Q' + K_2^{\text{conF}}\end{array}}{\Gamma, x{:}\mathit{bool}; Q \vdash \mathit{if}\ x\ \mathit{then}\ e_t\ \mathit{else}\ e_f : (A, Q')}\;(\text{T:COND}) \qquad \frac{\begin{array}{c}\Gamma, x_1{:}A_1, x_2{:}A_2; P \vdash e : (B, P') \\ P + K_1^{\text{matP}} = Q \quad P' = Q' + K_2^{\text{matP}}\end{array}}{\Gamma, x{:}A; Q \vdash \mathit{match}\ x\ \mathit{with}\ (x_1, x_2) \to e : (B, Q')}\;(\text{T:MATP})$$

$$\frac{Q = Q' + K^{\text{pair}}}{x_1{:}A_1, x_2{:}A_2; Q \vdash (x_1, x_2) : ((A_1, A_2), Q')}\;(\text{T:PAIR}) \qquad \frac{q_0 = K^{\text{nil}} \quad q'_{\vec{0}} = 0}{\emptyset; Q \vdash \mathit{nil} : (L(A), Q')}\;(\text{T:NIL}) \qquad \frac{q_0 = K^{\text{leaf}} \quad q'_{\vec{0}} = 0}{\emptyset; Q \vdash \mathit{leaf} : (T(A), Q')}\;(\text{T:LEAF})$$

$$\frac{Q = \lhd_L(Q') + K^{\text{cons}}}{x_h{:}A, x_t{:}L(A); Q \vdash \mathit{cons}(x_h, x_t) : (L(A), Q')}\;(\text{T:CONS}) \qquad \frac{Q = \lhd_T(Q') + K^{\text{node}}}{x_0{:}A, x_1{:}T(A), x_2{:}T(A); Q \vdash \mathit{node}(x_0, x_1, x_2) : (T(A), Q')}\;(\text{T:NODE})$$

$$\frac{\begin{array}{c}\Gamma; R \vdash e_1 : (B, R') \quad R + K_1^{\text{matN}} = \pi_0^{\Gamma}(Q) \\ R' = Q' + K_2^{\text{matN}} \quad \Gamma, x_h{:}A, x_t{:}L(A); P \vdash e_2 : (B, P') \quad P + K_1^{\text{matC}} = \lhd_L(Q) \quad P' = Q' + K_2^{\text{matC}}\end{array}}{\Gamma, x{:}L(A); Q \vdash \mathit{match}\ x\ \mathit{with}\ \mid \mathit{nil} \to e_1 \mid \mathit{cons}(x_h, x_t) \to e_2 : (B, Q')}\;(\text{T:MATL})$$

$$\frac{\begin{array}{c}\Gamma; R \vdash e_1 : (B, R') \quad R + K_1^{\text{matTL}} = \pi_0^{\Gamma}(Q) \\ R' = Q' + K_2^{\text{matTL}} \quad \Gamma, x_0{:}A, x_1{:}T(A), x_2{:}T(A); P \vdash e_2 : (B, P') \quad P + K_1^{\text{matTN}} = \lhd_T(Q) \quad P' = Q' + K_2^{\text{matTN}}\end{array}}{\Gamma, x{:}T(A); Q \vdash \mathit{match}\ x\ \mathit{with}\ \mid \mathit{leaf} \to e_1 \mid \mathit{node}(x_0, x_1, x_2) \to e_2 : (B, Q')}\;(\text{T:MATT})$$

$$\frac{\Gamma, x{:}A, y{:}A; P \vdash e : (B, Q') \quad Q = \curlyvee(P)}{\Gamma, z{:}A; Q \vdash e[z/x, z/y] : (B, Q')}\;(\text{T:SHARE}) \qquad \frac{\Gamma; P \vdash e : (B, P') \quad Q \geq P \quad Q' \leq P'}{\Gamma; Q \vdash e : (B, Q')}\;(\text{T:WEAKEN})$$

$$\frac{\Gamma; P \vdash e : (B, P') \quad Q = P + c \quad Q' = P' + c}{\Gamma; Q \vdash e : (B, Q')}\;(\text{T:OFFSET}) \qquad \frac{\Gamma; P \vdash e : (B, P') \quad \forall i \in I(\Gamma){:}\ \ p_i = q_{(i,0)}}{\Gamma, x{:}A; Q \vdash e : (B, Q')}\;(\text{T:AUGMENT})$$

Figure 2. Type rules for annotated types.

Lemma 6 is a consequence of Corollary 1. Moreover, the coefficients $c_k^{(i,j)}$ can be computed effectively and are *natural* numbers. For a context $\Gamma, x_1{:}A, x_2{:}A; Q$ we define $\curlyvee(Q)$ to be the Q' from Lemma 6.

Type Rules Fig. 2 shows the annotated type rules for RAML expressions. We assume a fixed global signature Σ that we omit from the rules. The last four rules are structural rules that apply to every expression. The other rules are syntax-driven and there is one rule for every construct of the syntax. In the implementation we incorporated the structural rules in the syntax-driven ones. The most interesting rules are explained below.

T:SHARE has to be applied to expressions that contain a variable twice (z in the rule). The sharing operation $\curlyvee(P)$ transfers the annotation P for the context $\Gamma, x{:}A, y{:}A$ into an annotation Q for the context $\Gamma, z{:}A$ without loss of potential (Lemma 6). This is crucial for the accuracy of the analysis since instances of T:SHARE are quite frequent in typical examples. The remaining rules are affine linear in the sense that they assume that every variable occurs at most once.

T:CONS assigns potential to a lengthened list. The additive shift $\lhd_L(Q')$ transforms the annotation Q' for a list type into an annotation for the context $x_h{:}A, x_t{:}L(A)$. Lemma 4 shows that potential is neither gained nor lost by this operation. The potential Q of the context has to pay for both the potential Q' of the resulting list and the resource cost K^{cons} for list cons.

T:MATL shows how to treat pattern matching of lists. The initial potential defined by the annotation Q of the context $\Gamma, x{:}L(A)$ has to be sufficient to pay the costs of the evaluation of e_1 or e_2 (depending on whether the matched list is empty or not) and the potential defined by the annotation Q' of the result type. To type the expression e_1 of the nil case we use the projection $\pi_0^{\Gamma}(Q)$ that results in an annotation for the context Γ. Since the matched list is empty in this case no potential is lost by the discount of the annotations $q_{(i,j)}$ of Q where $j \neq 0$. To type the expression e_2 of the cons case we rely on the shift operation $\lhd_L(Q)$ for lists that results in an annotation for the context $\Gamma, x_h{:}A, x_t{:}L(A)$. Again there is no loss of potential (see Lemma 4). The equalities relate the potential before and after the evaluation of e_1 or e_2, to the potential before the and after the evaluation of the match operation by incorporating the respective resource cost for the matching.

T:NODE and T:MATT are similar to the corresponding rules for lists but use the shift operator $\lhd_T$ for trees (see Lemma 5).

T:LET comprises essentially an application of Proposition 2 (with $f = e_1$ and $C = \Gamma_2$) followed by an application of Proposition 1 (with f being the parallel composition of e_1 and the identity on Γ_2 and g being e_2). Of course, the rigorous soundness proof takes into account partiality and additional constant costs for dispatching a let. It is part of the inductive soundness proof for the entire type system (Theorem 1).

The derivation of the type judgment $\Gamma_1, \Gamma_2; Q \vdash \mathit{let}\, x = e_1\, \mathit{in}\, e_2 : (B, Q')$ can be explained in two steps. The first starts with the derivation of the judgment $\Gamma_1; P \vdash e_1 : (A, P')$ for the sub-expression e_1. The annotation P corresponds to the potential that is exclusively attached to Γ_1 by the annotation Q plus some resource cost for the *let*, namely $P = \pi_{\vec{0}}^{\Gamma_1}(Q) + K_1^{\text{let}}$. Now we derive the judgment $\Gamma_2, x{:}A; R \vdash e_2 : (B, R')$. The potential that is assigned by R to $x{:}A$ is the potential that resulted from the judgment for e_1 plus some cost that might occur when binding the variable x to the value of e_1, namely $P' = \pi_{\vec{0}}^{x:A}(R) + K_2^{\text{let}}$. The potential that is assigned by R to Γ_2 is essentially the potential that is assigned by to Γ_2 by Q, namely $\pi_{\vec{0}}^{\Gamma_2}(Q) = \pi_0^{\Gamma_2}(R)$. The second step of the derivation is to relate the annotations in R that refer to mixed potential between $x{:}A$ and Γ_2 to the annotations in Q that refer to potential that is mixed between Γ_1 and Γ_2. To this end we remember that we can derive from a judgment $\Gamma_1; S \vdash e_1 : (A, S')$ that $\Phi(\Gamma_1; S) \geq \Phi(v{:}(A, S'))$ if e_1 evaluates to v. This inequality remains valid if multiplied with a potential for $\phi_{\Gamma_2} = \Phi(\Gamma_2; T)$, i.e., $\Phi(\Gamma_1; S) \cdot \phi_{\Gamma_2} \geq \Phi(v{:}(A, S')) \cdot \phi_{\Gamma_2}$. To relate the mixed potential annotations we thus derive a cost-free judgment $\Gamma_1; P_j \stackrel{\text{cf}}{\vdash} e_1 : (A, P_j')$ for every $\vec{0} \neq j \in I(\Gamma_2)$. (We use cost-free judgments to avoid paying multiple times for the evaluation of e_1.) Then we equate P_j to the corresponding annotations in Q and equate P_j' to the corresponding annotations in R, i.e., $P_j = \pi_j^{\Gamma_1}(Q)$ and $P_j' = \pi_j^{x:A}(R)$. The intuition is that j corresponds to ϕ_{Γ_2}. Note that we use a fresh signature Σ in the derivation of each cost-free judgment for e_1.

Soundness The main theorem of this paper states that type derivations establish correct bounds: an annotated type judgment for an expression e shows that if e evaluates to a value v in a well-formed environment then the initial potential of the context is an upper bound on the watermark of the resource usage and the difference between initial and final potential is an upper bound on the consumed resources.

Note that it is possible to prove that the bounds also hold for non-terminating evaluations as we did for the univariate system [17] in a companion paper (see the discussion in §3).

Theorem 1 (Soundness) *Let* $\mathcal{H} \vDash \mathcal{V}{:}\Gamma$ *and* $\Sigma; \Gamma; Q \vdash e{:}(A, Q')$. *If* $\mathcal{V}, \mathcal{H} \vdash e \rightsquigarrow v, \mathcal{H}' \mid (p, p')$ *then* $p \leq \Phi_{\mathcal{V},\mathcal{H}}(\Gamma; Q)$ *and* $p - p' \leq \Phi_{\mathcal{V},\mathcal{H}}(\Gamma; Q) - \Phi_{\mathcal{H}'}(v{:}(A, Q'))$.

Theorem 1 is proved by a nested induction on the derivation of the evaluation judgment $\mathcal{V}, \mathcal{H} \vdash e \rightsquigarrow v, \mathcal{H}' \mid (p, p')$ and the type judgment $\Gamma; Q \vdash e{:}(A, Q')$. The inner induction on the type judgment is needed because of the structural rules. There is one proof for all possible instantiations of the resource constants. It is technically involved but conceptually unsurprising. Compared to earlier works [16], further complexity arises from the new rich potential annotations. It is mainly dealt with in Lemmas 4, 5, and 6 and the concept of projections as explained in Propositions 2 and 3.

7. Type Inference and Experiments

Type Inference The type-inference algorithm for RAML extends the algorithm that we have developed for the univariate polynomial system [17]. It is not complete with respect to the type rules in §6 but it works well for the example programs we tested.

Its basis is a classic type inference generating simple linear constraints for the annotations that are collected during the inference, and that can be solved later by linear programming. In order to obtain a finite set of constraints one has to provide a maximal degree of the resource bounds. If the degree is too low then the generated linear program is unsolvable. The maximal degree can either be specified by the user or can be incremented successively after an unsuccessful analysis.

A main challenge in the inference is the handling of resource-polymorphic recursion which we believe to be of very high complexity if not undecidable in general. To deal with it practically, we employ a heuristic that has been developed for the univariate system.

In a nutshell, a function is allowed to invoke itself recursively with a type different from the one that is being justified (polymorphic recursion) provided that the two types differ only in lower-degree terms. In this way, one can successively derive polymorphic type schemes for higher and higher degrees; for details, see [17]. The generalisation of this approach to the multivariate setting poses no extra difficulties.

The number of multivariate polynomials our type system takes into account (e.g., $nm, n\binom{m}{2}, n\binom{m}{3}, m\binom{n}{2}, m\binom{n}{3}, \binom{n}{2}\binom{m}{2}$ for a pair of integer lists if the max. degree is 4) grows exponentially in the maximal degree. Thus the number of inequalities we collect for a fixed program grows also exponentially in the given maximal degree. Moreover, one often has to analyze function applications context-sensitively with respect to the call stack. Recall, e.g., the expression *filter(a,filter(b,l))* from §2 where we had to use two different types for *filter*.

Experimental Evaluation In our prototype implementation we collapse the cycles in the call graph and analyze each function once for every path in the resulting graph. For larger programs this can lead to large linear constraint systems if the maximal degree is high. Sometimes they are infeasible for the LP solver[6] we use.

Our emphasis was on correctness of the prototype, not on performance. There certainly is room for improvement, either by tuning the configuration of the current LP solver[7] or by experimenting with alternative solvers. Further improvement is possible by finding a suitable heuristic that is in between the (maybe too) flexible method we use here and the inference for the univariate system that also works efficiently with high maximal degree for large programs. For example, we could set certain coefficients q_i to zero before even generating the constraints. Alternatively, we could limit the number of different types for each function.

However, we are satisfied with the performance of the prototype on the example programs that do not require high degrees. For instance, we successfully analyzed longer examples with up to degree 4 (multiplication of a list of matrices).

Table 1 shows a compilation of the computation of evaluation-step bounds for several example functions. All computed bounds are asymptotically tight. The run-time of the analysis varies from 0.02 to 1.96 seconds on an 3.6 GHz Intel Core 2 Duo iMac with 4 GB RAM depending on the needed degree and the complexity of the source program.

Our experiments show that the constant factors in the computed bounds are generally quite tight and even match the measured

[6] lp_solve version 5.5.0.1

[7] Currently, we use the standard configuration with no additional options.

Function	Computed Evaluation-Step Bound	Simplified Computed Bound	Act. Behav.	Run Time
isortlist:$L(L(int))\to L(L(int))$	$\sum_{1\leq i<j\leq n} 16m_i+16\binom{n}{2}+12n+3$	$8n^2m+8n^2-8nm+4n+3$	$O(n^2m)$	0.91 s
nub:$L(L(int))\to L(L(int))$	$\sum_{1\leq i<j\leq n} 12m_i+18\binom{n}{2}+12n+3$	$6n^2m+9n^2-6nm+3n+3$	$O(n^2m)$	0.97 s
transpose:$L(L(int))\to L(L(int))$	$\sum_{1\leq i\leq n} 32m_i+2n+13$	$32nm+2n+13$	$O(nm)$	0.04 s
mmult:$(L(L(int)))^2\to L(L(int))$	$(\sum_{1\leq i\leq x} y_i)(32+28n)+14n+2x+21$	$28xyn+32xy+2x+14n+21$	$O(nxy)$	1.96 s
dyade:$(L(int),L(int))\to L(L(int))$	$10nx+14n+3$	$10nx+14n+3$	$O(nx)$	0.03 s
lcs:$(L(int),L(int))\to int$	$39nx+6x+21n+19$	$39nx+6x+21n+19$	$O(nx)$	0.36 s
subtrees:$T(int)\to L(T(int))$	$8\binom{n}{2}+23n+3$	$4n^2+19n+3$	$O(n^2)$	0.06 s
eratos:$L(int)\to L(int)$	$16\binom{n}{2}+12n+3$	$8n^2+4n+3$	$O(n^2)$	0.02 s

Table 1. The computed evaluation-step bounds, the actual worst-case time behavior, and the run time of the analysis in seconds. All computed bounds are asymptotically tight and the constant factors are close to the worst-case behavior. In the bounds n is the size of the first argument, m_i are the sizes of the elements of the first argument, x is the size of the second argument, y_i are the sizes of the elements of the second argument, $m = \max_{1\leq i\leq n} m_i$, and $y = \max_{1\leq i\leq x} y_i$.

worst-case running times of many functions. The univariate analysis [16, 17] infers identical bounds for the functions *subtrees* and *eratos*. In contrast, it can infer bounds for the other functions only after manual source-code transformations. Even then, the resulting bounds are not asymptotically tight.

We present the experimental evaluation of two functions below. The source code and the experimental validation for the other examples is available online[8]. It is also possible to download the source code of the prototype and to analyze user generated examples directly on the web.

Example 1: Lexicographic Sorting of Lists of Lists The following RAML code implements the well-known sorting algorithm insertion sort that lexicographically sorts lists of lists. To lexicographically compare two lists one needs linear time in length of the shorter one. Since insertion sort does quadratic many comparisons in the worst-case it has a running time of $O(n^2m)$ if n is the length of the outer list and m is the maximal length of the inner lists.

```
leq (l1,l2) = match l1 with | nil -> true
  | (x::xs) -> match l2 with | nil -> false
      | (y::ys) -> (x<y) or ((x == y) and leq (xs,ys));


insert (x,l) = match l with | nil -> [x]
               | (y::ys) -> if leq(x,y) then x::y::ys
                            else y::insert(x,ys);

isortlist l = match l with | nil -> nil
               | (x::xs) -> insert (x,isortlist xs);
```

Below is the analysis' output for the function *isortlist* when instantiated to bound the number of needed evaluation steps. The computation needs less then a second on typical desktop computers.

```
isortlist: L(L(int)) --> L(L(int))
Positive annotations of the argument
0     --> 3.0           2     --> 16.0
1     --> 12.0          [1,0] --> 16.0

The number of evaluation steps consumed by isortlist
is at most: 8.0*n^2*m + 8.0*n^2 - 8.0*n*m + 4.0*n + 3.0
where
  n is the length of the input
  m is the length of the elements of the input
```

The more precise bound implicit in the positive annotations of the argument is presented in mathematical notation in Table 1.

[8] http://raml.tcs.ifi.lmu.de

We manually identified inputs for which the worst-case behavior of *isortlist* emerges (namely reversely sorted lists with similar inner lists). Then we measured the needed evaluation steps and compared the results to our computed bound. Fig. 3 shows a plot of this comparison. Our experiments indicate that the computed bound exactly matches the actual worst-case behavior.

Example 2: Longest Common Subsequence An example of dynamic programming that can be found in many textbooks is the computation of (the length of) the longest common subsequence (LCS) of two given lists (sequences). If the sequences $a_1,\ldots,a_n$ and $b_1,\ldots,b_m$ are given then an $n\times m$ matrix (here a list of lists) A is successively filled such that $A(i,j)$ contains the length of the LCS of $a_1,\ldots,a_i$ and $b_1,\ldots,b_j$. The following recursion is used in the computation.

$$A(i,j)=\begin{cases} 0 & \text{if } i=0 \text{ or } j=0 \\ A(i-1,j-1)+1 & \text{if } i,j>0 \text{ and } a_i=b_j \\ \max(A(i,j-1),A(i-1,j)) & \text{if } i,j>0 \text{ and } a_i\neq b_j \end{cases}$$

The run time of the algorithm is thus $O(nm)$. Below is the RAML implementation of the algorithm.

```
lcs(l1,l2) = let m = lcstable(l1,l2) in
    match m with | nil -> 0
      | (l1::_) -> match l1 with | nil -> 0
                     | (len::_) -> len;

lcstable (l1,l2) = match l1 with | nil -> [firstline l2]
      | (x::xs) -> let m = lcstable (xs,l2) in
              match m with | nil -> nil
                | (l::ls) -> (newline (x,l,l2))::l::ls;

newline (y,lastline,l) = match l with | nil -> nil
  | (x::xs) -> match lastline with | nil -> nil
      | (belowVal::lastline') ->
          let nl = newline(y,lastline',xs) in
          let rightVal = right nl in
          let diagVal = right lastline' in
          let elem = if x == y then diagVal+1
                     else max(belowVal,rightVal)
          in elem::nl;

firstline(l) = match l with | nil -> nil
               | (x::xs) -> 0::firstline xs;

right l = match l with | nil -> 0 | (x::xs) -> x;
```

The analysis of the program takes less then a second on a usual desktop computer and produces the following output for the function *lcs*.

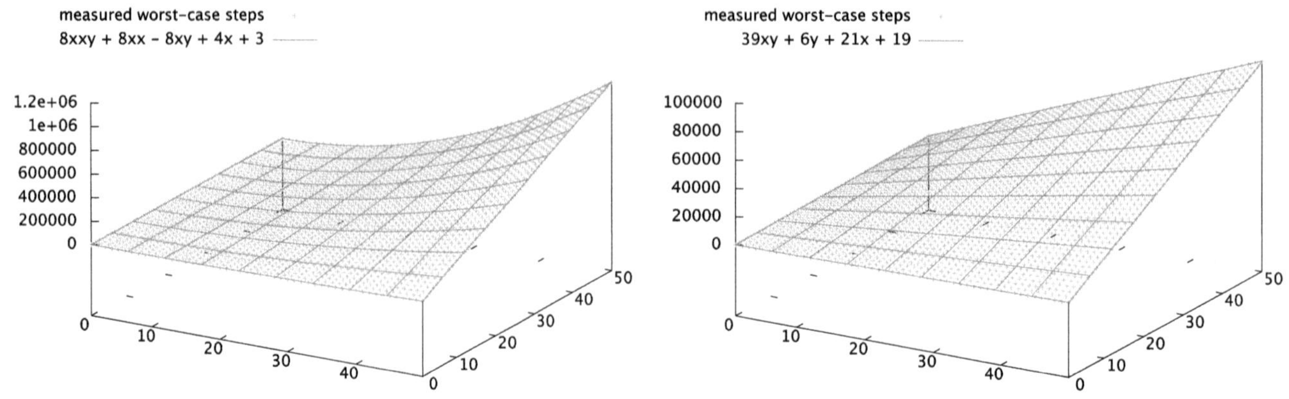

Figure 3. The computed evaluation-step bound (lines) compared to the actual worst-case number of evaluation-steps for sample inputs of various sizes (crosses) used by *isortlist* (on the left) and *lcs* (on the right).

```
lcs: (L(int),L(int)) --> int
Positive annotations of the argument
(0,0) --> 19.0        (1,0) --> 21.0
(0,1) --> 6.0         (1,1) --> 39.0

The number of evaluation steps consumed by lcs is at
most:       39.0*m*n + 6.0*m + 21.0*n + 19.0
where
    n is the length of the first component of the input
    m is the length of the second component of the input
```

Fig. 3 shows that the computed bound is close to the measured number of evaluation steps needed. In the case of *lcs* the run time exclusively depends on the lengths of the input lists.

8. Related Work

Most closely related is the previous work on automatic amortized analysis [17, 16, 18, 19, 20, 23, 24] (see §1). This paper describes the first system that can compute multivariate polynomial bounds.

Other resource analyses that can in principle obtain polynomial bounds are approaches based on recurrences pioneered by Grobauer [12] and Flajolet [11]. In those systems, an a priori unknown resource bounding function is introduced for each function in the code; by a straightforward intraprocedural analysis a set of recurrence equations or inequalities for these functions is then derived. Even for relatively simple programs the resulting recurrences are quite complicated and difficult to solve with standard methods.

In the COSTA project [1, 2, 3] progress has been made with the solution of those recurrences. In an automatic complexity analysis for higher-order Nuprl terms Benzinger uses Mathematica to solve the generated recurrence equations [5]. The size measures used in these approaches (like the length of the longest path in the input data) are less precise for nested data structures than our resource polynomials which comprise the sizes of all inner data structures. As a result, our method can deal with compositions of functions more accurately and is able to express a wider range of relations between parts of the input. We also find that amortization yields better results in cases where resource usage of intermediate functions depends on factors other than input size, e.g., sizes of partitions in quick sort.

A successful method to estimate time bounds for C++ procedures with loops and recursion was recently developed by Gulwani et al. [15, 13] in the SPEED project. They annotate programs with counters and use automatic invariant discovery between their values using off-the-shelf program analysis tools which are based on abstract interpretation. A recent innovation for non-recursive programs is the combination of disjunctive invariant generation via abstract interpretation with proof rules that employ SMT-solvers [14]. In contrast to our method, these techniques can not fully automatically analyze iterations over data structures. Instead, the user needs to define numerical "quantitative functions". This seems to be less modular for nested data structures where the user needs to specify an "owner predicate" for inner data structures. It is also unclear if quantitative functions can represent complex mixed bounds such as $\sum_{1\leq i<j\leq n}(10m_i+2m_j)+16\binom{n}{2}+12n+3$ for *isortlist*. Moreover, our method infers tight bounds for functions such as insertion sort that admit a worst-case time usage of the form $\sum_{1\leq i\leq n} i$. In contrast, [15] indicates that a nested loop on $1 \leq i \leq n$ and $1 \leq j \leq i$ is over-approximated with the bound n^2.

A methodological difference to techniques based on abstract interpretation is that we infer (using linear programming) an abstract potential function which indirectly yields a resource-bounding function. The potential-based approach may be favorable in the presence of compositions and data scattered over different locations (partitions in quick sort). As any type system, our approach is naturally compositional and lends itself to the smooth integration of components whose implementation is not available. Moreover, type derivations can be seen as certificates and can be automatically translated into formalized proofs in program logic [6]. On the other hand, our method does not model the interaction of integer arithmetic with resource usage.

Other related works use type systems to validate resource bounds. Crary and Weirich [9] presented a (monomorphic) type system capable of specifying and certifying resource consumption. Danielsson [10] provided a library, based on dependent types and manual cost annotations, that can be used for complexity analyses of purely functional data structures and algorithms. In contrast, our focus is on the inference of bounds.

Another related approach is the use of sized types [22, 21, 8] which provide a general framework to represent the size of the data in its type. Sized types are a very important concept and we also employ them indirectly. Our method adds a certain amount of data dependency and dispenses with the explicit manipulation of symbolic expressions in favour of numerical potential annotations.

Polynomial resource bounds have also been studied in [25] that addresses the derivation of polynomial size bounds for functions whose exact growth rate is polynomial. Besides this strong restriction, the efficiency of inference remains unclear.

9. Conclusion and Directions for Future Work

We have introduced a quantitative amortized analysis for first-order functions with multiple arguments. For the first time, we have been able to fully automatically derive complex multivariate resource bounds for recursive functions on nested inductive data structures such as lists and trees. Our experiments have shown that the analysis is sufficiently efficient for the functions we have tested, and that the resulting bounds are not only asymptotically tight but are also surprisingly precise in terms of constant factors.

The system we have developed will be the basis of various future projects. A challenging unsolved problem we are interested in is the computation of precise heap-space bounds in the presence of automatic memory management.

We have first ideas for extending the type system to derive bounds that contain not only polynomial but also involve logarithmic and exponential functions. The extension of linear amortized analysis to polymorphic and higher-order programs [24] seems to be compatible with our system and it would be interesting to integrate it. Finally, we plan to investigate to what extent our multivariate amortized analysis can be used for programs with cyclic data structures (following [19, 20, 4]) and recursion (including loops) on integers. For the latter it might be beneficial to merge the amortized method with successful existing techniques on abstract interpretation [15, 3].

Another very interesting and rewarding piece of future work would be an adaptation of our method to imperative languages without built-in inductive types such as C. One could try to employ pattern-based discovery of inductive data structures as is done, e.g., in separation logic.

References

[1] E. Albert, P. Arenas, S. Genaim, G. Puebla, and D. Zanardini. Cost Analysis of Java Bytecode. In *16th Euro. Symp. on Prog. (ESOP'07)*, pages 157–172, 2007.

[2] E. Albert, P. Arenas, S. Genaim, and G. Puebla. Automatic Inference of Upper Bounds for Recurrence Relations in Cost Analysis. In *15th Static Analysis Symp. (SAS'08)*, pages 221–237, 2008.

[3] E. Albert, P. Arenas, S. Genaim, M. Gómez-Zamalloa, G. Puebla, D. Ramírez, G. Román, and D. Zanardini. Termination and Cost Analysis with COSTA and its User Interfaces. *Electr. Notes Theor. Comput. Sci.*, 258(1):109–121, 2009.

[4] R. Atkey. Amortised Resource Analysis with Separation Logic. In *19th Euro. Symp. on Prog. (ESOP'10)*, pages 85–103, 2010.

[5] R. Benzinger. Automated Higher Order Complexity Analysis. *Theor. Comput. Sci.*, 318(1-2):79–103, 2004.

[6] L. Beringer, M. Hofmann, A. Momigliano, and O. Shkaravska. Automatic Certification of Heap Consumption. In *Log. f. Prog., AI, and Reas., 11th Conf. (LPAR'04)*, pages 347–362, 2004.

[7] B. Campbell. Amortised Memory Analysis using the Depth of Data Structures. In *18th Euro. Symp. on Prog. (ESOP'09)*, pages 190–204, 2009.

[8] W.-N. Chin and S.-C. Khoo. Calculating Sized Types. *High.-Ord. and Symb. Comp.*, 14(2-3):261–300, 2001.

[9] K. Crary and S. Weirich. Resource Bound Certification. In *27th ACM Symp. on Principles of Prog. Langs. (POPL'00)*, pages 184–198, 2000.

[10] N. A. Danielsson. Lightweight Semiformal Time Complexity Analysis for Purely Functional Data Structures. In *35th ACM Symp. on Principles Prog. Langs. (POPL'08)*, pages 133–144, 2008.

[11] P. Flajolet, B. Salvy, and P. Zimmermann. Automatic Average-case Analysis of Algorithms. *Theoret. Comput. Sci.*, 79(1):37–109, 1991.

[12] B. Grobauer. Cost Recurrences for DML Programs. In *6th Int. Conf. on Funct. Prog. (ICFP'01)*, pages 253–264, 2001.

[13] B. S. Gulavani and S. Gulwani. A Numerical Abstract Domain Based on Expression Abstraction and Max Operator with Application in Timing Analysis. In *Comp. Aid. Verification, 20th Int. Conf. (CAV '08)*, pages 370–384, 2008.

[14] S. Gulwani and F. Zuleger. The Reachability-Bound Problem. In *Conf. on Prog. Lang. Design and Impl. (PLDI'10)*, pages 292–304, 2010.

[15] S. Gulwani, K. K. Mehra, and T. M. Chilimbi. SPEED: Precise and Efficient Static Estimation of Program Computational Complexity. In *36th ACM Symp. on Principles of Prog. Langs. (POPL'09)*, pages 127–139, 2009.

[16] J. Hoffmann and M. Hofmann. Amortized Resource Analysis with Polynomial Potential. In *19th Euro. Symp. on Prog. (ESOP'10)*, pages 287–306, 2010.

[17] J. Hoffmann and M. Hofmann. Amortized Resource Analysis with Polymorphic Recursion and Partial Big-Step Operational Semantics. In *8th Asian Symp. on Prog. Langs. (APLAS'10)*, 2010. To appear.

[18] M. Hofmann and S. Jost. Static Prediction of Heap Space Usage for First-Order Functional Programs. In *30th ACM Symp. on Principles of Prog. Langs. (POPL'03)*, pages 185–197, 2003.

[19] M. Hofmann and S. Jost. Type-Based Amortised Heap-Space Analysis. In *15th Euro. Symp. on Prog. (ESOP'06)*, pages 22–37, 2006.

[20] M. Hofmann and D. Rodriguez. Efficient Type-Checking for Amortised Heap-Space Analysis. In *18th Conf. on Comp. Science Logic (CSL'09)*. LNCS, 2009.

[21] J. Hughes and L. Pareto. Recursion and Dynamic Data-structures in Bounded Space: Towards Embedded ML Programming. In *4th Int. Conf. on Funct. Prog. (ICFP'99)*, pages 70–81, 1999.

[22] J. Hughes, L. Pareto, and A. Sabry. Proving the Correctness of Reactive Systems Using Sized Types. In *23th ACM Symp. on Principles of Prog. Langs. (POPL'96)*, pages 410–423, 1996.

[23] S. Jost, H.-W. Loidl, K. Hammond, N. Scaife, and M. Hofmann. Carbon Credits for Resource-Bounded Computations using Amortised Analysis. In *16th Symp. on Form. Meth. (FM'09)*, pages 354–369, 2009.

[24] S. Jost, K. Hammond, H.-W. Loidl, and M. Hofmann. Static Determination of Quantitative Resource Usage for Higher-Order Programs. In *37th ACM Symp. on Principles of Prog. Langs. (POPL'10)*, pages 223–236, 2010.

[25] O. Shkaravska, R. van Kesteren, and M. C. van Eekelen. Polynomial Size Analysis of First-Order Functions. In *Typed Lambda Calc. Apps. (TLCA'07)*, pages 351–365, 2007.

[26] R. E. Tarjan. Amortized Computational Complexity. *SIAM J. Algebraic Discrete Methods*, 6(2):306–318, 1985.

[27] R. Wilhelm et al. The Worst-Case Execution-Time Problem — Overview of Methods and Survey of Tools. *ACM Trans. Embedded Comput. Syst.*, 7(3), 2008.

Symmetric Lenses

Martin Hofmann
Ludwig-Maximilians-Universität
München, Germany

Benjamin Pierce
University of Pennsylvania
Pennsylvania, USA

Daniel Wagner
University of Pennsylvania
Pennsylvania, USA

Abstract

Lenses—bidirectional transformations between pairs of connected structures—have been extensively studied and are beginning to find their way into industrial practice. However, some aspects of their foundations remain poorly understood. In particular, most previous work has focused on the special case of *asymmetric lenses*, where one of the structures is taken as primary and the other is thought of as a projection, or view. A few studies have considered symmetric variants, where each structure contains information not present in the other, but these all lack the basic operation of *composition*. Moreover, while many domain-specific languages based on lenses have been designed, lenses have not been thoroughly explored from an algebraic perspective.

We offer two contributions to the theory of lenses. First, we present a new symmetric formulation, based on *complements*, an old idea from the database literature. This formulation generalizes the familiar structure of asymmetric lenses, and it admits a good notion of composition. Second, we explore the algebraic structure of the space of symmetric lenses. We present generalizations of a number of known constructions on asymmetric lenses and settle some longstanding questions about their properties—in particular, we prove the existence of (symmetric monoidal) tensor products and sums and the *non*-existence of full categorical products or sums in the category of symmetric lenses. We then show how the methods of universal algebra can be applied to build *iterator lenses* for structured data such as lists and trees, yielding lenses for operations like mapping, filtering, and concatenation from first principles. Finally, we investigate an even more general technique for constructing mapping combinators, based on the theory of *containers*.

Categories and Subject Descriptors D.3.2 [*Programming Languages*]: Language Classifications—Specialized application languages

General Terms Design, Languages, Theory

Keywords lens, view-update, algebra, category theory

1. Introduction

The electronic world is rife with partially synchronized data—replicated structures that are not identical but share some common parts, and where the shared parts need to be kept up to date as the structures change. Examples include databases and materialized views, in-memory and on-disk representations of heap structures, connected components of user interfaces, and models representing different aspects of the same software system.

In current practice, the propagation of changes between connected structures is mostly handled by *ad hoc* methods. Given a pair of structures X and Y, we write one transformation that maps changes to X into changes to Y and a separate transformation that maps Y changes to X changes. However, when the structures involved are complex, managing such pairs of transformations manually can be a maintenance nightmare.

This has led to a burgeoning interest in *bidirectional programming languages*, in which every expression denotes a related pair of transformations. A great variety of bidirectional languages have been proposed (see [8, 13] for recent surveys), and these ideas are beginning to see commercial application, e.g., in RedHat's system administration tool, Augeas [21].

One particularly well-studied class of bidirectional programming languages is the framework of *lenses* [11]. Prior work on lenses and lens-like structures has mostly been carried out in specific domains—designing combinators for lenses that work over strings [5, 7, 12], trees [11, 17, 20, 25], relations [6], graphs [16], or software models [9, 10, 15, 26, 27, 31]. By contrast, our aim in this paper is to advance the *foundations* of lenses in two significant respects.

First, we show that lenses can be generalized from their usual asymmetric presentation—where one of the structures is always a "view" of the other—to a fully *symmetric* version where each of the two structures may contain information that is not present in the other (Section 2). This generalization is significantly more expressive than any previously known: although symmetric variants of lenses have been studied [10, 23, 28], they all lack a notion of sequential composition of lenses, a significant technical and practical limitation (see Section 10). As we will see, the extra structure that we need to support composition is nontrivial; in particular, constructions involving symmetric lenses need to be proved correct modulo a notion of *behavioral equivalence* (Section 3).

Second, we undertake a systematic investigation of the *algebraic structure* of the space of lenses, using the concepts of elementary category theory as guiding and organizing principles. (Our presentation is self contained, but some prior familiarity with basic concepts of category theory will be helpful. Most proofs are omitted for brevity; they can be found in a long version of the paper, available from the second author's web page.)

We begin this algebraic investigation with some simple generic constructions on symmetric lenses: composition, dualization, terminal lenses, simple bijections, etc. (Section 4). We then settle some basic questions about products and sums (Sections 5 and 6). In particular, it was previously known that asymmetric lenses admit constructions intuitively corresponding to pairing and projection [7] and another construction that is intuitively like a sum [11].

POPL'11, January 26–28, 2011, Austin, Texas, USA.

However, these constructions were not very well understood; in particular, it was not known whether the pairing and projection operations formed a full categorical product, while the injection arrows from X to $X + Y$ and from Y to $X + Y$ were not definable at all in the asymmetric setting. We prove that the category of symmetric lenses does *not* have full categorical products or sums, but does have "symmetric monoidal" structures with many of the useful properties of products and sums.

Next, we consider how to build lenses over more complex data structures such as lists and trees (Section 7). We first observe that the standard construction of algebraic datatypes can be lifted straightforwardly from the category of sets to the category of lenses. For example, from the definition of lists as the least solution of the equation $L(X) \simeq \mathit{Unit} + X \times L(X)$ we obtain a lens connecting the set $L(X)$ with the set $\mathit{Unit} + X \times L(X)$; the two directions of this lens correspond to the *unfold* and *fold* operations on lists. Moreover, the familiar notion of *initial algebra* also generalizes to lenses, giving us powerful iterators that allow for a modular definition of many symmetric lenses on lists and trees—e.g., mapping a symmetric lens over a list, filtering, reversing, concatenating, and translating between lists and trees.

Finally, we briefly investigate an even more general technique for constructing "mapping lenses" that apply the action of a given sublens to all the elements of some data structure (Section 8). This technique applies not only to algebraic data structures but to an arbitrary *container* in the sense of Abbot, Altenkirch, and Ghani [2]. This extends the variety of list and tree mapping combinators that we can construct from first principles to include non-inductive datatypes such as labeled dags and graphs.

We carry out these investigations in the richer space of symmetric lenses, but many of the results and techniques should also apply to the special case of asymmetric lenses. Indeed, we can show (Section 9) that asymmetric lenses form a subcategory of symmetric ones in a natural way: every asymmetric lens can be embedded in a symmetric lens, and many of the algebraic operators on symmetric lenses specialize to known constructions on asymmetric lenses. Conversely, a symmetric lens can be factored into a "back to back" assembly of two asymmetric ones.

Sections 10 and 11 discuss related and future work.

2. Fundamental Definitions

Asymmetric Lenses To set the stage, let's review the standard definition of asymmetric lenses. (Other definitions can be given, featuring weaker or stronger laws, but this version is widely accepted. We discuss variants in Section 10.) Suppose X is some set of source structures (say, the possible states of a database) and Y a set of target structures (views of the database). An asymmetric lens from X to Y has two components:

$$\begin{aligned} get &\in X \to Y \\ put &\in Y \times X \to X \end{aligned}$$

The get component is the forward transformation, a total function from X to Y. The put component takes an old X and a modified Y and yields a correspondingly modified X. These components must obey two "round-tripping" laws for every $x \in X$ and $y \in Y$:

$$put\ (get\ x)\ x = x \qquad \text{(GETPUT)}$$

$$get\ (put\ y\ x) = y \qquad \text{(PUTGET)}$$

It is also useful to be able to create an element of x given just an element of y, with no "original x" to put it into; in order to handle this in a uniform way, each lens is also equipped with a function $create \in Y \to X$, and we assume one more axiom:

$$get\ (create\ y) = y \qquad \text{(CREATEGET)}$$

Complements The key step toward symmetric lenses is the notion of *complements*. The idea dates back to a famous paper in the database literature on the view update problem [4] and was adapted to lenses in [5] (and, for a slightly different definition, [22]), and it is quite simple. If we think of the get component of a lens as a sort of projection function, then we can find another projection from X into some set C that keeps all the information discarded by get. Equivalently, we can think of get as returning two results—an element of Y and an element of C—that together contain all the information needed to reconstitute the original element of X. Now the put function doesn't need a whole $x \in X$ to recombine with some updated $y \in Y$; it can just take the complement $c \in C$ generated from x by the get, since this will contain all the information that is missing from y. Moreover, instead of a separate $create$ function, we can simply pick a distinguished element $missing \in C$ and define $create(y)$ as $put(y, missing)$.

Formally, an *asymmetric lens with complement* mapping between X and Y consists of a set C, a distinguished element $missing \in C$, and two functions

$$\begin{aligned} get &\in X \to Y \times C \\ put &\in Y \times C \to X \end{aligned}$$

obeying the following laws for every $x \in X$, $y \in Y$, and $c \in C$:[1]

$$\frac{get\ x = (y, c)}{put\ (y, c) = x} \qquad \text{(GETPUT)}$$

$$\frac{get\ (put\ (y, c)) = (b', c')}{b' = y} \qquad \text{(PUTGET)}$$

Note that the type is just "lens from X to Y": the set C is an internal component, not part of the externally visible type. In symbols, $Lens(X, Y) = \exists C.\ \{missing : C,\ get : X \to Y \times C,\ put : Y \times C \to X\}$.

Symmetric Lenses Now we can symmetrize. First, instead of having only get return a complement, we make put return a complement too, and we take this complement as a second argument to get. So we have $get \in X \times C_Y \to Y \times C_X$ and $put \in Y \times C_X \to X \times C_Y$. Intuitively, C_X is the "information from X that is discarded by get," and C_Y is the "information from Y that is discarded by put." Next we observe that we can, without loss of generality, use the same set C as the complement in both directions. So now we have $get \in X \times C \to Y \times C$ and $put \in Y \times C \to X \times C$. Intuitively, we can think of the combined complement C as $C_X \times C_Y$—that is, each complement contains some "private information from X" and some "private information from Y"; by convention, the get function reads the C_Y part and writes the C_X part, while the put reads the C_X part and writes the C_Y part. Lastly, now that everything is symmetric, the get/put distinction is not helpful, so we rename the functions to $putr$ and $putl$. This brings us to our core definition.

2.1 Definition [Symmetric lens]: A lens ℓ from X to Y (written $\ell \in X \leftrightarrow Y$) has three parts: a set of complements C, a distinguished element $missing \in C$, and two functions

$$\begin{aligned} putr &\in X \times C \to Y \times C \\ putl &\in Y \times C \to X \times C \end{aligned}$$

satisfying the following round-tripping laws:

[1] We can convert back and forth between the two presentations; in particular, if $(get, put, create)$ are the components of a traditional lens, then we define a canonical complement by $C = \{f \in Y \to X \mid \forall y.\ get(f(y)) = y\}$. We then define the components $missing'$, get', and put' of an asymmetric lens with complement as $missing' = create$ and $get'(x) = (get(x), \lambda y.put(y, x))$ and $put'(y, f) = f(y)$.

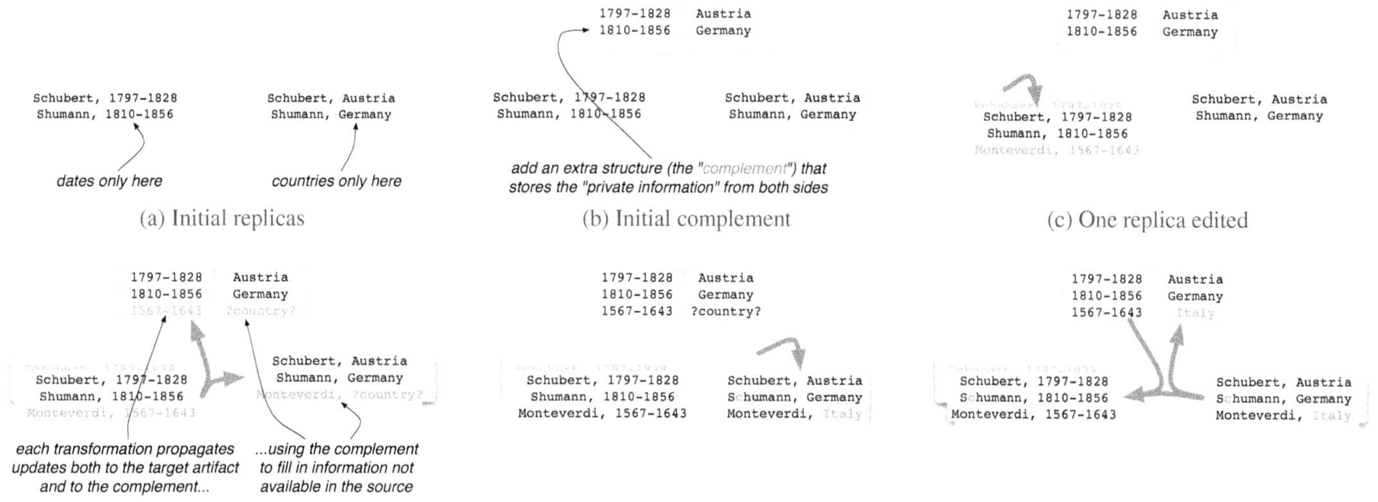

(a) Initial replicas (b) Initial complement (c) One replica edited

(d) Propagating the edit (e) Second replica is edited (f) This change is propagated

Figure 1. Behavior of a symmetric lens

$$\frac{putr(x,c) = (y,c')}{putl(y,c') = (x,c')} \qquad \text{(PUTRL)}$$

$$\frac{putl(y,c) = (x,c')}{putr(x,c') = (y,c')} \qquad \text{(PUTLR)}$$

When several lenses are under discussion, we use record notation to identify their parts, writing $\ell.C$ for the complement set of ℓ, etc.

The force of the PUTRL and PUTLR laws is to establish some "consistent" or "steady-state" triples (x, y, c), for which *puts* of x from the left or y from the right will have no effect—that is, will not change the complement. The conclusion of each rule has the same variable c' on both sides of the equation to reflect this. We will use the equation $putr(x, c) = (y, c)$ to characterize the steady states. In general, a *put* of a new x' from the left entails finding a y' and a c' that restore consistency. Additionally, we often wish this process to involve the complement c from the previous steady state; as a result, it can be delicate to choose a good value of *missing*. This value can often be chosen compositionally; each of our primitive lenses and lens combinators specify one good choice for *missing*.

One can imagine other laws. In particular, the long version of the paper considers symmetric forms of the asymmetric "PUTPUT" laws, which specify that two *put* operations in a row should have the same effect as the second one alone. As with asymmetric lenses, these laws appear too strong to be desirable in practice.

Examples Figure 1 illustrates the use of a symmetric lens. The structures in this example are lists of textual records describing composers. The partially synchronized records (a) have a name and two dates on the left and a name and a country on the right. The complement (b) contains all the information that is discarded by both *puts*—all the dates from the left-hand structure and all the countries from the right-hand structure. (It can be viewed as a pair of lists of strings, or equivalently as a list of pairs of strings; the way we build list lenses later actually corresponds to the latter.) If we add a new record to the left hand structure (c) and use the *putr* operation to propagate it through the lens (d), we copy the shared information (the new name) directly from left to right, store the private information (the new dates) in the complement, and use a default string to fill in both the private information on the right and the corresponding right-hand part of the complement. If we now update the right-hand structure to fill in the missing information and correct a typo in one of the other names (e), then a *putl* operation will propagate the edited country to the complement, propagate the edited name to the other structure, and use the complement to restore the dates for all three composers.

Viewed more abstractly, the connection between the information about a single composer in the two tables is a lens from $X \times Y$ to $Y \times Z$, with complement $X \times Z$—let's call it e. Its *putr* component is given (x, y) as input and has (x', z) in its complement; it constructs a new complement by replacing x' by x to form (x, z), and it constructs its output by pairing the y from its input and the z from its complement to form (y, z). The *putl* component does the opposite, replacing the z part of the complement and retrieving the x part. Then the top-level lens in Figure 1—let's call it $e^\star$—abstractly has type $(X \times Y)^\star \leftrightarrow (Y \times Z)^\star$ and can be thought of as the "lifting" of e from elements to lists.

There are several plausible implementations of $e^\star$, with slightly different behaviors when list elements are added and removed—i.e., when the input and complement arguments to *putr* or *putl* are lists of different lengths. One possibility is to take $e^\star.C = (e.C)^\star$ and maintain the invariant that the complement list in the output is the same length as the input list. When the lists in the input have different lengths, we can restore the invariant by either truncating the complement list or padding it with $e.missing$. For example, taking $X = \{a, b, c, \ldots\}$, $Y = \{1, 2, 3, \ldots\}$, $Z = \{A, B, C, \ldots\}$, and $e.missing = (m, M)$, and writing $\langle a, b, c\rangle$ for the sequence with the three elements a, b, and c, we could have:

$$\begin{aligned} & putr(\langle(a,1)\rangle\,,\ \langle(p,P),(q,Q)\rangle) \\ = \ & putr(\langle(a,1)\rangle\,,\ \langle(p,P)\rangle) \qquad \text{(truncating)} \\ = \ & (\langle(1,P)\rangle\,,\ \langle(a,P)\rangle) \end{aligned}$$

$$\begin{aligned} & putr(\langle(a,1),(b,2)\rangle\,,\ \langle(a,P)\rangle) \\ = \ & putr(\langle(a,1),(b,2)\rangle\,,\ \langle(a,P),(m,M)\rangle) \qquad \text{(padding)} \\ = \ & (\langle(1,P),(2,M)\rangle\,,\ \langle(a,P),(b,M)\rangle) \end{aligned}$$

Notice that, after the first *putr*, the information in the second element of the complement list (q, Q) is lost. The second *putr* creates a brand new second element for the list, so the value Q is gone forever; what's left is the default value M.

Another possibility—arguably better behaved—is to keep an *infinite* list of complements. Whenever we do a *put*, we use (and update) a prefix of the complement list of the same length as the current value being *put*, but we keep the infinite tail so that, later, we have values to use when the list being *put* is longer.

$$\begin{array}{rl} & putr(\langle(a,1)\rangle\,,\ \langle(p,P),(q,Q),(m,M),(m,M),\ldots\rangle) \\ = & (\langle(1,P)\rangle\,,\ \langle(a,P),(q,Q),(m,M),(m,M),\ldots\rangle) \\ & putr(\langle(a,1),(b,2)\rangle\,,\ \langle(a,P),(q,Q),(m,M),(m,M),\ldots\rangle) \\ = & (\langle(1,P),(2,Q)\rangle\,,\ \langle(a,P),(b,Q),(m,M),\ldots\rangle) \end{array}$$

We call the first form the *forgetful* list mapping lens and the second the *retentive* list mapping lens. We will see, later, that the difference between these two precisely boils down to a difference in the behavior of the lens-summing operator $\oplus$ in the specification $e^\star \simeq id_{Unit} \oplus (e \otimes e^\star)$ of the list mapping lens.

Figure 2 illustrates another use of symmetric lenses. The structures in this example are lists of categorized data; each name on the left is either a composer (tagged `inl`) or an author (tagged `inr`), and each name on the right is either a composer or an actor. The lens under consideration will synchronize just the composers between the two lists, leaving the authors untouched on the left and the actors untouched on the right. The synchronized state (a) shows a complement with two lists, each with holes for the composers. If we re-order the right-hand structure (b), the change in order will be reflected on the left by swapping the two composers. Adding another composer on the left (c) involves adding a new hole to each complement; on the left, the location of the hole is determined by the new list, and on the right it simply shows up at the end. Similarly, if we remove a composer (d), the final hole on the other side disappears.

Abstractly, to achieve this behavior we need to define a lens $comp$ between $(X+Y)^\star$ and $(X+Z)^\star$. To do this, it is convenient to first define a lens that connects $(X+Y)^\star$ and $X^\star \times Y^\star$; call this lens $partition$. The complement of the $partition$ is a list of booleans telling whether the corresponding element of the left list is an X or a Y. The $putr$ function is fairly simple: we separate the $(X+Y)$ list into X and Y lists by checking the tag of each element, and set the complement to exactly match the tags. For example:

$$putr(\langle \mathsf{inl}\ a, \mathsf{inl}\ b, \mathsf{inr}\ 1\rangle\,, c) = ((\langle a,b\rangle\,, \langle 1\rangle), \langle \mathsf{false}, \mathsf{false}, \mathsf{true}\rangle)$$
$$putr(\langle \mathsf{inl}\ a, \mathsf{inr}\ 1, \mathsf{inl}\ b\rangle\,, c) = ((\langle a,b\rangle\,, \langle 1\rangle), \langle \mathsf{false}, \mathsf{true}, \mathsf{false}\rangle)$$

These examples demonstrate that $putr$ ignores the complement entirely, fabricating a completely new one from its input. The $putl$ function, on the other hand, relies entirely on the complement for its ordering information. When there are extra entries (not accounted for by the complement), it adds them at the end. Consider taking the output of the second $putr$ above and adding c to the X list and 2 to the Y list:

$$\begin{array}{l} putl((\langle a,b,c\rangle\,, \langle 1,2\rangle), \langle \mathsf{false}, \mathsf{true}, \mathsf{false}\rangle) = \\ \quad (\langle \mathsf{inl}\ a, \mathsf{inr}\ 1, \mathsf{inl}\ b, \mathsf{inl}\ c, \mathsf{inr}\ 2\rangle\,, \\ \quad \langle \mathsf{false}, \mathsf{true}, \mathsf{false}, \mathsf{false}, \mathsf{true}\rangle) \end{array}$$

The $putl$ fills in as much of the beginning of the list as it can, using the complement to indicate whether to draw elements from $X^\star$ or from $Y^\star$. (How the remaining X and Y elements are interleaved is a free choice, not specified by the lens laws, since this case only arises when we are *not* in a round-tripping situation. The strategy shown here, where all new X entries precede all new Y entries, is just one possibility.)

Given $partition$, we can obtain $comp$ by composing three lenses in sequence: from $(X+Y)^\star$ we get to $X^\star \times Y^\star$ using $partition$, then to $X^\star \times Z^\star$ using a variant of the lens e discussed above, and finally to $(X+Z)^\star$ using a "backwards" $partition$.

Alignment One important *non*-goal of the present paper is dealing with the (important) issue of *alignment* [5, 7]. We consider only the simple case of lenses that work "positionally." For example, the lens $e^\star$ in the example will always use e to propagate changes between the first element of x and the first element of y, between the second element of x and the second of y, and so on. This amounts to assuming that the lists are edited either by editing individual elements in place or by adding or deleting elements at the end of the list; if an actual edit inserts an element at the head of one of the lists, positional alignment will produce surprising (and probably distressing) results. We see two avenues for incorporating richer notions of alignment: either we can generalize the mechanisms of *matching lenses* [5] to the setting of symmetric lenses, or we can refine the whole framework of symmetric lenses with a notion of *delta propagation*; see Section 11.

3. Equivalence

Since each lens carries its own complement—and since this need not be the same as the complement of another lens with the same domain and codomain—we now need to define what it means for two lenses to be indistinguishable, in the sense that no user could ever tell the difference between them by observing just the X and Y parts of their outputs. We will use this relation pervasively in what follows: indeed, most of the laws we would like our constructions to validate—even things as basic as associativity of composition—will not hold "on the nose," but only up to equivalence.

3.1 Definition: Given X, Y, C_f, C_g and a relation $R \subset C_f \times C_g$, we say that functions $f \in X \times C_f \to Y \times C_f$ and $g \in X \times C_g \to Y \times C_g$ are *R-similar*, written $f \sim_R g$, if they take inputs with R-related complements to equal outputs with R-related complements:

$$\frac{(c_f, c_g) \in R \qquad f(x, c_f) = (y_f, c_f') \qquad g(x, c_g) = (y_g, c_g')}{y_f = y_g \wedge (c_f', c_g') \in R}$$

3.2 Definition [Lens equivalence]: Two lenses k and ℓ are *equivalent* (written $k \equiv \ell$) if there is a relation $R \in k.C \times \ell.C$ with

1. $(k.missing, \ell.missing) \in R$
2. $k.putr \sim_R \ell.putr$
3. $k.putl \sim_R \ell.putl$.

We write $X \Longleftrightarrow Y$ for the set of equivalence classes of lenses from X to Y. When ℓ is a lens, we write $[\ell]$ for the equivalence class of ℓ (that is, $\ell \in X \leftrightarrow Y$ iff $[\ell] \in X \Longleftrightarrow Y$). Where no confusion results, we abuse notation and drop these brackets, using ℓ for both a lens and its equivalence class.

We show in the long version that this definition of lens equivalence coincides with a more "observational" definition where two lenses are equivalent iff they always give the same sequence of outputs when presented with the same sequence of inputs, starting with a $missing$ complement.

4. Basic Constructions

With the basic definitions in hand, we can start defining lenses. We begin in this section with several relatively simple constructions.

4.1 Definition [Identity lens]: Let $Unit$ be a distinguished singleton set and $()$ its only element.

$$id_X \in X \leftrightarrow X$$

$$\begin{array}{lcl} C & = & Unit \\ missing & = & () \\ putr(x, ()) & = & (x, ()) \\ putl(x, ()) & = & (x, ()) \end{array}$$

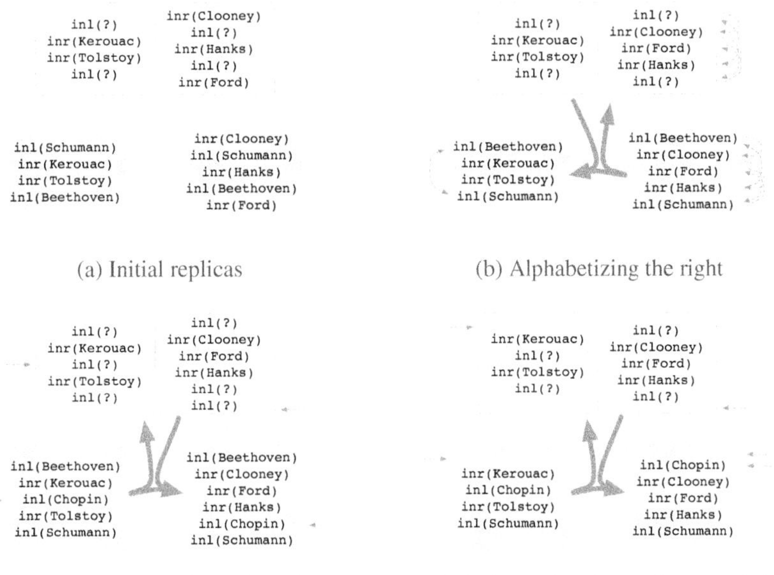

(a) Initial replicas

(b) Alphabetizing the right

(c) Inserting Chopin on the left

(d) Deleting Beethoven from the left

Figure 2. Synchronizing lists of sums

To check that this definition is well formed, we must show that the components defined in the lower box satisfy the round-trip laws implied by the upper box. This proof and analogous ones for later lens definitions are given in full in the long version.

4.2 Definition [Lens composition]:

$$\frac{k \in X \leftrightarrow Y \qquad \ell \in Y \leftrightarrow Z}{k;\ell \in X \leftrightarrow Z}$$

$$\begin{array}{lcl}
C & = & k.C \times \ell.C \\
missing & = & (k.missing, \ell.missing) \\
putr(x,(c_k,c_\ell)) & = & \text{let } (y,c_k') = k.putr(x,c_k) \text{ in} \\
 & & \text{let } (z,c_\ell') = \ell.putr(y,c_\ell) \text{ in} \\
 & & (z,(c_k',c_\ell')) \\
putl(z,(c_k,c_\ell)) & = & \text{let } (y,c_\ell') = \ell.putl(z,c_\ell) \text{ in} \\
 & & \text{let } (x,c_k') = k.putl(y,c_k) \text{ in} \\
 & & (x,(c_k',c_\ell'))
\end{array}$$

This definition specifies what it means to compose two lenses. To show that this definition lifts to equivalence classes of lenses, we need to check the following congruence property. We include the proof to give a taste of the technique; proofs of similar lemmas for the other operators on lenses defined below are deferred to the long version.

4.3 Lemma [Composition preserves equivalence]: If $k \equiv k'$ and $\ell \equiv \ell'$, then $k;\ell \equiv k';\ell'$.

4.4 Definition: The following function on relations is convenient here:

$$R_1 \times R_2 = \{((c_1,c_2),(c_1',c_2')) \mid (c_1,c_1') \in R_1 \wedge (c_2,c_2') \in R_2\}$$

Proof of 4.3: If the simulation R_k witnesses $k \equiv k'$ and R_ℓ witnesses $\ell \equiv \ell'$ then it is straightforward to verify that $R = R_k \times R_\ell$ witnesses $k;\ell \equiv k';\ell'$. There are three things to show.

1. We wish to show the first line:

$$\begin{array}{l}
(k;\ell).missing\ R\ (k';\ell').missing \\
\iff (k.missing, \ell.missing)\ R\ (k'.missing, \ell'.missing) \\
\iff k.missing\ R_k\ k'.missing \wedge \ell.missing\ R_\ell\ \ell'.missing
\end{array}$$

   But the final line is certainly true, since R_k and R_ℓ are simulation relations.
2. We must show that $(k;\ell).putr \sim_R (k';\ell').putr$. So take $c_k, c_\ell, c_{k'}, c_{\ell'}$ such that $(c_k,c_\ell)\ R\ (c_{k'},c_{\ell'})$ and choose an input x. Define the following:

$$\begin{array}{rcl}
(y,c_k') & = & k.putr(x,c_k) \\
(z,c_\ell') & = & \ell.putr(y,c_\ell) \\
(y',c_{k'}') & = & k'.putr(x,c_{k'}) \\
(z',c_{\ell'}') & = & \ell'.putr(y',c_{\ell'})
\end{array}$$

   We can then compute:

$$\begin{array}{rcl}
(k;\ell).putr(x,(c_k,c_\ell)) & = & (z,(c_k',c_\ell')) \\
(k';\ell').putr(x,(c_{k'},c_{\ell'})) & = & (z',(c_{k'}',c_{\ell'}'))
\end{array}$$

   We need to show that $z = z'$ and that $(c_k',c_\ell')\ R\ (c_{k'}',c_{\ell'}')$. Since $c_k\ R_k\ c_{k'}$, we can conclude that $y = y'$ and $c_k'\ R_k\ c_{k'}'$; similarly, since $c_\ell\ R_\ell\ c_{\ell'}$ and $y = y'$, we know that $z = z'$ (discharging one of our two proof burdens) and $c_\ell'\ R_\ell\ c_{\ell'}'$. Combining the above facts, we find that $(c_k',c_\ell')\ R\ (c_{k'}',c_{\ell'}')$ by definition of R (discharging the other proof burden).
3. The proof that $(k;\ell).putl \sim_R (k';\ell').putl$ is similar to the $putr$ case. □

4.5 Lemma [Associativity of composition]: $j;(k;\ell) \equiv (j;k);\ell$. (The equivalence is crucial here: $j;(k;\ell)$ and $(j;k);\ell$ are not the same lens because their complements are structured differently.)

4.6 Lemma [Identity arrows]: The identity lens is a left and right identity for composition: $id_X;\ell \equiv \ell; id_Y \equiv \ell$.

Thus symmetric lenses form a category, LENS, with sets as objects and equivalence classes of lenses as arrows. The identity arrow for a set X is $[id_X]$. Composition is $[k];[\ell] = [k;\ell]$.

4.7 Proposition [Bijective lenses]:

$$\frac{f \in X \to Y \qquad f \text{ bijective}}{bij_f \in X \leftrightarrow Y}$$

$$\begin{array}{lcl} C & = & Unit \\ missing & = & () \\ putr(x, ()) & = & (f(x), ()) \\ putl(y, ()) & = & (f^{-1}(y), ()) \end{array}$$

(If we were designing *syntax* for a bidirectional language, we might not want to include bij, since we would then need to offer programmers some notation for writing down bijections in such a way that we can verify that they *are* bijections and derive their inverses. However, even if it doesn't appear in the surface syntax, we will see several places where bij is useful in talking about the algebraic theory of symmetric lenses.)

This transformation (and several others we will see) respects much of the structure available in our category. Formally, bij is a functor. Recall that a *covariant* (respectively, *contravariant*) *functor* between categories $\mathcal{C}$ and $\mathcal{D}$ is a pair of maps—one from objects of $\mathcal{C}$ to objects of $\mathcal{D}$ and the other from arrows of $\mathcal{C}$ to arrows of $\mathcal{D}$—that preserve typing, identities, and composition:

- The image of any arrow $f : X \to Y$ in $\mathcal{C}$ has the type $F(f) : F(X) \to F(Y)$ (respectively, $F(f) : F(Y) \to F(X)$) in $\mathcal{D}$.
- For every object X in $\mathcal{C}$, we have $F(id_X) = id_{F(X)}$ in $\mathcal{D}$.
- If $f;g = h$ in $\mathcal{C}$, then $F(f); F(g) = F(h)$ (respectively, $F(g); F(f) = F(h)$) in $\mathcal{D}$.

Covariant functors are simply called functors. When it can be inferred from the arrow mapping, the object mapping is often elided.

4.8 Lemma: The bij operator forms a functor from the category ISO, whose objects are sets and whose arrows are isomorphic functions, to LENS—that is, $bij_{id_X} = id_X$ and $bij_f; bij_g = bij_{f;g}$.

4.9 Definition [Dual of a lens]:

$$\frac{\ell \in X \leftrightarrow Y}{\ell^{op} \in Y \leftrightarrow X}$$

$$\begin{array}{lcl} C & = & \ell.C \\ missing & = & \ell.missing \\ putr(y, c) & = & \ell.putl(y, c) \\ putl(x, c) & = & \ell.putr(x, c) \end{array}$$

It is easy to see that $(-)^{op}$ is involutive—that is, that $(\ell^{op})^{op} = \ell$ for every ℓ—and that $bij_{f^{-1}} = bij_f^{op}$ for any bijective f. Recalling that an endofunctor is a functor whose source and target categories are identical, we can easily show the following lemma.

4.10 Lemma: The $(-)^{op}$ operation can be lifted to a contravariant endofunctor on the category LENS, mapping each arrow $[\ell]$ to $[\ell^{op}]$.

4.11 Corollary: The category LENS is self dual, i.e., equivalent to its own opposite. (Note that this does not mean that each arrow is its own inverse!)

Proof: The arrow part of $(-)^{op}$ is bijective. □

The lenses we have discussed so far maintain all the information in the domain and codomain. It is sometimes useful to discard some information in one direction of the lens. The terminal lens does this, recording the discarded information in the complement so that the other direction of the lens can restore it.

4.12 Definition [Terminal lens]:

$$\frac{x \in X}{term_x \in X \leftrightarrow Unit}$$

$$\begin{array}{lcl} C & = & X \\ missing & = & x \\ putr(x', c) & = & ((), x') \\ putl((), c) & = & (c, c) \end{array}$$

4.13 Proposition [Uniqueness of terminal lens]: Lenses with the same type as a terminal lens are equivalent to a terminal lens. More precisely, suppose $k \in X \leftrightarrow Unit$ and $k.putl((), k.missing) = (x, c)$. Then $k \equiv term_x$.

Of course, there may be many (pairwise non-equivalent) terminal lenses of a particular type; for any two $x, y \in X$ with $x \neq y$, it's clear that $term_x \not\equiv term_y$. Proposition 4.13 tells us that there are exactly as many arrows $\ell : X \Longleftrightarrow Unit$ as there are elements of X.

4.14 Definition [Disconnect lens]:

$$\frac{x \in X \qquad y \in Y}{disconnect_{xy} \in X \leftrightarrow Y}$$

$$disconnect_{xy} \;=\; term_x; term_y^{op}$$

The disconnect lens does not synchronize its two sides at all. The complement, $disconnect.C$, is $X \times Y$; inputs are squirreled away into one side of the complement, and outputs are retrieved from the other side of the complement.

5. Products

A few additional notions from elementary category theory will be useful for giving us ideas about what sorts of properties to look for and for structuring the discussion of which of these properties hold and which fail for lenses.

The *categorical product* of two objects X and Y is an object $X \times Y$ and arrows $\pi_1 : X \times Y \to X$ and $\pi_2 : X \times Y \to Y$ such that for any two arrows $f : Z \to X$ and $g : Z \to Y$ there is a unique arrow $\langle f, g\rangle : Z \to X \times Y$—the *pairing* of f and g—satisfying $\langle f, g\rangle; \pi_1 = f$ and $\langle f, g\rangle; \pi_2 = g$. It is well known that, if a categorical product exists at all, it is unique up to isomorphism. If a category $\mathcal{C}$ has a product for each pair of objects, we say that $\mathcal{C}$ has products.

5.1 Theorem: LENS does not have products.

Proof idea: Suppose we have lenses $k \in Z \Longleftrightarrow X$ and $\ell \in Z \Longleftrightarrow Y$. Informally, the lens k includes a way to take any Z and choose a corresponding X and a way to take any X and find a corresponding Z. Many common categories with products include the former, but the latter is somewhat unique to lens categories, so we focus on the return trip here.

The lenses k and ℓ together mean we have a way to take any X and choose a corresponding Z, and we have a (separate) way to take any Y and choose a corresponding Z. Assume temporarily that the object part of the product of two objects is simply the Cartesian product. To complete the product, we must construct $\langle k, \ell\rangle \in Z \Longleftrightarrow X \times Y$, that is, we must find a way to take an X and a Y and choose a Z that corresponds to both simultaneously. But there may not be any such Z—the Z that k gives us from X may not be the same as the Z that ℓ gives us from Y.

To complete the proof, we simply choose X and Y carefully to rule out the possibility of a corresponding Z, regardless of whether we choose $X \times Y$ to be the Cartesian product or to be some other construction.

Proof: Uniqueness of pairing shows that there is exactly one lens from $Unit$ to $Unit \times Unit$ (whatever this may be). Combined with Prop. 4.13 this shows that $Unit \times Unit$ is a one-element set. Again by Prop. 4.13 this then means that lenses between $Unit \times Unit$ and any other set X are constant which leads to cardinality clashes once $|X| > 1$. (A more detailed proof appears in the full paper.) □

However, LENS *does* have a similar (but weaker) structure: a *tensor product*—i.e., an associative, two-argument functor. For any two objects X and Y, we have an object $X \otimes Y$, and for any two arrows $f : A \to X$ and $g : B \to Y$, an arrow $f \otimes g : A \otimes B \to X \otimes Y$ such that $(f_1; f_2) \otimes (g_1; g_2) = (f_1 \otimes g_1); (f_2 \otimes g_2)$ and $id_X \otimes id_Y = id_{X \otimes Y}$. Furthermore, for any three objects X, Y, Z there is a natural isomorphism $\alpha_{X,Y,Z} : (X \otimes Y) \otimes Z \to X \otimes (Y \otimes Z)$ satisfying certain coherence conditions (which specify that all ways of re-associating a quadruple are equal).

A categorical product is always a tensor product (by defining $f \otimes g = \langle \pi_1; f, \pi_2; g \rangle$), and conversely a tensor product is a categorical product if there are natural transformations $\pi_1, \pi_2, diag$

$$\begin{aligned} \pi_{1,X,Y} &\in X \otimes Y \to X \\ \pi_{2,X,Y} &\in X \otimes Y \to Y \\ diag_X &\in X \to X \otimes X \end{aligned}$$

such that (suppressing subscripts to reduce clutter)

$$(f \otimes g); \pi_1 = \pi_1; f \quad (1)$$
$$(f \otimes g); \pi_2 = \pi_2; g \quad (2)$$
$$diag; (f \otimes f) = f; diag \quad (3)$$
$$diag; \pi_1 = id \quad (4)$$
$$diag; \pi_2 = id \quad (5)$$
$$diag; (\pi_1 \otimes \pi_2) = id \quad (6)$$

for all arrows f and g. Building a categorical product from a tensor product is not the most familiar presentation, but it can be shown to be equivalent (see Proposition 13 in [3], for example).

In the category LENS, we can build a tensor product and can also build projection lenses with reasonable behaviors. However, these projections are not quite natural transformations—laws 1 and 2 above hold only with an additional indexing constraint for particular f and g. More seriously, while it seems we can define some reasonable natural transformations with the type of $diag$ (that is, arrows satisfying law 3), none of them satisfy the final three laws.

5.2 Definition [Tensor product lens]:

$$\frac{k \in X \leftrightarrow Z \qquad \ell \in Y \leftrightarrow W}{k \otimes \ell \in X \times Y \leftrightarrow Z \times W}$$

$$\begin{aligned} C &= k.C \times \ell.C \\ missing &= (k.missing, \ell.missing) \\ putr((x, y), (c_k, c_\ell)) &= \text{let } (z, c_k') = k.putr(x, c_k) \text{ in} \\ &\quad\ \text{let } (w, c_\ell') = \ell.putr(y, c_\ell) \text{ in} \\ &\quad\ ((z, w), (c_k', c_\ell')) \\ putl((z, w), (c_k, c_\ell)) &= \text{let } (x, c_k') = k.putl(z, c_k) \text{ in} \\ &\quad\ \text{let } (y, c_\ell') = \ell.putl(w, c_\ell) \text{ in} \\ &\quad\ ((x, y), (c_k', c_\ell')) \end{aligned}$$

The verification that this forms a lens is straightforward.

5.3 Lemma [Product bijection]: For bijections f and g,

$$bij_f \otimes bij_g \equiv bij_{f \times g}.$$

In fact, the particular tensor product defined above is very well behaved: it induces a *symmetric monoidal category*—i.e., a category with a unit object 1 and the following natural isomorphisms:

$$\begin{aligned} \alpha_{X,Y,Z} &: (X \otimes Y) \otimes Z \to X \otimes (Y \otimes Z) \\ \lambda_X &: 1 \otimes X \to X \\ \rho_X &: X \otimes 1 \to X \\ \gamma_{X,Y} &: X \otimes Y \to Y \otimes X \end{aligned}$$

These are known as the *associator*, *left-unitor*, *right-unitor*, and *symmetry*, respectively. In addition to the equations implied by these being natural isomorphisms, they must also satisfy some coherence conditions (given in the full version).

5.4 Proposition [LENS,$\otimes$ is a symmetric monoidal category]: In the category SET, the Cartesian product is a bifunctor with $Unit$ as unit, and gives rise to a symmetric monoidal category. Let $\alpha^\times, \lambda^\times, \rho^\times, \gamma^\times$ be associator, left-unitor, right-unitor, and symmetry natural isomorphisms. Then the $\otimes$ bifunctor also gives rise to a symmetric monoidal category of lenses, with $Unit$ as unit and $\alpha^\otimes = bij \circ \alpha^\times$, $\lambda^\otimes = bij \circ \lambda^\times$, $\rho^\otimes = bij \circ \rho^\times$, and $\gamma^\otimes = bij \circ \gamma^\times$ as associator, left-unitor, right-unitor, and symmetry, respectively.

Knowing that LENS is a symmetric monoidal category is useful for several reasons. First, it tells us that, even though it is not quite a full-blown product, the tensor construction is algebraically quite well behaved. Second, it justifies a convenient intuition where lenses built from multiple tensors are pictured as graphical "wiring diagrams," and suggests a possible syntax for lenses that shuffle product components (which we briefly discuss in Section 11).

5.5 Definition [Projection lenses]: In LENS, the projection is parametrized by an extra element to return when executing a $putl$ with a $missing$ complement.

$$\frac{y \in Y}{\pi_{1y} \in X \times Y \leftrightarrow X}$$

$$\pi_{1y} = (id_X \otimes term_y); \rho_X^\otimes$$

The other projection is defined similarly.

Returning to the example in the introduction, recall that we wish to create a lens $e : X \times Y \leftrightarrow Y \times Z$ with missing elements $m \in X$ and $M \in Z$. We now have the machinery necessary to construct this lens:

$$e = \pi_{2m} ; \pi_{1M}^{op}$$

The extra parameter to the projection (e.g. m or M above) needs to be chosen with some care. Some sets may have clear neutral elements; for example, a projection from $A \times B^\star \to A$ will likely use the empty list $\langle\rangle$ as its neutral element. Other projections may need additional domain knowledge to choose a good neutral element—for example, a projection $A \times \text{Country} \to A$ might use the country with the most customers as its default.

In some cases, the algebraic laws that one wants the projection to satisfy may guide the choice as well. The extra parameter prevents full naturality from holding, and therefore prevents this from being a categorical product, but the following "indexed" version of the naturality law does hold.

5.6 Lemma [Naturality of projections]: Suppose $k \in X_k \leftrightarrow Y_k$ and $\ell \in X_\ell \leftrightarrow Y_\ell$ and choose some initial value $y_i \in Y_\ell$. Define $(x_i, c_i) = \ell.putl(y_i, \ell.missing)$. Then $(k \otimes \ell); \pi_{1y_i} \equiv \pi_{1x_i}; k$.

The most serious problem, though, is that there is no diagonal. There are, of course, lenses with the *type* we need for *diag*—for example, *disconnect*. Or, more usefully, the lens that coalesces the copies of X whenever possible, preferring the left one when it cannot coalesce (this is essentially the *merge* lens from [11])

$$diag \in X \to X \times X$$

$$\begin{array}{lcl} C & = & \mathit{Unit} + X \\ \mathit{missing} & = & \mathsf{inl}\,() \\ \mathit{putr}(x, \mathsf{inl}\,()) & = & ((x,x), \mathsf{inl}\,()) \\ \mathit{putr}(x, \mathsf{inr}\,x') & = & ((x,x'), \mathit{eq}(x,x')) \\ \mathit{putl}((x,x'),c) & = & (x, \mathit{eq}(x,x')) \end{array}$$

where here the eq function tests its arguments for equality—$eq(x, x')$ yields $\mathsf{inl}\,()$ if $x = x'$ and yields x' if not. However, neither of these proposals satisfy all the required laws.

6. Sums and Lists

The status of sums has been even more mysterious than that of products. In particular, the *injection arrows* from A to $A + B$ and B to $A + B$ do not even make sense in the asymmetric setting; as functions, they are not surjective, so they cannot satisfy PUTGET.

A *categorical sum* of two objects X and Y is an object $X + Y$ and arrows $inl : X \to X + Y$ and $inr : Y \to X + Y$ such that for any two arrows $f : X \to Z$ and $g : Y \to Z$ there is a unique arrow $[f, g] : X + Y \to Z$—the *choice* of f or g—satisfying $inl; [f, g] = f$ and $inr; [f, g] = g$. As with products, if a sum exists, it is unique up to isomorphism.

Since products and sums are dual, Corollary 4.11 and Theorem 5.1 imply that LENS does not have sums. But we do have a tensor whose object part is a set-theoretic sum—in fact, there are at least two interestingly different ones—and we can define useful associated structures, including a choice operation on lenses. As with products, a tensor can be extended to a sum by providing injection and *co-diagonal* natural transformations satisfying a family of equations, but these constructions are even farther away from being categorical sums than what we saw with products.

The two tensors, which we called *retentive* and *forgetful* in Section 2, differ in how they handle the complement when the new value being put is from a different branch of the sum than the old value that was put. The retentive sum keeps complements for *both* sublenses in its own complement and switches between them as needed. The forgetful sum keeps only one complement, corresponding to whichever branch was last put. If the next put switches sides, the complement is replaced with $missing$. We give just the retentive sum here, since it seems more useful; the forgetful sum can be found in the long version.

6.1 Definition [Retentive tensor sum lens]:

$$\frac{k \in X \leftrightarrow Z \qquad \ell \in Y \leftrightarrow W}{k \oplus \ell \in X + Y \leftrightarrow Z + W}$$

$$\begin{array}{lcl} C & = & k.C \times \ell.C \\ \mathit{missing} & = & (k.\mathit{missing}, \ell.\mathit{missing}) \\ \mathit{putr}(\mathsf{inl}\,x, (c_k, c_\ell)) & = & \mathsf{let}\,(z, c_k') = k.\mathit{putr}(x, c_k)\,\mathsf{in} \\ & & (\mathsf{inl}\,z, (c_k', c_\ell)) \\ \mathit{putr}(\mathsf{inr}\,y, (c_k, c_\ell)) & = & \mathsf{let}\,(w, c_\ell') = \ell.\mathit{putr}(y, c_\ell)\,\mathsf{in} \\ & & (\mathsf{inr}\,w, (c_k, c_\ell')) \\ \mathit{putl}(\mathsf{inl}\,z, (c_k, c_\ell)) & = & \mathsf{let}\,(x, c_k') = k.\mathit{putl}(z, c_k)\,\mathsf{in} \\ & & (\mathsf{inl}\,x, (c_k', c_\ell)) \\ \mathit{putl}(\mathsf{inr}\,w, (c_k, c_\ell)) & = & \mathsf{let}\,(y, c_\ell') = \ell.\mathit{putl}(y, c_\ell)\,\mathsf{in} \\ & & (\mathsf{inr}\,y, (c_k, c_\ell')) \end{array}$$

6.2 Lemma [Sum bijection]: For bijections f and g,

$$bij_f \oplus bij_g \equiv bij_{f+g}$$

6.3 Proposition [LENS,$\oplus$ is a symmetric monoidal category]: In SET, the disjoint union gives rise to a symmetric monoidal category with $\emptyset$ as unit. Let $\alpha^+, \lambda^+, \rho^+, \gamma^+$ be associator, left-unitor, right-unitor, and symmetry natural isomorphisms. Then the $\oplus$ bifunctor gives rise to a symmetric monoidal category of lenses with $\emptyset$ as unit and $\alpha^\oplus = bij \circ \alpha^+$, $\lambda^\oplus = bij \circ \lambda^+$, $\rho^\oplus = bij \circ \rho^+$, and $\gamma^\oplus = bij \circ \gamma^+$ as associator, left-unitor, right-unitor, and symmetry, respectively.

The types of these natural isomorphisms are:

$$\begin{array}{rcl} \alpha^\oplus_{X,Y,Z} & \in & (X+Y)+Z \leftrightarrow X+(Y+Z) \\ \lambda^\oplus_X & \in & \emptyset + X \leftrightarrow X \\ \rho^\oplus_X & \in & X + \emptyset \leftrightarrow X \\ \gamma^\oplus_{X,Y} & \in & X+Y \leftrightarrow Y+X \end{array}$$

Unlike the product unit, there are no interesting lenses whose domain is the sum's unit, so this cannot be used to define the injection lenses; we have to do it by hand.

6.4 Definition [Injection lenses]:

$$\frac{x \in X}{inl_x \in X \leftrightarrow X + Y}$$

$$\begin{array}{lcl} C & = & X \times (\mathit{Unit} + Y) \\ \mathit{missing} & = & (x, \mathsf{inl}\,()) \\ \mathit{putr}(x, (x', \mathsf{inl}\,())) & = & (\mathsf{inl}\,x, (x, \mathsf{inl}\,())) \\ \mathit{putr}(x, (x', \mathsf{inr}\,y)) & = & (\mathsf{inr}\,y, (x, \mathsf{inr}\,y)) \\ \mathit{putl}(\mathsf{inl}\,x, c) & = & (x, (x, \mathsf{inl}\,())) \\ \mathit{putl}(\mathsf{inr}\,y, (x, c)) & = & (x, (x, \mathsf{inr}\,y)) \end{array}$$

We also define $inr_y = inl_y; \gamma^\oplus_{Y,X}$.

6.5 Proposition: The injection lenses are not natural.

As with products, where we have a useful lens of type $X \leftrightarrow X \times X$ that is nevertheless not a diagonal lens, we can craft a useful conditional lens of type $X + X \leftrightarrow X$ that is nevertheless not a codiagonal lens. In fact, we define a more general lens $union \in X + Y \leftrightarrow X \cup Y$. Occasionally, a value that is both an X and a Y may be put to the left across one of these union lenses. In this situation, the lens may legitimately choose either an inr tag or an inl tag. The $union$ lens uses the most recent unambiguous put to break the tie. (In the long version, we also define a variant that looks back to the last tagged value that was put to the right that was in both sets.)

6.6 Definition [Union lens]:

$$union_{XY} \in X + Y \leftrightarrow X \cup Y$$

$$\begin{array}{lcl} C & = & \mathit{Bool} \\ \mathit{missing} & = & \mathsf{false} \\ \mathit{putr}(\mathsf{inl}\,x, c) & = & (x, \mathsf{false}) \\ \mathit{putr}(\mathsf{inr}\,y, c) & = & (y, \mathsf{true}) \\ \mathit{putl}(xy, c) & & \\ \quad = \begin{cases} (\mathsf{inl}\,xy, \mathsf{false}) & xy \notin Y \vee (xy \in X \wedge \neg c) \\ (\mathsf{inr}\,xy, \mathsf{true}) & xy \notin X \vee (xy \in Y \wedge c) \end{cases} & & \end{array}$$

This definition is not symmetric in X and Y, because $putl$ prefers to return an inl value if there have been no tie breakers yet. Because of this preference, $union$ cannot be used to construct a true codiagonal. However, there are two useful related constructions:

6.7 Definition [Switch lens]:

$$switch_X \in X + X \leftrightarrow X$$

$$switch_X \;=\; union_{XX}$$

6.8 Definition [Retentive case lens]:

$$\frac{k \in X \leftrightarrow Z \qquad \ell \in Y \leftrightarrow Z}{case_{k,\ell} \in X + Y \leftrightarrow Z}$$

$$case_{k,\ell} = (k \oplus \ell); switch_X$$

A forgetful case lens appears in the long version.

Lists We can also define a variety of lenses operating on lists. We only consider mapping here, because in the next section we show how to obtain this and a whole variety of other functions on lists as instances of a powerful generic theorem, but it is useful to see one concrete instance first!

Write $X^\star$ for the set of lists with elements from the set X. Write $\langle\rangle$ for the empty list and $x{:}xs$ for the list with head x and tail xs. Write X^ω for the set of infinite lists over X. When $x \in X$ and $ss \in X^\omega$, write $x{:}ss \in X^\omega$ for the infinite list with head x and tail ss. Write $x^\omega \in X^\omega$ for the infinite list of x's.

6.9 Definition [Retentive list mapping lens]:

$$\frac{\ell \in X \leftrightarrow Y}{map(\ell) \in X^\star \leftrightarrow Y^\star}$$

$$\begin{array}{lll}
C & = & (\ell.C)^\omega \\
missing & = & (\ell.missing)^\omega \\
putr(x,c) & = & \mathsf{let}\ \langle x_1,\ldots,x_m\rangle = x\ \mathsf{in} \\
 & & \mathsf{let}\ \langle c_1,\ldots\rangle = c\ \mathsf{in} \\
 & & \mathsf{let}\ (y_i,c_i') = \ell.putr(x_i,c_i)\ \mathsf{in} \\
 & & (\langle y_1,\ldots,y_m\rangle, \langle c_1',\ldots,c_m',c_{m+1},\ldots\rangle) \\
putl & & \text{(similar)}
\end{array}$$

As we saw in Section 2, there is also a forgetful variant of the list mapping lens. Indeed, this is the one that corresponds to the known list mapping operator on asymmetric lenses [7, 11]. Additionally, the map lens gives us the machinery we need to complete the first example in the introduction: simply define $e^\star = map(e)$.

7. Iterators

In functional programming, mapping functionals are usually seen as instances of more general "fold patterns," or defined by general recursion. In this section, we investigate to what extent this path can be followed in the world of symmetric lenses.

Allowing general recursive definitions for symmetric lenses may be possible, but in general, complements change when unfolding a recursive definition; this means that the structure of the complement of the recursively defined function would itself have to be given by some kind of fixpoint construction. Preliminary investigation suggests that this is possible, but it would considerably clutter the development—on top of the general inconvenience of having to deal with partiality.

Therefore, we choose a different path. We identify a "fold" combinator for lists, reminiscent of the view of lists as initial algebras. We show that several important lenses on lists—including mapping—can be defined with the help of a fold, and that, due to the self-duality of lenses, folds can be composed back-to-back to yield general recursive patterns in the style of *hylomorphisms* [24]. We also discuss iteration patterns on trees and argue that the methodology carries over to other polynomial inductive datatypes.

7.1 Lists

Let $fold \in Unit + (X \times X^\star) \to X^\star$ be the bijection between "unfolded" lists and lists; $fold$ takes $\mathsf{inl}\ ()$ to $\langle\rangle$ and $\mathsf{inr}\ (x, xs)$ to $x{:}xs$. Note that $bij_{fold} \in Unit + (X \times X^\star) \Longleftrightarrow X^\star$ is then a bijective arrow in the category LENS.

7.1.1 Definition: An X*-list algebra* on a set Z is an arrow $\ell \in Unit + (X \times Z) \Longleftrightarrow Z$ and a function $w \in Z \to \mathbb{N}$ such that $\ell.putl(z,c) = (\mathsf{inr}\ (x,z'),c')$ implies $w(z') < w(z)$. We write $T_X^\star$ for the functor that sends any lens k to $id_{Unit} \oplus (id_X \otimes k)$.

The function w here plays the role of a termination measure. We will be iterating $\ell.putl$, producing a stream of values of type Z, which we would like to guarantee eventually ends.

7.1.2 Theorem: For X-list algebra ℓ on Z, there is a unique arrow $It(\ell) \in X^\star \Longleftrightarrow Z$ such that the following diagram commutes:

$$\begin{array}{ccc}
T_X^\star(X^\star) & \xrightarrow{\;bij_{fold}\;} & X^\star \\
{\scriptstyle T_X^\star(It(\ell))}\big\downarrow & & \big\downarrow{\scriptstyle It(\ell)} \\
T_X^\star(Z) & \xrightarrow[\;\ell\;]{} & Z
\end{array}$$

Proof sketch: We choose the complement of $It(\ell)$ to be $\ell.C^\omega$, so that the complements of the two arms of the commuting square are isomorphic. We then take commutativity of the diagram as a suggestion for a recursive definition of both $putr$ and $putl$. The length of the list in the case of $putr$ and the weight function in the case of $putl$ are used as ranking functions establishing totality of the recursive definitions. One must then prove, again by induction on these ranking functions, that the square does indeed commute.

To show uniqueness, we take another lens k which satisfies the above commutativity diagram. The diagram induces an "unfolding" of k's complement into an infinite sequence of complements that satisfy a pairwise correspondence property with the infinite sequence in $It(\ell)$'s complement. We can then show that $putr$ and $putl$ preserve this correspondence, which lets us construct a relation witnessing the equivalence of k and $It(\ell)$. □

In the terminology of universal algebra, an algebra for a functor F from some category to itself is simply an object Z and an arrow $F(Z) \to Z$. An arrow between F-algebras (Z, f) and (Z', f') is an arrow $u \in Z \to Z'$ such that $f; u = F(u); f'$. The F-algebras thus form a category themselves. An initial F-algebra is an initial object in that category (an initial object has exactly one arrow to each other object, and is unique up to isomorphism). F-algebras can be used to model a wide variety of inductive datatypes, including lists and various kinds of trees [29]. Using this terminology, Theorem 7.1.2 says that bij_{fold} is an initial object in the subcategory consisting of those $T_X^\star$-algebras for which a weight function w is available.

Let us consider some concrete instances of the theorem. First, if $k \in X \Longleftrightarrow Y$ is a lens, then we can form an X-list algebra ℓ on $Y^\star$ by composing $id_{Unit} \oplus (k \otimes id_{Y^\star}) \in Unit + (X \times Y^\star) \Longleftrightarrow Unit + (Y \times Y^\star)$ with $bij_{fold} \in Unit + (Y \times Y^\star) \Longleftrightarrow Y^\star$. A suitable weight function is given by $w(ys) = length(ys)$. The induced lens $It(\ell) \in X^\star \Longleftrightarrow Y^\star$ is the lens analog of the familiar list mapping function. In fact, substituting the lens $e \in X \times Y \Longleftrightarrow Y \times Z$ (from the introduction) for k in the above diagram, we find that $It(\ell)$ is the sneakier variant of the lens $e^\star$. (Again, we are ignoring the important question of alignment here. A hand-written map lens could perform a more sophisticated alignment analysis to associate "similar" items in a sequence of puts and recover more appropriate data from the complement; the process described above results in a simple positional alignment scheme.)

Second, suppose that $X = X_1 + X_2$ and let Z be $X_1^\star \times X_2^\star$. Writing X_i^+ for $X_i \times X_i^\star$, we can define isomorphisms

$$\begin{array}{rcl} f & \in & (X_1 + X_2) \times X_1^\star \times X_2^\star \\ & \to & (X_1^+ + X_2^+) + (X_1^+ \times X_2^+ + X_1^+ \times X_2^+) \\ g & \in & Unit + ((X_1^+ + X_2^+) + X_1^+ \times X_2^+) \\ & \to & X_1^\star \times X_2^\star \end{array}$$

by distributing the sum and unfolding the list type for f and by factoring the polynomial and folding the list type for g. Then we can create

$$\ell \in Unit + ((X_1 + X_2) \times Z) \leftrightarrow Z$$

$$\begin{array}{rcl} \ell & = & (id_{Unit} \oplus bij_f); \\ & & (id_{Unit} \oplus (id_{X_1^+ + X_2^+} \oplus switch_{X_1^+ \times X_2^+})); \\ & & bij_g \end{array}$$

A suitable weight function for ℓ is given by $w((xs_1, xs_2)) = length(xs_1) + length(xs_2)$. The lens $It(\ell) \in (X_1 + X_2)^\star \Longleftrightarrow X_1^\star \times X_2^\star$ that we obtain from iteration partitions the input list in one direction and uses a stream of booleans from the state to put them back in the right order in the other direction. Indeed, $It(\ell)$ is exactly the *partition* lens described in the introductory examples. Composing it with a projection yields a filter lens. (Alternatively, the filter lens could be obtained directly by iterating a slightly trickier ℓ.) Consequently, we now have the machinery we need to define *comp* from the introduction:

$$filter = partition; \pi_{1\langle\rangle}$$
$$comp = filter; filter^{op}$$

7.1.3 Corollary: Suppose k^{op} is an X-list algebra on W and ℓ is an X-list algebra on Z. Then there is a lens $Hy(k, \ell) \in W \Longleftrightarrow Z$ such that the following diagram commutes:

$$\begin{array}{ccc} T_X^\star(W) & \xleftarrow{\;k\;} & W \\ {\scriptstyle T_X^\star(Hy(k,\ell))}\downarrow & & \downarrow{\scriptstyle Hy(k,\ell)} \\ T_X^\star(Z) & \xrightarrow[\;\ell\;]{} & Z \end{array}$$

Proof: Define $Hy(k, \ell)$ as the composition $It(k^{op})^{op}; It(\ell)$. □

One can think of $Hy(k, \ell)$ as a recursive definition of a lens. The lens k tells whether a recursive call should be made, and if so, produces the argument for the recursive call and some auxiliary data. The lens ℓ then describes how the result is to be built from the result of the recursive call and the auxiliary data. This gives us a lens version of the hylomorphism pattern from functional programming [24]. Unfortunately, we were unable to prove or disprove the uniqueness of $Hy(k, \ell)$.

We have not formally studied the question of whether $It(\ell)$ is actually an initial algebra, i.e., whether it can be defined and is unique even in the absence of a weight function. However, this seems unlikely, because then it would apply to the case where Z is the set of finite and infinite X lists and ℓ the obvious bijective lens. The *putl* component of $It(\ell)$ would then have to truncate an infinite list, which would presumably break the commuting square.

7.2 Other Datatypes

Analogs of Theorem 7.1.2 and Corollary 7.1.3 are available for a number of other functors, in particular those that are built up from variables by $+$ and $\times$. All of these can also be construed as containers (see Section 8), but the iterator and hylomorphism patterns provide more powerful operations for the construction of lenses than the mapping operation available for general containers. Moreover, the universal property of the iterator provides a modular proof method, allowing one to deduce equational laws which can be cumbersome to establish directly because of the definition of equality as behavioral equivalence. For instance, we can immediately deduce that list mapping is a functor. Containers, on the other hand, subsume datatypes such as labeled graphs that are not initial algebras.

Iterators with multiple arguments The list iterator allows us to define a lens between $X^\star$ and some other set Z, but Theorem 7.1.2 cannot be directly used to define a lens between $X^\star \times Y$ and Z (think of Y as modeling parameters). In standard functional programming, a map from $X^\star \times Y$ to Z is tantamount to a map from $X^\star$ to $Y \to Z$, so iteration with parameters is subsumed by the parameterless case. Unfortunately, LENS does not seem to have the function spaces required to play this trick.

Therefore, we introduce the functor $T_{X,Y}^\star(Z) = Y + X \times Z$ and notice that $T_{X,Y}^\star(X^\star \times Y) \simeq X^\star \times Y$. Just as before, an algebra for that functor is a lens $\ell \in T_{X,Y}^\star(Z) \leftrightarrow Z$ together with a function $w : Z \to \mathbb{N}$ such that $\ell.putl(z, c) = (\mathsf{inr}\ (x, z'), c')$ implies $w(z') < w(z)$.

As an example, let $Y = Z = X^\star$ and define

$$\ell \in X^\star + X \times X^\star \leftrightarrow X^\star$$

$$\begin{array}{lcl} C & = & Bool \\ missing & = & \mathsf{true} \\ \ell.putr(\mathsf{inl}\ xs, b) & = & (xs, \mathsf{true}) \\ \ell.putr(\mathsf{inr}\ (x, xs), b) & = & (x{:}xs, \mathsf{false}) \\ \ell.putl(\langle\rangle, b) & = & (\mathsf{inl}\ \langle\rangle, \mathsf{true}) \\ \ell.putl(x{:}xs, \mathsf{true}) & = & (\mathsf{inl}\ (x{:}xs), \mathsf{true}) \\ \ell.putl(x{:}xs, \mathsf{false}) & = & (\mathsf{inr}\ (x, xs), \mathsf{false}) \end{array}$$

Iteration yields a lens $X^\star \times X^\star \leftrightarrow X^\star$ that can be seen as a bidirectional version of list concatenation. The commuting square for the iterator corresponds to the familiar recursive definition of concatenation: $concat(\langle\rangle, ys) = ys$ and $concat(x{:}xs, ys) = x{:}concat(xs, ys)$. In the bidirectional case considered here the complement will automatically retain enough information to allow splitting in the *putl*-direction.

We can use a version of Corollary 7.1.3 for this data structure to implement tail recursive constructions. Consider, for instance, the $T_{Unit,X^\star}^\star$-algebra $k : X^\star + X^\star \times X^\star \leftrightarrow X^\star \times X^\star$ where

$$\begin{array}{lcl} k.putl((acc, \langle\rangle), \mathsf{true}) & = & (\mathsf{inl}\ acc, \mathsf{true}) \\ k.putl((acc, x{:}xs), \mathsf{true}) & = & (\mathsf{inr}\ (x{:}acc, xs), \mathsf{true}) \\ k.putl((acc, xs), \mathsf{false}) & = & (\mathsf{inr}\ (acc, xs), \mathsf{false}). \end{array}$$

Together with the $T_{Unit,X^\star}^\star$-algebra $switch_{X^\star} : X^\star + X^\star \leftrightarrow X^\star$, this furnishes a bidirectional version of the familiar tail recursive list reversal that sends (acc, xs) to $xs^{rev}\ acc$.

Trees For set X let $Tree(X)$ be the set of binary X-labeled trees given inductively by $leaf \in Tree(X)$ and $x \in X, \ell \in Tree(X), r \in Tree(X) \Rightarrow node(x, \ell, r) \in Tree(X)$. Consider the endofunctor $T_X^{Tree}(Z) = Unit + X \times Z \times Z$. Let $c \in T_X^{Tree}(Tree(X)) \leftrightarrow Tree(X)$ denote the obvious bijective lens.

An X-tree algebra is a lens $\ell \in T_X^{Tree}(Z) \leftrightarrow Z$ and a function $w \in Z \to \mathbb{N}$ with the property that if $\ell.putl(z, c) =$

(inr $(x, z_l, z_r), c'$) then $w(z_l) < w(z)$ and $w(z_r) < w(z)$. The bijective lens c is then the initial object in the category of X-tree algebras; that is, every X-tree algebra on Z defines a unique lens in $Tree(X) \leftrightarrow Z$.

Consider, for example, the concatenation lens $concat : X^\star \times X^\star \leftrightarrow X^\star$. Let $concat' : Unit + X \times X^\star \times X^\star \leftrightarrow X^\star$ be the lens obtained from $concat$ by precomposing with the fold-isomorphism and the terminal lens $term_{\langle\rangle}$. Intuitively, this lens sends inl () to $\langle\rangle$ and x, xs, xs' to $x{:}xs@xs'$, using the complement to undo this operation properly. This lens forms an example of a tree algebra (with number of nodes as weight functions) and thus iteration furnishes a lens $Tree(X) \leftrightarrow X^\star$ which does a pre-order traversal, keeping enough information in the complement to rebuild a tree from a modified traversal.

The hylomorphism pattern can also be applied to trees, yielding the ability to define symmetric lenses by divide-and-conquer, i.e., by dispatching one call to two parallel recursive calls whose results are then appropriately merged.

8. Containers

The previous section suggests a construction for a variety of operations on datatypes built from polynomial functors. Narrowing the focus to the very common "map" operation, we can generalize still further, to any kind of *container functor* [1], i.e. a *normal functor* in the terminology of Hasegawa [14] or an *analytic functor* in the terminology of Joyal [19]. (These structures are also related to the *shapely types* of Jay and Cockett [18].)

8.1 Definition [Container]: A *container* consists of a set I together with an I-indexed family of sets $B \in I \to Set$.

Each container (I, B) gives rise to an endofunctor $F_{I,B}$ on SET whose object part is defined by $F_{I,B}(X) = \sum_{i \in I} B(i) \to X$. For example, if $I = \mathbb{N}$ and $B(n) = \{0, 1, \dots, n-1\}$, then $F_{I,B}(X)$ is $X^\star$ (up to isomorphism). Or, if $I = Tree(Unit)$ is the set of binary trees with trivial labels and $B(i)$ is the set of nodes of i, then $F_{I,B}(X)$ is the set of binary trees labeled with elements of X. In general, we can think of I as a set of shapes and, for each shape $i \in I$, we can think of $B(i)$ as the set of "positions" in shape i. So an element $(i, f) \in F_{I,B}(X)$ consists of a shape i and a function f assigning an element $f(p) \in X$ to each position $p \in B(i)$. The arrow part of $F_{I,B}$ maps a function $u \in X \to Y$ to a function $F_{I,B}(u) \in F_{I,B}(X) \to F_{I,B}(Y)$ given by $(i, f) \mapsto (i, f; u)$.

Now, we would like to find a way to view a container as a functor on the category of lenses. In order to do this, we need a little extra structure.

8.2 Definition: A *container with ordered shapes* is a pair (I, B) satisfying these conditions:

1. I is a partial order with binary meets. We say i is a *subshape* of j whenever $i \leq j$.
2. B is a functor from $(I, \leq)$ viewed as a category (with one object for each element and an arrow from i to j iff $i \leq j$) into SET. When B and i are understood, we simply write $b|i'$ for $B(i \leq i')(b)$ if $b \in B(i)$ and $i \leq i'$.
3. If i and i' are both subshapes of a common shape j and we have positions $b \in B(i)$ and $b' {\in} B(i')$ with $b|j = b'|j$, then there must be a unique $b_0 {\in} B(i {\wedge} i')$ such that $b = b_0|i$ and $b' = b_0|i'$. Thus such b and b' are really the same position. In other words, every diagram of the following form is a pullback:

$$\begin{array}{ccc} B(i \wedge i') & \xrightarrow{B(i \wedge i' \leq i)} & B(i) \\ {\scriptstyle B(i \wedge i' \leq i')}\downarrow & & \downarrow{\scriptstyle B(i \leq j)} \\ B(i') & \xrightarrow[B(i' \leq j)]{} & B(j) \end{array}$$

If $i \leq j$, we can apply the instance of the pullback diagram where $i = i'$ and hence $i \wedge i' = i$ and deduce that $B(i \leq j) \in B(i) \to B(j)$ is always injective.

For example, in the case of trees, we can define $t \leq t'$ if every path from the root in t is also a path from the root in t'. The arrow part of B then embeds positions of a smaller tree canonically into positions of a bigger tree. The meet of two trees is the greatest common subtree starting from the root.

8.3 Definition [Container mapping lens]:

$$\frac{\ell \in X \leftrightarrow Y}{F_{I,B}(\ell) \in F_{I,B}(X) \leftrightarrow F_{I,B}(Y)}$$

$C =$
  $\{t \in \prod_{i \in I} B(i) \to \ell.(C) \mid$
  $\forall i, i'.\ i \leq i' \supset \forall b {\in} B(i).\ t(i')(b|i') = t(i)(b)\}$
$missing(i)(b) \ = \ \ell.missing$
$putr((i, f), t) \ =$
  let $f'(b) \ = \ \mathsf{fst}(\ell.putr(f(b), t(i)(b)))$ in
  let $t'(j)(b) \ =$
    if $\exists b_0 \in B(i \wedge j).\ b_0|j = b$
    then $\mathsf{snd}(\ell.putr(f(b_0|i), t(j)(b)))$ in
    else $t(j)(b)$
  $((i, f'), t')$
$putl$ (similar)

(Experts will note that C is the limit of the contravariant functor $i \mapsto (B(i) \to \ell.(C))$. Alternatively, we can construe C as the function space $D \to \ell.(C)$ where D is the colimit of the functor B. Concretely, D is given by $\sum_{i \in I} B(i)$ modulo the equivalence relation $\sim$ generated by $(i, b) \sim (i', b')$ whenever $i \leq i'$ and $b' = B(i \leq i')(b)$.)

For the case of lists, this mapping lens coincides with the retentive map that we obtained from the iterator in Section 7. In general, two pieces of data synchronized by one of these mapping lenses will have exactly the same shape; any shape change to one of the sides will be precisely mirrored in the other side. For example, the tree version of this lens will transport the deletion of a node by deleting the node in the same position on the other side. We believe it should also be possible to define a forgetful version where the complement is just $F_{I,B}(\ell.C)$.

9. Asymmetric Lenses as Symmetric Lenses

The final step in our investigation is to formalize the connection between symmetric lenses and the more familiar asymmetric ones, and to show how known constructions on asymmetric lenses correspond to the constructions we have considered.

Write $X \overset{a}{\leftrightarrow} Y$ for the set of asymmetric lenses from X to Y (using the first presentation of asymmetric lenses from Section 2, with get, put, and $create$ components).

9.1 Definition: Every asymmetric lens can be embedded in a symmetric one.

$$\frac{\ell \in X \overset{a}{\leftrightarrow} Y}{\ell^{sym} \in X \leftrightarrow Y}$$

$$\begin{array}{lcl} C & = & \{f \in Y \to X \mid \forall y \in Y.\ \ell.get(f(y)) = y\} \\ missing & = & \ell.create \\ putr(x, f) & = & (\ell.get(x), f_x) \\ putl(y, f) & = & \text{let } x = f(y) \text{ in } (x, f_x) \end{array}$$

(Here, $f_x(y)$ means $\ell.put(y, x)$.) Viewing X as the source of an asymmetric lens (and therefore as having "more information" than Y), we can understand the definition of the complement here as being a value from X stored as a closure over that value. The presentation is complicated slightly by the need to accommodate the situation where a complete X does not yet exist—i.e. when defining *missing*—in which case we can use *create* to fabricate an X value out of a Y value if necessary.

9.2 Definition [Asymmetric lenses]: Here are several useful asymmetric lenses, based on string lenses from [7]. (We give only their names and types here; full definitions appear in the long version.) We use $\ell_{X,Y}$ to stand for any asymmetric lens $\ell \in X \overset{a}{\leftrightarrow} Y$.

$$\begin{array}{rcl} copy_X & \in & X \overset{a}{\leftrightarrow} X \\ \ell_{X,Y}; \ell_{Y,Z} & \in & X \overset{a}{\leftrightarrow} Z \\ aconst_x & \in & X \overset{a}{\leftrightarrow} Unit \text{ whenever } x \in X \\ \ell_{X,Y} \cdot \ell_{Z,W} & \in & X \times Z \overset{a}{\leftrightarrow} Y \times W \\ \ell_{X,Y} | \ell_{Z,W} & \in & X + Z \overset{a}{\leftrightarrow} Y \cup W \\ \ell^{\star}_{X,Y} & \in & X^{\star} \overset{a}{\leftrightarrow} Y^{\star} \end{array}$$

9.3 Theorem: The symmetric embeddings of these lenses correspond nicely to definitions from earlier in this paper:

$$\begin{array}{rcll} copy_X^{sym} & \equiv & id_X & (1) \\ (k; \ell)^{sym} & \equiv & k^{sym}; \ell^{sym} & (2) \\ aconst_x^{sym} & \equiv & term_x & (3) \\ (k \cdot \ell)^{sym} & \equiv & k^{sym} \otimes \ell^{sym} & (4) \\ (k|\ell)^{sym} & \equiv & (k^{sym} \oplus^f \ell^{sym}); union & (5) \\ (\ell^{\star})^{sym} & \equiv & map^f(\ell^{sym}) & (6) \end{array}$$

The first two show that $(-)^{sym}$ is a functor. The $\oplus^f$ operator is the forgetful variant of $\oplus$; see the long version for the full definition.

We suspect that there might be an asymmetric *fold* construction similar to our iteration lens above satisfying an equivalence like

$$fold(\ell)^{sym} \equiv It(\ell^{sym}),$$

but have not explored this carefully.

The $(-)^{sym}$ functor is not *full*—that is, there are some symmetric lenses which are not the image of any asymmetric lens. Injection lenses, for example, have no analog in the category of asymmetric lenses, nor do either of the example lenses presented in the introduction. However, we *can* characterize symmetric lenses in terms of asymmetric ones in a slightly more elaborate way.

9.4 Theorem: Given any arrow ℓ of LENS, there are asymmetric lenses k_1, k_2 such that $(k_1^{sym})^{op}; k_2^{sym} = \ell$.

To see this, we need to know how to "asymmetrize" a symmetric lens. We can view a symmetric lens as a pair of asymmetric lenses joined "tail to tail" whose common domain is consistent triples. For any lens $\ell \in X \leftrightarrow Y$, define $S_\ell = \{(x, y, c) \in X \times Y \times \ell.C \mid \ell.putr(x, c) = (y, c)\}$. Now define:

$$\frac{\ell \in X \leftrightarrow Y}{\ell_r^{asym} \in S_\ell \overset{a}{\leftrightarrow} X}$$

$$\begin{array}{lcl} get((x, y, c)) & = & x \\ put(x', (x, y, c)) & = & \text{let } (y', c') = \ell.putr(x', c) \\ & & \text{in } (x', y', c') \\ create(x) & = & \text{let } (y, c) = \ell.putr(x, \ell.missing) \\ & & \text{in } (x, y, c) \end{array}$$

The definition of $\ell_l^{asym} \in S_\ell \overset{a}{\leftrightarrow} Y$ is similar.

Proof of 9.4: Given $[\ell]$, choose $k_1 = \ell_r^{asym}$ and $k_2 = \ell_l^{asym}$. □

10. Related Work

There is a large literature on lenses and related approaches to propagating updates between connected structures. We discuss only the most closely related work here; good general surveys of the area can be found in [8, 13]. Connections to the literature on *view update* in databases are surveyed in [11].

The first symmetric approach to update propagation was proposed by Meertens [23] and followed up by Stevens [26], Diskin [10], and Xiong, et al [30].

Meertens suggests modeling synchronization between two sets X and Y by a *consistency relation* $R \subseteq X \times Y$ and two *consistency maintainers* $\lhd : X \times Y \to X$ and $\rhd : X \times Y \to Y$ such that $(x \lhd y)\ R\ y$ and $x\ R\ (x \rhd y)$ always hold, and such that $x\ R\ y$ implies $x \lhd y = x$ and $x \rhd y = y$.

The main advantage of symmetric lenses over consistency maintainers is their closure under composition. Indeed, all of the aforementioned authors note that, in general, consistency maintainers do not compose and view this as a drawback. Suppose that we have relations $R \subseteq X \times Y$ and $R' \subseteq Y \times Z$ maintained by $\rhd, \lhd$ and $\rhd', \lhd'$, resp. If we want to construct a maintainer for the composition $R; R'$, we face the problem that, given $x \in X$ and $z \in Z$, there is no canonical way of coming up with a $y \in Y$ that will allow us to use either of the existing maintainer functions. Concretely, Meertens gives the following counterexample. Let X be the set of nonempty context free grammars over some alphabet, and let Y be the set of words over that same alphabet. Let $R \subseteq X \times Y$ be given by $G\ R\ x \iff x \in L(G)$. It is easy to define computable maintainer functions making this relation a constraint maintainer. Composing this relation with its opposite yields an undecidable relation (namely, whether the intersection of two context-free grammars is nonempty), so there cannot be computable maintainer functions.

We can transform any constraint maintainer into a symmetric lens as follows: take the relation R itself (viewed as a set of pairs) as the complement, and define $putl(x', (x, y)) = (x' \rhd y, (x', x' \rhd y))$ and similarly for $putr$. If we compose such a symmetric lens with its opposite we obtain $R \times R^{op}$ as the complement and, for example, $putr(x', ((x_1, y_1), (y_2, x_2))) = (x_2 \lhd (x' \rhd y_1), ((x', x' \rhd y_1), (x' \rhd y_1, x_2 \lhd (x' \rhd y_1))))$. For Meertens' counterexample, we would have complements of the form $((G_1, w_1), (w_2, G_2))$, with $w_1 \in L(G_1)$ and $w_2 \in L(G_2)$; "$putr$"-ing a new grammar G_1' through the composed lens yields the complement $((G_1', w_1'), (w_1', G_2'))$, where w_1' is w_1 if $w_1 \in L(G_1)$ and some default otherwise, and where $G_2' = G_2$ if $w_1' \in L(G_2)$ and $S \to w_1'$ (where S is the start state) otherwise. We observe that there is a property of lenses analogous to Meertens' requirement that $x\ R\ y$ implies $x \lhd y = x$. This property is not necessarily preserved by composition, and in particular the lens described above for synchronizing languages does not have it. Meertens recommends using a *chain* of consistency maintainers in such a situation to achieve a similar effect; however, the properties of such chains have not been explored.

For asymmetric lenses, a number of alternative laws have been explored. Some of these are weaker than ours; for example, a number of papers from a community of researchers based in Tokyo replace the PUTGET law with a somewhat looser PUTGETPUT law, permitting a broader range of useful behaviors for lenses that duplicate information. It would be interesting to see what kind of categorical structures arise from these choices. The proposal by Matsuda et al.[22] is particularly interesting because it also employs the idea of complements. Conversely, stronger laws can be imagined, such as the PUTPUT law discussed by Foster et al. [11].

A different foundation for defining lenses by recursion was explored by Foster et al. [11], using standard tools from domain theory to define monotonicity and continuity for lens combinators parametrized on other lenses. The main drawback of this approach is that the required (manual) proofs that such recursive lenses are total tend to be somewhat intricate. By contrast, we expect that our initial-algebra approach can be equipped with automatic proofs of totality (that is, choices of the weight function w) in many cases of interest.

11. Conclusions and Future Work

We have proposed the first notion of symmetric bidirectional transformations that supports composition. Composability opens up the study of symmetric bidirectional transformations from a category-theoretic perspective. We have explored the category of symmetric lenses, which is self-dual and has the category of bijections and that of asymmetric lenses each as full subcategories. We have surveyed the structure of this category and found it to admit tensor product structures that are the Cartesian product and disjoint union on objects. We have also investigated datatypes both inductively and as "containers" and found the category of symmetric lenses to support powerful mapping and folding constructs.

Syntax Although we have focused here on semantic and algebraic foundations, many of our constructions have a straightforward syntactic realization. In particular, it is easy to give a string-transformation interpretation to all the constructions in Sections 4 to 6 (including lenses over lists); these could easily be used to build a symmetric version of Boomerang [7]. More interesting would be to eliminate Boomerang's built-in lists and instead obtain lenses over lists and other structures (mapping, reversing, flattening of lists, transforming trees into lists) solely by using the combinators derived from the category-theoretic structure we have exhibited. To accomplish this, two further fine points need to be considered. First, we would want an automatic way for discovering weight functions for iterators. We believe that a straightforward termination analysis based on unfolding (similar to the one built into Coq) could help, but the details remain to be checked. And second, we must invent a formal syntax for programming with containers. Surprisingly, the existing literature does not seem to contain such a proposal.

More speculatively, it is a well-known folklore result that symmetric monoidal categories are in 1-1 correspondence with wiring diagrams and with first-order linear lambda calculus. We would like to exploit this correspondence to design a lambda-calculus-like syntax for symmetric lenses and perhaps also a diagrammatic language. The linear lambda calculus has judgments of the form $x_1{:}A_1, \dots, x_n{:}A_n \vdash t : A_0$, where $A_0, \dots, A_n$ are sets or possibly syntactic type expressions and where t is a linear term made up from basic lenses, lens combinators, and the variables $x_1, \dots, x_n$. This could be taken as denoting a symmetric lens $A_1 \otimes \cdots \otimes A_n \leftrightarrow A_0$. For example, here is such a term for the lens $concat'$ from Section 7.2:

$$z{:}Unit \oplus A \otimes A^\star \otimes A^\star \vdash \mathit{match}\ z\ \mathit{with} \\ \mid \mathsf{inl}\ () \mapsto term^{op}_{()} \\ \mid \mathsf{inr}\ (a, al, ar) \mapsto concat(a{:}al, ar)$$

The interpretation of such a term in the category of lenses then takes care of the appropriate insertion of bijective lenses for regrouping and swapping tensor products.

Complements as States One benefit of treating complements explicitly is that it opens the way to a *stateful* presentation of lenses. The idea is that the complement of a lens can be thought of as its local storage—the part of the heap that belongs to it. An obvious next step is that, instead of the lens components taking the local storage as an argument and returning an updated version as a result, they can just hang onto it themselves, internally, in mutable variables. The types of the put operations then become just $\ell.putr \in A \to B$ and $\ell.putl \in B \to A$, where the $\to$ is now a "programming language function type," with the usual implicit treatment of the heap. This avoids destructing the given C each time we propagate an update and rebuilding a new C to yield as a result, improving the efficiency of the implementation. An additional improvement comes from the next potential extension.

Alignment and Delta Lenses As we mentioned in Section 2, dealing correctly with alignment of structured information is crucial in practice. This issue has been extensively explored in the context of asymmetric lenses, and it seems it should be possible to adapt existing ideas such as *dictionary lenses* [7] and *matching lenses* [5] to symmetric lenses. An even better approach might be to change the fundamental nature of lenses so that, instead of working directly with entire *structures*, they work with *deltas*—descriptions of changes to the structures. These deltas can arise from simple positional judgments, as in this paper, from diff-like heuristics, from cues within the data itself, or perhaps even from user interaction—the lens itself doesn't need to know anything about this.

Many of our basic constructions can be adapted to deltas by taking the domain and codomain of a lens to be monoids (of edit operations) instead of sets, and then, for each lens construction, defining an appropriate edit monoid from the monoids of its components. For example, an edit for a pair lens is a pair of edits for the left- and right-hand sides of the pair. However, more thought is required to make this scheme really work: applying this idea naively leads to insufficiently expressive edit languages for structures like lists. In particular, we would like to see insertion and deletion as edit operations on lists (and rotations and the like for trees, etc.). Currently, we believe that containers are a promising framework for this endeavour.

Algebraic Structure We have shown that the category of symmetric lenses does not have products or sums. One reviewer suggests that it may be interesting to explore placing a partial order on the the homsets of our category (the sets of arrows between pairs of objects). Perhaps this extra structure would allow us to define variants of products and sums in which the required equations do not hold as equalities, but as inequalities.

Acknowledgments We are grateful to Nate Foster for productive discussions of many points, especially about the category of lenses, and to both Nate and Alexandre Pilkiewicz for helpful comments on drafts of the paper. Our work is supported by the National Science Foundation under grant IIS-0534592 *Linguistic Foundations for XML View Update*.

References

[1] M. Abbott, T. Altenkirch, and N. Ghani. Categories of containers. In *Foundations of Software Science and Computation Structures*, pages 23–38. Springer, 2003.

[2] Michael Abbott, Thorsten Altenkirch, and Neil Ghani. Containers: constructing strictly positive types. *Theor. Comput. Sci.*, 342(1):3–27, 2005.

[3] Samson Abramsky and Nikos Tzevelekos. Introduction to categories and categorical logic. In Bob Coecke, editor, *New Structures for Physics*. Springer, 2010.

[4] François Bancilhon and Nicolas Spyratos. Update semantics of relational views. *ACM Transactions on Database Systems*, 6(4):557–575, December 1981.

[5] Davi M. J. Barbosa, Julien Cretin, Nate Foster, Michael Greenberg, and Benjamin C. Pierce. Matching lenses: Alignment and view update. In *ACM SIGPLAN International Conference on Functional Programming (ICFP), Baltimore, Maryland*, September 2010.

[6] Aaron Bohannon, Jeffrey A. Vaughan, and Benjamin C. Pierce. Relational lenses: A language for updateable views. In *Principles of Database Systems (PODS)*, 2006. Extended version available as University of Pennsylvania technical report MS-CIS-05-27.

[7] Aaron Bohannon, J. Nathan Foster, Benjamin C. Pierce, Alexandre Pilkiewicz, and Alan Schmitt. Boomerang: Resourceful lenses for string data. In *ACM SIGPLAN–SIGACT Symposium on Principles of Programming Languages (POPL), San Francisco, California*, January 2008.

[8] Krzysztof Czarnecki, J. Nathan Foster, Zhenjiang Hu, Ralf Lämmel, Andy Schürr, and James F. Terwilliger. Bidirectional transformations: A cross-discipline perspective. In Richard F. Paige, editor, *ICMT*, volume 5563 of *Lecture Notes in Computer Science*, pages 260–283. Springer, 2009. ISBN 978-3-642-02407-8.

[9] Z. Diskin, K. Czarnecki, and M. Antkiewicz. Model-versioning-in-the-large: algebraic foundations and the tile notation. In *Proceedings of the 2009 ICSE Workshop on Comparison and Versioning of Software Models*, pages 7–12. IEEE Computer Society, 2009.

[10] Zinovy Diskin. Algebraic models for bidirectional model synchronization. In Krzysztof Czarnecki, Ileana Ober, Jean-Michel Bruel, Axel Uhl, and Markus Völter, editors, *MoDELS*, volume 5301 of *Lecture Notes in Computer Science*, pages 21–36. Springer, 2008. ISBN 978-3-540-87874-2.

[11] J. Nathan Foster, Michael B. Greenwald, Jonathan T. Moore, Benjamin C. Pierce, and Alan Schmitt. Combinators for bi-directional tree transformations: A linguistic approach to the view update problem. *ACM Transactions on Programming Languages and Systems*, 29 (3):17, May 2007. Extended abstract in *Principles of Programming Languages* (POPL), 2005.

[12] J. Nathan Foster, Alexandre Pilkiewicz, and Benjamin C. Pierce. Quotient lenses. In *ACM SIGPLAN International Conference on Functional Programming (ICFP), Victoria, Canada*, September 2008.

[13] John Nathan Foster. *Bidirectional Programming Languages*. PhD thesis, University of Pennsylvania, December 2009.

[14] R. Hasegawa. Two applications of analytic functors. *Theoretical Computer Science*, 272(1-2):113–175, 2002.

[15] S. Hidaka, Z. Hu, H. Kato, and K. Nakano. A compositional approach to bidirectional model transformation. In *New Ideas and Emerging Results Track of 31st International Conference on Software Engineering (ICSE 2009, NIER Track)*, 2009.

[16] S. Hidaka, Z. Hu, K. Inaba, H. Kato, K. Matsuda, and K. Nakano. Bidirectionalizing graph transformations. In *ACM SIGPLAN International Conference on Functional Programming (ICFP), Baltimore, Maryland*, September 2010.

[17] Zhenjiang Hu, Shin-Cheng Mu, and Masato Takeichi. A programmable editor for developing structured documents based on bidirectional transformations. In *Partial Evaluation and Program Manipulation (PEPM)*, pages 178–189, 2004. Extended version to appear in *Higher Order and Symbolic Computation*, 2008.

[18] C. Barry Jay and J. Robin B. Cockett. Shapely types and shape polymorphism. In Donald Sannella, editor, *ESOP*, volume 788 of *Lecture Notes in Computer Science*, pages 302–316. Springer, 1994. ISBN 3-540-57880-3.

[19] A. Joyal. Foncteurs analytiques et especes de structures. *Combinatoire énumérative*, pages 126–159, 1986.

[20] Dongxi Liu, Zhenjiang Hu, and Masato Takeichi. Bidirectional interpretation of xquery. In *ACM SIGPLAN Symposium on Partial Evaluation and Semantics-based Program Manipulation (PEPM), Nice, France*, pages 21–30, New York, NY, USA, 2007.

[21] David Lutterkort. Augeas: A Linux configuration API, February 2007. Available from `http://augeas.net/`.

[22] K. Matsuda, Z. Hu, K. Nakano, M. Hamana, and M. Takeichi. Bidirectionalization transformation based on automatic derivation of view complement functions. In *ACM SIGPLAN International Conference on Functional Programming (ICFP)*, pages 47–58. ACM Press New York, NY, USA, 2007.

[23] Lambert Meertens. Designing constraint maintainers for user interaction, 1998. Manuscript.

[24] E. Meijer, M. Fokkinga, and R. Paterson. Functional programming with bananas, lenses, envelopes and barbed wire. In *Functional Programming Languages and Computer Architecture*, pages 124–144. Springer, 1991.

[25] Shin-Cheng Mu, Zhenjiang Hu, and Masato Takeichi. An algebraic approach to bi-directional updating. In *ASIAN Symposium on Programming Languages and Systems (APLAS)*, pages 2–20, November 2004.

[26] Perdita Stevens. Bidirectional model transformations in QVT: Semantic issues and open questions. In *International Conference on Model Driven Engineering Languages and Systems (MoDELS), Nashville, TN*, volume 4735 of *Lecture Notes in Computer Science*, pages 1–15. Springer-Verlag, 2007. ISBN 978-3-540-75208-0.

[27] Perdita Stevens. A landscape of bidirectional model transformations. *Postproceedings of GTTSE*, 7, 2008.

[28] Perdita Stevens. Towards an algebraic theory of bidirectional transformations. In *Graph Transformations: 4th International Conference, Icgt 2008, Leicester, United Kingdom, September 7-13, 2008, Proceedings*, page 1. Springer, 2008.

[29] Varmo Vene. *Categorical Programming with Inductive and Coinductive Types*. PhD thesis, Universitatis Tartuensis, 2000.

[30] Y. Xiong, H. Song, Z. Hu, and M. Takeichi. Supporting parallel updates with bidirectional model transformations. *Theory and Practice of Model Transformations*, pages 213–228, 2009.

[31] Yingfei Xiong, Dongxi Liu, Zhenjiang Hu, Haiyan Zhao, Masato Takeichi, and Hong Mei. Towards automatic model synchronization from model transformations. In *IEEE/ACM International Conference on Automated Software Engineering (ASE), Atlanta, GA*, pages 164–173, 2007.

Regular Expression Containment: Coinductive Axiomatization and Computational Interpretation

Fritz Henglein Lasse Nielsen

DIKU, University of Copenhagen

{ henglein, lnielsen }@diku.dk

Abstract

We present a new sound and complete axiomatization of regular expression containment. It consists of the conventional axiomatization of concatenation, alternation, empty set and (the singleton set containing) the empty string as an idempotent semiring, the fixed-point rule $E^* = 1 + E \times E^*$ for Kleene-star, and a general coinduction rule as the only additional rule.

Our axiomatization gives rise to a natural computational interpretation of regular expressions as simple types that represent parse trees, and of containment proofs as *coercions*. This gives the axiomatization a Curry-Howard-style constructive interpretation: Containment proofs do not only certify a language-theoretic containment, but, under our computational interpretation, constructively transform a membership proof of a string in one regular expression into a membership proof of the same string in another regular expression.

We show how to encode regular expression equivalence proofs in Salomaa's, Kozen's and Grabmayer's axiomatizations into our containment system, which equips their axiomatizations with a computational interpretation and implies completeness of our axiomatization. To ensure its soundness, we require that the computational interpretation of the coinduction rule be a hereditarily total function. Hereditary totality can be considered the mother of syntactic side conditions: it "explains" their soundness, yet cannot be used as a conventional side condition in its own right since it turns out to be undecidable.

We discuss application of *regular expressions as types* to bit coding of strings and hint at other applications to the wide-spread use of regular expressions for substring matching, where classical automata-theoretic techniques are *a priori* inapplicable.

Neither regular expressions as types nor subtyping interpreted coercively are novel *per se*. Somewhat surprisingly, this seems to be the first investigation of a general proof-theoretic framework for the latter in the context of the former, however.

Categories and Subject Descriptors F.4.3 [*Formal languages*]: Regular sets; D.1.1 [*Applicative (functional) programming*]

General Terms Languages, Theory

Keywords axiomatization, coercion, coinduction, computational interpretation, containment, equivalence, regular expression, type

1. Introduction

What is *regular expression matching*? In classical theoretical computer science it is the problem of *deciding* whether a string belongs to the regular *language* denoted by a regular expression; that is, it is *membership testing*. In this sense, *abdabc* matches `((ab)(c|d)|(abc))*`, but *abdabb* does not. This interpretation is used for most theoretical computer science results: NFA-generation, DFA-generation by subset construction, DFA-minimization, the Myhill-Nerode Theorem, the Pumping Lemma, closure properties, the Star Height Problem, Brzozowski derivatives, fast regular expression equivalence algorithms and matching algorithms, coalgebraic characterizations, bisimulation, etc. If membership testing is all we are interested in, regular expressions and finite automata denoting the same *language* are completely interchangeable. In that case we may as well implement regular expression matching using a state-minimized DFA and forget about the original regular expression.

In *programming*, however, membership testing is rarely good enough: We do not only want a yes/no answer, we also want to obtain proper *matches* of substrings against the constituents of a regular expression so as to *extract* parts of the input for processing. In a *Perl Compatible Regular Expression (PCRE)*[1] matcher, for example, matching *abdabc* against $E =$ `((ab)(c|d)|(abc))*` yields a substring match for each of the 4 parenthesized subexpressions: They match *abc*, *ab*, *c*, and ϵ (the empty string), respectively. If we use a POSIX matcher (Institute of Electrical and Electronics Engineers (IEEE) 1992) instead, we get *abc*, ϵ, ϵ, *abc*, however. How is this possible? The reason is that $((ab)(c|d)|(abc))*$ is *ambiguous*: the string *abc* can match the left or the right alternative of $(ab)(c|d)|(abc)$, and returning substring matches makes this difference observable. In a membership testing setting ambiguity is not observable and thus not much studied.

An oddity and limitation of Perl-style matching is that we only get one match under Kleene star, the last one. This is why we get a match of *abc* above, but not *abd*. Intuitively, we would like to get the *list* of matches under the Kleene star, not just a single one. This is possible, with *regular expression types* (Hosoya et al. 2005b): Each group can be named by a variable, and the output may contain multiple bindings to the same variable. For a variable under *two* Kleene stars, however, we cannot discern the bindings between the different level-1 Kleene-star groups. An even more refined notion of matching is thus *regular expression parsing*: Returning a parse tree of the input string under the regular expression read as a *grammar*.

A little noticed fact is that the parse trees for a regular expression are isomorphic to the elements of the regular expression read as a *type*; e.g. the type interpretation $\mathcal{T}[\![E]\!]$ of regular expression $E = ((ab)(c|d)|(abc))*$ is $((a \times b) \times (c + d) +$

[1] See `http://www.pcre.org`.

$a \times (b \times c))$ list with a, b, c, d being singleton types identified with the respective values a, b, c, d they contain. The *values* $p_1 = [\text{inl}((a, b), \text{inr}\, d), \text{inr}\,(a, (b, c))]$ and $p_2 = [\text{inl}((a, b), \text{inr}\, d), \text{inl}((a, b), \text{inl}\, c)]$ are elements of $((a \times b) \times (c+d) + a \times (b \times c))$ list, representing two different parse trees of the same type. Since their *flattening* (unparsing) yields the same string *abdabc*, this shows that $((ab)(c|d)|(abc))^*$ is grammatically ambiguous.

When we have a parsed representation of a string we sometimes need to transform it into a parsed representation of another regular expression. Consider for example E_d = `(ab(c|d))*`, which is equivalent to E. E_d corresponds to a DFA that can be used to match a string efficiently. But what if we need a parsed representation of the string with respect to E? We need a *coercion*, a function that maps parse trees under one regular expression (here E_d) into parse trees under another regular expression (here E) such that the underlying string is preserved. Since E is ambiguous there are different coercions for doing this. The choice of coercion thus incorporates a particular ambiguity resolution strategy; in particular, we may need to make sure that it always returns the *greedy left-most* parse, as in PCRE matching, or the *longest prefix* parse, as in POSIX matching. Also, we will be interested in favoring *efficient* coercions over less efficient ones amongst extensionally equivalent ones; e.g., for coercing E to E, we prefer the constant-time coercion that copies a reference to its input instead of the linear-time coercion that traverses its input and returns a copy of it. Even if coercions are not used to transform parse trees, they are useful for regular expressions under their language (membership testing) interpretation: The existence of a well-typed coercion from $\mathcal{L}[\![E]\!]$ to $\mathcal{L}[\![F]\!]$ is a proof object that logically certifies that E is contained in F. Once it is constructed, it can be *checked* efficiently for ascertaining that E is contained in F instead of embarking on search of a proof of that each time the containment needs to be checked.[2]

The purpose of this paper is to develop the basic theory of *regular expressions as types* with *coercions* interpreting containment as a conceptual and technical framework for regular expression based programming where the classic language-theoretic view is insufficient.

1.1 Contributions

Before delving into the details we summarize our contributions.

1.1.1 Regular expressions as types

The interpretation of regular expressions as types built from empty, unit, singleton, sum, product, and list types was introduced by Frisch and Cardelli (2004) for the purpose of regular expression matching. We allow ourselves to observe and point out that the elements of regular expressions as types correspond exactly to the parse trees of regular expressions understood as grammars. Frisch and Cardelli refer to types as describing "a concrete structured representation of values", but do not verbalize that those representations are essentially parse trees. Conversely, Brabrand and Thomsen (2010) as well as other works define an inference system for parse trees, but do not make explicit that that is tantamount to a type-theoretic interpretation of regular expressions.

1.1.2 Proofs of containment by coercion

We observe that containment can be *characterized* by finding a *coercion*, a function mapping every parse tree under one regular expression to a parse tree with same underlying string in the other regular expression.

[2] The size of a coercion will necessarily be exponential in the sizes of E and F for complexity-theoretic reasons in the worst case, but it *may* be small in many cases.

This means that proving a containment amounts to finding a coercion for the corresponding regular types, allowing us to bring functional programming intuitions to bear. For example, $E \times E^* \leq E^* \times E$ for all E can be proved by defining the obvious function `f`

```
fun f : 'a * 'a list -> 'a list * 'a
```

that retains the elements in the input.

The idea of a coercion interpretation of an axiomatically given subtyping relation is not new. Our observation expresses something more elementary and "syntax-free", however: The existence of a coercion between regular types, however specified, implies containment of the corresponding regular expressions. Note the direction of reasoning: from existence of coercion to containment.

1.1.3 Coinductive regular expression containment axiomatization with computational interpretation

We give a general coinductive axiomatization of regular expression containment and show how to interpret containment proofs computationally as string-preserving transformations on parse trees. Each rule in our axiomatization corresponds to a natural functional programming construct. Specifically, the coinduction rule corresponds to the principle of definition by recursion, where the side condition guarantees that the resulting function is total.

We show that the derivations of the axiomatizations by Salomaa (1966), Kozen (1994) and Grabmayer (2005) can be coded as coercion judgements in our inference system. This provides a natural computational interpretation for their axiomatizations.

As far as we know, no previous regular expression *axiomatization* has explicitly been given a sound and complete computational interpretation, where *all* derivations are interpreted computationally. Sulzmann and Lu (2007) come close, however. They provide what can be considered the first coercion synthesis algorithm, implemented in an extension of Haskell. They show how to construct an explicit coercion for each valid regular expression containment by providing a computational interpretation of Antimirov's algorithm (Antimirov 1996; Antimirov and Mosses 1995) for deciding regular expression containment. They show that their treatment is sound (Sulzmann and Lu 2007, Lemma A.3), and state that it is complete. We observe that, being based on the construction of deterministic linear forms, their work can be thought of as implementing a proof search using Antimirov's algorithm in Grabmayer's axiomatization.

1.1.4 Parametric completeness

Let us define $E[X_1, \ldots, X_m] \leq F[X_1, \ldots, X_m]$ if the containment holds for all substitutions of X_i with (closed) regular expressions. Our axiomatization is not only complete, but *parametrically complete* for infinite alphabets:
If $E[X_1, \ldots, X_m] \leq F[X_1, \ldots, X_m]$ for all regular expressions $X_1, \ldots, X_m$ then there exists c such that $\vdash c : E[X_1, \ldots, X_m] \leq F[X_1, \ldots, X_m]$. As a consequence, a schematic axiom such as $E \times E^* \leq E^* \times E$ is *derivable*, not just admissible in our axiomatization: we can prove it once and use the *same* proof for all instances of E.

We observe that Kozen's axiomatization (Kozen 1994) is also parametrically complete, but neither Salomaa's (Salomaa 1966) nor Grabmayer's (Grabmayer 2005) appear to be so: In Salomaa's case we need to make a case distinction as to whether the regular expression E substituted for X has the empty word property; and in Grabmayer's case the proofs use the derivatives of E, which are syntax dependent.

1.1.5 Application: Bit coding

We believe regular expressions as types with coercions have numerous applications in programming, both conceptually—how to *think* about regular expressions—and technically. We sketch one potential application: how *bit coding* can be used to compactly represent parse trees and thus strings. This can be thought of as a regular expression specific string representation that often can be compressed more than the original string. A thorough investigation of this and other applications requires separate treatment, however.

1.2 Prerequisites

We assume basic knowledge of regular expressions as in Hopcroft and Ullman (1979), and denotational semantics as in Winskel (1993).

1.3 Notation and terminology

$\mathcal{A}$ denotes an *alphabet*, a possibly infinite set of *symbols* $\{a_i\}_{i \in I}$. The *strings* over $\mathcal{A}$ is the set of finite sequences $\{s, t, \ldots\}$ with elements from $\mathcal{A}$. The *length* of a string s is denoted by $|s|$. The n-ary concatenation of $s_1, \ldots, s_n$ is denoted by their juxtaposition $s_1 \ldots s_n$; for $n = 0$ it denotes the empty string ϵ.

We use inl and inr as the tags distinguishing the elements of a disjoint sum of two sets such that $X + Y = \{\text{inl}\, v \mid v \in X\} \cup \{\text{inr}\, w \mid w \in Y\}$. We treat recursive types *iso-recursively*, where $(\text{fold}^{-1}, \text{fold})$ denotes the isomorphism between a recursive type and its unrolling. In particular, we define the list type X^* by $\mu Y.1 + X \times Y$. The empty list $[]$ is an abbreviation for fold (inl ()); and cons (x, y) stands for fold (inr (x, y)). The list notation $[x_1, \ldots, x_n]$ is syntactic sugar for cons $(x_1, \ldots, \text{cons}\,(x_n, []))$.

We say a unary predicate P *universally implies* another unary predicate Q if $\forall x.(P(x) \Rightarrow Q(x))$.

2. Regular expressions as types and coercions

In this section we show that a regular expression E can be interpreted as an ordinary *type* and regular expression containment as the existence of a *coercion* between such types. The elements of the types correspond to *proofs* of membership of strings in the regular language denoted by E, which in turn are the parse trees for E viewed as a right-regular *grammar*. A coercion then is any function that transforms parse trees without changing the underlying string.

DEFINITION 1 (Regular expression). *The*regular expressions $\text{Reg}_{\mathcal{A}}$ *is the set of abstract syntax tree defined by the following regular tree grammar:*

$$E, F, G, H ::= 0 \mid 1 \mid a \mid E + F \mid E \times F \mid E^*$$

where $a \in \mathcal{A}$.

In anticipation of our interpretation of regular expressions as types we write $\times$ instead of the more customary juxtaposition or $\cdot$ for concatenation. Our notational convention is that $^*, \times, +$ bind in decreasing order; e.g. $a + a \times b$ stands for $a + (a \times b)$.

2.1 Regular expressions as languages

The *language interpretation* of $\text{Reg}_{\mathcal{A}}$ maps regular expressions to *regular languages* (Kleene 1956). This is also called the *standard interpretation* of $\text{Reg}_{\mathcal{A}}$ since it is isomorphic to the free Kleene algebra over $\mathcal{A}$ (Kozen 1994).

DEFINITION 2 (Language interpretation). *The* language $\mathcal{L}[\![E]\!]$ *is the set of strings compositionally defined by:*

$$\begin{array}{lllllll} \mathcal{L}[\![0]\!] & = & \emptyset & \quad & \mathcal{L}[\![E+F]\!] & = & \mathcal{L}[\![E]\!] \cup \mathcal{L}[\![F]\!] \\ \mathcal{L}[\![1]\!] & = & \{\epsilon\} & & \mathcal{L}[\![E \times F]\!] & = & \mathcal{L}[\![E]\!] \cdot \mathcal{L}[\![F]\!] \\ \mathcal{L}[\![a]\!] & = & \{a\} & & \mathcal{L}[\![E^*]\!] & = & \bigcup_{i \geq 0} (\mathcal{L}[\![E]\!])^i \end{array}$$

where $S \cdot T = \{st \mid s \in S \wedge t \in T\}$, $E^0 = \{\epsilon\}$, $E^{i+1} = E \cdot E^i$.

We write $\models s \in E$ *if* $s \in \mathcal{L}[\![E]\!]$; $\models E \leq F$ *if* $\mathcal{L}[\![E]\!] \subseteq \mathcal{L}[\![F]\!]$; *and* $\models E = F$ *if* $\mathcal{L}[\![E]\!] = \mathcal{L}[\![F]\!]$.

$$\frac{}{\epsilon \in 1} \qquad \frac{}{a \in a} \qquad \frac{s \in E}{s \in E + F} \qquad \frac{s \in F}{s \in E + F} \qquad \frac{s \in E \quad t \in F}{st \in E \times F} \qquad \frac{s \in 1 + E \times E^*}{s \in E^*}$$

a) Regular expression matching

$$\frac{}{() : 1} \qquad \frac{}{a : a} \qquad \frac{v : E}{\text{inl}\, v : E + F} \qquad \frac{w : F}{\text{inr}\, w : E + F} \qquad \frac{v : E \quad w : F}{(v, w) : E \times F} \qquad \frac{v : 1 + E \times E^*}{\text{fold}\, v : E^*}$$

b) Type inhabitation

Figure 1. Matching relation and type inhabitation

As expected, $\mathcal{L}[\![E^*]\!]$ is the set of all finite concatenations of strings from $\mathcal{L}[\![E]\!]$:

$$\mathcal{L}[\![E^*]\!] = \{s_1 \ldots s_n \mid n \geq 0 \wedge s_i \in \mathcal{L}[\![E]\!] \text{ for all } 1 \leq i \leq n\}.$$

DEFINITION 3 (Constant part). *The* constant part $o(E)$ *of* E *is defined as* $o(E) = 1$ *if* $\epsilon \in \mathcal{L}[\![E]\!]$ *and* $o(E) = 0$ *otherwise.*

DEFINITION 4 (Matching). *We say* s matches E *and write* $\vdash s \in E$ *if the statement* $s \in E$ *is derivable in the inference system in Figure 1a.*

Matching is sound and complete for membership testing:

PROPOSITION 5. $\models s \in E$ *if and only if* $\vdash s \in E$.

The *derivation* of a matching statement $s \in E$ describes a *parse tree* for s under E understood as a regular grammar. This paper is about studying the parse trees, not just the regular language denoted by E.

2.2 Regular expressions as types

Parse trees are in one-to-one correspondence with regular expressions interpreted as *types*; that is, all we need to do is interpret the regular expression constructors as type constructors and we obtain *exactly* the parse trees.

DEFINITION 6 (Type interpretation). *The* type interpretation $\mathcal{T}[\![.]\!]$ *compositionally maps a regular expression* E *to a set of structured values:*

$$\begin{array}{llll} \mathcal{T}[\![0]\!] = \emptyset & \mathcal{T}[\![E+F]\!] & = & \mathcal{T}[\![E]\!] + \mathcal{T}[\![F]\!] \\ \mathcal{T}[\![1]\!] = \{()\} & \mathcal{T}[\![E \times F]\!] & = & \mathcal{T}[\![E]\!] \times \mathcal{T}[\![F]\!] \\ \mathcal{T}[\![a]\!] = \{a\} & \mathcal{T}[\![E^*]\!] & = & \{[v_1, \ldots, v_n] \mid v_i \in \mathcal{T}[\![E]\!]\} \end{array}$$

We write $\models v : E$ *if* $v \in \mathcal{T}[\![E]\!]$.

Note that this is the ordinary interpretation of the regular expression constructors as type constructors: 0 is the empty type, 1 the unit type, a (as a type) the singleton type $\{a\}$, $+$ the sum type constructor, $\times$ the product type constructor, and $.^*$ the list type constructor.

DEFINITION 7 (Inhabitation). *We say* v inhabits E *and write* $\vdash v : E$ *if the statement* $v : E$ *is derivable in the inference system in Figure 1b.*

Inhabitation is sound and complete for type membership:

PROPOSITION 8. $\models v : E$ *if and only if* $\vdash v : E$.

By inspection of Figures 1a and 1b we can see that a value v such that $\vdash v : E$ corresponds to a unique derivation of $s \in E$ for a string s that is uniquely determined by *flattening* v.

DEFINITION 9. *The* flattening *function* flat(.) *from values to strings is defined as follows:*

$$\begin{array}{rclrcl} \text{flat}(()) & = & \epsilon & \text{flat}(a) & = & a \\ \text{flat}(\text{inl}\, v) & = & \text{flat}(v) & \text{flat}(\text{inr}\, w) & = & \text{flat}(w) \\ \text{flat}((v,w)) & = & \text{flat}(v)\,\text{flat}(w) & \text{flat}(\text{fold}\, v) & = & \text{flat}(v) \end{array}$$

In particular we have:

THEOREM 10. $\mathcal{L}[\![E]\!] = \{\text{flat}(v) \mid v \in \mathcal{T}[\![E]\!]\}$

2.3 Regular expression containment as type coercion

Since each regular expression can be thought of as an ordinary type whose elements are all the parse trees for all its strings under the language interpretation, we can characterize regular language containment as the problem of transforming parse trees under one regular expression into parse trees under the other regular expression.

DEFINITION 11 (Coercion). *A function* $f \in \mathcal{T}[\![E]\!] \rightarrow \mathcal{T}[\![F]\!]_\bot$ *is a* partial coercion from E to F *if* $\text{flat}(v) = \text{flat}(f(v))$ *for all* $v \in \mathcal{T}[\![E]\!]$ *whenever* $f(v) \neq \bot$. *It is a* total coercion *(or just* coercion*) if* $f(v) \neq \bot$ *for all* $v \in \mathcal{T}[\![E]\!]$.

We write $\mathcal{T}[\![E \leq F_\bot]\!]$ *for the set of partial coercions from* E *to* F*; and* $\mathcal{T}[\![E \leq F]\!]$ *for the set of total coercions from* E *to* F.

In other words, a coercion from E to F is a function that transforms every parse tree under E to a parse tree under F for the same underlying string. Clearly, if there exists a coercion from E to F then $\models E \leq F$: the coercion takes any membership proof of a string in $\mathcal{L}[\![E]\!]$ to a membership proof for the same string in $\mathcal{L}[\![F]\!]$. Conversely, if $\models E \leq F$, we can define a coercion from E to F by mapping any value $v : E$ to a value $w : F$ where $\text{flat}(v) = \text{flat}(w)$.

THEOREM 12 (Containment by coercion). $\models E \leq F$ *if and only if there exists a coercion from* E *to* F.

An immediate corollary is that two regular expressions are equivalent if and only if there is a pair of coercions between them:

COROLLARY 13 (Equivalence by coercion pairs). $\models E = F$ *if and only if there exists a pair of coercions* (f, g) *such that* $f \in \mathcal{T}[\![E \leq F]\!]$ *and* $g \in \mathcal{T}[\![F \leq E]\!]$.

It may be tempting to expect such pairs to be isomorphisms; that is, $f \circ g = \text{id}_{\mathcal{T}[\![F]\!]}$ and $g \circ f = \text{id}_{\mathcal{T}[\![E]\!]}$). This is generally not the case, however: We have $\models a = a + a$, but there is no isomorphism between them, since there are two values for $a + a$ but only one value for a.

Theorem 12 provides a simple and amazingly useful method for proving regular expression containments by *functional programming*: Find a function from E to F (as *types*!) and make sure that it terminates, outputs each part of the input exactly once and in the same left-to-right order. The latter is usually easily checked when using pattern matching in the definition of the function.

EXAMPLE 14. *We prove the* denesting *rule (Kozen 1997)* $\models (a + b)^* = a^* \times (b \times a^*)^*$. *In one direction, find a function* $f : (a+b)^* \rightarrow a^* \times (b \times a^*)^*$ *and make sure that it terminates, uses each part of the input exactly once and outputs them in the same left-to-right order as in the input.*

$$\begin{array}{rcl} f([]) & = & ([], []) \\ f(\text{inl}\, u :: \vec{z}) & = & \textbf{let}\, (\vec{x}, \vec{y}) = f(\vec{z})\, \textbf{in}\, (u :: \vec{x}, \vec{y}) \\ f(\text{inr}\, v :: \vec{z}) & = & \textbf{let}\, (\vec{x}, \vec{y}) = f(\vec{z})\, \textbf{in}\, ([], (v, \vec{x}) :: \vec{y}) \end{array}$$

We can see that f *terminates since it is called recursively with smaller sized arguments, and the output contains the input components in the same left-to-right order. Consequently,* f *defines a coercion, and by Theorem 12 this constitutes a proof that the regular language* $\mathcal{L}[\![(a + b)^*]\!]$ *is contained in* $\mathcal{L}[\![a^* \times (b \times a^*)^*]\!]$. *The other direction is similar.*

In this example we defined an element of the function space $\mathcal{T}[\![E]\!] \rightarrow \mathcal{T}[\![F]\!]_\bot$ and then verified manually that it belongs to the subspace $\mathcal{T}[\![E \leq F]\!]$. The following section is about designing a *language* of functions each of which is guaranteed to be a coercion (soundness) and that furthermore is expressive enough so that it contains a term denoting a coercion from E to F whenever $\models E \leq F$ (completeness).

3. Declarative coinductive axiomatization

At the core of all axiomatizations of regular expression equivalence are the axiomatization of product ($\times$), sum ($+$), empty (0) and unit (1) as the free idempotent semiring over $\mathcal{A}$. See Figures 2 and 3. We add the familiar *fold/unfold* axiom for Kleene-star in Figure 4, which models that E^* is a fixed point of $X = 1 + E \times X$. Let us call the resulting inference system *weak equivalence*. It is a sound, but incomplete axiomatization of regular expression equivalence. In particular, we have $\models (a + 1)^* = a^*$, but they are not weakly equivalent (Salomaa 1966, Remark 4).

Intuitively, this is because weak equivalence does not allow invoking *recursively* what we want to prove. The basic idea in our axiomatization is to add recursion by way of a general *finitary coinduction* rule

$$\frac{\begin{array}{c}[E = F] \\ \vdots \\ E = F\end{array}}{E = F} \quad (*)$$

Here $[E = F]$ is a *hypothetical assumption*: It may be used an arbitrary number of times in deriving the premise, but is *discharged* when applying the inference step.

Since the premise is the same as the conclusion, without a side condition $(*)$ restricting its applicability this rule is blatantly unsound: We could simply satisfy the premise by immediately concluding $E = F$ from the hypothetical assumption. By the coinduction rule $E = F$ for arbitrary E, F would be derivable.

The key idea of this paper is to make the side condition not a property of the premise, but of the *derivation* of the premise. To this end we switch from axiomatizing equivalence to axiomatizing containment and equip our inference system with names for the rules, arriving at a type-theoretic formulation with explicit *proof terms*. These proof terms can be computationally interpreted as *coercions* as defined in Section 2.

The coinduction rule then suggestively reads

$$\frac{\begin{array}{c}[f : E \leq F] \\ \vdots \\ c : E \leq F\end{array}}{\text{fix} f. c : E \leq F} \quad (*)$$

as in Brandt and Henglein (1998, Section 4.4), where the side condition is a syntactic condition specific to recursive subtyping. The *computational interpretation* of $\text{fix} f. c$ is the *recursively defined* partial coercion f such that $f = c$ where c may contain free occurrences of f. For soundness all we need is for the coercion to be total, that is terminate on all inputs. This leads us to the side condition in its most general form:

The computational interpretation of $\text{fix} f. c$ must be *total*.

$$E + (F + G) = (E + F) + G \quad (1)$$
$$E + F = F + E \quad (2)$$
$$E + 0 = E \quad (3)$$
$$E + E = E \quad (4)$$
$$E \times (F \times G) = (E \times F) \times G \quad (5)$$
$$1 \times E = E \quad (6)$$
$$E \times 1 = E \quad (7)$$
$$E \times (F + G) = (E \times F) + (E \times G) \quad (8)$$
$$(E + F) \times G = (E \times G) + (F \times G) \quad (9)$$
$$0 \times E = 0 \quad (10)$$
$$E \times 0 = 0 \quad (11)$$

Figure 2. Axioms for idempotent semirings

$$E = E \qquad \frac{E = F}{F = E} \qquad \frac{E = F \quad F = G}{E = G}$$
$$\frac{E = G \quad F = H}{E + F = G + H} \qquad \frac{E = G \quad F = H}{E \times F = G \times H}$$

Figure 3. Rules of equality

$$E^* = 1 + E \times E^* \quad (12)$$

Figure 4. Fold/unfold rule for Kleene-star

$$\Gamma \vdash \text{shuffle} : E + (F + G) = (E + F) + G$$
$$\Gamma \vdash \text{retag} : E + F = F + E$$
$$\Gamma \vdash \text{untagL} : 0 + F = F$$
$$\Gamma \vdash \text{untag} : E + E \leq E$$
$$\Gamma \vdash \text{tagL} : E \leq E + F$$
$$\Gamma \vdash \text{assoc} : E \times (F \times G) = (E \times F) \times G$$
$$\Gamma \vdash \text{swap} : E \times 1 = 1 \times E$$
$$\Gamma \vdash \text{proj} : 1 \times E = E$$
$$\Gamma \vdash \text{abortR} : E \times 0 = 0$$
$$\Gamma \vdash \text{abortL} : 0 \times E = 0$$
$$\Gamma \vdash \text{distL} : E \times (F + G) = (E \times F) + (E \times G)$$
$$\Gamma \vdash \text{distR} : (E + F) \times G = (E \times G) + (F \times G)$$
$$\Gamma \vdash \text{wrap} : 1 + E \times E^* = E^*$$
$$\Gamma \vdash \text{id} : E = E$$

$$\frac{\Gamma \vdash c : E \leq E' \quad \Gamma \vdash d : E' \leq E''}{\Gamma \vdash c; d : E \leq E''}$$

$$\frac{\Gamma \vdash c : E \leq E' \quad \Gamma \vdash d : F \leq F'}{\Gamma \vdash c + d : E + F \leq E' + F'}$$

$$\frac{\Gamma \vdash c : E \leq E' \quad \Gamma \vdash d : F \leq F'}{\Gamma \vdash c \times d : E \times F \leq E' \times F'}$$

$$\Gamma, f : E \leq F, \Gamma' \vdash f : E \leq F$$

$$\frac{\Gamma, f : E \leq F \vdash c : E \leq F}{\Gamma \vdash \text{fix} f.c : E \leq F} \text{(coinduction rule)}$$

Figure 5. Declarative coercion inference system for regular expressions as types. With suitable side conditions for the coinduction rule this is sound and complete for regular expression containment. See Sections 3.2 and 3.3 for side conditions.

Unfortunately, totality turns out to be undecidable, and we present efficiently checkable syntactic conditions that entail totality and yet are expressive enough to admit completeness.

3.1 Axiomatization

Consider the coercion inference system in Figure 5. Each axiom of the form $\Gamma \vdash p : E = F$ is a short-hand for two containment axioms: $\Gamma \vdash p : E \leq F$ and $\Gamma \vdash p^{-1} : F \leq E$.

DEFINITION 15 (Coercion judgement). *Let* Γ *be a sequence of* coercion assumptions *of the form* $f : E \leq F$, *with no* f *repeated. A* coercion judgement *is a statement of the form* $\Gamma \vdash c : E \leq F$ *that is derivable in the inference system of Figure 5.*

If Γ *is empty we may omit it and write* $\vdash c : E \leq F$.

By induction on its derivation, a coercion judgement $f_1 : E_1 \leq F_1, \ldots, f_n : E_n \leq F_n \vdash c : E \leq F$ can be interpreted coherently as a continuous function $\mathcal{F}[\![\Gamma \vdash c : E \leq F]\!] : \mathcal{T}[\![E_1 \leq F_{1\perp}]\!] \times \ldots \times \mathcal{T}[\![E_n \leq F_{n\perp}]\!] \to \mathcal{T}[\![E \leq F_\perp]\!]$, which is specified by the equations in Figure 6. For example, the clauses for retag should be understood as

$$\mathcal{F}[\![\Gamma \vdash \text{retag} : E + F \leq F + E]\!](f_1, \ldots, f_n) = \lambda x.\textbf{case}\ x\ \textbf{of}\ \text{inl}\ v \Rightarrow \text{inr}\ v \mid \text{inr}\ v \Rightarrow \text{inl}\ v.$$

The interpretation of fix$f.c$ is defined to be the least fixed point of a continuous function on $\mathcal{T}[\![E \leq F_\perp]\!]$, which always exists since $\mathcal{T}[\![E \leq F_\perp]\!]$ is empty or a cpo with bottom. The interpretation of abortL, abortR, abortL^{-1}, abortR^{-1} is the empty function since the type interpretation of their domain is empty. Formally:

DEFINITION 16 (Computational interpretation).
The computational interpretation

$$\mathcal{F}[\![f_1 : E_1 \leq F_1, \ldots, f_n : E_n \leq F_n \vdash c : E \leq F]\!]$$

of a coercion judgement is the (domain-theoretically least) continuous function that maps partial coercions from E_i *to* F_i *bound to the* f_i *to a partial coercion from* E *to* F *satisfying the equations of Figure 6.*

We can interpret all computation judgements, but without a side condition controlling the use of the coinduction rule, the coercion inference system is unsound for deducing regular expression containments. To wit, we can trivially derive $\vdash \text{fix} f.f : E \leq F$ for any E, F. We might hope that a simple *guarding rule* would ensure soundness.

DEFINITION 17 (Left-guarded). *Let* $\Gamma \vdash \text{fix} f.c : E \leq F$ *be a coercion judgement. We say an occurrence of* f *in* c *is* left-guarded by d *if* c *contains a subterm of the form* $d \times d'$ *and the particular occurrence of* f *is in* d'. *We call* fix$f.c$ left-guarded *if for each occurrence of* f *there is a* d *that left-guards* f.

Left-guardedness is not sufficient for soundness, however. Consider

$$\vdash \text{fix} f.(\text{proj}^{-1}; (\text{id}_1 \times f); \text{proj}) : E \leq F,$$

which is derivable for all E and F. (For emphasis, we have annotated id with a subscript indicating which regular expression it operates on.) Computationally, this coercion judgement does not terminate on any input. This is an instructive case: It contains *both*

$\text{shuffle}(\text{inl}\, v)$	$=$	$\text{inl}\,(\text{inl}\, v)$
$\text{shuffle}(\text{inr}\,(\text{inl}\, v))$	$=$	$\text{inl}\,(\text{inr}\, v)$
$\text{shuffle}(\text{inr}\,(\text{inr}\, v))$	$=$	$\text{inr}\, v$
$\text{shuffle}^{-1}(\text{inl}\,(\text{inl}\, v))$	$=$	$\text{inl}\, v$
$\text{shuffle}^{-1}(\text{inl}\,(\text{inr}\, v))$	$=$	$\text{inr}\,(\text{inl}\, v)$
$\text{shuffle}^{-1}(\text{inr}\, v)$	$=$	$\text{inr}\,(\text{inr}\, v)$
$\text{retag}(\text{inl}\, v)$	$=$	$\text{inr}\, v$
$\text{retag}(\text{inr}\, v)$	$=$	$\text{inl}\, v$
retag^{-1}	$=$	retag
$\text{untagL}\,(\text{inr}\, v)$	$=$	v
$\text{untag}\,(\text{inl}\, v)$	$=$	v
$\text{untag}\,(\text{inr}\, v)$	$=$	v
$\text{tagL}\,(v)$	$=$	$\text{inl}\, v$
$\text{assoc}(v, (w, x))$	$=$	$((v, w), x)$
$\text{assoc}^{-1}((v, w), x)$	$=$	$(v, (w, x))$
$\text{swap}(v, ())$	$=$	$((), v)$
$\text{swap}^{-1}((), v)$	$=$	$(v, ())$
$\text{proj}((), w)$	$=$	w
$\text{proj}^{-1}(w)$	$=$	$((), w)$
$\text{distL}(v, \text{inl}\, w)$	$=$	$\text{inl}\,(v, w)$
$\text{distL}(v, \text{inr}\, x)$	$=$	$\text{inr}\,(v, x)$
$\text{distL}^{-1}(\text{inl}\,(v, w))$	$=$	$(v, \text{inl}\, w)$
$\text{distL}^{-1}(\text{inr}\,(v, x))$	$=$	$(v, \text{inr}\, x)$
$\text{distR}(\text{inl}\, v, w)$	$=$	$\text{inl}\,(v, w)$
$\text{distR}(\text{inr}\, v, x)$	$=$	$\text{inr}\,(v, x)$
$\text{distR}^{-1}(\text{inl}\,(v, w))$	$=$	$(\text{inl}\, v, w)$
$\text{distR}^{-1}(\text{inr}\,(v, x))$	$=$	$(\text{inr}\, v, x)$
$\text{wrap}\,(v)$	$=$	$\text{fold}\, v$
$\text{wrap}^{-1}(v)$	$=$	$\text{fold}^{-1}\, v$
$\text{id}(v)$	$=$	v
id^{-1}	$=$	id
$(c; d)(v)$	$=$	$d(c(v))$
$(c + d)(\text{inl}\, v)$	$=$	$\text{inl}\,(c(v))$
$(c + d)(\text{inr}\, w)$	$=$	$\text{inr}\,(d(w))$
$(c \times d)(v, w)$	$=$	$(c(v), d(w))$
$(\text{fix} f.c)(v)$	$=$	$c[\text{fix} f.c/f](v)$

Figure 6. Computational interpretation of coercions

a proj^{-1} coercion *and* an f that is left-guarded "only" by (a coercion operating on) a regular expression,, in this case 1, whose language contains the empty string.

3.2 Soundness

We have seen that, without a side condition on the coinduction rule, the coercion inference system is unsound for deducing regular expression containments. The key idea now is this: Impose a side condition that guarantees that the coercion in the conclusion of the coinduction rule is total. Since all other rules preserve totality of coercions, this yields a sound axiomatization of regular expression containment by Theorem 12. Since our coercions may contain free variables, we need to generalize totality to second-order coercions:

DEFINITION 18 (Hereditary totality). *We say coercion judgement* $\Gamma \vdash c : E \leq F$ *for* $\Gamma = f_1 : E_1 \leq F_1, \ldots, f_n : E_n \leq F_n$ *is* hereditarily total *if* $\mathcal{F}[\![\Gamma \vdash c : E \leq F]\!](f_1, \ldots, f_n)$ *is total whenever* f_i *is a total coercion from* E_i *to* F_i *for all* $i = 1, \ldots, n$.

We are now ready to define sound restrictions of the coercion inference system. Instead of formulating a specific side condition, we parameterize over side conditions for the coinduction rule to express, generally, what is necessary for such a side condition to guarantee soundness.

DEFINITION 19 (Coercion inference system with side condition). *Consider the coercion inference system of Figure 5 where the coinduction rule is equipped with a side condition P, a predicate on the coercion judgement in the conclusion:*

$$\frac{\Gamma, f : E \leq F \vdash c : E \leq F}{\Gamma \vdash \text{fix} f.c : E \leq F} \quad (P(\Gamma \vdash \text{fix} f.c : E \leq F)).$$

We write $\Gamma \vdash_P c : E \leq F$*, if each application of the coinduction rule in the derivation of* $\Gamma \vdash c : E \leq F$ *satisfies* P.

We arrive at the Master Soundness Theorem, which provides a general criterion for sound side conditions:

THEOREM 20 (Soundness). *Let* P *be any predicate on coercion judgements that universally implies hereditary totality.*
Then $\vdash_P d : E \leq F$ *implies* $\models E \leq F$ *for all* d, E, F.

This theorem shows that hereditary totality is an "upper bound" for how liberal the side condition can be without the risk of losing sound computational interpretation of a regular expression containment proof as a coercion. Interestingly, allowing *partial* coercions does not *necessarily* make the resulting inference system unsound for proving regular expression containment. If we define the side condition

$$P^t(\Gamma \vdash \text{fix} f.c : E \leq F) \iff \models E \leq F,$$

the resulting inference system is trivially sound and complete since $\vdash \text{fix} f.f : E \leq F$ is derivable for those E, F such that $\models E \leq F$. Clearly, $\mathcal{F}[\![\vdash \text{fix} f.f : E \leq F]\!]$ is computationally completely useless, however: it never terminates.

Unfortunately, hereditary totality itself is undecidable even for the restricted language of coercions denotable by coercion judgements:[3]

THEOREM 21. *Whether or not* $\Gamma \vdash c : E \leq F$ *is hereditarily total is undecidable.*

PROOF Even totality of $\vdash c : 1 \leq 1$ is undecidable. This follows from the undecidability of $\vdash c : 1^* \times 1^* \leq 1^* \times 1^*$, which in turn follows from encoding Minsky machines (2-register machines) as closed coercion judgements, using a unary coding of natural numbers. □

This makes hereditary totality inapplicable as a conventional side condition in an axiomatization, where valid instances of an inference rule are expected to be decidable. Below we provide polynomial-time decidable side conditions that are sufficient to encode existing derivations in previous axiomatizations (see Section 3.3). In each case their soundness follows from application of Theorem 20. In this sense, hereditary totality can be considered the "mother of all side conditions", even though it itself is "too extensional" to be used as a conventional side condition.

DEFINITION 22 (Syntactic side conditions S_i). *Define predicates* S_1, S_2, S_3 *and* S_4 *on coercion judgements of the form* $\Gamma \vdash \text{fix} f.c : E \leq F$ *as follows:*

- $S_1(\Gamma \vdash \text{fix} f.c : E \leq F)$ *if and only if each occurrence of* f *in* c *is left-guarded by a* d *where* $\Gamma, \ldots \vdash d : E' \leq F'$ *is the coercion judgement for* d *occurring in the derivation of* $\Gamma \vdash \text{fix} f.c : E \leq F$ *and* $o(E') = 0$ *(from Definition 3).*
- $S_2(\Gamma \vdash \text{fix} f.c : E \leq F)$ *if and only if each occurrence of* f *in* c *is left-guarded and for each subterm of the form* $c_1; c_2$ *in* c *at least one of the following conditions is satisfied:*

[3] Proved by Eijiro Sumii, Yasuhiko Minamide, Naoki Kobayashi, Atsushi Igarashi and Fritz Henglein at the IFIP TC 2 Working Group 2.8 meeting at Shirahama, Japan, April 11-16, 2010

- c_1 *is closed and* proj^{-1}*-free;*
- c_2 *is closed.*

- $S_3(\Gamma \vdash \mathrm{fix} f.c : E \leq F)$ *if* c *is of the form* $\mathrm{wrap}^{-1}; (\mathrm{id} + \mathrm{id} \times f); d$ *where* d *is closed.*
- $S_4 = S_1 \vee S_3$.

It is easy to see that S_1, S_2, S_3 and S_4 are polynomial-time checkable. They furthermore imply hereditary totality:

LEMMA 23 (Hereditary totality for S_i). *Let* $\Gamma \vdash \mathrm{fix} f.c : E \leq F$ *such that* $S_i(\Gamma \vdash \mathrm{fix} f.c : E \leq F)$ *with* $i \in \{1, 2, 3, 4\}$.
Then $\Gamma \vdash \mathrm{fix} f.c : E \leq F$ *is hereditarily total.*

PROOF (Sketch) Side condition S_3 is a special case of S_2. The case of S_4 follows from S_1 and S_3. We have formulated S_3 separately since S_4 is sufficient to code all derivations in Salomaa's and Grabmayer's axiomatizations. S_2 by itself, without S_1, is sufficient for Kozen's axiomatization.

The general idea behind the side conditions S_1, S_2 is that they ensure that every recursive call f in the body c of a recursively defined coercion $\mathrm{fix} f.c$ is called with an argument whose *size* is properly smaller than the size of the original call. The difference between the two conditions is the definition of size in each case.

Consider S_1. Define the 0-*size* $|v|_0$ of a value by $|v|_0 = |\mathrm{flat}(v)|$; that is, it is the length of the underlying string. Values containing $()$ may be of 0-size 0, e.g. $|((), ())|_0 = 0$, and the size of a component of a pair may be the same as the size of the pair: $|((), v)|_0 = |v|_0$. Consider a call of $\mathrm{fix} f.c$ to a value v of 0-size n. The predicate S_1 ensures that all recursive calls to f in c are only applied to a value constructed from the second component of some pair, where the first component has size at least 1. Since coercions never increase the size this guarantees that the recursive call is applied to a value of 0-size at most $n - 1$.

Now consider S_2. Define the 1-size $|v|_1$ of v as follows:

$$
\begin{array}{rclcrcl}
|()|_1 & = & 1 & \quad & |a|_1 & = & 1 \\
|\mathrm{inl}\, v|_1 & = & |v|_1 & & |\mathrm{inr}\, v|_1 & = & |v|_1 \\
|\mathrm{fold}\, v|_1 & = & |v|_1 & & |(v, w)|_1 & = & |v|_1 + |w|_1
\end{array}
$$

Note that if we had defined $|()|_1$ to be 0 then this would be just the 0-size (hence our terminology).

The idea for ensuring termination of a recursively defined coercion is the same as before, but for 1-size instead of 0-size. With 1-size we have the important property that each component of a pair is *properly* smaller than the pair, in particular $|w|_1 < |(v, w)|_1$ for *all* v. We say a coercion c is *nonexpansive* if $|c(v)|_1 < |v|_1$. All primitive coercions *except for* proj^{-1} are nonexpansive, and the inference rules preserve nonexpansiveness. Side condition S_2 guarantees that each recursive call is applied to an argument of size properly smaller than the original call. Informally, this is because S_2 guarantees that a recursive call of f is never applied to a value (constructed from) the *output* (return value) of a proj^{-1}-call. □

From Theorem 20, Lemma 23 and Theorem 12 we obtain:

COROLLARY 24 (Soundness for side conditions S_i). *Let* S_1, S_2, S_3, S_4 *as in Definition 22,* $i \in \{1, 2, 3, 4\}$.
Then $\vdash_{S_i} d : E \leq F$ *implies* $\models E \leq F$.

3.3 Completeness

We show now how to code derivations in Salomaa's, Kozen's and Grabmayer's axiomatizations of regular expression equivalence in our coercion inference system (Figure 5) with side condition S_4 (Salomaa, Grabmayer) or S_2 (Kozen). This provides a computational interpretation for each of these systems. Furthermore, it implies that coercion axiomatization with either S_2 or S_4 is complete. More precisely, we encode every derivation of $\vdash E = F$ as a pair of coercion judgements $\vdash c : E \leq F$ and $\vdash d : F \leq E$, which provides a computational interpretation of a regular expression equivalence as a pair of coercions that witness $\vdash E = F$ according to Corollary 13.

$$
\frac{E = F}{E^* = F^*}
$$

$$
E^* \quad = \quad (1 + E)^*
$$

$$
\frac{E = F \times E + G}{E = F^* \times G} \qquad (\text{if } o(F) = 0)
$$

Figure 7. Salomaa's rules for axiomatization F_1

Even though they are for regular expression *equivalence*, these codings also provide completeness of our coercion axiomatization for regular expression *containment*. Assume $\models E \leq F$. This holds if and only if $\models E + F = F$. By completeness of the regular expression equivalence axiomatizations, $E + F = F$ is derivable, and we can construct a coercion judgement of $\vdash c : E + F \leq F$. Composed with $\mathtt{tagL}$ this yields $\vdash \mathtt{tagL}\, ; c : E \leq F$, and we are done.

THEOREM 25 (Completeness). *Let* P *be either* S_2 *or* S_4.
If $\models E \leq F$ *then there exists* c *such that* $\vdash_P c : E \leq F$.

It follows that any side condition logically "between" S_2 or S_4 on the one hand and hereditary totality on the other hand yields a sound and complete coercion axiomatization of regular expression containment.

COROLLARY 26 (Soundness and completeness). *Let* P *be such that either* S_2 *or* S_4 *universally implies* P*, and* P *universally implies hereditary totality. Then* $\vdash_P c : E \leq F$ *if and only if* $\models E \leq F$.

Whereas hereditary totality is the natural "upper" bound we suspect that there are natural weaker "lower" bounds than S_2 and S_4.

3.3.1 Salomaa

Salomaa's System F_1 (Salomaa 1966) arises from adding the rules of Figure 7 to the axiomatization of weak equivalence (Figures 2, 3 and 4).[4] The side condition of the inference rule in Figure 7 is called the "no empty word property".

To be precise, we prove by induction on derivations of $E = F$ in System F_1 that there exist coercion judgements $\vdash_{S_4} c : E \leq F$ and $\vdash_{S_4} d : F \leq E$. This is straightforward for the weak equivalence rules. We thus concentrate on the rules in Figure 7.

Consider $\dfrac{E = F}{E^* = F^*}$. By induction hypothesis there exist $\vdash_{S_4} c : E \leq F$ and $\vdash_{S_4} d : F \leq E$. We reason as follows: Assume $E^* \leq F^*$ and call this assumption f.

$$
\begin{array}{rcll}
E^* & \leq & (1 + E \times E^*) & \text{by } \mathrm{wrap}^{-1} \\
 & \leq & (1 + F \times F^*) & \text{by } \mathrm{id} + c \times f \\
 & \leq & F^* & \text{by } \mathrm{wrap}
\end{array}
$$

This shows that

$$
f : E^* \leq F^* \vdash_{S_4} (\mathrm{wrap}^{-1}; \mathrm{id} + c \times f; \mathrm{wrap}) : E^* \leq F^*.
$$

Note that $\vdash \mathrm{fix} f.(\mathrm{wrap}^{-1}; \mathrm{id} + c \times f; \mathrm{wrap}) : E^* \leq F^*$ satisfies side condition S_3 and thus S_4. Its computational interpretation is the map-function on lists. With S_4 satisfied we can ap-

[4] Technically, this is the "left-handed" dual due to Grabmayer (2005) to Salomaa's original "right-handed" formulation, where the fold-unfold rule for Kleene star is axiomatized as $E^* = 1 + E^* \times E$.

ply the coinduction rule to conclude $\vdash_{S_4}$ fix$f$.(wrap^{-1}; id $+ c \times f$; wrap) : $E^* \leq F^*$. Similarly, we get $\vdash_{S_4}$ fix g.(wrap^{-1}; id $+ d \times g$; wrap) : $F^* \leq E^*$.

Consider $E^* = (1+E)^*$. The case $E^* \leq (1+E)^*$ follows from the rule above since $E \leq 1+E$. For the converse containment assume $f : (1+E)^* \leq E^*$. We have:

$$\begin{array}{lll} (1+E)^* & \leq 1+(1+E)\times(1+E)^* & \text{by wrap}^{-1} \\ & \leq 1+(1+E)\times E^* & \text{by } f \\ & \leq 1+1\times E^* + E\times E^* & \text{by distR} \\ & \leq 1+E^*+E\times E^* & \text{by proj} \\ & \leq 1+E\times E^*+E^* & \text{by retag} \\ & \leq E^*+E^* & \text{by wrap} \\ & \leq E^* & \text{by untag} \end{array}$$

We are a bit informal here: We have left associativity, congruence and identity steps implicit. Let us consider $\vdash$ fix$f.c : (1+E)^* \leq E^*$ now. Without displaying c in full detail, from the derivation above we can see that f satisfies side condition S_3 and thus S_4, and we can conclude $\vdash_{S_4}$ fix$f.c : (1+E)^* \leq E^*$ by the coinduction rule. Operationally, $\mathcal{F}[\![\vdash \text{fix}f.c : (1+E)^* \leq E^*]\!]$ traverses its input list of type $\mathcal{T}[\![(1+E)^*]\!]$, removes all occurrences of inl () and returns the v's for each inr v in the input.

Finally, consider $\dfrac{E = F\times E + G}{E = F^*\times G}$ (if $o(F)=0$).

Our induction hypothesis is $\vdash_{S_4} c_1 : E \leq F\times E+G$ and $\vdash_{S_4} d_1 : F\times E+G \leq E$. Let us consider $F^*\times G \leq E$ first. Assume $f : F^*\times G \leq E$, and we can calculate $d_2 : F^*\times G \leq E$ as follows:

$$\begin{array}{lll} F^*\times G & \leq (1+F\times F^*)\times G & \text{by wrap}^{-1} \\ & \leq 1\times G+F\times F^*\times G & \text{by distR} \\ & \leq G+F\times F^*\times G & \text{by proj} \\ & \leq G+F\times E & \text{by } f \\ & \leq F\times E+G & \text{by retag} \\ & \leq E & \text{by } d_1 \end{array}$$

We can see that $\vdash$ fix$f.d_2 : F^*\times G \leq E$ satisfies S_2 and, since $o(F)=0$, also S_1 and thus S_4. We can thus conclude $\vdash_{S_4}$ fix$f.d_2 : F^*\times G \leq E$ by the coinduction rule. Observe that $\vdash$ fix$f.d_2 : F^*\times G \leq E$ is hereditarily total, whether or not $o(F)=0$, since S_2 is also satisfied.

For the other direction, assume $\vdash_{S_4} g : E \leq F^*\times G$, and we can calculate $c_2 : E \leq F^*\times G$ essentially in the reverse direction to the above calculation.

$$\begin{array}{lll} E & \leq F\times E+G & \text{by } c_1 \\ & \leq G+F\times E & \text{by retag} \\ & \leq G+F\times F^*\times G & \text{by } g \\ & \leq 1\times G+F\times F^*\times G & \text{by proj}^{-1} \\ & \leq (1+F\times F^*)\times G & \text{by distR}^{-1} \\ & \leq F^*\times G & \text{by wrap} \end{array}$$

Here, the coercion judgement $\vdash$ fix$g.c_2 : E \leq F^*\times G$ may computationally be nonterminating: Choose, e.g., $c_1 = \text{proj}^{-1}$; tagL : $E \leq 1\times E+0$. For $o(F)=0$, however, $\vdash$ fix$g.c_2 : E \leq F^*\times G$ satisfies side condition S_1 and thus S_4; in particular, it always terminates. We can conclude $\vdash_{S_4}$ fix$g.c_2 : E \leq F\times E+G$ by the coinduction rule.

3.3.2 Kozen

Kozen (1994) has shown that adding the rules in Figure 8 to weak equivalence is sound and complete for regular expression equivalence. Formally, a containment $E \leq F$ in his axiomatization is an abbreviation for $E+F=F$. We show now that all derivations in his system can be coded as coercion judgements with side condition S_2.

$$1+(E^*\times E) \quad \leq \quad E^*$$

$$\frac{E\times F \leq F}{E^*\times F \leq F} \qquad \frac{E\times F \leq E}{E\times F^* \leq E}$$

Figure 8. Kozen's rules for axiomatization of Kleene Algebras

$$\begin{array}{rcll} 0_{a_i} & = & 0 & \\ 1_{a_i} & = & 0 & \\ (a_i)_{a_i} & = & 1 & \\ (a_j)_{a_i} & = & 0 & (i \neq j) \\ (E+F)_{a_i} & = & E_{a_i}+F_{a_i} & \\ (E\times F)_{a_i} & = & E_{a_i}\times F & (o(E)=0) \\ (E\times F)_{a_i} & = & E_{a_i}\times F+F_{a_i} & (o(E)=1) \\ (E^*)_{a_i} & = & E_{a_i}\times E^* & \end{array}$$

Figure 9. Definition of Brzozowski-derivative

Consider $1+(E^*\times E) \leq E^*$. It is sufficient to construct a coercion judgement $\vdash_{S_2} c : E^*\times E \leq E\times E^*$, since we then have $\vdash_{S_2}$ id $+ c$; wrap : $1\times E^*\times E \leq E^*$, as desired.

Assume $f : E^*\times E \leq E\times E^*$. We can calculate $c : E^*\times E \leq E\times E^*$ as follows:

$$\begin{array}{lll} E^*\times E & \leq (1+E\times E^*)\times E & \text{by wrap}^{-1} \\ & \leq 1\times E+E\times E^*\times E & \text{by distR} \\ & \leq 1\times E+E\times E\times E^* & \text{by } f \\ & \leq E\times 1+E\times E\times E^* & \text{by swap} \\ & \leq E\times(1+E\times E^*) & \text{by distL}^{-1} \\ & \leq E\times E^* & \text{by wrap} \end{array}$$

Writing c explicitly, we have

$$\begin{array}{l} c = (\text{wrap}^{-1}\times \text{id}); \text{distR}; \\ \quad \text{swap} + (\text{assoc}^{-1}; \text{id}\times f); \\ \quad \text{distL}^{-1}; \text{id}\times \text{wrap} \end{array}$$

Observe that $\vdash$ fix$f.c : E^*\times E \leq E\times E^*$ satisfies side condition S_2, and we can conclude $\vdash_{S_2}$ fix$f.c : E^*\times E \leq E\times E^*$ by the coinduction rule.

Consider the rule $\dfrac{E\times F \leq F}{E^*\times F \leq F}$. Our induction hypothesis is that there exists $\vdash_{S_2} d : E\times F \leq F$. Assume $f : E^*\times F \leq F$, and we calculate $c : E^*\times F \leq F$ as follows:

$$\begin{array}{lll} E^*\times F & \leq (1+E\times E^*)\times F & \text{by wrap}^{-1} \\ & \leq 1\times F+E\times E^*\times F & \text{by distR} \\ & \leq 1\times F+E\times F & \text{by } f \\ & \leq F+E\times F & \text{by proj} \\ & \leq F+F & \text{by } d \\ & \leq F & \text{by untag} \end{array}$$

Note that $\vdash$ fix$f.c : E^*\times F \leq F$ satisfies side condition S_2, and we can apply the coinduction rule to conclude $\vdash_{S_2}$ fix$f.c : E^*\times F \leq F$.

The rule $\dfrac{E\times F \leq E}{E\times F^* \leq E}$ is similar to the previous rule, with an additional step involving $E^*\times E \leq E\times E^*$.

3.3.3 Grabmayer

The following results hold for all alphabets, but for convenience we assume that $\mathcal{A}$ is finite in this section.

The *Brzozowski-derivative* E_a (Antimirov 1996; Brzozowski 1964; Conway 1971; Rutten 1998; Salomaa 1966) for regular expression E and $a \in \mathcal{A}$ is defined in Figure 9.

$$\dfrac{\begin{matrix}[E = F] & & [E = F] \\ \vdots & \cdots & \vdots \\ E_{a_1} = F_{a_1} & & E_{a_n} = F_{a_n}\end{matrix}}{E = F} \quad (o(E) = o(F))$$

Figure 10. Grabmayer's coinduction rule COMP/FIX

Grabmayer (2005) recognized that Brzozowski-derivatives can be combined with the ACI-properties of $+$ and the coinductive fixed point rule for recursive types of Brandt and Henglein (1998) to give a *coinductive* axiomatization of regular expression equivalence. His rule COMP/FIX is given in Figure 10. Indeed, it can be seen that in the presence of a transitivity rule of equational logic, the compatibility-with-context-rules, and ACI-axioms, only the rule COMP/FIX is needed to obtain a complete system for regular expression equivalence, without the other rules of Grabmayer's inference system $\mathbf{cREG}_0(\Sigma)$. A sequent style presentation of COMP/FIX is as follows:

$$\frac{\Gamma, E = F \vdash_G E_a = F_a \text{ for all } a \in \mathcal{A}, \quad o(E) = o(F)}{\Gamma \vdash_G E = F}$$

Let us write $\Gamma_{\leq}$ and $\Gamma_{\geq}$ for Γ where all occurrences of $=$ in Γ are replaced by $\leq$, respectively $\geq$. We can show by rule induction that for each derivation of $\Gamma \vdash_G E = F$ there exist coercion judgements $\Gamma_{\leq} \vdash_{S_4} c : E \leq F$ and $\Gamma_{\geq} \vdash_{S_4} d : F \leq E$.

The only interesting rule to consider is COMP/FIX. By induction hypothesis, we have $\Gamma_{\leq}, f : E \leq F \vdash c_a : E_a \leq F_a$ and $\Gamma_{\geq}, g : F \leq E \vdash d_a : F_a \leq E_a$ for all $a \in \mathcal{A}$, where $o(E) = o(F)$. Note that $\models E = o(E) + \sum_{a \in \mathcal{A}} a \times E_a$. Salomaa (1966) shows that $E = o(E) + \sum_{a \in \mathcal{A}} a \times E_a$ is derivable from the rules for weak equivalence (Figures 2, 3 and 4), extended with Salomaa's Axiom A_{11}: $F^* = (1+F)^*$. (See also Grabmayer (2005, Lemma 5, p. 189).) A_{11} is only required for what Frisch and Cardelli (2004) call *problematic* regular expressions, regular expressions of the form G^* where $o(G) = 1$.

By applying the derivation coding of Salomaa's axiomatization from Subsection 3.3.1 to the derivation of $E = o(E) + \sum_{a \in \mathcal{A}} a \times E_a$, we know that there exist $\vdash_{S_4} c_E : o(E) + \sum_{a \in \mathcal{A}} a \times E_a \leq E$ and $\vdash_{S_4} d_E : E \leq o(E) + \sum_{a \in \mathcal{A}} a \times E_a$. This gives us the following derivable coercion judgements:

$$\Gamma_{\leq}, f : E \leq F \vdash_{S_4} d_E; (\mathrm{id}_{o(E)} + \textstyle\sum_{a \in \mathcal{A}} \mathrm{id}_a \times c_a); c_F : E \leq F$$
$$\Gamma_{\geq}, g : F \leq E \vdash_{S_4} d_F; (\mathrm{id}_{o(F)} + \textstyle\sum_{a \in \mathcal{A}} \mathrm{id}_a \times d_a); c_E : F \leq E$$

We can observe that they satisfy side condition S_1 and thus S_4. By the coinduction rule we can thus conclude:

$$\Gamma_{\leq} \vdash_{S_4} \mathrm{fix} f.d_E; (\mathrm{id}_{o(E)} + \textstyle\sum_{a \in \mathcal{A}} \mathrm{id}_a \times c_a); c_F : E \leq F$$
$$\Gamma_{\geq} \vdash_{S_4} \mathrm{fix} g.d_F; (\mathrm{id}_{o(F)} + \textstyle\sum_{a \in \mathcal{A}} \mathrm{id}_a \times d_a); c_E : F \leq E$$

This provides an alternative proof to the one based on coding Salomaa's System F_1 for concluding that $\models E \leq F$ implies $\vdash_{S_4} E \leq F$.

3.4 Examples

We give examples of coercion judgements for regular expression containments.

EXAMPLE 27 (Denesting as coercion). *We continue Example 14 by implementing the function proving $(a+b)^* \leq a^* \times (b \times a^*)^*$ in the coercion language.*

Abbreviate $E = (a+b)^*$ and $F = a^* \times (b \times a^*)^*$. We can calculate $(a+b)^* \leq a^* \times (b \times a^*)^*$ as follows.

$$\begin{array}{rcll}
E & \leq & 1 + (a+b) \times E & \textit{by } \mathrm{wrap}^{-1} \\
& \leq & 1 + (a+b) \times F & \textit{by } f \\
& \leq & 1 + (b+a) \times F & \textit{by } \mathrm{retag} \\
& \leq & 1 + ((b \times F) + (a \times F)) & \textit{by } \mathrm{distR} \\
& \leq & 1 + (((b \times a^*) \times (b \times a^*)^*) + (a \times F)) & \textit{by } \mathrm{assoc} \\
& \leq & (1 + (b \times a^*) \times (b \times a^*)^*) + ((a \times F)) & \textit{by } \mathrm{shuffle} \\
& \leq & (b \times a^*)^* + (a \times F) & \textit{by } \mathrm{wrap} \\
& \leq & (b \times a^*)^* + ((a \times a^*) \times (b \times a^*)^*) & \textit{by } \mathrm{assoc} \\
& \leq & (b \times a^*)^* + ((1 + a \times a^*) \times (b \times a^*)^*) & \textit{by } \mathrm{tagR} \\
& \leq & (b \times a^*)^* + F & \textit{by } \mathrm{wrap} \\
& \leq & 1 \times (b \times a^*)^* + F & \textit{by } \mathrm{proj}^{-1} \\
& \leq & (1 + a \times a^*) \times (b \times a^*)^* + F & \textit{by } \mathrm{tagL} \\
& \leq & F + F & \textit{by } \mathrm{wrap} \\
& \leq & F & \textit{by } \mathrm{untag}
\end{array}$$

Writing it out in full, the coercion coercion judgement is

$$\begin{array}{ll}
\vdash \mathrm{fix} f. & \mathrm{wrap}^{-1}; \mathrm{id} + \mathrm{retag} \times f; \mathrm{id} + \mathrm{distR}; \\
& \mathrm{id} + (\mathrm{assoc} + \mathrm{assoc}); \mathrm{shuffle}; \mathrm{wrap} + \mathrm{id}; \\
& \mathrm{id} + (\mathrm{tagR}\,; \mathrm{wrap}) \times \mathrm{id}; \mathrm{proj}^{-1} + \mathrm{id}; \\
& (\mathrm{tagL}\,; \mathrm{wrap}) \times \mathrm{id} + \mathrm{id}; \mathrm{untag} \ : \\
& \qquad (a+b)^* \leq a^* \times (b \times a^*)^*
\end{array}$$

In the above example, the coercion is, operationally, basically the function f defined in Example 14: It folds a constant-time computable function over its input list and therefore runs in linear time. Kozen (1994, Proposition 2.7) gives a proof of the same inclusion in his axiomatization of Kleene algebra. When encoding it as in Section 3.3.2 we obtain a similar, linear-time coercion. This raises the question whether computational interpretation of *all* proofs of the *same* containment in the axiomatizations of Salomaa, Kozen and Grabmayer yield coercions of the same, linear-time complexity. Remarkably, this is not the case, as illustrated by the next example.

EXAMPLE 28 (Coercion efficiency). *Consider $a^* \times a^{**} \leq a^*$. The simplest way to prove this with Kozen's rules is to start from $a \times a^* \leq a^*$ proved by* tagR ; wrap. *By the left inference rule in Figure 8 we then get $a^* \times a^* \leq a^*$. By the right inference rule in Figure 8 we finally obtain $a^* \times a^{**} \leq a^*$.*

Let us consider the computational interpretation of this proof. We have two (nested) applications of the (left and right, respectively) inference rule from Figure 8. This gives quadratic *runtime. It is unclear to us whether there exists a proof using Kozen's rules whose computational interpretation as a functional program runs in linear time. It is possible to construct a linear-time coercion for $a^* \times a^{**} \leq a^*$ in our coercion inference system, however. This can be systematically obtained by encoding the (minimal) proof in Grabmayer's axiomatization. In fact, the encoding of any proof in Grabmayer's axiomatization will have linear run time. This is because the only admissible application of recursion in Grabmayer's axiomatization is of the form $\mathrm{fix} f.d_E; (\mathrm{id} + \Sigma_{a \in \mathcal{A}} \mathrm{id}_a \times c_a); c_F$, where f does not occur in d_E and c_F, which entails that only constant amount of processing occurs for each constant part of the input.*

3.5 Parametric completeness

Let us extend regular expressions by adding variables that can be bound to arbitrary regular sets. Formally,

$$E, F, G, H ::= 0 \mid 1 \mid a \mid X \mid E + F \mid E \times F \mid E^*$$

where X ranges over a denumerable set of *(formal) variables* $\{X_i\}_{i \in \mathbb{N}}$. Such a regular expression is *closed* if it contains no formal variables. We define $\models \forall X_1, \ldots, X_m.E[X_1, \ldots, X_m] \leq$

$F[X_1, \ldots, X_m]$ if the containment holds for all substitutions of X_i with (closed) regular expressions.

Our axiomatization is immediately applicable to regular expressions with free variables. Without change, it is not only complete, but *parametrically complete* for infinite alphabets:

THEOREM 29 (Parametric completeness). *Let $\mathcal{A}$ be infinite. Let the side condition P for the coinduction rule in Figure 5 be either total hereditariness or S_2. Then: $\models \forall X_1, \ldots, X_m. E \leq F$ if and only if $\vdash_P c : E \leq F$.*

PROOF Only if: By rule induction, coercion axiomatization is closed under substitution, with total hereditariness or S_2 as side condition. Note that this is not the case for S_4. (Technically, S_1 is not even defined for regular expressions with variables, since $o(X)$ is undefined.)

If: Assume $\models \forall X_1, \ldots, X_n. E \leq F$. Let $b_1, \ldots, b_n$ be n distinct alphabet symbols not occurring in E or F. (Since $\mathcal{A}$ is infinite, they exist.) By definition of $\models \forall X_1, \ldots, X_n. E \leq F$, we have $\models E\{X_1 \mapsto b_1, \ldots, X_n \mapsto b_n\} \leq F\{X_1 \mapsto b_1, \ldots, X_n \mapsto b_n\}$. By Theorem 25 (completeness), there is a derivable coercion judgement $\vdash_P c : E\{X_1 \mapsto b_1, \ldots, X_n \mapsto b_n\} \leq F\{X_1 \mapsto b_1, \ldots, X_n \mapsto b_n\}$. Since coercion axiomatization with hereditary totality or S_2 as side condition is closed under substitution, the $b_1, \ldots, b_n$ can be replaced by arbitrary regular expressions $E_1, \ldots, E_n$, respectively, such that $\vdash c : E\{b_1 \mapsto E_1, \ldots, b_n \mapsto E_n\} \leq F\{b_1 \mapsto E_1, \ldots, b_n \mapsto E_n\}$. In particular, we can choose $X_1, \ldots, X_n$ for $E_1, \ldots, E_n$ and thus obtain $\vdash c : E \leq F$. □

As a consequence of Theorem 29, a schematic containment such as $E \times E^* \leq E^* \times E$ is *derivable*, not just *admissible* in our axiomatization: we can synthesize a *single* coercion judgement for it and use it for all instances of E. For finite alphabets our axiomatization is incomplete, however: $\models \forall X. (X \leq (a+b)^*)$ holds for $\mathcal{A} = \{a, b\}$, but $X \leq (a+b)^*$ is not derivable.

We observe that Kozen's axiomatization (Kozen 1994) is also parametrically complete for infinite alphabets, but not for finite alphabets. Neither Salomaa's (Salomaa 1966) nor Grabmayer's (Grabmayer 2005) appear to be parametrically complete: In Salomaa's case we need to make a case distinction as to whether the regular expression E substituted for X has the empty word property; and in Grabmayer's case E needs to be differentiated, the proof of which depends on the syntax of E.

4. Application: Compact bit representations of parse trees

If the regular expressions are statically known in a program we can code their elements, more precisely their parse trees, compactly as bit strings.

4.1 Bit coded strings

Intuitively, a *bit coding* of a parse tree p factors p into its static part, the regular expression E it is a member of, and its dynamic part, a bit sequence that uniquely identifies p as a particular element of E.

Consider for example the string $s = abaab$ as an element of $H_1 = (a+b)^*$. It has the unique parse tree corresponding to

$$p_s = [\text{inl}\, a, \text{inr}\, b, \text{inl}\, a, \text{inl}\, a, \text{inr}\, b]$$

with $\vdash p_s : H_1$, which shows that $\text{flat}(p_s) = abaab$ is an element of $\mathcal{L}[\![H_1]\!]$.

Figures 11 and 12 define regular-expression directed coding and decoding functions from parse trees to their *(canonical) bit codings* and back. Informally, the bit coding of a parse tree consists of listing the inl- and inr-constructors in preorder traversal, where inl is mapped to 0 and inr is mapped to 1. No bits are generated

$$\begin{array}{lcl}
\text{code}(() : 1) & = & \epsilon \\
\text{code}(a : a) & = & \epsilon \\
\text{code}(\text{inl}\, v : E + F) & = & 0\ \text{code}(v : E) \\
\text{code}(\text{inr}\, w : E + F) & = & 1\ \text{code}(w : F) \\
\text{code}((v, w) : E \times F) & = & \text{code}(v : E)\ \text{code}(w : F) \\
\text{code}(\text{fold}\, v : E^*) & = & \text{code}(v : 1 + E \times E^*)
\end{array}$$

Figure 11. Type-directed encoding function from parse trees (values) to bit sequences

$$\begin{array}{lcl}
\text{decode}'(d : 1) & = & ((), d) \\
\text{decode}'(d : a) & = & (a, d) \\
\text{decode}'(0d : E + E') & = & \textbf{let}\ (v, d') = \text{decode}'(d : E) \\
 & & \textbf{in}\ (\text{inl}\, v, d') \\
\text{decode}'(1d : E + E') & = & \textbf{let}\ (w, d') = \text{decode}'(d : E) \\
 & & \textbf{in}\ (\text{inr}\, w, d') \\
\text{decode}'(d : E \times E') & = & \textbf{let}\ (v, d') = \text{decode}'(d : E) \\
 & & \quad (w, d'') = \text{decode}'(d' : E') \\
 & & \textbf{in}\ ((v, w), d'') \\
\text{decode}'(d : E^*) & = & \textbf{let}\ (v, d') = \text{decode}'(d : 1 + E \times E^*) \\
 & & \textbf{in}\ (\text{fold}\, v, d') \\
\text{decode}(d : E) = & = & \textbf{let}\ (w, d') = \text{decode}'(d : E) \\
 & & \textbf{in}\ \textbf{if}\ d' = \epsilon\ \textbf{then}\ w\ \textbf{else}\ \mathit{error}
\end{array}$$

Figure 12. Type-directed decoding function from bit sequences to parse trees (values)

for the other constructors. For example, the bit coding b_s for p_s is 10 11 10 10 11 0.

We can think of the bit coding of a parse tree p as a bit coding of the underlying string $\text{flat}(p)$. Note that the bit coding of a string is not unique. It depends on

- which regular expression it is parsed under; and
- if the regular expression is ambiguous, which parse tree is chosen for it.

As an illustration of the first effect, the bit representation b'_s of s under $H_2 = 1 + (a+b)^* \times (a+b)$ is 1 10 11 10 10 0 1. Since both H_1 and H_2 are unambiguous there are no other bit representations of s under either H_1 or H_2.

4.2 Bit code coercions

So what if we have a bit representation of a run-time string under one regular expression and we need to transform it into a bit representation under another regular expression? This arises if the branches of a conditional expression each return a bit-coded string, but under different regular expressions E_1, E_2, and we need to ensure that the result of the conditional is a bit coding in a common regular expression F that contains the E_1 and E_2.

Let us consider s again and how to transform b_s into b'_s. As we have seen in Section 3.3, E^* is contained in $1 + (E^* \times E)$ for all E and there is a parametric polymorphic coercion $c_1 : \forall X. X^* \leq 1 + (X^* \times X)$ mapping any value $\vdash p : E^*$ representing a parse tree for string $s' = \text{flat}(p)$ to a parse tree $\vdash p' : 1 + E^* \times E$ for s'. In particular applying c_1 to p_s yields p'_s.

We can compose c_1 with code and decode from Figures 11 and 12 to compute a function $\hat{c}_1$ operating on bit codings:

$$\hat{c}_1 = \text{code} \cdot c_1 \cdot \text{decode}.$$

Instead of converting to and from values we can define a *bit coding coercion* by providing a computational interpretation of

$$
\begin{array}{lcl}
\text{retag}(0d) & = & 1d \\
\text{retag}(1d) & = & 0d \\
\text{retag}^{-1} & = & \text{retag} \\
\text{tagL}\,(d) & = & 0d \\
\text{untag}\,(bd) & = & d \\
\text{shuffle}(0d) & = & 00d \\
\text{shuffle}(10d) & = & 01d \\
\text{shuffle}(11d) & = & 1d \\
\text{shuffle}^{-1}(00d) & = & 0d \\
\text{shuffle}^{-1}(01d) & = & 10d \\
\text{shuffle}^{-1}(1d) & = & 11d \\
\text{swap}(d) & = & d \\
\text{swap}^{-1} & = & \text{swap} \\
\text{proj}(d) & = & d \\
\text{proj}^{-1}(d) & = & d \\
\text{assoc}(d) & = & d \\
\text{assoc}^{-1}(d) & = & d \\
\text{distL}(d : E \times (F + G)) & & \\
 & = & \textbf{let}\,(d_1, bd_2) = \text{split}(d : E) \\
 & & \textbf{in}\, bd_1 d_2 \\
\text{distL}^{-1}(bd : (E \times F) + (E \times G)) & & \\
 & = & \textbf{let}\,(d_1, d_2) = \text{split}(d : E) \\
 & & \textbf{in}\, d_1 bd_2 \\
\text{distR}(d) & = & d \\
\text{distR}^{-1}(d) & = & d \\
\text{wrap}\,(d) & = & d \\
\text{wrap}^{-1}(d) & = & d \\
(c + c')(0d) & = & 0\ c(d) \\
(c + c')(1d') & = & 1\ c'(d')) \\
(c \times c')(d : E \times F) & = & \textbf{let}\,(d_1, d_2) = \text{split}(d : E) \\
 & & \textbf{in}\, c(d_1)\ c'(d_2) \\
(c; c')(d) & = & c'(c(d)) \\
\text{id}(d) & = & d \\
(\text{fix}\, f.c)(d) & = & c[\text{fix}\, f.c/f](d)
\end{array}
$$

Figure 13. Coercions operating on typed bit sequence representations instead of values

$$
\begin{array}{lcl}
\text{split}(d : 1) & = & (\epsilon, d) \\
\text{split}(d : a) & = & (\epsilon, d) \\
\text{split}(0d : E + E') & = & \textbf{let}\,(d_1, d_2) = \text{split}(d : E) \\
 & & \textbf{in}\,(0d_1, d_2) \\
\text{split}(1d' : E + E') & = & \textbf{let}\,(d_1, d_2) = \text{split}(d' : E') \\
 & & \textbf{in}\,(1d_1, d_2) \\
\text{split}(d : E^*) & = & \text{split}(d : 1 + E \times E^*) \\
\text{split}(d : E \times E') & = & \textbf{let}\,(d_1, d_2) = \text{split}(d : E) \\
 & & \quad (d_3, d_4) = \text{split}(d_2 : E') \\
 & & \textbf{in}\,(d_1 d_3, d_4)
\end{array}
$$

Figure 14. Type-directed function for splitting bit sequence into subsequences corresponding to components of product type

$$
\frac{v : \alpha[\mu X.\alpha/X]}{\text{fold}\, v : \mu X.\alpha}
$$

Figure 15. Inhabitation rule for μ

coercion judgements that operates directly on bit coded strings. See Figure 13. It uses the type-directed function split from Figure 14 for splitting a bit sequence into a pair of bit sequences.

Consider for example the coercion $\vdash c_0 : E^* \times E$ to $E \times E^*$ from Section 3.3. By interpreting c_0 according to Figure 13 we arrive at the following highly efficient function g_E, which transforms bit codings of values of $E^* \times E$ into corresponding bit representations for $E \times E^*$.

$$
\begin{array}{lcl}
g_E(0d) & = & 0d \\
g_E(1d) & = & 1\, f_E(d) \\
f_E(0d) & = & d0 \\
f_E(1d) & = & \textbf{let}\,(d_1, d_2) = \text{split}_E(d)\textbf{in}\, d_1\, 1\, f_E(d_2)
\end{array}
$$

The bit coded version of $c_1 : E^* \leq 1 + E^* \times E$ gives us a linear-time function h_E that operates directly on bit codings of (parse trees) of strings in E^* and transforms them to bit codings in $1 + E^* \times E$:

$$
\begin{array}{lcl}
h_E(0d) & = & 0d \\
h_E(1d) & = & 1\, g_E(d)
\end{array}
$$

Note that $h_{(a+b)}$ is the bit coding coercion from H_1 to H_2. It transforms 10 11 10 10 11 0 into 1 10 11 10 10 0 1 without ever materializing a string or value.

4.3 Tail-recursive μ-types

The presented bit sequences are compact, but their sizes depend on the regular expression used. Thus it is necessary to use *reasonable* regular expressions to obtain compact bit sequences. In fact the most compact representations can be found only by generalizing regular expressions to *tail-recursive μ-types*. We will use the remainder of this section to study this extension and the compression it allows.

A common representation of strings over an alphabet $\Sigma = \{a_1, \ldots, a_{255}\}$ of 255 characters from the Latin-1 (ISO/IEC 8859-1:1998) alphabet employs a sequence of 8-bit bytes representing each of the 255 different characters and uses the remaining byte to indicate the end of the string. This gives a total size of $8 \cdot (n + 1)$ bits to represent a string of length n.

Consider now the size of the bit sequence from Section 4.1 of a string under regular expression E_Σ^* where E_Σ is a sum type holding all the 255 characters in Σ. This can be written in many ways using permutations and associations of the characters. For example, if we define E_Σ as $a_1 + (a_2 + (a_3 + \ldots + a_{255}) \ldots)$ this means that the size of the bit coding of a_k is k bits long. This can be improved by ensuring that the type is balanced such that each path to a character has the same length. As there are 255 characters this means we will use 8 bits to represent each characters, leaving one path unused (so one character only uses 7 bits). Now we can look at the space required for the bit coding of a string under type E_Σ^*. Since E_Σ^* is unfolded to $1 + E_\Sigma \times E_\Sigma^*$ the representation of the empty string requires 1 bit, while the representation of other strings is 1 bit plus 8 bits for representing the first character, plus the bits to represent the rest of the string for the type E_Σ^*. Thus up to $9 \cdot n + 1$ bits are used to represent a string of length n.

The reason why bit codings for regular types use one bit more per character is due to the very restrictive recursion in regular expressions. The extra bit is used to say for each character that we do not want to end the string yet. This is because we can only use the $.^*$ constructor to define recursive types, and a regular expression E^* always unfolds to $1 + E \times E^*$. Therefore we use one bit for each character to choose the right hand side after the unfold. This is equivalent to using a unary integer representation to state how many times the E inside the $.^*$ is used, which leaves room for optimization.

We now generalize the recursion to *tail-recursive μ-types* in order to obtain more compact bit codings. Consider the language of expressions $\text{UnReg}^{\mu}_{\Sigma}$ over a finite alphabet $\Sigma = \{a_1, \dots, a_n\}$:

$$\alpha ::= 0 \mid 1 \mid a \mid \alpha_1 + \alpha_2 \mid \alpha_1 \times \alpha_2 \mid \mu X.\alpha \mid X$$

We define the free variables of α to be the set of variables X that occur in α without a binder μX. If there are no free variables in α then we say that α is closed. We call α tail-recursive if α_1 is closed in all subterms of the form $\alpha_1 \times \alpha_2$.

We can now define the language $\text{Reg}^{\mu}_{\Sigma}$ as the closed, tail-recursive expressions from $\text{UnReg}^{\mu}_{\Sigma}$.

We need to define semantics, type-interpretation and inhabitation for the new expressions, but we can reuse the definitions from regular expressions ($\mathcal{L}[\![]\!], \mathcal{T}[\![]\!], v : E$), simply by adding new rules for the new μ and X constructs.

We can extend the type-interpretation from Definition 6 with an environment σ, and replace the definition of $\mathcal{T}[\![E^*]\!]$ with

$$\mathcal{T}[\![X]\!]_\sigma = \sigma(X) \text{ and } \mathcal{T}[\![\mu X.\alpha]\!]_\sigma = \bigcup_{i \ge 0} \mathcal{T}[\![\alpha]\!]_{\sigma^{(i)}} \text{ where } \sigma^{(0)} = \sigma[X \mapsto \emptyset] \text{ and } \sigma^{(n+1)} = \sigma[X \mapsto \mathcal{T}[\![\alpha]\!]_{\sigma^{(n)}}].$$

Similarly, $\mathcal{L}[\![.]\!]$ can be extended to $\text{Reg}^{\mu}_{\Sigma}$.

Finally, we can use the inhabitation rules from Figure 1, except the fold rule is replaced with the rule for μ in Figure 15.

We can now prove that $\text{Reg}^{\mu}_{\Sigma}$ expresses exactly the same languages as Reg_{Σ}:

THEOREM 30 (Conservativity of tail-recursive μ-types).

1. *For all $E \in Reg_{\Sigma}$ there is $\alpha \in Reg^{\mu}_{\Sigma}$ such that* $\{\text{flat}(v) \mid \vdash v : E\} = \{\text{flat}(v) \mid \vdash v : \alpha\}$.
2. *For all $\alpha \in Reg^{\mu}_{\Sigma}$ there is $E \in Reg_{\Sigma}$ such that* $\{\text{flat}(v) \mid \vdash v : \alpha\} = \{\text{flat}(v) \mid \vdash v : E\}$.

PROOF (Sketch) The first statement is proved by encoding E^* as $\mu X.1 + \alpha \times X$ where α is the encoding of E. The second statement is proved by first rewriting μ-types to the form $\mu X.(\alpha \times X + \beta)$, where X is not free in α or β. Now it can be seen that $\mathcal{L}[\![\mu X.(\alpha \times X + \beta)]\!] = \mathcal{L}[\![E^* \times F]\!]$ where E is a regular expression encoding of α and F is an encoding of β. □

The equivalence of regular expressions with right-regular grammars is well known (Chomsky 1959). Tail-recursive μ-types are like right-regular grammars, but do not *exactly* correspond to them: tail-recursive μ-types lack mutual recursion, but offer locally scoped recursion, where grammars only provide top-level recursion. [5]

Even though $\text{Reg}^{\mu}_{\Sigma}$ expresses exactly the same languages as Reg_{Σ}, the new expressions allow us to define $(a + b + c)^*$ as $\mu X.(1 + a \times X) + (b \times X + c \times X)$ and thus saving us one bit per character we need to express.

Using this optimization the representation of any string with respect to the generalized regular expression type α_{Σ} will use eight bits per Latin-1 character plus eight bits to terminate the string. This is exactly the same size as the standard Latin1-representation. In fact the bit-representations for this type will be exactly the same as the bit-representations for the standard Latin-1 representation if the same permutation of characters is chosen in α_{Σ}.

It may not seem very impressive to reinvent the Latin-1 representation this way, but it can guarantee that bit coding uses at most as much space as the Latin-1 representation. The benefit of bit coding comes when we no longer consider all Latin-1 strings, but a subset specified by a regular expression. In this case the bit codings will generally be more compact. The ultimate example of this is when the regular expression allows exactly one string. For example the bit sequence of `'abcbcba'` under regular expression $a \times b \times c \times b \times c \times b \times a$ uses *zero* bits since its value contains no inl/inr-choices. Of course the program needs to know the regular expression in order to interpret the bit sequences, but that can be shared across interpretation of multiple bit sequences.

We end this section with two examples showing the bit sizes of strings under different regular expressions.

EXAMPLE 31. *In the table below Z denotes a designated end-of-string character; and characters a, b, c their 8-bit Latin-1 codings.*

Regular expression	*Representation*	*Size*
Latin1	*abcbcbaZ*	*64*
Σ^*	*1a1b1c1b1c1b1a0*	*64*
$((a+b)+(c+d))^*$	*1001011101011101011000*	*22*
$((a+b)+c)^*$	*10010111101111011000*	*20*
$a \times (b+c)^* \times a$	*10111011100*	*11*
$a \times b \times c \times b \times c \times b \times a$		*0*

The following is a more realistic example, where we also consider the data size before and after text compression.

EXAMPLE 32 (Sizes for XML record collection string). *Consider the following regular expression, corresponding to a regular XML schema ($\times$ and associativity have been omitted for simplicity).*

```
<CATALOG>
 (<CD><TITLE>Σ*</TITLE><ARTIST>Σ*</ARTIST>
      <COUNTRY>Σ*</COUNTRY><COMPANY>Σ*</COMPANY>
      <PRICE>Σ*</PRICE><YEAR>Σ*</YEAR>
 </CD>)*
</CATALOG>
```

This regular expression describes an XML-format for representing a list of CDs. We have found the sizes for representing a specific list containing 26 CDs to be as follows:

	Uncompressed	*Compressed*
Latin-1	*32760*	*7248*
bit representation using E_{Σ}	*11187*	*6654*
bit representation using α_{Σ}	*9947*	*6552*

As we can see, there is almost a factor 3 reduction in the space requirement when using the regular expression specific bit codings. The benefit is reduced by compression of the bit codes with bzip (Seward) but an 8% space reduction is still obtained.

5. Discussion

Regular expressions are fundamental to computer science with numerous applications in semi-structured text processing, natural language processing, program analysis, graph querying, shortest path computation, compilers, program verification, bioinformatics and more.

Salomaa (1966) and, independently, Aanderaa provided the first sound and complete axiomatizations of regular expression equivalence , based on a unique fixed point rule, with Krob (1990), Pratt (1990) (for extended regular expressions), and Kozen (1994) providing alternatives in the 90s.

Recently, coinductive axiomatizations based on finitary cases of Rutten's coinduction principle (Rutten 1998) for simulation relations have become popular: Grabmayer (2005) for regular expressions; Chen and Pucella (2004) and Kozen (2008) for Kleene Algebra with Tests. Silva, Bonsangue and Rutten show how to specialize their coalgebraic framework to regular languages and how to translate regular languages into so-called *deterministic expressions*

[5] Milner (1984) presents a sound and complete axiomatization of behavioral equivalence of μ-terms denoting labeled transition systems. Behavioral equivalence is properly weaker than regular expression equivalence, however. Crucially, distributivity $E \times (F + G) = E \times F + E \times G$ does not hold.

(Silva et al. 2010, Example 3.4). Such expressions appear to correspond to (nondeterministic) linear forms (Antimirov 1996), which in turn represent ϵ-free nondeterministic automata. (Their particular translation may generate exponentially bigger expressions than the original regular expressions, however, which may limit practical applicability.)

Grabmayer's axiomatization (Grabmayer 2005) is based on Brzozowski derivatives (Antimirov 1996; Brzozowski 1964), which allow automata constructions and pairwise regular expression rewriting (Antimirov 1995; Ginzburg 1967; Lu and Sulzmann 2004) to be understood as proof search.

In this paper we present a *declarative* coinductive axiomatization of regular expression containment, generalizing Grabmayer's *algorithmic* coinductive axiomatization of regular expression equality.[6] Ours is the first axiomatization of regular expression containment with a Curry-Howard-style computational interpretation of containment proofs as functions (coercions) operating on regular expressions read as *regular types*. Like Kozen's (noncoinductive) axiomatization, but unlike Salomaa's (noncoinductive) and Grabmayer's (coinductive) it is parametrically complete for infinite alphabets: If $E[X] \leq F[X]$ for all X, then there is a parametric polymorphic coercion $c : \forall X. E[X] \leq F[X]$.

Frisch and Cardelli (2004) were, as far we know, the first to state the precise connection between regular expressions as languages and regular expressions as types (Section 2.2 in this paper).

Coinductive axiomatizations with a Curry-Howard style computational interpretation have been introduced by Brandt and Henglein (1998) for recursive type equivalence and subtyping, expounded on by Gapeyev et al. (2002), as an alternative to the axiomatization of Amadio and Cardelli (1993), which uses the unique fixed point principle. In this fashion, classical unification closure can be understood as proof search for a type isomorphism, and the product automaton construction of Kozen et al. (1995) as search for the coercion embedding a subtype into another type. Di Cosmo et al. (2005) provide a coinductive characterization of recursive subtyping with associative-commutative products, but it is not a proper *axiomatization* since it appeals directly to bisimilarity.[7] Recursive type isomorphisms have also been studied by Abadi and Fiore (1996); Fiore (2004, 1996) and have been used for stub generation (Auerbach et al. 1999).

The (finitary) coinduction rule in its most general form is

$$\frac{\Gamma, P \vdash P}{\Gamma \vdash P}$$

It requires a side condition for soundness, which is usually specific to the syntax of the formulae P and the particular logical system at hand. Numerous syntactic variations may be possible, and care must be applied to retain soundness; e.g. by not allowing a transitivity rule (Gapeyev et al. 2002). This work represents the end of a quest for a general *semantic* side condition, at least for containment formulae: Interpret a *proof* of containment computationally as a function, and let the side condition be that the conclusion (now with explicit proof object) under this interpretation be (hereditarily) total. For regular expression containment, hereditary totality turns out to be undecidable, but it justifies the soundness of our side conditions S_2 and S_4, which each yield sound and complete axiomatizations of regular expression containment. Their disjunction is expressive enough to facilitate a compositional encoding of derivations in Salomaa's, Kozen's and Grabmayer's axiomatizations.

[6] Here, "declarative" and "algorithmic" are used in the same sense as in Benjamin Pierce's book *Types and Programming Languages*, MIT Press.

[7] Bisimilarity is coinductively defined (that is, as a greatest fixed point), but not necessarily *finitarily* as required in an ordinary (recursive) axiomatization.

Brandt and Henglein (1998, Section 4.3) discuss how the finitary coinduction rule can be understood as a rule for finding a *finite* set of formulae that are intrinsically consistent. Intuitively this corresponds to constructing proofs of such formulae that are finite, but may be circular: they may contain occurrences of formulae to be proved as assumptions. This is also the essence of circular coinduction for behavioral equivalences (Rosu and Goguen 2000). Rosu and Lucanu (2009) provide a general proof-theoretic framework for applying circular coinduction soundly. It allows marking certain equations as *frozen* to prevent them from being applied prematurely, which would lead to unsound conclusions. Our approach is fundamentally different in the following sense: We allow circular equations without any restriction. An equation is interpreted as a pair of potentially partial functions, whose definition depends on the particular (circular) proof of the equation. An equation is *valid* (sound), however, only if the two functions making up its computational interpretation are total.

Our regular-expression specific bit representation of (parse trees of) strings corresponds to composing regular expression parsing with the flattening function of Jansson and Jeuring (1997), who attribute the technique to work in the 80s on text compression with syntactic source information models (see references in their paper). Bit coding captures the idea that only choices made—the tags of sum types—need to be encoded, which is also the key idea of oracle-based coding in proof-carrying code (Necula and Rahul 2001). Our direct compilation of containment proofs to bit manipulation functions appears to be novel, however. It should be noted that compaction by bit coding is orthogonal to statistical text data compression. As we have illustrated, combining them may yield significantly shorter bit strings than either technique by itself.

Type- and coercion-theoretic techniques appear to be applicable to *regular expression types* (Hosoya et al. 2005a,b; Nielsen 2008; Sulzmann and Lu 2007) and other nonregular extensions, notably context-free languages.[8] This remains to be investigated thoroughly, however. Note that regular expression types are a proper extension of regular expressions *as* types.

There are also numerous practically motivated topics to investigate: Inference of regular type containments and search for practically *efficient* coercions implementing them; disambiguation of regular expressions by annotating them; instrumenting automata constructions for fast input processing that yields parse trees; and more. We hope that this may lead the way to putting logic and computer science into a new generation of expressive, generally applicable high-performance regular expression processing tools.

Acknowledgements

We would like to thank the anonymous reviewers for their comprehensive critical and constructive comments, and for detailed recommendations for improvement. Any remaining problems are solely the authors' responsibility. The alphabetically first author is grateful to Eijiro Sumii, Yasuhiko Minamide, Naoki Kobayashi, and Atsushi Igarashi for jointly solving the question of decidability of hereditary totality (Theorem 21). We would like to thank Dexter Kozen for sharing many insights on Kleene Algebras as part of a mini-course held at DIKU, as well as for ideas and suggestions for the present–and for further–work. Thanks also to Alexandra Silva for explaining and commenting her work on Kleene coalgebras and its relation to regular expressions. Finally we would like to thank the participants of our graduate course "Topics in Programming Languages: Theory and Practice of Regular Expressions", held at DIKU in Spring 2010, for exploring some of the applications of regular expressions as types.

[8] Completeness is out of the question, of course, since context-free grammar containment is not recursively enumerable.

References

M. Abadi and M. P. Fiore. Syntactic considerations on recursive types. In *Proc. 1996 IEEE 11th Annual Symp. on Logic in Computer Science (LICS), New Brunswick, New Jersey*. IEEE Computer Society Press, June 1996.

R. M. Amadio and L. Cardelli. Subtyping recursive types. *ACM Transactions on Programming Languages and Systems (TOPLAS)*, 15(4):575–631, September 1993.

V. Antimirov. Rewriting regular inequalities. In *Proc. 10th International Conference, FCT '95 Dresden, Germany*, volume 965 of *Lecture Notes in Computer Science (LNCS)*, pages 116–125. Springer-Verlag, August 1995.

V. Antimirov. Partial derivatives of regular expressions and finite automaton constructions. *Theor. Comput. Sci.*, 155(2):291–319, 1996. ISSN 0304-3975. doi: http://dx.doi.org/10.1016/0304-3975(95)00182-4.

V. M. Antimirov and P. D. Mosses. Rewriting extended regular expressions. *Theor. Comput. Sci.*, 143(1):51–72, 1995. doi: http://dx.doi.org/10.1016/0304-3975(95)80024-4.

J. S. Auerbach, C. Barton, M. Chu-Carroll, and M. Raghavachari. Mockingbird: Flexible stub compilation from pairs of declarations. In *ICDCS*, pages 393–402, 1999.

C. Brabrand and J. Thomsen. Typed and unambiguous pattern matching on strings using regular expressions. In *Proc. 12th International ACM SIGPLAN Symposium on Principles and Practice of Declarative Programming (PPDP)*, 2010.

M. Brandt and F. Henglein. Coinductive axiomatization of recursive type equality and subtyping. *Fundamenta Informaticae*, 33:309–338, 1998.

J. A. Brzozowski. Derivatives of regular expressions. *J. ACM*, 11(4):481–494, 1964. ISSN 0004-5411. doi: http://doi.acm.org/10.1145/321239.321249.

H. Chen and R. Pucella. A coalgebraic approach to Kleene algebra with tests. *Theor. Comput. Sci.*, 327(1-2):23–44, 2004.

N. Chomsky. On certain formal properties of grammars*. *Information and control*, 2(2):137–167, 1959.

J. H. Conway. *Regular Algebra and Finite Machines*. Printed in GB by William Clowes & Sons Ltd, 1971. ISBN 0-412-10620-5.

R. Di Cosmo, F. Pottier, and D. Remy. Subtyping recursive types modulo associative commutative products. In *Proc. Seventh International Conference on Typed Lambda Calculi and Applications (TLCA 2005)*, 2005.

M. Fiore. Isomorphisms of generic recursive polynomial types. *SIGPLAN Not.*, 39(1):77–88, 2004. ISSN 0362-1340. doi: http://doi.acm.org/10.1145/982962.964008.

M. P. Fiore. A coinduction principle for recursive data types based on bisimulation. *Information and Computation*, 127:186–198, 1996. Conference version: Proc. 8th Annual IEEE Symp. on Logic in Computer Science (LICS), 1993, pp. 110-119.

A. Frisch and L. Cardelli. Greedy regular expression matching. In *Proc. 31st International Colloquium on Automata, Languages and Programming (ICALP)*, volume 3142 of *Lecture notes in computer science*, pages 618–629, Turku, Finland, July 2004. Springer.

V. Gapeyev, M. Y. Levin, and B. C. Pierce. Recursive subtyping revealed. *J. Funct. Program.*, 12(6):511–548, 2002.

A. Ginzburg. A procedure for checking equality of regular expressions. *J. ACM*, 14(2):355–362, 1967. ISSN 0004-5411. doi: http://doi.acm.org/10.1145/321386.321399.

C. Grabmayer. Using proofs by coinduction to find "traditional" proofs. In *Proc. 1st Conference on Algebra and Coalgebra in Computer Science (CALCO)*, number 3629 in Lecture Notes in Computer Science (LNCS). Springer, September 2005.

J. Hopcroft and J. Ullman. *Introduction to Automata Theory, Languages, and Computation*. Addison-Wesley, 1979.

H. Hosoya, A. Frisch, and G. Castagna. Parametric polymorphism for XML. In J. Palsberg and M. Abadi, editors, *POPL*, pages 50–62. ACM, 2005a. ISBN 1-58113-830-X.

H. Hosoya, J. Vouillon, and B. C. Pierce. Regular expression types for XML. *ACM Trans. Program. Lang. Syst.*, 27(1):46–90, 2005b.

Institute of Electrical and Electronics Engineers (IEEE). *Standard for information technology — Portable Operating System Interface (POSIX) — Part 2 (Shell and utilities), Section 2.8 (Regular expression notation)*. New York, 1992. IEEE Standard 1003.2.

P. Jansson and J. Jeuring. Polyp—a polytypic programming language extension. In *Proceedings of the 24th ACM SIGPLAN-SIGACT Symposium on Principles of Programming Languages (POPL)*, page 482. ACM, 1997.

S. C. Kleene. Representation of events in nerve nets and finite automata. *Automata Studies*, 1956.

D. Kozen. A completeness theorem for Kleene algebras and the algebra of regular events. *Information and Computation*, 110(2):366–390, May 1994.

D. Kozen. Kleene algebra with tests. *Transactions on Programming Languages and Systems*, 19(3):427–443, May 1997.

D. Kozen. On the coalgebraic theory of Kleene algebra with tests. Technical report, Computing and Information Science, Cornell University, March 2008. URL `http://hdl.handle.net/1813/10173`.

D. Kozen, J. Palsberg, and M. Schwartzbach. Efficient recursive subtyping. *Mathematical Structures in Computer Science (MSCS)*, 5(1), 1995. Conference version presented at the 20th Annual ACM SIGPLAN-SIGACT Symp. on Principles of Programming Languages (POPL), 1993.

D. Krob. A complete system of b-rational identities. In M. Paterson, editor, *ICALP*, volume 443 of *Lecture Notes in Computer Science*, pages 60–73. Springer, 1990. ISBN 3-540-52826-1.

K. Z. M. Lu and M. Sulzmann. Rewriting regular inequalities. In *Proc. Second Asian Symposium, APLAS 2004, Taipei, Taiwan, November 4-6, 2004*, volume 3302 of *Lecture Notes in Computer Science (LNCS)*, pages 57–73. Springer, November 2004.

R. Milner. A complete inference system for a class of regular behaviours. *J. Comput. Syst. Sci.*, 28(3):439–466, 1984.

G. C. Necula and S. P. Rahul. Oracle-based checking of untrusted software. In *POPL*, pages 142–154, 2001.

L. Nielsen. A coinductive axiomatization of XML subtyping. Graduate term project report, DIKU, University of Copenhagen, 2008.

V. Pratt. Action logic and pure induction. In *Proc. Logics in AI: European Workshop JELIA*, volume 478 of *Lecture Notes in Computer Science (LNCS)*, pages 97–120. Springer, 1990.

G. Rosu and J. Goguen. Circular coinduction. In *Proc. International Joint Conference on Automated Reasoning*, 2000.

G. Rosu and D. Lucanu. Circular coinduction: A proof theoretical foundation. In *Proc. 3rd Conference on Algebra and Coalgebra in Computer Science (CALCO)*, number 5728 in Lecture Notes in Computer Science (LNCS), pages 127–144. Springer, September 2009. ISBN 978-3-642-03740-5.

J. J. M. M. Rutten. Automata and coinduction (an exercise in coalgebra). In D. Sangiorgi and R. de Simone, editors, *CONCUR*, volume 1466 of *Lecture Notes in Computer Science*, pages 194–218. Springer, 1998. ISBN 3-540-64896-8.

A. Salomaa. Two complete axiom systems for the algebra of regular events. *J. ACM*, 13(1):158–169, 1966. ISSN 0004-5411. doi: http://doi.acm.org/10.1145/321312.321326.

J. Seward. Bzip. URL `http://www.bzip.org/`.

A. Silva, M. M. Bonsangue, and J. J. M. M. Rutten. Non-deterministic Kleene coalgebras. *Logical Methods in Computer Science*, 6(3), 2010. URL `http://arxiv.org/abs/1007.3769`.

M. Sulzmann and K. Z. M. Lu. XHaskell - adding regular expression types to Haskell. In O. Chitil, Z. Horváth, and V. Zsók, editors, *IFL*, volume 5083 of *Lecture Notes in Computer Science*, pages 75–92. Springer, 2007. ISBN 978-3-540-85372-5.

G. Winskel. *The Formal Semantics of Programming Languages: An Introduction*. Foundations of Computing series. MIT Press, Feb. 1993. ISBN 0-262-23169-7.

Making Prophecies with Decision Predicates

Byron Cook
Microsoft Research &
Queen Mary, University of London
bycook@microsoft.com

Eric Koskinen
University of Cambridge
ejk39@cam.ac.uk

Abstract

We describe a new algorithm for proving temporal properties expressed in LTL of infinite-state programs. Our approach takes advantage of the fact that LTL properties can often be proved more efficiently using techniques usually associated with the branching-time logic CTL than they can with native LTL algorithms. The caveat is that, in certain instances, nondeterminism in the system's transition relation can cause CTL methods to report counterexamples that are spurious with respect to the original LTL formula. To address this problem we describe an algorithm that, as it attempts to apply CTL proof methods, finds and then removes problematic nondeterminism via an analysis on the potentially spurious counterexamples. Problematic nondeterminism is characterized using *decision predicates*, and removed using a partial, symbolic determinization procedure which introduces new prophecy variables to predict the future outcome of these choices. We demonstrate—using examples taken from the PostgreSQL database server, Apache web server, and Windows OS kernel—that our method can yield enormous performance improvements in comparison to known tools, allowing us to automatically prove properties of programs where we could not prove them before.

Categories and Subject Descriptors D.2.4 [*Software Engineering*]: Software/Program Verification—Model checking; Correctness proofs; Reliability; D.4.5 [*Operating Systems*]: Reliability—Verification; F.3.1 [*Logics and Meanings of Programs*]: Specifying and Verifying and Reasoning about Programs; F.3.2 [*Logics and Meanings of Programs*]: Semantics of Programming Languages—Program analysis

General Terms Verification, Theory, Reliability

Keywords Linear temporal logic, formal verification, termination, program analysis, model checking

1. Introduction

The common wisdom amongst users and developers of tools that prove temporal properties of systems is that the linear specification logic LTL [33] is more intuitive than CTL [10], but that properties expressed in the universal fragment of CTL (∀CTL) without fairness constraints are often easier to prove than their LTL cousins [3, 32, 44][1]. Properties expressed in CTL without fairness can be proved in a purely syntax-directed manner using state-based reasoning techniques, whereas LTL requires deeper reasoning about whole sets of traces and the subtle relationships between families of them.

In this paper we aim to make an LTL prover for infinite-state programs with performance closer to what one would expect from a CTL prover. We use the observation that ∀CTL without fairness can be a useful abstraction of LTL. The problem with this strategy is that the pieces don't always fit together: there are cases when, due to some instances of nondeterminism in the transition system, ∀CTL alone is not powerful enough to prove an LTL property.

In these cases our LTL prover works around the problem using something we call *decision predicates*, which are used to characterize and treat such instances of nondeterminism. A decision predicate is represented as a pair of first-order logic formulae (a, b), where the formula a defines the decision predicate's presupposition (*i.e. when* the decision is made), and b characterizes the binary choice made when this presupposition holds. Any transition from state s to state s' in the system that meets the constraint $a(s) \wedge b(s')$ is distinguished by the decision predicate (a, b) from $a(s) \wedge \neg b(s')$.

We use decision predicates as the basis of a partial symbolic determinization procedure: for each predicate we introduce a new prophecy variable [3] to predict the future outcome of the decision. After partially determinizing with respect to these prophecy variables, we find that CTL proof methods succeed, thus allowing us to prove LTL properties with CTL proof techniques in cases where this strategy would have previously failed. To synthesize the decision predicates we employ a form of symbolic execution on spurious ∀CTL counterexamples together with an application of Farkas' lemma [23].

With our new approach we can automatically prove properties of infinite-state programs in minutes or seconds which were intractable using existing tools. Examples include code fragments drawn from the PostgreSQL database server, the Apache web server, and the Windows OS kernel.

Limitations. In practice, the applicability and performance of our technique is dependent on the heuristic used to choose new decision predicates when given an abstract representation of a specific point in a spurious counterexample. The predicate synthesis mechanism implemented in our tool is applicable primarily to infinite-state programs over arithmetic variables with commands that only contain linear arithmetic. However, no matter which predicate selection mechanism is used, our predicate-based determinization strategy is sound. Thus, unsound approximations to predicate synthesis could potentially be used in instances where the systems considered do not meet the constraints given above. Our technique is also based

[1] Abadi and Lamport [3] make this point using the terminology of "refinement mappings" and "trace equivalence" instead of phrasing it in the context of temporal logics.

POPL'11, January 26–28, 2011, Austin, Texas, USA.

on an ∀CTL prover for infinite-state systems, which itself cannot be complete.

A further limitation is that our procedure is not well suited for finite-state model checking. The problem is that introducing prophecy variables greatly increases the number of state-holding elements required in usual finite-state encodings: Each prophecy variable must be capable of counting up to a number larger than the system's diameter [12]. The problem is further exacerbated when we introduce multiple prophecy variables, as the nth prophecy variable must range over values as large as the diameter of the system which has been augmented with the first $n-1$ prophecy variables. In contrast, when using proof tools for infinite-state systems the performance cost for adding additional infinite-state variables is usually low.

Finally, our procedure critically depends on the full structure of counterexamples to ∀CTL properties, which are in the form of trees. Unfortunately, with only a few exceptions [13, 17] tools do not return whole tree counterexamples.

Related work. Our method complements more classical automata-theoretic approaches [34, 45] in which fairness constraints are used to encode linear-temporal conditions and then language emptiness—*a.k.a.* fair termination—is proved of the resulting system. The difficulty with language emptiness for infinite state systems (*e.g.* as implemented in previous work [15]) is that the mechanisms that allow us to ignore infinite executions not accepted by the fairness constraints are effectively the same as the expensive techniques used for proving termination. Thus, in practice, our previous tool [15] relies too heavily on termination proving machinery. In contrast, our new approach uses syntax-directed techniques for ∀CTL that depend much less on the performance of the underlying termination proving infrastructure. However, our strategy does rely on the assumption that, on average, the subtle correlations that are tracked only on-demand in our approach do not occur frequently. In cases where this assumption is not true, the cost of on-demand inference of decision predicates may be higher than simply using traditional techniques. We will see an example of this later in Section 6.

It is well known that determinization addresses the subtle semantic distinctions between linear-time and branching-time logics [39]. However, for infinite-state systems, open questions still remain if we hope to develop a practical determinization-based strategy: a) *what* to determinize, since complete determinization does not lead to a viable automatic tool for infinite-state systems, and b) *how* to determinize in a way that facilitates the application of current formal verification tools. We address these two questions in this paper.

Others have considered this trade-off between linear-time specifications and efficient branching-time verification procedures. For example, Cadence SMV [1] reduces LTL to CTL using additional fairness constraints [9, 14]. This technique still relies heavily on reasoning about fairness. This is a sensible engineering choice for finite-state systems for the reasons discussed above, but not for infinite-state systems. Schneider describes a method of translating an LTL formula into a semantically equivalent CTL formula [41]. However, this leads to an exponential blowup in the size of the CTL formula, and requires a modification to the model checking algorithm. Maidl identifies the subset of ∀CTL (called $\forall CTL^{det}$) which is expressible in LTL. Consequentially, for such formulae, an ∀CTL prover can be used [31]. By contrast, our decision predicate-based technique allows one to verify any LTL formula using branching-time proof techniques in such a way that performance is affected only in cases where tracking subtle correlations between traces is actually required.

Previous work has also examined different methods of representing systems [4, 6, 43] in order to facilitate proving linear-time temporal properties or proving linear-time properties of abstractions (*e.g.* pushdown systems [21, 42]). When model-checking is performed using explicit-state techniques [25, 28, 29] then the converse of our assumption is true: linear-time traces are in fact more naturally explored than branching-time executions in this context.

Our procedure uses several techniques found in the literature: namely prophecy variables [3] and Farkas' lemma [23]. We are of course not the first to use these techniques in applications related to the one addressed here. Prophecy variables have been used for many years to resolve nondeterminism in proofs, including some recent work [27, 38]. Our use of Farkas' lemma is similar to its use in rank function synthesis [35] and invariant generation [40].

```
PROVE (M,φL) :
  Ω := ∅
  let φC = APPROXIMATE(φL) in
  while true do
      let M^Ω = DETERMINIZE(M,Ω) in
      match PROVE∀CTL(M^Ω,φC) with
        | Succeed -> return Succeed
        | Fail(χ) ->
          let Ω' = REFINE(χ) in
              if(Ω' = ∅)
                let π ∈ χ in return Fail(π)
              else
                Ω := Ω ∪ Ω'
  done
```

Figure 1: Algorithm based on predicate determinization which implements LTL model checking (*i.e.* $M \models_L \varphi_L$). The procedures APPROXIMATE, DETERMINIZE, REFINE and $\text{PROVE}_{\forall CTL}$ are defined in later sections.

2. Algorithm

Our LTL proof procedure, PROVE_{LTL}, is given in Figure 1. The algorithm is designed to iteratively find a sufficient set of decision predicates Ω such that proof tools for CTL can be used to prove an LTL property φ_L of the system M. The algorithm is based on four procedures which are each defined in later sections of the paper:

- APPROXIMATE (Section 3) is a simple procedure which approximates an LTL formula with an analogous ∀CTL formula in which universal operators are added in (*e.g.* F becomes AF, and G becomes AG). Without loss of generality we assume that negations have been pushed to the atomic propositions of the formula.
- DETERMINIZE (Section 4) takes a transition system and a set of decision predicates Ω and returns a new partially determinized system in which newly introduced prophecy variables are used to make predictions about the valuations of the decision predicates in Ω.
- REFINE (Section 5) takes an ∀CTL counterexample χ and, in the case that χ represents multiple distinct paths through the system, returns decision predicates which characterize the nondeterminism that distinguishes between the different paths. In the case that χ represents only a single path through the system then REFINE returns ∅.
- $\text{PROVE}_{\forall CTL}$(Section 6) is an ∀CTL-prover.

When $\Omega = \varnothing$, $\text{DETERMINIZE}(M, \Omega) = M$. Thus, on the first iteration of the loop our procedure is attempting to prove φ_L via a simple approximation φ_C together with the original system M. When given a non-empty set of decision predicates, DETERMINIZE builds M^Ω by conjoining the original transition relation of M with a relation that specifies the behavior of a prophecy variable for each decision predicate. For any set of decision predicates Ω, if φ_C holds, then φ_L also holds. Thus, whenever we find a sufficient set of predicates to prove φ_C, we have proved φ_L.

REFINE is used to determine if an $\forall$CTL-counterexample found by PROVE$_{\forall CTL}$ represents a real LTL-counterexample or something spurious. At first glance there is a formidable semantic gap between the two types of counterexamples: $\forall$CTL-counterexamples are trees, whereas LTL-counterexamples are traces. However, if all of the paths through the counterexample χ represent the same path or its prefixes, then any one of these paths is a legitimate counterexample to φ_L. In this case REFINE returns $\varnothing$. Otherwise, if χ represents more than one path in the program, REFINE returns a non-empty set of new decision predicates.

Example. Consider the LTL property $\mathsf{FG}(\mathsf{x} = 1)$, which informally can be read *"for every trace of the system,* $\mathsf{x} = 1$ *will eventually become true and stay true."* The meaning of the analogous $\forall$CTL property $\mathsf{AFAG}(\mathsf{x} = 1)$ is slightly more operational: *"On all paths emanating from an initial state, the system eventually reaches a state such that along all paths starting from this state,* $\mathsf{x} = 1$ *will be true and stay true."* For every transition system, if $\mathsf{AFAG}(\mathsf{x} = 1)$ holds, then $\mathsf{FG}(\mathsf{x} = 1)$ holds. Furthermore, our experience leads us to believe that proving $\mathsf{AFAG}(\mathsf{x} = 1)$ is often an efficient method of proving $\mathsf{FG}(\mathsf{x} = 1)$.

However, consider the following program, where $*$ represents nondeterministic choice:

```
1   x := 1;
2   while (*) {
3       skip;
4   }
5   x := 0;
6   x := 1;
7   while (true) {
8       skip;
9   }
```

In this case $\mathsf{FG}(\mathsf{x} = 1)$ is valid, but unfortunately $\mathsf{AFAG}(\mathsf{x} = 1)$ is not. $\mathsf{FG}(\mathsf{x} = 1)$ is valid because, *for every individual program trace*, it is valid. For example, if a trace never leaves the loop at line 2, then the property is valid because $\mathsf{x} = 1$ before entering the loop. For the traces that do leave the loop, $\mathsf{x} = 1$ will become true at the command on line 6 and then remain true. The $\forall$CTL property is valid only if we can find a set of states that are eventually reached from the program's initial states such that $\mathsf{AG}(\mathsf{x} = 1)$ holds. In this case *no such set of states exists*, and tools for $\forall$CTL verification will return counterexamples to $\mathsf{AFAG}(\mathsf{x} = 1)$ that seemingly have no relation to to the original property $\mathsf{FG}(\mathsf{x} = 1)$.

The heart of the problem is the nondeterministic choice between the transition from line 2 to 3, and the transition from line 2 to 5: when we are in the loop at line 2 we cannot know if we will eventually leave the loop or not. We struggle when trying to decide if a state at location 2 is the point at which $\mathsf{x} = 1$ will be global true, as it is only *after* considering a full program trace that we would know (*i.e.* in this case we need to be looking at sets of traces, not sets of states).

We now illustrate the procedure in Figure 1 on this example. Let $\varphi_\mathsf{L} = \mathsf{FG}(\mathsf{x} = 1)$ and M be the example program from above. Our procedure approximates φ_L with APPROXIMATE$(\varphi_\mathsf{L}) = \varphi_\mathsf{C} = \mathsf{AFAG}(\mathsf{x} = 1)$. As we described above, the program M does not respect the property φ_C. The counterexample χ to φ_C in M is an infinite tree which can be represented as a finite graph of transitions between program locations:

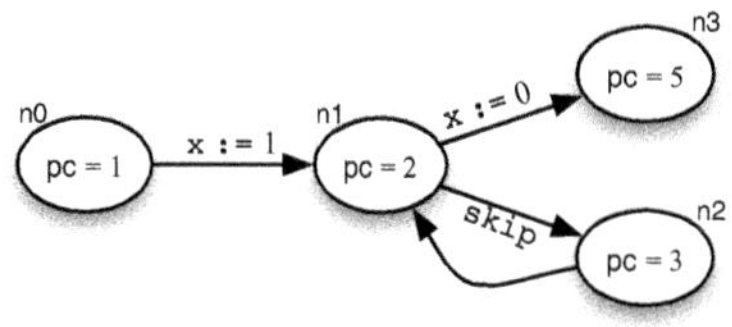

In this graph $\mathsf{pc} = 5$ indicates that the execution is at a state in which the program counter is at line 5. Our procedure uses REFINE to simultaneously symbolically simulate all possible paths through this graph and try to unify them into a single path through M. In this case it would begin its execution by visiting first $\mathsf{pc} = 1$ and then $\mathsf{pc} = 2$, after which it would discover that, for all paths of the graph to represent the same path, it must unify $\mathsf{pc} = 5$ and $\mathsf{pc} = 3$, which cannot be done. Thus, in this case, the $\forall$CTL counterexample χ will be deemed spurious to the LTL property and the decision predicate $(\mathsf{pc} = 2, \mathsf{pc} = 5)$ will be included in the Ω' refinement[2]. This decision predicate $(\mathsf{pc} = 2, \mathsf{pc} = 5)$ characterizes the choice: "when $\mathsf{pc} = 2$, will $\mathsf{pc}' = 5$ or not?" Notice also that, in this particular case, the predicates selected are over program locations, but this is not true in general (see Example 10 in Section 5).

The procedure then uses DETERMINIZE to generate M^Ω, which is effectively the cross product of M and a new transition relation which updates a new prophecy variable ρ based on the valuations of the decision predicate $(\mathsf{pc} = 2, \mathsf{pc} = 5)$:

$$\bigwedge \left\{ \begin{array}{l} s(\mathsf{pc}) = 2 \wedge s'(\mathsf{pc}) \neq 5 \Rightarrow s(\rho) \neq 0 \wedge s'(\rho) = s(\rho) - 1 \\ s(\mathsf{pc}) = 2 \wedge s'(\mathsf{pc}) = 5 \Rightarrow s(\rho) = 0 \wedge s'(\rho) \in \mathbb{Z} \\ s(\mathsf{pc}) \neq 2 \Rightarrow s'(\rho) = s(\rho) \end{array} \right\}$$

We might try to express M^Ω in textual program code form as

```
ρ := *;
x := 1;
while (*) {
    assume(ρ ≠ 0);
    ρ := ρ - 1;
    skip;
}
assume(ρ = 0);
ρ := *;
x := 0;
x := 1;
while (true) {
    skip;
}
```

This new prophecy variable ρ predicts the outcomes of the decision predicate $(\mathsf{pc} = 2, \mathsf{pc} = 5)$. We initialize ρ to be an integer. For every given trace of the system, the concrete number chosen at the command "$\rho := *$" predicts the number of instances of the transition $s(\mathsf{pc}) = 2 \wedge s'(\mathsf{pc}) \neq 5$ before we see a transition $s(\mathsf{pc}) = 2 \wedge s'(\mathsf{pc}) = 5$. The choice of a negative number (*e.g.* -1) represents the case where the execution will never see a $s(\mathsf{pc}) = 2 \wedge s'(\mathsf{pc}) = 5$ transition (*i.e.* non-termination)[3]. Whenever the program makes a transition $s(\mathsf{pc}) = 2 \wedge s'(\mathsf{pc}) \neq 5$ it knows that $\rho \neq 0$, because the prophecy made previously does not allow it. The program also decrements ρ whenever we see a $s(\mathsf{pc}) = 2 \wedge s'(\mathsf{pc}) \neq 5$ transition, for we know that (if we are going to see it at all) we are one step closer to seeing $s(\mathsf{pc}) = 2 \wedge s'(\mathsf{pc}) = 5$. If and when a

[2] An additional decision predicate will also be returned by our procedure, but it is not important for this example.

[3] In later sections we use a special element $\perp$ instead of negative numbers to represent non-termination, but for the purpose of this illustration negative numbers are easier.

$s(\mathsf{pc}) = 2 \wedge s'(\mathsf{pc}) = 5$ transition finally occurs, we know that $\rho = 0$. The program then predicts how many $s(\mathsf{pc}) = 2 \wedge s'(\mathsf{pc}) \neq 5$ transitions will be visited the next time around until seeing another $s(\mathsf{pc}) = 2 \wedge s'(\mathsf{pc}) = 5$ transition (which will never occur in this example). Because the old prediction is not needed again, we can re-use the same variable ρ for the new prophecy.

With the prophecy variable ρ in place, there is now a set of states where $\mathsf{AG}(x = 1)$ holds:

$$\{s \mid (s(\rho) < 0 \wedge s(\mathsf{pc}) = 2) \vee s(\mathsf{pc}) = 6\}$$

Furthermore we can prove that this set of states is eventually reached. So we can now use ∀CTL where it previously failed. On the second iteration of the procedure from Figure 1, no ∀CTL-counterexample will be found in M^{Ω} and thus the LTL property φ_{L} has been proved of M.

Note that if we remove the second `x := 1` command from the example, then the property φ_{L} is false. In this case the variable ρ will uniquely determine the number of iterations through the first loop, and the counterexample returned will instead involve the second loop. From this ∀CTL counterexample, we can construct a valid LTL counterexample.

Preliminaries

In the later sections of this paper we define each of the sub-procedures used in Figure 1 (*i.e.* APPROXIMATE in Section 3, DETERMINIZE in Section 4, etc). However, before moving to these more detailed descriptions we must develop some terminology and definitions that will be shared later. More details on any of our formalities, including a Coq proof script, can be found in our companion technical report [16].

States, sets, relations. We assume a domain D of states and, in the context of programs, will often treat it as a mapping from variables V to values. We will let s and t range over states, and S represent a set of states. We assume that no two states are indistinguishable. R will often be used to represent relations. When R is represented symbolically (*i.e.* expressed as a formula) it will be over the unprimed variables V and primed variables V'. For a state predicate p, the meaning $[\![p]\!]^{\mathsf{S}}$, is defined as the set of concrete states that respect p. The relational meaning of a formula p over primed and unprimed variables, $[\![p]\!]^{\mathsf{R}}$ is defined in the usual way. When it is clear from the context that we mean the real relation as opposed to the symbolic formula representation, we will drop the $[\![\ ]\!]^{\mathsf{R}}$ brackets. The notations Π^1 and Π^2 mean the first and second projection, respectively, of a relation. In cases where we are representing programs with control-flow graphs we will assume that states include a variable pc that represents the program counter and whose value is taken from a finite domain $\mathcal{L} = \{\ell_1, ..., \ell_n\}$.

Transition systems. We define a machine $M = (S, R, I)$ where $I \subseteq S$ is the set of initial states and $R \subseteq S \times S$ is the transition relation. In this paper we will be constructing new systems by adding variables and equating them to their original versions. Thus, it is convenient to build in a notion of internal and external state elements. We assume that $S = S^{\mathsf{ex}} \times S^{\mathsf{in}}$ (*i.e.* states consist of an external (visible) component and an internal component). We refer to an individual state as $\langle s, s^{\mathsf{in}}\rangle \in S$ and when a machine has no internal components, we omit the $\langle\rangle$ brackets.

Traces and paths. We define a *trace* to be a sequence of states

$$\pi = (\langle s_0, s_0^{\mathsf{in}}\rangle, \langle s_1, s_1^{\mathsf{in}}\rangle, ...)$$
$$\text{such that } \langle s_0, s_0^{\mathsf{in}}\rangle \in I \wedge \forall i \geq 0.(\langle s_i, s_i^{\mathsf{in}}\rangle, \langle s_{i+1}, s_{i+1}^{\mathsf{in}}\rangle) \in R$$

We denote $\mathsf{traces}(I, R)$ as the set of all such traces. For convenience, we do not allow finite traces – the transition relation must be such that every state s has at least one successor state. This is without a loss of generality, as final states can be encoded as states that loop back to themselves in the transition relation. With coinductive reasoning we can show that there exists an infinite trace from every state.

We use the notation $\pi|_{\mathsf{ext}}$ to denote the projection of π where internal components are removed:

$$(\langle s_0, s_0^{\mathsf{in}}\rangle, \langle s_1, s_1^{\mathsf{in}}\rangle, ...)|_{\mathsf{ext}} \triangleq (s_0, s_1, ...)$$

$\mathsf{traces}(I, R)|_{\mathsf{ext}}$ is similarly defined. We say that two systems are trace equivalent, notationally $\cong$, if their sets of projected traces are equivalent. We define an *abstract trace* to be a sequence of state abstractions. A *path* is a special case of an abstract trace in which only the pc-valuations are given. A path or an abstract trace is *spurious* if there does not exist a concrete trace from which we can construct the path via a projection.

Decision predicate vector. Formally we will treat Ω as a vector of pairs. Each element in the decision predicate vector Ω is a predicate pair denoted (a, b). We will use the vector index i to refer to a particular pair within Ω, and a_i, b_i denote the components of the ith pair. We use the notation $a_i(s)$ to indicate that s is in the set of states where a_i holds (i.e. $s \in [\![a_i]\!]$) and similar for $b_i(s)$.

$$\frac{\alpha(\pi_0|_{\mathsf{ext}})}{\pi \vDash_{\mathsf{L}} \alpha} \qquad \frac{\pi \vDash_{\mathsf{L}} \varphi_{\mathsf{L}} \ \vee\ \pi \vDash_{\mathsf{L}} \psi_{\mathsf{L}}}{\pi \vDash_{\mathsf{L}} \varphi_{\mathsf{L}} \vee \psi_{\mathsf{L}}} \qquad \frac{\pi \vDash_{\mathsf{L}} \varphi_{\mathsf{L}} \quad \pi \vDash_{\mathsf{L}} \psi_{\mathsf{L}}}{\pi \vDash_{\mathsf{L}} \varphi_{\mathsf{L}} \wedge \psi_{\mathsf{L}}}$$

$$\frac{\forall i \geq 0.\pi^i \vDash_{\mathsf{L}} \varphi_{\mathsf{L}}}{\pi \vDash_{\mathsf{L}} \mathsf{G}\varphi_{\mathsf{L}}} \qquad \frac{\exists i \geq 0.\pi^i \vDash_{\mathsf{L}} \varphi_{\mathsf{L}}}{\pi \vDash_{\mathsf{L}} \mathsf{F}\varphi_{\mathsf{L}}}$$

$$\frac{\forall i \geq 0.\pi^i \vDash_{\mathsf{L}} \varphi_{\mathsf{L}} \ \vee\ \exists j \geq 0.\pi^j \vDash_{\mathsf{L}} \psi_{\mathsf{L}} \wedge \forall i < j.\pi^i \vDash_{\mathsf{L}} \varphi_{\mathsf{L}}}{\pi \vDash_{\mathsf{L}} \varphi_{\mathsf{L}} \mathsf{W} \psi_{\mathsf{L}}}$$

Figure 2: Semantics of LTL: $\vDash_{\mathsf{L}}$

$$\frac{\alpha(s|_{\mathsf{ext}})}{s \vDash_{\mathsf{C}} \alpha} \qquad \frac{s \vDash_{\mathsf{C}} \varphi_{\mathsf{C}} \quad s \vDash_{\mathsf{C}} \psi_{\mathsf{C}}}{s \vDash_{\mathsf{C}} \varphi_{\mathsf{C}} \wedge \psi_{\mathsf{C}}} \qquad \frac{s \vDash_{\mathsf{C}} \varphi_{\mathsf{C}} \ \vee\ s \vDash_{\mathsf{C}} \psi_{\mathsf{C}}}{s \vDash_{\mathsf{C}} \varphi_{\mathsf{C}} \vee \psi_{\mathsf{C}}}$$

$$\frac{\forall (s_0, s_1, ...) \in \mathsf{traces}(I, R).\exists i \geq 0.\ s_0 = s \Rightarrow s_i \vDash_{\mathsf{C}} \varphi_{\mathsf{C}}}{s \vDash_{\mathsf{C}} \mathsf{AF}\varphi_{\mathsf{C}}}$$

$$\frac{\forall (s_0, s_1, ...) \in \mathsf{traces}(I, R).\forall i \geq 0.\ s_0 = s \Rightarrow s_i \vDash_{\mathsf{C}} \varphi_{\mathsf{C}}}{s \vDash_{\mathsf{C}} \mathsf{AG}\varphi_{\mathsf{C}}}$$

$$\frac{\begin{array}{c}\forall (s_0, s_1, ...) \in \mathsf{traces}(I, R).\\ \forall i \geq 0.\ s_i \vDash_{\mathsf{C}} \varphi_{\mathsf{C}} \ \vee\ \exists j \geq 0.\ s_j \vDash_{\mathsf{C}} \psi_{\mathsf{C}} \wedge \forall 0 \leq i < j.\ s_i \vDash_{\mathsf{C}} \varphi_{\mathsf{C}}\end{array}}{s \vDash_{\mathsf{C}} \mathsf{A}[\varphi_{\mathsf{C}} \mathsf{W} \psi_{\mathsf{C}}]}$$

Figure 3: Semantics of ∀CTL: $\vDash_{\mathsf{C}}$

3. APPROXIMATE: Proving LTL with ∀CTL

In this section we describe APPROXIMATE, which defines a sound over-approximation of LTL formulae with formulae in ∀CTL.

3.1 Linear Temporal Logic (LTL)

We use the following LTL grammar:

$$\varphi_{\mathsf{L}} \ ::= \ \alpha \mid \varphi_{\mathsf{L}} \wedge \varphi_{\mathsf{L}} \mid \varphi_{\mathsf{L}} \vee \varphi_{\mathsf{L}} \mid \mathsf{G}\varphi_{\mathsf{L}} \mid \mathsf{F}\varphi_{\mathsf{L}} \mid \varphi_{\mathsf{L}} \mathsf{W} \varphi_{\mathsf{L}}$$

We have not included U, R, X or ¬. Without loss of generality we assume that negations appear only in atomic propositions (*i.e.* instances of ¬ have been pushed to the leaves of the formula). In the context of programs X is relatively useless and is easily subsumed by F. U and R can be encoded as: $\varphi_L \mathsf{U} \psi_L \triangleq \mathsf{F}\psi_L \wedge (\varphi_L \mathsf{W} \psi_L)$ and $\varphi_L \mathsf{R} \psi_L \triangleq \psi_L \mathsf{W}(\varphi_L \wedge \psi_L)$. The LTL semantics, notationally $\vDash_L$, are given in Figure 2. The notation π^i indicates a *suffix* of a trace starting at the ith state in the sequence. We use π_0 to denote the first element in π. The superscript binds tighter than the subscript, i.e. $\pi_0^i = (\pi^i)_0$.

An atomic proposition α is from some abstract domain D, and we assume that true, false $\in D$ and that D is closed under negation (*i.e.* $\forall \alpha \in D.\ \exists \beta \in D.\ [\![\beta]\!]^S = [\![\neg\alpha]\!]^S$). The operator $\mathsf{G}\varphi_L$ specifies that φ_L globally holds along all traces. The operator $\mathsf{F}\varphi_L$ specifies that along every trace, eventually a suffix will be reached where φ_L holds. Finally, the $\varphi_L \mathsf{W} \psi_L$ operator specifies that φ_L holds forever or φ_L holds until ψ_L holds.

The LTL entailment relation $\vDash_L$ is defined on traces: the relation $\pi \vDash_L \varphi_L$ indicates that φ_L holds for a given trace π. We now lift $\vDash_L$ to machines.

Definition 3.1 (LTL Machine Entailment). *Assume that $M = (S, R, I)$. We define LTL-entailment, notationally $M \vDash_L \varphi_L$, as*

$$\forall \pi \in \mathit{traces}(I, R)\ .\ \pi \vDash_L \varphi_L$$

3.2 Computation Tree Logic ($\forall$CTL)

We now review existential-free computation tree logic:

$$\varphi_C ::= \alpha \mid \varphi_C \wedge \varphi_C \mid \varphi_C \vee \varphi_C \mid \mathsf{AG}\varphi_C \mid \mathsf{AF}\varphi_C \mid \mathsf{A}[\varphi_C \mathsf{W} \varphi_C]$$

The semantics of $\forall$CTL $\vDash_C$ are given in Figure 3. Unlike the trace-based LTL semantics, $\forall$CTL's semantics are state-based. By this we mean that the temporal operators are state-based in structure—the derivation of a given formula is per-state and depends on the derivation of subformulae for subsequent states. The operator $\mathsf{AG}\varphi_C$ specifies that φ_C globally holds in all reachable future states. The operator $\mathsf{AF}\varphi_C$ specifies that across all computation sequences from the current state, that there is a reachable state in which φ_C holds. Finally, the $\mathsf{A}[\varphi_C \mathsf{W} \psi_C]$ operator specifies that φ_C holds in every state where ψ_C does not hold yet.

Definition 3.2 ($\forall$CTL Machine Entailment). *As we did for $\vDash_L$, we lift $\vDash_C$ to machines. Assume $M = (S, R, I)$. We define $\forall$CTL-entailment, notationally $M \vDash_C \varphi_C$, to be*

$$\forall s \in I\ .\ R, s \vDash_L \varphi_L$$

3.3 Over-approximating LTL with $\forall$CTL

We describe a simple syntactic conversion from a formula in LTL to its corresponding over-approximation in $\forall$CTL.

Definition 3.3. *(*APPROXIMATE*) For all φ_L,*

$$\begin{array}{lcl}
\text{APPROXIMATE}(\alpha) & = & \alpha \\
\text{APPROXIMATE}(\varphi_L \wedge \psi_L) & = & \text{APPROXIMATE}(\varphi_L) \\
 & \wedge & \text{APPROXIMATE}(\psi_L) \\
\text{APPROXIMATE}(\varphi_L \vee \psi_L) & = & \text{APPROXIMATE}(\varphi_L) \\
 & \vee & \text{APPROXIMATE}(\psi_L) \\
\text{APPROXIMATE}(G\varphi_L) & = & AG\ \text{APPROXIMATE}(\varphi_L) \\
\text{APPROXIMATE}(F\varphi_L) & = & AF\ \text{APPROXIMATE}(\varphi_L) \\
\text{APPROXIMATE}(\varphi_L W \psi_L) & = & A[\text{APPROXIMATE}(\varphi_L) \\
 & & \quad W\ \text{APPROXIMATE}(\psi_L)]
\end{array}$$

Lemma 3.1. *($\forall$CTL Approximation) For a machine M and LTL property φ_L,*

$$M \vDash_C \text{APPROXIMATE}(\varphi_L) \quad \Rightarrow \quad M \vDash_L \varphi_L$$

Proof. By corresponding structural induction on the formulae APPROXIMATE(φ_L) and φ_L. We first unlift $\vDash_C$ and $\vDash_L$. Since traces is defined over I, we are free to pick a state $s \in I$ such that $s \vDash_C \varphi_C$. We now pick a trace $\pi \in \mathsf{traces}(\{s\}, R)$ and the appropriate case from the CTL semantics. For example, in the $s \vDash_C \mathsf{AF}\varphi_C{}'$ case the universal quantification tells us that for $\pi = (s_0, s_1, ...)$ that $\exists n. s_n \vDash_C \varphi_C{}'$. By the inductive hypothesis for all $\tilde{\pi} \in \mathsf{traces}(\{s_n\}, R)$, we have that $\tilde{\pi} \vDash_L \varphi_L{}'$. and thus we have established the criteria for $\pi \vDash_L \mathsf{F}\varphi_L{}'$. For further details, see our companion technical report [16]. □

$$\text{DETERMINIZE}((S,R,I),\Omega) = (S^\Omega, R^\Omega, I^\Omega) \text{ where}$$

$$\begin{array}{lcl}
S^\Omega & = & S \times \overrightarrow{\mathbb{N}_\bot} \qquad \text{denoted } \langle s, \rho \rangle \\
I^\Omega & = & I \times \overrightarrow{\mathbb{N}_\bot} \\
R^\Omega & = & \{(\langle s,\rho\rangle, \langle s', \rho'\rangle) \mid (s,s') \in R \wedge \forall (a_i, b_i) \in \Omega.
\end{array}$$

$$\begin{array}{rcll}
[a_i(s) \wedge \rho_i = \bot & \Rightarrow & b_i(s') \wedge \rho_i' = \bot] & (1) \\
\wedge[a_i(s) \wedge \rho_i > 0 & \Rightarrow & b_i(s') \wedge \rho_i' = \rho_i - 1] & (2) \\
\wedge[a_i(s) \wedge \rho_i = 0 & \Rightarrow & \neg b_i(s') \wedge \rho_i' \in \mathbb{N}_\bot] & (3) \\
\wedge[\neg a_i(s) & \Rightarrow & \rho_i' = \rho_i]\} & (4)
\end{array}$$

and $\mathbb{N}_\bot \triangleq \mathbb{N} \cup \{\bot\}$.

Figure 4: The DETERMINIZE procedure which, when given a vector of predicate pairs Ω, constructs the corresponding predicate-determinized machine.

4. DETERMINIZE: Decision Predicate Determinization

In this section we describe the procedure DETERMINIZE, which uses decision predicates as it performs a symbolic form of partial determinization.

Partially determinized machines. Figure 4 contains the definition for DETERMINIZE, which is designed to return a partially determinized machine when given a vector of predicates Ω and a machine:

$$M^\Omega = \text{DETERMINIZE}(M, \Omega)$$

The new machine M^Ω includes additional prophecy variables denoted ρ_i. These correspond to the predicate pairs (a_i, b_i) in the vector Ω. In accordance with I^Ω these variables are free to be a positive integer or zero or $\bot$ in the initial state. We will see that the choice of initial values (and the choice in Eqn. 3 from Figure 4) is the driving force behind determinization. For simplicity we used $\mathbb{Z}$ instead of $\mathbb{N}_\bot$ in Section 2. We also now define the update relation differently than we did in Section 2, in the sense that in Figure 4 the unprimed variables appear only to the left of $\Rightarrow$ and primed variables appear only to the right. While the two formalizations are equivalent, the encoding in Figure 4 is conceptually more operational and easier to implement within a tools setting, where in practice we are modifying the existing transition relation of M.

Transitions in R^Ω are made in accordance with R, but constrained by the values of ρ when states are reached that match a decision predicate (a_i, b_i) in Ω. Specifically, when a state is reached where a_i holds and the prophecy variable $\rho_i = \bot$, then b_i must hold in the next state and ρ_i is unchanged (Eqn. 1 of Figure 4). This rule corresponds to behaviors where a $a_i(s)$ state is visited infinitely often. Alternatively, if $\rho_i > 0$ (Eqn. 2) then b_i must also hold in the next state, except that ρ_i is decremented. When ρ_i reaches zero, then $\neg b_i$ must hold in the next state and ρ_i is free to take a new value from $\mathbb{N}_\bot$, starting the process all over (Eqn. 3). Finally, when a_i doesn't hold of a particular state, ρ_i is unchanged (Eqn. 4).

The prophecy variables introduced here trade *nondeterminism in the transition relation R* for a larger, *nondeterministic state space*. The state space nondeterminism is either determined at machine initialization by the initial choice of values for ρ given by I^Ω, or else later in a trace (Eqn. 3) by choosing new nondeterministic values for ρ. This lazy selection of nondeterministic values means that M^Ω needn't consist of infinitely many prophecy variables for each predicate pair. This formulation restricts us to treat programs with only countable nondeterminism. One could conceive of more powerful forms of nondeterminism, but we intend to use this technique in the context of programs for which countable nondeterminism is sufficient.

Theorem 4.1. *For all* Ω, $M^\Omega \cong M$.

Proof. The theorem holds if each of the conditions **P1**, **P2**, **P3** and **P4** and **PB** described below are met. These conditions are a variation of Proposition 5 from Abadi and Lamport [3]. Conditions **P1**, **P2**, **P3** and **P4** directly match Abadi and Lamport's conditions. We omit Condition **P5** as it involves liveness restrictions on the behavior of machines and we assume that our machines have no liveness restrictions. We loosen the restriction of Abadi and Lamport's **P6** with **PB** (detailed below), as our prophecy variables do not respect the condition of finite nondeterminism. The new condition **PB** is in fact a consequence of **P6**: in the second part of the proof, Abadi and Lamport show that all the behaviors of M are contained within M^Ω (note that regardless of superscript, $P = M$ because $L = \mathsf{true}$). Part 2.1 defines a directed graph, and then introduces Claim 2.1, which is not true in our setting. However, Claim 2.1 is only used in conjunction with Claim 2.2 and König's Lemma in order to prove Claim 2.3. In our setting we have simply included Claim 2.3 as condition **PB**. We now describe why each condition holds:

(P1) $S^\Omega \subseteq S \times S^P$ for some S^P. $\surd$

(P2) $I^\Omega = \Pi_p^{-1}(I)$ where Π_p^{-1} maps $S \times S^\Omega$ onto S. $\surd$

(P3) If $((s,p),(s',p')) \in R^\Omega$ then $(s,s') \in R$ or $s = s'$. This holds by construction of R^Ω from R. $\surd$

(P4) If $(s,s') \in R$ and $(s',p') \in S^\Omega$ then there exists $p \in S^\Omega$ such that $((s,p),(s',p')) \in R^\Omega$. Again, this holds by construction of R^Ω from R, case splitting on the value of p' and quantifying over $i \in \Omega$. $\surd$

(PB) For every $(s_0, s_1, \ldots) \in \mathsf{traces}(I,R)$ there exists $(p_0, p_1, \ldots)$ such that $((s_0,p_0),(s_1,p_1),\ldots) \in \mathsf{traces}(I^\Omega, R^\Omega)$.
Proof: Quantifying over each $i \le |\Omega|$, consider all of the (possibly infinitely many) transitions (s_j, s_{j+1}) such that $a_i(s_j)$ holds. Now for each transition $b_i(s_{j+1})$ may or may not hold. This can be modeled by:

$$(\exists m.\ b_i^m \neg b_i)^{\infty|*}(b_i^\infty)$$

i.e. a head $(\exists m \ge 0.\ b_i^m \neg b_i)^{\infty|*}$ consisting of repeated instances of finitely many b_i-states and a single $\neg b_i$-state, and a tail consisting of infinitely many b_i-states. So we can choose ρ_i accordingly, setting $\rho_i = m$ in each (potentially zero or infinitely many) instances of the head, and setting $\rho_i = \bot$ in the tail. $\surd$

Further details are available [16]. □

Example 5. *(Nondeterministic Choice) Consider the following machine:*

$$\begin{array}{rcl} S & = & [\begin{smallmatrix}\mathbb{N}\\ \mathbb{N}\end{smallmatrix}] \quad \textit{denoted} \quad [\begin{smallmatrix}\mathsf{x}\\ \mathsf{y}\end{smallmatrix}] \\ I & = & [\begin{smallmatrix}0\\ 0\end{smallmatrix}] \\ R & = & \{([\begin{smallmatrix}0\\ 0\end{smallmatrix}],[\begin{smallmatrix}1\\ 0\end{smallmatrix}]),\ ([\begin{smallmatrix}0\\ 0\end{smallmatrix}],[\begin{smallmatrix}0\\ 1\end{smallmatrix}]),\ ([\begin{smallmatrix}1\\ 0\end{smallmatrix}],[\begin{smallmatrix}1\\ 0\end{smallmatrix}]),\ ([\begin{smallmatrix}0\\ 1\end{smallmatrix}],[\begin{smallmatrix}0\\ 1\end{smallmatrix}])\} \end{array}$$

In this transition relation there is nondeterminism in the first transition. We can determinize this with the predicates $a = (\mathsf{x} = 0 \wedge \mathsf{y} = 0)$ *and* $b = (\mathsf{x} = 1)$. *With these predicates we can construct the corresponding* M^Ω.

$$\begin{array}{rcl} S^\Omega & = & [\begin{smallmatrix}\mathbb{N}\\ \mathbb{N}\end{smallmatrix}] \times \mathbb{N}_\bot \quad \textit{denoted} \quad \langle [\begin{smallmatrix}\mathsf{x}\\ \mathsf{y}\end{smallmatrix}], \rho\rangle \\ I^\Omega & = & \langle [\begin{smallmatrix}0\\ 0\end{smallmatrix}], \mathbb{N}_\bot\rangle \\ R^\Omega & = & \{(\langle[\begin{smallmatrix}0\\ 0\end{smallmatrix}],1\rangle,\langle[\begin{smallmatrix}1\\ 0\end{smallmatrix}],0\rangle),(\langle[\begin{smallmatrix}0\\ 0\end{smallmatrix}],0\rangle,\langle[\begin{smallmatrix}0\\ 1\end{smallmatrix}],\mathbb{N}_\bot\rangle), \\ & & (\langle[\begin{smallmatrix}1\\ 0\end{smallmatrix}],0\rangle,\langle[\begin{smallmatrix}1\\ 0\end{smallmatrix}],0\rangle),(\langle[\begin{smallmatrix}0\\ 1\end{smallmatrix}],\mathbb{N}_\bot\rangle,\langle[\begin{smallmatrix}0\\ 1\end{smallmatrix}],\mathbb{N}_\bot\rangle)\} \end{array}$$

The first two transitions have now been determinized: from the initial state, depending on the initial choice of ρ, *either* $(\mathsf{x} = 1)$ *or* $\neg(\mathsf{x} = 1)$ *will hold in the next state. In this example, since the nondeterministic transition only happens once, the (external) behaviors when* $\rho > 1$ *or* $\rho = \bot$ *in the initial state are all equivalent to* $\rho = 1$ *in the initial state so, for presentation purposes, we have omitted them. The additional behaviors will be used in the next example.*

Example 6. *(Termination) Consider the following infinite-state system which we represent symbolically*

$$\begin{array}{rcl} S & = & \mathbb{N} \quad \textit{denoted} \quad \mathsf{x} \\ I & = & \mathbb{N} \\ R & = & [\![(\mathsf{x} > 0 \wedge \mathsf{x}' = \mathsf{x} + 1) \vee (\mathsf{x} > 0 \wedge \mathsf{x}' = 0) \vee (\mathsf{x} = 0 \wedge \mathsf{x}' = 0)]\!]^R \end{array}$$

In this transition relation, when $\mathsf{x} > 0$ *initially, there is nondeterminism in how many times the first transition is chosen before the second transition is chosen. We can determinize this with the predicates* $a = (\mathsf{x} > 0)$ *and* $b = (\mathsf{x} > 0)$, *constructing the corresponding* M^Ω *as follows:*

$$\begin{array}{rcl} S^\Omega & = & \mathbb{N} \times \mathbb{N}_\bot \\ I^\Omega & = & \mathbb{N} \times \mathbb{N}_\bot \\ R^\Omega & = & [\![(\mathsf{x} > 0 \wedge \rho = \bot \wedge \mathsf{x}' = \mathsf{x} + 1 \wedge \rho' = \bot) \vee \\ & & (\mathsf{x} > 0 \wedge \rho > 0 \wedge \mathsf{x}' = \mathsf{x} + 1 \wedge \rho' = \rho - 1) \vee \\ & & (\mathsf{x} > 0 \wedge \rho = 0 \wedge \mathsf{x}' = 0 \wedge \rho' \in \mathbb{N}_\bot) \vee \\ & & (\mathsf{x} = 0 \wedge \rho \in \mathbb{N}_\bot \wedge \mathsf{x}' = 0 \wedge \rho' \in \mathbb{N}_\bot)]\!]^R \end{array}$$

In M^Ω *the first choice of how many times a transition from* $[\![\mathsf{x} > 0 \wedge \mathsf{x}' = \mathsf{x} + 1]\!]^R$ *is taken is given by the choice of an initial value for* ρ. *Any finite number of iterations corresponds to an arbitrarily chosen numeric value of* ρ. *The case where the transition is taken infinitely many times corresponds to the initial choice of* $\bot$ *for* ρ.

Example 7. *(Running example) For the example given in Section 2, the state space of the original program is* $S = \{\ell_1, \ldots, \ell_9\} \times \{0, 1\}$ *denoted* pc, x. *For* $\Omega = \{(\mathsf{pc} = \ell_2, \mathsf{pc} = \ell_5)\}$, *we have one prophecy variable denoted* ρ, *so* $S^\Omega = S \times \mathbb{N}_\bot$ *and* $I^\Omega = \{\ell_1\} \times \{1\} \times \mathbb{N}_\bot$. *The transition relation (omitting some uninteresting arcs) is defined as follows:*

$$\begin{array}{rcl} R^\Omega & = & [\![(\mathsf{x} = 1 \wedge \mathsf{pc} = \ell_2 \wedge \rho = \bot \wedge \mathsf{x}' = 1 \wedge \mathsf{pc}' = \ell_2 \wedge \rho' = \bot) \vee \\ & & (\mathsf{x} = 1 \wedge \mathsf{pc} = \ell_2 \wedge \rho > 0 \wedge \mathsf{x}' = 1 \wedge \mathsf{pc}' = \ell_2 \wedge \rho' = \rho - 1) \vee \\ & & (\mathsf{x} = 1 \wedge \mathsf{pc} = \ell_2 \wedge \rho = 0 \wedge \mathsf{x}' = 1 \wedge \mathsf{pc}' = \ell_5 \wedge \rho' \in \mathbb{N}_\bot) \vee \\ & & \ldots]\!]^R \end{array}$$

4.1 Proving LTL with ∀CTL and determinization

Lemma 3.1 shows that one can prove LTL properties with an ∀CTL verifier and an unmodified transition relation. We now extend this to show that one can prove (*perhaps even more*) LTL properties with ∀CTL and a predicate-determinized machine.

Theorem 4.2. *(∀CTL Approximation with Determinization) For a machine* M, *LTL property* φ_L *and predicates* Ω,

$$M^\Omega \models_C \text{APPROXIMATE}(\varphi_L) \quad \Rightarrow \quad M \models_L \varphi_L$$

Proof. Lemma 3.1 says that $M \models_C$ APPROXIMATE$(\varphi_L) \Rightarrow M \models_L \varphi_L$. The process of predicate determinization constructs machine M^Ω from M such that $M^\Omega \cong M$. Since the two machines are trace equivalent and it is known that trace-equivalent machines have the same LTL-behavior, Lemma 3.1 applies to the new machine and hence the theorem holds. Further details are available [16]. □

5. REFINE: Decision Predicate Refinement

We now describe REFINE, our procedure which examines counterexamples from a branching-time verification tool and discovers predicates which characterize the nondeterministic branching within them if any nondeterminism exists.

∀CTL counterexamples. Counterexamples in ∀CTL are trees [13]. The shape of the tree depends on the shape of the property which is violated. While most tools typically do not annotate their counterexamples with subformula, they could be made to do so. We formalize an ∀CTL counterexample tree as follows:

Definition 5.1. *(∀CTL tree counterexample)*

$$\begin{array}{rcl} \chi & ::= & CEX_\alpha \text{ of } \pi \\ & | & CEX_\wedge \text{ of } \chi \\ & | & CEX_\vee \text{ of } \chi \times \chi \\ & | & CEX_{AG} \text{ of } \pi \times \chi \\ & | & CEX_{AF} \text{ of } \pi \times \pi \times \chi \\ & | & CEX_W \text{ of } \pi \times \chi \times \chi \end{array}$$

In the above definition there is a constructor for each structural element of an ∀CTL formula. A counterexample to an atomic proposition CEX_α is a (single state) trace where the atomic proposition does not hold of the first element. A counterexample to a conjunction $\mathsf{CEX}_\wedge$ is a counterexample to one of the conjuncts. A counterexample to a disjunction $\mathsf{CEX}_\vee$ is comprised of two counterexamples, one for each disjunct. A counterexample CEX_{AG} is a path to a state in which a counterexample exists for the subformula. A counterexample CEX_{AF} is a "stem" path to an infinite "lasso" loop where a counterexample exists for the subformula. A counterexample CEX_W is a path to a state where a counterexample exists for both subformulae. For example, the counterexample to the property $\mathsf{AF}((\mathsf{AG}p) \vee (\mathsf{AG}q))$ consists of a stem and loop (for the AF subformula), and from within the loop a stem for each AG subformula.

Equality $\doteq$ between counterexamples is inductively defined, lifting equality between traces. We denote by $\chi|_{\text{ext}}$ the counterexample which consists of the external projection of paths in all components. Often counterexamples from model checking tools may contain less information than actual concrete traces (*e.g.* SLAM returns abstract traces that include the valuations of pc together with the valuations of the predicates used during the failed proof attempt).

In the AF rule, the counterexample is represented as a "stem" with an infinitely-repeated "lasso" path, along which every subtree is a counterexample to the subformula. In reality, not all counterexamples to termination can be represented this way. There are some rare programs that do not terminate but whose counterexamples cannot be represented as a infinitely-repeated "lasso path." For example:

```
while (x > 0) {
   y := x;
   x := x + 1;
   while (y > 0) { y := y - 1; }
}
```

In this case we assume an approximation of the real counterexample has been found and has been encoded using CEX_{AF}. In some instances this could potentially lead to divergence in our tool.

Counterexample control-flow graphs. From a given counterexample χ, we can construct a corresponding counterexample flow-graph (CEFG) Γ which represents all paths in the counterexample. We use a standard graph-based notation, where nodes $\mathsf{n} \in \mathbb{N}$

$$\mathrm{PSYNTH}_D(R, R') = \begin{cases} \{(a,b),(a,\neg b)\} & \text{such that } R \subseteq [\![a \wedge b']\!]^{\mathsf{R}} \\ & \text{and } R' \subseteq [\![a \wedge \neg b']\!]^{\mathsf{R}} \\ \varnothing & \text{if no such } a, b \text{ exist} \end{cases}$$

Figure 5: Specification of PSYNTH_D which, when given symbolic representations of two relations, returns predicate pairs that distinguishes them. An implementation of this procedure is described in Section 6.

```
REFINE(χ) :
    S := ∅
    N := {n₀}
    let Γ = cefg(χ|ext) in
    while true do
         let N' = {n' | n ∈ N ∧ ∃(n,r,n') ∈ Γ} in
         let T = {r | n ∈ N ∧ ∃n'.(n,r,n') ∈ Γ} in
         let Ω = ⋃_{r,r'∈T} PSYNTH_D(r,r') in
           if Ω = ∅ then
              if N' ∪ S = S then
                 return ∅
              else
                 N := N'
                 S := S ∪ N'
           else
                 return Ω
    done
```

Figure 6: The REFINE procedure walks down a counterexample flow-graph, at each step simultaneously exploring all possible next steps. If any pair of possible next steps are distinguishable via a predicate from PSYNTH_D then that predicate is immediately returned.

$\mathtt{cefg}(\mathsf{n}_0,\chi) \triangleq$ match χ with

| $\mathsf{CEX}_\alpha\ s$	$\longrightarrow$	$(\mathsf{n}_0, Id, \mathsf{n}_0)$
| $\mathsf{CEX}_\wedge\ \chi_1$	$\longrightarrow$	$\mathtt{cefg}(\mathsf{n}_0,\chi_1)$
| $\mathsf{CEX}_\vee\ \chi_1,\chi_2$	$\longrightarrow$	$\mathtt{cefg}(\mathsf{n}_0,\chi_1) \cup \mathtt{cefg}(\mathsf{n}_0,\chi_2)$
| $\mathsf{CEX}_{AG}\ \pi,\chi_1$	$\longrightarrow$	$\mathtt{cefg}_\pi(\mathsf{n}_0,\mathsf{n}_x) \cup \mathtt{cefg}(\mathsf{n}_x,\chi_1)$
| $\mathsf{CEX}_{AF}\ \pi,\bar{\pi},\chi_1$	$\longrightarrow$	$\mathtt{cefg}_\pi(\mathsf{n}_0,\mathsf{n}_1) \cup \mathtt{cefg}_{\bar{\pi}}(\mathsf{n}_1,\mathsf{n}_1) \cup \mathtt{cefg}(\mathsf{n}_1,\chi_1)$
| $\mathsf{CEX}_W\ \pi,\chi_1$	$\longrightarrow$	$\mathtt{cefg}_\pi(\mathsf{n}_0,\mathsf{n}_x) \cup \mathtt{cefg}(\mathsf{n}_x,\chi_1)$

where $\mathsf{n}_x, \mathsf{n}_1$ are fresh.

$$\mathtt{cefg}_\pi(\mathsf{n}_0,\mathsf{n}_x) \triangleq \{(\mathsf{n}_i, r, \mathsf{n}_{i+1}) \mid 0 \le i < |\pi| \wedge (\pi_0^i, \pi_0^{i+1}) \in [\![r]\!]^{\mathsf{R}}\}$$

where each n_i is fresh and $\mathsf{n}_x = \mathsf{n}_{|\pi|}$

Figure 7: The `cefg` procedure consumes a counterexample and constructs a counterexample flow graph, using $\mathtt{cefg}_\pi$ to convert a path π to a graph component.

correspond to states in the counterexample, and edges are triples $(\mathsf{n}_1, r, \mathsf{n}_2)$ consisting of a starting node, a transition relation r from the counterexample and a destination node. Even when we are working with programs, these CEFGs are different from program CFGs because they represent possible state transitions: there may be multiple CEFG transitions for a single CFG transition (e.g. when the program involves nondeterministic assignment) and there maybe multiple CEFG nodes which have the same CFG node. A counterexample flow graph can be constructed from a counterexample via the translation shown in Figure 7.

Predicate synthesis. The procedure $\text{PSYNTH}_D(r, r')$ is specified in Figure 5. It consumes two transition relations R, R' and returns *two* pairs of decision predicates: both (a, b) and $(a, \neg b)$. We return both pairs because it is difficult to know *a priori* which will be more useful to the LTL proving procedure, as the information tracked by (a, b) differs slightly from that tracked by $(a, \neg b)$. Moreover, there are cases where tracking only (a, b) will result in divergence, whereas $(a, \neg b)$ does not.

The details of the implementation of PSYNTH_D will differ, depending on the context (*i.e.* finite-state systems expressed at the bit-level, infinite-state systems expressed over linear arithmetic, etc). We assume that for a given domain D (a) that D is capable of distinguishing two states and (b) that PSYNTH_D is capable of discovering sufficient elements in D to do so. If these assumptions do not hold then in some instances our technique may be unable to sufficiently determinize. In our implementation, described in Section 6, we use constraint-solving techniques to find predicates which are monomials over linear inequalities.

Symbolic tree execution. The recursive procedure REFINE, given in Figure 6, consumes an $\forall$CTL counterexample and returns a set of predicates which distinguish nondeterministic branching. This involves first constructing a counterexample flow-graph, and iteratively exploring the frontier. REFINE simultaneously steps down each possible branch of the counterexample, ensuring that all of the next states are equivalent using PSYNTH_D (see the PSYNTH_D specification in Figure 5) to find distinguishing predicates. When distinct states are found, the corresponding predicates are returned, so that they can be added to Ω and the main algorithm can reiterate.

Progress. We now show that for a given counterexample χ, if REFINE discovers predicates, then our algorithm produces a new machine for which $\chi|_{\mathsf{ext}}$ is not a counterexample. We also show that, if no predicates are found by REFINE, then a real counterexample to the original LTL property can be constructed from $\chi|_{\mathsf{ext}}$.

Lemma 5.1. *(Counterexample elimination) For a machine M^{Ω}, property φ_L,*

$$\text{if } \chi \text{ is a counterexample to } M^{\Omega} \vDash_C \text{APPROXIMATE}(\varphi_L)$$
$$\text{then } \nexists \text{ counterexample } \chi' \text{ to } M^{\Omega'} \vDash_C \text{APPROXIMATE}(\varphi_L)$$
$$\text{such that } \chi|_{ext} \doteq \chi'|_{ext}$$

where $\Omega' = \Omega \cup \text{REFINE}(\chi)$ and $\text{REFINE}(\chi) \neq \varnothing$.

Proof. Let $(a_i, b_i) \in \text{REFINE}(\chi)$. By definition of REFINE in Figure 6 this predicate pair must have come from a subcomponent of the counterexample χ flow graph of the form $(\mathsf{n}, r, \mathsf{n}'), (\mathsf{n}, r', \mathsf{n}'')$. Moreover $a_i(\Pi^1(r))$, $b_i(\Pi^2(r))$ and $\neg b_i(\Pi^2(r'))$. Now, in the new machine the prophecy vector is augmented with a new element ρ_i. So the set of states denoted $\langle \Pi^1(r), \rho \rangle$ have either $\rho_i = 0$ or $\rho_i \in \{\bot, 1, 2, ...\}$. According to $R^{\Omega'}$, either $(\langle \Pi^1(r), \rho \rangle, \langle \Pi^2(r), \rho \rangle)$ is enabled or else $(\langle \Pi^1(r), \rho \rangle, \langle \Pi^2(r'), \rho \rangle)$ is enabled, but not both. Hence, there is no valid counterexample χ' such that $\chi|_{\mathsf{ext}} \doteq \chi'|_{\mathsf{ext}}$. Further details are available [16]. □

Remark on completeness. There are a few impediments to making a completeness claim. First, for a given $\forall$CTL counterexample χ, the routine PSYNTH_D must be able to discover predicates to characterize nondeterminism in χ. However, since we use approximation (*e.g.* with linear arithmetic), it will not always be able to discover sufficient predicates when they exist.

Second, even when we have a perfect PSYNTH_D routine, some $\forall$CTL counterexamples may be spurious, as the underlying $\forall$CTL also supports only overapproximation in linear arithmetic. Consequently, when $\text{REFINE}(\chi) = \varnothing$ we cannot necessarily claim that we have a valid LTL counterexample. Furthermore, as mentioned previously, there are some non-terminating programs that do not have a infinitely-repeated "lasso path." In these instances, the $\forall$CTL tool itself will either hang or return spurious counterexamples.

Finally, it is unclear whether our refinement loop will discover a finite number of decision predicates. With an infinite predicate vector Ω^{∞}, all nondeterminism can be represented (given a sufficient predicate domain), but one would hope that for each program/property there is a finite predicate vector.

Example 8. *(Running Example) For the example in Section 2, an $\forall$CTL prover may generate the following counterexample:*

$$(\mathsf{CEX}_{\mathsf{AF}}\ [\begin{smallmatrix}1\\1\end{smallmatrix}] :: [\begin{smallmatrix}2\\1\end{smallmatrix}], [\begin{smallmatrix}2\\1\end{smallmatrix}] :: [\begin{smallmatrix}3\\1\end{smallmatrix}] :: [\begin{smallmatrix}2\\1\end{smallmatrix}], \mathsf{CEX}_{\alpha}\ [\begin{smallmatrix}5\\0\end{smallmatrix}])$$

where a state is represented as $[\begin{smallmatrix}pc\\x\end{smallmatrix}]$. From this counterexample, we use `cefg` to construct the counterexample flow-graph Γ given in Section 2. Each arc represents a possible transition within the counterexample tree. the procedure REFINE *then walks all possible paths of the control-flow graph simultaneously, starting from the first node as follows:*

Iteration 1:	$N = \{n0\}$,	$S = \varnothing$
Iteration 2:	$N = \{n1\}$,	$S = \{n0, n1\}$
Iteration 3:	$N = \{n2, n3\}$,	$S = \{n0, n1, n2, n3\}$

After the first and second iterations PSYNTH_D does not discover a predicate to distinguish the two branches, but after the third call to REFINE*, the predicate pairs $(pc = \ell_2, pc = \ell_3)$ and $(pc = \ell_2, pc \neq \ell_3)$ are discovered, which distinguish paths that remain in the loop or exit the loop. A new machine is then constructed with prophecy variables corresponding to these decisions, and for this new machine an $\forall$CTL verifier can prove that the property holds.*

Example 9. *Consider the following program for which we would like to prove $\varphi_L = (FG\, y = 1) \vee (F\, x \geq t)$:*

```
ℓ0: x = y = 0; t = *;
    while(*)
ℓ1:    x++;
ℓ2: t = *;
ℓ3: if (x<t)
ℓ4:    y-1;
    while (true)
ℓ5:    skip;
```

The machine representing this program can be encoded as follows:

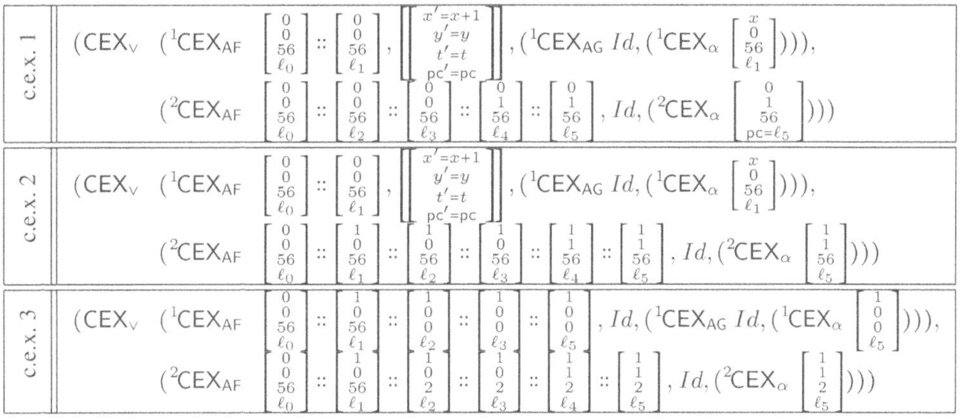

Figure 8: Counterexamples for each of the three iterations of proving Example 9. The notation Id indicates the identity transition (arising from the loop at line ℓ_5).

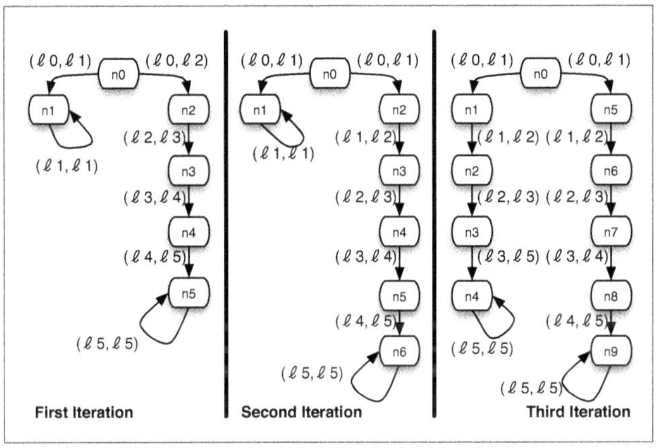

Figure 9: The counterexample flow graphs that are constructed at each iteration of proving Example 9.

$$S = \begin{bmatrix} \mathbb{N} \\ \mathbb{N} \\ \mathbb{N} \\ \mathcal{L} \end{bmatrix} \quad \textit{denoted} \quad \begin{bmatrix} x \\ y \\ t \\ pc \end{bmatrix} \qquad I = \begin{bmatrix} 0 \\ 0 \\ \mathbb{N} \\ \ell_0 \end{bmatrix}$$

$$\begin{aligned} R = \ & [\![(pc = \ell_0 \wedge pc' = \ell_1 \wedge x' = x \wedge y' = y \wedge t' = t) \vee \\ & (pc = \ell_0 \wedge pc' = \ell_2 \wedge x' = x \wedge y' = y \wedge t' = t) \vee \\ & (pc = \ell_1 \wedge pc' = \ell_1 \wedge x' = x + 1 \wedge y' = y \wedge t' = t) \vee \\ & (pc = \ell_1 \wedge pc' = \ell_2 \wedge x' = x + 1 \wedge y' = y \wedge t' = t) \vee \\ & (pc = \ell_2 \wedge pc' = \ell_3 \wedge x' = x \wedge y' = y \wedge t' \in \mathbb{N}) \vee \\ & (pc = \ell_3 \wedge pc' = \ell_4 \wedge x < t \wedge x' = x \wedge y' = y \wedge t' = t) \vee \\ & (pc = \ell_3 \wedge pc' = \ell_5 \wedge x \geq t \wedge x' = x \wedge y' = y \wedge t' = t) \vee \\ & (pc = \ell_4 \wedge pc' = \ell_5 \wedge x' = x \wedge y' = 1 \wedge t' = t) \vee \\ & (pc = \ell_5 \wedge pc' = \ell_5 \wedge x' = x \wedge y' = y \wedge t' = t)]\!]^R \end{aligned}$$

Using an $\forall$CTL prover, we may obtain the first counterexample in Figure 8. From this counterexample, we use `cefg` *to construct the first counterexample flow graph in Figure 9. Each arc represents a possible transition within the counterexample tree. The procedure* REFINE *then walks all possible paths of the control-flow graph simultaneously, starting from* n0 *as follows:*

Iteration 1: $N = \{n0\}$, $S = \emptyset$

In this iteration, REFINE *finds that $N' = \{n1,n2\}$ and that $R = \{(\ell_0,\ell_1),(\ell_0,\ell_2)\}$. Taking the (only) pair of relations from R,* PSYNTH$_D$ *generates the predicate pairs ($pc = \ell_0, pc = \ell_1$) and ($pc = \ell_0, pc \neq \ell_1$). Corresponding prophecy variables are created, and the $\forall$CTL verifier is used on the newly constructed machine, resulting in the next counterexample in Figure 8. We then get the second counterexample flow graph in Figure 9 and the* REFINE *explores it as follows:*

Iteration 1: $N = \{n0\}$, $S = \emptyset$
Iteration 2: $N = \{n1,n2\}$, $S = \{n0,n1,n2\}$

After the first iteration, PSYNTH$_D$ *does not discover any predicates to distinguish the two branches, but after the second iteration the predicate pairs ($pc = \ell_1, pc = \ell_1$) and ($pc = \ell_1, pc \neq \ell_1$) are discovered, which distinguish paths that remain in the loop or exit the loop. The $\forall$CTL verifier is executed once again, resulting in the third counterexample in Figure 8. The counterexample flow-graph is given in Figure 9 and* REFINE *explores it as follows:*

Iteration 1: $N = \{n0\}$, $S = \emptyset$
Iteration 2: $N = \{n1,n5\}$, $S = \{n0,n1,n5\}$
Iteration 3: $N = \{n2,n6\}$, $S = \{n0,n1,n5,n2,n6\}$
Iteration 4: $N = \{n3,n7\}$, $S = \{n0,n1,n5,n2,n6,n3,n7\}$

In the final iteration, PSYNTH$_D$ *discovers the predicate pairs ($pc = \ell_2, t \geq x$) and ($pc = \ell_2, t < x$). Notice that the second predicate is over a program variable other than* pc *– in the next example we will see that* pc *is not always sufficient to distinguish paths. Running the $\forall$CTL verifier one more time yields no counterexamples. Hence the original LTL property holds.*

Example 10. *In the examples above, almost all predicates were over the program counter variable* pc. *In many cases, the program counter serves as a convenient way of distinguishing paths through the program. However, this is not always the case. Consider proving the property ($G\, x = 0$) $\vee$ ($F\, x = 20$) for the following program:*

```
ℓ0: x = 0;
    while(x<20)
ℓ1:     x := (x==0)*{0,1} + (x==1)*20;
    while(true)
ℓ2:     skip
```

The notation {0,1} represents nondeterministic choice between 0 or 1. The LTL property holds because in traces where this nondeterministic choice is always 0, the property $G\, x = 0$ holds. For any trace in which the nondeterministic choice is 1, the property $F\, x = 20$ holds.

We shall represent the state as $\left[\begin{smallmatrix} x \\ \ell \end{smallmatrix}\right]$ *where* $x \in \mathbb{N}$. *An* $\forall$*CTL prover will generate the following counterexample to* $(\mathsf{AG}\ x = 0) \vee (\mathsf{AF}\ x = 20)$*:*

$$\begin{array}{ll}(\mathsf{CEX}_{\vee} & (\mathsf{CEX}_{\mathsf{AG}} \left[\begin{smallmatrix} 0 \\ \ell_0 \end{smallmatrix}\right] :: \left[\begin{smallmatrix} 0 \\ \ell_1 \end{smallmatrix}\right] :: \left[\begin{smallmatrix} 1 \\ \ell_1 \end{smallmatrix}\right], (\mathsf{CEX}_{\wedge} \left[\begin{smallmatrix} 1 \\ \ell_1 \end{smallmatrix}\right])) \\ & (\mathsf{CEX}_{\mathsf{AF}} \left[\begin{smallmatrix} 0 \\ \ell_0 \end{smallmatrix}\right] :: \left[\begin{smallmatrix} 0 \\ \ell_1 \end{smallmatrix}\right] :: \left[\begin{smallmatrix} 0 \\ \ell_1 \end{smallmatrix}\right], Id, (\mathsf{CEX}_{\wedge} \left[\begin{smallmatrix} 0 \\ \ell_1 \end{smallmatrix}\right])))\end{array}$$

For this counterexample REFINE *would explore the corresponding CEFG, and discover the decision predicate pairs* $(x = 0, x = 1)$ *and* $(x = 0, x \neq 1)$ *which distinguish the transition* $(\left[\begin{smallmatrix} 0 \\ \ell_1 \end{smallmatrix}\right], \left[\begin{smallmatrix} 1 \\ \ell_1 \end{smallmatrix}\right])$ *from* $(\left[\begin{smallmatrix} 0 \\ \ell_1 \end{smallmatrix}\right], \left[\begin{smallmatrix} 0 \\ \ell_1 \end{smallmatrix}\right])$*. Importantly, there is no predicate over the program counter variable alone which distinguishes these two transitions. We can now synthesize a prophecy variable corresponding to this decision predicate and an* $\forall$*CTL prover will discover a proof of the* $\forall$*CTL property, implying that the original LTL property holds.*

6. Implementation

In this section we discuss some details of our implementation of the algorithm in Figure 1, our implementation of an $\forall$CTL prover, and the results of our tool when applied to example programs.

Predicate synthesis. In Section 5, we have assumed the existence of a predicate synthesis mechanism PSYNTH_D that met the constraints given in Figure 5:

$$\text{PSYNTH}_D(R, R') = \begin{cases} \{(a,b),(a,\neg b)\} & \text{such that } R \subseteq [\![a \wedge b']\!]^{\mathsf{R}} \\ & \text{and } R' \subseteq [\![a \wedge \neg b']\!]^{\mathsf{R}} \\ \varnothing & \text{if no such } a, b \text{ exist} \end{cases}$$

Depending on the configuration of the systems considered by the tool, PSYNTH_D will need to be implemented in different ways. Here we describe a particular method of synthesizing predicates for counterexamples drawn from the style of programs typically accepted by modern model checking tools for infinite-state programs.

As is true in many symbolic model checking tools for software, we will assume that counterexamples are sequences of commands drawn from a path in the program. We will assume that these commands are over a finite set of arithmetic variables, and that the conditional checks and assignment statements only use linear arithmetic. Given this context, an implementation can represent the relations passed to PSYNTH_D as conjunctions of inequalities using variables. For example, the command sequence

$$\begin{array}{ll} \ell_{41}: & \mathsf{x} := \mathsf{x} - 1; \\ \ell_{21}: & \mathtt{assume}(\mathsf{x} > 0); \\ \ell_{10}: & \mathsf{y} := \mathsf{x}; \end{array}$$

which might represent a piece of a counterexample can be represented as a relation from valuations on $(\mathsf{x}, \mathsf{y}, \mathsf{pc})$ to valuations on $(\mathsf{x}', \mathsf{y}', \mathsf{pc}')$ where

$$\exists \mathsf{x}_1, \mathsf{x}_0, \mathsf{y}_1, \mathsf{y}_0. \bigwedge \left\{ \begin{array}{c} \mathsf{pc} = \ell_{41} \wedge \mathsf{pc}' = \ell_{10} \wedge \mathsf{x} = \mathsf{x}_0 \wedge \mathsf{x}' = \mathsf{x}_1 \wedge \mathsf{y} = \mathsf{y}_0 \wedge \mathsf{y}' = \mathsf{y}_1 \\ \mathsf{x}_1 = \mathsf{x}_0 - 1 \wedge \mathsf{x}_1 > 0 \wedge \mathsf{y}_1 = \mathsf{x}_1 \end{array} \right\}$$

We can reduce the search for predicates in this setting to the search for functions satisfying a set of constraints. In this instance we hope to find families of affine functions f and g such that the following conditions are true

1. $(\exists V'.R_1 \wedge \exists V'.R_2) \Rightarrow \bigwedge_{i \in \mathsf{dom}(f)} f_i(V) > 0$
2. $R_1 \Rightarrow \bigwedge_{i \in \mathsf{dom}(g)} g_i(V') > 0$
3. $R_2 \Rightarrow \neg(\bigwedge_{i \in \mathsf{dom}(g)} \cdot g_i(V') > 0)$

The set of pre-states common to both relations R_1 and R_2 are given $S \equiv \exists V'.R_1 \wedge \exists V'.R_2$, *i.e.* we are existentially quantifying out the post-states by quantifying out the variables that are used to represent them. We then find an over-approximation of S that is expressible as the conjunction of inequalities using f. The second and third constraints force the function g—which is expressed only over the primed variables—to distinguish between two transitions.

As done elsewhere [35], we can apply Farkas' lemma [23] and an SMT solver (*e.g.* Z3 [2] or Yices [20]) to find linear functions f_i and g_i that satisfy the above constraints. Thus, to implement $\text{PSYNTH}_D(R_1, R_2)$ we find families f and g satisfying the above constraints. We then return the predicate pairs (a, b) and $(a, \neg b)$ where

$$a \equiv \bigwedge_{i \in \mathsf{dom}(f)} f_i(V) > 0 \qquad \text{and} \qquad b \equiv \bigwedge_{i \in \mathsf{dom}(g)} g_i(V) > 0$$

A witness to $\exists V'.R_1 \wedge \exists V'.R_2$ can be computed using a quantifier elimination procedure, or alternatively, an additional application of Farkas' lemma. In practice, however, a good guess is simply to take the valuation of pc from both R_1 and R_2, *i.e.* $S \equiv \mathsf{pc} = \ell$, where $R_1 \Rightarrow \mathsf{pc} = \ell$ and $R_2 \Rightarrow \mathsf{pc} = \ell$.

Proving $\forall$CTL for infinite-state systems. We use $\forall$CTL verification tool for infinite-state programs, described elsewhere [17]. Our $\forall$CTL prover works by reducing the task of $\forall$CTL verification, via a program transformation, to an interprocedural program analysis problem. Thus, we can use known safety analysis tools [5, 11, 19, 26] combined with techniques for refining termination arguments [7, 8, 18, 22, 37] to obtain an $\forall$CTL verification tool whose power is limited only by the power of these underlying tools. The transformation uses recursion and nondeterminism in such a way that when these tools are applied to the transformed program, they effectively perform the necessary reasoning (*e.g* backtracking, eventuality checking, tree counterexamples, abstraction, abstraction-refinement, etc.) to prove branching-time behaviors of the original program. Formally, our transformation $\mathcal{T}$ works as follows: For a program P and an $\forall$CTL property φ_{C},

$$\exists \mathcal{M}.\ \mathcal{T}(P, \mathcal{M}, \varphi_{\mathsf{C}}) \text{ cannot return false} \quad \Rightarrow \quad P \vDash_{\mathsf{C}} \varphi_{\mathsf{C}}$$

where $\mathcal{M}$ is assumed to be a finite set of disjunctively well-founded relations [36]. The new program $\mathcal{T}(P, \mathcal{M}, \varphi_{\mathsf{C}})$ is constructed by recursively walking the structure of φ_{C}. Instances of $\mathsf{AF}(p)$ is syntactically decomposed into proving termination to a set of states in which p holds; $\mathsf{AG}(p)$ can be decomposed into checking that p holds at each line of the program, etc. $\mathcal{M}$ can be thought of as the argument of progress when proving φ_{C}. Once a suitable set $\mathcal{M}$ has been found, proving that $\mathcal{T}(P, \mathcal{M}, \varphi_{\mathsf{C}})$ cannot return false can be accomplished with existing interprocedural analysis tools. Satisfying instances of $\mathcal{M}$ can be found using the same technique as is used in TERMINATOR [18]. In our implementation we use SLAM [5] as the underlying safety prover, and RANKFINDER [35] as the method of finding new ranking functions f from spurious counterexamples χ.

Experiments. We have drawn out a set of LTL challenge problems from industrial code bases. Examples were taken from code models of the I/O subsystem of the Windows kernel, the back-end infrastructure of the PostgreSQL database server, and the Apache web server. We also include a few toy examples, as well as the example from Figure 8 in [15]. Further details on our benchmarks, including sources are available in our companion technical report [16].

In many cases, heap-commands from the original sources have been abstracted away using the approach due to Magill *et al.* [30]. This abstraction introduces new arithmetic variables that track the sizes of recursive predicate found as a byproduct of a successful memory safety analysis using an abstract domain based on separation logic. This abstraction also may introduce extra nondeterminism into the transition relation which, in more complex cases, may force our method to synthesize decision predicates.

Program	LOC	Property	Fair termination tool [15] Time (s)	|M|	Result	Decision predicates tool (Figure 1) Time (s)	|M|	|Ω|	Result
Example from Section 2	5	$\mathsf{FG}p$	2.32	1	✓	1.98	1	1	✓
Example from Fig. 8 of [15]	34	$\mathsf{G}(p \Rightarrow \mathsf{F}q)$	209.64	1	✓	27.94	0	0	✓
Toy acquire/release example	14	$\mathsf{G}(p \Rightarrow \mathsf{F}q)$	103.48	3	✓	14.18	1	0	✓
Toy linear arith. 1	13	$p \Rightarrow \mathsf{F}q$	126.86	1	✓	34.51	1	0	✓
Toy linear arith. 2	13	$p \Rightarrow \mathsf{F}q$	**T.O.**	1+	???	6.74	1	0	✓
PostgreSQL strmsrv	259	$\mathsf{G}(p \Rightarrow \mathsf{FG}q)$	**T.O.**	5+	???	9.56	0	0	✓
PostgreSQL strmsrv+bug	259	$\mathsf{G}(p \Rightarrow \mathsf{FG}q)$	87.31	0	χ	47.16	1	0	χ
PostgreSQL pgarch	61	$\mathsf{FG}p$	31.50	2	✓	15.20	0	0	✓
PostgreSQL dropbuf	152	$\mathsf{G}p$	**T.O.**	2+	???	1.14	0	0	✓
PostgreSQL dropbuf	152	$\mathsf{G}(p \Rightarrow \mathsf{F}q)$	53.99	1	✓	27.54	2	0	✓
Apache `accept()` liveness	314	$\mathsf{G}p \Rightarrow \mathsf{GF}q$	**T.O.**	1+	???	197.41	1	2	✓
Apache progress	314	$\mathsf{G}(p \Rightarrow (\mathsf{F}q_1 \vee \mathsf{F}q_2))$	685.34	0	✓	684.24	0	0	✓
Windows OS fragment 1	180	$\mathsf{G}(p \Rightarrow \mathsf{F}q)$	901.81	2	✓	539.00	2	0	✓
Windows OS fragment 2	158	$\mathsf{FG}p$	16.47	0	✓	52.10	3	3	✓
Windows OS fragment 2+bug	158	$\mathsf{FG}p$	26.15	0	χ	30.37	0	0	χ
Windows OS fragment 3	14	$\mathsf{FG}p$	4.21	0	✓	15.75	1	1	✓
Windows OS fragment 4	327	$\mathsf{G}(p \Rightarrow \mathsf{F}q)$	**T.O.**	7+	???	1,114.18	1	0	✓
Windows OS fragment 4	327	$(\mathsf{F}a) \vee (\mathsf{F}b)$	1,223.96	5	✓	100.68	1	0	✓
Windows OS fragment 5	648	$\mathsf{G}(p \Rightarrow \mathsf{F}q)$	**T.O.**	1+	???	**T.O.**	0	0	???
Windows OS fragment 6	13	$\mathsf{FG}p$	149.41	2	✓	59.56	1	0	✓
Windows OS fragment 6+bug	13	$\mathsf{FG}p$	6.06	0	χ	22.12	0	0	χ
Windows OS fragment 7	13	$\mathsf{GF}p$	**T.O.**	1+	???	55.77	1	0	✓
Windows OS fragment 8	181	$\mathsf{FG}p$	**T.O.**	1+	???	5.24	1	0	✓

Table 1: Comparison of fair termination based LTL prover [15] to decision predicate based algorithm from Figure 1 . Examples drawn from PostgreSQL database server, Apache web server, as well as the I/O subsystem of the Windows OS. The property column indicates the shape of the temporal properties, where p and q are atomic propositions specific to the program. A ✓ indicates that the tool has proved the property, whereas a χ indicates that a valid LTL counterexample has been found. $|\Omega|$ indicates the number of decision predicates needed, and $|\mathrm{M}|$ the number of progress measures required. **T.O.** indicates that the experiment timed out after 4 hours, and in such cases we specify at least how many termination arguments were needed (denoted +).

The only previously known tool for automatically proving LTL-like properties of infinite-state programs is described in [15], which is a TERMINATOR-like [18] procedure with an extension for fairness. LTL2BA [24] is used to convert LTL formulae to Büchi automata. As we have done in our implementation of Figure 1, the implementation of [15] uses SLAM as the underlying safety model checker, and RANKFINDER [35] as the rank function synthesis tool.

Table 1 reports the results of our experiments. The first column describes the code artifact. We added bugs into several of the examples. The second column "LOC" reports the number of lines of code for each example. We studied the results for properties of differing shapes (e.g. $\mathsf{G}(p \Rightarrow Fq)$, $\mathsf{FG}p$, $\mathsf{GF}p$, etc.). Experiments were run using Windows Vista and an Intel 2.66GHz processor.

For both tools we report the total time, the number of ranking functions required (denoted $|\mathrm{M}|$), and the result for each of the benchmarks. A ✓ indicates that the tool proved the property, and χ is used to denote cases where bugs were found. In the case that the tool exceeded the timeout threshold of 4 hours, "**T.O.**" is used to represent the time, the result is listed as "**???**", and we simply report the current size of $|\mathrm{M}|$ at the time that the tool was killed together with a "+" symbol.

For our approach we report the number of decision predicates required $|\Omega|$. For these examples relatively few prophecy variables are usually required. This confirms our assumption that faster CTL-based techniques *usually* work, so long as we have a fast method for evaluating the potential spuriousness of CTL counterexamples, and an effective strategy of refinement when CTL methods fail. We also observe that $|\mathrm{M}|$ is typically smaller when using the decision predicates based tool.

We implemented support for fairness in our decision predicate based approach tool in order to support Figure 8 of [15]. This is due to the fact that one of the fairness constraints actually comes from an environment assumption and thus must still be modeled. Our support for fairness uses essentially the same recipe as given in [15], combined with the source-to-source transformation.

As mentioned in Section 1, a limitation to our approach is that there are cases when we see a minor performance penalty for our strategy of only tracking correlations on demand (*e.g.* in "Windows OS fragment 2.") We also see some minor overhead when computing real counterexamples (*e.g.* in "Windows OS fragment 2+bug").

The most dramatic aspect of Table 1 is the overall result: our decision predicate based LTL prover was able to prove/disprove all but 1 example in usually a fraction of a minute, whereas the fair termination based tool fails on nearly a quarter of the benchmarks. This is due to our strategy of first trying to use ∀CTL proof strategies, and only tracking subtle relationships between families of traces on demand using decision predicates. Without our approach we could not reliably use an ∀CTL-based proof strategy with precision equal to native LTL-based approaches. In each of these **T.O.** cases but one our decision predicate based tool proves all of the examples with reasonable runtimes (resulting in a ✓). Furthermore, our tool reported no spurious counterexamples: in the cases where a purely ∀CTL-based approach would have been incomplete for LTL (resulting in a spurious counterexample), our refinement procedure quickly found and then symbolically shifted the problematic nondeterminism into the state-space of the system.

7. Conclusion

We have described a new algorithm for proving LTL properties of infinite-state systems. Our algorithm searches for instances of nondeterminism that preclude the use of CTL-based proof methods. We characterize these instances of nondeterminism using decision predicates, and then symbolically shift them into the state-space using a partial-determinization procedure. The advantage to this approach is that CTL proof methods can be used where they would have previously failed. We find in practice that most instances of nondeterminism is harmless to CTL proof methods. Thus, in many cases, we see performance improvements when using this strategy.

Acknowledgments. We thank Josh Berdine, Matko Botinčan, Axel Legay, Peter O'Hearn, Matthew Parkinson, Nir Piterman, Moshe Vardi and Hongseok Yang for their comments and thoughtful discussions. Stephen Magill provided several of the examples from Table 1. We also thank the Gates Cambridge Scholarship program for funding Eric Koskinen's Ph.D.

References

[1] Cadence SMV. `http://www.kenmcmil.com/smv.html`.

[2] The Z3 Theorem Prover. research.microsoft.com/projects/Z3.

[3] ABADI, M., AND LAMPORT, L. The existence of refinement mappings. *Theoretical Computer Science 82*, 2 (1991), 253–284.

[4] ABDULLA, P. A., JONSSON, B., NILSSON, M., D'ORSO, J., AND SAKSENA, M. Regular model checking for LTL(MSO). In *CAV* (2004).

[5] BALL, T., BOUNIMOVA, E., COOK, B., LEVIN, V., LICHTENBERG, J., MCGARVEY, C., ONDRUSEK, B., RAJAMANI, S., AND USTUNER, A. Thorough static analysis of device drivers. *ACM SIGOPS Operating Systems Review 40*, 4 (2006), 85.

[6] BOUAJJANI, A., LEGAY, A., AND WOLPER, P. Handling liveness properties in (ω-) regular model checking. *Electronic Notes in Theoretical Computer Science 138*, 3 (2005), 101–115.

[7] BRADLEY, A., MANNA, Z., AND SIPMA, H. Termination of polynomial programs. In *VMCAI* (2005).

[8] BRADLEY, A. R., MANNA, Z., AND SIPMA, H. B. Linear ranking with reachability. In *CAV* (2005).

[9] BURCH, J., CLARKE, E., MCMILLAN, K., DILL, D., AND HWANG, L. Symbolic model checking: 10 to the 20 states and beyond. *Information and Computation 98*, 2 (1992).

[10] CLARKE, E., EMERSON, E., AND SISTLA, A. Automatic verification of finite-state concurrent systems using temporal logic specifications. *TOPLAS 8*, 2 (1986), 263.

[11] CLARKE, E., GRUMBERG, O., JHA, S., LU, Y., AND VEITH, H. Counterexample-guided abstraction refinement for symbolic model checking. *JACM 50*, 5 (2003), 794.

[12] CLARKE, E., GRUMBERG, O., AND PELED, D. *Model checking*. Springer, 1999.

[13] CLARKE, E., JHA, S., LU, Y., AND VEITH, H. Tree-like counterexamples in model checking. In *LICS* (2002).

[14] CLARKE, E. M., GRUMBERG, O., AND HAMAGUCHI, K. Another look at LTL model checking. *Form. Methods Syst. Des. 10*, 1 (1997), 47–71.

[15] COOK, B., GOTSMAN, A., PODELSKI, A., RYBALCHENKO, A., AND VARDI, M. Y. Proving that programs eventually do something good. In *POPL* (2007).

[16] COOK, B., AND KOSKINEN, E. Making prophecies with decision predicates. Tech. Rep. UCAM-CL-TR-789, University of Cambridge, Computer Laboratory, Jan. 2011.

[17] COOK, B., KOSKINEN, E., AND VARDI, M. Branching-time reasoning for programs. Tech. Rep. UCAM-CL-TR-788, University of Cambridge, Computer Laboratory, Jan. 2011.

[18] COOK, B., PODELSKI, A., AND RYBALCHENKO, A. Termination proofs for systems code. In *PLDI* (2006).

[19] COUSOT, P., COUSOT, R., FERET, J., MAUBORGNE, L., MINÉ, A., MONNIAUX, D., AND RIVAL, X. The ASTREE analyzer. In *ESOP* (2005).

[20] DUTERTRE, B., AND DE MOURA, L. M. A fast linear-arithmetic solver for dpll(t). In *CAV* (2006), T. Ball and R. B. Jones, Eds., vol. 4144 of *LNCS*, Springer, pp. 81–94.

[21] ESPARZA, J., KUCERA, A., AND SCHWOON, S. Model-checking LTL with regular valuations for pushdown systems. In *TACS* (2001).

[22] FANG, Y., PITERMAN, N., PNUELI, A., AND ZUCK, L. Liveness with invisible ranking. *International Journal on Software Tools for Technology Transfer (STTT) 8*, 3 (2006), 261–279.

[23] FARKAS, J. Uber die theorie der einfachen ungleichungen. *Journal fur die Reine und Angewandte Mathematik 124* (1902), 1–27.

[24] GASTIN, P., AND ODDOUX, D. Fast LTL to Büchi automata translation. In *CAV* (July 2001).

[25] HAVELUND, K., AND PRESSBURGER, T. Model checking Java programs using Java pathfinder. *International Journal on Software Tools for Technology Transfer (STTT) 2*, 4 (2000), 366–381.

[26] HENZINGER, T. A., JHALA, R., MAJUMDAR, R., NECULA, G. C., SUTRE, G., AND WEIMER, W. Temporal-safety proofs for systems code. In *CAV* (2002).

[27] HOBOR, A., APPEL, A. W., AND NARDELLI, F. Z. Oracle semantics for concurrent separation logic. In *ESOP* (2008).

[28] HOLZMANN, G. J. The model checker SPIN. *IEEE Trans. Software Eng. 23*, 5 (1997), 279–295.

[29] KWIATKOWSKA, M., NORMAN, G., AND PARKER, D. PRISM: Probabilistic symbolic model checker. *LNCS 2324* (2002), 200–204.

[30] MAGILL, S., BERDINE, J., CLARKE, E., AND COOK, B. Arithmetic strengthening for shape analysis. *LNCS 4634* (2007), 419.

[31] MAIDL, M. The common fragment of CTL and LTL. In *FOCS* (2000).

[32] NAIN, S., AND VARDI, M. Branching vs. linear time: Semantical perspective. In *ATVA* (2007).

[33] PNUELI, A. The temporal logic of programs. In *18th Annual Symposium on Foundations of Computer Science* (1977), IEEE, pp. 46–57.

[34] PNUELI, A., AND ZAKS, A. PSL model checking and run-time verification via testers. In *FM* (2006), J. Misra, T. Nipkow, and E. Sekerinski, Eds., vol. 4085 of *LNCS*, Springer, pp. 573–586.

[35] PODELSKI, A., AND RYBALCHENKO, A. A Complete Method for the Synthesis of Linear Ranking Functions. *LNCS* (2003), 239–251.

[36] PODELSKI, A., AND RYBALCHENKO, A. Transition invariants. In *LICS* (2004), pp. 32–41.

[37] PODELSKI, A., AND RYBALCHENKO, A. ARMC: the logical choice for software model checking with abstraction refinement. In *PADL* (2007).

[38] QADEER, S., SEZGIN, A., AND TASIRAN, S. Back and forth: Prophecy variables for static verification of concurrent programs. Tech. Rep. MSR-TR-2009-142, Microsoft, 2009.

[39] SAFRA, S. On the complexity of omega -automata. In *SFCS* (1988).

[40] SANKARANARAYANAN, S., SIPMA, H., AND MANNA, Z. Constraint-based linear-relations analysis. In *SAS* (2004).

[41] SCHNEIDER, K. Model checking on product structures. *FMCAD* (1998).

[42] SCHUPPAN, V., AND BIERE, A. Liveness checking as safety checking for infinite state spaces. In *Workshop on Verification of Infinite-State Systems (INFINITY)* (2005).

[43] VARDHAN, A., SEN, K., VISWANATHAN, M., AND AGHA, G. Using language inference to verify Omega-regular properties. In *TACAS* (2005).

[44] VARDI, M. Branching time vs. linear time: Final showdown. In *TACAS* (2001).

[45] VARDI, M. Y., AND WOLPER, P. An automata-theoretic approach to automatic program verification (preliminary report). In *LICS* (1986).

Delay-Bounded Scheduling

Michael Emmi
LIAFA, Université Paris Diderot, France
mje@liafa.jussieu.fr

Shaz Qadeer
Microsoft Research, Redmond, WA, USA
qadeer@microsoft.com

Zvonimir Rakamarić
University of British Columbia, Canada
zrakamar@cs.ubc.ca

Abstract

We provide a new characterization of scheduling nondeterminism by allowing deterministic schedulers to delay their next-scheduled task. In limiting the delays an otherwise-deterministic scheduler is allowed, we discover concurrency bugs efficiently—by exploring few schedules—and robustly—i.e., independent of the number of tasks, context switches, or buffered events. Our characterization elegantly applies to any systematic exploration (e.g., testing, model checking) of concurrent programs with dynamic task-creation. Additionally, we show that certain delaying schedulers admit efficient reductions from concurrent to sequential program analysis.

Categories and Subject Descriptors D.2.4 [*Software Engineering*]: Software/Program Verification; D.2.5 [*Software Engineering*]: Testing and Debugging

General Terms Algorithms, Reliability, Testing, Verification

Keywords Concurrency, Asynchronous programs, Delay, Sequentialization

1. Introduction

A concurrent program is a transition system combined with a (nondeterministic) scheduler. The program's semantics is easy to describe: the scheduler repeatedly chooses an enabled state-altering transition to execute, executes it, then chooses another transition, and so on. This inherently nondeterministic semantics is the root cause of Heisenbugs—i.e., programming errors that manifest rarely, and are hard to reproduce and repair. A class of techniques known as *model checking* [8] systematically explore this nondeterminism in order to discover, or occasionally prove the absence of, such bugs.

Although systematically exploring (or *searching*) a concurrent program's behavior is a simple and intuitively appealing idea, the exploration is computationally expensive. For programs in which the only source of nondeterminism is the scheduler, the combinatorial cost is determined by two factors: the maximum number I of scheduler invocations, and the maximum number C of choices available to the scheduler at each invocation. Given these two factors, the cost of exploration is $\mathcal{O}(C^I)$. While I naturally corresponds to the length of program executions, C corresponds to the number of concurrently executing tasks. Both C and I grow rapidly in realistic programs, causing a combinatorial explosion in the exploration cost.

PoPL'11, January 26–28, 2011, Austin, Texas, USA.

Search prioritization is a basic strategy to combat the explosion. In general, one characterizes a subset of the search space by a bounding parameter p. More behaviors are explored as p is increased, and in the limit all behaviors are explored. A prioritization is effective when useful information (e.g., the presence of bugs) is obtained by examining few behaviors (i.e., low values of p).

In this work we introduce *delay-bounding*: an effective search prioritization strategy for concurrent programs that handles both statically-known and dynamically-created tasks. We begin by quantifying scheduler nondeterminism with the concept of *delay*. Our main insight is captured by the premise:

> A deterministic scheduler is made sufficiently nondeterministic with the ability to delay its next-scheduled task.

In other words, we can quantify—and thus limit—scheduling nondeterminism by allotting a finite delay-budget.

More concretely, delay-bounding parameterizes the search space by a deterministic scheduler M, and a delay-bound K. When $K = 0$, exploration is limited to the unique execution produced by M. When $K > 0$, the scheduler may deviate from its usual schedule a total of K times over an entire execution. For instance, a round-based delaying scheduler executes all of its scheduled tasks to completion in a given round i, before advancing to the next round, where the tasks delayed in round i are again scheduled; as the total number of exercised delays is bounded by K, the number of rounds is bounded by $K + 1$. The search space for any deterministic scheduler and delay-bound K is bounded by I^K.

Delay-bounding is endowed with many appealing properties:

- Delay-bounding is a canonical characterization, and a means of limiting, scheduling nondeterminism. Since the bound is chosen independently of the number of tasks, the approach naturally handles both statically-known and dynamically-created tasks.
- The cost of delay-bounded exploration is polynomial in I. Our preliminary experiments discover (previously unknown) bugs in real programs with small delay-bounds, suggesting that delay-bounded search does provide adequate coverage in practice.
- The choice of a deterministic scheduler is independent of the delay-bound, and *every* reasonable scheduler discovers *any* given bug at some cost. To minimize exploration cost it is even possible to perform parallel exploration using various deterministic schedulers—perhaps even chosen at random.
- It is possible, with certain deterministic schedulers, to capture a concurrent program's delay-bounded semantics as a sequential program. Theoretically, the *scheduling complexity* of these schedulers is reduced from undecidable (with preemptible tasks), or EXPSPACE-complete (with non-preemptible tasks), to NP-complete (with or without preemption). In practice, the reduction allows us to leverage the numerous existing tools and techniques for sequential-program verification, including symbolic model checking, and symbolic exploration with SMT solvers.

1.1 Contributions

Our contributions are summarized as follows:

- We introduce a canonical characterization of scheduling non-determinism, allowing a simple, elegant, and unified approach for prioritized exploration of concurrent programs with dynamic task-creation.
- We show that delaying deterministic schedulers can efficiently discover both known and previously-undiscovered bugs by systematic exploration (e.g., testing).
- We give concurrent-to-sequential program translations using clever encodings of certain delaying schedulers. The encodings rely on insightful extensions of Lal and Reps [27]'s guess and constrain methodology, and ultimately lead to practical verification algorithms.
- We identify an NP-complete analysis problem: state-reachability under a particular delaying scheduler. The complexity is lower than related bounded reachability problems.

1.2 Comparison to Related Search Prioritizations

Delay-bounding represents a convergence of a progression over the last decade of search prioritization techniques for concurrent programs. Given a number I of scheduler invocations and C of choices available to the scheduler at each invocation—recall the cost of complete search is $\mathcal{O}(C^I)$:

Depth-bounding limits the number of scheduler invocations by a *depth-bound* d, reducing the search complexity to $\mathcal{O}(C^d)$. Though this approach is taken by VERISOFT [17], it is clearly not effective as d approaches I. In practical terms, errors manifested deeply in a program execution remain difficult to discover.

Context-bounding [34] labels the choices available to the scheduler by distinct (task) identifiers, and bounds the number of label changes in executions by a *context-bound* c. Here the complexity is reduced to $\mathcal{O}((IC)^c)$; the polynomial dependence on execution length alleviates, to a large extent, the aforementioned problem with depth-bounding. Empirically, low context-bound values are sufficient for finding many bugs in real programs [27, 35]. However, in many cases, bugs are exhibited only after each of the, say C, tasks have a chance to execute. (In practice this dependence arises in, e.g., initialization patterns, round-robin protocols, etc.) Consequently, the exponential dependence on c in $\mathcal{O}((IC)^c)$ is practically an exponential dependence on C as well. Worse yet, when tasks are created dynamically, context-bounding suffers the same ill fate as depth-bounding: errors manifested deeply in a task-creation chain are discovered only for high values of c.

Preemption-bounding [29] also labels scheduler choices with distinct identifiers, but only bounds the number of *preemptive* label changes (by p); label changes due to blocking or completion are not budgeted. Preemption-bounded search addresses the main problem with context-bounding, as each task gets the opportunity to complete its execution. Unfortunately, the number of label changes is *expected to* depend on C, rendering the search complexity, $\mathcal{O}((IC)^{p+C})$, prohibitive for large values of C.

As we can see, when tasks are numerous or dynamically created, the existing prioritized exploration techniques are ineffective. Delay-bounding fixes these problems by allowing an unbounded number of tasks to execute, and bounding instead the degree of variation from a deterministic scheduling order. The exploration cost using K delays is I^K, which is independent of the number of (dynamically-created) tasks.

2. Asynchronous Programs

So that our approach handles dynamic task-creation *by design*, we begin with a model of simple asynchronous programs corresponding to the style of single-threaded event-driven programming. The style is typically used as a lightweight technique for adding reactivity to single-threaded applications by breaking up long-running computations into a collection of *tasks*. In this model, control begins with a non-empty *task buffer* of pending tasks from which a *dispatcher* picks a single task to execute. The dispatcher transfers control to the task, which is essentially a sequential program that can read from and write to global storage, and *post* additional tasks to the task buffer. When a task completes its execution, control returns to the dispatcher, which picks another task from the task buffer, and so on. When the dispatcher has control and the task buffer is empty, the program terminates. This model forms the basis of (client-side) web applications [15], and has been shown useful for building fast servers [32], routers [22], and embedded sensor networks [18].

In what follows we generalize the usual notion [37] of task-buffer dispatch (i.e., choosing any pending task) by exposing a *scheduler*, by which we parameterize a simple program semantics.

To capture programs with interruptible tasks (or, alternatively, concurrently running tasks on sequentially consistent processors/threads), we extend the simple asynchronous model to permit arbitrary task interruption with the **yield**-statement. Although the extension may seem modest, the resulting language is powerful enough to model concurrent programs with arbitrary preemption and synchronization, e.g., by inserting a **yield**-statement before every shared variable access. The model particularly resembles typical operating-systems kernel code and device drivers, which are often implemented as a collection of preemptible task-handlers [9, 31].

2.1 The Scheduler

For the moment, let Tasks and Vals be uninterpreted sets, and $\mathsf{blocked} : \mathsf{Tasks} \times \mathsf{Vals} \to \mathbb{B}$ be an uninterpreted predicate. Intuitively, each element $w \in \mathsf{Tasks}$ is a task to be scheduled, each element $g \in \mathsf{Vals}$ is a global state, and $\mathsf{blocked}(w, g)$ holds when w is not enabled in the global state g.

A *scheduler* $M = \langle D, \mathsf{empty}, \mathsf{give}, \mathsf{take} \rangle$ consists of a data-type D of *scheduler objects* $m \in D$, a scheduler *constructor* $\mathsf{empty} \in D$, and scheduler update functions $\mathsf{give} : D \times \mathsf{Tasks} \to D$ to receive posted tasks, and $\mathsf{take} : D \times \mathsf{Vals} \to \wp(D \times \mathsf{Tasks})$ to determine which tasks can be scheduled next. The scheduler M is *deterministic* when for all $m \in D$ and $g \in \mathsf{Vals}$, $\mathsf{take}(m, g)$ contains at most one element, and is *non-blocking* when for all $w \in \mathsf{Tasks}$, $g \in \mathsf{Vals}$, and $m, m' \in D$, $\mathsf{blocked}(w, g)$ implies $\langle m', w \rangle \notin \mathsf{take}(m, g)$. In general, non-blocking schedulers must be aware of the program state; hence the argument $g \in \mathsf{Vals}$ to take.

Fix $m \in D$ and $g \in \mathsf{Vals}$. A task w is *pending (in m)* if there is a sequence $m_1 w_2 m_2 w_3 m_3 \ldots w_j m_j$ such that $m_1 = m$, $w_j = w$, and for $1 < i \leq j$, $\langle m_i, w_i \rangle \in \mathsf{take}(m_{i-1}, g)$; in other words, w is pending when w can eventually be taken from m. A task w is *schedulable (by m)* when there exists m' such that $\langle m', w \rangle \in \mathsf{take}(m, g)$.

Scheduler 1 (The bag scheduler). The multiset-based scheduler bag is defined on the multiset domain D_{bag} of tasks as[1]

$$\begin{aligned} \mathsf{empty}_{\mathsf{bag}} &\stackrel{\text{def}}{=} \emptyset \\ \mathsf{give}_{\mathsf{bag}}(m, w) &\stackrel{\text{def}}{=} m \cup \{w\} \\ \mathsf{take}_{\mathsf{bag}}(m, g) &\stackrel{\text{def}}{=} \{\langle m \setminus \{w\}, w \rangle : w \in m\}. \end{aligned}$$

The bag scheduler is non-deterministic, since all pending tasks are returned by each application of $\mathsf{take}_{\mathsf{bag}}$.

[1] Here $\cup$ and $\setminus$ are the *multiset* union and difference operators.

$$
\begin{array}{rl}
P ::= & \mathbf{var}\ \mathtt{g} : T\ H^* \\
H ::= & \mathbf{proc}\ p\ (\mathbf{var}\ \mathtt{l} : T)\ s \\
s ::= & s;\ s \\
| & x := e \\
| & \mathbf{skip} \\
| & \mathbf{assume}\ e \\
| & \mathbf{if}\ e\ \mathbf{then}\ s\ \mathbf{else}\ s \\
| & \mathbf{while}\ e\ \mathbf{do}\ s \\
| & \mathbf{call}\ x := p\ e \\
| & \mathbf{return}\ e \\
| & \mathbf{post}\ p\ e \\
x ::= & \mathtt{g} \mid \mathtt{l}
\end{array}
$$

Figure 1. The grammar of simple asynchronous programs.

We consider only schedulers M that refine the bag scheduler, i.e., schedulers satisfying the property:

Property 1. *Any sequence of* give *and* take *operations allowed by* M *are also allowed by* bag.

Note that a scheduler can be *lossy*—i.e., can drop pending tasks—though is not allowed to "pull tasks out of thin air," i.e., schedule tasks that have not been posted. The following is an example of a lossy scheduler that refines the bag scheduler.

Scheduler 2 (The bounded bag scheduler). *The K-bounded bag scheduler* bb is defined on the multiset domain D_{bb} of tasks as

$$
\begin{aligned}
\mathsf{empty}_{\mathsf{bb}} &\stackrel{\text{def}}{=} \emptyset \\
\mathsf{give}_{\mathsf{bb}}(m, w) &\stackrel{\text{def}}{=} \begin{cases} m \cup \{w\} & \text{if } m(w) < K \\ m & \text{otherwise} \end{cases} \\
\mathsf{take}_{\mathsf{bb}}(m, g) &\stackrel{\text{def}}{=} \{\langle m \setminus \{w\}, w\rangle : w \in m\}.
\end{aligned}
$$

The bounded bag scheduler is non-deterministic, since all pending tasks are returned by each application of $\mathsf{take}_{\mathsf{bb}}$. It is lossy since it will drop posted tasks if its bound K has been reached.

2.2 Program Syntax

Let Procs be a set of procedure names, Vals a set of values containing `true` and `false`, and T the type of values. The grammar of Figure 1 describes our language of *simple asynchronous programs*, where p ranges over procedure names. We intentionally leave the syntax of expressions e unspecified, though we do insist the set of expressions Exprs contains Vals and the *(nullary) choice operator* $\star$. A *simple (synchronous) program*, or *sequential program*, is a simple asynchronous program which does not contain **post**-statements.

Each program declares a single type-T global variable g, and a sequence of procedures $p_1 \dots p_n \in \mathsf{Procs}^*$. Each procedure p has single type-T parameter `l`, and a top-level statement denoted s_p. The set of program statements s is denoted Stmts.

We assign the statements of simple asynchronous programs their usual meaning. In particular, **post** p e is an asynchronous call to procedure p with argument e, which returns immediately with the expectation that p is invoked at a later time; the **assume** e statement proceeds only when e evaluates to `true`. (Later on we use the **assume**-statement to block undesired executions in a reduction to sequential programs.)

2.3 Program Semantics

For the remainder of this section we fix a predicate blocked : Tasks $\times$ Vals $\to \mathbb{B}$ and a scheduler $M = \langle D, \mathsf{empty}, \mathsf{give}, \mathsf{take}\rangle$.

A *frame* $\langle \ell, s\rangle$ is a valuation $\ell \in$ Vals to the procedure-local variable `l` with a statement s. A *task* w is a sequence of frames, and the set $(\mathsf{Vals} \times \mathsf{Stmts})^*$ of tasks is denoted Tasks. A *configuration* $c = \langle g, w, m\rangle$ is a valuation $g \in$ Vals of the global variable g with a task $w \in$ Tasks, and a scheduler object $m \in D$. We say a task w is *blocked* in a configuration $\langle g, w', m\rangle$ (alternatively, in a global state g) when $\mathsf{blocked}(w, g) = \mathtt{true}$.

For expressions without program variables, we assume the existence of an evaluation function $[\![\cdot]\!] : \mathsf{Exprs} \to \wp(\mathsf{Vals})$ such that $[\![\star]\!] = \mathsf{Vals}$. For convenience, we define

$$
e(\langle g, \langle \ell, s\rangle\, w, m\rangle) \stackrel{\text{def}}{=} e(g, \ell) \stackrel{\text{def}}{=} [\![e[g/\mathtt{g}, \ell/\mathtt{l}]]\!]
$$

—since g and `l` are the only variables, the expression $e[g/\mathtt{g}, \ell/\mathtt{l}]$ has no free variables. A *statement context* S is a term derived from the grammar

$$
S ::= \diamond \mid S;\ s.
$$

We write $S[s]$ for the statement obtained by substituting a statement s for the unique occurrence of $\diamond$ in S, and write $\langle g, \langle \ell, S\rangle\, w, m\rangle\, [s]$ to denote the configuration $\langle g, \langle \ell, S[s]\rangle\, w, m\rangle$.

Figure 2 gives the scheduler-parameterized semantics of simple asynchronous programs as a set of operational steps on configurations. The choice operator $\star$ is used in the CALL and RETURN-SYNC rules only as a placeholder for an undetermined value. The ASSUME rule restricts the set of valid executions: a step is only allowed when the predicated expression e evaluates to `true`. (This statement—usually confined to intermediate languages—is crucial for our reduction to sequential programs in Section 5.) A task w' in a POST-step is said to be *posted*, and a task w in a DISPATCH-step is said to be *dispatched*. We refer to the semantics instantiated by a scheduler M as the M*-semantics*. The "natural" bag-semantics (see Scheduler 1) corresponds to the usual asynchronous program semantics [37]. We call the semantics of synchronous programs—i.e., those without **post**-statements—the *synchronous semantics*, which is in fact independent of the scheduler.

A configuration $\langle g, \langle \ell, s; \mathbf{return}\ \star\rangle, \mathsf{empty}\rangle$, where s does not contain **return**-statements, is called M*-initial*. An M*-execution (to c_j)* is a configuration sequence $h = c_1 c_2 \dots c_j$ where

- c_1 is M-initial, and
- $c_i \to c_{i+1}$ for $1 \le i < j$.

(The initial statement s begins the execution by posting tasks; if no tasks are posted by s, the execution ends when s completes.) We say a configuration $c = \langle g, w, m\rangle$ (alternatively, the global value g) is M*-reachable* when there exists an M-execution to c, and is M*-final* when in addition $w = \varepsilon$ and $\mathsf{take}(m) = \emptyset$.

For a scheduler M and program P, the M*-value set on* P is the set of values $\mathtt{g}(c)$ of the global variable g such that c is M-final.[2] The M-semantics on P is g*-equivalent* to the M'-semantics on P' when the M-value set on P is equal to the M'-value set on P'.

Although we have not made task identifiers explicit, we may assume that a set $U \subseteq \mathbb{N}$ of *task identifiers* is defined by an execution $h = c_1 c_2 \dots c_j$ such that $u \in U$ is the task identifier of a task dispatched[3] by $c_{u-1} \to c_u$. With an execution in mind, there is no ambiguity when referring to the frame or execution of a task by its identifier. We say u is *posted* (resp., *dispatched*) in h when there exists $1 \le i < j$ such that the task identified by u is posted (resp., dispatched) in $c_i \to c_{i+1}$.

[2] In the presence of the **assume**-statement, only the values of completed executions are guaranteed to be valid.

[3] We could also define task identifiers by their tasks' posting-points in h.

SKIP
$$\frac{}{c[\textbf{skip}; s] \to c[s]}$$

ASSUME
$$\frac{\texttt{true} \in e(c)}{c[\textbf{assume}\ e] \to c[\textbf{skip}]}$$

IF-THEN
$$\frac{\texttt{true} \in e(c)}{c[\textbf{if}\ e\ \textbf{then}\ s_1\ \textbf{else}\ s_2] \to c[s_1]}$$

IF-ELSE
$$\frac{\texttt{false} \in e(c)}{c[\textbf{if}\ e\ \textbf{then}\ s_1\ \textbf{else}\ s_2] \to c[s_2]}$$

LOOP-DO
$$\frac{\texttt{true} \in e(c)}{c[\textbf{while}\ e\ \textbf{do}\ s] \to c[s; \textbf{while}\ e\ \textbf{do}\ s]}$$

LOOP-END
$$\frac{\texttt{false} \in e(c)}{c[\textbf{while}\ e\ \textbf{do}\ s] \to c[\textbf{skip}]}$$

ASSIGN-GLOBAL
$$\frac{g' \in e(g, \ell)}{\langle g, \langle \ell, S[\mathbf{g} := e] \rangle\, w, m \rangle \to \langle g', \langle \ell, S[\textbf{skip}] \rangle\, w, m \rangle}$$

ASSIGN-LOCAL
$$\frac{\ell' \in e(g, \ell)}{\langle g, \langle \ell, S[\mathbf{l} := e] \rangle\, w, m \rangle \to \langle g, \langle \ell', S[\textbf{skip}] \rangle\, w, m \rangle}$$

CALL
$$\frac{\ell' \in e(g, \ell)}{\langle g, \langle \ell, S[\textbf{call}\ x := p(e)] \rangle\, w, m \rangle \to \langle g, \langle \ell', s_p \rangle \langle \ell, S[x := \star] \rangle\, w, m \rangle}$$

RETURN-SYNC
$$\frac{v \in e(g, \ell)}{\langle g, \langle \ell, \textbf{return}\ e \rangle \langle \ell', S[x := \star] \rangle\, w, m \rangle \to \langle g, \langle \ell', S[x := v] \rangle\, w, m \rangle}$$

POST
$$\frac{\ell' \in e(g, \ell) \qquad w' = \langle \ell', s_p \rangle}{\langle g, \langle \ell, S[\textbf{post}\ p(e)] \rangle\, w, m \rangle \to \langle g, \langle \ell, S[\textbf{skip}] \rangle\, w, \mathsf{give}(m, w') \rangle}$$

DISPATCH
$$\frac{\langle m', w \rangle \in \mathsf{take}(m, g) \qquad \neg \mathsf{blocked}(w, g)}{\langle g, \varepsilon, m \rangle \to \langle g, w, m' \rangle}$$

RETURN-ASYNC
$$\frac{}{\langle g, \langle \ell, \textbf{return}\ e \rangle, m \rangle \to \langle g, \varepsilon, m \rangle}$$

Figure 2. The operational semantics of simple asynchronous programs, parameterized by the scheduler $M = \langle D, \mathsf{empty}, \mathsf{give}, \mathsf{take} \rangle$.

2.4 Programs with Preemption

The language of *preemptive asynchronous programs* extends the grammar of Figure 1 with the production

$$s ::= \textbf{yield},$$

and the semantics of Figure 2 with the rule

YIELD
$$\frac{w' = \langle \ell, S[\textbf{skip}] \rangle\, w}{\langle g, \langle \ell, S[\textbf{yield}] \rangle\, w, m \rangle \to \langle g, \varepsilon, \mathsf{give}(m, w') \rangle},$$

allowing arbitrary task resumptions—not simply single frames—to be added to, and later dispatched from, the task buffer.

2.5 Synchronization and Blocking

Our model of preemptive asynchronous programs (i.e., with the **yield**-statement) can express arbitrary synchronization disciplines.

Example 1 (Locking). Lock-based mutual exclusion can be modeled by adding an additional global variable `lock`. Critical sections are surrounded with the *lock acquire* operation, encoded by

$$(\textbf{while}\ \texttt{lock} = \texttt{true}\ \textbf{do}\ \textbf{yield}); \texttt{lock} := \texttt{true},$$

and the *lock release* operation, encoded by `lock := false`. The $\mathsf{blocked}(w, g)$ predicate is defined to hold if and only if $w = \langle \ell, S[\textbf{while}\ \texttt{lock} = \texttt{true}\ \textbf{do}\ \textbf{yield}] \rangle\, w'$ and $\texttt{lock}(g, \ell) = \texttt{true}$; i.e., w is waiting for a lock that is in use. Although the mere presence of these primitives does not imply that critical sections are mutually exclusive, ensuring mutual exclusion in their presence is a well-studied, and orthogonal problem [28].

Since exploration deadlocks when blocked tasks are scheduled, we are generally interested in non-blocking schedulers.

Example 2 (Non-blocking lock scheduling). A deterministic non-blocking scheduler for the lock-based mutual exclusion encoding of Example 1 can be defined by differentiating between *ready* tasks, and tasks *waiting* for the lock; the scheduler must not pick a waiting task when $\texttt{lock}(g, \ell) = \texttt{true}$.

3. Delay-Bounded Scheduling

To limit the nondeterminism present in a scheduler, and thus the number of executions explored—while at the same time retaining the ability to consider "interesting" executions!—we allow deterministic schedulers to exercise a limited (and parameterized) number of deviations from their deterministic schedules. We define a *delaying scheduler* as a tuple $M = \langle D, \mathsf{empty}, \mathsf{give}, \mathsf{take}, \mathsf{delay} \rangle$, where D, empty, give, and take are defined as before for schedulers, and the delay : $D \times \mathsf{Tasks} \to D$ function is intended to inform the scheduler of task-postponement. The definitions of *deterministic*, *non-blocking*, *pending*, and *schedulable* remain unchanged.

We extend the semantics of Figure 2 with a postponing rule

DELAY
$$\frac{\langle m', w \rangle \in \mathsf{take}(m, g)}{\langle g, \varepsilon, m \rangle \to \langle g, \varepsilon, \mathsf{delay}(m', w) \rangle}$$

which we henceforth refer to as a *delay (operation)*, and we say w is *delayed*. Note that the delay operation occurs at the point when tasks are usually dispatched, not the at point when they are posted. We say an execution h is K*-delay-bounded* when the number of delay operations in h is at most K. A delaying scheduler M is *limit sound* when for any bag-reachable global value g, there exists $K \in \mathbb{N}$ such that g is M-reachable in a K-delay-bounded execution.

Limit soundness has an operational characterization. When h is an execution to c, we say w is *blocked* (resp., *pending*) in h when w is blocked (resp., pending) in c. A delaying scheduler M is *lossless* when for any M-execution h and task w posted[4] in h, w is either dispatched, pending, or blocked in h; otherwise we say M is *lossy*. A delaying scheduler M is *delay-accessible* when for every reachable configuration c_1 with non-blocked, pending task w, there exists a sequence $c_1 \to \ldots \to c_j$ of DELAY-steps such that w is schedulable in c_j.

Lemma 1. *A delaying scheduler M is limit sound if M is lossless and delay-accessible.*

[4] Here we assume w is uniquely identified by its task identifier.

Intuitively, a lossless and delay-accessible scheduler can always spend delays to access any task pending in the bag scheduler, since bag-pending tasks are also pending in lossless schedulers. A detailed proof appears in our extended technical report [13].

As a consequence of Lemma 1, our approach will discover any bug, with some delay-bound, using any well-behaved (i.e., lossless & delay-accessible) deterministic scheduler—though the delay-bound required to uncover a given bug depends on the scheduler. Since the number of explored schedules is exponential in the delay-bound, in practice one may want to hand-craft the scheduler to fit a particular program- or bug-domain. Alternatively, it is also possible to run several explorations with different schedulers in parallel with the same (small) delay-bound, or even to choose schedulers at random.

Here we highlight a couple of simple deterministic delaying schedulers to compare with existing exploration techniques, and as a basis for defining practical exploration algorithms.

3.1 Round-Robin Scheduling

One simple scheduler cycles through tasks in task-creation order. The scheduler advances to the next task when the current task either (i) completes execution, (ii) yields, and is blocked, or (iii) is delayed.

Scheduler 3 (The round-robin scheduler). Let rr be the list-based delaying scheduler $\langle \mathsf{Tasks}^* \times \mathbb{N}, \langle \varepsilon, 0\rangle, \mathsf{give}, \mathsf{take}, \mathsf{delay}\rangle$, where the $\mathsf{give}(\langle m, i\rangle, w)$ operation is defined by[5]

1. if $w = \langle \ell, s_p\rangle$ for some procedure p, then append w to m;
2. else (w is a yielding task): insert w into m at position i,

the $\mathsf{delay}(\langle m, i\rangle, w)$ operation is defined by

1. insert w into m at position i;
2. increment i modulo $|m|$,

and the $\mathsf{take}(\langle m, i\rangle, g)$ operation is defined by

1. if $m(j)$ is blocked in g for all $j \in 0 \ldots |m| - 1$, return $\emptyset$;
2. while $m(i)$ is blocked in g, increment i modulo $|m|$;
3. remove w from m at position i;
4. return w.

It is easy to see that rr is deterministic, lossless, delay-accessible, and non-blocking.

The round-robin scheduler demonstrates that delay-bounded scheduling captures context-bounded scheduling [34].

Example 3 (Context-bounding). In the rr-scheduler, each delay operation simulates a context-switch to the next task; context-switching to any of n tasks generally requires n successive delay operations. Given a "context-bound" K and a program with n tasks, the set of nK-delay-bounded rr-executions contains the set of K-context-bounded executions.

From the perspective of limiting scheduling choice, context-bounding does not give a direct bound: the number of choices nK is also dependent on the number of tasks. (In contrast, K-delay-bounded exploration requires only K choices.)

3.2 Depth-First Scheduling

Another simple scheduler schedules all tasks posted by a given task u before scheduling tasks that were pending when u was dispatched, in a stack-based discipline. This scheduler is particularly appealing since, as we show in Section 5, for any delay-bound K and asynchronous program P, we can encode the K-delay-bounded depth-first semantics of P compactly as a sequential program!

[5] We define the give, delay, and take operations by destructively mutating and returning the scheduler object.

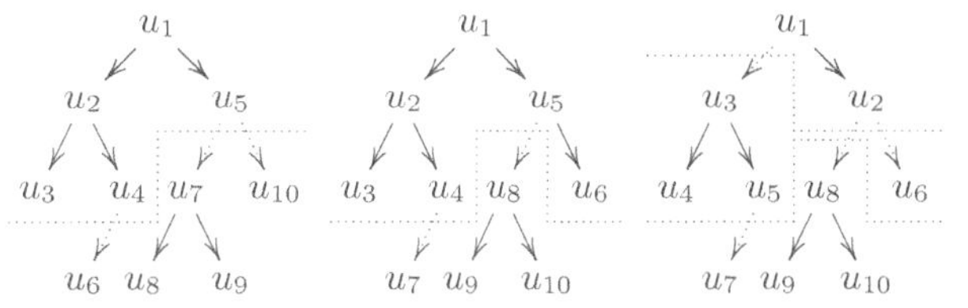

Figure 4. Depth-first traversals of round-partitioned asynchronous call forests with task identifiers $u_1, \ldots, u_{10}$. Arrows indicate task-posting, dotted arrows indicate delays, and the dotted line separates rounds. The traversal-order is $u_1, u_2, \ldots, u_{10}$.

Scheduler 4 (The depth-first scheduler). Let dfs be the stack-based scheduler $\langle \mathsf{Tasks}^* \times \mathsf{Tasks}^* \times \mathsf{Tasks}^*, \langle \varepsilon, \varepsilon, \varepsilon\rangle, \mathsf{give}, \mathsf{take}, \mathsf{delay}\rangle$ —for a scheduler object $\langle q_h, q_r, q_d\rangle$, we call q_h, q_r and q_d the *handler-*, *round-*, and *delay-stacks*—where the $\mathsf{give}(\langle q_h, q_r, q_d\rangle, w)$ operation is defined by

1. push w to q_h,

the $\mathsf{delay}(\langle q_h, q_r, q_d\rangle, w)$ operation is defined by

1. push w to q_d,

and the $\mathsf{take}(\langle q_h, q_r, q_d\rangle, g)$ operation is defined by

1. empty q_h into q_r;
2. if $q_r = \varepsilon$ then empty q_d into q_r;
3. if $q_r = \varepsilon$ then return $\emptyset$;
4. pop w from q_r;
5. return w.

Figure 3 shows the dfs-execution of a simple asynchronous program. It is easy to see that dfs is deterministic, lossless, and delay-accessible, though is not generally non-blocking.

To understand the task-execution order in depth-first scheduling, we view executions as trees, where nodes are tasks, and the parent relation corresponds to the *posting* relation on tasks. Let h be an execution and U a set of task identifiers from h. We define the *asynchronous call forest*[6] as the ordered forest F with nodes labeled by the identifiers $u \in U$ of tasks posted in h. When u was posted by a task u' in h, u is a child of u' in F; children are ordered by the order they are posted. We capture yielding by viewing task-resumptions as newly-posted tasks. Note that synchronous calls are not explicit in F: the tasks posted along the synchronous execution of u appear directly as children of u.

The dfs-execution of a program proceeds in a sequence of "rounds," ending when a take operation encounters both q_h and q_r empty. With this nomenclature, we schedule each delayed task w in the round $i+1$ following the round i where w is delayed, after all pending non-delayed tasks of round i have been scheduled.

A *round partitioning* of an asynchronous call forest F with nodes U is a labeling $R : U \to \mathbb{N}$ on the nodes of F such that $R(u_1) \leq R(u_2)$ whenever u_1 is an ancestor of u_2. Given an execution h, we can think of the round partitioning as a partition of F into asynchronous call forests $\{F_0, F_1, \ldots\}$ where each task u is in the forest $F_{R(u)}$ corresponding to the round in which it executes. The depth-first scheduler traverses the asynchronous call forest in a round-by-round depth-first preorder (see Figure 4). In this order, yielding tasks u are rescheduled only after the tasks that u has posted before yielding, have been scheduled.

[6] We consider forests rather than trees since more than one task may be posted initially—or as we encounter shortly, at the beginning of each "round" in certain delaying schedulers.

var g : T
proc p_1 (var l : T)
  s_1; post p_2 e_1;
  s_2; post p_3 e_2; s_3
proc p_2 (var l : T) s_4
proc p_3 (var l : T) s_5

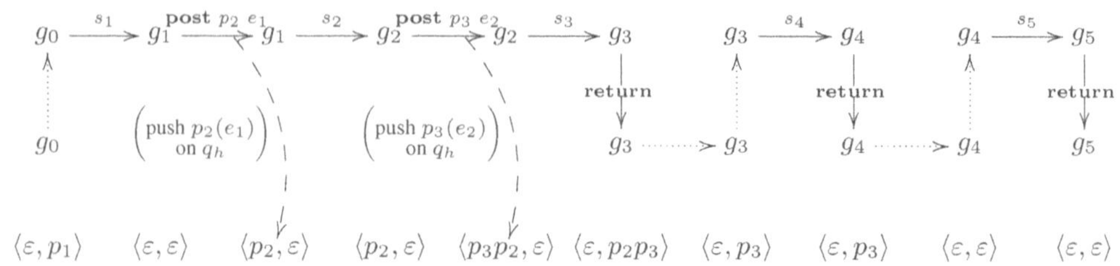

Figure 3. The no-delay dfs-execution of a simple asynchronous program. The scheduler objects $\langle q_h, q_r \rangle$—since there are no delays, q_d is omitted—are given below the corresponding points in the execution which are labeled with the global values. Solid lines indicate procedure control, and dotted lines indicate dispatcher control. Note that the bag scheduler allows one additional execution, where p_3 executes before p_2.

4. Delay-Bounded Testing

In concurrency analyses which explicitly enumerate execution schedules (e.g., systematic testing), using delay-bounded deterministic schedulers has a clear scalability advantage over existing bounded exploration approaches. For instance, the number of p-preemption-bounded executions [29] of a program using n tasks is exponential in n, since a complete execution must apply at least $\max(n, p)$ label changes; the number of k-delay-bounded executions does not depend on n. Here we demonstrate that although delay-bounding explores much fewer schedules than preemption-bounding (with the same bound), existing bugs caught with p preemptions are also caught with p delays. Furthermore, delay-bounded exploration is able to discover bugs which have not been caught by bounding preemptions—due to the exponential increase in schedules with respect to the number of tasks.

To demonstrate this advantage, we have implemented the delaying round-robin scheduler (Scheduler 3) in the CHESS concurrency testing tool [30] to directly compare preemption- and delay-bounding on three programs: *CCR*, *Futures* (both written by Microsoft product groups), and *Region Ownership* (written by Peter Müller of ETH Zurich). We feel the round-robin scheduler is appropriate for comparison with preemption-bounding since it minimizes preemptions. We observe:

1. Every bug found with p preemptions is also found with p delays.
2. Delay-bounding explores significantly fewer schedules before discovering a buggy execution.
3. Delay-bounding can discover at least one bug that cannot be found with preemption-bounding, under similar time-constraints.

As a systematic testing tool, CHESS repeatedly executes each test case to completion until all possible schedules—for each test case—have been explored. During the exploration, CHESS has no control over the number of tasks created, nor the number of steps taken by the input program. Thus, each test case is expected to drive the program to termination under any schedule.

CCR Microsoft's Concurrency and Coordination Runtime provides a concurrent programming model with high-level primitives for data- and work-coordination without the use of explicit threading and synchronization. We evaluate a suite of 42 test cases exercising various parts of CCR. Each test case takes between 82–255 steps to complete, and creates at most 3 tasks, before exhibiting a known bug (found with CHESS); 41 of these bugs were discovered with 1 preemption, and the remaining one with 2 preemptions. The delaying rr-scheduler discovers each of these bugs with the same budget of delays, but fewer schedules. Figure 5 compares the number of schedules explored to discover each 1-preemption bug. Discovering the remaining bug required exploring 8,895 schedules using 2 preemptions, and only 2,728 schedules using 2 delays.

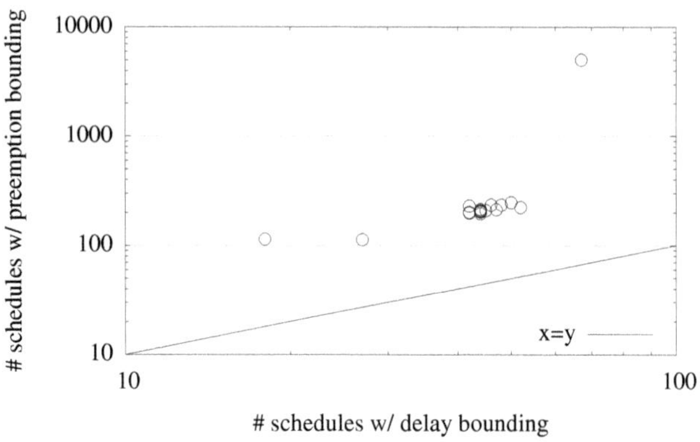

Figure 5. Comparing the number of schedules explored between preemption- and delay-bounding before discovering known bugs in 41 tests of Microsoft's Concurrency and Coordination Runtime (CCR). CHESS found each of these bugs with 1 preemption/delay.

Futures Microsoft's Futures library provides a synchronization primitive based on a proxy value for a computation whose result is not yet known. We find two previously-discovered (with CHESS) 1-preemption bugs, also with 1 delay. Both the livelock and uncaught exception are exposed after the program has spawned 4 tasks:

Bug	# steps	# schedules (PB)	# schedules (DB)
Livelock	1075	259	45
Exception	1152	1899	320

Region Ownership Peter Müller's region ownership library manages concurrency and coordination based on objects grouped into regions that communicate with each other via asynchronous procedure calls. The library is accompanied by a single test case comprising a one-producer one-consumer system. During testing, at most 5 tasks are created, and at most 284 execution steps taken. Preemption-bounding with 0 and 1 preemptions terminates without finding a bug; with 2 preemptions, CHESS generates 340,000 schedules over several hours without terminating, after which we manually killed it. Bounding delays to 0, 1, and 2 did not expose any bugs, though a delay-bound of 3 discovered a previously unknown bug after exploring only 132,507 schedules.

To determine whether this bug can be discovered with 2 preemptions, we re-ran CHESS, focusing preemptions [3] to the methods interrupted in our (delay-bounded) error trace. After exploring 128,998 schedules, CHESS finishes without discovering the bug. Thus, this is the first bug CHESS has ever found in a real-world program that requires at least 3 preemptions!

5. Sequentialization of Depth-First Scheduling

The depth-first scheduling order (i.e., of Scheduler 4) has a rather nice property: the stack of pending tasks used for a depth-first traversal of the asynchronous call forest (see Section 3.2) can be combined with a synchronous program's call stack (i.e., of activation records). In this section we exploit that fact to compactly encode a program's delay-bounded dfs semantics as a sequential program. (A similar encoding is possible for reverse depth-first scheduling—i.e., where each task's children are traversed in reverse order.)

In Section 5.1 we reveal the most basic encoding of no-delay depth-first scheduling for simple asynchronous programs. In Sections 5.2 and 5.3, we orthogonally extend the basic encoding to handle delaying and preemption. To improve clarity we leverage the syntactic extensions of Appendix A, which each reduce to the original syntax of asynchronous programs.

5.1 No-Delay Depth-First Scheduling

We begin by defining the function $[\![\cdot]\!]^0_{\mathsf{dfs}}$ which translates a simple asynchronous program P into a synchronous program $[\![P]\!]^0_{\mathsf{dfs}}$ which encodes the no-delay depth-first scheduler:

$$
\begin{aligned}
[\![\mathbf{var}\ \mathtt{g} : T\ \vec{H}]\!]^0_{\mathsf{dfs}} &\stackrel{\text{def}}{=} \mathbf{var}\ \mathtt{g} : T,\ \bar{\mathtt{g}} : T\ \overrightarrow{[\![H]\!]^0_{\mathsf{dfs}}} \\
[\![\mathbf{proc}\ p\ (\mathbf{var}\ \mathtt{l} : T)\ s]\!]^0_{\mathsf{dfs}} &\stackrel{\text{def}}{=} \mathbf{proc}\ p\ (\mathbf{var}\ \mathtt{l} : T)\ [\![s]\!]^0_{\mathsf{dfs}} \\
[\![s_1;\ s_2]\!]^0_{\mathsf{dfs}} &\stackrel{\text{def}}{=} [\![s_1]\!]^0_{\mathsf{dfs}};\ [\![s_2]\!]^0_{\mathsf{dfs}} \\
[\![x := e]\!]^0_{\mathsf{dfs}} &\stackrel{\text{def}}{=} x := e \\
[\![\mathbf{skip}]\!]^0_{\mathsf{dfs}} &\stackrel{\text{def}}{=} \mathbf{skip} \\
[\![\mathbf{assume}\ e]\!]^0_{\mathsf{dfs}} &\stackrel{\text{def}}{=} \mathbf{assume}\ e \\
[\![\mathbf{if}\ e\ \mathbf{then}\ s_1\ \mathbf{else}\ s_2]\!]^0_{\mathsf{dfs}} &\stackrel{\text{def}}{=} \mathbf{if}\ e\ \mathbf{then}\ [\![s_1]\!]^0_{\mathsf{dfs}}\ \mathbf{else}\ [\![s_2]\!]^0_{\mathsf{dfs}} \\
[\![\mathbf{while}\ e\ \mathbf{do}\ s]\!]^0_{\mathsf{dfs}} &\stackrel{\text{def}}{=} \mathbf{while}\ e\ \mathbf{do}\ [\![s]\!]^0_{\mathsf{dfs}} \\
[\![\mathbf{call}\ x := p\ e]\!]^0_{\mathsf{dfs}} &\stackrel{\text{def}}{=} \mathbf{call}\ x := p\ e \\
[\![\mathbf{return}\ e]\!]^0_{\mathsf{dfs}} &\stackrel{\text{def}}{=} \mathbf{return}\ e \\
[\![\mathbf{post}\ p\ e]\!]^0_{\mathsf{dfs}} &\stackrel{\text{def}}{=} \mathbf{let}\ \mathtt{g}_{\mathtt{tmp}} : T = \mathtt{g}\ \mathbf{in} \\
&\qquad \mathbf{let}\ \bar{\mathtt{g}}_? : T\ \mathbf{in} \\
&\qquad\quad \mathtt{g} := \bar{\mathtt{g}}; \\
&\qquad\quad \bar{\mathtt{g}} := \bar{\mathtt{g}}_?; \\
&\qquad\quad \mathbf{call}\ \_ := p\ e; \\
&\qquad\quad \mathbf{assume}\ \mathtt{g} = \bar{\mathtt{g}}_?; \\
&\qquad\quad \mathtt{g} := \mathtt{g}_{\mathtt{tmp}}.
\end{aligned}
$$

The initial configuration is translated as

$$[\![\langle g, \langle \ell, s; \mathbf{return}\ e\rangle, m\rangle]\!]^0_{\mathsf{dfs}} \stackrel{\text{def}}{=} \langle g', \langle \ell, s'; \mathbf{return}\ e\rangle, m\rangle,$$

with the initial global value $g' \stackrel{\text{def}}{=} \{\mathtt{g} = g, \bar{\mathtt{g}} = \star\}$, and the initial statement s' given by

$$
\begin{aligned}
s' \stackrel{\text{def}}{=}\ & \mathbf{let}\ \bar{\mathtt{g}}_?\ \mathbf{in} \\
&\quad \bar{\mathtt{g}} := \bar{\mathtt{g}}_?; \\
&\quad [\![s]\!]^0_{\mathsf{dfs}}; \\
&\quad \mathbf{assume}\ \mathtt{g} = \bar{\mathtt{g}}_?; \\
& \mathtt{g} := \bar{\mathtt{g}}.
\end{aligned}
$$

The key mechanism enabling the encoding is the introduction of *guessed global values* in the form of unconstrained symbolic constants $\bar{\mathtt{g}}_?$. These are essentially prophecy variables [1] whose values will be available only later in the sequential execution. Once the appropriate global values are available, the corresponding guesses are suitably constrained.

In the translation, we replace **post**-statements with **call**-statements, and introduce the following variables to ensure the correct global values are observed along the mimicked dfs-execution:

- $\mathtt{g}_{\mathtt{tmp}}$ caches the global value of a *posting* task, so that the *posted* task can observe its future global value in g, and the posting task can resume from its current global value without interference.
- $\bar{\mathtt{g}}_?$ stores the (guessed) global value reached when each posted task completes.
- $\bar{\mathtt{g}}$ stores the (guessed) global value reached after all tasks that have been posted thus far (i.e., that have appeared on the call-stack) have completed.

Example 4. The dfs-encoding of the program in Figure 3 is

$$
\begin{aligned}
&\mathbf{var}\ \mathtt{g} : T,\ \bar{\mathtt{g}} : T \\
&\mathbf{proc}\ p_1\,(\mathbf{var}\ \mathtt{l} : T) \\
&\quad s_1; \\
&\quad \left.\begin{aligned}
&\mathbf{let}\ \mathtt{g}_{\mathtt{tmp}} : T = \mathtt{g}\ \mathbf{in}\ \mathbf{let}\ \bar{\mathtt{g}}_? : T\ \mathbf{in} \\
&\quad \mathtt{g} := \bar{\mathtt{g}};\ \bar{\mathtt{g}} := \bar{\mathtt{g}}_?; \\
&\quad \mathbf{call}\ \_ := p_2\ e_1; \\
&\quad \mathbf{assume}\ \mathtt{g} = \bar{\mathtt{g}}_?;\ \mathtt{g} := \mathtt{g}_{\mathtt{tmp}};
\end{aligned}\right\}
\begin{aligned}
&= [\![\mathbf{post}\ p_2\ e_1]\!]^0_{\mathsf{dfs}} \\
&\mathtt{g}_{\mathtt{tmp}} = g_1, \bar{\mathtt{g}}_? = g_4
\end{aligned} \\
&\quad s_2; \\
&\quad \left.\begin{aligned}
&\mathbf{let}\ \mathtt{g}_{\mathtt{tmp}} : T = \mathtt{g}\ \mathbf{in}\ \mathbf{let}\ \bar{\mathtt{g}}_? : T\ \mathbf{in} \\
&\quad \mathtt{g} := \bar{\mathtt{g}};\ \bar{\mathtt{g}} := \bar{\mathtt{g}}_?; \\
&\quad \mathbf{call}\ \_ := p_3\ e_2; \\
&\quad \mathbf{assume}\ \mathtt{g} = \bar{\mathtt{g}}_?;\ \mathtt{g} := \mathtt{g}_{\mathtt{tmp}};
\end{aligned}\right\}
\begin{aligned}
&= [\![\mathbf{post}\ p_3\ e_2]\!]^0_{\mathsf{dfs}} \\
&\mathtt{g}_{\mathtt{tmp}} = g_2, \bar{\mathtt{g}}_? = g_5
\end{aligned} \\
&\quad s_3 \\
&\mathbf{proc}\ p_2\,(\mathbf{var}\ \mathtt{l} : T)\ s_4 \\
&\mathbf{proc}\ p_3\,(\mathbf{var}\ \mathtt{l} : T)\ s_5,
\end{aligned}
$$

where we assume s_1–s_5 do not contain **post**-statements. To the right of the braces we indicate the values stored in the let-bound variables $\mathtt{g}_{\mathtt{tmp}}$ and $\bar{\mathtt{g}}_?$, which are the same values used below. This program has the following unique, sequential execution:

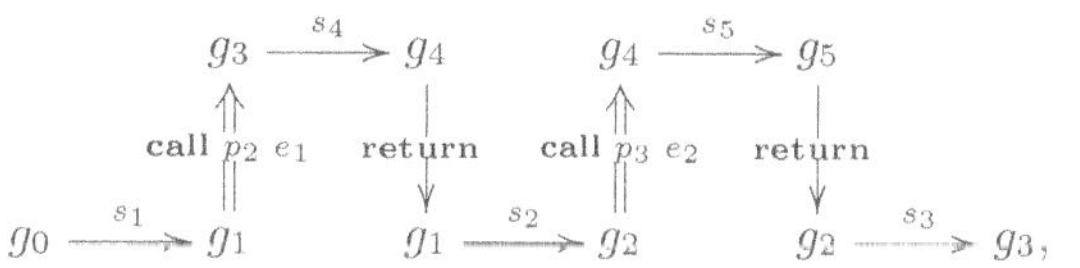

where the double lines indicate part of a $[\![\mathbf{post}\ \ldots]\!]^0_{\mathsf{dfs}}$-translation (i.e., up to the **call**). Here each global value g_i matches that of the (asynchronous) dfs-execution (of Figure 3). Execution begins with an initial guess for $\bar{\mathtt{g}}$ of g_3, i.e., the global value after p_1 executes. The latter guessed values for $\bar{\mathtt{g}}$ of g_4 and g_5 are the global values after the execution of p_2 and p_3. The final global value is g_5.

Lemma 2. *Let P be a simple asynchronous program. The synchronous semantics of $[\![P]\!]^0_{\mathsf{dfs}}$ is g-equivalent to the no-delay dfs-semantics of P.*

Proof sketch. Let h be a dfs-execution of P, and consider the asynchronous call forest F of h with tasks $U = \{u_1, u_2, \ldots u_j\}$. Furthermore, without loss of generality, suppose the dispatch order $\sqsubset$ of tasks in h is $u_1 \sqsubset u_2 \sqsubset \ldots \sqsubset u_j$. Since the dfs-schedule corresponds to a preorder depth-first traversal of the forest F, each task u's children u' are executed before any other pending task or task to be posted later in u's execution. In this way, the order $\sqsubset$ corresponds exactly to the execution of *synchronously* executed tasks—i.e., the order in which tasks would execute had they been *called* instead of *posted*—except that the tasks would observe not the semantically-consistent global state at the end of the current task's execution, but an intermediate global state. To ensure that tasks observe the semantically-consistent global state, we rely on the following invariant of the synchronous semantics of $[\![P]\!]^0_{\mathsf{dfs}}$:

> The value of $\bar{\mathtt{g}}$ at the beginning of execution for each task u_{i+1} is equal to the final value of $\mathtt{g}$ at the end of execution for the task u_i immediately preceding u_{i+1} in the order $\sqsubset$.

Combining the invariant with the coincidence of task-execution order in the dfs-schedule of P and the synchronous program $[\![P]\!]^0_{\mathsf{dfs}}$, we have the sequence $g_0 g_1 g_2 \ldots g_j$ of global values during dispatch points of h (i.e., when control is given to the dispatcher) is equal to the sequence $\bar{g}_0 \bar{g}_1 \bar{g}_2 \ldots \bar{g}_j$ of global values before the synchronous execution of each task, and after all tasks have executed. Finally, the last statement to be executed in $[\![P]\!]^0_{\mathsf{dfs}}$ sets the global value to $\bar{g}_j$, ensuring the final global states of P and $[\![P]\!]^0_{\mathsf{dfs}}$ are equal. □

Note that in general, for an arbitrary deterministic scheduler, algorithmic delay-bounded exploration is not possible. For example, even no-delay scheduling with the round-robin scheduler (Scheduler 3) is undecidable, by reduction from the state-reachability problem for Turing-complete Queue machines. From an automata-theoretic point of view, delay-bounded depth-first scheduling remains decidable since the asynchronous task-buffer is a stack which can be combined with the synchronous activation stack.

5.2 Delaying Depth-First Scheduling

The function $[\![\cdot]\!]^K_{\mathsf{dfs}}$ translates a simple asynchronous program P into a synchronous program $[\![P]\!]^K_{\mathsf{dfs}}$ which encodes the K-delay bounded depth-first scheduler:

$$
\begin{aligned}
[\![\mathbf{var}\ \mathtt{g} : T\ \vec{H}]\!]^K_{\mathsf{dfs}} &\stackrel{\text{def}}{=} \mathbf{var}\ \mathtt{g} : T,\ \bar{\mathtt{G}} : T^{K+1},\ \mathtt{k_{delay}} : \mathbb{N} \\
&\qquad \overrightarrow{[\![H]\!]^K_{\mathsf{dfs}}} \\
[\![\mathbf{proc}\ p\ (\mathbf{var}\ \mathtt{l} : T)\ s]\!]^K_{\mathsf{dfs}} &\stackrel{\text{def}}{=} \mathbf{proc}\ p\ (\mathbf{var}\ \mathtt{l} : T, \mathtt{k_{round}} : \mathbb{N})\ [\![s]\!]^K_{\mathsf{dfs}} \\
[\![\mathbf{call}\ x := p\ e]\!]^K_{\mathsf{dfs}} &\stackrel{\text{def}}{=} \mathbf{call}\ x := p\ (e, \mathtt{k_{round}}) \\
[\![\mathbf{post}\ p\ e]\!]^K_{\mathsf{dfs}} &\stackrel{\text{def}}{=} \mathbf{let}\ \mathtt{g_{tmp}} : T = \mathtt{g}\ \mathbf{in} \\
&\quad \mathbf{let}\ \bar{\mathtt{g}}_? : T\ \mathbf{in} \\
&\qquad \mathbf{var}\ \mathtt{k} : \mathbb{N} := \mathtt{k_{round}}; \\
&\qquad \mathbf{while}\ \star\ \mathbf{and}\ \mathtt{k_{delay}} > 0\ \mathbf{do} \\
&\qquad\quad \mathtt{k_{delay}} := \mathtt{k_{delay}} - 1; \\
&\qquad\quad \mathtt{k} := \mathtt{k} + 1 \\
&\qquad \mathtt{g} := \bar{\mathtt{G}}[\mathtt{k}]; \\
&\qquad \bar{\mathtt{G}}[\mathtt{k}] := \bar{\mathtt{g}}_?; \\
&\qquad \mathbf{call}\ \_ := p\ (e, \mathtt{k}); \\
&\qquad \mathbf{assume}\ \mathtt{g} = \bar{\mathtt{g}}_?; \\
&\qquad \mathtt{g} := \mathtt{g_{tmp}},
\end{aligned}
$$

where the omitted statements are translated exactly as in the no-delay translation $[\![\cdot]\!]^0_{\mathsf{dfs}}$. The initial configuration is translated as

$$[\![\langle g, \langle \ell, s; \mathbf{return}\ e\rangle, m\rangle]\!]^K_{\mathsf{dfs}} \stackrel{\text{def}}{=} \langle g', \langle \ell', s'; \mathbf{return}\ e\rangle, m\rangle,$$

where the initial global and local values g' and ℓ' are

$$
\begin{aligned}
g' &\stackrel{\text{def}}{=} \{\mathtt{g} = g, \bar{\mathtt{G}} = [\star, \star, \ldots], \mathtt{k_{delay}} = K\}, \text{ and} \\
\ell' &\stackrel{\text{def}}{=} \{\mathtt{l} = \ell, \mathtt{k_{round}} = \star\},
\end{aligned}
$$

and the initial statement s' is given by

$$
\begin{aligned}
s' \stackrel{\text{def}}{=}\ & \mathbf{let}\ \mathtt{k_{round}} : \mathbb{N} = 0\ \mathbf{in} \\
& \quad \mathbf{let}\ \bar{\mathtt{G}}_? : T^{K+1}\ \mathbf{in} \\
& \qquad \bar{\mathtt{G}} := \bar{\mathtt{G}}_?; \\
& \qquad [\![s]\!]^K_{\mathsf{dfs}}; \\
& \qquad \mathbf{assume}\ \mathtt{g} = \bar{\mathtt{G}}_?[0]; \\
& \qquad \mathbf{assume}\ \bar{\mathtt{G}}[0] = \bar{\mathtt{G}}_?[1]; \\
& \qquad \ldots \\
& \qquad \mathbf{assume}\ \bar{\mathtt{G}}[K-1] = \bar{\mathtt{G}}_?[K]; \\
& \quad \mathtt{g} := \bar{\mathtt{G}}[K].
\end{aligned}
$$

The K-delay-bounded encoding extends the no-delay encoding in two important ways. First, the schedule proceeds in $K+1$ rounds; we must note which round each task executes in, and separately accumulate the perceived global values in each round. Second, each time a task is posted, there is the possibility of delay; we must keep track of how many delays have been spent. To accomplish this, we introduce the following auxiliary variables:

- $\mathtt{g_{tmp}}$ and $\bar{\mathtt{g}}_?$ are used exactly as before, to cache the posting task's observed global value, and store the global value reached at the end of the posted task.
- $\bar{\mathtt{G}}$ is the multi-round extension to $\bar{\mathtt{g}}$: each $\bar{\mathtt{G}}[i]$ stores the global value reached after all tasks that have been posted thus far, and are executed in round i, have completed.
- $\mathtt{k_{delay}}$ stores the remaining budget of delays.
- $\mathtt{k_{round}}$ indicates which round a given task executes in.
- $\mathtt{k}$ is incremented once per delay of the posted task, then passed as the round-indicator ($\mathtt{k_{round}}$).

Note that a task may be delayed more than once, and we simulate all the delays of a given task instantaneously.

Example 5. The 1-delay-bounded dfs-encoding of the program of Figure 3, allows the following (sequential) execution:

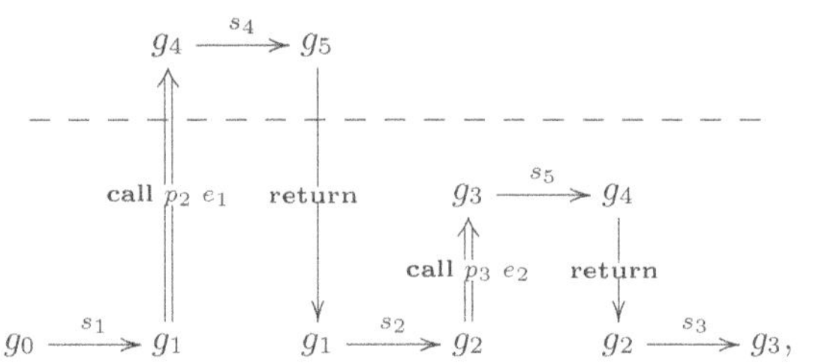

where p_2 executes before p_3. This execution mimics two rounds, separated by a dashed line: p_3, though posted second, executes with p_1 in the first round, while p_2 executes alone in the second. Thus $\bar{\mathtt{G}}[0]$ takes the values g_3, g_4, and $\bar{\mathtt{G}}[1]$ takes the values g_4, g_5. The final global value is g_5.

Lemma 3. *Let P be a simple asynchronous program. The synchronous semantics of $[\![P]\!]^K_{\mathsf{dfs}}$ is* g*-equivalent to the K-delay* dfs*-semantics of P.*

Proof sketch. As in the proof sketch of Lemma 2, there is a correspondence between the K-delay-bounded dfs-execution order of tasks in P and $[\![P]\!]^K_{\mathsf{dfs}}$, except in this case the order is a round-by-round depth-first preorder. Here, we adapt the previous invariant to the K-round case:

> The value of $\bar{\mathtt{G}}[k]$ at the beginning of execution for each task u_{i+1} of round k is equal to the value of $\mathtt{g}$ at the end of execution for the task u_i immediately preceding u_{i+1} in the order $\sqsubset$.

For adjacently executed tasks $u_i \sqsubset u_{i+1}$ in differing rounds k_a and k_b, the resulting global value of u_i is guaranteed to be in $\bar{\mathtt{G}}[k_a]$, which is in turn guaranteed to be equal the initial global value $\bar{\mathtt{G}}_?[k_b]$ of task u_{i+1}. □

$$
\begin{aligned}
[\![\mathbf{var}\ \mathtt{g} : T\vec{H}]\!]^0_{\mathsf{dfs}} &\stackrel{\text{def}}{=} \mathbf{var}\ \mathtt{g} : T,\ \bar{\mathtt{g}} : T\ \overrightarrow{[\![H]\!]^0_{\mathsf{dfs}}} \\
[\![\mathbf{proc}\ p\ (\mathbf{var}\ \mathtt{l} : T)\ s]\!]^0_{\mathsf{dfs}} &\stackrel{\text{def}}{=} \mathbf{proc}\ p\ (\mathbf{var}\ \mathtt{l}, \bar{\mathtt{g}}_? : T)\ [\![s]\!]^0_{\mathsf{dfs}} \\
[\![\mathbf{call}\ x := p\ e]\!]^0_{\mathsf{dfs}} &\stackrel{\text{def}}{=} \mathbf{call}\ (x, \bar{\mathtt{g}}_?) := p\ (e, \bar{\mathtt{g}}_?) \\
[\![\mathbf{return}\ e]\!]^0_{\mathsf{dfs}} &\stackrel{\text{def}}{=} \mathbf{return}\ (e, \bar{\mathtt{g}}_?) \\
[\![\mathbf{post}\ p\ e]\!]^0_{\mathsf{dfs}} &\stackrel{\text{def}}{=} \mathbf{let}\ \mathtt{g}_{\mathtt{tmp}} : T = \mathtt{g}\ \mathbf{in} \\
&\quad\ \mathbf{let}\ \bar{\mathtt{g}}'_? : T\ \mathbf{in} \\
&\qquad \mathtt{g} := \bar{\mathtt{g}}; \\
&\qquad \bar{\mathtt{g}} := \bar{\mathtt{g}}'_?; \\
&\qquad \mathbf{call}\ (\_, \bar{\mathtt{g}}'_?) := p\ (e, \bar{\mathtt{g}}'_?); \\
&\qquad \mathbf{assume}\ \mathtt{g} = \bar{\mathtt{g}}'_?; \\
&\qquad \mathtt{g} := \mathtt{g}_{\mathtt{tmp}} \\
[\![\mathbf{yield}]\!]^0_{\mathsf{dfs}} &\stackrel{\text{def}}{=} \mathbf{assume}\ \mathtt{g} = \bar{\mathtt{g}}_?; \\
&\quad\ \bar{\mathtt{g}}_? := \star; \\
&\quad\ \mathtt{g} := \bar{\mathtt{g}}; \\
&\quad\ \bar{\mathtt{g}} := \bar{\mathtt{g}}_?
\end{aligned}
$$

Figure 6. The symbolic encoding of no-delay depth-first scheduling with yields extending the symbolic encoding of Section 5.1. The translation of the missing control-flow statements and initial configuration is identical to the yield-free encoding.

5.3 Depth-First Scheduling with Preemption

Perhaps surprising is the fact that our symbolic encodings of delaying depth-first schedulers can be extended to preemptive asynchronous programs. The encoding of Figure 6 extends the no-delay depth-first scheduler encoding of Section 5.1 to handle **yield**-statements. The key difference is that the guess ($\bar{\mathtt{g}}_?$) of the post-state of each handler should not be verified only at the end of a handler's execution; instead, the guess is validated if a handler yields, at which point a new guess is made, and the new guess will be validated either at the next yield point—if one exists—or at the end of the handler's execution. To allow multiple guesses throughout a handler's execution, we simply ensure the guess-variable $\bar{\mathtt{g}}_?$ is in scope throughout by making it a parameter to every procedure.

The extension to delaying depth-first scheduling is straightforward; extending to multiple rounds is orthogonal to handling yields, and is done exactly according to the extension of Section 5.2. In particular, occurrences of $\bar{\mathtt{g}}$ are replaced by their multi-round counterparts $\bar{\mathtt{G}}$`[k]`, and incrementing the round counters also happens at yield-points. We omit the full definition of $[\![P]\!]^K_{\mathsf{dfs}}$ for preemptive asynchronous programs P, since it is redundant.

Lemma 4. *Let P be a preemptive asynchronous program. The synchronous semantics of $[\![P]\!]^K_{\mathsf{dfs}}$ is* g*-equivalent to the K-delay* dfs*-semantics of P.*

5.4 Complexity of Depth-First Scheduling

Thus far we have given sequentializations that reduce delay-bounded depth-first semantics to sequential semantics. Since the number of program variables in the resulting sequential program is $\mathcal{O}(K)$, the worst-case complexity of program-state exploration using this reduction (for programs with finite-data domains) is exponential in K. What remains is the question of whether the exploration via this reduction is (asymptotically) optimal. Here we find that a sub-exponential algorithm is unlikely. The proofs of these results are quite technical, and can be found in our extended technical report [13].

For the remainder of this section we assume the data-domain of asynchronous programs (i.e., the set Vals) is finite-state. We show that delay-bounded depth-first state-reachability is an NP-complete problem.[7] Though this exploration corresponds to an *under*approximation of the program semantics, the complexity is lower than the precise EXPSPACE-complete explorations of Sen and Viswanathan [37] and Jhala and Majumdar [19] for non-preemptive asynchronous programs. Additionally, our underapproximation has a lower complexity than the PSPACE-hard underapproximation [5] used by Jhala and Majumdar [19]'s algorithm, which corresponds to our (non-preemptive) bounded bag semantics (see Scheduler 2). Note in the case of preemptive programs, the analysis problem is generally undecidable [36].

Interestingly, delay-bounded depth-first exploration has the same NP-complete complexity as context-bounding for a finite number of tasks [27], even though delay-bounded scheduling explores an unbounded number of tasks.

Problem 1 (Delay-bounded depth-first scheduling). *For a given $K \in \mathbb{N}$,[8] initial configuration c_0, and global value g of an asynchronous program P, does there exist a K-delay-bounded* dfs*-execution to g?*

By reduction from the Circuit Satisfiability problem [33], we show our exponential algorithm for delay-bounded depth-first scheduling is likely to be asymptotically optimal.

Theorem 1. *Delay-bounded depth-first scheduling is NP-hard.*

To show membership in NP for the non-preemptive case, we give an algorithm that validates a nondeterministically-guessed execution witness to the target global value, given by the sequence of tasks delayed in, and a global value reached at the end of, each round. For a delay-bound K, we validate the guess by applying $K+1$ polynomial-time sequential program analyses to sequential encodings of each round of execution—the initial conditions of each round are determined by the delayed tasks and final global state of the previous round. Validation ensures that each round can indeed reach the guessed global value while delaying exactly the guessed delayed tasks.

Theorem 2. *Delay-bounded depth-first scheduling for simple asynchronous programs is in NP.*

In fact we can extend the proof of Theorem 2 to the preemptive case. The presence of yields poses an additional technical challenge: a naïve extension of the execution witnesses to record delayed task-*resumptions* does not work, because the resumptions' activation stacks have no bound. We solve this problem essentially by realizing the activation stacks of preempted tasks need not be stored across rounds; instead we may re-execute tasks to recreate their stacks from scratch—the same so-called "lazy" sequentialization technique pioneered by La Torre et al. [23].

Theorem 3. *Delay-bounded depth-first scheduling for preemptive asynchronous programs is in NP.*

Thus we achieve tight complexity-bounds on depth-first scheduling.

Corollary 1. *Delay-bounded depth-first scheduling is NP-complete.*

[7] Since we are interested in measuring the *scheduling* complexity (rather than complexity arising from program data), we have restricted the program syntax so that a fixed number of variables is in scope at any moment. Indeed, the reachability problem is EXPTIME-complete in the number of variables (even with only a single recursive task), due to the logarithmic encoding of states in the corresponding pushdown system.

[8] We assume the delay-bound K is written in unary.

6. Delay-Bounded Verification

The sequentialization of Section 5 allows any sequential analysis algorithm to be lifted, immediately, to a concurrent analysis algorithm: a sequential analysis of $[\![P]\!]_{\mathsf{dfs}}^{K}$ is exposed to all concurrent behaviors of P with a K-delay-bounded depth-first scheduler (an underapproximation of P's concurrent semantics). The additional implementation effort is minimal since only the source-to-source translation is required.

As a proof-of-concept, we have implemented a source-to-source symbolic encoding of the delaying depth-first scheduler in the STORM [26] concurrent C-program checker. STORM analyzes *closed* concurrent software modules (i.e., each module is closed from below using stubs for external procedures, and closed from above using a test driver with symbolic inputs). While CHESS *concretely* executes a closed concurrent program with a single input vector (see Section 4), STORM *symbolically* verifies a closed concurrent program on a (potentially unbounded) set of input vectors. To analyze the input program precisely, STORM unfolds loops and recursive procedure calls up to a user-provided bound.

Prior to this work, STORM implemented context-bounded verification for programs with a finite number of statically declared tasks. Our experience applying STORM to realistic programs indicated that the theoretical exponential complexity in the number of execution contexts does manifest in practice [26]. Furthermore, many concurrency errors in realistic programs require a large (i.e., > 3) number of tasks to be executed, and the number of tasks required to manifest a concurrency error is a lower bound on the number of required contexts. In these cases, context-bounded discovery becomes prohibitively expensive.

In contrast, delay-bounded scheduling discovers these errors with very few delays—typically 1 or 2. The reason depth-first scheduling works well (despite the fact that it is an artificial ordering) is that the majority of these tasks need not participate in any intricate interaction; they simply need to be executed in causal order to reach a program point which manifests the bug. Thus, our implementation of delay-bounded scheduling improves STORM in two important ways: we enable STORM to handle programs with dynamic task-creation, and to find a thus-far elusive class of bugs at low computational cost.

The (end-to-end) implementation works in three phases. In the first phase, we translate a concurrent C program into a concurrent BOOGIE [11] program—though BOOGIE was originally intended as an intermediate language for representing the semantics of simple imperative sequential programs, we have extended the syntax and semantics to express concurrent behavior. In the second phase, we transform the concurrent BOOGIE program into a sequential BOOGIE program encoding the delay-bounded depth-first semantics. It is noteworthy that our algorithm was very easy to implement with simple, minimal extensions to STORM. Finally, we verify the resulting sequential BOOGIE program using the triumvirate of field abstraction [26], verification-condition generation [4], and satisfiability-modulo-theory (SMT) solving [10].

We have applied our implementation to symbolic exploration of over 20 preemptible event-driven device drivers with 1K–30K lines of code. In the process we have found 4 previously unknown bugs with a maximum delay-budget of 2; the developers of these drivers have confirmed the accuracy of these bugs. More importantly, with the ability to handle dynamic task-creation, we can precisely model the asynchrony in the device driver's execution environment (e.g., interrupts, deferred procedure calls, timers, driver request cancellation and completion, etc.), thereby qualitatively extending the applicability and precision of STORM.

7. Related Work

The programming models considered in this paper have received plenty of attention from researchers interested in stack-based, finite-data abstractions of concurrent programs. The preemptive model has not been so heavily studied, primarily because the reachability problem is known to be undecidable [36]—even with a finite number of tasks—due to interference between multiple stacks. More attention has been paid to the non-preemptive model of asynchronous programs. Sen and Viswanathan [37] introduced the model explicitly to reason about event-driven programs, and showed that control-state reachability is EXPSPACE-hard; Ganty and Majumdar [14] tightened this result to show that the problem is EXPSPACE-complete. To combat this high worst-case theoretical complexity, Jhala and Majumdar [19] suggest a scheme that combines an underapproximate and an overapproximate computation of the reachable states.

Context-bounded verification [34, 35] explores only those executions of a concurrent program in which the number of context switches is bounded globally by a user-supplied value. However, the idea of context-bounding does not make intuitive sense for programs with large or unbounded number of tasks. This problem is well-known, and other researchers have proposed various fixes. Atig et al. [2] suggested stratified context-bounding that allows an unbounded number of context switches without sacrificing decidability. La Torre et al. [24] exploit the nondeterministic round-robin scheduling scheme of Lal and Reps [27] to achieve unbounded number of context switches for parameterized concurrent programs.

Exploiting sequential verifiers for concurrent program verification is also an active area. The KISS verifier [35] pioneered this approach by providing a source-to-source transformation from multithreaded programs into sequential programs that underapproximates the set of behaviors of the original program. Lal and Reps [27] achieved a breakthrough by providing the first source-to-source translation that computes a context-bounded underapproximation for any context-bound. This approach also pioneered the idea of guessing future-values and constraining them later at an appropriate control point in the execution; we exploit this idea in our transformation as well. A key weakness of Lal and Reps [27]'s so-called "eager" approach is that control states unreachable in the original concurrent program may be explored in the transformed sequential program; La Torre et al. [23]'s "lazy" technique addresses this weakness by repeatedly re-executing to the control points where guessed values would have been used; Ghafari et al. [16] empirically compared the two approaches in the verification-condition-checking paradigm where, as opposed to model-checking, benefits of laziness are unclear since the eager approach in fact outperforms the lazy one. Kidd et al. [21] have introduced a reduction from concurrent programs with priority-preemptive schedulers to sequential programs, though the construction requires a bound on the number of tasks. Although none of these sequentializations handle dynamic task-creation, La Torre et al. [25] have recently introduced a sequentialization of their parameterized model-checking algorithm [24] which does handle an unbounded number of tasks.

Finally, runtime-schedule "fuzzers" such as CONTEST [12] and CALFUZZER [20] introduce delays by adding sleep statements; PCT [7] introduces delays by randomly perturbing task priorities. These techniques share with delay-bounding the ability to scale to many tasks. In fact, a derandomized version of the PCT algorithm provides a scheduling complexity that is independent of the number of program tasks [6]; the mechanism for achieving this scalability is based on their characterization of a bug's *depth* as the minimum number of events that must occur in a certain order to reveal the bug. Bug-depth attempts, like delay-bounding, to canonize the effort required to discover a given bug, but is defined with respect to ordering constraints rather than deviations from a deterministic scheduler.

8. Conclusion

We have introduced a canonical characterization of scheduling nondeterminism by considering deterministic schedulers with the ability to delay their next-scheduled task. We demonstrate that delay-bounding is an effective search prioritization strategy for concurrent programs by extending the applicability of existing prioritization techniques. Furthermore, we identify a lower-complexity concurrent analysis problem via delay-bounded depth-first scheduling, and we show that our depth-first delaying schedulers admit practical sequential reductions, allowing us to lift existing sequential analyses to concurrent analyses. Our approach is generally applicable to concurrent programs with dynamic task-creation, and arbitrary preemption and synchronization.

Acknowledgments

We thank Ahmed Bouajjani, Pierre Ganty, Rupak Majumdar, and Gennaro Parlato for providing helpful insight, and the anonymous reviewers for their numerous comments and suggestions.

References

[1] M. Abadi and L. Lamport. The existence of refinement mappings. *Theor. Comput. Sci.*, 82(2):253–284, 1991.

[2] M. F. Atig, A. Bouajjani, and S. Qadeer. Context-bounded analysis for concurrent programs with dynamic creation of threads. In *TACAS '09: Proc. 15th International Conference on Tools and Algorithms for the Construction and Analysis of Systems*, volume 5505 of *LNCS*, pages 107–123. Springer, 2009.

[3] T. Ball, S. Burckhardt, K. E. Coons, M. Musuvathi, and S. Qadeer. Preemption sealing for efficient concurrency testing. In *TACAS '10: Proc. 16th International Conference on Tools and Algorithms for the Construction and Analysis of Systems*, volume 6015 of *LNCS*, pages 420–434. Springer, 2010.

[4] M. Barnett and K. R. M. Leino. Weakest-precondition of unstructured programs. In *PASTE '05: Proc. ACM SIGPLAN-SIGSOFT Workshop on Program Analysis For Software Tools and Engineering*, pages 82–87. ACM, 2005.

[5] A. Bouajjani and R. Majumdar. Personal communication, July 2010.

[6] S. Burckhardt and M. Musuvathi. Personal communication, November 2010.

[7] S. Burckhardt, P. Kothari, M. Musuvathi, and S. Nagarakatte. A randomized scheduler with probabilistic guarantees of finding bugs. In *ASPLOS '10: Proc. 15th International Conference on Architectural Support for Programming Languages and Operating Systems*, pages 167–178. ACM, 2010.

[8] E. M. Clarke and E. A. Emerson. Design and synthesis of synchronization skeletons using branching-time temporal logic. In *Logic of Programs*, volume 131 of *LNCS*, pages 52–71. Springer, 1981.

[9] J. Corbet, A. Rubini, and G. Kroah-Hartman. *Linux Device Drivers*. O'Reilly Media, Inc., 3rd edition, 2005.

[10] L. M. de Moura and N. Bjørner. Z3: An efficient SMT solver. In *TACAS '08: Proc. 14th International Conference on Tools and Algorithms for the Construction and Analysis of Systems*, volume 4963 of *LNCS*, pages 337–340. Springer, 2008.

[11] R. DeLine and K. R. M. Leino. BoogiePL: A typed procedural language for checking object-oriented programs. Technical Report MSR-TR-2005-70, Microsoft Research, 2005.

[12] O. Edelstein, E. Farchi, E. Goldin, Y. Nir, G. Ratsaby, and S. Ur. Framework for testing multi-threaded Java programs. *Concurrency and Computation: Practice and Experience*, 15(3-5):485–499, 2003.

[13] M. Emmi, S. Qadeer, and Z. Rakamarić. Delay-bounded scheduling: A canonical characterization of scheduler nondeterminism. Technical Report MSR-TR-2010-123, Microsoft Research, 2010. `http://research.microsoft.com/apps/pubs/?id=138569`.

[14] P. Ganty and R. Majumdar. Algorithmic verification of asynchronous programs. *CoRR*, abs/1011.0551, 2010. `http://arxiv.org/abs/1011.0551`.

[15] J. J. Garrett. Ajax: A new approach to web applications, February 2005. `http://www.adaptivepath.com/ideas/essays/archives/000385.php`.

[16] N. Ghafari, A. J. Hu, and Z. Rakamarić. Context-bounded translations for concurrent software: An empirical evaluation. In *SPIN '10: Proc. 17th International Workshop on Model Checking Software*, volume 6349 of *LNCS*, pages 227–244. Springer, 2010.

[17] P. Godefroid. Model checking for programming languages using VeriSoft. In *POPL '97: Proc. 24th ACM SIGPLAN-SIGACT Symposium on Principles of Programming Languages*, pages 174–186. ACM, 1997.

[18] J. L. Hill, R. Szewczyk, A. Woo, S. Hollar, D. E. Culler, and K. S. J. Pister. System architecture directions for networked sensors. In *ASPLOS '00: Proc. 9th International Conference on Architectural Support for Programming Languages and Operating Systems*, pages 93–104. ACM, 2000.

[19] R. Jhala and R. Majumdar. Interprocedural analysis of asynchronous programs. In *POPL '07: Proc. 34th ACM SIGPLAN-SIGACT Symposium on Principles of Programming Languages*, pages 339–350. ACM, 2007.

[20] P. Joshi, M. Naik, C.-S. Park, and K. Sen. CalFuzzer: An extensible active testing framework for concurrent programs. In *CAV '09: Proc. 21st International Conference on Computer Aided Verification*, volume 5643 of *LNCS*, pages 675–681. Springer, 2009.

[21] N. Kidd, S. Jagannathan, and J. Vitek. One stack to run them all: Reducing concurrent analysis to sequential analysis under priority scheduling. In *SPIN '10: Proc. 17th International Workshop on Model Checking Software*, volume 6349 of *LNCS*, pages 245–261. Springer, 2010.

[22] E. Kohler, R. Morris, B. Chen, J. Jannotti, and M. F. Kaashoek. The Click modular router. *ACM Trans. Comput. Syst.*, 18(3):263–297, 2000.

[23] S. La Torre, P. Madhusudan, and G. Parlato. Reducing context-bounded concurrent reachability to sequential reachability. In *CAV '09: Proc. 21st International Conference on Computer Aided Verification*, volume 5643 of *LNCS*, pages 477–492. Springer, 2009.

[24] S. La Torre, P. Madhusudan, and G. Parlato. Model-checking parameterized concurrent programs using linear interfaces. In *CAV '10: Proc. 22nd International Conference on Computer Aided Verification*, volume 6174 of *LNCS*, pages 629–644. Springer, 2010.

[25] S. La Torre, P. Madhusudan, and G. Parlato. Sequentializing parameterized programs, 2010. Under submission.

[26] S. K. Lahiri, S. Qadeer, and Z. Rakamarić. Static and precise detection of concurrency errors in systems code using SMT solvers. In *CAV '09: Proc. 21st International Conference on Computer Aided Verification*, volume 5643 of *LNCS*, pages 509–524. Springer, 2009.

[27] A. Lal and T. W. Reps. Reducing concurrent analysis under a context bound to sequential analysis. *Formal Methods in System Design*, 35(1): 73–97, 2009.

[28] L. Lamport. Proving the correctness of multiprocess programs. *IEEE Trans. Software Eng.*, 3(2):125–143, 1977.

[29] M. Musuvathi and S. Qadeer. Iterative context bounding for systematic testing of multithreaded programs. In *PLDI '07: Proc. ACM SIGPLAN Conference on Programming Language Design and Implementation*, pages 446–455. ACM, 2007.

[30] M. Musuvathi, S. Qadeer, T. Ball, G. Basler, P. A. Nainar, and I. Neamtiu. Finding and reproducing Heisenbugs in concurrent programs. In *OSDI '08: Proc. 8th USENIX Symposium on Operating Systems Design and Implementation*, pages 267–280. USENIX Association, 2008.

[31] W. Oney. *Programming the Microsoft Windows Driver Model*. Microsoft Press, 2nd edition, 2002.

[32] V. S. Pai, P. Druschel, and W. Zwaenepoel. Flash: An efficient and portable web server. In *USENIX '99: Proc. General Track of the USENIX Annual Technical Conference*, pages 199–212. USENIX, 1999.

[33] C. H. Papadimitriou. *Computational Complexity*. Addison Wesley, 1993.

[34] S. Qadeer and J. Rehof. Context-bounded model checking of concurrent software. In *TACAS '05: Proc. 11th International Conference on Tools and Algorithms for the Construction and Analysis of Systems*, volume 3440 of *LNCS*, pages 93–107. Springer, 2005.

[35] S. Qadeer and D. Wu. KISS: Keep it simple and sequential. In *PLDI '04: Proc. ACM SIGPLAN Conference on Programming Language Design and Implementation*, pages 14–24. ACM, 2004.

[36] G. Ramalingam. Context-sensitive synchronization-sensitive analysis is undecidable. *ACM Trans. Program. Lang. Syst.*, 22(2):416–430, 2000.

[37] K. Sen and M. Viswanathan. Model checking multithreaded programs with asynchronous atomic methods. In *CAV '06: Proc. 18th International Conference on Computer Aided Verification*, volume 4144 of *LNCS*, pages 300–314. Springer, 2006.

A. Syntactic Sugar

The following syntactic extensions are reducible to the original syntax of asynchronous programs of Section 2.2. Here we freely assume the existence of various type- and expression-constructors. This does not present a problem since our program semantics does not restrict the language of types nor expressions.

Multiple types. Multiple type labels $T_1, \ldots, T_j$ can be encoded by systematically replacing each T_i with the sum-type $T = \sum_{i=1}^{j} T_i$. This allows local and global variables with distinct types.

Multiple variables. Additional variables $\mathtt{x}_1 : T_1, \ldots, \mathtt{x}_j : T_j$ can be encoded with a single record-typed variable $\mathtt{x} : T$, where T is the record type $\{\mathtt{f}_1 : T_1, \ldots, \mathtt{f}_j : T_j\}$, and all occurrences of $\mathtt{x}_i$ are replaced by $\mathtt{x.f}_i$. When combined with the extension allowing multiple types, this allows each procedure to declare any number and type of local variable parameters, distinct from the number and type of global variables.

Local variable declarations. Additional (non-parameter) local variable declarations $\mathbf{var}\ \mathtt{l}' : T$ to a procedure p can be encoded by adding $\mathtt{l}'$ to the list of parameters, and systematically adding an initialization expression (e.g., the choice expression $\star$, or `false`) to the corresponding position in the list of arguments at each call site of p to ensure that $\mathtt{l}'$ begins correctly (un)initialized.

Unused values. Call assignments $\mathbf{call}\ x := p\ e$, where x is not subsequently used, can be written as $\mathbf{call}\ \_ := p\ e$, where $\_ : T$ is an additional unread local variable, or simpler yet as $\mathbf{call}\ p\ e$.

Let bindings. Let bindings of the form $\mathbf{let}\ x : T = e\ \mathbf{in}$ can be encoded by declaring x as a local variable $\mathbf{var}\ x : T$ immediately followed by an assignment $x := e$. This construct is used to explicate that the value of x remains constant once initialized. The binding $\mathbf{let}\ x : T\ \mathbf{in}$ is encoded by the binding $\mathbf{let}\ x : T = \star\ \mathbf{in}$, where $\star$ is the choice expression.

Tuples. Assignments $(x_1, \ldots, x_j) := e$ to a tuple of variables $x_1, \ldots, x_j$ are encoded by the sequence $\mathbf{let}\ \mathtt{r} : \{\mathtt{f}_1 : T_1, \ldots, \mathtt{f}_j : T_j\} = e\ \mathbf{in}\ x_1 := \mathtt{r.f}_1; \ldots; x_j := \mathtt{r.f}_j$, where $\mathtt{r}$ is a fresh variable. A tuple expression $(x_1, \ldots, x_j)$ occurring in a statement s is encoded as $\mathbf{let}\ \mathtt{r} : \{\mathtt{f}_1 : T_1, \ldots, \mathtt{f}_j : T_j\} = \{\mathtt{f}_1 = x_1, \ldots, \mathtt{f}_j = x_j\}\ \mathbf{in}\ s[\mathtt{r}/(x_1, \ldots, x_j)]$, where $\mathtt{r}$ is a fresh variable, and $s[e_1/e_2]$ replaces all occurrences of e_2 in s with e_1. When a tuple-element x_i on the left-hand side of an assignment is unneeded (e.g., from the return value of a $\mathbf{call}$), we may replace the occurrence of x_i with the $\_$ variable—see the "unused values" desugaring.

Arrays. Finite T^j-arrays with j elements of type T can be encoded as records of type $T' = \{\mathtt{f}_1 : T, \ldots, \mathtt{f}_j : T\}$, where $\mathtt{f}_1, \ldots, \mathtt{f}_j$ are fresh names. Occurrences of terms `a[i]` are replaced by $\mathtt{a.f}_i$, and array-expressions $[e_1, \ldots, e_j]$ are replaced by record-expressions $\{\mathtt{f}_1 = e_1, \ldots, \mathtt{f}_j = e_j\}$.

On Interference Abstractions

Nishant Sinha
NEC Laboratories America
nishants@nec-labs.com

Chao Wang
NEC Laboratories America
chaowang@nec-labs.com

Abstract

Interference is the bane of both concurrent programming and analysis. To avoid considering all possible interferences between concurrent threads, most automated static analysis employ techniques to approximate interference, e.g., by restricting the thread scheduler choices or by approximating the transition relations or reachable states of the program. However, none of these methods are able to reason about interference directly. In this paper, we introduce the notion of *interference abstractions* (IAs), based on the models of shared memory consistency, to reason about interference efficiently. IAs differ from the known abstractions for concurrent programs and cannot be directly modeled by these abstractions. Concurrency bugs typically involve a small number of unexpected interferences and therefore can be captured by small IAs. We show how IAs, in the form of both over- and under-approximations of interference, can be obtained syntactically from the axioms of sequential consistency. Further, we present an automatic method to synthesize IAs suitable for checking safety properties. Our experimental results show that small IAs are often sufficient to check properties in realistic applications, and drastically improve the scalability of concurrent program analysis in these applications.

Categories, Subject Descriptors: D.2.4 [Software/Program Verification]: Model Checking, Formal Methods.

General Terms: Algorithms, Verification.

1. Introduction

Analyzing shared memory concurrent programs is difficult due to the fact that constituent program threads may *interfere* with each other via shared variables. Multiple formalisms have been developed to model and reason about interference, e.g., the Mazurkiewicz traces [1] model the program behaviors as a partial order over events while the *context-switching* model utilizes a scheduler to generate all possible thread interleavings. Because analyzing all possible interferences is intractable in practice, these models employ *reduction* techniques to focus on a subset of interferences, e.g., partial-order reduction [2–6] or context-bounding [7–9].

In this paper, we develop a new formalism based on *memory consistency* models [10] for analyzing shared memory concurrent programs efficiently. A memory consistency (MC) model prescribes rules on when a read to a shared location may observe some write to the same location, and hence determines the set of feasible executions of a concurrent program. Concurrent program analysis based on MC models has received considerable attention recently, both for the *relaxed* MC models which allow instruction reorderings [11, 12] by the compiler or hardware, as well as for high-level static analysis [13]. Using a MC model is particularly attractive because it allows us to reason about correlations between reads and writes of program threads directly, inside a reasoning framework for partially-ordered events, similar to Mazurkiewicz traces.

In this work, we focus on the well-known MC model of *sequential consistency* (SC) [10, 14], which is both intuitive as well as simpler to analyze. The SC model prescribes the following rules (more formally, axioms in first-order logic) of interference for correct program executions: (i) each read must observe some write to the same shared location (interfering write), and (ii) a read may only observe the *last* such write in the causal order. Note, however, that enforcing these rules for all reads and corresponding interfering writes in a program, again leads to an intractable analysis.

To obtain a scalable analysis, we introduce *interference abstraction* (IA), a new concurrency abstraction to reason about thread interference using the memory consistency models. One way to obtain an IA is by *weakening* the SC rules, e.g., by permitting a read to not observe any interfering write. In other words, we allow program executions where the read may obtain any value independent of the values of the interfering writes. This form of weakening leads to an *over*-approximation of interference (denoted as an OIA). Alternatively, we may *strengthen* the SC rules, e.g., by forcing a read to observe only a *subset* of all possible interfering writes. Consequently, executions where the read may observe writes outside the subset are ruled out. Such strengthening leads to an *under*-approximation of interference (denoted as an UIA). Employing either of these approximations (obtained by weakening or strengthening the SC rules) makes analysis more tractable. Intuitively, an IA enforces *fewer* dependency relationships among reads and writes than ordained by the SC rules. Many concurrent safety errors, e.g., data races, deadlocks and atomicity violations, typically occur due to a small amount of unexpected interference between threads [15]. This fact is captured formally by IAs, i.e., there often exist *small* IAs sufficient to detect these errors.

We present a formal framework to characterize IAs in an uniform manner by exploiting the axiomatic formulation of SC rules. More precisely, we show how to obtain a wide variety of IAs in a *syntactic* manner by selectively instantiating the SC axioms. The framework models not only OIA's and UIA's but also mixed IAs (MIA's) containing both over- and under-approximations of interference, in a seamless manner. Further, we show how several informal notions of concurrency abstractions for checking properties can be formally captured in the uniform framework of IAs.

Given our unified framework of IAs, the key problem is to synthesize IAs suitable for checking a property. To this goal, we present an iterative refinement scheme which starts from a coarse IA and gradually refines it in a property-driven manner. Most traditional abstraction/refinement schemes (e.g. [4, 16–19]) work with either over- or under-approximations to obtain proofs or witnesses

POPL'11, January 26–28, 2011, Austin, Texas, USA.

respectively. In contrast, our algorithm works directly on a mixed approximation, i.e., mixed IAs, and iteratively steers the mixed IA to an OIA (if a proof exists) or an UIA (if a witness exists).

We implemented our approach in the FUSION platform, which is a collection of tools for concurrent program verification (e.g. [13, 20–23]). We evaluated the effectiveness of IAs for checking embedded assertions and data races on medium sized programs. Our results show that small IAs are sufficient to decide many of the properties, and our iterative refinement procedure enables drastically improved analysis of these benchmarks. Further, we have been able to check larger benchmarks that were intractable without using IAs.

To sum up, this paper makes the following contributions:

- We introduce the notion of *interference abstraction* to reason about interferences based on memory consistency models. These IAs may over- or under-approximate the thread interference, or represent their combination. (Sec. 5). We show that these IAs formally capture common concurrency bug patterns and as well as correctness proofs (Sec. 5.3).
- We present a unified framework for obtaining these IAs from the axioms of sequential consistency [10, 14] (Sec. 4, 5). The framework of IAs provides a flexible mechanism for approximating interference among reads and writes, guided by the memory consistency axioms.
- We formalize the set of IAs as a complete lattice and present an iterative approach to synthesize IAs for checking properties based on a symbiotic combination of over- and under-approximate IAs (Sec. 6). A set of focusing heuristics are also presented to make the iterative algorithm practical.

2. Preliminaries

We start with formalizing concurrent programs.

2.1 Concurrent Programs

A *concurrent program* consists of a finite set of *threads* $T_0, \ldots, T_k$ communicating via a set SV of *shared variables*. Each thread T_i has a set of local variables LV_i and is represented by a control flow graph (defined below). Threads are allowed to fork other threads in a bounded manner, i.e., the total number of threads is finite. Let T_0 denote the main thread and $V_i = SV \cup LV_i$ denote the set of variables accessible to thread T_i.

We represent a concurrent program using a concurrent control flow graph (CCFG), which may be viewed as an extension of control flow graphs (CFGs) for sequential programs. A CCFG $C{=}(N, E)$ consists of a set of nodes N and a set of edges E. We use two special types of nodes $fork$ and $join$ to model thread creation and thread join respectively. A program thread T_i corresponds to a sub-graph (N_i, E_i) of the CCFG, where N_i consists of nodes representing program locations in thread T_i and E_i consists of edges representing the program statements. Assume that N_i contains unique *entry* and *exit* nodes of T_i. For each T_i $(i \neq 0)$ the entry node has a single incoming edge from a $fork$ node and the exit node has a single outgoing edge to a $join$ node.

Each edge in E_i is labeled by one of the following actions:

- guarded assignment $(\mathsf{assume}(c), asgn)$, where c is a condition over V_i, and $asgn = \{w := exp\}$ is a set of parallel assignments, where $w \in V_i$ and exp is an expression over V_i. Intuitively, the assignments proceed iff condition c is true.
- $fork(j)$, where $0 < j \leq k$ and $j \neq i$, starts the execution of child thread T_j.
- $join(j)$, where $0 < j \leq k$ and $j \neq i$, waits for child thread T_j to terminate.
- $\mathsf{assert}(c)$, where c is a condition over V_i, asserts c.

Thread T_0
```
      int x = 0;
      int y = 0;
      pthread_t t1, t2;
      main() {
t1      pthread_create(&t1,0,foo,0);
t2      pthread_create(&t2,0,bar,0);
t3      pthread_join(t2,0);
t4      pthread_join(t1,0);
t5      assert( x != y);
      }
```

Thread T_1
```
      foo() {
        int a;
t11     a=y;
t12     if (a==0) {
t13       x=1;
t14       a=x+1;
t15       x=a;
t16     }else
t17       x=0;
t18   }
```

Thread T_2
```
      bar() {
        int b;
t21     b=x;
t22     if (b==1) {
t23       y=1;
t24       b=y+1;
t25       y=b;
t26     }else
t27       y=0;
t28   }
```

Figure 1. A multi-threaded C program with an assertion.

By defining expressions suitably and using code transformations, the above formulation can model all statements in standard programming languages like Java and multi-threaded C. The details on modeling generic language constructs such as pointers and structures are omitted since they are not directly related to concurrency. For more information on language modeling, please refer to recent efforts including [24–26].

The guarded assignment action $(\mathsf{assume}(c), asgn)$ may have the following variants: (1) when $c = \mathsf{true}$, it represents normal assignments; (2) when the set $asgn$ is empty, $assume(c)$ itself can represent the `then`-branch of an `if(c)-then-else` statement, while $assume(\neg c)$ can represent the `else`-branch; and (3) with both guard and assignments, it represents an atomic *check-and-set*, which can be used as the foundation of all kinds of synchronization primitives. For example, acquiring the lock lk in thread T_i is modeled as $(\mathsf{assume}(lk = \bot), \{lk := i\})$ and releasing the lock is modeled as $(\mathsf{assume}(lk = i)\{lk := \bot\})$. Here the value of lk indicates the lock owner's thread index ($\bot$ means the lock is free). Similarly, acquiring the counting semaphore se is modeled as $(\mathsf{assume}(se > 0), \{se := se - 1\})$.

2.2 Bounded Concurrent Programs

Static analysis of concurrent programs with loops and/or recursion is known to be undecidable even with finite data. Our goal, however, is to analyze real-life programs where data structures are precisely modeled. We, therefore, focus on analyzing *bounded* concurrent programs, whose analysis is decidable. Intuitively, a *structurally* bounded program is obtained by finitely unwinding the loops and recursion in an arbitrary real-life concurrent program. Bounded programs are also obtained in the context of symbolic predictive analysis (e.g., [21, 22]), by generalizing from the sequence of program statements executed in a particular trace. This form of bounding finitizes the number of program threads and the heap. Further, if the underlying program theory is decidable, then the analysis becomes decidable. A bounded program under-approximates the sets of paths of the original program and hence the violations found by the analysis are real. However, the proofs (absence of violations) found may not generalize to the original program.

We represent bounded programs using CCFGs. For ease of presentation, we assume that all function calls in the program have been inlined. However, the presented technique can be directly extended to handle function calls modularly [13].

Example. Fig. 1 shows an example of a multi-threaded C program with two shared variables x and y. The main thread T_0 creates threads T_1 and T_2, which in turn execute functions `foo` and `bar`, respectively. Thread T_0 waits for T_1, T_2 to terminate and join back, before asserting $(x \neq y)$. Here `pthread_create` and `pthread_join` are routines in *PThreads* library, directly corresponding to *fork/join* in our model. (Since this particular example does not have loops and recursion, the bounded and the original programs are same.)

The assertion at t_5 defines the correctness property, which holds in some, but not in all, execution traces of the program. In particular, the execution trace $\rho = (t_1 t_2)(\{t_{11}–t_{15}\}t_{18})(t_{21}t_{26}t_{27}t_{28})\{t_3–t_5\}$ does not violate the assertion ($x = 2, y = 0$ at t_5), whereas the execution trace $\rho' = (t_1 t_2)(\{t_{11}\text{-}t_{14}\})(t_{21} - t_{25}t_{28})(t_{15}t_{18})\{t_3\text{-}t_5\}$ violates the assertion ($x = 2, y = 2$ at t_5).

2.3 Gated Single Static Assignment

Recall that a sequential program can be encoded in a standard manner using the gated single static assignment (GSA) form [27], which combines the classic single static assignment (SSA) form (each variable is defined exactly once) with conditions under which a particular definition of a variable may reach a *join* node. For example, consider the following C code:

```
l1 : if (c1) { z = 1; }    // z1
l2 : else z = 2;           // z2
l3 : y = z + 3;            // y1
```

The SSA form renames the writes to z at l_1 and l_2 in terms of new *definitions* of z_1 and z_2, respectively. The *use* of z in l_3 is then rewritten using the ϕ function as $\phi(z_1, z_2)$, which, by definition, may evaluate to either z_1 or z_2. Consequently, l_3 is rewritten as $y_1 = \phi(z_1, z_2) + 3$, where y_1 is a fresh definition of y. Note that the ϕ operator does not contain information about the conditions under which definition z_1 or z_2 may be chosen, and therefore cannot be used for precise encoding of the bounded program. The GSA representation solves the problem by replacing $\phi(z_1, z_2)$ with $ite(c_1, z_1, z_2)$ where ite stands for the *if-then-else* operator. That is, $y_1 = z_1 + 3$ when condition c_1 is true; otherwise $y_1 = z_2 + 3$.

3. Symbolic Analysis of Bounded Programs

We say that two memory accesses interfere if both access the same memory location and at least one of them is a write. To avoid worrying about whether the accesses are concurrent or not, we use the term *interference* in a generic manner, both for access pairs occurring in the same thread or occurring concurrently.

In order to check properties of a bounded CCFG C, we encode it as a first-order logic formula in a step-wise manner. First the program statements in C are encoded in an *interference-modular* manner by ignoring the interference between all reads and writes (denoted Φ_C). The read-write interference in C is then encoded using sequential consistency axioms (denoted Π), which corresponds to composing the program threads. The property, e.g., existence of an assertion violation, data race, or atomicity violation, is encoded as a formula Φ_{PRP}. The combined formula

$$\Phi := \Phi_C \wedge \Pi \wedge \Phi_{PRP}$$

is then checked for satisfiability using an off-the-shelf constraint solver, e.g., an SMT solver [28, 29]. The formula Φ is satisfiable iff there exists an execution of the program that violates the property.

3.1 Interference-Modular Encoding

We show how to encode all the edges of the CCFG C without modeling the interference between the global reads and writes. The encoding in this section is similar to our previous works [13, 21]; we review the main details here. Although the GSA form can encode sequential programs (cf. Sec. 2.3), it cannot directly encode a program thread in a concurrent context. This is due to possibility of *interference* on shared variables by concurrent threads, i.e., a read of a shared variable (a global read, in short) must take into account all possible interferences from concurrent writes. To ignore modeling such interferences, each global read of variable z is assigned a fresh symbolic value rz (also called a *placeholder*). Using these fresh values, we can now encode the threads in the CCFG using the standard GSA encoding [1].

We say that a program edge is *global* if it accesses a shared variable; otherwise it is *local*. Both local and global edges participate in the data flow inside a thread; however, only global edges participate in data flow across the threads. Hence, we encode the local and global edges separately: this enables us to only consider global edges for encoding the thread interleavings, or more precisely, the interference between threads. Our encoding, denoted by Φ_C, consists of a local component Φ_L and a global component Φ_G:

$$\Phi_C := \Phi_L \wedge \Phi_G$$

We now discuss how Φ_L and Φ_G are obtained.

3.1.1 Encoding Local Edges (Φ_L)

Given the program in the GSA form together with placeholders for global reads, we can encode each program assignment of form $w := exp$ on a local edge as a formula ($w = exp$). The local encoding Φ_L is obtained by conjoining the formula obtained from local edges. Fig. 2 (left) shows the GSA encoding of the running example in Fig. 1. The local variable a is defined in t_{11} and t_{14}. At t_{18} the value of a is either a_1 (defined in t_{11}) or a_2 (defined in t_{14}), depending on the condition ($a_1 \neq 0$).

3.1.2 Encoding Global Edges(Φ_G)

We first compute the enabling condition for each edge.

Path conditions. The path condition for an edge t_i in the CCFG C is denoted by $g(t_i)$: t_i executes iff $g(t_i)$ is satisfiable. Let t_{first} and t_{last} be the unique first and last edge in C respectively. Starting with $g(t_{first}) := true$, the path conditions are computed iteratively for each t_i via CCFG traversal as follows. We distinguish between CCFG nodes having multiple predecessors: if the predecessors are in the same thread, the node is said to be an *intra-thread* join; otherwise it is an *inter-thread* join.

- If the source of t_i is an *intra-thread join* node with incoming edges t_j and t_k, then $g(t_i) = g(t_j) \vee g(t_k)$.
- If the source of t_i is an *inter-thread join* node with incoming edges t_j and t_k, then $g(t_i) = g(t_j) \wedge g(t_k)$.
- If t_i is a branching statement with condition c and t_j precedes t_i, then $g(t_i) = g(t_j) \wedge c$.
- In all other cases, the source of t_i has a single incoming edge t_j and $g(t_i) = g(t_j)$.

Fig. 2 (center) shows the path conditions in the example CCFG.

Global accesses. Each global edge is encoded using the notion of a *global access*. The global access a for an edge e is a tuple ($Addr, Val, En$), where $Addr(a)$ is the memory location accessed, $Val(a)$ is the value read or written, and $En(a)$ is the condition under which e is enabled. For example, edge t_{11} (cf. Fig. 2) is encoded as an access $r_{11} = (y, ry_1, g(t_{11}))$. Similarly, edge t_{15} is encoded as a global access $w_{15} = (x, a_1, g(t_{15}))$. The global access a captures all the information about the execution of the corresponding global edge e succinctly.

Interference Skeleton. Observe that to model all interferences in the CCFG C precisely, we not only need the values of global accesses, but also their relative order in C. Let $\sqsubset$ denote the partial order among global accesses induced by the CCFG (called *program order*). For accesses a_1 and a_2, if $a_1 \sqsubset a_2$ holds, then a_1 must happen before a_2 in all program executions. The set of global accesses in C, say RW, together with their program order, denoted

[1] We will later see that introducing such placeholders is, in fact, an instance of interference abstraction (Sec.5).

GSA Form:

$t_0 : x_0{=}0 \wedge y_0{=}0\ [\mathbf{w_{00}}, \mathbf{w_{01}}]$
$t_1 :$
$t_2 :$
$t_{11} : a_1 = ry^1\ [\mathbf{r_{11}}]$
$t_{12} :$
$t_{13} : x_1 = 1\ [\mathbf{w_{13}}]$
$t_{14} : a_2 = rx^1 + 1\ [\mathbf{r_{14}}]$
$t_{15} : x_2 = a_2\ [\mathbf{w_{15}}]$
$t_{16} :$
$t_{17} : x_3 = 0\ [\mathbf{w_{17}}]$
$t_{18} : a_3 = ite(a_1 \neq 0, a_1, a_2)$
$t_3 :$
$t_4 :$
$t_5 :$ assert$(rx^3 \neq ry^3)\ [\mathbf{r_{50}}, \mathbf{r_{51}}]$

$t_{21} : b_1 = rx^2\ [\mathbf{r_{21}}]$
$t_{22} :$
$t_{23} : y_1 = 1\ [\mathbf{w_{23}}]$
$t_{24} : b_2 = ry^2 + 1\ [\mathbf{r_{24}}]$
$t_{25} : y_2 = b_2\ [\mathbf{w_{25}}]$
$t_{26} :$
$t_{27} : y_3 = 0\ [\mathbf{w_{27}}]$
$t_{28} : b_3 = ite(b_1 \neq 1, b_1, b_2)$

Path Conditions of all Edges:

$g(t_1) = \mathsf{true}$
$g(t_2) = g(t_1)$
$g(t_{11}) = g(t_1)$
$g(t_{12}) = g(t_{11}) \wedge (a_1 = 0)$
$g(t_{13}) = g(t_{12})$
$g(t_{14}) = g(t_{13})$
$g(t_{15}) = g(t_{14})$
$g(t_{16}) = g(t_{11}) \wedge (a_1 \neq 0)$
$g(t_{17}) = g(t_{16})$
$g(t_{18}) = g(t_{15}) \vee g(t_{17})$
$g(t_3) = g(t_2) \wedge g(t_{28})$
$g(t_4) = g(t_3) \wedge g(t_{18})$
$g(t_5) = g(t_4)$

$g(t_{21}) = g(t_2)$
$g(t_{22}) = g(t_{21} \wedge (b_1 = 1)$
$g(t_{23}) = g(t_{22})$
$g(t_{24}) = g(t_{23})$
$g(t_{25}) = g(t_{24})$
$g(t_{26}) = g(t_{21}) \wedge (b_1 \neq 1)$
$g(t_{27}) = g(t_{26})$
$g(t_{28}) = g(t_{25}) \vee g(t_{27})$

Interference Skeleton:

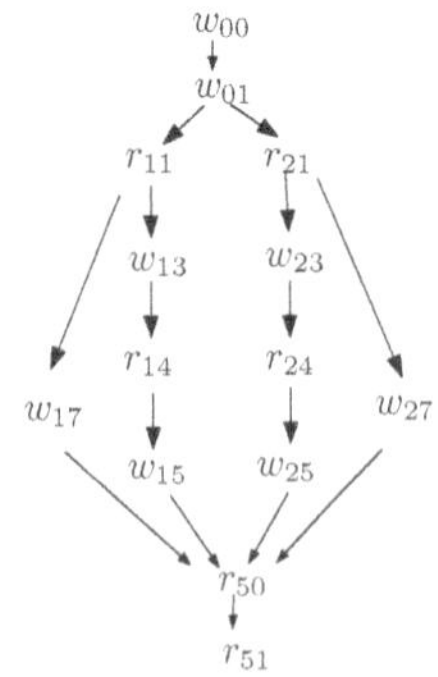

Figure 2. The symbolic encoding of the bounded program in Fig. 1. The global edges are labeled by the corresponding global accesses (e.g., t_{11} by $[\mathbf{r_{11}}]$). Edges t_0 is labeled by write accesses on x ($\mathbf{w_{00}}$)and y ($\mathbf{w_{01}}$) respectively. Edge t_5 is labeled similarly.

$(RW, \sqsubset)$, is called the *interference skeleton* (IS) of C. Fig. 2 (right) shows the IS (as a graph) for the running example: each node corresponds to an access $a = (Addr, Val, En)$ modeling the location, value and the enabling condition respectively, and the edges model the program order. Note that the IS models all the global accesses and their mutual ordering precisely.

To encode the IS $(RW, \sqsubset)$ in first-order logic, we introduce a new type called *Acc*, and the following operators over the type: a *must-happen-before* predicate HB over pairs of *Acc* elements and operators $addr$, val, and en which map an *Acc* element to its location, value and enabling condition, respectively. Now IS is encoded as Φ_G:

$$\Phi_G = \Phi_{Acc} \wedge \Phi_{PO}$$

where Φ_{Acc} encodes the set of accesses RW,

$$\Phi_{Acc} := \bigwedge_{a \in RW} \begin{array}{l}(addr(a) = Addr(a) \wedge en(a) = En(a) \wedge \\ val(a) = Val(a))\end{array}$$

and Φ_{PO} encodes $\sqsubset$:

$$\Phi_{PO} := \bigwedge_{(a_i, a_j) \in \sqsubset} (HB(a_i, a_j))$$

We also refer to Φ_{PO} as *program order constraints*.

3.2 Encoding Properties

Generic programming errors may be modeled as embedded assertions in the CCFG. The formula Φ_{PRP} then captures the condition under which a given assertion is violated. For an assertion $assert(c)$ in transition t, Φ_{PRP} is defined as

$$\Phi_{PRP} := g(t) \wedge \neg c$$

denoting that the condition c must hold if t is executed. In our running example in Fig. 2, fresh variables $rx^1, rx^2, rx^3, ry^1, ry^2, ry^3$ are added to denote the values of the six global reads, and the property sub-formula is defined as $\Phi_{PRP} := g(t_5) \wedge \neg(rx^3 \neq ry^3)$

Besides assertion violations, we can encode standard concurrency errors such as data races and atomicity violations directly as a set of happens-before constraints. Suppose we want to check the three-access atomicity violation [30, 31] involving global accesses c, c' and r, where c and c' are in the same thread and are intended to execute atomically, r is executed in another thread and interferes with both c and c'. (An example of such violation is given later in Fig. 7.) The property formula is defined as follows:

$$\Phi_{PRP} := en(c) \wedge en(r) \wedge en(c') \wedge HB(c, r) \wedge HB(r, c')$$

4. Axiomatic Composition

Given the skeleton IS = $(RW, \sqsubset)$ obtained from the interference-modular encoding of the CCFG C, we can now encode the interference (both intra- and inter-thread) using the axioms for sequential consistency (SC) over the set of global accesses RW in C. Intuitively, the SC axioms *link* the read accesses in RW to appropriate write accesses in RW to obtain feasible program executions. The basis of axiomatic composition is the *link* relation.

DEFINITION 1 (Link Relation). *The predicate $link(r, w)$ denotes that the read r observes write w, i.e., the value retrieved by the read access r is the same as the value set by the write access w. The $link$ relation is* exclusive, *i.e.,* $link(r, w) \Rightarrow \forall w' \neq w.\ \neg link(r, w')$.

The SC axioms [11, 13, 32], denoted as Π, can be modeled in typed first order logic using operators HB, *addr*, val and en and quantified variables r, w and w' over type *Acc* (cf. Sec. 3.1). The formula $\Pi := \Pi_1 \wedge \Pi_2 \wedge \Pi_3$, where

$$\begin{array}{l}\Pi_1 := \forall r\ .\ \exists w\ .\ \ en(r) \Leftrightarrow (en(w) \wedge link(r, w)) \\ \Pi_2 := \forall r\ .\ \forall w\ .\ \ link(r, w) \Rightarrow HB(w, r) \wedge \\ \qquad (addr(r) = addr(w)) \wedge (val(r) = val(w)) \\ \Pi_3 := \forall r\ .\ \forall w\ .\ \forall w'\ .\ \ (link(r, w) \Rightarrow \\ \qquad (\ en(w') \wedge \neg HB(w', w) \wedge \neg HB(r, w') \Rightarrow \\ \qquad addr(r) \neq addr(w')\ )\end{array}$$

Formula Π_1 models that if a read r is enabled, then r must be linked to some enabled write w, and vice versa. Formula Π_2 models the data flow and relative order between r and w when r links with w, i.e., both the value and address of r and w must be same and w executes before r. Formula Π_3 says that if r links with w then no other write w' to the *same address* as r should be executed between w and r, i.e., w' executes either before w or after r.

Fig. 3 shows the hierarchical encoding of Φ. When checking properties, the Π axioms interact subtly with the property violation condition Φ_{PRP}: the condition Φ_{PRP} identifies well-formed paths in the CCFG that lead to a property violation and enables the reads and writes along those paths; the axioms Π then make sure that reads and writes along those paths can be appropriately linked to obtain a feasible thread interleaving.

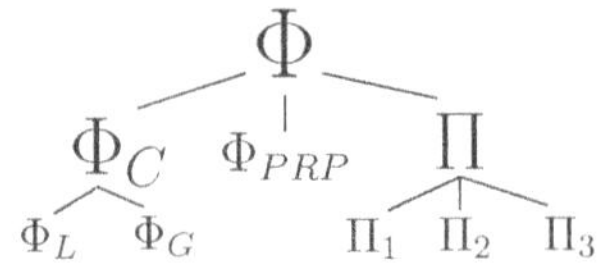

Figure 3. Hierarchical Encoding of the CCFG.

4.1 Full instantiation of SC axioms

Let $\mathbb{R}$ and $\mathbb{W}$ denote the set of all reads and writes in RW respectively. Given $\mathbb{R}$ and $\mathbb{W}$, Π can be encoded directly by instantiating the quantifiers for all reads in $\mathbb{R}$ and writes in $\mathbb{W}$. Recall from

Sec. 3.1 that the values of $addr(a)$, $val(a)$ and $en(a)$ for each access a are already encoded in Φ_G. Additional constraints are required to encode the exclusivity of $link$ and that HB is a strict partial order. Here, we exploit the theory of uninterpreted functions: rewrite $link(r, w)$ as $Id(r)$=$Id(w)$, where Id is an indexing function which maps each access to an unique integer. All writes w are initialized with unique $Id(w)$ values. Similarly, rewrite $HB(a, b)$ as $Clk(a) < Clk(b)$, where the Clk function assigns an integer time-stamp to each access and the operator $<$ encodes the partial order over integer time-stamps.

Example. The SC constraints for the running example (with substituted values for en, val, $addr$ and HB in Π_2 and Π_3) are

$$
\begin{aligned}
\Pi_1 := {} & (en(r_{14}) \Leftrightarrow \bigvee_{j \in \{00,13,15,17\}} (en(w_j) \wedge link(r_{14}, w_j)) \wedge \\
& (en(r_5) \Leftrightarrow \bigvee_{j \in \{01,23,25,27\}} (en(w_j) \wedge link(r'_5, w_j)) \wedge \\
& \ldots \\
\Pi_2 := {} & link(r_{14}, w_{00}) \Rightarrow Clk(w_{00}) < Clk(r_{14}) \wedge rx^1 = 0) \wedge \\
& link(r_{14}, w_{13}) \Rightarrow Clk(t_{13}) < Clk(t_{14}) \wedge rx^1 = 1) \wedge \\
& link(r_{14}, w_{15}) \Rightarrow Clk(t_{15}) < Clk(t_{14}) \wedge rx^1 = a_1) \wedge \\
& \ldots \\
\Pi_3 := {} & link(r_{14}, w_{00}) \Rightarrow \\
& \qquad \neg(g(t_{13}) \wedge Clk(w_{00}) < Clk(w_{13}) < Clk(r_{14})) \wedge \\
& \qquad \neg(g(t_{15}) \wedge Clk(w_{00}) < Clk(w_{15}) < Clk(r_{14})) \wedge \\
& \qquad \neg(g(t_{17}) \wedge Clk(w_{00}) < Clk(w_{17}) < Clk(r_{14})) \wedge \\
& \ldots
\end{aligned}
$$

Let $\widehat{\Pi}$ denote the quantifier-free formula obtained by instantiating Π for all accesses in $\mathbb{R}$ and $\mathbb{W}$. Note that the number of constraints in the worst case is cubic in the sizes of $\mathbb{R}$ and $\mathbb{W}$.

The following theorem captures the idea that the solutions of $\widehat{\Pi}$ correspond to the feasible executions of the program that violate the checked property.

THEOREM 1. *[13] Suppose we have an encoding Φ_C of a bounded CCFG C and a property encoding Φ_{PRP}. The formula $\Phi := \Phi_C \wedge \widehat{\Pi} \wedge \Phi_{PRP}$ is satisfiable iff there exists a feasible execution of C which violates the property.*

For convenience, if Φ is satisfiable then we say that a witness exists; otherwise we say that a (unsatisfiability) proof exists. Instead of always referring to Φ for a given CCFG and a property, we say $\widehat{\Pi}$ is satisfiable (has a witness) or is unsatisfiable (has a proof).

We now characterize the satisfying models of Π using the notion of a *read-write match* and an *interference relation*.

DEFINITION 2 (Read-Write Match). *Given set of reads $\mathbb{R}$ and writes $\mathbb{W}$, a* read-write match *(match, in short) is a partial function $M : \mathbb{R} \rightarrow \mathbb{W}$.*

DEFINITION 3 (Interference Relation (IR)). *An* interference relation *is a tuple $(R_\mathcal{I}, W_\mathcal{I}, M, \sqsubset)$ where $R_\mathcal{I} \subseteq \mathbb{R}$, $W_\mathcal{I} \subseteq \mathbb{W}$, M is a match and $\sqsubset$ is a partial order over the set $\mathbb{R} \cup \mathbb{W}$.*

DEFINITION 4 (IR Satisfying $\widehat{\Pi}$). *If $\widehat{\Pi}$ is satisfiable with a model Θ, then there exists an unique IR $\mathcal{I} = (R_\mathcal{I}, W_\mathcal{I}, M, \sqsubset)$* satisfying *$\widehat{\Pi}$ defined as follows:*

- *$R_\mathcal{I}$ and $W_\mathcal{I}$ are respectively the enabled reads and writes in Θ, i.e., ($r \in R_\mathcal{I} \Leftrightarrow en(r)$) and ($w \in W_\mathcal{I} \Leftrightarrow en(w)$).*
- *$M : R_\mathcal{I} \rightarrow W_\mathcal{I}$ is well-defined for all $r \in R_\mathcal{I}$ with co-domain $W_\mathcal{I}$. Moreover, $M(r) = w$ iff $link(r, w)$ holds in Θ.*
- *$\sqsubset = \{(a, b) \mid a, b \in (R_\mathcal{I} \cup W_\mathcal{I}) \wedge HB(a, b)$ holds in Θ \}.*

Intuitively, if $\widehat{\Pi}$ is satisfiable, then we can extract a match M by recording which of the $link(r, w)$ predicates hold in the current solution and the partial order $\sqsubset$ induced by the HB predicate. Note that the exclusivity of the $link$ constraints ensures that M is a well-defined function.

For the running example in Fig. 2, $\widehat{\Pi}$ has a satisfying IR $\mathcal{I}$ = $(R_\mathcal{I}, W_\mathcal{I}, M, \sqsubset)$ where $R_\mathcal{I} = \{r_{11}, r_{14}, r_{50}, r_{51}, r_{21}, r_{24}\}$, $W_\mathcal{I} = \{w_{00}, w_{01}, w_{13}, w_{15}, w_{23}, w_{25}\}$, $M = \{(r_{11}, w_{01}), (r_{14}, w_{13}), (r_{50}, w_{15}), (r_{21}, w_{13}), (r_{24}, w_{23}), (r_{51}, w_{25})\}$ and $\sqsubset$ consists of program order constraints (Φ_{PO} in Sec. 3.1) together with ($w_{13} \sqsubset r_{21}$) and ($r_{21} \sqsubset w_{15}$). Note that w_{17} and w_{27} are disabled and hence not in $W_\mathcal{I}$. An execution trace $\rho = (t_1 t_2)(\{t_{11} - t_{14}\})(t_{21} - t_{25}\ t_{28})(t_{15} t_{18})\{t_3\text{-}t_5\}$ corresponds to $\mathcal{I}$ and violates the assertion.

4.2 Redundant Instantiation of SC axioms

As mentioned earlier, Π may give rise to a large number (cubic in the reads/writes) of constraints; in practice, many of these are redundant. For example, if a read r precedes write w in the program order, instantiating Π for $link(r, w)$ is wasteful and can be avoided. Redundant constraints also occur in a more obscure manner, e.g., suppose the given property can be violated by executing the program threads sequentially without interleaving them. In this case, most constraints linking reads in one thread to concurrent writes in another thread are unnecessary for checking the property. Pruning redundant constraints is the key to making our problem tractable.

Interestingly, the syntactic formulation of Π offers insights on how to prune redundant constraints. Let us consider a few pruning methods. Suppose, for example, we pick a subset of reads and writes, say $R \subseteq \mathbb{R}$ and $W \subseteq \mathbb{W}$ respectively, and instantiate Π_2 only for R and W to obtain, say, Π^+. Note that Π^+ is an *over-approximation* of $\widehat{\Pi}$ because $\widehat{\Pi} = \Pi^+ \wedge F$, where F corresponds to the pruned constraints. Hence, a witness to Π^+ may not correspond to any feasible program execution; however, a proof for Π^+ implies that the property is never violated in P. On pruning constraints as above, we are able to *over-approximate* the interference, and hence the program behaviors axiomatically. Clearly, such an over-approximation is cheaper to check if we can discover small R and W sets, which are sufficient for proving the absence of violation.

Consider another form of pruning, again based on the syntactic structure of the axioms. Observe that instantiating Π_1 leads to a disjunction of $link(r, w)$ formula for each read $r \in \mathbb{R}$ and write $w \in \mathbb{W}$. If $\mathbb{W}$ is large, we must explore a large number of choices to find an appropriate read-write match. This naturally leads to another approximation: pick a subset of writes $W \subseteq \mathbb{W}$ for each read r and instantiate Π_1 (similarly Π_2 and Π_3) only for pairs (r, w) where $w \in W$. By pruning the disjunctions, we obtain an *under-approximation* of the interference (denoted by Π^-) which is cheaper to analyze. This under-approximation preserves witnesses, i.e., a witness found using Π^- corresponds to a concrete witness in the program P. Again, the usefulness of Π^- depends on obtaining a small W sufficient for computing a witness.

Each of the approximations above relies on either weakening or strengthening the SC axioms by *decoupling* reads and writes; hence we refer to them as *interference abstractions* (IAs). The above two examples show how the syntactic structure of the SC axioms may be exploited to obtain approximations (under- or over-) of thread interference. In fact, the abundance of quantifiers in Π allows us to build a complex array of abstractions systematically, where the under- and over-approximations of interference are intricately combined. We now define interference abstractions obtained in this manner formally.

5. Interference Abstractions

To formally represent the interference abstractions, we first define the *link set* for a read.

DEFINITION 5 (Link Set). *Given a set of reads $R \subseteq \mathbb{R}$, let $\mathcal{W} : R \rightarrow 2^{\mathbb{W}}$ map each read $r \in R$ to a set of writes which r may link with. We say that $\mathcal{W}(r)$ is the link set of r.*

Let $\widehat{\mathcal{W}}$ denote the default link set such that $\widehat{\mathcal{W}}(r)$ contains all possible writes that r may link with statically. For example, in Fig. 2,

$\widehat{\mathcal{W}}(r_{14}) = \{w_{00}, w_{13}, w_{15}, w_{17}\}$ because r_{14} reads variable x. Let Λ and Σ denote the (r, w) pairs and (r, w, w') triplets for which Π_2 and Π_3 are instantiated respectively. Now, we can reformulate the SC axioms Π as follows.

$$\begin{aligned}
\Pi_1 &:= \forall r \in R \,.\, \exists w \in \mathcal{W}(r) \,.\ \ \phi_1(r, w) \\
\Pi_2 &:= \forall (r, w) \in \Lambda \,.\ \ \phi_2(r, w) \\
\Pi_3 &:= \forall (r, w, w') \in \Sigma \,.\ \ \phi_3(r, w, w') \\
\Pi &:= \Pi_1 \wedge \Pi_2 \wedge \Pi_3
\end{aligned}$$

where

$$\begin{aligned}
\phi_1(r, w) &:= && en(r) \Leftrightarrow (en(w) \wedge link(r, w)) \\
\phi_2(r, w) &:= && link(r, w) \Rightarrow (HB(w, r) \wedge \\
& && addr(r) = addr(w) \wedge val(r) = val(w)) \\
\phi_3(r, w, w') &:= && link(r, w) \Rightarrow \\
& && (en(w') \wedge \neg HB(w', w) \wedge \neg HB(r, w') \\
& && \Rightarrow addr(r) \neq addr(w'))
\end{aligned}$$

To model Λ and Σ, we introduce functions λ and σ as follows.

$$\lambda(R, \mathcal{W}) = \{(r, w) \mid r \in R, w \in \mathcal{W}(r)\}$$

$$\sigma(R, \mathcal{W}, \mathcal{W}') = \{(r, w, w') \mid r \in R, w \in \mathcal{W}(r), w' \in \mathcal{W}'(r)\}$$

Given R, $\mathcal{W}$ and $\mathcal{W}'$ the functions λ and σ model the set of (r, w) pairs and (r, w, w') triples that Π_2 and Π_3 are instantiated for, respectively. The complete instantiation $\widehat{\Pi}$ of Π corresponds to $R = \mathbb{R}$, $\mathcal{W} = \widehat{\mathcal{W}}$, $\Lambda = \lambda(R, \widehat{\mathcal{W}})$ and $\Sigma = \sigma(R, \widehat{\mathcal{W}}, \widehat{\mathcal{W}})$.

5.1 Syntactic IAs

An interference abstraction (IA) is characterized by an *incomplete* instantiation of Π axioms. We say that the IAs thus obtained are *syntactic* because they are obtained by restricting the instantiations of SC axioms syntactically.

DEFINITION 6 (Syntactic Interference Abstraction (IA)). *Given Π as above and the set of all global reads $\mathbb{R}$, an interference abstraction α is defined to be a tuple $\langle R, \mathcal{W}, \Lambda, \Sigma\rangle$ such that: (i) $R \subseteq \mathbb{R}$, (ii) $\mathcal{W} \subseteq \widehat{\mathcal{W}}$, (iii) $\Lambda \subseteq \lambda(R, \widehat{\mathcal{W}})$, and (iv) $\Sigma \subseteq \sigma(R, \widehat{\mathcal{W}}, \widehat{\mathcal{W}})$.*

We say that α is a *proper* IA if at least one of R, $\mathcal{W}$, Λ or Σ is a proper subset. We refer to R, $\mathcal{W}$, Λ and Σ as components or dimensions of α. The *size* of α is defined to be the sum of the sizes of components of α.

Each IA $\alpha = (R, \mathcal{W}, \Lambda, \Sigma)$ corresponds to an instantiation of Π, denoted by Π^α, consisting of sub-formulas Π_1^α, Π_2^α and Π_3^α. Intuitively, an IA corresponds to first fixing a set of reads R and the set of writes $\mathcal{W}(r)$ that each read $r \in R$ may link to, and then instantiating Π_1 for each (r, w) in $\lambda(R, \mathcal{W})$, and Π_2 and Π_3 for subsets of $\lambda(R, \widehat{\mathcal{W}})$ and $\sigma(R, \widehat{\mathcal{W}}, \widehat{\mathcal{W}})$ respectively. Note that replacing read values by placeholders (during interference-modular encoding, cf. Sec. 3.1) is the coarsest IA, where a read does not link with any write, i.e., may assume an arbitrary value.

An IA α is said to be *under*-approximate (UIA) iff $\Pi^\alpha \Rightarrow \widehat{\Pi}$. Similarly, α is said to be *over*-approximate (OIA) iff $\widehat{\Pi} \Rightarrow \Pi^\alpha$. Otherwise we say that α is a *mixed* IA (MIA). As expected, an UIA is useful for obtaining witnesses while an OIA helps obtain proofs. We now show how the OIA and UIA as defined above in a semantic manner can be obtained *syntactically*.

DEFINITION 7 (Syntactic OIA). *An IA $\alpha = (R, \mathcal{W}, \Lambda, \Sigma)$ is an OIA iff $\mathcal{W} = \widehat{\mathcal{W}}$.*

In other words, an OIA is obtained if Π_1 is instantiated for all writes in the default link set $\widehat{\mathcal{W}}(r)$ of each read $r \in R$. However, Π_1 need not be instantiated for all reads and Π_2/Π_3 may not be instantiated for all reads and writes. The following lemma shows that a syntactic OIA is also a *semantic* OIA and hence preserves proofs.

LEMMA 1. *Given a syntactic OIA α, $\widehat{\Pi} \Rightarrow \Pi^\alpha$.*

Syntactic UIA's are more tricky to define.

DEFINITION 8 (Syntactic UIA). *An IA $\alpha = (R, \mathcal{W}, \Lambda, \Sigma)$ is an UIA iff (i) $R = \mathbb{R}$, (ii) $\Lambda = \lambda(R, \mathcal{W})$ and (iii) $\Sigma = \sigma(R, \mathcal{W}, \widehat{\mathcal{W}})$.*

Intuitively, an UIA is obtained if Π_1 is instantiated for all reads $r \in \mathbb{R}$ but only for a subset $\mathcal{W}$ of the default link set of each read. Moreover, Π_2 must be instantiated for all pairs $(r, w) \in \lambda(R, \mathcal{W})$ and Σ consists of all triples (r, w, w') where w is drawn from $\mathcal{W}(r)$ but w' ranges over the default set $\widehat{\mathcal{W}}(r)$. All the above constraints are critical for constructing an UIA which preserves witnesses.

LEMMA 2. *Given a syntactic UIA $\alpha = (R, \mathcal{W}, \Lambda, \Sigma)$, $\Pi^\alpha \Rightarrow \widehat{\Pi}$.*

A subtle difference between an OIA $\alpha = (R, \mathcal{W}, \Lambda, \Sigma)$ and an UIA $\beta = (R', \mathcal{W}', \Lambda', \Sigma')$ must be noted. Suppose for some $r \in \mathbb{R}$, $r \notin R$ in α. In the UIA β, $R' = \mathbb{R}$ and hence $r \in R'$; however, let $\mathcal{W}'(r)$ be empty. Although these two cases appear similar, they correspond to different instantiations of Π. For the OIA α, Π_1 will not be instantiated for r at all; however, for the UIA β, Π_1 will be instantiated as $\neg en(r)$. In other words, not including a read r in an OIA allows r to be enabled in any witness of Π^α without linking to any write; in contrast, setting $\mathcal{W}'(r) = \emptyset$ in an UIA amounts to disabling r in all witnesses of Π^β.

A full instantiation $\widehat{\Pi}$ of Π corresponds to both an OIA and an UIA. Also, an IA $\alpha = (R, \mathcal{W}, \Lambda, \Sigma)$ is an mixed IA (MIA), if α is neither an OIA nor an UIA. In particular, if $R \neq \mathbb{R}$ and $\mathcal{W} \neq \widehat{\mathcal{W}}$, then α is an MIA. Intuitively, in an MIA, some reads may not be linked to any writes while other reads may link to a restricted set of writes. We next discuss how to visualize the set of syntactic IAs.

5.2 Visualizing Syntactic IAs

As mentioned above, an IA α corresponds to instantiating Π only for a subset of all possible reads and/or writes. Note that even though Π_1 is instantiated for $\lambda(R, \mathcal{W})$, Π_2 and Π_3 may be instantiated independent of Π_1, for different subsets of reads and writes from R and $\mathcal{W}$. The possible choice of read and write subsets gives rise to a complex space of IAs. To better visualize this space, consider Fig. 4 which shows the components as four independent dimensions, R, $\mathcal{W}$, Λ and Σ. Intuitively, the $\mathcal{W}$ dimension corresponds to an under-approximation, while the other dimensions correspond to over-approximations. Moving away from the center along any dimension corresponds to *reducing* the approximation corresponding to that dimension. Note also that the dimensions are somewhat inter-dependent, i.e., it makes sense to select values for Λ and Σ only after we finish selecting the values for R and $\mathcal{W}$.

The IA space shown in Fig. 4 is, in fact, even more complex, e.g., we may instantiate only the order constraints $HB(w, r)$ in Π_2 without instantiating the data flow constraints $val(r){=}val(w)$. Consequently, we may obtain even more fine-grained OIA's, corresponding to sub-dimensions of the Λ-axis in the figure. We show later that the space of syntactic IAs directly corresponds to a complete lattice. We now show that these syntactic IAs indeed have a practical significance, i.e., they correspond to some common semantic notions useful for reasoning about concurrent programs.

5.3 Useful Semantic Interference Abstractions

Many popular techniques for reasoning about concurrent programs incorporate some form of *semantic* interference abstraction. Many of these abstractions can be readily modeled by our syntactic IAs.

Let us first examine the meaning of instantiating Π incompletely. Not instantiating Π_1 for some read r and write w disallows linking r with w in any execution. Formula Π_2 corresponds to *local* consistency: not instantiating Π_2 for some (r, w) implies that

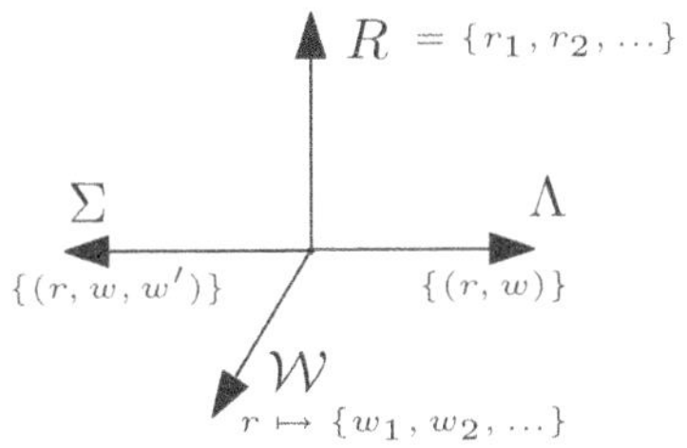

Figure 4. The Space of Syntactic Interference Abstractions.

Thread T_1		Thread T_2	
t_1	lock(A)	t_{11}	lock(B)
t_2	x = 1;	t_{12}	a = y;
t_3	lock(B)	t_{13}	lock(A)
t_4	y = 1;	t_{14}	b = x;
t_5	unlock(B)	t_{15}	unlock(A)
t_6	z = 1;	t_{16}	z = 2;
t_7	unlock(A)	t_{17}	unlock(B)

no interleaving can reach t_6 and t_{16} simultaneously

...　　...

t_6　　t_{16}

...

Figure 5. A control-state reachability analysis can prove the absence of data race (between t_6 and t_{16}).

Thread T_i	
t_1	lock(A)
t_2	if (x == 0)
t_3	unlock(A)
t_4	y = 1;
t_5	unlock(A)

Thread T_i	
$t_1 \to t_2$	assert(A $\neq i$)
	assume (A $= \perp$) { A := i; }
$t_2 \to t_3$	assume (x = 1)
$t_2 \to t_4$	assume (x $\neq$ 1)
$t_3 \to t_4$	assert(A= i) { A: = $\perp$; }
$t_4 \to t_5$	{ y = 1; }
$t_5 \to t_6$	assert(A= i) { A: = $\perp$; }

Figure 6. The assertion failure at t_5, caused by double unlock, can be detected in a serial execution.

Thread T_1	Thread T_2	a feasible interleaving
		...
$t_1 : p := \&a;$		t_1
{		t_2
t_2 : if $(p \neq 0)$		t_4
$t_3 : \quad *(p) := 10$		t_5
}		
	$t_4 : p := 0;$	t_3
	$t_5 : a := 0;$	...

Figure 7. Any serial execution of block t_2, t_3 is non-erroneous.

in any execution, r may link with w irrespective of their values, addresses and execution order. The formula Π_3 corresponds to *global* consistency: not instantiating Π_3 for some (r, w, w') implies that in any execution where r links with w, any other interfering w' is allowed to interleave in between r and w.

5.3.1 Control-State Reachability

Sometimes we can prove a property using a control-state reachability analysis [23, 31] where the control flow structure and the synchronization operations (such as *lock-unlock* and *signal-wait*) are modeled precisely, whereas the other data flow is ignored. This reasoning corresponds to a *semantic* IA defined as follows: partition the set of all reads $\mathbb{R}$ on shared variables SV in the program into two disjoint subsets: R_{sync} and $(\mathbb{R} \setminus R_{sync})$. The subset R_{sync} consists of all the variables modeling the synchronization primitives. The subset $(\mathbb{R} \setminus R_{sync})$ consists of the remaining global variables, which will be ignored in the IA. Given a default write map $\widehat{\mathcal{W}}$ for the reads in the program, this semantic IA can be obtained syntactically as

$$\alpha = \langle R_{sync}, \widehat{\mathcal{W}}, \lambda(R_{sync}, \widehat{\mathcal{W}}), \sigma(R_{sync}, \widehat{\mathcal{W}}, \widehat{\mathcal{W}}) \rangle$$

The IA α is an OIA by definition ($\mathcal{W} = \widehat{\mathcal{W}}$ and $R_{sync} \subseteq \mathbb{R}$) and hence a proof obtained with α still holds when the SC axioms are fully enforced.

Consider Fig. 5 as an example. The two concurrent threads T_1, T_2 communicate through locks A, B and shared variables x, y, z. The property of interest is that whether the writes to z at t_6 and t_{16} cause a data race. We can show that no data race exists by using a control-state reachability analysis based on locks A and B only; the rest of the variables x, y and z may be ignored because of the following reason. Transitions t_6 and t_{16} cannot be enabled at the same time, because thread T_1 must acquire A in order to reach t_6, but if A is held by T_1, then thread T_2 cannot reach t_{16} because it cannot acquire A at t_{13}. We can capture this reasoning precisely by including reads on only A and B variables in R_{sync} in the IA α above and therefore can prove the absence of data race with α.

5.3.2 Serial or Largely Serial Execution

Sometimes program bugs are insensitive to thread scheduling, i.e., they appear even in executions where the threads execute serially or interleave sporadically [7, 9]. Thread-local bugs fall in this category, e.g., as in Fig. 6 (left), where $x = 0$ initially. Here lock A may be released twice. Recall (cf. Sec. 2) that we encode locks using guarded assignments to shared variables as in Fig. 6 (right). Additional assertions are added to t_1 for checking double-locking errors, and to t_3, t_5 for checking double-unlocking errors. The assertion at t_5 is violated due to double unlocking. We can detect this violation by only considering a serial execution of threads T_i.

This form of reasoning can be captured by an UIA $\alpha = (R, \mathcal{W}, \Lambda, \Sigma)$, where R contains reads on x which are only linked with writes inside the same thread or an initial write. More precisely, the read of x at t_2 links with the initial write $x = 0$, the read of A at t_5 links with the write at either t_1 or t_3, and so on. Note that restricting the set of writes to link makes $\mathcal{W}(r) \subset \widehat{\mathcal{W}}(r)$ for $r \in R$, and hence results in an UIA. Checking this UIA for satisfiability corresponds to checking only serial executions.

Sometimes all the serial executions are good, but an interleaved execution involving only a small amount of interference may lead to a bug. Fig. 7 shows one such bug due to atomicity violation[2]. The transitions t_2, t_3 in thread T_1 are intended to be executed atomically; however, the programmer fails to enforce it. If t_4 is interleaved in between t_2 and t_3, a NULL dereference occurs. Again, an UIA α is sufficient to detect such bugs. Note that if we force each global read to copy from the preceding intra-thread write, we will not be able to detect the bug. Therefore, the UIA should allow the read of p at t_3 to link with t_4 (besides t_1). Inferring such reduced set of writes ($\mathcal{W}$) automatically is, however, the prime challenge.

6. Exploring the IA Space

We now focus on finding an efficient exploration strategy over the IA space to discover IAs of small size, which are precise enough for checking the given property. Let $\mathcal{A}$ denote the set containing all possible IAs. We define an order relation on $\mathcal{A}$ as follows.

DEFINITION 9 (Order of IAs). *Given two IAs $\alpha = (R, \mathcal{W}, \Lambda, \Sigma)$ and $\beta = (R', \mathcal{W}', \Lambda', \Sigma')$, we say that $\alpha \prec \beta$ if $R \subseteq R'$, $\mathcal{W} \subseteq \mathcal{W}'$, $\Lambda \subseteq \Lambda'$, $\Sigma \subseteq \Sigma'$, and at least one of $R, \mathcal{W}, \Lambda$ is a proper subset of the corresponding $R, \mathcal{W}', \Lambda'$.*

[2] For modeling pointers/structures, please refer to our previous work [13].

Figure 8. Semantic Interpretation of IAs. The bold circle denotes the full instantiation of Π.

If $\alpha \prec \beta$, then we say that β *refines* α. The poset $(\mathcal{A}, \prec)$ is a complete lattice with component-wise set union and intersection as the join and meet operators. The top element of the lattice $(\mathbb{R}, \widehat{\mathcal{W}}, \lambda(\mathbb{R}, \widehat{\mathcal{W}}), \sigma(\mathbb{R}, \widehat{\mathcal{W}}, \widehat{\mathcal{W}}))$ corresponds to a full instantiation ($\Pi^\alpha = \widehat{\Pi}$) while the bottom element $(\emptyset, \emptyset, \emptyset, \emptyset)$ corresponds to not instantiating Π at all ($\Pi^\alpha = true$).

6.1 Exploring the Lattice

Given a property P, we say that an α is *minimal* for P if α is an OIA (UIA) which proves (falsifies) P, and there exists no $\beta \prec \alpha$ such that β proves(falsifies) P. Since computing a minimal IA is at least as hard as checking the property itself, we are only interested in practically efficient algorithms to compute *small* IAs.

The formulation of syntactic IAs suggests two naive strategies to obtain small IAs. Starting with a UIA α, one may iteratively augment the sets $\mathcal{W}$, Λ and Σ until an actual witness is obtained. Similarly, one may start with an OIA α and iteratively instantiate constraints until a proof is obtained. Both these refinement strategies introduce new constraints in a *lazy* manner. Semantically, this form of refinement corresponds to increasing coupling or interference between threads and checking if a witness or a proof persists as the coupling increases.

The two refinement strategies presented above have a number of issues. First, these strategies are suitable either for finding proofs (using OIA's) or witnesses (using UIA's), but not both. Second, since the two IAs are disjoint, the proof-directed strategy does not gain from the witness-directed strategy, and vice versa. Ideally, we desire of a refinement method where both OIA's and UIA's could work in unison and assist each other. A natural way to combine OIA's and UIA's is via an MIA.

Fig. 8 depicts and compares the semantics of OIA's, UIA's and MIA's in a visual manner. Recall that the full instantiation $\widehat{\Pi}$ models sequential consistency precisely and hence corresponds to all feasible thread interleavings. An OIA removes interference constraints from $\widehat{\Pi}$ and therefore leads to more interleavings (infeasible ones) than allowed by $\widehat{\Pi}$. In contrast, an UIA adds interference constraints to $\widehat{\Pi}$, leading to fewer interleavings than allowed by $\widehat{\Pi}$. An MIA contains both an OIA and an UIA, and therefore omits some interleavings from $\widehat{\Pi}$ while allowing some infeasible ones.

Although MIA's combine the advantages of both OIA's and UIA's, neither models nor proofs of MIA's may provide conclusive results because of combined over- and under-approximation in an MIA. We now examine the sufficient conditions under which a model (proof) of an MIA may be an actual model (proof) for $\widehat{\Pi}$.

6.2 Models and Proofs of (Mixed) IAs

Given an MIA α, we define the interference relation (IR) $\mathcal{I}$ satisfying Π^α (model of the MIA) in a manner similar to Defn. 4: in the solution of Π^α, $R_\mathcal{I}$ and $W_\mathcal{I}$ are enabled reads and writes respectively, $M(r) = w$ iff $link(r, w)$ holds and $\sqsubset$ consists of (r, w)-pairs satisfying HB relation. Each IR $\mathcal{I}$, in turn, corresponds to an induced IA defined as follows. Intuitively, if an IR $\mathcal{I}$ satisfies Π^α, then the induced IA, IA($\mathcal{I}$), models the subset of SC constraints relevant to $\mathcal{I}$. The hope is that IA($\mathcal{I}$) is an UIA; in that case, $\mathcal{I}$ is a true witness.

	Thread T_1		Thread T_2
r_1 :	$assume(l = \bot)$;	r_2 :	$assume(l = \bot)$;
w_1 :	$l := 1$;	w_2 :	$l := 2$;
	...		...
w_1' :	$l := \bot$;	w_2' :	$l := \bot$;

Figure 9. Example with concurrent lock/unlock.

DEFINITION 10 (IR-induced IA). *Given an interference relation $\mathcal{I} = (R_\mathcal{I}, W_\mathcal{I}, M, \sqsubset)$, the IA $\beta = (R, \mathcal{W}, \Lambda, \Sigma)$ induced by $\mathcal{I}$, denoted by IA($\mathcal{I}$), is defined as follows.*

- *(i) $R = R_\mathcal{I}$,*
- *(ii) $\mathcal{W}(r) = \{M(r)\}$ if $M(r)$ is defined, else $\mathcal{W}(r) = \emptyset$,*
- *(iii) $\Lambda = M$,*
- *(iv) $\Sigma = \{(r, w, w') \mid (r, w) \in M \wedge w' \in W_\mathcal{I} \wedge w \sqsubset w' \sqsubset r\}$.*

However, in general, $\mathcal{I}$ may not correspond to a true witness of $\widehat{\Pi}$ because of approximation in MIA: all the constraints IA($\mathcal{I}$) relevant to the $\mathcal{I}$ may not be enforced by (contained in) the current MIA. On enforcing the missing constraints (from the set IA($\mathcal{I}$)), if $\mathcal{I}$ is no longer a witness, then we say that $\mathcal{I}$ is Π-inconsistent.

DEFINITION 11 (Π-inconsistent IR). *Suppose an IR $\mathcal{I}$ induces IA β = IA($\mathcal{I}$). We say that $\mathcal{I}$ is Π-inconsistent if Π^β is unsatisfiable.*

An IR $\mathcal{I} = (R_\mathcal{I}, W_\mathcal{I}, M, \sqsubset)$ may be Π-inconsistent (invalid witness) due to multiple reasons. For example, M may not be defined for some enabled $r \in R_\mathcal{I}$. Instantiating Π_1 for such r is unsatisfiable because antecedent $en(r)$ is true but the consequent is false. We say that $\mathcal{I}$ is Π_1-inconsistent here. Similarly, instantiating Π_2 for a subset of r-w pairs in M may be unsatisfiable. In this case, we say $\mathcal{I}$ is Π_2-inconsistent. We define Π_3-inconsistent similarly. Note that, in general, we may need to instantiate a combination of Π_1, Π_2 and Π_3 constraints for $\mathcal{I}$ to detect if $\mathcal{I}$ is Π-inconsistent.

The following lemma is crucial to finding actual witnesses using IAs: it shows that to find an actual witness, i.e., an IR satisfying $\widehat{\Pi}$, it is sufficient to compute a Π-consistent IR.

LEMMA 3. *If an IR $\mathcal{I}$ is Π-consistent, then $\mathcal{I}$ satisfies $\widehat{\Pi}$.*

Example. Consider the example in Fig. 9 with two threads T_1 and T_2, each containing a pair of lock/unlock statements on the lock l. The lock/unlock statements are transformed into guarded statements (cf. Sec. 2) and note that each lock/unlock pair is associated with a triple of lock accesses, e.g., (r_1, w_1, w_1') for T_1. Here, the link set of r_1 is $\mathcal{W}(r_1) = \{w_2, w_2'\}$. Similarly, $\mathcal{W}(r_2) = \{w_1, w_1'\}$. Consider an IR $\mathcal{I} = (R_\mathcal{I}, W_\mathcal{I}, M, \sqsubset)$, where $R_\mathcal{I}$ and $W_\mathcal{I}$ contain all reads and writes respectively, $M = \{(r_1, w_2'), (r_2, w_1')\}$ and $\sqsubset$ contains program order relation, i.e., $r_1 \sqsubset w_1 \sqsubset w_1'$ and $r_2 \sqsubset w_2 \sqsubset w_2'$. Clearly, match M violates lock semantics. More precisely, M is Π_2-inconsistent, i.e., on instantiating Π_2 for pairs in M, the IR $\mathcal{I}$ becomes unsatisfiable because the transitivity of HB relation is violated. Consider another IR $\mathcal{I}'$ with ordering: $r_1 \sqsubset w_1 \sqsubset w_1' \sqsubset r_2 \sqsubset w_2 \sqsubset w_2'$. Suppose the match M' links r_2 with w_1. The IR $\mathcal{I}'$ is Π_3-inconsistent: if r_2 links with w_1 then the interfering write w_2' should not occur in between, and hence $\mathcal{I}'$ violates Π_3.

Dual to the notion of a Π-consistent IR (a valid witness) is the idea of a *valid proof*, i.e. a subset of constraints of Π^α, which does not mention any reads whose link sets are under-approximated.

DEFINITION 12 (Valid Proof). *Suppose the instantiation Π^α for an IA $\alpha = (R, \mathcal{W}, \Lambda, \Sigma)$ is unsatisfiable and P is a proof of unsatisfiability. We say that P is valid if P contains no r such that $\mathcal{W}(r) \subset \widehat{\mathcal{W}}(r)$.*

We say that a read r *invalidates* a proof P, if P contains r and $\mathcal{W}(r) \subset \widehat{\mathcal{W}}(r)$. The following lemma shows that to prove absence of errors, it is sufficient to find an IA having a valid proof P.

LEMMA 4. *Let the instantiation Π^α of an IA $\alpha = (R, \mathcal{W}, \Lambda, \Sigma)$ have a valid proof P. Then P is also a proof for $\widehat{\Pi}$.*

6.3 Refinement of Mixed IA's

We now present our refinement procedure REF which tries to automatically compute an IA precise enough for either proving the property or finding a violating witness. REF works directly on an mixed IA (MIA) and iteratively refines the MIA to obtain either a valid proof or a Π-consistent IR (cf. Sec. 6.2). Fig. 10 provides an overview of our refinement procedure. The procedure starts with an initial IA $\alpha = (R, \mathcal{W}, \Lambda, \Sigma)$ by choosing sets R, $\mathcal{W}$, Λ and Σ. Then, REF checks if Π^α conjoined with the CCFG and property encodings, Φ_C and Φ_{PRP} respectively (cf. Sec. 3.1), is satisfiable. If Π^α is satisfiable and the IR $\mathcal{I}$ obtained from the solution is Π-consistent, the algorithm terminates with a valid witness. If $\mathcal{I}$ is not Π-consistent, then α must contain an over-approximation due to either R, Λ or Σ (cf. Sec. 6.2). Therefore, Π^α is refined to reduce the over-approximation (using procedure RED-O). Otherwise Π^α is unsatisfiable: if Π^α has a valid proof P, the algorithm terminates. If P is not valid, i.e., it contains an under-approximation due to $\mathcal{W}(r)$ for some r, then Π^α is refined to reduce the under-approximation (using procedure RED-U).

Note the advantage of working with an MIA: upon termination, the final IA may not be an OIA or an UIA; obtaining a Π-consistent IR or a valid proof is sufficient to obtain a conclusive result. We now describe the details of the RED-O and RED-U steps. The pseudo code is listed as follows.

RED-O :

Let $\alpha = (R, \mathcal{W}, \Lambda, \Sigma)$. Let the Π-inconsistent IR be $\mathcal{I} = (R_\mathcal{I}, W_\mathcal{I}, M, \sqsubset)$. Refine α by performing one of the following operations to reduce the over-approximation in α:

- Pick $r \in R_\mathcal{I} \setminus R$ and $W \subseteq \widehat{\mathcal{W}}(r)$. Set $R := R \cup \{r\}$ and $\mathcal{W}(r) := W$.
- Set $\Lambda := \Lambda \cup M$
- Set $\Sigma := \Sigma \cup \{(r, w, w') \mid (r, w) \in M \wedge w \sqsubset w' \sqsubset r\}$

RED-U :

Since Π^α is unsatisfiable, obtain the set of invalidating reads $R' \subseteq R$ in the proof of unsatisfiability of Π^α. Refine α by setting $\mathcal{W}(r) = \widehat{\mathcal{W}}(r)$ for each $r \in R'$ to reduce the under-approximation in α.

In words, RED-O analyzes the IR $\mathcal{I}$ and then chooses to refine α by updating one or more of R or Λ or Σ depending on the reason of Π-inconsistency (cf. Sec. 6.2). Similarly, RED-U checks if Π^α is unsatisfiable due to under-approximation in $\mathcal{W}(r)$ for some r; in that case, RED-U removes the approximation by setting $\mathcal{W}(r) := \widehat{\mathcal{W}}(r)$.

Checking if the IR $\mathcal{I}$ is Π-inconsistent is done by adding constraints IA($\mathcal{I}$) related to $\mathcal{I}$ incrementally and checking if the result is satisfiable. Note that both RED-O and checking Π-consistency involve adding constraints to reduce the over-approximation. Therefore, we combine them in practice using a layered instantiation strategy (Sec. 7.2). Besides disambiguating the choices in RED-O as presented above, the strategy also avoids adding irrelevant constraints.

Note how REF exploits the uniform representation of IAs in form of MIA's to check properties using a symbiotic combination of OIA's and UIA's. Also, the refinement is guided both by unsatisfiability proofs and witnesses obtained at intermediate iterations and hence is property-directed. The algorithm REF terminates in finite number of steps because the height of the IA lattice is finite and each iteration of REF ascends the lattice by one or more steps.

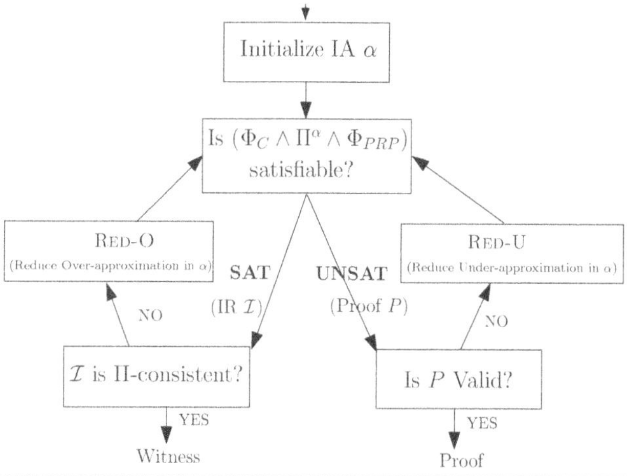

Figure 10. Flow diagram for the refinement procedure REF.

The refinement procedure can be implemented efficiently using an incremental SMT solver [28, 29] by iteratively adding new constraints. Moreover, using an MIA during refinement enables sharing the learned information between the constituent OIA's and UIA's inside the MIA, thus allowing the OIA's and UIA's to assist each other for computing both proofs and witnesses.

For the example in Fig. 2, we initialize MIA $\alpha = (R, \mathcal{W}, \Lambda, \Sigma)$ as follows. R includes all reads $r_{11}, r_{14}, r_{21}, r_{24}, r_{50}, r_{51}$. $\mathcal{W}$ is initialized so that the link set of each read contains no concurrent writes: $\mathcal{W}(r_{11}) = \{w_{01}\}$, $\mathcal{W}(r_{14}) = \{w_{13}, w_{17}\}$, $\mathcal{W}(r_{50}) = \{w_{15}, w_{17}\}$ and so on. Suppose we instantiate $\Lambda = \lambda(R, \mathcal{W})$, i.e., for all writes in the link set of each read. Let $\Sigma = \emptyset$. The IA α is an MIA because, e.g., $\mathcal{W}(r_{14}) \subset \widehat{\mathcal{W}}(r_{14})$ (under-approximation) and $\Sigma = \emptyset$ (over-approximation).

On checking Π^α (with Φ_C and Φ_{PRP}), the result is unsatisfiable because r_{11} links with w_{01} and r_{21} links w_{00}. Hence, the *then* branch in T_1 executes while the *else* branch in T_2 executes. Therefore, r_{50} gets value 2 and r_{51} gets value 0 so that the assertion is never violated. The proof of unsatisfiability mentions r_{11} and r_{21}. Suppose the procedure RED-U then expands $\mathcal{W}$ for r_{21} to $\widehat{\mathcal{W}}(r_{21}) = \{w_{00}, w_{13}, w_{15}, w_{17}\}$ and Λ is updated with the corresponding pairs. In the next iteration, suppose we obtain an IR $\mathcal{I}$ which links r_{21} with w_{13}, but $\mathcal{I}$ has $w_{13} \sqsubset w_{15} \sqsubset r_{21}$ in $\mathcal{I}$. Here, $\mathcal{I}$ is not Π-consistent because it violates Π_3. Therefore, REF updates $\Sigma = \{(r_{21}, w_{15}, w_{13})\}$ using RED-O, which finally results in a Π-consistent IR with $w_{13} \sqsubset r_{21} \sqsubset w_{15}$.

Note how a combination of over- and under-approximation was exploited by REF to arrive at a Π-consistent IR. Further, even though we check bounded programs (where paths in each thread or number of threads have been under-approximated), over-approximating interference is orthogonal and does not work against the previous under-approximation. In fact, it may assist in finding the bug quickly in many cases (cf. above example) or obtaining a proof early by avoiding redundant constraints.

7. Focused Refinement

The procedure REF proceeds iteratively by ascending the lattice of IAs based on the current satisfying solution or an infeasibility proof. Since the size of the lattice is exponential in the number of reads and writes, the basic refinement strategy may not converge quickly to a desirable small IA on its own. In particular, it may add redundant constraints guided by the model from the solver, thus making the intermediate IA larger and the subsequent iterations more expensive. We propose a set of heuristics to focus the refinement on relevant constraints.

7.1 Static Focusing

We first describe heuristics to guide REF by removing redundant constraints or adding useful lemmas statically.

(S0) Interference Pruning. For each read r, compute a small $\widehat{\mathcal{W}}(r)$, not containing any writes that r may never link with. For example, a r cannot link with w if $HB(r, w)$ holds statically, or if $HB(w, r)$ and there exist interfering writes w' along each path from w to r. Such writes may be detected by performing a static analysis on the interference skeleton (IS) (cf. Sec. 3.1).

(S1) Biased Initialization. To obtain IAs with lesser concurrent interference, we initialize $\mathcal{W}(r)$ for each r with only writes in the same thread or initial writes. This ensures that if a serial or largely serial execution (cf. Sec. 5.3) violates the property, then few refinement iterations will be sufficient. We also bias the initial IA to couple reads and writes on synchronization variables only. This forces REF to start with only those IAs where the above interference conditions must hold.

(S2) Lock Lemmas. A number of optimizations are possible for locks. **(S2a)** Consider the program shown in Fig. 9 again. The read in the initial assume statement (r_1) may link with either w_2 or w_2'. However note that if $link(r_1, w_2)$ holds then $val(r_1) = val(w_2) = 2$, making the guard ($l = \bot$) as $false$, which in turn blocks the execution of T_1. Therefore, we reduce the link set $\widehat{\mathcal{W}}(r_1)$ by removing w_2 from it. **(S2b)** Let $\mathcal{L}$ denote the set of matching lock/unlock statements in the whole program and the accesses to the lock variable for each $L_i \in \mathcal{L}$ be (r_i, w_i, w_i'). For each $L_1, L_2 \in \mathcal{L}$, either the statement block denoted by L_1 executes before the block denoted by L_2 or vice-versa. This fact can be captured by the constraints $\forall i.\forall j.\ (HB(w_i', r_j) \vee HB(w_j', r_i))$, which are quadratic in the size of $\mathcal{L}$ (better than the original cubic size).

(S3) Although instantiating Π_2 eagerly for all pairs of reads/writes $\Lambda = \lambda(\mathbb{R}, \widehat{\mathcal{W}})$ is expensive, instantiating only a portion of Π_2 for Λ incurs lesser cost both in terms of constraints size and solving times. We can therefore instantiate only a portion of Π_2, e.g., $link(r, w) \Rightarrow HB(w, r)$ for all $(r, w) \in \Lambda$ eagerly. This is especially useful if the ordering constraints are sufficient for checking the property. Formally, this form of instantiation corresponds to further partitioning the components of an α and instantiating some of those partitions eagerly.

7.2 Layered Instantiation

Note that in RED-O, updating Σ adds far more (quadratic in number of reads and writes) constraints than updating Λ (linear in size of reads R). We, therefore, perform a layered refinement towards the goal of adding fewer redundant constraints. Given an IR $\mathcal{I} = (R, W, M, \sqsubset)$ satisfying Π^α, we first check if $\mathcal{I}$ is Π_2-consistent (cf. Sec. 6.2). If $\mathcal{I}$ is not Π_2-consistent, we update Λ and continue to the next iteration. Only when we find a Π_2-consistent IR, we check if $\mathcal{I}$ is Π_3-consistent. In this way, we bias the refinement towards Λ. Similarly, we update the set R only when the current match M is both Π_2- and Π_3-consistent.

8. Experiments

We implemented the algorithm REF and evaluated it on concurrent benchmarks in the FUSION framework [20, 21]. Although our method can be applied to arbitrary bounded concurrent programs, in these experiments, we focus on analyzing concurrent program slices obtained by run-time analysis of the FUSION tool. Our benchmarks consist of Java program slices obtained from the various publicly available programs [33–35]. We check for errors such as assertion violations and data races. Many of these program slices are difficult to analyze, because they contain multiple threads (with forks and joins), each having a large number of global accesses, together with *assume* statements containing guards for branches taken during run-time. Our goal was to investigate if the hardest subset of available benchmarks could be checked using small IAs.

We initialize the refinement scheme with an IA containing all reads in the CCFG and the link set of each read with only writes which are non-concurrent with the read. Lock lemmas were also added to improve refinement. We observed that lemma **S2a** had a much larger impact than lemma **S2b**, although **S2b** also helped reduce run-times in a few cases. Further, we used biased refinement (7.2) strategy for reducing over-approximation. We focus on showing the effectiveness of IAs and that MIA's can perform better than OIA's or UIA's. All experiments were conducted on 2.33GHz Intel Xeon machine with 16GB memory.

Fig. 11 compares the full instantiation with the refinement (REF) procedure on a set of properties of the hard benchmarks. In this table, Columns 1-3 show the name of each test case, the number of threads, and whether there is a bug (T) or a proof (F). Columns 4-6 show the number of reads, the number of writes, and the average size of the link sets. The remaining columns compare the run-times and the IA sizes obtained with and without interference abstraction. The IAs computed by REF are drastically smaller than full instantiation both for satisfiable and unsatisfiable benchmarks. This confirms the belief that only a small amount of interference need be considered for checking many properties. Moreover, small IAs lead to much lesser run-times than with the full instantiation. We observed that for obtaining proofs, REF needed to instantiate Π_2 only a few times for each r-w pair in the initial IA. Finding witnesses is more challenging than finding proofs: REF goes through a number of iterations for reducing both the under- and over-approximation present in the initial IA.

Fig. 12 shows the advantage of using combined MIA's in REF vs using only OIA's or only UIA's. These are scatter plots where the x-axis is the run-time with only OIA's or only UIA's, and the y-axis is the run-time with MIA's. The data points correspond to checking several data race properties in benchmark (syncBench.1119). We observe that MIA's clearly outperform OIA's implying that under-approximated IAs are essential for efficiency. In contrast, MIA's may not be always better than only UIA's: however, the over-approximation in MIA's improves the performance in most cases.

The procedure REF for finding small IAs may be viewed as an automated quantifier instantiation (AQI) technique specific to the domain of SC axioms where the variables are quantified over finite domains. Although a number of SMT solvers support asserting quantified formula and include generic AQI heuristics, we found that such approach did not perform well even on small benchmarks (we used Yices [28] with default settings). We believe it is due to the following reasons: first, the solver must be provided with large number (at least quadratic in the number of reads and writes) of non-interference constraints derived from static pruning (cf. Sec. 7.1), without which these benchmarks become intractable. Secondly, generic AQI heuristics often lead to eager redundant instantiation which severely hurts performance. Most importantly, it is difficult for generic heuristics to infer a biased initialization of the MIA's: the initialization exploits knowledge about the typical behaviors of concurrent programs, which is unavailable to the solver.

We are aware that a number of improved AQI heuristics have been implemented in Z3 [36]. We believe that these recent improvements are complementary, and, if exploited correctly, could assist REF in converging faster. Note that an SMT solver also uses a combination of under- and over-approximations internally during

Bm	N	SAT	R	W	Avg. $\lvert\mathcal{W}\rvert$	Full Instantiation		With IAs (REF)	
						T(s)	IA Size	T (s)	IA Size
barrierB.653	13	F	285	269	9	29	2.7K / 2.7K / 91K	2	249 / 285 / 0
barrierB.653	13	T	285	269	9	30	2.7K / 2.7K / 91K	22	350 / 382 / 3.2K
syncBench.722	13	F	270	289	3	4	891 / 891 / 8.5K	2	259 / 270 / 0
syncBench.722	13	T	270	289	3	4	891 / 891 / 8.5K	2	254 / 270 / 55
syncBench.1119	16	F	496	457	24	902	12K / 12K / 1M	3	477 / 496 / 0
syncBench.1119	16	T	496	457	24	741	12K / 12K / 1M	149	533 / 498 / 12K
syncBench.1954	19	F	1012	856	48	>1hr	49K / 49K / 8M	15	989 / 1012 / 0
syncBench.1954	19	T	1012	856	48	>1hr	49K / 49K / 8M	258	1056 / 1023 / 20K
daisy1	3	F	496	798	19	117	10K / 10K / 0.4M	5	370 / 495 / 0
daisy1	3	T	496	798	19	681	10K / 10K / 0.4M	396	370 / 30 / 850
elevator1	4	F	829	615	3	202	3K / 3K / 29K	38	824 / 0 / 0
elevator1	4	T	829	615	3	82	3K / 3K / 29K	23	824 / 30 / 0
elevator2	4	F	2259	1491	10	>1hr	24K / 24K / 0.7M	15	2204 / 0 / 0
elevator2	4	T	2259	1491	10	>1hr	24K / 24K / 0.7M	14	2204 / 39 / 215

Figure 11. Experimental Results. R (W) = number of reads (writes). IA size denotes the size of the IA $\alpha = (R', \mathcal{W}, \Lambda, \Sigma)$ when the check terminates, in form (A/B/C) where A = $\sum_r |\mathcal{W}(r)|$, B = $|\Lambda|$ and C = $|\Sigma|$. nK and nM are shorthand for $n * 10^3$ and $n * 10^6$ respectively.

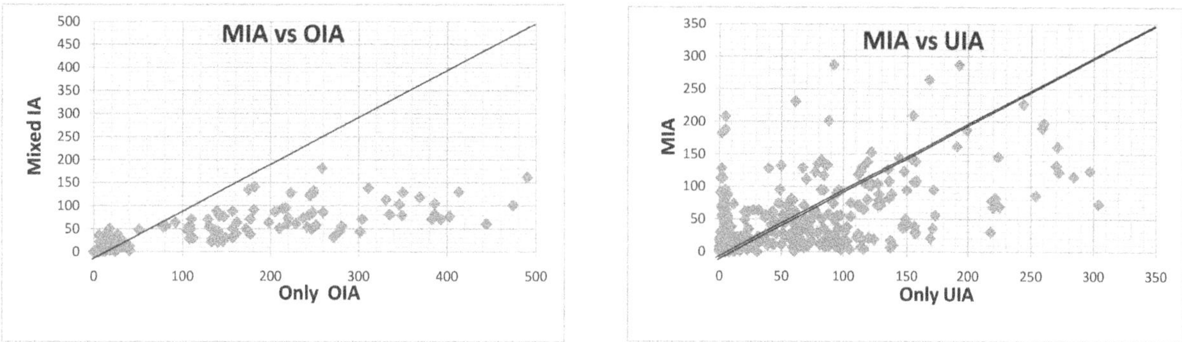

Figure 12. Run-times using MIA's vs. only OIA's or only UIA's on benchmark syncBench.1119.

constraint solving, which is unfortunately ineffective in handling the full instantiation directly. In other words, the solver is unable to focus on the concurrent facts relevant to the property by itself; the presented refinement scheme, in contrast, has the concurrency-specific knowledge (e.g., to compute an initial biased IA) and is able to steer the solver towards the relevant facts.

9. Related Work

Automated reasoning about concurrent programs with shared memory has been traditionally done by systematically restricting the thread scheduler [2, 4, 5, 37, 38] based on partially-ordered traces [1] with dependency relation (Mazurkiewicz (M-) traces). In particular, the work in [4] uses iterative enlargements of scheduler under-approximations to find bugs based on proofs from a SAT solver. Automated compositional methods have also employed abstractions of both transition relations [39, 40] and state spaces [41] of individual threads. IAs, in contrast, build upon the axioms of memory consistency instead of M-traces (cf. [42]). Note that the notion of IAs is orthogonal to abstractions of transition relations: IAs abstract only the correlations between reads and writes without modifying the transition relations of individual threads. The notion of *field abstraction* introduced in [26] for removing reads and writes to selected structure fields may be viewed as a form of OIA. However, field refinement links each field read with *all* possible writes, thus hampering its scalability. As our experiments show, the combination of OIA's with UIA's is important.

Iterative abstraction-refinement methods [16, 17] for sequential software using predicate abstraction [18, 19] have been investigated widely. Mixed abstractions of transition systems containing both *may* and *must* transitions to preserve universal and existential properties respectively have also been studied and applied to sequential software (cf. [43] for a nice overview). Recent work has also combined may- and must-summaries of procedures to obtain a more scalable analysis of sequential software [44]. Decision procedures for bit-vectors [45] also employ mixed abstractions of formula.

Automatic quantifier instantiation (AQI) inside SMT solvers is an active research topic. The most prevalent AQI strategy [28, 29], introduced in Simplify [46], employs *triggers* [36, 46]: to enable QI, subterms (triggers) of quantified assertions are matched (unified) with the ground terms in the partial model of the solver. However, such heuristics are in general incomplete and often cause a large number of redundant instantiations. Leino *et al.* proposed to handle quantified assertions via a separate module [47] similar to a theory module in an SMT solver. However, lack of tight integration between the quantifier module and the main solver leads to duplicate theory reasoning as well as restrained learning.

10. Conclusions

We presented a new form of concurrency abstraction for shared memory programs called interference abstractions (IAs) based on the axioms of sequential consistency. The framework of IAs provides an automated and flexible mechanism for approximating interference. An iterative algorithm to synthesize IAs for checking concurrent properties was presented and shown to yield small IAs for practical benchmarks. IAs may be extended in multiple ways, e.g., we can *cluster* multiple reads and/or writes into a single access and reason about these access sets simultaneously. These extensions, in contrast to pure IAs, may also violate the program order. Extending the notion of IAs to relaxed memory models is also an interesting direction. We also plan to compare with automated quantifier instantiation inside constraint solvers, handle unbounded programs, and investigate rely-guarantee reasoning using interference abstractions.

Acknowledgments. We thank the anonymous reviewers for their careful reading and valuable suggestions. We are also indebted to Yeting Ge and Cesare Tinelli for useful discussions.

References

[1] Mazurkiewicz, A.W.: Trace theory. In: Advances in Petri Nets. (1986) 279–324

[2] Godefroid, P.: Partial-Order Methods for the Verification of Concurrent Systems: An Approach to the State-Explosion Problem. Springer-Verlag New York, Inc., Secaucus, NJ, USA (1996)

[3] Peled, D.: Partial order reduction: Model-checking using representatives. In: MFCS. (1996) 93–112

[4] Grumberg, O., Lerda, F., Strichman, O., Theobald, M.: Proof-guided underapproximation-widening for multi-process systems. In: POPL. (2005) 122–131

[5] Musuvathi, M., Qadeer, S., Ball, T., Basler, G., Nainar, P.A., Neamtiu, I.: Finding and reproducing heisenbugs in concurrent programs. In: OSDI. (2008) 267–280

[6] Kahlon, V., Wang, C., Gupta, A.: Monotonic partial order reduction: An optimal symbolic partial order reduction technique. In: CAV. (2009) 398–413

[7] Qadeer, S., Rehof, J.: Context-bounded model checking of concurrent software. In: TACAS. (2005) 93–107

[8] Musuvathi, M., Qadeer, S.: Iterative context bounding for systematic testing of multithreaded programs. In: PLDI. (2007) 446–455

[9] Lal, A., Touili, T., Kidd, N., Reps, T.W.: Interprocedural analysis of concurrent programs under a context bound. In: TACAS. (2008) 282–298

[10] Adve, S.V., Gharachorloo, K.: Shared memory consistency models: A tutorial. IEEE Computer **29**(12) (1996) 66–76

[11] Burckhardt, S., Alur, R., Martin, M.M.K.: Checkfence: checking consistency of concurrent data types on relaxed memory models. In: PLDI. (2007) 12–21

[12] Torlak, E., Vaziri, M., Dolby, J.: Memsat: checking axiomatic specifications of memory models. In: PLDI. (2010) 341–350

[13] Sinha, N., Wang, C.: Staged concurrent program analysis, FSE 2010

[14] Lamport, L.: How to make a multiprocessor computer that correctly executes multiprocess programs. IEEE Trans. Computers **28**(9) (1979) 690–691

[15] Lu, S., Park, S., Seo, E., Zhou, Y.: Learning from mistakes: a comprehensive study on real world concurrency bug characteristics. SIGARCH Comput. Archit. News **36**(1) (2008) 329–339

[16] Kurshan, R.P.: Computer-aided verification of coordinating processes: the automata-theoretic approach. Princeton University Press (1994)

[17] Clarke, E.M., Grumberg, O., Jha, S., Lu, Y., Veith, H.: Counterexample-guided abstraction refinement for symbolic model checking. Journal of the ACM (JACM) **50**(5) (2003) 752–794

[18] Ball, T., Majumdar, R., Millstein, T.D., Rajamani, S.K.: Automatic predicate abstraction of C programs. In: PLDI. Volume 36(5)., ACM Press (June 2001) 203–213

[19] Henzinger, T.A., Jhala, R., Majumdar, R., McMillan, K.L.: Abstractions from proofs. In: POPL. (2004) 232–244

[20] Wang, C., Chaudhuri, S., Gupta, A., Yang, Y.: Symbolic pruning of concurrent program executions. In: FSE 2009. 23–32

[21] Wang, C., Kundu, S., Ganai, M.K., Gupta, A.: Symbolic predictive analysis for concurrent programs. In: FM. (2009) 256–272

[22] Wang, C., Limaye, R., Ganai, M., Gupta, A.: Trace-based symbolic analysis for atomicity violations. In: TACAS, Springer (2010) 328–342

[23] Kahlon, V., Wang, C.: Universal Causality Graphs: A precise happens-before model for detecting bugs in concurrent programs. In: CAV, Springer (2010) 434–445

[24] Clarke, E., Kroening, D., Lerda, F.: A tool for checking ANSI-C programs. In Jensen, K., Podelski, A., eds.: TACAS. Volume 2988 of LNCS., Springer (2004) 168–176

[25] Ivancic, F., Yang, Z., Ganai, M.K., Gupta, A., Shlyakhter, I., Ashar, P.: F-soft: Software verification platform. In: CAV. (2005) 301–306

[26] Lahiri, S.K., Qadeer, S., Rakamaric, Z.: Static and precise detection of concurrency errors in systems code using smt solvers. In: CAV. (2009) 509–524

[27] Ballance, R.A., Maccabe, A.B., Ottenstein, K.J.: The program dependence web: A representation supporting control, data, and demand-driven interpretation of imperative languages. In: PLDI'90. 257–271

[28] Dutertre, B., de Moura, L.: A fast linear-arithmetic solver for DPLL(T). In: CAV. (2006) 81–94

[29] de Moura, L., Bjørner, N.: Z3: An efficient smt solver. In: TACAS. (2008) 337–340

[30] Lu, S., Tucek, J., Qin, F., Zhou, Y.: AVIO: detecting atomicity violations via access interleaving invariants. In: ASPLOS. (2006) 37–48

[31] Farzan, A., Madhusudan, P., Sorrentino, F.: Meta-analysis for atomicity violations under nested locking. In: CAV. (2009) 248–262

[32] Yang, Y., Gopalakrishnan, G., Lindstrom, G., Slind, K.: Nemos: A framework for axiomatic and executable specifications of memory consistency models. In: IPDPS. (2004)

[33] `http://www.javagrande.org/`: The Java Grande Forum Benchmark Suite.

[34] Havelund, K., Pressburger, T.: Model checking Java programs using Java PathFinder. International Journal on Software Tools for Technology Transfer (STTT) **2**(4) (2000)

[35] von Praun, C., Gross, T.R.: Static detection of atomicity violations in object-oriented programs. Object Technology **3**(6) (2004)

[36] de Moura, L.M., Bjørner, N.: Efficient e-matching for smt solvers. In: CADE. (2007) 183–198

[37] Flanagan, C., Godefroid, P.: Dynamic partial-order reduction for model checking software. In: POPL. (2005) 110–121

[38] Clarke, E., Grumberg, O., Peled, D.: Model Checking. MIT Press.

[39] Flanagan, C., Qadeer, S.: Thread-modular model checking. In: SPIN. (2003) 213–224

[40] Henzinger, T.A., Jhala, R., Majumdar, R., Qadeer, S.: Thread-modular abstraction refinement. In: CAV. Volume 2725., Springer-Verlag (2003) 262–274

[41] Cohen, A., Namjoshi, K.S.: Local proofs for global safety properties. Formal Methods in System Design **34**(2) (2009) 104–125

[42] Şerbănuţă, T.F., Chen, F., Roşu, G.: Maximal causal models for sequentially consistent multithreaded systems. Technical report, University of Illinois (2010)

[43] Wei, O., Gurfinkel, A., Chechik, M.: Mixed transition systems revisited. In: VMCAI. (2009) 349–365

[44] Godefroid, P., Nori, A.V., Rajamani, S.K., Tetali, S.: Compositional may-must program analysis: unleashing the power of alternation. In: POPL. (2010) 43–56

[45] Bryant, R.E., Kroening, D., Ouaknine, J., Seshia, S.A., Strichman, O., Brady, B.A.: An abstraction-based decision procedure for bit-vector arithmetic. STTT **11**(2) (2009) 95–104

[46] Detlefs, D., Nelson, G., Saxe, J.B.: Simplify: a theorem prover for program checking. J. ACM **52**(3) (2005) 365–473

[47] Leino, K.R.M., Musuvathi, M., Ou, X.: A two-tier technique for supporting quantifiers in a lazily proof-explicating theorem prover. In: TACAS. (2005) 334–348

Dynamic Multirole Session Types

Pierre-Malo Deniélou   Nobuko Yoshida

Imperial College London

Abstract

Multiparty session types enforce structured safe communications between several participants, as long as their number is fixed when the session starts. In order to handle common distributed interaction patterns such as peer-to-peer protocols or cloud algorithms, we propose a new role-based multiparty session type theory where roles are defined as classes of local behaviours that an arbitrary number of participants can dynamically join and leave. We offer programmers a polling operation that gives access to the current set of a role's participants in order to fork processes. Our type system with universal types for polling can handle this dynamism and retain type safety. A multiparty locking mechanism is introduced to provide communication safety, but also to ensure a stronger progress property for joining participants that has never been guaranteed in previous systems. Finally, we present some implementation mechanisms used in our prototype extension of ML.

Categories and Subject Descriptors D.3.1 [*Programming Languages*]: Formal Definitions and Theory; F.3.2 [*Semantics of Programming Languages*]: Process models

General Terms Theory, Types, Design

Keywords communications, roles, multiparty, session types, mobile processes, dynamic protocols, join-leave, peer-to-peer, auction.

1. Introduction

As a type foundation for structured distributed, communication-centred programming, *session types* [18, 31] have been studied over the last decade for a wide range of process calculi and programming languages. The original binary theory has been generalised to *multiparty session types* [19] in order to guarantee stronger conformance to stipulated session structures between cooperating multiple end-point participants. Since the first work [19] was proposed, the multiparty session type theory has been developed in process calculi [4, 10, 14, 22], and used in several different contexts such as distributed object communication optimisations [29], security [5, 9], design by contract [6], parallel and web service programming [25, 35, 36] and medical guidelines [23], some of which initiated industrial collaborations (see § 6 and 7). While many interaction patterns can be captured in the existing multiparty sessions framework, there are significant limitations for describing and validating *loosely-coupled, ungoverned, dynamic protocols*, since the number of participants is required to be fixed both when the session is designed and when the session execution starts. This makes it unable to express interaction patterns frequently found in messaging oriented middleware and service-oriented computing.

POPL'11, January 26–28, 2011, Austin, Texas, USA.

The central underpinning of multiparty session types is that critical properties, such as communication safety (essentially a correspondence between send and receive) and deadlock-freedom, are guaranteed by the combination of two means: first, a static type-checking methodology based on the existence of a *global type* (a description of a multiparty protocol from a global viewpoint) and of its *end-point projections* — the global type is projected to end-point types against which processes can be efficiently type-checked; second, a synchronisation mechanism which ensures that all the well-behaved (i.e. well-typed) participants are actually present when the session starts. This paper introduces a new role-based multiparty type system and synchronisation mechanism that, together, can specify, verify and govern dynamically evolving protocols.

In the rest of this section, we illustrate our motivation, approach and solutions through protocols of increasing complexity: **(1) Map/Reduce** (introduction of the notion of roles and universal quantification); **(2) P2P chat** (projection challenges) and **(3) Auction** (branching and communication safety).

(1) Map/Reduce We imagine a server that wants a task to be computed on a cluster made of three cluster clients: the server sends them jobs and they give back their answers. We give a picture illustrating this communication pattern and the corresponding *global multiparty session type* written in the original theory [19].

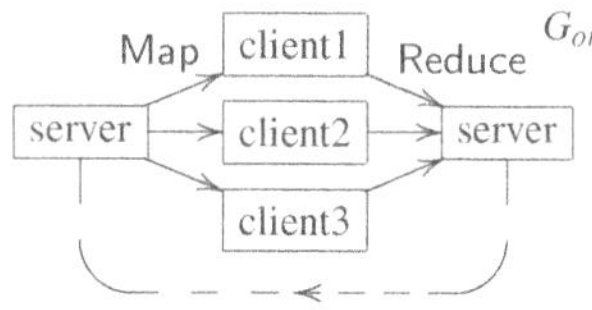

$$G_{org} = \mu\mathbf{x}.(\mathsf{server}\to\mathsf{client1}\langle\mathsf{Map}\rangle;\ \mathsf{server}\to\mathsf{client2}\langle\mathsf{Map}\rangle;\ \mathsf{server}\to\mathsf{client3}\langle\mathsf{Map}\rangle;\ \mathsf{client1}\to\mathsf{server}\langle\mathsf{Reduce}\rangle;\ \mathsf{client2}\to\mathsf{server}\langle\mathsf{Reduce}\rangle;\ \mathsf{client3}\to\mathsf{server}\langle\mathsf{Reduce}\rangle);\mathbf{x}$$

This session starts with the server sending asynchronously the messages Map to participants client1, client2 and client3. Each of them answers back with a message Reduce.[1] Recursion $\mu\mathbf{x}$ denotes an unbounded number of repeated interactions.

The problem here is that such a session cannot start without one of the clients and, once running, is not able to handle a fourth client joining or one of the current clients leaving. In the original multiparty sessions, any of these scenarios requires ending the session, writing an appropriate global type for the new situation, and starting a fresh session again.

This paper proposes a theory of *dynamic multirole session types* that can describe global interactions between *roles*, which are classes of participants that share a common behaviour (e.g. the clients in the above example). Dynamism is disciplined by a simple *universally quantified type* that allows to spawn further interactions by polling the set of participants currently playing a given role.

In the above session, we notice that the three clients have the exact same behaviour (receiving a Map message and sending a Reduce message). We call this behaviour the client role and now expect a varying number of participants to inhabit it. On the other hand, the server role is as usual instantiated by exactly one participant and the session does not start without its presence. The follow-

[1] Since the previous multiparty session types [4, 19] do not support explicit parallelism, we rely on asynchrony to express the desired behaviour.

ing picture illustrates this dynamic protocol. Its global type features the new universal type.

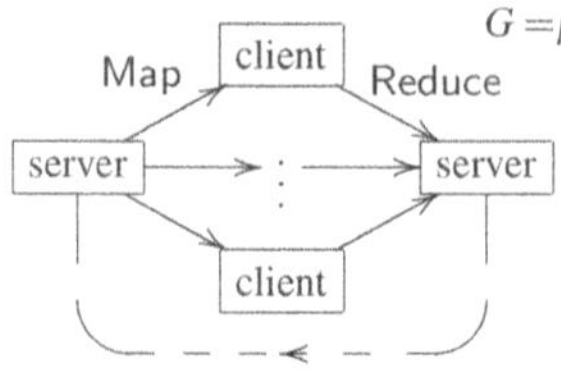

$$G = \mu\mathbf{x}.\forall x\!:\!\mathsf{client}.\{\mathsf{server}{\to}x\langle\mathsf{Map}\rangle;\; x{\to}\mathsf{server}\langle\mathsf{Reduce}\rangle\};\mathbf{x}$$

The repeated interaction in the global type G involves a Map message to be sent by the server to every participants x of the client role; the server then expects a message Reduce in answer.

At the type level, such an operation is specified using a universal quantification:

> $\forall x : r.G'$ polls the current participants $p_1, ..., p_n$ of role r and, in parallel processes, binds x to each in the subsequent interaction, as in $G'\{p_1/x\} \mid ... \mid G'\{p_n/x\}$

In our example, $G' = \mathsf{server}{\to}x\langle\mathsf{Map}\rangle; x{\to}\mathsf{server}\langle\mathsf{Reduce}\rangle$ is executed in parallel for each client x. Then, the recursion variable $\mathbf{x}$ points the interaction back to its beginning.

Local types Since the implementation, written here in a variant of the π-calculus, is distributed, the typing system first *projects* the global type to each end-point (local) type. For each role, the projection algorithm computes a local type that describes the behaviour of any participant that wants to play it. The local types for this session are the following:

$$T_{\mathsf{client}} = \mu\mathbf{x}.?\langle\mathsf{server},\mathsf{Map}\rangle;\,!\,\langle\mathsf{server},\mathsf{Reduce}\rangle;\mathbf{x}$$

$$T_{\mathsf{server}} = \mu\mathbf{x}.\forall x\!:\!\mathsf{client}.\{\,!\,\langle x,\mathsf{Map}\rangle;?\langle x,\mathsf{Reduce}\rangle\};\mathbf{x}$$

First, the client behaviour T_{client} is straightforward as it is only involved in two messages at each iteration with the server. The local type of the client expresses that it expects a message Map from the server ($?\langle\mathsf{server},\mathsf{Map}\rangle$) and that it sends a message Reduce as an answer ($!\,\langle\mathsf{server},\mathsf{Reduce}\rangle$). The server role is involved in all the messages of this session. We note the presence of the quantification over all x playing the client role.

Processes We write some process examples that would be well typed against the local types. The session identifier s denotes an active session:

$$P_{\mathsf{client}}(z) = a[z\!:\!\mathsf{client}](s).\mu X.s?\langle\mathsf{server},\mathsf{Map}\rangle;s!\,\langle\mathsf{server},\mathsf{Reduce}\rangle;X$$

$$P_{\mathsf{server}}(z) = a[z\!:\!\mathsf{client}](s).\mu X.s\forall(x\!:\!\mathsf{client}).\{s!\,\langle x,\mathsf{Map}\rangle;s?\langle x,\mathsf{Reduce}\rangle\};X$$

A session starts through the join operation ($a[z\!:\!\mathsf{client}](s)$) which gets the session name s of a running session advertised on a. A participant z playing the client with $P_{\mathsf{client}}(z)$ is simply exchanging messages Map and Reduce with the server through sending ($s!$) and receiving ($s?$) operations. The server needs to fork subprocesses for its interactions with each client. To this effect, the polling operation $s\forall(x\!:\!\mathsf{client}).\{s!\,\langle x,\mathsf{Map}\rangle;s?\langle x,\mathsf{Reduce}\rangle\}$ creates as many processes $s!\,\langle x,\mathsf{Map}\rangle;s?\langle x,\mathsf{Reduce}\rangle$ as there are participants x playing the client role. Note that late joining client participants are incorporated in the session at each iteration: the repetition of the polling operation $s\forall(x\!:\!\mathsf{client})$ is able to ensure a safe interaction between all parties.

(2) Peer-to-peer chat In this session, there is only one role, the client, whose behaviour is to always broadcast its messages to all the other clients. We give the global type and a representation of the interaction when four clients are present.

$$G = \mu\mathbf{x}.(\forall x\!:\!\mathsf{client}.\forall y\!:\!\mathsf{client}\setminus x.\{x{\to}y\,\mathsf{Msg}\langle\mathsf{string}\rangle\});\mathbf{x}$$

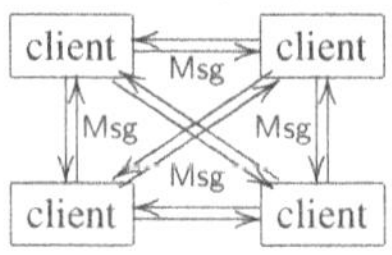

This type features a double quantification which specifies that each pair of clients x, y will interact in the form of a unique Msg. The explicit exclusion of x from the list of clients y prevents self-sent messages.

This second example shows the projection difficulties that arise from quantification.

Local types To illustrate the projection of nested quantifiers, we first rely on our intuition: each client should send a message Msg to every other client and, concurrently, should expect a message Msg from each of them.

$$T_{\mathsf{client}}(z) = \mu\mathbf{x}.(\forall y\!:\!\mathsf{client}\setminus z.\{\,!\,\langle y\!:\!\mathsf{client},\mathsf{Msg}\langle\mathsf{string}\rangle\rangle\} \mid \forall x\!:\!\mathsf{client}\setminus z.\{?\langle x\!:\!\mathsf{client},\mathsf{Msg}\langle\mathsf{string}\rangle\rangle\});\mathbf{x}$$

Let us examine how the projection algorithm gives this local type. Suppose we project for a generic client z. The first quantifier $\forall x$: client of the global type necessarily involves z, meaning that among these parallel processes there is exactly one where x is z. In the other parallel processes, although x is not z, z can still be involved. The projection of the second nested quantifier $\forall y\!:\!\mathsf{client}\setminus x$ works in the same way. This is why the first parallel part is $\forall y\!:\!\mathsf{client}\setminus z.\{\,!\,\langle y\!:\!\mathsf{client},\mathsf{Msg}\langle\mathsf{string}\rangle\rangle\}$, which explicitly excludes the possible $!\,\langle z,\mathsf{Msg}\langle\mathsf{string}\rangle\rangle$.[2]

Process Once the local types are known, the client processes have a similar structure, including the explicit polling operator, written $s\forall(y\!:\!\mathsf{client}\setminus z)$.

$$P_{\mathsf{client}}(z) = a[z\!:\!\mathsf{client}](s).\mu X.(s\forall(y\!:\!\mathsf{client}\setminus z).\{s!\,\langle y,\mathsf{Msg}\langle m\rangle\rangle\} \mid s\forall(x\!:\!\mathsf{client}\setminus z).\{s?\langle x,\mathsf{Msg}\langle w\rangle\rangle\});X$$

(3) Auction We now illustrate the expressiveness of our universal types when combined with instantiation of participant identities and branching session. In this session, we have three roles: the multiple buyers (here participants `alice`, `alex`, `alan`) and sellers (here `bob`, `ben`) which all connect to a single broker. This broker will then form matching pairs (x,y) of buyers and sellers who will then continue their interaction Price-Order separately.

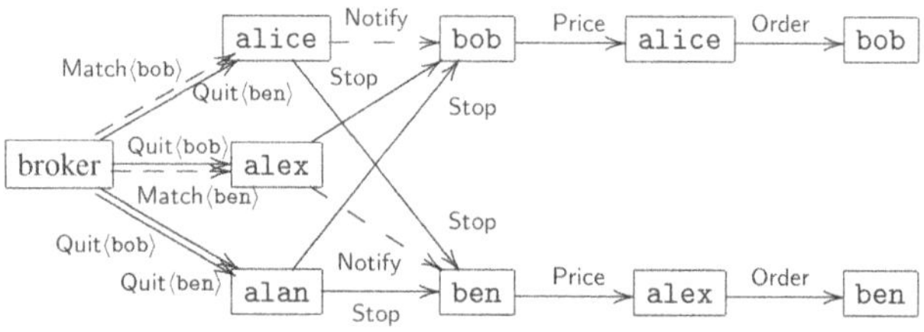

$$G = \forall x\!:\!\mathsf{buyer}.\forall y\!:\!\mathsf{seller}.\; \mathsf{broker}{\to}x\{\mathsf{Match}\langle y\rangle.x{\to}y\langle\mathsf{Notify}\rangle.y{\to}x\langle\mathsf{Price}\rangle.x{\to}y\langle\mathsf{Order}\rangle,\; \mathsf{Quit}\langle y\rangle.\,x{\to}y\,\langle\mathsf{Stop}\rangle\};\mathsf{end}$$

The quantifications $\forall x\!:\!\mathsf{buyer}.\forall y\!:\!\mathsf{seller}$ specify that every possible association between buyers and sellers is considered by the broker when he makes his choices. For each pair (x,y) of buyer and seller, the broker selects to send to x either a message $\mathsf{Match}\langle y\rangle$ if he has found y to be a match for x, or a message $\mathsf{Quit}\langle y\rangle$ otherwise. If the message Match was sent, x notifies y and the interaction Price-Order proceeds. In the other branch, x needs to warn y by the message Stop that the broker chose the second branch.

For this example, we just write a process for a buyer:

$$P_{\mathsf{buyer}}(z) = a[z\!:\!\mathsf{buyer}](s).s\forall(y\!:\!\mathsf{seller}).\{ s?\langle\mathsf{broker},\{\mathsf{Match}\langle y\rangle.s!\,\langle y,\mathsf{Notify}\rangle.s?\langle y,\mathsf{Price}\rangle.s!\,\langle y,\mathsf{Order}\rangle,\; \mathsf{Quit}\langle y\rangle.s!\,\langle y,\mathsf{Stop}\rangle\}\rangle\};\mathtt{quit}\langle s\rangle$$

From the above process, we can see the importance of the communication of the participant identity y with the messages Match and Quit. The adjunction of y to the messages is necessary for x to know to which y to send the Notify message. Note that the y in $\mathsf{Match}\langle y\rangle$ is not a regular payload as all the sellers y are already known by x: at reception, x matches his known y against the one coming along Match or Quit.

This example presents a non-recursive session where all participants leave the session (through the expression $\mathtt{quit}\langle s\rangle$) at the end of their interaction. Since late joiners always start at the beginning of the session, they cannot safely interact with the participants that have already proceeded. To guarantee progress, we require that late

[2] If we want our global type to include those self-sent message, it can be done explicitly by writing a global type: $\mu\mathbf{x}.(\forall x\!:\!\mathsf{client}.(x{\to}x\,\mathsf{Msg}\langle\mathsf{string}\rangle \mid \forall y\!:\!\mathsf{client}.x{\to}y\,\mathsf{Msg}\langle\mathsf{string}\rangle);\mathbf{x}$.

joiners wait for the current participants to end before joining themselves and beginning their actions. To provide consistent synchronisation, we introduce a *multiparty locking mechanism* to protect the global session executions.

Main contributions

(§ **2**) A new role-based multiparty session type framework where participants can play several roles in a session. Its semantics allows participants to dynamically join and leave a running session, and create new parallel sessions.

(§ **3**, § **4**) Introduction of a universal type for polling participants, along with explicit parallel compositions, and a type system that provides subject reduction (Theorem 4.2) and type safety (Corollary 4.3: no type error for values and labels). The endpoint projection and the well-formedness conditions of global types deal with the subtle interplay between universal quantifiers, parallel compositions, branching and instantiations of participant identities.

(§ **5**) A semantics and type system with a simple locking mechanism by which communication safety (Theorem 5.4: every receiver has a corresponding sender with the right type), progress (Theorem 5.6: processes in a single multiparty session always progress) and join progress (Theorem 5.8: late joiners can always join to an existing session and progress) are established.

(§ **5.5**) Practical implementation techniques used in our prototype extension of ML.

The proofs, detailed definitions, additional examples and the prototype implementation are available from [3].

2. Multirole session calculus

We describe here an extension of the multiparty session calculus presented in [4]. Our new system handles roles and allows programs to participate in protocols that include multiple parallel interactions and dynamic role instantiation.

$u ::= x \mid a \mid b \mid \ldots$	Shared channel
$p ::= \mathtt{p}{:}r \mid x{:}r$	Participant with role
$\vec{p} ::= \mathtt{p}{::}\vec{p} \mid x{::}\vec{p} \mid \varepsilon$	Participant list
$c ::= s[p] \mid y$	Session channel
$e ::= v \mid x \mid e \wedge e \mid \ldots$	Expression
$v ::= a \mid s[\mathtt{p}{:}r] \mid \text{true} \mid \ldots$	Values
$P ::=$	Processes
$\mid u\langle G\rangle$	Session initialisation
$\mid u[p](y).P \mid \mathtt{quit}\langle c\rangle$	Join, Quit
$\mid c!\langle p, l\langle\vec{p}\rangle\langle e\rangle\rangle$	Send
$\mid c?\langle p, \{l_i\langle\vec{p}_i\rangle(x_i).P_i\}_{i\in I}\rangle$	Receive
$\mid c\forall(x{:}r\setminus\vec{p}).\{P\}$	Poll
$\mid P \mid P \mid P;P$	Parallel, Sequential
$\mid \text{if } e \text{ then } P \text{ else } P$	Conditional
$\mid \mu X.P \mid X$	Recursion, Variable
$\mid \mathbf{0} \mid (\nu\, a{:}G)P$	Null, Restriction
$\mid (\nu\, s)P \mid s{:}h$	Session restriction, Buffer
$\mid a\langle s\rangle[\mathtt{R}]$	Registry
$\mathtt{R} ::= r_1{:}\mathtt{P}_1, \ldots, r_n{:}\mathtt{P}_n$	Role set
$h ::= \varepsilon \mid h\cdot(\mathtt{p}_0{:}r_0, \mathtt{p}_1{:}r_1, l\langle\vec{\mathtt{p}}\rangle\langle v\rangle)$	Buffer

Figure 1. Multirole session calculus

Syntax We give in Figure 1 the syntax of the processes of our session variant of the π-calculus.

A session is always initialised by a process of the form $u\langle G\rangle$ where G is a global type (formally defined in § 3). Session initialisation attributes a particular global interaction pattern G to a shared channel u. Once the session has been initialised on channel u, participants can join with $u[p](y).P$ where p designates a participant identity $\mathtt{p}$ or x associated with a particular role name r. Joining binds the variable y with the session channel that this particular participant can use when he plays the role r. Leaving the session is done by $\mathtt{quit}\langle c\rangle$, where c is the session channel corresponding to the participant and role.

The asynchronous emission $c!\langle p, l\langle\vec{p}\rangle\langle e\rangle\rangle$ allows to send to p a value e labelled by a constant l and participant names $\vec{p}$. The reception $c?\langle p, \{l_i\langle\vec{p}_i\rangle(x_i).P_i\}_{i\in I}\rangle$ expects from p a message with a label among the $\{l_i\}_{i\in I}$ with participants $\vec{p}_i$. The message payload is then received in variable x_i, which binds in P_i. Messages are always labelled. The list of participants $\vec{p}_i$ enriches the label l_i in order for the receiver to be able to disambiguate messages that have the same sender and label, but different continuations.

The polling operation $c\forall(x{:}r\setminus\vec{p}).\{P\}$ is the main way to interact with the participants that instantiate a given role: P is replicated for each participant x playing role r, with the exception of the participants mentioned in $\vec{p}$.

Parallel and sequential composition are standard, as are the conditional and recursion. The creation of a shared rendez-vous name is done by $(\nu\, a{:}G)P$. This fresh name can then be used as a reference for future instances of a session specified by G.

Once a session is running, our semantics uses some artifacts that are not directly accessible to the programmer. First, session instances are represented by session restriction $(\nu\, s)P$. Second, the message buffer $s{:}h$ stores the messages in transit for the session s. Last, the session registry $a\langle s\rangle[\mathtt{R}]$ records the current association between participants and roles in the running session s.

For simplicity, we write $c?\langle p, l\langle\vec{p}\rangle(x_i)\rangle.P$ if there is a unique branch. Similarly, we omit the empty list of participant ($\langle\varepsilon\rangle$) and unit payloads (e.g. $c!\langle p, l\rangle$). We also do not write $\mathbf{0}$, and roles r (e.g. in $x{:}r$) if they are clear from the context.

We use syntactic sugar for the special roles that cannot be multiply instantiated. Polling is done implicitly for these roles. Their participants' names ($\mathtt{p}$ or x) do not have to be explicitly mentioned: the mention of the role r is sufficient and unambiguous. In the Map/Reduce example from § 1, server is such a role.

We call a process which does not contain free variables and runtime syntax *initial*.

Semantics Figure 2 lists the reduction rules. The ⌊Init⌋ rule proceeds to a session initialisation by reducing $a\langle G\rangle$. It creates a fresh session channel s and two processes. First, the session registry $a\langle s\rangle[\mathtt{R}]$ is an entity that centralises the association between participants and roles in the particular instance s of a session. Initially, $\mathtt{R}$ does not record any participant for any of the roles of G. The second process is the session's message buffer $s{:}\varepsilon$, which is also initially empty.

The rule ⌊Join⌋ governs the registration of a participant to a running session. The participant asks with $a[\mathtt{p}:r](y).P$ to join the session advertised on channel a and specifies his identity $\mathtt{p}$ and which role r he wants to play. This information is added to the session registry $a\langle s\rangle[\mathtt{R}\cdot r:\mathtt{P}\uplus\{\mathtt{p}\}]$ and the session channel $s[\mathtt{p}{:}r]$ is communicated. The rule ⌊Quit⌋ manages the departure of a participant from a session: $\mathtt{quit}\langle s[\mathtt{p}{:}r]\rangle$ forces the deletion of $\mathtt{p}{:}r$ from the registry.

The rule ⌊Send⌋ describes asynchronous sending, which appends its labelled message to the buffer $s{:}h$. In rule ⌊Recv⌋, the reception takes from the session buffer the first message $(\mathtt{p}'{:}r', \mathtt{p}{:}r, l_k\langle\vec{\mathtt{p}}_k\rangle\langle v\rangle)$ that has a proper address, label and participant list and selects the matching continuation P_k. The rule ⌊Poll⌋ details the reduction of the polling process $s[\mathtt{p}{:}r']\forall(x{:}r\setminus\vec{\mathtt{p}}).\{P\}$. The set

$$
\begin{array}{rcll}
a\langle G\rangle & \rightarrow & (\nu\, s)(a\langle s\rangle[\mathtt{R}] \mid s:\varepsilon) & (\forall r_i \in G, \mathtt{R}(r_i)=\varnothing)\ \lfloor\textsc{Init}\rfloor\\
a[\mathtt{p}:r](y).P \mid a\langle s\rangle[\mathtt{R}\cdot r:\mathtt{P}] & \rightarrow & P\{s[\mathtt{p}:r]/y\} \mid a\langle s\rangle[\mathtt{R}\cdot r:\mathtt{P}\uplus\{\mathtt{p}\}] & \lfloor\textsc{Join}\rfloor\\
\mathtt{quit}\langle s[\mathtt{p}:r]\rangle \mid a\langle s\rangle[\mathtt{R}\cdot r:\mathtt{P}] & \rightarrow & a\langle s\rangle[\mathtt{R}\cdot r:\mathtt{P}\setminus\mathtt{p}] & \lfloor\textsc{Quit}\rfloor\\
s[\mathtt{p}:r]!\langle \mathtt{p}':r', l\langle\vec{\mathtt{p}}\rangle\langle v\rangle\rangle \mid a\langle s\rangle[\mathtt{R}] \mid s:h & \rightarrow & a\langle s\rangle[\mathtt{R}] \mid s:h\cdot(\mathtt{p}:r,\ \mathtt{p}':r',\ l\langle\vec{\mathtt{p}}\rangle\langle v\rangle) & (\mathtt{p}\in\mathtt{R}(r)\wedge\mathtt{p}'\in\mathtt{R}(r'))\ \lfloor\textsc{Send}\rfloor\\
s[\mathtt{p}:r]?\langle \mathtt{p}':r', \{l_i\langle\vec{\mathtt{p}}_i\rangle(x_i).P_i\}_{i\in I}\rangle \mid a\langle s\rangle[\mathtt{R}] \mid s:(\mathtt{p}':r',\ \mathtt{p}:r,\ l_k\langle\vec{\mathtt{p}}_k\rangle\langle v\rangle)\cdot h & \rightarrow & P_k\{v/x_k\} \mid a\langle s\rangle[\mathtt{R}] \mid s:h & (\mathtt{p}\in\mathtt{R}(r)\wedge k\in I)\ \lfloor\textsc{Recv}\rfloor\\
s[\mathtt{p}:r']\forall(x:r\setminus\vec{\mathtt{p}}).\{P\} \mid a\langle s\rangle[\mathtt{R}] & \rightarrow & P\{\mathtt{p}_1/x\} \mid \ldots \mid P\{\mathtt{p}_k/x\} \mid a\langle s\rangle[\mathtt{R}] & (\mathtt{R}(r)\setminus\vec{\mathtt{p}}=\{\mathtt{p}_1,..,\mathtt{p}_k\}\wedge\mathtt{p}\in\mathtt{R}(r'))\ \lfloor\textsc{Poll}\rfloor
\end{array}
$$

$$
\text{if true then } P \text{ else } Q \rightarrow P \quad \lfloor\textsc{IfT}\rfloor \qquad\qquad \text{if false then } P \text{ else } Q \rightarrow Q \quad \lfloor\textsc{IfF}\rfloor
$$

$$
P \mid Q \rightarrow P' \mid Q' \Longrightarrow \mathscr{E}[P] \mid Q \rightarrow \mathscr{E}[P'] \mid Q' \quad \lfloor\textsc{Par}\rfloor \qquad P \rightarrow P' \Longrightarrow \mathscr{E}[P] \rightarrow \mathscr{E}[P'] \quad \lfloor\textsc{Ctxt}\rfloor \qquad P\equiv P' \rightarrow Q' \equiv Q \Longrightarrow P \rightarrow Q \quad \lfloor\textsc{Cong}\rfloor
$$

$$
\mathscr{E} \ ::= \ [\_] \mid \mathscr{E} \mid P \mid \mathscr{E};P \mid (\nu\, a)\mathscr{E} \mid (\nu\, s)\mathscr{E} \mid s[\mathtt{p}:r]!\langle \mathtt{p}':r', l\langle\vec{\mathtt{p}}\rangle\langle\mathscr{E}\rangle\rangle \mid \text{if } \mathscr{E} \text{ then } P \text{ else } P \mid \mathscr{E}\wedge e \mid v\wedge\mathscr{E} \mid \ldots
$$

Figure 2. Reduction rules for the multirole session calculus

of participants $\{\mathtt{p}_1,...,\mathtt{p}_k\}$ that play role r (once the ones in $\vec{\mathtt{p}}$ are removed) is received from the session registry and the process P is forked accordingly, with x appropriately substituted. In $\lfloor\textsc{Par}\rfloor$, bound names in $\mathscr{E}$ and free names in Q are disjoint.

The reduction is defined modulo the standard structural equivalence $\equiv$. We just mention here the session garbage collection rule $(\nu\ a:G,s)(a\langle s\rangle[\mathtt{R}] \mid s:\varepsilon)\equiv\mathbf{0}$ (when $\forall r_i\in G, \mathtt{R}(r_i)=\varnothing$) and the permutation rule $s:(q,p,l\langle\vec{p_1}\rangle\langle v\rangle)\cdot(q',p',l'\langle\vec{p_2}\rangle\langle v'\rangle)\cdot h \equiv s:(q',p',l'\langle\vec{p_2}\rangle\langle v'\rangle)\cdot(q,p,l\langle\vec{p_1}\rangle\langle v\rangle)\cdot h$ which allows to put forward in the session buffers the messages that have different senders, recipients, labels or participants lists. Others are standard.

Reduction example We take the process $P_{\text{client}}(z)$ from the peer-to-peer chat mentioned in the introduction (§ 1(2)). Figure 3 gives reduction steps of a situation where we have two client processes $P_{\text{client}}(\mathtt{p}_1)$ and $P_{\text{client}}(\mathtt{p}_2)$ that want to interact on session channel a. We call $Q(z)$ the process $\mu X.(s[z]\forall(y:\text{client}\setminus z).\{s[z]!\langle y, \mathsf{Msg}\langle m\rangle\rangle\} \mid s[z]\forall(x:\text{client}\setminus z).\{s[z]?\langle x, \mathsf{Msg}(w)\rangle\});X$ and abbreviate the registry $a\langle s\rangle[\text{client}:\{\mathtt{p}_1,\mathtt{p}_2\}]$ by R.

$$
\begin{array}{ll}
 & (\nu\, a)(a\langle \mathrm{G}\rangle \mid P(\mathtt{p}_1) \mid P(\mathtt{p}_2))\\
\lfloor\textsc{Init}\rfloor & \rightarrow (\nu\, a)((\nu\, s)(a\langle s\rangle[\text{client}:\varnothing] \mid s:\varepsilon) \mid P(\mathtt{p}_1) \mid P(\mathtt{p}_2)))\\
\lfloor\textsc{Join}\rfloor & \rightarrow (\nu\, a,s)(a\langle s\rangle[\text{client}:\{\mathtt{p}_1\}] \mid s:\varepsilon \mid Q(\mathtt{p}_1) \mid P(\mathtt{p}_2))\\
\lfloor\textsc{Join}\rfloor & \rightarrow (\nu\, a,s)(a\langle s\rangle[\text{client}:\{\mathtt{p}_1,\mathtt{p}_2\}] \mid s:\varepsilon \mid Q(\mathtt{p}_1) \mid Q(\mathtt{p}_2))\\
\lfloor\textsc{Poll}\rfloor & \rightarrow (\nu\, a,s)(R \mid s:\varepsilon \mid Q(\mathtt{p}_2) \mid (s[\mathtt{p}_1]!\langle \mathtt{p}_2, \mathsf{Msg}\langle m\rangle\rangle \mid\\
 & \qquad s[\mathtt{p}_1]\forall(x:\text{client}\setminus\mathtt{p}_1).\{s[\mathtt{p}_1]?\langle x, \mathsf{Msg}(w)\rangle\});Q(\mathtt{p}_1))\\
\lfloor\textsc{Send}\rfloor & \rightarrow (\nu\, a,s)(R \mid s:(\mathtt{p}_1,\mathtt{p}_2,\mathsf{Msg}\langle m\rangle) \mid Q(\mathtt{p}_2) \mid\\
 & \qquad (s[\mathtt{p}_1]\forall(x:\text{client}\setminus\mathtt{p}_1).\{s[\mathtt{p}_1]?\langle x, \mathsf{Msg}(w)\rangle\});Q(\mathtt{p}_1))\\
\lfloor\textsc{Poll}\rfloor & \rightarrow (\nu\, a,s)(R \mid s:(\mathtt{p}_1,\mathtt{p}_2,\mathsf{Msg}\langle m\rangle)) \mid Q(\mathtt{p}_2) \mid\\
 & \qquad s[\mathtt{p}_1]?\langle \mathtt{p}_2, \mathsf{Msg}(w)\rangle;Q(\mathtt{p}_1))\\
\lfloor\textsc{Poll}\rfloor & \rightarrow (\nu\, a,s)(R \mid s:(\mathtt{p}_1,\mathtt{p}_2,\mathsf{Msg}\langle m\rangle) \mid s[\mathtt{p}_1]?\langle \mathtt{p}_2, \mathsf{Msg}(w)\rangle;Q(\mathtt{p}_1) \mid\\
 & \qquad (s[\mathtt{p}_2]!\langle \mathtt{p}_1, \mathsf{Msg}\langle m\rangle\rangle \mid\\
 & \qquad\quad s[\mathtt{p}_2]\forall(x:\text{client}\setminus\mathtt{p}_2).\{s[\mathtt{p}_2]?\langle x, \mathsf{Msg}(w)\rangle\});Q(\mathtt{p}_2))\\
\lfloor\textsc{Send}\rfloor & \rightarrow (\nu\, a,s)(R \mid s:(\mathtt{p}_1,\mathtt{p}_2,\mathsf{Msg}\langle m\rangle)\cdot(\mathtt{p}_2,\mathtt{p}_1,\mathsf{Msg}\langle m\rangle) \mid\\
 & \qquad s[\mathtt{p}_1]?\langle \mathtt{p}_2, \mathsf{Msg}(w)\rangle;Q(\mathtt{p}_1) \mid\\
 & \qquad\quad s[\mathtt{p}_2]\forall(x:\text{client}\setminus\mathtt{p}_2).\{s[\mathtt{p}_2]?\langle x, \mathsf{Msg}(w)\rangle\};Q(\mathtt{p}_2))\\
\lfloor\textsc{Poll}\rfloor & \rightarrow (\nu\, a,s)(R \mid s:(\mathtt{p}_1,\mathtt{p}_2,\mathsf{Msg}\langle m\rangle)\cdot(\mathtt{p}_2,\mathtt{p}_1,\mathsf{Msg}\langle m\rangle) \mid\\
 & \qquad s[\mathtt{p}_1]?\langle \mathtt{p}_2, \mathsf{Msg}(w)\rangle;Q(\mathtt{p}_1) \mid s[\mathtt{p}_2]?\langle \mathtt{p}_1, \mathsf{Msg}(w)\rangle;Q(\mathtt{p}_2))\\
\lfloor\textsc{Recv}\rfloor & \rightarrow (\nu\, a,s)(R \mid s:(\mathtt{p}_2,\mathtt{p}_1,\mathsf{Msg}\langle m\rangle) \mid\\
 & \qquad s[\mathtt{p}_1]?\langle \mathtt{p}_2, \mathsf{Msg}(w)\rangle;Q(\mathtt{p}_1) \mid Q(\mathtt{p}_2))\\
\lfloor\textsc{Recv}\rfloor & \rightarrow (\nu\, a,s)(R \mid s:\varepsilon \mid Q(\mathtt{p}_1) \mid Q(\mathtt{p}_2))
\end{array}
$$

Figure 3. Reduction for the peer-to-peer chat example

3. Multirole session types

In this section, we present the multirole session types which specify the communication patterns that are to be enforced. We start with the definition of global and local types and follow with projection and well-formedness properties.

$$
\begin{array}{rll}
G ::= & & \text{Global types}\\
 & \mid\ p\rightarrow p'\{l_i\langle\vec{p}_i\rangle\langle U_i\rangle.G_i\}_{i\in I} & \quad\text{Labelled messages}\\
 & \mid\ \forall x:r\setminus\vec{p}.G & \quad\text{Universal quantification}\\
 & \mid\ G \mid G' \ \mid\ G;G' & \quad\text{Parallel, Sequential}\\
 & \mid\ \mu\mathbf{x}.G \ \mid\ \mathbf{x} & \quad\text{Recursion, variable}\\
 & \mid\ \varepsilon \ \mid\ \text{end} & \quad\text{Inaction, End}\\
T ::= & & \text{Local types}\\
 & \mid\ !\langle p, \{l_i\langle\vec{p}_i\rangle\langle U_i\rangle.T_i\}_{i\in I}\rangle & \quad\text{Selection}\\
 & \mid\ ?\langle p, \{l_i\langle\vec{p}_i\rangle\langle U_i\rangle.T_i\}_{i\in I}\rangle & \quad\text{Branching}\\
 & \mid\ \forall x:r\setminus\vec{p}.T & \quad\text{Universal quantification}\\
 & \mid\ T \mid T' \ \mid\ T;T' & \quad\text{Parallel, Sequential}\\
 & \mid\ \mu\mathbf{x}.G \ \mid\ \mathbf{x} \ \mid\ \varepsilon \ \mid\ \text{end} & \quad\text{Recursion, inaction, end}\\
U ::= & S \ \mid\ T & \text{Message types}\\
S ::= & \langle G\rangle \ \mid\ \text{bool} \ \mid\ \text{unit} \ \mid\ \ldots & \text{Sorts}
\end{array}
$$

Figure 4. Global and local types

3.1 Global and local types

Global types G describe role-based global scenarios between multiple participants as a type signature. When a participant agrees with a global type G, his behaviour is defined by a local protocol (called *local type* T_i) that is generated by the projection of G to the role he wants to play. If each of the local programs $P_1,...,P_n$ can be type-checked against the corresponding projected local types $T_1,..,T_n$, then they are automatically guaranteed to interact properly, following the intended scenario. The grammar of global types $(G,G',...)$ and local types $(T,T',...)$ is given in figure 4. There are four key extensions from the standard multiparty session types [4]: (1) association of each participant to a role; (2) universal quantifiers to bind participants identities; (3) parallel compositions for local types; and (4) labels that can be extended by lists of participants.

In the global types $(G,G',...)$, a global interaction can be a labelled message exchange $(p\rightarrow p'\{l_i\langle\vec{p}_i\rangle\langle U_i\rangle.G_i\}_{i\in I})$, where p and p' denote the sending and receiving participants with roles (recall that p denotes either $\mathtt{p}:r$ or $x:r$), $\vec{p}_i$ is a list of participants, U_i is the payload type of the message and G_i the interaction that follows the choice of label l_i (I is a finite set of integers). Value types S include shared channel types $\langle G\rangle$ or base types (bool, unit, ...). Message types U are either value types S or local types T (which correspond to the behaviour of one of the session participants) for delegation.

Parallel composition is written as $G \mid G'$, and $G;G'$ denotes sequential composition. $\mu\mathbf{x}.G$ is a recursive type where type variable $\mathbf{x}$ is guarded in the standard way (they only appear under some prefix). Inaction ε marks the absence of communication, while end denotes the end of the session for all roles. The *universal quantification* is written $\forall x:r\setminus\vec{p}.G$ where the participants of role r bind free occurrences x in G. It corresponds to the operational semantics of $s[\mathrm{p}:r']\forall(x:r\setminus\vec{p}).\{P\}$ (see § 2), i.e. a parallel composition $G\{\mathrm{p}_1/x\} \mid ... \mid G\{\mathrm{p}_k/x\}$ for some list of participants $\{\mathrm{p}_1,...,\mathrm{p}_k\}$ playing the role r (which is decided at runtime), from which the list of participants $\vec{p}$ has been excluded.

In local types T, selection expresses the transmission to p of a label l_i taken from a set $\{l_i\}_{i\in I}$ with a list of participants $\vec{p}_i$ and a message type U_i, followed by T_i. Branching is its dual counterpart. The other local types are similar to their global versions.

We consider global and local types modulo the following equalities. For local types, we define: $(T \mid \varepsilon) = (\varepsilon \mid T) = (\varepsilon;T) = T$, $(T \mid \mathrm{end}) = (\mathrm{end} \mid T) = T$, $(T \mid T');\mathrm{end} = (T;\mathrm{end} \mid T';\mathrm{end})$ and $!\langle p,\{l_i\langle\vec{p}_i\rangle\langle U_i\rangle.T_i\}_{i\in I}\rangle;\mathrm{end} = !\langle p,\{l_i\langle\vec{p}_i\rangle\langle U_i\rangle.T_i;\mathrm{end}\}_{i\in I}\rangle$. Similar equalities are applied to global types. We also use similar abbreviations for global and local types as the ones for processes (mentioned in § 2). In particular, we write $p\to q\, l\langle\vec{p}'\rangle\langle U\rangle;G$ or $!\langle p,l\langle\vec{q}\rangle\langle U\rangle\rangle;T$ for a single branching, and $p\to q\langle l\rangle$ if the list of participant is empty and the payload type is unit. end is also often eluded.

EXAMPLE 3.1 (Global types). To give some additional clarity to the semantics of global session types, we give here several variations on an additional example. We imagine a chat protocol (similar in spirit to the peer-to-peer chat session) where the clients must interact through a single server. We have thus two roles: the unique server and the multiple clients. Each client's behaviour is to send a message to the server who will then broadcast it to all the others. In the following picture, we only represent the Msg that one client sends to the server and that is followed by the server broadcasting its content (in message Spread) to all the other clients.

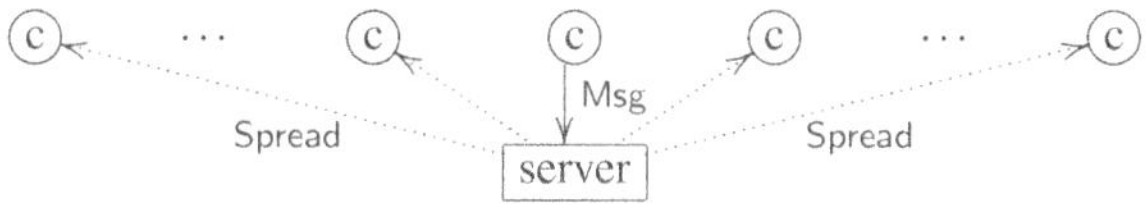

The global type for this session relies on the sequentiality that links each Msg to its following Spread. We write it as:

$$G_1 = \mu\mathbf{x}.\forall x{:}\mathrm{client}.\{x\to\mathrm{server}\langle\mathsf{Msg}\rangle.\forall y{:}\mathrm{client}\setminus x.\{\mathrm{server}\to y\langle\mathsf{Spread}\rangle\}\};\mathbf{x}$$

It starts with a quantification over all clients x. Upon reception by the server of a message from x, the global type specifies that Spread should be sent to all the other clients: $\forall y:\mathrm{client}\setminus x.\mathrm{server}\to y\langle\mathsf{Spread}\rangle$.

An alternate chat server could be one where the server collects all incoming messages and then sends a digest to all clients. In that case, the global type would be written:

$$G_2 = \mu\mathbf{x}.\forall x{:}\mathrm{client}.\{x\to\mathrm{server}\langle\mathsf{Msg}\rangle\};\forall y{:}\mathrm{client}.\{\mathrm{server}\to y\langle\mathsf{Spread}\rangle\};\mathbf{x}$$

The central synchronisation between the two quantified types is important in our model. The semantics is radically different if this synchronisation is removed.

$$G_3 = \mu\mathbf{x}.\forall x{:}\mathrm{client}.\{x\to\mathrm{server}\langle\mathsf{Msg}\rangle;\mathrm{server}\to x\langle\mathsf{Spread}\rangle\};\mathbf{x}$$

The global type G_3 means that, independently for each client, the server first collects a message Msg and then immediately sends back to this same client a message Spread.

3.2 Projection from multirole global types to local types

We now define the projection operation, which, for any participant z playing a role r in a session G, computes the local type it has to conform to. We say *an end-point projection of G onto $z:r$*, written $G\upharpoonright z:r$, is the local type that the participant z should respect to play the role r in session G.

As mentioned in § 1, the main difficulty lies in the projection of the quantifiers. Let us first consider informally the global type $\forall x:r.G$. This global type has the same semantics as $G\{\mathrm{p}_1/x\} \mid ... \mid G\{\mathrm{p}_k/x\}$ for some $\mathrm{p}_1,...,\mathrm{p}_k$ playing the role r. If we write the projection of $\forall x:r.G$ for a participant p_i playing role r (written as $\forall x:r.G\upharpoonright \mathrm{p}_i:r$), we can single out the instance corresponding to p_i:

$$(G\{\mathrm{p}_1/x\}\upharpoonright \mathrm{p}_i:r) \mid ... \mid (G\{\mathrm{p}_k/x\}\upharpoonright \mathrm{p}_i:r) = (G\{\mathrm{p}_i/x\}\upharpoonright \mathrm{p}_i:r) \mid \forall x:r\setminus \mathrm{p}_i.(G\upharpoonright \mathrm{p}_i:r)$$

Based on this intuition behind the projection of quantifiers, we give the projection definition in figure 5. Projection is role-based, i.e. for each role r of a session G, a local type $T = G\upharpoonright p$ is computed with $p = z:r$. The case $p = \mathrm{p}:r$ is defined by replacing z by p.

$$p\to p'\{l_i\langle\vec{p}_i\rangle\langle U_i\rangle:G_i\}_{i\in I}\upharpoonright p = !\langle p',\{l_i\langle\vec{p}_i\rangle\langle U_i\rangle.G_i\upharpoonright p\}_{i\in I}\rangle$$
$$p'\to p\{l_i\langle\vec{p}_i\rangle\langle U_i\rangle:G_i\}_{i\in I}\upharpoonright p = ?\langle p',\{l_i\langle\vec{p}_i\rangle\langle U_i\rangle.G_i\upharpoonright p\}_{i\in I}\rangle$$
$$p\to p\{l_i\langle\vec{p}_i\rangle\langle U_i\rangle:G_i\}_{i\in I}\upharpoonright p = !\langle p,\{l_i\langle\vec{p}_i\rangle\langle U_i\rangle.?\langle p,l_i\langle\vec{p}_i\rangle\langle U_i\rangle.G_i\upharpoonright p\rangle\}_{i\in I}\rangle$$
$$p'\to p''\{l_i\langle\vec{p}_i\rangle\langle U_i\rangle.G_i\}_{i\in I}\upharpoonright p = \textstyle\bigsqcup_{i\in I}\{G_i\upharpoonright p\}$$
$$(\forall x:r\setminus\vec{p}.G)\upharpoonright z:r = G\{z/x\}\upharpoonright z:r \mid \forall x:r\setminus z::\vec{p}.(G\upharpoonright z:r) \quad (z\notin\vec{p})$$
$$(\forall x:r\setminus\vec{p}.G)\upharpoonright p = \forall x:r\setminus\vec{p}.(G\upharpoonright p) \qquad \text{(otherwise)}$$
$$(G \mid G)\upharpoonright p = (G\upharpoonright p \mid G\upharpoonright p) \quad (G;G)\upharpoonright p = (G\upharpoonright p;G\upharpoonright p)$$
$$\mu\mathbf{x}.G\upharpoonright p = \mu\mathbf{x}.(G\upharpoonright p) \quad \mathbf{x}\upharpoonright p = \mathbf{x} \qquad \varepsilon\upharpoonright p = \varepsilon \quad \mathrm{end}\upharpoonright p = \mathrm{end}$$

Figure 5. Projection

The projection of communication leads to a case analysis: if the participant projected to (i.e. p) is the sender, then the projection is a selection sent to p'; if p is the receiver then the projection is an input from p'; if participant p is both sender and receiver then the projection is an output followed by an input; otherwise, the communication is not observed locally and is skipped. The operator $\sqcup$ then merges the different remote branches (this operation was introduced in [35, § 4]). Roughly speaking, it makes sure that the locally observable behaviours are either independent of the remotely chosen branch or can be properly identified through their labels. It is defined by $T\sqcup T = T$ and the following equality:

$$?\langle p,\{l_i\langle\vec{p}_i\rangle\langle U_i\rangle.T_i\}_{i\in I}\rangle \sqcup ?\langle p,\{l_j\langle\vec{p}_j'\rangle\langle U_j'\rangle.T_j'\}_{j\in J}\rangle$$
$$= ?\langle p,\{l_k\langle\vec{p}_k\rangle\langle U_k\rangle.T_k\}_{k\in I\setminus J} \cup \{l_k\langle\vec{p}_k'\rangle\langle U_k'\rangle.T_k\}_{k\in J\setminus I}$$
$$\cup\{l_k\langle\vec{p}_k\rangle\langle U_k\rangle.T_k\sqcup T_k'\}_{k\in I\cap J}\rangle \quad \text{when } \forall k\in I\cap J, \vec{p}_k = \vec{p}_k' \wedge U_k = U_k'$$

Note that the merging operation may not return a result if the session uses labels ambiguously. An example can be found in § 3.3.

Finally, the most critical rules define the projection of a quantified global type $(\forall x:r\setminus\vec{p}.G)\upharpoonright p$. The first rule applies only when the quantification acts on the same role r as the projection, and when p is not in the exclusion list $\vec{p}$. In that case, as explained above, the local type is the parallel composition of G where $x:r$ is substituted by p, projected for p, and a quantification excluding p. The second rule sees the projection acting homomorphically through the quantification on a different role, or if p is in $\vec{p}$. Other rules are homomorphic as well. We say that G is *projectable* if G can be projected (i.e. projection gives a result) for each of its roles.

EXAMPLE 3.2 (Projection). **(1) Peer-to-peer chat example.** We give an example of projection for the peer-to-peer chat session from § 1, which features nested quantifiers. The local type $T(z{:}\mathrm{client})$ is calculated in the following way (p is $z{:}\mathrm{client}$):

$$(\mu\mathbf{x}.(\forall x{:}\mathrm{client}.\forall y{:}\mathrm{client}\setminus x.x\to y\,\mathsf{Msg}\langle\mathrm{string}\rangle);\mathbf{x})\upharpoonright z{:}\mathrm{client}$$
$$= \mu\mathbf{x}.((\forall x{:}\mathrm{client}.\forall y{:}\mathrm{client}\setminus x.x\to y\,\mathsf{Msg}\langle\mathrm{string}\rangle)\upharpoonright z{:}\mathrm{client});\mathbf{x}$$
$$= \mu\mathbf{x}.((\forall y{:}\mathrm{client}\setminus z.z\to y\,\mathsf{Msg}\langle\mathrm{string}\rangle)\upharpoonright z{:}\mathrm{client} \mid$$
$$\forall x{:}\mathrm{client}\setminus z.(\forall y{:}\mathrm{client}\setminus x.x\to y\,\mathsf{Msg}\langle\mathrm{string}\rangle)\upharpoonright z{:}\mathrm{client});\mathbf{x}$$
$$= \mu\mathbf{x}.(\forall y{:}\mathrm{client}\setminus z.(z\to y\,\mathsf{Msg}\langle\mathrm{string}\rangle)\upharpoonright z{:}\mathrm{client} \mid$$
$$\forall x{:}\mathrm{client}\setminus z.((x\to z\,\mathsf{Msg}\langle\mathrm{string}\rangle)\upharpoonright z{:}\mathrm{client} \mid$$
$$\forall y{:}\mathrm{client}\setminus z.(x\to y\,\mathsf{Msg}\langle\mathrm{string}\rangle)\upharpoonright z{:}\mathrm{client}));\mathbf{x}$$
$$= \mu\mathbf{x}.(\forall y{:}\mathrm{client}\setminus z.!\langle y,\mathsf{Msg}\langle\mathrm{string}\rangle\rangle \mid$$
$$\forall x{:}\mathrm{client}\setminus z.(?\langle x,\mathsf{Msg}\langle\mathrm{string}\rangle\rangle \mid \forall y{:}\mathrm{client}\setminus z.\varepsilon));\mathbf{x}$$
$$\equiv \mu\mathbf{x}.(\forall y{:}\mathrm{client}\setminus z.!\langle y,\mathsf{Msg}\langle\mathrm{string}\rangle\rangle \mid \forall x{:}\mathrm{client}\setminus z.?\langle x,\mathsf{Msg}\langle\mathrm{string}\rangle\rangle);\mathbf{x}$$

(2) Chat-server from example 3.1. We give the projections for each of the three global types. The projection of G_1 for the server and client roles gives:

$$T_1(z{:}\mathrm{server}) = \mu\mathbf{x}.(\forall x{:}\mathrm{client}.\{?\langle x{:}\mathrm{client},\mathsf{Msg}\rangle;$$
$$\forall y{:}\mathrm{client}\setminus x.!\langle y{:}\mathrm{client},\mathsf{Spread}\rangle\});\mathbf{x}$$
$$T_1(z{:}\mathrm{client}) = \mu\mathbf{x}.(!\langle\mathrm{server},\mathsf{Msg}\rangle \mid \forall x{:}\mathrm{client}\setminus z.\{?\langle\mathrm{server},\mathsf{Spread}\rangle\});\mathbf{x}$$

Note that the sequentiality between Msg and Spread is rightly present in the server's local type. The projection of G_2 results in:

$$T_2(z\!:\!\text{server}) = \mu\mathbf{x}.\ \forall x\!:\!\text{client}.\{?\langle x\!:\!\text{client}, \text{Msg}\rangle\};\ \forall y\!:\!\text{client}.\{!\langle y\!:\!\text{client}, \text{Spread}\rangle\};\mathbf{x}$$

$$T_2(z\!:\!\text{client}) = \mu\mathbf{x}.(!\langle\text{server}, \text{Msg}\rangle \mid \forall x\!:\!\text{client} \setminus z.\{?\langle\text{server}, \text{Spread}\rangle\});\mathbf{x}$$

We note that the server's local type represents a behaviour which first collects all incoming messages and then sends a digest to all clients. On the other hand, the client behaviour is the same as in session G_1. The projection of G_3 is given as:

$$T_3(z\!:\!\text{server}) = \mu\mathbf{x}.\forall x\!:\!\text{client}.\{?\langle x\!:\!\text{client}, \text{Msg}\rangle; !\langle y\!:\!\text{client}, \text{Spread}\rangle\};\mathbf{x}$$

$$T_3(z\!:\!\text{client}) = \mu\mathbf{x}.!\langle\text{server}, \text{Msg}\rangle; ?\langle\text{server}, \text{Spread}\rangle;\mathbf{x}$$

In the above types, for each client, the server first collects a message Msg and then immediately sends back a message Spread to this client.

3.3 Well-formedness

For type-checking to work, global types need to follow a set of rules that will ensure a reliable and unambiguous session behaviour.

Syntax correctness We apply kinding rules [3] to construct syntactically correct types. A first point that is verified is that every participant variable x is bound by a quantifier and that it is consistently used with the same role. Then, we check that recursion variables do not appear under quantification or explicit parallel composition. Formally, if a global type is of the form $\forall x\!:\!r \setminus \vec{p}.G$ or $G \mid G'$, then G and G' are required not to contain any free recursion variables. This condition prevents any race condition between different iterations of the same loop. We give a few examples of correct and incorrect global session types.

× $G_1 = \mu\mathbf{x}.(\text{server}\to\text{client}\langle\text{Msg}\rangle;\mathbf{x} \mid \text{server}\to\text{broker}\langle\text{Notify}\rangle;\mathbf{x})$
√ $G_2 = \mu\mathbf{x}.(\text{server}\to\text{client}\langle\text{Msg}\rangle \mid \text{server}\to\text{broker}\langle\text{Notify}\rangle);\mathbf{x}$
√ $G_3 = \mu\mathbf{x}.\text{server}\to\text{client}\langle\text{Msg}\rangle;\mathbf{x} \mid \mu\mathbf{y}.\text{server}\to\text{broker}\langle\text{Notify}\rangle;\mathbf{y}$

Other checks include the verification that the position of end is indeed correct. For example, $(G;\text{end});(G';\text{end})$ is not well-formed.

Projectability As seen in § 3.2, projection does not always return a local type, due to the verification made when branches are merged. The merging operation verifies that each branch is properly labelled and that no local process can be confused about which branch to follow. We thus require that any global session type G should be projectable.

× $G_4 = \text{broker}\to\text{buyer}\{\text{Notify}.\text{buyer}\to\text{seller}\langle\text{Msg}\rangle;\text{seller}\to\text{buyer}\langle\text{Pay}\rangle, \text{Quit}.\text{buyer}\to\text{seller}\langle\text{Msg}\rangle\}$
√ $G_5 = \text{broker}\to\text{buyer}\{\text{Notify}.\text{buyer}\to\text{seller}\langle\text{Price}\rangle;\text{seller}\to\text{buyer}\langle\text{Pay}\rangle, \text{Quit}.\text{buyer}\to\text{seller}\langle\text{Stop}\rangle\}$

The seller in G_4 cannot distinguish the two Msg sent by the buyer. In G_5, the seller knows which branch has been taken by the broker since the upper one is labelled by Price and the lower one by Stop.

Linearity The concept of linearity is introduced in [19] but, in our case, we use a relaxed version to allow flexible parallel compositions (explicit or through quantification) and branching. It makes sure that messages are always labelled in a way that prevents communication mix-ups.

To verify the linearity of a global type G, we first need to transform the quantifiers into explicit parallel compositions. To this effect, we associate to each role r of G a (big enough) list of participant names $\mathtt{p}_0, \mathtt{p}_1, \ldots$. Then, we compute for each role r the local type $T_r = G \upharpoonright \mathtt{p}_0 : r$ and homomorphically replace every subterm of T_r of the form[3] $\forall x\!:\!r \setminus \vec{p}.T_0$ by $T_0\{\mathtt{p}_i/x\} \mid T_0\{\mathtt{p}_j/x\}$ with $\mathtt{p}_i, \mathtt{p}_j$ the first two participant names for role r that do not appear in $\vec{p}$. This transformation is called dequantification.

[3] We leave the implicit quantifiers of the singly instantiated roles untouched.

DEFINITION 3.3 (Linearity). We say that a well-labelled global type G is *linear* if, for all roles r of G, the dequantification T_r' of $T_r = G \upharpoonright \mathtt{p}_0 : r$ satisfies: If $?\langle\mathtt{p}, \{l_i\langle\vec{p}_i\rangle\langle U_i\rangle.T_i\}_{i\in I}\rangle$ and $?\langle\mathtt{p}, \{l_j'\langle\vec{p}_j'\rangle\langle U_j'\rangle.T_j'\}_{j\in J}\rangle$ are both subterms of T_r', then, $\forall i,j \in I\times J$, $l_i = l_j' \Rightarrow (\{l_i\}_{i\in I} = \{l_j'\}_{j\in J} \wedge U_i = U_j' \wedge (\vec{p}_i = \vec{p}_j' \Rightarrow T_i = T_j'))$.

This definition checks that if two receptions exist in the local type of a role r, then either they share no label (and thus cannot be confused), or they share exactly the same set of message labels, with identical payload types, in which case they should only differ by the distinguishing lists of participants: these lists allow to reliably target different continuation types even when concurrent threads expect messages with the same labels.

× $G_6 = \forall x\!:\!\text{buyer}.\forall y\!:\!\text{seller}.\{\text{broker}\to x\langle\text{Msg}\rangle.x\to y\langle\text{Notify}\rangle\}$
√ $G_7 = \forall x\!:\!\text{buyer}.\forall y\!:\!\text{seller}.\{\text{broker}\to x\langle\text{Msg}\langle y\rangle\rangle.x\to y\langle\text{Notify}\rangle\}$

The dequantification of $G_6 \upharpoonright \mathtt{p}_0 : \text{seller}$ is (buyers are $\mathtt{p}_0, \mathtt{p}_1$, sellers are $\mathtt{q}_0, \mathtt{q}_1$):

$$?\langle\text{broker}, \langle\text{Msg}\rangle.!\langle\mathtt{q}_0, \langle\text{Notify}\rangle\rangle\rangle \mid ?\langle\text{broker}, \langle\text{Msg}\rangle.!\langle\mathtt{q}_1, \langle\text{Notify}\rangle\rangle\rangle$$

These two concurrent threads have identical guards but different continuations. The dequantification of $G_7 \upharpoonright \mathtt{p}_0 : \text{seller}$ is:

$$?\langle\text{broker}, \langle\text{Msg}\langle\mathtt{q}_0\rangle\rangle.!\langle\mathtt{q}_0, \langle\text{Notify}\rangle\rangle\rangle \mid ?\langle\text{broker}, \langle\text{Msg}\langle\mathtt{q}_1\rangle\rangle.!\langle\mathtt{q}_1, \langle\text{Notify}\rangle\rangle\rangle$$

In that case, the participant identity $\langle y\rangle$ is added to the label Msg and is able to disambiguate the concurrent receptions.

Well-formedness We now give the formal version of the well-formedness condition. Note that it is decidable.

DEFINITION 3.4 (Well-formed global types). *We say that a global type G is* well-formed *if the following conditions hold:*

1. *(Syntactically correct) G is syntactically correct [3].*
2. *(Projectability) $G \upharpoonright z\!:\!r$ is defined for each role r of G.*
3. *(Linearity) G is linear (Definition 3.3).*

EXAMPLE 3.5 (Well-formedness). We test the well-formedness of the auction example from § 1 (the numbers below correspond to the well-formedness conditions). Recall the global type G:

$$G = \forall x\!:\!\text{buyer}.\forall y\!:\!\text{seller}.\text{broker}\to x\{\text{Match}\langle y\rangle.x\to y\langle\text{Notify}\rangle.y\to x\langle\text{Price}\rangle.x\to y\langle\text{Order}\rangle, \text{Quit}\langle y\rangle.\ x\to y\ \langle\text{Stop}\rangle\};\text{end}$$

The syntax correctness (1) is checked easily: there is no recursion, participant variables are bound and used for a unique role, and end is well-positioned. G is projectable (2) since the two branches (Match, Quit) do not forget to use different labels (Notify, Stop) to propagate to the seller y the choice that the broker makes. Concerning linearity (3), the potential problem is in the first message: when a buyer x receives a message Match or Quit from the broker, x should know which parallel instance it concerns among the ones the quantification $\forall y\!:\!\text{seller}$ creates. We only give below the verification details for the buyer. With buyers $\mathtt{p}_0, \mathtt{p}_1$ and sellers $\mathtt{q}_0, \mathtt{q}_1$, the result of the dequantification of $G \upharpoonright \mathtt{p}_0 : \text{buyer}$ is:

$$\begin{aligned}&?\langle\text{broker}, \{\text{Match}\langle\mathtt{q}_0\rangle.!\langle\mathtt{q}_0, \langle\text{Notify}\rangle.?\langle\mathtt{q}_0, \langle\text{Price}\rangle.!\langle\mathtt{q}_0, \langle\text{Order}\rangle\rangle\rangle\rangle, \text{Quit}\langle\mathtt{q}_0\rangle.!\langle\mathtt{q}_0, \langle\text{Stop}\rangle\rangle\}\rangle\\ \mid\ &?\langle\text{broker}, \{\text{Match}\langle\mathtt{q}_1\rangle.!\langle\mathtt{q}_1, \langle\text{Notify}\rangle.?\langle\mathtt{q}_1, \langle\text{Price}\rangle.!\langle\mathtt{q}_1, \langle\text{Order}\rangle\rangle\rangle\rangle, \text{Quit}\langle\mathtt{q}_1\rangle.!\langle\mathtt{q}_1, \langle\text{Stop}\rangle\rangle\}\rangle\end{aligned}$$

For $G \upharpoonright \mathtt{q}_0 : \text{seller}$, the dequantification result gives:

$$?\langle\mathtt{p}_0, \{\text{Notify}.!\langle\mathtt{p}_0, \langle\text{Price}\rangle.?\langle\mathtt{p}_0, \langle\text{Order}\rangle\rangle\rangle, \text{Stop}\}\rangle \mid ?\langle\mathtt{p}_1, \{\text{Notify}.!\langle\mathtt{p}_1, \langle\text{Price}\rangle.?\langle\mathtt{p}_1, \langle\text{Order}\rangle\rangle\rangle, \text{Stop}\}\rangle$$

We check linearity by looking at the different occurrences of the same label (for example Match in $G \upharpoonright \mathtt{p}_0 : \text{buyer}$) being received from the same participant (e.g. broker): we verify that the lists of participant identities are different whenever the continuations are different. Linearity is thus only achieved here thanks to the communication of the disambiguating y in messages Match and Quit, as it can be seen in the buyer's case. The seller's and broker's (here omitted) linearity verifications are trivial.

4. Multirole session typing system

This section introduces the typing system and proves subject reduction (Theorem 4.2) and type safety (Corollary 4.3). There are three main differences with previous session systems. First, a participant x can appear free in environments, types and processes, and is necessarily bound by universal quantifiers. Second, previous systems did not allow any parallel composition of types which use common channels. Since the projection of a universal quantified type generates parallel compositions, we relax this restriction. Thanks to the well-formedness of the global types (Definition 3.4), the typing system for initial processes is kept simple. Third, our runtime typing system needs to track parallel behaviours by forks and joins.

4.1 Typing systems

Environments We start with the grammar of environments.

$$\Gamma ::= \emptyset \mid \Gamma, u:S \mid \Gamma, y:r \mid \Gamma, X:\Delta \qquad \Delta ::= \emptyset \mid \Delta, c:T$$

Γ is the *standard environment* which associates variables to sort types or roles, shared names to global types, and process variables to session types. Δ is the *session environment* which associates channels to session types. We write $\Gamma, u:S$ only if $u \notin dom(\Gamma)$. Similarly for other variables. We define the sequential ; and parallel $\circ$ compositions for types as follows:

$$\begin{aligned}\Delta \sharp \Delta' = \;& \Delta \backslash dom(\Delta') \cup \Delta' \backslash dom(\Delta) \\ & \cup \{c : \Delta(c) \sharp \Delta'(c) \mid c \in dom(\Delta) \cap dom(\Delta')\}\end{aligned}$$

where $\sharp \in \{\circ, ;\}$ and $\Delta(c) \sharp \Delta'(c)$ is syntactically well-formed.

Typing systems for initial processes We detail the typing system for expressions and processes in figure 6. The judgement for expression typing is given as $\Gamma \vdash e : S$. The judgement for process typing is given as $\Gamma \vdash P \triangleright \Delta$ which can be read as: "under the environment Γ, process P has session type Δ".

Rules [BOOL,OR,ID] are standard. $\Gamma \vdash \mathsf{Env}$ means that Γ is well-formed, and $\Gamma \vdash S \triangleright \mathsf{Type}$ means S is well-formed under Γ. Since a participant variable with role can appear both in types and environments, we need to use kinding techniques to make sure that types with free variables do not appear before the variables' declarations and ensure well-formedness (see Definition 3.4). Rules [RL,RLV] are introduction rules for participants associated with roles.

Rule [INIT] types the initialisation of a session with global type G. The judgement $\Gamma \vdash \Delta$: end means that Δ only contains end or ε [18, 19]. The rule ensures the initialisation is not bound by the prefix. Rule [JOIN] types a joining process that follows the projection to p. A leaving process is typed if the remaining session type is completed (i.e. end).

Rule [SEL] is for the selection of label l_i, participants $\vec{p}_i$ and payload e. We first infer the destination p from Γ. If e is an atomic type (e.g. bool) or a shared channel type, then it is typed as in standard selection rules [4, 19] for the expression by recording participants $\vec{p}_i$ in the resulting type. This way, we can preserve the dependency between the participants during polling and session communications. Rule [SELS] is a session delegation rule [4, 19]. Rule [BRA] is the dual of the selection rules. Note that the participants p and $\vec{p}_i$ in $c?\langle p, \{l_i\langle\vec{p}_i\rangle(y_i).P_i\}_{i \in I}\rangle$ are free so that they are bound by the polling and dynamically instantiated by reductions. Rules [PAR,SEQ] assume $\Delta \circ \Delta'$ and $\Delta;\Delta'$ are defined. Rule [POLLING] is the introduction rule for the universal quantification. It only concerns a single session (otherwise other sessions are copied after forking). The other rules are standard [4, 19].

Since checking well-formedness is decidable, following the standard method [19, § 4], we have:

PROPOSITION 4.1. *Assuming the bound names and variables in P are annotated (i.e. processes whose bound variables are annotated by types), type-checking of* $\Gamma \vdash P \triangleright \emptyset$ *terminates.*

Typing runtime processes While the session typing systems for initial processes are simple, typing runtime (which keeps tracking intermediate invariants to prove the theorems) is not trivial due to parallel processes and participant instantiations generated by polling. We first extend the syntax of types T to include *message selection* type $!\langle \mathrm{p} : r, l\langle\vec{\mathrm{p}}\rangle\langle U\rangle\rangle$, which is an intermediate type for labelled values stored in the message buffer.

To type runtime processes, we need to extend judgements to $\Gamma \vdash_\Sigma P \triangleright \Delta$, which means that P contains the message buffers whose session names are in Σ. We only show the most interesting typing rule for the register:

$$\frac{\Gamma \vdash a : \langle G\rangle \quad \{r_i\}_{i\in I} = dom(\mathrm{R}) \quad G \upharpoonright x_i : r_i = T_i}{\Gamma \vdash_\emptyset a\langle s\rangle[\mathrm{R}] \triangleright \{s[\mathrm{p}_{ji} : r_i] : T_i\{\mathrm{p}_{ji}/x_i\}\}_{i \in I, \mathrm{p}_{ji} \notin \mathrm{R}(r_i)}}\,[\text{RGST}]$$

$$\frac{\Gamma \vdash_{\Sigma_i} P_i \triangleright \Delta_i \; (i = 1,2)}{\Gamma \vdash_{\Sigma_1 \uplus \Sigma_2} P_1 \mid P_2 \triangleright \Delta_1 * \Delta_2}\,[\text{GPAR}]$$

[RGST] assigns to the registry a type which holds a set of projected local types for all roles with participants which are *not* recorded in R. Session typing $s[r_i : \mathrm{p}_{ji}] : T_i\{\mathrm{p}_{ji}/x_i\}$ is erased once it interacts with the initialisation process $a[\mathrm{p}_{ji} : r_i](y).P$ (see rule [JOIN] in figure 2), and the resulting $P\{s[\mathrm{p}_{ji} : r_i]/y\}$ holds $s[r_i : \mathrm{p}_{ji}] : T_i\{\mathrm{p}_{ji}/x_i\}$ (see the proof of Subject reduction theorem in [3]).

When two runtime processes are put in parallel (rule [GPAR]) a queue associated to the same session does not appear twice ($\Sigma_1 \cap \Sigma_2 = \emptyset$). For composing the two session environments, either (1) we sequence a message type T and a local type T' for the same session channel as $s[\mathrm{p} : r] : T;T'$ or (2) we check whether $s[\mathrm{p} : r] : T$ and $s[\mathrm{p} : r] : T'$ can be parallel composed as $s[\mathrm{p} : r] : (T \mid T')$ by checking the linearity condition for $T \mid T'$ following Definition 3.3; and otherwise (3) undefined. Then we define $\Delta * \Delta'$ replacing $\sharp$ by $*$ in the definition of $\Delta \sharp \Delta'$.

4.2 Subject reduction

As session participants join, interact and leave, runtime session types need to follow. This dynamism is formalised by a type reduction relation $\Rightarrow$ on session environments as follows.

1. $\{s[\mathrm{q} : r'] : !\langle \mathrm{p} : r, \{l_i\langle\vec{\mathrm{p}}_i\rangle\langle U_i\rangle.T_i\}_{i \in I}\rangle\} \Rightarrow \{s[\mathrm{q} : r'] : !\langle \mathrm{p} : r, l_k\langle\vec{\mathrm{p}}_i\rangle\langle U_k\rangle.T_k\rangle\}$
2. $s[\mathrm{p} : r] : !\langle \mathrm{q} : r', l_k\langle\vec{\mathrm{p}}_k\rangle\langle U_k\rangle\rangle.s[\mathrm{q} : r'] : ?\langle \mathrm{p} : r, \{l_i\langle\vec{\mathrm{p}}_k\rangle\langle U_i\rangle.T_i\}_{i \in I}\rangle$
   $\Rightarrow s[\mathrm{p} : r] : \varepsilon, s[\mathrm{q} : r'] : T_k \quad \text{if } k \in I$
3. $s[\mathrm{p} : r] : !\langle \mathrm{p} : r, l_k\langle\vec{\mathrm{p}}_k\rangle\langle U_k\rangle\rangle; ?\langle \mathrm{p} : r, \{l_i\langle\vec{\mathrm{p}}_i\rangle\langle U_i\rangle.T_i\}_{i \in I}\rangle \to s[\mathrm{p} . r] : T_k \text{ if } k \in I$
4. $s[\mathrm{p} : r] : \forall x : r_i \setminus \vec{\mathrm{p}}.T \Rightarrow s[\mathrm{p} : r] : (T\{\mathrm{p}_1/x\} \mid .. \mid T\{\mathrm{p}_k/x\}) \quad \text{with } \mathrm{p}_i \notin \vec{\mathrm{p}}$
5. $s[\mathrm{p} : r] : \mathscr{E}[T] \cup \Delta \Rightarrow s[\mathrm{p} : r] : \mathscr{E}[T'] \cup \Delta' \quad \text{if} \quad s[\mathrm{p} : r] : T \cup \Delta \Rightarrow s[\mathrm{p} : r] : T' \cup \Delta'$
6. $\Delta \cup \Delta'' \Rightarrow \Delta' \cup \Delta'' \quad \text{if} \quad \Delta \to \Delta'$

In the above type reduction rules, message selection types are considered modulo the type equivalence relation $\equiv$ and $\mathscr{E}$ is a type evaluation context (i.e. $\mathscr{E} ::= [\_] \mid \mathscr{E} \mid T \mid T \mid \mathscr{E} \mid \mathscr{E};T$).

Rule (1) corresponds to the choice of label l_i. Rule (2) corresponds to the exchange of a labelled value from participant $\mathrm{p} : r$ to participant $\mathrm{q} : r'$. Rule (3) is about self-sending and receiving. Rule (4) governs universal quantifiers and forks types with respect to the participants which are not in the exclusion list $\vec{p}$. Rules (5,6) are congruent rules.

Hereafter we assume all processes are derived from the initial processes (§ 2) (i.e. subterms of those who are reduced from initials). Using the above definitions,

THEOREM 4.2 (Subject reduction). *Suppose* $\Gamma \vdash_\Sigma P \triangleright \Delta$ *and* $P \to^* P'$. *Then,* $\Gamma \vdash_\Sigma P' \triangleright \Delta'$ *for some* Δ' *such that* $\Delta \Rightarrow^* \Delta'$.

We say P has ***a type error*** if expressions in P contain either a type error for a value or constant in the standard sense (e.g. if 3 then P else Q) or a label error (e.g. the sender sends a value with label l_0 while the receiver does not expect label l_0). From the

$$\frac{\Gamma \vdash \mathsf{Env}}{\Gamma \vdash \mathrm{true}\ ,\mathrm{false}\ :\mathrm{bool}}\,[\textsc{Bool}] \qquad \frac{\Gamma \vdash e_i:\mathrm{bool}\ (i=1,2)}{\Gamma \vdash e_1 \vee e_2:\mathrm{bool}}\,[\textsc{Or}] \qquad \frac{\Gamma \vdash \mathsf{Env}}{\Gamma \vdash \mathtt{p}:r}\,[\textsc{Rl}] \qquad \frac{\Gamma \vdash \mathsf{Env} \quad y:r\in\Gamma}{\Gamma \vdash y:r}\,[\textsc{Rlv}] \qquad \frac{\Gamma \vdash S \triangleright \mathsf{Type} \quad u:S\in\Gamma}{\Gamma \vdash u:S}\,[\textsc{Id}]$$

$$\frac{\Gamma, a:\langle G\rangle \vdash P \triangleright \Delta}{\Gamma \vdash (\nu a:G)P \triangleright \Delta}\,[\textsc{New}] \qquad \frac{\Gamma \vdash a:\langle G\rangle \quad \Gamma \vdash \Delta:\mathsf{End}}{\Gamma \vdash a\langle G\rangle \triangleright \Delta}\,[\textsc{Init}] \qquad \frac{\Gamma \vdash u:\langle G\rangle \quad \Gamma \vdash P \triangleright \Delta, y:G\uparrow p}{\Gamma \vdash u[p](y).P \triangleright \Delta}\,[\textsc{Join}] \qquad \frac{\Gamma \vdash P \triangleright \Delta, c:\mathsf{end}}{\Gamma \vdash \mathtt{quit}\langle c\rangle;P \triangleright \Delta, c:\mathsf{end}}\,[\textsc{Leave}]$$

$$\frac{\Gamma \vdash p \quad \Gamma \vdash \vec{p}_j \quad \Gamma \vdash e:S_j \quad \Gamma \vdash P \triangleright \Delta, c:T_j \quad j\in I}{\Gamma \vdash c!\langle p, l_j\langle \vec{p}_j\rangle\langle e\rangle\rangle;P \triangleright \Delta, c:!\langle p,\{l_i\langle\vec{p}_j\rangle\langle S_i\rangle.T_i\}_{i\in I}\rangle}\,[\textsc{Sel}] \qquad \frac{\Gamma \vdash p \quad \Gamma \vdash \vec{p}_j \quad \Gamma \vdash P \triangleright \Delta, c:T_j \quad j\in I}{\Gamma \vdash c!\langle p, l_j\langle \vec{p}_j\rangle\langle c'\rangle\rangle;P \triangleright \Delta, c:!\langle p,\{l_i\langle\vec{p}_j\rangle\langle T\rangle.T_i\}_{i\in I}\rangle, c':T}\,[\textsc{SelS}]$$

$$\frac{\Gamma \vdash p \quad \forall i\in I \quad \Gamma \vdash \vec{p}_i \qquad \begin{array}{r}\Gamma, y_i:S_i \vdash P_i \triangleright \Delta, c:T_i \quad (U_i=S_i)\\ \text{or}\quad \Gamma \vdash P_i \triangleright \Delta, c:T_i, y_i:T_i' \quad (U_i=T_i')\end{array}}{\Gamma \vdash c?\langle p,\{l_i\langle\vec{p}_i\rangle(y_i).P_i\}_{i\in I}\rangle \triangleright \Delta, c?\langle p,\{l_i\langle\vec{p}_i\rangle\langle U_i\rangle.T_i\}_{i\in I}\rangle}\,[\textsc{Bra}] \qquad \frac{\Gamma, x:r \vdash P \triangleright c:T \quad \Gamma \vdash \vec{p}}{\Gamma \vdash c\forall(x:r\setminus\vec{p}).\{P\} \triangleright c:\forall x:r\setminus\vec{p}.T}\,[\textsc{Polling}] \qquad \frac{\Gamma \vdash \Delta:\mathsf{End}}{\Gamma \vdash \mathbf{0} \triangleright \Delta}\,[\textsc{Nil}]$$

$$\frac{\Gamma \vdash e:\mathrm{bool} \quad \Gamma \vdash P_i \triangleright \Delta\ (i=1,2)}{\Gamma \vdash \text{if } e \text{ then } P_1 \text{ else } P_2 \triangleright \Delta}\,[\textsc{If}] \qquad \frac{\Gamma \vdash P \triangleright \Delta \quad \Gamma \vdash Q \triangleright \Delta'}{\Gamma \vdash P \mid Q \triangleright \Delta \circ \Delta'}\,[\textsc{Par}] \qquad \frac{\Gamma \vdash P \triangleright \Delta \quad \Gamma \vdash Q \triangleright \Delta'}{\Gamma \vdash P;Q \triangleright \Delta;\Delta'}\,[\textsc{Seq}] \qquad \frac{\Gamma, X:\Delta \vdash P \triangleright \Delta}{\Gamma \vdash \mu X.P \triangleright \Delta}\,[\textsc{Rec}] \qquad \frac{\Gamma, X:\Delta \vdash \mathsf{Env}}{\Gamma, X:\Delta \vdash X \triangleright \Delta}\,[\textsc{RVar}]$$

Figure 6. Multirole session typing for initial processes

subject reduction theorem and the well-formedness of global types (Definition 3.4), we can prove:

COROLLARY 4.3 (Type safety). *Suppose* $\Gamma \vdash P \triangleright \Delta$. *For any* P' *such that* $P \rightarrow^* P'$, P' *has no type error.*

5. Communication safety and progress

This section discusses the difficulties that a distributed session semantics creates when participants can dynamically join, leave and poll. We illustrate two limitations of the semantics and typing system presented so far and propose a solution based on multiparty locking that allows more flexibility for leaving a session and guarantees communication safety. We give two progress properties, one of which goes beyond existing achievements.

5.1 Limitations

Leaving a session While our operational semantics (⌊QUIT⌋ in figure 2) allows a participant to leave a session at any time, the typing rule ([LEAVE] in figure 6) only allows a participant to leave when its local type is end.

Recall the peer-to-peer chat example from § 1 (2), G is of the form $\mu\mathbf{x}.G_0;\mathbf{x};\mathrm{end}$ with $G_0 = \forall x:\mathrm{client}.\forall y:\mathrm{client}\setminus x.\{x\to y\,\mathsf{Msg}\langle\mathrm{string}\rangle\}$. The recursive type prevents any participant from ever leaving since a process will never reach type end. We however remark that a client can play just one interaction round (i.e. G_0) and leave safely before another session iteration occurs. If the starting and ending points of global types are known, some participants are able to leave a session safely while others stay.

Communication safety and progress In traditional multiparty sessions, the subject reduction theorem immediately brings *communication safety* and *progress* (in a single session) [19]. The reason is that standard multiparty session initiation ensures that all parties are eventually present (it waits for the expected fixed number of participants to join), while the typing system guarantees the safety of the communications when they start. This does not hold in our system due to the interplay between joining, leaving and polling.

We illustrate this point with the peer-to-peer chat example from § 1. In that global type, every client is broadcasting Msg to all the others. Recall the client process $P_{\mathrm{client}}(z)$ from § 1.

$$\begin{array}{l} a[z:\mathrm{client}](s).\mu X.(s\forall(y:\mathrm{client}\setminus z).\{s!\langle y,\mathsf{Msg}\langle m\rangle\rangle\} \\ \qquad\qquad \mid s\forall(x:\mathrm{client}\setminus z).\{s?\langle x,\mathsf{Msg}(w)\rangle\});X \end{array}$$

At each iteration, every client does exactly two polling operations. Now suppose that a client does the first polling operation (to send Msg) before another client joins. It means that this new client will not receive the message it expects. More generally, the polls that correspond to the emissions need to always give the exact same result as the reception polls. This suggests that some mechanism to synchronise distributed polling processes is required to guarantee consistent polling results.

5.2 Multiparty locking for polling synchronisation

This subsection shows that a simple locking policy that can be automatically computed from the global type is able to ensure a safe synchronisation to allow flexible session departure and consistent polling results. The key point is to temporarily *block* late participants from joining in the middle of a session execution in order to prevent any interference with polling. This is simply done by automatically surrounding global types by locks: $\mathtt{lock}\{G\}$ means that the *interactions specified by G are protected from late joiners* and is called a *locked global type*. This condition is easily implementable using a standard two phase commitment protocol which minimises the necessary synchronisation between processes (figure 7) and is easily implementable in ML (§ 5.5).

The peer-to-peer chat example from § 1 is now defined by $\mu\mathbf{x}.\mathtt{lock}\{\forall x:\mathrm{client}.\forall y:\mathrm{client}.x\to y\,\mathsf{Msg}\langle\mathrm{string}\rangle\};\mathbf{x}$. This type allows participants to join at each recursive iteration, preventing interferences while the exchange of Msg is under way.

Syntax We first extend the syntax of processes (figure 1) as:

$$\begin{array}{l} P ::= \ldots \mid c\ \mathtt{lock} \mid c\ \mathtt{unlock} \mid a^{\circ}[\mathtt{R},\Lambda] \mid a^{\bullet}[\mathtt{R},\Lambda] \\ \Lambda ::= \varnothing \mid \Lambda \cup \{\mathtt{p}:r\} \end{array}$$

The process syntax is extended to locking and unlocking operations. The registry has two new states: $a^{\circ}[\mathtt{R},\Lambda]$ represents a registry that is in the process of being locked (so far by participants Λ), while $a^{\bullet}[\mathtt{R},\Lambda]$ represents a registry that is locked (and where participants Λ are still involved).

Semantics The operational semantics with multiparty locking is given in figure 7. It defines the relations between the three states of the registry and is based on a standard two phase locking protocol commonly found in distributed applications.

The first phase is the *registration state*: if the registry is of the form $a\langle s\rangle[\mathtt{R}]$, participants can join and leave the session through ⌊JOIN⌋ and ⌊QUIT⌋. The only other reduction rule that can be applied is ⌊LOCK⌋, which puts the registry in its second state, the *locking state* $a^{\circ}[\mathtt{R},\ell:\Lambda]$. Then, the session can only wait for all the current participants in R to activate their locks by the rules ⌊UP, TOP⌋. A new process can asynchronously join by ⌊JOIN2⌋, and a current process can finally decide to leave ⌊QUIT2⌋ from the active session. The difference between ⌊UP⌋ and ⌊TOP⌋ lies in the side condition:

$$
\begin{array}{rcll}
a\langle G\rangle & \rightarrow & (\nu\, s)(a\langle s\rangle[\mathtt{R}] \mid s{:}\varepsilon) & (\forall r_i \in G, \mathtt{R}(r_i) = \varnothing) \quad \lfloor\textsc{Init}\rfloor \\
a[\mathtt{p}{:}r](y).P \mid a\langle s\rangle[\mathtt{R}\cdot r{:}\mathtt{P}] & \rightarrow & P\{s[\mathtt{p}{:}r]/y\} \mid a\langle s\rangle[\mathtt{R}\cdot r{:}\mathtt{P}\uplus\{\mathtt{p}\}] & \lfloor\textsc{Join}\rfloor \\
a[\mathtt{p}{:}r](y).P \mid a^{\circ}\langle s\rangle[\mathtt{R}\cdot r{:}\mathtt{P},\Lambda] & \rightarrow & P\{s[\mathtt{p}{:}r]/y\} \mid a^{\circ}\langle s\rangle[\mathtt{R}\cdot r{:}\mathtt{P}\uplus\{\mathtt{p}\},\Lambda] & (\mathtt{p}{:}r \notin \Lambda) \quad \lfloor\textsc{Join2}\rfloor \\
\mathtt{quit}\langle s[\mathtt{p}{:}r]\rangle \mid a\langle s\rangle[\mathtt{R}\cdot r{:}\mathtt{P}] & \rightarrow & a\langle s\rangle[\mathtt{R}\cdot r{:}\mathtt{P}\setminus\{\mathtt{p}\}] & \lfloor\textsc{Quit}\rfloor \\
\mathtt{quit}\langle s[\mathtt{p}{:}r]\rangle \mid a^{\circ}\langle s\rangle[\mathtt{R}\cdot r{:}\mathtt{P},\Lambda] & \rightarrow & a^{\circ}\langle s\rangle[\mathtt{R}\cdot r{:}\mathtt{P}\setminus\{\mathtt{p}\},\Lambda] & (\mathtt{p}{:}r \notin \Lambda) \quad \lfloor\textsc{Quit2}\rfloor \\
s[\mathtt{p}{:}r]\mathtt{lock} \mid a\langle s\rangle[\mathtt{R}] & \rightarrow & a^{\circ}\langle s\rangle[\mathtt{R},\{\mathtt{p}{:}r\}] & \lfloor\textsc{Lock}\rfloor \\
s[\mathtt{p}{:}r]\mathtt{lock} \mid a^{\circ}\langle s\rangle[\mathtt{R},\Lambda] & \rightarrow & \begin{cases} a^{\circ}\langle s\rangle[\mathtt{R},\Lambda\uplus\{\mathtt{p}{:}r\}] \\ a^{\bullet}\langle s\rangle[\mathtt{R},\Lambda\uplus\{\mathtt{p}{:}r\}] \end{cases} & \begin{array}{l} (\mathtt{R} \not\approx \Lambda\uplus\{\mathtt{p}{:}r\}) \quad \lfloor\textsc{Up}\rfloor \\ (\mathtt{R} \approx \Lambda\uplus\{\mathtt{p}{:}r\}) \quad \lfloor\textsc{Top}\rfloor \end{array} \\
s[\mathtt{p}{:}r]\mathtt{unlock} \mid a^{\bullet}\langle s\rangle[\mathtt{R},\Lambda\uplus\{\mathtt{p}{:}r\}] & \rightarrow & \begin{cases} a^{\bullet}\langle s\rangle[\mathtt{R},\Lambda] \\ a\langle s\rangle[\mathtt{R}] \end{cases} & \begin{array}{l} (\Lambda \neq \varnothing) \quad \lfloor\textsc{Down}\rfloor \\ (\Lambda = \varnothing) \quad \lfloor\textsc{Unlock}\rfloor \end{array} \\
s[\mathtt{p}{:}r]!\langle \mathtt{p}'{:}r', l\langle\vec{\mathtt{p}}\rangle\langle v\rangle\rangle \mid a^{\bullet}\langle s\rangle[\mathtt{R},\Lambda] \mid s{:}h & \rightarrow & a^{\bullet}\langle s\rangle[\mathtt{R},\Lambda] \mid s{:}h\cdot(\mathtt{p}{:}r,\ \mathtt{p}'{:}r',\ l\langle\vec{\mathtt{p}}\rangle\langle v\rangle) & (\mathtt{p}\in\mathtt{R}(r) \wedge \mathtt{p}'\in\mathtt{R}(r')) \quad \lfloor\textsc{Send}\rfloor \\
s[\mathtt{p}{:}r]?\langle \mathtt{p}'{:}r', \{l_i\langle\vec{\mathtt{p}}_i\rangle(x_i).P_i\}_{i\in I}\rangle \mid a^{\bullet}\langle s\rangle[\mathtt{R}] \mid s{:}(\mathtt{p}'{:}r',\ \mathtt{p}{:}r,\ l_k\langle\vec{\mathtt{p}}_k\rangle\langle v\rangle)\cdot h & \rightarrow & P_k\{v/x_k\} \mid a^{\bullet}\langle s\rangle[\mathtt{R}] \mid s{:}h & (\mathtt{p}\in\mathtt{R}(r) \wedge k\in I) \quad \lfloor\textsc{Recv}\rfloor \\
s[\mathtt{p}{:}r]\forall(x{:}r\setminus\vec{\mathtt{p}}).\{P\} \mid a^{\bullet}\langle s\rangle[\mathtt{R}\cdot r{:}\mathtt{P},\Lambda] & \rightarrow & P\{\mathtt{p}_1/x\} \mid .. \mid P\{\mathtt{p}_k/x\} \mid a^{\bullet}\langle s\rangle[\mathtt{R}\cdot r{:}\mathtt{P},\Lambda] & (\mathtt{R}(r)\setminus\vec{\mathtt{p}} = \{\mathtt{p}_1,..,\mathtt{p}_k\} \wedge \mathtt{p}\in\mathtt{R}(r')) \quad \lfloor\textsc{Poll}\rfloor
\end{array}
$$

Other rules are from 2.

Figure 7. Operational semantics with multiparty lock

$\mathtt{R} \approx \Lambda$ holds when $\forall \mathtt{p}{:}r.(\Lambda = \Lambda' \uplus \{\mathtt{p}{:}r\} \Leftrightarrow \mathtt{R} = \mathtt{R}'\cdot r{:}\mathtt{P}\uplus\{\mathtt{p}\})$. Consequently, $\lfloor$TOP$\rfloor$ is only triggered when the set Λ contains the exact same combinations of participants and role as the set $\mathtt{R}$, meaning that all participants have activated their locks.

The application of rule $\lfloor$TOP$\rfloor$ marks the beginning of the *interaction state*, with a registry of the form $a^{\bullet}\langle s\rangle[\mathtt{R},\ell:\Lambda]$. Only in this state can the rules $\lfloor$ SEND, RECV, POLL$\rfloor$ be safely applied. The registry goes back to its registration state by the application of rule $\lfloor$UNLOCK$\rfloor$ which can occur only when everyone besides one participant has activated the `unlock` operation by rule $\lfloor$DOWN$\rfloor$.

Types and typing The syntax of global and local types are extended from figure 4 as follows:

$$G ::= \ldots \mid \mathtt{lock}\{G\} \qquad T ::= \ldots \mid \mathtt{lock} \mid \mathtt{unlock}$$

We say that a global type G is *terminable* if there exists at least one finite path (whose leaf is ε) up to the unfolding of G. A terminable type can be easily defined by a kinding system: ε is terminable; $p{\rightarrow}p'\{l_i\langle\vec{p}_i\rangle\langle U_i\rangle.G_i\}_{i\in I}$ is terminable if for some $k\in I$, G_k is terminable; and others are defined homomorphically (see [3]). For example, $\mu\mathbf{x}.p{\rightarrow}p'\{l_1\langle U_1\rangle.\varepsilon, l_2\langle U_2\rangle.\mathbf{x}\}$ is terminable, but $\mu\mathbf{x}.p{\rightarrow}p'\{l_1\langle U_1\rangle.\mathbf{x}, l_2\langle U_2\rangle.\mathbf{x}\}$ is not. We define the condition for global types and environments.

DEFINITION 5.1 (Well-locked and persistently well-locked). We say that a global type G is *well-locked* if G is closed (i.e. no free participant and recursive type variables) and of the form $\mathtt{lock}\{G_0\};\mathtt{end}$, and G_0 does not include any `lock`. We say that a closed global type G is *persistently well-locked* if G is of the form $\mu\mathbf{x}.\mathtt{lock}\{G_0\};\mathbf{x};\mathtt{end}$, with $\mathtt{lock}\{G_0\};\mathtt{end}$ well-locked and G_0 is terminable. We call Γ *well-locked* if for all $\Gamma(u) = \langle G\rangle$, G is either well-locked or persistently well-locked. We call Γ *persistently well-locked* if for all $\Gamma(u) = \langle G\rangle$, G is persistently well-locked.

Type $\mathtt{lock}\{G_0\}$ means that a single multiparty session is locked. Type $\mu\mathbf{x}.\mathtt{lock}\{G_0\};\mathbf{x}$ states a multiparty session is *persistently* (repeatedly) locked. The persistent lock ensures if a new participant p wants to join, it can join at the beginning of the interaction G_0, and if one wishes to quit, it can quit at the end of the session. Consequently, it requires the global type to be of the form $\mu\mathbf{x}.G_0;\mathbf{x}$ with a well-locked G_0 that does not contain any infinite loop which would prevent from reaching a new iteration (`unlock`). The persistent condition is needed for the final strong join progress discussed later.

Local types `lock` and `unlock` come from the projection:

$$\mathtt{lock}\{G\} \upharpoonright z{:}r \quad = \quad \mathtt{lock};(G \upharpoonright z{:}r);\mathtt{unlock}$$

This way, correct locks are automatically inserted at the right points of the local types. Typing `lock` and `unlock` is straightforward.

$$\frac{\Gamma \vdash \mathsf{Env}}{\Gamma \vdash c\ \mathtt{lock} \triangleright c{:}\mathtt{lock}} \qquad \frac{\Gamma \vdash \mathsf{Env}}{\Gamma \vdash c\ \mathtt{unlock} \triangleright c{:}\mathtt{unlock}}$$

We add the following rule which types $\mathtt{quit}\langle c\rangle$ as some projection of session $\langle G\rangle$ in the environment.

$$\frac{\Gamma \vdash P \triangleright \Delta, c{:}\mathtt{end} \quad \Gamma \vdash u{:}\langle G\rangle}{\Gamma \vdash \mathtt{quit}\langle c\rangle;P \triangleright \Delta, c{:}G \upharpoonright p}$$

The above rule is useful when G is persistently well-locked. Suppose $G = \mu\mathbf{x}.\mathtt{lock};G_0;\mathbf{x};\mathtt{end}$. By the above rule, we can type $\mathtt{lock};Q;\mathtt{unlock};\mathtt{quit}\langle c\rangle$ if Q has type $G_0 \upharpoonright p$ since $G \upharpoonright p \approx G_0 \upharpoonright p; G \upharpoonright p$ where $T \approx T'$ means T is isomorphic to T'; once session is unlocked, one can leave the active session at c instead of repeating the same session $G \upharpoonright p$.

As a simple example, recall the peer-to-peer chat server from § 1. The following client leaves a session after one interaction, which is typable under $G = \mu\mathbf{x}.\mathtt{lock}\{G_0\};\mathbf{x};\mathtt{end}$ with $G_0 = \forall x:\mathrm{client}.\forall y:\mathrm{client}\setminus x.\{x{\rightarrow}y\,\mathsf{Msg}\langle\mathrm{string}\rangle\}$.

$$\begin{array}{l} P_{\mathrm{client}}(\mathtt{p}) = a[\mathtt{p}.\mathrm{client}](s).(s\forall(y{:}\mathrm{client}\setminus z).\{s!\langle y, \mathsf{Msg}\langle m\rangle\rangle\} \mid \\ \qquad\qquad s\forall(x{:}\mathrm{client}\setminus z).\{s?\langle x, \mathsf{Msg}(w)\rangle\});\mathtt{quit}\langle s\rangle \end{array}$$

5.3 Communication safety and progress

We first state communication safety. It states that, in a session execution, no receiver waits for a message that will never come; and that there is no messages sent but never received.

DEFINITION 5.2 (Communication-safety). We say P is ***communication safe*** if:

- $P \equiv \mathscr{E}[Q]$ with $Q = s[\mathtt{p}{:}r]?\langle\mathtt{p}'{:}r', \{l_i\langle\vec{\mathtt{p}}_i\rangle(x).P_i\}_{i\in I}\rangle$ implies that there exists $\mathscr{E}[Q] \rightarrow^* \mathscr{E}'[Q \mid s{:}(\mathtt{p}'{:}r',\ \mathtt{p}{:}r,\ l_k\langle\vec{\mathtt{p}}_k\rangle\langle v\rangle)\cdot h]$ with $k\in I$; and
- $P \equiv \mathscr{E}[Q]$ with $Q = s{:}(\mathtt{p}'{:}r',\ \mathtt{p}{:}r,\ l_k\langle\vec{\mathtt{p}}_k\rangle\langle v\rangle)\cdot h$ implies that there exists $\mathscr{E}[Q] \rightarrow^* \mathscr{E}'[Q \mid s[\mathtt{p}{:}r]?\langle\mathtt{p}'{:}r', \{l_i\langle\vec{\mathtt{p}}_i\rangle(x).P_i\}_{i\in I}\rangle]$ with $k\in I$.

The first statement means that branching processes can always find out a correct element in the message buffer; and the second one is its dual. Note that combining with Type safety, the receiver will input a value v of the expected type.

DEFINITION 5.3 (Single-session join). We write $\Gamma \vdash^* P \triangleright \Delta$ if P is typable and with a type derivation where the session typing in the premise and the conclusion of each prefix rule is restricted to be at most a singleton (more precisely, $\Delta = \varnothing$ in [JOIN,LEAVE,SEL,BAR] and Δ contains at most one element in $\Delta;\Delta'$ in [SEQ], $\Delta \circ \Delta'$ in [PAR,SEQ], Δ in [IF,NEW,REC,RVAR] in figure 6, deleting [SELS]). We say $Q = a[p](y).Q'$ is a *single-session* join if $a:\langle G\rangle \vdash^* Q \triangleright \varnothing$ and Q' does not contain shared name restriction and any join process.

$\Gamma \vdash^* P \triangleright \Delta$ ensures that P contains (several) join processes each of which holds a single session, while single-session join $a[p](y).Q'$ has only one active point a, and once the session initiated at a, Q' can only perform session communication at that initiated session. We prove the communication safety in a single multiparty session.

THEOREM 5.4 (Communication safety). *Suppose $a:\langle G\rangle \vdash^* P \triangleright \varnothing$ and P is initial. Assume $a:\langle G\rangle$ is well-locked*[4]*. and P does not contain any shared name restriction. For any P' such that $P \longrightarrow^* P'$, P' is communication safe.*

The proof starts by a definition of coherent environments (a certain kind of duality relation over multiple participants [4, § 3]). Then, we prove a stronger subject reduction theorem that shows the reduction of well-locked processes preserves the coherency of the resulting environment. We note that session fidelity [19, Corollary 5.6] comes also as a corollary.

Now we prove the *progress* property in a single multiparty session as in [19, Theorem 5.12], i.e. if a program P starts from one session, the reductions at session channels do not get stuck.

DEFINITION 5.5 (Progress property). We say $\Gamma \vdash P \triangleright \varnothing$ can progress, or satisfies the ***progress property***, if, whenever $P \longrightarrow^* P'$, then either $P' \equiv \mathbf{0}$, $P' \longrightarrow R$ or for some single-session join $a:\langle G\rangle \vdash Q$ with $a:\langle G\rangle \in \Gamma$ such that $P' \mid Q \longrightarrow R$ and R can progress.

The above definition means that a process satisfies the progress property if it can never reach a deadlock state, i.e., if it never reduces to a process which contains active sessions (this amounts to containing waiting process at some session channel) and which is irreducible in any inactive context with single-session join Q running in parallel.

THEOREM 5.6 (Progress). *Suppose $\Gamma \vdash^* P \triangleright \varnothing$ and P is initial. Assume Γ is well-locked and P does not contain any shared name restriction. Then P can progress.*

5.4 Join progress

The above standard progress property is not strong enough, since all late joiners cannot participate to existing sessions. This subsection states a new progress property, not found in the literature.

Recall the (1) map-reduce example from § 1, and change the position of the recursion in the global type to:

$$G_0 = \forall x\!:\!\mathsf{client.server}{\to}x\langle\mathsf{Map}\rangle;\mu\mathbf{x}.x{\to}\mathsf{server}\langle\mathsf{Reduce}\rangle;\mathbf{x}$$

From G_0, we have the following well-typed processes:

$$P_0(s,z\!:\!\mathsf{client}) \;=\; s?\langle\mathsf{server},\mathsf{Map}\rangle;\mu X.s!\langle\mathsf{server},\mathsf{Reduce}\rangle;X$$
$$P_0(s,z\!:\!\mathsf{server}) \;=\; s\forall(x\!:\!\mathsf{client}).\{s!\langle x,\mathsf{Map}\rangle;\mu X.s?\langle x,\mathsf{Reduce}\rangle;X\}$$

While the interaction between them is communication safe, the problem is that a late client will never be listened to by *the existing server* because the server's polling operation is not repeated to include him. In other words, the late client cannot join an existing, already running session. Persistent locking ensures this situation does not happen.

[4] The property can be generalised to Γ from $\{a:\langle G\rangle\}$ if we compose a parallel composition of single-session processes to $\mathscr{E}[Q]$ in Definition 5.2 as Definition 5.5. A similar generalisation is possible for Definition 5.7.

Below we write $P \xrightarrow{s[\mathsf{p}:r]} Q$ if $P \longrightarrow Q$ and $P \longrightarrow Q$ is derived using ⌊QUIT⌋, ⌊QUIT2⌋, ⌊SEND⌋, ⌊RECV⌋ or ⌊POLL⌋ at $s[\mathsf{p}:r]$ with ⌊PAR,CTX,CONG⌋, i.e. P interacts with a queue or registry through $s[\mathsf{p}:r]$.

DEFINITION 5.7 (Join progress property). We say that $a:\langle G\rangle \vdash P \triangleright \varnothing$ satisfies the ***join progress property*** if:

- P can progress; and
- if $P \longrightarrow^* (\nu\ s)(P' \mid a\langle s\rangle[\mathrm{R}])$ then, for any single-session join $a:\langle G\rangle \vdash a[\mathsf{p}:r](y).Q \triangleright \varnothing$ with $\mathsf{p}:r$ fresh, and for any R such that $P' \mid a\langle s\rangle[\mathrm{R}] \mid a[\mathsf{p}:r](y).Q \longrightarrow^* a^\bullet\langle s\rangle[\mathrm{R}'] \mid R = Q'$,
  - if $s[\mathsf{p}:r] \in R$, then there exists $Q' \longrightarrow^* \xrightarrow{s[\mathsf{p}:r]} R'$; and
  - $(\nu\ s)Q'$ satisfies the join progress property.

The above definition says that a fresh joiner ($a[\mathsf{p}:r](y).Q$) can always join the existing (unlocked) session s in P'. In addition, it can always progress at the created session channel s by interacting with P'. More intuitively, once some participants under any role start a session, the late joiner can still join that session and interact with earlier joiners, progressing further. Note that we can consider *any* single-session join $a[\mathsf{p}:r](y).Q$ to make a process progress, which contrasts with the definition of the progress property (Definition 5.5) where P is only composed of single-session joining processes.

THEOREM 5.8 (Join progress). *Suppose $a:\langle G\rangle \vdash^* P \triangleright \varnothing$ and P is initial. Assume $a:\langle G\rangle$ is persistently well-locked and P does not contain any shared name restriction. Then P satisfies the join progress property.*

We have for our examples:

PROPOSITION 5.9 (Properties of the examples). *Assume that each global type G in the protocols (1–3) of § 1 is replaced by $\mathsf{lock}\{G\}$. Then all examples are type/communication safe and can always progress. Moreover if each global type in the protocols (1,2) of § 1 inside the recursive type, i.e. $\mu\mathbf{x}.G;\mathbf{x}$ is replaced by $\mu\mathbf{x}.\mathsf{lock}\{G\};\mathbf{x}$, then they additionally satisfy the join progress property.*

5.5 Implementation

Prototype implementation The multirole calculus has been implemented as an extension of ML. Following the technique used in [5, 13], the global types that the programmer writes are compiled into an end-point function for each role. This choice allows to replace the implementation of the typing system by an automated generation of well-typed processes that can be used, through an API, by the programmer. The session semantics is thus entirely generated and implemented by communication libraries.

A distributed implementation The main issue for our compiler is to distribute as much as possible the centralised aspects of the semantics of figures 2 and 7. First concerned, the message buffers are completely distributed and implemented on the sender side: a thread is spawned to asynchronously make sure that the message gets across the TCP channel. Second, the registries can be partially distributed with one registry per role that deals with the corresponding joining, leaving and polling activities. These distributed registries however need to stay in contact to synchronise the global locking events (rules ⌊LOCK, TOP, UNLOCK⌋). Registries are attributed to participants by age: the first joiner for a role plays the registry as well, until he quits, in which case the registry is transmitted to the second older.

Extension Singly instantiated roles, like the server or broker from examples in § 1, are modelled through an inefficient implicit quantification. Our implementation gives a special status to these roles. We use the fact that they play their own registry. As a consequence, no separate polling is necessary to send them messages and the extra messages required by the quantification can be avoided.

Efficiency To gain performances, we propose an implementation with optimised messaging and improved asynchrony.

First, since the slowest operation is communication, our implementation tries to minimise the number of messages that are exchanged. The main illustration is that if two messages are specified to be sent in a row between the same participants, they are automatically concatenated.

A more radical change is to do the polling only once for every participant, at the beginning of each locked part of the session execution. The advantages are to limit the number of sent messages and to remove in effect the global synchronisation point of rule ⌊UNLOCK⌋. As soon as all polling operations are done, the distributed session execution can safely proceed until the list of participants of the next iteration is synchronised (rule ⌊TOP⌋).

6. Related work

The first motivation for the present work is a strong need to extend session type theory with *dynamic reconfiguration* of multiparty sessions and *role*-based abstraction to support a wider range of communication protocols found in practice.

The inspiration for multiparty session types comes from the design of high-level global protocol signatures for Web Services Choreography Description Language [1]. In CDL, types of participants (participantType) are declared as instances of types of roles (roleType) which represent collections of interaction behaviours. Later, some of the members of the W3C CDL working group have started developing a language called Scribble [17, 28] based on the theory of multiparty session types [4, 19]. Scribble is currently being experimented with for several different application domains in distributed systems [2, 24, 27] including business and financial protocols [32]. Our auction example in § 1(3) was extracted from the Scribble specification document.

The need for roles in session programming is also substantiated by our experiences in implementing web service usecases [1] and parallel algorithms for high-performance clusters [25] using Session Java (SJ) [20, 21]. In this work, we first describe communications between processes in a global topology (e.g. a multidimensional mesh or a ring) in the form of parameterised multiparty session types [35]. The compatibility between [35] and our present work is yet to be investigated as complex topologies with dynamic features need sophisticated distributed synchronisation algorithms (see also § 7).

The second motivation for the present work is the incorporation of dynamic features most suited to and compatible with existing multiparty session types [4–6, 9, 14, 19, 22, 23, 29, 35, 36]. The Conversation Calculus [8, 33] models distributed behaviours among "places" using new primitives such as conversation contexts (i.e. shared interaction points) and up (↑) communication (similar to [7, 12]). A conversation models the interactions between a client and various services, with dynamic joining into a conversation, for a possibly unknown number of processes. While both their work and ours aim to support dynamic natures for sessions, the two join mechanisms are quite different. Their join is encoded by base primitives for late joining into a point of conversation, which more closely resembles the late asynchronous session initiation in [20, 35]. On the other hand, our join mechanism is *role-based*, and articulated at the level of *global types*, by declaring a single type construct which binds participants to a role. In contrast to [8], the process which controls joining might be a sender or listener, depending on the result of the projection (i.e. the position of polling). This flexibility enables direct modelling and clear articulation (i.e. without encoding) of different patterns of dynamic parallel protocols including symmetric peer-to-peer chats (§ 1 and Examples 3.1 and 3.2) by types. In [8], they proposed a sophisticated typing system that builds a well-founded order on events (similar to the line of [34]), to guarantee progress for processes under the assumption that all communications are matched with sufficient joiners. They do not, however, explore type inference for progress (decidability of a generation of well-formed ordering) [33]. Our progress can be, on the other hand, guaranteed by well-formedness of global types, with an automatic insertion of locks (which means a typing system with progress is decidable with Proposition 4.1). This leads to a simple but practical prototype implementation as discussed in § 5.5. A strong joining property has not been studied in [8].

Contracts [11] record abstract interaction behaviours of processes, and typable processes themselves may not always satisfy the properties of session types such as progress: it is proved *later* by checking whether a whole contract conforms to a certain form. Proving properties with contracts requires an exploration of all possible interleaved or non-deterministic paths of a protocol, see [35, § 5].

The first suggestion to use roles to model dynamic conversations in the context of session types was made in [16]. This idea is further developed in a master's thesis [26] which formalises a Java-like core calculus for role-based session interactions. A session structure is described as a collection of binary session types for broadcast channels (used to send messages to role participants). New participants can only join a conversation before it starts. Type structures for global protocols and their induced properties (in particular progress) are not studied in [26].

For further comparisons of session types with other service-oriented calculi and behaviour typing systems, see [15] for a wide ranging survey of the related literature.

7. Conclusion and future work

This work introduced a multirole session type discipline for validating dynamic behaviours among an unspecified number of participants, answering a well-known open problem of multiparty session types [4, 6, 9, 14, 19, 22, 29, 35]. Dynamism is formalised through a powerful universal type construct which can represent many collective communications protocols, ranging over parallel computations, P2P networking, chat protocols and e-commerce auctions. Despite the greater expressiveness, projection and type checking are decidable. Global types offer a practical guideline for a correct multiparty synchronisation mechanism, by which the theorems (properties) are articulated as: (1) $\forall x.G$ (subject reduction and type safety with dynamic join and leave semantics), (2) well-locked $\mathtt{lock}\{G\}$ (communication safety and progress); and (3) persistently well-locked $\mu\mathbf{x}.\mathtt{lock}\{G\};\mathbf{x}$ (join progress). Our prototype implementation demonstrates the direct applicability of the present theory.

To realise the full potential of the multirole session type theory, several challenges need to be addressed. First, the theory can be integrated with the multiparty session exceptions developed in [10] in order to handle system failure and fault-tolerance in a larger class of distributed protocols, preserving type safety. It is especially useful to directly express more complex and dynamic topologies, in combination with the parameterised type theory from [35].

One extension that comes immediately to mind is the addition of an explicit existential $\exists x{:}r.G$. It however raises many semantic issues. Consider $G' = \forall x : \text{client}.\{\exists y : \text{server}.x{\to}y\langle\mathsf{Msg}\rangle\}$. In that example, every client contacts a server (the intuition is that each x chooses his y). The question is: how can we ensure by local typing that servers will be listening to the right number of requests? The difficulty is that a server y can be potentially chosen by every client x or by none, and that this choice is distributed (and thus very hard to locally type check). Consequently, the global existential quantification rather abstracts complex distributed election algorithms. A different solution is an extension to subtyping between roles $r_1 <: r_2$ by which we can represent a protocol with memberships, e.g. a client sends a message to a subset of subscribers.

Second, type-based approaches for correct locking has been widely studied, including [30] in a framework of linear program analysis and types. Our aim in § 5.2 is to propose a simple way to realise synchronisation, articulated by global types, suggesting another use of global descriptions for different purposes. One such instance is studied in [14], where multiparty session types lead to an efficient buffer analysis, along with automatically guaranteed communication and buffer safety. A benefit of using global types (i.e. a choreography framework [1]) is that the analysis can be done solely based on global types, without directly analysing (possibly distributed) end-point types or processes since we can assume all processes agree with that global specification. An integration with global and local locking [30] is, however, an interesting future topic from the viewpoint of local refinements [22].

Third, we are currently collaborating with several industry partners working on open standardisations for financial protocols [32] and messaging middleware [2], governance architectures [27] and cyberinfrastructures [24] to attest the practical use and expressiveness of the session framework, for which an integration with multiparty logic [6] and security [5, 9] for monitoring, is our next task.

Acknowledgement We are grateful to Luís Caires, Marco Carbone, Søren Debois, Kohei Honda, Raymond Hu, Kohei Suenaga, Hugo Vieira and Vasco Vasconcelos for their helpful comments. We thank the anonymous reviewers for their precise questions and suggestions. This work was supported by EPSRC EP/F003757/01 and G015635/01.

References

[1] Web Services Choreography Description Language. http://www.w3.org/2002/ws/chor/.

[2] Advanced Message Queueing Protocols. http://www.amqp.org/confluence/display/AMQP/Advanced+Message+Queuing+Pr%otocol.

[3] On-line Appendix of this paper. http://www.doc.ic.ac.uk/~pmalo/dynamic.

[4] L. Bettini et al. Global Progress in Dynamically Interfered Multiparty Sessions. In *CONCUR'08*, volume 5201 of *LNCS*, pages 418–433. Springer, 2008.

[5] K. Bhargavan, R. Corin, P.-M. Deniélou, C. Fournet, and J. Leifer. Cryptographic protocol synthesis and verification for multiparty sessions. In *CSF*, pages 124–140, 2009.

[6] L. Bocchi, K. Honda, E. Tuosto, and N. Yoshida. A theory of design-by-contract for distributed multiparty interactions. In *CONCUR'10*, volume 6269 of *LNCS*, pages 162–176. Springer, 2010.

[7] M. Bugliesi, G. Castagna, and S. Crafa. Access control for mobile agents: The calculus of boxed ambients. *TOPLAS*, 26(1):57–124, 2004.

[8] L. Caires and H. T. Vieira. Conversation types. In *ESOP*, volume 5502 of *LNCS*, pages 285–300. Springer, 2009. A full version will appear in TCS.

[9] S. Capecchi, I. Castellani, M. Dezani-Ciancaglini, and T. Rezk. Session Types for Access and Information Flow Control. In *CONCUR'10*, volume 6269 of *LNCS*, pages 237–252. Springer, 2010.

[10] S. Capecchi, E. Giachino, and N. Yoshida. Global escape in multiparty session. In *30th FSTTCS'10*, LIPICS, 2010. To appear.

[11] G. Castagna and L. Padovani. Contracts for mobile processes. In *CONCUR*, number 5710 in LNCS, pages 211–228, 2009.

[12] G. Castagna, J. Vitek, and F. Z. Nardelli. The seal calculus. *Inf. Comput.*, 201(1):1–54, 2005.

[13] R. Corin and P. Deniélou. A protocol compiler for secure sessions in ML. In *TGC*, volume 4912 of *LNCS*, pages 276–293. Springer, 2008.

[14] P.-M. Deniélou and N. Yoshida. Buffered communication analysis in distributed multiparty sessions. In *CONCUR'10*, volume 6269 of *LNCS*, pages 343–357. Springer, 2010. Full version, Prototype at http://www.doc.ic.ac.uk/~pmalo/multianalysis.

[15] M. Dezani-Ciancaglini and U. de' Liguoro. Sessions and Session Types: an Overview. In *WS-FM'09*, volume 6194 of *LNCS*, pages 1–28. Springer, 2010.

[16] E. Giachino, M. Sackman, S. Drossopoulou, and S. Eisenbach. Softly safely spoken: role playing for session types. Preliminary on-line preproceeding, 64–69 pages, http://gloss.di.fc.ul.pt/places09/preproceedings.pdf.

[17] K. Honda, A. Mukhamedov, G. Brown, T.-C. Chen, and N. Yoshida. Scribbling interactions with a formal foundation. In *ICDCIT*, LNCS. Springer, 2011. To appear.

[18] K. Honda, V. T. Vasconcelos, and M. Kubo. Language primitives and type disciplines for structured communication-based programming. In *ESOP'98*, volume 1381 of *LNCS*, pages 22–138. Springer, 1998.

[19] K. Honda, N. Yoshida, and M. Carbone. Multiparty Asynchronous Session Types. In *POPL*, pages 273–284, 2008.

[20] R. Hu, D. Kouzapas, O. Pernet, N. Yoshida, and K. Honda. Type-Safe Eventful Sessions in Java. In *ECOOP'10*, volume 6183 of *LNCS*, pages 329–353. Springer, 2010.

[21] R. Hu, N. Yoshida, and K. Honda. Session-Based Distributed Programming in Java. In *ECOOP'08*, volume 5142 of *LNCS*, pages 516–541, 2008.

[22] D. Mostrous, N. Yoshida, and K. Honda. Global principal typing in partially commutative asynchronous sessions. In *ESOP'09*, volume 5502 of *LNCS*, pages 316–332, 2009.

[23] L. Nielsen, N. Yoshida, and K. Honda. Multiparty symmetric sum-types. Technical Report 8, Department of Computing, Imperial College London, 2009. To appear in Express'10. Apims Project at: http://www.thelas.dk/index.php/apims.

[24] Ocean Observatories Initiative (OOI). http://www.oceanleadership.org/programs-and-partnerships/ocean-observin%g/ooi/.

[25] O. Pernet, N. Ng, R. Hu, N. Yoshida, and Y. Kryftis. Safe Parallel Programming with Session Java. Technical Report 14, Department of Computing, Imperial College London, 2010.

[26] A. Raad. *Smelling of Roses: ROles, Specification, Specification and Scrutiny*. DoC master's thesis, Imperial College London, 2010.

[27] Savara JBoss Project. http://www.jboss.org/savara.

[28] Scribble Project. http://www.jboss.org/scribble.

[29] K. C. Sivaramakrishnan, K. Nagaraj, L. Ziarek, and P. Eugster. Efficient session type guided distributed interaction. In *Coordination'10*, volume 6116 of *LNCS*, pages 152–167. Springer, 2010.

[30] K. Suenaga. Type-based deadlock-freedom verification for non-block-structured lock primitives and mutable references. In *APLAS*, volume 5356 of *LNCS*, pages 155–170, 2008.

[31] K. Takeuchi, K. Honda, and M. Kubo. An interaction-based language and its typing system. In *PARLE'94*, volume 817 of *LNCS*, pages 398–413. Springer, 1994.

[32] UNIFI. International Organization for Standardization ISO 20022 UNIversal Financial Industry message scheme. http://www.iso20022.org.

[33] H. Viera. *A Calculus for Modeling and Analyzing Conversations in Service-Oriented Computing*. PhD thesis, University Nova de Lisboa, 2010.

[34] N. Yoshida. Graph types for monadic mobile processes. In *FSTTCS*, volume 1180 of *LNCS*, pages 371–386, 1996.

[35] N. Yoshida, P.-M. Deniélou, A. Bejleri, and R. Hu. Parameterised multiparty session types. In *FoSSaCs*, volume 6014 of *LNCS*, pages 128–145, 2010.

[36] N. Yoshida, V. T. Vasconcelos, H. Paulino, and K. Honda. Session-based compilation framework for multicore programming. In *FMCO'08*, volume 5751 of *LNCS*, pages 226–246. Springer, 2009.

Practical Affine Types

Jesse A. Tov Riccardo Pucella
Northeastern University, Boston, Massachusetts, USA
{tov,riccardo}@ccs.neu.edu

Abstract

Alms is a general-purpose programming language that supports practical affine types. To offer the expressiveness of Girard's linear logic while keeping the type system light and convenient, Alms uses expressive kinds that minimize notation while maximizing polymorphism between affine and unlimited types.

A key feature of Alms is the ability to introduce abstract affine types via ML-style signature ascription. In Alms, an interface can impose stiffer resource usage restrictions than the principal usage restrictions of its implementation. This form of sealing allows the type system to naturally and directly express a variety of resource management protocols from special-purpose type systems.

We present two pieces of evidence to demonstrate the validity of our design goals. First, we introduce a prototype implementation of Alms and discuss our experience programming in the language. Second, we establish the soundness of the core language. We also use the core model to prove a principal kinding theorem.

Categories and Subject Descriptors D.3.3 [*Programming Languages*]: Language Constructs and Features

General Terms Languages

Keywords Affine types, linear logic, type systems, polymorphism, modules

1. A Practical Affine Type System

Alms is a practical, general-purpose programming language with affine types. *Affine types* enforce the discipline that some values are not used more than once, which in Alms makes it easy to define new, resource-aware abstractions. *General-purpose* means that Alms offers a full complement of modern language features suitable for writing a wide range of programs. *Practical* means that Alms is neither vaporware nor a minimal calculus—it is possible to download Alms today and try it out.

Rationale. Resource-aware type systems divide into two camps: foundational calculi hewing closely to linear logic, and implementations of special-purpose type systems designed to solve special problems. We argue that a general, practical type system based on Girard's linear logic (1987) can naturally and directly express many of the special cases, such as region-based memory management, aliasing control, session types, and typestate. To this end, the language must satisfy several desiderata:

PoPL'11, January 26–28, 2011, Austin, Texas, USA.


```
module type RW_LOCK = sig
  type (α, β) array    — array of α identified by β
  type excl            — exclusive access
  type shared          — shared access
  type β@γ : A         — grants γ-level access to array β

  val new      : int → α → ∃β. (α, β) array

  val acquireW : (α, β) array → β@excl
  val acquireR : (α, β) array → β@shared
  val release  : (α, β) array → β@γ → unit

  val set : (α, β) array → int → α → β@excl → β@excl
  val get : (α, β) array → int → β@γ → α × β@γ
end
```

Figure 1. An interface for reader-writer locks (§2)

Convenience. Unlimited values are the common case, so working with them is as smooth as in a conventional language.

Expressiveness. A wide variety of resource-aware type systems appear naturally as idioms.

Familiarity. It is easy to use and understand.

Pragmatics. It provides the trappings of a modern, high-level programming language, such as algebraic datatypes, pattern matching, exceptions, concurrency, and modules.

Soundness. It has a clear theoretical foundation.

We show that Alms meets these criteria.

Alms employs a dependent kind system to determine whether a particular type is affine or unlimited and to support polymorphism over affine and unlimited types. This approach may sound complicated, but in practice it is no stranger or harder to understand than the type systems of other functional programming languages.

Affine types, a weakening of linear types, forbid duplication of some values; unlike with linear types, all values may be dropped. This flexibility is appropriate to a high-level, garbage-collected language, and it interacts better with other features such as exceptions.

Our Contributions. This paper introduces the programming language Alms, its implementation, and its basic theory:

- We describe the design of Alms, whose novel features include precise kinds for affine type constructors, and demonstrate how it expresses a variety of resource-aware idioms (§2).
- Our implementation is a usable, full-featured prototype in which we have written several thousand lines of code (§3).
- Alms rests on a firm theoretical basis. We provide a formal model (§4) and establish essential theoretical properties (§5).

Our implementation and full proofs are available at www.ccs.neu.edu/~tov/pubs/alms.

2. Learn Alms in 2.5 Pages

Alms is a typed, call-by-value, impure functional language with algebraic data types, pattern matching, reference cells, threads, exceptions, and modules with opaque signature ascription. Alms reads like Ocaml (Leroy et al. 2008) but is explicitly typed. In most cases local type inference renders explicit type instantiation unnecessary.

We introduce Alms through a series of examples. Consider a simple Alms function, *deposit*, that updates one element of an array by adding an integer:

```
let deposit (a: int Array.array) (acct: int) (amount: int) =
  Array.set a acct (Array.get a acct + amount)
```

This function has a race condition between the read and the write, so we may want to use a lock to enforce mutual exclusion:

```
let deposit (a: int Array.array) (acct: int)
            (amount: int) (lock: Lock.lock) =
  Lock.acquire lock;
  Array.set a acct (Array.get a acct + amount);
  Lock.release lock
```

Affine data. Locks can ensure mutual exclusion, but using them correctly is error-prone. A rather coarse alternative to ensure mutual exclusion is to forbid aliasing of the array altogether. If we have the only reference to an array then no other process can operate on it concurrently. In Alms, we do this by declaring an interface that includes a new, abstract array type:

```
module type AF_ARRAY = sig
  type α array : A
  val new : int → α → α array
  val set  : α array → int -A→ α -A→ α array
  val get  : α array → int -A→ α × α array
end
module AfArray : AF_ARRAY = struct ... end
```

The notation ": **A**" specifies that type α AfArray.array has kind **A**, as in *affine*, which means that any attempt to duplicate a reference to such an array is a type error. Two points about the types of *AfArray.get* and *AfArray.set* are worth noting:

- Each must return an array because the caller cannot reuse the reference to the array supplied as an argument.
- Type $\tau_1 \xrightarrow{\mathsf{A}} \tau_2$ has kind **A**, which means that it may be used at most once.[1] This is necessary because reusing a function partially applied to an affine value would reuse that value.

We now rewrite *deposit* to use the AF_ARRAY interface:

```
let deposit (a: int AfArray.array) (acct: int) (amt: int) =
  let (balance, a) = AfArray.get a acct in
    AfArray.set a acct (balance + amt)
```

If we attempt to use an AfArray.array more than once without single-threading it, a type error results:

```
let deposit (a: int AfArray.array) (acct: int) (amt: int) =
  let (balance,_) = AfArray.get a acct in
    AfArray.set a acct (balance + amt)
```

Alms reports that the affine variable *a* is duplicated.

Implementing *AfArray* is just a matter of wrapping the primitive array type and operations, and sealing the module with an opaque signature ascription:

```
module AfArray : AF_ARRAY = struct
  type α array = α Array.array
  let new = Array.new
  let set (a: α array) (ix: int) (v: α) = Array.set a ix v; a
  let get (a: α array) (ix: int) = (Array.get a ix, a)
end
```

The original array type α Array.array has kind **U**, as in *unlimited*, because it places no limits on duplication. We can use it to represent an abstract type of kind **A**, however, because **U** is a subkind of **A**, and Alms's kind subsumption rule allows assigning an abstract type a greater kind than that of its concrete representation. This is somewhat akin to Standard ML's treatment of equality types (Milner et al. 1997) and Ocaml's treatment of type constructor variance (Leroy et al. 2008). In SML, eqtype is subsumed by type, in that signature matching can abstract an equality type to a non-equality type but not vice versa.

We need not change *new* at all, and *get* and *set* are modified slightly to return the array as required by the interface.

Affine capabilities. The affine array interface is quite restrictive. Because it requires single-threading an array through the program, it cannot support operations that do not actually require exclusive access to the array. However, Alms supports creating a variety of abstractions to suit our needs. One way to increase our flexibility is to separate the reference to the array from the *capability* to read and write the array. Only the latter needs to be affine.

For example, we may prefer an interface that supports "dirty reads," which do not require exclusive access but are not guaranteed to observe a consistent state:

```
module type CAP_ARRAY = sig
  type (α, β) array
  type β cap : A
  val new: int → α → ∃β. (α, β) array × β cap
  val set : (α, β) array → int → α → β cap → β cap
  val get : (α, β) array → int → β cap → α × β cap
  val dirtyGet : (α, β) array → int → α
end
```

In this signature, (α, β) array is now unlimited and β cap is affine. Type array's second parameter, β, is a "stamp" used to tie it to its capability, which must have type β cap (where β matches). In particular, the type of *new* indicates that it returns an existential containing an array and a capability with matching stamps. The existential guarantees that the stamp on an array can only match the stamp on the capability created by the same call to *new*.

Operations *set* and *get* allow access to an array only when presented with the matching capability. This ensures that *set* and *get* have exclusive access with respect to other *set*s and *get*s. They no longer return the array, but they do need to return the capability. On the other hand, *dirtyGet* does not require a capability and should not return one.

For example, the CAP_ARRAY interface allows us to shuffle an array while simultaneously computing an approximate sum:

```
let shuffleAndDirtySum (a: (α, β) CapArray.array)
                       (cap: β CapArray.cap)     =
  let th1 = Thread.fork (λ_ → inPlaceShuffle a cap) in
  let th2 = Thread.fork (λ_ → dirtySumArray a) in
    (Thread.wait th1, Thread.wait th2)
```

To implement CAP_ARRAY, we need suitable representations for its two abstract types. We represent CAP_ARRAY's arrays by the primitive array type, and capabilities by type unit, which is adequate because these capabilities have no run-time significance.

[1] It is tempting to call this an affine function, but standard terminology says that an affine function uses its *argument* at most once, whereas here we have the type of a function *itself* usable at most once. Whether an Alms function is affine is determined by the kind of the type of its formal parameter.

```
module A = Array
module CapArray : CAP_ARRAY = struct
  type (α, β) array = α A.array
  type β cap        = unit
  let new (size: int) (init: α) = (A.new size init, ())
  let set (a: α A.array) (ix: int) (v: α) _ = A.set a ix v
  let get (a: α A.array) (ix: int) _ = (A.get a ix, ())
  let dirtyGet = A.get
end
```

Type unit has kind **U**, but as in the previous example, we can abstract it to **A** to match the kind of β CapArray.cap. The implementation of the operations is in terms of the underlying array operations, with some shuffling to ignore capability arguments (in *set* and *get*) and to construct tuples containing () to represent the capability in the result (in *new* and *get*).[2]

Capabilities are values. Capabilities such as β CapArray.cap often represent the state of a resource, but in Alms they are also ordinary values. They may be stored in immutable or mutable data structures, packed into exceptions and thrown, or sent over communication channels like any other value. For example, suppose we would like a list of array capabilities. Lists are defined thus in the standard library:

```
type α̂ list = Nil | Cons of α̂ × α̂ list
```

The type variables we have seen until now could only be instantiated with unlimited types, but the diacritic on type variable $\hat\alpha$ indicates that $\hat\alpha$ may be instantiated to any type, whether affine or unlimited.

Whether a list should be treated as affine or unlimited depends on whether the contents of the list is affine or unlimited. Alms represents this fact by giving the list type constructor a dependent kind, where kind $\langle\hat\alpha\rangle$ denotes the kind of $\hat\alpha$:

$$\hat\alpha \text{ list} : \langle\hat\alpha\rangle \qquad\qquad \text{— list } \textit{has kind } \Pi\hat\alpha.\,\langle\hat\alpha\rangle$$

That is, the kind of a list is the same as the kind of its element type: type int list has kind **U**, whereas β CapArray.cap list has kind **A**.

In general, the kind of a type is the least upper bound of the kinds of the types that occur directly in its representation. For example:

```
type (α̂, β̂) r = α̂ × β̂                      — ⟨α̂⟩ ⊔ ⟨β̂⟩
type (α̂, β̂) s = int × β̂                    —       ⟨β̂⟩
type (α̂, β̂) t = T₁ of α̂ | T₂ of (β̂, α̂) t   — ⟨α̂⟩ ⊔ ⟨β̂⟩
type (α̂, β̂) u = U₁ | U₂ of (β̂, α̂) u        —       U
type (α̂, β̂) v = α̂ × (unit → β̂)            — ⟨α̂⟩
type (α̂, β̂) w = α̂ × (unit -⟨β̂⟩-> unit)    — ⟨α̂⟩ ⊔ ⟨β̂⟩
```

Because both $\hat\alpha$ and $\hat\beta$ are part of the representation of $(\hat\alpha, \hat\beta)$ r, it must be affine if either of its parameters is affine. On the other hand, the phantom parameter $\hat\alpha$ is not part of the representation of $(\hat\alpha, \hat\beta)$ s, so that has kind $\langle\hat\beta\rangle$. The kinds of t and u are the least solutions to these inequalities:

$$\kappa((\hat\alpha,\hat\beta)\,\mathsf{t}) \sqsupseteq \kappa(\hat\alpha) \qquad \kappa((\hat\alpha,\hat\beta)\,\mathsf{u}) \sqsupseteq \mathbf{U}$$
$$\kappa((\hat\alpha,\hat\beta)\,\mathsf{t}) \sqsupseteq \kappa((\hat\beta,\hat\alpha)\,\mathsf{t}) \qquad \kappa((\hat\alpha,\hat\beta)\,\mathsf{u}) \sqsupseteq \kappa((\hat\beta,\hat\alpha)\,\mathsf{u})$$

The kind of each type must be at least as restrictive as the kinds of all of its alternatives.

For $(\hat\alpha, \hat\beta)$ v, the kind of $\hat\beta$ does not appear because the domain and codomain of a function type are not part of the function's representation. Instead, function types have their kind in a superscript as in the definition of type w. We saw this in the *AfArray* example, where the superscripts were all **A**. (When the kind is **U**, we often omit it.) We discuss the kinds of function types and their subtyping in more depth in §4.3.

More possibilities. The rules of Alms are flexible enough to express a wide variety of designs. For example, the ability to store capabilities in data structures allows us to create a more dynamic interface than the static capabilities of *CapArray*:

```
module type CAP_LOCK_ARRAY = sig
  include CAP_ARRAY
  val new     : int → α → ∃β. (α, β) array
  val acquire : (α, β) array → β cap
  val release : (α, β) array → β cap → unit
end
```

This signature changes the type of *new* to return an array (with unique tag β) but no capability. To operate on the array, one needs to request a capability using *acquire*. Subsequent attempts to acquire a capability for the same array block until the capability is *released*.

We implement CAP_LOCK_ARRAY in terms of *CapArray* without any privileged knowledge about the representation of its capabilities. The implementation relies on mvars, synchronized variables based Id's *M-structures* (Barth et al. 1991). An $\hat\alpha$ mvar may hold a value of type $\hat\alpha$ or it may be *empty*. While an mvar may contain an affine value, the mvar itself is always unlimited. This is safe because calling *take* on a non-empty mvar removes the value and returns it, while *take* on an empty mvar blocks until another thread *puts* a value in it.

To implement CAP_LOCK_ARRAY we now represent an array as a pair of the underlying (α, β) CapArray.array and an mvar to store its capability:

```
module CapLockArray : CAP_LOCK_ARRAY = struct
  module A = CapArray
  type (α, β) array = (α, β) A.array × β cap MVar.mvar
  let new (size: int) (init: α) =
    let (β, a, cap) = A.new size init in
      (a, MVar.new cap)
  let acquire ((_, mvar): (α, β) array) = MVar.take mvar
  let release ((_, mvar): (α, β) array) (cap: β cap) =
    MVar.put mvar cap
  let set ((a,_): (α, β) array) = A.set a
  let get ((a,_): (α, β) array) = A.get a
  ...
end
```

The *new* operation creates a new array-capability pair and stores the capability in an mvar. Operations *acquire* and *release* use the mvar component of the representation, while the old operations such as *set* must be lifted to project out the underlying CapArray.array.

There are many more possibilities. Figures 1 and 2 show two interfaces for reader-writer locks, which at any one time allow either exclusive read-write access or shared read-only access. Signature RW_LOCK (figure 1 on the first page) describes dynamic reader-writer locks. The signature declares nullary types excl and shared and an affine, binary type constructor $(\cdot\,@\,\cdot)$. Capabilities now have type $\beta@\gamma$, where β ties the capability to a particular array and γ records whether the lock is exclusive or shared. Operation *set* requires an exclusive lock (β@excl), but *get* allows γ to be shared or excl.

Signature FRACTIONAL (figure 2) describes static reader-writer locks based on fractional capabilities (Boyland 2003). As in the previous example, the capability type (β, γ) cap has a second parameter, which in this case represents a fraction of the whole

[2] If you think this unit shuffling is unnecessary, we agree (§7).

```
module type FRACTIONAL = sig
  type (α, β) array
  type 1
  type 2
  type γ/δ
  type (β, γ) cap : A
  val new : int → α → ∃β. (α, β) array × (β, 1) cap
  val split: (β, γ) cap → (β, γ/2) cap × (β, γ/2) cap
  val join : (β, γ/2) cap × (β, γ/2) cap → (β, γ) cap
  val set  : (α, β) array → int → α →
               (β, 1) cap → (β, 1) cap
  val get  : (α, β) array → int →
               (β, γ) cap → α × (β, γ) cap
end
```

Figure 2. Another interface for reader-writer locks

capability. The fraction is represented using type constructors 1, 2, and $(\cdot\,/\,\cdot)$. A capability of type $(\beta, 1)$ cap grants exclusive access to the array with tag β, while a fraction less than 1 such as 1/2 or 1/2/2 indicates shared access. There are operations *split*, which splits a capability whose fraction is γ into two capabilities of fraction $\gamma/2$, and *join*, which combines two $\gamma/2$ capabilities back into one γ capability. Again, *set* requires exclusive access but *get* does not.

Syntax matters. Given *CapLockArray* as defined above, we can rewrite *deposit* to take advantage of it:

```
open CapLockArray
let deposit (a: (int, β) array) (acct: int) (amt: int) =
  let cap            = acquire a in
  let (balance, cap) = get a acct cap in
  let cap            = set a acct (balance + amt) cap in
    release a cap
```

While this gets the job done, the explicit threading of the capability can be inconvenient and hard to read. To address this, Alms provides preliminary support for an alternative syntax inspired by a proposal by Mazurak et al. (2010):

```
let deposit (a: (int, β) array) (acct: int) (amt: int) =
  let !cap = acquire a in
    set a acct (get a acct cap + amt) cap;
    release a cap
```

The pattern !*cap* bound by **let** marks *cap* as an "imperative variable," which means that within its scope, functions applied to *cap* are expected to return a pair of their real result and the new version of *cap*. Alms transforms this code into the explicitly-threaded version above. Currently this transformation happens before type checking, which means that it cannot compromise soundness but also cannot exploit type information.

3. Implementation and Experience

Our prototype, implemented in 16k lines of Haskell, is available at www.ccs.neu.edu/~tov/pubs/alms. Besides a usable interpreter, it includes all the example code from this paper and other Alms examples illustrating a variety of concepts:

- A capability-based interface to Berkeley Sockets ensures that the protocol to set up a socket is followed correctly. This library also shows how exceptions may be used for error recovery in the presence of affine capabilities.
- An echo server is built on top of the socket library.
- Two session types (Gay et al. 2003) libraries demonstrate different approaches to alternation: one uses anonymous sums and the other uses algebraic datatypes for named branches.
- Our version of Sutherland and Hodgman (1974) re-entrant polygon clipping uses session types to connect stream transducers.
- The Alms standard library implements higher-order coercions for checked downcasts which can, for example, turn a function of type (unit $\xrightarrow{\mathsf{U}}$ unit) $\xrightarrow{\mathsf{U}}$ thread into a function of type (unit $\xrightarrow{\mathsf{A}}$ unit) $\xrightarrow{\mathsf{U}}$ thread by adding a dynamic check.

These examples are not the last word on what can be done in a language like Alms. Haskell's type classes (Wadler and Blott 1989), a general mechanism invented to solve specific problems, have since found myriad unanticipated uses. Similarly, a practical, general form of substructural types as offered by Alms likely has many applications waiting to be uncovered.

We have now written several thousand lines of code in Alms, and this experience has led to improvements in both its design and our skill at using what it has to offer. For example, an earlier version of Alms had only unlimited ($\xrightarrow{\mathsf{U}}$) and affine ($\xrightarrow{\mathsf{A}}$) arrows, but Alms's behavioral contract library motivated the introduction of arrows whose kinds involve type variables (*e.g.*, $\xrightarrow{\langle\hat{\alpha}\rangle}$). In particular, we found ourselves writing the same function multiple times with different qualifiers in the argument types, and the addition of usage qualifier expressions eliminates this redundancy.

4. The Calculus ${}^a\lambda_{ms}$

We model Alms with a calculus based on System $F^{\omega}_{<:}$, the higher-order polymorphic λ calculus with subtyping (Pierce 2002). Our calculus, ${}^a\lambda_{ms}$, makes several important changes to $F^{\omega}_{<:}$:

- Our type system's structural rules are limited. In particular contraction, which duplicates variables in a typing context to make them accessible to multiple subterms, applies only to variables whose type is of the unlimited kind. Variables of affine or polymorphic kind cannot be contracted.
- Our kind system is enriched with dependent kinds.
- Our kind system is also enriched with variance on type operators (Steffen 1997), which allows abstract type constructors to specify how their results vary in relation to their parameters.
- Type operators are limited to first-order kinds—that is, type operators may not take type operators as parameters.
- Universally-quantified type variables are bounded only by a kind, not by a type.
- The subtyping relation is induced by the subtyping rule for functions, whereby an unlimited-use function may be supplied where a one-use function is expected.

The calculus ${}^a\lambda_{ms}$ also includes more types and terms than a minimal presentation of $F^{\omega}_{<:}$. Because we are interested in practical issues, we think it is important that our model include products,[3] sums, mutable references, and non-termination.

We do not model modules directly in ${}^a\lambda_{ms}$, but its higher-kinded type abstraction makes ${}^a\lambda_{ms}$ a suitable target for the first-order fragment of Rossberg et al.'s (2010) "F-ing modules" translation.

[3] In linear logic terms, our calculus (like Alms) supplies multiplicative products ($\otimes$) and additive sums ($\oplus$) directly. Additive products ($\&$) are easily encoded by

$$\tau_1 \,\&\, \tau_2 \triangleq \forall\alpha{:}\mathsf{A}.\,(\tau_1 \xrightarrow{\mathsf{A}} \alpha) + (\tau_2 \xrightarrow{\mathsf{A}} \alpha) \xrightarrow{\varphi_1 \sqcup \varphi_2} \alpha$$

$$[e_1, e_2] \triangleq \Lambda\alpha{:}\mathsf{A}.\,\lambda k.\ \mathsf{case}\ k\ \mathsf{of}\ \iota_1\, x_1 \to x_1\, e_1;\ \iota_2\, x_2 \to x_2\, e_2,$$

where φ_1 and φ_2 are the kinds of τ_1 and τ_2.

$$
\begin{aligned}
\varphi &::= \mathsf{q} \mid \langle\alpha\rangle \mid \varphi_1 \sqcup \varphi_2 \mid \varphi_1 \sqcap \varphi_2 && \textit{(usage qualifiers)}\\
\kappa &::= \varphi \mid \Pi\alpha^{\mathfrak{v}}.\kappa && \textit{(kinds)}\\
\tau &::= \alpha \mid \lambda\alpha.\tau \mid \tau_1\,\tau_2 \mid \forall\alpha{:}\kappa.\tau \mid \tau_1 \xrightarrow{\varphi} \tau_2 && \textit{(types)}\\
&\quad\mid 1 \mid (+) \mid (\times) \mid \mathsf{aref}\\
e &::= x \mid \lambda x{:}\tau.e \mid e_1\,e_2 \mid \Lambda\alpha{:}\kappa.v \mid e[\tau] && \textit{(terms)}\\
&\quad\mid \langle\rangle \mid \langle e_1, e_2\rangle \mid \mathsf{case}\ e_1\ \mathsf{of}\ \langle x_1, x_2\rangle \to e_2\\
&\quad\mid \iota_1\ e \mid \iota_2\ e \mid \mathsf{case}\ e\ \mathsf{of}\ \iota_1\ x \to e_1;\ \iota_2\ y \to e_2\\
&\quad\mid \mathsf{fix}\ e \mid \mathsf{new}\ e \mid \mathsf{swap}\ e_1\,e_2 \mid \mathsf{delete}\ e \mid \mathsf{ptr}\ \ell\\
v &::= \lambda x{:}\tau.e \mid \Lambda\alpha{:}\kappa.v \mid \langle\rangle \mid \langle v_1, v_2\rangle && \textit{(values)}\\
&\quad\mid \iota_1\ v \mid \iota_2\ v \mid \mathsf{ptr}\ \ell\\
\Gamma, \Sigma &::= \cdot \mid \alpha{:}\kappa \mid x{:}\tau \mid \ell{:}\tau \mid \Gamma_1, \Gamma_2 && \textit{(typing contexts)}
\end{aligned}
$$

$(\mathsf{q}, \sqsubseteq, \sqcup, \sqcap)$

(qual. constants)

$(\mathfrak{v}, \sqsubseteq, \sqcup, \sqcap)$

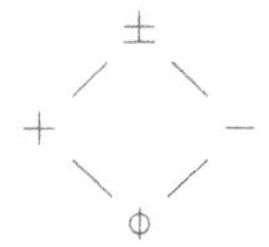

(variances)

$\mathfrak{v}_1 \cdot \mathfrak{v}_2 = \mathfrak{v}$

·	±	−	+	ϕ
±	±	±	±	ϕ
−	±	+	−	ϕ
+	±	−	+	ϕ
ϕ	ϕ	ϕ	ϕ	ϕ

(variance composition)

Figure 3. Syntax of ${}^a\lambda_{ms}$

$\boxed{s; e \longmapsto s'; e'}$ (small-step reduction)

$$
\begin{aligned}
s; (\lambda x{:}\tau.e)\, v &\longmapsto s; [v/x]e\\
s; (\Lambda\alpha{:}\kappa.v)[\tau] &\longmapsto s; [\tau/\alpha]v\\
s; \mathsf{fix}\ v &\longmapsto s; v\,(\mathsf{fix}\ v)\\
s; \mathsf{new}\ v &\longmapsto s \uplus \{\ell \mapsto v\}; \mathsf{ptr}\ \ell\\
s \uplus \{\ell \mapsto v_1\}; \mathsf{swap}\,(\mathsf{ptr}\ \ell)\, v_2 &\longmapsto s \uplus \{\ell \mapsto v_2\}; \langle \mathsf{ptr}\ \ell, v_1\rangle\\
s \uplus \{\ell \mapsto v\}; \mathsf{delete}\,(\mathsf{ptr}\ \ell) &\longmapsto s; \langle\rangle
\end{aligned}
$$

$$
\frac{s; e \longmapsto s'; e'}{s; E[e] \longmapsto s'; E[e']}
$$

$$
\begin{aligned}
E &::= [\,] \mid E\,e \mid v\,E \mid E[\tau] \mid \langle E, e\rangle \mid \langle v, E\rangle && \textit{(evaluation contexts)}\\
&\quad\mid \mathsf{case}\ E\ \mathsf{of}\ \langle x_1, x_2\rangle \to e \mid \iota_1\ E \mid \iota_2\ E\\
&\quad\mid \mathsf{case}\ E\ \mathsf{of}\ \iota_1\ x \to e_1;\ \iota_2\ y \to e_2\\
&\quad\mid \mathsf{fix}\ E \mid \mathsf{new}\ E \mid \mathsf{swap}\ E\,e \mid \mathsf{swap}\ v\,E \mid \mathsf{delete}\ E\\
s &::= \{\} \mid \{\ell \mapsto v\} \mid s_1 \uplus s_2 && \textit{(stores)}
\end{aligned}
$$

Figure 4. Operational semantics (selected rules)

4.1 Syntax

We begin with the syntax of ${}^a\lambda_{ms}$ in figure 3. Terms (e) include the usual terms from System F (variables, abstractions, applications, type abstractions, and type applications), several forms for data construction and elimination (nil, pairs, pair elimination, sum injections, and sum elimination), recursion (fix e), and several operations on reference cells (allocation, linear swap, and deallocation). Location names (ptr ℓ) appear at run time but are not present in source terms. Values (v) are standard.

Types (τ) include type variables, type-level abstraction and application, universal quantification, function types, and type constructor constants for unit, sums, products, and references. As in Alms, the function arrow carries a *usage qualifier* (φ), which specifies whether the function is unlimited or one-use.

The two constant usage qualifiers (q), U for unlimited and A for affine, are the bottom and top of the two-element lattice in figure 3. Now consider the K combinator $\Lambda\alpha{:}\langle\alpha\rangle.\Lambda\beta{:}\langle\beta\rangle.\lambda x{:}\alpha.\lambda y{:}\beta.x$ partially applied to a value: $\mathrm{K}[\tau_1][\tau_2]\ v$. Whether it is safe to duplicate this term depends on whether it is safe to duplicate v, and this is reflected in the instantiation of α. To express this relationship, we introduce usage qualifier expressions (φ), which form a bounded, distributive lattice over type variables with U and A as bottom and top. We can thus give K type $\forall\alpha{:}\langle\alpha\rangle.\forall\beta{:}\langle\beta\rangle.\alpha \xrightarrow{\mathsf{U}} \beta \xrightarrow{\langle\alpha\rangle} \alpha$.

Qualifier expressions are the base kinds of ${}^a\lambda_{ms}$—that is, the kinds that classify proper types that may in turn classify values. To classify type operators, kinds (κ) also include dependent product kinds, written $\Pi\alpha^{\mathfrak{v}}.\kappa$. This is the kind of a type operator that, when applied to a type with kind φ, gives a type with kind $[\varphi/\alpha]\kappa$. For example, the kind of the Alms list type constructor in §2 is $\Pi\alpha^{+}.\langle\alpha\rangle$, which means that list τ has the same kind as τ.[4]

The superscript $+$ in kind $\Pi\alpha^{+}.\langle\alpha\rangle$ means that list is a covariant (or monotone) type constructor: if τ_1 is a subtype of τ_2 then list τ_1 is a subtype of list τ_2. Variances ($\mathfrak{v}$) form a four-point lattice (figure 3). A type operator may also be contravariant ($-$), where the result varies inversely with the argument; omnivariant (ϕ), where argument may vary freely without affecting the result; or invariant ($\pm$) where the argument may not vary at all without producing a subtyping-unrelated result. We define a composition operation ($\cdot$) on variances, where $\mathfrak{v}_1 \cdot \mathfrak{v}_2$ is the variance of the composition of type operators having variances $\mathfrak{v}_1$ and $\mathfrak{v}_2$.

The kinds of the type constructors for sums and references may aid understanding. The sum type constructor $(+)$ has kind $\Pi\alpha^{+}.\Pi\beta^{+}.\langle\alpha\rangle \sqcup \langle\beta\rangle$. This means that the kind of a sum type is at least as restrictive as the kinds of its disjuncts. It is covariant in both arguments, which means that $\tau_1 + \tau_2$ is a subtype of $\tau_1' + \tau_2'$ if τ_1 is a subtype of τ_1' and τ_2 is a subtype of τ_2'. The reference type constructor, on the other hand, has kind $\Pi\alpha^{\pm}.\mathsf{A}$. This means that reference cells are always affine and that their types do not support subtyping in either direction.

Typing contexts (Γ or Σ) associate type variables with their kinds, variables with their types, and locations with the types of their contents. By convention, we use Γ for typing contexts that include neither affine variables nor locations, and we use Σ for typing contexts that may include locations and affine (or indeterminate) variables. We use $\mathrm{dom}(\Gamma)$ to refer to the type variables, variables, and locations mapped by a context.

We define the free type variables in a variety of syntactic forms ($\mathrm{ftv}(e)$, $\mathrm{ftv}(\tau)$, $\mathrm{ftv}(\kappa)$, etc.) in the standard way. We use $\mathrm{locs}(e)$ to denote the set of location names present in term e. There are no binders for locations.

4.2 Operational Semantics

The operational semantics of ${}^a\lambda_{ms}$ is mostly a standard call-by-value reduction semantics. We give a selection of rules in figure 4. The reduction relation ($\longmapsto$) relates configurations ($s; e$) comprising a store and a term. A store maps locations (ℓ) to values (v). Stores are taken to be unordered and do not repeat location names.

The rules for reference operations are worth noting. In store s, new v chooses a fresh location ℓ, adding v to the store at location ℓ and reducing to the reference ptr ℓ. The operation swap (ptr ℓ) v_2 requires that the store have location ℓ holding some value v_1. It swaps v_2 for v_1 in the store, returning a pair of a reference to ℓ and value v_1. Finally, delete (ptr ℓ) also requires that the store contain ℓ, which it then removes from the store. This means that freeing a location can result in a dangling pointer, which would cause subsequent attempts to access that location to get stuck. Our type system prevents this.

[4] Whereas Alms uses ML's conventional postfix notation for type-level application, ${}^a\lambda_{ms}$ uses prefix application.

$\Gamma \vdash \kappa$	kind κ is well formed	(fig. 6)
$\Gamma \vdash \kappa_1 <: \kappa_2$	kind κ_1 is subsumed by κ_2	(fig. 6)
$\Gamma \vdash \alpha \in \tau \updownarrow \mathfrak{v}$	type τ varies $\mathfrak{v}$-ly when α increases	(fig. 7)
$\Gamma \vdash \tau : \kappa$	type τ has kind κ	(fig. 7)
$\Gamma \vdash \tau_1 <:^{\mathfrak{v}} \tau_2$	type τ_1 is $\mathfrak{v}$-related to type τ_2	(fig. 7)
$\Gamma \vdash \Sigma \preceq \varphi$	context Σ is bounded by qualifier φ	(fig. 8)
$\vdash (\Gamma_0; \Sigma_0), \Sigma' \rightsquigarrow \Gamma; \Sigma$	extending $\Gamma_0; \Sigma_0$ with Σ' gives $\Gamma; \Sigma$	(fig. 8)
$\Gamma; \Sigma \rhd e : \tau$	term e has type τ	(fig. 9)
$\Sigma_1 \rhd s : \Sigma_2$	store s has type Σ_2	(fig. 10)
$\rhd\, s; e : \tau$	configuration $s; e$ has type τ	(fig. 10)

Figure 5. Type system judgments

$\boxed{\Gamma \vdash \kappa}$ (kind well-formedness)

OK-QUAL
$$\frac{\mathrm{ftv}(\varphi) \subseteq \mathrm{dom}(\Gamma)}{\Gamma \vdash \varphi}$$

OK-ARR
$$\frac{\Gamma, \alpha{:}\langle\alpha\rangle \vdash \kappa \qquad \text{if } \alpha \in \mathrm{ftv}(\kappa) \text{ then } + \sqsubseteq \mathfrak{v}}{\Gamma \vdash \Pi\alpha^{\mathfrak{v}}.\kappa}$$

$\boxed{\Gamma \vdash \kappa_1 <: \kappa_2}$ (subkinding)

KSUB-QUAL
$$\frac{\Gamma \models \varphi_1 \sqsubseteq \varphi_2}{\Gamma \vdash \varphi_1 <: \varphi_2}$$

KSUB-ARR
$$\frac{\mathfrak{v}_1 \sqsubseteq \mathfrak{v}_2 \qquad \Gamma, \alpha{:}\langle\alpha\rangle \vdash \kappa_1 <: \kappa_2}{\Gamma \vdash \Pi\alpha^{\mathfrak{v}_1}.\kappa_1 <: \Pi\alpha^{\mathfrak{v}_2}.\kappa_2}$$

Figure 6. Statics (i): kinds

4.3 Static Semantics

Our type system involves a large number of judgments, which we summarize in figure 5. In several cases, we omit premises concerning well-formedness of contexts, which clutter the presentation and do not add anything of interest. The omitted premises appear in the extended version of this paper.

Kind judgments. Judgments on kinds appear in figure 6. The first judgment, $\Gamma \vdash \kappa$, determines whether a kind κ is well formed in typing context Γ. A base kind (*i.e.*, a usage qualifier expression) is well formed provided that Γ specifies a kind for all of its free variables. A dependent product kind $\Pi\alpha^{\mathfrak{v}}.\kappa$ is well formed if Γ maps all of its free variables, provided it satisfies a second condition: whenever the bound type variable α is free in κ—that is, when the kind is truly dependent—then variance $\mathfrak{v}$ must be $+$ or $\pm$. This rules out incoherent kinds such as $\Pi\alpha^{-}.\langle\alpha\rangle$ that classify no useful type operator but whose presence breaks the kinding relation's monotonicity property (see lemma 4).

The second judgment is subkinding: $\Gamma \vdash \kappa_1 <: \kappa_2$. As we will see, if a type has kind κ_1, then it may be used where κ_1 or any greater kind is expected. For dependent product kinds the subkinding order is merely the product order on the variance and the result kind, but for base kinds the relation relies on an interpretation of qualifier expressions.

We interpret qualifier expressions via a valuation $\mathcal{V}$, which is a map from type variables to qualifier constants. We extend $\mathcal{V}$'s domain to qualifier expressions:

$$\mathcal{V}(\mathfrak{q}) = \mathfrak{q} \qquad \mathcal{V}(\varphi_1 \sqcup \varphi_2) = \mathcal{V}(\varphi_1) \sqcup \mathcal{V}(\varphi_2)$$
$$\mathcal{V}(\langle\alpha\rangle) = \mathcal{V}(\alpha) \qquad \mathcal{V}(\varphi_1 \sqcap \varphi_2) = \mathcal{V}(\varphi_1) \sqcap \mathcal{V}(\varphi_2)$$

We need to interpret qualifier expressions under a typing context:

Definition 1 (Consistent valuations)**.** *A valuation $\mathcal{V}$ is **consistent with** a typing context Γ if for all $\alpha{:}\varphi \in \Gamma$, $\mathcal{V}(\alpha) \sqsubseteq \mathcal{V}(\varphi)$.*

Thus, a valuation is consistent with a context if it corresponds to a potential instantiation of the type variables, given that context.

Definition 2 (Qualifier subsumption)**.** *We say that φ_1 **is subsumed by** φ_2 in Γ, written $\Gamma \models \varphi_1 \sqsubseteq \varphi_2$, if for all valuations $\mathcal{V}$ consistent with Γ, $\mathcal{V}(\varphi_1) \sqsubseteq \mathcal{V}(\varphi_2)$.*

In other words, in all possible instantiations of the type variables in Γ, qualifier φ_1 being A implies that φ_2 is A.

Kinding and variance. The first two judgments in figure 7, for computing variances and giving kinds to types, are defined by mutual induction. It should be clear on inspection that the definitions are well-founded. Judgment $\Gamma \vdash \alpha \in \tau \updownarrow \mathfrak{v}$ means that type variable α appears in type τ at variance $\mathfrak{v}$, or in other words, that type operator $\lambda\alpha.\tau$ has variance $\mathfrak{v}$. Rules V-VAR and V-BOT say that type variables appear positively with respect to themselves and omnivariantly with respect to types in which they are not free. Rule V-ABS says that a type variable appears in a type operator $\lambda\beta.\tau$ at the same variance that it appears in the body τ. The remaining three rules are more involved:

- By rule V-APP, the variance of a type variable in a type application comes from both the operator and the operand. The variance of α in $\tau_1\,\tau_2$ is at least the variance of α in τ_1 and at least the variance of α in the τ_2 composed with the variance of operator τ_1. This makes sense: if τ is a contravariant type operator, then α appears negatively in $\tau\,\alpha$ but positively in $\tau\,(\tau\,\alpha)$.
- By rule V-ALL, the variance of α in $\forall\beta{:}\kappa.\tau$ is at least its variance in τ. However, if α appears in κ then it is invariant in $\forall\beta{:}\kappa.\tau$. This reflects the fact that universally-quantified types are related only if their bounds (κ) match exactly, so changing a type variable that appears in κ produces an unrelated type. (This means that ${}^{a}\lambda_{ms}$ is based on the *kernel* variant of $\mathrm{F}^{\omega}_{<:}$ (Pierce 2002).)
- By rule V-ARR, the variance of α in a function type $\tau_1 \xrightarrow{\varphi} \tau_2$ is at least its variance in the codomain τ_2 and at least the opposite (composition with $-$) of its variance in the domain τ_1. This reflects function argument contravariance. The variance of α is at least $+$ if it appears in the qualifier expression φ.

The second judgment, $\Gamma \vdash \tau : \kappa$, assigns kinds to well formed types. Rule K-VAR merely looks up the kind of a type variable in the context. Rules K-ABS and K-APP are the usual rules for dependent abstraction and application, with two small changes in rule K-ABS. First, it associates α with *itself* in the context, as $\alpha{:}\langle\alpha\rangle$, which ensures that occurrences of α in τ can be reflected in κ. Second, it appeals to the variance judgment to determine the variance of the type operator. Rule K-ALL assigns a universal type the same kind as its body, but with A replacing α. This is necessary because the resulting kind is outside the scope of α. Qualifier A is a safe bound for any instantiation of α, and no terms have types that lose precision by this choice. The kind of an arrow type, in rule K-ARR, is just the qualifier expression attached to the arrow. The remaining rules give kinds for type constructor constants.

Type equivalence and dereliction subtyping. The last judgment in figure 7 is subtyping. The subtyping relation is parametrized by a variance $\mathfrak{v}$, which gives the direction of the subtyping: $\Gamma \vdash \tau_1 <:^{+} \tau_2$ is the usual direction, judging τ_1 a subtype of τ_2. In terms of subsumption, this means that values of type τ_1 may be used where values of type τ_2 are expected. The other variances are useful in defining the relation in the presence of $\mathfrak{v}$-variant type operators: $(<:^{-})$ gives the inverse of the subtyping relation, $(<:^{\pm})$ relates only equivalent types, and $(<:^{\phi})$ relates all types. We can see how this works this in rule TSUB-APP. To determine whether $\tau_{11}\,\tau_{12}$ is a

$\boxed{\Gamma \vdash \alpha \in \tau \updownarrow \mathfrak{v}}$ (variance of type variables with respect to types)

$$\text{V-VAR}\quad \frac{}{\Gamma \vdash \alpha \in \alpha \updownarrow +} \qquad \text{V-BOT}\quad \frac{\alpha \notin \mathrm{ftv}(\tau)}{\Gamma \vdash \alpha \in \tau \updownarrow \phi} \qquad \text{V-ABS}\quad \frac{\Gamma, \beta{:}\langle\beta\rangle \vdash \alpha \in \tau \updownarrow \mathfrak{v}}{\Gamma \vdash \alpha \in \lambda\beta.\tau \updownarrow \mathfrak{v}}$$

$$\text{V-APP}\quad \frac{\Gamma \vdash \alpha \in \tau_1 \updownarrow \mathfrak{v}_1 \qquad \Gamma \vdash \alpha \in \tau_2 \updownarrow \mathfrak{v}_2 \qquad \Gamma \vdash \tau_1 : \Pi\beta^{\mathfrak{v}_3}.\kappa_3}{\Gamma \vdash \alpha \in \tau_1\,\tau_2 \updownarrow \mathfrak{v}_1 \sqcup (\mathfrak{v}_2 \cdot \mathfrak{v}_3)}$$

$$\text{V-ALL}\quad \frac{\Gamma, \beta{:}\kappa \vdash \alpha \in \tau \updownarrow \mathfrak{v}_1 \qquad \mathfrak{v}_2 = \text{if } \alpha \in \mathrm{ftv}(\kappa) \text{ then } \pm \text{ else } \phi}{\Gamma \vdash \alpha \in \forall\beta{:}\kappa.\tau \updownarrow \mathfrak{v}_1 \sqcup \mathfrak{v}_2}$$

$$\text{V-ARR}\quad \frac{\Gamma \vdash \alpha \in \tau_1 \updownarrow \mathfrak{v}_1 \qquad \Gamma \vdash \alpha \in \tau_2 \updownarrow \mathfrak{v}_2 \qquad \mathfrak{v}_3 = \text{if } \alpha \in \mathrm{ftv}(\varphi) \text{ then } + \text{ else } \phi}{\Gamma \vdash \alpha \in \tau_1 \xrightarrow{\varphi} \tau_2 \updownarrow -\mathfrak{v}_1 \sqcup \mathfrak{v}_2 \sqcup \mathfrak{v}_3}$$

$\boxed{\Gamma \vdash \tau : \kappa}$ (kinding of types)

$$\text{K-VAR}\quad \frac{\alpha{:}\kappa \in \Gamma}{\Gamma \vdash \alpha{:}\kappa} \qquad \text{K-ABS}\quad \frac{\Gamma, \alpha{:}\langle\alpha\rangle \vdash \tau : \kappa \qquad \Gamma, \alpha{:}\langle\alpha\rangle \vdash \alpha \in \tau \updownarrow \mathfrak{v}}{\Gamma \vdash \lambda\alpha.\tau : \Pi\alpha^{\mathfrak{v}}.\kappa} \qquad \text{K-APP}\quad \frac{\Gamma \vdash \tau_1 : \Pi\alpha^{\mathfrak{v}}.\kappa \qquad \Gamma \vdash \tau_2 : \varphi}{\Gamma \vdash \tau_1\,\tau_2 : [\varphi/\alpha]\kappa}$$

$$\text{K-ALL}\quad \frac{\Gamma, \alpha{:}\kappa \vdash \tau : \varphi}{\Gamma \vdash \forall\alpha{:}\kappa.\tau : [\mathsf{A}/\alpha]\varphi} \qquad \text{K-ARR}\quad \frac{\Gamma \vdash \tau_1 : \varphi_1 \qquad \Gamma \vdash \tau_2 : \varphi_2}{\Gamma \vdash \tau_1 \xrightarrow{\varphi} \tau_2 : \varphi} \qquad \text{K-UNIT}\quad \frac{}{\Gamma \vdash 1 : \mathsf{U}}$$

$$\text{K-SUM}\quad \frac{}{\Gamma \vdash (+) : \Pi\alpha^{+}.\Pi\beta^{+}.\langle\alpha\rangle \sqcup \langle\beta\rangle} \qquad \text{K-PROD}\quad \frac{}{\Gamma \vdash (\times) : \Pi\alpha^{+}.\Pi\beta^{+}.\langle\alpha\rangle \sqcup \langle\beta\rangle} \qquad \text{K-REF}\quad \frac{}{\Gamma \vdash \mathsf{aref} : \Pi\alpha^{\pm}.\mathsf{A}}$$

$\boxed{\Gamma \vdash \tau_1 <:^{\mathfrak{v}} \tau_2}$ (subtyping)

$$\text{TSUB-EQ}\quad \frac{\tau_1 \equiv \tau_2}{\Gamma \vdash \tau_1 <:^{\mathfrak{v}} \tau_2} \qquad \text{TSUB-TRANS}\quad \frac{\Gamma \vdash \tau_1 <:^{\mathfrak{v}} \tau_2 \qquad \Gamma \vdash \tau_2 <:^{\mathfrak{v}} \tau_3}{\Gamma \vdash \tau_1 <:^{\mathfrak{v}} \tau_3} \qquad \text{TSUB-OMNI}\quad \frac{}{\Gamma \vdash \tau_1 <:^{\phi} \tau_2}$$

$$\text{TSUB-CONTRA}\quad \frac{\Gamma \vdash \tau_2 <:^{-\mathfrak{v}} \tau_1}{\Gamma \vdash \tau_1 <:^{\mathfrak{v}} \tau_2} \qquad \text{TSUB-ABS}\quad \frac{\Gamma, \alpha{:}\langle\alpha\rangle \vdash \tau_1 <:^{\mathfrak{v}} \tau_2}{\Gamma \vdash \lambda\alpha.\tau_1 <:^{\mathfrak{v}} \lambda\alpha.\tau_2}$$

$$\text{TSUB-APP}\quad \frac{\Gamma \vdash \tau_{11} : \Pi\alpha^{\mathfrak{v}_1}.\kappa_1 \qquad \Gamma \vdash \tau_{21} : \Pi\alpha^{\mathfrak{v}_2}.\kappa_2 \qquad \Gamma \vdash \tau_{11} <:^{\mathfrak{v}} \tau_{21} \qquad \Gamma \vdash \tau_{12} <:^{\mathfrak{v}\cdot(\mathfrak{v}_1 \sqcup \mathfrak{v}_2)} \tau_{22}}{\Gamma \vdash \tau_{11}\,\tau_{12} <:^{\mathfrak{v}} \tau_{21}\,\tau_{22}}$$

$$\text{TSUB-ALL}\quad \frac{\Gamma, \alpha{:}\kappa \vdash \tau_1 <:^{\mathfrak{v}} \tau_2}{\Gamma \vdash \forall\alpha{:}\kappa.\tau_1 <:^{\mathfrak{v}} \forall\alpha{:}\kappa.\tau_2} \qquad \text{TSUB-ARR}\quad \frac{\Gamma \vdash \tau_{11} <:^{-\mathfrak{v}} \tau_{21} \qquad \Gamma \vdash \tau_{12} <:^{\mathfrak{v}} \tau_{22} \qquad \Gamma \vdash \varphi_1 <:^{\mathfrak{v}} \varphi_2}{\Gamma \vdash \tau_{11} \xrightarrow{\varphi_1} \tau_{12} <:^{\mathfrak{v}} \tau_{21} \xrightarrow{\varphi_2} \tau_{22}}$$

Figure 7. Statics (ii): types

subtype of $\tau_{21}\,\tau_{22}$, we take $\mathfrak{v}$ to be $+$, yielding

$$\frac{\Gamma \vdash \tau_{11} : \Pi\alpha^{\mathfrak{v}_1}.\kappa_1 \qquad \Gamma \vdash \tau_{21} : \Pi\alpha^{\mathfrak{v}_2}.\kappa_2 \qquad \Gamma \vdash \tau_{11} <:^{+} \tau_{21} \qquad \Gamma \vdash \tau_{12} <:^{\mathfrak{v}_1 \sqcup \mathfrak{v}_2} \tau_{22}}{\Gamma \vdash \tau_{11}\,\tau_{12} <:^{+} \tau_{21}\,\tau_{22}}.$$

This means that for the subtyping relation to hold:

- The operators must be related in the same direction, so that τ_{11} is a subtype of τ_{21}.
- The operands must be related in the direction given by the variances of the operators. For example, if both operators are covariant, then the operands must vary in the same direction, so that τ_{12} is a subtype of τ_{22}. If both operators are contravariant, then the operands must vary in the opposite direction. If the operators are invariant then the operands cannot vary at all, but if they are omnivariant then $\tau_{11}\,\tau'_{12}$ is a subtype of $\tau_{21}\,\tau'_{22}$ for any τ'_{12} and τ'_{22}.

Rule TSUB-EQ says that subtyping includes type equivalence ($\tau_1 \equiv \tau_2$), which is merely β equivalence on types. Rule TSUB-OMNI allows any pair of types to be related by ϕ-variant subtyping, and rule TSUB-CONTRA says that the opposite variance sign gives the inverse relation. Rules TSUB-ABS and TSUB-ALL specify that type operators and universally-quantified types are related if their bodies are.

Rule TSUB-ARR is more than the usual arrow subtyping rule. Beyond the usual contravariance for arguments and covariance for results, it requires that qualifiers φ_1 and φ_2 relate in the same direction. This rule is the source of non-trivial subtyping in ${}^{a}\lambda_{ms}$, without which subtyping would relate only equivalent types. The rule has two important implications.

First, an unlimited-use function can always be used where a one-use function is expected. This corresponds to linear logic's usual dereliction rule, which says that the ! ("of course!") modality may always be removed. ILL (Bierman 1993) has a rule:

$$\frac{\Delta \vdash e : !A}{\Delta \vdash \mathsf{derelict}\ e : A}\ \text{DERELICTION}.$$

Dereliction is syntax-directed in this rule, but for practical programming we consider that as too inconvenient. Thus, our subtyping relation supports dereliction as needed.

For example, the function for creating a new thread in Alms, *Thread.fork*, has type $\forall\hat\alpha.\ (\mathsf{unit} \xrightarrow{\mathsf{A}} \hat\alpha) \xrightarrow{\mathsf{U}} \hat\alpha\ \mathsf{thread}$, which means that *Thread.fork* will not call its argument more than once. However, this should not stop us from passing an unlimited-use function to *Thread.fork*, and indeed we can. Dereliction subtyping allows us to use a value of type $\mathsf{unit} \xrightarrow{\mathsf{U}} \hat\alpha$ where a value of type $\mathsf{unit} \xrightarrow{\mathsf{A}} \hat\alpha$ is expected. Alternatively, by domain contravariance, we can use *Thread.fork* where a value of type $\forall\hat\alpha.\ (\mathsf{unit} \xrightarrow{\mathsf{U}} \hat\alpha) \xrightarrow{\mathsf{U}} \hat\alpha\ \mathsf{thread}$ is expected. In this case subsumption allows us to forget *Thread.fork*'s promise not to reuse its argument.

The other important implication of dereliction subtyping will become clearer once we see how qualifier expressions are assigned to function types. Subsumption makes it reasonable to always assign functions the most permissive safe usage qualifier, because

$\boxed{\Gamma \vdash \Sigma \preceq \varphi}$ (bound of typing context)

$$\frac{}{\Gamma \vdash \cdot \preceq \mathsf{U}}\ \text{B-NIL} \qquad \frac{\Gamma \vdash \Sigma \preceq \varphi_1 \qquad \Gamma \vdash \kappa}{\Gamma \vdash \Sigma, \alpha{:}\kappa \preceq \varphi_1}\ \text{B-CONSA}$$

$$\frac{\Gamma \vdash \Sigma \preceq \varphi_1 \qquad \Gamma \vdash \tau : \varphi_2}{\Gamma \vdash \Sigma, x{:}\tau \preceq \varphi_1 \sqcup \varphi_2}\ \text{B-CONSX} \qquad \frac{\Gamma \vdash \Sigma \preceq \varphi_1 \qquad \Gamma \vdash \tau : \varphi_2}{\Gamma \vdash \Sigma, \ell{:}\tau \preceq \mathsf{A}}\ \text{B-CONSL}$$

$\boxed{\vdash (\Gamma_0; \Sigma_0), \Sigma' \rightsquigarrow \Gamma_1; \Sigma_1}$ (typing context extension)

$$\frac{}{\vdash (\Gamma; \Sigma), \cdot \rightsquigarrow \Gamma; \Sigma}\ \text{X-NIL}$$

$$\frac{\Gamma_0 \vdash \tau : \mathsf{U} \qquad \vdash (\Gamma_0, x{:}\tau; \Sigma_0), \Sigma' \rightsquigarrow \Gamma; \Sigma}{\vdash (\Gamma_0; \Sigma_0), x{:}\tau, \Sigma' \rightsquigarrow \Gamma; \Sigma}\ \text{X-CONSU} \qquad \frac{\Gamma_0 \vdash \tau : \varphi \qquad \vdash (\Gamma_0; \Sigma_0, x{:}\tau), \Sigma' \rightsquigarrow \Gamma; \Sigma}{\vdash (\Gamma_0; \Sigma_0), x{:}\tau, \Sigma' \rightsquigarrow \Gamma; \Sigma}\ \text{X-CONSA}$$

Figure 8. Statics (iii): typing contexts

subsumption then allows us to use them in a less permissive context. Dereliction subtyping applies only to function types because in both the $^a\lambda_{ms}$ calculus and Alms language only function types carry qualifiers. For instance, Alms has no separate types int^U for unlimited integers and int^A for affine integers. Integers are always unlimited. If a programmer wants an affine version of int, she can create it in Alms using the module system.

Context judgments. Figure 8 defines two judgments on contexts. Judgment $\Gamma \vdash \Sigma \preceq \varphi$, which will be important in typing functions, computes an upper bound φ on the qualifiers of all the types in context Σ. If a context contains any locations, it is bounded by A; otherwise, its bound is the least upper bound of the qualifiers of all the types of variables in the context.

The second judgment shows how environments are extended by variable bindings. The typing judgment for terms will use two typing contexts: Γ holds environment information that may be safely duplicated, such as type variables and variables of unlimited type, whereas Σ holds information, such as location types and affine variables, that disallows duplication. Given contexts Γ_0 and Σ_0, judgment $\vdash (\Gamma_0; \Sigma_0), \Sigma' \rightsquigarrow \Gamma; \Sigma$ extends them by the variables and types in Σ' to get Γ and Σ. Any variables may be placed in Σ, but only variables whose types are known to be unlimited may be placed in Γ, since Γ may be duplicated.

Term judgment. The typing judgment for terms appears in figure 9. The judgment, $\Gamma; \Sigma \rhd e : \tau$, uses two typing contexts in the style of DILL (Barber 1996): the unlimited environment Γ and the affine environment Σ. When typing multiplicative terms such as application, we distribute Γ to both subterms but partition Σ between the two:

$$\frac{\Gamma; \Sigma_1 \rhd e_1 : \tau_1 \xrightarrow{\varphi} \tau_2 \qquad \Gamma; \Sigma_2 \rhd e_2 : \tau_1}{\Gamma; \Sigma_1, \Sigma_2 \rhd e_1\, e_2 : \tau_2}\ \text{T-APP}$$

Unlike DILL, not all types in Σ are necessarily affine. Since types whose usage qualifier involves type variables are not known to be unlimited, we place those in Σ, to ensure that we do not duplicate values that *might* turn out to be affine once universally-quantified types are instantiated.

The other multiplicative rules are T-PAIR for product introduction, T-UNPAIR for product elimination, and T-SWAP for reference updates. Note that T-SWAP does not require that the type of the reference in its first parameter match the type of the value in its second—in other words, swap performs a *strong update*. To type the term case e of $\langle x_1, x_2 \rangle \to e_1$, rule T-UNPAIR first splits the affine environment into Σ_1 for typing subterm e and Σ_2 for subterm e_1. It invokes the context extension relation (figure 8) to extend Γ and Σ_2 with bindings for x_1 and x_2 in order to type e_1. The context extension relation requires that variables not known to be unlimited be added to Σ_2.

The rule for sum elimination, T-CHOOSE, is both multiplicative and additive: the affine context is split between the term being destructed and the branches of the case expression. However, the portion of the context given to the branches is shared between them, because only one or the other will be evaluated. Rule T-CHOOSE also uses the context extension relation to bind the pattern variables for the branches.

Rules T-NEW and T-DELETE introduce and eliminate reference types in the usual way. Likewise, the sum introduction rules T-INk and type abstraction rule T-TABS are standard. Rules T-VAR, T-PTR, and T-UNIT are standard for an affine calculus but not a linear one, as they implicitly support weakening by allowing Σ to contain unused bindings. Rule T-FIX is also standard, modulo the reasonable constraint that its parameter function be unlimited, since the reduction rule for fix makes a copy of the parameter.

The type application rule T-TAPP supports subkinding, because it requires only that the kind of the actual type parameter be a subkind of that of the formal parameter. This is the rule that supports the sort of type abstraction that we used in our examples of §2 to construct affine capabilities. For example, the rule lets us instantiate affine type variable α with unlimited unit type 1:

$$\frac{\Gamma; \Sigma \rhd (\Lambda\alpha{:}\mathsf{A}.\,\lambda x{:}\alpha.\,e) : \forall\alpha{:}\mathsf{A}.\,\alpha \xrightarrow{\varphi} \tau \qquad \Gamma \vdash 1 : \mathsf{U} \qquad \Gamma \vdash \mathsf{U} <: \mathsf{A}}{\Gamma; \Sigma \rhd (\Lambda\alpha{:}\mathsf{A}.\,\lambda x{:}\alpha.\,e)[1] : 1 \xrightarrow{\varphi} \tau}\ \text{T-TAPP}$$

Within its scope, α is considered *a priori* affine, regardless of how it may eventually be instantiated. This term types only if x appears in affine fashion in e.

This brings us finally to T-ABS, the rule for typing term-level λ abstractions. To type a term $\lambda x{:}\tau_1.e$, rule T-ABS uses the context extension relation to add $x{:}\tau_1$ to its contexts and types the body e in the extended contexts. It also must determine the qualifier φ that decorates the arrow. Because abstractions close over their free variables, duplicating a function also duplicates the values of its free variables. Therefore, the qualifier of a function type should be at least as restrictive as the qualifiers of the abstraction's free variables. To do this, rule T-ABS appeals to the context bounding judgment (figure 8) to find the least upper bound of the usage qualifiers of variables in the affine environment, and it requires that the function type's qualifier be equally restrictive.

This refines linear logic's usual promotion rule, which says that the ! modality may be added to propositions that in turn depend only on !-ed resources. In ILL, we have

$$\frac{!\Delta \vdash e : A}{!\Delta \vdash \mathsf{promote}\ e : !A}\ \text{PROMOTION},$$

where $!\Delta$ is a context in which all assumptions are of the form $x : !B$. As with dereliction, in our system it only makes sense to apply promotion to function types.

Our treatment of promotion indicates why we need the explicit weakening rule T-WEAK, which allows discarding unused portions of the affine environment. In order to give a function type the best qualifier possible, we need to remove from Σ any unused variables or locations that might otherwise raise the bound on Σ, and the algorithmic version of the type system as implemented in

$\boxed{\Gamma;\Sigma \rhd e : \tau}$ (typing of terms)

T-SUBSUME
$$\frac{\Gamma;\Sigma \rhd e : \tau' \qquad \Gamma \vdash \tau' <:^{+} \tau}{\Gamma;\Sigma \rhd e : \tau}$$

T-WEAK
$$\frac{\Gamma;\Sigma \rhd e : \tau}{\Gamma;\Sigma,\Sigma' \rhd e : \tau}$$

T-VAR
$$\frac{x{:}\tau \in \Gamma,\Sigma}{\Gamma;\Sigma \rhd x : \tau}$$

T-PTR
$$\frac{\ell{:}\tau \in \Sigma}{\Gamma;\Sigma \rhd \mathsf{ptr}\ \ell : \mathsf{aref}\ \tau}$$

T-ABS
$$\frac{\begin{array}{c}\vdash (\Gamma;\Sigma), x{:}\tau_1 \rightsquigarrow \Gamma';\Sigma' \\ \Gamma';\Sigma' \rhd e : \tau_2 \qquad \Gamma \vdash \Sigma \preceq \varphi\end{array}}{\Gamma;\Sigma \rhd \lambda x{:}\tau_1.e : \tau_1 \xrightarrow{\varphi} \tau_2}$$

T-APP
$$\frac{\Gamma;\Sigma_1 \rhd e_1 : \tau_1 \xrightarrow{\varphi} \tau_2 \qquad \Gamma;\Sigma_2 \rhd e_2 : \tau_1}{\Gamma;\Sigma_1,\Sigma_2 \rhd e_1\, e_2 : \tau_2}$$

T-TABS
$$\frac{\Gamma,\alpha{:}\kappa;\Sigma \rhd v : \tau}{\Gamma;\Sigma \rhd \Lambda\alpha{:}\kappa.v : \forall\alpha{:}\kappa.\tau}$$

T-TAPP
$$\frac{\Gamma;\Sigma \rhd e : \forall\alpha{:}\kappa.\tau \qquad \Gamma \vdash \tau' : \kappa' \qquad \Gamma \vdash \kappa' <: \kappa}{\Gamma;\Sigma \rhd e[\tau'] : [\tau'/\alpha]\tau}$$

T-UNIT
$$\frac{}{\Gamma;\Sigma \rhd \langle\rangle : 1}$$

T-PAIR
$$\frac{\Gamma;\Sigma_1 \rhd e_1 : \tau_1 \qquad \Gamma;\Sigma_2 \rhd e_2 : \tau_2}{\Gamma;\Sigma_1,\Sigma_2 \rhd \langle e_1, e_2\rangle : \tau_1 \times \tau_2}$$

T-UNPAIR
$$\frac{\Gamma;\Sigma_1 \rhd e : \tau_1 \times \tau_2 \qquad \vdash (\Gamma;\Sigma_2), x_1{:}\tau_1, x_2{:}\tau_2 \rightsquigarrow \Gamma';\Sigma' \qquad \Gamma';\Sigma' \rhd e_1 : \tau}{\Gamma;\Sigma_1,\Sigma_2 \rhd \mathsf{case}\ e\ \mathsf{of}\ \langle x_1, x_2\rangle \to e_1 : \tau}$$

T-INk $(k \in \{1,2\})$
$$\frac{\Gamma;\Sigma \rhd e : \tau_k}{\Gamma;\Sigma \rhd \iota_k\ e : \tau_1 + \tau_2}$$

T-CHOOSE
$$\frac{\Gamma;\Sigma \rhd e : \tau_1 + \tau_2 \qquad \vdash (\Gamma;\Sigma'), x_1{:}\tau_1 \rightsquigarrow \Gamma_1;\Sigma_1 \qquad \Gamma_1;\Sigma_1 \rhd e_1 : \tau \qquad \vdash (\Gamma;\Sigma'), x_2{:}\tau_2 \rightsquigarrow \Gamma_2;\Sigma_2 \qquad \Gamma_2;\Sigma_2 \rhd e_2 : \tau}{\Gamma;\Sigma,\Sigma' \rhd \mathsf{case}\ e\ \mathsf{of}\ \iota_1\ x_1 \to e_1;\ \iota_2\ x_2 \to e_2 : \tau}$$

T-FIX
$$\frac{\Gamma;\Sigma \rhd e : \tau \xrightarrow{\mathsf{U}} \tau}{\Gamma;\Sigma \rhd \mathsf{fix}\ e : \tau}$$

T-NEW
$$\frac{\Gamma;\Sigma \rhd e : \tau}{\Gamma;\Sigma \rhd \mathsf{new}\ e : \mathsf{aref}\ \tau}$$

T-SWAP
$$\frac{\Gamma;\Sigma_1 \rhd e_1 : \mathsf{aref}\ \tau_1 \qquad \Gamma;\Sigma_2 \rhd e_2 : \tau_2}{\Gamma;\Sigma_1,\Sigma_2 \rhd \mathsf{swap}\ e_1\, e_2 : \mathsf{aref}\ \tau_2 \times \tau_1}$$

T-DELETE
$$\frac{\Gamma;\Sigma \rhd e : \mathsf{aref}\ \tau}{\Gamma;\Sigma \rhd \mathsf{delete}\ e : 1}$$

Figure 9. Statics (iv): terms

$\boxed{\Sigma_1 \rhd s : \Sigma_2}$ (store typing)

S-NIL
$$\frac{}{\Sigma_1 \rhd \{\} : \cdot}$$

S-CONS
$$\frac{\Sigma_{11} \rhd s : \Sigma_2 \qquad \cdot;\Sigma_{12} \rhd v : \tau}{\Sigma_{11},\Sigma_{12} \rhd s \uplus \{\ell \mapsto v\} : \Sigma_2, \ell{:}\tau}$$

$\boxed{\rhd s; e : \tau}$ (configuration typing)

CONF
$$\frac{\Sigma_1 \rhd s : \Sigma_1,\Sigma_2 \qquad \cdot;\Sigma_2 \rhd e : \tau}{\rhd s; e : \tau}$$

Figure 10. Statics (v): stores and configurations

Alms does just that. In §5 we show that our implicit promotion mechanism selects the best usage qualifier for function types.

Store and configuration judgments. In order to prove our type soundness theorem, we need to lift our typing judgments to stores and run-time configurations.

The type of a store is a typing context containing the names of the store's locations and the types of their contents. The store typing judgment $\Sigma_1 \rhd s : \Sigma_2$ gives store s type Σ_2 in the context of Σ_1, which is necessary because values in the store may refer to other values in the store. Rule S-CONS shows that the resources represented by context Σ_1 (*i.e.*, Σ_{11}, Σ_{12}) are split between the values in s.

Our preservation lemma concerns typing judgments on configurations, $\rhd s; e : \tau$, which means that e has type τ in the context of store s. To type the configuration by rule CONF, we type the store, splitting its type into Σ_1, which contains locations referenced from the store, and Σ_2, which contains locations referenced from e.

5. Theoretical Results

We now state our two main theorems—principal qualifiers and type soundness—and sketch their proofs. Full versions of our proofs may be found in an extended version of this paper available at www.ccs.neu.edu/~tov/pubs/alms.

Principal qualifiers. Alms and ${}^{a}\lambda_{ms}$ go to a lot of trouble to find the best usage qualifier expressions for function types. To make programming with affine types as convenient as possible, we want to maximize polymorphism between one-use and unlimited versions of functions. While writing the Alms standard library, we found that usage qualifier constants **A** and **U**, even with dereliction subtyping, were insufficient to give a principal type to some terms.

For example, consider function *default*, an eliminator for option types, sans function argument types:

```
let default (def: ...) (opt: ...) =
  match opt with
  | Some x → x
  | None   → def
```

Without usage qualifier expressions, *default* has at least two incomparable types:

$$default_1 : \forall\hat{\alpha}.\, \hat{\alpha} \xrightarrow{\mathsf{U}} \hat{\alpha}\ \mathsf{option} \xrightarrow{\mathsf{A}} \hat{\alpha}$$
$$default_2 : \forall\alpha.\, \alpha \xrightarrow{\mathsf{U}} \alpha\ \mathsf{option} \xrightarrow{\mathsf{U}} \alpha.$$

In the first case, because $\hat{\alpha}$ *might* be affine, the partial application of $default_1$ must be a one-use function, but in the second case we know that α is unlimited so partially applying $default_2$ and reusing the result is safe. Formally, these types are incomparable because the universally-quantified type variable $\hat{\alpha}$ in the former has a different kind than α in the latter, and Alms uses the *kernel* variant of rule TSUB-ALL. However, even were we to replace rule TSUB-ALL with a rule analogous to $F^{\omega}_{<:}$'s *full* variant,

$$\frac{\Gamma,\alpha{:}\kappa \vdash \tau_1 <:^{\mathfrak{v}} \tau_2 \qquad \Gamma,\alpha{:}\kappa \vdash \kappa_1 <:^{-\mathfrak{v}} \kappa_2}{\Gamma \vdash \forall\alpha{:}\kappa_1.\tau_1 <:^{\mathfrak{v}} \forall\alpha{:}\kappa_2.\tau_2}\ \text{TSUB-ALL}_{\text{FULL}},$$

the types would not be related by the subtyping order. More importantly, neither type is preferable in an informal sense. The type of *default*$_1$ allows $\hat{\alpha}$ to be instantiated to an affine or unlimited type, but the result of partially applying it is a one-use function even if $\hat{\alpha}$ is known to be unlimited:

default$_1$ 5 : int option $\xrightarrow{\mathsf{A}}$ int
default$_1$ (*aref 5*) : int aref option $\xrightarrow{\mathsf{A}}$ int aref.

If we choose *default*$_2$, the result of partial application is unlimited, but attempting to instantiate α to an affine type is a type error:

default$_2$ 5 : int option $\xrightarrow{\mathsf{U}}$ int
default$_2$ (*aref 5*) : *Type error!*

Alms avoids both problems and instead discovers that the best usage qualifier for the arrow is the kind of the type variable:

default : $\forall\hat{\alpha}.\,\hat{\alpha} \xrightarrow{\mathsf{U}} \hat{\alpha}$ option $\xrightarrow{\langle\hat{\alpha}\rangle} \hat{\alpha}$
default 5 : int option $\xrightarrow{\mathsf{U}}$ int
default (*aref 5*) : int aref option $\xrightarrow{\mathsf{A}}$ int aref.

Because this is an important property, we prove a theorem that every typeable ${}^{a}\lambda_{ms}$ function has a principal usage qualifier.

Theorem 3 (Principal qualifiers). *If* $\Gamma;\Sigma \rhd \lambda x{:}\tau.e : \tau_1 \xrightarrow{\varphi} \tau_2$, *then it has a least qualifier expression* φ_0*; that is,*

- $\Gamma;\Sigma \rhd \lambda x{:}\tau.e : \tau_1 \xrightarrow{\varphi_0} \tau_2$ *and*
- $\Gamma \vdash \varphi_0 <: \varphi'$ *for all* φ' *such that* $\Gamma;\Sigma \rhd \lambda x{:}\tau.e : \tau_1 \xrightarrow{\varphi'} \tau_2$.

Proof sketch. We obtain the principal qualifier φ_0 as follows. Let Σ_0 be the restriction of Σ to exactly the free variables and locations of $\lambda x{:}\tau.e$. Let φ_0 be the unique bound of Σ_0 given by $\Gamma \vdash \Sigma_0 \preceq \varphi_0$. By strengthening, $\Gamma;\Sigma_0 \rhd \lambda x{:}\tau.e : \tau_1 \xrightarrow{\varphi_0} \tau_2$, and by rule T-WEAK we can get the same type in Σ.

A derivation of $\Gamma;\Sigma \rhd \lambda x{:}\tau.e : \tau_1 \xrightarrow{\varphi'} \tau_2$ always involves rule T-ABS using some portion of Σ, followed by some number of subsumptions and weakenings. Subsumption will never let φ' be less than φ_0. However, weakening might allow us to type $\lambda x{:}\tau.e$ with a different portion of Σ than Σ_0. We know that any superset of Σ_0 has bound no less than φ_0, and while a non-superset of Σ_0 may have a smaller bound, we chose Σ_0 so that only Σ_0 and its supersets are suitable to type the term and then weaken to Σ. □

Thus, for a function in any given context, there is a least usage qualifier, and our implementation can find the least qualifier by considering only the portion of Σ that pertains to the free identifiers of the λ term, as suggested by the algorithmic rule

(T-ABS$_{\text{ALG}}$)

$$\frac{\vdash (\Gamma;\Sigma), x{:}\tau_1 \rightsquigarrow \Gamma';\Sigma' \qquad \Gamma';\Sigma' \rhd e : \tau_2 \qquad \varphi_0 = \begin{cases} \mathsf{A} & \text{if locs}(e) \neq \varnothing \\ \bigsqcup\{\varphi \mid x \in \text{fv}(e), \Gamma \vdash \Sigma(x) : \varphi\} & \text{otherwise}\end{cases}}{\Gamma;\Sigma \rhd \lambda x{:}\tau_1.e : \tau_1 \xrightarrow{\varphi_0} \tau_2}.$$

Type soundness. The key obstacle in our type soundness proof is establishing a substitution lemma, which in turn relies on showing that the kind of the type of any value accurately reflects the resources contained in that value, which itself comes as a corollary to the proposition that the kinds of subtypes are themselves subkinds:

Lemma 4 (Monotonicity of kinding). *If* $\Gamma \vdash \tau_1 <:^{+} \tau_2$ *where* $\Gamma \vdash \tau_1 : \varphi_1$ *and* $\Gamma \vdash \tau_2 : \varphi_2$, *then* $\Gamma \vdash \varphi_1 <: \varphi_2$.

This lemma is the reason for the premise in rule OK-ARR that for a kind $\Pi\alpha^{\mathfrak{v}}.\kappa$, variance $\mathfrak{v}$ must be at least $+$ if $\alpha \in \text{ftv}(\kappa)$. Otherwise, we could construct a counterexample to lemma 4:

- $\beta{:}\Pi\alpha^{-}.\langle\alpha\rangle \vdash \beta\,(1 \xrightarrow{\mathsf{A}} 1) <:^{+} (1 \xrightarrow{\mathsf{U}} 1)$,
- $\beta{:}\Pi\alpha^{-}.\langle\alpha\rangle \vdash \beta\,(1 \xrightarrow{\mathsf{A}} 1) : \mathsf{A}$, and
- $\beta{:}\Pi\alpha^{-}.\langle\alpha\rangle \vdash \beta\,(1 \xrightarrow{\mathsf{U}} 1) : \mathsf{U}$,
- but $\beta{:}\Pi\alpha^{-}.\langle\alpha\rangle \vdash \mathsf{A} <: \mathsf{U}$ is not the case.

The kind well-formedness judgment rules out kinds like $\Pi\alpha^{-}.\langle\alpha\rangle$.

Proof for lemma 4. We define an extension of the subkinding relation, $\Gamma \vdash \kappa_1 \lessapprox \kappa_2$, which is insensitive to the variances decorating Π kinds. Observe that on qualifier expressions this new relation coincides with subkinding. We generalize the induction hypothesis—if $\Gamma \vdash \tau_1 <:^{+} \tau_2$ where $\Gamma \vdash \tau_1 : \kappa_1$ and $\Gamma \vdash \tau_2 : \kappa_2$, then $\Gamma \vdash \kappa_1 \lessapprox \kappa_2$—and complete the proof by induction on the structure of the subtyping derivation. □

Corollary 5 (Kinding finds locations). *Suppose that* $\Gamma;\Sigma \rhd v : \tau$ *and* $\Gamma \vdash \tau : \varphi$ *where* $\text{dom}(\Sigma)$ *contains only locations* (ℓ). *If any locations appear in* v *then* $\Gamma \vdash \mathsf{A} <: \varphi$.

Proof sketch. By induction on the typing derivation. We use the previous lemma in the case for the subsumption rule T-SUBSUME:

$$\textbf{Case}\ \frac{\Gamma;\Sigma \rhd v : \tau' \qquad \Gamma \vdash \tau' <:^{+} \tau \qquad \Gamma \vdash \tau : \varphi}{\Gamma;\Sigma \rhd v : \tau}.$$

By the induction hypothesis, $\Gamma \vdash \tau' : \mathsf{A}$, and by lemma 4, $\Gamma \vdash \mathsf{A} <: \varphi$. □

Corollary 5 lets us prove our substitution lemma. Then progress, preservation, and type soundness are standard:

Theorem 6 (Type soundness). *If* $\rhd \{\}; e : \tau$ *then either e diverges or there exists some store s and value v such that* $\{\}; e \xrightarrow{*} s; v$ *and* $\rhd s; v : \tau$.

6. Related Work

In prior work, we showed how an Alms-like affine language may safely interoperate with a conventional (non-affine) language (Tov and Pucella 2010). In particular, the languages may freely share values, including functions. Attempts by the conventional language to subvert the affine language's invariants are prevented by dynamic checks in the form of behavioral software contracts. That paper focused specifically on multi-language interaction, using a predecessor of Alms.

System F°. Mazurak et al. (2010) describe a calculus of "lightweight linear types." Their primary motivation is similar to ours: to remove needless overhead and provide a "simple foundation for practical linear programming."

System F° and the prior iteration of Alms independently introduced several new ideas:

- Both use kinds to distinguish linear (in Alms, affine) types from unlimited types, where F°'s kinds $\circ$ and $\star$ correspond to our A and U, and their subkinding relation $\star \leq \circ$ corresponds to our $\mathsf{U} \sqsubseteq \mathsf{A}$.
- F° uses existentials and subkinding to abstract unlimited types into linear types. Alms (the language) uses modules and ${}^{a}\lambda_{ms}$ (the calculus) uses higher-kinded type abstraction to define abstract affine types, including type constructors with parameters. Mazurak et al. mention the possibility of extending F° with abstraction over higher kinds but do not show the details.

- They sketch out a convenient notation for writing linear computations. This inspired our different implicit threading syntax, which is implemented in Alms as mentioned at the end of §2.

There are also notable differences:

- F° has linear types, which disallow weakening, whereas Alms has affine types, which support it. This is a trade-off. Linear types make it possible to enforce liveness properties, which may be useful, for instance, to ensure that manual memory management does not leak. On the other hand, we anticipate that safely combining linearity with exceptions requires a type-and-effect system to track when raising an exception would implicitly discard linear values. Alms can support explicit deallocation so long as failure to do so is backed up by a garbage collector.
- Alms's unlimited-use function type is a subtype of its one-use function type. F° does not provide subtyping, though they do show how η expansion can explicitly perform the coercion that our subtyping does implicitly. Experience with our implementation confirms that dereliction subtyping is valuable, though we admit it comes at the cost of complexity.
- F° requires annotating abstractions ($\lambda^\kappa x{:}\tau.e$) to specify the kind of the resulting arrow type, which may only be $\star$ or $\circ$. Alms refines this with qualifier expressions and selects the least kind automatically.
- Mazurak et al. give a resource-aware semantics and prove that they can encode regular protocols. We do neither but conjecture that our system enjoys similar properties, except that weakening makes it possible to bail out of a protocol at any point.
- Their sketch of rules for algebraic datatypes is similar to how ours work, though ours are strictly stronger. For example, an option type in F° would have two versions:

  $$\mathsf{optionLin} : \circ \Rightarrow \circ \qquad \mathsf{optionUn} : \star \Rightarrow \star.$$

  Our dependent kinds in Alms let us define one type constructor whose kind subsumes both:

  $$\mathsf{option} : \Pi\hat{\alpha}^+.\,\langle\hat{\alpha}\rangle.$$

Clean. At first glance, Clean's uniqueness types *appear* to be dual to affine types. Uniqueness types are descriptive—they indicate that a particular reference is unique—while affine (and linear) types are prescriptive, since they restrict what may be done to some reference in the future but do not necessarily know where it's been. Similarly, Clean's subtyping relation, which allows forgetting that a value is unique, appears dual to Alms's, which allows pretending that an unlimited value is affine. However, the duality breaks down in the higher-order case. When a partially applied function captures some unique free variable, Clean's type system must *prohibit* aliasing of the function in order to maintain descriptive uniqueness when the function is fully applied (Plasmeijer and Eekelen 2002). In Clean's terminology, function types with the unique attribute are "essentially unique," but we might call them "affine."

There is a strong similarity between our kinding judgment and Clean's uniqueness propagation rules that relate the uniqueness of data structures to that of their constituent parts. While Clean supports subtyping, it does not have a subkinding relation analogous to Alms or F°'s. In particular, Clean requires that the uniqueness attributes declared for an abstract type in a module's interface exactly match the uniqueness attributes in the module's implementation.

Use types and qualifiers. Wadler (1991) discusses several variants of linear type systems. He proposes something akin to dereliction subtyping (*i.e.*, $!A \le A$) and points out that in such a system, terms such as $\lambda f.\lambda x.f\,x$ have several unrelated types. (We made a similar observation in §5.) In order to recover principal types, he introduces use types, which decorate the exponential modality with a *use variable* i: $!^i$. The use variable ranges over 0 and 1, where $!^0A = A$ and $!^1A = !A$. This provides principal types, but at the cost of adding use-variable inequality constraints to type schemes.

A use-variable inequality of the form $i \le j$ is essentially an implication $i \supset j$, where 1 is truth and 0 is falsity. De Vries et al. (2008) show, in the setting of uniqueness types, how such inequalities may be represented instead using Boolean logic. For example, if we have a type

$$\ldots\,!^i\,\ldots\,!^j\quad\ldots,[i \le j],$$

we can discard the inequality constraint and represent it instead as

$$\ldots\,!^i\,\ldots\,!^{i\vee k}\,\ldots,$$

because $i \le (i \vee k)$. In general, any collection of use-variable inequalities (or uniqueness-attribute constraints) may be eliminated by replacing some of the use variables with propositional formulae over use variables. This insight is the source of Alms's usage qualifier expressions.

If we follow use types to their logical conclusion, we reach λ^{URAL} (Ahmed et al. 2005), wherein each type is composed of a pretype that describes its representation and a qualifier that gives its usage. Alms does not follow this approach because we insist that qualified types are too verbose for a user-visible type system. Their system's qualifier lattice includes two more than ours, R for relevant types that allow duplication but not discarding, and L for linear types. This results in a rich and elegant system, but we do not believe R and L would be useful in a language like Alms.

However, there is an interesting correspondence between our kinding rules and their type rules. For example, our product type constructor $(\times)$ has kind $\Pi\alpha^+.\Pi\beta^+.\langle\alpha\rangle \sqcup \langle\beta\rangle$, which means that the kind of a product type is the least upper bound of the kinds of its components. The product typing rule in λ^{URAL} enforces a similar constraint, that the qualifier of a product type, ξ, must upper bound the qualifiers of its components τ_1 and τ_2.

$$\frac{\begin{array}{ll}\Delta \vdash \Gamma \rightsquigarrow \Gamma_1 \boxplus \Gamma_2 & \Delta \vdash \xi : \mathsf{QUAL} \\ \Delta;\Gamma_1 \vdash v_1 : \tau_1 & \Delta \vdash \tau_1 \preceq \xi \\ \Delta;\Gamma_2 \vdash v_2 : \tau_2 & \Delta \vdash \tau_2 \preceq \xi\end{array}}{\Delta;\Gamma \vdash \langle v_1, v_2\rangle : {}^{\xi}(\tau_1 \otimes \tau_2)}\ (\textsc{MPair}).$$

Vault. DeLine and Fähndrich's Vault (2001) is a safe, low-level language with support for typestate. It tracks *keys*, which associate static capabilities with the identity of run-time objects, in the same manner that Alms uses existentially-quantified type variables to tie values to capabilities. This allows static enforcement of a variety of protocols. As an example, DeLine and Fähndrich give a tracked version of the Berkeley Sockets API. In previous work on Alms we show how Alms expresses the same interface.

Vault's treatment of capabilities may be more convenient to use than Alms's, because while Alms requires explicit threading of capability values, Vault's key sets are tracked automatically within function bodies. On the other hand, because capabilities in Alms appear as ordinary values, we may combine them using the native intuitionistic logic of Alms's type system. Instead, Vault must provide a simple predicate calculus for expressing pre- and postconditions. For more complicated logic, Vault allows embedding capabilities in values, but since the values are untracked, extracting a capability from a value requires a dynamic check. Alms's type system eliminates the need for such checks for affine values stored in algebraic datatypes, though it also allows dynamic management of affine values by storing them in reference cells.

Notably, Alms can also express Fähndrich and DeLine's *adoption and focus* (2002).

Sing#. Microsoft's experimental Singularity operating system is written in Sing#, a high-level systems programming language that extends Spec# (Fähndrich et al. 2006). Sing# has built-in support for *channel contracts,* which are a form of session type providing static checking of communication protocols between device drivers and other services. Unlike more idealistic linear systems, the design acknowledges the need to allow for failure: every protocol implicitly includes branches to close the channel at any point.

Sing# processes do not share memory but can allocate tracked objects on a common *exchange heap*. Only one process has access to an exchange heap object at a given time, but a process may give up access and transmit the object over a channel to another process, which then claims ownership of it.

Alms's library includes two different implementations of session types supporting different interfaces, and the exchange heap concept is easily expressible as well.

7. Future Work and Conclusion

We already enjoy programming in Alms, but we are not done yet.

Unit subsumption. In §2, we found that adding capabilities to an existing interface often involves wrapping the old version of a function to ignore a new argument of type unit or construct a tuple containing unit for its result. This is unnecessary. While the client outside the abstraction barrier needs to see types that involve the affine capabilities, the implementation has no use for them.

To eliminate much of this noise, we can extend our subtyping relation to take advantage of the fact that unit is, well, a unit:

$$\frac{\Gamma \vdash \tau_2 \text{ singleton}}{\Gamma \vdash \tau_1 <:^{\mathfrak{u}} \tau_1 \times \tau_2} \qquad \frac{\Gamma \vdash \tau_2 \text{ singleton}}{\Gamma \vdash \tau_1 <:^{\mathfrak{u}} \tau_2 \times \tau_1}$$

$$\frac{\Gamma \vdash \tau_2 \text{ singleton}}{\Gamma \vdash \tau_1 \xrightarrow{\varphi} \tau_2 \xrightarrow{\varphi} \tau_3 <:^{\mathfrak{u}} \tau_1 \xrightarrow{\varphi} \tau_3}$$

This is implementable via a type erasure technique such as intensional polymorphism (Crary et al. 2002). Not representing compile-time capabilities at run time has performance benefits as well.

Type inference. Alms's local type inference eliminates most explicit type applications, but needing to annotate all function arguments is irksome. To fix this, we are exploring possibilities for type inference. While we suspect that our limited subtyping should not impede full Damas-Milner–style inference (Damas and Milner 1982), Alms has several idioms that rely on existential types. We are exploring whether an extension for first-class polymorphism, such as HML (Leijen 2009), would be suitable for Alms.

Alms is not finished, but our prototype is at this point usable for experimentation. It is based on a calculus, ${}^{a}\lambda_{ms}$, whose type system we have proved sound. While some parts of the type system are complex, we have seen in practice that Alms types are tractable and Alms programs do not look very different from the functional programs to which we are accustomed. It currently implements algebraic datatypes, exceptions, pattern matching, concurrency, and opaque signature ascription. The language is rich enough to express Vault-style typestate, a variety of static and dynamic locking protocols, checked downcasts of one-use functions to unlimited-use functions, session types, and more.

Acknowledgments

We wish to thank J. Daniel Brown, Bryan Chadwick, Matthias Felleisen, Sam Tobin-Hochstadt, Vincent St-Amour, and the anonymous referees for their helpful comments, discussion, and corrections. This research was supported in part by AFOSR grant FA9550-09-1-0110.

References

A. Ahmed, M. Fluet, and G. Morrisett. A step-indexed model of substructural state. In *ICFP'05*, pages 78–91. ACM, 2005.

A. Barber. Dual intuitionistic linear logic. Technical Report ECS-LFCS-960347, U. of Edinburgh, 1996.

P. S. Barth, R. S. Nikhil, and Arvind. M-structures: Extending a parallel, non-strict, functional language with state. In *Proc. FPCA'91*, volume 523 of *LNCS*. Springer, 1991.

G. M. Bierman. *On Intuitionistic Linear Logic*. PhD thesis, U. of Cambridge, 1993.

J. Boyland. Checking interference with fractional permissions. In *SAS'03*, volume 2694 of *LNCS*. Springer, 2003.

K. Crary, S. Weirich, and G. Morrisett. Intensional polymorphism in type-erasure semantics. *JFP*, 12(06):567–600, 2002.

L. Damas and R. Milner. Principal type-schemes for functional programs. In *POPL'82*, pages 207–212. ACM, 1982.

R. DeLine and M. Fähndrich. Enforcing high-level protocols in low-level software. In *PLDI'01*. ACM, 2001.

M. Fähndrich and R. DeLine. Adoption and focus: Practical linear types for imperative programming. In *PLDI'02*. ACM, 2002.

M. Fähndrich, M. Aiken, C. Hawblitzel, O. Hodson, G. Hunt, J. R. Larus, and S. Levi. Language support for fast and reliable message-based communication in Singularity OS. In *EuroSys'06*, pages 177–190. ACM, 2006.

S. J. Gay, V. T. Vasconcelos, and A. Ravara. Session types for inter-process communication. Technical Report TR-2003-133, U. of Glasgow, 2003.

J.-Y. Girard. Linear logic. *Theoretical Computer Science*, 50:1–102, 1987.

D. Leijen. Flexible types: Robust type inference for first-class polymorphism. In *POPL'09*, pages 66–77. ACM, 2009.

X. Leroy, D. Doligez, J. Garrigue, D. Rémy, and J. Vouillon. *The Objective Caml system*. INRIA, 3.11 edition, 2008.

K. Mazurak, J. Zhao, and S. Zdancewic. Lightweight linear types in System F°. In *TLDI'10*, pages 77–88. ACM, 2010.

R. Milner, M. Tofte, R. Harper, and D. MacQueen. *The Definition of Standard ML*. MIT, revised edition, 1997.

B. C. Pierce. *Types and Programming Languages*. MIT, 2002.

R. Plasmeijer and M. van Eekelen. *Clean Language Report, Version 2.1*. Dept. of Software Technology, U. of Nijmegen, 2002.

A. Rossberg, C. V. Russo, and D. Dreyer. F-ing modules. In *TLDI'10*, pages 89–102. ACM, 2010.

M. Steffen. *Polarized Higher Order Subtyping*. PhD thesis, Universität Erlangen-Nürnberg, 1997.

I. E. Sutherland and G. W. Hodgman. Reentrant polygon clipping. *CACM*, 17(1):32–42, 1974.

J. A. Tov and R. Pucella. Stateful contracts for affine types. In *ESOP'10*, volume 6012 of *LNCS*, pages 550–569. Springer, 2010.

E. de Vries, R. Plasmeijer, and D. M. Abrahamson. Uniqueness typing simplified. In *IFL'07*, pages 201–218. Springer, 2008.

P. Wadler. Is there a use for linear logic? In *PEPM'91*, pages 255–273. ACM, 1991.

P. Wadler and S. Blott. How to make ad-hoc polymorphism less ad hoc. In *POPL'89*, pages 60–76. ACM, 1989.

Dynamic Inference of Static Types for Ruby

Jong-hoon (David) An[†] Avik Chaudhuri[‡] Jeffrey S. Foster[⋆] Michael Hicks[⋆]
rockalizer@gmail.com achaudhu@adobe.com jfoster@cs.umd.edu mwh@cs.umd.edu
[†]Epic Systems Corporation [‡]Advanced Technology Labs, Adobe Systems [⋆]University of Maryland, College Park

Abstract

There have been several efforts to bring static type inference to object-oriented dynamic languages such as Ruby, Python, and Perl. In our experience, however, such type inference systems are extremely difficult to develop, because dynamic languages are typically complex, poorly specified, and include features, such as `eval` and reflection, that are hard to analyze.

In this paper, we introduce *constraint-based dynamic type inference*, a technique that infers static types based on dynamic program executions. In our approach, we wrap each run-time value to associate it with a type variable, and the wrapper generates constraints on this type variable when the wrapped value is used. This technique avoids many of the often overly conservative approximations of static tools, as constraints are generated based on how values are used during actual program runs. Using wrappers is also easy to implement, since we need only write a constraint resolution algorithm and a transformation to introduce the wrappers. The best part is that we can eat our cake, too: our algorithm will infer *sound* types as long as it observes every path through each method body—note that the number of such paths may be dramatically smaller than the number of paths through the program as a whole.

We have developed Rubydust, an implementation of our algorithm for Ruby. Rubydust takes advantage of Ruby's dynamic features to implement wrappers as a language library. We applied Rubydust to a number of small programs and found it to be both easy to use and useful: Rubydust discovered 1 real type error, and all other inferred types were correct and readable.

Categories and Subject Descriptors F.3.2 [*Logics and Meaning of Programs*]: Semantics of Programming Languages—Program analysis; F.3.3 [*Logics and Meaning of Programs*]: Studies of Program Constructs—Type structure

General Terms Languages, Theory, Verification

Keywords Dynamic type inference, static types, Ruby, dynamic languages

1. Introduction

Over the years, there have been several efforts to bring static type inference to object-oriented dynamic languages such as Ruby, Python, and Perl [2–5, 7, 10, 12, 16, 18, 24, 27]. Static type inference has the potential to provide the benefits of static typing—well-typed programs don't go wrong [17]—without the annotation burden of pure type checking.

However, based on our own experience, developing a static type inference system for a dynamic language is extremely difficult. Most dynamic languages have poorly documented, complex syntax and semantics that must be carefully reverse-engineered before any static analysis is possible. Dynamic languages are usually "specified" only with a canonical implementation, and tend to have many obscure corner cases that make the reverse engineering process tedious and error-prone. Moreover, dynamic language programmers often employ programming idioms that impede precise yet sound static analysis. For example, programmers often give variables flow-sensitive types that differ along different paths, or add or remove methods from classes at run-time using dynamic features such as reflection and `eval`. Combined, these challenges make developing and maintaining a static type inference tool for a dynamic language a daunting prospect.

To address these problems, this paper introduces *constraint-based dynamic type inference*, a technique to infer static types using information gathered from dynamic runs. More precisely, at run time we introduce type variables for each position whose type we want to infer—specifically fields, method arguments, and return values. As values are passed to those positions, we *wrap* them in a proxy object that records the associated type variable. The user may also supply trusted type annotations for methods. When wrapped values are used as receivers or passed to type-annotated methods, we generate *subtyping constraints* on those variables. At the end of the run, we solve the constraints to find a valid typing, if one exists.

We have implemented this technique for Ruby, as a tool called Rubydust (where "dust" stands for dynamic unraveling of static types). Unlike standard static type systems, Rubydust only conflates type information at method boundaries (where type variables accumulate constraints from different calls), and not within a method. As such, Rubydust supports flow-sensitive treatment of local variables, allowing them to be assigned values having different types. Since Rubydust only sees actual runs of the program, it is naturally path-sensitive and supports use of many dynamic features. Finally, Rubydust can be implemented as a library by employing common introspection features to intercept method calls; there is no need to reverse-engineer any subtle parsing or elaboration rules and to build a separate analysis infrastructure. In sum, Rubydust is more precise than standard static type inference, and sidesteps many of the engineering difficulties of building a static analysis tool suite.

Although Rubydust is based purely on dynamic runs, we can still prove a soundness theorem. We formalized our algorithm on a core subset of Ruby, and we prove that if the training runs on which types are inferred cover every path in the control-flow graph (CFG) of every method of a class, then the inferred types for that class's fields and methods are sound for all possible runs. In our formalism, all looping occurs through recursion, and so the number of required

POPL'11, January 26–28, 2011, Austin, Texas, USA.

paths is at most exponential in the size of the largest method body in a program. Notice that this can be dramatically smaller than the number of paths through the program as whole.

Clearly, in practice it is potentially an issue that we need test cases that cover all method paths for fully sound types. However, there are several factors that mitigate this potential drawback.

• Almost all software projects include test cases, and those test cases can be used for training. In fact, the Ruby community encourages test-driven development, which prescribes that tests be written before writing program code—thus tests will likely be available for Rubydust training right from the start.

• While loops within methods could theoretically yield an unbounded number of paths, in our experimental benchmarks we observed that most loop bodies use objects in a type-consistent manner within each path within the loop body. Hence, typically, observing all paths within a loop body (rather that observing all possible iterations of a loop) suffices to find correct types. We discuss this more in Section 4.

• Even incomplete tests may produce useful types. In particular, the inferred types will be sound for any execution that takes (within a method) paths that were covered in training. We could potentially add instrumentation to identify when the program executes a path not covered by training, and then blame the lack of coverage if an error arises as a result [10]. Types are also useful as documentation. Currently, the Ruby documentation includes informal type signatures for standard library methods, but those types could become out of sync with the code (we have found cases of this previously [12]). Using Rubydust, we could generate type annotations automatically from code using its test suite, and thus keep the type documentation in-sync with the tested program behaviors.

Our implementation of Rubydust is a Ruby library that takes advantage of Ruby's rich introspection features; no special tools or compilers are needed. Rubydust wraps each object o at runtime with a proxy object that associates o with a type variable α that corresponds to o's position in the program (a field, argument, or return-value). Method calls on o precipitate the generation of constraints; e.g., if the program invokes o.m(x) then we generate a constraint indicating that α must have a method m whose argument type is a supertype of the type of x. Rubydust also consumes trusted type annotations on methods; this is important for giving types to Ruby's built-in standard library, which is written in C rather than Ruby and hence is not subject to our type inference algorithm.

We evaluated Rubydust by applying it to several small programs, the largest of which was roughly 750 LOC, and used their accompanying test suites to infer types. We found one real type error, which is particularly interesting because the error was uncovered by solving constraints from a passing test run. All other programs were found to be type correct, with readable and correct types. The overhead of running Rubydust is currently quite high, but we believe it can be reduced with various optimizations that we intend to implement in the future. In general we found the performance acceptable and the tool itself quite easy to use.

In summary, our contributions are as follows:

- We introduce a novel algorithm to infer types at run-time by dynamically associating fields and method arguments and results with type variables, and generating subtyping constraints as those entities are used. (Section 2)
- We formalize our algorithm and prove that if training runs cover all syntactic paths through each method of a class, then the inferred type for that class is sound. (Section 3)
- We describe Rubydust, a practical implementation of our algorithm that uses Ruby's rich introspection features. Since Rubydust piggybacks on the standard Ruby interpreter, we can naturally handle all of Ruby's rather complex syntax and semantics without undue effort. (Section 4)
- We evaluate Rubydust on a small set of benchmarks and find it to be useful. (Section 5)

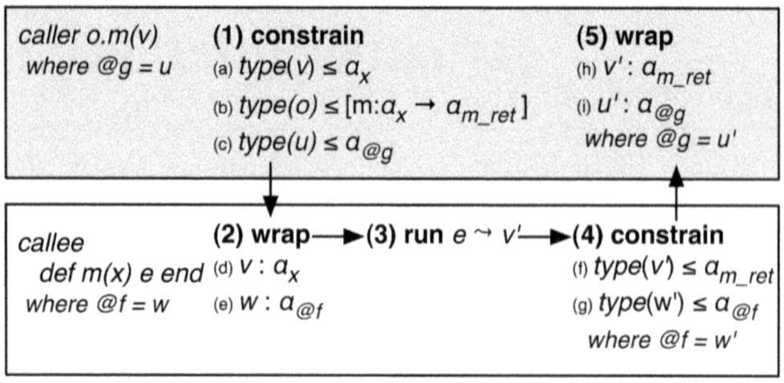

Figure 1. Dynamic instrumentation for a call o.m(v)

We believe that Rubydust is a practical, effective method for inferring useful static types in Ruby, and that the ideas of Rubydust can be applied to other dynamic languages.

2. Overview

Before presenting our constraint-based dynamic type inference algorithm formally, we describe the algorithm by example and illustrate some of its key features. Our examples below are written in Ruby, which is a dynamically typed, object-oriented language inspired by Smalltalk and Perl. In our discussion, we will try to point out any unusual syntax or language features we use; more complete information about Ruby can be found elsewhere [28].

2.1 Method call and return

In our algorithm, there are two kinds of classes: *annotated classes*, which have trusted type signatures, and *unannotated classes*, whose types we wish to infer. We assign a type variable to each field, method argument, and method return value in every unannotated class. At run time, values that occupy these positions are associated with the corresponding type variable. We call this association *wrapping* since we literally implement it by wrapping the value with some metadata. When a wrapped value is used, e.g., as a receiver of a method call, or as an argument to a method with a trusted type signature, we generate a subtyping constraint on the associated variable. At the end of the training runs, we solve the generated constraints to find solutions for those type variables (which yield field and method types for unannotated classes), or we report an error if no solution exists. Note that since all instances of a class share the same type variables, use of any instance contributes to inferring a single type for its class.

Before working through a full example, we consider the operation of our algorithm on a single call to an unannotated method. Figure 1 summarizes the five steps in analyzing a call o.m(v) to a method defined as **def** m(x) e **end**, where x is the formal argument and e is the method body. In this case, we create two type variables: α_x, to represent x's type, and α_{m_ret}, to represent m's return type.

In step (1), the caller looks up the (dynamic) class of the receiver to find the type of the called method. In this case, method m has type $\alpha_x \to \alpha_{m\_ret}$. The caller then generates two constraints. The constraint labeled (a) ensures the type of the actual argument is a subtype of the formal argument type. Here, $\mathtt{type}(x)$ is the type of an object, either its actual type, for an unwrapped object, or the type variable stored in the wrapper. In the constraint (b), the type $[m : \ldots]$ is the type of an object with a method m with the

```
 1 # Numeric : [...+ : Numeric → Numeric...]
 2
 3 class A
 4   # foo : α_w × α_u → α_foo_ret
 5   def foo(w,u)         # w = (b : α_w), u = (1 : α_u)
 6     w.baz()            #                     α_w ≤ [baz : () → ()]
 7     y = 3 + u          # y = (4 : Numeric)   α_u ≤ Numeric
 8     return bar(w)      # ret = (7 : α_bar_ret)  α_w ≤ α_x
 9   end                  #                     α_bar_ret ≤ α_foo_ret
10   # bar : α_x → α_bar_ret
11   def bar(x)           # x = (b : α_x)
12     x.qux()            #                     α_x ≤ [qux : () → ()]
13     return 7           #                     Numeric ≤ α_bar_ret
14   end
15 end
16
17 A.new.foo(B.new,1)     # B.new returns a new object b
18                        # B ≤ α_w
19                        # Numeric ≤ α_u
20                        # ret = (7 : α_foo_ret)
```

Figure 2. Basic method call and return example

given type. Hence by width-subtyping, constraint (b) specifies that o has at least an m method with the appropriate type. We generate this constraint to ensure o's static type $\texttt{type}(o)$ is consistent with the type for m we found via dynamic lookup. For now, ignore the constraint (c) and the other constraints (e), (g), and (i) involving fields @f and @g; we will discuss these in Section 2.3.

In step (2) of analyzing the call, the callee wraps its arguments with the appropriate type variables immediately upon entry. In this case, we set x to be $v : \alpha_x$, which is our notation for the value v wrapped with type α_x.

Then in step (3), we execute the body of the method. Doing so will result in calls to other methods, which will undergo the same process. Moreover, as $v : \alpha_x$ may be used in some of these calls, we will generate constraints on $\texttt{type}(v : \alpha_x)$, i.e., α_x, that we saw in step (1). In particular, if $v : \alpha_x$ is used as a receiver, we will constrain α_x to have the called method; if $v : \alpha_x$ is used as an argument, we will constrain it to be a subtype of the target method's formal argument type.

At a high-level, steps (1) and (2) maintain two critical invariants:

- Prior to leaving method n to enter another method m, we generate constraints to capture the flow of values from n to m (Constraints (a) and (b)).
- Prior to entering a method m, all values that could affect the type of m are wrapped (Indicated by (d)).

Roughly speaking, constraining something with a type records how it was used in the past, and wrapping something with a type observes how it is used in the future.

Returning from methods should maintain the same invariants as above but in the reverse direction, from callee to caller. Thus, in step (4), we generate constraint (f) in the callee that the type of the returned value is a subtype of the return type, and in step (5), when we return to the caller we immediately wrap the returned value with the called method's return type variable.

2.2 Complete example

Now that we have seen the core algorithm, we can work through a complete example. Consider the code in Figure 2, which defines a class A with two methods foo and bar, and then calls foo on a fresh instance of A on line 17.

This code uses Ruby's Numeric class, which is one of the built-in classes for integers. Because Numeric is built-in, we make it an annotated class, and supply trusted type signatures for all of its methods. A portion of the signature is shown on line 1, which indicates Numeric has a method + of type Numeric→Numeric.[1]

As in the previous subsection, we introduce type variables for method arguments and returns, in this case α_w, α_u, and α_{foo_ret} for foo, and α_x and α_{bar_ret} for bar. Then we begin stepping through the calls. At the call on line 17, we pass in actual arguments b (the object created by the call to B.new on the same line) and 1. Thus we constrain the formal argument types in the caller (lines 18 and 19) and wrap the actuals in the callee (line 5).

Next, on line 6, we use a wrapped object, so we generate a constraint; here we require the associated type variable α_w contains a no-argument method baz. (For simplicity we show the return type as (), though as it is unused it could be arbitrary.)

On line 7, we call 3 + u. The receiver object is 3, which has actual class is Numeric, an annotated class. Thus, we do the normal handling in the caller (the shaded box in Figure 1), but omit the steps in the callee, since the annotation is trusted. Here, we generate a constraint $\alpha_u \leq$ Numeric between the actual and formal argument types. We also generate a constraint (not shown in the figure) $\texttt{type}(3) \leq [+ : \ldots]$, but as $\texttt{type}(3) =$ Numeric, this constraint is immediately satisfiable; in general, we need to generate such constraints to correctly handle cases where the receiver is not a constant. Finally, we wrap the return value from the caller with its annotated type Numeric.

Next, we call method bar. As expected, we constrain the actuals and formals (line 8), wrap the argument inside the callee (line 11), and generate constraints during execution of the body (line 12). At the return from bar, we constrain the return type (line 13) and wrap in the caller (yielding the wrapped value $7 : \alpha_{bar\_ret}$ on line 8). As that value is immediately returned by foo, we constrain the return type of foo with it (line 9) and wrap in the caller (line 20).

After this run, we can solve the generated constraints to infer types. Drawing the constraints from the example as a directed graph, where an edge from x to y corresponds to the constraint $x \leq y$, we have:

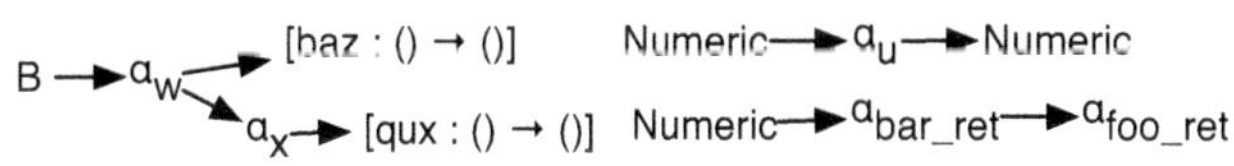

(Here we duplicated Numeric for clarity; in practice, it is typically represented by a single node in the graph.) As is standard, we wish to find the *least solution* (equivalent to a most general type) for each method. Since arguments are contravariant and returns are covariant, this corresponds to finding *upper bounds* (transitive successors in the constraint graph) for arguments and *lower bounds* (transitive predecessors) for returns. Intuitively, this is equivalent to inferring argument types based on how arguments are used within a method, and computing return types based on what types flow to return positions. For our example, the final solution is

$$\alpha_w = [\text{baz} : () \to (), \text{qux} : () \to ()] \qquad \alpha_x = [\text{qux} : () \to ()]$$

$$\alpha_u = \text{Numeric} \qquad \alpha_{bar\_ret} = \alpha_{foo\_ret} = \text{Numeric}$$

Notice that w must have bar and qux methods, but x only needs a qux method. For return types, both bar and foo always return Numeric.

2.3 Local variables and fields

In the previous example, our algorithm generated roughly the same constraints that a static type inference system might generate. How-

[1] In Ruby, the syntax $e_1 + e_2$ is shorthand for $e_1.+(e_2)$, i.e., calling the + method on e_1 with argument e_2.

```
21 class C
22   def foo(x)
23     z = x;  z.baz();
24     z = 3; return z + 5;
25   end
26 end
27 class D
28   def bar(x)  @f = x        end
29   def baz()   y = 3 + @f end
30   def qux()   @f = "foo"  end
31   def f() bar("foo") end
32 end
```

Figure 3. Example with local variables and fields

```
class E
  def foo(x, p)
    if p then x.qux() else x.baz() end
  end
  def bar(p)
    if p then y = 3 else y = "hello" end
    if p then y + 6 else y.length end
  end
end
```

(a) Paths and path-sensitivity

```
class F
  def foo(x)
    return ( if x then 0 else "hello" end)
  end
  def bar(y,z)
    return ( if y then foo(z) else foo(!z) end)
  end
end
f = F.new
```

(b) Per-method path coverage

Figure 4. Additional Examples

ever, because our algorithm observes only dynamic runs, in many cases it can be more precise than static type inference.

Consider class C in Figure 3. On entry to foo, we wrap the actual argument v as $v : \alpha_x$, where α_x is foo's formal argument type. At the assignment on line 23, we do nothing special—we allow the language interpreter to copy a reference to $v : \alpha_x$ into z. At the call to baz, we generate the expected constraint $\alpha_x \leq [\mathsf{baz} : () \to ()]$. More interestingly, on line 24, we reassign z to contain 3, and so at the call to z's + method, we do not generate any constraints on α_x. Thus, our analysis is *flow-sensitive* with respect to local variables, meaning it respects the order of operations within a method.

To see why this treatment of local variable assignment is safe, it helps to think in terms of compiler optimization. We are essentially performing inference over a series of execution traces. We can view each trace as a straight-line program. Consider the execution trace of foo (which is the same as the body of the function, in this case). If we apply copy propagation (of x and 3) to the trace we get `z=x; x.baz(); z=3; return 3 + 5;` Since z is a local variable inaccessible outside of the scope of foo, it is dead at the end of the method, too, so we can apply dead code elimination to reduce the trace to "`x.baz(); return 3+5;`". The constraints we would generate from this trace are equivalent to those we would generate with our approach.

Instance fields in Ruby are not visible outside an object, but they are shared across all methods of an object. Thus, we need to treat them differently than locals. To see why, consider the class D in Figure 3, which uses the instance variable @f (all instance variables begin with @ in Ruby). Suppose that we treated fields the same way as local variables, i.e., we did nothing special at assignments to them. Now consider inferring types for D with the run `bar(1); baz(); qux()`. During the call bar(1), we would generate the constraint $\mathsf{Numeric} \leq \alpha_x$ (the type variable for x) and store $1 : \alpha_x$ in @f. Then during baz(), we would generate the constraint $\alpha_x \leq \mathsf{Numeric}$, and the call to qux() would generate no constraints. Thus, we could solve the constraints to get $\alpha_x = \mathsf{Numeric}$, and we would think this class has type $[\mathsf{bar} : \mathsf{Numeric} \to (), \mathsf{baz} : () \to (), \mathsf{qux} : () \to ()]$. But this result is clearly wrong, as the "well-typed" sequence `qux(); baz()` produces a type error.

To solve this problem, we need to introduce a type variable $\alpha_{@f}$ for the field, and then generate constraints and wrap values accordingly. It would be natural to do this at writes to fields, but that turns out to be impossible with a Ruby-only, dynamic solution, as there is no dynamic mechanism for intercepting field writes.[2] Fortunately, we can still handle fields safely by applying the same principles we saw in Figure 1 for method arguments and returns. There, we needed two invariants: (1) when we switch from method m to method n, we need to capture the flow of values from m to n, and (2) when we enter a method n, we need to wrap all values that could affect the type of n. Translating this idea to fields, we need to ensure:

- When we switch from m to n, we record all field *writes* performed by m, since they might be read by n. This is captured by constraints (c) and (g) in Figure 1.
- When we enter n, we need to wrap all fields n may use, so that subsequent field *reads* will see the wrapped values. This is captured by constraints (e) and (i) in Figure 1.

Adding these extra constraints and wrapping operations solves the problem we saw above. At the call bar(1), we generate the constraint $\mathsf{Numeric} \leq \alpha_x$, as before. However, at the end of bar, we now generate a constraint $\alpha_x \leq \alpha_{@f}$ to capture the write. At the beginning of baz, we wrap @f so that the body of baz will now generate the constraints $\alpha_{@f} \leq \mathsf{Numeric}$. Then qux generates the constraint $\mathsf{String} \leq \alpha_{@f}$. We can immediately see the constraints $\mathsf{String} \leq \alpha_{@f} \leq \mathsf{Numeric}$ are unsatisfiable, and hence we would correctly report a type error.

Notice that this design also allows a small amount of flow-sensitivity for fields: A field may temporarily contain a value of a different type, as long as it is overwritten before calling another method or returning. We do not expect that this yields much additional precision in practice, however.

Our implementation handles class variables similarly to instance variables. Note that we assume single-threaded execution—if accesses of such variables by other threads are interleaved, the inferred constraints may be unsound.

2.4 Path, path-sensitivity, and path coverage

As our algorithm observes dynamic runs, to infer sound types we need to observe all possible paths through branching code sequences. For example, we can infer types for the foo method in Figure 4(a) if we see an execution such as `foo(a, true); foo(b, false);`.

[2] Recall we wish to avoid using static techniques, including program rewriting, because they require complex front-ends that understand program semantics. For example, even ordering of assignment operations in Ruby can be non-obvious in some cases [11].

In this case, we will generate $\alpha_x \leq$ [qux : ...] from the first call, and $\alpha_x \leq$ [baz : ...] from the second.

One benefit of observing actual dynamic runs is that we never model unrealizable program executions. For example, consider the bar method in Figure 4(a). In a call bar(**true**), line 38 assigns a Numeric to y, and in a call bar(**false**), it assigns a String to y. Typical path-insensitive static type inference would conflate these possibilities and determine that y could be either a Numeric or String on line 39, and hence would signal a potential error for both the calls to + and to length. In contrast, in our approach we do not assign any type to local y, and we observe each path separately. Thus, we do not report a type error for this code.

Our soundness theorem (Section 3) holds if we observe all possible paths within each method body. To see why this is sufficient, rather than needing to observe all possible *program* paths, consider the code in Figure 4(b). Assuming bar is the entry point, there are four paths through this class, given by all possible truth value combinations for y and z. However, to observe all possible *types*, we only need to explore two paths. If we call f.bar(**true**, **true**) and f.bar(**false** , **true**), we will generate the following constraints:[3]

f.bar(true, true)	f.bar(false, true)
Boolean $\leq \alpha_y$	Boolean $\leq \alpha_y$
Boolean $\leq \alpha_z$	Boolean $\leq \alpha_z$
$\alpha_z \leq \alpha_x$	Boolean $\leq \alpha_x$
Numeric $\leq \alpha_{foo\_ret}$	String $\leq \alpha_{foo\_ret}$
$\alpha_{foo\_ret} \leq \alpha_{bar\_ret}$	$\alpha_{foo\_ret} \leq \alpha_{bar\_ret}$

Thus, we can deduce that bar may return a Numeric or a String. (Note that our system supports union types, so we can express this return type as String ∪ Numeric.)

The reason we only needed two paths is that type variables on method arguments and returns act as join points, summarizing the possible types of all paths within a method. In our example, both branches of the conditional in bar have the same type, α_{foo_ret}. Thus, the other possible calls, f.bar(**true**, **false**) and f.bar(**false** , **false**), do not affect what types bar could return.

2.5 Dynamic features

Another benefit of our dynamic type inference algorithm is that we can easily handle dynamic features that are very challenging for static type inference. For example, consider the following code, which occurred in one of our experimental benchmarks:

```
def initialize (args)
  args.keys.each do | attrib |
    self.send("#{attrib}=", args[ attrib ])
end end
```

This constructor takes a hash args as an argument, and then for each key-value pair (k, v) uses reflective method invocation via send to call a method named after k with the argument v. Or, consider the following code:

```
ATTRIBUTES = ["bold", "underscore", ... ]
ATTRIBUTES.each do |attr|
  code = "def #{attr}(&blk) ... end"
  eval code
end
```

For each element of the string array ATTRIBUTES, this code uses eval to define a new method named after the element.

[3] Note that an **if** generates no constraints on its guard as any object may be supplied (**false** and **nil** are false, and any other object is true). Also, here and in our implementation, we treat **true** and **false** as having type Boolean, though in Ruby they are actually instances of TrueClass and FalseClass, respectively.

$$
\begin{array}{rrcl}
\text{expressions} & e & ::= & \mathsf{nil} \mid \mathsf{self} \mid x \mid @f \mid x = e \\
 & & \mid & @f = e \mid A.\mathsf{new} \mid e.m(e') \mid e; e' \\
 & & \mid & \mathsf{if}^{\ell}\ e\ \mathsf{then}\ e'\ \mathsf{else}\ e'' \\
\text{methods} & d & ::= & \mathsf{def}\ m(x) = e \\
\text{classes} & c & ::= & \mathsf{class}\ A = d^{\star} \\
\text{programs} & \mathcal{P} & ::= & c^{\star} \rhd e \\
 & & & \\
\text{types} & \tau & ::= & A.@f \mid A.m \mid A.\overline{m} \mid \bot \mid \top \\
 & & \mid & A \mid [m : A.m \to A.\overline{m}] \mid \tau \cup \tau' \mid \tau \cap \tau'
\end{array}
$$

$$
\begin{array}{rcl@{\qquad}rcl}
x & \in & \text{local variables} & A & \in & \text{class names} \\
@f & \in & \text{field names} & \ell & \in & \text{labels} \\
m & \in & \text{method names} & & &
\end{array}
$$

Figure 5. Syntax of source language

We encountered both of these code snippets in earlier work, in which we proposed using run-time profiling to gather concrete uses of send, eval, and other highly dynamic constructs, and then analyzing the profile data statically [10]. In the dynamic analysis we propose in the current paper, no separate profiling pass is needed: we simply let the language interpreter execute this code and observe the results during type inference. Method invocation via send is no harder than normal dynamic dispatch; we just do the usual constraint generation and wrapping, which, as mentioned earlier, is actually performed inside the callee in our implementation. Method creation via eval is also easy, since we add wrapping instrumentation by dynamically iterating through the defined methods of unannotated classes; it makes no difference how those methods were created, as long as it happens before instrumentation.

3. Formal development

In this section, we describe our dynamic type inference technique on a core Ruby-like source language.

The syntax is shown in Figure 5. Expressions include nil, self, variables x, fields $@f$, variable assignments $x = e$, field assignments $@f = e$, object creations A.new, method calls $e.m(e')$, sequences $e; e'$, and conditionals $\mathsf{if}^{\ell}\ e$ then e' else e''. Conditionals carry labels ℓ to allow us to reason about path coverage. Conceptually, labels may be thought of as logical propositions—literals of the form ℓ and $\neg\ell$ represent a branch taken or not taken, respectively, at run time. We assume that all labels are distinct.

The form def $m(x) = e$ defines a method m with formal argument x and body e. Classes c are named collections of methods. A program consists of a set of classes and a single expression that serves as a *test*. Typically, we run a test on a collection of classes to "train" the system—i.e., infer types—and, in our proofs, run other tests to "monitor" the system—i.e., show that the inferred types are sound. In the formalism, we use only a single test e to train the system, but we can always represent a set of tests by sequencing them together into a single expression.

The syntax of types requires some explanation. Type variables are "tagged" to avoid generating and accounting for fresh variables. Thus, $A.@f$ is a type variable that denotes the type of the field $@f$ of objects of class A; similarly, $A.m$ and $A.\overline{m}$ are type variables that denote the argument and result types of the method m of class A. In addition, we have nominal types A for objects of class A, and structural types $[m : A.m \to A.\overline{m}]$ for objects with method m whose argument and result types can be viewed as $A.m$ and $A.\overline{m}$. Finally, we have the bottom type $\bot$, the top type $\top$, union types $\tau \cup \tau'$, and intersection types $\tau \cap \tau'$.

$$\begin{array}{rcl}
\text{values } v & ::= & l \mid \mathsf{nil} \\
\text{wrapped values } \omega & ::= & v : \tau \\
\text{field maps } \mathcal{F} & ::= & (@f \mapsto \omega)^{\star} \\
\text{method maps } \mathcal{M} & ::= & (m \mapsto \lambda(x)e)^{\star} \\
\text{class maps } \mathcal{C} & ::= & (A \mapsto \mathcal{M})^{\star} \\
\text{heaps } \mathcal{H} & ::= & (l \mapsto A\langle\mathcal{F}\rangle)^{\star} \\
\text{environments } \mathcal{E} & ::= & (x \mapsto \omega)^{\star}, (\mathsf{self} \mapsto l : A)^{?} \\
\text{literals } p & ::= & (\ell \mid \neg\ell) \\
\text{paths } \phi & ::= & p^{\star} \\
\text{constraints } \Pi & ::= & (\tau \leq \tau')^{\star}, \phi^{\star}
\end{array}$$

Figure 6. Auxiliary syntax

3.1 Training semantics

We now define a semantics for training. The semantics extends a standard semantics with some instrumentation. The instrumentation does not affect the run-time behavior of programs; it merely records run-time information that later allows us to infer types and argue about their soundness.

To define the semantics, we need some auxiliary syntax to describe internal data structures, shown in Figure 6. Let l denote heap locations. Values include heap locations and nil. Such values are *wrapped* with types for training. A field map associates field names with wrapped values. A method map associates method names with abstractions. A class map associates class names with method maps. A heap maps locations to objects $A\langle\mathcal{F}\rangle$, which denote objects of class A with field map $\mathcal{F}$. An environment maps variables to wrapped values and, optionally, self to a location wrapped with its run-time type. Formally, the run-time type of a value under a heap is defined by $\texttt{runtype}_{\mathcal{H}}(l) = A$ if $\mathcal{H}(l) = A\langle\mathcal{F}\rangle$ and $\texttt{runtype}_{\mathcal{H}}(\mathsf{nil}) = \bot$.

A path ϕ is a list of label literals ℓ or $\neg\ell$, denoted by p, that mark conditionals encountered in a run. Constraints Π include standard subtyping constraints $\tau \leq \tau'$ and coverage constraints ϕ, meaning that the path ϕ is traversed during some call in the run.

The rules shown in Figure 7 derive big-step reduction judgments of the form $\mathcal{H}; \mathcal{E}; e \longrightarrow_{\mathcal{C}} \mathcal{H}'; \mathcal{E}'; \omega \mid \Pi; \phi$, meaning that given class map $\mathcal{C}$, expression e under heap $\mathcal{H}$ and environment $\mathcal{E}$ reduces to wrapped value ω, covering path ϕ, generating constraints Π, and returning heap $\mathcal{H}'$ and environment $\mathcal{E}'$. We define the following operations on wrapped values: if $\omega = v : \tau$ then $\texttt{val}(\omega) = v$, $\texttt{type}(\omega) = \tau$, and $\omega \bullet \tau' = v : \tau'$. In the rules, we use an underscore in any position where an arbitrary quantity is allowed, and we write empty set as $\{\}$ to avoid confusion with ϕ.

By (TNIL), the type assigned to nil is $\bot$, which means that nil may have any type. (TSELF) is straightforward. In (TNEW), the notation $A\langle \_ \mapsto \mathsf{nil} : \bot\rangle$ indicates an instance of A with all possible fields mapped to nil. (As in Ruby, fields need not be explicitly initialized before use, and are nil by default.) (TVAR) and (TVAR=) are standard, and generate no constraint nor perform any wrapping, as discussed in Section 2.3.

As explained in Section 2, we permit some flow-sensitivity for field types. Thus, (FIELD) and (FIELD=) are like (VAR) and (VAR=) in that they generate no constraint and perform no wrapping.

(TSEQ) is straightforward. By (TCOND), either ℓ or $\neg\ell$ is recorded in the current path, depending on the branch traversed for the conditional with label ℓ. Note that ℓ and $\neg\ell$ can never appear in the same path: looping in the formal language occurs only via recursive calls, and callee paths are not included in caller paths. That said, the conditional itself may be visited on many occasions during the training run, so that both ℓ and $\neg\ell$ may eventually appear in coverage constraints.

(TNIL)

$$\mathcal{H}; \mathcal{E}; \mathsf{nil} \longrightarrow_{\mathcal{C}} \mathcal{H}; \mathcal{E}; \mathsf{nil} : \bot \mid \{\}; \{\}$$

(TSELF)

$$\frac{\mathcal{E}(\mathsf{self}) = l : A}{\mathcal{H}; \mathcal{E}; \mathsf{self} \longrightarrow_{\mathcal{C}} \mathcal{H}; \mathcal{E}; l : A \mid \{\}; \{\}}$$

(TNEW)

$$\frac{l \text{ fresh} \qquad \mathcal{H}' = \mathcal{H}\{l \mapsto A\langle \_ \mapsto \mathsf{nil} : \bot\rangle\}}{\mathcal{H}; \mathcal{E}; A.\mathsf{new} \longrightarrow_{\mathcal{C}} \mathcal{H}'; \mathcal{E}; l : A \mid \{\}; \{\}}$$

(TVAR)

$$\frac{\mathcal{E}(x) = \omega}{\mathcal{H}; \mathcal{E}; x \longrightarrow_{\mathcal{C}} \mathcal{H}; \mathcal{E}; \omega \mid \{\}; \{\}}$$

(TVAR =)

$$\frac{\mathcal{H}; \mathcal{E}; e \longrightarrow_{\mathcal{C}} \mathcal{H}'; \mathcal{E}'; \omega \mid \Pi; \phi \qquad \mathcal{E}'' = \mathcal{E}'\{x \mapsto \omega\}}{\mathcal{H}; \mathcal{E}; x = e \longrightarrow_{\mathcal{C}} \mathcal{H}'; \mathcal{E}''; \omega \mid \Pi; \phi}$$

(TFIELD)

$$\frac{\mathcal{E}(\mathsf{self}) = \omega \qquad l = \texttt{val}(\omega) \qquad \mathcal{H}(l) = \_\langle\mathcal{F}\rangle \qquad \mathcal{F}(@f) = \omega}{\mathcal{H}; \mathcal{E}; @f \longrightarrow_{\mathcal{C}} \mathcal{H}; \mathcal{E}; \omega \mid \{\}; \{\}}$$

(TFIELD =)

$$\frac{\begin{array}{c}\mathcal{H}; \mathcal{E}; e \longrightarrow_{\mathcal{C}} \mathcal{H}'; \mathcal{E}'; \omega \mid \Pi; \phi \\ \mathcal{E}'(\mathsf{self}) = \omega' \qquad l = \texttt{val}(\omega') \\ \mathcal{H}'(l) = A\langle\mathcal{F}\rangle \qquad \mathcal{H}'' = \mathcal{H}'\{l \mapsto A\langle\mathcal{F}\{@f \mapsto \omega\}\rangle\}\end{array}}{\mathcal{H}; \mathcal{E}; @f = e \longrightarrow_{\mathcal{C}} \mathcal{H}''; \mathcal{E}'; \omega \mid \Pi; \phi}$$

(TSEQ)

$$\frac{\begin{array}{c}\mathcal{H}; \mathcal{E}; e \longrightarrow_{\mathcal{C}} \mathcal{H}'; \mathcal{E}'; \_ \mid \Pi; \phi \\ \mathcal{H}'; \mathcal{E}'; e' \longrightarrow_{\mathcal{C}} \mathcal{H}''; \mathcal{E}''; \omega \mid \Pi'; \phi'\end{array}}{\mathcal{H}; \mathcal{E}; (e; e') \longrightarrow_{\mathcal{C}} \mathcal{H}''; \mathcal{E}''; \omega \mid \Pi, \Pi'; \phi, \phi'}$$

(TCOND)

$$\frac{\begin{array}{c}\mathcal{H}; \mathcal{E}; e \longrightarrow_{\mathcal{C}} \mathcal{H}'; \mathcal{E}'; \omega \mid \Pi; \phi \\ p = \ell, e_p = e' \text{ if } \texttt{val}(\omega) \neq \mathsf{nil} \\ p = \neg\ell, e_p = e'' \text{ if } \texttt{val}(\omega) = \mathsf{nil} \\ \mathcal{H}'; \mathcal{E}'; e_p \longrightarrow_{\mathcal{C}} \mathcal{H}''; \mathcal{E}''; \omega' \mid \Pi'; \phi'\end{array}}{\mathcal{H}; \mathcal{E}; \mathsf{if}^{\ell}\ e \ \mathsf{then}\ e' \ \mathsf{else}\ e'' \longrightarrow_{\mathcal{C}} \mathcal{H}''; \mathcal{E}''; \omega' \mid \Pi, \Pi'; \phi, p, \phi'}$$

(TCALL)

$$\frac{\begin{array}{c}\mathcal{H}; \mathcal{E}; e \longrightarrow_{\mathcal{C}} \mathcal{H}'; \mathcal{E}'; \omega \mid \Pi; \phi \qquad \tau = \texttt{type}(\omega) \\ \mathcal{H}'; \mathcal{E}'; e' \longrightarrow_{\mathcal{C}} \mathcal{H}''; \mathcal{E}''; \omega' \mid \Pi'; \phi' \qquad \tau' = \texttt{type}(\omega') \\ l = \mathcal{E}''(\mathsf{self}) \qquad \bar{l} = \texttt{val}(\omega') \\ \mathcal{H}''(\bar{l}) = A\langle\_\rangle \qquad \mathcal{C}(A) = \mathcal{M} \qquad \mathcal{M}(m) = \lambda(x)e'' \\ \Pi'' = \tau' \leq [m : A.m \rightarrow A.\overline{m}], \tau \leq A.m, \texttt{constrain}_{l}(\mathcal{H}'') \\ \mathcal{H}''' = \texttt{wrap}_{\bar{l}}(\mathcal{H}'') \qquad \mathcal{E}''' = \{\mathsf{self} \mapsto \omega' \bullet A, x \mapsto \omega \bullet A.m\} \\ \mathcal{H}'''; \mathcal{E}'''; e'' \longrightarrow_{\mathcal{C}} \overline{\mathcal{H}}; \_; \overline{\omega} \mid \overline{\Pi}; \overline{\phi} \qquad \overline{\tau} = \texttt{type}(\overline{\omega}) \\ \overline{\Pi}' = \overline{\tau} \leq A.\overline{m}, \texttt{constrain}_{\bar{l}}(\overline{\mathcal{H}}), \overline{\phi} \\ \overline{\mathcal{H}}' = \texttt{wrap}_{l}(\overline{\mathcal{H}}) \qquad \overline{\omega}' = \overline{\omega} \bullet A.\overline{m}\end{array}}{\mathcal{H}; \mathcal{E}; e'.m(e) \longrightarrow_{\mathcal{C}} \overline{\mathcal{H}}'; \mathcal{E}''; \overline{\omega}' \mid \Pi, \Pi', \Pi'', \overline{\Pi}, \overline{\Pi}'; \phi, \phi'}$$

Figure 7. Training semantics

(TCALL) performs the actions introduced in Figure 1. First, the type of the receiver ω' is constrained to be a subtype of $[m : A.m \rightarrow A.\overline{m}]$, and the type of the argument ω is constrained to be a subtype of $A.m$, the argument type of the callee. We evaluate the body e'' with argument x mapped to $\omega \bullet A.m$, which is the argument wrapped with method argument's type variable. The type of the result $\overline{\omega}$ is constrained to be a subtype of the result type $A.\overline{m}$, and returned wrapped with that type. Furthermore (TCALL) relates the current path to the set of paths stored as coverage constraints. In particular, while ϕ, ϕ' records the current path traversed in the caller, the path $\overline{\phi}$ traversed by the callee is recorded as a coverage constraint in $\overline{\Pi}'$. In addition, (TCALL) involves wrapping and generation of subtyping constraints for fields of the caller and the callee objects. Let $\mathcal{H}(l) = A\langle\mathcal{F}\rangle$. We define

- $\texttt{wrap}_l(\mathcal{H}) = \mathcal{H}\{l \mapsto A\langle\{@f \mapsto \omega \bullet A.@f \mid @f \mapsto \omega \in \mathcal{F}\}\rangle\}$
- $\texttt{constrain}_l(\mathcal{H}) = \{\texttt{type}(\omega) \leq A.@f \mid @f \mapsto \omega \in \mathcal{F}\}$

As discussed in Section 2, we constrain the fields of the caller object and wrap the fields of the callee object before the method call, and symmetrically, constrain the fields of the callee object and wrap the fields of the caller object after the method call.

Finally, the following rule describes training with programs.

(TRAIN)

$$\frac{\mathcal{C} = \texttt{classmap}(c^\star) \qquad \{\}, \{\}, e \longrightarrow_{\mathcal{C}} \_; \_; \_ \mid \Pi; \_}{c^\star \rhd e \uparrow \texttt{solve}(\texttt{subtyping}(\Pi)); \texttt{coverage}(\Pi)}$$

where we define:

$$\begin{aligned} \texttt{classmap}(c^\star) &= \{A \mapsto \texttt{methodmap}(d^\star) \mid \mathsf{class}\ A = d^\star \in c^\star\} \\ \texttt{methodmap}(d^\star) &= \{m \mapsto \lambda(x)e \mid \mathsf{def}\ m(x) = e \in d^\star\} \\ \texttt{coverage}(\Pi) &= \{\phi \mid \phi \in \Pi\} \end{aligned}$$

We assume that $\texttt{solve}(\texttt{subtyping}(\Pi))$ externally solves the subtyping constraints in Π to obtain a mapping $\mathcal{T}$ from type variables to concrete types (possibly involving $\top$ and $\bot$, and unions and intersections of nominal types and structural types). We discuss the solving algorithm we use in our implementation in Section 4; however, our technique is agnostic to the choice of algorithm or even to the language of solved types.

The crucial soundness measure for the inferred types is $\Phi = \texttt{coverage}(\Pi)$, which collects all the coverage constraints in the run. The key soundness theorem states that any run whose paths are a subset of Φ must use types that are consistent with Φ. As a corollary, we show that if all possible paths are covered during inference, then all runs are type safe.

3.2 Monitoring semantics

To argue about the soundness of inferred types, next we define a monitoring semantics. This semantics slightly extends a standard semantics with monitoring of calls at the top level, and monitoring of conditionals. This affects the run-time behavior of programs—we enforce a contract between the run-time type of the argument and the inferred argument type for any call at the top level, and require that the monitoring run only traverses paths that have already been traversed by the training run. A top-level call is simply one that calls into any of the classes for which we have inferred types from outside; a call from within a typed class (either to its own method or to one of other typed class) is considered internal.

To define the monitoring semantics, we modify the syntax of expressions, field maps, class maps, and environments as follows.

$$\begin{aligned} \text{expressions } e &::= \ \ldots \mid \underline{e'.m(e)} \\ \text{class maps } \mathcal{C} &::= \ (A \mapsto \mathcal{M})^\star, \mathcal{T}, \Phi \\ \text{field maps } \mathcal{F} &::= \ (@f \mapsto v)^\star \\ \text{environments } \mathcal{E} &::= \ (x \mapsto v)^\star, (\mathsf{self} \mapsto l)^? \end{aligned}$$

Expressions of the form $\underline{e'.m(e)}$ denote method calls at the top level. Class maps additionally carry the solution $\mathcal{T}$ of the subtyping constraints collected during training, and the coverage Φ of the training run. Field maps and environments no longer map to types.

The rules shown in Figure 8 derive big-step reduction judgments of the form $\mathcal{H}; \mathcal{E}; e \mid \phi \longrightarrow_{\mathcal{C}} \mathcal{H}'; \mathcal{E}'; v \mid \phi'$, where ϕ is the prescribed path to be traversed and ϕ' is the suffix of ϕ that remains.

(NIL)

$$\mathcal{H}; \mathcal{E}; \mathsf{nil} \mid \phi \longrightarrow_{\mathcal{C}} \mathcal{H}; \mathcal{E}; \mathsf{nil} \mid \phi$$

(SELF)

$$\frac{\mathcal{E}(\mathsf{self}) = l}{\mathcal{H}; \mathcal{E}; \mathsf{self} \mid \phi \longrightarrow_{\mathcal{C}} \mathcal{H}; \mathcal{E}; l \mid \phi}$$

(NEW)

$$\frac{l \text{ fresh} \qquad \mathcal{H}' = \mathcal{H}\{l \mapsto A\langle\_ \mapsto \mathsf{nil}\rangle\}}{\mathcal{H}; \mathcal{E}; A.\mathsf{new} \mid \phi \longrightarrow_{\mathcal{C}} \mathcal{H}'; \mathcal{E}; l \mid \phi}$$

(VAR)

$$\frac{\mathcal{E}(x) = v}{\mathcal{H}; \mathcal{E}; x \mid \phi \longrightarrow_{\mathcal{C}} \mathcal{H}; \mathcal{E}; v \mid \phi}$$

(VAR =)

$$\frac{\mathcal{H}; \mathcal{E}; e \mid \phi \longrightarrow_{\mathcal{C}} \mathcal{H}'; \mathcal{E}'; v \mid \phi' \qquad \mathcal{E}'' = \mathcal{E}'\{x \mapsto v\}}{\mathcal{H}; \mathcal{E}; x = e \mid \phi \longrightarrow_{\mathcal{C}} \mathcal{H}'; \mathcal{E}''; v \mid \phi'}$$

(FIELD)

$$\frac{\mathcal{E}(\mathsf{self}) = l \qquad \mathcal{H}(l) = \_\langle\mathcal{F}\rangle \qquad \mathcal{F}(@f) = v}{\mathcal{H}; \mathcal{E}; @f \mid \phi \longrightarrow_{\mathcal{C}} \mathcal{H}; \mathcal{E}; v \mid \phi}$$

(FIELD =)

$$\frac{\begin{array}{c}\mathcal{H}; \mathcal{E}; e \mid \phi \longrightarrow_{\mathcal{C}} \mathcal{H}'; \mathcal{E}'; v \mid \phi' \qquad \mathcal{E}'(\mathsf{self}) = l \\ \mathcal{H}'(l) = A\langle\mathcal{F}\rangle \qquad \mathcal{H}'' = \mathcal{H}'\{l \mapsto A\langle\mathcal{F}\{@f \mapsto v\}\rangle\}\end{array}}{\mathcal{H}; \mathcal{E}; @f = e \mid \phi \longrightarrow_{\mathcal{C}} \mathcal{H}''; \mathcal{E}'; v \mid \phi'}$$

(SEQ)

$$\frac{\begin{array}{c}\mathcal{H}; \mathcal{E}; e \mid \phi \longrightarrow_{\mathcal{C}} \mathcal{H}'; \mathcal{E}'; \_ \mid \phi' \\ \mathcal{H}'; \mathcal{E}'; e' \mid \phi' \longrightarrow_{\mathcal{C}} \mathcal{H}''; \mathcal{E}''; v \mid \phi''\end{array}}{\mathcal{H}; \mathcal{E}; (e; e') \mid \phi \longrightarrow_{\mathcal{C}} \mathcal{H}''; \mathcal{E}''; v \mid \phi''}$$

(CALL)

$$\frac{\begin{array}{c}\mathcal{H}; \mathcal{E}; e \mid \phi \longrightarrow_{\mathcal{C}} \mathcal{H}'; \mathcal{E}'; v \mid \phi' \\ \mathcal{H}'; \mathcal{E}'; e' \mid \phi' \longrightarrow_{\mathcal{C}} \mathcal{H}''; \mathcal{E}''; l \mid \phi'' \\ \mathcal{H}''(l) = A\langle\_\rangle \qquad \mathcal{C}(A) = \mathcal{M} \qquad \mathcal{M}(m) = \lambda(x)e'' \\ \overline{\phi} \in \mathcal{C} \qquad \mathcal{H}''; \{\mathsf{self} \mapsto l, x \mapsto v\}; e'' \mid \overline{\phi} \longrightarrow_{\mathcal{C}} \mathcal{H}'''; \_; v' \mid \_\end{array}}{\mathcal{H}; \mathcal{E}; e'.m(e) \mid \phi \longrightarrow_{\mathcal{C}} \mathcal{H}'''; \mathcal{E}''; v' \mid \phi''}$$

(MCOND)

$$\frac{\begin{array}{c}\mathcal{H}; \mathcal{E}; e \mid \phi \longrightarrow_{\mathcal{C}} \mathcal{H}'; \mathcal{E}'; v \mid p, \phi' \\ p = \ell, e_p = e' \text{ if } v \neq \mathsf{nil} \qquad p = \neg\ell, e_p = e'' \text{ if } v = \mathsf{nil} \\ \mathcal{H}', \mathcal{E}'; e_p \mid \phi' \longrightarrow_{\mathcal{C}} \mathcal{H}''; \mathcal{E}''; v' \mid \phi''\end{array}}{\mathcal{H}; \mathcal{E}; \mathsf{if}^\ell\ e \ \mathsf{then}\ e' \ \mathsf{else}\ e'' \mid \phi \longrightarrow_{\mathcal{C}} \mathcal{H}''; \mathcal{E}''; v' \mid \phi''}$$

(MCALL)

$$\frac{\begin{array}{c}\mathcal{H}; \mathcal{E}; e \mid \phi \longrightarrow_{\mathcal{C}} \mathcal{H}', \mathcal{E}'; v \mid \phi' \\ \mathcal{H}'; \mathcal{E}'; e' \mid \phi' \longrightarrow_{\mathcal{C}} \mathcal{H}''; \mathcal{E}''; l \mid \phi'' \\ \mathcal{H}''(l) = A\langle\_\rangle \qquad \mathcal{C}(A) = \mathcal{M} \\ \mathcal{M}(m) = \lambda(x)e'' \qquad \texttt{runtype}_{\mathcal{H}''}(v) \leq \mathcal{C}(A.m) \\ \overline{\phi} \in \mathcal{C} \qquad \mathcal{H}''; \{\mathsf{self} \mapsto l, x \mapsto v\}; e'' \mid \overline{\phi} \longrightarrow_{\mathcal{C}} \mathcal{H}'''; \_; v'' \mid \_\end{array}}{\mathcal{H}; \mathcal{E}; \underline{e'.m(e)} \mid \phi \longrightarrow_{\mathcal{C}} \mathcal{H}'''; \mathcal{E}''; v'' \mid \phi''}$$

Figure 8. Monitoring semantics

(NIL), (SELF), (NEW), (VAR), (FIELD), (VAR=), (FIELD=), and (SEQ) are derived from the corresponding rules for training, simply by erasing types, paths, and constraints. (CALL) is similar, but in addition, it (non-deterministically) picks a path from the coverage of the training run, which is carried by $\mathcal{C}$, and prescribes that the call should traverse that path by including it in the environment under which that call is run.

By (MCOND), a particular branch p of a conditional may be traversed only if the path prescribes that branch, i.e., it begins with p. The branch is then run under a residual path ϕ'.

By (MCALL), a top level call requires that the run-time type of the argument v is a subtype of the argument type of the method, as prescribed by the solution carried by $\mathcal{C}$, which we write as $\mathcal{C}(A.m)$.

The following rule describes monitoring of programs.

(RUN)

$$\frac{\mathcal{C} = \texttt{classmap}(c^\star), \mathcal{T}, \Phi \qquad \{\}, \{\}, \texttt{monitor}(e) \mid \{\} \longrightarrow_{\mathcal{C}} \_; \_; \_ \mid \{\}}{c^\star \rhd e \downarrow}$$

where $\texttt{monitor}(e')$ is e' but with any method call underlined.

Of course, reduction may be stuck in several ways, so we do not expect to derive such a judgment for every program. In particular, we do not care when reduction is stuck due to calls on nil, violations of argument type contracts for top-level calls, and violation of coverage contracts for conditionals: these correspond to a failed null check, a type-incorrect program, and an inadequately monitored program, respectively. However, we do care about "method not found" errors, since they would reveal that our inferred types, even for paths we have monitored, are unsound. The following rule (along with other versions of the monitoring rules augmented with error propagation, not shown) derives error judgments of the form $\mathcal{H}; \mathcal{E}; e \mid \phi \,\lightning_{\mathcal{C}}$.

(ERROR)

$$\frac{\begin{array}{c}\mathcal{H}; \mathcal{E}; e \mid \phi \longrightarrow_{\mathcal{C}} \mathcal{H}'; \mathcal{E}'; v \mid \phi' \\ \mathcal{H}'; \mathcal{E}'; e' \mid \phi' \longrightarrow_{\mathcal{C}} \mathcal{H}''; \mathcal{E}''; l \mid \phi'' \\ \mathcal{H}''(l) = A\langle \_ \rangle \qquad \mathcal{C}(A) = \mathcal{M} \qquad m \notin \texttt{dom}(\mathcal{M})\end{array}}{\mathcal{H}; \mathcal{E}; e'.m(e) \mid \phi \,\lightning_{\mathcal{C}}}$$

Finally, the following rule defines program error judgments of the form $\mathcal{T}; \Phi \vdash c^\star \rhd e \,\lightning$.

(MONITOR)

$$\frac{\mathcal{C} = \texttt{classmap}(c^\star), \mathcal{T}, \Phi \qquad \{\}, \{\}, \texttt{monitor}(e) \mid \{\} \,\lightning_{\mathcal{C}}}{\mathcal{T}; \Phi \vdash c^\star \rhd e \,\lightning}$$

3.3 Soundness

We prove the following key soundness theorem.

Theorem 3.1 (Soundness). *Suppose that $c^\star \rhd e_1 \uparrow \mathcal{T}; \Phi$ for some e_1. Then there cannot be e_2 such that $\mathcal{T}; \Phi \vdash c^\star \rhd e_2 \,\lightning$.*

Informally, if we infer types $\mathcal{T}$ with a test that covers paths Φ, then as long as we run other tests that only traverse paths in Φ and satisfy the type contracts in $\mathcal{T}$, we cannot have "method-not-found" errors. In particular, this implies the following corollary.

Corollary 3.2. *If we infer types with a test that covers all possible paths, then our types are always sound.*

We sketch our proof below. Our monitoring semantics constrains execution to follow only paths traversed in the training run—this guarantees that if some expression in the methods of $c^\star$ is visited in the monitoring run, then it must be visited by the training run. Our proof is by simulation of the executions of such expressions between these runs.

We define the following simulation relation between heaps and environments of the training run (marked by subscript $\cdot_1$) and those of the monitoring run (marked by subscript $\cdot_2$).

Definition 3.3 (Simulation). *$\mathcal{H}_1; \mathcal{E}_1$ simulates $\mathcal{H}_2; \mathcal{E}_2$ under types $\mathcal{T}$, denoted by $\mathcal{H}_1; \mathcal{E}_1 \sim_{\mathcal{T}} \mathcal{H}_2; \mathcal{E}_2$, iff the following hold:*

- *$\mathcal{E}_1 \sim_{\mathcal{T}} \mathcal{E}_2$, i.e., $\mathcal{E}_1(x) = \omega_1$ if and only if $\mathcal{E}_2(x) = v_2$ such that $\texttt{runtype}_{\mathcal{H}_2}(v_2) \leq \mathcal{T}(\texttt{type}(\omega_1))$, and $\mathcal{E}_1(\mathsf{self}) = l_1 : A$ if and only if $\mathcal{E}_2(\mathsf{self}) = l_2 : A$.*
- *$\mathcal{H}_1(\mathcal{E}_1(\mathsf{self})) = A\langle \mathcal{F}_1 \rangle$ such that $\mathcal{F}_1(@f) = \omega_1$ if and only if $\mathcal{H}_2(\mathcal{E}_2(\mathsf{self})) = A\langle \mathcal{F}_2 \rangle$ such that $\mathcal{F}_2(@f) = v_2$ and $\texttt{runtype}_{\mathcal{H}_2}(v_2) \leq \mathcal{T}(\texttt{type}(\omega_1))$.*
- *whenever $\mathcal{H}_1(l_1) = A\langle \mathcal{F}_1 \rangle$ such that $\mathcal{F}_1(@f) = \omega_1$ and $l_1 \neq \mathcal{E}_1(\mathsf{self})$, we have $\texttt{type}(\omega_1) = A.@f$; and whenever $\mathcal{H}_2(l_2) = A\langle \mathcal{F}_2 \rangle$ such that $\mathcal{F}_2(@f) = v_2$ and $l_2 \neq \mathcal{E}_2(\mathsf{self})$, we have $\texttt{runtype}_{\mathcal{H}_2}(v_2) \leq \mathcal{T}(\texttt{type}(A.@f))$.*

Informally, let us say that a value v_2 in the monitoring run agrees with a type τ_1 associated in the training run if the run-time type of v_2 is a subtype of the solution of τ_1. Then, we say that a training state (heap and environment) simulates a monitoring state (heap and environment) if the values of variables in the monitoring environment agree with their types in the training environment; the self objects in both environments have the same class; the fields of objects in the monitoring heap agree with their types in the training heap; and for all objects other than self, the fields of those objects in the training heap are of the form $A.@f$. This last requirement essentially says that while self fields may have flow-sensitive types, all other fields must be "stabilized" with their flow-insensitive types. We define this notion of stability for training and monitoring heaps below.

Definition 3.4 (Training heap stability). *$\mathcal{H}_1$ is training-stable iff, whenever $\mathcal{H}_1(l_1) = A_1\langle \mathcal{F}_1 \rangle$ such that $\mathcal{F}_1(@f) = \omega_1$, we have $\texttt{type}(\omega_1) = \texttt{type}(A_1.@f)$.*

Definition 3.5 (Monitoring heap stability). *$\mathcal{H}_2$ is monitoring-stable iff, whenever $\mathcal{H}_2(l_2) = A_2\langle \mathcal{F}_2 \rangle$ such that $\mathcal{F}_2(@f) = v_2$, we have $\texttt{runtype}_{\mathcal{H}_2}(v_2) \leq \mathcal{T}(\texttt{type}(A_2.@f))$.*

Monitoring and training heaps can be stabilized by the operations of constraining and wrapping, respectively, as shown by the lemmas below. Recall that these operations happen upon entry and exit of method calls; thus, we can ensure that the flow-sensitivity of field types does not "leak" across method calls. This is crucial for our proof, as shown later.

Lemma 3.6 (Constraining). *Suppose that $\mathcal{H}_1; \mathcal{E}_1 \sim_{\mathcal{T}} \mathcal{H}_2; \mathcal{E}_2$. Suppose that whenever $\tau \leq \tau' \in \texttt{constrain}_{\mathcal{E}_1(\mathsf{self})}(\mathcal{H}_1))$, we have $\mathcal{T}(\tau) \leq \mathcal{T}(\tau')$. Then $\mathcal{H}_2$ is monitoring-stable.*

Lemma 3.7 (Wrapping). *Suppose that $\mathcal{H}_1; \mathcal{E}_1 \sim_{\mathcal{T}} \mathcal{H}_2; \mathcal{E}_2$. Then $\texttt{wrap}_{\mathcal{E}_1(\mathsf{self})}(\mathcal{H}_1)$ is training-stable.*

We now have a neat way of establishing that a training state simulates a monitoring state. If both heaps are stabilized (say by constraining and wrapping), and furthermore, if the environments themselves satisfy the requirements for simulation, then the states are related by simulation.

Lemma 3.8 (Proof technique for simulation). *Suppose that $\mathcal{H}_1$ is training-stable; $\mathcal{H}_2$ is monitoring-stable; and $\mathcal{E}_1 \sim_{\mathcal{T}} \mathcal{E}_2$. Then $\mathcal{H}_1; \mathcal{E}_1 \sim_{\mathcal{T}} \mathcal{H}_2; \mathcal{E}_2$.*

This proof technique is used to show the following main lemma: if we run the same expression in both runs and the initial training heap simulates the initial monitoring heap, then we cannot have method-not-found errors in the monitoring run, the result of the monitoring run agrees with its type in the training run, and the final training heap simulates the final monitoring heap.

Lemma 3.9 (Preservation). *Suppose that $\_ \rhd \_ \uparrow \mathcal{T}, \Phi$, in particular deriving $\mathcal{H}_1; \mathcal{E}_1; e \longrightarrow_{\mathcal{C}_1} \_; \mathcal{H}_1'; \mathcal{E}_1'; \_ : \tau_1 \mid \phi$. Let $\mathcal{C}_2 = \mathcal{C}_1, \mathcal{T}, \Phi$. Let $\mathcal{H}_2$ and $\mathcal{E}_2$ be such that $\mathcal{H}_1; \mathcal{E}_1 \sim_{\mathcal{T}} \mathcal{H}_2; \mathcal{E}_2$. Then:*

- *We cannot have $\mathcal{H}_2; \mathcal{E}_2; e \,\lightning_{\mathcal{C}_2}$.*
- *If $\mathcal{H}_2; \mathcal{E}_2; e \longrightarrow_{\mathcal{C}_2} \mathcal{H}_2'; \mathcal{E}_2'; v_2$ with $\phi, \phi' \in \mathcal{E}_2$ and $\phi' \in \mathcal{E}_2'$ for some ϕ', then $\texttt{runtype}_{\mathcal{H}_2}(v_2) \leq \mathcal{C}_2(\tau_1)$ and $\mathcal{H}_1'; \mathcal{E}_1' \sim_{\mathcal{T}} \mathcal{H}_2'; \mathcal{E}_2'$.*

Proof. The proof is by induction on the monitoring run. The only difficult case is for method calls, which we sketch below. (Note that these method calls are internal, not top-level, since only environments for which self is defined can appear in the simulation.)

By the induction hypothesis we cannot have errors in the evaluation of the argument and the receiver; let us say they evaluate to v_2 and l_2. Furthermore, the simulation relation must hold for resulting states, say $\mathcal{H}_1; \mathcal{E}_1$ and $\mathcal{H}_2; \mathcal{E}_2$, and v_2 and l_2 must agree with the types τ_1 and τ_1' associated with the argument and receiver in the training run, respectively. Since τ_1' is a subtype of a structural type with method m, we cannot have a method-not-found error here.

The main complication now is that the method dispatched in the training run may not be the same as that in the monitoring run, although the latter method should be dispatched at some point in the training run. Thus, to apply our induction hypothesis for the method call, we need to show that the initial state for that method call in the monitoring run is simulated by the possibly unrelated initial state with which that method was called in the training run. However, at this point we can apply Lemmas 3.6, 3.7, and 3.8 to relate those states, since we constrain the initial state of the caller and wrap the initial state of the callee. Thus, now by induction hypothesis, the method expression evaluates to (say) v_2'', such that the simulation relation must hold for resulting states, say $\mathcal{H}_1''; \mathcal{E}_1''$ and $\mathcal{H}_2''; \mathcal{E}_2''$ and v_2'' must agree with the type τ_1'' associated with the result in the training run. Finally, as above, we apply Lemmas 3.6, 3.7, and 3.8 to show that the final state for the method call in the training run simulates the final state for the method call in the monitoring run, since we constrain the final state of the callee and wrap the final state of the caller. □

Now using Lemma 3.9, we can show that the following weaker state invariant is preserved at the top level of a monitoring run.

Definition 3.10. *At the top level,* $\texttt{invariant}(\mathcal{H}_2; \mathcal{E}_2)$ *holds iff:*

- *whenever* $\mathcal{H}_2(l) = A\langle\mathcal{F}\rangle$ *such that* $\mathcal{F}(@f) = v_2$, *we have* $\texttt{runtype}_{\mathcal{H}_2}(v_2) \leq \mathcal{C}_2(A.@f)$;
- $\mathcal{E}_2(\mathsf{self})$ *is undefined.*

Lemma 3.11. *Suppose that* $c^\star \rhd_{-} \uparrow \mathcal{T}; \Phi$ *with* $\mathcal{C}_1 = \texttt{classmap}(c^\star)$. *Let* $\mathcal{C}_2 = \mathcal{C}_1, \mathcal{T}, \Phi$. *Let* $\mathcal{H}_2$ *and* $\mathcal{E}_2$ *be such that* $\texttt{invariant}(\mathcal{H}_2; \mathcal{E}_2)$. *Then:*

- *We cannot have* $\mathcal{H}_2; \mathcal{E}_2; \texttt{monitor}(e_0) \not\downarrow_{\mathcal{C}_2}$.
- *If* $\mathcal{H}_2; \mathcal{E}_2; \texttt{monitor}(e_0) \longrightarrow_{\mathcal{C}_2} \mathcal{H}_2'; \mathcal{E}_2'; v_2$ *then we must have* $\texttt{invariant}(\mathcal{H}_2'; \mathcal{E}_2')$.

Theorem 3.1 follows by Lemma 3.11.

Perhaps the most interesting thing about this theorem is that it proves we do not need to train on all iterations of a loop (here formalized as recursive calls to a function), but rather just all paths within the loop body. Here is an example to provide some intuition as to why. Suppose a recursive method walks over an array and calls baz on each element, e.g.,

```
def foo(a, i)
  return if i == a.length
  a[i].baz
  foo(a, i+1)
end
```

Recall that a[i] is actually a method call to the [] method, i.e., a[i].baz is really a.[](i, baz). If α is the array's contents type variable (i.e., the array has type Array<α>), this call generates a constraint $\alpha \leq$ [baz : ...]. This constraint, generated from a single call to foo, affects *all* elements of a because when the array was created, we added constraints that each of its element types are compatible with α, e.g., $\tau_1 \leq \alpha$, $\tau_2 \leq \alpha$, etc. where the τ_i are the element types. (Thus the solution to α will contain $\tau_1 \cup \tau_2 \cup \ldots$)

```
65 class A
66   infer_types ()              # A is an unannotated class
67   def foo ... end
68   def bar ... end
69 end
70 class String                  # String is an annotated class
71   typesig (" insert : (Numeric, String) → String")
72   typesig ("+ : ([to_s : ()→String]) → String")
73   ...
74 end
75 class ATest
76   include Rubydust::RuntimeSystem::TestCase
77   def test_1 ... end   # test cases called by Rubydust
78   def test_2 ... end
79 end
```

Figure 9. Using Rubydust

We can also prove the following "completeness" theorem.

Theorem 3.12 (Completeness). *If there are* N *methods and a maximum of* K *labels in each method, and each label is reachable, then a program of size* $O(N \cdot 2^K)$ *is sufficient to ensure that the inferred types are sound over all runs.*

Proof. For any method m, there can be at most 2^K paths with the labels in m; and there can be at most N such methods. □

In practice, the completeness bound $N \cdot 2^K$ is likely quite loose. Of course, a tighter bound could be obtained by considering the actual number of labels K in each method. Furthermore, a method with K labels may induce far less paths than 2^K—indeed, we are estimating the number of nodes in a branching tree of height K, which may even be K if the tree is skewed as a list, as is the case for switch statements.

4. Implementation

In this section we describe Rubydust, an implementation of our dynamic type inference algorithm for Ruby. Rubydust comprises roughly 4,500 lines of code, and is written purely in standard Ruby.

Using Rubydust is straightforward, as illustrated with the example in Figure 9. To use a program with Rubydust, the programmer simply runs the program as `ruby rubydust.rb` ⟨*program*⟩. The Ruby script `rubydust.rb` in turn sets up the Ruby environment before running the target program ⟨*program*⟩. For each class whose types should be inferred, the programmer adds a call to Rubydust's infer_types method during the class definition (line 66). Note that in Ruby, class definitions are executed to create the class, and hence methods can be invoked as classes are defined.

For classes with annotated types, the programmer calls Rubydust's typesig method with a string for each type to be declared. For example, on line 71, we declare that String :: insert takes a Numeric and String and returns a String. As another example, on line 72, we declare that String::+ takes a argument that has a to_s method and returns a String. We support the full type annotation language from DRuby [12], including intersection types and generics (discussed below).

Finally, the programmer also needs to define several test cases, which are run when the program is executed by Rubydust. After Rubydust runs the test cases, it solves the generated constraints and outputs the inferred types (examples in Section 5).

Next, we briefly discuss details of the instrumentation process, constraint resolution, and some limitations of our implementation.

Instrumenting Unannotated Classes Wrapped objects $v : \tau$ are implemented as instances of a class Proxy that has three fields: the object that is being wrapped, its type, and the *owner* of the Proxy, which is the instance that was active when the Proxy was created. When a method is invoked on a Proxy, the object's method_missing method will be called; in Ruby, if such a method is defined, it receives calls to any undefined methods. Here method_missing does a little work and redirects the call to the wrapped object.

To implement the wrapping (with Proxy) and constraint generation operations, we use Ruby introspection to *patch* the unannotated class. In particular, we rename the current methods of each unannotated class and then add method_missing to perform work before and after delegating to the now-renamed method. We need to patch classes to bootstrap our algorithm, as the program code we're tracking creates ordinary Ruby objects whose method invocations we need to intercept.

On entry to and exit from a patched method, we perform all of the constraint generation and wrapping, according to Figure 1. Note that we perform both the caller and the callee's actions in the callee's method_missing. This is convenient, because it allows us rely on Ruby's built-in dynamic dispatch to find the right callee method, whereas if we did work in the caller, we would need to reimplement Ruby's dynamic dispatch algorithm. Moreover, it means we can naturally handle dispatches via send, which performs reflective method invocation.

Since we are working in the callee, we need to do a little extra work to access the caller object. Inside of each patched class, we add an extra field *dispatcher* that points to the Proxy object that most recently dispatched a call to this object; we set the field whenever a Proxy is used to invoke a wrapped-object method. Also recall that each Proxy has an owner field, which was set to **self** at the time the proxy was created. Since we wrap arguments and fields whenever we enter a method, this means all Proxy objects accessible from the current method are always owned by **self**. Thus, on entry to a callee, we can find the caller object by immediately getting its dispatching Proxy, and then finding the owner of that Proxy.

Finally, notice that the above discussion suggests we sometimes need to access the fields of an object from a different object. This is disallowed when trying to read and write fields normally, but there is an escape hatch: we can access field @f of o from anywhere by calling o. instance_eval ("@f"). In our formalism, we assumed fields were only accessible from within the enclosing object; thus, we may be unsound for Ruby code that uses instance_eval to break the normal access rules for fields (as we do!).

Instrumenting Annotated Classes As with unannotated classes, we patch annotated classes to intercept calls to them, and we perform constraint generation and wrapping for the caller side only, as in Figure 1. We also fully unwrap any arguments to the patched method before delegating to the original method. We do this to support annotations on Ruby's core library methods, which are actually implemented as native code and expect regular, rather than Proxy-wrapped, objects. The actual method annotations for classes are stored in the class object, and can thus be retrieved from the patched method by inspecting **self** . **class** . For some methods, the proxy forwards intercepted calls to the original method, unwrapping all the arguments. For example, we forward calls to eql? and hash so wrapped objects will be treated correctly within collections.

Rubydust includes support for polymorphic class and method types. If a class has a polymorphic type signature, e.g., A<t>, we instantiate its type parameters with fresh type variables whenever an instance is created. We store the instantiated parameters in the instance, so that we can substitute them in when we look up a method signature. For methods that are polymorphic, we instantiate their type parameters with fresh type variables at the call.

Lastly, we also support intersection types for methods, which are common in the Ruby core library [12]. If we invoke o.m(x), and o.m has signature $(A \to B) \cap (C \to D)$, we use the run-time type of x to determine which branch of the intersection applies. (Recall we trust type annotations, so if the branches overlap, then either branch is valid if both apply.)

Constraint solving and type reconstruction We train a program by running it under a test suite and generating subtyping constraints, which are stored in globals at run time. At the end, we check the consistency of the subtyping constraints and solve them to reconstruct types for unannotated methods. The type language for reconstruction is simple, as outlined in Section 3; we do not try to reconstruct polymorphic or intersection types for methods. Consequently, the algorithms we use are fairly standard.

We begin by computing the transitive closure of the subtyping constraints to put them in a *solved form*. Then, we can essentially read off the solution for each type variable. First, we set method return type variables to be the union of their (immediate) lower bounds. Then, we set method argument type variables to be the intersection of their (immediate) upper bounds. These steps correspond to finding the least type for each method. Then we set the remaining type variables to be either the union of their lower-bounds or intersection of their upper-bounds, depending on which is available. Finally, we check that our solved constraints, in which type variables are replaced by their solutions, are consistent.

Limitations There are several limitations of our current implementation, beyond what has been mentioned so far. First, for practicality, we allow calls to methods whose classes are neither marked with infer_types () nor provided with annotations; we do nothing special to support this case, and it is up to the programmer to ensure the resulting program behavior will be reasonable. Second, we do not wrap **false** and **nil**, because those two values are treated as false by conditionals, whereas wrapped versions of them would be true. Thus we may miss some typing constraints. However, this is unlikely to be a problem, because the methods of **false** and **nil** are rarely invoked. For consistency, we also do not wrap **true**. Third, Rubydust has no way to intercept the creation of Array and Hash literals, and thus initially Rubydust treats such a literal as having elements of type $\top$. The first time a method is invoked on an Array or Hash literal, Rubydust iterates through the container elements to infer a more precise type. Thus if an Array or Hash literal is returned before one of its methods is invoked, Rubydust will use the less precise $\top$ for the element type for the constraint on the return variable. (This limitation is an oversight we will address soon.)

Fourth, for soundness, we would need to treat global variables similarly to instance and class fields, we but do not current implement this. Fifth, Ruby includes looping constructs, and hence there are potentially an infinite number of paths through a method body with a loop. However, as the foo example at the end of Section 3 illustrates, if types of the loop-carried state are invariant, the number of loop iterations is immaterial as long as all internal paths are covered. We manually inspected the code in our benchmarks (Section 5) and found that types are in fact invariant across loops. Note that looping constructs in Ruby actually take a code block—essentially a first-class method—as the loop body. If we could assign type variables to all the inputs and outputs of such blocks, we could eliminate the potential unsoundness at loops. However, Ruby does not currently provide any mechanism to intercept code block creation or to patch the behavior of a code block.

Sixth, we currently do not support annotations on some low-level classes, such as IO, Thread, Exception, Proc, and Class. Also, if methods are defined during the execution of a test case, Rubydust will not currently instrument them. We expect to add handling of these cases in the future.

	LOC	TC	E(#)	LCov	MCov	P(#)	PCov	OT(s)	RT(s)	Solving(s)
ministat-1.0.0	96	10	7	75%	11 / 15	19	84%	0.00	11.19	57.11
finitefield-0.1.0	103	9	6	98%	12 / 12	14	93%	0.00	1.74	1.28
Ascii85-1.0.0	105	7	3	95%	2 / 2	67	28%	0.01	6.81	0.17
a-star	134	1	5	100%	20 / 24	41	62%	0.04	114.81	37.46
hebruby-2.0.2	178	19	8	81%	20 / 26	36	91%	0.01	19.97	19.08
style-0.0.2	237	12	1	75%	17 / 32	88	28%	0.01	8.46	0.28
Rubyk	258	1	4	69%	15 / 20	37	68%	0.00	7.33	0.56
StreetAddress-1.0.1	772	1	10	79%	33 / 44	23	88%	0.02	4.45	24.58

TC - test cases E - manual edits LCov - line coverage MCov - method coverage / total # of methods
P - paths PCov - path coverage OT - original running time RT - Rubydust running time

Figure 10. Results

Finally, in Rubydust, infer_types () is a class-level annotation—either all methods in a class have inferred types, or none do. However, it is fairly common for Ruby programs to patch existing classes or inherit from annotated classes. In these cases, we would like to infer method signatures for just the newly added methods; we plan to add support for doing so in the future.

5. Experiments

We ran Rubydust on eight small programs obtained from RubyForge and Ruby Quiz [23]. We ran on a Mac Pro with two 2.4Ghz quad core processors with 8GB of memory running Mac OS X version 10.6.5. Figure 10 tabulates our results. The column headers are defined at the bottom of the figure. The first group of columns shows the program size in terms of lines of code (via SLOCcount [30]), the number of test cases distributed with the benchmark, and the number of manual edits made, which includes rewriting Array and Hash literals, and inserting calls to infer_types . For the *ministat* benchmark, two of the edits ensure the test setup code is called only once across all tests; without this change, the constraint solver does not complete in a reasonable amount of time. For all benchmarks, when calculating the lines of code, number of methods, and manual edits made we excluded testing code. For *style*, we also did not count about 2,700 lines of the source file that occur after Ruby's __END__ tag, which tells the interpreter to ignore anything below that line. In this case, those lines contain static data that the program loads at run time by reading its own source file.

The next group of columns gives the line coverage from the test cases (computed by rcov [21]), the method coverage, the sum of the number paths in covered methods, and the percentage of these paths covered by the test cases. As rcov does not compute path coverage, we determined the last two metrics by hand—for each method, we inserted print statements on every branch of the program to record which branches were taken at run time. We then manually analyzed this information to determine path coverage. When considering paths, we tried to disregard infeasible paths (e.g., conditionals with overlapping guards) and paths that only flagged errors. The path coverage is generally high, with the exception of *Ascii85* and *style*, which have long methods with sequences of conditionals that create an exponential number of paths.

We manually inspected the source code of the benchmark programs, and we determined that for the methods that were covered, the type annotations inferred by Rubydust are correct. It is interesting that the annotations are correct even for the two programs with low path coverage; this suggests that for these programs, reasonable line coverage is sufficient to infer sound types. Rubydust also found one type error, which we discuss below.

Performance The last group of columns in Figure 10 reports Rubydust's running time, which we split into the time to instrument and run the instrumented program, and the time to solve the generated constraints. As we can see, the overhead of running under Rubydust, even excluding solving time, is quite high compared to running the original, uninstrumented program. Part of the reason is that we have not optimized our implementation, and our heavy use of wrappers likely impedes fast paths in the Ruby interpreter. For example, values of primitive types like numbers are not really implemented as objects, but we wrap them with objects. Nevertheless, we believe that some overhead is acceptable because inference need not be performed every time the program is run.

The solving time is high, but that is likely because our solver is written in Ruby, which is known to be slow (this is being addressed in newer versions of Ruby). We expect this solving time would decrease dramatically if we exported the constraints to a solver written in a different language.

Inferred Types We now describe the benchmark programs and show some example inferred types, as output by Rubydust.

Ministat generates simple statistical information on numerical data sets. As an example inferred type, consider the median method, which computes a median from a list of numbers:

```
median: ([sort !: () → Array<Numeric>;
          size : () → Numeric;
          '[]': (Numeric) → Numeric])
        → Numeric
```

The method takes an object that has sort!, size, and [] methods, and returns a Numeric. Thus, one possible argument would be an Array of Numeric. However, this method could be used with other arguments that have those three methods—indeed, because Ruby is dynamically typed, programmers are rarely required to pass in objects of exactly a particular type, as long as the passed-in objects have the right methods (this is referred to as "duck typing" in the Ruby community).

Finitefield, another mathematical library, provides basic operations on elements in a finite field. As an example type, consider the inverse method, which inverts a matrix:

```
inverse : (['>': (Numeric) → Boolean;
            '≪': (Numeric) → Numeric;
            '≫': (Numeric) → Numeric;
            '&': (Numeric) → Numeric;
            '^': (Numeric) → Numeric]) → Numeric ")
```

As above, we can see exactly which methods are required of the argument; one concrete class that has all these methods is Numeric.

Ascii85 encodes and decodes data following Adobe's binary-to-text Ascii85 format. There are only two methods in this program, both of which are covered by the seven test cases. Rubydust issues an error during the constraint solving, complaining that Boolean is not a subtype of [to_i : () → Numeric]. The offending parts of the code are shown below.

```
module Ascii85
  def self.encode(str, wrap_lines=80)
    ... if (! wrap_lines) then ... return end
```

```
    ... wrap_lines . to_i
  end ...
end
```

The author of the library uses wrap_lines as an optional argument, with a default value of 80. In one test case, the author passes in **false**, hence wrap_lines may be a Boolean. But as Boolean does not have a to_i method, invoking wrap_lines . to_i is a type error. For example, passing **true** as the second argument will cause the program to crash. It is unclear whether the author intends to allow **true** as a second argument, but clearly wrap_lines can potentially be an arbitrary non-integer, since its to_i method is invoked (which would not be necessary for an integer).

A-star is a solution for the A* search problem. It includes a class Tile to represent a position on a two-dimensional Map. Rubydust infers that two of the methods to Tile have types:

```
y: () → Numeric
x: () → Numeric
```

The Map class uses Tile, which we can see from the inferred types for two of Map's methods:

```
adjacent: ([y: () → Numeric; x: () → Numeric]) → Array<Tile>
find_route : () →
  [push: ([y: () → Numeric; x: () → Numeric]) → Array<Tile>;
   include ?: ([y: () → Numeric; x: () → Numeric]) → Boolean;
   pop: () → [y: () → Numeric; x : () → Numeric];
   to_ary : () → Array<Tile>]
```

The adjacent method computes a set of adjacent locations (represented as an Array<Tile>) given an input Tile. The find_route method returns an array of Tile, which is an instance of the slightly more precise structural type Rubydust infers. (Here the structural type is actually the type of a field returned by find_route .)

Hebruby is a program that converts Hebrew dates to Julian dates and vice versa. One method type we inferred is

```
leap?: (['*' : (Numeric) → Numeric]) → Boolean
```

This method determines whether the year is a leap year. This signature is interesting because the argument only needs a single method, $*$, which returns a Numeric. This is the only requirement because subsequent operations are on the return value of $*$, rather than on the original method argument.

Rubyk is a Rubik's Cube solver; as this program did not come with a test suite, we constructed a test case ourselves (one of the four edits we made to the program). Some of the inferred types are shown below.

```
visualize :() → Array<Array<String>>
initialize :() → Array<Array<String>>
```

We can see that the visualize and initialize methods return a representation of the cube faces as an Array<Array<String>>.

Style is a "surface-level analysis tool" for English. The program has several methods that determine characteristics of English text. Some sample inferred types are:

```
pronoun? :([downcase : () → String]) → Boolean
passive? :([each : () → Array<String>]) → Boolean
preposition ? :([downcase : () → String]) → Boolean
abbreviation ? :([downcase : () → String]) → Boolean
nominalization ? :([downcase : () → String]) → Boolean
interrogative_pronoun ? :([downcase : () → String]) → Boolean
normalize :([downcase : () → String]) → String
```

Here, most of the methods first downcase their argument, and then use the resulting String. The passive method takes an array of Strings, representing a sentence, and iterates through the array to determine whether the sentence is in the passive voice.

Finally, *StreetAddress* is a tool that normalizes U.S. street address into different subcomponents. As an example, the parse class method takes a String and returns an instance of the class, which is depicted in the following output:

```
class << StreetAddress::US; # define a class method
  parse: (String) → StreetAddress::US::Address
end
```

Notes We encountered all of Rubydust's limitations in these benchmark programs—there were tests that called out to unannotated and uninferred classes; that use **false** and **nil**; that use global variables; and that use unannotated low-level classes like IO. However, as already mentioned, the types Rubydust inferred were correct, and so these limitations did not affect the results.

We also encountered the use of reflective method invocation via send described in Section 2.5. We did not encounter uses of other dynamic features for classes whose types are inferred (though they do occur internally in the standard library).

6. Related work

There has been significant interest in the research community in bringing static type systems to dynamic languages. Much recent research has developed ways to mix typed and untyped code, e.g., via quasi-static typing [26], occurrence typing [29], gradual typing [25], and hybrid typing [13]. In these systems, types are supplied by the user. In contrast, our work focuses on type inference, which is complementary: we could potentially use our dynamic type inference algorithm to infer type annotations for future checking.

Several researchers have explored type inference for object-oriented dynamic languages, including Ruby [2, 3, 10, 12, 16, 18], Python [4, 7, 24], and JavaScript [5, 27], among others. As discussed in the introduction, these languages are complex and have subtle semantics typically only defined by the language implementation. This makes it a major challenge to implement and maintain a static type inference system for these languages. We experienced this firsthand in our development of DRuby, a static type inference system for Ruby [3, 10, 12].

There has also been work on type inference for Scheme [31], a dynamic language with a very compact syntax and semantics; however, these inference systems do not support objects.

Dynamic type inference has been explored previously in several contexts. Rapicault et al. describe a dynamic type inference algorithm for Smalltalk that takes advantage of introspection features of that language [20]. However, their algorithm is not very clearly explained, and seems to infer types for variables based on what types are stored in that variable. In contrast, we infer more general types based on usage constraints. For example, back in Figure 2, we discovered argument x must have a qux method, whereas we believe the approach of Rapicault et al would instead infer x has type B, which is correct, but less general.

Guo et al. dynamically infer abstract types in x86 binaries and Java bytecode [14]. Artzi et al. propose a combined static and dynamic mutability inference algorithm [6]. In both of these systems, the inferred types have no structure—in the former system, abstract types are essentially tags that group together values that are related by the program, and in the latter system, parameters and fields are either mutable or not. In contrast, our goal is to infer more standard structural or nominal types.

In addition to inferring types, dynamic analysis has been proposed to discover many other program properties. To cite three examples, Daikon discovers likely program invariants from dynamic runs [9]; DySy uses symbolic execution to infer Daikon-like invariants [8]; and Perracotta discovers temporal properties of programs [32]. In these systems, there is no notion of sufficient coverage to guarantee sound results. In contrast, we showed we can soundly infer types by covering all paths through each method.

There are several dynamic inference systems that, while they have no theorems about sufficient coverage, do use a subsequent checking phase to test whether the inferred information is sound. Rose et al. [22] and Agarwal and Stoller [1] dynamically infer types that protect against races. After inference the program is annotated and passed to a type checker to verify that the types are sound. Similarly, Nimmer and Ernst use Daikon to infer invariants that are then checked by ESC/Java [19]. We could follow a similar approach to these systems and apply DRuby to our inferred types (when coverage is known to be incomplete); we leave this as future work.

Finally, our soundness theorem resembles soundness for *Mix*, a static analysis system that mixes type checking and symbolic execution [15]. In *Mix*, blocks are introduced to designate which code should be analyzed with symbolic execution, and which should be analyzed with type checking. At a high-level, we could model our dynamic inference algorithm in *Mix* by analyzing method bodies with symbolic execution, and method calls and field reads and writes with type checking. However, there are several important differences: We use concrete test runs, where *Mix* uses symbolic execution; we operate on an object-oriented language, where *Mix* applies to a conventional imperative language; and we can model the heap more precisely than *Mix*, because in our formal language, fields are only accessible from within their containing objects.

7. Conclusion

In this paper we presented a new technique, constraint-based dynamic type inference, that infers types based on dynamic executions of the program. We have proved that this technique infers sound types as long as all possible paths through each method are traversed during inference. We have developed Rubydust, an implementation of our technique for Ruby, and have applied it to a number of small Ruby programs to find a real error and to accurately infer types in other cases. We expect that further engineering of our tool will improve its performance. We also leave the inference of more advanced types, including polymorphic and intersection types, to future work.

Acknowledgments

We would like to thank Mark T. Daly for his work on the type annotation parser. Most of this work was performed while the first and second authors were at the University of Maryland, College Park. This work was supported in part by DARPA ODOD.HR00110810-073, NSF CCF-0346982, CCF-0541036, and CCF-0915978.

References

[1] Rahul Agarwal and Scott D. Stoller. Type Inference for Parameterized Race-Free Java. In *VMCAI*, 2004.

[2] O. Agesen, J. Palsberg, and M.I. Schwartzbach. Type Inference of SELF. *ECOOP*, 1993.

[3] Jong-hoon (David) An, Avik Chaudhuri, and Jeffrey S. Foster. Static Typing for Ruby on Rails. In *ASE*, 2009.

[4] Davide Ancona, Massimo Ancona, Antonio Cuni, and Nicholas Matsakis. RPython: Reconciling Dynamically and Statically Typed OO Languages. In *DLS*, 2007.

[5] Christopher Anderson, Paola Giannini, and Sophia Drossopoulou. Towards Type Inference for JavaScript. In *ECOOP*, 2005.

[6] Shay Artzi, Adam Kiezun, David Glasser, and Michael D. Ernst. Combined static and dynamic mutability analysis. In *ASE*, 2007.

[7] John Aycock. Aggressive Type Inference. In *International Python Conference*, 2000.

[8] Christoph Csallner, Nikolai Tillmann, and Yannis Smaragdakis. Dysy: dynamic symbolic execution for invariant inference. In *ICSE*, 2008.

[9] Michael D. Ernst, Jeff H. Perkins, Philip J. Guo, Stephen McCamant, Carlos Pacheco, Matthew S. Tschantz, and Chen Xiao. The Daikon system for dynamic detection of likely invariants. *Sci. Comput. Program.*, 69(1-3), 2007.

[10] Michael Furr, Jong-hoon (David) An, and Jeffrey S. Foster. Profile-guided static typing for dynamic scripting languages. In *OOPSLA*, 2009.

[11] Michael Furr, Jong-hoon (David) An, Jeffrey S. Foster, and Michael Hicks. The Ruby Intermediate Language. In *Dynamic Language Symposium*, 2009.

[12] Michael Furr, Jong-hoon (David) An, Jeffrey S. Foster, and Michael Hicks. Static Type Inference for Ruby. In *OOPS Track, SAC*, 2009.

[13] J. Gronski, K. Knowles, A. Tomb, S.N. Freund, and C. Flanagan. Sage: Hybrid Checking for Flexible Specifications. *Scheme and Functional Programming*, 2006.

[14] Philip J. Guo, Jeff H. Perkins, Stephen McCamant, and Michael D. Ernst. Dynamic inference of abstract types. In *ISSTA*, 2006.

[15] Yit Phang Khoo, Bor-Yuh Evan Chang, and Jeffrey S. Foster. Mixing type checking and symbolic execution. In *PLDI*, 2010.

[16] Kristian Kristensen. Ecstatic – Type Inference for Ruby Using the Cartesian Product Algorithm. Master's thesis, Aalborg University, 2007.

[17] Robin Milner. A Theory of Type Polymorphism in Programming. *Journal of Computer and System Sciences*, 17, 1978.

[18] Jason Morrison. Type Inference in Ruby. Google Summer of Code Project, 2006.

[19] Jeremy W. Nimmer and Michael D. Ernst. Invariant Inference for Static Checking: An Empirical Evaluation. In *FSE*, 2002.

[20] Pascal Rapicault, Mireille Blay-Fornarino, Stéphane Ducasse, and Anne-Marie Dery. Dynamic type inference to support object-oriented reenginerring in Smalltalk. In *ECOOP Workshops*, 1998.

[21] rcov. rcov: code coverage for ruby, 2010. `http://eigenclass.org/hiki/rcov`.

[22] James Rose, Nikhil Swamy, and Michael Hicks. Dynamic inference of polymorphic lock types. *Sci. Comput. Program.*, 58(3), 2005.

[23] Ruby Quiz, 2010. `http://www.rubyquiz.com`.

[24] Michael Salib. Starkiller: A Static Type Inferencer and Compiler for Python. Master's thesis, MIT, 2004.

[25] Jeremy G. Siek and Walid Taha. Gradual typing for functional languages. In *Scheme and Functional Programming Workshop*, 2006.

[26] Satish Thatte. Quasi static typing. In *POPL*, 1990.

[27] Peter Thiemann. Towards a type system for analyzing javascript programs. In *ESOP*, 2005.

[28] Dave Thomas, Chad Fowler, and Andy Hunt. *Programming Ruby: The Pragmatic Programmers' Guide*. Pragmatic Bookshelf, 2004.

[29] Sam Tobin-Hochstadt and Matthias Felleisen. The Design and Implementation of Typed Scheme. In *POPL*, 2008.

[30] David A. Wheeler. Sloccount, August 2004. `http://www.dwheeler.com/sloccount/`.

[31] A.K. Wright and R. Cartwright. A practical soft type system for Scheme. *ACM TOPLAS*, 19(1), 1997.

[32] Jinlin Yang, David Evans, Deepali Bhardwaj, Thirumalesh Bhat, and Manuvir Das. Perracotta: mining temporal API rules from imperfect traces. In *ICSE*, 2006.

Robin Milner 1934–2010

Verification, Languages, and Concurrency

Andrew D. Gordon
Microsoft Research

Robert Harper
Carnegie Mellon University

John Harrison
Intel

Alan Jeffrey
Bell Labs

Peter Sewell
University of Cambridge

A special session of the symposium pays tribute to Robin Milner; the session features talks by Robert Harper (Carnegie Mellon University), John Harrison (Intel), and Alan Jeffrey (Bell Labs), and is organised by Andrew D. Gordon (Microsoft Research) and Peter Sewell (University of Cambridge).

Robin Milner was born near Plymouth in England. He was educated at Eton College, Windsor, and went up to King's College, Cambridge, in 1954. In between, his national service was with the Royal Engineers, in Egypt.

After university he was first a school teacher and then worked in London as a programmer at Ferranti, an early British computer company. In 1963 he took a job as lecturer at City University, and started research on the side—he never studied for a PhD. In 1968, he moved to Swansea to become a research assistant. He was excited by Scott's lectures in 1969 in Oxford on domain theory. During this time he learnt about Floyd's work on verification, and got to know Tony Hoare, and started trying to verify programs.

After meeting Zohar Manna during a visit to Carnegie Mellon University, he got a job with John McCarthy at Stanford in 1971. There he built the theorem proving system Stanford LCF, which he would later substantially refine with the addition of a metalanguage (ML) for constructing proofs.

> The interesting thing there was, they were just looking for somebody who would do something practical. Scott had recently produced a kind of logic of domains, a logic of the hierarchy of domains, a type-theoretic hierarchy. This to me seemed to be something which was practical. That is what LCF came out of. Since I was so interested in human-assisted – or I would say machine-assisted – proof, this seemed to be a wonderful opportunity for a program-oriented logic. It really took off for me when I realised that I could write down the syntax of a programming language in this logic and I could write the semantics in the logic.
>
> (*An interview with Robin Milner* by Martin Berger, 3 September 2003)

Moving to Scotland, Robin worked at the University of Edinburgh 1973–1994, as a professor from 1984. During this period he co-founded the LFCS, the Laboratory for Foundations of Computer Science, and served as its first director. This was also a time of amazing scientific productivity, for which he became a Fellow of the Royal Society and received the ACM A. M. Turing Award:

> For three distinct and complete achievements: 1) LCF, the mechanization of Scott's Logic of Computable Functions, probably the first theoretically based yet practical tool for machine assisted proof construction; 2) ML, the first language to include polymorphic type inference together with a type-safe exception-handling mechanism; 3) CCS, a general theory of concurrency. In addition, he formulated and strongly advanced full abstraction, the study of the relationship between operational and denotational semantics.
>
> (Citation for *1991 ACM A. M. Turing Award*)

We can now add to this list of his contributions Robin's refinement of CCS into the π-calculus, a more general theory of concurrency that takes into account dynamic generation and communication of names, and also bigraphs, a theory of ubiquitous computing.

He returned to England to occupy the first established Chair in Computer Science at the University of Cambridge. He was a member of the Computer Laboratory from 1995 onwards, serving as Head of the Laboratory 1996–1999. During the last year of his life, he resumed his Edinburgh connection as a part-time professor.

All three strands of his work have been enormously influential. Machine-assisted verification is now feasible for realistic systems software and for deep mathematics; Robin's concept of tactics is widely used in interactive provers such as HOL, Isabelle, and Coq, as is his idea of relying on a type-safe programming language to restrict the part of a prover that must be trusted to a small kernel.

ML itself is also still in use and has had a big impact on other programming languages: Robin gave us practical parametric polymorphism, now incorporated into most modern typed programming languages, and a push towards strongly typed languages and the use of operational semantics for language definition and metatheory.

His theories of concurrency underpin much work on verification (complementing the theory of sequential computable functions of Church and Turing) and are being applied to modelling processes from business to systems biology; Robin gave us the word bisimulation (while always taking care to credit David Park with the idea), and, more generally, a clear understanding of the role of observational congruences and coinductive proof methods.

He has left the subject a collection of elegant and finely honed intellectual tools, reified in mathematics and in software.

Robin and Lucy married in 1963 and died within weeks of each other in March 2010. They are survived by two children and two grandchildren.

Robin was always an inspirational teacher and colleague, and an unassuming and warm-hearted man; he will be greatly missed.

POPL'11, January 26–28, 2011, Austin, Texas, USA.
ACM 978-1-4503-0490-0/11/01.

Space Overhead Bounds for Dynamic Memory Management with Partial Compaction *

Anna Bendersky
Computer Science Department
Technion
Haifa 32000
Israel
annaben@cs.technion.ac.il

Erez Petrank
Computer Science Department
Technion
Haifa 32000
Israel
erez@cs.technion.ac.il

Abstract

Dynamic memory allocation is ubiquitous in today's runtime environments. Allocation and de-allocation of objects during program execution may cause fragmentation and foil the program's ability to allocate objects. Robson has shown that a worst case scenario can create a space overhead within a factor of $\log n$ of the space that is actually required by the program, where n is the size of the largest possible object. Compaction can eliminate fragmentation, but is too costly to be run frequently. Many runtime systems employ partial compaction, in which only a small fraction of the allocated objects are moved. Partial compaction reduces some of the existing fragmentation at an acceptable cost. In this paper we study the effectiveness of partial compaction and provide the first rigorous lower and upper bounds on its effectiveness in reducing fragmentation at a low cost.

Categories and Subject Descriptors D.1.5 [*Object-oriented Programming*]: Memory Management; D.3.3 [*Language Constructs and Features*]: Dynamic storage management; D.3.4 [*Processors*]: Memory management (garbage collection); D.4.2 [*Storage Management*]: Garbage Collection

General Terms Languages, Performance, Algorithms, Theory.

Keywords Runtime systems, Memory management, Storage allocation, Dynamic storage allocation, Compaction, Partial compaction.

1. Introduction

The study of the theoretical foundations of memory management has not been very extensive. In particular, not much is known about the theoretical potential and limitations of memory management functionalities. Previous work that we are aware of includes a study of fragmentation [18], a study of cache-conscious memory placement [13], and a study of the space limitations of conservative garbage collection and lazy reference counting [5, 6]. In this work we attempt to extend these foundations and study the potential and limitations of partial compaction.

Modern software employs dynamic memory allocation to support its memory needs. Allocation and de-allocation of memory create fragmentation: holes between the allocated objects in the memory may be too small to further satisfy future allocation. Fragmentation creates a space overhead, since the memory consumed may become larger than the memory required to satisfy the allocation requests when no fragmentation exists.

Robson [17, 18] studied the amount of space overhead that may be caused by fragmentation when no objects are moved. He showed that in the worst case, fragmentation causes quite a large space overhead. In particular, he presented a program (or an allocation and de-allocation sequence) that never keeps more than M words allocated simultaneously, but any allocator that attempts to satisfy this sequence would require a space of (almost) $\frac{1}{2}M\log n$ words. The parameter n stands for the largest possible allocated size in the system. Robson also provided a simple allocation strategy that can handle any allocation sequence in (approximately) $M\log n$ words.

Frequent compaction eliminates fragmentation completely. If one compacts the heap after each de-allocation, then no fragmentation appears at all and M words of space always suffice. However, full compaction is costly since a substantial fraction of the objects may be moved and all references need to be updated [1, 11, 12]. Therefore, modern systems tend to either use compaction infrequently, or employ partial compaction, moving some objects in an attempt to reduce fragmentation and keep its cost acceptable [2, 3, 8, 9, 14, 15]. Of course, the larger the space that is being compacted, the less fragmented the heap becomes; on the other hand, the overhead that is posed on the executing program increases. The question that arises is what is the trade-off between the amount of space the can be moved and the space overhead that may occur in the heap? In this work we provide the first lower and upper bounds for such a scenario.

Since the amount of moved space makes a difference, we need to bound the amount of relocated space. We choose to study a scenario in which a predetermined percentage of all allocated space can be moved. One could generalize the question to allow a quota of $B(S)$ movement for an arbitrary function B of the allocated space S. Other budgeting decisions are also possible; for example, one could limit the relocation according to the amount of live space, or the deleted space. All these make sense as well, but we felt that budgeting by a fraction of the allocated space is interesting, as the amount of allocation typically represents allocation "time" in the memory management literature, most notably for generational garbage collection.

* Supported by THE ISRAEL SCIENCE FOUNDATION grant No. 283/10.

POPL'11, January 26–28, 2011, Austin, Texas, USA.

In this work we present general results that bound the heap size required for allocation in the presence of partial compaction. Let the compaction budget at any point in the execution be $1/c$ of the space allocated so far by the program. To provide an upper bound, we present an allocation and compaction strategy. We show that for programs that never keep more than M words allocated simultaneously, it suffices to use a heap whose size is the minimum between $M \cdot (c+1)$ and $M \cdot \log n$, where n is the largest possible object that can be allocated. When the compaction budget is high, i.e., c is small, then the heap size can be significantly smaller than the heap size obtained when no compaction is used. The above is formally asserted in Theorem 1 in Section 3.

To show a lower bound on the space overhead, we present a program that incurs a large space overhead for any allocator (whose compaction budget is limited by $\frac{1}{c}$ of the allocated objects). This program never keeps more than M words allocated simultaneously, and it makes any allocator use a heap whose size is at least the minimum of $\frac{1}{10}M \cdot c$ and $\frac{1}{10}M \cdot \frac{\log n}{\log c+1}$ words. When the compaction budget is large (c is small), the minimum is obtained with $\frac{1}{10}M \cdot c$. When the compaction budget is tighter, the heap size is at least $\frac{1}{10}M \cdot \frac{\log n}{\log c+1}$. Thus, these asymptotic bounds show that partial compaction can reduce the heap size, but only to a limited extent, which depends on the compaction quota. This result is stated as Theorem 2 in Section 4.

The above results hold for any possible allocator. We continued this investigation with a study of a specific widely used memory allocator: the segregated free list allocator (used for example in [2, 7, 10]). Fixing a specific allocator allows a more accurate analysis and yields better bounds. We first examine this allocator when no compaction is allowed and improve Robson's bounds. It turns out that the bounds depend on the number of free-lists used by the allocation scheme. One extreme case is that the allocator maintains a free-list for any possible object size between 1 and n. In this case the required space becomes (almost) $\frac{4}{5}M\sqrt{n}$ words. This is much higher than the $\frac{1}{2}M \log n$ words presented in Robson's papers. The other extreme case is that a small number of free lists is allowed, specifically, one for each power of 2. In this case, we show a lower bound of $M \log n$ words, which is two times stronger than the lower bound for the general allocator. In practice, the number of free lists kept is somewhere in between, and our analysis can be applied to any specific choice of sizes to yield the corresponding lower bound. These results are formalized in Theorems 3 and 4 in Section 5.2.

Finally, we examine the effects of adding partial compaction to the segregated free list allocator. We show that a heap size of $M \cdot c + k \cdot n$ suffices in this case for any program, where k is the number of different free lists. So when the compaction budget is large, i.e., c is small, partial compaction helps reducing fragmentation. See Theorem 5 in Section 5.3. For the lower bound, the number of free lists employed is important. We first show that when using free lists for any object size, the space required is at least the minimum between $\frac{1}{6}M\sqrt{n}$ and $\frac{1}{12} \cdot M \cdot c$. So the true overhead is large if we don't allow a substantial compaction budget. If we only keep free lists for objects sizes that are powers of 2, then the heap size required is at least the minimum between $\frac{1}{4} \cdot M \cdot \log n$ and $\frac{1}{8} \cdot M \cdot c$. See Theorems 6 and 7 in Section 5.3.

This work initiates a study of the cost and effectiveness of partial compaction. New techniques are developed and novel bounds are shown. The results are asymptotic. They hold for any possible object size limit n, any possible live space bound M, and any possible compaction budget ratio c. However, although they represent the tightest known bounds, their applicability for specific realistic parameters of modern systems is limited. We hope that these techniques can be extended in future work to provide tighter bounds and help us better understand the behavior of memory managers in practice.

Organization. In Section 2 we survey previous results on fragmentation when no compaction is allowed, and formally define the compaction budget model used in this paper. In Section 3 we present and prove a simple upper bound on the effectiveness of partial compaction. In Section 4 we state and prove the lower bound on the effectiveness of partial compaction. We divide the proof into two parts. First, we prove the lower bound for the restricted case of aligned objects. This proof contains most of the ideas and is easier to follow. The full proof of the lower bound (with all the hairy details) follows. In Section 5 we study the specific segregated free list allocator and prove all the results stated above. We conclude in Section 6.

2. Problem Description

2.1 Framework and previous work

Dynamic storage allocation that does not move objects can suffer from fragmentation. J. M. Robson [17, 18] provided lower and upper bounds on the space overhead for a memory management system that allocates and deallocates, but cannot move objects. The lower bound demonstrates the existence of a "bad" program that makes *any* allocator use a lot of space overhead. The upper bound provides an allocator, whose space overhead is limited, for *any* program (including the bad program that demonstrates the lower bound). Clearly, if the program allocates a lot and does not de-allocate space, then a lot of space is required to satisfy the request. It is thus interesting to ask how much space is required to satisfy the allocation requests of a program that never keeps more than M words alive simultaneously. If compaction is frequently used, a space of M words suffices. The memory manager can simply compact the heap after each de-allocation. However, when no compaction is allowed, some allocation sequences demand a large space overhead in order to satisfy the allocation requests.

An allocator should be able to handle any allocation (and de-allocation) sequence, and for each allocator, we can ask what is the smallest heap that can handle all allocation sequences that never allow more than M words of memory simultaneously allocated. The bounds that are going to be derived depend on the size of the largest possible object in the system. We denote by n the size of such an object and assume that no allocation in the sequence requests more than n words for the allocated object.

Some allocators can move allocated objects in the memory. This is not always the case, as moving objects requires updating all pointers referencing them, and some runtime systems cannot always distinguish pointers from integers that hold the same values. Such systems do not move objects whose references cannot be identified. Other runtime systems avoid compaction because of its costs.

The interaction between the program and the memory allocator is divided into stages. Each stage consists of three parts:

1. *Deletion:* The program removes objects from the heap
2. *Compaction:* The memory allocator moves objects in the heap.
3. *Allocation:* The program makes allocation requests and the memory allocator returns the corresponding object addresses in the heap.

For the Upper and Lower bounds the program and the memory allocator can be viewed as opponents. The program objective is to make the memory allocator use as much space as possible. The memory allocator's objective is to allocate space in a way that will require as little space as possible. The upper and lower bounds for the case when is no compaction occurs were studied by Robson

[18]. He showed a tight connection between the upper and lower bounds. We define $\mathscr{P}(M,n)$ as the set of all programs that never keep more than M words of space allocated simultaneously, and never allocate an object larger than n words. The function $HS(A,P)$ is defined as the heap size necessary for allocator A to answer the allocation requests of a program P, so that $P \in \mathscr{P}(M,n)$. The upper and lower bounds Robson showed demand an overhead of $\times \frac{1}{2}\log n$ of the actual allocated space M, i.e.:

- *Upper bound:* For all $M,n > 0$ such that $n|M$, there exists an allocator A_o, such that for all programs $P \in \mathscr{P}(M,n)$, it holds that:
$$HS(A_o,P) \leq M \cdot \log n + M.$$
- *Lower bound:* For all $M,n > 0$ such that $n|M$, there exists a program $P_o \in \mathscr{P}(M,n)$, such that for all allocators A, it holds that:
$$HS(A,P_o) \geq M \cdot \frac{1}{2}\log n + M - n + 1.$$

In this work we investigate the effect of moving objects during the run. We allow the allocator to move a fraction of the objects, i.e. to perform partial compaction. We explore how partial compaction affects these bounds.

2.2 The compaction budget

Our objective in this work is to explore upper and lower bounds on the space required by allocators that apply partial compaction. We now define partial compaction. If there were no limit on how much space can be moved, the total heap size required for the allocation would be M, the largest amount of live space throughout the application run. One simple method of compaction that uses only M words could be: allocate sequentially using a bump pointer and compact all of the memory once the M boundary is reached. The problem with this approach is that compacting the memory incurs a high computation overhead and is unacceptable in real systems. Practical systems consider trade-offs between the amount of compaction executed and the space overhead. Therefore, we introduce a bound on the amount of space that can be moved. This space is denoted by $B(S)$, which is the partial compaction function. Specifically, after the program allocates a space S, the compactor may move $B(S) = \frac{1}{c} \cdot S$ space. c is a constant larger than 1. The $B(S)$ function is calculated incrementally: the quota is added to on every allocation, and reduced with every compaction. For example: $B(S) = \frac{1}{10}S$ means that after every allocation of S, the compactor can move $\frac{1}{10}$ of the space allocated. In this example, if there were allocations of 200 words (and maybe some deletions) without any compactions, space of size of $\frac{1}{10} \cdot 200 = 20$ could be moved. If only 8 words are moved - a quota of 12 words remains. We define an algorithm that works within the $B(S)$ limit as the $B(S)$-*bounded partial compaction*. In this document we always use the compaction threshold function $B(S) = \frac{1}{c} \cdot S$, for some constant $c > 1$.

2.3 The setting

To present our results we first specify what a program is, what an allocator is, in what way they are limited, and how we measure their interaction. We consider a program P that executes a sequence of allocations and de-allocations. The program's execution is adaptive in the sense that it may choose its upcoming allocation according to the locations in which the allocator chose to place its previous allocation. However, to save further quantification over the inputs, we assume that P already has some fixed embedded input, so that the allocation sequence depends only on P and the allocation decisions of the allocator (but not on any additional inputs of P). We also consider an allocator A that receives the sequence of allocations and de-allocations one by one (sequentially, or on-line) from the program and must satisfy each allocation request as it arrives.

Given a specific pair of a program P and an allocator A, their joint execution is well defined and we measure the size of the heap that the allocator A uses to satisfy the requests of P. We denote this heap size by $HS(A,P)$. Of course, for the same program P, there could be a non-space-efficient allocator A_1 that requires a large heap size $HS(A_1,P)$ and there could be a better allocator A_2 for which $HS(A_2,P)$ is much smaller. For a lower bound, we look for a program P for which $HS(A,P)$ is high for all allocators. For an upper bound, we look for an allocator A that can serve all programs with a low $HS(A,P)$.

Finally, we define $\mathscr{P}(M,n)$ as the set of all programs that never keep more than M words of space allocated simultaneously, and never allocate an object larger than n words.

3. The Upper Bound

We start with the upper bound, which is simpler to show. Formally, we state and prove the following theorem.

Theorem 1. (Upper bound.) *For any real number $c \geq 1$, there exists a memory manager A_c that satisfies the compaction bound $\frac{1}{c}S$, and for all $M,n > 0$, such that $n|M$, and all programs $P \in \mathscr{P}(M,n)$:*
$$HS(A_c,P) \leq \min\left(M(c+1), M \cdot \log n + M\right).$$

Proof. For any real number $c \geq 1$, we present a specific memory manager A_c, that never exceeds the compaction quota $\frac{1}{c} \cdot S$ and that uses a heap size of at most $M \cdot (c+1)$ words, i.e., $HS(A_c,P) \leq M \cdot (c+1)$ for any program $P \in \mathscr{P}(M,n)$. The memory manager A_c allocates objects sequentially by bumping a pointer. When the bump pointer reaches the $M(c+1)$ boundary, the live space is fully compacted to the beginning of the heap. A pseudo-code for the memory allocator A_c is presented in Algorithm 1.

Algorithm 1 Memory Manager A_c

Initially: The heap is empty, $free = 0$;
While (TRUE)
1: **Receive an allocation request for an object of size ℓ;**
2: **if** $free + \ell \geq M(c+1)$ **then**
3: Compact all allocated objects to the beginning;
4: $free \leftarrow$ first word after the allocated space;
5: **end if**
6: Allocate the object at address $free$;
7: $free \leftarrow free + \ell$;

Clearly, Algorithm 1 never uses more than $M \cdot (c+1)$ words. However, we need to show that there is enough compaction budget to execute Step 3, which compacts all live objects to the beginning of the heap. The required compaction quota for this step is at most $M - \ell$. Consider the time interval between any two compactions, denoted C_1 and C_2. Since $P \in \mathscr{P}(M,n)$, there are at most M allocated words at any point in time, and therefore, after the compaction C_1 there are at most M words allocated in the beginning of the heap, and $free$ is smaller than M. After executing C_1 and before starting to execute C_2, the allocator receives requests for allocations and deletions, until it fails to allocate ℓ words – when the $free$ pointer arrives at a point beyond $M(c+1) - \ell$ in the heap. The total size of the allocations executed between C_1 and C_2 must be at least $M(c+1) - M - \ell$, since this is (at least) the number of words that the free pointer has advanced between the two compactions. Therefore, the compaction quota at Step 3 is at least $\frac{1}{c} \cdot (M(c+1) - M - \ell) = M - \frac{\ell}{c}$. According to our assumptions, $c \geq 1$ (and $\ell \geq 0$), and therefore, $M - \frac{\ell}{c} \geq M - \ell$. Thus, enough budget is available in the quota so that all of the $M - \ell$ allocated words can be moved to the beginning of the heap.

This memory manager is effective when $c+1 \leq \log n$. Otherwise, c is large, i.e. the compaction budget is small, and then it is possible to obtain a good heap size without moving objects at all. We can use the allocator presented in Robson's paper, not use compaction at all, and consume at most $M \log n + M$ words for any possible program $P \in \mathscr{P}(M,n)$. This concludes the proof of Theorem 1. □

4. The Lower Bound

In this section we provide a specific program that can force any memory allocator to incur a space overhead. To simplify the presentation, we start with a program that assumes that the allocators respect some alignment restriction. We later extend this proof to eliminate the alignment restriction. Using a similar program, we provide a proof for Theorem 2. Due to paper size limitation, the proof details appear only in the full version of the paper.

4.1 Bounding the space consumption with aligned objects

We start by defining what aligned object allocation means. Aligned object allocation places a limitation on the memory allocator, which is not allowed to allocate objects in an arbitrary location, but only in an aligned manner. This constraint simplifies the proofs, and has fewer corner cases.

For the lower bound we only consider objects whose size is a power of two (because the program we build only allocates such sizes). Thus, it is fine to define alignment only with respect to objects of size 2^i for some integer i. Without loss of generality, we assume that the smallest object is of size 1. Otherwise, one could think of the object sizes as multiples of the smallest object size.

Definition 4.1. *We say that an object of size* 2^i *is* aligned *if it is located at address* $k \cdot 2^i$ *for some integer* k.

Definition 4.2. *We say that a memory allocator uses* aligned allocation *if all the objects it allocates are aligned.*

We present a specific program, called *Aligned-Waster* and denoted P_{AW}, and prove that any memory allocator that satisfies the compaction bound and uses aligned allocation, must incur a space overhead when supporting the allocation requests of P_{AW}. The program P_{AW} receives the compaction bound c, the largest object size n and the bound on the live space M as its input, and for any c, M, n it holds that $P_{AW}(c,M,n) \in \mathscr{P}(M,n)$. We will show that the program P_{AW} satisfies the following lemma.

Lemma 4.3. *For all* $c \geq 1$*, and all* $M \geq n > 4$*, there exists a program* $P_{AW} \in \mathscr{P}(M,n)$ *such that for all allocators A that use aligned allocation, and satisfy the compaction bound* $\frac{1}{c}(S)$*, the following holds:*

$$HS(A,P_{AW}) \geq \begin{cases} \frac{1}{6}M \cdot min\left(c, \frac{\log n}{\log c} - \frac{6n}{M}\right) & \text{if } c \leq 4\log n \\ \frac{1}{3}M \cdot \frac{\log n}{\log\log n} - n & \text{if } c > 4\log n \end{cases}$$

Note that this lemma is very much like Theorem 2, except that it is stated for aligned allocation and (therefore) the leading constants are better: a $1/6$ instead of a $1/10$.

We start with some intuition for constructing P_{AW} and then provide its algorithm. P_{AW} works in phases. In each phase, it generates a series of allocation requests and lets the allocator allocate the requests. Once it sees the locations of the allocated objects, it then decides which objects to delete.

The *Aligned-Waster* Algorithm follows. The idea is that at each phase i, for $i = 0, 1, 2, \ldots, \log n$ *Aligned-Waster* requests allocation of objects of size 2^i. It allocates as many of them as possible while keeping the allocated space below M. It then examines where the allocator places the objects and decides on object deletions. The deletion is intended to prevent space reuse in the next phase, Phase $i+1$. In the aligned setting, an allocated object of size 2^{i+1} must be placed on a full aligned interval of size 2^{i+1}. *Aligned-Waster* examines each such interval, and if it is not empty, *Aligned-Waster* makes sure that some object is kept there to avoid re-allocation of a new object on this interval in the next phase.

However, not leaving an aligned interval of length 2^{i+1} empty is not enough to prevent its reuse in the presence of partial compaction. The allocator may choose to move the objects on such an interval and clear it for re-allocation. Therefore, *Aligned-Waster* applies a stricter policy when deciding which objects to delete. In particular, it attempts to keep enough allocated space in each interval so that it will not be worthwhile for the allocator to waste its compaction budget and move all these objects out of the interval. Given the compaction bound ratio $\frac{1}{c}$, the Algorithm P_{AW} sets a density $\frac{1}{d} > \frac{1}{c}$, and when deleting objects, P_{AW} attempts to keep a density of $\frac{1}{d}$ in each of the aligned 2^{i+1}-sized interval. The algorithm follows.

Algorithm 2 Aligned-Waster Program

Input: M, n, and c.

Compute d as a function of c (to be determined).
for $i = 0$ to $\log n$ **do**
  { Deletion step: }
    Divide the memory into consecutive areas of size 2^i
    Remove as many objects as possible from each area,
      subject to leaving at least $2^i/d$ space occupied.
  { Allocation step: }
    Request allocation of as many objects as possible of
      size 2^i (not exceeding the overall allocated size M).
end for

By definition $P_{AW} \in \mathscr{P}(M,n)$ since it never allocates an object larger than n and its overall allocation space never exceeds M words.

We note that (intuitively) it does not make sense to set $d \geq c$. If the allocated space that remains in an interval is of size $2^i/c$ (or less), then it makes sense for the allocator to move these allocated objects away and make space for reuse. This costs the compaction budget $2^i/c$, but this budget is completely refilled when the 2^i-sized object is later allocated on the cleared interval. So if we want to make the allocator pay for a reuse, we must set $d < c$ or in other words, let P_{AW}'s deletion step leave more allocated space on each interval. We leave the setting of the density $1/d$ as a parameter, but one possible good setting sets d to be $c/2$. In this case, the deletion step of P_{AW} leaves enough allocated space on each interval so that not much reuse is possible within the given allocation budget. If reuse cannot be applied, then the allocator has to get more fresh space and increase the heap in order to satisfy the allocation requests of P_{AW}.

The rest of this section provides a rigorous analysis of P_{AW} showing that it outputs allocation and de-allocation requests that make any allocation strategy incur a space overhead as asserted in Lemma 4.3. Section 4.2 extends this algorithm and analysis for the non-aligned case, extending the analysis to obtain the proof of Theorem 2.

To bound the space required to satisfy the allocation requests, we bound, on one hand, the amount of space allocated by P_{AW} in the execution, and on the other hand, the amount of space that the allocator manages to reuse during the execution. Let $S(A, P_{AW})$ denote the total space allocated during an execution of the program

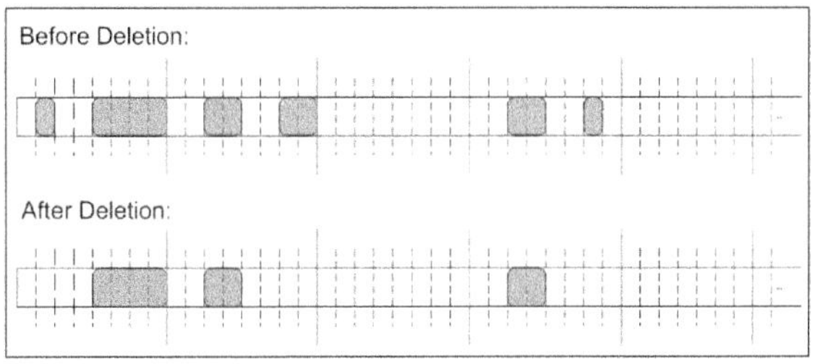

Figure 1. An example of deleting objects in *Aligned-Waster*, with parameter $1/d = 1/4$, and phase $i = 3$.

P_{AW} with an allocator A. Also, let $R(A, P_{AW})$ denote the total reused space. A space is considered reused if some object is allocated on it, the object is then deleted or relocated by the compaction, and later the same space is used for allocation of another object. The same space can be counted as reused more than once if more than two objects are placed on it during the execution. Clearly, during the execution of P_{AW} and A, the size of the heap required to allocate all objects is at least the total size of the allocated objects, minus the size of reuse that the allocator manages to make. Formally, we can state this claim as follows.

Claim 4.4. *For any program P and any allocator A, the space $HS(A,P)$ required by A to satisfy the allocation requests of P during their joint execution satisfies:*

$$HS(A,P) \geq S(A,P) - R(A,P).$$

We stress that Claim 4.4 holds not only for the specific program P_{AW}, or in the aligned setting. It holds for any program and any allocator.

To prove Lemma 4.3 we use Claim 4.4 and show that a lot of space is allocated and not much space is reused. In other words, we bound $S(A, P_{AW})$ from below, and $R(A, P_{AW})$ from above, for any possible allocator A.

We start with an upper bound on the space reuse $R(A, P_{AW})$. The intuition is that reuse can typically be done only after relocating the objects out of this area. For *Aligned-Waster*, there are not too many objects that can be moved out, as discussed earlier. Nonetheless, the actual proof is more complicated than this simple intuition, because as phases advance, different areas converge into a single one. An area of Phase i consists of eight areas from Phase $i-3$. Some of these eight areas may be empty, while others may be dense, still creating a sparse area of size 2^i.

Let $Q(A, P_{AW})$ denote the total size of compacted space (i.e., relocated objects) throughout the run of the program P_{AW} against a memory manager A that allocates in an aligned manner and satisfies the compaction threshold $\frac{1}{c}S$. Let d be the deletion threshold of *Aligned-Waster*. We show that the reuse $R(A, P_{AW})$ is bounded according to the following claim.

Claim 4.5. *For any allocator A that allocates objects in an aligned manner and satisfies the compaction bound $\frac{1}{c}S$, and a deletion factor $d \geq 1$ employed by P_{AW}, the following bound holds.*

$$R(A, P_{AW}) \leq Q(A, P_{AW}) \cdot d.$$

In the proof of this claim we use several definitions of areas, reuses and compaction quota that hold in the run of Program *Aligned-Waster*:

Definition 4.6. *If o is an object that is placed on the heap during the run of Program* Aligned-Waster, *then $|o|$ is its size. r_o is the space size reused by the allocation of the object o. r_o is defined as the total size of objects (and parts of objects) that existed in the space that is later occupied by object o. These objects were removed or compacted, but there was no object placed on top of them between their removal/compaction and until the allocation of Object o. Namely, the relocation was used for the reuse of o, and not for any previous reuse. q_o is the total size of objects that were located in the space occupied later by object o. These objects were compacted, but there was no object placed on top of them until the allocation of o.*

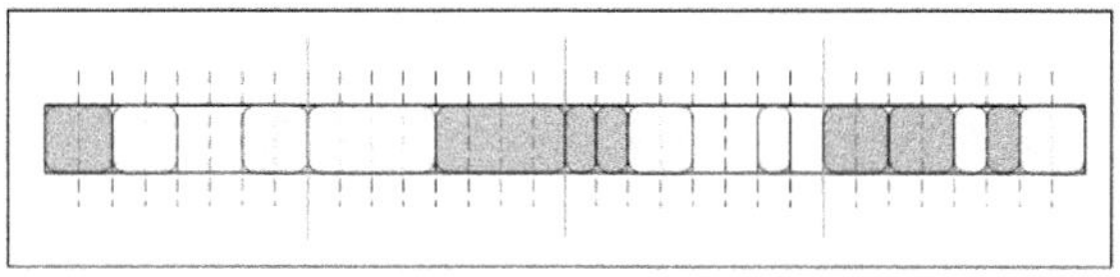

Figure 2. An example the definitions o, r_o and q_o in the execution of *Aligned-Waster*, with parameter $1/d = 1/4$, and phase $i = 5$.

An example of these definitions is in Figure 2. In this figure, a fraction of the heap of size 32 words is shown. This fraction of the heap is an empty aligned area, upon which an object o is placed in Phase 5 in the run of program *Aligned-Waster*. The dark gray squares represent words in the heap, that the last operation on this word was a compaction of an object. The light gray squares represent words in the heap, that the last operation on this word was a deletion of an object. The white squares are words on the heap that were empty since the beginning of the run of the program. In this example, q_o equals to the total size of the objects that were last compacted - i.e. to the total size of the dark words, 13 words. r_o equals to the total size of the deleted + compacted objects in this area, i.e. 27 words.

Proof of Claim 4.5. Fix an allocator A and consider a specific execution of P_{AW} with A. We break the amount of compaction on $Q(A, P_{AW})$ and the amount of reuse $R(A, P_{AW})$ into small increments. In particular, consider the space reuse in the execution. A reuse occurs when a new object is placed upon an empty aligned area that previously contained allocated objects. Consider each such allocation of an object o_j on an aligned area a of size 2^i. Just before the placement of o_j, we check the size of deletions and compactions that occurred in order to make space for the allocation. We show in Claim 4.7 below that $r_{o_j} \leq q_{o_j} \cdot d$ for any allocated object o_j. Now, summing over all allocations during in the execution of *Aligned-Waster*, we get:

$$R(A, P_{AW}) = \sum_j r_{o_j} \leq \sum_j q_{o_j} \cdot d \leq Q(A, P_{AW}) \cdot d \qquad (4.1)$$

The second inequality follows from Claim 4.7. The last inequality follows since any relocation that is later used for space reuse is part of the entire set of relocations executed by A during the execution. It remains to show that Claim 4.7 holds. □

Claim 4.7. *Consider any phase i during the execution of* Aligned-Waster. *Observe any object o just before it is being allocated in the heap during phase i. It holds:*

$$r_o \leq q_o \cdot d$$

Proof. We look at the area a where the object o is placed, just before the allocation of o in phase i. The space of a is empty at that time. This space can be sub-divided into aligned sub-areas of size 2^k for any k *s.t.* $0 < k < i$, using the Algorithm 3.

The result of Algorithm 3 is a list L that contains sub-areas of the area a. The sub-areas are distinct, their size is 2^k for $k \in \mathbb{N}, 0 \leq k \leq i$. The union of the sub-areas is exactly the area a. For every sub area that is the output of Algorithm 3, one of the following holds:

Algorithm 3 Division of an area a into sub-areas

Input: An area a of size 2^i.

List $L \leftarrow$ a new empty list
Stack $S \leftarrow$ a new empty stack
$S.Push(a, i)$
while S is not empty **do**
    $(x, k) \leftarrow S.Pop()$
    if $k = 1$ **then**
        $L.Push(x, k)$
    else
        Look at the removal step in phase k, during the run of *Aligned-Waster*. Check if there were any removals in area x during that step.
        if there was at least one removal **then**
            $L.Push(x, k)$
        else
            Divide x into its two equal sub areas x_1, x_2.
            $S.Push(x_1, k-1)$
            $S.Push(x_2, k-1)$
        end if
    end if
end while
return L.

1. The sub-area was either was always empty, or was occupied by an object that was compacted away. The sub-area size is 1.
2. The sub-area size is 2^k $s.t.$ $k \geq 1$, and last time objects were deleted from this sub-area happened during the deletion step of phase k in Algorithm *Aligned-Waster*.

The statement above follows directly from the behavior of Algorithm 3. An area of size 2^k is sub-divided only if it had no deletions in phase k. Therefore, when an area reaches size 1, it never had any deletions, and statement (1.) is true. Since Algorithm 3 divides each aligned area of size 2^k to its two equal halves, the resulting sub-areas are the exact same areas that Algorithm *Aligned-Waster* considered in phase $k-1$. The algorithm actually goes back from phase i back to phase 1 looking for the last deletion for each sub-area. For all sub-areas $sa(k)$ resulting from Algorithm 3, we examine cases (1.) and (2.).

In case (1.), it holds that there were no removals at all from the sub-area $sa(k)$. The reuse, if larger than 0, occurs since an object was allocated and later compacted (possibly more than once). In this case, the reuse in phase i of the sub-area $sa(k)$ equals to the size of the object that was last compacted away from this sub-area: $r_{sa(k)} = q_{sa(k)}$. Since $d \geq 1$, it holds that:

$$r_{sa(k)} \leq q_{sa(k)} \cdot d.$$

In case (2.), for each sub-area $sa(k)$, phase k captures the time of the last deletion from the sub area $sa(k)$. If the sub-area $sa(k)$ was not reused between phases k and i (the first allocation on sub-area $sa(k)$ after phase k, occurred in phase i), then we compute the reuse based on the following. According to the definition of the adversarial program *Aligned-Waster* behavior, for each such area, after each removal, at least $1/d$ of the area remains occupied, we denote these objects by q. These objects must be later compacted away from this sub-area, so that the space could be reused. Therefore, if we multiply the size of this compaction by d, we get the size of the sub-area $sa(k)$. The reuse size in this sub-area is smaller or equal to the sub-area size, therefore, in this case

$$r_{sa(k)} \leq q_{sa(k)} \cdot d.$$

Another option, is that the area was already reused (fully or partially) - an object was already placed on the sub-area $sa(k)$, and was later compacted away. In this case, it holds that the size that was compacted but never reused is at least $1/d$ of the sub-area $sa(k)$ size. This statement is true since after the last deletion, at least $1/d$ of the area remained occupied. If we notice only these locations in the heap, we can see that objects were compacted, and possibly partially reused by other objects between phases k and i, but these "reusing" objects were later compacted, as the sub-area is eventually empty. Therefore, in this case also there is always $1/d$ of the area that was compacted away, and not yet reused. So we get that:

$$r_{sa(k)} \leq q_{sa(k)} \cdot d.$$

This statement is true for all sub-areas. The sum of $r_{sa(k)}$, where k denotes the sub-area k of a, holds $r_a = \Sigma_k r_{sa(k)}$, and the sum of $q_{sa(k)}$, where k denotes the sub-area k of a, holds $q_a = \Sigma_k q_{sa(k)}$. Since the area a is exactly the location of the newly placed object o, it holds that

$$r_o \leq q_o \cdot d.$$

This concludes the proof of Claim 4.7 □

Claim 4.8. *Let A be any allocator that satisfies the compaction bound $\frac{1}{c}S$, such that $c \geq 1$. Let the deletion threshold of P_{AW} be $d \geq 1$ and let the total space allocated during the execution of P_{AW} with A be $S(A, P_{AW})$. It holds that:*

$$HS(A, P_{AW}) \geq S(A, P_{AW}) \left(1 - \frac{d}{c}\right).$$

Proof. By Claim 4.4, it holds that

$$HS(A, P_{AW}) \geq S(A, P_{AW}) - R(A, P_{AW}). \qquad (4.2)$$

By Claim 4.5, it holds that

$$R(A, P_{AW}) \leq Q(A, P_{AW}) \cdot d, \qquad (4.3)$$

where Q is the total compacted space. Furthermore, by the bound on the partial compaction we know that only $1/c$ of the allocated space can be compacted, i.e.,

$$Q(A, P_{AW}) \leq \frac{1}{c} \cdot S(A, P_{AW}). \qquad (4.4)$$

Using Equations 4.2, 4.3, and 4.4, we get:

$$HS(A, P_{AW}) \geq S(A, P_{AW}) - S(A, P_{AW}) \cdot \frac{d}{c}$$

as required, and we are done with the proof of Claim 4.8. □

We now return to Lemma 4.3, which asserts the lower bound (for the aligned case). We break the argument into its two different cases, according to the compaction bound range. We first state the two key claims, then derive the lower bound from them as a conclusion, and finally, provide the proofs of these two claims. The first claim considers the case of a small compaction allowance. In particular, the compaction ratio c and the density parameter d are larger than the logarithm of the largest object size n.

Claim 4.9. *For all allocators A such that A satisfies the compaction bound $\frac{1}{c}S$, s.t. $c > d \geq 2\log n$, and $M \geq n > 4$, it holds that:*

$$HS(A, P_{AW}) \geq \frac{1}{3} M \frac{\log n}{\log\log n} - 2n \left(1 - \frac{d}{c}\right).$$

The second key claim considers the general case in which more compaction can be executed and only requires that $c > d > 1$.

Claim 4.10. *For all allocators A such that A satisfies the compaction bound $\frac{1}{c}S$, for all $M \geq n > 2$, and for all $c > d > 1$, it holds that:*

$$HS(A, P_{AW}) \geq min\left(\frac{1}{3}Md, \left(\frac{1}{3}M\frac{\log n}{\log d} - 2n\right) \cdot \left(1 - \frac{d}{c}\right)\right).$$

Having stated these two key claims, we now show that they imply Lemma 4.3, which is the main focus of this section. To this end we choose the density parameter d for P_{AW} to be $d = \frac{c}{2}$. Claim 4.9 holds for $d \geq 2\log n$, and therefore, for $c \geq 4\log n$. In this case we get

$$HS(A, P_{AW}) \geq \frac{1}{3} \cdot M \cdot \frac{\log n}{\log\log n} - n.$$

For the case that $c \leq 4\log n$ we can use Claim 4.10 and deduce that

$$HS(A, P_{AW}) \geq \frac{1}{6} \cdot M \cdot min\left(c, \frac{\log n}{\log c} - \frac{6n}{M}\right).$$

These two equations yield the lower bound of Lemma 4.3 exactly, as required.

To finish the proof of the lower bound, we need to prove Claims 4.9 and 4.10. We start with some properties of areas as induced by the activity of the program P_{AW}.

Claim 4.11. *Consider any execution of P_{AW} with any allocator A, and any Phase i, $0 \leq i \leq \log n$. Let d be the deletion threshold. Just after the deletion step in Phase i, any non-empty aligned area of size 2^i has one of the following two possible configurations:*

1. *The allocated space in the area is smaller than $\frac{2^i}{d} \cdot 2$ (and each object size is smaller than $\frac{2^i}{d}$).*
2. *The area contains exactly one object that is larger or equal to $\frac{2^i}{d}$.*

Proof. Recall that the deletion in Phase i attempts to delete as much space as possible, while still leaving a space of at least $\frac{2^i}{d}$ words allocated. Suppose that after the deletion we have an object whose size is at least $\frac{2^i}{d}$. Then before the deletion this object existed in the area and if the deletion left this object allocated, then it must delete all other objects in the area and this object must be the only object alone in this area, satisfying the second case.

Otherwise, after the deletion all objects are of size smaller than $\frac{2^i}{d}$. Let the smallest of the remaining objects be of size 2^j for some $j \leq i$. Removing this object was not possible in the deletion step, therefore, the occupied space in this area can be at most $\frac{2^i}{d} + 2^j - 1$, which is smaller than $\frac{2^i}{d} \cdot 2$. □

The above claim shows that small objects must be sparsely allocated after a deletion step. In particular, objects smaller than $\frac{2^i}{d}$ must be allocated on an area with density smaller than $\frac{2}{d}$. We generalize this sparseness of small objects in the next claim. Let i be the phase number, and let $k \leq d$ be a size threshold, i.e., we consider objects of size $\frac{2^i}{k}$ as small objects. Denote by $x_i(k)$ the total space consumed by small objects after Phase i. The following claim asserts that the heap size must be large enough to accommodate these small objects.

Claim 4.12. *Consider an execution of P_{AW} against any allocator A. Let $k \leq d$ be a size threshold, and $x_i(k)$ be the total space consumed by objects that are smaller than $2^i/k$ after the deletion step in Phase i. After the deletion step of any Phase i in the execution, it holds that:*

$$HS(A, P_{AW}) \geq \begin{cases} x_i(k) \cdot k & \textit{if } k \leq \frac{1}{2}d \\ x_i(k) \cdot \frac{1}{2} \cdot k & \textit{if } \frac{1}{2}d \leq k \leq d \end{cases}$$

Proof. Consider the state of the heap after the deletion step in any Phase i. In this phase the areas considered for allocation and deletion are of size 2^i. All objects that are smaller than $\frac{2^i}{k}$ belong to $x_i(k)$. Consider any area that holds an object in $x_i(k)$. According to Claim 4.11, either there is only one object in the area and its size lies between $\frac{2^i}{d}$ and $\frac{2^i}{k}$, or the size of all remaining objects in the area is at most $\frac{2^i}{d} \cdot 2$. If $k \leq \frac{1}{2}d$, then the size of the area is larger by a factor of at least k than the occupied space on this area with objects from $x_i(k)$. If $\frac{1}{2}d \leq k \leq d$, then the size of the area is larger by a factor of at least $\frac{1}{2}k$ than the occupied space on this area with objects from $x_i(k)$. The size of the heap must be at least the sum of all areas containing objects in $x_i(k)$. Therefore, we get $HS(A, P_{AW}) \geq x_i(k) \cdot k$ or $HS(A, P_{AW}) \geq x_i(k) \cdot \frac{1}{2}k$ as required. Note that the heap size is monotone, because the heap size required for Phases $1, \ldots, i, i+1$ is at least the space required for Phases $1, \ldots, i$. Therefore, the obtained bound holds for the heap size of the entire execution. □

We now prove the key claims. Intuitively, it can be argued that either there is a point in the run of the program with many small objects that are so sparsely allocated that the lower bound follows easily, or there is no such point. In the latter case, there must be many memory allocations during the execution of P_{AW} with A, i.e., $S(A, P_{AW})$ is large, and therefore, Claim 4.8 implies the correctness of the lower bound.

Proof of Claim 4.9. We need show that if $\frac{1}{2}d > \log n$, then

$$HS(A, P_{AW}) \geq \frac{1}{3} \cdot M \cdot \frac{\log n}{\log\log n} - 2n\left(1 - \frac{d}{c}\right).$$

We use Claim 4.12, and set the size bound k to be $\log n$, which is smaller than $\frac{1}{2}d$. This means that in Phase i we consider an object to be small if it is smaller than $\frac{2^i}{\log n}$. We divide the analysis into two cases. In one case there is a phase in which a lot of small objects are allocated, and in the other case all phases do not have a large number of small objects allocated. So let α be some fraction, $0 < \alpha < 1$ (to be set later) and consider the case in which the execution has a Phase i for which small objects (smaller than $\frac{2^i}{\log n}$) occupy more than $(1-\alpha)M$ words. Then by Claim 4.12, the heap size at this point (and on) is larger than $(1-\alpha)M \cdot \log n$. Otherwise, in each of the Phases $i = 0, \ldots, \log n$, after every allocation phase i, the total space occupied in the heap is at least $M - 2^i$. It holds that more than $\alpha \cdot M - 2^i$ of the heap consists of objects that are larger than $\frac{2^i}{\log n}$. The size of the object tells us when it was allocated. Objects smaller than $\frac{2^i}{\log n}$ words were allocated in phases that are at least $\log\log n$ earlier than the current phase, whereas large objects were created in the last $\log\log n$ phases. This means that at least $\alpha \cdot M - 2^i$ of the live space must consist of objects that were created in the last $\log\log n$ phases. An execution consists of $\log n$ phases. We divide the execution into discrete sections of $\log\log n$ phases. In the last phase of each such section, at least $\alpha \cdot M - 2^i$ of the allocated space must have been allocated during this section. This is true for all sections. Therefore, if we compute the amount of space allocated in all $\frac{\log n}{\log\log n}$ sections, we get that that the amount of space allocated in the entire execution, $S(A, P_{AW})$, satisfies

$$S(A, P_{AW}) \geq \alpha M \frac{\log n}{\log\log n} - \sum_{i=\log\log n}^{\log n} 2^i \geq \alpha M \frac{\log n}{\log\log n} - 2n.$$

According to the relation between the amount of allocation and the heap size, shown in Claim 4.8, we get that

$$\begin{aligned} HS(A, P_{AW}) &\geq S(A, P_{AW}) \cdot \left(1 - \tfrac{d}{c}\right) \\ &\geq \left(\alpha M \cdot \tfrac{\log n}{\log\log n} - 2n\right) \cdot \left(1 - \tfrac{d}{c}\right). \end{aligned}$$

Setting $\alpha = \frac{1}{3(1-\frac{d}{c})}$, and using the fact that $d \le \frac{c}{2}$, we get that

$$HS(A, P_{AW}) \ge \frac{1}{3} M \cdot \log n$$

in the first case and that

$$HS(A, P_{AW}) \ge \frac{1}{3} M \cdot \frac{\log n}{\log\log n} - 2n\left(1 - \frac{d}{c}\right)$$

in the second case and we are done with the proof of Claim 4.9. □

Proof of Claim 4.10. We need to show that

$$HS(A, P_{AW}) \ge min\left(\frac{1}{3}Md, \left(\frac{1}{3}M\frac{\log n}{\log d} - 2n\right) \cdot \left(1 - \frac{d}{c}\right)\right).$$

Similarly to the proof of Claim 4.9, we use Claim 4.12. This time we set $k = d$, implying that in Phase i objects are considered small if they are smaller than $\frac{2^i}{d}$. If there is a Phase i where more than $\frac{2}{3}M$ of the live space consists of objects smaller than $\frac{2^i}{d}$, then the total heap size is larger than $\frac{2}{3}M \cdot \frac{1}{2}d = \frac{1}{3}Md$. Otherwise, in every phase i in the execution, it holds that more than $\frac{1}{3}M - 2^i$ of the live space consists of objects that are larger than $\frac{2^i}{d}$. Partitioning the execution into disjoint consecutive sections of $\log d$ phases, we get that in each such section, at least $\frac{1}{3}M - 2^i$ space was allocated. Therefore,

$$S(A, P_{AW}) \ge \frac{1}{3} M \cdot \frac{\log n}{\log d} - \sum_{i=\log\log d}^{\log d} 2^i \ge \frac{1}{3} M \cdot \frac{\log n}{\log d} - 2n.$$

And again, according to Claim 4.8, we get that

$$HS(A, P_{AW}) \ge \left(\frac{1}{3} M \cdot \frac{\log n}{\log d} - 2n\right) \cdot \left(1 - \frac{d}{c}\right).$$

One of these cases must hold, and therefore, the heap size satisfies:

$$HS(A, P_{AW}) \ge min\left(\frac{1}{3}Md, \left(\frac{1}{3}M\frac{\log n}{\log d} - 2n\right) \cdot \left(1 - \frac{d}{c}\right)\right),$$

as required and we are done with the proof of Claim 4.10. □

4.2 Bounding the space consumption when the objects are not necessarily aligned

In the general form of the allocation problem, there are no alignment constraints on the memory allocator, and the objects can be allocated anywhere. This requires a modification of the *Aligned-Waster* program and an extension of the proofs. The details become more hairy and are omitted due to space limitation. The proofs are available in the full version of this paper [4]. The main problem that comes up in the proof is that a new allocation does not necessarily cover an aligned area, and so we cannot analyze reuse in a clean manner as we did above. The solution is to consider smaller areas in the delete step. If we consider aligned areas whose size is a quarter of the allocated object size, then we can be sure that at least three of them are completely covered by the newly allocated object. The proof details appear in the full version of the paper. Here we only state the main theorem.

Theorem 2. (Lower bound.) *For all $c \ge 1$, and all $M \ge n > 4$, there exists a program $P_W \in \mathscr{P}(M, n)$ such that for all allocators A that satisfy the compaction bound $\frac{1}{c}(S)$ the following holds:*

$$HS(A, P_W) \ge \begin{cases} \frac{1}{10} M \cdot min\left(c, \frac{\log n}{\log c + 1} - \frac{5n}{M}\right) & \textit{if } c \le 4\log n \\ \frac{1}{6} M \cdot \frac{\log n}{\log\log n + 2} - \frac{n}{2} & \textit{if } c > 4\log n \end{cases}$$

5. Segregated Free List Allocator

In the previous section we presented a specific program that manages to create a large space overhead for any possible memory allocation method. In practice, systems implement specific allocators that can be specifically studied. It is possible that a program can cause more overhead to a given specific allocator. One very common memory allocator is the *segregated free list* allocator, and in particular, the one that is block-oriented (e.g., [2, 7, 10]). In this section we study limits of this specific allocator and prove tighter lower bounds based on its specific behavior. We start by defining this segregated free list allocation method. We then show bounds on the space requirement when no compaction is allowed, and finally, in Section 5.3, we show bounds on the space requirements when partial compaction is used to aid in reducing fragmentation for a segregated free list allocation.

5.1 Definition of a Segregated Free List Allocator

A segregated free list allocator divides the free list into several subsets, according to the size of the free chunks. Each subset forms a list of free chunks of the same size (or a small range of sizes) and an array of pointers is used to index the various free lists. A freed object is placed on the appropriate list according to its size. An allocation request is serviced from the appropriate list.

Segregated free lists are typically implemented in a block oriented manner [2, 7, 10]. The heap is partitioned into blocks (typically, of a page size, i.e., 4KB) and each block may only contain objects of one size. Whenever a full block is freed, it is returned to the pool of free blocks. Whenever an allocation is requested for an object whose free list is empty, a free block is pulled from the block pool, it is partitioned into as many free chunks as possible in an aligned manner, and then the new chunks are added to the appropriate free list to allow allocation.

The free lists are known as buckets. Each bucket is characterized by the chunk size (or range of chunk sizes) that can be allocated in it. The allocation within each bucket is executed in a first-fit manner, in the first free chunk in the bucket's list that can satisfy the allocation. The simplicity of this method comes with a cost. This method is susceptible to high external fragmentation, as shown below.

In the following sections we simplify the discussion by assuming that the maximal object size, n, equals the block size. This is close to what happens in practice, and small adjustments, e.g., if the block size is $2n$, have small impact on the results. As before, we denote by M the total space that can be allocated simultaneously.

5.2 Memory usage without compaction

Let us start with the case that no compaction is used. The general lower bound of Robson [17, 18] holds in this case, implying that an overhead factor of at least $\times \frac{1}{2}\log n$ can occur in practice for the worst fragmenting program. We extend this bound for the specific segregated free list allocator. Denote by $s_1, \ldots, s_k$ the different maximal object sizes inside each bucket, and assume for simplicity that the program only allocates objects whose sizes are one of $s_1, \ldots, s_k$. (When proving a lower bound, it is enough to show that there exists one bad program.) A block contains objects of the same size, but this can be any size as long as $s_k \le n$. As stated earlier, for simplicity we also assume that $n = s_k$.

Different segregated free list allocators have different segregation policies, which are determined by the size vector $s_1, \ldots, s_k$. We study two rather extreme cases by looking at an allocator that keeps a bucket for each possible object size (i.e., a lot of buckets) and an allocator that has buckets for exponential object sizes, i.e., sizes that increase by a factor of two. Typical implementations use something in between these extreme cases and the tools developed here can be used to explore each specific set of sizes.

We first look at the allocator SFL_{all} that implements the segregated free list method, with a full assortment of bucket sizes: $s_1 = 1, s_2 = 2, s_3 = 3, s_4 = 4, ..., s_n = n$. Let the class $\mathscr{P}(M, [s_1, \ldots, s_n])$ be the class of all programs that always keep the allocated space smaller or equal to M, and allocates objects only of the sizes $s_1, ..., s_n$. The theorems below show that with no compaction, the space overhead is quite large. It is of the order of the square root of n. This is much higher than the logarithmic factor that was shown for the general allocator.

Theorem 3. *There exists a program $P \in \mathscr{P}(M, [s_1, \ldots, s_n])$, and the heap size required for allocator SFL_{all} to execute the allocation requests of P satisfies:*

$$HS(SFL_{all}, P) \geq \frac{4}{5} M \sqrt{n} - n.$$

The result for the smaller set of buckets is very different. Particularly, let SFL_{log} be an allocator that implements the segregated free list method, with a logarithmic assortment of bucket sizes: $s_1 = 1, s_2 = 2, s_3 = 4, s_4 = 8, ..., s_{\log n+1} = n$. Let $\mathscr{P}(M, [s_1, \ldots, s_{\log n+1}])$ be a set of programs that always keep the live space smaller or equal to M, and allocates objects only of the sizes $s_1, ..., s_{\log n+1}$.

Theorem 4. *There exists a program $P \in \mathscr{P}(M, [s_1, \ldots, s_{\log n+1}])$, and the heap size required for allocator SFL_{log} to execute the allocation requests of P satisfies:*

$$HS(SFL_{log}, P) \geq M \log n - \frac{4}{3} M - n.$$

Note that Theorems 3 and 4 improve on the general results obtained by Robson [17, 18]. Robson could only show an overhead of $\frac{1}{2} \log n$ since he needed to work with a general allocator, unlike the segregated free list allocator that we assume in this section.

The proofs of the theorems are omitted for lack of space and are available in the full version of this paper [4]. Below we only present the "bad" program that causes large space overheads for any allocator that employs the segregated free list allocation method.

Algorithm 4 Program P_{BW} with bucket sizes $s_1, \ldots, s_k$.

```
1: for i = 1 to k do do
2:     Allocate as many object as possible of size s_i
3:     Deallocate as many objects as possible subject to leaving
       exactly one object in each allocated block.
4: end for
```

According to the definition of Program P_{BW}, after each deallocation step, there will be a single object in each allocated block. Moreover, this single object will not be deleted until the end of the execution. This property makes the algorithm use a large heap. In the full version of this paper [4] we prove that the heap size in phase k, HS_k depends on the total space size available for allocation in each of the phases, M_i, and on the choice for bucket sizes s_i, in the following way:

$$HS_k = \sum_{i=1}^{k} \left\lceil \frac{\left\lfloor \frac{M_i}{s_i} \right\rfloor}{\left\lfloor \frac{n}{s_i} \right\rfloor} \right\rceil \cdot n. \quad (5.1)$$

Equation 5.1 implies that the more phases there are during the program execution, and the more memory remaining for allocation in every one of them, the larger the heap is. The total space size available for allocation in each of the phases, M_i, satisfies:

$$M_{i+1} \geq M_i - \left\lceil \frac{\left\lfloor \frac{M_i}{s_i} \right\rfloor}{\left\lfloor \frac{n}{s_i} \right\rfloor} \right\rceil \cdot s_i. \quad (5.2)$$

Equation 5.2 represents the connection between object sizes in the different buckets and the memory remaining for allocation in every phase of the Program 4 execution. The larger the range of object sizes is, the more memory remains for future phases. Consequently, according to Equation 5.1, the total heap size becomes larger. Simplification of the above equations, and assignment of the s_i parameter yields the proofs of Theorems 3, 4.

5.3 Space overheads with compaction

In Section 5.2, we built P_{BW} that wasted many blocks by leaving a single object in each. With no compaction that program created a lot of fragmentation. Modern collectors employ partial compaction especially for such scenarios, and they clear sparse blocks by moving their elements to a different block. The evacuated blocks can then be used for further allocations. In this section we first discuss a simple upper bound on the heap usage by looking at a simple compaction strategy (which is similar to what is used in actual systems in practice). We then provide a program that makes the allocator waste blocks by leaving enough allocated space on them so that the compaction budget will not allow effective defragmentation.

5.3.1 The Upper Bound

Our memory manager allocates in a (block-oriented) segregated free list manner as before, but it also has a compacting strategy. We call this memory manager a *Compacting Segregated Free List* allocator and denote it by *CSFL*. We specify the compaction strategy, and later show that using this compaction strategy the following upper bound on the heap size holds.

Theorem 5. *Let c be the compaction threshold, k be the number of buckets, and n be the block size. The maximal heap size required for CSFL to execute any program P that never uses more than M words of allocated space simultaneously and never allocates an object larger than n satisfies:*

$$HS(CSFL, P) \leq M \cdot c + k \cdot n.$$

In order to prove this upper bound, we first present the compaction strategy of *CSFL*, show that it is consistent (always has enough budget for compaction), and finally prove the bound in Theorem 5.

The definition below assumes a *last block* in any bucket. Between all blocks that are allocated for the bucket, the last block is the one that was most recently allocated for this bucket. By the behavior of the segregated free list allocator, all slots in other blocks were exhausted before the last one was allocated.

Definition 5.1 (*CSFL* Compaction Strategy)**.** *We denote by b, a block that contains objects of size i. CSFL will compact all objects within Block b to other block(s), if Block b holds the following constraints:*

1. *Block b is not the last block for objects of size i,*
2. *At most 1/c of the space in Block b is allocated,*
3. *There is enough free space in blocks containing objects of size i to contain all of the objects that are currently placed in Block b.*

Claim 5.2. *CSFL with the compaction strategy of Definition 5.1 has enough compaction budget to execute all required compaction.*

Proof. We show that enough space was allocated on this block alone to provide the budget for compacting it at the appropriate time in the execution. By the allocation strategy of the segregated free list, any block that is not the last block, was filled with objects at some point in the execution. Otherwise, the next block would not have been allocated. There were no compactions made on this block since it was taken from the pool, according to the algorithm (by which every compaction frees an entire block and returns it to the blocks pool). Since this block was taken from the blocks pool, the accumulated compaction quota due to allocations on this block is at least $1/c$ of the block size. (It can be larger if space on this block was reused.) At the execution point in which compaction is triggered on this block, at most $1/c$ of the block is allocated, therefore all this space can be moved using only budget in the quota that originated from allocations on this block. After all of the objects in this block are compacted away, the block is returned to the block pool and can be reused in the future for other bucket sizes. □

Proof of Theorem 5. According to Claim 5.2, all blocks (except maybe the last block) are at least $1/c$ full (otherwise, the block would have been cleared using compaction). Therefore, the total heap size required for these blocks is at most: $c \cdot M_1$, where M_1 is the total space in all blocks except the last ones in each bucket size. Therefore, the total heap size required is at most $c \cdot M + k \cdot n$, where k is the number of different possible sizes, and n is the block size. □

5.3.2 The Lower Bound

We now construct a program that creates a lot of fragmentation for the compacting segregated free list allocator. As before, we look at a *CSFL* that uses a large number of buckets and at a *CSFL* that uses a small number of buckets. We provide lower bounds for these two extreme cases, and the same techniques can be used to work with any specific bucket sizes employed in any practical system.

Denote by $\mathscr{P}(M,[s_1,\ldots,s_k])$ the set of programs that never allocate more than M words simultaneously and allocate only objects whose size is in the set $\{s_1,...,s_n\}$. The following theorems assert the two lower bounds.

Theorem 6. *Let $CSFL_{all}$ be an allocator that implements the segregated free list method and keeps the compaction bound of $\frac{1}{c}\cdot S$ for $c \geq 4$. Let its bucket object sizes be the complete assortment of: $s_1 = 1, s_2 = 2, s_3 = 3, s_4 = 4, ..., s_n = n$ for $n \geq 2$. Then there exists a program $P \in \mathscr{P}(M,[s_1,\ldots,s_n])$, such that the heap size required for allocator $CSFL_{all}$ to execute the allocations and deallocations of P, $HS(CSFL_{all},P)$, satisfy:*

$$HS(CSFL_{all},P) \geq \begin{cases} \frac{1}{6}\cdot M\cdot\sqrt{n}+\frac{1}{16}M & \text{if } c \geq 2\sqrt{n} \\ \frac{1}{12}\cdot M\cdot c+\frac{1}{16}M & \text{if } c \leq 2\sqrt{n}\,. \end{cases}$$

Theorem 7. *Let $CSFL_{log}$ be an allocator that implements the segregated free list method and keeps the compaction bound of $\frac{1}{c}\cdot S$. Let its bucket object sizes be the logarithmic assortment of bucket sizes: $s_1 = 1, s_2 = 2, s_3 = 4, s_4 = 8, ..., s_{\log n+1} = n$. Then there exists a program $P \in \mathscr{P}(M,[s_1,\ldots,s_{\log n+1}])$, such that the heap size required for the allocator $CSFL_{log}$ to execute all allocations and deallocations of P, $HS(CSFL_{log},P)$, satisfy:*

$$HS(CSFL_{log},P) \geq \begin{cases} \frac{1}{4}\cdot M\cdot\log n-2M & \text{if } c \geq 2\log n \\ \frac{1}{8}\cdot M\cdot c-2M & \text{if } c \leq 2\log n \end{cases}$$

We now present the program *Segregated-Waster*, denoted P_{SW}, that creates a large fragmentation for the compacting segregated free list allocator.

Algorithm 5 Program *Segregated-Waster* for the compacting segregated free list allocator

Compute d as a function of the input compaction threshold c.
for $i = 1$ to k do **do**
    Allocate as many objects as possible of size s_i
    In each block, deallocate as many objects as possible subject to leaving at least $1/d$ of the space allocated in this block.
end for

Algorithm 5 is similar to Algorithm 4 presented in Section 5.2 in its allocation steps, but differs in its deallocation steps. The difference is that Algorithm 5 keeps the allocated space remaining in each block larger than $1/d$ of the space allocated within this block. Leaving more allocated space in a block makes it difficult to compact away all of the objects in it. A block can be used for allocating objects of a different size only when all of the objects in it are moved away.

Below we investigate the joint run of *CSFL* and P_{SW} and provide claims that lead to the proof of the Theorems 6 and 7. Note the difference between the execution of *CSFL* against a program P (with compaction enabled), and the execution of *SFL* against it (with compaction disabled). The difference is the fact that in the compacting scenario space can be reused. After objects on a block are compacted away, this same block can be reused for objects of larger sizes. Therefore, it will be necessary to calculate the heap size depending on compaction as well as allocation. The compaction is the reason why in Algorithm 5, deletions leave $1/d$ of the space in a block, where d is chosen according to the value of c. This is done in order to make the compaction more costly, but it has another effect: less deletion leaves less space for future allocations. Below, we present some claims that lead to the proof of Theorems 6 and 7 presented above.

Claim 5.3. *Consider the execution of a CSFL allocator with the program P_{SW}. For any phase i in the execution, let M_i denote the space available for allocation in Phase i, and let s_i denote the object size allocated in Phase i. Let k denote the number of phases in the execution. The heap size required for the execution of P_{SW} with CSFL satisfies:*

$$HS_k(CSFL,P_{SW}) \geq \frac{1}{2}\sum_{i=1}^{k} M_i - \frac{1}{2}\sum_{i=1}^{k} s_i.$$

Proof. According to the definition of P_{SW}, the program run consists of phases. In each phase the space available for allocation is M_i. The program requests allocations of as many objects as it can of size s_i. The number of allocation requests is, therefore, $\left\lfloor \frac{M_i}{s_i} \right\rfloor$, and the total space allocated in Phase i is $\left\lfloor \frac{M_i}{s_i} \right\rfloor \cdot s_i$. The total space allocated from the beginning of the run until (including) Phase k is

$$S_k = \sum_{i=1}^{k} \left\lfloor \frac{M_i}{s_i} \right\rfloor \cdot s_i \geq \sum_{i=1}^{k} M_i - \sum_{i=1}^{k} s_i. \tag{5.3}$$

The total quota for compaction is $S_k \cdot \frac{1}{c}$.

In each phase, the program removes as many objects as it can, subject to leaving at least $1/d$ of the space already allocated in each block. In order to free a bucket for reuse, all the objects in this block must be moved to another block. Therefore, the total space reuse during the execution is at most d times the space compacted, which is at most $d \cdot S_k \cdot \frac{1}{c}$. Setting $d = \frac{c}{2}$ in P_{SW}, we get that the space reuse is at most $\frac{1}{2}S_k$. The total heap size necessary is at least the space allocated, S_k, minus the space reused, which is at most $\frac{1}{2}S_k$. Now using the Inequality 5.3 for S_k gets the desired bound. □

Claim 5.4. *Consider the execution of a CSFL allocator with the Program P_{SW}. Let k be the number of phases in the execution, let M_i be the total space size available for allocation in Phase i, let s_i be the size of objects allocated in Phase i, let n be the block size, and let d be the density threshold. Then in all phases $1 \leq i < k$ it holds that:*

$$M_{i+1} \geq M_i\left(1 - \frac{1}{d} - \frac{s_i}{n - s_i}\right).$$

We omit the proof of this claim due to the constraints of the paper length. The proof appears in the full version of the paper [4].

Claim 5.5. *Consider the execution of a CSFL allocator with the program P_{SW}. Let M_i be the size of the space available for allocation in Phase i, let s_i be the objects size in Phase i, let n be the block size, and let d be the density threshold. In all phases $2 \le i \le k$ it holds that:*

$$M_i \ge M - M \cdot \left(\frac{i-1}{d} + \sum_{j=1}^{i-1} \frac{s_j}{n - s_j} \right).$$

Proof. By removing the recursion from the result of Claim 5.4, we get:

$$M_i \ge M \prod_{j=1}^{i-1} \left(1 - \frac{1}{d} - \frac{s_i}{n - s_i} \right).$$

We use the fact that for any positive $\alpha_1, \ldots, \alpha_i$ it holds that

$$\prod_{j=1}^{i} (1 - \alpha_j) \ge 1 - \sum_{j=1}^{i} \alpha_j. \tag{5.4}$$

to simplify the equation above. The result is:

$$M_i \ge M \left(1 - \sum_{j=1}^{i-1} \left(\frac{1}{d} + \frac{s_i}{n - s_i} \right) \right).$$

Which is what we wanted to prove. □

Claim 5.6. *Consider the execution of a CSFL allocator with the program P_{SW}. Let HS_k be the total heap size required for the allocations of CSFL until the end of phase k. The heap size can be bounded by:*

$$\begin{aligned} HS_k(CSFL, P_{SW}) \ & \ge \frac{1}{2} Mk - M \cdot \frac{k(k-1)}{4d} \\ & - \frac{1}{2} M \sum_{i=1}^{k-1} \frac{(k-i-1)s_i}{n - s_{k-1}} - \frac{1}{2} \sum_{i=1}^{k} s_i. \end{aligned}$$

Proof. According to Claim 5.3, the total heap size until Phase k is:

$$HS_k(CSFL, P_{SW}) \ge \frac{1}{2} \sum_{i=1}^{k} M_i - \frac{1}{2} \sum_{i=1}^{k} s_i.$$

Substituting the value of M_i with the result of Claim 5.5, we get:

$$\begin{aligned} & HS_k(CSFL, P_{SW}) \ge \\ & \ge \frac{1}{2} \sum_{i=1}^{k} \left(M - M \left(\frac{i-1}{d} + \sum_{j=1}^{i-1} \frac{s_j}{n - s_j} \right) \right) - \frac{1}{2} \sum_{i=1}^{k} s_i \\ & \ge \frac{1}{2} Mk - M \cdot \frac{k(k-1)}{4d} - \frac{1}{2} M \sum_{i=1}^{k-1} \frac{(k-i-1)s_i}{n - s_i} - \frac{1}{2} \sum_{i=1}^{k} s_i. \end{aligned}$$

By substituting $-s_i$ in the denominator, with the maximal value of s_i, which is s_{k-1}, we get the claim. □

We now use the above claims to prove Theorems 6 and 7.

Proof of Theorem 6. The object sizes in this case are: $s_1 = 1, s_2 = 2, s_3 = 3, s_4 = 4, \ldots, s_n = n$. We set these sizes in the expression of Claim 5.6:

$$\begin{aligned} HS_k(CSFL_{all}, P_{SW}) \ & \ge \frac{1}{2} Mk - M \frac{k(k-1)}{4d} \\ & - \frac{1}{2} M \sum_{i=1}^{k-1} \frac{(k-i-1)i}{n-k+1} - \frac{1}{2} \sum_{i=1}^{k} i. \end{aligned}$$

Using the closed sum for squares:

$$\sum_{i=1}^{k} i^2 = \frac{k(k+1)(2k+1)}{6} \tag{5.5}$$

and some algebra we get:

$$\begin{aligned} HS_k(CSFL_{all}, P_{SW}) \ge & \ \tfrac{1}{2} Mk - M \frac{k(k-1)}{4d} \\ & - M \frac{(k-1)(k-2)(k-3)}{6(n-k+1)} - \frac{k(k+1)}{4}. \end{aligned}$$

The above bound is correct for any phase k, $1 \le k \le \sqrt{n}$, but the quality of the bound is best at where the computation actually stops. We divide into two possible cases. The first case is when $d \ge \sqrt{n}$. In this case, we choose $k = \frac{\sqrt{n}}{2}$ and get:

$$\begin{aligned} HS_{\frac{\sqrt{n}}{2}}(CSFL_{all}, P_{SW}) \ge & \ \tfrac{1}{4} M \sqrt{n} - M \cdot \frac{\sqrt{n}(\sqrt{n}-2)}{16d} \\ & - M \frac{(\sqrt{n}-2)(\sqrt{n}-4)(\sqrt{n}-6)}{48(n - \frac{\sqrt{n}}{2} + 1)} - \frac{\sqrt{n}(\sqrt{n}+2)}{16}. \end{aligned}$$

Since we assume that $d \ge \sqrt{n}$, we can bound $\frac{\sqrt{n}}{d}$ from above by 1. Note also that for $n \ge 2$

$$\frac{(\sqrt{n}-2)(\sqrt{n}-4)(\sqrt{n}-6)}{(n - \frac{\sqrt{n}}{2} + 1)} \le \sqrt{n} - 6.$$

Therefore,

$$\begin{aligned} HS_{\frac{\sqrt{n}}{2}}(CSFL_{all}, P_{SW}) \ge & \ \frac{1}{4} M \sqrt{n} - M \frac{\sqrt{n}-2}{16} \\ & - \frac{1}{48} M (\sqrt{n} - 6) - \frac{n + 2\sqrt{n}}{16}. \end{aligned}$$

According to our definition $M \ge n$. Therefore, we can replace the last $n + 2\sqrt{n}$ with $3M$, and get that:

$$HS_{\frac{\sqrt{n}}{2}}(CSFL_{all}, P_{SW}) \ge \frac{1}{6} M \sqrt{n} + \frac{1}{16} M.$$

The other case is when $d \le \sqrt{n}$. In this case, we choose $k = \frac{d}{2}$. Therefore:

$$\begin{aligned} & HS_{\frac{d}{2}}(CSFL_{all}, P_{SW}) \ge \\ & \tfrac{1}{4} Md - M \cdot \frac{(d-2)}{16} - M \frac{(d-2)(d-4)(d-6)}{48(n - \frac{d}{2} + 1)} - \frac{d(d+2)}{16}. \end{aligned}$$

Since $\sqrt{n} \ge d$, we can replace n with d^2. We also use the fact that for $d \ge 2$,

$$\frac{(d-2)(d-4)(d-6)}{(d^2 - \frac{d}{2} + 1)} \le d - 6.$$

Therefore,

$$HS_{\frac{d}{2}}(CSFL_{all}, P_{SW}) \ge \frac{1}{4} Md - M \cdot \frac{d-2}{16} - M \frac{d-6}{48} - \frac{d^2 + 2d}{16}.$$

Since $M \ge n \ge d^2$, we can replace the last $d^2 + 2d$ with $3M$, and get that:

$$HS_{\frac{d}{2}}(CSFL_{all}, P_{SW}) \ge \frac{1}{6} Md + \frac{1}{16} M$$

setting $d = c/2$ the claim holds. □

Proof of Theorem 7. The object sizes in this case are: $s_1 = 1, s_2 = 2, s_3 = 4, s_4 = 8, \ldots, s_n = 2^n$. Setting the object sizes in the expression of Claim 5.6 we get:

$$\begin{aligned} HS_k(CSFL_{log}, P_{SW}) \ & \ge \tfrac{1}{2} Mk - M \cdot \frac{k(k-1)}{4d} \\ & - \tfrac{1}{2} M \sum_{i=1}^{k-1} \frac{(k-i-1)2^i}{n - 2^{k-1}} - \frac{1}{2} \sum_{i=1}^{k} 2^i. \end{aligned}$$

Using the following equation:

$$\sum_{i=1}^{k-1} i 2^i = 2^k (k-2) + 2 \tag{5.6}$$

and some algebra, we get:

$$\begin{aligned} HS_k(CSFL_{log}, P_{SW}) &\geq \tfrac{1}{2}Mk - M \cdot \frac{k(k-1)}{4d} \\ &\quad -M \cdot \frac{2^{k-1}-k}{n-2^{k-1}} - \tfrac{1}{2}(2^{k+1}-1). \end{aligned}$$

We split the analysis into two possible cases. First, assume that $d \leq \log(n)$. In this case we look at the phase $k = \log n$. In this case, we get:

$$\begin{aligned} HS_{\log n}(CSFL_{log}, P_{SW}) &\geq \tfrac{1}{2}M \log n - M \cdot \frac{\log n(\log n - 1)}{4d} \\ &\quad -M \cdot \frac{\frac{n}{2} - \log n}{n - \frac{n}{2}} - \tfrac{1}{2}(2n-1) \\ &\geq \tfrac{1}{2}M \log n - M \cdot \frac{\log n(\log n - 1)}{4d} \\ &\quad -M + M \cdot \frac{2\log n}{n} - n + \tfrac{1}{2}. \end{aligned}$$

Since $d \geq \log n$, we can bound $\frac{\log n}{d}$ from above by 1. Also, we use the fact that $M \geq n \geq 1$ to get:

$$\begin{aligned} HS_{\log n}(CSFL_{log}, P_{SW}) &\geq \tfrac{1}{2}M \log n - M \cdot \frac{(\log n - 1)}{4} \\ &\quad -M + M \cdot \frac{2\log n}{n} - n + \tfrac{1}{2} \\ &\geq \tfrac{1}{4}M \log n - 2M. \end{aligned}$$

The other case is that $d \leq \log n$. In this case, we choose $k = d$ and obtain:

$$\begin{aligned} HS_d(CSFL_{log}, P_{SW}) &\geq \tfrac{1}{2}Md - M \cdot \frac{d(d-1)}{4d} \\ &\quad -M \cdot \frac{2^{d-1}-d}{n-2^{d-1}} - \tfrac{1}{2}(2^{d+1}-1). \end{aligned}$$

We replace n with 2^d, and use the fact that $M \geq n \geq 2^d$ to get:

$$\begin{aligned} HS_d(CSFL_{log}, P_{SW}) &\geq \tfrac{1}{2}Md - M\frac{(d-1)}{4} \\ &\quad -M \cdot \frac{2^{d-1}-d}{2^d - 2^{d-1}} - 2^d + \tfrac{1}{2} \\ &\geq \tfrac{1}{4}Md - 2M \end{aligned}$$

and again, setting $d = c/2$, the claim holds. □

6. Conclusion

In this work we studied the effectiveness of partial compaction for reducing the space overhead of dynamic memory allocation. We developed techniques for showing lower bounds on how much space must be used when the amount of compaction is limited by a given budget. It was shown that partial compaction can reduce fragmentation, but up to a limit, determined by the compaction budget. We also studied the effectiveness of partial compaction for a specific common allocator: the segregated free list allocator. Tighter bounds have been shown based on the specific behavior of this allocator.

This work extends our understanding of the underlying theory behind memory management with compaction. We hope that the techniques developed herein can be further extended in future work to achieve even tighter bounds and improve our understanding of the effectiveness of partial compaction for modern systems.

References

[1] Diab Abuaiadh, Yoav Ossia, Erez Petrank, and Uri Silbershtein. An efficient parallel heap compaction algorithm. In *Proceedings of the Nineteenth ACM SIGPLAN Conference on Object-Oriented Programming, Systems, Languages, and Applications*, ACM SIGPLAN Notices 39(10), pages 224–236, Vancouver, Canada, October 2004.

[2] David F. Bacon, Perry Cheng, and V.T. Rajan. A real-time garbage collector with low overhead and consistent utilization. In *Conference Record of the Thirtieth Annual ACM Symposium on Principles of Programming Languages*, ACM SIGPLAN Notices 38(1), pages 285–298, New Orleans, LA, USA, January 2003.

[3] Ori Ben-Yitzhak, Irit Goft, Elliot Kolodner, Kean Kuiper, and Victor Leikehman. An algorithm for parallel incremental compaction. In Hans-J. Boehm and David Detlefs, editors, *Proceedings of the Third International Symposium on Memory Management (June, 2002)*, ACM SIGPLAN Notices 38(2 supplement), pages 100–105, Berlin, Germany, February 2003.

[4] Anna Bendersky and Erez Petrank. Space overhead bounds for dynamic memory management with partial compaction. A full version of this paper is available at http://www.cs.technion.ac.il/ erez/papers.html, 2010.

[5] Hans-Juergen Boehm. Bounding space usage of conservative garbage collectors. In POPL 2002 [16], pages 93–100.

[6] Hans-Juergen Boehm. The space cost of lazy reference counting. In *Proceedings of the Thirty-First Annual ACM Symposium on Principles of Programming Languages*, ACM SIGPLAN Notices 39(1), pages 210–219, Venice, Italy, January 2004.

[7] Hans-Juergen Boehm and Mark Weiser. Garbage collection in an uncooperative environment. *Software Practice and Experience*, 18(9):807–820, 1988.

[8] Cliff Click, Gil Tene, and Michael Wolf. The Pauseless GC algorithm. In Michael Hind and Jan Vitek, editors, *Proceedings of the First ACM SIGPLAN/SIGOPS International Conference on Virtual Execution Environments*, pages 46–56, Chicago, IL, USA, June 2005.

[9] David Detlefs, Christine Flood, Steven Heller, and Tony Printezis. Garbage-first garbage collection. In David F. Bacon and Amer Diwan, editors, *Proceedings of the Fourth International Symposium on Memory Management*, pages 37–48, Vancouver, Canada, October 2004. ACM Press.

[10] Tamar Domani, Elliot K. Kolodner, Ethan Lewis, Elliot E. Salant, Katherine Barabash, Itai Lahan, Erez Petrank, Igor Yanover, and Yossi Levanoni. Implementing an on-the-fly garbage collector for Java. In Craig Chambers and Antony L. Hosking, editors, *Proceedings of the Second International Symposium on Memory Management*, ACM SIGPLAN Notices 36(1), pages 155–166, Minneapolis, MN, October 2000.

[11] Richard E. Jones. *Garbage Collection: Algorithms for Automatic Dynamic Memory Management*. Wiley, Chichester, July 1996. With a chapter on Distributed Garbage Collection by R. Lins.

[12] Haim Kermany and Erez Petrank. The Compressor: Concurrent, incremental and parallel compaction. In Michael I. Schwartzbach and Thomas Ball, editors, *Proceedings of the ACM SIGPLAN Conference on Programming Language Design and Implementation*, ACM SIGPLAN Notices 41(6), pages 354–363, Ottawa, Canada, June 2006.

[13] Erez Petrank and Dror Rawitz. The hardness of cache conscious data placement. In POPL 2002 [16], pages 101–112.

[14] Filip Pizlo, Daniel Frampton, Erez Petrank, and Bjarne Steensgard. STOPLESS: A real-time garbage collector for multiprocessors. In Greg Morrisett and Mooly Sagiv, editors, *Proceedings of the Sixth International Symposium on Memory Management*, pages 159–172, Montréal, Canada, October 2007. ACM Press.

[15] Filip Pizlo, Erez Petrank, and Bjarne Steensgaard. A study of concurrent real-time garbage collectors. In Rajiv Gupta and Saman P. Amarasinghe, editors, *Proceedings of the ACM SIGPLAN Conference on Programming Language Design and Implementation*, ACM SIGPLAN Notices 43(6), pages 33–44, Tucson, AZ, USA, June 2008.

[16] *Conference Record of the Twenty-ninth Annual ACM Symposium on Principles of Programming Languages*, ACM SIGPLAN Notices 37(1), Portland, OR, USA, January 2002.

[17] J. M. Robson. An estimate of the store size necessary for dynamic storage allocation. *Journal of the ACM*, 18(3):416–423, July 1971.

[18] J. M. Robson. Bounds for some functions concerning dynamic storage allocation. *Journal of the ACM*, 21(3):419–499, July 1974.

Laws of Order: Expensive Synchronization in Concurrent Algorithms Cannot be Eliminated

Hagit Attiya
Technion
hagit@cs.technion.il

Rachid Guerraoui
EPFL
rachid.guerraoui@epfl.ch

Danny Hendler
Ben-Gurion University
hendlerd@cs.bgu.ac.il

Petr Kuznetsov
TU Berlin/Deutsche Telekom Labs
pkuznets@acm.org

Maged M. Michael
IBM T. J. Watson Research Center
magedm@us.ibm.com

Martin Vechev
IBM T. J. Watson Research Center
mtvechev@us.ibm.com

Abstract

Building correct and efficient concurrent algorithms is known to be a difficult problem of fundamental importance. To achieve efficiency, designers try to remove unnecessary and costly synchronization. However, not only is this manual trial-and-error process ad-hoc, time consuming and error-prone, but it often leaves designers pondering the question of: is it inherently impossible to eliminate certain synchronization, or is it that I was unable to eliminate it on this attempt and I should keep trying?

In this paper we respond to this question. We prove that it is impossible to build concurrent implementations of classic and ubiquitous specifications such as sets, queues, stacks, mutual exclusion and read-modify-write operations, that completely eliminate the use of expensive synchronization.

We prove that one cannot avoid the use of either: i) read-after-write (RAW), where a write to shared variable A is followed by a read to a different shared variable B without a write to B in between, or ii) atomic write-after-read (AWAR), where an atomic operation reads and then writes to shared locations. Unfortunately, enforcing RAW or AWAR is expensive on all current mainstream processors. To enforce RAW, memory ordering–also called fence or barrier–instructions must be used. To enforce AWAR, atomic instructions such as compare-and-swap are required. However, these instructions are typically substantially slower than regular instructions.

Although algorithm designers frequently struggle to avoid RAW and AWAR, their attempts are often futile. Our result characterizes the cases where avoiding RAW and AWAR is impossible. On the flip side, our result can be used to guide designers towards new algorithms where RAW and AWAR can be eliminated.

Categories and Subject Descriptors D.1.3 [*Concurrent Programming*]; E.1 [*Data*]: Data Structures

General Terms Algorithms, Theory

Keywords Concurrency, Algorithms, Lower Bounds, Memory Fences, Memory Barriers

1. Introduction

The design of concurrent applications that avoid costly synchronization patterns is a cardinal programming challenge, requiring consideration of algorithmic concerns and architectural issues with implications to formal testing and verification.

Two common synchronization patterns that frequently arise in the design of concurrent algorithms are *read after write* (RAW) and *atomic write after read* (AWAR).

The RAW pattern consists of a process writing to some shared variable A, followed by the same process reading a different shared variable B, without that process writing to B in between. The AWAR pattern consists of a process reading some shared variable followed by the process writing to a shared variable (the write could be to the same shared variable as the read), where the entire read-write sequence is atomic. Examples of the AWAR pattern include read-modify-write operations such as a Compare-and-Swap [26] (CAS).

Unfortunately, on all mainstream processor architectures, the RAW and AWAR patterns are associated with expensive instructions. Modern processor architectures use relaxed memory models, where guaranteeing RAW order among accesses to independent memory locations requires the execution of memory ordering instructions–often called *memory fences* or *memory barriers*–that enforce RAW order.[1] Guaranteeing the atomicity of AWAR requires the use of atomic instructions. Typically, fence and atomic instructions are substantially slower than regular instructions, even under the most favorable caching conditions.

Due to these high overheads, designers of concurrent algorithms aim to avoid both RAW and AWAR patterns. However, such attempts are often unsuccessful: in many cases, even after multiple attempts, it turns out impossible to avoid these patterns while ensuring correctness of the algorithm.

This raises an interesting and important practical question:

Can we discover and formalize the conditions under which avoiding RAW and AWAR, while ensuring correctness, is futile?

In this paper, we answer this question formally. We show that implementations of a wide class of concurrent algorithms must involve RAW or AWAR. In particular, we focus on two widely used

[1] RAW order requires the use of explicit fences or atomic instructions even on strongly ordered architectures (e.g., X86 and SPARC TSO) that automatically guarantee other types of ordering (read after read, write after read, and write after write).

specifications: linearizable objects [23] and mutual exclusion [11]. Our results are applicable to any algorithm claiming to satisfy these specifications.

Main Contributions. The main contributions of this paper are the following:

- We prove that it is impossible to build a linearizable implementation of a strongly non-commutative method that satisfies a deterministic sequential specification, in a way that sequential executions of the method are free of RAW and AWAR (Section 5).
- We prove that common methods on ubiquitous and fundamental abstract data types–such as sets, queues, work-stealing queues, stacks, and read-modify-write objects–are strongly non-commutative and are subject to our results (Section 6).
- We prove that it is impossible to build an algorithm that satisfies mutual exclusion, is deadlock-free and avoids both RAW and AWAR (Section 4).

Practical Implications. Our results have several implications:

- Designers of concurrent algorithms can use our results to determine when looking for a design without RAW and AWAR is futile. Conversely, our results indicate when avoidance of these patterns may be possible.
- For processor architects, our result indicates the importance of optimizing the performance of atomic operations such as compare-and-swap and RAW fence instructions, which have historically received little attention for optimization.
- For synthesis and verification of concurrent algorithms, our result is potentially useful in the sense that a synthesizer or a verifier need not generate or attempt to verify algorithms that do not use RAW and AWAR for they are certainly incorrect.

The remainder of the paper is organized as follows. We present an overview of our results with illustrative examples in Section 2. In Section 3, we present the necessary formal machinery. We present our result for mutual exclusion in Section 4 and for linearizable objects in Section 5. In Section 6, we show that many widely used specifications satisfy the conditions outlined in Section 5 and hence are subject to our result. We discuss related work in Section 7 and conclude the paper with Section 8.

2. Overview

In this section we explain our results informally, give an intuition of the formal proof presented in later sections and show concurrent algorithms that exemplify our result.

As mentioned already, our result focuses on two practical specifications for concurrent algorithms: mutual exclusion [11, 31] and linearizability [23].

Informally, our result states that if we are to build a mutual exclusion algorithm or a linearizable algorithm, then in certain sequential executions of that algorithm, we must use either RAW or AWAR. That is, if all executions of the algorithm do not use RAW or AWAR, then the algorithm is incorrect.

2.1 Mutual Exclusion

Consider the classic mutual exclusion template shown in Fig. 1. Here we have N processes ($N > 1$), with each process acquiring a lock, entering the critical section, and finally releasing the lock. The specification for mutual exclusion states that we cannot have multiple processes in their critical section at the same time. The template does not show the actual code that each process must execute in its lock, critical, and unlock sections. Further, the code executed by different processes need not be identical.

Process 0:	Process 1:		Process N-1:
$lock_0$: ...	$lock_1$: ...	.....	$lock_{N-1}$: ...
CS_0: ...	CS_1: ...	.....	CS_{N-1}: ...
$unlock_0$: ...	$unlock_1$: ...	.....	$unlock_{N-1}$: ...

Figure 1. N-process mutual exclusion template, for $N > 1$.

```
lock_i:
  while ( ¬ CAS(Lock,FREE,BUSY) );
```

Figure 2. Illustrating AWAR: a simplified snippet of a test-and-set lock acquire.

```
lock_i:
  flag[i] = true;
  while (flag[¬i])...
```

Figure 3. Illustrating RAW: simplified snippet from the lock section of Dekker's 2-way mutual exclusion algorithm (here $0 \leq i < 2$).

Our result states that whenever a process has sequentially executed its $lock$ section, then this execution must use RAW or AWAR. Otherwise, the algorithm does not satisfy the mutual exclusion specification and is incorrect.

2.1.1 Informal Proof Explanation

Let us now give an intuition for the proof on a simplified case where the system is in its initial state, i.e., all processes are just about to enter their respective $lock$ sections, but have not yet done so. Let us pick an arbitrary process i, $0 \leq i < N$, and let process i sequentially execute its $lock_i$ section, enter the critical section CS_i, and then stop. Let us assume that process i did not perform a shared write when it executed its $lock_i$ section.

Now, let us select another process $j \neq i$, $0 \leq j < N$. As process i did not write to the shared state, there is no way for process j to know where process i is. Therefore, process j can fully execute its own $lock_j$ section and enter the critical section CS_j. Now, both processes are inside the critical section, violating mutual exclusion. Therefore we have shown that each process must perform a shared write in its $lock$ section.

Let us now repeat the same exercise and assume that all processes are in the initial state, where they are all just about to enter their respective $lock$ sections, but have not yet done so. We know that each process must write to shared memory in the sequential execution of its lock section. Let us again pick process i to execute its $lock_i$ section sequentially. Assume that process i writes to shared location named X. Now, let us assume that the $lock_i$ section is executed by process i sequentially without using RAW and AWAR. Since there is no AWAR, it means that the write to X cannot be executed atomically with a previous shared read (be it a read from X or another shared location). There could still be a shared read in $lock_i$ that precedes the write to X, but that read cannot execute atomically with the write to X. Let us now have process i execute until it is about to perform its first shared write operation, and then stop. Now, let process j perform a full sequential execution of its $lock_j$ section (this is possible as process i has not yet written to shared memory so process j is not perturbed). Process j now enters its critical section CS_j and stops. Process i now resumes its $lock_i$

section and immediately performs the shared write to X. Once process i writes to X, it over-writes any changes to X that process j made. This means that if process i is to know where process j is, it must read a shared memory location other than X. However, we assumed that there is no RAW which means that process i cannot read a shared location other than X, without previously having written to that location. In turn, this implies that process i cannot observe where process j is, that is, process j cannot influence the execution of process i. Hence, process i continues and completes its $lock_i$ section and enters its critical section, leading to a violation of mutual exclusion. Therefore, any sequential execution of a $lock$ section requires the use of either AWAR or RAW.

2.1.2 Examples

Here, we show several examples of mutual exclusion algorithms that indeed use either RAW or AWAR in their lock sections. These examples are specific implementations that highlight the applicability of our result, namely that implementation of algorithms that satisfy the mutual exclusion specification cannot avoid both RAW and AWAR.

One of the most common lock implementations is based on the test-and-set atomic sequence. Its lock acquire operation boils down to an AWAR pattern, by using an atomic operation, e.g., CAS, to atomically read a lock variable, check that it represents a free lock, and if so replace it with an indicator of a busy lock. Fig. 2 shows a simplified version of a test-and-set-lock. Similar pattern is used in all other locks that require the use of read-modify-write atomic operations in every lock acquire [2, 18, 36].

On the other hand, a mutual exclusion lock algorithm that avoids AWAR [6, 11, 41], must use RAW. For example, Fig. 3 shows a simplified snippet from the lock section of Dekker's algorithm [11] for 2-process mutual exclusion. A process that succeeds in entering its critical section must first raise its own flag and then read the other flag to check that the other process's flag is not raised. Thus, the lock section involves a RAW pattern.

2.2 Linearizability

The second part of our result discusses linearizable algorithms [23]. Intuitively, an algorithm is linearizable with respect to a sequential specification if each execution of the algorithm is equivalent to some sequential execution of the specification, where the order between the non-overlapping methods is preserved. The equivalence is defined by comparing the arguments and results of method invocations.

Unlike mutual exclusion where *all* sequential executions of a certain method (i.e., the $lock$ section) must use either RAW or AWAR, in the case of linearizability, only *some* sequential executions of specific methods must use either RAW or AWAR. We quantify these methods and their executions in terms of properties on *sequential* specifications. Any algorithm implementation that claims to satisfy these properties on the sequential specifications is subject to our results. The two properties are:

- *Deterministic sequential specifications*: Informally, we say that a sequential specification is deterministic if a method executes from the same state will always produce the same result. Many classic abstract data types have deterministic specifications: sets, queues, etc.
- *Strongly non-commutative methods*: Informally, a method m_1 is said to be strongly non-commutative if there exists some state in the specification from which m_1 executed sequentially by process p can influence the result of a method m_2 executed sequentially by process q, $q \neq p$, and vice versa, m_2 can influence the result of m_1 from the same state. Note that m_1 and m_2 are performed by different processes.

$$\{\mathcal{S} = \mathcal{A}\} \quad \texttt{contains}(k) \quad \{ret = k \in \mathcal{A} \wedge \mathcal{S} = \mathcal{A}\}$$

$$\{\mathcal{S} = \mathcal{A}\} \quad \texttt{add}(k) \quad \{ret = k \notin \mathcal{A} \wedge \mathcal{S} = \mathcal{A} \cup \{k\}\}$$

$$\{\mathcal{S} = \mathcal{A}\} \quad \texttt{remove}(k) \quad \{ret = k \in \mathcal{A} \wedge \mathcal{S} = \mathcal{A} \setminus \{k\}\}$$

Figure 4. Sequential specification of a set. $\mathcal{S} \subset \mathbb{N}$ denotes the contents of the set. ret denotes the return value.

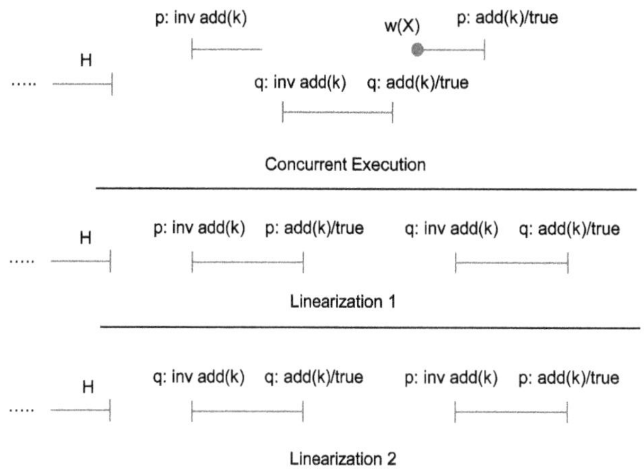

Figure 5. Illustration of the reasoning for why RAW is required in linearizable algorithms.

Our result states that if we have an implementation of a strongly non-commutative method m, then there are *some sequential* executions of m that must use RAW or AWAR. That is, if all sequential executions of m do not use RAW or AWAR, then the algorithm implementation is not linearizable with respect to the given sequential specification.

Let us illustrate these concepts with an example: a Hoare-style sequential specification of a classic Set, shown in Fig. 4 where each method can be executed by more than one process.

First, this simple sequential specification is deterministic: if an `add`, `remove` or `contains` execute from a given state, they will always return the same result.

Second, both methods, `add` and `remove` are strongly non-commutative. For `add`, *there exists* an execution of the specification by a process such that `add` can influence the result of `add` which is executed by another process. For example, let us begin with $\mathcal{S} = \emptyset$. Then, if process p performs an `add(5)`, it will return *true* and a subsequent `add(5)` will return *false*. However, if we change the order, and the second `add(5)` executes first, then it will return *true* while the first `add(5)` will return *false*. That is, `add` is a strongly non-commutative method as there exists another method where both method invocations influence each other's result starting from some state (i.e.,$\mathcal{S} = \emptyset$). In this case it happens to be another `add` method, but in general the two methods could be different. Similar reasoning shows why `remove` is strongly non-commutative. However, `contains` is *not* a strongly non-commutative method, as even though its result can be influenced by a preceding `add` or `remove`, its execution cannot influence the result of any of the three methods `add`, `remove` or `contains`, regardless of the state from which `contains` starts executing.

For the Set specification, our result states that *any* linearizable implementation of the strongly non-commutativie methods `add` and `remove` *must* use RAW or AWAR in *some sequential* execution of the implementation. For example, let us consider a sequential execution of `add(k)` starting from a state where $k \notin \mathcal{S}$. Then this sequential execution must use RAW or AWAR. However, our result does not apply to the sequential execution of `add(k)` where $k \in \mathcal{S}$. In that case, regardless of whether `add(k)` is performed, the result of any other subsequent method performed right after `add(k)` is unaffected.

2.2.1 Informal Proof Explanation

The proof steps in the case of linearizable implementations are very similar to the ones already outlined in the case of mutual exclusion implementations. Intuitively, if a method is strongly non-commutative, then any of its sequential executions must perform a shared write. Otherwise, there is no way for the method to influence the result of any other method that is executed after it, and hence the method cannot be strongly non-commutative. Let us illustrate how we reason about why RAW or AWAR should be present on our set example.

By contradiction, let us assume that RAW and AWAR are not present. Consider the concurrent execution in Fig. 5. Here, some prefix of the execution marked as H has completed and at the end of H, $k \notin \mathcal{S}$. Then, process p invokes method `add(k)` and executes it up to the first shared write (to a location called X), and then p is preempted. Then, another process q performs a full sequential execution of `add(k)` (for the same k) which returns *true*. After that, p resumes its execution and immediately performs the shared write, and completes its execution of `add(k)` and also returns *true*. The reason why both returned *true* is similar to the case for mutual exclusion: the write to X by p overwrites any writes to X that q has made and as we assumed that RAW is not allowed, it follows that process p cannot read any locations other than X in its subsequent steps without having previously written to them. Hence, both `add(k)`'s return the same value *true*.

Now, if the algorithm is linearizable, there could only be two valid linearizations as shown in Fig. 5. However, it is easy to see that both linearizations are incorrect as they do not conform to the specification: if $k \notin \mathcal{S}$ at the end of H, then according to the set specification, executing two `add(k)`'s sequentially in a row cannot lead to both `add(k)`'s returning the same result. Therefore, either RAW or AWAR must be present in some sequential executions of `add(k)`.

More generally, as we will see in Section 5, we show this for any deterministic specification, not only for sets. We will see that the central reason why both linearizations are not allowed is because the result of `add(k)` executed by process q is not influenced by the preceding `add(k)` executed by process p, violating the assumption that `add()` is a strongly non-commutative method.

2.2.2 Practical Implications

While our result shows when it is impossible to eliminate both RAW and AWAR, the result can also be used to guide the search for linearizable algorithms where it may be possible to eliminate RAW and AWAR, by changing one or more of the following dimensions:

- *Deterministic Specification*: change the sequential specification, perhaps by considering non-deterministic specifications.
- *Strong Non-Commutativity*: focus on methods that are not strongly non-commutative, i.e.,`contains` instead of `add`.
- *Single-Owner*: restrict the specification such that a method can only be performed by a single process, instead of multiple processes (as we will see later, technically, this is also part of the strong non-commutativity definition).

```
    bool WFCAS(Val ev, Val nv) {
14:  if (ev == nv) return WFRead()==ev;
15:  Blk b = L;
16:  b.X = p;
17:  if (b.Y) goto 27;
     ...
```

Figure 6. Adapted snippet from Luchagco et al.'s [34] wait-free CAS algorithm.

- *Execution Detectors*: design efficient detectors that can identify executions which are known to be commutative.

The first three of these pertain to the specification and we illustrate two of them (deterministic specification and single-owner) in the examples that follow. The last one is focused on the implementation. As mentioned already, for linearizability our result holds for *some sequential* executions. However, when implementing an algorithm, it may be difficult to differentiate the sequential executions of a given method for which the result holds and those for which it does not. However, if a designer is able to come up with an efficient mechanism to identify these cases, it may be possible to avoid RAW and AWAR in the executions where it may not be required. For instance, if the method can check that $k \in \mathcal{S}$ before `add(k)` is performed, then for those sequential executions of `add(k)` it may not need to use neither RAW nor AWAR.

Even though our result only talks about *some* sequential executions, in practice, it is often difficult to design efficient tests that differentiate sequential executions, and hence, it often ends up the case that RAW or AWAR is used on *all* sequential executions of a strongly non-commutative linearizable method.

2.3 Examples: Linearizable Algorithms

Next, we illustrate the applicability of our result in practice via several well-known linearizable algorithms.

2.3.1 Compare and Swap

We begin with the universal compare-and-swap (CAS) construct, whose sequential specification is deterministic, and the method is strongly non-commutative (for a formal proof, see Section 6). The sequential specification of CAS(m, o, n) says that it first compares $[m]$ to o and if $[m] = o$, then n is assigned to $[m]$ and CAS returns *true*. Otherwise, $[m]$ is unchanged and CAS returns *false*. Here we use the operator [] to denote address dereference.

The CAS specification can be implemented trivially with a linearizable algorithm that uses an atomic hardware instruction (also called CAS) and in that case, the implementation inherently includes the AWAR pattern.

Alternatively, the CAS specification can be implemented by a linearizable algorithm using reads, writes, and hardware CAS, with the goal of avoiding the use of the hardware CAS in the *common* case of no contention. Such a linearizable algorithm is presented by Luchangco et al. [34]. Fig. 6 shows an adapted code snippet of the common path of that algorithm. While the algorithm succeeds in avoiding the AWAR pattern in the common case, the algorithm does indeed include the RAW pattern in its common path. To ensure correctness, the write to `b.X` in line 16 *must* precede the read of `b.Y` in line 17.

Both examples confirm our result: AWAR or RAW was necessary. Knowing that RAW or AWAR cannot be avoided in implementing CAS correctly is important as CAS is a fundamental building block for many classic concurrent algorithms.

```
    WorkItem take() {
1:    b = bottom;
2:    CircularArray a = activeArray;
3:    b = b - 1;
4:    bottom = b;
5:    t = top;
      ...
```

Figure 7. Snippet adapted from the `take` method of Chase-Lev's work stealing algorithm [10].

```
WorkItem take() {
  h = head;
  t = tail;
  if (h = t) return EMPTY;
  task = tasks.array[h%tasks.size];
  head = h+1;
  return task;
}
```

Figure 8. The `take` method from Michael et al.'s idempotent work stealing FIFO queue [38].

2.3.2 Work Stealing Structures

Concurrent work stealing algorithms are popular algorithms for implementing load balancing frameworks.

A work stealing structure holds a collection of work items and it has a single process as its owner. It supports three main methods: `put`, `take`, and `steal`. Only the owner can insert and extract work items via methods `put` and `take`. Other processes (thieves) may extract work items using `steal`.

In designing algorithms for work stealing, the highest priority is to optimize the owner's methods, especially the common paths of such methods, as they are expected to be the most frequently executed parts of the methods. Examining known work stealing algorithms that avoid the AWAR pattern (i.e., avoid the use of complex atomic operations) in the common path of the owner's methods [3, 16, 19, 20], reveals that they all contain the RAW pattern in the common path of the `take` method that succeeds in extracting work items.

The work stealing algorithm by Chase and Lev [10] is representative of such algorithms. Fig. 7 shows a code snippet adapted from the common path of the `take` method of that algorithm, with minor changes for the sake of consistency in presentation. The variables `bottom` and `top` are shared variables, and `bottom` is written only by the owner but may be read by other processes. The key pattern in this code snippet is the RAW pattern in lines 4 and 5. The order of the write to `bottom` in line 4 followed by the read of `top` in line 5 is necessary for the correctness of the algorithm. Reversing the order of these two instructions results in an incorrect algorithm. In subsequent sections, we will see why correct implementations of the `take` and `steal` methods must use either RAW or AWAR.

From deterministic to non-deterministic specifications Our result dictates that in the standard case where we have the expected deterministic sequential specification of a work-stealing structure, it is impossible to avoid both RAW and AWAR. However, as mentioned earlier, our result can guide us towards finding practical cases where we can indeed eliminate RAW and AWAR. Indeed, relaxing the deterministic specification may allow us to come up with algorithms that avoid both RAW and AWAR. Such a relaxation is exemplified by the idempotent work stealing introduced by Michael et al. [38]. This concept relaxes the semantics of work stealing to require that each inserted item is eventually extracted *at least once* instead of *exactly once*. Under this notion the authors managed to design algorithms for idempotent work stealing that avoid both the AWAR and RAW patterns in the owner's methods.

Our result explains the underlying reason of why the elimination of RAW and AWAR was possible: because the sequential specification of idempotent structures is necessarily non-deterministic, our result now indicates that it may be possible to avoid RAW and AWAR. Indeed, this is confirmed by the algorithms in [38]. Fig. 8 shows the `take` method of one of the idempotent algorithms. Note the absence of both AWAR and RAW in this code. The shared variables `head`, `tail`, and `tasks.array[]` are read before writing to `head`, and no reads need to be atomic with the subsequent write.

2.3.3 FIFO Queue Example

In examining concurrent algorithms for multi-consumer FIFO queues, one notes that either locking or CAS is used in the common path of nontrivial `dequeue` methods that return a dequeued item. However, as we mentioned already, our result proves that mutual exclusion locking requires each sequential execution of a successful lock acquire to include AWAR or RAW. All algorithms that avoid the use of locking in `dequeue` include a CAS operation in the common path of each nontrivial `dequeue` execution. Fig. 9 shows the simplified code snippet from the `dequeue` method of the classic Michael and Scott's lock-free FIFO queue [37]. Note that every execution that returns an item must execute CAS.

We observe that algorithms for *multi-consumer* `dequeue` include directly or indirectly at least one instance of the AWAR or RAW patterns (i.e., use either locking or CAS).

From Multi-Owner to Single-Owner Our results suggest that if we want to eliminate RAW and AWAR, we can focus on restricting the processes that can execute a method. For instance, we can specify that `dequeue` can be executed only be a single process. Indeed, when we consider single-consumer FIFO queues, where no more than one process can execute the `dequeue` method, we can obtain a correct implementation of `dequeue` which does not require RAW and AWAR.

```
Data dequeue() {
  h = head;
  t = tail;
  next = h.next;
  if head ≠ h goto 1;
  if next = null return EMPTY;
  if h = t {CAS(tail,t,next) ; goto 1; }
  d = next.data;
  if ¬CAS(head,h,next) goto 1;
  return d;
}
```

Figure 9. Simplified snippet of `dequeue` on lock-free FIFO queue [37].

```
Data dequeue() {
  if (tail = head) return EMPTY;
  Data data = Q[head mod m];
  head = head +1 mod m;
  return data;
}
```

Figure 10. Single-consumer `dequeue` method adapted from Lamport's FIFO queue which does not use RAW and AWAR [30].

$$
\begin{array}{rclll}
x, y & \in & Var & & \\
m & \in & MID & & \\
l & \in & Lab & & \\
B & \in & BExp & ::= & \ldots \\
E & \in & NExp & ::= & \ldots \\
C & \in & Com & ::= & l : x = E \mid l : x = G[E] \mid \\
 & & & & l : G[E] = E \mid l : \textbf{if } B \textbf{ goto } l \mid \\
 & & & & l : \textbf{beg-atomic} \mid l : \textbf{end-atomic} \\
 & & & & l : \textbf{entry } m\, \vec{x} \mid l : \textbf{exit } m\, x \\
 & & & & C; C \\
P & & & ::= & C \parallel \ldots \parallel C
\end{array}
$$

Figure 11. Language Syntax

Fig. 10 shows a single-consumer `dequeue` method, adapted from Lamport's single-producer single-consumer FIFO queue [30].[2] Note that the code avoids both RAW and AWAR. The variable `head` is private to the single consumer and its update is done by a regular write. Once again, this example demonstrates a case where we used our result to guide the implementation. In particular, by changing the specification of a method of the abstract data type–namely from multi-consumer to single-consumer–it enabled us to create an implementation of the method (i.e., `dequeue`) where we did not need RAW and AWAR.

3. Preliminaries

In this section, we present the formal machinery necessary to specify and prove our results later.

3.1 Language

The language shown in Fig. 11 is a basic assembly language with labeled statements: assignments, sequencing and conditional goto's. We do not elaborate on the construction of numerical and boolean expressions, which are standard. The language is also equipped with the following features:

- Statements for beginning and ending of atomic sections. Using these, one can implement various universal constructs such as compare-and-swap.
- Parallel composition of sequential commands.
- We use *G* to model global memory via a one dimensional array.
- Two statements are used to denote the start (i.e., entry statement) and end of a method (i.e., exit statement).

We use Var to denote the set of local variables for each process, *MID* to denote a finite set of method identifiers, *Lab* the set of program labels and *PID* a finite set of process identifiers. We assume the set of values obtained from expression evaluation includes at least the integers and the booleans.

3.2 Semantics

A *program state* σ is a tuple $\langle pc, locals, G, inatomic \rangle \in \Sigma$:

- $\Sigma = PC \times Locals \times Globals \times InAtomic$
- $PC = PID \rightharpoonup Lab$
- $Locals = PID \times Var \rightharpoonup Val$
- $Globals = Val \rightharpoonup Val$
- $InAtomic = PID \cup \bot$

[2] The restriction or the lack of restriction on the number of concurrent producers does not affect the algorithm for the `dequeue` method.

A state σ tracks the program counter for each process (*pc*), a mapping from process local variables to values ($locals$), the contents of global memory (*G*) and whether a process executes atomically ($inatomic$). If no process executes atomically then $inatomic$ is set to $\bot$. We denote the set of initial states as $Init \subseteq \Sigma$ (Initially $inatomic$ is set to $\bot$ for all states in $Init$).

Transition Function We assume standard small-step operational semantics given in terms of transitions between states [45]. The behavior of a program is determined by a partial transition function $TF \colon \Sigma \times PID \rightharpoonup \Sigma$. Given a state σ and a process p, $TF(\sigma, p)$ returns the unique state, if it exists, that the program will evolve into once p executes its enabled statement. When convenient, we sometimes use the function TF as a relation.

For a transition $t \in TF$, we denote its source state by $src(t)$, its executing process by $proc(t)$, its destination state by $dst(t)$, its executing statement by $stmt(t)$. A program transition represents the intuitive fact that starting from a state $src(t)$, process $proc(t)$ can execute the statement $stmt(t)$ and end up in a state $dst(t)$, that is, $TF(src(t), proc(t)) = dst(t)$. We say that a transition t performs a global read (resp. write) if $stmt(t)$ reads from *G* (resp. writes to) and use $mloc(t)$ to denote the global memory location that the transition accesses. If the transition does not read or write a global location, then $mloc(t)$ returns $\bot$. That is, only in the case where a transition t accesses a global memory location does $mloc(t)$ return a non-$\bot$ value, otherwise, $mloc(t)$ always returns $\bot$.

We enforce strong atomicity semantics: for any state σ, process p can make a transition from σ only if $inatomic_\sigma = \bot$ or $inatomic_\sigma = p$. For a transition t, if $stmt(t) =$ **beg-atomic**, then $inatomic_{dst(t)} = proc(t)$. Similarly, if $stmt(t) =$ **end-atomic**, $inatomic_{dst(t)} = \bot$. We use $enabled_\sigma$ to denote the set of processes that can make a transition from σ. If $inatomic_\sigma \neq \bot$, then $enabled_\sigma = \{inatomic_\sigma\}$, otherwise $enabled_\sigma = PID$.

The statement **entry** $m\,\vec{x}$ is used to denote the start of a method invoked with a sequence of variables which contain the arguments to the method (denoted by $\vec{x}$). The statement **exit** $m\,x$ is used to denote the end of a method m. These statements do not affect the program state (except the program counter). The meaning of the other statements in the language is standard.

Executions An execution π is a (possibly infinite) sequence of transitions $\pi_0, \pi_1, \ldots$, where $\forall i \geq 0,\ \pi_i \in TF$ and $\forall j \geq 1.\ dst(\pi_{j-1}) = src(\pi_j)$. We use $first(\pi)$ as a shortcut for $src(\pi_0)$, i.e., the first state in the execution π, and, $last(\pi)$ to denote the last state in the execution π, i.e., $last(\pi) = dst(\pi_{|\pi|-1})$. If a transition t is performed in an execution π then $t \in \pi$ is *true*, otherwise it is *false*.

For a program Prog, we use $[\![\text{Prog}]\!]$ to denote the set of executions for that program starting from initial states (e.g. states in $Init$). Next, we define what it means for an execution $\pi \in [\![\text{Prog}]\!]$ to be *atomic*:

Definition 3.1 (Atomic Execution). *We say that an execution π is executed atomically by process p when:*

- *All transitions are performed by p:* $\forall i.\ 0 \leq i < |\pi|.\ proc(\pi_i) = p$.
- *All transitions are atomic:* $|\pi| = 1$ *or* $\forall i.\ 1 \leq i < |\pi|,\ inatomic_{src(\pi_i)} = p$.

We use $\pi_{(i,j)}$ to denote the substring of π occurring between positions i and j (including the transitions at i and j).

Definition 3.2 (Maximal Atomic Cover). *Given an execution π and a transition $\pi_k \in \pi$, the* maximal atomic cover *of π_k in π is the unique substring $\pi_{(i,j)}$ of π, where:*

- *$\pi_{(i,j)}$ is executed atomically by $proc(\pi_k)$, where $i \leq k \leq j$.*

- $inatomic_{src(\pi_i)} = \bot$.
- $inatomic_{dst(\pi_j)} = \bot$.

Intuitively, we can understand the maximal atomic cover as taking a transition and extending it in both directions until we reach a leftmost state and a rightmost state where no process is inside an atomic section in either of these two states.

Next, we define read-after-write executions:

Definition 3.3 (Read After Write Execution). *We say that a process p performs a* read-after-write *in execution* π, *if* $\exists i, j.\ 0 \leq i < j < |\pi|$ *such that:*

- π_i *performs a global write by process p.*
- π_j *performs a global read by process p.*
- $mloc(\pi_i) \neq mloc(\pi_j)$ *(the memory locations are different).*
- $\forall k.\ i < k < j$, *if* $proc(\pi_k) = p$, *then* $mloc(\pi_k) \neq mloc(\pi_j)$.

Intuitively, these are executions where somewhere in the execution the process writes to global memory location A and then, sometimes later, reads a global memory location B that is different from A, and in-between the process does not access B. Note that there could be transitions in π performed by processes other than p. Note that in this definition there is no restriction on whether the global accesses are performed atomically or not, the definition only concerns itself with the ordering of accesses and not their atomicity.

We introduce the predicate $\texttt{RAW}(\pi, p)$ which evaluates to *true* if p performs a *read-after-write* in execution π and to *false* otherwise.

Next, we define atomic write-after-read executions. These are executions where a process first reads from a global memory location and then, sometimes later, writes to a global memory location and these two accesses occur atomically, that is, in-between these two accesses, no other process can perform any transitions. Note that unlike read-after-write executions, here, the global read and write need *not* access different memory locations.

Definition 3.4 (Atomic Write After Read Execution). *We say that a process p performs an* atomic write-after-read *in execution* π, *if* $\exists i, j.\ 0 \leq i < j < |\pi|$ *such that:*

- *process p performs a global read in* π_i.
- *process p performs a global write in* π_j.
- $\pi_{(i,j)}$ *is executed atomically by process p.*

We introduce the predicate $\texttt{AWAR}(\pi, p)$ which evaluates to *true* if process p performs an atomic write-after-read in execution π and to *false* otherwise.

3.3 Specification

3.3.1 Histories

A *history* H is defined as a finite sequence of actions, i.e., $H = \psi; \psi ...; \psi$, where an action denotes the start and end of a method:

$$\psi = (p, \textbf{entry}\ m\ \vec{a}) \mid (p, \textbf{exit}\ m\ r)$$

where $p \in PID$ is a process identifier, $m \in MID$ is a method identifier, $\vec{a}$ is a sequence of arguments to the method and r is the return value. For an action ψ, we use $proc(\psi)$ to denote the process, $kind(\psi)$ to denote the kind of the action (entry or exit), and $m(\psi)$ to denote the name of the method. We use H_i to denote the action at position i in the history, where $0 \leq i < |H|$. For a process p, $H\downharpoonright_p$ is used to denote the subsequence of H consisting only of the actions of process p. For a method m, $H\downharpoonright_m$ is used to denote the subsequence of H consisting only of the actions of method m.

A method entry $(p, \textbf{entry}\ m_1\ \vec{a_1})$ is said to be *pending* in a history H if it has no matching exit, that is, $\exists i.\ 0 \leq i < |H|$ such that $proc(H_i) = p$, $kind(H_i) = entry$, $m(H_i) = m_1$ and $\forall j.\ i < j < |H|$, $proc(H_j) \neq p$ or $kind(H_j) \neq exit$ or $m(H_j) \neq m_1$. A history H is said to be *complete* if it has no pending calls. We use *complete*(H) to denote the set of histories resulting after extending H with matching exits to a subset of entries that are pending in H and then removing the remaining pending entries.

A history H is *sequential* if H is empty ($H = \epsilon$) or H starts with an entry action, i.e., $kind(H_0) = entry$ and if $|H| > 1$, entries and exits alternate. That is, $\forall i.\ 0 \leq i < |H| - 1, kind(H_i) \neq kind(H_{i+1})$ and each exit is matched by an entry that occurs immediately before it in H, i.e., $\forall i.\ 1 \leq i < |H|$, if $kind(H_i) = exit$ then $kind(H_{i-1}) = entry$ and $proc(H_i) = proc(H_{i-1})$. A complete sequential history H is said to be a *complete invocation* of a method m_1 iff $|H| = 2$, $m(H_0) = m_1$ and $m(H_1) = m_1$. In the case where H is a complete sequential invocation, we use $entry(H)$ to denote the entry action in H and $exit(H)$ to denote the exit action in H. A history H is *well-formed* if for each process $p \in PID$, $H\downharpoonright_p$ is sequential. In this work, we consider only well-formed histories.

3.4 Histories and Executions

Given an execution π, we use the function $hs(\pi)$ to denote the history of π. $hs(\pi)$ takes as input an execution π and produces a sequence of actions by iterating over each transition $t \in \pi$ in order, and extracting $proc(t)$ and $stmt(t)$. If $stmt(t)$ is an entry statement of a method m, then the transition t contributes the action $(proc(t), \textbf{entry}\ m\ \vec{a})$, where $\vec{a}$ is the sequence of values obtained from evaluating the variables used in the sequence $stmt(t)$, in state $src(t)$. Similarly, for exit statements. If the transition t does not perform an entry or an exit statement, then it contributes ϵ.

For a program Prog, we define its corresponding set of histories as $[\![\text{Prog}]\!]_H = \{hs(\pi) \mid \pi \in [\![\text{Prog}]\!]\}$. We use $[\![\text{Prog}]\!]_{HS}$ to denote the sequential histories in $[\![\text{Prog}]\!]_H$.

A transition $t \in \pi$ is said to be a *method* transition if it is performed in-between method entry and exit. That is, there exists a preceding transition $t_{prev} \in \pi$ that performs an entry statement with $proc(t_{prev}) = proc(t)$, such that $proc(t)$ does not perform an exit statement in-between t_{prev} and t in π. We say that t_{prev} is a matching entry transition for t. Note that t_{prev} may be the same as t. A transition that is not a method transition is said to be a *client* transition.

Definition 3.5 (Well-formed Execution). *We say that an execution* π *is well-formed if:*

- $hs(\pi)$ *is well-formed.*
- *Any client transition* $t \in \pi$:
  - $mloc(t) = \bot$.
  - $stmt(t) \neq$ ***beg-atomic*** *and* $stmt(t) \neq$ ***end-atomic***.
- *For any transition* $t \in \pi$, *if* $stmt(t)$ *is an exit statement, then* $inatomic_{src(t)} = \bot$.
- *For any transition* $t_r \in \pi$, *if* t_r *is a method transition that reads a local variable other than the variables specified in the statement of its matching entry transition* t_m, *then there exists a transition* t_w *performed by process* $proc(t)$, *in-between* t_m *and* t_r, *such that* t_w *writes to that local variable.*

That is, a well-formed execution is one where its history is well-formed, only method transitions are allowed to access global memory or perform atomic statements, when a method exit statement is performed, the $inatomic$ should be $\bot$, and methods must initialize local variables which are not used for argument passing before using them.

We say that π is a *complete sequential execution* of a method m by process p, if π is a well-formed execution and $hs(\pi)$ is a complete invocation of m by process p. Note that π may contain client transitions (both by process p and other processes).

A program Prog is *well-formed* if $[\![\text{Prog}]\!]$ contains only well-formed executions. In this paper, we only consider well-formed programs.

4. Synchronization in Mutual Exclusion

In this section, we consider implementations that provide mutually exclusive access to a critical section among a set of processes. We show that every deadlock-free mutual exclusion implementation incurs either the RAW or the AWAR pattern in certain executions.

A mutual exclusion implementation exports the following methods: $MID = \{lock_0, unlock_0, \ldots, lock_{n-1}, unlock_{n-1}\}$, where $n = |PID|$. In this setting, we strengthen the definition of well-formed executions by requiring that each process $p \in PID$ only invokes methods $lock_p$ and $unlock_p$ in an alternating fashion. That is, for any execution $\pi \in [\![\text{Prog}]\!]$ and for any process $p \in PID$, $hs(\pi)\downharpoonright_p$ is such that lock and unlock operations alternate, i.e., $lock_p, unlock_p, lock_p, \ldots$.

Given an execution $\pi \in [\![\text{Prog}]\!]$ and $H = hs(\pi)\downharpoonright_p$, we say that p is in its trying section if it has started, but not yet completed a $lock_p$ operation, i.e., $m(H_{|H|-1}) = lock_p$ and $kind(H_{|H|-1}) = entry$. We say that p is in its critical section if it has completed $lock_p$ but has not yet started $unlock_p$, that is, $m(H_{|H|-1}) = lock_p$ and $kind(H_{|H|-1}) = exit$. We say that p is in its exit section if it has started $unlock_p$ but has not yet finished it, that is, $m(H_{|H|-1}) = unlock_p$ and $kind(H_{|H|-1}) = entry$. Otherwise we say that p is in the remainder section (initially all processes are in their remainder sections). A process is called *active* if it is in its trying or exit section.

For the purpose of our lower bound, we assume the following weak formulation of the mutual exclusion problem [11, 31]. In addition to the classical mutual exclusion requirement, we only require that the implementation is *deadlock-free*, i.e., if a number of active processes concurrently compete for the critical section, at least one of them succeeds.

Definition 4.1 (Mutual Exclusion). *A deadlock-free mutual exclusion implementation Prog guarantees:*

- *Safety: For all executions $\pi \in [\![Prog]\!]$, it is always the case that at most one process is in its critical section at a time, that is, for all $p, q \in$ PID, if p is in its critical section in $\text{hs}(\pi)\downharpoonright_p$ and q is in its critical section in $\text{hs}(\pi)\downharpoonright_q$, then $p = q$.*
- *Liveness: In every execution in which every active process takes sufficiently many steps: i) if at least one process is in its trying section and no process is in its critical section, then at some point later some process enters its critical section, and ii) if at least one process is in its exit section, then at some point later some process enters its remainder section.*

Theorem 4.2 (RAW or AWAR in Mutual Exclusion). *Let Prog be a deadlock-free mutual exclusion implementation for two or more processes ($|\text{PID}| > 1$). Then, for every complete sequential execution π of $lock_p$ by process p:*

- $\mathtt{RAW}(\pi, p) = \text{true}$, *or*
- $\mathtt{AWAR}(\pi, p) = \text{true}$

Proof. Let $\pi_{base} \cdot \pi \in [\![\text{Prog}]\!]$ such that π is a complete sequential execution of $lock_p$ by process p. It follows that no process $q \in PID$, $q \neq p$, is in its critical section in $hs(\pi_{base})\downharpoonright_q$ (otherwise mutual exclusion would be violated). It also follows that p is not active in $hs(\pi_{base})\downharpoonright_p$.

By contradiction, assume that π does not contain a global write. Consider an execution $\pi_{base} \cdot \rho$ such that process p does not perform transitions in ρ and every active process takes sufficiently many steps in ρ until some process $q \neq p$ completes its $lock_q$ section, i.e., q is in its critical section in $hs(\pi_{base} \cdot \rho)\downharpoonright_q$. The execution $\pi_{base} \cdot \rho \in [\![\text{Prog}]\!]$ since Prog is deadlock-free.

Since p does not write to a shared location in π, $G_{last(\pi_{base})} = G_{last(\pi_{base} \cdot \pi)}$. Further, the local state of all processes other than p in $last(\pi_{base})$ is the same as their local state in $last(\pi_{base} \cdot \pi)$, i.e., $\forall q \in PID, \forall var \in Var$, if $q \neq p$, then $locals_{last(\pi_{base})}(q, var) = locals_{last(\pi_{base} \cdot \pi)}(q, var)$. Also, we know $enabled_{last(\pi_{base})} = enabled_{last(\pi_{base} \cdot \pi)}$ as transitions by process p do not access local variables of other processes. Hence, we can build the execution $\pi_{nc} = \pi_{base} \cdot \pi \cdot \rho'$ where ρ' is the execution with the same sequence of statements as ρ (i.e., process p does not perform transitions in ρ'). Hence, $hs(\pi_{nc})\downharpoonright_q = hs(\pi_{base} \cdot \rho)\downharpoonright_q$, that is, q is in its critical section in $hs(\pi_{nc})\downharpoonright_q$. But p is also in its critical section in $hs(\pi_{nc})\downharpoonright_p$ — a contradiction.

Thus, π contains a global write, and let t_w be the *first* global write transition in π. Let $\pi = \pi_f \cdot \pi_w \cdot \pi_l$, where π_w is the maximal atomic cover of t_w in π. We proceed by contradiction and assume that $\mathtt{RAW}(\pi, p) = \mathit{false}$ and $\mathtt{AWAR}(\pi, p) = \mathit{false}$. Since $\mathtt{AWAR}(\pi, p) = \mathit{false}$ and t_w is the first write transition in π, it follows that t_w is the first global transition in π_w.

Since π_f contains no global writes, $G_{first(\pi_f)} = G_{last(\pi_f)}$. Applying the same arguments as before, there exists an execution $\pi_{base} \cdot \pi_f \cdot \tau \in [\![\text{Prog}]\!]$ such that some process q, $q \neq p$, is in its critical section in $hs(\pi_{base} \cdot \pi_f \cdot \tau)\downharpoonright_q$.

The assumption $\mathtt{RAW}(\pi, p) = \mathit{false}$ implies that no global read transition by process p in $\pi_w \cdot \pi_l$ accesses a variable other than $mloc(t_w)$ without having previously written to it. Note that t_w overwrites the only location that can be read by p in $\pi_w \cdot \pi_l$. Thus, applying the same arguments as before, there exists an execution $\pi_c = \pi_{base} \cdot \pi_f \cdot \tau \cdot \pi'_w \cdot \pi'_l$ in $[\![\text{Prog}]\!]$ such that q is in its critical section in $hs(\pi_c)\downharpoonright_q$ and p is in its critical section in $hs(\pi_c)\downharpoonright_p$ —a contradiction.

Thus, either $\mathtt{RAW}(\pi, p) = \mathit{true}$ or $\mathtt{AWAR}(\pi, p) = \mathit{true}$. □

5. Synchronization in Linearizable Algorithms

In this section we state and prove that certain sequential executions of strongly non-commutative methods of algorithms that are linearizable with respect to a deterministic sequential specification must use RAW or AWAR.

5.1 Linearizability

Following [21, 23] we define linearizable histories. A history H induces an irreflexive partial order $<_H$ on actions in the history: $a <_H b$ if $kind(a) = exit$ and $kind(b) = entry$ and $\exists i, j.\ 0 \leq i < j < |H|$ such that $H_i = a$ and $H_j = b$. That is, exit action a precedes entry action b in H. A history H is said to be *linearizable* with respect to a sequential history S if there exists a history $H' \in complete(H)$ such that:

1. $\forall p \in PID, H'\downharpoonright_p = S\downharpoonright_p$
2. $<_H \subseteq <_S$.

We can naturally extend this definition to a set of histories. Let $Spec$ be a *sequential specification*, a prefix-closed set of sequential histories (that is, if s is a sequential history in $Spec$, then any prefix of s is also in $Spec$). Then, given a set of histories $Impl$, we say that $Impl$ is linearizable with respect to $Spec$ if for any history $H \in Impl$ there exists a history $S \in Spec$ such that H is linearizable with respect to S.

We say that a program Prog is linearizable with respect to a sequential specification $Spec$ when $[\![\text{Prog}]\!]_H$ is linearizable with respect to $Spec$.

5.2 Deterministic Sequential Specifications

In this paper, similarly to [8], we define deterministic sequential specifications. Given two sequential histories s_1 and s_2, let $\mathtt{maxprefix}(s_1, s_2)$ denote the longest common prefix of the two histories s_1 and s_2.

Definition 5.1 (Deterministic Sequential Specifications). *A sequential specification Spec is deterministic, if for all* $s_1, s_2 \in Spec$, $s_1 \neq s_2$ *and* $\hat{s} = \mathtt{maxprefix}(s_1, s_2)$, *we have* $\hat{s} = \epsilon$ *or* $kind(\hat{s}_{|\hat{s}|-1}) \neq entry$.

That is, a specification is deterministic, if we cannot find two different histories whose longest common prefix ends with an entry. If we can find such a prefix, then that would mean that there was a point in the execution of the two histories s_1 and s_2 up to which they behaved identically, but after they both performed the same entry, they produced different results (or one had no continuation).

5.3 Strong Non-Commutativity

We define a *strongly non-commutative* method as follows:

Definition 5.2 (Strongly Non-Commutative Method). *We say that a method* m_1 *is* strongly non-commutative *in a sequential specification Spec if there exists a method* m_2 *(possibly the same as* m_1*), and there exist histories base,* s_1, s_2, s_3, s_4 *such that:*

1. s_1 *and* s_4 *are complete invocations of* m_1 *with* $entry(s_1) = entry(s_4)$ *and* $exit(s_1) \neq exit(s_4)$.
2. s_2 *and* s_3 *are complete invocations of* m_2 *with* $entry(s_2) = entry(s_3)$ *and* $exit(s_2) \neq exit(s_3)$.
3. $proc(entry(s_1)) \neq proc(entry(s_2))$.
4. *base is a complete sequential history in Spec.*
5. $base \cdot s_2 \cdot s_4 \in Spec$.
6. $base \cdot s_1 \cdot s_3 \in Spec$.

In other words, the method m_1 is strongly non-commutative if there is another method m_2 and a history *base* in $Spec$ such that we can distinguish whether m_1 is applied right after *base* or right after m_2 (which is applied after *base*). Similarly we can distinguish whether m_2 is applied right after *base* or right after m_1 (which is applied after *base*). Note that m_2 may be the same method as m_1.

In this work we focus on programs where the specification $Spec$ can be determined by the sequential executions of the program.

Assumption 1. $Spec = [\![Prog]\!]_{HS}$.

5.4 RAW and AWAR for Linearizability

Next, we state and prove the main result of this section:

Theorem 5.3 (RAW or AWAR in Linearizable Algorithms). *Let* m_1 *be a strongly non-commutative method in a deterministic sequential specification Spec and let* $Prog$ *be a linearizable implementation of Spec. Then there exists a complete sequential execution* π_a *of* m_1 *by process p such that:*

- $RAW(\pi_a, p) =$ true, *or*
- $AWAR(\pi_a, p) =$ true

Proof. From the premise that m_1 is a strongly non-commutative method and Assumption 1, we know that there exist executions $\pi_{base_1} \cdot \pi_a \cdot \pi_c \in [\![\text{Prog}]\!]$ and $\pi_{base_2} \cdot \pi_b \cdot \pi_d \in [\![\text{Prog}]\!]$ such that:

1. $hs(\pi_{base_1})$ and $hs(\pi_{base_2})$ are complete sequential histories.
2. $hs(\pi_{base_1}) = hs(\pi_{base_2})$.
3. π_a and π_d are complete sequential executions of m_1.
4. π_b and π_c are complete sequential executions of m_2.
5. $entry(hs(\pi_a)) = entry(hs(\pi_d))$.
6. $entry(hs(\pi_b)) = entry(hs(\pi_c))$.
7. $exit(hs(\pi_a)) \neq exit(hs(\pi_d))$.
8. $exit(hs(\pi_b)) \neq exit(hs(\pi_c))$.
9. $proc(entry(hs(\pi_a))) \neq proc(entry(hs(\pi_b)))$.

From the fact that executions in the program are well-formed, we know that if π, $\rho \in [\![\text{Prog}]\!]$ and $hs(\pi)$, $hs(\rho)$ are complete sequential invocations such that $entry(hs(\pi)) = entry(hs(\rho))$, and $G_{first(\pi)} = G_{first(\rho)}$, it follows that $hs(\pi) = hs(\rho)$ and $G_{last(\pi)} = G_{last(\rho)}$. That is, if a process completes the same method invocation from two program states with identical global memory, the method will always produce the same result and global memory (Fact 1). Fact 1 follows directly from the fact that transitions are deterministic, processes cannot access the local state of another process, arguments to both methods are the same, and the starting global states are the same.

From Fact 1 and $hs(\pi_{base_1})$, $hs(\pi_{base_2})$ being complete sequential histories, we can show that $G_{last(\pi_{base_1})} = G_{last(\pi_{base_2})}$. That is, from $first(\pi_{base_1}) = first(\pi_{base_2})$ (both are initial states), we can inductively show that any complete sequential invocation preserves the fact that the global state in the last states of the two executions are the same. From $G_{last(\pi_{base_1})} = G_{last(\pi_{base_2})}$, it follows that $G_{first(\pi_a)} = G_{first(\pi_b)}$.

Let $p = proc(entry(hs(\pi_a)))$ and $q = proc(entry(hs(\pi_b)))$. We first prove that a method transition performed by process p must perform a global write in π_a. Let us assume the execution π_a does not contain a method transition where process p performs a global write. As π_a is well-formed, we know that any client transitions performed in π_a do not access global memory. It then follows that $G_{first(\pi_a)} = G_{last(\pi_a)}$. However, from the premise we know that $G_{last(\pi_a)} = G_{first(\pi_c)}$ and hence $G_{first(\pi_a)} = G_{first(\pi_c)}$. Transitively, we know that $G_{first(\pi_b)} = G_{first(\pi_c)}$. From item 4 above we know that π_b and π_c are complete sequential executions of m_2 with $entry(hs(\pi_b)) = entry(hs(\pi_c))$ (item 6). Then, it follows from Fact 1 that $exit(hs(\pi_b)) = exit(hs(\pi_c))$ which contradicts with item 8. Therefore, there must exist a method transition in π_a by process p that performs a global write.

Let us proceed by contradiction and assume that both $\mathtt{RAW}(\pi_a, p) = false$ and $\mathtt{AWAR}(\pi_a, p) = false$. Let $\pi_a = \pi_f \cdot \pi_w \cdot \pi_\ell$, where t_w is the *first* method transition in π_a that writes to global memory and π_w is the maximal atomic cover of t_w in π_a. As π_a is well-formed, we know that all transitions in π_w are method transitions. Since $\mathtt{AWAR}(\pi_a, p) = false$ and t_w is the first global write transition in π_a, it follows that there can be no global read transitions in π_w that occur before t_w (otherwise we would contradict AWAR). This means that t_w is the first *global* read or write transition in π_w.

As π_f does not contain global writes, it follows that $G_{first(\pi_a)} = G_{last(\pi_f)}$. From the premise we know that $G_{first(\pi_a)} = G_{first(\pi_b)}$ and hence $G_{first(\pi_b)} = G_{last(\pi_f)}$. As π_w is a maximal atomic cover, we know that $inatomic_{last(\pi_f)} = \bot$.

From the fact that client transitions cannot synchronize (they cannot execute atomic statements or access global memory), and that a process cannot access the local variables of another process, it follows that process q can execute m_2 concurrently with m_1 from state $last(\pi_f)$. That is, there exists an execution $\pi_{base_1} \cdot \pi_f \cdot \pi'_b \in [\![\text{Prog}]\!]$ where π'_b is a complete sequential execution of m_2 by process q such that $entry(hs(\pi_b)) = entry(hs(\pi'_b))$. As $G_{first(\pi'_b)} = G_{last(\pi_f)}$, it follows that $G_{first(\pi'_b)} = G_{first(\pi_b)}$. Then, by Fact 1, it follows that $hs(\pi'_b) = hs(\pi_b)$.

As $p \in enabled_{first(\pi'_b)}$ and π'_b is a complete sequential execution by process q, it follows that $p \in enabled_{last(\pi'_b)}$. Process p can now continue execution of method m_1 and build the execution $\pi_{base_1} \cdot \pi_{conc} \in [\![\text{Prog}]\!]$ where $\pi_{conc} = \pi_f \cdot \pi'_b \cdot \pi'_w \cdot \pi'_\ell$.

By assumption, we know that $\texttt{RAW}(\pi_a, p)$ and $\texttt{AWAR}(\pi_a, p)$ are *false* and it follows that $\pi_w \cdot \pi_\ell$ does not contain a method transition which reads a global memory location other than $mloc(t_w)$ without previously having written to it. In both, π_w and π'_w, process p overwrites the only global memory location $mloc(t_w)$ that it can read without previously having written to it. Then, $\pi_w \cdot \pi_\ell$ and $\pi'_w \cdot \pi'_\ell$ will contain the same sequence of statements, with all global transitions accessing and reading/writing identical values. Thus, $hs(\pi_{conc}) \lfloor_{m_1} = hs(\pi_a)$.

Given that the implementation is linearizable the two possible linearizations of $\pi_{base_1} \cdot \pi_{conc}$ are:

1. $hs(\pi_{base_1}) \cdot hs(\pi_{conc}) \lfloor_{m_1} \cdot hs(\pi'_b)$. We already established that $hs(\pi_{conc}) \lfloor_{m_1} = hs(\pi_a)$ and $hs(\pi'_b) = hs(\pi_b)$, and hence by substitution we get $hs(\pi_{base_1}) \cdot hs(\pi_a) \cdot hs(\pi_b)$. From the premise, we know that $hs(\pi_{base_1}) \cdot hs(\pi_a) \cdot hs(\pi_c) \in Spec$. As the specification is deterministic, it follows that $hs(\pi_b) = hs(\pi_c)$, a contradiction with item 8.
2. $hs(\pi_{base_1}) \cdot hs(\pi'_b) \cdot hs(\pi_{conc}) \lfloor_{m_1}$. We already established that $hs(\pi_{conc}) \lfloor_{m_1} = hs(\pi_a)$ and $hs(\pi'_b) = hs(\pi_b)$ and hence by substitution we get $hs(\pi_{base_1}) \cdot hs(\pi_b) \cdot hs(\pi_a)$. From the premise, we know that $hs(\pi_{base_2}) \cdot hs(\pi_b) \cdot hs(\pi_d) \in Spec$ and $hs(\pi_{base_1}) = hs(\pi_{base_2})$. As the specification is deterministic, it follows that $hs(\pi_a) = hs(\pi_d)$, a contradiction with item 7.

Therefore, $\texttt{RAW}(\pi_a, p) = true$ or $\texttt{AWAR}(\pi_a, p) = true$. □

5.5 A Note on Commutativity and Idempotency

The notion of strongly non-commutative method is related to traditional notions of non-commutative methods [44] and non-idempotent methods. Let us again consider Definition 5.2.

Non-Idempotent Method vs. Strongly Non-Commutative Method If it is the case that method m_2 is the same as method m_1, then the definition instantiates to *non-idempotent* methods. That is, given *base*, if we apply m_1 twice in a row, the second invocation will return a different result than the first. Consider again the Set specification in Fig. 4. The method `add` is non-idempotent. As discussed in the example in Section 2, we can start with $S = \emptyset$ and $base = \epsilon$. Then, if we perform two methods `add(5)` in a row, each one of the `add(5)`'s will return a different result.

Classic Non-Commutativity vs. Strong Non-Commutativity In the classic notion of non-commutativity [44], it is enough for one of the methods to not commute with the other, while here, it is required that both methods do not commute from the *same* prefix history. In the classic case, if two methods do not commute, it does not mean that either of them is a strongly non-commutative method. However, if a method is strongly non-commutative, then it is always the case that there exists another method with which it does not commute (by definition). Consider again the Set specification in Fig. 4. Although `add` and `contains` do not commute, `contains` is not a strongly non-commutative method. That is, `add` influences the result of `contains`, but `contains` does *not* influence the result of `add`.

6. Strongly Non-Commutative Specifications

In this section we provide a few examples of well-known sequential specifications that contain strongly non-commutative methods as defined in Definition 5.2.

6.1 Stacks

Definition 6.1 (Stack Sequential Specification). *A stack object S supports two methods: push and pop. The state of a stack is a sequence of items $S = \langle v_0, ..., v_k \rangle$. The stack is initially empty. The push and pop methods induce the following state transitions of the sequence $S = \langle v_0, \ldots, v_k \rangle$, with appropriate return values:*

- *push(v_{new}): changes S to be $\langle v_0, ..., v_k, v_{new} \rangle$ and returns* ack.
- *pop(): if S is non-empty, changes S to be $\langle v_0, ..., v_{k-1} \rangle$ and returns v_k. If S is empty, returns empty and S remains unchanged.*

We let $Spec_s$ denote the sequential specification of a stack object as defined above.

Lemma 6.2 (Pop is Strongly Non-Commutative). *The* pop *stack method is strongly non-commutative.*

Proof. Let $base \in Spec_s$ be a complete sequential history after which $S = \langle v \rangle$ for some v. Let p and q be two processes, let s_1 and s_4 be complete invocations of *pop* by p, and let s_2 and s_3 be complete invocations of *pop* by q. From Definition 6.1, $\{base \cdot s_1 \cdot s_3, base \cdot s_2 \cdot s_4\} \subset Spec_s$, $ret(s_1) = ret(s_2) = v$, and $ret(s_3) = ret(s_4) = empty$. The claim now follows from Definition 5.2. □

It also follows from Definition 5.2 that *push* methods are not strongly non-commutative.

6.2 Work Stealing

As we now prove, the (non-idempotent) work stealing object, discussed in section 2.2, is an example of an object for which two different methods are strongly non-commutative.

Definition 6.3 (Work Stealing Sequential Specification). *A work stealing object supports three methods: put, take, and steal. The state of each process i is a sequence of items $Q_i = \langle v_0^i, ..., v_{k_i}^i \rangle$. All queues are initially empty. The put and take methods are performed by each process i on its local queue Q_i and induce on it the following state transitions, with appropriate return values:*

- *put(v_{new}): changes Q_i to be $\langle v_{new}, v_0^i, ..., v_{k_i}^i \rangle$ and returns* ack.
- *take(): if Q_i is non-empty, it changes Q_i to be $\langle v_1^i, ..., v_{k_i}^i \rangle$ and returns v_0^i. If Q_i is empty, it returns empty and Q_i remains unchanged.*

The steal *method is performed by each process i on some queue $Q_j = \langle v_0^j, ..., v_{k_j}^j \rangle$ for $j \neq i$. if Q_j is non-empty, it changes Q_j to be $\langle v_0^j, ..., v_{k_j-1}^i \rangle$ and returns $v_{k_j}^j$. If Q_j is empty, it returns empty and Q_j remains unchanged. We let $Spec_{ws}$ denote the sequential specification of a work stealing object as defined above.*

Lemma 6.4 (Take & Steal are Strongly Non-Commutative). *The* take *and* steal *methods are strongly non-commutative.*

Proof. Let $base \in Spec_{ws}$ be a complete sequential history after which $Q_j = \langle v \rangle$ for some value v and process j. Let $i \neq j$ be some process other than j, let s_1 and s_4 be complete invocations of *steal* by process i on Q_j, and let s_2 and s_3 be complete invocations of *take* by process i. From Definition 6.3, $\{base \cdot s_1 \cdot s_3, base \cdot s_2 \cdot s_4\} \subset Spec_s$, $ret(s_1) = ret(s_2) = v$, and $ret(s_3) = ret(s_4) = empty$. The claim now follows from Definition 5.2. □

It is easily shown that specifications for *queues*, *hash-tables* and *sets* have strongly non-commutative methods. The proofs are essentially identical to the proofs of Lemmas 6.2 and 6.4 and are therefore omitted.

6.3 Compare-and-Swap (CAS)

We now prove that *CAS* is strongly non-commutative.

Definition 6.5 (Compare-and-swap Sequential Specification). *A compare-and-swap object C supports a single method called CAS and stores a scalar value over some domain $\mathcal{V}$. The method CAS(exp,new), for $exp, new \in \mathcal{V}$, induces the following state transition of the compare-and-swap object. If C's value is exp, C's value is changed to new and the method returns true; otherwise, C's value remains unchanged and the method returns false.*
We let $Spec_C$ denote the sequential specification of a compare-and-swap object as defined above.

Lemma 6.6 (CAS is Strongly Non-Commutative). *The CAS method is strongly non-commutative.*

Proof. Let $base \in Spec_C$ be a complete sequential history after which C's value is v, let i and j be two processes, let s_1 and s_4 be complete invocations of CAS(v,v') by process i, for some $v \neq v' \in \mathcal{V}$, and let s_2 and s_3 be complete invocations of CAS(v,v') by process j. From Definition 6.5, $\{base \cdot s_1 \cdot s_3, base \cdot s_2 \cdot s_4\} \subset Spec_C$, $ret(s_1) = ret(s_2) = true$, and $ret(s_3) = ret(s_4) = false$. The claim now follows from Definition 5.2. □

It follows from lemma 6.6 that any software implementation of CAS is required to use either AWAR or RAW. Proving a similar result for all non-trivial read-modify-write specifications (such as fetch-and-add, swap, test-and-set and load-link/store-conditional) is equally straightforward.

7. Related Work

Numerous papers present implementations of concurrent data structures, several of these are cited in Section 2. We refer the reader to Herlihy and Shavit's book [22] for many other examples.

Modern architectures often execute instructions issued by a single process out-of-order, and provide *fence* or *barrier* instructions to order the execution (cf. [1, 33]). There is a plethora of fence and barrier instructions (see [35]). For example, DEC Alpha provides two different fence instructions, a memory barrier (`MB`) and a write memory barrier (`WMB`). PowerPC provides a lightweight (`lwsync`) and a heavyweight (`sync`) memory ordering fence instructions, where `sync` is a full fence, while `lwsync` guarantees all other orders except RAW. SPARC V9 RMO provides several flavors of fence instructions, through a MEMBAR instruction that can be customized (via four-bit encoding) to order a combination of previous read and write operations with respect to future read and write operations. Pentium 4 supports load fence (`lfence`), store fence (`sfence`) and memory fence (`mfence`) instructions. The `mfence` instruction can be used for enforcing the RAW order.

Herlihy [22] proved that linearizable wait-free implementations of many widely-used concurrent data-structures, such as counters, stacks and queues, must use AWAR. These results do not mention RAW and do not apply to obstruction-free [15] implementations of such objects or to implementations of mutual exclusion, however, whereas our results do.

Recently, there has been a renewed interest in formalizing memory models (cf. [40, 42, 43]), and model checking and synthesizing programs that run on these models [29]. Our result is complementary to this direction: it states that we may need to enforce certain order, i.e., RAW, regardless of what weak memory model is used. Further, our result can be used in tandem with program testing and verification: if both RAW and AWAR are missing from a program that claims to satisfy certain specifications, then that program is certainly incorrect and there is no need test it or verify it.

Kawash's PhD thesis [28] (also in papers [24, 25]) investigates the ability of *weak consistency* models to solve mutual exclusion, with only reads and writes. This work shows that many weak models (Coherence, Causal consistency, P-RAM, Weak Ordering, SPARC consistency and Java Consistency) cannot solve mutual exclusion. Processor consistency [17] can solve mutual exclusion, but it requires multi-write registers; for two processes, solving mutual exclusion requires at least three variables, one of which is multi-writer. In contrast, we show that particular orders of operations or certain atomicity constraints must be enforced, regardless of the memory model; moreover, our results apply beyond mutual exclusion and hold for a large class of important linearizable objects.

Boehm [7] studies when memory operations can be reordered with respect to PThread-style locks, and shows that it is not safe to move memory operations into a locked region by delaying them past a lock call. On the other hand, memory operations can be moved into such a region by advancing them to be before an unlock call. However, Boehm's paper does not address the central subject of our paper, namely, the necessity that certain ordering patterns (RAW or AWAR) must be present *inside* the lock operations.

Our proof technique employs the *covering* technique, originally used by Burns and Lynch [9] to prove a lower bound on the number of registers needed for solving mutual exclusion. This technique had many applications, both with read / write operations [4, 5, 12, 14, 27, 39], and with non-trivial atomic operations, such as compare&swap [13]. Some steps of our proofs can be seen as a formalization of the arguments Lamport uses to derive a fast mutual exclusion algorithm [32].

In terms of our result for mutual exclusion, while one might guess that some form of RAW should be used in the entry code of read/write mutual exclusion, we are not aware of any prior work that states and proves this claim. Burns and Lynch [9] show that you need to have *n* registers, and as part of their proof show that a process needs to write, but they do not show that after it writes, the process must read from a different memory location. Lamport [32] also only hints to it. These works neither state nor prove the claim we are making (and they also do not discuss AWAR).

8. Conclusion and Future Work

In this work, we focused on two common synchronization idioms: read-after-write (RAW) and atomic write after read (AWAR). Unfortunately, enforcing any of these two patterns is costly on all current processor architectures.

We showed that it is impossible to eliminate both RAW and AWAR in the sequential execution of a lock section of any mutual exclusion algorithm. We also proved that RAW or AWAR must be present in some of the sequential executions of strongly non-commutative methods that are linearizable with respect to a deterministic sequential specification. Further, we proved that many classic specifications such as stacks, sets, hash tables, queues, work-stealing structures and compare-and-swap operations have strongly non-commutative operations, making implementations of these specifications subject to our result. Finally, as RAW or AWAR cannot be avoided in most practical algorithms, our result suggests that it is important to improve the hardware costs of store-load fences and compare-and-swap operations, the instructions that enforce RAW and AWAR.

An interesting direction for future work is taking advantage of our result by weakening its basic assumptions in order to build useful algorithms that do not use RAW and AWAR.

9. Acknowledgements

We thank Bard Bloom and the anonymous reviewers for valuable suggestions which improved the quality of the paper. Hagit Attiya's research is supported in part by the *Israel Science Foundation* (grants number 953/06 and 1227/10). Danny Hendler's research is supported in part by the *Israel Science Foundation* (grants number 1344/06 and 1227/10).

References

[1] Sarita V. Advee and Kourosh Gharachorloo. Shared memory consistency models: A tutorial. *IEEE Computer*, 29(12):66–76, 1996.

[2] Thomas E. Anderson. The performance of spin lock alternatives for shared-money multiprocessors. *IEEE Trans. Parallel Distrib. Syst.*, 1(1):6–16, 1990.

[3] Nimar S. Arora, Robert D. Blumofe, and C. Greg Plaxton. Thread scheduling for multiprogrammed multiprocessors. In *Proceedings of the Tenth Annual ACM Symposium on Parallel Algorithms and Architectures, SPAA*, pages 119–129, June 1998.

[4] Hagit Attiya, Faith Fich, and Yaniv Kaplan. Lower bounds for adaptive collect and related objects. In *Proceedings of the Twenty-Third Annual ACM Symposium on Principles of Distributed Computing*, pages 60–69, 2004.

[5] Hagit Attiya, Alla Gorbach, and Shlomo Moran. Computing in totally anonymous asynchronous shared memory systems. *Information and Computation*, 173(2):162–183, March 2002.

[6] Yoah Bar-David and Gadi Taubenfeld. Automatic discovery of mutual exclusion algorithms. In *Proceedings of the 17th International Conference on Distributed Computing, DISC*, pages 136–150, 2003.

[7] Hans-J. Boehm. Reordering constraints for pthread-style locks. In *Proceedings of the Twevelth ACM SIGPLAN Symposium on Principles and Practice of Parallel Programming, PPoPP*, pages 173–182, 2007.

[8] Sebastian Burckhardt, Chris Dern, Madanlal Musuvathi, and Roy Tan. Line-up: a complete and automatic linearizability checker. In *PLDI '10: Proceedings of the 2010 ACM SIGPLAN conference on Programming language design and implementation*, pages 330–340, New York, NY, USA, 2010. ACM.

[9] James Burns and Nancy Lynch. Bounds on shared memory for mutual exclusion. *Information and Computation*, 107(2):171–184, December 1993.

[10] David Chase and Yossi Lev. Dynamic circular work-stealing deque. In *Proceedings of the Seventeenth Annual ACM Symposium on Parallelism in Algorithms and Architectures, SPAA*, pages 21–28, July 2005.

[11] Edsger W. Dijkstra. Solution of a problem in concurrent programming control. *Commun. ACM*, 8(9):569, 1965.

[12] Faith Ellen, Panagiota Fatourou, and Eric Ruppert. Time lower bounds for implementations of multi-writer snapshots. *Journal of the ACM*, 54(6):30, 2007.

[13] Faith Fich, Danny Hendler, and Nir Shavit. On the inherent weakness of conditional primitives. *Distributed Computing*, 18(4):267–277, 2006.

[14] Faith Fich, Maurice Herlihy, and Nir Shavit. On the space complexity of randomized synchronization. *Journal of the ACM*, 45(5):843–862, September 1998.

[15] Faith Fich, Victor Luchangco, Mark Moir, and Nir Shavit. Obstruction-free step complexity: Lock-free dcas as an example. In *DISC*, pages 493–494, 2005.

[16] Matteo Frigo, Charles E. Leiserson, and Keith H. Randall. The implementation of the cilk-5 multithreaded language. In *Proceedings of the ACM SIGPLAN 1998 Conference on Programming Language Design and Implementation, PLDI*, pages 212–223, June 1998.

[17] James R. Goodman. Cache consistency and sequential consistency. Technical report, 1989. Technical report 61.

[18] Gary Graunke and Shreekant S. Thakkar. Synchronization algorithms for shared-memory multiprocessors. *IEEE Computer*, 23(6):60–69, 1990.

[19] Danny Hendler, Yossi Lev, Mark Moir, and Nir Shavit. A dynamic-sized nonblocking work stealing deque. *Distributed Computing*, 18(3):189–207, 2006.

[20] Danny Hendler and Nir Shavit. Non-blocking steal-half work queues. In *Proceedings of the Twenty-First Annual ACM Symposium on Principles of Distributed Computing*, pages 280–289, July 2002.

[21] Maurice Herlihy. Wait-free synchronization. *ACM Trans. Program. Lang. Syst.*, 13(1):124–149, 1991.

[22] Maurice Herlihy and Nir Shavit. *The art of multiprocessor programming*. Morgan Kaufmann, 2008.

[23] Maurice Herlihy and Jeannette Wing. Linearizability: a correctness condition for concurrent objects. *ACM Trans. Program. Lang. Syst.*, 12(3):463–492, 1990.

[24] Lisa Higham and Jalal Kawash. Java: Memory consistency and process coordination. In *DISC*, pages 201–215, 1998.

[25] Lisa Higham and Jalal Kawash. Bounds for mutual exclusion with only processor consistency. In *DISC*, pages 44–58, 2000.

[26] *IBM System/370 Extended Architecture, Principles of Operation*, 1983. Publication No. SA22-7085.

[27] Prasad Jayanti, King Tan, and Sam Toueg. Time and space lower bounds for nonblocking implementations. *SIAM Journal on Computing*, 30(2):438–456, 2000.

[28] Jalal Kawash. *Limitations and Capabilities of Weak Memory Consistency Systems*. PhD thesis, University of Calgary, January 2000.

[29] Michael Kuperstein, Martin Vechev, and Eran Yahav. Automatic inference of memory fences. In *Formal Methods in Computer Aided Design*, 2010.

[30] Leslie Lamport. Specifying concurrent program modules. *ACM Trans. Program. Lang. Syst.*, 5(2):190–222, April 1983.

[31] Leslie Lamport. The mutual exclusion problem: part II - statement and solutions. *J. ACM*, 33(2):327–348, 1986.

[32] Leslie Lamport. A fast mutual exclusion algorithm. *ACM Trans. Comput. Syst.*, 5(1):1–11, 1987.

[33] Jaejin Lee. *Compilation Techniques for Explicitly Parallel Programs*. PhD thesis, Department of Computer Science, University of Illinois at Urbana-Champaign, 1999.

[34] Victor Luchangco, Mark Moir, and Nir Shavit. On the uncontended complexity of consensus. In *Proceedings of the 17th International Conference on Distributed Computing*, pages 45–59, October 2003.

[35] Paul E. McKenney. Memory barriers: a hardware view for software hackers. Linux Technology Center, IBM Beaverton, June 2010.

[36] John M. Mellor-Crummey and Michael L. Scott. Algorithms for scalable synchronization on shared-memory multiprocessors. *ACM Trans. Comput. Syst.*, 9(1):21–65, 1991.

[37] Maged M. Michael and Michael L. Scott. Simple, fast, and practical non-blocking and blocking concurrent queue algorithms. In *Proceedings of the Fifteenth Annual ACM Symposium on Principles of Distributed Computing*, pages 267–275, May 1996.

[38] Maged M. Michael, Martin T. Vechev, and Vijay Saraswat. Idempotent work stealing. In *Proceedings of the Fourteenth ACM SIGPLAN Symposium on Principles and Practice of Parallel Programming, PPoPP*, pages 45–54, February 2009.

[39] Shlomo Moran, Gadi Taubenfeld, and Irit Yadin. Concurrent counting. *Journal of Computer and System Sciences*, 53(1):61–78, August 1996.

[40] Scott Owens, Susmit Sarkar, and Peter Sewell. A better x86 memory model: x86-tso. In *TPHOLs*, pages 391–407, 2009.

[41] Gary L. Peterson. Myths about the mutual exclusion problem. *Inf. Process. Lett.*, 12(3):115–116, 1981.

[42] Vijay A. Saraswat, Radha Jagadeesan, Maged M. Michael, and Christoph von Praun. A theory of memory models. In *Proceedings of the 12th ACM SIGPLAN Symposium on Principles and Practice of Parallel Programming, PPOPP*, pages 161–172, March 2007.

[43] Susmit Sarkar, Peter Sewell, Francesco Zappa Nardelli, Scott Owens, Tom Ridge, Thomas Braibant, Magnus O. Myreen, and Jade Alglave. The semantics of x86-cc multiprocessor machine code. In *POPL*, pages 379–391, 2009.

[44] William E. Weihl. Commutativity-based concurrency control for abstract data types. *IEEE Trans. Computers*, 37(12):1488–1505, 1988.

[45] Glynn Winskel. *The Formal Semantics of Programming Languages*. MIT Press, 1993.

Complexity of Pattern-based Verification for Multithreaded Programs *

Javier Esparza
Fakultät für Informatik, Technische Universität München, Germany.
esparza@model.in.tum.de

Pierre Ganty
The IMDEA Software Institute, Madrid, Spain.
pierre.ganty@imdea.org

Abstract

Pattern-based verification checks the correctness of the program executions that follow a given *pattern*, a regular expression over the alphabet of program transitions of the form $w_1^* \dots w_n^*$. For multithreaded programs, the alphabet of the pattern is given by the synchronization operations between threads. We study the complexity of pattern-based verification for *abstracted* multithreaded programs in which, as usual in program analysis, conditions have been replaced by nondeterminism (the technique works also for boolean programs). While unrestricted verification is undecidable for abstracted multithreaded programs with recursive procedures and PSPACE-complete for abstracted multithreaded while-programs, we show that pattern-based verification is NP-complete for both classes. We then conduct a multiparameter analysis in which we study the complexity in the number of threads, the number of procedures per thread, the size of the procedures, and the size of the pattern. We first show that no algorithm for pattern-based verification can be polynomial in the number of threads, procedures per thread, or the size of the pattern (unless P=NP). Then, using recent results about Parikh images of regular languages and semilinear sets, we present an algorithm exponential in the number of threads, procedures per thread, and size of the pattern, but polynomial in the size of the procedures.

Categories and Subject Descriptors: D.2.4 [Software Engineering]: Software/Program Verification.
General Terms: Verification, Languages, Algorithms, Reliability.
Keywords: concurrent programming, safety, context-free languages.

1. Introduction

The analysis and verification of multithreaded programs is one of the most active research areas in software model checking. This is due, on the one hand, to the increasing relevance of multicore architectures, and, on the other hand, to the difficulty of conceiving, reasoning about, and debugging concurrent software. Automated analysis tools must cope with the very untractable nature of the analysis problems. Multithreaded programs with possibly recursive procedures communicating through global variables are Turing powerful even for programs having only two threads and three variables, all of them boolean. If communication takes place through message passing, the programs are Turing powerful even after applying the usual program analysis abstraction that replaces all conditions in alternative constructs and loops by nondeterminism.

Context-bounding, proposed by Qadeer and Rehof in [25], is the most successful proposal to date for overcoming untractability. It restricts the problem further by exploring only those computation with a bounded, fixed number of *contexts*. A *context* is a segment of the computation during which only one thread accesses the global variables; a *context switch* takes place when the identity of this thread changes. Reachability of a program point by a computation with at most k context switches (the *context-bounded reachability problem*) is NP-complete when k is given in unary, and can be checked by means of an algorithm polynomial in the size of the program and exponential in k [20, 21, 25] . Context-bounding has been implemented in several model checkers, like CHESS, SPIN, SLAM, jMoped, and others [1, 5, 20, 28, 30], and experiments with these tools have provided evidence that many concurrency errors manifest themselves in computations with few context switches.

While context bounding has been very successful, it also has important limitations. In particular, it restricts the number of communications between threads. While a thread can perform arbitrarily many reads and writes to the global variables during a context, these writes are not observed by the other threads, and so only the value of the variable immediately before the context switch amounts to a communication. So in a computation with k context switches threads communicate at most k times. In this paper we study a more flexible technique, introduced by Kahlon in [15], that applies the theory of *bounded languages* developed in the mid-sixties by Ginsburg and Spanier [11] to the verification problem. Kahlon uses the theory to prove decidability of safety analysis for multithreaded programs whose executions conform to a *pattern*, a regular expression of the form $w_1^* \dots w_n^*$ over the alphabet of program instructions. Observe that the executions of such a program can be arbitrarily long. An equivalent, but in our opinion more fruitful point to view is to consider a pattern as a class of executions specified by the verifier. The executions of the program may conform to the pattern or not, but we can automatically verify whether those executions conforming to the pattern satisfy the property. In other words, the programmer specifies by means of a pattern those executions she/he is interested in. We call this point of view *pattern-based verification*.

The claim of [15] is that pattern-based verification provides a good compromise between expressivity and complexity. The ex-

* This research was sponsored by the Comunidad de Madrid's Program PROMETIDOS-CM (S2009TIC-1465), by the PEOPLE-COFUND's program AMAROUT (PCOFUND-2008-229599), and by the Spanish Ministry of Science and Innovation (TIN2010-20639).

POPL'11, January 26–28, 2011, Austin, Texas, USA.

pressivity point has been considered in some detail in [9], where it is shown there that the pattern-based approach is strictly more expressive than context-bounding.[1] In this paper we study the computational complexity of pattern-based verification, thus completing the theoretical analysis. In a nutshell, we show that pattern-based verification, like context-bounding, is NP-complete, and we identify an interesting (and in a certain sense unique) polynomial case.

For the complexity analysis we reduce the reachability problem for multithreaded programs to a language theory problem called *non-Disjointness Modulo a Pattern*, or nDMP for short: checking non-emptiness of the intersection of a given set of context-free grammars *and* a given pattern. By putting together classical results by Ginsburg and Spanier [11] and more recent results by Verma, Seidl, and Schwentick [31] we first show that, like context-bounded reachability, nDMP is NP-complete. Interestingly, the algorithm we derive from the easiness proof relies on satisfiability checking of a Presburger formula, which contrasts with the fixed point evaluation used in context-bounding. In the second and main part of the paper, we conduct a multiparameter analysis of nDMP. The size of an instance of nDMP is a function of four parameters: the number of threads, the maximal number of procedures per thread, the maximal size of a procedure, and the size of the pattern. For every subset of parameters we determine the complexity of nDMP when the parameters in the subset (and no others) have a fixed value. While this gives 16 possible cases, the results can be easily summarized: apart from some trivial cases, in which the problem can be solved in constant time (for instance, when all four parameters have fixed values), the problem remains NP-complete for all subsets *except one*: the case in which the number of threads, procedures per thread and the size of the pattern are fixed, but the size of the procedures is not. We prove that this case is polynomial. The proof uses several recent results about Parikh images of regular languages and complexity of semilinear sets [19, 29].

The paper is organized as follows. Section 2 contains preliminaries. Section 3 presents our program and formal models, an analysis of the context-bounding technique, and the reduction of the pattern-based verification problem to nDMP. Section 4 shows that nDMP is NP-complete. Section 5 contains our multiparameter analysis of nDMP. The NP-hard cases are covered by means of reductions from different NP-complete problems. Our main result, the polynomial case mentioned above, is contained in Section 5.3. Finally, Section 6 contains conclusions and discusses related work.

2. Preliminaries

An *alphabet* Σ is a finite non-empty set of symbols. We assume the reader is familiar with the basics of language theory, including regular and context-free languages (see e.g. [13]).

Context-free Languages. A *context-free grammar* is a tuple $G = (\mathcal{X}, \Sigma, \mathcal{P}, S)$ where $\mathcal{X}$ is a finite non-empty set of *variables*, Σ is an alphabet, $\mathcal{P} \subseteq \mathcal{X} \times (\Sigma \cup \mathcal{X})^*$ is a finite set of *productions* (the production (X, w) may also be noted $X \to w$) and $S \in \mathcal{X}$ is the *axiom*. Given two strings $u, v \in (\Sigma \cup \mathcal{X})^*$ we write $u \Rightarrow v$ if there exists a production $(X, w) \in \mathcal{P}$ and some words $y, z \in (\Sigma \cup \mathcal{X})^*$ such that $u = yXz$ and $v = ywz$. We use $\Rightarrow^*$ to denote the reflexive transitive closure of $\Rightarrow$. The language of a grammar is the set $L(G) = \{w \in \Sigma^* \mid S \Rightarrow^* w\}$. A language L is *context-free* if $L = L(G)$ for some context-free grammar G. A context-free grammar is *regular* if each production is in $\mathcal{X} \times \Sigma^*(\mathcal{X} \cup \{\varepsilon\})$. A language L is *regular* if $L = L(G)$ for some regular grammar G.

[1] This is achieved by exhibiting a family of two-thread programs, parameterized by a number n, such that reachability analysis for a *fixed* pattern proves reachability of a program point for all n, but such that the number of context switches needed to reach the program point goes to infinity when n grows.

We sometimes use $L_X(G)$ with $X \in \mathcal{X}$ to denote the language $\{w \in \Sigma^* \mid X \Rightarrow^* w\}$.

Multisets. A *multiset* $\mathbf{m} \colon \Sigma \mapsto \mathbb{N}$ maps each symbol of Σ to a natural number. $\mathbb{M}[\Sigma]$ denotes the set of all multisets over Σ. We sometimes use the following notation: $[\![q_1, q_1, q_3]\!]$ denotes the multiset $\mathbf{m}$ such that $\mathbf{m}(q_1) = 2$, $\mathbf{m}(q_3) = 1$ and $\mathbf{m}(x) = 0$ for all $x \in \Sigma \setminus \{q_1, q_3\}$. The empty multiset is denoted $\emptyset$. The size of a multiset $\mathbf{m}$ is $|\mathbf{m}| = \sum_{\sigma \in \Sigma} \mathbf{m}(\sigma)$. Given two multisets $\mathbf{m}, \mathbf{m}' \in \mathbb{M}[\Sigma]$ and we define $\mathbf{m} \oplus \mathbf{m}' \in \mathbb{M}[\Sigma]$ as the multiset satisfying $(\mathbf{m} \oplus \mathbf{m}')(a) = \mathbf{m}(a) + \mathbf{m}'(a)$ for every $a \in \Sigma$. Given $\mathbf{m} \in \mathbb{M}[\Sigma]$ and $c \in \mathbb{N}$, we define $c \cdot \mathbf{m}$ as the multiset satisfying $(c \cdot \mathbf{m})(a) = c \cdot \mathbf{m}(a)$ for every $a \in \Sigma$. By fixing a linear order on Σ, every multiset $\mathbf{m}$ can be seen as a vector of $\mathbb{N}^k$ where $k = |\Sigma|$, and vice versa.

3. Model and decision problem

3.1 Program model

We model a sequential program by a *system of flowgraphs*, a tuple of flowgraphs containing one flowgraph for each procedure. *Nodes* of a flowgraph correspond to *control points* of the program, and edges to *sequential statements*. A sequential statement is either a *condition* (a boolean combination of expressions $x \le e$), an *assignment* $x := e$, or a *procedure call*. Each flowgraph has a unique node without incoming edges, the *initial node*, and a unique node without outgoing edges, the *final node*, different from the initial node. All nodes are reachable from the initial node and co-reachable from the final node.

A multithreaded program is modeled by a tuple of systems of flowgraphs, one for each program thread. Each system of flowgraphs uses a set of *channels* to send or receive messages; abusing language, we call a system of flowgraphs together with the set of channels it uses a *thread*. We denote by Ch_i the set of channels used by the i-th thread, and the set of all channels by Ch. The edges of the flowgraphs are labeled by sequential statements, by *send statements* $a!x$, indicating that the thread is willing to send the value of x through channel $a \in Ch$, or by *receive statements* $a?y$, indicating that the thread is willing to receive a value through channel a and assign it to variable y. We assume that each channel is *owned* by a thread: the owner of channel a can only contain send statements $a!x$, and all other threads can only contain receive statements $a?y$. Channels work as in CSP: they have capacity 0, i.e., a message is exchanged through channel a only if its owner executes a send statement, and all other threads having a in their sets of channels simultaneously execute a matching receive statement. So we allow multiparty synchronization. Figure 1 shows a model of a program with three threads. Each of the threads, contains only one flowgraph, with channels $\{a, b, c\}$, $\{a, b\}$, and $\{b, c\}$, respectively. The first thread owns channels a and c, the second thread owns channel b and the third owns no channel.

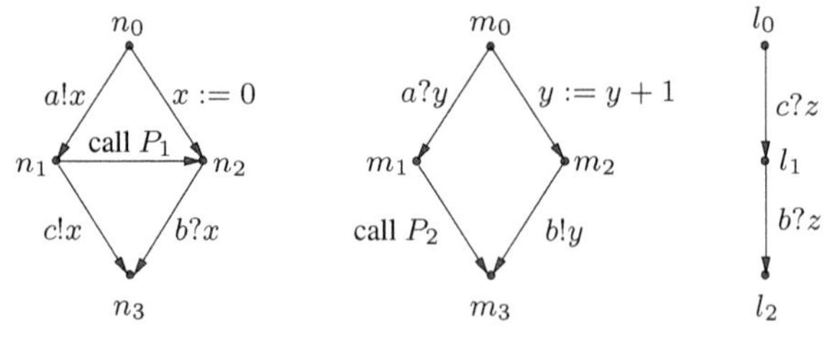

Figure 1. A model of a program with three threads.

During a program execution threads exchange values through channels. A *trace* of the program is the sequence of channels used along some *full* execution. For instance, $aacb$ is a trace of the program of Figure 1 corresponding to (among others) the execution $(a!x, a?y)$ $callP_1$ $callP_2$ $(a!x, a?y)$ $(c!x, c?z)$ $callP_2$ $y := y + 1$ $(b?x, b!y, b?z)$.

Using standard techniques, verification of safety properties can be reduced to the reachability of some program point, which can be reduced to nonemptiness of the set of traces of a modified program (notice that the set of traces is nonempty iff the program can terminate, i.e, all threads can simultaneously reach their final node). Since this problem is undecidable even for single-thread while-programs, further restrictions are unavoidable. The classical program analysis abstraction consists of replacing all condition statements by non deterministic choice, which amounts to ignoring data, since data do not longer influence control-flow. We call the result an *abstracted program*. Unfortunately, trace emptiness is still undecidable for abstracted multithreaded programs [26], and PSPACE-complete for multithreaded while-programs. For this reason we restrict the problem further. However, before doing so we define a formal model for abstracted multithreaded programs.

Remark. Context-bounding is formulated in [24, 25] for *boolean programs*, programs in which all variables are boolean. In boolean programs data influences control, and so one could think that there is a deep conceptual difference with the program analysis abstraction. However, this is not the case. Since the number of valuations of the variables of a boolean program is finite, the program can be easily transformed into a dataless program whose program points are pairs consisting of a program point of the boolean program and a valuation of the variables. This is in fact how the context-bounding technique proceeds, since it models a boolean program as a pushdown system, a dataless formal model. In our presentation we stick to the program analysis abstraction for convenience and clarity, but the technique can be equally well applied to predicate abstractions and boolean programs.

3.2 Formal model

Let P be an abstracted multithreaded program with threads $t_1, \ldots, t_n$ communicating over a set Ch of channels. We assign to P a tuple $G_1, \ldots, G_n$ of context-free grammars over the alphabet Ch, such that w is a trace of P iff w belongs to $\bigcap_{i=1}^n L(G_i)$. We proceed in two steps. First we assign to P grammars $G'_1, \ldots, G'_n$ with alphabets $Ch_1, \ldots, Ch_n$ such that w is a trace of P iff for every $1 \leq i \leq n$ the projection of w onto Ch_i belongs to $L(G'_i)$. In a second step we transform these grammars into the final grammars $G_1, \ldots, G_n$.

The grammar G'_i over the alphabet Ch_i generates the interprocedurally valid traces of t_i. These are the traces that t_i can generate in an environment always ready to match its send and receive statements. G'_i has a variable for each node of t_i, a production for each edge, and a further production for the final node of t_i. The production corresponding to an edge leading from node X to node Y and labelled by ℓ is defined as follows:

- if ℓ is a condition or an assignment, the production is $X \to Y$;
- if $\ell = call\ P$, the production is $X \to P_0Y$, where P_0 is the initial node of procedure P;
- if $\ell = a!x$ or $\ell = a?y$, the production is $X \to aY$;
- the production for the final node Z of t is $Z \to \varepsilon$.

The three grammars for the program of Figure 1 have variables $\{n_0, \ldots, n_3\}$, $\{m_0, \ldots, m_3\}$, $\{l_0, l_1, l_2\}$, terminals $\{a, b, c\}$, $\{a, b\}$, $\{b, c\}$, and productions:

$$\begin{array}{lll} n_0 \to an_1 \mid n_2 & m_0 \to am_1 \mid m_2 & l_0 \to cl_1 \\ n_1 \to cn_3 \mid n_0n_2 & m_1 \to m_0m_3 & l_1 \to bl_2 \\ n_2 \to bn_3 & m_2 \to bm_3 & l_2 \to \varepsilon \\ n_3 \to \varepsilon & m_3 \to \varepsilon & \end{array}$$

Observe that the number of "proper" procedures (procedures that can be called, unlike P_3 in our example) is equal to the number of variables Z for which there is a production of the form $X \to ZY$. We call them *procedure variables*. In our example, those variables are n_0, m_0. It is easy to see that the traces of P under the program analysis abstraction are the words $w \in Ch^*$ satisfying the following property: for every thread t_i, the projection of w onto Ch_i is a word of $L(G'_i)$. This completes the first step.

For the second step, we slightly modify each G'_i: we set its alphabet to Ch, and add new productions. For each variable X of G'_i and for each channel a that *does not appear in* G'_i, we add a new production $X \to aX$. The grammar so obtained is denoted by G_i. In our example, we add productions $m_j \to cm_j$ to the second grammar for $j \in \{0, \ldots, 3\}$, and productions $l_j \to al_j$ to the third grammar for $j \in \{0, \ldots, 2\}$. Observe that a grammar G_i is in a particular *program normal form*: all productions are of the form $X \to a\alpha$ or $X \to \beta\gamma$, where α is a variable and β, γ is either a variable or ε. All grammars now have Ch as alphabet. Since every channel is owned by some thread, it is easy to see that the set of traces of an abstracted program with threads $t_1, \ldots, t_n$ is equal to $\bigcap_{i=1}^n L(G_i)$.

Since reachability of a program point can be easily reduced to checking nonemptiness of the set of traces of a modified program, our formal model reduces the reachability problem for abstracted programs to the nonemptiness problem for the intersection of context-free languages. Since this problem is undecidable, this does not immediately provide any algorithmic advantage. For this reason we restrict the problem and introduce pattern-based verification.

3.3 Pattern-based verification

Kahlon [15] has recently proposed to only explore the traces of a multithreaded program having a certain *shape*. Inspired by the work of Ginsburg and Spanier [11], he suggests to only explore traces conforming to what we call in this paper *communication patterns* (or just *patterns* for short). Patterns are regular expressions of the form $w_1^* w_2^* \ldots w_n^*$, where $w_i \in Ch^* \setminus \{\varepsilon\}$[2]. We study the problem of deciding, given an abstract multithreaded program P and a pattern $\boldsymbol{p}$, whether some word of $L(\boldsymbol{p})$ is a trace of P. Given the formal model given above, this verification problem reduces to the following language-theoretic problem:

DEFINITION 1. ***Non Disjointness Modulo a Pattern (nDMP)***
Instance: *Context-free grammars $G_1, \ldots, G_g$ in program normal form over an alphabet Σ, and a pattern $\boldsymbol{p}$ over Σ.*
Question: *Is $\bigcap_{i=1}^g L(G_i) \cap L(\boldsymbol{p}) \neq \varnothing$?*

3.4 Context bounding as pattern-based verification

Recall that in context bounding, instead of asking whether a given multithreaded program has a trace, we ask if it has a trace with at most k context switches. Before studying the complexity of nDMP, we sketch an argument showing that context bounding can be seen as a special case of pattern-based verification. We do not formalize the reduction, which would be very technical and tedious, but describe it in enough detail in order to (we hope) convince the reader.

[2] The languages of patterns are called *bounded languages* in the literature.

Consider a multithreaded boolean program P communicating through shared variables. Without loss of generality (see [24, 25] for details) we assume that P has one single shared variable g which can take v different values. We first show how to simulate P by a multithreaded program P' whose threads communicate through message passing. Let $t_1, \ldots, t_n$ be the threads of P. The program P' has threads $t'_1, \ldots, t'_n$. Each thread t'_i has a variable g_i that acts as a local "copy" of g.[3] At any given moment in time, every thread of P' is either *active* or *passive*. Loosely speaking, when t'_i is active it simulates the thread t_i; when it goes passive, it suspends the simulation, until its next active phase. More precisely, from its passive state a thread t'_i can either send a signal to all other threads through a channel a_i, by which it becomes active, or receive a signal through a channel a_j for some $j \neq i$, by which it remains passive. After one of the two happens, t'_i behaves as follows: (1) If t'_i has become active, then it resumes its simulation of t_i. Thread t'_i simulates t_i using the most recent value of g which is available from g_i. At any point t'_i may nondeterministically decide to suspend the simulation. In this case, t'_i communicates to all other processes the current value of g (available through g_i), say u, by sending a signal through a channel $b_{i,u}$. After sending this signal, t'_i becomes passive. (2) If t'_i has remained passive, then it waits for a signal through some channel $b_{j,u}$, where $j \neq i$, and when the signal arrives it updates the value of g_i to u.

Observe that a context of P is simulated by an "activity cycle" of P', i.e., a segment of the computation of P' starting at the moment a thread becomes active, and ending when it switches to the passive state. Since the trace of an activity cycle has length 2 (during a cycle the active thread sends exactly two signals), the traces of P' simulating computations of P with at most k contexts have length at most $2k$.

The problem of deciding if P has a full computation with at most k context switches can now be reduced to an instance of nDMP. The grammars of the instance are the result of applying the translation of Section 3.2 to P'. For the pattern, let $W = \{w_1, \ldots, w_{nv}\}$ be the set of all sequences of length 2 of the form $a_i b_{i,u}$ (there are nv of them), and let $\boldsymbol{p} = (w_1^* \ldots w_{nv}^*)^k$. Clearly, $L(\boldsymbol{p})$ contains (among others) all sequences obtained by concatenating at most k words of W. So all full computations of P with at most k contexts are simulated by computations of P' whose traces belong to $L(\boldsymbol{p})$. Therefore, if P has a full computation with at most k contexts, then the intersection of the languages of the grammars obtained from P' and $\boldsymbol{p}$ is nonempty. (The converse does not hold, but this only shows that the instance of nDMP explores *more* computations of P that context bounding with k context switches.)

4. NP-completeness of nDMP

The decidability of nDMP was proved in [11]. We show it is NP-complete. But we first define the size of an instance of nDMP, since this requires some care. The size $|w|$ of a word w is its length $|w|$. The size of a pattern $\boldsymbol{p} = w_1^* \ldots w_n^*$ is $|\boldsymbol{p}| = \sum_{i=1}^{n} |w_i|$. Defining the size of a grammar requires a bit of care. The seemingly natural choice would be to define the size of a grammar $G = (\mathcal{X}, \Sigma, \mathcal{P}, S)$ as $|\mathcal{X}| + |\mathcal{P}|$. However, recall that the grammar G_t for a thread t is constructed in two steps: in a first step, a grammar G'_t is constructed that matches the behaviour of the thread is defined; in a second step, loop productions of the form $X \to aX$ are added for every variable X and every channel a that does not appear in t. In pathological cases the number of these productions could be much larger than the number of "true" productions, artificially increasing the size of the grammar. For this reason, when a grammar has productions $X \to aX$ for every variable X and some terminal a, we define that all those productions count as one single production for determining the size. We denote the size of a grammar G, so defined, by $|G|$.

[3] Since our multithreaded programs are dataless, the local variable g_i is actually encoded into the nodes of the program as explained in a previous remark.

4.1 nDMP is NP-hard

We show[4] that nDMP is NP-hard even for regular grammars and fixed pattern $\boldsymbol{p} = a^*$. From a programming point of view, this means that the verification problem is already NP-hard for multithreaded procedureless programs, and the simplest pattern.

THEOREM 1. *The following problem is NP-hard:*
Instance: *Regular grammars $G_1, \ldots, G_g$ in program normal form.*
Question: *Is $\bigcap_{i=1}^{g} L(G_i) \cap L(\boldsymbol{p}) \neq \varnothing$ for the pattern $\boldsymbol{p} = a^*$?*

PROOF: The proof is by reduction from 3-CNF-SAT. Let Ψ be a propositional formula with n variables and m clauses $c_1, \ldots, c_m$. We define for each clause c_i a regular grammar G_i over the alphabet $\{a\}$ such that $\bigcap_{i=1}^{m} L(G_i) \neq \varnothing$ iff Ψ is satisfiable.

We need some preliminaries. Assign to each variable v a prime number n_v, and assign to each clause c the number n_c obtained by multiplying the primes of the three variables occurring in c. (This requires to construct n primes in time $p(n)$ for some polynomial p. It is well-known that the i-th prime number p_i satisfies $p_i < i \ln i + i \ln \ln i$, and so one can compute n primes by applying a primality test to each number from 1 to $n \ln n + n \ln \ln n$. Notice that the primality test can take exponential time, because the size of the number k is $\mathcal{O}(\ln k)$.) Given a clause c and a variable v, we say that a number $0 \leq k$ is a *(c, v)-witness* if v appears positively in c and $k \equiv 0 \mod n_v$, or v appears negatively in c and $k \not\equiv 0 \mod n_v$. Further, k is a *c-witness* if it is a (c, x)-witness, or a (c, y)-witness, or a (c, z)-witness where x, y and z are the three variables occurring in c. For instance, if $c = x \vee \neg y \vee z$ and $n_x = 2, n_y = 3, n_z = 5$, then k is a c-witness if $k \equiv 0 \mod 2$, or $k \not\equiv 0 \mod 3$, or $k \equiv 0 \mod 5$, i.e., if $k \neq 3, 9, 21, 27$. Given an assignment ϕ to the variables of Ψ, let n_ϕ be the product of the numbers of the variables set to **true** by ϕ. It is easy to see that ϕ satisfies c iff n_ϕ is a c-witness.

Now, for each clause c we define a grammar G_c in program normal form over the alphabet $\{a\}$. The grammar G_c has the numbers $0, 1, 2, \ldots, n_c - 1$ as grammar variables, 0 as axiom, productions $k \to a\ (k \oplus_c 1)$ for every $0 \leq k \leq n_c - 1$, where $\oplus_c$ is addition modulo n_c, and a further production $k \to \epsilon$ for each c-witness $k \leq n_c - 1$. We have $L(G_c) = \{a^k \mid k \text{ is a } c\text{-witness}\}$, and so an assignment ϕ satisfies c iff $a^{n_\phi} \in L(G_c)$. So $\bigcap_{i=1}^{m} L(G_{c_i}) \neq \varnothing$ iff Ψ is satisfiable, and so $\bigcap_{i=1}^{m} L(G_{c_i}) \cap L(\boldsymbol{p}) \neq \varnothing$ holds for $\boldsymbol{p} = a^*$ iff Ψ is satisfiable. □

4.2 nDMP is in NP

We show that nDMP is in NP. The direct approach would be to show that if $\bigcap_{i=1}^{g} L(G_i) \cap L(\boldsymbol{p}) \neq \varnothing$, then there is a witness $w \in \bigcap_{i=1}^{g} L(G_i) \cap L(\boldsymbol{p})$ of polynomial length. However, it is easy to construct instances of size k for which the shortest witness is the word a^{2^k} (see also Lemma 2). So we proceed differently, in two steps: first we polynomially reduce nDMP to a problem about Parikh images of context-free grammars, and then we show that this problem is in NP.

The *Parikh image* of a word $w \in \Sigma^*$ is the multiset $\Pi(w) : \Sigma \mapsto \mathbb{N}$ that assigns to each $a \in \Sigma$ the number of occurrences of a in w. The Parikh image of a language L, denoted by $\Pi(L)$, is the set of Parikh images of its words. We consider the following problem:

[4] The proof is due to Mikołaj Bojańczyk.

DEFINITION 2. ***Non Disjointness of Parikh Images (nDPK)***
Instance: *Context-free grammars $G_1, \ldots, G_g$ in program normal form.*
Question: *Is $\bigcap_{i=1}^{g} \Pi(L(G_i)) \neq \varnothing$?*

The reduction from nDMP to nDPK relies on a classical result by Ginsburg and Spanier [11]: Given context-free languages $L_1, \ldots, L_g$ and a pattern $\boldsymbol{p} = w_1^* \ldots w_n^*$ over an alphabet Σ, there exist context-free languages $L'_1, \ldots, L'_g$ such that

$$\textstyle\bigcap_{i=1}^{g} L_i \cap L(\boldsymbol{p}) \neq \varnothing \quad \text{iff} \quad \bigcap_{i=1}^{g} \Pi(L'_i) \neq \varnothing \ . \tag{1}$$

The proof can be easily sketched: take a new alphabet $\widetilde{\Sigma} = \{a_1, \ldots, a_n\}$, and consider the homomorphism $h \colon \widetilde{\Sigma} \to \Sigma^*$ given by $h(a_i) = w_i$ for every $1 \leq i \leq n$. Since context-free languages are closed under intersection with regular languages and under inverse homomorphism, the language $L'_i = h^{-1}(L_i \cap L(\boldsymbol{p})) \cap L(a_1^* \ldots a_n^*)$ is context-free and satisfies property (1). Moreover, using the constructions underlying these closure properties we can easily construct from a grammar G_i for L_i a grammar G'_i for L'_i in polynomial time.

However, for the complexity analysis in Sect. 5.3 we also need to establish a relation between the number of procedure variables of G_i and G'_i. For this reason we provide our own direct construction.

4.2.1 A polynomial time reduction from nDMP to nDPK

The following lemma contains the main properties of our construction.

LEMMA 1. *Given $\boldsymbol{p} = w_1^* \ldots w_n^*$ over Σ, an alphabet $\widetilde{\Sigma} = \{a_1, \ldots, a_n\}$, a homomorphism $h \colon \widetilde{\Sigma} \to \Sigma^*$, and a grammar G in program normal form, we can compute in polynomial time a grammar G^f over $\widetilde{\Sigma}$ in program normal such that:*

- *$L(G^f) = h^{-1}(L(G) \cap L(\boldsymbol{p})) \cap L(a_1^* \ldots a_n^*)$;*
- *If pr is the number of procedure variables in G, then G^f has $\mathcal{O}(pa^2 \cdot pr)$ procedure variables where pa is the size of $\boldsymbol{p}$.*

PROOF: (Sketch.) Let $G^{\boldsymbol{p}}$ be a regular grammar with $\mathcal{O}(pa)$ variables such that $L(G^{\boldsymbol{p}}) = L(\boldsymbol{p})$ (this grammar clearly exists). The variables of G^f are triples $[q_1 X q_2]$, where X is a variable of G and q_1, q_2 are variables of $G^{\boldsymbol{p}}$ such that q_2 is reachable from q_1. The productions are chosen to satisfy that $[q_1 X q_2] \Rightarrow^* w$ holds in G^f iff there exists $u \subset \Sigma^*$ such that (1) $w \subset h^{-1}(u) \cap L(a_1^* \ldots a_n^*)$, (2) $X \Rightarrow^* u$ holds in G, and (3) $q_1 \Rightarrow^* u \cdot q_2$ in $G^{\boldsymbol{p}}$. This is achieved in two steps. First, a grammar $G^{\bowtie}$ is constructed that satisfies $[q_1 X q_2] \Rightarrow^* u$ iff conditions (2) and (3) above hold. The construction is similar to the triple construction used to transform a pushdown automaton into an equivalent context-free grammar. In the second step we adjust the terminals in the productions of $G^{\bowtie}$: the productions used to generate the letters of the words $w_1, \ldots, w_n$ are modified so that they generate no terminal at all, with the exception of those productions generating the last letter of one the words $w_1, \ldots, w_n$, say, the word w_i: these that are modified so that they generate the letter $a_i = h^{-1}(w_i)$ instead. For the number of process variables, notice that by the above construction each procedure variable in G yields $\mathcal{O}(pa^2)$ procedure variables in G^f, hence if pr is the number of procedure variables in G we find that the number of procedure variables in G^f is $\mathcal{O}(pa^2 \cdot pr)$.

A detailed proof of this lemma is given in an appendix. □

4.2.2 nDPK is in NP

The proof relies on results of [11, 23, 31], showing that Parikh images of context-free languages are semilinear sets, that semilinear sets are exactly the sets definable by (existential) Presburger formulas, and that satisfiability of existential Presburger formulas is NP-complete. We briefly recall these notions.

Given $k \geq 1$, $c \in \mathbb{N}^k$, and $P = \{p_1, \ldots, p_m\} \subseteq \mathbb{N}^k$, we denote by $L(c; P)$ the subset of $\mathbb{N}^k$ defined as follows

$$\begin{aligned} L(c; P) = \{\mathbf{m} \in \mathbb{N}^k \mid \exists \lambda_1, \ldots, \lambda_m \in \mathbb{N}: \\ \mathbf{m} = c \oplus (\lambda_1 \cdot p_1) \oplus \cdots \oplus (\lambda_m \cdot p_m)\} \ . \end{aligned}$$

A set $S \subseteq \mathbb{N}^k$ is *linear* if $S = L(c; P)$ for some $c \in \mathbb{N}^k$ and some finite $P \subseteq \mathbb{N}^k$. A *semilinear set* is a finite union of linear sets.

Existential Presburger formulas ϕ are defined by the following grammar and interpreted over natural numbers:

$$\begin{aligned} t &::= 0 \mid 1 \mid x \mid t_1 + t_2 \\ \phi &::= t_1 = t_2 \mid t_1 > t_2 \mid \phi_1 \wedge \phi_2 \mid \phi_1 \vee \phi_2 \mid \exists x \cdot \phi_1 \ . \end{aligned}$$

Given an existential Presburger formula ϕ, we denote by $[\![\phi]\!]$ the set of valuations of the free variables of ϕ that make ϕ true; ϕ is satisfiable if $[\![\phi]\!]$ is nonempty. Satisfiability of existential Presburger formulas is an NP-complete problem (see e.g. [31, Lemma 5]).

A set $S \subseteq \mathbb{N}^k$ is (existential) Presburger definable if $S = [\![\phi]\!]$ for some existential Presburger formula ϕ. It is well known that a set is Presburger definable iff it is existential Presburger definable iff it is semilinear.

We use the following result of [31, Th. 4]: given a context-free grammar G over Σ, one can compute in linear time an existential Presburger formula ϕ_G such that $[\![\phi_G]\!] = \Pi(L(G))$. We briefly sketch the proof for future reference. Let $G = (\mathcal{X}, \Sigma, \mathcal{P}, S)$. A result of [7] characterizes $\Pi(L(G))$ as the set of all multisets $\mathbf{m} \in \mathbb{M}[\mathcal{P}]$ that are solution of a certain system of linear equations, and for which a certain derived graph is connected. Then, [31, Th. 4] shows that this set of multisets is Presburger definable by explicitly constructing an existential Presburger formula in linear time in the size of G.

THEOREM 2. *nDMP is in NP.*

PROOF: By Lemma 1 it suffices to show that nDPK is in NP. Let $G_1, \ldots, G_g$ be an instance of nDPK, and let ϕ_{G_i} be the existential Presburger formula of [31, Th. 4] defining $\Pi(L(G_i))$. Let $\Psi = \phi_{G_1} \wedge \ldots \wedge \phi_{G_g}$. We have $[\![\Psi]\!] = \bigcap_{i=1}^{g} \Pi(L(G_i))$, and so Ψ is satisfiable iff $\bigcap_{i=1}^{g} \Pi(L(G_i)) \neq \varnothing$. Since existential formulas are closed under conjunction, Ψ is an existential Presburger formula. Since satisfiability of existential Presburger formulas is NP-complete (see e.g. [31]), the result follows. □

5. Multiparameter analysis

From a verification point of view, it is important to analyze whether nDMP remains NP-complete or becomes polynomial for programs in which one or more of the following parameters is fixed: the number of threads, the maximal size of a procedure, the maximum number of procedures per thread, and the size of the pattern. In the formal model, these parameters correspond to the number of grammars g, the maximal size of a grammar sg, the maximal number of procedure variables in each grammar pr, and the size of the pattern pa. Since each parameter can be fixed or not, there are in principle 16 possible cases. We use $\widehat{p}$ to denote that a parameter p is fixed, and p to denote that it is not fixed. So, for instance, the case in which g and pr are fixed but sg and pa are not, is denoted by nDMP($\widehat{g}, sg, \widehat{pr}, pa$). Section 5.1 consider the cases in which the size of a grammar sg is *fixed*. Sections 5.2 and 5.3 deal with the more involved cases in which sg is not fixed, i.e., threads can have arbitrary size.

5.1 Fixed-sized grammars

In this section we assume that sg is fixed. Recall that the size of a grammar in program normal form is equal to the number of variables plus the number of productions, but when for some terminal a the grammar contains a production $X \to aX$ for every variable X, then all those productions count together as one.

Observe that fixing the size sg of a grammar immediately fixes pr (the number of procedure variables of a grammar cannot be larger than its size). This leaves four cases, corresponding to the four combinations for fixed/nonfixed g and pa.

We first observe that if on top of sg and pr we fix at least another parameter (viz. g or pa), then each instance of nDMP can be reduced to one out of a constant number of nDPK instances, and so the problem can be trivially solved in polynomial time. So the only non-trivial case is nDMP($g, \widehat{sg}, \widehat{pr}, pa$), which corresponds to small but arbitrarily many threads, and an arbitrary pattern. This case remains NP-complete.

THEOREM 3. *The following problem is NP-hard:*
Instance: *Regular grammars $G_1, \ldots, G_g$ in program normal form of fixed size, and a pattern* $\mathbf{p}$.
Question: *Is* $\bigcap_{i=1}^{g} L(G_i) \cap L(\mathbf{p}) \neq \varnothing$?

PROOF: (Sketch.) By reduction from 3-CNF-SAT. Let Ψ be a propositional formula with n variables $x_1, \ldots, x_n$ and m clauses $c_1, \ldots, c_m$. We define for each clause c_i a regular grammar G_i such that $\bigcap_{i=1}^{m} L(G_i) \cap L(\mathbf{p}) \neq \varnothing$ iff Ψ is satisfiable. Let $c_i = \ell_{i_1} \vee \ell_{i_2} \vee \ell_{i_3}$ where $1 \leq i_1 < i_2 < i_3 \leq n$ and $\ell_i \in \{x_i, \overline{x}_i\}$. We define G_i as a regular grammar for the language $\Sigma^* \ell_{i_1} \Sigma^* \ell_{i_2} \Sigma^* \ell_{i_3} \Sigma^*$, where $\Sigma = \{x_k, \overline{x}_k \mid k \notin \{i_1, i_2, i_3\}\}$. Observe that we can easily give a regular grammar G_i with four variables and four productions, plus productions of the form $X \to aX$, which are not counted in the size of the grammar. It is now easy to see that $\bigcap_{i=1}^{m} L(G_i)$ is the set of words $\ell_1 \ldots \ell_n$ that correspond to a satisfying assignment of Ψ, and so by taking $\mathbf{p} = x_1^* (\overline{x}_1)^* \ldots x_n^* (\overline{x}_n)^*$ we are done. □

5.2 Grammars of arbitrary size: NP-hard cases

Since sg is not fixed, there are three parameters, namely g, pr, and pa, that can still be fixed or not. We show that if *at least one* of these three parameters is *not* fixed, then nDMP remains NP-complete. In Section 5.3 we complete the analysis by proving that if *all three* parameters are fixed, then nDMP becomes polynomial.

We have already dealt with one case: Theorem 1 shows that nDMP($g, sg, \widehat{pr}, \widehat{pa}$) is NP-complete (in the theorem the grammars are regular, and so $pr = 0$, and the pattern is always a^*, and so $pa = 1$). This leaves two cases: nDMP($\widehat{g}, sg, pr, \widehat{pa}$), and nDMP($\widehat{g}, sg, \widehat{pr}, pa$). For nDMP($\widehat{g}, sg, pr, \widehat{pa}$) we show that nDMP remains NP-complete for two grammars and fixed pattern a^* by a reduction from the 0-1 Knapsack problem.

DEFINITION 3 (0–1 Knapsack Problem).
Instance: *(1) A set of objects $\{o_1, \ldots, o_m\}$ and their associated weights $\{w_1, \ldots, w_m\}$, which are positive integer given in binary. (2) A positive integer W given in binary.*
Question: *Is there a subset $S \subseteq \{o_1, \ldots, o_m\}$ such that the total weight of S is equal to W ?*

THEOREM 4. *The following problem is NP-hard:*
Instance: *Two context-free grammars G_1, G_2 in program normal form over the alphabet $\{a\}$.*
Question: *Is $L(G_1) \cap L(G_2) \cap L(\mathbf{p}) \neq \varnothing$ for pattern $\mathbf{p} = a^*$?*

PROOF: The proof is by reduction from the 0-1 Knapsack problem: Let $\{o_1, \ldots, o_m\}, \{w_1, \ldots, w_m\}, W$ be an instance of the 0-1 Knapsack problem, and let n be the maximum number of bits needed to encode any of the integers $\{w_1, \ldots, w_m, W\}$. Define G to be the grammar over unary alphabet $\{a\}$ with productions given by the union of the sets (2) through (7) shown below. Intuitively, a derivation of G nondeterministically selects a subset of objects as follows. The object o_i is selected by applying the production $S_i \to S_i^{(n)}$ (2), and omitted by applying $S_i \to S_{i+1}$ (3). If o_i has been selected, then the derivation outputs a^{w_i} through the variable $S_i^{(n)}$ using the productions in (4) and (5), and then comes back to S_{i+1} using production (6). Formally, we have $S_i^{(n)} \Rightarrow^* a^{w_i} \cdot S_{i+1}$. Indeed, observe that $w_i = \sum_{j=0}^{n} j\text{th bit of } w_i \times 2^j$, and the productions of (4)-(5) follow the binary encoding of w_i: if the j-th bit is 0 then the derivation moves to the next bit, and if it is 1, then the grammar outputs a^{2^j} through A_j. The productions of (7) make use of a well-known encoding to ensure $L_{A_k}(G) = \left\{a^{2^k}\right\}$ for every $0 \leq k \leq n$. Finally, the axiom of G is S_1.

$$\left\{S_i \to S_i^{(n)} : 1 \leq i \leq m\right\} \tag{2}$$

$$\{S_i \to S_{i+1} : 1 \leq i \leq m-1\} \cup \{S_m \to \varepsilon\} \tag{3}$$

$$\left\{ S_i^{(k)} \to A_k \cdot S_i^{(k-1)} : \begin{array}{c} 1 \leq i \leq m \\ 1 \leq k \leq n \\ \text{bit } k \text{ of } w_i \text{ is } 1 \end{array} \right\} \tag{4}$$

$$\left\{ S_i^{(k)} \to S_i^{(k-1)} : \begin{array}{c} 1 \leq i \leq m \\ 1 \leq k \leq n \\ \text{bit } k \text{ of } w_i \text{ is } 0 \end{array} \right\} \tag{5}$$

$$\left\{S_i^{(0)} \to S_{i+1} : 1 \leq i \leq m-1\right\} \cup \left\{S_m^{(0)} \to \varepsilon\right\} \tag{6}$$

$$\{A_k \to A_{k-1}A_{k-1} : 1 \leq k \leq n\} \cup \{A_0 \to aZ\} \cup \{Z \to \varepsilon\} \tag{7}$$

We now turn to W, and define the grammar G_W by:

$$\left\{ W^{(k)} \to A_k \cdot W^{(k-1)} : \begin{array}{c} 1 \leq k \leq n \\ \text{bit } k \text{ of } W \text{ is } 1 \end{array} \right\} \tag{8}$$

$$\left\{ W^{(k)} \to W^{(k-1)} : \begin{array}{c} 1 \leq k \leq n \\ \text{bit } k \text{ of } W \text{ is } 0 \end{array} \right\} \cup \left\{W^{(0)} \to \varepsilon\right\} \tag{9}$$

where $W^{(n)}$ is the axiom. From the reasoning above we find that $L(G) = \{a^W\}$.

Clearly, G and G_W can be computed in polynomial time, and are in program normal form. Moreover, it is easily seen that $L(G) \cap L(G_W) \cap L(\mathbf{p}) \neq \varnothing$ iff there is a subset $S \subseteq \{o_1, \ldots, o_m\}$ such that the total weight of S is W. □

For nDMP($\widehat{g}, sg, \widehat{pr}, pa$), we show that nDMP remains NP-complete for three grammars, each of them with at most one procedure variable. The proof is by reduction from the bounded Post Correspondence Problem [10].

DEFINITION 4 (Bounded Post Correspondence Problem).
Instance. *Two sequences $a = (a_1, \ldots, a_n)$ and $b = (b_1, \ldots, b_n)$ of words over an alphabet Σ, and a positive integer $K \leq n$.*
Question: *Is there a non-empty sequence $i_1, \ldots, i_k$ of $k \leq K$ (not necessarily distinct) positive integers, each between 1 and n, such that $a_{i_1} a_{i_2} \ldots a_{i_k} = b_{i_1} b_{i_2} \ldots b_{i_k}$.*

THEOREM 5. *The following problem is NP-hard:*
Instance: *Two context-free grammars G_1, G_2 in program normal form, each of them with 1 procedure variable, a regular grammar R in program normal form, and a pattern* $\mathbf{p}$.
Question: *Is* $L(G_1) \cap L(G_2) \cap L(R) \cap L(\mathbf{p}) \neq \varnothing$?

PROOF:(Sketch.) Let a, b, K be an instance of the bounded Post Correspondence Problem. Define $\Gamma = \{1, \ldots, n\}$ and assume it is disjoint from Σ. We construct the context-free grammars $G_1 = (\{X\}, \Sigma \cup \Gamma, \mathcal{P}_1, X)$, where

$$\mathcal{P}_1 = \{X \rightarrow a_i \cdot X \cdot i \mid i \in \Gamma\} \cup \{X \rightarrow \varepsilon\} ,$$

$G_2 = (\{Y\}, \Sigma \cup \Gamma, \mathcal{P}_2, Y)$, where

$$\mathcal{P}_2 = \{Y \rightarrow b_i \cdot Y \cdot i \mid i \in \Gamma\} \cup \{Y \rightarrow \varepsilon\} ,$$

the regular grammar R such that $L(R) = \Sigma^* \cdot \bigcup_{i=1}^{K} \Gamma^i$, and the pattern $\boldsymbol{p} = (a_1^* \ldots a_n^*)^K (1^* \ldots n^*)^K$. Observe that, since $K \leq n$, the size of $\boldsymbol{p}$ is polynomial in the size of the instance. Notice that G_1 and G_2 can be easily put in program normal form: replace a production $X \rightarrow a_i \cdot X \cdot i$ by productions $X \rightarrow a_i \cdot X_i', X_i' \rightarrow X \cdot X_i'', X_i'' \rightarrow i \cdot Z, Z \rightarrow \varepsilon$, where X_i', X_i'' and Z are fresh variables. Finally, observe that X is the only procedure variable. It follows easily from the construction that $L(G_1) \cap L(G_2) \cap L(R) \cap L(\boldsymbol{p}) \neq \varnothing$ iff the bounded PCP instance is positive. □

Notice that in this reduction, neither the number of words in $\boldsymbol{p}$ nor their length is fixed. By mean of a more involved reduction it is possible to show NP-hardness with a single word only (but arbitrarily long). This reduction is presented next.

5.2.1 A finer analysis

We have defined the size of a pattern $\boldsymbol{p} = w_1^* \ldots w_n^*$ as $\sum_{i=1}^{n} |w_i|$. We can now zoom in and consider the size as a function of two parameters, the number n of words in the pattern, and the maximal length of a pattern. Since the reduction of Theorem 5 requires a pattern with a large number of words ($2n$ in the worst case), we study whether nDMP stays NP-complete if on top of the number of grammars g and the number pr of procedures also the number of words n in the pattern $\boldsymbol{p} = w_1^* \ldots w_n^*$ is fixed, but not their length. We show that nDMP remains NP-hard by reduction to the 0-1 Knapsack problem of Def. 3.

Consider the reduction from 0-1 Knapsack shown in Th. 4. It does not yield a grammar with a fixed number of procedure variables because of the sets (7), (4), and (8) of productions.

To solve this problem we first construct a grammar $G^\sharp$ with a fixed number of procedure variables that can still be used to encode big numbers, albeit by means of a more complicated encoding. Fix a number $n \geq 1$ and an alphabet $\Sigma = \{a_0, a_1, \ldots, a_n\} \cup \{b_1, \ldots, b_n\}$, and let $w = a_n b_n \cdots a_1 b_1 a_0$. We encode the number $k \leq 2^n$ by the word w^k. The grammar $G^\sharp = (\mathcal{X}^\sharp, \Sigma, \mathcal{P}^\sharp, X)$ has variables $\mathcal{X}^\sharp = \{X\} \cup \{A_1, \ldots, A_n\}$ (X is the only procedure variable), and productions $\mathcal{P}^\sharp$ given by the union of the sets (10) to (14):

$$\{X \rightarrow A_n\} \tag{10}$$
$$\{X \rightarrow b_k A_{k-1} \mid 1 \leq k \leq n\} \tag{11}$$
$$\{A_k \rightarrow a_k X A_{k-1} \mid 1 \leq k \leq n\} \tag{12}$$
$$\{A_k \rightarrow a_j b_j A_k \mid n \geq j, k \geq 0 \wedge j > k\} \tag{13}$$
$$\{A_0 \rightarrow a_0\} \tag{14}$$

$G^\sharp$ can also be obtained as follows. We first apply the construction of Sect. 3.2 to the program shown in Figure 2. This returns a context-free grammar in program normal form. Second, some productions are merged for better readability.

Consider the pattern $\boldsymbol{p} = w^*$. Our first lemma shows that the language $L_{A_k}(G^\sharp) \cap L(\boldsymbol{p})$ consists of a unique word given by 2^k repetitions of w.

LEMMA 2. *$L_{A_k}(G^\sharp) \cap L(\boldsymbol{p}) = \left\{w^{2^k}\right\}$ for every $0 \leq k \leq n$.*

PROOF: The proof is by induction on k.

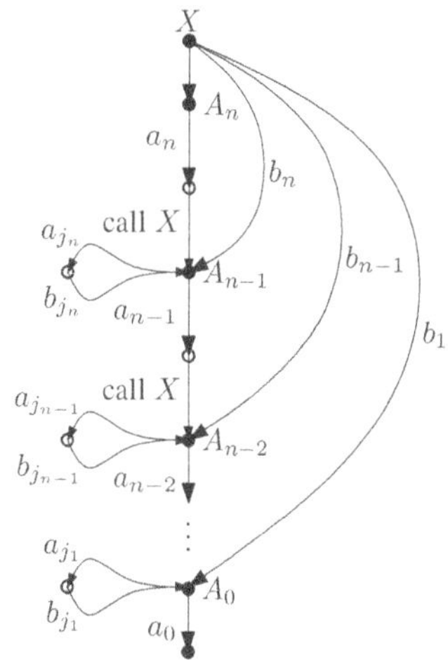

Figure 2. The abstracted program defining $G^\flat$. For every $i \in \{1, \ldots, n\}$ we have $j_i \in \{i, \ldots, n\}$ as in (13).

k = 0. The only word which can be derived from A_0 and follows $\boldsymbol{p}$ is given by $A_0 (\Rightarrow^{(13)})^* a_n b_n \ldots a_1 b_1 A_0 \Rightarrow^{(14)} a_n b_n \ldots a_1 b_1 a_0 = w^{2^0}$.

k > 0. We distinguish two cases: $k < n$ and $k = n$. For $k < n$, consider the following partial leftmost derivation:

$$\begin{array}{lll} A_k & (\Rightarrow^{(13)})^* & a_n b_n \ldots a_{k+1} b_{k+1} A_k \\ & \Rightarrow^{(12)} & a_n b_n \ldots a_{k+1} b_{k+1} a_k X A_{k-1} \\ & \Rightarrow^{(11)} & a_n b_n \ldots a_{k+1} b_{k+1} a_k b_k A_{k-1} A_{k-1} \\ & (\Rightarrow^{(12)} \Rightarrow^{(11)})^* & a_n b_n \cdots a_1 b_1 A_0 A_0 A_1 \ldots A_{k-1} \\ & \Rightarrow^{(14)} & a_n b_n \cdots a_1 b_1 a_0 A_0 A_1 \ldots A_{k-1} \\ & = & w \cdot A_0 A_1 \ldots A_{k-1} \end{array}$$

For the case $k = n$, consider

$$\begin{array}{lll} A_n & (\Rightarrow^{(12)} \Rightarrow^{(11)})^* & a_n b_n \ldots a_1 b_1 A_0 A_0 A_1 \ldots A_{n-1} \\ & \Rightarrow^{(14)} & w \cdot A_0 A_1 \ldots A_{n-1} \ . \end{array}$$

We only need these two partial derivations, because every leftmost derivation that does not start like one of the two does not generates a word of $L(\boldsymbol{p})$ either. To conclude, we apply the induction hypothesis on $A_0 A_1 \ldots A_{k-1}$ to show that $A_k \Rightarrow^* w \cdot w^{2^0} \cdot w^{2^1} \cdots w^{2^{k-1}}$, hence that $A_k \Rightarrow^* w^{2^k}$ since $1 + \sum_{i=0}^{k-1} 2^i = 2^k$. □

Using this lemma we can already obtain a first reduction from the 0-1 Knapsack problem to nDMP in polynomial time. If in the reduction of Th. 4 the set (7) is replaced by the set $\mathcal{P}^\sharp$, we get $L(G) \cap L(G_W) \cap L(\boldsymbol{p}) \neq \varnothing$ iff there exists $S \subseteq \{o_1, \ldots, o_m\}$ such that S's weight is W. However, this reduction is not yet adequate because the variables $\{A_1, \ldots, A_n\}$ are procedures variables (see the sets (4) and (8) of productions). To fix this problem, we need a second lemma:

LEMMA 3. *(1) $L(G^\sharp) \cap L(\boldsymbol{p}) = \left\{w^{2^n}\right\}$.*

(2) $\left(\{a_n b_n \ldots a_{k+1}\} \cdot L(G^\sharp)\right) \cap L(\boldsymbol{p}) = \left\{w^{2^k}\right\}$ for all $1 \leq k \leq n-1$.

PROOF: (1) Any derivation of $G^\sharp$ that generates a word of $L(\boldsymbol{p})$ must use the production (10) first, so that $X \Rightarrow^{(10)} A_n$. Applying Lem. 2 we get $L(G^\sharp) \cap L(\boldsymbol{p}) = L_{A_n}(G) \cap L(\boldsymbol{p}) = \left\{w^{2^n}\right\}$.

(2) Any derivation of $G^\sharp$ generating a word u such that $a_n b_n \ldots a_{k+1} u$ belongs to $L(\boldsymbol{p})$ must start with $X \Rightarrow^{(11)} b_{k+1} \cdot A_k$. As shown in

the proof of Lem. 2, the derivation must continue with $X \Rightarrow^{(11)} b_{k+1} \cdot A_k \Rightarrow^* w \cdot A_0 A_1 \cdots A_{k-1}$, and so finally lead to w^{2^k}. □

We the help of this lemma we can now proceed as follows. Recall that we have already replaced set (7) in the reduction of Th. 4 by $\mathcal{P}^\sharp$. Now we replace the set (4) by

$$\left\{ S_i^{(k)} \to a_n b_n \cdots a_{k+1} \cdot X \cdot S_i^{(k-1)} : \begin{array}{c} 1 \leq i \leq m \\ 1 \leq k \leq n \\ \text{bit } k \text{ of } W \text{ is } 1 \end{array} \right\}$$

and the set (8) by

$$\left\{ W^{(k)} \to a_n b_n \cdots a_{k+1} \cdot X \cdot W^{(k-1)} : \begin{array}{c} 1 \leq k \leq n \\ \text{bit } k \text{ of } W \text{ is } 1 \end{array} \right\}$$

This gives two grammars $G_1^{\bowtie}$ and $G_2^{\bowtie}$ with S_1 and $W^{(n)}$ as axioms, respectively. We have:

THEOREM 6. *The following problem is NP-hard:*
Instance: *Two context-free grammars G_1, G_2 in program normal form over alphabet Σ, each of them with 1 procedure variable, and a pattern $\mathbf{p} = w^*$ consisting of a single word $w \in \Sigma^*$.*
Question: *Is $L(G_1) \cap L(G_2) \cap L(\mathbf{p}) \neq \varnothing$?*

PROOF: The proof is by reduction to 0-1 Knapsack. We construct $G_1^{\bowtie}, G_2^{\bowtie}$ and $\mathbf{p}$ as above. The proof of correctness for the reduction essentially follows the one of Th. 4 where the result of Lem. 3 is used when needed. We thus obtain that $L(G_1^{\bowtie}) \cap L(G_2^{\bowtie}) \cap L(\mathbf{p}) \neq \varnothing$ iff a subset of $\{o_1, \ldots, o_m\}$ has weight W.

It is routine to check the following: given a 0-1 Knapsack instance (1) $G_i^{\bowtie}$ is computable in polynomial time, (2) X is the only procedure of $G_i^{\bowtie}$ where $i \in \{1,2\}$ and (3) $\mathbf{p} = w^*$ is computable in polynomial time. Note that $G_i^{\bowtie}$ are not in program normal form, but can easily be brought into it by adding new variables and productions. The transformation does not add any procedure variable. □

5.3 Grammars of arbitrary size: a polynomial case

We present the most involved result of the paper, a polynomial algorithm for nDMP($\widehat{g}, sg, \widehat{pr}, \widehat{pa}$). Notice that the reduction of nDMP to satisfiability of existential Presburger formulas of Th. 2 does not help, because it yields formulas of arbitrary size that, to the best of our knowledge, do not fall immediately into any polynomial class described in the literature (see e.g. [12, 22, 27]). However, using some recent results of [19, 29] we show how to compute in polynomial time an equisatisfiable formula that belongs to the polynomial class of [27].

As a first step we observe that, because of the reduction from nDMP to nDPK shown in Section 4.2, it suffices to provide a polynomial algorithm for nDPK, and in fact only for the instances of nDPK with a fixed number g of grammars over an alphabet of fixed size al, and a fixed number of procedure variables pr', i.e., a polynomial procedure for nDPK($\widehat{g}, sg, \widehat{al}, \widehat{pr'}$). Indeed, Lem. 1 shows that (1) al, the size of the alphabet in the reduced nDPK instance, is fixed, because pa is fixed in nDMP, and (2) that pr', the number of procedure variables in the reduced nDPK instance, is fixed since pa and pr are fixed.

Let $G_1, \ldots, G_g$ be an instance of nDPK($\widehat{g}, sg, \widehat{al}, \widehat{pr}$). The polynomial algorithm proceeds in two steps: first, for each $i \in \{1, \ldots, g\}$ the algorithm computes a regular grammar (or non-deterministic automaton) A_i such that $\Pi(L(A_i)) = \Pi(L(G_i))$; then, the algorithm checks if $\bigcap_{i=1}^{g} \Pi(L(A_i)) = \varnothing$. The difficulty consists of showing that both steps can be carried out in polynomial time. For this we prove two facts. First, if $G_i = (\mathcal{X}, \Sigma, \mathcal{P}, S)$, then the algorithm constructs A_i in $\mathcal{O}(|G_i|^{f(pr)})$ time and space for some function f. Second, given automata $A_1, \ldots, A_g$ over an alphabet of size al, the algorithm performs the check $\bigcap_{i=1}^{g} \Pi(L(A_i)) = \varnothing$ in $\mathcal{O}((|A_1| + \cdots + |A_g|)^{h(g,al)})$ time for some function h. Since g, pr, and al have fixed values, so do $f(pr)$ and $h(g, al)$.

Step 1. We show that given a context-free grammar G in program normal form with pr variables, we can construct a regular grammar A_G satisfying $\Pi(L(A_G)) = \Pi(L(G))$ in $\mathcal{O}(|G_i|^{f(pr)})$ time and space (for some function f). For this we strengthen a recent result of [8], which shows that such a grammar can be constructed in $\mathcal{O}(|G|^{f(v)})$ time and space, where v is the *total* number of variables of G. We start by defining the grammar A_G.

DEFINITION 5. *Let $G = (\mathcal{X}, \Sigma, \mathcal{P}, S)$ be a context-free grammar in program normal form, and let pr be the number of procedure variables of G. We define the regular grammar $A_G = (\mathcal{Q}, \Sigma, \delta, q)$ as follows:*

- *$\mathcal{Q}$ is the set of all multisets $\mathbf{m} \in \mathbb{M}[\mathcal{X}]$ of at most $(pr + 2)$ elements, and q, the axiom, is given by $[\![S]\!]$;*
- *$\delta = \{\emptyset \to \epsilon\} \cup \delta'$, where δ' contains a production $\mathbf{m} \to \alpha \cdot \mathbf{m}'$ iff $\mathcal{P}$ contains a production $X \to \alpha\beta$, such that $\alpha \in \Sigma^*$, $\beta \in \mathcal{X}^*$, and $\mathbf{m}' \oplus [\![X]\!] = \mathbf{m} \oplus \Pi(\beta)$.*

Observe that $|\mathcal{Q}| = \mathcal{O}(|\mathcal{X}|^{pr+2})$ and $|\delta| \leq |\mathcal{Q}|^2 \cdot al$. We set out to prove the following result (see Theorem 7 in the next page) by means of several lemmas:

> Let $G = (\mathcal{X}, \Sigma, \mathcal{P}, S)$ be a context-free grammar in program normal form. The regular grammar A_G of Def. 5 satisfies $\Pi(L(G)) = \Pi(L(A_G))$.

We first introduce some new notation. Given $L_1, L_2 \subseteq \Sigma^*$, we write $L_1 =_\Pi L_2$, respectively $L_1 \subseteq_\Pi L_2$, to denote that the Parikh image of L_1 is equal to, respectively included in, the Parikh image of L_2. Also, given $w, w' \in \Sigma^*$, we abbreviate $\{w\} =_\Pi \{w'\}$ to $w =_\pi w'$. Using this notation we can rewrite our proof goal $\Pi(L(G)) = \Pi(L(A_G))$ as $L(A_G) =_\Pi L(G)$.

The proof is a modification of the one given in [8]. The inclusion $L(A_G) \subseteq_\Pi L(G)$ is proved in [8, Prop 2.1]. Establishing $L(G) \subseteq_\Pi L(A_G)$ is done through the chain of inclusions $L(G) \subseteq_\Pi L^{(pr+2)}(G) \subseteq_\Pi L(A_G)$, where $L^{(i)}(G)$ is the index-i approximation of $L(G)$, defined as follows.

DEFINITION 6. *A derivation $S = \alpha_0 \Rightarrow \cdots \Rightarrow \alpha_m$ of $G = (\mathcal{X}, \Sigma, \mathcal{P}, S)$ has index k if for every $i \in \{0, \ldots, m\}$ at most k symbols of α_i are variables. The set of words derivable through derivations of index k is denoted by $L^{(k)}(G)$.*

The inclusion $L^{(pr+2)}(G) \subseteq_\Pi L(A_G)$ is proved in [8, Lem. 2.4]. To prove $L(G) \subseteq_\Pi L^{(pr+2)}(G)$ we need a few preliminaries.

DEFINITION 7. *Let $G = (\mathcal{X}, \Sigma, \mathcal{P}, S)$ be a context-free grammar in program normal form. We inductively define the set Tr of finite labelled trees as follows:*

- *if $(X, \varepsilon) \in \mathcal{P}$ then the tree t labelled by production (X, ε) and consisting of one single node is a tree of Tr, and its yield $\Delta(t)$ is equal to ε;*
- *if $(X, a \cdot Y) \in \mathcal{P}$, then the tree t labelled by $(X, a \cdot Y)$ and having as only child a tree $t' \in Tr$ labelled by some $(Y, \alpha) \in \mathcal{P}$ is a tree of Tr, and $\Delta(t) = a \cdot \Delta(t')$;*
- *if $(X, Y) \in \mathcal{P}$, then the tree t labelled by (X, Y) and having as only child a tree $t' \in Tr$ labelled by some $(Y, \alpha) \in \mathcal{P}$ is a tree of Tr, and $\Delta(t) = \Delta(t')$;*
- *if $(X, Z \cdot Y) \in \mathcal{P}$, then the tree t labelled by $(X, Z \cdot Y)$ and having two children labelled by some (Z, α_1) (left) and (Y, α_2) (right) is also a tree of Tr, and $\Delta(t) = \Delta(t_1) \cdot \Delta(t_2)$.*

A tree $t \in Tr$ is a derivation tree *if it is labelled by a production $(S, \alpha) \in \mathcal{P}$ for some α. The set of all derivation trees of G is* *denoted by T_G. The* yield $\Delta(T)$ *of a countable set* $T \subseteq Tr$ *of trees is defined by* $\Delta(T) = \bigcup_{t \in T} \Delta(t)$. *In the following, we mean* derivation tree *whenever we say* tree.

LEMMA 4 (Easy). *Let* $G = (\mathcal{X}, \Sigma, \mathcal{P}, S)$ *be a context-free grammar in program normal form. Then* $L(G) = \Delta(T_G)$.

By Lem. 4, proving $L(G) \subseteq_\Pi L^{(pr+2)}(G)$ reduces to proving $\Delta(T_G) \subseteq_\Pi L^{(pr+2)}(G)$. We now introduce the notion of dimension of a tree.

DEFINITION 8. *The* dimension $d(t)$ *of a tree* t *is inductively defined as follows:*

1. *If* t *has no children, then* $d(t) = 0$;
2. *If* t *has exactly one child* t_1, *then* $d(t) = d(t_1)$;
3. *If* t *has exactly two children* t_1 *and* t_2, *then*

$$d(t) = \begin{cases} d(t_1) + 1 & \text{if } d(t_1) = d(t_2) \\ \max(d(t_1), d(t_2)) & \text{if } d(t_1) \neq d(t_2). \end{cases}$$

The set of all derivation trees of dimension k *for grammar* G *is denoted by* T_G^k.

The next lemma goes along the lines of [8, Lem. 2.1], but with many small changes.

LEMMA 5. *Let* $G = (\mathcal{X}, \Sigma, \mathcal{P}, S)$ *be a context-free grammar in program normal form with* pr *procedure variables. Then* $\Delta(T_G) \subseteq_\Pi \bigcup_{i=0}^{pr+1} \Delta(T_G^i)$.

PROOF: In this proof we write $t = t_1 \cdot t_2$ to denote that t_1 is a derivation tree except that exactly one leaf ℓ is labelled by a production of the form (A, α) with $\alpha \neq \varepsilon$; t_2 is a derivation tree labelled (A, α') for some α'; and the tree t is obtained from t_1 and t_2 by replacing the leaf $\ell = (A, \alpha)$ of t_1 by t_2.

We want to prove that for every tree $t \in T_G$, there exists a tree t' such that $\Delta(t) =_\Pi \Delta(t')$ and $d(t') \leq pr + 1$. Let a tree t be *compact* if $d(t) \leq L(t)$, where $L(t) = 1 + L'(t)$ and $L'(t)$ is the number of distinct procedure variables in t. We find that $L'(t) \leq pr$ for every $t \in T_G$, hence $L(t) \leq pr + 1$. To establish the above result, it suffices to show that for every tree t, there exists a compact tree t' such that $\Delta(t) =_\Pi \Delta(t')$.

The proof is by induction on the number of nodes of t. In the base case, t has just one node labelled (S, ε), so $d(t) = 0 < 1 \leq L(t)$, hence t is compact, and we are done. In the following, assume that t has more than one node and $d(t) > L(t)$ holds. If t has exactly one child t_1 then $d(t) = d(t_1) > L(t)$. Since t_1 has one node less than t, induction hypothesis shows that t_1 can be made compact, i.e. $d(t_1) \leq L(t_1)$. Next we conclude from the definition of L and the structure of t that $L(t_1) \leq L(t)$, also that $d(t) = d(t_1)$ and finally that $d(t) \leq L(t)$ and we are done. Let us turn to the case where t has two children t_1 and t_2. We assume w.l.o.g. that $d(t) \geq d(t_1) \geq d(t_2)$. Finally, by the induction hypothesis, we can further assume that t_1 and t_2 are compact, i.e. $d(t_i) \leq L(t_i)$ for $i = 1, 2$.

From the definition of dimension and L, t_1 is a subtree of t, and $d(t) > L(t)$ we find that: $L(t) + 1 \leq d(t) \leq d(t_1) + 1 \leq L(t_1) + 1 \leq L(t) + 1$. We conclude from above that $d(t_1) = L(t)$ and $d(t) = d(t_1) + 1$, hence that $d(t_1) = d(t_2)$ by definition of dimension and finally that $d(t_1) = d(t_2) = L(t) = L(t_1) = L(t_2)$ since t_1, t_2 are compact subtrees of t. We now prove the following claim: there is a path in t_2 from the root to a leaf such that two nodes are labelled by (Z, α) and (Z, α') where Z is a procedure variable.

Our proof is by contradiction. Observe that for derivation tree t with child t' such that $d(t) > d(t')$, the definition of dimension and program normal form shows that t is labelled by $(X, Z \cdot Y)$ for some variables X, Z and Y. If $d(t) = k$ then the rooted path that goes down through the left child whenever possible has at least k nodes with label of the form (Z, α) where Z is a procedure variable. Finally since $d(t_2) = L(t_2) = L'(t_2) + 1$ where $L'(t_2)$ is the number of distinct procedure variables in t_2, we find that two nodes are labelled (Z, α) and (Z, α') where Z is a procedure variable, hence a contradiction.

So t_2 can be factored into $t_2^a \cdot (t_2^b \cdot t_2^c)$ such that t_2^b and t_2^c have their root labelled (Z, α) and (Z, α') where Z is a procedure variable.

As $L(t) = L(t_1) = L(t_2)$, we also find a node of t_1 labelled (Z, α) where Z is a procedure variable which allows us to write $t_1 = t_1^a \cdot t_1^b$ where t_1^b has its root labelled (Z, α) where Z is a procedure variable.

Now we cut out the middle part t_2^b of t_2, and insert it between the two parts t_1^a and t_1^b of t_1, so that we get $t_1' = t_1^a \cdot (t_2^b \cdot t_1^b)$ and $t_2' = t_2^a \cdot t_2^c$. We then have $L(t_1') = L(t_1) = L(t_2) \geq L(t_2')$. By induction, t_1' and t_2' can be made compact, so $d(t_1') \leq L(t_1') = d(t_1) = d(t_2) \geq L(t_2') \geq d(t_2')$. Consider the tree t' obtained from t by replacing t_1 by t_1' and t_2 by t_2'. Clearly, $\Delta(t) =_\Pi \Delta(t')$. If $d(t_1') < d(t_1)$ or $d(t_2') < d(t_2)$, then $d(t') \leq d(t) - 1 = L(t) = L(t')$ by definition of dimension, and we are done because t' is compact. Otherwise, we have $d(t_1') = d(t_2') = L(t') = L(t_1') = L(t_2')$. So we can iterate the above procedure and insert a part of t_2' into t_1'. This procedure terminates, because the transfer of nodes from the second child to the first cannot proceed forever. □

By this lemma, proving $\Delta(T_G) \subseteq_\Pi L^{(pr+2)}(G)$ reduces to showing $\Delta(T_G) \subseteq_\Pi \bigcup_{i=0}^{pr+1} \Delta(T_G^i) \subseteq_\Pi L^{(pr+2)}(G)$. To conclude the proof we show $\bigcup_{i=0}^{pr+1} \Delta(T_G^i) \subseteq L^{(pr+2)}(G)$.

LEMMA 6. *For every* $k \geq 0$: $\Delta(T_G^k) \subseteq L^{(k+1)}(G)$.

PROOF: Let t be a derivation tree of dimension k. The proof is by induction on the structure of t.

Base. t consists of a node labelled (S, ε), hence $k = 0$ and $S \Rightarrow \varepsilon$ is of index 1.

Step. W.l.o.g. t has two children t_1 and t_2 such that $d(t) \geq d(t_1) \geq d(t_2)$. By the definition of dimension we have $d(t_2) \leq k - 1$. Let A, A_1 and A_2 be the roots of t, t_1 and t_2, respectively. Then $A \to A_1 A_2$ is a production of the grammar. By induction hypothesis, there are derivations $A_1 \Rightarrow^* w_1$ of index $k + 1$ and $A_2 \Rightarrow^* w_2$ of index k. So there is a derivation $A \Rightarrow A_1 A_2 \Rightarrow^* A_1 w_2 \Rightarrow^* w_1 w_2$ of index $k + 1$. □

Collecting the results above, we get:

THEOREM 7. *For every context-free grammar* G *in program normal form with* pr *procedure variables,* $\Pi(L(A_G)) = \Pi(L(G))$.

PROOF: In [8, Prop 2.1], $L(A) \subseteq_\Pi L(G)$ has been proved. For the reverse inclusion:

$$\begin{aligned} L(G) &= \Delta(T_G) && \text{Lem. 4} \\ &\subseteq_\Pi \textstyle\bigcup_{i=0}^{pr+1} \Delta(T_G^i) && \text{Lem. 5} \\ &\subseteq L^{(pr+2)}(G) && \text{Lem. 6} \\ &\subseteq_\Pi L(A_G) && \text{[8, Lem. 2.4]} \end{aligned}$$

□

COROLLARY 1. *Given a context-free grammar* G *with* pr *procedure variables, we can construct in* $\mathcal{O}(|G|^{(pr+2)})$ *time a regular grammar* A_G *such that* $\Pi(L(G)) = \Pi(L(A_G))$.

PROOF: Follows immediately from the fact that the number of variables of the regular grammar A_G of Def.5 for a context-free grammar G with n variables and pr procedure variables is $\mathcal{O}(n^{pr+2})$. □

Step 2. Given regular grammars $A_1, \ldots, A_g$ over an alphabet of size al, we show that $\bigcap_{i=1}^{g} \Pi(L(A_i)) = \emptyset$ can be checked in time $\mathcal{O}((|A_1| + \cdots + |A_g|)^{h(g,al)})$ for a function h.

It is well known that for every regular grammar A, the set $\Pi(L(A))$ is semilinear. It has been recently proved that $\Pi(L(A))$ is "small".

THEOREM 8. **[29, Th. 4.1]** *Let A be a regular grammar with n variables over alphabet Σ of size al. There exists a representation of $\Pi(L(A)) \subseteq \mathbb{N}^{al}$ as a union of linear sets $\bigcup_{j=1}^{m} L(c_j; P_j)$, where m is polynomial in n and exponential in al, the maximum entry of each c_j is polynomial in n and exponential in al, the number of periods in each P_j is at most al, and the maximum entry of each period is at most n. Furthermore, this is computable in time polynomial in n and exponential in al.*

This theorem suggests the following procedure to check $\bigcap_{i=1}^{g} \Pi(L(A_i)) = \emptyset$ for fixed g. First, compute for each A_i a representation of $\Pi(L(A_i))$ as given above. This is done in polynomial time in the number of variables of A_i since Σ is of fixed size. Then, for each tuple $\langle L(c_1; P_1), \ldots, L(c_g; P_g)\rangle$, where $L(c_i; P_i)$ is a linear set of $\Pi(L(A_i))$, check if $\cap_{i=1}^{g} L(c_i; P_i) = \emptyset$. Since g and al are fixed, the number of tuples is polynomial, and so in order to obtain a polynomial procedure we just need to prove that $\cap_{i=1}^{g} L(c_i; P_i) = \emptyset$ can be checked in polynomial time. For this we first reduce the problem to solving a system of linear equations over the natural numbers.

DEFINITION 9. *Let $t = \langle L(c_1; P_1), \ldots, L(c_g; P_g)\rangle$ be a tuple of linear sets of dimension al, where $P_i = \left\{p_i^{(1)}, \ldots, p_i^{(j_i)}\right\}$. The existential Presburger formula Φ_t is given by*

$$\exists x_1^{(1)}, \ldots, x_1^{(j_1)}, \ldots, x_g^{(1)}, \ldots, x_g^{(j_g)} : \bigwedge_{\substack{1 \le id \le g-1 \\ 1 \le \ell \le al}} \phi(id, id+1, \ell)$$

where $\phi(id, id', \ell)$ denotes the formula

$$c_{id}(a_\ell) + \sum_{i=1}^{j_{id}} x_{id}^{(i)} * p_{id}^{(i)}(a_\ell) = c_{id'}(a_\ell) + \sum_{i=1}^{j_{id'}} x_{id'}^{(i)} * p_{id'}^{(i)}(a_\ell) \ .$$

In the above definition, the subformula $\phi(id, id', \ell)$ has the following interpretation: $\phi(id, id', \ell)$ is satisfiable iff there exist $v \in L(c_{id}; P_{id})$ and $v' \in L(c_{id'}; P_{id'})$ such that $v(\ell) = v'(\ell)$. Therefore $\bigwedge_{1 \le \ell \le al} \phi(id, id', \ell)$ is satisfiable iff $L(c_{id}; P_{id})$ and $L(c_{id'}; P_{id'})$ have a common vector, i.e., iff $L(c_{id}; P_{id}) \cap L(c_{id'}; P_{id'}) \neq \emptyset$. So $\bigwedge_{1 \le id \le g-1} \bigwedge_{1 \le \ell \le al} \phi(id, id+1, \ell)$ is satisfiable iff $\cap_{i=1}^{g} L(c_i; P_i) \neq \emptyset$. Hence the following result.

LEMMA 7. *Let $t = \langle L(c_1; P_1), \ldots, L(c_g; P_g)\rangle$ be a tuple of linear sets. We have $\cap_{i=1}^{g} L(c_i; P_i) \neq \emptyset$ iff Φ_t is satisfiable.*

Assume now that the maximum entries and number of periods of the linear sets in the tuple t of Def. 9 are as given in Th. 8. An inspection of the formula Φ_t in Def. 9 shows that in this case the number of variables of Φ_t is at most $g * al$, and so that Φ_t is an existential Presburger formula with $g * al$ quantifiers and no free variables. Since g and al are fixed parameters, $g * al$ is also fixed. It follows that the satisfiability of Φ_t can be determined in polynomial time by means of the Lenstra-Scarpellini's algorithm [22, 27] (see also [12]).

This concludes the proof that given regular grammars $A_1, \ldots, A_g$ over an alphabet of size al, whether $\bigcap_{i=1}^{g} \Pi(L(A_i)) \neq \emptyset$ holds or not can be determined in polynomial time.

6. Conclusions

We have studied the complexity of pattern-based verification, an approach to the verification of multithreaded programs essentially introduced by Kahlon in [15]. The approach asks the programmer to supply a pattern, a regular expression of the form $w_1^* \ldots w_n^*$ over the alphabet of channels (and possibly other program instructions). The verification tool then analyzes whether the program has some execution that uses the channels conforming to the pattern.

The expressivity of pattern-based verification was first investigated in [9], where it was shown that context bounding, the technique introduced by Qadeer and Rehof in [25] and implemented in CHESS, SPIN, SLAM, jMoped, and other tools [1, 5, 20, 28, 30], is a special case of pattern-based verification. In this paper we provide a further analysis and give a explicit reduction.

We have reduced the pattern-based verification problem to nDMP, the problem of deciding whether the intersection of a given set of context-free grammars and a pattern is nonempty. Putting together classical results by Ginsburg and Spanier [11] about bounded context-free languages; the characterization of the Parikh images of context-free languages given in [7]; the encoding of this characterization into existential Presburger arithmetic presented in [31]; and the fact that existential Presburger arithmetic reduces to solving a system of linear Diophantine equations (well-known to be in NP [32]) we have shown that nDMP is NP-complete. Since context bounding is also NP-complete, the additional expressivity of pattern-based verification does not come at an extra cost in terms of asymptotic complexity.

We have conducted a multiparameter analysis of nDMP on the number of threads, the maximum number of procedures per thread, the maximal size of a procedure, and the size of the pattern. By requiring the value of a parameter to be fixed or not, we get 16 cases. We have shown that all *except one* are either trivially polynomial or still NP-complete. The analysis of the remaining case (all parameters fixed except the maximal size of a procedure) is the main technical contribution of the paper. Using a novel constructive proof of Parikh's theorem and recent results about the Parikh images of nondeterministic automata [19, 29], we have shown that this case is polynomial. Given the high complexity of automatic verification of multithreaded procedural programs (unless strong constraints like absence of communication between threads or restriction to local properties of a thread are imposed) we think that this is a remarkable result.

Two comments about our model are in order. First, while we have only considered abstracted programs (i.e., we assume that all program paths with (1) correct nesting of procedure calls and returns, and (2) correct synchronization over channels, are feasible), our approach can also be applied to boolean programs at the price of an increase in the size of the procedures and the number of procedures per thread. Notice that context bounding and other techniques face the same problem. Second, we have opted for a communication model based on rendez-vous à la CSP. The reason is convenience: the connection between the verification problem and the emptiness problem for the intersection of context-free grammars is easier to describe in this model. Our approach can also be applied to other communication mechanisms by suitably choosing the alphabet of the patterns.

Related work. The automatic verification of safety properties for multithreaded programs with possibly recursive procedures has been intensively studied in the last years. The program is usually modeled as a set of pushdown systems communicating by some means. Several special cases with restricted communication have been proved decidable, including communication through locks satisfying certain conditions, linearly ordered multi-pushdown systems, and systems with acyclic communication structure (also satisfying some additional conditions) [2, 3, 14–17]. Several recent papers study the automatic verification of parametric programs with an arbitrary number of procedures [18] and with dynamic creation of procedures [4, 6], two features that we have not considered in this paper. From a complexity point of view, pattern-based verification lies together with context-bounding and communication through locks at the lower end of the spectrum. Other approaches require exponential time, but do not belong to NP (or this is not known), or are superexponential. The only other case we know of a problem with polynomial complexity in the size of the program is the verification of single-index properties (close to local reachability) in systems communicating through locks [17].

Acknowledgement. Many thanks to Mikołaj Bojańczyk for providing the proof of Theorem 1, to Anthony Widjaja To for suggesting a more direct polynomial time algorithm using [22, 27], to Michael Luttenberger and Andrey Rybalchenko for helpful discussions, and finally to the anonymous reviewers for their helpful comments and to Tomas Poch for pointing typos in the manuscript.

References

[1] CHESS: Find and reproduce heisenbugs in concurrent programs. URL `http://research.microsoft.com/en-us/projects/CHESS/`.

[2] M. F. Atig, B. Bollig, and P. Habermehl. Emptiness of multi-pushdown automata is 2EXPTIME-complete. In *DLT '08: Proc. 12th Int. Conf. on Developments in Language Theory*, volume 5257 of *LNCS*, pages 121–133. Springer, 2008.

[3] M. F. Atig, A. Bouajjani, and T. Touili. On the reachability analysis of acyclic networks of pushdown systems. In *CONCUR '08: Proc. 19th Int. Conf. on Concurrency Theory*, volume 5201 of *LNCS*, pages 356–371. Springer, 2008.

[4] M. F. Atig, A. Bouajjani, and S. Qadeer. Context-bounded analysis for concurrent programs with dynamic creation of threads. In *TACAS '09: Proc. 15th Int. Conf. on Tools and Algorithms for the Construction and Analysis of Systems*, volume 5505 of *LNCS*, pages 107–123. Springer, 2009.

[5] T. Ball and S. K. Rajamani. The SLAM project: debugging system software via static analysis. In *POPL '02: Proc. 29th ACM SIGPLAN-SIGACT Symp. on Principles of Programming Languages*, pages 1–3. ACM Press, 2002.

[6] A. Bouajjani, M. Müller-Olm, and T. Touili. Regular symbolic analysis of dynamic networks of pushdown systems. In *CONCUR '05: Proc. 16th Int. Conf. on Concurrency Theory*, volume 3653 of *LNCS*, pages 473–487. Springer, 2005.

[7] J. Esparza. Petri nets, commutative context-free grammars, and basic parallel processes. *Fundamenta Informaticae*, 31:13–26, 1997.

[8] J. Esparza, P. Ganty, S. Kiefer, and M. Luttenberger. Parikh's theorem: A simple and direct construction. *CoRR*, 1006.3825, 2010.

[9] P. Ganty, B. Monmege, and R. Majumdar. Bounded underapproximations. In *CAV '10: Proc. 20th Int. Conf. on Computer Aided Verification*, volume 6174 of *LNCS*, pages 600–614. Springer, 2010.

[10] M. R. Garey and D. S. Johnson. *Computers and Intractability, A Guide to the Theory of NP-Completeness*. New York, 1979.

[11] S. Ginsburg and E. H. Spanier. Semigroups, presburger formulas, and languages. *Pacific Journal of Mathematics*, 16(2):285–296, 1966.

[12] E. Graedel. Subclasses of presburger arithmetic and the polynomial-time hierarchy. *Theoretical Computer Science*, 56(3):289 – 301, 1988.

[13] J. E. Hopcroft and J. D. Ullman. *Introduction to Automata Theory, Languages and Computation*. Addison-Wesley, 1st edition, 1979.

[14] V. Kahlon. Boundedness vs. unboundedness of lock chains: Characterizing decidability of pairwise cfl-reachability for threads communicating via locks. In *LICS '09: Proc. 24th Annual IEEE Symp. on Logic in Computer Science*, pages 27–36. IEEE Computer Society, 2009.

[15] V. Kahlon. Tractable dataflow analysis for concurrent programs via bounded languages. Patent WO/2009/094439, July 2009.

[16] V. Kahlon and A. Gupta. On the analysis of interacting pushdown systems. In *POPL '03: Proc. 30th ACM SIGPLAN-SIGACT Symp. on Principles of Programming Languages*, pages 303–314. ACM, 2007.

[17] V. Kahlon, F. Ivancic, and A. Gupta. Reasoning about threads communicating via locks. In *CAV '05: Proc. 17th Int. Conf. on Computer Aided Verification*, volume 3576 of *LNCS*, pages 505–518. Springer, 2005.

[18] A. Kaiser, D. Kroening, and T. Wahl. Dynamic cutoff detection in parameterized concurrent programs. In *CAV '10: Proc. 20th Int. Conf. on Computer Aided Verification*, volume 6174 of *LNCS*. Springer, 2010.

[19] E. Kopczyński and A. W. To. Parikh images of grammars: Complexity and applications. In *LICS'10: Proc. 25th Annual IEEE Symp. on Logic in Computer Science*. IEEE, 2010.

[20] A. Lal and T. Reps. Reducing concurrent analysis under a context bound to sequential analysis. In *CAV '08: Proc. 20th Int. Conf. on Computer Aided Verification*, volume 5128 of *LNCS*, pages 37–51. Springer, 2008.

[21] A. Lal, T. Touili, N. Kidd, and T. W. Reps. Interprocedural analysis of concurrent programs under a context bound. In *TACAS '08: Proc. 14th Int. Conf. on Tools and Algorithms for the Construction and Analysis of Systems*, volume 4963 of *LNCS*, pages 282–298. Springer, 2008.

[22] J. Lenstra, H. W. Integer programming with a fixed number of variables. *Mathematics of Operations Research*, 8(4):538–548, 1983.

[23] R. J. Parikh. On context-free languages. *Journal of the ACM*, 13(4): 570–581, 1966.

[24] S. Qadeer. The case for context-bounded verification of concurrent programs. In *SPIN '08: Proc. of 15th Int. Model Checking Software Workshop*, volume 5156 of *LNCS*, pages 3–6. Springer, 2008.

[25] S. Qadeer and J. Rehof. Context-bounded model checking of concurrent software. In *TACAS '05: Proc. 11th Int. Conf. on Tools and Algorithms for the Construction and Analysis of Systems*, volume 3440 of *LNCS*, pages 93–107. Springer, 2005.

[26] G. Ramalingam. Context-sensitive synchronization-sensitive analysis is undecidable. *ACM TOPLAS*, 22(2):416–430, 2000.

[27] B. Scarpellini. Complexity of subcases of presburger arithmetic. *Trans. of the American Mathematical Society*, 284(1):203–218, 1984.

[28] D. Suwimonteerabuth, J. Esparza, and S. Schwoon. Symbolic context-bounded analysis of multithreaded java programs. In *SPIN '08: Proc. of 15th Int. Model Checking Software Workshop*, volume 5156 of *LNCS*, pages 270–287. Springer, 2008.

[29] A. W. To. Parikh images of regular languages: Complexity and applications. *CoRR*, 1002.1464, 2010.

[30] S. La Torre, G. Parlato, and P. Madhusudan. Reducing context-bounded concurrent reachability to sequential reachability. In *CAV'09: Proc. 21st Int. Conf. on Computer Aided Verification*, volume 5643 of *LNCS*, pages 477–492. Springer, 2009.

[31] K. N. Verma, H. Seidl, and T. Schwentick. On the complexity of equational horn clauses. In *CADE '00: 20th Int. Conf. on Automated Deduction*, volume 1831 of *LNCS*, pages 337–352. Springer, 2005.

[32] J. von zur Gathen and M. Sieveking. A bound on solutions of linear integer equalities and inequalities. *Proc. of the American Mathematical Society*, 72:155–158, 1978.

A. Reduction of nDMP to nDPK

A.1 Construction of the grammar G^f

Let $\mathbf{p} = w_1^* \dots w_n^*$, and let $w_i = b_1^{(i)} \dots b_{j_i}^{(i)}$ for every $1 \le i \le n$. Let $G^{\mathbf{p}} = (\mathcal{X}^{\mathbf{p}}, \Sigma, \delta^{\mathbf{p}}, q_1^{(1)})$ be the regular grammar where

$$\begin{aligned} \mathcal{X}^{\mathbf{p}} &= \left\{ q_r^{(s)} \mid 1 \le s \le n \wedge 1 \le r \le j_s \right\} \\ \delta^{\mathbf{p}} &= \left\{ q_i^{(s)} \to b_i^{(s)} q_{i+1}^{(s)} \mid 1 \le s \le n \wedge 1 \le i < j_s \right\} \cup \\ & \left\{ q_{j_s}^{(s)} \to b_{j_s}^{(s)} q_1^{(s')} \mid 1 \le s \le s' \le n \right\} \cup \\ & \left\{ q_1^{(s)} \to \varepsilon \mid 1 \le s \le n \right\} . \end{aligned}$$

It is routine to check that $\bigcup_{i=1}^n L_{q_1^{(i)}}(G^{\mathbf{p}}) = L(w_1^* \dots w_n^*)$.

Given $G^{\mathbf{p}}$ and a grammar $G = (\mathcal{X}, \Sigma, \mathcal{P}, S)$ in program normal form our goal is to define a grammar for the language

$$h^{-1}(L(G) \cap L(\mathbf{p})) \cap L(a_1^* \dots a_n^*) .$$

We first define $G^{\bowtie} = (\mathcal{X}^{\bowtie}, \Sigma, \mathcal{P}^{\bowtie}, X_0)$ which, as we prove later, satisfies $L(G^{\bowtie}) = L(G) \cap L(\mathbf{p})$:

- $\mathcal{X}^{\bowtie} = \{X_0\} \cup \left\{ [q_r^{(s)} X q_y^{(x)}] \mid X \in \mathcal{X}, q_r^{(s)}, q_y^{(x)} \in \mathcal{X}^{\mathbf{p}}, s \le x \right\}$
- $\mathcal{P}^{\bowtie}$ is the set containing for every $1 \le s \le x \le n$ a production $X_0 \to [q_1^{(s)} S q_1^{(x)}]$ and:
  - for every production $X \to \varepsilon \in \mathcal{P}$ of G and for every $1 \le s \le n$, $1 \le r \le j_s$ a production
  $$[q_r^{(s)} X q_r^{(s)}] \to \varepsilon \; ; \tag{15}$$
  - for every production $X \to Y \in \mathcal{P}$ of G and for every $1 \le s \le u \le n$, $1 \le r \le j_s$, $1 \le v \le j_u$ a production
  $$[q_r^{(s)} X q_v^{(u)}] \to [q_r^{(s)} Y q_v^{(u)}] \; ; \tag{16}$$
  - for every production $X \to \gamma \cdot Y \in \mathcal{P}$ of G with $\gamma \in \Sigma$ and for every $1 \le s \le u \le n$, $1 \le r \le j_s$, $1 \le v \le j_u$ productions
  $$[q_r^{(s)} X q_v^{(u)}] \to \gamma \cdot [q_{r+1}^{(s)} Y q_v^{(u)}] \quad \text{if } r < j_s \text{ and } \gamma = b_r^{(s)}; \text{ and} \tag{17}$$
  $$[q_{j_s}^{(s)} X q_v^{(u)}] \to \gamma \cdot [q_1^{(s')} Y q_v^{(u)}] \in \mathcal{P}^{\bowtie} \quad \text{if } \gamma = b_{j_s}^{(s)} \text{ and } s \le s' \le u \tag{18}$$
  - for every production $X \to ZY \in \mathcal{P}$ of G and for every $1 \le s \le u \le x \le n$, $1 \le r \le j_s$, $1 \le v \le j_u$, $1 \le y \le j_x$ a production
  $$[q_r^{(s)} X q_y^{(x)}] \to [q_r^{(s)} Z q_v^{(u)}][q_v^{(u)} Y q_y^{(x)}] \; . \tag{19}$$

In what follows, we use $X \underset{G}{\Rightarrow} \alpha$ to indicate that the derivation is carried out using the productions of the grammar G.

LEMMA 8. *Let $w \in \Sigma^*$. We have $[q_r^{(s)} X q_v^{(u)}] \underset{G^{\bowtie}}{\Rightarrow}^* w$ iff $q_r^{(s)} \underset{G^{\mathbf{p}}}{\Rightarrow}^* w \cdot q_v^{(u)}$ and $X \underset{G}{\Rightarrow}^* w$.*

PROOF: The proof for the only if direction is by induction on the length of the derivation of $[q_r^{(s)} X q_v^{(u)}] \Rightarrow^* w$.

$\mathbf{i = 1}$. Then $[q_r^{(s)} X q_r^{(s)}] \Rightarrow \varepsilon$. The definition of $G^{\bowtie}$ shows that $X \to \varepsilon \in \mathcal{P}$, and so $X \Rightarrow \varepsilon$.

$\mathbf{i > 1}$. We do a case analysis according to the definition of $G^{\bowtie}$.

- $[q_r^{(s)} X q_v^{(u)}] \Rightarrow [q_r^{(s)} Y q_v^{(u)}] \Rightarrow^* w$. It is trivially solved using the induction hypothesis.
- $[q_r^{(s)} X q_v^{(u)}] \Rightarrow \gamma \cdot [q_{r+1}^{(s)} Y q_v^{(u)}] \Rightarrow^* \gamma w'$. The definition of $G^{\bowtie}$ shows that $\gamma = b_r^{(s)}$ for some $r < j_s$. The production $q_r^{(s)} \to b_r^{(s)} \cdot q_{r+1}^{(s)} \in \delta^{\mathbf{p}}$ and induction hypothesis show that $q_r^{(s)} \Rightarrow b_r^{(s)} \cdot q_{r+1}^{(s)} \Rightarrow^* b_r^{(s)} w' \cdot q_v^{(u)}$. Also the production $X \to \gamma \cdot Y \in \mathcal{P}$ and induction hypothesis show that $X \Rightarrow \gamma \cdot Y \Rightarrow^* \gamma \cdot w'$ and we are done since $\gamma = b_r^{(s)}$.
- $[q_{j_s}^{(s)} X q_v^{(u)}] \Rightarrow b_{j_s}^{(s)} \cdot [q_1^{(s')} Y q_v^{(u)}] \Rightarrow^* b_{j_s}^{(s)} \cdot w'$. The production $q_{j_s}^{(s)} \to b_{j_s}^{(s)} \cdot q_1^{(s')} \in \delta^{\mathbf{p}}$ and induction hypothesis show that $q_{j_s}^{(s)} \Rightarrow b_{j_s}^{(s)} \cdot q_1^{(s')} \Rightarrow^* b_{j_s}^{(s)} w' \cdot q_v^{(u)}$. Also the production $X \to \gamma \cdot Y \in \mathcal{P}$ where $\gamma = b_{j_s}^{(s)}$ and the induction hypothesis show that $X \Rightarrow \gamma \cdot Y \Rightarrow^* \gamma \cdot w'$ and we are done.
- $[q_r^{(s)} X q_y^{(x)}] \Rightarrow [q_r^{(s)} Z q_v^{(u)}][q_v^{(u)} Y q_y^{(x)}] \Rightarrow^* w_1 \cdot [q_v^{(u)} Y q_y^{(x)}] \Rightarrow^* w_1 w_2 = w$. By induction hypothesis, we have $q_r^{(s)} \Rightarrow^* w_1 \cdot q_v^{(u)}$ and $Z \Rightarrow^* w_1$. Also $q_v^{(u)} \Rightarrow^* w_2 \cdot q_y^{(x)}$ and $Y \Rightarrow^* w_2$. Hence we find that $q_r^{(s)} \Rightarrow^* w_1 w_2 \cdot q_y^{(x)}$ and $X \Rightarrow^* w_1 w_2$ since $X \to Z \cdot Y \in \mathcal{P}$ which concludes this case since $w = w_1 w_2$.

Using a similar induction on the length of $X \Rightarrow^* w$, the "if" direction is easily proved. □

We now obtain a grammar G^f by slightly modifying $G^{\bowtie}$. We change the productions of (17) and (18) respectively to

$$[q_r^{(s)} X q_v^{(u)}] \to [q_{r+1}^{(s)} Y q_v^{(u)}] \text{ and } [q_{j_s}^{(s)} X q_v^{(u)}] \to a_s \cdot [q_1^{(s')} Y q_v^{(u)}]$$

where $a_s \in \widetilde{\Sigma}$. Because of this change, G^f has alphabet $\widetilde{\Sigma}$. Also, it is routine to check that this change amounts to applying the inverse homomorphism h^{-1} and taking the intersection with $L(a_1^* \dots a_n^*)$.

A.2 Proof of Lemma. 1

Given $\mathbf{p} = w_1^* \dots w_n^*$ and a grammar G in program normal form, we have that G^f satisfies each of the following properties:

- $L(G^f) \subseteq \widetilde{\Sigma}^*$ where $\widetilde{\Sigma} = \{a_1, \dots, a_n\}$;
- $L(G^f) = h^{-1}(L(G) \cap L(\mathbf{p})) \cap L(a_1^* \dots a_n^*)$;
- G^f is in program normal form;
- G^f is computable in polynomial time;
- If pr is the number of procedure variables in G, then G^f has $\mathcal{O}(pa^2 \cdot pr)$ procedure variables where pa is the size of $\mathbf{p}$.

PROOF: The first item is obvious from the definition of G^f. Let $G^f = (\mathcal{X}^f, \widetilde{\Sigma}, \mathcal{P}^f, X_0)$. If follows directly from Lem. 8 that for every $w \in \Sigma^*$, $X_0 \underset{G^{\bowtie}}{\Rightarrow}^* w$ iff $q_1^{(s)} \underset{G^{\mathbf{p}}}{\Rightarrow}^* w \cdot q_1^{(x)}$ where $1 \le s \le x \le n$ and $S \underset{G}{\Rightarrow}^* w$. The productions $\left\{ q_1^{(s)} \to \varepsilon \mid 1 \le s \le n \right\} \subseteq \delta^{\mathbf{p}}$ of $G^{\mathbf{p}}$ shows that the equivalence can be rewritten as follows: $X_0 \underset{G^{\bowtie}}{\Rightarrow}^* w$ iff $q_1^{(s)} \underset{G^{\mathbf{p}}}{\Rightarrow}^* w$ where $1 \le s \le n$ and $S \underset{G}{\Rightarrow}^* w$. We conclude from the definition of $G^{\mathbf{p}}$ that $L(\mathbf{p}) = \bigcup_{i=1}^n L_{q_1^{(i)}}(G^{\mathbf{p}})$, hence that $L(G^{\bowtie}) = L(G) \cap L(\mathbf{p})$, and finally that $L(G^f) = h^{-1}(L(G^{\bowtie})) \cap L(a_1^* \dots a_n^*)$.

The second item is immediate from the definition of G^f and that G is in program normal form. The third item is clear from the definition of $G^{\bowtie}$ and G^f. For the fourth item, we have that since pa is the size of $\mathbf{p}$, pa is also the size of $\mathcal{X}^{\mathbf{p}}$ by definition of $G^{\mathbf{p}}$. Also (19) shows that each procedure variable in G yields $\mathcal{O}(pa^2)$ procedure variables in G, hence if pr is the number of procedure variables in G we find that the number of procedure variables in $G^{\bowtie}$, hence G^f is $\mathcal{O}(pa^2 \cdot pr)$. □

EigenCFA: Accelerating Flow Analysis with GPUs

Tarun Prabhu, Shreyas Ramalingam, Matthew Might, Mary Hall
University of Utah, Salt Lake City, Utah, USA
{tarunp,sramalin,might,mhall}@cs.utah.edu

Abstract

We describe, implement and benchmark EigenCFA, an algorithm for accelerating higher-order control-flow analysis (specifically, 0CFA) with a GPU. Ultimately, our program transformations, reductions and optimizations achieve a factor of 72 speedup over an optimized CPU implementation.

We began our investigation with the view that GPUs accelerate high-arithmetic, data-parallel computations with a poor tolerance for branching. Taking that perspective to its limit, we reduced Shivers's abstract-interpretive 0CFA to an algorithm synthesized from linear-algebra operations. Central to this reduction were "abstract" Church encodings, and encodings of the syntax tree and abstract domains as vectors and matrices.

A straightforward (dense-matrix) implementation of EigenCFA performed slower than a fast CPU implementation. Ultimately, sparse-matrix data structures and operations turned out to be the critical accelerants. Because control-flow graphs are sparse in practice (up to 96% empty), our control-flow matrices are also sparse, giving the sparse matrix operations an overwhelming space and speed advantage.

We also achieved speedups by carefully permitting data races. The monotonicity of 0CFA makes it sound to perform analysis operations in parallel, possibly using stale or even partially-updated data.

Categories and Subject Descriptors D.3.4 [*Programming Languages*]: Processors and Optimization

General Terms Languages

Keywords abstract interpretation, EigenCFA, program analysis, flow analysis, lambda calculus, GPU, CPS, matrix

1. Introduction

GPUs excel at obtaining speedups for algorithms over continuous domains with low-control, high-arithmetic kernels. Flow analyses [22, 24, 25], on the other hand, tend to be fixed-point algorithms over discrete domains with high-control, low-arithmetic kernels, such as abstract interpretations [7, 8]. At first glance, GPUs seem ill-suited to accelerating flow analyses. Yet, with a shift in algorithmic perspective and the right data structures, GPUs make the bedrock flow analysis for higher-order programs—0CFA—nearly two orders of magnitude faster.

POPL'11, January 26–28, 2011, Austin, Texas, USA.

1.1 Motivation

After nearly a quarter century, higher-order control-flow analysis [11, 25] remains an important analysis for highly-optimizing, whole-program compilers of functional languages. Yet, the analysis also remains stubbornly expensive. Even one of its simplest formulations, 0CFA, is still "nearly" cubic in complexity: $O(n^3/\log n)$ [6, 19].

With CPU clock cycles no longer growing, this complexity places a *de facto* upper bound on the size of programs that can be analyzed in a reasonable amount of time. To analyze large programs, higher-order control-flow analysis must exploit the ever-increasing parallelism available on modern systems. Toward that end, we develop a GPU-accelerated algorithm for 0CFA—EigenCFA—that achieves a factor of 72 speedup over existing CPU techniques.

1.2 High-level methodology

To develop EigenCFA, we imagined the GPU as a platform for accelerating non-branching, data-parallel algorithms composed entirely of linear-algebra operations. So, we reduced Shivers' abstract-interpretive 0CFA to a data-parallel, non-branching algorithm composed entirely of matrix operations: matrix multiplication, matrix addition and matrix transposition. There are five key insights to this reduction:

1. **Canonicalization to binary continuation-passing style.**

   To achieve good data-parallelism on a GPU, we need control-flow uniformity among the GPU threads, *i.e.*, to avoid branching operations. In flow analysis, the key step to parallelize is the propagation of flow information at each call site. To eliminate branching from this propagation routine, we transform our programs into a canonical form: binary continuation-passing style (binary CPS). In binary CPS, every call site provides two arguments, and every function accepts two arguments. By eliminating the need to discriminate on the "instruction type" (there is only one: function call) and on the number of arguments, binary CPS eliminates branching from the propagation sub-routine.

2. **Abstract Church encodings.**

   One could use Church encodings to reduce every program construct (*e.g.*, `if`, `letrec`, `set!`) to binary continuation-passing style. But, these desugarings obscure control-flow. For instance, desugaring `set!` requires a global store-passing transform, and the Y combinator fogs up recursion. An abstract Church encoding exploits the approximation in 0CFA so that the encoded program has the same abstract control-flow as the original program, if no longer the same concrete behavior. For example:

   ```
   (set! x 10)
   ```

   is equivalent (as far as 0CFA is concerned) to:

   ```
   (let ((x 10)) #void)
   ```

3. **Matrix-vector encoding of the syntax tree.**

We use binary continuation-passing style to provide uniformity to program syntax, but we still need a GPU-friendly way to encode the syntax tree of a program. We encode the syntax tree of a program as a collection of selector functions, which are themselves represented as matrices. Individual program terms are then encoded as vectors. (We'll write $\langle\!\langle t \rangle\!\rangle$ to mean the vector that encodes term t.) For instance, every call site has three components: the procedure expression, its first argument expression and its second argument expression. So, there are three selector matrices that operate on call sites: $\mathbf{Fun}$, $\mathbf{Arg}_1$ and $\mathbf{Arg}_2$. For example, for a call site $(f\ e_1\ e_2)$:

$$\langle\!\langle (f\ e_1\ e_2) \rangle\!\rangle \times \mathbf{Fun} = \langle\!\langle f \rangle\!\rangle$$
$$\langle\!\langle (f\ e_1\ e_2) \rangle\!\rangle \times \mathbf{Arg}_1 = \langle\!\langle e_1 \rangle\!\rangle$$
$$\langle\!\langle (f\ e_1\ e_2) \rangle\!\rangle \times \mathbf{Arg}_2 = \langle\!\langle e_2 \rangle\!\rangle.$$

4. **Matrix encoding of the abstract store.**

In 0CFA, the abstract store (also known as the abstract heap) maps variable names to sets of values. It is the primary data structure used during the execution of 0CFA, so it must be encoded in a GPU-friendly way. Fortunately, it is straightforward to represent this data structure as a matrix. One axis of the store matrix represents variables; the other axis represents lambda terms. If the entry for variable i, lambda j is non-zero, this indicates that (a closure over) lambda j may get bound to variable i. Thus, if the matrix $\boldsymbol{\sigma}$ is an abstract store in matrix form, and v is a variable, then the vector $\langle\!\langle v \rangle\!\rangle \times \boldsymbol{\sigma}$ describes the possible values of the variable v.

5. **Linear-algebraic encoding of the transfer function.**

Once the syntax tree of the program is described in terms of selection matrices, the next step is to describe the action of the small-step transition relation for 0CFA in terms of linear-algebraic operations. Examination of the small-step transition relation (Section 2.4) finds only three operations beyond syntactic selection: function lookup, join over functions and functional extension. We reduce function lookup to matrix-vector multiplication, join to matrix addition and functional extension to a combination of matrix addition, matrix multiplication and matrix transposition.

1.3 Key insights for acceleration: Sparseness and races

For the implementation, there are two insights that lead to acceleration: a sparse-matrix representation of the abstract store, and a tolerance of benign (monotonic) races that allows the analysis of call sites in parallel.

1. **Exploiting sparseness.**

In practice, most control-flow graphs are sparse. In our matrix encoding of the store, the sparseness of this matrix is linked to the sparseness of the control-flow graph. Thus, sparse-matrix algorithms have a performance advantage over dense-matrix algorithms for all but the most pathological programs: programs which tend toward completeness in their control-flow graphs—programs in which any point may jump to any other point.

2. **Exploiting monotonicity to permit benign race conditions.**

When analyzing call sites in parallel, they may both attempt to read from and/or write to the same location in the abstract store. Fortunately, the monotonic growth of the abstract store during an abstract transition guarantees us that these races are benign: if properly engineered, once an entry is set to a non-zero value in the abstract store, no other thread will set it back to zero. Monotonicity *also* guarantees soundness when a thread works with a stale or partially updated store.

1.4 Contributions

- Our *primary* contribution is the formulation of GPU-accelerated flow analysis. To the best of our knowledge, EigenCFA is the first such formulation.
- Our secondary claims are the reductions that made this formulation possible: the encoding of the syntax tree as selection matrices, abstract Church encodings and the reduction to linear algebra of the abstract semantics for 0CFA.

1.5 Outline

Theory and implementation cleave this work in halves:

- **Theory.**

  Section 2 is a brief review of the small-step formulation of Shivers' 0CFA for continuation-passing style. Section 3 defines EigenCFA, a linear-algebraic formulation of 0CFA. Section 4 describes abstract Church encodings—program transformations that are meaning-preserving only for the *abstract semantics* of our analysis, which more precisely and efficiently handle language constructs such as mutation, recursion, termination, basic values and conditionals.

- **Implementation.**

  Section 5 describes how we map the algorithm for EigenCFA down to a (CUDA-enabled) GPU. In fact, this section describes three different approaches for performing the mapping: two of these end up slower than or only as fast as the CPU version, but the final implementation, which uses sparse matrices, achieves the desired speedup. Section 6 gives the results of our empirical evaluation. We tested two (GPU) implementations of EigenCFA against two (CPU) implementations of 0CFA, and found a factor of 72 speedup.

2. Background: Binary CPS and 0CFA

We are going to accelerate Shivers's original 0CFA for continuation-passing style (CPS). To enable high performance on the GPU, we are going to specialize it for a canonicalized form: binary continuation-passing style. In this section, we'll define binary CPS and briefly review 0CFA. Readers familiar with 0CFA may wish to skip this section. Our definition of 0CFA is taken from Might and Shivers's recent small-step reformulations. (We refer readers to [20] for details such as abstraction maps and proofs of soundness.)

Binary CPS is a canonicalized variant of the continuation-passing style λ-calculus in which every procedure accepts exactly two arguments. We use binary, as opposed to unary, CPS because the CPS transform on lambda terms introduces an additional argument—the continuation argument—and CPS cannot use Currying to handle multiple arguments, since it violates the "no procedure may return" principle. We are using binary, instead of variadic, CPS because we want to eliminate branching from the small-step transition relation we're about to define; branches interfere with data-parallel single-instruction, multiple-thread (SIMT) operations in the GPU.

The uniformity in binary CPS also has the benefit of making our forthcoming matrix encodings of syntax trees predictably structured. This predictable structure is amenable to the arithmetic optimizations and compressions presented in section 5.

2.1 Binary CPS

The grammar for binary CPS contains calls and expressions, and expressions are either lambda terms or variables:

$$call \in \mathsf{Call} ::= (f\ e_1\ e_2)$$
$$f, e \in \mathsf{Exp} = \mathsf{Var} + \mathsf{Lam}$$
$$v \in \mathsf{Var} \text{ is a set of identifiers}$$
$$lam \in \mathsf{Lam} ::= (\lambda\ (v_1\ v_2)\ call).$$

2.2 Concrete semantics

The simplest small-step concrete semantics for binary CPS uses just three domains in its state-space, Σ:

$$\varsigma \in \Sigma = \mathsf{Call} \times Env$$
$$\rho \in Env = \mathsf{Var} \rightharpoonup Clo$$
$$clo \in Clo = \mathsf{Lam} \times Env,$$

and one transition rule, $(\Rightarrow) \subseteq \Sigma \times \Sigma$:

$$
\begin{aligned}
(\llbracket (f\ e_1\ e_2) \rrbracket, \rho) &\Rightarrow (call, \rho''), \text{ where} \\
(\llbracket (\lambda\ (v_1\ v_2)\ call) \rrbracket, \rho') &= \mathcal{E}(f, \rho) \\
clo_1 &= \mathcal{E}(e_1, \rho) \\
clo_2 &= \mathcal{E}(e_2, \rho) \\
\rho'' &= \rho'[v_1 \mapsto clo_1, v_2 \mapsto clo_2],
\end{aligned}
$$

where the function $\mathcal{E} : \mathsf{Exp} \times Env \rightharpoonup Clo$ evaluates expressions:

$$\mathcal{E}(v, \rho) = \rho(v)$$
$$\mathcal{E}(lam, \rho) = (lam, \rho).$$

2.3 Abstract state-space for 0CFA

Might and Shivers reformulated 0CFA as an abstract interpretation of the concrete semantics just given [20]. The core of the abstraction is the elimination of environments from the semantics, and the use of an abstract store to represent all environments. So, abstract states ($\hat{\Sigma}$) pair the current call site with the abstract store, and closures lose their environments:

$$\hat{\varsigma} \in \hat{\Sigma} = \mathsf{Call} \times \widehat{Store}$$
$$\hat{\sigma} \in \widehat{Store} = \mathsf{Var} \to \widehat{Lams}$$
$$\hat{L} \in \widehat{Lams} = \mathcal{P}(\mathsf{Lam}).$$

We assume the natural partial orders on these sets: lambda sets are ordered by inclusion, abstract stores are ordered point-wise by inclusion, and abstract states use a product ordering. For instance, $(\hat{\sigma}_1 \sqcup \hat{\sigma}_2)(v) = \hat{\sigma}_1(v) \cup \hat{\sigma}_2(v)$.

2.4 0CFA Abstract Semantics

The transition relation for the abstract semantics, $(\leadsto) \subseteq \hat{\Sigma} \times \hat{\Sigma}$, mirrors that of the concrete semantics:

$$
\begin{aligned}
(\llbracket (f\ e_1\ e_2) \rrbracket, \hat{\sigma}) &\leadsto (call, \hat{\sigma}'), \text{ where} \\
\llbracket (\lambda\ (v_1\ v_2)\ call) \rrbracket &\in \hat{\mathcal{E}}(f, \hat{\sigma}) \\
\hat{L}_1 &= \hat{\mathcal{E}}(e_1, \hat{\sigma}) \\
\hat{L}_2 &= \hat{\mathcal{E}}(e_2, \hat{\sigma}) \\
\hat{\sigma}' &= \hat{\sigma} \sqcup [v_1 \mapsto \hat{L}_1, v_2 \mapsto \hat{L}_2],
\end{aligned}
$$

as does the argument evaluator, $\hat{\mathcal{E}} : \mathsf{Var} \times \widehat{Store} \to \mathcal{P}(\mathsf{Lam})$:

$$\hat{\mathcal{E}}(v, \hat{\sigma}) = \hat{\sigma}(v)$$
$$\hat{\mathcal{E}}(lam, \hat{\sigma}) = \{lam\}.$$

A notable change in the abstract semantics is the nondeterminism that results from branching to the set of possible lambda terms for the procedure argument (note the appearance of $\in$).

2.5 Computing 0CFA

To compute classical, flow-insensitive 0CFA with the small-step transition relation, we need a family of functions that computes the output store with respect to each call site $call$, $\hat{f}_{call} : \widehat{Store} \to \widehat{Store}$:

$$\hat{f}_{call}(\hat{\sigma}) = \bigsqcup \{\hat{\sigma}' : (call, \hat{\sigma}) \leadsto (\_, \hat{\sigma}')\}.$$

Then, we can construct the "pass" function, $\hat{F} : \widehat{Store} \to \widehat{Store}$, which performs one full pass of the analysis by considering the effect on the store of every call site in the program, $call_1, \ldots, call_n$:

$$\hat{F}(\hat{\sigma}) = (\hat{f}_{call_1} \circ \cdots \circ \hat{f}_{call_n})(\hat{\sigma}).$$

Because the function $\hat{F}$ is continuous and monotonic, and the height of the abstract store lattice is finite, the result of 0CFA is least fixed point of the function $\hat{F}$:

$$\text{lfp}(\hat{F}) = \hat{F}^n(\bot_{\widehat{Store}}) \text{ for some finite } n,$$

where the bottom store maps everything to the empty set:

$$\bot_{\widehat{Store}} = \lambda v.\emptyset.$$

Complexity If the function $\hat{F}$ adds one entry to the abstract store per application, there can be at most $|\mathsf{Var}| \times |\mathsf{Lam}|$ applications before it saturates the abstract store and must terminate. Since the cost of each application is proportional to $|\mathsf{Call}|$, the complexity of this 0CFA is cubic, as expected.

3. EigenCFA: A linear encoding of 0CFA

In this section, we discuss our linear-algebra encoding of both binary CPS and 0CFA. In brief, individual program terms will be represented as vectors. The structure of the syntax tree will be compiled into static selection matrices that operate on these term vectors. Finally, the pass function ($\hat{F}$) from 0CFA will be encoded as a function operating on stores represented as matrices.

Running example. Throughout the remainder of this paper, all of the examples will be with respect to this program (the call-sites $c_1, c_2, \ldots$ are explicitly labelled for future reference):

$$
\begin{aligned}
((\lambda_1\ (v_1\ v_1')\ &(v_1\ \ v_1\ \ v_1')_{c_1}) \\
&(\lambda_2\ (v_2\ v_2')\ (v_2'\ \ v_2\ \ v_2')_{c_2}) \\
&(\lambda_3\ (v_3\ v_3')\ (v_3\ \ v_3\ \ v_3)_{c_3}))_{c_4}
\end{aligned}
$$

and the same abstract store, $\hat{\sigma}$:

$$
\begin{aligned}
\hat{\sigma}(v_1) &= \{\lambda_2\} \\
\hat{\sigma}(v_2) &= \{\lambda_2\} \\
\hat{\sigma}(v_3) &= \{\lambda_2\} \\
\hat{\sigma}(v_1') &= \{\lambda_3\} \\
\hat{\sigma}(v_2') &= \{\lambda_3\} \\
\hat{\sigma}(v_3') &= \{\lambda_3\}.
\end{aligned}
$$

We do this to improve presentation and to emphasize the differences between each data representation strategy in Section 5.

3.1 Encoding terms as vectors

We encode each program term (a lambda term, a variable or a call site) as a vector over the set $\{0, 1\}$. Every term in the program will have a unique vector representation.[1] For convenience, we write the vector encoding of term t as $\langle\!\langle t \rangle\!\rangle$.

We'll have vectors of two lengths: expression vectors (of length $|\mathsf{Exp}|$) and call vectors (of length $|\mathsf{Call}|$). Formally:

$$\begin{aligned} \vec{e} &\in \overrightarrow{\mathsf{Exp}} = \{0,1\}^{|\mathsf{Exp}|} \\ \vec{call} &\in \overrightarrow{\mathsf{Call}} = \{0,1\}^{|\mathsf{Call}|} \\ \vec{v} &\in \overrightarrow{\mathsf{Var}} \subset \overrightarrow{\mathsf{Exp}} \\ \vec{lam} &\in \overrightarrow{\mathsf{Lam}} \subset \overrightarrow{\mathsf{Exp}}. \end{aligned}$$

We can assign each expression a number from 1 to $|\mathsf{Exp}|$, so that the expression vector with 1 at slot i is the expression vector for expression i. We can do likewise for call sites.

More specifically, variables are represented as vectors of size $|\mathsf{Exp}|$ (notably not of size $|\mathsf{Var}|$). λ-terms are also represented as vectors of size $|\mathsf{Exp}|$ (also notably not of size $|\mathsf{Lam}|$). The first $|\mathsf{Var}|$ entries of an expression vector represent variables, and the last $|\mathsf{Lam}|$ entries represent lambda terms.

Running example. Here is the expression vector representing lambda term λ_2:

$$\begin{array}{ccccccccc} v_3' & v_2' & v_1' & v_3 & v_2 & v_1 & \lambda_3 & \lambda_2 & \lambda_1 \end{array}$$
$$\left[\begin{array}{ccccccccc} 0 & 0 & 0 & 0 & 0 & 0 & 0 & 1 & 0 \end{array}\right]$$

And, here is the expression vector representing variable v_2:

$$\begin{array}{ccccccccc} v_3' & v_2' & v_1' & v_3 & v_2 & v_1 & \lambda_3 & \lambda_2 & \lambda_1 \end{array}$$
$$\left[\begin{array}{ccccccccc} 0 & 0 & 0 & 0 & 1 & 0 & 0 & 0 & 0 \end{array}\right]$$

It's worth asking why we don't split expressions into two vector types—one for variables, and one for lambda terms. We took this approach because it allows us to eliminate branching from argument evaluation later on. As it is formulated in the abstract semantics, the argument evaluator $\hat{\mathcal{E}}$ must look up its expression argument if it is a variable and return its argument if it is a lambda term. We'll be able to construct a single linear operator that has the effect of the argument evaluator $\hat{\mathcal{E}}$—no branching necessary.

3.2 Encoding the syntax tree as matrices

To encode the syntax tree, we'll use selectors encoded as static matrices to destructure syntax terms. That is, given a term vector $\langle\!\langle t \rangle\!\rangle$, to figure out the syntactic children of term t, we'll have a matrix for each type of child (e.g. first formal parameter, second argument) that maps $\langle\!\langle t \rangle\!\rangle$ to that child. For instance, the matrix **Call** maps lambda terms to their call site, so that $\langle\!\langle (\lambda\ (v_1\ v_2)\ call) \rangle\!\rangle \times \mathbf{Call} = \langle\!\langle call \rangle\!\rangle$.

There are six static syntax matrices:

$$\begin{array}{rll} \mathbf{Fun}: & \overrightarrow{\mathsf{Call}} \to \overrightarrow{\mathsf{Exp}} & \textit{(function applied in a call site)} \\ \mathbf{Arg}_1: & \overrightarrow{\mathsf{Call}} \to \overrightarrow{\mathsf{Exp}} & \textit{(the first argument in a call site)} \\ \mathbf{Arg}_2: & \overrightarrow{\mathsf{Call}} \to \overrightarrow{\mathsf{Exp}} & \textit{(the second argument in a call site)} \\ \mathbf{Call}: & \overrightarrow{\mathsf{Lam}} \to \overrightarrow{\mathsf{Call}} & \textit{(the call site of a } \lambda\textit{-term)} \\ \mathbf{Var}_1: & \overrightarrow{\mathsf{Lam}} \to \overrightarrow{\mathsf{Exp}} & \textit{(the first formal of a } \lambda\textit{-term)} \\ \mathbf{Var}_2: & \overrightarrow{\mathsf{Lam}} \to \overrightarrow{\mathsf{Exp}} & \textit{(the second formal of a } \lambda\textit{-term)} \end{array}$$

These matrices are constructed once per program and remain constant through the duration of the analysis.

[1] We could formulate the analysis more generally in terms of any orthogonal basis vectors for terms, but there doesn't seem to be any performance advantage to doing so.

Running example. The **Fun** matrix determines the function being applied at a call site for our running example:

$$\begin{array}{c} \\ c_1 \\ c_2 \\ c_3 \\ c_4 \end{array} \begin{array}{c} \begin{array}{ccccccccc} v_3' & v_2' & v_1' & v_3 & v_2 & v_1 & \lambda_3 & \lambda_2 & \lambda_1 \end{array} \\ \left[\begin{array}{ccccccccc} 0 & 0 & 0 & 0 & 0 & 1 & 0 & 0 & 0 \\ 0 & 1 & 0 & 0 & 0 & 0 & 0 & 0 & 0 \\ 0 & 0 & 0 & 1 & 0 & 0 & 0 & 0 & 0 \\ 0 & 0 & 0 & 0 & 0 & 0 & 0 & 0 & 1 \end{array}\right] \end{array}$$

Running example. In order to look up the function being applied at call site labelled c_2, we multiply the vector representing c_2 with the **Fun** matrix. The result is the vector representing the variable v_2':

$$\begin{array}{c} \begin{array}{cccc} c_1 & c_2 & c_3 & c_4 \end{array} \\ \left[\begin{array}{cccc} 0 & 1 & 0 & 0 \end{array}\right] \end{array}$$

$$\times \begin{array}{c} \begin{array}{ccccccccc} v_3' & v_2' & v_1' & v_3 & v_2 & v_1 & \lambda_3 & \lambda_2 & \lambda_1 \end{array} \\ \left[\begin{array}{ccccccccc} 0 & 0 & 0 & 0 & 0 & 1 & 0 & 0 & 0 \\ 0 & 1 & 0 & 0 & 0 & 0 & 0 & 0 & 0 \\ 0 & 0 & 0 & 1 & 0 & 0 & 0 & 0 & 0 \\ 0 & 0 & 0 & 0 & 0 & 0 & 0 & 0 & 1 \end{array}\right] \end{array}$$

$$= \begin{array}{c} \begin{array}{ccccccccc} v_3' & v_2' & v_1' & v_3 & v_2 & v_1 & \lambda_3 & \lambda_2 & \lambda_1 \end{array} \\ \left[\begin{array}{ccccccccc} 0 & 1 & 0 & 0 & 0 & 0 & 0 & 0 & 0 \end{array}\right] \end{array}$$

3.3 Encoding flow sets as vectors

0CFA manipulates flow sets; flow sets are sets of lambda terms ($\widehat{Lams}$). We also need to represent these as linear-algebraic values. A natural encoding of flow sets is to use bit vectors of length $|\mathsf{Lam}|$:

$$\vec{L} \in \overrightarrow{\mathsf{Lam}^\star} = \{0,1\}^{|\mathsf{Lam}|}.$$

In some sense, we appear to be breaking with the uniform representation of expressions by creating a special encoding of lambda terms. However, it is more accurate to think of the set $\overrightarrow{\mathsf{Lam}^\star}$ as representing sets of abstract closures than sets of lambda terms. Moreover, we can (and do) efficiently interconvert values between the set $\overrightarrow{\mathsf{Lam}}$ and the set $\overrightarrow{\mathsf{Lam}^\star}$ simply by adding or ignoring 0-padding on the front of the vector.

For a set of lambda terms, $\hat{L}$, we write their vector encoding as $\langle\!\langle \hat{L} \rangle\!\rangle$, and we expect the following property to hold:

$$\langle\!\langle \{lam_1, \ldots, lam_n\} \rangle\!\rangle = \langle\!\langle lam_1 \rangle\!\rangle + \cdots + \langle\!\langle lam_n \rangle\!\rangle,$$

where the operator $+$ is element-wise Boolean-OR.

3.4 Encoding abstract stores as matrices

Now that we have a representation for syntactic domains and for flow sets, we need a matrix representation for the abstract store. Fortunately, the store is a map from variables to flow sets, and a linear operator (encoded as a matrix) is a natural way of representing such a map.

We do have a design choice here, and the right answer is not immediately obvious. We *could* use a $|\mathsf{Var}|$-by-$|\mathsf{Lam}|$ matrix to represent stores; but we'll be able to eliminate a branch during argument evaluation if we make all stores into slightly larger $|\mathsf{Exp}|$-by-$|\mathsf{Lam}|$ matrices. So, formally:

$$\sigma \in \mathbf{Store} = \overrightarrow{\mathsf{Exp}} \to \overrightarrow{\mathsf{Lam}^\star},$$

We write the matrix-encoding of an abstract store $\hat{\sigma}$ as $\langle\!\langle \hat{\sigma} \rangle\!\rangle$. And, we define the encoding by relating abstract and matrix stores:

$$\langle\!\langle lam \rangle\!\rangle \times \boldsymbol{\sigma} = \langle\!\langle lam \rangle\!\rangle$$
$$\langle\!\langle v \rangle\!\rangle \times \langle\!\langle \hat{\sigma} \rangle\!\rangle = \langle\!\langle \hat{\sigma}(v) \rangle\!\rangle,$$

where the operator $\times$ is actually Boolean matrix multiplication.

According to these rules, the lower portion of all stores (the part that corresponds the lambda portion of expression vectors) must be the identity matrix.

Running example. The matrix representation of the store is:

$$\begin{array}{c} \\ v_3' \\ v_2' \\ \vdots \\ v_1 \\ \\ \lambda_3 \\ \lambda_2 \\ \lambda_1 \end{array} \begin{array}{c} \begin{array}{ccc} \lambda_3 & \lambda_2 & \lambda_1 \end{array} \\ \left[\begin{array}{ccc} 1 & 0 & 0 \\ 1 & 0 & 0 \\ \vdots & \vdots & \vdots \\ 0 & 1 & 0 \\ \hline 1 & 0 & 0 \\ 0 & 1 & 0 \\ 0 & 0 & 1 \end{array}\right] \end{array}$$

Under this encoding of stores, the evaluation of an expression takes a single matrix multiplication:

Theorem 3.1. $\langle\!\langle \hat{\mathcal{E}}(e, \hat{\sigma}) \rangle\!\rangle = \langle\!\langle e \rangle\!\rangle \times \langle\!\langle \hat{\sigma} \rangle\!\rangle$.

Proof. By case-wise analysis and the rules for the encoding. □

Running example. Here's the look-up of variable v_2':

$$\begin{array}{c} \begin{array}{cccccc} v_3' & v_2' & \cdots & v_1 & \lambda_3 & \cdots \end{array} \\ \left[\begin{array}{cccccc} 0 & 1 & \cdots & 0 & 0 & \cdots \end{array}\right] \end{array} \times \begin{array}{c} \\ v_3' \\ v_2' \\ \vdots \\ v_1 \\ \\ \lambda_3 \\ \lambda_2 \\ \lambda_1 \end{array} \begin{array}{c} \begin{array}{ccc} \lambda_3 & \lambda_2 & \lambda_1 \end{array} \\ \left[\begin{array}{ccc} 1 & 0 & 0 \\ 1 & 0 & 0 \\ \vdots & \vdots & \vdots \\ 0 & 0 & 1 \\ \hline 1 & 0 & 0 \\ 0 & 1 & 0 \\ 0 & 0 & 1 \end{array}\right] \end{array}$$

$$= \begin{array}{c} \begin{array}{ccc} \lambda_3 & \lambda_2 & \lambda_1 \end{array} \\ \left[\begin{array}{ccc} 1 & 0 & 0 \end{array}\right] \end{array}$$

3.4.1 Updates on the store

During the abstract transition, we make updates to stores of the form:

$$\hat{\sigma}' = \hat{\sigma} \sqcup [v_1 \mapsto \hat{L}_1, v_2 \mapsto \hat{L}_2].$$

We need matrix operations that correspond to this update operation.

First, we have to construct a store representing a single mapping: $[v \mapsto \hat{L}]$. Fortunately, matrix transposition and matrix multiplication make this straightforward:

Lemma 3.1. $\langle\!\langle [v \mapsto \hat{L}] \rangle\!\rangle = \langle\!\langle v \rangle\!\rangle^{\top} \times \langle\!\langle \hat{L} \rangle\!\rangle + \langle\!\langle \bot_{Store} \rangle\!\rangle$.

It's also the case that Boolean-OR acts as join on stores:

Lemma 3.2. $\langle\!\langle \hat{\sigma}_1 \sqcup \hat{\sigma}_2 \rangle\!\rangle = \langle\!\langle \hat{\sigma}_1 \rangle\!\rangle + \langle\!\langle \hat{\sigma}_2 \rangle\!\rangle$.

And, these two lemmas give us store update:

Theorem 3.2 (Store Update Theorem)**.**

$$\langle\!\langle \hat{\sigma} \sqcup [v_1 \mapsto \hat{L}_1, v_2 \mapsto \hat{L}_2] \rangle\!\rangle$$
$$= \langle\!\langle \hat{\sigma} \rangle\!\rangle + \langle\!\langle v_1 \rangle\!\rangle^{\top} \times \langle\!\langle \hat{L}_1 \rangle\!\rangle + \langle\!\langle v_2 \rangle\!\rangle^{\top} \times \langle\!\langle \hat{L}_2 \rangle\!\rangle.$$

Proof. By the prior two lemmas. □

3.4.2 Running example: Store update

This example shows all the moving parts for store update.

Running example. To update with λ_2 flowing to variable v_2', we multiply the vectors representing λ_2 and v_2' and add the result, $\boldsymbol{\sigma}_{\text{frag}}$, to the current store:

$$\begin{array}{c} v_3' \\ v_2' \\ \vdots \\ v_1 \\ \\ \lambda_3 \\ \lambda_2 \\ \lambda_1 \end{array} \left[\begin{array}{c} 0 \\ 1 \\ \vdots \\ 0 \\ \hline 0 \\ 0 \\ 0 \end{array}\right] \times \begin{array}{c} \begin{array}{ccc} \lambda_3 & \lambda_2 & \lambda_1 \end{array} \\ \left[\begin{array}{ccc} 0 & 1 & 0 \end{array}\right] \end{array} = \begin{array}{c} \\ v_3' \\ v_2' \\ \vdots \\ v_1 \\ \\ \lambda_3 \\ \lambda_2 \\ \lambda_1 \end{array} \begin{array}{c} \begin{array}{ccc} \lambda_3 & \lambda_2 & \lambda_1 \end{array} \\ \left[\begin{array}{ccc} 0 & 0 & 0 \\ 0 & 1 & 0 \\ \vdots & \vdots & \vdots \\ 0 & 0 & 0 \\ \hline 0 & 0 & 0 \\ 0 & 0 & 0 \\ 0 & 0 & 0 \end{array}\right] \end{array}$$

$$\begin{array}{c} \\ v_3' \\ v_2' \\ \vdots \\ v_1 \\ \\ \lambda_3 \\ \lambda_2 \\ \lambda_1 \end{array} \begin{array}{c} \boldsymbol{\sigma}_{\text{frag}} \\ \left[\begin{array}{ccc} 0 & 0 & 0 \\ 0 & 1 & 0 \\ \vdots & \vdots & \vdots \\ 0 & 0 & 0 \\ \hline 0 & 0 & 0 \\ 0 & 0 & 0 \\ 0 & 0 & 0 \end{array}\right] \end{array} + \begin{array}{c} \boldsymbol{\sigma}_{\text{curr}} \\ \left[\begin{array}{ccc} 1 & 0 & 0 \\ 1 & 0 & 0 \\ \vdots & \vdots & \vdots \\ 0 & 1 & 0 \\ \hline 1 & 0 & 0 \\ 0 & 1 & 0 \\ 0 & 0 & 1 \end{array}\right] \end{array} = \begin{array}{c} \boldsymbol{\sigma}_{\text{new}} \\ \left[\begin{array}{ccc} 1 & 0 & 0 \\ 1 & 1 & 0 \\ \vdots & \vdots & \vdots \\ 0 & 1 & 0 \\ \hline 1 & 0 & 0 \\ 0 & 1 & 0 \\ 0 & 0 & 1 \end{array}\right] \end{array}$$

3.5 Linear encoding of the transfer function

Earlier, we constructed a family of transfer functions, $\hat{f}_{call}$, which produced the effect of the transition relation on the store for a given call site. We can construct an equivalent linearized function, $\mathbf{f}_{call} : \mathbf{Store} \to \mathbf{Store}$,

$$\mathbf{f}_{call}(\boldsymbol{\sigma}) = \boldsymbol{\sigma}'$$
$$\vec{L} = \langle\!\langle call \rangle\!\rangle \times \mathbf{Fun} \times \boldsymbol{\sigma}$$
$$\vec{L}_1 = \langle\!\langle call \rangle\!\rangle \times \mathbf{Arg}_1 \times \boldsymbol{\sigma}$$
$$\vec{L}_2 = \langle\!\langle call \rangle\!\rangle \times \mathbf{Arg}_2 \times \boldsymbol{\sigma}$$
$$\vec{v}_1 = \vec{L} \times \mathbf{Var}_1$$
$$\vec{v}_2 = \vec{L} \times \mathbf{Var}_2$$
$$\boldsymbol{\sigma}' = \boldsymbol{\sigma} + \left(\vec{v}_1^{\top} \times \vec{L}_1\right) + \left(\vec{v}_2^{\top} \times \vec{L}_2\right).$$

3.6 Soundness

We can prove that the linearized transfer function is equivalent to the traditional one, under our matrix-vector encoding:

Theorem 3.3 (Soundness)**.** $\langle\!\langle \hat{f}_{call}(\hat{\sigma}) \rangle\!\rangle = \mathbf{f}_{call} \langle\!\langle \hat{\sigma} \rangle\!\rangle$.

Proof. The proof proceeds bidirectionally. First, show that every entry in $\langle\!\langle \hat{f}_{call}(\hat{\sigma}) \rangle\!\rangle$ must be in $\mathbf{f}_{call} \langle\!\langle \hat{\sigma} \rangle\!\rangle$, and then *vice versa*. In both directions, it's easiest to split into cases: the one in which the entry exists in $\hat{\sigma}$, and the one in which it is fresh. □

3.7 EigenCFA: The Algorithm

Algorithm 1 gives the high-level algorithm for EigenCFA. The algorithm assumes that the store σ is empty at the start.

while σ *changes* **do**
  foreach *call* **do**
    // Lookup function and arguments in *call*
    $\vec{L} := (\langle\langle call\rangle\rangle \times \mathbf{Fun}) \times \sigma$
    $\vec{L}_1 := (\langle\langle call\rangle\rangle \times \mathbf{Arg}_1) \times \sigma$
    $\vec{L}_2 := (\langle\langle call\rangle\rangle \times \mathbf{Arg}_2) \times \sigma$

    // Formal arguments of function, $\vec{L}$
    $\vec{v}_1 := (\vec{L} \times \mathbf{Var}_1) \times \sigma$
    $\vec{v}_2 := (\vec{L} \times \mathbf{Var}_2) \times \sigma$

    // Update store
    $\sigma := \sigma + \underbrace{\vec{v}_1^{\top} \times \vec{L}_1}_{Bind\ L_1\ to\ v} + \underbrace{\vec{v}_2^{\top} \times \vec{L}_2}_{Bind\ L_2\ to\ v'}$
  end
end

Algorithm 1: EigenCFA

4. Abstract Church encodings

It's possible to transform any program into binary CPS using mechanisms like Church encodings and the Y combinator. Some encodings, like transforming the term `(let ((`v e`))` *body*`)` into the term `((λ (`v`)` *body*`)` e`)` are benign. But, because some encodings transform data-flow into control-flow, they obscure the control-flow of the original program. Even Church-encoded integers raise thorny control-flow issues. Yet, handling forms like `set!` or `letrec` as special cases in the transfer function is not practical: this would force conditional tests and branching, disrupting the data-parallelism that we have carefully engineered and protected.

To avoid branching but preserve precision, we turn to "abstract Church encodings." An *abstract Church encoding* is a program transformation that is meaning-preserving for an *abstract* semantics, but not for the concrete semantics.

Caution The abstract Church encodings in this section work for the abstract semantics of 0CFA and the simple linear model of EigenCFA. Some of the forthcoming GPU optimizations require alphatization of the program, a constraint that these encodings violate. Where violations occur, we will note how to adapt.

4.1 Abstracting termination as non-termination

We actually *need* abstract Church encodings to handle program termination: notice that our CPS language has no `halt` form. So to encode `halt`, we'll use *non*-termination; that is, we use the non-terminating program Omega as the abstract encoding for termination. In other words, we apply the following rewrite rule after conversion to a binary CPS that contains a `halt` primitive:

```
halt ⟹
    (λ (a b) ((λ (f g) (f f f))
      (λ (f g) (f f f))
      (λ (f g) (f f f))))
```

This works because once an abstract interpreter hits Omega, that branch won't contribute any more changes to the abstract store, so the abstract interpretation can reach a fixed point.

4.2 Abstracting mutation as binding

To Church encode a construct like `set!`, we'd have to (1) perform cell boxing on all mutable variables, and then (2) eliminate all cells with a store-passing-style transformation. These kinds of global transforms alter the control-flow and data-flow behavior of the program. Yet, 0CFA has a single abstract store that represents *all* program environments. As a result, `let` and `set!` have *exactly the same effect on the abstract store*; so we can apply a rewriting rule:

`(set!` v e`)` ⟹ `(let ((`v e`)) #void)`

From the abstract store's perspective, these terms are equivalent.

4.3 Encoding recursion as mutation

Now that we can handle mutation, we can avoid using the Y combinator (or a grisly polvariadic, mutually recursive variant thereof) to handle recursion. `Letrec` normally desugars into "`let`s and `set!`s." But, since `let` has the same effect as `set!`, we can actually turn `letrec` into `let` with an abstract rewrite rule:

`(letrec ((`v_1 lam_1`)` $\ldots$ `(`v_n lam_n`))` e`)`
⟹ `(let ((`v_1 lam_1`)` $\ldots$ `(`v_n lam_n`))` e`)`

0CFA does not distinguish their effects on the abstract store.

4.4 Abstracting basic values as non-termination

Most CFAs encode all numbers as a single abstract value. In fact, most even convert *all* basic values into a single abstract value. We can do the same, using the `halt` function from before as the single abstract value. (Any attempt to apply a basic value shouldn't allow the program to continue normal execution.) All primitive operations that operate on basic values ignore their arguments and return this basic value.

4.5 Abstractly encoding conditionals

Most CFAs do not attempt to evaluate conditionals; their behavior is to always branch in both directions at an `if`. We could Church encode Booleans and conditionals, but this introduces a level of indirection, as conditionals appear to interprocedurally flow through their Church-encoded condition. Or, we could exploit the fact that flow sets merge in 0CFA to simulate the non-determinism of the conditional with the non-determinism of procedure call. So, after we CPS transform `if` forms, we can abstractly encode them with a `let`-based rewrite:

```
(if e call₁ call₂)
⟹ (let ((next (λ () call₁)))
      (let ((next (λ () call₂)))
        (next)))
```

It's safe to drop the conditional expression e, because after the CPS transform, this expression is atomic, and it makes no changes to the store. By the time the analysis reaches the call site `(next)`, both continuations will have been bound to `next` in the abstract store.

5. Our GPU implementation narrative

In this section, we discuss the details of mapping our high-level algorithm for EigenCFA down to the nuts and bolts of a GPU implementation. It took effort to discover which optimizations and data structures were the right ones, so we will discuss both the right turns and the wrong ones on the road to EigenCFA. We present three iterations of our implementation: (1) naïve, (2) dense and (3) sparse.

We wrote a pre-processor in Racket which transformed the input program and generated the static syntax matrices. These matrices were passed to a C program which copied them into the GPU memory and launched the CUDA (GPU) kernels that performed the analysis. (For a brief summary of CUDA and the high-level architecture of the GPU we targeted, see the appendix.) All three of our implementations picked up at this point.

5.1 Attempt 1: Naïve implementation with CUBLAS

Our first implementation of EigenCFA used NVidia's CUBLAS library for linear algebra to perform the matrix operations. This implementation was an almost verbatim transliteration of Algorithm 1, and it turned out to be *slower* than our CPU implementation. We identified several problems:

- **Dense matrix computations.**

  Although most of the matrices in our analysis were sparse, the CUBLAS library is written for accelerating dense-matrix operations. Since the matrices are all quadratic in the size of the program, they consumed all of the parallel processing facilities of the GPU, even for small programs.

- **Memory requirements.**

  The matrices and vectors in EigenCFA only contain boolean values. Use of 4-byte floats as required by the CUBLAS libraries for each element was wasteful. As we describe in Section 5.2, using one bit per entry yielded large constant-factor speedups and substantial memory savings.

- **Redundant operations.**

  The static syntax matrix lookups (each a large multiplication) were repeated in each iteration. Eventually, we were able to compress these matrices and simplify their application.

5.2 Attempt 2: Bit-packed matrix implementation

To overcome some of the limitations of the naïve approach, we optimized the matrix and vector representations.

5.2.1 Bit-packing

Since the vectors and matrices contain Boolean entries, one obvious way to reduce the sizes of the matrices was to use bit-vectors for terms and values, and bit matrices for the abstract store and the syntactic matrices. Once encoded as bit-packed data structures, we also gain word-level parallelism by shifting from Boolean to bitwise-logical operations.

Running example. Here is the same store lookup from earlier, with bit-packed matrices:

$$\begin{bmatrix} 0 & 128 \end{bmatrix} \otimes \begin{bmatrix} 1 & 0 & 0 \\ 196 & 58 & 1 \end{bmatrix} = \begin{bmatrix} 1 & 0 & 0 \end{bmatrix}$$

Each column of the store has been compressed. To make this example small but interesting, we assume that the size of each word is eight bits. The $\otimes$ operator is bitwise matrix-multiplication that works on our bit-packing scheme: the multiplication and addition in conventional matrix multiplication algorithm become bitwise-AND and bitwise-OR.

In our implementation, the word size is 32 bits—the word size on the GPU on which we ran the analysis. This means that all vectors are padded to bring their size to the nearest multiple of 32. This bit-packing reduced the size of the matrices by almost a factor of 32. (The word-alignment padding is why the reduction in size isn't always *exactly* a factor of 32.)

Running example. Here is bit-packed store update:

$$\begin{bmatrix} 0 \\ 128 \end{bmatrix} \times \begin{bmatrix} 0 & 1 & 0 \end{bmatrix} = \begin{bmatrix} 0 & 0 & 0 \\ 0 & 128 & 0 \end{bmatrix}$$

$$\oplus \begin{bmatrix} 1 & 0 & 0 \\ 196 & 58 & 1 \end{bmatrix} = \begin{bmatrix} 1 & 0 & 0 \\ 196 & 186 & 1 \end{bmatrix}$$

(The $\oplus$ operator performs a bitwise-OR.)

5.2.2 Compressing static syntax matrices

Each static syntax matrix is quadratic in the size of the program. Transferring them to and manipulating them on the GPU imposes significant time and memory costs. Fortunately, we can exploit the uniformity of binary CPS to compress them and optimize their application at the same time.

By choosing the numbering scheme for variables and lambda terms carefully, we compressed the operators $\mathbf{Var}_1$ and $\mathbf{Var}_2$ into small, explicit formulae. Specifically, if the lambda term λ_n is the nth lambda term, then in an expression vector, $(n + |\mathsf{Lam}|)$ is the expression number of its first formal, and $(n + 2|\mathsf{Lam}|)$ is the expression number of it second formal.

Now, each expression vector has three distinct segments: the $\mathbf{Lam}$ segment for the lambda terms; the $\mathbf{Var}_1$ segment for formals in the first position; and the $\mathbf{Var}_2$ segment for formal in the second position. With this scheme, we can determine $\langle\!\langle v_k \rangle\!\rangle$ and $\langle\!\langle v'_k \rangle\!\rangle$ from the representation of λ_k without any matrix multiplication.

Running example. If v_k and v'_k are, respectively, the first and second formal arguments for λ_k, these are the vectors representing λ_2, v_2 and v'_2:

$$\langle\!\langle \lambda_2 \rangle\!\rangle = \begin{bmatrix} \overset{\lambda_2}{0} & \overset{\lambda_2}{1} & \overset{\lambda_1}{0} \end{bmatrix}$$

$$\langle\!\langle v_2 \rangle\!\rangle = \begin{bmatrix} \overset{v'_3}{0} & \overset{v'_2}{0} & \overset{v'_1}{0} & | & \overset{v_3}{0} & \overset{v_2}{1} & \overset{v_1}{0} & | & \overset{\lambda_3}{0} & \overset{\lambda_2}{0} & \overset{\lambda_1}{0} \end{bmatrix}$$

$$\langle\!\langle v'_2 \rangle\!\rangle = \begin{bmatrix} 0 & 1 & 0 & | & 0 & 0 & 0 & | & 0 & 0 & 0 \end{bmatrix}$$

The $\mathbf{Call}$ matrix disappears after making the observation that there is exactly one call site for every λ-term. That is, the *same vector* (suitably truncated) can represent both the λ-term and its corresponding call site. (When we shift to a sparse-matrix implementation, we will be able to compress the remaining static syntax matrices.)

Caution: Abstract Church encodings The compression strategy we have chosen implicitly alphatizes the program, so that each variable has a unique lambda term that binds it. Some of the abstract Church encodings carefully exploit the behavior of 0CFA on non-alphatized code. There are two ways to resolve this problem: (1) more sophisticated abstract Church encodings or (2) a look-up table in the GPU implementation:

1. The encoding approach adds a procedure for every variable v:

   $$\texttt{write-}v = (\lambda\ (v\ q)\ (q))$$

   All mutation of the variable v must pass through this procedure.

2. The lookup-table approach creates a $2|\mathsf{Lam}|$-entry table in which entry n contains the expression number of the first formal and the entry $n + |\mathsf{Lam}|$ contains the expression number of the second formal for the nth lambda term.

5.2.3 Store update optimization

Under the encoding described in the previous section, the store is also logically divided into the same three equal-sized segments: the $\mathbf{Lam}$ region, the $\mathbf{Var}_1$ region and the $\mathbf{Var}_2$ region. As a result, we determined that store update, which adds $\vec{v}^{\top} \times \vec{L}$, can only modify a (known) third of the store: the region in which the variables in the vector $\vec{v}$ live. (Recall that, in the abstract semantics, updates for first-argument formals are carried out separately from updates for second-argument formals.) Exploiting this knowledge cuts the number of operations on update by two-thirds.

5.2.4 GPU-only optimizations

A few optimizations in our second implementation apply only to the GPU:

- **Reducing the number of kernel calls.**

  The CPU initiates parallel operations on the GPU through kernel invocations. Each kernel call has non-trivial overhead, so kernels should be combined whenever synchronization between them is unnecessary. We performed the calculations for $\vec{L}$, $\vec{L}_1$ and $\vec{L}_2$ (see Algorithm 1) within the same kernel. Combined with the static matrix compression and the store update optimization, the total number of kernel calls per iteration dropped from 14 to 3.

- **Constant memory.**

  Since we were iterating over all call sites in the program, there was strong locality in the syntax matrix lookup, and this data was read-only on the GPU. Therefore, it was a good candidate to use the GPU's constant memory, which unlike the global memory, is cached for low latency memory accesses. Although the constant memory on the GPU was not large enough to store the entire static matrix, we could leverage this locality and store only that part of the matrix which we knew would be used at any point of time. This increased speed by 40% compared to the scheme without constant memory.

- **Aligning thirds of the vectors to word boundaries.**

  In order to efficiently implement static syntax matrix compression (Section 5.2.2), we aligned each segment of the expression vectors—$\mathbf{Lam}$, $\mathbf{Var}_1$ and $\mathbf{Var}_2$—along word boundaries.

Running example. The figure below shows 0-padded vectors where $|\mathsf{Lam}| = 3$ and the word size is 4.

$$\overbrace{\begin{bmatrix} \overset{\lambda_d}{\mathbf{0}} & \overset{\lambda_3}{0} & \overset{\lambda_2}{1} & \overset{\lambda_1}{0} \end{bmatrix}}^{\langle\langle \lambda_2 \rangle\rangle}$$

$$\overbrace{\begin{bmatrix} \cdots & \overset{v'}{0} & \cdots & | & \overset{v_d}{\mathbf{0}} & \overset{v_3}{0} & \overset{v_2}{1} & \overset{v_1}{0} & | & \cdots & \overset{\lambda}{0} & \cdots \end{bmatrix}}^{\langle\langle v_2 \rangle\rangle}$$

$$\overbrace{\begin{bmatrix} \overset{v'_d}{\mathbf{0}} & \overset{v'_3}{0} & \overset{v'_2}{1} & \overset{v'_1}{0} & | & \cdots & \overset{v}{0} & \cdots & | & \cdots & \overset{\lambda}{0} & \cdots \end{bmatrix}}^{\langle\langle v'_2 \rangle\rangle}$$

We also padded the store to take into account this change in the size of the vectors.

Running example. The corresponding 0-padded store is below. When creating the store, we need to add blank rows corresponding to the pads:

	λ_d	λ_3	λ_2	λ_1
v'_d	**0**	**0**	**0**	**0**
$\vdots$	$\vdots$	$\vdots$	$\vdots$	$\vdots$
v'_1	**0**	1	0	0
v_d	**0**	**0**	**0**	**0**
$\vdots$	$\vdots$	$\vdots$	$\vdots$	$\vdots$
v_1	**0**	0	1	0
λ_d	**1**	**0**	**0**	**0**
λ_3	**0**	1	0	0
λ_2	**0**	0	1	0
λ_1	**0**	0	0	1

- **Shared memory.**

  In our implementation of matrix multiplication, each thread calculates the value of exactly one cell in the result. We arranged the threads so that all threads within a block write to adjacent cells within the same row of the result. This means that all of the threads will read from exactly the same part of the vectors being multiplied. This yields significant data reuse. So, we copied the relevant segments of the vectors into shared memory and observed a 25% reduction in the running-time.

5.2.5 Limitations of this approach

To our surprise, these optimizations only barely beat the performance of our CPU implementation of 0CFA. Through debugging, we narrowed the cause of the poor performance down to a few principal factors:

- **Unnecessary operations.**

  The first phase of the store update operation generates a new store which contains new bindings; the second phase then adds this new store to the old store. Not only does this waste memory on a second store, the update only impacts a small number of locations, yet we pay a cost proportional to the size of the store—*twice*.

- **Failure to exploit "superposition."**

  EigenCFA can do things 0CFA can't: EigenCFA can represent multiple terms, *e.g.*, call sites, in the same vector, simply by setting additional bits. This gives EigenCFA control over a different kind of parallelism—the ability to act on "superimposed" terms. Yet, our implementation ignores this ability.

- **Unutilized parallelism.**

  Since the analysis is flow-insensitive, all of the call sites could be evaluated in parallel and their effects then merged. However, since we were using dense-matrix operations, performing large matrix multiplications for each call site consumed the storage capacity of the GPU. To process each call site required a return to the CPU to retrieve the partial solution from the GPU, and copy the input data for the next call site, sequentializing the computation.

5.3 Success: Sparse matrix implementation

Before constructing our third implementation, we observed that the abstract store tended to be sparse. In fact, 96% of all entries in the final store matrix contained zeros. And, on average, each variable was bound to about two lambda terms. Using a dense matrix to encode the store is inefficient. So, we switched to using a sparse matrix representation of the store, and this optimization turned out to be the critical accelerant for EigenCFA.

5.3.1 A sparse representation

The sparse matrix representation we use is essentially ELL form, in which the sparse matrix has a fixed maximum number of columns. Each row has a header indicating how many cells in that row are active, and an auxiliary array indicates the column for each nonzero element.[5] ELL is best suited to sparse matrices that have roughly comparable numbers of non-zero elements, and lends itself to computationally efficient access to the sparse matrix. This scheme is not as memory-efficient as the more commonly used CSR (Compressed Sparse Row) representation [3], but it has a smaller memory footprint than the dense representation and it retains, for our purposes, the performance advantages.

We allocate our initial store matrix by allocating a fixed number of columns to each row in the store. Initially, we assume no flow set will hold more than 4% of all lambda terms in the program. If, during the course of the analysis, this number proves to be insufficient, we save the store, terminate the analysis and restart with a twice as many columns.

The header cell of each row is the index of the first free slot available in that row. Each entry in a flow set row is the assigned number of the lambda term in the flow set, *e.g.*, if row i contains n, then λ_n may flow to variable v_i.

Running example. We sketch the sparse store representation for our running example below:

$$\begin{array}{c} v'_3 \\ v'_2 \\ \vdots \\ v_1 \\ \\ \lambda_3 \\ \lambda_2 \\ \lambda_1 \end{array} \left[\begin{array}{c|cccc} 2 & 3 & \_ & \_ \\ 3 & 3 & 2 & \_ \\ \vdots & \vdots & \vdots & \vdots \\ 2 & 2 & \_ & \_ \\ \hline 2 & 3 & \_ & \_ \\ 2 & 2 & \_ & \_ \\ 2 & 1 & \_ & \_ \end{array}\right]$$

In order to add λ_2 to the flow set for v_1, we append the number corresponding to λ_2 to the row vector representing v_1, now a linear-time operation. (It's a linear-time operation because we check for membership before appending.)

5.3.2 Optimizing the static matrices

In addition to sparsifying the store, we also compressed the remaining static syntax matrices. Since every variable and λ-term has an assigned row in the store, when evaluating the function and argument expressions of a given call site, all EigenCFA needs is the corresponding row number in the store. With this insight, we reduced the **Fun**, $\mathbf{Arg}_1$ and $\mathbf{Arg}_2$ matrices to look-up vectors of size |Call|. This eliminates the need to perform a true matrix multiplication in the argument-lookup phase of Algorithm 1.

Running example. The **Fun** matrix becomes the vector:

$$\begin{array}{cccc} c_1 & c_2 & c_3 & c_4 \\ \end{array}$$
$$\left[\begin{array}{cccc} 5 & 1 & 3 & 8 \end{array}\right]$$

5.3.3 Parallelizing call-site evaluation

Since the store-update operation was simplified, we freed up enough GPU resources to parallelize each iteration across call sites.

5.3.4 Tolerating race conditions

Since global synchronization on a GPU is expensive, it's important to engineer store update to behave correctly in the presence of races once call sites are analyzed in parallel. It will likely be the case that one GPU thread sees a store has been only partially updated by another GPU thread. Fortunately, abstract transfer functions in 0CFA are monotonic, which means that flow sets only get larger. More importantly, it means that 0CFA is information-preserving during each iteration: working with stale data does not affect the soundness.

We ensure that the store grows monotonically by writing to it only when a GPU thread has new information to add. And, for overall efficiency, we tolerate some rare inefficiencies: a row may have more than one copy of the same lambda term if they race on trying to add the same lambda at the same time. This prevents threads with stale data from overwriting any changes to the store, without the cost of global synchronization.

For instance, let's say that two call sites c_1 and c_2 are being evaluated in parallel and c_2 reads from a row before c_1 updates it. If the evaluation of c_1 does not yield any new store bindings, nothing will be written to the store and the updates of c_2 will be preserved. In the next iteration, these updates will be visible during the evaluation of c_1 and the final result will still be correct.

Robustness against races from monotonicity We can argue more formally that 0CFA is robust in the presence of stale or partially completed stores and out-of-order analysis for call sites. Suppose that the current abstract store $\hat{\sigma}$ is reset at some point to an arbitrarily chosen weaker store, $\hat{\sigma}'$, so that $\hat{\sigma}' \sqsubseteq \hat{\sigma}$. This represents acting on stale or partially completed data. We can show that the analysis will still reach the most precise result:

Theorem 5.1. *If* $\hat{\sigma}' \sqsubseteq \mathrm{lfp}(\hat{F})$ *then* $\hat{F}^{\infty}(\hat{\sigma}') = \mathrm{lfp}(\hat{F})$.

Proof. By definition, $\hat{\sigma}' = \mathrm{lfp}(\hat{F}) \sqcap \hat{\sigma}'$. Applying $\hat{F}^{\infty}$ to both sides yields $\hat{F}^{\infty}(\hat{\sigma}') = \mathrm{lfp}(\hat{F}) \sqcap \hat{F}^{\infty}(\hat{\sigma}')$. By Kleene's fixed-point theorem, $\hat{F}^{\infty}(\hat{\sigma}')$ must also be a fixed point. Tarski-Knaster guarantees this fixed point will be equal to or greater than the least fixed point. Thus, $\mathrm{lfp}(\hat{F}) \sqcap \hat{F}^{\infty}(\hat{\sigma}') = \mathrm{lfp}(\hat{F})$. □

We can also analyze calls in any order—also on partially completed or stale data. We show this by proving that applying the transfer function for any call site to a point below the least fixed point remains consistent with the least fixed point:

Theorem 5.2. *If* $\hat{\sigma}' \sqsubseteq \mathrm{lfp}(\hat{F})$ *then* $\hat{f}_{call}(\hat{\sigma}') \sqsubseteq \mathrm{lfp}(\hat{F})$, *for any call site call.*

Proof. By contradiction, and cases: (1) $\hat{f}_{call}(\hat{\sigma}') \sqsupseteq \mathrm{lfp}(\hat{F})$ and (2) $\hat{f}_{call}(\hat{\sigma}') \not\sqsubseteq \mathrm{lfp}(\hat{F})$ and $\hat{f}_{call}(\hat{\sigma}') \not\sqsupseteq \mathrm{lfp}(\hat{F})$. □

5.4 GPU-specific optimization: Texture memory

A final GPU-specific tweak led to additional speedup. The selection matrices (which had by now been reduced to a linear array) were all stored in texture memory, a way of designating read-only data in global memory so that it is cached for low-latency memory access. We did this because texture data doesn't have the size restrictions of constant memory. The use of texture memory resulted in a roughly 20% speedup over the use of global memory.

6. Empirical evaluation

In total, we created four implementations to evaluate and compare. In case it is not clear, EigenCFA and 0CFA have exactly the same precision, so time is the only relevant metric for comparison. *Ultimately, our fastest GPU implementation was a factor of 72 faster than our fastest CPU implementation at scale.* We compared two CPU implementations against two GPU implementations:

- **CPU (S)**: A fast CPU implementation of 0CFA in Racket. We implemented a traditional small-step version of 0CFA according to best practices.
- **CPU (Sp)**: A sparse-matrix CPU implementation of EigenCFA in C. Since many of our optimizations to the sparse-matrix implementation were not GPU-specific, and many good sparse matrix algorithms for the CPU exist, we had to make sure that merely representing 0CFA as a sparse matrix algorithm was not the sole cause of the speedup. We implemented this CPU version of the sparse-matrix algorithm in order to show that the speedups from the GPU mattered. In fact, this matrix CPU version beat our Racket CPU version in performance, so we report our relative speedup against this sparse-matrix CPU implementation instead.
- **GPU (D)**: A dense-matrix implementation of EigenCFA on the GPU. It performed terribly. We implemented this version as a cautionary point of comparison. (This implementation corresponds to Attempt 2.)
- **GPU (Sp)**: A sparse-matrix implementation of EigenCFA on the GPU. We implemented this version to measure the speedup over the fastest CPU version, which ended up being a factor of 72.

6.1 Platform

We evaluated our implementations on an NVidia GTX-480 "Fermi" GPU with 1.5 GB of memory. The host machine (on which we also ran the CPU implementations) was equipped with an Intel i7 CPU running at 2.79 GHz.

6.2 Benchmarks

To benchmark our implementations across a range of program sizes, we exploited Van Horn and Mairson's recent work on the complexity of control-flow analyses [26, 27]. Because Van Horn and Mairson offer *constructive* proofs of complexity, we can extract a "benchmark generator" from these proofs that emits a program of the requested size that will be worst-case to analyze for k-CFA when $k \geq 1$. For 0CFA, the programs it generates are difficult but not worst-case. Might, Smaragdakis and Van Horn's recent work on the complexity of k-CFA also used this generator, and their empirical results provide a sense of its verisimilitude to hand-written benchmarks [21]. In short, these benchmarks are about an order of magnitude harder to analyze than code written by humans.

6.3 Measurements

Table 1 presents the running time of the analysis for each implementation. The first column is the number of terms in the program. A time of "∞" indicates that the analysis took longer than 6 hours to complete. Figure 1 is a plot of the same data. Note the logarithmic scale on the time-axis. As programs grow larger, the sparse-matrix GPU implementation of EigenCFA has a significant advantage over the other implementations.

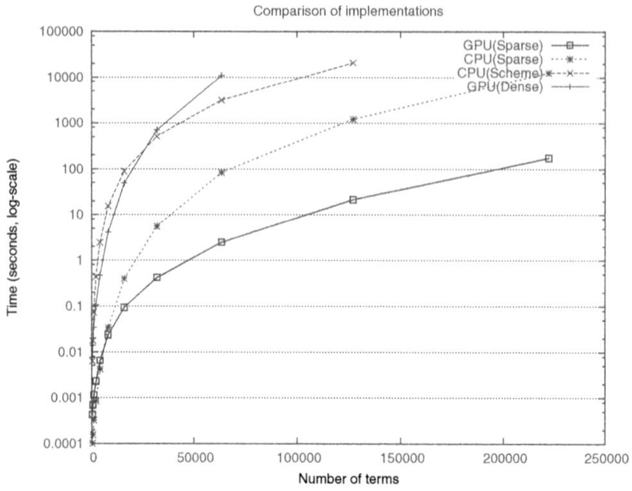

Figure 1. Comparison of implementations: Running times versus number of terms. Note that the time axis is **log-scale**. The sparse-matrix GPU implementation of EigenCFA clearly dominates.

Terms	GPU (Sp)	CPU (Sp)	CPU (S)	GPU (D)
297	0.4 ms	0.1 ms	6.3 ms	7.7 ms
545	0.7 ms	0.16 ms	18 ms	13.9 ms
1,041	1.15 ms	0.33 ms	74.3 ms	34.2 ms
2,033	2.27 ms	0.84 ms	433 ms	0.11 s
4,017	6.51 ms	4.2 ms	2.46 s	0.47 s
7,985	24.01 ms	34.7 ms	15.53 s	4.13 s
15,921	94.48 ms	0.4 s	1m 30s	49.16 s
31,793	0.4 s	5.6 s	8m 30s	11m 43s
63,537	2.49 s	1m 24s	52 min	3hr 2m
127,025	21.3 s	20 min	5hr 46m	∞
222,257	2m 53s	3hr 30 m	∞	∞

Table 1. Analysis running times versus number of terms. (∞ means greater than 6 hours.)

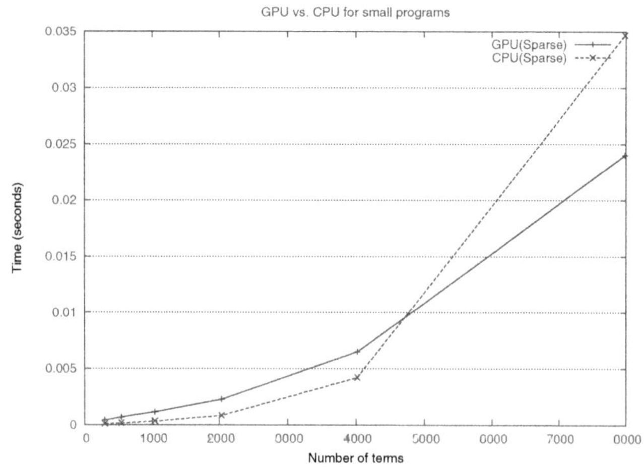

Figure 2. Comparison of GPU and CPU at smaller program sizes. Up to 4500 program terms, the CPU implementation beats the GPU implementation.

In the interest of showing trade-offs, Figure 2 compares the performance of the sparse-matrix implementation of the analysis running on the CPU and the GPU for smaller program sizes. For small programs (less than 4500 terms), the CPU (barely) outperforms the GPU for the following reasons:

- **Kernel invocation cost.**

  There is a fixed cost associated with each invocation of a kernel on a GPU. At smaller program sizes, since the number of iterations and the time taken per iteration is small, the start-up cost becomes a significant percentage of the total running time.

- **Faster CPU clock.**

  The CPU clock runs twice as fast as the GPU (2.8 GHz against 1.4Ghz). In small programs, there isn't as much parallelism that can be exploited by the GPU. In this situation, the slower clock of the GPU limits speed.

- **Fewer CPU iterations.**

  On larger program sizes, the number of iterations is large enough that in the limit, both the serial and parallel algorithms converge in exactly the same number of iterations. For the smaller programs, this isn't true and the GPU often takes twice as many iterations to converge.

Figure 3 is a plot of the speedup obtained by the sparse-matrix GPU implementation of EigenCFA over the CPU. Negative speedup values (barely visible at the left side of the chart) indicate a slowdown. Figure 2 shows this territory of the chart in more detail.

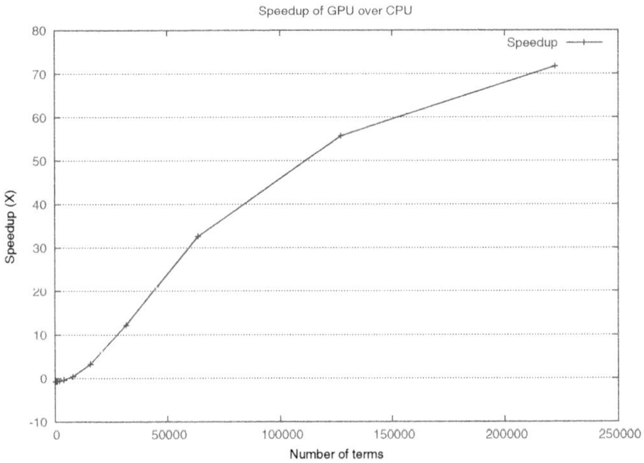

Figure 3. Speedup (in multiples) of GPU over CPU versus the number of program terms.

7. Related Work

Our work in flow analysis descends from a long line of research, beginning with the Cousots' foundational work on abstract interpretation [7, 8], continuing through Jones' work on control-flow analysis [11] and, most recently, through Shivers' work on *k*-CFA [20, 24, 25].

The literature on parallelizing static analyses is sparse. To the best of our knowledge, there haven't been any efforts to parallelize higher-order control-flow analyses. Notable very recent contributions include Mendez-Lojo *et al.*'s use of multicore architectures to accelerate classical inclusion-based points-to analysis [18] and Lopes *et al.*'s framework for distributed software model checking [16]. Given that 0CFA can also be phrased as an inclusion-based analysis, Mendez-Lojo's techniques are likely applicable.

Most of the prior work in parallelizing static analyses have been focused on data-flow analysis for first-order, imperative programs. Classically, data-flow analyses have been performed by iterative methods such as those originally proposed by Kildall [12] and Hecht [10], elimination methods [2, 23] or hybrid algorithms which combine both approaches [17]. Most efforts at parallelizing data flow analysis have involved parallelizing these algorithms. Zobel [28] and Gupta [9] parallelized Allen-Cocke's interval analysis. Ryder [15] improved on the graph partitioning scheme from [2] which led to a more effective parallel algorithm. Lee implemented the hybrid approach for MIMD architectures using message passing between the processors [14]. Gupta et al. moved away from parallelizing existing algorithms to developing specific techniques for parallel program analysis. In [13], they convert the control-flow graph of a program into a DAG and solve the data-flow problem for each node of the graph in parallel.

The GPU has been used to accelerate static analysis most notably by Banterle and Giacobazzi [4] who implemented the Octagon Abstract Domain (OAD) on a GPU. Since OAD computations are based on matrices, it was easily mapped to the GPU.

8. Future Work

There are at least two promising avenues for future work: adapting our techniques to pointer analysis and exploiting "superposition" within EigenCFA to achieve a genuinely new kind of flow analysis.

8.1 Accelerating pointer analyses

Given recent results unearthing the connection between control-flow and pointer analyses [21], we believe that the techniques presented here can be adapted to pointer analyses as well. Pointer analyses face additional hurdles, such as the fact that its small-step transition relation is much more complex, and a reduction to binary CPS seems out of the question. But these problem do not seem insurmountable.

8.2 Exploiting "superposition"

Using matrices to represent the store and vectors allows "superposition" to be used as another potential source of parallelism. This parallelism is implicit in the structure of the matrices themselves, so it could be exploited in addition to the explicit parallelism that was described in section 5.3.

8.3 Phased analysis

It took a lot of syntactic normalization and abstract Church encodings to impose control-flow uniformity on the abstract transfer function. We hypothesize that a better approach would be to allow different syntactic forms, and then process each kind of form in parallel—to process all function calls in parallel, then all `set!` statements in parallel, then all conditionals, and so on, in each pass of the analysis.

A. The GPU and CUDA

In this section, we provide a brief, high-level description of the architecture, memory hierarchy and programming model of the GPU. CUDA (Compute Unified Device Architecture) is a general purpose parallel computing architecture that leverages the parallel compute engine in NVidia GPUs. The parallel programming model provides three levels of abstraction—a hierarchy of thread groups, shared memories and barrier synchronization [1].

Threads on a GPU are organized into groups called blocks. Only threads within a block can be synchronized cheaply. Synchronization of threads across blocks would have to be done on the host which can be quite expensive. Threads are scheduled and executed in groups of parallel threads called warps. Divergence in execution paths of threads within a warp can have an adverse impact on performance. The GPU has different types of memories:

- **Global memory**: is large, global, read-write, uncached DRAM.
- **Shared Memory**: is small, private to each block, read-write memory whose access time is potentially as low as register access time
- **Constant Memory**: is small, global, read-only[3] and cached.
- **Texture Memory**: is read-only[3] and cached. It is optimized for 2D spatial locality which means that certain memory access patterns can be very efficient.

Data placement in memory and divergent execution in threads must be carefully controlled to maximize performance.

References

[1] *NVIDIA CUDA Programming Guide 2.3*, Aug. 2009.

[2] F. E. Allen and J. Cocke. A program data flow analysis procedure. *Commun. ACM*, 19(3):137+, 1976. ISSN 0001-0782.

[3] S. Balay, K. Buschelman, V. Eijkhout, W. Gropp, D. Kaushik, M. Knepley, L. C. McInnes, B. Smith, and H. Zhang. Sparse Matrices. In *PETSc Users Manual*, chapter 3, pages 55–66. 3.0.0 edition, Dec. 2008.

[4] F. Banterle and R. Giacobazzi. A Fast Implementation of the Octagon Abstract Domain on Graphics Hardware. In H. R. Nielson and G. Filé, editors, *Static Analysis*, volume 4634 of *Lecture Notes in Computer Science*, chapter 20, pages 315–332. Springer Berlin Heidelberg, Berlin, Heidelberg, 2007. ISBN 978-3-540-74060-5.

[5] N. Bell and M. Garland. Implementing sparse matrix-vector multiplication on throughput-oriented processors. In *SC '09: Proceedings of the Conference on High Performance Computing Networking, Storage and Analysis*, pages 1–11, New York, NY, USA, 2009. ACM. ISBN 9781-605-5874-4-8.

[6] S. Chaudhuri. Subcubic algorithms for recursive state machines. In *Proceedings of the 35th annual ACM SIGPLAN-SIGACT Symposium on Principles of Programming Languages*, POPL '08, pages 159–169, New York, NY, USA, 2008. ACM. ISBN 9781-595-9368-9-9.

[7] P. Cousot and R. Cousot. Abstract interpretation: A unified lattice model for static analysis of programs by construction or approximation of fixpoints. In *Conference Record of the Fourth ACM Symposium on Principles of Programming Languages*, pages 238–252, New York, NY, USA, 1977. ACM Press.

[8] P. Cousot and R. Cousot. Systematic design of program analysis frameworks. In *POPL '79: Proceedings of the 6th ACM SIGACT-SIGPLAN Symposium on Principles of Programming Languages*, pages 269–282, New York, NY, USA, 1979. ACM.

[9] R. Gupta, L. Pollock, and M. L. Soffa. Parallelizing data flow analysis. 1990.

[10] M. S. Hecht. *Flow Analysis of Computer Programs*. Elsevier Science Inc., New York, NY, USA, 1977. ISBN 0-444-00216-2.

[11] N. D. Jones. Flow Analysis of Lambda Expressions (Preliminary Version). In *Proceedings of the 8th Colloquium on Automata, Languages and Programming*, pages 114–128, London, UK, 1981. Springer-Verlag. ISBN 3-540-10843-2.

[12] G. A. Kildall. A unified approach to global program optimization. In *POPL '73: Proceedings of the 1st annual ACM SIGACT-SIGPLAN symposium on Principles of programming languages*, pages 194–206, New York, NY, USA, 1973. ACM.

[13] R. Kramer, R. Gupta, and M. L. Soffa. The Combining DAG: A Technique for Parallel Data Flow Analysis. *IEEE Transactions on Parallel and Distributed Systems*, 5(8):805–813, Aug. 1994. ISSN 1045-9219.

[14] Y. F. Lee, T. J. Marlowe, and B. G. Ryder. Performing data flow analysis in parallel. In *Supercomputing '90: Proceedings of the 1990 ACM/IEEE conference on Supercomputing*, pages 942–951, Los Alamitos, CA, USA, 1990. IEEE Computer Society Press. ISBN 0-89791-412-0.

[15] Y. F. Lee, B. G. Ryder, and M. E. Fiuczynski. Region Analysis: A Parallel Elimination Method for Data Flow Analysis. *IEEE Trans. Softw. Eng.*, 21(11):913–926, 1995. ISSN 0098-5589.

[16] N. P. Lopes and A. Rybalchenko. Distributed and Predictable Software Model Checking. In *Proc. of the 12th International Conference on Verification, Model Checking, and Abstract Interpretation (VMCAI)*, Jan. 2011.

[17] T. J. Marlowe and B. G. Ryder. An efficient hybrid algorithm for incremental data flow analysis. In *POPL '90: Proceedings of the 17th ACM SIGPLAN-SIGACT symposium on Principles of programming languages*, pages 184–196, New York, NY, USA, 1990. ACM. ISBN 0-89791-343-4.

[18] M. Méndez-Lojo, A. Mathew, and K. Pingali. Parallel inclusion-based points-to analysis. In *Proceedings of the ACM International Conference on Object Oriented Programming Systems languages and Applications*, OOPSLA '10, pages 428–443, New York, NY, USA, 2010. ACM. ISBN 9781-450-3020-3-6.

[19] J. Midtgaard and D. Van Horn. Subcubic control flow analysis algorithm. *Higher-Order and Symbolic Computation*, To appear.

[20] M. Might and O. Shivers. Improving flow analyses via ΓCFA: Abstract garbage collection and counting. In *ICFP '06: Proceedings of the Eleventh ACM SIGPLAN International Conference on Functional Programming*, pages 13–25, New York, NY, USA, 2006. ACM. ISBN 1-59593-309-3.

[21] M. Might, Y. Smaragdakis, and D. V. Horn. Resolving and exploiting the k-CFA paradox: illuminating functional vs. object-oriented program analysis. In *PLDI '10: Proceedings of the 2010 ACM SIGPLAN Conference on Programming Language Design and Implementation*, pages 305–315, New York, NY, USA, 2010. ACM. ISBN 9781-450-3001-9-3.

[22] J. Palsberg. Closure analysis in constraint form. *ACM Transactions on Programming Languages and Systems*, 17(1):47–62, Jan. 1995. ISSN 0164-0925.

[23] B. G. Ryder and M. C. Paull. Elimination algorithms for data flow analysis. *ACM Comput. Surv.*, 18(3):277–316, 1986. ISSN 0360-0300.

[24] O. Shivers. Control flow analysis in Scheme. In *Proceedings of the ACM SIGPLAN 1988 Conference on Programming Language Design and Implementation*, volume 23, pages 164–174, New York, NY, USA, July 1988. ACM. ISBN 0-89791-269-1.

[25] O. G. Shivers. *Control-Flow Analysis of Higher-Order Languages*. PhD thesis, Carnegie Mellon University, 1991.

[26] D. Van Horn and H. G. Mairson. Relating complexity and precision in control flow analysis. In *ICFP '07: Proceedings of the 12th ACM SIGPLAN International Conference on Functional Programming*, pages 85–96, New York, NY, USA, 2007. ACM. ISBN 9781-59593-815-2.

[27] D. Van Horn and H. G. Mairson. Deciding k-CFA is complete for EXPTIME. In *ICFP '08: Proceeding of the 13th ACM SIGPLAN International Conference on Functional Programming*, pages 275–282, New York, NY, USA, 2008. ACM. ISBN 978-1-59593-919-7.

[28] A. Zobel. Parallel interval analysis of data flow equations. volume II. The Penn State University press, Aug. 1990.

[3] For code running on the GPU, this memory is read-only. Code running on the host, i.e. the CPU, can write to it.

Bisimulation for Quantum Processes *

Yuan Feng

Centre for Quantum Computation and Intelligent Systems, University of Technology Sydney, Australia

State Key Laboratory of Intelligent Technology and Systems, TNList, Department of Computer Science and Technology, Tsinghua University, Beijing, China

yuan.feng@uts.edu.au

Runyao Duan Mingsheng Ying

Centre for Quantum Computation and Intelligent Systems, University of Technology Sydney, Australia

State Key Laboratory of Intelligent Technology and Systems, TNList, Department of Computer Science and Technology, Tsinghua University, Beijing, China

runyao.duan@uts.edu.au
mingsheng.ying@uts.edu.au

Abstract

Quantum cryptographic systems have been commercially available, with a striking advantage over classical systems that their security and ability to detect the presence of eavesdropping are provable based on the principles of quantum mechanics. On the other hand, quantum protocol designers may commit much more faults than classical protocol designers since human intuition is much better adapted to the classical world than the quantum world. To offer formal techniques for modeling and verification of quantum protocols, several quantum extensions of process algebra have been proposed. One of the most serious issues in quantum process algebra is to discover a quantum generalization of the notion of bisimulation, which lies in a central position in process algebra, preserved by parallel composition in the presence of quantum entanglement, which has no counterpart in classical computation. Quite a few versions of bisimulation have been defined for quantum processes in the literature, but in the best case they are only proved to be preserved by parallel composition of purely quantum processes where no classical communications are involved.

Many quantum cryptographic protocols, however, employ the LOCC (Local Operations and Classical Communications) scheme, where classical communications must be explicitly specified. So, a notion of bisimulation preserved by parallel composition in the circumstance of both classical and quantum communications is crucial for process algebra approach to verification of quantum cryptographic protocols. In this paper we introduce a novel notion of bisimulation for quantum processes and prove that it is congruent with respect to various process algebra combinators including parallel composition even when both classical and quantum communications are present. We also establish some basic algebraic laws for this bisimulation. In particular, we prove uniqueness of the solutions to recursive equations of quantum processes, which provides a powerful proof technique for verifying complex quantum protocols.

Categories and Subject Descriptors D.3.1 [*Programming Languages*]: Formal Definitions and Theory; F.3.1 [*Logics and Meanings of Programs*]: Specifying and Verifying and Reasoning about Programs

General Terms Languages, Theory, Verification

Keywords Quantum communication, quantum computing, quantum process algebra, bisimulation, congruence

1. Introduction

Quantum computing offers the potential of considerable speedup over classical computing for some important problems such as prime factoring [16] and unsorted database search [7]. However, functional quantum computers which can harness this potential in dealing with practical applications are extremely difficult to implement. On the other hand, quantum cryptography, of which the security and ability to detect the presence of eavesdropping are provable based on the principles of quantum mechanics, has been developed so rapidly that quantum cryptographic systems are already commercially available by a number of companies such as Id Quantique, Cerberis, MagiQ Technologies, SmartQuantum, and NEC.

As is well known, it is very difficult to guarantee correctness of classical communication protocols at the design stage, and some simple protocols were finally found to have fundamental flaws. Since human intuition is much worse adapted to the quantum world than the classical world, quantum protocol designers may commit much more faults than classical protocol designers, especially when more and more complicated quantum protocols can be implemented by future physical technology. With the purpose of cloning the success classical process algebras achieve in analyzing and verifying classical communication protocols and even distributed computing, various quantum process algebras have been proposed independently by several research groups. Jorrand and Lalire [10] defined a language QPAlg (Quantum Process Algebra) by extending a classical CCS-like process algebra. A branching bisimulation which identifies quantum processes associated with graphs having the same branching structure was also presented [12]. The bisimulation is, however, not congruent: it is not preserved by parallel composition. Gay and Nagarajan [6] defined a language CQP (Communicating Quantum Processes), which combines the communication primitives of pi-calculus [13] with primitives for unitary transformations and measurements. One distinctive feature of

* Partially supported by Australian ARC grant DP110103473, National Natural Science Foundation of China (Grant Nos: 60736011) and FANEDD grant 200755).

CQP is a type system which guarantees the physical realizability of quantum processes. However, no notion of equivalence between processes was presented.

Authors of the current paper proposed a model named qCCS [5] for quantum communicating systems by adding quantum input/output and quantum operation/measurement primitives to classical value-passing CCS [8, 9]. The semantics of quantum input and output was carefully designed to describe the communication of quantum systems which have been entangled with other systems. A bisimulation was defined for finite processes, and a simplified version of congruence property was proved, in which parallel composition is only permitted when the participating processes are free of quantum input, or free of quantum operations and measurement. In [18] the same authors studied a purely quantum version of qCCS where no classical data is explicitly involved, aiming at providing us a suitable framework to observe the interaction of computation and communication in quantum systems. A bisimulation was defined for this purely quantum qCCS and shown to be fully preserved by parallel composition. It is worth noting that, however, the bisimulation proposed in [18] cannot be directly extended to general qCCS where classical data as well as probabilistic behaviors are included.

In this paper, we combine the two models proposed in [5] and [18] together to involve both classical data and quantum data. This general model, which we still call qCCS for coherence, accommodates all classical process constructors (especially recursive definitions) as well as quantum primitives. As a consequence, both sequential and distributed quantum computing, quantum communication protocols, and quantum cryptographic systems can be formally modeled and rigorously analyzed in the framework of qCCS. We also design a bisimulation for processes in qCCS and an equivalence relation based on it, which turns out to be a congruence. This bisimulation has several distinctive features compared with those proposed in the literature: Firstly, it takes local quantum operations into account in a weak manner, but at the same time fits well with recursive definitions. Lalire's bisimulation cannot distinguish different operations on a quantum system which will never be output: quantum states are only compared when they are input or output. Bisimulation defined in [5] works well only for finite processes since quantum states are required to be compared after all the actions have been performed. Note that no state comparison is needed in [18] since all local quantum operations are regarded as visible actions, and the resulted bisimulation is a very strong one – it distinguishes two different sequences of local operations even when they have the same effect as a whole. Secondly, entanglement between the input/output system and the remaining systems is fully considered in our definition. Bisimulation presented in [12] totally ignores this correlation by only considering the reduced state of the input/output system. In [5] this consideration is implicitly made by the state comparison after the processes terminating. Again, it does not work for infinite processes. Finally, but most importantly, the bisimulation presented here is preserved by parallel composition, and the equivalence derived by the bisimulation is a congruence, making them suitable for equational reasoning in verifying quantum communication and cryptographic systems. Lalire's bisimulation is not preserved by parallel composition. The bisimulation in [5] is not preserved by restriction, and whether it is preserved by parallel composition still remains open, although the positive answer is affirmed in two special cases. The bisimulation proposed in [18] is indeed a congruence. However, since no classical data is involved in that model, many important quantum communication protocols such as superdense coding and teleportation cannot be described. This restricts the scope of its application.

The paper is organized as follows: in Section 2, we review some basic notions from linear algebra and quantum mechanics. The syntax and operational semantics of qCCS are presented in Section 3. To illustrate the expressiveness of qCCS, we describe with it the well-known quantum superdense coding and teleportation protocols. We also show how to encode quantum unitary gates and measurement gates, which are two basic elements of quantum circuits, by qCCS. Section 4 defines the notion of bisimulations for configurations as well as quantum processes. Equivalence relation based on bisimularity is also defined and proved to be fully preserved by all process constructors of qCCS. The validity of examples in Section 3 is proved by using the notion of bisimilarity defined in this section. Various properties such as monoid laws, static laws, the expansion law, as well as uniqueness of solutions of process equations are also examined. We outline the main results in Section 5 and point out some problems for further study.

2. Preliminaries

For convenience of the reader, we briefly recall some basic notions from linear algebra and quantum theory which are needed in this paper. For more details, we refer to [14].

2.1 Basic linear algebra

A *Hilbert space* $\mathcal{H}$ is a complete vector space equipped with an inner product

$$\langle\cdot|\cdot\rangle : \mathcal{H}\times\mathcal{H}\rightarrow \mathbf{C}$$

such that

(1) $\langle\psi|\psi\rangle \geq 0$ for any $|\psi\rangle \in \mathcal{H}$, with equality if and only if $|\psi\rangle = 0$;

(2) $\langle\phi|\psi\rangle = \langle\psi|\phi\rangle^*$;

(3) $\langle\phi|\sum_i \lambda_i|\psi_i\rangle = \sum_i \lambda_i\langle\phi|\psi_i\rangle$,

where $\mathbf{C}$ is the set of complex numbers, and for each $\lambda \in \mathbf{C}$, λ^* stands for the complex conjugate of λ. For any vector $|\psi\rangle \in \mathcal{H}$, its length $|||\psi\rangle||$ is defined to be $\sqrt{\langle\psi|\psi\rangle}$, and it is said to be *normalized* if $|||\psi\rangle|| = 1$. Two vectors $|\psi\rangle$ and $|\phi\rangle$ are *orthogonal* if $\langle\psi|\phi\rangle = 0$. An *orthonormal basis* of a Hilbert space $\mathcal{H}$ is a basis $\{|i\rangle\}$ where each $|i\rangle$ is normalized and any pair of them are orthogonal.

Let $\mathcal{L}(\mathcal{H})$ be the set of linear operators on $\mathcal{H}$. For any $A \in \mathcal{L}(\mathcal{H})$, A is *Hermitian* if $A^\dagger = A$ where $A^\dagger$ is the adjoint operator of A such that $\langle\psi|A^\dagger|\phi\rangle = \langle\phi|A|\psi\rangle^*$ for any $|\psi\rangle, |\phi\rangle \in \mathcal{H}$. The fundamental *spectrum theorem* states that the set of all normalized eigenvectors of a Hermitian operator in $\mathcal{L}(\mathcal{H})$ contains an orthonormal basis for $\mathcal{H}$. That is, there exists a so-called spectral decomposition for each Hermitian A such that

$$A = \sum_i \lambda_i|i\rangle\langle i| = \sum_{i\in spec(A)} \lambda_i E_i$$

where the set $\{|i\rangle\}$ constitute an orthonormal basis of $\mathcal{H}$, $spec(A)$ denotes the set of eigenvalues of A, and E_i is the projector to the corresponding eigenspace of λ_i. A linear operator $A \in \mathcal{L}(\mathcal{H})$ is *unitary* if $A^\dagger A = AA^\dagger = I_\mathcal{H}$ where $I_\mathcal{H}$ is the identity operator on $\mathcal{H}$. In this paper, we will use some well-known unitary operators listed as follows: the quantum control-not operator performed on two qubits with the matrix representation

$$CN = \begin{pmatrix} 1 & 0 & 0 & 0 \\ 0 & 1 & 0 & 0 \\ 0 & 0 & 0 & 1 \\ 0 & 0 & 1 & 0 \end{pmatrix}$$

under the computational basis, and the 1-qubit Hadamard operator H and Pauli operators $\sigma^0, \sigma^1, \sigma^2, \sigma^3$ defined respectively as

$$H = \frac{1}{\sqrt{2}}\begin{pmatrix} 1 & 1 \\ 1 & -1 \end{pmatrix}, \quad \sigma^0 = I = \begin{pmatrix} 1 & 0 \\ 0 & 1 \end{pmatrix},$$

$$\sigma^1 = \begin{pmatrix} 0 & 1 \\ 1 & 0 \end{pmatrix}, \sigma^2 = \begin{pmatrix} 1 & 0 \\ 0 & -1 \end{pmatrix}, \sigma^3 = \begin{pmatrix} 0 & -i \\ i & 0 \end{pmatrix}.$$

The *trace* of $A \in \mathcal{L}(\mathcal{H})$ is defined as $\mathrm{tr}(A) = \sum_i \langle i|A|i\rangle$ for some given orthonormal basis $\{|i\rangle\}$ of $\mathcal{H}$. It is worth noting that trace function is actually independent of the orthonormal basis selected. It is also easy to check that trace function is linear and $\mathrm{tr}(AB) = \mathrm{tr}(BA)$ for any operators $A, B \in \mathcal{L}(\mathcal{H})$.

Let $\mathcal{H}_1$ and $\mathcal{H}_2$ be two Hilbert spaces. Their *tensor product* $\mathcal{H}_1 \otimes \mathcal{H}_2$ is defined as a vector space consisting of linear combinations of the vectors $|\psi_1\psi_2\rangle = |\psi_1\rangle|\psi_2\rangle = |\psi_1\rangle \otimes |\psi_2\rangle$ with $|\psi_1\rangle \in \mathcal{H}_1$ and $|\psi_2\rangle \in \mathcal{H}_2$. Here the tensor product of two vectors is defined by a new vector such that

$$\left(\sum_i \lambda_i|\psi_i\rangle\right) \otimes \left(\sum_j \mu_j|\phi_j\rangle\right) = \sum_{i,j} \lambda_i\mu_j|\psi_i\rangle \otimes |\phi_j\rangle.$$

Then $\mathcal{H}_1 \otimes \mathcal{H}_2$ is also a Hilbert space where the inner product is defined as the following: for any $|\psi_1\rangle, |\phi_1\rangle \in \mathcal{H}_1$ and $|\psi_2\rangle, |\phi_2\rangle \in \mathcal{H}_2$,

$$\langle\psi_1 \otimes \psi_2|\phi_1 \otimes \phi_2\rangle = \langle\psi_1|\phi_1\rangle_{\mathcal{H}_1}\langle\psi_2|\phi_2\rangle_{\mathcal{H}_2}$$

where $\langle\cdot|\cdot\rangle_{\mathcal{H}_i}$ is the inner product of $\mathcal{H}_i$. For any $A_1 \in \mathcal{L}(\mathcal{H}_1)$ and $A_2 \in \mathcal{L}(\mathcal{H}_2)$, $A_1 \otimes A_2$ is defined as a linear operator in $\mathcal{L}(\mathcal{H}_1 \otimes \mathcal{H}_2)$ such that for each $|\psi_1\rangle \in \mathcal{H}_1$ and $|\psi_2\rangle \in \mathcal{H}_2$,

$$(A_1 \otimes A_2)|\psi_1\psi_2\rangle = A_1|\psi_1\rangle \otimes A_2|\psi_2\rangle.$$

The *partial trace* of $A \in \mathcal{L}(\mathcal{H}_1 \otimes \mathcal{H}_2)$ with respected to $\mathcal{H}_1$ is defined as $\mathrm{tr}_{\mathcal{H}_1}(A) = \sum_i \langle i|A|i\rangle$ where $\{|i\rangle\}$ is an orthonormal basis of $\mathcal{H}_1$. Similarly, we can define the partial trace of A with respected to $\mathcal{H}_2$. Partial trace functions are also independent of the orthonormal basis selected.

A linear operator $\mathcal{E}$ on $\mathcal{L}(\mathcal{H})$ is *completely positive* if it maps positive operators in $\mathcal{L}(\mathcal{H})$ to positive operators in $\mathcal{L}(\mathcal{H})$, and for any auxiliary Hilbert space $\mathcal{H}'$, the trivially extended operator $\mathcal{I}_{\mathcal{H}'} \otimes \mathcal{E}$ also maps positive operators in $\mathcal{L}(\mathcal{H}' \otimes \mathcal{H})$ to positive operators in $\mathcal{L}(\mathcal{H}' \otimes \mathcal{H})$. Here $\mathcal{I}_{\mathcal{H}'}$ is the identity operator on $\mathcal{L}(\mathcal{H}')$. The elegant and powerful *Kraus representation theorem* [11] of completely positive operators states that a linear operator $\mathcal{E}$ is completely positive if and only if there are some set of operators $\{E_i\}$ with appropriate dimension such that

$$\mathcal{E}(A) = \sum_i E_i A E_i^\dagger$$

for any $A \in \mathcal{L}(\mathcal{H})$. The operators E_i are called Kraus operators of $\mathcal{E}$. A linear operator is said to be a *super-operator* if it is completely positive and trace-nonincreasing. Here an operator $\mathcal{E}$ is *trace-nonincreasing* if $\mathrm{tr}(\mathcal{E}(A)) \leq \mathrm{tr}(A)$ for any positive $A \in \mathcal{L}(\mathcal{H})$, and it is said to be *trace-preserving* if the equality always holds. Then a super-operator (resp. a trace-preserving super-operator) is a completely positive operator with its Kraus operators E_i satisfying $\sum_i E_i^\dagger E_i \leq I$ (resp. $\sum_i E_i^\dagger E_i = I$).

2.2 Basic quantum mechanics

According to von Neumann's formalism of quantum mechanics [17], an isolated physical system is associated with a Hilbert space which is called the *state space* of the system. A *pure state* of a quantum system is a normalized vector in its state space, and a *mixed state* is represented by a density operator on the state space. Here a density operator ρ on Hilbert space $\mathcal{H}$ is a positive linear operator such that $\mathrm{tr}(\rho) = 1$. Another equivalent representation of density operator is probabilistic ensemble of pure states. In particular, given an ensemble $\{(p_i, |\psi_i\rangle)\}$ where $p_i \geq 0$, $\sum_i p_i = 1$, and $|\psi_i\rangle$ are pure states, then $\rho = \sum_i p_i[|\psi_i\rangle]$ is a density operator. Here $[|\psi_i\rangle]$ denotes the abbreviation of $|\psi_i\rangle\langle\psi_i|$. Conversely, each density operator can be generated by an ensemble of pure states in this way.

It is mathematically convenient to allow the trace of a density operator to be less than 1, which makes it possible to represent both the actual state (by the normalized density operator) and the probability with which the state is reached (by its trace) in a single expression [15]. Then the set of (partial) density operators on $\mathcal{H}$ can be defined as

$$\mathcal{D}(\mathcal{H}) = \{\ \rho \in \mathcal{L}(\mathcal{H})\ :\ \rho \text{ is positive and } \mathrm{tr}(\rho) \leq 1\}.$$

The state space of a composite system (for example, a quantum system consisting of many qubits) is the tensor product of the state spaces of its components. For a mixed state ρ on $\mathcal{H}_1 \otimes \mathcal{H}_2$, partial traces of ρ have explicit physical meanings: the density operators $\mathrm{tr}_{\mathcal{H}_1}\rho$ and $\mathrm{tr}_{\mathcal{H}_2}\rho$ are exactly the reduced quantum states of ρ on the second and the first component system, respectively. Note that in general, the state of a composite system cannot be decomposed into tensor product of the reduced states on its component systems. A well-known example is the 2-qubit state

$$|\Psi\rangle = \frac{1}{\sqrt{2}}(|00\rangle + |11\rangle)$$

which appears repeatedly in our examples of this paper. This kind of state is called *entangled state*. To see the strangeness of entanglement, suppose a measurement $M = \lambda_0[|0\rangle] + \lambda_1[|1\rangle]$ is applied on the first qubit of $|\Psi\rangle$ (see the following for the definition of quantum measurements). Then after the measurement, the second qubit will definitely collapse into state $|0\rangle$ or $|1\rangle$ depending on whether the outcome λ_0 or λ_1 is observed. In other words, the measurement on the first qubit changes the state of the second qubit in some way. This is an outstanding feature of quantum mechanics which has no counterpart in classical world, and is the key to many quantum information processing tasks such as teleportation [4] and superdense coding [3].

The evolution of a closed quantum system is described by a unitary operator on its state space: if the states of the system at times t_1 and t_2 are ρ_1 and ρ_2, respectively, then $\rho_2 = U\rho_1U^\dagger$ for some unitary operator U which depends only on t_1 and t_2. In contrast, the general dynamics which can occur in a physical system is described by a super-operator on its state space. Note that the unitary transformation $U(\rho) = U\rho U^\dagger$ is a trace-preserving super-operator.

A quantum *measurement* is described by a collection $\{M_m\}$ of measurement operators, where the indices m refer to the measurement outcomes. It is required that the measurement operators satisfy the completeness equation $\sum_m M_m^\dagger M_m = I_{\mathcal{H}}$. If the system is in state ρ, then the probability that measurement result m occurs is given by

$$p(m) = \mathrm{tr}(M_m^\dagger M_m\rho),$$

and the state of the post-measurement system is $M_m\rho M_m^\dagger/p(m)$.

A particular case of measurement is *projective measurement* which is usually represented by a Hermitian operator. Let M be a Hermitian operator and

$$M = \sum_{m \in spec(M)} mE_m$$

its spectral decomposition. Obviously, the projectors $\{E_m : m \in spec(M)\}$ form a quantum measurement. If the state of a quantum system is ρ, then the probability that result m occurs when measuring M on the system is $p(m) = \mathrm{tr}(E_m\rho)$, and the post-measurement state of the system is $E_m\rho E_m/p(m)$. Note that for each outcome m, the map

$$\mathcal{E}_m(\rho) = E_m\rho E_m$$

is again a super-operator by Kraus Theorem; it is not trace-preserving in general.

3. Basic definitions of qCCS

In this section, we give the basic definitions of qCCS, which is a combination of those proposed in [5] and [18], involving classical data as well as quantum data, all classical process constructors (especially the recursive definition) as well as quantum primitives. The reader is referred to [5] and [18] for further examples and explanations of the language.

3.1 Syntax

For simplicity, only two types of data are considered in qCCS: real numbers Real for classical data and qubits Qbt for quantum data. Let $cVar$, ranged over by $x, y, \dots$, be the set of classical variables and $qVar$, ranged over by $q, r, \dots$, the set of quantum variables. It is assumed that $cVar$ and $qVar$ are both countably infinite. Let Exp, ranged over by e, be the set of expressions with the value domain Real. Let $cChan$ be the set of classical channel names, ranged over by $c, d, \dots$, and $qChan$ the set of quantum channel names, ranged over by $\mathsf{c}, \mathsf{d}, \dots$. Let $Chan = cChan \cup qChan$. A relabeling function f is a one to one function from $Chan$ to $Chan$ such that $f(cChan) \subseteq cChan$ and $f(qChan) \subseteq qChan$.

We often abbreviate the indexed set $\{q_1, \dots, q_n\}$ to $\widetilde{q}$ when $q_1, \dots, q_n$ are distinct quantum variables and the dimension n is understood. Sometimes we also use $\widetilde{q}$ to denote the string $q_1 \dots q_n$. We assume a set of process constant schemes, ranged over by $A, B, \dots$. Assigned to each process constant scheme A there is a non-negative integer $ar(A)$. If $\widetilde{q}$ is a tuple of distinct quantum variables with $|\widetilde{q}| = ar(A)$, then $A(\widetilde{q})$ is called a process constant.

Based on these notations, we now propose the syntax of qCCS as follows.

DEFINITION 3.1. (Quantum process) The set of quantum processes $qProc$ and the free quantum variable function $qv : qProc \to 2^{qVar}$ are defined inductively by the following formation rules:

(1) **nil** $\in qProc$, and $qv(\textbf{nil}) = \emptyset$;
(2) $A(\widetilde{q}) \in qProc$, and $qv(A(\widetilde{q})) = \widetilde{q}$;
(3) $\tau.P \in qProc$, and $qv(\tau.P) = qv(P)$;
(4) $c?x.P \in qProc$, and $qv(c?x.P) = qv(P)$;
(5) $c!e.P \in qProc$, and $qv(c!e.P) = qv(P)$;
(6) $\mathsf{c}?q.P \in qProc$, and $qv(\mathsf{c}?q.P) = qv(P) - \{q\}$;
(7) If $q \notin qv(P)$ then $\mathsf{c}!q.P \in qProc$, and $qv(\mathsf{c}!q.P) = qv(P) \cup \{q\}$;
(8) $\mathcal{E}[\widetilde{q}].P \in qProc$, and $qv(\mathcal{E}[\widetilde{q}].P) = qv(P) \cup \widetilde{q}$;
(9) $M[\widetilde{q}; x].P \in qProc$, and $qv(M[\widetilde{q}; x].P) = qv(P) \cup \widetilde{q}$;
(10) $P + Q \in qProc$, and $qv(P + Q) = qv(P) \cup qv(Q)$;
(11) If $qv(P) \cap qv(Q) = \emptyset$ then $P \| Q \in qProc$, and $qv(P \| Q) = qv(P) \cup qv(Q)$;
(12) $P[f] \in qProc$, and $qv(P[f]) = qv(P)$;
(13) $P \backslash L \in qProc$, and $qv(P \backslash L) = qv(P)$;
(14) **if** b **then** $P \in qProc$, and $qv(\textbf{if } b \textbf{ then } P) = qv(P)$,

where $P, Q \in qProc$, $c \in cChan$, $x \in cVar$, $\mathsf{c} \in qChan$, $q \in qVar$, $\widetilde{q} \subseteq qVar$, $e \in Exp$, τ is the silent action, $A(\widetilde{q})$ is a process constant, f is a relabeling function, $L \subseteq Chan$, b is a boolean-valued expression, $\mathcal{E}$ and M are respectively a trace-preserving super-operator and a Hermitian operator applying on the Hilbert space associated with the systems $\widetilde{q}$. Furthermore, for each process constant $A(\widetilde{q})$, there is a defining equation

$$A(\widetilde{q}) \stackrel{def}{=} P$$

where $P \in qProc$ with $qv(P) \subseteq \widetilde{q}$. When $\widetilde{q} = \emptyset$, we simply denote $A(\widetilde{q})$ as A.

The notion of free classical variables in quantum processes can be defined in the usual way with a unique modification that quantum measurement $M[\widetilde{q}; x]$ has binding power on x. A quantum process P is closed if it contains no free classical variables, *i.e.*, $fv(P) = \emptyset$.

3.2 Operational semantics

To present the operational semantics of qCCS, some further notations are necessary. For each quantum variable $q \in qVar$, we assume a 2-dimensional Hilbert space $\mathcal{H}_q$ to be the state space of the q-system. For any $S \subseteq qVar$, we denote

$$\mathcal{H}_S = \bigotimes_{q \in S} \mathcal{H}_q.$$

In particular, $\mathcal{H} = \mathcal{H}_{qVar}$ is the state space of the whole environment consisting of all the quantum variables. Note that $\mathcal{H}$ is a countably infinite-dimensional Hilbert space.

Suppose P is a closed quantum process. A pair of the form $\langle P, \rho \rangle$ is called a configuration, where $\rho \in \mathcal{D}(\mathcal{H})$ is a density operator on $\mathcal{H}$. The set of configurations is denoted by Con. We sometimes let $\mathcal{C}, \mathcal{D}, \dots$ range over Con to ease notations.

Let $D(Con)$ be the set of finite-support probability distributions over Con; that is,

$$D(Con) = \{\mu : Con \to [0,1] \mid \mu(\mathcal{C}) > 0 \text{ for finitely many } \mathcal{C}, \text{ and } \sum_{\mu(\mathcal{C})>0} \mu(\mathcal{C}) = 1\}.$$

For any $\mu \in D(Con)$, we denote by $supp(\mu)$ the support set of μ, *i.e.*, the set of configurations $\mathcal{C}$ such that $\mu(\mathcal{C}) > 0$. When μ is a simple distribution such that $supp(\mu) = \{\mathcal{C}\}$ for some $\mathcal{C}$, we abuse the notation slightly to denote μ by $\mathcal{C}$. Sometimes we find it convenient to denote a distribution μ by an explicit form $\mu = \boxplus_{i \in I} p_i \bullet \mathcal{C}_i$ (or $\mu = \boxplus p_i \bullet \mathcal{C}_i$ when the index set I is understood) where $\mathcal{C}_i$ are distinct configurations, $supp(\mu) = \{\mathcal{C}_i : i \in I\}$, and $\mu(\mathcal{C}_i) = p_i$ for each $i \in I$.

Given $\mu_1, \dots, \mu_n \in D(Con)$ and $p_1, \dots, p_n \in [0,1]$, $\sum_i p_i = 1$, we define the combined distribution, denoted by $\sum_{i=1}^n p_i \mu_i$, to be a new distribution μ such that $supp(\mu) = \bigcup_i supp(\mu_i)$, and for any $\mathcal{D} \in supp(\mu)$, $\mu(\mathcal{D}) = \sum_i p_i \mu_i(\mathcal{D})$.

It is worth pointing out the difference between the two notations $\boxplus_{i \in I} p_i \bullet \mathcal{C}_i$ and $\sum_{i \in I} p_i \mathcal{C}_i$: the former is the explicit form of a distribution, so it is required that $p_i > 0$ for each $i \in I$, and $\mathcal{C}_i \neq \mathcal{C}_j$ for $i \neq j$; while the latter is a combined distribution of the simple distributions $\mathcal{C}_i$ with the probability weights p_i, so p_i may be zero for some $i \in I$, and $\mathcal{C}_i$ are not necessarily distinct.

Let $\mu = \boxplus_{i \in I} p_i \bullet \langle P_i, \rho_i \rangle$. We denote by $qv(\mu)$ the free variables of μ; that is, $qv(\mu) = \bigcup_{i \in I} qv(P_i)$. We write $\text{tr}(\mu) = \sum_{i \in I} p_i \text{tr}(\rho_i)$, and $\mathcal{E}(\mu) = \boxplus_{i \in I} p_i \bullet \langle P_i, \mathcal{E}(\rho_i) \rangle$ when $\mathcal{E}$ is a super-operator.

Let

$$Act = \{\tau\} \cup \{c?v, c!v \mid c \in cChan, v \in \mathsf{Real}\} \cup \{\mathsf{c}?r, \mathsf{c}!r \mid \mathsf{c} \in qChan, r \in qVar\}.$$

For each $\alpha \in Act$, we define the bound quantum variable $bv(\alpha)$ of α as $bv(\mathsf{c}?r) = \{r\}$ and $bv(\alpha) = \emptyset$ if α is not a quantum input. The channel name used in action α is denoted by $cn(\alpha)$; that is, $cn(c?v) = cn(c!v) = \{c\}$, $cn(\mathsf{c}?r) = cn(\mathsf{c}!r) = \{\mathsf{c}\}$, and $cn(\tau) = \emptyset$.

The semantics of qCCS is given by the probabilistic labeled transition system $(Con, Act, \longrightarrow)$, where $\longrightarrow \subseteq Con \times Act \times D(Con)$ is the smallest relation satisfying the rules defined in Figs. 1 and 2 (For brevity, we write $\langle P, \rho \rangle \stackrel{\alpha}{\longrightarrow} \mu$ instead of $(\langle P, \rho \rangle, \alpha, \mu) \in \longrightarrow$. The symmetric forms for Rules **Inp-Int**, **Oth-Int**, and **Sum** are omitted).

$$\textbf{Tau}: \quad \frac{}{\langle \tau.P, \rho\rangle \xrightarrow{\tau} \langle P, \rho\rangle}$$

$$\textbf{C-Inp}: \quad \frac{}{\langle c?x.P, \rho\rangle \xrightarrow{c?v} \langle P\{v/x\}, \rho\rangle}, \quad v \in \mathsf{Real}$$

$$\textbf{C-Outp}: \quad \frac{}{\langle c!e.P, \rho\rangle \xrightarrow{c!v} \langle P, \rho\rangle}, \quad v = [\![e]\!]$$

$$\textbf{C-Com}: \quad \frac{\langle P_1, \rho\rangle \xrightarrow{c?v} \langle P_1', \rho\rangle, \quad \langle P_2, \rho\rangle \xrightarrow{c!v} \langle P_2', \rho\rangle}{\langle P_1 \| P_2, \rho\rangle \xrightarrow{\tau} \langle P_1' \| P_2', \rho\rangle}$$

$$\textbf{Q-Inp}: \quad \frac{}{\langle c?q.P, \rho\rangle \xrightarrow{c?r} \langle P\{r/q\}, \rho\rangle}, \quad r \notin qv(c?q.P)$$

$$\textbf{Q-Outp}: \quad \frac{}{\langle c!q.P, \rho\rangle \xrightarrow{c!q} \langle P, \rho\rangle}$$

$$\textbf{Q-Com}: \quad \frac{\langle P_1, \rho\rangle \xrightarrow{c?r} \langle P_1', \rho\rangle, \quad \langle P_2, \rho\rangle \xrightarrow{c!r} \langle P_2', \rho\rangle}{\langle P_1 \| P_2, \rho\rangle \xrightarrow{\tau} \langle P_1' \| P_2', \rho\rangle}$$

$$\textbf{Oper}: \quad \frac{}{\langle \mathcal{E}[\widetilde{r}].P, \rho\rangle \xrightarrow{\tau} \langle P, \mathcal{E}_{\widetilde{r}}(\rho)\rangle}$$

$$\textbf{Meas}: \quad \frac{}{\langle M[\widetilde{r}; x].P, \rho\rangle \xrightarrow{\tau} \sum_{i\in I} p_i \langle P\{\lambda_i/x\}, E^i_{\widetilde{r}}\rho E^i_{\widetilde{r}}/p_i\rangle}$$

where M has the spectrum decomposition $M = \sum_{i\in I} \lambda_i E^i$ and $p_i = \mathrm{tr}(E^i_{\widetilde{r}}\rho)/\mathrm{tr}(\rho)$

Figure 1. Inference rules for qCCS (Part 1)

The transition relation $\longrightarrow$ can be lifted to $D(Con) \times Act \times D(Con)$ by writing $\mu \xrightarrow{\alpha} \nu$ if for any $\mathcal{C} \in supp(\mu)$, $\mathcal{C} \xrightarrow{\alpha} \nu_{\mathcal{C}}$ for some $\nu_{\mathcal{C}}$, and $\nu = \sum_{\mathcal{C}\in supp(\mu)} \mu(\mathcal{C})\nu_{\mathcal{C}}$.

For any $S \subseteq qVar$ we denote by $\overline{S}$ the complement set of S in $qVar$. The following lemmas can be easily observed from the inference rules defined above.

LEMMA 3.1. *If* $\langle P, \rho\rangle \xrightarrow{\alpha} \mu$, *then* $qv(\mu) \subseteq qv(P) \cup \{bv(\alpha)\}$.

LEMMA 3.2. *If* $\langle P, \rho\rangle \xrightarrow{\alpha} \mu$, *then*

(1) $\mathrm{tr}(\rho) = \mathrm{tr}(\mu)$;

(2) there exist a set of super operators $\{\mathcal{E}_i : i \in I\}$ *acting on* $\mathcal{H}_{qv(P)}$ *such that for any* $\sigma \in \mathcal{D}(\mathcal{H})$,

$$\langle P, \sigma\rangle \xrightarrow{\alpha} \boxplus_{i\in I} q_i^\sigma \bullet \langle P_i, \mathcal{E}_i(\sigma)/q_i^\sigma\rangle$$

where $q_i^\sigma = \mathrm{tr}(\mathcal{E}_i(\sigma))/\mathrm{tr}(\sigma)$;

(3) for any super-operator $\mathcal{E}$ *acting on* $\mathcal{H}_{\overline{qv(P)}}$,

$$\langle P, \mathcal{E}(\rho)\rangle \xrightarrow{\alpha} \mathcal{E}(\mu).$$

3.3 Examples

To illustrate the expressiveness of qCCS, we give some examples.

EXAMPLE 3.1. Superdense coding [3] is a quantum protocol using which two bits of classical information can be faithfully transmitted by sending only one qubit, provided that a maximally entangled state is shared *a priori* between the sender and the receiver. The protocol goes as follows. Let $|\Psi\rangle = (|00\rangle + |11\rangle)/\sqrt{2}$ be the entangled state shared between the sender Alice and the receiver Bob. Alice applies a Pauli operator on her qubit of $|\Psi\rangle$ according to which information among the four possibilities she wishes to

$$\textbf{Inp-Int}: \quad \frac{\langle P_1, \rho\rangle \xrightarrow{c?r} \langle P_1', \rho\rangle, \ r \notin qv(P_2)}{\langle P_1 \| P_2, \rho\rangle \xrightarrow{c?r} \langle P_1' \| P_2, \rho\rangle}$$

$$\textbf{Oth-Int}: \quad \frac{\langle P_1, \rho\rangle \xrightarrow{\alpha} \boxplus_{i\in I} p_i \bullet \langle P_i', \rho_i\rangle, \ \alpha \neq c?r}{\langle P_1 \| P_2, \rho\rangle \xrightarrow{\alpha} \boxplus_{i\in I} p_i \bullet \langle P_i' \| P_2, \rho_i\rangle}$$

$$\textbf{Sum}: \quad \frac{\langle P, \rho\rangle \xrightarrow{\alpha} \mu}{\langle P + Q, \rho\rangle \xrightarrow{\alpha} \mu}$$

$$\textbf{Rel}: \quad \frac{\langle P, \rho\rangle \xrightarrow{\alpha} \boxplus p_i \bullet \langle P_i, \rho_i\rangle}{\langle P[f], \rho\rangle \xrightarrow{f(\alpha)} \boxplus p_i \bullet \langle P_i[f], \rho_i\rangle}$$

$$\textbf{Res}: \quad \frac{\langle P, \rho\rangle \xrightarrow{\alpha} \boxplus p_i \bullet \langle P_i, \rho_i\rangle, \ cn(\alpha) \notin L}{\langle P \backslash L, \rho\rangle \xrightarrow{\alpha} \boxplus p_i \bullet \langle P_i \backslash L, \rho_i\rangle}$$

$$\textbf{Cho}: \quad \frac{\langle P, \rho\rangle \xrightarrow{\alpha} \mu, \ [\![b]\!] = \mathsf{true}}{\langle \textbf{if } b \textbf{ then } P, \rho\rangle \xrightarrow{\alpha} \mu}$$

$$\textbf{Def}: \quad \frac{\langle P\{\widetilde{r}/\widetilde{q}\}, \rho\rangle \xrightarrow{\alpha} \mu, \ A(\widetilde{q}) \stackrel{def}{=} P}{\langle A(\widetilde{r}), \rho\rangle \xrightarrow{\alpha} \mu}$$

Figure 2. Inference rules for qCCS (Part 2)

transmit, and sends her qubit to Bob. With the two qubits in hand, Bob performs a perfect discrimination among the possible states (they are actually the four Bell states $\{\sigma^i \otimes I|\Psi\rangle : i = 0, 1, 2, 3\}$ where σ^i are defined in Section 2) and retrieves the information Alice has sent.

We now show how to describe the protocol of superdense coding with qCCS. Let M be a 2-qubit measurement such that $M = \sum_{i=0}^{3} i|\tilde{i}\rangle\langle\tilde{i}|$, where $\tilde{i}$ is the binary expansion of i. Let CN be the controlled-not operator and H Hadamard operator. Then the quantum processes participated in superdense coding protocol can be defined as follows:

$$\begin{aligned} Alice_s &= c?x. \sum_{0\le i\le 3} \left(\textbf{if } x = i \textbf{ then } \sigma^i[q_1].\mathsf{e}!q_1.\textbf{nil}\right), \\ Bob_s &= \mathsf{e}?q_1.CN[q_1, q_2].H[q_1].M[q_1, q_2; x].d!x.\textbf{nil}, \\ Sdc &= (Alice_s \| Bob_s)\backslash\{\mathsf{e}\}. \end{aligned}$$

For any $\rho \in \mathcal{D}(\mathcal{H}_{\overline{\{q_1, q_2\}}})$ and $v \in \{0, 1, 2, 3\}$, we have the transitions

$$\begin{aligned} & \langle Sdc, [|\Psi\rangle]_{q_1,q_2} \otimes \rho\rangle \\ \xrightarrow{c?v} \ & \langle\left(\left(\sum_{0\le i\le 3} (\textbf{if } v = i \textbf{ then } \sigma^i[q_1].\mathsf{e}!q_1.\textbf{nil})\right) \| Bob_s\right)\backslash\{\mathsf{e}\}, \\ & [|\Psi\rangle]_{q_1,q_2} \otimes \rho\rangle \\ \xrightarrow{\tau} \ & \langle(\mathsf{e}!q_1.\textbf{nil} \| Bob_s)\backslash\{\mathsf{e}\}, \sigma^v_{q_1}([|\Psi\rangle]) \otimes \rho\rangle \\ \xrightarrow{\tau} \ & \langle(\textbf{nil} \| CN[q_1, q_2].H[q_1].M[q_1, q_2; x].d!x.\textbf{nil})\backslash\{\mathsf{e}\}, \\ & \sigma^v_{q_1}([|\Psi\rangle]) \otimes \rho\rangle \\ \xrightarrow{\tau} \ & \langle(\textbf{nil} \| H[q_1].M[q_1, q_2; x].d!x.\textbf{nil})\backslash\{\mathsf{e}\}, \\ & CN_{q_1,q_2}(\sigma^v_{q_1}([|\Psi\rangle])) \otimes \rho\rangle \\ \xrightarrow{\tau} \ & \langle(\textbf{nil} \| M[q_1, q_2; x].d!x.\textbf{nil})\backslash\{\mathsf{e}\}, [|\widetilde{v}\rangle]_{q_1,q_2} \otimes \rho\rangle \qquad (1) \\ \xrightarrow{\tau} \ & \langle(\textbf{nil} \| d!v.\textbf{nil})\backslash\{\mathsf{e}\}, [|\widetilde{v}\rangle]_{q_1,q_2} \otimes \rho\rangle \\ \xrightarrow{d!v} \ & \langle(\textbf{nil} \| \textbf{nil})\backslash\{\mathsf{e}\}, [|\widetilde{v}\rangle]_{q_1,q_2} \otimes \rho\rangle. \end{aligned}$$

Here Eq.(1) is calculated as follows:

$$H_{q_1}(CN_{q_1,q_2}(\sigma^v_{q_1}([|\Psi\rangle]))) =$$

$$\begin{cases} H_{q_1}(CN_{q_1,q_2}([\frac{|00\rangle+|11\rangle}{\sqrt{2}}])) = [|00\rangle], \text{ if } v=0 \\ H_{q_1}(CN_{q_1,q_2}([\frac{|10\rangle+|01\rangle}{\sqrt{2}}])) = [|01\rangle], \text{ if } v=1 \\ H_{q_1}(CN_{q_1,q_2}([\frac{|00\rangle-|11\rangle}{\sqrt{2}}])) = [|10\rangle], \text{ if } v=2 \\ H_{q_1}(CN_{q_1,q_2}([\frac{|01\rangle-|10\rangle}{\sqrt{2}}])) = [|11\rangle], \text{ if } v=3. \end{cases}$$

EXAMPLE 3.2. Quantum teleportation [4] is one of the most important protocols in quantum information theory which can make use of a maximally entangled state shared between the sender and the receiver to teleport an unknown quantum state by sending only classical information. It serves as a key ingredient in many other communication protocols. The protocol goes as follows. Let $|\Psi\rangle_{q_1,q_2}$ be the entanglement state shared between the sender Alice and the receiver Bob, with Alice holding q_1 and Bob holding q_2. Let q be the quantum system whose state Alice want to transmit to Bob. Alice first applies a quantum control-not operations on q and q_1, with q the control qubit and q_1 the target, followed by a Hadamard operator H on q. She then measures q and q_1 according to the computational basis, and sends the measurement outcome to Bob. Upon receiving the classical bits from Alice, Bob applies a corresponding Pauli operator on his qubit q_2 to recover the original state of q.

Let M, CN, H, and σ^i, $i = 0, \ldots, 3$ be as defined in Example 3.1. Then the quantum processes participated in teleportation protocol can be defined as follows:

$$\begin{aligned} Alice_t &= \mathsf{c}?q.CN[q,q_1].H[q].M[q,q_1;x].e!x.\mathbf{nil}, \\ Bob_t &= e?x.\sum_{0\le i\le 3}(\textbf{if } x=i \textbf{ then } \sigma^i[q_2].\mathsf{d}!q_2.\mathbf{nil}), \\ Tel &= (Alice_t \| Bob_t)\backslash\{e\}, \end{aligned}$$

For any $\rho \in \mathcal{D}(\mathcal{H}_{\overline{\{q_1,q_2\}}})$, we have

$$\begin{aligned} & \langle Tel, [|\Psi\rangle]_{q_1,q_2}\otimes\rho\rangle \\ \xrightarrow{\mathsf{c}?r} & \langle (CN[r,q_1].H[r].M[r,q_1;x].c!x.\mathbf{nil}\|Bob_t)\backslash\{e\}, \\ & \quad [|\Psi\rangle]_{q_1,q_2}\otimes\rho\rangle \\ \xrightarrow{\tau} & \langle (H[r].M[r,q_1;x].c!x.\mathbf{nil}\|Bob_t)\backslash\{e\}, \\ & \quad CN_{r,q_1}([|\Psi\rangle]_{q_1,q_2}\otimes\rho)\rangle \\ \xrightarrow{\tau} & \langle (M[r,q_1;x].c!x.\mathbf{nil}\|Bob_t)\backslash\{e\}, \\ & \quad \sum_{0\le j\le 3}\frac{1}{4}[|\widetilde{j}\rangle]_{r,q_1}\otimes\sigma^j_{q_2}(\rho)\rangle \qquad (2) \\ \xrightarrow{\tau} & 1/4\bullet\langle (c!0.\mathbf{nil}\|Bob_t)\backslash\{e\},[|00\rangle]_{r,q_1}\otimes\rho\rangle \\ & \boxplus 1/4\bullet\langle (c!1.\mathbf{nil}\|Bob_t)\backslash\{e\},[|01\rangle]_{r,q_1}\otimes\sigma^1_{q_2}(\rho)\rangle \\ & \boxplus 1/4\bullet\langle (c!2.\mathbf{nil}\|Bob_t)\backslash\{e\},[|10\rangle]_{r,q_1}\otimes\sigma^2_{q_2}(\rho)\rangle \\ & \boxplus 1/4\bullet\langle (c!3.\mathbf{nil}\|Bob_t)\backslash\{e\},[|11\rangle]_{r,q_1}\otimes\sigma^3_{q_2}(\rho)\rangle, \end{aligned}$$

and for $0 \le j \le 3$,

$$\begin{aligned} & \langle (c!j.\mathbf{nil}\|Bob_t)\backslash\{e\},[|\widetilde{j}\rangle]_{r,q_1}\otimes\sigma^j_{q_2}(\rho)\rangle \\ \xrightarrow{\tau} & \langle (\mathbf{nil}\|\sum_{0\le i\le 3}(\textbf{if } j=i \textbf{ then } \sigma^i[q_2].\mathsf{d}!q_2.\mathbf{nil}))\backslash\{e\}, \\ & \quad [|\widetilde{j}\rangle]_{r,q_1}\otimes\sigma^j_{q_2}(\rho)\rangle \\ \xrightarrow{\tau} & \langle (\mathbf{nil}\|\mathsf{d}!q_2.\mathbf{nil})\backslash\{e\},[|\widetilde{j}\rangle]_{r,q_1}\otimes\rho\rangle \\ \xrightarrow{\mathsf{d}!q_2} & \langle (\mathbf{nil}\|\mathbf{nil})\backslash\{e\},[|\widetilde{j}\rangle]_{r,q_1}\otimes\rho\rangle. \end{aligned}$$

Here Eq.(2) is calculated as follows. Notice that any $\rho \in \mathcal{D}(\mathcal{H}_{\overline{\{q_1,q_2\}}})$ can be decomposed as $\rho = \sum_{0\le i\le 3}\gamma_i[|\psi_i\rangle]_r\otimes\rho_i$ where $|\psi_0\rangle = |0\rangle$, $|\psi_1\rangle = |1\rangle$, $|\psi_2\rangle = |+\rangle = (|0\rangle+|1\rangle)/\sqrt{2}$, and $|\psi_3\rangle = |-\rangle = (|0\rangle-|1\rangle)/\sqrt{2}$. Then it is easy to derive that

$$\begin{aligned} & H_r(CN_{r,q_1}([|\Psi\rangle]_{q_1,q_2}\otimes\rho)) \\ = & \frac{\gamma_0}{4}[|000\rangle+|011\rangle+|100\rangle+|111\rangle]_{r,q_1,q_2}\otimes\rho_1 \\ & +\frac{\gamma_1}{4}[|001\rangle+|010\rangle-|101\rangle-|110\rangle]_{r,q_1,q_2}\otimes\rho_2 \\ & +\frac{\gamma_2}{4}[|00+\rangle+|01+\rangle+|10-\rangle-|11-\rangle]_{r,q_1,q_2}\otimes\rho_3 \\ & +\frac{\gamma_3}{4}[|00-\rangle-|01-\rangle+|10+\rangle+|11+\rangle]_{r,q_1,q_2}\otimes\rho_4 \\ = & \frac{1}{4}[|00\rangle]_{r,q_1}\otimes\rho+\frac{1}{4}[|01\rangle]_{r,q_1}\otimes\sigma^1_{q_2}(\rho) \\ & +\frac{1}{4}[|10\rangle]_{r,q_1}\otimes\sigma^2_{q_2}(\rho)+\frac{1}{4}[|11\rangle]_{r,q_1}\otimes\sigma^3_{q_2}(\rho). \end{aligned}$$

EXAMPLE 3.3. (Encode quantum circuits with qCCS) Quantum circuits consist of two different types of gates: unitary gates and quantum measurements. We now show how to encode them using qCCS. To ease the notations, we allow quantum channels to input and output multiple qubits. We write the quantum channel c as c^n if n qubits can be communicated through c simultaneously. In other words, the quantum capacity of c^n is n qubits.

- Unitary gate. Suppose U is a unitary operator acting on n qubits. Then the unitary gate which implements U can be defined as a process constant $\mathcal{U}(U)$, $qv(\mathcal{U}(U)) = \emptyset$, with the defining equation

  $$\mathcal{U}(U) \stackrel{def}{=} \mathsf{c}^n?\widetilde{q}.U[\widetilde{q}].\mathsf{d}^n!\widetilde{q}.\mathcal{U}(U).$$

  We denote $ar(\mathcal{U}(U)) = n$.
- Measurement gate. Suppose M is a quantum measurement acting on n qubits. Then the measurement gate which implements M can be defined as

  $$\mathcal{M}(M) \stackrel{def}{=} \mathsf{c}^n?\widetilde{q}.M[\widetilde{q};x].e!x.\mathsf{d}^n!\widetilde{q}.\mathcal{M}(M).$$

  We denote $ar(\mathcal{M}(M)) = n$.

For any $\rho \in \mathcal{D}(\mathcal{H})$, we have

$$\begin{aligned} \langle \mathcal{U}(U),\rho\rangle & \xrightarrow{\mathsf{c}^n?\widetilde{r}} \langle U[\widetilde{r}].\mathsf{d}^n!\widetilde{r}.\mathcal{U}(U),\rho\rangle \\ & \xrightarrow{\tau} \langle \mathsf{d}^n!\widetilde{r}.\mathcal{U}(U),U_{\widetilde{r}}\rho U^\dagger_{\widetilde{r}}\rangle \\ & \xrightarrow{\mathsf{d}^n!\widetilde{r}} \langle \mathcal{U}(U),U_{\widetilde{r}}\rho U^\dagger_{\widetilde{r}}\rangle \end{aligned}$$

and

$$\begin{aligned} \langle \mathcal{M}(M),\rho\rangle & \xrightarrow{\mathsf{c}^n?\widetilde{r}} \langle M[\widetilde{r};x].e!x.\mathsf{d}^n!\widetilde{r}.\mathcal{M}(M),\rho\rangle \\ & \xrightarrow{\tau} \boxplus_{i\in I}p_i\bullet\langle e!\lambda_i.\mathsf{d}^n!\widetilde{r}.\mathcal{M}(M),E^i_{\widetilde{r}}\rho E^i_{\widetilde{r}}/p_i\rangle \end{aligned}$$

where $M = \sum_{i\in I} \lambda_i E^i$ and $p_i = \mathrm{tr}(E^i_{\tilde{r}}\rho)/\mathrm{tr}(\rho)$. Now for each $i \in I$,

$$\begin{aligned} & \langle e!\lambda_i.\mathsf{d}^n!\widetilde{r}.\mathcal{M}(M), E^i_{\widetilde{r}}\rho E^i_{\widetilde{r}}/p_i\rangle \\ \xrightarrow{e!\lambda_i} & \langle \mathsf{d}^n!\widetilde{r}.\mathcal{M}(M), E^i_{\widetilde{r}}\rho E^i_{\widetilde{r}}/p_i\rangle \\ \xrightarrow{\mathsf{d}^n!\widetilde{r}} & \langle \mathcal{M}(M), E^i_{\widetilde{r}}\rho E^i_{\widetilde{r}}/p_i\rangle. \end{aligned}$$

Suppose $\mathcal{G}_1$ and $\mathcal{G}_2$ are two (unitary or measurement) gates with $ar(\mathcal{G}_1) = ar(\mathcal{G}_2) = n$. The sequential composition of $\mathcal{G}_1$ and $\mathcal{G}_2$ can be defined as

$$\mathcal{G}_1 \circ \mathcal{G}_2 \stackrel{def}{=} (L_s\|\mathcal{G}_1[\mathsf{e}^n/\mathsf{c}^n, \mathsf{f}^n/\mathsf{d}^n]\|\mathcal{G}_2[\mathsf{f}^n/\mathsf{c}^n, \mathsf{g}^n/\mathsf{d}^n]\|R_s)\backslash \{c, \mathsf{e}^n, \mathsf{f}^n, \mathsf{g}^n\}$$

where $L_s \stackrel{def}{=} \mathsf{c}^n?\widetilde{q}.\mathsf{e}^n!\widetilde{q}.c?x.L_s$ and $R_s \stackrel{def}{=} \mathsf{g}^n?\widetilde{q}.\mathsf{d}^n!\widetilde{q}.c!0.R_s$.

If $ar(\mathcal{G}_1) = m$ and $ar(\mathcal{G}_2) = n$, then the parallel composition of $\mathcal{G}_1$ and $\mathcal{G}_2$ is defined as

$$\mathcal{G}_1 \otimes \mathcal{G}_2 \stackrel{def}{=} (L_p\|\mathcal{G}_1[\mathsf{e}_1^m/\mathsf{c}^m, \mathsf{f}_1^m/\mathsf{d}^m]\|\mathcal{G}_2[\mathsf{e}_2^n/\mathsf{c}^n, \mathsf{f}_2^n/\mathsf{d}^n] \|R_p)\backslash\{c, \mathsf{e}_1^m, \mathsf{f}_1^m, \mathsf{e}_2^n, \mathsf{f}_2^n\}$$

where $L_p \stackrel{def}{=} \mathsf{c}^{m+n}?\widetilde{q}.\mathsf{e}_1^m!l(\widetilde{q}).\mathsf{e}_2^n!r(\widetilde{q}).c?x.L_p$,

$$R_p \stackrel{def}{=} \mathsf{f}_1^m?\widetilde{r}_1.\mathsf{f}_2^n?\widetilde{r}_2.\mathsf{d}^{m+n}!(\widetilde{r}_1\widetilde{r}_2).c!0.R_p,$$

$l(\widetilde{q})$ denotes the prefix of $\widetilde{q}$ with length m while $r(\widetilde{q})$ the postfix of $\widetilde{q}$ with length n, and $\widetilde{r}_1\widetilde{r}_2$ is the concatenation of $\widetilde{r}_1$ and $\widetilde{r}_2$.

4. (Weak) Bisimulation between quantum processes

To present the notion of bisimulation which abstracts the internal actions caused by local quantum operations and (classical or quantum) communications, we first extend the transition relation defined in Section 3.

DEFINITION 4.1. We define the relation $\Longrightarrow \subseteq Con \times D(Con)$ as the smallest relation satisfying the following conditions:

(1) $\mathcal{C} \Longrightarrow \mathcal{C}$;

(2) if $\mathcal{C} \xrightarrow{\tau} \boxplus_{i\in I} p_i \bullet \mathcal{C}_i$ and $\mathcal{C}_i \Longrightarrow \mu_i$ for each $i \in I$, then $\mathcal{C} \Longrightarrow \sum p_i\mu_i$.

Similar to $\longrightarrow$, we can also lift $\Longrightarrow$ to $D(Con) \times D(Con)$ by writing $\mu \Longrightarrow \nu$ if for each $\mathcal{C} \in supp(\mu)$, $\mathcal{C} \Longrightarrow \nu_{\mathcal{C}}$ for some $\nu_{\mathcal{C}}$ such that $\nu = \sum_{\mathcal{C}\in supp(\mu)} \mu(\mathcal{C})\nu_{\mathcal{C}}$.

For any $\mu, \nu \in D(Con)$ and $s = \alpha_1 \ldots \alpha_n \in Act^*$, we say that μ can evolve into ν by a weak s-transition, denoted by $\mu \stackrel{s}{\Longrightarrow} \nu$, if there exist $\mu_1, \ldots, \mu_{n+1}, \nu_1, \ldots, \nu_n \in D(Con)$, such that $\mu \Longrightarrow \mu_1$, $\mu_{n+1} = \nu$, and for each $i = 1, \ldots, n$, $\mu_i \xrightarrow{\alpha_i} \nu_i$ and $\nu_i \Longrightarrow \mu_{i+1}$.

LEMMA 4.1. *Let $\mu = \boxplus_{i\in I} p_i \bullet \mathcal{C}_i$ and $s \in Act^*$. Then $\mu \stackrel{s}{\Longrightarrow} \nu$ if and only for each $i \in I$, $\mathcal{C}_i \stackrel{s}{\Longrightarrow} \nu_i$ for some ν_i such that $\sum_{i\in I} p_i\nu_i = \nu$.*

Note that $\mu \Longrightarrow\xrightarrow{\alpha} \nu$ and $\mu \stackrel{\alpha}{\Longrightarrow} \nu$ are different since in the former the last action of every execution branch from μ to ν must be α while in the latter the action α appeared in each branch is not necessarily the last one.

With these notations, we can extend Lemma 3.2 to the weak transition case.

LEMMA 4.2. *If $\langle P, \rho\rangle \stackrel{s}{\Longrightarrow} \mu$, then*

(1) $\mathrm{tr}(\rho) = \mathrm{tr}(\mu)$;

(2) there exist a set of super-operators $\{\mathcal{E}_i : i \in I\}$ acting on $\mathcal{H}_{qv(P)\cup bv(s)}$ where $bv(\alpha_1 \ldots \alpha_n) = bv(\alpha_1) \cup \cdots \cup bv(\alpha_n)$, such that for any $\sigma \in \mathcal{D}(\mathcal{H})$;

$$\langle P, \sigma\rangle \stackrel{s}{\Longrightarrow} \boxplus_{i\in I} q_i^\sigma \bullet \langle P_i, \mathcal{E}_i(\sigma)/q_i^\sigma\rangle$$

where $q_i^\sigma = \mathrm{tr}(\mathcal{E}_i(\sigma))/\mathrm{tr}(\sigma)$;

(3) for any super-operator $\mathcal{E}$ acting on $\mathcal{H}_{\overline{qv(P)\cup bv(s)}}$, we have $\langle P, \mathcal{E}(\rho)\rangle \stackrel{s}{\Longrightarrow} \mathcal{E}(\mu)$.

4.1 Bisimulation

To present the notion of bisimulation, we need a definition from [2].

DEFINITION 4.2. Let $\mathcal{R} \subseteq Con \times Con$, and $\mu, \nu \in D(Con)$. A weight function for (μ, ν) w.r.t. $\mathcal{R}$ is a function $\delta : supp(\mu) \times supp(\nu) \rightarrow [0, 1]$ which satisfies

(1) For all $\mathcal{C}, \mathcal{D} \in Con$,

$$\sum_{\mathcal{D}\in supp(\nu)} \delta(\mathcal{C}, \mathcal{D}) = \mu(\mathcal{C}), \qquad \sum_{\mathcal{C}\in supp(\mu)} \delta(\mathcal{C}, \mathcal{D}) = \nu(\mathcal{D});$$

(2) If $\delta(\mathcal{C}, \mathcal{D}) > 0$, then $(\mathcal{C}, \mathcal{D}) \in \mathcal{R}$.

We write $\mu\mathcal{R}\nu$ if there exists a weight function for (μ, ν) w.r.t. $\mathcal{R}$.

LEMMA 4.3. *Let $\mu, \nu \in D(Con)$. Then $\mu\mathcal{R}\nu$ if and only if $\mu = \sum_{i\in I} p_i\mathcal{C}_i$ and $\nu = \sum_{i\in I} p_i\mathcal{D}_i$ such that $\mathcal{C}_i\mathcal{R}\mathcal{D}_i$ for each $i \in I$. In particular, if $\mathcal{C}\mathcal{R}\mu$ then $\mathcal{C}\mathcal{R}\mathcal{D}$ for each $\mathcal{D} \in supp(\mu)$.*

Note that when we write $\mu = \sum_{i\in I} p_i\mathcal{C}_i$, then $\mathcal{C}_i$ denotes a simple distribution. As a consequence, the $\mathcal{C}_i$s are not necessarily distinct.

DEFINITION 4.3. A relation $\mathcal{R} \subseteq Con \times Con$ is called a bisimulation if for any $\langle P, \rho\rangle, \langle Q, \sigma\rangle \in Con$, $\langle P, \rho\rangle\mathcal{R}\langle Q, \sigma\rangle$ implies that $qv(P) = qv(Q)$, $\mathrm{tr}_{qv(P)}(\rho) = \mathrm{tr}_{qv(Q)}(\sigma)$, and

(1) whenever $\langle P, \rho\rangle \xrightarrow{c?q} \mu$, then $\langle Q, \sigma\rangle \Longrightarrow\xrightarrow{c?q} \nu$ for some ν such that for any super-operator $\mathcal{E}$ acting on $\mathcal{H}_{\overline{qv(\mu)-\{q\}}}$, $\mathcal{E}(\mu)\mathcal{R}\mathcal{E}(\nu)$;

(2) whenever $\langle P, \rho\rangle \xrightarrow{\alpha} \mu$ where α is not a quantum input, then there exists ν such that $\langle Q, \sigma\rangle \stackrel{\widehat{\alpha}}{\Longrightarrow} \nu$ and $\mu\mathcal{R}\nu$;

(3) whenever $\langle Q, \sigma\rangle \xrightarrow{c?q} \nu$, then $\langle P, \rho\rangle \Longrightarrow\xrightarrow{c?q} \mu$ for some μ such that for any super-operator $\mathcal{E}$ acting on $\mathcal{H}_{\overline{qv(\nu)-\{q\}}}$, $\mathcal{E}(\mu)\mathcal{R}\mathcal{E}(\nu)$;

(4) whenever $\langle Q, \sigma\rangle \xrightarrow{\alpha} \nu$ where α is not a quantum input, then there exists μ such that $\langle P, \rho\rangle \stackrel{\widehat{\alpha}}{\Longrightarrow} \mu$ and $\mu\mathcal{R}\nu$.

Here for any $s \in Act^*$, $\widehat{s}$ is the string obtained from s by deleting all the occurrences of τ.

DEFINITION 4.4. (1) Two quantum configurations $\langle P, \rho\rangle$ and $\langle Q, \sigma\rangle$ are bisimilar, denoted by $\langle P, \rho\rangle \approx \langle Q, \sigma\rangle$, if there exists a bisimulation $\mathcal{R}$ such that $\langle P, \rho\rangle\mathcal{R}\langle Q, \sigma\rangle$;

(2) Two quantum processes P and Q are bisimilar, denoted by $P \approx Q$, if for any quantum state $\rho \in \mathcal{D}(\mathcal{H})$ and any indexed set $\widetilde{v}$ of classical values, $\langle P\{\widetilde{v}/\widetilde{x}\}, \rho\rangle \approx \langle Q\{\widetilde{v}/\widetilde{x}\}, \rho\rangle$. Here $\widetilde{x}$ is the set of free classical variables contained in P and Q.

Some design decisions made in Definition 4.3 deserve justification and explanation:

- Recall that in the definition of bisimulations proposed in [5], a clause

$$\text{If } \langle P, \rho\rangle \not\longrightarrow \text{ and } \langle Q, \sigma\rangle \not\longrightarrow, \text{ then } \rho = \sigma \qquad (3)$$

  is presented to guarantee that the quantum operations applied by P and Q, which give rise only to invisible actions, are the same. That definition, however, does not fit well with recursive definitions since recursively defined processes will generally never reach a terminating process.

In Definition 4.3, we solve this problem by requiring instead that

$$\mathrm{tr}_{qv(P)}(\rho) = \mathrm{tr}_{qv(Q)}(\sigma). \quad (4)$$

Obviously, when $\langle P, \rho\rangle \not\longrightarrow$ and $\langle Q, \sigma\rangle \not\longrightarrow$, and P and Q do not hold any quantum variables, Eqs. (3) and (4) are equivalent. However, Eq.(4) can deal with processes which have infinite behaviors. For example, let

$$A \stackrel{def}{=} \mathsf{c}?q.Set_0[q].\mathsf{c}!q.A$$

and

$$B \stackrel{def}{=} \mathsf{c}?q.M_{0,1}[q;x].\sum_{i=0}^{1}(\textbf{if } x = \lambda_i \textbf{ then } \sigma^i[q].\mathsf{c}!q.B),$$

where Set_0 is the super-operator which sets the target qubit to $|0\rangle$, and $M_{0,1}$ is the measurement according to the computational basis; that is, $M_{0,1} = \lambda_0|0\rangle\langle 0| + \lambda_1|1\rangle\langle 1|$. Intuitively, B can be regarded as an implementation of A specifying how to set the input qubit to $|0\rangle$. We now show $A \approx B$ indeed holds under our definition of bisimulation. Let

$$\begin{aligned} Con_{0,\rho} &= \{\langle A, \rho\rangle, \langle B, \rho\rangle\} \\ Con_{1,q,\rho} &= \{\langle A_{1q}, \rho\rangle, \langle A_{2q}, \rho_0\rangle, \langle B_{1q}, \rho\rangle, \\ &\qquad \langle B_{2qj}, \rho_j\rangle, \langle B_{3q}, \rho_0\rangle : j = 0, 1\} \end{aligned}$$

where $A_{1q} = Set_0[q].\mathsf{c}!q.A$, $A_{2q} = \mathsf{c}!q.A$,

$$B_{1q} = M_{0,1}[q;x].\sum_{i=0}^{1}(\textbf{if } x = \lambda_i \textbf{ then } \sigma^i[q].\mathsf{c}!q.B),$$

$$B_{2qj} = \sum_{i=0}^{1}(\textbf{if } \lambda_j = \lambda_i \textbf{ then } \sigma^i[q].\mathsf{c}!q.B),$$

$B_{3q} = \mathsf{c}!q.B$, and $\rho_j = [|j\rangle]_q \otimes \mathrm{tr}_q\rho$. Let $\mathcal{R} \subseteq Con \times Con$ such that $\langle P, \sigma\rangle\mathcal{R}\langle Q, \eta\rangle$ if and only if there exist $q \in qVar$ and $\rho \in \mathcal{D}(\mathcal{H})$ such that $\langle P, \sigma\rangle$ and $\langle Q, \eta\rangle$ are simultaneously included in $Con_{0,\rho}$ or $Con_{1,q,\rho}$. Then it is not difficult to prove that $\mathcal{R}$ is a bisimulation. Thus $A \approx B$.

- Furthermore, by replacing Eq.(3) with Eq.(4), the derived bisimilarity will be preserved by restriction. Take the example in [5]. Let U_1, U_2, V_1, V_2 be unitary operators such that $U_2U_1 = V_2V_1$ but $U_1 \neq V_1$. Let

$$P = U_1[q].\mathsf{c}!0.U_2[q].\textbf{nil}, Q = V_1[q].\mathsf{c}!0.V_2[q].\textbf{nil}.$$

Then P and Q are bisimilar but $P\backslash\{c\}$ and $Q\backslash\{c\}$ are not if Eq.(3) is required in the definition. However, in our definition presented here, $P\backslash\{c\}$ and $Q\backslash\{c\}$ are also bisimilar since in Eq.(4) we only need to consider the reduced states on the systems $\overline{qv(P)} = \overline{qv(Q)}$. The "unfinished" quantum operations, which are blocked by the restriction, are not taken into account when comparing the accompanying quantum states.

- Another question one may ask is that why we require $qv(P) = qv(Q)$ in the definition, which excludes the pair

$$P = I[q].\textbf{nil} \quad \text{and} \quad Q = \textbf{nil}$$

to be bisimilar. The reason is, although P and Q have the same effect (they both do nothing at all) on the environment, they are indeed different under parallel composition. For example, if $q \in qv(R)$, then the process $Q\|R$ is valid while $P\|R$ is not.

- In Clause (1), we require $\mathcal{E}(\mu)\mathcal{R}\mathcal{E}(\nu)$ for any super-operator $\mathcal{E}$ acting on $\mathcal{H}_{\overline{qv(\mu)-\{q\}}}$. The reason for this rather strange requirement is as follows. To check whether two configurations are bisimilar, we have to feed them with all possible inputs. In classical process algebra, this is realized by requiring that the input value is arbitrarily chosen. In quantum process algebra, however, since the state of all environmental systems is fixed for a given configuration, only requiring the arbitrariness of the input system is not sufficient. Note that the state-preparation operation and the swap operation are both special super-operators. Our definition actually includes the possibility of inputing an arbitrary system which lies in an arbitrary state.

Furthermore, this requirement is also essential in proving the congruence property of the derived bisimilarity (See Theorem 4.3).

EXAMPLE 4.1. (Superdense coding revisited) This example is devoted to proving rigorously that the protocol presented in Example 3.1 indeed sends two bits of classical information from Alice to Bob by transmitting a qubit, with the help of a maximally entangled state. Let

$$Sdc_{spec} = c?x.Set_x[q_1, q_2].d!x.\textbf{nil}$$

be the specification of superdense coding protocol, where

$$Set_x[q_1, q_2].d!x.\textbf{nil} = \sum_{i=0}^{3}(\textbf{if } x = i \textbf{ then } Set_i[q_1, q_2].d!x.\textbf{nil}),$$

and Set_i, $i = 0, \ldots, 3$, is the 2-qubit super-operator which sets the target qubits to $|\widetilde{i}\rangle$; that is, for any $\rho \in \mathcal{D}(\mathcal{H})$,

$$Set_{i,q,q'}(\rho) = [|\widetilde{i}\rangle]_{q,q'} \otimes \mathrm{tr}_{q,q'}(\rho).$$

We have $Set_x[q_1, q_2]$ in the specification simply for technical reasons: to make $qv(Sdc_{spec}) = qv(Sdc)$ and to set q_1, q_2 to the required final states. For any $\rho \in \mathcal{D}(\mathcal{H}_{\overline{\{q_1, q_2\}}})$, and $v \in \{0, 1, 2, 3\}$,

$$\begin{aligned} &\langle Sdc_{spec}, [|\Psi\rangle]_{q_1,q_2} \otimes \rho\rangle \\ \xrightarrow{c?v} \; &\langle Set_v[q_1, q_2].d!v.\textbf{nil}, [|\Psi\rangle]_{q_1,q_2} \otimes \rho\rangle \\ \xrightarrow{\tau} \; &\langle d!v.\textbf{nil}, [|\widetilde{v}\rangle]_{q_1,q_2} \otimes \rho\rangle \\ \xrightarrow{d!v} \; &\langle \textbf{nil}, [|\widetilde{v}\rangle]_{q_1,q_2} \otimes \rho\rangle. \end{aligned}$$

We can easily prove

$$\langle Sdc, [|\Psi\rangle]_{q_1,q_2} \otimes \rho\rangle \approx \langle Sdc_{spec}, [|\Psi\rangle]_{q_1,q_2} \otimes \rho\rangle$$

by checking that

$$\begin{aligned} \mathcal{R} = \; &\{(\langle Sdc, \rho_\Psi\rangle, \langle Sdc_{spec}, \rho_\Psi\rangle)\} \\ &\cup\{(\langle P, \eta\rangle, \langle Set_v[q_1, q_2].d!v.\textbf{nil}, \rho_\Psi\rangle) : v = 0, \ldots, 3, \\ &\quad \langle Sdc, \rho_\Psi\rangle \stackrel{c?v}{\Longrightarrow} \langle P, \eta\rangle, \text{ and } qv(P) \neq \emptyset\} \\ &\cup\{(\langle(\textbf{nil}\|d!v.\textbf{nil})\backslash\{\mathsf{e}\}, \rho_{\widetilde{v}}\rangle, \langle d!v.\textbf{nil}, \rho_{\widetilde{v}}\rangle) : v = 0, \ldots, 3\} \\ &\cup\{(\langle(\textbf{nil}\|\textbf{nil})\backslash\{\mathsf{e}\}, \rho_{\widetilde{v}}\rangle, \langle \textbf{nil}, \rho_{\widetilde{v}}\rangle) : v = 0, \ldots, 3\} \end{aligned}$$

is a bisimulation, where $\rho_\psi = [|\psi\rangle]_{q_1,q_2} \otimes \rho$.

Note that $Sdc \approx Sdc_{spec}$ does not hold in general since superdense coding protocol needs the assistance of a maximally entangled state to realize the intended task.

EXAMPLE 4.2. (Teleportation revisited) This example is devoted to proving rigorously that the protocol presented in Example 3.2 indeed teleports any unknown quantum state from Alice to Bob, again with the help of a maximally entangled state. To employ our notion of bisimulation, we need to modify the original definition of Alice's protocol in Example 3.2 as follows:

$$Alice'_t = \mathsf{c}?q.CN[q, q_1].H[q].M[q, q_1; x].Set_\Psi[q, q_1].\mathsf{e}!x.\textbf{nil}$$

and $Tel' = (Alice'_t \| Bob_t)\backslash c$ where Set_Ψ is similar to Set_x in the previous example. Let

$$Tel_{spec} = \mathsf{c}?q.SWAP_{1,3}[q, q_1, q_2].\mathsf{d}!q_2.\mathbf{nil}$$

be the specification of teleportation protocol, where $SWAP_{1,3}$ is a 3-qubit unitary operator which exchanges the states of the first and the third qubits, keeping the second qubit untouched. Again, we involve qubit q_1 here just for technique reason: to make $qv(Tel_{spec}) = qv(Tel')$. Then for any $\rho \in \mathcal{D}(\mathcal{H}_{\overline{\{q_1,q_2\}}})$ and $r \neq q_1, q_2$,

$$\begin{aligned}
&\langle Tel_{spec}, [|\Psi\rangle]_{q_1,q_2} \otimes \rho\rangle \\
\xrightarrow{\mathsf{c}?r}\ &\langle SWAP_{1,3}[r, q_1, q_2].\mathsf{d}!q_2.\mathbf{nil}, [|\Psi\rangle]_{q_1,q_2} \otimes \rho\rangle \\
\xrightarrow{\tau}\ &\langle \mathsf{d}!q_2.\mathbf{nil}, [|\Psi\rangle]_{q_1,r} \otimes \rho\rangle \\
\xrightarrow{\mathsf{d}!q_2}\ &\langle \mathbf{nil}, [|\Psi\rangle]_{q_1,r} \otimes \rho\rangle.
\end{aligned}$$

We can now prove

$$\langle Tel', [|\Psi\rangle]_{q_1,q_2} \otimes \rho\rangle \approx \langle Tel_{spec}, [|\Psi\rangle]_{q_1,q_2} \otimes \rho\rangle$$

by checking that

$$\begin{aligned}
\mathcal{R} = \ &\{(\langle Tel', \rho_\Psi^{q_1,q_2}\rangle, \langle Tel_{spec}, \rho_\Psi^{q_1,q_2}\rangle)\} \\
&\cup\{(\langle P, \eta\rangle, \langle SWAP_{1,3}[r, q_1, q_2].\mathsf{d}!q_2.\mathbf{nil}, \sigma_\Psi^{q_1,q_2}) : \\
&\quad \langle Tel', \sigma_\Psi^{q_1,q_2}\rangle \stackrel{\mathsf{c}?r}{\Longrightarrow} \langle P, \eta\rangle, \sigma \in \mathcal{D}(\mathcal{H}_{\overline{\{q_1,q_2\}}}), \\
&\quad qv(P) = \{r, q_1, q_2\}, \text{ and } r \neq q_1, q_2\} \\
&\cup\{(\langle P, \eta\rangle, \langle \mathsf{d}!q_2.\mathbf{nil}, \sigma_\Psi^{q_1,r}) : \\
&\quad \langle Tel', \sigma_\Psi^{q_1,q_2}\rangle \stackrel{\mathsf{c}?r}{\Longrightarrow} \mu \text{ with } \langle P, \eta\rangle \in supp(\mu), \\
&\quad \sigma \in \mathcal{D}(\mathcal{H}_{\overline{\{q_1,q_2\}}}), qv(P) = \{q_2\}, \text{ and } r \neq q_1, q_2\} \\
&\cup\{(\langle(\mathbf{nil}\|\mathbf{nil})\backslash\{c\}, \sigma_\Psi^{q_1,r}\rangle, \langle \mathbf{nil}, \sigma_\Psi^{q_1,r}\rangle) : \sigma \in \mathcal{D}(\mathcal{H}_{\overline{\{q_1,r\}}})\}
\end{aligned}$$

is a bisimulation, where $\sigma_\psi^{q,q'} = [|\psi\rangle]_{q,q'} \otimes \sigma$.

Again, $Tel' \approx Tel_{spec}$ does not hold in general since Teleportation protocol is valid only when a maximally entangled state is provided and consumed.

The following example shows the bimilarity between quantum processes.

EXAMPLE 4.3. (Encode quantum circuits by qCCS, revisited) Using the notion presented in Example 3.3, we can prove the following properties considering the sequential composition and parallel composition of quantum gates:

(1) $\mathcal{U}(U) \circ \mathcal{U}(V) \approx \mathcal{U}(VU)$;
(2) $\mathcal{U}(U) \circ \mathcal{G}(M) \approx \mathcal{G}(U^\dagger MU) \circ \mathcal{U}(U)$;
(3) $\mathcal{U}(U) \otimes \mathcal{U}(V) \approx \mathcal{U}(V \otimes V)$.

The proof is straightforward, and we only take (1) as an example. Let

$$\begin{aligned}
\mathcal{R} = \ &\{(\langle \mathcal{U}(U) \circ \mathcal{U}(V), \rho\rangle, \langle \mathcal{U}(VU), \rho\rangle) : \rho \in \mathcal{D}(\mathcal{H})\} \\
\cup\ &\{(\langle P, \sigma\rangle, \langle Q, \eta\rangle) : \langle \mathcal{U}(U) \circ \mathcal{U}(V), \rho\rangle \stackrel{c''?\widetilde{r}}{\Longrightarrow} \langle P, \sigma\rangle \text{ and} \\
&\langle \mathcal{U}(VU), \rho\rangle \stackrel{c''?\widetilde{r}}{\Longrightarrow} \langle Q, \eta\rangle \text{ where } \widetilde{r} \subseteq qVar \text{ and } \rho \in \mathcal{D}(\mathcal{H})\} \\
\cup\ &\{(\langle P, \sigma\rangle, \langle Q, \eta\rangle) : \langle \mathcal{U}(U) \circ \mathcal{U}(V), \rho\rangle \stackrel{c''?\widetilde{r}, d''!\widetilde{r}}{\Longrightarrow} \langle P, \sigma\rangle \text{ and} \\
&\langle \mathcal{U}(VU), \rho\rangle \stackrel{c''?\widetilde{r}, d''!\widetilde{r}}{\Longrightarrow} \langle Q, \eta\rangle \text{ where } \widetilde{r} \subseteq qVar \text{ and } \rho \in \mathcal{D}(\mathcal{H})\}.
\end{aligned}$$

It is easy to check that $\mathcal{R}$ is a bisimulation. So we have $\langle \mathcal{U}(U) \circ \mathcal{U}(V), \rho\rangle \approx \langle \mathcal{U}(VU), \rho\rangle$ for all $\rho \in \mathcal{D}(\mathcal{H})$ and then $\mathcal{U}(U) \circ \mathcal{U}(V) \approx \mathcal{U}(VU)$.

To conclude this section, we prove some properties of bisimilarity which are useful in the rest of this paper.

LEMMA 4.4. *If $\langle P, \rho\rangle \approx \langle Q, \sigma\rangle$, then for any super-operator $\mathcal{E}$ acting on $\mathcal{H}_{\overline{qv(P)}}$, we have $\mathrm{tr}(\mathcal{E}(\rho)) = \mathrm{tr}(\mathcal{E}(\sigma))$. In particular, $\mathrm{tr}(\rho) = \mathrm{tr}(\sigma)$.*

THEOREM 4.1. *$\approx$ is a bisimulation on Con, and it is an equivalence relation.*

THEOREM 4.2. *For any configurations $\langle P, \rho\rangle$ and $\langle Q, \sigma\rangle$, $\langle P, \rho\rangle \approx \langle Q, \sigma\rangle$ if and only if $qv(P) = qv(Q)$, $\mathrm{tr}_{qv(P)}(\rho) = \mathrm{tr}_{qv(Q)}(\sigma)$, and*

(1) whenever $\langle P, \rho\rangle \xrightarrow{\mathsf{c}?q} \mu$, then $\langle Q, \sigma\rangle \stackrel{\mathsf{c}?q}{\Longrightarrow} \nu$ for some ν such that for any super-operator $\mathcal{E}$ acting on $\mathcal{H}_{\overline{qv(\mu)-\{q\}}}$, $\mathcal{E}(\mu) \approx \mathcal{E}(\nu)$;
(2) whenever $\langle P, \rho\rangle \xrightarrow{\alpha} \mu$ where α is not a quantum input, then there exists ν such that $\langle Q, \sigma\rangle \stackrel{\widehat{\alpha}}{\Longrightarrow} \nu$ and $\mu \approx \nu$;

and the symmetric conditions of (1) and (2).

4.2 Bisimilarity congruence

We now turn to prove the congruence properties of bisimulation. First, we show that the bisimulation for configurations is preserved by all *static* constructors.

THEOREM 4.3. *If $\langle P, \rho\rangle \approx \langle Q, \sigma\rangle$ then*

(1) $\langle P\|R, \rho\rangle \approx \langle Q\|R, \sigma\rangle$;
(2) $\langle P[f], \rho\rangle \approx \langle Q[f], \sigma\rangle$;
(3) $\langle P\backslash L, \rho\rangle \approx \langle Q\backslash L, \sigma\rangle$;
*(4) $\langle$**if** b **then** $P, \rho\rangle \approx \langle$**if** b **then** $Q, \sigma\rangle$.*

Proof. Let us prove (1); other cases are simpler. Let

$$\begin{aligned}
\mathcal{R} = \ &\{(\langle P\|R, \mathcal{E}(\rho)\rangle, \langle Q\|R, \mathcal{E}(\sigma)\rangle) : \langle P, \rho\rangle \approx \langle Q, \sigma\rangle \text{ and} \\
&\mathcal{E} \text{ is a super-operator acting on } \mathcal{H}_{\overline{qv(P)}}\}.
\end{aligned}$$

It suffices to show that $\mathcal{R}$ is a bisimulation. Suppose $(\mathcal{C}, \mathcal{D}) \in \mathcal{R}$ where $\mathcal{C} = \langle P\|R, \mathcal{E}(\rho)\rangle$ and $\mathcal{D} = \langle Q\|R, \mathcal{E}(\sigma)\rangle$ for some $\langle P, \rho\rangle \approx \langle Q, \sigma\rangle$, and $\mathcal{E}$ is a super-operator acting on $\mathcal{H}_{\overline{qv(P)}}$. Then $qv(P) = qv(Q)$ and $\mathrm{tr}_{qv(P)}(\rho) = \mathrm{tr}_{qv(Q)}(\sigma)$ by Theorem 4.2. Thus $qv(P\|R) = qv(Q\|R)$ and

$$\mathrm{tr}_{qv(P\|R)}(\mathcal{E}(\rho)) = \mathrm{tr}_{qv(Q\|R)}(\mathcal{E}(\sigma)).$$

Let $\langle P\|R, \mathcal{E}(\rho)\rangle \xrightarrow{\alpha} \mu$ for some α and μ. There are three cases to consider.

I: The transition is caused by P solely. We need to further consider two subcases:

i: $\alpha = \mathsf{c}?q$ is a quantum input. Then there exists a transition $\langle P, \rho\rangle \xrightarrow{\mathsf{c}?q} \langle P', \rho\rangle$ and $\mu = \langle P'\|R, \mathcal{E}(\rho)\rangle$. By the assumption that $\langle P, \rho\rangle \approx \langle Q, \sigma\rangle$, we have

$$\langle Q, \sigma\rangle \Longrightarrow \boxplus_{i\in I} p_i \bullet \langle Q'_i, \sigma_i\rangle \xrightarrow{\mathsf{c}?q} \boxplus_{i\in I} p_i \bullet \langle Q_i, \sigma_i\rangle$$

such that for any super-operator $\mathcal{F}$ acting on $\mathcal{H}_{\overline{qv(P')-\{q\}}}$,

$$\langle P', \mathcal{F}(\rho)\rangle \approx \langle Q_i, \mathcal{F}(\sigma_i)\rangle \qquad (5)$$

holds for any $i \in I$. Then $\langle Q, \mathcal{E}(\sigma)\rangle \Longrightarrow \boxplus_{i\in I} p_i \bullet \langle Q'_i, \mathcal{E}(\sigma_i)\rangle$ by Lemma 4.2(3), from which we further derive

$$\langle Q, \mathcal{E}(\sigma)\rangle \stackrel{\mathsf{c}?q}{\Longrightarrow} \boxplus_{i\in I} p_i \bullet \langle Q_i, \mathcal{E}(\sigma_i)\rangle$$

and

$$\langle Q\|R, \mathcal{E}(\sigma)\rangle \stackrel{\mathsf{c}?q}{\Longrightarrow} \nu = \boxplus_{i\in I} p_i \bullet \langle Q_i\|R, \mathcal{E}(\sigma_i)\rangle.$$

For any super-operator $\mathcal{F}'$ acting on $\mathcal{H}_{\overline{qv(P'\|R)-\{q\}}}$, we obtain from Lemma 3.1 that the composite map $\mathcal{F}' \circ \mathcal{E}$ is a super-operator acting on $\mathcal{H}_{\overline{qv(P')-\{q\}}}$. Now using Eq.(5) we have

$$\langle P', \mathcal{F}'(\mathcal{E}(\rho))\rangle \approx \langle Q_i, \mathcal{F}'(\mathcal{E}(\sigma_i))\rangle,$$

and thus $\langle P'\|R, \mathcal{F}'(\mathcal{E}(\rho))\rangle\mathcal{R}\langle Q_i\|R, \mathcal{F}'(\mathcal{E}(\sigma_i))\rangle$. That is, $\mathcal{F}'(\mu)\mathcal{R}\mathcal{F}'(\nu)$ as required.

ii: α is not a quantum input. Then there exists a transition $\langle P, \rho\rangle \xrightarrow{\alpha} \mu_1 = \boxplus_{i\in I} p_i \bullet \langle P_i, \rho_i\rangle$ and $\mu = \boxplus_{i\in I} p_i \bullet \langle P_i\|R, \mathcal{E}(\rho_i)\rangle$ by Lemma 3.2(3). From the assumption that $\langle P, \rho\rangle \approx \langle Q, \sigma\rangle$, we have

$$\langle Q, \sigma\rangle \stackrel{\widehat{\alpha}}{\Longrightarrow} \nu_1 = \boxplus_{j\in J} q_j \bullet \langle Q_j, \sigma_j\rangle$$

and $\mu_1 \approx \nu_1$ by Theorem 4.2. Noting that $\mathcal{E}$ is a super-operator on $\mathcal{H}_{\overline{qv(Q)}}$, we have $\langle Q, \mathcal{E}(\sigma)\rangle \stackrel{\widehat{\alpha}}{\Longrightarrow} \boxplus_{j\in J} q_j \bullet \langle Q_j, \mathcal{E}(\sigma_j)\rangle$ by Lemma 4.2(3). So it holds that

$$\langle Q\|R, \mathcal{E}(\sigma)\rangle \stackrel{\widehat{\alpha}}{\Longrightarrow} \nu = \boxplus_{j\in J} q_j \bullet \langle Q_j\|R, \mathcal{E}(\sigma_j)\rangle.$$

Now for each $i \in I$ and $j \in J$, $\langle P_i, \rho_i\rangle \approx \langle Q_j, \sigma_j\rangle$ implies $\langle P_i\|R, \mathcal{E}(\rho_i)\rangle\mathcal{R}\langle Q_j\|R, \mathcal{E}(\sigma_j)\rangle$ since from Lemma 3.1, $\mathcal{E}$ is also a super-operator acting on $\mathcal{H}_{\overline{qv(P_i)}}$. Thus we have $\mu\mathcal{R}\nu$ by Lemma 4.3, by noting that $\mu_1 \approx \nu_1$.

II: The transition is caused by R solely. We also need to further consider two subcases:

i: $\alpha = c?q$ is a quantum input where $q \notin qv(P)$. Then we have $\langle R, \mathcal{E}(\rho)\rangle \xrightarrow{c?q} \langle R', \mathcal{E}(\rho)\rangle$ for some R', and $\mu = \langle P\|R', \mathcal{E}(\rho)\rangle$. Thus $\langle R, \mathcal{E}(\sigma)\rangle \xrightarrow{c?q} \langle R', \mathcal{E}(\sigma)\rangle$. By inference rule **Inp-Int**, we have $\langle Q\|R, \mathcal{E}(\sigma)\rangle \xrightarrow{c?q} \langle Q\|R', \mathcal{E}(\sigma)\rangle$ since $q \notin qv(Q)$. Now for any super-operator $\mathcal{F}$ acting on $\mathcal{H}_{\overline{qv(P\|R')-\{q\}}}$, the composite map $\mathcal{F}\circ\mathcal{E}$ is a super-operator acting on $\mathcal{H}_{\overline{qv(P)}}$ from the fact that $qv(P\|R') - \{q\} \supseteq qv(P) - \{q\} = qv(P)$. Thus

$$\langle P\|R', \mathcal{F}(\mathcal{E}(\rho))\rangle\mathcal{R}\langle Q\|R', \mathcal{F}(\mathcal{E}(\sigma))\rangle$$

from the definition of $\mathcal{R}$.

ii: α is not a quantum input. Then by Lemma 3.2(2), there exists a transition $\langle R, \mathcal{E}(\rho)\rangle \xrightarrow{\alpha} \boxplus p_i \bullet \langle R_i, \mathcal{E}_i(\mathcal{E}(\rho))/p_i\rangle$ where $\mathcal{E}_i$ is a super-operator on $\mathcal{H}_{qv(R)}$,

$$p_i = \mathrm{tr}(\mathcal{E}_i(\mathcal{E}(\rho)))/\mathrm{tr}(\mathcal{E}(\rho)),$$

and $\mu = \boxplus p_i \bullet \langle P\|R_i, \mathcal{E}_i(\mathcal{E}(\rho))/p_i\rangle$. Then we derive

$$\langle R, \mathcal{E}(\sigma)\rangle \xrightarrow{\alpha} \boxplus q_i \bullet \langle R_i, \mathcal{E}_i(\mathcal{E}(\sigma))/q_i\rangle$$

where $q_i = \mathrm{tr}(\mathcal{E}_i(\mathcal{E}(\sigma)))/\mathrm{tr}(\mathcal{E}(\sigma))$, again by Lemma 3.2(2). Thus

$$\langle Q\|R, \mathcal{E}(\sigma)\rangle \xrightarrow{\alpha} \nu = \boxplus q_i \bullet \langle Q\|R_i, \mathcal{E}_i(\mathcal{E}(\sigma))/q_i\rangle.$$

Notice that for any i, we have $p_i = q_i$ by Lemma 4.4, and

$$(\langle P\|R_i, \mathcal{E}_i(\mathcal{E}(\rho))\rangle, \langle Q\|R_i, \mathcal{E}_i(\mathcal{E}(\sigma))\rangle) \in \mathcal{R}$$

since the composite map $\mathcal{E}^i \circ \mathcal{E}$ is a super-operator acting on $\mathcal{H}_{\overline{qv(P)}}$ ($qv(R) \cap qv(P) = \emptyset$ by the validity of $P\|R$). Then it follows that $\mu\mathcal{R}\nu$ from Lemma 4.3.

III: The transition is caused by a communication between P and R. Without loss of generality, we assume that

$$\langle P, \rho\rangle \xrightarrow{c?q} \langle P', \rho\rangle, \quad \langle R, \rho\rangle \xrightarrow{c!q} \langle R', \rho\rangle,$$

and $\mu = \langle P'\|R', \mathcal{E}(\rho)\rangle$. Other cases are simpler. Then $q \notin qv(P)$ by the validity of $P\|R$, and $\langle R, \eta\rangle \xrightarrow{c!q} \langle R', \eta\rangle$ for any $\eta \in \mathcal{D}(\mathcal{H})$. From the assumption that $\langle P, \rho\rangle \approx \langle Q, \sigma\rangle$, we have

$$\langle Q, \sigma\rangle \Longrightarrow \boxplus_{i\in I} p_i \bullet \langle Q_i', \sigma_i\rangle \xrightarrow{c?q} \boxplus_{i\in I} p_i \bullet \langle Q_i, \sigma_i\rangle$$

such that for any $i \in I$ and any super-operator $\mathcal{F}$ acting on $\mathcal{H}_{\overline{qv(P')-\{q\}}}$, it holds that $\langle P', \mathcal{F}(\rho)\rangle \approx \langle Q_i, \mathcal{F}(\sigma_i)\rangle$. In particular, we have

$$\langle P', \mathcal{E}(\rho)\rangle \approx \langle Q_i, \mathcal{E}(\sigma_i)\rangle \tag{6}$$

since $qv(P) \supseteq qv(P') - \{q\}$. Noting that $\mathcal{E}$ is a super-operator on $\mathcal{H}_{\overline{qv(Q)}}$, we have $\langle Q, \mathcal{E}(\sigma)\rangle \Longrightarrow \boxplus_{i\in I} p_i \bullet \langle Q_i', \mathcal{E}(\sigma_i)\rangle$ by Lemma 4.2(3), from which we derive further

$$\langle Q, \mathcal{E}(\sigma)\rangle \Longrightarrow\xrightarrow{c?q} \boxplus_{i\in I} p_i \bullet \langle Q_i, \mathcal{E}(\sigma_i)\rangle,$$

and

$$\langle Q\|R, \mathcal{E}(\sigma)\rangle \Longrightarrow\xrightarrow{\tau} \nu = \boxplus_{i\in I} p_i \bullet \langle Q_i\|R', \mathcal{E}(\sigma_i)\rangle.$$

Furthermore, for any $i \in I$, we have

$$(\langle P'\|R', \mathcal{E}(\rho)\rangle, \langle Q_i\|R', \mathcal{E}(\sigma_i)\rangle) \in \mathcal{R}$$

by Eq.(6). That is, $\mu\mathcal{R}\nu$ as required.

The symmetric form when $\langle Q\|R, \mathcal{E}(\sigma)\rangle \xrightarrow{\alpha} \nu$ can be similarly proved. So $\mathcal{R}$ is a bisimulation on Con. The result follows by noting that the identity transformation is also a super-operator on $\mathcal{H}_{\overline{qv(P)}}$. □

From Theorem 4.3, the superdense coding protocol and teleportation protocol presented in Section 3 is still valid in any quantum process context which consists only of parallel composition, relabeling, restriction, and conditional.

The configuration bisimulation is not preserved, however, by *dynamic* constructors such as prefix and summation. A counterexample is as follows. Let $P = M_{0,1}[q; x].\mathbf{nil}$ where $M_{0,1} = \lambda_0[|0\rangle] + \lambda_1[|1\rangle]$ is the 1-qubit measurement according to the computational basis, $Q = I[q].\mathbf{nil}$, and $\rho = [|0\rangle]_q \otimes \sigma$ where $\sigma \in \mathcal{D}(\mathcal{H}_{\overline{q}})$. Then $\langle P, \rho\rangle \approx \langle Q, \rho\rangle$, but $\langle H[q].P, \rho\rangle \not\approx \langle H[q].Q, \rho\rangle$ where H is the Hadamard operator.

Nevertheless, similar to standard classical CCS, the bisimulation for quantum processes is preserved by all the combinators of qCCS except for summation.

THEOREM 4.4. *If $P \approx Q$ then*

(1) $a.P \approx a.Q$, $a \in \{\tau, c?x, c!e, c?q, c!q, \mathcal{E}[\widetilde{q}], M[\widetilde{q}; x]\}$;
(2) $P\|R \approx Q\|R$;
(3) $P[f] \approx Q[f]$;
(4) $P\backslash L \approx Q\backslash L$;
(5) **if** *b* **then** *$P \approx$* **if** *b* **then** *Q.*

4.3 Congruent equivalence of quantum processes

As in classical process algebra, the bisimilarity $\approx$ is not preserved by summation combinator " + ". To deal with this problem, we introduce the notion of equality between quantum processes based on $\approx$.

DEFINITION 4.5. Two configurations $\langle P, \rho\rangle$ and $\langle Q, \sigma\rangle$ are said to be equal, denoted by $\langle P, \rho\rangle \simeq \langle Q, \sigma\rangle$, if $qv(P) = qv(Q)$, $\mathrm{tr}_{qv(P)}(\rho) = \mathrm{tr}_{qv(Q)}(\sigma)$, and

(1) whenever $\langle P, \rho\rangle \xrightarrow{c?q} \mu$, then $\langle Q, \sigma\rangle \Longrightarrow\xrightarrow{c?q} \nu$ for some ν such that for any super-operator $\mathcal{E}$ acting on $\mathcal{H}_{\overline{qv(\mu)-\{q\}}}$, $\mathcal{E}(\mu) \approx \mathcal{E}(\nu)$;

(2) whenever $\langle P, \rho\rangle \xrightarrow{\alpha} \mu$ where α is not a quantum input, then there exists ν such that $\langle Q, \sigma\rangle \stackrel{\alpha}{\Longrightarrow} \nu$ and $\mu \approx \nu$;

and the symmetric conditions of (1) and (2).

The only difference between the definitions of $\approx$ and $\simeq$ is that in the latter the $\overset{\widehat{\alpha}}{\Longrightarrow}$ transition in Clause (2) is replaced by $\overset{\alpha}{\Longrightarrow}$; that is, the matching action for a τ-move has to be at least one τ-move.

Furthermore, we lift the definition of equality to quantum processes as follows. For $P, Q \in qProc$, $P \simeq Q$ if and only if for any quantum state $\rho \in \mathcal{D}(\mathcal{H})$ and any indexed set $\widetilde{v}$ of classical values, $\langle P\{\widetilde{v}/\widetilde{x}\}, \rho\rangle \simeq \langle Q\{\widetilde{v}/\widetilde{x}\}, \rho\rangle$ where $\widetilde{x} = fv(P) \cup fv(Q)$.

It is worth noting that all the bisimulation relations proved in the examples of previous subsections are also valid when $\approx$ is replaced by $\simeq$. Now we prove that the equality relation is preserved by various process constructors of qCCS.

THEOREM 4.5. *If $P \simeq Q$ then*

(1) $a.P \simeq a.Q$, $a \in \{\tau, c?x, c!e, c?q, c!q, \mathcal{E}[\widetilde{q}], M[\widetilde{q}; x]\}$;
(2) $P + R \simeq Q + R$;
(3) $P\|R \simeq Q\|R$;
(4) $P[f] \simeq Q[f]$;
(5) $P\backslash L \simeq Q\backslash L$;
(6) **if** b **then** $P \simeq$ **if** b **then** Q.

The monoid laws and the static laws in classical CCS can also be generalized to qCCS.

THEOREM 4.6. *For any $P, Q, R \in qProc$, $K, L \subseteq Chan$, any relabeling functions f, f', and any action prefix a, we have*

(1) $P + \mathbf{nil} \simeq P$;
(2) $P + P \simeq P$;
(3) $P + Q \simeq Q + P$;
(4) $P + (Q + R) \simeq (P + Q) + R$;
(5) $P\|\mathbf{nil} \simeq P$;
(6) $P\|Q \simeq Q\|P$;
(7) $P\|(Q\|R) \simeq (P\|Q)\|R$;
(8) $(a.P)\backslash L \simeq \begin{cases} \mathbf{nil}, & \text{if } cn(a) \in L \\ a.P\backslash L, & \text{otherwise} \end{cases}$
(9) $(a.P)[f] \simeq f(a).P[f]$;
(10) $(P + Q)\backslash L \simeq P\backslash L + Q\backslash L$;
(11) $(P + Q)[f] \simeq P[f] + Q[f]$;
(12) $P\backslash L \simeq P$ *if* $cn(P) \cap L = \emptyset$, *where $cn(P)$ is the set of free channel names used in P;*
(13) $(P\backslash K)\backslash L \simeq P\backslash(K \cup L)$;
(14) $(P\|Q)\backslash L \simeq P\backslash L\|Q\backslash L$, *if* $cn(P) \cap cn(Q) \cap L = \emptyset$;
(15) $P[f]\backslash L \simeq P\backslash f^{-1}(L)[f]$;
(16) $P[Id] \simeq P$ *where Id is the identity relabeling function;*
(17) $P[f] \simeq P[f']$ *if the restrictions of f and f' on $cn(P)$ coincide;*
(18) $P[f][f'] \simeq P[f' \circ f]$;
(19) $(P\|Q)[f] \simeq P[f]\|Q[f]$ *if the restriction of f on $cn(P) \cup cn(Q)$ is one-to-one.*

In the following theorem, we simply write $P \xrightarrow{\alpha} P'$ if for any $\rho \in \mathcal{D}(\mathcal{H})$, $\langle P, \rho\rangle \xrightarrow{\alpha} \langle P', \rho\rangle$.

THEOREM 4.7. *(Expansion Law) Let*

$$P = (P_1[f_1]\|\cdots\|P_n[f_n])\backslash L.$$

Then

$$\begin{aligned}
P \simeq & \sum\{f_i(\alpha).(P_1[f_1]\|\cdots\|P_i'[f_i]\|\cdots\|P_n[f_n])\backslash L : \\
& \qquad P_i \xrightarrow{\alpha} P_i' \text{ and } f_i(cn(\alpha)) \notin L\} \\
+ & \sum\{f_i(c?x).(P_1[f_1]\|\cdots\|P_i'[f_i]\|\cdots\|P_n[f_n])\backslash L : \\
& \qquad P_i \xrightarrow{c?v} P_i'\{v/x\} \text{ for any } v, \text{ and } f_i(c) \notin L\} \\
+ & \sum\{\mathcal{E}[\widetilde{q}].(P_1[f_1]\|\cdots\|P_i'[f_i]\|\cdots\|P_n[f_n])\backslash L : \\
& \qquad \langle P_i, \rho\rangle \xrightarrow{\tau} \langle P_i', \mathcal{E}_{\widetilde{q}}(\rho)\rangle \text{ for any } \rho\} \\
+ & \sum\{M[\widetilde{q}; x].(P_1[f_1]\|\cdots\|P_i'[f_i]\|\cdots\|P_n[f_n])\backslash L : \\
& \qquad \langle P_i, \rho\rangle \xrightarrow{\tau} \boxplus_{j\in J} p_j \bullet \langle P_i'\{\lambda_j/x\}, K_{j,\widetilde{q}}\rho K_{j,\widetilde{q}}/p_j\rangle \\
& \qquad \text{for any } \rho, \text{ and } M = \sum_{j\in J} \lambda_j K_j\} \\
+ & \sum\{\tau.(P_1[f_1]\|\cdots\|P_i'[f_i]\|\cdots\|P_j'[f_j]\|\cdots\|P_n[f_n])\backslash L : \\
& \qquad P_i \xrightarrow{\alpha} P_i', P_j \xrightarrow{\beta} P_j', i < j, f_i(cn(\alpha)) = f_j(cn(\beta)), \text{ and} \\
& \qquad \text{among } \alpha \text{ and } \beta \text{ there is exactly one input and one output}\}.
\end{aligned}$$

We now turn to examine the properties of the congruence relation $\simeq$ under recursive definitions. To this end, we assume a set of process variable schemes, ranged over by $X, Y, \ldots$. Assigned to each process variable scheme X there is a non-negative integer $ar(X)$. If $\widetilde{q}$ is an indexed set of distinct quantum variables with $|\widetilde{q}| = ar(A)$, then $X(\widetilde{q})$ is called a process variable.

Process expressions may be defined by adding the following clause into Definition 3.1 (and replacing the word "process" by the phrase "process expression" and "qProc" by "qExp"):

(15) $X(\widetilde{q}) \in qExp$, and $qv(X(\widetilde{q})) = \widetilde{q}$

where $X(\widetilde{q})$ is a process variable. We use metavariables $E, F, \ldots$ to range over process expressions. Suppose that E is a process expression, and $\{X_i(\widetilde{q_i}) : i \in I\}$ is a family of process variables. If $\{P_i : i \in I\}$ is a family of processes such that $qv(P_i) \subseteq \widetilde{q_i}$ for all i, then we write

$$E\{P_i/X_i(\widetilde{q_i}) : i \in I\}$$

for the process obtained by replacing simultaneously $X_i(\widetilde{q_i})$ in E with P_i for all $i \in I$.

DEFINITION 4.6. Let E and F be process expressions containing at most process variables $\{X_i(\widetilde{q_i}) : i \in I\}$. Then E and F are equal, denoted by $E \simeq F$, if for all family $\{P_i : i \in I\}$ of quantum processes with $qv(P_i) \subseteq \widetilde{q_i}$, we have

$$E\{P_i/X_i(\widetilde{q_i}) : i \in I\} \simeq F\{P_i/X_i(\widetilde{q_i}) : i \in I\}.$$

The next theorem shows that $\simeq$ is also preserved by recursive definitions.

THEOREM 4.8. *(1) If $A(\widetilde{q}) \overset{def}{=} P$, then $A(\widetilde{q}) \simeq P$;*
(2) Let $\{E_i : i \in I\}$ and $\{F_i : i \in I\}$ be two families of process expressions containing at most process variables $\{X_i(\widetilde{q_i}) : i \in I\}$, and $E_i \simeq F_i$ for each $i \in I$. If $\{A_i(\widetilde{q_i}) : i \in I\}$ and $\{B_i(\widetilde{q_i}) : i \in I\}$ be two families of process constants such that

$$\begin{aligned}
A_i(\widetilde{q_i}) &\overset{def}{=} E_i\{A_j(\widetilde{q_j})/X_j(\widetilde{q_j}) : j \in I\} \\
B_i(\widetilde{q_i}) &\overset{def}{=} F_i\{B_j(\widetilde{q_j})/X_j(\widetilde{q_j}) : j \in I\},
\end{aligned}$$

then $A_i(\widetilde{q_i}) \simeq B_i(\widetilde{q_i})$ for all $i \in I$.

Finally, the uniqueness of solutions of equations can be proved for process expressions in qCCS.

DEFINITION 4.7. Given a process variable $X(\widetilde{q})$ and a process expression E, we call

- $X(\widetilde{q})$ is sequential in E if every subexpression of E which contains $X(\widetilde{q})$, excluding $X(\widetilde{q})$ itself, is of the form $a.F$, $\sum_{i\in I} F_i$, or **if** b **then** F;
- $X(\widetilde{q})$ is guarded in E if each occurrence of $X(\widetilde{q})$ is within some subexpression $a.F$ of E where a is a (classical or quantum) input or output.

THEOREM 4.9. *Let $\{E_i : i \in I\}$ be a family of process expressions containing at most process variables $\{X_i(\widetilde{q_i}) : i \in I\}$, and each $X_j(\widetilde{q_j})$ is sequential and guarded in each E_i. Let $\{P_i : i \in I\}$ and $\{Q_i : i \in I\}$ be two families of quantum processes such that $qv(P_i) \cup qv(Q_i) \subseteq \widetilde{q_i}$ for each i, and*

$$P_i \simeq E_i\{P_j/X_j(\widetilde{q_j}) : j \in I\}$$
$$Q_i \simeq E_i\{Q_j/X_j(\widetilde{q_j}) : j \in I\},$$

then $P_i \simeq Q_i$ for all $i \in I$.

To illustrate the power of the theorems proved in this section, let us reconsider Example 4.3. We will provide another proof for $\mathcal{U}(U) \circ \mathcal{U}(V) \simeq \mathcal{U}(VU)$ using the expansion law and the uniqueness of solutions of equations. For simplicity, we only consider the special case where U and V are both 1-qubit unitary operators. Recall the definition of $\mathcal{U}(U) \circ \mathcal{U}(V)$ in Example 3.3:

$$\mathcal{U}(U) \circ \mathcal{U}(V) \stackrel{def}{=} (L_s \| \mathcal{U}(U)[\mathsf{e}/\mathsf{c}, \mathsf{f}/\mathsf{d}] \| \mathcal{U}(V)[\mathsf{f}/\mathsf{c}, \mathsf{g}/\mathsf{d}] \| R_s) \backslash L$$

where $L = \{c, \mathsf{e}, \mathsf{f}, \mathsf{g}\}$. Then from Theorem 4.8(1), and repeatedly using Theorems 4.7 and 4.5, we have

$$\mathcal{U}(U) \circ \mathcal{U}(V) \simeq \mathsf{c}?q.\tau.U[q].\tau.V[q].\tau.\mathsf{d}!q.\tau.\mathcal{U}(U) \circ \mathcal{U}(V)$$

where the first τ action is caused by interaction between L_s and $\mathcal{U}(U)[\mathsf{e}/\mathsf{c}, \mathsf{f}/\mathsf{d}]$, the second one between $\mathcal{U}(U)[\mathsf{e}/\mathsf{c}, \mathsf{f}/\mathsf{d}]$ and $\mathcal{U}(V)[\mathsf{f}/\mathsf{c}, \mathsf{g}/\mathsf{d}]$, the third one between $\mathcal{U}(V)[\mathsf{f}/\mathsf{c}, \mathsf{g}/\mathsf{d}]$ and R_s, while the last one between R_s and L_s.

On the other hand, by Theorem 4.8(1) we have

$$\mathcal{U}(VU) \simeq \mathsf{c}?q.VU[q].\mathsf{d}!q.\mathcal{U}(VU).$$

Now let X be a quantum process variable with $qv(X) = \emptyset$, and

$$E = \mathsf{c}?q.\tau.U[q].\tau.V[q].\tau.\mathsf{d}!q.\tau.X, \quad F = \mathsf{c}?q.VU[q].\mathsf{d}!q.X$$

be two quantum process expressions. Then E and F are both sequential and guarded, and $E \simeq F$. So we have $\mathcal{U}(U) \circ \mathcal{U}(V) \simeq \mathcal{U}(VU)$ from Theorem 4.9.

5. Conclusions and further work

In this paper, we propose a formal model qCCS, which is a quantum extension of classical value-passing CCS, to model and rigorously analyze the behaviors of quantum distributed computing and quantum communication protocols. We define a notion of equivalence, based on bisimulation, for quantum processes in qCCS, and prove that it is preserved by all process constructors, including parallel composition, restriction, and recursive definitions. This is the first congruence relation for process algebras proposed so far aiming at modeling quantum communicating systems. Various examples are fully examined to show the expressiveness as well as the proof techniques of qCCS.

We conclude this paper by pointing out some topics for further study. In the present paper, only *exact* bisimulation is presented where two quantum processes are either bisimilar or non-bisimilar. Obviously, such a bisimulation cannot capture the idea that a quantum process *approximately* implements its specification. Note that this approximation, or imprecision, is especially essential for quantum process algebra since quantum operations constitute a continuum and exact bisimulation is not always practically suitable for their physical implementation. To provide techniques and tools for approximate reasoning, a quantified version of bisimulation, which defines for each pair of quantum processes a bisimulation-based distance characterizing the extent to which they are bisimilar, has already been proposed for purely quantum processes in [18]. We plan to extend it to qCCS defined in this paper.

Another interesting direction worthy of being researched is to expand the application scope of qCCS to model and analyze the *security properties* of quantum cryptographic systems. By introducing cryptographic primitives, such as constructors for encryption and decryption, into pi-calculus, the Spi calculus [1] has been very successful in cryptographic protocol analysis. We believe that a similar extension of our qCCS will provide tools for analyzing quantum cryptographic protocols such as BB84 quantum key distribution protocol.

References

[1] M. Abadi and A. Gordon. A calculus for cryptographic protocols: the spi calculus, 1997.

[2] C. Baier and M. Kwiatkowska. Domain equations for probabilistic processes. *Mathematical Structure in Computer Science*, 1999.

[3] C. H. Bennett and S. J. Wiesner. Communication via one- and two-particle operators on einstein-podolsky-rosen states. *Physical Review Letters*, 69(20):2881–2884, 1992.

[4] C. H. Bennett, G. Brassard, C. Crepeau, R. Jozsa, A. Peres, and W. Wootters. Teleporting an unknown quantum state via dual classical and epr channels. *Physical Review Letters*, 70:1895–1899, 1993.

[5] Y. Feng, R. Duan, Z. Ji, and M. Ying. Probabilistic bisimulations for quantum processes. *Information and Computation*, 205(11):1608–1639, 2007.

[6] S. J. Gay and R. Nagarajan. Communicating quantum processes. In J. Palsberg and M. Abadi, editors, *Proceedings of the 32nd ACM SIGPLAN-SIGACT Symposium on Principles of Programming Languages (POPL)*, pages 145–157, 2005.

[7] L. K. Grover. Quantum mechanics helps in searching for a needle in a haystack. *Physical Review Letters*, 78(2):325, 1997.

[8] M. Hennessy. A proof system for communicating processes with value-passing. *Formal Aspects of Computer Science*, 3:346–366, 1991.

[9] M. Hennessy and A. Ingólfsdóttir. A theory of communicating processes value-passing. *Information and Computation*, 107(2):202–236, 1993.

[10] P. Jorrand and M. Lalire. Toward a quantum process algebra. In P. Selinger, editor, *Proceedings of the 2nd International Workshop on Quantum Programming Languages, 2004*, page 111, 2004.

[11] K. Kraus. *States, Effects and Operations: Fundamental Notions of Quantum Theory*. Springer, Berlin, 1983.

[12] M. Lalire. Relations among quantum processes: Bisimilarity and congruence. *Mathematical Structures in Computer Science*, 16(3): 407–428, 2006.

[13] R. Milner, J. Parrow, and D. Walker. A calculus of mobile processes, parts i and ii. *Information and Computation*, 100:1–77, 1992.

[14] M. Nielsen and I. Chuang. *Quantum computation and quantum information*. Cambridge university press, 2000.

[15] P. Selinger. Towards a quantum programming language. *Mathematical Structures in Computer Science*, 14(4):527–586, 2004.

[16] P. W. Shor. Algorithms for quantum computation: discrete log and factoring. In *Proceedings of the 35th IEEE FOCS*, pages 124–134, 1994.

[17] J. von Neumann. *Mathematical Foundations of Quantum Mechanics*. Princeton University Press, Princeton, NJ, 1955.

[18] M. Ying, Y. Feng, R. Duan, and Z. Ji. An algebra of quantum processes. *ACM Transactions on Computational Logic (TOCL)*, 10 (3):1–36, 2009.

Safe Nondeterminism in a Deterministic-by-Default Parallel Language

Robert L. Bocchino Jr.[1] Stephen Heumann[2] Nima Honarmand[2] Sarita V. Adve[2]
Vikram S. Adve[2] Adam Welc[3] Tatiana Shpeisman[4]

[1]Carnegie Mellon University rbocchin@cs.cmu.edu [2]University of Illinois at Urbana-Champaign dpj@cs.uiuc.edu [3]Adobe Systems awelc@adobe.com [4]Intel Labs tatiana.shpeisman@intel.com

Abstract

A number of deterministic parallel programming models with strong safety guarantees are emerging, but similar support for nondeterministic algorithms, such as branch and bound search, remains an open question. We present a language together with a type and effect system that supports nondeterministic computations with a deterministic-by-default guarantee: nondeterminism must be explicitly requested via special parallel constructs (marked nd), and any deterministic construct that does not execute any nd construct has deterministic input-output behavior. Moreover, deterministic parallel constructs are always equivalent to a sequential composition of their constituent tasks, even if they enclose, or are enclosed by, nd constructs. Finally, in the execution of nd constructs, interference may occur only between pairs of accesses guarded by atomic statements, so there are no data races, either between atomic statements and unguarded accesses (strong isolation) or between pairs of unguarded accesses (stronger than strong isolation alone). We enforce the guarantees at compile time with modular checking using novel extensions to a previously described effect system. Our effect system extensions also enable the compiler to remove unnecessary transactional synchronization. We provide a static semantics, dynamic semantics, and a complete proof of soundness for the language, both with and without the barrier removal feature. An experimental evaluation shows that our language can achieve good scalability for realistic parallel algorithms, and that the barrier removal techniques provide significant performance gains.

Categories and Subject Descriptors D.1.3 [*Software*]: Concurrent Programming—Parallel Programming; D.3.1 [*Software*]: Formal Definitions and Theory; D.3.2 [*Software*]: Language Classifications—Concurrent, distributed, and parallel languages; D.3.2 [*Software*]: Language Classifications—Object-oriented languages; D.3.3 [*Software*]: Language Constructs and Features—Concurrent Programming Structures

General Terms Languages, Verification, Performance

1. Introduction

Widely used parallel programming models today (Java, C#, Posix, Win32) are based on a low-level and error-prone concept of threads. These models provide few or no guards against parallel programming errors such as data races, deadlocks, or atomicity violations. Some higher-level programming models are available, or are emerging, that prevent these kinds of errors. However, these models achieve their safety guarantees by greatly restricting side effects, either through functional programming (e.g., STM Haskell [31]) or through dataflow or data-parallel styles of programming (e.g., Concurrent Collections [23], Ct [30]).

There is much recent interest in supporting *deterministic* algorithms within general imperative languages, via static type systems [17], runtime-supported language mechanisms [10, 11, 24, 45, 49, 50], or largely transparent runtime techniques [14, 15, 27, 43]. For algorithms that have deterministic input-output behavior, such models can provide major benefits compared with traditional thread-based programming [18, 38].

There are also important algorithms, however, that do *not* have deterministic input-output behavior, and are not supported by these techniques. Some examples include clustering algorithms, optimization algorithms like branch-and-bound solvers, and graph algorithms like Delaunay mesh refinement. A common feature of such algorithms is that they permit any of multiple possible outputs to be produced for a given input. Such outputs must usually be derived from a controlled set of choices, typically from different, schedule-dependent, orders of evaluating parallel tasks, e.g., evaluating different groups of neighboring points in clustering algorithms. Importantly, the nondeterminism should not simply derive from unpredictable behavior due to data races and atomicity violations. Such behavior is not only potentially erroneous but can also can make proram executions difficult to reason about, e.g., by producing non-sequentially-consistent results. Furthermore, real-world applications are composed of a (potentially large) number of different algorithms, likely to be a mixture of deterministic and nondeterministic ones. Therefore, it is essential to be able to compose deterministic and nondeterministic algorithms in a way that is easy to reason about.

These observations pose two challenges for a safe and realistic parallel programming model: (1) How do we express nondeterminism itself in a disciplined manner that simplifies reasoning about program behavior? (2) How do we allow nondeterministic and deterministic computations to be composed without weakening the deterministic guarantees for the latter?

In this work, we present a Java-based parallel language that supports both deterministic and nondeterministic parallel code in a disciplined manner. Our language has the following major features:

1. *Deterministic parallel operations.* We provide operations that describe deterministic parallel composition of tasks. A deterministic parallel operation enforces *noninterference* between its component tasks (i.e., there are no conflicting reads or writes in any pair of tasks), ensuring that the whole operation behaves like a sequential (and therefore deterministic) composition of

POPL'11, January 26–28, 2011, Austin, Texas, USA.

its component tasks. The noninterference property is enforced *at compile time*. This part is derived from previous work [17].

2. *Nondeterministic parallel operations.* We provide operations that describe potentially nondeterministic parallel composition of tasks. These operations allow interference between tasks, but any such interference is subject to the following guarantees, again enforced *at compile time*. This part is entirely new.

   (a) *Race freedom and sequential consistency.* No execution of a valid program in our language can ever produce a data race. This property is very important, even for nondeterministic codes, because in the Java memory model, race freedom implies sequential consistency, which makes parallel programs much easier to reason about.

   (b) *Strong isolation.* Our language provides an *atomic statement* `atomic` S that executes the enclosed statement S in isolation, i.e., as if there were no interleaving with concurrently executing tasks. The isolation is *strong*, i.e., isolation is provided with respect to *all* concurrent operations, not just other ones occurring in atomic statements. Novel effect system features enable our language to be built on top of an "off the shelf" runtime, such as software transactional memory, that provides only weak isolation. Previous work [6, 31, 42] has also used effects to enforce strong isolation but, as discussed in Section 7, our language is less restrictive, and our guarantees are stronger.

   (c) *Composition of deterministic and nondeterministic operations.* A deterministic parallel operation always behaves as an isolated and sequential composition of its component tasks, *even if the operation encloses, or is enclosed in, a nondeterministic parallel operation.* This property allows local, compositional reasoning about deterministic operations, which we view as essential for a language that supports both deterministic and nondeterministic operations.

   (d) *Determinism by default.* Nondeterminism occurs *only where requested by an explicit nondeterministic operation*, and cannot occur "by accident." Specifically, if a deterministic construct does not encounter any nondeterministic construct for a given input heap state in some execution, then it has deterministic input-output behavior (i.e., it produces the same output heap state and other results in all executions, for that input heap state).

For the deterministic parallel operations (1), we build on Deterministic Parallel Java (DPJ) [17]. In DPJ, the programmer partitions the heap into *regions*, and writes *effect summaries* on methods that describe the method's read and write operations on the regions. The compiler uses the regions and effect summaries to enforce noninterference of parallel tasks at compile time. However, by design, DPJ *completely disallows nondeterministic parallel algorithms*. To provide the nondeterministic operations (2) and their associated guarantees, we must extend DPJ.

For the isolation guarantee 2(b), we build on software transactional memory (STM) [37]. STM is not the only choice here, but it is a good one, as it runs on all platforms (as opposed to hardware transactions, which require special hardware) and provides relatively strong guarantees (isolation and deadlock freedom) with very low programming overhead. However, STM alone is insufficient for our purposes. First, STM implementations usually provide only *weak isolation*, and we want strong isolation. Second, even strong isolation is not enough: it allows data races between accesses outside of transactions, and we want to disallow such data races. Finally, STM introduces significant runtime overheads, including scalar overhead and false conflicts (due to over-synchronization), which can cause poor scalability.

To solve these technical challenges, we extend the DPJ effect system in several ways. First, we add a new kind of effect called an *atomic effect* for tracking when memory accesses occur inside an atomic statement. The atomic effects allow the compiler to guarantee both race freedom (property 2(a)) and strong isolation (2(b)), by prohibiting conflicting memory operations *unless each operation is in an atomic statement*. Second, we introduce new effect checking rules to enforce composition of operations (2(c)) and determinism by default (2(d)). For composition of operations, the extended effect system disallows interference between a deterministic operation and any other concurrent operation *unless the whole deterministic operation is enclosed in an atomic statement*. For determinism by default, the interference is disallowed for deterministic parallel operations, but allowed for nondeterministic parallel operations. Third, to reduce STM overhead, we introduce *atomic regions*, so that the programmer can identify which regions may be accessed in an interfering manner. For operations to other regions, the compiler can remove or simplify the STM synchronization, because such operations never cause conflicts.

Overall, this work makes the following contributions:

1. We present a language that provides the compile-time guarantees 1 through 2(d) stated above. To our knowledge, *no previous language or system has provided all these properties for shared-memory parallel programs through any mechanisms, static or dynamic.* Our language includes novel extensions to the DPJ effect system as discussed above for enforcing race freedom, strong isolation, and determinism by default; and for reducing the runtime overhead of the underlying STM implementation.
2. We formalize our ideas using three formal languages: the first has only deterministic parallel operations, the second adds nondeterministic parallel operations, and the third adds atomic regions. We have developed a full syntax, static semantics, and dynamic semantics for all three languages. Further, we have formally stated the soundness properties given informally above, and proved that the properties follow from the semantic definitions. Here we summarize the key features of the formal language and the essential soundness results; the full details, including proofs, may be found in the lead author's Ph.D. thesis [19].
3. We describe our experience using our language to implement three nondeterministic algorithms: *Delaunay Mesh Refinement* from the Lonestar benchmarks [1], the *traveling salesman problem* (TSP), and *OO7* [25], a synthetic database benchmark. Our experience shows that porting these algorithms form "pure" Java into our language was relatively straightforward and required neither redesign of existing data structures nor restructuring of the algorithms themselves. The language naturally expresses all these algorithms, although the speedups achieved vary depending on the inherent parallelism in the algorithms and performance limitations of the underlying STM. Additionally, judicious use of atomic regions eliminated a large fraction of the STM-related overhead in two out of three benchmarks.

2. Background

In this work, we build on a language called Deterministic Parallel Java (DPJ) [17]. DPJ uses an effect system to enforce deterministic semantics for explicitly parallel programs via compile-time type checking. This section briefly explains the key constructs of DPJ; the details may be found in [17, 19]. In the rest of this paper, we refer to the preexisting language as *basic DPJ*.

DPJ provides a fork-join parallel model: the programmer creates parallel tasks using either a `foreach` statement (for a parallel loop) or `cobegin` block (for a group of mutually parallel statements). DPJ's effect system guarantees that in a well-typed parallel program, any two parallel tasks have *noninterfering effects*. An effect is a set of operations on memory. Two effects interfere if they both access a common memory location and at least one of them writes to that location. The noninterference guarantee for parallel tasks implies deterministic input-output semantics for the computation.

The DPJ effect system works as follows. The programmer assigns every object field and array cell to a *region* and annotates every method with a *method effect summary* stating (a superset of) the reads or write operations performed by the method, in terms of regions. The compiler checks two things: (1) that the effect summaries are a superset of the actual effects in the method body; and (2) that no two parallel statements are interfering. The effect summaries on method definitions enable modular checking of effects.

```
1  class Node<region P> {
2    region L, R;
3    double mass in P;
4    Node<P:L> left in P:L;
5    Node<P:R> right in P:R;
6    void setMass(double mass) writes P {
7      this.mass = mass;              // writes P
8    }
9    void setMassOfChildren(double mass) writes P:* {
10       cobegin {
11         if (left != null) left.setMass(mass);    // writes P:L
12         if (right != null) right.setMass(mass);  // writes P:R
13       }
14   }
15 }
```

Figure 1. Some features of basic DPJ for deterministic parallelism.

Figure 1 illustrates the use of regions and effects in basic DPJ. In line 1, we declare class `Node` to have one region parameter `P`. Line 3 declares field `mass` in region `P`; the actual region of the field is determined when the class is instantiated into a type, as shown in lines 4 and 5. Line 2 declares names `L` and `R` that have static scope (i.e., they are shared by all instances of class `Node`). Lines 4 and 5 declare fields `left` and `right` and place them in regions `P:L` and `P:R`, respectively. The form `P:L` is called a *region path list*, or RPL, and it expresses the hierarchical structure of regions: intuitively, `P:L` and `P:R` are both nested under `P`. The use of `L` and `R` puts the two fields in different regions, while the use of `P` allows different `Node` objects instantiated with different bindings to `P` to have their fields in different regions. Because `L` and `R` are distinct names, `P:L` and `P:R` are guaranteed to refer to different regions, for any common binding to `P`.

Lines 6 and 9 illustrate the use of method effect summaries. Method `setMass` (line 6) has declared effects `writes P`, while `setMassOfChildren` (line 9) has declared effects `writes P:*`, where the `*` is a wildcard representing any sequence of names. If an effect declaration is omitted, it defaults to most general effect (writes the whole heap).

The compiler performs checks (1) and (2) stated above by accumulating the effects of a method, `foreach` statement, or `cobegin` statement. The analysis is simple and local because, at each call site, the declared effects of the invoked method provide the effects of the invocation, after substituting actual for formal region parameters. For example, the effect of `left.setMass(mass)` in line 11 is `writes P:L`, obtained by substituting `P:L` (from the type of left) for the class parameter `P` in the declared method effect `writes P` (the read of field `left` is subsumed because in DPJ, write effects imply read effects). Similarly, the compiler infers the effect of a field access or assignment to $e.f$ by substituting the region named in the type of e for the parameter in the declared region of the field f.

As an example of check (1) (correct method effects), the effect of `setMass` is legal because the method body writes to field `mass` in region `P` and has no other heap effects. As an example of check (2) (parallel noninterference), the compiler infers that the effect of lines 11 and 12 are `writes P:L` and `writes P:R`, respectively. Because `P:L` and `P:R` must be disjoint regions, for any common binding to `P`, the effects are noninterfering.

Although this example is somewhat simplistic, these and other features of DPJ can express a range of realistic parallel idioms [17], including parallel updates on arrays of objects, parallel traversals and updates of a tree, in-place divide-and-conquer on arrays, and commutative operations within parallel tasks.

3. Language Support for Nondeterminism

We now informally describe the language mechanisms for nondeterministic parallel control, parallel safety guarantees, and optimization support. We illustrate the new language features with a running example of the *traveling salesman problem* (TSP). Section 4 describes the language more formally.

3.1 The TSP Computation

The traveling salesman problem, or TSP, is the well-known problem of finding a shortest cycle in a weighted graph that visits all the nodes once (i.e., a Hamiltonian cycle). TSP can be solved by *branch and bound search*, a common algorithm for solving optimization problems and a classical example of a nondeterministic computation. Figures 2–4 show simplified Java-like pseudocode for TSP. The global data (lines 1–13) include a weighted graph that is the input to the program; a priority queue for storing the paths being explored; and a "best" (i.e., shortest) tour, which is refined as the computation progresses, eventually storing the answer. Two regions are used to hold the data: `ReadOnly` for fields that will not be modified during the computation, and `Mutable` for those that will be. The priority queue's type `PriorityQueue<Path<ReadOnly>, Mutable>` indicates that it contains objects of type `Path<ReadOnly>`, and that the internal data used to represent the queue itself is in region `Mutable`. The main computation loop (lines 15–23) iterates in parallel over several worker tasks. Each task generates a prefix to search (using the pseudocode in Figure 3) and adds it to a priority queue. When all prefixes have been generated, the tasks remove prefixes from the priority queue and search them (using the pseudocode in Figure 4), until there are no more prefixes to search.

3.2 Nondeterministic Parallel Control

To express nondeterministic parallel computations, we introduce a parallel loop denoted `foreach_nd`, where `nd` stands for "nondeterministic." Line 15 in Figure 2 shows an example. This construct is identical to `foreach` in basic DPJ [17], except it says explicitly that conflicting accesses, and therefore potential nondeterminism, are allowed between the loop iterations of `foreach_nd`. We also introduce a `cobegin_nd` construct corresponding to `cobegin` in basic DPJ. Collectively, we refer to these four (`foreach`, `foreach_nd`, `cobegin`, and `cobegin_nd`) as *parallel constructs*.

The resulting parallel control structure is just fork-join parallelism and can be represented as a static task graph, where each node or *task* is a single iteration of a parallel loop (`foreach` or `foreach_nd`) or a single statement in a `cobegin` or `cobegin_nd`. All four parallel constructs have an implicit "join" synchronization at the end of the construct for the tasks of the construct. The (directed) edges in the task graph represent either program order, or forking at the start of a parallel construct, or the "join" synchronization at the end of a parallel construct. Two tasks are *concurrent* if they are not ordered in the task graph. Two memory accesses are concurrent if they occur in concurrent tasks.

```
1  /* Regions for partitioning data */
2  region ReadOnly, atomic Mutable;
3
4  /* Graph we are working on; immutable */
5  Graph<ReadOnly> graph in ReadOnly = the TSP graph;
6
7  /* Priority queue for tour prefix paths */
8  final PriorityQueue<Path<ReadOnly>, Mutable> priorityQueue =
9      new PriorityQueue<Path<ReadOnly>, Mutable>();
10 priorityQueue.add(new Path<ReadOnly>(startNode));
11
12 /* The answer */
13 Path<ReadOnly> bestTour in Mutable = infinite path;
14
15 foreach_nd(int i in 0, NWORKERS) {
16     Path<ReadOnly> prefix = null;
17     do {
18         atomic {
19             prefix = generateNextPrefix();
20         }
21         if (prefix != null) searchAllToursWithPrefix(prefix);
22     } while (prefix != null);
23 }
```

Figure 2. Global data and main computation for the Traveling Salesman Problem.

```
Path generateNextPrefix() reads ReadOnly writes Mutable {
    while (!priorityQueue.isEmpty() &&
           priorityQueue.best().length() < bestTour.length()) {
        Path<ReadOnly> prefix = priorityQueue.removeBest();
        if (prefix.nodeCount() > PREFIX_CUTOFF) {
            return prefix;
        } else {
            for (each edge edge that can be added to prefix
                 while staying under bestTour.length()) {
                Path<ReadOnly> newPrefix =
                    new Path<ReadOnly>(prefix, edge);
                priorityQueue.add(newPrefix);
            }
        }
    }
    return null;
}
```

Figure 3. Generating the next tour prefix.

```
1  void searchAllToursWithPrefix(Path<ReadOnly> prefix)
2      reads ReadOnly writes atomic Mutable {
3      for (each Hamilton cycle tour in graph with prefix prefix) {
4          atomic {
5              if (tour.length() < bestTour.length()) {
6                  bestTour = tour;
7              }
8          }
9      }
10 }
```

Figure 4. Searching all tours with a given prefix.

The specific parallel constructs used to fork and join tasks are not fundamental to our work. The language mechanisms used to enforce safety properties (described next) can be applied directly to other fork-join parallel programming languages, e.g., Cilk [16], a large subset of OpenMP [4], and potentially other parallel languages in which the compiler can identify all groups of concurrent tasks. Distinguishing the constructs that permit interference (i.e., may be nondeterministic) from those that do not (and so are deterministic) is a useful property, but again, not necessary for any of our other guarantees.

3.3 Safety Properties for Nondeterministic Code

As stated in the introduction, the goal of our language design and type system is to achieve four safety guarantees for nondeterministic and deterministic code: (i) data race freedom; (ii) strong isolation for nondeterministic parallel constructs; (iii) sequential equivalence for deterministic parallel constructs; and (iv) a property we call *determinism by default*, defined below. These four properties give programmers a simple, elegant execution model for reasoning about partly nondeterministic programs. Below, we discuss the language mechanisms for expressing synchronization, the effect system features for enforcing the properties, and the resulting execution model seen by programmers.

Synchronization: To ensure correctly synchronized accesses in the presence of interference (defined in Section 2), we add an *atomic statement* to the language. This construct is similar to previous work [8, 28, 32, 33], except that in conjunction with our effect system, discussed below, our atomic statements provide stronger guarantees. A statement `atomic` S indicates that S is to be run as if *all other concurrent execution* were suspended while S is executing. This is called strong isolation [40, 47].

With reference to the TSP example, in Figure 2 each call to `generateNextPrefix` is enclosed by an atomic statement that protects the accesses to the shared priority queue. Note that while the calls to `generateNextPrefix` are effectively serialized, each worker can start its call to `searchAllToursWithPrefix` as soon as its call to `generateNextPrefix` is done, in a pipelined manner. This pattern can achieve good speedups because most of the work in this code is done in `searchAllToursWithPrefix`. In Figure 4, an atomic statement protects the concurrent updates to `bestTour`.

An atomic statement may appear inside any of the four parallel constructs, as well as inside other atomic statements. Two nested atomic statements in the same task are "flattened": that is, the inner `atomic` becomes a no-op, and atomicity is enforced entirely at the outer `atomic`. If a parallel task created in an atomic statement contains a nested atomic statement, then the nesting behaves in the standard way: the inner `atomic` enforces isolation with regard to other tasks created by the immediately enclosing parallel construct, while the outer `atomic` enforces isolation as to tasks created by any outer enclosing parallel construct.

Effect System: We now discuss how our effect system enforces the four safety properties stated at the outset of this section.

Data Race Freedom and Strong Isolation: We use the following strategy to ensure both data race freedom and strong isolation. First, a transactional runtime guarantees at least weak isolation of atomic statements (i.e., isolation between different atomic statements, but not between atomic statements and unguarded code). Second, the effect system ensures that for any pair of conflicting memory accesses, each access occurs inside an atomic statement. For example, in Figure 4, any two concurrent accesses to `bestTour` are both enclosed in instances of the atomic block at line 4 (the concurrency is created by the `foreach_nd` at line 15 of Figure 2). This requirement ensures strong isolation, because no conflicts between unguarded memory accesses and atomic statements are allowed. It also ensures race freedom, because no conflicts between pairs of unguarded accesses are allowed.

Notice two things about our strategy. First, our language may be built on top of a standard software transactional memory (STM) implementation, which typically guarantees only weak isolation for performance reasons. Second, our strategy prohibits all data races. Even TM systems with strong isolation generally allow data races between pairs of accesses occurring outside any transaction.

To accomplish the effect checking, we extend the DPJ effect system to distinguish effects that are *atomic* (meaning the effect occurred inside an atomic statement) from effects that are *nonatomic* (meaning the effect occurred outside any atomic statement). The compiler ensures that interference occurs *only between atomic effects*.

To enable sound modular reasoning about method invocations, we make atomic effects explicit in method effect summaries. For example, the effect `writes atomic Mutable` in the summary for `searchAllToursWithPrefix` (Figure 4) says that any possible writes to region `Mutable` occur inside atomic blocks in the body of the method or its callees. In checking method effect summaries, our system is sound but conservative: it is correct to summarize a write to region R occurring inside an `atomic` block as either `writes atomic` R or simply `writes` R; the latter is more conservative than necessary but is correct. However, it is not correct to summarize an access occurring outside any atomic section as an atomic effect, because such an effect would report a transactional guard when in fact there is none.

For example, the effect system can verify that all interfering accesses within the `foreach_nd` in Figure 2 are atomic effects. First, the variable `prefix` is local to each task and so generates no conflicts across tasks. Second, according to the effect summary for `generateNextPrefix` (Figure 3), the method invocation in line 19 produces conflicting effects on region `Mutable`. These effects are enclosed within the atomic statement starting at line 18 and so are recorded as atomic effects that may interfere. Third, the call to `searchAllToursWithPrefix` is not within an atomic statement; but according to its effect summary it generates only read effects (which do not interfere with themselves) and atomic write effects (which are allowed to interfere with themselves, and are to a different region from the read effects).

Sequential Equivalence for Deterministic Constructs: An important property we wish to preserve from basic DPJ is *sequential equivalence* for deterministic constructs: that is, `foreach` and `cobegin` are equivalent to the sequential execution of their constituent tasks in program order. To enforce this property, we obviously need to disallow interference between `cobegin` or `foreach` branches, even if the interfering effects are atomic. For example, this program is not allowed:

```
cobegin {
  atomic x = 0;
  atomic x = 1;
}
```

For this we just have a simple typing rule that interference between atomic effects is allowed only inside `foreach_nd` or `cobegin_nd`.

However, that is not enough, because interference can also occur between a deterministic task and a concurrent nondeterministic task. For example, consider the following program:

```
z = 0;
cobegin_nd {
  cobegin { atomic x = z; atomic y = z; } // S1, S2
  atomic z = 1;   // S3
}
```

This program could produce the result $x = 1, y = 0$ by executing `S2; S3; S1`. This result violates sequential equivalence of `cobegin`, because it does not correspond to any sequentially consistent execution of the program where the `cobegin` block is executed in program order. Instead, we wish to ensure that a `foreach` or `cobegin` executes in isolation, even if it appears inside `foreach_nd` or `cobegin_nd`.

Our solution to this problem is to convert atomic effects occurring inside a deterministic construct to non-atomic effects when propagating them to the outer context. In the example above, when checking interference, the compiler sees *nonatomic* reads to `z` in the first `cobegin_nd` branch: those reads occurred in atomic statements, but became nonatomic when passing outwards across the `cobegin`. On the other hand, the second branch has atomic writes to `z`. Therefore the `cobegin_nd` branches have illegal read-write interference (i.e., not both guarded by atomic) on `z`. To write this program legally in our language, the programmer could put the whole `cobegin` in an atomic statement.

Determinism by Default: Finally, by virtue of the isolation of deterministic constructs, and the noninterference between their internal tasks, both discussed above, we have the following property: if a deterministic construct does not dynamically execute any nondeterministic construct, then the execution of the deterministic construct is, in fact, deterministic. That is, a given input heap state to the deterministic construct always produces a fixed result value and fixed output heap state. We refer to this property as *determinism by default*: nondeterministic input-output behavior may be introduced *only* by the execution of an explicit nondeterministic construct.

Implications for Programmers: The properties discussed above, and treated more formally in the next section, provide two key benefits for programmers. First, concurrency errors such as data races or unintentional nondeterminism will be detected via compile-time type checking; this benefit existed in base DPJ for deterministic programs and has now been extended to nondeterministic ones. Second, once a program has been type checked, the above properties greatly simplify how programmers can reason about the possible (nondeterministic) execution behaviors.

With regard to the second point, many programmers and testing tools analyze program behavior by reasoning about the possible interleavings (or schedules) of parallel operations. The above properties simplify this reasoning in several important ways (we focus on `cobegin` here without loss of generality; `foreach` is analogous):

1. We only need to consider interleavings of isolated `atomics`, `cobegins`, and unguarded accesses, because of strong isolation and sequential equivalence of `cobegin`. The `nd` constructs do not constrain interleavings.
2. We can reason about the tasks of a `cobegin` sequentially: the first task can be fully evaluated without any intervening accesses from elsewhere, immediately followed by a complete evaluation of the second task.
3. `cobegin_nd` provides the only source of nondeterminism. Even within such a construct, the effect system guarantees that any block of code that is outside an atomic statement and does not execute any atomic statement (call this an *atomic-free section*) cannot interfere with any concurrent task. Therefore, programmers need not consider interactions between any atomic-free sections when reasoning about program behavior.

Put together, these observations mean that *the only source of multiple interleavings is from different orderings of atomic sections*, thereby significantly reducing the number of interleavings that programmers must consider. Furthermore, programmers can control the granularity of the atomic sections to control the number of possible interleavings.

The following example illustrates these observations (assume the `S` terms are all atomic-free statements).

```
cobegin_nd {
  { S11; S12; atomic S13 }
  { S21; atomic S22; S23 }
}
```

Even if all the statements are primitive operations (reads or writes), if sequential consistency is not guaranteed, then up to $6! = 720$ different interleavings are possible. If sequential consistency holds, then there are still up to 20 different interleavings. In our language, however, *we may consider only two sequentially consistent interleavings*: one with `atomic S13` appearing before `atomic S22`, and vice versa. For example, any execution generated by our language is equivalent to executing the entire first `cobegin_nd` branch before the entire second branch, or vice versa.

3.4 Performance: Removing Unneeded Barriers

We use a Software Transactional Memory (STM) runtime system to implement the `atomic` construct because STM provides weak atomicity, better composability than locks, and potentially better scalability because of optimistic rather than pessimistic synchronization. One key drawback of STMs is the overhead due to *transactional read and write barriers* for every load or store to shared data (e.g., see [52]). These barriers are snippets of code, often automatically inserted by a transactions-aware compiler, that invoke the STM runtime to implement some transactional concurrency control protocol. The barriers can either read and write shared memory directly (so-called *in-place update* STM) and *undo* all transactional operations when a transaction aborts, or they can buffer updates into a private data structure (so-called *write buffering* STM) and apply all the buffered changes into shared memory when a transaction successfully commits. In both cases, barriers can incur significant overhead and minimizing them is essential for performance.

We observe that we can use the region and effect system to remove unnecessary STM barriers, where there is no interference. However, the effect system as described so far does not carry enough information to perform this analysis locally. For example, suppose a method m reads a variable x inside an atomic section. Then the read needs a barrier if and only if m is invoked in some context where there is interference on x. There is no information in the method body that enables the compiler to make that judgment; interprocedural analysis would be required.

However, with a slight extension to the effect system, we can enable *local* reasoning about this kind of noninterference. Specifically, we have the effect system distinguish two kinds of regions: those that may interfere (and so need barriers everywhere) and those that cannot (and so do not need read barriers anywhere). We call the first kind *atomic regions*. The programmer can declare a region to be `atomic`, such as region `Mutable` on line 2 of Figure 2.

The key benefit is that, for a non-atomic region, the compiler can remove read barriers entirely and, assuming STM using in-place updates, it can turn write barriers into logging-only barriers (synchronization is not needed, because there is no interference, but transactions must still log the old value on writes, in case the transaction aborts). This completely eliminates the barrier overheads for read-only shared data. It also substantially reduces the barrier overheads for task-local data and noninterfering shared data.

To enable sound reasoning about atomic regions and barrier elimination, we require some constraints on the use of these regions. Any region declaration (field region, local region, or region parameter) may be declared to be atomic. We impose the following requirements:

- When instantiating a type, an atomic (respectively, non-atomic) region parameter may only be passed an atomic (respectively, non-atomic) region name as the argument. This is straightforward to enforce using the region declarations.
- A region that is involved in interfering effects must be declared atomic. This is enforced by the compiler as described below.

The barrier elimination also requires a refinement in the semantics of atomic effects described in the previous section. An effect in an atomic statement is marked atomic *only if it operates on an atomic region*. For example, the read of region `ReadOnly` in Figure 4 (due to the operation `tour.length()`) does not generate an atomic effect, even though it is inside the `atomic` block at line 4. The write to region `Mutable` does generate an atomic effect. If region `Mutable` had *not* been declared `atomic`, the write to `bestTour` would generate a non-atomic effect. The compiler would then flag the effect declaration at line 2 of Figure 4 as an error because an atomic effect does not cover a non-atomic effect, as noted earlier.

We can now explain how the last rule above is enforced. If a region is not marked atomic but has an effect that causes interference in some parallel construct, the compiler will detect an error either at the parallel construct or at the method effect summary. For example, if region `Mutable` were not marked `atomic`, the write to `bestTour` would generate a normal effect `writes Mutable`. This would cause the effect summary at line 2 of Figure 4 to be flagged as an error, as noted above. If the effect summary were changed to not mark the write effect atomic, then the call to `searchAllToursWithPrefix` at line 21 of Figure 2 would generate a nonatomic effect, and the compiler would report the interference there.

Programs	$\mathcal{P}$	::=	$\mathcal{R}^*\ \mathcal{C}^*\ e$
Classes	$\mathcal{C}$	::=	`class` C<ρ> $\{\ F^*\ M^*\ \}$
Region Names	$\mathcal{R}$	::=	`region` r
Fields	F	::=	$T\ f$ `in` R
Methods	M	::=	$T\ m(T\ x)\ E\ \{\ e\ \}$
Regions	R	::=	$r \mid \rho$
Types	T	::=	C<R>
Effects	E	::=	$\emptyset$ | `reads` R | `writes` R | $E \cup E$
Expressions	e	::=	`this.`f | `this.`f`=`e | e`.`$m(e)$ | v | `new` T | `seq(`e,e`)` | `cobegin(`e,e`)`
Variables	v	::=	`this` | x

Figure 5. Core language syntax. C, ρ, f, m, and x are identifiers.

4. Formal Semantics and Soundness

To make precise the ideas discussed in the previous section, we have studied three variants of the same formal language, each one building on the last:

1. The first variant, which we call the *deterministic language*, is a simple expression language with regions, effects, and deterministic parallel composition. It is a version of Core DPJ [17] simplified to focus on the key elements for this work.
2. The second variant, which we call the *deterministic-by-default language*, adds nondeterministic parallel composition, atomic expressions, and atomic effects to the deterministic language.
3. The third variant, which we call the *atomic regions language*, adds atomic regions for removing or simplifying transactional barriers.

Without loss of generality, we only include `cobegin` and `cobegin_nd` in these simple languages; the treatment for `foreach` and `foreach_nd` is similar.

4.1 Overview of Language Variants

We first explain the syntactic structure of all three languages, and we summarize the soundness guarantees that each one provides. In the following subsections, we explain the formal semantics of each language variant, state the soundness guarantees more formally, and sketch how the guarantees follow from the semantic definitions. The full details, including all the semantics rules and proofs of all the claims, may be found in the lead author's Ph.D. thesis [19].

Deterministic Language: Figure 5 gives the syntax of the deterministic language. A program $\mathcal{P}$ consists of zero or more region declarations, zero or more class definitions, and an expression to evaluate. A class $\mathcal{C}$ consists of a class name C, a region parameter ρ, zero or more field declarations, and zero or more method declarations. A field F specifies a type, a field name, and a region. A method M consists of a return type, a method name, a formal parameter type, a formal parameter, an effect, and an expression to

Effects	E	::=	... | atomic reads R | atomic writes R
Expressions	e	::=	... | cobegin_nd(e,e) | atomic e

Figure 6. Syntax of the deterministic-by-default language (extends Figure 5).

Regions	$\mathcal{R}$	::=	... | atomic region r
Classes	C	::=	... | class C<atomic ρ> { F^* M^* }

Figure 7. Syntax of the atomic regions language (extends Figure 6).

evaluate. A region R is either a region name r or a region parameter ρ. A type T is a class instantiated with a region parameter, C<R>. An effect E is a possibly empty union of read effects and write effects on regions.

For expressions e, we model field access, field assignment, method invocation, variables, new objects, sequential composition (`seq`), and deterministic parallel composition (`cobegin`). A variable v is `this` or a method formal parameter x. The operational semantics of the first five expressions in Figure 5 is exactly as in Java. The last two expressions evaluate both component expressions (either sequentially or in parallel) and return the value of the second component as the value of the entire expression.

The deterministic language provides the following semantic guarantees, stated more formally as Theorems 1–2 in Section 4.2. They follow from the fact that the executions of the two branches of any `cobegin` expression are required to be noninterfering:

1. *Equivalence of `cobegin` and `seq`:* In terms of the final result (final value produced and final heap state), there is no difference between executing `cobegin(`e,e'`)` and `seq(`e,e'`)`. As a consequence, the entire program is guaranteed to behave like a sequential program (the one that results by replacing `cobegin` everywhere with `seq`).
2. *Determinism:* If an expression e evaluates to completion, then the value it produces is deterministic. Moreover, if e is evaluated in a sequential context (i.e., not inside a `cobegin`), then the final heap state is deterministic. In particular, the final heap produced by a terminating execution of the whole program is deterministic.

Deterministic-by-Default Language: Figure 6 shows the additional syntax for the deterministic-by-default language. We extend the syntax of effects to record atomic effects. We also add (1) `cobegin_nd`, which is the same as `cobegin`, except that it allows interference guarded by atomic expressions; and (2) expressions `atomic` e, which signal that expression e should be executed in *isolation*: that is, as if it were executed all at once, with no interleavings from the rest of the execution.

The deterministic-by-default language provides the following semantic guarantees, stated more formally as Theorems 3–6 in Section 4.3:

1. *Race freedom and sequential consistency:* Program execution contains no data race. This result follows because the effect system requires that all parallel interference occur between pairs of accesses guarded by atomic expressions. Further, in the Java memory model, race freedom implies sequential consistency, i.e., one can reason about execution as a *program-ordered* interleaving of memory operations.
2. *Strong isolation:* For the same reason that the program is race free, expressions `atomic` e execute e in isolation, *even if the underlying implementation guarantees only weak isolation*. Moreover, the effect system disallows any interference between the `cobegin` and concurrent operations that would violate isolation of the `cobegin`. Therefore, every `cobegin` expression executes in isolation. Together, race freedom and strong isolation imply that execution is a sequentially consistent interleaving *of isolated expressions*.
3. *Equivalence of `cobegin` and `seq`:* Because `cobegin(`e,e'`)` executes in isolation, it is equivalent to an isolated execution of `seq`, i.e., `atomic seq(`e,e'`)`. As discussed in Section 3.3, for the deterministic-by-default language, we make `cobegin` behave like `atomic seq`, and not just `seq`, to guarantee that `cobegin` executes deterministically, *even inside a `cobegin_nd`.*
4. *Determinism by default:* Both atomic and cobegin expressions execute deterministically in the same sense as discussed for the deterministic language, *even inside a `cobegin_nd`, unless* they contain a dynamic instance of `cobegin_nd`.

Atomic Regions Language: The third variant of the formal language allows some regions to be marked `atomic`, and *only operations on those regions generate atomic effects.* Operations on nonatomic regions *never generate atomic effects, even in an atomic expression.* Figure 7 shows the new syntax.

The execution semantics of this language variant is identical to that of the deterministic-by-default language, except that the compiler can distinguish, and potentially optimize, operations within an atomic expression that never interfere with concurrent tasks. In Section 5, we discuss a prototype compiler that uses these rules to optimize our STM by omitting or simplifying barriers (inside an atomic expression) for such noninterfering operations.

4.2 Deterministic Language

Static Semantics: The typing is done with respect to an environment Γ, which consists of elements (v, T) stating that variable v has type T. The key rule for *subeffects* (i.e., when one effect conservatively summarizes another, written $\Gamma \vdash E \subseteq E'$), is that a write effect on region r covers a read effect on the same region r:

$$\text{SE-READS-WRITES} \quad \frac{}{\Gamma \vdash \texttt{reads}\ R \subseteq \texttt{writes}\ R}$$

The rules for typing programs, classes, fields, etc., are straightforward. The rule for typing methods enforces *effect subsumption*: that is, that a method's actual effect must be a subeffect of its declared effect:

$$\text{METHOD} \quad \frac{\Gamma \vdash T_r \quad \Gamma \vdash T_x \quad \Gamma \vdash E \quad \Gamma \cup (x, T_x) \vdash e : T_r, E' \quad \Gamma \vdash E' \subseteq E}{\Gamma \vdash T_r\ m(T_x\ x)\ E\ \{\ e\ \}}$$

The key rules for *noninterfering effects* (i.e., effects that may safely go in parallel, with deterministic composition, written $\Gamma \vdash E \# E'$) are that reads never interfere with reads, and writes never interfere with reads or writes to different regions:

$$\text{NI-READS} \quad \frac{}{\Gamma \vdash \texttt{reads}\ r \# \texttt{reads}\ r'} \qquad \text{NI-WRITES} \quad \frac{r \neq r'}{\Gamma \vdash \texttt{writes}\ r \# \texttt{writes}\ r'}$$

$$\text{NI-READS-WRITES} \quad \frac{r \neq r'}{\Gamma \vdash \texttt{reads}\ r \# \texttt{writes}\ r'}$$

As in Core DPJ [17, 19], every expression has a type and an effect. The rules for typing expressions e with type T and effect E ($\Gamma \vdash e : T, E$) are straightforward. The most important rule says that in parallel composition, the effects of the expressions being evaluated in parallel must be noninterfering:

$$\text{COBEGIN} \quad \frac{\Gamma \vdash e : T, E \quad \Gamma \vdash e' : T', E' \quad \Gamma \vdash E \# E'}{\Gamma \vdash \texttt{cobegin}(e, e') : T', E \cup E'}$$

Dynamic Semantics: We give a small-step operational semantics describing the recursive reduction of expressions.

Execution State: The execution state is (e, H), consisting of an expression to evaluate and a heap. A heap H is a partial function from object references to pairs (O, T), where O is an object, and T is the type of O. An object O is a mapping from field names f to object references o. null is a special reference that is in $\mathsf{Dom}(H)$ but does not map to an object. Attempting to invoke a method of null causes the execution to fail. We extend the static syntax of expressions to represent computations:

$$e ::= \ldots \mid o \mid (e, \Sigma, E) \mid e_i$$

The additional expressions have the following meanings: object references o are the values produced by reducing expressions; a *local execution state* (e, Σ, E) records an expression e to evaluate, an environment Σ containing the bindings for the free variables in e, and an effect E of reducing e; and the indices i enable us to say unambiguously which expression is reduced in a given execution step, as explained below.

A program execution is a sequence of steps

$$((e_{\mathcal{P}}, \emptyset, \emptyset)_i, \mathsf{null}) \rightarrow^* (e_i, H),$$

for some i, e, and H, where $e_{\mathcal{P}}$ is the main program expression, i is an arbitrary index denoting the top-level expression in the reduction, e_i is the evolution of expression $(e_{\mathcal{P}}, \emptyset, \emptyset)_i$, and H is the evolved heap (represented as a domain containing `null` plus all object references o added during the execution). A terminating execution has $e_i = (o, \emptyset, E)_i$, where o is the "answer" computed by the program, and E is the union of all effects on H done in the execution.

Expression Semantics: Field access and assignment work in the standard way, except that we track dynamic effects, to state and prove the soundness results. As an example of the effect tracking, we give the rule for field access:

DYN-FIELD-ACCESS
$$\frac{(\mathtt{this}, o) \in \Sigma \quad H(o) = (O, C\texttt{<}r\texttt{>}) \quad F(C, f) = T\ f\ \mathtt{in}\ R}{((\mathtt{this}.f, \Sigma, \emptyset), H) \rightarrow ((O(f), \Sigma, \mathtt{reads}\ \sigma_{C<r>}(R)), H)}$$

The function $\sigma_{C<r>}$ substitutes the region argument r for the parameter ρ of class C. The rule for field assignment is similar, except that the right-hand-side subexpression is evaluated first, the heap is updated, and the effect is a write instead of a read.

For evaluation of subexpressions, we use the following standard rule:

DYN-SUBEXP
$$\frac{(e, H) \rightarrow (e', H')}{(e'', H) \rightarrow (e''[e_i \leftarrow e'_i], H')}$$

It says that if we can reduce expression e to e' starting with heap H, and e appears with index i as a subexpression of e'', then we can reduce e'' by rewriting the subexpression e_i in place and updating the heap.

The rules for `cobegin` illustrate subexpression evaluation:

DYN-COBEGIN-EVAL
$$\frac{\mathsf{fresh}(i) \quad \mathsf{fresh}(j)}{((\mathtt{cobegin}(e,e'), \Sigma, \emptyset), H) \rightarrow (\mathtt{cobegin}((e, \Sigma, \emptyset)_i, (e', \Sigma, \emptyset)_j), H)}$$

DYN-COBEGIN-ACCUMULATE
$$\frac{}{(\mathtt{cobegin}((o, \Sigma, E)_i, (o', \Sigma, E')_j), H) \rightarrow ((o', \Sigma, E \cup E'), H)}$$

DYN-COBEGIN-EVAL creates two new subexpressions with fresh indices i and j for evaluation in environment Σ. The evaluation steps of e_i and e_j can be arbitrarily interleaved, via rule DYN-SUBEXP. This interleaving models the parallelism. When both are done, DYN-COBEGIN-ACCUMULATE accumulates the results into the top-level expression. Field assignment, method invocation, and sequential composition are similar, except that the subexpressions are evaluated in a fixed sequential order (so there is no parallelism, except inside a `cobegin`). The rules are entirely standard, and are stated in full in the thesis.

Soundness Results: As summarized in Section 4.1, there are two main soundness results for the core deterministic language. To state the results, we call out the reduction of a particular expression inside the evolution of the whole program. We write

$$((e, \Sigma, \emptyset)_i, H) \rightsquigarrow_{\mathcal{P}} (e'_i, H')$$

to denote a *reduction of expression* i occurring in program execution. That means $\mathcal{P}$ is well-typed with main expression $e_{\mathcal{P}}$, and there is a program execution

$$((e_{\mathcal{P}}, \emptyset, \emptyset)_j, \mathsf{null}) \rightarrow^* (e''_j, H) \rightarrow^* (e'''_j, H'),$$

such that e''_j contains $(e, \Sigma, \emptyset)_i$, which is the first appearance of expression i in the execution; and e'''_j contains e'_i. (e''_j, H) is called the *initial state* of the reduction, and (e'_j, H') is called the *final state*.

Our first result states that there is no semantic difference in this language between `seq` and `cobegin`: at any point in the execution that is an initial state for a `cobegin` reduction, we can replace `cobegin` with `seq` and get exactly the same results. The proof follows directly from the noninterference property guaranteed by the static and dynamic semantics.

Theorem 1 (Equivalence of `cobegin` and `seq`).

$$((\mathit{cobegin}(e, e'), \Sigma, \emptyset)_i, H) \rightsquigarrow_{\mathcal{P}} ((o, \Sigma, E)_i, H')$$

if and only if

$$((\mathit{seq}(e, e'), \Sigma, \emptyset)_i, H) \rightsquigarrow_{\mathcal{P}} ((o, \Sigma, E)_i, H')$$

with the same initial state, except that expression i is as shown.

The second result states that expression evaluation is input-output deterministic, up to the choice of object reference names. The proof follows from the fact that once `cobegin` is replaced by `seq` everywhere according to Theorem 1, the only nondeterminism left in the rules is the choice of reference names and expression indices.

Theorem 2 (Input-Output Determinism). *If $((e, \Sigma, \emptyset)_j, H) \rightsquigarrow_{\mathcal{P}} ((o, \Sigma, E)_j, H')$ and $((e, \Sigma, \emptyset)_j, H) \rightsquigarrow_{\mathcal{P}} ((o', \Sigma, E')_j, H'')$ with the same initial state, then $o \cong o'$, where $\cong$ denotes equivalence up to renaming object references, and $E = E'$. Moreover, if $(e, \Sigma, \emptyset)_j$ is not a subexpression of any* `cobegin` *expression, then $H \cong H'$.*

4.3 Deterministic-by-Default Language

Static Semantics: Figure 8 gives the static semantics of atomic effects. Rule SE-ATOMIC-1 formally expresses the idea that non-atomic effects cover atomic effects: that is, if E occurred in an atomic expression, then we can summarize the effect as either `atomic` E or E. Note that the converse is not true, because we cannot soundly report an atomic effect where there is no atomic expression. Rule SE-ATOMIC-2 provides the subeffect relation for two atomic effects. Rule NI-ATOMIC says that an atomic effect is noninterfering if the underlying effect is.

The judgment $\Gamma \vdash \mathsf{nondet}(E, E')$ states that it is safe to run expressions with effects E and E' nondeterministically in parallel, inside a `cobegin_nd`. Figure 8 gives the key rules for making the judgment.

Figure 9 gives the rules for typing nondeterministic parallel composition and atomic expressions. Rule COBEGIN_ND is similar to COBEGIN, except that interfering effects are allowed if they

$\boxed{\Gamma \vdash E \subseteq E'}$

SE-ATOMIC-1 $\dfrac{\Gamma \vdash E \subseteq E'}{\Gamma \vdash \texttt{atomic}\ E \subseteq E'}$ SE-ATOMIC-2 $\dfrac{\Gamma \vdash E \subseteq E'}{\Gamma \vdash \texttt{atomic}\ E \subseteq \texttt{atomic}\ E'}$

$\boxed{\Gamma \vdash E \# E'}$ NI-ATOMIC $\dfrac{\Gamma \vdash E \# E'}{\Gamma \vdash \texttt{atomic}\ E \# E'}$

$\boxed{\Gamma \vdash \mathsf{nondet}(E, E')}$ NONDET-NI $\dfrac{\Gamma \vdash E \# E'}{\Gamma \vdash \mathsf{nondet}(E, E')}$

NONDET-ATOMIC $\dfrac{}{\Gamma \vdash \mathsf{nondet}(\texttt{atomic}\ E, \texttt{atomic}\ E')}$

Figure 8. Static semantics of atomic effects (selected rules).

$\boxed{\Gamma \vdash e : T, E}$

COBEGIN_ND $\dfrac{\Gamma \vdash e : T, E \quad \Gamma \vdash e' : T', E' \quad \Gamma \vdash \mathsf{nondet}(E, E')}{\Gamma \vdash \texttt{cobegin\_nd}(e,e') : T', E \cup E'}$

ATOMIC $\dfrac{\Gamma \vdash e : T, E \quad \Gamma \vdash \mathsf{atomic}(E) = E'}{\Gamma \vdash \texttt{atomic}\ e : T, E'}$

COBEGIN $\dfrac{\Gamma \vdash e : T, E \quad \Gamma \vdash e' : T', E' \quad \Gamma \vdash E \# E'}{\Gamma \vdash \texttt{cobegin}(e,e') : T', \mathsf{nonatomic}(E \cup E', \Gamma)}$

$\boxed{\Gamma \vdash \mathsf{atomic}(E) = E'}$ ATOMIC-READS $\dfrac{}{\Gamma \vdash \mathsf{atomic}(\texttt{reads}\ R) = \texttt{atomic reads}\ R}$

$\boxed{\mathsf{nonatomic}(E, \Gamma)}$ NONATOMIC-ATOMIC $\dfrac{}{\Gamma \vdash \mathsf{nonatomic}(\texttt{atomic}\ E) = E}$

Figure 9. Static semantics of `cobegin_nd` and atomic expressions (selected rules). The judgment $\Gamma \vdash \mathsf{atomic}(E) = E'$ says that E' is the effect obtained after adding `atomic` from all reads and writes in E; and $\Gamma \vdash \mathsf{nonatomic}(E)$ is the reverse.

are both guarded by atomic expressions. Rule ATOMIC collects the effect E of the expression e, then marks all the constituent read and write effects atomic, to reflect the fact that E is occurring in an atomic expression. Finally, rule COBEGIN has changed. In addition to checking noninterference, as in the basic language, the new rule converts all atomic effects occurring inside the `cobegin` to ordinary effects using the judgment $\Gamma \vdash \mathsf{nonatomic}(E) = E'$. This ensures that *no atomic effects are ever propagated outward from inside a* `cobegin`. The last rule is key to ensuring that `cobegin` executes in isolation, as discussed in Section 3.3.

Dynamic Semantics: We describe the dynamic semantics of the nondeterministic language in two parts, the first operational and the second non-operational. The first, operational, part is just the same semantics as for the basic language (Section 4.2), with a few minor adjustments to accommodate the new features. The second, non-operational part, describes a *weak isolation constraint* on execution histories generated by the operational part. The overall dynamic semantics comprises all execution histories described by the operational semantics that also satisfy weak isolation. In practice, weak isolation would be enforced by a runtime implementation (such as software transactional memory [37]).

Operational Semantics of Expressions: The operational semantics is identical to the one described in Section 4.2, with three changes. First, we add a rule to execute `cobegin_nd`; it is identical to the rule for `cobegin` shown in Section 4.2 (i.e., in the operational semantics, there is no difference between executing `cobegin_nd` and `cobegin` — the difference is all in the static semantics).

Second, we add a rule for executing an expression `atomic` e. We execute e, then mark all its effects atomic, for purposes of effect tracking:

DYN-ATOMIC-EVAL
$$\frac{\mathsf{fresh}(i)}{((\texttt{atomic}\ e, \Sigma, \emptyset), H) \to (\texttt{atomic}\ (e, \Sigma, \emptyset)_i, H)}$$

DYN-ATOMIC-MARK-EFFECTS
$$\frac{\emptyset \vdash \mathsf{atomic}(E) = E'}{(\texttt{atomic}\ (o, \Sigma, E)_i, H) \to ((o, \Sigma, E'), H)}$$

Finally, we modify the rule DYN-COBEGIN-ACCUMULATE (shown in Section 4.2) to mark the effects of a `cobegin` expression non-atomic:

DYN-COBEGIN-ACCUMULATE
$$\frac{\emptyset \vdash \mathsf{nonatomic}(E \cup E') = E''}{(\texttt{cobegin}((o, \Sigma, E)_i, (o', \Sigma, E')_j), H) \to ((o', \Sigma, E''), H)}$$

Weak Isolation Constraint: To state the weak isolation constraint, we need the concept of a *reduction history* $\mathbf{H}$, which is a sequence of program execution steps witnessing $((e, \Sigma, \emptyset)_i, H) \rightsquigarrow_{\mathcal{P}} (e'_i, H)$. If $((e, \Sigma, \emptyset)_i), H)$ is the initial program state, then we call $\mathbf{H}$ a *program execution history* and write $\mathbf{H}_{\mathcal{P}}$. Two histories occur *in parallel under* `cobegin` (or `cobegin_nd`) if they each occur in reducing different branches of the same `cobegin` (or `cobegin_nd`) expression, in the same program execution.

Definition 1 (Conflict relation on atomic expressions). *Fix a program execution history $\mathbf{H}_{\mathcal{P}}$, and let I be the set of expression indices appearing in $\mathbf{H}_{\mathcal{P}}$ that label atomic expressions (i.e., expressions introduced by rule* DYN-ATOMIC-EVAL*). The* ***conflict relation on atomic expressions in*** $\mathbf{H}_{\mathcal{P}}$ *is the transitive closure of the following relation on $I \times I$: (i, j) is in the relation if $i \neq j$, and there are conflicting memory accesses a_i and a_j such that (a) a_i occurs in the reduction of an atomic expression e_i; (b) a_j occurs in the reduction of an atomic expression e_j; (c) the reductions of e_i and e_j occur in parallel under* `cobegin_nd`*, and (d) a_i precedes a_j in $\mathbf{H}_{\mathcal{P}}$.*

Notice that we put the relation *only on operations under* `cobegin_nd`*, not under* `cobegin`; and we *do not include any conflicts occurring outside of atomic expressions*. That is because the type system will ensure there are no conflicts between `cobegin` tasks or outside of atomic expressions; this is the soundness result that we state below.

Now we can define the weak isolation constraint on executions in the language. For the remainder of this section, we assume an implementation that guarantees weakly isolated program execution histories $\mathbf{H}_{\mathcal{P}}$.

Definition 2 (Weakly isolated histories). *Let $\mathbf{H}$ be a history. If the conflict relation on atomic expressions in $\mathbf{H}$ is a partial order, then we say that $\mathbf{H}$ is* ***weakly isolated****.*

Soundness Results: As summarized in Section 4.1, there are three main soundness results for the nondeterministic language: race freedom, strong isolation, and determinism by default.

Race Freedom: The first result says that the language is race free, assuming that pairs of memory accesses in different atomic expressions are well-synchronized (which is true of any transactional implementation). The proof follows from the fact that the type system disallows parallel interference, except for pairs of accesses both occurring in atomic expressions.

Theorem 3 (Race freedom). *If $\vdash \mathcal{P}$, then a history $\mathbf{H}_{\mathcal{P}}$ that has synchronization orderings consistent with the conflict relation stated in Definition 1, contains no data race.*

Strong Isolation: To state the strong isolation result formally, we use the well-known concept of *serializable histories* [44]. We say that a history $\mathbf{H}$ witnessing $((e, \Sigma, \emptyset)_i, H) \leadsto_{\mathcal{P}} (e'_i, H')$ is *serial with respect to expression* i if every step in the history transforms expression i or a subexpression of expression i. We say that $\mathbf{H}$ is *serializable with respect to expression* i if it is possible to generate a history $\mathbf{H}'$ with the same initial and final states as $\mathbf{H}$ that contains a serial history witnessing $((e, \Sigma, \emptyset)_i, H'') \leadsto_{\mathcal{P}} (e'_i, H''')$, for some heaps H'' and H'''. In other words, an expression reduction is serializable if we "could have done it serially," with the same results.

The following theorem says that a history is serializable if it does not occur in a `cobegin_nd`; or it does not reduce any atomic expression; or it reduces a `cobegin` or atomic expression. The proof follows from the type system's guarantees of noninterference for `cobegin` tasks, and noninterference for `cobegin_nd` tasks except where guarded by atomic expressions; together with the weak isolation assumption for atomic expressions.

Theorem 4 (Strong isolation). *Suppose $\vdash \mathcal{P}$, let $\mathbf{H}_{\mathcal{P}}$ be a weakly isolated history executing $\mathcal{P}$, and let $\mathbf{H}$ be a history witnessing $((e, \Sigma, \emptyset)_i, H) \leadsto_{\mathcal{P}} (e'_i, H')$ contained in $\mathbf{H}_{\mathcal{P}}$. Then $\mathbf{H}$ is serializable with respect to expression i if (1) $(e, \Sigma, \emptyset)_i$ is not a subexpression of any `cobegin_nd` expression; or (2) no atomic expression appears in $\mathbf{H}$; or (3) e is a `cobegin` or atomic expression.*

Determinism by Default: Finally, we show that the nondeterministic language is deterministic by default. First we show the equivalent of Theorem 1 for the nondeterministic language: there is no difference between `cobegin` e and `atomic seq` e. Note that we need the `atomic` here because in general a `seq` occurring under a `cobegin_nd` can interfere with the other branch of the `cobegin_nd`. The result follows directly from Theorem 1 and Theorem 4. ("Initial state" is defined before Theorem 1.)

Theorem 5 (Semantic equivalence of `cobegin` and `atomic seq`).

$$((\mathit{cobegin}(e, e'), \Sigma, \emptyset)_i, H) \leadsto_{\mathcal{P}} ((o, \Sigma, E)_i, H')$$

if and only if

$$((\mathit{atomic\ seq}(e, e'), \Sigma, \emptyset)_i, H) \leadsto_{\mathcal{P}} ((o, \Sigma, E)_i, H')$$

with the same initial state, except that expression i is as shown.

Second, we show the equivalent of Theorem 2 for the nondeterministic language: for the expressions called out by Theorem 4 as having serializable reductions, the execution of such expressions is also input-output deterministic, *unless* there is explicit nondeterminism via `cobegin_nd`. The proof follows from Theorem 2, together with the definition of a serializable history.

Theorem 6 (Determinism by default). *Suppose $\vdash \mathcal{P}$, and let $\mathbf{H}$ be a history witnessing $((e, \Sigma, \emptyset)_i, H) \leadsto_{\mathcal{P}} ((o, \Sigma, E)_i, H')$ that is serializable with respect to expression i, where no `cobegin_nd` expression ever appears in expression i. If $((e, \Sigma, \emptyset)_i, H) \leadsto_{\mathcal{P}} ((o', \Sigma, E')_i, H'')$ with the same initial state as in $\mathbf{H}$, then $o \cong o$, where $\cong$ denotes equivalence up to renaming object references, and $E = E'$. Moreover, if $(e, \Sigma, \emptyset)_i$ is not a subexpression of any `cobegin` or `cobegin_nd` expression, then $H' \cong H''$.*

4.4 Atomic Regions Language

Static Semantics: First, the rules for constructing types require that atomic regions bind only to region parameters declared `atomic`, and non-atomic regions bind only to region parameters not declared `atomic`. This requirement ensures that memory regions are treated consistently across method invocation. Second, we refine the judgment $\Gamma \vdash \mathsf{atomic}(E) = E'$ so that an atomic expression "makes an effect atomic" only if the effect is on an atomic region. This rule ensures that, in applying rule COBEGIN_ND to check a `cobegin_nd` expression, the compiler will never allow effects on non-atomic regions to interfere. The rules are stated in full in the thesis.

Dynamic Semantics and Soundness: The dynamic semantics of this language is exactly as given in the previous section, with two changes. First, marking effects in rule DYN-ATOMIC-MARK-EFFECTS happens according to the refined definition of $\emptyset \vdash \mathsf{atomic}(E) = E'$: that is, effects are marked atomic only if they operate on atomic regions. Second, we redefine the conflict relation on atomic expressions (Definition 1) so that only conflicts involving accesses to statically identifiable atomic regions (i.e., region names r or region parameters ρ marked `atomic`) are synchronized by the implementation. The soundness result says that Theorems 3–6 hold for this language variant; the proofs, given in the thesis, are entirely straightforward.

5. Prototype Implementation

To implement our new mechanisms, we extended the compiler used for basic DPJ. It is a modified version of Sun's `javac`, which translates DPJ code to standard Java. The compiler implements DPJ's parallelism constructs by generating calls to the `ForkJoinTask` library [2], which schedules tasks onto a pool of worker threads; further details are available in [17].

In this work, we extended the compiler to implement atomic blocks using the Deuce STM library [3]. We used the well-respected Transactional Locking II (TL2) algorithm [28]. TL2 is a write-buffering (i.e., lazy versioning) algorithm with optimistic reads. Deuce supports concurrency control at the object field level, and uses a light-weight, custom reflection mechanism to access object fields inside transactions.

We selected this STM system for pragmatic reasons of ease of implementation, and because it implements a well-known high-performance STM algorithm. We have not attempted to maximize absolute performance in our implementation; it could be improved significantly by using a different STM system, such as one integrated with the JVM [46]. Our method is applicable to other types of STM systems and algorithms (including those utilizing in-place updates).

For each atomic block, the compiler generates code to execute the body of the atomic block as a transaction, retrying until the transaction commits successfully. Nested atomic blocks are flattened. Methods that are transitively callable within atomic blocks are cloned; versions containing barriers are used when they are called within atomic blocks. Within atomic blocks, the compiler inserts normal read and write barriers for accesses to fields in atomic regions. As discussed in section 3.4, the compiler omits barriers for read accesses to non-atomic regions, and it generates logging-only barriers for write accesses.

We modified the TL2 implementation in Deuce to support these optimized logging-only barriers. However, because TL2 is a write-buffering algorithm, we would have to use read-barriers to obtain correct values in the read-after-write cases. To avoid read barriers entirely, we modified the algorithm to perform in-place updates for these locations and we maintain a separate undo log to revert effects of such updates in case the transaction aborts. Reads to such locations do not need barriers because they can now obtain their values directly from the original memory location.

6. Evaluation

The ideas presented in this paper raise four key questions for experimental investigation: (1) Can the language express nondeterministic algorithms in a natural way? (2) Can the algorithms expressed in the language give good performance? (3) How effective is the optimization of STM barriers? (4) What is the annotation overhead of the language?

We used four nondeterministic algorithms to evaluate these questions: two different versions of TSP, Delaunay mesh triangulation from the *Lonestar Benchmarks* [1], and *OO7*, a synthetic database benchmark that has been used in previous studies of parallel performance [47, 51]. These codes are discussed further below.

6.1 Benchmarks and Expressing Parallelism

Traveling Salesman Problem: We studied two versions of the TSP algorithm, which we call **TSP-PQ** and **TSP-R**. TSP-PQ is the algorithm described in Section 3. As discussed there, the algorithm proceeds in two phases: the first phase breaks the problem up into subproblems and adds them to a priority queue, and the second phase concurrently removes items from the queue and processes each one using sequential recursive search. The priority queue orders the work, so that more promising subtrees are explored first.

TSP-R is a variant that eliminates the priority queue and uses recursion to express the entire algorithm. At each level of the tree, the algorithm computes a bound for each subtree and compares the bound against the global current best tour. Bounds that are definitely no better than the current best are excluded, while bounds that may be better are explored recursively. The recursion occurs in parallel until a specified depth of the tree; in our studies we used a depth varying with the log of the number of threads. TSP-R is a simpler algorithm than TSP-PQ, but it potentially suffers from more contention, as the global best tour must be read before every recursive descent into a subtree to avoid exploring too many bad paths. By contrast, because TSP-PQ uses a priority queue to order the paths, it can read the global best tour less often (once per tree level).

We adapted both versions of TSP from code that was used in previous studies of STM performance [46, 47]. Our TSP-PQ code uses the identical algorithm to the original code, and expresses the parallelism in the same way. The original code had a data race, and we added one extra atomic block to eliminate that race. Our TSP-R code is a transformation of TSP-PQ that eliminates the priority queue, checks the bound at each level of the tree, and parallelizes the recursion.

Delaunay Mesh Refinement: This code uses Chew's algorithm [26, 36] to find and eliminate "bad triangles," i.e., those that do not satisfy some quality constraint from a Delaunay triangulation of a mesh of points. The program is nondeterministic since different orders of processing of bad elements lead to different meshes, although all such meshes satisfy the quality constraints [26]. The program uses a `foreach_nd` loop, and each iteration of the loop spawns a new worker thread (at most one per core). Each worker thread has a private worklist of bad triangles. In each iteration of the worklist loop, the worker selects one bad triangle from the work list, forms a *cavity* around it, re-triangulates the cavity, and adds any new bad triangles back to the worklist. Cavity finding and re-triangulating code sections access the shared mesh data structure and are enclosed in atomic blocks.

OO7: OO7 simulates a number of clients, each performing a fixed number of queries on an in-memory database. Each query is enclosed in an atomic block. The performance metric is the throughput (queries per unit time), and we measure how this scales by varying the number of clients while keeping the number of queries performed by each one constant. The program uses a `foreach_nd` loop, with one iteration corresponding to each client. We configured it to use a number of clients equal to the number of worker threads, so there is always one thread per client. Thus, the total amount of work performed is proportional to the number of threads.

Expressing Parallelism: We successfully expressed *all* the parallelism that did not use data races, in these four nondeterministic algorithms. As discussed above, we eliminated a race in TSP-PQ that was presumably there to avoid synchronization; we could have also written TSP-R with a similar race. The four codes do not use any deterministic algorithms but such algorithms do not incur any runtime performance overheads in our language; such overheads are dominated by that of atomic sections in nondeterministic components. The performance and expressivity of the language for deterministic algorithms were studied previously [17].

6.2 Performance

To evaluate performance, we measured the self-relative speedup (i.e., the speedup compared to running the transactional code on one thread) achieved by the three codes. We focused on self-relative speedup rather than absolute speedup because (a) optimizing the code generation for atomic statements has not been a focus of this paper, and (b) the Deuce STM, although using a good *algorithm*, lacks many many essential performance features of a high performance Java STM [46]. Self-relative speedups have the effect of "factoring out" some of the performance impact of the STM implementation while capturing the scalability of the benchmarks.

We ran and measured the codes on a 24-core system using four Intel Xeon E7450 processors (each with six cores), running Windows Server 2008. Figure 10 shows the self-relative speedups with barrier optimizations enabled, using running times for Delaunay and TSP, and throughput scaling for OO7. Because the runtimes are nondeterministic, we averaged 5–10 runs for each data point, using an interquartile method to exclude a few extreme outliers. For both TSP variants, we used the one-thread version of TSP-PQ, which was the faster of the two, as the baseline. Both versions of TSP show good scaling, and OO7 shows moderately good scaling, throughout the range of numbers of threads t we examined. TSP-R shows better (superlinear) speedup for smaller t; this is because the parallel algorithm is very efficient in that range: it rules out subtrees quickly, and so visits only about $1/4$ of the tree nodes at $t = 2$ compared to $t = 1$. However, the scaling curve for TSP-R flattens out as t increases, most likely due to higher contention than TSP-PQ.

The speedup curve for Delaunay is poor: it flattens out and reaches only 3x on 22 threads. We profiled the code to understand the source of this behavior and traced it to the method `System.identityHashcode()` in the JVM. This standard Java function is extensively used in Deuce to index into lock tables. We observed that the time spent in this function grows with the number of threads. In Delaunay, which has large transactions, this overhead negatively affected the speedup curve. This problem can by solved by modifying the JVM, but we leave that (and other optimizations for `atomic`) to future work.

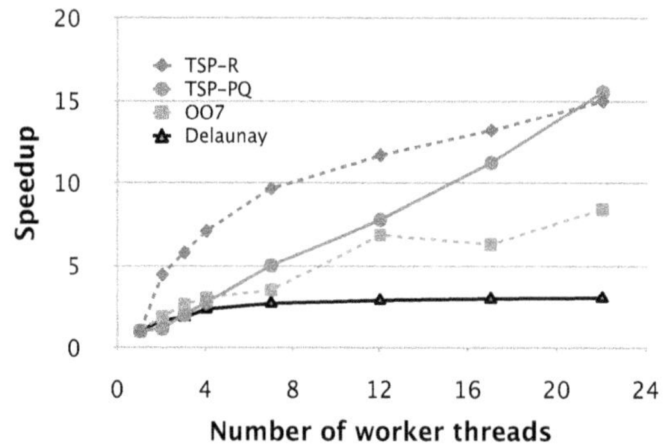

Figure 10. Self-relative speedups. For OO7, we scaled the amount of work with the number of worker threads, and measured speedup based on throughput scaling (number of queries done per unit time). The barrier optimization was enabled for all of these benchmarks.

6.3 Impact of Barrier Elimination

We compared the performance of two versions of the parallel code for each benchmark: with and without the barrier simplification optimization for non-atomic regions. Figure 11 shows the improvement in running time for the optimized code compared to the unoptimized code. Figure 12 shows the reduction in the number of dynamically-executed barriers due to our optimizations.

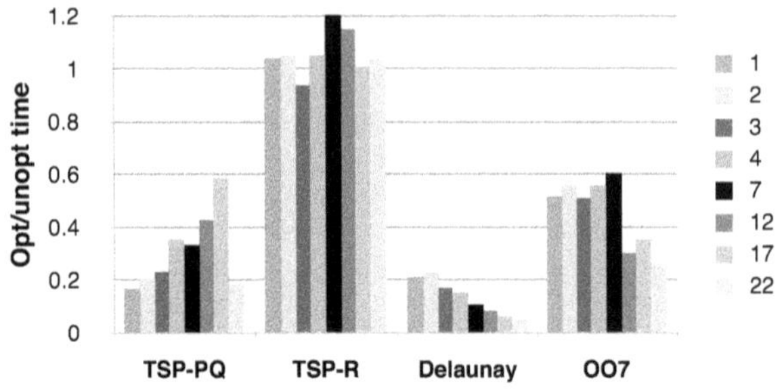

Figure 11. Ratio of optimized runtimes (with barrier elimination) to unoptimized runtimes (without barrier elimination). A value lower than 1 means the optimization increased performance.

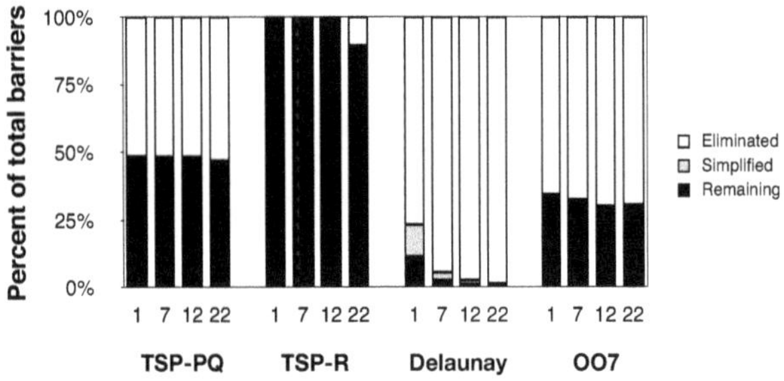

Figure 12. Reduction in barriers due to optimizations, showing the proportion of barriers from the unoptimized version that are eliminated entirely, simplified to log-only write barriers, or that remain as full barriers in the optimized version, for each of the three benchmarks with 1, 7, 12, and 22 worker threads.

The optimization has a substantial impact on performance for three of the four benchmarks (TSP-PQ, Delaunay, and OO7). The performance improvements correlate well with the barrier reductions. The optimizations give essentially no improvement for TSP-R, because the transactions are very short (reads and read-modify-write operations on the best tour). As a result (1) there are few if any barriers to remove; and (2) transactional overhead is not a significant component of the overall runtime. On the other hand, TSP-PQ, OO7, and Delaunay use longer transactions, providing more opportunities for reducing overhead.

Our optimizations can eliminate barriers both by actually removing barrier operations on certain statements and also by reducing the number of times that transactions must be retried. The latter effect occurs because removing unnecessary barriers reduces the number of false conflicts incurred by the STM system. As shown in Table 1, this effect is more pronounced with larger numbers of worker threads, so our optimizations not only reduce scalar overheads but also improve scalability. For example, in Delaunay, the optimization changed this ratio from 0.944 to 0.999 on 2 threads but from 0.244 to 0.944 on 22 threads.

	Delaunay		OO7	
threads	opt	unopt	opt	unopt
2	0.999	0.944	0.944	0.932
3	0.975	0.848	0.877	0.872
4	0.998	0.810	0.822	0.560
7	0.993	0.647	0.700	0.210
12	0.996	0.405	0.539	0.100
17	0.995	0.291	0.442	0.071
22	0.994	0.244	0.369	0.071

Table 1. Ratio of committed transactions to started transactions for Delaunay and OO7. Lower numbers indicate more aborted transactions. For both versions of TSP, all numbers are 1.000.

Program	Total SLOC	Annotated SLOC	Region Decls	RPLs	Params	Effect Summ.
TSP-PQ	433	77 (17.8%)	2(1)	101(4)	6(2)	14/20
TSP-R	200	34 (17%)	2(1)	42(4)	2(0)	6/12
OO7	1570	105 (6.7%)	4(1)	76(7)	6(0)	52/104
Delaunay	1994	302 (15.1%)	3(1)	374(3)	21(7)	165/216
Total	4197	518 (12.3%)	11(4)	593(18)	35(9)	237/352

Table 2. Annotation counts for the four benchmarks. In the middle columns, the numbers in parentheses represent the number of annotations marked `atomic`. In the last column, x/y means of y total method definitions in the program, x were annotated with effect summaries.

6.4 Annotation Overhead

Table 2 provides a quantitative measure of the annotation overhead of writing the four benchmarks in our language. Column 1 after the vertical bar shows the total number of non-blank, non-comment lines of source code, counted by `sloccount`. Column 2 gives the count of annotated lines, as an absolute number and as a percentage of the total lines. The following three columns show the number of region declarations, RPLs (including arguments to `in`, arguments to types and methods, and arguments to effect summaries), and region parameters. The number of annotations marked `atomic` is shown in parentheses after the main number. The last column shows the number of effect summaries before the slash, and the number of method definitions after the slash.

While the average number of annotated lines (12.3%) is nontrivial, we believe it is not unduly high, given the strong safety properties of the programming model. As in our prior work [17], most of the RPL annotations were arguments to types. The overhead could be reduced by inferring some of the annotations [48], but we leave that for future work.

Our approach does impose the limitation that if a programmer wishes to use a class region parameter as an atomic region in some context and a non-atomic region in some other context, then the class must be *cloned*: the programmer must create two copies of the class, one with the atomic parameter and one with the non-atomic parameter. The cloning is required because different barriers must be generated for methods of the class that operate transactionally on the parameter, depending on whether the region bound to the parameter is atomic. The cloning could be done automatically by the compiler, similarly to what C++ does for templates. While we have not implemented this approach, we believe it does not raise any significant technical issues.

In the benchmarks we studied, only Delaunay required class cloning. In Delaunay, we needed both atomic and non-atomic versions of the list and map structures used in the benchmark.

7. Related Work

Type and Effect Systems: Several researchers have described effect systems for enforcing a locking discipline in nondeterministic programs that prevents data races and deadlocks [5, 20, 34] or guarantees isolation for critical sections [29]. Matsakis et al. [41] have recently proposed a type system that guarantees race-freedom for locks and other synchronization constructs using a construct called an "interval" for expressing parallelism. While there is some overlap with our work in the guarantees provided (race freedom, deadlock freedom, and isolation), the mechanisms are very different (explicit synchronization vs. atomic statements supported by STM). Further, these systems do not provide determinism by default. Finally, there is no other effect system we know of that provides both race freedom *and* strong isolation together.

STM Correctness (Language): STM Haskell [31] provides an isolation guarantee, but for a pure functional language that uses monads to limit effects to the transactional store, unlike our imperative shared-memory language. Moore and Grossman [42] and Abadi et al. [6] use types and effects to guarantee strong isolation for an imperative language, but their languages permit races where neither access occurs in a transaction. Finally, none of these languages allows both transactional and non-transactional effects to the same memory, as our language does.

Beckman et al. [12] show how to use a form of alias control called *access permissions* [21] to verify that the placement of atomic blocks in a threaded program respects the invariants of a specification written by the programmer — for example, that a condition is checked and acted upon atomically. This approach is complementary to ours: we provide guarantees of race freedom, strong isolation, and determinism by default for all programs in our language; on top of that one could check that additional programmer-specified invariants are satisfied.

STM Correctness (Compiler and Runtime): Several STMs guarantee strong isolation by preventing interference between transactions and non-transactional accesses at runtime. Most of these systems use a combination of sophisticated static whole-program analysis, runtime optimizations, and other runtime techniques like page protection to optimize strong isolation [7, 22, 46, 47]. While these techniques can significantly reduce the cost of strong isolation, they cannot completely eliminate it. In contrast, our language-based approach provides strong isolation without imposing extra runtime overhead.

Reducing STM Overheads: Much research has been devoted to reducing the cost of compiler-generated STM barriers on transactional memory accesses. Early work [8, 32] showed how to eliminate several classes of transactional overhead including redundant barriers, barriers for accesses to provably immutable memory locations, and certain barriers for accesses to objects allocated in a transaction. Recent work by Afek et al. [9] uses the logic of program reads and writes within a transaction to reduce STM overhead: for example, a shared variable that is read several times can be be read once and cached locally. These optimizations complement ours, as they target different kinds of STM overhead from our work.

Beckman et al. [13] show how to use access permissions to remove STM synchronization overhead. While the goals are the same as ours, the mechanisms are different (alias control vs. type and effect annotations). The two mechanisms have different tradeoffs in expressivity and power: for example, Beckman et al.'s method can eliminate write barriers only if an object is accessed through a unique reference, whereas our system can eliminate barriers for access through shared references, so long as the access does not cause interfering effects. However, alias restrictions can express some patterns (such as permuting unique references in a data structure) that our system cannot. As future work, it would be interesting to explore these tradeoffs further.

Finally, several researchers have eliminated STM overhead for accesses to thread-local data using whole-program static escape analysis [47] and programmer annotations to specify code blocks that do not require instrumentation [52]. Unlike our work, this work either requires whole-program analysis, or it relies on unverified programmer annotations.

Nondeterministic Parallel Programming: Several research efforts are developing parallel models for nondeterministic codes with irregular data access patterns, such as Delaunay mesh refinement. Galois [36] provides a form of isolation, but with iterations of parallel loops (instead of atomic statements) as the isolated computations. Concurrency is increased by detecting conflicts at the level of method calls, instead of reads and writes, and using semantic commutativity properties. Lublinerman et al. [39] have proposed *object assemblies* as an alternative model for expressing irregular, graph-based computations.

These models are largely orthogonal to our work. In Galois, strong isolation holds if all shared data is accessed through well-defined APIs, but this property is not enforced, either statically or at runtime. We believe that our type and effect mechanisms could be applied to Galois to ensure this property. The object assemblies model may have stronger isolation guarantees than Galois, but it is very specialized to irregular graph computations, in contrast to the more general fork-join model we present here.

Kulkarni et al. [35] have recently proposed *task types* as a way of enforcing a property they call *pervasive atomicity*. This work shares with ours the broad goal of reducing the number of concurrent interleavings the programmer must consider. However, Kulkarni et al. adopt an actor-inspired approach, in which data is non-shared by default, and sharing musk occur through special "task objects." This is in contrast to our approach of allowing familiar shared-memory patterns of programming, but using effect annotations to enforce safety properties. Finally, none of the work discussed above provides any deterministic-by-default guarantee.

8. Conclusion

We have shown how to design a type and effect system that, together with a weakly atomic runtime system, achieves our stated goals of providing disciplined and safe nondeterminism, including race freedom, strong isolation of atomic operations and deterministic parallel operations, compositional reasoning about deterministic and nondeterministic operations, and determinism by default. We have also shown how to leverage the system to remove unnecessary barriers from the transactional implementation, thereby enhancing performance.

Acknowledgements

This work was supported by the National Science Foundation under grants CCF 07-02724 and CNS 07-20772, and by Intel, Microsoft, and the University of Illinois through UPCRC Illinois. An anonymous reviewer encouraged us to study TSP-R. Dan Grossman and Brad Chamberlain provided helpful suggestions on a draft of this paper and the supporting proofs.

References

[1] `http://iss.ices.utexas.edu/lonestar/`.

[2] `http://gee.cs.oswego.edu/dl/concurrency-interest`.

[3] `http://http://sites.google.com/site/deucestm`.

[4] OpenMP Application Program Interface, Version 3.0. http://www.openmp.org/mp-documents/spec30.pdf, 2008.

[5] M. Abadi et al. Types for safe locking: Static race detection for Java. *TOPLAS*, 2006.

[6] M. Abadi et al. Semantics of transactional memory and automatic mutual exclusion. In *POPL*, 2008.

[7] M. Abadi et al. Transactional memory with strong atomicity using off-the-shelf memory protection hardware. In *PPoPP*, 2009.

[8] A.-R. Adl-Tabatabai et al. Compiler and runtime support for efficient software transactional memory. In *PLDI*, 2006.

[9] Y. Afek et al. Lowering STM overhead with static analysis. In *LCPC*, 2010.

[10] M. D. Allen et al. Serialization sets: A dynamic dependence-based parallel execution model. In *PPOPP*, 2009.

[11] A. Aviram et al. Efficient system-enforced deterministic parallelism. 2010.

[12] N. E. Beckman et al. Verifying correct usage of atomic blocks and typestate. In *OOPSLA*, 2008.

[13] N. E. Beckman et al. Reducing STM overhead with access permissions. In *IWACO*, 2009.

[14] T. Bergan et al. CoreDet: A compiler and runtime system for deterministic multithreaded execution. In *Int'l. Conf. on Arch. Support for Programming Langs. and Operating Systs. (ASPLOS)*, 2010.

[15] E. D. Berger et al. Grace: Safe Multithreaded Programming for C/C++. In *OOPSLA*, 2009.

[16] R. D. Blumofe et al. Cilk: An efficient multithreaded runtime system. *PPOPP*, 1995.

[17] R. L. Bocchino et al. A type and effect system for Deterministic Parallel Java. In *OOPSLA*, 2009.

[18] R. L. Bocchino et al. Parallel programming must be deterministic by default. In *HotPar*, 2009.

[19] R. L. Bocchino Jr. *An Effect System and Language for Deterministic-by-Default Parallel Programming*. PhD thesis, University of Illinois, Urbana-Champaign, IL, 2010.

[20] C. Boyapati et al. Ownership types for safe programming: Preventing data races and deadlocks. In *OOPSLA*, 2002.

[21] J. Boyland. Checking interference with fractional permissions. *SAS*, 2003.

[22] N. G. Bronson et al. Feedback-directed barrier optimization in a strongly isolated STM. In *POPL*, 2009.

[23] Z. Budimlic et al. Multicore implementations of the concurrent collections programming model. In *CPC*, 2009.

[24] S. Burckhardt et al. Concurrent programming with revisions and isolation types. In *OOPSLA*, 2010.

[25] M. J. Carey et al. A status report on the OO7 OODBMS benchmarking effort. In *OOPSLA*, 1994.

[26] L. P. Chew. Guaranteed-quality mesh generation for curved surfaces. In *SCG*, 1993.

[27] J. Devietti et al. DMP: Deterministic Shared Memory Multiprocessing. In *ASPLOS*, 2009.

[28] D. Dice et al. Transactional locking II. In *DISC*, 2006.

[29] C. Flanagan et al. Types for atomicity: Static checking and inference for Java. *TOPLAS*, 2008.

[30] A. Ghuloum et al. Ct: A flexible parallel programming model for tera-scale architectures. Intel White Paper, 2007.

[31] T. Harris et al. Composable memory transactions. In *PPoPP*, 2005.

[32] T. Harris et al. Optimizing memory transactions. In *PLDI*, 2006.

[33] T. Harris and K. Fraser. Language support for lightweight transactions. In *OOPSLA*, 2003.

[34] B. Jacobs et al. A programming model for concurrent object-oriented programs. *TOPLAS*, 2008.

[35] A. Kulkarni et al. Task types for pervasive atomicity. In *OOPSLA*, 2010.

[36] M. Kulkarni et al. Optimistic parallelism requires abstractions. In *PLDI*, 2007.

[37] J. Larus and R. Rajwar. *Transactional Memory (Synthesis Lectures on Computer Architecture)*. Morgan & Claypool Publishers, 2007.

[38] E. A. Lee. The problem with threads. *Computer*, 2006.

[39] R. Lublinerman et al. Parallel programming with object assemblies. In *OOPSLA*, 2009.

[40] M. Martin, C. Blundell, and E. Lewis. Subtleties of transactional memory atomicity semantics. *IEEE Comp. Arch. Letters*, 5(2):17, 2006.

[41] N. D. Matsakis and T. R. Gross. A time-aware type system for data-race protection and guaranteed initialization. In *OOPSLA*, 2010.

[42] K. F. Moore and D. Grossman. High-level small-step operational semantics for transactions. In *POPL*, 2008.

[43] M. Olszewski et al. Kendo: Efficient deterministic multithreading in software. In *ASPLOS*, 2009.

[44] C. Papadimitriou. *The theory of database concurrency control*. Computer Science Press, Inc., 1986.

[45] M. C. Rinard and M. S. Lam. The design, implementation, and evaluation of Jade. *TOPLAS*, 1998.

[46] F. T. Schneider, V. Menon, T. Shpeisman, and A.-R. Adl-Tabatabai. Dynamic optimization for efficient strong atomicity. In *OOPSLA*, 2008.

[47] T. Shpeisman et al. Enforcing isolation and ordering in STM. In *PLDI*, 2007.

[48] M. Vakilian et al. Inferring Method Effect Summaries for Deterministic Parallel Java. Technical Report UIUCDCS-R-2009-3038, U. Illinois, 2009.

[49] C. von Praun et al. Implicit parallelism with ordered transactions. In *PPOPP*, 2007.

[50] A. Welc et al. Safe futures for Java. In *OOPSLA*, 2005.

[51] A. Welc et al. Revocation techniques for Java concurrency. *Concurrency and Computation: Practice and Experience*, 2006.

[52] R. M. Yoo et al. Kicking the tires of software transactional memory: Why the going gets tough. In *SPAA*, 2008.

Loop Transformations: Convexity, Pruning and Optimization

Louis-Noël Pouchet
The Ohio State University
pouchet@cse.ohio-state.edu

Uday Bondhugula
IBM T.J. Watson Research Center
ubondhug@us.ibm.com

Cédric Bastoul
University of Paris-Sud 11
cedric.bastoul@inria.fr

Albert Cohen
INRIA
albert.cohen@inria.fr

J. Ramanujam
Louisiana State University
jxr@ece.lsu.edu

P. Sadayappan
The Ohio State University
saday@cse.ohio-state.edu

Nicolas Vasilache
Reservoir Labs, Inc.
vasilache@reservoir.com

Abstract

High-level loop transformations are a key instrument in mapping computational kernels to effectively exploit resources in modern processor architectures. However, determining appropriate compositions of loop transformations to achieve this remains a significantly challenging task; current compilers may achieve significantly lower performance than hand-optimized programs. To address this fundamental challenge, we first present a convex characterization of all distinct, semantics-preserving, multidimensional affine transformations. We then bring together algebraic, algorithmic, and performance analysis results to design a tractable optimization algorithm over this highly expressive space. The framework has been implemented and validated experimentally on a representative set of benchmarks run on state-of-the-art multi-core platforms.

Categories and Subject Descriptors D 3.4 [*Programming languages*]: Processor — Compilers; Optimization

General Terms Algorithms; Performance

Keywords Compilation; Compiler Optimization; Parallelism; Loop Transformations; Affine Scheduling

1. Introduction

Loop nest optimization continues to drive much of the ongoing research in the fields of optimizing compilation [8, 27, 33], high-level hardware synthesis [22], and adaptive library generation [19, 47]. Loop nest optimization attempts to map the proper granularity of independent computation to a complex hierarchy of memory, computing, and interconnection resources. Despite four decades of research and development, it remains a challenging task for compiler designers and a frustrating experience for programmers — the performance gap, between expert-written code for a given machine and that optimized and parallelized automatically by a compiler, is *widening* with newer generations of hardware.

One reason for this widening gap is due to the way loop nest optimizers attempt to decompose the global optimization problem into simpler sub-problems. Recent results in feedback-directed optimization [33] indicate that oversimplification of this decomposition is largely responsible for the failure. The polyhedral compiler framework provides a convenient and powerful abstraction to apply composite transformations in one step [20, 24]. However, the space of affine transformations is extremely large. Linear optimization in such a high-dimensional space raises complexity issues and its effectiveness is limited by the lack of accurate profitability models.

This paper makes fundamental progresses in the understanding of polyhedral loop nest optimization. It is organized as follows. Section 2 formalizes the optimization problem and contributes a complete, convex characterization of all distinct, semantics-preserving, multidimensional affine transformations. Focusing on one critical slice of the transformation space, Section 3 proposes a general framework to reason about all distinct, semantics-preserving, multidimensional statement interleavings. Section 4 presents a complete and tractable optimization algorithm driven by the iterative evaluation of these interleavings. Section 5 presents experimental data. Related work is discussed in Section 6.

2. Problem Statement and Formalization

The formal semantics of a language allows the definition of program transformations and equivalence criteria to validate these transformations. Denotational semantics can be used as an abstraction to decide on the functional equivalence of two programs. But operational semantics is preferred to express program transformations themselves, especially in the case of transformations impacting the detailed interaction with particular hardware. Program optimization amounts to searching for a particular point in a space of semantics-preserving transformations. When considering optimizing compilation as a whole, the space has no particular property that makes it amenable to any formal characterization or optimization algorithm. As a consequence, compilers decompose the problem into sub-problems that can be formally defined, and for which complexity results and effective optimization algorithms can be derived.

The ability to encompass a large set of program transformations into a single, well understood optimization problem is the strongest asset of the polyhedral compilation model. In the polyhedral model, transformations are validated against dependence relations among dynamic instances of individual statements of a loop nest. The dependence relation is the denotational abstraction that defines functional equivalence. This dependence relation may not be statically

POPL'11, January 26–28, 2011, Austin, Texas, USA.

computable, but (conservative) abstractions may be (finitely) represented through systems of affine inequalities, or unions of parametric polyhedra [2, 16, 22]. Two decades of work in polyhedral compilation has demonstrated that the main loop nest transformations can be modeled and effectively constructed as multidimensional affine schedules, mapping dynamic instances of individual statements to lexicographically sorted vectors of integers (or rational numbers) [6, 8, 17, 20, 24, 38]. Optimization in the polyhedral model amounts to selecting a good multidimensional affine schedule for the program.

In this paper, we make the following contributions:

- We take this well defined optimization problem, and provide a *complete, convex formalization* for it. This convex set of semantics-preserving, distinct, affine multidimensional schedules opens the door to more powerful linear optimization algorithms.
- We propose a decomposition of the general optimization problem over this convex polyhedron into sub-problems of much lower complexity, introducing the powerful *fusibility* concept. The fusibility relation generalizes the legality conditions for loop fusion, abstracting a large set of multidimensional, affine, fusion-enabling transformations.
- We demonstrate that exploring fusibility opportunities in a loop nest reduces to the enumeration of total preorders, and to the existence of pairwise compatible loop permutations. We also study the transitivity of the fusibility relation.
- Based on these results, we design a multidimensional affine scheduling algorithm targeted at achieving portable high performance across modern processor architectures.
- Our approach has been fully implemented in a source-to-source compiler and validated on representative benchmarks.

2.1 Loop optimization challenge

Let us illustrate the challenge of loop optimization from the standpoint of performance portability through a simple example, ThreeMatMat, shown in Figure 1. We seek the best combination of loop transformations—expressed as a multidimensional affine schedule—to optimize a sequence of three matrix-products for a given target platform.

```
   for (i1 = 0; i1 < N; ++i1)
     for (j1 = 0; j1 < N; ++j1)
       for (k1 = 0; k1 < N; ++k1)
R:       C[i1][j1] += A[i1][k1] * B[k1][j1];
   for (i2 = 0; i2 < N; ++i2)
     for (j2 = 0; j2 < N; ++j2)
       for (k2 = 0; k2 < N; ++k2)
S:       F[i2][j2] += D[i2][k2] * E[k2][j2];
   for (i3 = 0; i3 < N; ++i3)
     for (j3 = 0; j3 < N; ++j3)
       for (k3 = 0; k3 < N; ++k3)
T:       G[i3][j3] += C[i3][k3] * F[k3][j3];
```

Figure 1. ThreeMatMat: $C = AB$, $F = DE$, $G = CF$

We set $N = 512$ and computed 5 different versions of ThreeMatMat using combinations of loop transformations including tiling. We experimented on two platforms (quad-Xeon E7450 and quad-Opteron 8380), using the Intel ICC 11.0 compiler with aggressive optimization flags. The framework developed in this paper enables us to outperform ICC by a factor 2.28× and 1.84×, respectively, for the Intel and AMD machines. We observe that the best version found depends on the target machine: for the Intel system, the best found loop fusion structure is shown in Figure 2(b), on which further polyhedral tiling and parallelization were applied (not shown in Figure 2). But on the AMD machine, distributing all statements and individually tiling them performs best, 1.23× better than 2(b).

The efficient eecution of a computation kernel on a modern multi-core architecture requires the synergistic operation of many hardware resources, via the exploitation of thread-level parallelism; the memory hierarchy, including prefetch units, different cache levels, memory buses and interconnect; and all available computational units, including SIMD units. Because of the very complex interplay between all these components, it is currently infeasible to *guarantee at compile-time* which set of transformatios leads to maximal performance.

To maximize performance, one must carefully tune for the trade-off between the different levels of parallelism and the usage of the local memory components. This can be performed via loop fusion and distribution choices, that drive the success of subsequent optimizations such as vectorization, tiling or parallelization. It is *essential to adapt the fusion structure* to the program and target machine. However, the state-of-the-art provides only rough models of the impact of loop transformations on the actual execution. To achieve performance portability across a wide variety of architectures, empirical evaluation of several fusion choices is an alternative, but requires the construction and traversal of a search space of all possible fusion/distribution structures. To make the problem sound and tractable, we develop a complete framework to reason and optimize in the space of all semantics-preserving combinations of loop structures.

2.2 Background and notation

The *polyhedral model* is a flexible and expressive representation for loop nests. It captures the linear algebraic structure of statically predictable control flow, where loop bounds and conditionals are affine functions of the surrounding loop iterators and invariants (a.k.a. parameters, unknown at compilation time) [15, 20]; but it is not restricted to static control flow [2, 4].

The set of all executed instances of each statement is called an *iteration domain*. These sets are represented by affine inequalities involving the loop iterators and the global variables. Considering the ThreeMatMat example in Figure 1, the iteration domain of R is:

$$\mathcal{D}_R = \{(i,j,k) \in \mathbb{Z}^3 \mid 0 \le i < \mathrm{N} \wedge 0 \le j < \mathrm{N} \wedge 0 \le k < \mathrm{N}\}$$

$\mathcal{D}_R$ is a (parametric) integer polyhedron, that is a subset of $\mathbb{Z}^3$. The *iteration vector* $\vec{x}_R$ is the vector of the surrounding loop iterators, for R it is (i,j,k) and takes value in $\mathcal{D}_R$.

In this work, a given loop nest optimization is defined by a multidimensional affine schedule, which is an affine form of the loop iterators and global parameters [18, 20].

DEFINITION 1 (Affine multi-dimensional schedule). *Given a statement S, an affine schedule Θ^S of dimension m is an affine form on the d outer loop iterators $\vec{x}_S$ and the p global parameters $\vec{n}$. $\Theta^S \in \mathbb{Z}^{m\times(d+p+1)}$ can be written as:*

$$\Theta^S(\vec{x}_S) = \begin{pmatrix} \theta_{1,1} & \dots & \theta_{1,d+p+1} \\ \vdots & & \vdots \\ \theta_{m,1} & \dots & \theta_{m,d+p+1} \end{pmatrix} \cdot \begin{pmatrix} \vec{x}_S \\ \vec{n} \\ 1 \end{pmatrix}$$

The scheduling function Θ^S maps each point in $\mathcal{D}_S$ with a multidimensional timestamp of dimension m, such that in the transformed code the instances of S defined in $\mathcal{D}_S$ will be executed following the lexicographic ordering of their associated timestamp. Multidimensional timestamps can be seen as logical clocks: the first dimension corresponds to days (most significant), next one is hours (less significant), the third to minutes, and so on. Note that every static control program has a multidimensional affine schedule [18], and that any composition of loop transformation can be represented in the polyhedral representation [20, 50]. The full program optimization is a collection of affine schedules, one for each syntactical program statement. Even seemingly non-linear transformations like loop tiling (a.k.a. blocking) and unrolling can be modeled [20, 38].

Finally, syntactic code is generated back from the polyhedral representation on which the optimization has been applied; CLooG is the state-of-the art algorithm and code generator [3] to perform this task.

2.3 Semantics-preserving transformations

A program transformation must preserve the semantics of the program. The legality of affine loop nest transformations is defined at the level of dynamic statement instances. As a starting point for transformation space pruning, we build a *convex, polyhedral characterization of all semantics-preserving multidimensional affine schedules for a loop nest.*

Two statements instances are in *dependence relation* if they access the same memory cell and at least one of these accesses is a write. Given two statements R and S, a *dependence polyhedron* $\mathcal{D}_{R,S}$ is a subset of the Cartesian product of $\mathcal{D}_R$ and $\mathcal{D}_S$: $\mathcal{D}_{R,S}$ contains all pairs of instances $\langle \vec{x}_R, \vec{x}_S \rangle$ such that $\vec{x}_S$ depends on $\vec{x}_R$, for a given array reference. Hence, for a transformation to preserve the program semantics, it must ensure that

$$\Theta^R(\vec{x}_R) \prec \Theta^S(\vec{x}_S),$$

where $\prec$ denotes the *lexicographic ordering.*[1]

To capture all program dependences we build a set of dependence polyhedra, one for each pair of array references accessing the same array cell (scalars being a particular case of array), thus possibly building several dependence polyhedra per pair of statements. The *polyhedral dependence graph* is a multi-graph with one node per statement, and an edge $e^{R \to S}$ is labeled with a dependence polyhedron $\mathcal{D}_{R,S}$, for all dependence polyhedra.

The schedule constraints imposed by the precedence constraint are expressible as finding all non-negative functions over the dependence polyhedra [17]. It is possible to express the set of affine, non-negative functions over $\mathcal{D}_{R,S}$ thanks to the affine form of the Farkas lemma [39].

LEMMA 1 (Affine form of Farkas Lemma). *Let $\mathcal{D}$ be a nonempty polyhedron defined by the inequalities $A\,\vec{x} + \vec{b} \geq \vec{0}$. Then any affine function $f(\vec{x})$ is non-negative everywhere in $\mathcal{D}$ iff it is a positive affine combination:*

$$f(\vec{x}) = \lambda_0 + \vec{\lambda}^T(A\vec{x} + \vec{b}), \text{ with } \lambda_0 \geq 0 \text{ and } \vec{\lambda}^T \geq \vec{0}.$$

λ_0 and $\vec{\lambda}^T$ are called Farkas multipliers.

Since it is a necessary and sufficient characterization, the Farkas Lemma offers a loss-less linearization of the constraints from the dependence polyhedron into direct constraints on the schedule coefficients. For instance considering the first time dimension (the first row of the scheduling matrices, that is, we set $p = 1$ in the following equation), to preserve the precedence relation we have:

$$\forall \mathcal{D}_{R,S},\ \forall \langle \vec{x}_R, \vec{x}_S \rangle \in \mathcal{D}_{R,S},\quad \Theta^S_p(\vec{x}_S) - \Theta^R_p(\vec{x}_R) \geq \delta_p^{\mathcal{D}_{R,S}} \qquad (1)$$
$$\delta_p^{\mathcal{D}_{R,S}} \in \{0,1\}$$

We resort to variable $\delta_1^{\mathcal{D}_{R,S}}$ to model the dependence satisfaction. A dependence $\mathcal{D}_{R,S}$ can be either *weakly satisfied* when $\delta_1^{\mathcal{D}_{R,S}} = 0$, permitting $\Theta^S_1(\vec{x}_S) = \Theta^R_1(\vec{x}_R)$ for some instances in dependence, or *strongly satisfied* when $\delta_1^{\mathcal{D}_{R,S}} = 1$, enforcing strict precedence (at the first time dimension) for all instances in dependence.

This model extends to multidimensional schedules, observing that once a dependence has been strongly satisfied, it does not contribute to the semantics preservation constraints for the subsequent time dimensions. Furthermore, for a schedule to preserve semantics, it is sufficient for every dependence to be strongly satisfied at least once. Following these observations, one may state a sufficient condition for semantics preservation (adapted from Feautrier's formalization [18]).

LEMMA 2 (Semantics-preserving affine schedules). *Given a set of affine schedules $\Theta^R, \Theta^S \ldots$ of dimension m, the program semantics is preserved if:*

$$\forall \mathcal{D}_{R,S},\ \exists p \in \{1,\ldots,m\},\ \delta_p^{\mathcal{D}_{R,S}} = 1 \wedge \left(\forall j < p,\ \delta_j^{\mathcal{D}_{R,S}} = 0\right) \wedge$$
$$\left(\forall j \leq p, \forall \langle \vec{x}_R, \vec{x}_S \rangle \in \mathcal{D}_{R,S},\ \Theta^S_j(\vec{x}_S) - \Theta^R_j(\vec{x}_R) \geq \delta_j^{\mathcal{D}_{R,S}}\right)$$

The proof directly derives from the lexicopositivity of dependence satisfaction [18].

Regarding the schedule dimensionality m, it is sufficient to pick $m = d$ to guarantee the existence of a legal schedule (the maximum program loop depth is d). Obviously, any schedule implementing the original execution order is a valid solution [18].

This formalization involves an "oracle" to select the dimension p at which each dependence should be strongly satisfied. To avoid the combinatorial selection of this dimension, we conditionally nullify constraint (1) on the schedules *when the dependence was strongly satisfied at a previous dimension.* To nullify the constraint, we may always pick a lower bound lb for $\Theta^S_k(\vec{x}_S) - \Theta^R_k(\vec{x}_R)$. Without any loss of generality, we assume (parametric) loop bounds are non-negative. Vasilache [44] proposed a method to evaluate this lower bound when the coefficients of Θ are bounded: lb is greater or equal to the sum of the maximal coefficient values times the (possibly parametric) loop bounds. We can always select a large enough K such that [32]

$$\Theta^S_k(\vec{x}_S) - \Theta^R_k(\vec{x}_R) \geq -K.\vec{n} - K \qquad (2)$$

Note that this lower bound can also be linearized into constraints on Θ^R, Θ^S thanks to the Farkas Lemma. To obtain the schedule constraints we reinsert this lower bound in the previous formulation [44], such that either the dependence has not been previously strongly satisfied and then the lower bound is (1), or it has been and the lower bound is (2). We thus derive the convex form of semantics-preserving affine schedules of dimension m for a program as a corollary of Lemma 2.

LEMMA 3 (Convex form of semantics-preserving affine schedules). *Given a set of affine schedules $\Theta^R, \Theta^S \ldots$ of dimension m, the program semantics is preserved if the three following conditions hold:*

$$(i) \qquad \forall \mathcal{D}_{R,S},\ \forall p,\ \delta_p^{\mathcal{D}_{R,S}} \in \{0,1\}$$

$$(ii) \qquad \forall \mathcal{D}_{R,S},\ \sum_{p=1}^{m} \delta_p^{\mathcal{D}_{R,S}} = 1 \qquad (3)$$

$$(iii) \qquad \forall \mathcal{D}_{R,S},\ \forall p \in \{1,\ldots,m\},\ \forall \langle \vec{x}_R, \vec{x}_S \rangle \in \mathcal{D}_{R,S}, \qquad (4)$$
$$\Theta^S_p(\vec{x}_S) - \Theta^R_p(\vec{x}_R) \geq -\sum_{k=1}^{p-1} \delta_k^{\mathcal{D}_{R,S}}.(K.\vec{n} + K) + \delta_p^{\mathcal{D}_{R,S}}$$

One can then build the set $\mathcal{L}_m$ of all (bounded) legal affine multidimensional schedules of dimension m by encoding the affine constraints given by Lemma 3 into a problem with m binary variables per dependence and $m \times (dim(\vec{x}_S) + dim(\vec{n}) + 1)$ variables per statement S. For an efficient construction of the constraints for

[1] $(a_1,\ldots,a_n) \prec (b_1,\ldots,b_m)$ iff there exists an integer $1 \leq i \leq min(n,m)$ s.t. $(a_1,\ldots,a_{i-1}) = (b_1,\ldots,b_{i-1})$ and $a_i < b_i$.

semantics-preservation, one should proceed dependence by dependence. Building the constraints of the form of (4) is done for each dependence, then the Farkas multipliers are eliminated for instance with a scalable Fourier-Motzkin projection technique [33]. The set of constraints obtained for each schedules are then intersected, and the process is replicated for all dimensions.

2.4 Finding a schedule for the program

We achieved completeness: an Integer Linear Program operating on $\mathcal{L}_m$ can exhibit the best affine schedule according to a given objective function. Yet solving an arbitrary ILP on $\mathcal{L}_m$ is NP-complete [39]. Given the high dimensionality of this space on the larger loop nests, our convex formalization induces a serious tractability challenge. To address this challenge and reduce the complexity effect of the problem, we propose to decouple the optimization into two sub-problems:

1. the problem of selecting how statements are interleaved — this is traditionally viewed as selecting a proper combination of loop fusion, loop distribution and code motion;
2. the problem of selecting an affine schedule compatible with the statement interleaving selected at the previous step.

Selecting a statement interleaving that maximizes a fusion criterion is still an NP-complete problem in general [12], but its complexity is dramatically reduced from the high-dimensionality linear optimization problem. We focus our efforts on this simplified problem.

2.5 Encoding statement interleaving

Fusion and fusibility of statements In the polyhedral model, loop fusion is characterized by the fine-grain interleaving of statement instances [6, 24]. Two statements are fully distributed if the range of the timestamps associated to their instances never overlap. Syntactically, this results in distinct loops to traverse the domains. One may define fusion as the negation of the distribution criterion. For such a case we say that two statements R, S are fused if there exists at least one pair of iterations for which R is scheduled before S, and another pair of iterations for which S is scheduled before R. This is stated in Definition 2.

DEFINITION 2 (Fusion of two statements). *Consider two statements R, S and their schedules Θ^R and Θ^S. R and S are said to be fused at level p if, $\forall k \in \{1 \ldots p\}$, there exists at least three distinct executed instances $\vec{x}_R, \vec{x}_R{}'$ and $\vec{x}_S$ such that*

$$\Theta^R_k(\vec{x}_R) \leq \Theta^S_k(\vec{x}_S) \leq \Theta^R_k(\vec{x}_R{}'). \quad (5)$$

We now propose an encoding of Definition 2 such that we can determine, from the dependence graph, if it is possible to find a schedule leading to fuse the statements whatever additional transformation(s) may be required to enable fusion. This is called *fusibility*. The purpose is to exhibit sufficient affine constraints that can be added to $\mathcal{L}$ to keep in the solution space only the schedules which correspond to fusing the considered statements.

We rely on the fact that the first and last scheduled instances of R and S will conform to Definition 2 if the two statements are fused. These specific instances belong to the set of vertices of $\mathcal{D}_R$ and $\mathcal{D}_S$. Thus, to determine whether R and S are fusable or not, it is sufficient to enumerate all vertices of $\mathcal{D}_R$ and $\mathcal{D}_S$, and for each possible combinations of vertices plug their actual value into Eq (5) — leading to an affine constraint on the schedule coefficients — and test for the existence of a solution in the space of all semantics-preserving schedules $\mathcal{L}$ augmented with the new constraint. As soon as there is a solution to one of the problems formed, then the statements are fusable. This is stated in Definition 3.

DEFINITION 3 (Generalized fusibility check). *Given v_R (resp. v_S) the set of vertices of $\mathcal{D}_R$ (resp. $\mathcal{D}_S$). R and S are fusable at level p if, $\forall k \in \{1 \ldots p\}$, there exist two semantics-preserving schedules Θ^R_k and Θ^S_k such that*

$$\exists(\vec{x}_1, \vec{x}_2, \vec{x}_3) \in v_R \times v_S \times v_R, \quad \Theta^R_k(\vec{x}_1) \leq \Theta^S_k(\vec{x}_2) \leq \Theta^R_k(\vec{x}_3)$$

Note that in practice, the number of vertices of an iteration domain is often small (from 2 to 10), hence the number of cases to be checked is limited. We also present in Section 4.2 a specialization of this test to the case of non-negative schedule coefficients, which removes the need to enumerate the vertices.

Multidimensional statement interleaving Thanks to Lemma 3 and Definition 3, we can determine if a set of statements can be fused at a given level while preserving semantics. For our optimization problem, we are interested in building a space representing all ways to interleave the program statements.

To reason about statement interleaving, one may associate a vector ρ^S of dimension d (d being the maximal loop depth in the program) to each statement S, and order those vectors lexicographically. If some statement S is surrounded by less than d loops, ρ^S is post-padded with zeroes. Figure 2 gives an example of three possible optimizations for the ThreeMatMat example, as defined by different configurations of the ρ vectors. Note that to implement the interleaving specified by ρ several loop permutations may be required.

There exist an analogy between ρ^S and a standard encoding of multidimensional affine schedules where statement interleaving vectors are made explicit: for each statement S, one may constrain the rows of Θ^S to alternate between constant forms of a vector of dimension $d+1$ (usually denoted β [20]) and affine forms of the iteration and global parameter vectors. This $2d+1$-dimensional encoding does not incur any loss of expressiveness [11, 18, 20, 24]. However in this paper we explicitly give ρ important structural properties of the transformed loop nest:

1. if $\rho^R_k = \rho^S_k$, $\forall k \in \{1, \ldots, p\}$ then the statements share (at least) p common loops;
2. if $\rho^R_p \neq \rho^S_p$, then the statements do not share any common loop starting at depth p. We thus have

$$\rho^R_p \neq \rho^S_p \Rightarrow \rho^R_k \neq \rho^S_k, \ \forall k \in \{p+1, \ldots, m\}$$

Our objective to model all possible interleavings is to build a space containing all ρ vectors for which there exists a semantics-preserving affine transformation that implements the specified interleaving. To guarantee that the solution space contains only useful points, we need to address the problem that several choices of ρ vectors represent the same multidimensional statement interleaving. Intuitively, the problem arises because there exists an infinite number of vectors which have the same lexicographic ordering. In particular, the order is invariant to translation of all coefficients of ρ at a given dimension, or by multiplication of all its coefficients by a non-negative constant. To abstract away these equivalences, we now formally define the concept of multidimensional statement interleaving.

DEFINITION 4 (Multidimensional statement interleaving). *Consider a set of statements $\mathcal{S}$ enclosed within at most d loops and their associated vectors $\mathcal{R} = \{\rho^S\}_{S \in \mathcal{S}}$. For a given $k \in \{1, \ldots, d\}$, the one-dimensional statement interleaving of $\mathcal{S}$ at dimension k defined by $\mathcal{R}$ is the partition of $\mathcal{S}$ according to the coefficients ρ^S_k. The multidimensional statement interleaving of $\mathcal{S}$ at dimension k defined by $\mathcal{R}$ is the list of partitions at dimension k.*

```
  for (t1 = 0; t1 < N; ++t1) {
    for (t3 = 0; t3 < N; ++t3)
      for (t5 = 0; t5 < N; ++t5)
R       C[t3][t1] += A[t3][t5] * B[t5][t1];
    for (t3 = 0; t3 < N; ++t3)
      for (t5 = 0; t5 < N; ++t5)
S       F[t1][t3] += D[t1][t5] * E[t5][t3];
    for (t3 = 0; t3 < N; ++t3)
      for (t5 = 0; t5 < N; ++t5)
T       G[t5][t3] += C[t5][t1] * F[t1][t3];
  }
```

$$\mathbf{L}_R = \begin{pmatrix} 0 & 1 & 0 \\ 1 & 0 & 0 \\ 0 & 0 & 1 \end{pmatrix} \mathbf{L}_S = \begin{pmatrix} 1 & 0 & 0 \\ 0 & 1 & 0 \\ 0 & 0 & 1 \end{pmatrix} \mathbf{L}_T = \begin{pmatrix} 0 & 0 & 1 \\ 0 & 1 & 0 \\ 1 & 0 & 0 \end{pmatrix}$$

$$\rho_R = \begin{pmatrix} 0 \\ 0 \\ 0 \end{pmatrix} \quad \rho_S = \begin{pmatrix} 0 \\ 1 \\ 1 \end{pmatrix} \quad \rho_T = \begin{pmatrix} 0 \\ 2 \\ 2 \end{pmatrix}$$

(a)

```
  for (t1 = 0; t1 < N; ++t1)
    for (t3 = 0; t3 < N; ++t3)
      for (t5 = 0; t5 < N; ++t5) {
S       F[t1][t3] += D[t1][t5] * E[t5][t3];
R       C[t1][t3] += A[t1][t5] * B[t5][t3];
      }
  for (t1 = 0; t1 < N; ++t1)
    for (t3 = 0; t3 < N; ++t3)
      for (t5 = 0; t5 < N; ++t5)
T       G[t1][t3] += C[t1][t3] * F[t3][t5];
```

$$\mathbf{L}_R = \begin{pmatrix} 1 & 0 & 0 \\ 0 & 1 & 0 \\ 0 & 0 & 1 \end{pmatrix} \mathbf{L}_S = \begin{pmatrix} 1 & 0 & 0 \\ 0 & 1 & 0 \\ 0 & 0 & 1 \end{pmatrix} \mathbf{L}_T = \begin{pmatrix} 1 & 0 & 0 \\ 0 & 1 & 0 \\ 0 & 0 & 1 \end{pmatrix}$$

$$\rho_R = \begin{pmatrix} 0 \\ 0 \\ 0 \end{pmatrix} \quad \rho_S = \begin{pmatrix} 0 \\ 0 \\ 0 \end{pmatrix} \quad \rho_T = \begin{pmatrix} 1 \\ 1 \\ 1 \end{pmatrix}$$

(b)

```
  for (t1 = 0; t1 < N; ++t1)
    for (t3 = 0; t3 < N; ++t3)
      for (t5 = 0; t5 < N; ++t5)
R       C[t1][t3] += A[t1][t5] * B[t5][t3];
  for (t1 = 0; t1 < N; ++t1)
    for (t3 = 0; t3 < N; ++t3)
      for (t5 = 0; t5 < N; ++t5) {
S       F[t3][t1] += D[t3][t5] * E[t5][t1];
T       G[t5][t1] += C[t5][t3] * F[t3][t1];
      }
```

$$\mathbf{L}_R = \begin{pmatrix} 1 & 0 & 0 \\ 0 & 1 & 0 \\ 0 & 0 & 1 \end{pmatrix} \mathbf{L}_S = \begin{pmatrix} 0 & 1 & 0 \\ 1 & 0 & 0 \\ 0 & 0 & 1 \end{pmatrix} \mathbf{L}_T = \begin{pmatrix} 0 & 0 & 1 \\ 1 & 0 & 0 \\ 0 & 1 & 0 \end{pmatrix}$$

$$\rho_R = \begin{pmatrix} 0 \\ 0 \\ 0 \end{pmatrix} \quad \rho_S = \begin{pmatrix} 1 \\ 1 \\ 1 \end{pmatrix} \quad \rho_T = \begin{pmatrix} 1 \\ 1 \\ 1 \end{pmatrix}$$

(c)

Figure 2. Three possible legal transformations for $C = AB$, $F = DE$, $G = CF$

The structural properties of statement interleaving indicate that equivalence classes at dimension k correspond to statements that share common loops at depth k in the transformed loop nest.

DEFINITION 5 (Total preorder). *A total preorder on a set $\mathcal{S}$ is a relation $\lhd$ which is reflexive, transitive, and such that for any pair of elements $(S_1, S_2) \in \mathcal{S}$, either $S_1 \lhd S_2$ or $S_2 \lhd S_1$ or both.*

An important result is that any preorder of a set $\mathcal{S}$ is isomorphic to a partial order of some equivalence classes of $\mathcal{S}$. Applying this result to the structural properties of statement interleavings yields the following lemma.

LEMMA 4 (Structure of statement interleavings). *Each one-dimensional statement interleaving corresponds to a unique total preorder of the statements and reciprocally.*

3. Semantics-Preserving Statement Interleavings

We now propose a convex, complete characterization of multidimensional statement interleavings which serves as a basis to encode the space of valid ρ vectors.

3.1 Convex encoding of total preorders

We first present a solution for the problem of total preorders of scalar elements, that corresponds to one-dimensional interleavings.

One-dimensional case For a given set of n elements, we define $\mathcal{O}$ as the set of all and distinct total preorders of its n elements. The key problem is to model $\mathcal{O}$ as a convex polyhedron.[2]

To the best of our knowledge, uniqueness of orderings cannot be modeled in a convex fashion on a set with a linear number of variables. We propose to model the ordering of two elements i, j with three *binary* decision variables, defined as follows. $p_{i,j} = 1$ iff i precedes j, $e_{i,j} = 1$ iff i equals j and $s_{i,j} = 1$ iff i succeeds j. To model the entire set, we introduce three binary variables for each ordered pair of elements, i.e., all pairs (i, j) such that $1 \leq i < j \leq n$. This models a set with $3 \times n(n-1)/2$ variables.

$$\left\{ \begin{array}{c} 0 \leq p_{i,j} \leq 1 \\ 0 \leq e_{i,j} \leq 1 \\ 0 \leq s_{i,j} \leq 1 \end{array} \right\}$$

[2] This problem is not a straight adaptation of standard order theory: we look for the *set* of *all distinct* total preorders of n elements, in contrast to classical work defining counting functions of this set [41].

For instance, the outer-most interleaving $\rho_1^R = 0$, $\rho_1^S = 0$, $\rho_1^T = 1$ of Figure 2(b) is represented by:

$$e_{R,S} = 1,\ e_{R,T} = 0,\ e_{S,T} = 0$$
$$p_{R,S} = 0,\ p_{R,T} = 1,\ p_{S,T} = 1$$
$$s_{R,S} = 0,\ s_{R,T} = 0,\ s_{S,T} = 0$$

From there, one may easily recompute the corresponding total preorder $\{\rho_1^R = 0, \rho_1^S = 0, \rho_1^T = 1\}$, e.g., by computing the lexicographic minimum of a system $\mathcal{W}$ of 3 non-negative variables that replicate the ordering defined by all $p_{i,j}$, $e_{i,j}$ and $s_{i,j}$.

The first issue is the consistency of the model: an inconsistent preorder would make $\mathcal{W}$ infeasible, e.g., setting $e_{1,2} = 1$ and $p_{1,2} = 1$. The second issue is the totality of the relation. These two conditions can be merged into the the following equality, capturing both mutual exclusion and totality:

$$p_{i,j} + e_{i,j} + s_{i,j} = 1 \tag{6}$$

To simplify the system, we immediately get rid of the $s_{i,j}$ variables, thanks to (6). We also relax (6) to get:

$$p_{i,j} + e_{i,j} \leq 1$$

Mutually exclusive decision variables capture the consistency of the model for a single pair of elements. However, one needs to insert additional constraints to capture transitivity.

To enforce transitivity, the following rule must hold true for all triples of statements (i, j, k):

$$e_{i,j} = 1 \wedge e_{i,k} = 1 \Rightarrow e_{j,k} = 1.$$

Similarly, we have:

$$e_{i,j} = 1 \wedge e_{j,k} = 1 \Rightarrow e_{i,k} = 1.$$

These two rules set the basic transitivity of e variables. Since we are dealing with binary variables, the implications can be easily modeled as affine constraints:

$$\left\{ \begin{array}{ll} \forall k \in]j,n], & e_{i,j} + e_{i,k} \leq 1 + e_{j,k} \\ & e_{i,j} + e_{j,k} \leq 1 + e_{i,k} \end{array} \right\}$$

Slightly more complex transitivity patterns are also required. For instance, we also have transitivity conditions imposed by a connection between the value for some e coefficients and some p ones. For instance, $i < j$ and $j = k$ implies $i < k$. The general rules for those cases are:

$$e_{i,j} \wedge p_{i,k} \Rightarrow p_{j,k}$$
$$e_{i,j} \wedge p_{j,k} \Rightarrow p_{i,k}$$
$$e_{k,j} \wedge p_{i,k} \Rightarrow p_{i,j}$$

These three rules set the complex transitivity between the p and e variables. They can be modeled equivalently by following affine constraints:

$$\left\{\begin{array}{ll} \forall k \in]j,n] & e_{i,j}+p_{i,k} \leq 1+p_{j,k} \\ & e_{i,j}+p_{j,k} \leq 1+p_{i,k} \\ \forall k \in]i,j[& e_{k,j}+p_{i,k} \leq 1+p_{i,j} \end{array}\right\} \quad (7)$$

Generalizing this reasoning, we collect all constraints to enforce the transitivity of the total preorder relation. Those constraints are gathered in the following system, for $1 \leq i < j < n$, defining the convex set of all, distinct total preorders of n elements $\mathcal{O}$:

$$\left\{\begin{array}{lll} & \left.\begin{array}{r} 0 \leq p_{i,j} \leq 1 \\ 0 \leq e_{i,j} \leq 1 \end{array}\right\} & \text{Variables are binary} \\ & \left. p_{i,j}+e_{i,j} \leq 1 \right\} & \text{Relaxed mutual exclusion} \\ \forall k \in]j,n] & \left.\begin{array}{r} e_{i,j}+e_{i,k} \leq 1+e_{j,k} \\ e_{i,j}+e_{j,k} \leq 1+e_{i,k} \end{array}\right\} & \text{Basic transitivity on } e \\ \forall k \in]i,j[& \left. p_{i,k}+p_{k,j} \leq 1+p_{i,j} \right\} & \text{Basic transitivity on } p \\ \forall k \in]j,n] & \left.\begin{array}{r} e_{i,j}+p_{i,k} \leq 1+p_{j,k} \\ e_{i,j}+p_{j,k} \leq 1+p_{i,k} \end{array}\right. & \text{Complex} \\ \forall k \in]i,j[& \left.\begin{array}{r} e_{k,j}+p_{i,k} \leq 1+p_{i,j} \end{array}\right\} & \text{transitivity on } p \text{ and } e \\ \forall k \in]j,n] & \left. e_{i,j}+p_{i,j}+p_{j,k} \leq 1+p_{i,k}+e_{i,k} \right\} & \text{Complex transitivity on } s \text{ and } p \end{array}\right.$$

The following lemma is proved in [32, appendix A].

LEMMA 5 (Completeness and correctness of $\mathcal{O}$). *The set $\mathcal{O}$ contains one and only one element per distinct total preorder of n elements.*

Multidimensional case $\mathcal{O}$ encodes all possible total preorders (or, statement interleaving) for a given loop level. To extend to the multidimensional interleaving case, we first replicate $\mathcal{O}$ for each dimension of the ρ vectors. However, further constraints are needed to also achieve consistency and uniqueness of the characterization across dimensions. Intuitively, if a statement is distributed at dimension k, then for all remaining dimensions it will also be distributed. This is modeled with the following equations:

$$\forall l > k,\ \left(p^k_{i,j} = 1 \Rightarrow p^l_{i,j} = 1\right) \wedge \left(s^k_{i,j} = 1 \Rightarrow s^l_{i,j} = 1\right)$$

The final expression of the set $\mathcal{I}$ of all, distinct d-dimensional statement interleavings is:

$$\left\{\begin{array}{ll} \forall k \in \{1,\ldots,d\}, \quad \text{constraints on } \mathcal{O}^k \Big\} & \text{Total preorders at level } k \\ \left.\begin{array}{r} p^k_{i,j} \leq p^{k+1}_{i,j} \\ e^{k+1}_{i,j}+p^{k+1}_{i,j} \leq p^k_{i,j}+e^k_{i,j} \end{array}\right\} & \text{Statement interleaving uniqueness} \end{array}\right.$$

It is worth noting that each $\mathcal{O}^k$ contains numerous variables and constraints; but when it is possible to determine — thanks to the dependence graph for instance — that a given ordering of two elements i and j is impossible, some variables and constraints are eliminated. Our experiments indicate that these simplifications are quite effective, improving the scalability of the approach significantly.

3.2 Pruning for semantics preservation

The set $\mathcal{I}$ contains all and only distinct multi-level statement interleavings. A pruning step is needed to remove all interleavings that does not preserve the semantics. The algorithm proceeds level-by-level, from the outermost to the innermost. Such a decoupling is possible because we have encoded multi-dimensional interleaving constraints in $\mathcal{I}$, and that fusion at level k implies fusion at all preceding levels. In addition, leveraging Lemma 3 and Definition 3 we can determine the *fusibility* of a set of statements at a given level by exposing sufficient conditions for fusion on the schedules.

The general principle is to detect all the smallest possible sets of p unfusable statements at level k, and for each of them, to update $\mathcal{I}^k$ by adding an affine constraint of the form:

$$e^k_{S_1,S_2} + e^k_{S_2,S_3} + \ldots + e^k_{S_{p-1},S_p} < p-1 \quad (8)$$

thus preventing them (and any super-set of them) to be fused all together. We note $\mathcal{F}$ the final set with all pruning constraints for legality, $\mathcal{F} \subseteq \mathcal{I}$. A naive approach could be to enumerate all unordered subsets of the n statements of the program at level k, and check for fusibility, while avoiding to enumerate a super-set of an unfusable set. Instead, we leverage the polyhedral dependence graph to reduce the test to a much smaller set of structures.

The first step of our algorithm is to build a graph G to facilitate the enumeration of sets of statements to test for, with one node per statement. Sets of statements to test for fusibility will be represented as nodes connected by a path in that graph. Intuitively, if G is a complete graph then we can enumerate all unordered subsets of the n statements: enumerating all paths of length 1 gives all pairs of statements by retrieving the nodes connected by a given path, all paths of length 2 gives all triplets, etc. We aim at building a graph with less edges, so that we lower the number of sets of statements to test for fusibility. We first check the fusibility of all possible pairs of statements, and add an edge between two nodes only if (1) there is a dependence between them, and (2) either they must be fused together or they can be fused and distributed at that level. When two statements must be fused, they are merged to ensure all schedule constraints are considered when checking for fusibility.

The second step is to enumerate all paths of length ≥ 2 in the graph. Given a path p, the nodes in p represent a set of statements that has to be tested for fusibility. Each time they are detected to be not fusable, all paths with p as a sub-path are discarded from enumeration, and $\mathcal{F}^k$ is updated with an equation in the form of (8). The complete algorithm is shown in Figure 3.

Procedure `buildLegalSchedules` computes the space of legal schedules $\mathcal{L}$ according to Lemma 3, for the set of statements given in argument. Procedure `mustDistribute` tests for the emptiness of $\mathcal{L}$ when augmented with fusion conditions from Definition 3 up to level d. If there is no solution in the augmented set of constraints, then the statements cannot be fused at that level and hence must be distributed. Procedure `mustFuse` checks if it is legal to distribute the statements R and S. The check is performed by inserting a *splitter* at level d. This splitter is a constant one-dimensional schedule at level d, to force the full distribution of statement instances at that level. If there is no solution in this set of constraints, then the statements cannot be distributed at that level and hence must be fused. Procedure `canDistributeAndSwap` tests if it is legal to distribute R and S at level d and to execute S before R. The latter is required to compute the legal values of the $s_{R,S}$ variables at that level. The check is performed in a similar fashion as with `mustFuse`, except the splitter is made to make R execute after S. Finally procedure `mergeNodes` modifies the graph edges after the merging of two nodes R and S such that: (1) if for T there was an edge $e^{T\rightarrow R}$ and not $e^{T\rightarrow S}$ or vice-versa, $e^{T\rightarrow R}$ is deleted, and $e_{S,T} = 0$, this is to remove triplets of trivially unfusable sets;

```
PruneIllegalInterleavings: Compute ℱ
Input:
  pdg: polyhedral dependence graph
  n: number of statements
  maxDepth: maximum loop depth
Output:
  ℱ : the space of semantics-preserving distinct interleavings

ℱ ← I
unfusable ← ∅
for d ← 1 to maxDepth do
  G ← newGraph(n)
  forall pairs of dependent statements R,S do
    ℒ_{R,S} ← buildLegalSchedules({R,S}, pdg)
    if mustFuse(ℒ_{R,S}, d) then
      ℱ^d ← ℱ^d ∩ {e^d_{R,S} = 1}
    elseif mustDistribute(ℒ_{R,S}, d) then
      ℱ^d ← ℱ^d ∩ {e^d_{R,S} = 0}
    else
      if ¬ canDistributeAndSwap(ℒ_{R,S}, d) then
        ℱ^d ← ℱ^d ∩ {e^d_{R,S} + p^d_{R,S} = 1}
      end if
      addEdge(G, R, S)
    end if
  end for
  forall pairs of statements R,S such that e^d_{R,S} = 1 do
    mergeNodes(G, R, S)
  end for
  for l ← 2 to n-1 do
    forall paths p in G of length l such that
           there is no prefix of p in unfusable do
      ℒ_{nodes(p)} ← buildLegalSchedules({nodes(p)}, pdg)
      if mustDistribute(ℒ_{nodes(p)}, d) then
        ℱ^d ← ℱ^d ∩ {∑_p e^d_{pairs in p} < l-1}
        unfusable ← unfusable ∪ p
      end if
    end for
  end for
end for
```

Figure 3. Pruning algorithm

(2) if there are 2 edges between T and RS, one of them is deleted and its label is added to the remaining one existing label; (3) the label of the edge $e^{R\to S}$ is added to all remaining edges to/from RS, and $e^{R\to S}$ is deleted.

Applications The first motivation of building a separate search space of multidimensional statement interleavings is to decouple the selection of the interleaving from the selection of the transformation that enables this interleaving. One can then focus on building search heuristics for the fusion/distribution of statements only, and through the framework presented in this paper compute a schedule that respects this interleaving. Additional schedule properties such as parallelism and tilability can then be exploited without disturbing the outer level fusion scheme. We present in the following a complete technique to optimize programs based on iterative interleaving selection, leading to parallelized and tiled transformed programs. This technique is able to automatically adapt to the target framework, and successfully discovers the best performing fusion structure, whatever the specifics of the program, compiler and architecture.

Another motivation of building I is to enable the design of objective functions on fusion with the widest degree of applicability. For instance one can maximize fusion at outer level, by maximizing $\sum_{i,j} e^1_{i,j}$ or similarly distribution by minimizing the same sum. One can also assign a weight to the coefficients $e_{i,j}$ to favor fusion for statements carrying more reuse, for instance. This formulation allows to devise further pruning algorithms, offering to the optimization the most relevant choice of legal interleavings for a given target.

4. Optimizing for Locality and Parallelism

The previous sections define a general framework for multi-level statement interleaving. We address now the problem of *specializing* this framework to provide a complete optimization algorithm that integrates tiling and parallelization, along with the possibility to iteratively select different interleavings.

The optimization algorithm proceeds recursively, from the outermost level to the innermost. At each level of the recursion, we *select* the associated schedule dimension by instantiating its values. Then, we build the set of semantics-preserving interleavings at that level, pick one and proceed to the next level until a full schedule is instantiated. We present in Section 4.1 additional conditions on the schedules to improve the performance of the generated transformation, by integrating parallelism and tilability as criteria. Then we define in Section 4.2 a new fusibility criterion for a better performance impact, while restricting it to non-negative schedule coefficients. In Section 4.3, we show how to construct the set of legal interleaving without resorting on testing the set of legal schedules for sets larger than a pair of statements. Finally we present the complete optimization algorithm in Section 4.4.

4.1 Additional constraints on the schedules

Tiling (or blocking) is a crucial loop transformation for parallelism and locality. Bondhugula et al. developed a technique to compute an affine multidimensional schedule such that parallel loops are brought to the outer levels, and loops with dependences are pushed inside [6, 8]; at the same time, the number of dimensions that can be tiled are maximized. We extend and recast their technique into our framework.

Legality of tiling Tiling along a set of dimensions is legal if it is legal to proceed in fixed block sizes along those dimensions: this requires dependences not to be backward along those dimensions, thus avoiding a dependence path going out of and coming back into a tile; this makes it legal to execute the tile atomically. Irigoin and Triolet showed that a sufficient condition for a schedule Θ to be tilable [23], given R the dependence cone for the program, is that

$$\Theta.R \geq \vec{0}$$

In other words, this is equivalent to saying that all dependences must be weakly satisfied for each dimension Θ_k of the schedule. Such a property for the schedule is also known as Forward Communication Only property [21]. Returning to Lemma 3, it is possible to add an extra condition such that the p first dimensions of the schedules are permutable, a sufficient condition for the p first dimensions to be tilable. This translates into the following additional constraint on schedules, to enforce permutability of schedule dimensions.

DEFINITION 6 (Permutability condition). *Given two statements R,S. Given the conditions for semantics-preservation as stated by Lemma 3. Their schedule dimensions are permutable up to dimension k if in addition:*

$$\forall \mathcal{D}_{R,S},\ \forall p \in \{1,\ldots,k\},\ \forall \langle \vec{x}_R, \vec{x}_S\rangle \in \mathcal{D}_{R,S},$$
$$\Theta^S_p(\vec{x}_S) - \Theta^R_p(\vec{x}_R) \geq \delta_p^{\mathcal{D}_{R,S}}$$

To translate k into actual number of permutable *loops*, the k associated schedule dimensions must express non-constant schedules.

Rectangular tiling Selecting schedules such that each dimension is independent with respect to all others enables a more efficient tiling. Rectangular or close to rectangular blocks are achieved when possible, avoiding complex loop bounds which may arise in the case of arbitrarily shaped tiles. We resort to augmenting the constraints, level-by-level, with independence constraints. Hence, to compute schedule dimension k, we need *instantiate* first a schedule for all previous dimensions 1 to $k-1$. This comes from the fact that orthogonality constraints are not linear or convex and cannot be modeled as affine constraints directly. In its complete form, adding orthogonality constraints leads to a non-convex space, and ideally, all cases have to be tried and the best among those kept. When the number of statements is large, this leads to a combinatorial explosion. In such cases, we restrict ourselves to the sub-space of the orthogonal space where all the constraints are non-negative (that is, we restrict to have $\theta_{i,j} \in \mathbb{N}$). By just considering a particular convex portion of the orthogonal sub-space, we discard solutions that usually involve loop reversals or combination of reversals with other transformations; however, we believe this does not make a strong difference in practice. For the rest of this paper, **we now assume** $\theta_{i,j} \in \mathbb{N}$.

Inner permutable loops If it is not possible to express permutable loops for the first level, Bondhugula proposed to split the statements into distinct blocks to increase the possibility to find outer permutable loops [8]. Since our technique already supports explicitly the selection of any semantics-preserving possibility to split statements into blocks via the statement interleaving, we propose instead to enable the construction of *inner* permutable loops, by choosing to maximize the number of dependences solved at the first levels until we (possibly) find permutable dimensions at the current level. Doing so increases the freedom for the schedule at inner dimensions when it is not possible to express permutable loops at the outer levels. Maximizing the number of dependences solved at a given level was introduced by Feautrier [18] and we use a similar form:

$$S^i = \max \sum_{\mathcal{D}_{R,S}} \delta_k^{\mathcal{D}_{R,S}} \tag{9}$$

This cost function replaces the permutability condition, when it is not possible to find a permutable schedule for a given dimension k.

Dependence distance minimization There are infinitely many schedules that may satisfy the permutability criterion from Definition 6 as well as (9). An approach that has proved to be simple, practical, and powerful has been to find those schedules that have the shortest dependence components along them [6]. For polyhedral code, the distance between dependent iterations can always be bounded by an affine function of the global parameters, represented as a p-dimensional vector $\vec{n}$.

$$\mathbf{u}.\vec{n} + w \geq \Theta^S(\vec{x}_S) - \Theta^R(\vec{x}_R) \quad \langle \vec{x}_R, \vec{x}_S \rangle \in \mathcal{D}_{R,S} \qquad \mathbf{u} \in \mathbb{N}^p, w \in \mathbb{N} \tag{10}$$

In order to maximize data locality, one may include read-after-read dependences in the set of dependences $\mathcal{D}_{R,S}$ considered in the bounding function (10). We showed in (2) that there always exists a parametric form $-K.\vec{n} - K$ for the lower bound of the schedule latency. Reciprocally, $\mathbf{u}$ and w can always be selected large enough for $\mathbf{u}.\vec{n} + w$ to be an upper-bound on the schedule latency. So considering read-after-read dependences in the bounding function does not prevent from finding a legal schedule.

The permutability and bounding function constraints are recast through the affine form of the Farkas Lemma such that the only unknowns left are the coefficients of Θ and those of the bounding function, namely $\mathbf{u}$, w. Coordinates of the bounding function are then used as the minimization objective to obtain the unknown coefficients of Θ.

$$\text{minimize}_{\prec} \left(\mathbf{u}, w, \ldots, \theta_{i,1}, \ldots\right) \tag{11}$$

The resulting transformation is a complex composition of multidimensional loop fusion, distribution, interchange, skewing, shifting and peeling. Eventually multidimensional tiling is applied on all permutable bands, and resulting tiles can be executed in parallel or at worse with a pipeline-parallel schedule [8]. Tile sizes are computed such that data accessed by each tile roughly fits in the L1 cache.

4.2 Fusability check

We presented in Section 2.5 a generalized check for fusibility which guarantees at least one instance of the iteration domains are fused. But for fusion to have a stronger performance impact, a better criterion is preferred to guarantee that at most x instances are *not* finely interleaved. In general, computing the exact set of interleaved instances requires complex techniques. A typical example is schedules generating a non-unit stride in the supporting lattice of the transformed iteration domain. For such cases, computing the exact number of non-fused instances could be achieved using the Ehrhart quasi-polynomial of the intersection of the image of iteration domains by the schedules [10]. However, this refined precision is not required to determine if a schedule represents a potentially interesting fusion. We allow for a lack of precision to present an easily computable test for fusibility based on an *estimate* of the number of instances that are not finely interleaved.

For the sake of simplicity, we assume that loop bounds have been normalized such that $\vec{0}$ is the first iteration of the domain. When considering non-negative coefficients, the lowest timestamp assigned by a schedule Θ_k^R is simply $\Theta_k^R(\vec{0})$. One can recompute the corresponding timestamp by looking at the values of the coefficients attached to the parameters and the constant. Hence, the timestamp interval c between the two first scheduled instances by Θ_k^R and Θ_k^S is simply the difference of the (parametric) constant parts of the schedules. In addition, to avoid the case where Θ_k^R and/or Θ_k^S are (parametric) constant schedules, we force the linear part of the schedule to be non-null. This is formalized in Definition 7.

DEFINITION 7 (Fusability restricted to non-negative coefficients). *Given two statements R,S such that R is surrounded by d^R loops, and S by d^S loops. They are fusable at level p if, $\forall k \in \{1 \ldots p\}$, there exist two semantics-preserving schedules Θ_k^R and Θ_k^S such that:*

$$(i) \quad -c < \Theta_k^R(\vec{0}) - \Theta_k^S(\vec{0}) < c$$

$$(ii) \quad \sum_{i=1}^{d^R} \theta_{k,i}^R > 0, \; \sum_{i=1}^{d^S} \theta_{k,i}^S > 0$$

The constant c is an indicator on the timestamp difference between the first scheduled instance of R and the first scheduled instance of S. By tuning the allowed size for this interval, one can range from full, aligned fusion ($c = 0$) to full distribution (with c greater than the schedule latency of R or S). Note that Definition 7 is independent from any composition of affine transformations that may be needed to enable the fusion of the statements. The schedules that implement the fusion (hence modeling also the fusion-enabling sequence of transformations) are simply solutions in the space of semantics-preserving non-negative schedules augmented with the fusibility constraints.

4.3 Computation of the set of interleavings

We have now restricted $\theta_{i,j} \in \mathbb{N}$. A consequence is the design of a *specialized* version of our generic algorithm to compute the set of semantics-preserving interleavings. This specialized version leverages new results on the transitivity of fusibility for the case of non-negative schedule coefficients, as shown below. Furthermore, it does not require computing with $\mathcal{L}$, which significantly improves the overall complexity of the procedure.

Fusability is the capability to exhibit a semantics-preserving schedule such that some of the instances are fused, according to Definition 7. First let us remark that fusibility is not a transitive relation. As an illustration, consider the sequence of matrix-by-vector products $x = Ab$, $y = Bx$, $z = Cy$. While it is possible to fuse them 2-by-2, it is not possible to fuse them all together. When considering fusing loops for $x = Ab$, $y = Bx$, one has to permute loops in $y = Bx$. When considering fusing loops for $y = Bx$, $z = Cy$, one has to keep loops in $y = Bx$ as is. We now present a sufficient condition to determine the transitivity of fusibility, based on the existence of compatible pairwise permutations.

First we introduce a decomposition of *one-dimensional schedules* in two sub-parts, with the objective of isolating loop permutation from the other transformations embedded in the schedule. One can decompose a one-dimensional schedule Θ_k^R with coefficients in $\mathbb{N}$ into two sub-schedules μ^R and λ^R such that:

$$\Theta_k^R = \mu^R + \lambda^R, \quad \mu_i^R \in \mathbb{N}, \; \lambda_i^R \in \mathbb{N}$$

without any loss of expressiveness. Such a decomposition is always possible because of the distributivity of the matrix multiplication over the matrix addition. For our purpose, we are interested in modeling one-dimensional schedules which are *not* constant schedules. This is relevant as we do not want to consider building a schedule for fusion that would translate only into statement interleaving. On the contrary we aim at building a schedule that performs the interleaving of statements *instances*, hence the linear part of the schedule must be non-null. For R surrounded by d loops, we enforce μ to be a linear form of the d loop iterators:

$$\mu^R(\vec{x}_R) = \begin{pmatrix}\mu_1^R & \dots & \mu_d^R & \vec{0} & 0\end{pmatrix}.\begin{pmatrix}i_1 & \dots & i_d & \vec{n} & 1\end{pmatrix}^t$$

To model non-constant schedules, we add the additional constraint $\sum_{i=1}^{d} \mu_i^R = 1$. Note that by constraining μ to have only one coefficient set to 1, this does not prevent to model any compositions of slowing or skewing: these would be embedded in the λ part of the schedule, as shown in the example below.

The μ part of the schedule models different cases of loop permutations. For instance for statement R surrounded by 3 loops in the ThreeMatMat example, μ^R can take only three values:

$$\mu^R(\vec{x}_R) = \begin{pmatrix}1 & 0 & 0 & 0 & 0\end{pmatrix}.\begin{pmatrix}i & j & k & N & 1\end{pmatrix}^t = (i)$$
$$\mu^R(\vec{x}_R) = \begin{pmatrix}0 & 1 & 0 & 0 & 0\end{pmatrix}.\begin{pmatrix}i & j & k & N & 1\end{pmatrix}^t = (j)$$
$$\mu^R(\vec{x}_R) = \begin{pmatrix}0 & 0 & 1 & 0 & 0\end{pmatrix}.\begin{pmatrix}i & j & k & N & 1\end{pmatrix}^t = (k)$$

while λ^R can take arbitrary values. For better illustration let us now build the decomposition of the schedule $\Theta_k^R = (2.j + k + 2)$. Θ_k^R is the composition of a permutation, a non-unit skewing and a shifting, and can be decomposed as follows:

$$\mu^R = \begin{pmatrix}0 & 1 & 0 & 0 & 0\end{pmatrix}$$
$$\lambda^R = \begin{pmatrix}0 & 1 & 1 & 0 & 2\end{pmatrix}$$
$$\Theta_k^R(\vec{x}_R) = (\mu^R + \lambda^R)(\vec{x}_R) = (2.j + k + 2)$$

One may note that another possible decomposition is $\mu^R(\vec{x}_R) = (k)$, $\lambda^R(\vec{x}_R) = (2j + 2)$. In general, when the schedule contains skewing it is possible to embed either of the skewing dimensions in the μ part of the schedule. For the sake of coherency we add an extra convention for the decomposition: μ matches the first non-null iterator coefficient of the schedule. Returning to the example, $\mu^R(\vec{x}_R) = (j)$, $\lambda^R(\vec{x}_R) = (j + k + 2)$ is thus the only valid decomposition of Θ_k^R.

Note that this decomposition prevents modeling of compositions of loop permutations in the λ part. For λ to represent a loop permutation, λ must have values in $\mathbb{Z}$, as shown in the following example:

$$\mu^R(\vec{x}_R) = \begin{pmatrix}1 & 0 & 0 & 0 & 0\end{pmatrix}.\begin{pmatrix}i & j & k & N & 1\end{pmatrix}^t = (i)$$

$$(\mu^R + \lambda)(\vec{x}_R) = (j) \Rightarrow \lambda = \begin{pmatrix}-1 & 1 & 0 & 0 & 0\end{pmatrix}$$

which is not possible as we have constrained $\lambda_i \in \mathbb{N}$. Hence, when considering arbitrary compositions of permutation, (parametric) shifting, skewing and peeling, the $\mu + \lambda$ decomposition separates permutation (embedded in the μ part of the schedule) from the other transformations (embedded in the λ part of the schedule). We now show it is possible to determine if a set of statements are fusable only by looking at the possible values for the μ part of their schedules.

Considering three statements R, S, T that are fusable while preserving the semantics at level k. Then there exist $\Theta_k^R = \mu^R + \lambda^R$, $\Theta_k^S = \mu^S + \lambda^S$, $\Theta_k^T = \mu^T + \lambda^T$ leading to fusing those statements. Considering now the sub-problem of fusing only R and S, we build the set $\mathcal{M}_{R,S}$ of all possible values of μ^R, μ^S for which there exist a λ^R, λ^S leading to fuse R and S. Obviously, the value of μ^R, μ^S leading to fusing R, S, T are in $\mathcal{M}_{R,S}$, and μ^S, μ^T are also in $\mathcal{M}_{S,T}$. Similarly μ^R, μ^T are in $\mathcal{M}_{R,T}$. We derive a sufficient condition for fusibility based on pairwise loop permutations for fusion.

LEMMA 6 (Pairwise sufficient condition for fusibility). *Given three statements R, S, T such that they can be 2-by-2 fused and distributed. Given $\mathcal{M}_{R,S}$ (resp. $\mathcal{M}_{R,T}$, resp. $\mathcal{M}_{S,T}$) the set of possible tuples μ^R, μ^S (resp. μ^R, μ^T, resp. μ^S, μ^T) leading to fusing R and S (resp. R and T, resp. S and T) such that the full program semantics is respected. R, S, T are fusable if there exists μ^R, μ^S, μ^T such that:*

$$\mu^R, \mu^S \in \mathcal{M}_{R,S}$$
$$\mu^R, \mu^T \in \mathcal{M}_{R,T}$$
$$\mu^S, \mu^T \in \mathcal{M}_{S,T}$$

Proof. Given the schedule $\Theta_k^R = \mu^R + \lambda^R, \Theta_k^S = \mu^S + \lambda^S$ leading to fusing R and S, $\Theta_k^{'R} = \mu^R + \lambda^{'R}, \Theta_k^T = \mu^T + \lambda^T$ leading to fusing R and T, and $\Theta_k^{'S} = \mu^S + \lambda^{'S}, \Theta_k^{'T} = \mu^T + \lambda^{'T}$ leading to fusing S and T, such that they all preserve the full program semantics.

The schedule $\Theta_k^{*R} = \mu^R + \lambda^R + \lambda^{'R}, \Theta_k^{*S} = \mu^S + \lambda^S + \lambda^{'R}$ is legal, as adding $\lambda^{'R}$ consists in performing additional compositions of skewing and shifting, which cannot make the dependence vectors lexicographically negative. It cannot consist in performing a parametric shift (resulting in a loop distribution), Θ_k^R is a schedule fusing R and S and $\Theta_k^{'R}$ is a schedule fusing R and T. As Θ_k^{*R} is a non-constant schedule, it leads to fusing R and S. Generalizing this reasoning we can exhibit the following semantics-preserving schedule leading to the fusion of R, S, T:

$$\Theta_k^{*R} = \mu^R + \lambda^R + \lambda^{'R} + \lambda^S + \lambda^{'S} + \lambda^T + \lambda^{'T}$$
$$\Theta_k^{*S} = \mu^S + \lambda^R + \lambda^{'R} + \lambda^S + \lambda^{'S} + \lambda^T + \lambda^{'T}$$
$$\Theta_k^{*T} = \mu^T + \lambda^R + \lambda^{'R} + \lambda^S + \lambda^{'S} + \lambda^T + \lambda^{'T}$$

As all statements are fused 2-by-2, they are fused all together. As the three statements can be distributed 2-by-2, there is no dependence cycle. ∎

To stress the importance of Lemma 6, let us return to the ThreeMatMat example. We can compute the pairwise permutations for fusion sets at the outermost level:

$$\mathcal{M}_{R,S} = \{(i,i); (i,j); (i,k); (j,i); (j,j); (j,k); (k,i); (k,j); (k,k)\}$$
$$\mathcal{M}_{R,T} = \{(i,i); (j,k)\}$$
$$\mathcal{M}_{S,T} = \{(i,k); (j,j)\}$$

These sets are computed by iteratively testing, against the set of constraints for semantics-preservation augmented with fusion and orthogonality constraints, for the existence of solutions with a non-null value for each of the coefficients associated with the statement iterators *for only the two considered statements*. This is in contrast to the general algorithm which requires to consider the whole set of candidate statements for fusion. Here we can decide that R,S,T are fusable, as the solution $\mu^R = j$, $\mu^S = i$, $\mu^T = k$ respects the conditions from Lemma 6. This solution is presented in Figure 2(a).

To improve further the tractability, we rely on two more standard properties on fusion. Given two statements R and S:

1. if R and S are not fusable, then any statement on which R transitively depends on is not fusable with S and any statement transitively depending on S;
2. reciprocally, if R and S must be fused, then any statement depending on R and on which S depends must also be fused with R and S.

These properties cut the number of tested sequences dramatically, in particular, in highly constrained programs such as loop-intensive kernels. They are used at each step of the optimization algorithm.

4.4 Optimization algorithm

We now present our optimization algorithm. The algorithm explores possible interleavings of dimension *maxExploreDepth*, and generates a collection of program schedules, each of them being a candidate for the optimization. We use iterative compilation to select the best performing one. For each candidate program schedule we generate back a syntactic C code, compile it and run it on the target machine.

The structure and principle of the optimization algorithm, shown in Figure 4, matches that of the pruning algorithm of Figure 3, as it also aims at computing a set of feasible interleavings at a given level. It is in essence a *specialization* of the pruning algorithm for our optimization problem instance. To decide the fusibility of a set of statements, we put the problem in a form matching the applicability conditions of Lemma 6. We merge nodes that must be 2-by-2 fused to guarantee that we are checking for the strictest set of program-wise valid μ values when considering fusibility.

Procedure `buildLegalOptimizedSchedules` computes, for a given pair of statements R,S, the set $\mathcal{T}_{R,S}$ of semantics-preserving non-negative schedules augmented with permutability and orthogonality constraints as defined in the previous Section, given the previously computed rows of Θ. Procedures `mustDistribute`, `mustFuse`, `mergeNodes` operate in a similar fashion as in the general case. Procedure `computeLegalPermutationsAtLevel` computes $\mathcal{M}_{R,S}$ the set of all valid permutations μ^R,μ^S leading to fusion. To check if a given permutation μ^R,μ^S is valid and leading for fusion at level d, the set of constraints is tested for the existence of a solution where the schedule coefficients of row d corresponding to μ^R and μ^S is not 0. This is sufficient to determine the existence of the associated λ part. Procedure `existCompatiblePermutation` collects the sets $\mathcal{M}$ of the pairs of statements connected by the path p, and tests for the existence of μ values according to Lemma 6. If there is no compatible permutation, then an additional constraint is added to $\mathcal{F}^d$ such that it is not possible to fuse the statements in p all together. The constraint sets that the $e_{i,j}$ variables, for all pairs i,j in the path p, cannot be set to 1 all together. Procedure `embedInterleaving` instantiate a schedule row Θ_{2d} that implements the interleaving i, using only the scalar coefficients of the schedule. Procedure `computeOptimizedSchedule` instantiates a schedule row Θ_{2d+1} at the current interleaving dimension d, for all statements. The interleaving is given by i, and individually for each group of statements to be fused under a common loop, a schedule is computed to maximize fusion and to enforce permutability if possible. To select the coefficient values we resort to the objective function (11). Finally, procedure `finalizeOptimizedSchedule` computes the possibly remaining schedule dimensions, when *maxEploreDepth* is lower than the maximum program loop depth. Note that in this case, maximal fusion is used to select the interleaving, hence we do not need to build a set of interleavings for the remaining depths.

```
OptimizeRec: Compute all optimizations
Input:
  Θ: partial program optimization
  pdg: polyhedral dependence graph
  d: current level for the interleaving exploration
  n: number of statements
  maxExploreDepth: maximum level to explore for interleaving
Output:
  Θ: complete program optimization

G ← newGraph(n)
F^d ← O
unfusable ← ∅
forall pairs of dependent statements R,S in pdg do
   T_{R,S} ← buildLegalOptimizedSchedules({R,S}, Θ, d, pdg)
   if mustDistribute(T_{R,S}, d) then
      F^d ← F^d ∩ {e_{R,S} = 0}
   else
      if mustFuse(T_{R,S}, d) then
         F^d ← F^d ∩ {e_{R,S} = 1}
      end if
      F^d ← F^d ∩ {s_{R,S} = 0}
      M_{R,S} ← computeLegalPermutationsAtLevel(T_{R,S}, d)
      addEdgeWithLabel(G, R, S, M_{R,S})
   end if
end for
forall pairs of statements R,S such that e_{R,S} = 1 do
   mergeNodes(G, R, S)
end for
for l ← 2 to n−1 do
   forall paths p in G of length l such that
     there is no prefix of p in unfusable do
      if ¬ existCompatiblePermutation(nodes(p)) then
         F^d ← F^d ∩ {∑_p e_{pairs in p} < l−1}
         unfusable ← unfusable ∪ p
      end if
   end do
end for
forall i ∈ F^d do
   Θ_{2d} ← embedInterleaving(Θ, d, i)
   Θ_{2d+1} ← computeOptimizedSchedule(Θ, pdg, d, i)
   if d < maxExploreDepth then
      OptimizeRec(Θ, pdg, d+1, n, maxExploreDepth)
   else
      finalizeOptimizedSchedule(Θ, pdg, p)
       output Θ
   end if
end for
```

Figure 4. Optimization Algorithm

In practice this algorithm proved to be very fast, and for instance computing the set $\mathcal{F}^1$ of all semantics-preserving interleavings at the first dimension takes less than 0.5 second for the benchmark ludcmp, pruning I^1 from about 10^{12} structures to 8, on an initial space with 182 binary variables to model all total preorders. Subsequently traversing $\mathcal{F}^1$ and computing a valid transformation for all interleavings takes an additional 2.1 second.

5. Experimental Results

Studies performed on the performance impact of selecting schedules at various levels highlighted the higher impact of carefully selecting outer loops [32, 33]. The selection of the statement interleaving at the outermost level captures the most significant difference in terms of locality and communication. We can limit the recursive traversal of interleavings to the outer level only, while obtaining significant performance improvement and a wide range of transformed codes. Nevertheless, when the number of candidates in $\mathcal{F}^1$ is very small, typically because of several loop-dependent dependences at the outer level, it is relevant to build $\mathcal{F}^2$ and further.

				$\mathcal{O}$			$\mathcal{F}^1$						
Benchmark	#loops	#stmts	#refs	#dim	#cst	#points	#dim	#cst	#points	Time	Pb. Size	perf-Intel	perf-AMD
advect3d	12	4	32	12	58	75	9	43	26	0.82s	300x300x300	1.47×	5.19×
atax	4	4	10	12	58	75	6	25	16	0.06s	8000x8000	3.66×	1.88×
bicg	3	4	10	12	58	75	10	52	26	0.05s	8000x8000	1.75×	1.40×
gemver	7	4	19	12	58	75	6	28	8	0.06s	8000x8000	1.34×	1.33×
ludcmp	9	14	35	182	3003	$\approx 10^{12}$	40	443	8	0.54s	1000x1000	1.98×	1.45×
doitgen	5	3	7	6	22	13	3	10	4	0.08s	50x50x50	15.35×	14.27×
varcovar	7	7	26	42	350	47293	22	193	96	0.09s	1000x1000	7.24×	14.83×
correl	5	6	12	30	215	4683	21	162	176	0.09s	1000x1000	3.00×	3.44×

Table 1. Search space statistics and performance improvement

Note that in the experiments presented in this paper we traverse exhaustively only $\mathcal{F}^1$.

Search space statistics Several $e_{i,j}$ and $p_{i,j}$ variables are set during the pruning of $\mathcal{O}$, so several consistency constraints are made useless and are not built, significantly helping to reduce the size of the space to build. Table 1 illustrates this by highlighting, for our benchmarks considered, the properties of the polytope $\mathcal{O}$ in terms of the number of dimensions (#dim), constraints (#cst) and points (#points) when compared to $\mathcal{F}^1$, the polytope of possible interleavings *for the first dimension only*. For each benchmark, we list #loops the number of loops, #stmts the number of statements, #refs the number of array references, as well as the time to build all candidate interleavings from the input source code (that is, including all analysis) on an Intel Xeon 2.4GHz. We also report the dataset size we used for the benchmarks (Pb. Size).

Performance evaluation The automatic optimization and parallelization approach has been implemented in PoCC, the *Polyhedral Compiler Collection*, a complete source-to-source polyhedral compiler based on available free software for polyhedral compilation.[3] The time to compute the space, select a candidate and compute a full transformation is negligible with respect to the compilation and execution time of the tested versions. In our experiments, the full process takes a few seconds for the smaller benchmarks, and up to about 2 minutes for correl on an Intel Xeon processor.

Extensive performance characterization is beyond the scope of this paper. The reader is referred to other publications [32, 34] for a more comprehensive analysis of the performance issues that are successfully addressed by our iterative framework on various high-end multi-core architectures. Nevertheless, to illustrate the benefit of our approach, we report in Table 1 the performance improvement obtained by our iterative process. We used Intel ICC 11.0 with options `-fast -parallel -openmp` as the baseline on the original code, and also to compile all our optimized programs. We report the performance improvement achieved over ICC with automatic parallelization enabled on the original code, under the column perf-Intel for a 4-socket Intel hex-core Xeon E7450 (Dunnington), running at 2.4GHz with 64GB of memory (24 cores, 24 hardware threads), and perf-AMD for a 4-socket AMD quad-core Opteron 8380 (Shanghai) running at 2.50GHz (16 cores, 16 hardware threads) with 64GB of memory.

Beyond absolute performance improvement, another motivating factor for iterative selection of fusion structures is performance portability. Because of significant differences in design, in particular in SIMD units' performance and cache behavior, a transformation has to be tuned for a specific machine. This leads to a significant variation in performance across tested frameworks. To illustrate this, we show in Figure 5 the relative performance normalized with respect to icc-par for gemver, for the Xeon and Opteron. The version index is plotted on the x axis; 1 represents maximal fusion while 8 corresponds to maximal distribution. For the Xeon, the best found version performs 10% better than the best fusion configuration for the Opteron. Optimizing for the Opteron, the best version performs 20% better than the best fusion structure for the Xeon.

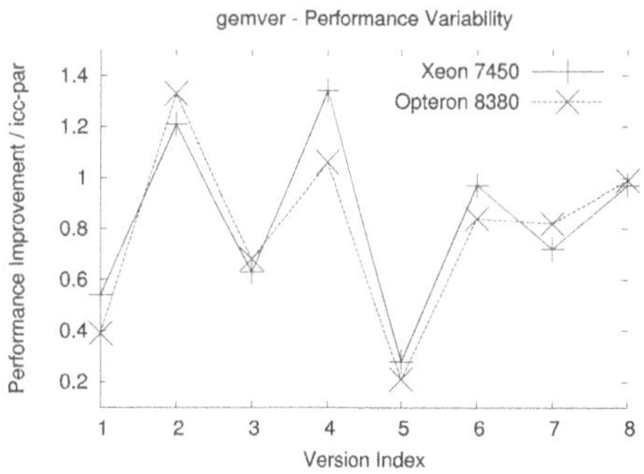

Figure 5. Performance variability for gemver

Tuning the trade-off between fusion and distribution is a relevant approach to drive a complete high-level optimization framework. The main motivation is the difficulty to design a portable heuristic to select the best interleaving, as the best fusion structure is machine-dependent and even depends on the back-end compiler used. Also, as shown in Figure 2, the interleaving selection can dramatically impact the transformations required to implement the interleaving (e.g., loop interchange) and subsequently drives the optimization process.

Our technique is able to automatically adapt to the target framework, and thanks to empirical search successfully discovers the best fusion structure, whatever the specifics of the program, compiler and architecture.

6. Related Work

Traditional approaches to loop fusion [25, 29, 40] are limited in their ability to handle compositions of loop transformations. This is mainly due to the lack of a powerful representation for dependences and transformations. Hence, non-polyhedral approaches typically study fusion in isolation from other transformations. Megiddo and Sarkar [30] presented a solution to the problem of loop fusion in parallel programs that performs fusion while preserving the parallelism in the input program. We believe that several interesting solutions are not obtained when fusion is decoupled from parallelization in those frameworks where legal fusion choices are left out of the framework. Darte et al. [13, 14] studied the combination of loop shifting and fusion for parallelization. In contrast to all of these works, the search space explored in this paper includes fusion in the presence of all polyhedral transformations.

Heuristics for loop fusion and tiling have been proposed in loop-nest optimizers [26, 35, 45, 48]. Those heuristics have also been revisited in the context of new architectures with non-uniform mem-

[3] PoCC is available at `http://pocc.sourceforge.net`

ory hierarchies and heterogeneous computing resources [37]. The polyhedral model is complementary to these efforts, opening many more opportunities for optimization in loop nest optimizers and parallelizing compilers. Note that the polyhedral model is currently being integrated into production compilers, including GCC[4], IBM XL and LLVM/Polly.

A heuristic that integrates loop fusion and tiling in the polyhedral model that subsumes a number of transformations such as interchange, skewing and loop shifting was presented in Bondhugula et al. [6, 8]. Their work builds complex sequences of transformations that enable communication-minimal tiling of imperfectly nested loops that generalizes the prior work on tiling perfectly-nested loops [21, 23, 36, 49] and is helpful in identifying parallelism-locality trade-offs. Bondhugula et al. [7] refined their static cost model for fusion by incorporating utilization of hardware prefetch stream buffers, loss of parallelism, and constraints imposed by privatization and code expansion. However, these techniques do not model a closed space of all and only distinct fusion structures, instead they operate on the entire space of valid fusion structures and select a specific one that minimizes a static cost function.

Across a broad range of machine architectures and compiler transformations, iterative compilation has proven to be effective in deriving significant performance benefits [1, 5, 19, 31, 33, 35, 37, 42, 46]. Nevertheless, none of iterative compilation approaches achieved the expressiveness and the ability to apply complex sequences of transformations presented in this paper, while focusing the search only on semantics-preserving transformation candidates.

Several powerful semi-automatic frameworks based on the polyhedral model [9, 11, 20, 24, 43] have been proposed; these frameworks are able to capture fusion structures, but do not construct profitable parallelization and tiling strategies using a model-based heuristic.

R-Stream is a source-to-source, auto-parallelizing compiler developed by Reservoir Labs, Inc. R-Stream is based on the polyhedral model and targets modern heterogeneous multi-core architectures, including multiprocessors with caches, systems with accelerators, and distributed memory architectures that require explicit memory management and data movement [28]. The affine scheduler in R-Stream builds on contributions from Feautrier [18], Megiddo and Sarkar [30] and Bondhugula et al. [8]. It introduced the concept of affine fusion to enable a single formulation for the joint optimization of cost functions representing tradeoffs between amount of parallelism and amount of locality at various depths in the loop nest hierarchy. Scheduling algorithms in R-Stream search an optimization space that is either constructed on a depth-by-depth basis as solutions are found or based on the convex space of all legal multi-dimensional schedules as had been illustrated by Vasilache [44]. R-Stream allows direct optimization of the tradeoff function using Integer Linear Programming (ILP) solvers as well as iterative exploration of the search space. Redundant solutions in the search space are implicitly pruned out by the combined tradeoff function as they exhibit the same overall cost. In practice, a solution to the optimization problem represents a whole class of equivalent scheduling functions with the same cost.

7. Conclusions

The selection of a profitable composition of loop transformations is a hard combinatorial problem. We proposed a complete, non-redundant characterization of multidimensional affine transformations as a convex space. We then pruned this polyhedron, focusing on multidimensional statement interleavings corresponding to a generalized combination of loop fusion, loop distribution and code motion. We proposed a practical optimization algorithm to explore the pruned polyhedron, while heuristically building a profitable, semantics-preserving, affine enabling transformation. This algorithm was applied to relevant benchmarks, demonstrating good scalability and strong performance improvements over state-of-the-art multi-core architectures and parallelizing compilers.

Acknowledgments We are grateful to Paul Feautrier for providing the foundations for multidimensional affine scheduling, and the simplification of Vasilache's original convex formulation of all semantics-preserving schedules that we presented in this paper.

This work was supported in part by the U.S. Defense Advanced Research Projects Agency through AFRL Contract FA8650-09-C-7915, the U.S. National Science Foundation through awards 0541409, 0811457, 0811781, 0926687 and 0926688, by the U.S. Army through contract W911NF-10-1-0004, and by the European Commission through the FP7 project TERAFLUX id. 249013.

References

[1] F. Agakov, E. Bonilla, J. Cavazos, B. Franke, G. Fursin, M. F. P. O'Boyle, J. Thomson, M. Toussaint, and C. K. I. Williams. Using machine learning to focus iterative optimization. In *Proc. of the Intl. Symposium on Code Generation and Optimization (CGO'06)*, pages 295–305, Washington, 2006.

[2] D. Barthou, J.-F. Collard, and P. Feautrier. Fuzzy array dataflow analysis. *Journal of Parallel and Distributed Computing*, 40:210–226, 1997.

[3] C. Bastoul. Code generation in the polyhedral model is easier than you think. In *IEEE Intl. Conf. on Parallel Architectures and Compilation Techniques (PACT'04)*, pages 7–16, Juan-les-Pins, France, Sept. 2004.

[4] M.-W. Benabderrahmane, L.-N. Pouchet, A. Cohen, and C. Bastoul. The polyhedral model is more widely applicable than you think. In *Intl. Conf. on Compiler Construction (ETAPS CC'10)*, LNCS 6011, pages 283–303, Paphos, Cyprus, Mar. 2010.

[5] F. Bodin, T. Kisuki, P. M. W. Knijnenburg, M. F. P. O'Boyle, and E. Rohou. Iterative compilation in a non-linear optimisation space. In *W. on Profile and Feedback Directed Compilation*, Paris, Oct. 1998.

[6] U. Bondhugula, M. Baskaran, S. Krishnamoorthy, J. Ramanujam, A. Rountev, and P. Sadayappan. Automatic transformations for communication-minimized parallelization and locality optimization in the polyhedral model. In *International conference on Compiler Construction (ETAPS CC)*, Apr. 2008.

[7] U. Bondhugula, O. Gunluk, S. Dash, and L. Renganarayanan. A model for fusion and code motion in an automatic parallelizing compiler. In *Proc. of the 19th Intl. conf. on Parallel Architectures and Compilation Techniques (PACT'10)*, pages 343–352, 2010.

[8] U. Bondhugula, A. Hartono, J. Ramanujam, and P. Sadayappan. A practical automatic polyhedral program optimization system. In *ACM SIGPLAN Conference on Programming Language Design and Implementation*, June 2008.

[9] C. Chen, J. Chame, and M. Hall. CHiLL: A framework for composing high-level loop transformations. Technical Report 08-897, U. of Southern California, 2008.

[10] P. Clauss. Counting solutions to linear and nonlinear constraints through ehrhart polynomials: applications to analyze and transform scientific programs. In *Proc. of the Intl. Conf. on Supercomputing*, pages 278–285. ACM, 1996.

[11] A. Cohen, S. Girbal, D. Parello, M. Sigler, O. Temam, and N. Vasilache. Facilitating the search for compositions of program transformations. In *ACM International conference on Supercomputing*, pages 151–160, June 2005.

[12] A. Darte. On the complexity of loop fusion. *Parallel Computing*, pages 149–157, 1999.

[13] A. Darte and G. Huard. Loop shifting for loop parallelization. Technical Report RR2000-22, ENS Lyon, May 2000.

[4] Graphite framework: `http://gcc.gnu.org/wiki/Graphite`.

[14] A. Darte, G.-A. Silber, and F. Vivien. Combining retiming and scheduling techniques for loop parallelization and loop tiling. *Parallel Proc. Letters*, 7(4):379–392, 1997.

[15] P. Feautrier. Parametric integer programming. *RAIRO Recherche Opérationnelle*, 22(3):243–268, 1988.

[16] P. Feautrier. Dataflow analysis of scalar and array references. *Intl. J. of Parallel Programming*, 20(1):23–53, Feb. 1991.

[17] P. Feautrier. Some efficient solutions to the affine scheduling problem, part I: one dimensional time. *Intl. J. of Parallel Programming*, 21(5):313–348, Oct. 1992.

[18] P. Feautrier. Some efficient solutions to the affine scheduling problem, part II: multidimensional time. *Intl. J. of Parallel Programming*, 21(6):389–420, Dec. 1992.

[19] F. Franchetti, Y. Voronenko, and M. Püschel. Formal loop merging for signal transforms. In *ACM SIGPLAN Conf. on Programming Language Design and Implementation*, pages 315–326, 2005.

[20] S. Girbal, N. Vasilache, C. Bastoul, A. Cohen, D. Parello, M. Sigler, and O. Temam. Semi-automatic composition of loop transformations. *Intl. J. of Parallel Programming*, 34(3):261–317, June 2006.

[21] M. Griebl. Automatic parallelization of loop programs for distributed memory architectures. Habilitation thesis. Facultät für Mathematik und Informatik, Universität Passau, 2004.

[22] A.-C. Guillou, F. Quilleré, P. Quinton, S. Rajopadhye, and T. Risset. Hardware design methodology with the Alpha language. In *FDL'01*, Lyon, France, Sept. 2001.

[23] F. Irigoin and R. Triolet. Supernode partitioning. In *ACM SIGPLAN Principles of Programming Languages*, pages 319–329, 1988.

[24] W. Kelly. *Optimization within a Unified Transformation Framework*. PhD thesis, Univ. of Maryland, 1996.

[25] K. Kennedy and K. McKinley. Maximizing loop parallelism and improving data locality via loop fusion and distribution. In *Languages and Compilers for Parallel Computing*, pages 301–320, 1993.

[26] I. Kodukula, N. Ahmed, and K. Pingali. Data-centric multi-level blocking. In *ACM SIGPLAN'97 Conf. on Programming Language Design and Implementation*, pages 346–357, Las Vegas, June 1997.

[27] M. Kudlur and S. Mahlke. Orchestrating the execution of stream programs on multicore platforms. In *ACM SIGPLAN Conf. on Programming Language Design and Implementation (PLDI'08)*, pages 114–124. ACM Press, 2008.

[28] R. Lethin, A. Leung, B. Meister, N. Vasilache, D. Wohlford, M. Baskaran, A. Hartono, and K. Datta. R-stream compiler. In D. Padua, editor, *Encyclopedia of Parallel Computing*. Springer, 1st edition., 2011, 50 p. in 4 volumes, not available separately., hardcover edition, June 2011.

[29] K. S. McKinley, S. Carr, and C.-W. Tseng. Improving data locality with loop transformations. *ACM Trans. Program. Lang. Syst.*, 18(4):424–453, 1996.

[30] N. Megiddo and V. Sarkar. Optimal weighted loop fusion for parallel programs. In *symposium on Parallel Algorithms and Architectures*, pages 282–291, 1997.

[31] A. Nisbet. GAPS: A compiler framework for genetic algorithm (GA) optimised parallelisation. In *HPCN Europe 1998: Proc. of the Intl. Conf. and Exhibition on High-Performance Computing and Networking*, pages 987–989, London, UK, 1998. Springer-Verlag.

[32] L.-N. Pouchet. *Interative Optimization in the Polyhedral Model*. PhD thesis, University of Paris-Sud 11, Orsay, France, Jan. 2010.

[33] L.-N. Pouchet, C. Bastoul, A. Cohen, and J. Cavazos. Iterative optimization in the polyhedral model: Part II, multidimensional time. In *ACM SIGPLAN Conf. on Programming Language Design and Implementation (PLDI'08)*, pages 90–100. ACM Press, 2008.

[34] L.-N. Pouchet, U. Bondhugula, C. Bastoul, A. Cohen, J. Ramanujam, and P. Sadayappan. Combined iterative and model-driven optimization in an automatic parallelization framework. In *Conf. on SuperComputing (SC'10)*, New Orleans, LA, Nov. 2010. To appear.

[35] A. Qasem and K. Kennedy. Profitable loop fusion and tiling using model-driven empirical search. In *Proc. of the 20th Intl. Conf. on Supercomputing (ICS'06)*, pages 249–258. ACM press, 2006.

[36] J. Ramanujam and P. Sadayappan. Tiling multidimensional iteration spaces for multicomputers. *Journal of Parallel and Distributed Computing*, 16(2):108–230, 1992.

[37] M. Ren, J. Y. Park, M. Houston, A. Aiken, and W. J. Dally. A tuning framework for software-managed memory hierarchies. In *Intl. Conf. on Parallel Architectures and Compilation Techniques (PACT'08)*, pages 280–291. ACM Press, 2008.

[38] L. Renganarayanan, D. Kim, S. Rajopadhye, and M. M. Strout. Parameterized tiled loops for free. *SIGPLAN Notices, Proc. of the 2007 PLDI Conf.*, 42(6):405–414, 2007.

[39] A. Schrijver. *Theory of linear and integer programming*. John Wiley & Sons, 1986.

[40] S. Singhai and K. McKinley. A Parameterized Loop Fusion Algorithm for Improving Parallelism and Cache Locality. *The Computer Journal*, 40(6):340–355, 1997.

[41] N. J. A. Sloane. Sequence a000670. The On-Line Encyclopedia of Integer Sequences.

[42] M. Stephenson, S. Amarasinghe, M. Martin, and U.-M. O'Reilly. Meta optimization: improving compiler heuristics with machine learning. *SIGPLAN Not.*, 38(5):77–90, 2003.

[43] A. Tiwari, C. Chen, J. Chame, M. Hall, and J. K. Hollingsworth. A scalable autotuning framework for computer optimization. In *IPDPS'09*, Rome, May 2009.

[44] N. Vasilache. *Scalable Program Optimization Techniques in the Polyhedra Model*. PhD thesis, University of Paris-Sud 11, 2007.

[45] S. Verdoolaege, F. Catthoor, M. Bruynooghe, and G. Janssens. Feasibility of incremental translation. Technical Report CW 348, Katholieke Universiteit Leuven Department of Computer Science, Oct. 2002.

[46] Y. Voronenko, F. de Mesmay, and M. Püschel. Computer generation of general size linear transform libraries. In *Intl. Symp. on Code Generation and Optimization (CGO'09)*, Mar. 2009.

[47] R. C. Whaley, A. Petitet, and J. J. Dongarra. Automated empirical optimization of software and the atlas project. *Parallel Computing*, 27(1–2):3–35, 2001.

[48] M. Wolf, D. Maydan, and D.-K. Chen. Combining loop transformations considering caches and scheduling. In *MICRO 29: Proceedings of the 29th annual ACM/IEEE international symposium on Microarchitecture*, pages 274–286, 1996.

[49] M. Wolfe. More iteration space tiling. In *Proceedings of Supercomputing '89*, pages 655–664, 1989.

[50] M. Wolfe. *High performance compilers for parallel computing*. Addison-Wesley Publishing Company, 1995.

The Essence of Compiling with Traces

Shu-yu Guo Jens Palsberg

UCLA Computer Science Department
University of California, Los Angeles, USA
{shu,palsberg}@cs.ucla.edu

Abstract

The technique of trace-based just-in-time compilation was introduced by Bala et al. and was further developed by Gal et al. It currently enjoys success in Mozilla Firefox's JavaScript engine. A trace-based JIT compiler leverages run-time profiling to optimize frequently-executed paths while enabling the optimized code to "bail out" to the original code when the path has been invalidated. This optimization strategy differs from those of other JIT compilers and opens the question of *which trace optimizations are sound*. In this paper we present a framework for reasoning about the soundness of trace optimizations, and we show that some traditional optimization techniques are sound when used in a trace compiler while others are unsound. The converse is also true: some trace optimizations are sound when used in a traditional compiler while others are unsound. So, traditional and trace optimizations form incomparable sets. Our setting is an imperative calculus for which tracing is explicitly spelled out in the semantics. We define optimization soundness via a notion of bisimulation, and we show that sound optimizations lead to confluence and determinacy of stores.

Categories and Subject Descriptors D.2.4 [*Program Verification*]: Correctness proofs, formal methods; D.3.4 [*Processors*]: Compilers; F.3.2 [*Semantics of Programming Languages*]: Operational semantics

General Terms Languages, Theory

Keywords just-in-time compilation, compiler correctness, bisimulation

1. Introduction

With the advent of "Web 2.0", the web browser has become a platform that delivers rich interactive applications. The technology central to this transformation of the web browser is JavaScript. JavaScipt's dynamic nature has since then become a performance bottleneck. The performance of dynamic languages is much worse than statically typed languages, and JavaScript is no exception. Moreover, traditional just-in-time (JIT) compilation techniques designed for static, typed languages are ill-fitted for JavaScript.

The work of Bala et al. [1] was adapted as a novel JIT compilation technique called trace compilation [2–4, 7, 8]. A trace-based JIT compiler uses run-time profiling to approximate the "hot" execution paths (loops) in the program and compiles only those paths [4, 7, 8]. The rarely executed bits of code are interpreted. The idea is quite intuitive: if there is a repeatedly executed section of the code, that section should be top priority for compiling to native code. For example, a micro-blogging web application might take many rows of data and transform them into a news feed format. This loop would be where the program spends the majority of its time; a trace-enabled JIT detects that this loop is a hot execution path and compiles it to native code.

Tracing JIT compilers are amenable to JavaScript and enjoy their greatest success in Mozilla Firefox's JavaScript engine (TraceMonkey). It is available in versions 3.5 and greater, and Mozilla metrics report that approximately 94 million people in the world are using the tracing JIT [13].[1]

Tracing JIT compilers differ greatly in technique from many other JIT techniques. It opens the following question:

Which trace optimizations are sound?

We distill the essence of trace compilation to a simple imperative calculus with an operational semantics. This allows us to formally investigate notions of correctness of trace-based JIT compilers and the properties that trace optimizations must satisfy to be sound. We present a bisimulation-based soundness criterion for trace optimizations, and we prove a determinism theorem: whether one traces or not, the final store will be the same.

Our framework is modular in two ways. First, an optimization designer needs only prove that a given optimization satisfies our correctness criterion; the determinism theorem then follows. Second, the composition of two sound optimizations is itself sound. We leverage the first kind of modularity to easily prove soundness of the folding of free loop variables and dead branch elimination. Proving optimizations unsound is equally simple. We show that dead store elimination is unsound with an easy-to-check counterexample. Readers can easily proceed like we did to prove additional trace optimizations sound.

Our proof of the determinism theorem has the following coarse steps. First we prove that an unoptimized, recorded trace of the loop is "behaviorally correct", or bisimilar, to the original loop. We then prove that the original program with the new trace stitched in place of the old loop is bisimilar to the original program. This then sets the stage for sound optimizations: sound optimizations are those that do not invalidate this behavioral correctness guarantee had from bisimilarity. Finally, we put the pieces together and prove confluence and determinacy of stores via a diamond lemma and a strip lemma.

Our framework shows, surprisingly, that "traditional" whole-function optimizations and tracing JIT optimizations *do not stand in a subset relation in either direction*. In one direction, it is clear

POPL'11, January 26–28, 2011, Austin, Texas, USA.

[1] The exact average of daily usage from January 1, 2010 until July 12, 2010 of versions 3.5, 3.6, 3.7, and 4.0 is 93,977,941.

that traditional optimizations are not subsumed by trace optimizations. Informally, trace optimizations are not obliged to be correct for all possible executions and contexts. They are obliged to be correct only for a *particular* execution and a *particular* context. For instance, in the paper we prove folding of variables that are not assigned to be sound for tracing but unsound in general in a traditional setting. In the other direction, trace optimizations are also not subsumed by traditional optimizations. The reason for this is more subtle: the domain of trace optimizations is restricted to *only* the trace. The code surrounding the trace is unavailable to the optimizer. Traditional optimizations, on the other hand, are privy to both the prefix and the suffix of the trace in that their domain *is* the entire procedure. In other words, those optimizations can prove properties on entire procedures while trace optimizations cannot. For one, whole-function optimizations know that their local variables are dead after the function exits. Trace optimizations cannot make the same assumption about their local variables after the trace exits. In the paper we show dead store elimination to be unsound as a trace optimization.

To expand upon the incomparability of the two sets of optimizations, it is illuminating to spell out the differences between our work and recent prominent works in compiler correctness [11, 12]. The program equivalence condition (Lemma 1) found in Lacey et al. [11] basically states classical bisimilarity as the condition under which to judge the correctness of optimizations. An optimized program must be bisimilar to the original and their respective final stores must contain the same values for all variables. In their framework, optimizations are formulated as rewrite rules with side conditions expressed in temporal logic. Despite this difference, we can make the following fruitful comparisons. We write $m \approx n \textit{ for } \sigma$ to mean that the program m is bisimilar to n when their initial stores are σ. Suppose there is an optimization function O. Their correctness criterion describes traditional optimizations and is extensional: for all p, $p \approx O(p) \textit{ for all stores}$. Our correctness criterion describes tracing optimizations and is intensional. Suppose the program p decomposes into two components, w (the traced loop) and k (the rest of the program). The criterion is then: for all w, k, σ, $w\ k \approx O(w, \sigma)\ k \textit{ for } \sigma$. Note how our optimization function takes a state σ in addition to a program to produce an optimized program guaranteed to be correct when the initial store is fixed to be that store and the rest of the program is fixed to be k. This succinctly captures that trace optimizations may not be straightforwardly used in a classical setting.

The correctness criterion in Chambers et al. [12] raises yet more differences between classical optimization soundness and trace optimization soundness. At the heart of their formulation of soundness is contextual equivalence. However, note that we have said that trace optimization correctness is intensionalized to a particular computation suffix. This necessarily precludes trace optimization correctness from being contextual equivalence. Classical optimizations speculate about the behavior of a program to substitute optimized portions for the original portions *before* execution. Trace optimizations, on the other hand, know exactly the behavior for which they need to optimize and substitute optimized portions *during* execution. This departure also highlights that the input to trace optimizations is mercurial: we do not know *a priori* what loops are hot. The input to classical optimization on the other hand is fixed. In Chambers et al. and Lacey et al. [11, 12], this input is the entire program. As mentioned before, the domains of the two kinds of optimizations are simply different.

The remainder of this paper is organized as follows. In section 2 we introduce our language, its operational semantics, and discuss certain properties of compiling with traces. In section 3 we show that the operational semantics of our language is correct up to weak bisimulation and relate the results to confluence. In section 4 we explore various optimizations, both provably correct and provably incorrect, pluggable into the framework. In section 5 we discuss related work. Section 6 concludes.

2. Compiling with Traces

What is essential to the trace compilation technique? What features must our calculus contain? At its core, it is a method of compiling often-executed loops. We must therefore have loops. More specifically, it is a technique of recording loop bodies at run-time and optimizing them. The second essential part must thus be the ability to record execution. What is optimized, then, is not the text of the loop but a run-time execution path *through* the loop. In other words, we are optimizing some fixed execution. So, when the execution diverges from the recorded path, there must exist a mechanism to return us to the original program. The third and final component is this bail-out mechanism. In the literature of trace compilation, these are called side-exits [8].

We forego modeling the many other features of the technique that exist in implementations. For instance, we shall not model the heuristics in how one actually detects a hot path of execution, we will simply build in the ability to record a path of execution nondeterministically. This nondeterminism will be realized via overlapping reduction rules. Nor shall we model implementation details, such as trace trees and their interactions [7]. We aim to keep the calculus minimal yet high-level, safe—and even desirable—for human consumption.

2.1 The Language and Its Baseline Execution

We first present the syntax and small-step operational semantics for a simple imperative language with two of the three essential ingredients: loops and the ability to "bail out" modeled by continuations.

The syntax of our language, inspired by the calculus presented in Moll [9], is shown in figure 1. Concretely, traces are a subset of normal statements. They are meant to be straightline sections of code with side-exits, so there are only no-ops, assignments, and side-exits.

We use x to range over variables, i to range over non-negative integers, σ, ρ to range over stores, and l, m, n, k, s, p to range over statements throughout the rest of the paper.

The baseline transition rules are shown in figure 2. Assume $\oplus$ is the "real" addition operator on integers. We use a labeled transition system where labels correspond to store updates. We assume the reader is familiar with such systems as they are used in the literature of concurrency [14]. The only observable transitions are store updates, which are labeled by the "store delta". All other transitions are silent, labeled τ, and are unobservable. The subscript $_B$ denotes baseline transition rules. The subscript $_A$ denotes a strict subset of the baseline transition rules that will be used in the upcoming proofs. The subscript $_T$ denotes tracing transition rules. The baseline rules in figure 2 are common to both.

The baseline rules do the usual things. BailTrue is the rule that applies continuations in the **bail**s. It says to clobber the current reduct with the packaged continuation s.

2.2 Recording Traces

We extend the baseline execution with the ability to record traces. The set of baseline rules is a proper subset of the tracing rules, i.e. $\longrightarrow_B \subset \longrightarrow_T$. The abstract syntax is the same between the two languages. The additional transition rules are shown in figure 3.

Starting Traces We start a trace at the beginning of a **while** loop. For technical reasons for the proof of correctness, we record when we have already unfolded at least one iteration of the loop.

Also note that Trace puts the reduction rules in *recording mode*, which is represented syntactically as 4-tuples. The components are,

$$
\begin{array}{rll}
e ::= n \mid x+1 & & \text{expressions} \\
b ::= x = 0 \mid x \neq 0 & & \text{boolean expressions} \\
w ::= \textbf{while } b \textbf{ do } s & & \text{loops} \\
s ::= \epsilon \mid c\ s & & \text{statements} \\
c ::= \textbf{skip}; \mid x := e; \mid w \mid \textbf{if } b \textbf{ then } s \mid \textbf{bail } b \textbf{ to } s & & \text{commands} \\
\\
t ::= \epsilon \mid c_t\ t & & \text{traces} \\
c_t ::= \textbf{skip}; \mid x := e; \mid \textbf{bail } b \textbf{ to } s & & \text{recorded commands}
\end{array}
$$

Figure 1. Syntax of the Simple Imperative Language and Traces

$$
\hat{\sigma}(e) = \begin{cases} n & \text{if } e = n \\ \sigma(x) \oplus 1 & \text{if } e = x+1 \end{cases}
\qquad
\hat{\sigma}(b) = \begin{cases} \textit{true} & \text{if } b \text{ is } x = 0 \wedge \sigma(x) = 0 \\ \textit{false} & \text{if } b \text{ is } x = 0 \wedge \sigma(x) \neq 0 \\ \textit{true} & \text{if } b \text{ is } x \neq 0 \wedge \sigma(x) \neq 0 \\ \textit{false} & \text{if } b \text{ is } x \neq 0 \wedge \sigma(x) = 0 \end{cases}
$$

$$
\begin{array}{rl}
\delta ::= x/i \mid x/\textbf{true} \mid x/\textbf{false} & \text{store updates} \\
\alpha ::= \tau \mid \delta & \text{actions}
\end{array}
$$

$$\langle \sigma, x := e; k \rangle \xrightarrow{\delta}_{T,B,A} \langle \sigma[x/\hat{\sigma}(e)], k \rangle \quad \text{where } \delta = x/\hat{\sigma}(e) \qquad \text{(Assign)}$$

$$\langle \sigma, \textbf{skip}; k \rangle \xrightarrow{\tau}_{T,B,A} \langle \sigma, k \rangle \qquad \text{(Seq)}$$

$$\langle \sigma, (\textbf{if } b \textbf{ then } s)\ k \rangle \xrightarrow{\tau}_{T,B,A} \langle \sigma, k \rangle \quad \text{if } \hat{\sigma}(b) = \textit{false} \qquad \text{(IfFalse)}$$

$$\langle \sigma, (\textbf{if } b \textbf{ then } s)\ k \rangle \xrightarrow{\tau}_{T,B,A} \langle \sigma, s\ k \rangle \quad \text{if } \hat{\sigma}(b) = \textit{true} \qquad \text{(IfTrue)}$$

$$\langle \sigma, (\textbf{while } b \textbf{ do } s)\ k \rangle \xrightarrow{\tau}_{T,B,A} \langle \sigma, (\textbf{if } b \textbf{ then } (s \textbf{ while } b \textbf{ do } s))\ k \rangle \qquad \text{(While)}$$

$$\langle \sigma, (\textbf{bail } b \textbf{ to } s)\ k \rangle \xrightarrow{\tau}_{T,B,A} \langle \sigma, k \rangle \quad \text{if } \hat{\sigma}(b) = \textit{false} \qquad \text{(BailFalse)}$$

$$\langle \sigma, (\textbf{bail } b \textbf{ to } s)\ k \rangle \xrightarrow{\tau}_{T,B} \langle \sigma, s \rangle \quad \text{if } \hat{\sigma}(b) = \textit{true} \qquad \text{(BailTrue)}$$

Figure 2. Shared Transition Rules

$$
\neg b = \begin{cases} x = 0 & \text{if } b \text{ is } x \neq 0 \\ x \neq 0 & \text{if } b \text{ is } x = 0 \end{cases}
$$

$$\langle \sigma, (\textbf{if } b \textbf{ then } (s\ (\textbf{while } b \textbf{ do } s)))\ k \rangle \xrightarrow{\tau}_{T} \langle \sigma, (\textbf{while } b \textbf{ do } s)\ k, \epsilon, s\ (\textbf{while } b \textbf{ do } s)\ k \rangle \quad \text{if } \hat{\sigma}(b) = \textit{true} \qquad \text{(Trace)}$$

$$\langle \sigma, k_w, t, x := e; k \rangle \xrightarrow{\delta}_{T} \langle \sigma[x/\hat{\sigma}(e)], k_w, t\ (x := e;), k \rangle \quad \text{where } \delta = x/\hat{\sigma}(e) \qquad \text{(RecordAssign)}$$

$$\langle \sigma, k_w, t, \textbf{skip}; k \rangle \xrightarrow{\tau}_{T} \langle \sigma, k_w, t\ (\textbf{skip};), k \rangle \qquad \text{(RecordSeq)}$$

$$\langle \sigma, k_w, t, (\textbf{if } b \textbf{ then } s)\ k \rangle \xrightarrow{\tau}_{T} \langle \sigma, k_w, t\ (\textbf{bail } b \textbf{ to } (s\ k)), k \rangle \quad \text{if } \hat{\sigma}(b) = \textit{false} \qquad \text{(RecordIfFalse)}$$

$$\langle \sigma, k_w, t, (\textbf{if } b \textbf{ then } s)\ k \rangle \xrightarrow{\tau}_{T} \langle \sigma, k_w, t\ (\textbf{bail } \neg b \textbf{ to } k), s\ k \rangle \quad \text{if } \hat{\sigma}(b) = \textit{true} \qquad \text{(RecordIfTrue)}$$

$$\langle \sigma, k_w, t, (\textbf{while } b \textbf{ do } s)\ k \rangle \xrightarrow{\tau}_{T} \langle \sigma, k_w, t\ (\textbf{skip};), (\textbf{if } b \textbf{ then } (s \textbf{ while } b \textbf{ do } s))\ k \rangle \quad \text{if } k_w \neq (\textbf{while } b \textbf{ do } s)\ k \qquad \text{(RecordWhile)}$$

$$\langle \sigma, k_w, t, (\textbf{while } b \textbf{ do } s)\ k \rangle \xrightarrow{\tau}_{T} \langle \sigma, O(\textbf{while } b \textbf{ do } t, \sigma)\ k \rangle \quad \text{if } k_w = (\textbf{while } b \textbf{ do } s)\ k \qquad \text{(Stitch)}$$

$$\langle \sigma, k_w, t, k \rangle \xrightarrow{\alpha}_{T} \langle \sigma', k' \rangle \quad \text{if } \langle \sigma, k \rangle \xrightarrow{\alpha}_{T} \langle \sigma', k' \rangle \wedge k_w \neq k \qquad \text{(Abort)}$$

Figure 3. Tracing Transition Rules

in order, the store, the stopping point of the trace, the trace thus far, and the current program being reduced.

Recording Traces The recording rules record one command at a time and concatenate it to the end of the trace. Concatenation is simple juxtaposition. The trace itself is a straightline section of code, so we install side-exits (pieces of code that jump back to untraced code when the condition we traced no longer holds) when we record conditionals.

To ease the task of proving correctness, RecordWhile appends a **skip** to the trace while unrolling the loop. Its side condition is to ensure that we are recording an *inner* loop inside the current loop we are tracing, and that we have not come full circle and finished tracing. The work for finishing up a trace is done in Stitch, whose side condition is mutually exclusive with that of RecordWhile.

Ending Well-Behaved Traces We end the trace and stitch it back into the program using Stitch when we finish tracing the body of the loop. We know we have finished when we come back to reducing the same loop that started the trace.

We "compile" the loop that was traced into the same language.[2] The actual optimization is immaterial to the semantics; we assume that there is a sound optimization function O : (*Statement* $\times$ *Store*) $\rightarrow$ *Statement*. What soundness entails here will be made precise when we investigate correctness. Informally, soundness means that the output of the O function "does the same thing" as the original code, as far as observable behavior (store updates) goes.

Ending Badly-Behaved Traces We are not guaranteed to finish tracing the body of the loop. That loop body might never terminate! Consider the following example; assume s_2 never changes b to 0.

```
a := 1;
b := 1;
while a ≠ 0 do
    s1
    while b ≠ 0 do
        s2
```

If we start tracing the *outer* loop, once we start executing the *inner* loop we will *never finish the outer loop body*, and thus never finish tracing. Implementations of trace compilation, then, must use heuristics to end the trace if it is continuing on for too long.

In our semantics, we model this by introducing another nondeterministic rule that prematurely stops the trace, Abort. This rule shares the same premises with *all* Record_ rules, where "_" is a wildcard. Note that there are no axioms for recording **bails**—what this means is that instead of the semantics getting stuck when trying to trace a trace, we abort the trace (that is, we do not model higher-order tracing). Also note that Abort's[3] side condition is mutually exclusive with Stitch, which is intuitively the "good" situation of a successful trace. In this way the rule models the semantics of bailing out of tracing mode for all "bad" situations.

2.3 Example Trace Recording

To help illustrate the tracing rules and to build some concrete intuition, consider the following contrived example.

Example Input

```
1  x := 0;
2  while x = 0 do
3      y := 0;
4      while y = 0 do
5          y := 1;
6      z := 1;
7      b := a + 1;
```

There are two loops; the inner loop only iterates once. The variable a is computed at some earlier point in the program. We give a rule-by-rule walkthrough of tracing the outer loop. We build up the trace in tandem with our walking through of the reduction rules; each snippet that the Record_ rules append to the trace is displayed one by one.

To start, line 1 of the input is matched by Assign, so we reduce by Assign. Line 2 is a **while** loop, which we reduce by While. While converts the loop into an **if** statement testing the condition $x = 0$. This is indeed true by how we mutated the store in line 1, so we can reduce by IfTrue or Trace. In the interest of demonstrating tracing, we reduce by Trace. The trace built thus far is empty, or ϵ. We've only entered recording mode, but we haven't actually recorded any commands yet.

Line 3 in the input is an assignment, which is matched by RecordAssign. RecordAssign appends the assignment itself onto the trace:

Example Trace

```
y := 0;
```

Line 4 in the input is the inner loop, and we will now see how the tracing rules deal with recording loops. The loop itself will first reduce to an **if** via RecordWhile, which appends a no-op **skip;** to the trace. In reducing the resulting **if**, we are testing the condition $y = 0$. It is true, so we reduce using RecordIfTrue. The result is that we append a side-exit as a **bail** to the trace. The computation that would have been executed *had the condition been false* gets packaged up as a continuation and gets put into the body of the **bail** (shown indented in the listing):

```
skip;
bail y ≠ 0 to
    z := 1;
    b := a + 1;
    while x = 0 do
        y := 0;
        while y = 0 do
            y := 1;
        z := 1;
        b := a + 1;
```

Now that we have installed the side-exit for entering into the inner loop, we trace the body of the inner loop as straightline code. Line 5 in the input is another assignment, which we record using RecordAssign.

```
y := 1;
```

After the body of the inner loop we attempt to reduce the next iteration of that loop. Again, the loop will first reduce to an **if** by RecordWhile. This appends a **skip;**. Unlike the last time, however, the condition $y = 0$ is now false, so we instead reduce using RecordIfFalse. We append another side-exit as before, but the packaged continuation is different. Since the condition was false in the actual execution, we need to include the statement that would have been executed if the condition were true. After that statement we package the rest of the iteration of the outer loop and append it:

```
skip;
bail y = 0 to
    y := 1;
    while y = 0 do
```

[2] Note that this is a simplification in our model. In actual tracing JITs, the compiled code is in machine language.

[3] The rule is modeled as presented instead of the viable alternative of $\langle \sigma, k_w, t, k\rangle \xrightarrow{\tau}_T \langle \sigma, k\rangle$ if $k_w \neq k$ for a cleaner proof of correctness.

$$FV : \textit{Statement} \rightarrow \textit{Variables}$$

$$FV(s) = \{x \mid x \text{ is free in } s\}$$

$$F : ((\textit{Expression} + \textit{Statement} + \textit{Command}) \times \textit{Store} \times \mathcal{V}) \rightarrow \textit{Statement}$$

$$F(e, \sigma, v) = \begin{cases} n & \text{if } e = n \\ \sigma(x) \oplus 1 & \text{if } e = x + 1 \wedge x \in v \\ e & \text{if } e = x + 1 \wedge x \notin v \end{cases}$$

$$F(s, \sigma, v) = \begin{cases} s & \text{if } s = \epsilon \\ F(c, \sigma, v)\ F(s_1, \sigma, v) & \text{if } s = c\ s_1 \end{cases}$$

$$F(c, \sigma, v) = \begin{cases} x := F(e, \sigma, v) & \text{if } c = x := e \\ c & \text{otherwise} \end{cases}$$

$$O : (\textit{Statement} \times \textit{Store} \times \mathcal{V}) \rightarrow \textit{Statement}$$

$$O(s, \sigma) = \begin{cases} \textbf{while } b \textbf{ do } F(s_1, \sigma, FV(s_1)) & \text{if } s = \textbf{while } b \textbf{ do } s_1 \\ s & \text{otherwise} \end{cases}$$

Figure 4. Variable Folding O

```
17            y := 1;
18        z := 1;
19        b := a + 1;
20        while x = 0 do
21            y := 0;
22            while y = 0 do
23                y := 1;
24            z := 1;
25            b := a + 1;
```

Finally, we apply RecordAssign twice to lines 6–7 and append the assignments to the trace.

```
26  z := 1;
27  b := a + 1;
```

Having successfully traced an iteration of the loop, we now reduce by Stitch to stitch the trace back into the program using the identity as the O function. Abbreviating the continuations for the side-exits as k_i, the final stitched traced loop is as follows.

Abbreviated Stitched and Traced Example Loop

```
1  while x = 0 do
2      y := 0;
3      skip;
4      bail y ≠ 0 to k1
5      y := 1;
6      skip;
7      bail y = 0 to k2
8      z := 1;
9      b := a + 1;
```

2.4 Example O

We have seen the output of tracing, but we obviously want to do more than that. We want to optimize. Consider optimization shown in figure 4 that folds away variables that we never assign to inside a traced loop. First we define a function that calculates the "free" (in the sense of never-assigned-to) variables of a statement. It is assumed to be defined in the usual way. Next we define a helper function F that does the actual optimization. $\mathcal{V}$ is the set of free variables. Finally the O function is just a wrapper around F that calculates and passes in the free variables.

If we apply it to our running example where $a \mapsto 41$, we fold the assignment to b on line 9 of the abbreviated stitch example:

```
9      b := 42;
```

The main benefit of run-time optimization is that we can be more aggressive than with ahead-of-time optimization. Here we presented a simple conservative folding of free loop variables. The idea is that free variables in the loop bodycan be treated as constants and folded until we break out of the loop. We cannot be so bold with a static version of this kind of folding, as we can only do so if we know that the variables we want to fold are constants for the entirety of program execution. Here, however, we only need to know that the variable's value does not change *until the loop is finished*.[4]

3. Correctness

What does it mean for a trace to be correct? First, correctness of the traced code is behavioral correctness—the trace has to "do the same thing" as the original code. Attempting to prove confluence of the program text such as in Pfenning [16] is unfruitful, as there are no guarantees in trace compilation of the traced code converging back to the same text as the original program. In a reactive user-interface, for instance, we might trace-compile many inner loops, and those compiled inner loops might execute forever, waiting for user input. But even in those cases of infinite execution we still want to reason about correctness. The need for infinite executions suggests the tool of bisimilarity.

Second, correctness of the traced code is intensional correctness. Unlike ahead-of-time compiler correctness, we cannot say that an optimized trace is observationally equivalent, or has the same sequence of observable reductions, to the original loop in the traditional, extensional sense. Specifically, an optimized trace need *not* be observationally equivalent to the original loop under all stores. Consider the following version of our little example:

```
x := 0;
while x = 0 do
    b := a + 1;
```

A reasonable trace-based optimization if $a \mapsto 41$, as we have seen, would be to replace the loop body with $b := 42$. But this code is

[4] In our simple model, the trace is effectively discarded after the loop exits. There is no way to re-enter a traced loop once it exits. This is not the case in practice, where constructs such as methods allow compiled traces to be called multiple times. In those cases the tracing JIT has to add in more guards and side-exits to guard the folded values. We omit this complexity.

most definitely not observationally equivalent to the original: the original has a free variable, a, and the optimized code $b := 42$ does not. Side-exits are also problematic. How do we ensure that we jump back to the right place in the original code?

We retain the familiar notion of observational equivalence, but parameterize it over stores and computation suffixes. Namely, a trace is correct if it is observationally equivalent to the original loop *for the store that the original loop is currently reducing under* and *for the rest of the program that the original loop would have reduced under*.

To formalize these intuitions, we model correctness using intensionalized bisimulations over stores. Intensionalizing to a particular suffix will be made formal in the definition of O soundness in section 3.3. Bisimulation techniques see popular use in process calculi [14]. There is also existing work in the analysis and correctness proofs of program transformation [6, 21, 22].

The definitions here are built upon, but slightly different from, the standard notions found in the concurrency literature [14], as they are defined over a store. Observational equivalence also becomes formally defined as the notion of bisimilarity. Let the set of labels be defined as follows.

$$Act = \{\delta \mid \delta \text{ is a store update}\} \cup \{\tau\}$$

Definition. If $r \in Act^*$, then $\hat{r}$ is the sequence whereby all occurrences of τ are removed.

Definition. If $r = \alpha_1 \cdots \alpha_n \in Act^*$, we write $m \stackrel{r}{\Longrightarrow} m'$ to mean

$$m \stackrel{\tau}{\longrightarrow}^* \cdot \stackrel{\alpha_1}{\longrightarrow} \cdot \stackrel{\tau}{\longrightarrow}^* \cdots \stackrel{\tau}{\longrightarrow}^* \cdot \stackrel{\alpha_n}{\longrightarrow} \cdot \stackrel{\tau}{\longrightarrow}^* m'$$

That is, there may be any number of intervening silent transitions between the observable sequences. In this particular system, the primary observable entity is the store itself, so the intuitive meaning of a program becomes the sequence of store updates it performs.

We only concern ourselves with closed program-store pairs in this paper, where the definition of *closed* is as follows.

Definition. For a store σ and a program m, we say m is σ-closed if for all variables that appear in m, $\hat{\sigma}(x)$ is defined.

For the rest of the paper, when we say "for any store" or "for all stores", we mean for all stores that form closed program-store pairs with the programs under consideration.

Definition (Bisimulation)**.** A *bisimulation* for two reduction relations X, Y is a relation $\mathcal{R}$ such that $\mathcal{R}(\sigma, m, n)$ implies

1. Whenever $\langle\sigma, m\rangle \stackrel{\alpha}{\longrightarrow}_X \langle\sigma', m'\rangle$ then, for some n', $\langle\sigma, n\rangle \stackrel{\hat{\alpha}}{\Longrightarrow}_Y \langle\sigma', n'\rangle$ and $\mathcal{R}(\sigma', m', n')$
2. Whenever $\langle\sigma, n\rangle \stackrel{\alpha}{\longrightarrow}_Y \langle\sigma', n'\rangle$ then, for some m', $\langle\sigma, m\rangle \stackrel{\hat{\alpha}}{\Longrightarrow}_X \langle\sigma', m'\rangle$ and $\mathcal{R}(\sigma', m', n')$

In the above definition we abuse notation and let m, m', n, and n' range over both statements and triples of statements. That is, since it does not add to the discussion to distinguish between 2-tuples and 4-tuples in the definition, we use a single metavariable to range over both.

The traditional notion of bisimilarity is a special case of this one: two programs are bisimilar in the traditional sense if they are bisimilar for all stores.

Definition. m is said to be *bisimilar* to n under reduction relations X, Y for a store σ, written $m \;{}_X{\approx}_Y\; n$ *for* σ, if $\mathcal{R}(\sigma, m, n)$ for some bisimulation $\mathcal{R}$ on X, Y. In other words,

$${}_X{\approx}_Y = \bigcup\{\mathcal{R} \mid \mathcal{R} \text{ is a bisimulation for } X, Y\}$$

Lemma 3.1. Bisimilarity is an equivalence relation.

Before stating the main lemma, we note that all nondeterministic rules in our system step to the same store. We prove this later in lemma 3.7. For simplicity in stating the main lemma, we simply say that the two branching stores are always the same.

We are now ready to state the main lemma. In the literature, diamond lemmas are usually single diamonds. The trace calculus, however, has a modal flavor with 2-tuples as one mode and 4-tuples as the other mode. As such, our calculus has six diamonds up to symmetry.

Lemma 3.2 (Diamond Lemma)**.** All of the following hold. For diamonds 4–6, $\langle\rho, k_w, t, p\rangle$ is well-formed, a notion we will expound upon in section 3.1.

1. If $R : \langle\rho, p\rangle \stackrel{\alpha}{\longrightarrow}_T \langle\sigma, m\rangle$ and $R' : \langle\rho, p\rangle \stackrel{\alpha}{\longrightarrow}_T \langle\sigma, n\rangle$, then $m \;{}_T{\approx}_T\; n$ for σ.

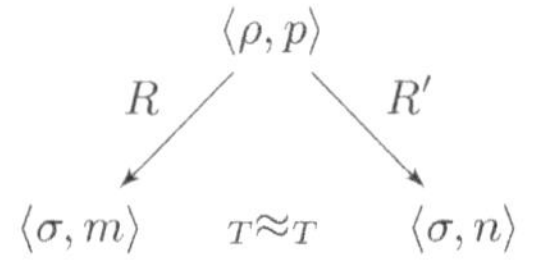

2. If $R : \langle\rho, p\rangle \stackrel{\alpha}{\longrightarrow}_T \langle\sigma, k_w, t, m\rangle$ and $R' : \langle\rho, p\rangle \stackrel{\alpha}{\longrightarrow}_T \langle\sigma, k'_w, t', n\rangle$, then $\langle k_w, t, m\rangle \;{}_T{\approx}_T\; \langle k'_w, t', n\rangle$ for σ.

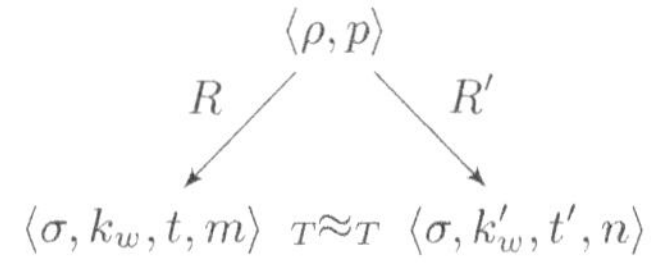

3. If $R : \langle\rho, p\rangle \stackrel{\alpha}{\longrightarrow}_T \langle\sigma, m\rangle$ and $R' : \langle\rho, p\rangle \stackrel{\alpha}{\longrightarrow}_T \langle\sigma, k_w, t, n\rangle$, then $m \;{}_T{\approx}_T\; \langle k_w, t, n\rangle$ for σ.

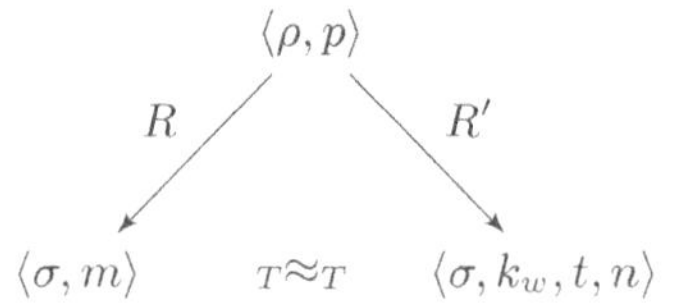

4. If $R : \langle\rho, k_w, t, p\rangle \stackrel{\alpha}{\longrightarrow}_T \langle\sigma, m\rangle$ and $R' : \langle\rho, k_w, t, p\rangle \stackrel{\alpha}{\longrightarrow}_T \langle\sigma, n\rangle$, then $m \;{}_T{\approx}_T\; n$ for σ.

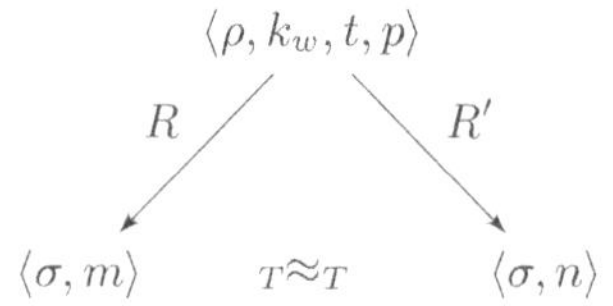

5. If $R : \langle\rho, k_w, t, p\rangle \stackrel{\alpha}{\longrightarrow}_T \langle\sigma, k'_w, t', m\rangle$ and $R' : \langle\rho, k_w, t, p\rangle \stackrel{\alpha}{\longrightarrow}_T \langle\sigma, k''_w, t'', n\rangle$, then $\langle k'_w, t', m\rangle \;{}_T{\approx}_T\; \langle k''_w, t'', n\rangle$ for σ.

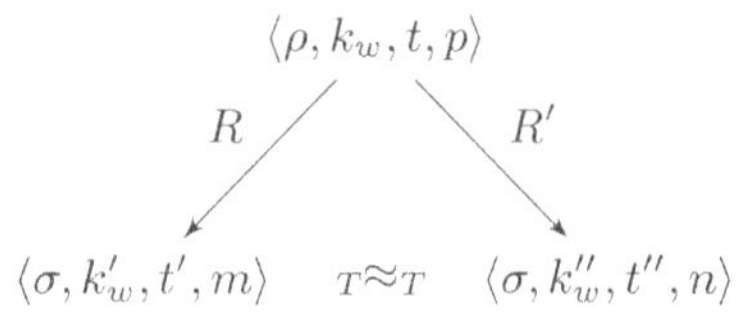

6. If $R : \langle\rho, k_w, t, p\rangle \stackrel{\alpha}{\longrightarrow}_T \langle\sigma, m\rangle$ and $R' : \langle\rho, k_w, t, p\rangle \stackrel{\alpha}{\longrightarrow}_T \langle\sigma, k'_w, t', n\rangle$, then $m \;{}_T{\approx}_T\; \langle k'_w, t', n\rangle$ for σ.

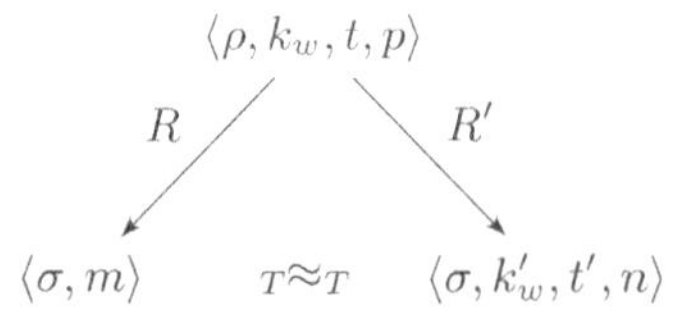

This lemma says that should execution branch into two branches, both branches will do the same thing, at least observationally. We aim to use the main lemma to arrive at a more familiar place: confluence of stores, namely corollary 3.10.

The rest of this section is organized as follows. Section 3.1 introduces the idea of well-formedness for the 4-tuples, or the tracing rules. Section 3.2 introduces the correctness criterion of the unoptimized trace. Section 3.3 proves the main lemma. Section 3.4 explores the relationship between confluence and our bisimulation result.

Many proofs in this section are omitted for brevity. The reader may find them in the full version of the paper at `http://www.cs.ucla.edu/~palsberg/paper/popl11.pdf`.

3.1 Well-Formedness of 4-Tuples

When the calculus decides to initiate a trace, it steps to a configuration in the shape of a 4-tuple. The four components are, in order, the store, the point in the original code when we started tracing, the trace so far, and the statement currently being reduced. Not all 4-tuples are created equal, however, as not all 4-tuples are *well-formed*. Intuitively, well-formedness is something like an incremental version of correctness. Only well-formed 4-tuples eventually become fully correct unoptimized traces. Thus, we want it to be an invariant of the computation.

Well-formedness is a tight and intricate relationship between the original loop, the trace thus far, and the current reduct. Informally, we need the trace thus far to be a recording of all the steps that the original loop took just before it reached the current reduct. Before we formally define well-formedness, we formalize what it means to be a "trace thus far".

Definition (Partial Trace Relation)**.** A *partial trace relation* is a relation $\mathcal{T}$ such that $\mathcal{T}(\sigma, t, l)$ implies that whenever $\langle \sigma, t\rangle \xrightarrow{\alpha}_B \langle \sigma', t'\rangle$ then, for some l', $\langle \sigma, l\rangle \xrightarrow{\alpha}_B \langle \sigma', l'\rangle$ and

1. If t stepped by BailTrue, $t' = l'$
2. Otherwise, $\mathcal{T}(\sigma', t', l')$

The constituents are as follows: t is the trace and l is the original code. Recall that both t and l are just statements. The formalization is a variation on the standard simulation relation and captures the two properties that a partially constructed trace intuitively satisfies. First, BailTrue models jumping back to the original code, so we expect the descendants to be exactly equal. Second, the partial trace is *partial*, so it can terminate before the original code does, signifying that the rest has not yet been traced.

Definition. We call t a *partial trace* to l for a store σ, written $t \precapprox l$ for σ, if $\mathcal{T}(\sigma, t, l)$ for some partial trace relation $\mathcal{T}$. In other words,

$$\precapprox = \bigcup\{\mathcal{T} \mid \mathcal{T} \text{ is a partial trace relation}\}$$

For the definition of well-formedness and subsequent lemmas we will be working with the reduction relation A, which we have not used yet, as well as a notion of being "stuck". Recall that the reduction relation $A = B \setminus \{\text{BailTrue}\}$.

Definition. For a reduction relation X, we say a configuration $\langle \sigma, m\rangle$ is *not X-stuck* iff $m = \epsilon$ or $\langle \sigma, m\rangle \xrightarrow{\alpha}_X \langle \sigma', m'\rangle$ for some σ', m'.

Definition (Well-Formedness)**.** A 4-tuple $\langle \sigma_0, k_w, t, m\rangle$ is *well-formed* iff all the following hold.

1. $k_w = (\textbf{while } b_0 \textbf{ do } l_0)\ k_0$
2. For all σ, either

$$\langle \sigma, t\rangle \xrightarrow{r}{}^{*}_{A} \langle \sigma', \epsilon\rangle \text{ and } \langle \sigma, l_0\ k_w\rangle \xrightarrow{r}{}^{*}_{A} \langle \sigma', m\rangle$$

or for some t',

$$\langle \sigma, t\rangle \xrightarrow{r'}{}^{*}_{A} \langle \sigma'', t'\rangle \text{ and } t' \text{ is } A\text{-stuck but not } B\text{-stuck}$$

3. For all σ, $t \precapprox l_0\ k_w$ for σ.

This property formalizes the invariant we wish computation to preserve. First, k_w must be the loop where we started tracing. Second, the trace t must do one of two things. It must either "go far enough" by terminating in the same reduction sequence that body of the original loop undergoes to reduce to the current statement, m, or it must eventually step to some descendant that can only reduce by BailTrue. Third, t must be a partial trace to the original loop for all stores.

We now prove that the reduction relation T preserves this invariant. We will do this in two steps. First, we prove that the tracing rules themselves—the rules that step from a 4-tuple to another 4-tuple—preserve well-formedness.

Lemma 3.3. Let $p = \langle \sigma_0, k_w, t, m\rangle$. If p is well-formed and $p \xrightarrow{\alpha}_T p'$ such that p' is a 4-tuple, then p' is also well-formed.

Proof. The first conjunct holds trivially because no rules change k_w, and we proceed to prove the next two conjuncts together by case analysis on the structure of the reduction relation. □

Second, we prove that whenever we initiate a trace—whenever we step from a 2-tuple to a 4-tuple—the resulting 4-tuple is well-formed.

Lemma 3.4. If $\langle \sigma, m\rangle \xrightarrow{\alpha}_T p'$ where p' is a 4-tuple, then p' is well-formed.

Proof. By inversion the only rule that results in a 4-tuple is Trace. Let $w = \textbf{while } b \textbf{ do } s$. We have

$$\langle \sigma, (\textbf{if } b \textbf{ then } (s\ w))\ k\rangle \xrightarrow{\tau}_T \langle \sigma, w\ k, \epsilon, s\ w\ k\rangle$$

The first two conjuncts are clearly satisfied. It remains to prove conjunct 3, that $\epsilon \precapprox s\ w\ k$ for all σ. It suffices to exhibit a partial trace relation $\mathcal{T}$ such that for all σ, $\mathcal{T}(\sigma, \epsilon, s\ w\ k)$. Since $t = \epsilon$, we exhibit the empty relation $\emptyset$ as one such $\mathcal{T}$. □

Lemmas 3.3 and 3.4 lead us to a more general lemma about the transitive, reflexive closure of the T reduction relation. This lemma is not used in the rest of the section, but does clearly convey that well-formedness is a property preserved by computation in our calculus.

Lemma 3.5. If $\langle \sigma, m\rangle \xrightarrow{r}{}^{*}_{T} p'$ where p' is a 4-tuple, then p' is well-formed.

3.2 Correctness of the Unoptimized Trace

Recall that the intuition for well-formedness is that it is an incremental correctness. With it we can now build up a bisimulation relation.[5]

Lemma 3.6 (Stitch Lemma)**.** For some t, let $w = \textbf{while } b_0 \textbf{ do } l_0$ and $w' = \textbf{while } b_0 \textbf{ do } t$. If for some k, $t \precapprox l_0\ w\ k$ for all σ and (*) holds of $t, l_0\ w\ k, \sigma$ then, $w'\ k\ {}_B{\approx}_B\ w\ k$ for all σ.

(*) For all σ, either

$$\langle \sigma, t\rangle \xrightarrow{r}{}^{*}_{A} \langle \sigma', \epsilon\rangle \text{ and } \langle \sigma, l_0\ w\ k\rangle \xrightarrow{r}{}^{*}_{A} \langle \sigma', w\ k\rangle$$

[5] The unoptimized trace is in fact strongly bisimilar to the original code. Since we are simply recording some execution path command-for-command, it shouldn't be surprising that the resulting trace is exactly equivalent to the original path. In the interest of less mechanism and since weak bisimilarity subsumes strong bisimilarity, we will directly prove weak bisimilarity.

or for some t',

$$\langle \sigma, t \rangle \xrightarrow{r'}{}^{*}_{A} \langle \sigma'', t' \rangle \text{ and } t' \text{ is } A\text{-stuck but not } B\text{-stuck}$$

This lemma is the correctness property we want to express of unoptimized traces. In prose, w is the original loop, and w' is the new loop with the trace stitched in. The $t \precsim l_0\ w\ k$ for all σ and (*) conditions are what hold of $t, l_0\ w\ k, \sigma$ per well-formedness at the point of stitching.

The lemma says once we come full circle and stitch the recorded trace into the original program, that trace is actually equivalent to the original loop. The reader should bear in mind that this is an almost extensional equivalence, a stronger notion than intensional equivalence. The insight here is since we have proven a more restrictive property than we need, we can relax it. For fruitful optimization we need to make the relation larger, relaxing extensional bisimilarity to the intensional version.

Proof. By exhibition of a bisimulation relation $\mathcal{R}$ under the relations B, B such that $\mathcal{R}(\sigma, w'\ k, w\ k)$ for all σ. □

3.3 Proof of the Diamond Lemma

With the tool of bisimilarity under our belt, we can now make precise the notion of the soundness of O. This definition will be crucial for the proof of the diamond lemma.

Definition (O-Soundness). An O function is *sound* iff for any w, w', k, σ such that $w'\ k\ {}_B{\approx}_B\ w\ k$ for all stores, $O(w', \sigma)\ k\ {}_B{\approx}_B\ w\ k$ for σ.

Proof of the diamond lemma. If R and R' are the same, then we are done as $m = n$ or $\langle k_w, t, n \rangle = \langle k'_w, t', n' \rangle$. It is straightforward to verify that $R = R'$ for diamonds 1, 2, 4, and 5, which are deterministic, so we only need to prove diamonds 3 and 6. We can rewrite these diamonds more precisely below.

3. The nondeterministic rules are IfTrue and Trace. We have $m = n$ by inversion. Further, by lemma 3.4 $\langle \sigma, k_w, t, n \rangle$ is well-formed.
   If $R : \langle \rho, p \rangle \xrightarrow{\alpha}_T \langle \sigma, m \rangle$ and $R' : \langle \rho, p \rangle \xrightarrow{\alpha}_T \langle \sigma, k_w, t, n \rangle$, then $m\ {}_T{\approx}_T\ \langle k_w, t, n \rangle$ for σ.

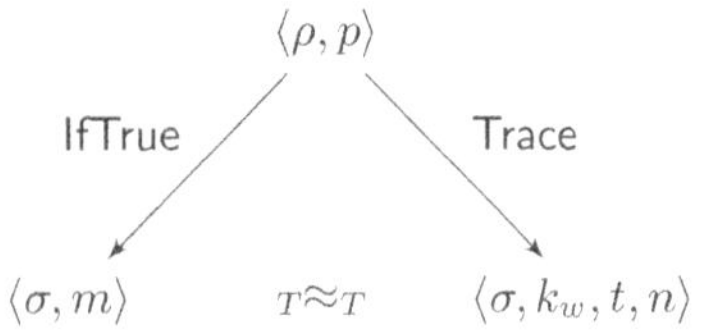

6. The nondeterministic rules are Record_ and Abort. We have $k_w = k'_w$ and $m = n$ by inversion. Similarly, by lemma 3.3 $\langle \sigma, k_w, t', n \rangle$ is well-formed.
   If $R : \langle \rho, w, t, p \rangle \xrightarrow{\alpha}_T \langle \sigma, m \rangle$ and $R' : \langle \rho, k_w, t, p \rangle \xrightarrow{\alpha}_T \langle \sigma, k'_w, t', n \rangle$, then $m\ {}_T{\approx}_T\ \langle k'_w, t', n \rangle$ for σ.

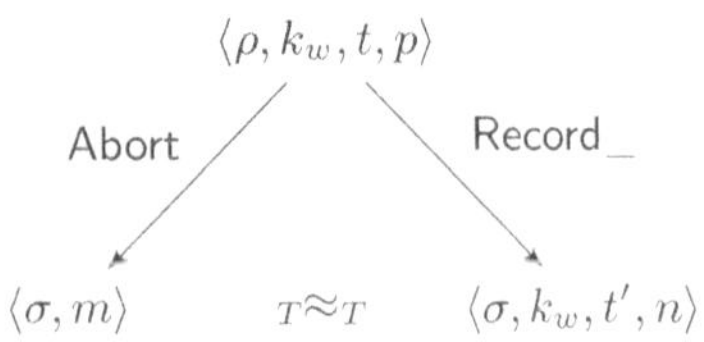

To show that ${}_T{\approx}_T$ holds for both diamonds, it suffices to exhibit a bisimulation relation $\mathcal{R}$ under the reductions T, T such that $\mathcal{R}(\sigma, m, \langle k_w, t, n \rangle)$ and $\mathcal{R}(\sigma, m, \langle k_w, t', n \rangle)$ hold.

We claim the following relation is a bisimulation for any $m, n, u, k_v, k_w, t, \sigma$.

$$\begin{aligned}
\mathcal{R} = \{(\sigma, m, n) \quad & \mid m\ {}_B{\approx}_B\ n \text{ for } \sigma\} \\
\cup \{(\sigma, m, \langle k_v, u, n \rangle) \quad & \mid m\ {}_B{\approx}_B\ n \text{ for } \sigma \text{ and} \\
& \quad \langle \sigma, k_v, u, n \rangle \text{ is well-formed } \} \\
\cup \{(\sigma, \langle k_w, t, m \rangle, n) \quad & \mid m\ {}_B{\approx}_B\ n \text{ for } \sigma \text{ and} \\
& \quad \langle \sigma, k_w, t, m \rangle \text{ is well-formed } \}
\end{aligned}$$

The rest is omitted for brevity. □

3.4 From Bisimulation to Confluence

This section aims to be the interface between bisimulation and confluence. As correctness is often studied in terms of determinacy and confluence, we seek here to prove something akin to confluence of stores to show the adequacy of our operational semantics. Traditionally, confluence theorems are proven from the bottom up using a diamond lemma, iterating that diamond lemma to build a strip lemma, and finally using the strip lemma to construct confluence [16]. Bisimilarity, however, allows us to skip the iteration of the single-step diamond lemma. Indeed, there is no analog to an iterable diamond lemma here. We instead use bisimilarity to directly obtain a strip lemma. Nevertheless, the techniques and diagrams in this section are strongly influenced by the clear and readable approach of Pfenning [16].

First we prove the assumption needed for all cases of the diamond lemma, that nondeterministic branching always branches to configurations with the same store.

Lemma 3.7. If $\langle \sigma, m \rangle \xrightarrow{\alpha}_T \langle \sigma', m' \rangle$ and $\langle \sigma, m \rangle \xrightarrow{\alpha'}_T \langle \sigma'', m'' \rangle$, then $\sigma' = \sigma''$ and $\alpha = \alpha'$.

Proof. Straightforward case analysis. □

Lemma 3.8 (Strip Lemma). If $R : \langle \sigma, m \rangle \longrightarrow_T \langle \sigma', m' \rangle$ and $R^{*\prime} : \langle \sigma, m \rangle \longrightarrow^*_T \langle \sigma'', m'' \rangle$, then for some ρ, n', n'', $\langle \sigma', m' \rangle \longrightarrow^*_T \langle \rho, n' \rangle$ and $\langle \sigma'', m'' \rangle \longrightarrow^*_T \langle \rho, n'' \rangle$ such that $n'\ {}_T{\approx}_T\ n''$ for ρ.

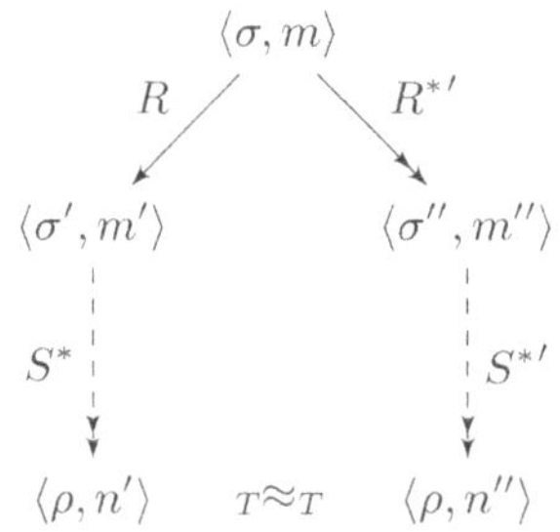

Proof. By case analysis on the structure of R^* and the definition of ${}_T{\approx}_T$. □

Now we can prove the diamond property for stores on the multistep reduction, which we call *store confluence*.

Theorem 3.9 (Store Confluence). If $R^* : \langle \sigma, m \rangle \longrightarrow^*_T \langle \sigma', m' \rangle$ and $R^{*\prime} : \langle \sigma, m \rangle \longrightarrow^*_T \langle \sigma'', m'' \rangle$, then for some ρ, n', n'', $\langle \sigma', m' \rangle \longrightarrow^*_T \langle \rho, n' \rangle$ and $\langle \sigma'', m'' \rangle \longrightarrow^*_T \langle \rho, n'' \rangle$ such that $n'\ {}_T{\approx}_T\ n''$ for ρ.

$$
\begin{array}{ccccc}
 & & \langle \sigma, m \rangle & & \\
 & {\scriptstyle R^*} \swarrow & & \searrow {\scriptstyle R^{*\prime}} & \\
\langle \sigma', m' \rangle & & & & \langle \sigma'', m'' \rangle \\
{\scriptstyle S^*} \Big\downarrow & & & & \Big\downarrow {\scriptstyle S^{*\prime}} \\
\langle \rho, n' \rangle & & {}_T{\approx}_T & & \langle \rho, n'' \rangle
\end{array}
$$

Proof. By induction on the structure of R^*. □

Finally, theorem 3.9 implies the familiar notion of store determinacy for terminating programs.

Corollary 3.10. If $\langle \sigma, m \rangle \longrightarrow_T^* \langle \sigma', \epsilon \rangle$ and $\langle \sigma, m \rangle \longrightarrow_T^* \langle \sigma'', \epsilon \rangle$, then $\sigma' = \sigma''$.

4. Sound and Unsound Optimizations

We have achieved our project of proving the essence of trace compilation correct, yet at the same time that result is largely interesting due to its modularity with respect to the O function. In this section we show the example O from section 2.4 to be sound and explore which kinds of O functions are sound and which are not sound.

4.1 Soundness of Variable Folding

Let F, FV, and O be the ones presented in figure 4. For brevity we assume that $FV(s)$ is defined in the usual way and correctly generates the set of free variables for s. That is, for some store σ, $FV(s)$ the set of variables which s never writes to in σ during reduction.

Lemma 4.1. $\longrightarrow_B^*$ is deterministic.

Proof. $\longrightarrow_B$ has no points of nondeterminism. □

Lemma 4.2. O is sound.

Proof. Assuming we have for some w, w', k such that $w'\ k\ {}_B{\approx}_B\ w\ k$ for all stores, we want to show that $O(w', \sigma)\ k\ {}_B{\approx}_B\ w\ k$ for σ.

Our technique will be showing that $O(w', \sigma)\ k\ {}_B{\approx}_B\ w'\ k$, and then obtaining the desired result via transitivity of ${}_B{\approx}_B$.

We proceed by case analysis on the O function.

Case: $s = \textbf{while}\ b\ \textbf{do}\ s_1$.

We want to show that

$$(\textbf{while}\ b\ \textbf{do}\ F(s_1, \sigma, FV(s_1)))\ k\ {}_B{\approx}_B\ (\textbf{while}\ b\ \textbf{do}\ s_1)\ k$$

It suffices to exhibit a bisimulation relation $\mathcal{R}$ such that

$$\mathcal{R}(\sigma, (\textbf{while}\ b\ \textbf{do}\ F(s_1, \sigma, FV(s_1)))\ k, (\textbf{while}\ b\ \textbf{do}\ s_1)\ k)$$

Let $s_1' = F(s_1, \sigma, FV(s_1))$. We claim the following relation is a bisimulation relation for any m, ρ, σ'. Note that σ and the loops are fixed from the assumption.

$$
\begin{aligned}
\mathcal{R} = {} & \{(\rho, m, m)\} \\
& \cup \{(\sigma, (\textbf{while}\ b\ \textbf{do}\ s_1')\ k, \\
& \qquad (\textbf{while}\ b\ \textbf{do}\ s_1)\ k)\} \\
& \cup \{(\sigma, (\textbf{if}\ b\ \textbf{then}\ (s_1'\ \textbf{while}\ b\ \textbf{do}\ s_1'))\ k, \\
& \qquad (\textbf{if}\ b\ \textbf{then}\ (s_1\ \textbf{while}\ b\ \textbf{do}\ s_1))\ k)\} \\
& \cup \{(\sigma', (F(n, \sigma, FV(s_1))\ \textbf{while}\ b\ \textbf{do}\ s_1')\ k, \\
& \qquad (n\ \textbf{while}\ b\ \textbf{do}\ s_1)\ k) \\
& \qquad \mid \sigma'(x) = \sigma(x) \text{ for all free variables in } s_1\}
\end{aligned}
$$

We proceed by case analysis on the left-side reduction step.

Subcase: The left side and right side are the same.

By lemma 4.1 B is deterministic, both sides step using the same rule, producing the same descendants. But then they are in $\mathcal{R}$ by construction.

$$
\begin{array}{ccc}
\langle \rho, m \rangle & \mathcal{R} & \langle \rho, m \rangle \\
\Big\downarrow {\scriptstyle \alpha} & & {\scriptstyle \alpha} \Big\downarrow \\
\langle \rho', m' \rangle & \mathcal{R} & \langle \rho', m' \rangle
\end{array}
$$

Subcase: The left side is $(\textbf{while}\ b\ \textbf{do}\ s_1')\ k$ and the right side is $(\textbf{while}\ b\ \textbf{do}\ s_1)\ k$. Both sides reduce by way of While.

Their descendants are in $\mathcal{R}$ by construction.

$$
\begin{array}{ccc}
\langle \sigma, (\textbf{while}\ b\ \textbf{do}\ s_1')\ k \rangle & \mathcal{R} & \langle \sigma, (\textbf{while}\ b\ \textbf{do}\ s_1)\ k \rangle \\
{\scriptstyle \mathsf{While}} \Big\downarrow {\scriptstyle \tau} & & {\scriptstyle \tau} \Big\downarrow {\scriptstyle \mathsf{While}} \\
\langle \sigma', (\textbf{if}\ b\ \textbf{then}\ (s_1' \cdots)\ k \rangle & \mathcal{R} & \langle \sigma', (\textbf{if}\ b\ \textbf{then}\ (s_1 \cdots)\ k \rangle
\end{array}
$$

Subcase: The left side is

$$\langle \sigma, (\textbf{if}\ b\ \textbf{then}\ (s_1'\ \textbf{while}\ b\ \textbf{do}\ s_1'))\ k \rangle$$

and the right side is

$$\langle \sigma, (\textbf{if}\ b\ \textbf{then}\ (s_1\ \textbf{while}\ b\ \textbf{do}\ s_1))\ k \rangle$$

Suppose the left side reduce by IfFalse, then both sides step to k, which is already in $\mathcal{R}$ by way of the first subrelation.

$$
\begin{array}{ccc}
\langle \sigma, (\textbf{if}\ b\ \textbf{then}\ (s_1' \cdots)\ k \rangle & \mathcal{R} & \langle \sigma, (\textbf{if}\ b\ \textbf{then}\ (s_1 \cdots)\ k \rangle \\
{\scriptstyle \mathsf{IfFalse}} \Big\downarrow {\scriptstyle \tau} & & {\scriptstyle \tau} \Big\downarrow {\scriptstyle \mathsf{IfFalse}} \\
\langle \sigma, k \rangle & \mathcal{R} & \langle \sigma, k \rangle
\end{array}
$$

Subcase: The left side is

$$\langle \sigma, (\textbf{if}\ b\ \textbf{then}\ (s_1'\ \textbf{while}\ b\ \textbf{do}\ s_1'))\ k \rangle$$

and the right side is

$$\langle \sigma, (\textbf{if}\ b\ \textbf{then}\ (s_1\ \textbf{while}\ b\ \textbf{do}\ s_1))\ k \rangle$$

Suppose the left side reduce by IfTrue, we can then fill out the diagram as follows. The descendants are in $\mathcal{R}$ by way of the fourth subrelation, as

$$s_1' = F(s_1, \sigma, FV(s_1))$$

$$
\begin{array}{ccc}
\langle \sigma, (\textbf{if}\ b\ \textbf{then}\ (s_1' \cdots)\ k \rangle & \mathcal{R} & \langle \sigma, (\textbf{if}\ b\ \textbf{then}\ (s_1 \cdots)\ k \rangle \\
{\scriptstyle \mathsf{IfTrue}} \Big\downarrow {\scriptstyle \tau} & & {\scriptstyle \tau} \Big\downarrow {\scriptstyle \mathsf{IfTrue}} \\
\langle \sigma, (s_1' \cdots)\ k \rangle & \mathcal{R} & \langle \sigma, (s_1 \cdots)\ k \rangle
\end{array}
$$

Subcase: The left side is

$$(F(n, \sigma, FV(s_1)) \textbf{ while } b \textbf{ do } s_1')\ k$$

and the right side is

$$(n \textbf{ while } b \textbf{ do } s_1)\ k$$

The left side steps by way of Assign. By inversion, $n = c\, n'$ and

$$F(n, \sigma, FV(s_1)) = F(c, \sigma, FV(s_1))\ F(n', \sigma, FV(s_1))$$

Further, $c = x := e$. For brevity let $n'' = F(n', \sigma, FV(s_1))$.

By case analysis on e we have two subcases. In the case where $e = n$, we have an identity. In the case where $e = x' + 1 \wedge x' \in v$, $e = \sigma(x') \oplus 1$. We know that $\sigma(x')$ is defined from assumption that the left side steps at all. This means the left side step looks like the following. The call to F is abbreviated due to space.

$$\langle \sigma', (c'\ n''\ \cdots)\ k\rangle \xrightarrow{\delta}_B \langle \sigma'[x/\sigma(x') \oplus 1], (n'' \cdots)\ k\rangle$$
$$\text{where } \delta = x/\sigma(x') \oplus 1$$

By inversion then we see that the right side, starting with c, also steps by Assign. By the definition of $\hat{\sigma}'$ we have the following reduction for the right side

$$\langle \sigma', (c\, n' \cdots)\ k\rangle \xrightarrow{\delta'}_B \langle \sigma'[x/\sigma'(x') \oplus 1], (n' \cdots)\ k\rangle$$
$$\text{where } \delta' = x/\sigma'(x') \oplus 1$$

For these two descendants to be in $\mathcal{R}$, we need $\sigma'(x') = \sigma(x')$. We know this to hold for all free variables in s_1, as their freeness guarantees them to be never written to during s_1's reduction. We assumed that FV correctly generates the set of free variables for a statement. It is easy to see that c is a descendant of s_1, thus $x \in FV(s_1)$ and $\sigma'(x') = \sigma(x')$ holds.

Since FV is correct, x is not free in s_1. Therefore,

$$\sigma'[x/\sigma'(x') \oplus 1](y) = \sigma(y)$$

for all y free in s_1. This finally gives us

$$\mathcal{R}(\sigma'[x/\sigma'(x') \oplus 1], n'', n')$$

which holds by way of the fourth subrelation.

For the diagram below, let $v = \sigma(x') \oplus 1$.

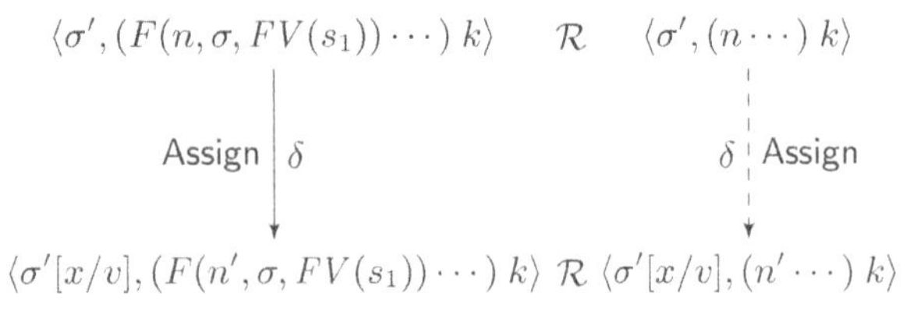

All other cases (where s is something other than a **while** loop) are identities. The proofs for the converses are symmetric.

We have shown $O(w', \sigma)\ k\ {}_B{\approx}_B\ w'\ k$ for σ. By transitivity, we have the desired result of $O(w', \sigma)\ k\ {}_B{\approx}_B\ w\ k$. □

The most interesting part of the proof is that in every subcase we relied on the right side to be able to mirror the left side's move exactly in a single step. This is a stronger property than required by the bisimulation definition, which says only *visible* moves need to be mirrored.

4.2 Soundness of Dead Branch Elimination

What kinds of optimizations only mirror visible moves? One can imagine that during tracing we may generate many spurious side-exits. Suppose we extend our variable folding example to also eliminate "dead", or always-*false* **bail**s. The modifications needed for F are shown in figure 5.

For example, considered the following example trace with a dead side-exit. Clearly x is free in the body of the traced loop, and the boolean expression $x \neq 0$ is always going to be *false*.

Example Trace with Dead Bail

while $x = 0$ **do**
    bail $x \neq 0$ **to** k_1
    $z := 1;$

Plugging the above example into the extended O function will output the following.

Example Trace with Dead Bail Optimized Away

while $x = 0$ **do**
    $z := 1;$

Such an optimization does not generate code that exactly mirrors the original. This fails to hold if we wholly excise dead conditionals, as the original code would still need to take a step to evaluate the conditional to false before skipping it. To show that this new optimization is still bisimilar, let us extend lemma 4.2 with the proof sketch of a new subcase and its converse.

New subcase and its converse for lemma 4.2.

Subcase: The left side is

$$(F(n, \sigma, FV(s_1)) \textbf{ while } b \textbf{ do } s_1')\ k$$

and the right side is

$$(n \textbf{ while } b \textbf{ do } s_1)\ k$$

The left side takes some step. Let $n = c\, n'$ and

$$F(n, \sigma, FV(s_1)) = F(n', \sigma, FV(s_1))$$

We are concerned with the case when $c = \textbf{bail } b' \textbf{ to } k' \wedge F(b', \sigma, FV(s_1)) = \textit{false}$, all other cases for c are identities. For brevity let $n'' = F(n', \sigma, FV(s_1))$.

The left side step looks like the following for some n'''. The call to F is abbreviated due to space.

$$\langle \sigma', (n''\ \cdots)\ k\rangle \xrightarrow{\alpha}_B \langle \sigma'', (n''' \cdots)\ k\rangle$$

By inversion we know that $\hat{\sigma}(b') = \textit{false}$. Since we assumed that FV correctly generates the set of free variables for s_1 and c is a s_1-descendant, so $\hat{\sigma}'(b') = \textit{false}$. By inversion then we see that the right side, starting with c, steps by BailFalse.

$$\langle \sigma', (c\, n' \cdots)\ k\rangle \xrightarrow{\tau}_B \langle \sigma', (n' \cdots)\ k\rangle$$

It remains to show that n' can take a step to match the left side step that $F(n', \sigma, FV(s_1))$ took. We again decompose n' into its first command and continuation. We iteratively apply the same reasoning we just underwent until the first command is not **bail** b'' **to** $k'' \wedge F(b'', \sigma, FV(s_1)) = \textit{false}$. For these other cases F acts as an identity for the first command and as congruence for the continuation, so clearly it will take the same α step.

In the diagram below, let $^+$ mean "1 or more times".

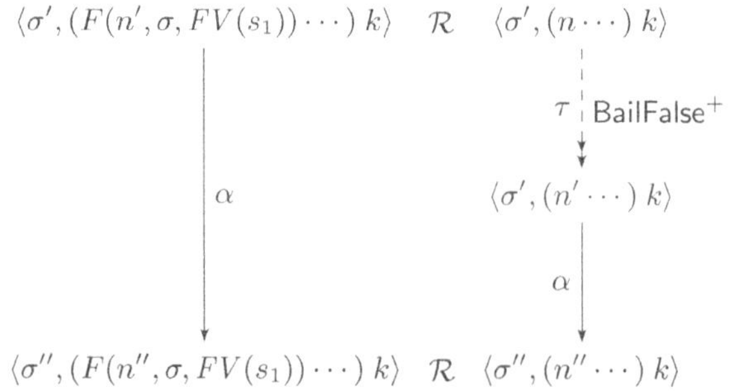

$$F(b,\sigma,v) = \begin{cases} \textit{true} & \text{if } b = x = 0 \wedge x \in v \wedge \sigma(x) = 0 \\ \textit{false} & \text{if } b = x = 0 \wedge x \in v \wedge \sigma(x) \neq 0 \\ \textit{true} & \text{if } b = x \neq 0 \wedge x \in v \wedge \sigma(x) \neq 0 \\ \textit{false} & \text{if } b = x \neq 0 \wedge x \in v \wedge \sigma(x) = 0 \\ \textit{undef} & \text{otherwise} \end{cases}$$

$$F(c,\sigma,v) = \begin{cases} \ldots & \\ \epsilon & \text{if } c = \textbf{bail } b \textbf{ to } s_1 \wedge F(b,\sigma,v) = \textit{false} \\ \ldots & \end{cases}$$

Figure 5. Variable Folding extended with Dead Branch Elimination

$$F(c,\sigma,v) = \begin{cases} \ldots & \\ \epsilon & \text{if } c = x := e \wedge x \text{ has no use sites in the trace} \\ \ldots & \end{cases}$$

Figure 6. Variable Folding extended with Dead Branch and Dead Store Elimination

The converse is considerably simpler. We have the case where the right side steps by BailFalse. By the same reasoning above concerning free variables, we see that the left side would have had its **bail** optimized away into ϵ, thus we can complete the diagram by using *Id*.

$$\begin{array}{ccc} \langle \sigma', (F(n',\sigma,FV(s_1))\cdots)\; k\rangle & \mathcal{R} & \langle \sigma', (n\cdots)\; k\rangle \\ \Big\downarrow \mathit{Id} & & \Big\downarrow \tau\ \mathsf{BailFalse} \\ \langle \sigma', (F(n',\sigma,FV(s_1))\cdots)\; k\rangle & \mathcal{R} & \langle \sigma', (n'\cdots)\; k\rangle \end{array}$$

All other cases are still identities. □

4.3 Unsoundness of Dead Store Elimination

Finally, we want to explore what kinds of optimizations are simply unsafe in the tracing framework. Put formally, we want to ask what kind of optimizations do not produce bisimilar code. Continuing with our existing O function, suppose we were to extend it with dead store elimination. That is, suppose variables that we assign to but have no use sites inside the trace body are simply excised. This is shown informally in figure 6.

For example, consider the following example trace with a dead assignment. The variable z is assigned but never used.

Example Trace with Dead Assignment

```
while x = 0 do
    z := 1;
```

Plugging the above example into the extended O function will output the following.

Example Trace with Dead Assignment Optimized Away

```
while x = 0 do
    ε
```

Intuitively this is unsafe because even though z is dead inside the trace, there very well may be use sites of z after the trace! This intuition is reflected formally. Taking our example above, we need to show that $z := 1$; takes a step that can be mirrored by ϵ. For some σ, by inversion $z := 1$ can step only by Assign: $\langle \sigma, z := 1\rangle \xrightarrow{\tau}_B \langle \sigma[z/1], \epsilon\rangle$. ϵ needs to be able to match this move, but $\langle \sigma, \epsilon\rangle \not\xRightarrow{\hat{\tau}}_B \langle \sigma[z/1], s\rangle$ for any s. In fact, it does not step at all.

In this fashion this optimization does not output bisimilar code, and is not safe for use inside the tracing framework.

4.4 Soundness of Composition

One property that correct optimizations enjoy in our framework is that the composition of two correct optimizations also yield a correct optimization. We give the following two lemmas to demonstrate this property.

Lemma 4.3. Let I : (*Statement* $\times$ *Store*) $\rightarrow$ *Statement* be the identity function on its first argument. I is sound.

Proof. Trivial by the definition of O-soundness. □

Lemma 4.4. Let F, G : (*Statement* $\times$ *Store*) $\rightarrow$ *Statement* be two sound optimizations. Let their composition be defined as

$$F \circ G = \lambda(s,\sigma).F(G(s,\sigma),\sigma)$$

$F \circ G$ is sound.

Proof. We want to show that for any w, w', k such that $w'\ k\ {}_B{\approx}_B\ w\ k$ for all stores, $(F \circ G)(w',\sigma)\ k\ {}_B{\approx}_B\ w\ k$ for σ.

By soundness of G on w, w', k we know that

$$G(w',\sigma)\ k\ {}_B{\approx}_B\ w\ k$$

By soundness of F on $w, G(w',\sigma), k$ we then know that

$$F(G(w',\sigma),\sigma)\ k\ {}_B{\approx}_B\ w\ k$$

But $F(G(w',\sigma),\sigma)\ k = (F \circ G)(w',\sigma)$, so we are done. □

5. Related Work

The work carried out in this paper depends on both compiler-correctness and concurrency techniques. Though the corpora of both communities are large, there is a dearth of truly relevant papers that explore purely operational compiler correctness of JIT compilers from as a high-level as ours. Nevertheless, we have taken inspiration as well as fruitful comparisons with several works.

Relevant is Wand's work on parallel compiler correctness [20]. We believe Wand's enterprise to be, though also employing bisimulations to prove compiler-correctness, of a different flavor than our own. His approach is the combination of (syntax-directed) denotational semantics and essentially β-convertibility. His picture is also closer to the traditional picture of compiler correctness [5]—that is, the compilation process preserves denotation up to bisimulation—than ours, as his compiler is an ahead-of-time compiler. The elegance of Wand's work is that he recognized that β-convertibility *induces* bisimilarity; in the conclusion he admits that almost all the required reasoning is done in the λ-caculus and as such, he can re-use work already done in sequential compiler correctness.

Unlike Wand's work, our vision of correctness is purely syntax-directed: the translation itself (if the JIT tracing can be seen as such) becomes a non-instantaneous process since we have to spell it out in the operational semantics. This is what makes the enterprise nontrivial. Our notion of convertibility informally becomes something akin to "store-convertiblity", but this is much less powerful than β-convertibility as it does not directly imply bisimilarity. We also do not have the luxury of bringing to bear the entirety of the λ-calculus machinery, so our technique here, while still using bisimulations, is at once more basic and less elegant.

There is also a breadth of literature exploring using bisimulation to show program equivalence by way of contextual equivalence in Pierce et al., Lassen et al., and Wand et al. [10, 17–19]. Though the topics of their specific investigations differ, they all concern themselves with using bisimulation as a more tractable proof technique to prove contextual equivalence without having to universally quantify over all contexts. Their setting is higher-ordered, modeled within the λ-calculus. Pierce et al. [19], for instance, aims to prove bisimiliarity sound and complete with respect to contextual equivalence for a modified λ-calculus with recursive types. Wand [10] aims to improve the proof technique and reasons about a λ-calculus extended with explicit stores. These works are basic investigations into the nature of the proof technique. Ours is an application of the technique to prove equivalence of a dynamically transformed program. We also arrived at bisimiliarity by an entirely different motivation, that of proving determinism of a JIT compiler that performs the dynamic transform. We are not met with the difficulty of universally quantifying contexts; in fact, we fix our correctness to hold for one context only.

Myreen's method of creating formally correct JIT compilers for x86 [15] is at the much lower level of abstraction: machine language. They use Hoare logic, and so still retain a flavor of the denotational. We are much farther from the "bare metal" than they are.

6. Conclusions and Future Work

We have demonstrated a paradigm for high-level, purely operational correctness of the tracing JIT compilation technique via bisimulation and confluence. Unlike traditional ahead-of-time compiler correctness where the translation process from the source language to the target language is an opaque function, trace compiler-correctness requires the translation—the tracing—to be spelled out explicitly. We overcome this difficulty by using bisimulations, though we strive to maintain continuity with existing purely operational correctness approaches by returning to confluence.

We hope that the theoretical framework we have provided will prove useful in reasoning about trace compilers at a high level. We hope that we have opened up a wealth of possible future research in the foundational differences betweens traditional and trace optimizations. Though a different problem, we also feel applying the trace compilation technique to an applicative setting, namely the λ-calculus, will be a worthy venture. It is also interesting to further explore O and the question of just what exactly is observable in computation. We also hope to look at deriving tools from the techniques described here in the future.

Acknowledgements. We thank Michael Bebenita and the Mozilla JavaScript team for enlightening discussions about the implementation of trace compilers. We also thank Jonathan Lee, Oren Freiberg, Kannan Goudan, Dave Herman, Dimitris Vardoulakis, and the anonymous reviewers for draft reading and helpful discussions.

References

[1] Vasanth Bala, Evelyn Duesterwald, and Sanjeev Banerjia. Dynamo: A transparent dynamic optimization system. In *PLDI '00*, pages 1–12. ACM, 2000.

[2] Michael Bebenita, Florian Brandner, Manuel Fahndrich, Francesco Logozzo, Wolfram Schulte, Nikolai Tillmann, and Herman Venter. SPUR: A trace-based JIT compiler for CIL. In *OOPSLA '10*, 2010.

[3] Michael Bebenita, Mason Chang, Gregor Wagner, Christian Wimmer, Andreas Gal, and Michael Franz. Trace-based compilation in execution environments without interpreters. In *PPPJ '10*, 2010.

[4] Mason Chang, Edwin W. Smith, Rick Reitmaier, Michael Bebenita, Andreas Gal, Christian Wimmer, Brendan Eich, and Michael Franz. Tracing for web 3.0: trace compilation for the next generation web applications. In *VEE*, pages 71–80, 2009.

[5] Joëlle Despeyroux. Proof of translation in natural semantics. In *LICS*, pages 193–205, 1986.

[6] Cormac Flanagan and Matthias Felleisen. The semantics of future and its use in program optimization. In *POPL '95*, pages 209–220. ACM, 1995.

[7] Andreas Gal. *Efficient bytecode verification and compilation in a virtual machine*. PhD thesis, 2006. Adviser: Michael Franz.

[8] Andreas Gal, Brendan Eich, Mike Shaver, David Anderson, David Mandelin, Mohammad R. Haghighat, Blake Kaplan, Graydon Hoare, Boris Zbarsky, Jason Orendorff, Jesse Ruderman, Edwin W. Smith, Rick Reitmaier, Michael Bebenita, Mason Chang, and Michael Franz. Trace-based just-in-time type specialization for dynamic languages. In *PLDI '09*, pages 465–478. ACM, 2009.

[9] A. J. Kfoury, Michael A. Arbib, and Robert N. Moll. *A Programming Approach to Computability*. Springer-Verlag, 1982.

[10] Vasileios Koutavas and Mitchell Wand. Small bisimulations for reasoning about higher-order imperative programs. In *POPL '06*, pages 141–152. ACM, 2006.

[11] David Lacey, Neil D. Jones, Eric Van Wyk, and Carl Christian Frederiksen. Proving correctness of compiler optimizations by temporal logic. In *POPL '02*, pages 283–294. ACM, 2002.

[12] Sorin Lerner, Todd Millstein, and Craig Chambers. Automatically proving the correctness of compiler optimizations. In *PLDI '03*, pages 220–231. ACM, 2003.

[13] Mozilla Metrics. Firefox usage: https://metrics.mozilla.com/.

[14] Robin Milner. *Communication and Concurrency*. Prentice Hall, 1995.

[15] Magnus O. Myreen. Verified just-in-time compiler on x86. In *POPL '10*, pages 107–118. ACM, 2010.

[16] Frank Pfenning. A proof of the Church-Rosser theorem and its representation in a logical framework. *Journal of Automated Reasoning*, 1993.

[17] Kristian Støvring and Soren B. Lassen. A complete, co-inductive syntactic theory of sequential control and state. In *POPL '07*, pages 161–172. ACM, 2007.

[18] Eijiro Sumii and Benjamin C. Pierce. A bisimulation for dynamic sealing. In *POPL '04*, pages 161–172. ACM, 2004.

[19] Eijiro Sumii and Benjamin C. Pierce. A bisimulation for type abstraction and recursion. In *POPL '05*, pages 63–74. ACM, 2005.

[20] Mitchell Wand. Compiler correctness for parallel languages. In *FPCA*, pages 120–134, 1995.

[21] Mitchell Wand and William D. Clinger. Set constraints for destructive array update optimization. *Journal of Functional Programming*, 11(3):319–346, 2001.

[22] Mitchell Wand and Igor Siveroni. Constraint systems for useless variable elimination. In *POPL '99*, pages 291–302. ACM, 1999.

Resourceable, Retargetable, Modular Instruction Selection Using a Machine-Independent, Type-Based Tiling of Low-Level Intermediate Code

Norman Ramsey
Department of Computer Science, Tufts University
nr@cs.tufts.edu

João Dias
Department of Computer Science, Tufts University
dias@cs.tufts.edu

Abstract

We present a novel variation on the standard technique of selecting instructions by tiling an intermediate-code tree. Typical compilers use a different set of tiles for every target machine. By analyzing a formal model of machine-level computation, we have developed a single set of tiles that is *machine-independent* while retaining the expressive power of machine code. Using this tileset, we reduce the number of tilers required from one per machine to one per architectural family (e.g., register architecture or stack architecture). Because the tiler is the part of the instruction selector that is most difficult to reason about, our technique makes it possible to retarget an instruction selector with significantly less effort than standard techniques. Retargeting effort is further reduced by applying an earlier result which generates the machine-dependent implementation of our tileset automatically from a declarative description of instructions' semantics. Our design has the additional benefit of enabling modular reasoning about three aspects of code generation that are not typically separated: the semantics of the compiler's intermediate representation, the semantics of the target instruction set, and the techniques needed to generate *good* target code.

Categories and Subject Descriptors D.3.4 [*Processors*]: Code generation; D.3.4 [*Processors*]: Retargetable compilers

General Terms Algorithms, Theory

1. Introduction

Since compilers were first written, researchers have worked toward the goal of implementing N programming languages on M target machines with only $O(N+M)$ work instead of the $O(N \times M)$ work required to write a compiler for each language on each machine (Conway 1958; Strong et al. 1958). This goal has led to years of fruitful work on retargetable compilers, and at the current state of the art, the major $O(N \times M)$ component of a retargetable compiler is the *instruction selector*, which maps compiler-specific intermediate code to target-specific machine code. We have developed a new way of selecting instructions which reduces N to the number of compiler infrastructures and reduces M to the number of architectural families supported. Our implementation supports one compiler infrastructure and two architectural families (register machines and stack machines).

POPL'11, January 26–28, 2011, Austin, Texas, USA.

Our compiler infrastructure is built on C--, an abstraction that encapsulates an optimizing code generator so it can be reused with multiple source languages and multiple target machines (Peyton Jones, Ramsey, and Reig 1999; Ramsey and Peyton Jones 2000). C-- accommodates multiple source languages by providing two main interfaces: the C-- *language* is a machine-independent, language-independent target language for front ends; the C-- *run-time interface* is an API which gives the run-time system access to the states of suspended computations.

C-- is *not* a universal intermediate language (Conway 1958) or a "write-once, run-anywhere" intermediate language encapsulating a rigidly defined compiler and run-time system (Lindholm and Yellin 1999). Rather, C-- encapsulates compilation techniques that are well understood, but expensive to implement. Such techniques include instruction selection, register allocation, implementation of procedure calling conventions, instruction scheduling, scalar optimizations, and loop optimizations.

To accomodate a variety of source languages, the C-- language is very expressive. The implementation of a code generator for C-- therefore presents an unusual challenge: ensuring that the code generator accepts all valid input programs is harder than usual, and the compiler writer's job of mapping the language to target-machine code is bigger than usual. In this paper we present a new *tileset* for machine-level computation, which helps address both problems. Our work makes these contributions:

- We have developed a new variation on a standard model of machine-level computation: register transfers. By formalizing and analyzing register transfers, we have found a way of decomposing register transfers into *tiles*, where a tile represents a simple operation such as a sign-extending load or a three-register arithmetic operation (Section 5.2). The decomposition is the same for every target machine and is implemented once.
- By contrast with current techniques, which require a compiler writer to show that tiling is correct and complete for each new target machine, our techniques require the compiler writer to show correctness and completeness just once per architectural family. We argue informally that our tiling algorithm is correct and complete for the family of register machines (Section 6).
- We show that the syntax and type structure of register transfers, which are almost trivially simple, nevertheless provide enough structure around which to design an instruction selector.
- Finally, our design enables modular reasoning about a code generator that emits quality code; in particular, we decouple knowledge of the compiler's intermediate code from knowledge of the target machine, simplifying the task of retargeting the instruction selector to the point where most of the work can be done automatically (Dias and Ramsey 2010).

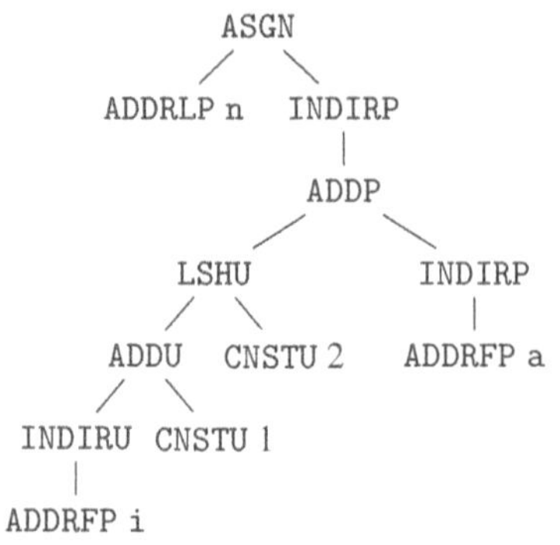

Figure 1. `lcc` IR for `n = a[i+1];`

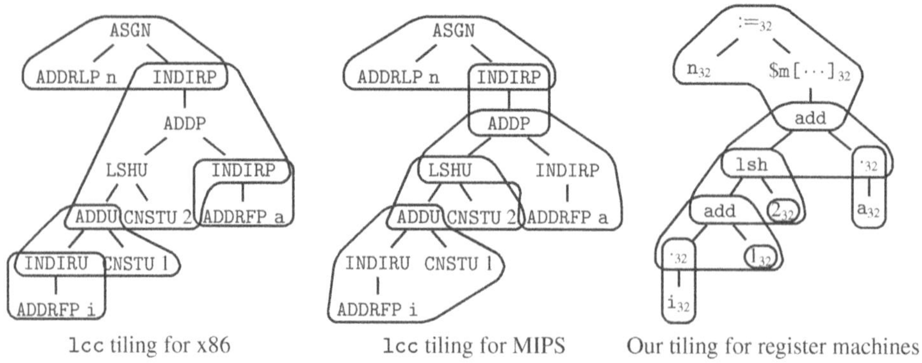

Figure 2. Multiple tilings of the tree from Figure 1

2. Background

The problem we solve is the mapping from a compiler's low-level intermediate code to target machine instructions: *instruction selection*. For a compiler that generates code for more than one target, instruction selection should be easily *retargetable*.

2.1 Related work: Instruction selection by tiling

Instruction selection is usually treated as a *tiling* problem. For each target machine, the compiler writer defines a set of *tiles*, where each tile maps a tree of the compiler's intermediate code (an *IR tree*) to an effective address or to one or more machine instructions. Using the tiles, the instruction selector covers the tree so that the root of one tile is a leaf of another tile, and so on. Such a covering is called a *tiling*. Postorder traversal of a tiling produces a sequence of instructions that implements the tree.

Figure 1 shows an IR tree created by the `lcc` compiler (Fraser and Hanson 1995) from the C assignment `n = a[i+1]`, where `i` is an unsigned integer, `n` is a signed integer, and `a` is a pointer to an array of signed integers. If you are not familiar with `lcc`'s IR, suffix `P` or `U` indicates the result is a pointer or an unsigned integer. `lcc` assumes that all variables are in memory, so a use of a variable is an `INDIR` node above an `ADDRF` (formal parameter) or `ADDRL` (local variable) node. A later pass may convert some `INDIR`/`ADDR` combinations to `REG`. The example tree also includes constants (`CNST`), operations (`ADD`, `LSH`), and an assignment (`ASGN`).

In a typical compiler, each target machine requires its own unique set of tiles or *tileset*. Figure 2 shows tilings of the tree in Figure 1 using three different tilesets. The left-hand tiling uses `lcc`'s x86 tileset. The middle tiling uses `lcc`'s MIPS tileset. The right-hand tiling uses our register-machine tileset, which works for both x86 and MIPS as well as other typical register machines such as ARM and PowerPC. (Our tiling, instead of `lcc`'s IR, shows the IR used by our Quick C-- compiler: the tree is the same, but the nodes are labeled differently. In particular, $\cdot_{32}$ labels a fetch from a variable.)

Given a tileset, there is often more than one way to tile a particular tree. The way is computed by a *tiling algorithm*, of which there are two common families: bottom-up rewriting and maximal munch.

Bottom-up rewriting, often called BURS or BURG, computes an optimal tiling. A bottom-up rewriter uses dynamic programming, and it is usually built using a code-generator generator: the compiler writer defines the tiles using a domain-specific language, and the code-generator generator uses the tiles to build a bottom-up tree matcher (Pelegrí-Llopart and Graham 1988; Aho, Ganapathi, and Tjiang 1989; Fraser, Henry, and Proebsting 1992; Proebsting 1992; Fraser, Hanson, and Proebsting 1992).

Maximal munch is a greedy tiling algorithm that works by top-down pattern-matching on the IR tree (Cattell 1980; Appel 1998). The tiling may not be optimal, but the algorithm is easy to implement by hand. Our compiler uses maximal munch.

2.2 Retargeting is surprisingly complicated

To the uninitiated, writing an instruction selector for a new machine seems simple: just define a tile for each machine instruction. But the task is more complicated than it seems:

- *A tile does not describe an instruction's semantics.* A tile might map a small IR tree to a machine instruction that implements the tree. But it is not safe to assume that the instruction performs *only* the computation described by the IR tree. For example, it is common to have a tile that maps an addition operation to a machine instruction that performs not only the addition but also an extra assignment to a condition-code register. To use such an instruction, the compiler writer must reason about whether the extra assignments are safe.
- *Having one tile for each machine instruction may not be sufficient to generate code.* The instruction selector must be able to tile *any* IR tree. Consequently, it is not possible to define a set of tiles without reasoning about what IR trees can be covered by the tiles. For example, on a 32-bit RISC machine, there is no instruction that loads a 32-bit immediate constant into a register. If the tileset contains only one tile for each machine instruction, the compiler will not be able to generate code for an IR tree that loads an immediate constant.

  The load-immediate problem is an instance of a general problem: to make sure that every IR tree can be covered, the compiler writer must define tiles that map to *sequences* of machine instructions, not just single instructions. To discover these tiles, it's not enough to think about the instruction set; the compiler writer has to think about the instruction set *and* about the structure of IR trees—and about what IR trees can occur during compilation.
- *Having one tile for each IR node may not be sufficient to generate* good *code.* To generate efficient code, you might need multiple tiles that can cover the same IR tree using different machine instructions. The x86 tiling on the left of Figure 2 shows two examples in which an addition is tiled using something other than the obvious `add` instruction. The small tile implementing `ADDU(INDIRU(···), CNSTU 1)` uses the x86 *load effective address* instruction, which has a small binary encoding and which doesn't affect condition codes. As another example, the largest tile, which performs a left shift, an add, and a fetch

(INDIRP), uses the indexed addressing mode to do the addition in the x86 addressing unit. This instruction not only has a small binary encoding but also frees up an integer unit for some other computation, enhancing instruction-level parallelism.

These complications arise because the standard approach to instruction selection, mapping IR fragments to machine instructions, inhibits modular reasoning: a compiler writer must reason about interactions among the compiler's IR, the target instruction set, and the optimizer. Such reasoning requires broad expertise. Worse, for each new machine, crafting new tiles requires that similar reasoning be repeated using somewhat different but equally broad expertise.

3. A modular approach to instruction selection

To reduce the effort required to write a code generator for a new target machine, we have developed a new, modular approach to instruction selection. Our approach separates concerns about the compiler from concerns about the machine and concerns about low-level optimization. We separate these concerns by refactoring the compiler in two ways: we optimize code *after* translating IR to machine instructions, and we divide tiling into separate machine-dependent and machine-independent components.

3.1 Related work: Optimizing machine codes

To separate the concerns of choosing machine instructions and generating efficient code, we adapt the approach developed by Davidson and Fraser (1984). In this approach, the compiler writer maps IR trees to *naïve* machine code, represented using *register-transfer lists*, also called RTLs (Section 4). RTLs are later improved by an optimizer. The optimizer is *machine-independent*, but it improves the program under the machine-dependent constraint that each RTL represents a single machine instruction: the *machine invariant*. The machine invariant is enforced by a predicate called the *recognizer*. Optimizing RTLs does not rule out other optimizations that operate on IR trees or on even higher-level representations, but Davidson has shown that many optimizations which are typically performed on IR are better performed on RTLs, where they help generate particularly efficient code (Benitez and Davidson 1988, 1994).

To ensure that the compiler emits efficient machine instructions, the optimizer includes a machine-independent peephole optimizer. Because the peephole optimizer translates the tiler's naïve machine code into efficient machine code, this way of organizing a compiler is sometimes called instruction selection by peephole optimization, and the peephole optimizer is sometimes called the instruction selector. This organization is used not only in Davidson's vpo compiler but also in gcc.

In Davidson and Fraser's original design, the mapping from low-level IR to RTLs satisfying the machine invariant is done by a component called the *code expander*. The expander is so named because it maps a typical IR tree to a long sequence of simple RTLs, expanding the code. Davidson and Fraser (1984) note that code expanders are simple and easy to to implement; to add a new machine, compiler writers are advised to clone and modify the expander for a similar machine. But since 1984, IRs, machines, and expanders have become more complex, and having an expander for each combination of source language and target machine creates maintenance problems: when bugs are discovered, there is not a single point of truth about how to do the translation. In our adaptation of the design, the code expander is split into three parts:

- A language-dependent part maps the compiler's low-level IR to RTLs that respect only the word size and byte order of the target machine—*not* the machine invariant.
- The tiler described in this paper expands these RTLs to RTLs that conform to the shapes described in Section 5.2 below.
- A machine-dependent implementation, which can be generated automatically (Dias and Ramsey 2010), computes a representation of each shape using RTLs that represent machine instructions—i.e., RTLs that respect the machine invariant.

We changed Davidson and Fraser's original design in a modest way: we took a single component and split it into three. This change, although modest, has a big impact: the number of components that have to be maintained drops from $N \times M$ to $N + M$, and the M machine-dependent components can be generated automatically from declarative descriptions of the target-machine semantics.

A big payoff of Davidson's approach is that responsibility for producing efficient machine code is isolated in the optimizer. The tiler is responsible not for performance but only for mapping IR trees to simple machine instructions. The naïveté of our tiler's output can be seen in Figure 2: compared to lcc's locally optimal, machine-dependent tilings, Quick C-- uses eight tiles instead of five. This naïve code is improved by the optimizer.

3.2 Modularity through machine-independent tiling of RTLs

Davidson's body of work shows that we can build an excellent compiler by first generating naïve machine code, then improving it. But even when we don't need to generate *good* machine code, writing a traditional tiler still requires that we reason simultaneously about the semantics of machine instructions and about the compiler's intermediate representation. In this paper, we show a novel alternative, which supports modular reasoning:

- Low-level IR may be translated to almost any well-typed RTLs. Unlike earlier compilers, which require that all RTLs satisfy the machine invariant, our compiler requires only that RTLs respect the byte order and word size of the target machine. This innovation frees the front end from having to reason about the target instruction set.
- Provided there is a machine-dependent recognizer, RTLs support machine-independent optimization. The recognizer decouples reasoning about *optimization* from reasoning about the instruction set. Dias and Ramsey (2006) show how to generate a recognizer from a description of instructions' semantics.
- RTLs are language-neutral: no matter what the source language, if the source code can be compiled to a low-level intermediate representation, that representation can easily be translated into RTLs. Reasoning about the source language is therefore confined to the front end, which emits RTLs.
- Part of our strategy of language-neutrality is to avoid high-level types. Instead, we use a type system that treats values only as bit vectors or Booleans, much as the hardware does (Section 4.1). This simple type system leads us to the centerpieces of our design: a single, machine-independent tileset that can be reused for any register machine (Section 5.2), and a tiling algorithm that reduces control-flow graphs to that tileset (Section 6).
- A compiler writer can reuse our tileset and tiling algorithm unchanged for any register machine. For each new target machine, all the compiler writer has to do is implement our machine-independent tileset using machine instructions. Our tiles are simple enough that this process can be automated by using a *tileset generator* (Dias and Ramsey 2010).

  Our tileset is *almost* target-neutral: while not suitable for *any* machine, it is suitable for any machine that provides roughly interchangeable *registers*. (We have defined another tileset for *stack* machines, but it has been used only to generate code for the x86 legacy floating-point unit.)

Using our modular approach, it is significantly easier to add a new target machine: because the tileset doesn't change, you don't have to design tiles, and you know our tileset will cover any IR tree. Even if you don't use our tileset generator, our experience shows that it is easy to implement the tileset by hand. Finally, our modular approach does not affect the code ultimately generated by the compiler; like any other Davidson/Fraser compiler, our compiler generates high-quality code if and only if the optimizer used after instruction selection is of high quality.

Using machine-independent intermediate forms to improve modularity is standard practice; prominent examples include the Java Virtual Machine (Lindholm and Yellin 1999) and LLVM (Lattner and Adve 2004). Some of these intermediate forms are very close to machine instructions. Our innovation is not that the intermediate form is machine-independent or low-level; rather, it is that

- As described below, the intermediate form is derived in a principled way from the type system of a metalanguage used to describe instructions' *semantics* (Ramsey and Davidson 1998).
- As described by Dias and Ramsey (2010), the intermediate form *eliminates* the need for the compiler writer to specify how each tile is implemented by machine instructions—the implementations can be discovered automatically by heuristic search.

Below, we present the ideas that lead to our design: we explain RTLs (Section 4); we discuss their static semantics (Section 4.1); we analyze their types (Section 4.2); we show how types suggest tiles (Section 5); and we present a tiling algorithm (Section 6).

4. Register-transfer lists and control-flow graphs

Register-transfer lists (RTLs) provide a simple but precise representation of the effects of machine instructions. A register-transfer list denotes a function from machine states to machine states. A machine state is represented as a collection of *storage spaces*, each of which we designate with a lower-case letter. For example, on the popular x86 architecture, we write `m` for memory, `r` for general-purpose registers, `f` for legacy floating-point registers, `x` for SSE registers (`%xmm`*n*), and `c` for control registers (including flags and the instruction pointer). Each storage space is divided into *cells*; a cell is the smallest natural unit with which the hardware reads and writes the storage. On the x86, for example, the cell size is 8 bits for memory, 32 bits for general-purpose registers, and 80 bits for legacy floating-point registers. (Access to a "register" like AL or AH is treated as access to an internal "slice" of a full cell like EAX.)

After program variables have been mapped to machine locations, RTLs are represented using the syntax shown in Figure 3.

- A register-transfer list is a list of guarded effects. Each effect represents the transfer of a value into a storage location, i.e., an assignment. The transfer occurs only if the guard (an expression) evaluates to true (**T**). Effects in a list take place simultaneously, as in Dijkstra's multiple-assignment statement; an RTL represents a single change of state. For example, an RTL can represent a swap instruction without introducing temporaries.
- A location may be a single cell or an aggregate of consecutive cells within a storage space. For example, four 8-bit bytes may be aggregated to form a location holding a 32-bit word, as in $\$\mathtt{m}_{\text{BIG},8}\,\mathtt{[}addr\mathtt{]}_{32}$, which specifies a big-endian word starting at address *addr*. In an aggregate, byte order is explicit.

  Some storage spaces stand for "temporary registers," or *temporaries*. Eventually the register allocator replaces temporaries with hardware registers (Dias and Ramsey 2006, §2.1).
- Values are computed by expressions that have no side effects. An expression may be a compile-time constant (k_w, **T**, or **F**), a link-time constant L, a fetch from a location l_w, or an application of an *RTL operator* $\oplus_\tau$ to a list of expressions.

a	Aggregation order (big-endian, little-endian, or ID)
c	Cell width of storage space
e, g	Expression (aka *guard*)
G	Control-flow graph
k	Literal integer or bit vector
l	Location
L	Label
$\oplus$	RTL operator
τ	Type
w	Width in bits

$$
\begin{array}{lll}
RTL & \Rightarrow & [g \rightarrow \mathit{effect}\ \{\ \mid g \rightarrow \mathit{effect}\}] \\
\mathit{effect} & \Rightarrow & l :=_w e \\
l & \Rightarrow & \$space_{a,c}\,\mathtt{[}e\mathtt{]}_w \\
e & \Rightarrow & k_w \mid \mathbf{T} \mid \mathbf{F} \mid L \mid l_w \mid \oplus_\tau(e_1,\ldots,e_n) \\
G & \Rightarrow & \varepsilon \mid RTL \mid G_1;G_2 \mid L\!: \mid \mathbf{goto}\ e \mid L_T \lhd g \rhd L_F
\end{array}
$$

Figure 3. Syntax of RTLs and control-flow graphs

RTLs are themselves composed into *control-flow graphs G*, whose syntax is also shown in Figure 3. Straight-line code includes the empty graph ε, a single RTL, or a sequence of graphs. Control flow is represented using labels and branches. (We take one liberty with the syntax; instead of writing $L\!::G$, we write the clearer $L\!:G$.) For conditional branches, we use the nonstandard notation $L_T \lhd g \rhd L_F$, which means the same as "**if** g **then goto** L_T **else goto** L_F." This notation makes the inference rules in Section 6 easier to read.

As part of instruction selection, each conditional and unconditional branch in a control-flow graph is associated with a machine instruction, which is represented by an RTL that assigns to the program counter (PC). For example, a conditional branch is represented by an assignment like $\$\mathtt{r[4]} > 0 \rightarrow PC := L$. For computational instructions, the PC is updated implicitly, as formally specified elsewhere (Ramsey and Cifuentes 2003).

A control-flow graph can represent any code from a single statement all the way up to an entire procedure body. For example, on a 32-bit big-endian machine, the C statement `n = a[i+1]` could be translated to a flow graph consisting of the RTL

$$\mathtt{n}_{32} :=_{32} \$\mathtt{m}_{\text{BIG},8}\,\mathtt{[add}_{\tau32}\mathtt{(a}_{32}\mathtt{,shl}_{\tau32}\mathtt{(add}_{\tau32}\mathtt{(i}_{32}\mathtt{,1}_{32}\mathtt{),2}_{32}\mathtt{))]}_{32}$$

where $\tau32 = 32\ \mathtt{bits} \times 32\ \mathtt{bits} \rightarrow 32\ \mathtt{bits}$.

In contrast to RTLs used in some earlier work, C--'s RTLs have a precise semantics independent of any particular machine. The details are not relevant to the contribution of this paper, but you can imagine the simplest possible denotational semantics:

- A syntactic location l denotes a function from a machine state to a hardware location holding a bit vector. The location may be a single cell or a sequence of cells in a storage space.
- A syntactic expression e denotes a function from a machine state to a value, which is either a Boolean or a bit vector.
- A syntactic effect or a syntactic RTL denotes a function from a machine state to another machine state. If two effects in the same RTL mutate the same cell, the parallel composition of those effects denotes the constant wrong function ($\perp$). Denotations are strict, so if a computation goes wrong, it stays wrong.
- An RTL operator denotes a pure function on values.

As usual, the dynamic semantics describes the observable effects of a program. These effects must be preserved by the tiling algorithm, just as by any other instruction selector. The algorithm, however, is inspired not by the dynamic semantics but by the static semantics.

n	A width variable
w	A literal width
w_M	The width of an address on the target machine
n `bits`	A value that is n bits wide
n `loc`	A location containing an n-bit value
`bool`	A Boolean condition

$\boxed{\Delta \vdash_\tau \tau}$ (τ is a well-formed type)

$$\frac{n \in \Delta}{\Delta \vdash_\tau n\,\mathtt{bits}} \qquad \frac{n \in \Delta}{\Delta \vdash_\tau n\,\mathtt{loc}} \qquad \frac{w \in \mathbb{N}}{\Delta \vdash_\tau w\,\mathtt{bits}} \qquad \frac{w \in \mathbb{N}}{\Delta \vdash_\tau w\,\mathtt{loc}}$$

$$\frac{}{\Delta \vdash_\tau \mathtt{bool}} \qquad \frac{\Delta, n \vdash_\tau \tau}{\Delta \vdash_\tau \forall n.\tau} \qquad \frac{\Delta \vdash_\tau \tau_i \qquad \Delta \vdash_\tau \tau}{\Delta \vdash_\tau \tau_1 \times \ldots \times \tau_n \rightarrow \tau}$$

Figure 4. Types and type-formation rules

4.1 Static semantics of RTLs

Our RTLs are typed, but not as expressively as typed intermediate languages or assembly languages. Our type system tells us how *wide* something is—how many bits are in a value or a location—and whether an expression computes a bit vector or a Boolean.

Our type system is inspired by System F (Girard 1986), but it is both extended and restricted:

- Our system is extended by allowing a type to be quantified over an *integer*. The integer is a *width* and tells how many bits are in a value or in a location.
- Our system is restricted in ways that might remind you of the Hindley-Milner system (Milner 1978): The only polymorphic types are prenex-quantified type schemes, and only RTL operators, which are named and bound in the environment Γ_0, may have polymorphic types. At each use, a type scheme is fully instantiated, so the type of any *term* in the RTL language (from Figure 3) is always monomorphic.

Types and type-formation rules are shown in Figure 4. Rules for typing operators, locations, and expressions are shown in Figure 5. The side condition "w_s indexes s" says that storage space s is indexed by an an address or register number that is w_s bits wide. If s refers to main memory, then w_M indexes s.

By giving two distinct rules for literal constants k, we emphasize a design decision: unlike many other intermediate representations, our RTLs do not distinguish signed integers, unsigned integers, floating-point numbers, and pointers. In this paper, we pretend k is an integer, and we show two side conditions under which an integer k can be said to fit in w bits. In our implementation, a compile-time constant k has an abstract type, and the side conditions are imposed by the operations used to create values of this type.

The important part of the type system is the specialization of width-polymorphic RTL operators, as shown in the judgment form $\Gamma_0 \vdash_{op} \oplus : \tau$. In this judgment, Γ_0 represents the collection of operators defined in the C-- language specification (Ramsey, Peyton Jones, and Lindig 2005). This collection represents a *union machine*: it includes any operator we think might be used to describe a machine instruction on a current or future target. For example, the collection includes `popcnt`, which returns the number of 1 bits in a word. This operator is native to Intel architectures; on other machines, we use algebraic laws to rewrite it as a composition of other operators, much in the spirit of Warren (2003). Thinking about all the machine-level operators we ever heard of—and their types—led us to our new tiling for code generation.

$\boxed{\vdash l : \tau}$

$$\frac{\vdash e : w_s\,\mathtt{bits} \qquad w_s \text{ indexes } s \qquad c = w}{\vdash \$s_{\mathrm{ID},c}[e]_w : w\,\mathtt{loc}} \qquad \frac{\vdash e : w_s\,\mathtt{bits} \qquad w_s \text{ indexes } s \qquad a \in \{\mathrm{BIG}, \mathrm{LITTLE}\} \qquad c \text{ divides } w}{\vdash \$s_{a,c}[e]_w : w\,\mathtt{loc}}$$

$\boxed{\vdash e : \tau}$

$$\frac{0 \le k < 2^w}{\vdash k_w : w\,\mathtt{bits}} \qquad \frac{-2^{w-1} \le k < 2^{w-1}}{\vdash k_w : w\,\mathtt{bits}} \qquad \frac{}{\vdash L : w_M}$$

$$\frac{\vdash l : w\,\mathtt{loc}}{\vdash l_w : w\,\mathtt{bits}} \qquad \frac{\Gamma_0 \vdash_{op} \oplus : \tau_1 \times \ldots \times \tau_n \rightarrow \tau \qquad \vdash e_i : \tau_i}{\vdash \oplus_{\tau_1 \times \ldots \times \tau_n \rightarrow \tau}(e_1, \ldots, e_n) : \tau}$$

$\boxed{\Gamma_0 \vdash_{op} \oplus : \tau}$ (operator $\oplus$ can be instantiated at type τ)

$$\frac{\oplus \in \operatorname{dom} \Gamma_0}{\Gamma_0 \vdash_{op} \oplus : \Gamma_0(\oplus)} \qquad \frac{\Gamma_0 \vdash_{op} \oplus : \forall n.\tau}{\Gamma_0 \vdash_{op} \oplus : \tau[n \mapsto w]}$$

Figure 5. Typing rules for locations and selected expressions

4.2 Classifying RTL operators by type

Although the C-- language specification lists 81 RTL operators (28 floating-point operators and 53 integer and bitwise operators), these operators have only 14 distinct types (Table 6). Before explaining how these types help classify RTLs (Section 5 below), we put the 14 types into just 5 groups:

- A *standard value operator* takes some bit vectors of reasonable width and returns a result of that width. (The width is typically the width of one word on the target machine.) These operators are summarized in the first two rows of Table 6. Binary operators include two's-complement addition and subtraction, signed and unsigned division, quotient and remainder, bitwise Boolean operations, and rotations and shifts. Unary operators include bitwise complement, two's-complement negation, population count, and floating-point absolute value and negation.
- A *weird value operator* takes some bit vectors of reasonable width, but also takes an argument or returns a result of another ("weird") width. Such operators require special treatment during tiling. Most floating-point operators are weird value operators because in addition to their ordinary operands, they take a 2-bit rounding mode. The other weird value operators are extended multiplies (which double the width of their operands), nullary rounding-mode "operators" like `round_down`, and multiprecision operators such as carry, borrow, add with carry, and add with borrow.
- A *size-changing operator* widens or narrows a bit vector. The integer size-changing operators are sign extension (`sx`), zero extension (`zx`), and extraction of least-significant bits (`lobits`). Conversions between integers and floating-point values, and between floating-point values of different sizes (`f2f`), are also size-changing operators. Size-changing operators help formalize machine instructions, such as sign-extending loads, that convert values between representations of different sizes.
- A *comparison operator* takes two bit vectors and returns a Boolean. Comparison operators include the usual integer and floating-point comparisons.
- A *Boolean operator* takes one or more Booleans and returns a Boolean. The Boolean operators are `conjoin`, `disjoin`, and `not`.

These groups provide a starting point from which to classify RTLs.

5. From graphs to tiles via types

Before explaining how groups of operators influence the design of our tileset, we consider how to tile an arbitrary control-flow graph using a small set of tiles. As explained in Section 6.1 below, our tiling algorithm reduces every control-flow graph to a composition of graphs in which each node is either a single assignment, an unconditional branch, or a conditional branch on the results of a comparison operator. But even a single assignment or branch can contain an arbitrarily large expression on the right-hand side. To tile these nodes, we use a restricted subset of graphs, where the restrictions are motivated by common properties of register machines (Section 5.1). We then build on the groups of operators identified above to classify the restricted graphs and to identify tiles, using a new idea we call *shape* (Section 5.2).

5.1 Restricting graphs in the tileset

We would like as few graphs as possible to be tiles, because the fewer tiles there are and the simpler the tiles are, the easier it is to implement the tileset. But enough graphs need to be tiles to cover any single assignment or branch. In particular, because every RTL operator can appear in either an assignment or a branch, we need at least one tile for every RTL operator. We have designed our tileset around a fundamental assumption about register machines: if the target machine can compute operator $\oplus$, then the machine can apply $\oplus$ to arguments in registers, and it can place the result in a register (or if the result is Boolean, it can use the result to determine control flow).

We get our tiles by restricting the graphs and RTLs from Figure 3:

- A graph must be a single RTL, a label, **goto** L, **goto** t, or a conditional branch.
- An RTL must have exactly one assignment,[1] and its guard must be the literal **T**.
- If a graph or RTL refers to a memory location, the location's address must be stored in a register. (A memory location is one in which the actual location can be computed at run time or at link time. A register is a location that must be encoded in the instruction word at compile time.)
- The arguments of an RTL operator must be in locations, and except for size-changing operators, those locations must be registers. (Because putting a "weird" value into a register can be expensive, we also permit that a weird argument may be a compile-time constant.)

Any single assignment or branch can be tiled using these restricted graphs. For example (leaving widths and byte order implicit),

$$r_1 := r_2 + (r_3 \times 12)$$

can be reduced to this sequence of tiles:

$$\begin{aligned} t_1 &:= 12 \\ t_2 &:= r_3 \times t_1 \\ r_1 &:= r_2 + t_2. \end{aligned}$$

The reduction introduces fresh temporaries t_1 and t_2 to hold the values of subexpressions of the original RTL.

5.2 Using types to give shapes to tiles

The restrictions above still permit the formation of more than 90 tiles. To simplify both the explanation and the implementation of our tileset, we group tiles into equivalence classes we call *shapes*.

[1] We except procedure calls (not otherwise covered in this paper), which both capture and update the program counter, requiring two assignments.

Type of operator	*Number of operators*	*Sample*
$\forall n.n$ `bits` $\times\ n$ `bits` $\rightarrow n$ `bits`	17	`add`
$\forall n.n$ `bits` $\rightarrow n$ `bits`	5	`com`
$\forall n.n$ `bits` $\times\ n$ `bits` $\times$ 1 `bits` $\rightarrow n$ `bits`	2	`addc`
$\forall n.n$ `bits` $\times\ n$ `bits` $\times$ 1 `bits` $\rightarrow$ 1 `bits`	2	`carry`
$\forall n.n$ `bits` $\times\ n$ `bits` $\times$ 2 `bits` $\rightarrow n$ `bits`	4	`fadd`
$\forall n.n$ `bits` $\times$ 2 `bits` $\rightarrow n$ `bits`	1	`fsqrt`
$\forall n.n$ `bits` $\times\ n$ `bits` $\rightarrow 2n$ `bits`	3	`fmulx`
$\forall n.n$ `bits`	4	`mzero`
2 `bits`	4	`round_down`
$\forall n,m.n$ `bits` $\rightarrow m$ `bits`	5	`sx`
$\forall n,m.n$ `bits` $\times$ 2 `bits` $\rightarrow m$ `bits`	3	`f2f`
$\forall n.n$ `bits` $\times\ n$ `bits` $\rightarrow$ `bool`	24	`eq`
`bool` $\times$ `bool` $\rightarrow$ `bool`	2	`conjoin`
`bool` $\rightarrow$ `bool`	1	`not`

Table 6. Types of selected RTL operators

t	Any temporary or hardware register
m	Any hardware memory space
k	Any literal integer, bit vector, or other compile-time constant
L	Any label or other link-time constant
$\oplus$	An RTL value operator
r	A hardware register
rm	A floating-point rounding mode
$\omega, \hat{r}, \hat{t}$	A weird value, like a carry bit, in all or part of a register
$?$	Any RTL comparison operator

Table 7. Notational conventions for metavariables

A shape is characterized by a control-flow graph in which locations, literals, and operators may be represented by the metavariables in Table 7. Shapes for a register machine, which are inspired both by our restrictions on graphs and RTLs and by our grouping of RTL operators by type, are shown in Figure 8. The graphs with these shapes constitute our *tileset*. (We have also defined shapes for stack machines, such as the x86 floating-point unit; these shapes are sketched in Appendix A.) To simplify the presentation, we omit nonlocal control constructs such as call and return. We also omit some shapes that involve sign-extending or zero-extending a narrow result ω instead of storing it in a narrow location like ω_1.

A tile is a control-flow graph that can be obtained by substituting for metavariables in the tile's shape: we replace the metavariable $\oplus$ (if any) with an actual RTL operator of an appropriate type, and we replace metavariables r and t by hardware registers or temporaries appropriate to the context in which they appear. For example, given the `binop` shape $t := \oplus(t_1, t_2)$, we get a shift-left tile by using `shl` in place of $\oplus$ and by using temporaries that stand for general-purpose registers. As another example, the `store` tile might require an address or integer register for temporary t_1 but should support any register t as the value to be stored.

5.3 Tiling through a code-generation interface

Each shape in Figure 8 is labeled with a name. The names identify functions in our *code-generation interface*, which encapsulates a machine-dependent implementation of every tile. Our instruction selector works as follows:

- The tiler expects an input control-flow graph in which each node contains a well-typed RTL. Moreover, the RTLs in an input graph may contain only trivially true guards. (The C-- language cannot express nontrivial guards.) Nontrivial Boolean

Standard and weird value operators

$t := \oplus(t_1, t_2)$	`binop`	(a binary ALU operation)
$t := \oplus(t_1)$	`unop`	(a unary ALU operation)
$t := \oplus(t_1, t_2, rm)$	`binrm`	(a binary floating-point operation)
$t := \oplus(t_1, rm)$	`unrm`	(a unary floating-point operation or conversion)
$t := \oplus(t_1, t_2, \omega)$	`wrdop`	(a weird value operation, like add with carry)
$\omega_1 := \oplus(t_1, t_2, \omega_2)$	`wrdrop`	(a weird value/result operation, like carry)
$t_{hi}, t_{lo} := t_1 \otimes t_2$	`dblop`	(an extended multiply operation)

Size-changing operators

$t := \mathtt{sx}(m[t_1])$	`sxload`	(load signed byte/halfword)
$t := \mathtt{zx}(m[t_1])$	`zxload`	(load unsigned byte/halfword)
$m[t_1] := \mathtt{lobits}_n(t)$	`lostore`	(store byte/halfword)

Data movement (most tiles transfer exactly one word)

$m[t_1] := t$	`store`	
$t := m[t_1]$	`load`	
$m[t_1] := m[t_2]$	`block_copy`	(any number of bytes)
$t_1 := t_2$	`move`	
$t := \omega$	`hwget`	
$\omega := t$	`hwset`	
$t := k$ or $t := L$	`li`	(load immediate constant)

Control flow (including comparison operators)

goto L	`b`	(branch)
goto t	`br`	(branch register)
$L_T \lhd t_1 ? t_2 \rhd L_F ; L_F$:	`bc`	(branch conditional)

Figure 8. Shapes of tiles for a register machine

expressions g appear only in conditional branches $L_T \lhd g \rhd L_F$. (If a target machine supports guarded assignments, aka "predicated instructions," the proper RTLs can be found by standard optimizations *after* instruction selection.)

- The tiler covers each input graph with tiles. For each tile, the tiler identifies the shape, then calls the function in the code-generation interface which implements that shape. The tiler passes arguments which correspond to the metavariables shown in Figure 8; metavariables typically identify locations and an operator. The code-generation function returns a machine-dependent control-flow graph that implements the tile. This graph may contain RTLs with nontrivial guards.

  For example, to get a control-flow graph implementing the tile $r_1 := r_2 + t_2$, the tiler would call

  ```
  CG.binop ('r',1) ("add",[32]) ('r',2) ('t',2)
  ```

  The `binop` function would return a small control-flow graph, probably containing one RTL representing an add instruction. (In the example, the `[32]` in `("add", [32])` is the list of widths with which the polymorphic operator `add` is instantiated.)

- The tiler produces an output control-flow graph in which each node contains a well-typed RTL that is representable by a single instruction on the target machine.

The code-generation interface also associates each operator with a machine-dependent *context*, which tells the tiler what registers and temporaries may be operands or results of that operator.

5.4 Implementation of tilesets

The functions in the code-generation interface must be implemented for every target machine. Each function corresponds to a shape and must implement all tiles of that shape. The implementation of a tile may have side effects not called for in the interface, but these effects must be limited to *scratch registers*—which can't be named by any program—and to compiler temporaries. The implementor of the tileset decides which registers are scratch registers.

It is not difficult to implement a tileset by hand, but we have developed an algorithm for automatically generating a tileset from a declarative machine description (Dias and Ramsey 2010). Although the problem is undecidable in principle, our tileset generator produces complete tilesets for the x86, PowerPC, and ARM.

6. Specification of a machine-independent tiler

Our tiler takes as input a control-flow graph G' and returns a new graph G, which has the same observable effect as G', but which is composed entirely of RTLs that represent machine instructions. As shown in the example tiling in Section 5.1, RTLs in G may have side effects on locations not mentioned in G'. We therefore write the tiling transformation using the judgment form

$$G \overset{\mathscr{L}}{\subseteq} G',$$

which states that executing control-flow graph G has the same effect as executing graph G', except that G may also overwrite any location in the set $\mathscr{L}$. As shorthand, we say that G *implements* G'.

Graph G and set $\mathscr{L}$ satisfy important properties: G is made from tiles; $\mathscr{L}$ contains all the locations assigned by G, which we write $defs(G)$; and $defs(G)$ includes $defs(G')$. Any locations in $\mathscr{L}$ that are *not* in $defs(G')$ must be scratch registers or compiler temporaries, which cannot be observed by a program, so that G and G' have the same observable effect. These properties are established by metatheoretic reasoning.

We represent calls to the code-generation interface by a very similar judgment: $G \subseteq^{\mathscr{L}}{}_M G'$ says that graph G implements graph G', and moreover, every RTL in G is implementable by a single instruction on the target machine M. The $\subseteq^{\mathscr{L}}{}_M$ relation is significant for another reason: judgment $G \subseteq^{\mathscr{L}}{}_M G'$ appears only when G' is a tile.

The tiler satisfies two properties:

- *Soundness*: If $G \subseteq^{\mathscr{L}} G'$, then G is equivalent to G', modulo assignments to unobservable locations in $\mathscr{L}$.
- *Machine invariant*: If $G \subseteq^{\mathscr{L}} G'$, then G contains only RTLs implementable on the target machine.

These properties follow by inspection of the rules. Ideally the tiler would satisfy a third property:

- *Completeness*: If G' is composed of well-typed RTLs that use operators only at the word size of the target machine,[2] then there exist a G and an $\mathscr{L}$ such that $G \subseteq^{\mathscr{L}} G'$.

Like most compiler writers, we don't prove that our code generator is complete. Instead, we follow typical best practices: we reason informally about the completeness of the tiler, and we supplement that reasoning with regression tests. One advantage of our approach is that we have to do the reasoning just *once*, and the results apply to any register machine. The current state of the art is that the completeness of an instruction selector must be established once *per target machine*.

[2] The restriction on widths of integer and bitwise operators can be relaxed to permit values smaller than a machine word (Redwine and Ramsey 2004).

PAR

$$\frac{G_1 \overset{\mathscr{L}_1}{\subseteq} l_1 := e_1 \qquad \forall i > 1 : \mathscr{L}_1 \parallel uses(e_i) \qquad G_2 \overset{\mathscr{L}_2}{\subseteq} l_2 := e_2 \mid \cdots \mid l_n := e_n \qquad \mathscr{L}_2 \parallel \{l_1\}}{G_1; G_2 \overset{\mathscr{L}_1 \cup \mathscr{L}_2}{\subseteq} l_1 := e_1 \mid \cdots \mid l_n := e_n}$$

BREAKCYCLE

$$\frac{t\ \texttt{fresh} \qquad G \overset{\mathscr{L}}{\subseteq} t := e_1 \mid l_2 := e_2 \mid \cdots \mid l_n := e_n \,;\, l_1 := t}{G \overset{\mathscr{L}}{\subseteq} l_1 := e_1 \mid \cdots \mid l_n := e_n}$$

SEQ

$$\frac{G_1 \overset{\mathscr{L}_1}{\subseteq} G_1' \qquad G_2 \overset{\mathscr{L}_2}{\subseteq} G_2' \qquad \mathscr{L}_1 \setminus defs(G_1') \parallel uses(G_2') \qquad \mathscr{L}_2 \parallel defs(G_1') \setminus defs(G_2')}{G_1; G_2 \overset{\mathscr{L}_1 \cup \mathscr{L}_2}{\subseteq} G_1'; G_2'}$$

Figure 9. Rules to eliminate parallel assignments and sequences

Techniques for proving completeness would represent a significant advance over the state of practice. An even greater advance would be to formalize the idea of architectural family and to prove completeness for an entire family. Both problems are beyond the scope of this paper.

The rest of this section presents rules for the tiling transformation. Although widths and byte order play a role in the tiling, they complicate the exposition of the algorithm, so we omit them except when they are crucial. This treatment is consistent with the treatment of widths and byte order in the C-- language itself: a C-- compiler infers widths when possible, so they are rarely needed in surface syntax. Widths are also inferred in our machine descriptions (Ramsey and Davidson 1998). Similarly, byte order is fixed for each storage space and so is inferred from the space.

6.1 Reducing graphs to RTLs

A single assignment can be covered by tiles whose shapes are given in Figure 8. But as noted in Section 4, an RTL can contain more than one assignment: to be able to express the semantics of machine instructions, RTLs must be able to express parallel assignments. In C--, we have chosen to make that expressive power available to front ends. Our compiler must therefore handle parallel assignments.

One way to handle a parallel assignment is to present it to the machine-dependent recognizer; if the RTL is accepted, it satisfies the machine invariant and it need not be tiled. If the recognizer does *not* accept a parallel assignment, we use the rules in Figure 9.

Rule PAR takes a parallel assignment, extracts a single assignment $l_1 := e_1$, and executes it before the remaining assignments. This transformation preserves semantics only if an important side condition holds: for all $i > 1$, the value of e_i does not depend on the contents of l_1. The rule uses the slightly stronger condition $\mathscr{L}_1 \parallel uses(e_i)$, where writing $\parallel$ between two sets means they are disjoint. The stronger condition requires in addition that graph G_1, which computes $l_1 := e_1$, does not reuse temporaries that appear free in e_i. There is an additional side condition that graph G_2 does not change the value of l_1.

Because parallel composition of assignments is associative and commutative, rule PAR can be applied to a parallel assignment as long as some location l_i can be changed without affecting the value of any other expression e_j, $j \neq i$. Otherwise, all assignments have cyclic data dependencies, and we apply the BREAKCYCLE rule, which breaks a cycle by introducing a fresh temporary.

Finally, the SEQ rule shows that graphs in a sequence are tiled independently. This rule expresses a standard code-generation technique: additional locations modified by G_1 (beyond what G_1' modifies) may not affect values computed in G_2, and similarly G_2 may not overwrite any observable locations modified by G_1.

6.2 Rules for value operators

To tile a single assignment of a value operator (Figure 10), we use the first group of shapes in Figure 8. The BINOP rule is representative; its task is to tile the assignment $t := \oplus(e_1, e_2)$. The first step is to allocate fresh temporaries to hold the values of e_1 and e_2 and to tile those RTLs recursively, producing graphs G_1 and G_2. The side condition $\mathscr{L}_1 \parallel uses(e_2)$ ensures that graph G_1 does not mutate any location on which the value of e_2 depends. Then, the judgment $G \subseteq^{\mathscr{L}}{}_M\, t := \oplus(t_1, t_2)$ calls the code-generation interface to get a machine-dependent implementation of the binary operator $\oplus$. The result of the tiling is the sequence $G_1; G_2; G$. All of the rules in Figure 10 work along similar lines, but a few are noteworthy.

In rules BINRM through WRDROPZX, we use hat signs to indicate "weird" values, that is, values that aren't the same width as a register. For example, in the BINRM rule, expression $\hat{e}_3$ denotes an IEEE floating-point rounding mode (RM), which is only two bits wide. The hatted temporary $\hat{t}_3$ means something a little different: $\hat{t}_3$ stands for a standard register containing the value of $\hat{e}_3$ in its least significant two bits. In the weird-operator rules, one-bit carries and borrows are treated similarly. (Our tiler does some extra work not shown in the rules: it keeps track of whether the high bits of register $\hat{t}_3$ are zero, are copies of bit 1, or are unknown. Our tiler uses this information to tile sign-extension and zero-extension operations more efficiently.)

The last noteworthy rule in Figure 10 is the DBLOP rule, which handles extended-multiply operators. An extended multiply takes two operands of equal width and produces a result of twice that width. In hardware, that result is expected to be split over two registers, as enforced by the code-generation interface in the judgment $G_3 \subseteq^{\mathscr{L}_3}{}_M\, t_{hi}, t_{lo} := \otimes(t_1, t_2)$. In C--, however, it is not possible to express an assignment of a single result to a register pair, so in a well-typed RTL, the assignment must be to memory. The addresses of the most and least significant words (*hiaddr* and *loaddr*) depend on byte order.

6.3 Rules for tiling size-changing operators

To tile a single assignment of a size-changing operator, we use the second group of shapes in Figure 8. We show rules for integer size-changing operators only; there are similar rules for changing the sizes of floating-point values and for converting between integer and floating point. Our intermediate language uses integer size-changing operators in two contexts: when transferring bytes (or halfwords, etc.) between registers and memory (Figure 11), and when transferring small values between special-purpose hardware registers and ordinary registers (Figure 12). Both groups of rules use the same techniques: when transferring a value from a narrow location to a wide location, the value must be sign-extended or zero-extended; when transferring a value from a wide location to a narrow location, only the least significant n bits are transferred. Both groups of rules allocate fresh temporaries to hold the values of subexpressions, which are tiled recursively.

6.4 Rules for data-movement tiles

To tile a single, data-movement assignment (Figure 13), we use the third group of shapes in Figure 8. Rules STORE and LOAD

BINOP

$$\frac{\begin{array}{c} t_1, t_2 \texttt{ fresh} \\ \oplus : \forall n.n\ bits \times n\ bits \to n\ bits \qquad \mathscr{L}_1 \parallel uses(e_2) \\ G_1 \overset{\mathscr{L}_1}{\subseteq} t_1 := e_1 \qquad G_2 \overset{\mathscr{L}_2}{\subseteq} t_2 := e_2 \qquad G \overset{\mathscr{L}}{\subseteq}_M t := \oplus(t_1, t_2) \end{array}}{G_1; G_2; G \overset{\mathscr{L} \cup \mathscr{L}_1 \cup \mathscr{L}_2}{\subseteq} t := \oplus(e_1, e_2)}$$

UNOP

$$\frac{\begin{array}{c} t' \texttt{ fresh} \\ \oplus : \forall n.n\ bits \to n\ bits \qquad G \overset{\mathscr{L}}{\subseteq} t' := e \qquad G' \overset{\mathscr{L}'}{\subseteq}_M t := \oplus(t') \end{array}}{G; G' \overset{\mathscr{L} \cup \mathscr{L}'}{\subseteq} t := \oplus(e)}$$

BINRM

$$\frac{\begin{array}{c} t_1, t_2, \hat{t}_3 \texttt{ fresh} \\ \oplus : \forall n.n\ bits \times n\ bits \times 2\ bits \to n\ bits \qquad G_1 \overset{\mathscr{L}_1}{\subseteq} t_1 := e_1 \\ G_2 \overset{\mathscr{L}_2}{\subseteq} t_2 := e_2 \qquad G_3 \overset{\mathscr{L}_3}{\subseteq} \hat{t}_3 := \hat{e}_3 \qquad G \overset{\mathscr{L}}{\subseteq}_M t := \oplus(t_1, t_2, \hat{t}_3) \\ \mathscr{L}_1 \parallel uses(e_2) \cup uses(\hat{e}_3) \qquad \mathscr{L}_2 \parallel uses(\hat{e}_3) \end{array}}{G_1; G_2; G_3; G \overset{\mathscr{L} \cup \mathscr{L}_1 \cup \mathscr{L}_2 \cup L_3}{\subseteq} t := \oplus(e_1, e_2, \hat{e}_3)}$$

UNRM

$$\frac{\begin{array}{c} t_1, \hat{t}_2 \texttt{ fresh} \\ \oplus : \forall n.n\ bits \times 2\ bits \to n\ bits \qquad \mathscr{L}_1 \parallel uses(\hat{e}_2) \\ G_1 \overset{\mathscr{L}_1}{\subseteq} t_1 := e_1 \qquad G_2 \overset{\mathscr{L}_2}{\subseteq} \hat{t}_2 := \hat{e}_2 \qquad G \overset{\mathscr{L}}{\subseteq}_M t := \oplus(t_1, \hat{t}_2) \end{array}}{G_1; G_2; G \overset{\mathscr{L} \cup \mathscr{L}_1 \cup \mathscr{L}_2}{\subseteq} t := \oplus(e_1, \hat{e}_2)}$$

WRDOP

$$\frac{\begin{array}{c} t_1, t_2, \hat{t}_3 \texttt{ fresh} \\ \oplus : \forall n.n\ bits \times n\ bits \times 1\ bit \to n\ bits \qquad G_1 \overset{\mathscr{L}_1}{\subseteq} t_1 := e_1 \\ G_2 \overset{\mathscr{L}_2}{\subseteq} t_2 := e_2 \qquad G_3 \overset{\mathscr{L}_3}{\subseteq} \hat{t}_3 := \hat{e}_3 \qquad G \overset{\mathscr{L}}{\subseteq}_M t := \oplus(t_1, t_2, \hat{t}_3) \\ \mathscr{L}_1 \parallel uses(e_2) \cup uses(\hat{e}_3) \qquad \mathscr{L}_2 \parallel uses(\hat{e}_3) \end{array}}{G_1; G_2; G_3; G \overset{\mathscr{L} \cup \mathscr{L}_1 \cup \mathscr{L}_2 \cup L_3}{\subseteq} t := \oplus(e_1, e_2, \hat{e}_3)}$$

WRDROPSX

$$\frac{\begin{array}{c} t_1, t_2, \hat{t}_3 \texttt{ fresh} \qquad \oplus : \forall n.n\ bits \times n\ bits \times 1\ bit \to 1\ bit \\ G_1 \overset{\mathscr{L}_1}{\subseteq} t_1 := e_1 \qquad G_2 \overset{\mathscr{L}_2}{\subseteq} t_2 := e_2 \\ G_3 \overset{\mathscr{L}_3}{\subseteq} \hat{t}_3 := \hat{e}_3 \qquad G \overset{\mathscr{L}}{\subseteq}_M \hat{t} := \texttt{sx}(\oplus(t_1, t_2, \hat{t}_3)) \\ \mathscr{L}_1 \parallel uses(e_2) \cup uses(\hat{e}_3) \qquad \mathscr{L}_2 \parallel uses(\hat{e}_3) \end{array}}{G_1; G_2; G_3; G \overset{\mathscr{L} \cup \mathscr{L}_1 \cup \mathscr{L}_2 \cup \mathscr{L}_3}{\subseteq} \hat{t} := \texttt{sx}(\oplus(e_1, e_2, \hat{e}_3))}$$

WRDROPZX

$$\frac{\begin{array}{c} t_1, t_2, \hat{t}_3 \texttt{ fresh} \qquad \oplus : \forall n.n\ bits \times n\ bits \times 1\ bit \to 1\ bit \\ G_1 \overset{\mathscr{L}_1}{\subseteq} t_1 := e_1 \qquad G_2 \overset{\mathscr{L}_2}{\subseteq} t_2 := e_2 \\ G_3 \overset{\mathscr{L}_3}{\subseteq} \hat{t}_3 := \hat{e}_3 \qquad G \overset{\mathscr{L}}{\subseteq}_M \hat{t} := \texttt{zx}(\oplus(t_1, t_2, \hat{t}_3)) \\ \mathscr{L}_1 \parallel uses(e_2) \cup uses(\hat{e}_3) \qquad \mathscr{L}_2 \parallel uses(\hat{e}_3) \end{array}}{G_1; G_2; G_3; G \overset{\mathscr{L} \cup \mathscr{L}_1 \cup \mathscr{L}_2 \cup \mathscr{L}_3}{\subseteq} \hat{t} := \texttt{zx}(\oplus(e_1, e_2, \hat{e}_3))}$$

DBLOP

$$\frac{\begin{array}{c} t_1, t_2, t_{lo}, t_{hi} \texttt{ fresh} \qquad \otimes : \forall n.n\ bits \times n\ bits \to 2n\ bits \\ G_1 \overset{\mathscr{L}_1}{\subseteq} t_1 := e_1 \qquad G_2 \overset{\mathscr{L}_2}{\subseteq} t_2 := e_2 \qquad G_3 \overset{\mathscr{L}_3}{\subseteq}_M t_{hi}, t_{lo} := \otimes(t_1, t_2) \\ G_4 \overset{\mathscr{L}}{\subseteq} \$m[loaddr(m,e,n)] := t_{lo} \mid \$m[hiaddr(m,e,n)] := t_{hi} \\ \mathscr{L}_1 \parallel uses(e_2) \cup uses(e) \qquad \mathscr{L}_2 \parallel uses(e) \qquad \mathscr{L}_3 \parallel uses(e) \end{array}}{G_1; G_2; G_3; G \overset{\mathscr{L} \cup \mathscr{L}_1 \cup \mathscr{L}_2 \cup L_3}{\subseteq} \$m[e] := \otimes(e_1, e_2)}$$

Figure 10. Tiling rules for standard and weird value operators

SXLOAD

$$\frac{\begin{array}{c} t' \texttt{ fresh} \\ G \overset{\mathscr{L}}{\subseteq} t' := e \qquad G' \overset{\mathscr{L}'}{\subseteq}_M t := \texttt{sx}(\$m[t']) \qquad \mathscr{L} \parallel \{\$m[e]\} \end{array}}{G; G' \overset{\mathscr{L} \cup \mathscr{L}'}{\subseteq} t := \texttt{sx}(\$m[e])}$$

ZXLOAD

$$\frac{\begin{array}{c} t' \texttt{ fresh} \\ G \overset{\mathscr{L}}{\subseteq} t' := e \qquad G' \overset{\mathscr{L}'}{\subseteq}_M t := \texttt{zx}(\$m[t']) \qquad \mathscr{L} \parallel \{\$m[e]\} \end{array}}{G; G' \overset{\mathscr{L} \cup \mathscr{L}'}{\subseteq} t := \texttt{zx}(\$m[e])}$$

LOSTORE

$$\frac{\begin{array}{c} t_1, t_2 \texttt{ fresh} \qquad \mathscr{L}_2 \parallel uses(e_1) \qquad G_1 \overset{\mathscr{L}_1}{\subseteq} t_1 := e_1 \\ G_2 \overset{\mathscr{L}_2}{\subseteq} t_2 := e_2 \qquad G \overset{\mathscr{L}}{\subseteq}_M \$m[t_1] := \texttt{lobits}_\texttt{n}(t_2) \end{array}}{G_2; G_1; G \overset{\mathscr{L}_1 \cup \mathscr{L}_2 \cup \mathscr{L}}{\subseteq} \$m[e_1] := \texttt{lobits}_\texttt{n}(e_2)}$$

Figure 11. Size-changing rules (registers $\leftrightarrow$ memory)

HWGETSX

$$\frac{G \overset{\mathscr{L}}{\subseteq}_M t := \texttt{sx}(r)}{G \overset{\mathscr{L}}{\subseteq} t := \texttt{sx}(r)}$$

HWGETZX

$$\frac{G \overset{\mathscr{L}}{\subseteq}_M t := \texttt{zx}(r)}{G \overset{\mathscr{L}}{\subseteq} t := \texttt{zx}(r)}$$

HWSET

$$\frac{t \texttt{ fresh} \qquad G \overset{\mathscr{L}}{\subseteq} t := e \qquad G' \overset{\mathscr{L}'}{\subseteq}_M r := \texttt{lobits}_\texttt{n}(t)}{G; G' \overset{\mathscr{L} \cup \mathscr{L}'}{\subseteq} r := \texttt{lobits}_\texttt{n}(e)}$$

Figure 12. Size-changing rules (registers $\leftrightarrow$ small registers)

transfer words between registers and memory. Rule BLOCKCOPY copies data from one memory location to another, and it is not limited to a single word: a block copy can move any number of bytes (where a "byte" is the cell size of the memory space). Rule MOVEREG moves a word between registers; rule LI loads a compile-time constant into a register; and rule LI-LABEL loads a link-time constant into a register. Finally, rule MOVEEXP accounts for hardware restrictions on registers and operators. For example, if the result of an integer computation e is placed in a floating-point register t, the tiler introduces a fresh integer temporary t' to hold the result of the integer computation. Use of rule MOVEEXP reduces the burden on the implementor of the tileset: although the implementation must include a tile for every RTL operator (see, for example, rules BINOP and UNOP), it is sufficient that for each RTL operator, there is *some* set of registers in which the tiler can place the operands, and there is some set of registers in which the tiler can expect the result. It is not necessary to implement so many tiles that the result of *any* operator can be placed into *any* register. Our code-generation interface includes a mapping from each RTL operator into a data structure which identifies what kinds of registers or temporaries may be used as arguments and results for that operator.

6.5 Tiling control flow

To tile control flow (Figure 14), we use the final group of shapes in Figure 8. As with sequential control flow in Figure 9, the rules in Figure 14 express standard code-generation techniques. For example, if the target of an unconditional branch is known statically

STORE

$$\frac{t_1, t_2\ \texttt{fresh} \qquad \mathscr{L}_2 \parallel \mathit{uses}(e_1) \qquad G_1 \overset{\mathscr{L}_1}{\subseteq} t_1 := e_1 \qquad G_2 \overset{\mathscr{L}_2}{\subseteq} t_2 := e_2 \qquad G \overset{\mathscr{L}}{\subseteq}_M \$m[t_1] := t_2}{G_2; G_1; G \overset{\mathscr{L}_1 \cup \mathscr{L}_2 \cup \mathscr{L}}{\subseteq} \$m[e_1] := e_2}$$

LOAD

$$\frac{t'\ \texttt{fresh} \qquad G \overset{\mathscr{L}}{\subseteq} t' := e \qquad G' \overset{\mathscr{L}'}{\subseteq}_M t := \$m[t'] \qquad \mathscr{L} \parallel \{\$m[e]\}}{G; G' \overset{\mathscr{L} \cup \mathscr{L}'}{\subseteq} t := \$m[e]}$$

BLOCKCOPY

$$\frac{t_1, t_2\ \texttt{fresh} \qquad \mathscr{L}_1 \parallel \{\$m[e_2]\} \qquad \mathscr{L}_2 \parallel \mathit{uses}(e_1) \cup \{\$m[e_2]\} \qquad G_1 \overset{\mathscr{L}_1}{\subseteq} t_1 := e_1 \qquad G_2 \overset{\mathscr{L}_2}{\subseteq} t_2 := e_2 \qquad G \overset{\mathscr{L}}{\subseteq}_M \$m[t_1] := \$m[t_2]}{G_2; G_1; G \overset{\mathscr{L}_1 \cup \mathscr{L}_2 \cup \mathscr{L}}{\subseteq} \$m[e_1] := \$m[e_2]}$$

MOVEREG

$$\frac{G \overset{\mathscr{L}}{\subseteq}_M t_1 := t_2}{G \overset{\mathscr{L}}{\subseteq} t_1 := t_2}$$

LI

$$\frac{G \overset{\mathscr{L}}{\subseteq}_M t := k}{G \overset{\mathscr{L}}{\subseteq} t := k}$$

LI-LABEL

$$\frac{G \overset{\mathscr{L}}{\subseteq}_M t := L}{G \overset{\mathscr{L}}{\subseteq} t := L}$$

MOVEEXP

$$\frac{t'\ \texttt{fresh} \qquad G \overset{\mathscr{L}}{\subseteq} t' := e \qquad G' \overset{\mathscr{L}'}{\subseteq}_M t := t'}{G; G' \overset{\mathscr{L} \cup \mathscr{L}'}{\subseteq} t := e}$$

Figure 13. Tiling rules for data movement

BRANCHL

$$\frac{G \overset{\mathscr{L}}{\subseteq}_M \textbf{goto}\ L}{G \overset{\mathscr{L}}{\subseteq} \textbf{goto}\ L}$$

BRANCHR

$$\frac{t\ \texttt{fresh} \qquad G \overset{\mathscr{L}}{\subseteq} t := e \qquad G' \overset{\mathscr{L}'}{\subseteq}_M \textbf{goto}\ t}{G; G' \overset{\mathscr{L} \cup \mathscr{L}'}{\subseteq} \textbf{goto}\ e}$$

COMPARE

$$\frac{t_1, t_2\ \texttt{fresh} \qquad ? : \forall n. n\ \mathit{bits} \times n\ \mathit{bits} \rightarrow \texttt{bool} \qquad G_1 \overset{\mathscr{L}_1}{\subseteq} t_1 := e_1 \qquad G_2 \overset{\mathscr{L}_2}{\subseteq} t_2 := e_2 \qquad \mathscr{L}_1 \parallel \mathit{uses}(e_2) \qquad G \overset{\mathscr{L}}{\subseteq}_M L_T \triangleleft t_1 ? t_2 \triangleright L_F}{G_1; G_2; G \overset{\mathscr{L}_1 \cup \mathscr{L}_2 \cup \mathscr{L}}{\subseteq} L_T \triangleleft e_1 ? e_2 \triangleright L_F}$$

Figure 14. Rules for tiling control flow

we use the **goto** L tile; otherwise we use the tiler to put the address into a fresh temporary t, then use the **goto** t tile, which typically corresponds to a "branch register" instruction.

The interesting rule in Figure 14 is the COMPARE rule: it applies only when the condition is a comparison. But in general, a condition can be any Boolean expression. If we look at the last block of Table 6 on page 6, we see that a Boolean expression can be produced not only by comparison operators, but also by Boolean constants or operators. The rules in Figure 15 show how to reduce any conditional branch to a control-flow graph in which every branch is either unconditional or is conditioned on the results of a comparison. These rules formalize standard techniques used when compil-

TRUE

$$\frac{G \overset{\mathscr{L}}{\subseteq}_M \textbf{goto}\ L_T}{G \overset{\mathscr{L}}{\subseteq} L_T \triangleleft \mathbf{T} \triangleright L_F}$$

FALSE

$$\frac{G \overset{\mathscr{L}}{\subseteq}_M \textbf{goto}\ L_F}{G \overset{\mathscr{L}}{\subseteq} L_T \triangleleft \mathbf{F} \triangleright L_F}$$

NOT

$$\frac{G \overset{\mathscr{L}}{\subseteq} L_F \triangleleft e \triangleright L_T}{G \overset{\mathscr{L}}{\subseteq} L_T \triangleleft \texttt{not}(e) \triangleright L_F}$$

CONJOIN

$$\frac{L\ \texttt{fresh} \qquad G \overset{\mathscr{L}}{\subseteq} L \triangleleft e_1 \triangleright L_F \qquad G' \overset{\mathscr{L}'}{\subseteq} L_T \triangleleft e_2 \triangleright L_F \qquad \mathscr{L} \parallel \mathit{uses}(e_2)}{G; L\!: G' \overset{\mathscr{L} \cup \mathscr{L}'}{\subseteq} L_T \triangleleft \texttt{conjoin}(e_1, e_2) \triangleright L_F}$$

DISJOIN

$$\frac{L\ \texttt{fresh} \qquad G \overset{\mathscr{L}}{\subseteq} L_T \triangleleft e_1 \triangleright L \qquad G' \overset{\mathscr{L}'}{\subseteq} L_T \triangleleft e_2 \triangleright L_F \qquad \mathscr{L} \parallel \mathit{uses}(e_2)}{G; L\!: G' \overset{\mathscr{L} \cup \mathscr{L}'}{\subseteq} L_T \triangleleft \texttt{disjoin}(e_1, e_2) \triangleright L_F}$$

Figure 15. Rules to eliminate Boolean operators

ing Boolean expressions in a control-flow context. By considering every RTL operator whose return type is `bool`, we can be confident that these rules are complete.

We have formulated the COMPARE rule in a way which glosses over the fact that a conditional-branch *node* in a control-flow graph must be reduced to a *sequence* of machine instructions. The COMPARE rule shows an *unserialized* control-flow graph, in which the true and false labels L_T and L_F are treated symmetrically. But the `bc` shape in Figure 8 does not treat the labels symmetrically; when the condition is not true, the shape falls through to the successor instruction. The judgment $G \subseteq^{\mathscr{L}}{}_M L_T \triangleleft t_1 ? t_2 \triangleright L_F$ actually provides *two* tiles, one of which is chosen when the flow graph is serialized. The graph may be serialized either as $L_T \triangleleft t_1 ? t_2 \triangleright L'; L'\!: \textbf{goto}\ L_F$, where L' is fresh, or as $L_F \triangleleft \neg(t_1 ? t_2) \triangleright L'; L'\!: \textbf{goto}\ L_T$, where L' is again fresh. Each of these serializations uses a tile of the `bc` shape and a tile of the `b` (unconditional branch) shape. The basic blocks of a control-flow graph are serialized using a reverse postorder depth-first traversal, which in most cases allows the serializer to drop the fresh label L' and the unconditional branch.

6.6 Informal argument about completeness

Our tiler addresses a different problem from the instruction selectors found in most compilers. Most code-generation problems start with a known source language and an intermediate code tailored to that language, and all programs in the source language must be compiled. But C-- is not a source language: it is a low-level target language for compilers. It resembles low-level intermediate codes used in compilers, but it is not tailored to any particular source language; rather, it is tailored to express today's architectural consensus on floating-point computation, integer computation, and bitwise computation—on words of any width. Our code-generation problem starts with an *unknown* source language, which compiles to a *subset* of C--, which we must tile to machine instructions.

We do not expect to compile all well-typed C-- programs. For example, a program that uses 17-bit bytes and 73-bit arithmetic may be well typed, but we cannot compile it. We compile only code that respects the *memory-cell size*, *byte order*, and *word size* of the target machine. For example, code intended to run on the SPARC should use 8-bit cells (bytes) in memory, big-endian loads and stores, and 32-bit RTL operators. Code intended to run on a PDP-10 should use 36-bit cells (words) in memory, 36-bit loads and stores, and 36-bit RTL operators.

With integer and bitwise operations, we are more flexible: a compiler pass called the *widener* converts narrow operations to operations at the word size of the target machine. For example, the widener can translate 32-bit code to 64-bit code while minimizing sign extensions and zero extensions (Redwine and Ramsey 2004).

If a control-flow graph G contains only well-typed RTLs which use the proper memory size, byte order, and word size, and which have trivial guards, our tiler reduces G to tiles, and thence to machine instructions. We argue by structural induction over the graph. Section 6.1 shows how sequences and parallel assignments are reduced to individual graphs and single assignments. Section 6.5 shows how a control-flow graph containing a nontrivial guard is reduced to conditional-branch tiles. The most complex part of the induction is over assignments. Given only value operators and data movement, our rules cover all the type schemes of all the C-- operators. A new RTL operator can easily be added without changing the tiler, provided the operator has the same type as an existing RTL operator. In all cases, the side conditions on $\mathscr{L}$ can be satisfied by choosing a combination of fresh temporaries and scratch registers.

The difficult part of the argument lies with size-changing operators. We believe that our tiler is complete for C-- programs in which values are sign-extended or zero-extended to at most the word size, and low bits are extracted from words, not from larger values. Unfortunately, these restrictions rule out cases of practical interest. For example, on the SPARC, it can be necessary to convert a double-precision floating-point number to a 64-bit integer, then transfer the most and least significant words of that integer to two 32-bit integer registers. This case is supported by the Quick C-- compiler, but we do not have a general algorithm for translating size-changing operators when operands or results are larger than one word, so the tiling rules for this case are omitted from this paper.

7. Discussion

Our main result is a machine-independent tileset and tiling algorithm that can be used with any register machine. The tileset and algorithm are implemented in our Quick C-- compiler, as are a similar tileset and algorithm for stack machines. Experimental results are good, although they reflect the immaturity of Quick C--'s optimizer: our generated code outperforms code generated by `lcc` or by gcc with optimization turned off, but it is not as good as code generated by gcc with optimization turned on. Details of these results have already been published (Dias and Ramsey 2010). Our results, together with Benitez and Davidson's (1994) demonstration that standard scalar and loop optimizations can be implemented in a compiler very similar to Quick C--, indicate that our tiler could be used in a high-quality optimizing compiler.

Our approach to instruction selection is built around two ideas:

- Instead of designing a new tileset for every target machine, design a single, machine-independent tileset that is reused for every machine in a big architectural family.
- Let the design of the tileset follow from a formal model of machine-level computation (RTLs), which expresses the consensus common to the architectural family.

These ideas make it possible to reduce the intellectual work required to add support for new target machines.

The consensus common to the architectural family of register machines includes flat memory addressing, a preferred word size and byte order, and groups of interchangeable registers; these features are expected to be found in all possible targets, and in those aspects our design is a classic *intersection machine*. But our design also supports a rich and extensible set of computational operators, and in that aspect our design is a classic *union machine*.

We establish the correctness and completeness of the tiling algorithm just once per architectural family, instead of once per target machine. While arguing about completeness can be difficult, the work we do per machine—to show that our tileset is implemented correctly and completely—is trivially easy. The reduction in overall work represents a significant advance over prior art. To illustrate the work, we conclude by discussing how you might create an infrastructure, add new languages, add new target machines, and add new optimizations, and how our techniques (together with those of Davidson and Fraser) will help you separate concerns.

To create an infrastructure, you will define representations of RTLs and control-flow graphs, and you will define an interface that allows a front end to create control-flow graphs. You will specify a code-generation interface for our tileset. If you wish to generate code for the x86 legacy floating-point unit or for some other stack machine, you will also specify an interface for a stack-machine tileset, perhaps like the one in Appendix A. You will implement the tiler. And if you choose to generate machine-dependent components from declarative machine descriptions (Ramsey and Davidson 1998), you will implement a recognizer generator and a tileset generator that understand your representation of RTLs (Dias and Ramsey 2006, 2010).

To add a new language, you will build a front end that translates your language to low-level, imperative intermediate code. For example, if your language includes first-class, nested functions, you will write a front end that performs closure conversion, defunctionalization, or some other translation to first-order code. Your primary concern will be the semantics of your language, but you will also need a thorough grasp of machine-level computation, and your front end will need to generate code that matches the word size and byte order of the target machine. You will be insulated from all other details of the target machine's instruction set.

To add a new target machine, you will need to implement a recognizer and our tileset for that machine. You can do this by hand, or you can generate a recognizer and an implementation of the tileset from a declarative machine description. Your primary concern will be to know what target-machine instructions are useful and what their semantics are. You will be insulated from details of optimization and from the front end. If your infrastructure generates the recognizer and the implementation of our tileset, you will also be insulated from the details of your compiler's intermediate representation and from the details of writing the recognizer and implementing the tileset—and you may be able to reuse a machine description written by someone else.

To add an optimization, you will write a code-improving transformation on RTLs. Most likely your primary concern will be to implement a machine-independent code improvement—ideally one that can improve almost any RTL and so will be effective on many target machines. But you may instead be concerned with implementing a machine-independent transformation which is intended to be effective only on particular machines, for example, a vectorizing transformation. Either way, you will be insulated from irrelevant details of the target-machine architecture: the recognizer will ensure that your optimization preserves the machine invariant and is safe to run on any machine.

This plan of building an infrastructure and then adding to it incrementally, which we have done with Quick C--, does not require radical departures from established ways of doing things, and it is not limited to a particular source language, intermediate representation, or target machine. Indeed, our design can be thought of as a modest refactoring of a Davidson/Fraser compiler. And yet, as with many good ideas in software design, modest changes yield significant benefits: our design separates front end from back end and IR from target machine to a degree not achieved in previous compilers. When combined with automatic generation of machine-dependent components, our plan offers a uniquely cost-effective way of building quality compilers.

Acknowledgments

Kevin Redwine carefully scrutinized the tiling rules. Eddie Aftandilian helped improve the presentation. The anonymous referees provided invaluable feedback about the presentation and the work. In particular, referee A's review showed extraordinary depth, insight, and attention to detail.

The work was funded by a grant from Intel Corporation and by NSF awards 0838899 and 0311482.

References

Alfred V. Aho, Mahadevan Ganapathi, and Steven W. K. Tjiang. 1989 (October). Code generation using tree matching and dynamic programming. *ACM Transactions on Programming Languages and Systems*, 11 (4):491–516.

Andrew W. Appel. 1998. *Modern Compiler Implementation*. Cambridge University Press, Cambridge, UK. Available in three editions: C, Java, and ML.

Manuel E. Benitez and Jack W. Davidson. 1988 (July). A portable global optimizer and linker. *Proceedings of the ACM SIGPLAN '88 Conference on Programming Language Design and Implementation*, in *SIGPLAN Notices*, 23(7):329–338.

Manuel E. Benitez and Jack W. Davidson. 1994 (March). The advantages of machine-dependent global optimization. In *Programming Languages and System Architectures*, *LNCS* volume 782, pages 105–124. Springer Verlag.

Roderic G. G. Cattell. 1980 (April). Automatic derivation of code generators from machine descriptions. *ACM Transactions on Programming Languages and Systems*, 2(2):173–190.

Melvin E. Conway. 1958 (October). Proposal for an UNCOL. *Communications of the ACM*, 1(10):5–8.

Jack W. Davidson and Christopher W. Fraser. 1984 (October). Code selection through object code optimization. *ACM Transactions on Programming Languages and Systems*, 6(4):505–526.

João Dias and Norman Ramsey. 2006 (March). Converting intermediate code to assembly code using declarative machine descriptions. In *15th International Conference on Compiler Construction (CC 2006)*, *LNCS* volume 3923, pages 217–231.

João Dias and Norman Ramsey. 2010 (January). Automatically generating back ends using declarative machine descriptions. In *Proceedings of the 37th ACM Symposium on the Principles of Programming Languages*, pages 403–416.

Christopher W. Fraser and David R. Hanson. 1995. *A Retargetable C Compiler: Design and Implementation*. Benjamin/Cummings.

Christopher W. Fraser, David R. Hanson, and Todd A. Proebsting. 1992 (September). Engineering a simple, efficient code-generator generator. *ACM Letters on Programming Languages and Systems*, 1(3):213–226.

Christopher W. Fraser, Robert R. Henry, and Todd A. Proebsting. 1992 (April). BURG—fast optimal instruction selection and tree parsing. *SIGPLAN Notices*, 27(4):68–76.

Jean-Yves Girard. 1986. The System F of variable types, fifteen years later. *Theoretical Computer Science*, 45(2):159–192.

Chris Lattner and Vikram Adve. 2004. LLVM: A compilation framework for lifelong program analysis & transformation. In *CGO '04: Proceedings of the International Symposium on Code Generation and Optimization*, pages 75–86.

Tim Lindholm and Frank Yellin. 1999. *Java Virtual Machine Specification*. Addison-Wesley, second edition.

Robin Milner. 1978 (December). A theory of type polymorphism in programming. *Journal of Computer and System Sciences*, 17:348–375.

Eduardo Pelegrí-Llopart and Susan L. Graham. 1988 (January). Optimal code generation for expression trees: An application of BURS theory. In *Conference Record of the 15th Annual ACM Symposium on Principles of Programming Languages*, pages 294–308.

Simon L. Peyton Jones, Norman Ramsey, and Fermin Reig. 1999 (September). `C--`: A portable assembly language that supports garbage collection. In *International Conference on Principles and Practice of Declarative Programming*, *LNCS* volume 1702, pages 1–28. Springer Verlag.

Todd A. Proebsting. 1992 (June). Simple and efficient BURS table generation. *Proceedings of the ACM SIGPLAN '92 Conference on Programming Language Design and Implementation*, in *SIGPLAN Notices*, 27 (7):331–340.

Norman Ramsey and Cristina Cifuentes. 2003 (March). A transformational approach to binary translation of delayed branches. *ACM Transactions on Programming Languages and Systems*, 25(2):210–224.

Norman Ramsey and Jack W. Davidson. 1998 (June). Machine descriptions to build tools for embedded systems. In *ACM SIGPLAN Workshop on Languages, Compilers, and Tools for Embedded Systems (LCTES'98)*, *LNCS* volume 1474, pages 172–188. Springer Verlag.

Norman Ramsey, Simon Peyton Jones, and Christian Lindig. 2005 (February). The C-- language specification Version 2.0 (CVS revision 1.128). See `http://www.cminusminus.org/code.html#spec`.

Norman Ramsey and Simon L. Peyton Jones. 2000 (May). A single intermediate language that supports multiple implementations of exceptions. *Proceedings of the ACM SIGPLAN '00 Conference on Programming Language Design and Implementation*, in *SIGPLAN Notices*, 35 (5):285–298.

Kevin Redwine and Norman Ramsey. 2004 (April). Widening integer arithmetic. In *13th International Conference on Compiler Construction (CC 2004)*, *LNCS* volume 2985, pages 232–249.

J. Strong, J. H. Wegstein, A. Tritter, J. Olsztyn, Owen R. Mock, and T. Steel. 1958. The problem of programming communication with changing machines: A proposed solution (Part 2). *Communications of the ACM*, 1 (9):9–16.

Henry S. Warren. 2003. *Hacker's Delight*. Addison-Wesley.

A. Shapes of tiles for a stack machine

These shapes are used in our tiler for the x86 legacy floating-point unit. The stack pointer is `st`, and the stack grows downward.

Standard and weird value operators

$f[\mathtt{st}] := \oplus(f[\mathtt{st}])$	`stackop`
$f[\mathtt{st}+1] := \oplus(f[\mathtt{st}], f[\mathtt{st}+1]) \mid \mathtt{st} := \mathtt{st}+1$	`stackop`
$f[\mathtt{st}] := \oplus(f[\mathtt{st}], rm)$	`stackop_rm`
$f[\mathtt{st}+1] := \oplus(f[\mathtt{st}], f[\mathtt{st}+1], rm) \mid \mathtt{st} := \mathtt{st}+1$	`stackop_rm`

Size-changing operators

$m[t_1] := \oplus(f[\mathtt{st}]) \mid \mathtt{st} := \mathtt{st}+1$	`store_pop_cvt`
$f[\mathtt{st}-1] := \oplus(m[t_1]) \mid \mathtt{st} := \mathtt{st}-1$	`push_cvt`
$m[t_1] := \oplus(f[\mathtt{st}], rm) \mid \mathtt{st} := \mathtt{st}+1$	`store_pop_cvt_rm`
$f[\mathtt{st}-1] := \oplus(m[t_1], rm) \mid \mathtt{st} := \mathtt{st}-1$	`push_cvt_rm`

Data movement (most tiles transfer exactly one word)

$m[t_1] := f[\mathtt{st}] \mid \mathtt{st} := \mathtt{st}+1$	`store_pop`
$f[\mathtt{st}-1] := m[t_1] \mid \mathtt{st} := \mathtt{st}-1$	`push`
$f[\mathtt{st}-1] := k \mid \mathtt{st} := \mathtt{st}-1$	`pushk`
$f[\mathtt{st}-1] := \oplus(k) \mid \mathtt{st} := \mathtt{st}-1$	`pushk_cvt`

Control flow (including comparison operators)

$L_T \triangleleft f[\mathtt{st}]?\, f[\mathtt{st}+1] \triangleright L_F; L_F:$	`bc_stack`

Verifying Higher-Order Functional Programs with Pattern-Matching Algebraic Data Types

C.-H. Luke Ong
Oxford University Computing Laboratory
lo@comlab.ox.ac.uk

Steven J. Ramsay
Oxford University Computing Laboratory
ster@comlab.ox.ac.uk

Abstract

Type-based model checking algorithms for higher-order recursion schemes have recently emerged as a promising approach to the verification of functional programs. We introduce *pattern-matching recursion schemes* (PMRS) as an accurate model of computation for functional programs that manipulate algebraic data-types. PMRS are a natural extension of higher-order recursion schemes that incorporate pattern-matching in the defining rules.

This paper is concerned with the following (undecidable) verification problem: given a correctness property φ, a functional program $\mathcal{P}$ (*qua* PMRS) and a regular input set $\mathcal{I}$, does every term that is reachable from $\mathcal{I}$ under rewriting by $\mathcal{P}$ satisfy φ? To solve the PMRS verification problem, we present a sound *semi-algorithm* which is based on model-checking and counterexample guided abstraction refinement. Given a no-instance of the verification problem, the method is guaranteed to terminate.

From an order-n PMRS and an input set generated by a regular tree grammar, our method constructs an order-n *weak* PMRS which over-approximates *only* the first-order pattern-matching behaviour, whilst remaining completely faithful to the higher-order control flow. Using a variation of Kobayashi's type-based approach, we show that the (trivial automaton) model-checking problem for weak PMRS is decidable. When a violation of the property is detected in the abstraction which does not correspond to a violation in the model, the abstraction is automatically refined by 'unfolding' the pattern-matching rules in the program to give successively more and more accurate weak PMRS models.

Categories and Subject Descriptors D.2.4 [*Software Engineering*]: Software/Program Verification; F.3.1 [*Logics and Meanings of Programs*]: Specifying and Verifying and Reasoning about Programs

General Terms Languages, Verification

1. Introduction

In the past decade, huge strides have been made in the development of finite-state and pushdown model checking for software verification. Though highly effective when applied to first-order, imperative programs such as C, these techniques are much less useful for higher-order, functional programs. In contrast, the two standard approaches to the verification of higher-order programs are *type-based program analysis* on the one hand, and *theorem-proving* and *dependent types* on the other. The former is sound, but often imprecise; the latter typically requires human intervention.

Recently, a model-checking approach, based on *higher-order recursion schemes* (HORS), has emerged as a verification methodology that promises to combine accurate analysis and push-button automation. HORS are a form of simply-typed lambda-calculus with recursion and uninterpreted function symbols that is presented as a grammar and used as a generator of (possibly infinite) trees. Ong showed that the trees generated by HORS have a decidable modal mu-calculus theory [14] and Kobayashi introduced a novel approach to the verification of higher-order functional programs by reduction to their model-checking problems [6].

This method has been applied successfully to the Resource Usage Verification Problem [3] (and, through it, to such problems as reachability and control-flow analysis) for a simply typed functional language with finite data-types and dynamic resource creation and resource access primitives. The method relies on the existence of certain transformations which, given a functional program and a resource usage specification, reduce the corresponding verification problem to the question of whether the computation tree of the program, generated by a HORS, satisfies a resource-wise specification encoded by an automaton on infinite trees. Despite the high worst-case time complexity of the modal mu-calculus model-checking problem for recursion schemes, which is n-EXPTIME complete for order-n schemes, an implementation of this approach, TRecS, performs remarkably well on realistic inputs [7].

From a verification perspective, a serious weakness of the HORS approach is its inability to naturally model functional programs with infinite data structures, such as integers and algebraic data-types. This severely limits the potential impact of this programme as functions defined by cases on algebraic data types are ubiquitous in functional programming.

A model of functional programs. Our first contribution is the introduction of *pattern-matching recursion schemes*, which are HORS extended with a notion of pattern matching. A PMRS is a kind of restricted term-rewriting system. We believe that PMRS have a very natural syntax into which large classes of functional programs can readily be translated. A typical rule, which is required to be well typed, has the shape:

$$F\, x_1 \cdots x_m\, p(y_1, \cdots, y_k) \longrightarrow t$$

where the variables $x_1, \cdots, x_m$ are (possibly higher-order) formal parameters of the non-terminal (or *defined operator*) F. The expression $p(y_1, \cdots, y_k)$, which takes the place of the final parameter, is a *pattern* constructed from terminal (or *constructor*) symbols and variables $y_1, \cdots, y_k$.

POPL'11, January 26–28, 2011, Austin, Texas, USA.

Example 1. The following PMRS defines a function $Merge : \mathbf{ablist} \to \mathbf{ablist} \to \mathbf{ablist}$ that merges two lists of $\mathtt{a}$ and $\mathtt{b}$ by recursively destructing them.

$$\begin{array}{lcl} Merge\ x\ \mathtt{nil} & \longrightarrow & x \\ Merge\ x\ (\mathtt{cons\ a}\ y) & \longrightarrow & \mathtt{cons\ a}\ (Merge\ y\ x) \\ Merge\ x\ (\mathtt{cons\ b}\ y) & \longrightarrow & \mathtt{cons\ b}\ (Merge\ y\ x) \end{array}$$

The patterns in the second argument position are used both to decompose compound data structures (so as to select the required components), and to determine control flow. Selected components are communicated to the right-hand side of the chosen rule by means of binding to the variables in the pattern.

Remark 1. Our work is not the first to propose a pattern-matching extension to HORS. A recent paper by Kobayashi, Tabuchi and Unno [9] introduces an extension of HORS called *higher-order multi-parameter tree transducers* (HMTT). HMTT model functions that may employ pattern matching but, in return, must satisfy a rigid type constraint. An HMTT function takes tree arguments of input sort $\mathtt{i}$ (which are trees that can only be destructed) and returns a tree of sort $\mathtt{o}$ (which are trees that can only be constructed). Pattern matching is only allowed on trees of sort $\mathtt{i}$. Consequently HMTT functions are not compositional in the natural way. We believe our PMRS model to be both simpler and more natural.

A verification problem. This paper is concerned with the following verification problem. Given a correctness property φ, a functional program $\mathcal{P}$ (*qua* deterministic PMRS) and a regular set $\mathcal{I}$ of input (constructor) terms, does every term that is reachable from $\mathcal{I}$ under rewriting by $\mathcal{P}$ satisfy φ? It is straightforward to see that the problem is undecidable.

Example 2. Consider the PMRS $\mathcal{P}$ which, when started from $Main$ takes as input a list of natural numbers and returns the same list with all occurrences of the number zero removed. The defining rules of $\mathcal{P}$ are given by:

$$Main\ m \longrightarrow Filter\ Nz\ m$$

$$\begin{array}{lcl} If\ a\ b\ \mathtt{true} & \longrightarrow & a \\ If\ a\ b\ \mathtt{false} & \longrightarrow & b \end{array}$$

$$\begin{array}{lcl} Nz\ \mathtt{z} & \longrightarrow & \mathtt{false} \\ Nz\ (\mathtt{s}\ n) & \longrightarrow & \mathtt{true} \end{array}$$

$$\begin{array}{l} Filter\ p\ \mathtt{nil} \longrightarrow \mathtt{nil} \\ Filter\ p\ (\mathtt{cons}\ x\ xs) \longrightarrow \\ \qquad If\ (\mathtt{cons}\ x\ (Filter\ p\ xs))\ (Filter\ p\ xs)\ (p\ x) \end{array}$$

The input set $\mathcal{I}$ is given by a regular tree grammar $\mathcal{G}$ (equivalently order-0 recursion scheme). The defining rules of $\mathcal{G}$ are:

$$S \longrightarrow ListN$$

$$\begin{array}{l} N \longrightarrow \mathtt{z} \\ N \longrightarrow \mathtt{s}\ N \end{array}$$

$$\begin{array}{l} ListN \longrightarrow \mathtt{nil} \\ ListN \longrightarrow \mathtt{cons}\ N\ ListN \end{array}$$

As usual, the start symbol of $\mathcal{G}$ is taken to be S. The correctness property φ is: "any outcome of the program is a list containing no zeros". This is easily expressible as a trivial automaton $\mathcal{A}$, whose definition is omitted.

An algorithmic solution. Our second contribution is a sound but incomplete semi-algorithm for solving the problem, which is based on a counterexample-guided abstraction refinement loop [2, 11]. The input to the algorithm consists of a PMRS $\mathcal{P}$ representing the program, a regular tree grammar $\mathcal{G}$ (equivalently an order-0 recursion scheme) representing the set $\mathcal{I}$ of possible inputs to the program and a trivial tree automaton $\mathcal{A}$ (which is to say, an automaton on infinite trees with a trivial acceptance condition) representing a specification φ of good behaviour. The algorithm proceeds according to the diagram in Figure 1.

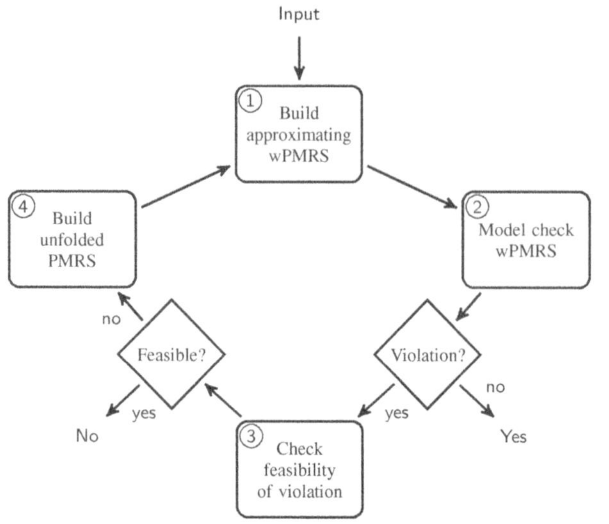

Figure 1. Counterexample-guided abstraction-refinement loop.

In step (1) we compute a sound abstraction of the behaviour of $\mathcal{P}$ when started from terms in $\mathcal{I}$. From an order-n PMRS $\mathcal{P}$ and an order-0 recursion scheme $\mathcal{G}$, we build an order-n *weak pattern-matching recursion scheme* (wPMRS) which over-approximates the set of terms that are reachable from $\mathcal{I}$ under rewriting by $\mathcal{P}$. A wPMRS is similar to a PMRS, except that its pattern matching mechanism is only able to determine control flow; it is unable to decompose data structure.

Our method is a kind of flow analysis. The first – and key – stage of the algorithm is a *binding analysis* which is inspired by Jones and Andersen [5]. It performs a fixpoint construction of a *finite* set Ξ of variable-term bindings such that, for every variable x (formal parameter of rewrite rule), every term that is ever bound to x during the computation is derivable from Ξ. In the second stage, we use the fixpoint set Ξ to build rules of the over-approximating wPMRS. These rules model the bindings of all non-pattern-matching (including all higher-order) variables *precisely*; they only approximate the binding behaviours of the pattern-matching variables. This is in contrast to Jones and Andersen's algorithm, which builds a regular tree grammar that over-approximates the binding set of *every* variable. For an order-n PMRS, our algorithm produces an order-n wPMRS $\widetilde{\mathcal{P}_{\mathcal{G}}}$ as an abstraction, which is a tighter approximation of the order-n PMRS being analysed than regular tree grammars (which are equivalent to order-0 wPMRS). To our knowledge, our algorithm gives the most accurate reachability / flow analysis of its kind.

The weakened pattern-matching mechanism of wPMRS makes it possible to decide a model checking problem for it, which is the content of step (2). Given a wPMRS $\mathcal{W}$, a closed term t and a Büchi automaton with a trivial acceptance condition $\mathcal{A}$, we decide if every (possibly infinite) tree generated by $\mathcal{W}$ on input t is accepted by $\mathcal{A}$. The proof uses a variation of Kobayashi's type-based approach.

If the model-checker fails to find any violation of the property then, since the approximating wPMRS $\widetilde{\mathcal{P}_{\mathcal{G}}}$ defines a superset of the terms reachable under $\mathcal{P}$ from $\mathcal{I}$, the loop in Figure 1 will terminate because $\mathcal{P}$ satisfies $\mathcal{A}$ on $\mathcal{I}$. However, if the model-checker reports a counterexample, then it may be that $\mathcal{P}$ also violates the property (for some term in $\mathcal{I}$), but it may also be that the counterexample is an artifact of an inaccuracy in the abstraction. To determine which of these possibilities is the case, in step (3) we analyse the non-determinism introduced in the abstraction to see whether, in this particular counterexample, it behaves well or behaves badly.

In step (4) the abstraction process is refined. Due to the fact that the abstractions only ever approximate the (first-order) pattern matching variables, whilst remaining faithful to all the others, there is a simple notion of automatic abstraction-refinement, whereby patterns are "unfolded" to a certain depth in the PMRS $\mathcal{P}$, forming a new PMRS $\mathcal{P}'$. In the abstraction $\widetilde{\mathcal{P}'_{\mathcal{G}}}$ of $\mathcal{P}'$, the rules that define the approximation will be more accurate and, in particular, the spurious counterexample will no longer be present. Since any rule in a wPMRS abstraction $\widetilde{\mathcal{P}'_{\mathcal{G}}}$ is *perfectly* accurate whenever the pattern parameter contains no free variables, this method of unfolding gives rise to a semi-completeness property. Given any no-instance of the PMRS verification problem, the loop in Figure 1 will eventually terminate with the answer "No".

Returning to Example 2, whilst performing step (1) we obtain an over-approximation of the binding behaviour of the variables in the program Ξ. This fixpoint set contains, amongst others, the bindings: $x \mapsto N$ and $xs \mapsto ListN$. From this set, we construct an approximating wPMRS $\widetilde{\mathcal{P}_{\mathcal{G}}}$, whose rule-set contains the following:

$$\begin{array}{l} \mathit{Filter}\ p\ \mathtt{nil} \longrightarrow \mathit{Nil} \\ \mathit{Filter}\ p\ (\mathtt{cons}\ x\ xs) \longrightarrow \\ \qquad \mathit{If}\ (\mathit{Cons}\ X\ (\mathit{Filter}\ p\ XS))\ (\mathit{Filter}\ p\ XS)\ (p\ X) \end{array}$$

$$\begin{array}{l} X \longrightarrow N \\ XS \longrightarrow \mathit{ListN} \end{array}$$

together with, amongst others, all the $\mathcal{P}$ and $\mathcal{G}$ rules in Example 2 except those for *Filter*. Unfortunately the wPMRS is too coarse to be useful: there are trees (representing lists) that are obtained by rewriting from '*Main S*' that are not accepted by the trivial automaton $\mathcal{A}$. However, these are spurious counterexamples. For an illustration, consider the error trace in the wPMRS:

$$\begin{array}{l} \mathit{Main}\ S \\ \rightarrow^* \mathit{Main}\ (\mathtt{cons}\ (\mathtt{s}\ \mathtt{z})\ \mathtt{nil}) \\ \rightarrow^* \mathit{Filter}\ \mathit{Nz}\ (\mathtt{cons}\ (\mathtt{s}\ \mathtt{z})\ \mathtt{nil}) \\ \rightarrow \mathit{If}\ (\mathit{Cons}\ X\ (\mathit{Filter}\ \mathit{Nz}\ XS))\ (\mathit{Filter}\ \mathit{Nz}\ XS)\ (\mathit{Nz}\ X) \\ \rightarrow^* \mathit{If}\ (\mathtt{cons}\ \mathtt{z}\ (\mathit{Filter}\ \mathit{Nz}\ \mathtt{nil}))\ (\mathit{Filter}\ \mathit{Nz}\ XS)\ (\mathit{Nz}\ (\mathtt{s}\ \mathtt{z})) \\ \rightarrow^* \mathtt{cons}\ \mathtt{z}\ (\mathit{Filter}\ \mathit{Nz}\ \mathtt{nil}) \\ \rightarrow^* \mathtt{cons}\ \mathtt{z}\ \mathtt{nil} \end{array}$$

The problem can be traced to the second clause of *Filter* in the wPMRS: when replacing the *variable* x by the *non-terminal* X, the connection between the two occurrences of x in the RHS is lost, as the reduction of one occurrence of X is independent of that of the other.

The refinement algorithm produces a new, unfolded PMRS $\mathcal{P}'$ that replaces the two defining rules of *Filter* by five new rules. The two rules that cover the case when the list is a singleton are shown below:

$$\begin{array}{l} \mathit{Filter}\ p\ (\mathtt{cons}\ \mathtt{z}\ \mathtt{nil}) \longrightarrow \\ \qquad \mathit{If}\ (\mathtt{cons}\ \mathtt{z}\ (\mathit{Filter}\ p\ \mathtt{nil}))\ (\mathit{Filter}\ p\ \mathtt{nil})\ (p\ \mathtt{z}) \\ \mathit{Filter}\ p\ (\mathtt{cons}\ (\mathtt{s}\ v_2)\ \mathtt{nil}) \longrightarrow \\ \qquad \mathit{If}\ (\mathtt{cons}\ (\mathtt{s}\ v_2)\ (\mathit{Filter}\ p\ \mathtt{nil}))\ (\mathit{Filter}\ p\ \mathtt{nil})\ (p\ (\mathtt{s}\ v_2)) \end{array}$$

Applying the approximation algorithm to PMRS $\mathcal{P}'$ (and input grammar $\mathcal{G}$), we obtain a wPMRS $\widetilde{\mathcal{P}'_{\mathcal{G}}}$ that does accurately capture the set of reachable terms.

$$\frac{}{\Gamma, x : \sigma \vdash x : \sigma}\ (\textsc{Var}) \qquad \frac{\xi : \sigma \in \Sigma \cup \mathcal{N}}{\Gamma \vdash \xi : \sigma}\ (\textsc{Const})$$

$$\frac{\Gamma \vdash t_0 : \sigma \to \tau \qquad \Gamma \vdash t_1 : \sigma}{\Gamma \vdash t_0\, t_1 : \tau}\ (\textsc{App})$$

Figure 2. A simple type system for applicative terms.

Outline. The rest of the paper is organised as follows. Section 2 introduces PMRS, wPMRS and other technical preliminaries. In Section 3, the abstraction algorithm, which takes a program (PMRS) and an input set (order-0 recursion scheme) and returns a wPMRS, is presented; termination and soundness of the approximation are proved. Section 4 presents a type-inference algorithm for deciding if every tree generated by a given wPMRS is accepted by a trivial automaton. The abstraction refinement algorithm is the topic of Section 5. Finally Section 6 presents related work. Note: a long version of the paper is available [15], which contains the proofs and additional material.

2. Preliminaries

We introduce PMRS, a model for functional programs manipulating algebraic data types; wPMRS, a restriction of PMRS with good algorithmic properties and the PMRS Verification Problem, whose solution is the subject of the remainder of this work.

2.1 Types, terms and substitutions

Fix a finite set $(b, o \in)$ $\mathbb{B}$ of *base types*. The *simple types* $(\sigma, \tau \in)$ $\mathbb{S}$ are those expressions that can be constructed from the base types using the arrow:

$$\sigma, \tau \quad ::= \quad b \mid \sigma \to \tau.$$

We adopt the usual convention that arrows associate to the right and omit parenthesis accordingly. The *order* of a type τ, denoted $\mathbf{ord}(\tau)$, is a measure of the nestedness of the arrow constructor on the left; it is defined by $\mathbf{ord}(b) = 0$ and $\mathbf{ord}(\sigma \to \tau) = \max\{\mathbf{ord}(\sigma) + 1, \mathbf{ord}(\tau)\}$.

Applicative terms. Fix a finite, simply-typed alphabet $(f, g, a \in)$ Σ of first-order *terminal symbols* (or *constructors*), a finite, simply-typed alphabet $(F, G, H \in)$ $\mathcal{N}$ of (arbitrary-order) *non-terminal symbols* (or *defined operators*) and a denumerable set $(x, y, z \in)$ $\mathcal{V}$ of *variables*.

- The *constructor terms* $T(\Sigma)$ are those expressions that can be built from terminals using application.
- The *closed terms* $T(\Sigma, \mathcal{N})$ are those expressions that can be built from terminals and non-terminals using application.
- The *patterns* are those expressions p, q of base type that can be built from variables of base type and terminals.
- The *applicative terms* $T(\Sigma, \mathcal{N}, \mathcal{V})$ are those expressions that can be built from terminals, non-terminals and variables using application.

We denote the free variables of a term t by $\mathsf{FV}(t)$.

Standardly, applicative terms may be assigned simple types via a formal system of typing judgements, $\Gamma \vdash s : \tau$ (where Γ is a finite set of *type bindings*) defined by the rules in Figure 2. When an applicative term t can be assigned a simple type $\tau_1 \to \cdots \to \tau_m \to b$ we say that it has *arity* m and write $\mathsf{ar}(t) = m$. Henceforth, by *term* we shall mean well-typed, applicative term.

Labelled trees. Given a ranked alphabet Ω, an *Ω-labelled tree* t is a map from $\{1, \cdots, m\}^*$ to Ω, where m is the largest arity of symbols in Ω, such that $\mathbf{dom}(t)$ is prefix-closed, and if $t(x) = f$ then $\{ i \mid x\,i \in \mathbf{dom}(t) \} = \{ 1, \cdots, \mathsf{ar}(f) \}$. Standardly we identify $T(\Sigma)$ with finite Σ-labelled trees, and write $T^\infty(\Sigma)$ for the collection of (possibly infinite) Σ-labelled trees.

Let $\Sigma^\perp$ be $\Sigma \cup \{ \perp \}$ with $\mathsf{ar}(\perp) = 0$. Given a closed term t, we write $t^\perp$ for the finite, $\Sigma^\perp$-labelled tree defined by recursion as follows: for $m \geq 0$

$$(\xi\ s_1\ \cdots\ s_m)^\perp := \begin{cases} \perp & \text{if } \xi = F \in \mathcal{N} \\ f\, s_1^\perp \cdots s_m^\perp & \text{otherwise } \xi = f \in \Sigma \end{cases}$$

E.g. $(f(g(G\,a))b)^\perp = f(g\perp)b$. $\Sigma^\perp$-labelled trees can be endowed with a natural complete partial order $\sqsubseteq$ in which, for all trees t, $\perp \sqsubseteq t$ and $f\ s_1\ \cdots\ s_m \sqsubseteq f\ t_1\ \cdots\ t_m$ iff for all i, $s_i \sqsubseteq t_i$.

Substitutions. A *substitution* is just a partial function θ in $\mathcal{V} \to T(\Sigma, \mathcal{N}, \mathcal{V})$. By convention, we do not distinguish between a substitution and its homomorphic extension to the free algebra $T(\Sigma, \mathcal{N}, \mathcal{V})$ and we will write the application of both using prefix juxtaposition. A term t is said to *match* a term u precisely when there exists a substitution θ such that $t = \theta u$. We shall say that a substitution θ is *closed* whenever every term in its image is closed.

2.2 Pattern-matching recursion scheme (PMRS)

A *pattern-matching recursion scheme* (PMRS) is a quadruple $\mathcal{P} = \langle \Sigma, \mathcal{N}, \mathcal{R}, \mathit{Main} \rangle$ with Σ and $\mathcal{N}$ as above. $\mathcal{R}$ is a finite set of rewrite rules, each of which is one of the following shapes ($m \geq 0$):

$$\begin{array}{ll} (\textit{pure}) & F\ x_1\ \cdots\ x_m \longrightarrow t \\ (\textit{pattern-matching}) & F\ x_1\ \cdots\ x_m\ p \longrightarrow t \end{array}$$

where p is a pattern (which may be trivial). $\mathit{Main} : b \to o$ is a distinguished non-terminal symbol whose defining rules are always pattern-matching rules. In this paper we will assume that the variables appearing as formal parameters to defining rules in a PMRS will always be distinct.

A pure rule $F\ x_1\ \cdots\ x_m \longrightarrow t$ is well-typed when $F : \tau_1 \to \cdots \to \tau_m \to o \in \mathcal{N}$ and the judgement:

$$x_1 : \tau_1, \ldots, x_m : \tau_m \vdash t : o$$

is provable. A pattern-matching rule $F\ x_1\ \cdots\ x_m\ p \longrightarrow t$ is well-typed when $F : \tau_1 \to \cdots \to \tau_m \to b \to o \in \mathcal{N}$ and there exist base-types $b_1, \ldots, b_k$ such that the judgements:

$$y_1 : b_1, \ldots, y_k : b_k \vdash p : b \qquad \text{and}$$
$$x_1 : \tau_1, \ldots, x_m : \tau_m, y_1 : b_1, \ldots, y_k : b_k \vdash t : o$$

are provable. We say that a PMRS is *well-typed* just when each of its rules is well-typed. We will only consider well-typed PMRS in the following.

We define the *order* of a PMRS to be the maximum order of (the type of) any of the non-terminal symbols in $\mathcal{N}$. Since a pure rule can be simulated by a pattern-matching rule with a trivial pattern (e.g. a nullary terminal of a distinguished base type), we shall sometimes find it convenient to treat all PMRS rules as pattern-matching rules.

Reduction. We associate with each PMRS a notion of reduction as follows. A *redex* is a term of the form $F\ \theta x_1\ \cdots\ \theta x_m\ \theta p$ whenever θ is a closed substitution and $F\ x_1\ \cdots\ x_m\ p \longrightarrow t$ is a rule in $\mathcal{P}$. The *contractum* of the redex is $\theta\, t$. We define the one-step reduction relation, $\Rightarrow\ \subseteq T(\Sigma, \mathcal{N}) \times T(\Sigma, \mathcal{N})$, by $C[s] \Rightarrow C[t]$ whenever s is a redex, t is its contractum and C is a one-hole context.

We say that a PMRS is *deterministic* just if, given some redex $F\ s_1\ \cdots\ s_n$ there is exactly one rule $l \longrightarrow r \in \mathcal{R}$ such that $F\ s_1\ \cdots\ s_n = \theta l$ for some θ.

Given a PMRS $\mathcal{P} = \langle \Sigma, \mathcal{N}, \mathcal{R}, \mathit{Main} \rangle$, let $s \in T(\Sigma, \mathcal{N})$ be a closed term of base type. We write $\mathcal{L}(\mathcal{P}, s)$ to mean the language of $\Sigma^\perp$-labelled trees obtained by infinitary rewriting of the term s. More precisely, define $\mathcal{L}(\mathcal{P}, s)$ as the collection of $\Sigma^\perp$-labelled trees t such that there are $\langle t_i \rangle_{i \in \omega}$ with $s \Rightarrow t_1 \Rightarrow t_2 \Rightarrow t_3 \cdots$ a *fair* reduction sequence (in the sense that for each i, every outermost redex in t_i is eventually contracted) and $t = \bigsqcup \{ t_i^\perp \mid i \in \omega \}$. In case $\mathcal{P}$ is a deterministic PMRS, $\mathcal{L}(\mathcal{P}, s)$ is a singleton set; we write the unique $\Sigma^\perp$-labelled tree as $[\![s]\!]_\mathcal{P}$.

Example 3. Let $\Sigma = \{\mathtt{zero} : \mathbf{nat}, \mathtt{succ} : \mathbf{nat} \to \mathbf{nat}, \mathtt{nil} : \mathbf{natlist}, \mathtt{cons} : \mathbf{nat} \to \mathbf{natlist} \to \mathbf{natlist}\}$ and $\mathcal{N} = \{\mathit{Rev} : \mathbf{natlist} \to \mathbf{natlist}, \mathit{RevA} : \mathbf{natlist} \to \mathbf{natlist} \to \mathbf{natlist}\}$. The following deterministic, order-1 PMRS contains rewrite rules that implement list reversal with an accumulating parameter:

$$\mathit{Main}\ zs \longrightarrow \mathit{RevA}\ \mathtt{nil}\ zs$$

$$\begin{array}{lll} \mathit{RevA}\ xs\ \mathtt{nil} & \longrightarrow & xs \\ \mathit{RevA}\ xs\ (\mathtt{cons}\ y\ ys) & \longrightarrow & \mathit{RevA}\ (\mathtt{cons}\ y\ xs)\ ys \end{array}$$

When started from the term $t = \mathtt{cons\ z\ nil}$, the only possible reduction sequence is:

$$\mathit{Main}\ t \Rightarrow \mathit{RevA}\ \mathtt{nil}\ t \Rightarrow \mathit{RevA}\ t\ \mathtt{nil} \Rightarrow t$$

and hence $[\![\mathit{Main}\ t]\!]_\mathcal{P} = t$, as expected.

2.3 Weak pattern matching recursion schemes (wPMRS)

A *weak pattern-matching recursion scheme* (wPMRS) is a quadruple $\mathcal{W} = \langle \Sigma, \mathcal{N}, \mathcal{R}, \mathit{Main} \rangle$ with $\Sigma, \mathcal{N}$ and Main as for PMRS. The (finite) set $\mathcal{R}$ consists of rewrite rules of the shape ($m \geq 0$):

$$\begin{array}{ll} (\textit{pure}) & F\ x_1\ \cdots\ x_m \longrightarrow t \\ (\textit{weak-matching}) & F\ x_1\ \cdots\ x_m\ p \longrightarrow t \end{array}$$

in which $\mathsf{FV}(p) \cap \mathsf{FV}(t) = \emptyset$. A pure rule is well typed according to the same criteria as for pure PMRS rules. A weak-matching rule $F\ x_1\ \cdots\ x_m\ p \longrightarrow t$ is well-typed just when $F : \tau_1 \to \cdots \to \tau_m \to b \to o \in \mathcal{N}$ and there exist base-types $b_1, \ldots, b_k$ such that the judgements:

$$y_1 : b_1, \ldots, y_k : b_k \vdash p : b$$
$$\text{and} \quad x_1 : \tau_1, \ldots, x_m : \tau_m \vdash t : o$$

are provable (note that none of the pattern-matching variables y_j occurs in t). Henceforth we will only consider wPMRS with well-typed rules.

wPMRS have exactly the same notion of reduction as PMRS: a *redex* is a term of the form $F\ \theta x_1\ \cdots\ \theta x_m\ \theta p$ whenever θ is a substitution and $F\ x_1\ \cdots\ x_m\ p \longrightarrow t$ is a rule in $\mathcal{P}$. The *contractum* of the redex is $\theta\, t = t[\theta\, x_1/x_1] \cdots [\theta\, x_m/x_m]$ (as the pattern-matching variables do not occur in t). The one-step reduction relation, $\to$, is defined as for PMRS.

We define the order, determinism and language of a wPMRS analogously with PMRS.

2.4 A verification problem

We are interested in solving the following verification problem. Given a program in the form of a PMRS $\mathcal{P}$, a regular set $\mathcal{I}$ of "input" terms, and a correctness property φ, does the output $[\![\mathit{Main}\ t]\!]$ of the program '$\mathit{Main}\ t$' satisfy φ, for every input $t \in \mathcal{I}$? To propose a solution, we require two further stipulations, both of which concern the representation of the entities involved.

Higher-order recursion schemes. A *higher-order recursion scheme* (HORS) is a quadruple $\mathcal{G} = \langle \Sigma, \mathcal{N}, \mathcal{R}, S \rangle$ with Σ and $\mathcal{N}$ as before and $\mathcal{R}$ is a finite set of well-typed, pure wPMRS rewrite rules. The component S is a distinguished non-terminal called the "start symbol". The reduction relation for HORS, $\to$, is just that of wPMRS, noting that all redexes will necessarily be of the form $F\ \theta x_1\ \cdots\ \theta x_m$ since there are no pattern-matching arguments. We can associate with a recursion scheme $\mathcal{G}$ its language $\mathcal{L}(\mathcal{G})$ of terms in $T(\Sigma)$ that can be derived from the start symbol S by rewriting away all occurrences of non-terminals. More precisely, we make the following definition:

$$\mathcal{L}(\mathcal{G}) := \{\, t \mid S \to^* t,\ t \in T(\Sigma)\,\}$$

We define the *order* of a recursion scheme analogously with PMRS and wPMRS. Note that (as generators of finite ranked trees) order-0 recursion schemes are equivalent to regular tree grammars.

Trivial automata. Let Σ be as before. A *Büchi tree automaton with a trivial acceptance condition* (or simply, *trivial automaton*) is a quadruple $\mathcal{A} = \langle \Sigma, Q, \Delta, q_0\rangle$ where Σ is as before, Q is a finite set of states, $q_0 \in Q$ is the initial state, and Δ, the transition relation, is a subset of $Q \times \Sigma \times Q^*$ such that if $(q, f, q_1 \cdots q_n) \in \Delta$ then $n = \mathsf{ar}(f)$. A Σ-labelled tree t is *accepted* by $\mathcal{A}$ if there is a Q-labelled tree r such that

(i) $\mathbf{dom}(t) = \mathbf{dom}(r)$,

(ii) for every $x \in \mathbf{dom}(r)$, $(r(x), t(x), r(x\,1) \cdots r(x\,m)) \in \Delta$ where $m = \mathsf{ar}(t(x))$.

The tree r is called a *run-tree* of $\mathcal{A}$ over t. We write $\mathcal{L}(\mathcal{A})$ for the set of Σ-labelled trees accepted by $\mathcal{A}$.

The PMRS Verification Problem. Given a deterministic PMRS $\mathcal{P} = \langle \Sigma, \mathcal{N}_\mathcal{P}, \mathcal{R}_\mathcal{P}, \mathit{Main}\rangle$, a (non-deterministic) order-0 recursion scheme $\mathcal{G} = \langle \Sigma, \mathcal{N}_\mathcal{G}, \mathcal{R}_\mathcal{G}, S\rangle$, and a Büchi tree automaton with a trivial acceptance condition $\mathcal{A} = \langle \Sigma, Q, \Delta, q_0\rangle$, we write:

$$\vDash (\mathcal{P}, \mathcal{G}, \mathcal{A}) \quad \text{iff} \quad \forall t \in \mathcal{L}(\mathcal{G}) \cdot [\![\mathit{Main}\ t]\!]_\mathcal{P} \in \mathcal{L}(\mathcal{A})$$

The *PMRS Verification Problem* is to decide the truth of $\vDash(\mathcal{P}, \mathcal{G}, \mathcal{A})$.

3. Constructing an abstraction

In this section we will present an algorithm which, given an order-n deterministic PMRS $\mathcal{P}$ and an order-0 recursion scheme $\mathcal{G}$, constructs an order-n wPMRS $\widetilde{\mathcal{P}_\mathcal{G}}$ whose language of Σ-labelled trees is an over-approximation of the set of Σ-labelled trees reachable from $\mathcal{L}(\mathcal{G})$ under rewriting by $\mathcal{P}$.

At the heart of the algorithm is an analysis of the composite PMRS $\mathcal{P}_\mathcal{G} := \langle \Sigma, \mathcal{N}_\mathcal{G} \cup \mathcal{N}_\mathcal{P}, \mathcal{R}_\mathcal{G} \cup \mathcal{R}_\mathcal{P}, \mathit{Main}\rangle$. Since every term s reachable from $\mathcal{L}(\mathcal{G})$ under rewriting by $\mathcal{P}$ (i.e. $\mathit{Main}\ t \Rightarrow^*_\mathcal{P} s$, for some $t \in \mathcal{L}(\mathcal{G})$) is certainly reachable from S under rewriting by $\mathcal{P}_\mathcal{G}$ (i.e. $\mathit{Main}\ S \Rightarrow^*_{\mathcal{P}_\mathcal{G}} \mathit{Main}\ t \Rightarrow^*_{\mathcal{P}_\mathcal{G}} s$), it suffices to look only at the behaviours of $\mathcal{P}_\mathcal{G}$ in order to construct a safe abstraction of those of $\mathcal{P}$. We detail the nature of this analysis and its properties separately before showing how it underlies the construction of the approximating wPMRS $\widetilde{\mathcal{P}_\mathcal{G}}$.

Some nomenclature. A *simple term* is a subterm of the RHS of a $\mathcal{P}_\mathcal{G}$-rule or is the "starting term" $\mathit{Main}\ S$. A *compound term* has the shape $\xi\, t_1 \cdots t_m$ with $m \geq 0$, where the head symbol ξ is either a variable, or a terminal, or a non-terminal, and each t_i is simple. It follows from the definition that a simple term is compound, but the converse is not true.

3.1 Binding analysis

In a PMRS, the pattern matching rules use pattern matching both to determine control flow (by selecting which of a number of defining rules is used to reduce a redex) as well as to decompose compound data structure (by binding components to variables in the pattern that then occur on the RHS of the rule). However, the weak pattern matching mechanism in a wPMRS exhibits only the former capability: although patterns are matched, since there are no pattern-matching variables on the RHS of defining rules, data structures cannot be decomposed. Therefore, to build an effective abstraction of a PMRS requires some knowledge of the substitutions that can occur in redex/contractum pairs during PMRS reduction.

To this end, we define a *binding analysis*, which determines a (finitary) over-approximation Ξ to the set of variable-term bindings $\bigcup\{\, \theta \mid \mathit{Main}\ S \Rightarrow^* C[F\ \theta x_1\ \cdots\ \theta x_m\ \theta p] \Rightarrow C[\theta t]\,\}$ which occur in redex/contractum substitutions θ arising in $\mathcal{P}_\mathcal{G}$-reductions from '$\mathit{Main}\ S$'. The analysis is based on the observation that every such redex is either '$\mathit{Main}\ S$', or arises as an instance of a simple term. It proceeds by an iterative process in which bindings, by which instances of simple terms can be derived, give rise to redexes which in turn give rise, via contraction, to more bindings, until the desired set Ξ is reached in the limit.

Before we give the details of the analysis, let us make precise what it means for a set of bindings $\mathcal{S}$ to give rise to an instance of a term. Given such a set $\mathcal{S}$, we define the relation $s \preccurlyeq_\mathcal{S} t$, which is a subset of $T(\Sigma, \mathcal{N}, \mathcal{V}) \times T(\Sigma, \mathcal{N})$, inductively, by the system RS:

(R) $t \preccurlyeq_\mathcal{S} t$

(S) If $x \mapsto s \in \mathcal{S}$ and $C[s] \preccurlyeq_\mathcal{S} t$, then $C[x] \preccurlyeq_\mathcal{S} t$

where C ranges over one-hole contexts. We say that an instance of rule (S) is a *head-instance* just if the hole in $C[\,]$ occurs in head position.

Example 4. Let $\mathcal{S}_1 = \{x \mapsto y\ \mathtt{b},\ x \mapsto N,\ y \mapsto \mathtt{f}\ z,\ z \mapsto \mathtt{a}\}$. Then, using the system RS, it is possible to derive:

$$F\ x\ z \preccurlyeq_{\mathcal{S}_1} F\ (\mathtt{f\ a\ b})\ \mathtt{a} \qquad \text{and} \qquad F\ x\ z \preccurlyeq_{\mathcal{S}_1} F\ N\ \mathtt{a}$$

Note that the form of rule (S) does not constrain bindings to be used consistently within non-linear terms. Let $\mathcal{S}_2 = \{x \mapsto \mathtt{f}\ y\ z,\ y \mapsto z,\ y \mapsto \mathtt{a},\ z \mapsto \mathtt{b}\}$. Then we have, for example:

$$F\ x\ (G\ x) \preccurlyeq_{\mathcal{S}_2} F\ (\mathtt{f\ a\ b})\ (G\ (\mathtt{f\ b\ b}))$$

in which the binding $y \mapsto \mathtt{a}$ has been used in the derivation of the first argument of F whereas $y \mapsto z$ has been used in the derivation of the second argument.

To ensure that the analysis is computable, we cannot afford to work with instances of simple terms directly. We instead work with terms in which bindings have been applied only where strictly necessary in order to uncover new redexes. The construction of such terms is the purpose of the function head.

The head function. Given a set $\mathcal{S}$ of bindings, we define the *head function*, $\mathsf{head}_\mathcal{S} : T(\Sigma, \mathcal{N}, \mathcal{V}) \longrightarrow 2^{T(\Sigma, \mathcal{N}, \mathcal{V})}$ given by:

$$\mathsf{head}_\mathcal{S}(\xi\ t_1\ \cdots\ t_m) = \{\, \delta\ t_1\ \cdots\ t_m \mid \delta \in \mathsf{hs}_\mathcal{S}(\xi, \emptyset)\,\}$$

where $\mathsf{hs}_\mathcal{S}$ is an auxiliary function defined by the following:

$\mathsf{hs}_\mathcal{S}(k, X) = \{k\}$ (whenever $k \in \Sigma \cup \mathcal{N}$)

$\mathsf{hs}_\mathcal{S}(x, X) = \text{if } x \in X \text{ then } \emptyset \text{ else}$

$$\{\, \delta\ t_1\ \cdots\ t_m \mid x \mapsto \zeta\ t_1\ \cdots\ t_m \in \mathcal{S},\ \delta \in \mathsf{hs}_\mathcal{S}(\zeta, X \cup \{x\})\,\}$$

Thus $\mathsf{head}_\mathcal{S}(u)$ is the set of terms that are obtainable from u by iteratively replacing the head symbol—provided it is a variable—by a term bound to it in $\mathcal{S}$. The second argument of $\mathsf{hs}_\mathcal{S}$ disregards any cyclic chain of bindings. For example, let $\mathcal{S} = \{\, x \mapsto y, y \mapsto x\,\}$, then: $\mathsf{head}_\mathcal{S}(x) = \mathsf{hs}_\mathcal{S}(x, \emptyset) = \mathsf{hs}_\mathcal{S}(y, \{\,x\,\}) = \mathsf{hs}_\mathcal{S}(x, \{\,x, y\,\}) = \emptyset$

Example 5. Let $\mathcal{S}_1$ and $\mathcal{S}_2$ be as in Example 4. Then:

$$\mathsf{head}_{\mathcal{S}_1}(x\ \mathtt{c}) = \{\, N\ \mathtt{c},\ \mathtt{f}\ z\ \mathtt{b}\ \mathtt{c}\,\}$$

$$\mathsf{head}_{\mathcal{S}_2}(x\ \mathtt{c}) = \{\mathtt{f}\ y\ z\ \mathtt{c}\} \quad \mathsf{head}_{\mathcal{S}_2}(F\ x\ (G\ x)) = \{F\ x\ (G\ x)\}$$

Notice that since head performs variable-substitutions according to bindings from $\mathcal{S}$, its behaviour is consistent with a strategy for constructing initial prefixes of derivations in the system RS. Each use of the recursive clause of $\mathsf{hs}_\mathcal{S}$ corresponds to a head-instance of rule (S). A consequence of this relationship is made precise by the following lemma.

Lemma 1. *If $u \preccurlyeq_\mathcal{S} \xi\ v_1\ \cdots\ v_m$ then there is a compound term $\xi\ u_1\ \cdots\ u_m \in \mathsf{head}_\mathcal{S}(u)$ and, for all $1 \leq i \leq m$, $u_i \preccurlyeq_\mathcal{S} v_i$.*

One final property to note about head is that, whenever its argument is compound and all the variables in $\mathcal{S}$ are bound to simple terms, the terms in (sets in) its image are all compound. This is due to the fact that, in this case, the action of the head function is to construct new, compound terms by prepending old, simple terms into head position. This limited behaviour of the head-function will contribute towards guaranteeing the termination of the analysis.

Lemma 2. *We say that a set of bindings $\mathcal{S}$ is image-simple just if every term in the image of $\mathcal{S}$ is simple. Suppose $\mathcal{S}$ is image-simple. If u is compound, then every term in $\mathsf{head}_\mathcal{S}(u)$ is compound.*

The goal of the analysis is to discover the possible redexes $F\theta x_1\ \cdots\ \theta x_m\ \theta p$ that occur during reduction sequences of $\mathcal{P}_\mathcal{G}$ starting from $Main\ S$. The head function $\mathsf{head}_\mathcal{S}(u)$ is able to determine, in a way that is computable, when an F-redex is an instance (according to $\mathcal{S}$) of a simple term u. In this case, according to Lemma 1, a term of the shape $F\ t_1\ \cdots\ t_m\ s$ is an element of $\mathsf{head}_\mathcal{S}(u)$. However, to know which defining rule of F is triggered, it is necessary to find out which patterns are matched by residuals of instances of s.

The approximate reduction. To this end, we introduce a new notion of reduction $\rhd_\mathcal{S}\ \subseteq\ T(\Sigma,\mathcal{N},\mathcal{V}) \times T(\Sigma,\mathcal{N},\mathcal{V})$ parametrised by a set of bindings $\mathcal{S}$. This reduction approximates the usual PMRS reduction by performing redex/contractum substitutions only where absolutely necessary and only when the relevant bindings are contained in $\mathcal{S}$. A *$\rhd_\mathcal{S}$-redex* is a term of the form $F\ \theta x_1\ \cdots\ \theta x_m\ \theta p$ whenever there is a $\mathcal{P}_{\mathcal{G}_0}$-rule of the form $F\ x_1\ \cdots\ x_m\ p \longrightarrow t$ and θ is a substitution (not necessarily closed). The contractum of the redex is t, no substitution is performed upon contraction.

We define the one step reduction $\rhd_\mathcal{S}$ by the following rules. Let C range over one-hole contexts.

$$\frac{(s,t)\text{ a }\rhd\text{-redex/contractum pair}}{C[s] \rhd_\mathcal{S} C[t]} \qquad \frac{t \in \mathsf{head}_\mathcal{S}(x\,t_1\ \cdots\ t_m)}{C[x\,t_1\ \cdots\ t_m] \rhd_\mathcal{S} C[t]}$$

As is standard, we write $\rhd^*_\mathcal{S}$ to mean the reflexive, transitive closure of $\rhd_\mathcal{S}$, and $\rhd^n_\mathcal{S}$ to mean a n-long chain of $\rhd_\mathcal{S}$.

Example 6. Consider the composite PMRS $\mathcal{P}_\mathcal{G}$ constructed from the PMRS and grammar given in Example 2 and let $\mathcal{S}$ contain the bindings $p \mapsto Nz$ and $x \mapsto N$. Then the following:

$$p\ x \rhd_\mathcal{S} Nz\ x \rhd_\mathcal{S} Nz\ N\ \ \rhd_\mathcal{S} Nz\ (\mathtt{s}\ N) \rhd_\mathcal{S} \mathtt{true}$$

is a $\rhd_\mathcal{S}$-reduction. Observe how, as demonstrated by the third step, approximate reduction is accurate for order-0 $\mathcal{G}$-rules.

Given a substitution θ and a pattern p, we say that a $\rhd_\mathcal{S}$-reduction $s \rhd^i_\mathcal{S} \theta p$ is *minimal* just if it is *not* the case that there exist $j < i$ and substitution θ' such that $s \rhd^j_\mathcal{S} \theta' p$. Consider the two rules defining $\rhd_\mathcal{S}$-reduction. In the RHS of the conclusion of each rule is the term t. In both cases, assuming $\mathcal{S}$ is image simple, t is a compound term. Since there are only finitely many such terms t and since there are only finitely many patterns (drawn from the PMRS) p, the problem of finding such *minimal* reductions is computable.

Lemma 3. *Assume $\mathcal{S}$ is image-simple. Given a compound term s and a pattern p drawn from the defining rules of $\mathcal{P}_\mathcal{G}$, the problem of finding a substitution θ and a minimal reduction $s \rhd^*_\mathcal{S} \theta p$ is computable.*

The fixpoint construction. Let $\mathcal{S}$ be a set of bindings. We define $\mathcal{F}(\mathcal{S})$ as the least set X of bindings that contains $\mathcal{S}$ and is closed under *Rule* **C**: if

(i) u is simple term of base type,

(ii) $F\ t_1\ \cdots\ t_m\ s \in \mathsf{head}_\mathcal{S}(u)$,

(iii) $F\ x_1\ \cdots\ x_m\ p \longrightarrow t$ is a $\mathcal{P}_{\mathcal{G}_0}$-rule,

(iv) there is a minimal reduction $s \rhd^*_\mathcal{S} \theta\, p$

then $\theta \cup \{\, x_i \mapsto t_i \mid 1 \leq i \leq m \,\} \subseteq X$.

Thus $\mathcal{F} : 2^{\mathcal{V}\times T(\Sigma,\mathcal{N},\mathcal{V})} \longrightarrow 2^{\mathcal{V}\times T(\Sigma,\mathcal{N},\mathcal{V})}$ is, by construction, a monotone (endo)function on the complete lattice $2^{\mathcal{V}\times T(\Sigma,\mathcal{N},\mathcal{V})}$ ordered by subset-inclusion. By the Tarski-Knaster Fixpoint Theorem, the least fixpoint of $\mathcal{F}$, which we shall denote Ξ, exists, and is constructable as the supremum of the chain

$$\emptyset \subseteq \mathcal{F}\,\emptyset \subseteq \mathcal{F}(\mathcal{F}\,\emptyset) \subseteq \mathcal{F}(\mathcal{F}(\mathcal{F}\,\emptyset)) \subseteq \cdots$$

Example 7. Consider again the composite PMRS $\mathcal{P}_\mathcal{G}$ composed from the PMRS $\mathcal{P}$ and tree grammar $\mathcal{G}$ given in Example 2. We shall apply the fixpoint construction to this structure.

Initially, the only fruitful choice of simple term is the "starting term" $Main\ S$ which otherwise trivially satisfies the premises of Rule **C** and yields the single binding $m \mapsto S$. Subsequently, taking $u = Filter\ Nz\ m$ matches both the defining rules for $Filter$ after approximate-reductions of:

$$m \rhd^*_{\{m\mapsto S\}} \mathtt{nil} \qquad \text{and} \qquad m \rhd^*_{\{m\mapsto S\}} \mathtt{cons}\ N\ ListN$$

respectively. This choice adds the bindings $p \mapsto Nz$, $x \mapsto N$ and $xs \mapsto ListN$. Examining the term $p\ x$ in the RHS of the second defining rule for $Filter$ then gives $n \mapsto N$. Finally, taking u as the entire RHS of the second defining rule for $Filter$ and approximate-reducing $p\ x$ as in Example 6 gives bindings $a \mapsto \mathtt{cons}\ x\ (Filter\ p\ xs)$ and $b \mapsto Filter\ p\ xs$. In this case, no other choices of simple term yield any new bindings, so the fixpoint Ξ is obtained as:

$$\begin{gathered} m \mapsto S, \quad p \mapsto Nz, \quad x \mapsto N, \quad xs \mapsto ListN \\ n \mapsto N, \quad a \mapsto \mathtt{cons}\ x\ (Filter\ p\ xs), \quad b \mapsto Filter\ p\ xs \end{gathered}$$

Though the complete lattice $2^{\mathcal{V}\times T(\Sigma,\mathcal{N},\mathcal{V})}$ is infinite, the least fixpoint Ξ is finitely constructable (i.e. the closure ordinal of $\mathcal{F}$ is finite); it is in fact a finite set. Observe that, in Example 7, the form of every binding in the fixpoint is $v \mapsto t$ in which t is a simple term. This is the key to showing the convergence of the analysis. Since every term $F\ t_1\ \cdots\ t_m\ s \in \mathsf{head}_\mathcal{S}(u)$ is compound (whenever $\mathcal{S}$ is image-simple and u is compound) so every binding $x_i \rightarrow t_i$ is image-simple. Since, whenever $\mathcal{S}$ is image-simple, every $\rhd_\mathcal{S}$-contractum is compound, so the bindings due to θp are image-simple. Since there are only finitely many simple terms, termination follows.

Theorem 1 (Termination)**.** *The least fixpoint of $\mathcal{F}$, Ξ, is a finite set.*

To see that this finite set of bindings Ξ is sufficient to describe all the all the substitutions that occur during redex contractions in reduction sequences of $\mathcal{P}_\mathcal{G}$ starting from $Main\ S$, one should first notice that the approximate reduction, when instantiated with the fixpoint, acts on simple terms in a way which is consistent with the way PMRS reduction acts on their instances in a trivial context.

Lemma 4. *Assume θt is a contractum and u is a simple term. If $s \Rightarrow^+ \theta t$ and $u \preccurlyeq_\Xi s$, then $u \rhd^*_\Xi t$ and $t \preccurlyeq_\Xi \theta t$.*

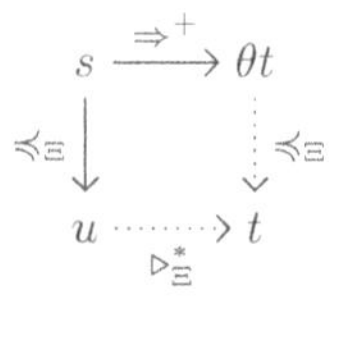

To lift this fact to the level of arbitrary reduction sequences starting from $Main\ S$, it is enough to observe that any redex in such a sequence (apart from the first), can be seen either to be itself a simple term or to arise as a subterm of some previous contractum, regardless of the context in which the redex occurs. As a consequence of Lemma 4, the variable-term bindings necessary to derive the redex as an instance of the corresponding simple term will already be contained in the fixpoint. Hence, if the reduction sequence reaches any contractum, the fixpoint will contain the bindings necessary to reconstruct the substitution associated with the contraction.

Lemma 5. *Assume θt is a contractum. If $Main\ S \Rightarrow^+ C[\theta t]$ is a $\mathcal{P}_\mathcal{G}$-reduction sequence then $t \preccurlyeq_\Xi \theta t$.*

3.2 Construction of the over-approximating wPMRS

We are now ready to define the wPMRS which is an abstraction of the composite PMRS $\mathcal{P}_\mathcal{G} = \langle \Sigma, \mathcal{N}, \mathcal{R}, Main \rangle$. Let Ξ be the fixpoint set of bindings and let $\mathcal{N}_\mathcal{V} = \{ V_x \mid x \in \mathcal{V} \}$ and $\mathcal{N}_\Sigma = \{ K_\mathsf{a} \mid \mathsf{a} \in \Sigma \}$ be two sets of fresh non-terminal symbols which we call *pattern-symbols* and *accounting-symbols* respectively. We define the approximating wPMRS:

$$\widetilde{\mathcal{P}_\mathcal{G}} := \langle \Sigma,\ \mathcal{N} \cup \mathcal{N}_\mathcal{V} \cup \mathcal{N}_\Sigma,\ \mathcal{R}',\ Main \rangle$$

where $\mathcal{R}'$ consists of the following three kinds of rules:

I. *Weak pattern-matching rules.* For each (pure or pattern-matching) $\mathcal{P}_\mathcal{G}$-rule $F\,x_1 \cdots x_m\,p \longrightarrow t$, $\mathcal{R}'$ contains the following rule:
$$F\,x_1 \cdots x_m\,p \longrightarrow t^\dagger$$

II. *Instantiation rules.* For each binding $x \mapsto t$ in Ξ where $\mathsf{FV}(t^\dagger) = \{ x_1, \cdots, x_l \}$, $\mathcal{R}'$ contains the following rule:
$$V_x\,z_1 \cdots z_{\mathsf{ar}(x)} \longrightarrow (t^\dagger[V_{x_1}/x_1] \cdots [V_{x_l}/x_l])\,z_1 \cdots z_{\mathsf{ar}(x)}$$
where each z_i is a fresh variable of the appropriate types.

III. *Accounting rules.* For each terminal symbol $\mathsf{a} : b_1 \to \cdots \to b_n \to o$ in Σ, $\mathcal{R}'$ contains the following rule:
$$K_\mathsf{a}\,z_1\ \cdots\ z_n \longrightarrow \mathsf{a}\,z_1\ \cdots\ z_n$$
where each z_i is a fresh variable of type b_i.

where we have written $t^\dagger$ to denote the term t in which every occurrence of a pattern matching variable $y \in \mathsf{FV}(p)$ has been replaced by the corresponding pattern-symbol V_y and every occurrence of a terminal symbol a has been replaced by the corresponding accounting-symbol K_a.

Example 8. Consider the following order-2 PMRS, whose defining rules are given by:

$$Main\ m \longrightarrow Map2\ KZero\ KOne\ m$$

$$\begin{aligned} Map2\ \varphi\ \psi\ \mathtt{nil} &\longrightarrow \mathtt{nil} \\ Map2\ \varphi\ \psi\ (\mathtt{cons}\ x\ xs) &\longrightarrow \mathtt{cons}\ (\varphi\ x)\ (Map2\ \psi\ \varphi\ xs) \end{aligned}$$

$$\begin{aligned} KZero\ x_1 &\longrightarrow \mathtt{0} \\ KOne\ x_2 &\longrightarrow \mathtt{1} \end{aligned}$$

and input grammar $\mathcal{G}$ consisting of two rules:

$$S \longrightarrow \mathtt{nil} \mid \mathtt{cons}\ \mathtt{0}\ S$$

The function $Map2$ behaves like the standard Map function, except that it swaps the first two function arguments as it filters through the successive elements of the list argument. The reachable constructor terms are finite lists that are prefixes of `[0 1 0 1 0 1 ···]`.

After applying the fixpoint construction to this example, the set of bindings Ξ consists of the following:

$$\begin{array}{lllllllll} m & \mapsto & S & \varphi & \mapsto & KZero & \varphi & \mapsto & \psi \\ x & \mapsto & \mathtt{0} & \psi & \mapsto & KOne & \psi & \mapsto & \varphi \\ x_1 & \mapsto & x & x_2 & \mapsto & x & xs & \mapsto & S \end{array}$$

and hence the approximating wPMRS $\widetilde{\mathcal{P}_\mathcal{G}}$ is as follows.

$$Main\ m \longrightarrow Map2\ KZero\ KOne\ M$$

$$\begin{aligned} Map2\ \varphi\ \psi\ \mathtt{nil} &\longrightarrow Nil \\ Map2\ \varphi\ \psi\ (\mathtt{cons}\ x\ xs) &\longrightarrow Cons\ (\varphi\ X)\ (Map2\ \psi\ \varphi\ XS) \end{aligned}$$

$$\begin{aligned} KZero\ x_1 &\longrightarrow Zero \\ KOne\ x_2 &\longrightarrow One \end{aligned}$$

$$\begin{aligned} M &\longrightarrow S \\ X &\longrightarrow Zero \\ XS &\longrightarrow S \\ S &\longrightarrow Nil \mid Cons\ Zero\ S \end{aligned}$$

$$\begin{aligned} Zero &\longrightarrow \mathtt{0} \\ One &\longrightarrow \mathtt{1} \\ Nil &\longrightarrow \mathtt{nil} \end{aligned}$$

$$Cons\ v_1\ v_2 \longrightarrow \mathtt{cons}\ v_1\ v_2$$

Since φ, ψ, x_1 and x_2 are not pattern-matched variables, the rules for V_φ, V_ψ, V_{x_1} and V_{x_2} are, in this case, never used and so play no part in the approximation process: they have been omitted. It is easy to see that the constructor terms in $\mathcal{L}(\widetilde{\mathcal{P}_\mathcal{G}}, Main\ S)$ are exactly the finite prefixes of `[0 1 0 1 ···]` i.e. the approximation is exact in this case.

Given any $\mathcal{P}_\mathcal{G}$-reduction $Main\ S \Rightarrow^+ t$, the reduction can be faithfully simulated in the abstraction $\widetilde{\mathcal{P}_\mathcal{G}}$ using the weak pattern-matching rules and the instantiation rules. Whenever the $\mathcal{P}_\mathcal{G}$-reduction contracts a $\mathcal{P}$-rule which binds data θy to a pattern matching variable y, the simulation can contract the corresponding redex using a weak pattern-matching rule and, by Lemma 5, can then reconstruct the bound data θy from V_y using the instantiation rules.

Theorem 2 (Soundness). *Let the composite PMRS $\mathcal{P}_\mathcal{G}$ and the approximating wPMRS $\widetilde{\mathcal{P}_\mathcal{G}}$ be as before. Then $\mathcal{L}(\mathcal{P}_\mathcal{G}, Main\ S) \subseteq \mathcal{L}(\widetilde{\mathcal{P}_\mathcal{G}}, Main\ S)$.*

The third class of rules is not essential to the achieving soundness. The purpose of the accounting rules is to enforce a strict correspondence between the length of a $\widetilde{\mathcal{P}_\mathcal{G}}$ reduction sequence and the maximum size of any constructor term created within it. This eases the justification of the semi-completeness property of refinement in Section 5.

4. Model checking by type inference

In this section, we exhibit an algorithm to decide the *wPMRS Model Checking Problem*: given a non-deterministic wPMRS $\mathcal{W} = \langle \Sigma, \mathcal{N}, \mathcal{R}, Main \rangle$ in which $Main : b \to o$, a closed term $t : b$ and a trivial automaton $\mathcal{A}$, is $\mathcal{L}(\mathcal{W}, Main\ t) \subseteq \mathcal{L}(\mathcal{A})$? Following work by Kobayashi [6] and Kobayashi and Ong [8], we characterise the model checking problem as a type inference problem in a particular, finitary intersection type system induced by the automaton.

Eliminating non-determinism. The first step we take is to simplify the problem at hand by eliminating the non-determinism in $\mathcal{W}$. To this end we construct a new wPMRS $\mathcal{W}^\#$ in which multiple defining rules for a given non-terminal are collapsed using a family $\mathcal{B} := \{ \mathtt{br}_b \mid b \in \mathbb{B} \}$ of "non-deterministic choice" terminal symbols $\mathtt{br}_b$ of type $b \to b \to b$. We define:

$$\mathcal{W}^\# := \langle \Sigma \cup \mathcal{B}, \mathcal{N}, \{ l \longrightarrow \mathtt{BR}(l) \mid \exists r \cdot l \longrightarrow r \in \mathcal{R} \}, Main \rangle$$

in which, by way of a short-hand, we define:

$$\mathtt{BR}(F\, t_1 \cdots t_n) := \mathtt{br}_b\, r_1\, (\mathtt{br}_b\, r_2\, (\cdots (\mathtt{br}_b\, r_{m-1}\, r_m) \cdots))$$

where $\{ r_1, \ldots, r_m \} = \{ r \mid F\, t_1 \cdots t_n \longrightarrow r \in \mathcal{R} \}$ and the type of F is of the form $\tau_1 \to \cdots \to \tau_n \to b$. We must modify the automaton $\mathcal{A}$ accordingly, so we define:

$$\mathcal{A}^\# := \langle \Sigma \cup \mathcal{B}, Q, \Delta \cup \{ (q, \mathtt{br}_b, q\, q \mid q \in Q, b \in \mathbb{B} \}, q_0 \rangle$$

Lemma 6. *For all terms t of base-type:*

$$\mathcal{L}(\mathcal{W}, Main\ t) \subseteq \mathcal{L}(\mathcal{A}) \quad \textit{iff} \quad [\![Main\ t]\!]_{\mathcal{W}^\#} \in \mathcal{L}(\mathcal{A}^\#)$$

Model checking as type inference. We first introduce recursion schemes with weak definition-by-cases, which is a term rewriting system similar to (in fact, equi-expressive with) wPMRS; the difference is that (weak) matching is explicitly provided by a case construct. Assume for each base type b, an exhaustive and non-overlapping family of patterns $P_b = \{ p_1, \cdots, p_k \}$. A *recursion scheme with weak definition-by-cases* (wRSC) is a quadruple $\mathcal{G} = \langle \Sigma, \mathcal{N}, \mathcal{R}, S \rangle$ where $\Sigma, \mathcal{N}$, and S are as usual, and $\mathcal{R}$ is a set of (pure) rules of the form

$$F\, x_1 \cdots x_m \longrightarrow t$$

We write $\mathbf{rhs}(F) = \lambda x_1 \cdots x_m.t$. The set of applicative terms is defined as before, except that it is augmented by a definition-by-cases construct $\mathsf{case}_b(t; t_1, \cdots, t_k)$ with typing rule:

$$\frac{\Gamma \vdash t : b \qquad \Gamma \vdash t_i, o\ (\text{for } 1 \le i \le k)}{\Gamma \vdash \mathsf{case}_b(t; t_1, \cdots, t_k) : o}$$

We say that $\mathcal{G}$ is deterministic just if there is one rule for each $F \in \mathcal{N}$. There are two kinds of redexes:

(i) $F\, s_1 \cdots s_m$ which contracts to $t[s_1/x_1] \cdots [s_m/x_m]$ for each rule $F\, x_1 \cdots x_m \longrightarrow t$ in $\mathcal{R}$

(ii) $\mathsf{case}_b(t; t_1, \cdots, t_k)$ which contracts to t_i, provided t of base type b matches pattern $p_i \in P_b = \{ p_1, \cdots, p_k \}$.

We define evaluation contexts E as follows

$$E ::= [\,] \mid f\, t_1 \cdots t_{i-1}\, E\, t_{i+1} \cdots t_{\mathsf{ar}(f)}$$

and write $\to$ for the one-step reduction relation $E[\Delta] \to E[\underline{\Delta}]$ where $(\Delta, \underline{\Delta})$ ranges over redex/contractum pairs and E over evaluation contexts. Assuming $\mathcal{G}$ is deterministic, we define the $\Sigma^\perp$-labelled tree generated by $\mathcal{G}$ by infinitary rewriting from S as $[\![\mathcal{G}]\!] := \{ t^\perp \mid S \to^* t \}$.

Lemma 7. *Deterministic wPMRS and deterministic wRSC are equi-expressive as generators of Σ-labelled trees.*

We present an intersection type system for characterising the model checking problem. The *intersection types* of the system are given by the grammar:

$$\sigma, \tau \quad ::= \quad q \mid p \mid \bigwedge_{i=1}^{m} \tau_i \to \tau$$

where $q \in Q$ and p is one of the finitely many patterns associated with a definition by cases in the scheme $\mathcal{G}$. Judgements of the type system are sequents of the form $\Gamma \vdash t : \tau$, in which Γ is simply a set of type bindings $\xi : \sigma$ where $\xi \in \mathcal{N} \cup \mathcal{V}$. The defining rules of the system are as follows:

$$\frac{}{\Gamma, x : \tau \vdash x : \tau} \quad (\text{VAR})$$

$$\frac{(q, f, q_1 \cdots q_n) \in \Delta_{\mathcal{A}^\#}}{\Gamma \vdash f : q_1 \to \cdots \to q_n \to q} \quad (\text{TERM})$$

$$\frac{\exists \theta \cdot s\, p_1 \cdots p_n = \theta\, p}{\Gamma \vdash s : p_1 \to \cdots \to p_n \to p} \quad (\text{MATCH})$$

$$\frac{\Gamma \vdash t : p_i \qquad \Gamma \vdash t_i : \tau}{\Gamma \vdash \mathsf{case}_b(t; t_1, \cdots, t_i, \cdots, t_n) : \tau} \quad (\text{CASE})$$

$$\frac{\Gamma \vdash s : \bigwedge_{i=1}^{n} \tau_i \to \tau \qquad \Gamma \vdash t : \tau_i \quad (\text{for each } 1 \le i \le n)}{\Gamma \vdash s\, t : \tau} \quad (\text{APP})$$

$$\frac{\Gamma, x : \tau_1, \cdots, x : \tau_n \vdash t : \tau}{\Gamma \vdash \lambda x.t : \bigwedge_{i=1}^{n} \tau_i \to \tau} \quad (\text{ABS})$$

Note that we have the following derived rule from (Match): if a term s (of the appropriate type) matches the pattern p, then $\Gamma \vdash s : p$.

We write $\vdash_{\mathcal{A}} \mathcal{G} : \Gamma$ if $\Gamma \vdash \mathbf{rhs}(F) : \tau$ is provable for every $F : \tau \in \Gamma$. A wRSC is *well-typed*, written $\vdash_{\mathcal{A}} \mathcal{G}$, just if there exists Γ such that (i) $\vdash_{\mathcal{A}} \mathcal{G} : \Gamma$, (ii) $S : q_0 \in \Gamma$, (iii) for each $F : \tau \in \Gamma$, $\tau :: \kappa$, where $F : \kappa \in \mathcal{N}$, meaning that τ is an intersection type *compatible* with type κ (as assigned to F by the wRSC), which is defined by: (i) $q :: o$, (ii) $p :: b$ for each $p \in P_b$, (iii) $\bigwedge_{i=1}^{k} \tau_i \to \tau :: \kappa' \to \kappa$ if $\tau :: \kappa$ and for each $1 \le i \le k$, $\tau_i :: \kappa'$.

Theorem 3. *Let $\mathcal{A}$ be a trivial automaton, and $\mathcal{G}$ be wRSC. Then $\vdash_{\mathcal{A}} \mathcal{G}$ if and only if $[\![\mathcal{G}]\!] \in \mathcal{L}(\mathcal{A})$.*

The proof is omitted as it is very similar to the proof of the soundness and completeness theorems in [6].

Corollary 1. *The wPMRS model checking problem is decidable.*

Proof. This follows from Lemma 6, Lemma 7 and Theorem 3, and the decidability of typability $\vdash_{\mathcal{A}} \mathcal{G}$. The latter follows from the fact that for each non-terminal, there are only finitely many candidate intersection types compatible with a given type. □

5. Abstraction refinement

When the model checking stage reports a counterexample in the form of an error trace, the trace may be "feasible", that is, it corresponds to a concrete reduction sequence in the original PMRS $\mathcal{P}$, or it may be "spurious": an artifact of the abstraction process. In the case the counterexample is spurious, we will want to ignore it and perform the process again, but in a new setting in which we are guaranteed never again to encounter this unwanted trace. To achieve this we restart the cycle from a modified PMRS $\mathcal{P}'$, which has had some of its defining rules unfolded, so as to reduce the amount of non-determinism in the corresponding wPMRS abstraction.

5.1 Counterexamples and feasibility.

When the model-checker reports a violation of the property, a counterexample error trace is returned. This error trace is a reduction sequence in the abstract wPMRS $\widetilde{\mathcal{P}_\mathcal{G}}$. Since $\widetilde{\mathcal{P}_\mathcal{G}}$ is not completely faithful to the PMRS $\mathcal{P}$, it is necessary to determine whether such a counterexample trace corresponds to a reduction sequence in $\mathcal{P}$ which itself witnesses the violation or whether it is an artifact of the abstraction.

Anatomy of a counterexample. It is useful to highlight two important features of any given counterexample trace, namely, (i) the shape of the last term in the reduction sequence and (ii) the "type" of each constituent reduction .

Any counterexample trace must end in a term t which witnesses the violation of the property φ. Since the property is a collection of (possibly infinite) Σ-labelled trees, the witnessing term can be seen to be of the form θq where q is a pattern which does not match any prefix of a tree $t \in \varphi$. We say that the pattern q which witnesses the violation of the property is the *error witness*.

In any $\widetilde{\mathcal{P}_\mathcal{G}}$ reduction sequence, each reduction $u \to v$ can be classified into one of two kinds based on the head symbol occurring in the redex. In case we want to emphasise that the head symbol is a non-terminal belonging to $\mathcal{P}$ we say the contraction of this redex is an *abstract $\mathcal{P}$-reduction* and write $u \to_\mathcal{P} v$. Otherwise the head symbol is either a pattern-symbol, an accounting-symbol or it belongs to $\mathcal{G}$. In this case we say that the head symbol in question is a *live-symbol* and that the contraction of this redex is an *abstract $\widetilde{\mathcal{P}_\mathcal{G}}$-reduction*; we write $u \to_{\widetilde{\mathcal{P}_\mathcal{G}}} v$.

Example 9. Consider the following abstract error trace which is derived from the abstraction $\widetilde{\mathcal{P}_\mathcal{G}}$ of the PMRS $\mathcal{P}$ and grammar $\mathcal{G}$ given in Example 2:

$$
\begin{aligned}
& \mathit{Main}\ S \\
\to\ & \mathit{Filter}\ \mathit{Nz}\ M \\
\to^*\ & \mathit{Filter}\ \mathit{Nz}\ (\mathtt{cons}\ N\ \mathit{ListN}) \\
\to\ & \mathit{If}\ (\mathit{Cons}\ X\ (\mathit{Filter}\ \mathit{Nz}\ \mathit{XS}))\ (\mathit{Filter}\ \mathit{Nz}\ \mathit{XS})\ (\mathit{Nz}\ X) \\
\to^*\ & \mathit{If}\ (\mathit{Cons}\ X\ (\mathit{Filter}\ \mathit{Nz}\ \mathit{XS}))\ (\mathit{Filter}\ \mathit{Nz}\ \mathit{XS})\ (\mathit{Nz}\ (\mathtt{s}\ N)) \\
\to\ & \mathit{If}\ (\mathit{Cons}\ X\ (\mathit{Filter}\ \mathit{Nz}\ \mathit{XS}))\ (\mathit{Filter}\ \mathit{Nz}\ \mathit{XS})\ \mathit{True} \\
\to^*\ & \mathit{Cons}\ X\ (\mathit{Filter}\ \mathit{Nz}\ \mathit{XS}) \\
\to\ & \mathtt{cons}\ X\ (\mathit{Filter}\ \mathit{Nz}\ \mathit{XS}) \\
\to^*\ & \mathtt{cons}\ \mathtt{z}\ (\mathit{Filter}\ \mathit{Nz}\ \mathit{XS})
\end{aligned}
$$

which violates the property since it is the start of a list that contains a zero. The *error-witness* for this trace is $\mathtt{cons}\ \mathtt{z}\ v$ (for some variable v). The first reduction is an *abstract $\mathcal{P}$-reduction*, as is the reduction written over lines 3 and 4 and that of lines 5 and 6. All the other reductions in the sequence are *abstract $\widetilde{\mathcal{P}_\mathcal{G}}$-reductions*.

The trace in the above example is spurious since there are no reduction sequences of the PMRS $\mathcal{P}$ (starting from terms in $\mathcal{L}(\mathcal{G})$) from Example 2 which result in a list headed by a zero. Intuitively, we can see that this trace is infeasible because the non-determinism introduced by the abstraction has been resolved in an inconsistent way during the sequence. The data bound by the pattern match for *Filter*, which is given as N (i.e. some number) has been resolved on the one hand (line 5) to a non-zero number and on the other hand (line 9) to zero.

In the following, we define a process of labelling of the counterexample trace that will reveal information about the resolution of non-determinism that has been introduced as a consequence of the abstraction. The information that is exposed will allow us to see whether or not this abstract trace in $\widetilde{\mathcal{P}_\mathcal{G}}$ has any corresponding trace in $\mathcal{P}$ starting form $\mathcal{I}$, that is, whether the trace is feasible.

Labelling. The labelling procedure, labelSeq, keeps track of how non-determinism is resolved in an abstract reduction sequence by annotating each live-symbol X with a set of (possibly open) terms, which represent all the closed terms to which it reduces. When the terms are given by the set l, we write the annotated term X^l and we identify an unlabelled live-symbol X with $X^\emptyset$. Given a term t which may include labelled subterms, we define the *resolution* of t, which is a set of terms $\bar{t}$, defined as follows:

$$
\bar{t} = \begin{cases} \{\mathsf{a}\} & \text{when } t = \mathsf{a} \in \Sigma \\ \{F\} & \text{when } t = F \text{ is not a live-symbol} \\ \hat{l} & \text{when } t = F^l \text{ is a live-symbol} \\ \{\, u\ v \mid u \in \overline{t_0},\ v \in \overline{t_1}\,\} & \text{when } t = t_0\ t_1 \end{cases}
$$

where $\hat{l}$ denotes the set l when l is non-empty and $\{z\}$ for some fresh variable z otherwise. If any pattern-symbol reduces to two incompatible terms or to a term which is inconsistent with the term that it represents in the matching, then the procedure will detect a conflict and record it in the set Failures.

labelSeq($\mathit{Main}\ S$)

> If S is labelled by l and there is a term $t \in \mathcal{L}(\mathcal{G})$ which is an instance of mgci(l) then do nothing else add (Main, l) to Failures.

labelSeq($\mathit{Main}\ S \to^* u \to v$)

1. Analyse the reduction $u \to v$:

   $C[F\ \theta x_1\ \cdots\ \theta x_m] \to_{\widetilde{\mathcal{P}_\mathcal{G}}} C[t\ \theta x_1\ \cdots\ \theta x_m]$:
   Label the head symbol F by $\bar{t}$.

   $C[F\ \theta x_1\ \cdots\ \theta x_m\ \theta p] \to_\mathcal{P} C[\theta t^\dagger]$:
   For each $y \in \mathsf{FV}(p)$, let $\{V_y^{l_1}, \ldots, V_y^{l_k}\}$ be the labelled pattern-symbols in v created by the contraction. Perform labelTm(θy)($\bigcup\{l_1, \ldots, l_k\}$) on the corresponding occurrence of θy in θp. If labelTm fails, then add $(F, \bigcup\{l_1, \ldots, l_k\})$ to Failures.

2. For each occurrence of an unlabelled live-symbol N in u, let $\{N_1^{l_1}, \ldots, N_k^{l_k}\}$ be the set of labelled descendants in v. Label this occurrence of N with $\bigcup\{l_1, \ldots, l_k\}$.
3. Perform labelSeq($\mathit{Main}\ S \to^* u$).

where the procedure labelTm, which is designed to resolve the data bound in a pattern match and the data created by the abstraction, is given by:

labelTm(t)($\{s_1, \ldots, s_k\}$)

> Analyse the form of t:
>
> $t = \mathsf{a}$**:** If $\forall i$ a matches s_i then do nothing else fail.
>
> $t = F$**:** If F is not a live-symbol and $\forall i$ F matches s_i then do nothing else, if F is a live-symbol and $w =$ mgci($\{s_1, \ldots, s_k\}$) exists then label F by $\{w\}$ else fail.
>
> $t = t_0\ t_1$**:** If $\forall i$ either s_i is a variable or $s_i = s_{i_0}\ s_{i_1}$ then (let $s_{j_0} = z_0$ and $s_{j_1} = z_1$ for fresh z_1, z_2 whenever s_j is a variable) and perform labelTm(t_0)($\{s_{1_0}, \ldots, s_{k_0}\}$) and perform labelTm($t_1$)($\{s_{1_1}, \ldots, s_{k_1}\}$) else fail.

where mgci(l) denotes the most general common instance (MGCI) of the set of terms l (regarding a single fresh variable as the MGCI of the empty set)[1]. We call a counterexample trace that has been labelled by labelSeq a *labelled trace*.

[1] For the purposes of calculating MGCIs, terms are considered as first order entities constructed from atomic constants and a single (silent) application operator.

Example 10. Consider again the abstract reduction sequence in Example 9, after performing $\mathsf{labelSeq}$ the following labelled trace is produced (the set bracket notation has been elided since all labels are singleton sets):

$\mathit{Main}\ S^{\mathtt{cons}\ v_1\ v_2}$

$\rightarrow\ \ \mathit{Filter}\ \mathit{Nz}\ M^{\mathtt{cons}\ v_1\ v_2}$

$\rightarrow^*\ \mathit{Filter}\ \mathit{Nz}\ (\mathtt{cons}\ N\ \mathit{ListN}^{v_2})$

$\rightarrow\ \ \mathit{If}\ (\mathit{Cons}^{\mathtt{cons}}\ X^{\mathtt{z}}\ (\mathit{Filter}\ \mathit{Nz}\ \mathit{XS}))\ (\mathit{Filter}\ \mathit{Nz}\ \mathit{XS})\ (\mathit{Nz}\ X^{\mathtt{s}\ v_0})$

$\rightarrow^*\ \mathit{If}\ (\mathit{Cons}^{\mathtt{cons}}\ X^{\mathtt{z}}\ (\mathit{Filter}\ \mathit{Nz}\ \mathit{XS}))\ (\mathit{Filter}\ \mathit{Nz}\ \mathit{XS})\ (\mathit{Nz}\ (\mathtt{s}\ N^{v_0}))$

$\rightarrow\ \ \mathit{If}\ (\mathit{Cons}^{\mathtt{cons}}\ X^{\mathtt{z}}\ (\mathit{Filter}\ \mathit{Nz}\ \mathit{XS}))\ (\mathit{Filter}\ \mathit{Nz}\ \mathit{XS})\ \mathit{True}^{\mathtt{true}}$

$\rightarrow^*\ \mathit{Cons}^{\mathtt{cons}}\ X^{\mathtt{z}}\ (\mathit{Filter}\ \mathit{Nz}\ \mathit{XS})$

$\rightarrow\ \ \mathtt{cons}\ X^{\mathtt{z}}\ (\mathit{Filter}\ \mathit{Nz}\ \mathit{XS})$

$\rightarrow^*\ \mathtt{cons}\ \mathtt{z}\ (\mathit{Filter}\ \mathit{Nz}\ \mathit{XS})$

After labelling, we have $\mathsf{Failures} = \{(\mathit{Filter}, \{\mathtt{z}, \mathtt{s}\ v_0\})\}$. Observe that there are no labels on N in line 2, due to the fact that $\mathsf{labelTm}$ failed.

Feasibility. For a trace α in $\widetilde{\mathcal{P}_{\mathcal{G}}}$ to be feasible two properties are required. First, the non-determinism introduced by the abstraction should be well behaved and second, there should be a term in the input that is able to trigger the trace, i.e. when given as an argument to Main, the rest of the trace follows. The first of these conditions is the subject of the step case in $\mathsf{labelSeq}$, the second is the subject of the base case. Hence, if after performing $\mathsf{labelSeq}(\alpha)$ it is the case that $\mathsf{Failures} = \emptyset$, then we say α is *feasible*. The justification is the following lemma.

Lemma 8. *Let α be a feasible reduction sequence in $\widetilde{\mathcal{P}_{\mathcal{G}}}$ with error-witness q. Then there exists a term $t \in \mathcal{L}(\mathcal{G})$ and a finite reduction sequence $\mathit{Main}\ t \Rightarrow \cdots$ in $\mathcal{P}$ with error witness q.*

The witness to soundness, which appears in the proof of Theorem 2, will always be feasible. We say that any trace that is not feasible is *spurious*.

5.2 Refinement

When a reduction sequence in $\widetilde{\mathcal{P}_{\mathcal{G}}}$ is shown to be spurious, the problem can always be traced back to an occurrence of pattern-matching (notice that, by definition, the single parameter of the defining rule for Main is always a pattern). Since the only loss of accuracy in the abstraction is in the way that data bound in pattern matches is handled during reduction, our remedy for infeasibility is to increase precision in the pattern matching rules of $\widetilde{\mathcal{P}_{\mathcal{G}}}$.

Our strategy is based on the observation that, due to the particular way in which the abstract wPMRS is constructed from the composite PMRS, the terminal symbol-labelled parts of each pattern are accurately preserved in the RHS of the defining rules of the abstraction. Based on the depth of pattern matches in the counterexample trace, we unfold patterns in the defining rules of $\mathcal{P}$ in a way that preserves the the set of possible reduction sequences.

Pattern-matching depth. To determine how much to unfold we define a measure $\mathsf{depth} : T(\Sigma, \mathcal{N}, \mathcal{V}) \rightarrow \mathbb{N}$, which quantifies the extent to which a term can be matched, as follows:

$$\mathsf{depth}(x) = 0$$
$$\mathsf{depth}(F\ t_1\ \cdots\ t_m) = 1$$
$$\mathsf{depth}(a\ t_1\ \cdots\ t_m) = 1 + \bigsqcup_{\mathbb{N}}\{\,\mathsf{depth}(t_i) \mid 1 \leq i \leq m\,\}$$

Given a set of non-terminals $\mathcal{N}$, a *depth profile* for $\mathcal{N}$ is a map $\mathcal{N} \rightarrow \mathbb{N}$. We assign a depth profile to a set of rules to quantify, for each non-terminal F, how accurately the defining rules for F model pattern-matching. Given a set of rules $\mathcal{R}$ defining non-terminals from $\mathcal{N}$, let the depth profile of $\mathcal{R}$, denoted $\mathsf{dp}(\mathcal{R})$, be the function:

$$\mathsf{dp}(\mathcal{R})(F) = \bigsqcup_{\mathbb{N}}\{\,\mathsf{depth}(p) \mid F\ x_1\ \cdots\ x_m\ p \longrightarrow t \in \mathcal{R}\,\}$$

Depth profiles can be naturally ordered pointwise, so that if d and d' are depth profiles over the same domain $\mathcal{N}$, then $d \leq d'$ iff $d(F) \leq d'(F)$ for all $F \in \mathcal{N}$.

Unfolding. To capture the result of unfolding we first introduce two auxiliary definitions. To aid readability, in each of them we will annotate fresh variables with their implied types by a superscript. The set of *atomic patterns* of type b, $\mathbb{A}_b$ is the set $\{\,a\ z_1^{b_1}\ \cdots\ z_{\mathsf{ar}(a)}^{b_{\mathsf{ar}(a)}} \mid a : b_1 \rightarrow \cdots \rightarrow b_{\mathsf{ar}(a)} \rightarrow b \in \Sigma\,\}$. For each $n \in \mathbb{N}$ we define the non-overlapping, exhaustive set of patterns of type b and depth n, $\mathsf{pats}_b(n)$:

$$\mathsf{pats}_b(0) = \{z^b\}$$
$$\mathsf{pats}_b(n+1) = \{\,p[q_1, \ldots, q_m/x_1^{b_1}, \cdots, x_m^{b_m}] \mid \varphi\,\}$$

where φ stands for the conjunction:

$$p \in \mathsf{pats}_b(n)\ \ \&\ \ \mathsf{FV}(p) = \{x_1^{b_1}, \ldots, x_m^{b_m}\}\ \ \&\ \ \forall i\, q_i \in \mathbb{A}_{b_i}$$

Hence, the depth 2 family of patterns of type $\mathbf{natlist}$ are given by (n, x and xs arbitrary variables):

$$\mathtt{nil},\quad \mathtt{cons\ z\ nil},\quad \mathtt{cons\ z}\ (\mathtt{cons}\ x\ xs),$$
$$\mathtt{cons}\ (\mathtt{s}\ n)\ \mathtt{nil},\quad \mathtt{cons}\ (\mathtt{s}\ n)\ (\mathtt{cons}\ x\ xs)$$

To unfold the rules of a PMRS $\mathcal{P}$ according to a depth profile d, one constructs a new PMRS $\mathcal{P}'$ whose rule-set is enlarged so that, for a given non-terminal F of type $\tau_1 \rightarrow \cdots \rightarrow \tau_m \rightarrow b \rightarrow o$, there is a number of defining rules which is equal to the number of patterns of type b and depth $d(F)$. For each of these rules the corresponding right-hand side is constructed by using the existing $\mathcal{P}$ rules as a template.

Let $\mathcal{P} = \langle \Sigma, \mathcal{N}, \mathcal{R}, \mathit{Main} \rangle$ be a PMRS and let d be a depth profile with domain $\mathcal{N}$ such that $\mathsf{dp}(\mathcal{R}) \leq d$. The d-unfolding of $\mathcal{P}$ is the PMRS $\langle \Sigma, \mathcal{N}, \mathcal{R}', \mathit{Main} \rangle$, where $\mathcal{R}'$ is the set such that, for all substitutions σ, $F\ x_1\ \cdots\ x_m\ \sigma p \longrightarrow \sigma t \in \mathcal{R}'$ iff:

(i) $F\ x_1\ \cdots\ x_m\ p \longrightarrow t \in \mathcal{R}$

(ii) and p is of type b

(iii) and $q \in \mathsf{pats}_b(d(F))$

(iv) and $q = \sigma p$

Example 11. Let $\mathcal{P}$ be as in Example 2 and let d be the depth profile given by the following rule:

$$d(F) = \begin{cases} 2 & \text{when } F = \mathit{Filter} \\ \mathsf{dp}(\mathcal{R})(F) & \text{otherwise} \end{cases}$$

Then the d-unfolding of $\mathcal{P}$ is the PMRS $\mathcal{P}'$, whose rules are the same as $\mathcal{P}$ except that the two rules for Filter have been replaced by the five rules in Figure 3.

Consider an abstraction $\widetilde{\mathcal{P}'_{\mathcal{G}}}$ of the PMRS $\mathcal{P}'$ in Example 11 (with $\mathcal{G}$ as given in Example 2). The only non-determinism that is introduced in constructing the abstraction is in replacing the pattern-matching variables in the right-hand sides of the defining rules by pattern-symbols. Due to the unfolding of the Filter rules in $\mathcal{P}'$ (and hence in $\widetilde{\mathcal{P}'_{\mathcal{G}}}$), there is no longer a possibility to make the problematic reduction:

$\mathit{Filter}\ (\mathit{Nz}\ (\mathtt{cons}\ N\ \mathit{ListN})$

$\rightarrow\ \mathit{If}\ (\mathit{Cons}\ X\ (\mathit{Filter}\ \mathit{Nz}\ \mathit{XS}))\ (\mathit{Filter}\ \mathit{Nz}\ \mathit{XS})\ (\mathit{Nz}\ X)$

since the unfolded rules require more of the non-determinism (in the non-terminal symbols N and ListN) to be resolved earlier.

$$\begin{aligned}
\mathit{Filter}\ p\,\texttt{nil} &\longrightarrow \texttt{nil}\\
\mathit{Filter}\ p\,(\texttt{cons z nil}) &\longrightarrow \mathit{If}\ (\texttt{cons z}\ (\mathit{Filter}\ p\,\texttt{nil}))\ (\mathit{Filter}\ p\,\texttt{nil})\ (p\,\texttt{z})\\
\mathit{Filter}\ p\,(\texttt{cons z}\ (\texttt{cons}\ v_0\ v_1)) &\longrightarrow \mathit{If}\ (\texttt{cons z}\ (\mathit{Filter}\ p\,(\texttt{cons}\ v_0\ v_1)))\ (\mathit{Filter}\ p\,(\texttt{cons}\ v_0\ v_1))\ (p\,\texttt{z})\\
\mathit{Filter}\ p\,(\texttt{cons}\ (\texttt{s}\ v_2)\ \texttt{nil}) &\longrightarrow \mathit{If}\ (\texttt{cons}\ (\texttt{s}\ v_2)\ (\mathit{Filter}\ p\,\texttt{nil}))\ (\mathit{Filter}\ p\,\texttt{nil})\ (p\,(\texttt{s}\ v_2))\\
\mathit{Filter}\ p\,(\texttt{cons}\ (\texttt{s}\ v_3)\ (\texttt{cons}\ v_4\ v_5)) &\longrightarrow \mathit{If}\ (\texttt{cons}\ (\texttt{s}\ v_3)\ (\mathit{Filter}\ p\,(\texttt{cons}\ v_4\ v_5)))\ (\mathit{Filter}\ p\,(\texttt{cons}\ v_4\ v_5))\ (p\,(\texttt{s}\ v_3))
\end{aligned}$$

Figure 3. Depth-2 unfolding of the defining rules for *Filter*.

Refinement. Given a PMRS $\mathcal{P}$ and an infeasible error trace α in the abstraction of $\mathcal{P}$, we can obtain refined abstractions by unfolding the rules of $\mathcal{P}$ according to the depths of terms in the Failures set, then using the unfolded PMRS as the input to the next cycle of the abstraction-refinement loop.

Lemma 9. *Let $\mathcal{P} = \langle \Sigma, \mathcal{N}, \mathcal{R}, Main\rangle$ be a PMRS and $\widetilde{\mathcal{P}_\mathcal{G}}$ be the abstraction of $\mathcal{P}$ (starting from terms in $\mathcal{L}(\mathcal{G})$). Let α be a counterexample trace of $\widetilde{\mathcal{P}_\mathcal{G}}$ which is spurious with* Failures *set S. Let d be the depth profile with domain $\mathcal{N}$ defined by:*

$$d(F) = \mathsf{dp}(\mathcal{R})(F) + \bigsqcup_{\mathbb{N}}\{\,\mathsf{depth}(t) \mid (F, P) \in S,\ t \in P\,\}$$

and let $\mathcal{P}'$ be the d-unfolding of $\mathcal{P}$. Then α is not a reduction sequence in the abstraction $\widetilde{\mathcal{P}'_\mathcal{G}}$ of $\mathcal{P}'$.

Although it is clear that, given any spurious trace in some abstraction $\widetilde{\mathcal{P}_\mathcal{G}}$, it is possible to construct a refinement that eliminates it from any future abstraction $\widetilde{\mathcal{P}'_\mathcal{G}}$, the set of traces of $\widetilde{\mathcal{P}_\mathcal{G}}$ and the set of traces of $\widetilde{\mathcal{P}'_\mathcal{G}}$ are incomparable since, in general, there are new pattern-variables introduced in the refinement and hence new pattern-symbols into $\widetilde{\mathcal{P}'_\mathcal{G}}$. However, there is a very close relationship between the depth of a PMRS and the feasibility of reduction sequences in its abstraction.

Lemma 10. *Fix $n \in \mathbb{N}$. Then given any PMRS $\mathcal{P}$ and input grammar $\mathcal{G}$, there is a depth-profile d such that, if $\widetilde{\mathcal{P}'_\mathcal{G}}$ is the abstraction of the d-unfolding of $\mathcal{P}$, then all length-$m \leq n$ reduction sequences in $\widetilde{\mathcal{P}'_\mathcal{G}}$ are feasible.*

A consequence of this close relationship between depth and feasibility is that, under the assumption that the model-checker always reports the shortest counterexample trace, if the PMRS $\mathcal{P}$ (when run from a term in $\mathcal{I}$) does violate the property then eventually the abstraction-refinement cycle will produce a feasible counterexample trace demonstrating the fact.

Theorem 4 (Semi-completeness). *Let $(\mathcal{P}, \mathcal{I}, \mathcal{A})$ be a no-instance of the verification problem. Then the algorithm terminates with a feasible counterexample trace.*

6. Related work

We compare and contrast our work with a number of topics in the literature broadly related to flow analysis and verification of functional programs.

Higher-order multi-parameter tree transducer. As discussed in the Introduction, Kobayashi [6] introduced a type-based verification method for temporal properties of higher-order functional programs generated from finite base types. In a follow-up paper [9], Kobayashi et al. introduced a kind of tree transducer, called HMTT, that uses pattern-matching, taking trees as input and returning an output tree. They studied the problem of whether the tree generated by a given HMTT meets the output specification, assuming that the input trees meet the input specification, where both input and output specifications are regular tree languages. A sound but incomplete algorithm has been proposed for the HMTT verification problem by reduction to a model checking problem for recursion schemes with finite data domain (which can then be solved by a variation of Kobayashi's type-based algorithm). Though our algorithm in the present paper solves a similar kind of verification problem, it is not straightforward to compare it with the HMTT work [9]. It would appear that PMRS is a more general (and natural) formalism than HMTT. What is clear is that our approach to the over-approximation is very different: we use binding analysis to obtain a wPMRS which generates an over-approximation of the reachable term-trees, whereas Kobayashi et al. use automaton states to approximate input trees.

Approximating collecting semantics and flow analysis. In a seminal paper [5], Jones and Andersen studied the (data) flow analysis of functional programs by safely approximating the behaviour of a certain class of untyped, first-order, term rewriting systems with pattern matching. Their algorithm takes a regular set $\mathcal{I}$ of input terms, a program $\mathcal{P}$ and returns a regular tree grammar which is a "safe" description of the set of all reachable (constructor) terms of the computation of $\mathcal{P}$ with inputs form $\mathcal{I}$. Precisely, the algorithm computes a safe approximation of the *collecting semantics* of $\mathcal{P}$ relative to $\mathcal{I}$, which assigns to each rewrite rule a set of pairs (θ, g_θ) such that θ is a substitution (*realisable* in the course of such a computation) of actual parameters to the formal parameters of the rule, and g_θ is a term reachable from the RHS of the rule with the substitution θ. The collecting semantics is undecidable in general. Jones and Andersen was able to obtain, for each rewrite rule, a regular over-approximation of the set of realisable bindings $\{\, x \mapsto \theta\, x \mid \text{realisable } \theta \,\}$ for each formal parameter x of the rule, and the set of reachable terms $\{\, g_\theta \mid \text{realisable } \theta \,\}$, by decoupling the pair (θ, g_θ).

There are two directions in which Jones and Andersen's algorithm may be refined. Consider the setting of simply-typed functional programs with pattern-matching algebraic data types. Recent advances in the model checking of higher-order recursion schemes (notably the decidability of MSO theories of trees generated by higher-order recursion schemes [14]) indicate that the bindings of *non* pattern-matching variables, whether higher-order or not, can be precisely analysed algorithmically (though with extremely high asymptotic complexity). Jones and Andersen's algorithm builds a regular approximation of the binding set of every variable. A natural question is whether one can improve it by approximating *only* the bindings of pattern-matching variables, while analysing other variables (including all higher-order variables) precisely using the method in [14]. The work presented here offers a positive answer to the question. Another direction worth investigating is to seek to preserve, for each rewrite rule, as much of the connection between realisable substitutions θ and reachable terms g_θ as one can get away with. In an recent dissertation [10], Kochems has presented just such an algorithm using a kind of linear indexed tree grammars (which are equivalent to context-free tree grammars) whereby the indices are the realisable substitutions.

To compare our algorithm with Jones and Andersen's, it is instructive to apply their algorithm to our Example 8. Their framework can be extended to simply-typed and higher-order programs. It is an old idea in functional programming that an higher-order expression, such as an "incompletely applied" function $(\cdots(f\,e_1)\cdots)e_m$ where the type of f has arity greater than m, may be viewed as a closure. (Indeed, closures are a standard implementation technique.) From this viewpoint, a higher-order non-terminal is regarded, not as a defined operator, but as a constructor, and closures are formed using a *binary closure-forming operator* @. Thus, the second clause of $Map2$ is written in their system as

$$@\,(@\,(@\,Map2\;\varphi)\;\psi)\;(\mathtt{cons}\;x\;xs)\;\longrightarrow\;\mathtt{cons}\;(@\;\varphi\;x)\;(@\;(@\;(@\;Map2\;\psi)\;\varphi)\;xs)$$

Observe that in this setting, $Map2$ is a constructor (i.e. terminal) symbol, and the expression $(@\;(@\;Map2\;\varphi)\;\psi)$ a pattern. Call the *binding set* of a variable the set of terms that may be bound to it at some point in the course of a computation. The approximating grammar produced by Jones and Andersen's algorithm is always regular (equivalently an order-0 recursion scheme). This is achieved by over-approximating the binding set of *every* variable (including higher-order ones, such as φ). The resultant grammar generates all finite lists of 0's and 1's, which is less precise than our algorithm.

Control flow analysis. Established in the 80's by Jones [4], Shivers [17] and others, *Control Flow Analysis (CFA)* of functional programs has remained an active research topic ever since (see e.g. Midtgaard's survey [12] and the book by Nielson et al. [13]). The aim of CFA is to approximate the flow of control within a program phrase in the course of a computation.

In a functional computation, control flow is determined by a sequence of function calls (possibly unknown at compile time); thus CFA amounts to approximating the values that may be substituted for bound variables during the computation. Since these values are (denoted by) pieces of syntax, CFA reduces to an algorithm that assigns *closures* (subterms of the examined term paired with substitutions for free variables) to bound variables. Reachability analysis and CFA are clearly related: for example, the former can aid the latter because unreachable parts of the term can be safely excluded from the range of closure assignment. There are however important differences: on one hand, CFA algorithms are *approximation algorithms* designed to address a more general problem; on the other, because CFA considers terms in isolation of its possible (program) contexts, the corresponding notion of reachability essentially amounts to reachability in the reduction graph.

Functional reachability. Based on the fully abstract game semantics, *traversals* [1, 14] are a (particularly accurate) model of the flow of control within a term; they can therefore be viewed as a CFA method. Using traversals, a new notion of reachability of higher-order functional computation (in the setting of PCF) is studied in [16], called *Contextual Reachability*: given a PCF term M of type A and a subterm N^α with occurrence α, is there a program context $C[-]$ such that $C[M]$ is a closed term of ground type and the evaluation of $C[M]$ causes control to flow to N^α?

7. Conclusion

Recursion schemes with pattern matching (PMRS) are an accurate and natural model of computation for functional programs have pattern-matching algebraic data types. We have given an algorithm that, given a PMRS $\mathcal{P}$ and a regular set $\mathcal{I}$ of input terms, constructs a *recursion scheme with weak pattern-matching* (wPMRS) that (i) over-approximates the set of terms reachable from under rewriting from $\mathcal{P}$ (ii) has a decidable model checking problem (relative to trivial automata). Finally, because of the precise analysis at higher-orders, we show that there is a simple notion of automatic abstraction-refinement, which gives rise to a semi-completeness property.

For future work, we plan to build an implementation of the verification algorithm for a real functional programming language. We shall be especially interested in investigating the scalability of our approach.

Acknowledgements. We would like to thank the anonymous reviewers for many useful comments.

References

[1] W. Blum and C.-H. L. Ong. Path-correspondence theorems and their applications. Preprint, 2009.

[2] E. M. Clarke, O. Grumberg, S. Jha, Y. Lu, and H. Veith. Counterexample-guided abstraction refinement. In *CAV '00: Proceedings of the 12th International Conference on Computer Aided Verification*, pages 154–169, London, UK, 2000. Springer-Verlag.

[3] A. Igarashi and N. Kobayashi. Resource usage analysis. *ACM Trans. Program. Lang. Syst.*, 27(2):264–313, 2005.

[4] N. D. Jones. Flow analysis of lambda expressions (preliminary version). In *Proceedings of the 8th Colloquium on Automata, Languages and Programming*, pages 114–128. Springer-Verlag, 1981. ISBN 3-540-10843-2.

[5] N. D. Jones and N. Andersen. Flow analysis of lazy higher-order functional programs. *Theoretical Computer Science*, 375:120–136, 2007.

[6] N. Kobayashi. Types and higher-order recursion schemes for verification of higher-order programs. In *Proceedings of POPL 2009*, pages 416–428. ACM Press, 2009.

[7] N. Kobayashi. Model-checking higher-order functions. In *PPDP*, pages 25–36, 2009.

[8] N. Kobayashi and C.-H. L. Ong. A type theory equivalent to the modal mu-calculus model checking ofhigher-order recursion schemes. In *Proceedings of LICS 2009*. IEEE Computer Society, 2009.

[9] N. Kobayashi, N. Tabuchi, and H. Unno. Higher-order multi-parameter tree transducers and recursion schemes for program verification. In *POPL*, pages 495–508, 2010.

[10] J. Kochems. Approximating reachable terms of functional programs. University of Oxford MMathsCompSc thesis, 2010.

[11] R. P. Kurshan. *Computer Aided Verification of Coordinating Processes*. Princeton University Press, 1994.

[12] J. Midtgaard. Control-flow analysis of functional programs. Technical Report BRICS RS-07-18, DAIMI, Department of Computer Science, University of Aarhus, Aarhus, Denmark, Dec 2007. URL `http://www.brics.dk/RS/07/18/BRICS-RS-07-18.pdf`.

[13] F. Nielson, H. R. Nielson, and C. Hankin. *Principles of Program Analysis*. Springer-Verlag New York, 1999.

[14] C.-H. L. Ong. On model-checking trees generated by higher-order recursion schemes. In *Proceedings 21st Annual IEEE Symposium on Logic in Computer Science, Seattle*, pages 81–90. Computer Society Press, 2006. Long version (55 pp.) downloadable at `users.comlab.ox.ac.uk/luke.ong/`.

[15] C.-H. L. Ong and S. J. Ramsay. Verifying higher-order functional programs with pattern-matching algebraic data types. Long version, available from: `https://mjolnir.comlab.ox.ac.uk/papers/pmrs.pdf`.

[16] C.-H. L. Ong and N. Tzevelekos. Functional reachability. In *LICS*, pages 286–295, 2009.

[17] O. Shivers. *Control-flow analysis of higher-order languages*. PhD thesis, Carnegie-Mellon University, 1991.

Streaming Transducers for Algorithmic Verification of Single-pass List-processing Programs *

Rajeev Alur
University of Pennsylvania
alur@cis.upenn.edu

Pavol Černý
IST Austria
pavol.cerny@ist.ac.at

Abstract

We introduce *streaming data string transducers* that map input data strings to output data strings in a single left-to-right pass in linear time. Data strings are (unbounded) sequences of data values, tagged with symbols from a finite set, over a potentially infinite data domain that supports only the operations of equality and ordering. The transducer uses a finite set of states, a finite set of variables ranging over the data domain, and a finite set of variables ranging over data strings. At every step, it can make decisions based on the next input symbol, updating its state, remembering the input data value in its data variables, and updating data-string variables by concatenating data-string variables and new symbols formed from data variables, while avoiding duplication. We establish that the problems of checking functional equivalence of two streaming transducers, and of checking whether a streaming transducer satisfies pre/post verification conditions specified by streaming acceptors over input/output data-strings, are in PSPACE.

We identify a class of imperative and a class of functional programs, manipulating lists of data items, which can be effectively translated to streaming data-string transducers. The imperative programs dynamically modify a singly-linked heap by changing next-pointers of heap-nodes and by adding new nodes. The main restriction specifies how the next-pointers can be used for traversal. We also identify an expressively equivalent fragment of functional programs that traverse a list using syntactically restricted recursive calls. Our results lead to algorithms for assertion checking and for checking functional equivalence of two programs, written possibly in different programming styles, for commonly used routines such as insert, delete, and reverse.

Categories and Subject Descriptors D.2.4 [*Software Engineering*]: Software/Program Verification—Formal Methods, Model Checking; F.3.1 [*Logics and Meanings of Programs*]: Specifying and Verifying and Reasoning about Programs—Mechanical verification

General Terms Verification, Theory, Algorithms

Keywords transducers, algorithmic software verification, lists

* This research was partially supported by NSF grants CCF 0915777 and CCF 0905464.

POPL'11, January 26–28, 2011, Austin, Texas, USA.

1. Introduction

We propose streaming transducers as an abstract and analyzable model for programs that access and modify sequences of data items in a single pass. The idea of using transducers for modeling such programs is a natural one. However, the class of regular transductions, which has appealing theoretical properties such as MSO characterization, is defined by two-way transducers. As an example, consider the *reverse* transduction that reverses the input string. It is not definable using classical one-way transducers (such as Mealy machines), we need a second (backward) pass during which the output is produced. On the other hand, this transduction can easily be computed by a single-pass program that traverses a list both in the settings of imperative programs manipulating heap-allocated lists and functional programs using tail recursion. Our streaming transducer model can capture such computations naturally. Furthermore, we show that verification problems such as checking functional equivalence, assertion checking, and checking correctness with respect to pre/post conditions, are decidable for this transducer model, even in the presence of values from an unbounded data domain.

In the proposed model, a (deterministic) *streaming data-string transducers* map input data strings to output data strings in a single left-to-right pass in linear time. A *data string* is a sequence of items of type `data` $\times$ `tag`, where `data` is a potentially infinite set of data values, and `tag` is a finite set of labels. The only operations allowed on the type `data` are tests for equality and ordering, and this restriction is essential for decidability. The transducer uses a finite set of states, a finite set of variables ranging over `data`, and a finite set of variables ranging over data strings. At every step, it can make decisions based on the current state, the tag of the next input symbol, and the ordering relationship of the data of the next input symbol with the data values stored in data variables. It can update the state, modify data variables using the input data value, and update the data-string variables using assignments whose right-hand-sides are concatenations of data-string variables and new symbols formed using data variables. A key restriction is that a data-string variable can be used at most once in a right-hand-side expression at each step. Multiple data-string variables are necessary for the transducer to compute different possible chunks of the output, and the restriction on how they can be used ensures that at every step there is merely a rearrangement of outputs computed so far without duplication.

We consider the following two decision problems for streaming transducers: (1) *Equivalence:* given two streaming transducers, do they define the same (partial) functions? (2) *Pre-post condition checking:* given a streaming transducer, a pre-condition and a post-condition, both expressed by similarly defined streaming acceptors over data strings, is it the case that for every input satisfying the pre-condition, the corresponding transducer output satisfies the postcondition? We show both problems to be in PSPACE. We also show that extending the model along several possible directions leads quickly to undecidability of basic problems such as reachability.

We then identify a class of programs that precisely correspond to the streaming data-string transducers. The input to a program is a single list with elements of type `data` × `tag`, possibly with additional arguments of types `data`, `tag`, and `bool`, and the output is a single list, possibly with additional returned values of types `data`, `tag`, and `bool`. The key restriction, needed for decidability of verification problems, is that the program computes the output in a single pass processing the next item of the list at each step. A number of commonly used routines such as insertion, deletion, membership, reversal, sorting with respect to tags (but not data values), naturally satisfy this restriction.

For heap-manipulating imperative programs, the input list is stored in a heap of nodes each of which can store a tag, a data value, and a next-node pointer. During the computation of the program, the next-pointers induce an unranked forest structure over the nodes. The program accesses the heap using a finite number of pointer variables and uses a finite number of data variables. The program can add new nodes to the heap, change values stored at nodes referenced by pointer variables, and also modify next-pointers of such nodes. A key restriction on the traversal of the heap using next-pointers is that the only legal use of the next-field on the right-hand-side is in the assignment *curr* := *curr.next*, where *curr* is the unique pointer initially pointing to the head of the input list. We also show that for this class of programs, a variety of assertion checking problems (such as "is a program location reachable," and "does the heap stay acyclic") are solvable in PSPACE.

Finally, we present a class of list-processing functional programs which traverse an input list from left to right using recursive calls. The key restriction is that a call to the function f with input list l can recursively call f with input `tail l`, and returns value obtained by composing its input arguments and the values returned by the recursive call without examining them. We show that this class precisely corresponds to the streaming data string transducers. Thus, the results of this paper show how to automatically compile two list-processing programs, one written in imperative style, and one written in functional style, into an intermediate low-level transducer model, and algorithmically check if the two are semantically equivalent.

2. Streaming transducers

2.1 Data strings and transductions

A *data domain* is a totally ordered, possibly infinite, set D of data values. We will use $<$ to denote the strict total order over D. Throughout this paper, assume D to be fixed. A *data symbol* over Σ, where Σ is a finite set of symbols or *tags*, is a pair (σ, d) with $\sigma \in \Sigma$ and $d \in D$. A *data string* w over Σ is a finite sequence $(\sigma_1, d_1), (\sigma_2, d_2), \ldots (\sigma_k, d_k)$ of data symbols over Σ. A *data language* over Σ is a set L of data strings over Σ. A *(deterministic) data transduction* from an input alphabet Σ to an output alphabet Γ is a partial function F from data strings over Σ to data strings over Γ. For a data transduction F from an input alphabet Σ to an output alphabet Γ, the *domain* of F is the data language over Σ consisting of data strings w such that $F(w)$ is defined.

As an example, let D be the set of strings over ASCII characters ordered by the standard lexicographic ordering. Let Σ contain two tags *private* and *public*. A data symbol denotes an entry in an address-book consisting of a name tagged either as private or public. A data string represents an address-book. Here are a few examples of data languages: language L_1 consists of all data strings in which names appear in the alphabetic order (that is, data symbols are sorted in an increasing order according to $<$ over data values); and language L_2 consists of all data strings that do not contain duplicate entries. A few examples of useful data transductions are: transduction F_1 maps a data string to its reverse; transduction F_2 maps a data string w to $w_1.w_2$, where w_1 is the subsequence of w containing private entries, and w_2 is the subsequence of w containing public entries; and transduction F_3 deletes an entry (*private*,d) from the input data string if the string also contains (*public*,d). To model operations such as insertion and deletion that take data values/symbols as inputs in addition to a data string, we can encode all inputs in a single data string. For example, the transduction F_4, given an input data string $(\sigma, d).w$ checks if names appear in the alphabetic order in the tail w, and if so, it returns w with (σ, d) inserted in the correct position to maintain the output string sorted (F_4 is undefined if the input string is empty, or if the tail of the input string is not sorted).

2.2 Transducer definition

We now describe our model of deterministic transducers. The transducer reads an input data string left-to-right in a single pass, and computes an output data string. The transducer uses a finite set of states, a finite set of data variables that range over data values, and a finite set of data string variables that range over data strings over the output alphabet. At each step, the transducer reads the next data symbol of the input string, and chooses a transition depending on the current state, the tag of the input symbol, and the ordering relationship of the data value of the input symbol with values of all its data variables. The transition updates the state, updates the data variables possibly using the input data value, and updates the data string variables in parallel using assignments whose right-hand-sides are concatenations of data string variables and new data symbols formed using data variables. When the transducer consumes the entire input string, the final output string is produced by similarly concatenating data string and data variables. A key restriction is that a data string variable can be used at most once in a right-hand-side expression in a transition, and thus, at every step, there is merely a rearrangement of output chunks computed so far, without duplication.

We now define the model formally. A *(deterministic) streaming data-string transducer* (SDST) S from an input alphabet Σ to an output alphabet Γ consists of a finite set of states Q, an initial state $q_0 \in Q$, a finite set of data variables V, a data variable *curr* $\in V$ used to refer to the data value of the current input symbol, a finite set of data string variables X, a partial output function O from Q to $((\Gamma \times V) \cup X)^*$, a finite set E of transitions of the form $(q, \sigma, \varphi, q', \alpha)$, where $q \in Q$ is a source state, $\sigma \in \Sigma$ is an input tag, φ is a Boolean formula over atomic constraints of the form $v <$ *curr* and *curr* $< v$ with $v \in V$, $q' \in Q$ is a target state, and α is an assignment mapping data variables V to V and data string variables X to $((\Gamma \times V) \cup X)^*$. It is required that (1) for each $q \in Q$ and $x \in X$, there is at most one occurrence of x in $O(q)$, and (2) for each transition $(q, \sigma, \varphi, q', \alpha)$, for each $x \in X$, x appears at most once in the set of strings $\{\alpha(y) \mid y \in X\}$, and (3) for each pair of transitions $(q, \sigma, \varphi, q', \alpha)$ and $(q, \sigma, \varphi', q'', \alpha')$ with the same source state and input tag, the tests φ and φ' are mutually exclusive (that is, $\varphi \wedge \varphi'$ is unsatisfiable).

A *valuation* β for such a transducer S is a *partial* function over data and data string variables such that for each data variable $v \in V$, either $\beta(v)$ is undefined or is a data value in D, and for each data string variable $x \in X$, either $\beta(x)$ is undefined or is a data string over the output alphabet Γ. Such a valuation naturally extends to a partial Boolean function to evaluate tests. Each test φ is a Boolean formula over atomic constraints of the form $v <$ *curr* and *curr* $< v$ with $v \in V$. The value $\beta(\varphi)$ is defined if $\beta(v)$ is defined for all data variables v occurring in φ, and if so, φ is evaluated using the values β assigns to these data variables. A valuation β also extends to strings in $((\Gamma \times V) \cup X)^*$: given a string u in $((\Gamma \times V) \cup X)^*$, the valuation $\beta(u)$ is defined when β is defined for all the data and data string variables occurring in u, and if so, $\beta(u)$ is the data string over the output alphabet Γ obtained by replacing each data string variable x in u with the data string $\beta(x)$ and each data variable v in u with the data value $\beta(v)$.

Given an SDST S, a *configuration* of S is a pair (q, β), where q is a state in Q, and β is a valuation for S. The initial configuration is (q_0, β_0) where q_0 is the initial state of S, $\beta_0(v)$ is undefined for each data variable v, and $\beta_0(x)$ is the empty string for each data string variable x. The one-step transition relation over the set of configurations is defined as follows. Consider a configuration (q, β) and an input data symbol (σ, d). The transducer first updates the valuation β to β' by setting *curr* to the input data value d. Next, let $(q, \sigma, \varphi, q', \alpha)$ be a transition such that β' satisfies the test φ. If there is such a transition, then the updated state is q', and the updated value of each data and data string variable x is obtained by evaluating the right-hand-side $\alpha(x)$ according to the valuation β'. That is, if there exists a transition $(q, \sigma, \varphi, q', \alpha)$ such that $\beta'(\varphi) = 1$, for $\beta' = \beta[curr \mapsto d]$, then $(q, \beta) \xrightarrow{\sigma, d} (q', \beta' \cdot \alpha)$. Determinism ensures that each configuration has at most one successor for a given input data symbol. The transition relation extends to a multi-step relation over input data strings in the natural way. Given an input data string w over Σ, $(q_0, \beta_0) \xrightarrow{w} (q, \beta)$ means that the configuration of the transducer after reading the input data string w is (q, β) (if no such configuration exists that means no transition is enabled at some step). The semantics of S is then defined to be the transduction $[\![S]\!]$ defined as: for an input data string w over Σ, if $(q_0, \beta_0) \xrightarrow{w} (q, \beta)$ and $O(q)$ is defined then $[\![S]\!](w)$ is defined to be $\beta(O(q))$, otherwise $[\![S]\!](w)$ is undefined.

We call a data transduction F from an input alphabet Σ to an output alphabet Γ to be *streaming-regular* if there exists an SDST S such that $[\![S]\!] = F$.

2.3 Examples

To illustrate our definition of transducers, let us consider the transductions mentioned in Section 2.1. The transduction F_1 to reverse the input data string can be implemented by a streaming data-string transducer S_1 with a single state, a single data variable *curr*, and a single data string variable x. The input tag σ is processed by the self-loop transition with update $x := (\sigma, curr).x$ (by default, a variable that is not explicitly updated, remains unchanged; we omit such assignments for readability). The output function outputs x. No tests on input data values are needed. Notice that classical definitions of transducers allow adding output symbols only at the end of the output computed so far. Adding a symbol to the front of the string variable x at each step is crucial to implement reverse in a single left-to-right pass.

Now let us consider the transduction F_2 that maps a data string w to $w_1.w_2$, where w_1 and w_2 are the subsequences of w containing private and public entries, respectively. This can be implemented by an SDST S_2 that maintains two data string variables x_1 and x_2, and a single data variable *curr*. At each step, if the tag of current input symbol is *private*, the symbol is added to x_1 (the precise assignment is $[x_1, x_2] := [x_1.(private, curr), x_2]$), otherwise the symbol is added to x_2 in a symmetric manner. The output function outputs the concatenation $x_1.x_2$. Note that it is not possible to implement this transduction by an SDST using just one variable.

The transduction F_3 deletes a private entry from the input data string if the string also contains a public entry with a matching data value. When reading an input symbol with data value d, the streaming algorithm needs to figure out if a private entry with the same data value has been encountered before. An SDST with k variables can effectively use only k data values for tests at any step,

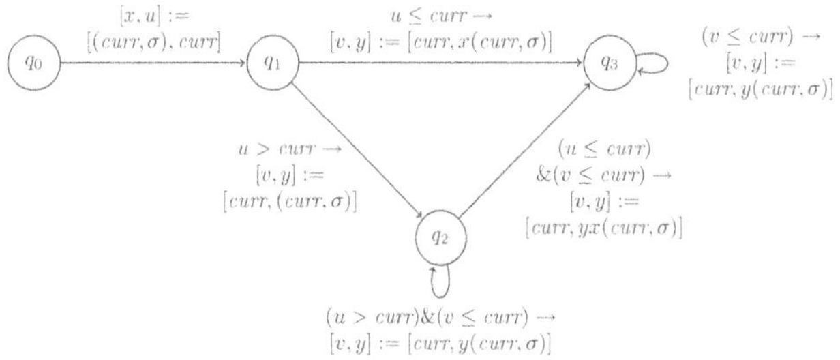

Figure 1. Transduction F_4

and since the number of possible data values in an input string is unbounded, F_3 is not streaming-regular.

Consider the transduction F_4 that inserts the head symbol of the input string in its tail, provided that the tail is sorted. The transducer S_4 uses three data variables: u to remember the head data value, v to remember the previous data value, and *curr* to refer to the current data value. It uses a data string variable x to remember the first data symbol, and y to compute the output. The transducer is shown in Figure 1. The transducer is in state q_0 initially, in state q_1 after reading one symbol, in state q_2 after reading 2 or more symbols provided the tail so far is sorted and all its data values are smaller than the head data value (stored in u), and in state q_3 after reading 2 or more symbols provided the tail so far is sorted and the head symbol has already been inserted in the output. In states q_2 and q_3, the variable v stores the previous data value, and the test $v \leq curr$ checks for sortedness of the input (v gets updated to *curr* at each step). If this test does not hold, no transition is enabled, and the output will be undefined. The transition to q_3 inserts the data symbol stored in x in the output y. The output function is undefined in state q_0, and is x in state q_1, $y.x$ in state q_2, and y in state q_3.

2.4 Streaming acceptors

A *streaming data-string acceptor* (SDSA) is a streaming data-string transducer S with an empty set of data string variables. Such an acceptor S has a finite set of data variables that can remember the data values from the input string, and can make decisions based on their relative ordering. The output alphabet plays no role in the behavior of an acceptor. Given an input data string w, either the output $[\![S]\!](w)$ is defined or undefined, and the domain of the transducer is the data language associated with the acceptor S. This is the same as saying that the output function O marks states of S as accepting or rejecting based on whether the output function O is defined or undefined at a state. We call a data language L over an alphabet Σ to be *streaming-regular* if L is accepted by a streaming data-string acceptor.

The data language L_1 consisting of sorted data strings can be defined by such an acceptor using one data variable that remembers the previous data value, along with the data variable *curr* needed to refer to the data value of the currently read symbol. Thus L_1 is a streaming-regular data language. The data language L_2 consisting of data strings without duplicate entries is not streaming-regular by an argument similar to the one for the transduction F_3.

Among different types of automata over data strings that have been studied, *data automata* [3] have emerged as a good candidate for the notion of regularity for languages of data strings. However, data automata are too expressive for our purpose as they have an undecidable emptiness problem in the presence of ordering on data values [3].

2.5 Properties

In this section, we note some properties of streaming transducers aimed at understanding their expressiveness. First, observe that a streaming data-string transducer S cannot output "new" data values. That is, for every input data string w, any data value appearing in the output data string $[\![S]\!](w)$ must appear in some symbol in w. Second, streaming transducers are *bounded* in the sense that the length of the output string is within at most a constant factor of the length of the input string.

Proposition 1. *If F is a streaming-regular transduction from Σ to Γ, then for all input data strings w over Σ, $|F(w)| = O(|w|)$.*

The boundedness depends on the fact that the parallel assignment at each step is copyless: each variable can appear in a right-hand-side expression at most once. Not only this is crucially needed for decidability of the equivalence problem, it also allows an efficient implementation: if the data strings corresponding to variables are stored in linked lists, then the assignment can be executed by only changing a constant number of pointers (proportional to the description of the transducer, but independent of the lengths of the data strings they store, and thus, independent of the length of the input string).

Proposition 2. *If F is a streaming-regular data-string transduction, then given an input string w, the output $F(w)$ can be computed in time $O(|w|)$.*

This also means that the sorting transduction that maps an input data string to its sorted version is not streaming-regular due to well-known lower bounds for sorting. Obviously streaming transducers cannot capture all linear-time streaming algorithms. As a specific example, let us revisit the transduction F_2 that maps a data string w to $w_1.w_2$, where w_1 and w_2 are the projections of w containing private and public entries, respectively. Consider the variation F_2' that maps w to a *merge* of the two projections w_1 and w_2 taking elements from the two lists in an alternate manner. This can be easily implemented in linear-time if we maintain two read-heads over the input string, one corresponding to private entries and one corresponding to public entries. Note that the emptiness problem of finite automata with multiple read-heads is undecidable, and the traversal allowed for streaming transducers is restricted by design to ensure decidability of key analysis problems. In particular, F_2' is not streaming-regular.

Let us now consider some closure properties for the class of streaming-regular transducers. Given two data transductions F_1 and F_2, and a test L as a data language, suppose we want to compute $F_1(w)$ when $w \in L$ and $F_2(w)$ otherwise. If all of F_1, F_2, and L are specified using SDSTs then we can construct an SDST for the desired transduction by a suitably modified product construction.

Proposition 3. *If F_1 and F_2 are streaming-regular data transductions from Σ to Γ, and L is a streaming-regular data language over Σ, then the following data transduction F is streaming-regular: for an input data string w over Σ, if $w \in L$ then $F(w) = F_1(w)$ else $F(w) = F_2(w)$.*

It turns out that streaming-regular data transductions are not closed under functional composition. That is, given two SDSTs S_1 and S_2, we cannot always construct an SDST S such that $S(w) = S_2(S_1(w))$.

Proposition 4. *There exist streaming-regular data transductions F_1 and F_2 from Σ to Σ such that the following data transduction F is not streaming-regular: for an input data string w over Σ, $F(w) = F_2(F_1(w))$.*

Proof. We choose Σ to be a singleton set, and thus, it plays no role. Consider the transduction F_1 that maps a data string $d_1 d_2 \cdots d_k$ to its reverse $d_k d_{k-1} \cdots d_1$. F_1 is streaming-regular. Consider the transduction F_2 that maps a data string $d_1 d_2 \cdots d_k$ to $(d_1)^k$. That is, F_2 just repeats the first data value for each input symbol read. It is easy to implement F_2 by an SDST. Now consider the composition $F = F_1 \cdot F_2$. The transduction F maps an input data string $d_1 d_2 \cdots d_k$ to $(d_k)^k$. We can prove that F is not streaming-regular. □

Note that the above proof crucially uses the fact that the data domain D is unbounded, and we can always find a "fresh" data value that has not appeared in the input string before. If we make D finite, then the streaming-regular transducers are closed under composition.

3. Imperative Programs Updating Linked Lists

We consider a class of imperative programs that manipulate heap-allocated singly-linked list data structures. Each node of the heap stores a tag, a data value, and a pointer to another node. For clarity, in this section, we will assume that the output alphabet is the same as the input alphabet, so we need to consider tags of only one type. The input data string is stored in such a heap using one node for each position (null pointer indicates the end of the list). A list-processing program is invoked with the reference to the head-node of the list as input. The program traverses the list using next-pointers, and computes using variables that range over tags, over data values, over booleans, and over pointers into the heap. It can create new nodes and add them to the heap, and can also manipulate the shape of the heap by updating the next-pointers of the nodes referenced by its pointer variables. The output data string is returned using a pointer-variable that points to the head of the list storing that output. During the computation of the program, next-pointers of two heap-nodes may point to the same node, and thus, the heap in general has a structure of an unordered forest. Since the output is computed by possibly reusing the nodes that store the input, we need careful syntactic restrictions to allow a single-pass traversal of the input list, while disallowing repeated or nested traversals. We require that a typical traversal assignment $x := y.next$ for pointer variables x and y is disallowed. The only legal use of the next-field on the right-hand-side is in the assignment *curr* := *curr.next*, where *curr* is the unique input pointer. Assignments of the form x.*next* := y to update the heap structure are allowed, provided x and *curr* are not referencing the same heap-node. An attempt to execute x.*next* := y in a state where x and *curr* reference the same heap-node, causes a runtime error (alternatively we can require each such assignment to be syntactically guarded by the boolean condition $x \neq curr$).

A program can have additional input and output parameters, and each such input/output parameter can be a data value, a boolean value, or a tag. Before we describe the syntax and the semantics in detail, let us first consider a couple of examples. The following function reverses a list in-place, and corresponds to the data transduction F_1:

```
function Reverse
  input ref curr;  output ref result := curr;
  local ref prev := curr;
  if curr ≠ nil then {
    curr := curr.next;
    while curr ≠ nil {
      result := curr;   curr := curr.next;
      result.next := prev;   prev := result;
  } }.
```

Suppose given an input data string w and an input data symbol d, we want to delete each symbol in w whose data value equals d, and return the resulting data string along with a boolean flag that indicates whether or not some symbol was actually deleted. The following function implements this:

```
function Delete
  input ref curr;  input data v;
  output ref result;  output bool b := 0;
  local ref prev;
  while (curr ≠ nil) & (curr.data = v) {
    curr := curr.next;   b := 1;
  }
  result := curr;   prev :=curr;
  if curr ≠ nil then {
    curr := curr.next;   prev.next := nil;
    while curr ≠ nil {
      if curr.data = v then {
        curr := curr.next;   b := 1;
      } else {
        prev.next := curr;   prev := curr;
        curr := curr.next;   prev.next := nil;
  }; }; }.
```

3.1 Syntax

Types: Variables are typed. The possible types are: `bool` for Boolean-valued variables, `tag` for variables ranging over the alphabet Σ, `data` for variables ranging over the data domain D along with an "undefined" value denoted $\perp$, and `ref` for reference variables that index into the data heap along with the null reference `nil`.

Variable declarations: A program variable is declared along with its type (`bool`, `tag`, `data`, or `ref`) and an annotation which can be either `local`, `input`, or `output`. The `input` annotation means that the variable is an input to the function. A function has exactly one input variable of type `ref`, and can have multiple input variables of other types. We will use *curr* to name this unique input reference variable. The `output` annotation means that the variable is an output of the function, and `local` annotation means that the variable is neither an input nor an output. There is exactly one output variable of type `ref` which is used to return a single data string. The declaration of each output and local variable has an associated value. The initial value of a variable of type `bool` or `tag` can be either a constant or an input variable of matching type. The initial value of a data variable can be either $\perp$ or an input data variable. The initial value of a pointer variable can be either *curr* or `nil`.

Data expressions and assignments: A data expression is of the form (1) a variable of type `data`, or (2) $r.data$, where r is a variable of type `ref`, denoting the data value stored in the heap-node indexed by r. A data assignment statement assigns a data expression to a data variable.

Tag expressions and assignments: A tag expression is of the form (1) a variable of type `tag`, (2) a constant σ from the alphabet Σ, or (3) $r.tag$, where r is a variable of type `ref`, denoting the tag value stored in the heap-node indexed by r. A tag assignment statement assigns a tag expression to a tag variable.

Reference expressions and assignments: A reference expression re is either a variable of type `ref` or the constant `nil`. A reference assignment statement is either (1) $r := re$, where r is a local or a output variable of type `ref` and re is a reference expression, (2) $r.next := re$, where r is of type `ref` and re is a reference expression, (3) $r := \texttt{new}(te, de, re)$, where r is a local or a output variable of type `ref` and te is a tag expression, de is a data expression, re is a reference expression, or (4) $curr := curr.next$. The first assignment allows reassignment of reference variables, except for the input variable *curr*. The second assignment updates the heap by changing the next-pointer of the heap-node indexed by r, provided r and *curr* do not point to the same heap-node. The third assignment creates a new heap-node with tag value given by te, data value given by de, and next-pointer given by re. The last assignment allows traversal, and is syntactically restricted to ensure that only the unique input reference variable is used to traverse the input list.

Boolean expressions and assignments: An atomic boolean expression is either a boolean constant (0/1), or tests equality between two tag expressions, or tests equality or ordering between two data expressions, or tests equality between two reference expressions. A boolean expression is formed from atomic boolean expressions using standard logical connectives for negation, conjunction, and disjunction. A boolean assignment statement assigns a boolean expression to a boolean variable.

Statements: An assignment statement is either a data assignment statement, a tag assignment statement, a reference assignment statement, or a boolean assignment statement. A statement s is either (1) an assignment statement, (2) a conditional statement of the form `if` *be* `then` s or `if` *be* `then` s_1 `else` s_2, where *be* is a boolean expression, (3) a while statement of the form `while` *be* $\{ s \}$, where *be* is a boolean expression, or (4) a finite sequence of statements.

Program: A *single-pass list processing program* P consists of a sequence of variable declarations followed by a statement.

3.2 Semantics

Recall that a program has a single input variable of type `ref` and a single output variable of type `ref`. The semantics of a program is defined as a partial function from an input data string together with values for input data/tag/boolean variables to an output data string together with values for output data/tag/boolean variables. For example, the semantics of `Delete` is a partial function from $(\Sigma \times D)^* \times D$ to $(\Sigma \times D)^* \times \{0,1\}$.

Configurations: Given a program P, its configuration is completely described by (1) the values of its data, tag, boolean, and reference variables, (2) the program counter indicating the next statement to be executed, and (3) the data-heap. Let *Loc* be the set of locations in P (this can be the set of vertices in the control-flow graph of the program). A data heap h consists of a finite set N of heap-nodes, a data function $f_d : N \mapsto D$ that gives the data element stored at each node, a tag function $f_t : N \mapsto \Sigma$ that gives the tag element stored at each node, and a next-pointer function $f_n : N \mapsto N_\perp$ that gives the next-pointer of each node, where $N_\perp$ is the set N together with the constant `nil`. A program-configuration c of P then consists of a location $\ell \in Loc$, a data heap $h = (N, f_d, f_t, f_n)$, and a partial function β over all the program variables that maps each data variable to D, each reference variable to N, each boolean variable to $\{0,1\}$, and each tag variable to Σ.

Initialization: Given an input data string $(\sigma_1, d_1) \cdots (\sigma_k, d_k)$, the initial heap h_0 consists of the set $N = \{n_1, \ldots n_k\}$ of nodes, one per each data symbol of the input string. The data function is given by $f_d(n_i) = d_i$, the tag function is given by $f_t(n_i) = \sigma_i$, and the next-pointer function is given by $f_n(n_i) = n_{i+1}$ for $i < k$ and $f_n(n_k) = \texttt{nil}$. The initial location ℓ_0 is the unique entry location of the control-flow graph. For the initial valuation β_0, $\beta_0(curr) = n_1$. For all other input variables x, $\beta_0(x)$ is set to the corresponding input value. For all local and output variables x, $\beta_0(x)$ is defined according to the initialization in the declaration for x. The initial configuration c_0 of the program is (ℓ_0, h_0, β_0).

Transition relation over configurations: The operational semantics of programs is defined by a transition relation over the configurations. First, given a configuration $c = (\ell, (N, f_d, f_t, f_n), \beta)$, there is a natural way to evaluate a data expression de to obtain a data value $c(de) \in D$, a tag expression te to obtain a tag value $c(te) \in \Sigma$, a reference expression re to obtain a value $c(re) \in N_\perp$, and a boolean expression be to obtain a boolean value $c(be)$. Every program configuration $c = (\ell, (N, f_d, f_t, f_n), \beta)$ can have at most one successor configuration, determined by the statement s at location ℓ. The details are standard, and we illustrate them using a few cases.

Suppose the statement is a conditional statement ℓ : `if` b `then` ℓ_1 : s_1 `else` ℓ_2 : s_2. Then, if $c(b) = 1$ then the successor configuration of c is (ℓ_1, h, β), and if $c(b) = 0$ then the successor configuration of c is (ℓ_2, h, β).

Suppose the statement s is a reference assignment statement $\ell : r := \texttt{new}(te, de, re)$. The effect of executing the statement s updates the control location from ℓ to the unique successor location ℓ' of the statement s. For the updated data heap h', the set of nodes is $N \cup \{n\}$, where $n \notin N$ is a "new" heap-node, the data function is $f_d[n \mapsto c(de)]$, the tag function is $f_t[n \mapsto c(re)]$, and the next-pointer function is $f_n[n \mapsto c(re)]$. The updated valuation β' is $\beta[r \mapsto n]$.

Suppose the statement s is a reference assignment statement $\ell : r.next := re$. If $c(r) = c(curr)$ then this is an error and the configuration c has no successor. Otherwise, the successor configuration is c' such that the location ℓ' is the unique successor location of ℓ in the control-flow graph, the valuation β stays unchanged, and the updated heap is $(N, f_d, f_t, f_n[c(r) \mapsto c(re)])$ (that is, the next-pointer of the node $c(r)$ in the heap changes to $c(re)$ which may be `nil` or a heap-node).

Termination and output: An execution of the program is obtained by starting in the initial configuration c_0 and continuing with the successor configuration as long as possible. If this execution is infinite, then the program is non-terminating, and the output is undefined. Suppose the execution is finite and ends in the configuration $c_f = (\ell_f, h_f, \beta_f)$. If the location ℓ_f is not the unique exit location of the control-flow graph, then again the output is undefined. Otherwise, the returned value of each output data/tag/boolean variable is given by the final valuation β_f of program variables. For the unique output reference variable r, let $(\sigma_1, d_1)(\sigma_2, d_2)\cdots$ be the unique sequence of tag/data values stored in the heap h_f starting at the node $\beta_f(r)$ following the next-pointers until the `nil` value is encountered. If this sequence is infinite, this indicates that the program created a cycle in the heap during its computation, and the output is again undefined. If this sequence is finite, it is the returned output data string.

3.3 Streaming transducers with ϵ-transitions

We extend the model of streaming data-string transducers by allowing the transducer to update its state, data variables, and data string variables using an ϵ-transition that does not consume an input symbol. We will first show that it is possible to eliminate such ϵ-transitions, and then we will translate list-processing programs to transducers with ϵ-transitions.

The definition of a (deterministic) streaming data-string transducer S with ϵ-transitions extends the definition of SDSTs as follows: in a transition $(q, \sigma, \varphi, q', \alpha)$, σ can now also be ϵ, provided there is no transition of the form $(q, \sigma', \varphi', q'', \alpha')$ with $\sigma' \in \Sigma$. The restriction is needed for ensuring determinism: in a state q, either all outgoing transitions are ϵ-transitions, or all outgoing transitions have non-ϵ tags (and thus consume the next input symbol). Note that the original determinism requirement still applies: if there are multiple transitions with same source state and same input tag (which now may be ϵ), their tests must be mutually exclusive.

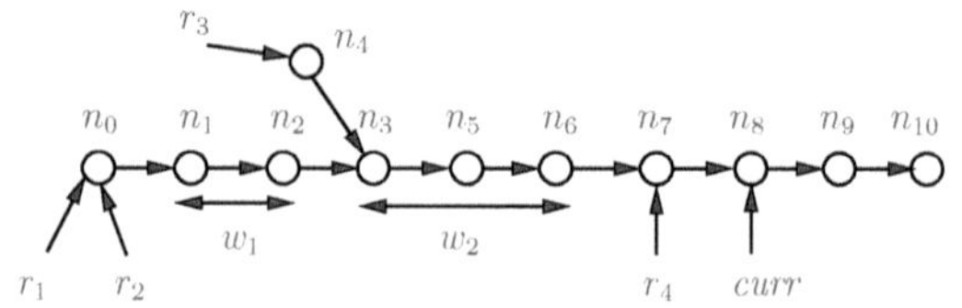

Figure 2. Storing heap in data strings

As in case of SDSTs, a configuration consists of a state q and a valuation β for the data and data string variables. The definition of the transition relation $(q, \beta) \xrightarrow{\sigma, d} (q', \beta')$, for $\sigma \in \Sigma$ and $d \in D$, is unchanged. The ϵ-transitions are defined by: if there exists a transition $(q, \epsilon, \varphi, q', \alpha)$ such that $\beta(\varphi) = 1$ then $(q, \beta) \xrightarrow{\epsilon} (q', \beta \cdot \alpha)$. A run over the input data string w is obtained by starting in the initial configuration (q_0, β_0), and applying either an ϵ-transition or a transition corresponding to the next input data symbol until all the input data symbols are consumed and no more ϵ-transitions are possible. This ensures determinism: for a given input string w, there is at most one configuration (q, β) such that (1) $(q_0, \beta_0) \xrightarrow{w} (q, \beta)$ and (2) (q, β) has no ϵ-successor. The semantics $[\![S]\!](w)$ is defined to be $\beta(O(w))$ in such a case, provided $O(q)$ is defined, and is undefined otherwise. Note that it is possible that such a transducer keeps on executing ϵ-transitions without terminating, and in such a case, the corresponding output is undefined.

It turns out this extension does not add to the expressiveness:

Proposition 5. *Given a streaming data-string transducer S with ϵ-transitions, one can effectively construct a streaming data-string transducer (without ϵ-transitions) S' such that $[\![S]\!] = [\![S']\!]$ with the same number of states, same number of data variables, and the same number of data string variables.*

3.4 From single-pass programs to streaming transducers

In this section, we describe how to translate single-pass list processing programs to streaming data-string transducers. The first step is to view the semantics of a single-pass list processing program as a partial function from data strings to data strings. To associate such a data string transduction $[\![P]\!]$ with a program P, we encode input parameters in the same manner as described in Sec. 2.1. If P has k_i input boolean/data/tag variables and k_o output boolean/data/tag variables, then we prefix the input data string with k_i symbols each encoding one input argument, and prefix the output data string with k_o symbols each encoding one output value.

The main challenge in the construction is to store the information in the data heap used by the program P using a bounded number of data and data string variables in the corresponding transducer S. Figure 2 shows a possible configuration of the data heap that the program accesses using the reference variables $curr$ and r_1, r_2, r_3, r_4. The first observation is that the heap-nodes that are not accessible from any of the reference variables are not relevant to the execution of the program, and can be ignored. Second, nodes such as n_9 and n_{10} that are accessible from $curr.next$ can contain only input symbols that the program has not processed so far. These nodes have not influenced the execution of the program so far, and information in these nodes does not need to be stored. When the program executes the statement $curr := curr.next$, the node n_9 becomes relevant. This step is analogous to the transducer S processing the next input symbol.

Compressing the heap using a bounded number of strings is achieved using an encoding similar to [13]. A node is called a referenced node if a reference variable points to it. In the example, n_0, n_4, n_7 and n_8 are referenced nodes. Information in such nodes needs to be stored explicitly by S. For each reference variable r of P, S maintains a data variable d_r and a tag variable t_r storing the information in the node that r points to. A node such as n_3 is called an interruption node as two nodes point to it (and both these nodes are accessible from the program's reference variables). If P has k reference variables, then there can be at most $2k-1$ interruption nodes. The stretches n_1, n_2 and n_3, n_5, n_6 are uninterrupted heap segments. In each such segment (1) the first node is either an interruption node, or is the next-successor of a referenced node, (2) the next-pointer of each node in the sequence points to the next node in the sequence, (3) no node other than the first is an interruption or a referenced node, and (4) the next-pointer of the last node is either `nil` or points to an interruption or a referenced node. If P has k reference variables, then there can be at most $2k-1$ uninterrupted heap segments. The sequence of data symbols stored in an uninterrupted heap segment is stored in a data string variable by S. In our example, the data string w_1 stores the data symbols in n_1, n_2 and the data string w_2 stores the data symbols in n_3, n_4, n_5. The finite-state control of S remembers the *shape* of the heap: r_1 and r_2 point to the same node, the next-pointer of the r_1-referenced node points to the data string stored in w_1, the next-pointers of the node referenced by r_3 and of the last node of w_1 point to w_2, w_2 is followed by the r_4-referenced node, which is followed by the *curr*-referenced node. Such a shape can be captured by a function $f_n : Y \mapsto Y_\perp$, where Y contains all the reference variables of P and all the data string variables of S that store the data strings in uninterrupted heap segments. If P executes the assignment $r_3.next := curr$, then n_3 is no longer an interruption node, and in this case, the two uninterrupted heap segments collapse into one. This is achieved by S by the assignment $[w_1, w_2] := [w_1.w_2, \varepsilon]$ to the data string variables, updating the tag/data variable corresponding to r_3, and changing the shape by updating $f_n(w_1)$ to r_4 and $f_n(r_3)$ to *curr*.

Proposition 6. *Given a single-pass list-processing program P one can effectively construct a streaming data-string transducer S with ϵ-transitions such that $[\![P]\!] = [\![S]\!]$. If P has m locations, k_r reference variables, k_b boolean variables, k_t tag variables, and k_d data variables, then S has $k_d + k_r$ data variables, $2k_r$ data string variables, and $O(m \cdot 2^{k_b} \cdot k_r^{k_r} \cdot |\Sigma|^{k_t+k_r})$ states.*

Proof. The transducer S has a data variable for each data variable for P, and also for each reference variable of P (to store the data values in referenced nodes in the heap). It has $2k_r$ data string variables to store uninterrupted heap segments. The state of S stores (1) the location of control of P, (2) the boolean value of each boolean variable of P, (3) the tag value of each tag variable of P, (4) a partition of the reference variables of P (two reference variables are in the same partition if they point to the same heap-node), (5) for each equivalence class in the partition, either a tag value stored at the node referenced, or `nil`, and (6) for each data string variable and each equivalence class of the partition, a next value that gives either a data string variable or an equivalence class of the partition. The last component stores the shape of the heap. The bound on the possible number of states follows by a simple counting argument.

If P has data, boolean, or tag input variables, the transducer S first scans the initial prefix of data symbols setting up the initial values using ϵ-transitions. Then the transducer processes the first input symbol, assigning the tag-component corresponding to *curr* in its state to tag of the input symbol, and assigning the data variable corresponding to *curr* to data of the input symbol. After this phase, the control location is set to the unique entry location, all output strings are empty (there are no uninterrupted heap segments in the initial heap), and the partition has only two classes (some reference variables are `nil` and some are in the class that contains *curr*).

We now describe transitions of S corresponding to statements of P. The only statement that causes a non-ϵ transition is the statement *curr* := *curr.next*. The transition that corresponds to this statement in S: (1) changes the stored control location of P, (2) changes the partition of reference variables into equivalence classes: *curr* is split from its current equivalent class, (3) a new tag value is stored for the new equivalence class of *curr*, (4) for each reference variable p from the previous equivalence class of *curr* the new next value of p (i.e. $f_n(p)$) will be *curr*, (5) if for any data string variable x (that stores an uninterrupted heap segment) of S we have $(f_n(x) = curr)$ then we append the current data symbol (from before the transition is executed) to x. All other statements are captured by an ϵ-transition, as they do not correspond to the move of the head of the automaton. Boolean, tag, and data assignments can be simulated directly. We have already described using an example how a statement *r.next* = *curr* can affect the shape of the heap, and how this is captured by assignments that S can perform in its transitions. □

In Section 2.5, we have mentioned that the assignments that a streaming transducer performs on its data string variables can be executed by only changing a constant number of pointers. A list-processing program equivalent to a transducer stores data strings in list segments on the heap, and keeps pointers to the first and last nodes of the segment. To perform an assignment of the form $x := xy$, the program performs commands $xl.next := yf; xl := yl$, where xf (xl) is a reference to the first (last) node representing x (and similarly for y). We obtain the following proposition:

Proposition 7. *Given a streaming data string transducer S, one can effectively construct a single-pass list-processing program P such that $[\![S]\!] = [\![P]\!]$.*

4. Functional programs on lists

We consider a simply typed functional language with types `bool`, `tag`, `data`, list, and function types, with `letrec` recursion and pair and list constructors. As in the previous section, we assume that $\Sigma = \Gamma$ for ease of presentation. The terms are defined by:

```
t:=    true | false | isTrue t | isFalse t
     | S | isS (for all S ∈ tag)
     | x | fun x:T.t | t t | if t then t else t
     | x = x | x < x | {t,t} | t.1 | t.2
     | nil | cons t t | append t t
     | isnil t | head t | tail t
     | let x=t in t | letrec x:T=t in t
```

The operators `=` and `<` apply to terms of type `data`. The lists are of type (`list (tag` × `data)`), or `list` for short. The list and pair terms are standard.

We defined a class of functional programs that intuitively captures single-pass functions that process a list by recursing through it from left to right. The recursion restriction we define is a minor generalization of tail recursive functions, where we allow the caller to perform operations on, but not test, the values that the callee returns. This allows capturing common routines such as insert, delete, and reverse (both tail-recursive and non-tail recursive). We allow wrapper functions in order to enable the standard programming style for tail recursive functions.

A function is a *single-pass list processing function* iff it is defined by the following term:

```
fun a:list × T1.
  letrec f:((list × T1 × T2) → (list × T)) = t
  in (f a initValues)
```

This term encodes a wrapper function that can pass some additional arguments to a recursive function `f`. The following conditions are required to hold:

- *one list*: Let us denote the first argument to `f` (by definition of type `list`) by `l`. The list `l` is the only list accessed by `isnil`, `head` and `tail`. The contents of the other list variables are thus not examined. However, it is possible to use `cons` or `append` with these variables.
- *type restrictions*: The types `T1` and `T` are products of types `bool`, `tag`, `data`, with possibly more than one component of each type. These are input and output arguments of the list processing function. The type `T2` is a product of types `bool`, `tag`, `data`, and `list`, with possibly more than one component of each type. Intuitively, these are buffers where the recursive function can store results.
- *recursion restriction*: The first argument to any recursive call is the term `(tail l)`, where `l` is the first argument to `f`. Every recursive call to `f` is enclosed in an expression `e` defined by `let r =(f (tail l) a) in t`. Furthermore, `e` is the last expression the caller evaluates, i.e. `t` is the caller's result. Using the type restriction above, we have that $\mathtt{r} \equiv \mathtt{l}_1, \mathtt{r}_1, \ldots, \mathtt{r}_n$, and $\mathtt{a} \equiv \mathtt{a}_1 \ldots \mathtt{a}_n$, and $\mathtt{t} \equiv \mathtt{l}_2, \mathtt{t}_1, \ldots \mathtt{t}_n$, where $\mathtt{l}_1$ is a list and $\mathtt{l}_2$ is a list expression, each of $\mathtt{r}_1, \ldots \mathtt{r}_n$ and $\mathtt{t}_1, \ldots \mathtt{t}_n$ is of type `bool`, `tag` or `data`, and each of $\mathtt{a}_1, \ldots \mathtt{a}_n$ is of type `bool`, `tag`, `data`, or `list`. We have the following restrictions on these subexpressions: (i) a list variable of `f` can appear in at most one expression $\mathtt{a}_i$ or $\mathtt{t}_j$ (this is similar to the restriction that requires the assignments of SDSTs to be "copyless"), (ii) if $\mathtt{t}_i$ is of type `bool`, then the only variable from `r` it can use is $\mathtt{r}_i$, (iii) if $\mathtt{t}_i$ is of type `tag` or `data`, then we have $\mathtt{t}_i = \mathtt{r}_i$, (iv) the only variable from `r` that $\mathtt{l}_2$ can use is $\mathtt{l}_1$.
- *term t*: The term `t` is of the form `fun x: (list` $\times$ `T1` $\times$ `T2). t'`, where $\mathtt{t}'$ does not contain the function definition term `fun` or the recursive definition term `letrec`.
- *initValues*: The expression `initValues` is of type `T2`. If `T2` contains `list` types, the corresponding values in `initValues` are `nil`.

Note that all the above conditions can be checked syntactically.

4.1 Examples

The data transduction F_1 that reverses a list can be encoded as a single-pass list processing function as follows:

```
fun l:list.
  letrec reverse: (list × list → list)
      = fun l:list. fun result:list.
    if (isnil l) then result
    else (reverse (tail l) (cons (head l) result))
  in (reverse l nil)
```

A function that given a list l and a data value d deletes all occurrences of d in l is encoded as follows:

```
fun l:list. d:data.
  letrec FuncDelete: (list × data → list)
      = fun l:list. fun d:data.
    if (isnil l) then nil
    else
      if (head l).data = d
        then (FuncDelete (tail l) d)
        else (cons (head l)
                   (FuncDelete (tail l) d))
  in (FuncDelete l d)
```

One of the recursive calls in `FuncDelete` is enclosed in an expression that adds a cell to the front of the list: `(cons (head l) (FuncDelete (tail l) d))`. This recursive call is not tail recursive, as the caller function applies an operation to the result returned by the callee. However, the recursive call satisfies the recursion restriction from our definition of single-pass list processing functions (and it satisfies the other restrictions as well).

The constructions in this paper lead to an algorithm to check if the imperative function `Delete` of Section 3 and the above function `FuncDelete` are semantically equivalent (i.e., specify the same transduction). Such a check can be used for full functional verification of one using the other as the specification.

4.2 From list processing functions to streaming transducers

Semantics The simply-typed functional language we defined contains standard terms. The values of the language, as well as the typing rules, and the evaluation relation $\mathtt{t}_1 \rightarrow \mathtt{t}_2$ for all the terms are omitted here, as they can be found in a standard textbook [16]. The operational semantics is given by a transition system, whose states are subterms of `f`, whose transitions are given by the evaluation relation $\mathtt{t}_1 \rightarrow \mathtt{t}_2$, and whose initial state is the term `f`.

As for imperative programs, the semantics of a single-pass list processing function can be viewed as a data string transduction, that is, a partial function from data strings to data strings. To associate a transduction $[\![\mathtt{f}]\!]$ with a single-pass list processing function $\mathtt{f}$: $(\mathtt{list} \times \mathtt{T}_1) \rightarrow \mathtt{T}$, we encode input parameters in the same way as in Section 3. Given a data string w, its first k_i symbols can represent k_i input boolean/data/tag variables, and the rest represents the input list (converting a data string to a list term of type `list` is straightforward). Given a data string, the function $decode\_param(w, k_i)$ returns the parameter values, and the function $decode\_list(w, k_i)$ returns the tail of the input string represented as a list term. Similar encoding to data strings can be used for output values and output lists. Given a tuple $\{\mathtt{l}_1, \mathtt{r}_1, \ldots, \mathtt{r}_n\}$ of type $\mathtt{list} \times \mathtt{T}$, $enc\_res(\{\mathtt{l}_1, \mathtt{r}_1, \ldots, \mathtt{r}_n\})$ returns the corresponding data string. Given a single-pass list processing function `f`, we have that $[\![\mathtt{f}]\!](w) = w'$ iff $(\mathtt{f}\ decode\_list(w)\ decode\_param(w)) \rightarrow^* \{l_1, r_1, \ldots, r_n\}$ and $enc\_res(l_1, r_1, \ldots, r_n) = w$.

Proposition 8. *Given a single-pass list processing function* $\mathtt{f}$: $(\mathtt{list} \times \mathtt{T}_1) \rightarrow \mathtt{T}$, *one can effectively construct a streaming data string transducer* S, *such that* $[\![\mathtt{f}]\!] = [\![S]\!]$. *Let* `g` *be the recursive function used by* `f`. *If* `g` *has* k_b *boolean variables,* k_t *tag variables,* k_d *data variables, and* k_l *list variables, then* S *has* $O(2^{k_b} \cdot |\Sigma|^{k_t})$ *states,* k_d *data variables, and* $k_l + 1$ *data string variables.*

We note that the construction used in the proof of Proposition 8 is more direct than the one used in the proof of Proposition 6. The list variables (apart from the list that is traversed) and data variables are modeled directly by data string variables and data variables of the transducer, and the control state of the transducer encodes the value of boolean and tag variables.

Given an SDST S, we can construct an equivalent list-processing program `f`. We first describe the arguments of the recursive function `g` the function `f` uses: its boolean arguments encode state of S, its data arguments correspond to data variables of S, and its list arguments correspond to the data string variables of S. A transition $(q, \sigma, \varphi, q', \alpha)$ is translated by making the function g test whether the current boolean arguments correspond to q, whether the current tag is σ, and whether φ holds for the current data arguments. If so, the function makes a recursive call with parameters encoding q' and the assignments from α. The function we obtain in this way is tail recursive. The next proposition follows:

Proposition 9. *Given a single-pass data string transducer* S, *one can effectively construct a single-pass list processing function* `f`, *such that* $[\![S]\!] = [\![\mathtt{f}]\!]$.

5. Decision Problems

In this section, we prove that the equivalence problem and the pre/post condition checking problem are decidable for streaming data string transducers. We also show that, for a number of extensions of the streaming transducer model, already the basic analysis problem of reachability is undecidable.

5.1 Sound and complete abstraction for order and equality

In proofs of decidability of equivalence and pre/post condition checking of SDSTs that operate on an infinite data domain D, we will construct finite state systems that do not store values of the data variables of the SDSTs, but only keep track of order and equality predicates. In order to prove that such an abstraction is both sound and complete for analysis problems, we will need the lemma presented in this subsection.

Let V be a set of variables that range over D. We fix V and an infinite D for this subsection. We will consider pairs of the form (V^d, ρ), where the set $V^d \subseteq V$ represents the set of variables with a defined value, and where ρ is an *ec-order* on V^d (short for order on equivalence classes). An ec-order $\rho = (\equiv_\rho, <_\rho)$ is a pair where the first component is an equivalence relation on V^d, and the second component is a strict total order on equivalence classes of $\equiv_\rho$. For data variables v_1, v_2, we write $v_1 <_\rho v_2$, if v_1 belongs to an equivalence class c_1, v_2 belongs to an equivalence class c_2, and $c_1 <_\rho c_2$. For example, if $V = \{v_1, v_2, v_3\}$, all variables have a defined value, then a possible ec-order on V^d can be represented as $v_1 \equiv_\rho v_3 <_\rho v_2$. Let β be a valuation of data variables as in the definition of SDSTs. A pair (V^d, ρ) represents a set of valuations. We write $\beta \models (V^d, \rho)$ iff β is defined precisely for the variables in V^d, and for all $v_1, v_2 \in V^d$ we have that $\beta(v_1) < \beta(v_2)$ iff $v_1 <_\rho v_2$, and $\beta(v_1) = \beta(v_2)$ iff $v_1 \equiv_\rho v_2$. Let φ be a Boolean combination of constraints of the form $v_1 < v_2$ and $v_1 = v_2$ for variables $v_1, v_2 \in V$. Let α be a map from V to V modeling assignments, as in the definition of transitions of SDSTs. We write $\beta_1 \xrightarrow{(\varphi,\alpha)} \beta_2$, if β_1 satisfies φ and $\beta_2 = \beta_1 \cdot \alpha$, similarly to the definition of SDSTs. For pairs (V^d, ρ), we define a transition relation $(V^d, \rho) \xrightarrow{(\varphi,\alpha)} (V'^d, \rho')$ iff (a) V'^d contains the variables which were assigned to by α from variables in V^d, (b) ρ implies φ, and (c) ρ' is the ec-order obtained from ρ by executing α. Let u^a be a sequence of pairs $(V_1^d, \rho_1)(V_2^d, \rho_2)\ldots(V_n^d, \rho_n)$. Let u be a sequence of valuations $\beta_1\beta_2\ldots\beta_n$. Let *upd* be a sequence of pairs $(\varphi_1, \alpha_1)(\varphi_2, \alpha_2)\ldots(\varphi_{n-1}, \alpha_{n-1})$. The sequence u^a *conforms* to the sequence *upd* if for all i if $1 \leq i < n$, then $(V_i^d, \rho_i) \xrightarrow{(\varphi_i,\alpha_i)} (V_{i+1}^d, \rho_{i+1})$. Similarly, the sequence u *conforms* to the sequence *upd* if for all i if $1 \leq i < n$, then $\beta_i \xrightarrow{(\varphi_i,\alpha_i)} \beta_{i+1}$.

The proof of the following lemma crucially uses the fact that the infinite totally-ordered data domain D contains chains, that is, sequences of elements in an increasing order, of unbounded length. The proof is omitted here in the interest of space. A similar proof is a part of the proof of Theorem 1 of [2].

Lemma 10. *Let upd be a sequence of pairs $(\varphi_1, \alpha_1)(\varphi_2, \alpha_2)\ldots(\varphi_{n-1}, \alpha_{n-1})$. Let u^a be a sequence of pairs $(V_1^d, \rho_1)(V_1^d, \rho_1)\ldots(V_n^d, \rho_n)$, such that u^a conforms to upd. Then there exists a sequence of valuations $u = \beta_1\beta_2\ldots\beta_n$ such that u conforms to upd and for all i, if $1 \leq i \leq n$, then $u_i \models u_i^a$.*

5.2 Equivalence checking

Given two streaming data-string transducers S_1 and S_2 from Σ to Γ, the *streaming transducer equivalence problem* is to determine whether $[\![S_1]\!] = [\![S_2]\!]$.

In order to show that the problem can be solved in PSPACE we reduce the problem to a reachability problem in 1-counter machines. A 1-counter machine M is a tuple $(Q_M, \delta_M, q_0^M, F_M)$, where Q_M is a set of states, q_0^M is the initial state, and $F_M \subseteq Q_M$ is a set of final states. The transition relation δ_M is a relation in $Q_M \times Q_M \times \{-1, 0, 1\}$. Note that 1-counter machines do not test the content of the counter. A configuration of the 1-counter machine is a pair in $Q \times Z$, that is, it consists of a state and the value of a counter. A transition relation $\rightarrow$ on configurations is defined as follows: $(q, z) \rightarrow (q', z')$ iff $(q, q', c) \in \delta_M$ and $z' = z + c$. The 1-counter 0-reachability problem is to decide whether there exists a state $q \in F_M$ such that $(q_0^M, 0) \rightarrow^* (q, 0)$. This is a special case of the empty-stack reachability problem for pushdown automata. While the latter is PTIME-complete, the following lemma shows that the former is in NLOGSPACE.

Lemma 11. *The* 1*-counter* 0*-reachability problem is in* NLOGSPACE.

Proof. Consider a 1-counter machine $M = (Q_M, \delta_M, q_0^M, F_M)$. We observe that for all $q, q' \in Q_M$, if there is a path $(q, 0) \rightarrow^* (q', 0)$, then there is such a path with stack depth bounded by n^2. This is a consequence of a summarization-based reachability algorithm (easily adapted from summarization-based reachability algorithm for pushdown automata), which computes summaries for pairs (q, q'). The iteration in which a pair (q, q') gets added is the minimum absolute value of counter needed to reach from $(q, 0)$ to $(q', 0)$. The number of iterations is at most the number of summaries, that is, n^2. Note that this observation holds for all pushdown automata.

We can thus assume that the counter ranges over $(-n^2, n^2)$. State of a 1-counter machine is (q, z), where z is the value of a counter. Therefore we need to consider only $O(n^3)$ possible configurations. (This statement does not hold for general pushdown automata). Thus our reachability problem is a reachability problem in a graph with $O(n^3)$ states. The problem can be therefore solved in space $O(\log n^3)$. □

Theorem 12. *The streaming data-string transducer equivalence problem is in* PSPACE.

Proof. Let us consider two streaming data-string transducers S_1 and S_2 from Σ to Γ. They are not equivalent if there exists an input data string w over Σ such that one of the following three conditions hold: (i) $[\![S_1]\!](w)$ is defined, but $[\![S_2]\!](w)$ is not (or vice-versa), (ii) $[\![S_1]\!](w)$ and $[\![S_2]\!](w)$ are defined, but have different lengths, (iii) $[\![S_1]\!](w)$ and $[\![S_2]\!](w)$ are defined and have the same lengths, but there exists a position p such that the data strings $[\![S_1]\!](w)$ and $[\![S_2]\!](w)$ differ at the position p.

We construct a 1-counter automaton and designate a state q such that q is 0-reachable in M if and only if S_1 and S_2 are not equivalent. The automaton M nondeterministically chooses which type of difference (of the three described above) it will find. We only describe here how M can determine that there is an input string such that the p-th output symbol of S_1 is different from the p-th output symbol of S_2. The construction for the other two cases uses similar ideas and is simpler.

The automaton M nondeterministically simulates S_1 and S_2 running in parallel. It keeps track of states of S_1 and S_2 precisely, but only keeps some information on the data and data string variables. Intuitively, M guesses during the course of simulation of S_1 (resp. S_2) where the position p in the output is, and uses its counter to check that the guess is the same for S_1 and S_2.

For each data string variable, M guesses (at each step) where the contents of the variable will appear in the output with respect to the position p. More concretely, for each data string variable x of both S_1 and S_2, M guesses which of the following categories the variable is in: (i) left of p (Class L), (ii) center, i.e. position p

is in this string (Class C), (iii) right of p (Class R), (iv) x does not contribute to the output (Class N).

Maintaining consistency of assignment of data string variables into these four classes is straightforward. First, consider the case when at a particular step, S_1 performs an assignment $y := (a, v_1)z(b, v_2)$ and M guesses that the contents y will appear to the left of the position p in the output of M_1. To verify that this guess is consistent with previous guesses, M checks that in the previous step, z was in Class L. The assignment caused two output symbols (a, v_1) and (b, v_2) to appear to the left of the position p, therefore M increases its counter by 2 (outputs of S_2 are taken into account by decreasing the counter rather than increasing). Second, if at a particular step, S_1 performs an assignment $x := (a, v_1)y(b, v_2)z$, and M guesses that the symbol (b, v_2) in this assignment will be at the position p, then: (i) M verifies that at the previous step, y was in Class L, and z was in Class R, (ii) M increases its counter by two in order to simulate the fact that S_1 outputs (a, v_1) and (b, v_2) (as before, when simulating S_2, M decreases the counter), and (iii) M assigns x to Class C. Note that initially, no variable is assigned to Class C, and at each step, at most one variable is in Class C, because of the copyless assignment restriction. The cases when M guesses that a variable to which S_1 (resp. S_2) assigns is in Class R or Class N are similar.

In the remainder of the proof, we assume that the data domain D is infinite. If it is finite, the automaton can directly store values from D in its finite-state control, and the construction is simpler.

For data variables, M keeps track of which variable is defined, and for the defined variables, it keeps track of the ordering and equality information. More precisely, let us consider the following set of variables $V = (V_1 \setminus \{curr^1\}) \cup (V_2 \setminus \{curr^2\}) \cup \{vp_1, vp_2, curr\}$, where V_1 and V_2 are the sets of data variables of S_1 and S_2, and vp_1 and vp_2 are used by M to store information about the data value S_1 and S_2 output at position p. The automaton M stores a pair (V^d, ρ), where $V^d \subseteq V$ that contains all of the variables whose values are defined in computation of S_1 and S_2, and ρ is an ec-order on V^d. The pair (V^d, ρ) is updated as steps of S_1 and S_2 are simulated and their transitions are executed. Note that M maintains only one variable *curr* common to M_1 and M_2 because the two automata are running on the same input. The final part of the construction is the maintenance of vp_1, the variable used to store the output of S_1 at position p. When M guesses that the output symbol of S_1 at position p will be one in the right-hand side of the assignment (such as $x := (a, v_1)y(b, v_2)z$) it is simulating currently, it assigns x to Class C as above, and if it guesses that at position p is the symbol (b, v_2), then : (i) the value b from Σ is stored in the finite state control of M, and (ii) vp_1 is added to V^d, the set of defined variables, and vp_1 is added to the equivalence class of v_2 in ρ. The construction for vp_2 is analogous.

To summarize, a state of M consists of (1) a state of S_1, (2) a state of S_2, (3) a set $V^d \subseteq V$ representing the defined variables, (4) an ec-order ρ, (5) a partition of the data string variables of S_1 and S_2 to classes (as described above) and a symbol from Γ at position p for S_1 and S_2 (if M guessed that the output to position p was already performed). The set of states of M is thus a product: $Q_1 \times Q_2 \times 2^V \times \rho \times Q_B$, with the components corresponding to items (1) to (5). The initial state of M is the tuple containing initial states of S_1 and S_2, with the set V^d empty — all the variables are undefined, and the component (5) has a special value i. From this state there are nondeterministic transitions which choose the initial assignments of data string variables to classes. The other transitions are as described above. The set of final states consists of states where either the variables vp_1 and vp_2 are defined, but ρ does *not* imply $vp_1 = vp_2$ or the Γ symbols stored in the finite-state control of M for position p in output strings of S_1 and S_2 differ.

We now prove that a final state of M is 0-reachable iff there exists an input data string w and a position p, such that $[\![S_1]\!](w)$ and $[\![S_2]\!](w)$ differ at position p. We will need the following notion that relates configurations of M to configurations of S_1 and S_2. Let $c_1 = (q_1, \beta_1)$ be a configuration of S_1, let $c_2 = (q_2, \beta_2)$ be a configuration of S_2 and let $c_M = ((q_1^M, q_2^M, V^d, \rho, q_B), e)$ be a configuration of M (e is the value of the counter). The configuration c_M is an abstraction of configurations (c_1, c_2) (denoted by $\alpha((c_1, c_2)) = c_M$) iff the following conditions hold:

- States: the states of S_1 and S_2 are the same in c_1 and c_2 as they are in c_M.
- Data variables: β_1 or β_2 are defined for each of the variables in V^d, and the values β_1 and β_2 assign to variables in V^d are consistent with ρ
- Data string variables: Let e_L^1 be the number of symbols in the data string variables of S_1 that are assigned to Class L in Q_B. Class C in Q_B contains by construction at most one data string variable of S_1. If Class C contains a data string variable x_1 of S_1, then we can designate a position p_1 in the data string in x_1. Let e_C^1 be the number of characters to the left of p_1 in x_1. The values e_L^2 and e_C^2 are defined analogously for S_2 and a position p_2 in a data string variable x_2. The following equality is required to hold: $e_L^1 + e_C^1 - (e_L^2 + e_C^2) = e$, where e is the counter value in c_M. Furthermore, let d_1 be the data value at position p_1. We have that the equality and order relations that ρ contains on vp_1 and the other data variables hold for d_1 and the values of these data variables given by β_1 and β_2. An analogous condition holds for the data value at position p_2.

Claim 1 The automaton M can reach the configuration $c_M = ((q_1, q_2, V^d, \rho, Q_B), e)$ in k steps iff there exists an input string w of length k, such that S_1 (S_2), after traversing this input, reaches a configuration c_1 (c_2), and $\alpha((c_1, c_2)) = c_M$.

The claim is proven by induction on k. The more difficult part of the proof of the claim is the left-to-right implication, where we are required to find an input string w that satisfies the condition. We need to find a sequence of valuations β that is the same as the sequence of pairs (V^d, ρ) given by the sequence of configurations of M. It is here that Lemma 10 is used.

Using Claim 1, we now prove that a final state of M is 0-reachable implies that there exists an input data string w and a position p, such that $[\![S_1]\!](w)$ and $[\![S_2]\!](w)$ differ at position p. A final state of M is a state where we do not have $vp_1 = vp_2$ or where the Γ symbols stored for positions p_1 and p_2 differ. By Claim 1, this means that there is a position p_1 in the output of S_1 and a position p_2 in the output of S_2 where the data values or the Γ symbols differ. If such a state is 0-reachable, (using Claim 1) we get that $e_L^1 + e_C^1 - (e_L^2 + e_C^2) = 0$, which implies $p_1 - p_2 = 0$, which implies that $p_1 = p_2$. The other implication can be also easily shown using Claim 1.

Complexity Checking whether a particular final state of M is 0-reachable can be done in NLOGSPACE (Lemma 11). A nondeterministic algorithm first guesses which final state is reachable, and then checks its reachability in NLOGSPACE. The number of states of the 1-counter automaton M we constructed is linear in the number of states of S_1 and S_2 and exponential in the number of data string and data variables of S_1 and S_2. Furthermore, given two states of M, one can decide (in polynomial time in the number of variables), whether there is a transition between the two states. We thus have that the streaming transducer equivalence problem is in PSPACE.

□

Theorem 12 implies that checking equivalence is in PSPACE for list-processing programs from Section 3 and list-processing functions defined in Section 4. The reason is that the number of data and output variables of the resulting transducer is linear in the size of the program (more precisely, in the number of data and reference variables of the program).

5.3 Checking pre/post conditions and assertions

Let S be a streaming data string transducer S from Σ to Γ. Let A_1 be a streaming data string acceptor on Σ, and let A_2 be a streaming data string acceptor on Γ. The triple $\{A_1\}S\{A_2\}$ holds iff for all input data strings w over Σ we have that if A_1 accepts w and $[\![S]\!](w) = w'$, then A_2 accepts w'. The *pre/post condition problem* for SDSTs is to determine, given A_1, S, and A_2, whether $\{A_1\}S\{A_2\}$ holds. Pre-post condition checking is useful in the context of verification, because we can, for example, ask whether a transducer that takes a sorted list (with respect to an ordering on Σ) as an input returns a sorted list (with respect to an ordering on Γ) as an output. The upper bound in the following theorem is obtained by reduction to the emptiness problem in nondeterministic finite automata (NFAs).

Theorem 13. *The pre/post condition problem for SDSTs is in* PSPACE.

The above definition of pre/post condition checking corresponds to partial correctness. We can also check total correctness: there is a PSPACE algorithm to check, given S, A_1, and A_2, is it the case that for all input strings w accepted by A_1, $[\![S]\!](w)$ is defined and A_2 accepts $[\![S]\!](w)$.

The constructions discussed so far can also be used to solve a number of *assertion checking* problems for single-pass list-processing programs.

Reachability Given a single-pass list processing program P, a location ℓ of P, and a streaming data string acceptor A, is there a data string w accepted by A such that starting from the initial heap that stores w, there is an execution of P leading to a configuration with location ℓ? For this, we need to construct the SDST corresponding to P as discussed in Section 3.4, and simulate it on an input together with A. The complexity is PSPACE. The same construction can be used if additional constraints are specified on boolean and tag variables of P at the end of the execution.

Pointer analysis Given a single-pass list processing program P, two pointer variables x and y, and a streaming data string acceptor A, is there a data string w accepted by A such that starting from the initial heap that stores w, there is an execution of P leading to a configuration in which both x and y point to the same heap-node? Recall that the compilation of programs into SDSTs keeps track of such aliasing relationships, and has the necessary information to answer such a query. We can also check if a pointer variable r is guaranteed to be non-null whenever it is dereferenced (using expressions such as *r.next* and *r.data*).

Heap-cycles detection Given a single-pass list processing program P and a streaming data string acceptor A, is there a data string w accepted by A such that starting from the initial (acyclic) heap that stores w, there is an execution of P leading to a configuration in which the heap contains a cycle (formed by next-pointers of heap-nodes)? Again, the compilation of programs into SDSTs keeps track of the heap shape, and can be used to solve this problem in PSPACE.

5.4 Undecidable extensions

Two-way data string transducers A *two-way (deterministic) data string transducer* (2DST) is an extension of the streaming data string transducer model, where at each step, the transducer can decide whether to move left or to move right or to stay put. More precisely, a transition of a 2DST is defined by a a tuple $(q, \sigma, \varphi, q', \alpha, \zeta)$, where q, σ, φ, q' and α are as for SDSTs, and ζ is in $\{\leftarrow, \downarrow, \rightarrow\}$. For 2DSTs, we assume that the input data string is enclosed by two special symbols $\vdash$, $\dashv$. The machine stops when it reaches a final state. If the machine never reaches a final state, or if it tries to move left while the tag is $\vdash$ or it tries to move right when the tag is $\dashv$, then the output undefined. Given a 2DST S and a state q of S, the *2DST reachability problem* is to determine whether there exists a data string w such that S enters the state q while processing w.

Theorem 14. *The 2DST reachability problem is undecidable.*

The theorem is proven by reduction from the undecidable problem of emptiness for two-counter automata. The main step of the proof is to show that a 2DST can recognize whether the input data string encodes a computation of a two-counter machine. The proof uses the fact that the data domain is ordered.

Programs with multiple traversing pointers The class of imperative list processing programs considered in Section 3 restricts how next pointers of heap nodes can be traversed: there is one special pointer variable *curr*, and it is the only pointer variable that can traverse the next pointer. Now consider the class of programs, denoted by PMTP (short for programs with multiple traversal pointers), obtained by lifting this restriction, and allowing assignments $x := y.next$ for any two pointer variables x and y. Given a program P from the class PMTP and a location ℓ, the *PMTP reachability problem* is to determine whether there exists a data string w such that starting from the initial heap that stores w, there is an execution of P leading to a configuration with location ℓ.

Theorem 15. *The PMTP reachability problem is undecidable.*

The proof of the undecidability is again by a reduction from the reachability problem for two-counter automata. The basic observation is that if multiple pointers can traverse the heap simultaneously, the program can check whether two successive parts of the heap encode two successive configurations of the two-counter machine.

Data string variable equality While a number of analysis problems for SDSTs, and assertion checking problems for single-pass list-processing programs, are decidable, checking whether the transducer/program can reach a configuration where the contents of two string variables are the same, is undecidable. Given an SDST S, a state q of S, and two data string variables x and y of S, the *data string variable equality problem* is to determine whether there exists a data string w such that S reaches a configuration where $x = y$ and the state is q. The following theorem is proven using a reduction from Post's correspondence problem.

Theorem 16. *The data string variable equality problem is undecidable.*

6. Related Work

We are not aware of any prior decidability results for checking semantic equivalence of list processing programs, even for the restricted case of bounded data domains.

The decidability of safety properties for programs with lists was investigated in [7]. The negative result in [7] holds for a very restricted class of programs: programs with only non-nested loops which do not modify the list data structure. Compared to the model of [7], we do not allow general traversal assignments of the form $x := y.next$, but allow only one pointer variable *curr* to traverse the next pointers of the heap nodes. We also assume that the initial heap is acyclic (but analysis algorithms can detect if cycles get introduced during program execution). In previous work [8], we have presented decidability results for a class of concurrent list accessing programs. The two models are different: the model in [8] allows concurrency and nondeterminism, but is not able to capture for example the list reversal transduction. The restrictions in [8] are rather intricate, and that is what triggered this study in search of a robust automata-theoretic model. Extending the streaming transducer model to capture concurrency is an interesting research direction. There is an emerging literature on automata and logics over data strings [3, 15] and algorithmic analysis of programs accessing data strings [2]. While existing literature studies acceptors and languages of data strings, we want to handle destructive methods that e.g. delete elements, and thus, a model of transducers is needed.

A number of automata-based techniques have been proposed for shape analysis [4, 5] (see also [9] for a survey). In particular, the *regular model checking* approach [4] employs transducers to reason about heap-manipulating programs in the following manner. The set of heaps feasible at a program point is represented by either a string automaton or a tree automaton, and the transformation on the heap due to a single statement is captured by a corresponding transducer model. The transformation of the entire program, then, corresponds to iterated composition of such transducers. Given a regular initial set of heaps, the set of heaps reachable after one transition will be regular. However, regular languages are not closed under unbounded union, so the set of all reachable heaps need not be regular. Consider a program that given an input list w outputs the list ww (note that data values do not play an important role in this transduction). For such a program, the iterative fixpoint procedure to compute the set of all reachable configurations does not terminate (in fact, the set of reachable configurations is not regular, and cannot be represented by a finite-state automaton). However, a streaming transducer that computes such a transduction can be easily defined. It is important to note that our decision procedures do not attempt to compute the set of reachable configurations (or heap contents). The literature on regular model checking provides several techniques for over-approximations of the set of reachable heaps to ensure termination, such as widening [20] and specialized abstractions using counters [6].

Analyzing programs that manipulate dynamic linked data structures is a widely studied problem commonly described as *shape analysis* [19]. Proving assertions of such programs is undecidable [12, 18], and the bulk of the literature consists of abstraction-based techniques for verification (see e.g. [10, 14, 17]). The core problem these techniques focus on is computation of invariants that often need to quantify over the nodes in the heap. Let us consider function `Delete` from Section 3. If the function was called with the parameter d, a natural postcondition is that all nodes reachable from `result` have values different from d. A quantified invariant needed to prove the postcondition could be automatically computed using for example the approach described in [17]. However, we emphasize that in contrast to the sound-but-not-complete abstraction-based methods for checking safety properties, our approach is sound and complete for a well-defined class of programs and, in addition to checking of assertions and pre/post conditions, we presented an algorithm for checking equivalence of programs.

7. Conclusions

We have introduced a streaming transducer model, and showed that it can serve as a foundational model of single-pass list processing programs. Our results lead to algorithms for checking functional equivalence of two programs, written possibly in different programming styles, for commonly used routines for processing lists of data items. We are not aware of any prior decidability results for checking semantic equivalence of list processing programs, even for the restricted case of bounded data domains.

We also believe that the streaming transducer model introduced in this paper is of independent theoretical interest. We have started the investigation of expressiveness and related theoretical properties of the transducer model when the data domain is bounded. Classical string-to-string finite-state transducers need to be "two-way" to implement an operation such as reverse. In a subsequent paper, we showed that the streaming string transducer model is expressively equivalent to two-way transducers [1], and thus, to MSO-definable string transductions [11]. Learning streaming string transducers from input/output examples, and defining a similar streaming transducer model for tree-structured data are potential fruitful directions for future research.

References

[1] R. Alur and P. Černý. Expressivness of streaming string transducers. Invited paper. In *FSTTCS*, 2010.

[2] R. Alur, P. Černý, and S. Weinstein. Algorithmic analysis of array-accessing programs. In *CSL*, pages 86–101, 2009.

[3] M. Bojańczyk, A. Muscholl, T. Schwentick, L. Segoufin, and C. David. Two-variable logic on words with data. In *LICS*, pages 7–16, 2006.

[4] A. Bouajjani, B. Jonsson, M. Nilsson, and T. Touili. Regular model checking. In *CAV*, pages 403–418, 2000.

[5] A. Bouajjani, P. Habermehl, P. Moro, and T. Vojnar. Verifying programs with dynamic 1-selector-linked structures in regular model checking. In *TACAS*, pages 13–29, 2005.

[6] A. Bouajjani, M. Bozga, P. Habermehl, R. Iosif, P. Moro, and T. Vojnar. Programs with lists are counter automata. In *CAV*, pages 517–531, 2006.

[7] M. Bozga and R. Iosif. On flat programs with lists. In *VMCAI*, pages 122–136, 2007.

[8] P. Černý, A. Radhakrishna, D. Zufferey, S. Chaudhuri, and R. Alur. Model checking of linearizability of concurrent list implementations. In *CAV*, pages 465–479, 2010.

[9] S. Chakraborty. Reasoning about heap manipulating programs using automata techniques. To appear in *IISc-World Scientific Review Volume on Modern Applications of Automata Theory*.

[10] D. Distefano, P. O'Hearn, and H. Yang. A local shape analysis based on separation logic. In *TACAS*, pages 287–302, 2006.

[11] J. Engelfriet and H. Hoogeboom. MSO definable string transductions and two-way finite-state transducers. *ACM Trans. Comput. Log.*, 2(2): 216–254, 2001.

[12] W. Landi. Undecidability of static analysis. *LOPLAS*, 1(4):323–337, 1992.

[13] R. Manevich, E. Yahav, G. Ramalingam, and S. Sagiv. Predicate abstraction and canonical abstraction for singly-linked lists. In *VMCAI*, pages 181–198, 2005.

[14] R. Manevich, J. Berdine, B. Cook, G. Ramalingam, and M. Sagiv. Shape analysis by graph decomposition. In *TACAS*, pages 3–18, 2007.

[15] F. Neven, T. Schwentick, and V. Vianu. Finite state machines for strings over infinite alphabets. *ACM Trans. Comput. Logic*, 5(3):403–435, 2004.

[16] B. Pierce. *Types and programming languages*. MIT Press, 2002.

[17] A. Podelski and T. Wies. Counterexample-guided focus. In *POPL*, pages 249–260, 2010.

[18] G. Ramalingam. The undecidability of aliasing. *ACM Trans. Program. Lang. Syst.*, 16(5):1467–1471, 1994.

[19] S. Sagiv, T. Reps, and R. Wilhelm. Parametric shape analysis via 3-valued logic. *ACM Trans. Program. Lang. Syst.*, 24(3):217–298, 2002.

[20] T. Touili. Regular model checking using widening techniques. *Electr. Notes Theor. Comput. Sci.*, 50(4), 2001.

Decidable Logics Combining Heap Structures and Data

P. Madhusudan
University of Illinois at Urbana-Champaign, USA
madhu@illinois.edu

Gennaro Parlato
LIAFA, CNRS and University of Paris Diderot, France
gennaro@liafa.jussieu.fr

Xiaokang Qiu
University of Illinois at Urbana-Champaign, USA
qiu2@illinois.edu

Abstract

We define a new logic, STRAND, that allows reasoning with heap-manipulating programs using deductive verification and SMT solvers. STRAND logic ("STRucture ANd Data" logic) formulas express constraints involving heap structures and the data they contain; they are defined over a class of pointer-structures $\mathcal{R}$ defined using MSO-defined relations over trees, and are of the form $\exists\vec{x}\forall\vec{y}\varphi(\vec{x},\vec{y})$, where φ is a monadic second-order logic (MSO) formula with additional quantification that combines structural constraints as well as data-constraints, but where the data-constraints are only allowed to refer to $\vec{x}$ and $\vec{y}$.

The salient aspects of the logic are: (a) the logic is powerful, allowing existential and universal quantification over the nodes, and complex combinations of data and structural constraints; (b) checking Hoare-triples for linear blocks of statements with pre-conditions and post-conditions expressed as Boolean combinations of existential and universal STRAND formulas reduces to satisfiability of a STRAND formula; (c) there are powerful decidable fragments of STRAND, one semantically defined and one syntactically defined, where the decision procedure works by combining the theory of MSO over trees and the quantifier-free theory of the underlying data-logic. We demonstrate the effectiveness and practicality of the logic by checking verification conditions generated in proving properties of several heap-manipulating programs, using a tool that combines an MSO decision procedure over trees (MONA) with an SMT solver for integer constraints (Z3).

Categories and Subject Descriptors F.3.1 [*Logics and Meanings of Programs*]: Specifying and Verifying and Reasoning about Programs: Mechanical Verification; D.2.4 [*Software Engineering*]: Software/Program Verification: Assertion checkers; F.1.1 [*Theory of Computation*]: Models of Computation: Automata

General Terms Algorithms, Reliability, Theory, Verification

Keywords heap analysis, SMT solvers, monadic second-order logic, combining decision procedures, automata, decidability

1. Introduction

A fundamental component of analysis techniques for complex programs is logical reasoning. The advent of efficient SMT solvers (satisfiability modulo theory solvers) have significantly advanced the techniques for the analysis of programs. SMT solvers check satisfiability in particular theories (e.g. integers, arrays, theory of uninterpreted functions, etc.), and are often restricted to *quantifier-free* fragments of first-order logic, but support completely automated and efficient decision procedures for satisfiability. Moreover, by using techniques that *combine* theories, larger decidable theories can be obtained. The Nelson-Oppen framework [22] allows generic combinations of *quantifier-free* theories, and has been used in efficient implementations of combinations of theories using a SAT solver that queries decision procedures of component theories.

Satisfiability solvers for theories are tools that advance several analysis techniques. They are useful in test-input generation, where the solver is asked whether there exists an input to a program that will drive it along a particular path; see for example [12]. SMT solvers are also useful in static-analysis based on abstract interpretation, where the solver is asked to compute precise abstract transitions (for example see SLAM [2] for predicate abstraction and TVLA [17, 27] for shape-analysis). Solvers are also useful in classical deductive verification, where Hoare-triples that state pre-conditions and post-conditions can be transformed into verification conditions whose validity is checked by the solver; for example BOOGIE [3] and ESC/Java [11] use SMT solvers to prove verification conditions.

One of the least understood classes of theories, however, are theories that combine heap-structures and the data they contain. Analysis of programs that manipulate dynamically allocated memory and perform destructive pointer-updates while maintaining data-structure invariants (like a binary search tree), requires reasoning with heaps with an *unbounded* number of nodes with data stored in them. Reasoning with heap structures and data poses fundamental challenges due to the unboundedness of the data-structures. First, for a logic to be useful, it must be able to place constraints on all parts of the structure (e.g. to say a list is sorted), and hence some form of universal quantification over the heap is absolutely necessary. This immediately rules out classical combinations of theories, like the Nelson-Oppen scheme [22], which caters only to quantifier-free theories. Intuitively, given a constraint on heap structures and data, there may be an *infinite* number of heaps that satisfy the structural constraints, and checking whether any of these heaps can be extended with data to satisfy the constraint cannot be stated over the data-logic (even if it has quantification).

There have been a few breakthroughs in combining heap structures and data recently. For instance, HAVOC [16] supports a logic that ensures decidability using a highly restrictive syntax, and CSL [7] extends the HAVOC logic mechanism to handle constraints on sizes of structures. However, both these logics have very awkward syntax that involve the domain being partially ordered with respect to *sorts*, and the logics are heavily curtailed so that the decision procedure can move down the sorted structures hierarchically and hence terminate. Moreover, these logics cannot express even simple properties on trees of unbounded depth, like the property

POPL'11, January 26–28, 2011, Austin, Texas, USA.

that a tree is a binary search tree. More importantly, the technique for deciding the logic is encoded in the *syntax*, which in turn narrowly aims for a fast reduction to the underlying data-logic, making it hard to extend or generalize.

In this paper, we propose a new fundamental technique for deciding theories that combine heap structures and data, for fragments of a logic called STRAND.

The logic STRAND: We define a new logic called STRAND (for "STRucture ANd Data"), that combines a powerful heap-logic with an arbitrary data-logic. STRAND formulas are interpreted over a class of *data-structures* $\mathcal{R}$, and are of the form $\exists\vec{x}\forall\vec{y}\varphi(\vec{x},\vec{y})$, where φ is a formula that combines a complete monadic second-order logic over the heap-structure (and can have additional quantification), and a data-logic that can constrain the data-fields of the nodes referred to by $\vec{x}$ and $\vec{y}$.

The heap-logic in STRAND is derived from the rich logic tradition of designing decidable monadic second-order logics over graphs, and is extremely expressive in defining structural shapes and invariants. STRAND formulas are interpreted over a recursively defined class of data-structures $\mathcal{R}$, which is defined using a regular set of *skeleton* trees with MSO-defined edge-relations (pointer-relations) between them. This way of recursively defining data-structures is not new, and was pioneered by the PALE system [20], which reasons with purely structural properties of heaps defined in a similar manner. In fact, the notion of *graph types* [14] is a convenient and simple way to define data-structure types and invariants, and is easily expressible in our scheme. Data-structures defined over skeleton trees have enough expressive power to state most data-structure invariants of recursively defined data-structures, including nested lists, threaded trees, cyclic and doubly-linked lists, and separate or loosely connected combinations of these structures. Moreover, they present a class of graphs that have a decidable MSO theory, as MSO on these graphs can be *interpreted* using MSO over trees, which is decidable. In fact, graphs defined this way are one of the largest classes of graphs that have a decidable MSO theory.

As we show in this paper, the STRAND logic is well-suited to reasoning with programs. In particular, assume we are given a (straight-line) program P, a pre-condition on the data-structure expressed as a set of recursive structures $\mathcal{R}$, and a pre-condition and a post-condition expressed in a sub-fragment of STRAND that allows Boolean combinations of the existential and universal fragments. We show that checking the invalidity of the associated Hoare-triple reduces to the satisfiability problem of STRAND over a new class of recursive structures $\mathcal{R}_P$.

Note that despite its relative expressiveness in allowing quantification over nodes, STRAND formulas cannot express certain constraints such as those that constrain the *length* of a list of nodes (e.g., to express that the number of black nodes on all paths in a red-black tree are the same), nor express the *multi-set* of data-values stored in a data-structure (e.g., to express that one list's data contents are the same as that of another list). We hope that future work will extend the results in this paper to handle such constraints.

Decidable fragments of STRAND: The primary contribution of this paper is in identifying decidable fragments of STRAND. We define two such fragments, one which is a *semantic* fragment $\text{STRAND}^{sem}_{dec}$ that defines the largest class that can exploit our combination mechanism for decidability, and the other a smaller but *syntactic* fragment STRAND_{dec}.

The decision procedures work through a notion called *satisfiability-preserving embeddings*. Intuitively, for two heap structures (without data) S and S', *S satisfiability-preservingly embeds* in S' with respect to a STRAND formula ψ if there is an embedding of the nodes of S in S' such that *no matter how the data-logic constraints are interpreted*, if S' satisfies ψ, then so will the submodel S satisfy ψ, by inheriting the data-values. We define the notion of satisfiability-preserving embeddings so that it is entirely structural in nature, and is definable using MSO on an underlying graph that simultaneously represents S, S', and the embedding of S in S'.

If S satisfiability-preservingly embeds in S', then clearly, when checking for satisfiability, we can ignore S' if we check satisfiability for S. More generally, the satisfiability check can be done only for the *minimal* structures with respect to the partial-order (and well-order) defined by satisfiability-preserving embeddings.

The semantic decidable fragment $\text{STRAND}^{sem}_{dec}$ is defined to be the class of all formulas for which the set of minimal structures with respect to satisfiability-preserving embeddings is *finite*, and where the quantifier-free theory of the underlying data-logic is decidable. Though this fragment of STRAND is semantically defined, we show that it is syntactically checkable. Given a STRAND formula ψ, we show that we can build a regular finite representation of all the minimal models with respect to satisfiability-preserving embeddings, even if it is an infinite set, using automata-theory. Then, checking whether the number of minimal models is finite is decidable. If the set of minimal models is finite, we show how to enumerate the models, and reduce the problem of checking whether they admit a data-extension that satisfies ψ to a formula in the *quantifier-free* fragment of the underlying data-logic, which can then be decided.

We also define a *syntactic* decidable fragment of STRAND, STRAND_{dec}, which is a subfragment of the semantic class $\text{STRAND}^{sem}_{dec}$. In this fragment, we distinguish two kinds of binary relations in the heap, *elastic* and *non-elastic* relations. Intuitively, a relation is elastic if for every model M and submodel M', the relation holds on a pair of nodes of M' iff the relation holds for the corresponding pair of nodes in M. Given a relation R, we show it is also decidable whether R is an elastic relation. STRAND_{dec} formulas are then of the form $\exists\vec{x}\forall\vec{y}\varphi(\vec{x},\vec{y})$, where (a) φ has no additional quantification, and (b) the atomic non-elastic structural relations in φ compare only variables in $\vec{x}$. We show that STRAND_{dec} formulas always have a finite number of minimal models with respect to satisfiability-preserving embeddings, and are hence decidable using the decision procedure for the semantic fragment $\text{STRAND}^{sem}_{dec}$.

We report also on an implementation of the above decision procedures. For the structural phase, we use MONA [13], a powerful tool for deciding MSO over trees which, despite its theoretical non-elementary worst-case complexity, works very efficiently on realistic examples, by combining a variety of techniques including tree-automata minimization, BDDs, and guided tree automata. The quantifier-free data-logic we use is the quantifier-free logic of linear arithmetic, and we use the SMT solver Z3 to handle these constraints. We have proved several heap-manipulating programs correct including programs that search and insert into sorted lists, reverse sorted lists, and perform search, insertion, and rotation on binary-search trees.

In each of these cases, the verification conditions were always expressible in the syntactic fragment STRAND_{dec}, and hence in the semantic decidable fragment $\text{STRAND}^{sem}_{dec}$, supporting our thesis that the decidable fragment is natural and useful.

In summary, we present a general decidability technique for combining heap structures and data, identify semantically a decidable fragment $\text{STRAND}^{sem}_{dec}$, demonstrate a syntactically-defined subfragment STRAND_{dec}, and present experimental evaluation to show that the decidable combination is expressive and efficiently solvable. We believe that this work breaks new ground in combining heap structures and data, and the technique may also pave the way for defining decidable fragments of other logics, such as separation logic, that combine structures and data.

2. Motivating examples and logic design

The goal of this section is to present an overview of the issues involved in finding decidable logics that combine heap structure and data, which sets the stage for defining the decidable fragments of the logic STRAND, and motivates the choices in our logic design using simple examples on lists.

Let us consider lists in this section, where each node u has a data-field $d(u)$ that can hold a value (say an integer), and with two variables `head` and `tail` pointing to the first and last nodes of the list, respectively. Consider first-order logic, where we are allowed to quantify over the nodes of the list, and further, for any node x, allowed to refer to the *data-field* of x using the term $d(x)$. Let $x \rightarrow y$ denote that y is the successor of x in the list, and let $x \rightarrow^* y$ denote that x is the same as y or precedes y in the list.

EXAMPLE 2.1. *Consider the formula:*

$$\varphi_1: \quad d(\texttt{head}){=}c_1 \ \wedge\ d(\texttt{tail}){=}c_2 \ \wedge \\ \forall y_1 \forall y_2 ((y_1 \rightarrow^* y_2) \Rightarrow d(y_1) \leq d(y_2))$$

The above says that the list must be *sorted* and that the head of the list must have value c_1 and the tail must have value c_2. Note that the formula is satisfiable iff $c_1 \leq c_2$, and in which case it is actually satisfied by a list containing *just two elements,* pointed to by `head` and `tail`, with values c_1 and c_2, respectively.

In fact, the property that the formula is satisfiable by a two-element list has *nothing* really to do with the data-constraints involved in the above formula. Assume that we have no idea as to what the data-constraints mean, and hence look upon the above formula by replacing all the data-constraints using uninterpreted predicates $p_1, p_2, \ldots$ to get the formula:

$$\widehat{\varphi}_1: \quad p_1(d(\texttt{head})) \ \wedge p_2(d(\texttt{tail})) \ \wedge \\ \forall y_1 \forall y_2 ((y_1 \rightarrow^* y_2) \Rightarrow p_3(d(y_1), d(y_2)))$$

Now, we do not know whether the formula is satisfiable (for example, p_1 may be unsatisfiable). But we still do know that two-element lists are *always sufficient.* In other words, *if there is a list that satisfies the above formula, then there is a two-element list that satisfies it.* The argument is simple: take any list l that satisfies the formula, and form a new list l' that has only the head and tail of the list l, with an edge from head to tail, and with data values inherited from l (see figure below). It is easy to see that l' satisfies the formula as well, since whenever two nodes are related by $\rightarrow^*$ in the list l', the corresponding elements in l are similarly related. This property,

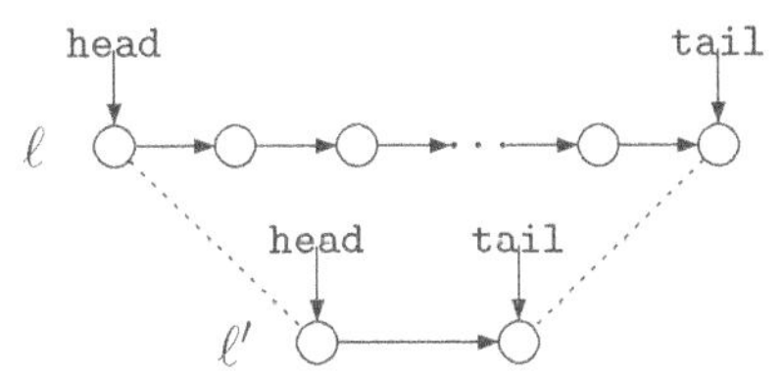

of course, does not hold on all formulas, as we see in the example below.

EXAMPLE 2.2. *Consider the formula:*

$$\varphi_2: \quad d(\texttt{head}){=}c_1 \ \wedge\ d(\texttt{tail}){=}c_2 \ \wedge \\ \forall y_1 \forall y_2 ((y_1 \rightarrow y_2) \Rightarrow d(y_2) = d(y_1) + 1)$$

The above says that the values in the list increase by one as we go one element down the list, and that the head and tail of the list have values c_1 and c_2, respectively. This formula is satisfiable iff $c_1 < c_2$. However, there is no bound on the size of the minimal model that is *independent* of the data-constraints. For example, if $c_1 = 1$ and $c_2 = 10^6$, then the smallest list that satisfies the formula has a million nodes. In other words, the data-constraints place arbitrary lower bounds on the *size* of the minimal structure that satisfies the formula.

Intuitively, the formula φ_2 refers to *successive* elements in the list, and hence a large model that satisfies the formula is not necessarily contractible to a smaller model. The formula φ_1 in the sortedness example (Example 2.1) refers to pairs of elements that were reachable, leading to contraction of large models to small ones.

Recall that the design principle of the decidable fragment of STRAND is to examine the structural constraints in a formula φ, and enumerate a *finite* set of structures such that the formula is satisfiable iff it one of these structures can be populated with values to satisfy the formula. This strategy necessarily fails for the above formula φ_2, as there is no class of finite structures that adequately captures all models of the formula, independent of the data-constraints. The *sortedness* formula φ_1 in the first example is part of the decidable fragment of STRAND, while φ_2 is outside of it.

EXAMPLE 2.3. *Consider the formula:*

$$\varphi_3: \quad d(\texttt{head}){=}c_1 \ \wedge\ d(\texttt{tail}){=}c_2 \ \wedge \\ \forall y_1 ((y_1 \neq \texttt{tail}) \Rightarrow \exists y_2 (d(y_2) = d(y_1) + 1))$$

This formula says that for any node n except the tail, there is some node n' that has the value $d(n) + 1$. Notice that the formula is satisfiable if $c_1 < c_2$, but still there is no a priori bound on the minimal model that is independent of the data-constraints. In particular, if $c_1 = 0$ and $c_2 = 10^6$, then the smallest model is a list with 10^6 nodes. Moreover, the reason why the bounded structure property fails is not because of the data-constraints referring to successive elements as in Example 2.2, but rather because the above formula has a $\forall\exists$ prefix quantification of data-variables. Formulas where an existential quantification follows a universal quantification in the prefix seldom have bounded models, and STRAND hence only allows formulas with $\exists^*\forall^*$ quantification prefixes. Note that quantification of *structure variables* (variables that quantify over nodes but whose data-field is not referenced in the formula) can be arbitrary, and in fact we allow STRAND formulas to even have *set quantifications* over nodes.

The Bernays-Schönfinkel-Ramsey class: Having motivated formulas with the $\exists^*\forall^*$ quantification, it is worthwhile to examine this fragment in classical first-order logic (over arbitrary infinite universes), which is known as the Bernays-Schönfinkel-Ramsey class, and is a classical decidable fragment of first-order logic [6].

Consider first a purely relational vocabulary (assume there are no functions and even no constants). Then, given a formula $\exists\vec{x}\forall\vec{y}\varphi(\vec{x}, \vec{y})$, let M be a model that satisfies this formula. Let v be an interpretation for $\vec{x}$ such that M under v satisfies $\forall\vec{y}\varphi(\vec{x}, \vec{y})$. Then it is not hard to argue that the submodel obtained by picking only the elements used in the interpretation of $\vec{x}$ (i.e. $v(\vec{x})$), and projecting each relation to this smaller set, satisfies the formula $\exists\vec{x}\forall\vec{y}\varphi(\vec{x}, \vec{y})$ as well [6]. Hence a model of size at most k always exists that satisfies φ, if the formula is satisfiable, where k is the size of the vector of existentially quantified variables $\vec{x}$. This *bounded model property* extends to when constants are present as well (the submodel should include all the constants) but fails when more than two functions are present. Satisfiability hence reduces to propositional satisfiability, and this class is also called the *effectively propositional* class, and SMT solving for this class exists [8].

The decidable fragment of STRAND is fashioned after a similar but more complex argument. Given a subset of nodes of a model, the subset itself may not form a valid graph/data-structure. We define a notion of *submodels* that allows us to extract proper subgraphs that contain certain nodes of the model. However, the relations (edges) in the submodel will *not* be the projection of edges in the larger model. Consequently, the submodel may not satisfy a formula, even though the larger model does.

We define a notion called *satisfiability-preserving embeddings* that allows us to identify when a submodel S of T is such that, whenever T satisfies ψ under some interpretation of the data-logic, S can *inherit* values from T to satisfy ψ as well. This is considerably more complex and is the main technical contribution of the paper. We then build decision procedures to check the minimal models according to this embedding relation.

3. Recursive data-structures

We now define recursive data-structures using a formalism that defines the nodes and edges using MSO formulas over a regular set of trees. Intuitively, a set of data-structures is defined by taking a regular class of trees that acts as a *skeleton* over which the data-structure will be defined. The precise set of nodes of the tree that corresponds to the nodes of the data-structure, and the edges between these nodes (which model pointer fields) will be captured using MSO formulas over these trees. We call such classes of data-structures *recursively defined data-structures*.

Recursively defined data-structures are very powerful mechanisms for defining invariants of data-structures. The notion of *graph types* [14] is a very similar notion, where again data-structure invariants are defined using a tree-backbone but where edges are defined using *regular path expressions*. Graph types can be modeled directly in our framework; in fact, our formalism is more powerful.

The framework of recursively defined data-structures is also interesting because they define classes of graphs that have a *decidable monadic second-order theory*. In other words, given a class $\mathcal{C}$ of recursively defined data-structures, the satisfiability problem for MSO formulas over $\mathcal{C}$ (i.e. the problem of checking, given φ, whether there is some structure $R \in \mathcal{C}$ that satisfies φ) is decidable. The decision procedure works by interpreting the MSO formula on the tree-backbone of the structures. In fact, our framework can capture all graphs definable using *edge-replacement grammars*, which are one of the most powerful classes of graphs known that have a decidable MSO theory [10].

3.1 Graphs and monadic second-order logics

A labeled (directed) graph G over a finite set of vertex-labels L_v and a finite set of edge labels L_e is a 6-tuple, $G = (V, E, \mu, \nu, L_v, L_e)$, where V is a non-empty finite set of nodes, $E \subseteq V \times V$ is a set of edges, $\mu : V \rightarrow 2^{L_v}$ assigns a subset of labels to each vertex, and $\nu : E \rightarrow 2^{L_e}$ assigns a subset of labels to each edge.

Monadic second-order logic (MSO) on graphs over the labels (L_v, L_e) is the standard MSO on structures of the form $(U, E, \{Q_a\}_{a\in L_v}, \{E_b\}_{b\in L_e})$ where U represents the universe, E is a binary relation capturing the edge relation, Q_a is a monadic predicate that captures all nodes whose labels contain a, and E_b is a binary relation that captures all edges whose label contain b (note that $E_b \subseteq E$, for every $b \in L_e$). However, we also allow Boolean variables and quantification over them[1].

Let us fix a countable set of first-order variables FV (first-order variables will be denoted by s, t, etc.) and a countable set of set-variables SV (set-variables will be denoted by S, T, etc.). Let us also fix a countable set of Boolean variables BV(denoted by p, q, etc.) The syntax of the logic is:

$$\varphi ::= p \mid Q_a(s) \mid E(s,t) \mid E_b(s,t) \mid s = t \mid s \in S \mid$$
$$\varphi \vee \varphi \mid \neg\varphi \mid \exists s.\varphi \mid \exists p.\varphi \mid \exists S.\varphi$$

where $a \in L_v$, $b \in L_e$, $s, t \in FV$, $S \in SV$, and $p \in BV$.

3.2 Recursively defined data-structures

Let Σ be a finite alphabet. For any $k \in \mathbb{N}$, let $[k]$ denote the set $\{1, \ldots k\}$.

A k-ary Σ-labeled tree is a pair (V, λ), where $V \subseteq [k]^*$, and V is non-empty and prefix-closed, and $\lambda : V \rightarrow \Sigma$. The edges of the tree are implicitly defined: that is $u.i$ is the i'th child of u, for every $u, u.i \in V$, where $u \in [k]^*$ and $i \in [k]$. Trees are seen as graphs with Σ-labeled vertices and edge relations $E_i(x, y)$ that define the i'th-child edges. Monadic second-order logic over trees is the MSO logic over these graphs.

Formally, we define classes of recursively defined data-structures as follows.

DEFINITION 3.1. *A class $\mathcal{C}$ of* recursively defined data-structures *is specified by a tuple $\mathcal{R} = (\psi_{Tr}, \psi_U, \{\alpha_a\}_{a\in L_v}, \{\beta_b\}_{b\in L_e})$, where ψ_{Tr} is an MSO sentence, ψ_U is a unary predicate defined in MSO, and each α_a and β_b are monadic and binary predicates defined using MSO, where all MSO formulas are over k-ary trees, for some $k \in \mathbb{N}$, .* ■

Let $\mathcal{R} = (\psi_{Tr}, \psi_U, \{\alpha_a\}_{a\in L_v}, \{\beta_b\}_{b\in L_e})$ and T be a k-ary Σ-labeled tree. Then $T = (V, \{E_i\}_{i\in[k]})$ defines (according to $\mathcal{R}$) a graph $Graph(T) = (N, E, \mu, \nu, L_v, L_e)$ defined as follows:

- $N = \{s \in V \mid \psi_U(s)$ *holds in* $T\}$
- $E = \{(s, s') \mid \beta_b(s, s')$ *holds in* T *for some* $b \in L_e\}$
- $\mu(s) = \{a \in L_v \mid \alpha_a(s)$ *holds in* $T\}$
- $\nu((s, s')) = \{b \in L_e \mid \beta_b(s, s')$ *holds in* $T\}$.

The class of graphs defined by $\mathcal{R}$ is the set $Graph(\mathcal{R}) = \{Graph(T) \mid T \models \psi_{Tr}\}$.

EXAMPLE 3.2. *Let us define a class of recursive data-structures that consists of trees where the leaves of the tree are connected by a linked list. The class of trees will be the class of binary trees (with edges E_1 and E_2 representing left- and right-child relations), and we define the next-edge relation for the list using an MSO predicate:*

$$E_{next}(s,t) \equiv leaf(s) \wedge leaf(t) \wedge \exists z_1, z_2, z_3(E_1(z_3, z_1) \wedge E_2(z_3, z_2) \wedge RightMostPath(z_1, s) \wedge LeftMostPath(z_2, t))$$

where $leaf(x)$ is a subformula that checks if x is a leaf, and $RightMostPath(x, y)$ (and $LeftMostPath(x, y)$) is a formula that checks if y is in the right-most (left-most, respectively) path from x.

4. STRAND: A logic over heap structures and data

4.1 Definition of STRAND

We now introduce our logic STRAND ("STRucture ANd Data"). STRAND is a two-sorted logic interpreted on program heaps with both locations and their carried data. Given a first-order theory $\mathcal{D}$ of sort $Data$, and given $\mathcal{L}$, a monadic second-order (MSO) theory over (L_v, L_e)-labeled graphs, of sort Loc, the syntax of STRAND is presented in Figure 1. STRAND is defined over the two-sorted signature $\Gamma(\mathcal{D}, \mathcal{L}) = Sig(\mathcal{D}) \cup Sig(\mathcal{L}) \cup \{data\}$, where $data$ is a function of sort $Loc \rightarrow Data$. STRAND formulas are of the form $\exists\vec{x}\forall\vec{y}\varphi(\vec{x}, \vec{y})$, where $\vec{x}$ and $\vec{y}$ are $\exists$DVar and $\forall$DVar, respectively, of sort Loc (we also refer to both as DVar), φ is an MSO formula with atomic formulas of the form either $\gamma(e_1, \ldots, e_n)$ or $\alpha(v_1, \ldots, v_n)$. $\gamma(e_1, \ldots, e_n)$ is an atomic $\mathcal{D}$-formula in which the data carried by Loc-variables can be referred as $data(x)$ or $data(y)$. $\alpha(v_1, \ldots, v_n)$ is just an atomic formula from $\mathcal{L}$. Note that additional variables are allowed in $\varphi(\vec{x}, \vec{y})$, both first-order and second-order, but $\gamma(e_1, \ldots, e_n)$ is only allowed to refer to $\vec{x}$ and $\vec{y}$.

A model for STRAND is a structure $\mathcal{M} = \langle \mathcal{M}_{Loc}, \mathcal{M}_{Data}, M_{map}\rangle$. $\mathcal{M}_{Loc}$ is an $\mathcal{L}$-model (i.e. a labeled graph) with M_{Loc} as the underlying set of nodes, and $\mathcal{M}_{Data}$ is a $\mathcal{D}$-model with M_{Data} as the underlying set. M_{map} is an interpretation for the function $data$ of sort $M_{Loc} \rightarrow M_{Data}$. The semantics of STRAND formulas is the natural extension of the logics $\mathcal{L}$ and $\mathcal{D}$.

[1] Classical definitions of MSO do not allow such Boolean quantification, but we will find it useful in our setting. These variables can be easily removed; e.g. instead of quantifying over a Boolean variable p, we can quantify over a set X and convert every occurrence of p to a formula that expresses that X is empty.

∃DVar	x	$\in$	Loc
∀DVar	y	$\in$	Loc
GVar	z	$\in$	Loc
Variable	v	$::=$	$x \mid y \mid z$
Set − Variable	S	$\in$	2^{Loc}
Constant	c	$\in$	$Sig(\mathcal{D})$
Function	g	$\in$	$Sig(\mathcal{D})$
$\mathcal{D}$−Relation	γ	$\in$	$Sig(\mathcal{D})$
$\mathcal{L}$−Relation	α	$\in$	$Sig(\mathcal{L})$
Expression	e	$::=$	$data(x) \mid data(y) \mid c \mid g(e_1, \ldots, e_n)$
AFormula	φ	$::=$	$\gamma(e_1, \ldots, e_n) \mid \alpha(v_1, \ldots, v_n)$
			$\mid \neg\varphi \mid \varphi_1 \wedge \varphi_2 \mid \varphi_1 \vee \varphi_2$
			$\mid \exists z.\varphi \mid \forall z.\varphi \mid \exists S.\varphi \mid \forall S.\varphi$
∀Formula	ω	$::=$	$\varphi \mid \forall y.\omega$
Formula	ψ	$::=$	$\omega \mid \exists x.\psi$

Figure 1. Syntax of STRAND

We will refer to an $\mathcal{L}$-model as a *graph-model*. A *data-extension* of a graph model $\mathcal{M}_{Loc}$ is a STRAND model $\langle \mathcal{M}_{Loc}, \mathcal{M}_{Data}, M_{map} \rangle$.

Undecidability. STRAND is an expressive logic, as we will show below, but it is undecidable in general, even if both its underlying theories $\mathcal{D}$ and $\mathcal{L}$ are decidable. Let $\mathcal{D}$ be linear integer arithmetic and $\mathcal{L}$ be the standard MSO logic over lists. It is easy to model an execution of a 2-counter machine using a list with integers. Each configuration is represented by two adjacent nodes, which are labeled by the current instruction. The data fields of the two nodes hold the value of the two registers, respectively. Then a halting computation can be expressed by a STRAND formula. Hence the satisfiability of the STRAND logic is undecidable, even though the underlying logics $\mathcal{L}$ and $\mathcal{D}$ are decidable.

4.2 Examples

We now show various examples to illustrate the expressiveness of STRAND. We sometimes use $d()$ instead of $data()$, for brevity.

EXAMPLE 4.1 (Binary search tree). *In* STRAND, *a* binary search tree *(BST) is interpreted as a binary tree data structure with an additional* key *field for each node. The keys in a BST are always stored in such a way as to satisfy the binary-search-tree property, expressed in* STRAND *as follows:*

$leftsubtree(y_1, y_2) \equiv \exists z(left(y_1, z) \wedge z \rightarrow^* y_2)$
$rightsubtree(y_1, y_2) \equiv \exists z(right(y_1, z) \wedge z \rightarrow^* y_2)$
$\psi_{bst} \equiv \forall y_1 \forall y_2(\ (leftsubtree(y_1, y_2) \Rightarrow d(y_2) < d(y_1)) \wedge ((rightsubtree(y_1, y_2) \Rightarrow d(y_1) \geq d(y_2))\ )$

Note that ψ_{bst} has an existentially quantified variable z in GVar after the universal quantification of y_1, y_2. However, as z is a structural quantification (whose data-field cannot be referred to), this formula is in STRAND.

EXAMPLE 4.2 (Two disjoint lists). *In* separation logic*[26], a novel binary operator* $*$, *or* separating conjunction, *is defined to assert that the heap can be split into two disjoint parts where its two arguments hold, respectively. Such an operator is useful in reasoning with* frame conditions *in program verification. Thanks to the powerful expressiveness of MSO logic, the separating conjunction is also expressible in* STRAND. *For example,* $(\mathtt{head}_1 \rightarrow^* \mathtt{tail}_1) * (\mathtt{head}_2 \rightarrow^* \mathtt{tail}_2)$ *states, in separation logic, that there are two disjoint lists such that one list is from* $\mathtt{head}_1$ *to* $\mathtt{tail}_1$, *and the other is from* $\mathtt{head}_2$ *to* $\mathtt{tail}_2$. *This formula can be written in* STRAND *as:*

$$\exists S_1 \exists S_2(disjoint(S_1, S_2) \wedge \mathtt{head}_1 \in S_1 \wedge \mathtt{tail}_1 \in S_1 \wedge \mathtt{head}_2 \in S_2 \wedge \mathtt{tail}_2 \in S_2 \wedge \mathtt{head}_1 \rightarrow^* \mathtt{tail}_1 \wedge \mathtt{head}_2 \rightarrow^* \mathtt{tail}_2) \wedge (\forall z(\mathtt{head}_1 \rightarrow^* z \wedge z \rightarrow^* \mathtt{tail}_1) \Rightarrow z \in S_1) \wedge (\forall z(\mathtt{head}_2 \rightarrow^* z \wedge z \rightarrow^* \mathtt{tail}_2) \Rightarrow z \in S_2)$$

where $disjoint(S_1, S_2) \equiv \neg\exists z(z \in S_1 \wedge z \in S_2)$.

5. Deciding STRAND fragments

5.1 Removing existential quantification:

Given a STRAND formula $\exists\vec{x}\forall\vec{y}\varphi(\vec{x}, \vec{y})$ over a class of recursively defined data-structures $\mathcal{R} = (\psi_{Tr}, \psi_U, \{\alpha_a\}_{a \in L_v}, \{\beta_b\}_{b \in L_e})$, we can transform this to an *equisatisfiable* formula $\forall\vec{x}\forall\vec{y}\varphi'(\vec{x}, \vec{y})$ over a *different* class of recursive data-structures $\mathcal{R}'$, where data-structures in $\mathcal{R}'$ are data-structures in $\mathcal{R}$ with new unary predicates that give a valuation for the variables in $\vec{x}$. We won't define this formally, but this is an easy transformation: we modify ψ_{Tr} to accept trees with extra labelings a_i that give (an arbitrary) singleton valuation of each $x_i \in \vec{x}$ that satisfies ψ_U, and introduce new unary predicates $Val_i(x) = Q_{a_i}(x)$, and define $\varphi'(\vec{x}, \vec{y})$ to be $(\wedge_i Val_i(x_i)) \Rightarrow \varphi(\vec{x}, \vec{y})$. It is easy to see there is a graph in *Graph*($\mathcal{R}$) that satisfies $\exists\vec{x}\forall\vec{y}\varphi(\vec{x}, \vec{y})$ iff there is a graph in *Graph*($\mathcal{R}'$) that satisfies $\forall\vec{x}\forall\vec{y}\varphi'(\vec{x}, \vec{y})$. The latter is a STRAND formula with no existential quantification of variables whose data is referred to by the formula. Let us refer to these formulas with no leading existential quantification on data-variables as *universal* STRAND *formulas*; we will now outline techniques to solve the satisfiability problem of a certain class of universal STRAND formulas.

5.2 Submodels

Let us fix a class of recursively defined data-structures $\mathcal{R} = (\psi_{Tr}, \psi_U, \{\alpha_a\}_{a \in L_v}, \{\beta_b\}_{b \in L_e})$ for the rest of this section.

We first need to define the notion of *submodels* of a model. The definition of a submodel will depend on the particular class of recursively defined data-structures we are working with, since we want to exploit the tree-representation of the models, which in turn will play a crucial role in deciding fragments of STRAND, as it will allow us to check satisfiability-preserving embeddings. In fact, we will define the submodel relation between trees that satisfy ψ_{Tr}.

DEFINITION 5.1. *Let* $T = (V, \lambda)$ *be a tree that satisfies* ψ_{Tr}, *and let* $S \subseteq V$. *Then we say that* S *is* a valid subset *of* V *if the following hold:*

- *S is non-empty, and least-ancestor closed (i.e. for any $s, s' \in S$, the least common ancestor of s and s' in T also belongs to S).*
- *The* subtree *defined by S, denoted Subtree(T, S), is the tree with nodes S, and where the i'th child of a node $u \in S$ is the (unique) node $u' \in S$ closest to u that is in the subtree rooted at the i'th child of u. (This is uniquely defined since S is least-ancestor closed.) Then we require that Subtree(T, S) also satisfies ψ_{Tr}.*
- *We also require that for every $s \in S$, if $\psi_U(s)$ holds in Subtree(T, S), then $\psi_U(s)$ holds in T as well.*

A tree $T' = (V', \lambda')$ *is said to be a* submodel *of* $T = (V, \lambda)$ *if there is a valid subset* S *of* V *such that* T' *is isomorphic to Subtree*(T, S). ∎

Note that a submodel is necessarily a valid data-structure.

Intuitively, $T' = (V', \lambda')$ is a submodel of $T = (V, \lambda)$ if the vertices of T' can be embedded in T, preserving the tree-structure. The nodes of the *Graph*(T'), are a subset of the nodes of *Graph*(T) (because of the last condition in the definition of a submodel), and, given a valid subset S, there is in fact an injective mapping from the nodes of *Graph*(T') to *Graph*(T). For technical convenience, we will work with valid subsets mostly, as fixing the precise embedding helps in the decision procedures.

5.3 Structural abstractions of STRAND formulas

Let $\psi = \forall \vec{y}\ \varphi(\vec{y})$ be a universal STRAND formula.

We now define the *structural abstraction* of ψ as follows. Let $\gamma_1, \gamma_2, \ldots, \gamma_r$ be the *atomic* relational formulas of the data-logic in φ. Note that each of these relational formulas will be over the data fields of variables in $\vec{y}$ only (since the data-logic is restricted to working over the terms $data(y)$, where $y \in \vec{y}$).

Consider evaluating ψ over a particular model. After fixing a particular valuation of $\vec{y}$, notice that the data-relations γ_i get all fixed, and evaluate to true or false. Moreover, once the values of γ_i are fixed, the rest of the formula is purely *structural* in nature. Now, if ψ is to hold in the model, then no matter how we choose to evaluate $\vec{y}$ over the nodes of the model, the γ_i relations must evaluate to true or false in such a way that φ holds.

Since we want, in the first phase, to *ignore* the data-constraints entirely, we will abstract ψ using a purely structural formula by using Boolean variables $b_1, \ldots b_r$ instead of the data-relations $\gamma_1, \gamma_2, \ldots, \gamma_r$. However, since these Boolean variables get determined only *after* the valuation of $\vec{y}$ gets determined, and since we are solving for satisfiability, we existentially quantify over these Boolean variables and quantify them *after* the quantification of $\vec{y}$. Formally[2],

DEFINITION 5.2. *Let $\psi = \forall \vec{y}\ \varphi(\vec{y})$ be a universal* STRAND *formula, and let the atomic relational formulas of the data-logic that occur in φ be $\gamma_1, \gamma_2, \ldots, \gamma_r$. Then its structural abstraction $\widehat{\psi}$ is defined as the pure MSO formula on graphs:*

$$\forall \vec{y}\ \exists b_1 \ldots b_r\ \ \varphi'(\vec{y}, \vec{b})$$

where φ' is φ with every occurrence of γ_i replaced with b_i. ∎

For example, consider the sortedness formula ψ_{sorted} from Example 2.1. Then

$$\widehat{\psi}_{sorted}:\ \ \forall y_1 \forall y_2\ \exists b_1\ (d(\texttt{head}){=}c_1\ \wedge\ d(\texttt{tail}){=}c_2\ \wedge\ ((y_1 \rightarrow^* y_2) \Rightarrow b_1)$$

Note that each Boolean variable b_i replaces an atomic relational formula γ_i, where γ_i places some data-constraint on the data-fields of some of the universally quantified variables.

The following proposition is obvious; it says that if a universal STRAND formula ψ is satisfiable, then so is its structural abstraction $\widehat{\psi}$. The proposition is true because the values for the Boolean variables can be set in the structural abstraction precisely according to how the relational formulas γ_i evaluate in ψ:

PROPOSITION 5.3. *Let $\psi = \forall \vec{y} \varphi(\vec{y})$ be a universal* STRAND *formula, and $\widehat{\psi}$ be its structural abstraction. If ψ is satisfiable over a set of recursive data-structures $\mathcal{R}$, then the MSO formula on graphs (with no constraints on data) $\widehat{\psi}$ is also satisfiable over $\mathcal{R}$.*

[2] The definition of structural abstractions can be strengthened in two ways. First, if γ_i and γ_j are of the same arity and over $\vec{z}$ and $\vec{z}\,'$, respectively, and further uniformly replacing z_i with z_i' in γ_i yields γ', then we can express the constraint $((\vec{z_i} = \vec{z_i}') \Rightarrow (b_i \Leftrightarrow b_j))$, in the inner formula φ'. Second, if a constraint γ_i involves only existentially quantified variables in $\vec{x}$, then we can move the quantification of b_i outside the universal quantification. Doing these steps gives a more accurate structural abstraction, and in practice, restricts the number of models created. We use these more precise abstractions in the experiments, but use the less precise abstractions in the theoretical narrative. The proofs in this section, however, smoothly extend to the more precise abstractions.

5.4 Satisfiability-preserving embeddings

We are now ready to define satisfiability-preserving embeddings using structural abstractions. Given a model defined by a tree $T = (V, \lambda)$ satisfying ψ_{Tr}, and a valid subset $S \subseteq V$, and a universal STRAND formula ψ, we would like to define the notion of when the submodel defined by S satisfiability-preservingly embeds in the model. The most crucial requirement for the definition is that if S satisfiability-preservingly embeds in T, then we require that if there is a data-extension of *Graph*(T) that satisfies ψ, then the nodes of the submodel defined by S, *Graph*(*Subtree*(T, S)), can inherit the data-values and also satisfy ψ. The notion of structural abstractions defined above allows us to define such a notion.

Intuitively, if a model satisfies ψ, then it would satisfy $\widehat{\psi}$ too, as for every valuation of $\vec{y}$, there is some way it would satisfy the atomic data-relations, and using this we can pull out a valuation for the Boolean variables to satisfy $\widehat{\psi}$ (as in the proof of Proposition 5.3 above). Now, since the data-values in the submodel are *inherited* from the larger model, the atomic data-relations would hold *in the same way* as they do in the larger model. However, the submodel may not satisfy ψ if the conditions on the truth- and false-hood of these atomic relations demanded by ψ are not the same.

For example, consider a list and a sublist of it. Consider a formula that demands that for any two successor elements y_1, y_2 in the list, the data-value of y_2 is the data-value of y_1 incremented by 1 (as in the *successor* example in Section 2):

$$\psi \equiv \forall y_1 \forall y_2(\ (y_1 \rightarrow y_2) \Rightarrow (d(y_2) = d(y_1) + 1)\ )$$

Now consider two nodes y_1 and y_2 that are successors in the sublist but not successors in the list. The list hence could satisfy the formula by setting the data-relation $\gamma : d(y_2) = d(y_1) + 1$ to false. Since the sublist inherits the data values, γ would be false in the sublist as well, but the sublist will *not* satisfy the formula ψ. We hence want to ensure that *no matter how the larger model satisfies the formula* using some valuation of the atomic data-relations, the submodel will be able to satisfy the formula using the *same valuation of the atomic data-relations*. This leads us to the following definition:

DEFINITION 5.4. *Let $\psi = \forall \vec{y}\ \varphi(\vec{y})$ be a universal* STRAND *formula, and let its structural abstraction be $\widehat{\psi} = \forall \vec{y}\ \exists \vec{b}\ \varphi'(\vec{y}, \vec{b})$. Let $T = (V, \lambda)$ be a tree that satisfies ψ_{Tr}, and let a submodel be defined by $S \subseteq V$. Then S is said to* satisfiability-preservingly embed *into T wrt ψ if for every possible valuation of $\vec{y}$ over the elements of S, and for every possible Boolean valuation of $\vec{b}$, if $\varphi'(\vec{y}, \vec{b})$ holds in the graph defined by T under this valuation, then the submodel defined by S, Graph(Subtree(T, S)), also satisfies $\varphi'(\vec{y}, \vec{b})$ under the same valuation.* ∎

The satisfiability-preserving embedding relation can be seen as a *partial order* over trees (a tree T' satisfiability-preservingly embeds into T if there is a subset S of T such that S satisfiability-preservingly embeds into T and *Subtree*(T, S) is isomorphic to T'); it is easy to see that this relation is reflexive, anti-symmetric and transitive.

It is now not hard to see that if S satisfiability-preservingly embeds into T wrt ψ, and *Graph*(T) satisfies ψ, then *Graph*(*Subtree*(T, S)) also necessarily satisfies ψ, which is the main theorem we seek.

THEOREM 5.5. *Let $\psi = \forall \vec{y} \varphi(\vec{y})$ be universal* STRAND *formula. Let $T = (V, \lambda)$ be a tree that satisfies ψ_{Tr}, and S be a valid subset of T that satisfiability-preservingly embeds into T wrt ψ. Then, if there is a data-extension of Graph(T) that satisfies ψ, then there is a data-extension of Graph(Subtree(T, S)) that satisfies ψ.*

Notice that the above theorem crucially depends on the formula being universal over data-variables. For example, if the formula was of the form $\forall y_1 \exists y_2 \gamma(y_1, y_2)$, then we would have no way of knowing *which* nodes are used for y_2 in the data-extension of *Graph*(T) to satisfy the formula. Without knowing the precise meaning of the data-predicates, we would not be able to declare that whenever a data-extension of *Graph*(T) is satisfiable, a data-extension of a strict submodel S is satisfiable (even over lists).

The above notion of *satisfiability preserving embeddings* is the property that will be used to decide if a formula falls into our decidable fragment.

5.5 STRAND$_{dec}^{sem}$: A semantic decidable fragment of STRAND

We are now ready to define STRAND$_{dec}^{sem}$, the most general decidable fragment of STRAND in this paper. This fragment is semantically defined (but syntactically checkable, as we show below), and intuitively contains all STRAND formulas that have a *finite number of minimal models* with respect to the partial-order defined by satisfiability-preserving embeddings.

Formally, let $\psi = \forall \vec{y} \varphi(\vec{y})$ be a universal STRAND formula, and let $T = (V, \lambda)$ be a tree that satisfies ψ_{Tr}. Then we say that T is *a minimal model* with respect to ψ if there is no strict valid subset S of V that satisfiability-preservingly embeds in T.

DEFINITION 5.6. *Let $\mathcal{R}$ be a recursively defined set of data-structures.*

A universal formula $\psi = \forall \vec{y}\ \varphi(\vec{y})$ is in STRAND$_{dec}^{sem}$ iff the number of minimal models with respect to $\mathcal{R}$ and ψ is finite.

A STRAND formula of the form $\psi = \exists \vec{x}\ \forall \vec{y}\ \varphi(\vec{x}, \vec{y})$ is in STRAND$_{dec}^{sem}$ iff the corresponding equi-satisfiable universal formula ψ' over set of data-structure $\mathcal{R}'$ (as defined in Section 5.1) is in STRAND$_{dec}^{sem}$. ∎

We now show that we can *effectively check* if a STRAND formula belongs to the decidable fragment STRAND$_{dec}^{sem}$. The idea, intuitively, is to express that a model is a minimal model with respect to satisfiability-preserving embeddings, and then check, using automata theory, that the number of minimal models is finite.

Let $\psi = \forall \vec{y} \varphi(\vec{y})$ be universal STRAND formula, and let its structural abstraction be $\widehat{\psi} = \forall \vec{y}\ \exists \vec{b}\ \varphi'(\vec{y}, \vec{b})$.

We now show that we can define an MSO formula $MinModel_\psi$, such that it holds on a tree $T = (V, \lambda)$ iff T defines a minimal model with respect to satisfiability-preserving embeddings.

Before we do that, we need some technical results and notation. Let $\mathcal{R} = (\psi_{Tr}, \psi_U, \{\alpha_a\}_{a \in L_v}, \{\beta_b\}_{b \in L_e})$.

We first show that any (pure) MSO formula δ on (L_v, L_e)-labeled graphs can be *interpreted* on trees. Formally, we show that any (pure) MSO formula δ on (L_v, L_e)-labeled graphs can be transformed syntactically to a (pure) MSO formula δ' on trees such that for any tree $T = (V, \lambda)$, *Graph*(T)) satisfies δ iff T satisfies δ'.

This is not hard to do, since the graph is defined using MSO formulas on the trees, and we can adapt these definitions to work over the tree instead. The transformation is given by the following function *interpret*; the predicates for edges, and the predicates that check vertex labels and edges labels are transformed according to their definition, and all quantified variables are restricted to quantify over nodes that satisfy ψ_U.

- $interpret(p) = p$
- $interpret(Q_a(s)) = \alpha_a(s)$, for every $a \in L_v$
- $interpret(E(s,t)) = \bigvee_{b \in L_e} \beta_b(s,t)$
- $interpret(E_b(s,t)) = \beta_b(s,t)$, for every $b \in L_e$
- $interpret(s = t) = (s = t)$
- $interpret(s \in W) = s \in W$
- $interpret(\varphi_1 \vee \varphi_2) = interpret(\varphi_1) \vee interpret(\varphi_2)$
- $interpret(\neg\varphi) = \neg(interpret(\varphi))$
- $interpret(\exists s.\varphi) = \exists s.(\psi_U(s) \wedge interpret(\varphi))$
- $interpret(\exists W.\varphi) = \exists W.((\forall s.(s \in W \Rightarrow \psi_U(s))) \wedge interpret(\varphi))$

It is not hard to show that for any formula δ on (L_v, L_e)-labeled graphs *Graph*(T) satisfies δ iff T satisfies *interpret*(δ).

Now, we give another transformation, that transforms an MSO formula δ on trees to a formula $\delta'(X)$ on trees, over a free set-variable X, such that for any tree $T = (V, \lambda)$ and any valid subset $S \subseteq V$, *Subtree*(T, S) satisfies δ iff T satisfies $\delta'(X)$ when X is interpreted to be S. In other words, we can transform a formula that expresses a property of a subtree to a formula that expresses the same property on the subtree defined by the free variable X. The transformation is given by the following function *tailor*; the crucial transformation are the edge-formulas, which has to be interpreted as the edges of the subtree defined by X.

- $tailor_X(p) = p$
- $tailor_X(Q_a(s)) = Q_a(s)$, for every $a \in L_v$
- $tailor_X(E_i(s,t)) = \exists s'\ \ [E_i(s,s') \wedge s' \leq t \wedge \forall t'. ((t' \in X \wedge s' \leq t') \Rightarrow t \leq t')]$, for every $i \in [k]$.
- $tailor_X(s = t) = (s = t)$
- $tailor_X(s \in W) = s \in W$
- $tailor_X(\varphi_1 \vee \varphi_2) = tailor(\varphi_1) \vee tailor(\varphi_2)$
- $tailor_X(\neg\varphi) = \neg(tailor(\varphi))$
- $tailor_X(\exists s.\varphi) = \exists s.(s \in X \wedge tailor(\varphi))$
- $tailor_X(\exists W.\varphi) = \exists W.(W \subseteq X \wedge tailor(\varphi))$

The above transformation satisfies the following property. For any MSO sentence δ on k-ary trees, for any tree $T = (V, \lambda)$ and for any valid subset $S \subseteq V$, *Subtree*(T, S) satisfies δ iff T satisfies $tailor_X(\delta)$ when X is interpreted to be S.

Note that the above transformations can be combined. For any MSO formula δ on (L_v, L_e) labeled graphs, consider the formula $tailor_X(interpret(\delta))$. Then for any tree $T = (V, \lambda)$ and for any valid subset $S \subseteq V$, *Graph*(*Subtree*(T, S)) satisfies δ iff T satisfies $tailor_X(interpret(\delta))$, where X is interpreted as S.

Expressing minimal models in MSO. First, we can also express, with an MSO formula *ValidSubModel*(X), with a free set variable X, that holds in a tree $T = (V, \lambda)$ iff X is interpreted as a valid submodel of T:

$$ValidSubModel(X) \equiv$$
$$\forall s,t,u\,((s \in X \wedge t \in X \wedge lca(s,t,u)) \Rightarrow u \in X) \wedge tailor_X(\psi_{Tr}) \wedge (\forall s(s \in X \wedge tailor_X(\psi_U(s))) \ \Rightarrow\ \psi_U(s))$$

where $lca(s,t,u)$ is an MSO formula that checks whether u is the least-common ancestor of s and t in the tree; this expresses the requirements in Definition 5.1.

We are now ready to define the MSO formula on k-ary trees $MinModel_\psi$ that captures minimal models. Let the structural abstraction of ψ be $\widehat{\psi} = \forall \vec{y}\ \exists \vec{b}\ \varphi'(\vec{y}, \vec{b})$, then

$$MinModel_\psi \equiv \neg\exists X.(\ ValidSubModel(X) \wedge \exists s.(s \in X)\ \wedge\ \exists s.(s \notin X)\ \wedge (\ \forall \vec{y}\, \forall \vec{b}\, ((\wedge_{y \in \vec{y}}(y \in X \wedge \psi_U(y)) \wedge interpret(\varphi'(\vec{y}, \vec{b}))) \Rightarrow tailor_X(interpret(\varphi'(\vec{y}, \vec{b})))))$$

The above formula when interpreted on a tree T says that there does not exists a set X that defines a non-empty valid strict subset of the nodes of T, which defines a model *Graph*(*Subtree*(T, X)) that further satisfies the following: for every valuation of $\vec{y}$ over the nodes of *Graph*(*Subtree*(T, S)) and for every valuation of the Boolean variables $\vec{b}$ such that the structural abstraction of φ holds in

Graph(T), the same valuation also makes the structural abstraction of φ hold in *Graph*(*Subtree*(T,S)).

Note that the above is a *pure* MSO formula on trees, and encodes the properties required of a minimal model with respect to satisfiability-preserving embeddings. Using the classical logic-automaton connection [6], we can transform the MSO formula $MinModel_\psi \wedge \psi_{Tr} \wedge \widehat{\psi}$ to a tree automaton that accepts precisely those trees that define data-structures that satisfy the structural abstraction and are minimal models. Since the finiteness of the language accepted by a tree automaton is decidable, we can check whether there are only a finite number of minimal models wrt satisfiability-preserving embeddings, and hence decide membership in the decidable fragment $\text{STRAND}^{sem}_{dec}$.

THEOREM 5.7. *Given a sentence $\exists\vec{x}\forall\vec{y}\ \varphi(\vec{x},\vec{y})$, the problem of checking whether the sentence belongs to the fragment $\text{STRAND}^{sem}_{dec}$ is decidable.*

In fact, we develop, using the tool MONA, the decision procedure above (see Section 7).

Deciding formulas in $\text{STRAND}^{sem}_{dec}$. We now give the decision procedure for satisfiability of sentences in $\text{STRAND}^{sem}_{dec}$ over a recursively defined class of data-structures. First, we transform the satisfiability problem to that of satisfiability of universal formulas of the form $\psi = \forall\vec{y}\ \varphi(\vec{y})$. Then, using the formula $MinModel_\psi$ described above, and by transforming it to tree automata, we extract the set of *all* trees accepted by the tree-automaton in order to get the tree-representation of all the minimal models. Note that this set of minimal models is finite, and the sentence is satisfiable iff it is satisfiable in some data-extension of one of these models.

We can now write a quantifier-free formula over the data-logic that asserts that one of the minimal models has a data-extension that satisfies ψ. This formula will be a disjunction of m sub-formulas $\eta_1,\ldots,\eta_m$, where m is the number of minimal models. Each formula η_i will express that there is a data-extension of the i'th minimal model that satisfies ψ. First, since a minimal model has only a finite number of nodes, we create one data-variable for each of these nodes, and associate them with the nodes of the model. It is now not hard to transform the formula ψ to this model using no quantification. The universal quantification over $\vec{y}$ translates to a conjunction of formulas over all possible valuations of $\vec{y}$ over the nodes of the fixed model. Existential (universal) quantified variables are then "expanded" using disjunction (conjunction, respectively) of formulas for all possible valuations over the fixed model. The edge-relations between nodes in the model are interpreted on the tree using MSO formulas in $\mathcal{R}$, which are then expanded to conditions over the fixed set of nodes in the model. Finally, the data-constraints in the STRAND formula are directly written as constraints in the data-logic.

The resulting formula is a pure data-logic formula without quantification that is satisfiable if and only if ψ is satisfiable over $\mathcal{R}$. This is then decided using the decision procedure for the data-logic.

THEOREM 5.8. *Given a sentence $\exists\vec{x}\forall\vec{y}\ \varphi(\vec{x},\vec{y})$ over $\mathcal{R}$ in $\text{STRAND}^{sem}_{dec}$, the problem of checking whether ψ is satisfiable reduces to the satisfiability of a quantifier-free formula in the data-logic. Since the quantifier-free data-logic is decidable, the satisfiability of $\text{STRAND}^{sem}_{dec}$ formulas is decidable.*

5.6 STRAND_{dec}: A syntactic decidable fragment of STRAND

We utilize the semantically defined decidable class in the previous section to define a logic that has a simple syntactic restriction and is entirely decidable. The decidable fragment allows only formulas of the kind $\exists\vec{x}\forall\vec{y}\varphi$ where φ has *no further quantification*. Moreover, some of the structural edge relations R on the data-structure are classified as *elastic* relations. In φ, elastic relations are allowed to relate any pair of variables, while non-elastic relations are allowed only to relate existentially quantified variables in $\vec{x}$.

A relation R is elastic if, intuitively, for any model M and a submodel M' of M, R holds on a pair of nodes of M' iff R holds for the corresponding pair of nodes in M.

More formally, let us fix a class of recursively defined data-structures $\mathcal{R} = (\psi_{Tr}, \psi_U, \{\alpha_a\}_{a\in L_v}, \{\beta_b\}_{b\in L_e})$. Let E_b denote the edge-relation defined by β_b. Then we say E_b is *elastic* if the following holds: for every tree $T = (V, \{E_i\}_{i\in[k]})$ satisfying ψ_{Tr}, for every valid subset S of V, and for every pair of nodes u, v in the model $M' =$ *Graph*(*Subtree*(T,S)), $E_b(u,v)$ holds in M' iff $E_b(u,v)$ holds in *Graph*(T).

For example, over trees, the $\leq$ relation relating a node with any of its descendants is an elastic relation; however, the relation that relates a node to its parent is not elastic, as we can take two nodes u and v in a subtree *Subtree*(S,T) where u is the parent of v, but u is not the parent of v in T.

We can express the property that R_b is elastic in MSO over a particular tree T using the following formula:

$$\forall S\forall u\forall v((ValidSubModel(S) \wedge u{\in}S \wedge v{\in}S \wedge tailor_S(\psi_U(u)) \\ \wedge tailor_S(\psi_U(v))) \Rightarrow (\beta_b(u,v) \Leftrightarrow tailor_S(\beta_b(u,v))))$$

Hence, we can *decide* whether a relation is elastic or not, by checking the validity of the above formula over all trees satisfying ψ_{Tr}.

The syntactic decidable fragment STRAND_{dec} is defined as the class of all STRAND formulas of the form $\exists\vec{x}\forall\vec{y}\varphi$ such that (a) φ has no quantification, (b) every occurrence of an atomic relation in φ is of the form $R(z_1, z_2)$ where either R is an elastic relation or z_1 and z_2 are in $\vec{x}$, or are constants. We can now show:

THEOREM 5.9. *Over any class of recursively defined structures $\mathcal{R}$, STRAND_{dec} is decidable.*

We omit the proof for lack of space; it's gist is as follows. When all relations are elastic, for any valid subset S, $tailor_S(\varphi)$ holds on any valuation of variables over S iff φ holds on the same valuation over T (since the atomic relations are elastic). Hence the submodel can always inherit the data-values from the model to satisfy the formula. The minimal models with respect to satisfiability-preserving embeddings are hence a subset of the minimal models with respect to the submodel-relation, which we can show is finite. When all relations are not elastic, the proof is much more complex, and relies on the fact that the non-elastic relations define only a finite number of equivalence classes of relationships over $\vec{x}$.

All of verification conditions in our experiments turn out to be in the syntactic decidable class STRAND_{dec}.

6. Program Verification Using STRAND

In this section we show how STRAND can be used to reason about the correctness of programs, in terms of verifying Hoare-triples where the pre- and post-conditions express both the structure of the heap as well as the data contained in them. The pre- and post-conditions that we allow are STRAND formulas that consist of Boolean combinations of the formulas with pure existential or pure universal quantification over the data-variables (i.e. Boolean combinations of formulas of the form $\exists\vec{x}\varphi$ and $\forall\vec{y}\varphi$); let us call this fragment $\text{STRAND}_{\exists,\forall}$.

Given a straight-line program P that does destructive pointer-updates and data updates, we model a Hoare-triple as a tuple $(\mathcal{R}, Pre, P, Post)$, where the pre-condition is given by the data-structure constraint $\mathcal{R}$ with the $\text{STRAND}_{\exists,\forall}$ formula Pre, and the post-condition is given by the $\text{STRAND}_{\exists,\forall}$ formula $Post$ (note that structural constraints on the data-structure for the post-condition are also expressed in $Post$, using MSO logic).

In this section, we show that given such a Hoare-triple, we can reduce checking whether the Hoare-triple is *not* valid can be reduced to a satisfiability problem of a STRAND formula over a class of recursively defined data-structures $\mathcal{R}_P$. This then allows us to use STRAND$_{\exists,\forall}$ to verify programs (where, of course, loop-invariants are given by the programmer, which breaks down verification of a program to verification of straight-line code). Intuitively, this reduction *augments* the structures in $\mathcal{R}$ with extra nodes that could be created during the execution of P, and models the *trail* the program takes by logically defining the configuration of the program at each time instant. Over this trail, we then express that the pre-condition holds and the post-condition fails to hold. We also construct formulas that check if there is any memory access violation during the run of P (e.g. free-ing locations twice, dereferencing a null pointer, etc.).

Syntax of programs. Let us define the syntax of a basic programming language manipulating heaps and data; more complex constructs can be defined by combining these statements appropriately. Let *Var* be a countable set of *pointer variables*, F be a countable set of *structural pointer fields*, and `data` be a *data field*. A *condition* is defined as follows: (for technical reasons, negations are pushed all the way in):

$$\psi \in \texttt{Cond} ::= \gamma(q^1.\texttt{data},\ldots,q^k.\texttt{data}) \mid \neg\gamma(q^1.\texttt{data},\ldots,q^k.\texttt{data}) \mid p == q \mid p \neq q \mid p == nil \mid p \neq nil \mid \psi_1 \wedge \psi_2 \mid \psi_1 \vee \psi_2$$

where $p, q, q^1, \ldots, q^k \in Var$, and γ is a predicate over data values. The set of statements `Stmt` defined over *Var*, F, and `data` is defined as follows:

$$s \in \texttt{Stmt} ::= p := new \mid free(p) \mid assume(\psi) \mid p := nil \mid p := q \mid p.f := q \mid p := q.f \mid p.\texttt{data} := h(q^1.\texttt{data},\ldots,q^k.\texttt{data})$$

where $p, q, q^1, \ldots, q^k \in Var$, $f \in F$, h is a function over data, and ψ is a condition. A *program* P over *Var*, F, and `data` is a non empty finite sequence of statements $s_1; s_2; \ldots; s_m$, with $s_i \in \texttt{Stmt}$.

The semantics of a program is the natural one and we skip its definition.

Let $\mathcal{R}$ be a recursive data-structure, Pre, $Post$ be two STRAND$_{\exists,\forall}$ formulas, and $P ::= s_1; s_2; \ldots; s_m$ be a program. The configuration of the program at any point is given by a heap modeled as a graph, where nodes of the graph are assigned data values. For a program with m statements, let us fix the configurations to be $G_0, \ldots, G_m$.

The trail. The idea is to capture the entire computation starting from a particular data-structure using a single data-structure. The main intuition is that if we run P over a graph $G_0 \in Graph(\mathcal{R})$ then a new class of recursive data-structures $\mathcal{R}_P$ will define a graph G_{trail} which encodes in it G_0, as well as all the graphs G_i, for every $i \in [m]$. G_{trail} has the nodes of G_0 plus m other fresh nodes (these nodes will be used to model newly created nodes P creates as well as to hold new data-values of variables that are assigned to in P). Each of these new nodes are pointed by a distinguished pointer variable new_i. Initially, these additional nodes are all inactive in G_0. We build an MSO-defined unary predicate $active_i$ that captures at each step i the precise set of active nodes in the heap. To capture the pointer variables at each step of the execution, we define a new unary predicate p_i, for each $p \in Var$ and $i \in [0, m]$. Similarly, we create MSO-defined binary predicates f_i for each $f \in F$ and $i \in [0, m]$, to capture structural pointer fields at step i. The heap G_i at step i is hence the graph consisting of all the nodes x of G_{trail} such that $active_i(x)$ holds true, and the pointers and edges of G_i are defined by p_i and f_i predicates, respectively.

Formally, fix a recursively defined data-structure $\mathcal{R} = (\psi_{Tr}, \psi_U, \{\alpha_p\}_{p\in Var}, \{\beta_f\}_{f\in F})$, with a monadic predicate α_{xnil}, which evaluates to a unique NIL node in the data-structure. Then its trail with respect to the program P is defined as $\mathcal{R}_P = (\psi'_{Tr}, \psi'_U, \{\alpha'_p\}_{p\in Var'}, \{\beta'_f\}_{f\in F'})$ where:

- ψ'_{Tr} is designed to hold on all trees in which the first subtree of the root satisfies ψ_{Tr} and the second child of the root has a chain of $m-1$ nodes where each of them is the second child of the parent.
- ψ'_U holds true on the root, on all the second child descendent of the root, and on all first child descendent on which ψ_U holds true.
- $Var' = \{new_i | i \in [m]\} \cup \{p_i | p \in Var, i \in [0, m]\}$, and
-(1) α'_{new_1} holds only on the root, and α'_{new_i} holds true only on the $i+1$'th descendent of the second child of the root, for every $i \in [m-1]$.
-(2) for every $p \in Var$ and $i \in [m]$, $\alpha'_{p_0} = \alpha_p$ and α'_{p_i} is defined as in Figure 2.
- $F' = \{f_i | f \in F, i \in [0, m]\}$, and for every $f \in F$ and $i \in [m]$, $\beta'_{f_0} = \beta_f$ and β'_{f_i} is defined as in Figure 2.

In Figure 2, the MSO formulas α'_{p_i} and β'_{f_i} are derived in the natural way from the semantics of the statements, except for the statement $p.\texttt{data} := h(q^1.\texttt{data},\ldots,q^k.\texttt{data})$. Although the semantics for this statement does not involve any structural modification of the graph (it changes only the data value associated p), we represent this operation by making a *new version* of the node pointed by p in order to represent explicitly the change for the data value corresponding to that node. We deactivate the node pointed by p_{i-1} and activate the dormant node pointed by new_i. All the edges in the graph and the pointers are rearranged to reflect this exchange of nodes.

In Figure 2, we also define two more MSO formulas, $active_i$ and $error_i$, which are not part of the trail, where the first models the active nodes at step i, and the second expresses when an error occurs due to the dereferencing of a variable pointing to $xnil$, respectively.

Handling data constraints. The trail $\mathcal{R}_P$ captures all the structural modifications made to the graph during the execution P. However, data constrains entailed by *assume* statements and data-assignments cannot be expressed in the trail as they are not expressible in MSO. We impose them in the STRAND formula. We define a formula φ_i for each statement index $i \in [m]$, where if s_i is not an assume or a data-assignment statement, then $\varphi_i = \texttt{true}$. Otherwise, there are two cases:
<u>*Handling assume assignments.*</u> If s_i is the statement $assume(\psi)$, then φ_i is the STRAND formula obtained by *adapting* the constraint φ to the i'th stage of the trail. This is not hard, but is tedious, and we skip its definition. Constraints on data-variables asserted in the formula using data-logic constraints.
<u>*Handling data-assignments.*</u> The STRAND formula φ_i for a data-assignment statement $p.\texttt{data} := h(q^1.\texttt{data},\ldots,q^k.\texttt{data})$ is:

$$\varphi_i \quad := \quad \exists ex, ex_1, \ldots, ex_k.\ p_i(ex) \wedge$$
$$\Big(\bigwedge_{i\in[k]} q^j_{i-1}(ex_j)\Big) \wedge \texttt{data}(ex) = h(\texttt{data}(ex_1),\ldots,\texttt{data}(ex_k))$$

which translates s_i into STRAND making sure that it refers to the heap at step i–1.

Adapting pre- and post-conditions to the trail. The last ingredient that we need is to express the STRAND$_{\exists,\forall}$ formulas Pre and the negation of the $Post$ on the trail $\mathcal{R}_P$. More specifically, we need to

[$p := new$]:

$$\alpha'_{p_i}(x)=\alpha'_{new_i}(x),\quad \alpha'_{q_i}(x) = \alpha'_{q_{i-1}}(x),\ \ \forall q \in Var \setminus \{p\},$$
$$\beta'_{f_i}(x,y)=\beta'_{f_{i-1}}(x,y),\ \ active_i(x) = active_{i-1}(x) \vee \alpha'_{new_i}(x)$$
$$error_i = \texttt{false}$$

[$free(p)$]:

$$\alpha'_{z_i}(x) = (\alpha'_{z_{i-1}}(x) \wedge (\alpha'_{xnil_{i-1}}(x) \vee \neg\alpha'_{p_{i-1}}(x))) \vee (\alpha'_{xnil_{i-1}}(x) \wedge \neg\alpha'_{z_{i-1}}(x))$$
$$\beta'_{f_i}(x,y) = (\beta'_{f_{i-1}}(x,y) \wedge \neg\alpha'_{p_{i-1}}(x)) \vee (\alpha'_{xnil_{i-1}}(y) \wedge \exists ex.\ (\beta'_{f_{i-1}}(x,ex) \wedge \alpha'_{p_{i-1}}(ex)))$$
$$active_i(x) = active_{i-1}(x) \wedge \neg\alpha'_{p_{i-1}}(x)$$
$$error_i = \exists x.(\alpha'_{p_{i-1}}(x) \wedge \alpha'_{xnil_{i-1}}(x))$$

[$p := nil$]:

$$\alpha'_{p_i(x)} = \alpha'_{xnil_{i-1}}(x),\ \ \alpha'_{z_i}(x) = \alpha'_{z_{i-1}}(x),\ \ \forall z \in Var \setminus \{p\}$$
$$\beta'_{f_i}(x,y) = \beta'_{f_{i-1}}(x,y),\ \ active_i(x)=active_{i-1}(x),\ \ error_i=\texttt{false}$$

[$p := q$]:

$$\alpha'_{p_i}(x) = \alpha'_{q_{i-1}}(x),\ \ \alpha'_{z_i}(x) = \alpha'_{z_{i-1}}(x),\ \ \forall z \in (Var \setminus \{p\})$$
$$\beta'_{f_i}(x,y) = \beta'_{f_{i-1}}(x,y),\ \ active_i(x)=active_{i-1}(x),\ \ error_i=\texttt{false}$$

[$p.f := q$]:

$$\alpha'_{z_i}(x) = \alpha'_{z_{i-1}}(x),\qquad \forall z \in Var$$
$$\beta'_{f_i}(x,y) = (\neg\alpha'_{p_{i-1}}(x) \wedge \beta'_{f_{i-1}}(x,y)) \vee (\alpha'_{p_i-1}(x) \wedge \alpha'_{q_{i-1}}(y))$$
$$\alpha'_{g_i}(x,y) = \alpha'_{g_{i-1}}(x,y),\qquad \forall g \in (F \setminus \{f\})$$
$$active_i(x) = active_{i-1}(x),\ \ error_i=\exists x.(\alpha'_{p_{i-1}}(x) \wedge \alpha'_{xnil_{i-1}}(x))$$

[$p := q.f$]:

$$\alpha'_{p_i(x)} = \exists ex.\ (\alpha'_{q_{i-1}}(ex) \wedge \beta'_{f_{i-1}}(ex,x))$$
$$\alpha'_{q_i}(x) = \alpha'_{q_{i-1}}(x),\qquad \forall q \in (Var \setminus \{p\})$$
$$\beta'_{f_i}(x,y) = \beta'_{f_{i-1}}(x,y)$$
$$\alpha'_{g_i}(x,y) = \alpha'_{g_{i-1}}(x,y),\qquad \forall g \in (F \setminus \{f\})$$
$$active_i(x) = active_{i-1}(x),\ \ error_i=\exists x.\ (\alpha'_{q_{i-1}}(x) \wedge \alpha'_{xnil_{i-1}}(x))$$

[$assume(\psi)$]:

$$\alpha'_{q_i}(x) = \alpha'_{q_{i-1}}(x), \forall q \in Var,\quad \beta'_{f_i}(x,y) = \beta'_{f_{i-1}}(x,y), \forall f \in F$$
$$active_i(x) = active_{i-1}(x),\ \ error_i=\exists x.\bigvee_{p \in Var^{\psi}}(\alpha'_{p_{i-1}}(x) \wedge \alpha'_{xnil_{i-1}}(x))$$

where Var^{ψ} is the set of all variables occurring in ψ.

[$p.\texttt{data} := h(q^1.\texttt{data}, \ldots, q^k.\texttt{data})$]:

$$\alpha'_{p_i}(x) = \alpha'_{new_i}(x),\quad \alpha'_{q_i}(x) = \alpha'_{q_{i-1}}(x),\ \ \forall q \in Var \setminus \{p\}$$
$$\beta'_{f_i}(x,y) = (\beta'_{f_{i-1}}(x,y) \wedge \neg\alpha'_{p_{i-1}}(x)) \vee (\alpha'_{new_i}(y) \wedge \exists ex.\ (\beta'_{f_{i-1}}(x,ex) \wedge \alpha'_{p_{i-1}}(ex)))$$
$$active_i(x) = (active_{i-1}(x) \wedge \neg p_{i-1}(x)) \vee \alpha'_{new_i}(x)$$
$$error_i = \exists x.(\bigvee_{z \in \{p,q^1,\ldots,q^k\}} (\alpha'_{z_{i-1}}(x) \wedge \alpha'_{xnil_{i-1}}(x)))$$

Figure 2. Predicates defining the new data-structure.

adapt Pre to the trail for index 0, which corresponds to the original graph, i.e. the predicates p are replaced with p_0, for every $p \in Var$, and the edge predicates f with f_0, for every $f \in F$. Moreover, whenever we refer to a node in the graph we need to be sure that node is active which can be done by using the predicate $active_0(x)$ which holds true if x is in the first subtree of the root and $\psi'_U(x)$ holds. A similar transformation is done for the formula $\neg Post$, where now we consider pointers, edge labels, and active nodes at the last step m. Let $Pre_{\mathcal{R}_P}$ (resp., $Post_{\mathcal{R}_P}$) be the STRAND formula corresponding to the adaptation of Pre (resp., $Post$)

Reduction to satisfiability problem on the trail. It is easy to see that an error occurs during the execution of P on a graph defined through $\mathcal{R}$ that satisfies Pre if the following STRAND formula is satisfiable on the trail $\mathcal{R}_P$:

$$Error = \bigvee_{i \in [m]}(Pre_{\mathcal{R}_P} \wedge \bigwedge_{j \in [i-1]} \varphi_j \quad \wedge \quad error_i)$$

Similarly, the Hoare-triple is not valid iff the following STRAND formula is satisfiable on the trail:

$$Violate_{Post} = Pre_{\mathcal{R}_P} \wedge (\bigwedge_{j \in [m]} \varphi_j) \wedge \neg Post_{\mathcal{R}_P}$$

THEOREM 6.1. *Let P be a program, $\mathcal{R}$ be a recursive data-structure, and Pre, $Post$ be two STRAND$_{\exists,\forall}$ formulas over Var, F, and* data. *Then, there is a graph $G \in Graph(\mathcal{R})$ that satisfies Pre and where either P terminates with an error or the obtained graph G' does not satisfy $Post$ iff the STRAND formula $Error \vee Violate_{Post}$ is satisfiable on the trail $\mathcal{R}_P$.*

7. Evaluation

7.1 Implementation

In this section, we demonstrate the effectiveness and practicality of the decision procedures for STRAND by checking verification conditions generated in proving properties of several heap-manipulating programs. Given pre-conditions, post-conditions and loop-invariants, each linear block of statements of a program yields a Hoare-triple, which is manually translated into a STRAND formula ψ over trees and integer arithmetic, as a verification condition.

The decision procedure for STRAND implements the decision procedure for the semantically defined fragment STRAND$^{sem}_{dec}$. Given a STRAND formula, our procedure will first determine if it is in the semantic decidable fragment, and if not, will halt and report that satisfiability of the formula is not checkable. When given a formula in the syntactic fragment STRAND$_{dec}$, this procedure will always succeed, and the decision procedure will determine satisfiability of the formula.

The decision procedure consists of a structural phase, where we determine whether the number of minimal models is finite, and if so, determine a bound on the size of the minimal models. This phase is effected by using MONA [13], a monadic second-order logic solver over (strings and) trees. In the second data-constraint solving phase, the finite set of minimal models, if any, are examined by the data-solver Z3 [9] to check if they can be extended with data-values to satisfy the formula.

Instead of building an automaton representing the minimal models and then checking it for finiteness, we check the finiteness formula $MinModel_{\psi}$ using WS2S, supported by MONA, which is a monadic second-order logic over *infinite* trees with set-quantification restricted to finite sets. By quantifying over a finite universe U, and transforming all quantifications to be interpreted over U, we can interpret $MinModel_{\psi}$ over all finite trees. Let us denote this emulation as $MinModel'_{U,\psi}$. The finiteness condition can now be checked by asking if *there exists a finite set B* such that any minimal model for ψ is contained within the nodes of B:

$$\exists\ Bound\ \forall U\ \ \forall Q_{a(a \in \Sigma)}\ (MinModel'_{U,\psi} \Rightarrow (U \subseteq Bound))$$

This formula has no free-variables, and hence either holds on the infinite tree or not, and can be checked by MONA. This formula evaluates to `true` iff the formula is in STRAND$^{sem}_{dec}$.

We also follow a slightly different procedure to synthesize the data-logic formula. Instead of extracting each minimal model, and

Program	Verification condition	Structural solving (MONA)					Data-constraint Solving (Z3 with QF-LIA)			
		in $\text{STRAND}_{dec}^{sem}$? (finitely-many minimal models)	#States	Final BDD size	Time(s)	Graph model exists?	Bound (#Nodes)	Formula size (KB)	Satisfiable?	Time(s)
sorted-list-search	before-loop	Yes	67	264	0.34	No	-	-	-	-
	in-loop	Yes	131	585	0.59	No	-	-	-	-
	after-loop	Yes	67	264	0.18	No	-	-	-	-
sorted-list-insert	before-head	Yes	73	298	1.66	Yes	5	6.2	No	0.02
	before-loop	Yes	259	1290	0.38	No	-	-	-	-
	in-loop	Yes	1027	6156	4.46	No	-	-	-	-
	after-loop	Yes	146	680	13.93	Yes	7	14.5	No	0.02
sorted-list-insert-error	before-loop	Yes	298	1519	0.34	Yes	7	9.5	Yes	0.02
sorted-list-reverse	before-loop	Yes	35	119	0.24	No	-	-	-	-
	in-loop	Yes	513	2816	2.79	No	-	-	-	-
	after-loop	Yes	129	576	0.35	No	-	-	-	-
bubblesort	loop-if-if	Yes	2049	13312	7.70	No	-	-	-	-
	loop-if-else	Yes	1025	6144	6.83	No	-	-	-	-
	loop-else	Yes	1033	6204	2.73	Yes	8	22.2	No	0.02
bst-search	before-loop	Yes	52	276	5.03	No	-	-	-	-
	in-loop	Yes	160	1132	32.80	Yes	9	7.7	No	0.02
	after-loop	Yes	52	276	3.27	No	-	-	-	-
bst-insert	before-loop	Yes	36	196	1.34	No	-	-	-	-
	in-loop	Yes	68	452	9.84	No	-	-	-	-
	after-loop	Yes	20	84	1.76	No	-	-	-	-
left/right-rotate	bst-preserving	Yes	29	117	1.59	Yes	19	70.3	No	0.05

Figure 3. Results of program verification

checking if there is a data-extension for it, we obtain a *bound* on the size of minimal models, and ask the data-solver to check for any model within that bound. This is often a much simpler formula to feed to the data-solver.

In our current implementation, the MONA constraints are encoded manually, and once the bound is obtained, we write a program that outputs the Z3 constraints for the verification condition and the bound. The translation from STRAND to MONA formulas and the translation from STRAND formulas to Z3 formulas for any bound can be automated, and is a plan for the future.

7.2 Experiments

Figure 3 presents the evaluation of our tools on checking a set of programs that manipulate sorted singly-linked lists and binary search trees. Note that the binary search trees presented here are out of the scope of the logics HAVOC [16] and CSL [7].

The programs `sorted-list-search` and `sorted-list-insert` search and insert a node in a sorted singly-linked list, respectively, while `sorted-list-insert error` is the insertion program with an intended error. The program `sorted-list -reverse` is a routine for in-place reversal of a sorted singly-linked list, which results in a reverse-sorted list, and `bubblesort` is the code for Bubble-sort of a list. The routines `bst-search` and `bst-insert` search and insert a node in a binary search tree, respectively, while the programs `left-rotate` and `right-rotate` perform rotations (for balancing) in a binary search tree.

For all these examples, a set of partial correctness properties including both structural and data requirements is checked. For example, assuming a node with value k exists, we check if both `sorted-list-search` and `bst-search` return a node with value k. For `sorted-list-insert`, we assume that the inserted value does not exist, and check if the resulting list contains the inserted node, and the sortedness property continues to hold. In the program `bst-insert`, assuming the tree does not contain the inserted node in the beginning, we check whether the final tree contains the inserted node, and the binary-search-tree property continues to hold. In `sorted-list-reverse`, we check if the output list is a valid list that is reverse-sorted. The code for `bubblesort` is checked to see if it results in a sorted list. And the `left-rotate` and `right-rotate` codes are checked to see whether they maintain the property that maintain the binary search-tree property.

Note that each program requires checking several verification conditions (typically for the linear block from the beginning of the program to a loop, for the loop invariant linear block, and for the block from the loop invariant to the end of the program).

The experiments were conducted on a 2.2GHz, 4GB machine running Windows 7, and the formulas and results are available at `http://www.cs.uiuc.edu/~qiu2/strand`.

For the structural solving phase, we report first whether the verification condition falls within our semantic decidable fragment $\text{STRAND}_{dec}^{sem}$. *In fact, it turns out that all of our verification conditions can be written entirely in the* syntactic *decidable fragment* STRAND_{dec}*!*

We also report the number of states, the BDD sizes to represent automata, and the time taken by MONA to compute the minimal models. We report whether there were *any* models found; note that if the formula is unsatisfiable and there are no models, the Z3 phase is skipped (these are denoted by "-" annotations in the table for Z3).

For the data-constraint solving phase, we first report the number of nodes of the tree (or string) that is an upper bound for all minimal models. The Z3 formulas are typically large (but simple) as one can see from the size of the formulas in the table. We report whether Z3 found the formula to be satisfiable or not (all cases were unsatisfiable, except `sorted-list-insert-error`, as the Hoare-triples verified were correct), and the time it took to determine this.

The experimental results show that natural verification conditions tend to be expressible in the syntactic decidable fragment STRAND_{dec}. Moreover, the expressiveness of our logic allows us to write complex conditions involving structure and data, and yet are handled well by MONA and Z3. We believe that a full-fledged engineering of an SMT solver for $\text{STRAND}_{dec}^{sem}$ that answers queries involving heap structures and data is a promising future direction. Towards this end, an efficient *non-automata theoretic* decision procedure (unlike MONA) that uses search techniques (like SAT) instead of representing the class of all models (like BDDs and automata) may yield more efficient decision procedures.

8. Related Work

We first discuss related work that can reason with combinations of heaps and data. In handling heaps, first-order theories that can reason with restricted forms of the reachability relation for ensuring decidability are the most common. The work most closely related to our work is the logic in HAVOC, called LISBQ [16], that offers a reasoning with generic heaps combined with an arbitrary data-logic. The logic has restricted reachability predicates and universal quantification, but is syntactically severely curtailed, to obtain decidability. We find the restrictions on the syntax quite awkward, with *sort*-based restrictions in the logic. Furthermore, the logic cannot handle even simple constraints over trees with unbounded depth where the nodes are of the same sort (like a tree being a binary search tree). However, the logic is extremely efficient, as it uses no structural solver, but translates the structure-solving also to (the Boolean aspect of) the SMT solver. We gained a lot of insight into decidability by studying the expressive power of HAVOC, and we believe that STRAND generalizes some of the underlying ideas present in HAVOC to a much more powerful technique for decidability. The logic CSL [7] has a similar flavor as HAVOC, with similar sort-restrictions on the syntax, but generalizes to handle doubly linked lists, and allows size constraints on structures. The work reported in [5] gives a logic that extends an LTL-like syntax to define certain decidable logic fragments on heaps.

Rakamarić et al [23] propose an inference rule system for reasoning with restricted reachability (but this logic does not have universal quantification and cannot express disjointness constraints), and an SMT solver based implementation has been reported [24]. Restricted forms of reachability were first axiomatized in early work by Nelson [21]. Several mechanisms without quantification exist, including the work reported in [1, 25]. Automatic decision procedures that approximate higher-order logic using first-order logic, using approximate logics over sets and their cardinalities, have been proposed [15].

There is a rich literature on heap analysis without data. Since first-order logic over graphs is undecidable, decidable logics must either restrict the logic or the class of graphs. The closest work to ours in this realm is PALE [20], which restricts structures to be definable over tree-skeletons, similar to STRAND, and reduces problems to the MONA system [13]. Several approximations of first-order axiomatizations of reachability have been proposed: axioms capturing *local* properties [19], a logic on regular patterns that is decidable [28], among others.

Finally, separation logic [26] has emerged as a convenient logic to express heap properties of programs, and a decidable fragment (without data) on lists is known [4]. However, not many extensions of separation logics handle data constraints (see [18] which combines this logic for linked lists with arithmetic).

Acknowledgments

We thank Christof Löding for the fruitful discussions we had when we started this project a few years back. This work is partially funded by NSF CAREER award #0747041 and French ANR-09-SEGI project Veridyc.

References

[1] I. Balaban, A. Pnueli, and L. D. Zuck. Shape analysis by predicate abstraction. In *VMCAI'05*, volume 3385 of *LNCS*, pages 164–180. Springer, 2005.

[2] T. Ball, R. Majumdar, T. Millstein, and S. K. Rajamani. Automatic predicate abstraction of C programs. In *PLDI'01*, pages 203–213. ACM, 2001.

[3] M. Barnett, B.-Y. E. Chang, R. DeLine, B. Jacobs, and K. R. M. Leino. Boogie: A modular reusable verifier for object-oriented programs. In *FMCO'05*, volume 4111 of *LNCS*, pages 364–387. Springer, 2005.

[4] J. Berdine, C. Calcagno, and P. W. O'Hearn. A decidable fragment of separation logic. In *FSTTCS'04*, volume 3328 of *LNCS*, pages 97–109. Springer, 2004.

[5] N. Bjørner and J. Hendrix. Linear functional fixed-points. In *CAV'09*, volume 5643 of *LNCS*, pages 124–139. Springer, 2009.

[6] E. Börger, E. Grädel, and Y. Gurevich. *The Classical Decision Problem*. Springer, 2001.

[7] A. Bouajjani, C. Dragoi, C. Enea, and M. Sighireanu. A logic-based framework for reasoning about composite data structures. In *CONCUR'09*, volume 5710 of *LNCS*, pages 178–195. Springer, 2009.

[8] L. M. de Moura and N. Bjørner. Deciding effectively propositional logic using DPLL and substitution sets. In *IJCAR'08*, volume 5195 of *LNCS*, pages 410–425. Springer, 2008.

[9] L. M. de Moura and N. Bjørner. Z3: An efficient SMT solver. In *TACAS'08*, volume 4963 of *LNCS*, pages 337–340. Springer, 2008.

[10] J. Engelfriet. Context-free graph grammars. In *Handbook of Formal Languages*, volume 3, pages 125–214. Springer, 1997.

[11] C. Flanagan, K. R. M. Leino, M. Lillibridge, G. Nelson, J. B. Saxe, and R. Stata. Extended static checking for Java. In *PLDI'02*, pages 234–245. ACM, 2002.

[12] P. Godefroid, N. Klarlund, and K. Sen. DART: directed automated random testing. In *PLDI'05*, pages 213–223. ACM, 2005.

[13] N. Klarlund and A. Møller. *MONA*. BRICS, Department of Computer Science, Aarhus University, January 2001. Available from `http://www.brics.dk/mona/`.

[14] N. Klarlund and M. I. Schwartzbach. Graph types. In *POPL'93*, pages 196–205. ACM, 1993.

[15] V. Kuncak. *Modular Data Structure Verification*. PhD thesis, Massachusetts Institute of Technology, 2007.

[16] S. Lahiri and S. Qadeer. Back to the future: revisiting precise program verification using SMT solvers. In *POPL'08*, pages 171–182. ACM, 2008.

[17] T. Lev-Ami and S. Sagiv. Tvla: A system for implementing static analyses. In *SAS'00*, volume 1824 of *LNCS*, pages 280–301. Springer, 2000.

[18] S. Magill, M.-H. Tsai, P. Lee, and Y.-K. Tsay. THOR: A tool for reasoning about shape and arithmetic. In *CAV'08*, volume 5123 of *LNCS*, pages 428–432. Springer, 2008.

[19] S. McPeak and G. C. Necula. Data structure specifications via local equality axioms. In *CAV'05*, volume 3576 of *LNCS*, pages 476–490. Springer, 2005.

[20] A. Møller and M. I. Schwartzbach. The pointer assertion logic engine. In *PLDI'01*, pages 221–231. ACM, 2001.

[21] G. Nelson. Verifying reachability invariants of linked structures. In *POPL'83*, pages 38–47. ACM, 1983.

[22] G. Nelson and D. C. Oppen. Simplification by cooperating decision procedures. *ACM Trans. Program. Lang. Syst.*, 1:245–257, 1979.

[23] Z. Rakamarić, J. D. Bingham, and A. J. Hu. An inference-rule-based decision procedure for verification of heap-manipulating programs with mutable data and cyclic data structures. In *VMCAI'07*, volume 4349 of *LNCS*, pages 106–121. Springer, 2007.

[24] Z. Rakamarić, R. Bruttomesso, A. J. Hu, and A. Cimatti. Verifying heap-manipulating programs in an SMT framework. In *ATVA'07*, volume 4762 of *LNCS*, pages 237–252. Springer, 2007.

[25] S. Ranise and C. Zarba. A theory of singly-linked lists and its extensible decision procedure. In *SEFM'06*, pages 206–215. IEEE-CS, 2006.

[26] J. Reynolds. Separation logic: a logic for shared mutable data structures. In *LICS'02*, pages 55–74. IEEE-CS, 2002.

[27] G. Yorsh, T. W. Reps, and S. Sagiv. Symbolically computing most-precise abstract operations for shape analysis. In *TACAS'04*, volume 2988 of *LNCS*, pages 530–545. Springer, 2004.

[28] G. Yorsh, A. M. Rabinovich, M. Sagiv, A. Meyer, and A. Bouajjani. A logic of reachable patterns in linked data-structures. In *FoSSaCS'06*, volume 3921 of *LNCS*, pages 94–110. Springer, 2006.

A Technique for the Effective and Automatic Reuse of Classical Compiler Optimizations on Multithreaded Code

Pramod G. Joisha, Robert S. Schreiber, Prithviraj Banerjee, Hans-J. Boehm, Dhruva R. Chakrabarti
Hewlett-Packard Laboratories, Palo Alto, California, USA
{pramod.joisha, rob.schreiber, prith.banerjee, hans.boehm, dhruva.chakrabarti}@hp.com

Abstract

A large body of data-flow analyses exists for analyzing and optimizing sequential code. Unfortunately, much of it cannot be directly applied on parallel code, for reasons of correctness. This paper presents a technique to automatically, aggressively, yet safely apply sequentially-sound data-flow transformations, *without change*, on shared-memory programs. The technique is founded on the notion of program references being "siloed" on certain control-flow paths. Intuitively, siloed references are free of interference from other threads within the confines of such paths. Data-flow transformations can, in general, be unblocked on siloed references.

The solution has been implemented in a widely used compiler. Results on benchmarks from SPLASH-2 show that performance improvements of up to 41% are possible, with an average improvement of 6% across all the tested programs over all thread counts.

Categories and Subject Descriptors D.3.4 [*Programming Languages*]: Processors—Compilers, Optimization

General Terms Algorithms, Languages, Theory

Keywords Data-Flow Analysis, Parallel-Program Optimization

1. Introduction

It has long been known that *classical* compiler optimizations, i.e., sequentially-sound transformations based on data-flow analysis frameworks [16], cannot be directly applied on parallel code, even under conditions that would be correct for the sequential case [22, 17, 19, 26, 30, 3]. The problem stems from asynchronous updates. Classical methods were not designed to reason about them under a multiplicity of interleavings [17, 30]. Parallel-code optimization has hence been specially addressed, in mainly two ways:

- Devise analyses and optimizations from the ground up, or adapt existing sequential analyses and optimizations, often using specialized program representations [35, 17, 31, 19, 26, 30].
- Assume the program to be *well-synchronized*, i.e., free of data races, and restrict the scope of classical transformations to the *synchronization-free regions* (SFRs) of the code.

The first has been used to analyze and optimize the so-called *explicitly parallel program* (EPP). An EPP is shared-memory code in which parallelism is expressed using the `cobegin/coend` construct, or some equivalent. The second is how all production C/C++ compilers that we are aware of, such as the GNU C/C++ Compiler (`gcc`) and Open64, currently optimize multithreaded code.

The SFR approach promises *sequential consistency* (SC) [18] to the programmer, if the code is data-race free. The EPP approach usually gives "full SC", i.e., SC even in the presence of data races.

1.1 Limitations of Past Approaches

Since the EPP approach ensures interleaving semantics, it can produce overly conservative results on well-synchronized programs. The reason is that to assure full SC, all *conflicting accesses* that *could* be performed by two threads, without them performing intervening synchronizations, have to be modeled [36].[1] Such accesses do not exist in well-synchronized code, since they would be data races. Thus, it would be easier to deduce in well-synchronized code, for example, whether the expression `x+x` is even.

Second, neither Pthreads [13] nor OpenMP [27] currently define semantics under data races. Neither do the current drafts of the C and C++ standards.[2] Implementations already take advantage of this fact, for example, by reordering memory operations on possibly shared locations. Therefore, it appears wasteful to artificially restrict an analysis not to do the same.

Third, since the EPP approach typically relies on IRs (intermediate representations) that go beyond traditional sequential IRs, it can incur high infrastructure costs. For instance, an EPP IR may include special nodes like ψ- and π-functions [35, 19]. It may include edges to reflect properties peculiar to a parallel setting, such as conflicts [19] and synchronizations [31, 26]. To exploit the information borne by these new nodes and edges, existing transformations will have to be reworked. Hence, incorporating the approach into a compiler either means a from-scratch enterprise, or extending a serial compiler's phase or recasting it to a parallel IR. Whichever way, the undertaking is expensive. In contrast, this paper's approach allows for the *direct* reuse of existing data-flow transformations.

In the SFR approach, *data statements* (i.e., synchronization-free statements [1]) are modeled without concurrency considerations. For example, may-definition may_{def} and may-use may_{use} sets, which form the basis of data-flow analyses, do *not* account for concurrent accesses at data statements. These accesses are considered only at synchronizations. In compilers like `gcc`, this presently happens automatically, albeit exceedingly conservatively, because synchronizations are viewed as fully opaque. It should be emphasized that data-race freedom is essential for this approach.

POPL'11, January 26–28, 2011, Austin, Texas, USA.

[1] Accesses of the same location, all of which are not reads, conflict [34].

[2] Java and .NET presently do define limited semantics for data races, though it remains unclear whether this can be done usefully and fully correctly [33]. The approach presented here would require adjustment for those languages.

```
                 X == Y == 0
Thread h1                          | Thread h2
0 t1 := X                          | 0' do { pthread_mutex_lock(l)
1 pthread_mutex_lock(l)            | 1'     t4 := Y
2 Y := 1                           | 2'     pthread_mutex_unlock(l)
3 pthread_mutex_unlock(l)          | 3' } while (t4 == 0)
4 do { pthread_mutex_lock(l)       | 4' X := 11
5      t2 := Y                     | 5' pthread_mutex_lock(l)
6      pthread_mutex_unlock(l)     | 6' Y := 2
7 } while (t2 == 1)                | 7' pthread_mutex_unlock(l)
8 t3 := t1                         |
9 print(t3)                        |
```

Figure 1. The two snippets comprise the program, which always prints 0. If X were copy propagated from Line 0 to Line 8, the result would be data-race free, but 11 would always be printed instead.

```
LOCK(G_Memory->count_lock);
my_id = G_Memory->id;
LockedPrint("%d\n", my_id);
G_Memory->id++;
LockedPrint(...);
UNLOCK(G_Memory->count_lock);
            ⇓
0 t1 := G_Memory
1 t2 := &(t1->count_lock)
2 pthread_mutex_lock(t2)
3 t' := χ(G_Memory)
  ⋮
4 t3 := t'->id
5 LockedPrint("%d\n", t3)
6 t'' := χ(G_Memory)
  ⋮
7 t4 := t''->id
8 t5 := t4+1
9 t''->id := t5
10 LockedPrint(...)
11 t''' := χ(G_Memory)
  ⋮
12 t6 := &(t'''->count_lock)
13 pthread_mutex_unlock(t6)
```

Figure 2. A critical section originally from SPLASH-2's FMM program, and its lowered HSSA Form. Lowering hides the equivalence of the pointers t_2 and t_6. A challenge is to recover such knowledge under multithreading, by safely applying classical methods.

1.1.1 The Pitfall of Simply Extending Optimization Scopes

Consider the multithreaded program in Figure 1, which uses the Pthreads library [13]. The snippets in the columns, along with initialization and termination code, fully constitute the program. The left and right snippets are only executed by threads h_1 and h_2 respectively. The only shared variables X and Y are initialized to 0. Despite accesses of X not being protected by a lock, the program is data-race free. (The two threads coordinate on Y, which is always accessed with a lock held.) This program always outputs 0.

In the left snippet, the only access of X is the read on Line 0. A compiler, on examining it in isolation, might conclude that an opportunity to propagate through critical sections exists, from Line 0 to Line 8. Interestingly, this would preserve data-race freedom, unlike many past examples of invalid transformations, such as bitfield manipulations and register promotion [3]. Nevertheless, it is incorrect since the transformed program would always output 11.[3]

The root of the problem is that the right snippet updates X when running concurrently with the left snippet. Because detecting this requires more analysis, and potentially of a whole-program nature, current compilers follow the SFR approach and safely avoid the problem because a synchronization like `pthread_mutex_lock`, as well as any procedure that may transitively call it, is regarded as having a possible side-effect on all globally visible data.

1.1.2 Benefits of Judiciously Extending Optimization Scopes

The opaque treatment of synchronizations has the adverse consequence that legally exploitable opportunities could, at the same time, get blocked. For instance, consider another hypothetical program consisting of the left snippet in Figure 1 but a different right snippet, one that does not update X. As before, assume that only h_1 executes the left snippet and h_2 the right snippet. In this situation, it would be correct to copy propagate X from Line 0 to Line 8.

We now discuss an example, derived from real code, where synchronization opacity hinders the recovery of useful knowledge that is obfuscated by IR lowering. Figure 2 displays a critical section originally from SPLASH-2's FMM benchmark [41]. The only difference from the original are the calls to the `LockedPrint` procedure, which FMM itself provides. `LockedPrint` writes to `stdout`, under the protection of a lock. The calls have been randomly inserted to illustrate the additional complexities posed by an arbitrary number of nested critical sections to the recovery process.

Modern compilers often work with a variant of the Static Single Assignment (SSA) Form that takes into account aliasing effects and indirect memory operations, such as the HSSA Form by Chow et al [7]. gcc's Memory SSA Form is akin to HSSA [25]. Therefore, for pedagogical reasons, we base our discussions on HSSA.

Figure 2 also shows the critical section's lowered HSSA Form, in which special constructs, called "χ assignments" and "μ operations", denote ambiguous definitions and uses [7]. The χ assignments on Lines 3, 6 and 11 are examples—they signify that a possible side-effect of the preceding calls, including *concurrent effects*, is the changed global variable `G_Memory`.[4] Since these calls can have other side-effects, such as changed heap objects, there can be more χ assignments between Lines 3 and 4, 6 and 7, and 11 and 12.

All lines except 2, 5, 10 and 13 are purely data statements. Under data-race freedom, concurrent effects need not be accounted for against them, because the χ assignments against synchronizations account for these effects. This, however, stymies a classical optimizer from establishing the equivalence of t_2 and t_6. A standard application of a pointer analysis will not uncover this equivalence. If t_2 and t_6 had nonsingleton may-points-to sets, nothing can be said about their equivalence.[5] Likewise, no equivalence conclusions can be drawn if t_2 and t_6 have empty must-points-to sets. We shall later see, in Section 4.5.1, how a classical optimizer can be transparently empowered to safely regain such knowledge.

1.2 A New Approach: The Siloed-References (SR) Technique

This paper presents a two-step technique for extending the scope of arbitrary classical optimizations *across* synchronizations. First, program references to objects that can be statically proved to be free of cross-thread interference are determined. The specific attribute our analysis identifies is the siloed property. Informally, an object reference is "siloed" on a procedure f if no other thread writes (reads or writes) the object whenever a thread is executing a path in f in which it reads (writes) the object. Second, the IR's may_{def} and may_{use} sets are narrowed using these siloed references—this unveils previously blocked classical transformation opportunities. Since these abstractions are only narrowed, the outcome of the technique is not the same as synchronization removal [6, 29].

Our methods use two existing compiler algorithms, designed for sequential programs, as building blocks. They are a flow-insensitive interprocedural pointer analysis, and a transformation to an HSSA-like form. The former is used to derive aliasing information. Its usage is valid because it is known that flow-insensitive schemes re-

[3] The example assumes a fair scheduler, so the program is guaranteed to make progress. It would have to be modified for the case of a nonpreemptive uniprocessor scheduler, by suitably inserting thread-yielding operations.

[4] For brevity, μ operations have not been shown.

[5] A *sound* may-points-to set is never ∅ because a pointer will always point to something. ("Special" pointer values, such as `NULL`, are modeled by separate targets.) So nonsingleton here means two or more elements.

tain correctness in a multithreaded context [30, Page 71]. The usage of the latter is also valid because synchronizations are, by default, treated as opaque procedure calls. They can hence affect all globally visible memory. By generating new symbols at these calls, the HSSA conversion phase conservatively models the asynchronous updates that could occur in a data-race-free program.

1.2.1 Advantages

Because the SR Technique sharpens key data-flow abstractions, it permits arbitrary *bidirectional* classical data-flow analyses across synchronizations, in well-synchronized programs. As far as we know, this is a first. Previous work on program transformations for the data-race-free model only considered what was effectively *forward* data-flow through a lock synchronization, and *backward* data-flow through an unlock synchronization [33]. This is insufficient, for instance, to expose the equivalence of t_2 and t_6 in Figure 2. And in previous work for the full SC model, synchronization knowledge was only used to eliminate conflict edges in the EPP IR [26, 36].

The second important advantage is that the technique needs no new IR constructs, no modifications to the semantics of existing constructs, and no changes to existing phases. In fact, existing phases are treated as black boxes. Because the technique only prunes may_{def} and may_{use} sets, dropping a phase that implements it into a serial compiler's phase-pipeline will automatically "energize" downstream data-flow phases to better optimize parallel code.

1.3 Paper Overview

The rest of this article is organized as follows. Section 2 lays out the requisites for our work. Section 3 shows how to build an abstraction called the Procedural Concurrency Graph (PCG) that enables the calculation of concurrency and interference information. Siloed references are computed from the PCG, using the algorithm presented in Section 4. This section also explains how a data-flow analysis can take advantage of the computed information. An important tradeoff involving interference is described in Section 5. Experiments on an implementation in gcc are reported in Section 6. Finally, Section 7 discusses related work, and Section 8 concludes.

2. Preliminaries

The term "object" in this paper has the sense used in the C Standard—it means any named piece of storage in the execution environment [14]. To simplify the presentation, our usage of this term will encompass procedures. Two objects are distinct if either their lifetimes or address ranges are not identical. Thus, if `x` is a `struct` variable with field `f`, then `x` and `x.f` are distinct objects (although the first contains the second). As in the C Standard, we use the term *lvalues* for syntactic expressions that refer to objects, such as `x` and `x.f`. Specific and arbitrary lvalues will be displayed, respectively, with typewriter and italicized fonts.

2.1 The Program's Call Universe

A program comprises parts for which an IR is available, and parts for which it is not—we call the former *user code*. A procedure invoked in user code is either *defined*, *abstracted* or *inscrutable*. It is defined if its IR is known, abstracted if undefined but with a summary capable of describing its effects at call sites, and inscrutable if undefined and not abstracted. These classes form the sets $\mathscr{F}_d$, $\mathscr{F}_a$ and $\mathscr{F}_{inscr}$—together, they constitute the program's call universe.

If $STMTS(f)$ is the set of statements in a defined procedure f, then $\mathscr{U} = \cup_{f \in \mathscr{F}_d} STMTS(f)$ is the set of all user-code statements. An $s \in \mathscr{U}$ is either non-call code or a call.[6] The function *proc* maps a call to the callee in $\mathscr{F}_d \cup \mathscr{F}_a \cup \mathscr{F}_{inscr}$, and non-call code to $\top$.

[6] Indirect calls are modeled as sets of direct calls to possible targets. This is to simplify the presentation; the implementation retains indirect calls as is.

2.2 Synchronizations

It is posited that a subset of $\mathscr{F}_a \cup \mathscr{F}_{inscr}$ are *synchronizing procedures*, and that the program utilizes them to attain *data-race freedom* [1]. A "synchronization" is a synchronizing-procedure call.

Let $\mathscr{U}_{sync}$ be the set of all synchronizations in $\mathscr{U}$. Statements in a fixed subset $\mathring{\mathscr{U}}_{sync}$ of $\mathscr{U}_{sync}$ are postulated to have changeable may_{def} and may_{use} sets. All other user-code statements, i.e., $\mathscr{U} - \mathring{\mathscr{U}}_{sync}$, have fixed may_{def} and may_{use} sets—these will be referred to as the program's "unaffected statements".

There is full latitude in choosing $\mathring{\mathscr{U}}_{sync}$. As will be shown in Section 5, the choice influences the precision of the PCG and depends on the PCG's intended use. For instance, if unblocking optimization opportunities is the goal, $\mathring{\mathscr{U}}_{sync}$ consists of synchronizations whose may_{def} and may_{use} sets are to be sharpened. $\mathring{\mathscr{U}}_{sync}$ are then the "interesting synchronizations", as far as this goal is concerned.

2.3 On Lvalues

An lvalue can refer to several objects. For example, if `r` is a pointer variable that is only assigned the returned value of a `malloc` call, then the lvalue `*r` denotes all objects created at that allocation site.

2.3.1 Aliasing

Lvalues *alias* if they name overlapping objects. For instance, if `p` and `q` are pointer variables, `*p` and `*q` alias if `p` and `q` target overlapping objects. By this definition, `p` and `q` themselves do not alias because they name nonoverlapping objects in C. Hence, aliasing in this paper is not a points-to relation. The predicate $x \sim y$ is true if the lvalues x and y may alias. We use the *set-aliasing operator* $\approx$ to find the may-aliases in the lvalue sets X and Y:

$$X \approx Y = \{z \mid \exists x \in X, \exists y \in Y. (x \sim y \wedge (z \equiv x \vee z \equiv y))\}, \quad (1)$$

where $u \equiv v$ is true iff u and v are identical lvalues. As an example, if $*\mathtt{p} \sim \mathtt{y}$, $*\mathtt{p} \not\sim *\mathtt{q}$, $*\mathtt{q} \not\sim \mathtt{x}$, then $\{*\mathtt{p}, \mathtt{x}\} \approx \{*\mathtt{q}, \mathtt{y}\} = \{*\mathtt{p}, \mathtt{y}\}$.

2.3.2 Renaming Assumptions

Without loss of generality, local variables in user code are assumed to be appropriately renamed so that no two defined procedures declare local variables with the same name. Also assumed is an SSA-based IR for defined procedures that takes into consideration aliasing effects and indirect memory operations, such as HSSA [7]. For instance, HSSA renames two occurrences of `*r` to different versions if `r` is redefined between them, even if `*r` is not redefined. These two assumptions ensure that identical lvalues, irrespective of where they occur in user code, always name the same set of objects.

2.3.3 Important Lvalue Sets

Suppose $\mathscr{L}$ is the set of all lvalues that may be accessed in user code. An object is either *user-visible* or *user-invisible*, depending on whether there is an lvalue in $\mathscr{L}$ that refers to it. Not all objects existent in a run are user-visible. For example, external library state that cannot be referred to by any lvalue in $\mathscr{L}$ is user-invisible.

Our analyses are underpinned by a bunch of lvalue sets: $\mathscr{L}_h$, $\mathscr{L}_{inscr}$, R_i, W_i, $\overline{R}_i$, $\overline{W}_i$, $SYNC$ and $\overline{SYNC}$. Most of them, as well as sets derived from them, contain only lvalues for user-visible objects. This is because the SR Technique prunes may_{def} and may_{use} sets, which normally are subsets of $\mathscr{L}$.[7] Exceptions are the $SYNC$ and $\overline{SYNC}$ sets, which may include *virtual lvalues* for covering sync objects strictly internal to undefined procedures.

$\mathscr{L}_h$: User-visible objects allocated on the heap. We represent by $\mathscr{L}_h$ a subset of $\mathscr{L}$ that covers all user-visible objects that may be

[7] It may sometimes be more convenient to model all user-invisible objects with a single virtual lvalue ui, and to define $\mathscr{L}$ as including ui.

allocated on the heap. To ascertain $\mathscr{L}_h$, only undefined-procedure calls need to be considered. It is assumed we are given a set $\mathscr{H} \subseteq \mathscr{L}$ covering all user-visible heap objects that may be allocated by abstracted-procedure calls. For instance, if `malloc` is an abstracted procedure, and if `r` is assigned its result, then `*r` is in $\mathscr{H}$. When inscrutable-procedure calls are absent, $\mathscr{H}$ is a safe choice for $\mathscr{L}_h$. But not when they are present, since they could allocate heap objects and later expose them to user code in myriad ways. Since exposure implies being accessible through some pointer-type lvalue in $\mathscr{L}$, the following is a conservative formulation for $\mathscr{L}_h$:

$$\mathscr{L}_h = \begin{cases} \mathscr{H} & \text{if } proc(s) \notin \mathscr{F}_{inscr} \forall s \in \mathscr{U}, \\ \{*x \mid x \in \mathscr{L} \wedge (\text{type of } x \text{ is } \texttt{T*} \\ \quad \text{where } \texttt{T} \text{ is not } \texttt{void})\} & \text{otherwise.} \end{cases} \quad (2)$$

It should be stressed that the second case in Equation (2) is very conservative. For example, if none of the invoked inscrutable procedures have pointer parameters or return pointers, and if none of the pointer variables in $\mathscr{L}$ have *external linkage* [14], then choosing just $\mathscr{H}$ for the second case is also safe.

***$\mathscr{L}_{inscr}$*: User-visible objects immediately accessible in inscrutable procedures.** Let $\mathscr{L}_{addr} \subseteq \mathscr{L}$ be the set of all variables and procedures whose addresses are taken in user code. Let $\mathscr{L}_e \subseteq \mathscr{L}$ be the set of all variables and procedures that have external linkage. An lvalue is *immediately accessed* in a procedure f if a memory operation m in f reads or writes it. m is then an immediate access. The following lvalue set conservatively covers user-visible objects that may be immediately accessed in any inscrutable procedure:

$$\mathscr{L}_{inscr} = \mathscr{L}_{addr} \cup \mathscr{L}_e \cup \mathscr{L}_h. \quad (3)$$

There is potential for greater accuracy by calculating $\mathscr{L}_{inscr}$ differently for different categories of inscrutable procedures. For instance, inscrutable procedures that belong to external libraries predating the user code can never *explicitly* access lvalues in $\mathscr{L}_e$. Therefore, $\mathscr{L}_{inscr}$ for that category can be set to just $\mathscr{L}_{addr} \cup \mathscr{L}_h$.

The static call graph models both defined and undefined procedures. For an inscrutable-procedure call-graph node, procedure lvalues in $\mathscr{L}_{inscr}$ will cover all of its immediate successors.

***R_i, W_i, $\overline{R}_i$, $\overline{W}_i$*: User-visible objects that may be immediately accessed.** We denote the sets of lvalues that may be immediately read and immediately written at a statement s as $R_i(s)$ and $W_i(s)$. Determining these sets is simple when $proc(s) \in \{\top\} \cup \mathscr{F}_d$.

But when an undefined procedure g is called at s, there is the issue of accounting for the accesses that occur in it and procedures that it reaches in the call graph. Our approach is to include in $R_i(s)$ and $W_i(s)$ the reads and writes immediate to procedures that lie in a call-graph path of undefined procedures starting at g. In other words, the treatment is as if g, along with any undefined procedure that it may reach in the call graph without going through a defined procedure, were inlined at the call site s. Thus, the effects of undefined-procedure calls are accounted for on the caller's side. This is basically a context-sensitization—it avoids spuriously conflating the undefined procedure's effects over several call sites.

An example is the call `pthread_mutex_lock(l)`. Its $R_i(s) = \{l, *l\}$ and $W_i(s) = \{*l\}$. (A synchronization is a read, and conservatively, also a write since the state of the operated-on sync object can change.) Another example is `r := scanf(p, q)`. Its $R_i(s) = \{\texttt{p}, \texttt{q}, *\texttt{p}, \texttt{stdin}, *\texttt{stdin}\}$ and $W_i(s) = \{\texttt{r}, *\texttt{q}, *\texttt{stdin}\}$.[8]

We postulate the existence of the partial functions $\check{R}_i$ and $\check{W}_i$ that give the immediate read and immediate write sets when s is either an abstracted-procedure call (such as the previous `scanf` and `pthread_mutex_lock` invocations) or not a call. These functions can be used to compute $R_i(s)$ and $W_i(s)$ for any s, as shown below:

$$R_i(s) = \begin{cases} largs(s) & \text{if } proc(s) \in \mathscr{F}_d, \\ largs(s) \cup \mathscr{L}_{inscr} & \text{else if } proc(s) \in \mathscr{F}_{inscr}, \\ \check{R}_i(s) & \text{otherwise,} \end{cases} \quad (4)$$

$$W_i(s) = \begin{cases} \{ret(s)\} & \text{if } proc(s) \in \mathscr{F}_d, \\ \{ret(s)\} \cup \mathscr{L}_{inscr} & \text{else if } proc(s) \in \mathscr{F}_{inscr}, \\ \check{W}_i(s) & \text{otherwise.} \end{cases} \quad (5)$$

The first two cases in Equations (4) and (5) are when s invokes a defined or inscrutable procedure. They use the partial functions *largs* and *ret*, which give the set of argument lvalues and the lvalue assigned the returned result for an invocation s. That is, if s is `z := f(x1, x2, ..., xk)`, then $largs(s) = \{x_1, x_2, \ldots, x_k\}$ and $ret(s) = z$. Because the second case in both equations coincides with an inscrutable-procedure invocation, $\mathscr{L}_{inscr}$ is included in $R_i(s)$ and $W_i(s)$. The third case is when $proc(s) \notin \mathscr{F}_d \cup \mathscr{F}_{inscr}$. Since this corresponds to either non-call code or an abstracted-procedure call, $R_i(s)$ and $W_i(s)$ can be simply expressed as $\check{R}_i(s)$ and $\check{W}_i(s)$.

Lvalues that are immediately accessed at the granularity of a defined procedure f can be computed as follows:

$$\overline{R}_i(f) = \bigcup_{s \in STMTS(f)} R_i(s), \quad \overline{W}_i(f) = \bigcup_{s \in STMTS(f)} W_i(s). \quad (6)$$

***SYNC*, *$\overline{SYNC}$*: Sync objects.** Synchronizations communicate using sync objects. Locks, barriers and condition variables are examples of sync objects. A partial function *SYNC* is posited that gives an lvalue set covering the user-visible and user-invisible sync objects that may be immediately or *transitively* accessed at a synchronization.[9] *SYNC* can be used to find $\overline{SYNC}(f)$, the set of lvalues for all sync objects that may be accessed by a thread executing f:

$$\overline{SYNC}(f) = \bigcup_{s \in \mathscr{U}_{sync} \cap STMTS(f)} SYNC(s). \quad (7)$$

Although user-invisible sync objects are not exposed to user code, they may be needed for analysis, such as when building the PCG. They will then be named by the virtual lvalue ui_{sync}.

2.4 Notational Conventions

Names of program-wide sets use a calligraphic font for the main lettering—e.g., $\mathscr{F}_d$, $\mathscr{F}_{FOLLOW}$ and $\mathscr{L}_h$. Functions with a procedure domain may sometimes have names that share common letters with other names—e.g., $\overline{R}_i$ and R_i, $\overline{W}_i$ and W_i, and $\overline{I}_i$ and I_i. A bar on top is then used to distinguish them. A subscript i is used when a set only consists of immediately accessed lvalues. An index that maps a notation to its pertinent equation and/or section is in the appendix.

3. Building the Procedural Concurrency Graph

The PCG indicates whether a pair of procedures may concurrently execute, and if so, objects accessed in one that may "interfere" with objects accessed in the other. Our approach to building the PCG is to begin with a solution that is possibly imprecise but assuredly correct, and to then subject it to a series of transformations, called refinements, that progressively improve its precision.

3.1 PCG Definition

A PCG is the labeled undirected graph $G_p = (\mathscr{F}_d, E, I_i)$, where $I_i : E \mapsto 2^{\mathscr{L}}$ is the *immediate interference function*. Nodes in $\mathscr{F}_d$ correspond to the defined procedures in user code. An edge $(a, b) \in$

[8] `*q` may not be written, for instance, if assignment suppression is used [14]. But including `*q` in $W_i(s)$ is safe since these sets encode "may information".

[9] An object is transitively accessed at a call site s if it is immediately accessed in a procedure that lies in a call-graph path from the callee at s.

E means that the execution of a by one thread may overlap with an execution of b by a different thread—this is the standard MHP (may-happen-in-parallel) relation [23]. Then, $I_i((a,b))$ is the set of lvalues on which a and b may immediately interfere. Since a could run in parallel with itself, G_p can have self-loops.

3.1.1 Immediate Interference

The *overlapping regions* of two control-flow graph (CFG) paths P and P', executed by different threads, are subpaths p_1p_2 in P and p_3p_4 in P'—where p_1 through p_4 are points—such that p_1 abuts p_3 and p_2 abuts p_4 in some interleaving. Given this, two procedures f and f' are said to *immediately interfere* on an lvalue x if there exist two immediate accesses, m of x in f and m' of an lvalue x' in f', for which the following conditions simultaneously hold:

C1. m and m' conflict—i.e., at least one is a write, and x aliases x'.

C2. m and m' either lie in the overlapping regions of paths in f and f' that are executed by different threads, or there are no *unaffected statements* whose may_{def} and may_{use} sets prevent them from ending up in such regions due to a sequentially-sound transformation based on *data-flow analysis frameworks* [16].

From the above definition, f and f' also immediately interfere on x'. Therefore, immediate interference is a special kind of conflict [34]. We say that f and f' "may immediately interfere" on x (and x') if each of the above conditions only *may* hold.

Condition C2 is a disjunction of two clauses. The first covers the situation of an interleaving in which m and m' abut, and are executed by different threads. The second conservatively anticipates the emergence of such situations after a class of sequentially-sound transformations. Recall from Section 2.2 that for an unaffected statement, the may_{def} and may_{use} sets are fixed. So an unaffected statement *always* prevents the movement of an access m'' across it if the lvalue involved in m'' belongs to its may_{def} set, or if m'' is a write and the lvalue involved belongs to its may_{use} set.

For the may-immediately-interfere case, Condition C2 is assumed true unless there is evidence to the contrary. Refinement 3 exemplifies how evidence to the contrary falsifies the condition.

3.2 The Initial PCG

The initial PCG $G_p^0 = (\mathscr{F}_d, E^0, I_i^0)$ is a complete graph with self-loops, and has an I_i^0 that is set so that

$$I_i^0((a,b)) = (\overline{R}_i(a) \approx \overline{W}_i(b)) \cup (\overline{W}_i(a) \approx (\overline{R}_i(b) \cup \overline{W}_i(b))) \quad (8)$$

for all $(a,b) \in E^0$, where $\approx$ is as defined by Equation (1).

Equation (8) finds all lvalues that may satisfy Condition C1; these approximate the may-immediate interference between a and b because Condition C2 can always be regarded to hold for them.

Observe that accesses in defined procedures called from a or b do not affect $I_i^0((a,b))$. As an example, if b invokes $c \in \mathscr{F}_d$, then the immediate accesses in c do not affect $I_i^0((a,b))$. These accesses interfere with those in a only if c and a can execute in parallel.[10] But then, $I_i^0((a,c))$ would capture this interference.

3.3 Iteratively Improving a PCG's Precision

A *refinement* maps a PCG $G_p^j = (\mathscr{F}_d, E^j, I_i^j)$ to G_p^{j+1}. Thus, given an initial G_p^0, a sequence $G_p^1, G_p^2, \ldots$ can be generated by successively applying refinements. All refinements, by definition, possess the following two properties: $E^{j+1} \subseteq E^j$, and $I_i^{j+1}(e) \subseteq I_i^j(e)$ for all $e \in E^{j+1}$. Hence, the PCG sequence converges.

A refinement is a *concurrency type* if $I_i^{j+1} = I_i^j / E^{j+1}$, where '$F/A$' denotes the restriction of a function F to a subset A of its domain. It is a *purely interference type* if $E^{j+1} = E^j$. While the two types are not mutually exclusive, the identity refinement is the only one that is both a concurrency type and a purely interference type. This paper only explores refinements that are one of these two types. But clearly, there could be other types of refinements depending on how E^{j+1} and I_i^{j+1} are related to E^j and I_i^j.

3.3.1 A Thread-Based Classification of Procedures

Several of the refinements in this paper are formulated using a special classification of a program's invoked procedures. This classification, which is specific to a POSIX-like threading model, categorizes every invoked procedure, whether defined or undefined, into one or more of the following groups: "start routines", spawners, spawnees and "follow routines". A procedure is a *start routine* if it may be the entry point of a spawned thread. It is a *spawnee* if it may be executed by a spawned thread. It is a *spawner* if it may create a thread and return with the created thread still running. It is a *follow routine* if a thread may invoke it after that thread returns from a spawner. These categories are respectively represented by the sets $\mathscr{F}_{START}$, $\mathscr{F}_{SPAWNEE}$, $\mathscr{F}_{SPAWNER}$ and $\mathscr{F}_{FOLLOW}$.

Start routines are often easily recognizable. For instance, they are targeted by the third argument of a `pthread_create` call.

Start routines, and every procedure they *call-reach* (i.e., reach in the static call graph), are conservatively marked spawnees.

Procedures that call-reach a spawner are conservatively also spawners. This is a recursive definition—its base case is every undefined procedure that is a spawner, such as `pthread_create`. A procedure does not become a spawner by the mere act of spawning a thread. It is not a spawner if the created threads are not existent on its return. Thus, procedures that create threads and wait for them to exit before returning are not spawners.

A conservative set of follow routines can be obtained thus: (1) a procedure whose call site lies in a control-flow path that starts just after a spawner's call site is a follow routine;[11] and (2) procedures call-reachable from follow routines are also follow routines.

3.3.2 Concurrency-Type Refinements

Refinements 1 and 2 below are of the concurrency type. Because their only effect on the immediate interference function is to restrict it to the new edge set E^{j+1}, they can be formally stated by just describing their effects on E^j. All of the refinements in this paper are provably sound—i.e., the new PCG never omits an immediate interference or happens-in-parallel event that occurs at run time. Soundness proofs for all the refinements are available in a technical report [15]; the proof for Refinement 4 is reproduced in this paper.

Refinement 1.

$$E^{j+1} = E^j - \{(a,b) \mid a \notin \mathscr{F}_{SPAWNEE} \wedge b \notin \mathscr{F}_{SPAWNEE}\}.$$

Refinement 2.

$$E^{j+1} = E^j - \{(a,b) \mid a \notin (\mathscr{F}_{SPAWNEE} \cup \mathscr{F}_{SPAWNER} \cup \mathscr{F}_{FOLLOW})\}.$$

The above refinements go after different concurrency-paring opportunities. Refinement 1 removes an edge if the involved procedures can only be executed by the main thread. Refinement 2 addresses opportunities in which a spawned thread may execute at most one of the procedures in an edge. The refinements do not depend on knowledge pertaining to synchronization orders or thread termination. More concurrency-type refinements can be devised if calls to other thread-related procedures, such as `pthread_join` and `pthread_cond_wait`, are not handled opaquely.[12]

[10] It is also possible for c and a to not execute in parallel—e.g., a and b begin running together, a finishes before b, and b invokes c after a finishes.

[11] Because the path starts just after the spawner's call site, spawners themselves are not follow routines unless they are called in the path.

[12] If some thread-related procedure is not modeled, it should be treated opaquely, and not ignored, in order to ensure correctness.

```
0 GetArguments();                    4 CREATE(ParallelExecute,...);
1 InitGlobalMemory();                5 WAIT_FOR_END(...);
2 InitExpTables();                   6 printf(...);
3 CreateDistribution(...);           7 PrintTimes();
```

Figure 3. An excerpt from the `main` procedure of SPLASH-2's FMM benchmark. Calls preceding `CREATE` perform initialization tasks. Calls after `WAIT_FOR_END` are to output procedures.

3.3.3 Demonstrations of Refinements 1 and 2 on Real Code

Figure 3 shows a code fragment from the `main` procedure of SPLASH-2's FMM benchmark [41]. The macros `CREATE` and `WAIT_FOR_END` expand to calls to `pthread_create` and `pthread_join`. Only the main thread executes the procedures invoked on Lines 0 to 3, and on Line 7. Therefore, these procedures cannot execute concurrently with each other. Refinement 1 detects this since none of them belong to $\mathscr{F}_{SPAWNEE}$. Indeed, Refinement 1 also determines that none of them can happen in parallel with themselves.

The first argument to `CREATE` is a start routine. Since the procedures invoked on Lines 0 to 3 are neither spawnees, spawners nor belong to $\mathscr{F}_{FOLLOW}$, Refinement 2 discovers that none of them can execute in parallel with `ParallelExecute` or any procedure call-reachable from `ParallelExecute`.

This example also shows the complementarity of Refinements 1 and 2. That is, Refinement 1 will not detect that `ParallelExecute` and its call-descendants cannot run in parallel with the procedures invoked on Lines 0 to 3. And because `PrintTimes` is in $\mathscr{F}_{FOLLOW}$, Refinement 2 will not uncover that it is never concurrent with itself.

3.3.4 Purely Interference-Type Refinements

As remarked in Section 3.3, purely interference-type refinements only affect the immediate interference function I_i. Our first purely interference-type refinement is based on the observation that lvalues that are only accessed before spawner call sites, in procedures that are only executed by the main thread, can never interfere with accesses that occur in concurrent procedures *if* the spawner call sites are unaffected statements. Our second purely interference-type refinement is based on the observation that under a certain condition, two procedures that do not synchronize on common sync objects cannot interfere in a data-race-free program.

A flow-sensitive refinement. A statement s_2 "follows" a statement s_1 if s_2 occurs in a control-flow path that starts just after s_1. Given a set of statements S', we use $follow(S')$ to designate the set of all statements each of which follows some statement in S'. Let $spawner(f)$ be the set of all statements that invoke spawners in a defined procedure f. If the spawner call sites all belong to $\mathscr{U} - \mathring{\mathscr{U}}_{sync}$, their MOD-REF sets (which correspond to may_{def} and may_{use} sets) will ensure that any *unsafe* movement of shared-object accesses across them by a data-flow analysis is blocked. This presents a pruning opportunity, formalized in Refinement 3, because lvalues that are not accessed after spawner call sites can never satisfy Condition C2. Notice that no edge-set effects are shown because for purely interference-type refinements, $E^{j+1} = E^j$.

Refinement 3. If spawner call sites are unaffected statements, then

$$I_i^{j+1}(e) = I_i^j(e) - \{x \mid x \notin R_i(s) \cup W_i(s) \forall s \in follow(spawner(a))\},$$

where $e = (a,b) \in E^j$, and $a \notin \mathscr{F}_{SPAWNEE} \cup \mathscr{F}_{FOLLOW}$.

The expression $follow(spawner(a))$ above can be ascertained by finding basic blocks reachable in the CFG from spawner invocation sites. It can also be used to calculate the program's $\mathscr{F}_{FOLLOW}$. That is, suppose $RTC(f)$ is the set of all immediate successors of a procedure f in the reflexive transitive closure of the static call graph. Then, $f \in \mathscr{F}_{FOLLOW}$ if there exists a procedure f' such that $f \in RTC(f')$ and a call site of f' belongs to some $follow(spawner(a))$.

A refinement based on data-race freedom. Consider two procedures a and b that may execute simultaneously. Equation (7) gives their $\overline{SYNC}$ sets. If none of the lvalues in $\overline{SYNC}(a)$ and $\overline{SYNC}(b)$ can alias each other, then a and b cannot immediately interfere with each other, provided the no-chain condition specified in the statement of Refinement 4 holds. a and b can make conflicting accesses of a data object (i.e., non-sync object) when they do not overlap during execution.[13] If the conflicting accesses were to occur when their executions overlap, an interleaving exists in which the accesses are adjacent. But then, the program has a data race.

Refinement 4. If the program is data-race free and $(a,b) \in E^j$, then

$$I_i^{j+1}((a,b)) = \varnothing \text{ if } \overline{SYNC}(a) \approx \overline{SYNC}(b) = \varnothing,$$

and the "no-chain" condition holds, i.e., there are no procedures $f_1 f_2 \dots f_n$ $(n > 2)$ that satisfy three clauses: (1) $f_1 = a$ (or b), $f_n = b$ (or a) *can* happen in parallel, (2) for at least one k, $\overline{SYNC}_i(f_k) \approx \overline{SYNC}_i(f_{k+1}) \neq \varnothing$ and f_k, f_{k+1} can happen in parallel, and (3) for all other k, a call of f_k precedes a call of f_{k+1} in program order. ($\overline{SYNC}_i(f)$ is the set of immediately accessed sync objects in f.)

Soundness Proof. We show by contradiction that $I_i^{j+1}((a,b))$ can be set to $\varnothing$. Assume a and b immediately interfere on x—thus, by Conditions C1 and C2, there can be an execution instance in which accesses of x in a and b conflict and lie in overlapping regions. Then, there must be a happens-before relation $\overset{hb}{\rightarrow}$ between an $s_a \in STMTS(a)$ and an $s_b \in STMTS(b)$—otherwise, the program has a data race on x [2]. Happens-before is the irreflexive transitive closure of the program order $\overset{po}{\rightarrow}$ and synchronization order $\overset{so}{\rightarrow}$ relations [2]. Without loss of generality, let $s_a \overset{hb}{\rightarrow} s_b$. Then, there is a chain of statements $s_1 s_2 \dots s_m$ such that $s_1 = s_a$, $s_m = s_b$, and either $s_k \overset{so}{\rightarrow} s_{k+1}$ or $s_k \overset{po}{\rightarrow} s_{k+1}$. If $s_k \overset{so}{\rightarrow} s_{k+1}$, then there exist procedures f_k and f_{k+1} such that $\overline{SYNC}_i(f_k) \approx \overline{SYNC}_i(f_{k+1}) \neq \varnothing$ and f_k and f_{k+1} can happen in parallel. If $s_k \overset{po}{\rightarrow} s_{k+1}$, then s_k and s_{k+1} belong to procedures f_k and f_{k+1} that either are the same, or f_k is called before f_{k+1} in program order. Now, $s_k \overset{so}{\rightarrow} s_{k+1}$ for at least one k—otherwise, an interleaving can be constructed that has a data race on x. Hence, there is a set of procedures that violates the no-chain condition. Thus, a and b cannot immediately interfere on x. □

The no-chain condition holds if any of the three clauses is false. It is not checked by our current implementation, though for all our tested SPLASH-2 benchmarks, it holds whenever Refinement 4 is applied. That is, some clause is false whenever $\overline{SYNC}(a) \approx \overline{SYNC}(b) = \varnothing$ by the time Refinement 4 is applied.

The no-chain condition, as presented, is conservative. It can be tightened if other procedure-level information is used—e.g., the absence of spinning synchronizations inside procedures.

3.3.5 Demonstrations of Refinements 3 and 4 on Real Code

The `InitExpTables` call on Line 2 in Figure 3 initializes `Zero` and `One`, which are two global `struct` variables. Various procedures call-reachable from `ParallelExecute` use these variables. `InitExpTables` is sufficiently small that `gcc` inlines it when the `-O3` switch is turned on. Because `ParallelExecute` and all of its call-descendants may run concurrently with `main`, Equation (8) includes `Zero` and `One` in the initial immediate interference sets between `main` and procedures in RTC(`ParallelExecute`) that access these variables. Nevertheless, `main` is neither a spawnee nor a follow routine, and statements in $follow(spawner($`main`$))$ do not

[13] For instance, by acquiring a common lock before calling a and b.

access these variables. Hence, Refinement 3 removes `Zero` and `One` from all of the above immediate interference sets.

We illustrate Refinement 4 by considering `InitBox` and `CreateBoxes`, two procedures call-reachable from `ParallelExecute`. Both write into a global array called `Local`, so the initial immediate interference set for the pair is nonempty.

Now, `pthread_mutex_lock` and `pthread_mutex_unlock` are the only synchronizations performed when `InitBox` and `CreateBoxes` are active. `InitBox` performs them through the callee `LockedPrint`. The locks held are all different, however, and `InitBox` and `CreateBoxes` satisfy the no-chain condition. (FMM invokes a barrier between `CreateBoxes` and `InitBox`, ensuring that the two cannot happen in parallel.) So Refinement 4 reduces the immediate interference between them to the empty set.

3.4 Dealing with Inscrutable Procedures

The description thus far of the PCG construction algorithm is adequate for handling programs in which only defined and abstracted procedures are called. We now show that the algorithm works even when there are inscrutable-procedure calls, e.g., into arbitrary third-party libraries distributed as pure binaries. The issue boils down to understanding the effects of inscrutable-procedure calls on the construction of the initial PCG and on Refinements 1 to 4.

3.4.1 Effect on Building the Initial PCG

Inscrutable procedures do not affect the PCG's node set $\mathscr{F}_d$. From Equations (4) and (5), R_i and W_i are well defined in the presence of undefined-procedure calls. Therefore, from Equation (6), $\overline{R}_i(f)$ and $\overline{W}_i(f)$ are well defined for all $f \in \mathscr{F}_d$. Since Equation (8) remains operable, inscrutable procedures pose no problems to building G^0_p.

3.4.2 Effect on Refinements 1 to 3

But inscrutable-procedure calls may affect sets such as $\mathscr{F}_{SPAWNER}$, $\mathscr{F}_{SPAWNEE}$ and $\mathscr{F}_{FOLLOW}$; these, in turn, affect Refinements 1 to 3:

- $\mathscr{F}_{SPAWNER}$: In the absence of information to the contrary, inscrutable procedures must be regarded as spawners. Then, every inscrutable procedure g, and every procedure that call-reaches g, must be added to $\mathscr{F}_{SPAWNER}$.
- $\mathscr{F}_{START}$: Suppose $\mathscr{F}_{START}$ is initially the set of start routines, obtained by ignoring all inscrutable-procedure calls. If there is even one such call, every procedure in $\mathscr{L}_{inscr}$ whose function type is indicative of a start routine must be added to $\mathscr{F}_{START}$.
- $\mathscr{F}_{SPAWNEE}$: $\mathscr{F}_{SPAWNEE}$ is just $\cup_{f \in \mathscr{F}_{START}} RTC(f)$.
- $\mathscr{F}_{FOLLOW}$: Let $\mathscr{F}'_{FOLLOW}$ be initially the set of follow routines, ignoring all inscrutable-procedure calls. If there is a call to an inscrutable procedure g, every procedure in $\mathscr{L}_{inscr}$ would have to be included in $\mathscr{F}'_{FOLLOW}$ because g could invoke all of them after spawning a thread. $\mathscr{F}_{FOLLOW}$ can then be obtained by applying the algorithm in Section 3.3.1 using $\mathscr{F}'_{FOLLOW}$.

3.4.3 Effect on Refinement 4

The weak-ordering model of memory consistency prescribes an algorithm for safely distinguishing synchronizations in a data-race-free program [1, Page 75]. The idea is to mark a statement as a synchronization if treating it as a data operation *could* lead to a data race. We assume that inscrutable-procedure calls have been appositely marked as synchronizations using this algorithm.

For instance, if $\mathscr{L}_{inscr}$ is the empty set, then inscrutable-procedure invocations need not be regarded as synchronizations. But in the situation that a call to an inscrutable procedure g should be treated as a synchronization, the $\overline{SYNC}$ set of every defined procedure that call-reaches g will include the virtual lvalue ui_{sync}.

Refinement 4 does not require a special handling of the above two situations. It automatically will *not* apply in the latter situation since $\overline{SYNC}(a) \approx \overline{SYNC}(b)$ will then be nonempty.

4. Enabling Optimizations on Siloed References

PCGs have several applications. One is determining a class of *references* (i.e., accesses) in a multithreaded program on which classical optimization opportunities can be safely unblocked. Members of this class have the read- and write-siloed properties on certain intraprocedural paths. More precise may_{def} and may_{use} sets can be obtained by leaving out these references. This section proves that the resulting sets *always* remain sound for a data-flow analysis.

4.1 The Read-Siloed and Write-Siloed Properties

Let P be a control-flow path between two program points. We say that an lvalue x is "read-siloed in a thread h on P" if once h enters P, no other thread writes an object named by x until h exits P. This definition is best understood by considering an execution interleaving, such as the one below:

$$\ldots\ s'_1\ s'_2\ \mathbf{s_1}\ s'_3\ s'_4\ s'_5\ \mathbf{s_2}\ s'_6\ \mathbf{s_3}\ s'_7\ s'_8\ \ldots\ \mathbf{s_n}\ s'_m\ s'_{m+1}\ \ldots$$

The boldface symbols $\mathbf{s_1}$ to $\mathbf{s_n}$ are instructions executed by h, and form the path P. $\mathbf{s_1}$ and $\mathbf{s_n}$ are also the first and last instructions in P. The lightface symbols are instructions executed by other threads. If x is read-siloed in h on P, then any write of x by another thread would have to precede s'_2 or succeed s'_m.[14] Similarly, x is said to be "write-siloed in h on P" if no other thread reads or writes x once h enters P and until it exits P. If these definitions were true for all h, we would just say that x is "read- or write-siloed on P". P would then be a *read-* or *write-siloed path* with respect to x.

There are numerous points about these definitions. First, they do not mention an occurrence of x in P. An lvalue x can be read-siloed in h even on a stretch of code free of x, so long as no other thread updates x when h is at any point in this code stretch. Second, write-siloed is a stronger property than read-siloed. If x is write-siloed in h on P, then it is also read-siloed in h on P. Third, an lvalue y that is read-siloed (write-siloed) on P in all threads has the salient quality that a write (read or write) of y by any thread outside P can only occur when no other thread is within the confines of P. This trait is stronger than read- or write-siloed references within P being just data-race free. It means accesses of y in P, including those involving proper synchronization, are free of cross-thread effects.

4.2 The Siloed-on-a-Procedure Property

The siloed concept can be extended to whole procedures. Let $stmts(P)$ be the set of statements in a path P. Then, an lvalue z is said to be "siloed on a procedure f" if two conditions are met:

S1. z is write-siloed on every path P in f in which it may be immediately written at a statement s and is not in $may_{def}(s') \cup may_{use}(s')$ of any unaffected statement s' in $stmts(P) - \{s\}$.

S2. z is read-siloed on every path P in f in which it may be immediately read at a statement s and is not in $may_{def}(s')$ of any unaffected statement s' in $stmts(P) - \{s\}$.

The set $SOP_i(f)$ consists of lvalues siloed on f. As our work is the first treatment of the siloed concept, the focus will be on this simpler procedure-level variant, although working with the concept at a finer granularity will likely yield more powerful results. In this paper, *siloed* without qualification means siloed on a procedure.

[14] To preclude data races, s'_2 and s'_m should not be writes of x.

4.3 Computing Siloed Lvalues

Let $MHP(f)$ be the set of neighbors of a procedure f in the program's PCG. Then f's *overall immediate interference* is

$$\overline{I}_i(f) = \bigcup_{f' \in MHP(f)} I_i((f, f')). \tag{9}$$

From Equation (9), it is clear that for every $x \in \overline{I}_i(f)$, there is some $f' \in MHP(f)$ such that f and f' may immediately interfere on x. So lvalues in $\overline{I}_i(f)$ may not be siloed on f. But those in

$$S_i(f) = (\overline{R}_i(f) \cup \overline{W}_i(f)) - \overline{I}_i(f) \tag{10}$$

will be, as Theorem 1 shows. The subscript i, as usual, signifies that only immediately accessed lvalues comprise the *siloed-lvalue set*.

Theorem 1. *$S_i(f) \subseteq SOP_i(f)$.*

Proof. If $x \in S_i(f)$, then $x \notin \overline{I}_i(f)$ by Equation (10). We prove that if P is a path in f with a possible immediate write-access m of x at a statement s, and $x \notin may_{def}(s') \cup may_{use}(s')$ for all unaffected statements s' in $stmts(P) - \{s\}$, then x must be write-siloed on P. If not, there exist threads h and h' such that when h is in P in some execution instance, h' performs an access m' of an alias x' of x. Now, m' is immediate to some $f' \in \mathscr{F}_d$ and is in a path P' in f'. Since none of the unaffected statements in $stmts(P) - \{s\}$ define or use x, a data-flow transformation *could* move m to any point in P. Then, because m and m' also conflict, Conditions C1 and C2 can both hold for x. Thus, $x \in I_i((f, f'))$. So by Equation (9), $x \in \overline{I}_i(f)$, a contradiction. Condition S2 can be similarly proved for paths that may immediately read x. Therefore, $x \in SOP_i(f)$. □

There is an important case for Equations (9) and (10) that we highlight. If lvalues in $\overline{SYNC}(f)$ do not alias with lvalues in $\overline{SYNC}(f')$ for all $f' \in MHP(f)$, then $\overline{I}_i(f)$ will be $\varnothing$ if the program is given to be data-race free and if f and f' satisfy the no-chain condition in Refinement 4. This is because Refinement 4 will force all $I_i((f, f'))$ to $\varnothing$; $S_i(f)$ will then equal $\overline{R}_i(f) \cup \overline{W}_i(f)$. Since $SOP_i(f) \subseteq \overline{R}_i(f) \cup \overline{W}_i(f)$, we would then have $S_i(f) = SOP_i(f)$.

4.4 A More Accurate May-Definition Set

Let $DU(s)$ be the set of all user-code lvalues z for which there is an intraprocedural path from a potential access of z to the statement s, or from s to a potential access of z.[15] From a data-flow analysis standpoint, it is enough if $may_{def}(s)$ includes two groups of lvalues when s is a synchronization: (1) those in $\mathscr{L}$ that could be written at s by a thread h executing s; and (2) those in $DU(s)$ that could be concurrently written when h is executing s. The first group is drawn from $\mathscr{L}$, and not the possibly smaller $DU(s)$, because *isolated* definitions may be used, or may kill definitions, in concurrent threads. But only those concurrent definitions that may kill definitions in the current thread, or that may be later killed or used in the current thread, need to be factored into $may_{def}(s)$—hence, $DU(s)$ is the superset for the second group. This suggests that

$$may^t_{def}(s) = W(s) \cup (DU(s) \cap CW(s)) \subseteq may_{def}(s) \tag{11}$$

is a more precise may-definition set for synchronizations, where

$$W(s') = \{x \mid x \in \mathscr{L} \wedge (\text{the thread executing } s' \text{ may immediately or transitively write } x \text{ at } s')\}, \tag{12}$$

$$CW(s') = \{x \mid x \in \mathscr{L} \wedge (\text{an execution exists wherein when a thread is at } s', \text{ another thread writes } x)\} \tag{13}$$

for *any* statement s'.

[15] Interprocedural definition-use flow can also be modeled, by expediently adding artificial assignments and uses to the CFG's entry and exit nodes.

It is easy to calculate $W(s')$ using the immediate-write sets W_i and $\overline{W}_i$, which were defined in Equations (5) and (6):

$$W(s') = W_i(s') \cup \begin{cases} \varnothing & \text{if } proc(s') = \top, \\ \bigcup_{f' \in RTC(proc(s'))} \overline{W}_i(f') & \text{otherwise.} \end{cases} \tag{14}$$

The first case in the above coincides with non-call code. The second case coincides with a call. Besides $W_i(s')$, it includes the $\overline{W}_i$ set of every defined or undefined procedure that is call-reachable from s'.

$CW(s')$ models the parallel writes at s'. Lemma 1 states that for any synchronization s, $DU_i(s) \cap CW(s)$ and $SOP_i(f)$ are disjoint. (Lemma 1 is proved in [15].) $DU_i(s)$, which is a subset of $DU(s)$, comprises lvalues $z \in \mathscr{L}$ for which a potential immediate access of z at a statement s' reaches just before s, or is reached from just after s, by a path P in f in which the unaffected statements among $stmts(P) - \{s\}$ do not access z. Theorem 2 uses Lemma 1 to prove an "upper bound" on $may^t_{def}(s)$ that is better than $may_{def}(s)$.

Lemma 1. *For all synchronizations s in f,*

$$DU_i(s) \cap CW(s) \cap SOP_i(f) = \varnothing.$$

Theorem 2. *For all synchronizations s in f,*

$$(may_{def}(s) - (DU_i(s) \cap SOP_i(f))) \cup W(s) \supseteq may^t_{def}(s).$$

Proof. Let $x \in may^t_{def}(s)$. Then $x \in may_{def}(s)$. By Equation (11), $x \in W(s) \cup (DU(s) \cap CW(s))$. If $x \notin DU(s) \cap CW(s)$, then $x \in W(s)$. If $x \in DU(s) \cap CW(s)$, then x is either in or not in $DU_i(s) \cap CW(s)$. If in, then $x \notin SOP_i(f)$ by Lemma 1. If not in, then $x \notin DU_i(s)$, since $DU_i(s) \subseteq DU(s)$. Either way, $x \notin DU_i(s) \cap SOP_i(f)$. So $x \in (may_{def}(s) - (DU_i(s) \cap SOP_i(f))) \cup W(s)$ always holds. □

Theorem 2 can only be used to tighten the may_{def} sets of interesting synchronizations, since the siloed-on-a-procedure notion is stipulated on the other synchronizations (i.e., unaffected statements) having fixed may_{def} and may_{use} sets. Thus, by using Theorems 1 and 2, $may_{def}(s)$ of an interesting synchronization s can be replaced by $(may_{def}(s) - (DU_i(s) \cap S_i(f))) \cup W(s)$.

There is a similar result for a more accurate may_{use} set [15].

4.5 Examples

We now show how identifying siloed lvalues in some of the previous code fragments can expose optimization opportunities in them.

4.5.1 A Value-Numbering Opportunity

The critical section in Figure 2 is from FMM's `ParallelExecute` procedure. Now, `InitGlobalMemory` is the only FMM procedure that writes `G_Memory`. As discussed in Section 3.3.3, the PCG reveals that `InitGlobalMemory` cannot happen in parallel with `ParallelExecute`. So `ParallelExecute`'s overall immediate interference will not contain `G_Memory`. Equation (10) then ascertains that `G_Memory` is siloed on `ParallelExecute`. Hence, by Theorem 2, the χ assignments on Lines 3, 6 and 11 can be removed, and t', t'' and t''' can be replaced by `G_Memory`. A value-numbering pass will now be able to catch the equivalence of t_2 and t_6.

4.5.2 A Copy Propagation Opportunity

Assume that the left and right snippets in Figure 1 are from procedures a and b respectively (a and b could be the same). Then, there will be an edge between a and b in the PCG. By Equation (9), `X` and `Y` will be in the overall immediate interference of both a and b. Hence, by Equation (10), both `X` and `Y` will not be in either $S_i(a)$ or $S_i(b)$. So no optimization opportunities on `X` or `Y` get unblocked.

For the second hypothetical program, from Section 1.1.2 (same left snippet, but a different right snippet, one in which `X` is not

f_a:	a:	f_b:	b:
1.0 LOCK(L_x)	*2.0* t_a := x	*3.0* LOCK(L_y)	*4.0* t_b := y
1.1 LOCK(L_y)	*2.1* y := ...	*3.1* LOCK(L_z)	*4.1* z := ...
1.2 ...y...	*2.2* UNLOCK(L_y)	*3.2* ...z...	*4.2* UNLOCK(L_z)
1.3 a(...)	*2.3* ...t_a...	*3.3* b(...)	*4.3* ...t_b...
1.4 UNLOCK(L_x)	*2.4* return	*3.4* UNLOCK(L_y)	*4.4* return

Figure 4. A program in which different optimization opportunities exist, depending on whether the UNLOCK on Line 2.2 in procedure a is an interesting synchronization or an unaffected statement.

updated), X will be in both $S_i(a)$ and $S_i(b)$. So a copy propagation opportunity involving X will get unblocked in the left snippet.

5. A Tradeoff Involving Interference

The reason for Condition C2's second clause is that data-flow information conservatively killed at an interesting synchronization s, due to $may_{def}(s)$ and $may_{use}(s)$, could later flow through s, since $may_{def}(s)$ and $may_{use}(s)$ are alterable. This could allow the movement of one or both of the accesses mentioned in Section 3.1.1, into an overlapping region of execution. Thus, the fewer the interesting synchronizations among $\mathscr{U}_{sync}$, the more the unaffected statements in user code, and so the less the chance of two procedures immediately interfering as a result of a data-flow transformation.

On the other hand, not designating a synchronization s as interesting could result in s unnecessarily killing useful data-flow information. Therefore, there is a tradeoff between immediate interference and the marking of synchronizations as interesting.

As an example, spawner call sites can be marked as interesting synchronizations, since spawning imposes a synchronization order [1]. But then, an unconditional application of Refinement 3 would not be guaranteed sound, because subsequent changes to a spawner call site's may_{def} and may_{use} sets could lift a killing effect, which may allow the movement of an access across the site, which in turn could change a noninterfering access into an interfering one. Therefore, spawner call sites must belong to $\mathscr{U} - \mathring{\mathscr{U}}_{sync}$ for Refinement 3 to be applicable.

Another example is in Figure 4. The only shared data objects are x, y and z, which are always accessed holding the locks L_x, L_y and L_z respectively. Procedures a and b are always invoked with the respective lock pairs L_x, L_y and L_y, L_z held. Specimen invocations are shown on Lines 1.3 and 3.3. Now, irrespective of whether the UNLOCK on Line 2.2 is an unaffected statement, the read of x on Line 2.0 cannot satisfy Condition C2. Hence, x $\notin \overline{I}_i$(a) for the perfect $\overline{I}_i$(a). So if Line 2.2 were an interesting synchronization, this would permit the SR Technique to drop x from $may_{def}(s_{2.2})$, thus enabling the copy propagation of x from Line 2.0 to Line 2.3.

On the other hand, marking Line 2.2 as an interesting synchronization means a and b may immediately interfere on y. This is because there would then be no unaffected statements that block the movement of y across Line 2.2. If Line 2.2 were instead an unaffected statement, the accesses of y on Lines 2.1 and 4.0 cannot satisfy Condition C2. Then, y $\notin \overline{I}_i$(b) for the perfect $\overline{I}_i$(b). This would allow the SR Technique to drop y from $may_{def}(s_{4.2})$, if Line 4.2 were an interesting synchronization. This, in turn, would permit the copy propagation of y from Line 4.0 to Line 4.3.

6. Experimental Results

We have implemented the SR Technique in revision 148810 of gcc, a pre-release of version series 4.5 of the compiler. This section reports measurements demonstrating how our implementation fared on benchmarks from the SPLASH-2 suite [41]. Our test bed was a four-socket 64-bit server, in which each socket was a 2.40GHz quad-core Intel Xeon E7330 processor having a 1066MHz front-side bus. A socket has two dies, with two cores per die. The per-core L1 instruction and data cache sizes were 32KB each. The per-die L2 cache was 3MB. The system ran Redhat Enterprise Linux 5 (kernel release 2.6.18), and had 32GB of available memory.

6.1 Compilation Details

In all our experiments, the `-O3` switch was turned on. Our prototype operates in gcc's whole-program compilation mode. This is turned on by the `-combine` and `-fwhole-program` flags, which require all source files to be on a single command-line. Until recently, it was the only way to do a whole-program interprocedural analysis (IPA) in gcc. New LTO (Link-Time Optimization) support in the current release series of gcc (4.5) should remove this deficiency.

6.1.1 Design of the SR Phase

An IPA-based SR phase was created to implement the SR Technique. To evaluate, we focused on opportunities enabled by the technique in some of gcc's existent phases that implement fundamental and commonly used optimizations. In particular, we quantified exposed opportunities in the following five *arbitrarily* selected intraprocedural phases: `pass_ccp` (conditional constant propagator), `pass_fre` (full-redundancy eliminator), `pass_copy_prop` (copy propagator), `pass_merge_phi` (phase that merges directly linked ϕ-nodes), and `pass_dce` (dead-code eliminator). When invoked from within the SR phase, these were executed in the given order, as part of an `opts_on_srefs` pass list.

The SR phase is structured as a loop. In each iteration, the SR Technique is applied once, followed by an application of `opts_on_srefs`. This "SR loop" is repeated until the IR no longer changes. Applying the technique once means building the PCG using the algorithm of Section 3, and sharpening data-flow abstractions using the algorithm of Section 4. Thus, the SR phase aims to unfetter a *maximal* set of opportunities in `opts_on_srefs`.[16]

6.1.2 'Enabled' and 'Baseline' Executables

Just prior to the SR phase, `opts_on_srefs` is repeatedly applied until the IR reaches quiescence. Hence, executables produced with and without the SR phase differ in the optimizations enabled by the SR phase. We will refer to these executables as *enabled* and *baseline* respectively. It should be noted that optimization effects unblocked in phases downstream from the SR phase are included in the enabled executables. These are due to a one-time use of siloed information, unlike those unblocked in the `opts_on_srefs` phases.

6.2 Benchmark Details

Table 1 shows the eight SPLASH-2 benchmarks used in our experiments: `m-fmm` (Fast Multipole Method), `ocean-c` (Contiguous Ocean), `barnes` (Barnes-Hut), `wr-spl` (Water-Spatial), `wr-nsq` (Water-Nsquared), `lu-c` (Contiguous LU), `radix` (Radix), and `fft` (FFT). The SPLASH-2 suite has a total of 12 "application" and "kernel" benchmarks. The remaining four did not successfully compile with the `-combine`/`-fwhole-program` combination.[17]

`m-fmm` is a slightly modified version of SPLASH-2's implementation of the Fast Multipole Method. The modification was to outline two adjacent loops into their own procedure. This was done to overcome a limitation in gcc's IRA (Integrated Register Allocator) phase, and is explained further in Section 6.4.1.

The 'Problem Size' column displays the inputs to our benchmarks. These were always above the original defaults [41], and

[16] "Maximal" because for a different `opts_on_srefs` pass order, a different set of opportunities may be unfettered by the time the IR stops changing.

[17] The failures seem to be related to cross-file IPA not being a routinely used feature in gcc. This will likely change with LTO coming online.

Program	Problem Size	Program Size				Static Synchronization Statistics				$\lvert\overline{R}_i\rvert_{\max}$	$\lvert\overline{W}_i\rvert_{\max}$
		LOC	Files	BBS	$\lvert\mathscr{F}_d\rvert$	Transitive Callers	Direct Callers	Sync Sites	Critical Sections		
`m-fmm`	1048576 particles	4381	17	969	86	32	19	52	17	43	36
`ocean-c`	4098×4098 grid	4774	10	1670	35	4	4	37	4	129	185
`barnes`	1048576 particles	2887	15	465	50	7	7	21	5	50	50
`wr-spl`	1331 molecules	2670	23	447	35	7	7	37	8	64	51
`wr-nsq`	4096 molecules	2063	23	324	34	6	6	41	8	59	51
`lu-c`	6000×6000 matrix, 16×16 blocks	911	1	301	26	4	4	11	1	33	28
`radix`	335544320 integers	833	1	212	18	2	2	31	6	34	29
`fft`	67108864 data points	899	1	250	24	3	3	13	1	40	38

Table 1. The SPLASH-2 benchmarks used in our experiments. 'LOC' means total lines of code. 'BBS' is the total number of basic blocks on entry to the SR phase. 'Transitive Callers' are defined procedures that transitively reach a Pthreads procedure. 'Direct Callers' are the direct invokers among them. 'Sync Sites' are the counts of the Pthreads call sites. $\lvert\overline{R}_i\rvert_{\max}$ and $\lvert\overline{W}_i\rvert_{\max}$ are the largest $\overline{R}_i$ and $\overline{W}_i$ set sizes.

Program	Average $\lvert S_i\rvert$ after Refinements 1 to k				Reductions	
	$k=1$	$k=2$	$k=3$	$k=4$	Edges	Intf.
`m-fmm`	0.53	1.28	1.37	4.96	813	362
`ocean-c`	8.05	11.95	28.41	42.67	186	113
`barnes`	2.51	4.81	5.05	8.89	664	71
`wr-spl`	1.03	2.05	3.53	4.29	112	27
`wr-nsq`	0.84	1.81	3.11	3.70	109	19
`lu-c`	1.10	1.10	1.10	5.39	15	12
`radix`	0.54	0.54	0.54	2.33	3	2
`fft`	0.90	0.90	0.90	2.79	10	6

Table 2. Metrics showing how the S_i set precision accrues with additional refinements. 'Edges' are edges removed by Refinements 1 and 2. 'Intf.' are the $I_i(e)$ sets pared by Refinements 3 and 4.

Program	Propagations		ϕ-Node Merges	Eliminations	Lock Pointer Equivalences
	Constant	Copy			
`m-fmm`	48	190	7	449	17
`ocean-c`	146	1334	2	2040	4
`barnes`	4	145	2	246	3
`wr-spl`	228	265	0	621	6
`wr-nsq`	317	311	93	677	8
`lu-c`	0	200	0	273	1
`radix`	0	187	0	277	6
`fft`	1	152	2	299	1

Table 3. Static metrics on a maximal set of optimization opportunities that were enabled by the SR phase in `opts_on_srefs`.

were chosen, to the extent possible, to make the 16-thread execution times measurably significant; 16 was the maximum number of threads used. The 'Program Size' section states benchmark sizes in terms of total lines of source code, number of source files, and the following at the start of the SR phase: total number of basic blocks, and total number of defined procedures. Therefore, the 'Files' column is indicative of the length of a compilation command-line with the `-combine/-fwhole-program` combination.

The 'Static Synchronization Statistics' section reflects the static usage intensity of undefined synchronizing procedures. For SPLASH-2, these are Pthreads library calls. For instance, 37% of `m-fmm`'s 86 defined procedures are 'Transitive Callers'—these procedures eventually reach the Pthreads library in the static call graph. (By that measure, `m-fmm` is among SPLASH-2's most Pthreads-intensive programs.) Therefore, their data-flow abstractions, such as MOD-REF sets, may be more conservative than necessary.

Among the synchronizations, `pthread_mutex_lock` and `pthread_mutex_unlock` were the only ones treated as interesting.

There is built-in support in `gcc` for certain procedures, such as `puts` and `strtol`. These are defined procedures, and are counted in $\lvert\mathscr{F}_d\rvert$. All other external library procedures used by SPLASH-2 can be abstracted, since they have specifications—e.g., Pthreads.

6.3 Static Metrics of Improvement

Table 2 is a quantification of the effectiveness of our refinement-based approach to constructing the PCG. We measured the size of the S_i set, averaged over $\lvert\mathscr{F}_d\rvert$. From Equations (9) and (10), we observe that as the PCG is refined, the overall immediate interference tends to decrease, which tends to increase the size of the siloed-lvalue set. Thus, the average $\lvert S_i\rvert$ and the precision of S_i are correlated. To check how the refinements affect this precision, we measured the average $\lvert S_i\rvert$ over multiple compilations, successively turning on the four refinements in this paper. The column '$k=1$' shows these measurements with just Refinement 1 turned on, the column '$k=2$' shows them with *both* Refinements 1 and 2 turned on, and so on. From these numbers, we observe that the average increase in $\lvert S_i\rvert$ across all tested programs is 62%, 37% and 170% on moving from $k=1$ to $k=4$. Refinement 4 is the most powerful by this measure, at least for the benchmarks studied.

The last two columns show absolute reductions. The reductions can also be expressed as percentages. For example, since the number of edges in G_p^0 is $\lvert\mathscr{F}_d\rvert(\lvert\mathscr{F}_d\rvert+1)/2$, the percentage edge reductions follow from Table 1: 22%, 30%, 52%, 18%, 4%, 2%, 3%.

The measurements in Table 2 were made on the last iteration of the SR loop. They are therefore a conservative representation of the improvements, which tend to be higher in the initial iterations.

Table 3 shows the total number of opportunities that were enabled in `opts_on_srefs`, at the end of the SR phase. An "opportunity" is an instance of an optimizing transformation. For example, 'Constant' and 'Copy' are unblocked propagations of constants and copies. 'ϕ-Node Merges' are unblocked opportunities in `pass_merge_phi`. 'Eliminations' is the sum of unblocked opportunities in `pass_fre` and `pass_dce`. Since the numbers do not include opportunities unblocked in downstream phases, Table 3 is a conservative reflection of all the enabled opportunities.

The 'Lock Pointer Equivalences' column displays the number of uncovered lock-pointer equivalences, of the kind discussed in Section 4.5.1. Every such equivalence is indicative of a critical section. We were therefore able to detect all of the critical sections in the source code, except for two each in `barnes` and `wr-spl`. Although the missed ones in `wr-spl` were because of an imprecision

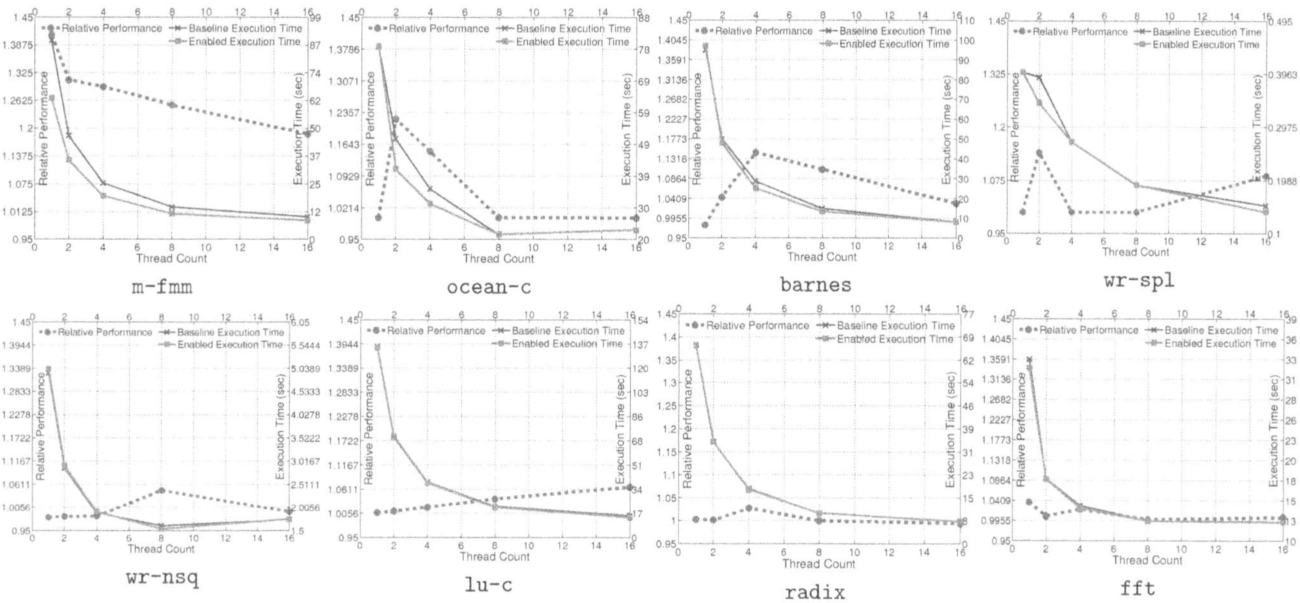

Figure 5. Relative performances of the enabled and baseline executables. Each graph's right axis measures T_B and T_E, the execution times in seconds of the baseline and enabled executables of a benchmark at thread counts 1, 2, 4, 8 and 16. The left axis measures T_B/T_E.

in our may-alias information, the undetected ones in `barnes` were due to lock-pointer accesses done through `volatile` variables.

6.4 Execution-Time Improvements

Figure 5 shows the execution times T_B and T_E of the baseline and enabled executables, and the relative performance T_B/T_E. Each reported time is the average of the last five of an eight-run experiment. The graphs show that improvements can sometimes be substantial, as in the `m-fmm` case, where it ranged from 41% to 19%.

In all of the tested benchmarks except two, relative improvements of 5% or more were seen at one or more thread counts. As an example, `ocean-c` exhibited improvements of 22% and 15% at two and four threads. It uses a red-black Gauss-Seidel multigrid solver; we suspect this benefits more from the enabled optimizations at those thread counts. `wr-spl` showed 14% and 9% improvements at two and 16 threads. Another example is `barnes`, which registered 15% and 11% improvements at four and eight threads.

The gains on `fft` and `radix` were at most 4% and 3%. Although `radix` has six critical sections, they are all in one procedure.

While `m-fmm`'s relative performance decreases with increasing thread count, `lu-c`'s increases, from 1% to 7%. For the others, there is no specific trend. Using simple arguments based on serial fractions, it can be shown that even when the enabled performance is always better than the baseline performance, the relative performance trend can be either increasing, decreasing, or flat [15].

The average improvements across all the tested programs at thread counts 1, 2, 4, 8, 16 were 5%, 9%, 8%, 6%, 5% respectively. Thus, the average improvement over all threads was 6%.

Since 37% of `m-fmm`'s defined procedures ultimately touch a synchronization, it is perhaps unsurprising that the SR Technique benefits it the most. A serial compiler would normally be unduly conservative on opportunities associated with those procedures.

6.4.1 Impact of Enabled Optimizations on Register Pressure

A secondary effect of enabling optimizations is that live ranges generally become longer. Hence, register pressure can increase. Register allocators typically cope with register pressure by spilling to memory. Because spilled code has costs, the enabling of optimizations can negatively influence the quality of the generated code. Register allocation in `gcc` happens in the IRA phase, which is a fairly recent addition—it replaced the old allocator in release series 4.4 [9], the series preceding our revision. In the original FMM program, the SR phase exposed a number of common-subexpression opportunities in `VListInteraction`, its hottest procedure. Several of these were between expressions involving field-based array-element accesses, in which one was deep inside a loop and the other was outside of it, with another loop in between. Unblocking them resulted in the extension of live ranges across entire loops; this sufficiently strained the IRA phase that improvements from the enabled optimizations were masked. We suppressed this register-allocation artifact by outlining the two loops into their own procedure. In the absence of the SR phase, the run time of this modified FMM program, i.e., `m-fmm`, does not perceptibly change. Its statistical execution profile also remains essentially the same.

Program	Baseline Time (B)	SR Technique Statistics			$\frac{A}{B}$
		Total Time	No. of Applications	Average Time (A)	
m-fmm	9.36	0.88	3	0.29	3%
ocean-c	26.88	9.95	4	2.49	9%
barnes	6.68	0.58	3	0.19	3%
wr-spl	5.93	0.87	3	0.29	5%
wr-nsq	5.22	2.97	11	0.27	5%
lu-c	2.47	0.36	3	0.12	5%
radix	1.93	0.56	4	0.14	7%
fft	1.75	0.33	3	0.11	6%

Table 4. Measurements of compilation times, in seconds. 'B' is the time to produce the baseline executables. 'A' is the average time per application of the SR Technique within the SR phase.

6.5 Compile-Time Measurements

Table 4 shows the times for producing the baseline versions. The 'SR Technique Statistics' section displays data on compiling into the enabled versions. Shown is the number of times the SR loop iterated before the IR reached quiescence. This is exactly the number of times the SR Technique was applied for a benchmark. 'Total Time' is the aggregate time over all these applications. An average per-application time for the SR Technique can therefore be obtained—this is shown in column 'A'. We thus see that the SR Technique increases baseline compilation times by 5% on average.

7. Related Work

There have been numerous works in the broad area of multithreaded-program optimization. Some were discussed in Section 1. This section covers other works in the area that are relevant to our effort.

7.1 Concurrency Analyses

Past analyses have utilized a variety of techniques for discovering whether code fragments may execute in parallel. An early one, by Bristow et al., built the Interprocess Precedence Graph, an abstraction for denoting the synchronization-imposed execution ordering among processes [4]. They modeled synchronization using event variables. Taylor proposed a state-based technique for generating, via simulation, an Ada program's "concurrency history" [37]. The resulting state space, however, can be exponential in the number of "tasks", i.e., groups of computations that may concurrently execute.

A few projects calculated the MHP relation for Java [24, 20]. These were based on an abstraction called the Parallel Execution Graph (PEG). A drawback with PEGs is that they combine the CFGs of individual threads. Therefore, not only do they require a bound on the number of coincident threads modeled, but they also potentially grow in size with this bound.

Several projects tackled the concurrency-determination problem by deducing complementary knowledge, such as partial execution orders and the Cannot-Happen-Together (CHT) relation [5, 8, 21]. Of these, the "nonconcurrency" analysis by Masticola and Ryder is perhaps closest to our refinement-based method of constructing PCGs [21]. Their work computes the CHT relation by progressively improving an approximation through a series of refinements. But they diverge in several crucial ways from our work:

- ***No notion of interference.*** Ascertaining only the CHT relation means that interference is at best either "none" or "anything".
- ***The assumption of single-instance tasks.*** Their initial CHT solution is $Task(s) - \{s\}$ for each statement s, where $Task(s)$ is the set of statements in the task containing s. This is premised on there being at most one instance of a task at any moment. In a POSIX-like threading model, however, statements reachable from a start routine may belong to multiple coincident tasks.
- ***Refinements specific to alternative parallel-programming models.*** Their refinements were primarily designed for Ada's rendezvous synchronization mechanism and binary semaphores.

7.2 Interference on Shared Data

A past abstraction probably closest to the PCG is the Concurrency Graph (CG), by Zhang et al [42]. Like the PCG, it is a labeled undirected graph in which edges represent the MHP relation. Nodes, however, stand for critical sections. But more importantly, the CG has a coarse notion of interference. An edge is labeled I if conflicting accesses exist between the corresponding critical sections, and labeled N otherwise. Zhang et al. used CGs for a purpose different from in our work—to assign locks to critical sections. They assumed CGs to be given, and manually constructed them [42].

Rodríguez et al. presented extensions to the Java Modeling Language for specifying the noninterference of methods [28]. They informally described two kinds of interference: "internal" and "external". Internal interference is when a concurrent thread alters program invariants between a method's entry and exit. External interference is when pre- and post-conditions are violated due to changes by a concurrent thread between a call and method entry, and between a method exit and caller resumption. Their work did not address the issue of automatically inferring interference.

In Hendren and Nicolau's analysis of recursive data structures, the concept of interference is synonymous with conflict [11]. Other authors have considered interference as conflict combined with the MHP relation [17, 30]. In our work, this would be analogous to an edge in the PCG plus Condition C1.

There is a family of static analyses for determining whether an object may *thread-escape*, e.g., [6]. An object o thread-escapes if it could be accessed by more than one thread. This definition lacks temporality. That is, even if o is accessed by threads in disjoint time intervals, it still escapes. Although thread-escaping is not the same as interference, the idea is nonetheless complementary because threads can never interfere on objects that do not thread-escape.

Praun and Gross devised a static analysis for Java to determine conflicting object accesses [39]. This was based on an abstraction called the Object Use Graph (OUG), which is built per abstract object using symbolic execution. Conflict in their terminology has the sense of interference in our work. There are, however, important differences. Some of them are: (1) there is no counterpart to Condition C2's second clause; (2) to establish pairs of conflicting accesses, OUGs need to be processed for pairs of conflicting events.

7.3 Preserving SC on Weakly Consistent Hardware

There have been efforts on mapping code written for a memory model that is presumably easy to reason about, e.g., SC, to more relaxed memory models offered by the hardware [34, 22, 36]. Their solution has been to insert special instructions, called "memory barriers" (e.g., IBM POWER3's `sync` and Intel x86's `fence`), so as to suppress the compiler and hardware from reordering code. These efforts differ from the SR approach in a number of ways:

- ***Problem solved is different.*** Their goal is to provide the appearance of SC, even in the presence of data races. The SR approach is about effectively reusing classical optimizations on data-race-free SC code, preserving both SC and data-race freedom.
- ***No reordering across synchronizations.*** Synchronization knowledge is only used to remove IR conflict edges, since doing so improves the results of the barrier-insertion analysis [34].
- ***A solution may not always be possible.*** There are programs, such as the IRIW example [3], for which inserting barriers is insufficient to realize SC on certain platforms.

7.4 Rule-Based Transformations for Data-Race-Free Models

There is work on *syntactic* elimination and reordering rules that are safe on *sequences* (i.e., traces) of memory-related operations in data-race-free programs [33]. Because of its phrasing as transformation rules on sequences, it is unclear how to incorporate the work into the existing phases of a serial compiler without nontrivial engineering. A more significant point is that the rules only consider opportunities that do not require information on cross-thread interactions. In particular, the lock/unlock-related rules only allow for the movement of code *into* critical sections, not out of them [33].

7.5 OpenMP Program Optimization

Optimizations for OpenMP programs, in general, either have used the EPP approach [32, 12] or have been restricted to within parallel constructs [38]. Satoh et al. used an IR called the Parallel Flow Graph to model the intra- and cross-thread flow of information [32]. They developed data-flow analyses for reaching definitions, memory synchronizations and cross-loop data dependences. Huang et al. observed that it is easier to optimize a high-level version of an

OpenMP program than a lowered threaded version; they used an IR called the Parallel Control Flow Graph for this purpose [12].

7.6 Extending Sequential Optimizations to Parallel Code

Praun et al. showed how classical SSAPRE can be changed (manually) to consume conflict information derived from OUGs [40]. Heffner et al. described modifications to three sequential object-oriented optimizations in order to improve their effectiveness in the presence of concurrency [10]. The modified versions were based on a field-access analysis that maps every field *fld* to the duple $\langle locks, threads \rangle$, in which *locks* is the set of locks held on every access of *fld*, and in which *threads* is essentially a Boolean that indicates whether a single thread or multiple threads access *fld*. No distinction was made between read and write accesses. Moreover, the results of the field-access analysis were consumed by the modifications in ways that were specific to each extended optimization.

8. Conclusions

We presented an interprocedural static analysis that allows classical optimizations to be applied on data-race-free multithreaded programs in more cases than when synchronizations are viewed as opaque operations. We have shown that the additional precision is useful for optimization, and produces superior performance.

It may also be possible to use a version of this analysis in a static concurrency-bug detection tool, where viewing synchronizations as opaque could obscure essential information.

Much of the precision of our analysis comes from Refinement 4, which exploits the fact that C and C++ do not define semantics for data races. The coming standards for these languages will likely forbid them. As stated, Refinement 4 does not apply in all cases in which it could. In particular, it does not yet account for differences in behavior between synchronization primitives. For example, two procedures that both acquire but do not release the same lock, and that perform no other synchronization on common sync objects, must have empty interference sets, since any real interference would reflect a data race. This probably has little bearing on most existing code, but a C++ analog is likely to be important for two procedures both reading the same C++0x `atomic<T>` variable.

Acknowledgments

We thank the anonymous referees for their keen and valuable feedback on earlier drafts of this paper, which helped improve the work.

References

[1] ADVE, S. V., AND GHARACHORLOO, K. Shared Memory Consistency Models: A Tutorial. *IEEE Computer 29*, 12 (Dec. 1996), 66–76.

[2] ADVE, S. V., AND HILL, M. D. Weak Ordering—A New Definition. In *Proc. International Symposium on Computer Architecture* (May 1990), pp. 2–14.

[3] BOEHM, H.-J., AND ADVE, S. V. Foundations of the C++ Concurrency Memory Model. In *Proc. Conference on Programming Language Design and Implementation* (June 2008), pp. 68–78.

[4] BRISTOW, G., DREY, C., EDWARDS, B., AND RIDDLE, W. Anomaly Detection in Concurrent Programs. In *Proc. International Conference on Software Engineering* (Sept. 1979), pp. 265–273.

[5] CALLAHAN, D., AND SUBHLOK, J. Static Analysis of Low-level Synchronization. In *Proc. ACM Workshop on Parallel and Distributed Debugging* (May 1988), pp. 100–111.

[6] CHOI, J.-D., GUPTA, M., SREEDHAR, V. C., AND MIDKIFF, S. P. Escape Analysis for Java. In *Proc. Conference on Object-Oriented Programming, Systems, Languages and Applications* (Nov. 1999), pp. 1–19.

[7] CHOW, F., CHAN, S., LIU, S.-M., LO, R., AND STREICH, M. Effective Representation of Aliases and Indirect Memory Operations in SSA Form. In *Proc. International Conference on Compiler Construction* (Apr. 1996), vol. 1060 of *Lecture Notes in Computer Science*, Springer, pp. 253–267.

[8] DUESTERWALD, E., AND SOFFA, M. L. Concurrency Analysis in the Presence of Procedures Using a Data-Flow Framework. In *Proc. Symposium on Testing, Analysis and Verification* (Oct. 1991), pp. 36–48.

[9] GCC 4.4 Release Series—Changes, New Features, and Fixes. At `http://gcc.gnu.org/gcc-4.4/changes.html`.

[10] HEFFNER, K., TARDITI, D., AND SMITH, M. D. Extending Object-Oriented Optimizations for Concurrent Programs. In *Proc. International Conference on Parallel Architectures and Compilation Techniques* (Sept. 2007), pp. 119–129.

[11] HENDREN, L. J., AND NICOLAU, A. Parallelizing Programs with Recursive Data Structures. *IEEE Transactions on Parallel and Distributed Systems 1*, 1 (Jan. 1990), 35–47.

[12] HUANG, L., SETHURAMAN, G., AND CHAPMAN, B. Parallel Data Flow Analysis for OpenMP Programs. In *Proc. International Workshop on OpenMP* (June 2007), vol. 4935 of *Lecture Notes in Computer Science*, Springer, pp. 138–142.

[13] THE IEEE AND THE OPEN GROUP. *IEEE Standard 1003.1*, 2004.

[14] C Standard ISO/IEC 9899. At `http://www.open-std.org/JTC1/`.

[15] JOISHA, P. G., SCHREIBER, R. S., BANERJEE, P., BOEHM, H.-J., AND CHAKRABARTI, D. R. A Technique for the Effective and Automatic Reuse of Classical Compiler Optimizations on Multithreaded Code. Technical Report HPL-2010-81R1, Hewlett-Packard Laboratories, July 2010.

[16] KAM, J. B., AND ULLMAN, J. D. Monotone Data Flow Analysis Frameworks. *Acta Informatica 7*, 3 (Sept. 1977), 305–317.

[17] KNOOP, J., AND STEFFEN, B. Parallelism for Free: Efficient and Optimal Bitvector Analyses for Parallel Programs. *ACM Transactions on Programming Languages and Systems 18*, 3 (May 1996), 268–299.

[18] LAMPORT, L. How to Make a Multiprocessor Computer That Correctly Executes Multiprocess Programs. *IEEE Transactions on Computers C-28*, 9 (Sept. 1979), 690–691.

[19] LEE, J., MIDKIFF, S. P., AND PADUA, D. A. Concurrent Static Single Assignment Form and Constant Propagation for Explicitly Parallel Programs. In *Proc. International Workshop on Languages and Compilers for Parallel Computing* (Aug. 1997), vol. 1366 of *Lecture Notes in Computer Science*, Springer, pp. 114–130.

[20] LI, L., AND VERBRUGGE, C. A Practical MHP Information Analysis for Concurrent Java Programs. In *Proc. International Workshop on Languages and Compilers for Parallel Computing* (Sept. 2004), vol. 3602 of *Lecture Notes in Computer Science*, Springer, pp. 194–208.

[21] MASTICOLA, S. P., AND RYDER, B. G. Non-concurrency Analysis. In *Proc. Symposium on Principles and Practices of Parallel Programming* (May 1993), pp. 129–138.

[22] MIDKIFF, S. P., AND PADUA, D. A. Issues in the Optimization of Parallel Programs. In *Proc. International Conference on Parallel Processing* (Aug. 1990), vol. II, The Pennsylvania State University Press, pp. 105–113.

[23] NAUMOVICH, G., AND AVRUNIN, G. S. A Conservative Data Flow Algorithm for Detecting All Pairs of Statements that May Happen in Parallel. In *Proc. Symposium on Foundations of Software Engineering* (Nov. 1998), pp. 24–34.

[24] NAUMOVICH, G., AVRUNIN, G. S., AND CLARKE, L. A. An Efficient Algorithm for Computing MHP Information for Concurrent Java Programs. In *Proc. Symposium on Foundations of Software Engineering* (Sept. 1999), pp. 338–354.

[25] NOVILLO, D. Memory SSA—A Unified Approach for Sparsely Representing Memory Operations. In *Proc. GCC Developers' Summit* (July 2007), pp. 97–110.

[26] NOVILLO, D., UNRAU, R., AND SCHAEFFER, J. Concurrent SSA Form in the Presence of Mutual Exclusion. In *Proc. International Conference on Parallel Processing* (Aug. 1998), IEEE Computer Society Press, pp. 356–364.

[27] OPENMP ARCHITECTURE REVIEW BOARD. *OpenMP Application Program Interface*, version 3.0 ed., May 2008.

[28] RODRÍGUEZ, E., DWYER, M., FLANAGAN, C., HATCLIFF, J., LEAVENS, G. T., AND ROBBY. Extending JML for Modular Specification and Verification of Multi-threaded Programs. In *Proc. European Conference on Object-Oriented Programming* (July 2005), vol. 3586 of *Lecture Notes in Computer Science*, Springer, pp. 551–576.

[29] RUF, E. Effective Synchronization Removal for Java. In *Proc. Conference on Programming Language Design and Implementation* (June 2000), pp. 208–218.

[30] RUGINA, R., AND RINARD, M. C. Pointer Analysis for Structured Parallel Programs. *ACM Transactions on Programming Languages and Systems 25*, 1 (Jan. 2003), 70–116.

[31] SARKAR, V. Analysis and Optimization of Explicitly Parallel Programs Using the Parallel Program Graph Representation. In *Proc. International Workshop on Languages and Compilers for Parallel Computing* (Aug. 1997), vol. 1366 of *Lecture Notes in Computer Science*, Springer, pp. 94–113.

[32] SATOH, S., KUSANO, K., AND SATO, M. Compiler Optimization Techniques for OpenMP Programs. *Scientific Programming 9*, 2/3 (Aug. 2001), 131–142.

[33] ŠEVČÍK, J. *Program Transformations in Weak Memory Models*. PhD thesis, University of Edinburgh, 2008.

[34] SHASHA, D., AND SNIR, M. Efficient and Correct Execution of Parallel Programs that Share Memory. *ACM Transactions on Programming Languages and Systems 10*, 2 (Apr. 1988), 282–312.

[35] SRINIVASAN, H., HOOK, J., AND WOLFE, M. Static Single Assignment for Explicitly Parallel Programs. In *Proc. Symposium on Principles of Programming Languages* (Jan. 1993), pp. 260–272.

[36] SURA, Z., FANG, X., WONG, C.-L., MIDKIFF, S. P., LEE, J., AND PADUA, D. A. Compiler Techniques for High Performance Sequentially Consistent Java Programs. In *Proc. Symposium on Principles and Practices of Parallel Programming* (June 2005), pp. 2–13.

[37] TAYLOR, R. N. A General-Purpose Algorithm for Analyzing Concurrent Programs. *Communications of the ACM 26*, 5 (May 1983), 362–376.

[38] TIAN, X., BIK, A., GIRKAR, M., GREY, P., SAITO, H., AND SU, E. Intel OpenMP C++/Fortran Compiler for Hyper-Threading Technology: Implementation and Performance. *Intel Technology Journal 6*, 1 (Feb. 2002), 36–46.

[39] VON PRAUN, C., AND GROSS, T. R. Static Conflict Analysis for Multi-Threaded Object-Oriented Programs. In *Proc. Conference on Programming Language Design and Implementation* (June 2003), pp. 338–349.

[40] VON PRAUN, C., SCHNEIDER, F., AND GROSS, T. R. Load Elimination in the Presence of Side Effects, Concurrency and Precise Exceptions. In *Proc. International Workshop on Languages and Compilers for Parallel Computing* (Oct. 2003), vol. 2958 of *Lecture Notes in Computer Science*, Springer, pp. 390–405.

[41] WOO, S. C., OHARA, M., TORRIE, E., SINGH, J. P., AND GUPTA, A. The SPLASH-2 Programs: Characterization and Methodological Considerations. In *Proc. International Symposium on Computer Architecture* (June 1995), pp. 24–36.

[42] ZHANG, Y., SREEDHAR, V. C., ZHU, W., SARKAR, V., AND GAO, G. R. Optimized Lock Assignment and Allocation: A Method for Exploiting Concurrency among Critical Sections. CAPSL Technical Memo Revised 65, University of Delaware, Mar. 2007.

Notation Index

Author Index

www.ingramcontent.com/pod-product-compliance
Ingram Content Group UK Ltd.
Pitfield, Milton Keynes, MK11 3LW, UK
UKHW051418290926
15471UKWH00009B/1665

9 781450 304900